HARRIS

MILITARY CRIMINAL JUSTICE: PRACTICE AND PROCEDURE

FOURTH EDITION

DAVID A. SCHLUETER
Professor of Law
St. Mary's University
San Antonio, Texas

MICHIE
Law Publishers
CHARLOTTESVILLE, VIRGINIA

COPYRIGHT © 1996
BY
MICHIE
A Division of Reed Elsevier Inc.
and Reed Elsevier Properties Inc.

Library of Congress Catalog Card No. 96-076705
ISBN 1-55834-344-X

All rights reserved.

The views of the author do not purport to reflect the views of the Department of the Army or Department of Defense.

6692811

"Michie" and the Open Book and Gavel logo are trademarks of Michie, a division of Reed Elsevier Inc.

To Linda, Jennifer, and Jonathan

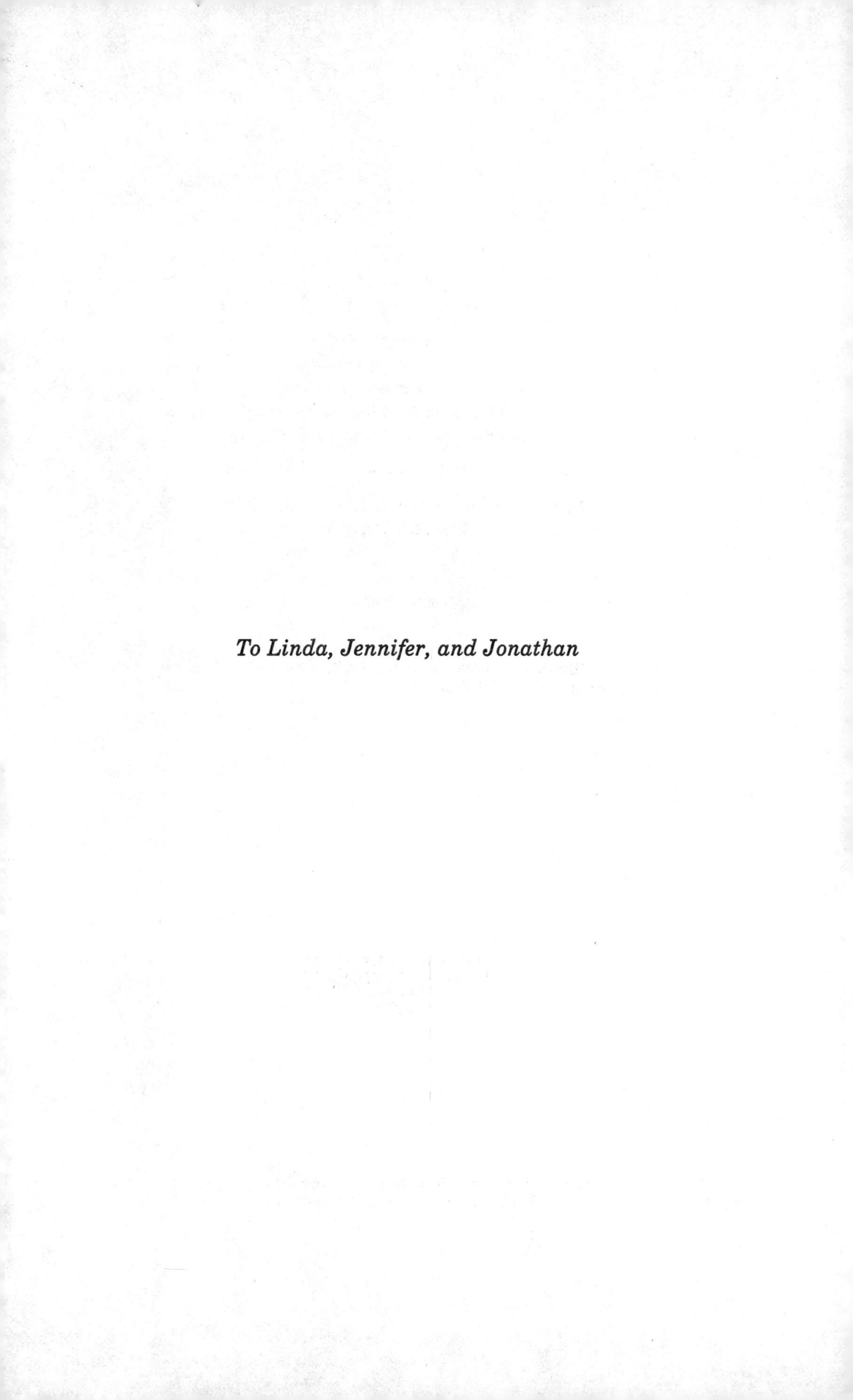

PREFACE and ACKNOWLEDGMENTS

This text is designed to lead readers through the maze of procedural and substantive rules, military acronyms, and related practices unique to military criminal law, with citations to pertinent caselaw, statutory and regulatory authority.

The sheer volume of cumulative supplements to the third edition indicated that the time was ripe for a new edition. Amendments to the Uniform Code of Military Justice, changes in the *Manual for Courts-Martial*, developing military case law in a number of key areas, and name changes for the military courts, also indicated that some expansion and reorganization was appropriate. Throughout, the text has been edited and arranged to make it more usable for the harried reader looking for a particular topic. Discussion for the most part has been kept short and to the point, in order to keep the size manageable. Because of the increased length of the book, the Appendices have been trimmed to make room for additional caselaw citations and commentary, and still keep the book in its one-volume format.

This text is neither a defense of military justice nor a call for reform of the system. In the 25 years that I have been associated with military criminal law, I have become a firm believer in the high quality of the system and those who practice within it. Although I have included some editorial analysis in this text, I have left to other forums, commentators, and speakers the task of addressing the concerns raised by critics of the system. This text is intended to be a thorough reference—a no-nonsense approach to military justice, a system that predates the Constitution. It is my firm belief that those practicing within the system are able ambassadors of the quality of the system. If they do the job right, the quality of military justice will remain high. This text is an attempt to help those practicing military justice, both civilian and military, to do it right. But the text should also assist students of the system in understanding what military justice is all about, in the hope that they will have a better appreciation of its strengths.

I owe a deep debt of gratitude to a number of individuals who assisted in this fourth edition. In addition to those who helped prepare the previous editions, a number deserve special recognition here. Captain Ken Arnold, Commander Gary Palmer, and Major Dwight Sullivan provided invaluable editorial assistance in reviewing the Chapter on Nonjudicial Punishment. Ms. Linda Perez provided assistance in checking citations of authority and, with the assistance of LTC Rob Minor and his office, provided indispensable aid in compiling the Appendices. Dan Schlueter prepared the flow chart at Appendix 4. The manuscript was prepared with the expert assistance of Maria Klatt, Cecelia Aguilar, and Kathy Worthington. Finally, Professor Gerry Beyer provided untold assistance in solving whatever computer problems arose during the process.

PREFACE & ACKNOWLEDGMENTS

In the hope that I can in some small measure express thanks for the patience, sacrifices, and encouragement of my wife and children, it is to them that I dedicate this work.

Dave Schlueter
San Antonio, Texas

June 1996

SUMMARY TABLE OF CONTENTS

Preface and Acknowledgments v
Table of Contents ix

Chapter 1. The Military Criminal Justice System 1
Chapter 2. Military Crimes 55
Chapter 3. Nonjudicial Punishment: A Comparative Analysis 113
Chapter 4. Jurisdiction 149
Chapter 5. The Commander's Investigation, Pretrial Restraints, and Confinement 209
Chapter 6. Preferral and Forwarding of Charges; Command Influence 269
Chapter 7. The Article 32 Investigation and the Pretrial Advice 317
Chapter 8. Convening of a Court-Martial, Detailing Participants, and the Referral Process 337
Chapter 9. Plea Bargaining and Other Pretrial Negotiations 369
Chapter 10. Notice, Disclosure and Discovery 387
Chapter 11. Production of Witnesses and Evidence 413
Chapter 12. The Article 39(a) Pretrial Session 447
Chapter 13. Motions Practice 479
Chapter 14. Pleas 573
Chapter 15. Trial Procedures 609
Chapter 16. Sentencing 703
Chapter 17. Review of Courts-Martial 763

Appendices 845
Table of Cases 999
Index 1183

TABLE OF CONTENTS

Preface and Acknowledgments v
Summary Table of Contents vii

CHAPTER 1. THE MILITARY CRIMINAL JUSTICE SYSTEM 1

PART I. INTRODUCTION

§ 1-1.	A Separate System: Justice or Discipline?	2
	§ 1-1(A). Constitutional Underpinnings	5
	§ 1-1(B). Military Due Process: The Hierarchy	6
§ 1-2.	Using This Book	9
	§ 1-2(A). A Foreword	9
	§ 1-2(B). Frontal Analysis	9
	§ 1-2(C). Discussion	10
	§ 1-2(D). Annotated Bibliography	10
	§ 1-2(E). Glossary	10
	§ 1-2(F). Appendices	10
§ 1-3.	Researching Military Criminal Law Issues	10
	§ 1-3(A). The Uniform Code of Military Justice (UCMJ)	10
	§ 1-3(B). The Manual for Courts-Martial, United States: The MCM	11
	§ 1-3(C). Service Supplements to the MCM	12
	§ 1-3(D). Military Case Law	13
	§ 1-3(D)(1). Court-Martial Reports	13
	§ 1-3(D)(2). Military Justice Reporter	13
	§ 1-3(D)(3). Citator	14
	§ 1-3(E). Military Legal Periodicals	14

PART II. HISTORICAL ROOTS OF THE COURT-MARTIAL

§ 1-4.	The Early European Models	15
§ 1-5.	The British System	19
	§ 1-5(A). General	19
	§ 1-5(B). The Court of Chivalry: The Constable's Court	19
	§ 1-5(C). The "Council of War"	21
	§ 1-5(D). The Mutiny Act	24
§ 1-6.	The American Court-Martial	25
	§ 1-6(A). The Formative Years: 1775 to 1800	26
	§ 1-6(B). The Period From 1800 to 1900: Quiet Growth	29
	§ 1-6(C). From 1900 to Present: Rapid Change	33

PART III. THE PRESENT SYSTEM: A PROLOGUE

§ 1-7.	An Overview	37

§ 1-8.	The Commander's Options: Prosecutorial Discretion	40
§ 1-8(A).	General	40
§ 1-8(B).	Nonpunitive Measures	40
§ 1-8(C).	Nonjudicial Punishment	41
§ 1-8(D).	Court-Martial	41
§ 1-8(D)(1).	Summary Court-Martial	41
§ 1-8(D)(2).	Special Court-Martial	42
§ 1-8(D)(3).	General Court-Marial	43

Appendix References 44
Annotated Bibliography 44

CHAPTER 2. MILITARY CRIMES — 55

§ 2-1.	Introduction	56
§ 2-2.	Absence Offenses	56
§ 2-2(A).	General	56
§ 2-2(B).	Desertion	57
§ 2-2(C).	Absence Without Leave	59
§ 2-2(C)(1).	Failing to Go to Place of Duty	59
§ 2-2(C)(2).	Leaving Place of Duty	60
§ 2-2(C)(3).	Absence Without Leave	60
§ 2-2(D).	Missing Movement	63
§ 2-2(E).	Defenses to Absence Offenses	64
§ 2-2(E)(1).	Impossibility	64
§ 2-2(E)(2).	Justification or Necessity	65
§ 2-2(E)(3).	Duress	65
§ 2-2(E)(4).	Mistake of Fact	66
§ 2-2(E)(5).	Civilian Detention	66
§ 2-2(E)(6).	Statute of Limitations	67
§ 2-2(E)(7).	Moral Grounds or Beliefs	67
§ 2-3.	Disrespect Offenses	68
§ 2-3(A).	Disrespect Toward Officers	69
§ 2-3(B).	Insubordination Toward Petty, Warrant, or Noncommissioned Officers	69
§ 2-3(C).	Defenses to Disrespect Offenses	70
§ 2-4.	Disobedience Offenses	71
§ 2-4(A).	General	71
§ 2-4(B).	Disobedience of a Superior's Orders	74
§ 2-4(C).	Violation of General Orders or Regulations	75
§ 2-4(D).	Disobedience of Other Orders	77
§ 2-4(E).	Dereliction of Duty	77
§ 2-4(F).	Defenses to Disobedience Offenses	78
§ 2-5.	Article 133: Conduct Unbecoming an Officer and a Gentleman	80
§ 2-6.	Article 134: The General Article	82
§ 2-6(A).	Disorders and Neglects to the Prejudice of Good Order and Discipline	83

TABLE OF CONTENTS

§ 2-6(B).	Conduct Bringing Discredit Upon the Armed Forces	85
§ 2-6(C).	Crimes and Offenses Not Capital: Federal Crimes	86
§ 2-7.	Drug Offenses	87
§ 2-7(A).	Charging Drug Offenses	87
§ 2-7(B).	Proving Wrongfulness; Defenses	89
§ 2-7(C).	Evidentiary Issues; Proving Identity of the Drugs	91
§ 2-8.	Fraternization	93
§ 2-8(A).	In General	93
§ 2-8(B).	Fraternization and the General Articles	94
§ 2-8(C).	Fraternization and Regulations or Orders	97
§ 2-8(D).	Fraternization and the Constitution	98
§ 2-9.	AIDS and HIV-Related Offenses	99
§ 2-9(A).	General	99
§ 2-9(B).	Violating "Safe Sex" Orders	100
§ 2-9(C).	Prosecuting HIV-Related Offenses Under Other U.C.M.J. Provisions	102
§ 2-9(C)(1).	Murder, Manslaughter, and Assault	103
§ 2-9(C)(2).	Rape and Sodomy	104
§ 2-9(C)(3).	"Catch-All" Offenses Under Articles 133 and 134	105
§ 2-9(D).	Constitutionality of Prosecuting HIV-Related Conduct	105
Appendix References		108
Annotated Bibliography		108

CHAPTER 3. NONJUDICIAL PUNISHMENT: A COMPARATIVE ANALYSIS ... 113

§ 3-1.	Introduction	114
§ 3-2.	Applicable Policies	115
§ 3-3.	Authority to Impose Punishment	115
§ 3-3(A).	Who May Impose?	116
§ 3-3(B).	Who May Be Punished?	117
§ 3-3(C).	"Minor" Offenses	118
§ 3-4.	The Right to Demand Trial	120
§ 3-5.	Procedural Rules for Imposing Nonjudicial Punishment	122
§ 3-5(A).	General	122
§ 3-5(B).	Army Procedures	123
§ 3-5(B)(1).	Preliminary Inquiry	123
§ 3-5(B)(2).	Notice	124
§ 3-5(B)(3).	Hearing	125
§ 3-5(B)(4).	Appeals	126
§ 3-5(C).	Air Force Procedures	127
§ 3-5(C)(1).	Preliminary Inquiry	127
§ 3-5(C)(2).	Notice	128
§ 3-5(C)(3).	Hearing	129

	§ 3-5(C)(4).	Appeals	130
§ 3-5(D).	Navy and Marine Corps Procedures		131
	§ 3-5(D)(1).	Preliminary Inquiry	132
	§ 3-5(D)(2).	Notice	132
	§ 3-5(D)(3).	Hearing	133
	§ 3-5(D)(4).	Appeals	134
§ 3-5(E).	Coast Guard Procedures		135
	§ 3-5(E)(1).	Preliminary Inquiry	135
	§ 3-5(E)(2).	Notice	136
	§ 3-5(E)(3).	Hearing	136
	§ 3-5(E)(4).	Appeals	138
§ 3-6.	Punishments		138
	§ 3-6(A).	General	138
	§ 3-6(B).	Reduction in Grade	139
	§ 3-6(C).	Deprivation of Liberty	139
		§ 3-6(C)(1). Correctional Custody	139
		§ 3-6(C)(2). Extra Duties	140
		§ 3-6(C)(3). Restriction	140
		§ 3-6(C)(4). Arrest in Quarters	140
		§ 3-6(C)(5). Confinement on Bread and Water	140
	§ 3-6(D).	Forfeiture of Pay	141
	§ 3-6(E).	Censure	141
	§ 3-6(F).	Combination of Punishments	142
	§ 3-6(G).	Effective Dates of Punishments	142
§ 3-7.	Effect of Errors in Imposition		143
§ 3-8.	Consequences of Nonjudicial Punishment		144
	§ 3-8(A).	Filing Requirements: Military Career	144
	§ 3-8(B).	Use at Court-Martial or Administrative Proceedings	144
Appendix References			147
Annotated Bibliography			147

CHAPTER 4. JURISDICTION 149

Part I. Introduction

§ 4-1.	General	150
§ 4-2.	The Nature of Court-Martial Jurisdiction	151
	§ 4-2(A). A Creature of Statute	151
	§ 4-2(B). Requisites of Jurisdiction	152
§ 4-3.	Jurisdictional Limits of Courts-Martial	152
	§ 4-3(A). General Court-Martial	152
	§ 4-3(B). Special Court-Martial	152
	§ 4-3(C). Summary Court-Martial	153

TABLE OF CONTENTS

PART II. PERSONAL JURISDICTION

§ 4-4.	General	153
§ 4-5.	Inception of Jurisdiction: A Change of Status	154
§ 4-5(A).	Enlistment: Voluntary Entry	154
§ 4-5(A)(1).	Valid Enlistments	155
§ 4-5(A)(2).	Void Enlistments: Minors; Involuntary; Incompetent	156
§ 4-5(A)(3).	Effect of Recruiter Misconduct	158
§ 4-5(A)(4).	Constructive Enlistment	158
§ 4-5(B).	Induction: Involuntary Entry	160
§ 4-5(C).	Appointment of Officers	161
§ 4-6.	Jurisdiction Over Reservists and Members of National Guard	161
§ 4-7.	Jurisdiction Over Civilians	164
§ 4-7(A).	In Wartime	165
§ 4-7(B).	In Peacetime	166
§ 4-8.	Termination of Personal Jurisdiction	166
§ 4-8(A).	Continuing Jurisdiction	167
§ 4-8(B).	General Rule; Discharge Termination Status	168
§ 4-8(C).	Exceptions to the General Rule	169
§ 4-8(C)(1).	Reenlistment Discharges	169
§ 4-8(C)(2).	Article 3(a) Offenses	169
§ 4-8(C)(3).	Fraudulent Discharge	170
§ 4-8(C)(4).	Deserters	174
§ 4-8(C)(5).	Persons in Custody	174
§ 4-8(D).	Retired Members	174
§ 4-9.	Pleading and Proving Personal Jurisdiction	175

PART III. JURISDICTION OVER THE OFFENSE

§ 4-10.	Introduction	176
§ 4-11.	The Service Connection Requirement: 1969-1987	177
§ 4-11(A).	Applying the *Relford* Factors	179
§ 4-11(B).	Military Retreat from the *Relford* Ad Hoc Analysis	183
§ 4-11(C).	*Solorio v. United States*: The Demise of the Service Connection Requirement	184
§ 4-11(C)(1).	The Constitutional Implications of *Solorio*	186
§ 4-11(C)(2).	The Practical Implications of *Solorio*	188
§ 4-12.	Exclusive, Reciprocal, and Concurrent Jurisdiction	188
§ 4-12(A).	State and Federal Courts	189
§ 4-12(B).	Foreign Courts	190

PART IV. CONVENING AND COMPOSITION OF COURTS-MARTIAL; REFERRAL OF CHARGES

§ 4-13. General 192
§ 4-14. Authority to Convene a Court-Martial 192
    § 4-14(A). The Convening Authority 193
        § 4-14(A)(1). Statutory Authorization 193
        § 4-14(A)(2). Disqualifications 193
        § 4-14(A)(3). Delegation of Authority 195
    § 4-14(B). Convening Orders 195
§ 4-15. Properly Composed Court-Martial 196
    § 4-15(A). Military Judge 196
    § 4-15(B). Counsel 197
    § 4-15(C). Court Members 197
§ 4-16. Charges Properly Referred to Court-Martial 199
Appendix References 201
Annotated Bibliography 201

CHAPTER 5. THE COMMANDER'S INVESTIGATION, PRETRIAL RESTRAINTS, AND CONFINEMENT   209

PART I. THE COMMANDER'S INVESTIGATION

§ 5-1. Introduction 210
§ 5-2. The Commander's Investigation: In General 210
§ 5-3. Searches and Seizures 211
    § 5-3(A). The Servicemember's Reasonable Expectation of Privacy 212
    § 5-3(B). Probable Cause Searches 214
    § 5-3(C). Nonprobable Cause Searches 216
        § 5-3(C)(1). In General 216
        § 5-3(C)(2). Searches of Government Property 216
        § 5-3(C)(3). Gate Searches; Border Searches 217
        § 5-3(C)(4). Searches in Jails and Restricted Areas 217
        § 5-3(C)(5). Emergency Searches 218
        § 5-3(C)(6). Consent Searches 218
        § 5-3(C)(7). Searches Incident to Apprehension 219
        § 5-3(C)(8). Searches Incident to Lawful Stop 220
        § 5-3(C)(9). Other Nonprobable Cause Searches 220
    § 5-3(D). Other Reasonable Searches 221
        § 5-3(D)(1). Inspections and Inventories 221
        § 5-3(D)(2). Body Views and Intrusions 224
    § 5-3(E). Seizures 225
    § 5-3(F). Exclusionary Rule; Exceptions 225
§ 5-4. The Right Against Self-Incrimination, Interrogation, and Immunity 227

TABLE OF CONTENTS

§ 5-4(A).	The Right Against Self-Incrimination	227
§ 5-4(A)(1).	In General	227
§ 5-4(A)(2).	Reporting Requirements	228
§ 5-4(A)(3).	Comments on Invoking the Right	229
§ 5-4(B).	Interrogation of Suspects; Rights Warnings	229
§ 5-4(C).	Grants of Immunity	237
§ 5-5.	Eyewitness Identification	239

PART II. PRETRIAL RESTRAINTS AND CONFINEMENT

§ 5-6.	In General	240
§ 5-7.	Apprehension	240
§ 5-8.	Pretrial Restraints	242
§ 5-8(A).	In General	242
§ 5-8(B).	Conditions on Liberty	244
§ 5-8(C).	Restriction in Lieu of Arrest	245
§ 5-8(D).	Arrest	245
§ 5-9.	Pretrial Confinement	245
§ 5-9(A).	In General	245
§ 5-9(B).	Initial Decision to Confine	246
§ 5-9(C).	Review by Commander	248
§ 5-9(D).	Review of Commander's Decision to Confine	248
§ 5-9(E).	Judicial Review	252
§ 5-10.	Illegal Pretrial Punishment and Restraints	254
§ 5-10(A).	In General	254
§ 5-10(B).	Pretrial Punishment Other Than Restraint	255
§ 5-10(C).	Pretrial Restraints Constituting Illegal Punishment	256
§ 5-10(D).	Remedies; Waiver	257
Appendix References		263
Annotated Bibliography		263

CHAPTER 6. PREFERRAL AND FORWARDING OF CHARGES; COMMAND INFLUENCE 269

PART I. PREFERRAL AND FORWARDING OF CHARGES

§ 6-1.	Preferring Sworn Charges	270
§ 6-1(A).	The Charge Sheet	275
§ 6-1(B).	General Rules of Pleading	275
§ 6-1(B)(1).	Pleading Jurisdiction	277
§ 6-1(B)(2).	Amendments to Pleadings	277
§ 6-1(B)(3).	Additional Charges	278
§ 6-1(C).	Defective Pleadings	279
§ 6-1(C)(1).	Misjoinder	281
§ 6-1(C)(2).	Duplicitous Specifications	282
§ 6-1(C)(3).	Multiplicity	284

§ 6-2.	Forwarding of Charges		290
	§ 6-2(A).	Immediate Commander	290
	§ 6-2(B).	Summary Court-Martial Convening Authority	291
	§ 6-2(C).	Special Court-Martial Convening Authority	291
	§ 6-2(D).	General Court-Martial Convening Authority	292

PART II. COMMAND INFLUENCE

§ 6-3.	Command Influence; In General		292
	§ 6-3(A).	The Perpetual Problem of Unlawful Command Influence	292
	§ 6-3(B).	Lawful and Unlawful Influence Distinguished	294
	§ 6-3(C).	Actual, Apparent, and Perceived Unlawful Command Influence	295
§ 6-4.	Pretrial Command Influence		296
	§ 6-4(A).	The Preliminary Inquiry and Preferring Charges	297
	§ 6-4(B).	Command Influence on Article 32 Investigations	297
	§ 6-4(C).	Command Influence on Referral of Charges	298
	§ 6-4(D).	Command Influence in Selecting Court Members	299
	§ 6-4(E).	Pretrial Comments and Actions	299
§ 6-5.	Command Influence on Courts-Martial		300
	§ 6-5(A).	Command Influence on Court Members, Judges, and Counsel	300
	§ 6-5(B).	Command Influence on Witnesses	303
	§ 6-5(C).	Commander's "Presence" at Trial	306
§ 6-6.	Post-Trial Command Influence		307
	§ 6-6(A).	Clemency Matters	307
	§ 6-6(B).	Comments on Outcome of Case	308
	§ 6-6(C).	Discouraging Witness Testimony in Other Cases	308
§ 6-7.	Appellate Review of Command Influence		309
§ 6-8.	Minimizing the Potential for Unlawful Command Influence		311
Appendix References			314
Annotated Bibliography			314

CHAPTER 7. THE ARTICLE 32 INVESTIGATION AND THE PRETRIAL ADVICE ... 317

§ 7-1.	General		317
§ 7-2.	The Article 32 Investigation		317
	§ 7-2(A).	The Parties to the Investigation	319
		§ 7-2(A)(1). The Investigating Officer	319
		§ 7-2(A)(2). Counsel	321
	§ 7-2(B).	The Accused's Rights	322
		§ 7-2(B)(1). Notice of Charges	322
		§ 7-2(B)(2). Right to Counsel	322
		§ 7-2(B)(3). Right to be Present	323
		§ 7-2(B)(4). Right to Confront Witnesses	323
		§ 7-2(B)(5). Right to Examine Evidence	325

TABLE OF CONTENTS

§ 7-2(B)(6).	Right to Production of Witnesses	325
§ 7-2(B)(7).	Right to Present Other Evidence	326
§ 7-2(B)(8).	Right to Remain Silent	326
§ 7-2(C).	Article 32 Investigation Procedures	326
§ 7-2(D).	Investigating Officer's Report	327
§ 7-2(E).	Defects in the Investigation	329
§ 7-3.	The Staff Judge Advocate's Pretrial Advice	330
§ 7-3(A).	Contents of the Pretrial Advice	331
§ 7-3(B).	Defective Pretrial Advice	333
Appendix References		334
Annotated Bibliography		334

CHAPTER 8. CONVENING OF A COURT-MARTIAL, DETAILING PARTICIPANTS, AND THE REFERRAL PROCESS ... 337

§ 8-1.	General	337
§ 8-2.	Convening the Court-Martial	338
§ 8-2(A).	The Convening Authority	338
§ 8-2(B).	The Convening Order	339
§ 8-3.	Detailing the Participants	340
§ 8-3(A).	The Military Judge	340
§ 8-3(B).	Trial and Defense Counsel	345
§ 8-3(B)(1).	Qualifications of Counsel	345
§ 8-3(B)(2).	Detailing Military Counsel	347
§ 8-3(B)(3).	Requests for Individual Military Counsel	348
§ 8-3(B)(4).	Obtaining Civilian Counsel	351
§ 8-3(C).	Members of the Court	352
§ 8-3(C)(1).	Qualifications of Members	352
§ 8-3(C)(2).	Requests for Enlisted Members	354
§ 8-3(C)(3).	Constitutional Challenges to Composition	356
§ 8-3(C)(4).	Selecting the Members	356
§ 8-3(D).	Changes in Composition of Court	359
§ 8-4.	Referral of Charges to a Court-Martial	361
§ 8-5.	Withdrawal of Charges	363
§ 8-6.	Service of Charges Upon the Accused	365
Appendix References		366
Annotated Bibliography		366

CHAPTER 9. PLEA BARGAINING AND OTHER PRETRIAL NEGOTIATIONS ... 369

§ 9-1.	General	369
§ 9-2.	Pretrial Agreements	369
§ 9-2(A).	Procedures	371
§ 9-2(A)(1).	Initiation of Negotiations and Terms	371

	§ 9-2(A)(2).	Submission and Acceptance of Offer	372
	§ 9-2(A)(3).	Informal Agreements	373
§ 9-2(B).	Conditions and Terms		373
	§ 9-2(B)(1).	Valid Conditions	374
	§ 9-2(B)(2).	Invalid Terms	379
§ 9-2(C).	Withdrawal From the Agreement		380
§ 9-2(D).	Judicial Review of the Agreement		381

§ 9-3. Confessional Stipulations 381
§ 9-4. Discharge in Lieu of Court-Martial 383
Appendix References 385
Annotated Bibliography 385

CHAPTER 10. NOTICE, DISCLOSURE AND DISCOVERY ... 387

§ 10-1. General 387
§ 10-2. Notice Requirements 388
    § 10-2(A). Notice by the Prosecution 389
    § 10-2(B). Notice by the Defense 390
§ 10-3. Discovery: General Rules 392
    § 10-3(A). Protected Information 392
    § 10-3(B). Equal Access to Evidence 393
    § 10-3(C). Failure to Call a Witness 393
    § 10-3(D). Continuing Duty to Disclose 394
    § 10-3(E). Reciprocal Discovery 394
    § 10-3(F). The Ethical Duty to Disclose 395
§ 10-4. Defense Discovery 396
    § 10-4(A). Automatic Prosecutorial Disclosure 396
        § 10-4(A)(1). Charges and Allied Papers 396
        § 10-4(A)(2). Names of Prosecution Witnesses 397
        § 10-4(A)(3). Prior Convictions 397
        § 10-4(A)(4). Favorable Evidence: The Constitutional Mandate 398
    § 10-4(B). Defense Requests for Discovery 399
        § 10-4(B)(1). The *Brady* Request 399
        § 10-4(B)(2). Tangibles and Documents 400
        § 10-4(B)(3). Reports, Tests, and Results 401
        § 10-4(B)(4). Sentencing Evidence 401
        § 10-4(B)(5). Jencks Act Materials 402
    § 10-4(C). Reciprocal Discovery 404
§ 10-5. Prosecution Discovery 405
    § 10-5(A). Automatic Defense Disclosure 405
        § 10-5(A)(1). Names of Defense Witnesses 405
        § 10-5(A)(2). Notice of Alibi Defense 406
        § 10-5(A)(3). Notice of Lack of Mental Responsibility Defense 407
        § 10-5(A)(4). Notice of Defense of Innocent Ingestion 407

TABLE OF CONTENTS

§ 10-5(B).	Prosecution Requests for Discovery	407
§ 10-5(C).	Reciprocal Discovery	408
§ 10-6.	Judicial Control of Discovery: Remedies	408
Appendix References		410
Annotated Bibliography		410

CHAPTER 11. PRODUCTION OF WITNESSES AND EVIDENCE ... 413

§ 11-1.	General	413
§ 11-2.	Production of Witnesses	414
§ 11-2(A).	General Rules	414
§ 11-2(A)(1).	Equal Access: The Right to Witnesses	414
§ 11-2(A)(2).	Unavailable Witnesses	416
§ 11-2(A)(3).	Employing Expert Witnesses	417
§ 11-2(A)(4).	Adequate Substitutes for Testimony	420
§ 11-2(B).	Requests for Witnesses	421
§ 11-2(B)(1).	Defense Witnesses	421
§ 11-2(B)(2).	Prosecution Witnesses	424
§ 11-2(C).	Production of Military Witnesses	424
§ 11-2(D).	Production of Civilian Witnesses	425
§ 11-2(D)(1).	General	425
§ 11-2(D)(2).	Use of the Subpoena	425
§ 11-2(D)(3).	Sanctions for Failure to Appear	427
§ 11-2(E).	Immunity for Witnesses	427
§ 11-2(E)(1).	General	427
§ 11-2(E)(2).	Immunity for Prosecution Witnesses	429
§ 11-2(E)(3).	Immunity for Defense Witnesses	430
§ 11-2(F).	Refusal to Testify	434
§ 11-3.	Depositions	435
§ 11-3(A).	In General	435
§ 11-3(B).	Procedures for Depositions	435
§ 11-3(B)(1).	In General	436
§ 11-3(B)(2).	Procedures for Oral Depositions	438
§ 11-3(B)(3).	Procedures for Written Depositions	439
§ 11-3(C).	Use of Depositions at Trial	440
§ 11-4.	Production of Evidence	441
Appendix References		444
Annotated Bibliography		444

CHAPTER 12. THE ARTICLE 39(a) PRETRIAL SESSION ... 447

§ 12-1.	Introduction	447
§ 12-2.	Preliminary Matters	449
§ 12-2(A).	Calling the Court to Order	449
§ 12-2(B).	Announcing the Convening Orders, Referral, and Service of Charges	450
§ 12-2(C).	Accounting for Parties Present and Absent	451

§ 12-2(D). Noting the Detail of a Court Reporter and an Interpreter 452
§ 12-2(E). Announcing the Detail and Qualifications of the Trial Counsel 453
§ 12-2(F). Announcing the Detail and Qualifications of the Defense Counsel and the Judge's Inquiry Concerning the Accused's Rights to Counsel 454
  § 12-2(F)(1). Detail and Qualifications of Counsel ... 454
  § 12-2(F)(2). The *Donohew* Inquiry 455
  § 12-2(F)(3). The *Breese* Inquiry and Conflicts of Interest 456
  § 12-2(F)(4). The *Faretta* Inquiry and Self-Representation 458
  § 12-2(F)(5). Accused's Election of Counsel 461
§ 12-2(G). Administering the Oaths and Announcing the Detail of the Military Judge 461
§ 12-2(H). Challenges for Cause to the Military Judge 462
§ 12-3. Military Judge's Inquiries Concerning the Accused's Decisions Regarding Composition of the Court 466
  § 12-3(A). Accused's Request for Trial by Judge Alone 467
  § 12-3(B). Accused's Request for Enlisted Members on the Court 470
§ 12-4. Arraignment 472
§ 12-5. Conference 474
Appendix References 477
Annotated Bibliography 477

CHAPTER 13. MOTIONS PRACTICE 479
§ 13-1. Introduction 480
§ 13-2. Procedural Aspects of Motions Practice 480
  § 13-2(A). Timing of Motions 481
  § 13-2(B). Waiver of Motions 482
  § 13-2(C). Notice and Service of Motions 483
  § 13-2(D). Burden of Proof on Motions 483
  § 13-2(E). Rulings on Motions 484
  § 13-2(F). Reconsideration of Rulings 485
  § 13-2(G). Appeal of Rulings 486
    § 13-2(G)(1). Defense Appeals: Extraordinary Writs 486
    § 13-2(G)(2). Government Appeals 487
§ 13-3. Motions to Dismiss 492
  § 13-3(A). Lack of Jurisdiction 493
  § 13-3(B). Statute of Limitations 493
  § 13-3(C). Speedy Trial 495
    § 13-3(C)(1). Sixth Amendment and Due Process Standards 496

TABLE OF CONTENTS

§ 13-3(C)(2). U.C.M.J. Requirements: The *Burton* 90-Day Rule (1972-1993) 497
§ 13-3(C)(3). The Manual's 120-Day Speedy Trial Rule 503
§ 13-3(C)(4). Interstate Agreement on Detainers Act (IADA) 514
§ 13-3(C)(5). Remedies for Speedy Trial Violations .. 515
§ 13-3(D). Lack of Mental Responsibility 515
§ 13-3(E). Former Jeopardy 517
§ 13-3(F). Failure to Allege an Offense 519
§ 13-3(G). Former Punishment 520
§ 13-3(H). Grant of Immunity 521
§ 13-3(I). Constructive Condonation of Desertion 523
§ 13-3(J). Multiplicity 523
§ 13-3(K). Defective Specification That Misled the Accused ... 525
§ 13-3(L). Presidential Pardon 525
§ 13-3(M). Selective or Vindictive Prosecution: Prosecutorial Misconduct 526
§ 13-3(N). Constitutional Challenges to the Underlying Statute, Regulation, or Order 528
§ 13-3(N)(1). Equal Protection 529
§ 13-3(N)(2). Vagueness: Lack of Fair Notice 533
§ 13-3(N)(3). First Amendment: Speech, Religion, and Association 535
§ 13-3(N)(4). Rights of Privacy 544
§ 13-3(N)(5). *Ex Post Facto* Laws 546
§ 13-4. Motions to Suppress 547
§ 13-4(A). Pretrial Statements of the Accused 549
§ 13-4(B). Illegal Searches and Seizures 550
§ 13-4(C). Eyewitness Identification 551
§ 13-5. Motions to Grant Appropriate Relief 551
§ 13-5(A). Accused Incompetent to Stand Trial 552
§ 13-5(B). Pretrial Restraint 554
§ 13-5(C). Change of Location of Trial 555
§ 13-5(D). Defective Pretrial Investigation or Pretrial Advice 556
§ 13-5(E). Defective Pleadings: Motions to Cure or Amend 556
§ 13-5(F). Motion for a Bill of Particulars 557
§ 13-5(G). Motions to Sever 560
§ 13-5(G)(1). Severance of Accuseds 560
§ 13-5(G)(2). Severance of Charges 561
§ 13-5(G)(3). Severance of Duplicitous Specification 562
§ 13-5(H). Requests Concerning Individual Military Counsel or Retention of Detailed Military Counsel 562
§ 13-5(I). Request for Witnesses 563
§ 13-5(J). Discovery 564
§ 13-5(K). Continuance 564

§ 13-5(L). Motions to Obtain Rulings on Evidentiary Matters; Motions *in Limine* 565
Appendix References 568
Annotated Bibliography 568

CHAPTER 14. PLEAS 573
§ 14-1. Introduction 573
§ 14-2. Not Guilty Pleas 574
§ 14-3. Guilty Pleas 575
    § 14-3(A). Effects of Guilty Plea 576
        § 14-3(A)(1). Waiver of Rights 577
        § 14-3(A)(2). Waiver of Issues 578
        § 14-3(A)(3). Plea as to a Lesser Offense 579
        § 14-3(A)(4). Effect of Guilty Plea on Later Proceedings 579
    § 14-3(B). The *Care* Providency Inquiry 580
        § 14-3(B)(1). Advice Regarding Rights 581
        § 14-3(B)(2). Determining the Accuracy of the Plea 582
        § 14-3(B)(3). Determining the Voluntariness of the Plea 587
        § 14-3(B)(4). Admissibility of Accused's Statements 589
    § 14-3(C). The *Green-King* Pretrial Agreement Inquiry 590
    § 14-3(D). Improvident Guilty Pleas 593
        § 14-3(D)(1). In General 593
        § 14-3(D)(2). *Alford* Pleas 593
        § 14-3(D)(3). Misunderstanding of Sentence 593
        § 14-3(D)(4). Factual and Legal Inconsistencies 595
        § 14-3(D)(5). Procedural Consequences of an Improvident Plea 597
    § 14-3(E). Entry of Findings 599
    § 14-3(F). Informing the Members of the Accused's Plea of Guilty 600
    § 14-3(G). Withdrawal of Guilty Plea 602
§ 14-4. Conditional Pleas of Guilty 603
§ 14-5. Irregular Pleas 605
Appendix References 606
Annotated Bibliography 606

CHAPTER 15. TRIAL PROCEDURES 609

Part I. Introduction

§ 15-1. General 610
§ 15-2. The Participants 611
    § 15-2(A). The Accused 611
    § 15-2(B). The Defense Counsel 612

TABLE OF CONTENTS

§ 15-2(B)(1).	In General	613
§ 15-2(B)(2).	Representation of Multiple Accused, and Conflicts of Interest	613
§ 15-2(B)(3).	Ineffective Assistance of Counsel	614
§ 15-2(B)(4).	Defense Counsel and the Perjurious Client	626
§ 15-2(C).	The Trial Counsel	627
§ 15-2(D).	The Military Judge	627
§ 15-2(E).	The Court Members	630
§ 15-2(F).	The Court Reporter	631
§ 15-2(G).	The Interpreter	631
§ 15-3.	Courts-Martial and the Media: Public Trials	632
§ 15-4.	Motions at Trial	634
§ 15-4(A).	Continuances	634
§ 15-4(B).	Mistrial	635
§ 15-4(C).	Motion for Finding of Not Guilty	637
§ 15-4(D).	Motions for Inquiring Into Accused's Sanity	638
§ 15-5.	Contempts	638
§ 15-6.	Trial Procedure Guides — Uniform Rules of Practice	640

PART II. PROCEDURES FOR GENERAL AND SPECIAL COURTS-MARTIAL

§ 15-7.	General	640
§ 15-8.	Introduction and Swearing of the Participants	641
§ 15-9.	Assembly of the Court	642
§ 15-10.	Voir Dire and Challenges of Court Members	643
§ 15-10(A).	Voir Dire of Court Members	643
§ 15-10(B).	Grounds for Challenging Court Members	647
§ 15-10(C).	Challenges of Court Members	653
§ 15-10(C)(1).	Challenge of the Selection Process	653
§ 15-10(C)(2).	Challenges for Cause	655
§ 15-10(C)(3).	Peremptory Challenges	657
§ 15-11.	Opening Statements	660
§ 15-12.	Presentation of the Cases-in-Chief	660
§ 15-12(A).	Examination of the Witnesses	661
§ 15-12(B).	Questions by the Court	662
§ 15-12(C).	Exhibits	663
§ 15-12(D).	Views and Inspections of Places and Objects	664
§ 15-13.	Closing Arguments	664
§ 15-14.	Instructions to the Court Members	669
§ 15-14(A).	General	669
§ 15-14(B).	*Sua Sponte* Instructions	672
§ 15-14(C).	Instructions Upon Request	675
§ 15-14(D).	Review of Instructions Errors	676
§ 15-15.	Deliberations	677
§ 15-16.	Verdict; Announcement of Findings	679
§ 15-16(A).	General Findings	679

§ 15-16(B). Impeaching the Findings 682
§ 15-16(C). Special Findings by the Military Judge 683
§ 15-17. Sentencing Procedures 684

Part III. Evidentiary Rules

§ 15-18. General 684
§ 15-19. Military Rules of Evidence 685
§ 15-20. Presumptions and Inferences 686
§ 15-21. Stipulations 687
§ 15-22. Depositions 689
§ 15-23. Objections and Preserving Error 690
§ 15-24. Evidentiary Instructions During Trial 690

Part IV. Summary Courts-Martial Procedures

§ 15-25. General 691
§ 15-26. The Summary Court-Martial Participants 692
§ 15-26(A). The Summary Court-Martial Officer 692
§ 15-26(B). The Accused 692
§ 15-26(C). Counsel 692
§ 15-27. Pretrial Conference 693
§ 15-28. Trial on the Merits and Sentencing 693
§ 15-29. Post-Trial Procedures 694
Appendix References 695
Annotated Bibliography 695

CHAPTER 16. SENTENCING 703
§ 16-1. In General 703
§ 16-2. Maximum Authorized Punishments 704
§ 16-2(A). Jurisdictional Limits on the Sentence 704
§ 16-2(B). Nature of Proceeding as Limitation 705
§ 16-2(C). Manual for Courts-Martial Limitations 706
§ 16-2(D). Multiplicity 707
§ 16-2(E). Escalator Provisions 708
§ 16-2(F). "Footnote Five" Limitations 709
§ 16-2(G). Equivalent Punishments 710
§ 16-3. Permissible Punishments 711
§ 16-3(A). Death Penalty 711
§ 16-3(B). Punitive Separations 715
§ 16-3(C). Deprivation of Liberty 715
§ 16-3(D). Deprivation of Pay 716
§ 16-3(E). Reduction in Grade 718
§ 16-3(F). Loss of Numbers 719
§ 16-3(G). Reprimand 719
§ 16-4. Sentencing Procedures 719
§ 16-4(A). In General 719

	§ 16-4(B).	Applicability of Rules of Evidence	720
§ 16-5.	Prosecution Evidence		721
	§ 16-5(A).	Data From the Charge Sheet	722
	§ 16-5(B).	Data Concerning the Accused's Prior Service	722
	§ 16-5(C).	Evidence of Prior Convictions	725
	§ 16-5(D).	Evidence in Aggravation	727
	§ 16-5(D)(1).	In General	727
	§ 16-5(D)(2).	Evidence of Circumstances Surrounding Offenses	729
	§ 16-5(D)(3).	Evidence of Impact of Offense on Victim and Community	730
	§ 16-5(D)(4).	Evidence Addressing Rehabilitative Potential	732
	§ 16-5(D)(5).	Evidence of Uncharged Misconduct	735
§ 16-6.	Defense Evidence		738
§ 16-7.	Rebuttal and Surrebuttal		741
§ 16-8.	Arguments on Sentencing		742
	§ 16-8(A).	In General	742
	§ 16-8(B).	Prosecution Arguments on Sentencing	743
	§ 16-8(C).	Defense Counsel's Argument on Sentencing	746
§ 16-9.	Instructions on Sentencing		748
§ 16-10.	Deliberations on Sentencing		751
§ 16-11.	Announcement of the Sentence		753
§ 16-12.	Advice on Appellate Rights		755
§ 16-13.	Adjournment		757
Appendix References			758
Annotated Bibliography			758

CHAPTER 17. REVIEW OF COURTS-MARTIAL 763

Part I. General

§ 17-1.	Introduction		764
§ 17-2.	Post-Trial Duties of Counsel		765
	§ 17-2(A).	Trial Counsel's Duties	765
	§ 17-2(B).	Defense Counsel's Duties	765
	§ 17-2(B)(1).	Advice on Appellate Rights	766
	§ 17-2(B)(2).	Request for Deferment of Confinement, Forfeiture of Pay and Reduction in Grade	767
	§ 17-2(B)(3).	Submission of Matters to the Convening Authority	769
	§ 17-2(B)(4).	Review of the Staff Judge Advocate's Post-Trial Recommendation	773
§ 17-3.	Post-Trial Proceedings		774
	§ 17-3(A).	Revision Proceedings	775
	§ 17-3(B).	Article 39(a) Post-Trial Sessions	776

§ 17-4.	Records of Trial	778
	§ 17-4(A). Authentication of the Record	781
	§ 17-4(B). Service of Record on Accused	782
§ 17-5.	Confinement Pending Review	783
§ 17-6.	Military Corrections	784

PART II. INITIAL REVIEW BY THE CONVENING AUTHORITY

§ 17-7.	Introduction	784
§ 17-8.	Legal Review of Courts-Martial	785
	§ 17-8(A). General Matters	785
	§ 17-8(B). Post-Trial Recommendation	786
	§ 17-8(B)(1). Format and Contents of Recommendation	788
	§ 17-8(B)(2). Defective Recommendations	791
	§ 17-8(B)(3). Service of Recommendation on Defense Counsel	793
§ 17-9.	Convening Authority's Powers	796
	§ 17-9(A). General Matters	796
	§ 17-9(B). Qualified and Disqualified Convening Authorities	800
	§ 17-9(C). Actions and Execution of Sentences	802
	§ 17-9(D). Power to Suspend	803
	§ 17-9(E). Other Clemency Powers	805
§ 17-10.	Promulgating Orders	806
§ 17-11.	Post-Trial Delays	806

PART III. APPELLATE REVIEW

§ 17-12.	General	808
§ 17-13.	Waiver or Withdrawal of Appeals	808
§ 17-14.	Appellate Counsel	810
§ 17-15.	United States Courts of Criminal Appeals	812
	§ 17-15(A). Jurisdiction	813
	§ 17-15(B). Scope of Review and Actions	814
	§ 17-15(C). Procedural Rules	817
§ 17-16.	The United States Court of Appeals for the Armed Forces	818
	§ 17-16(A). General	818
	§ 17-16(B). Jurisdiction	819
	§ 17-16(C). Scope of Review	820
	§ 17-16(D). Procedures	821
§ 17-17.	Review by the Supreme Court of the United States	821

PART IV. OTHER FORMS OF REVIEW

§ 17-18.	General	823
§ 17-19.	Extraordinary Writs in the Military Courts	823
§ 17-20.	Review in the Offices of the Judge Advocates General	828

TABLE OF CONTENTS

§ 17-21. Petition for New Trial	829
§ 17-22. Administrative Relief	831
§ 17-22(A). Boards for the Correction of Military Records	831
§ 17-22(B). Discharge Review Boards	832
§ 17-23. Review in the Federal Courts	832
§ 17-23(A). In General	832
§ 17-23(B). The Exhaustion of Remedies Requirement	833
§ 17-23(C). Forms of Collateral Review	834
§ 17-23(C)(1). Habeas Corpus	835
§ 17-23(C)(2). *Mandamus*	835
Appendix References	836
Annotated Bibliography	936

Appendices	845
Table of Cases	999
Index	1183

CHAPTER 1

THE MILITARY CRIMINAL JUSTICE SYSTEM

PART I
INTRODUCTION

§ 1-1.   A Separate System: Justice or Discipline?
    § 1-1(A).   Constitutional Underpinnings.
    § 1-1(B).   Military Due Process: The Hierarchy.
§ 1-2.   Using This Book.
    § 1-2(A).   A Foreword.
    § 1-2(B).   Frontal Analysis.
    § 1-2(C).   Discussion.
    § 1-2(D).   Annotated Bibliography.
    § 1-2(E).   Glossary.
    § 1-2(F).   Appendices.
§ 1-3.   Researching Military Criminal Law Issues.
    § 1-3(A).   The Uniform Code of Military Justice (UCMJ).
    § 1-3(B).   The Manual for Courts-Martial, United States: The MCM.
    § 1-3(C).   Service Supplements to the MCM.
    § 1-3(D).   Military Case Law.
        § 1-3(D)(1).   Court-Martial Reports.
        § 1-3(D)(2).   Military Justice Reporter.
        § 1-3(D)(3).   Citator.
    § 1-3(E).   Military Legal Periodicals.

PART II
HISTORICAL ROOTS OF THE COURT-MARTIAL

§ 1-4.   The Early European Models.
§ 1-5.   The British System.
    § 1-5(A).   General.
    § 1-5(B).   The Court of Chivalry: The Constable's Court.
    § 1-5(C).   The "Council of War."
    § 1-5(D).   The Mutiny Act.
§ 1-6.   The American Court-Martial.
    § 1-6(A).   The Formative Years: 1775 to 1800.
    § 1-6(B).   The Period From 1800 to 1900: Quiet Growth.
    § 1-6(C).   From 1900 to Present: Rapid Change.

PART III
THE PRESENT SYSTEM: A PROLOGUE

§ 1-7.   An Overview.
§ 1-8.   The Commander's Options: Prosecutorial Discretion.
    § 1-8(A).   General.
    § 1-8(B).   Nonpunitive Measures.
    § 1-8(C).   Nonjudicial Punishment.
    § 1-8(D).   Court-Martial.
        § 1-8(D)(1).   Summary Court-Martial.
        § 1-8(D)(2).   Special Court-Martial.
        § 1-8(D)(3).   General Court-Martial.

Appendix References.
Annotated Bibliography.

Part I

Introduction

§ 1-1. A Separate System: Justice or Discipline?

During discussions on military justice, the conversation will occasionally turn to queries concerning the justice, or lack thereof, for servicemembers tried by a court-martial. And occasionally the more celebrated courts-martial of General Billy Mitchell,[1] Lieutenant William Calley,[2] Private Eddie Slovick,[3] Private Robert Garwood,[4] or more recently, the trial of Michael New,[5] will be referred to in support of, or rejection of, any number of arguments for and against the military criminal legal system. Often lost in the discussion is the breadth of the military justice system. These few widely publicized and analyzed courts-martial draw the public's attention for only a brief time to a separate system of justice — a system mandated by Congress and recognized by the United States Supreme Court as legitimately unique.[6]

---

1. General Mitchell, a strong advocate of air power, was tried and convicted by a general court-martial in 1926 for being critical of War Department policies. Major General Douglas McArthur sat as a member on the court that convicted Mitchell.
2. Accused of killing unarmed Vietnamese civilians in the village of My Lai, Republic of South Vietnam, Calley was tried and convicted by general court-martial at Fort Benning, Georgia. His conviction was affirmed first in the military appellate courts and then in the federal court system. *See* United States v. Calley, 22 C.M.A. 534, 48 C.M.R. 19 (1973); Calley v. Callaway, 519 F.2d 184 (5th Cir. 1975), *cert. denied*, 425 U.S. 911 (1976). *See generally* Calley, *Lieutenant Calley: His Own Story* (1971); Greenhaw, *The Making of a Hero: The Story of Lieutenant William Calley, Jr.* (1971); Hammer, *The Court-Martial of William Calley* (1971). Addicott & Hudson, "The Twenty-Fifth Anniversary of My Lai: A Time to Inculcate the Lessons," 139 MIL. L. REV. 153 (1993).
3. Private Slovick was court-martialled and executed by a firing squad in France, 1945, for desertion. An account of his case is recounted in Huie, *The Execution of Private Slovick* (1970).
4. United States v. Garwood, 16 M.J. 863 (N.M.C.M.R. 1983), *aff'd*, 20 M.J. 148 (C.M.A. 1985), *cert. denied*, 106 S. Ct. 524 (1985). Garwood, who had served as a servicemember in Vietnam, was convicted in February 1981 of aiding the enemy (Art. 104) and misconduct as a prisoner (Art. 105). Charges of unauthorized absence (Art. 86), desertion (Art. 85), and solicitation (Art. 82) were dismissed at the trial level. His conviction was affirmed by the Navy-Marine Corps Court of Military Review.
5. New was court-martialled in Germany in 1996 for refusing an order to don United Nations insignia and markings when his unit was deployed on a peace-keeping mission. He argued unsuccessfully before the trial court that the order was illegal because he had taken an oath to defend and support the United States Constitution, not the United Nations Charter. The case received significant sympathetic treatment from conservative members of Congress and the media.
6. *See, e.g.*, Middendorf v. Henry, 425 U.S. 25 (1976); Chappell v. Wallace, 462 U.S. 296 (1983). For a general discussion of the separate and unique nature of military justice, *see* United States v. Newak, 15 M.J. 541 (A.F.C.M.R. 1982) (Miller, J., concurring). *Cf.* Fidell, "If a Tree Falls in the Forest — Publication and Digesting Policies and the Potential Contribution of Military Courts to American Law," 22 JAG J. 1 (1983).

Some have expressed the concern that military justice is becoming even more "civilianized" by adoption of rules used in the civilian system of criminal justice. For example, in United States v. Ralston, 24 M.J. 709 (A.C.M.R. 1987), the court concluded that under the facts the accused could agree as part of a plea bargain to waive a trial by court members. The appendix to the courts opinion includes the following observation by Judge Raby:

This unique legal system is among those few systems that do not look to the civilian courts to dispose of military justice problems. The system is separate: separate crimes, procedures, and sanctions.

The reasons for a separate system are primarily grounded on the rationale that world-wide deployment of large numbers of military personnel with unique disciplinary requirements mandates a flexible, separate jurisprudence capable of operating in times of peace or conflict. When confronted with arguments from a convicted servicemember that the military justice system was incompatible with the Fifth Amendment guarantee of due process and that no justification existed for a separate system, the Court of Appeals for the District of Columbia stated:

> The need for national defense mandates an armed force whose discipline and readiness is not unnecessarily undermined by the often deliberately cumbersome concepts of civilian jurisprudence. Yet, the dictates of individual liberty clearly require some check on military authority in the conduct of courts-martial. The provisions of the Uniform Code of Military Justice with respect to court-martial proceedings represent a congressional attempt to accommodate the interests of justice, on the one hand, with the demands for an efficient, well-disciplined military, on the other.[7]

The uniqueness of the military's system of criminal law is often erroneously equated with an inflexible, archaic system of justice.[8] In fact, the military system has been innovative in many areas of criminal law and in many respects provides greater protection for an accused than does the civilian system.

The flavor of a rigid military criminal practice is no doubt left in part by a passing view of myriad statutes and regulations governing the military. However, those same statutes and regulations, when properly applied, present a flexible, yet highly predictable, system that moves quickly and efficiently.

Skepticism toward military criminal justice is also generated by a general distrust of things military, especially discipline. Indeed, the term "military

---

> [I] wish to muse whether we gatekeepers of military law are not inadvertently finding more and more novel ways in which gradually to ease line officers and commanders out of the military system — moving it ever closer to the civilian justice model. Quarere: If this trend continues, could we reach a point, in futuro, where the military justice system is no longer unique, and thus is no longer necessary?

Assuming that Judge Raby is correct and that the military justice system is becoming civilianized and no longer unique, it does not necessarily follow that it would become unnecessary. That is, the fact that military procedures are modeled after civilian rules does not mean that civilian authorities would manage the military justice system. For some additional comments on the issue of "civilianization," see Cox, "The Army, The Courts, and The Evolution of Military Justice," 118 MIL. L. REV. 1, 28-30 (1987).

7. Curry v. Secretary of Army, 595 F.2d 873, 877 (D.C. Cir. 1979) (footnotes omitted).

8. *See generally* Schlueter, "Military Justice in the 1990s: A Legal System Looking for Respect," 133 MIL. L. REV. 1 (1991) (noting several reasons why military justice is often viewed with suspicion).

justice" has been labeled an "oxymoron"[9] — the apparent reference to the fact that military discipline and justice are inconsistent dimensions, not unlike the oft-debated concept of citizen soldiers. But the concepts of discipline and justice are not inconsistent. True, the strength of the military depends heavily on disciplined individuals ready to fight and win wars.[10] In *United States ex rel. Toth v. Quarles*,[11] the Supreme Court observed:

> [I]t is the primary business of armies and navies to fight or be ready to fight wars should the occasion arise. But trial of soldiers to maintain discipline is merely incidental to an army's primary fighting function. To the extent that those responsible for performance of this primary function are diverted from it by the necessity of trying cases, the basic fighting purpose of armies is not served.... [M]ilitary tribunals have not been and probably never can be constituted in such a way that they can have the same kind of qualifications that the Constitution has deemed essential to fair trials of civilians in federal courts.

But a criminal system that metes out sanctions for both major and minor delicts, some of which are not recognized in the civilian legal systems, must also do so with procedures that accord due process. The fact that the procedures seem foreign, rigid, mechanical, or even unfair, does not detract from the fact that due process is afforded and in many cases now reflects current federal criminal practices.[12]

The question of whether military justice is primarily a discipline tool or a means of dispensing justice has been long debated. Interestingly, Paragraph 3 of the Preamble to the 1984 *Manual* recognizes the dual purposes of military justice and lists first the function of "justice":

> 3. Nature and purpose of military law.
>
> Military law consists of the statutes governing the military establishment and regulations issued thereunder, the constitutional powers of the President and regulations issued thereunder, and the inherent authority of military commanders. Military law includes jurisdiction exercised by courts-martial and the jurisdiction exercised by commanders with respect to nonjudicial punishment. *The purpose of military law is to promote efficiency and effectiveness in the military establishment, and thereby to strengthen the national security of the United States* (emphasis added).

---

9. *See* Spak, "Military Justice: The Oxymoron of the 1980s," 20 CAL. W.L. REV. 436 (1984).

10. *See* United States Navy-Marine Corps Court of Military Review v. Carlucci, 26 M.J. 328, 333 (C.M.A. 1988) (a major objective of the military justice system is to obtain obedience by subordinates to orders of their superiors).

Cf. R. Rivkin, *GI Rights and Army Justice: The Serviceman's Guide to Military Life and Law*, 336-38 (1970) (studies indicate that in combat setting the fear of punishment is not a significant motivation).

11. 350 U.S. 11, 17 (1955).

12. See the Introduction to the Drafters' Analysis for the 1984 Manual for Courts-Martial, which indicates that the new *Manual* was intended to adopt as much of the federal criminal procedure rules as possible — and yet recognize the unique requirements of military justice.

In a Report to the Secretary of the Army in 1960 on the status of the UCMJ (The Powell Report), the Committee (composed of distinguished high-ranking Army officers) noted at 11, 12:

> Discipline — a state of mind which leads to a willingness to obey an order no matter how unpleasant or dangerous the task to be performed — is not a characteristic of a civilian community. Development of this state of mind among soldiers is a command responsibility and a necessity. In the development of discipline, correction of individuals is indispensable; in correction, fairness or justice is indispensable. Thus, it is a mistake to talk of balancing discipline and justice — the two are inseparable....

> Once a case is before a court-martial it should be realized by all concerned that the sole concern is to accomplish justice under the law. This does not mean justice as determined by the commander referring a case or by anyone not duly constituted to fulfill a judicial role. It is not proper to say that a military court-martial has a dual function as an instrument of discipline and as an instrument of justice. It is an instrument of justice and in fulfilling this function it will promote discipline.

Still another factor bears heavily on the perception of military justice: the role of the commander in the process. Although a number of changes over the years have limited the ability of the commander to orchestrate the entire military justice process, the specter of unlawful command influence raises its ugly head every few years. There should be no doubt that deliberate efforts to dictate the verdict or sentence of a court-martial are extremely rare. The more common incident arises where a commander in good faith, often with the considered advice of a judge advocate, passes along otherwise neutral observations about military justice and thereby sets in motion a chain of command responses that might very well result in a subordinate taking steps that he feels the "general" wants implemented. Although the outcome of any particular trial might not be affected in the least, the appearance of the evil alone is enough to reinforce the stereotypical observation, "typical military justice." The problem of command influence is discussed in more detail in Chapter 6.

However one views military criminal justice, this separate system, the fact of its constitutional legitimacy cannot be denied.

§ 1-1(A). Constitutional Underpinnings.

As discussed in succeeding sections that address the historical roots of the court-martial, the United States Constitution makes specific provision for rules and regulations governing military justice. For example, a number of the enumerated powers delegated to Congress in Article I address the authority to enact laws affecting armies, a Navy, and the militia.[13] In addition, Article II addresses the powers of the President, as Commander in Chief. The

---

13. *See* U.S. CONST., art. 1, § 8.

President is authorized, *inter alia*, to govern the armed forces and execute whatever laws Congress passes concerning conflicts and wars.[14] In reading the applicable constitutional provisions it must not be forgotten that the drafters were not writing in a vacuum; there was extant a code of military justice in the form of Articles of War that had been used during the Revolution.[15] Although these constitutional provisions are fundamental, as with many other areas of constitutional jurisprudence they only provide a sketchy guide for, and limitations on, military justice. The implementing role of the Constitution in relation to military due process is addressed in the next section.

§ 1-1(B). Military Due Process: The Hierarchy.

The concept of "military due process" is probably a misnomer [16] to the extent that it suggests that the due process outlined in the Fifth and Fourteenth Amendments of the Constitution has no relevance to military justice.[17] In the

---

14. *See* U.S. CONST., Art. 2.
15. *See* § 1-6(A).
16. *See* § 1 United States v. Kelly, 41 M.J. 833 (N.M.Ct.Crim.App. 1995) (en banc) (military due process is not a source of military law nor is it common law or natural law concept; it was a term coined by Court of Military Appeals to describe pattern of rights created by Congress in U.C.M.J. and as a means to determine when remedy was required; court said that before military due process may be applied, it must be shown that act of Congress, which grants fundamental right to an accused has been violated or that the government has engaged in outrageous conduct which gives rise to the functional equivalent of a recognized defense).
17. *See* United States v. Berrey, 28 M.J. 714 (N.M.C.M.R. 1989) (en banc), where the court concluded that intentional delay in notifying the accused of charges against him violated "military due process." The court indicated that showing a denial of military due process requires two elements: first, the accused must establish that Congress has granted a fundamental right; and second, that right was denied during the course of the trial. *Id.* at 717, *citing* United States v. Jerasi, 20 M.J. 719 (N.M.C.M.R. 1985), *aff'd*, 23 M.J. 162 (C.M.A. 1986). In a lengthy dissent, Judge Jones addressed the issue of military due process and the requirement of finding prejudice.

The very concept of due process is elusive. A rule violates substantive due process if its content, its effect, does not bear a reasonable or fair relationship to the object sought to be regulated. In the context of criminal procedure, the test is usually one of measuring whether the procedures used to deprive an accused of life, liberty, or property are fair. At a minimum, in a civilian setting, that usually requires notice of the accusations, right to counsel, and an opportunity to be heard. But the exact measure of procedural due process is flexible and more closely approximates a balancing of three interests:

> First, the private interest that will be affected by the official action; second, the risk of an erroneous deprivation of such interest through procedures used, and the probative value, in any, of additional or substitute procedural safeguards; and finally, the Government's interest, including the function involved, and the fiscal and administrative burdens that the additional or substitute procedural requirements would entail.

Illinois v. Batchelder, 463 U.S. 1112, 1117 (1983), *citing* Matthews v. Eldridge, 424 U.S. 319, 335 (1976). However, in United States v. Weiss, 114 S. Ct. 752 (1994), the Supreme Court indicated that the foregoing *Matthews* test was inapplicable in the military context. The applicable test, said the Court, is found in Middendorf v. Henry, 425 U.S. 25 (1976) where the question is whether the factors militating in favor of a particular right are so extraordinarily weighty as to overcome the balance struck by Congress.

114 S. Ct. at 761.

past that may have been the case. It was not always well-settled that the Constitution applied with equal vigor to military proceedings.[18] But the term is probably useful to the extent that it describes a sort of hierarchy of authority for those charged with dispensing military justice and protections for the individual servicemember.

As noted in § 1-1(A), the Constitution serves as the foundation for military justice. Relying upon its powers, both delegated and "necessary and proper,"[19] Congress has enacted the Uniform Code of Military Justice (U.C.M.J.),[20] and a variety of other statutes that govern the armed forces. That Code, applicable to all of the armed forces, in turn not only sets out certain procedural prerequisites and protections, but it also authorizes the President to prescribe more detailed rules governing pretrial, trial, and post-trial procedures.[21]

The President in turn has promulgated the Manual for Courts-Martial (MCM), which sets out specific Rules for Courts-Martial (R.C.M.), maximum punishments, and rules for imposition of nonjudicial punishment. The President has also delegated to the armed forces limited authority to promulgate regulations further implementing the *Manual*[22] and any other executive rules and regulations created through the President's role as Commander in Chief.[23]

The Constitution, which sets in motion a system of military criminal justice, also contains specified limitations on government infringement of individual rights. Military due process, as it is applied today, recognizes that the protections of the Constitution generally apply with equal force to servicemembers[24] and that the U.C.M.J., the Manual for Courts-Martial, and service regulations may provide greater protections than the Constitution.[25] If any of these three sources conflict with the Constitution and provide less protection, the burden rests upon the government to justify the different treat-

---

18. *See generally* Henderson, "Courts-Martial and the Constitution: The Original Understanding," 71 HARV. L. REV. 293 (1957); Quinn, "The United States Court of Military Appeals and Military Due Process," 35 ST. JOHN'S L. REV. 225 (1961) (author, formerly a member of the Court of Military Appeals, traces development of military due process and observes that the Constitution is only the starting point in determining what process is due a military accused). *See also* "Military Due Process: What Is It?," 6 VAND. L. REV. 251 (1953).

Additional materials addressing this issue are noted in the annotated bibliography at the end of this chapter.

19. U.S. CONST., art. 1-8, cl. 18.
20. 10 U.S.C. 801-940. *See also* § 1-3(A) and Appendix 3.
21. *See* Art. 36, U.C.M.J. *See* Loving v. United States, 116 S. Ct. 1737 (1996) (discussion of delegation of authority to President).
22. *See, e.g.,* MCM, Part IV, para. 2, which authorizes the service secretaries to prescribe the limit on imposition of nonjudicial punishment.
23. As Commander in Chief, the President should be able to rely upon his inherent rule-making powers, implied in the Constitution, to promulgate a wide range of rules and regulations governing the armed forces, as long as he does not entrench upon other specific powers of the Congress.
24. *See* Warren, "The Bill of Rights and the Military," 37 N.Y.U. L. REV. 181 (1962).
25. *See, e.g.,* United States v. Eshalomi, 23 M.J. 12 (C.M.A. 1986); United States v. Douglas, 1 M.J. 354 (C.M.A. 1976); United States v. Jacoby, 11 C.M.A. 428, 29 C.M.R. 244 (1960).

ment.[26] On the other hand, if they provide greater protection, the military courts are bound to extend the greater protection — absent changes to those sources of due process.[27] This coverage of protections is not unlike the ability of states to extend greater protection through their constitutions than is provided in the federal constitution.[28]

There is a final ingredient to military due process — military common law. Military courts, a term that includes not only courts-martial, but also the Courts of Criminal Appeals and the Court of Appeals for the Armed Forces, have over the years interpreted and created due process rights, some of which have been codified.[29]

The military courts, both trial and appellate, provide an important function not fully realized under prior codes. The current courts generally view themselves as having an important responsibility for filling gaps otherwise not addressed by the Code, the *Manual*, or regulations. Thus, they do more than simply interpret the meaning of the applicable rules. In many instances, they are called upon to address, in some cases in the first instance, the constitutionality of a procedure or rule not found in any of those main sources. To that extent, the Supreme Court's observation that military tribunals are incapable of dealing with the nice subtleties of constitutional law no longer remains valid.[30]

But a sort of tension exists because the President or Congress may attempt to limit judicial precedent through redrafting the U.C.M.J.[31] or the *Manual*.[32] The military courts may attempt to avoid the impact of a provision by concluding that *stare decisis*, not the *Manual*, dictates a particular result.[33] What

---

26. *See* Courtney v. Williams, 1 M.J. 267 (C.M.A. 1976).

27. This, of course, assumes that the President's changes to the *Manual* or Congress' changes to the U.C.M.J. comport with the Constitution.

28. *See generally* Schlueter, "Federalism and Supreme Court Review of Expansive State Court Decisions: A Response to Unfortunate Impressions," 11 HAST. CON. L.Q. 523 (1984).

29. *See, e.g.*, R.C.M. 707(d) which partially codifies the 90-day speedy trial rule first set out in United States v. Burton, 21 C.M.A. 112, 44 C.M.R. 166 (1971); *See also infra* § 13-3(C).

30. *See* O'Callaghan v. Parker, 395 U.S. 258, 265 (1969) (courts-martial as an institution are singularly inept in dealing with the nice subtleties of constitutional law). For further discussion of the *O'Callaghan* case and its progeny, see Chapter 4.

31. *See* § 4-5(A)(3), which addresses the 1979 amendment to Art. 2, U.C.M.J., which was intended to overrule military case law that had voided certain enlistments involving recruiter malpractice.

32. *See, e.g.*, R.C.M. 1001(b)(2), which governs the admissibility of prosecution sentencing evidence and which was drafted in a manner intended to limit the effect of United States v. Morgan, 15 M.J. 128 (C.M.A. 1983), which in the drafters' view promoted "gamesmanship." R.C.M. 1001(b)(2) Analysis.

33. United States v. Postle, 20 M.J. 632 (N.M.C.M.R. 1985) (in lengthy dicta the court ignored the clear mandate of Rule 315, Military Rules of Evidence, governing the definition of probable cause in favor of the Supreme Court's most recent ruling on the issue).

The Drafters of the *Manual* have included in the introduction to their Analysis a reminder of the binding effect of rules promulgated by the President:

[T]he user is reminded that the amendment of the *Manual* is the province of the President. Developments in the civilian sector that affect the underlying rationale for a rule do not affect the validity of the rule except to the extent otherwise required as a matter of statutory

the due process hierarchy dictates is that the more protective of the due process sources (the Constitution, the U.C.M.J., the *Manual,* the regulations, or military case law) must prevail.[34] In this way, the military justice system will be applied in a consistent, and more importantly, fair fashion. What seems clear is that the niggardly or slipshod application of protections accorded by military due process, whatever the source, does little to promote respect for a system that has always been considered suspect. Indeed, such applications usually only reinforce the notion that military tribunals will interpret the rules in such a way that the offender is disciplined, if necessary, at the cost of justice. Military criminal justice deserves better.

§ 1-2. Using This Book.

§ 1-2(A). A Foreword.

This book addresses the basics of the court-martial process. Emphasis is placed upon the practical aspects of handling criminal justice problems. The sequence of materials, with minor exceptions, follows the flow of a case from pretrial investigation through appellate disposition. Readers will not find a general treatise on "military law" that encompasses many other areas such as military applications of administrative, contract, and international law. The subject here is criminal law, specifically the procedural facets of court-martial practice. Related military justice topics are addressed, however. For example, chapters on non-judicial punishment and military crimes are included. The former is closely tied with court-martial practices, and the latter provides a brief review of those crimes without civilian counterparts. The following sections briefly highlight features of the book that should assist the reader in quickly locating treatment of a particular topic, and either finding the answer or discovering a source that can give the answer.

§ 1-2(B). Frontal Analysis.

At the beginning of each chapter, a frontal analysis provides the reader with a quick reference tool. By scanning this analysis, a particular topic may be quickly located and its relationship with related topics realized. To assist the reader, each major area has been divided into as many topics and subtopics as possible.

---

or constitutional law. The same is true with respect to rules derived from the decisions of military tribunals. Once incorporated into the Executive Order, such matters have an independent source of authority and are not dependent upon continued support from the judiciary.

34. United States v. Marrie, 39 M.J. 993 (A.F.C.M.R. 1994) (if rule of procedure conflicts with U.C.M.J., the latter controls).

§ 1-2(C). Discussion.

The text of each chapter contains a discussion of key points of military practice. Extensive footnoted references to applicable statutes, service regulations, manuals, and cases are intended to serve as a guide for additional research. In many instances, only the latest or most illustrative decision or provision is noted.

§ 1-2(D). Annotated Bibliography.

An annotated bibliography of selected books and periodicals appears at the end of each chapter. In many situations, the bibliography should direct the reader to more detailed discussions of topics that are only briefly addressed in the text.

§ 1-2(E). Glossary.

A glossary of military and military justice terms is included at Appendix 2. In addition, the text and footnotes include parenthetical explanations of terms and abbreviations. A separate list of abbreviations is at Appendix 1.

§ 1-2(F). Appendices.

In the appendices, the reader can find appropriate forms, guides, rules, and tables. In addition to the normal table of appendices, the reader will find at the end of each chapter an Appendix Reference list that will identify appropriate forms, tables, rules, and guides. In most instances, only exemplar forms or tables are included. Although the appendices were included on the basis of overall usefulness to readers, the fact that one form is included while another is omitted does not mean that it is of any greater value.

§ 1-3. Researching Military Criminal Law Issues.

Although researching a military criminal law question is in effect no different than the research required for any criminal law problem, the available references should be noted. Discussion here centers on the brief notation of each reference, or category of references; they serve not only as future research aids, but also as a further introduction to this book, which will cite liberally from each reference.

§ 1-3(A). The Uniform Code of Military Justice (UCMJ).

The indispensable skeletal framework, the U.C.M.J., is the starting point in any analysis of military criminal law issues. The U.C.M.J., found at 10 U.S.C.A. § 801-946, is included as an appendix in this book.[1] It is also at

---

1. *See* Appendix 3.

Appendix 2 to the Manual for Courts-Martial (see § 1-3(B) *infra*). Because almost all military law issues find some connection to this rather comprehensive statute, research of those issues may appropriately begin with an examination of its provisions.

§ 1-3(B). The Manual for Courts-Martial, United States: The MCM.

A significant recent change in military criminal law was the promulgation of the Manual for Courts-Martial (MCM), which was prescribed by Executive Order 12473 (13 Apr. 1984) pursuant to the President's authority under Article 36, U.C.M.J.[2] The *Manual,* which implements the U.C.M.J. and applies to all of the services, replaced the 1969 Manual for Courts-Martial. The 1969 *Manual* had been organized into twenty-nine chapters, and citations were to paragraphs.

The 1984 revision of the *Manual* was effective August 1, 1984 and consists of four parts. Part I is the Preamble and briefly states the sources of military jurisdiction, the exercise of that jurisdiction,[3] and the structure of the *Manual.* Part II is the largest portion and consists of the Rules for Courts-Martial (cited as R.C.M.). The R.C.M. are divided into thirteen chapters that prescribe the procedures for courts-martial and are organized in the chronology of a trial, i.e., pretrial processing through appellate review. The Rules are binding,[4] but the "Discussion" that accompanies each Rule is not binding.[5] Instead, it is designed to provide more guidance on implementing the Rules. The Discussion portions are not part of the implementing executive order, *supra,* and may be changed from time to time to reflect changes in applicable law.

The Military Rules of Evidence are located in Part III of the 1984 *Manual.* (They were formerly included in Chapter 27 of the 1969 *Manual*). They are cited as M.R.E. or MIL. R. EVID. The Rules are discussed in more detail in Chapter 15.

Part IV includes discussion of the punitive articles (Articles 77 to 134). The material in this part is arranged into paragraphs. For each offense, the *Manual* includes discussions of (a) the text of each punitive article, (b) the elements of the offense, (c) an explanation, (d) lesser included offenses, (e) the maximum punishment which may be imposed, and (f) sample specifications.

Nonjudicial punishment procedures (See Chapter 3, *infra*) are laid out in Part V of the *Manual.* Finally, appendices to the *Manual* include a Drafter's Analysis, tables, and forms.

---

2. 10 U.S.C.A. § 836. This provision is discussed in more detail at § 1-7 *infra. See generally* Milhizer & McShane, "Analysis of Change 6 to the 1984 Manual for Courts-Martial," ARMY LAW., May 1994, p. 40.
3. *See also* Chapter 4.
4. *See* United States v. Fisher, 37 M.J. 812 (N.M.C.M.R. 1993) (R.C.M.'s are binding; they are issued by the President pursuant to rule-making authority in Article 36, U.C.M.J.).
5. Manual for Courts-Martial, Part I, Para. 4. United States v. Fisher, 37 M.J. 812 (N.M.C.M.R. 1993).

In May 1995, the formal name of the 1984 Manual for Courts-Martial was changed to simply Manual for Courts-Martial, United States (19xx edition).[6] Any amendments to the *Manual* are no longer referred to as "Changes." Instead, they will simply be identified as *19xx Amendments to the Manual for Courts-Martial, United States.*[7] In 1994, the *Manual* was published as a softcover text, complete with changes 1 through 6.[8] An updated, softbound, version of the *Manual* will be published each year, with the most current amendment, thus ending the long-standing tradition of inserting looseleaf pages for each set of changes in the bulky maroon binder.[9]

Change 7[10] and the 1995 Amendments to the *Manual*[11] were included in the Fall 1995 re-publication of the *Manual.*

The *Manual* may be purchased directly from the Superintendent of Documents, U.S. Government Printing Office, Washington, D.C. 20402.

§ 1-3(C). Service Supplements to the MCM.

The Manual for Courts-Martial has been supplemented by each service to meet its individual needs. The Army turns to Army Regulation 27-10, Legal Services-Military Justice,[12] which covers myriad judicial and nonjudicial matters. The Navy and Marine Corps rely on the *Manual of the Judge Advocate General,*[13] and the Coast Guard looks to its *Military Justice Manual.*[14] AFPD 51-2, *Military Justice,*[15] serves as the Air Force's implementation of the MCM. These foregoing service regulations have the force and effect of law unless they conflict with the U.C.M.J. or MCM.[16] Because court-martial practices and procedures do vary slightly among the services, these individual regulations should be consulted for specific guidance where a variation does occur. Throughout this book references will be made, when necessary, to the individualized rules of each service as expressed in the supplemental regulations.

---

6. *See* Executive Order 12960, May 12, 1995 (change to Preamble of *Manual*).
7. *Id.*
8. The pertinent Executive Orders effecting the changes (now amendments) are included in their entirety at Appendix 23 in the *Manual.*
9. *See generally* Criminal Law Notes, ARMY LAW., Oct. 1994, at 58 (explaining changes in format of *Manual*).
10. *See* Executive Order 12936, Nov. 10, 1994 (effective December 9, 1994). *See generally* Borch, "Analysis of Change 7 to the 1984 Manual for Courts-Martial," ARMY LAW., Jan. 1995, at 22.
11. *See* Executive Order 12960, May 12, 1995. *See generally* Borch, "Analysis of the 1995 Amendments to the Manual for Courts-Martial," ARMY LAW., Apr. 1995, at 19.
12. May be cited as AR 27-10.
13. May be cited as JAGMAN 0101a(1) or JAGMAN A-1-b-(1).
14. Cited as Military Justice Manual (M.J.M.). Note that the Coast Guard is under the control of the Department of Transportation.
15. See also Air Force Instruction 51-202 (April 1994) for procedures used by the Air Force to impose nonjudicial punishment.
16. These regulations are promulgated pursuant to statutory authority authorizing the heads of the various departments to prescribe necessary rules and regulations. 5 U.S.C. § 301 (1988).

§ 1-3(D). Military Case Law.

§ 1-3(D)(1). Court-Martial Reports.

The uniqueness of the military system extends in part to its decisional law, which proves to be an invaluable resource. Although various Boards of Review prior to 1951 prepared unpublished written opinions of appellate dispositions of courts-martial, the formation in 1951 of the United States Court of Military Appeals, now the Court of Appeals for the Armed Forces[17] marked a major step in the development of military case law. The opinions of that court and selected opinions of the service appellate courts[18] were published between 1951 and 1975 by the Lawyers Cooperative Publishing Company in the Court-Martial Reports (C.M.R.).[19] The fifty volumes[20] of headnoted decisions are separately indexed.[21] Each volume contains a table of cases, table of court-martial cases cited, table of orders, laws, and regulations cited, and a topical index.

§ 1-3(D)(2). Military Justice Reporter.

Military decisions are now published (since 1977) in the *Military Justice Reporter* (M.J.), a West Publishing Company publication that employs the West key number system and is styled after the National Reporter System also published by West.[22] Again, all of the Court of Military Appeals (C.M.A.), now the Court of Appeals for the Armed Forces (C.A.A.F.) decisions and selected Courts of Military Review, now the Courts of Criminal Appeals, deci-

---

17. The formation of the Court was included as part of the Act implementing the Uniform Code of Military Justice, 64 Stat. 108 (1950). *See also* Chapter 17 for more information on the Court of Appeals for the Armed Forces, formerly the Court of Military Appeals.
18. The service appellate courts, discussed in Chapter 17, include the Army, Navy-Marine Corps (formerly Navy; N.C.M.R.), Air Force, and Coast Guard Courts of Criminal Appeals. From 1969 until 1994, they were called "Courts of Military Review." Before 1969, they were called "Boards of Review." An Army Board of Review opinion published in 1956 would be cited as follows: United States v. Boyd, 21 C.M.R. 395 (A.B.R. 1956).
19. In addition, the opinions of the United States Court of Military Appeals (C.M.A.) were separately published in the *United States Court of Military Appeals Reports*, Volumes 1-23 (Lawyers Coop.). Citations for those cases would be cited as follows: United States v. Mountain, 20 C.M.A. 319, 43 C.M.R. 159 (1971).
20. Advance Sheets for Volumes 51 and 52 were published but are not readily accessible. Those decisions were, however, included in Volumes 1 and 2 of the Military Justice Reporter (M.J.) discussed at § 1-3(D)(2). Volume 54, C.M.R. (interim) was the military's collection of the Court of Military Appeals decisions. Those decisions are also included in Volumes 1 and 2 of the Military Justice Reporter System.
21. The citator consists of two volumes (Vols. 1-25, 26-50).
22. Typical cites for the Court of Military Appeals and Court of Military Review decisions, before the names of those courts were changed in 1994, were as follows:

CMA: United States v. Fimmano, 8 M.J. 197 (C.M.A. 1980).
Army: United States v. Happel, 5 M.J. 908 (A.C.M.R. 1978).
Air Force: United States v. Lewis, 1 M.J. 904 (A.F.C.M.R. 1976).
Navy-Marine Corps: United States v. Lahman, 12 M.J. 513 (N.M.C.M.R. 1981).
Coast Guard: United States v. Allen, 6 M.J. 633 (C.G.C.M.R. 1978).

sions are included. Volume 1 contains Court of Military Review decisions that were also published in Volume 50 of the *Court-Martial Reports* and interim decisions rendered during the transition to the new reporter system.[23] Each volume of the Reporter includes a table of cases reported, table of military cases cited, table of statutes, rules and regulations construed, words and phrases, and a key number digest.

In 1994, the names of the military appellate courts were changed.[24] The United States Court of Military Appeals became the United States Court of Appeals for the Armed Forces. And the United States Courts of Military Review became the United States Courts of Criminal Appeals. The opinions of those courts are now cited as follows:

> United States Court of Appeals for the Armed Forces:
> United States v. Cage, 42 M.J. 139 (1995).
> United States Air Force Court of Criminal Appeals:
> United States v. Cox, 42 M.J. 647 (A.F.Ct.Crim.App. 1995).
> United States Army Court of Criminal Appeals:
> United States v. Henry, 42 M.J. 593 (Army Ct. Crim. App. 1995).
> United States Coast Guard Court of Criminal Appeals
> United States v. Bernier, 42 M.J. 521 (C.G. Ct. Crim. App. 1995).
> United States Navy-Marine Corps Court of Criminal Appeals:
> United States v. Williamson, 42 M.J. 613 (N.M. Ct. Crim. App. 1995)

§ 1-3(D)(3). Citator.

Shepard's Military Justice Citations, published quarterly, contains a compilation of citations to the various decisions of Appeals and the military courts, the U.C.M.J., the Manual for Courts-Martial, the military court rules,[25] and miscellaneous orders and regulations. It includes citations in the *Military Justice Reporter,* the *Court-Martial Reports,* the *National Reporter System,* the three Supreme Court reporter systems, and the *American Law Reports.*

§ 1-3(E). Military Legal Periodicals.

In addition to numerous military pamphlets and manuals,[26] three legal periodicals published by the Army, Air Force, and Navy provide timely discussion on military criminal law issues. The *Military Law Review,* a quarterly publication, is edited by the Army's Judge Advocate General's School.

---

23. *See supra* note 22.
24. The change was made in Section 924 of the Department of Defense Authorization Act for Fiscal Year 1995, Pub. L. 103-337, 108 Stat. 2663 (1994). The name change was effective October 5, 1994.
25. *See generally* Chapter 17, *infra.*
26. *See, e.g., Analysis of Contents Manual for Courts-Martial,* United States, 1969 (Rev. ed.), DA Pamphlet 27-2 (1970); *Military Justice Handbook — Guide for Summary Court-Martial — Trial Procedure,* DA Pamphlet 27-7 (1973); *Military Judges Benchbook,* DA Pamphlet 27-9 (1982); *Military Justice Handbook — Procedural Guide for Article 32(b) Investigating Officers,* DA Pamphlet 27-17 (1980); *Military Justice — Trial Procedure,* DA Pamphlet 27-173 (1978).

The *Air Force Law Review* (formerly *Air Force JAG Law Review*) is also published quarterly by the United States Air Force Judge Advocate General's School. *The Naval Law Review* (formerly *JAG Journal*) is published by the Judge Advocate General of the Navy. All three publications include discussion of matters in addition to criminal law subjects and may be purchased from the Superintendent of Documents, U.S. Government Printing Office, Washington, D.C. 20402.

Additionally, the Army's Judge Advocate General's School in Charlottesville, Virginia, publishes a monthly periodical entitled ARMY LAW.[27] The Army's Defense Appellate Division formerly published *The Advocate*, a bimonthly periodical containing valuable articles focused on defense issues.[28] And on a quarterly basis, the Air Force office of the Judge Advocate General publishes *The Reporter*, which includes military criminal law articles.[29]

PART II

HISTORICAL ROOTS OF THE COURT-MARTIAL

§ 1-4. The Early European Models.

The roots of the court-martial run deep.[1] They predate written military codes designed to bring order and discipline to an armed, sometimes barbarous, fighting force. Although some form of enforcement of discipline has always been a part of every military system, for our purposes we trace the roots only as far back as the Roman system.

In the Roman armies, justice was normally dispensed by the *magistri militum* or by the legionary tribunes who acted either as sole judges or with the assistance of councils.[2] The punishable offenses included cowardice, mutiny, desertion, and doing violence to a superior. While these offenses or their permutations have been carried forward to contemporary settings, many of the punishments imposed upon the guilty have long since been abandoned: decimation, denial of sepulture, maiming, and exposure to the elements. Other punishments remain, such as dishonorable discharge.[3] The Roman model was no doubt employed or observed by the later continental armies and is credited by most commentators as the template for later military codes. For

---

27. Individual issues and subscriptions are available through the Government Printing Office.

28. The articles now appear as a regular feature in ARMY LAW., along with articles of interest to military prosecutors.

29. Subscriptions and single copies may be obtained through the Government Printing Office.

1. The discussion of the courts-martial historical roots is an abridged version of an article written by the author and published at 87 MIL. L. REV. 129 (1980). Because the present court-martial finds its deepest roots in the development of the land forces, discussion here will not include an examination of the development of naval courts, which derived in large part from maritime law. Discussions of the history of naval courts-martial may be found in Byrne, *Military Law* (1981) and in J. Snedeker, *A Brief History of Courts-Martial* (1954). The present practice, with some minor exceptions, is uniform throughout all of the services.

2. *See* W. Winthrop, *Military Law and Precedents* 17, 45 (2d ed. 1920 reprint). *See generally* C. Brand, *Roman Military Law* (1969); G. Squibb, *The High Court of Chivalry* (1959).

3. Winthrop, *supra* note 2, at 17.

example, the military code of the Salic chieftains, circa fifth century, contained phrases closely approximating those in the Roman Twelve Tables. By the ninth century the Western Goths, Lombards, and Bavarians were also using written military codes.[4]

The early European courts-martial took on a variety of forms and usages. Typically, the early tribunals operated both in war and in peacetime conditions, the former occupying the greater part of an army's time. The Germans, in peacetime, conducted their proceedings before a court that was assisted by assemblages of freemen, and in war, before a duke or military chief. Later, courts of regiments, the "regiment" being a mace or staff serving as a symbol of judicial authority, were held by the commander or his delegate. For proceedings involving high-ranking commanders, the king formed courts composed of bishops and nobles.[5]

In Germany, courts-martial, or *militagerichts,* were formally established by Emperor Frederick III in 1487, specifically provided for in the penal code of Charles V in 1533, and refined still further under Maximillian II in 1570.[6] In France, although a military code existed as early as 1378, courts-martial, *conseils de guerre,* were not formally instituted by ordnnance until 1655.[7]

But the contribution of the German and French systems to the overall development of the court-martial is overshadowed by two contributions that were very different and yet very similar: the age of chivalry and the written military codes of King Gustavus Adolphus.

Although it has elusive origins, the age of chivalry is most often linked with the Middle Ages, those centuries after the fall of the Roman Empire and before the Renaissance. Amidst the intense rivalries for land and power and the usual accompanying dishonorable practices, "chevaliers" vowed to maintain order, and to uphold the values of honor, virtue, loyalty, and courage. The position and power of the chevalier rendered him an arbiter in matters affecting his peers, and also his dependents who held his estates under the feudal system. From this informal system arose the more formal court of chivalry.

The Duke of Normandy (William the Conqueror) vested the power and authority of his court of chivalry in his high officials; the particulars of this court will be discussed later. It was this system of military justice that he carried to England in the 11th century.[8]

The second contributing factor, the written military code of King Gustavus Adolphus of Sweden in 1621, was grounded on the need for honor, high morals, order, and discipline in a time when soldiers were generally considered barbarians and opportunists seeking the booty of war. King Adolphus was a born leader, deeply religious, and a man of modern thought. During the siege of Riga, Poland, in 1621, he issued his 167 articles for the maintenance

---

4. Winthrop, *supra* note 2, at 18. *See also* W. Aycock & S. Wurfel, *Military Law Under the Uniform Code of Military Justice* 4 (1955).
5. J. Snedeker, *A Brief History of Courts-Martial* 7 (1954).
6. Winthrop, *supra* note 2, at 18.
7. *Id.*
8. Aycock & Wurfel, *supra* note 4, at 4.

of order.[9] These provided for a regimental (lower) court-martial. The president of this court was the regimental commander, and the court's members were elected individuals from the regiment.

The standing court-martial (the "higher court") was presided over by the commanding general, and its members consisted of high-ranking officers.[10] If a gentleman or any officer was summoned before the lower court to answer for a matter affecting his life or his honor, the issue was referred to the higher or standing court for litigation.[11]

The code provided a detailed guide for conducting the courts[12] and contained a number of provisions for due process.[13] The regimental, lower court tried cases of theft, insubordination, and other minor offenses, and also exer-

---

9. See Winthrop, supra note 2, at 19. The entire code is printed as an appendix to Winthrop's work. Winthrop points out, and other writers allude to the point, that the code of Adolphus contributes in large part to later codes. He also notes that many English soldiers had served under Adolphus. Id. at 19, n. 15.

10. Article 142 provided:

In our highest Marshall Court, shall our General be President; in his absence our Field Marshall; when our General is present, his associates shall be our Field Marshall first, next him our General of the Ordnance, Serjeant-Major General, General of the Horse, Quarter-Master General; next to them shall sit our Muster-Masters and all our Colonells, and in their absence their Lieutenant Colonells, and these shall sit together when there is any matter of great importance in controversie.

11. Article 152. This provision contains one of many references throughout military history to a distinction between "officers" and "soldiers," the former presumably men of "honor" and entitled to greater privileges.

12. See Article 143, which reads:

Whensoever this highest Court is to be holden they shall observe this order; our great General as President, shall sit alone at the head of the Table, on his right hand our Field Marshall, on his left hand the General of the Ordnance, on the right hand next our Sergeant-Major General, on the left hand againe the General of the Horse, and then the Quarter-Master General on one hand, and the Muster-Master-General on the other; after them shall every Colonell sit according to his place as here follows; first the Colonell of our Life Regiment, or the Guards of our owne person; then every Colonell according to their places of antiquity. If there happen to be any great men in the Army of our subjects, that be of good understanding, they shall cause them to sit next these Officers; after these shall sit all of the Colonells of strange Nations, every one according to his antiquity of service.

Further, an oath was required of the participants:

All these Judges both of higher and lower Courts, shall under the blue Skies thus swear before Almighty God, that they will inviolably keep this following oath unto us: I.R.W. doe here promise before God upon his holy Gospell, that I both will and shall Judge uprightly in all things according to the Laws of God, or our Nation, and these Articles of Warre, so farre forth as it pleaseth Almighty God to give me understanding; neither will I for favour nor for hatred, for good will, feare, ill will, anger, or any gift or bribe whatsoever, judge wrongfully; but judge him free that ought to be free, and doom him guilty, that I find guilty; as the Lord of Heaven and Earth shall help my soule and body at the last day, I shall hold this oath truly.

Article 144.

13. For example, an appeal could be had to the higher court if the lower court was suspected of being partial. Articles 151, 153.

cised jurisdiction over minor civil issues.[14] The standing (higher) court exercised jurisdiction over treason, conspiracy, and other serious offenses.[15]

Those found guilty of misdemeanors were punished uniformly, without regard to status. If a regiment ran from a battle, its troops forfeited their goods or were decimated by hanging.[16] Other more common methods of dealing with the recalcitrants included confinement on bread and water,[17] being placed in shackles,[18] riding the wooden horses,[19] and forfeitures.[20]

The details and precise formula of the code and its intent of preserving the welfare of "our Native Countrey" are impressive.[21] In many respects, then, its foundation rested alongside the roots of the court of chivalry — a need to recognize honor, loyalty, and high morals, not just raw military discipline. In one notable respect, the code of King Adolphus differed from the Norman court of chivalry. Whereas the latter sanctioned trial by combat — the innocent being the victor — the former expressly forbade dueling.[22]

These two important factors, the development of the court of chivalry and the code of King Adolphus, marked significant benchmarks in the growth of the court-martial. Both recognized the need to maintain discipline and honor

---

14. Article 153.
15. Article 150.
16. *See* Articles 60, 66. Those lucky enough to survive were destined to "carry all the filth out of the Leaguer, until such time as they perform some exploit that is worthy to procure their pardon, after which time they shall be clear of their former disgrace." If any man could show through the testimony of ten men that he was not guilty of the charged cowardice, he would go free. While punishment for minor crimes and cowardice was harsh, rewards were specifically in store for those who served honorably. *See* Article 69.
17. Article 49.
18. Article 94.
19. Article 49. In this punishment, the miscreant was placed on a block or franie, with his back exposed, and was flogged. The block or frame resembled a sawhorse.
20. Article 80.
21. The closing article, which was Article 167, read:

 These Articles of warre we have made and ordained for the welfare of our Native Countrey, and doe command that they be read every moneth publickly before every Regiment, to the end that no man shall pretend ignorance. We further will and command all, whatsoever Officers higher or lower, and all our common souldiers, and all others that come into our Leaguer amongst the souldiers, that none presume to doe the contrary hereof upon paine of rebellion, and the incurring of our highest displeasure; For the firmer confirmation whereof, we have hereunto set our hand and seale.

Cf. Hagan, "Overlooked Textbooks Jettison Some Durable Military Law Legends," 113 MIL. L. REV. 163 (1986) (author indicates that much of what King Adolphus provided for in his code was simply a recodification of earlier codes and that he therefore is not due the accolades that many military writers have bestowed upon him).

22. Article 84 provided:

 No Duell or Combat shall be permitted to bee fought either in the Leaguer or place of Strength: if any offereth to wrong others, it shall bee decided by the Officers of the Regiment; he that challengeth the field of another shall answer it before the Marshal's Court. If any Captain, Lieutenant, Ancient, or other inferior officer, shall either give leave or permission unto any under their command, to enter combat, and doth not rather hinder them, [he] shall be presently cashiered from their charges, and serve afterwards as a Reformado or common souldier; but if any harm be done he shall answer it as deeply as he that did it.

and both recognized the requirements of the concept now labeled "due process."

§ 1-5. The British System.

§ 1-5(A). General.

The contribution of the British to the development of the court-martial is rich with tradition. As pointed out in the preceding section, the early European models of military courts contributed in some respects to the modern system used in the United States. It is to the British models, however, that commentators most often turn in discussing the history of the present court-martial. Indeed, the British system served as the first pattern for the American military justice system.

Because the British contribution is so complex and multifaceted, discussion here is limited to three general points or stages: the court of chivalry (or constable's court);[1] the era of martial law and councils of war;[2] and the Mutiny Act.[3] These three highlights of the British model will provide ample footing for later discussions of the American court-martial system.

§ 1-5(B). The Court of Chivalry: The Constable's Court.

The preceding discussion on the early European court-martial model noted the rise of the courts of honor, the court of chivalry, *curia militaris*. With his armies, William the Conqueror carried that system of justice to England and established it as his forum for administering military justice.[4]

The court is often referred to as the constable's or marshal's court — the name deriving from the titles of the principal participants in the court. William's supreme court, the *Aula Regis,* included within its jurisdiction, in its early years, the jurisdiction of the court of chivalry.[5] The court moved with the king, and thus proved to be an awkward and bulky affair until the reign of Edward I. He subdivided the court to provide a separate forum for litigation of matters concerned primarily with military discipline.[6]

The commander of the royal armies was the lord high constable. When he sat as the superior judge, he was assisted by the earl marshal, three doctors of civil law, and a clerk (who served as prosecutor). This court exercised jurisdiction over civil and criminal matters involving soldiers and camp followers.

---

1. *See* § 1-5(B).
2. *See* § 1-5(C).
3. *See* § 1-5(D).
4. W. Aycock & S. Wurfel, *Military Law Under the Uniform Code of Military Justice* 4 (1955). For discussions of the court of chivalry, see generally S.C. Pratt, *Military Law: Its Procedure and Practice* (1915), C. Fairman, *The Law of Martial Rule* (1943), and Squibb, *The High Court of Chivalry* (1959). An interesting account of a court of chivalry proceeding can be found at 3 *Corbett's Complete Collection of State Trials* 483 (1809). A chapter on procedure is included in Squibb's book.
5. Pratt, *supra* note 4, at 6; Fairman, *supra* note 4, at 1.
6. W. Winthrop, *Military Law and Precedents* 46 (2d ed. 1920 reprint).

The court also exercised jurisdiction over criminal acts that were subversive of discipline.[7]

The earl marshal was next in rank to the constable and bore the responsibility for managing the army's personnel. When he presided, the "constable's court" was considered a court of honor or military court. This arrangement survived until 1521, when Edward, Duke of Buckingham, constable during the reign of Henry VIII, was executed for treason.[8] The office of constable reverted to the crown and the constable's court became the "marshal's court." The office of marshal derived from royal appointment until 1533 when it became hereditary.[9]

The court was much more mobile than the *Aula Regis* and during periods of war followed the army. In its early forms, the court became somewhat of a standing or permanent forum, rendering summary punishment in accordance with the existing military code or articles of war.[10]

The court's supposed strength, that is, its jurisdictional powers over a wide range of civil and criminal matters, eventually became the thorn in its flesh. At several points in its history, limitations, both royal and legislative, were imposed to restrict its growing infringements upon the common law courts.[11]

---

7. Fairman, *supra* note 4, at 2 to 4.
8. Aycock & Wurfel, *supra* note 4, at 5.
9. *Id.*
10. *See* Pratt, *supra* note 4, at 6. The various articles of war promulgated by the crown during conflicts were drawn with the advice of the constable and marshal. For example, the preamble to Richard II's articles reads:

> These are the Statutes, Ordinances, and Customs, to be observed in the Army, ordained and made by good consultation and deliberation of our Most Excellent Lord the King Richard, John Duke of Lancaster, Seneschall of England, Thomas Earl of Essex and Buckingham, Constable of England, and Thomas de Mowbray, Earl of Nottingham, Marshall of England, and other Lords, Earls, Barons, Banneretts, and experienced Knights, whom they have thought proper to call unto them; then being at Durham the 17th day of the Month of July, in the ninth year of the Reign of our Lord the King Richard II.

The whole of Richard II's articles are reprinted in Winthrop, *supra* note 6, at 904.

11. Fairman notes that it was inherent in the nature of the military court to expand its jurisdiction whenever possible. Civil jurisdiction was restricted in 1384:

> And because divers Pleas concerning the Common Law, and which by the Common Law ought to be examined and discussed, are of late drawn before the Constable and Marshal of England, to the great Damage and Disquietness of the People; it is agreed and ordained, that all Pleas and Suits touching the Common Law, and which ought to be examined and discussed at the Common Law, shall not hereafter be drawn or holden by any Means before the foresaid Constable and Marshal, but that the court of the same Constable and Marshal shall have that which belongeth to the same Court, and that the Common Law shall be executed and used and have that which to it belongeth, and the same shall be executed and used as it was accustomed to be used in the Time of King Edward.

8 Richard II, stat. 1, c. 2. *See* Fairman, *supra* note 4, at 4, n.13.

Criminal jurisdiction was limited in 1399 by 1 Henry IV, c. 14, and in 1439 punishment for desertion was also limited to the common law courts. 18 Henry VI, c. 19. *See* Fairman, *supra* note 4, at 4.

The court eventually fell into disuse and by the 18th century ceased to exist as a military court.[12]

§ 1-5(C). The "Council of War."

With the decline of the court of chivalry (the constable's court or the marshal's court), the martial courts or councils held under the various articles or codes of war became more prominent.[13] Long before the court of chivalry had faded, the problem of maintaining military discipline in a widely dispersed army had prompted the formation of military courts by issuance of royal commissions, or through inclusion of special enabling clauses in the commissions of high-ranking commanders.[14] These tribunals eventually became the modern courts-martial and were convened by a general who also sat as presiding judge or president. The courts' powers were plenary, and were limited to wartime. Sentences were carried into execution without confirmation by higher authorities.[15]

As with the court of chivalry, the emerging councils of war or courts-martial frequently fell into abuse. More than once, royal prerogative expanded or attempted to expand, the jurisdiction of these tribunals over civilians or over soldiers in peacetime armies. For example, during the reigns of Edward VI, Mary, Elizabeth I, and Charles I, certain offenses, normally recognized only at common law in the civilian courts, could be punished under military law

---

12. After the fall of the constable's court in 1521, the marshal's court normally consisted of deputies assigned to hear cases. In 1640, Parliament resolved that the marshal's court was a "grievance." No formal act ended the court; it simply, as Fairman notes, suffered from atrophy. Winthrop notes that the last case was apparently tried in 1737. Winthrop, *supra* note 6, at 46, n.9 (Chambers v. Sir John Jennings, 7 Mod. 127). One writer states, however, that the court of chivalry (court of honor) was used as recently as 1954, in the case of Manchester Corp. v. Manchester Palace of Varieties, Ltd. [1955] p. 133. *See* Stuart-Smith, "Military Law: Its History, Administration and Practice," 85 L.Q. REV. 478 (1969). The case is discussed in detail in Squibb, *supra* note 4, at 123.

13. The more commonly cited articles of war, under a variety of titles, are those of Richard I, Richard II, Henry V, Henry VII, Charles II, and James II. *See generally* Winthrop, *supra* note 6, at 18, 19. Several of these codes are included as appendices in his work and are noted elsewhere in this section. The individual codes are thoroughly discussed in Clode, *Military and Martial Law* (London 1872).

14. *See generally* Pratt, *supra* note 4, at 7; Aycock & Wurfel, *supra* note 4, at 5. One of these "commissions" cited often is that given to Sir Thomas Baskerville, June 10, 1957 (to execute Marshall law, and, upon trial by an orderly court ... to inflict punishment....), cited in Aycock & Wurfel, *supra* note 4, at 6, and Fairman, *supra* note 4, at 6. A good discussion of the workings of the British courts-martial during this period is found in Clode, *supra* note 13, at chapter 11.

15. The exact origin of the term "court-martial" is open to some interpretation. Pratt states:

> The true derivation of the word "martial" opens out an interesting field of inquiry. Simmons and others hold that courts-martial derive their name from the Court of the Marshal; but there is a good deal to be said against this view, as the words "martial" and "military" are in some of the old records synonymous.

Pratt, *supra* note 4, at 7.

before courts-martial similar to those employed during times of war.[16] Parliament was rightfully very sensitive about these and other attempted encroachments upon the civilian populace. The struggle over court-martial jurisdiction simply fueled the fires. The only legislative aid to enforcing military discipline was found in various statutes that could be enforced only before civil courts.

From 1625 to 1628, Charles I attempted to use court-martial jurisdiction as a lever on the populace in hope of obtaining supplies. He failed and, in seeking the needed money from Parliament, was forced to assent to a Petition of Rights (1628), which, among other things, dissolved the commissions proceedings under military law. Charles agreed to imprison no one without due process of law, and never again to subject the people to courts-martial.[17] From the continuing struggle for control of the military, Parliament slowly gained a foothold on control of the conduct of military trials. In 1642, the first direct legislation affecting military law authorized the formation of military courts. A commanding general and 56 other officers were appointed as "commissioners" to execute military law. Twelve or more constituted a quorum and the body was empowered to appoint a judge advocate, provost marshal, and other necessary officers.[18]

---

16. *See generally*, Fairman, *supra* note 4, at 6.
17. 3 Charles I, c. 1. The petition provided in part:

Sec. VII. And whereas also by Authority of Parliament, in the five and twentieth Year of the Reign of King Edward the Third, it is declared and enacted, that no man shall be forejudged of Life or Limb against the Form of the Great Charter and the Law of the Land; (2) and by the said Great Charter and other the Laws and Statutes of this your Realm, no Man ought to be adjudged to Death but by the laws established in this your Realm, either by the Customs of the same Realm, or by the Acts of Parliament; (3) And Whereas no Offender of what Kind soever is exempted from the Proceedings to be used, and punishments to be inflicted by the laws and Statutes of this your Realm; Nevertheless of late Time divers Commissions under your Majesty's Great Seal have issued forth, by which certain Persons have been assigned and appointed Commissioners, with Power and Authority to proceed within the land, according to the Justice of Martial Law, against such Soldiers or Mariners, or other dissolute Persons joining with them, as should commit any Murder, Robbery, Felony, Mutiny or other Outrage or Misdemeanor whatsoever, and by such summary Course and Order as is agreeable to Martial Law, and as is used in Armies in Time of War, to proceed to the Trial and Condemnation of such Offenders, and them to cause to be executed and put to Death according to the Law Martial.

Sec. VIII. By Pretext whereof some of your Majesty's Subjects have been by some of the said Commissioners put to Death, when and where, if by the laws and Statutes of the land they had deserved Death, by the same Laws and Statutes also they might, and by no other ought to have been judged and executed.

Sec. X.... (5) And that the aforesaid Commissions, for proceeding by Martial Law, may be revoked and annulled; and that hereafter no Commissions of like Nature may issue forth to any Person or Persons whatsoever to be executed as aforesaid, lest by colour of them any of your Majesty's Subjects be destroyed, or put to death contrary to the laws and Franchise of the Land.

18. The act, Lord Essex's Code, established a Parliamentary Army. *See* D. Jones, *Notes on Military Law* 15 (London 1881). *See also* J. Snedeker, *A Brief History of Courts-Martial* 16.

Beginning in 1662 with articles of war issued by Charles II, there was a general recognition that a standing army[19] needed power to maintain peacetime discipline. There was also an increased interest in military due process as evidenced in various provisions of the myriad articles of war. For example, the 1686 code of "English Military Discipline" of James II included the following description of the procedure to be followed in conducting a *Councel of War*:

> If the Councel of War, or Court-martial be held to judge a Criminal, the President and Captains having taken their places and the Prisoner being brought before them, And the Information read, The President Interrogates the Prisoner about all the Facts whereof he's accused, and having heard his Defense, and the Proof made or alleged against him, He is ordered to withdraw, being remitted to the Care of the Marshal or Jaylor. Then every one judges according to his Conscience, and the Ordinances or Articles of War. The Sentence is framed according to the Plurality of Votes, and the Criminal being brought in again. The Sentence is Pronounced to him in the name of the Councel of War, or Court-Martial.
>
> When a Criminal is Condemned to any Punishment, the Provost Martial causes the Sentence to be put in Execution; And if it be a publick Punishment, the Regiment ought to be drawn together to see it, that thereby the Souldiers may be deterred from offending. Before a Souldier be punished for any infamous Crime, he is to be publickly Degraded from his Arms, and his coat stript over his ears.
>
> A Councel of War or Court Martial is to consist of Seven at least with the President, when so many Officers can be brought together; And if it so happen that there be no Captains enough to make up that Number, the inferior Officers may be called in.[20]

More detailed rules were set out two years later in the Articles of War of James II (1688), which also placed a limitation on certain punishments:

> All other faults, misdemeanours and Disorders not mentioned in these Articles, shall be punished according to the Laws and Customs of War, and discretion of the Court-Martial; Provided that no Punishment amounting to the loss of Life or Limb, be inflicted upon any Offender in time of Peace, although the same be allotted for the said Offence by these Articles, and the Laws and Customs of War.[21]

It was this closing phrase of the 1688 Articles of War, concerning limited punishments during peacetime, that in some part no doubt led to the enactment of the Mutiny Act.

---

19. The Parliament of the Restoration (1660) allowed Charles II to maintain an armed force of some 8,000 at his own expense. Parliament, for fear of being bound to support the army, declined to legislatively create courts-martial. Thus, Charles was left to govern his troops. *See* Clode, *supra* note 13; *see also* Jones, *supra* note 18, at 14.

20. Reprinted as an appendix to Winthrop, *supra* note 6, at 919.

21. Article LXIV, in the Rules and Articles for the Better Government of his Majesties Land Forces in Pay (1688), reprinted in Winthrop, *supra* note 6, at 920.

§ 1-5(D). The Mutiny Act.

In 1689, while William and Mary were asking the House of Commons to consider a bill that would allow the army to punish deserters and mutineers during peacetime and thereby ensure some degree of discipline,[22] there was a massive desertion of 800 English and Scottish dragoons who had received orders to proceed to Holland. Instead, they headed northward from Ipswich and sided with the recently deposed James II, who had recruited them.

No further royal pleading was required. Parliament quickly passed the bill known as the First Mutiny Act,[23] which added teeth to military discipline. The death penalty was allowed for the offenses of mutiny or desertion, with the proviso that:

> And noe Sentence of Death shall be given against any offender in such case by any Court Martiall unlesse nine of thirteene Officers present shall concur therein. And if there be a greater number of Officers present, then the judgement shall passe by the concurrence of the greater part of them soe sworne, and not otherwise; and noe Proceedings, Tryall, or Sentence of Death shall be had or given against any Offender, but betweene the hours of eight in the morning and one in the afternoone.[24]

Interestingly, the existing articles of war, which had been promulgated under James II, were not abrogated. Nor was any change made in the Crown's prerogative to issue articles of war or to authorize the death penalty for offenses committed abroad.[25] The act, at first limited to seven months' effective duration, simply provided for the death penalty for mutineers and deserters at home.

Until 1712, the successive Mutiny Acts did not cover offenses committed abroad. In the years that followed, the Act extended to Ireland, and to the colonies. In the 1717 Mutiny Act, the Parliament approved the practices of the Crown in issuing articles of war to extend the jurisdiction to the court-martial within the Kingdom.[26] In 1803, the Mutiny Act and the Articles of War were broadened to apply both at home and abroad.[27] A general statutory basis of authority was thus given to the Articles of War, which had to that point existed only by exercise of the royal prerogative. With the exception of a brief interval from 1698 to 1701, annual Mutiny Acts were passed until they, along with the Articles of War, were replaced in 1879 by the Army Discipline and Regulation Act, and finally, in 1881, by the Army Act.[28]

Several key themes have run through the British court-martial system.

---

22. Jones notes that at this point the soldiers were considered citizens and subject only to civil tribunals. *Supra* note 18, at 15. *See also* Clode, *supra* note 13.
23. 1 William & Mary, c. 5, reprinted in Winthrop, *supra* note 6, at 929.
24. Winthrop, *supra* note 6, at 930.
25. Aycock & Wurfel, *supra* note 4, at 8.
26. *See generally* Jones *supra* note 18, at 17.
27. Aycock & Wurfel, *supra* note 4, at 8.
28. For discussions of the act, see Jones, *supra* note 18, at 18, and Clode, *supra* note 13, at 43.

First, the struggle between the Crown on the one hand, and the Parliament on the other, over control of the military justice system, was classic. The British model typifies the reluctance of a populace to vest, or allow to be vested, too much control in the military courts. Development of the British model demonstrated the metamorphosis from a forum serving under total royal prerogative, the court of chivalry, to one acting pursuant to a legislative enactment — a blessing, of sorts, from the populace.

Second, over a period of approximately seven hundred years, the British court-martial developed a system of military due process. From the court of chivalry with its trial by combat, the system evolved to one that accorded more sophisticated rights to an accused: the rights to receive notice, to present his defense, and to argue his cause.

Third, the jurisdiction of the court-martial was gradually restricted to exercising its powers over soldiers only, as opposed to the general populace. When expansion of those powers was attempted, at least in later years, legislative limiting action was taken.

The formative years, actually centuries, in the British system served as a firm stepping stone for the American system that had its genesis in 1775.

§ 1-6. The American Court-Martial.

Much of the great credit for the development of the court-martial in America must go to the British military system. In its inception, the American court-martial drew from centuries of proud tradition, trial and error, and a keen sense of justice.[1]

---

1. Loving v. United States 116 S. Ct. 1737 (1996) (What framers distrusted were not courts-martial per se, but unchecked authority by commanders.) Not all would agree. Note the language from an article written by Brigadier General Samuel T. Ansell in 1919:

> I contend — and I have gratifying evidence of support not only from the public generally but from the profession — that the existing system of Military Justice is un-American, having come to us by inheritance and rather witless adoption out of a system of government which we regard as fundamentally intolerable; that it is archaic, belonging as it does to an age when armies were but bodies of armed retainers and bands of mercenaries, that it is a system arising out of and regulated by the mere power of military Command rather than Law; and that it has ever resulted, as it must ever result, in such injustice as to crush the spirit of the individual subjected to it, shock the public conscience and alienate public esteem and affection from the Army that insists upon maintaining it.

S. T. Ansell, "Military Justice," 5 CORNELL L.Q. (Nov. 1919), *reprinted at* Mil. L. Rev. Bicent. Issue 53, 55 (1975).

General Ansell was acting judge advocate general from 1917 to 1919, and campaigned vigorously for extensive revision of the Articles of War of 1916. His views were a generation ahead of their time; only minor changes were made in the military justice system until the present Uniform Code of Military Justice came into being with the Act of 5 May 1950, ch. 169, § 1, 65 Stat. 108. For accounts of General Ansell's struggle for reform, see Weiner, "The Seamy Side of the World War I Court-Martial Controversy," 123 MIL. L. REV. 109 (1989); T.W. Brown, "The Crowder-Ansell Dispute: The Emergence of General Samuel T. Ansell," 35 MIL. L. REV. 1 (1967); U.S. Dept. of the Army, ARMY LAW.: A History of the Judge Advocate General Corps, 1775-1975, at 114-15 (1975).

This section briefly examines three key periods in the development of the American court-martial. These are, first, the period from 1775 to 1800;[2] second, the period from 1800 to 1900;[3] and last, the period from 1900 to the present.[4] As in the preceding sections, the discussion here will center on the court-martial system for the land forces. We turn our attention first to the inception of the American court-martial.

§ 1-6(A). The Formative Years: 1775 to 1800.

The British system of military justice was an unwitting mid-wife to the American court-martial. At the outbreak of the Revolutionary War, the British soldiers were operating under the 1774 Articles of War. Ironically, even as American troops were fighting for independence, colonial leaders were embracing the British system of rendering military justice.

In April 1775, the Provisional Congress of Massachusetts Bay adopted, with little change, the 1774 British Articles of War, detailed prescription for conducting courts-martial and for otherwise maintaining military discipline.[5]

The American military was thus presented with its first written military code, the Massachusetts Articles of War.[6]

This code provided for two military courts: the "general" court-martial, to consist of at least 13 officers,[7] and a "regimental" court-martial, to consist of not less than five officers "except when that number cannot be conveniently assembled, then three shall be sufficient."[8] Other provisions included an eight-day confinement rule, a limitation on the number of "stripes" to be meted out as punishment,[9] and an admonition that "all the Members of a Court-Martial are to behave with calmness, decency, and impartiality, and in the giving of their votes are to begin with the youngest or lowest in commission."[10] Also included was a provision which survives, in form at least, to this day, that "No Officer or Soldier who shall be put in arrest or imprisonment, shall continue in his confinement more than eight days, or till such time as a Court-Martial can be conveniently assembled."[11]

---

2. *See* § 1-6(A).
3. *See* § 1-6(B).
4. *See* § 1-6(C).
5. *See* W. Aycock & S. Wurfel, *Military Law Under the Uniform Code of Military Justice* 5 (1955).
6. Similar articles were adopted within the following months by the Provincial Assemblies of Connecticut and Rhode Island, the Congress of New Hampshire, the Pennsylvania Assembly, and the Convention of South Carolina. *See* Winthrop, *Military Law and Precedents* 22 n.32 (2d ed. 1920 Reprint). The Massachusetts Articles of War are printed in Winthrop at 947.
7. Article 32.
8. Article 37.
9. Article 50. The number was limited to thirty-nine.
10. Article 34.
11. Article 41. The current U.C.M.J. provides:

   Art. 33. Forwarding of charges.

   When a person is held for trial by general court-martial the commanding officer shall, within eight days after the accused is ordered into arrest or confinement, if practicable, forward the

The Continental Congress appointed a committee in June 1775 to author rules for the regulation of the Continental Army.[12] The committee presented its report, and on June 30, 1775, the Congress adopted 69 articles based upon the British Articles of War of 1774 and the 1775 Massachusetts Articles of War.[13] In November of that same year, the articles were amended.[14] And again in 1776 the Articles of War were revised to reflect the growing American tradition of military justice.[15] The 1776 Articles of War were arranged in a manner similar to the British Articles of War, by sections according to specific topics.[16] These articles continued in force, with some minor amendments, until 1786, when some major revisions were accomplished.

The section dealing with the composition of general courts-martial was changed to reflect the need for smaller detachments to convene a general court with less than 13 members, the requisite number under the 1776 Articles. The new provision, Section 14, Administration of Justice, allowed a minimum of five officers.[17]

---

charges, together with the investigation and allied papers, to the officer exercising general court-martial jurisdiction. If that is not practicable, he shall report in writing to that officer the reasons for delay.

12. The committee was composed of George Washington, Philip Schuyler, Silas Deans, Thomas Cushing, and Joseph Hewes. It was tasked with preparing "rules and regulations for the government of the Army." Winthrop, *supra* note 6, at 21.
13. *See* Aycock & Wurfel, *supra* note 5, at 10.
14. *Id.*
15. The revision in 1776 resulted from a suggestion by General Washington. The revising committee included John Adams, Thomas Jefferson, John Rutledge, James Wilson, and R.R. Livingston. S.T. Ansell, acting Judge Advocate General of the Army from 1917 to 1919, harshly criticized the American System of military justice. *See* note 1, *supra*. According to Ansell, discussing the Articles of War of 1776, John Adams "was responsible for their hasty adoption ... to meet an emergency." Ansell also offers the following illuminating quotation from the writings of John Adams:

There was extant, I observed, one system of Articles of War which had carried two empires to the head of mankind, the Roman and the British; for the British Articles of War are only a literal translation of the Roman. It would be vain for us to seek in our own invention or the records of warlike nations for a more complete system of military discipline. I was, therefore, for reporting the British Articles of War totidem verbis.... So undigested were the notices of liberty prevalent among the majority of the members most zealously attached to the public cause that to this day I scarcely know how it was possible that these articles should have been carried. They were adopted, however, and they have governed our armies with little variation to this day.

3 J. Adams, *History of the Adoption of the British Articles of 1774 by the Continental Congress: Life and Works of John Adams* 68-82, quoted in S.T. Ansell, *supra* note 1, at 55-56.
16. For the first time in the American articles, no mention was made of the "Crown."
17. Article 1, sec. XIV. *See* Aycock & Wurfel, *supra* note 5, at 11, and Winthrop, *supra* note 6, at 23. The preamble to the resolution adopting the revisions stated:

Whereas, crimes may be committed by officers and soldiers serving with small detachments of the forces of the United States, and where there may be a sufficient number of officers to hold a general court-martial, according to the rules and articles of war, in consequence of which criminals may escape punishment, to the great injury of the discipline of the troops and the public service;

These early courts-martial were of three forms: general, regimental, and garrison. The general court-martial could be convened by a general officer or an "officer commanding the troops."[18] No sentence could be carried into execution until after review by the convening authority. In the case of a punishment in time of peace involving loss of life, or "dismissal" of a commissioned officer or a general officer (war or peace), congressional review was required.[19]

The "regiment" (or corps) court-martial could be convened by an officer commanding a regiment or corps.[20] Likewise, the commander of a "garrison, fort, barracks, or other place where the troops consist of different corps" could convene a "garrison" court-martial.[21] The membership of these two latter courts consisted of three officers, and the jurisdictional limits were as follows:

> No garrison or regimental court-martial shall have the power to try capital cases, or commissioned officers; neither shall they inflict a fine exceeding one month's pay, nor imprison, nor put to hard labor, any non-commissioned officer or soldier, for a longer time than one month.[22]

A judge advocate (lawyer) or his deputy was assigned to the court to prosecute in the name of the United States and to act as a counsel for the accused, object to leading questions (of any witness), and object to questions of the accused which might incriminate him.[23] In addition, no trials were to be held except between the hours of "8 in the morning and 3 in the afternoon, except in cases which, in the opinion of the officer appointing the court, require immediate example."[24]

This system of courts-martial was extant when the framers of the Constitution met to decide the fate of the military justice itself. Congress did not create the court-martial; it simply permitted its existence to continue. In effect, the court-martial is older than the Constitution and predates any other court authorized or instituted by the Constitution.

Of significance here is the point that the Constitution's framers provided that Congress, not the President, would "make rules for the Government and

---

Resolved, That the 14th Section of the Rules and Articles for the better government of the troops of the United States, and such other Articles as relate to the holding of courts-martial and the confirmation of the sentences thereof, be and they are hereby repealed;

Resolved, That the following Rules and Articles for the administration of justice, and the holding of courts-martial, and the confirmation of the sentences thereof, be duly observed and exactly obeyed by all officers and soldiers who are or shall be in the armies of the United States.

18. Article 2, sec. XIV.
19. *Id.*
20. Article 3, sec. XIV.
21. *Id.*
22. Article 4, sec. XIV.
23. Article 6. Winthrop discusses the dual role of counsel in these early proceedings and points out that the judge advocate could not act in a "personal" capacity as counsel for the accused because that would be inconsistent with his role as a prosecutor. Rather, the relationship was "official." Winthrop, *supra* note 6, at 197. This provision was carried forward to the 1874 Articles of War, under which the role of counsel was to exercise "paternal-like" care over an accused. *See* S. Ulmer, *Military Justice and the Right to Counsel* 23 (1970).
24. Article II, sec. XIV.

Regulation of the land and naval forces."[25] The President was named as "Commander in Chief of the Army and Navy of the United States...."[26] With these parameters drawn, the framers avoided much of the political-military power struggle that typified so much of the early history of the British court-martial system.[27] In 1797, the separateness of the military system of justice was further recognized in the Fifth Amendment provision that drew a distinction between civil and military offenses.[28]

§ 1-6(B). The Period From 1800 to 1900: Quiet Growth.

The Articles of War of 1776 (with amendments in 1789) remained in effect until 1806, when 101 articles were enacted by the Congress.[29] The composition and procedure for the court-martial changed little with the revised articles. The three courts, general, regimental, and garrison, remained, but some minor changes affected the power to convene a general court. While the 1786 amendment had allowed a general or other officer commanding the troops to convene a general court, the 1806 articles established the more particular requirement that "[a]ny general officer commanding an army, or [c]olonel commanding a separate department" could convene a general court.[30] The composition and jurisdictional limits of the three courts remained without change.

Further developments included a clause barring double jeopardy,[31] a two-year statute of limitations,[32] a provision allowing the accused to challenge members of the court-martial,[33] and a provision that a prisoner standing mute would be presumed to plead innocent.[34] Amidst these progressive procedural and substantive safeguards, one finds the provision: "The President of the United States shall have power to prescribe the uniform of the army."[35]

---

25. U.S. CONST., art. 1, § 8, cl. 14.
26. U.S. CONST., art. 2, § 2, cl. 1.
27. An early Supreme Court decision noted the effect of these Constitutional provisions:

   These provisions show that Congress has the power to provide for the trial and punishment of military and naval offenses in the manner then and now practiced by civilized nations; and that the power to do so is given without any connection between it and the 3d article of the Constitution defining the judicial power of the United States; indeed, that the two powers are entirely independent of each other.

Dynes v. Hoover, 61 U.S. 65, 79 (1857).

28. The Fifth Amendment states in part: "No person shall be held to answer for a capital, or otherwise infamous crime unless on a presentment or indictment of a Grand Jury, except in cases arising in the land or naval forces, or in the Militia, when in actual service in time of War or public danger."
29. 2 STAT. L. 359 (1806), *reprinted* in Winthrop, *supra* note 6, at 976.
30. Article 65.
31. Article 87.
32. Article 88.
33. Article 71.
34. Article 70.
35. Article 100.

The next seven decades were marked with little change to the composition of the court-martial or the procedures to be employed.[36] The relatively quiet movement of the court-martial as a tribunal was in contrast to the lusty growth of the United States and the attendant tensions that led in part to the Civil War.

Having established a government and army, the Congress of the Confederate States in October 1862 promulgated "An Act to organize Military Courts to attend the Army of the Confederate States in the Field and to define the Powers of Said Courts."[37] The court-martial under the Confederate States model was a permanent tribunal, not like the traditional (and modern) temporary forum, which was formed only for a specific case.

Each court consisted of three members, two constituting a quorum, a judge advocate,[38] a provost marshal, and a clerk. Initially, a court accompanied each army corps in the field and by later amendments courts were authorized military departments,[39] North Alabama,[40] any division of cavalry in the field,

---

36. As noted in a later discussion, periods of war during the 1700s and 1900s usually spurred prompt and major revisions to the Articles of War. Such was not the case in the 1800s, at least prior to 1874, when the country went through the War of 1812, the Mexican War, the Civil War, and part of the Indian Wars. During that century, only minor changes were made to the governing articles.

37. Act of Oct. 9, 1862, *reprinted in* Winthrop, *supra* note 3, at 1006, *and* 2 *Journal of the Congress of the C.S.A. 1861-1865*, at 452 (1905). For a very good discussion of courts-martial within the Confederate system, see Robinson, *Justice in Grey* 362-82 (1941). *See also* J.D. Peppers, Confederate Military Justice: A Statutory and Procedural Approach (May 1976) (unpublished M.A. thesis in library of Rice University, Houston, Texas). Mr. Peppers was concurrently pursuing a J.D. degree at the University of Houston College of Law when he wrote this master's thesis.

Mr. Peppers notes that the officer corps of the Confederate forces included many professional soldiers and sailors who had served in the United States Army or Navy. Because of this, the organization of the Confederate Army and Navy, including the Confederate system of military justice, for the most part was like that of the Union Forces. *Id.* at 7.

The Confederate constitution, like that of the United States, empowered the congress "to make rules for the government and regulation of the land and naval forces." *Id.* The Confederate congress exercised this power in its Act of March 6, 1861, establishing "Rules and Articles for the Government of the Confederate States." *Id.* at 17.

38. Trial judge advocates in the field were supposed to have knowledge of the law and also of military life. They were not explicitly required to be attorneys. J.D. Peppers, *supra* note 37, at 48.

The Confederate forces had no judge advocate general's corps, nor even a judge advocate general. President Jefferson Davis recommended to the Confederate congress the creation of both, but no action was taken. The work of reviewing records of trial was performed by an assistant secretary of war, and other work was handled by a "judge advocate's office" created within the office of the adjutant general, and headed by an assistant adjutant general. *Id.* at 57-59.

39. Act of May 1, 1863, *reprinted in* Winthrop, *supra*, note 6, at l007, *and* 3 *Journal of the Congress of the C.S.A. 1861-1865*, at 417 (1905).

The original creation of the new permanent courts-martial by the Act of Oct. 9, 1862, *supra* note 37, and subsequent expansions of their jurisdiction, were necessary to strengthen the military justice system of the Confederacy. J.D. Peppers, *supra* note 37, at 40. Although the Confederate military tactical leadership was very able, the Union Army as a whole was better disciplined, better equipped, and better organized by far than the Confederate forces. *Id* at 37. In the geographic areas of active military operations, the civil courts, intended to supplement the work of

---

40. Act of Feb. 13, 1864. Winthrop, *supra* note 6, at 1007.

and one for each State within a military department.[41] The legislative foundation also provided:

> Said courts shall attend the army, shall have appropriate quarters within the lines of the army, shall be always open for the transaction of business, and the final decisions and sentences of said courts in convictions shall be subject to review, mitigation, and suspension, as now provided by the Rules and Articles of War in cases of courts-martial.[42]

With the conclusion of the war, the short-lived era of the permanent court-martial faded.

The next major contribution to the development of the court-martial occurred in the American Articles of War of 1874.[43] The original three courts (general, regimental, garrison) were expanded to include a "field officer" court:

> In time of war a field-officer may be detailed in every regiment, to try soldiers thereof for offenses not capital; and no soldier serving with his regiment, shall be tried by a regimental or garrison court-martial when a field-officer of his regiment may be so detailed.[44]

The authority to convene a general court-martial was further delineated. A general officer commanding an "army, a Territorial Division or a Department, or colonel commanding a separate Department," could appoint a general court.[45] In time of war, the commander of a division or of a separate brigade

---

the military courts, often were not functioning, and the high mobility required of the Confederate forces made it difficult to convene courts-martial. Moreover, when courts-martial were convened, they apparently were prone to be very lenient toward accused, which was displeasing to senior commanders. *Id.* at 38-40. For a contemporary version of this issue, *see* United States v. McClain, 22 M.J. 124 (C.M.A. 1986).

The new military courts were permanent in the sense that they were required to be open for business continuously, not merely case by case. *Id.* at 41. Jurisdiction of the new courts as to persons accused and as to punishments authorized apparently was similar to that of the general courts-martial. The major difference was that jurisdiction extended not only to offenses recognized under military law, but also to all offenses defined as crimes by the laws of the Confederacy and of the various Confederate states, as well as certain common-law offenses committed outside the boundaries of the Confederacy. *Id.* at 42-43.

The old ad hoc courts-martial were not abolished by the act creating the new courts, however, and the Confederate Congress later had to define the boundaries between the courts' jurisdiction more precisely. This was done in the Act of Oct. 13, 1862; *The War of the Rebellion: A Compilation of the Official Records of the Union and Confederate Armies*, Series IV, at 1003-1004 (180-1901); and also in the Act of May 1, 1863, 3 *Journal of the Congress of the C.S.A. 1861-1865*, at 417 (1905).

41. Act of Feb. 16, 1864. Winthrop, *supra* note 6, at 1007, *and* 3 *Journal of the Congress of the C.S.A. 1861-1865*, at 754 (1905).
42. Section 5 of the original Act. *See* note 37, *supra*.
43. 18 STAT. 228 (1874).
44. Article 80.
45. Article 72. However, that article also placed a restriction on the authority to appoint a general court:

> But when any such commander is the accuser or prosecutor of any officer of his command the court shall be appointed by the President; and its proceedings and sentence shall be sent

could likewise convene a general court.[46]

In addition to new and expanded jurisdictional bounds applicable to certain offenses in time of war,[47] procedural changes included a provision allowing for the appointment of a judge advocate to any court-martial,[48] and a provision allowing for continuances:

> A court-martial shall, for reasonable cause, grant a continuance to either party, for such time, and as often as may appear to be just: Provided, That if the prisoner be in close confinement, the trial shall not be delayed for a period longer than sixty days.[49]

These 1874 changes marked an increased realization by Congress that due process considerations should apply. But the court-martial, at least to this point, was considered primarily as a function or instrument of the executive department to be used in maintaining discipline in the armed forces. It was, therefore, not a "court," as that term is normally used. There seemed to be a general reluctance to expand the accused's rights liberally. A feeling prevailed, and still prevails, that discipline would suffer as a result of any such expansion. If the court-martial was viewed as a judicial body, this would certainly have raised the problem of implementation of burdensome procedural and substantive rules. The truth is that, viewed in their entirety over time, the regulations and general orders were slowly converting the court-martial into a proceeding convened and conducted with meticulous care, sensitive to the individual's rights, as well as to the need for discipline. The statutory language looks barren, but in practice the court-martial during this period seems to have been considered by observers to be a fair and just means of litigating guilt and assessing appropriate punishment.[50]

A few statutory changes to court-martial practice between 1879 and 1900 are worthy of note. First, in 1890, Congress established the "summary" court-martial, which in time of peace was to replace the regimental or garrison

---

directly to the Secretary of War, by whom they shall be laid before the President, for his approval or orders in the case.

46. Article 73.
47. Article 58 provided:

In time of war, insurrection, or rebellion, larceny, robbery, burglary, arson, mayhem, manslaughter, murder, assault and battery with an intent to kill, wounding by shooting or stabbing, with an intent to commit murder, rape, or assault with an intent to commit rape, shall be punishable by the sentence of a general court-martial, when committed by persons in the military service of the United States, and the punishment in any such case shall not be less than the punishment provided, for the like offense, by the laws of the State, Territory, or district in which such offense may have been committed.

48. Article 74. But the role of the counsel remains unchanged from that espoused in the 1806 Articles. *See* Article 90. *See also supra* note 24.
49. This provision originated with the Act of March 3, 1863, ch. 75, sec. 29. *See* Winthrop, *supra* note 6, at 239.
50. *See generally* Winthrop, *supra* note 6. *See also* S.V. Benet, *A Treatise On Military Law and the Practice of Courts-Martial* (1862); J. Regan, *The Judge Advocate Recorder's Guide* (1877). Both of these sources provide fascinating reading and insight into the court-martial practice of the late 1800s.

court-martial in the trial of enlisted men for minor offenses.[51] Within twenty-four hours of arrest, the individual was brought before a one-officer court that determined guilt and appropriate punishments. This trial was a consent proceeding, however. The accused could object to trial by summary court and as a matter of right have his case heard by a higher-level court-martial where greater due process protections were available.

Another important step was taken in 1895 when, by executive order, a table of maximum punishments was promulgated.[52] Specific maximum sentences were made applicable to each punitive article or offense. Other specific guidance was given for considering prior convictions, assessing punitive discharges, and determining equivalent punishments.

§ 1-6(C). From 1900 to Present: Rapid Change.

If the nineteenth century was a time of relatively quiet changes in the American court-martial, the innovations marked by the twentieth century are by comparison revolutionary. Periods of drastic change occurred in 1916, 1920, 1948, 1951, 1968, and 1983-84.

Congress undertook a major revision of the Articles of War in 1916,[53] and for the first time the three existing courts-martial emerged: the general court-martial; the special court-martial; and the summary court,[54] which replaced the field officer's court that had been established in 1874.

The authority of a commander to convene a court was expanded. For example, a general court could be convened by the President and commanding officers down to the level of brigade commanders.[55] However, only commanding officers could convene special and summary courts.[56] Other important changes included:

  1. Mandatory appointment of a judge advocate to general and special courts-martial;[57]
  2. The right of the accused to be represented by counsel at general and special courts;[58]
  3. Explicit prohibition of compulsory self-incrimination;[59]
  4. Addition of a speedy trial provision, according to which the accused was to be tried within ten days,[60] and no person could be tried over objec-

---

51. Act of October 1, 1890. *Reprinted in* Winthrop, *supra* note 6, at 999. Traditionally, officers could be tried only by general court-martial.
52. The Executive Order by President Cleveland was published as General Order No. 16. *Reprinted in* Winthrop, *supra* note 6, at 1001.
53. 39 STAT. L. 619, at 650-70 (1916).
54. Article 3.
55. Article 8.
56. Articles 9, 10.
57. Article 11.
58. Article 17.
59. Article 24.
60. Article 70. The provision stated that the accused is to be served with a copy of the charges within eight days of his arrest, and tried within ten days thereafter, unless the necessities of the

tion (in peacetime) by a general court-martial within a period of five days subsequent to service of charges.[61]

The 1916 revisions did not wholly stand the testing fires of the global World War I. Troops, officers, and soldiers alike returned with bitter complaints about military justice. In the heated debates that followed in the press, in the halls of Congress, and in the War Department,[62] the whole system was reexamined. As a result, in 1920 the Congress enacted a new set of 121 Articles of War.[63] Key features included the following:

1. A general court-martial would consist of any number of officers not less than five.[64]
2. A trial judge advocate and defense counsel would be appointed for each general and special court-martial. (An accused could be represented by either a civilian counsel, reasonably available military counsel or appointed counsel.)[65]
3. A general court-martial convening authority could send the case to a special court-martial if it was in the interest of the service to do so.[66]
4. A thorough pretrial investigation was to be conducted. The accused was to be given full opportunity for cross-examination and to present matters in defense or mitigation.[67]
5. A board of review, consisting of three officers assigned to the office of the judge advocate general, was tasked with reviewing courts-martial, subject to presidential confirmation.[68]

Notwithstanding these changes, which most agreed represented a fair effort to improve military due process, a troublesome aspect remained. A single commander could prefer charges, convene the court, select the members and counsel, and review the case.[69] The spectre of unlawful command influence lingered. But in the quiet, peacetime years that followed the 1920 revision, this caused little concern. The citizen soldier returned to his work, the regular forces were involved in no major discipline problems, and the 1920 Articles of War seemed to function smoothly. With only minor amendments, these articles were those used by courts-martial during World War II.

Again, the massive influx of citizens into the armed forces, the widely scattered courts-martial, inexperienced leaders, and many reported instances of military "injustice" greatly concerned Congress. Again, there were hearings

---

service prevented such. In that case, trial was required within 30 days after the expiration of the ten-day period. Compare this with present speedy trial rules. *See* Chapter 13.

61. *Id.*
62. *See generally* Ulmer, *supra* note 23, at 20-45; Ansell, *supra* note 1.
63. 41 STAT. L. 787 (1920).
64. Article 4.
65. Articles 11, 17.
66. Article 12.
67. Article 70.
68. Article 50.
69. *See, e.g.,* Articles 70, 8, 11, 17, and 46.

and reports of advisory committees.[70] Again, there was a major revision, this time as an amendment to the Selective Service Act of 1948.[71] A number of changes, designed to rectify the growing complaints about the court-martial, were enacted.

For the first time, under the new provisions, the accused was entitled to be represented by counsel at all pretrial investigations.[72] To ensure that at least one member of the general court-martial was familiar with the judicial process, a provision was inserted that required that a member of the judge advocate general's department or an officer who was a member of the federal bar, or the bar of the highest court of a state, certified by the judge advocate general, be appointed to all general courts-martial.[73] For the first time, enlisted men and warrant officers were authorized to serve as members of general and special courts-martial.[74]

But before the new Act could cool, a move was under way to establish a code of military justice to apply to all the services, not just the Army. Under the leadership of Professor Edmund M. Morgan, Jr.,[75] the "Uniform Code of Military Justice" was approved by Congress in 1950,[76] with some amendments. The next major revision occurred in 1968[77] when Congress made a number of changes, the most significant being the provision for a presiding military judge at courts-martial.[78] The 1968 changes also resulted in a redrafting of the Manual for Courts-Martial (1969).

Major statutory changes were made in the Military Justice Act of 1983.[79] The Act, *inter alia*, modified the selection process for counsel[80] and judges,[81]

---

70. A War Department Advisory Committee on Military Justice noted that under the system of military justice "the innocent are almost never convicted and the guilty seldom acquitted." The committee, known as the Vanderbilt Committee, included in its membership, Chief Justice Arthur T. Vanderbilt (New Jersey), Judge Morris A. Soper of the United States Court of Appeals (4th Cir.), Justice Holtsoff (District of Columbia), and Judge Frederick Crane (New York). See Aycock & Wurfel, *supra* note 5, at 14, n.78.
71. 62 STAT. L. 604, at 627-44 (1948) (The Elston Act).
72. Article 46.
73. Article 8.
74. Article 4. The accused had to specifically request in writing, prior to the convening of the court, that enlisted soldiers be appointed to the court. The provision has been carried forward as a prerequisite to the present U.C.M.J.
75. *See generally* Morgan, "The Background of the Uniform Code of Military Justice," 6 VAND. L. REV. 169 (1953). A biographical sketch of Professor Morgan appears at 28 MIL. L. REV. 3 (1965).
76. 64 STAT. 198 (1950).
77. 82 STAT. 1335 (1968). The provisions of the U.C.M.J. had been earlier codified at 10 U.S.C. §§ 801-940. Thus, Article 1 of the U.C.M.J. is 10 U.S.C. § 801; Article 140 is 10 U.S.C. § 940, and so on. In military practice, as in this text, provisions of the Code are more commonly cited to the U.C.M.J. than to the United States Code. *See supra* § 1-3(A).
78. *See* Art. 26, U.C.M.J. (military judge is a commissioned officer of the armed forces who is a licensed attorney).
79. 97 STAT. 1393 (1983). *See generally* Cooke, "Highlights of The Military Justice Act of 1983," ARMY LAW. Feb. 1984, at 40.
80. *See* Art. 27, U.C.M.J.
81. Art. 26, U.C.M.J. For a discussion on the process of detailing counsel and judges, see Chapter 8.

abbreviated the contents of pretrial[82] and post-trial recommendations[83] from the staff judge advocate, permitted the prosecution to appeal certain rulings of the military judge,[84] and provided for direct review by the Supreme Court of the United States of decisions by the Court of Military Appeals.[85] The Act also established a nine-member commission[86] to examine the necessity and feasibility of providing tenure for military judges, sentencing by military judges alone, suspension powers of the military judge, possible Article III status for the Court of Military Appeals, now the Court of Appeals for the Armed Forces, and a retirement program for the judges of that Court.[87] Finally, as part of a comprehensive program to conform military practice to not only the amended

---

82. Art. 7, U.C.M.J.
83. Art. 60, U.C.M.J.
84. Art. 62, U.C.M.J. *See also* Chapter 13.
85. Art. 67(h), U.C.M.J. *See also* 28 U.S.C. 1259.
86. The commission consisted of members appointed by the Secretary of the Defense: Colonel Thomas L. Hemingway, USAF (Chairman); Captain Edward M. Burne, USN; Mr. Steven S. Honigman, Esq.; Colonel Charles H. Mitchell, USMC; Colonel Kenneth A. Raby, USA; Professor Kenneth F. Ripple; Professor Stephen A. Saltzburg; Captain William B. Steinbach, USCG; and Mr. Christopher Sterrit, Esq.
87. In December 1984, after hearing from 27 witnesses and conducting a number of surveys, the commission published its conclusions and recommendations in its Advisory Commission Report and Position Papers (published by the Government Printing Office). Its recommendations were as follows:

(A) That sentencing should not be exercised by military judge where the court-martial consists of members.

(B) That military judges and Courts of Military Review should not be given the power to suspend sentences.

(C) That the jurisdiction of the special court-martial should be expanded to permit adjudgement of sentences including confinement of up to one year: provided that, 1) a military judge and a certified defense counsel are required to be detailed to every special court-martial in which confinement in excess of six months may be adjudged; 2) no Article 32 investigation requirement for the special court-martial be created; and 3) no change to current appellate jurisdiction be made.

(D) That military judges, including those presiding at special and general courts-martial and those sitting on the Courts of Military Review, should not have a guaranteed term of office (tenure).

(E) That the United States Court of Military Appeals should be reconstituted as an Article III court under the U.S. Constitution: provided that, enacting legislation not alter the current jurisdiction of the Court and specify that the Court will not have jurisdiction over administrative discharges and nonjudicial punishment actions.

(F) That, if the recommendation to reconstitute the Court of Military Appeals as an Article III court is not followed, the Tax Court retirement system should be applied to judges of the Court of Military Appeals.

Although the Commission was not directed to study and make recommendations regarding the membership of the Court of Military Appeals, the Commission recommended that the membership of the Court of Military Appeals be increased from three to five judges regardless of which Article of the Constitution the Court is constituted under.

See generally Lonegran, "An Overview of the Military Justice Act of 1983 Advisory Commission Report," ARMY LAW, May 1985, at 35.

U.C.M.J., but also to federal criminal procedure, a new Manual for Courts-Martial was promulgated by the President in 1984.[88]

Several minor changes were made in 1992.[89] Most recently, Congress made a number of significant changes to the U.C.M.J. in the National Defense Authorization Act for Fiscal Year (FY) 1996.[90]

PART III

THE PRESENT SYSTEM: A PROLOGUE

§ 1-7. An Overview.

As a transition point between the foregoing introduction and the detailed discussions in the following chapters, a brief survey of contemporary practice is appropriate.

The foundations of the present court-martial practice, a far cry from practices of only a few decades ago, rest on the Constitutional provisions vesting Congress with the authority to regulate the armed forces.[1]

Congress has exercised its powers in formulating the Uniform Code of Military Justice,[2] the U.C.M.J., which in turn authorizes the President to promulgate rules of procedures before courts-martial.[3] These rules, for the most part, are found in the Manual for Courts-Martial, United States.[4] The respective services have promulgated "supplements" to the *Manual* to meet individualized needs or clarify service practices.[5]

The current court-martial remains a temporary tribunal, convened by a commander to hear a specific case. It is not a part of the federal judiciary, nor is it subject to direct judicial review in that system.[6] Instead, it is strictly a court of criminal jurisdiction, and its findings are binding on other federal courts.[7] In some points, the court-martial provides greater safeguards than its civilian counterparts, and a brief survey of the current practice bears this out.

---

88. *See* § 1-3(B), *supra*.

89. *See* Pub. L. No. 104-106, 110 STAT. 186 (1996), National Defense Authorization Act for Fiscal Year (FY) 1996. *See generally*. "Joint Service Committee on Military Justice Report," ARMY LAW., Mar. 1996, at 138.

90. The following Articles were amended: Art. 1 (Definitions); Art. 32 (Pretrial investigations); Art. 47(b) (Refusal to testify); Art. 57(a) (Effective date of punishments); Art. 57a (Deferment of matters to convening authority); Art. 62(a) (Appeals relating to disclosure of classified information); Art. 76b (Lack of competency or mental responsibility: commitment of accused for mental examination and treatment); Art. 95 (Resistance, flight, breach of arrest and escape); Art. 120 (Carnal knowledge); and Art. 137(a) (Time after accession for initial instruction in the Uniform Code of Military Justice). *See generally* "Joint Service Committee on Military Justice Report," ARMY LAW., Mar. 1996, at 138.

1. U.S. CONST., art. 1, § 8 details the power of Congress to regulate the armed forces.

2. 10 U.S.C. §§ 801-946 [hereinafter cited as U.C.M.J.].

3. Art. 36, U.C.M.J. *See* Appendix 3 for a complete text of the Uniform Code of Military Justice.

4. The Manual for Courts-Martial, United States prescribed by Executive Order No. 12473 (April 13, 1984). *See* § 1-3(B), *supra*.

5. *See* § 1-3(C), *supra*.

6. Burns v. Wilson, 346 U.S. 137 (1953); Hiatt v. Brown, 339 U.S. 103 (1950).

7. *See* Art. 76, U.C.M.J.

Before preferring and swearing to charges, a company commander is tasked with conducting a thorough and impartial inquiry into the charged offenses.[8] This almost always involves obtaining legal advice from a lawyer-judge advocate. Most commanders do not want to send a weak case to court. In an environment where law and lawyers are playing an increasingly vital role in military justice, few commanders are willing to run the risk of an acquitted servicemember returning to the unit and flaunting his "victory" over the command.

The current trend is to use *administrative discharges*[9] and other remedies, such as nonjudicial punishment,[10] rather than a court-martial. If a case goes to trial, the convening authority does select court members.[11] He *does not* select the counsel[12] or the judge,[13] however, and specific provisions within the U.C.M.J. prohibit attempts to control the proceedings.[14] The commander may also "plea bargain" with the accused.[15] At trial, the accused is entitled to virtually the same procedural protections he would have in a state or federal criminal court.[16]

The government must first establish that jurisdiction exists over the person[17] and the subject matter,[18] and that the court is properly convened.[19] The

---

8. Art. 30, U.C.M.J. A flow chart outlining the pretrial processing of court-martial charges is at Appendix 4.

9. For example, the Army utilizes a Discharge for the Good of the Service, Chapter 10, AR 635-200 (referred to as the "Chapter-10 Discharge"), which may be given in lieu of a court-martial under certain conditions. *See infra* § 9-4. *See also* § 1-5(B) for other "nonpunitive" measures.

10. *See infra* Chapter 3, for a discussion of nonjudicial punishment.

11. Art. 25, U.C.M.J. *See* Chapter 8.

12. Art. 27, U.C.M.J. *See* Chapter 8.

13. Art. 26, U.C.M.J. The "law officer" of the earlier Articles of War has been replaced by a military judge, certified by the Judge Advocate General of each service. The "president" of the court, for all practical purposes, is now the foreman of the jury. The accused may request trial before the judge alone. Art. 16, U.C.M.J. *See* Chapter 12.

14. Arts. 37, 98, U.C.M.J. *See* Chapter 6 and R.C.M. 104. The military judicial community is extremely sensitive to even the appearance of evil. The current military appellate courts may reverse a case if it appears that a superior commander has intentionally or unintentionally influenced the members of the court, the fact finders. *See* Chapter 6.

The role of the convening authority was in issue in Curry v. Secretary of the Army, 595 F.2d 873 (D.C. Cir. 1979). The court reviewed the reports of the legislative hearings on the matter, and examined the statutory protections designed to check unlawful command influence. The court found justification to reject Curry's arguments. 595 F.2d at 880. For an historical discussion of the commander's role, see West, "A History of Command Influence on the Military Judicial System," 18 U.C.L.A. L. REV. 1 (1970).

15. *See* Chapter 9 and Appendix 12.

16. An exception, of course, would be the right to a preliminary grand jury proceeding. At least one experienced civilian trial attorney prefers the court-martial over the existing civilian system. Speech by F. Lee Bailey, *reported in The Commercial Appeal* (Memphis), March 29, 1979, at 34-C.

17. Art. 2, U.C.M.J. Coleman v. Tennessee, 97 U.S. 509 (1879). *See* Chapter 4.

18. Provisions describing offenses that may be tried by court-martial are listed as "punitive" articles in the U.C.M.J. *See* Arts. 77-134, U.C.M.J. *See* Chapter 4 for discussion of subject matter jurisdiction.

19. The court-martial is considered to be a "creature of statute." If proper statutory procedures are not followed in appointing the Court, there is some authority for the proposition that the proceedings may be declared void *ab initio. See, e.g.,* United States v. White, 21 C.M.A. 583,

accused is entitled to a speedy trial[20] and carte blanche discovery rights. If the case is to be referred to a general court-martial, an intensive *pretrial investigation* is conducted[21] and written legal advice is prepared. The accused is entitled to counsel (civilian, selected individual military counsel, or appointed counsel), to present a defense, and to cross-examine witnesses. A copy of the record of the proceedings is presented, without cost, to the accused.

One provision of particular note is the right to defense witnesses,[22] a procedure much more liberal than found in most civilian jurisdictions.[23] Maximum limitations on punishments are specified.[24]

The appellate review system is unique and usually outside the critic's gaze. If the accused is convicted and sentenced, the convening authority reviews the case. Before approving a court-martial conviction and sentence, he must be satisfied beyond a reasonable doubt that the findings are supported by the evidence.[25] If the case was tried before a general court-martial he may not act without first obtaining the written legal opinion of his judge advocate.[26] Certain cases are forwarded for appeal to the various Service Courts of Criminal Appeals, where specialized appellate counsel, at no cost to the accused, review the record for errors and present written and oral arguments.[27] A case may be further appealed to the military's highest court, the United States Court of Appeals for the Armed Forces,[28] and the United States Supreme Court.[29]

---

45 C.M.R. 357 (1972). In that case, the accused failed to properly execute a written request for enlisted court members who sat on his court. This was a violation of Art. 25(c)(1), U.C.M.J.

20. Art. 10, U.C.M.J. provides in part:

When any person subject to this chapter is placed in arrest or confinement prior to trial, immediate steps shall be taken to inform him of the specific wrong of which he is accused and try him or to dismiss the charges and release him.

For a discussion of the military's speedy trial rules, see Chapter 13. Local regulations may provide for even more stringent speedy trial provisions. For example, soldiers stationed in Europe at one time had benefit of a 45-day speedy trial mandate. USAREUR Supplement 2 to Army Regulation 27-10, Military Justice (1963). *See* Chapter 13.

21. Art. 32, U.C.M.J. *See* Chapter 7.
22. Art. 46, U.C.M.J. *See also* Chapter 11.
23. *See, e.g.*, United States v. Daniels, 23 C.M.A. 94, 48 C.M.R. 655 (1974). In that case, the charges were dismissed because a material defense witness, the victim, was not produced. The line of cases supporting this rule obviously expands the Sixth Amendment right to present a defense to limits beyond those now reached by most state and federal decisions. *See* Chapter 11 for discussion of defense requests for witnesses.
24. *See* R.C.M. 1003, Manual for Courts-Martial, United States (1984). Authority of the President to prescribe maximum punishments is found in Art. 56, U.C.M.J. See Appendix 30 for a copy of the Maximum Punishment Chart.
25. Arts. 60, 64, U.C.M.J.
26. Art. 61, U.C.M.J.
27. Art. 66, U.C.M.J. The various service courts of military review are composed of senior judge advocates who exercise fact-finding powers and may approve, or disapprove wholly or in part, court-martial findings or sentences. Until the 1968 amendments, these courts were called "Boards of Military Review." In 1994, they were changed to Courts of Criminal Appeals. *See* Chapter 17.
28. Art. 67, U.C.M.J. Although the United States Court of Appeals for the Armed Forces is the highest court in the military system of courts, it is not itself a military court, but a federal civilian

---

29. *See* Art. 67(h), U.C.M.J. 28 U.S.C. § 1259.

One can readily see that throughout the entire process, lawyers are actively involved in either advising the commanders, representing the accused, sitting as military judges, reviewing records, or writing appellate opinions. On the whole, the changes in the court-martial system have kept pace with similar innovations in the civilian courts and as noted have often led the way for further changes.

§ 1-8. The Commander's Options: Prosecutorial Discretion.

§ 1-8(A). General.

Central to court-martial practice is the commander and the chain-of-command. Despite repeated proposals to modify the system,[1] the commander, whether at the company or corps level, still serves as the keystone for the operation of the military criminal process. As briefly noted in earlier discussions, the issue of command control is a sensitive topic, and the current system includes numerous statutory safeguards against unlawful command influence.[2]

A criminal offense may be disposed of in the military criminal system in any one of several forums. The commander who discovers an offense, upon investigation, may take no action, or he may use nonpunitive measures or nonjudicial punishment. In the alternative, he may prefer court-martial charges and forward them up the chain of command with recommendations for disposition at a court-martial. The *Manual for Courts-Martial* requires only that in exercising his prosecutorial discretion, the commander should seek resolution of the case at the lowest level consistent with the seriousness of the offense.[3] As an introduction to subsequent chapters detailing court-martial procedures, the following sections briefly discuss the options or forums available to the commander in the exercise of his prosecutorial discretion.

§ 1-8(B). Nonpunitive Measures.

In the past years, the use of nonpunitive measures[4] has steadily increased. Many commanders recognize the value of punishing violations of military standards through means other than the sometimes cumbersome nonjudicial or judicial proceedings. Although the specific availability or applicability of various nonpunitive options varies from service to service, the general nature remains. Options commonly employed include:

---

court created by Congress under Article I of the Constitution. *Id.*

Since its inception in 1951, the Court of Appeals, currently composed of five civilian judges, has played an expanding role in shaping the form and substance of courts-martial. *See, e.g.*, Cooke, "The United States Court of Military Appeals, 1975-1977: Judicializing the Military Justice System," 76 MIL. L. REV. 43 (1977). *See* Chapter 17 for discussion of appellate procedures.

1. *See, e.g.*, Schiesser & Benson, "A Proposal to Make Courts-Martial Courts: The Removal of Commanders from Military Justice," 7 TEX. TECH. L. REV. 559 (1976).
2. Arts. 37, 98, U.C.M.J. *See infra* § 6-3 and Appendix 3.
3. R.C.M. 306(b).
4. Nonpunitive measures are discussed at R.C.M. 306(c)(2).

a. Transfer in assignments,
b. Administrative discharges,[5]
c. Administrative reductions in rank,[6]
d. Extra training,[7]
e. Written or oral reprimands,[8] and
f. Withdrawal of privileges or passes.

§ 1-8(C). Nonjudicial Punishment.

This disciplinary procedure is discussed in greater detail in Chapter 3, but is briefly mentioned here as a viable option for the commander. Nonjudicial punishment, widely used in all of the services, is specifically addressed in Article 15 of the U.C.M.J. and is designed to allow a commander to quickly impose minor punishments for minor offenses committed by members of his command. The procedures and maximum punishments available are covered in Article 15, U.C.M.J.,[9] Part V of the Manual for Courts-Martial, and in the various service regulations.[10]

§ 1-8(D). Court-Martial.

Assuming that the commander decides that proper sanctions lie in a judicial forum, a number of additional options and procedures are available. The requisite procedural and substantive elements for trial of a case by court-martial will be discussed more fully in later chapters. Discussion here will briefly summarize the types and composition of the three types of court-martial: summary, special, and general.

§ 1-8(D)(1). Summary Court-Martial.

A summary court-martial, designed to dispose of minor offenses in a simplified proceeding, consists of one commissioned officer who may, but need not be, a lawyer.[11] The accused, whose consent is a prerequisite to the proceeding,[12] is normally not entitled to a detailed lawyer[13] but upon request may be

---

5. *See, e.g.*, AR 635-200, which allows administrative discharges for misconduct or unsuitability.
6. *See, e.g.*, AR 600-200.
7. There must be a nexus between the alleged deficiency in the servicemember's performance and the extra training or the remedy may be labelled as punishment. *See* United States v. Robertson, 17 C.M.R. 684 (A.F.B.R. 1954). *See generally* Kaczynski, "The School of the Soldier: Remedial Training or Prohibited Punishment?," ARMY LAW., June 1981, at 17.
8. Service regulations generally detail requirements for imposition and filing of written reprimands. *See, e.g.*, AR 640-10.
9. *See* Art. 15, U.C.M.J., in Appendix 3.
10. See Chapter 3 for discussion of various nonjudicial punishment procedures.
11. Art. 16, U.C.M.J.
12. Art. 20, U.C.M.J.
13. In Middendorf v. Henry, 425 U.S. 25 (1976), the Supreme Court held that presence of counsel was not required at a summary court-martial, which the Court characterized as a "disci-

represented by a civilian counsel, at no expense to the government, or by an individually requested military counsel. The procedures, outlined in the Manual for Courts-Martial[14] and discussed at § 15-25 *infra*, include examination of witnesses and application of the Military Rules of Evidence.[15] Only enlisted servicemembers may be tried by summary court-martial. The maximum punishment that may be imposed by a summary court includes confinement at hard labor for one month, forfeiture of two-thirds of one month's pay for one month, hard labor without confinement for forty-five days, or restriction for two months.[16]

§ 1-8(D)(2). Special Court-Martial.

The special court-martial, the intermediate court in the military's judicial structure, may be composed of either a military judge sitting alone, at least three members sitting without a judge, or a combination of a military judge and at least three members.[17] Both the trial counsel (the prosecutor) and defense counsel are appointed to the court.[18] In addition, the accused may be represented by civilian counsel or individually requested military counsel.[19] Any servicemember may be tried by a special court-martial for any noncapital offense.[20] Maximum punishments from this proceeding include confinement at hard labor for six months and forfeiture of two-thirds of one month's pay for six months. A bad-conduct discharge[21] may also be assessed if additional procedural protections are met: a military judge must be detailed,[22] a defense

---

plinary" proceeding. Summary courts, according to the Court, are limited to conduct not declared criminal in the civilian community. For discussions relating to the question of counsel at summary courts, see "Right to Counsel at a Summary Court-Martial: Middendorf v. Henry," 55 N.C. L. REV. 300 (1977); "'Military Justice—Right to Counsel' Servicemen Tried Before Summary Courts Have No Constitutional Right to Counsel." Middendorf v. Henry, 425 U.S. 25, 96 S. Ct. 1281, 47 L. Ed. 2d 566 (1976), 54 TEX. L. REV. 1471 (1976).

14. R.C.M. 1301 *et seq.* The Army uses DA Pam. 27-7, *Guide for Summary Court-Martial Procedure*.
15. *Id.* The Military Rules of Evidence are discussed at § 15-21.
16. Art. 20, U.C.M.J. For a discussion on sentencing, see Chapter 17.
17. Art. 16, U.C.M.J.
18. Art. 27, U.C.M.J.
19. Art. 30(b), U.C.M.J.
20. Art. 19, U.C.M.J. *See, e.g.*, United States v. Sykes, 32 M.J. 791 (N.M.C.M.R. 1990) (rape charges were capital and could not be referred to special court-martial without consent of the general court-martial convening authority; *see* R.C.M. 201(f)(2)(C)(ii)). In United States v. Castillo, 34 M.J. 1160 (N.M.C.M.R. 1992), the accused was tried by a special court-martial for disobeying an order, under Article 90, while assigned in Saudi Arabia. The accused argued that the court had no jurisdiction to try him because Article 90 is a capital offense during a time of war and that the general court-martial convening authority had not authorized the trial by special court-martial. In a lengthy discussion of the issue, the court concluded that the conflict with Iraq was, indeed, a time of war but that the President had not authorized the death penalty for Article 90 violations.
21. R.C.M. 1003(b)(10)(C) indicates that a bad-conduct discharge is appropriate as punishment for an accused who has been convicted repeatedly of minor offenses and whose punitive separation from the service appears to be necessary.
22. Art. 19, U.C.M.J. Article 19 allows, however, for a bad-conduct special court-martial without a military judge where one could not be detailed because of "physical conditions or military exigencies."

counsel, within the meaning of Article 27(b), U.C.M.J., must be detailed, and a verbatim record of trial must be prepared.[23]

§ 1-8(D)(3). General Court-Martial.

Before a general court-martial may be convened, a pretrial investigation into the offense must be conducted,[24] and a legal opinion as to the disposition of the charges must be given to the convening authority.[25] This forum, the highest trial level in military law, may be composed of a military judge sitting alone[26] or a combination of at least five members with a military judge presiding.[27] The only limits upon a general court-martial sentence are those set for each offense in Part IV of the *Manual*,[28] and may include the death penalty, a dishonorable or bad-conduct discharge, or a dismissal (for officers).[29]

---

23. Article 19, U.C.M.J.
24. Art. 32, U.C.M.J.
25. Art. 34, U.C.M.J.
26. Art. 16(1), U.C.M.J.
27. Art. 16(1), U.C.M.J.
28. *See* § 1-3(B). A copy of a chart setting out the maximum punishments is included at Appendix 30.
29. See Chapter 16 for a discussion of sentences and sentencing procedures.

APPENDIX REFERENCES

Appendix 1. Abbreviations.
Appendix 2. Glossary.
Appendix 3. Uniform Code of Military Justice
Appendix 4. Court-Martial Flow Chart.
Appendix 30. Maximum Punishment Chart.

ANNOTATED BIBLIOGRAPHY

BOOKS

Addleston, *The Rights of Veterans* (1978).

In handbook format, this short work presents many practical pointers and answers to questions concerning the rights of former servicemembers. Included are discussions of the offense of AWOL, the military's discharge program, and the consequences of a court-martial conviction.

Appleton, *Military Law for the Company Commander* (1944).

The author, a retired Warrant Officer in the United States Army, uses actual case scenarios to illustrate his points and provides an excellent reference source for practical, day-to-day use by company commanders. This book is a simple, yet concise and complete handbook that practically illustrates the company commander's role in the administration of military justice in the 1940s.

Bishop, *Justice Under Fire: A Study of Military Law* (1974).

This easy-reading introductory book to military justice presents a fine overview of selected topics: history of the court-martial, jurisdiction, the war powers, and the applicability of the Bill of Rights to servicemembers.

Byrne, *Military Law* (1981).

This third edition work is a good introductory text to military law. It includes text material, discussion cases, self-quizzes, and appendices which contain forms and tables. The discussion cases, although dated, cover significant areas of courts-martial practice.

DeHart, *Observations on Military Law and the Constitution and Practice of Courts-Martial* (1846).

Noting the inconsistencies wrought by the divergent authority in American and English military law, the author, then-acting Judge-Advocate of the Army, sets out the well-settled principles upon which American military law was based in the early 1800s. This book contains an excellent reference base to anyone interested in a historical perspective of military law in the early American Army.

Everett, *Military Justice in the Armed Forces of the United States* (1956).

This book, written by a former Chief Judge of the Court of Military Appeals, presents a very good, easy-to-read discussion of military criminal law as it was practiced before the 1968 changes to the U.C.M.J.

Finn, *Conscience and Command: Justice and Discipline in the Military* (1971).

In this collection of short essays, the authors explore and analyze the soldier's right of conscience with the United States armed forces. Some of the areas focused upon include an examination of military and civilian societies, an analysis of justice within the military, and the Army and the First Amendment. The book concludes with personal testimonies from several authors and individuals involved in this concept of conscience within the military.

Generous, *Swords and Scales: The Development of the Uniform Code of Military Justice* (1973).

Of some historical interest, this well-documented book traces the major steps in the development of the U.C.M.J. Of particular interest is an extensive bibliography containing 524 entries.

Gilligan & Lederer, *Court-Martial Procedure* (1991).

This two-volume book covers the court-martial process from apprehension through appellate review. The appendices include a copy of the Rules of Courts-Martial.

Ives, *Military Law* (1881).

Ives, then an assistant professor at the United States Military Academy, presents a text-book analysis of the changes and their concomitant interpretations that took place in the "Law Military" during the period of 1860-1880. This work was also intended to be used as a quick-reference tool by military officers who, according to the author, "[come] in daily [contact] with some question of military law."

Military Law Reporter.

This loose-leaf service, was formerly published by the Public Law Education Institute. The service consisted of six bimonthly issues per volume.

Moyer, *Justice and the Military* (1972).

This one-volume loose-leaf reference contains detailed discussions of the role of commanders, jurisdiction, military criminal procedure, First Amendment rights, substantive law, and collateral review of courts-martial by the civilian court system.

Rivkin, *The Rights of Military Personnel* (1977).

An ACLU handbook, this work discusses the rights of servicemembers facing military nonjudicial or judicial action. Included is a list of agencies that provide counseling or referral services.

Schiller, *Military Law and Defense Legislation* (1941).

Focusing upon selected general topics such as the constitutional extent of military power, the organization of the United States Army, military law, courts-martial organization, and the civil rights of armed forces members, the author provides an academic sourcebook that serves as a thorough introduction to military law and certain aspects of defense legislation.

Schug, *Cases and Materials on Constitutional Law, Courts-Martial, and the Rights of Servicemen* (1972).

Mr. Schug's book is in the case-book format and discusses a wide range of topics: the powers of Congress, jurisdiction, court-martial procedures, First Amendment claims, and review of court-martial convictions.

Sherrill, *Military Justice is to Justice As Military Music is to Music* (1970).

In this short, highly critical view of the military justice system, the author chronicles a number of well-known courts-martial where the rights of servicemembers were, in the author's view, trammeled in an effort to enforce military discipline.

Snedeker, *Military Justice Under the Uniform Code* (1953).

The author, a retired Brigadier General in the United States Marine Corps, provides a thorough overview of the law, sources, and relevant precedents under the U.C.M.J. Although published in 1953 prior to the influx of court decisions construing the Code, this book still provides a solid overall statement of military law as it then existed.

Snedeker, *A Brief History of Courts-Martial* (1954).

Although it does not contain footnotes or other reference materials, this sixty-five page book discusses the historical aspects of the court-martial. Particular attention is paid to the development of naval or maritime courts.

Solis, *Marines and Military Law in Vietnam: Trial by Fire* (1989).

This well-documented work closely examines the workings of the military justice system in Vietnam. The author, a retired Marine Corps lawyer, presents a concise and revealing history of the legal and practical problems of implementing the Uniform Code of Military Justice in a war zone.

Tilloston, *The Articles of War Annotated* (1943).

In this book, Colonel (Retired) Tilloston furnishes a detailed listing of the Articles of War as they appeared in 1943. Additionally, the author thoroughly annotates each Article with a discussion of key points, emphasis being made to other key Article provisions where necessary.

Walker, *Military Law* (1954).

The author, a former commissioner on the United States Court of Military Appeals, provides the reader with a thorough introduction to military law. This book was intended as both a teaching source and a reference point for those interested in military law. Particular emphasis is given to military criminal law, due in part to the author's belief that it is this area of military law that will provide the most litigation and discussion to both military and civilian lawyers.

West, *They Call it Justice* (1977).

Presenting what the author characterizes as the "darker side" of military justice, the book presents an interesting discussion of the military justice system. But the absence of citations, footnotes, and bibliography limits its value as a resource for further research.

Winthrop, *Military Law and Precedents* (1920 Reprint).

Clearly a classic work on military law, Colonel Winthrop's book presents an invaluable research tool for discovering the historical bases of military law. Now of historic value, it includes abstracts of some of the early military codes.

Zillman, Blaustein, & Sherman, *The Military in American Society* (1978).

This loose-leaf casebook represents the efforts of nine individuals familiar with the workings of the military system of justice. Valuable discussions include treatment of the American military establishment, entry into the military, the military justice system, individual rights of servicemembers, termination of military service, and the law of armed conflict. Selected cases are discussed and notes for further reading are located at the end of each chapter.

PERIODICALS

In General

Gerwig, "Viewpoints of Military Law, Civil and Criminal," 48 NOTRE DAME L. REV. 509 (1973).

In sixty-nine pages, the author does a fine job of covering the principles of both civil and criminal facets of military law. Under the heading of civil law, he covers such topics as military reservations, administrative discharges, civilian personnel, investigations, claims, and procurement. Of more interest here is his discussion of the criminal topics of jurisdiction, pretrial and trial procedures, and a brief item on recent issues of interest such as search and seizure, speedy trial, and rights warnings. A table of contents is included.

Morris, "Keystones of the Military Justice System: A Primer for Chiefs of Justice," ARMY LAW., Oct. 1994, at 15.

This 41-page article is an excellent guide for those charged with administering military criminal law, especially those with relatively little military justice experience. The article provides helpful checklists of issues and suggestions which often plague the administration of military justice and emphasizes the supervisory capacity of chiefs of military justice so that cases may be tried efficiently.

Sandel, "Other Than Honorable Military Administrative Discharges: Time for Confrontation," 21 SAN DIEGO L. REV. 839 (1984).

This comment examines current nonjudicial proceedings for imposing less than honorable discharges in terms of the due process rights of the servicemember. Because less than honorable discharges could have adverse effects upon a servicemember's entitlements and later employment opportunities, the author concludes that additional due process rights should be provided either within the present system or by removing the process to the military courts-martial system.

Westmoreland, "Military Justice — A Commander's Viewpoint," 10 AM. CRIM. L. REV. 5 (1971).

Written while Chief of Staff of the Army, General Westmoreland's article notes the commander's view of military justice and its impact on and relationship to "good order and discipline" in the Army. Only four pages in length, this article presents a perspective not usually found in "legal" discussions of military criminal law.

MILITARY CRIMINAL JUSTICE

Historical Perspectives

Bennett, "The Jacksonville Mutiny," 134 MIL. L. REV. 157 (1991).

In an interesting article, the author recounts the details of the mutiny trials and execution of six black soldiers in Jacksonville, Florida in 1865. Noting that most attention has been focused on the more familiar Houston Riots and the Brownsville Affray, the Jacksonville Mutiny remains an almost forgotten footnote in history.

Cooper, "Gustavus Adolphus," 92 MIL. L. REV. 129 (1981).

This article provides a general background of the influential military code imposed by the warrior king Gustavus Adolphus upon the Swedish military in 1691. This reform established specific military offenses and actual courts-martial with provisions for appeal, thus representing a great improvement over the arbitrary disciplinary practices of the time. Cooper also illustrates how many features of modern military justice find their origins in this code.

Cox, "The Army, The Courts, and the Constitution: The Evolution of Military Justice," 118 MIL. L. REV. 1 (1987).

The author, a judge on the Court of Military Appeals, presents an overview of the development of military justice in the United States and the applicability of the Constitution to various rules and practices. The author also addresses the issue of review of military justice decisions by the Article III courts, the possibility of the Court of Military Appeals becoming an Article III court, and the criticism that military justice has become "civilianized."

Crump, "Part I: A History of the Structure of Military Justice in the United States, 1775-1920," 16 A.F. L. REV. 41 (Winter 1974).

The author presents a review of the military justice system during the period of the Revolutionary War up through what the author refers to as the "period of modernization and reform" before and after World War I. This article, which is the first of two parts, does not address the military justice system used by the Confederate States during the Civil War.

Crump, "Part II: A History of the Structure of Military Justice in the United States, 1921-1966," 17 A.F. L. REV. 55 (Fall 1975).

This article, which is a continuation of an earlier article, *supra,* presents a brief overview of the military justice developments from the period following World War I until the period preceding the changes to the system in the 1968 changes to the U.C.M.J. and the 1969 *Manual for Courts-Martial.*

Hagan, "Overlooked Textbooks Jettison Some Durable Military Law Legends," 113 MIL. L. REV. 163 (1986).

In a careful and thoughtful analysis of early military codes, the author concludes that some heretofore assumptions about the roles of some of them should be reassessed. In particular, he challenges the oft-cited code of King Gustavus Adolphus of Sweden, which has been considered by some writers to be a model for much later codes. In his view, Adolphus has been incorrectly given the credit for originating many due process protections now found in modern codes. Adolphus, he maintains, was simply parroting earlier codes that have not gained widespread attention.

Lurie, "Military Justice 50 Years After Nuremberg: Some Reflections on Appearance v. Reality," 149 Mil. L. Rev. 189 (1995).

Professor Lurie, who serves as Historian to the Court of Appeals for the Armed Forces, surmises that perhaps the massive changes which have resulted in military justice systems throughout the world in the last 50 years may have resulted, at least in part, from the Nuremberg trials. Noting potential gaps between appearance and reality in several areas of military criminal justice, the author notes that the true potential of the system has not been completely fulfilled.

Lurie, "Andrew Jackson, Martial Law, Civilian Control of the Military, and American Politics: An Interesting Amalgam," 126 Mil. L. Rev. 133 (1989).

The author, the historian for the Court of Appeals for the Armed Forces, relates Andrew Jackson's imposition of martial law in New Orleans, his unsuccessful attempt to court-martial a federal judge, and the judge's later imposition of a $1,000.00 fine against Jackson for contempt of court.

Morton, "The Background of the Uniform Code of Military Justice," 6 Vand. L. Rev. 169 (1953).

Part of a symposium on military justice, this article presents an overview of the 1950 U.C.M.J. and the proposals leading to its enactment.

Nicholson, "Courts-Martial in the Legion Army: American Military Law in the Early Republic, 1792-1796," 144 Mil. L. Rev. 77 (1994).

The article briefly traces the history of American military law and discusses the application of military justice by Major General Anthony Wayne in the Legion Army, the major force of the United States Army along the Northwestern frontier, what later became the states of Indiana, Ohio, and Michigan.

Schlueter, "The Court-Martial: An Historical Survey," 87 Mil. L. Rev. 12 (1980).

Tracing the roots of the court-martial, this article addresses the development of this tribunal and the procedural changes reflected through various military codes from the Roman armies to the present day.

Weiner, "American Military Law in the Light of the First Mutiny Act's Tricentennial," 126 Mil. L. Rev. 1 (1989).

Colonel Weiner's article is an expanded version of a speech he gave at the Army's Judge Advocate General's School in April 1989. The article offers interesting insights into the history of military law, beginning with the First Mutiny Act and ending with some comments on the contemporary system and thoughts on the future of military justice.

Weiner, "The Seamy Side of the World War I Court-Martial Controversy," 123 Mil. L. Rev. 109 (1989).

Colonel Weiner, a distinguished commentator on military justice, presents a fascinating account of the "Crowder-Ansell" dispute concerning court-martial practices during World War I and its underlying currents. In his view, some of Ansell's vehement criticism of military justice, and especially of General Crowder who had always spoken highly of him, can be attributed to Ansell's fall from power and grace when his superiors lost faith in him.

Affirmation of Military Justice

Bishop, "The Case for Military Justice," 62 MIL. L. REV. 215 (1973).

Rejecting calls for abandonment of the military justice system, Professor Bishop discusses several arguments for continuation of a separate system. He notes the need for military justice under unique and far-flung situations, separate military crimes, and the concept of "discipline."

Everett, "The New Look in Military Justice," 1973 DUKE L.J. 648 (1973).

Responding to allegations of "drumhead justice" in the military, Professor Everett (later the Chief Judge of C.M.A.) suggests in his article that the arguments against military justice have been exaggerated and that major reforms, which were effected by the 1968 U.C.M.J., have precluded many criticisms against the system. He presents an interesting overview of some of the protections available to a servicemember and not otherwise available to a civilian defendant.

Latimer, "A Comparative Analysis of Federal and Military Criminal Procedure," 29 TEMP. L.Q. 1 (1955).

Judge Latimer, formerly of the Court of Military Appeals, compares federal and military criminal procedures and seeks to dispel the notion among civilian attorneys that military practice is arcane and disjunct from federal practice. Judge Latimer straight forwardly examines each step of the military judicial process, from the accusatory/investigatory stages to the trial and appellate processes, surveying the points at which the two systems run parallel and where they diverge. Although over 35 years old, this article is an excellent primer.

Moyer, "Procedural Rights of the Military Accused: Advantages Over a Civilian Defendant," 22 ME. L. REV. 105 (1970); 51 MIL. L. REV. 1 (1971).

This forty-page article compares the civilian and military criminal procedures such as pretrial investigation, interrogation, right to witnesses, right to counsel, and appellate review. The author concludes that the military accused enjoys greater procedural and substantive advantages than the civilian counterpart.

Nichols, "The Justice of Military Justice," 12 WM. & MARY L. REV. 482 (1971).

Offering "practical necessity" as a buttress for the historical and constitutional bases for military justice, the author discusses the need for a separate system, the comparisons made between military and civilian procedures, and finally comments on proposed changes.

Poydasheff & Suter, "Military Justice? Definitely!," 49 TUL. L. REV. 588 (1975).

The writers, in an attempt to dispel the misconception of a military justice system that operates to the prejudice of an accused, review some of the basic rights available. In doing so, they note that upon entry into the military the servicemember does not surrender his basic freedoms, although they must be occasionally limited by overriding military interests. The article is short (fifteen pages) but presents an easy-reading discussion of such rights as the right to counsel, speedy trial, search and seizure, and confessions.

THE MILITARY CRIMINAL JUSTICE SYSTEM

Calls for Reform

Fidell, "The Culture of Change in Military Law," 126 Mil. L. Rev. 125 (1989).

Noting that law reform has always been controversial, the author states that uniformed lawyers have a key role to play in fashioning military justice reform, including a better digesting system for military case law and a system of tenure for military trial and appellate judges.

Fidell, "If a Tree Falls in the Forest ...: Publication and Digesting Policies and the Potential Contribution of Military Courts to American Law," 22 JAG J. 1 (1983).

The author notes that the military criminal justice system has much to offer to the civilian legal system. To foster increased interaction between the two, he suggests that changes be made in publication and digesting of military decisions.

Rothblatt, "Military Justice: The Need for Change," 12 Wm. & Mary L. Rev. 455 (1971).

The author recognizes and rejects the often emotionally charged criticisms of the system, but does review and offer constructive comments that he feels will on the whole improve the military justice system.

Schlueter, "Military Justice in the 1990s: A Legal System in Search of Respect," 133 Mil. L. Rev. 1 (1991).

The author explores the criticisms often leveled at the military justice system and targets a number of areas where the system seems most vulnerable, such as size and composition of the courts-martial, and offers suggested changes.

Spak, "Military Justice: The Oxymoron of the 1980s," 20 Cal. W. L. Rev. 436 (1984).

In a critical analysis of expanding court-martial jurisdiction after *United States v. Trottier*, Professor Spak strongly asserts that military jurisdiction should be limited to purely military offenses. In support of his stance, he advocates four justifications: (1) military discipline does not require a broad military justice system that encroaches upon the constitutional rights of military personnel; (2) military jurisdiction unfairly attaches to military members fraudulently induced into joining the military; (3) military procedural law is inherently unfair; and (4) due to the inequity of military law, military jurisdiction should not attach to off-post offenses.

Military Justice: A Separate System

Barker, "Military Law — A Separate System of Jurisprudence," 36 U. Cin. L. Rev. 223 (1967).

Through an analysis of the military justice system as a separate judicial entity under the Constitution, the author provides a helpful perspective on the nature of its separation from the civilian legal system and the extent of its isolation from federal court review.

Cook, "Courts-Martial: The Third System in American Criminal Law," 1978 S. Ill. U. L.J. 1.

The author, a judge on the United States Court of Military Appeals, notes that the U.C.M.J. regulates the conduct of two million persons in the armed forces, more than the number of persons in eighteen of the fifty states. This third system is examined in the light of recent developments in two key areas: the responsibilities of the defense counsel and the role of the trial judge.

Hirschhorn, "The Separate Community: Military Uniqueness and Servicemen's Constitutional Rights," 62 N.C. L. REV. 177 (1984).

In this scholarly and massive article (77 pages), the author undertakes an exhaustive critique of the fundamental thesis of civilian/military judicial relations, i.e., that the military is a "separate community" by virtue of its peculiar needs. The author first describes the separate development of civilian and military constitutional jurisprudence, and finds that neither the Supreme Court majority, with its "reflexive" hands-off attitude, nor the minority, which minimizes the distinctiveness of military needs, properly balances all relevant interests. Professor Hirschhorn then delves into the aspects of this doctrine of separation and its relevance to the role and performance of the individual soldier. The author, in conclusion, finds that the "separate community" doctrine is a necessary and appropriate jurisprudential framework, with adequate political safeguards against abuse.

Karlen, "Civilianization of Military Justice: Good or Bad," 60 MIL. L. REV. 113 (1973).

Just because military justice is different from civilian justice does not mean that the former is inferior. So concludes Professor Karlen who, in comparing the time-consuming civilian process, argues against the "blind application" of civilian practices to the military system, which Karlen views as being efficient and fair.

Military Justice in War

Gates & Casida, "Report to The Judge Advocate General by the Wartime Legislation Team," 104 MIL. L. REV. 139 (1984).

In a response to the Judge Advocate General's concern that the military justice system may be rendered ineffective during wartime, the Wartime Legislation Team conducted a thorough study of the current military justice system. This study group concluded that although the system could operate during a low-intensity conflict, major revisions, which the authors discuss, are necessary for the system to properly operate in the midst of a general war.

Lasseter and Thwing, "Military Justice in Time of War," 68 A.B.A.J. 566 (May 1982).

These authors briefly review the changes in the military justice system over the past decades and conclude that the present model is not flexible enough to work well during times of war. They offer specific changes to various phases of the system and propose that a simplified *Manual for Courts-Martial* (Combat) and a U.C.M.J. (Combat) be established.

Westmoreland & Prugh, "Judges in Command: The Judicialized Uniform Code of Military Justice in Combat," 3 HARV. J. OF LAW & PUBLIC POLICY 1 (1980).

During the years following enactment of the 1950 U.C.M.J., the military courts have generally taken a course of civilianizing military justice, a step that the authors feel will greatly detract from the commander's powers to impose swift, sure discipline in time of war. In support of their position, they present a review of Court of Military Appeals' decisions that have tended to place additional "legal" burdens on the commander, and present views based upon their experiences in the combat environment.

Military Justice and the Constitution

Harrison, "Be All You Can Be (Without the Protection of the Constitution)," 8 HARV. BLACK LETTER J. 221 (1991).

Noting that the Supreme Court has at one time or another denied basic constitutional protections to various minority groups, the author argues that the Court's decision in *Solorio v. United States* has deprived servicemembers of their basic rights. That decision, he points out, should be of particular concern to minority groups because the current all-volunteer composition of the armed forces includes a high percentage of minorities.

Henderson, "Courts-Martial and the Constitution: The Original Understanding," 71 HARV. L. REV. 293 (1957).

Drawing from the Founding Fathers' original understanding, the author concludes that the Bill of Rights was to be applied to the military, a view now accepted, in part, by civilian and military courts.

Nunn, "The Fundamental Principles of the Supreme Court's Jurisprudence in Military Cases," 29 WAKE FOREST L. REV. 557 (1994).

Senator Sam Nunn, former Chairman of the Senate Armed Services Committee, presents an essay discussion of the constitutional structure of the military and the Supreme Court's approach to deciding cases involving military issues.

Warren, "The Bill of Rights and the Military," 37 N.Y.U. L. REV. 181 (1962).

The late Chief Justice Warren addresses the sensitive balance between the individual's rights and the need for a separate, but subordinate, military system of justice. Throughout the article he draws from Supreme Court decisions involving the military.

Weiner, "Courts-Martial and The Bill of Rights: The Original Practice I," 72 HARV. L. REV. 1 (1958).

Colonel Weiner examines the thesis that the Bill of Rights was intended to apply to courts-martial and concludes, relying on early writers, that they were not intended to apply. His thorough forty-six page article presents a fine historical analysis of the American military justice system. Emphasis in this, the first part of a two-part article, centers on the Sixth Amendment right to counsel.

Weiner, "Courts-Martial and The Bill of Rights: The Original Practice II," 72 HARV. L. REV. 266 (1958).

Continuing an earlier discussion of the applicability of the Bill of Rights to courts-martial, *supra,* Colonel Weiner examines the First, Fourth, Fifth, Eighth, and other Sixth Amendment rights.

Symposia

"Bibliography of Military Law," 10 AM. CRIM. L. REV. 175 (1971).

This extensive bibliography lists finding aids, books, symposiums, surveys, service publications, and selected writings in legal periodicals. Most entries predate the 1968 amendments to the U.C.M.J.

Mott, Hartnett & Morton, "A Survey of the Literature of Military Law — A Selective Bibliography," 6 VAND. L. REV. 333 (1953).

This valuable thirty-six page symposium article presents a selected bibliography (partially annotated) of primary sources of military literature including books, official and unofficial military publications, and legal periodical materials.

"Symposium, Military Law," 10 AM. CRIM. L. REV. 1 (1971).

This symposium issue covers a valuable range of topics pertinent to the practice of military criminal law. Included are articles on jurisdiction over civilian-type offenses, plea-bargaining, sentencing, discovery, appeals, and an article by General Westmoreland on the commander's perspective of military justice. Also included is a fine bibliography of books, articles, and listings of military law materials.

"A Symposium on Military Justice," 6 VAND. L. REV. (1953).

Although this material is dated, it does provide historical insight into the workings, theory, and shortcomings of the 1951 U.C.M.J. It contains articles by the then-judges of the Court of Military Appeals, an article on the background of the U.C.M.J., habeas corpus, the Court of Military Appeals, and a comparative study of reforms in the military justice systems in Britain and America. Of particular value is an article, listed separately here, presenting a survey of military law literature.

"Symposium, Uniform Code of Military Justice," 35 ST. JOHN's L. REV. 197 (1961).

Included in this issue are insightful articles on the background of the 1951 U.C.M.J., the appellate process, and on the "general articles," 133 and 134 of the Code.

The 1984 *Manual for Courts-Martial:* Significant Changes and Potential Issues, ARMY LAW., July 1984.

This 58-page article, prepared by the Instructors of the Criminal Law Division of the Army's Judge Advocate General's School, presents a concise explanation of the principal changes and potential problems of the 1984 Manual for Courts-Martial.

CHAPTER 2
MILITARY CRIMES

§ 2-1. Introduction.
§ 2-2. Absence Offenses.
    § 2-2(A). General.
    § 2-2(B). Desertion.
    § 2-2(C). Absence Without Leave.
        § 2-2(C)(1). Failing to Go to Place of Duty.
        § 2-2(C)(2). Leaving Place of Duty.
        § 2-2(C)(3). Absence Without Leave.
    § 2-2(D). Missing Movement.
    § 2-2(E). Defenses to Absence Offenses.
        § 2-2(E)(1). Impossibility.
        § 2-2(E)(2). Justification or Necessity.
        § 2-2(E)(3). Duress.
        § 2-2(E)(4). Mistake of Fact.
        § 2-2(E)(5). Civilian Detention.
        § 2-2(E)(6). Statute of Limitations.
        § 2-2(E)(7). Moral Grounds or Beliefs.
§ 2-3. Disrespect Offenses.
    § 2-3(A). Disrespect Toward Officers.
    § 2-3(B). Insubordination Toward Petty, Warrant, or Noncommissioned Officers.
    § 2-3(C). Defenses to Disrespect Offenses.
§ 2-4. Disobedience Offenses.
    § 2-4(A). General.
    § 2-4(B). Disobedience of a Superior's Orders.
    § 2-4(C). Violation of General Orders or Regulations.
    § 2-4(D). Disobedience of Other Orders.
    § 2-4(E). Dereliction of Duty.
    § 2-4(F). Defenses to Disobedience Offenses.
§ 2-5. Article 133: Conduct Unbecoming an Officer and a Gentleman.
§ 2-6. Article 134: The General Article.
    § 2-6(A). Disorders and Neglects to the Prejudice of Good Order and Discipline.
    § 2-6(B). Conduct Bringing Discredit Upon the Armed Forces.
    § 2-6(C). Crimes and Offenses Not Capital: Federal Crimes.
§ 2-7. Drug Offenses.
    § 2-7(A). Charging Drug Offenses.
    § 2-7(B). Proving Wrongfulness; Defenses.
    § 2-7(C). Evidentiary Issues; Identity of the Drugs.
§ 2-8. Fraternization.
    § 2-8(A). In General.
    § 2-8(B). Fraternization and the General Articles.
    § 2-8(C). Fraternization and Regulations or Orders.
    § 2-8(D). Fraternization and the Constitution.
§ 2-9. AIDS and HIV-Related Offenses.
    § 2-9(A). General.
    § 2-9(B). Violating "Safe Sex" Orders.
    § 2-9(C). Prosecuting HIV-Related Offenses Under Other U.C.M.J. Provisions.
        § 2-9(C)(1). Murder, Manslaughter, and Assault.
        § 2-9(C)(2). Rape and Sodomy.
        § 2-9(C)(3). "Catch-All" Offenses Under Articles 133 and 134.
    § 2-9(D). Constitutionality of Prosecuting HIV-Related Conduct.

Appendix References.
Annotated Bibliography.

§ 2-1. Introduction.

The uniqueness of the military criminal system is clearly evident in its proscription of conduct, or lack thereof, that may not find a counterpart in the civilian sector. Supporting this proscription is a deeply rooted argument that unchecked behavior may undermine discipline — an indispensable ingredient in the military's mission.[1] This chapter examines a variety of the so-called "military crimes." These crimes are among those listed in the punitive articles of the U.C.M.J.[2] Important to note is that the "military" itself does not define the elements for these unique offenses; they are delineated by Congress in the U.C.M.J. and discussed in the Manual for Courts-Martial.

Not addressed here are those offenses for which a civilian analog exists, although a quick review of the punitive articles section of the U.C.M.J. will reveal that many common-law offenses have been specifically incorporated into the military criminal law practice.[3]

Also not examined are some of the less common military or military-related crimes.[4] The emphasis here rests on those military crimes most often encountered in the court-martial process.

§ 2-2. Absence Offenses.

§ 2-2(A). General.

The military offenses generally involving a servicemember's absence from place of duty or organization are noted in Articles 85 to 87, U.C.M.J.[1] They include a wide range of "absences" ranging from desertion[2] to failing to go to

---

1. *See, e.g.*, Parker v. Levy, 417 U.S. 733 (1974), where the Court noted that "[A]n army is not a deliberative body. It is the executive arm. Its law is that of obedience. No question can be left open as to the right to command in the officer, or the duty of obedience in the soldier." See United States v. Stockman, 17 M.J. 530 (A.C.M.R. 1983), where the court ruled that by attempting to smuggle East Germans out of their country, the accused had breached the duty of responsive discipline. See generally Westmoreland, "Military Justice—A Commanders Viewpoint," 10 Am. Crim. L. Rev. 5 (1971).
2. The U.C.M.J. is included in this book at Appendix 3. The punitive articles run from Article 77 to Article 134.
3. For example, see Article 128 (assaults), Article 120 (rape), Article 121 (larceny), Article 122 (robbery), and Article 118 (murder).
4. *See, e.g.*, Article 94 (mutiny or sedition); Article 93 (cruelty and maltreatment), Article 117 (provoking words or gestures), Article 84 (effecting unlawful enlistment), Article 112 (drunk on duty), Article 115 (malingering).

Articles 99 through 106 generally proscribe combat or war-related offenses; misbehavior before the enemy (Art. 99); subordinate compelling surrender (Art. 100); improper use of countersign (Art. 101); forcing a safeguard (Art. 102); captured or abandoned property (Art. 103); aiding the enemy (Art. 104); misconduct as prisoner (Art. 105); spying (Art. 106).

1. The U.C.M.J. is included at Appendix 3.
2. Art. 85, U.C.M.J.

an appointed place of duty.[3] The elements for each of the offenses is discussed in the Manual for Courts-Martial[4] and the authorized maximum punishments are noted in the *Manual*'s Maximum Punishment Chart,[5] which appears in this book at Appendix 30.

§ 2-2(B). Desertion.

The offense of desertion,[6] a specific intent crime, may be committed under one of four circumstances. First, if a servicemember, without authority goes or remains absent from his unit, organization, or place of duty with the intent to remain away permanently, he has committed desertion.[7] This is the most common form of desertion and is completed at the point the specific intent to remain away permanently is formed.[8]

The second form of desertion is committed when a servicemember quits his unit, organization, or place of duty with intent to avoid hazardous duty[9] or shirk important service.[10] The third form is directed at commissioned officers

---

3. Art. 86, U.C.M.J.
4. For a general discussion of the Manual for Courts-Martial, see *supra* § 1-3(B).
5. The chart, which is now included as Appendix 12 of the MCM, notes the ceilings on punishments that may be imposed for conviction of the listed offenses. The ceilings may be further lowered by the jurisdictional limits of the court-martial. *See infra* Chapter 4.
6. Art. 85(a), U.C.M.J.
7. MCM, Part IV, para. 9. United States v. Holder, 7 C.M.A. 213, 22 C.M.R. 3 (1956). For an explanation of military case citations, see *supra* § 1-3(D).
8. United States v. Maslanich, 13 M.J. 611 (A.F.C.M.R. 1982) (intent to remain away permanently found even where accused was apprehended several hours later a short distance from the base).
9. United States v. Smith, 39 C.M.R. 46 (C.M.A. 1968).
10. Art. 85(a), U.C.M.J. United States v. Gonzales, 42 M.J. 469 (1995) (discussion of offense; whether accused intended to desert is subjective but question of whether service was important is objective one depending on surrounding facts and circumstances in expected military situation; fact that his unit was not actually deployed was no defense); United States v. Walker, 41 M.J. 462 (1995) (court rejected argument that order directing accused overseas violated Army's C.O. regulation; court also observed that soldier does not have a constitutional right to be discharged from service or to disobey orders because he is a conscientious objector); United States v. Thun, 36 M.J. 468 (C.M.A. 1993) (accused committed desertion to avoid service in Operation Desert Storm).
United States v. Johnson, 37 M.J. 982 (A.C.M.R. 1993) (accused not guilty of refusing to deploy to Saudi Arabia; the order to do so was invalid because the accused had attempted to seek status as C.O.); United States v. Wiley, 37 M.J. 885 (A.C.M.R. 1993) (accused not guilty of desertion; commander's order to deploy was unlawful because accused had filed request for C.O. status); United States v. Pruner, 37 M.J. 573 (A.C.M.R. 1993) (military intelligence with unit about to be deployed to Saudi Arabia was important service); United States v. Swanholm, 36 M.J. 743 (A.C.M.R. 1992) (medic's prospective service in Gulf War constituted important service); United States v. Kim, 35 M.J. 553 (A.C.M.R. 1992) (accused guilty of desertion where he avoided preparations to deploy to Saudi Arabia); United States v. Galloway, 34 M.J. 1017 (A.C.M.R. 1992) (government argued that specification alleging flight to avoid prosecution was broad enough to mean desertion to shirk important service; court did not decide issue. Trial judge impermissibly took legislative action in determining that specification alleged new offense of desertion).
United States v. Hocker, 32 M.J. 594 (A.C.M.R. 1991) (accused deserted in order to avoid deployment to Saudi Arabia); United States v. Walker, 26 M.J. 886 (A.F.C.M.R. 1988) (absence to avoid special court-martial was not "important service"); United States v. Wolff, 25 M.J. 752

who, after tender of a resignation and before its acceptance, quit their place of duty without leave and with the intent to remain away permanently.[11]

There is also a fourth type of desertion proscribed in Article 85 that apparently does not require a specific intent to desert. Article 85(a)(3) indicates that a servicemember may desert by enlisting, before being separated, in another armed force of the United States or in another nation's armed forces.[12]

Note that the key element of "intent" must be alleged and proved beyond a reasonable doubt.[13] If the prosecution should fail to establish the requisite intent, the court may still find the individual guilty of the lesser-included offense of unauthorized absence. The courts, in determining whether the specific intent was present, have considered a variety of factors, including statements and actions of the accused, length of absence, and method of terminating the absence.[14] For example, a lengthy absence, terminated by apprehension, while on orders to go to a war zone has been ruled sufficient to show intent.[15] A pattern of absences may also establish the accused's state of mind as to the intent element.[16]

If a desertion is terminated by apprehension, not only may the prosecution rely upon that fact to show intent, but the maximum punishment may be

---

(N.M.C.M.R. 1987) (absence to avoid serving summary court-martial sentence was not intentional avoidance of "important service").

See also United States v. Willingham, 2 C.M.A. 590, 10 C.M.R. 88 (1953) (overseas transfer to Korea during combat); United States v. Shull, 1 C.M.A. 177, 2 C.M.R. 83 (1952) (assignment to Korea); United States v. Merrow, 14 C.M.A. 265, 34 C.M.R. 45 (icebreaker duty); and United States v. Deller, 3 C.M.A. 409, 12 C.M.R. 165 (1953) (basic training where such was requirement for assignment to Korea). Infantry service in Vietnam was considered important service in United States v. Moss, 44 C.M.R. 298 (A.C.M.R. 1971).

11. Art. 85(b), U.C.M.J.
12. Art. 85(a)(3), U.C.M.J.
13. United States v. Huet-Vaughn, 43 M.J. 105 (1995) (discussion of element of intent vis-á-vis motive; court held that trial court did not err in instructing members that accused's motive for deserting was not relevant).
14. MCM, Part IV, para. 9c(1)(c). United States v. Care, 18 C.M.A. 535, 40 C.M.R. 247 (1969); United States v. Huet-Vaughn, 43 M.J. 105 (1995) (discussion of methods of proving intent of accused to desert).

United States v. Horner, 32 M.J. 576 (C.G.C.M.R. 1991) (144-day absence terminated by apprehension, accused did not have ID card or uniform when apprehended, and establishment of residence 3,000 miles away in Canada). *See also* United States v. Bindley, 23 M.J. 658 (A.F.C.M.R. 1986) (arresting detective permitted to offer "opinion" on issue of whether accused intended to return to base; the court noted that the detective's testimony was more in the nature of an explanation of inferences arising from accused's actions and statements); United States v. Logan, 18 M.J. 606 (A.F.C.M.R. 1984) (under the facts the court held that the evidence did not support the trial court's finding that the accused intended to desert; when apprehended he admitted his military status and the fact that he was AWOL and had in his possession various documents showing his true identity).

In addition, termination by apprehension may increase the maximum punishment from two to three years. *See* Appendix 30, Chart of Punishments. MCM, Part IV, para. 9e(2).

15. United States v. Thun, 36 M.J. 468 (C.M.A. 1993) (accused committed desertion to avoid service in Operation Desert Storm; while duration of accused's desertion was short, the timing of the absence was critical; the imminence of the overseas duty was considered a decisive factor); United States v. Mackey, 46 C.M.R. 754 (N.C.M.R. 1972).
16. United States v. Wallace, 19 C.M.A. 146, 41 C.M.R. 146 (1969).

§ 2-2(C)   MILITARY CRIMES   § 2-2(C)(1)

increased,[17] if the prosecution has properly alleged and proved the termination by apprehension.[18] This element is not applicable, however, to the form of desertion alleging absence with intent to avoid hazardous duty or important service.[19]

§ 2-2(C). Absence Without Leave.

The offense of absence without leave, recognized more commonly as "AWOL" or "UA" (unauthorized absence), and proscribed in Article 86, U.C.M.J., actually consists of three separate crimes: (1) failure to go to the appointed place of duty, (2) leaving the place of duty, and (3) absence without leave.[20] Each crime consists of different elements and is briefly discussed in the following sections. As a general rule these offenses require only a general intent.

§ 2-2(C)(1). Failing to Go to Place of Duty.

Article 86(1) and (2), U.C.M.J. proscribe the offense of failing to go to the place of duty and the offense of improperly leaving a place of duty.[21] The offense of failing to go to the place of duty, sometimes labelled as "failing to repair," is committed when a servicemember has been "appointed" to a specific place of duty at a specific time and thereafter fails to appear.[22] A specification[23] is deficient if it fails to allege a specific time and place,[24] and the proof will be deficient if the prosecution fails to show that the accused had either actual or constructive knowledge of the order.[25] Occasionally, a commander will give a direct order to go to a particular place and when the servicemember fails to do so, will attempt to charge the individual with disobedience of an order,[26] a more serious offense.[27] In that case, the maximum

---

17. The maximum is increased from two years confinement at hard labor to three years confinement at hard labor. MCM, Part IV, para. 9e(2).
18. United States v. Nickaboine, 3 C.M.A. 152, 11 C.M.R. 152 (1953); United States v. Washington, 24 M.J. 527 (A.F.C.M.R. 1987) (arrest by civilian police does not constitute apprehension for purposes of terminating desertion unless it was accomplished on behalf of the military or unless the accused was returned to the military for some reason other than the accused's request).
19. The maximum punishment for this form of desertion includes confinement at hard labor for five years. MCM, Part IV, para. 9e(1).
20. Art. 86, U.C.M.J. *See generally* Anderson, "Unauthorized Absences," ARMY LAW., June 1989, at 3; Lederer, "Absence Without Leave—The Nature of the Offense," ARMY LAW., March 1974, at 4.
21. Art. 86(1)(2), U.C.M.J. *See* Appendix 3.
22. MCM, Part IV, para. 10b(1). United States v. High, 39 M.J. 82 (C.M.A. 1994) (accused violated Art. 86(1) by failing to comply with nonjudicial punishment implementing order to report).
23. A "specification" is the military's vehicle for formally alleging criminal conduct on the charge sheet. A sample charge sheet is included at Appendix 6 and the charging process is discussed in Chapter 6 *infra*.
24. United States v. Sturkey, 50 C.M.R. 110 (A.C.M.R. 1975).
25. United States v. Gilbert, 23 C.M.R. 914 (A.F.B.R. 1957).
26. *See infra* § 2-4.
27. For example, if the servicemember were to be convicted for disobeying an officer's personal

punishment is limited to that which could be imposed for simply failing to go to his place of duty.[28]

§ 2-2(C)(2). Leaving Place of Duty.

This type of unauthorized absence[29] serves as a counterpart to failing to go to the place of duty. The requirement of specificity in the order to go to a particular place of duty again applies in this offense, which usually arises where the servicemember was originally at the proper place but at some point left without proper authority.[30]

§ 2-2(C)(3). Absence Without Leave.

"AWOL" or "UA" is proscribed in Article 86(3)[31] and is completed when the servicemember "absents himself or remains absent from his unit, organization, or place of duty."[32] The "place of duty," for purposes of what may be referred to as the standard AWOL, need not be as narrowly specified as that required in the offenses of failing to go to or going from the place of duty offenses discussed in the preceding sections.[33] The term "unit" usually refers to a company-sized unit, while the term "organization" refers to a larger command.[34] The specification is fatally defective if the prosecution fails to allege the current unit, organization, or place of duty,[35] or if it fails to allege

---

order to report to a place of duty, the maximum punishment would be a dishonorable discharge and five years of confinement at hard labor. Simple violation of Article 86(1), on the other hand, is punishable by no more than one month's confinement at hard labor. See Appendix 30, Chart of Maximum Punishments.

28. United States v. Baldwin, 49 C.M.R. 814 (A.C.M.R. 1975).
29. Art. 86(2), U.C.M.J. MCM, Part IV, para. 10b(2).
30. The accused must have known that he was at the proper place at the proper time. See United States v. Gilbert, 23 C.M.R. 914 (A.F.B.R. 1957).
31. See Appendix 3.
32. Id. See MCM, Part IV, para. 10b(3). For discussions on the question of charging absence offenses where the accused has failed to perform duties with his unit and stays in a barracks on the installation, see United States v. Smith, 37 M.J. 583 (N.M.C.M.R. 1993); United States v. Phillips, 28 M.J. 599 (N.M.C.M.R. 1989); United States v. Wargo, 11 M.J. 501 (N.C.M.R. 1981).
33. United States v. Horton, 36 M.J. 1039 (N.M.C.M.R. 1993) (place of duty for purposes of absence without leave, unlike appointed place of duty, is general place of duty similar to unit, organization, post, station, base, or camp); United States v. Brown, 24 C.M.R. 585 (A.B.R. 1957), petition denied, 24 C.M.R. 311 (C.M.A. 1951). Cf. United States v. Bement, 34 C.M.R. 648 (A.B.R. 1964) (accused was charged with violating Article 86(2) (see supra § 2-2(C)(2)), but court was improperly instructed on Article 86(3) offense).
34. See, e.g., United States v. Jack, 7 C.M.A. 235, 22 C.M.R. 25 (1956); United States v. Graham, 37 M.J. 603 (A.C.M.R. 1993) (Army can serve as organization for purpose of AWOL); United States v. Vidal, 45 C.M.R. 540 (A.C.M.R. 1972).
35. See United States v. Atkinson, 39 M.J. 462 (C.M.A. 1994) (accused may be absent from both assigned unit and attached unit); United States v. Stroud, 27 M.J. 765 (A.F.C.M.R. 1988) (accused was properly charged with absence from CONUS unit although he was in process of permanent change of station to Europe, where AF regulations indicated that "losing unit" would retain accountability until a stated effective date); United States v. Holmes, 43 C.M.R. 446 (A.C.M.R. 1970). See also United States v. Walls, 1 M.J. 734 (A.F.C.M.R. 1975).

that the accused was required to be at the place of duty.[36] Failure to allege that the absence was unauthorized is no longer fatal, however.[37] An accused may be absent from more than one unit.[38]

The offense of absence without leave is not a continuing offense and is completed at the time the servicemember leaves.[39] The length of the absence is a matter in aggravation.[40]

The absence is terminated when the servicemember returns to military control. Military case law has recognized myriad methods for terminating absences.[41] They include apprehension by civil authorities,[42] apprehension by military authorities,[43] surrender to military authorities,[44] and delivery to military authorities by anyone.[45] Mere telephonic contact will not constitute a

---

36. United States v. Kohlman, 21 C.M.R. 793 (A.B.R. 1956). *Cf.* United States v. Willis, 7 M.J. 827 (C.G.C.M.R. 1979).
37. United States v. Watkins, 21 M.J. 208 (C.M.A. 1986), *overruling* United States v. Fout, 3 C.M.A. 565, 13 C.M.R. 121 (1953).
38. United States v. Mitchell, 7 C.M.A. 238, 22 C.M.R. 28 (1956).
39. *See* MCM, Part IV, para. 10c(8). United States v. DiBello, 17 M.J. 77 (C.M.A. 1983); United States v. Jackson, 20 M.J. 83 (C.M.A. 1985) (offense of absence without leave is not a continuing offense and is complete on the date the accused unlawfully absents himself); United States v. Francis, 15 M.J. 424 (C.M.A. 1983); United States v. Lovell, 7 C.M.A. 445, 22 C.M.R. 235 (1956).

United States v. Kimbrell, 28 M.J. 542 (A.F.C.M.R. 1989); United States v. Jones, 26 M.J. 1009 (A.C.M.R. 1988) (judge could not change inception date to a later date and thereby save charge of AWOL from statute of limitations). The statute of limitations commences at the moment of the absence.

40. United States v. Lynch, 22 C.M.A. 457, 47 C.M.R. 498 (1973). The prosecution must show the duration of the absence in order to determine the maximum punishment authorized. Failure to do so usually results in a finding of only a one-day AWOL with a maximum punishment of one month's confinement and forfeiture of two-thirds of one month's pay for one month. *See* United States v. Simmons, 3 M.J. 398 (C.M.A. 1977). Note that the 1984 version of the *Manual* increased the maximum confinement for an absence lasting more than 30 days and terminated by apprehension from one year to eighteen months. *Cf.* United States v. Fielder, 21 M.J. 544 (A.F.C.M.R. 1985) (maximum punishment for AWOL from 1983-1985 and terminated by apprehension would be determined under provisions of 1969 MCM).
41. For a good review of the prerequisites for termination of an AWOL, see United States v. Coglin, 10 M.J. 670 (A.C.M.R. 1981). *See* MCM, Part IV, para. 10c(10).

Cf. United States v. Kimbrell, 28 M.J. 542 (A.F.C.M.R. 1989) (period of authorized leave did not interrupt or end period of unauthorized absence); United States v. Pettersen, 14 M.J. 608 (A.F.C.M.R. 1982) (accused's absence was not terminated when superiors gave orders to return to base and he refused; disobeying such orders is separate offense).

United States v. Ringer, 14 M.J. 979 (N.M.C.M.R. 1982) (accused's absence did not terminate with beginning of authorized leave).

42. United States v. Garner, 7 C.M.A. 578, 23 C.M.R. 42 (1957); United States v. Fritz, 31 M.J. 661 (N.M.C.M.R. 1990) (accused's confinement by civil authorities on DWI charges did not terminate AWOL).
43. United States v. Coates, 2 C.M.A. 625, 10 C.M.R. 123 (1953) (may be of different service).
44. United States v. Gudaitis, 18 M.J. 816 (A.F.C.M.R. 1984) (accused terminated his first AWOL when he presented himself to a security police sergeant and the AF could have determined by reasonable diligence that he was AWOL and the AF exercised control over him, although that was not necessary in this case. Military control is not required when the accused intends to surrender and presents himself to military authority); United States v. Zammit, 14 M.J. 554 (N.C.M.R. 1982) (accused turned himself in to VA hospital officials); United States v. Kitchen, 5 C.M.A. 541, 18 C.M.R. 165 (1955).
45. United States v. Lanphear, 23 C.M.A. 338, 49 C.M.R. 742 (1975) (AWOL terminated when civilian authorities made accused available for delivery to military authorities; failure of the

termination[46] nor will mere casual presence at a military installation.[47] A surrender to military authorities must be accompanied by a bona fide intent to return to duty.[48] Once the accused has indicated a desire to return to military control, authorities may not refuse to act.[49]

Occasionally the evidence at trial will show that what appears to be one continuous period of AWOL is in effect two, or three, separate absences. For example, the accused may have effectively terminated the absence by returning to military control and several days later started a new period of unauthorized absence. Under prior law,[50] absent a proper amendment to the charges and specifications by the prosecution,[51] the court entered a finding of guilty, by exceptions and substitutions,[52] to the first termination date. The *Manual* provides that an accused may be convicted of two or more separate absences so long as they fall within the period charged in the specification and the accused is not misled.[53] The maximum punishment, however, remains the same as if he was convicted of the single absence as charged.[54]

In addition to duration of the absence,[55] there are several other factors that may serve as "aggravating" factors and permit an increase in the maximum

---

latter to pick up accused constituted constructive termination of AWOL); United States v. Rayle, 6 M.J. 836 (N.C.M.R. 1979) (AWOL terminated when accused appeared at military medical facility to surrender). *Cf.* United States v. Asbury, 28 M.J. 595 (N.M.C.M.R. 1989) (a detainer request filed by the military with civilian authorities does not terminate an unauthorized absence).

46. United States v. Fritz, 31 M.J. 661 (N.M.C.M.R. 1990) (accused's phone call to NCO did not terminate absence); United States v. Anderson, 1 M.J. 688 (N.C.M.R. 1975).

47. United States v. Dubry, 12 M.J. 36 (C.M.A. 1981) (presence at reserve center); United States v. Acemoglu, 21 C.M.A. 561, 45 C.M.R. 335 (1972) (mere casual presence at American embassy was insufficient); United States v. Coleman, 34 M.J. 1020 (A.C.M.R. 1992) (accused's presence in assigned barracks after missing work was more than casual presence and terminated absence even though he did not report to anyone); United States v. Williams, 29 M.J. 504 (A.C.M.R. 1989) (temporary submission to military does not terminate absence unless accused discloses his status).

48. United States v. Claussen, 15 M.J. 660 (N.M.C.M.R. 1983) (absence not terminated when accused spoke with chaplain; the latter had authority to apprehend but did not do so and the accused had no intention of returning to military control); United States v. Self, 35 C.M.R. 557 (A.B.R. 1965).

49. United States v. Reeder, 22 C.M.A. 11, 46 C.M.R. 11 (1972).

50. *See* United States v. Lynch, 22 C.M.A. 457, 47 C.M.R. 498 (1973); United States v. Reeder, 22 C.M.A. 11, 46 C.M.R. 11 (1972).

51. *See* § 6-4(B)(2) for a discussion of amendments to the pleadings. For example, in United States v. Francis, 15 M.J. 424 (C.M.A. 1983) the court suggested that the prosecution could properly amend the specification at trial to allege only the first included absence and later attempt to try separately the accused on any later absences within the originally charged period.

52. *See* § 15-16 for a discussion on announcement of a verdict.

53. MCM, Part IV, para. 10c(11). The change is grounded on United States v. Francis, 15 M.J. 424 (C.M.A. 1983). *See also* United States v. Bush, 18 M.J. 685 (N.M.C.M.R. 1984) (accused could be found guilty of four separate specifications of unauthorized absence that were clearly within the single longer period originally charged).

54. MCM, Part IV, para. 10c(11).

55. A continuous absence of 24 hours or less is considered one day. United States v. Krutsinger, 15 C.M.A. 235, 35 C.M.R. 207 (1965).

Absences for three or more days and absences of more than 30 days are considered aggravated forms of absence without leave. *See* MCM, Part IV, para. 10c(4)(a), (b).

§ 2-2(D)   MILITARY CRIMES   § 2-2(D)

punishment.[56] Termination of the absence by apprehension is an aggravating factor if the absence is longer than 30 days.[57] Absence from guard, watch, or duty station with or without intent to abandon[58] and absence with intent to avoid maneuvers or field exercises[59] are also aggravating factors. These last two factors cover types of special duty and the specific intent in each must be pleaded and proved.[60]

§ 2-2(D). Missing Movement.

Designed to fill the gap between a mere absence without leave and desertion, the offense of "missing movement" is committed when a servicemember:

> [T]hrough neglect or design misses the movement of a ship, aircraft, or unit with which he is required in the course of duty to move....[61]

"Movement" under this offense depends on an application of several factors, such as duration, distance, and mission of the movement.[62] Actions such as practice marches of short duration or mere changes in locations at the same installation[63] generally do not constitute "movements." This offense was originally intended to cover those situations where servicemembers missed the departure of a troop ship, or flight,[64] and reported cases on the subject generally involve such situations.[65] The Court in *United States v. Graham*,[66] however, ruled that the clearly disjunctive language of Article 87 included cases where an accused missed his individual port call.[67]

---

56. MCM, Part IV, para. 10c(4). *See also* Appendix 30, Chart of Maximum Punishments.
57. MCM, Part IV, para. 10e(2)(d). United States v. Northern, 42 M.J. 638 (N.M.Ct.Crim.App. 1995) (accused's guilty plea to UA terminated by apprehension was provident; court concluded that accused revealed his military status to apprehending civilian authorities who questioned him; he did not voluntarily return to military control).
58. MCM, Part IV, para. 10c(4)(c), (d).
59. MCM, Part IV, para. 10c(4)(e).
60. MCM, Part IV, para. 10c(3).
61. Art. 87, U.C.M.J.
62. United States v. Quezada, 40 M.J. 109 (C.M.A. 1994) (missing movement for 8-hour dependents cruise on aircraft carrier was not minor; court noted that plain language of codal provision centered on accused's duty to move with ship, not on purpose for movement); United States v. Jones, 1 C.M.A. 276, 3 C.M.R. 10 (1952).
63. *Id.* United States v. Smith, 34 M.J. 1005 (A.C.M.R. 1992) (accused's failure to rejoin unit after he had initially moved with it was not a unit movement as contemplated by Article 87); United States v. Smith, 2 M.J. 566 (A.C.M.R. 1976) (on-post, two-day manuever and bivouac area 12 miles down range of unit's permanent headquarters was not a "movement" within meaning of statute), *aff'd on other grounds,* 4 M.J. 210 (C.M.A. 1978).
64. *See* United States v. Bisser, 27 M.J. 692 (N.M.C.M.R. 1988) (accused could be convicted of missing multiple movements where commander had divided Marine squadron into three separate "units" consisting of an advance party, the main body, and the fly-on unit).
65. *See, e.g.,* United States v. Blair, 24 M.J. 879 (A.C.M.R. 1987) (accused violated Article 87 even though the aircraft he was to board was a "commercial" airliner); United States v. Lemley, 2 M.J. 1196 (N.C.M.R. 1976).
66. 16 M.J. 460 (C.M.A. 1983). *See also* United States v. Johnson, 3 C.M.A. 174, 11 C.M.R. 174 (1953).
67. MCM, Part IV, para. 11c(2). United States v. Kapple, 40 M.J. 472 (C.M.A. 1994) (evidence insufficient to show that accused missed movement; government presented no evidence that

Note that the offense may be committed with intent (through "design") or through neglect. In the case of the former, the act must be knowing and purposeful.[68] Negligence, such as failing to allow sufficient time to report to the departure station, will also support a finding of guilty.[69] In either case, however, the prosecution must establish that the accused knew of the pending movement.[70]

§ 2-2(E). Defenses to Absence Offenses.

§ 2-2(E)(1). Impossibility.

A variety of circumstances amounting to impossibility to return may serve as a valid defense to the various unauthorized absence offenses. The circumstances must, however, be unforeseen and through no fault of the servicemember.[71] The impossibility may result from physical inability,[72] transportation problems,[73] acts of third parties,[74] or acts of God.[75]

---

accused was required to travel on specific aircraft; CMR opinion includes discussion of evolution of missing movement offense, 36 M.J. 1119 (A.F.C.M.R. 1993)); United States v. Smith, 26 M.J. 276 (C.M.A. 1988) (accused guilty of missing movement although he was permitted to travel individually when unit was moved from CONUS to Germany; court stated that it is the missed move which is significant, not the mode of moving); United States v. Ray, 37 M.J. 1052 (N.M.C.M.R. 1993) (discussion reuse of Article 87 to punish accused's failure to board commercial airline; court found nexus between accused's actions and foreseeable disruption of operations); United States v. Stroud, 27 M.J. 765 (A.F.C.M.R. 1988) (accused guilty of missing movement by failing to catch his commercial overseas flight); United States v. Blair, 24 M.J. 879 (A.C.M.R. 1987). *Cf.* United States v. Gibson, 17 M.J. 143 (C.M.A. 1984) (missing movement not committed where accused was given airline ticket and told to catch a flight).

68. *See* United States v. Bridges, 9 C.M.A. 121, 25 C.M.R. 383 (1958); United States v. Thompson, 2 C.M.A. 460, 9 C.M.R. 90 (1953).

69. *See* United States v. Mitchell, 3 M.J. 641 (A.C.M.R. 1977), *petition denied*, 8 M.J. 76 (C.M.A. 1979).

70. Knowledge of the pending movement may be established through circumstantial evidence. United States v. Chandler, 23 C.M.A. 193, 48 C.M.R. 945 (1974).

71. United States v. Smith, 34 M.J. 1005 (A.C.M.R. 1992) (accused's inability to see doctor, pick up his children and take them home, and return to unit at designated time did not raise defense of impossibility; these were matters within his control); United States v. Sprague, 25 M.J. 743 (A.C.M.R. 1987) (accused's absence was due to civil arrest triggered by his failure to comply with civil judge's order); United States v. Franklin, 4 M.J. 635 (A.F.C.M.R. 1977).

72. United States v. Barnes, 39 M.J. 230 (C.M.A. 1994) (evidence raised defense of physical inability to return; accused was allegedly victim of carjacking; court noted that defense may be defeated by showing that accused did not exert sufficient effort to overcome disability); United States v. Irving, 2 M.J. 967 (A.C.M.R. 1976), *petition denied*, 2 M.J. 197 (C.M.A. 1977). *Cf.* United States v. Bermudez, 47 C.M.R. 68 (A.F.C.M.R. 1973) (accused made no attempts to seek assistance from civilian or military authorities); United States v. Myhre, 9 C.M.A. 32, 25 C.M.R. 294 (1958) (voluntary intoxication not a defense).

73. The defense will not be available if the accused, for example, decides to remain with his car

---

74. Typical examples would include automobile accidents or traffic congestion not caused by the accused.

75. Of particular note, here, however, is the point that the defense may not be available where the act of God (or Nature) is expected, such as an approaching hurricane with accompanying winds and floods.

§ 2-2(E)(2). Justification or Necessity.

The defense of justification may be available to the accused, if he or she can show that their absence offense was in furtherance of a legal duty, established by a statute, order, or regulation.[76] The defense of necessity may be available where the accused can show that he or she committed the absence offense to avoid a greater evil.[77]

§ 2-2(E)(3). Duress.

The defense of duress is available where the servicemember reasonably fears that immediate death or serious bodily injury will occur if the act in question is not committed.[78] It may also be available in those situations where the servicemember fears that death or injury will occur to others.[79] Fear of a perilous duty[80] or fear of aggravating an existing injury[81] will normally not suffice, however. Likewise, fear of injury to reputation or property will not

---

while awaiting repairs for his convenience, United States v. Kessinger, 9 C.M.R. 261 (A.B.R. 1952), or where the accused through his own negligence misses his transportation, United States v. Mann, 12 C.M.R. 367 (A.B.R. 1953); United States v. Williams, 21 M.J. 360 (C.M.A. 1986) (accused unsuccessfully raised defense of "lost airline tickets" in 3-year AWOL); United States v. Kapple, 36 M.J. 1119 (A.F.C.M.R. 1993), *rev'd on other grounds*, 40 M.J. 472 (C.M.A. 1994) (defense not available to accused who claimed wreck of wife's car as reason for missing flight; the wreck occurred day before scheduled departure and he made no attempt to find alternate means of transportation; the court noted that the defense of impossibility had been construed narrowly); United States v. Lee, 14 M.J. 633 (A.C.M.R. 1982) (court rejected defense where accused argued that 40 hours' absence resulted from car trouble).

76. R.C.M. 916(c)(defense of justification).
77. *See* United States v. Huet-Vaughn, 43 M.J. 105 (1995) (citing cases).
78. See R.C.M. 916(h) for a general discussion of the defense of duress. United States v. Rankins, 34 M.J. 326 (C.M.A. 1992) (evidence did not raise defense of impossibility where accused failed to show that her husband's health problems raised a well-grounded fear); United States v. Mitchell, 34 M.J. 970 (A.C.M.R. 1992) (defense of duress not available where accused had concern for wife's mental stability and suicidal tendencies).
   In United States v. Roberts, 14 M.J. 671 (N.M.C.M.R. 1982), *rev'd as to one of appellants*, 15 M.J. 106 (C.M.A. 1983), the court held that the threat of an initiation ceremony, under the circumstances, was justification for a reasonably grounded fear of bodily injury.
   In United States v. Hullum, 15 M.J. 261 (C.M.A. 1983), the court extended this defense to racial harassments extending to threats on one's life.
   United States v. Campfield, 17 M.J. 715 (N.M.C.M.R. 1983) (defense not available where accused failed to report threats to his chain-of-command; therefore, he did not have reasonably grounded fear).
79. United States v. Jemmings, 1 M.J. 414 (C.M.A. 1976); United States v. Banks, 37 M.J. 700 (A.C.M.R. 1993) (distinction between defenses of necessity and duress; neither defense was available to accused who chose to stay with ill mother at completion of authorized leave). *Cf.* United States v. Roberts, 14 M.J. 671 (N.M.C.M.R. 1982), *rev'd as to husband*, 15 M.J. 106 (C.M.A. 1983) (husband's absence was not excused on ground that his wife, also a servicemember, feared for her safety).
80. *See, e.g.*, United States v. Wilson, 30 C.M.R. 630 (N.B.R. 1960).
81. United States v. Guzman, 3 M.J. 740 (N.C.M.R. 1977), *rev'd on other grounds*, 4 M.J. 115 (C.M.A. 1977).

support the defense of duress.[82] The defense of duress is only available where the source of the coercion is applied by a third person.[83]

§ 2-2(E)(4). Mistake of Fact.

In order for a servicemember to successfully assert the defense of mistake of fact, he must establish that his mistake is both reasonable and honest.[84] This defense is often raised in those situations where the servicemember is told to go home and await further orders[85] or discharge from the armed forces.[86]

§ 2-2(E)(5). Civilian Detention.

If a servicemember is unable to return to military control because of civilian detention, that circumstance may be available as a defense if he was turned over to civilian authorities,[87] or if while on proper leave he was detained, tried, but later acquitted.[88] This defense is actually a variation of the impossibility defense discussed earlier.[89] As a general rule, this defense is not available where the servicemember through his own actions ends up in civilian confinement.[90] Military authorities are required to seek the release of the servicemember if the civilians indicate that they are not going to prosecute.[91] Where the civilian authorities are willing to turn over a known absentee to the military, failure of the latter to assume custody will constructively terminate the absence.[92]

---

82. R.C.M. 916(h).
83. United States v. Collins, 37 M.J. 1072 (N.M.C.M.R. 1993) (defense not available to accused who claimed that he committed unauthorized absence because of pregnancy problems of fiancee); United States v. Rankins, 34 M.J. 326, 330, n. 2 (C.M.A. 1992); United States v. Mitchell, 34 M.J. 970 (A.C.M.R. 1992).
84. United States v. Scheunemann, 14 C.M.A. 479, 34 C.M.R. 259 (1964). When the defense is raised the prosecution must establish beyond a reasonable doubt that the mistake was not honest and reasonable. United States v. Thompson, 39 C.M.R. 537 (A.B.R. 1968). R.C.M. 916(b).
85. United States v. Davis, 22 C.M.A. 241, 46 C.M.R. 241 (1973) (accused went home to await orders to go to Vietnam).
86. *See* United States v. King, 27 M.J. 327 (C.M.A. 1989) (in dicta the court indicated that if the accused believed that he had returned to civilian status that it would be difficult for the government to show the requisite *mens rea*); United States v. Holder, 7 C.M.A. 213, 22 C.M.R. 3 (1956).
87. United States v. Northrup, 12 C.M.A. 487, 31 C.M.R. 73 (1961).
88. The accused must, however, make an attempt to return following the acquittal. *See* United States v. Grover, 10 C.M.A. 91, 27 C.M.R. 165 (1958).
89. *See supra* § 2-2(E)(1).
90. United States v. Myhre, 9 C.M.A. 32, 25 C.M.R. 294 (1958).
91. United States v. Lanphear, 23 C.M.A. 338, 49 C.M.R. 742 (1975).
92. *Id.* United States v. Asbury, 28 M.J. 595 (N.M.C.M.R. 1989) (termination of desertion). *See also supra* § 2-2(C) and accompanying notes for discussion of methods of terminating absences. *Cf.* United States v. Dubry, 12 M.J. 36 (C.M.A. 1981) (because accused was under a state appeal bond he was not available for return to unrestricted military control).

§ 2-2(E)(6). Statute of Limitations.

The statute of limitations[93] may be used as a defense to the absence offenses: five years for AWOL and desertion.[94] There is no statute of limitations for these offenses, however, in time of war.[95] What constitutes "war" is a question of fact. Both the Korean and Vietnam Conflicts were considered "wars" within the context of the availability of this defense.[96] Even in time of peace certain periods are excluded in computing the running of the statute: (1) When the servicemember is absent from the territory in which the United States has authority to apprehend him; (2) When the servicemember is in the custody of civil authorities, or (3) When the servicemember is in the custody of the enemy.[97]

Additionally, the statute is tolled when charges are preferred and endorsed by the summary court-martial convening authority.[98] Most jurisdictions in order to so toll the statute, will forward the charges, file them, and upon the accused's return to military control, add the termination date to the charges.[99] Although the statute may be waived,[100] the military judge has a responsibility to inform the accused of the right to interpose the statute.[101] The burden of showing timeliness is upon the government.[102]

§ 2-2(E)(7). Moral Grounds or Beliefs.

An accused charged with one of the absence offenses may attempt to assert that he absented himself, or refused to report to a particular location, on grounds that the order violated the accused's moral beliefs or conscience. For example in *United States v. Huet-Vaughn*,[103] the accused, a medical doctor,

---

93. See also infra § 13-3(b).
94. Art. 43(b), U.C.M.J. Before 1986, when Art. 43 was amended, the periods were two and three years, respectively.
95. Art. 43(a), U.C.M.J.
96. United States v. Anderson, 17 C.M.A. 588, 38 C.M.R. 386 (1968) (time of war ended on January 27, 1973 for hostilities in Vietnam); United States v. Shell, 7 C.M.A. 646, 23 C.M.R. 110 (1957) ("time of war" in Korea ended on February 27, 1953); United States v. Dienst, 16 M.J. 727 (A.F.C.M.R. 1983) (statute tolled where accused deserted during Vietnam conflict).
97. Art. 43(d), U.C.M.J.
98. Art. 43(c), U.C.M.J. See United States v. Johnson, 3 M.J. 623 (N.C.M.R. 1977). But the statute does bar prosecution where a new charge sheet is prepared after the statute has expired. See United States v. Arsneault, 6 M.J. 182 (C.M.A. 1979). Minor amendments may be made later without affecting the statute of limitations. United States v. Reeves, 49 C.M.R. 841 (A.C.M.R. 1975) (addition of AWOL termination date to previously sworn charge); United States v. Arbic, 16 C.M.A. 292, 36 C.M.R. 448 (1966). See also infra §§ 6-1(B)(2), 6-2(B).
99. United States v. Reeves, 49 C.M.R. 841 (A.C.M.R. 1975). See infra Chapter 6 for a discussion of forwarding of sworn charges through the summary court-martial convening authority.
100. United States v. Troxell, 12 C.M.A. 6, 30 C.M.R. 6 (1960).
101. United States v. Brown, 1 M.J. 1151 (N.C.M.R. 1977). See also United States v. Cooper, 16 C.M.R. 390, 37 C.M.R. 10 (1966) (judge has duty to advise accused of availability of statute of limitations where the accused has been found guilty of a lesser-included offense against which the statute has run).
102. United States v. Morris, 11 C.M.A. 16, 28 C.M.R. 240 (1959).
103. 43 M.J. 105 (1995).

absented herself after her reserve unit was ordered to deploy to Southwest Asia as part of Operation "Desert Storm." At trial on a charge of desertion, she argued that she was entitled to offer evidence of her moral and religious beliefs as a defense and also urged the so-called "Nuremburg defense" on grounds that the United States' actions were crimes against humanity and international law. The court concluded that an absence defense based upon conscience, religion, personal philosophies, ethical or professional factors is not a valid defense.[104] With regard to the "Nuremburg defense," the court concluded that that defense is only applicable to individual acts during wartime and not to the government's decision to wage war.[105] The accused, said the court, had not shown that she was ordered, as an individual, to commit a positive act which would have amounted to a war crime.[106] Her general challenge to the legality of the deployment itself, said the court, was a non-justiciable political question.[107]

§ 2-3. Disrespect Offenses.

At the core of the military's structure is the superior-subordinate relationship. Disrespect of the relationship or disobedience of orders coming from a superior is considered a potential threat to military discipline.[1] This section examines those punitive articles in the U.C.M.J. directed at proscribing disrespect. The following section[2] will discuss those offenses involving disobedience.

Within the general category of military disrespect offenses exist two primary offenses: disrespect to superior commissioned officers,[3] and insubordinate conduct toward petty or warrant officers or noncommissioned officers.[4] Discussion centers on these two, although the military system does recognize other forms of offenses that amount to disrespect of the superior-subordinate relationship. For example, officers are prohibited from expressing contempt toward officials[5] and mutiny and sedition are also offenses against superiors.[6] Note that disrespect offenses may be lesser-included offenses to other crimes.[7]

---

104. 43 M.J. at 115.
105. 43 M.J. at 114.
106. 43 M.J. at 114.
107. 43 M.J. at 115. United States v. Berrigan, 283 F. Supp. 336 (D. Md. 1968), aff'd, sub nom, United States v. Eberhardt, 417 F.2d 1009 (4th Cir. 1969) (discussion of "Nurnberg [sic.] defense.")
1. See Parker v. Levy, 417 U.S. 733 (1974), where court noted well-settled precedent for necessity of support for superior-subordinate relationship in the military society.
2. See infra § 2-4.
3. Art. 89, U.C.M.J. See infra § 2-3(A).
4. Art. 91, U.C.M.J. See infra § 2-3(B).
5. Art. 88, U.C.M.J.; MCM, Part IV, para. 12.
6. Art. 94, U.C.M.J.; MCM, Part IV, para. 18.
7. It may be a lesser-included offense to assault, United States v. Van Beek, 47 C.M.R. 98 (A.C.M.R. 1973), or threat, United States v. Ross, 40 C.M.R. 718 (A.C.M.R. 1969).

§ 2-3(A). Disrespect Toward Officers.

Article 89, U.C.M.J. proscribes a servicemember's behavior that constitutes "disrespect toward his superior commissioned officer."[8] The questioned behavior must be such that it detracts from the respect due to the superior officer and his authority.[9] To be guilty of this offense it is not necessary that the officer be executing his office, nor is it essential that the disrespectful behavior occur in the presence of the officer.[10] Mere difference in rank is not always determinative. An officer being disrespectful to another officer junior in rank but superior in the chain of command may be guilty of this offense.[11] It is essential that the prosecution establish that the accused had actual knowledge of the officer's status.[12] Finally, the disrespectful behavior may be either in the form of words[13] or actions.[14]

§ 2-3(B). Insubordination Toward Petty, Warrant, or Noncommissioned Officers.

An enlisted servicemember, noncommissioned officer (NCO), or warrant officer who treats with contempt, or is disrespectful in language or deportment toward, a noncommissioned officer, petty, or warrant officer may be guilty of insubordination under Article 91, U.C.M.J.[15] The words or actions must be in the presence of the victim[16] and with knowledge of the victim's status.[17] Additionally, the victim must be in the "execution of his office"[18] at

---

8. Art. 89, U.C.M.J.
9. MCM, Part IV, para. 13c(3). United States v. Merriweather, 13 M.J. 605 (A.F.C.M.R. 1982) (Air Force servicemember could not be guilty of disrespect to superior officers in the Navy where they were not in his chain of command. He was found guilty of disorderly conduct, a lesser-included offense). Cf. United States v. White, 39 M.J. 796 (N.M.C.M.R. 1994) (Navy enlisted servicemember guilty of disrespect to Air Force NCO).
10. *Id. See* United States v. Van Beek, 47 C.M.R. 98 (A.C.M.R. 1973) (detonation of chemical grenade on window of absent officer's quarters was disrespectful).
Normally, an accused will not be held accountable for disrespectful language in private conversations. *Cf.* United States v. Hoxsey, 17 M.J. 964 (A.F.C.M.R. 1984) (accused's disrespectful comments during phone conversation with NCO were not private).
11. United States v. Peoples, 6 M.J. 904 (A.C.M.R. 1979), *petition denied,* 7 M.J. 141 (C.M.A. 1979).
12. United States v. Ross, 40 M.C.R. 718 (A.C.M.R. 1969).
13. United States v. Montgomery, 11 C.M.R. 308 (A.B.R. 1953); United States v. Dornick, 16 M.J. 642 (A.F.C.M.R. 1983) (accused said "Hi, sweetheart" to his superior commissioned female officer).
14. United States v. Ferenczi, 10 C.M.A. 3, 27 C.M.R. 77 (1958) (accused walked away while superior was talking to him).
15. MCM, Part IV, para. 15.
16. MCM, Part IV, para. 15.
17. United States v. Lusk, 21 M.J. 695 (A.C.M.R. 1985) (defense of mistake of fact not available to accused charged with disobeying order by NCO); United States v. Ross, 40 C.M.R. 718 (A.C.M.R. 1969) (servicemember must be conditioned to err on the side of obedience).
18. United States v. Brooks, 44 C.M.R. 873 (A.C.M.R. 1971); United States v. White, 39 M.J. 796 (N.M.C.M.R. 1994) (extensive discussion of issue of whether enlisted member of one service can be found guilty of showing disrespect to servicemember in another service; court concluded that the offense does not occur simply because the victim is superior in rank to the accused; the

the time of the offense. In *United States v. Wasson*,[19] the court noted the distinction between disrespectful language and deportment. Where accused is charged with the former, the court may not consider the manner in which the words were spoken. Here, the accused's words, "I'm tired of this crap," were not in themselves disrespectful. The court observed:

> A word is not rendered inherently disrespectful merely because it is sometimes considered vulgar. The conditions surrounding the use of the word are important. Words which might be acceptable when spoken to a guard at Buckingham Palace might be disrespectful if spoken to the Queen. We are being unrealistic, and more restrictive than the law requires, to expect only pristine, courtly language to be used in the Air Force. While the appellant's use of the word "crap" showed a certain roughness in his language, we are not convinced beyond a reasonable doubt that the word is inherently disrespectful.

An accused may commit this offense even if he is superior in rank to the alleged victim.[20] If the victim is superior in rank to the accused, that fact may be an aggravating factor for punishment purposes if properly pleaded and proved.[21]

§ 2-3(C). Defenses to Disrespect Offenses.

The military courts have recognized several defenses to the foregoing disrespect offenses. First, contemptuous or other disrespectful words must be directed "toward" the victim. Simply uttering the words in the presence of the victim will not suffice.[22]

Second, the victim through words or actions may have abandoned his status as a superior.[23] For example, the victim may have invited the accused to

---

question is whether the victim was in a position of authority over the accused; here a Navy enlisted member was guilty of disrespect toward Air Force NCOs who were apprehending him). Note that an officer may be protected at any time. United States v. Montgomery, 11 C.M.R. 308 (A.B.R. 1953) (during poker game). "Acting" noncommissioned officers are not protected. *See* United States v. Sutton, 23 C.M.A. 231, 49 C.M.R. 248 (1974).

19. 26 M.J. 894 (A.F.C.M.R. 1988). *See also* United States v. Barber, 8 M.J. 153 (C.M.A. 1979) (relatively neutral words supported conviction); United States v. Klein, 42 C.M.R. 671 (A.C.M.R. 1970) (otherwise neutral words did not constitute disrespect to officer); United States v. Woltmann, 22 C.M.R. 737 (C.G.C.B.R. 1956) (words contained no epithet, no obscenity, nor denunciation).

20. This is a change from the 1969 *Manual,* para. 170, which suggested that a superior-subordinate relationship was necessary. *See* MCM, Part IV, para. 15(c)(1) Analysis.

21. Note that the victim's status as the accused's superior is *not* an aggravating factor where the victim is a warrant officer. A higher punishment already exists for contempt or disrespect to a warrant officer. *Compare* the Maximum Punishment Chart at Appendix 30.

22. *See, e.g.,* United States v. Wasson, 26 M.J. 894 (A.F.C.M.R. 1988) (words "I'm tired of this crap" suggested the accused's view of his situation and were not directed at any one person); United States v. Sorrells, 49 C.M.R. 44 (A.C.M.R. 1974).

23. MCM, Part IV, para. 13c(5) ("unprotected victim"); United States v. Middleton, 36 M.J. 835 (A.C.M.R. 1993) (divestiture defense was not available to assault upon NCO where accused argued that he and NCO were close friends and occasionally joked around; the court said the defense rests on conduct which is incompatible with rank or status); United States v. Collier, 27

§ 2-4   MILITARY CRIMES   § 2-4(A)

fight[24] or may have used profanity[25] or a racial slur[26] against the accused. However, an officer conducting an unwarranted search does not divest himself of his status,[27] nor does an NCO necessarily lose his status by attempting to control a drunk servicemember by forcing him into a cold shower.[28] Where an officer's actions have a military purpose, mere incompetence or poor judgment on the part of the officer do not divest that officer of his or her office.[29] Third, lack of knowledge of the victim's status is a defense.[30]

§ 2-4. Disobedience Offenses.

§ 2-4(A). General.

In addition to the absence offenses discussed in the preceding sections, a number of offenses, which may be generally labelled as disobedience offenses, are proscribed in Articles 90, 91, and 92 of the U.C.M.J.[1] Before proceeding with examination of each of those offenses, some general comments are in order regarding the legality of orders.

Orders and regulations are presumed to be lawful.[2] If defense evidence raises the issue, however, the prosecution must establish lawfulness.[3] If the

---

M.J. 806 (A.C.M.R. 1988) (warrant officer did not use language so shocking, out of the ordinary, or inappropriately challenging so as to divest himself of his status and thereby permit disobedience of order).

24. United States v. Struckman, 20 C.M.A. 493, 43 C.M.R. 333 (1971).

25. United States v. Sanders, 37 M.J. 628 (A.C.M.R. 1993), aff'd, 41 M.J. 485 (1995) (discussion of divestiture defense in assault case); United States v. Collier, 27 M.J. 806 (A.C.M.R. 1988) (although language used by warrant officer was not language used in polite society, it was typical of language "used daily in line units, motor pools, and the like by soldiers and their superiors"); United States v. Cheeks, 43 C.M.R. 1013 (A.F.C.M.R. 1971). See also United States v. Allen, 10 M.J. 576 (A.C.M.R. 1980).

26. See, e.g., United States v. Richardson, 7 M.J. 320 (C.M.A. 1979) (although the approved findings did not include status as an element, NCO's calling the accused a "boy" was considered as mitigating evidence to offense of assault).

27. United States v. Lewis, 7 M.J. 348 (C.M.A. 1979) (disrespectful conduct arose during apprehension and advising of rights when accused said, "Aw man, I don't have to listen to this").

28. United States v. McDaniel, 7 M.J. 522 (A.C.M.R. 1979) (NCO, in order to calm down the intoxicated and belligerent accused, used the "time-honored remedy" of the cold shower). If the NCO is properly exercising his duties, there is no abandonment of status. See United States v. Vallenthine, 2 M.J. 1170 (N.C.M.R. 1975).

29. United States v. Pratcher, 17 M.J. 388 (C.M.A. 1984) (officer's mismanagement of accused's financial problem, which resulted in heated discussion, did not divest officer of status); United States v. Pratcher, 14 M.J. 819 (A.C.M.R. 1982) (officer mishandled counselling session which led to disrespect by accused).

30. United States v. Ross, 40 C.M.R. 718 (A.C.M.R. 1969).

1. See Appendix 3. Art. 90, U.C.M.J. (disobedience of a superior's orders); Art. 91, U.C.M.J. (disobedience of orders of warrant, petty, or noncommissioned officer); Article 92, U.C.M.J. (disobedience of orders or regulations).

2. Unger v. Ziemniak, 27 M.J. 349 (C.M.A. 1989) (order to female officer to present urine sample in presence of another person did not appear to be unreasonable); United States v. Smith, 21 C.M.A. 231, 45 C.M.R. 5 (1972). See § 13-3(N) for constitutional challenges to regulations and orders.

3. Unger v. Ziemniak, 27 M.J. 349 (C.M.A. 1989) (if facts are undisputed as to lawfulness, the

§ 2-4(A) MILITARY CRIMINAL JUSTICE § 2-4(A)

authority giving the order is without authority to do so[4] or if the order is not related to "military duty,"[5] it is unlawful. It is this latter area that most often finds the concept of military order at loggerheads with private rights.[6] The military services may properly regulate conduct affecting military duties or service:

> All activities which are reasonably necessary to safeguard and protect the morale, discipline and usefulness of the members of a command and are directly connected with the maintenance of good order in the services are subject to the control of the officers upon whom the responsibility of the command rests.[7]

And in *United States v. Smith*,[8] the court noted that military duty may include activities which are:

> [r]easonably necessary to safeguard or promote the morale, discipline, and usefulness of the members of any particular command and which are directly connected with the maintenance of good order.[9]

Typically, lawful orders may be used to regulate hygiene,[10] dress[11] and grooming,[12] consumption of alcohol or drugs,[13] blackmarketing activities,[14] financial

---

trial judge decides the issue; but if they are controverted the fact-finder must find lawfulness beyond a reasonable doubt); United States v. Tiggs, 40 C.M.R. 352 (A.B.R. 1968).

4. United States v. Gray, 6 C.M.A. 615, 20 C.M.R. 331 (1956).

5. United States v. Horner, 32 M.J. 576 (C.G.C.M.R. 1991) (order to shower directly related to accused's duties as cook).

6. United States v. Flynn, 34 M.J. 1183 (A.F.C.M.R. 1992) (order requiring unit members to remain within 400-mile radius of base or be on pass maintained order and discipline by insuring reasonable accountability for duty purposes); United States v. Spencer, 29 M.J. 740 (A.F.C.M.R. 1989) (order from hospital commander to produce all civilian medical records was broader and more restrictive of private rights than required by military needs).

7. United States v. Martin, 1 C.M.A. 674, 676, 5 C.M.R. 102, 104 (1952).

8. 25 M.J. 545 (A.C.M.R. 1987) (an order to the accused to produce the title to a car purchased from her by a junior enlisted servicemember was legal where fraud and trickery were involved and the commander was attempting to end the resulting administrative problems).

9. 25 M.J. at 548.

10. United States v. Horner, 32 M.J. 576 (C.G.C.M.R. 1991) (order to take a shower).

11. United States v. Wartsbaugh, 21 C.M.A. 535, 45 C.M.R. 309 (1972) (prohibited wearing of bracelet); United States v. Yunque-Burgos, 3 C.M.A. 498, 13 C.M.R. 54 (1953) (prohibited wearing of civilian clothing).

12. *See, e.g.,* United States v. Verdi, 5 M.J. 330 (C.M.A. 1978) (regulation controlling length of hair and wearing of wigs); United States v. Young, 1 M.J. 433 (C.M.A. 1976) (standards of hair grooming).

13. The court in United States v. Blye, 37 M.J. 92 (C.M.A. 1993) discussed the legality of issuing orders not to consume alcohol and concluded that:

> a military member may be lawfully ordered not to consume alcoholic beverages as a condition of pretrial restriction if such order is reasonably necessary to protect the morale, welfare, and safety of the unit (or the accused); to protect victims or potential witnesses; or to ensure the accused's presence at the court-martial or pretrial hearings in a sober condition.

14. United States v. Lumagui, 31 M.J. 789 (A.F.C.M.R. 1990) (blackmarket regulation was not overbroad and was constitutional because it expressed a valid military interest in conforming with customs requirements).

matters,[15] production of urine or body evidence samples,[16] and association with other persons.[17]

But the mere fact that an order may legitimately relate to a military duty or purpose does not mean that the order is enforceable. Potential constitutional problems may arise where the order infringes upon a servicemember's constitutional rights. Where, for example, an order places restrictions on a servicemember's "speech," the lawfulness of the order is directly questioned.[18]

See also United States v. McMonagle, 34 M.J. 852 (A.C.M.R. 1992) (general order in Panama not to consume alcohol); United States v. Stewart, 33 M.J. 519 (A.F.C.M.R. 1991) (although order to refrain from drinking alcohol is not patently illegal it must have some connection to military duty; order to refrain could not be used as diagnostic tool for determining whether accused was alcoholic); United States v. McFatrich, 32 M.J. 1039 (A.C.M.R. 1991) (accused convicted for violating lawful general regulation against being on duty with more than a blood-alcohol level of .05%); United States v. Kochan, 27 M.J. 574 (N.M.C.M.R. 1988) (order to accused not to drink alcoholic beverages until he had reached state's drinking age was illegal because it was too broad and not related to military duties); United States v. Alexander, 26 M.J. 796 (A.F.C.M.R. 1988).

Cf. United States v. Roach, 29 M.J. 33 (C.M.A. 1989) (court concluded that order to refrain from consuming alcoholic beverages was in violation of Coast Guard regulations and did not address issue of whether there was a valid military need for the order); United States v. Green, 22 M.J. 711 (A.C.M.R. 1986) (regulation governing use of alcohol held void).

15. United States v. McClain, 10 M.J. 271 (C.M.A. 1981) (making loans prohibited).

16. United States v. Musguire, 9 C.M.A. 67, 25 C.M.R. 329 (1958) (order to submit to blood test was illegal); United States v. Ruiz, 23 C.M.A. 181, 48 C.M.R. 797 (1974) (order to urinate for drug testing was illegal). These decisions rested on the court's application of the right against self-incrimination provided in Article 31, U.C.M.J. The court has since held that blood and urine samples are not protected under that provision. United States v. Armstrong, 9 M.J. 374 (C.M.A. 1980). *See also* United States v. Lloyd, 10 M.J. 172 (C.M.A. 1981) (handwriting samples not protected); Murray v. Haldeman, 16 M.J. 74 (C.M.A. 1983); United States v. Blair, 29 M.J. 862 (A.F.C.M.R. 1989) (commander's order to present urine sample was based upon reasonable suspicion and was therefore lawful).

17. United States v. Flynn, 34 M.J. 1183 (A.F.C.M.R. 1992) (order that officer not have contact with female airman was reasonable and preserved good order and discipline within unit); United States v. McMonagle, 34 M.J. 852 (A.C.M.R. 1992) (general order in Panama not to consort with females); United States v. Hoard, 12 M.J. 563 (A.C.M.R. 1981) (fraternization). *See infra* § 2-8 for a discussion on the offense of fraternization.

United States v. Wheeler, 12 C.M.A. 387, 30 C.M.R. 387 (1961) (regulations restricting marriage of servicemembers assigned overseas to local nationals were legal); United States v. Button, 31 M.J. 897 (A.F.C.M.R. 1990) (order not to go to residence where victim resided was lawful); United States v. Wine, 28 M.J. 688 (A.F.C.M.R. 1989) (order to accused to disassociate himself from dependent friend's wife was lawful).

18. *See, e.g.,* Parker v. Levy, 417 U.S. 733 (1974) and United States v. Priest, 21 C.M.A. 564, 45 C.M.R. 338 (1972) (court balanced needs of military service against right of servicemembers to protest the Vietnam war).

See generally Boyce, "Freedom of Speech and the Military," 1968 Utah L. Rev. 240; Imwinkelried & Zillman, "An Evolution in the First Amendment: Overbreadth Analysis and Free Speech Within the Military Community," 54 Tex. L. Rev. 42 (1972); Lewis, "Freedom of Speech An Examination of the Civilian Test for Constitutionality and Its Application to the Military," 41 Mil. L. Rev. 55 (1968); Wolf, "Commentary: A Soldier's First Amendment Rights: The Art of Formally Granting and Practically Suppressing," 18 Wayne L. Rev. 665 (1972); Zillman & Imwinkelried, "Constitutional Rights and Military Necessity: Reflections on a Society Apart," 51 Notre Dame L. Rev. 396 (1976); Note, "Free Speech in the Military," 65 Marq. L. Rev. 660 (1982).

§ 2-4(B) MILITARY CRIMINAL JUSTICE § 2-4(B)

The courts, both military and civilian, tend to support reasonable limits upon a servicemember's activities but will not enforce orders that clearly conflict with a servicemember's constitutional or statutory rights.[19] For a discussion on constitutional challenges to orders and regulations, see § 13-3(N).

If conflicting orders have been given, the general rule is the last order should be obeyed,[20] in order to avoid the problem of requiring the accused to simultaneously comply with two orders.[21] No conflict, however, should exist where one order is a lawful specific order and the other is simply to perform regularly assigned duties.[22]

§ 2-4(B). Disobedience of a Superior's Orders.

Disobedience of a superior's direct, personal orders may be in violation of either Article 90(2) (orders of officers) or Article 91(2) (orders of warrant, petty, or noncommissioned officers).[23] Under either provision the order must be a positive command[24] directed personally to the accused,[25] who must have

---

19. In United States v. Austin, 27 M.J. 227 (C.M.A. 1988), the accused disobeyed two orders to draw a weapon and unsuccessfully argued in defense that at the time of the orders, he had applied for status as a conscientious objector and that the orders therefore violated AR 600-43. The court disagreed, finding that the first order was given after his first application had been denied and that the second order had been given before he properly submitted the second application.

20. United States v. Morse, 34 M.J. 677 (A.C.M.R. 1992) (order to deploy was not in conflict with regulation regarding filing of conscientious objector status); United States v. Hill, 26 M.J. 876 (N.M.C.M.R. 1988).

21. United States v. Patton, 41 C.M.R. 572 (A.C.M.R. 1969).

22. United States v. Hill, 26 M.J. 876 (N.M.C.M.R. 1988) (no conflict existed where a lawful order, enforcing his commander's order, took precedence over accused's responsibility to report for regularly assigned duties).

23. *See* MCM, Part IV, paras. 14, 15.

24. United States v. Mitchell, 6 C.M.A. 579, 20 C.M.R. 295 (1955). A directive that, for example, is mere advice, is not a positive command amounting to an "order."
United States v. Warren, 13 M.J. 160 (C.M.A. 1982) (officer telling soldier to "settle down and be quiet" not an order under these facts); United States v. Mantilla, 36 M.J. 621 (A.C.M.R. 1992) (although order must be positive command, the form of the order is immaterial; accused violated order to double-time); United States v. Claytor, 34 M.J. 1030 (N.M.C.M.R. 1992) (order to shut up, following disrespectful words by accused, was a specific order related to maintenance of good order and discipline); United States v. Victorian, 31 M.J. 830 (N.M.C.M.R. 1990) (ruling by NCO sitting as camp traffic court judge that barred accused from driving privileges did not amount to an "order" for which he could be prosecuted; he should have been prosecuted under Camp Regulation that prohibited him from driving while his privileges were suspended).
United States v. Beattie, 17 M.J. 537 (A.C.M.R. 1983) (officer's order to report to his "place of duty" was not, under the facts, a clear enough mandate to establish violation of Art. 90; the case includes a list of cases involving orders to go to training, duty, etc.); United States v. McLaughlin, 14 M.J. 908 (N.M.C.M.R. 1982) (accused charged with disobeying lawful order, *see* § 2-4(D); order valid even though preceded with a "please;" case contains good discussion of "orders" offenses).

25. United States v. Byers, 40 M.J. 321 (C.M.A. 1994) (no evidence that general did anything to lift his routine driving regulations above common ruck to make disobeying it a violation of Article 90); United States v. Wartsbaugh, 21 C.M.A. 535, 45 C.M.R. 309 (1972); United States v. Selman, 28 M.J. 627 (A.F.C.M.R. 1989) (letter requiring servicemembers in minimum custody to

had actual knowledge of the order[26] and then willfully disobeyed it.[27] Delay in compliance of the order does not necessarily constitute disobedience. For example, reasonable delay in complying with an order that states no specific time for compliance will probably not be an offense.[28]

For the maximum allowable punishments for disobedience of a superior's orders, see the Maximum Punishment Chart at Appendix 30.

§ 2-4(C). Violation of General Orders or Regulations.

"General" orders or regulations are those given or promulgated by either the President, the Secretary of Defense, the Secretary of Transportation (for Coast Guard), the Secretaries of the various military departments, general court-martial convening authorities, or general or flag officers in command.[29] In *United States v. Breault*,[30] a case of first impression, the court discussed the issue of who may be permitted to sign a general order. The court concluded that someone other than the commander may sign the order as long as the commander personally knows and approves of the contents of any order or regulation issued under his or her command line. In *United States v. Bartell*,[31] the court ruled that a general order was lawful even though it was not signed personally by a general. The court distinguished between decisional authority and signature authority and noted that the latter is only ministerial.

If violation of a regulation is involved, it must be *punitive* and must be directed at a group that includes the accused.[32] The regulation must purport to

---

follow certain procedures was a standing order directed at all prisoners and did not amount to a personal order to the accused).

26. United States v. Austin, 27 M.J. 227 (C.M.A. 1988) (court concluded that accused knew that he had a legal duty to obey order to draw weapon after his application of conscientious objector status was denied); United States v. Pettigrew, 19 C.M.A. 191, 41 C.M.R. 191 (1970); United States v. Payne, 29 M.J. 899 (A.C.M.R. 1989) (prosecution failed to show that accused was aware that order was given by superior noncommissioned officer).

27. United States v. Ferenczi, 10 C.M.A. 3, 27 C.M.R. 77 (1958). *Cf.* United States v. Young, 18 C.M.A. 324, 40 C.M.R. 36 (1969) (accused was intoxicated and may not have willfully acted against superior).

28. *See* United States v. Woodley, 20 C.M.A. 357, 43 C.M.R. 197 (1971) (time for compliance is question of fact); United States v. Schwabauer, 34 M.J. 709 (A.C.M.R. 1992) (a direct order to stop and come back here required immediate compliance); United States v. Dellarosa, 27 M.J. 860 (A.F.C.M.R. 1989) (accused's delay of five seconds in complying with order was not long enough to amount to disobedience. The case includes a good discussion of delays in compliance). If time is stated then a reasonable delay in compliance is not a crime. United States v. Clowser, 16 C.M.R. 543 (A.F.B.R. 1954).

Cf. United States v. Mauck, 17 M.J. 1033 (A.C.M.R. 1984) (immediate compliance is required unless order indicates that delay is authorized).

29. MCM, Part IV, para. 19. *See generally* Nagle, "Regulations in the Courtroom," 14 THE ADVOCATE 65 (1982).

30. 30 M.J. 833 (N.M.C.M.R. 1990); United States v. Webster, 37 M.J. 670 (C.G.C.M.R. 1993) (court was not satisfied that the Commandant had personally issued the general regulations in question).

31. 32 M.J. 295 (C.M.A. 1991).

32. United States v. Blanchard, 19 M.J. 196 (C.M.A. 1985) (regulation in question was punitive because it was directory in nature, authorized punitive action, applied to Air Force personnel, and specified prohibited conduct).

§ 2-4(C)

establish criminal sanctions[33] and must do more than simply establish guidelines for further implementation by subordinate commanders.[34]

The prosecution must allege that the order or regulation is "general"[35] and must also allege the manner of noncompliance.[36] In addition, the prosecution must establish, at trial, the existence and content of the order or regulation.[37] Although it need not show that the accused had actual knowledge,[38] there is some authority that if the regulation exempts certain classes or categories, the prosecution may be required to establish that the accused does not fall within one of those exemptions.[39]

United States v. Daniel, 42 M.J. 802 (N.M.Ct.Crim.App. 1995) (Navy Instruction on sexual harassment was not punitive regulation); United States v. Hecker, 42 M.J. 640 (A.F.Ct.Crim.App. 1995) (provision in Air Force regulation re standards of conduct was void for vagueness as a punitive provision); United States v. Goodwin, 37 M.J. 606 (A.C.M.R. 1993) (USAREUR regulation governing registration of firearms was punitive regulation even though it incorporated nonpunitive regulation); United States v. Asfeld, 30 M.J. 917 (A.C.M.R. 1990) (Army regulation setting out policy statements on sexual harassment was not punitive regulation and did not incorporate by reference another punitive regulation; punitive nature of regulation must be self-evident from entirety of regulation); United States v. Bright, 20 M.J. 661 (N.M.C.M.R. 1985) (court concluded that regulation governing traffic and vehicles was punitive in nature even though it contained administrative provisions); United States v. Jackson, 46 C.M.R. 1128 (A.C.M.R. 1973); United States v. Horton, 17 M.J. 1131 (N.M.C.M.R. 1984). *See generally* DeChiara, "Article 92: Judicial Guidelines for Identifying Punitive Orders and Regulations," 17 A.F. L. Rev. 61 (Summer 1975).

33. United States v. Nardell, 21 C.M.A. 327, 45 C.M.R. 101 (1972); United States v. Robinson, 37 M.J. 588 (A.F.C.M.R. 1993) (accused guilty of violating AF Reg. 30-30, standards of conduct, by using position and rank to make sexual advances); United States v. Finsel, 33 M.J. 739 (A.C.M.R. 1991) (commanding general's letter reuse of firearms during Operation Just Cause was general order; although the letter included the term "guidelines," it clearly regulated personal conduct, and the only implementation required by subordinate commanders was dissemination of the letter); United States v. Stewart, 2 M.J. 423 (A.C.M.R. 1975).

34. United States v. Tassos, 18 C.M.A. 12, 39 C.M.R. 12 (1968).

35. United States v. Baker, 17 C.M.A. 346, 38 C.M.R. 144 (1967); United States v. Watson, 40 C.M.R. 571 (A.B.R. 1969).

36. United States v. Sweitzer, 14 C.M.A. 39, 33 C.M.R. 251 (1963).

37. United States v. Williams, 3 M.J. 155 (C.M.A. 1977). *See also* United States v. Garcia, 21 M.J. 127 (C.M.A. 1985) (accused convicted for violating regulations governing amount of interest that may be charged).

38. United States v. Tinker, 10 C.M.A. 292, 27 C.M.R. 366 (1959); United States v. Davis, 13 M.J. 593 (A.F.C.M.R. 1982).

In United States v. Tolkach, 14 M.J. 239 (C.M.A. 1982), the court recognized that the government need not prove knowledge but that the accused could not be found guilty because the regulation had not yet been "published;" i.e., it had not been received in the base master publications library.

In United States v. Foster, 14 M.J. 246 (C.M.A. 1982), the court ruled that where an accused is charged with attempting to commit an act proscribed by a regulation, the prosecution need only prove that the accused had a specific intent to commit the act, not to violate the regulation. *See also* United States v. Davis, 16 M.J. 225 (C.M.A. 1983); United States v. Marsh, 21 M.J. 616 (A.F.C.M.R. 1985) (under 1969 MCM, the element of knowledge did not have to be plead in willful dereliction of duty specifications).

39. United States v. Verdi, 5 M.J. 330 (C.M.A. 1978). *See also* United States v. Vuitch, 402 U.S. 62 (1971). *Cf.* United States v. Cuffee, 10 M.J. 381 (C.M.A. 1981) (it is proper to place burden on the defense of going forward with evidence that accused was in an exempt category).

For a general discussion of the lawfulness of orders or regulations, see § 2-4(A) *supra*.

§ 2-4(D). Disobedience of Other Orders.

Article 92(2), U.C.M.J.[40] covers all orders not given as a personal direct order under Article 90(2) or 91(2), or violation of general orders discussed in preceding sections.[41] The "other" orders category includes orders not given by a superior but by someone in a status that imposes a duty to obey.[42] The orders may be either written or oral,[43] but the accused must have had actual knowledge of the order.[44]

§ 2-4(E). Dereliction of Duty.

Dereliction of duty, violation of Article 92(3), is committed through either willful or negligent acts or omissions.[45] The "duty" giving rise to the offense may rest in either regulation, order, or custom.[46] The accused need not have

---

40. *See* Appendix 3. MCM, Part IV, para. 16. United States v. Felix, 36 M.J. 903 (A.F.C.M.R. 1993), *aff'd*, 41 M.J. 356 (C.M.A. 1994) (order in question was vague; accused was charged with violating Correctee Honor System while in correctional custody; court said that order read more like civics lesson than a military order); United States v. Estrella, 35 M.J. 836 (A.C.M.R. 1992) (accused disobeyed orders not to reveal his location in Saudi Arabia during Desert Storm; accused sent letters to lover showing where his unit was located).
41. *See supra* § 2-4(B) and (C). *See, e.g.*, United States v. Gussen, 33 M.J. 736 (A.C.M.R. 1991) (although accused could not be convicted of disobedience of a superior commissioned officer orders concerning consumption of alcohol during Operation Just Cause, because they were not directed specifically to him, he could be convicted of disobeying orders under Article 92(2)).
42. United States v. Stovall, 44 C.M.R. 576 (A.F.C.M.R. 1971) (order of military policeman); United States v. McLaughlin, 14 M.J. 908 (N.M.C.M.R. 1982) (order given by assistant manager of enlisted men's club).
43. United States v. Wartsbaugh, 21 C.M.A. 535, 45 C.M.R. 309 (1972); United States v. Woodley, 20 C.M.A. 357, 43 C.M.R. 197 (1971); United States v. Selman, 28 M.J. 627 (A.F.C.M.R. 1989) (accused could be convicted of disobeying standing order in the form of a letter addressed to all prisoners).
44. United States v. Curtin, 9 C.M.A. 427, 26 C.M.R. 207 (1958). *See also* United States v. Payne, 29 M.J. 899 (A.C.M.R. 1989) (prosecution failed to prove that accused had actual knowledge that order had been given by person authorized to do so); United States v. Brown, 25 M.J. 793 (N.M.C.M.R. 1988) (specification alleging disobedience of order was defective where it failed to allege "knowledge"); United States v. Jordan, 21 C.M.R. 627 (A.F.B.R. 1955) (negligent disobedience warrants a finding of guilty), *rev'd on grounds that the order was illegal*, 7 C.M.A. 452, 22 C.M.R. 242 (1957).
45. MCM, Part IV, para. 16c(3). United States v. Rust, 41 M.J. 472 (1995) (accused doctor guilty of dereliction of duty re medical procedures; court noted that this is an example of conduct which in the military is considered an offense and in the civilian community is not); United States v. Powell, 32 M.J. 117 (C.M.A. 1991) (discussion of defense of ineptitude to charge of dereliction of duty).
46. *Id.* United States v. Tanksley, 36 M.J. 428 (C.M.A. 1993) (existence of duty must be established by evidence in record); United States v. Dallman, 34 M.J. 274 (C.M.A. 1992) (accused's self-imposed duty cannot give rise to dereliction of duty charge); United States v. Wilson, 33 M.J. 797 (A.C.M.R. 1991) (dereliction of duty to blow nose on U.S. flag while a member of flag-raising detail and charged with safeguarding and protecting flag); United States v. Moore, 21 C.M.R. 544 (N.B.R. 1956).

knowledge of the obligation to perform the duty unless the prosecution is alleging willful dereliction.[47] Typically, the prosecution proceeds on a negligence theory, that is, lack of ordinary care.[48] If the dereliction is based upon an order, it may be a lesser-included offense to a charge of disobedience of that order.[49]

§ 2-4(F). Defenses to Disobedience Offenses.

Several defenses apply to disobedience of orders offenses. If the order lacks content[50] or if it merely requires a servicemember to perform a pre-existing duty,[51] failure to comply will not normally constitute an offense under Article

---

In United States v. Heyward, 22 M.J. 35 (C.M.R. 1986), the accused, an NCO, was derelict in not following an Air Force regulation that required AF personnel to report drug activity. The court noted that the accused was not required to report his personal involvement with drugs, only use by other personnel. This excuse for noncompliance has become known as the *Heyward* defense. See § 5-4(A)(2).

United States v. Dupree, 24 M.J. 319 (C.M.A. 1987) (accused's conviction for dereliction of duty in failing to report offenses was excused on ground that the offenses were intertwined with his own delicts and therefore to report the offenses would implicate his right against self-incrimination). *See also* United States v. Thompson, 22 M.J. 40 (C.M.A. 1986); United States v. Dupree, 25 M.J. 659 (A.F.C.M.R. 1987) (accused could be convicted of dereliction of duty for not preventing or reporting drug use by subordinates; regulations and service customs imposed duty and provided notice to accused).

47. United States v. Pratt, 34 C.M.R. 731 (C.G.B.R. 1963) (when told of a boat in distress, the accused, who was the officer in charge of a rescue station, said "f—ck it" and went back to sleep); United States v. Ferguson, 40 M.J. 823 (N.M.C.M.R. 1994) (in lengthy discussion of issue; accused's actual knowledge must be pled and proven; court said that constructive knowledge may be shown, i.e., that accused reasonably should have known of the duties).

48. United States v. Lawson, 36 M.J. 415 (C.M.A. 1993) (simple negligence was proper standard for determining whether nonperformance of military duty to post road guards was dereliction of duty); United States v. Nickels, 20 M.J. 225 (C.M.A. 1985) (the accused's conviction for dereliction of duty was sustained although his conduct would not result in a permanent loss to the government); United States v. Grow, 3 C.M.A. 77, 11 C.M.R. 77 (1953); United States v. Ferguson, 12 C.M.R. 570 (A.B.R. 1953) (dereliction led to fatal accident).

49. United States v. Green, 47 C.M.R. 727 (A.F.C.M.R. 1973) (lesser-included offense to failure to obey order). *Cf.* United States v. Gonzales, 19 M.J. 951, 953 n.3 (A.F.C.M.R. 1985) (court noted that dereliction of duty would not be a lesser-included offense of Art. 92(1) because the former requires knowledge; not clear that proof of existence of nonpunitive general regulation gives rise to presumption of knowledge as required by Art. 92(3)).

50. United States v. Alexander, 26 M.J. 796 (A.F.C.M.R. 1988) (order not to "write any more checks" was too broad and unenforceable); United States v. Beattie, 17 M.J. 537 (A.C.M.R. 1983); United States v. Couser, 3 M.J. 561 (A.C.M.R. 1977); United States v. Oldaker, 41 C.M.R. 497 (A.C.M.R. 1969).

51. United States v. Brownlow, 39 M.J. 484 (C.M.A. 1994) (court rejected argument that order to board aircraft was not ultimate offense; gravamen of disobedience was flagrant defiance of order); United States v. Traxler, 39 M.J. 476 (C.M.A. 1994) (officer's order to board aircraft was specific mandate to perform particular act at specified time and place; order not given to enhance punishment); United States v. Peaches, 25 M.J. 364 (C.M.A. 1987) (court reversed conviction for disobedience of order where the order to report for routine duties was punishable under Article 86); United States v. Sidney, 23 C.M.A. 185, 48 C.M.R. 801 (1974) (order to comply with existing safety regulation should have been charged under Art. 92); United States v. Wartsbaugh, 21 C.M.A. 535, 45 C.M.R. 309 (1972) (order to comply with existing battalion regulation should have

§ 2-4(F)

90(a) or 91(2), although it may be punishable under another code provision.[52] Disobedience of a repeated order may not constitute an offense if the order was given solely to increase the punishment.[53] The military courts have also recognized the defense of "divestiture" of status through words or actions by the superior that would excuse compliance with the order.[54]

Additionally, the accused may, in an appropriate case, assert the defenses of justification,[55] necessity,[56] duress,[57] inability,[58] ignorance or mistake,[59] or in more limited circumstances, the so-called "Nuremburg defense."[60] That defense, as noted in § 2-2(E)(7), *supra*, is only available where the accused has

---

been charged under Article 92); United States v. Bratcher, 19 C.M.A. 125, 39 C.M.R. 125 (1969) (pre-existing military obligations).

United States v. Mitchell, 34 M.J. 1252 (A.C.M.R. 1992) (an order to obey the law or another order is not an order under Article 90; order to join unit to deploy to Saudi Arabia was lawful and not merely an attempt to exhort accused to obey law or to increase punishment).

United States v. Ebanks, 29 M.J. 926 (A.F.C.M.R. 1989) (court rejected argument that government was required to charge accused with Article 92 violation of safe sex order; mere fact that he could have been so charged does not require prosecution only under that article); United States v. Battle, 27 M.J. 781 (A.F.C.M.R. 1988) (extensive discussion of the issue); United States v. Caton, 23 M.J. 691 (A.F.C.M.R. 1986) (accused properly convicted of disobedience of order to remain on base even though he was already restricted to base pursuant to Article 15 punishment; commander gave order for reasons other than to increase the punishment). *Cf.* United States v. Petterson, 17 M.J. 69 (C.M.A. 1983), where an NCO issued a direct order to the accused (who was AWOL) to return to duty. The court ruled that the order was a lawful and "measured attempt to secure compliance with [the accused's] pre-existing obligations."

The difference in maximum punishments for violation of a direct, personal order, are higher than those that may be imposed for violating a regulation. *See* Appendix 30, Chart of Maximum Punishments.

52. As noted above, the offense might be chargeable under Article 92, U.C.M.J. and failure to comply might also be chargeable under any of the punitive articles addressing absences. *See supra* § 2-2.

53. United States v. Landwehr, 18 M.J. 355 (C.M.A. 1984) (order by commander to accused to return to his place of work was not designed solely to increase the punishment, but was instead issued to further a military function); United States v. Greene, 8 M.J. 796 (N.C.M.R. 1980); United States v. Tiggs, 40 C.M.R. 352 (A.B.R. 1968). On the other hand, an order given to bolster the first command may be legitimate. United States v. Bethea, 2 M.J. 892 (A.C.M.R. 1976).

54. *See, e.g.*, United States v. Collier, 27 M.J. 806 (A.C.M.R. 1988) (words used by warrant officer who gave order to accused were not sufficient to divest him of his status as a warrant officer). *See also* United States v. King, 29 M.J. 885 (A.C.M.R. 1989) (discussion of divestiture defense regarding assault on law enforcement officer). *See generally* Milhizer, "The Divestiture Defense and United States v. Collier," ARMY LAW., March 1990, at 3.

55. *See* R.C.M. 916(c). Because the defense of justification rests on the argument that the charged act was excused because the accused was acting pursuant to a legal duty, imposed by regulation, statute, or order, the defense in effect raises the question of conflicting "orders," discussed at § 2-4(A), *supra*.

56. *See* United States v. Huet-Vaughn, 43 M.J. 105, 114 (1995) (discussion of defense of necessity).

57. R.C.M. 916(h). This defense is not available to an accused charged with killing a person.

58. R.C.M. 916(i) (defense of inability). The defense may arise from a physical or financial inability to follow the order or perform the duty.

59. R.C.M. 916(j) (defense of ignorance or mistake).

60. United States v. Huet-Vaughn, 43 M.J. 105, 114 (1995).

been ordered, as an individual, to commit a positive act, which amounts to a war crime.[61]

§ 2-5. Article 133: Conduct Unbecoming an Officer and a Gentleman.

Traditionally, all military systems place special responsibilities and status upon officers.[1] The U.C.M.J. recognizes that not all officers will maintain an ideal moral standard, but does specifically proscribe conduct that either compromises his or her character as a gentleman or gentlewoman or seriously compromises his or her standing as an officer.[2] Not all misconduct is proscribed, but that which seriously compromises the officer is punishable.[3] It is

---

61. United States v. Huet-Vaughn, 43 M.J. 105, 114-115 (1995), *citing* United States v. Berrigan, 283 F. Supp. 336 (D. Md. 1968), *aff'd sub nom*, United States v. Eberhardt, 417 F.2d 1009 (4th Cir. 1969) (discussion of defense).
1. *See, e.g.*, Orloff v. Willoughby, 345 U.S. 83 (1953). *See also* Moyer, *Justice and the Military* (1972), and Nelson, "Conduct Expected of an Officer and a Gentleman: Ambiguity," 12 AF JAG L. Rev. 124 (1970).
2. *See* MCM, Part IV, para. 59. United States v. Hartwig, 39 M.J. 125 (C.M.A. 1994) (officer had fair notice that sending sexually suggestive material to student was prohibited; any reasonable officer would have recognized that such conduct would risk bringing disrepute on the profession); United States v. Maderia, 38 M.J. 494 (C.M.A. 1994) (publicly associating with known drug smuggler was conduct unbecoming an officer); United States v. Miller, 37 M.J. 133 (C.M.A. 1993) (accused officer's failure to report wife's abuse of their child and seek medical treatment was conduct unbecoming an officer and gentleman; decision includes discussion of offense vis-à-vis moral obligations); United States v. Frazier, 34 M.J. 194 (C.M.A. 1992) (officer's engaging in open relation with enlisted servicemember's wife was conduct unbecoming officer; court noted that it is critical that officer inspire trust and respect of enlisted soldiers who must obey officer and follow orders).
United States v. Czekala, 38 M.J. 566 (A.C.M.R. 1993), *aff'd on other grounds*, 42 M.J. 168 (1995) (accused's affair, dishonorably obtaining divorce, and failing to pay just debt amounted to conduct unbecoming an officer and a gentleman); United States v. Goosby, 36 M.J. 512 (A.F.C.M.R. 1992) (disobedience of superior's order restricting accused to city limits for 60 days; court rejected constitutional challenge of vagueness); United States v. Bilby, 34 M.J. 1191 (A.F.C.M.R. 1992) (accused officer guilty of soliciting distribution of child pornography); United States v. Dallman, 32 M.J. 624 (A.C.M.R. 1991) (discussion of the offense); United States v. Van Steenwyk, 21 M.J. 795 (N.M.C.M.R. 1985) (accused had adequate notice that his sexual liaisons with enlisted personnel was conduct unbecoming an officer and gentleman).
3. *Id. See, e.g.*, United States v. Lewis, 28 M.J. 179 (C.M.A. 1989) (officer convicted of charging fellow officer $2,000 for tutoring him in leadership skills; the court labelled this conduct "corrupt and demoralizing"); United States v. Guaglione, 27 M.J. 268 (C.M.A. 1988) (accused's visit to house of prostitution in Germany, without engaging in sex, did not constitute conduct unbecoming an officer under the facts; accused was not put on notice that his activity was proscribed); United States v. Norvell, 26 M.J. 477 (C.M.A. 1988) (officer, a nurse, was convicted under Article 133 for using catheter to inject saline solution into her bladder and presenting that as her drug test urine sample; she was also convicted for telling an enlisted servicemember how to do it).
United States v. Jenkins, 39 M.J. 843 (A.C.M.R. 1994) (officer's negligent act of writing 76 bad checks was conduct unbecoming an officer); United States v. Brunson, 30 M.J. 766 (A.C.M.R. 1990) (dishonorable failure to pay just debt); United States v. Shober, 26 M.J. 501 (A.F.C.M.R. 1986) (fornication with subordinate civilian employee was conduct unbecoming but taking nude pictures of her was not; court held that an offender's behavior must seriously expose him or her to public opprobrium).
United States v. Smith, 16 M.J. 694 (A.F.C.M.R. 1983) (the conduct must be unbecoming an officer and a gentleman); United States v. Clark, 15 M.J. 594 (A.C.M.R. 1983) (tardiness for

not necessary, however, that the officer's conduct be otherwise unlawful.[4] Note that Article 133 includes acts punishable by any other punitive article in the U.C.M.J. For example, an officer could be convicted under Article 133 for smoking marijuana in the presence of his or her enlisted subordinates; those same actions could serve as charges under other applicable punitive articles of the U.C.M.J.[5]

This practice, however, may lead to additional problems of multiplicity.[6] In *United States v. Timberlake*,[7] the accused was convicted of both Article 133 and the offense of forgery under Article 123. The Court of Military Appeals applied a multiplicity analysis and concluded that the forgery charge was a lesser-included offense of the Article 133 offense. Thus, the forgery charge was set aside. In his concurring opinion, Chief Judge Everett observed that the duplication of charges against officers is an anachronism carried over from practice under the Articles of War. Under Article of War 95, the sole punishment for an officer convicted of conduct unbecoming an officer and a gentleman was mandatory dismissal from the service. In order to increase the range of possible punishments, such as confinement, the government would also allege the violation of the underlying substantive offense. As Judge Everett observed, however, because current practice permits a court-martial to impose a wider range of punishments for violation of Article 133, "no legitimate advantage accrues to the Government from charging the same act as a violation both of Article 133 and of some other punitive article ..." while the accused suffers from the appearance of having committed two crimes.[8]

The better practice is to charge a violation of either an Article 133 or a substantive offense. But, as noted in the discussion at § 6-1(C)(3) *infra*, both charges may be pleaded and proved if the prosecution can demonstrate that multiplicious pleadings are necessary to meet the exigencies of proof. Otherwise, the judge should dismiss one of the charges before findings. The maxi-

---

formation not punishable; desertion was); United States v. Sheehan, 15 M.J. 724 (A.C.M.R. 1983) (failure to meet suspense date not punishable; intentional deception was).

United States v. Schumacher, 11 M.J. 612 (A.C.M.R. 1981) (charged with public drunkenness while in uniform); United States v. Bonar, 40 C.M.R. 482 (A.B.R. 1969) (conviction for violating state justice of the peace's order not to drive).

4. United States v. Bilby, 39 M.J. 467 (C.M.A. 1994) (accused could be convicted of conduct unbecoming for soliciting someone to violate federal child pornography statute without regard to constitutionality of that statute); United States v. Taylor, 23 M.J. 314 (C.M.A. 1987).

5. *See, e.g.,* United States v. Graham, 9 M.J. 556 (N.M.C.M.R. 1980). The prosecution will normally prefer "parallel" charges: the substantive offense (*i.e.,* use of drugs) and conduct unbecoming an officer (*i.e.,* wrongful use of drugs in presence of subordinates). *Cf.* United States v. Timberlake, 18 M.J. 371 (C.M.A. 1984) (concurring opinion by C.J. Everett that accused should not be charged with both Art. 133 violation and other substantive offense article).

6. *See infra* § 6-1(C)(3). United States v. Olson, 38 M.J. 597 (A.F.C.M.R. 1993) (where underlying conduct in Article 133 charge is defined by specific punitive article, the latter is treated as a lesser-included offense of conduct unbecoming an officer).

7. 18 M.J. 371 (C.M.A. 1984). *See also* United States v. Rodriquez, 18 M.J. 363 (C.M.A. 1984); United States v. Taylor, 23 M.J. 314 (C.M.A. 1987).

In United States v. Court, 25 M.J. 507 (A.F.C.M.R. 1987), the court indicated that the rationale of *Timberlake* would apply equally to those cases where the underlying offense was charged both as a violation of Article 133 and Article 134.

8. 18 M.J. at 377.

mum punishment for violation of this article, which was ruled constitutional by the Supreme Court in *Parker v. Levy*,[9] is dismissal from the service.[10]

§ 2-6. Article 134: The General Article.

One of the most controversial "crimes" in military practice is the deeply rooted general article— Article 134.[1] The article, which like Article 133 has been ruled constitutional,[2] actually consists of three categories of offenses[3] that will be individually addressed in the following subsections. The general article makes punishable all of those acts that are not specifically proscribed in the other punitive articles of the U.C.M.J.[4] Through the years various offenses have become associated with Article 134; counsel may find these commonly recognized offenses in Part IV of the Manual for Courts-Martial that discusses each offense and the elements necessary to establish guilt under Article 134.[5] Examples of these offenses include various assault offenses,[6]

---

9. 417 U.S. 733 (1974). *See generally* Bernard, "Structures of American Military Justice," 125 U. PA. L. REV. 307 (1976); Note, "Military Law The Standard of Constitutionality," 11 WAKE FOREST L. REV. 325 (1975); Ackroyd, "The General Articles, Articles 133 and 134 of the Uniform Code of Military Justice," 35 ST. JOHN'S L. REV. 264 (1961).
10. *See* MCM, Part IV, para. 59e; United States v. Hart, 30 M.J. 1176 (C.M.A. 1990) (confinement should not be in excess of that authorized for the most analogous offense for which a punishment is listed in the *Manual*, or if none is prescribed, one year of confinement).
1. Art. 134, U.C.M.J. *See* Appendix 3. An excellent discussion of Article 134 is contained in Moyer, *Justice and Military* (1972). *See also* Nichols, "The Devil's Article," 2 MIL. L. REV. 111 (1963).
2. Parker v. Levy, 417 U.S. 733 (1974). *Cf.* United States v. Peszynski, 40 M.J. 874 (N.M.C.M.R. 1994) (fact that Article 134 is constitutional does not relieve prosecution of alleging offense; in this case of alleged sexual harassment, no standard was given to court members to distinguish criminal from non-criminal behavior).
3. The three subcategories include (1) conduct to the prejudice of good order and discipline in the armed forces; (2) conduct of a nature to bring discredit upon the armed forces; and (3) conduct violating federal or state laws.
4. MCM, Part IV, para. 60. In United States v. Taylor, 23 M.J. 314 (C.M.A. 1987), the court noted that its earlier cases had not presented any "bright-line" guidelines on preemption but concluded that specific proscriptions against several types of solicitation did not preempt a charge under Article 134 for soliciting another to commit other offenses; United States v. Irvin, 21 M.J. 184 (C.M.A. 1986) (prosecution could not rely upon state child abuse statute and the Assimilative Crimes Act because the accused's conduct consisted of assaults which could have been charged under Art. 128).
United States v. Ventura, 36 M.J. 832 (A.C.M.R. 1993) (noting absence of bright-line test for determining preemption, court concluded that Congress did not intend to preempt field of forgery offenses by promulgating Article 123,U.C.M.J.); United States v. Williams, 26 M.J. 606 (A.C.M.R. 1988) (Article 95 does not preempt charges under Article 134 alleging resisting apprehension by Post Exchange employee).
In United States v. Wiegand, 23 M.J. 644 (A.C.M.R. 1986), the court indicated that application of the doctrine of "preemption" turns on two issues: whether Congress intended to limit prosecution of certain field of offenses to specific articles in the U.C.M.J. and whether the charged offense is "composed of a residuum of elements of a specific offense and is asserted as a violation of Article 133 ... or 134." *Id.* at 645.
5. MCM, Part IV, paras. 61 to 113.
6. MCM, Part IV, para. 64. Included are assaults with intent to commit murder, to commit voluntary manslaughter, to commit rape, to rob, and to commit sodomy.

indecent assault,[7] false swearing,[8] misprision of a serious offense,[9] bigamy,[10] and communicating a threat.[11]

The punishments for violation of Article 134 offenses are determined by first examining Part IV of the *Manual*[12] and locating the charged offense. If the offense is not listed there, the courts will attempt to align the Article 134 offense with an offense that is listed.[13] If that comparison is not possible, then the offense is punishable as authorized in the United States Code or as authorized by custom of the service.[14]

Because a servicemember's actions may constitute an offense under both an enumerated punitive article and Article 134, the prosecution may charge both offenses in the alternative, a suggestion made by the court in *United States v. Foster*.[15] In *Foster*, the court adopted the elements test for determining whether an offense is a lesser-included offense. It concluded that in military jurisprudence, the term necessarily included in Article 79[16] includes derivative offenses under Article 134. The court noted that it would be sound practice to charge both the enumerated offense and any analogous Article 134 offenses as an alternative. The court members would be instructed on the elements and told that the accused could not be convicted of both. If the court convicts him of the greater offense, no findings are entered with regard to the lesser offense and it is dismissed.

The following sections address each of the three categories of criminal conduct included within Article 134.

§ 2-6(A). Disorders and Neglects to the Prejudice of Good Order and Discipline.

This first category includes offenses that directly affect order and discipline in the military service. Potentially, any improper act or omission could be punished under this category. The intent, however, was to limit prosecution to those acts or omissions where the effect on discipline or order is real.[17] While

---

7. MCM, Part IV, para. 63. United States v. Burden, 2 C.M.A. 547, 10 C.M.R. 45 (1953).
8. MCM, Part IV, para. 79.
9. MCM, Part IV, para. 95.
10. MCM, Part IV, para. 65. *See* United States v. Pruitt, 17 C.M.A. 438, 38 C.M.R. 236 (1968).
11. MCM, Part IV, para. 110.
12. R.C.M. 1003(c)(A), (B).
13. *Id. See* United States v. Tatum, 34 M.J. 1115 (N.M.C.M.R. 1992) (no requirement that conduct be prohibited by an order, regulation or statute to fall within Article 134; here accused's failure to support family did not amount to violation of that Article); United States v. Jones, 5 M.J. 579 (A.C.M.R. 1978).
14. R.C.M. 1003(c)(B)(ii). If a state statute is assimilated and prosecuted under Article 134, see *infra* § 2-6(C).
15. 40 M.J. 140 (C.M.A. 1994).
16. Art. 79, U.C.M.J.
17. MCM, Part IV, para. 60c(2). Virtually any offense, not otherwise punishable under the U.C.M.J., may be charged under Article 134. United States v. Woods, 28 M.J. 318 (C.M.A 1989) (accused, who had tested positive for AIDS, was guilty of violating Article 134 by engaging in unprotected sexual intercourse). *See infra* § 2-9 for a discussion of prosecutions involving AIDS.

§ 2-6(A) MILITARY CRIMINAL JUSTICE § 2-6(A)

some acts, such as those involving moral turpitude,[18] are inherently prejudicial to good order and discipline,[19] other acts require a factual assessment.[20] Examples of offenses that could be so punished include negligent homicide,[21] careless discharge of firearms,[22] impersonating an officer,[23] disorderly conduct,[24] adultery,[25] use of drugs not otherwise covered by Article 112a,[26] or

---

United States v. Davis, 26 M.J. 445 (C.M.A. 1988) (Article 134 violation where accused, a male, dressed in woman's clothing); United States v. Harper, 22 M.J. 157 (C.M.A. 1986) (presence of drugs in accused's body while on active duty was prejudicial to good order and discipline); United States v. Bartole, 21 M.J. 234 (C.M.A. 1986) (kidnapping could be charged under either Art. 134(1) or (2)); United States v. Wright, 5 M.J. 106 (C.M.A. 1978); United States v. Alford, 32 M.J. 596 (A.C.M.R. 1991) (accused's pushing in mess hall line was not disorderly conduct and prejudicial to the good order and discipline); United States v. Guerrero, 31 M.J. 692 (N.M.C.M.R. 1990) (accused dressed as woman).

United States v. Herron, 39 M.J. 860 (N.M.C.M.R. 1994) (accused's utterance of profanity in angry and loud manner in public was not general disorder; extensive discussion of limits on using Article 134 for such conduct); United States v. Green, 39 M.J. 606 (A.C.M.R. 1994) (NCO's act of adultery with civilian in barracks); United States v. Warnock, 34 M.J. 567 (A.C.M.R. 1991) (accused's showing photograph of nude female officer did not have effect on discipline where only person seeing photograph testified that it did not bother him).

United States v. Thatch, 30 M.J. 623 (N.M.C.M.R. 1990) (mere drunkenness, without more, does not violate U.C.M.J.; incapacitation from properly answering call to duty might form the basis for prejudice to good order and discipline); United States v. Williams, 26 M.J. 606 (A.C.M.R. 1988) (wrongful flight to avoid arrest by Exchange detective was prejudicial to good order and discipline and service discrediting).

United States v. Smith, 25 M.J. 545 (A.C.M.R. 1987) ("disorder and neglect" language contemplates that misconduct is "directly and palpably," as distinguished from indirectly and remotely, prejudicial to good order and discipline; accused's failure to produce title to car purchased by junior enlisted servicemember constituted such an offense where fraud and trickery were involved).

Cf. United States v. Regan, 11 M.J. 745 (A.C.M.R. 1981) (throwing butter on mess hall ceiling was not covered by Article 134); United States v. Wickersham, 14 M.J. 404 (C.M.A. 1983) (unlawful entry). Additional acts are noted in Part IV of the *Manual* and in the *Manual's* Chart of Maximum Punishments. See Appendix 30.

18. United States v. Johnson, 39 M.J. 1033 (A.C.M.R. 1994); United States v. Greene, 34 M.J. 713 (A.C.M.R. 1992).

19. United States v. Johnson, 39 M.J. 1033 (A.C.M.R. 1994); United States v. Poole, 39 M.J. 819 (A.C.M.R. 1994).

20. United States v. Poole, 39 M.J. 819 (A.C.M.R. 1994).

21. *See, e.g.*, United States v. Martinez, 42 M.J. 327 (1995) (accused convicted of negligent homicide for permitting intoxicated servicemember to drive car and servicemember died as result of accident. The court indicated that Congress has determined that court-martial should decide whether the offense is a service disorder; the court also rejected the accused's argument that he did not have adequate notice of the offense).

22. *See, e.g.*, United States v. Potter, 15 C.M.A. 271, 35 C.M.R. 243 (1965).

23. United States v. Lane, 28 C.M.R. 749 (A.F.B.R. 1959).

24. MCM, Part IV, para. 73. United States v. Green, 33 M.J. 918 (A.C.M.R. 1991) (contentious NCO giving apparently legal order not guilty of disorderly conduct).

25. United States v. Poole, 39 M.J. 819 (A.C.M.R. 1994) (accused guilty of adultery under general article); United States v. Green, 39 M.J. 606 (A.C.M.R. 1994) (NCO committed adultery).

26. United States v. Deserano, 41 M.J. 678 (A.F.Ct.Crim.App. 1995) (wrongfully inhaling nitrous oxide gas punishable under first clause of Article 134 as simple disorder; Congress did not intend Article 112a as preemption of prosecution of other drug-related offenses).

being a peeping tom.[27] Note that in the past prosecution of marijuana offenses rested on this article.[28]

§ 2-6(B). Conduct Bringing Discredit Upon the Armed Forces.

The discussion in § 2-6(A) *supra* is also applicable here except that under this category, the term "discredit" means damage to the reputation of the armed forces.[29] Key here, is the fact that certain acts may lower the civilian community's esteem or may bring the armed forces into disrepute.[30] Typical acts punishable under this category would include dishonorable failure to pay debts, negligent homicide, and adultery.[31]

The relationship between the various clauses of Article 134 was addressed in *United States v. Sadler*,[32] where the accused was charged under the second clause of Article 134 on the grounds that he had violated New Mexico statutes concerning contributing to the delinquency of a minor and sexual exploitation of a minor at his off-base apartment. The court noted that using the third clause of Article 134, in tandem with the Assimilative Crimes Act, an accused may be charged with violations of state statutes that occur in an area under exclusive federal jurisdiction.[33] In this case the prosecution blended together an allegation of state statutes with a violation of the second clause of Article 134, which requires a showing that the acts alleged were service discrediting. Apparently that combination was not improper. But the trial court erred in not instructing the members that they must nonetheless find that the acts were actually service discrediting. The court noted that an accused could not be found guilty under Article 134 simply because the conduct violated a state or foreign law.[34]

---

27. United States v. Johnson, 4 M.J. 770 (A.C.M.R. 1978); United States v. Foster, 13 M.J. 789 (A.C.M.R. 1982) (window peeping; citations to other similar cases).
28. MCM, 1969 para. 213b; *see infra* § 2-7.
29. *See, e.g.,* United States v. Guerrero, 33 M.J. 295 (C.M.A. 1991) (although cross-dressing is not per se conduct prejudicial to good order and discipline, in this case it was, considering facts and circumstances); United States v. Davis, 26 M.J. 445 (C.M.A. 1988) (accused, a male, dressed in woman's clothing); United States v. Snyder, 1 C.M.A. 423, 4 C.M.R. 15 (1952); United States v. Chambers, 31 M.J. 776 (A.C.M.R. 1990) (drunk and disorderly).
30. MCM, Part IV, para. 60c(3). *See, e.g.,* United States v. Stone, 40 M.J. 420 (C.M.A. 1994) (accused's false official speech to high school students about his alleged role in Desert Storm violated Article 134); United States v. Henderson, 32 M.J. 941 (N.M.C.M.R. 1991) (recruiter's sexual acts with high school girls was not violative of general article; what may be service discrediting in moral sense is not necessarily criminal in legal sense); United States v. Mabie, 24 M.J. 711 (A.C.M.R. 1987) (accused convicted of committing indecent acts, i.e., sexual intercourse, with the dead body of the victim). *See also* United States v. Sanchez, 11 C.M.A. 216, 29 C.M.R. 32 (1960) (indecent bestial act with chicken).
31. *Id.* United States v. Carr, 28 M.J. 661 (N.M.C.M.R. 1989) (private consensual intercourse between unmarried persons does not fall within conduct bringing discredit upon the armed forces).
32. 29 M.J. 370 (C.M.A. 1990).
33. *See* § 2-6(C). United States v. Yancey, 36 M.J. 859 (A.C.M.R. 1993) (Assimilative Crimes Act not available where offense occurred at place not under exclusive or concurrent federal jurisdiction).
34. *See also* United States v. Wallace, 33 M.J. 561 (A.C.M.R. 1991) (accused's leaving children at home unattended was not service-discrediting; child neglect standing alone does not constitute an offense under Article 134).

§ 2-6(C). Crimes and Offenses Not Capital: Federal Crimes.

If the U.C.M.J. does not proscribe a particular course of conduct but federal law does, the military may prosecute the servicemember under Article 134 for committing an applicable federal (noncapital) offense.[35] This category of Article 134 may not be used to prosecute under a civilian statute if the same conduct is punishable under the U.C.M.J.[36] In *United States v. McGuinness*,[37] the court concluded that the *Manual's* preemption provision in Para. 60c(5) did not prohibit prosecution under Federal Espionage Act, 18 U.S.C. § 793(e), where the same acts could have been prosecuted under the U.C.M.J. as a violation of Navy regulation. Para 60c(5), said the court, provides that the preemption doctrine prohibits application of Article 134 to conduct covered by Articles 80 through 132. The court indicated that the test for determining whether preemption applies is to ask first, whether Congress intended to limit prosecution for wrongful conduct within a particular field to specific articles in the U.C.M.J. and second, whether the charged offense is composed of residuum elements of specific offense and asserted to be a violation of either Article 133 or Article 134.

The prosecution must prove that the offense charged was committed at a place subject to the exclusive or concurrent federal legislative jurisdiction and was thus within the maritime and territorial jurisdiction of the United States.[38]

If the charged offense occurred overseas the question of extraterritorial application of the federal statute must be addressed.[39] State law may not be included in this category unless the state law has been assimilated into fed-

---

35. MCM, Part IV, para. 60c(4). *See, e.g.,* United States v. Evans, 33 M.J. 309 (C.M.A. 1991) (possession of firearm during drug transaction was federal offense punishable under third clause of Article 134); United States v. Mitchell, 36 M.J. 882 (N.M.C.M.R. 1993) (accused could have been prosecuted under federal provision proscribing unauthorized reception of cable service); United States v. Canatelli, 5 M.J. 838 (A.C.M.R. 1978).

Only noncapital civilian offenses may be prosecuted under Article 134, MCM, Part IV, para. 60c(4). United States v. French, 10 C.M.A. 171, 27 C.M.R. 245 (1959).

36. United States v. Chattin, 33 M.J. 802 (N.M.C.M.R. 1991) (prosecution under Article 134 for violating Federal Espionage Act was not preempted by accused's guilty pleas to violating Navy regulations proscribing same general conduct).

37. 35 M.J. 149 (C.M.A. 1992).

38. 18 U.S.C. § 7. United States v. Williams, 17 M.J. 207 (C.M.A. 1984); United States v. Roberts, 32 M.J. 681 (A.F.C.M.R. 1991) (proprietary jurisdiction not sufficient to trigger assimilation of state criminal law); United States v. Dallman, 32 M.J. 624 (A.C.M.R. 1991) (plea of guilty admits this element); United States v. Geary, 30 M.J. 855 (N.M.C.M.R. 1990) (federal control may be established by testimony, documents, judicial notice, or stipulation); United States v. Harris, 27 M.J. 681 (A.C.M.R. 1988) (prosecution failed to establish that offense occurred at place subject to U.S. jurisdiction, and appellate court would not assume otherwise); United States v. Zupan, 17 M.J. 1039 (A.C.M.R. 1984).

39. *See, e.g.,* United States v. Pullen, 41 M.J. 886 (A.F.Ct.Crim.App. 1995) (court concluded that federal child pornography statute, 18 U.S.C. § 2252(a)(4)(A), was extraterritorial); United States v. Cuevas-Orvalle, 6 M.J. 284 (A.C.M.R. 1979) (Canal Zone kidnapping statute inapplicable to offense committed in Panama). For a thorough discussion of the problem of extraterritoriality. *See generally* Horbaly & Mullins, "Extraterritorial Jurisdiction and Its Effect on Military Criminal Justice Overseas," 71 MIL. L. REV. 1 (1976).

eral law under 18 U.S.C. § 13.[40] Note, however, that an act in violation of state law may be nonetheless prosecuted under either of the first two categories of Article 134.[41]

§ 2-7. Drug Offenses.

§ 2-7(A). Charging Drug Offenses.

A brief note should be made on the military's disposition of drug offenses. Although drug offenses are normally not considered traditional "military" offenses, such as disobedience or disrespect, a large portion of the military's criminal practice involves drug-related offenses. Under earlier practice drug offenses were charged under either Article 92 (violation of regulation),[1] or Article 134.[2] However, in the 1983 Military Justice Act,[3] Congress, recognizing the serious threat of drugs to a military environment, amended the U.C.M.J. specifically to provide for drug offenses. Article 112a states:

(a) Any person subject to this chapter who wrongfully uses, possesses, manufactures, distributes, imports into the customs territory of the United States, exports from the United States, or introduces into an installation, vessel, vehicle, or aircraft used by or under the control of the armed forces a substance described in subsection (b) shall be punished as a court-martial may direct.

(b) The substances referred to in subsection (a) are the following:

(1) opium, heroin, cocaine, amphetamine, lysergic acid diethylamide, methamphetamine, phencyclidine, barbituric acid, and marijuana, and any compound or derivative of any such substance.

(2) Any substance not specified in (1) that is listed on a schedule of controlled substances prescribed by the President for the purposes of this article.

---

40. MCM, Part IV, para. 60c(4). *See, e.g.,* United States v. Kline, 21 M.J. 366 (C.M.A. 1986) (MP is a "police officer" for purposes of Maryland Code, as incorporated by Assimilative Crimes Act); United States v. Picotte, 12 C.M.A. 196, 30 C.M.R. 196 (1961) (assimilated Colorado statute).

United States v. White, 39 M.J. 796 (N.M.C.M.R. 1994) (accused guilty of violating Hawaii open container law on military installation under Federal Assimilative Crimes Act, FACA); United States v. Mitchell, 36 M.J. 882 (N.M.C.M.R. 1993) (existence of specific federal criminal law prohibiting unauthorized reception of cable service prevented prosecution under Assimilative Crimes Act).

41. MCM, Part IV, para. 60c(4). United States v. Mayo, 12 M.J. 286 (C.M.A. 1982).

1. See *supra* § 2-4(C) for a discussion of violation of general orders or regulations. For a good background discussion of charging drug offenses in the military, see United States v. Reichenbach, 29 M.J. 128 (C.M.A. 1989). *See also* United States v. Ettleson, 13 M.J. 348 (C.M.A. 1982); United States v. Painter, 39 M.J. 578 (N.M.C.M.R. 1993) (accused charged with violating general regulation by possessing drug abuse paraphernalia; regulation not broad enough to cover possession of items not associated with use of drugs).

2. See *supra* § 2-6 for a discussion of using Article 134, U.C.M.J. to prosecute various offenses.

3. Pub. L. 98-209, § 8, 97 STAT. 1393 (1983).

(3) Any other substance not specified in clause (1) or contained on a list prescribed by the President under clause (2) that is listed in Schedules I through V of section 202 of the Controlled Substances Act (21 U.S.C. 812).

This provision should form the basis for virtually all drug offenses. It should also negate the equal protection arguments that formally existed where some servicemembers were prosecuted under Article 92 and others under 134. In *United States v. Courtney*,[4] the Court ruled that the constitutional infirmity existed because a particular drug offense might net a maximum sentence of two years under Article 92 and up to five years under Article 134.[5] Because a specific punitive article now covers certain drug offenses, the preemption doctrine generally prohibits reliance on Article 134.[6] But note that both Articles 134 and 92 may still be used where the drug-related offense is not covered by Article 112a.[7] For example, possession of drug paraphernalia (which is apparently not covered by Article 112a may be proscribed by service or local regulation and therefore chargeable under either of those two articles.[8]

The maximum punishments for drug offenses were completely restructured to compliment the new Article 112a. The maximum punishment now ranges up to 15 years confinement.[9] The maximum is increased by five years where the drug offense under Article 112a is committed while on duty as a sentinel or lookout, on board an armed forces vessel or aircraft, while receiving special pay under 37 U.S.C. § 310,[10] in a missile launch facility or during time of war.[11] Where the prosecution intends to seek an increased punishment under

---

4. 1 M.J. 438 (C.M.A. 1976). *See also* § 13-3(N)(1).
5. *See* MCM, 1969, Chart of Maximum Punishments. *Cf.* United States v. Batchelder, 442 U.S. 114 (1979) (where criminal act violates two criminal statutes, government may prosecute under either as long as it does not discriminate against class of defendants).
6. *See* MCM, Part IV, para. 60(5). *Cf.* United States v. Reichenbach, 29 M.J. 128 (C.M.A. 1989) (court held that enactment of Article 112a does not preempt prosecution under the third clause of Article 134 for drug-related misconduct proscribed under Title 21); United States v. Davis, 32 M.J. 951 (N.M.C.M.R. 1991) (promulgation of Article 112a did not preempt prosecution under Article 134 for possession of tetracycline, a prescription drug).
7. United States v. Reichenbach, 29 M.J. 128, 137 n. 8 (C.M.A. 1989) (Congress did not intend to preempt prosecution of other drug offenses); United States v. Deserano, 41 M.J. 678 (A.F.Ct.Crim.App. 1995) (accused could be prosecuted for inhaling nitrous oxide gas under Article 134 as a simple disorder).
8. *See supra* §§ 2-4(C) and 2-6. *See, e.g.,* United States v. Reichenbach, 29 M.J. 128 (C.M.A. 1989) (Article 134, clause 3, could be used to prosecute accused for offenses involving a new, unlisted drug called "Ecstasy"). Proceeding under Article 134 would depend on whether the possession of the items was (1) service discrediting; (2) conduct prejudicial to good order and discipline; or (3) a crime not capital and included in either the federal or applicable state criminal code; United States v. Caballero, 49 C.M.R. 594 (C.M.A. 1975). *See also* Hoffman Estates v. Flipside, 455 U.S. 489 (1981); United States v. Cannon, 13 M.J. 777 (A.C.M.R. 1982); United States v. Clarke, 13 M.J. 566 (A.C.M.R. 1982).
9. *See* MCM, Part IV, para. 37e. For an analysis of the changes, *see* ARMY LAW., Dec. 1982, at 1.
10. This provision provides for payment of special pay for being subject to hostile fire or imminent danger. *See, e.g.,* United States v. Pitt, 35 M.J. 478 (C.M.A. 1992) (accused possessed marijuana while posted as sentinel).
11. MCM, Part IV, para. 37e.

§ 2-7(B)   MILITARY CRIMES   § 2-7(B)

one of the foregoing factors, it must allege and prove it as an element of the offense.[12]

§ 2-7(B). Proving Wrongfulness; Defenses.

Litigation of drug offenses in the military generally parallels civilian practice. For example, the prosecution bears the burden of establishing the accused's conduct was wrongful and that the substance involved was indeed contraband. The prosecution also must be prepared to meet any defenses. This section briefly addresses the issues of wrongfulness and defenses.

Possession, use, distribution, etc. of a controlled substance may be inferred to be wrongful[13] unless the defense presents evidence raising a legal justification or authorization.[14] The *Manual* recognizes three exemptions, i.e., where the drug activity is not wrongful:

(A) Where the accused was acting pursuant to legitimate law enforcement activity;[15]

(B) Where the activity was part of medical activities;[16] or

(C) Where the accused lacked knowledge as to the contraband nature of the drugs.[17]

If a defense, or exemption, is raised the prosecution must prove that the defense is not available.[18] For example, the accused may argue that his possession was innocent[19] or unknowing[20] in nature. In *United States v. Mance*,[21]

---

12. MCM, Part IV, para. 37b.
13. MCM, Part IV, para. 37c(5). United States v. Commander, 39 M.J. 972 (A.F.C.M.R. 1994) (wrongfulness may be inferred in absence of evidence to contrary; inference not available if drugs were prescribed by physician); United States v. Birbeck, 35 M.J. 519 (A.F.C.M.R. 1992) (presence of controlled substance on accused permitted inference that it was possessed knowingly); United States v. Gardner, 29 M.J. 673 (A.F.C.M.R. 1989) (knowledge of possession may be inferred from fact of possession).
14. MCM, Part IV, para. 37c(5). United States v. Lancaster, 36 M.J. 1115 (A.F.C.M.R. 1993) (accused's use of prescription drug for another ailment was not wrongful).
15. MCM, Part IV, para. 37c(5)(A). United States v. Chambers, 24 M.J. 586 (N.M.C.M.R. 1987) (judge correctly instructed jury that accused's belief that he was transporting drugs as a part of an undercover operation must have been both genuine and reasonable).
16. MCM, Part IV, para. 37c(5)(B).
17. MCM, Part IV, para. 37c(5)(C).
18. MCM, Part IV, para 37c(5). *See* United States v. Cuffee, 10 M.J. 381 (C.M.A. 1981) (proper to place burden on the defense of going forward with evidence that exemption exists).
19. In United States v. Kunkle, 23 M.J. 213 (C.M.A. 1987), the court stated that a person's possession of drugs is not innocent if he intends to return the drugs to the owner, unless he feels that he would be in immediate physical harm if he did not return them.
United States v. Vega, 29 M.J. 892 (A.F.C.M.R. 1989) (accused's mistaken belief that he possessed marijuana was not defense in charges of possessing cocaine); United States v. Domingue, 24 M.J. 766 (A.F.C.M.R. 1987) (accused's guilty plea was improvident where stipulation of fact indicated that he was unaware that cigarette contained cocaine).
20. United States v. Rowe, 11 M.J. 11 (C.M.A. 1981); United States v. Ludlum, 20 M.J. 954 (A.F.C.M.R. 1985) (evidence insufficient to establish that the accused was guilty of knowing and conscious possession of drugs where the amount was small and was found in a jacket that the accused had loaned to another person and was found in the trunk of his car); United States v.

21. 26 M.J. 244 (C.M.A. 1988).

the court discussed extensively the issue of "knowledge" vis-à-vis wrongfulness and concluded that in prosecutions for wrongful use or possession:

> [T]he military judge should instruct the court members that, in order to convict, the accused must have known that he had custody of or was ingesting the relevant substance and also must have known that the substance was of a contraband nature — regardless whether he knew its particular identity.[22] The court added that this instruction must be given even in the absence of a defense request.[23]

The military uses the "subjective" test in determining whether the defendant has been entrapped. That is, the question is whether the defendant had the predisposition to commit the offense.[24]

Sorrell, 20 M.J. 684 (A.C.M.R. 1985) (because the critical element of the distribution of drugs offense is the accused's knowing delivery of illegal drugs to the possession of another, it is irrelevant that the person receiving the drugs is unaware of their presence or nature). *See also* United States v. Brown, 19 M.J. 63 (C.M.A. 1984); United States v. Adam, 20 M.J. 681 (A.F.C.M.R. 1985) (the court concluded that the evidence was insufficient to support a finding of constructive possession of drugs).

22. *Id.* at 256. *See also* United States v. Stringfellow, 32 M.J. 335 (C.M.A. 1991) (accused could be convicted of ingestion of drugs although he was not aware of exact identity of substance; it is sufficient if he knows that it is a controlled substance).

23. *Id.* United States v. Williams, 37 M.J. 972 (A.C.M.R. 1993) (discussion of lack of knowledge as defense).

24. *See* United States v. Harris, 41 M.J. 433 (1995) (no evidence that agents unfairly targeted servicemember in drug sting operation who had voluntarily enrolled in Army's ADAPCP for alcoholism, wishing to conceal his drug problem); United States v. LeMaster, 40 M.J. 178 (C.M.A. 1994) (agents conduct in offering inducements to unstable accused violated fundamental norms of military due process and was functional equivalent of entrapment); United States v. Lubitz, 40 M.J. 165 (C.M.A. 1994) (defense of entrapment not shown); United States v. Bell, 38 M.J. 358 (C.M.A. 1993) (per curiam) (lengthy dissent discusses defense of entrapment); United States v. Howell, 36 M.J. 354 (C.M.A. 1993) (defense includes two elements: governmental inducement and the accused had no predisposition to commit an offense; court properly refused to give entrapment instruction); United States v. Copper, 35 M.J. 417 (C.M.A. 1992) (on reconsideration of its earlier ruling, 33 M.J. 356, court indicated that accused was not entrapped and government conduct had not been outrageous); United States v. Whittle, 34 M.J. 206 (C.M.A. 1992) (accused was not entrapped; case includes discussion of entrapment defense); United States v. Cooper, 33 M.J. 356 (C.M.A. 1991) (extensive discussion of whether due process was violated when CID agent induced accused, who was already in drug rehabilitation program, to sell drugs; plurality opinion concluded that accused was not entrapped); United States v. Johnson, 18 M.J. 76 (C.M.A. 1984); United States v. Zickefoose, 17 M.J. 449 (C.M.A. 1984); United States v. Vanzandt, 14 M.J. 332 (C.M.A. 1982); United States v. Dayton, 29 M.J. 6 (C.M.A. 1989) (subjective test).

United States v. Kemp, 42 M.J. 839 (N.M.Ct.Crim.App. 1995) (accused not entrapped where evidence showed predisposition; court declined to decide whether "vicarious entrapment" exists under military law); United States v. Frazier, 30 M.J. 1231 (A.C.M.R. 1990) (use of reverse sting operation did not deny accused due process, nor was he entrapped); United States v. Anzalone, 40 M.J. 658 (N.M.C.M.R. 1994) (accused was not entrapped into transmitting information to Soviet Union); United States v. Hunt, 34 M.J. 765 (A.C.M.R. 1992) (prosecution did not show that accused was not entrapped); United States v. Massengill, 30 M.J. 800 (A.F.C.M.R. 1990) (accused was not entrapped); United States v. Cortes, 29 M.J. 946 (A.C.M.R. 1990) (although government originated drug offense, accused was predisposed to commit it); United States v. Eckhoff, 23 M.J. 875 (N.M.C.M.R. 1987) (court rejected argument that profit motive in itself defeats defense of entrapment; instead, it is one of several factors to be considered).

In the past, the defense of agency was sometimes available where the accused was charged with selling drugs.[25] The offense of sale of drugs is not included in Article 112a. Instead, the charge will now allege "transfer" and should thus preclude reliance on the agency defense.[26]

§ 2-7(C). Evidentiary Issues; Proving Identity of the Drugs.

Because much of the military's search and seizure law involves drug activity, counsel are likely to encounter situations where drug charges have followed a command-ordered search[27] or inspection[28] under the Military Rules of Evidence.[29] Such investigations might also include compulsory drug urinalysis programs, which have generally been approved by the military courts.[30] Thus, the defense typically may move to suppress the drugs as being the result of an illegal search or seizure.[31]

To prove the identity of the drugs, the prosecution usually relies upon properly authenticated laboratory reports[32] or upon the testimony of someone sufficiently familiar with the substance to identify the drugs as being contraband.[33]

From an evidentiary standpoint, counsel should pay particular attention to Military Rules of Evidence 803(6) and (8), which specifically include chain of custody documents[34] and laboratory reports as exceptions to the hearsay rule.[35] The prosecution will generally rely on these two documents to make its

---

25. *See* United States v. Steinruck, 11 M.J. 322 (C.M.A. 1981) (defenses of entrapment and agency (for buyer) may be used in same case); United States v. Fruscella, 21 C.M.A. 26, 44 C.M.R. 80 (1971) (accused was mere agent or conduit); United States v. Pettersen, 15 M.J. 934 (N.M.C.M.R. 1983) (discussion of agency defense).

26. *Cf.* United States v. Power, 20 M.J. 275 (C.M.A. 1985) (court concluded that the evidence submitted by the defense at trial did not raise the defense of agency, which would otherwise have been available because the accused was charged, before promulgation of Article 112a, with "sale" of drugs).

27. *See* Rule 315, MIL. R. EVID.

28. *See* Rule 313, MIL. R. EVID.

29. See Chapter 5 for a discussion on the commander's investigation.

30. MIL. R. EVID. 312(d); Murray v. Haldeman, 16 M.J. 74 (C.M.A. 1983).

31. *See* Chapter 13.

32. United States v. Hunt, 33 M.J. 345 (C.M.A. 1991) (prosecution failed to prove drug offense where it only offered lab report on accused's urine sample); United States v. Pinkston, 32 M.J. 555 (A.F.C.M.R. 1991) (proper foundation laid for laboratory report). *See generally* Rule 901, MIL. R. EVID.

33. *See, e.g.,* United States v. Evans, 16 M.J. 951 (A.F.C.M.R. 1983) (witness identified substance as marijuana by smell).

34. *See* Appendix 25 for the Military Rules of Evidence. United States v. Berry, 30 M.J. 134 (C.M.A. 1990) (insufficient foundation for chain of custody); United States v. Morris, 30 M.J. 1221 (A.C.M.R. 1990) (chain of custody on blood sample not required under facts); United States v. Carrott, 25 M.J. 823 (A.F.C.M.R. 1988) (insufficient chain of custody where it contained four-month gap). *See generally* Saltzburg, Schinasi & Schlueter, *Military Rules of Evidence Manual,* 882-883 (3d ed. 1991).

35. United States v. Harper, 32 M.J. 620 (A.C.M.R. 1991) (judge erred in admitting laboratory report as business record); United States v. Holman, 23 M.J. 565 (A.C.M.R. 1986) (lab report admissible). *Cf.* United States v. Broadnax, 23 M.J. 389 (C.M.A. 1987) (under circumstances, lab report on handwriting samples was inadmissible). The Federal Rules of Evidence, which served

§ 2-7(C) MILITARY CRIMINAL JUSTICE § 2-7(C)

case.[36] Where the government has used a confidential informant to ferret out drug activity the prosecution may rely on Military Rule of Evidence 507, which creates a limited privilege for the identity of informants.[37]

In *United States v. Murphy*,[38] the court held that if the prosecution is relying upon scientific evidence, such as urinalysis results,[39] not within the common knowledge or understanding of the court, the prosecution may not rely solely on the laboratory report to show use of drugs. Instead, counsel must present in-court expert testimony or some other lawful substitute to provide a rational basis that in turn may permit the fact finder to draw an inference that drugs were used.[40] This case greatly limits the ability of the prosecutor to prove drug use through a "paper case." In *United States v. Spann*,[41] however, the court indicated that a stipulation of fact could serve as a lawful substitute of expert testimony.

In *United States v. Ford*,[42] the court ruled that the prosecution may rely upon the inference of wrongfulness alone, arising from the urinalysis test and expert testimony explaining the results, to obtain a conviction. The court also noted that a conflict of evidence, for example, an accused's denial of conscious ingestion of a drug, does not prevent use of an inference of wrongfulness. The conflict simply requires the fact finder to resolve the conflict before deciding whether to draw the inference.[43]

---

as the template for the military rules, do not include such items as exceptions to the hearsay rule. *See* United States v. Oates, 560 F.2d 45 (2d Cir. 1977). The Court of Military Appeals has considered the lab report admissible as a business entry. United States v. Strangstalien, 7 M.J. 225 (C.M.A. 1979). *See* Saltzburg, Schinasi & Schlueter, *Military Rules of Evidence Manual* 797-799 (3d ed. 1991).

36. The documents themselves may be authenticated by relying upon MIL. R. EVID. 901 or 902.

37. *See* Saltzburg, Schinasi & Schlueter, *Military Rules of Evidence Manual* 595-601 (3d ed. 1991).

38. 23 M.J. 310 (C.M.A. 1987).

39. *See* United States v. Hagan, 24 M.J. 571 (N.M.C.M.R. 1987). *See also infra* § 5-2(A)(3).

40. United States v. Mack, 33 M.J. 251 (C.M.A. 1991) (scientific results of urinalysis testing can be substantially relied upon in courts-martial but only if they logically and demonstratively show drug use); United States v. Boulden, 29 M.J. 44 (C.M.A. 1989) (expert's testimony reasonably implied that presence of benzoylecgonine metabolite in urine was basis for showing use of cocaine); United States v. Murphy, 33 M.J. 248 (C.M.A. 1991) (judge could sua sponte judicially notice effects of cocaine on body).

United States v. Brown, 33 M.J. 706 (A.C.M.R. 1991) (court could judicially notice that cocaine is derived from cocoa plant, that when ingested into the human body it produces certain chemicals that are then excreted through urine; but fact that laboratory used particular testing procedures was not proper subject for judicial notice); United States v. Harper, 32 M.J. 620 (A.C.M.R. 1991) (judge erred in taking judicial notice of scientific principles and techniques without supporting information); United States v. Coleman, 32 M.J. 508 (A.C.M.R. 1990) (judge erred in taking judicial notice of documents relating to drug tests); United States v. Hagan, 24 M.J. 571 (N.M.C.M.R. 1987).

41. 24 M.J. 508 (A.F.C.M.R. 1987).

42. 23 M.J. 331 (C.M.A. 1987); United States v. Thompson, 34 M.J. 287 (C.M.A. 1992) (prosecution's evidence included expert testimony showing presence of benzoylecgonine in accused's urine sample and evidence negating tampering).

43. *See also* United States v. Spann, 24 M.J. 508 (A.F.C.M.R. 1987); United States v. Merritt, 23 M.J. 654 (N.M.C.M.R. 1986) (court may rely on permissible inferences to find wrongfulness); United States v. Williams, 23 M.J. 582 (N.M.C.M.R. 1986).

§ 2-8. Fraternization.

§ 2-8(A). In General.

Historically, the armed forces have recognized the distinction between officers and enlisted servicemembers and by custom have discouraged officers from fraternizing or associating with enlisted personnel on terms of military equality.[1] Early cases addressing fraternization often focused on financial transactions between officers and enlisted personnel. For example, officers were forbidden from entering into loan agreements with them.[2] On a few occasions the military courts addressed fact situations that amounted to improper socializing.[3] In recent years, with the growing influx of women into the main stream of military organizations, there has been a dramatic increase in the incidence of this controversial crime and a resulting increase in the interest and debate concerning the military's ability to regulate and punish fraternization.[4]

The underlying core for this brand of regulation of an individual's conduct is that fraternization is fatal to discipline.[5] Undue familiarity, most especially among members of the same command, tends to create disharmony and distrust. The subordinate member of the association may expect or actually receive favorable treatment. At a minimum, the rest of the command may perceive that the intimate association has resulted in favoritism at the expense to others similarly situated. These sorts of problems are certainly not unique to the military[6] but are clearly exacerbated when military order and discipline are at stake.

Fraternization is no longer limited to associations between officer and enlisted personnel but may arise in associations between officers of different

---

In United States v. Bassano, 23 M.J. 661 (A.F.C.M.R. 1986), the court held that para. 37 in Part IV of the MCM does not unconstitutionally shift the burden of proof to defense. The inference of wrongfulness is a permissible inference. See also § 15-20.

1. See MCM, Part IV, para. 87, Analysis. See generally Winthrop, *Military Law and Precedents*, 41 (2d ed. 1920 reprint). The problem has been serious enough to warrant a maximum punishment of dismissal, forfeiture of all pay and allowances, and confinement for two years. See MCM, Part IV, para. 83 (Article 133 or 134 violation). Similar punishments are assigned for acts of fraternization charged under Article 92. See infra § 2-8(C).
2. See, e.g., United States v. Mayne, 39 C.M.R. 628 (A.B.R. 1968); United States v. Light, 36 C.M.R. 579 (A.B.R. 1965).
3. United States v. Pitasi, 20 C.M.A. 601, 44 C.M.R. 31 (1971); United States v. Lovejoy, 20 C.M.A. 18, 42 C.M.R. 210 (1971); United States v. Free, 14 C.M.R. 466 (N.B.R. 1953).
4. See generally Carter, "Fraternization," 113 MIL. L. REV. 61 (1986); Mahoney, "Fraternization: Military Anachronism or Leadership Challenge," 28 A.F.L. REV. (1988); Jonas, "Fraternization: Time for a Rational Department of Defense Standard," 135 MIL. L. REV. 37 (1992); McDevitt, "Wrongful Fraternization As An Offense Under the Uniform Code of Military Justice," 33 CLEV. S.L. REV. 547 (1984-1985); Nelson, "Conduct Expected of an Officer and a Gentleman: Ambiguity," 12 A.F. JAG. L.R. 124 (1970); Davis, "'Fraternization' and the Enlisted Soldier: Some Considerations for the Defense," ARMY LAW., Oct. 1985, at 27; Flatten, "Fraternization," 10 THE REPORTER 109 (Aug. 1981).
5. MCM, Part IV, para. 83 Analysis, citing authorities. See also United States v. Adams, 19 M.J. 996 (A.C.M.R. 1985).
6. See, e.g., Camero v. United States, 345 F.2d 798 (Ct. Cl. 1965) (federal employee discharged for being too familiar with government contractors).

ranks and enlisted personnel of different ranks. Although the possibility is remote, the offense of fraternization might extend to an association between members of the same rank and status, one of whom is in a supervisory capacity over the other.[7]

Defining the offense is a delicate task because it now almost always involves intimate associations between members of the opposite sex,[8] and any attempt by the government to interfere with such liaisons is sometimes viewed as an unjustified infringement of various constitutional rights. As the following sections point out, the description of the proscribed conduct may determine whether the conduct is punishable under the General Articles, (Articles 133 and 134) or under one of the Articles proscribing disobedience of orders or regulations. The topic of possible constitutional attacks on regulation of personal associations is addressed in § 2-8(D) *infra*.

§ 2-8(B). Fraternization and the General Articles.

In addressing the offense of fraternization the Manual for Courts-Martial states in part:

> The gist of this offense is a violation of the custom of the armed forces against fraternization. Not all contact or association between officers and enlisted persons is an offense. Whether the contact or association in question is an offense depends on the surrounding circumstances. Factors to be considered include whether the conduct has compromised the chain of command, resulted in the appearance of partiality, or otherwise undermined good order, discipline, authority, or morale. The acts and circumstances must be such as to lead a reasonable person experienced in the problems of military leadership to conclude that the good order and discipline of the armed forces has been prejudiced by their tendency to compromise the respect of enlisted persons for the professionalism, integrity, and obligations of an officer.[9]

Thus, prosecution under either Article 133[10] or Article 134[11] should be considered only if it is clear that the accused had fair notice that the conduct in

---

7. The key here is that the undue familiarity between the two individuals lends itself to interoffice rivalry, distrust, and disrespect, as long as one of the individuals is in, or perceived to be in, a position to assist the other either through work assignments, efficiency reports or recommendations for promotion. Being of the same rank and status does not necessarily change that.

8. In United States v. Johanns, 20 M.J. 155, 160 (C.M.A. 1985), the court observed that part of the fraternization problem rests in the condonation by the military of officer-enlisted marriages. It is difficult, the court said, to see how premarital dating leading up to such a marriage could violate custom. *Cf.* United States v. Van Steenwyk, 21 M.J. 795 (N.M.C.M.R. 1985) (regulation governing housing for mixed-grade marriages cannot be construed as condonation of fraternization).

9. MCM, Part IV, para. 83. The last sentence was apparently derived from United States v. Free, 14 C.M.R. 466 (N.B.R. 1953).

10. *See supra* § 2-5. In United States v. Parrillo, 31 M.J. 886 (A.F.C.M.R. 1990), the court held

11. *See supra* § 2-6.

§ 2-8(B)

question was violative of the armed force's customs or policies.[12] In the absence of a clear custom or policy, prosecution under either of the general articles may be challenged as being void for vagueness. For example, in *United States v. Johanns*,[13] the Court reversed an Air Force officer's conviction for fraternization where he had engaged in sexual relations with female non-commissioned officers. Even under the flexible standards of *Parker v. Levy*,[14] said the court, the accused lacked the notice required by the fifth amendment due process clause. But the court observed that clear directives might remedy the notice problem.[15]

Subsequent cases have focused on the notice requirement and have concluded that such directives, or policy letters,[16] and even briefings[17] have provided ample notice that certain associations are forbidden. In at least one case, the court observed that the inclusion in the *Manual* of the topic of fraternization provided notice to the accused.[18]

---

that the government could properly charge a female officer under Article 133 for having private, consensual sexual relations with enlisted members within her command; the prosecution was thus not required to prove Air Force customs regarding fraternization. *Cf.* United States v. Arthen, 32 M.J. 541 (A.F.C.M.R. 1990) (alleging what was really a fraternization offense under Rule 133 failed to state offense where there was no supervisory relationship).

12. United States v. Cisler, 33 M.J. 503 (A.F.C.M.R. 1991) (regardless of whether fraternization offense is alleged under Article 133 or 134, prosecution must prove existence, notice, and violation of Air Force custom; court noted that in this case, the offense would not have been proved but that here the accused-officer's open and notorious adulterous acts with enlisted woman supported conviction).

13. 20 M.J. 155 (C.M.A.), *cert. denied*, 474 U.S. 850 (1985); United States v. Boyett, 42 M.J. 150 (1995) (court rejected argument that lower court had ignored stare decisis by implicitly overruling its earlier decision in *Johanns I*. The court noted sound reasons for the Court of Criminal Appeals changing its posture regarding fraternization customs in the Air Force).

14. 417 U.S. 733 (1974).

15. United States v. Johanns, 20 M.J. at 161 (C.M.A. 1985).

16. United States v. Adames, 21 M.J. 465 (C.M.A. 1986); United States v. Fox, 32 M.J. 747 (A.F.C.M.R. 1990) (evidence at trial established that accused's fraternization with his first sergeant violated Air Force custom). *Cf.* United States v. Wales, 31 M.J. 301 (C.M.A. 1990) (prosecution for private sexual intercourse between members of different command must be based upon specific punitive regulations forbidding that conduct); United States v. Moorer, 15 M.J. 520 (A.C.M.R. 1983) (policy letter). *See generally* Mahoney, "Fraternization: Military Anachronism or Leadership Challenge?", 28 A.F.L. Rev. 153 (1988).

17. United States v. Boyett, 42 M.J. 150 (1995) (under facts, officer was clearly on notice, for purposes of Article 133 conviction, that his dating of airman was fraternization; his pre-commissioning education informed him of the custom against dating enlisted persons and he was counseled twice about issue); United States v. Tedder, 24 M.J. 176 (C.M.A. 1987) (accused's conviction of fraternization affirmed where his statements to enlisted woman indicated that he was aware that he could not maintain an intimate sexual relationship; he also committed fraternization by encouraging other enlisted women to help him arrange a date); United States v. Mayfield, 21 M.J. 418 (C.M.A. 1986) (prosecution relied on more than "customs" of the service to establish notice). This case serves as a reminder that although the custom of a particular service might serve as sufficient notice, relying upon directives, as recommended in *Johanns*, generally is the more prudent route for the prosecution.

United States v. McCreight, 39 M.J. 530 (A.F.C.M.R. 1994) (customs of service provide notice to officer of what is prohibited; court concluded that officer knew that his actions were wrong).

18. United States v. Boyett, 42 M.J. 150, 152 n. 3 (1995) (Part IV, MCM discussion listing elements of fraternization constitutes explicit notice to servicemembers that fraternization is an

In *United States v. Wales*,[19] the Court again addressed the problem of fraternization in the Air Force, which according to the Court has tended to be more lenient about mingling of officers and enlisted personnel in living and social arrangements.[20] The Court indicated that if the services wish to prosecute fraternization on the basis of custom in the service, the prosecution must present testimony by a knowledgeable witness, subject to cross-examination.[21] The Court added that if the Air Force elects to punish private sexual conduct between officers and enlisted persons who are not in the chain of command or supervision, it must promulgate specific punitive regulations to that effect.[22] In *United States v. Appel*,[23] the Court addressed the issue of proving that a custom has been violated when the defendant has entered a plea of guilty. It concluded that the record must show "undisputed facts" that the accused violated a custom which prohibits an officer from fraternizing with someone he or she supervises.[24] The Court defined a supervisory relationship as follows:

> There must be a duty relationship which regularly or recurringly calls for or may call for direction, oversight, correction or evaluation of the enlisted member by the officer. It is not required that there be a formal supervisory relationship between the two.[25]

Whether Article 134 may be used for prosecuting enlisted personnel accused of fraternizing is doubtful. In *United States v. Stocken*,[26] the court held that

---

offense); United States v. Lowery, 21 M.J. 998 (A.C.M.R. 1986). *See also* United States v. Moultak, 21 M.J. 822 (N.M.C.M.R. 1985).

19. 31 M.J. 301 (C.M.A. 1990). *See also* United States v. Appel, 31 M.J. 314 (C.M.A. 1990) (accused officer pleaded guilty to fraternization with married enlisted subordinate).

20. 31 M.J. at 307.

21. 31 M.J. at 309. United States v. Fox, 34 M.J. 99 (C.M.A. 1992) (prosecution failed to prove custom; witness testimony was conclusory and circuitous); United States v. Blake, 35 M.J. 539 (A.C.M.R. 1992) (alleging custom of Army re fraternization between noncommissioned officers is essential element of the offense; failure to do so was fatal); United States v. Cottrell, 32 M.J. 675 (A.F.C.M.R. 1991) (absence of "undisputed facts" that accused and enlisted member were in supervisory relationship).

22. 31 M.J. at 307. United States v. Fox, 34 M.J. 99 (C.M.A. 1992) (fraternization conviction reversed where there was no supervisory relationship between accused officer and enlisted lover).

23. 31 M.J. 314 (C.M.A. 1990).

24. 31 M.J. at 320-321.

25. 31 M.J. at 317. *See also* United States v. Nunes, 39 M.J. 889 (A.F.C.M.R. 1994) (Colonel's relationship and activities with subordinate NCO in unit constituted unlawful fraternization; fact that there was no sexual relationship between the two men was utterly irrelevant); United States v. Arthen, 31 M.J. 539 (A.F.C.M.R. 1990) (accused's plea was improvident where she had no supervisory relationship with enlisted man; her admissions fell far short of "undisputed facts" required by *Appel*).

26. 17 M.J. 826 (A.C.M.R. 1984). Citing the Manual for Courts-Martial, Part IV, para. 83, one panel of the Army Court of Military Review in United States v. Clarke, 25 M.J. 631 (A.C.M.R. 1987), apparently disagreed with the decision in *Stocken*. Noting that that decision clouded the question of whether the NCO defendant had adequate notice that his sexual acts with an enlisted woman amounted to fraternization but indicated that "in the future ... noncommissioned officers are on notice that fraternization with enlisted subordinates is an offense punishable under the provisions of Article 134, U.C.M.J." *See also* United States v. Blake, 35 M.J. 539 (A.C.M.R. 1992) (court held that NCO fraternization could be prosecuted under Article 134); United States v.

enlisted accused, an NCO charged with various associations with female enlisted servicemembers, could not be prosecuted under Article 134. In the court's view, it would be an unwarranted extension of Article 134 to include acts such as smoking marijuana and fornication with junior enlisted personnel. The court observed that guidance from commanders and supervisors restricting such activity added nothing to military criminal law.[27] The court seemed concerned, not so much with whether the accused had notice that his activities were prohibited, but rather with what it considered to be an unwarranted extension of Article 134. Enlisted personnel may, however, be prosecuted under Article 92 for fraternizing in violation of regulations.

§ 2-8(C). Fraternization and Regulations or Orders.

The same directives, regulations, or orders that provide the necessary notice under Article 133 or 134 may also provide the basis for prosecution under one of the more specific punitive articles governing obedience of orders.[28] For example, most installations and commands that have a mission to train servicemembers now have specific regulations governing associations between cadre and students.[29] Violation of these orders or regulations can then be treated as an act of disobedience. The regulations in question are subject to the same sort of scrutiny as any other regulation governing conduct of military personnel.[30] Because such regulations involve private associations they should be narrowly tailored to meet the military's interests and should be as specific as possible in describing proscribed conduct.[31]

If there are not such orders or regulations in effect, the accused may nonetheless be prosecuted under other more specific offenses such as adultery,[32] drug-related activities,[33] or dereliction of duty.[34] In some cases it may be appropriate to meet the exigencies of proof to charge the act of fraternization as violation of a general article, a more specific article, and as a disobedience offense. In most cases these offenses would be multiplicious and subject to dismissal after findings.[35]

Carter, 23 M.J. 683 (N.M.C.M.R. 1986), where the court held that after August 1, 1987, enlisted fraternization offenses are punishable under Article 134, assuming that the accused has had sufficient notice that certain conduct is prohibited.

27. *Id.* at 829.
28. *See supra* § 2-4.
29. *See* United States v. Hoard, 12 M.J. 563 (A.C.M.R. 1981).
30. *See supra* § 2-4(C). United States v. Dowlat, 28 M.J. 958 (A.F.C.M.R. 1989) (applying well-known rules of statutory construction, the court concluded that the accused was not guilty of fraternizing by providing candy, soft-drinks, etc., to trainees).
31. United States v. Sartin, 24 M.J. 873 (A.C.M.R. 1987) (court rejected argument that regulation proscribing social fraternization was overly broad). *See infra* §§ 2-8(D) and 13-3(N).
32. *See, e.g.,* United States v. Callaway, 21 M.J. 770 (A.C.M.R. 1986) (officer charged with both adultery and fraternization with junior officer); United States v. Smith, 18 M.J. 786 (N.M.C.M.R. 1984) (adulterous relationship).
33. *See supra* § 2-7.
34. United States v. Hoard, 12 M.J. 563 (A.C.M.R. 1981).
35. *See infra* §§ 6-1(C)(3) and 13-3(J).

§ 2-8(D). Fraternization and the Constitution.

Although a number of constitutional challenges have been leveled at fraternization prosecutions, to date most have been rejected. The military courts have rejected the argument the proscriptions against fraternization infringe upon the freedom of speech,[36] the right to privacy,[37] or the right to equal protection.[38] However, a freedom of religion claim might prevail if the regulation in question prohibited joint attendance at a religious function.[39]

It should be noted that in most of the fraternization cases some activity other than mere socializing has been at the core of the case. In most, some sort of sexual activity, drug use, indecent acts, gambling, or drinking was involved.[40] Note, however, that charging both fraternization and the underlying offense may present multiplicity problems.[41] These sorts of activities, which generally promote neither harmony nor good order, can also give rise, as noted in § 2-8(C), to separate charges. When combined with the accompanying intimate association, a reasonable person should conclude that good order and discipline are not promoted. Thus, from a constitutional standpoint, the government should be able in most cases to argue effectively that the fraternizing conduct is not protected to the same extent as activities, such as religious functions, which tend to promote trust and respect.

As noted in § 2-8(B) *supra*, the facts in a particular case may give rise to a vagueness claim where the accused had inadequate notice. The topic of constitutional challenges to military rules and regulations is discussed in more detail at § 13-3(N).

---

36. *See, e.g.*, United States v. Hoard, 12 M.J. 563 (A.C.M.R. 1981) (the regulations govern conduct not speech).

37. United States v. Adams, 19 M.J. 996 (A.C.M.R. 1985). *See also* United States v. McFarlin, 19 M.J. 790 (A.C.M.R. 1985) (governmental interest in preventing sexual liaisons is sufficiently compelling). *Cf.* Bowers v. Hardwick, 478 U.S. 186 (1986); Dronenburg v. Zech, 741 F.2d 1388 (D.C. Cir. 1984) (homosexual conduct not protected by Constitution).

The right to associate is a concomitant penumbral right of both the First Amendment and the privacy right. This right might be implicated if the regulations operated to infringe substantially upon other important privacy rights such as decisions concerning procreation and intimate family matters. *See infra* § 13(N).

38. United States v. Moultak, 21 M.J. 822 (N.M.C.M.R. 1985), aff'd, 24 M.J. 316 (C.M.A. 1987) (but the court did not address the issue of equal protection).

39. United States v. Johanns, 20 M.J. 155 (C.M.A. 1985) (dicta).

40. *See, e.g.*, United States v. Pitasi, 20 C.M.A. 601, 44 C.M.R. 210 (1970) (officer engaged in lewd acts and sodomy with enlisted servicemember); United States v. Fox, 32 M.J. 747 (A.F.C.M.R. 1991) (commander committed adultery with member of his unit); United States v. Serino, 24 M.J. 848 (A.F.C.M.R. 1987) (officer using drugs with enlisted members). *Cf.* United States v. Nunes, 39 M.J. 889 (A.F.C.M.R. 1994) (Colonel's relationship and activities with subordinate NCO in unit constituted unlawful fraternization; fact that there was no sexual relationship between the two men was utterly irrelevant; court indicated that this case was a useful corrective to the common notion that fraternization perforce must include sexual hanky-panky).

41. *See* United States v. Jefferson, 21 M.J. 203 (C.M.A. 1986); United States v. Walker, 21 M.J. 74 (C.M.A. 1985); United States v. Caldwell, 23 M.J. 748 (A.F.C.M.R. 1987).

§ 2-9. AIDS and HIV-Related Offenses.

§ 2-9(A). General.

With the current threat of an AIDS[1] epidemic looming over society, the military has taken affirmative steps to thwart the spread of this disease by punishing those who knowingly risk transmission of the HIV[2] antibody, which causes AIDS.[3] The Court of Appeals for the Armed Forces has specifically stated the military has a "public duty of the highest order" to prevent its members from spreading the HIV antibody.[4] In an effort to perform this "duty," the military screens its applicants before they enter the service, educates its members about AIDS transmission and prevention, and conducts follow-up testing of its members on a regular basis.[5]

When servicemembers test positive for the HIV antibody, they receive mandatory counseling covering the significance of HIV positivity and how to minimize the risk of transmitting the antibody.[6] In conjunction with this counseling, medical personnel complete a medical and case history evaluation of HIV-positive members.[7] Information obtained during or as a result of these "epidemiological assessments" may not be used to support adverse actions against HIV-infected service members.[8] Therefore, HIV-related administrative and

---

1. The term AIDS stands for Acquired Immune Deficiency Syndrome.
2. HIV is the acronym for Human Immunodeficiency Virus. The most severe manifestation of HIV infection is AIDS. Milhizer, "Legality of the 'Safe-Sex' Order to Soldiers Having AIDS," ARMY LAW., Dec. 1988, at 4, n. 2.
3. *See, e.g.,* United States v. Dumford, 30 M.J. 137 (C.M.A. 1990) (HIV-infected member convicted for violating "safe sex" order); United States v. Johnson, 30 M.J. 53 (C.M.A. 1990) (accused convicted of aggravated assault for attempting unprotected anal intercourse while knowingly infected with HIV). *See generally* McLaughlin, "A 'Society Apart?' The Military's Response to the Threat of AIDS," ARMY LAW., October 1993, at 3.
4. United States v. Dumford, 30 M.J. 137, 138, n. 2 (C.M.A. 1990).
5. Secretary of Defense Memorandum, Policy on Identification, Surveillance, and Administration of Personnel Infected with Human Immunodeficiency Virus (Apr. 20, 1987) [hereinafter cited as DOD Memorandum].
6. DOD Memorandum, at para. B5a(1). *See also* Army Reg. 600-110, Identification, Surveillance, and Administration of Personnel Infected with Human Immunodeficiency Virus (HIV) (Mar. 11 1988) [hereinafter cited as AR 600-110].
7. DOD Memorandum, at paras. B3, 4, 5a(2), and 6. This Secretary of Defense Memorandum repeatedly stresses the need to obtain information regarding how the HIV infection may have been transmitted and to identify others who may have been exposed or be at risk of exposure. The memorandum emphasizes this information is vital to preventive medicine intervention and research aimed at minimizing further transmission of the infection.
8. National Defense Authorization Act of 1987, Pub. L. No. 99-661, § 705(c), 100 Stat. 3816, 3904 (1986). The text of § 705(c) can also be found in the Historical and Statutory Notes of 10 U.S.C.A. § 1074 (1991 Supp.). The Act stated that adverse actions include courts-martial, nonjudicial punishment, involuntary separations for other than medical reasons, reductions in grade, denials of promotion, unfavorable entries in personnel records, and bars to reenlistment. The military implemented this act with a DOD Memorandum, however, the Secretary of Defense added some caveats regarding the use of information obtained from "epidemiological assessments." He added such information could still be used for impeachment or rebuttal purposes or during actions based on independently derived evidence. DOD Memorandum, para. F. He also stated such information could be used for nonadverse personnel actions such as reassignment,

disciplinary actions usually do not arise until an infected member fails to comply with "lawfully ordered preventive medicine procedures."[9]

§ 2-9(B). Violating "Safe Sex" Orders.

In addition to the mandatory medical counseling, military commanders are required to issue orders to HIV-infected servicemembers that require them to inform sexual partners of their HIV positivity and to use a barrier method of protection during sex.[10] For example, the Air Force has mandated that commanders issue the following order to members who test positive for the HIV antibody:

ORDER TO FOLLOW
PREVENTIVE MEDICINE REQUIREMENTS

Because of the necessity to safeguard the overall health, welfare, safety, and reputation of this command, and to ensure unit readiness and the ability of the unit to accomplish its mission, certain behavior and unsafe health procedures must be proscribed for members who are diagnosed as positive for HIV infection.

As a military member who has been diagnosed as positive for HIV infection, you are hereby ordered: (1) to verbally inform sexual partners that you are HIV positive prior to engaging in sexual relations. This order extends to sexual relations with other military members, military dependents, civilian employees of [Department of Defense] (DOD) components or any other persons; (2) to use proper methods to prevent the transfer of bodily fluids during sexual relations, including the use of condoms; (3) in the event that you require emergency care, to inform personnel responding to your emergency that you are HIV positive; (4) when you seek medical or dental care, to inform health care providers that you are HIV positive before treatment is initiated; and, (5) not to donate blood, sperm, tissues, or other organs.

Violating the terms of this order may result in adverse administrative action or punishment under the Uniform Code of Military Justice.

Signature of Commander and Date

---

disqualification from personnel reliability program, changes in one's security clearance, or removal from flight status. *Id.*

9. *See* DOD Memorandum, para. D2 (HIV-positive military personnel not following preventive medicine procedures subject to administrative and disciplinary action). *See generally* Anderson, Kramer, and Shambley, "AIDS Issues in the Military", 32 A.F.L. Rev. 353 (1990); Milhizer, "Safe Sex ... or Else," 5 ABA Criminal Justice, Winter 1991, at 17; Wells-Petry, "Anatomy of an AIDS Case: Deadly Disease as an Aspect of Deadly Crime," Army Law., Jan. 1988, at 17.

10. Anderson, Kramer, and Shambley, "AIDS Issues in the Military," 32 A.F.L. Rev. 353, 362 (1990). *See also* AR 600-110, para. 2-17c (Mar. 11, 1988).

ACKNOWLEDGMENT

I have read and understand the terms of this order and acknowledge that I have a duty to obey this order. I understand that I must inform sexual partners, including other military members, military dependents, civilian employees of DOD components, or any other persons, that I am HIV positive prior to sexual relations; that I must use proper methods to prevent the transfer of bodily fluids while engaging in sexual relations, including the use of condoms; that if I need emergency medical care I will inform personnel responding to my emergency that I am HIV positive; that when I seek medical or dental care that I must inform health care providers that I am HIV positive before treatment is initiated; and, that I must not donate blood, sperm, tissues, or other organs. I understand that violations of this order may result in adverse administrative actions or punishment under the Uniform Code of Military Justice.

Signature of Member and Date[11]

Because these "safe sex" orders are issued by commissioned officers, the authority to enforce them stems from Article 90 of the Uniform Code of Military Justice.[12] Thus, when an HIV-infected member violates a "safe sex" order, he or she is subject to punishment under the military criminal justice system.

Although the legality of "safe sex" orders has been challenged on several occasions, the military courts have upheld them as lawful.[13] In *United States v. Womack*,[14] the Court noted that "safe sex" orders are valid if they are specific, definite, certain, and give the person ordered fair notice of the prohibited conduct.[15] Additionally, the order must have a valid military purpose, and an accused must have had actual knowledge of the order.[16] The court concluded that "safe sex" orders have a valid military purpose because the military has "a compelling interest in having those who defend the nation remain healthy and capable of performing their duty."[17]

---

11. Anderson, Kramer, and Shambley, "AIDS Issues in the Military," 32 A.F.L. Rev. 353, 363, n. 75 (1990).
12. United States v. Schoolfield, 36 M.J. 545 (A.C.M.R. 1992), *aff'd on other grounds*, 40 M.J. 132 (C.M.A. 1994) (accused convicted of violating safe-sex orders from succession of commanders by having sex with five different women). *See supra* § 2-4(B) for a discussion concerning disobedience of a superior's orders.
13. *See, e.g.,* United States v. Dumford, 30 M.J. 137 (C.M.A. 1990) ("safe sex" order mandating use of barrier protection during sex upheld even though case involved heterosexual, consensual sex with civilian); United States v. Womack, 29 M.J. 88 (C.M.A. 1989) ("safe sex" orders constitutional because they have a valid military purpose); United States v. Negron, 28 M.J. 775 (A.C.M.R.), *aff'd*, 29 M.J. 324 (C.M.A. 1989) (upheld order compelling HIV-positive member to forewarn sexual partners of his condition).
14. 29 M.J. 88 (C.M.A. 1989).
15. *Id.* at 90. *See generally* Milhizer, "Legality of the 'Safe Sex' Order to Soldiers Having AIDS," Army Law., Dec. 1988, at 5.
16. *Id.*
17. *Id.* at 90-91 (citing National Treasury Employees Union v. Von Raab, 489 U.S. 656 (1989)).

Much of the controversy surrounding the "safe sex" orders has centered on whether they really have a valid military purpose.[18] This is largely due to language in the *Manual* that states, "[t]he order may not, without a valid military purpose, interfere with private rights or personal affairs."[19] Because the valid military purpose set out in *Womack* only applied to an HIV-infected member having sexual relations with another service member, the Court of Military Appeals has expanded its view regarding the purpose behind a "safe sex" order. In *United States v. Dumford*,[20] the court held the military has a legitimate interest in limiting its HIV-infected members contacts with civilians in order to prevent the spread of infectious disease.[21] Whether this valid military purpose will extend into a marital relationship remains to be seen, and a brief discussion of this and other constitutional issues can be found in § 2-9(D) *infra*.

§ 2-9(C). Prosecuting HIV-Related Offenses Under Other U.C.M.J. Provisions.

Rather than punishing an HIV-infected servicemember under Article 90 for knowingly putting another at risk by engaging in unprotected or unwarned sexual intercourse after being ordered not to do so, the commander may wish to prosecute the accused for other violations of the U.C.M.J.[22] Several commentators have suggested that HIV-positive servicemembers might also be punished for attempted murder, rape, assault, and conduct that is prejudicial to good order and discipline.[23] In fact, the Court of Military Appeals has upheld the convictions of several HIV-infected servicemembers for aggravated assault[24] and conduct prejudicial to good order and discipline[25] because those

---

18. *See, e.g.,* United States v. Dumford, 30 M.J. 137 (C.M.A. 1990) ("safe sex" order challenged as having no valid military purpose); United States v. Sargeant, 29 M.J. 813 (A.C.M.R. 1989) (court upheld "safe sex" order because it had valid military purpose of promoting health and welfare of unit).
19. MCM, 1984, Part IV, para. 14c(2)(a)(iii).
20. 30 M.J. 137 (C.M.A. 1990).
21. *Id.* at 138. *Cf.* Jacobson v. Massachusetts, 197 U.S. 11 (1905) (state can force people to receive smallpox vaccinations to protect public health); United States v. Chadwell, 36 C.M.R. 741 (N.B.R. 1965) (upheld order requiring service member to obtain inoculation for certain diseases despite accused's conflicting religious beliefs).
22. *See* United States v. Ebanks, 29 M.J. 926 (A.F.C.M.R. 1989) (government not required to charge accused under any particular Article of U.C.M.J. for failing to obey "safe sex" order).
23. *See generally* Milhizer, "Safe Sex ... or Else," 5 ABA Criminal Justice, Winter 1991, at 17; Wells-Petry, "Anatomy of an AIDS Case: Deadly Disease as an Aspect of Deadly Crime," ARMY LAW., Jan. 1988, at 17.
24. *See, e.g.,* United States v. Johnson, 30 M.J. 53 (C.M.A. 1990) (accused convicted of aggravated assault for attempting unprotected anal intercourse); United States v. Stewart, 29 M.J. 92 (C.M.A. 1989) (aggravated assault conviction for knowingly exposing victim to HIV by engaging in unprotected sexual intercourse); United States v. Banks, 36 M.J. 1003 (A.C.M.R. 1993) (HIV-positive accused's unprotected sexual intercourse with three women constituted aggravated assault).
25. *See, e.g.,* United States v. Woods, 28 M.J. 318 (C.M.A. 1989) (unprotected and unwarned sexual conduct of HIV-positive member prejudicial to good order and discipline); United States v.

§ 2-9(C)(1) MILITARY CRIMES § 2-9(C)(1)

persons knowingly exposed others to the HIV antibody. Additionally, civilian courts and state legislatures have recognized that HIV-positive persons may be criminally liable for intentionally or knowingly exposing others to the virus.[26]

§ 2-9(C)(1). Murder, Manslaughter, and Assault.

The offenses of murder and manslaughter are proscribed by Articles 118[27] and 119[28] of the U.C.M.J., respectively. Due to the extended nature of the progression of the disease, death resulting from the servicemember's actions is not likely to occur until years later.[29] Therefore, charging an accused with murder or manslaughter is usually not a practical alternative for a military commander. Instead, a better solution would be to prosecute an accused for attempted murder[30] or attempted manslaughter.[31] At least one commentator has indicated these charges could provide a solid foundation for prosecuting certain HIV-related cases.[32]

The Court of Military Appeals has specifically approved of using the theory of aggravated assault under Article 128[33] to support the convictions of HIV-infected servicemembers.[34] Under Article 128, an accused is guilty of aggravated assault if he or she "commits an assault with a ... means ... *likely* to produce death or grievous bodily harm" (emphasis added).[35] In *United States*

Morris, 30 M.J. 1221 (A.C.M.R. 1990) (willfully and deliberately exposing another to HIV violates Article 134).

26. *See generally* Comment, "Criminalizing HIV Transmission: New Jersey Assembly Bill 966," 15 Seton Hall Legis. J. 193 (1991); Comment, "Imposing Criminal Liability on Those Who Knowingly Transmit the AIDS Virus: A Recommendation for Legislative Action," 13 U. Dayton L. Rev. 489 (Spring 1988).

27. *See* Appendix 3.

28. *Id.*

29. *See* Anderson, Kramer, and Shambley, "AIDS Issues in the Military," 32 A.F.L. Rev. 353, 355 (1990).

30. MCM, 1984, Part IV, para. 43d(3).

31. MCM, 1984, Part IV, para. 44d(1)(e).

32. Wells-Petry, "Anatomy of an AIDS Case: Deadly Disease as an Aspect of Deadly Crime," Army Law., Dec. 1988, at 20-22.

33. *See* Appendix 3.

34. United States v. Schoolfield, 40 M.J. 132 (C.M.A. 1994) (accused convicted of aggravated assault by having sex with five different women without warning them and failing to take precautions); United States v. Johnson, 30 M.J. 53 (C.M.A. 1990) (accused convicted of aggravated assault for attempting unprotected anal intercourse); United States v. Stewart, 29 M.J. 92 (C.M.A. 1989) (aggravated assault conviction for knowingly exposing victim to HIV by engaging in unprotected sexual intercourse); United States v. Reister, 40 M.J. 666 (N.M.C.M.R. 1994) (accused, who was infected with herpes, convicted of aggravated assault for having unprotected sex). *Cf.* United States v. Perez, 33 M.J. 1050 (A.C.M.R. 1991) (because victim did not learn of accused's HIV status until much later, evidence was not legally sufficient to support simple offer-type assault; and because accused was physically incapable of inserting AIDS virus in victim, he could not be guilty of assault consummated by a battery).

35. *See* Appendix 3. United States v. Joseph, 37 M.J. 392 (C.M.A. 1993) (HIV accused guilty of aggravated assault even though he was wearing condom); United States v. Bygrave, 40 M.J. 839 (N.M.C.M.R. 1994) (victim's consent to intercourse with HIV-infected accused was not defense to

v. Johnson,[36] the Court held the term "likely," as used in Article 128, means that "it must at least be more than a fanciful, speculative, or remote possibility."[37] Therefore, with proper expert testimony at trial on the likelihood of HIV transmission, prosecution under a theory of aggravated assault is also a viable option for military commanders.[38]

§ 2-9(C)(2). Rape and Sodomy.

Because HIV transmission most often occurs through sexual contact, military commanders may be able to punish unprotected and/or unwarned sexual relations as sex-related violations under the U.C.M.J. For example, an HIV-infected servicemember can undoubtedly be charged under Article 120 for nonconsensual intercourse with a woman other than his wife.[39] If he obtains actual consent, however, even though he fails to get informed consent by telling his partner of his HIV positivity, it is unlikely a court would convict on a rape charge.[40] Therefore, charging an HIV-positive member for rape would only be appropriate when the sexual partner did not consent to sexual relations at all.

An HIV-infected servicemember may be charged with the offense of sodomy, under Article 125,[41] when he or she engages in "unnatural carnal copulation"[42] with another person. If supported by the evidence, charging an accused with sodomy is a particularly attractive alternative for a commander because the offense of sodomy is not constitutionally protected.[43] Therefore, to avoid the chance that a "safe sex" order may be invalidated for some reason, commanders may also charge an accused with sodomy whenever the circumstances of a particular case warrant it.[44]

---

charge of aggravated assault; court said that seminal fluid containing HIV is means likely to produce death or grievous bodily harm).
36. 30 M.J. 53 (C.M.A. 1990).
37. *Id.* at 57.
38. United States v. Joseph, 37 M.J. 392 (C.M.A. 1993) (in case of first impression court held that accused was guilty of aggravated assault by having sexual relations with woman, without warning her, even though he was wearing a condom).
39. *See* Appendix 3.
40. *See* MCM, 1984, Part IV, para. 45c(1)(b) (if actual consent, although obtained by fraud, then there is no rape). *See also* Anderson, Kramer, and Shambley, "AIDS Issues in the Military," 32 A.F.L. REV. 353, 370 (1990); Wells-Petry, "Anatomy of an AIDS Case: Deadly Disease as an Aspect of Deadly Crime," ARMY LAW., Jan. 1988, at 22.
41. *See* Appendix 3.
42. MCM, 1984, Part IV, para. 51c states, "It is unnatural carnal copulation for a person to take into that person's mouth or anus the sexual organ of another person or of an animal; or to place that person's sexual organ in the mouth or anus of another person or of an animal; or to have carnal copulation in any opening of the body, except the sexual parts, with another person; or to have carnal copulation with an animal."
43. United States v. Johnson, 30 M.J. 53 (C.M.A. 1990) (sodomy not constitutionally protected conduct within the military). *Cf.* Bowers v. Hardwick, 478 U.S. 186 (1986) (Georgia statute criminalizing sodomy upheld).
44. In United States v. Womack, 29 M.J. 88 (C.M.A. 1989), the accused was charged and convicted under both Article 90 and Article 125.

§ 2-9(C)(3). "Catch-All" Offenses Under Articles 133 and 134.

When an HIV-positive service member who engages in unprotected and/or unwarned sex is an officer, Article 133 can be utilized.[45] As noted in § 2-5 *supra*, Article 133 is violated when an officer's actions or omissions constitute conduct unbecoming an officer and a gentleman.[46] Acts punishable by other, more specific articles, also amount to violations of Article 133, so long as those acts constitute conduct unbecoming an officer and a gentleman.[47] For a general discussion of Article 133, see § 2-5 *supra*.

As discussed in § 2-6 *supra*, Article 134 makes punishable all acts that are not specifically proscribed in other punitive articles of the U.C.M.J. Commonly recognized offenses that would be applicable under this article include adultery,[48] assault,[49] cohabitation,[50] fraternization,[51] indecent acts,[52] and prostitution.[53] Article 134 was specifically approved in *United States v. Woods*,[54] to support the conviction of a servicemember for engaging in unsafe sex. Therefore, it appears that an HIV-positive servicemember who is shown to have engaged in sexual relations without using barrier protection, or without informing his partner of his condition, may be punished under Article 134 without further evidence.[55]

§ 2-9(D). Constitutionality of Prosecuting HIV-Related Conduct.

Because the military places some restrictions on the manner in which its HIV-positive members must conduct themselves during sexual relations, those restrictions have been attacked as unconstitutional infringements of their right to privacy.[56] The United States Supreme Court has recognized that certain penumbral rights of privacy are implicitly guaranteed under express provisions of the Constitution.[57] While the Court has recognized that some aspects of sexual intimacy are constitutionally protected,[58] it has also stated

---

45. *See* Appendix 3.
46. MCM, Part IV, para. 59b.
47. MCM, Part IV, para. 59c(2).
48. MCM, Part IV, para. 62.
49. MCM, Part IV, para. 63-64.
50. MCM, Part IV, para. 69.
51. MCM, Part IV, para. 83.
52. MCM, Part IV, para. 87 and 90.
53. MCM, Part IV, para. 134.
54. 28 M.J. 318 (C.M.A. 1989).
55. *See* United States v. Morris, 30 M.J. 1221 (A.C.M.R. 1990).
56. *See, e.g.*, United States v. Womack, 29 M.J. 88 (C.M.A. 1989) (no right to privacy where accused engaged in nonconsensual, homosexual sodomy); United States v. Negron, 28 M.J. 775 (A.C.M.R.), *aff'd*, 29 M.J. 324 (C.M.A. 1989) (order to HIV-infected member to refrain from unprotected and unwarned sexual relations did not unnecessarily infringe on right to privacy).
57. Roe v. Wade, 410 U.S. 113, 152-53 (1973); Griswold v. Connecticut, 381 U.S. 479, 483-85 (1965).
58. *See, e.g.*, Eisenstadt v. Baird, 405 U.S. 438 (1972) (prohibition against unmarried persons access to contraceptives ruled unconstitutional); Griswold v. Connecticut, 381 U.S. 479 (1965) (regulating use of contraceptives in marital situations is unconstitutional).

§ 2-9(D)

that regulation of sexual conduct is permissible if the government demonstrates a compelling justification.[59] Keeping in step with this approach, the military courts have allowed the military to regulate the sexual conduct of its HIV-infected members because of the military's strong interest in preventing the spread of infectious disease among its members as well as the civilian population.[60] It still remains uncertain, however, whether this justification will allow the military to extend its control over an HIV-infected member's marital relationship.[61] Because the Supreme Court made it abundantly clear in *Griswold v. Connecticut*[62] that the marital relationship bears significant privacy interests, it is unlikely that the military could successfully prosecute an HIV-positive member for engaging in consensual, yet unprotected, sexual intercourse with his or her spouse.[63]

The other major constitutional challenge to prosecuting HIV-related misconduct involves claims of due process violations when the military charges such misconduct under general articles such as Articles 133 and 134.[64] The chief complaint under these claims is that these provisions do not provide fair notice of the prohibited conduct.[65] The Supreme Court, however, has previously rejected "void for vagueness" attacks on Articles 133 and 134 because the broad language in those articles is necessary for the military to respond to all potential threats to military discipline.[66] Furthermore, the military courts have held that the fair notice requirement is satisfied because HIV-positive members are aware that conduct that is prejudicial to good order and discipline is punishable under the U.C.M.J.[67] Because all HIV-positive service-

---

59. *See, e.g.*, Griswold v. Connecticut, 381 U.S. 479, 496 (1965) (Goldberg, J., concur.) (government cannot interfere with husband and wife sexual relationship absent compelling justification). *Cf.* Bowers v. Hardwick, 478 U.S. 186 (1986) (right to privacy cases do not "stand for the proposition that any kind of private sexual conduct between consenting adults is insulated from state proscription").

60. *See, e.g.*, United States v. Dumford, 30 M.J. 137 (C.M.A. 1990); United States v. Negron, 28 M.J. 775 (A.C.M.R.), *aff'd*, 29 M.J. 324 (C.M.A. 1989); United States v. Sargeant, 29 M.J. 813 (A.C.M.R. 1989).

61. As it currently reads, the Air Force "safe sex" order makes even marital sexual relations without a condom unlawful because the order includes sexual relations with military dependents or any other persons. *See supra* § 2-9(B).

62. 381 U.S. 479 (1965).

63. However, several court decisions indicate that the military may be able to invade the marital relationship if "nontraditional" sexual activity is occurring. *See, e.g.*, Bowers v. Hardwick, 478 U.S. 186 (1986) (although the Court specifically held homosexual sodomy was not protected, the Court upheld the Georgia statute that proscribed both homosexual and heterosexual sodomy); Lovisi v. Slayton, 363 F. Supp. 620 (E.D. Va. 1973), *aff'd*, 539 F.2d 349 (4th Cir. 1976) (married couple convicted for consensual sodomy in presence of third party even though in own home).

64. *See, e.g.*, United States v. Woods, 28 M.J. 318 (C.M.A. 1989) (accused alleged lack of fair notice that his conduct could be punishable under Article 134); United States v. Morris, 30 M.J. 1221 (A.C.M.R. 1990) (HIV-positive member claimed due process violated because he was charged under Article 134).

65. *Id.*

66. Parker v. Levy, 417 U.S. 733 (1974). *See also* §§ 2-5 and 2-6.

67. United States v. Woods, 28 M.J. 318 (C.M.A. 1989); United States v. Morris, 30 M.J. 1221 (A.C.M.R. 1990).

members are counselled regarding the negative "consequences" that may occur from engaging in unprotected or unwarned sexual relations,[68] their claims of "lack of fair notice" will necessarily fail.

For a more in-depth discussion of these due process challenges to military laws, see § 13-3(N)(2) *infra*.

---

68. *See supra* § 2-9(A).

APPENDIX REFERENCES

Appendix 1. Abbreviations.
Appendix 2. Glossary.
Appendix 3. Uniform Code of Military Justice
Appendix 4. Court-Martial Flow Chart.
Appendix 30. Maximum Punishment Chart.

ANNOTATED BIBLIOGRAPHY

BOOKS

Avins, *The Law of AWOL* (1957).

In a format that is, by the author's description, a casebook, a law review article, and a textbook, the author provides a comprehensive discussion of the offense of Absence Without Leave. Although much of this material is dated by more recent changes in military practice, much of it is very useful for historical purposes.

Byrne, *Military Law* (1981).

This third edition work is a good introductory text to military law. It includes text material, discussion cases, self-quizzes, and appendices that contain forms and tables. The discussion cases, although dated, cover significant areas of courts-martial practice.

Moyer, *Justice and the Military* (1972).

This one-volume loose-leaf reference contains detailed discussions of the role of commanders, jurisdiction, military criminal procedure, First Amendment rights, substantive law, and collateral review of courts-martial by the civilian court system.

Zillman, Blaustein, & Sherman, *The Military in American Society* (1978).

This loose-leaf case book represents the efforts of nine individuals familiar with the workings of the military system of justice. Valuable discussions include treatment of the American military establishment, entry into the military, the military justice system, individual rights of servicemembers, termination of military service, and the law of armed conflict. Selected cases are discussed and notes for further reading are located at the end of each chapter.

PERIODICALS

In General

Barto, "Sexual Harassment and the Uniform Code of Military Justice: A Primer for the Military Justice Practitioner," ARMY LAW., July 1995, at 3.

Noting that sexual harassment is a controversial topic and that there have been calls to specifically amend the U.C.M.J. to prohibit such conduct, the author briefly discusses the substantive criminal law elements of the offense, ambiguities that are likely to occur, and new developments.

Bernard, "Structures of American Military Justice," 125 U. PA. L. REV. 307 (1976).

The Supreme Court's decision in *Parker v. Levy*, 417 U.S. 733 (1974) serves as the keystone for this fascinating article. The author briefly addresses the court's rationale for a separate military system of justice and proceeds to examine the system using a "family" model of rules, sanctions, and interrelationships as a template.

"Bibliography of Military Law," 10 AM. CRIM. L. REV. 175 (1971).

This extensive bibliography lists finding aids, books, symposiums, surveys, service publications, and selected writings in legal periodicals. Most entries predate the 1968 amendments to the U.C.M.J.

DeChiara, "Article 92: Judicial Guidelines for Identifying Punitive Orders and Regulations," 17 A.F. L. REV. 61 (Summer 1975).

The author presents several tests for determining whether an untested regulation is "punitive" and thus enforceable under Article 92, U.C.M.J. He notes that although in practice regulations used as a basis for prosecution generally give fair notice, the military is vulnerable to the argument that Article 92 can be used to create criminal laws from regulations that appear to be nothing more than instructional.

Dunn, "Aspects of Malingering," 17 A.F. L. REV. 1 (Spring 1975).

This brief article discusses the military offense of malingering under Article 115 of the Uniform Code of Military Justice. Noting that the offense seems to be rarely charged, the author concludes that the offense is not well understood, and is difficult to detect and prove.

Note, "Military Law—The Standard of Constitutionality," 11 WAKE FOREST L. REV. 325 (1975).

This short article presents a good analysis of *Parker v. Levy*, 417 U.S. 733 (1979) which recognized the constitutionality of the military's "general" Articles, 133 and 134, which may be employed as punitive restrictions on wide-ranging conduct prejudicial to military standards.

Prescott & Snow, "Criminal Liability Under the Uniform Code of Military Justice for Sexual Relations During Psychotherapy," 135 MIL. L. REV. 21 (1991).

This article briefly recounts the problems experienced in both the civilian and military communities with sexual misconduct arising during treatment for psychological problems. The authors conclude that currently the U.C.M.J. provides victims of this type of offense a degree of protection matched by only a few other jurisdictions.

Soma, Banker & Smith, "Computer Crime: Substantive Statutes & the Technical & Legal Search Considerations," 39 A.F. L. REV. 225 (1996).

One of 17 articles in "The Master Criminal Law Edition" of the Air Force Law Review, this article includes a discussion on the search and seizures issues which may arise in investigating computer crimes.

Stevens, "Identifying and Charging Computer Crimes in the Military," 110 MIL. L. REV. 59 (1985).

With the explosion of computer technology in today's society, including the military sector, the author suggests that a concomitant rise in computer-related crime is inevitable. His article is an informative piece designed to provide the military prosecutor with the technological skill to efficiently, and more importantly, successfully prosecute computer crime in the military.

"Symposium, Military Law," 10 AM. CRIM. L. REV. 1 (1971).

This symposium issue covers a valuable range of topics pertinent to the practice of military criminal law. Included are articles on jurisdiction over civilian type offenses, plea bargaining, sentencing, discovery, appeals, and an article by General Westmoreland on the commander's perspective of military justice. Also included is a fine bibliography of books, articles, and listings of military law materials.

Trant, "The American Military Insanity Defense: A Moral, Philosophical, and Legal Dilemma," 99 MIL. L. REV. 1 (1983).

The author examines the military insanity defense, beginning with an overview of the defense's development in the United States and England and then analyzing the policies and procedures implicated in the American military insanity defense. The author concludes that a modification, similar to the "guilty but mentally ill" approach, be implemented along with a modified insanity test for the military.

Treanor, "Orchestrating the Successful Prosecution of Child Sexual Abuse Cases," 39 A.F. L. REV. 225 (1996).

Noting the complexity of trying child sexual abuse cases and the fact that such cases provide ample opportunities for mistakes, that author provides some general advice to judge advocates on being familiar with the dynamics of child abuse, preparing for such cases, interviewing the witnesses, and on trying the case.

Zillman & Imwinkelried, "Constitutional Rights and Military Necessity: Reflections on the Society Apart," 51 NOTRE DAME L. REV. 396 (1976).

The authors present an excellent discussion of the impact of the separateness of the military system. Particular attention is paid to areas that often find their way into the military justice practice through violation of regulations or orders: freedom of expression, religious belief, fraternization, control of drug use, personal appearance, and sex-related discrimination.

AIDS Offenses

Anderson, Kramer, and Shambley, "AIDS Issues in the Military," 32 A.F. L. REV. 353 (1990).

This article presents an overview of a wide variety of legal issues presented by the AIDS epidemic and specifically addresses criminal justice problems. A sample "safe-sex" order to HIV-infected servicemembers is included.

Fraternization

Carter, "Fraternization," 113 MIL. L. REV. 61 (1986).

This article presents a comprehensive study of the problem of fraternization, especially in the Army. The author presents an exhaustive treatment of early American fraternization policies, including a lengthy cataloguing and listing of early cases. In assessing current Army policy, the author notes the distinction between administrative relationships policies and criminal prohibition of fraternization. In his view, a more unified theory is appropriate, and to that end he offers a proposed fraternization regulation.

Flatten, "Fraternization," 10 THE REPORTER 109 (Aug. 1981).

This short article provides a good introduction to the problem of "fraternization" in the armed forces and specifically notes recommendations for handling the problem in the Air Force, including a copy of the Air Force OTJAG's opinion in 1971 concerning fraternization between officers and enlisted personnel (OPJAGAF 1971/69, 30 July 1971).

Jonas, "Fraternization: Time for a Rational Department of Defense Standard," 135 MIL. L. REV. 37 (1992).

In a lengthy article the author addresses the problems of fraternization and surveys not only the military rules but also the practices in other armed forces. He concludes that the only legitimate justification for regulating fraternization is the need to maintain the integrity of the chain of command. He concludes that the current custom-based fraternization rules lead to inconsistent results and recommends the adoption of a clear DOD regulation.

Mahoney, "Fraternization: Military Anachronism or Leadership Challenge?" 28 A.F. L. REV. 153 (1988).

This article provides an historical overview of the offense of fraternization in the Air Force and notes the demise of the Air Force "custom" prohibiting fraternization. The author also addresses the approaches taken by the other services to this offense and proposes changes to pertinent Air Force regulations. The article includes an interesting appendix that includes comments of senior Air Force officers about the offense of fraternization.

McDevitt, "Wrongful Fraternization as an Offense Under the Uniform Code of Military Justice," 33 CLEV. ST. L. REV. 547 (1985-86).

This note briefly summarizes the historical underpinnings of the offense of fraternization and the various avenues available to the military for punishing such behavior. The author observes the lack of cohesive guidance on the subject and that arbitrariness sometimes results. To alleviate the problem, the author offers a sample standard regulation.

Drug Offenses

Kaczynski, "America at War: Combatting Drugs in the Military," 19 NEW ENG. L. REV. 287 (1983-84).

Through a discussion of the issues involved in the detection and prosecution of drug offenders, this article provides a general overview of the major cases and procedures concerning the enforcement of drug laws and regulations by the military.

Raezer, "Needed Weapons in the Army's War on Drugs: Electronic Surveillance and Informants," 116 MIL. L. REV. 1 (1987).

The author notes the continuing problem of drug use in the Army and urges that in attacking the "supply" end of the problem, military authorities should make use of wired informants and reverse sting operations and should take steps to increase the "recruiting, rewarding, using, and protecting of informants as a necessary means of penetrating drug conspiracies in the Army."

CHAPTER 3

NONJUDICIAL PUNISHMENT: A COMPARATIVE ANALYSIS

§ 3-1. Introduction.
§ 3-2. Applicable Policies.
§ 3-3. Authority to Impose Punishment.
    § 3-3(A). Who May Impose?
    § 3-3(B). Who May Be Punished?
    § 3-3(C). "Minor" Offenses.
§ 3-4. The Right to Demand Trial.
§ 3-5. Procedural Rules for Imposing Nonjudicial Punishment.
    § 3-5(A). General.
    § 3-5(B). Army Procedures.
        § 3-5(B)(1). Preliminary Inquiry.
        § 3-5(B)(2). Notice.
        § 3-5(B)(3). Hearing.
        § 3-5(B)(4). Appeals.
    § 3-5(C). Air Force Procedures.
        § 3-5(C)(1). Preliminary Inquiry.
        § 3-5(C)(2). Notice.
        § 3-5(C)(3). Hearing.
        § 3-5(C)(4). Appeals.
    § 3-5(D). Navy and Marine Corps Procedures.
        § 3-5(D)(1). Preliminary Inquiry.
        § 3-5(D)(2). Notice.
        § 3-5(D)(3). Hearing.
        § 3-5(D)(4). Appeals.
    § 3-5(E). Coast Guard Procedures.
        § 3-5(E)(1). Preliminary Inquiry.
        § 3-5(E)(2). Notice.
        § 3-5(E)(3). Hearing.
        § 3-5(E)(4). Appeals.
§ 3-6. Punishments.
    § 3-6(A). General.
    § 3-6(B). Reduction in Grade.
    § 3-6(C). Deprivation of Liberty.
        § 3-6(C)(1). Correctional Custody.
        § 3-6(C)(2). Extra Duties.
        § 3-6(C)(3). Restriction.
        § 3-6(C)(4). Arrest in Quarters.
        § 3-6(C)(5). Confinement on Bread and Water.
    § 3-6(D). Forfeiture of Pay.
    § 3-6(E). Censure.
    § 3-6(F). Combination of Punishments.
    § 3-6(G). Effective Dates of Punishments.
§ 3-7. Effect of Errors in Imposition.
§ 3-8. Consequences of Nonjudicial Punishment.
    § 3-8(A). Filing Requirements: Military Career.
    § 3-8(B). Use at Court-Martial or Administrative Proceedings.
Appendix References.
Annotated Bibliography.

§ 3-1. Introduction.

Congress has long recognized the necessity to vest in commanders some authority to dispose of minor disciplinary infractions in a summary fashion. Article 15, U.C.M.J.,[1] which provides for "nonjudicial punishment," was intended to meet that need.[2] Often criticized,[3] nonjudicial punishment serves as a middle ground in the military justice process. It provides sanctions less onerous than a court-martial, yet more severe than nonpunitive measures. By its very nature and because it serves as a much-used alternative to more formalized judicial proceedings, the link between nonjudicial punishment and the court-martial process is direct.[4] This chapter examines the nature of nonjudicial punishment, its use among the various services, and the protections available to the servicemember. Throughout the general discussion references will be made to particular service practices; however, in the section on procedural rules each service receives separate treatment.[5]

As in any discussion of military criminal justice, the statutory framework for nonjudicial punishment (called an "Article 15" in the Air Force and Army, "Office Hours" in the Marine Corps, and "Captain's Mast" in the Navy and Coast Guard) rests on the Uniform Code of Military Justice.[6] Part V of the Manual for Courts-Martial provides amplified treatment of the subject but leaves some discretion to the individual services to promulgate particularized practices for imposing nonjudicial punishment.[7] Each service has exercised

---

1. *See* Appendix 3. *See also* S. Rep. No. 1911, 87th Cong., 2d Sess., U.S. Code Cong. & Ad. News pp. 2379, 2380-82 (1962):

    Article 15 ... provides a means whereby military commanders may impose nonjudicial punishment for minor infractions of discipline. Its use permits the services to reduce substantially the number of courts-martial for minor offenses, which result in stigmatizing and impairing the efficiency and morale of the person concerned.

2. For an excellent discussion on the historical development of Article 15, see Miller, "A Long Look at Article 15," 28 MIL. L. REV. 37 (1965). *See also* Carnahan, "Comment—Article 15 Punishments," 13 AF JAG L. REV. 270 (1971).

3. Critics of the system emphasize its summary nature and lack of due process. Commanders often criticize the procedures as too technical and administratively burdensome. For comparative analysis, see Comment, "The Unconstitutional Burden of Article 15," 82 YALE L.J. 1481 (1973) and Comment, "The Constitutionality of Article 15: A Rebuttal," 83 YALE L.J. 534 (1974).

   See also GAO Report to the Secretary of Defense, "Better Administration of Military Article 15 Punishments for Minor Offenses is Needed," September 2, 1980; Salisbury, "Nonjudicial Punishment Under Article 15 of the Uniform Code of Military Justice: Congressional Precept and Military Practice," 19 SAN DIEGO L. REV. 839 (1982).

4. The nonjudicial punishment option is one of those always available to a commander in exercising his prosecutorial discretion. The seriousness of the offense of course reduces the likelihood that nonjudicial punishment will be offered to an accused, but counsel representing any accused charged with a minor offense should consider suggesting the nonjudicial punishment option to a commander.

5. *See infra* § 3-5.

6. *See supra* § 1-3(A) for a brief introduction to the U.C.M.J.

7. For example, the services may further limit the types and amounts of Article 15 punishments. MCM, Part V, para. 5.

§ 3-2   NONJUDICIAL PUNISHMENT: A COMPARATIVE ANALYSIS   § 3-3

that discretion in its supplement to the *Manual*.[8]

Important to note is that a nonjudicial punishment proceeding is nonadversarial, and although the imposition of punishment does not constitute a federal conviction, a variety of due process protections are provided for what is essentially a consent proceeding.[9] Review of the imposition of nonjudicial punishment is not directed through normal military judicial appeals. Rather, the servicemember may seek relief through either chain-of-command or administrative channels.[10]

§ 3-2. Applicable Policies.

Nonjudicial punishment is designed to provide more than pure punishment for committing an offense. It is designed to be primarily corrective or rehabilitative.[1] Therefore, in deciding whether to proceed under Article 15, commanders are to consider the circumstances of the offense, and the age, intelligence, experience, and the military record of the servicemember;[2] Article 15 should be used, according to the *Manual,* only when nonpunitive measures are inadequate to meet disciplinary needs in the unit.[3] If punishment is imposed, commanders are urged to consider suspending all, or a portion, of the punishment.[4] Once punishment is imposed it may not be increased nor may another Article 15 be imposed for the same offense giving rise to the first action.[5] Generally, an offense previously punished in a state, federal, or foreign jurisdiction should not be the subject of nonjudicial punishment.[6]

§ 3-3. Authority to Impose Punishment.

According to Article 15, U.C.M.J., the general rule is that "any commanding officer may, in addition to or in lieu of admonition or reprimand, impose one or more ... disciplinary punishments, for minor offenses without the intervention of court-martial upon officers of his command and other personnel of

---

8. The service supplements (or regulations) noted briefly in § 1-3(C) will be heavily relied upon in this chapter. The citation format is as follows:

> *Army:* Army Regulation 27-10, Legal Services—Military Justice cited as AR 27-10.
> *Air Force:* Air Force Instruction 51-202, Nonjudicial Punishment Guide cited as AFI 51-202.
> *Coast Guard:* Military Justice Manual, COMDTDUST M5810.1 (series), cited as MJM.
> *Navy and Marine Corps:* The Manual of the Judge Advocate General cited as JAGMAN.

9. The servicemember has a right to demand trial in lieu of nonjudicial punishment unless he is attached to or embarked on a vessel. See *infra* § 3-4.
10. See *infra* § 3-7.
1. MCM, Part V, para. 1c. See also AR 27-10, para. 3-2; AFI 51-202, para. 1.1 and MJM, 1-B-2-a.
2. MCM, Part V, para. 1d(1).
3. MCM, Part V, para. 1d(1).
4. MCM, Part V, para. 1d(3).
5. MCM, Part V, para. 1f(1) to (3). If the offense is not a minor offense, however, the imposition of nonjudicial punishment will not ban a later court-martial. See *infra* § 3-3(C).
6. *See, e.g.,* MCM, Part V, para. 1f(5); AR 27-10, para. 4-2; and MJM, 1-A-5.

his command."[1] The question of authority to impose nonjudicial punishment actually addresses three separate issues: (1) Determining who is authorized to impose the punishment; (2) determining who may be punished; and (3) determining for what offenses nonjudicial punishment is appropriate. Each issue will be treated separately in the following sections.

§ 3-3(A). Who May Impose?

Article 15 authorizes commanding officers and warrant officers exercising command[2] to impose nonjudicial punishment but leaves to the various services the authority to designate the categories of commanding officers and warrant officers exercising command.[3] Each service has done so.[4] Key here is the requirement that the authority imposing the punishment be in the position of "command." For example, staff officers and platoon leaders are not normally considered commanding officers for purposes of nonjudicial punishment. An "officer-in-charge," however, is authorized to impose punishment.[5]

In imposing nonjudicial punishment, a commanding officer has wide discretion in determining whether to impose punishment and the amount of punishment unless that discretion, or authority, has been limited by Article 15, the *Manual,* service regulations, or by a superior. For example, Army Regulation 27-10 authorizes superior commanders to limit or withhold their subordinates' authority to impose punishment in a particular category of offenses,[6] personnel,[7] or in a particular case. These limitations may be accomplished through informal channels or in locally published supplements to AR 27-10.

Article 15(a) authorizes limited delegation of nonjudicial punishment authority by a "commanding officer exercising general court-martial jurisdiction or an officer of general or flag rank in command" to a principal assistant.[8] The

---

1. Art. 15(b), U.C.M.J. *See* Appendix 3.
2. Art. 15(a), U.C.M.J. Noncommissioned officers may *not* impose nonjudicial punishment even if serving as a "commander" or if delegated the authority by a commander competent to delegate his Article 15 powers. Note, however, that an enlisted officer in charge may impose nonjudicial punishment in the Coast Guard. This point is discussed in more detail at § 3-5(E), *infra.*
3. Art. 15(a), U.C.M.J.
4. *See, e.g.,* the Navy's JAGMAN, which permits a "multiservice" commander to designate a commissioned officer to impose nonjudicial punishment on specific units within his command. JAGMAN 0106d. *See also* AFI 51-202, para. 2.
5. Art. 15(c), U.C.M.J.; MCM, Part V, para. 2b. The position of "officer-in-charge" is available only in the Navy, Marine Corps, and Coast Guard, as that term is used in Article 15(c), U.C.M.J. *See* JAGMAN 0106b; MJM 1-A-2.a.
6. AR 27-10, para. 3-7c. The superior commander could, for example, withhold his subordinates' authority to impose nonjudicial punishment for A.W.O.L.'s in excess of three days in length. The Navy allows limitation on subordinates only if authorized by the Secretary of the Navy. JAGMAN 0106e. *See also* AFI 51-202, para. 2.6.
7. The commanding general of an installation, command, or division will normally reserve to himself the authority to impose Article 15's on officers in his or her command. *See also* JAGMAN 108a (commanding officers or officers-in-charge of units attached to ships should, as a matter of policy, refrain from imposing nonjudicial punishment while embarked in the ship and instead refer disciplinary matters to the ship's commanding officer).
8. MCM, Part V, para. 2c.

services have further defined the manner of delegation and the definition of "principal assistant."[9]

§ 3-3(B). Who May Be Punished?

The authority to impose nonjudicial punishment extends only to personnel of the commanding officer's "command."[10] Although the Manual for Courts-Martial does not further define the term "command," the services have addressed the classification of those military personnel who may receive nonjudicial punishment.[11] Generally speaking, a servicemember is a member of the command if he is assigned or attached to that command.[12] It is possible, due to temporary training or duty assignments, for an individual to be a member of more than one command for purposes of nonjudicial punishment. Punishment by one commander precludes punishment by any other commander who might otherwise have nonjudicial punishment jurisdiction over the servicemember.[13] If the servicemember leaves the command before punishment is imposed, the commander's jurisdiction ceases. He may, however, forward reports of investigations to the gaining commander who may in turn decide to proceed with nonjudicial punishment.[14]

Although only the Navy, Marine Corps, and Coast Guard originally provided for nonjudicial punishment jurisdiction over reservists during periods of training,[15] the *Manual* now explicitly authorizes such.[16]

Civilians are not subject to nonjudicial punishment,[17] and the services have traditionally followed a policy of restraining commanders from imposing nonjudicial punishment upon members of another service who may be assigned or attached to that commander's unit.[18] With the ever-increasing role of joint service operations, each service may establish procedures which allow com-

---

9. *See, e.g.,* the Navy's JAGMAN, para. 0106c which provides for delegation of authority to "a senior officer on his staff who is eligible to succeed to command in case of absence of such officer in command." *See also* AR 27-10, para. 3-7b; AFI 51-202, para. 2.3; and MJM, para. 1-A-2-d.
10. Art. 15(b), U.C.M.J.; MCM, Part V, para. 2a.
11. *See, e.g.,* AR 27-10, para. 3-8; AFI 51-202, para. 2.1.1; MJM, para. 1-A-3; JAGMAN 0107.
12. *Id.*
13. MCM, Part V, para. 1f(1).
14. *See, e.g.,* AR 27-10, para. 3-8b.
15. JAGMAN 0107b; MJM, para. 1-A-3.g. The Army and Air Force Judge Advocates General had expressed a "policy" that authorized U.C.M.J. jurisdiction over reservists on inactive duty training only where dangerous or expensive equipment was involved. *See, e.g.,* United States v. Abernathy, 48 C.M.R. 205 (C.G.C.M.R. 1974). In the Coast Guard, nonjudicial punishment for offenses committed by a reservist on active duty or inactive training may be imposed by either the commanding officer of the active duty or reserve unit. MJM 1-A-3.g.
16. *See* R.C.M. 204; MCM, Part V, para. 5e, f. The change resulted from a change to Articles 2 and 3 of the U.C.M.J. which extend jurisdiction to cover reservists on inactive duty training. *See* Chapter 4.
17. The *Manual* indicates that Article 15 powers extend to "military personnel." MCM, Part V, para. 2a. *See also* MJM, para. 1-A-3.d which specifically excludes civilians.
18. *See, e.g.,* AR 27-10, para. 3-8c; MJM, 1-A-3.c. But note JAGMAN 0108 which provides guidance on the authority of a commanding officer of a ship to impose nonjudicial punishment on units embarked on the ship.

manders of joint commands and joint task forces to impose punishment on members of other branches of the service.[19]

§ 3-3(C). "Minor" Offenses.

The final prong in discussing the authority to impose punishment under Article 15 turns on the requirement that punishment may only be imposed for "minor" offenses proscribed by the U.C.M.J.'s punitive articles.[20] The Manual for Courts-Martial in addressing the definition of minor offenses states:

> Whether an offense is minor depends on several factors: the nature of the offense and the circumstances surrounding its commission; the offender's age, rank, duty assignment, record, and experience; and the maximum sentence imposable for the offense if tried by general court-martial. Ordinarily, a minor offense is an offense for which the maximum sentence imposable would not include a dishonorable discharge or confinement for longer than 1 year if tried by general court-martial.[21]

The service supplements generally follow this guideline.[22] In practice, however, the commanding officer's authority is not limited to imposing punishment for only minor military offenses. And, in those few cases where the question of whether an offense was minor has been in issue, the military courts have recognized the commander's broad discretion.[23] One court has noted that normally possession of heroin is a "major" offense but that under the circumstances the possession may be a minor offense for purposes of Article 15.[24]

Few servicemembers who receive nonjudicial punishment for what may be characterized as a serious or major offense register complaints, at least while subject to court-martial jurisdiction. In those cases where a serious offense has occurred the only other feasible option available may well be a court-martial. Article 15, however, specifically provides that nonjudicial punishment for a serious crime or offense will not bar later court-martial proceedings for the

---

19. *See, e.g.*, AR 27-10, para. 3-8c (personnel of other armed forces); AFI 51-202, para. 2.2 (allows commander to impose NJP if the offense arises from joint origin or has joint forces implication); JAGMAN 0106d (authorizing multiservice commander or officer-in-charge to impose nonjudicial punishment upon members of the naval service under his command).

As a matter of policy, the Coast Guard generally prohibits imposing nonjudicial punishment on members of another armed force who are attached to a Coast Guard command unless authorized by interservice agreement. A commanding officer of another armed force may impose nonjudicial punishment on a Coast Guard member attached to their command if return to duty with the Coast Guard or temporary transfer to a nearby Coast Guard unit is not practicable and the need to discipline is urgent. MJM 1-A-3.c.

20. Arts. 77 through 134, U.C.M.J. *See* Appendix 3.

21. MCM, Part V, para. 1e.

22. *See* AR 27-10, para. 3-9; AFI 51-202, para. 2.1; MJM 1-A-4.

23. *See, e.g.*, United States v. Mahoney, 27 C.M.R. 898 (N.B.R. 1959). *Cf.* United States v. Fretwell, 11 C.M.A. 377, 29 C.M.R. 193 (1960) (officer drunk on duty was major offense); United States v. Wharton, 33 C.M.R. 729 (A.F.B.R. 1963) (involuntary manslaughter was major offense). *See also* Dobzynski v. Green, 16 M.J. 84, 86 (C.M.A. 1983).

24. United States v. Rivera, 45 C.M.R. 582, 584 n.3 (A.C.M.R. 1972).

same offense.[25] Punishment for a minor offense on the other hand will act as a bar.[26] In the case of the former, if the servicemember is later convicted by court-martial, the fact that nonjudicial punishment has been imposed must be considered by the court, if raised by the accused, in determining an appropriate sentence.[27]

---

25. Art. 15(f), U.C.M.J. United States v. Pierce, 27 M.J. 367 (C.M.A. 1989) (Article 15 punishment, which was imposed as part of division policy of "prompt discipline," did not preclude court-martial for serious offenses). *See* United States v. Joseph, 11 M.J. 333 (C.M.A. 1981); United States v. Fretwell, 11 C.M.A. 377, 29 C.M.R. 193 (1960). United States v. Hamilton, 36 M.J. 723 (A.C.M.R. 1992), *aff'd on other grounds*, 41 M.J. 32 (C.M.A. 1994) (accused prosecuted for aggravated assault for which unit commander imposed nonjudicial punishment).

26. R.C.M. 907(b) (2) (D) (iv). United States v. Sorby, 39 M.J. 914 (N.M.C.M.R. 1994) (offense of 23-day unauthorized absence was minor offense; failure of defense counsel to move to dismiss charges waived issue; the court, however, dismissed the specification).

27. Art. 15(f), U.C.M.J.; R.C.M. 1001(c)(1)(B). In United States v. Pierce, 27 M.J. 367 (C.M.A. 1989), the court indicated that it would violate due process for the government to exploit the prior Article 15 punishment, e.g., through MIL. R. EVID. 404(b); it should not be used for any purpose during the subsequent trial because it had no legal relevance. The court observed that in determining day-for-day credit for the prior Article 15 punishment, it would be helpful to have a comparison table similar to the Table of Equivalent Punishments which had appeared in the 1969 Manual for Courts-Martial. Finally, the court emphasized that it is the accused who must decide whether to reveal the prior Article 15 punishment to the court-martial and that the duty to give credit for that punishment cannot always be conferred on the court-martial. "Presumably," said the court, "the best place to repose the responsibility to ensure that credit is given is the convening authority." *Id.* at 369.

On remand, the Court of Military Review indicated that if the sentencing authority is the judge and he decides to give credit for the prior Article 15, he should state on the record what the credit was. 28 M.J. 1040 (A.C.M.R. 1989). The court also recognized that a commander could set aside the Article 15 if a credit was not later given.

United States v. Thompson, 41 M.J. 895 (Army Ct.Crim.App. 1995) (trial court erred in failing to assess appropriate administrative credit for prior Article 15 punishment covering same offense and in permitting the prosecution to use the Article 15 as aggravation evidence); United States v. Hudson, 39 M.J. 958 (N.M.C.M.R. 1994) (offense of communicating indecent language not minor; accused entitled to credit); United States v. Hall, 36 M.J. 770 (N.M.C.M.R. 1992) (prosecutor's introduction of NJP at sentencing was legitimate step to apprise judge that accused had received NJP punishment for offenses); United States v. Hamilton, 36 M.J. 723 (A.C.M.R. 1992), *aff'd on other grounds*, 41 M.J. 32 (C.M.A. 1994) (error for trial counsel to introduce prior Article 15 punishment for offenses which were later subject of court-martial; the court held that such punishments may not be used for any purpose at trial and decision to introduce that prior nonjudicial punishment is left to the accused); United States v. Strickland, 36 M.J. 569 (A.C.M.R. 1992) (sentence adjusted to ensure that accused received complete credit for prior nonjudicial punishment).

The Court of Appeals for the Armed Forces has also held that it is proper for the military judge to apply *Pierce* credit in determining the adjudged sentence. United States v. Edwards, 42 M.J. 381 (1995). If the judge does so, the convening authority need not take any further action.

See also United States v. Breland, 32 M.J. 801 (A.C.M.R. 1991) (although accused is entitled to appropriate and complete credit for prior nonjudicial punishment, no requirement that particular type of credit need be given in all cases; if trial court fails to make clear that credit has been given, convening authority should do so and document the record of trial. The court encouraged trial judges to make specific statements on the record that they have given appropriate credit); United States v. Moore, 32 M.J. 774 (A.C.M.R. 1991) (*Pierce* distinguished; accused's pretrial 110-day restriction to company area did not constitute punishment for the same offense by nonjudicial punishment); United States v. Collins, 30 M.J. 991 (A.C.M.R. 1990) (nonjudicial punishment was

Whether the offense was minor or not will normally not determine whether the Article 15 should be voided. Rather it is usually used to determine whether a subsequent court-martial was barred.[28] Note, however, that at least one federal court has ruled that the "minor offense" requirement is jurisdictional.[29] Similar reasoning was advanced by Chief Judge Everett in his dissenting opinion in *Dobzynski v. Green*.[30] In that case a Navy commander imposed Article 15 punishment for marijuana possession after the military judge granted a defense motion to suppress at the accused's special court-martial. Because the accused was attached to a vessel he could not decline the punishment.[31] Although the majority expressed concern about the appearance of injustice, it nonetheless concluded that "the court-martial charges were properly withdrawn and the Article 15 was properly imposed."[32] Chief Judge Everett opined that Article 15 and court-martial procedures are mutually exclusive[33] and that by deciding that court-martial charges should be referred in the first instance, the commander had determined that the drug offense was *not* minor. He was therefore not in a position to later impose Article 15 punishment.[34]

§ 3-4. The Right to Demand Trial.

Article 15, nonjudicial procedures are consensual in nature: Unless the right to demand trial is limited, a servicemember who is offered nonjudicial punishment may refuse to accept the procedures. The right is limited by Article 15(a), which provides that servicemembers who are "attached to or

---

admissible in part because it included offense for which accused had not been tried but was part of charged offense).

28. Art. 15(f) U.C.M.J.
29. Hagarty v. United States, 449 F.2d 352 (Ct. Cl. 1971) (suit to recover pay lost for reduction in grade was brought after the plaintiff was no longer on active duty).
30. 16 M.J. 84 (C.M.A. 1983).
31. *See infra* § 3-4.
32. Dobzynski v. Green, 16 M.J. at 86 (C.M.A. 1983); Jones v. Commander, Naval Air Force, 18 M.J. 198 (C.M.A. 1984) (the court denied extraordinary relief where the accused received an Article 15 after the prosecution had failed to prove its case against the accused in a court-martial). The court's reasoning should not extend to Article 15 punishment imposed *after* an accused has been tried and acquitted by a court-martial. In that case there would be a clear problem with double jeopardy. Here, the charges were withdrawn and Article 15 punishment imposed before evidence was presented on the merits.
See also Fletcher v. Covington, 42 M.J. 215 (1995) (misc. docket) (issuing stay of nonjudicial punishment where convening authority withdrew charges from court-martial and ordered a nonjudicial punishment hearing after military judge ordered government to provide defense with report on misconduct at laboratory that tested the defendant's sample). A week later, the Court vacated its stay as moot when the report was produced and the court-martial charges were dismissed. 42 M.J. 116 (1995) (misc. docket); Slater v. Kamrath, 33 M.J. 491 (C.M.A. 1991) (denying writ appeal petition seeking review of nonjudicial punishment proceeding). *See generally* § 8-5 for discussion on withdrawal of charges.
33. Dobzynski v. Green, 16 M.J. at 88 (C.M.A. 1983). That is true only where the offense is minor and the Article 15 punishment has actually been imposed before an accused is tried by a court-martial for the same offense.
34. Dobzynski v. Green, 16 M.J. at 88 (C.M.A. 1983).

embarked in a vessel" may *not* demand trial. This limitation does not deny those servicemembers of equal protection.[1] The *Manual* indicates that a person is attached to or embarked in a vessel if:

> at the time the nonjudicial punishment is imposed, that person is assigned or attached to the vessel, is on board for passage, or is assigned or attached to an embarked staff, unit, detachment, squadron, team, air group, or other regulatory organized body.[2]

The terms "assigned to or embarked in" and "vessel" have been litigated in both military and civilian proceedings.[3]

The demand for trial by court-martial does not require the commander to actually initiate charges.[4] It does, however, act as a bar to further Article 15 procedures.[5] Waiving the right to demand trial is not a plea of guilty; the servicemember is simply consenting to the procedures.

On the other hand, once a commander has offered nonjudicial punishment, the servicemember does not have a *right* to proceed under those procedures. The commander, for example, may determine at mid-stream that the offense is more serious than at first perceived and that court-martial procedures are more appropriate.[6] Or a superior commander may view the offense as inappropriate for nonjudicial punishment and order further investigation, the forwarding of the investigative files, and/or preferral of court-martial charges.[7]

---

1. *See, e.g.,* United States v. Penn, 4 M.J. 879 (N.C.M.R. 1978), *petition denied,* 5 M.J. 259 (C.M.A. 1978); United States v. Lecolst, 4 M.J. 800 (N.M.C.M.R. 1978).

2. MCM, Part V, para. 3.

3. *See, e.g.,* Bennett v. Tarquin, 466 F. Supp. 257 (D. Hawaii 1979) (servicemember attached to submarine although he was not actually present on vessel). In United States v. Forester, 8 M.J. 560 (N.C.M.R. 1979) the court delineated those vessels which may fit within the Article 15 exception prior to commissioning:

   1. "In service," as respects nuclear surface ships and submarines.
   2. "In commission, special," as respects nonnuclear surface ships.
   3. "In commission"/"in service," as respects nonnuclear submarines, as appropriate.

   In United States v. Edwards, 43 M.J. 619 (N.M.Ct.Crim.App.1995) the court concluded, in lengthy discussion of the issue, that accused could not demand trial because he was attached to vessel even though vessel was undergoing overhaul. The court rejected argument that term vessel means an "operational vessel."

4. *See* MCM, Part V, para. 4b(1). *See also* AR 27-10, para. 3-18f(3) (whether to prefer charges is within discretion of commander) and AFI 51-202, para. 6.2. For discussion of preferral of charges, see Chapter 6.

5. MCM, Part V, para. 4b(1).

6. Although a thorough pre-Article 15 investigation by the commander usually avoids the problem, it occasionally happens that during the proceedings the accused or one of the witnesses will indicate that all was not as it first appeared. Indeed, the *Manual* covers that possibility. It requires the commander to advise the accused that he has the right to remain silent and that any matters submitted by him may be used at a later court-martial. *See* MCM, Part V, para. 4c(1), (2).

7. *See* R.C.M. 307(a) and Chapter 6, *infra.* Where the offense is not a *minor* offense the superior commander could take such action even *after* the Article 15 punishments had been imposed and served. *See* § 3-3(C).

If the commander does prefer charges and they are referred to a summary court-martial, the servicemember may also refuse to be tried by that court.[8] In practice, commanders should not initiate Article 15 procedures unless they are reasonably sure that the available evidence would sustain a conviction at a court-martial.[9] Preferring charges to trial is generally not viewed as prosecutorial vindictiveness.[10]

§ 3-5. Procedural Rules for Imposing Nonjudicial Punishment.

§ 3-5(A). General.

Building on the skeletal frame of Article 15, U.C.M.J. and Part V of the Manual for Courts-Martial, the services have exercised the discretion, granted in those sources, to tailor nonjudicial punishment procedures to meet their unique needs. Notwithstanding the differences that in many instances constitute "fine tuning," there are some primary points of commonality. The common points consist of:

1. *Preliminary Inquiry.* The commanding officer is required to investigate the alleged offense and determine the appropriateness of nonjudicial punishment.[1]
2. *Notice.* The servicemember is to be informed that the commanding officer is considering punishment under Article 15 and that various rights and options are available.[2]
3. *Hearing.* The proceedings may include a nonadversarial "hearing." Evidence may be presented and the punishment may be announced at this time.[3]
4. *Appeals.* Each service has devised appellate procedures for reviewing nonjudicial punishment.[4]

These four points will serve as a template for more closely examining each service's practices in the following sections. There will be some redundancy in the discussions of each service's practices; the foregoing points of analysis are

---

8. Art. 20, U.C.M.J. This right accrues to all personnel whether or not they are attached to or embarked on a vessel. *See also infra* § 15-27, *et seq.*
9. *See* Dobzynski v. Green, 16 M.J. 84, 92 n.11 (C.M.A. 1983) (Everett, C.J., dissenting). *See also* AFI 51-202, para. 3.3 (commander must consider whether proof beyond a reasonable doubt is available before initiating action). *But see* JAGMAN 0110b (captain's mast or office hours that results in nonjudicial punishment is not criminal trial; it is a disciplinary measure and standard of proof is preponderance of the evidence).
10. United States v. Martino, 18 M.J. 526 (A.F.C.M.R. 1984) (no prosecutorial vindictiveness present where commander preferred charges after the accused declined to accept an Article 15). *See* United States v. Bass, 11 M.J. 545 (A.C.M.R. 1981); United States v. Blanchette, 17 M.J. 512 (A.F.C.M.R. 1983).
1. MCM, Part V, para. 4a; R.C.M. 303.
2. MCM, Part V, para. 4a.
3. MCM, Part V, para. 4c. United States v. Roppolo, 34 M.J. 820 (A.F.C.M.R. 1992) (nonjudicial punishment hearing was not a judicial proceeding).
4. Art. 15(e), U.C.M.J.; MCM, Part V, para. 7.

only broad guidelines, although there are obviously other similarities in the practices of each service. To assist the reader who may only be interested, for example, in Air Force procedures, that section is designed to provide a fairly comprehensive, yet somewhat independent, discussion of Air Force procedures.

In reading the entire section on procedural differences, the reader will, therefore, see some repetition of general rules. Note that the discussion of the various nonjudicial punishments is separately addressed in § 3-6 *infra*.

In addition to minor variations of practice between the services, there are often a variety of procedures within each service. The materials here present the usual or general procedure. To avoid confusion, the specific service supplement or regulation and any installation or command supplements should be reviewed.

§ 3-5(B). Army Procedures.

Nonjudicial punishment in the Army is more commonly recognized as the "Article 15." The specific procedural practices are detailed in Chapter 3 of Army Regulation 27-10, Legal Services — Military Justice.

The Army uses two forms of nonjudicial punishment: (1) summarized proceedings and (2) formal proceedings.

§ 3-5(B)(1). Preliminary Inquiry.

Prior to notifying the servicemember of his or her intent to offer either a summarized or formal Article 15, the commander is to have conducted a preliminary inquiry into the alleged offense.[1] This inquiry need not be conducted personally by the commander but should be more than simply building a case against the individual; evidence of a favorable nature should also be considered.[2] The amount of available evidence may range from a sketchy oral account of the offense to a detailed military police report. After the commander completes his inquiry and determines that nonjudicial punishment proceedings are appropriate, he notifies the servicemember of his intent to proceed with Article 15 proceedings.[3] If the commander concludes that his Article 15 authority is insufficient to mete an appropriate punishment, he may forward the file to a superior with a recommendation that the superior exercise his Article 15 authority.[4]

---

1. MCM, Part V, para. 4a; R.C.M. 303; AR 27-10, para. 3-14.
2. AR 27-10, para. 3-2 emphasizes the correctional and rehabilitative nature of Article 15. Commanders are expected to use nonpunitive measures to the maximum extent possible and are to use their personal discretion in determining whether to impose punishment.
3. AR 27-10, para. 3-16 (summarized proceedings), para. 3-18 (formal proceedings).
4. AR 27-10, para. 3-5. DA Form 5109-R is used to refer the matter to a superior officer.

§ 3-5(B)(2). Notice.

Where the commander intends to use *summarized* Article 15 proceedings,[5] the servicemember is so notified by the commander or another designated person.[6] The servicemember is orally informed of: (1) the commander's intent, (2) the maximum punishments, *see* § 3-5(B), (3) the right to remain silent, (4) the offenses alleged, (5) the right to demand trial, (6) the right to present and examine evidence, and (7) the right to appeal.[7] Upon request, the servicemember is given 24 hours to decide whether to accept the Article 15; there is no right to consult with counsel.[8]

If *formal* Article 15 proceedings[9] are to be used, the commander, or his designate,[10] presents the servicemember with DA Form 2627 (in effect a written notice) and also orally apprises[11] him of the available rights:

(a) The right to remain silent;[12]
(b) The right to demand trial;[13]
(c) The right to consult with counsel;[14]
(d) The right to an open, or public, hearing;[15]
(e) The right to the assistance of a spokesperson;[16]
(f) The right to examine available evidence and present witnesses and evidence.[17]

In this notice the commander may advise the servicemember of the maximum punishments that could be legally imposed under either an Article 15 or in a

---

5. *See* AR 27-10, para. 3-16b.
6. The commander may designate another subordinate officer or noncommissioned officer (NCO) who holds the pay grade of E-7 or above. This will normally be the unit's First Sergeant. The fact that notice was given is reflected on DA Form 2627-1 (summarized proceedings).
7. *See* AR 27-10, para. 3-16b.
8. *See* AR 27-10, para. 3-16c. If the servicemember fails to inform the commander of his decision, the commander may proceed with the Article 15.
The regulation indicates that there is no *right* to consult with counsel; this should not mean that the servicemember is barred from speaking with counsel. It does mean that the commander does not have to provide the means or extra time for the servicemember to consult with one. *Cf.* AR 27-10, para. 3-18c.
9. AR 27-10, para. 3-17.
10. AR 27-10, para. 3-18. The commander may designate another officer, warrant officer, or NCO (E-7 or above).
11. Most commanders use a sample guide or script for imposing Article 15 punishments, which is included as an appendix to AR 27-10.
12. *See* Article 15b, U.C.M.J. In United States v. McCullah, 8 M.J. 697 (A.F.C.M.R. 1981) the court stated that an accused presenting evidence to a commander during an Article 15 hearing is not being interrogated and Article 31 warnings would be pointless.
13. AR 27-10, para. 3-18d.
14. AR 27-10, para. 3-18c. *Cf.* United States v. Kendig, 36 M.J. 291 (C.M.A. 1993) (Article 15 proceedings do not constitute criminal prosecutions for purposes of Sixth Amendment right to counsel; thus Service regulations which provide opportunity to consult with counsel do not create a Sixth Amendment right to counsel and do not constitute appointment of counsel); United States v. Kelly, 41 M.J. 833 (N.M.Ct.Crim.App. 1995) (en banc) (no provision in U.C.M.J. or MCM requires that the service member has the right to consult with counsel).
15. AR 27-10, paras. 3-18e, 3-18g.
16. AR 27-10, para. 3-18e.
17. *Id.*

court-martial if convicted for the same offense.[18] If requested, the servicemember is given a reasonable time, normally 48 hours,[19] to consult with counsel[20] and determine whether he will accept the Article 15 and exercise any of the other available options. If at the end of the designated time the individual has not informed the commander of his decision, the latter may proceed with the Article 15.[21] If the servicemember demands trial, the proceedings must stop.[22]

§ 3-5(B)(3). Hearing.

If the servicemember decides to accept the Article 15 (summarized or formal), he is entitled to a personal appearance or hearing before the commander.[1] Normally, the request is granted. If such an appearance is not possible because of other extraordinary circumstances, the commander should appoint a commissioned officer to hold the hearing and make a written summary and recommendations.[2]

Hearings in a *summarized* Article 15 proceeding generally consist of the commander (1) considering the evidence (oral or written) against the servicemember, (2) letting the member examine that evidence and present his or her own evidence, (3) deciding the issue of guilt, (4) imposing punishment, and (5) advising the member concerning the right to appeal.[3]

If the servicemember decides to accept a *formal* Article 15,[4] he may request that the hearing be open to the public. Normally, that request is granted.[5] The hearing is really an opportunity for the servicemember to present his evidence to the commander. It is nonadversarial in nature,[6] with the servicemember or his spokesperson[7] being limited to presenting lines of questioning or inquiry unless the commander specifically allows either or both to ask questions of the witnesses.[8] Note that other than the rules governing privileges, the Military

---

18. AR 27-10, para. 3-18f(2). The commander will inform the soldier of maximum punishment upon soldier's request.
19. AR 27-10, para. 3-18f(1). The time may be extended for good cause.
20. AR 27-10, para. 3-18c. "Counsel" means: a judge advocate (JA), a Department of the Army civilian attorney, or an officer who is a member of a Federal court or of the highest court of a State. The last two categories must be under the supervision of either the USATDS (United States Army Trial Defense Service) or a staff or command judge advocate.
21. AR 27-10, para. 3-18f(4). The commander may also proceed if the servicemember refuses to complete the form and indicate his decision.
22. AR 27-10, para. 3-18f(3). *See also supra* § 3-4. The commander may, but need not, prefer court-martial charges.
1. MCM, Part V, para. 4c(1); AR 27-10, para. 3-16d, 3-18g.
2. AR 27-10, para. 3-18g(1).
3. AR 27-10, para. 3-16d.
4. AR 27-10, para. 3-17.
5. AR 27-10, para. 3-18g(2).
6. *Id.*
7. *See* AR 27-10, para. 3-18h. The spokesperson need not be a lawyer, although an accused may obtain a civilian counsel at no expense to the government. No travel fees nor other unusual costs may be charged to the government, and the spokesperson's presence is voluntary.
8. AR 27-10, para. 3-18h. The accused or his spokesperson may, however, indicate relevant lines of questioning. Commanders often find spokespersons helpful in sifting through the evidence and in dealing with any language difficulties.

Rules of Evidence do not apply to Article 15 proceedings.[9] Although the commander may coordinate the Article 15 with his legal advisor, the latter is not normally present at this hearing. In determining whether the servicemember is guilty beyond a reasonable doubt,[10] the commander may consider oral or written evidence, either sworn or unsworn. Any written statement or documentary evidence relied upon by the commander becomes a part of the original form.[11]

After the commander has considered the available evidence and if he determines that the individual is guilty of the offense, he may proceed immediately with imposing the punishments.[12] The individual is orally apprised of the punishments (they are also noted on the DA Form 2627) and informed of his right to appeal the punishments.[13]

§ 3-5(B)(4). Appeals.

At the time punishments are announced by the commander, the servicemember is advised that the right to appeal should be exercised within a reasonable period of time, usually five days,[14] to the appellate authority who is normally the next superior commander in the chain of command.[15] Simply checking the appropriate block on the DA Form 2627 or DA Form 2627-1 will initiate the appeal; the servicemember need not articulate any specific ground for appealing although it is advisable to do so.[16] In preparing any statements or other materials to forward with his appeal, the servicemember may seek the advice and assistance of an attorney in the JAGC office.

The appeal is first routed through the commander imposing the Article 15, who may himself take mitigating action on the Article 15,[17] or simply forward it to the appeal authority with his recommendations or comments.[18] Appeals of Article 15's including certain punishments must be first routed through a judge advocate for review before appellate action may be taken.[19]

---

9. MCM, Part V, para. 4c(3); AR 27-10, para. 3-18j.
10. AR 27-10 does not address the use of the beyond a reasonable doubt standard but the DA Form 2627 informs the servicemember that no punishment will be imposed unless the commander is convinced of his guilt beyond a reasonable doubt.
11. AR 27-10, para. 3-37a.
12. AR 27-10, para. 3-18l. The effective dates of the punishments are noted at AR 27-10, para. 3-21. *See also infra* § 3-6(G).
13. AR 27-10, para. 3-18m.
14. AR 27-10, para. 3-29a. If the appeal is not filed within five calendar days, it is presumed untimely, unless good cause is shown.
15. AR 27-10, para. 3-30a.
16. AR 27-10, para. 3-31. The accused should attach whatever evidence is appropriate to show that he is not guilty or that the punishment is too heavy.
17. AR 27-10, para. 3-31. If he does take such action he should so inform the accused and determine if he still desires to appeal. AR 27-10, para. 3-32.
18. AR 27-10, para. 3-32.
19. Art. 15(e), U.C.M.J. Those punishments include:

   (a) arrest in quarters for more than seven days;
   (b) correctional custody for more than seven days;

The appellate authority may not increase the punishment,[20] but he may take any of the following ameliorative actions: suspension of any or all of the punishment,[21] mitigation,[22] remission,[23] or setting aside the punishment.[24] Note that AR 27-10 specifically provides that even in the absence of a formal appeal any superior authority may take action on an Article 15.[25]

§ 3-5(C). Air Force Procedures.

The prescribed nonjudicial punishment procedures for the Air Force are detailed in Air Force Instruction 51-202, Nonjudicial Punishment.[26] As in the Army, nonjudicial punishment in the Air Force is referred to as the "Article 15." The major difference in the Air Force procedure is that it does not include summarized nonjudicial punishment.[27]

§ 3-5(C)(1). Preliminary Inquiry.

An Air Force commanding officer is to act only on the basis of reliable information and is to take temperate, well-conceived action that is just and conducive to good order and discipline.[28] Action should be initiated only when the commander is convinced that the offender committed the offense; if action is appropriate, the commander must decide whether he will initiate the Arti-

---

(c) forfeiture of more than seven days' pay;
(d) reduction of one or more pay grades from the fourth or a higher pay grade;
(e) extra duties for more than 14 days;
(f) restriction for more than 14 days; or
(g) detention of more than 14 days' pay.

20. MCM, Part V, para. 1f(2).
21. MCM, Part V, para. 6a. AR 27-10, para. 3-33. Suspension of the punishment may not extend beyond six months. The commander may vacate the suspension should the accused commit another offense. United States v. Covington, 10 M.J. 64 (C.M.A. 1980). Punishments of reduction or forfeiture may be suspended within a period of four months after the imposition of punishment. MCM, Part V, para. 6a(2). There is no appeal from the vacation of a suspended punishment. AR 27-10, para. 3-29b.
22. AR 27-10, para. 3-26. The unexecuted portion of the punishment may be reduced either in quantity or quality.
23. AR 27-10, para. 3-27. Only unexecuted punishments may be remitted. Discharge or separation from the service automatically remits the punishments.
24. AR 27-10, para. 3-28. Set aside action is appropriate where the punishment results from a "clear injustice." Property, privileges and rights affected by punishment are restored. This action should normally be taken within four months of the imposition. MCM, Part V, para. 6d. The regulation cautions that a "clear injustice" does not include a situation where the servicemember subsequently performs his duties in an exemplary fashion. The regulation also states that the servicemember's uncorroborated statement will not support setting aside a punishment.
25. AR 27-10, para. 3-35. Although para. 3-29 explicitly states that only one appeal is permissible, in theory the servicemember may ask any superior authority for relief after an unsuccessful appeal because para. 3-35 permits that authority to act whether or not an appeal has been filed.
26. Cited here as AFI 51-202.
27. Before 1 August 1984, the Air Force permitted "oral" Article 15's for certain offenses and personnel.
28. AFI 51-202, para. 3.1.

cle 15 himself or refer it to a superior officer.[29] In deciding what, if any, action should be taken, the commander is to confer with his staff judge advocate to determine whether nonjudicial punishment is appropriate, and how each offense should be alleged so as to state an offense under the U.C.M.J.[30] The legal office will type the specification language on the appropriate form, unless it is impractical to do so.[31] The Instruction states that nonjudicial punishment action should be initiated as soon as possible after an offense is committed.[32]

§ 3-5(C)(2). Notice.

If the commanding officer decides to proceed with an Article 15, he notifies the servicemember of the offense, the right to consult with counsel, the right to make a personal and/or a written presentation, the right to request a public hearing, and the right to demand trial by court-martial. The foregoing notice is accomplished through an AF Form 3070, which is a three-page document.[33]

In those cases where the commander intends to refer the action to a superior commander and it appears that the superior commander will not be able to personally hear the offender's presentation, the subordinate commander will personally serve the member with the AF Form 3070[34] to inform the offender of his Article 15 rights. In addition, the subordinate commander will hear the presentation and then summarize it in a written memorandum prepared for the superior commander.[35] If the commander later decides to dispose of the case personally before actually forwarding the AF Form 3070 to the superior commander, he must withdraw the form and execute a new one.[36] The servicemember is given at least three duty days to reply to the commander's notice.[37] During that time he is encouraged to meet and consult with an attorney to decide whether to accept the proceedings and if so, prepare matters in response to the commander's action.[38] Should he fail to indicate his

---

29. AFI 51-202, para. 4.1.
30. AFI 51-202, para. 4.1 and 4.3. The instruction notes that the decision to proceed rests on the commander, although it is the staff judge advocate's responsibility to advise and help the commander with evaluating the facts.
31. AFI 51-202, para. 4.3. Upon doing so the legal office will make a request for the Automated Justice Analysis and Management System (AMJAMS) Report on Individual Personnel (RIP).
32. AFI 51-202, para. 3.2. The regulation points out that commanders should offer nonjudicial punishment within 10 days of the commission of the earliest offense or be able to explain why that was not possible. Although the 10-day figure is not mandatory, commanders are encouraged to use that as a goal. This is only a suggested processing goal, however, and failure to meet it will not preclude the commander from initiating proceedings at a later date.
33. AFI 51-202, para. 4.4.1.
34. AFI 51-202, para. 4.4.2.
35. AFI 51-202, para. 4.4.2.
36. AFI 51-202, para. 4.4.3.
37. AFI 51-202, para. 4.7. The three-day period includes weekends and holidays if they are normally duty days for the servicemember. The initiating commander may grant an extension for good cause upon written request.
38. AFI 51-202, para. 4.7.1. United States v. Kendig, 36 M.J. 291 (C.M.A. 1993) (Article 15 proceedings do not constitute criminal prosecutions for purposes of Sixth Amendment right to

decision to the commander within the allotted time, the Article 15 punishment may be imposed, unless the commander believes that the failure to respond was for reasons beyond the control of the servicemember.[39] If the offender demands trial by court-martial, the commander may not further process the Article 15.[40] If the commander, however, decides to prefer court-martial charges, he is not limited to the charges listed on the AF Form 3070 and may change the form of the charges or even add new charges, regardless of whether those charges were used when the nonjudicial punishment procedures were initiated.[41]

§ 3-5(C)(3). Hearing.

If the servicemember has elected nonjudicial punishment, then the member is entitled to present matters in defense, mitigation, or extenuation before his commander.[42] Prior to doing so, the servicemember has a right to examine all statements and evidence available to the commander, unless they are privileged or restricted by law, regulation, or instruction.[43] The punishments[44] are noted on AF Form 3070.[45]

The offender is entitled to be informed of his Article 31, U.C.M.J. right to remain silent and say nothing in response to the charges.[46] He may be informed orally or in writing of the evidence relating to the alleged misconduct. Further, he is entitled to examine relevant documents the commander intends to rely upon, be accompanied by a spokesman, and have relevant witnesses present who can be obtained without legal process.[47] During this presentation, which may be open to the public,[48] the commander must carefully consider all matters submitted by the servicemember in defense, because acceptance of nonjudicial punishment proceedings is not a plea of guilty.[49] If the commander imposing the Article 15 is not located on the same base as the offender, the

---

counsel; thus Service regulations, which provide opportunity to consult with counsel do not create a Sixth Amendment right to counsel and do not constitute appointment of counsel).

39. AFI 51-202, para. 4.7.2.
40. MCM, Part V, para. 4b; AFI 51-202, para. 6.1. The commander is not required to prefer court-martial charges, however.
41. AFI 51-202, para. 6.2.
42. AFI 51-202, para. 4.8. This is also referred to as a personal appearance. The right is not absolute and may not apply if there are "extraordinary circumstances" or the imposing commander is unavailable. If the commander and the servicemember are not "collocated," the commander designates an officer to hear the presentation and prepare a memorandum for the absent commander.
43. AFI 51-202, para. 3.4.
44. See § 3-6 *infra* for a discussion of punishments.
45. AFI 51-202, para. 5.5. (referring to Attachment 3 to the Instruction which in turn sets out the format for the punishments to be entered on the form).
46. *See* AF Form 3070.
47. *Id.*
48. AFI 51-202, para. 4.8.1. The commander may open the hearing to the public even if the servicemember objects.
49. AFI 51-202, para. 4.9. The commander's considerations and the offender's reply are recorded on AF Form 3070.

commander will delegate an officer (senior in grade to the offender) to hear the presentation and to prepare a memorandum for the commander, summarizing the presentation.[50]

Any punishments that may be imposed are prepared and noted on AF Form 3070.[51] Unless otherwise stated by the commander, punishments are effective immediately upon notification.[52] Air Force Instruction 51-202 prescribes the permissible nonjudicial punishments and rules for imposing punishments under Article 15, U.C.M.J.[53]

§ 3-5(C)(4). Appeals.

If the offender considers his Article 15 "unjust or disproportionate" to the offense, he may appeal through command channels to the "next superior authority."[54] The member must indicate within five days if he or she desires an appeal.[55] A warning must be given to the offender that a failure to appeal within the prescribed time will cause a waiver of right to an appeal.[56] In addition, a decision not to appeal or to withdraw an appeal is *final*.[57] The "next superior authority" is either the immediate superior commander to the officer who imposed the nonjudicial punishment or the immediate commander superior to the commander who delegated power to the assistant who imposed nonjudicial punishment.[58] An appeal is an affirmative act by the servicemember; therefore he must clearly indicate that he is appealing.[59] Although the offender is entitled to consult with counsel on appeal issues, the offender is not entitled to a personal appearance with the appellate authority.[60] The initiating commander considers any written materials in support of the appeal and has the opportunity to grant relief.[61] If he does not grant the full relief requested, the commander includes all written materials considered before imposing punishment, a summary of the oral presentation (if applicable), and any written comments he feels are appropriate.[62] The commander

---

50. AFI 51-202, para. 4.8.
51. AFI 51-202, Attachment 3.
52. AFI 51-202, para. 5.1.
53. The enlisted punishments are noted in Table 1 of AFI 51-202, and punishments for officers are noted in Table 2 of AFI 51-202. *See also infra* § 3-6(G).
54. MCM, Part V, para. 7a.
55. AFI 51-202, para. 7.4.2. The commander may extend the time for good cause.
56. *Id.*
57. *Id.*
58. AFI 51-202, para. 7.1. If a squadron commander imposed punishment, however, appeals do not go to the squadron commander. Instead, they go to the squadron commander's superior commander.
59. AFI 51-202, para. 7.4.2 and 7.4.4. It is not an appeal if the servicemember does not clearly indicate he is appealing, if he indicates he will appeal in the future, or if he refuses to acknowledge receipt of the punishment.
60. AFI 51-202, para. 7.2.
61. AFI 51-202, para. 7.4.6.
62. AFI 51-202, para. 7.4.6 and 7.4.7.

will then send the record through the Staff Judge Advocate to the appellate authority.[63]

The appellate authority may not in any manner increase the punishments[64] but may take mitigating action that may assist in rehabilitating the offender — the primary objective of Article 15. Mitigating actions include suspension, remission, mitigation, or setting aside all or a portion of the Article 15 punishments.[65] *Suspension* is a postponement of punishment for a probationary period conditioned on its being remitted if the offender does not engage in further misconduct.[66] *Remission* occurs at any time before the execution of the punishment when a commander excuses the offender from the unexecuted portion.[67] *Mitigation* occurs prior to the complete execution of the punishment and the commander changes it to a less severe punishment.[68] Lastly, *setting aside* the punishment occurs when a commander decides that the guilt of the offender subsequently becomes questionable or "where it is in the best interests of the Air Force to clear the member's record."[69]

§ 3-5(D). Navy and Marine Corps Procedures.

Article 15 procedures in the Navy and Marine Corps (referred to as "Captain's Mast" and "Office Hours" respectively) are detailed in the Manual of the Judge Advocate General (the JAGMAN).[70] With minor exceptions, which may arise between these two services in imposing punishment, the nonjudicial punishment procedures are close enough in practice to warrant combined analysis in this section.

---

63. AFI 51-202, para. 7.4.6. The appellate authority is the next superior authority. *See also* AFI 51-202, para. 7.1 (outlines definition of next superior authority).
64. MCM, Part V, para. 1f(2).
65. AFI 51-202, para. 8. *See also* United States v. Covington, 10 M.J. 64 (C.M.A. 1980) (discusses due process requirements for vacating suspension).
66. AFI 51-202, para. 8.4. Suspension is often given to the first offender or when extenuating or mitigating matters are present. A suspension action will set a date when, unless vacated sooner, the suspension will terminate and the punishment will be remitted. The commander is to notify the offender of his rights using AF Form 366, Record of Proceedings of Vacation of Suspended Nonjudicial Punishment.
67. AFI 51-202, para. 8.6. The expiration of the current enlistment or term of service automatically remits any unexecuted punishments.
68. AFI 51-202, para. 8.5. The general nature of the punishment, however, must remain the same; correctional custody may not be mitigated to forfeitures, reduction in grade may be mitigated to forfeiture if taken within 4 months after the date of execution, and the mitigated punishment may not be for a greater time period than that remaining for the original punishment when mitigating arrest in quarters, correctional custody, and extra duties.
69. AFI 51-202, para. 8.7. This generally occurs when information later comes to the commander's attention that casts substantial doubt on the member's guilt or there is extenuation for the commission of the offense. Setting aside a punishment is not considered a rehabilitation tool. It restores the member to his position before punishment was taken, and if the action is taken, it should be taken within a reasonable time after the punishment has been executed, normally 4 months. The commander must consult with the servicing Staff Judge Advocate before setting aside a punishment.
70. MCM, Part V, para. 4, sets out the basic procedures for imposition of nonjudicial punishment in the Navy and Marine Corps. Additional guidance for completing the Marine Corps forms is provided in the Marine Corps Manual for Legal Administration (LEGALADMINMAN).

§ 3-5(D)(1). Preliminary Inquiry.

The preliminary inquiry normally consists of an informal examination of the available evidence. After a commander has received a report of an offense, he may appoint an investigation officer to gather evidence, interview witnesses, and make a recommendation for disposition. The report of the investigation is informally reviewed by the executive officer who may either dismiss the action or refer it to "Captain's Mast" or "Office Hours."[71] The screening process in the Marine Corps usually involves review by the unit's legal advisor.

In addition to this normal process, however, the Navy Department authorizes a commanding officer to impose nonjudicial punishment based upon facts elicited at a court of inquiry or other fact-finding body.[72] In order to rely upon those proceedings, the commander must be assured that the offender was afforded the rights of a party before that fact-finding body and that those rights were accorded with regard to the offense which is the subject of the nonjudicial punishment. If so, the commander may impose punishment without further proceedings, after giving the individual an opportunity to submit information in writing.[73]

§ 3-5(D)(2). Notice.

The JAGMAN requires that a commanding officer, prior to holding "captain's mast" or "office hours," ensure that the offender is fully advised of the following rights:

(a) The offense(s) that the accused is suspected of having committed.

(b) That the commanding officer is contemplating mast or office hours for the alleged offense(s).

(c) That, if the accused is not attached to or embarked on a vessel, he has the right to demand trial by courts-martial in lieu of mast or office hours.

(d) That, if the accused accepts mast or office hours, he has a right to a hearing at which time he will be accorded the following rights:

(i) To be present before the officer conducting the hearing.

(ii) To be advised of the offense(s) of which he is suspected.

(iii) To have his rights under Article 31(b) of the Uniform Code of Military Justice explained to him.

(iv) To be present during the presentation of all information against him, either by testimony of a witness in person or by the receipt of his written statement(s), copies of the latter being furnished to the accused.

---

71. JAGMAN 0110. This preliminary procedure in the Navy is noted on NAVPERS 1626/7, Report and Disposition of Offense(s). The corresponding Marine Corps form is NAVMC 10132, Unit Punishment Book, UPB.
72. JAGMAN 0110d.
73. Id.

(v) To have available for his inspection all items of information in the nature of physical or documentary evidence to be considered by the officer conducting the hearing.

(vi) To have full opportunity to present a personal representative, provided by the accused, to speak on his behalf; the personal representative may, but need not, be a lawyer.

(vii) To present matters in defense, extenuation, and mitigation orally, in writing, or both.

(viii) To have the proceedings open to the public unless the commanding officer determines that the proceedings should be closed for good cause.

(ix) To have witnesses attend the proceeding if their statements are relevant and they are reasonably available.[74]

Furthermore, the individual may be offered an opportunity to consult with an attorney if the right to demand trial by courts-martial exists. The commander's failure, however, to allow the offender to consult with counsel will not preclude the commander from imposing punishment.[75] Failure to allow such consultation before electing whether to accept nonjudicial punishment may, however, preclude the government from introducing the record of nonjudicial punishment at any later court-martial of the offender.[76] The offender's acknowledgement of receiving the foregoing notice is noted on the appropriate service forms.[77]

§ 3-5(D)(3). Hearing.

Part V, paragraph 4c, of the Manual for Courts-Martial prescribes the basic elements of the "hearing" (mast or office hours):

1. Presence of the accused before the officer conducting the mast.
2. Advice to the accused of the offenses of which he is suspected.
3. Explanation to the accused of his rights under Article 31(b) of the Uniform Code of Military Justice.
4. Presentation of the information against the accused, either by the testimony of witnesses in person or by the receipt of their written statements, copies of the latter being furnished to the accused.
5. Availability to the accused for his inspection all items of information in the nature of physical or documentary evidence which will be considered.
6. Full opportunity to the accused to present any matters in mitigation, extenuation, or defense of the suspected offenses. At the completion of the

---

74. JAGMAN 0109a. JAGMAN A-1-b, A-1-c. United States v. Kendig, 36 M.J. 291 (C.M.A. 1993) (Service regulations which provide opportunity to consult with counsel do not create a Sixth Amendment right to counsel and do not constitute appointment of counsel).
75. JAGMAN 0109.
76. See § 3-8(B).
77. NAVMC 118, Administrative Remarks may be used to record advisement of right and waiver of such.

hearing, the commanding officer may impose punishment under Article 15.

   7. To be accompanied by a spokesperson unless the punishment to be imposed will not exceed extra duty for 14 days, restriction for 14 days, and an oral reprimand.[78]

At the conclusion of the hearing, punishments, if any, may be imposed[79] and the offender is advised of his right to appeal.[80] See § 3-6 *infra* for a discussion of permissible punishments.

§ 3-5(D)(4). Appeals.

Appeals must be made within a reasonable period of time, i.e., submitted within 5 days unless the offender has received an extension of time, for good cause, from the commander who imposed the punishment.[81] The time for appealing commences to run from the date the punishment was imposed.[82] If the commander who imposed the nonjudicial punishment is in a Navy chain of command, the appeal is forwarded to the area coordinator authorized to convene general courts-martial or his designee.[83] Punishments meted by a commander in the chain of command of the Commandant of the Marine Corps are appealed to the commander next superior to the commander who imposed the punishment.[84] If the commander imposing the punishment is a commander of a multiservice command and is a Marine Corps officer, the appeal is sent to the nearest Marine Corps general officer in command.[85] Punishments imposed by a naval officer in command of a multiservice command are appealed to the nearest area coordinator.[86] In cases in which a multiservice commander has designated a naval officer in his command as a commanding officer for purposes of administering discipline under Article 15, that multiservice commander may retain the right to decide nonjudicial punishment appeals.[87]

---

   78. JAGMAN A-1-b, A-1-c. Note that in Conn. v. United States, 376 F.2d 878 (Ct. Cl. 1967), the failure to allow the accused to inspect the government's evidence voided the punishment imposed.
   79. The unsuspended punishments of reduction, forfeiture of pay, and detention of pay are effective on the date imposed. The unsuspended punishments of arrest in quarters, correctional custody, confinement on bread and water or diminished rations, extra duties, and restriction take effect the date imposed if the accused is attached to or embarked in a vessel. If not so attached the latter punishments may be delayed pending appeal (note that the punishment of confinement on bread and water or diminished rations is not authorized if the offender is not attached to or embarked in a vessel). JAGMAN 0113. *See also infra* § 3-6(G).
   80. JAGMAN 0110e.
   81. JAGMAN 0116a(1). Allowances shall be made for the time required to transmit communications pertaining to the imposition of nonjudicial punishment and an appeal through the mails.
   82. JAGMAN 0116a(1). The rule applies even if all or any part of the punishment imposed is suspended.
   83. JAGMAN 0117a.
   84. JAGMAN 0117b.
   85. JAGMAN 0117c.
   86. *Id.*
   87. JAGMAN 0117c(2).

The appeals must be made in writing and may include reasons for considering the punishment unjust or disproportionate.[88] According to the JAGMAN, the forwarding endorsement of the officer who imposed the nonjudicial punishment should normally include comments on the offender's assertion of facts in the appeal, the completed nonjudicial punishment forms, copies of all documents considered by the commander, and a copy of the offender's record of performance.[89] If the punishment exceeded that which could be imposed by a commanding officer in the grade of O-3, the reviewing authority must refer the appeal to a judge advocate for consideration and advice.[90]

The appellate authority, in accordance with paragraph 7 of Part V of the *Manual,* may not increase the punishment,[91] but may suspend, mitigate, remit, or set aside punishments.[92]

§ 3-5(E). Coast Guard Procedures.

The Coast Guard procedures for imposing nonjudicial punishment, labeled "Captain's Mast" are prescribed in Part 1 of the *Military Justice Manual* (MJM), the Coast Guard's supplement to the U.C.M.J. and the Manual for Courts-Martial. The procedures approximate those employed in both the Navy and Marine Corps.[93]

§ 3-5(E)(1). Preliminary Inquiry.

The preliminary inquiry is conducted in what the Coast Guard refers to as a "pre-mast" procedure.[94] The Article 15 proceedings are initiated with the accused being "booked" or "placed on report" — the methods for informing the commanding officer, or officer in charge,[95] that an offense may have been committed.[96] The form for accomplishing this is CG-4910, Report of Offense and Disposition.[97] Although the actual procedure for handling a case may

---

88. MCM, Part V, para. 7b.
89. JAGMAN 0116c(1) through (5).
90. Article 15(e), U.C.M.J. *See also* MCM, Part V, para. 7e.
91. JAGMAN 0117e, MCM, Part V, para. 7f(3).
92. JAGMAN 0118b, MCM, Part V, para. 7f(1).
93. *See supra* § 3-5(D). MCM, Part V, para. 4, notes the basic procedures for the Coast Guard.
94. MJM 1-C-1.a.
95. Officers in Charge of Coast Guard units may impose punishment upon personnel assigned to their units, unless that authority has been limited by an officer exercising general court-martial jurisdiction. MJM 1-A-2.a. By Coast Guard regulations, COMDTINST M5000.3(series) Article 4-3-1, an officer in charge of a unit, except Marine Inspection, is defined as a non-commissioned officer, warrant officer, petty officer, or civilian employee assigned to command the unit by the Commandant, area, district, of MLC commander. A civilian officer in charge does not have authority to impose nonjudicial punishment. The Coast Guard has over 200 enlisted personnel in pay grades E6 through E9 serving as officers in charge of small cutters, SAR stations, and aids to navigation teams. These personnel are drawn almost exclusively from the Boatswain Mate rating.
96. MJM 1-C-1.a.
97. Instructions for completing this form are located at Appendix 2a, Military Justice Manual (MJM). The MJM recommends that it be followed step-by-step.

vary with the unit, the normal procedure calls for the executive officer to review the report and refer it to a preliminary inquiry officer, through the administrative office that completes the "background data" portion on the CG-4910.[98] Unless waived, a representative is appointed to assist the servicemember prior to the time of referral of the case to the preliminary inquiry officer.[99]

Upon completing his investigation, the preliminary inquiry officer (PIO) notes his findings on the CG-4910 and recommends disposition of the case.[100] The executive officer again reviews the incident and either dismisses the action, if he has the authority, or recommends the offense be dismissed, disposed of at mast, referred to trial by court-martial, or recommends other measures.[101] If he recommends imposition of nonjudicial punishment, he must first advise the servicemember of the right to refuse "captain's mast" if that right is available.[102] The executive officer has no authority to impose nonjudicial punishment.[103]

§ 3-5(E)(2). Notice.

The "notice" to the accused of the pending nonjudicial punishment is actually accomplished at several stages. During the pre-mast proceedings the accused is advised of the suspected offense, his right to remain silent, and his various Article 15 rights.[104] During the pre-mast proceeding he is able to consult with his representative or his attorney who may also, but need not, be the representative.[105] The mast procedure itself, discussed in the next section, also provides for advisement of the accused's various rights.

§ 3-5(E)(3). Hearing.

The mast hearing, normally held in the wardroom or cabin aboard vessels or in the commander's office ashore, requires the presence of the accused before the commander.[106] Others present might include the executive officer,

---

98. MJM 1-C-3. Because the administrative office may be physically remote from the unit, the preliminary inquiry officer may, as a practical matter, personally obtain the background data from the member's Personnel Data Record held locally.
99. MJM 1-C-3.b.
100. MJM 1-C-4.b. Commanding officers may prescribe a particular format for the preliminary inquiry officer's report.
101. MJM 1-C-5. *See* MJM 1-D-3.a for other measures.
102. MJM 1-C-5.d. See § 3-4 for a general discussion of the right to demand trial.
103. MJM 1-C-5.b. Nonjudicial punishment authority rests solely on the commanding officer. However, the executive officer may administratively rebuke, censure, criticize, or warn a suspected offender.
104. MCM, Part V, para. 4(a), MJM 1-C-5.d.
105. MJM 1-C-5.d. United States v. Kendig, 36 M.J. 291 (C.M.A. 1993) (Service regulations which provide opportunity to consult with counsel before accepting Article 15 punishment do not create a Sixth Amendment right to counsel and do not constitute appointment of counsel). *See also* MJM 1-6.
106. MJM 1-D-1. Traditionally mast was held "before the mast," on the "quarterdeck." A mast held before unit personnel is not prohibited.

the offender's division officer, a master-at-arms, the offender's representative, and the witnesses.[107] Each mast hearing consists of a number of common elements, noted in detail in the Military Justice Manual (MJM). They are summarized here:

    a. *Opening Statement of the Commanding Officer.* The accused is advised of his procedural and substantive rights, including his right to refuse nonjudicial punishment, and the alleged offense.[108]

    b. *Inquiry of the Accused.* The accused is asked whether he chooses to admit or not admit the allegations against him. If the accused admits the allegations, no further evidence need be produced before punishment is imposed.

    c. *Examination of Witnesses.* If the accused chooses not to admit the allegations, the commanding officer examines the witnesses and then may allow the accused or his representative to examine them. The accused is given an opportunity to request additional witnesses.[109]

    d. *Statement by Accused.* The accused may waive his right to remain silent and make a statement in his own behalf.[110] The accused may also present matters in extenuation and mitigation.

    e. *Statements by Executive Officer, Division Officer, Department Head.* The commanding officer in reaching his decision may request comments from either or both the executive officer and the accused's division officer or department head.[111]

After hearing the case,[112] the commander may either dismiss the action, refer the matter to a court-martial or to a superior commander, or impose nonjudicial punishment.[113] Note that punishment may be based upon the findings of a court of inquiry or other investigative body in which the servicemember was accorded the rights of a party.[114]

The punishments, if any, are noted on CG-4910, Nonjudicial Punishment Report.[115] See § 3-6 *infra* for a general discussion of permissible nonjudicial punishments.

---

107. MJM 1-D-1.c. A Yeoman may be present to record the punishment imposed.
108. MJM 1-D-2 through 1-D-4.
109. MJM 1-D-5 through 1-D-6. The MJM further details for the commander general rules of evidence to be employed. MJM 1-D-5.d.
110. MJM 1-D-7.a.
111. MJM 1-D-11.
112. The commander may have to hold several sessions before completing the hearing, although that is unusual. MJM 1-D-8.
113. MJM 1-D-13. The commanding officer may also dismiss the action with a warning. This is *not* considered nonjudicial punishment and no service record entry is made.
114. MJM 1-H-1.
115. MJM 1-D-13. The effective dates of the punishments are stated in MJM 1-E-5. *See also infra* § 3-6(F).

§ 3-5(E)(4). Appeals.

The servicemember's appeal of the nonjudicial punishment must be made within five calendar days[116] and may be based upon either the argument that it was unjust or that it was disproportionate.[117] The appeal, which must be in writing, is first forwarded through the commander who imposed the punishment, who may either reduce the punishment or forward it to the appellate authority, the next superior commissioned officer in the commanding officer's chain of command who has a military lawyer regularly assigned, with an endorsement.[118] The endorsement should contain:

   (a) A statement outlining the proceedings held in the matter;
   (b) A statement of facts found by the commanding officer and considered by him in reaching his decision to impose punishment;
   (c) A statement of reasons as to why the appeal should not be granted;
   (d) The record of the mast (Nonjudicial Punishment Report, CG-4910); and
   (e) Copies of all written documents, statements, or reports relating to the case.[119]

The appeal may, in any case, be referred to a law specialist or lawyer for consideration, but must be referred to one of those individuals if the punishment includes one of those requiring mandatory review under Article 15(e), U.C.M.J.[120]

Upon review, the appellate authority may not increase the punishment[121] but may suspend, mitigate, remit, or set aside any or all of the punishment.[122]

§ 3-6. Punishments.

§ 3-6(A). General.

There are four general categories of punishments that may be imposed under Article 15: (1) reduction in grade; (2) deprivation of liberty; (3) deprivation of pay; and (4) censure. The maximum limits on these punishments are set out in Article 15,[1] but may be further limited by the services.[2] As a general rule, the maximum amount of punishment will depend upon the rank of the officer imposing the punishment and the grade or rank of the individual being

---

116. MCM, Part V, para. 7(d). An appeal shall be submitted within five (5) days of imposition of punishment, or the right to appeal shall be waived in the absence of good cause shown. MJM 1-E-11.
117. MJM 1-E-11.b and c.
118. MJM 1-E-11.d through g.
119. MJM 1-E-11.g. A copy of this endorsement is to be provided to the accused. MJM 1-E-11.h.
120. MJM 1-E-12.b.(1) through (6).
121. MCM, Part V, para. 7(3).
122. MJM 1-E-12.c.
1. *See* Appendix 3.
2. MCM, Part V, para. 5a.

punished. This section addresses the nature of the four categories of punishments and any special rules that may govern their imposition.

§ 3-6(B). Reduction in Grade.

Clearly one of the most severe punishments that may be imposed under Article 15, the reduction in grade both reduces the individual's pay and limits any authority or responsibility that may have been commensurate with his grade. The *Manual,* therefore, urges commanders to use this form of punishment with discretion.[3] In order to reduce an individual under Article 15, the commander must have the general authority to promote the individual to the grade from which he is being reduced.[4] The services have placed further restrictions or impositions on reduction in grade.[5]

§ 3-6(C). Deprivation of Liberty.

Within the general category of deprivation of liberty punishment there are four specific punishments that may be imposed under Article 15: correctional custody, extra duties, restriction, arrest in quarters, and confinement on bread and water or diminished rations.

§ 3-6(C)(1). Correctional Custody.

Correctional custody is defined by the *Manual* as physical restraint during duty or nonduty hours, or both, and may include extra duties, hard labor, or other fatigue duties.[6] Normally, those being punished with correctional custody should not be mingled with persons awaiting trial or those serving court-martial sentences.[7] The services have promulgated further limitations on imposition of this liberty punishment and the categories of individuals who may be placed in correctional custody.[8] Correctional custody does not constitute time lost nor is it confinement.[9]

---

3. MCM, Part V, para. 5c(7).
4. Art. 15(b) (2) (D), (H) (iv), U.C.M.J.; MCM, Part V, para. 5c(7).
5. *See, e.g.*, JAGMAN 0111e, only authorizes reduction to the next inferior grade. The Coast Guard only authorizes reduction for those personnel below the pay grade of E-6, and only to the next inferior grade, MJM 1-E-3.h. An enlisted officer in charge may not impose reduction as a punishment.
The Army has a similar policy. *See* AR 600-200 (servicemembers in grade of E-7 and above may not be reduced by Article 15). The Air Force policy is also similar. *See* AFI 51-202, para. 5.4 and Table 1, Enlisted Punishments.
6. MCM, Part V, para. 5c(4). United States v. Felix, 36 M.J. 903 (A.F.C.M.R. 1993) (correctional custody is form of physical restraint; fact that person is subject to periods of moral restraint does not change inherent status of physical restraint). The Court of Appeals affirmed the decision, on other grounds, 40 M.J. 356 (C.M.A. 1994). The court noted that a servicemember ordered to a facility which did not provide for physical restraint, is not in correctional custody. The court found it unnecessary to speculate as to the true nature of the facility involved in *Felix,* because the accused had admitted to having been placed in correctional custody.
7. MCM, Part V, para. 5c(4).
8. *See, e.g.*, JAGMAN 0111b (limiting punishment to those below grade of E-4). The Army provision is AR 27-10, para. 3-19b(1) (punishment may not be imposed on soldiers in grades PFC

9. 10 U.S.C. § 972 (1994). United States v. Shamel, 22 C.M.A. 361, 47 C.M.R. 116 (1973)

§ 3-6(C)(2)　　　　　MILITARY CRIMINAL JUSTICE　　　　　§ 3-6(C)(5)

§ 3-6(C)(2). Extra Duties.

An individual punished under Article 15 may be required to perform extra duties, i.e., duties in addition to his normally assigned duties. Extra duties may include fatigue duties. But where they are being assessed against noncommissioned or petty officers or other enlisted personnel in a position of responsibility, the extra duties should not demean that position of responsibility.[10]

§ 3-6(C)(3). Restriction.

"Restriction" is the least severe deprivation of liberty punishment and involves moral as opposed to physical restraint.[11] The commanding officer should note, in imposing the punishment, both the length and the designated place for serving the punishment.

§ 3-6(C)(4). Arrest in Quarters.

This punishment is reserved for officers and warrant officers and may be imposed only by general or flag officers in command.[12] The restraint, as in the case of restriction, consists of a moral restraint. The limits of restraint are the individual's "quarters" which, according to the *Manual*, may consist of the individual's "military residence, whether a tent, stateroom, or other quarters assigned to him, or a private residence when government quarters have not been provided."[13]

§ 3-6(C)(5). Confinement on Bread and Water.

Although the punishment of confinement on bread and water, or diminished

---

or above). Any Army commander may impose correctional custody as an Article 15 punishment unless that authority is otherwise withheld or limited. AR 190-34 details the policies and procedures for imposing correctional custody in the Army. The Coast Guard limits the punishment to those below the grade of E-3. *See* MJM, Chapter 1-E-2 and Personnel Manual, COMDINST M1000.6 (series), Chapter 8-E. *See also* AFR 111-9, para. 5, table 1, Table of Permissible Nonjudicial Punishments.

(correctional custody is not confinement; accused not entitled to counsel under Argersinger v. Hamlin, 407 U.S. 25 (1972)); United States v. Felix, 36 M.J. 903 (A.F.C.M.R. 1993), *aff'd on other grounds*, 40 M.J. 356 (C.M.A. 1994) (court concluded that correctional custody places accused under physical restraint whenever he or she has been committed to a designated correctional custody setting (a centralized base facility or designated area within a facility) under the supervision of a monitor, and with knowledge he or she is not to leave except under specified circumstances).

10. MCM, Part V, para. 5c(6). The Coast Guard limits this punishment to those in a grade below E-6, MJM 1-E-2. *See also* JAGMAN 0111d; AFI 51-202, para.5.4 and Tables 1 and 2, Enlisted and Officer Punishments. United States v. Dellarosa, 30 M.J. 255 (C.M.A. 1990) (court doubted whether commander was correct in assuming that extra duties could be imposed for eight hours a day; court noted that prior to changes in 1963, only two hours a day were permitted).
11. MCM, Part V, para. 5c(2).
12. Art. 15(b) (1), U.C.M.J.; MCM, Part V, para. 5c(3).
13. MCM, Part V, para. 5c(3).

rations, is no longer an authorized punishment for a court-martial sentence,[14] it is still a valid form of nonjudicial punishment. It involves confinement in places where the person so confined may communicate only with authorized persons.[15] This punishment may only be imposed on enlisted members who are attached to or embarked in a vessel.[16] If the punishment is to be imposed, a medical officer must first render an opinion that the individual will not suffer serious injury to his health.[17]

§ 3-6(D). Forfeiture of Pay.

"Forfeiture" means a permanent loss of entitlement to the pay forfeited.[18] "Pay" refers only to basic pay plus any sea or foreign duty pay. It does not include special pay such as hazardous duty pay, proficiency pay, or subsistence or quarters allowance.[19] If a forfeiture is imposed in conjunction with a reduction in grade, the amount of forfeiture, expressed in whole dollars only and not in a number of days' pay or fractions of monthly pay, must be computed on the basis of the lower grade.[20]

Before the promulgation of the 1984 changes to the *Manual*, commanders could also impose a punishment of detention of pay, which amounted to a temporary loss of pay; a commander could order that a portion of the servicemember's pay be detained and returned to the individual at the end of the designated period.[21] The drafters of the *Manual*, however, deleted the punishment "because under current centralized pay systems, detention of pay is cumbersome, ineffective, and seldom used."[22]

§ 3-6(E). Censure.

The censure may take the form of either an admonition or reprimand.[23] In the case of an officer, this punishment must be executed in writing.[24] For other personnel, the punishment may be oral unless otherwise prescribed by

---

14. In 1995, the Manual for Courts-Martial was amended to eliminate confinement on bread and water as an authorized court-martial punishment. R.C.M. 1003 Analysis. *See also* § 16-3(C) (Deprivation of Liberty).
15. Art. 15(b) (2) (A), U.C.M.J.; MCM, Part V, para. 5c(5).
16. Article 15(b)(2)(A); MCM, Part V, para. 5b(2)(B)(1). The Court of Appeals has held that a ship undergoing long-term repairs is not a vessel for purposes of confinement on bread and water. United States v. Lorance, 35 M.J. 382 (C.M.A. 1992).
17. MCM, Part V, para. 5c(5). JAGMAN 0111(c) limits this punishment to individuals below the grade of E-4. In the Department of Navy, diminished rations consists of a diet of 2100 calories per day. SECNAVINST 1640.9. *See also* AR 27-10, para. 3-19b. The Coast Guard does not authorize this punishment, MJM 1-E-3.e, nor does the Air Force. *See* table 1, Enlisted Punishments, note 3, AFI 51-202, para. 5.4.
18. MCM, Part V, para. 5c(8).
19. *Id.*
20. *Id.*
21. 1969 MCM, para. 131c(9).
22. MCM, Part V, para. 5 Analysis.
23. MCM, Part V, para. 5c(1).
24. MCM, Part V, para. 5c(1).

the services. Note that this punishment may be administered as a nonpunitive measure in lieu of nonjudicial punishment.[25]

§ 3-6(F). Combination of Punishments.

Subject to some limitations, the *Manual* permits combination of punishments. For example, a typical punishment might include a reduction in grade, extra duties, and forfeitures. The ability to combine punishments is limited by paragraph 5d which provides that:

> d. Limitations on combination of punishments.
>
> (1) Arrest in quarters may not be imposed in combination with restriction;
>
> (2) Confinement on bread and water or diminished rations may not be imposed in combination with correctional custody, extra duties, or restriction;
>
> (3) Correctional custody may not be imposed in combination with restriction or extra duties;
>
> (4) Restriction and extra duties may be combined to run concurrently, but the combination may not exceed the maximum imposable for extra duties;
>
> (5) Subject to the limits in subparagraphs d(l) through (4) all authorized punishments may be imposed in a single case in the maximum amounts.

In addition, the services may place additional restrictions on the ability to combine certain punishments.[26]

The 1969 *Manual* contained a Table of Equivalent Punishments which guided commanders in apportioning punishments.[27] But the drafters of the 1984 amendments to the *Manual* removed the concept of apportionment, because they viewed it as "unnecessary and confusing."[28] Thus that Table was also considered unnecessary.

§ 3-6(G). Effective Dates of Punishments.

Regarding the effective date and execution of punishments, the Manual for Courts-Martial simply states:

> Reduction and forfeiture of pay, if unsuspended, take effect on the date the commander imposes the punishments. Other punishments, if unsuspended, will take effect and be carried into execution as prescribed by the Secretary concerned.[29]

---

25. *Id.* Note that JAGMAN 0114 provides a detailed guide for imposing "censure." *See also* JAGMAN A-1-g (sample punitive letter). The Coast Guard MJM 1-E-3.a (Admonition or Reprimand) provides a form to be used. *See also* MJM 1-F-1, nonpunitive censure, as an administrative measure independent of Article 15.
26. *See, e.g.,* AR 27-10, para. 3-19b(8); JAGMAN 0111; MJM 1-E-2-d.
27. 1969 MCM, para. 131d (Combination and Apportionment).
28. MCM, Part V, para. 5 Analysis.
29. MCM, Part V, para. 5g.

This provision is deceptively simplistic; the services have further prescribed the effective dates and execution of certain punishments.[30] Though the practice varies, some general rules may be noted. Normally, an appeal will either toll or interrupt the imposition of punishments other than reduction or deprivation of pay punishments.[31] Those assigned to vessels may have those punishments deferred until arrival of the vessel in port, and a similar punishment still in effect will defer imposition of the punishment.[32]

§ 3-7. Effect of Errors in Imposition.

The fact that impositions of nonjudicial punishment are not directly reviewed in the military's judicial arena[1] does not mean that relief is not available to a servicemember who has received an improperly imposed punishment. Not every error in the process mandates relief, however. Paragraph 1h of Part V of the *Manual* states:

> *Effect of Errors.* Failure to comply with any of the procedural provisions of Part V of this Manual shall not invalidate a punishment imposed under Article 15, unless the error materially prejudiced a substantial right of the servicemember on whom the punishment was imposed.

Assuming that an error has occurred and the processing of the punishment through the prescribed appellate procedure has not purged the error and its effect, the servicemember has additional avenues of relief. In addition to Article 138, U.C.M.J., Complaints of Wrong,[2] each service has internal measures for examining nonjudicial punishment procedures to ensure compliance with Article 15, the *Manual*, and the service's supplemental manual or regulations.[3] Administrative boards for correction of military records may also provide relief[4] and the federal judicial system, although costly and time-consuming, may order corrective action.[5]

---

30. For specific guidance on the effective dates of the various punishments see AR 27-10, para. 3-21 (Army); AFI 51-202, para. 7.4.1; JAGMAN 0113 (Navy and Marine Corps); MJM 1-E-5 (Coast Guard).

31. *See, e.g.*, AR 27-10, para. 3-21; JAGMAN 0113. *Cf.* Article 15(e), UCMJ (punishment may be imposed during appeal); United States v. Dellarosa, 30 M.J. 255 (C.M.A. 1990). *But see* AFI 51-202, para. 11.2.2 (practical effect of appeal is that collection of forfeitures is delayed).

32. *See, e.g.*, JAGMAN 0113 and MJM 1-E-12 (punishment deferred pending resolution of an appeal may continue to be deferred after final action until arrival of the vessel in port following an underway period). In the case of persons serving on vessels, the execution of the punishment of restriction may be delayed until arrival in port, whether appealed or not. MJM 1-E-3.b.(2). Once commenced, however, restriction runs continuously and cannot be interrupted. MJM 1-E-3.b.(3).

1. The military courts have traditionally declined to grant extraordinary relief to servicemembers challenging nonjudicial punishments. Stewart v. Stevens, 5 M.J. 220 (C.M.A. 1978). *See also infra* Chapter 17. *Cf.* Fletcher v. Covington, 42 M.J. 116 (1995) (misc. docket) (vacating stay of nonjudicial punishment previously granted by Court, 42 M.J. 215, and dismissing petition for extraordinary relief as being moot).

2. *See* Appendix 3.

3. *See, e.g.*, MJM, 1-B.

4. 10 U.S.C. 1552 (1994) authorizes the Secretary of each service to establish procedures to correct any military record.

5. *See, e.g.*, Bennett v. Tarquin, 466 F. Supp. 257 (D. Hawaii 1979) (seven servicemembers

§ 3-8. Consequences of Nonjudicial Punishment.

The imposition of nonjudicial punishment, in addition to the obvious effect of either reducing the servicemember's grade or depriving him of liberty or pay, creates other and longer-lasting effects which should be briefly addressed. Specifically, the servicemember should be aware of the possible impact on his military career and of the fact that the record of the nonjudicial punishment may be later used against him at subsequent administrative board or court-martial proceedings.

§ 3-8(A). Filing Requirements: Military Career.

Unlike a court-martial conviction, which is a federal conviction and may adversely affect a servicemember's ability to find civilian employment, the imposition of nonjudicial punishment (which is not a conviction) is strictly a military record and does not follow the servicemember upon discharge. It may affect the individual's future military service, however.[1] Important here then are the individual service provisions that detail the filing requirements for records of nonjudicial punishment. Because of the complexities of each service's system and the great variance within each service, the pertinent supplements to the *Manual* should be consulted.[2] As a general rule, the services recognize the intent of Article 15, that is, the policy to employ nonjudicial punishment as primarily a corrective or rehabilitative measure. They are, therefore, more likely to provide for only temporary filing of records of nonjudicial punishment for first offenders.[3] Individuals who have had their Article 15 punishments permanently filed may find their opportunities for promotion to higher grades greatly affected. Officers who have received nonjudicial punishment are almost sure to see adverse effects on their careers.

§ 3-8(B). Use at Court-Martial or Administrative Proceedings.

Potential use of the record of the nonjudicial punishment at a later court-martial or administrative proceeding must also be weighed by the servicemember in deciding whether to refuse the offered nonjudicial punishment. This is especially true if the servicemember is aware of pending administrative elimination actions where his prior military record may very well have

---

sought writ of habeas corpus, writ of prohibition, and declaratory judgment).

1. A reduction in grade, for example, that removes the accused from a position of responsibility has an immediate effect. And depending on the service's filing system, the record of nonjudicial punishment may be filed in career management files or other files that are routinely examined by promotion boards.

2. *See, e.g.,* AR 27-10, para. 3-16f Army (summarized); para. 3-36 *et seq.* (formal, DA Form 2627) (permanent or temporary depending on amount of punishment and decision by commander); AFI 51-202, para. 14 (Air Force: The disposition of records of nonjudicial punishment is governed by AFMAN 37-139); JAGMAN 0119 (Navy and Marine Corps: Punishments are noted in the Unit Punishment Book); MJM 1-F-2 (Coast Guard: "Conduct marks").

3. *See, e.g.,* AR 27-10, para. 3-6.

§ 3-8(B) NONJUDICIAL PUNISHMENT: A COMPARATIVE ANALYSIS § 3-8(B)

an impact on his retention in the service.[4]

The possible use of the nonjudicial punishment record at a later court-martial does not normally weigh heavily in the servicemember's decision to accept or refuse nonjudicial punishment. But it is a factor that the command considers in initiating and processing nonjudicial punishment. If an individual is convicted by court-martial, the prosecutor may, subject to service limitations, introduce in evidence during sentencing the accused's military service record which may contain records of nonjudicial punishment.[5] The introduction of such aggravating evidence was addressed in *United States v. Booker.*[6] The court endorsed the importance of nonjudicial punishment[7] but in order to ensure due process, placed parameters on use of nonjudicial punishment records at a court-martial. Before the record of nonjudicial punishment may be admitted, the military judge must be satisfied that the accused fully understood the implications of waiving the right to demand trial by court-martial and did so voluntarily after consulting with a legally trained person.[8] The court also noted that this waiver must be in writing,[9] and if the document did

---

4. The particular service's administrative discharge regulations or instructions should be consulted to determine if records of nonjudicial punishment may be considered in determining the questions of retention and type of discharge.

5. R.C.M. 1001(b)(2) permits the prosecution to present evidence of personal data and the character of prior military service by the accused. That provision specifically mentions punishments under Article 15. *See also* United States v. Brown, 23 M.J. 149 (C.M.A. 1987) (Article 15 punishment is not a prior conviction); United States v. Johnson, 19 C.M.A. 464, 42 C.M.R. 66 (1970); United States v. Edwards, 39 M.J. 528 (A.F.C.M.R. 1994) (record of nonjudicial punishment inadmissible because it did not comport with AF regulations regarding retention of records).

In United States v. Hamilton, 36 M.J. 723 (A.C.M.R. 1992), the Court of Criminal Appeals held that it was error for trial counsel to introduce prior Article 15 punishment for offenses which were later subject of court-martial. Citing United States v. Pierce, 27 M.J. 367 (C.M.A. 1989), the court held that such punishments may not be used for any purpose at trial. The court indicated that the decision to introduce the prior nonjudicial punishment is left to the accused. The Court of Appeals affirmed on other grounds, 41 M.J. 32 (C.M.A. 1994). United States v. Joslin, 47 C.M.R. 271 (A.F.C.M.R. 1973); (vacation of suspended proceedings are part of Article 15 proceedings). See Chapter 16 for discussion of sentencing proceedings.

6. 5 M.J. 238 (C.M.A. 1978) (orig. pub. at 3 M.J. 443 (1971)). The *Booker* decision applies only to those cases tried or retried after the date of the decision, October 11, 1977. United States v. Cannon, 5 M.J. 198 (C.M.A. 1978).

7. The court stated:

We wholeheartedly express our firm belief that those exercising the command function need the disciplinary action provided for under Article 15 ... to meet and complete their military mission.

United States v. Booker, 5 M.J. at 242 (C.M.A. 1978).

8. *See* United States v. Henderson, 7 M.J. 817 (N.C.M.R. 1979) (accused did not validly waive right to demand trial where legal advice was given by a third-year law student serving as a summer intern). *Cf.* United States v. Kelly, 41 M.J. 833 (N.M.Ct.Crim.App. 1995) (en banc) (relying on Nichols v. United States, 114 S.Ct. 1921 (1994), the court concluded that no provision in U.C.M.J. or MCM requires that the servicemember has the right to consult with counsel; court indicated it was time to overrule *Booker*).

9. The court noted that the "writing" should be more than a mere check in a block. United States v. Becker, 5 M.J. at 244 (C.M.A. 1978). *Cf.* United States v. Wheaton, 18 M.J. 159 (C.M.A. 1984) (accused's signature on Art. 15 form that listed the various rights available to him and in the absence of an indication that he elected to be tried by court-martial instead, supported

not establish a knowing and intelligent waiver, the military judge was to conduct an inquiry into the matter.[10]

To meet these requirements, the services either revised their nonjudicial punishment forms or instituted use of separate waiver forms that became a part of the existing forms.[11] At least one court has noted that failure to follow the *Booker* requirements did not invalidate the nonjudicial punishment but rather only affected the later admissibility of the record of punishment.[12] *Booker* was later refined in *United States v. Mack*.[13] Although the court preferred that advice to be in writing, evidence of an oral advice would be sufficient. And, in *United States v. Sauer*,[14] the Court relied upon *Estelle v. Smith*[15] in ruling that the judge's questioning of an accused concerning his prior record of nonjudicial punishment violated his rights against self-incrimination.[16]

Litigation has also centered on illegible or incomplete forms — they will usually be inadmissible at a later court-martial on timely objection by counsel.[17]

---

inference that the accused had waived that right). *See, e.g.,* MJM 1-C-5.d. and enclosures 4a and 4b.

10. United States v. Booker, 5 M.J. at 244 (C.M.A. 1978).

11. Several service appellate court decisions concluded that their service's existing forms were adequate to meet the *Booker* requirements. *See, e.g.,* United States v. Huff, 4 M.J. 731 (A.F.C.M.R. 1978) (AF Form 3070); United States v. Howard, 7 M.J. 962 (A.C.M.R. 1970).

12. United States v. Lemon, 5 M.J. 750 (A.F.C.M.R. 1978).

13. 9 M.J. 300 (C.M.A. 1980). United States v. Wiggers, 25 M.J. 587 (A.C.M.R. 1987) (defense objection to Article 15 should have alerted trial judge to inquire into whether accused had been afforded the opportunity to see counsel).

14. 15 M.J. 113 (C.M.A. 1983), *overruling* United States v. Mathews, 6 M.J. 357 (C.M.A. 1979), *and* United States v. Spivey, 10 M.J. 7 (C.M.A. 1980). *Cf.* United States v. McGary, 12 M.J. 760 (A.C.M.R. 1981) (counsel waived defects under Rule 103(a), MIL. R. EVID.).

United States v. Adolph, 13 M.J. 775 (A.C.M.R. 1982) (defects in stating nonjudicial punishment offense not sufficient to preclude admissibility at trial). *See also* United States v. Atchison, 13 M.J. 798 (A.C.M.R. 1982).

15. 451 U.S. 454 (1981).

16. *See also* United States v. Nichols, 13 M.J. 154 (C.M.A. 1982).

17. *See, e.g.,* United States v. Yarbough, 33 M.J. 122 (C.M.A. 1991) (court rejected arguments that Navy nonjudicial punishment, which was pending appeal, should not have been admitted during sentencing; court rejected argument that the form itself was illegal; court noted that R.C.M. 1001(b) (2) contemplates that Service Secretaries have discretion as to the forms used); United States v. Blair, 10 M.J. 54 (C.M.A. 1980) (incomplete appellate advice); United States v. Guerro, 10 M.J. 52 (C.M.A. 1980) (no SJA review on form); United States v. Carmas, 10 M.J. 50 (C.M.A. 1980) (signatures missing); United States v. Burl, 10 M.J. 48 (C.M.A. 1980) (appellate action block was blank); United States v. Cross, 10 M.J. 34 (C.M.A. 1980) (signatures indiscernible); United States v. Gordon, 10 M.J. 31 (C.M.A. 1980) (no appellate action shown); United States v. Negrone, 9 M.J. 171 (C.M.A. 1980) (appellate review incomplete).

United States v. Sink, 27 M.J. 920 (A.C.M.R. 1989) (Article 15 form admissible despite absence of indication on form of the method used by accused to present evidence in extenuation and mitigation); United States v. Merrill, 25 M.J. 501 (A.F.C.M.R. 1987) (nonjudicial punishment form was admissible despite fact that accused's written response to commander's intent to impose punishment was missing); United States v. Balcom, 20 M.J. 558 (A.C.M.R. 1985) (on appeal the court reassessed the sentence when it was demonstrated through appellate exhibits that an Article 15 admitted at trial had afterwards been removed from the accused's records as a result of an ABCMR ruling).

APPENDIX REFERENCES

Appendix 1. Abbreviations.
Appendix 2. Glossary.
Appendix 3. U.C.M.J.
Appendix 4. Court-Martial Flow Chart.
Appendix 5. Nonjudicial Punishment Forms.
Appendix 30. Maximum Punishment Chart.

ANNOTATED BIBLIOGRAPHY

BOOKS

Byrne, *Military Law* (1981).

    This third edition work is a good introductory text to military law. It includes text material, discussion cases, self-quizzes, and appendices that contain forms and tables. The discussion cases, although now dated, cover significant areas of courts-martial practice.

PERIODICALS

"Bibliography of Military Law," 10 Am. Crim. L. Rev. 175 (1971).

    This extensive bibliography lists finding aids, books, symposiums, surveys, service publications, and selected writings in legal periodicals. Most entries predate the 1968 amendments to the U.C.M.J.

Imwinkelried & Gilligan, "The Unconstitutional Burden of Article 15: A Rebuttal," 83 Yale L.J. 534 (1974).

    In rebutting an earlier article on Article 15 *infra*, the authors present a good overview of nonjudicial punishment and reject any arguments that the process is constitutionally infirm. Finally, the authors take issue with proposed alternatives to Article 15 because they would in the long run work to the detriment of the servicemember.

Miller, "A Long Look at Article 15," 28 Mil. L. Rev. 37 (1965).

    This article presents a comprehensive overview of the use of Article 15 punishments in the Army. Covered are the topics of the historical underpinnings of nonjudicial punishment, a brief examination of constitutional protections extended to or withheld from the accused, and the types of punishments that might be imposed. The author concludes that Article 15 presents commanders with a much-needed disciplinary tool.

Note, "A Sixth Amendment Right to Counsel Under Article 15 of the Uniform Code of Military Justice," 72 Mich. L. Rev. 1431 (1974).

    The author briefly reviews the constitutional underpinnings of *Argersinger v. Hamlin*, 407 U.S. 25 (1972), and presents arguments for requiring counsel at an Article 15 proceeding where correctional custody is imposed. His position is grounded on the rationale that correctional custody amounts to confinement — a conclusion rejected in *United States v. Shamel,* 22 C.M.A. 361, 47 C.M.R. 116 (1973).

Note, "The Unconstitutional Burden of Article 15," 82 YALE L.J. 1481 (1973).

The author addresses the dilemma faced by an accused offered nonjudicial punishment — waive the right to demand a trial and the accompanying constitutional protections, or demand trial and risk much more severe punishment. In conclusion the author suggests four alternatives to Article 15: (1) Congress could abolish Article 15; (2) Congress could eliminate the right to a special court-martial; (3) Congress could provide all procedural rights at the Article 15 level; or (4) Congress could maintain the special court-martial, but limit its maximum punishment to that of the level initially chosen by the commander.

Salisbury, "Nonjudicial Punishment Under Article 15 of the Uniform Code of Military Justice: Congressional Precept and Military Practice," 19 SAN DIEGO L. REV. 839 (1982).

Arguing that the military has used Article 15 nonjudicial punishment procedures in a manner not intended, the author maintains that the procedures, especially in the Navy, are used to bypass jurisdiction requirements and that the imposition of punishment unduly stigmatizes the servicemember. The author proposes, *inter alia,* that records of nonjudicial punishment be destroyed, that no use be made of such punishments at courts-martial, and some modifications be made in the provisions governing the ability of servicemembers assigned to ships to demand trial by court-martial.

CHAPTER 4

JURISDICTION

Part I
Introduction

§ 4-1. General.
§ 4-2. The Nature of Court-Martial Jurisdiction.
    § 4-2(A). A Creature of Statute.
    § 4-2(B). Requisites of Jurisdiction.
§ 4-3. Jurisdictional Limits of Courts-Martial.
    § 4-3(A). General Court-Martial.
    § 4-3(B). Special Court-Martial.
    § 4-3(C). Summary Court-Martial.

Part II
Personal Jurisdiction

§ 4-4. General.
§ 4-5. Inception of Jurisdiction: A Change of Status.
    § 4-5(A). Enlistment: Voluntary Entry.
        § 4-5(A)(1). Valid Enlistments.
        § 4-5(A)(2). Void Enlistments: Minors; Involuntary; Incompetent.
        § 4-5(A)(3). Effect of Recruiter Misconduct.
        § 4-5(A)(4). Constructive Enlistment.
    § 4-5(B). Induction: Involuntary Entry.
    § 4-5(C). Appointment of Officers.
§ 4-6. Jurisdiction Over Reservists and Members of National Guard.
§ 4-7. Jurisdiction Over Civilians.
    § 4-7(A). In Wartime.
    § 4-7(B). In Peacetime.
§ 4-8. Termination of Personal Jurisdiction.
    § 4-8(A). Continuing Jurisdiction.
    § 4-8(B). General Rule: Discharge Terminates Status.
    § 4-8(C). Exceptions to the General Rule.
        § 4-8(C)(1). Reenlistment Discharges.
        § 4-8(C)(2). Article 3(a) Offenses.
        § 4-8(C)(3). Fraudulent Discharge.
        § 4-8(C)(4). Deserters.
        § 4-8(C)(5). Persons in Custody.
    § 4-8(D). Retired Members.
§ 4-9. Pleading and Proving Personal Jurisdiction.

Part III
Jurisdiction Over the Offense

§ 4-10. Introduction.
§ 4-11. The Service Connection Requirement: 1969-1987.
    § 4-11(A). Applying the *Relford* Factors.
    § 4-11(B). Military Retreat from the *Relford* Ad Hoc Analysis.
    § 4-11(C). *Solorio v. United States:* The Demise of the Service Connection Requirement.
        § 4-11(C)(1). The Constitutional Implications of *Solorio.*
        § 4-11(C)(2). The Practical Implications of *Solorio.*
§ 4-12. Exclusive, Reciprocal, and Concurrent Jurisdiction.

§ 4-12(A). State and Federal Courts.
§ 4-12(B). Foreign Courts.

PART IV

CONVENING AND COMPOSITION OF COURTS-MARTIAL;
REFERRAL OF CHARGES TO COURT

§ 4-13. General.
§ 4-14. Authority to Convene a Court-Martial.
    § 4-14(A). The Convening Authority.
        § 4-14(A)(1). Statutory Authorization.
        § 4-14(A)(2). Disqualifications.
        § 4-14(A)(3). Delegation of Authority.
    § 4-14(B). Convening Orders.
§ 4-15. Properly Composed Court-Martial.
    § 4-15(A). Military Judge.
    § 4-15(B). Counsel.
    § 4-15(C). Court Members.
§ 4-16. Charges Properly Referred to Court-Martial.
Appendix References.
Annotated Bibliography.

PART I

INTRODUCTION

§ 4-1. General.

At the very heart of any court-martial lies the requirement of jurisdiction — the power of a court to try and determine a case and to render a valid judgment.[1] The sources of court-martial jurisdiction rest in the Constitution, specifically Article I, which authorizes Congress to promulgate rules for the government and regulation of the armed forces;[2] consequently, courts-martial are not considered a part of the Article III system of United States courts. Further, they are recognized in the Fifth Amendment, which expressly exempts

---

1. This chapter addresses the power, the jurisdiction, of the military establishment to govern itself through "military law." MCM, Part 1, para. 2(a)(1). A principal agency for exercising that power is the court-martial. But military law is only one of four recognized methods of exercising military jurisdiction. The second means of exercising such power is through "military government," which may be established by a belligerent occupying enemy lands. MCM, Part 1, para. 2(a)(3). The authority for such power derives from the power of the occupying country to protect its resources and to maintain order under principles of international law. See Madsen v. Kinsella, 343 U.S. 341 (1952); Mechanics' & Traders' Bank v. Union Bank, 89 U.S. (22 Wall.) 276 (1875). The third means is through "martial law," which generally consists of a government exercising temporary control over its own civilian populace — usually in times of public necessity caused by civil war or invasion. MCM, Part 1, para. 2(a)(2). See Ex parte Milligan, 71 U.S. (4 Wall.) 2 (1866) (no jurisdiction to try civilian by military commission when state courts were operating). The fourth method of exercising military jurisdiction is by enforcement of the laws of war—usually war crimes cases. MCM, Part 1, para. 2(a)(4). See, e.g., Ex parte Quirin, 317 U.S. 1 (1942) (trial of German saboteurs who landed in U.S.); In re Yamashita, 327 U.S. 1 (1946) (trial of Japanese general).

2. See U.S. CONST. art. 1, § 8.

those cases "arising in the land and naval forces" from the requirements of presentment and indictment by a grand jury.[3]

The Congress, with its constitutional mandate, has provided "jurisdiction" articles in the Uniform Code of Military Justice (U.C.M.J.).[4] For example, Articles 2 and 3 enumerate those individuals who are subject to court-martial jurisdiction, and Articles 16 to 21 prescribe the jurisdictional limits of general, special, and summary courts-martial. This chapter addresses those statutory provisions, the pertinent Manual for Courts-Martial language, and the case law that continues to fashion court-martial jurisdiction.

§ 4-2. The Nature of Court-Martial Jurisdiction.

Courts-martial are solely disciplinary, or penal, in nature.[1] They may try only criminal cases and adjudge only criminal sentences.[2] They have no authority to adjudge civil remedies such as the payment of damages or the collection of private debts.[3] Unlike the federal courts, the location of the offense need not dictate the place of trial.[4] An exception to that general rule would be for those federal or state offenses prosecuted under Article 134, U.C.M.J.[5] when the court would be required to sit within the territorial limits of the particular statute. Nor is it necessary for court-martial jurisdiction that the offense occurred within the geographical limits of the United States; the U.C.M.J. applies in all places.[6]

§ 4-2(A). A Creature of Statute.

The courts, in referring to the nature of the court-martial, often label it as a "creature of statute,"[7] a phrase that sets the appropriate tone for any discussion of court-martial jurisdiction. Practitioners working within the system of military justice must be ever cognizant that only after a variety of jurisdictional prerequisites have been satisfied may a court-martial properly hear a case and render a valid judgment. The opportunities for jurisdictional defects are many and the effect of any such defect is the same: the court-martial is void.

---

3. U.S. CONST., Amend. V. The Air Force is included within this provision. *See, e.g.,* United States v. Naar, 2 C.M.R. 739 (A.F.B.R. 1951).
4. *See* Appendix 3.
1. *See* R.C.M. 201(a)(1).
2. R.C.M. 201(a).
3. R.C.M. 201(a)(1). A summary court-martial, however, is authorized to administer the affairs of deceased servicemembers, 10 U.S.C. § 4712 (1988) and conduct inquests, 10 U.S.C. § 4711 (1988).
4. R.C.M. 201(a)(1). *See, e.g.,* United States v. Gravitt, 5 C.M.A. 249, 17 C.M.R. 249 (1954). Venue is not a jurisdictional issue. United States v. Lahman, 12 M.J. 513 (N.M.C.M.R. 1981); United States v. Moody, 10 M.J. 845 (N.C.M.R. 1981).
5. *See supra* § 2-6.
6. Art. 5, U.C.M.J. *Cf. infra* § 4-10.
7. McClaughry v. Deming, 186 U.S. 49 (1902).

§ 4-2(B). Requisites of Jurisdiction.

In every court-martial there are three primary elements or requisites that must be met in order for jurisdiction to vest:

(1) The court-martial must have personal jurisdiction over the accused;
(2) The court-martial must have jurisdiction over the offense; and
(3) The court-martial must be properly convened and composed and the charges before it must have been properly referred to it.

These three prerequisites[8] form the analytical framework for discussion in Parts II, III, and IV of this chapter.

§ 4-3. Jurisdictional Limits of Courts-Martial.

In addition to the requisites of jurisdiction noted in the preceding section, Congress has outlined limits of jurisdiction for each of the three courts-martial: general, special, and summary. Those limits extend to persons who may be tried, the cognizable offense, and the maximum amount of punishment which may be imposed by each court. For a comparison of the limits on the punishments that may be imposed by each type of court, see Appendix 31.

§ 4-3(A). General Court-Martial.

Unless otherwise indicated by regulations, anyone subject to the Uniform Code of Military Justice may be tried, for any offense, by general court-martial (GCM).[1] The general court-martial may also try civilian personnel charged with committing war crimes.[2] The jurisdictional limits or permissible punishments are normally set for each offense in Part IV of the Manual for Courts-Martial.[3] Certain punishments are mandatory,[4] however, while others are specifically excluded.[5]

§ 4-3(B). Special Court-Martial.

A special court-martial (SPCM), unless otherwise limited by regulations, may try any person subject to the U.C.M.J. for noncapital offenses.[6] Unless lower limits are set by the *Manual*,[7] no special court-martial may impose a sentence that exceeds a bad conduct discharge, confinement for more than six

---

8. The three are sometimes broken into five categories, the third being further separated into the elements of (a) properly convened, (b) properly composed, and (c) properly referred to trial. *See* R.C.M. 101(b).
1. Art. 18, U.C.M.J.
2. *Id.* R.C.M. 202(b).
3. *See* §§ 16-2 and 16-3 and Appendix 30.
4. *See, e.g.,* Arts. 106, 118(1) and (4) where the death penalty is mandatory. *See also* Art. 51(b)(1), U.C.M.J.
5. Cruel and unusual punishments are prohibited. Art. 55, U.C.M.J.
6. Art. 19, U.C.M.J.; R.C.M. 201(f).
7. *See* Appendix 30 and Part IV, MCM.

months, hard labor without confinement for three months, or forfeiture of two-thirds pay per month for six months.[8] A bad-conduct discharge may be imposed as part of a special court-martial sentence only if: (1) a military judge was detailed to the trial, (2) a qualified defense counsel was detailed to represent the accused, and (3) a verbatim record of the proceedings was prepared.[9] The Army specifies an additional requirement: A bad-conduct discharge may be adjudged only if a general court-martial convening authority has convened the special court.[10]

§ 4-3(C). Summary Court-Martial.

The summary court-martial (SCM) may try only enlisted personnel, with their consent, for any offenses not capital.[11] The maximum permissible punishment that may be adjudged may not exceed confinement for more than one month, hard labor without confinement for more than forty-five days, restriction for more than two months, or forfeiture of more than two-thirds of one month's pay.[12] If more than one form of deprivation of liberty is to be imposed, there must be an apportionment of the punishments.[13] Note that if the accused is in the fourth enlisted grade (E-4), or higher, the summary court may not impose any form of confinement, hard labor without confinement, or reduction except to the next inferior grade.[14]

PART II

PERSONAL JURISDICTION

§ 4-4. General.

To be valid, a court-martial must have personal jurisdiction over the accused: The accused must have been subject to the U.C.M.J. both at the time of the offense and at the time of trial without any valid intervening termination of military service.[1] A court-martial that is properly convened and constituted has the power to try any accused subject to the Uniform Code of Military

---

8. Art. 19, U.C.M.J.
9. Art. 19, U.C.M.J. Counsel must meet the qualifications of Article 17(b), U.C.M.J. An exception to the requirement for the presence of a military judge is allowed if physical conditions or military exigencies prevent such; the convening authority of that case must present a detailed written explanation as to why a military judge was not detailed. The Army does not apply this exception to those situations where the Judge Advocate General has permitted a GCM convening authority, who otherwise does not exercise that authority, to convene a BCD SPCM. *See* AR 27-10, para. 5-25.
10. Army Reg. 27-10, para. 5-24.
11. Art. 10, U.C.M.J.; R.C.M. 201(f). *See* Middendorf v. Henry, 411 U.S. 25 (1976) for a discussion of nature of the summary court-martial. *See also* United States v. Booker, 5 M.J. 246 (C.M.A. 1978). See generally Chapter 15, part IV for summary court-martial procedures.
12. Art. 20, U.C.M.J.; R.C.M. 202(f), 1301(c).
13. *See* R.C.M. 1003(b)(6), (7), (9).
14. R.C.M. 1301(d)(2).
1. *See infra* § 4-8.

Justice.[2] The fact that the accused is not a member of the convening authority's command does not divest the court of jurisdiction.[3] Personal jurisdiction is a question of "status."[4] That is, the accused must possess the legal status of a servicemember, or a person otherwise subject to the U.C.M.J. before personal jurisdiction may vest. Article 2, U.C.M.J., generally defines those individuals who are subject to the U.C.M.J.:

> Members of a regular component of the armed forces, including those awaiting discharge after expiration of their terms of enlistment; volunteers from the time of their muster or acceptance into the armed forces; inductees from the time of their actual induction into the armed forces; and other persons lawfully called or ordered into, or to duty in or for training in, the armed forces, from the dates when they are required by the terms of the call or order to obey it.[5]

The remaining portions of Article 2 delineate specific categories of individuals who are also subject to the U.C.M.J.[6]

The discussion in this part will center on the inception and termination of personal jurisdiction. Also addressed are brief discussions of jurisdiction over reservists, members of the National Guard, and civilians.

§ 4-5. Inception of Jurisdiction: A Change of Status.

A change of status, from civilian to servicemember, occurs when an individual enters military service. The change, which affects all persons, may be voluntary, as in the enlistment process, or involuntary, as in the induction process. In all cases, the change of status is effective upon the taking of the applicable oath.[1]

§ 4-5(A). Enlistment: Voluntary Entry.

An enlistment provides the means for voluntarily changing one's status from civilian to servicemember. The vehicle for "enlisting" is the enlistment

---

2. United States v. Murphy, 30 M.J. 1040 (A.C.M.R. 1990).
3. *Id.* Service regulations may provide guidance on attachment of an accused to a particular command for purposes of court-martial jurisdiction. *See, e.g.,* AR 27-10, para. 5-2 (commanders involved should concur in the attachment).
4. Toth v. Quarles, 350 U.S. 11 (1955).
5. Art. 2(a), U.C.M.J.
6. United States v. Odegard, 25 M.J. 140 (C.M.A. 1987) (trial of Air Force Academy cadet). Although Article 2(a)(2) provides that "Cadets, aviation cadets and midshipmen" are amenable to court-martial jurisdiction; ROTC cadets are not. Woodrick v. Divich, 24 M.J. 147 (C.M.A. 1987); United States v. Sassaman, 32 M.J. 687 (A.F.C.M.R. 1991) (trial of Air Force Academy cadet).
1. Art. 2(b), U.C.M.J. (enlistment); Billings v. Truesdell, 321 U.S. 542 (1944) (induction). *Cf.* United States v. Cline, 29 M.J. 83 (C.M.A. 1989) (reservist ordered to active duty for two weeks was subject to jurisdiction one minute after midnight on the day he was supposed to report for duty; the court rejected the argument that he was not subject to court-martial jurisdiction until he actually departed for his duty station).

contract[2] or agreement, which in many respects is comparable to a contract for personal services.[3] But the enlistment is unique. In addressing its nature and effect, the Supreme Court in *In re Grimley*[4] compared the enlistment to a marriage and stated that in the process of enlisting

> something more is involved than the making of a contract, whose breach exposes to an action for damages. Enlistment is a contract; but it is one of those contracts which changes the status....[5]

In the succeeding years the military courts have emphasized the change of status language,[6] while the civilian courts have emphasized the contractual nature of the enlistment.[7]

The law of enlistments is complex. It generally involves both administrative and criminal issues, the two not always coinciding. A material breach of contract by the government, for example, may give rise to grounds for a valid administrative discharge.[8] It will not, however, necessarily relieve an accused from first being court-martialed for criminal conduct.[9] For the most part, any analysis tends to turn on a few basic requirements: Was the enlistment valid at its inception? If not, did the accused at some later point voluntarily effect a "constructive enlistment"?[10] If the answer is "yes" to either of these questions, there will normally be court-martial jurisdiction.

§ 4-5(A)(1). Valid Enlistments.

There are two requirements for a valid enlistment: voluntariness and competency.[11] The accused must have voluntarily enlisted and at the time of enlistment must have been competent to so enlist. The simplicity of the for-

---

2. The enlistment contract is contained in DD Form 4.
3. *See generally* Schlueter, "The Enlistment Contract: A Uniform Approach," 77 MIL. L. REV. 1 (1977). *See also* Casella, "Armed Forces Enlistment: The Use and Abuse of Contract," 39 U. CHI. L. REV. 783 (1972).
4. 137 U.S. 147 (1890).
5. In re Grimley, 137 U.S. at 151 (1890).
6. *See, e.g.,* United States v. Blanton, 7 C.M.A. 664, 23 C.M.R. 128 (1957).
7. *See, e.g.,* Bemis v. Whalen, 341 F. Supp. 1289 (S.D. Cal. 1912).
8. *See, e.g.,* Novak v. Rumsfeld, 423 F. Supp. 971 (N.D. Cal. 1976); Woodrick v. Divich, 24 M.J. 147 (C.M.A. 1987) (court noted that although accused might have requested discharge in lieu of court-martial, he was taking the position that he was not even in the armed services because of a material misrepresentation in his enlistment contract). *See generally* Dilloff, "A Contractual Analysis of the Military Enlistment," 8 U. RICH. L. REV. 121 (1974).
9. *See, e.g.,* Woodrick v. Divich, 24 M.J. 147 (C.M.A. 1987); United States v. Davis, 8 M.J. 575 (A.C.M.R. 1979), *citing* Dickenson v. Davis, 245 F.2d 317 (10th Cir. 1951); United States v. Imler, 17 M.J. 1021 (N.M.C.M.R. 1984) (accused unsuccessfully argued that material breach of his enlistment contract precluded jurisdiction).
10. *See infra* § 4-5(A)(4).
11. These two requirements are derived from the Supreme Court's decision in *In re Grimley*, 137 U.S. 147 (1890).

mula ends there because Congress, in exercising its "war powers," has prescribed the requirements for "competency":

> No person who is insane, intoxicated, or a deserter from an armed forces or who has been convicted of a felony, may be enlisted in any armed force. However, the Secretary concerned may authorize exceptions, in meritorious cases for the enlistment of deserters and persons convicted of felonies.[12]

Congress has also limited enlistments to individuals who are at least seventeen but less than thirty-five years of age,[13] and who meet citizenship requirements.[14] The various services in their recruiting regulations or manuals have further defined those categories of qualified individuals who may enlist.[15] Failure to meet either the statutory or regulatory criteria does not automatically void the enlistment. Nor does it necessarily spell the absence of personal jurisdiction, although uncured void enlistments, discussed in the next section, normally will not support jurisdiction.

§ 4-5(A)(2). Void Enlistments: Minors; Involuntary; Incompetent.

An enlistment may be void for purposes of personal jurisdiction if the accused, at the time of enlistment, was a minor,[15] was "incompetent,"[16] or enlisted involuntarily.[17] Each of these nonwaivable disqualifications may be

---

12. 10 U.S.C. § 505 (1994).
13. 10 U.S.C. § 504 (1994).
14. 10 U.S.C. § 3253 (1994).
15. *See, e.g.,* Army Reg. 601-210, Regular Army Enlistment Program.
15. Morrisey v. Perry, 137 U.S. 157 (1890); United States v. Blanton, 7 C.M.A. 664, 23 C.M.R. 128 (1957). An enlistment by an individual between the ages of 17 and 18 must have parental consent. Lack of consent creates a voidable enlistment. 10 U.S.C. § 1170 (1988). *See also* United States v. Bean, 13 C.M.A. 203, 32 C.M.R. 203 (1962); United States v. Scott, 11 C.M.A. 655, 29 C.M.R. 471 (1960).
16. "Incompetency" is generally limited here to those defects amounting to the inability to mentally assent to military status, *i.e.,* insanity and intoxication, although that term is often used to describe a broader range of disqualifying defects. *See, e.g.,* United States v. Hirsch, 26 M.J. 800 (A.C.M.R. 1988) (accused unsuccessfully argued that he was mentally incompetent to enlist); United States v. Julian, 45 C.M.R. 876 (N.C.M.R. 1971) (servicemember intoxicated at time of enlistment but later formed constructive enlistment); In re Judge's Petition, 148 F. Supp. 80 (S.D. Cal. 1956) (servicemember must show that he was insane on date of enlistment). *See also* 39 Comp. Gen. 742 (1960) (no basis for regarding servicemember as insane unless he has been subject of prior judicial determination of mental incompetence). Low entrance scores and mild mental retardation do not necessarily amount to lack of mental capacity to enlist. United States v. Jones, 50 C.M.R. 92 (A.C.M.R. 1975).
17. Typically, the involuntary enlistment arises in the "Join The Army or Go to Jail" enlistments. *See, e.g.,* United States v. Catlow, 23 C.M.A. 142, 48 C.M.R. 758 (1974) (coerced volunteer).

United States v. Ghiglieri, 25 M.J. 687 (A.C.M.R. 1987) (accused was placed on unsupervised probation provided he enlisted in armed forces; court noted its "grave concern" that civilian authorities are again using military service as an alternative to prosecution or confinement on civilian charges); United States v. Hurd, 8 M.J. 555 (N.C.M.R. 1979) (deceived recruit's service was involuntary). *Cf.* United States v. Wagner, 5 M.J. 461 (C.M.A. 1978) (accused's enlistment in

§ 4-5(A)(2)   JURISDICTION   § 4-5(A)(2)

later cured by a voluntary constructive enlistment, discussed in § 4-5(A)(4) *infra*. Normally, an enlistment violative of a service regulation will not be void.[18]

Amendments to Article 2, U.C.M.J., in 1979[19] reduced, in theory, the number of disqualifying factors. Subsection (b) of Article 2 now provides:

> The voluntary enlistment of any person who has the capacity to understand the significance of enlisting in the armed forces shall be valid for purposes of jurisdiction under subsection (a) of this section, and a change of status from civilian to member of the armed forces shall be effective upon the taking of the oath of enlistment.

Arguably, this provision ignores the age and competency requirements noted in § 4-5(A) *supra*. Congress intended, in amending Article 2, to reaffirm the Supreme Court's decision in *In re Grimley*[20] by requiring only two elements for a valid enlistment: (1) capacity to understand the significance of enlisting, and (2) voluntary taking of the oath of enlistment.[21] Again, even absent these two criteria, a valid constructive enlistment may be later effected.[22]

Taking a slightly different tack from the foregoing statutory provision is a line of military cases which declares as void those enlistments where intentional recruiter misconduct smoothed the enlistment path for an accused with

---

lieu of civilian trial was not involuntary); United States v. Hosford, 11 M.J. 762 (N.M.C.M.R. 1981) (voluntary enlistment to avoid charges).

In United States v. Jarrell, 12 M.J. 917 (N.M.C.M.R. 1982), the court rejected the argument that the service's inability to assign him to a specialty noted in his enlistment contract gave rise to an involuntary enlistment. If there was in fact a breach of contract, the accused could seek administrative or habeas relief. *See generally* § 17-23.

In United States v. Bachand, 16 M.J. 896 (A.C.M.R. 1983), the court rejected the accused's arguments that because he enlisted reluctantly to avoid civilian charges his enlistment was involuntary. *See generally* Dilloff, "The Involuntary Volunteer: Coerced Military Enlistments," 25 Am. U. L. Rev. 437 (1976).

18. *See, e.g.*, United States v. Wagner, 5 M.J. 461 (C.M.A. 1978); United States v. Lightfoot, 4 M.J. 262 (C.M.A. 1978).

19. Articles 2 and 36, U.C.M.J., were amended by Congress in the Defense Authorization Act for FY 1980 (S. 418), Pub. L. No. 96-107 (9 Nov. 1979). The amendment to Article 2 and its potential effect on court-martial jurisdiction are discussed in detail at Schlueter, "Personal Jurisdiction Under Article 2, U.C.M.J.: Whither Catlow, Russo, and Brown?", ARMY LAW., Dec. 1979, at 3.

In United States v. McDonagh, 14 M.J. 415 (C.M.A. 1983), the court ruled that the 1979 amendments to Article 2 would apply retroactively to offenses not military in nature; for military offenses *ex post facto* problems would arise because the amendments eliminated the *Catlow-Russo* rule, which was in effect a "defense" to the government's allegation that the accused possessed military status. *See also* United States v. Marsh, 15 M.J. 252 (C.M.A. 1983) (crime of unauthorized absence was military in nature and Art. 2 amendments may not be applied retroactively as to accused); United States v. McGinnis, 15 M.J. 345 (C.M.A. 1983); United States v. Robertson, 21 M.J. 747 (N.M.C.M.R. 1985).

See Ross, "Russo Revitalized," ARMY LAW., May 1983, at 9.

20. 137 U.S. 147 (1890).

21. Senate Report 96-197, Defense Authorization Act, 1980 (S. 428) at 121. United States v. Hirsch, 26 M.J. 800 (A.C.M.R. 1988) (there was ample evidence to support the trial judge's conclusion that the accused voluntarily and knowingly took his oath of enlistment and thus changed his status from civilian to servicemember).

22. *See infra* § 4-5(A)(4).

a nonwaivable defect. The next section addresses the effect of recruiter misconduct on the enlistment process.

§ 4-5(A)(3). Effect of Recruiter Misconduct.

Relying on public policy grounds, the Court of Military Appeals in *United States v. Russo*[23] ruled that where a recruiter has intentionally enlisted a disqualified recruit, the resulting enlistment is void *ab initio*. The government, according to the court, could not enter into illegal enlistment contracts and then "rely upon the change of status doctrine as a shield to avoid judicial scrutiny."[24] The *Russo* doctrine was applied in a variety of settings, the emphasis resting upon the recruiter's misconduct.[25] The court, however, has modified the *Russo* rule to apply only in those cases where the conduct of the recruiter is intentional and where the defect goes only to nonwaivable criteria.[26]

Amendments to Article 2, U.C.M.J., in 1979 spurred to some extent by *Russo* and its progeny, were intended to override the *Russo* doctrine, which had voided personal jurisdiction in a number of courts-martial.[27]

§ 4-5(A)(4). Constructive Enlistment.

The constructive enlistment rests on a legal doctrine of implied contracts; the courts will give effect to the mutual intent of the parties notwithstanding

---

23. 1 M.J. 134 (C.M.A. 1975). Russo suffered from dyslexia, which impaired his ability to read. The recruiter assisted him by providing the answers to the entrance tests. This, said the court, amounted to violation of the fraudulent enlistment article (Art. 84, U.C.M.J.) and rendered the enlistment void, on public policy grounds.
24. United States v. Russo, 1 M.J. at 137 (C.M.A. 1975).
25. *See, e.g.*, United States v. Torres, 7 M.J. 102 (C.M.A. 1979); United States v. Little, 1 M.J. 476 (C.M.A. 1976); United States v. Muniz, 1 M.J. 151 (C.M.A. 1975); United States v. Cronier, 14 M.J. 1 (C.M.A. 1982).
26. United States v. Stone, 8 M.J. 140 (C.M.A. 1979). In reaching its decision the court made no reference to the statutory change to Article 2, U.C.M.J. which had occurred barely a month earlier. *See also* United States v. Buckingham, 11 M.J. 184 (C.M.A. 1981); United States v. Long, 17 M.J. 661 (N.M.C.M.R. 1983); United States v. Andrews, 17 M.J. 717 (N.M.C.M.R. 1983); United States v. Matthews, 13 M.J. 501 (A.C.M.R. 1982) (en banc).
27. In discussing the *Russo* doctrine the Senate Armed Services Committee stated in part:

> The committee strongly believes that these doctrines serve no useful purpose, and severely undermine discipline and command authority. No military member who voluntarily enters the service and served routinely for a time should be allowed to raise for the first time after committing an offense defects in his or her enlistment, totally escaping punishment for offenses as a result. That policy makes a mockery of the military justice system in the eyes of those who serve in the military services.

Senate Report 96-197, Defense Authorization Act, 1980 (S. 428) at 121. *See also* Woodrick v. Divich, 24 M.J. 147, 150 (C.M.A. 1987) (noting fact that *Russo* was criticized in some quarters). For a discussion of that criticism, see Schlueter, "The Enlistment Contract: A Uniform Approach," 77 MIL. L. REV. 1 (1977).

defects in the enlistment process.[28] Factors from which a constructive enlistment may be inferred include (1) receipt of pay and benefits, (2) voluntary submission to military authority, (3) acceptance of service by the military, and (4) actual performance of military duties. Time spent involuntarily in the service, such as periods of confinement, does not normally constitute a constructive enlistment.[29] The doctrine was codified in 1979 as an amendment to Article 2, U.C.M.J.,[30] Subsection (c), of that Article now provides:

Notwithstanding any other provision of law, a person serving with an armed force who—

(1) submitted voluntarily to military authority;
(2) met the mental competency and minimum age qualifications of section 504 and 505 of this title at the time of voluntary submission to military authority;
(3) received military pay or allowances; and
(4) performed military duties;

is subject to this chapter until such person's active service has been terminated in accordance with law or regulations promulgated by the Secretary concerned.

The amendment was designed to overrule those military decisions that had estopped the prosecution from showing a constructive enlistment where recruiters had fraudulently enlisted an accused.[31] Note that the two common elements of voluntariness and competency, discussed in § 4-5(A)(1) *supra*, are also present in subsection (c). Again the language is broad and generally registers the Congressional intent to allow court-martial jurisdiction over individuals who might otherwise be serving under defective enlistments.[32]

---

28. United States v. King, 11 C.M.A. 19, 28 C.M.R. 243 (1959). *See also* United States v. Hirsch, 26 M.J. 800 (A.C.M.R. 1988) (accused effected constructive enlistment); United States v. Ghiglieri, 25 M.J. 687 (A.C.M.R. 1987) (constructive enlistment found where accused initially entered Army under nonwaivable moral disqualification in recruiting regulations—accused had been given choice of entering Army or going to jail).

29. *See, e.g.*, United States v. Santiago, 1 C.M.R. 365 (A.B.R. 1951). Likewise, five days of service has been held to be too short to constitute a constructive enlistment. United States v. Williams, 39 C.M.R. 471 (A.B.R. 1968).

30. Defense Authorization Act for FY 1980 (S. 428). Pub. L. No. 96-197 (9 Nov. 1979).

31. *See, e.g.*, United States v. Brown, 13 C.M.A. 162, 48 C.M.R. 778 (1974). Senate Report 96-197 Defense Authorization Act, 1980 (S. 428) at 122.

32. The provision was considered broad enough to support personal jurisdiction over a reserve officer who had been placed on active duty in violation of Air Force directives in United States v. Ernest, 32 M.J. 135 (C.M.A. 1991). The Senate Report indicated that:

A person who initially does not voluntarily submit to military authority or who lacks the capacity to do so may do so successfully at a later time and jurisdiction shall attach at that moment. As a result, an individual who fails to meet the minimum age requirements set forth by statute, 17 years of age at present, may form a constructive enlistment upon reaching that age. Similarly, an individual who initially submits to military authority because he or she is given a choice between jail or military service and who subsequently does not protest the enlistment, make any effort to secure his or her release, and accepts pay or allowances may effect a constructive enlistment for jurisdictional purposes.

§ 4-5(B). Induction: Involuntary Entry.

Inductees are amenable to court-martial jurisdiction from the time of their "actual induction."[33] The "involuntariness" of the induction process draws close scrutiny from the courts and the cases where the validity of the induction, and thus court-martial jurisdiction, has been questioned, generally center on three areas: (1) the induction itself; (2) the standards for a valid induction; and (3) waiver of defects.

As to the induction itself, a number of accuseds have argued that they never properly completed the induction ceremony.[34] Those arguments generally present a factual question to be determined by the courts.[35] The military courts have found what amounts to constructive induction, however, where the accused went through an induction ceremony (although defective) and then voluntarily submitted to military status.[36]

The second area goes to the question of what effect, if any, the failure to meet induction requirements might have on personal jurisdiction. Attempts to void inductions on arguments that the pertinent statutory requirements[37] have not been satisfied have met with mixed results. In most cases the inquiry will turn on the question of whether the particular requirement was intended for the benefit of the government or the inductee.[38]

The third category of cases addresses the issue of waiver of the right to assert defects or exemptions. If, for example, an accused is entitled to an exemption from induction and fails to assert that exemption prior to committing an offense, the courts will normally rule that the accused has waived the

---

Senate Report 96-197 Defense Authorization Act, 1980 (S. 428) at 123. *See also* United States v. McDonagh, 10 M.J. 698 (A.C.M.R. 1981); United States v. Boone, 10 M.J. 715 (A.C.M.R. 1981).

33. Billings v. Truesdell, 321 U.S. 641 (1944); Mayborn v. Heflebower, 145 F.2d 864 (5th Cir. 1944), *cert. denied*, 315 U.S. 864 (1945); United States v. Scheunemann, 14 C.M.A. 479, 34 C.M.R. 259 (1964).

34. Billings v. Truesdell, 311 U.S. 541 (1944); Mayborn v. Heflebower, 145 F.2d 864 (5th Cir. 1944), *cert. denied*, 315 U.S. 854 (1945); United States v. Scheunemann, 14 C.M.A. 479, 34 C.M.R. 259 (1964); United States v. Ornelas, 2 C.M.A. 96, 6 C.M.R. 96 (1952).

35. United States v. Ornelas, 2 C.M.A. 96, 6 C.M.R. 96 (1952).

36. United States v. Rodriguez, 2 C.M.A. 101, 6 C.M.R. 101 (1952). *Cf.* United States v. Hall, 17 C.M.A. 88, 37 C.M.R. 352 (1967) (no constructive induction where there was no induction ceremony and accused never voluntarily served in spite of accepting pay and benefits).

37. The standards are prescribed in the Military Selective Service Act, 50 U.S.C. § 451 *et seq. See also* 32 C.F.R. Chapter XVI.

38. *See, e.g.,* United States v. Martin, 9 C.M.A. 568, 26 C.M.R. 348 (1958) (failure to meet minimum test score did not render accused ineligible for induction); Korte v. United States, 260 F.2d 633 (9th Cir. 1958), *cert. denied*, 358 U.S. 928 (1959) (prior felony conviction could be waived by the armed forces). A good discussion of the law of "conscription" and the attendant problems is presented in Chapter 2 of Zillman, Blaustein & Sherman, *The Military in American Society* (1978).

exemption.[39] In *United States v. McNeill*,[40] the accused was entitled to an exemption, but the court, in finding jurisdiction over the accused, stated:

> [H]e failed to show for any reason for an exemption; he reported for duty; he was housed, fed, clothed, and possibly paid for six weeks, and then, when selected for possible overseas duty, he went absent. To allow such an exemption to be exercised in that manner and at that late date would allow an inductee to enter upon his duties as a soldier and then abandon the service according to his own whims without fear of punishment.[41]

In *United States v. Burden*,[42] however, the Court of Appeals voided an induction where the failure to pass the entrance exam and the inability to read and write English constituted a nonwaivable bar. This, coupled with recruiter misconduct, rendered the induction void.[43]

§ 4-5(C). Appointment of Officers.

Personal jurisdiction may also be exercised over officers who have received appointments in the armed forces and ordered to active duty.[44] The process of appointment, which changes the individual's "status" and which may be accomplished either by the President or the Secretary concerned, consists of three elements: (1) making of the appointment by proper authority; (2) tender of the appointment to the individual; and (3) acceptance of the appointment by the individual.[45] The effective date of the appointment is normally the date of acceptance, although the pertinent service regulations should be consulted for special situations. Article 2, U.C.M.J., provides that jurisdiction over the officer will vest at the time of being ordered to active duty.[46]

§ 4-6. Jurisdiction Over Reservists and Members of National Guard.

Personal jurisdiction may exist over reservists on active duty[1] or during periods of inactive duty for training (IDT),[2] and members of a state's National

---

39. *See, e.g.*, Pickens v. Cox, 181 F.2d 784 (10th Cir. 1960).
40. 2 C.M.A. 383, 9 C.M.R. 13 (1953).
41. United States v. McNeill, 2 C.M.A. at 387, 9 C.M.R. at 17 (1953).
42. 1 M.J. 89 (C.M.A. 1975).
43. The court relied upon its rationale in United States v. Russo, 1 M.J. 134 (C.M.A. 1975). *See* § 4-5(A)(3).
44. Art. 2, U.C.M.J.
45. The President's authority to appoint officers derives from Article II of the U.S. Constitution. For a discussion of the appointment process, see DA Pamphlet 27-11, Military Administrative Law.
46. United States v. Davis, 8 M.J. 575 (A.C.M.R. 1979).
1. "Active duty" is defined in 10 U.S.C. § 101(22) (1988) as:

> "[f]ull-time duty in the active military service of the United States. It includes duty on the active list, full-time training duty, annual training duty and attendance, while in the active military service, at a school designated as a service school by law or by the Secretary of the military department concerned."

---

2. Art. 2(a)(3) U.C.M.J.

Guard may be subject to court-martial jurisdiction while on active duty for training (ADT).[3]

With respect to jurisdiction over reservists, the services are unanimous in exercising jurisdiction over individuals who are on "active duty." Historically, there was a split, however, on the question of exercising jurisdiction over those individuals who are on inactive duty for training. In the past the Army and the Air Force, as a matter of policy, exercised court-martial jurisdiction under Article 2(a)(3) only in situations where the reservist was using expensive or dangerous equipment.[4] The Navy, Coast Guard, and Marines exercised jurisdiction in all situations involving reserve training.[5] Article 2(a)(3), U.C.M.J.,[6] now explicitly extends jurisdiction over:

> Members of a reserve component while on inactive duty training, but in the case of members of the Army National Guard of the United States or the Air National Guard of the United States only when in federal service.

In those instances where court-martial jurisdiction is being exercised, the prosecution must establish that (1) the individual was actually on inactive duty training; (2) the training was performed pursuant to written orders; (3) the orders stated that the individual was subject to the U.C.M.J.; and (4) the individual voluntarily accepted those orders.[7] In the past if the government intended to prosecute a reservist on inactive duty training, it had to do so during a period of drill where the foregoing elements were met.[8] The ability to invoke the foregoing statutory provisions was limited if the reservist's period of active, or inactive, duty was interrupted. In *United States v. Caputo*,[9] the accused, a Naval reservist, committed an offense while on his two-week ADT. After his release from that period of duty, the government processed charges

---

United States v. Lwin, 42 M.J. 279 (1995) (accused properly ordered to active duty during mobilization; Executive orders tolled processing of application for conscientious objector status). In United States v. Cline, 29 M.J. 83 (C.M.A. 1989), the court concluded that notwithstanding the accused's active duty orders, which required him to report for duty at 1600 hours, he was subject to court-martial jurisdiction for an offense committed at 0830 hours. The court distinguished active duty status and active duty service and noted that his status changed at 0001 hours on the date of his self-executing orders, the date of his offense.

3. 10 U.S.C. § 511 (1988).
4. United States v. Abernathy, 48 C.M.R. 205, 206 (C.G.C.M.R. 1974).
5. *Id. See also* Duncan v. Usher, 23 M.J. 29 (C.M.A. 1986); United States v. Caputo, 18 M.J. 269 (C.M.A. 1984) (thorough discussion of jurisdiction over reservists); United States v. Schuering, 16 C.M.A. 324, 36 C.M.R. 480 (1966).
6. *See* Appendix 3.
7. United States v. Abernathy, 48 C.M.R. 205 (C.G.C.M.R. 1974).
8. Wallace v. Chafee, 451 F.2d 1374 (9th Cir. 1911); United States v. Schuering, 16 C.M.A. 314, 36 C.M.R. 480 (1966). *See generally* Partington, "Court-Martial Jurisdiction over the Weekend Reservist: Wallace v. Chafee," 7 U. SAN FRAN. L. REV. 57 (1972); Comment, "The Weekend Warrior and the Uniform Code of Military Justice: Does the Military Have Jurisdiction Over Weekend Reservists?," 7 CAL. W.L. REV. 238 (1970); Note, "Constitutional Law: Military Jurisdiction Over Inactive Reservists," 27 JAG J. 129 (1972); "Recent Decision, *Wallace v. Chafee*," 23 CASE W. RES. L. REV. 668 (1972).
9. 18 M.J. 259 (C.M.A. 1984). *See generally* Partington, "Court-Martial Jurisdiction Over Weekend Reservists After *United States v. Caputo*," 37 NAV. L. REV. 183 (1988).

and when the accused reported for his regularly scheduled IDT, he was advised of his rights, informed of the charges, and placed in pretrial confinement. Although it found no constitutional deficiency in Article 2(a)(3), U.C.M.J., the court relied in part on the 1969 *Manual*[10] for the proposition that once a reservist's period of ADT or IDT ends, any jurisdiction that the government might have had over offenses within that period is interrupted and is saved only by several recognized exceptions — none of which applied here.[11]

The court also suggested that if the government had acted with a view toward trial during the accused's two-week ADT, that his subsequent release would not have terminated jurisdiction.[12] Noting some practical problems of extending ADT or IDT status, the court commented that Congress might wish to consider amending the U.C.M.J. to provide for ordering a "reservist to active duty for purposes of court-martial."[13]

Congress responded in 1986 by amending both Articles 2 and 3, U.C.M.J.[14] There is now statutory authority to order a reservist to active duty involuntarily for purposes of nonjudicial punishment,[15] an Article 32 investigation,[16] or trial by court-martial[17] for offenses committed while on active duty or inactive duty training.[18] Further, termination of the period of active duty or inactive duty training does not terminate jurisdiction.[19] Reservists who fail to

---

10. 1969 MCM, para. 11a.

11. *See infra* § 4-8. United States v. Poole, 20 M.J. 598 (N.M.C.M.R. 1985) (once the accused, a reservist, had been released from his active duty for training period, personal jurisdiction lapsed as to offenses committed during that period of active duty).

12. United States v. Caputo, 18 M.J. at 293 (C.M.A. 1984), *citing* United States v. Schuering, 16 C.M.A. 324, 36 C.M.R. 480 (1966); United States v. Rubenstein, 7 C.M.A. 523, 36 C.M.R. 313 (1957). *See also* Duncan v. Usher, 23 M.J. 29 (C.M.A. 1986) (reservist's release from active duty terminated jurisdiction over offenses committed while on active duty—even though there had been no break in his reserve status and he was back on active duty several days later. In dissent, Judge Cox criticized the "Jack-in-the-Box" approach to personal jurisdiction).

13. United States v. Caputo, 18 M.J. at 267 (C.M.A. 1984).

14. *See* Appendix 3.

15. Art. 2(d)(1)(C), U.C.M.J. *See also* Chapter 3.

16. Art. 2(d)(1)(A), U.C.M.J. *See, e.g.,* Murphy v. Garrett, 29 M.J. 469 (C.M.A. 1990) (Marine reserve officer ordered to active duty for Article 32 investigation of charges committed while on active duty). *See also* Chapter 7.

17. Art. 2(d)(1)(B), U.C.M.J.

18. Art. 2(d)(2), U.C.M.J. The changes also apply to members of the National Guard only when in federal service. *Id.* In Murphy v. Dalton, 81 F.3d 343 (3rd Cir. 1996), the court concluded that no jurisdiction existed over a Marine reserve officer who had been charged with offenses committed during his service as a member in the regular component of the Marine Corps. The court interpreted the term "active duty" in Article 2(d)(2)(A) refers to active duty as a reservist, not to active duty served in another component of the armed forces.

19. Art. 3(d), U.C.M.J. This assumes that the servicemember is still a member of the armed forces. In Murphy v. Garrett, 29 M.J. 469 (C.M.A. 1990), the court held that a Marine officer's discharge did not preclude jurisdiction for offenses committed while he was still on active duty; the court noted but did not decide the constitutional challenges. Significant here was the fact that the accused had maintained some contact with the Marine Corps Reserve after his discharge. *See also infra* § 4-8. The Court of Appeals for the Third Circuit later concluded, however, that the Marine officer's discharge from the regular component effectively terminated jurisdiction and

satisfactorily perform their military duties during periods of inactive duty training (IDT) may be involuntarily ordered to active duty.[20] Where the government has prosecuted servicemembers who were so ordered to active duty, the courts will closely examine the required statutory and regulatory process. Failure of the government to follow its own regulations will normally void jurisdiction[21] unless the servicemember waived the defect prior to committing an offense.[22]

Members of the National Guard[23] may be ordered to "active duty for training" (ADT) as prescribed by 10 U.S.C. § 511 (1994).[24] During that period, which normally runs for a time sufficient in length for the individual to successfully complete a designated phase of training, the individual is subject to court-martial jurisdiction.[25] The individual may not be initially ordered to active duty or retained beyond the scheduled training period without the consent of the "governor or other appropriate authority of the State."[26]

The state's "consent" extends to a guardsman's retention on active duty in accordance with regulations and statutes then in effect.[27] It includes travel time authorized by joint travel regulation.[28]

§ 4-7. Jurisdiction Over Civilians.

Article 2, U.C.M.J., specifically provides for jurisdiction over "persons serving with or accompanying an armed force in the field" in time of war[1] and also provides for jurisdiction over "persons serving with, employed by, or accompanying the armed forces outside the United States...."[2] In effect, these two provisions attempt to subject civilians to the U.C.M.J. The attempt has only been successful in part.[3]

---

rejected the arguments that personal jurisdiction existed under Article 2(d) or Article 3(a). Murphy v. Dalton, 81 F.3d 343 (3rd Cir. 1996).

20. 10 U.S.C. § 673(a) (1988). *See* Hoersch v. Froehlke, 382 F. Supp. 1235 (E.D. Pa. 1974). In 1980, the Army discontinued the involuntary activation process, deciding to rely instead on available administrative, nonjudicial, and judicial methods of enforcing discipline. United States v. Arthur, 2 M.J. 481 (A.C.M.R. 1975). See generally "Involuntary Activation," 10 The Advocate 1 (1980); Baldwin & McMenis, "Disciplinary Infractions Involving USAR Enlisted Personnel: Some Thoughts for Commanders and Judge Advocates," ARMY LAW., Feb. 1981, at 5.

21. *See, e.g.*, United States v. Kilbreth, 22 C.M.A. 390, 47 C.M.R. 327 (1973).

22. United States v. Barraza, 5 M.J. 230 (C.M.A. 1978).

23. The term "National Guard" means the Army National Guard and the Air Force National Guard. 32 U.S.C. § 191 (1994).

24. *See also* 32 U.S.C. § 101 *et seq.* (1994) for organization and training of National Guard. Convening and composition of courts-martial for National Guard not in federal service is addressed in 32 U.S.C. §§ 326 to 329.

25. *See, e.g.*, United States v. Self, 13 M.J. 132 (C.M.A. 1982). In re Taylor, 160 F. Supp. 932 (W.D. Mo. 1958).

26. 10 U.S.C. § 672(d) (1988). United States v. Peel, 4 M.J. 28 (C.M.A. 1977). *Cf.* United States v. Hudson, 5 M.J. 413 (C.M.A. 1978).

27. United States v. Self, 13 M.J. 132 (C.M.A. 1982).

28. United States v. Pearson, 13 M.J. 140 (C.M.A. 1982).

1. Art. 2(a)(1), U.C.M.J.

2. Art. 2(a)(11), U.C.M.J.

3. *See* Gibson, "Lack of Extraterritorial Jurisdiction Over Civilians: A New Look at an Old Problem," 148 MIL. L. REV. 114 (1995); Everett & Hourck, "Crime Without Punishment—Ex-Servicemen, Civilian Employees, and Dependents," 13 JAG L. REV. 184 (1971).

The ability to exert military jurisdiction is of some concern because of the vital functions that civilian technicians and support personnel often provide the government in overseas stations. Because jurisdiction over civilians in peacetime is nonexistent, see § 4-7(B), there is no effective deterrent for essential civilian personnel to remain at their posts overseas when world tensions indicate that war is imminent. Several proposals have been considered, including the possibility of amending Articles 85 and 86 to hold such employees accountable for desertion or absence without leave under limited circumstances.[4]

§ 4-7(A). In Wartime.

The courts, both civilian and military, have recognized as constitutional the provisions of Article 2(a)(10), which subjects civilians to court-martial jurisdiction if they are serving or accompanying an armed force, in the field, in a time of war. The courts have generally focused on the terms "in the field"[5] and "accompany"[6] and have sustained court-martial jurisdiction over a civilian, for example, who was engaged in transporting supplies and troops to a battle zone.[7] In *United States v. Averette*,[8] however, the court reversed a court-martial conviction of a civilian employee working with the armed forces in Vietnam. The court declared that the term "time of War" in Article 2 means a war formally declared in Congress. The court stated:

> We emphasize our awareness that the fighting in Vietnam qualifies as a war as that word is generally used and understood. By almost any standard of comparison — the number of persons involved, the level of casualties, the ferocity of the combat, the extent of the suffering, and the impact on our nation — the Vietnamese armed conflict is a major military action. But such a recognition should not serve as a shortcut for a formal declaration of war, at least in the sensitive area of subjecting civilians to military jurisdiction.[9]

The "sensitive area of subjecting civilians to military jurisdiction" during times of war has not been directly confronted by the Supreme Court, but in

---

4. *See generally* Gates & Casida, "Report to The Judge Advocate General by the Wartime Legislation Team," 104 MIL. L. REV. 139, 147-49 (1984).
5. *See* R.C.M. 202(a) Analysis, which indicates that "in the field" relates to "military operations with a view to the enemy," citing 14 Op. Att'y Gen. 22 (1872). *See also* Hines v. Mikell, 259 F. 28 (4th Cir. 1919) (activity, not locality, is determinative); In re Berue, 54 F. Supp. 252 (S.D. Ohio 1944); McCune v. Kilpatrick, 53 F. Supp. 80 (E.D. Va. 1943) (merchant ship transporting troops and supplies).
6. *See* R.C.M. 202(a) Analysis. In re DiBartolo, 50 F. Supp. 929 (S.D.N.Y. 1943). A civilian may be subject to jurisdiction even though not formally employed by the government.
7. *See, e.g.,* McCune v. Kilpatrick, 53 F. Supp. 80 (E.D. Va. 1943). *See also* Latney v. Ignatius, 416 F.2d 821 (D.D.C. 1969).
8. 19 C.M.A. 363, 41 C.M.R. 363 (1970).
9. *Id.* at 365, 41 C.M.R. at 365. *Cf.* United States v. Anderson, 17 C.M.A. 588, 38 C.M.R. 386 (1968) (Vietnam hostilities were time of war for purposes of statute of limitations). *See supra* § 2-2(E)(5).

decisions affecting civilians during peacetime, *see* § 4-7(B), the Court has implied that during wartime, the commander's broad powers of punishment might be properly exercised in those extraordinary circumstances present in an area of actual fighting.[10]

§ 4-7(B). In Peacetime.

The Supreme Court has directly addressed the validity of Article 2(a)(11), U.C.M.J., which provides for jurisdiction over persons "serving with, employed by, or accompanying" the armed forces outside the United States.[11] In a series of decisions, the Court has ruled as invalid any attempts, during peacetime, to provide for court-martial jurisdiction over civilians[12] for capital[13] and noncapital[14] offenses committed overseas. The cases have turned on the rationale that the requisite "status" was lacking.[15]

§ 4-8. Termination of Personal Jurisdiction.

The servicemember's status is determinative in personal jurisdiction questions. He must have been subject to the U.C.M.J. when he committed the offense and must be subject when he is tried, and in the interim the status must not have been terminated. This section examines the concept of continuing jurisdiction,[1] the general rule that "discharge" terminates jurisdiction,[2] and the exceptions to that rule.[3] Finally, the question of jurisdiction over retired members will be addressed.[4]

---

10. In Reid v. Covert, 354 U.S. 1, 33 (1957), the Court stated that:

    In the face of a hostile enemy, military commanders have broad power over persons on the battlefront. From a time prior to the adoption of the Constitution the extraordinary circumstances present in an area of actual fighting have been considered sufficient to permit punishment of some civilians in that area by military courts under military rules (citations omitted).

11. Article 2(a)(11) also attempts to extend jurisdiction over civilians accompanying the armed forces and outside the United States, the Canal Zone, Puerto Rico, Guam, and the Virgin Islands.
12. No distinction has been made by the courts between civilian dependents and civilian employees. *See, e.g.,* Grisham v. Hagan, 361 U.S. 278 (1960).
13. Grisham v. Hagan, 361 U.S. 278 (1960) (employee); Reid v. Covert, 354 U.S. 1 (1957) (dependent); Kinsella v. Krueger, 359 U.S. 1 (1957) (dependent).
14. Kinsella v. United States *ex rel.* Singleton, 361 U.S. 234 (1960) (dependent); McElroy v. United States *ex rel.* Guagliardo, 361 U.S. 281 (1960) (employee); Wilson v. Bohlender, 361 U.S. 281 (1960) (employee).
15. *See generally supra* § 4-4.
1. § 4-8(A) *infra.*
2. § 4-8(B) *infra.*
3. § 4-8(C) *infra.*
4. § 4-8(D) *infra.*

§ 4-8(A). Continuing Jurisdiction.

The mere expiration of an individual's enlistment (a designated period of military service) does not in itself terminate jurisdiction.[5] Article 2(a)(1), U.C.M.J., specifically provides that servicemembers remain subject to the U.C.M.J. while "awaiting discharge after expiration of their terms of enlistment."[6] The Manual for Courts-Martial amplifies this by noting that court-martial jurisdiction may attach and continue past the scheduled expiration date if action, prior to discharge, is initiated to try the servicemember.[7] Action with a view to trial includes apprehension, arrest, confinement, or filing of charges.[8] If after expiration of the enlistment, however, the servicemember demands a discharge and no action is taken by the government (within a reasonable time) to try him, jurisdiction may not vest.[9] In *United States v. Poole*,[10] the court concluded that jurisdiction exists despite delay, even unreasonable delay, by the government in discharging an accused at the end of his enlistment. The court rejected the argument that a "constructive discharge" takes place when a servicemember is retained beyond the enlistment. The court noted, however, that an accused in that position might have a defense to some military offenses.

---

5. United States v. Klunk, 3 C.M.A. 92, 11 C.M.R. 92 (1953); United States v. Douse, 12 M.J. 473 (C.M.A. 1982); R.C.M. 202(c)(1).
6. *See* Appendix 3.
7. R.C.M. 202(c). United States v. Fairchild, 16 M.J. 746 (A.F.C.M.R. 1983) (accused's discharge and reenlistment was a nullity but preferral of charges prior to expiration of enlistment provided continuing jurisdiction). *See generally* Zeigler, "The Termination of Jurisdiction over the Person and the Offense," 10 Mɪʟ. L. Rᴇᴠ. 139 (1960).
8. *Id. See* United States v. Self, 13 M.J. 132 (C.M.A. 1982) (Army took sufficient action where accused was targeted as a suspect; he was summoned for an interview, apprised of the charges and advised of his rights); United States v. Handy, 14 M.J. 202 (C.M.A. 1982) (government preferred charges); United States v. Fitzpatrick, 14 M.J. 394 (C.M.A. 1983) (charges preferred after accused protested continued status); United States v. Weise, 7 M.J. 993 (A.C.M.R. 1979); United States v. Beard, 7 M.J. 452 (C.M.A. 1979); United States v. Wheeley, 6 M.J. 220 (C.M.A. 1979). *See also* United States v. Morrison, 22 M.J. 743 (N.M.C.M.R. 1986) (preferral of charges and pretrial restraint); United States v. Brown, 11 M.J. 769 (N.M.C.M.R. 1981) (notice to accused that he would be tried was sufficient to continue his status).

The servicemember's status may be continued under the U.C.M.J. even in the absence of compliance with service regulation requiring affirmative action to do so. United States v. Hutchins, 4 M.J. 190 (C.M.A. 1978); United States v. Williams, 21 M.J. 524 (A.C.M.R. 1985).

A servicemember may consent to remain on active duty. *See, e.g.*, United States v. Bowman, 9 M.J. 676 (A.C.M.R. 1980) (servicemember consented to remain on active duty while civil action was pending in German courts).

9. United States v. Hutchins, 4 M.J. 190 (C.M.A. 1978). *See also* United States v. Hout, 19 C.M.A. 299, 41 C.M.R. 299 (1970); United States v. Douse, 12 M.J. 473 (C.M.A. 1982) (jurisdiction continued where prosecution proceeded at fairly rapid pace in bringing charges); United States v. McDowell, 34 M.J. 719 (N.M.C.M.R. 1992) (accused actually or impliedly consented to continuation on active duty by signing notice accepting assignment in reserve program).
10. 30 M.J. 149 (C.M.A. 1990).

§ 4-8(B). General Rule: Discharge Terminates Status.

The general rule seems clear. Delivery[11] of the discharge certificate[12] terminates status notwithstanding service regulations that may allow for a later "effective" time for the discharge.[13] After delivery is made,[14] status is terminated and may not be revived unless an exception exists. Those exceptions are noted in the following sections.

---

11. United States v. King, 42 M.J. 79 (1995) (citing three prongs of *King* requirements for valid discharge, court held that in personam jurisdiction existed where accused had neither picked up paycheck nor completed clearing process prior to his apprehension). In United States v. Brunton, 24 M.J. 566 (N.M.C.M.R. 1987), the court attempted to distinguish the "delivery" rule in *Howard*. The accused in *Brunton* received his discharge certificate while on leave at home several days before its effective date but was informed only hours later that the discharge was not effective. The court noted that the delivery in this case was in contravention of Navy regulations that indicate that discharge certificates should not be issued until the actual date of separation. Moreover, he had not received his final pay and when he returned to his command he consented to an "extension" of his enlistment.

Cf. United States v. Palumbo, 27 M.J. 565 (A.C.M.R. 1988) (preparation of discharge paper and showing it to accused did not amount to "delivery").

12. In United States v. Garvin, 26 M.J. 194 (C.M.A. 1988), the court, in three separate opinions, concluded that the mistaken delivery of a bad-conduct discharge that had no legal effect and that had been revoked did not end court-martial jurisdiction over the accused. The court noted that the delivery of the discharge certificate had not been accomplished with the intent required to deliver a valid discharge.

13. United States v. Howard, 20 M.J. 353 (C.M.A. 1985); United States v. Cortte, 36 M.J. 767 (N.M.C.M.R. 1992) (citing *King*, court held that no jurisdiction existed to try accused for offenses committed in prior enlistment; accused was discharged and reenlisted the next day); United States v. Thompson, 21 M.J. 854 (A.C.M.R. 1986); United States v. Scott, 11 C.M.A. 646, 29 C.M.R. 462 (1960). Note that the service regulations generally indicate that the discharge is effective at midnight on the day of delivery of the discharge. *Cf.* United States v. Meadows, 13 M.J. 165 (C.M.A. 1982); United States v. Barbeau, 9 M.J. 569 (A.F.C.M.R. 1980), *petition denied*, 9 M.J. 277 (C.M.A. 1980) (in dicta the court notes that the time stated in regulations is controlling).

A different rule exists with regard to discharges delivered solely for the purpose of reenlisting. In that case, not only must there be delivery of a valid discharge certificate, but there must also be a final accounting of pay and out-processing in accordance with service regulations. United States v. King, 27 M.J. 327 (C.M.A. 1989).

14. Where the servicemember is being discharged pursuant to "self-executing" orders, the effective date for termination of jurisdiction will normally be the effective date on the orders. *See, e.g.*, United States v. Smith, 4 M.J. 265 (C.M.A. 1978). *See also* United States v. Mansbarger, 20 C.M.R. 449 (A.B.R. 1955); United States v. Hamm, 36 C.M.R. 656 (A.B.R. 1966).

United States v. Meadows, 13 M.J. 165 (C.M.A. 1982) (enlistee in Regular Army received what appeared to be "self-executing orders"; court questioned whether those orders contemplated further steps toward actual separation).

Cf. United States v. Batchelder, 41 M.J. 337 (1994) (distinguishing Howard, court held that delivery of discharge certificate did not terminate jurisdiction because the commander did not make an informed decision to release the accused because the records clerk did not follow the instructed procedures, that the documents clearly stated that discharge would not occur until a later date, and the document was given to the accused as a matter of administrative convenience).

§ 4-8(C). Exceptions to the General Rule.

The U.C.M.J. makes provision for exception to the general rule that discharge terminates the military status of a servicemember.

The first exception rests on judicial interpretation of what constitutes a "discharge." The next three are specifically noted in Article 3, U.C.M.J, and the fifth finds its basis in judicial interpretations of Article 2(a)(8), U.C.M.J.

§ 4-8(C)(1). Reenlistment Discharges.

It has been common practice to discharge a servicemember at the expiration of a period of enlistment, or earlier, and then immediately reenlist him. Under what became known as the *Ginyard* rule,[15] any discharge terminated jurisdiction. This rule was abandoned to some extent in *United States v. Clardy*.[16] Thus, if the servicemember is discharged solely for purposes of reenlisting, and there is no interruption in his military status, jurisdiction will not lapse for offenses committed during the prior enlistment.[17] In *United States v. King*,[18] the accused was delivered a discharge certificate so that he could reenlist but upon receipt refused to do so. Noting a distinction between discharges issued at the end of completed enlistment obligations and those issued solely for the purposes of reenlistment, the court held that to accomplish an early discharge, three elements must be met: (1) a valid discharge certificate or Certificate of Release (DD 214) must be delivered; (2) there must be a final accounting of pay; and (3) the servicemember must have been "cleared" in accordance with service regulations.

If there is an interruption then the prosecution must rely on one of the other exceptions, *infra*.

§ 4-8(C)(2). Article 3(a) Offenses.

Article 3(a), U.C.M.J., as amended in 1992,[19] provides that discharge of a servicemember will not bar jurisdiction over him for offenses committed during a prior period of service, if he is currently subject to court-martial jurisdic-

---

15. United States v. Ginyard, 16 C.M.A. 512, 37 C.M.R. 132 (1967). For a good discussion of this rule and its implications, see Woodruff, "The Rule in Ginyard's Case—Congressional Intent or Judicial Field Expedient?," 21 A.F. L. Rev. 285 (1979).
16. 13 M.J. 308 (C.M.A. 1982), overruling United States v. Ginyard, 16 C.M.A. 512, 37 C.M.R. 132 (1967). The rule is to be applied prospectively. *See also* United States v. Calhoun, 13 M.J. 322 (C.M.A. 1982) (*Clardy* does not apply to short-term discharges on or before July 12, 1982).
17. *See, e.g.*, United States v. Clark, 35 M.J. 730 (A.F.C.M.R. 1992) (record established that court had jurisdiction over accused for offense committed in prior enlistment; court noted that reenlistment records need not be introduced in every case involving reenlistment but court and counsel should carefully examine charge sheet to note any potential problems); United States v. Fairchild, 33 M.J. 970 (A.F.C.M.R. 1991) (accused was subject to jurisdiction of court for offense committed in prior enlistment; court used term "*Clardy* gap"); United States v. Moore, 22 M.J. 523 (N.M.C.M.R. 1986).
18. 27 M.J. 327 (C.M.A. 1989).
19. See National Defense Authorization Act for Fiscal Year 1993, Pub. L. No. 102-484, 106 Stat. 2315, 2505 (1992). See also R.C.M. 202(a) Discussion.

tion.[20] Before 1992, Article 3(a) indicated that a discharge would not bar jurisdiction over offenses committed prior to a discharge, if the offense was not triable in a civilian court and was punishable by five or more years confinement at hard labor.[21] That provision still applies for any offense occurring prior to October 23, 1992.[22] The key here, under either the former or current provision, is that the servicemember is subject to the Uniform Code of Military Justice at the time of trial, whether by reentry into the military or otherwise.[23] In this regard it is important to note that the Supreme Court in *Toth v. Quarles*[24] ruled that Article 3(a) was unconstitutional to the extent that it attempts to provide for jurisdiction over individuals who were servicemembers at the time of the offense but are civilians at the time of trial.[25]

Whether Article 3(a) allows for jurisdiction over inactive reservists who have been discharged has not been settled.[26]

§ 4-8(C)(3). Fraudulent Discharge.

Article 3(b), U.C.M.J., provides for jurisdiction over an individual who has been discharged but who obtained that discharge fraudulently.[27] That provision further notes that if convicted for the fraudulent, the individual may also be tried for any offenses committed prior to the discharge.[28]

---

20. Art. 3(a), U.C.M.J. R.C.M. 202(a) Discussion.
21. As a practical matter, an actual interruption in active duty precluded jurisdiction because many offenses that might net more than five years' confinement had a separate civilian analog and were triable in a state or federal court. Purely military offenses generally did not meet the five-year confinement requirement. There was authority for the proposition that if the offense continued into a new enlistment, jurisdiction existed. United States v. Gladue, 4 M.J. 1 (C.M.A. 1977); United States v. Gonzales, 12 M.J. 747 (A.F.C.M.R. 1981). The same held true for offenses occurring overseas. United States v. Gladue, 4 M.J. 1 (C.M.A. 1977); United States v. Mosely, 14 M.J. 852 (A.C.M.R. 1982).
22. R.C.M. 202(a) Discussion, Subsection 2(B)(ii).
23. The *Manual* does not specify the basis for the servicemember's status at the time of trial.
24. 350 U.S. 11 (1950).
25. The civilian in *Toth* was a discharged member of the Air Force who was arrested by military authorities and returned to Korea for court-martial; he was convicted of murdering a Korean national.
26. *See* United States v. Caputo, 18 M.J. 259 (C.M.A. 1984). *See also* United States v. Wheeler, 28 C.M.R. 212 (C.M.A. 1959); United States v. Brown, 31 C.M.R. 279 (C.M.A. 1962). What seems clear is that jurisdiction does not end where, for example, an officer holding a reserve commission on active duty is relieved from that commission to accept a commission in a Regular Component. In that case, there is no break in an active status. R.C.M. 101 Discussion. *See also* Art. 3(d), U.C.M.J. and § 4-6, *supra*.
27. Art. 3(b), U.C.M.J.
28. Art. 3(b), U.C.M.J. In United States v. Spradley, 41 M.J. 827 (N.M.Ct.Crim.App. 1995), the accused was convicted of larceny of chapel funds, sentenced to a punitive discharge but administratively discharged after he allegedly made restitution. When his check bounced, he was ordered to return to active duty to serve sentence. The Court of Criminal Appeals concluded that there was no jurisdiction over the accused. Once he was discharged, his unexecuted court-martial sentence was automatically remitted. Citing Article 3, the court held that while a fraudulent separation is an invalid separation, a court must first convict a person for obtaining the fraudulent discharge before jurisdiction attaches for any additional charges may be tried.

In *Wickham v. Hall*,[29] the Court of Appeals for the Armed Forces for the first time squarely addressed the constitutionality of Article 3(b) to a situation where the accused had allegedly obtained a fraudulent discharge. Drawing distinctions between this case and *Toth v. Quarles*,[30] Judge Cook concluded that the accused was subject to court-martial jurisdiction; Judge Fletcher concurred in the result, but Chief Judge Everett dissented.

The Court of Appeals addressed the issue again in *United States v. Cole*,[31] where the accused presented a falsified DA Form 137 (Installation Clearance Record), which in turn led to delivery of a DD Form 214 (Certificate of Release or Discharge from Active Duty).[32] That form indicated that he was obligated to serve an additional four years as a reservist. Several months later he was arrested and returned to military control. Ultimately, he was convicted by general court-martial of obtaining a fraudulent separation from the armed services.[33]

Judge Sullivan, writing for the court, concluded, first, that Congress is constitutionally permitted to designate a court-martial as an appropriate forum for determining whether an individual's discharge is valid.[34] In *Toth*, Judge Sullivan noted, there was no question about the validity of the discharge, and in this case the accused was only released from active duty, not discharged — the implication being that the accused retained some connection with the military and was thus at least amenable to a military judicial decision about his exact status. He also noted the absence of any authority for the proposition that a court-martial does not have the power to decide the issue of personal jurisdiction. In a footnote he suggested that the *Toth* issue should be raised initially in an Article 39(a) session.[35] Second, Judge Sullivan focused on the narrow question of whether a person who has fraudulently obtained his separation is nonetheless actually a member of the armed services. In answering that question in the affirmative, he noted that the Supreme Court has declined to adopt any bright-line rules and that the Court has also recognized jurisdiction over persons serving court-martial sentences after their discharge.[36] Finally, Judge Sullivan noted the distinctions between Article 3(a), which was ruled in *Toth* to be unconstitutional insofar as it related to civil-

---

29. 12 M.J. 145 (C.M.A. 1981). Miss Wickham was properly discharged through administrative channels without being court-martialed, although the Court of Appeals for the Fifth Circuit agreed that she was properly subject to court-martial jurisdiction. See Wickham v. Hall, 706 F.2d 713 (5th Cir. 1983).

30. 350 U.S. 11 (1955).

31. 24 M.J. 18 (C.M.A. 1987). *See also* Murphy v. Garrett, 29 M.J. 469 (C.M.A. 1990) (court noted but did not decide question of whether accused, who was being investigated for obtaining a fraudulent discharge, was subject to jurisdiction because of that fact; the court found jurisdiction under Article 2(d)).

32. Delivery of this form effects the discharge of an individual regardless of whether service regulations indicate a different effective date or time. United States v. Howard, 20 M.J. 353 (C.M.A. 1985). *See also supra* § 4-8(B).

33. Art. 83, U.C.M.J. *See* Appendix 3.

34. 24 M.J. at 20.

35. 24 M.J. at 21, n.2. *See also infra* Chapters 12 and 13.

36. 24 M.J. at 22, *citing* Kahn v. Anderson, 255 U.S. 1 (1921) (jurisdiction over prisoner who had been dishonorably discharged).

ians, and Article 3(b). He concluded that the latter is not inconsistent with the language in *Toth* that court-martial jurisdiction should be limited to the "least possible power adequate to the end proposed."[37] Under Article 3(a), many civilians had been exposed to possible jurisdiction for a variety of offenses. Article 3(b), on the other hand, is narrower and, at least initially, only addresses the issue of whether the discharge was fraudulent.[38]

Judge Cox completely agreed with the opinion by Judge Sullivan, but wrote separately to emphasize that courts-martial possess the authority to decide the issue of personal jurisdiction and need not, as the dissent suggested, await a ruling by an Article III court.[39] Judge Cox also indicated that the Court is "not at all interested in permitting civilians to be tried by courts-martial in violation of long-standing Supreme Court decisions."[40]

In dissent, Chief Judge Everett reiterated his position in *Wickham v. Hall*, that Article 3(b) is unconstitutional in light of *Toth v. Quarles*.[41] Here, said Judge Everett, the accused did not forge his discharge,[42] nor did the military take any steps prior to his discharge to attach jurisdiction on the charges for which he was tried.[43] Instead, the procedures used in this case — arresting the accused while living in the civilian community and then bringing him before a court-martial — were in Judge Everett's view disturbing and inconsistent with the bright line test of *Toth*. First, the prosecution of the accused in this case did not further the primary function of the military to "fight or to be ready to fight wars."[44] Second, upholding the validity of Article 3(b) would actually and potentially sweep within military jurisdiction "a great number of persons not otherwise subject to military law."[45] Third, permitting a court-martial to exercise jurisdiction under Article 3(b) would not be the "least possible power adequate to the end proposed."[46] Judge Everett believed that the jurisdictional question presented in this case was an appropriate one for

---

37. 24 M.J. at 23, *citing* Toth v. Quarles, 350 U.S. at 23.
38. Under Article 83, once a court-martial determines that an accused has fraudulently obtained his separation, he may be tried for any additional offenses committed during his active duty. The statutory provision provides some protection here because it requires that further prosecution for those other offenses may be pursued only after conviction on the fraudulent separation charge.
39. 24 M.J. at 26.
40. 24 M.J. at 27, *citing* United States v. Howard, 20 M.J. 353 (C.M.A. 1985).
41. 350 U.S. 11 (1955).
42. 24 M.J. at 28. Judge Everett indicated that if the accused had forged his discharge certificate he would fully agree with the majority, because in that event the accused would not have been separated from the service. That seems to be a very fine distinction and one not intended by Congress. A transcript of hearings on Article 3(b), attached to the opinion as an Appendix, indicates that Article 3(b) was applicable whether the accused actually forged the discharge or obtained it by some other fraudulent act. Here, for example, the facts indicated that the accused falsified another form which was necessary to obtain issuance of the DD Form 214. In either case, the accused's status has been potentially altered through his own unlawful actions and not solely by the good faith mistakes of the military.
43. 24 M.J. at 28. For a discussion of continuing jurisdiction, see § 4-8(A) *supra*.
44. 24 M.J. at 28, *citing* Toth v. Quarles, 350 U.S. at 17, 22-23.
45. 24 M.J. at 29, *citing* Toth v. Quarles, 350 U.S. at 19-20, 22-23.
46. 24 M.J. at 29, *citing* Toth v. Quarles, 350 U.S. at 23. The rationale supporting this oft-cited quote is that there is a general distrust of providing too much authority to military courts.

the civilian courts, which should have ruled in the first instance whether the discharge was valid. Only upon a finding by a civilian court that it was void could the military courts proceed.[47]

The dissent and the majority positions may not be that far apart on the issue of whether a fraudulent discharge terminates jurisdiction. Both seem to agree in principle that such a separation does not forever terminate the ability of the military to try the individual. The real disagreement seems to lie in the issue of who should make the initial determination that jurisdiction exists.

The court's conclusion in this case that Article 3(b) is constitutional seems to be sound and one not likely to be set aside by the Supreme Court. First, as noted by Judge Sullivan, the precedential strength of *Toth v. Quarles* is diminished where the accused has fraudulently procured his separation, an act as noted by Congress to be tantamount to desertion,[48] especially where, as in this case, the accused has maintained some ties as a reservist. Perhaps more importantly, the Supreme Court has implicitly recognized that a discharge is not an absolute bar to jurisdiction.[49] Third, courts-martial are capable of determining whether they even have jurisdiction, a decision subject to review not only in the Court of Appeals, but also in the Supreme Court.[50] This point seems even more important in light of the Supreme Court's decision in *Solorio v. United States*,[51] where the Court noted its great deference for Congressional decisions concerning military affairs.[52]

Considering this broad and growing deference, it would not be at all surprising if *Toth* itself would be decided differently by the current Supreme Court. The tone of earlier, and generally more restrictive, opinions of the Supreme Court regarding court-martial jurisdiction rested in large part on the general distrust of military courts' ability to decide constitutional issues. An argument can be made that with an implicit blessing in *Solorio* of military courts themselves, the underlying distrust is muted and Congressional decisions concerning jurisdiction would be left untouched absent a blatant abuse of constitutional authority, even to the point of providing for jurisdiction over ex-servicemembers. The underlying argument in *Toth*, that servicemembers are denied the right to jury trials and grand jury indictment, also provided the underpinnings several years later for the *O'Callahan-Relford* service connection requirement. That requirement was explicitly abandoned in *Solorio*.[53]

---

47. 24 M.J. at 31.
48. *See* 24 M.J. at 24 (Appendix to opinion).
49. Kahn v. Anderson, 255 U.S. 1 (1921) (jurisdiction over dishonorably discharged prisoner). An argument might be made, however, that even in those cases the accused is still a "part" of the military by virtue of the fact that as a prisoner he is literally within the custody and control of the military.
50. See § 17-23 *infra* for a discussion of Supreme Court review of decisions by the Court of Military Appeals.
51. 483 U.S. 435 (1987). *See also* § 4-11(C).
52. 483 U.S. at 447-48.
53. See § 4-11(C).

§ 4-8(C)(4). Deserters.

Court-martial jurisdiction also exists over servicemembers who have deserted but are later able to obtain a discharge.[54] The discharge does not relieve the servicemember of accountability for the offense of desertion.[55]

§ 4-8(C)(5). Persons in Custody.

A servicemember convicted by court-martial who receives a sentence that includes a punitive discharge and confinement may receive delivery of that discharge while serving the confinement portion of the sentence. Article 2(a)(7), U.C.M.J., provides in effect that the discharge will not relieve that individual of court-martial jurisdiction if while in custody he commits an offense.[56] This provision has been deemed valid by both the Court of Appeals for the Armed Forces and the federal courts.[57]

§ 4-8(D). Retired Members.

Article 2, U.C.M.J., provides that retired members of the armed forces may be subject to court-martial jurisdiction while in a retired status. Specifically, Article 2 provides for jurisdiction over three categories of retirees: (1) retired members of a regular component of the armed forces who are entitled to pay;[58] (2) retired members of a reserve component who are receiving hospitalization from an armed force;[59] and (3) members of the Fleet Reserve and Fleet Marine Corps Reserve.[60] The first category, retired members entitled to pay, was

---

54. Art. 3(b), U.C.M.J.; see Appendix 3.
55. See United States v. Huff, 7 C.M.A. 247, 22 C.M.R. 37 (1956).
56. The Supreme Court has sustained the constitutionality of a similar provision. See Kahn v. Anderson, 255 U.S. 1 (1921); United States v. Harry, 25 M.J. 513 (A.F.C.M.R. 1987) (accused as sentenced prisoner still subject to court-martial jurisdiction).
57. See, e.g., Ragan v. Cox, 320 F.2d 815 (10th Cir. 1963). See generally, Bishop, "Court-Martial Jurisdiction Over Military-Civilian Hybrids: Retired Regulars, Reservists, and Discharged Prisoners," 112 U. PA. L. REV. 317 (1964).
58. Art. 2(a)(4), U.C.M.J. See, e.g., United States v. Sloan, 35 M.J. 4 (C.M.A. 1992) (trial of retired master sergeant for offenses committed while on active duty; court noted that after accused was tried, Army issued regulation indicating that retired members could be tried only with the prior approval of the Secretary); United States v. Allen, 33 M.J. 209 (C.M.A. 1991) (retired servicemember was tried under Article 2(a)(4) on espionage charges). Sands v. Colby, 35 M.J. 620 (A.C.M.R. 1992) (court rejected mandamus petition from accused who was retired from active duty; he received orders recalling him to active duty in accordance with Army Regulation 27-10 after he became a suspect in death of his wife).
59. Art. 2(a)(5), U.C.M.J.
60. Art. 2(a)(6), U.C.M.J. See, e.g., United States v. Overton, 20 M.J. 998 (N.M.C.M.R. 1985) (jurisdiction existed under Article 2(a)(6) over civilian employee who was member of U.S. Marine Corps Fleet Reserve; when he had completed 22 years of active duty, he was "transferred" to the Reserve where he continued to receive a retainer. He was subject to recall).
See also United States v. Bowie, 14 C.M.A. 631, 34 C.M.R. 411 (1964); Hooper v. United States, 326 F.2d 982 (Ct. Cl. 1964), cert. denied, 377 U.S. 977 (1964); United States v. Fenno, 167 F.2d 593 (2d Cir. 1948).

tested in *United States v. Hooper*[61] and found to be valid. The Court turned its decision on the conclusion that retired members entitled to receive pay are a part of the "land or naval forces."[62] Historically, the courts have considered retirees to be a part of the armed forces.[63] The holding in *Hooper* was reaffirmed by the Court in *Pearson v. Bloss*,[64] where a retired master sergeant was entitled to receive pay; the court held that he possessed the requisite status for court-martial jurisdiction.

Jurisdiction over the third category, members of the Fleet Reserve and Fleet Marine Corps Reserve, was addressed in *United States v. Overton*.[65] In *Overton*, the accused had retired after 22 years of active duty and was transferred to the Fleet Marine Corps Reserve. While working as a civilian employee for the Navy, he was court-martialed for various larcenies of government property. The court concluded that the personal jurisdiction over the accused was neither novel nor arbitrary[66] and noted that he was subject to recall; he was subject to some annual active duty, and he was receiving a retainer for his status.[67]

§ 4-9. Pleading and Proving Personal Jurisdiction.

The government may meet its burden of pleading personal jurisdiction[1] by including in the specification a statement of the individual's rank, unit, and armed force. If the accused is subject to court-martial jurisdiction under the provisions of Article 2(a)(3) through Article 2(a)(12), Article 3, or Article 4,[2] the specifications should include a description of the status upon which the government is relying for personal jurisdiction.[3]

At trial, the government's burden of establishing the court's jurisdiction over the accused is an interlocutory matter;[4] the military judge must upon a defense motion to dismiss for lack of personal jurisdiction, apply the prepon-

---

61. 9 C.M.A. 637, 26 C.M.R. 417 (1958). *See also* Hooper v. United States, 326 F.2d 982 (Ct. Cl. 1964), *cert. denied*, 377 U.S. 977 (1964).
62. United States v. Hooper, 9 C.M.A. at 645, 26 C.M.R. at 425 (1958). The decision includes a thorough discussion of the court-martial jurisdiction over retirees in general.
63. *See, e.g.*, United States v. Tyler, 145 U.S. 244 (1882).
64. 28 M.J. 764 (A.F.C.M.R. 1989).
65. 24 M.J. 309 (C.M.A. 1987), *cert. denied*, 484 U.S. 976 (1987). *See also* Notes and Comments, "The Retired Regular Officer: Status, Duties, and Responsibilities," 26 A.F. JAG L. Rev. 111 (1987).
66. 24 M.J. at 311.
67. *Id. See* 10 U.S.C. § 6485(a) (subject to recall); § 6485(b) (possible active duty commitment); § 6330(c)(1) (retainer pay).
1. *See* United States v. Alef, 3 M.J. 414 (C.M.A. 1977). *See also infra* § 13-2(D).
2. *See* Appendix 3.
3. *See* R.C.M. 307 Discussion. In United States v. Hatley, 14 M.J. 890 (N.M.C.M.R. 1982), the court held that a specification was not totally deficient because it failed to note that the accused was a reservist on active duty.
4. United States v. Bailey, 6 M.J. 965 (N.C.M.R. 1979) (good discussion of procedure and burden of proof). *See also* United States v. Buckingham, 9 M.J. 514 (A.F.C.M.R. 1980), *aff'd on other grounds*, 11 M.J. 184 (C.M.A. 1981); United States v. Jessie, 5 M.J. 573 (A.C.M.R. 1978), *petition denied*, 5 M.J. 300 (C.M.A. 1978). *See generally* Thorne, "Jurisdictional Issues at Trial and Beyond," Army Law., Sept. 1980, at 15.

derance of the evidence standard.[5] Should the military judge rule that the accused is subject to court-martial jurisdiction, the defense may still raise the issue of status before the fact-finders.[6] They must find beyond a reasonable doubt that the accused possesses military status where that status is an underlying element of the charged offense.[7]

PART III

JURISDICTION OVER THE OFFENSE

§ 4-10. Introduction.

The Supreme Court has ruled that every effort should be made "to restrict military tribunals to the narrowest jurisdiction deemed absolutely essential to maintaining discipline among the troops in active service."[1] This theme runs throughout any discussion of subject matter jurisdiction of courts-martial and is primarily based upon the fact that servicemembers tried by court-martial are not entitled to the Fifth Amendment right to indictment by grand jury and a trial by jury.[2] As noted in Chapter 1, the military system of criminal justice is recognized as a legitimately separate system and until 1969 was granted very broad discretion in prosecuting cases; the only qualifying factor was the need for military "status."[3]

That changed with the Supreme Court's opinion in *O'Callahan v. Parker*.[4] Justice Douglas, writing for the majority, reviewed the historical reluctance of governments to vest too much jurisdiction in military courts, especially when the civilian courts were open and operating and the offense involved could be tried in those courts. Noting that a court-martial is not "yet an independent instrument of justice," but rather a mechanism for preserving discipline, Justice Douglas stated:

> While the Court of Military Appeals takes cognizance of some constitutional rights of the accused who are court-martialed, courts-martial as an

---

5. United States v. Bailey, 6 M.J. 965 (N.C.M.R. 1979).

6. *Id.* at 969. The matter is not raised anew as a motion to dismiss but rather as a matter of defense. *See also* United States v. Ornelas, 2 C.M.A. 96, 6 C.M.R. 96 (1952).

7. For example, the purely military offenses of absence without leave and desertion include an underlying element of military status. *See* United States v. Buckingham, 9 M.J. 514 (A.F.C.M.R. 1980), *aff'd on other grounds,* 11 M.J. 184 (C.M.A. 1981). In United States v. Laws, 11 M.J. 475 (C.M.A. 1981), the court found no reversible error in a bifurcated proceeding: the judge did not submit the issue of guilt to the court until after it returned with a finding of personal jurisdiction. *See also* United States v. McDonagh, 14 M.J. 415, 422 (C.M.A. 1983).

1. Toth v. Quarles, 350 U.S. 11, 22 (1955).

2. *Id.* O'Callahan v. Parker, 395 U.S. 258 (1969).

3. *See generally* Rice, "*O'Callahan v. Parker:* Court-Martial Jurisdiction, 'Service Connection,' Confusion, and the Serviceman," 51 MIL. L. REV. 41 (1971).

4. 395 U.S. 258 (1969). The decision was not made retroactive. Gosa v. Mayden, 413 U.S. 665 (1973).

institution are singularly inept in dealing with the nice subtleties of constitutional law.[5]

Thus, to insure limitation on the powers of courts-martial, the Court limited subject matter jurisdiction to those offenses that were *service-connected.*

In the sections that follow, the discussion focuses on the evolution of the "service connection" requirement, how it was interpreted by the Supreme Court in *Relford v. Commandant,*[6] applied by the military courts,[7] and finally abandoned by the Supreme Court in *Solorio v. United States.*[8]

§ 4-11. The Service Connection Requirement: 1969-1987.

Shortly after its decision in *O'Callahan,* the Supreme Court again addressed the question of a court-martial's subject matter jurisdiction in *Relford v. Commandant.*[1] In finding jurisdiction, a unanimous Court identified for future use what became popularly characterized as the twelve *Relford* factors.[2] Those

---

5. A similar lack of confidence in military justice had been expressed earlier by Justice Black in Toth v. Quarles, 350 U.S. 11, 17 (1955):

   We find nothing in the history or constitutional treatment of military tribunals which entitles them to rank along with Article III courts as adjudicators of the guilt or innocence of people charged with offenses for which they can be deprived of their life, liberty or property. Unlike courts, it is the primary business of armies and navies to fight or be ready to fight wars should the occasion arise. But trial of soldiers to maintain discipline is merely incidental to an army's primary fighting function. To the extent that those responsible for performance of this primary function are diverted from it by the necessity of trying cases, the basic fighting purpose of armies is not served. And conceding to military personnel that high degree of honesty and sense of justice which nearly all of them undoubtedly have, it still remains true that military tribunals have not been and probably never can be constituted in such way that they can have the same kind of qualifications that the Constitution has deemed essential to fair trials of civilians in federal courts.

   Cf. Schlesinger v. Councilman, 420 U.S. 738, 758 (1975) ("it must be assumed that the military court system will vindicate servicemen's rights").
6. 401 U.S. 355 (1971). *See infra* § 4-11.
7. *See* § 4-11.
8. 483 U.S. 435 (1987). *See* § 4-11.
1. 401 U.S. 355 (1971).
2. The twelve factors listed by the Court are:

   1. The serviceman's proper absence from the base.
   2. The crime's commission away from base.
   3. Its commission at a place not under military control.
   4. Its commission within our territorial limits and not in an occupied zone of a foreign country.
   5. Its commission in peacetime and its being unrelated to authority stemming from the war powers.
   6. The absence of any connection between the defendant's military duties and the crime.
   7. The victim's not being engaged in the performance of any duty relating to the military.
   8. The presence and availability of a civilian court in which the case can be prosecuted.
   9. The absence of any flouting of military authority.
   10. The absence of any threat to a military post.
   11. The absence of any violation of military property.

factors were to serve as a template for the lower court's use in determining in an ad hoc fashion of whether an offense was service connected. In addition, the Court stressed a number of other factors to be considered by the courts.[3] The essence of the foregoing factors was condensed in *Schlesinger v. Councilman*.[4] The Supreme Court, expressing confidence in the military criminal system,[5] stated that the task of determining service connection is largely a question of:

(1) Measuring the impact of the offense on military discipline and effectiveness;

(2) Determining whether the military interest in deterring the offense is distinct from and greater than that of civilian society; and

(3) Deciding whether that interest can be adequately vindicated in the civilian courts.[6]

The Court added that these "are matters of judgment that will often turn on the precise facts in which the offense occurred" and that they are issues that fall within the expertise of military courts.[7]

---

12. The offense being among those traditionally prosecuted in civilian courts.

Relford v. Commandant, 401 U.S. at 367-69 (1971). These factors were gleaned in large part from the Court's *O'Callahan* decision and tend to emphasize the civilian interest in jurisdiction over the offense.

3. The Court noted that the following factors should also be considered:

(1) The essential and obvious interest of the military in the security of persons and of property on the military enclave; (2) the responsibility of the military commander for maintenance of order in the command and the commander's authority to maintain that order; (3) the impact and adverse effect that a crime committed against a person or property on a military base, thus violating the base's very security, has upon the morale, discipline, reputation and integrity of the base itself, upon its personnel, and upon the military operation and the military mission; (4) Article 1, section 8, clause 14, of the Constitution of the United States vesting in Congress the power "to make Rules for the Government and Regulation of the land and naval forces," means, in appropriate areas beyond the purely military offense, more than the mere power to arrest a servicemember-offender and turn that person over to the civil authorities; (5) the distinct possibility that civil courts, particularly non-federal courts, will have less than complete interest, concern, and capacity for all the cases that vindicate the military's disciplinary authority within its own community; (6) the presence of factors such as geographical and military relationships which have important significance in favor of service-connection; (7) historically, a crime against the person of one associated with the post was subject even to the General Article; (8) the misreading and undue restriction of *O'Callahan* if it were interpreted as confining the court-martial to the purely military offenses that have no counterpart in nonmilitary criminal law; (9) the inability appropriately and meaningfully to draw any line between a post's strictly military areas and its nonmilitary areas, or between a servicemember's duty and off-duty activities and hours on the post. In addition, the effect of the offense on the reputation and morale of the Armed Services is an appropriate consideration in determining service-connection.

401 U.S. at 367-68.

4. 420 U.S. 738 (1975).

5. *Id.* at 758.

6. *Id.* at 760.

7. *Id.* In a separate opinion Justice Brennan questioned the ability of military courts to determine whether "a common everyday practice carried on by civilians becomes service-connected when carried on by servicemembers." 420 U.S. at 764-65. He also indicated that such constitu-

§ 4-11(A). Applying the *Relford* Factors.

The *Relford* criteria initially had a negligible effect on restricting subject matter jurisdiction. Generally, the military courts had little difficulty in finding the requisite service connection; offenses committed on a military installation were automatically service connected.[8] If an off-post offense involved a servicemember as a victim or if the accused used his military status to further the crime, service connection was found; off-post drug offenses were also service connected.[9]

Beginning in 1976, however, the Court of Appeals for the Armed Forces emphasized that the *Relford* criteria could not be subjected to any generalized or *per se* formulas for finding service connection. Rather, lower military courts were instructed to apply the *Relford* factors on an *ad hoc* basis.[10] What developed was a highly structured analysis of the service connection requirement and careful application of the *Relford* criteria. Many of the cases focused on four main factors.

First, if the crime was committed on a military installation, service connection was found.[11] This "situs" rule apparently did not apply to those offenses committed just off the military installation,[12] and mere on-post preparation to commit an off-post offense did not always provide service connection.[13] The

---

tional questions are rarely confronted by military courts. 420 U.S. at 765, n.3. In response, Justice Powell, writing for the majority, presented a more positive and realistic image of military courts when he said:

> We express no opinion whether the offense with which respondent in this case was charged is in fact service connected. But we have no doubt that military tribunals do have both experience and expertise that qualify them to determine the facts and to evaluate their relevance to military discipline, morale, and fitness.

Id. U.S. at 761, n.34 (emphasis in original).

8. United States v. Wills, 20 C.M.A. 8, 42 C.M.R. 200 (1970). *See generally* Zillman, "*Relford v. Commandant:* On-Post Offenses and Military Jurisdiction," 52 Mil. L. Rev. 169 (1971).

9. *See, e.g.,* United States v. Everson, 19 C.M.A. 70, 41 C.M.R. 70 (1969) (military victim); United States v. Wolfson, 21 C.M.A. 549, 45 C.M.R. 323 (1972) (use of Military ID card); United States v. Beeker, 18 C.M.A. 563, 40 C.M.R. 275 (1969) (drug offenses).

10. *See, e.g.,* United States v. McCarthy, 2 M.J. 26 (C.M.A. 1976); United States v. Tucker, 1 M.J. 463 (C.M.A. 1976); United States v. Hedlund, 2 M.J. 11 (C.M.A. 1976). *See generally* Cooper, "*O'Callahan* Revisited: Severing the Service Connection," 76 Mil. L. Rev. 165 (1977).

11. United States v. Hedlund, 2 M.J. 11 (C.M.A. 1976); United States v. Rogers, 7 M.J. 274 (C.M.A. 1979) (service connection over rape committed at VA hospital on military installation). The situs of the offense, not the trial itself, is determinative. United States v. Bowers, 47 C.M.R. 516 (A.C.M.R. 1973).

12. United States v. Klink, 5 M.J. 404 (C.M.A. 1978) (no jurisdiction over drug offenses occurring 30 feet off installation).

Cf. United States v. Mauck, 17 M.J. 1033 (A.C.M.R. 1984) (jurisdiction found where assaults committed 15 feet outside installation boundary). *See also* United States v. Williams, 17 M.J. 207 (C.M.A. 1984); United States v. Daye, 17 M.J. 555 (A.C.M.R. 1983); United States v. Brauchler, 15 M.J. 755 (A.F.C.M.R. 1983).

13. United States v. McCollum, 6 M.J. 224 (C.M.A. 1979) (accused was charged with substantive offense, not conspiracy to commit it).

In United States v. Scott, 15 M.J. 589 (A.C.M.R. 1983), service connection was found where the murder had its basis in on-post conduct and involved servicemembers.

§ 4-11(A)   MILITARY CRIMINAL JUSTICE   § 4-11(A)

courts, however, found service connection where the agreement to later sell or transfer drugs off-post occurred on-post.[14] Where the offense commenced off-post but continued to the post, service connection was also found.[15]

Second, the courts focused on the question of whether the accused had abused his or her status as a servicemember. But simply presenting a military identification card to cash a forged check at an off-post bank was not always sufficient.[16] The use of status factor, often linked with the flouting of authority factor, was sufficient, however, in a case where a military doctor's ability to obtain fraudulent drug prescriptions at an off-base pharmacy was facilitated by his "status."[17] Status was also determinative where the accused's ability to wrongly collect military death benefits turned on the fact that he was a member of the armed forces.[18]

Third, the courts focused on the *Relford* "military duties" factor. There were really two *Relford* factors represented in this category of cases; connection between the accused's military duties and the offense, and whether the victim, if any, was engaged in a duty relating to the military. The "duties" factors were relied upon in *United States v. Whatley*[19] to sustain jurisdiction over an off-post larceny committed by a military policeman who, during the performance of his duties as an MP, learned of the absence of the military victim from his residence. The mere fact that the accused performed police duties did not always equate with service connection.[20] The courts required a nexus

---

14. *See, e.g.,* United States v. Hardin, 7 M.J. 399 (C.M.A. 1979); United States v. Strangstalien, 7 M.J. 225 (C.M.A. 1979); United States v. Chambers, 7 M.J. 24 (C.M.A. 1979) (off-post sale of drugs where accused knew they were going to the military installation could be service connected). *But see* United States v. McCollum, 6 M.J. 224 (C.M.A. 1979) (mere on-post planning not sufficient).

15. United States v. Seivers, 8 M.J. 63 (C.M.A. 1979); United States v. Escobar, 7 M.J. 197 (C.M.A. 1979); United States v. Goins, 20 M.J. 673 (A.F.C.M.R. 1985) (off-post aggravated assault and conspiracy to commit assault were service connected where the offenses were part of a continuous chain of events that began on the installation and where the military had an overriding interest in this case because it arose from the victim's reporting an offense to his first sergeant).

16. *See, e.g.,* United States v. Sims, 2 M.J. 109 (C.M.A. 1977); United States v. Hopkins, 4 M.J. 260 (C.M.A. 1978). *Cf.* United States v. Lockwood, 15 M.J. 1 (C.M.A. 1983) (indicating that *Sims* and *Hopkins* may not be controlling).

17. United States v. Pollack, 7 M.J. 627 (A.F.C.M.R. 1979), *petition denied*, 7 M.J. 376 (C.M.A. 1979). *See also* United States v. Wierzba, 11 M.J. 742 (A.F.C.M.R. 1981) (accused used status as active duty officer to prey upon civil air patrol victims).

18. United States v. Moore, 1 M.J. 448 (C.M.A. 1976); United States v. Kyles, 20 M.J. 571 (N.M.C.M.R. 1985) (accused's offense of bigamy was service connected in light of the fact that both wives sought military assistance or benefits and considerable time was spent by military authorities sorting through the administrative problems. The court took judicial notice of the fact that if the accused had died or become disabled, unnecessary delay and hardship would have resulted in determining who should have received his benefits).

19. 5 M.J. 39 (C.M.A. 1978); United States v. Roa, 20 M.J. 867 (A.F.C.M.R. 1985) (service connection over off-base burglaries of officers' quarters was found where one of the culprits in the theft ring had access to a duty roster and used it to plan the crimes).

20. *See, e.g.,* United States v. Conn, 6 M.J. 351 (C.M.A. 1979) (MP lieutenant using drugs in presence of subordinate off-post was not service connected); United States v. Saulter, 5 M.J. 281 (C.M.A. 1978) (MPs engaged in off-post, after hours, drug offenses while in civilian clothes not service connected).

§ 4-11(A) JURISDICTION § 4-11(A)

between the duties and the offense.[21] Both the victim's and accused's duties were considered by the court in *United States v. Brown*,[22] where the homosexual relationship between the accused and the victim was, according to the court, "inextricably bound up" with the duty performance of both individuals.[23]

Fourth, the courts tended to find service connection if the accused's actions had posed a threat to the military. For example, obscene phone calls to a servicemember's wife,[24] possession of stolen government explosives,[25] and sale of drugs intended for later on-post distribution[26] were considered threats to the military community. The Court of Military Appeals indicated that a servicemember's off-post use or possession of drugs in itself potentially constituted a threat to the military.[27]

The military courts did recognize two main exceptions to the service connection requirement. Both rested in part on the basis of the Supreme Court's decision in *O'Callahan*. *O'Callahan v. Parker*[28] rested in large part on the fact that servicemembers tried by courts-martial are not entitled to the constitutional protections of indictment by grand jury and jury trial. If those two rights would not be otherwise available if the servicemember were to be tried in a civilian court, then there was arguably no need to show service connection. Accordingly, a number of court decisions stated that if the offense was a petty offense the prosecution of which did not require application of those two rights, no service connection was required.[29] By the same token, offenses committed by servicemembers while assigned overseas were normally not subject to the service connection requirements; those offenses are usually not within the jurisdictional limits of any civilian court. The exception to the overseas rule rested in the possibility that extraterritorial application of the federal

---

21. A nexus was found in United States v. Graham, 9 M.J. 556 (N.C.M.R. 1980) (drug use by officer in presence of subordinates violated duty to enforce laws and regulations and set a good example).

22. 8 M.J. 501 (A.F.C.M.R. 1979), *petition denied*, 8 M.J. 234 (C.M.A. 1980).

23. *Id.* at 503. United States v. Shorte, 18 M.J. 518 (A.F.C.M.R. 1984) (service connection found where accused assaulted another servicemember off-base but confrontation began on base, the military had a distinct and greater interest in the prosecution, and the victim was unable to perform his duties for 12 days).

24. United States v. Respess, 7 M.J. 566 (A.C.M.R. 1979). *See also* United States v. Herring, 20 M.J. 1002 (A.F.C.M.R. 1985) (threat to servicemember).

25. United States v. Regan, 7 M.J. 600 (N.C.M.R. 1979).

26. United States v. Tomlinson, 7 M.J. 667 (A.C.M.R. 1979).

27. *See* United States v. Norman, 9 M.J. 355 (C.M.A. 1980) (dicta).

28. 395 U.S. 258 (1969).

29. *See, e.g.*, United States v. Sharkey, 19 C.M.A. 26, 41 C.M.R. 26 (1969) (accused tried for being drunk in civilian bar); United States v. Wentzel, 50 C.M.R. 690 (A.F.C.M.R. 1975) (attempted arson of car).

The Court of Appeals had rejected the argument that offenses tried by a special court-martial authorized to adjudge a bad-conduct discharge need not be service connected because the accused has no constitutional right to a jury—the maximum confinement that may be assessed is six months. The Court noted that a punitive discharge is itself a severe punishment exceeding the equivalent of six months. United States v. Smith, 9 M.J. 359, 360, n.1 (C.M.A. 1980). The question of whether the court would reach a different conclusion in a special court-martial not authorized to adjudge a punitive discharge was never answered.

penal code might exist.[30] Thus, if the overseas offense could have been prosecuted in a United States federal court, and the accused would be entitled to the right to indictment and jury trial, the military prosecutor was required to establish service connection over the offense.[31]

Finally, in all cases the prosecution was required to allege in its sworn charges those facts upon which subject matter jurisdiction was based.[32] Failure to do so could lead to a defense motion at trial to clarify the pleadings so as to properly allege the basis.[33] Generally the pleading requirement was met by alleging the applicable *Relford* factors in the specification.[34] Inclusion of the *Relford* factors was more in the nature of a "notice" pleading. The prosecution could generally make amendments to these factors at trial without changing the gravamen of the offense.[35] The pleading requirement could be waived,[36] and the question of whether the court had subject matter jurisdiction was an interlocutory question to be decided by the military judge; it was not submitted to the fact-finders.[37]

---

30. For example, in United States v. Lazzaro, 2 M.J. 76 (C.M.A. 1976), the accused was charged with stealing government funds from a commissioned officers' mess in Japan. The offense could have been tried in a U.S. district court because 18 U.S.C. 641 (larceny of U.S. funds) could be applied overseas. The court nonetheless found service connection. *See also* United States v. Black, 1 M.J. 340 (C.M.A. 1976); United States v. Holman, 19 M.J. 784 (A.C.M.R. 1984) (overseas exception did not apply where accused's offenses were punishable under a federal statute that has extraterritorial effect; court nonetheless found service connection). In footnote, the court indicated that it is not clear if the language recognizable in a civilian court is based upon theoretical or practical considerations.

31. For an excellent discussion of impact of extraterritorial federal penal statutes on subject matter jurisdiction see Horbaly & Mullins, "Extraterritorial Jurisdiction and its Effect on the Administration of Military Criminal Justice Overseas," 71 Mɪʟ. L. Rᴇᴠ. 1 (1976).

In United States v. Adams, 13 M.J. 728 (A.C.M.R. 1982), the court rejected the argument that the United States Court for Berlin was an available federal court. That court has tried only one case, United States v. Tiede & Rusk, 86 F.R.D. 227 (U.S. Court for Berlin 1979), and has no authority to try servicemembers.

32. United States v. Alef, 3 M.J. 414 (C.M.A. 1977).

33. *Id.* at 419, n.18. The Court suggested that motions for relief should be phrased in terms of a Bill of Particulars or motions to quash—terms at that time foreign to military practice. *See* § 13-5(F). No particular form or language was required to obtain the desired changes in the pleadings. *See generally* § 6-4(D)(5).

34. In United States v. George, 14 M.J. 990 (N.M.C.M.R. 1982), the court stated that with regard to drug offenses, the *Alef* pleading requirements could be met by simply alleging drug involvement. *See generally* Cooper, "Turning Over a New *Alef:* A Modest Proposal," Aʀᴍʏ Lᴀᴡ., Mar. 1982, at 8.

35. United States v. Graham, 9 M.J. 556 (N.C.M.R. 1980) (*Relford* factors were surplusage); United States v. Lewis, 5 M.J. 712 (A.C.M.R. 1978) (amendment did not change offense).

36. United States v. Ross, 9 M.J. 726 (A.C.M.R. 1980).

37. United States v. Rollins, 7 M.J. 125 (C.M.A. 1979). *See also supra* § 4-9. The military judge was to employ the preponderance of the evidence standard.

§ 4-11(B). Military Retreat from the *Relford* Ad Hoc Analysis.

In 1980 the Court of Military Appeals modified its narrow reading of *Relford* in *United States v. Trottier*,[38] a case involving drug sales. The court emphasized the threat that drugs pose to the military and its ability to perform its mission.[39] Drawing from Commerce Clause and War Powers jurisprudence the court concluded that virtually every drug offense would be service connected.[40] Three years later, in *United States v. Lockwood*,[41] The Court of Military Appeals indicated that it would be applying a broader template for service connection. There the court found service connection over two off-post offenses where an ID card, stolen from another servicemember on base, was used to commit an off-post theft and forgery. The court focused on the issue of whether the off-post offense had a significant effect on the military enclave and concluded that it did impact upon intangibles such as morale of service personnel and the installation's reputation.[42] The court further indicated that although the theory of pendant jurisdiction would not apply where on-post (clearly service connected) offenses were charged along with off-post offenses, the benefits to both the military *and* the accused would favor a single trial and provide another reason for finding service connection.[43] That single trial, said the court, should preferably be military, because of the inability of the civilian courts to adequately protect the military's interests and provide a convicted servicemember with the necessary rehabilitation.[44]

While the foregoing cases demonstrated a retreat from rigid application of *Relford*, the military courts never completely abandoned the rule. Nor did

---

38. 9 M.J. 337 (C.M.A. 1980). The decision includes a fine discussion on historical application of the *O'Callahan* and *Relford* decisions in military practice. See Schutz, "*Trottier* and the War Against Drugs: An Update," ARMY LAW., Feb. 1983, at 20.

39. United States v. Trottier, 9 M.J. at 345-48 (C.M.A. 1980).

40. *Id.* at 350. Subsequent cases found service connection where the servicemember had traces of drugs in his urine or blood when he reported back to the installation. See, e.g., Murray v. Haldeman, 16 M.J. 74 (C.M.A. 1983) (use of a "psychoactive drug," even while on extended leave, was service connected if the accused later enters a military installation and is under influence of the drug) United States v. Osburn, 23 M.J. 903 (N.M.C.M.R. 1987) (service connection over marijuana use while on extended leave); United States v. Walker, 23 M.J. 740 (A.C.M.R. 1987) (off-post sale of drugs was service connected); United States v. Malik, 23 M.J. 607 (A.F.C.M.R. 1986); United States v. Brown, 19 M.J. 826 (N.M.C.M.R. 1984) (positive test for drugs indicated a "physiological effect" of the drugs); United States v. Frost, 19 M.J. 509 (A.F.C.M.R. 1984) (use of drugs in "North America" established service connection).

41. 15 M.J. 1 (C.M.A. 1983).

42. *Id.* at 8-10. *See also* United States v. Pirraglia, 24 M.J. 671 (A.F.C.M.R. 1987) (bad check offenses damaged relationship between civilian and military communities and made it more difficult for servicemembers to get local support); United States v. Scott, 24 M.J. 578 (N.M.C.M.R. 1987) (adverse publicity generated by local newspaper publicizing accused's offenses of attempting to set up prostitution ring); United States v. Henderson, 23 M.J. 860 (A.C.M.R. 1987) (court considered adverse impact of bad credit reputation of command in community); United States v. Clarke, 23 M.J. 519 (A.F.C.M.R. 1986) (off-base rape of servicemember's wife had adverse impact on command); United States v. Blake, 20 M.J. 614 (A.F.C.M.R. 1985) (service connection existed over accused's theft of funds from public affairs community relations activities); United States v. Householder, 21 M.J. 613 (A.F.C.M.R. 1985).

43. United States v. Lockwood, 15 M.J. at 7-8 (C.M.A. 1983).

44. *Id.*

they endorse a wholesale adoption of *per se* service connection rules.[45] What emerged through the years was a variety of decisions from all of the military courts creating a grand collage of service connection.

The service connection requirement was finally abrogated by the Supreme Court in *Solorio v. United States*.[46]

§ 4-11(C). *Solorio v. United States*: The Demise of the Service Connection Requirement.

In his dissent in *O'Callahan v. Parker*, Justice Harlan predicted that "infinite permutations of possibly relevant factors are bound to create confusion and proliferate litigation over the [court-martial] jurisdiction issue."[47] His observation was prophetic. As the preceding discussion demonstrates, the military courts struggled again and again with the service connection requirement and in several instances dramatically shifted position on whether certain offenses should be treated as service connected.[48] The service connection requirement was finally abandoned by the Supreme Court in *Solorio v. United States*.[49] The accused, a member of the Coast Guard, had committed various acts of sexual abuse against two minor daughters of other members of the Coast Guard while he was stationed in Juneau, Alaska. Because there was no Coast Guard base or installation in Juneau, most of the servicemembers lived in civilian housing, and these offenses were committed in the privately owned residences of the victims' parents. The accused's offenses were not discovered, however, until after he had been reassigned to Governors Island, New York, and after he had committed similar offenses on minor daughters of other servicemembers in military housing at his new assignment.

At the accused's court-martial in New York, the trial judge ruled that the Alaska offenses were not service connected and dismissed those charges for lack of subject matter jurisdiction. On a government appeal of that ruling, the Coast Guard Court of Military Review reversed and reinstated the Alaska charges.[50] The Court of Military Appeals affirmed.[51] The court noted that "sex offenses against young children ... have a continuing effect on the victims and their families and ultimately on the morale of any military unit or organization to which the family member is assigned."[52] In concluding that there was

---

45. *Cf.* United States v. Chitwood, 12 M.J. 535 (A.F.C.M.R. 1981), where the court abandoned an *ad hoc* application of *Relford* and held that offenses by servicemembers against military property were service connected.
46. 483 U.S. 435 (1987).
47. 395 U.S. 258, 284 (1969).
48. See § 4-11(A) for a discussion of the *Relford* factors and how the military courts changed position several times over two decades.
49. 483 U.S. 435 (1987).
50. 21 M.J. 512 (C.G.C.M.R. 1985). Following affirmance by the United States Supreme Court, the charges were reinstated and Solorio was convicted by a general court-martial. United States v. Solorio, 29 M.J. 510 (C.G.C.M.R. 1989).
51. 21 M.J. 251 (C.M.A. 1986).
52. *Id.* at 256. *See also* United States v. Scott, 21 M.J. 345 (C.M.A. 1986) (jurisdiction over off-base sexual offenses on minors); United States v. Clarke, 23 M.J. 519 (A.F.C.M.R. 1986) (off-base

service connection, the court also evaluated the benefits to both the government and the accused in trying the Alaska and New York charges at the same trial, the adverse impact of returning some of the victims to Alaska to testify at a civilian trial, and the level of the Alaska civilian prosecutor's interest in prosecuting the accused.[53]

On certiorari review, the Supreme Court of the United States affirmed.[54] Chief Justice Rehnquist, writing for five members of the Court, indicated that the jurisdiction of a court-martial depends entirely on the status of the defendant as a member of the armed forces. It does not depend on service connection. In overruling *O'Callahan*, the Court noted that in that case the majority had departed from a long-standing precedent that status was the key and that the majority had also applied a less-than-accurate reading of the historical limits on court-martial jurisdiction. Instead, said the Court, there was support for Justice Harlan's dissent in *O'Callahan* that Article 1, § 8, cl. 14 of the Constitution grants Congress plenary authority to determine the extent of military jurisdiction. Comparing that power to Congress' plenary Commerce Clause powers, the Court noted that it has deferred to Congress in a variety of contexts where the individual rights of servicemembers were implicated.[55]

Justice Stevens concurred in the result but disagreed with the majority's decision to completely reevaluate *O'Callahan*. In his view, the opinion of the Court of Military Appeals had demonstrated that there was service connection in this case and unless the Court disagreed with that holding "it has no business reaching out to reexamine the decisions in [*O'Callahan* and *Relford*]."[56]

In dissent, Justice Marshall challenged the Court's historical analysis of court-martial jurisdiction and noted that it had completely ignored the underlying rationale of *O'Callahan* that courts-martial deny servicemembers the rights to indictment and trial by jury. He recognized that application of the *Relford* factors had been difficult and time-consuming and that it required narrow lines but that it was necessary because "[t]he trial of any person before a court-martial encompasses a deliberate decision to withhold procedural protections guaranteed by the Constitution."[57] Applying the *Relford* factors to the facts, he concluded that there was no service connection over the off-base Alaska offenses. Finally, he concluded that the Court's opinion dem-

---

rape of servicemember's wife had adverse impact on combat readiness of command where servicemember had to be removed from flight crew); United States v. Brenton, 24 M.J. 562 (A.F.C.M.R. 1987) (jurisdiction over accused's sexual offenses on stepdaughter).

Cf. United States v. Avila, 24 M.J. 501 (A.F.C.M.R. 1987) (en banc) (no jurisdiction over off-base sexual offenses on four-year-old stepdaughter); United States v. Barber, 23 M.J. 751 (A.F.C.M.R. 1987) (no jurisdiction over off-base sodomy of minor son); United States v. Dale, 23 M.J. 598 (A.F.C.M.R. 1986) (no jurisdiction over off-base sexual offenses against minor daughter of accused).

53. *Id.*
54. 483 U.S. 435 (1987).
55. *Id.* at 447. *See, e.g.*, Goldman v. Weinberger, 475 U.S. 503 (1986) (upholding Air Force regulation which placed some restriction on servicemember's free exercise of religion).
56. 483 U.S. at 451.
57. *Id.* at 466.

onstrated "contempt, both for the members of our armed forces and for the constitutional safeguards intended to protect us all."[58]

The Court did not indicate whether its decision would be applied retroactively, but at least one military court has indicated that it is retroactive.[59]

§ 4-11(C)(1). The Constitutional Implications of *Solorio*.

The Court in *Solorio* did not discuss in any depth the constitutional underpinnings of the service connection requirement found to be so crucial in *O'Callahan*. Nor did it address the constitutionality of the military criminal justice system itself.[60] Instead, it noted that in the area of military affairs it will generally defer to Congress when it comes to balancing a servicemember's constitutional rights against the requirements of the military. Thus, the fact that a servicemember might be denied the Fifth Amendment right to indictment by a grand jury and the Sixth Amendment right to a jury trial is not enough reason to require any special or individualized analysis of service connection. Congress has the prerogative to determine whether on balance those rights were applicable to servicemembers charged with "civilian" crimes.

Although it might be argued that the Court implicitly blessed the military justice system, it is probably safer to conclude that the Court only decided the narrower question of whether the service connection was required by the Constitution. The *Solorio* opinion provided an opportunity for the Supreme Court to review a criminal justice system that has changed dramatically in the past two decades and that had been so severely criticized by Justice Douglas in *O'Callahan*. Some of that same tenor was apparent in Justice Marshall's dissent. Although he commended the trial judge for his careful analysis of the *Relford* factors, he chastised the majority for showing contempt for servicemembers by not requiring service connection. Apparently in his view the military is still incapable of protecting constitutional rights.

Rather than expressing trust in the military justice system, the Court seems content for the time being with letting Congress run the system as it wills. Thus, various aspects of the military criminal justice system are still subject to constitutional scrutiny — by both military and Article III courts. Considering the Court's extremely deferential review of Congressional actions in recent years, it seems unlikely that the Court will find a part of the system constitutionally defective as long as Congress had any basis whatsoever for including it within the system.

It is important to note that the service connection requirement may be yet revived in other contexts. First, in *Loving v. United States*,[61] the Supreme

---

58. *Id.*
59. United States v. Avila, 27 M.J. 62 (C.M.A. 1988) (*Solorio* is retroactive). *See also* United States v. Starks, 24 M.J. 857 (A.C.M.R. 1987).
60. The accused apparently raised a due process challenge to court-martial jurisdiction in his arguments before the Court of Appeals for the Armed Forces but failed to raise it again before the Supreme Court. 483 U.S. 435, 451 n.18.
61. 116 S.Ct. 1737 (1996).

§ 4-11(C)(1) JURISDICTION § 4-11(C)(1)

Court concluded that Manual for Courts-Martial provisions for imposing the death penalty were not unconstitutional.[62] Observing that the service member had not challenged the power of the court-martial to try him for a capital offense, Justice Stevens in a concurring opinion (joined by three other Justices) observed:

> It is important to add to this observation that petitioner's first victim was a member of the Armed Forces on active duty and that the second was a retired serviceman who gave petitioner a ride from the barracks on the same night as the first killing. On these facts, this does not appear to be a case in which petitioner could appropriately have raised the question whether the holding in *Solorio v. United States*, should be extended to reach the imposition of the death penalty for an offense that did not have the "service connection" required prior to the change in the law effected in that case.
>
> The question whether a "service connection" requirement should obtain in capital cases is an open one both because *Solorio* was not a capital case, and because *Solorio's* review of the historical materials would seem to undermine any contention that a military tribunal's power to try capital offenses must be as broad as its power to try non-capital ones. Moreover, the question is a substantial one because, when the punishment may be death, there are particular reasons to ensure that the men and women of the Armed Forces do not by reason of serving their country receive less protection than the Constitution provides for civilians.
>
> As a consequence of my conclusion that the "service connection" requirement has been satisfied here, I join not only the Court's analysis of the delegation issue, but also its disposition of the case. By joining in the Court's opinion, however, I do not thereby accept the proposition that our decision in *Solorio* must be understood to apply to capital offenses. Nor do I understand the Court's decision to do so. That question, as I have explained, remains to be decided.[63]

Second, the full constitutional impact of *Solorio* may eventually be felt in the area of personal jurisdiction questions. As noted in the discussion on personal jurisdiction over civilians at § 4-7, and on jurisdiction over fraudulently discharged servicemembers at § 4-8(C)(3), the question of whether they should be subject to court-martial jurisdiction turns to some extent upon whether they would be deprived of the same constitutional protections which originally gave rise to the service connection requirement in *O'Callahan* — the right to indictment by grand jury and a jury trial. Does *Solorio* signal a shift in position on those issues and justify congressional attempts to expand personal jurisdiction as well? Probably not. The Court seemed careful in *Solorio* to indicate that jurisdiction depends on the status of the accused as a member of the armed forces at the time of the offense. Thus, it would probably

---
62. *See* § 16-3(A).
63. 116 S.Ct. at 1751.

stretch that opinion to conclude that previously invoked limitations on jurisdiction over civilians are also in jeopardy.

§ 4-11(C)(2). The Practical Implications of *Solorio*.

The *Solorio* opinion creates a broader category of concurrent jurisdiction between military and civilian authorities where a servicemember has committed an offense in the civilian community. As noted in § 4-12(A), when there is concurrent jurisdiction, the issue of priority of jurisdiction is largely a matter of comity and the subject of delicate negotiations. Civilian prosecutors may be sensitive to local public demands that a particular servicemember be tried in the local courts, and military prosecutors may fear that those courts will not adequately punish the individual or take into account specialized military needs or interests.

The defendant, of course, cannot choose the forum that will try him. But defense counsel may in some cases be able to tip the balance through attractive offers of plea bargaining in one forum or the other. In any event, *Solorio* has provided an opportunity to reevaluate military-civilian cooperation among prosecutors and to educate civilian prosecutors and defense counsel in the advantages, or disadvantages, of prosecuting the servicemember in the military courts.

Finally, it would be a mistake to assume that the *Solorio* decision means that every offense committed by a servicemember at any time is subject to court-martial jurisdiction. To be triable by a court-martial, the offense must have been committed by a person subject to the Uniform Code of Military Justice, while that person held that status.[64]

§ 4-12. Exclusive, Reciprocal, and Concurrent Jurisdiction.

Courts-martial have exclusive jurisdiction over purely military offenses.[1] But when the offense is violative of both the U.C.M.J. and a civilian code, concurrent, or nonexclusive, jurisdiction may exist. Further, Article 21, U.C.M.J.,[2] provides that court-martial jurisdiction may be concurrent with the jurisdiction of "military commissions, provost courts, or other military tribunals" with respect to offenses or persons which may be tried by those forums. For example, Article 106, U.C.M.J., provides that individuals accused of spying may be tried by court-martial or military commission. The more common concurrent jurisdiction questions center on those offenses that could be tried in either a state, federal, or foreign court.

Note that each of the armed forces has reciprocal jurisdiction over all persons subject to the U.C.M.J.[3] Thus, a Navy seaman may in theory be tried by

---

64. *See, e.g.*, United States v. Chodara, 29 M.J. 943 (A.C.M.R. 1990) (prosecution failed to show that reservist had ingested cocaine while on active duty).
1. R.C.M. 201(d).
2. *See* Appendix 3.
3. *See* R.C.M. 201(e)(1).

an Army court-martial. As a matter of policy, however, the *Manual* limits such exercises of jurisdiction to situations where:

> (A) The court-martial is convened by a commander of a joint command or joint task force who has been specifically empowered by the President, the Secretary of Defense, or a superior commander under the provisions of subsection (e)(2) of this rule to refer such cases for trial by courts-martial; or
>
> (B) The accused cannot be delivered to the armed force of which the accused is a member without manifest injury to the armed forces.[4]

As a matter of practice, exercises of reciprocal jurisdiction are rare.

§ 4-12(A). State and Federal Courts.

When an offense is punishable in both the military and civilian courts, the question of priority of prosecution is a matter of comity.[5] Generally, the particular military installation or command may have a negotiated memorandum of understanding with the state authorities detailing assessment of primary jurisdiction. In 1955, the Departments of Defense and Justice executed a Memorandum of Understanding that details each Department's responsibilities with regard to both the investigation and prosecution of crimes over which they have concurrent jurisdiction.[6] Additionally, Article 14, U.C.M.J., provides that the services may promulgate regulations prescribing the method of turning over to civilian authorities those servicemembers accused of a civilian offense.[7] Should a servicemember be tried first by a federal court for an offense over which the military also has jurisdiction, the federal trial will, under double jeopardy principles, bar a later military trial.[8] That rule

---

[4]. R.C.M. 201(e)(3). The Discussion portion of this Rule indicates that "manifest injury" does not mean minor inconvenience or expense.

[5]. *See, e.g.,* United States v. Herrington, 33 C.M.R. 814 (A.F.B.R. 1963). *See also* Fletcher, "Federal Criminal Prosecutions on Military Installations," ARMY LAW., Aug. 1987, at 21 (Part I) and Sept. 1987, at 5 (Part II).

[6]. *See* MCM, Appendix 3. The court in United States v. Duncan, 34 M.J. 1232 (A.C.M.R. 1992), aff'd on other grounds, 38 M.J. 476 (C.M.A. 1993), provided a detailed discussion of the problems associated with concurrent jurisdiction and concluded that the accused was denied a speedy trial where military authorities delayed prosecution until after the completion of a prosecution of the accused by the Department of Justice. The court concluded that an agreement of understanding between DOJ and DOD cannot extinguish court-martial jurisdiction or grant DOJ the authority to delay court-martial proceedings. The court agreed that the federal and military prosecutions had to be tried serially. But it also concluded that Article 30 and R.C.M. 401(b) and 707 and the statute of limitations dictated that the military prosecution should have come first.

[7]. *See* Air Force Instruction 51-201 para. 2.5, which prohibits courts-martial following civilian convictions unless the Secretary of the Air Force specifically approves such. United States v. Lorenc, 26 M.J. 793 (A.F.C.M.R. 1988) (approval not required where civil and military offenses were sufficiently dissimilar); United States v. Olsen, 24 M.J. 669 (A.F.C.M.R. 1987) (conviction reversed where no approval was obtained). *See also infra* § 13-3(G).

[8]. R.C.M. 907(b)(2)(C). *See, e.g.,* United States v. Chavez, 6 M.J. 615 (A.C.M.R. 1978) (trial by federal magistrate could bar court-martial for same offense). *See also infra* § 13-3(E).

does not apply to trials first held in a state court.[9] A convening authority's referral of charges to a court-martial is contrary to regulations governing prior trials in state or federal courts, is not a jurisdictional defect.[10]

§ 4-12(B). Foreign Courts.

The issue of concurrent or exclusive court-martial jurisdiction with regard to foreign courts is specifically addressed in applicable treaties between the United States (sending state) and the host nation (receiving state). Under principles of international law, the host nation has jurisdiction to try offenses committed within its borders unless it waives its jurisdiction.[11] For example, in Article VII of the Agreement Between the Parties to the North Atlantic Treaty Regarding the Status of their Forces (NATO SOFA), the United States has exclusive jurisdiction over those offenses punishable under United States law but not punishable under the law of the receiving state.[12] Where there is concurrent jurisdiction the treaty specifies those offenses for which each state may exercise primary right to exercise jurisdiction.[13] The issue of whether the

---

9. R.C.M. 907(b)(2)(C). United States v. Sloan, 35 M.J. 4 (C.M.A. 1992) (court rejected argument that accused had due process right not be tried by court-martial following civilian trial).

10. In United States v. Kohut, 41 M.J. 565 (N.M.Ct.Crim.App. 1994) the convening authority's failure to obtain prior approval from Judge Advocate General before referring charges to trial, where accused had already been convicted in state court, was not jurisdictional error. The court set out four factors to be considered in determining whether a service regulation has restricted a convening authority's discretion to refer charges: (1) policy is typically not law; (2) accused may assert regulation only if it is intended to protect an accused's right; (3) a court s duty to enforce agency regulation is clearest where compliance is required by Constitution or federal law; and (4) court has duty to enforce regulation if accused has relied upon it and will suffer substantially if regulation is not followed. *See also* United States v. Brown, 40 M.J. 625 (N.M.C.M.R. 1994) (setting out test).

11. This is part and parcel of the well-established "Visiting Forces Doctrine" first recognized in Schooner Exchange v. McFaddon, 11 U.S. (7 Cranch) 116 (1812). *See generally* Snee & Pye, *Status of Forces Agreements and Criminal Jurisdiction* (1957); United States v. Singleton, 15 M.J. 579 (A.C.M.R. 1983).

12. Article VII provides in part:

2. (a) The military authorities of the sending State shall have the right to exercise exclusive jurisdiction over persons subject to the military law of that State with respect to offenses, including offenses relating to its security, punishable by the law of sending State, but not by the law of the receiving State.

(b) The authorities of the receiving State shall have the right to exercise exclusive jurisdiction over members of a force or civilian component and their dependents with respect to offenses, including offenses relating to the security of that State, punishable by its law but not by the law of the sending State.

(c) For the purposes of this paragraph and of paragraph 3 of this Article a security offense against a State shall include

(i) treason against the State;

(ii) sabotage, espionage or violation of any law relating to official secrets of that State, or secrets relating to the national defense of that State.

13. Paragraph 3 of Article VII states:

In cases where the right to exercise jurisdiction is concurrent the following rules shall apply:

trial by one of the nations constitutes double jeopardy is also addressed in the treaty.[14] The treaty further provides a number of rights to servicemembers tried in the foreign court.[15] Note that an accused does not have any right to participate in the decision as to who will exercise jurisdiction[16] unless the decision denies him a fair trial.[17]

(a) The military authorities of the sending State shall have the primary right to exercise jurisdiction over a member of a force or of a civilian component in relation to
(i) offenses solely against the property or security of that State, or offenses solely against the person or property of another member of the force or civilian component of that State or of a dependent;
(ii) offenses arising out of any act of omission done in the performance of official duty.
(b) In the case of any other offense the authorities of the receiving State shall have the primary right to exercise jurisdiction.
(c) If the State having the primary right decides not to exercise jurisdiction, it shall notify the authorities of the other state as soon as practicable. The authorities of the State having the primary right shall give sympathetic consideration to a request from the authorities of the other State for a waiver of its right in cases where that other State considers such waiver to be of importance.

United States v. Murphy, 18 M.J. 220 (C.M.A. 1984) (sovereign nation has exclusive jurisdiction over offenses committed within its borders unless it has relinquished some jurisdiction to another country—citing Wilson v. Girard, 354 U.S. 524 (1957)).

14. *See* Article XVIII. *See also* United States v. Cadenhead, 14 C.M.A. 271, 34 C.M.R. 51 (1963) (discussion of double jeopardy provision in agreement with Japan); United States v. Stokes, 12 M.J. 229 (C.M.A. 1982) (court-martial following trial for a customs offense in Spanish contraband court did not constitute double jeopardy).
In United States v. Green, 14 M.J. 461 (C.M.A. 1983), the court noted that language in para. 8 of Art. VII, NATO SOFA, bars dual prosecutions by the receiving and sending States. Holding that an accused has standing to raise violations of that provision, the court concluded that British charges did not encompass the court-martial charges.
In United States v. Miller, 16 M.J. 169 (C.M.A. 1983), the court concluded that under the Korean SOFA the accused had not been subjected to double jeopardy when he was first convicted by a Korean court and then later tried by court-martial.
15. Paragraph 9, Article VII provides that:

Whenever a member of a force or civilian component or a dependent is prosecuted under the jurisdiction of a receiving State he shall be entitled —
(a) to a prompt and speedy trial;
(b) to be informed of the specific charge or charges made against him;
(c) to be confronted with the witnesses against him;
(d) to have compulsory process for obtaining witnesses in his favour, if they are within the jurisdiction of the receiving State;
(e) to have legal representation of his own choice for his defence or to have free or assisted legal representation under the conditions prevailing for the time being in the receiving State;
(f) if he considers it necessary, to have the services of a competent interpreter; and
(g) to communicate with a representative of the Government of the sending State and, when the rules of the court permit, to have such a representative present at his trial.

16. R.C.M. 201(d). Girard v. Wilson, 354 U.S. 524 (1957); United States v. Murphy, 36 M.J. 1137 (A.C.M.R. 1993) (accused had no standing to challenge his capital murder trial by court-martial rather than German courts); Porter v. Eggers, 32 M.J. 583 (A.C.M.R. 1990) (accused

---

17. Ponzi v. Fessenden, 258 U.S. 254 (1922); United States v. Murphy, 30 M.J. 1040 (A.C.M.R. 1990); United States v. Evans, 6 M.J. 577 (A.C.M.R. 1978).

PART IV

CONVENING AND COMPOSITION OF COURTS-MARTIAL;
REFERRAL OF CHARGES

§ 4-13. General.

The third and final requirement of court-martial jurisdiction, which focuses on the court-martial itself, has three elements: first, the court must be properly convened;[1] second, the court-martial must be properly composed, with regard to the qualifications and requisite number of participants;[2] and third, the charges must have been properly referred to the court.[3] The manner of meeting these requirements is crucial to the court's validity. If the court-martial is not structured in compliance with the U.C.M.J.'s mandates, any resulting conviction may be a nullity[4] and attempts to later ratify the court's existence and judgment may be fruitless.[5] Not every defect in the convening process or composition, however, is necessarily fatal to a court-martial's jurisdiction. This is especially true in defects arising from precatory language in the Manual for Courts-Martial that fleshes out the U.C.M.J. requirements for convening a court. But the three "jurisdictional" bases, noted above, must be touched in the process. These related, yet distinct, elements serve as the focus of discussion in the following sections.

Note that the actual process of convening a court, selecting the participants, and referring charges to it are discussed in more detail in Chapter 8. The material here emphasizes the jurisdictional elements of that process.

§ 4-14. Authority to Convene a Court-Martial.

The power to create a court-martial may be traced directly from the Constitution which delegates to Congress the power to prescribe the rules for the government of the armed forces; the U.C.M.J. meets that mandate and in turn prescribes the statutory requisites for creating a court-martial. The Manual for Courts-Martial further details the actual process of creation. Important to note here is that the court-martial is transitory in nature. Unlike civilian courts which exercise continuing jurisdiction, the military courts are authorized to hear only those cases which have been referred to it by the key figure in this process the "convening authority."

---

lacked standing to contest decision that United States and not Panama would exercise jurisdiction); United States v. Murphy, 30 M.J. 1040 (A.C.M.R. 1990) (accused had no standing to participate in discussions between Germany and United States on issue of jurisdiction, thus he had no right to representation by counsel in those discussions; the jurisdiction decision is not a critical stage in the trial).

1. R.C.M. 201(b)(1). *See also* Chapter 8.
2. R.C.M. 201(b)(2). *See also* Chapter 8.
3. R.C.M. 201(b)(3). *See also* Chapter 8.
4. McClaughry v. Deming, 186 U.S. 49 (1902); United States v. Emerson, 1 C.M.A. 43, 1 C.M.R. 43 (1951); United States v. O'Quin, 16 M.J. 650 (A.F.C.M.R. 1983). *Cf.* United States v. Allgood, 41 M.J. 492 (1995). *See generally* Tomes, "A Properly Convened Court — The Third Leg of the Jurisdictional Tripod," ARMY LAW., June 1981, at 3.
5. United States v. Genesee, 26 C.M.R. 845 (A.F.B.R. 1958).

§ 4-14(A). The Convening Authority.

The convening authority creates the court-martial. Procedurally, the process is simple: he or she appoints the court members[1] and refers the case to them for adjudication. If properly accomplished, the finding of the court stands on its own. It is not simply an investigation conducted on behalf of the convening authority.[2] The U.C.M.J. specifies those individuals who may convene a court and further allows the President and the Secretaries of the services to grant the requisite authority to other commanders.[3]

§ 4-14(A)(1). Statutory Authorization.

Articles 22, 23, and 24, U.C.M.J.[4] enumerate those commanders who have the authority to convene, respectively, general, special, and summary courts-martial. The authority granted by the U.C.M.J. is an attribute of command and is not dependent upon the rank of the commander.[5] Unless a superior has limited the commander's authority to convene a court, or he is otherwise disqualified, it is his authority alone to exercise; it may not be delegated.[6] If in his absence his command devolves to the next senior officer, that temporary commander possesses the authority to convene courts-martial.[7]

---

1. Prior to August 1, 1984 the convening authority also appointed the military judge, trial and defense counsels. That appointment process was for all practical purposes a formality because in most instances those individuals were predetermined by availability or attorney-client relationships.

2. *See, e.g.,* Mangsen v. Snyder, 1 M.J. 287 (C.M.A. 1976).

3. Articles 22, 23 and 24, U.C.M.J. United States v. Almy, 37 M.J. 465 (C.M.A. 1993) (Secretary of Transportation's designation in 1987 of all commanding officers in Coast Guard was not an improper delegation of authority to appoint convening authorities).
United States v. Bellett, 36 M.J. 563 (A.F.C.M.R. 1992) (convening order which cites ostensibly valid authority is prima facie evidence that convening authority was authorized to convene court).

4. *See* Appendix 3. United States v. DeBarrows, 41 M.J. 710 (C.G.Ct.Crim.App. 1995) (Coast Guard commanding officer of District 11 Reserve Stationkeepers authorized under Article 23 to convene court); United States v. Almy, 34 M.J. 1082 (C.G.C.M.R. 1992) (commander was authorized to convene special court-martial; in 1987, Secretary of Transportation designated commanding officers of all Coast Guard units as special court-martial convening authorities); United States v. Brinston, 28 M.J. 631 (A.F.C.M.R. 1989) (neither the commander of an Air Logistics Center nor the commander of an air base group were authorized to convene the general courts-martial which tried the accused).

5. *See, e.g.,* United States v. Williams, 6 C.M.A. 243, 19 C.M.R. 369 (1955). *See also* United States v. Ridley, 22 M.J. 43 (C.M.A. 1986) (no jurisdictional defect where CA junior in rank to accuser); United States v. McKillop, 38 M.J. 701 (A.C.M.R. 1993) (no jurisdictional defects in court convened by commander of USAG, Fort Dix; only change of name was involved).

6. United States v. Newcomb, 5 M.J. 4 (C.M.A. 1978).

7. United States v. Yates, 28 M.J. 60 (C.M.A. 1989) (no jurisdictional error where deputy post commander amended convening order although an officer more senior to him was present for duty at the same post); United States v. Bunting, 4 C.M.A. 84, 15 C.M.R. 84 (1954).
United States v. Radimecky, 25 M.J. 505 (A.F.C.M.R. 1987) (wing commander was not authorized to convene a court-martial because he had not been properly appointed in accordance with Air Force Regulations); United States v. Pazdernik, 22 M.J. 503 (A.F.C.M.R. 1986) (jurisdictional error where convening authority had not properly resumed command).

§ 4-14(A)(2). Disqualifications.

A general or special court-martial convening authority is disqualified from appointing a court if he is an *accuser*; the case must be referred to a superior competent authority for disposition.[8] Failure to do so, however, is a nonjurisdictional error.[9] An *accuser* is:

> [a] person who signs and swears to charges, any person who directs that charges nominally be signed and sworn to by another, and any other person who has an interest other than an official interest in the prosecution of the accused.[10]

The case law has amplified upon this proscription to include those convening authorities who are victims of an offense,[11] those connected with the prosecu-

---

United States v. Jette, 25 M.J. 16 (C.M.A. 1987) (commander's failure to resume command in accordance with Air Force Regulations did not divest him of his statutory authority to convene a court-martial); United States v. Harrington, 23 M.J. 788 (A.C.M.R. 1987) (because the next senior officer at the installation was the SJA, it was improper for the deputy post commander to assume command, and the court-martial he convened was therefore without jurisdiction; the deputy commander should have been temporarily appointed to command).

United States v. Miner, 23 M.J. 694 (A.F.C.M.R. 1986) (*en banc*) (applying Air Force regulations, the court concluded that a commander's mere return from a temporary absence was insufficient to reinstate his convening authority powers where in his short absence another commander had been "appointed" to the command); United States v. Bierley, 23 M.J. 557 (A.F.C.M.R. 1986) (commander was not properly reappointed to command before convening court).

United States v. Guidry, 19 M.J. 984 (A.F.C.M.R. 1985) (court lacked jurisdiction because the substitute convening authority who convened the court had not properly assumed command).

8. Art. 22(b), U.C.M.J., United States v. Jeter, 35 M.J. 442 (C.M.A. 1992) (accused waived nonjurisdictional error where court-martial was convened by subordinate of accuser).

9. United States v. Shiner, 40 M.J. 155 (C.M.A. 1994) (failure to forward case was nonjurisdictional error which accused waived); United States v. Jeter, 35 M.J. 442 (C.M.A. 1992).

10. Art. 1(9), U.C.M.J. *See* United States v. Shiner, 40 M.J. 155 (C.M.A. 1994) (ship's captain may have been accuser); United States v. Jeter, 35 M.J. 442 (C.M.A. 1992) (general who had been blackmailed by accused was considered accuser; nonjurisdictional error to have case referred to trial by subordinate; court held that accused had waived issue by putting general in position of having an interest in the case); United States v. Corcoran, 17 M.J. 137 (C.M.A. 1984) (CA ordered charges preferred and had personal interest in case); United States v. Shelton, 26 M.J. 787 (A.F.C.M.R. 1988) (convening authority not authorized to refer charges to court where he had ordered subordinate to prefer charges); United States v. Azevedo, 24 M.J. 559 (C.G.C.M.R. 1987) (convening authority's interest was official rather than personal).

In United States v. Beauchamp, 17 M.J. 590 (A.C.M.R. 1983), the CA was disqualified because the accused was charged with disobeying a direct order given by the CA. United States v. O'Quin, 16 M.J. 650 (A.F.C.M.R. 1983) (accused's first trial was a nullity because convening authority had acted earlier as the accuser; no double jeopardy to accused because of second trial).

Cf. United States v. Deachin, 22 M.J. 611 (A.C.M.R. 1986) (accused waived objection to CA who had personal interest in case; the accused had committed a sexual offense on the minor daughter of the CA's deputy commander).

11. United States v. Gordon, 1 C.M.A. 255, 2 C.M.R. 161 (1952). *See also* United States v. Marsh, 3 C.M.A. 48, 11 C.M.R. 48 (1953); United States v. Byers, 34 M.J. 923 (A.C.M.R. 1992), *rev'd on other grounds*, 40 M.J. 321 (C.M.A. 1994) (convening authority disqualified as accuser where accused was charged with order issued by him; the court indicated that the jurisdictional error of an accuser convening the court is different from cases involving lawfully convened courts which may be subject to unlawful command influence).

tion of the case,[12] and those connected with the pretrial investigation.[13] The proscription does not apply to summary court-martial convening authorities.[14]

§ 4-14(A)(3). Delegation of Authority.

The authority to convene a court-martial is personal and may not be delegated. Until recently it was common practice for convening authorities to delegate to their legal officers the authority to select or excise the parties to the court-martial. In a series of decisions the Court of Appeals for the Armed Forces emphasized the codal requirement that the convening authority, in exercising prosecutorial discretion powers, must personally appoint the court.[15] The same rule applies to the authority to refer charges to a particular court. Improper delegation voids the court-martial.[16]

§ 4-14(B). Convening Orders.

The vehicle for appointing a court-martial is the convening order,[17] which is almost always written, but may be oral.[18] If oral orders are used, written confirming orders should follow.[19] It is not the format of the orders that controls, but rather the information included. The orders indicate the type of court-martial and identify the members. A quick review of the order will normally answer questions concerning composition. The courts may, however, look behind the order if it appears that the convening authority has not personally selected the members.[20] If either the order or its amendments is defective, the court-martial may also be void.[21]

---

12. *See, e.g.*, Brookins v. Cullins, 23 C.M.A. 216, 49 C.M.R. 5 (1974); United States v. Cox, 37 M.J. 543 (N.M.C.M.R. 1993) (convening authority did not become accuser simply because he had ordered restriction which accused was charged with breaking; he had only official interest in case); United States v. Beauchamp, 17 M.J. 590 (A.C.M.R. 1983) (accused charged with disobeying immunity order given by CA).
13. United States v. Hammork, 13 C.M.R. 385 (A.B.R. 1953). Granting immunity to witnesses does not disqualify the convening authority from referring charges. *See* United States v. Hernandez, 3 M.J. 916 (A.C.M.R. 1977), *petition denied,* 4 M.J. 122 (C.M.A. 1977). *Cf.* § 8-8(B) *infra.*
14. R.C.M. 1302(b).
15. United States v. Ryan, 5 M.J. 97 (C.M.A. 1978). *Cf.* United States v. Allgood, 41 M.J. 492 (1995) (convening authority may adopt selection made by predecessor in command; court noted that although the procedure used was unusual in terms of regulatory form or procedure, it did not have codal or jurisdictional significance).
16. *Id.* at 101.
17. United States v. Bellett, 36 M.J. 563 (A.F.C.M.R. 1992) (convening order which cites ostensibly valid authority is prima facie evidence that convening authority was authorized to convene court). See a sample convening order at Appendix 9. See also Chapter 8 for a discussion of the procedures for referring charges to trial.
18. United States v. Napier, 20 C.M.A. 422, 43 C.M.R. 262 (1971). The U.C.M.J. is silent as to the format of the convening order but the MCM and the service supplements contain sample formats.
19. *See, e.g.*, United States v. Broadus, 2 M.J. 438 (A.C.M.R. 1975).
20. The Government is generally permitted to rely upon a presumption of regularity. United States v. Saunders, 6 M.J. 731 (A.C.M.R. 1978); United States v. Holmes, 17 M.J. 611

---

21. *See, e.g.*, United States v. Griffin, 13 C.M.A. 213, 32 C.M.R. 213 (1962). *Cf.* United States v.

§ 4-15. Properly Composed Court-Martial.

In examining the question of whether the court-martial is properly composed, the practitioner must determine whether the proper number of individuals were appointed and whether those individuals are competent to act in their appointed capacity. The three categories of participants include (1) the military judge, (2) counsel, and (3) court members. Although not all defects in composition are necessarily jurisdictional, the appellate courts consistently admonish those at the trial level to pay particular attention to the process of appointing the participants. Discussion here will briefly address the prerequisites for proper composition of the court-martial.

§ 4-15(A). Military Judge.

The court-martial proceedings and judgment are void unless the military judge meets the statutory qualifications of Article 26, U.C.M.J.: The military judge must be (1) a commissioned officer of the armed forces, (2) a member of the bar of a federal court or a member of the bar of the highest court of a State, and (3) certified to be qualified for duty as a military judge by The Judge Advocate General of the judge's armed forces. A military judge is *ineligible* to sit on a case if he is the accuser or a witness for the prosecution or has acted as an investigating officer or counsel in the same case.[1]

Before August 1, 1984 only the convening authority could appoint the military judge.[2] Now, Article 16(a), U.C.M.J. envisions that the judge will be appointed through judicial channels in accordance with service regulations.[3]

Replacement of the military judge after assembly of the court without a showing of good cause may result in jurisdictional error.[4] Jurisdictional error may result where the accused has not properly requested trial by the military judge alone an option provided by Article 16 of the U.C.M.J.[5] In the past,

---

(N.M.C.M.R. 1983) (written confirmation is not required where there was no indication that convening authority lacked power to modify convening order). *Cf.* United States v. Emerson, 12 M.J. 512 (N.M.C.M.R. 1981) (court declined to presume that jurisdictional prerequisites were met).

Good, 39 M.J. 615 (A.C.M.R. 1994) (administrative error in convening order's date was nonjurisdictional, administrative error); United States v. Otero, 26 M.J. 546 (A.F.C.M.R. 1988) (discrepancy in date on convening order and date reflected in referral section of charge sheet not jurisdictional error); United States v. Blascak, 17 M.J. 1081 (A.F.C.M.R. 1984) (typographical-administrative error on charge sheet was of little consequence and nonjurisdictional). *See also* United States v. Fields, 17 M.J. 1070 (A.F.C.M.R. 1984); United States v. Shepardson, 17 M.J. 793 (A.F.C.M.R. 1983); United States v. Smiley, 17 M.J. 790 (A.F.C.M.R. 1983).

1. If the judge is statutorily competent but "ineligible," the proceedings will generally not be void, but a rehearing may be required. An accused may waive a judge's "eligibility." *See* United States v. Airhart, 23 C.M.A. 124, 48 C.M.R. 685 (1974).
2. United States v. Newcomb, 5 M.J. 4 (C.M.A. 1978).
3. R.C.M. 503(b). *See* § 8-3(A).
4. R.C.M. 505(e). United States v. Smith, 3 M.J. 490 (C.M.A. 1975).
5. United States v. Dean, 20 C.M.A. 212, 43 C.M.R. 52 (1970). The approval of a request for trial by judge alone need not be in writing. United States v. Bowman, 49 C.M.R. 406 (A.C.M.R. 1974).

failure to properly note the appointment of the trial judge in the appropriate orders could be fatal to the jurisdiction of the court.[6] More recent caselaw, however, indicates that "administrative missteps" in appointing a judge will not be considered a jurisdictional defect. And counsel's failure to object to the detailing of a particular judge may be waived,[7] or as one court has indicated, "forfeited."[8] The difference in attitude may have resulted, at least in part, from the fact that currently judges are detailed by the judiciary, and not the convening authority.[9] Indeed, there is authority for the proposition that errors in detailing of a military judge will not rise to the level of plain error if the judge meets the statutory qualifications set out in Article 26(a), U.C.M.J.[10]

§ 4-15(B). Counsel.

Failure to properly appoint a trial counsel (prosecutor) and defense counsel is apparently not fatal. The Court of Appeals for the Armed Forces has ruled that because counsel are not an "integral" part of the court-martial, defects in their appointments are matters of procedure to be examined for prejudice.[11] The qualifications and role of counsel are discussed in more detail in §§ 8-3, 12-2(F) and 15-2.

§ 4-15(C). Court Members.

The court members are the military's equivalent of the civilian jury. To be competent to serve as a court member, the individual must be a servicemember on active duty and in a category of personnel authorized to hear cases involving officers, warrant officers, and enlisted personnel.[12] A member is not competent to serve if he is "the accuser or a witness for the prosecution or has acted as an investigating officer or as counsel in the same case."[13] The Manual for Courts-Martial and the service regulations provide additional guidelines for competency to serve.[14] Service of an unqualified

---

6. *See* United States v. Singleton, 21 C.M.A. 432, 45 C.M.R. 206 (1972).
7. United States v. Hawkins, 24 M.J. 257 (C.M.A. 1987) (accused waived objection to substitution of judge by affirmatively requesting trial by new judge; court saw no basis for conferring jurisdictional significance on "such nonmomentous events.").
8. United States v. Robinson, 43 M.J. 501 (A.F.Ct.Crim.App. 1995) (accused forfeited any challenge to substitute judge by not making appropriate motion); United States v. Pagel, 40 M.J. 771, 776 (A.F.C.M.R. 1994) (noting distinction between waiver and forfeiture of issue).
9. United States v. Dixon, 18 M.J. 310, 312 (C.M.A. 1984) (noting 1983 change in Article 26(a), U.C.M.J.).
10. United States v. Robinson, 43 M.J. 501, 504 (A.F. Ct. Crim. App. 1995).
11. United States v. Wright, 2 M.J. 9 (C.M.A. 1976); United States v. Daigneault, 18 M.J. 503 (A.F.C.M.R. 1984) (defects in appointment of trial counsel is a procedural matter which must be tested for prejudice); United States v. Bartlett, 12 M.J. 880 (A.F.C.M.R. 1981); R.C.M. 503(c) (Analysis).
12. Art. 25, U.C.M.J.; R.C.M. 502(a). Note that Article 25 does not specifically disqualify aliens as members. *See* United States v. Yager, 7 M.J. 171, 173, n. 6 (C.M.A. 1979).
13. Art. 25(d)(2), U.C.M.J.
14. *See* R.C.M. 503(a).

§ 4-15(C)　　　　　MILITARY CRIMINAL JUSTICE　　　　　§ 4-15(C)

member may be a jurisdictional defect,[15] although there are cases that apply the waiver doctrine [16] or require a showing of prejudice where the disqualification is not a fundamental defect.[17]

If the commander is otherwise qualified to act as a convening authority, it is not jurisdictional error for him to convene a court-martial that was selected by his predecessor.[18] If one or more appointed members is missing when the court is assembled, that absence, whether excused or unexcused,[19] is probably not a

---

15. *See, e.g.,* United States v. Gebhart, 34 M.J. 189 (C.M.A. 1992) (convening authority's relieving member and appointing him in same amending order was harmless, nonjurisdictional, administrative error; accused waived error by not objecting).

United States v. Hood, 37 M.J. 784 (A.C.M.R. 1993) (failure of accused to make personal election of enlisted members on court was jurisdictional error).

United States v. Smith, 37 M.J. 773 (A.C.M.R. 1993) (convening authority's direction to SJA to select only certain ranks of enlisted members from particular units amounted to an impermissible grade-based shortcut to obtain members qualified under Article 25; court thus lacked jurisdiction).United States v. Brookins, 33 M.J. 793 (A.C.M.R. 1991) (counsel's written request for enlisted members on court did not satisfy jurisdictional requirement that accused do so personally); United States v. Caldwell, 16 M.J. 575 (A.C.M.R. 1983) (court ruled that the trial was a nullity because one of the court members was an "interloper" and not properly appointed to the court); United States v. Beeks, 9 C.M.R. 743 (A.F.B.R. 1953); United States v. Wells, 4 C.M.R. 501 (C.G.B.R. 1952). *Cf.* United States v. Gebhart, 32 M.J. 634 (A.C.M.R. 1991) (irregularities in appointing two members to court were not jurisdictional errors; court cautioned trial participants to pay close attention to convening orders).

See also United States v. Brandt, 20 M.J. 74 (C.M.A. 1985) (court was without jurisdiction where the accused's request for enlisted members was signed by counsel rather than the accused). *See infra* § 12-3(B).

Cf. United States v. Sonnenfeld, 41 M.J. 765 (N.M. Ct. Crim. App. 1994) (whether servicemember has been appointed to court is question of convening authority's intent; here, confusing set of convening orders and amendments left some question about status of member who actually sat on case; court placed emphasis on apparent construction of orders by trial participants who took no exception to member's presence).

16. United States v. Bland, 6 M.J. 565 (N.C.M.R. 1978) (Medical Service Corps officer was ineligible under Navy regulations but accused waived defect); United States v. Wilson, 16 M.J. 678 (A.C.M.R. 1983) (accused waived objection that an enlisted member was in the same unit as the accused in violation of Art. 25(c)(1), U.C.M.J.; the case also contains citations to other cases applying the waiver doctrine). *See generally* Laverdure & Arberg, "Determining Unit 'Membership' for Appointment of Enlisted Personnel to Courts Martial," ARMY LAW. Aug. 1984 at 15. *Cf.* United States v. Morris, 9 C.M.R. 786 (A.F.B.R. 1953) (mere failure to challenge disqualified member was not waiver).

17. *See, e.g.,* United States v. Stafford, 25 M.J. 609 (A.C.M.R. 1987) (no jurisdictional error where SJA failed to memorialize instructions from convening authority to add alternate members to the court); United States v. Forehand, 8 C.M.R. 564 (N.B.R. 1953).

In United States v. Emerson, 12 M.J. 512 (N.M.C.M.R. 1981), the court assumed that one of the members had not been properly appointed but did not find the special court-martial jurisdictionally defective because at least three properly appointed members remained.

United States v. McGee, 15 M.J. 1004 (N.M.C.M.R. 1983) (appointment of members junior to the accused, in violation of Art. 25(d)(1), was not jurisdictional and accused was not prejudiced).

18. *See* United States v. Bianchi, 25 M.J. 557 (A.C.M.R. 1987). *Cf.* United States v. Yates, 25 M.J. 582 (A.C.M.R. 1987) (commander could not ratify or adopt unauthorized substitution of court members by deputy post commander who had no authorization to convene courts-martial). *See also infra* § 8-3(C)(4).

19. United States v. Colon, 6 M.J. 73 (C.M.A. 1978); United States v. Allen, 5 C.M.A. 626, 18 C.M.R. 250 (1955); United States v. Malczewskyj, 26 M.J. 995 (A.F.C.M.R. 1988) (*en banc*). The absence of members, however, may result in denial of military due process under *Malczewskyj*, *supra*.

jurisdictional defect as long as the minimum number of members is present.[20]

§ 4-16. Charges Properly Referred to Court-Martial.

The Manual for Courts-Martial specifically includes, as a separate jurisdictional prerequisite, the requirement that each charge before the court-martial must be properly referred to it by a competent authority.[1] The process of referring charges to a court is discussed in more detail at § 8-4. The Drafters' Analysis for that provision notes that the language was included:

> [T]o reflect the distinction long recognized in military justice, between creating a court-martial by convening it, and extending to the court-martial the power to resolve certain issues by referring charges to it. Thus, a court-martial has power to dispose only of those offenses which a convening authority has referred to it.[2]

The significance of the distinction was not clearly spelled out in the 1969 *Manual*. Consequently, a number of cases involving irregular referral of charges were decided on a nonjurisdictional basis.[3] That is, defects in the referral process were considered largely procedural.[4] Where defects were found, the courts could find that the charges had been "constructively referred"[5] or that the convening authority had later "ratified" the referral.[6] Those cases were distinguished, however, in *United States v. Wilkins*,[7] where the accused entered a guilty plea, with the knowledge of the convening authority, to a charge that had not been referred to the court-martial.[8] Citing the *Manual*, the court concluded that the prior theories of waiver,[9] ratification,[10] and constructive referral[11] were no longer viable and that the specifica-

---

20. *See* § 1-8(D).
1. R.C.M. 202(b)(3). United States v. Allgood, 41 M.J. 492 (1995) (charges properly referred by commander of newly designated unit to court established by convening order promulgated by predecessor commander; court noted that such procedure was unusual in terms of regulatory form or procedure).
2. R.C.M. 202(b) Analysis.
3. United States v. Stinson, 34 M.J. 233 (C.M.A. 1992) (omission in convening authority's referral indorsement on charge sheet was administrative defect); United States v. Wilkins, 28 M.J. 992 (A.C.M.R. 1989) (citing cases).
4. If the error is considered nonjurisdictional, it can usually be waived. Jurisdictional errors can be raised at any time and cannot be waived. See § 13-3(A) regarding motions to dismiss based upon lack of jurisdiction.
5. *See* United States v. Michaels, 3 M.J. 846 (A.C.M.R. 1977); United States v. Clark, 49 C.M.R. 192 (A.C.M.R. 1974).
6. United States v. Clark, 49 C.M.R. 192 (A.C.M.R. 1974).
7. 28 M.J. 992 (A.C.M.R. 1989).
8. *Id.* The accused had been charged with larceny offenses but he pleaded guilty, as part of a pretrial agreement, to offenses of receiving stolen property. Significantly, this latter offense is not a lesser included offense of larceny.
9. *Id.* at 996.
10. *Id.* at 997.
11. *Id.* at 996. The court did not consider the issue to be one of jurisdiction, but rather one of pleading guilty to what was substantially the same offense, *i.e.*, use of a contraband drug.

tions to which he pleaded guilty had never been properly referred to trial.[12]

However, the court concluded that the convening authority's acceptance of the defendant's proposed plea agreement relating to an entirely different charge amounted to the "functional equivalent of an order by the convening authority that the charges be referred to the court-martial for trial."[13] The court added that in this case the accused had waived the requirements that the convening authority consider the Staff Judge Advocate's pretrial advice and that the charges be sworn. By recommending the offense to the convening authority, said the court, the defendant had acted as the "accuser."

Apparently not all defects in the referral process will be considered jurisdictional.[14] For example, in *United States v. King*,[15] the convening authority intended to refer the charges to one court, but some unknown person changed the referral to another court.[16] Although this was a legally "erroneous error," the court concluded that this type of error was nonjurisdictional.[17]

See also United States v. Cooper-Tyson, 37 M.J. 481 (C.M.A. 1993) (although charge may be referred by means of a pretrial agreement, that is functional equivalent of convening authority's order doing so; in this case, the pretrial agreement mentioned an offense completely different from the one to which the accused pled guilty; the court noted that while referral is a jurisdictional prerequisite, the form of the order is not); United States v. Longmire, 39 M.J. 536 (A.C.M.R. 1994) (postarraignment amendment was major change requiring rereferral; jurisdictional defect); United States v. Moore, 36 M.J. 795 (A.C.M.R. 1993) (court had no jurisdiction where convening authority had not indorsed, the charges entered into a pretrial agreement on the charges, or in some other way personally ordered the charges be heard by a particular court-martial).

12. *Id.* at 994. *Cf.* United States v. Cornelius, 29 M.J. 501 (A.C.M.R. 1989) (distinguishing *Wilkins* and holding that accused could plead guilty to unreferred charge of adultery although it was not a lesser-included offense to referred charge of rape).

13. 29 M.J. 421 (C.M.A. 1990).

14. *See, e.g.,* United States v. Palmer, 41 M.J. 747 (N.M.Ct.Crim.App. 1994) (incorrect notation on referral block to convening order 54-93 instead of 51-93 was nonjurisdictional, nonprejudicial, scrivener s error); United States v. Good, 39 M.J. 615 (A.C.M.R. 1994) (erroneous date on convening order was administrative, nonjurisdictional error); United States v. Thompson, 37 M.J. 601 (A.C.M.R. 1993) (error in dating convening order did not amount to jurisdictional error); United States v. Hudson, 27 M.J. 734 (A.C.M.R. 1988); United States v. Whitfield, 35 M.J. 535 (A.C.M.R. 1992) (typographical error in SJA recommendation was nonjurisdictional).

15. 28 M.J. 397 (C.M.A. 1989).

16. *Id.* at 399.

17. *Id.* The court did not refer to R.C.M. 202(b)(3). *See also* United States v. Glover, 15 M.J. 419 (C.M.A. 1983); United States v. Ryan, 5 M.J. 97 (C.M.A. 1978); United States v. Randle, 35 M.J. 789 (A.C.M.R. 1992) (trial by court different from one to which it was referred was administrative error where convening authority appointed members of both courts); United States v. Choy, 33 M.J. 1080 (A.C.M.R. 1992) (discrepancy in trial counsel's announcement of convening order, the convening order itself and the charge were not jurisdictional defects; the court noted that such discrepancies may destroy presumption of regularity which normally attaches to such documents); United States v. Knight, 33 M.J. 896 (A.F.C.M.R. 1991) (publishing written order day after date of referral of charges is not jurisdictional defect; date written order was authenticated administratively is inconsequential for purposes of R.C.M. 601(a)); United States v. Thompson, 31 M.J. 667 (A.C.M.R. 1990) (accused waived irregularities in pretrial processing).

APPENDIX REFERENCES

Appendix 1. Abbreviations.
Appendix 2. Glossary.
Appendix 3. U.C.M.J.
Appendix 9. Court-Martial Convening Order.
Appendix 31. Punishments Chart.

ANNOTATED BIBLIOGRAPHY

BOOKS

Moyer, *Justice and the Military* (1972).

> This one-volume loose-leaf reference contains detailed discussions of the role of commanders, jurisdiction, military criminal procedure, First Amendment rights, substantive law, and collateral review of courts-martial by the civilian court system.

Zillman, Blaustein & Sherman, *The Military in American Society* (1978).

> This loose-leaf casebook represents the efforts of nine individuals familiar with the workings of the military system of justice. Valuable discussions include treatment of the American military establishment, entry into the military, the military justice system, individual rights of servicemembers, termination of military service, and the law of armed conflict. Selected cases are discussed and notes for further reading are located at the end of each chapter.

PERIODICALS

In General

"Bibliography of Military Law," 10 10 AM. CRIM. L. REV. 175 (1971).

> This extensive bibliography lists finding aids, books, symposiums, surveys, service publications, and selected writings in legal periodicals. Most entries predate the 1968 amendments to the U.C.M.J.

Hodgson, "Limiting Court-Martial Jurisdiction: A Continuing Process," 20 A.F. L. REV. 256 (1978).

> The author presents a brief historical overview of the military justice system in the United States and notes that court-martial jurisdiction has been limited to what was needed. Examining more closely the civilian and military decisions which have restricted jurisdiction, the author questions whether it is now too restrained.

Schlueter, "Court-Martial Jurisdiction: An Expansion of the Least Possible Power," 73 J. CRIM. L. & CRIMINOLOGY 74 (Spring 1982).

> This article examines the recent statutory and judicial developments which have apparently expanded military jurisdiction. Serving as the core for this discussion

is the amendment to Article 2, UCMJ and the Court of Military Appeals' decision in United States v. Trottier, 9 M.J. 337 (C.M.A. 1980).

Spak, "Military Justice: The Oxymoron of the 1980s," 20 CAL. W. L. REV. 436 (1984).

In a critical analysis of expanding court-martial jurisdiction after *United States v. Trottier*, Professor Spak strongly asserts that military jurisdiction should be limited to purely military offenses. In support of his stance, he advocates four justifications: (1) military discipline does not require a broad military justice system that encroaches upon the constitutional rights of military personnel; (2) military jurisdiction unfairly attaches to military members fraudulently induced into joining the military; (3) military procedural law is inherently unfair; and (4) due to the inequity of military law, military jurisdiction should not attach to off-post offenses.

Personal Jurisdiction: Inception and Termination

Dilloff, "The Involuntary Volunteer: Coerced Military Enlistments," 25 AM. U. L. REV. 437 (1976).

This is a thorough and valuable discussion, albeit dated by recent legislative and judicial changes, of the problem of involuntary enlistment. The author describes various factual permutations that give rise to attacks on court-martial jurisdiction on the grounds of coerced enlistment, and the void/voidable dichotomy created by the courts to deal with these varying situations. The author calls for greater control and discipline of recruiters, and increased vigilance by the courts to ensure that no recruit enter the military involuntarily.

Woodruff, "The Rule in Ginyard's Case—Congressional Intent or Judicial Field Expedient," 21 A.F. L. REV. 285 (1979).

Article 3(a), U.C.M.J. provides that after a servicemember has been discharged he may only be court-martialed for offenses punishable by five or more years confinement and that cannot be tried in any other civilian court. He must, of course, be on active duty at the time of trial. This article presents a critical analysis of the military courts' interpretation of what terminates "status" for purposes of Article 3(a) specifically United States v. Ginyard, 16 C.M.A. 512, 37 C.M.R. 132 (1967), wherein the court ruled that discharges for the purpose of reenlisting with no actual break in status, are nonetheless terminations of status. The author suggests that this rule unduly limits court-martial jurisdiction and should be overruled judicially or through legislative changes to Article 3(a).

Ziegler, "The Termination of Jurisdiction Over the Person and the Offense," 10 MIL. L. REV. 139 (1960).

The author begins this discussion of paragraph 11 of the 1969 Manual for Courts-Martial, which provided for the termination of court-martial jurisdiction upon a person's separation from the service, by posing several hypothetical situations designed to explore the periphery of the paragraph's applicability. After a thorough discussion of the analytical problems presented by these scenarios, Ziegler concludes that paragraph 11 should be amended so as to allow consistent jurisdiction over persons who depart but rejoin the service or otherwise come under military control.

Personal Jurisdiction: Reservists

Gates & Casida, "Report to The Judge Advocate General by the Wartime Legislation Team," 104 MIL. L. REV. 139 (1984).

In a response to the Judge Advocate General's concern that the military justice system may be rendered ineffective during wartime, the Wartime Legislation Team conducted a thorough study of the current military justice system. This study group concluded that although the system could operate during a low-intensity conflict, major revisions, including jurisdiction over civilians, which the authors discuss, are necessary for the system to properly operate in the midst of a general war.

Moore, "Disciplinary and Administrative Discharge Authority of Reserve and National Guard Commanders," 16 A.F. L. REV. 65 (1974).

This short article presents a fine thumbnail sketch of the powers of a Reserve or National Guard commander to proceed with court-martial charges or administrative action against a servicemember who fails to satisfactorily perform his duties.

Partington, "Court-Martial Jurisdiction Over Weekend Reservists After *United States v. Caputo*," 37 NAV. L. REV. 183 (1988).

This article supercedes the author' s earlier article, *infra*, at 7 U.S.F. L. Rev. 57 (1972) which addressed the same topic. The author traces the historical development of jurisdiction over reservists including the 1986 amendment to the U.C.M.J. which attempted to broaden jurisdiction. The author concludes that the amendment left several important questions unanswered and recommends that Congress clarify that change.

Partington, "Court-Martial Jurisdiction Over the Weekend Reservist: Wallace v. Chafee," 7 U.S.F. L. REV. 57 (1972).

The author examines the 9th Circuit's interpretation of Art. 2(3), U.C.M.J., in which the court, *inter alia*, refused to apply a strict waiver-of-right standard to the voluntariness of an inactive duty reservist's acceptance of orders that subjected him to court-martial jurisdiction. The author argues that the decision, by liberally conferring jurisdiction, runs counter to both judicial preference for narrow application of military jurisdiction and the Article Congressional background. The legislative history of the Article is included as an appendix.

Reed and Jarlenski, "Procedures and Issues Relating to the Court-Martial of Reservists," 32 A.F. L. REV. 331 (1990).

This short article, which sets out a step-by-step process for prosecuting reservists, is designed to assist those responsible for investigating and prosecuting reservists on active or inactive duty training. The article includes five helpful appendices which contain actual case studies.

Saxon, "The Weekend Warrior and the Uniform Code of Military Justice: Does the Military Have Jurisdiction Over the Weekend Reservist?," 7 CAL. W. L. REV. 238 (1970).

> The author describes the 1970 donnybrook that led to the court-martial and conviction of 15 marine reservists for failure to obey an order to get regulation haircuts, and, in anticipation of the 9th Circuit's disposition of the appeal arising from these convictions (*Wallace v. Chafee*), identifies and discusses the relevant case law, policies, and other considerations that will influence that decision on the issue of military jurisdiction over inactive duty reservists. After surveying the different approaches the services take to this problem, the author concludes that the military clearly does have court-martial jurisdiction over such personnel, but that reserve commanders should be given the flexibility to deal with disciplinary problems through administrative channels.

Personal Jurisdiction: Civilians

Bishop, "Court-Martial Jurisdiction Over Military-Civilian Hybrids: Retired Regulars, Reservists, and Discharged Prisoners," 112 U. PA. L. REV. 317 (1964).

> This is an extensive 60-page survey of the law as applied to three groups of persons that cannot be easily classified as either military or civilian for the purpose of extending court-martial jurisdiction. In an entertaining style, the author reviews historical materials and the development of case law as to each category and concludes that greater consistency in result might be obtained by lessening the fixation on status and examining to a greater degree other factors such as the circumstances of the offense and its punishment.

Everett & Hourck, "Crime Without Punishment-Ex-Servicemen, Civilian Employees, and Dependents," 13 JAG L. REV. 184 (1971).

> The authors address the problem of civilians who escape punishment for crimes committed abroad because local authorities decline to prosecute and the military courts are precluded from exercising jurisdiction over non-military and discharged persons. After examining a number of incidents illustrating the problems posed by the jurisdiction gap, the article evaluates different proposals to extend jurisdiction and the constitutional aspects of imposing military jurisdiction on civilians.

Gibson, "Lack of Extraterritorial Jurisdiction Over Civilians: A New Look at an Old Problem," 148 MIL. L. REV. 114 (1995).

> This lengthy article addresses the problem of exercising United States' jurisdiction over civilians working with the military in overseas locations. The author recommends that Congress expand slightly the jurisdiction of a court-martial to extend to civilians who are deployed on military operations. In her view, the expansion would pass constitutional muster.

Giovagnoni, "Jurisdiction: Minus a Uniform," 14 A.F. L. REV. 190 (1973).

> This article provides a detailed historical survey of the major cases and constitutional issues surrounding military jurisdiction over civilian ancillaries. The analysis contained here also includes a realistic evaluation of the contemporary scope of

military-civilian jurisdiction and an informed prediction of future trends in this area.

Grishman, "Commentary—Refining Military Jurisdiction Over Civilians," 19 CATH. U.L. REV. 351 (1970).

This brief article explores the historical framework, statutory and case law, for jurisdiction over civilians and concludes that Congress could refine Article 2(10), U.C.M.J., which provides for jurisdiction over civilians in time of war.

Bartley, "Military Law in the 1970s: The Effects of *Schlesinger v. Councilman*," 17 A.F. L. REV. 65 (Winter 1975).

In this short article, written shortly after *Schlesinger* was decided, the author argues that in its holding the Supreme Court, by failing to define when, if ever, federal courts may exercise equitable jurisdiction over the decisions of military courts, and by failing to establish a manageable analysis for determining "service-connection," missed the opportunity to avert extensive confusion among the courts.

Blumenfeld, "Court-Martial Jurisdiction over Civilian-Type Crimes," 10 AM. CRIM. L. REV. 81 (1971).

This 30-page work contains an excellent analysis of court-martial jurisdiction over civilian-type crimes as affected by *O'Callahan v. Parker*. The writer isolates the major issues concerning the determination of jurisdiction and realistically evaluates the arguments and authorities supporting the different positions on those issues.

Cooper, "*O'Callahan* Revisited: Severing the Service Connection," 76 MIL. L. REV. 165 (1977).

While reviewing both civilian and military court interpretations of *O'Callahan*, the writer illustrates the inconsistencies arising from the difficulties presented by the service connection standard.

Droddy, "King Richard to *Solorio*: The Historical and Constitutional Bases for Court-Martial Jurisdiction in Criminal Cases," 30 A.F. L. REV. 91 (1989).

The author provides an historical review of the issue of court-martial jurisdiction over servicemembers and civilians and concludes that there is ample authority for the latter. He briefly addresses changes in the military justice system that have occurred since the Supreme Court's decision in *O'Callahan* and concludes that "military due process" will remain equal to, or better than, civilian due process.

Harrison, "Be All You Can Be (Without the Protection of the Constitution)," 8 HARV. BLACK LETTER J. 221 (1991).

Noting that the Supreme Court has at one time or another denied basic constitutional protections to various minority groups, the author argues that the Court's decision in *Solorio v. United States* has deprived servicemembers of their basic rights. That decision, he points out, should be of particular concern to minority groups because the current all-volunteer composition of the armed forces includes a high percentage of minorities.

Hoffman, "Court-Martial Jurisdiction and the Constitution: An Historical and Textual Analysis," 21 CREIGHTON L. REV. 43 (1987).

Noting a certain hostility against things military, the author recounts the historical evolution of court-martial jurisdiction and concludes that the Supreme Court's decision in *Solorio* is consistent with constitutional principles and that because courts-martial are outside the federal judiciary, created by Article III, Congress has plenary power to determine the scope of court-martial jurisdiction.

Horbaly and Mullins, "Extraterritorial Jurisdiction and its Effect on the Administration of Military Criminal Justice Overseas," 71 MIL. L. REV. 1 (Winter 1976).

This article explores the ramifications for military justice administration stemming from extraterritorial application of federal criminal laws by the Criminal Justice Reform Act of 1975. Major cases concerning extraterritorial jurisdiction over servicemen are analyzed and related to new congressional laws designed to subject civilians and servicemen acting in civilian capacity to the jurisdiction of the U.S. federal courts.

Morrow, "*Solorio v. United States:* The Death and Burial of 'Service Connection' Jurisdiction," 28 A.F. L. REV. 201 (1989).

This short article provides an overview and analysis of the Supreme Court's decision in *Solorio v. United States,* which terminated the service connection requirement for determining whether a particular offense was subject to court-martial jurisdiction.

Rice, "*O'Callahan v. Parker:* Court-Martial Jurisdiction, 'Service Connection,' Confusion, and the Serviceman," 51 MIL. L. REV. 41 (1971).

This article presents a broad criticism of the holding of the Supreme Court in *O'Callahan* that court-martial jurisdiction does not extend to offenses that are not "service-connected." It contests the historical and precedential bases of the decision and concludes that the Court has ignored the teaching of history and its previous decisions and usurped the constitutional prerogative of Congress to define the scope of court-martial jurisdiction. Arguing that the "service-connection" standard is judicially unworkable, the author closes with the hope that the replacement of Warren and Fortas with Burger and Blackmun will spur a reconsideration.

"Symposium, Military Law," 10 AM. CRIM. L. REV. 1 (1971).

This symposium issue covers a valuable range of topics pertinent to the practice of military criminal law. Included are articles on jurisdiction over civilian type offenses, plea bargaining, sentencing, discovery, appeals, and an article by General Westmoreland on the commander's perspective of military justice. Also included is a fine bibliography of books, articles, and listings of military law materials.

Tomes, "The Imagination of the Prosecutor: The Only Limitation to Off-Post Jurisdiction Now, Fifteen Years After *O'Callahan v. Parker,*" 25 A.F. L. REV. 1 (1985).

The author reviews the development of military jurisdictional law since *O'Callahan* and observes that the broad status orientation that *O'Callahan* purported to restrict by requiring "service-connection" has been largely reinstated by the accretion of relaxed jurisdictional rules in particular circumstances. The current state of the law, according to the author, is that a "potentially adverse effect" on military interests, and that, in fact, *O'Callahan* stood for the principle, only recently understood, that proof of status alone, without some showing that military interests are negatively implicated by the conduct, is insufficient to confer jurisdiction.

CHAPTER 5

THE COMMANDER'S INVESTIGATION, PRETRIAL RESTRAINTS, AND CONFINEMENT

PART I
THE COMMANDER'S INVESTIGATION

§ 5-1. Introduction.
§ 5-2. The Commander's Investigation: In General.
§ 5-3. Searches and Seizures.
    § 5-3(A). The Servicemember's Reasonable Expectation of Privacy.
    § 5-3(B). Probable Cause Searches.
    § 5-3(C). Nonprobable Cause Searches.
        § 5-3(C)(1). In General.
        § 5-3(C)(2). Searches of Government Property.
        § 5-3(C)(3). Gate Searches; Border Searches.
        § 5-3(C)(4). Searches in Jails and Restricted Areas.
        § 5-3(C)(5). Emergency Searches.
        § 5-3(C)(6). Consernt Searches.
        § 5-3(C)(7). Searches Incident to Apprehension.
        § 5-3(C)(8). Searches Incident to Lawful Stop.
        § 5-3(C)(9). Other Nonprobable Cause Searches.
    § 5-3(D). Other Reasonable Searches.
        § 5-3(D)(1). Inspections and Inventories.
        § 5-3(D)(2). Body Views and Intrusions.
    § 5-3(E). Seizures.
    § 5-3(F). Exclusionary Rule; Exceptions.
§ 5-4. The Right Against Self-Incrimination, Interrogation, and Immunity.
    § 5-4(A). The Right Against Self-Incrimination.
        § 5-4(A)(1). In General.
        § 5-4(A)(2). Reporting Requirements.
        § 5-4(A)(3). Comments on Invoking the Right.
    § 5-4(B). Interrogation of Suspects; Rights Warnings.
    § 5-4(C). Grants of Immunity.
§ 5-5. Eyewitness Identification.

PART II
PRETRIAL RESTRAINTS AND CONFINEMENT

§ 5-6. In General.
§ 5-7. Apprehension.
§ 5-8. Pretrial Restraints.
    § 5-8(A). In General.
    § 5-8(B). Conditions on Liberty.
    § 5-8(C). Restriction in Lieu of Arrest.
    § 5-8(D). Arrest.
§ 5-9. Pretrial Confinement.
    § 5-9(A). In General.
    § 5-9(B). Initial Decision to Confine.
    § 5-9(C). Review by Commander.
    § 5-9(D). Review of Commander's Decision to Confine.
    § 5-9(E). Judicial Review.
§ 5-10. Illegal Pretrial Punishment and Restraints.
    § 5-10(A). In General.

§ 5-10(B). Pretrial Punishment Other Than Restraint.
§ 5-10(C). Pretrial Restraints Constituting Illegal Punishment.
§ 5-10(D). Remedies; Waiver.
Appendix References.
Annotated Bibliography.

PART I

THE COMMANDER'S INVESTIGATION

§ 5-1. Introduction.

In almost all cases the disposition of a suspected offense begins with an investigation by the commander which often includes coordination with military law enforcement personnel. In most cases, the commander will consider whether some sort of pretrial restraint is required to ensure that the accused servicemember is present for trial.

Both of these topics are the focus of this chapter, which in turn is the first chapter in a series dealing with pretrial procedures that generally reflect an important screening process. That process is designed to protect servicemembers from baseless charges and is enforced not only through external judicial action but also through self-imposed internal controls because few commanders are willing to take a weak case to court and risk an acquittal. Additionally, as the following discussion makes clear, military lawyers are playing a greater role in the initial stages of the investigation and in the decision to restrain a servicemember pending charges.

§ 5-2. The Commander's Investigation: In General.

The accused's immediate commander is charged with conducting an informal inquiry of the reported offense.[1] Information that an offense has been committed can come through both informal and formal sources. The more serious offenses will have probably first been investigated by one of the several investigative branches in the armed forces,[2] and in those cases the commander's "inquiry" will normally involve simply reviewing sworn statements and the investigator's formal report. In many cases, however, the commander will receive an informal report from someone in his unit that criminal acts have been or are being committed. In those instances the commander's responsibility may include a personal investigation or direction to a third party to gather more information and make a report.[3]

---

1. R.C.M. 303.
2. For example, the Army's investigative arm is the Criminal Investigation Department (CID), the Air Force uses its Office of Special Investigation (OSI) and the Navy and Marine Corps rely upon the Naval Criminal Investigative Service. Where an offense leads to concurrent jurisdiction by the Department of Defense and Department of Justice, the Memorandum of Understanding entered by those agencies is consulted. Pertinent extracts of that agreement are included in the *Manual* at Appendix 3.
3. *See* R.C.M. 303.

Because commanders do exercise limited law enforcement functions, the investigation may include actually authorizing or conducting searches and seizures and may include personal interrogation of a suspect or an accused. In those situations, the commander's actions must be carefully measured against applicable constitutional, statutory, and regulatory standards.

§ 5-3. Searches and Seizures.

It is generally accepted that the Fourth Amendment's protections are available to servicemembers.[1] Nonetheless, the unique military environment has traditionally permitted some limitation in its application.[2] The U.C.M.J. provides no specific guidance here, but the Military Rules of Evidence[3] and numerous judicial interpretations provide ample definition of the amendment's protections as applied in military practice. For the most part, the methodology of analyzing Fourth Amendment questions in the civilian sector is applicable in the military setting. For example, questions of standing[4] and probable cause[5] and questions concerning whether the search was governmental in nature[6] are generally resolved in the same manner. The differences tend to center on the degree of expectation of privacy, which is generally more limited in the military,[7] and the power of a commander to intrude into areas under his control.[8] As long as the military commander remains neutral and detached he may act as a magistrate and authorize searches and seizures of persons and property in his unit.[9] In addition, he may personally conduct inspections and

---

1. United States v. Ezell, 6 M.J. 307 (C.M.A. 1979); United States v. Jacoby, 11 C.M.A. 428, 29 C.M.R. 244 (1960); United States v. French, 38 M.J. 420 (C.M.A. 1993) (foreign search of accused's residence by British officers was not conducted, instigated, or participated in by military personnel; thus Constitutional protections not available). *See generally* Saltzburg, Schinasi & Schlueter, *Military Rules of Evidence Manual* (3d ed. 1991). *Cf.* Lederer & Borch, "Does the Fourth Amendment Apply to Armed Forces?" 144 MIL. L. REV. 110 (1994).
2. *See, e.g.,* United States v. McCarthy, 38 M.J. 398 (C.M.A. 1993) (discussion of different levels of privacy in military setting); United States v. Middleton, 10 M.J. 123 (C.M.A. 1981). The burden of showing that military conditions require a rule different from the prevailing civilian rule rests on the government. Courtney v. Williams, 1 M.J. 267, 270 (C.M.A. 1976). In United States v. Fagan, 28 M.J. 64 (C.M.A. 1989), the court indicated that servicemembers knowingly accept limits on their liberty and privacy and it would be unrealistic to "incorporate civilian standards of freedom of movement wholesale into the military setting." *Id.* at 69.
3. Rules 311 to 317, MIL. R. EVID.
4. *See* Rule 311(a)(2). United States v. Parrillo, 34 M.J. 112 (C.M.A. 1992) (standing to suppress evidence obtained by investigators overhearing telephone conversation turns on reasonable expectation of privacy).
5. Rule 315, MIL. R. EVID.
6. MIL. R. EVID. 311(a).
7. *See* United States v. McCarthy, 38 M.J. 398 (C.M.A. 1993).
8. *See, e.g.,* United States v. Chapple, 36 M.J. 410 (C.M.A. 1993) (commanding officer not empowered to authorize off-base search of accused's overseas apartment).
9. *See infra* § 5-2(A)(1). United States v. Moreno, 23 M.J. 622 (A.F.C.M.R. 1986) (installation commander was not magistrate under Right to Financial Privacy Act to authorize search of credit union records).

investigatories to ensure the fitness and readiness of his command.[10]

The material that follows provides a brief overview of some of the more commonly encountered Fourth Amendment issues and potential intrusions.

§ 5-3(A). The Servicemember's Reasonable Expectation of Privacy.

One of the threshold issues in analyzing search and seizure issues is to first determine whether the accused's reasonable expectation of privacy has been intruded upon.[11] And the other threshold issue is whether the intrusion was effected by governmental action.[12]

With regard to the first issue, the military courts have generally followed civilian caselaw precedent in framing the issue of expectations of privacy. That is, the courts will apply both a subjective and objective assessment of the expectation of privacy; the accused must have believed that he had a reasonable expectation of privacy and his belief must be supported by a finding that a reasonable person, i.e., the public, would perceive the expectation to be reasonable. If either component is missing, there is no reasonable expectation of privacy. That is, the accused has no standing to contest the legality of the search or seizure.[13]

On the other hand, the court may conclude that although the accused was claiming an expectation of privacy, that expectation was not reasonable. This is the more commonly confronted situation. Although the courts address the issue on a case by case basis,[14] some generalizations are possible. An accused probably does have a reasonable expectation of privacy in body fluids and substances,[15] personal property,[16] living quarters,[17] and the curtilage for the property,[18] and his own vehicle.[19] He probably does not have a reasonable

---

Where the command is located overseas, the commander's authority may extend to searches of foreign quarters occupied by his unit. *See* United States v. Bunkley, 12 M.J. 240 (C.M.A. 1981); United States v. Whiting, 12 M.J. 253 (C.M.A. 1982).

10. *See infra* § 5-2(A)(3).
11. *See* MIL. R. EVID. 311(a)(1).
12. *See* MIL. R. EVID. 311(a).
13. MIL. R. EVID. 311(a).
14. *See, e.g.*, United States v. Moore, 38 M.J. 490 (C.M.A. 1994) (no right of privacy in recorded conversations between accused and lover); United States v. Britton, 33 M.J. 238 (C.M.A. 1991) (accused had no reasonable expectation of privacy in gymnasium locker that he was not permitted to use).

United States v. Maxwell, 42 M.J. 568 (A.F.Ct.Crim.App. 1995) (court concluded that accused had reasonable expectation of privacy in e-mail messages stored in America Online computers); United States v. Baker, 28 M.J. 902 (A.C.M.R. 1989) (no expectation of privacy in large cardboard box that could easily be opened).

15. United States v. Pond, 36 M.J. 1050 (A.F.C.M.R. 1993) (urine).
16. United States v. Mancini, 8 F.3d 104 (1st Cir. 1993) (expectation of privacy in box).
17. United States v. Thatcher, 28 M.J. 20 (C.M.A. 1989). *Cf.* United States v. Moore, 23 M.J. 295, 299 (C.M.A. 1987) (Cox, J., concurring) (questioning whether servicemembers have any expectation of privacy in barracks).
18. United States v. Kaliski, 37 M.J. 105 (C.M.A. 1993) (curtilage protected).
19. The courts recognize that the expectation is limited, however. California v. Carney, 471 U.S. 386 (1985). The fact that an accused has a reasonable expectation of privacy in his or her vehicle will not end the inquiry, however, because the courts have recognized the "automobile exception" for the warrant requirement.

expectation of privacy in property he has abandoned,[20] bank records,[21] external body characteristics or markings,[22] open fields,[23] someone else's living quarters[24] or vehicles,[25] property located in common areas,[26] government property,[27] in property relinquished to third persons,[28] or in cordless telephone conversations.[29] The courts have also concluded that an accused does not have a reasonable expectation of privacy in odors[30] or heat[31] given off by certain substances.

Assuming that the accused can demonstrate that he had a reasonable expectation of privacy in the area searched, or the property seized, he must still show that the intrusion was effected by governmental authority, i.e., military,[32] federal,[33] or state officials.[34] Intrusions by private persons acting in a nongovernmental capacity are not prohibited.[35] Nor are intrusions conducted

---

20. *See, e.g.*, United States v. Sanford, 12 M.J. 170 (C.M.A. 1981) (accused denied ownership).
21. United States v. Wooten, 34 M.J. 141 (C.M.A. 1992) (bank records).
22. United States v. Fagan, 28 M.J. 64 (C.M.A. 1989) (no expectation of privacy in fingerprints); United States v. Repp, 23 M.J. 589 (A.F.C.M.R. 1986) (accused had no expectation of privacy in his forearms which were examined for needle marks). *See generally* Schlueter, "Investigative Detentions for Purposes of Fingerprinting," ARMY LAW., Oct. 1988, at 10.
23. United States v. Dunn, 480 U.S. 294 (1987); Oliver v. United States, 466 U.S. 170 (1984). *See also* MIL. R. EVID. 314(j) (searches of open fields and woodlands).
24. United States v. Foust, 17 M.J. 85 (C.M.A. 1983) (another's apartment).
25. United States v. Phillips, 38 M.J. 593 (N.M.C.M.R. 1993) (another's car).
26. United States v. McCarthy, 38 M.J. 398 (C.M.A. 1993) (private but common area provided no reasonable expectation of privacy; accused had no reasonable expectation of privacy from apprehension in barracks room); United States v. Battles, 25 M.J. 58 (C.M.A. 1987) (no expectation of privacy in berthing area of naval vessel); United States v. Watkins, 32 M.J. 1054 (A.C.M.R. 1991) (no expectation of privacy in attic which was accessible by anyone from common stairwell).
27. United States v. Muniz, 23 M.J. 201 (C.M.A. 1987) (although a servicemember may acquire an expectation of privacy in government property assigned to him for his use, the accused had no expectation of privacy in his government-owned credenza vis-à-vis his commander who was looking for information in an attempt to locate the accused); United States v. Craig, 32 M.J. 614 (A.C.M.R. 1991) (accused had no expectation of privacy in his desk owned by government, which could not be locked, others shared the office, and accused had been told not to lock it and to remove personal items).
28. United States v. Visser, 40 M.J. 86 (C.M.A. 1994) (no reasonable expectation of privacy in household goods voluntarily given to moving company); United States v. Ayala, 26 M.J. 190 (C.M.A. 1988) (accused had no expectation of privacy in former residence).
29. United States v. Sullivan, 38 M.J. 746 (A.C.M.R. 1993) (no expectation of privacy in cordless telephone calls; such calls are not subject to Wiretap Act).
30. United States v. Place, 457 U.S. 1104 (1983) (dog sniffing luggage); United States v. Alexander, 34 M.J. 121 (C.M.A. 1992) (use of drug-detection dog).
31. United States v. Ford, 34 F.3d 992 (11th Cir. 1994) (use of thermal imaging device not a search; no reasonable expectation of privacy in heat coming from home).
32. MIL. R. EVID. 311(c)(1). *See, e.g.*, United States v. Jacobs, 31 M.J. 138 (C.M.A. 1990) (entry into accused's off-base apartment by NCO during off-duty hours was nonetheless official).
33. MIL. R. EVID. 311(c)(2). United States v. Baker, 30 M.J. 262 (C.M.A. 1990) (search conducted by store detective working for post exchange was considered a search by a government agent).
34. MIL. R. EVID. 311(c)(2); United States v. Porter, 36 M.J. 812 (A.C.M.R. 1993) (military policeman's involvement in blood-alcohol test of accused by Panamanian authorities constituted participation and was thus United States action).
35. *See, e.g.*, United States v. Sullivan, 42 M.J. 360 (1995) (accused's neighbor was acting in private capacity when he intercepted accused's cordless telephone calls; court noted that at time

by foreign officers who are, not working at the behest, or with the participation of, United States officers.[36]

§ 5-3(B). Probable Cause Searches.

As noted in the introductory comments to this section, the requirement of probable cause is equally applicable in the military setting. When the commander has relied upon a probable cause to support a search, the prosecution must be prepared to show that the "totality of the circumstances" test of *Illinois v. Gates*[37] has been satisfied.[38]

Although there is no shortage of military case law addressing the question of whether probable cause was present,[39] there are fewer cases touching the question of whether the commander who made the probable cause determination and authorized the search was neutral and detached.[40] Military caselaw has indicated that a commander's prior law enforcement activities in a partic-

---

of interception, federal statute did not extend to cordless telephone calls); United States v. Hodges, 27 M.J. 754 (A.F.C.M.R. 1988) (intrusion by private freight carrier employee).

36. MIL. R. EVID. 311(c)(3).

37. 462 U.S. 213 (1983). In *Gates* the Supreme Court abandoned the two-prong test of Aguilar v. Texas, 378 U.S. 108 (1964). MIL. R. EVID. 315(f), which reflected the *Aguilar* test, was subsequently amended in 1984 to reflect the newer, more flexible *Gates* test.

United States v. Strozier, 31 M.J. 283 (C.M.A. 1990) (commander had probable cause to order seizure of accused's urine for testing); United States v. Poole, 30 M.J. 271 (C.M.A. 1990) (commander had insufficient probable cause to conduct successive urinalysis testing of the accused); United States v. Moore, 23 M.J. 295 (C.M.A. 1987) (there was no probable cause to search barracks for stolen stereo equipment).

United States v. Johnson, 23 M.J. 209 (C.M.A. 1987) (court applied *Illinois v. Gates* test although MIL. R. EVID. 315 in effect at the time of the search required the more rigid *Aguilar* two-pronged test).

United States v. Kabelka, 30 M.J. 1136 (A.F.C.M.R. 1990) (accused's possession of drugs at off-base location did not provide probable cause, standing alone, to search his on-base quarters 15 miles away).

Cf. Stevens, "New Jersey v. T.L.O.: Towards A More Reasonable Standard for Military Search Authorizations," 25 A.F. L. REV. 338 (1985) (author suggests that probable cause standard should be partially eliminated).

38. The *Gates* test for probable cause is located in Rule 315, MIL. R. EVID. United States v. Washington, 39 M.J. 1014 (A.C.M.R. 1994) (search authorization not supported by probable cause; commander lacked sufficient information on reliability of informant).

39. *See, e.g.,* United States v. Mix, 35 M.J. 283 (C.M.A. 1992) (commander had probable cause, even under the two-pronged *Aguilar-Spinelli* test, to authorize search of accused's car); United States v. Figueroa, 35 M.J. 54 (C.M.A. 1992) (commander had substantial basis for believing that accused's quarters contained weapons); United States v. Breseman, 26 M.J. 398 (C.M.A. 1988) (probable cause to search desk and room); United States v. Jones, 24 M.J. 294 (C.M.A. 1987) (authorization for urinalysis test); United States v. Mix, 32 M.J. 974 (A.C.M.R. 1991) (under facts commander had probable cause to authorize search of accused's car).

40. United States v. Freeman, 42 M.J. 239 (1995) (commander was neutral and detached at time he ordered seizure of accused's urine; court indicated that commander is only disqualified where he has acted in a law enforcement capacity or has been actively involved in process of gathering evidence); United States v. Lazenby, 42 M.J. 702 (C.G.Ct.Crim.App. 1995) (commander was neutral and detached; he did not know accused, had no interest in investigation and was acting solely as officer responsible for quarters).

ular case preclude him from later authorizing a probable cause search.[41] Mere presence at the scene, however, will not disqualify a commander.[42]

A commander's authority to authorize a search will extend to those persons and places over which the commander exercises control.[43]

Assuming that the search required issuance of a search authorization by the commander[44] or a search warrant by a civilian judicial authority,[45] the authorities may dispense with that authorization or warrant if exigencies required immediate action.[46] Such exigencies may exist if there is insufficient time,[47] if military "operational necessity" prevents communication with the person who would authorize the search,[48] if the search is of an operational vehicle,[49] or if the Constitution permits a warrantless search.[50]

To date, the military courts have not required a written affidavit, but the information given to the commander to support probable cause should preferably be under oath.[51] Normally, search authorizations [52] are informally given by the commander of the unit wherein the sought evidence is located,[53] although military judges may be authorized by the Secretary of their service to

---

41. United States v. Ezell, 6 M.J. 307 (C.M.A. 1979); United States v. Rivera, 10 M.J. 55 (C.M.A. 1980) (commander personally investigated tip in attempt to find probable cause); United States v. Cordero, 11 M.J. 210 (C.M.A. 1981) (commander took active part in setting up drug buy); United States v. Washington, 39 M.J. 1014 (A.C.M.R. 1994) (commander who relied only on police statement without determining facts was not impartial for purposes of good faith exception; court noted that commander's impartiality is an important and delicate role).

United States v. Allen, 31 M.J. 572 (N.M.C.M.R. 1990) (admiral's ongoing briefings and knowledge of case did not render him partial or less than neutral); United States v. Sloan, 30 M.J. 741 (A.F.C.M.R. 1990) (base commander was neutral and detached and did not instigate or devise the plan to ensnare the accused).

See generally Rule 315(d), MIL. R. EVID.; Cooke, "*United States v. Ezell*: Is the Commander a Magistrate? Maybe," ARMY LAW., Aug. 1979, at 9; Bender, "C.O.M.A. and the Commander's Power to Authorize Searches," ARMY LAW., July 1980, at 1.

42. United States v. Middleton, 10 M.J. 123 (C.M.A. 1981); United States v. Powell, 8 M.J. 260 (C.M.A. 1980).

43. MIL. R. EVID. 315(d). See, e.g., United States v. Chapple, 36 M.J. 410 (C.M.A. 1993) (commander not authorized to issue search authorization for off-base apartment).

44. MIL. R. EVID. 315(b)(1) (search authorization by commander).

45. MIL. R. EVID. 315(b)(2) (search warrants by competent civilian authority). See, e.g., United States v. Visser, 40 M.J. 86 (C.M.A. 1994) (civilian search warrant was sufficiently specific); United States v. Modesto, 39 M.J. 1055 (A.C.M.R. 1994) (US magistrate issued search warrant not overbroad).

46. MIL. R. EVID. 315(g) (exigencies).

47. MIL. R. EVID. 315(g)(1) (insufficient time).

48. MIL. R. EVID. 315(g)(2) (lack of communications).

49. MIL. R. EVID. 315(g)(3) (search of operational vehicle).

50. MIL. R. EVID. 315(g)(4) (other warrantless searches).

51. United States v. Stuckey, 10 M.J. 347 (C.M.A. 1981).

52. The term *search authorization* is used to describe a commander's direction to search and the term *search warrant* is used to describe a civilian-authorized search. See Rule 315(b). United States v. Phillips, 38 M.J. 593 (N.M.C.M.R. 1993) (civilian search warrant of military accused's residence was amply supported by probable cause).

53. See Rule 315(d)(1), MIL. R. EVID. United States v. Evans, 35 M.J. 306 (C.M.A. 1992) (applying automobile exception to search of accused's car by agents; original search authorization only extended to residence).

issue such authorizations.[54] The commander may only delegate his authority to conduct and authorize searches to magistrates and military judges.[55]

§ 5-3(C). Nonprobable Cause Searches.

§ 5-3(C)(1). In General.

Military practice also recognizes a variety of intrusions not requiring probable cause. Rule 314, Military Rules of Evidence, spells out these commonly recognized nonprobable cause searches. Included within that Rule are searches of government property,[56] gate searches,[57] border searches,[58] searches in jails and restricted areas,[59] emergency searches,[60] consent searches,[61] searches incident to a lawful apprehension,[62] frisks incident to a lawful stop,[63] and searches of open fields.[64] Rule 314 also includes a catch-all provision for other constitutionally permissible non-probable cause searches which may not be specifically mentioned in the Rules.[65] These intrusions are addressed in the following discussion.

§ 5-3(C)(2). Searches of Government Property.

The Rules of Evidence and military caselaw recognize that probable cause is normally not needed to conduct searches of government property.[66] Actually, the ability of the government to conduct such intrusions really goes to the question of the accused's expectation of privacy. That is, the accused normally cannot argue that he or she had a reasonable expectation in someone else's property, in this case the government's. Thus, a suppression motion addressing this type of search usually fails because the accused has no standing to

---

54. Rule 315(d)(3), MIL. R. EVID. *See, e.g.*, Army Regulation 27-10, Chapter 9 (permitting military judges to authorize searches of designated persons and places). That same chapter generally addresses particular Army rules governing searches and seizures. United States v. Schoolfield, 36 M.J. 545 (A.C.M.R. 1992) (search of accused's room approved by military magistrate).
55. Rule 315(d)(2), MIL. R. EVID. In United States v. Kalscheuer, 11 M.J. 373 (C.M.A. 1981), the Court of Military Appeals greatly restricted the commander's authority to delegate his search powers. The delegation should be preferably in writing.
56. Rule 314(d).
57. Rule 314(c).
58. Rule 314(b).
59. Rule 314(h).
60. Rule 314(i).
61. Rule 314(e), MIL. R. EVID. United States v. Castro, 23 C.M.A. 166, 48 C.M.R. 782 (1974).
62. Rule 314(b).
63. Rule 314(f).
64. MIL. R. EVID. 314(j).
65. MIL. R. EVID. 314(k).
66. *See* R.C.M. 314(d); United States v. Weshenfelder, 20 C.M.A. 416, 43 C.M.R. 256 (1971); United States v. Whalen, 15 M.J. 872 (A.C.M.R. 1983).

§ 5-3(C)(3)   THE COMMANDER'S INVESTIGATION   § 5-3(C)(4)

challenge the intrusion. In theory, however, a servicemember may have an expectation of privacy vis-a-vis particular persons.[67]

§ 5-3(C)(3). Gate Searches; Border Searches.

Under Rule of Evidence 314(c), the government may conduct nonprobable cause "gate searches." These searches may be conducted upon either entry[68] or exit[69] from United States installations,[70] aircraft,[71] or vessels abroad.[72] The government's authority to conduct this type of nonprobable cause intrusion is grounded on a theory similar to that asserted for border searches, *infra*[73]: That is, the government should be able to respond to threats to its property and interests.[74]

Rule 314 also addresses the use of border searches by the military.[75] These nonprobable cause intrusions require Congressional approval, and are less frequently used in the military setting.[76]

§ 5-3(C)(4). Searches in Jails and Restricted Areas

Government agents may conduct searches in jails and other restricted areas, without the need for probable cause.[77] The justification for these intrusions is grounded on the recognition that on balance, individual interests are subordinated to the overriding interests in security.[78] Such intrusions must still be reasonable, however.[79]

---

67. United States v. Muniz, 23 M.J. 201 (C.M.A. 1987) (accused might have reasonable expectation of privacy in government desk as to persons other than his commander).
68. Mil. R. Evid. 314(c). United States v. Jones, 24 M.J. 294 (C.M.A. 1987) (command authorized inspection of cars entering installation).
69. *See* United States v. Zachary, 10 M.J. 628 (A.C.M.R. 1980) (searches of persons leaving overseas military installations may also be permitted).
70. Mil. R. Evid. 314(c).
71. *Id.*
72. *See generally* United States v. Villamonte-Marquez, 462 U.S. 579 (1983).
73. United States v. Stringer, 37 M.J. 120 (C.M.A. 1993) (gate search at installation in foreign country is equivalent of border for purposes of Fourth Amendment and is presumed to be reasonable even if gate guards have broad discretion; no requirement that authorization to conduct such intrusions be in writing).
74. United States v. Harris, 5 M.J. 44 (C.M.A. 1978) (use of gate search to deter introduction of contraband onto military installation is eminently reasonable response to serious military problem).
75. Mil. R. Evid. 314(b). United States v. Ayala, 43 M.J. 296 (1995) (search by customs agents of package sent by accused amounted to permissible border search; no reasonable cause required). United States v. Rivera, 4 M.J. 215 (C.M.A. 1978).
76. Mil. R. Evid. 314(b).
77. Mil. R. Evid. 314(h). *See, e.g.*, United States v. Mix, 35 M.J. 283 (C.M.A. 1992) (accused's incriminating letter inspected at pretrial confinement facility); United States v. Maglito, 20 C.M.A. 456, 43 C.M.R. 296 (1971).
78. *See generally* Saltzburg, Schinasi & Schlueter, *Military Rules of Evidence Manual*, 328 (3d Ed. 1991).
79. *See also* Bell v. Wolfish, 441 U.S. 520 (1979).

§ 5-3(C)(5). Emergency Searches.

If officers in good faith believe that a life is threatened or that some harm might result,[80] they may conduct nonprobable cause searches to render aid, to seek additional information in order to render such aid, or to prevent injury.[81] A desire to preserve evidence will normally not be considered an emergency search.[82]

§ 5-3(C)(6). Consent Searches.

As an alternative to a probable cause search, officers may seek the accused's consent to conduct a search.[83] A person may consent to a search of his own person,[84] including body fluids,[85] his quarters,[86] property,[87] or of that property which he has,[88] or shares, control.[89] The military courts recognize that officers

---

80. MIL. R. EVID. 314(i).
81. United States v. Korda, 36 M.J. 578 (A.F.C.M.R. 1992) (warrantless search of accused's apartment justified by belief that he had committed, or would commit, suicide); United States v. Jackson, 34 M.J. 1145 (A.C.M.R. 1992) (sufficient exigent circumstances to justify warrantless apprehension of accused at motel); United States v. Yarborough, 50 C.M.R. 149 (A.F.C.M.R. 1975). *See generally* "Search and Seizure: A Primer, Part Nine—Open Fields and Bona Fide Emergency," 14 The Advocate 110 (1982).
82. United States v. Pond, 36 M.J. 1050 (A.F.C.M.R. 1993) (no exigent circumstances supported warrantless seizure of accused's urine by civilian police); United States v. Porter, 36 M.J. 812 (A.C.M.R. 1993) (blood-alcohol testing was not exigent search).
83. MIL. R. EVID. 314(c); Schneckloth v. Bustamonte, 412 U.S. 218 (1973); "Search and Seizure: A Primer (Consent)," 12 THE ADVOCATE 353 (1980).
84. United States v. Phillips, 32 M.J. 955 (A.F.C.M.R. 1991) (accused voluntarily consented to search of handbag); United States v. Roberts, 32 M.J. 681 (A.F.C.M.R. 1991) (accused consented to body search).
85. United States v. Avery, 40 M.J. 325 (C.M.A. 1994) (accused voluntarily consented to urinalysis); United States v. McClain, 31 M.J. 130 (C.M.A. 1990) (consent to urinalysis testing was lacking; involuntary consent cannot be ignored simply because there was sufficient probable cause to obtain a search authorization); United States v. Whipple, 28 M.J. 314 (C.M.A. 1989) (accused's consent to urinalysis was voluntary); United States v. Cook, 27 M.J. 858 (C.M.A. 1989) (consent to urinalysis was based on inadequate advice and therefore involuntary); United States v. White, 27 M.J. 264 (C.M.A. 1988) (accused's consent to give a urine sample was involuntary). United States v. McClendon, 41 M.J. 882 (A.F.Ct.Crim.App. 1994) (accused voluntarily consented to urinalysis); United States v. Pabon, 37 M.J. 836 (A.F.C.M.R. 1993) (consent to provide urine sample voluntary); United States v. Rachel, 32 M.J. 669 (A.F.C.M.R. 1991) (accused consented to urinalysis); United States v. Peoples, 28 M.J. 686 (A.F.C.M.R. 1989) (consent to urinalysis was involuntary); United States v. Simmons, 26 M.J. 667 (A.F.C.M.R. 1988) (valid consent to urinalysis test); United States v. Pellman, 24 M.J. 672 (A.F.C.M.R. 1987) (consent to provide urine sample was invalid where commander implied that he could order the accused to produce a sample); United States v. Spann, 24 M.J. 508 (A.F.C.M.R. 1987) (accused voluntarily consented to provide urine sample).
86. United States v. Kitts, 43 M.J. 23 (1995) (accused voluntarily consented to search of quarters); United States v. Goudy, 32 M.J. 88 (C.M.A. 1991) (consent to search of quarters).
87. United States v. Frazier, 34 M.J. 135 (C.M.A. 1992) (accused consented to searches of his wallet); United States v. Goudy, 32 M.J. 88 (C.M.A. 1991) (consent to search of locker, car and quarters was voluntary).
88. United States v. Reister, 40 M.J. 666 (N.M.C.M.R. 1994) (house sitter had authority to consent to search of accused's quarters).
89. United States v. Camanga, 38 M.J. 249 (C.M.A. 1993) (nonowner with joint control and

may count on a person's apparent authority to provide consent.[90] The consent may be limited in scope of time or place[91] and may be withdrawn at any time.[92] The burden rests upon the government to prove by clear and convincing evidence[93] that the consent was voluntarily given.[94] Whether the consent was voluntary will depend on the circumstances;[95] the fact that a person merely submitted to color of authority will not constitute a voluntary consent.[96]

While it is not necessary for officers to first advise a servicemember of the right to refuse to give consent, in many instances, they will do so simply to insure voluntariness.[97] Military caselaw also recognizes that officers need not give rights warnings in obtaining consent, because the request for consent is normally not an interrogation and giving consent is not normally considered to be a statement.[98]

§ 5-3(C)(7). Searches Incident to Apprehension.

Military practice authorizes searches of persons who have been lawfully apprehended.[99] These nonprobable cause searches are grounded in large part on safety concerns for the persons making the apprehension.[100] Thus, Military

---

access may lawfully consent to search of property); United States v. Clow, 26 M.J. 176 (C.M.A. 1988) (accused's estranged husband gave consent to search her belongings); United States v. Fish, 25 M.J. 732 (A.F.C.M.R. 1987) (accused's estranged husband could consent to search of accused's quarters).

90. Illinois v. Rodriguez, 110 S. Ct. 2793 (1990) (officers may rely on apparent authority of person giving consent to search); United States v. White, 40 M.J. 257 (C.M.A. 1994) (police reasonably relied upon apparent authority of accused's roommate to give consent to search).
91. MIL. R. EVID. 314(c)(3) (scope of consent).
92. MIL. R. EVID. 314(c)(3) (withdrawal of consent).
93. MIL. R. EVID. 314(c)(5).
94. MIL. R. EVID. 314(c)(5) (burden of proof).
95. MIL. R. EVID. 314(c)(4).
96. MIL. R. EVID. 314(c)(4). United States v. Jenkins, 24 M.J. 846 (A.F.C.M.R. 1987) (accused's consent to search room was not mere submission to official authority); United States v. Pellman, 24 M.J. 672 (A.F.C.M.R. 1987) (consent to provide urine sample was invalid where commander implied that he could order the accused to produce a sample).
97. MIL. R. EVID. 314(c)(4) (prosecution not required to show that accused knew of right to refuse to give consent). United States v. Cook, 27 M.J. 858 (A.F.C.M.R. 1989) (consent invalid where accused was not apprised of consequences of failing to give consent); United States v. Pellman, 24 M.J. 672 (A.F.C.M.R. 1987) (consent invalid where commander misled accused).
98. United States v. Murphy, 39 M.J. 486 (C.M.A. 1994) (failure to give Article 31 warnings did not affect voluntariness of consent); United States v. Burns, 33 M.J. 316 (C.M.A. 1991) (pretrial request for consent to search did not require advice of rights to counsel; the request is not an interrogation and consent is not a statement); United States v. Cannon, 29 M.J. 549 (A.F.C.M.R. 1980) (a consent to search is not a statement). *See generally* Caddell, "Article 31(b) Warnings Revisited: The COMA Does a Double Take," ARMY LAW., September 1993, p. 14.
99. MIL. R. EVID. 314(g). Chimel v. California, 395 U.S. 752 (1969). See also United States v. Pond, 36 M.J. 1050 (A.F.C.M.R. 1993) (search incident to arrest). *See generally* "Search and Seizure: A Primer, Part Five Search Incident to a Lawful Apprehension," 13 THE ADVOCATE 285 (1981).
100. Chimel v. California, 395 U.S. 752 (1969).

Rule of Evidence 314(g) indicates that the scope of the search is limited to looking for weapons or destructible evidence which is within the "immediate control" of the person being apprehended, i.e., the area which the person conducting the search reasonably believes could be reached by the apprehended person with a sudden movement.[101] Rule 314 also permits contemporaneous searches of the passenger compartments of automobiles even though the person being apprehended is no longer in the vehicle.[102] Under Rule 314(g)(3)(A), officers may conduct protective sweeps for other persons who might pose a threat to the officers,[103] if they have reasonable suspicion that such persons are present.[104] They may also conduct searches of what the rule labels "attack area"[105] as a precautionary measure, without reasonable suspicion or probable cause.[106]

§ 5-3(C)(8). Searches Incident to Lawful Stop.

If officers[107] have lawfully stopped[108] a servicemember to investigate what appears to be criminal activity,[109] they may conduct a protective "frisk" of that person if they have reason to believe that the servicemember is armed and poses a danger to the officers.[110] Similar safety concerns will support a search of the passenger compartment of a vehicle for weapons where the driver has been lawfully stopped.[111]

§ 5-3(C)(9). Other Nonprobable Cause Searches

Military Rule of Evidence 314 contains a sort of catch-all provision for other nonprobable cause searches.[112] Rule 314(k) permits searches, in addition to those specifically listed in the rule, which may be otherwise constitutional.[113]

---

101. MIL. R. EVID. 314(g)(2). United States v. Chadwick, 433 U.S. 1 (1977); United States v. Wallace, 34 M.J. 353 (C.M.A. 1992) (search of accused's wallet following apprehension); United States v. Acosta, 11 M.J. 307 (C.M.A. 1981) (servicemember's pillow and bed were within immediate control).
102. MIL. R. EVID. 314(g)(2). New York v. Belton, 453 U.S. 454 (1981).
103. MIL. R. EVID. 314(g)(3)(A).
104. MIL. R. EVID. 314(g)(3)(A).
105. MIL. R. EVID. 314(g)(3)(B). Maryland v. Buie, 494 U.S. 325 (1990).
106. MIL. R. EVID. 314(g)(3)(B).
107. MIL. R. EVID. 314(f). The person effecting the stop must be authorized to apprehend under R.C.M. 302(b) or authorized to perform law enforcement duties. *Id.*
108. MIL. R. EVID. 314(f). For a discussion of what constitutes a stop, *see* Saltzburg, Schinasi & Schlueter, *Military Rules of Evidence Manual*, 326-27 (3d Ed. 1991).
109. MIL. R. EVID. 314(f). Terry v. Ohio, 392 U.S. 1 (1968).
110. MIL. R. EVID. 314(f)(2) (purpose of frisk). United States v. Yandell, 13 M.J. 616 (A.F.C.M.R. 1982) (search of box being carried by accused was not unreasonable as part of frisk of accused); United States v. Garrett, 15 M.J. 601 (N.M.C.M.R. 1982) (scope of *Terry* exceeded where military policeman ordered accused to produce corn cob pipe he was trying to put in pocket).
111. MIL. R. EVID. 314(f)(3) (frisk of motor vehicles).
112. MIL. R. EVID. 314(k).
113. *Id.*

§ 5-3(D) THE COMMANDER'S INVESTIGATION § 5-3(D)(1)

That provision has been extended, for example, to the military's compulsory urinalysis program[114] and a military police customs inspection.[115]

§ 5-3(D). Other Reasonable Searches.

§ 5-3(D)(1). Inspections and Inventories.

The commander's broad authority to inspect persons and property within his unit and inventory property is set out in Military Rule of Evidence 313.[116] With few exceptions,[117] the military courts have traditionally recognized the broad powers of a commander to closely examine his unit to determine its readiness and fitness.[118] An inspection is defined in Military Rule of Evidence 313(b) as follows:

> An "inspection" is an examination of the whole or part of a unit, organization, installation, vessel, aircraft, or vehicle, including an examination conducted at entrance and exit points, conducted as an incident of command the primary purpose of which is to determine and to ensure the security, military fitness, or good order and discipline of the unit, organization, installation, vessel, aircraft, or vehicle.[119]

Although Rule 313 nowhere includes the term, the typical "health-and-welfare" inspection generally focuses on examination of the unit for sanitation, fitness of the servicemembers, and the maintenance of their equipment.[120] The only limit on this sort of intrusion apparently is that it be conducted in a

---

114. Murray v. Haldeman, 16 M.J. 74 (C.M.A. 1983).
115. United States v. Williamson, 28 M.J. 511 (A.C.M.R. 1989) (pre-shipment customs search on household goods being shipped from Germany to United States).
116. *See generally* Peluso, "Administrative Intrusions," ARMY LAW., Sept. 1985, at 24.
117. *See, e.g.*, United States v. Roberts, 2 M.J. 31 (C.M.A. 1976); United States v. Thomas, 1 M.J. 397 (C.M.A. 1976).
118. *See* United States v. Turner, 33 M.J. 40 (C.M.A. 1991) (inspection is commander's "tool" for ensuring overall fitness of unit); United States v. Daskam, 31 M.J. 77 (C.M.A. 1990) (compulsory random urinalysis is inspection); United States v. Evans, 37 M.J. 867 (A.F.C.M.R. 1993) (squadron commander had authority to order inspection of accused's unit even though administrative control of unit remained within control of parent reserve unit); United States v. Pompey, 32 M.J. 547 (A.F.C.M.R. 1990) (unit sweep was inspection rather than command directed urinalysis); United States v. Flowers, 26 M.J. 463 (C.M.A. 1988) (court upheld "brow" inspection of accused's property as he left ship).
Cf. United States v. Moore, 23 M.J. 295 (C.M.A. 1987) (commander's search of barracks for stolen goods was apparently not intended to be an inspection under Rule 313); United States v. Middleton, 10 M.J. 123 (C.M.A. 1981); United States v. Lange, 15 C.M.A. 486, 35 C.M.R. 458 (1965).
See generally Hunt, "Inspections," 54 MIL. L. REV. 225 (1971); Smith, "Administrative Inspections in the Armed Forces after *New York v. Burger*," ARMY LAW., Aug. 1988, at 9; Anderson, "Permissible Law Enforcement Discretion in Administrative Searches," ARMY LAW., Sept. 1987, at 26.
119. Rule 313(b), MIL. R. EVID. Wallis, "Military Rule of Evidence 313(b)," ARMY LAW., July 1988, at 52.
120. *See* United States v. Brown, 12 M.J. 420 (C.M.A. 1982) (classic example of militarily necessary health-and-welfare inspection); United States v. Tena, 15 M.J. 728 (A.C.M.R. 1983).

§ 5-3(D)(1)   MILITARY CRIMINAL JUSTICE   § 5-3(D)(1)

reasonable manner. What is reasonable will depend on the circumstances.[121] Factors such as timing and scope should be considered. Although the civilian community might never tolerate an otherwise lawful inspection of a regulated industry[122] at 5 a.m., doing so in the military may be perfectly reasonable if reveille is normally at that hour. Under Rule 313, there is no requirement that the inspection be based upon probable cause or reasonable suspicion.[123] The "inspectors" must be faithful, however, to the bounds of an inspection in terms of both scope and purpose.[124]

Note that Rule 313 provides that an inspection conducted for the primary purpose for obtaining evidence to be used in a court-martial or other disciplinary proceedings is not a valid inspection. The problem here is one of assessing the commander's subjective reasoning through objective facts. Rule 313 recognizes that if the purpose of the inspection was to locate weapons or contraband (e.g., drugs), some factors may indicate a forbidden motive of simply obtaining incriminating evidence.[125] In that case the government must prove by clear

---

121. *See generally* Saltzburg, Schinasi & Schlueter, *Military Rules of Evidence Manual*, 299 (3d ed. 1991).

122. *See, e.g.*, Donovan v. Dewey, 452 U.S. 594 (1981) (mining industry); United States v. Biswell, 406 U.S. 311 (1972); Colonnade Catering Corp. v. United States, 397 U.S. 73 (1970).

123. In the original version of Rule 313, reasonable suspicion would support an inspection for contraband if the inspection was not previously scheduled. That language was dropped from the 1984 amended version, however, because it tended to make Rule 313 inflexible; absent previous scheduling and reasonable suspicion, no legitimate, immediate, contraband inspections were permitted. See Rule 313, MIL. R. EVID. Drafter's Analysis. In United States v. Shepherd, 24 M.J. 596 (A.F.C.M.R 1987), the court indicated that nothing in Rule 313 precludes an inspection where there is some suspicion that contraband is present and that it was not error to inspect those individuals who had been suspected of using drugs.

124. United States v. Ellis, 24 M.J. 370 (C.M.A. 1987) (inspector did not exceed purpose and scope of inspection ordered for purpose of determining neatness and cleanliness of new barracks building when he opened accused's shaving kit, which he found hanging on headboard of accused's bed); United States v. Brown, 12 M.J. 420 (C.M.A. 1982).

United States v. Burris, 25 M.J. 846 (A.F.C.M.R. 1988) (although drug testing need not be conducted on random basis, the fact that it was establishes that accused was not singled out).

The issue of randomness—who determines just when or how inspections will be conducted—has been addressed in several opinions. In United States v. Johnston, 24 M.J. 271 (C.M.A. 1987), the court ruled that there was no violation of a Navy regulation that required "random" urinalysis testing where petty officer with law enforcement duties selected the date on which the test would be run. The court noted that some discretion is permitted in conducting inspections as long as the inspectors do so in accordance with standard criteria and on some basis other than suspicion of criminal activity.

In United States v. Jones, 24 M.J. 294 (C.M.A. 1987), the court again addressed the issue of "discretion." Rejecting its earlier opinion in United States v. Harris, 5 M.J. 44 (C.M.A. 1978) to the extent that that opinion indicates that no discretion is permitted, the court approved a vehicle inspection scheme which permitted the inspecting officer to determine randomness.

125. The three factors noted in the Rule itself are that (1) the inspection immediately followed a specific offense, (2) specific individuals were targeted, or (3) not all individuals were examined in a similar manner. These factors are not foolproof but do establish some objective criteria by which the commander's true purpose may be measured. *See, e.g.*, United States v. Daskam, 31 M.J. 77 (C.M.A. 1990) (urinalysis of accused was not valid inspection where he was not within group of individuals subject to testing).

United States v. Bickel, 30 M.J. 277 (C.M.A. 1990) (policy of retesting those who had tested positive in drug test was not based upon predetermined reasonable suspicion nor individualized

§ 5-3(D)(1) THE COMMANDER'S INVESTIGATION § 5-3(D)(1)

and convincing evidence that the inspection was not for such a purpose.[126] If those factors are missing, the government need only prove by a preponderance of evidence that the inspection met all of the legal requirements of Rule 313.[127] The point here is that although the commander's powers are broad, the military courts will not condone those inspections that are mere subterfuges for searches.[128]

The case law[129] and Rule 313[130] also recognize that drug detection dogs and other technological aids may be used during the inspection. Those same sources recognize the authority of the commander to authorize compulsory urinalysis testing[131] under this rule as long as it meets the "purpose" test applied to other inspections.[132]

---

suspicion and was reasonable); United States v. Patterson, 39 M.J. 678 (N.M.C.M.R. 1993) (urinalysis report was not result of valid inspection; commander apparently targeted accused for testing); United States v. Evans, 37 M.J. 867 (A.F.C.M.R. 1993) (inspection not subterfuge as search for servicemembers who had been involved in earlier drug offenses); United States v. Pappas, 30 M.J. 513 (A.F.C.M.R. 1990) (any distinction in selecting certain individuals for inspection must be based upon conscious command decision in order to trigger clear and convincing evidence standard).

126. *See* MIL. R. EVID. 313(b). The "clear and convincing" test falls between the "beyond a reasonable doubt" standard and the "preponderance of the evidence"standards *See also* MIL. R. EVID. 314(e)(5) and 316(d)(2).

127. United States v. Moore, 41 M.J. 812 (N.M.Ct.Crim.App. 1995) (preponderance of evidence is burden of proof unless one of factors stated in Rule 313 is present).

128. *See, e.g.*, United States v. Konieczka, 31 M.J. 289 (C.M.A. 1990) (officer's decision to forward accused's urine sample for additional testing converted inspection into impermissible search); United States v. Thatcher, 28 M.J. 20 (C.M.A. 1989) (intrusion was a search rather than an inspection); United States v. Middleton, 10 M.J. 123 (C.M.A. 1981).

United States v. Shover, 42 M.J. 753 (A.F.Ct.Crim.App. 1995)(commander's unit-wide urinalysis was not for purpose of prosecution); United States v. Neal, 41 M.J. 855 (A.F.Ct.Crim.App. 1994) (looking through accused's belongings was not valid inspection; applying search and seizure rules, court concluded that portions of the process were illegal); United States v. Alexander, 32 M.J. 664 (A.F.C.M.R. 1991) (inspection that immediately followed report of crime was nonetheless valid); United States v. Murphy, 28 M.J. 758 (A.F.C.M.R. 1989) (commander implicitly adopted legitimate nonprosecutorial purpose in conducting urinalysis testing where he testified that he was simply "filling the square," i.e., carrying out Air Force policy of testing for drugs).

In United States v. Rodriquez, 23 M.J. 896 (A.C.M.R. 1987), the commander stated during the suppression hearing that he had conducted the urinalysis testing to implement the Army's policy of controlling drug abuse and that he believed that disciplinary action might be appropriate for those testing positive. The trial judge ruled that under MIL. R. EVID. 313(b), the testing was a subterfuge for a search and that the results were inadmissible. On a Government appeal, *see* § 13-2(G)(2), the court overruled the judge, stating that multiple purposes for an inspection will not per se void it as an inspection. Here the primary purpose was for a reason other than instituting disciplinary action. *See also* United States v. Johnston, 24 M.J. 271 (C.M.A. 1987); United States v. Vincent, 15 M.J. 613 (N.M.C.M.R. 1982).

129. United States v. Alexander, 34 M.J. 121 (C.M.A. 1992) (canine sniff by well-trained narcotics dog in public place is not search); United States v. Middleton, 10 M.J. 123 (C.M.A. 1981); United States v. Grosskreutz, 5 M.J. 344 (C.M.A. 1978).

130. MIL. R. EVID. 313(b). Pottoroff, "Canine Narcotics Detection in the Military: A Continuing Bone of Contention?," ARMY LAW., July 1984, at 73.

131. United States v. Gardner, 41 M.J. 189 (C.M.A. 1994) (command-directed urinalysis was permissible; inspection court noted that administrative purpose was unquestionable); United

---

132. See also MIL. R. EVID. 312(d) concerning extraction of body fluids. An order to produce a

Inventories are also sometimes relied upon to support the lawful seizure and later admissibility of contraband.[133] For example, it is common for the commander, pursuant to regulation, to inventory the personal belongings of a servicemember who has been AWOL for a specified length of time.[134] Should the commander discover contraband in his belongings it would normally be admissible at any later trial. As in the case of an inspection, an inventory may not be used for the purpose of obtaining evidence.[135] The inventory must be a reasonable, administrative intrusion.[136]

§ 5-3(D)(2). Body Views and Intrusions.

The Military Rules of Evidence provide a unique rule concerning searches and seizures of body evidence.[137] Rule 312 governs visual examination of the body,[138] intrusion into body cavities,[139] extraction of body fluids,[140] other intrusive searches of the body,[141] and medical intrusions.[142]

States v. Campbell, 41 M.J. 177 (C.M.A. 1994) (invalid inspection; command relied upon its suspicions of drug activity as basis for ordering urinalysis); United States v. Taylor, 41 M.J. 168 (C.M.A. 1994) (commander's decision to conduct urinalysis testing of portion of unit was not subterfuge for search); United States v. Williams, 35 M.J. 323 (C.M.A. 1992) (results of command-directed urinalysis); Murray v. Haldeman, 16 M.J. 74 (C.M.A. 1983); United States v. Pollard, 26 M.J. 947 (C.G.C.M.R. 1988) (mandatory drug testing was reasonable); United States v. Brown, 35 M.J. 877 (A.F.C.M.R. 1992) (wing commander acted within authority in delegating execution of random urinalysis inspections to social actions officer; failure to follow directives exactly was not fatal); United States v. Valenzuela, 24 M.J. 934 (A.C.M.R. 1987) (the standard is reasonableness).

---

urine specimen is not an "extraction." Murray v. Haldeman, 16 M.J. 74 (C.M.A. 1983). *Cf.* United States v. Parker, 27 M.J. 522 (A.F.C.M.R. 1988) (evidence resulting from urinalysis was inadmissible because commander had ordered inspection for disciplinary purposes).

133. South Dakota v. Opperman, 428 U.S. 364 (1976) (auto inventory); Illinois v. Lafayette, 462 U.S. 640 (1983) (inventory upon incarceration); United States v. Dulus, 16 M.J. 324 (C.M.A. 1983) (auto inventory); United States v. Mons, 14 M.J. 575 (N.M.C.M.R. 1982) (inventory of accused's bloody clothing). See Anderson, "Inventory Searches," 110 MIL. L. REV. 95 (1985).

134. United States v. Jasper, 16 M.J. 786 (A.C.M.R. 1983).

135. See MIL. R. EVID. 313(c).

136. In United States v. McCormick, 13 M.J. 900 (N.M.C.M.R. 1982), the court recognized, however, that an inventory is not limited to inanimate objects and approved examination and notation of the accused's bodily condition. See United States v. Jasper, 16 M.J. 786 (A.C.M.R. 1983) (inventory may not include general rummaging around in accused's belongings).

137. MIL. R. EVID. 312. *See generally* Schlueter, "Bodily Evidence and Rule 312, M.R.E.," ARMY LAW., May 1980, at 35.

138. MIL R. EVID. 312(b).

139. MIL R. EVID. 312(c).

140. MIL R. EVID. 312(d). United States v. Fitten, 42 M.J. 179 (1995) (forced catherization of hospitalized accused did not violate the fourth amendment, due process, or Rule 312; the test was reasonably necessary for diagnosis and was minimally intrusive); United States v. Pond, 36 M.J. 1050 (A.F.C.M.R. 1993) (court applied Schmerber and Fourth Amendment standards in concluding that seizure of accused's urine by civilian officer was improper).

141. MIL R. EVID. 312(e).

142. United States v. Maxwell, 38 M.J. 148 (C.M.A. 1993) (blood-alcohol test was medically necessary). *See generally* Note, "Significant Medical Intrusions Under the Military Rules of Evidence," 67 VA. L. REV. 1069 (1981).

§ 5-3(E). Seizures.

The rules governing seizures of persons and property are set out in Military Rule of Evidence 316.[143] That rule addresses seizure of property,[144] apprehensions,[145] abandoned property,[146] consensual seizures,[147] seizure of government property,[148] seizure of property in plain view,[149] seizure of property pursuant to a search authorization or warrant,[150] seizure of property under exigent circumstances,[151] temporary detention of property,[152] and the question of who has authority to seize property.[153] The rule also contains a catch-all provision which provides that the permissible constitutional seizures may be recognized.[154]

§ 5-3(F). Exclusionary Rule; Exceptions.

If a search or seizure is not conducted in accordance with the Constitution or the Military Rules of Evidence, the evidence discovered pursuant to that intrusion may be excluded.[155] Military Rule of Evidence 311(a)[156] indicates that "[e]vidence obtained as a result of an unlawful search or seizure made by a person acting in a governmental capacity is inadmissible against an accused" if a timely objection is made[157] and the accused had a reasonable expectation of privacy in the person, place, or property searched.[158] Failure to follow applicable regulations in conducting the search or inspection will not necessarily result in exclusion.[159]

---

143. MIL. R. EVID. 316.
144. MIL. R. EVID. 316(b).
145. MIL. R. EVID. 316(c).
146. MIL. R. EVID. 316(d)(1).
147. MIL. R. EVID. 316(d)(2).
148. MIL. R. EVID. 316(d)(3).
149. MIL. R. EVID. 316(d)(4)(C). Arizona v. Hicks, 480 U.S. 321 (1987); United States v. Mix, 35 M.J. 283 (C.M.A. 1992) (accused's incriminating letter seized at pretrial confinement facility; letter was certainly evidence of crime); United States v. Schmitt, 33 M.J. 24 (C.M.A. 1991) (presence of military property in plain view provided probable cause for MP's to believe that it was stolen and to enter car to retrieve it); United States v. Jacobs, 31 M.J. 138 (C.M.A. 1990).
150. MIL. R. EVID. 316(d)(4)(A).
151. MIL. R. EVID. 316(d)(4)(B).
152. MIL. R. EVID. 316(d)(5).
153. MIL. R. EVID. 316(e).
154. MIL. R. EVID. 316(f).
155. Rule 311(a), MIL. R. EVID. United States v. Wooten, 34 M.J. 141 (C.M.A. 1992) (civil remedies under Right to Financial Privacy Act were exclusive and evidence obtained in violation of Act were not excluded in court-martial); United States v. Thompson, 33 M.J. 218 (C.M.A. 1991) (court noted in dicta that violation of statute or regulation does not necessarily give rise to operation of exclusionary rule).
156. Rule 311, MIL. R. EVID.
157. Rule 311(a)(1), MIL. R. EVID.
158. Rule 311(a)(2), MIL. R. EVID.
159. *See, e.g.*, United States v. Timoney, 34 M.J. 1108 (A.C.M.R. 1992) (government's failure to follow own regulations in labelling urine specimen bottles did not render evidence inadmissible).

If the court determines that a violation has occurred, any derivative evidence, such as an accused's statements,[160] may also be excluded.[161] Such evidence may be admissible if the prosecution can show, inter alia, by a preponderance of the evidence,[162] that the evidence was not obtained as a result of the illegal activity, i.e., that any taint was attenuated.[163]

Military practice, however, recognizes several exceptions to the exclusionary rule.[164] The "good-faith" exception recognized by the Supreme Court in *United States v. Leon*[165] is now codified in Military Rules of Evidence 311(b)(3) and extends to search authorizations issued by commanders as well as search warrants issued by civilian authorities.[166] The military also recognizes the impeachment exception[167] and the inevitable discovery exception.[168]

---

160. Brown v. Illinois, 422 U.S. 590 (1975) (four pronged test for determining whether taint from illegal fourth amendment action was attenuated); United States v. Washington, 39 M.J. 1014 (A.C.M.R. 1994) (statement was tainted by illegal search).

161. MIL. R. EVID. 311(e)(2) (admissibility of derivative evidence).

162. MIL. R. EVID. 311(e)(2) (1993 amendment addressing admissibility of accused's statements following apprehension which violates R.C.M. 302(d)(2)); New York v. Harris, 110 S.Ct. 1640 (1990) (defendant's statements at police station following improper arrest at home were admissible; the Court indicated that the illegal arrest was based upon probable cause and the statement was not the fruit of the illegality).

163. New York v. Harris, 110 S. Ct. 1640 (1990); Brown v. Illinois, 422 U.S. 590 (1975); United States v. Ravine, 11 M.J. 325 (C.M.A. 1981) (evidence having only slight or attenuated connection with the illegal conduct is admissible).

164. *See generally* MIL. R. EVID. 311(b).

165. 468 U.S. 897 (1984). *See also* Illinois v. Krull, 480 U.S. 340 (1987).

166. MIL. R. EVID. 311(b)(3)(A), (B). United States v. Lopez, 35 M.J. 35 (C.M.A. 1992) (in lengthy discussion, court applied good faith exception to search authorization by accused's commanding officer). *See* United States v. Morris, 28 M.J. 8 (C.M.A. 1989); United States v. Queen, 26 M.J. 136 (C.M.A. 1988).

United States v. Washington, 39 M.J. 1014 (A.C.M.R. 1994) (good faith exception not available where commander had abandoned impartial role by simply counting on police statement without determining factual basis; police did not act in good faith; blind faith is not good faith for purposes of exception); United States v. Pond, 36 M.J. 1050 (A.F.C.M.R. 1993) (court declined to apply good faith exception to warrantless seizure of accused's urine by civilian police); United States v. Evans, 32 M.J. 1016 (N.M.C.M.R. 1991) (court applied good faith exception in MIL. R. EVID. 311 to search authorized by commanding general); United States v. Mix, 32 M.J. 974 (A.C.M.R. 1991) (court applied good faith exception to probable cause search of car authorized by commander although car was outside his area of control); United States v. Lopez, 32 M.J. 924 (A.F.C.M.R. 1991) (possible application of good faith exception to search by commander); United States v. Sharrock, 30 M.J. 1003 (A.F.C.M.R. 1990) (good faith exception not available where commander was not neutral and detached); United States v. Thompson, 30 M.J. 577 (A.C.M.R. 1990) (commander did not have substantial basis for ordering urinalysis test so good faith exception was not available).

167. MIL. R. EVID. 311(b)(1). United States v. Havens, 444 U.S. 962 (1980). Note that the military provision only permits impeachment of the accused, a result recently reached by the Supreme Court in James v. Illinois, 493 U.S. 307 (1990).

168. Rule 311(b)(2), MIL. R. EVID. Nix v. Williams, 467 U.S. 431 (1984); United States v. Campbell, 41 M.J. 177 (C.M.A. 1994) (confession would not have been inevitably discovered); United States v. Allen, 34 M.J. 228 (C.M.A. 1992) (evidence would have been inevitably discovered); United States v. Kozak, 12 M.J. 389 (C.M.A. 1982). *See also* United States v. Roa, 24 M.J. 297 (C.M.A. 1987); United States v. Lawless, 18 M.J. 255 (C.M.A. 1984); United States v. Chick, 30 M.J. 658 (A.F.C.M.R. 1990) (discovery of contraband was not inevitable); United States v.

The independent source doctrine is also recognized for determining whether sufficient independent information, after excising tainted information, supported a finding of probable cause.[169]

§ 5-4. The Right Against Self-Incrimination, Interrogation, and Immunity.

§ 5-4(A). The Right Against Self-Incrimination.

§ 5-4(A)(1). In General.

The military's authoritarian environment has often prompted military courts to interpret servicemembers' rights against self-incrimination in broad fashion.[1] Servicemembers benefit not only from the Fifth Amendment protections, but also from Article 31(a), U.C.M.J., which prevents the use of compulsion to obtain incriminating information.[2]

While the Supreme Court has generally limited the Fifth Amendment protections only to testimonial evidence, the military courts have extended the statutory protection in the U.C.M.J. to actions constituting statements, i.e. verbal acts.[3] Thus, any attempts by a commander or law enforcement personnel to "compel" the production of evidence in furtherance of an investigation may result in the exclusion of that evidence and its fruits.[4] Servicemembers may be compelled to submit blood[5] and urine samples,[6] handwriting[7] and voiceprint exemplars,[8] and may be required to exhibit external body characteristics.[9] They may also be required to surrender evidence where there is an independent duty to make an accounting.[10]

Peoples, 28 M.J. 686 (A.F.C.M.R. 1989) (prosecution failed to show that discovery of drugs would have been inevitable); United States v. Tallon, 28 M.J. 635 (A.F.C.M.R. 1989).

169. United States v. Camanga, 38 M.J. 249 (C.M.A. 1993).

1. *See, e.g.*, United States v. Ruiz, 23 C.M.A. 181, 48 C.M.R. 797 (1974). See Saltzburg, Schinasi & Schlueter, *Military Rules of Evidence Manual* 102-03 (3d ed. 1991).

2. Art. 31, U.C.M.J. See Appendix 3.

3. *See, e.g.*, United States v. Whipple, 4 M.J. 773 (C.G.C.M.R. 1978); United States v. Hay, 3 M.J. 654 (A.C.M.R. 1977); United States v. Kinane, 1 M.J. 309, 311, n.1 (C.M.A. 1976).

4. Article 31(d), U.C.M.J., Rule 301, Mɪʟ. R. Evɪᴅ.

5. United States v. Armstrong, 9 M.J. 374 (C.M.A. 1980) (Article 31 protections parallel Fifth Amendment protections).

6. Murray v. Haldeman, 16 M.J. 74 (C.M.A. 1983) (urine samples).

7. United States v. Harden, 18 M.J. 81 (C.M.A. 1984).

8. United States v. Chandler, 17 M.J. 678 (A.C.M.R. 1983). *See also* United States v. Davenport, 9 M.J. 364 (C.M.A. 1980).

9. United States v. Cain, 5 M.J. 844 (A.C.M.R. 1978); United States v. Martin, 9 M.J. 731 (N.C.M.R. 1979).

10. *See infra* § 5-4(A)(2). In United States v. Jones, 31 M.J. 189 (C.M.A. 1990), the court reiterated that the required records doctrine is not an exception to Article 31 where the military suspect was not acting in a representative capacity. Thus, unwarned questioning of the accused, who was a suspect at the time, regarding certain merchandise transactions was prejudicial error. United States v. Sellers, 12 C.M.A. 262, 30 C.M.R. 262 (1961); United States v. Haskins, 11 C.M.A. 365, 29 C.M.R. 181 (1960).

§ 5-4(A)(2). Reporting Requirements.

In the military setting servicemembers may be required in the normal course of their duties to make an accounting of their activities, both personal and professional. For example, a servicemember might be required to report any contacts with agents of a foreign government,[11] accidents,[12] criminal activity of other servicemembers,[13] or purchases of goods abroad.[14] Occasionally, there are challenges to military regulatory reporting schemes on grounds that the requirement places the servicemember in the position of incriminating himself. Those challenges have generally failed because of strong public policy considerations underlying the reporting requirement.[15] The military courts, however, have recognized the *Heyward* defense: A servicemember is exempt from complying with a required reporting requirement that he report criminal activity if he was either a principal or accessory to the illegal activity he was charged with reporting.[16] Note that while a suspect may lawfully be compelled

---

United States v. Smalls, 30 M.J. 666 (A.F.C.M.R. 1990) (regulation requiring accounting of certain tax free items); United States v. Hilton, 29 M.J. 1036 (A.F.C.M.R. 1990) (regulation requiring servicemembers to account for tax exempt property in Philippines). *See generally* Saltzburg, Schinasi, & Schlueter, *Military Rules of Evidence Manual* 105-06 (3d ed. 1991).

11. *See, e.g.*, United States v. Kelliher, 35 M.J. 320 (C.M.A. 1992) (regulation requiring accused to report contacts with citizens of communist-controlled or hostile countries did not violate right against self-incrimination; servicemember does not commit offense by merely having contact); United States v. Kauffman, 14 C.M.A. 283, 34 C.M.R. 63 (1963); United States v. Anzalone, 40 M.J. 658 (N.M.C.M.R. 1994) (requirement to report contacts with Soviet Union not violative of self-incrimination privilege; individuals are not required to report criminal activity, only contacts); United States v. Kelliher, 31 M.J. 701 (N.M.C.M.R. 1990) (requiring accused to report his contacts with Soviets did not require him to report his criminal acts).
12. United States v. Smith, 9 C.M.A. 240, 26 C.M.R. 20 (1958).
13. United States v. Medley, 30 M.J. 879 (A.F.C.M.R. 1990) (accused could be required to report drug activity of subordinates in which she was not personally involved).
14. *See generally* United States v. Gregorio, 32 M.J. 401 (C.M.A. 1991) (conviction for violation of reporting requirement, "show and tell," reversed where suspect was questioned about tax-exempt property without first being warned of his rights under Article 31); United States v. Smalls, 32 M.J. 398 (C.M.A. 1991) (accused's Fifth Amendment and Article 31 rights were not violated when he was asked to comply with reporting requirement and account for tax-exempt property, where he was not a suspect at the time); United States v. Hilton, 32 M.J. 393 (C.M.A. 1991) (person suspected of violating regulations governing tax-exempted property could not be required to account for property absent rights warnings; court rejected distinction between general and individual suspect); United States v. Williams, 29 M.J. 112 (C.M.A. 1989) (court concluded that the reporting requirement of a USFK Regulation, which was designed to stop black-marketing activities in Korea, did not on its face require the accused to incriminate himself); United States v. Kretchmer, 33 M.J. 617 (A.F.C.M.R. 1991) (accused waived his self-incrimination rights in responding to show and tell requirements).
15. Baltimore City Department of Social Services v. Bouknight, 100 S. Ct. 900 (1990); California v. Beyers, 402 U.S. 424 (1971); United States v. French, 14 M.J. 510 (A.F.C.M.R. 1982); United States v. Lindsay, 11 M.J. 550 (A.C.M.R. 1981).
16. United States v. Heyward, 22 M.J. 35 (C.M.A. 1986). See also United States v. Medley, 33 M.J. 75 (C.M.A. 1991) (under facts, accused-NCO could not invoke *Heyward* rule to charges that she was derelict in not reporting drug activity of friends); United States v. Reed, 24 M.J. 80 (C.M.A. 1987) (the providence inquiry failed to disclose whether the accused failed to comply with reporting requirements because he was himself guilty); United States v. Bland, 39 M.J. 921 (N.M.C.M.R. 1994) (accused convicted of failing to report theft and attempted theft committed by

to turn over incriminating information pursuant to an independent duty to do so, at some point he may be entitled to Article 31 warnings,[17] which would in effect advise him that he does not have to incriminate himself.[18]

§ 5-4(A)(3). Comments on Invoking the Right.

If during an investigation a suspect or accused invokes the right to remain silent, the prosecutor's ability to use that silence against the accused at a later trial is restricted. If the suspect's "silence" occurs after rights warnings were given, and in the face of official questioning, that silence clearly may not be commented upon at a later trial.[19] If the silence in question arises before rights warnings were given, the prosecutor may be able to comment upon it.[20] Silence at the trial itself is clearly out-of-bounds for comment.[21]

§ 5-4(B). Interrogation of Suspects; Rights Warnings.

If during the investigation of an offense a commander intends to personally question a "suspect,"[22] or accused, he may be required to give rights warnings. The military courts generally adopt a two-pronged test in determining

---

friends, even though doing so might have led investigators to discover that he had assaulted victims earlier); United States v. Brunton, 24 M.J. 566 (N.M.C.M.R. 1987) (distinguishing *Heyward*, court held that right against self-incrimination excused accused from reporting criminal activity in which he was involved). *See generally* Saltzburg, Schinasi & Schlueter, *Military Rules of Evidence Manual*, 106-107 (3d ed. 1991).

17. *See generally* Saltzburg, Schinasi & Schlueter, *Military Rules of Evidence Manual* 106 (3d ed. 1991).
18. *See infra* § 5-4(B).
19. Doyle v. Ohio, 426 U.S. 610 (1976); United States v. Fitzpatrick, 14 M.J. 394 (C.M.A. 1983); United States v. Earnesty, 34 M.J. 1179 (A.F.C.M.R. 1992) (prejudicial error for prosecutor to comment on accused's invocation of rights to silence and assistance of counsel); United States v. Jackson, 23 M.J. 841 (A.F.C.M.R. 1987) (admission of evidence that accused refused to take a polygraph examination was reversible error). *See also* United States v. Cloyd, 25 C.M.R. 908 (A.F.B.R. 1958); United States v. Ortiz-Vergara, 24 C.M.R. 315 (A.B.R. 1957); United States v. Langford, 15 M.J. 1090 (A.C.M.R. 1983); Annotation, "Lie Detector Test—Willingness," 95 A.L.R.2d 819 (1963). *See also infra* § 15-13.
20. *Compare* Fletcher v. Weir, 455 U.S. 603 (1982) (permissible) *and* Jenkins v. Anderson, 447 U.S. 231 (1980) (permissible) *with* United States v. Noel, 3 M.J. 328 (C.M.A. 1977) (impermissible). Note that *Noel* predates both *Fletcher* and *Jenkins*. *See also* United States v. Garrett, 24 M.J. 413 (C.M.A. 1987) (curative instructions to court members removed any possible prejudice resulting from prosecutor's unintentional elicitation from witness that accused had invoked his rights); United States v. Wynn, 23 M.J. 726 (A.F.C.M.R. 1986) (accused's silence in face of unofficial accusations by base exchange employee was admissible).
21. *See* Rule 301(f)(1), Mil. R. Evid.; United States v. Langford, 15 M.J. 1090 (A.C.M.R. 1983); United States v. Abrecht, 4 M.J. 573 (A.C.M.R. 1977). *See also infra* § 15-13. For a discussion of dealing with the problem of an accused invoking his right to remain silent during cross-examination by the prosecution, see United States v. Castillo, 29 M.J. 145 (C.M.A. 1989). *See generally* Saltzburg, Schinasi & Schlueter, *Military Rules of Evidence Manual* 111 (3d ed. 1991). For discussion of the issue of witnesses invoking the right against self-incrimination on cross-examination, see United States v. Moore, 36 M.J. 329 (C.M.A. 1993) (invocation of right against self-incrimination on direct examination warranted striking portions of her testimony).
22. *See* Rule 305, Mil. R. Evid.

whether a questioned individual was a suspect. That is, the first inquiry is whether the questioner believed that the individual was a suspect. If not, the next inquiry is objective, i.e., whether a reasonable person would have considered the individual to be a suspect.[23]

The military recognizes not only the well-recognized *Miranda* right to counsel warnings,[24] but also statutory rights warnings required by Article 31(b), U.C.M.J.[25] Military rights warnings cards and forms used by investigators and commanders normally merge the *Miranda* and Article 31(b) warnings so that the suspect or accused is advised of:

(1) The offense of which he is suspected;[26]

---

23. *See, e.g.*, United States v. Meeks, 41 M.J. 150 (C.M.A. 1994) (accused not suspect at time of interview with commander); United States v. Brown, 40 M.J. 152 (C.M.A. 1994) (commander did not suspect and could not have reasonably suspected that accused was involved in criminal conduct at time of counseling session); United States v. Davis, 36 M.J. 337 (C.M.A. 1993), *aff'd on other grounds*, 114 S. Ct. 2350 (1994) (whether person is suspect is question of law; accused not suspect at time of initial questioning); United States v. Kendig, 36 M.J. 291 (C.M.A. 1993) (accused not a suspect at time of questioning); United States v. Good, 32 M.J. 105 (C.M.A. 1991) (although accused was not a "suspect" at time of first interrogation, by the second interrogation session the investigator should have reasonably suspected him); United States v. Morris, 13 M.J. 297 (C.M.A. 1982); United States v. Lewis, 12 M.J. 205 (C.M.A. 1982); United States v. Lavine, 13 M.J. 150 (C.M.A. 1982); United States v. Leiffer, 13 M.J. 337 (C.M.A. 1982).

United States v. Pownall, 42 M.J. 682 (Army Ct.Crim.App. 1995)(accused not suspect at time of non-investigatory questions by first sergeant); United States v. Brosius, 37 M.J. 652 (A.C.M.R. 1993) (accused not a suspect at time of initial questioning); United States v. Goldsmith, 29 M.J. 979 (A.F.C.M.R. 1990) (no warnings required where accused was not suspect at time of questioning).

United States v. Briley, 26 M.J. 977 (A.F.C.M.R. 1988) (accused was not suspected of drug use when first questioned but should have received rights warnings when it became apparent to investigators that he was more than just a witness); United States v. Tibbetts, 1 M.J. 1024 (N.C.M.R. 1976).

24. Rule 305, MIL. R. EVID. Miranda v. Arizona, 384 U.S. 436 (1966) has been applied to the military by United States v. Tempia, 16 C.M.A. 629, 37 C.M.R. 249 (1967). See generally Lederer, "Miranda v. Arizona—The Law Today," 78 MIL. L. REV. 197 (1977); Schlueter, "Tempia, Turner, McOmber and the Military Rules of Evidence: A Right to Counsel Trio With the New Look," ARMY LAW., Apr. 1980, at 1; Grendell, "Problem of Custodial Questioning After Dunaway v. New York," ARMY LAW., Sept. 1980, at 8.

25. See Appendix 3. Article 31 generally addresses the right against self-incrimination. Article 31(a) provides the right not to incriminate one's self (compare with Fifth Amendment right not to be a "witness" against one's self); Article 31(b) provides for statutory warnings; Article 31(c) provides what is now a dead letter attempt to protect witnesses from being embarrassed by nonmaterial questioning (*see* MIL. R. EVID. 303); Article 31(d) is a codified rule of exclusion. *See generally* Lederer, "Rights Warnings in the Armed Services," 72 MIL. L. REV. 1 (1976); Burnette, "Article 31(b)—A New Crop in a Fertile Field," ARMY LAW., Apr. 1986, at 32.

In United States v. Miller, 30 M.J. 703 (A.C.M.R. 1990), the court declined to adopt a rule that would require the civilian police to give Article 31(b) warnings to deserter.

26. United States v. Quintana, 5 M.J. 484 (C.M.A. 1978) (adequate advice); United States v. Erie, 29 M.J. 1008 (A.C.M.R. 1990) (warnings only need apprise suspect of general nature of offense being investigated and legal sufficiency is determined by totality of circumstances; warnings that he was being investigated for use of hashish were sufficient to cover all subsequent statements regarding controlled substances).

United States v. Huelsman, 27 M.J. 511 (A.C.M.R. 1988) (rights warning inadequate as to drug offense); United States v. Willeford, 5 M.J. 634 (A.F.C.M.R. 1978) (inadequate advice as to offense).

(2) The right to remain silent;[27]

(3) The consequence of speaking;[28] and

(4) The various rights to counsel.[29]

Technically, although the two rights warnings are almost always combined as above, the *Miranda* right to counsel warnings are only required after the servicemember has been placed in custody or after charges have been preferred.[30] Failure to give the necessary warnings usually results in exclusion.[31]

The exclusionary rule is inapplicable, however, where the statement would have been inevitably discovered,[32] where the statement resulted from an independent source,[33] or where the nexus between the offered statement and the inadmissible evidence has become attenuated so as to dissipate the taint.[34] Otherwise inadmissible statements may also be used for impeachment pur-

---

Note that the *Miranda* right to counsel warnings do not include a requirement that the suspect be advised of the offense. *Cf.* United States v. McCray, 643 F.2d 323 (5th Cir. 1981) (failure to so advise may under some circumstances result in an invalid waiver).

27. The interrogator may not interpret this right as simply the right not to incriminate one's self. *See, e.g.*, United States v. Williams, 2 C.M.A. 430, 9 C.M.R. 60 (1953). It is an absolute right not to say, or possibly do, anything, whether or not it might be incriminatory.

28. This warning may be negated if the questioner later leads the suspect to believe that whatever he says will be held in confidence. *See, e.g.*, United States v. Hanna, 2 M.J. 69 (C.M.A. 1976) (Just between you and me, did you do it?); United States v. Erie, 29 M.J. 1008 (A.C.M.R. 1990) (investigator vitiated warnings by giving impression that statements would not be used against suspect).

29. This includes the right to consult with counsel, have counsel present, and the appointment of counsel. Note that unlike the civilian warning, MIL. R. EVID. 305, which lays out the warning requirements, removes any requirement of indigency.

30. Rule 305, MIL. R. EVID. United States v. Lincoln, 42 M.J. 315 (1995)(accused not subjected to custodial interrogation); Note that this rule adopts a Sixth Amendment counsel warning, which is triggered after preferral of charges or imposition of pretrial confinement. See Brewer v. Williams, 430 U.S. 387 (1977); Messiah v. United States, 377 U.S. 201 (1964); United States v. Henry, 444 U.S. 824 (1980).

United States v. Langer, 41 M.J. 780 (A.F.Ct.Crim.App. 1995) (undercover questioning of accused following preferral of charges violated Sixth Amendment; statements excluded during prosecution's case-in-chief; admissible in rebuttal); United States v. Lincoln, 40 M.J. 679 (N.M.C.M.R. 1994) (accused not in custody at time of questioning; right to counsel warnings not required); United States v. Collier, 36 M.J. 501 (A.F.C.M.R. 1992) (accused not in custody when he told doctor what drugs he had given to wife-victim); United States v. Kelliher, 31 M.J. 701 (N.M.C.M.R. 1990) (failure to inform accused that charges had just been preferred against him did not void rights warnings and interrogation on unrelated charges); United States v. Miller, 30 M.J. 703 (A.C.M.R. 1990) (no right to counsel warnings required where accused not in custody).

31. Rule 304(b), MIL. R. EVID. Note that the Rule follows Harris v. New York, 401 U.S. 222 (1971), which provides that unwarned statements may be used for impeachment purposes. United States v. Kline, 35 M.J. 329 (C.M.A. 1992) (accused's statements were not product of earlier unwarned statements); United States v. McCoy, 31 M.J. 323 (C.M.A. 1990) (remedy of exclusion did not apply to coerced or unadvised statements obtained from other witnesses); United States v. Williams, 23 M.J. 362 (C.M.A. 1987) (failure to follow Article 31(b) requirements prevents use of statements for impeachment purposes); see also Article 31(d), U.C.M.J.

32. MIL. R. EVID. 304(b)(2) (exception).

33. Murray v. United States, 487 U.S. 533 (1988).

34. Oregon v. Elstad, 470 U.S. 298 (1985); Nardone v. United States, 308 U.S. 338 (1939); United States v. Marquardt, 39 M.J. 239 (C.M.A. 1994) (taint dissipated).

poses.[35] Evidence derived from an otherwise inadmissible statement may be admitted if the prosecution can prove by preponderance of the evidence that the statement was made voluntarily, that the evidence was not obtained by use of the statement, or that the evidence would have been obtained even if the statement had not been made.[36]

The military courts generally apply the same tests for "custody" as do the civilian courts.[37] A possible exception to that rule lies in the military's application of *Dunaway v. New York*.[38] In *Dunaway*, the Supreme Court ruled that a proper custodial interrogation must be based upon probable cause. In *United States v. Schneider*,[39] the Court of Military Appeals, now the Court of Appeals for the Armed Forces, observed that the obvious differences between civilian and military practice prevented literal application of *Dunaway*. The first question is whether the resulting confession was voluntary. The court will next determine whether the suspect was in custody and, if so, require the prosecution to establish probable cause.[40]

Not all conversations between a suspect and the commander or investigator need to be preceded by rights warnings.[41] But any "official" questioning,[42] by

---

35. MIL. R. EVID. 304(b)(1) (impeachment uses).
36. MIL. R. EVID. 304(b)(3) (derivative evidence).
37. What constitutes custody will depend on the facts. United States v. Harvey, 37 M.J. 140 (C.M.A. 1993) (Fifth Amendment rights to counsel not required where accused initiated conversations at sites she selected); United States v. McCarthy, 37 M.J. 595 (A.F.C.M.R. 1993) (accused not in custody at time of conversation with civilian investigator); United States v. Pond, 36 M.J. 1050 (A.F.C.M.R. 1993) (questioning of accused during traffic stop was not custodial). See United States v. Schake, 30 M.J. 314 (C.M.A. 1990) (test for custody is whether accused reasonably believed that he was not free to leave); United States v. Schneider, 14 M.J. 189 (C.M.A. 1982) (considered whether servicemember reported voluntarily, was a suspect or witness, and whether he was free to leave); United States v. Lonetree, 31 M.J. 849 (N.M.C.M.R. 1990) (accused was not in custody when he attended debriefings on information he had passed to Soviets; he attended meetings voluntarily and no restrictions were placed on his movements).
Note that Rule 305, MIL. R. EVID. apparently adopts an objective standard for measuring custody. *See also* Oregon v. Mathiason, 429 U.S. 492 (1977). *See generally* Saltzburg, Schinasi & Schlueter, *Military Rules of Evidence Manual* 199 (3d ed. 1991).
38. 439 U.S. 979 (1979).
39. 14 M.J. 189 (C.M.A. 1982).
40. *Id.* at 193. United States v. Scott, 22 M.J. 297 (C.M.A. 1986); United States v. Fagan, 24 M.J. 865 (N.M.C.M.R. 1987), *aff'd*, 28 M.J. 64 (C.M.A. 1989) (probable cause existed for custodial interrogation of accused who had been ordered by commander to report to the NIS offices).
41. *See* Saltzburg, Schinasi & Schlueter, *Military Rules of Evidence Manual*, 196 (3d ed. 1991). United States v. Britcher, 41 M.J. 806 (C.G.Ct.Crim.App. 1995) (statements to executive officer were not result of interrogation).
42. United States v. Bowerman, 39 M.J. 219 (C.M.A. 1994) (pediatrician's questions motivated by medical concerns); United States v. Harvey, 37 M.J. 140 (C.M.A. 1993) (noting that Article 31(b) must not be read literally, court concluded that subordinate, acting at request of OSI, was not required to give warnings to accused-supervisor; the meetings were initiated by the accused and would not have been viewed as inquiry by person acting in official capacity or law enforcement officer). United States v. Seay, 1 M.J. 201 (C.M.A. 1975). *See also* United States v. Dohle, 1 M.J. 223 (C.M.A. 1975) (applying "position of authority" test). In United States v. Duga, 10 M.J. 206 (C.M.A. 1981), the court indicated that Article 31(b) warnings were required only in those situations where the questioning was (1) official and (2) the suspect realized that it was official and not merely a casual conversation. In United States v. Loukas, 29 M.J. 385 (C.M.A. 1990), however, the court concluded that a crew chief's questioning of the accused, who had apparently

§ 5-4(B) THE COMMANDER'S INVESTIGATION § 5-4(B)

a person subject to the Uniform Code of Military Justice,[43] including informal

---

ingested drugs, was not for law-enforcement purposes and therefore no rights warnings were required. The questioning had been limited to the questioner's operational responsibilities and were not intended to evade constitutional or codal rights.

See also United States v. Good, 32 M.J. 105 (C.M.A. 1991) (questioning by accused's military superior was in official law enforcement or disciplinary capacity); United States v. Moore, 32 M.J. 56 (C.M.A. 1991) (questions by nurse regarding medical treatment of accused did not require warnings).

United States v. Lee, 25 M.J. 457 (C.M.A. 1988) (warnings required before requiring accused to document his overseas purchases pursuant to black market regulation); United States v. Toledo, 25 M.J. 270 (C.M.A. 1987) (clinical psychologist not required to give rights warnings where examination of defendant was at request of defense counsel); United States v. Jones, 24 M.J. 367 (C.M.A. 1987) (applying *Duga*, the court concluded that questioning by accused's former platoon sergeant while accused was standing in handcuffs was not official in nature).

United States v. Pownall, 42 M.J. 682 (Army Ct.Crim.App. 1995)(accused not suspect at time of non-investigatory questions by first sergeant); United States v. Dudley, 42 M.J. 528 (N.M.Ct.Crim.App. 1995) (questioning by Navy psychiatrist for diagnostic purposes did not require warnings); United States v. Williams, 39 M.J. 758 (A.C.M.R. 1994) (NCO's questioning, while escorting accused, was motivated by curiosity; warnings not required); United States v. Brown, 38 M.J. 696 (A.F.C.M.R. 1993) (treating physician and nurse not required to give rights warnings).

United States v. Schoolfield, 36 M.J. 545 (A.C.M.R. 1992) (nurse was not required to give rights warnings where questions were for legitimate health reasons); United States v. Collier, 36 M.J. 501 (A.F.C.M.R. 1992) (questions by accused's superior and physicians were not command disciplinary in nature; they were designed to obtain correct medical treatment).

United States v. Parrillo, 31 M.J. 886 (A.F.C.M.R. 1990) (although questioner was acting as agent for AFOSI investigators, suspect perceived conversation as personal); United States v. Thompson, 31 M.J. 781 (A.C.M.R. 1990) (under circumstances, conversation between accused and NCO concerning fraternization allegations was not an interrogation).

United States v. Carter, 26 M.J. 1002 (A.F.C.M.R. 1988) (official interrogation where two NCOs questioned the accused following entry into drug rehabilitation program).

43. *See* Art. 31(b), U.C.M.J., Rule 305(b), MIL. R. EVID. In United States v. Penn, 18 C.M.A. 194, 39 C.M.R. 194 (1969), the court indicated that there are two situations in which civilians might be required to give Article 31 rights warnings: where a military and civilian investigation have merged, and where the civilian is acting in furtherance of the military investigation or as an instrument of the military.

*See, e.g.,*United States v. French, 38 M.J. 420 (C.M.A. 1993) (minimal involvement of military officials with British investigation did not require British officers to give rights warnings); United States v. Raymond, 38 M.J. 136 (C.M.A. 1993) (civilian psychiatric social worker at military hospital not required to give accused rights warnings); United States v. Pittman, 36 M.J. 404 (C.M.A. 1993) (supervisor/friend not required to give warnings to accused; superiors in chain of command are normally presumed to be acting in official capacity); United States v. Miller, 36 M.J. 124 (C.M.A. 1992) (county child service investigator and court-appointed psychologist not required to give rights warnings); United States v. Moreno, 36 M.J. 107 (C.M.A. 1992) (civilian social worker not required to give warnings); United States v. Lonetree, 35 M.J. 396 (C.M.A. 1992) (intelligence agents were not required to give Article 31 warnings);United States v. Oakley, 33 M.J. 27 (C.M.A. 1991) (civilian officers who used NCO as liaison were not required to give rights warnings where questioning was essentially a civilian investigation); United States v. Moreno, 31 M.J. 935 (A.C.M.R. 1990) (state social worker not agent for police); United States v. Lonetree, 31 M.J. 849 (N.M.C.M.R. 1990) (Article 31 warnings were not required before interviews by intelligence agents—the civilian and military investigations were not one "indivisible entity" nor were the agents acting as instruments of the military); United States v. Quillen, 27 M.J. 312 (C.M.A. 1988) (civilian employee of Air Force Exchange Service was required to give warnings where her duties were governmental in nature and she in effect acted as an instrument of the military).

conversations designed to elicit a response,[44] may proceed only after proper warnings have been given and a waiver obtained.[45] Spontaneous utterances are exempted.[46] Questions motivated by concerns for public safety are also exempted.[47]

If at any time during the interrogation, the suspect indicates a desire to stop talking[48] or to see counsel,[49] questioning must cease. In the case of the latter

---

United States v. Mayhugh, 41 M.J. 657 (N.M.Ct.Crim.App.1994) (civilian detective not required to give warnings where military and civilian investigations had not merged); United States v. Gooden, 37 M.J. 1055 (N.M.C.M.R. 1993) (county social worker not required to give rights warnings).

See generally McDaniel, "Article 31(b) and the Defense Counsel Interview," ARMY LAW., May 1990, at 9.

44. Rule 305(b)(2), MIL. R. EVID. *See also* Rhode Island v. Innis, 440 U.S. 934 (1980); United States v. Leiker, 37 M.J. 418 (C.M.A. 1993) (no abuse of discretion to limit defense counsel's questions regarding general interrogation techniques); United States v. Schake, 30 M.J. 314 (C.M.A. 1990) (technique of conducting behavioral analysis interview can amount to interrogation); United States v. Byers, 26 M.J. 132 (C.M.A. 1988) ("lecture" by investigator amounted to interrogation that should have been preceded by warnings); United States v. Dowell, 10 M.J. 36 (C.M.A. 1980); United States v. Butner, 15 M.J. 139 (C.M.A. 1983).

United States v. Guron, 37 M.J. 942 (A.F.C.M.R. 1993) (nine-minute preface conversation with suspect was not functional equivalent of interrogation; court noted that first words out of mouth of questioner need not be rights warnings).

United States v. Kramer, 30 M.J. 805 (A.F.C.M.R. 1990) (investigator's informal interview or lecture that apprised defendant of the weight of evidence against him amounted to interrogation); United States v. Rollins, 23 M.J. 729 (A.F.C.M.R. 1986) (victim returning the accused's phone call at request of investigators did not amount to official interrogation); United States v. Hartsock, 14 M.J. 837 (A.C.M.R. 1982).

See generally Schlueter, "Tempia, Turner, McOmber and the Military Rules of Evidence: A Right to Counsel Trio With the New Look," ARMY LAW., Apr. 1980, at 1.

45. The waiver, which must be affirmative, need not be in writing although it is prudent to do so. The services provide standard rights-warnings/waiver forms. See United States v. Gay, 24 M.J. 304 (C.M.A. 1987) (permissible for investigators to obtain sworn statement from suspect assuming that proper rights warnings have been given and a waiver obtained).

46. United States v. Lichtenhan, 40 M.J. 466 (C.M.A. 1994) (accused's statements were spontaneous); United States v. Powell, 40 M.J. 1 (C.M.A. 1994) (accused statement was spontaneous); United States v. Shepard, 38 M.J. 408 (C.M.A. 1993) (statements were spontaneous admissions to unsuspected offense); United States v. Kendig, 36 M.J. 291 (C.M.A. 1993) (accused's spontaneous statements did not require warnings); United States v. Vitale, 34 M.J. 210 (C.M.A. 1992) (accused's statements were spontaneous and voluntary); United States v. Collier, 36 M.J. 501 (A.F.C.M.R. 1992) (accused's incriminating statements to superior were spontaneous); United States v. Tubbs, 34 M.J. 654 (A.C.M.R. 1992) (statements were unsolicited and voluntary); United States v. Foley, 12 M.J. 826 (N.M.C.M.R. 1981); United States v. Willeford, 5 M.J. 634 (A.F.C.M.R. 1978).

47. *See, e.g.*, United States v. Jones, 26 M.J. 353 (C.M.A. 1988); United States v. Collier, 36 M.J. 501 (A.F.C.M.R. 1992) (questions by accused's superior and physicians were not command disciplinary in nature; they were designed to obtain correct medical treatment); United States v. Shepard, 38 M.J. 408 (C.M.A. 1993) (questions by NCO were motivated for concern for accused's family).

48. *See, e.g.*, Michigan v. Mosley, 423 U.S. 96 (1975) (right to cut off questioning must be scrupulously honored); United States v. Watkins, 34 M.J. 344 (C.M.A. 1992) (there is no per se prohibition on reapproaching accused who has invoked the right to remain silent; the question is whether the accused's assertion of rights has been scrupulously honored); United States v.

---

49. United States v. Davis, 114 S. Ct. 2350 (1994) (military accused's comment, "Maybe I should talk to lawyer," followed by clarifying questions and then a statement, "No, I don't want a

§ 5-4(B)　　　　　THE COMMANDER'S INVESTIGATION　　　　　§ 5-4(B)

request, questioning may not be resumed until counsel has been provided or the suspect himself initiates further conversation or communication.[50]

Doucet, 43 M.J. 656 (N.M.C.Ct.Crim.App. 1995) (accused's refusal to signed a typed version of his statement was an invocation of right to remain silent; subsequent attempts to ask him to sign amounted to interrogation); United States v. Aikens, 16 M.J. 821 (N.M.C.M.R. 1983) (accused implied that he would decide whether to remain silent on a question-by-question basis).

---

lawyer" did not amount to invocation of right).

United States v. Morgan, 40 M.J. 389 (C.M.A. 1994) (accused's question re counsel was equivocal and investigators could ask clarifying questions; admonition to tell truth did not negate waiver).

United States v. Dock, 40 M.J. 112 (C.M.A. 1994) (request for counsel made to foreign officials does not necessarily apply to subsequent questioning by American officials)

United States v. Schroeder, 39 M.J. 471 (C.M.A. 1994) (accused's anticipatory invocation of right to counsel was too little and too early); United States v. Jordan, 38 M.J. 346 (C.M.A. 1993) (no error in civilian questioning where accused never invoked right to counsel; lengthy dissent by Chief Judge Sullivan pointed out several violations of right to counsel during interrogation process); United States v. McLaren, 38 M.J. 112 (C.M.A. 1993) (accused impliedly waived right to counsel after invoking it); United States v. Sager, 36 M.J. 137 (C.M.A. 1992) (accused not entitled to appointed military counsel for civilian investigation).

United States v. Moore, 38 M.J. 644 (A.F.C.M.R. 1993) (reversible error for interrogators to continue questioning after accused's equivocal reference to counsel); United States v. Brosius, 37 M.J. 652 (A.C.M.R. 1993) (accused's request for counsel to be present to look out for his interests was not request for counsel to assist him in murder investigation).

United States v. Joseph, 36 M.J. 846 (A.C.M.R. 1993) (accused's question whether he would have chance to see counsel was equivocal and ambiguous); United States v. Espronceda, 36 M.J. 535 (A.F.C.M.R. 1992) (accused waived right to counsel).

Cf. United States v. Vaughters, 42 M.J. 564 (A.F.Ct.Crim.App. 1995) (Edwards and its progeny is not broad enough to prohibit investigators from interrogating accused 19 days after he invoked right to counsel and was released from custody).

United States v. Sager, 32 M.J. 968 (A.C.M.R. 1991) (agent's reinstatement of interrogation on unrelated charges did not violate accused's right to counsel, in absence of invocation of that right).

50. Arizona v. Roberson, 486 U.S. 675 (1988); Edwards v. Arizona, 451 U.S. 477 (1981); Oregon v. Bradshaw, 462 U.S. 1039 (1983); Wyrick v. Fields, 459 U.S. 42 (1982).

United States v. Brabant, 29 M.J. 259 (C.M.A. 1989) (acting commander's attempt to speak with the accused after he had invoked his right to counsel amounted to an impermissible functional equivalent of interrogation); United States v. Fassler, 29 M.J. 193 (C.M.A. 1989) (questioning barred even if investigators do not know that accused requested to see counsel).

United States v. Coleman, 26 M.J. 451 (C.M.A. 1988) (interrogation by United States authorities not barred by accused's invocation of the right to counsel during previous interrogation by German police); United States v. Roa, 24 M.J. 297 (C.M.A. 1987) (request for consent to search did not violate accused's right to counsel).

United States v. Applewhite, 23 M.J. 196 (C.M.A. 1986) (investigator's request to take polygraph examination after accused invoked his right to counsel undermined accused's desire to see attorney).

United States v. McDavid, 37 M.J. 861 (A.F.C.M.R. 1993) (accused reinitiated conversations with interrogators); United States v. Grooters, 35 M.J. 659 (A.C.M.R. 1992) (knowledge that accused had requested counsel was imputed to another agent who later interviewed accused; court declined to adopt "good faith" exception to Edwards rule); United States v. Flynn, 34 M.J. 1183 (A.F.C.M.R. 1992) (accused initiated subsequent discussions with commander).

United States v. Watkins, 32 M.J. 1054 (A.C.M.R. 1991) (accused's right to counsel not violated where accused initiated conversation with agent following invocation of the right to counsel); United States v. Mathis, 31 M.J. 726 (A.F.C.M.R. 1990) (investigator cleared up suspect's ambiguous request to see counsel and obtained waiver).

Before 1994, a commander or investigator could question a suspect known (or reasonably should be known) to have counsel, only after first notifying that counsel of his intent to question the suspect and providing counsel a reasonable opportunity to be present.[51] That requirement was abrogated in a 1994 amendment to the *Military Rules of Evidence*.

Assuming that proper warnings have been given and a valid waiver obtained, the confession must still satisfy the due process requirement of voluntariness.[52] The procedures for challenging any pretrial statements made by an accused are addressed in § 13-4(A).

United States v. Lockwood, 31 M.J. 514 (A.C.M.R. 1990) (counsel provided to accused upon his request must be a lawyer certified under the U.C.M.J., i.e., a lawyer licensed by an American jurisdiction).

United States v. Smith, 30 M.J. 694 (A.C.M.R. 1990) (ambiguous request for counsel will be considered invoked); United States v. Granda, 29 M.J. 771 (A.C.M.R. 1989) (accused's waiver was presumptively invalid where he was reinterrogated at CID office at initiative of agents).

United States v. Brown, 27 M.J. 614 (A.C.M.R. 1988) (accused's request to speak with command prosecutor was not a request to see counsel).

United States v. Groh, 24 M.J. 767 (A.F.C.M.R. 1987) (no Edwards violation where accused initiated further conversation); United States v. Holliday, 24 M.J. 686 (A.C.M.R. 1987) (request for handwriting exemplars did not amount to functional equivalent of interrogation).

Cf. United States v. Vidal, 23 M.J. 319 (C.M.A. 1987) (request for counsel made to German investigators did not trigger *Edwards v. Arizona*); United States v. Harris, 16 M.J. 562 (A.C.M.R. 1983), rev'd, 21 M.J. 173 (C.M.A. 1985).

51. Rule 305(e), MIL. R. EVID. United States v. McOmber, 1 M.J. 380 (C.M.A. 1976); United States v. Sutherland, 16 M.J. 338 (C.M.A. 1983). This notice requirement was not grounded on the Sixth Amendment right to counsel but rather on a broad reading of Article 27, U.C.M.J., which provides for appointment of counsel. Rule 305(e), which codifies *McOmber*, expanded that case by extending the requirement to those situations where the investigator should know that the suspect or accused has counsel. Most of the subsequent case law centered on the issue of whether questioning about unrelated charges required notice. *See, e.g.,* United States v. Lewis, 36 M.J. 299 (C.M.A. 1993) (investigator's error in not following DA message requiring interrogators to ask suspects if they already have counsel did not require exclusion of statement; message was advisory in nature and was not a formal rule or regulation); United States v. Kendig, 36 M.J. 291 (C.M.A. 1993) (no notice required where interrogation was for different offenses); United States v. Sager, 36 M.J. 137 (C.M.A. 1992) (notice requirement is offense-specific).

Cf. United States v. LeMasters, 39 M.J. 490 (C.M.A. 1994) (accused waived right to have counsel notified of interrogation).United States v. Sutherland, 16 M.J. 338 (C.M.A. 1983); United States v. Lewis, 33 M.J. 758 (A.C.M.R. 1991) (interrogator not required to give notice of questioning to attorney representing accused on unrelated matter); United States v. Warren, 24 M.J. 656 (A.F.C.M.R. 1987) (offenses were factually unrelated); United States v. Lewis, 23 M.J. 508 (A.F.C.M.R. 1986) (no notice required where interrogation involved different offenses).

United States v. Holliday, 24 M.J. 686 (A.C.M.R. 1987) (counsel declined to appear at interrogation); United States v. Varraso, 15 M.J. 793 (A.C.M.R. 1983).

52. Rule 304(a), (c)(3), MIL. R. EVID. See, e.g., United States v. Martinez, 38 M.J. 82 (C.M.A. 1993) (confession during polygraph exam was result of psychological coercion).

United States v. Norfleet, 36 M.J. 129 (C.M.A. 1992) (accused's statements were voluntary); United States v. Lonetree, 35 M.J. 396 (C.M.A. 1992) (statements to intelligence agents were voluntary); United States v. Robinson, 26 M.J. 361 (C.M.A. 1988) (accused's statements were not involuntary despite length of interview and his weak character, considering fact that he was properly warned, there were no threats or promises, the time of the interrogation, and his experience and training); United States v. Jones, 26 M.J. 353 (C.M.A. 1988) (later statements were not tainted by earlier unwarned statements); United States v. Ravenel, 26 M.J. 344 (C.M.A. 1988) (failure to give warnings at initial interrogation created presumptive taint with regard to later

§ 5-4(C). Grants of Immunity.

Should a potential witness who possesses important information have a legitimate right to claim the privilege, the government may grant some form of immunity to that witness.[53] Normally, the general court-martial convening authority[54] may grant "use" or testimonial immunity which is the constitutional minimum.[55] That is, the witness is only promised that whatever he says, and any derivative evidence thereof, will not be used against him at any later trial. If the prosecution intends to later prosecute the witness, it bears a heavy burden of demonstrating at that subsequent trial that it is in no way using the fruits of the accused's earlier immunized statements.[56] Recent case

---

statements); United States v. Yeoman, 25 M.J. 1 (C.M.A. 1987). *See also* United States v. Stark, 24 M.J. 381 (C.M.A. 1987) (accused voluntarily returned to investigators' office for polygraph examination); United States v. Wheeler, 22 M.J. 76 (C.M.A. 1986) (appeal to religious beliefs); United States v. Murphy, 18 M.J. 220 (C.M.A. 1984) (inducement to confess to foreign authorities); United States v. Butner, 15 M.J. 139 (C.M.A. 1983) (threats rendered statement involuntary).

United States v. Sennett, 42 M.J. 787 (N.M. Ct. Crim. App. 1995) (investigators threatened accused); United States v. Washington, 42 M.J. 547 (A.F.Ct.Crim.App. 1995) (under facts, confession was voluntary; interrogation was business-like and included breaks, a meal, and an overnight break); United States v. Bubonics, 40 M.J. 734 (N.M.C.M.R. 1994) (confession involuntary where officers used, inter alia, "Mutt and Jeff" routine); United States v. Lincoln, 40 M.J. 679 (N.M.C.M.R. 1994) (summary of principles for determining whether statement is voluntary); United States v. Thomas, 39 M.J. 1094 (A.C.M.R. 1994) (accused's confession was voluntary even though he was tired and possibly intoxicated); United States v. Briggs, 39 M.J. 600 (A.C.M.R. 1994) (confession was voluntary under facts); United States v. Gill, 37 M.J. 501 (A.F.C.M.R. 1993) (accused's confession was voluntary although interrogator appealed to his religious beliefs).

United States v. Thrower, 36 M.J. 613 (A.F.C.M.R. 1992) (agent's ruse that he was psychic with special power to determine if accused was lying did not render confession involuntary; use of deception is permitted as long as it is not designed or calculated to produce untrue confession); United States v. Jones, 34 M.J. 899 (N.M.C.M.R. 1992) (confession not involuntary because accused was intoxicated); United States v. Branoff, 34 M.J. 612 (A.F.C.M.R. 1992) (statement was not involuntary because investigator told accused that honesty was the best policy).

United States v. Erie, 29 M.J. 1008 (A.C.M.R. 1990) (discussion of issue); United States v. Schuring, 16 M.J. 664 (A.C.M.R. 1983) (statement was voluntary although suspect was tired, had a headache, and questioning lasted six hours).

53. In lieu of immunity the prosecution may try to offer other forms or promises of clemency or leniency in hopes of obtaining the information. Such agreements require ungrudging enforcement. United States v. Brown, 13 M.J. 253 (C.M.A. 1982). *See also* § 11-2(E).

54. Only the general court-martial convening and the U.S. Attorney General may grant immunity. *See* R.C.M. 704(c)(2). In the case of immunity for a servicemember, the GCMCA may grant immunity after coordinating with federal authorities. In the case of a civilian witness, the GCMCA may act only after the grant is approved by the Attorney General, who may on his own authority also make the grant. Without such approval, the grant is invalid. *See* United States v. Andreas, 14 M.J. 483 (C.M.A. 1983).

55. Kastigar v. United States, 406 U.S. 441 (1972); Rule 301(c)(1), Mil. R. Evid. Transactional immunity promises the witness that he will not be prosecuted. United States v. Tagert, 11 M.J. 677 (N.M.C.M.R. 1981). Testimonial immunity is preferred over transactional because it permits later prosecution. *See generally* Green, "Grants of Immunity and Military Law, 1971-1976," 73 Mil. L. Rev. 1 (1976).

56. New Jersey v. Portash, 440 U.S. 450 (1979); United States v. Olivero, 39 M.J. 246 (C.M.A. 1994) (prosecution failed to prove by preponderance of evidence that non-evidentiary use of immunized testimony, i.e., decision to prosecute, was untainted by such testimony; court noted that

law[57] and changes to the Manual for Courts-Martial[58] should serve as a reminder of the dangers lurking in these procedures. For example, unauthorized grants of immunity may result in *de facto* immunity.[59] Because military grants of immunity are binding on other federal proceedings,[60] close coordination between the two entities is essential.[61] Military immunity affects state proceedings only insofar as the immunized testimony is inadmissible; it does not bar later state prosecutions.[62] If the grant of immunity, which amounts to

---

federal circuits are split on issue); Cunningham v. Gilevich, 36 M.J. 94 (C.M.A. 1992) (prosecution had burden of showing that evidence against accused was not tainted by coerced testimony of accused at investigation); United States v. Vith, 34 M.J. 277 (C.M.A. 1992) (SJA's use of immunized or derivative testimony to refute accused's claim in a post-trial clemency petition did not amount to a use of that testimony at a criminal trial for purposes of Fifth Amendment protections); United States v. England, 33 M.J. 37 (C.M.A. 1991) (government showed that evidence used against accused was independent of his earlier immunized testimony); United States v. Boyd, 27 M.J. 82 (C.M.A. 1988) (government did not sustain burden of proving lack of derivative use); United States v. Lucas, 25 M.J. 9 (C.M.A. 1987) (absent defense complaint, prosecution is not required to show that it has not utilized information or evidence derived from immunized testimony); United States v. Gardner, 22 M.J. 28 (C.M.A. 1986); United States v. Rivera, 1 M.J. 107 (C.M.A. 1975) (discouraging subsequent prosecutions); United States v. Whitehead, 5 M.J. 294 (C.M.A. 1978) (government's burden is more than simply negating taint); United States v. Daley, 3 M.J. 541 (A.C.M.R. 1977).

57. Cooke v. Orser, 12 M.J. 335 (C.M.A. 1982).
58. R.C.M. 704.
59. Samples v. Vest v. 38 M.J. 482 (C.M.A. 1994) (accused was not given enforceable promise of immunity); Cunningham v. Gilevich, 36 M.J. 94 (C.M.A. 1992) (accused not granted de facto tenure where commander told accused to testify before investigating board; commander did not believe anyone had committed a crime, accused was warned about lying, and commander was not acting with implicit approval of his superior; actions did amount to unlawful command influence); Cooke v. Orser, 12 M.J. 335 (C.M.A. 1982); United States v. Kimble, 33 M.J. 284 (C.M.A. 1991) (government was bound by de facto grant of immunity to accused); United States v. Conlon, 41 M.J. 800 (Army Ct.Crim.App. 1995) (accused not granted de facto immunity; court cited three-pronged test for such immunity and noted that although the commander manifested apparent authority to grant immunity and he apparently had the tacit approval of the GCM CA, the commander's statements did not require the accused to fulfill any condition; court rejected argument that his reenlistment was detrimental reliance); United States v. Wagner, 35 M.J. 721 (A.F.C.M.R. 1992) (accused entitled to de facto tenure where unit commander promised not to prosecute him for child sex abuse if he sought treatment); United States v. Zupkosfska, 34 M.J. 537 (A.F.C.M.R. 1991) (accused was not granted de facto immunity when investigator told him that he would not be charged).

United States v. Kershaw, 26 M.J. 723 (A.C.M.R. 1988) (statement by customs officer during meeting with accused and other officials, including IRS officer, that no one was interested in prosecuting him, does not amount to grant of immunity, but due process required suppression of statements); United States v. Whipple, 4 M.J. 773 (C.G.C.M.R. 1978); United States v. Brown, 13 M.J. 253 (C.M.A. 1982). The argument for enforcing otherwise defective promises of immunity or clemency generally rests on due process grounds. Enforcement will usually only extend to excluding any statements given in response to the promise. *Cf.* Cooke v. Orser, 12 M.J. 335 (C.M.A. 1982).

60. This is so because military courts are considered part of the same federal sovereignty. See Article 76, U.C.M.J., which makes binding on other federal agencies all actions taken pursuant to court-martial proceedings.
61. See R.C.M. 704.
62. Murphy v. Waterfront Common, 378 U.S. 52 (1964).

§ 5-5   THE COMMANDER'S INVESTIGATION   § 5-5

an order to testify, is valid, the witness faces possible criminal charges for failing to testify.[63]

§ 5-5. Eyewitness Identification.

The military rules governing eyewitness identification generally parallel those that guide civilian law enforcement personnel and center on two elements: the right to counsel, and due process. In military lineup procedures, the right to counsel attaches after preferral of charges or imposition of pretrial restraint.[1] Upon request for counsel the government is required to appoint, without regard to indigency, a JAG counsel. Military Rule of Evidence 321, which governs lineups, makes no mention of the right to individual military or civilian counsel.[2] But if the suspect requests the presence of a particular counsel, it would seem prudent for those conducting the lineup to wait until that counsel is present, barring an urgent need to proceed immediately.[3] The right to counsel can be waived.[4] Where counsel does appear, his role is limited to observing the procedures and offering suggestions.

There is no right to counsel at photographic identifications,[5] on-the-scene identifications,[6] or at accident viewings.[7] If there has been a denial of the right to counsel, the prosecution may still introduce an in-court identification if it can show by clear and convincing evidence that the identification is not the result of the first, illegal, identification.[8] Throughout, the procedure must not be so unnecessarily suggestive as to create a very substantial likelihood of

---

63. The grant of immunity is usually in the form of an order to testify. Thus, in addition to other provisions for generally failing to testify, see, e.g., R.C.M. 704(d) Discussion, the witness may be prosecuted under one of the several military disobedience offenses. Articles 90 or 92, U.C.M.J. See Chapter 2. See also § 13-3(H) (discusses motions to dismiss charges because of prior grants of immunity); § 11-2(E)(2) (discussion of notice to the defense of a grant of immunity to a prosecution witness); § 11-2(E)(3) (requests for immunity for defense witnesses).

1. Rule 321, MIL. R. EVID. Pretrial restraint, discussed in § 5-3, includes pretrial confinement, restriction, conditions on liberty, and arrest. Whether the restraint must still be in effect when the eyewitness identification takes place is not clear. The Drafters of Rule 321 apparently intended that mere apprehension or detention would not trigger the right to counsel. Rule 321(b)(2), MIL. R. EVID. Drafters' Analysis 1980.

For a general discussion on the right to counsel at military lineups, see Saltzburg, Schinasi & Schlueter, *Military Rules of Evidence Manual* 410-11 (3d ed. 1991); Gilligan & Hahn, "Eyewitness Identification in Military Law," 110 MIL. L. REV. 1 (1983); Gilligan, "Eyewitness Identification," 58 MIL. L. REV. 183 (1972); Oliphant, "The Lineup: The Sixth Amendment, Article 31 and the Right to Counsel," 31 Fed. B.J. (1972).

2. See Rule 321(b)(2)(A), MIL. R. EVID. The Drafters' Analysis to the Rule states that there is no right to civilian or individual military counsel under the Rule.

3. This would seem to be particularly true where an existing attorney-client relationship exists between the suspect and the counsel requested. The argument might be that the defendant was denied his Sixth Amendment right to counsel.

4. Rule 321(b)(2)(A), MIL. R. EVID. See Trant, "Defense-Requested Lineups," 11 THE ADVOCATE 161 (1979).

5. United States v. Ash, 413 U.S. 300 (1973); United States v. Gillespie, 3 M.J. 721 (A.C.M.R. 1977).

6. United States v. Smith, 2 M.J. 562 (A.C.M.R. 1976).

7. United States v. Young, 44 C.M.R. 670 (A.F.C.M.R. 1971).

8. United States v. Wade, 388 U.S. 218 (1967). Rule 321(d)(1), MIL. R. EVID.

misidentification; the test is whether the resulting identification is reliable.[9] The procedure for challenging pretrial identifications is discussed at § 13-4(C).

PART II
PRETRIAL RESTRAINTS AND CONFINEMENT

§ 5-6. In General.

A servicemember who is accused of committing an offense may be placed in pretrial restraint while charges are being processed. The method of taking a servicemember into custody is by "apprehension." Thereafter, depending on the offense and surrounding circumstances, the servicemember may be placed in one of the three forms of pretrial restraint: Conditions on Liberty, Restriction in Lieu of Arrest, and Pretrial Confinement. The following discussion addresses apprehension, the forms of pretrial restraint, and remedies for illegal restraint.

§ 5-7. Apprehension.

"Apprehension" is simply the placing of an individual in custody[1] and may be effected by all commissioned officers, warrant officers, petty officers, noncommissioned officers,[2] and military police, Air Force security policy, members of the shore patrol, and others who are performing police or guard duties.[3] Apprehension is accomplished by so notifying the individual[4] and in

---

9. Manson v. Brathwaite, 432 U.S. 98 (1977); Neil v. Biggers, 409 U.S. 188 (1972); United States v. Rhodes, 42 M.J. 287 (1995) (assuming that showup was suggestive, application of *Manson* factors indicated that trial identification was reliable); United States v. Fors, 10 M.J. 367 (C.M.A. 1981); United States v. Mueller, 40 M.J. 708 (A.C.M.R. 1994) (pretrial identification was not unnecessarily suggestive); United States v. Batzel, 15 M.J. 640 (N.M.C.M.R. 1982); Rule 321(b), MIL. R. EVID. *See generally* Gasperini, "Eyewitness Identification Under the Military Rules of Evidence," ARMY LAW., May 1980, at 42.

1. Art. 7(a), U.C.M.J. *See* Appendix 3.

2. The original Discussion to R.C.M. 302(b) indicated that normally NCOs and petty officers should not apprehend an officer unless directed to do so by another commissioned officer. The exception is where the apprehension is necessary to prevent a disgrace to the service or prevent an escape. Note that Article 7, which governs apprehensions, makes no such limitation but recognizes that the services will promulgate regulations further specifying who may apprehend. R.C.M. 302(b)(2) was amended in 1990 to permit commissioned, warrant, petty, and noncommissioned officers on inactive duty training to make apprehensions. That was apparently triggered by Military Justice Amendments of 1986, Title VIII, 804 National Defense Authorization for Fiscal Year 1987, Pub. L. No. 99-661, 100 Stat. 3905 (1986), which expanded jurisdiction over reservists. *See also* § 4-6.

United States v. Caver, 41 M.J. 556 (N.M.Ct.Crim.App.1994) (petty officers and master-at-arms personnel are authorized to apprehend and to issue any necessary and proper orders to effect the apprehension).

In United States v. Corriere, 24 M.J. 701 (A.C.M.R. 1987), a special court-martial convening authority apparently conducted a mass arrest. The court rejected the argument that this amounted to unlawful command influence and that it therefore denied the accused due process.

3. R.C.M. 302(b). In 1990 the *Manual* was amended to permit commissioned, warrant, petty, and noncomissioned officers on inactive duty training to make apprehensions.

4. R.C.M. 302(d)(1). United States v. Harris, 29 M.J. 169 (C.M.A. 1989) (military policeman's attempt to stop the accused for administrative reasons did not amount to an apprehension).

military parlance is the equivalent of an "arrest" in civilian practice.[5] On the other hand, a military arrest, as noted in § 5-8(D), is a form of moral restraint upon the servicemember's freedom to perform duties and move about.[6] The rules governing apprehension in the military generally parallel similar rules guiding civilian police. Thus, the apprehension must be based upon probable cause—reason to believe that the servicemember has committed or is committing an offense.[7] Generally, no warrant is required.[8] R.C.M. 302, which governs apprehensions, restricts the ability of military authorities to enter "private" dwellings to make apprehensions. Otherwise, the apprehension may be made at any place, off-post or on-post.[9] R.C.M. 302(e)(2) defines "private dwellings" as follows:

> A private dwelling includes dwellings, on or off a military installation, such as single family houses, duplexes, and apartments. The quarters may be owned, leased, or rented by the residents, or assigned, and may be occupied on a temporary or permanent basis. "Private dwelling" does not include the following, whether or not subdivided into individual units: living areas in military barracks, vessels, aircraft, vehicles, tents, bunkers, field encampments, and similar places.[10]

Assuming that authorities are not otherwise lawfully in a private dwelling, they may enter (1) with consent[11] or (2) upon probable cause coupled with exigent circumstances.[12] If neither of those is present, the procedure to be used for entering depends on whether the private dwelling is under military control (or in a foreign country) or is a civilian dwelling. In the case of private military dwellings or nonmilitary property overseas, military authorities need probable cause and authorization from a commander or military judge to

---

5. R.C.M. 302(a)(1) Discussion. United States v. Harris, 29 M.J. 169 (C.M.A. 1989) (apprehension is the equivalent to an arrest in civilian practice); United States v. Kinane, 1 M.J. 309 (C.M.A. 1976).
6. Art. 9, U.C.M.J. United States v. Harris, 29 M.J. 169 (C.M.A. 1989).
7. Art. 7, U.C.M.J.; R.C.M. 302(c); United States v. Camanga, 38 M.J. 249 (C.M.A. 1993) (probable cause to apprehend is measured by objective rather than subjective standard); United States v. Wallace, 34 M.J. 353 (C.M.A. 1992) (agents had probable cause to apprehend accused); United States v. Acosta, 11 M.J. 307 (C.M.A. 1981); United States v. Martin, 33 M.J. 599 (A.C.M.R. 1991) (MP had probable cause to apprehend accused based upon anonymous tip). See also Clevenger, "Present But Unarticulated Probable Cause to Apprehend," ARMY LAW., Nov. 1981, at 7.
8. R.C.M. 302(d)(2). The exception lies where the military authorities wish to apprehend an individual in a civilian dwelling. See R.C.M. 302(e)(2).
9. R.C.M. 302(e)(1).
10. R.C.M. 302(e)(2). United States v. McCarthy, 38 M.J. 398 (C.M.A. 1993) (warrant not required to apprehend servicemember in barracks).
11. R.C.M. 302(e)(2)(A). See also MIL. R. EVID. 314(e) and 316(d)(2). United States v. Sager, 30 M.J. 777 (A.C.M.R. 1990) (apprehension lawful where agent's presence in accused's quarters was based on consent provided by his wife); United States v. Davis, 30 M.J. 718 (A.F.C.M.R. 1990) (warrantless entry into accused's off-base home was unlawful).
12. R.C.M. 302(e)(2)(B). See also MIL. R. EVID. 315(g) and 316(d)(4)(B). United States v. Jackson, 34 M.J. 1145 (A.C.M.R. 1992) (sufficient exigent circumstances justified warrantless apprehension of accused at motel room).

apprehend a resident.[13] Where the person to be apprehended is not a resident in one of those dwellings, authorities also need authorization to enter the dwelling in the first instance.[14]

In the case of civilian private dwellings, civilian warrants are needed: an arrest warrant for a resident[15] and search and arrest warrants for someone not a resident.[16] Reasonable force may be used to effect an apprehension.[17] Upon a valid apprehension, the individual making the apprehension may search the servicemember and other areas within his immediate control for weapons and destructible evidence.[18]

A person should not remain under apprehension indefinitely.[19] At some point the servicemember's commander will decide whether to release him, turn him over to civilian authorities,[20] or impose one of the several forms of pretrial restraint.[21] Resisting apprehension is an offense[22] and should an apprehended accused escape before he can be placed in confinement, he may be charged with escape from custody.[23]

The Discussion to R.C.M. 302 points out that "apprehensions" and "investigative detentions" are not the same thing. The latter need not be supported by probable cause and will generally not support anything more than a "frisk" of the individual.[24]

§ 5-8. Pretrial Restraints.

§ 5-8(A). In General.

There are four recognized means of imposing "pretrial restraint" on servicemembers.[1] In order of the degree of restraint, beginning with the least, they are as follows:

(1) Conditions on Liberty;
(2) Restriction in Lieu of Arrest;

---

13. R.C.M. 302(e)(2)(C)(i). This practice follows Payton v. New York, 445 U.S. 573 (1980).
14. R.C.M. 302(e)(2)(C)(ii). See Stegald v. United States, 451 U.S. 204 (1981).
15. R.C.M. 302(e)(2)(D)(i). United States v. Carter, 31 M.J. 502 (C.M.A. 1990) (agents effected unlawful apprehension when they asked accused to step outside his off-base quarters and seized him).
16. R.C.M. 302(e)(2)(D)(ii).
17. R.C.M. 302(d)(3).
18. Mil. R. Evid. 314(g). United States v. Wallace, 34 M.J. 353 (C.M.A. 1992) (search of accused was conducted pursuant to lawful apprehension).
19. Art. 9(e), U.C.M.J.; R.C.M. 302(d) Discussion (person making apprehension should promptly notify the commanding officer).
20. See Art. 14, U.C.M.J. (delivery of offenders to civil authorities).
21. See infra § 5-3(B).
22. United States v. Burgess, 32 M.J. 446 (C.M.A. 1991) (resisting apprehension).
23. United States v. Felty, 12 M.J. 438 (C.M.A. 1982).
24. See Mil. R. Evid. 314(f). United States v. Peterson, 30 M.J. 946 (A.C.M.R. 1990) (initial encounter between police officer and accused, whose car was parked in high-crime area, was not seizure, especially since accused was not aware of officer's status).

1. See R.C.M. 304. See generally Boller, "Pretrial Restraint in the Military," 50 Mil. L. Rev. 71 (1970); Finnegan, "Pretrial Restraint and Pretrial Confinement," Army Law., Mar. 1985, at 15.

(3) Arrest; and
(4) Pretrial Confinement.

The first three are forms of moral restraint;[2] the fourth is physical restraint and is discussed in § 5-9. Before discussing each form and the applicable criteria, some general rules pertaining to pretrial restraint should be addressed.

First, only a commanding officer may order pretrial restraint of another officer or a civilian.[3] That authority may not be delegated.[4] Enlisted personnel may be ordered into pretrial restraint by any commissioned officer[5] or by any warrant, petty, or noncommissioned officer who has been delegated that authority by a commanding officer.[6] The delegation covers only enlisted personnel within control of that commanding officer.[7] A superior authority may limit a subordinate's authority to impose pretrial restraint.[8]

The basis for any of the forms of pretrial restraint is probable cause to believe that the individual has committed an offense triable by a court-martial and that pretrial restraint is required.[9] Restraint must be decided on a case-by-case basis, but certain factors should be considered in each case:[10] whether the individual presents a flight risk or danger to the unit because he may commit serious criminal acts.[11] Mere inconvenience to the unit will not suffice as a reason for imposing pretrial restraint.[12] Further, the imposing authority must have considered (but not necessarily imposed) lesser forms of restraint.[13]

Pretrial restraint, except pretrial confinement,[14] is imposed by informing the servicemember in writing or orally that he is in pretrial restraint.[15] He

---

2. Moral restraint is that which is imposed by an order from an authorized official. The servicemember in effect is ordered to stay at a certain place or refrain from going to a certain place.
3. Art. 9, U.C.M.J.; R.C.M. 304(b)(1).
4. R.C.M. 304(b)(3).
5. R.C.M. 304(b)(2).
6. R.C.M. 304(b)(3).
7. Id.
8. R.C.M. 304(b)(4).
9. R.C.M. 304(c). United States v. Acosta, 11 M.J. 307 (C.M.A. 1981).
10. R.C.M. 304(c) Discussion.
11. See R.C.M. 305(h)(2)(B). These same factors must be considered in deciding whether to impose pretrial confinement. Note that the nature and circumstances of the offense are a factor which should be considered. In theory, pretrial restraint may be imposed for minor offenses. Cf. Art. 10, U.C.M.J. (normally minor offenses should not result in pretrial confinement).
12. R.C.M. 305(h)(2)(B) Discussion makes it plain that a servicemember should not be confined for purposes of convenience or expedience; arguably, the same reasoning extends to the other three less rigorous forms of pretrial restraint. The justifications for pretrial restraint are sufficiently broad to affect most situations that might otherwise appear to be matters of convenience. See also United States v. Wallace, 2 M.J. 1 (C.M.A. 1976) (restriction should not be used as general preventive detention). Commanders are permitted to impose "administrative restraint" for purposes of training, for example, or medical treatment. See R.C.M. 304(h).
13. R.C.M. 304(c) Discussion citing R.C.M. 305(h)(2)(B).
14. See § 5-3(B)(4). Special rules govern the imposition procedures for pretrial confinement: it is imposed by delivery of the servicemember to the confinement facility pursuant to orders from a person authorized to impose pretrial confinement.
15. R.C.M. 304(d).

must be told of the conditions and limits of the restraint[16] and must also be informed of the offense for which he is being restrained.[17] The order of restraint must be delivered personally by the imposing authority or through others.[18] Notice as to offense itself apparently need not be given by the imposing authority.[19] Slightly different rules govern imposition of pretrial confinement. See § 5-9.

In no case may pretrial restraint constitute punishment,[20] and it should be no more rigorous than necessary to ensure the servicemember's presence.[21] Unless pretrial restraint is terminated by an authority authorized to impose such, it is automatically ended upon announcement of the sentence, acquittal of all charges, or dismissal of all charges.[22] Any offenses committed by the servicemember during pretrial restraint may be processed as any other charge.[23] In particular, escape from, or breach of, pretrial restraint may serve as the basis of additional charges.[24] For a discussion on illegal pretrial restraint *see* § 5-10, *infra*.

Note that imposition of restriction, arrest, and pretrial confinement starts the period for determining whether the accused has been denied a speedy trial[25] and also triggers the right to counsel at any subsequently held lineups.[26]

§ 5-8(B). Conditions on Liberty.

"Conditions on liberty" is the least restrictive of the four types of pretrial restraint. Although forms of this type of moral restraint have existed in the past,[27] it is now been officially recognized in the Manual for Courts-Martial.[28] Typically, this restraint consists of ordering the servicemember to avoid certain places or persons or to present himself to specified persons at certain

---

16. *Id.*
17. R.C.M. 304(e).
18. R.C.M. 304(d). For example, the First Sergeant (acting as an agent) could inform the accused that the commander had ordered him in pretrial restraint.
19. R.C.M. 304. This provides some flexibility as to who must tell the servicemember what crime he is supposedly linked to. Technical accuracy is not required; all that is required is that he be told of the "nature" of the offense.
20. Art. 13, U.C.M.J.; R.C.M. 304(f). A servicemember may receive "minor punishment," however, for minor infractions committed during the restraint. *Id.* This usually involves further restricting the accused's already limited liberty or denial of other privileges.
21. R.C.M. 304(c) Discussion.
22. R.C.M. 304(g). Frage v. Edington, 26 M.J. 927 (N.M.C.M.R. 1988) (continued pretrial confinement pending government appeal under Article 62 was not authorized where ruling being appealed had resulted in the charges being dismissed by trial judge).
23. *See* § 6-1.
24. *See, e.g.*, Art. 95, U.C.M.J. (resistance, breach of arrest, and escape); MCM, Part IV, para. 102 (breaking restriction).
25. R.C.M. 701; § 13-3(C).
26. Mil. R. Evid. 321. Apparently the right to counsel may also be triggered following imposition of "conditions on liberty."
27. See United States v. Heard, 3 M.J. 14 (C.M.A. 1977).
28. R.C.M. 304(a)(1).

times as a means of accounting for his presence.[29] Note that this form of restraint may be imposed in conjunction with arrest or restriction.[30]

§ 5-8(C). Restriction in Lieu of Arrest.

Restriction in lieu of arrest is less severe than arrest and generally consists of ordering the servicemember to stay within specific geographical limits.[31] For example, the commander may restrict an accused to the installation or to the company or battalion area except for purposes of a weekly visit to the chapel and postexchange. Unless the commander indicates otherwise in his order, the servicemember is expected to perform his regular duties.[32]

§ 5-8(D). Arrest.

Arrest in military practice is a form of moral, as opposed to physical, restraint.[33] Unlike restriction in lieu of arrest, discussed at § 5-8(C), the individual here may not be required to perform full military duties but may be required to take part in routine duties.[34] This form of restraint is generally more confining than restriction in lieu of arrest. Note that if the imposing authority, or a superior, orders the servicemember to perform duties inconsistent with his status as a person under arrest, the restraint automatically terminates.[35] This form of arrest is similar to but not identical to "arrest in quarters" which may be imposed on officers pursuant to nonjudicial punishment. *See* § 3-6(C)(4).

§ 5-9. Pretrial Confinement.

§ 5-9(A). In General.

The most rigorous form of pretrial restraint is pretrial confinement.[1] Consequently, the rules governing imposition of this form of restraint are compre-

---

29. For example, the commander may order the accused to report and sign in at specified times during duty hours. *See, e.g.*, United States v. Orback, 21 M.J. 610 (A.F.C.M.R. 1985) ("administrative freeze" on accused was not a condition on his liberty). In United States v. Bradford, 25 M.J. 181 (C.M.A. 1987), the court noted that, in theory, the "liberty risk" program is not a condition on liberty; but under some circumstances it could amount to restriction that might in turn trigger speedy trial issue. Here, the imposition of liberty risk (denying the accused the opportunity to leave the ship while it was in port) was more in the nature of an administrative protection of foreign relations.
30. R.C.M. 304(a)(1).
31. R.C.M. 304(a)(2).
32. *Id.*
33. Art. 9, U.C.M.J.; R.C.M. 304(a)(3).
34. *Id.*
35. *Id.*
1. Article 10, U.C.M.J. See generally Boller, "Pretrial Restraint in the Military," 50 Mil. L. Rev. 71 (1970); Owen, "A Hard Look at the Military Magistrate Pretrial Confinement Hearing: *Gerstein* and *Courtney* Revisited," 88 Mil. L. Rev. 3 (1980); Clevenger, "The Right to be Free from Pretrial Confinement," Army Law., Mar. 1986, at 19; Finnegan, "Pretrial Restraint and

hensive. Although the military has no system of bail, the servicemember is entitled to the same Fourth Amendment safeguards available to his civilian counterpart.[2]

Pretrial confinement, which is a form of physical restraint,[3] may be imposed by any person authorized to impose any other form of pretrial restraint.[4] *See* § 5-8(A). But the criteria and procedures for imposing pretrial confinement are more detailed. R.C.M. 305 presents a comprehensive guide for imposing pretrial confinement and generally incorporates much of the military case law that previously guided commanders in the decision to place and keep an accused in confinement.[5] The current procedures entail a four-step process: (1) the initial decision to place an accused in confinement; (2) the commander's decision to continue pretrial confinement; (3) review of the commander's decision by an impartial person; and (4) possible judicial review.[6]

§ 5-9(B). Initial Decision to Confine.

The initial decision to impose pretrial confinement need not be made by the accused's commander although in most cases it is.[7] The ability of another officer, for example, to confine immediately an enlisted servicemember provides some flexibility in the procedures where the commander is not readily available. But the initial decision must still be based upon probable cause and should include an examination of the factors that will be relied upon in deciding whether to keep the accused in confinement.[8] These include the fact that it is foreseeable that the accused presents either a flight risk or a danger to the military community[9] and that other lesser forms of restraint are inadequate.[10]

Pretrial Confinement," ARMY LAW., Mar. 1985, at 15. *See also* United States v. Davidson, 14 M.J. 81 (C.M.A. 1982) (discussions on nature of pretrial confinement).

2. *See* Courtney v. Williams, 1 M.J. 267, 271 (C.M.A. 1976).

3. Pretrial confinement is not "custody"; the latter is effected by apprehension and need not be physical in nature. See Art. 9(e), U.C.M.J.; R.C.M. 305(d) Discussion; United States v. Ellsey, 16 C.M.A. 455, 37 C.M.R. 75 (1966).

4. R.C.M. 305(c).

5. *See, e.g.,* United States v. Malia, 6 M.J. 65 (C.M.A. 1978); United States v. Heard, 3 M.J. 14 (C.M.A. 1977); Berta v. United States, 9 M.J. 390 (C.M.A. 1980); Courtney v. Williams, 1 M.J. 267 (C.M.A. 1976).

6. *See generally* R.C.M. 305.

7. *See* R.C.M. 304(b) as to who may impose pretrial confinement. R.C.M. 305 envisions that someone other than the accused's commanding officer may order pretrial confinement; if that is the case, the commanding officer is to be notified. R.C.M. 305(h). In United States v. Rexroat, 38 M.J. 292 (C.M.A. 1993), the Court held that the commander's initial probable cause decision to confine a person could satisfy the requirements of Gerstein if the commander is neutral and detached.

United States v. Lipscomb, 38 M.J. 608 (C.G.C.M.R. 1993) (commanding officer's initial probable cause decision to confine the accused satisfied both Gerstein and McLaughlin requirements).

8. R.C.M. 305(d) Discussion.

9. R.C.M. 305(h)(2)(B); United States v. Moore, 32 M.J. 56 (C.M.A. 1991) (defendant's action of

10. R.C.M. 305(h)(2)(B); United States v. Sharrock, 30 M.J. 1003 (A.F.C.M.R. 1990) (commander failed to show that he had considered other alternatives to pretrial confinement); United States v. Otero, 5 M.J. 781 (A.C.M.R. 1978). The commander is not required to have actually tried lesser forms of restraint.

§ 5-9(B)   THE COMMANDER'S INVESTIGATION   § 5-9(B)

Other factors that have been considered by courts and that are now listed in the Discussion portion of R.C.M. 305(h)(2)(B) include:

(1) The nature and circumstances of the offenses charged or suspected, including extenuating circumstances.

(2) The weight of the evidence against the accused;

(3) The accused's ties to the locale, including family, off-duty employment, financial resources, and length of residence;

(4) The accused's character and mental condition;

(5) The accused's service record, including any record of previous misconduct;

(6) The accused's record of appearance at or flight from other pretrial investigations, trials, and similar proceedings; and

(7) The likelihood that the accused can and will commit further serious criminal misconduct if allowed to remain at liberty.[11]

When the accused is confined, he must be advised of the nature of the offense involved,[12] his right to remain silent,[13] his right to military and civilian counsel,[14] and the procedures for reviewing the propriety of his pretrial confinement.[15] If someone other than the accused's commander has ordered pretrial confinement, notice of the confinement must be given to that commander within 24 hours.[16] Once confinement is ordered, it may be terminated only by a commander of the accused, a military judge, or an individual officially charged with reviewing the commander's decision to impose the confinement.[17]

---

speaking with wife resulted in her recanting accusations and warranted his pretrial confinement); United States v. Sharrock, 30 M.J. 1003 (A.F.C.M.R. 1990) (accused's earlier AWOL and other incidents of servicemembers in his unit going AWOL to avoid trial did not support pretrial confinement).

See also United States v. Heard, 3 M.J. 14 (C.M.A. 1977) (obstructing justice warrants pretrial confinement); United States v. Gaskins, 5 M.J. 772 (A.C.M.R. 1978) (future serious misconduct includes obstruction of justice); United States v. Shelton, 27 M.J. 540 (A.C.M.R. 1988); United States v. Rios, 24 M.J. 809 (A.F.C.M.R. 1987) (seriousness of crime alone is not sufficient grounds for imposing pretrial confinement).

11. These factors are derived from 18 U.S.C. § 3146(b). See R.C.M. 305(h)(2)(B) Analysis.

12. Art. 10, U.C.M.J.; R.C.M. 305(e)(1). *Cf.* United States v. Wallace, 14 M.J. 869 (C.G.C.M.R. 1982) (no notice required where the accused already knows).

13. R.C.M. 305(e)(2). *See also* Art. 31, U.C.M.J. and Mil. R. Evid. 305.

14. R.C.M. 305(e)(3), (f). The R.C.M. envisions that military counsel may be appointed for the sole purpose of representing the accused during pretrial confinement review procedures and before charges are preferred. This apparently is intended to ameliorate the problem of distance where the defense counsel are not in close proximity to the confinement facility. In many cases such limited representation will cause no prejudice to the accused. A different result might occur, however, where an attorney-client relationship already exists. United States v. Coburn, 42 M.J. 609 (N.M.Ct.Crim.App. 1995) (accused entitled to relief where government failed to provide counsel prior to initial review as required by R.C.M. 305(f); court stated that once accused has requested counsel, his silence at hearing did not amount to waiver of right to counsel.)

15. R.C.M. 305(e)(4).

16. R.C.M. 305(h)(1).

17. R.C.M. 305(g).

§ 5-9(C). Review by Commander.

Within 72 hours of ordering the accused into confinement or receiving notice that one of his personnel has been confined, the commander must decide whether to continue pretrial confinement.[18] He must consider, or reconsider as the case may be, whether the accused presents a flight risk or danger to the command and whether other lesser forms of restraint are adequate. Other factors, discussed *supra*, should also be considered.[19] If the commander decides that continued confinement is warranted, he must prepare a written memorandum detailing his reasons.[20] This memorandum, which may include backup materials such as police reports and witness statements, is then forwarded to a "reviewing officer" who in turn is charged with reviewing the commander's decision to continue confinement.

§ 5-9(D). Review of Commander's Decision to Confine.

Within 48 hours [21] of the date that pretrial confinement begins,[22] a "neutral

---

18. R.C.M. 305(h)(2). In United States v. Rexroat, 38 M.J. 292 (C.M.A. 1993), the court indicated that the Gerstein v. Pugh requirement of review by a neutral and detached magistrate could be accomplished by a neutral and detached commander. Change 6 to the Manual for Courts-Martial (Dec. 1993) amended R.C.M. 305(h) to make clear that the commander's responsibility to review a decision to confine arises in two situations: where the commander has ordered pretrial confinement, and where some other authority has ordered pretrial confinement. *See generally* Milhizer & McShane, "Analysis of Change 6 to the 1984 Manual for Courts-Martial," ARMY LAW., May 1994, p. 40. United States v. Shelton, 27 M.J. 540 (A.C.M.R. 1988) (record failed to show whether commander determined that further confinement was appropriate); United States v. Freeman, 24 M.J. 547 (A.C.M.R. 1987) (this requirement was met by the fact that it was the accused's commander who initially decided to impose pretrial confinement).
19. R.C.M. 305(h)(2)(B) Discussion.
20. The Army and Navy have had this requirement for some time. *See, e.g.*, AR 27-10, para. 9-5b(1), 16-5a; SECNAVINST 1640.10, para. 6. United States v. Beloney, 32 M.J. 639 (A.C.M.R. 1991) (properly completed checklist for pretrial confinement or any writing that memorializes decision and provides sufficient information for magistrate's review satisfies requirement of memorandum).
21. In United States v. Rexroat, 38 M.J. 292 (C.M.A. 1993), the court concluded that the 48-hour requirement of County of Riverside v. McLaughlin applied to military. The court noted that the requirement could be met by a neutral and detached commander's initial decision to confine under R.C.M. 305(d) or by an initial review under R.C.M. 305(h). The court rejected the argument that only a timely magistrate review under R.C.M. 305(i) would meet the requirements of *McLaughlin*. In reaching that conclusion the court rejected the argument that the Drafters' Analysis for R.C.M. 305 supported the position that a non-magistrate review of a decision to confine would not meet Gerstein's requirements; that analysis, said the court, was simply a reflection of the staff personnel who worked on the project, not necessarily the President's view. In dissent, Chief Judge Sullivan stated that the commander who initially orders confinement is not a neutral and detached magistrate for purposes of *Gerstein v. Pugh*.

United States v. Holloway, 38 M.J. 302 (C.M.A. 1993) (court concluded that Supreme Court's decision in County of Riverside v. McLaughlin applied to military).

United States v. Taylor, 36 M.J. 1166 (A.C.M.R. 1993) (accused entitled to have restriction amounting to confinement reviewed by a magistrate within 48 hours).

22. United States v. Rexroat, 38 M.J. 292 (C.M.A. 1993) (48-hour requirement of County of Riverside v. McLaughlin applies to military).

and detached" reviewing officer[23] must decide whether continued confinement is warranted;[24] this is the equivalent of a *Gerstein v. Pugh*[25] probable cause hearing conducted by civilian magistrates or judges.

If the accused has been confined in a civilian facility, the time limit also begins running at the time of confinement, if such was requested by military authorities.[26] In calculating whether the time requirement has been met, the date that confinement is imposed and the date of the review each count as one day.[27]

In United States v. Stuart, 36 M.J. 746 (A.C.M.R. 1993), the court indicated that the 48-hour time period involving pretrial confinement by civilian authorities on behalf of the Army begins when civilian authorities detain the servicemember with notice to, and approval of, military authorities. For good cause shown, the time for completion of the review may be extended to 7 days. As the Drafter's Analysis for this Rule points out, in most cases, the requirement will not be a problem because the reviewing officer will simply be reviewing the commander's memorandum and other written matters.

See, e.g., United States v. Ballesteros, 29 M.J. 14 (C.M.A. 1989) (detention by civilian authorities for military offense, with approval by military authorities, triggered requirement for magistrate's hearing).

United States v. Justice, 32 M.J. 599 (A.C.M.R. 1991) (defense counsel's inability to prepare for review before end of seventh day was good cause for delay).

United States v. Shelton, 27 M.J. 540 (A.C.M.R. 1988) (court declined to infer that good cause existed for tardy magistrate's review; if there is good cause it should be established and included in magistrate's memorandum); United States v. Dent, 26 M.J. 968 (A.C.M.R. 1988) (government bears burden of showing timely review).

United States v. DeLoatch, 25 M.J. 718 (A.C.M.R. 1987) (confinement in detention cell triggered right to have magistrate's review within 7 days).

23. *See also* United States v. Mcleod, 39 M.J. 278 (C.M.A. 1994) (per curiam) (review of accused's confinement by both brigade commander and SJA satisfied requirement that initial decision to confine must be reviewed by neutral and detached individual).

In United States v. Rexroat, 36 M.J. 708 (A.C.M.R. 1992) (en banc), aff'd on other grounds, 38 M.J. 292 (C.M.A. 1993), the court held that an attempt by the Army's Judge Advocate General to expand the definition of neutral and detached magistrate to include commanders was incorrect because AR 27-10 specifically limits that term to military judges and military magistrates.

United States v. Justice, 32 M.J. 599 (A.C.M.R. 1991) (magistrate not disqualified because he had previously authorized search warrant); United States v. Moore, 29 M.J. 819 (A.C.M.R. 1989) (magistrate was neutral and detached even though he had assumed prosecutorial duties at another command); United States v. Fals, 6 M.J. 713 (A.F.C.M.R. 1978) (special court-martial convening authority could review another commander's decision).

24. R.C.M. 305(i).
25. 420 U.S. 103 (1975).
26. *See* R.C.M. 305(i)(1). Change 6 to the Manual for Courts-Martial (Dec. 1993), R.C.M. 305(i) was intended to clarify that the review requirement applies to military confinement or civilian confinement requested by military authorities. The provision was also amended to require that in the case of civilian confinement, military authorities should take reasonable steps to bring the military prisoner within military control. The Drafters' Analysis to the 1993 change notes that any time spent in civilian confinement is subject to the "Allen" credit mandated by United States v. Allen, 17 M.J. 126 (C.M.A. 1984).

United States v. Scheffer, 41 M.J. 683 (A.F.Ct.Crim.App. 1995) (clock does not actually start until commander orders servicemember into confinement, not when accused was taken into custody). *See generally* Milhizer & McShane, "Analysis of Change 6 to the 1984 Manual for Courts-Martial," ARMY LAW., May 1994, at 40.

27. R.C.M. 305(i)(1).

Upon request[28] made known to military authorities,[29] the accused is entitled to counsel being provided before the review is conducted,[30] or within 72 hours,[31] whichever occurs first. Counsel may be assigned for the limited purpose of representing the accused during the pretrial confinement review process, before charges are referred to trial,[32] provided the accused is informed that counsel has been provided for that limited purpose.[33] Unless service regulations provide otherwise, the accused is not entitled to counsel of choice.[34]

The reviewing officer need not be a military judge and in most cases will not be. For example, in the past the Army has used "magistrates," JAGC officers, to perform this review. The court in *United States v. Lynch*[35] stated that neither a staff judge advocate nor a convening authority are neutral or detached. Those constitutionally qualified to act as a judicial officer to make a pretrial confinement decision are: (1) military judges, (2) military magistrates not connected with court-martial referral process, and (3) any person not directly or particularly involved in law enforcement function. Where these individuals are unavailable, as a matter of military necessity, Staff Judge Advocates and Convening Authorities may conduct the hearing.[36] The impartial reviewer must determine whether there is probable cause to believe that the accused committed an offense and that if he did whether confinement is necessary.[37] In reaching his decision the reviewing officer must review the commander's memorandum,[38] discussed *supra*, and any additional written matters. The accused and his counsel have a right to appear and may be permitted to make statements.[39] Counsel for the government, usually the prosecutor, may also be present.[40]

---

28. R.C.M. 305(f). There is no requirement that the request be in writing.
29. R.C.M. 305(f). United States v. Coburn, 42 M.J. 609 (N.M.Ct.Crim.App. 1995) (error to proceed without counsel, although accused had requested one).
30. *Id.*
31. *Id.* The timing requirement was added by Change 6 to the Manual for Courts-Martial (Dec. 1993), apparently because it is possible to obtain credit for violations of R.C.M. 305(f) and the Drafters believed that establishment of a standard for compliance was necessary. The Drafters also envisioned that the provision provides some protection for the government where the accused is in civilian confinement and the request is passed along to military authorities in an untimely manner, or is not passed along at all. See generally Milhizer & McShane, "Analysis of Change 6 to the 1984 Manual for Courts-Martial," ARMY LAW., May 1994, at 40.
32. See Chapter 8 for a discussion on the referral charges.
33. R.C.M. 305(f).
34. *Id.*
35. 13 M.J. 394 (C.M.A. 1982).
36. 13 M.J. at 397, n.4. United States v. McLeod, 39 M.J. 278 (C.M.A. 1994) (brigade commander authorized to conduct review where there was no evidence that he was directly or particularly involved in law enforcement function).
37. R.C.M. 305(i)(1). United States v. Fisher, 37 M.J. 812 (N.M.C.M.R. 1993) (test for probable cause vis-à-vis pretrial confinement is not Aguilar-Spinnelli test, but rather totality of circumstances test).
38. R.C.M. 305(i)(3)(B). United States v. Freeman, 24 M.J. 547 (A.C.M.R. 1987) (no need for commander to prepare memorandum where accused was released from pretrial confinement before the review could be accomplished).
39. *Id.* United States v. Coburn, 42 M.J. 609 (N.M.Ct.Crim.App. 1995) (error to proceed without

---

40. R.C.M. 305(i)(3)(B). United States v. Jackson, 5 M.J. 223 (C.M.A. 1978) (may be Sixth Amendment right to counsel).

The Military Rules of Evidence generally do not apply[41] and the standard of proof for determining whether confinement is appropriate is preponderance of the evidence.[42] It is not clear from R.C.M. 305 whether this hearing is to be adversarial in nature. In the past it has not been.[43] But the combination of the presence of counsel for both the accused and the government and the language that the "requirements for confinement ... must be proved by a preponderance of the evidence,"[44] may portend an adversarial proceeding in which the com-

---

counsel, although accused had requested one). The Rule permits such appearance and statements if it is "practicable" to do so. The Analysis for R.C.M. 305(i) gives no specifics on the interpretation of that term. But it would typically require a balancing of the mission and resources of the military and what, if anything, the accused or counsel can contribute in person to the proceeding. In order to review promptly the decision to confine, the reviewing officer will necessarily consider distance and transportation problems, attendant to a personal appearance. There is apparently no right to cross-examine witnesses.

The analysis for this Rule does point out that the review procedures are generally patterned after the revocation of parole procedures spelled out in Morrisey v. Brewer, 408 U.S. 471 (1972).

In United States v. Bell, 25 M.J. 676 (A.C.M.R. 1987), the magistrate held an *ex parte* conference with the accused's commander and trial counsel. *Citing* R.C.M. 305(i), the court concluded that a magistrate is not barred from holding ex parte proceedings. Noting that the magistrate had remained neutral, the court also concluded that the defendant had not been denied access to information considered by the magistrate.

United States v. Butler, 23 M.J. 702 (A.F.C.M.R. 1986) (the court held that the magistrate's refusal to delay the hearing until counsel could be present violated R.C.M. 305; the magistrate's reason, that two witnesses were scheduled to leave, was not sufficient). *See also* United States v. Duke, 23 M.J. 710 (A.F.C.M.R. 1986) (error to proceed without counsel; relying on lack of written request for delay is "elevating form over substance").

R.C.M. 305(f) indicates that upon request a military counsel must be provided to the accused before the magistrate reviews the decision to confine. In United States v. Freeman, 24 M.J. 547 (A.C.M.R. 1987), the court rejected the argument that there was a failure to comply with that provision where the accused had failed to make such a request.

41. R.C.M. 305(i)(3)(B). The exception is that the Rules governing privileges, MIL. R. EVID. 502-512 and Rules 302 (statements relating to mental responsibility) and 305 (rights warnings) are applicable. *See also* MIL. R. EVID. 1101(d) (stating that Rules are generally inapplicable to pretrial confinement proceedings).

Note that in United States v. Packer, 8 M.J. 785 (N.C.M.R. 1980), the court said that evidence seized illegally may be considered.

42. R.C.M. 305(i)(3)(C). United States v. Williams, 29 M.J. 570 (A.F.C.M.R. 1989) (commander erred by not preparing memorandum).

43. *See* Gerstein v. Pugh, 420 U.S. 103 (1975); *cf.* United States v. Heard, 3 M.J. 14, 25 (C.M.A. 1977) (Fletcher, C.J., concurring); United States v. Malia, 6 M.J. 65, 68 (C.M.A. 1978) (after counsel is appointed the proceeding is adversarial); United States v. Hanes, 34 M.J. 1168 (N.M.C.M.R. 1992) (pretrial confinement hearing before preferral of charges is not adversarial hearing or functional equivalent of custodial interrogation; nor is it a judicial proceeding which gives rise to Sixth Amendment right to counsel); United States v. Butler, 23 M.J. 702 (A.F.C.M.R. 1986) (pretrial confinement hearing is adversarial). The Drafters intended to make the hearing limited in nature. R.C.M. 305(i) Analysis. In their view the detailed procedures of R.C.M. 305, although not as protective in some respects as civilian analogs, still meet due process standards. *Cf.* United States v. Williams, 29 M.J. 570 (A.F.C.M.R. 1989) (pretrial confinement hearings are informal, non-adversary proceedings conducted by officers without legal training).

44. R.C.M. 305(i)(3)(C). As a practical matter there may be many cases where the command is not personally represented; rather the reviewing officer will be left to review written documents for the command's position.

mander, or his spokesman, carry a burden of showing the need for continued confinement.

The reviewing officer's decision, like that of the commander, must be reduced to writing and pertinent supporting documents attached.[45] It must also be provided to the government or the accused upon request.[46] The reviewing officer may later reconsider his decision to continue confinement if new, significant information is submitted by the accused.[47] It is important to add that service regulations may provide for more stringent review procedures.[48]

§ 5-9(E). Judicial Review.

The procedures discussed to this point are automatic and the accused need not initiate any of them. He may, however, initiate further judicial review of the decision to impose pretrial confinement. The vehicle for doing so is a motion for appropriate relief,[49] or seeking extraordinary relief from one of the military appellate courts.[50] The former is the more common avenue and should be used to avoid the possibility of waiver.[51] Note that under R.C.M. 305, the military judge's powers to review pretrial confinement arise after referral of charges to trial.[52] In the interim the confined accused is left with asking the reviewing officer to reconsider his ruling or seeking extraordinary relief.[53] The military judge may order release from confinement only if (1) the reviewing officer abused his discretion and there is no reason for continuing confinement, or (2) new information not presented to the reviewing officer requires release, or (3) there was no independent review by a reviewing officer and there is no reason for continuing confinement.[54]

---

45. R.C.M. 305(i)(6). In effect by this point in the proceedings a file memorializing each phase of the decision-making process has been formed, thus providing the military judge, who may review the procedures, with something more than the parties' oral statements as to what occurred. To some extent this was the practice before the 1984 revisions to the *Manual* required it. *See generally* United States v. Williams, 29 M.J. 570 (A.F.C.M.R. 1989) (nonprejudicial error for reviewing officer not to prepare report on his decision to keep accused in confinement).

46. R.C.M. 305(i)(6).

47. R.C.M. 305(i)(7).

48. *See, e.g.,* United States v. Marler, 7 M.J. 629 (A.F.C.M.R. 1979); United States v. White, 17 C.M.A. 211, 38 C.M.R. 9 (1967).

49. *See infra* § 13-5(B).

50. *See infra* § 13-2(G)(1).

51. *See infra* § 13-2(B). United States v. Warner, 33 M.J. 522 (A.F.C.M.R. 1991) (accused waived objections to magistrate's decision to leave him in pretrial confinement by not objecting at trial).

52. *See infra* § 8-3.

53. *See, e.g.,* Berta v. United States, 9 M.J. 390 (C.M.A. 1980). It is questionable whether a military judge has any authority to review a pretrial confinement decision prior to referral of charges. *See generally* Porter v. Richardson, 50 C.M.R. 910 (C.M.A. 1975); Bowler v. Wood, 1 M.J. 191 (C.M.A. 1975); Stevenson, "The Inherent Authority of the Military Judge," 17 A.F. L. Rev. 1 (1975). Note, however, that even after referral, the judge's review powers are not exclusive and the reviewing officer might reconsider his earlier ruling.

54. R.C.M. 305(j)(1). In United States v. Hitchman, 29 M.J. 951 (A.C.M.R. 1990), the court concluded that under the facts, the magistrate did not abuse his discretion in continuing confinement. The court noted that it would not follow approach taken by Air Force Court of Military

The hearing before the military judge, which does not constitute de novo review,[55] is clearly adversarial. Both sides should have the opportunity to present evidence and cross-examine witnesses.[56] If the judge determines that confinement is not warranted, he will order the accused's release and order administrative credit for the time improperly spent in pretrial confinement.[57]

Under some prior case law, if the reviewing officer (or magistrate) ordered the accused's release, the government could seek review by a military judge.[58] The judge could overrule the magistrate if the government proved that the confinement was lawful. But R.C.M. 305 makes no provision for that procedure. The Drafters' Analysis indicates that in order to give some degree of finality to the decision to release, reconfinement is not permitted unless new evidence is discovered or new misconduct takes place.[59]

In theory, the government is now left with asking the reviewing officer to reconsider his decision to release,[60] or possibly seeking an extraordinary writ from the military appellate courts.[61]

Review in United States v. Rios, 24 M.J. 809 (A.F.C.M.R. 1987), which determined whether the military magistrate abused his discretion in deciding whether military judge ruled correctly. That approach, said the court, would be inconsistent with permitting the defendant to litigate the issue de novo before the military judge.

United States v. Gaither, 41 M.J. 774 (A.F.Ct.Crim.App. 1995) (when deciding whether to order release of accused in pretrial confinement, judge reviews decision by magistrate by conducting de novo review; the abuse of discretion standard will be applied if the judge is determining whether confinement already served was proper).

In United States v. Lavalla, 24 M.J. 593 (A.F.C.M.R. 1987), the trial judge told accused first to exhaust his administrative remedies for release from confinement. Noting that it was not going to attempt to set out the judge's specific duties on this issue, the court concluded that even if the judge had reviewed the issue, he would not have concluded that release was required. The court added a lengthy admonishment for those dealing with the complicated issue of pretrial confinement, noting that application of R.C.M. 305 is often difficult.

United States v. Rios, 24 M.J. 809 (A.F.C.M.R. 1987) (under facts, magistrate did not abuse his discretion in approving pretrial confinement).

Note that the Rule makes no explicit allowance for minor technical violations of the procedures for imposing or reviewing pretrial confinement. Those violations do not necessarily make the pretrial confinement improper and require release. Instead, they should be tested for specific prejudice and appropriate remedial steps taken.

55. Some cases predating the 1984 revision of the *Manual* indicated that the judge's review was de novo in nature. See United States v. Van Slate, 14 M.J. 872 (N.M.C.M.R. 1982); United States v. Montford, 13 M.J. 829 (A.C.M.R. 1982); United States v. Dick, 9 M.J. 869 (N.C.M.R. 1980).

56. The review will normally take place at an Article 39(a) session when other motions are disposed of. See infra § 12-1. *See also* R.C.M. 802 (pretrial conference) and § 12-5 *infra*.

57. R.C.M. 305(i)(2), (k). See also infra § 5-10.

58. United States v. Montford, 13 M.J. 829 (A.C.M.R. 1982); United States v. Dick, 9 M.J. 869 (N.C.M.R. 1980).

59. R.C.M. 305(1) Analysis. United States v. Rolfe, 24 M.J. 756 (A.F.C.M.R. 1987) (accused properly reconfined after new magistrate in Nebraska, at accused's home installation, considered information not available to magistrate in California who released accused).

The provision is intended to remove the "revolving door" problem. Nonetheless, a rule permitting government-initiated review of an accused's release by a reviewing officer makes sense and would comport with other "government appeal" provisions in the *Manual. See, e.g.*, R.C.M. 908 and Art. 62, U.C.M.J. *See infra* § 13-2(G)(2).

60. R.C.M. 305(i)(7).

61. Government requests for extraordinary relief are of recent vintage and have generally been limited to requesting an appellate court to order a military judge to reverse his ruling as to

R.C.M. 305(m) states that certain specified exceptions to the foregoing rules may exist because of operational necessity[62] or because the person to be confined is at sea.[63]

§ 5-10. Illegal Pretrial Punishment and Restraints.

§ 5-10(A). In General.

Pretrial punishment is proscribed by Article 13, U.C.M.J., which prohibits punishment or penalty other than arrest or confinement pending trial.[1] The "punishment" may take the form of illegal restraint or confinement or it may take the form of imposing some condition on the servicemember.[2] What constitutes punishment will depend on the circumstances. In *Bell v. Wolfish*,[3] the Supreme Court provided a helpful template:

> A court must decide whether the disability has been imposed for the purpose of punishment or whether it is but an incident of some other legitimate governmental purpose.... [I]f a particular condition or restriction of pretrial detention is reasonably related to a legitimate governmental objective, it does not, without more, amount to "punishment." Conversely, if a restriction or condition is not reasonably related to a legitimate goal—if it is arbitrary or purposeless—a court permissibly may

---

dismissal of charges or admission of evidence. See generally § 17-19. Rather than ask the court to review the reviewing officer's decision, the prosecution should first ask the military judge to do so and if he refuses, ask the court to order the military judge to review the decision to release. *See* United States v. Dick, 9 M.J. 869 (N.C.M.R. 1980) (extraordinary relief denied but magistrate's release order stayed pending review by military judge at an Art. 39(a) session).

62. R.C.M. 305(m)(1) grants some exceptions when the Secretary of Defense decides that "operational requirements" make full compliance impracticable.

63. R.C.M. 305(m)(2).

1. *See* Appendix 3. *See, e.g.,* United States v. Nelson, 18 C.M.A. 177, 39 C.M.R. 177 (1969); United States v. Bayhand, 6 C.M.A. 762, 21 C.M.R. 84 (1956); United States v. Bruce, 14 M.J. 254 (C.M.A. 1982); United States v. Davidson, 14 M.J. 81 (C.M.A. 1982).

See also United States v. Davis, 30 M.J. 980 (A.C.M.R. 1990) (the court noted that the mere fact that illegal pretrial punishment occurred before charges were preferred does not preclude finding of illegal punishment; it is the nature of the treatment of the accused, not the formal date of preferral of charges which is important).

United States v. Hoover, 24 M.J. 874 (A.C.M.R. 1987) (Article 13 violated where accused was forced to sleep in pup tent surrounded by concertina wire).

Cf. United States v. Villamil-Perez, 32 M.J. 341 (C.M.A. 1991) (accused was not subjected to pretrial punishment where supervising officer posted on bulletin board a serious incident report listing the accused's offenses and prior record); United States v. Van Metre, 29 M.J. 765 (A.C.M.R. 1989) (removal of honor guard tab from uniform did not amount to illegal punishment); United States v. Southers, 12 M.J. 924 (N.M.C.M.R. 1982).

2. United States v. Allen, 33 M.J. 209 (C.M.A. 1991) (retired member was not unlawfully punished before trial where he did not receive full pay and allowances for his rank; he was compensable only at rate for retired member); United States v. Fogarty, 35 M.J. 885 (A.C.M.R. 1992) (extensive discussion of issue; court concluded that commingling of sentenced prisoners and pretrial confinees was due to limited facilities and did not constitute illegal pretrial punishment; further, ridicule of accused by facility guards did not amount to illegal punishment).

3. 441 U.S. 520, 538-39 (1979).

infer that the purpose of the governmental action is punishment that may not constitutionally be inflicted upon detainees qua detainees. (Citations and footnotes omitted).

Illegal pretrial punishment generally falls into one of two categories: illegal punishment which does not amount to restraint[4] and illegal punishment resulting from pretrial restraint, usually confinement.[5] If the court determines that the servicemember has been illegally punished before trial, several remedies are available.[6]

§ 5-10(B). Pretrial Punishment Other Than Restraint.

A servicemember may be subjected to illegal punishment through means which in some way affect his duty status or his standing in the military community. For example, in *United States v. Cruz*,[7] the court concluded that the defendant was subjected to illegal punishment where he had been apprehended during a mass formation, stripped of his unit crest, searched, and then placed in a special "Peyote Platoon." The court noted that a subsequent command investigation had concluded that this treatment violated Article 13 and remanded the case for a rehearing on the sentence. The court stated that "[c]learly, public denunciation by the commander and subsequent military degradation before the troops prior to courts-martial constitute unlawful pretrial punishment...."[8] The court rejected as "somewhat specious" the prosecution argument that this treatment was not punishment because it was intended to curb drug abuse.[9] The court in *United States v. Van Metre*,[10] concluded, however, that removal of the "Honor Guard" tab from the accused's uniform did not amount to a violation of Article 13. While the court indicated that it could not condone the tab's removal, the accused had not been subjected to the type of public denunciation exhibited in the *Cruz* decision. There was no evidence that the accused was "maltreated or ostracized by his fellow soldiers during the period after removal of the tab."[11] Typically, Article 13

---

4. *See* § 5-10(B).
5. *See* § 5-10(C).
6. *See* § 5-10(D).
7. 25 M.J. 326 (C.M.A. 1987).
8. 25 M.J. at 330. *See also* United States v. Washington, 42 M.J. 547 (A.F.Ct.Crim.App. 1995) (although, 'weeds and seeds' duties were not per se demeaning nor degrading, it appeared that commander intended them as punitive measures and there was no legitimate nonpunitive purpose); United States v. Stamper, 39 M.J. 1097 (A.C.M.R. 1994) (company commander's continuance and repeated disparaging remarks about accused resulted in credit for pretrial punishment); United States v. Latta, 34 M.J. 596 (A.C.M.R. 1992) (accused subjected to unlawful pretrial punishment when first sergeant called him to front of formation and sarcastically referred to him as "my favorite AWOL case"). *Cf.* United States v. Fogarty, 35 M.J. 885 (A.C.M.R. 1992) (extensive discussion of issue; ridicule of accused by facility guards did not amount to illegal punishment; none were made in public and although upsetting to accused, were personal and not official).
9. 25 M.J. at 331, n.4.
10. 29 M.J. 765 (A.C.M.R. 1989).
11. 29 M.J. at 767. *See also* United States v. Villamil-Perez, 32 M.J. 341 (C.M.A. 1991) (proscription against pretrial punishment covers officer outside accused's chain of command; public

violations center on illegal punishment resulting from the conditions of pretrial restraint or confinement.[12]

§ 5-10(C). Pretrial Restraints Constituting Illegal Punishment.

Article 13 violations generally center on illegal punishment resulting from the conditions of pretrial restraint or confinement. The general rule is that the restraint imposed should be no more restrictive than necessary to insure the accused's presence and prevent foreseeable serious misconduct.[13] Those restrained may not be required to perform punitive duties, wear special garb, or perform punitive training.[14] Generally, commingling with sentenced prisoners is also prohibited.[15] In assessing whether particular actions by govern-

---

posting of reports of suspected drug offenses was nonprejudicial, prohibited pretrial punishment; convening authority had taken mitigating action on sentence).

12. *Cf.* United States v. Coder, 39 M.J. 1006 (A.C.M.R. 1994) (court concluded that Article 58, not Article 13, governed arguments by accused that administrative sanctions imposed on his posttrial incarceration amounted to double punishment; court rejected his argument, noting that there was no authority to grant credit for those sanctions; Article 15 cases were inapposite).

13. R.C.M. 304(f). United States v. Carr, 37 M.J. 987 (A.C.M.R. 1993) (NCO accused subjected to illegal pretrial punishment; he was, *inter alia*, assigned to special processing unit, required to wear special garb, perform manual labor, and appeared to be a prisoner on work details; remedy was reduction of sentence on appeal). Whether Article 13 has been violated will turn on the circumstances surrounding the restraint. The Navy's Corrections Manual, SECNAVINST 1640.9 sets out a number of factors to be considered:

(1) Whether the accused is compelled to work with sentenced prisoners;
(2) Whether the accused is required to observe the same work schedules and duty hours as sentenced prisoners;
(3) Whether the type of work normally assigned to him is the same as that performed by persons serving sentences at hard labor;
(4) Whether the accused is dressed so as to distinguish him from those being punished;
(5) Whether it is the policy of the brig to have all prisoners governed by one set of instructions; and
(6) Whether there is any difference in the treatment accorded to the accused from that given to sentenced prisoners.

Note that some of these factors are now specifically proscribed by R.C.M. 304(f).

14. R.C.M. 304(f). United States v. Cruz, 25 M.J. 326 (C.M.A. 1987) (accused placed in "Peyote Platoon").
United States v. Stroud, 27 M.J. 765 (A.F.C.M.R. 1988) (under facts accused was not commingled with sentenced prisoners, even though he was housed in the same facility).
In United States v. Austin, 25 M.J. 639 (A.C.M.R. 1987), the court concluded that the accused had not been commingled with sentenced prisoners where he came into casual contact with them while he was performing work "necessary for the operation of the facility."
United States v. Marston, 22 M.J. 850 (A.F.C.M.R. 1986) (pretrial confined entitled to wear rank insignia).

15. *See, e.g.*, United States v. Palmiter, 20 M.J. 90 (C.M.A. 1985); United States v. Pringle, 19 C.M.A. 324, 41 C.M.R. 324 (1970); United States v. Bayhand, 6 C.M.A. 762, 21 C.M.R. 84 (1956); United States v. Huffman, 40 M.J. 225 (C.M.A. 1994) (*Bell v. Wolfish* standard applicable to deciding whether accused affirmatively requested to be mingled with sentenced prisoners); United States v. Fogarty, 35 M.J. 885 (A.C.M.R. 1992) (extensive discussion of issue; court concluded that commingling of sentenced prisoners and pretrial confinees was due to limited facilities and did not constitute illegal pretrial punishment).

mental officials amounted to impermissible "punishment" as part of the pretrial restraint, several cases have focused on whether the actions were intended as punishment. For example, in *United States v. Palmiter*,[16] the court stated that whether the accused has been subjected to punishment prior to trial will depend on whether the accused was commingled with prisoners and whether the pretrial confinement was intended to serve as punishment.[17] Citing *Bell v. Wolfish*,[18] the court held that where there is an absence of an intent to punish, courts must determine if the particular condition or restriction is really only an "incident of a legitimate nonpunitive governmental objective."[19]

Illegal punishment in a civilian jail, at the behest of the military, may also constitute a violation of Article 13.[20] In *United States v. Daniels*,[21] the court addressed a challenge to pretrial confinement served in a civilian jail pursuant to an agreement between civilian and military authorities. In denying an Article 13 challenge to this arrangement, the court indicated that civilian confinement that does not meet all of the Army regulations' requirements is not *per se* illegal. Instead, the confinement must be measured against the "general provisions of Article 13." Here, the absence of some of the amenities required by Army Regulation 190-47, such as access to a visitors' room or outside recreational areas, did not amount to a violation of Article 13.[22]

§ 5-10(D). Remedies; Waiver.

In *United States v. Sharrock*,[23] the court recognized the different ways in which lawfulness of pretrial confinement may be raised: First, the defense may file a pretrial motion for appropriate relief to be released from pretrial

---

16. 20 M.J. 90 (C.M.A. 1985).
17. In United States v. Herrin, 32 M.J. 983 (A.C.M.R. 1991), the court said that the intent of persons imposing pretrial detention is only one factor to be considered in deciding whether detention amounted to improper punishment. It concluded that the NCO-accused was subjected to improper punishment, even absent intent by confinement officials, where he was assigned menial tasks along with enlisted confinees who taunted him. The court provided a two-day credit for each of the 77 days in that condition.
18. 441 U.S. 520 (1979).
19. 20 M.J. at 95. See also United States v. Destefano, 20 M.J. 347 (C.M.A. 1985) (accused was not subject to illegal pretrial punishment where, in an attempt to subdue him in the pretrial confinement cell, the accused was accidentally burned; the brig personnel did not intend by their actions to punish him).
20. United States v. Phillips, 42 M.J. 346 (1995) (denial of Wiccan religious writings to accused was not violation of Article 13); United States v. James, 28 M.J. 214 (C.M.A. 1989) (accused's confinement conditions in civilian jail were related to orderly operation of facility and were no more stringent than necessary; court indicated that it would apply the same scrutiny to civilian confinement as to military confinement); United States v. Phillips, 38 M.J. 641 (A.C.M.R. 1993) (conditions in civilian jail, commingling with sentenced prisoners, giving accused recruit style haircut, and denying access to Wiccan bible did not amount to illegal pretrial punishment); United States v. Isler, 36 M.J. 1061 (A.F.C.M.R. 1993) (female accused's confinement in civilian jail did not constitute illegal punishment under Article 13).
21. 23 M.J. 867 (A.C.M.R. 1987).
22. 23 M.J. at 869.
23. 32 M.J. 326 (C.M.A. 1991).

confinement.[24] Second, the defense may seek credit toward the sentence for time spent in pretrial confinement through a sentencing motion for appropriate relief.[25] And third, the accused may seek to suppress any evidence seized as result of unlawful confinement.[26] Still another avenue of relief rests in seeking extraordinary relief from the military appellate courts.[27]

Assuming that counsel seeks sentencing relief for illegal pretrial punishment, the remedy is "meaningful sentence relief."[28] What amounts to meaningful relief may take several forms, however. First, with regard to illegal pretrial confinement, the remedies include an "administrative" day-for-day credit for pretrial confinement served.[29] That remedy is triggered by failure to provide counsel,[30] failure of the commander to review the initial decision to

---

24. See infra § 13-5(B).
25. R.C.M. 305(j)(2), (k). United States v. Rozier, 41 M.J. 707 (Army Ct.Crim.App. 1995) (judge abused discretion in denying defense request for relief for Article 13 violation; judge had denied hearing on grounds of timeliness when defense counsel noted that he had not learned that his client had been commingled with sentenced prisoners until just before the trial began).

In United States v. Fisher, 37 M.J. 812 (N.M.C.M.R. 1993), the court indicated that there are three types of administrative sentence credit for pretrial confinement: The day-for-day Allen credit for pretrial confinement, whether legal or illegal, actually served; the day-for-day credit for pretrial confinement served pursuant to an abuse of discretion, or violation of R.C.M. 305(f), (h), or (i); and, credit for other illegal pretrial confinement, which need not be day-for-day. The court noted that usually these credits are cumulative. It did not refer to the so-called Mason credit which may be given for pretrial restraint amounting to pretrial confinement.

26. 32 M.J. at 330. Judge Everett opined that although exclusionary rule may be invoked if commander lacked probable cause to confine an accused, exclusionary rule should not operate simply because commander erred in determining that pretrial confinement was required. 32 M.J. at 333. Judge Cox agreed, noting that confinement facility personnel had relied in good faith on commander's decision to confine. 32 M.J. at 334. See also infra § 13-4(B).

27. See infra § 17-19.

28. R.C.M. 304(f) Analysis; United States v. Carr, 37 M.J. 987 (A.C.M.R. 1993) (NCO accused subjected to illegal pretrial punishment for two months; remedy was reduction of sentence on appeal).

In United States v. Newberry, 35 M.J. 777 (A.C.M.R. 1992), (the court noted that there is no set formula for compensating for illegal pretrial confinement and that, under the facts, the defense counsel was not ineffective in obtaining 30-day credit); United States v. Bruce, 17 M.J. 1083 (A.F.C.M.R. 1984) (includes chart on remedies). Relief may include the judge ordering that administrative credit be granted on the accused's sentence. It may also include taking the illegality into account in arriving at a sentence. See, e.g., United States v. Hoover, 24 M.J. 874 (A.C.M.R. 1987) (relief consisted of dropping forfeitures from the approved sentence); United States v. Kimball, 50 C.M.R. 337 (A.C.M.R. 1975) (instruction should include reference to Article 13 and the rights violated); United States v. Whittier, 14 M.J. 606 (A.F.C.M.R. 1982) (judge failed to instruct).

See generally United States v. Pringle, 19 C.M.A. 324, 41 C.M.R. 324 (1970); United States v. Nelson, 18 C.M.A. 177, 39 C.M.R. 177 (1969).

29. R.C.M. 305(j)(2). In United States v. Davis, 29 M.J. 896 (A.F.C.M.R. 1989), the court acknowledged the trial court's innovative remedy of granting only ½ day of credit because the deficiency was not glaring. But the court noted that the one-day remedy was mandated by R.C.M. 305(k) and that anything less was not authorized by regulation.

United States v. Lavalla, 24 M.J. 593 (A.F.C.M.R. 1987) (confinement not illegal where sufficient grounds existed for believing that accused presented a danger).

30. R.C.M. 305(f). United States v. Coburn, 42 M.J. 609 (N.M.Ct.Crim.App. 1995) (because confinement adjudged had been served, appellate court credited 21 days worth of forfeitures).

confine,[31] failure to provide review by a reviewing officer,[32] or failing to comply with a military judge's order to release the accused from pretrial confinement.[33] This day-for-day credit may be in addition to any other *Allen* administrative day-for-day credit given for time served in pretrial confinement.[34] In

---

31. R.C.M. 305(h). United States v. Shelton, 27 M.J. 540 (A.C.M.R. 1988).
32. R.C.M. 305(i). United States v. McCants, 39 M.J. 91 (C.M.A. 1994) (accused entitled to credit for delays in magistrate's ruling and failure to provide accused with copy of that ruling); United States v. Ballesteros, 29 M.J. 14 (C.M.A. 1989) (accused entitled to additional administrative credit from the day on which the magistrate hearing should have been held).
  United States v. Mathieu, 29 M.J. 823 (A.C.M.R. 1989) (accused waived issue of credit for pretrial confinement; court repeated advice that trial counsel should inform trial court if magistrate has reviewed pretrial confinement within 7 days of imposition).
  United States v. Kuczaj, 29 M.J. 604 (A.C.M.R. 1989) (government is not required to affirmatively show that a review was conducted in the absence of the issue being raised by the defense).
  United States v. Williams, 29 M.J. 570 (A.F.C.M.R. 1989) (accused not entitled to additional administrative credit due to reviewing officer's failure to articulate in a memorandum the basis of his decision to continue confinement).
  United States v. Dent, 26 M.J. 968 (A.C.M.R. 1988) (government bears burden of proving that extension of time for review was granted); United States v. Hill, 26 M.J. 836 (A.C.M.R. 1988) (accused entitled to four days for failure to have timely magistrate review; at sentencing the trial counsel should announce whether magistrate had reviewed pretrial confinement).
  United States v. Chapman, 26 M.J. 515 (A.C.M.R. 1988) (although accused is entitled to Allen credit for time spent in civilian pretrial confinement imposed at request of military, he is not entitled to additional credit for noncompliance with R.C.M. 305 absent bad faith by military).
33. R.C.M. 305(o). The Analysis for R.C.M. 305(k) indicates that if one of the steps is omitted but the subsequent step is completed within the time limit for the omitted step, the illegality is cured.
34. *See* United States v. Allen, 17 M.J. 126 (C.M.A. 1984) (interpreting DOD Instruction 1325.4); United States v. Murray, 43 M.J. 507 (A.F.Ct.Crim.App. 1995) (Allen credit extends to any pretrial confinement served by accused in state facility, without regard to whether it was at the request of military authorities; court applied DOD Dir. 1325.4 (1988) which applies 18 U.S.C. § 3585(b) (1994)); United States v. Kersh, 34 M.J. 913 (N.M.C.M.R. 1992) (sentence credit for pretrial confinement extends only to time actually spent in pretrial confinement; court rejected argument that that period commences with apprehension); United States v. Fitzsimmons, 33 M.J. 710 (A.C.M.R. 1991) (Article 13 violated where accused was confined in pup tent outside charge of quarters for purposes of punishment; court said that only violations of Article 13 that result in substantial prejudice require remedial action; court noted that giving credit for illegal punishment does little to discourage it, court reassessed sentence and disapproved BCD); United States v. McCullough, 33 M.J. 595 (A.C.M.R. 1991) (accused was not entitled to *Allen* credit for time spent in civilian pretrial confinement; he was not being held there *solely* for the offenses for which he was ultimately sentenced by his court-martial); United States v. Peterson, 30 M.J. 946 (A.C.M.R. 1990) (accused entitled to administrative credit for civilian pretrial confinement imposed at behest of military); United States v. Ebanks, 29 M.J. 926 (A.F.C.M.R. 1989) (military judge was not required to give day-for-day credit for pretrial confinement; confinement authorities would do so without further direction. The court noted that military judges direct credit only for illegal pretrial confinement); United States v. Belmont, 27 M.J. 516 (N.M.C.M.R. 1988) (if credit for pretrial confinement exceeds confinement adjudged in sentence, it may not be applied to any other portion of the sentence; in those cases, as where confinement is not adjudged or approved, the *Allen* issue is moot).
  United States v. Williamson, 26 M.J. 835 (A.C.M.R. 1988) (pretrial confinement credit should be applied against sentence accused will have to serve, not against suspended portion of sentence).

effect, it is possible for an accused who has served 30 days in illegal pretrial confinement to receive 60 days administrative credit on his sentence.[35]

Second, where the illegal pretrial punishment has resulted from actions other than those involving actual confinement, the caselaw indicates that the matter should be presented to the sentencing authority to be considered in adjudging a fair sentence.[36]

The military courts have also extended the "administrative credit" remedy approach to pretrial restraint amounting to pretrial confinement[37] and have indicated that such restraint will be governed as though it were pretrial

---

35. These credits are applied first against any confinement adjudged and then, in order, against hard labor without confinement, restriction, fine, and forfeiture of pay. One day of confinement equals one day of forfeiture or a same amount of fine. *See also* R.C.M. 1003(b)(6), (7) for a conversion formula.

United States v. New, 23 M.J. 889 (A.C.M.R. 1987) (day-for-day credit for illegal pretrial confinement runs concurrently with *Mason* day-for-day credit; in determining credit, the first day of the restriction amounting to confinement is not counted but the last day is); United States v. Weddle, 28 M.J. 649 (A.C.M.R. 1989) (the *New* method of counting days only applies to calculations of timeliness provisions dealing with counsel, notification of action by commander, and review of pretrial confinement decision; all other time issues are calculated under the formula spelled out in United States v. DeLoatch, 25 M.J. 718 (A.C.M.R. 1987)).

36. *See, e.g.*, United States v. Cruz, 25 M.J. 326 (C.M.A. 1987); United States v. Latta, 34 M.J. 596 (A.C.M.R. 1992) (appellate court granted sentencing relief where accused was subjected to illegal pretrial punishment).

37. United States v. Mason, 19 M.J. 274 (C.M.A. 1985) (summary disposition); United States v. Walter, 39 M.J. 1067 (A.C.M.R. 1994) (tight restrictions on accused's movements did not amount to confinement); United States v. Lassiter, 35 M.J. 831 (A.C.M.R. 1992) (restriction did not amount to pretrial confinement); United States v. Richardson, 34 M.J. 1015 (A.C.M.R. 1992) (under totality of circumstances test, pretrial restraint was not tantamount to confinement); United States v. Calderon, 34 M.J. 501 (A.F.C.M.R. 1991) (totality of circumstances indicated that accused's pretrial restraint did not reflect kind of substantial impairment of the basic rights and privileges enjoyed by service members that is key to determining if credit is due. The court noted that this form of administrative credit is called the Mason credit, a term coined by Judge Raby on the Army Court of Military Review to reflect the rule in United States v. Mason, 19 M.J. 274 (C.M.A. 1985)); United States v. Russell, 30 M.J. 977 (A.C.M.R. 1990) (under test of totality of circumstances, pretrial restraint to bare barracks room amounted to pretrial confinement for which administrative credit was given because no magisterial review was conducted); United States v. Cahill, 23 M.J. 544 (A.C.M.R. 1986) (administrative credit given by appellate court).

See, e.g., United States v. DiMatteo, 19 M.J. 903 (A.C.M.R. 1985) (custody in a unit's storage room under onerous conditions amounted to pretrial confinement for which the accused should receive administrative credit).

In United States v. Smith, 20 M.J. 528 (A.C.M.R. 1985), the court held that the accused's pretrial restraint was restrictive enough in nature to constitute pretrial confinement and thus was entitled to administrative credit for that time; in dicta the court noted that the issue of administrative credit could be raised for the first time on appeal; illegality of pretrial confinement may not, however. The court's decision includes a list of the factors which should be considered in determining whether the restraint amounted to confinement and noted the cases going both ways.

United States v. McElyea, 22 M.J. 863 (A.C.M.R. 1986) (restriction did not amount to pretrial confinement); Wiggins v. Greenwald, 20 M.J. 823 (A.C.M.R. 1985) (post-trial request for extraordinary relief was proper procedure for requesting administrative credit for pretrial restraint allegedly amounting to confinement; on the merits the court concluded that it did not amount to confinement).

confinement.[38] But failure to raise the issue of pretrial restraint amounting to confinement at trial may constitute waiver.[39]

Attempts to have an accused waive the Article 13 limitations beforehand have generally not been successful.[40] Failure to raise the issue at the trial level may waive the issue.[41]

---

38. United States v. Gregory, 21 M.J. 952 (A.C.M.R. 1986) (failure to follow procedures for pretrial confinement where accused is in restriction tantamount to confinement requires additional administrative credit). *Cf.* United States v. Amos, 22 M.J. 798 (A.C.M.R. 1986).

39. *See* United States v. McCants, 39 M.J. 91 (C.M.A. 1994) (accused waived issue of entitlement to credit for failure to review decision to confine within 48 hours); United States v. Walter, 39 M.J. 1067 (A.C.M.R. 1994) (accused waived issue by not raising it until after sentencing; counsel deliberately waited until then in fear that court members would increase punishment if instructed that they must consider pretrial confinement served); United States v. Diaz, 30 M.J. 957 (C.G.C.M.R. 1990) (accused waived issue of credit for pretrial restraint); United States v. Walker, 27 M.J. 878 (A.C.M.R. 1989) (accused waived allegations that this pretrial confinement in a civilian jail constituted unlawful pretrial punishment by not raising it until 6 months after his trial); United States v. Bryant, 27 M.J. 811 (A.C.M.R. 1988) (defense waived the issue).
United States v. Guerrero, 25 M.J. 829 (A.C.M.R. 1988) (issue explicitly waived at trial); United States v. Ecoffey, 23 M.J. 629 (A.C.M.R. 1986) (court provided extended discussion of waiver and indicated that it would apply waiver doctrine 90 days after date of decision); United States v. Bennett, 23 M.J 664 (A.C.M.R. 1986) (failure to raise issue at trial is "strong evidence" that restriction was not tantamount to confinement).

40. United States v. Palmiter, 20 M.J. 90 (C.M.A. 1985) (a prisoner cannot waive an Article 13 violation, although "Work Program Request" forms are helpful to the accused in adjusting to pretrial confinement; the court also indicated that magistrates should keep an eye on these issues and as last resort, accused may seek extraordinary relief).
See also United States v. Bruce, 14 M.J. 254 (C.M.A. 1982) (Article 13 makes no provision for waiver and court was not inclined to find a waiver by implication); United States v. Thacker, 16 M.J. 841 (N.M.C.M.R. 1983) (any regulation purporting to authorize waiver of Article 13 is invalid; however, in this case mingling of the accused with sentenced prisoners was nonpunitive in nature); United States v. Murray, 16 M.J. 914 (N.M.C.M.R. 1983) (invalid waiver form was required for unrestricted participation in full rehabilitative program, i.e., recreational, religious, and educational activities); United States v. Watts, 36 M.J. 748 (A.C.M.R. 1993) (detainee cannot waive Article 13 violation during period of pretrial confinement by volunteering or otherwise consenting). *Cf.* United States v. Huffman, 40 M.J. 225 (C.M.A. 1994) (majority declined to find waiver of pretrial conditions but indicated that accused's desire to be placed with sentenced prisoners strengthened government's argument that it had not violated Article 13; dissent indicated that accused waived the issue by affirmatively requesting change in status and by not raising any objections at trial).

41. *See infra* § 13-2(B). United States v. Cruz, 25 M.J. 326 (C.M.A. 1987) (accused did not waive issue although he did not raise it until four months after trial and complained that pretrial punishment had induced him to plead guilty).
United States v. Folk, 37 M.J. 851 (A.F.C.M.R. 1993) (accused waived issue by not objecting at trial); United States v. Sanders, 36 M.J. 1013 (A.C.M.R. 1993) (accused waived issue of entitlement to administrative credit because no magistrate's review was conducted within 48 hours of her initial confinement); United States v. Watts, 36 M.J. 748 (A.C.M.R. 1993) (accused waived issue of illegal pretrial punishment by not raising it at trial); United States v. Foster, 35 M.J. 700 (N.M.C.M.R. 1992) (accused waived issue).
United States v. Wixon, 23 M.J. 570 (A.C.M.R. 1986) (failure to raise issue before the magistrate or military judge was a factor in denying appellate relief); United States v. Martinez, 19 M.J. 744 (A.C.M.R. 1984) (defense waived issue of illegal pretrial confinement by not raising it prior to appellate review of the case). *See also* United States v. Peacock, 19 M.J. 909 (A.C.M.R. 1985) (court permitted issue for the first time on appeal where it appeared that the accused had been mixed with sentenced prisoners because of a continuance in his trial).

Article 97, U.C.M.J. states that it is a punishable offense to unlawfully apprehend, arrest, or confine any person.[42] Thus, the military has at its disposal some means of disciplining those who impose illegal pretrial restraint or punishment. As a practical matter though, and despite words of caution from the courts about imposing illegal punishment,[43] there appear to be no reported cases on any servicemember being court-martialed for doing so.

Note that if the confinement is illegal, an accused cannot be convicted for escape from confinement.[44]

---

42. *See* Appendix 3. *See also* Article 98, U.C.M.J.

43. *See* United States v. Hoover, 24 M.J. 874, 878 n.4 (A.C.M.R. 1987) (calling upon those in authority to take action to preclude illegal forms of punishment).

44. United States v. Brown, 15 M.J. 501 (A.F.C.M.R. 1982); United States v. Wall, 15 M.J. 531 (A.F.C.M.R. 1982).

APPENDIX REFERENCES

Appendix 1. Abbreviations.
Appendix 2. Glossary.
Appendix 3. U.C.M.J.
Appendix 4. Court-Martial Flow Chart.
Appendix 11. Grant of Immunity.

ANNOTATED BIBLIOGRAPHY

BOOKS

Byrne, *Military Law* (1981).

> This third edition work is a good introductory text to military law. It includes text material, discussion cases, self-quizzes, and appendices that contain forms and tables. The discussion cases, although dated, cover significant areas of courts-martial practice.

Moyer, *Justice and the Military* (1972).

> This one volume loose-leaf reference contains detailed discussions of the role of commanders, jurisdiction, military criminal procedure, First Amendment rights, substantive law, and collateral review of courts-martial by the civilian court system.

Saltzburg, Schinasi, & Schlueter, *Military Rules of Evidence Manual* (3d ed. 1991).

> The authors have compiled the official text of the 1980 Military Rules of Evidence, the drafters' analysis to those rules, annotated cases, and an editorial comment for each rule that explains the rule, shows how it might be used, and discusses potential problem areas.

Zillman, Blaustein, & Sherman, *The Military in American Society* (1978).

> This loose-leaf case book represents the efforts of nine individuals familiar with the workings of the military system of justice. Valuable discussions include treatment of the American military establishment, entry into the military, the military justice system, individual rights of servicemembers, termination of military service, and the law of armed conflict. Selected cases are discussed and notes for further reading are located at the end of each chapter.

PERIODICALS

Anderson, "Inventory Searches," 110 MIL. L. REV. 95 (1985).

> This article rates the Supreme Court decisions relating to the inventory exception to the warrant requirement. The author extends his analysis to the military's application of the inventory exception, and examines the Court of Military Appeals' three-prong test for reasonableness as set forth in *United States v. Kazmierczak*.

Boller, "Pretrial Restraint in the Military," 50 MIL. L. REV. 71 (1970).

> Addressing the history of standard procedures, and the trends of pretrial confinement in military and civilian practice, the author presents a fine discussion on the

constitutional standards of probable cause and due process and suggests an approach to military pretrial confinement issues.

Clark, "Electronic Surveillance and Related Investigative Techniques," 128 MIL. L. REV. 155 (1990).

Noting that many practitioners may not be familiar with Electronic Surveillance (ELSUR) procedures and techniques, the author discusses the applicable definitions and terms and how approval is obtained for using it, procedures for consensual intercepts and jurisdictional concerns, and concludes with a discussion of the procedures for using specific types of ELSUR, i.e., video surveillance, tracking devices, and pagers.

Finnelly, "Inevitable Discovery, The Exclusionary Rule, and Military Due Process," 131 MIL. L. REV. 109 (1991).

The author posits that the current rules governing inevitable discovery are flawed because they permit the prosecution to use illegally seized evidence even if the police misconduct was willful. The article presents a survey of both federal and state practices and addresses the interplay of the constitutional issues presented by the exclusionary rule and the inevitable discovery exception.

Gilligan, "Eyewitness Identification," 58 MIL. L. REV. 183 (1972).

Building on the *Wade-Gilbert-Stovall* trilogy governing eyewitness identification, the author examines the pre-Military Rules of Evidence right to counsel threshold in the civilian and military practice. He also presents a discussion of the trial procedures for moving to suppress such evidence, and in conclusion presents a suggested format for service regulations designed to safeguard an accused's rights at a lineup.

Gilligan & Hahn, "Eyewitness Identification in Military Law," 110 MIL. L. REV. 1 (1985).

The authors present a comprehensive study of the constitutional and evidential issues relating to eyewitness identifications. They analyze the Fourth and Sixth Amendment issues, as well as the Military Rule of Evidence 321.

Hunt, "Inspections," 54 MIL. L. REV. 225 (1971).

This article presents a good discussion of the case law affecting both civilian and military "inspections." Now that inspections seem well established in military practice, see Rule 313, Military Rules of Evidence, this work offers good background material for understanding the nature of the military inspection.

Lederer & Borch, "Does the Fourth Amendment Apply to the Armed Forces," 144 MIL. L. REV. 110 (1994).

Observing that the Supreme Court has not ruled on the issue, the authors conclude that the Fourth Amendment does not apply in full to the armed forces. They note that if the amendment either does not apply at all, or only applies in a limited fashion, Military Rules of Evidence 311 to 317 could be revised in order to grant greater powers and flexibility to commanders who conduct searches.

Moyer, "Procedural Rights of the Military Accused: Advantages Over a Civilian Defendant," 22 ME. L. REV. 105 (1970); 51 Mil. L. Rev. 1 (1971).

This forty-page article compares the civilian and military criminal procedures such as pretrial investigation, interrogation, right to witnesses, right to counsel, and appellate review. The author concludes that the military accused enjoys greater procedural and substantive advantages than the civilian counterpart.

Oliphant, "The Lineup: The Sixth Amendment, Article 31, and The Right to Counsel," 31 FED. B.J. 58 (1972).

While providing a concise summary of the major cases concerning the right to counsel during pretrial identification procedure, this article also discusses the relevant sections of the U.M.C.J. in terms of the recent military cases interpreting a servicemember's Sixth Amendment right to counsel in a lineup.

Owen, "A Hard Look at the Military Magistrate Pretrial Confinement Hearing: *Gerstein* and *Courtney* Revisited," 88 MIL. L. REV. 3 (1980).

Each service has a regulation governing the imposition of pretrial confinement. The author critically reviews these requirements and measures them against the standards imposed by the Supreme Court and the Court of Military Appeals. Among his suggested changes, the author proposes that military magistrates be lawyers, that the time between imposition of confinement and the hearing be reduced, and that the Department of Defense promulgate reforms. The various service regulations governing pretrial confinement are included as appendices.

Quinn, "Some Comparisons Between Courts-Martial and Civilian Practice," 15 U.C.L.A. L. REV. 1240 (1968); 46 MIL. L. REV. 77 (1969).

Judge Quinn, Chief Judge of the Court of Military Appeals when this article was written, chronicles the key areas where the servicemember's rights are zealously guarded by military courts: interrogations, and searches and seizures.

Raezer, "Needed Weapons in the Army's War on Drugs: Electronic Surveillance and Informants," 116 MIL. L. REV. 1 (1987).

The author notes the continuing problem of drug use in the Army and urges that military authorities attack the "supply" side of the problem by using wired informants and reverse sting operations and take steps to increase "recruiting, rewarding, using, and protecting of informants as a necessary means of penetrating drug conspiracies in the Army."

Soma, Banker & Smith, "Computer Crime: Substantive Statutes & the Technical & Legal Search Considerations," 39 A.F. L. REV. 225 (1996).

One of 17 articles in "The Master Criminal Law Edition" of the Air Force Law Review, this article includes a discussion on the search and seizures issues which may arise in investigating computer crimes.

Stevens, "*New Jersey v. T.L.O.:* Towards a More Reasonable Standard for Military Search Authorizations," 25 A.F. L. REV. 338 (1985).

The author briefly reviews the basic rules governing the commander's authority to conduct searches and the Supreme Court's opinion in *New Jersey v. T.L.O.* He concludes that the Court's rationale requiring only a "reasonable suspicion" basis for searches in the school setting are also applicable to the military because of its unique and compelling interest in discipline.

Supervielle, "Article 31(b): Who Should Be Required to Give Warnings?," 123 MIL. L. REV. 151 (1989).

The author provides a comprehensive historical overview of Article 31 warnings, noting that since the effective date of that Article in 1951 the Court of Military Appeals has used four different tests in determining who should give the warnings.

Symposium, "Military Justice," ARMY LAW., March 1996.

This 127-page symposium contains a Foreword and 11 short articles on a wide range of military justice topics. They are as follows:

Morris, "Foreword."
Barto, "Developments in the Substantive Criminal Law Under the Uniform Code of Military Justice."
Frisk, "New Developments in Pretrial Confinement."
Frisk, "New Developments in Speedy Trial."
Winn, "Recent Developments in Military Pretrial and Trial Procedure."
Masterton, "Recent Developments in Urinalysis Law."
Kohlman, "Are You Ready for Some Changes? Five Fresh Views of the Fifth Amendment."
Wright, "Sex, Lies, and Videotape: Child Sexual Abuse Cases Continue to Create Appellate Issues and Other Developments in the Areas of the Sixth Amendment, Discovery, Mental Responsibility, and Nonjudicial Punishment."
Henley, "Caveat Criminale: The Impact of the New Military Rules of Evidence in Sexual Offense and Child Molestation Cases."
Henley, "Current Developments in Evidence Law."
Morris, "New Developments in Sentencing and Post-Trial Procedure."

Symposium, "The Military Rules of Evidence," ARMY LAW., May 1980.

This fifty-page symposium issue contains seven articles on the Military Rules of Evidence. They are as follows:

Schinasi, "The Military Rules of Evidence: An Advocate's Tool"
Basham, "Suppression Motions Under the Military Rules of Evidence"
Yustas, "Mental Evaluations of an Accused Under the Military Rules of Evidence: An Excellent Balance"
Eisenberg, "Fourth Amendment Practice and the Military Rules of Evidence"
Schlueter, "Bodily Evidence and Rule 312, M.R.E."
Gasperini, "Eyewitness Identification Under the Military Rules of Evidence"
Green, "The Military Rules of Evidence and the Military Judge"

Wright, "How to Improve Military Search and Seizure Law," 116 MIL. L. REV. 157 (1987).

The author reviews the history of search and seizure law in the military and draws upon the Supreme Court's opinion in *New Jersey v. T.L.O.*, 105 S. Ct. 733 (1985), to support his argument that the military should adopt the "discipline" exception to the warrant requirement. He also offers specific amendments to several of the Military Rules of Evidence to reflect that exception. One effect would be, as the author notes, to permit a squad leader to search a soldier whom he suspects of having contraband.

CHAPTER 6

PREFERRAL AND FORWARDING OF CHARGES; COMMAND INFLUENCE

Part I
Preferral and Forwarding of Charges

§ 6-1. Preferring Sworn Charges.
    § 6-1(A). The Charge Sheet.
    § 6-1(B). General Rules of Pleading.
        § 6-1(B)(1). Pleading Jurisdiction.
        § 6-1(B)(2). Amendments to Pleadings.
        § 6-1(B)(3). Additional Charges.
    § 6-1(C). Defective Pleadings.
        § 6-1(C)(1). Misjoinder.
        § 6-1(C)(2). Duplicitous Specifications.
        § 6-1(C)(3). Multiplicity.
§ 6-2. Forwarding of Charges.
    § 6-2(A). Immediate Commander.
    § 6-2(B). Summary Court-Martial Convening Authority.
    § 6-2(C). Special Court-Martial Convening Authority.
    § 6-2(D). General Court-Martial Convening Authority.

Part II
Command Influence

§ 6-3. Command Influence; In General.
    § 6-3(A). The Perpetual Problem of Unlawful Command Influence.
    § 6-3(B). Lawful and Unlawful Influence Distinguished.
    § 6-3(C). Actual, Apparent, and Perceived Unlawful Command Influence.
§ 6-4. Pretrial Command Influence.
    § 6-4(A). The Preliminary Inquiry and Preferring Charges.
    § 6-4(B). Command Influence on Article 32 Investigations.
    § 6-4(C). Command Influence on Referral of Charges.
    § 6-4(D). Command Influence in Selecting Court Members.
    § 6-4(E). Pretrial Comments and Actions.
§ 6-5. Command Influence on Courts-Martial.
    § 6-5(A). Command Influence on Court Members, Judges, and Counsel.
    § 6-5(B). Command Influence on Witnesses.
    § 6-5(C). Commander's "Presence" at Trial.
§ 6-6. Post-Trial Command Influence.
    § 6-6(A). Clemency Matters.
    § 6-6(B). Comments on the Outcome of Case.
    § 6-6(C). Discouraging Witness Testimony in Other Cases.
§ 6-7. Appellate Review of Command Influence.
§ 6-8. Minimizing the Potential for Unlawful Command Influence.
Appendix References.
Annotated Bibliography.

Part I

Preferral and Forwarding of Charges

§ 6-1. Preferring Sworn Charges.

The first formal step in prosecuting a military criminal case is *preferring* sworn charges against an accused. Anyone subject to the U.C.M.J.[1] may serve as an *accuser*[2] and prefer charges.[3] It is almost always the accused's immediate commanding officer, however, who after conducting a preliminary inquiry[4] directs that charges be drafted and a *charge sheet* prepared.[5] In some cases where the accused's commander has initially decided not to prefer charges, a superior commander may order that commander to prefer charges and forward them up the chain of command for review and action.[6] The accused's commander may decline to do so if he cannot truthfully swear, or affirm, that the charges, to the best of his knowledge, are true.[7] If charges are preferred in such a manner, the accused's commander is considered to be the *nominal accuser*,[8] and the superior who ordered him to prefer charges becomes

---

1. The term "subject to the U.C.M.J." requires that the person be subject to the jurisdiction of the U.C.M.J. Thus, a civilian employee working for the Department of Defense would ordinarily not be authorized to prefer charges. *See supra* § 4-7. For similar reasons a discharged servicemember could not prefer charges. *See supra* § 4-8(B).
2. *See* Art. 1(9), U.C.M.J.; Appendix 2 (Glossary). Persons serving as accusers are thereafter precluded from acting in a variety of roles, i.e., convening authority, pretrial investigating officer, trial counsel, defense counsel, interpreter, reporter, escort, bailiff, clerk, or orderly. *See* R.C.M. 405(d)(1), 502(d)(4), (e). *See also* §§ 4-4(A), 8-2(A). A convening authority who is an "accuser" is required to forward the charges to the next superior commander for action. Article 22(b), U.C.M.J., United States v. Nix, 40 M.J. 6 (C.M.A. 1994) (forwarding officer not disqualified if he was biased against accused).
3. Art. 30, U.C.M.J.; R.C.M. 307(a). If someone other than the accused's immediate commander prefers charges, they should be immediately forwarded to that commander for further action. United States v. Beckermann, 35 M.J. 842 (C.G.C.M.R. 1992) (Article 32 officer not disqualified from preferring charges after completing investigation; court noted that Article 30(a) includes reference to charges being preferred by someone who has investigated allegations).
4. *See supra* § 5-2.
5. The "charge sheet" is discussed at § 6-1(A) *infra*.
6. R.C.M. 307(a) Discussion. The Discussion to this R.C.M. notes that the practice of ordering a subordinate to prefer charges has existed for some time. However, note the difference between this procedure and one in which the superior commander simply orders the commander to (1) investigate the charges and forward the file for further action or (2) to take whatever action he feels appropriate. Either of these options are appropriate and are more palatable than ordering the commander to prefer charges.
7. R.C.M. 307(a) Discussion. In United States v. Miller, 33 M.J. 235 (C.M.A. 1991), the accused unsuccessfully argued that the court-martial lacked jurisdiction because the commander who swore to the charges did not believe she was guilty. The evidence showed that the commander, who had never preferred charges before, sought the advice of the SJA who informed him that if he did not prefer charges, a higher commander would. The court discussed the origins and purposes of the oath and concluded that the preferral of charges was not defective; there was nothing to indicate that the charges were frivolous or unfounded. The lower court had expressed concern about the possibility of unlawful command influence in such situations. United States v. Aue, 37 M.J. 528 (A.C.M.R. 1993) (signer testified that he did not believe that charges were true; accused waived any error in preferring sworn charges).
8. Art. 1(9), U.C.M.J. In other words the commander is an accuser in name only. United States v. Corcoran, 17 M.J. 137 (C.M.A. 1984); United States v. Shelton, 26 M.J. 787 (A.F.C.M.R. 1988).

§ 6-1 PREFERRAL AND FORWARDING OF CHARGES § 6-1

an *accuser*[9] and is thus barred from acting as either a special or general court-martial convening authority.[10] This disqualification does not exist for a summary court-martial convening authority.[11] This sort of "influence" on a subordinate commander has generally been approved as a form of lawful command influence[12] and is designed in part to prevent subordinate commanders from shelving a serious act of misconduct;[13] the accused receives limited protection because the superior authority is generally barred from referring or sending the charges to trial.[14]

The commander has broad discretion in deciding what charges to prefer.[15] Article 30, U.C.M.J., which governs preferral of charges, simply states that once charges are preferred, the proper authority will take immediate steps to determine what disposition is required in the interests of justice and discipline.[16] As a practical matter, before preferring charges the immediate com-

---

9. Art. 1(9), U.C.M.J. United States v. Corcoran, 17 M.J. 137 (C.M.A. 1984); United States v. Smith, 8 C.M.A. 178, 23 C.M.R. 402 (1957); United States v. Shelton, 26 M.J. 787 (A.F.C.M.R. 1988) (commander barred from referring case to trial because he ordered subordinate to prefer charges); United States v. Azevedo, 24 M.J. 559 (C.G.C.M.R. 1987) (the convening authority was not considered an accuser because his interest in the case was official, rather than personal). *See also supra* § 4-14(A)(2).

10. *See* Arts. 22(b), 23(b), U.C.M.J.; R.C.M. 307(a) Discussion. United States v. Johnston, 39 M.J. 242 (C.M.A. 1994) (court rejected argument that SJA's actions coerced subordinate into preferring charges; in any event her actions would only have disqualified special court-martial convening authority from convening case; case was convened by GCMCA).

11. R.C.M. 307(a) Discussion. Thus, a summary court-martial convening authority could order preferral of charges and upon receipt refer those charges to a summary court for trial.

12. *See also infra* § 6-3.

13. For example, a company commander might decide to dispose of a serious offense through nonjudicial punishment because of the accused's outstanding record. The battalion commander hears of the offense and feels that a court-martial is more appropriate. He thus orders the company commander to prefer charges. *See, e.g.,* United States v. Wharton, 33 C.M.R. 729 (A.F.B.R. 1963) (accused tried for manslaughter after commander imposed nonjudicial punishment).

14. *See* Arts. 22(b), 23(b); R.C.M. 307(a) Discussion, 1302(b).

15. *See* United States v. Baker, 14 M.J. 361, 365 (C.M.A. 1983). In commenting on the authority to charge violations of the U.C.M.J., the court indicated that the "convening authority ... is free to decide the number of offenses to charge...." The convening authority decides what charges, if any, of those preferred by the accuser should be referred to trial. United States v. Broussard, 35 M.J. 665 (A.C.M.R. 1992) (convening authority is free to decide the number of offenses to be charged when conduct violates more than one provision of U.C.M.J.; but discretion is not limitless). *See also infra* § 13-3(M).

United States v. Hagen, 25 M.J. 78 (C.M.A. 1987) (courts are hesitant to review decisions whether to prosecute and there is a strong presumption that convening authorities perform their function without bias); United States v. Anderson, 26 M.J. 555 (A.C.M.R. 1988) (command used alternatives to dealing with child sexual abuse before finally deciding to prosecute); United States v. Allen, 31 M.J. 572 (N.M.C.M.R. 1990) (extensive discussion of the "accuser concept" and how it is different from "unlawful command influence").

In a rare example of an appellate court reversing a case due to improper preferral of charges, the court in United States v. Asfeld, 30 M.J. 917 (A.C.M.R. 1990), noted that the commander's probable cause to prefer charges may be based upon incompetent, inadmissible, or even illegally obtained evidence but that the prosecution has a professional duty to ensure that baseless charges do not result in a denial of due process. The court concluded that under the facts of this case, the aggregation of legally and factually unsupportable charges denied due process even as to valid charges. In doing so, the court noted that the mere allegation of baseless charges may influence the fact-finder by suggesting that the accused is a bad character.

16. *See* Appendix 3. *See* Thomas v. Eddington, 26 M.J. 95 (C.M.A. 1988) (court did not resolve

mander has already decided that a court-martial is probably the most appropriate course to take. But the final decision as to whether the charges will be tried and what level of court will try the case is left to the convening authority who ultimately exercises prosecutorial discretion.[17]

The Manual for Courts-Martial provides some additional guidance on preferral of charges. First, the commander may prefer both minor and major offenses on the same charge sheet,[18] and he may prefer all known charges at the same time.[19] These two rules, which are a change from the 1969 *Manual*, obviously give the commander the discretion to reserve some charges as a bargaining chip for possible plea bargaining with the accused. It also permits him to dispose of all known charges at one proceeding, without regard to their severity, and avoid piecemeal litigation.[20] A commander may not, however, take what amounts to one criminal transaction and unreasonably multiply the charges against the accused.[21] Multiplicious charging is a frequent problem. The rules governing multiplicious charging are discussed at § 6-1(C)(3).

Note that some of the factors that a convening authority may take into account in deciding whether to refer a case to trial may, and should, be also considered by the commander when he decides what, if any, charges to prefer.[22] In reaching his decision, the commander will usually seek the advice of

---

allegation by defense that command deliberately delayed notifying the accused of the charges in order to delay the triggering of the speedy trial rules).

17. United States v. Baker, 14 M.J. 361, 365 (C.M.A. 1983); United States v. Taylor, 26 M.J. 816 (A.C.M.R. 1988) (failure of trial counsel to amend specification as directed by convening authority was nonjurisdictional error). R.C.M. 403, 404, 407, 601.

18. *See* R.C.M. 601(e)(2), 307(c)(4) Analysis. Under the 1969 *Manual*, commanders were discouraged from joining both minor and major offenses. *See* United States v. Yelverton, 40 C.M.R. 655 (A.B.R. 1969); United States v. Johnson, 49 C.M.R. 477 (A.C.M.R. 1974); United States v. Hypolite, 39 C.M.R. 830 (N.B.R. 1969); United States v. Healy, 39 C.M.R. 636 (A.B.R. 1968).

19. *See* R.C.M. 307(c)(4). *See, e.g.,* United States v. Whitfield, 35 M.J. 535 (A.C.M.R. 1992) (not abuse of discretion to proceed trial of some, but not all charges; apparently defense counsel deliberately did not seek joinder of offenses in order to argue speedy trial motion on some charges); United States v. Fahey, 33 M.J. 920 (A.C.M.R. 1991) (decision to consolidate charges is procedural matter within discretion of convening authority and all known charges need not be tried at one time; joinder not required where no evidence of government misconduct in referring one charge to separate trial).

In United States v. Alexander, 29 M.J. 877 (A.F.C.M.R. 1989), the court provided a long discussion on the history of trying all known charges at the same trial and concluded that it was not error to subject the accused to two trials where the charges leading the second trial were under investigation at the time of the first trial.

20. As a general rule preferring all known charges offers some of the same bargaining chips that might result if some charges are reserved for possible later referral, i.e., agreeing to dismiss some charges in return for plea bargain. *But see infra* § 6-1(C)(3). Commanders should be especially sensitive to speedy trial problems; R.C.M. 707(b)(4) addresses multiple charges and provides that the speedy trial clock commences with notice of preferral of each set of charges or imposition of restraint for those charges. *See, e.g.,* United States v. Honican, 27 M.J. 590 (A.C.M.R. 1988) (discussion of speedy trial problems vis-à-vis separate trial on certain charges). *See also infra* § 13-3(C).

21. United States v. Baker, 14 M.J. 361 (C.M.A. 1983); R.C.M. 307(c)(4) Discussion; 906(b)(12), and 1003(c)(I)(C).

22. For example, the commander should consider the accused's record, the seriousness of the offense, potential for rehabilitation, injury, if any, to a victim, and the availability of other

the military prosecutor. But the practice obviously varies. At some installations the "legal center" not only renders advice on what charges to prefer but also prepares the charge sheet and letters of transmittal for the forwarding process, discussed at § 6-2.

As a general rule, the military appellate courts will defer to the commander's broad discretion as to *what* charges should be preferred.[23] The preferral process is in some respect mechanical because the ultimate decision to prosecute, i.e., refer the charges to trial, is in the hands of the convening authority, not in the hands of the accuser—the person who prefers the charges. Indeed, until the charges have actually been referred to trial, the accused has little hope of judicial relief as to any defective charges.[24] Nonetheless, when judicial review is accomplished, either through a motion to dismiss or for appropriate relief,[25] the focus is not so much on whether the commander abused his discretion in *preferring* certain charges.[26] Rather, it is usually on the issue of whether the charges have been properly pleaded (which tends to be a technical question)[27] or on whether the convening authority abused his discretion in referring certain charges to a court for trial.[28]

After the charges are prepared, the commander signs the charge sheet[29] as the accuser and swears or affirms before an officer authorized to execute oaths[30] that he has personal knowledge of the charges or has investigated them and that they are true to the best of his knowledge and belief.[31] A ceremonial swearing is preferred but failure to raise the hand or read the oath aloud is not fatal;[32] nor is it critical that the signing precede the oath.[33] The key here is that someone has agreed to be accountable for preferring the charges.[34]

The requirement of *sworn* charges is critical because an accused cannot be tried on unsworn charges[35] over his objection. Failure to object constitutes

---

administrative or nonjudicial punishment options. *See supra* § 1-5. The commander may also consider the accused's status. *See* United States v. Means, 10 M.J. 162 (C.M.A. 1981) (commander considered accused's status as officer).

23. *See generally* United States v. Baker, 14 M.J. 361 (C.M.A. 1983).
24. Before charges are referred to a court-martial, the military judge has no authority to rule on any requests for relief by the accused. One option might be to seek extraordinary relief from one of the military appellate courts. *See, e.g.*, Dobzynski v. Green, 16 M.J. 84 (C.M.A. 1983).
25. *See infra* §§ 13-3(F), (J), (K), 13-5(E).
26. The military courts often blur the distinctions between preferral of charges and referral of charges in examining the issue of whether, for example, charges have been improperly joined or multiplied. *See, e.g., infra* §§ 6-1(C)(1), (3).
27. *See, e.g., infra* § 6-1(B)(1) (whether jurisdiction has been properly pleaded).
28. *See infra* § 8-4.
29. *See infra* § 6-1(A); Art. 30, U.C.M.J.; R.C.M. 304(b)(1).
30. Art. 30, U.C.M.J., R.C.M. 304(b)(2). Article 136, U.C.M.J., indicates who is authorized to administer oaths. *See* United States v. Johnson, 3 M.J. 623 (N.C.M.R. 1977).
31. R.C.M. 307(b)(2). United States v. Aue, 37 M.J. 528 (A.C.M.R. 1993) (signer testified that he did not believe that charges were true; accused waived any error by not objecting).
32. United States v. Koepke, 15 C.M.A. 542, 36 C.M.R. 40 (1965).
33. United States v. Autrey, 12 M.J. 547 (A.C.M.R. 1981) (substantial compliance is sufficient).
34. *See* R.C.M. 307(b) Analysis.
35. United States v. Marcy, 1 C.M.A. 176, 2 C.M.R. 82 (1952); United States v. Frage, 26 M.J. 924 (N.M.C.M.R. 1988); United States v. Clark, 49 C.M.R. 192 (A.C.M.R. 1974).

waiver.[36] The problem of unsworn charges does not usually arise in the original preferral of charges.[37] Rather, it arises most often when major amendments[38] or additional charges[39] are made during the forwarding process and the prosecution fails to have the new charges or specifications sworn or resworn as the case may be.

As a general rule, commanders are encouraged to prefer charges as promptly as possible.[40] In limited instances, they may delay charging an offense where, for example, an investigation is continuing and to do so would jeopardize further investigative fruits.[41] The commander should always be sensitive, however, to speedy trial and due process requirements[42] and the statute of limitations.[43] After the charges are prepared and sworn to, the commander[44] should immediately inform the accused of that fact.[45] The ac-

---

36. United States v. Aue, 37 M.J. 528 (A.C.M.R. 1993) (any error in preferring sworn charges was waived by failing to object at trial); United States v. Thompson, 31 M.J. 667 (A.C.M.R. 1990); United States v. Marcy, 1 C.M.A. 176, 2 C.M.R. 82 (1952).

37. *Cf.* Frage v. Moriarty, 27 M.J. 341 (C.M.A. 1988), in which the court, on an Article 62 appeal by the prosecution, held that the charges were properly dismissed where the officer was not authorized to administer oaths for purposes of military justice; thus, the statute of limitations had run. The court rejected a "good faith" exception to the requirement of properly sworn charges and noted that Article 30(a) was designed to avoid the problems associated with this case.

38. R.C.M. 603. *See infra* § 6-1(B)(2).

39. R.C.M. 601(e)(2).

40. R.C.M. 307(a) Discussion. United States v. Douglas, 32 M.J. 694 (A.F.C.M.R. 1991) (system encourages expeditious investigation and processing of charges).

41. In United States v. Douglas, 32 M.J. 694 (A.F.C.M.R. 1991), charges were not preferred until four months after the accused's apprehension, apparently to protect the identity of an informant who was still providing information. Noting that public officials have broad discretion in deciding when to prosecute, the court concluded that there was no due process violation in waiting. *See also* United States v. Porter, 50 C.M.R. 508 (N.C.M.R. 1975) (additional offense discovered just before trial for original offense).

42. *See infra* § 13-3(C); R.C.M. 707.

43. Art. 43, U.C.M.J. *See also infra* § 13-3(B).

44. *See* R.C.M. 308. This rule provides that the immediate commander should cause the accused to be informed of the charges; it is therefore not crucial that the commander himself personally inform the accused. United States v. Voyles, 28 M.J. 831 (N.M.C.M.R. 1989) (commander may use intermediaries to notify the accused).

45. R.C.M. 308. This Rule provides that the immediate commander should cause the accused to be informed of the charges; it is therefore not crucial that the commander himself personally inform the accused.

United States v. Maresca, 28 M.J. 328 (C.M.A. 1989) (although there is no bright line rule on the meaning of the language in R.C.M. 308, "as soon as practicable," the court indicated that an accused should be informed of the charges "as soon after they have been preferred as the accused can reasonably be found and informed thereof"; in this case, the court concluded that the accused was entitled to know of charges on the day they were preferred).

In an extensive discussion on the timing of the notice, the court in United States v. Beerey, 28 M.J. 714 (N.M.C.M.R. 1989) (en banc), concluded that intentionally delaying the giving of notice to avoid starting the speedy trial clock deprived the accused of military due process. The court concluded, however, that the commander is not required to give the notice as soon as he is physically able to do so and observed that there might be circumstances under which notification could legitimately be delayed.

United States v. Leamer, 29 M.J. 616 (C.G.C.M.R. 1989) (commander of accused's parent unit was not required to inform him of charges where accused paid an unofficial visit to that unit but

cused should also be told who served as his accuser.[46] Failure to provide this notice is not a jurisdictional error and may be corrected by appropriate relief.[47]

The vehicle for preferring charges, the charge sheet, rules, and defects in pleadings are discussed in the next sections.

§ 6-1(A). The Charge Sheet.

Charges for all types of courts-martial are drafted on a standard two-page *charge sheet*, DD Form 458, which is used by all of the services.[48] The first page consists of personal data on the accused, the nature and length of any pretrial restraint,[49] the charges, and the *preferral section*. In this section, the accuser, usually the commander, signs and swears or affirms that he has personal knowledge of the charges or that he has investigated them and that they are true. The second page contains an entry evidencing the fact that the accused has been informed of the charges. The remaining sections of page two are used for noting receipt of the charges by the summary court-martial convening authority[50] (which tolls the statute of limitations) and for referring the charges[51] to trial, and finally, for noting that the accused has been served with a copy of the completed charge sheet.[52] Note that this "service of charges" triggers a statutory delay in commencing trial.[53] *See* § 8-6.

Missing from the 1984 version of the charge sheet are notations as to witnesses, physical evidence, and an indication of whether the accused was offered nonjudicial punishment on the charges.[54] Further, the 1969 version served as the record of trial for any charges tried by summary court-martial. That proceeding is now recorded on DD Form 2329. *See* § 15-25 *et seq.*

§ 6-1(B). General Rules of Pleading.

In the military, allegations of criminal conduct are set out on the charge sheet in the form of "charges and specifications." The technical *charge* refers to the specific applicable punitive article[55] of the U.C.M.J. that has been

---

charges had already been transmitted to new unit for purpose of notifying him). *See generally* Pearson and Bowman, "Unreasonable Pre-preferral Delay," 10 A.F. JAG Rptr. 73 (June 1981).

46. R.C.M. 308(a).
47. R.C.M. 308(c). The Rule limits relief to a continuance or recess, assuming that the accused can demonstrate that he was hindered in preparing his defense. An example of hindrance might arise where the accused has not been informed that a superior authority ordered the preferral of charges and there is some question as to whether that individual is disqualified from acting as a convening authority.
48. *See* Appendix 6.
49. *See supra* § 5-3.
50. *See infra* § 6-2(B).
51. *See infra* § 8-3.
52. If by the time the charging process has been completed, the accused has a defense counsel, that counsel will generally also receive a copy of the charge sheet.
53. Art. 35, U.C.M.J.
54. *See* § 3-4.
55. *See* Arts. 77 to 134, U.C.M.J.

violated.[56] The *specification* states the specific facts and circumstances which the prosecution is relying upon to show the violation of the U.C.M.J.[57] Each specification, along with the charge, constitutes a separate accusation.[58]

Specifications are generally sufficient if they plead jurisdiction,[59] lay out the essential elements of the offense,[60] place the accused on notice of what he must defend,[61] and provide protection against double jeopardy.[62] A specification that fails to state an offense is subject to a motion to dismiss, and the proceedings with regard to that specification are a nullity.[63] The specifications may be attacked at any stage of the proceedings[64] and a guilty plea normally does not waive the issue.[65] The prosecution bears the burden of establishing valid pleadings.[66]

Appendix 6 of the 1969 Manual for Courts-Martial included sample forms for specifications, but failure to follow them was not necessarily fatal.[67] Nor did following them always guarantee a legally sufficient pleading.[68] The current *Manual* now provides some practical advice on drafting specifications in the Discussion accompanying R.C.M. 307(c)(3) and in Part IV of the *Manual* where each punitive article is discussed. As in the case of the 1969 *Manual*, the sample specifications in the current *Manual* may not guarantee a foolproof pleading.[69]

---

56. R.C.M. 307(c)(2).
57. R.C.M. 307(c)(3).
58. United States v. Weymouth, 43 M.J. 329 (1995).
59. *See infra* § 6-1(B)(1).
60. United States v. Brown, 42 C.M.R. 656 (A.C.M.R. 1970); United States v. Scott, 41 C.M.R. 773 (N.C.M.R. 1969). The specification may satisfactorily imply the offense. United States v. McCullom, 13 M.J. 127 (C.M.A. 1982). *See, e.g.*, United States v. Quarles, 50 C.M.R. 514 (N.C.M.R. 1975). *See generally* Dunn, "Military Pleading," 17 A.F. L. Rev. 17 (1975).
61. United States v. Curtiss, 19 C.M.A. 402, 42 C.M.R. 4 (1970).
62. United States v. Bolden, 40 C.M.R. 758 (A.C.M.R. 1969); United States v. Weems, 13 M.J. 609 (A.F.C.M.R. 1982).
63. United States v. Thompson, 1 M.J. 692 (N.C.M.R. 1975).
64. United States v. Culver, 22 C.M.A. 141, 46 C.M.R. 141 (1973).
65. United States v. Fout, 3 C.M.A. 565, 13 C.M.R. 121 (1953). *Cf.* United States v. Schwarz, 15 M.J. 109 (C.M.A. 1983) (where accused has entered guilty plea without challenging pleading, he may not successfully challenge the specification on the basis of a technical omission where the elements of the offense appear by implication).
66. United States v. Boswell, 45 C.M.R. 742 (A.C.M.R. 1972).
67. United States v. Quarles, 50 C.M.R. 514 (N.C.M.R. 1975).
68. United States v. Osborne, 31 M.J. 842 (N.M.C.M.R. 1990) (sample specification was defective re alleging carnal knowledge). *See, e.g.*, United States v. Alef, 3 M.J. 414 (C.M.A. 1977); United States v. Brice, 48 C.M.R. 368 (N.C.M.R. 1973).
69. In United States v. Vidal, 23 M.J. 319 (C.M.A. 1987), the court said that the standard form specification for the offense of rape was sufficient to charge the accused either as a principal or as an aider and abettor.

§ 6-1(B)(1). Pleading Jurisdiction.

The prosecution must affirmatively establish in the sworn charges the facts necessary to establish jurisdiction over the accused and offenses.[70] Alleging the accused's rank, armed force, and unit will normally be sufficient to allege jurisdiction.[71] Before the Supreme Court abandoned the service connection requirement in *Solorio v. United States*,[72] pleading subject matter jurisdiction required special consideration.[73] Now, a pleading will be sufficient to plead subject-matter jurisdiction if the specification states the servicemember's rank or grade and the proper elements of the alleged offense.[74] Because any jurisdictional language is normally considered surplusage, its inclusion at a later point is not considered an amendment which results in an unsworn charge.[75] The requirement to plead jurisdiction is procedural and may be waived.[76]

§ 6-1(B)(2). Amendments to Pleadings.

Pleadings in military practice are in the nature of an information and may, subject to some limitations, be amended at any time prior to findings if the accused is not prejudiced.[77] Before arraignment, minor changes may be made by anyone, except the Article 32 Investigation Officer,[78] who has acted upon or forwarded the charges.[79] After arraignment, the military judge must approve the changes and he may do so only if a substantial right of the accused is not prejudiced.[80] Amendments are normally used to cure minor deficiencies.[81]

---

70. R.C.M. 307(c)(3).
71. *See* R.C.M. 307(c)(3) Discussion. *Cf.* R.C.M. 203 Discussion, noting that it is not necessary to state the accused's armed force or unit if the accused is on active duty.
72. 483 U.S. 435 (1987).
73. United States v. Alef, 3 M.J. 414 (C.M.A. 1977). *See also* Chapter 4 and James, "Pleading and Practice Under United States v. Alef," 20 A.F. L. Rev. 22 (1978); Cooper, "United States v. Alef. Punishing the Pleader for Sins of Subject Matter Jurisdiction," Army Law., Nov. 1977, at 1.
74. R.C.M. 203 Discussion; R.C.M. 307(c)(3) Discussion.
75. United States v. Lewis, 5 M.J. 712 (A.C.M.R. 1978).
76. United States v. Adams, 13 M.J. 728 (A.C.M.R. 1982).
77. United States v. Alef, 3 M.J. 414 (C.M.A. 1977); United States v. Sullivan, 38 M.J. 746 (A.C.M.R. 1993) (amendment was minor and did not prejudice accused); United States v. Miller, 48 C.M.R. 446 (N.C.M.R. 1973).
78. R.C.M. 603(b). *See also* Chapter 7.
79. R.C.M. 603(b).
80. R.C.M. 603(c).
81. A minor change is defined in R.C.M. 603(a) as one which is not major. United States v. Sullivan, 42 M.J. 360 (1995) (amendment of specification from clause 3 to clause 1 of Article 134 amounted to a minor amendment); United States v. Loving, 41 M.J. 213 (1994) (changing information concerning employer of murder victims was minor change; focus of allegation was on identification of victim, not employer); United States v. Brown, 34 M.J. 105 (C.M.A. 1992) (change in date in specification of alleged offense was minor change made after arraignment); United States v. Brewster, 32 M.J. 591 (A.C.M.R. 1991) (changing designation of article violated was a minor amendment as was adding the word "wrongful").
United States v. Taylor, 26 M.J. 816 (A.C.M.R. 1988) (nonjurisdictional error for trial counsel not to make minor amendment to specification); United States v. Williams, 26 M.J. 606 (A.C.M.R.

Amendments are not permissible, however, if an additional or more serious offense is alleged, or if a substantial question as to the statute of limitations is raised, or if the accused is misled.[82] If the amendment results in a new charge, then it must be sworn to before proceeding and that may require a new Article 32 investigation,[83] and pretrial advice.[84] Failure to do so may result in a jurisdictional defect in the court-martial.[85] An accused may not be tried over objection on an unsworn charge.[86]

§ 6-1(B)(3). Additional Charges.

If after charges are preferred against an accused,[87] *see* § 6-1, he commits an offense or another offense is discovered, *additional* charges may be tried with the original charges if the requisite pretrial processing[88] has been completed prior to arraignment.[89] After arraignment, additional charges may be added only with the consent of the accused.[90] Note that for speedy trial purposes, the time runs separately for any additional charges.[91] If time permits, it is better practice to try all known offenses at once even though that may mean delay-

---

1988) (minor change where accused's conduct was the same under both versions and he was not misled).

For a discussion comparing minor and major changes, see United States v. Arbic, 16 C.M.A. 292, 36 C.M.R. 448 (1966). United States v. Bobroff, 23 M.J. 872 (N.M.C.M.R. 1987) (adding language that drug distribution involved money constituted minor change).

82. United States v. Krutsinger, 15 C.M.A. 235, 35 C.M.R. 207 (1965); United States v. Glenn, 29 M.J. 696 (A.C.M.R. 1989) (although a minor amendment to the charged offense properly alleged a lesser included offense it denied the accused the protection of the statute of limitations); United States v. Brown, 21 M.J. 995 (A.C.M.R. 1986) (amending specification to reflect lesser included offense was not a major change; lesser offense had longer statute of limitations); United States v. Blair, 21 M.J. 981 (N.M.C.M.R. 1986) (no major change where desertion charge was reinstituted); United States v. Moultak, 21 M.J. 822 (N.M.C.M.R. 1985) (error for prosecution to amend specification which had not previously stated an offense); United States v. Whitt, 21 M.J. 658 (A.C.M.R. 1985) (changing date of offense in specification was a major amendment because it raised a substantial question as to the statute of limitations).

83. *See* § 7-2.

84. *See* United States v. Longmire, 39 M.J. 536 (A.C.M.R. 1994) (postarraignment amendment was major change requiring re-referral; jurisdictional defect); United States v. Thompson, 31 M.J. 667 (A.C.M.R. 1990); United States v. Garrett, 17 M.J. 907 (A.F.C.M.R. 1984); United States v. Louder, 7 M.J. 548 (A.F.C.M.R. 1979). R.C.M. 603(d) Discussion. *See also* § 7-3.

85. United States v. Longmire, 39 M.J. 536 (A.C.M.R. 1994) (postarraignment amendment was major change requiring referral; jurisdictional defect).

86. United States v. Reeves, 49 C.M.R. 841 (A.C.M.R. 1975); United States v. Jones, 50 C.M.R. 724 (A.C.M.R. 1975). *See* § 6-1.

87. R.C.M. 601(e)(2).

88. The forwarding process, discussed in § 6-2, and any Article 32 Investigations, § 7-2, and Pretrial Advices, § 7-3, must be completed.

89. *See* § 12-4 for a discussion on arraignments. In United States v. Lee, 14 M.J. 983 (N.M.C.M.R. 1982), the court held that the limitation that additional charges may be consolidated before arraignment is not jurisdictional.

90. *See* R.C.M. 601(e)(2). United States v. Marsh, 19 M.J. 657 (A.C.M.R. 1984) (defense waived procedural error of adding charges after an arraignment; counsel avoided two convictions and the possibility of consecutive sentences).

91. R.C.M. 707(b)(4). *See* United States v. First, 2 M.J. 1266 (A.C.M.R. 1976); United States v. Ward, 1 M.J. 21 (C.M.A. 1975). *See generally* § 13-3(C).

ing the original charges and expediting the additional charges. The alternative is to try the original charges first and then the additional charges.[92]

Additional charges may be joined with the original charges without regard to whether it amounts to a joinder of a minor and major offense. Nor is it necessary that the charges be related.[93]

§ 6-1(C). Defective Pleadings.

A pleading that fails to state an offense is a nullity and may not be cured by waiver.[94] But a variety of lesser defects may appear in the pleadings and not render them legally deficient. For example, failure to allege the proper punitive article[95] and failure to allege the time and place of the offense are normally not fatal.[96] Nor is it necessarily fatal that the victim is not described.[97]

---

92. *See* United States v. Johnson, 14 M.J. 710 (N.M.C.M.R. 1982) (court denied defense motion to join subsequent offenses; government was anxious to avoid speedy trial problems).

93. R.C.M. 601(e)(2). These two limitations did exist under the 1969 Manual for Courts-Martial. *See* § 6-1.

94. United States v. Dear, 40 M.J. 196 (C.M.A. 1994) (specification adequately stated offense of maltreatment of subordinate by sexual harassment); United States v. Brecheen, 27 M.J. 67 (C.M.A. 1988) (specification sufficiently alleged wrongfulness of attempted drug distribution; element of wrongfulness was found by reasonable construction); United States v. McCollum, 13 M.J. 127 (C.M.A. 1982); United States v. Hoskins, 17 M.J. 134 (C.M.A. 1984); United States v. Watkins, 21 M.J. 208 (C.M.A. 1986) (court overruled United States v. Fout, 13 C.M.R. 121, to the extent that that case ruled that failure to allege "without authority" in Art. 86 violation is fatal). In United States v. Tallon, 28 M.J. 635 (A.F.C.M.R. 1989), the court, citing *Watkins*, noted that specifications which are challenged for the first time on appeal are not measured against strict common law pleading requirements, and that by pleading guilty the accused had waived any possible objections to the form of the specification.
United States v. Bryant, 28 M.J. 504 (A.C.M.R. 1989) (allegation of wrongfulness was implied in specification alleging "conspiracy"); United States v. Minor, 25 M.J. 898 (A.C.M.R. 1988) (specification alleging violation of Article 134, NCO loaning money to EM, failed to state offense; words of criminality do not in themselves allege an offense).
United States v. Simpson, 25 M.J. 865 (A.C.M.R. 1988) (omission of word "wrongful" from specification alleging violation of Article 112a was not fatal); United States v. Brown, 25 M.J. 793 (N.M.C.M.R. 1987) (specification alleging violation of orders under Article 92(2) void where knowledge of order not alleged; court noted apparently relaxed rules of pleadings in *Watkins*).
United States v. Cooley, 21 M.J. 968 (A.C.M.R. 1986) (specification alleging false official statement sufficient to state offense); United States v. Callaway, 21 M.J. 770 (A.C.M.R. 1986) (fraternization specification sufficient to state an offense where accused charged with conduct unbecoming an officer by entering into social relationship); United States v. Parrish, 20 M.J. 665 (N.M.C.M.R. 1985) (a specification alleging an Article 134 violation need not expressly allege that the accused's conduct was prejudicial to good order and discipline); United States v. Garcia, 18 M.J. 539 (A.C.M.R. 1984) (specification alleging possession of drugs was fatally defective because it did not include element of wrongfulness or criminality).

95. R.C.M. 307(d). The error is considered harmless unless the defect has prejudicially misled the accused. *See* United States v. Brewster, 32 M.J. 591 (A.C.M.R. 1991) (alleging wrong article was not fatal); United States v. Costello, 20 M.J. 659 (N.M.C.M.R. 1985); United States v. Parrish, 20 M.J. 665 (N.M.C.M.R. 1985) (specification incorrectly indicated a violation of Article 112a which had not yet gone into effect); United States v. Bluitt, 50 C.M.R. 675 (A.C.M.R. 1975).

96. Ledbetter v. United States, 170 U.S. 606 (1898) (unless date is essential element of offense, exact date is not required); United States v. Williams, 40 M.J. 379 (C.M.A. 1994) (specification of

---

97. United States v. Craig, 8 C.M.A. 218, 24 C.M.R. 28 (1957).

Misstatements of value are also generally not fatal, although failure to specify value may permit conviction of only a lesser included offense.[98] Common defects other than failure to state an offense are noted in the following discussion. Challenges to defective pleadings may be raised through a motion to dismiss[99] or motion for appropriate relief.[100]

In reviewing alleged errors in pleadings, the Court of Appeals for the Armed Forces has recognized a distinction between those cases where the defendant challenges the pleading before trial and pleads not guilty and those cases where the defendant pleads guilty and challenges the pleading for the first time on appeal.[101] In the case of the latter, the courts will generally be inclined to find the pleading sufficient if it alleges all of the necessary elements, either expressly or by implication.[102] And the defendant must show that the pleading was so obviously defective that by no reasonable construction could it be concluded that it alleges the crime for which the conviction was had.[103] Where the defendant has lodged a pretrial challenge and has not pled guilty, however, the courts will not view the pleading with such liberality.[104]

---

indecent acts and sodomy on 6-year old girl failed to include specific dates; accused had no Fifth Amendment right to have charges state exact date; he had adequate notice of allegations); United States v. Hunt, 37 M.J. 344 (C.M.A. 1993) (using on or about permitted). *Cf.* United States v. Brown, 25 M.J. 793 (N.M.C.M.R. 1987) (court questioned whether accused had sufficient notice where specification alleged incorrect date of violation of order); United States v. McKinney, 40 C.M.R. 1013 (A.F.B.R. 1969) (place of larceny); United States v. Brown, 4 C.M.A. 683, 16 C.M.R. 257 (1954).

98. United States v. May, 3 C.M.A. 703, 14 C.M.R. 121 (1954). *Cf.* United States v. Durham, 21 M.J. 232 (C.M.A. 1986) (failure to identify stolen property not fatal to charge of larceny).

99. *See* § 13-3.

100. *See* § 13-5.

101. United States v. Bryant, 30 M.J. 72 (C.M.A. 1990).

102. United States v. Bryant, 30 M.J. 72 (C.M.A. 1990); United States v. Johnson, 30 M.J. 930 (A.C.M.R. 1990) (failure to allege that accused committed offense was waived when accused failed to object); United States v. Brecheen, 27 C.M.A. 67 (C.M.A. 1988); United States v. Watkins, 21 M.J. 208 (C.M.A. 1986); United States v. Smythe, 37 M.J. 804 (C.G.C.M.R. 1993) (error raised for first time on appeal after pleading guilty; court found specification sufficient); United States v. Wrenn, 36 M.J. 1188 (N.M.C.M.R. 1993) (specification, as amended at trial, was sufficient to state an offense); United States v. Smith, 36 M.J. 754 (A.C.M.R. 1993) (specification included every essential element directly or by fair implication). One court has referred to this as the "greater tolerance" test. United States v. Morris, 30 M.J. 1221 (A.C.M.R. 1990) (accused did not challenge at trial; specification was sufficient in that it could be construed to allege a crime).

103. United States v. Bryant, 30 M.J. 72, 73 (C.M.A. 1990).

104. United States v. French, 31 M.J. 57 (C.M.A. 1990); United States v. Province, 42 M.J. 821 (N.M.C.Ct.Crim.App.1995) (accused challenged pleading at trial and entered plea of not guilty; court concluded that amendments to allegation of unauthorized absence resulted in trial of accused on unsworn, unpreferred, and unreferred charges). *Cf.* United States v. King, 32 M.J. 588 (A.C.M.R. 1991) (accused was on notice of offense, defended against it and suffered no prejudice); United States v. Berner, 32 M.J. 570 (A.C.M.R. 1991) (specification was sufficient where accused did not challenge specification, defended against it at trial, and suffered no prejudice).

§ 6-1(C)(1). Misjoinder.

Although commanders have always had some leeway in combining charges, under the 1969 *Manual* joinder of minor delicts with serious offenses was discouraged, but it was not improper per se.[105] A motion to dismiss rested on the sound discretion of the military judge.[106] Such joinder was appropriate, for example, where the minor offense explained the major[107] or where the accused had refused offered nonjudicial punishment and that offense was combined with a charge already preferred. If, however, the accused had been prejudiced by the misjoinder, then dismissal of the minor offense was appropriate.[108] The present *Manual*, however, specifically permits joinder of offenses without regard to whether they are minor or serious.[109] Consequently, most of the misjoinder of offense problems experienced under the 1969 *Manual* vanished with the expansion of the commander's discretion.[110]

A possible problem of joinder of offenses may arise when there is a danger that the court's determination of one charged offense may have an undesirable "spill over" onto another charged offense. For example, in *United States v. Haye*,[111] the accused was charged with adultery with one servicemember and fraternization with another. The lower court concluded that evidence offered to support the adultery conviction had been erroneously admitted and reversed that portion of the findings. The Court ultimately concluded that it was not clear that the conviction on the remaining fraternization charge was not impermissibly based upon evidence indicating a general criminal disposition.[112] The court noted that severances of charges are a rare creature in military practice,[113] but also noted:

> [W]here the criminal intent involved in two offenses is similar (although the offenses themselves are unrelated) and, significantly, where the proof of one would not be admissible to prove the other, there is a serious danger that overwhelming proof on one will "spill over" and prejudice a legitimate defense to another. One test that might be used in judging the possibility of spillover is to determine whether the evidence presented as to one charge would be independently admissible to prove the other.[114]

---

105. United States v. Haye, 29 M.J. 213 (C.M.A. 1989) (judge's instructions were insufficient to prevent "spill over effect" of adultery charge on fraternization charge); United States v. Yelverton, 40 C.M.R. 655 (A.B.R. 1969).
106. United States v. Johnson, 49 C.M.R. 477 (A.C.M.R. 1974).
107. United States v. Hypolite, 39 C.M.R. 830 (N.B.R. 1969); United States v. Healy, 39 C.M.R. 636 (A.B.R. 1968).
108. United States v. Yelverton, 40 C.M.R. 655 (A.B.R. 1969).
109. See R.C.M. 601(e)(2).
110. See § 6-1 for a discussion on the commander's discretion regarding charges. United States v. White, 19 M.J. 662 (C.G.C.M.R. 1984) (convening authority did not abuse discretion in joining disrespect and failure to obey offenses).
111. 29 M.J. 213 (C.M.A. 1989).
112. 29 M.J. at 214.
113. The court's explanation was twofold: First, motions to sever are usually futile, and second, unified sentencing favors joinder of all known offenses at one trial. 29 M.J. at 215.
114. 29 M.J. at 215. This sort of reasoning, however, could affect virtually any trial in which the accused is charged with multiple specifications of the same type of offense, e.g., numerous

The court noted that proper instructions might remedy the problem, but that in this case, given the factual presentation of the evidence against the accused, it would have been impossible for a rational factfinder, under any circumstances, to separate the evidence of one specification from the other.[115] Similar analysis should apply where one of several charges or specifications has been improperly referred to the court.[116]

Joint offenders—those committing an offense pursuant to a common interest—may be charged and tried together.[117] The key requirement here is that the offenders acted together.[118] The prosecution is not permitted to combine defendants who may have separately committed the same type of offense.[119] An accomplice whose testimony is necessary for a conviction, should not be joined with the other accused;[120] at a joint trial that accomplice would be an accused who could not take the stand unless he consented.[121] If co-accused have been improperly joined, the defense may seek relief through a pretrial motion to sever.[122] In ruling on the motion, the military judge must weigh the time and expense saved through a joint trial and the possible prejudice to the accused.[123]

§ 6-1(C)(2). Duplicitous Specifications.

A specification alleging more than one offense is duplicitous.[124] Offenses should not be charged in the alternative, and normally may not be charged in

---

drug offenses. There is always the danger of spill over and it should normally be handled through tightly worded and emphatic instructions to the court members. United States v. Curry, 31 M.J. 359 (C.M.A. 1990).

115. United States v. Schneider, 38 M.J. 387 (C.M.A. 1993) (accused could not be prejudiced by spillover if the evidence would have been admitted anyway; in addition, court gave limiting instruction on evidence of other acts); United States v. Kirks, 34 M.J. 646 (A.C.M.R. 1992) (severance not required where military judge, in effect, conducted bifurcated trial and instructed court members not to consider potential spillover evidence). *See also* United States v. Curry, 31 M.J. 359 (C.M.A. 1990) (no prejudice in joining two murder offenses where evidence of the other crime would have been admissible in each separate prosecution).

United States v. Silvis, 31 M.J. 707 (N.M.C.M.R. 1990) (joinder of rape offenses was not improper; court indicated that three factors should be considered: presence of an impermissible cross-over of strong evidence on one charge to a weaker charge, whether evidence of the other offenses would have been admissible although not charged, and whether there were limiting instructions). *See also* MIL. R. EVID. 105 (limiting instructions).

116. United States v. Rodriguez, 31 M.J. 150 (C.M.A. 1990) (improperly referred charge did not prejudice accused). *See also* United States v. Hogan, 20 M.J. 71 (C.M.A. 1985).

117. R.C.M. 307(c)(5). An accessory after the fact cannot be jointly charged with the principal. *Id.* at the Discussion.

118. R.C.M. 307(c)(5) Discussion.

119. *Id.*

120. *Id. See generally* Corrigan, "Prejudicial Joinder: The Crazy-Quilt World of Severances," 68 MIL. L. REV. 1 (1975).

121. *See* MIL. R. EVID. 301. *See also* MIL. R. EVID. 306 (statements of co-accused).

122. *See* § 13-5(G).

123. *Id.*

124. United States v. Paulk, 13 C.M.A. 456, 32 C.M.R. 456 (1963); United States v. Kim, 35 M.J. 553 (A.C.M.R. 1992) (pleading which alleged desertion with intent to remain away permanently and desertion with intent to avoid hazardous duty or shirk important service was duplici-

the conjunctive, unless two acts comprise a single offense or the offense was committed in several ways.[125] A specification containing allegations of a continuing course of conduct is not necessarily duplicitous;[126] nor is an allegation of an offense which includes lesser included offenses.[127] The appropriate remedy for a duplicitous pleading is severance into separate specifications.[128] In those cases where severance would increase the maximum authorized punishment, it may not be appropriate to sever.[129] A duplicitous pleading is grounds for reversal only where the defect has prejudiced the substantial rights of the accused.[130] Failure to object waives the defect.[131]

---

tous); United States v. Hiatt, 27 M.J. 818 (A.C.M.R. 1988) (specification alleged substantive offense and conspiracy to commit that offense).

125. United States v. Hart, 32 M.J. 101 (C.M.A. 1991) (three offenses arising out of single transaction were properly joined in single specification). In an extensive discussion on this point, the court in United States v. Mobley, 28 M.J. 1024 (A.F.C.M.R. 1989), concluded that a specification alleging murder by two different means, was not impermissibly duplicitous. United States v. Riggins, 2 C.M.A. 451, 9 C.M.R. 81 (1953) (alleging robbery by force and violence and placing in fear); United States v. Mincey, 42 M.J. 376 (1995) (court neither condoned nor condemned practice of joining numerous offenses into one specification for purposes of pleading and prosecution).

126. United States v. Means, 12 C.M.A. 290, 30 C.M.R. 290 (1961); United States v. Rupert, 25 M.J. 531 (A.C.M.R. 1987) (error to combine separate larcenies in one specification and then aggregate amounts stolen to allege a greater offense).

In United States v. Poole, 24 M.J. 539 (A.C.M.R. 1987), the court implicitly recognized the use of "mega-specs" which in this case permitted the government to combine 119 bad check offenses into only six specifications, something which the defense did not object to. But in determining the maximum punishment, the trial judge erred in totaling all the bad check amounts. Instead, he should have determined the maximum punishment for each specification by determining the dollar amount of the largest check in that specification. United States v. Jones, 15 C.M.R. 664 (A.B.R. 1954); United States v. Carter, 21 M.J. 665 (A.C.M.R. 1985) ("mega-spec" allegation of multiple offenses); United States v. Grubbs, 13 M.J. 594 (A.F.C.M.R. 1982) (16 acts of passing bad checks in one specification); United States v. Adams, 13 M.J. 728 (A.C.M.R. 1982) (pleading series of acts is permissible but new twist is added where some acts are outside court's jurisdiction; here no prejudice resulted).

127. United States v. Vigilito, 22 C.M.A. 394, 47 C.M.R. 331 (1973); United States v. King, 20 M.J. 706 (A.C.M.R. 1985) (allegation of both possession and distribution of drugs in the same specification did not make the specification duplicitous. R.C.M. 307(c)(3) Discussion. But doing so is contrary to R.C.M. 307(c)(4) which directs that each specification should state only one offense).

128. R.C.M. 906(b)(5). *Cf.* United States v. McNett, 21 M.J. 969 (A.C.M.R. 1986) (allegations of Arts. 92, 121, and 134 offenses in same specification were duplicitous; court treated as multiplicious for findings).

129. United States v. Taylor, 13 C.M.R. 201 (A.B.R. 1953); United States v. Davis, 16 C.M.A. 207, 36 C.M.R. 363 (1966).

130. United States v. Branford, 2 C.M.R. 489 (A.B.R. 1952).

131. United States v. Mincey, 42 M.J. 376 (1995) (failure to challenge duplicitous specification waived issue); United States v. Parker, 3 C.M.A. 541, 13 C.M.R. 97 (1953); United States v. Kim, 35 M.J. 553 (A.C.M.R. 1992) (accused waived defective pleading); United States v. Blucker, 30 M.J. 690 (A.C.M.R. 1990) (court noted that waiving objection to duplicitous specification often benefits accused); United States v. Hiatt, 27 M.J. 818 (A.C.M.R. 1988) (defense waived the issue by not moving to correct the duplicitous specification; but the error worked to the advantage of the accused because to have severed the charge would have increased the maximum punishment); United States v. Wakeman, 25 M.J. 644 (A.C.M.R. 1987) (accused waived objection by not raising it at trial); United States v. DeJonge, 16 M.J. 974 (A.F.C.M.R. 1983).

§ 6-1(C)(3). Multiplicity.

Multiplicious pleadings arise when a single criminal transaction is alleged in more than one specification.[132] Over the years the military courts have applied a variety of tests in determining whether a specification is multiplicious with no one test being dispositive. As a general rule, specifications are not multiplicious where each requires a showing of *different elements of proof*.[133] Even where different proof is required, however, the pleadings may be multiplicious where the offenses were a part of a *single integrated transaction*.[134] In assessing whether the offenses were integrated, the courts have considered the *unity of time*,[135] whether there was an *insistent flow of events*,[136] and whether the accused acted on a *single impulse*.[137] Nonetheless, even where the offenses are connected in proof, time, and circumstance they were nonetheless separately pleaded where they violated different duties[138] or societal standards.[139]

---

132. United States v. Gibson, 11 M.J. 434 (C.M.A. 1981); United States v. Rushing, 11 M.J. 95 (C.M.A. 1981); United States v. Ingham, 36 M.J. 990 (A.C.M.R. 1993) (multiple acts of sodomy charged by year were not multiplicious; government could have charged each and every act); United States v. Chisholm, 10 M.J. 795 (A.F.C.M.R. 1981); United States v. Hughes, 1 M.J. 346 (C.M.A. 1976) (multiplicious to charge drug offenses arising from possession of different drugs in same place). *See generally* Young, "Multiplicity and Lesser-Included Offenses", 39 A.F. L. Rev. 159 (1996); Youngblood, "Multiplicious Pleading," 8 Mil. L. Rev. 73 (1960).

133. Blockburger v. United States, 284 U.S. 299 (1931); United States v. Cashwell, 45 C.M.R. 748 (A.C.M.R. 1972). *E.g.*, coverups are not multiplicious with the offense, United States v. Harrison, 4 M.J. 332 (C.M.A. 1978).

134. United States v. Martin, 36 M.J. 315 (C.M.A. 1993) (ATM offenses were multiplicious); United States v. Hyska, 29 M.J. 122 (C.M.A. 1989) (attempt to distribute drugs and distribution of drugs were part of a single continuous transaction); United States v. Lyons, 33 M.J. 543 (A.F.C.M.R. 1991) (rape and adultery charges were multiplicious for findings where they arose out of single incident); United States v. Malone, 29 M.J. 1027 (A.C.M.R. 1990) (offenses were not multiplicious; although they arose out of continuing criminal scheme they did not arise from same act or transaction); United States v. Weaver, 20 C.M.A. 58, 42 C.M.R. 250 (1970) (escape from confinement, offering violence to officer, and assault upon an MP); United States v. Rosen, 9 C.M.A. 175, 25 C.M.R. 437 (1958) (thirteen specifications actually alleged only four separate offenses for punishment purposes).

135. United States v. Bashaw, 6 M.J. 179 (C.M.A. 1979); United States v. Irving, 3 M.J. 6 (C.M.A. 1977).

136. United States v. Burney, 21 C.M.A. 71, 44 C.M.R. 125 (1971); United States v. Dougal, 32 M.J. 863 (N.M.C.M.R. 1991) (specifications charging larceny and false claim are generally multiplicious for findings where false claim is mechanism for the larceny).

137. United States v. Flynn, 28 M.J. 218 (C.M.A. 1989) (assault with intent to commit rape and assault with intent to commit sodomy were not multiplicious where there were separate acts, there was a lapse of time, and the accused's intent with regard to each was different); United States v. Burney, 21 C.M.A. 71, 44 C.M.R. 125 (1971); United States v. Ignatko, 33 M.J. 571 (N.M.C.M.R. 1991) (attempted forgeries arising from accused's use of computer to generate two checks were multiplicious with each other and with larcenies arising from possession of the checks; the offenses were the result of a single intent to steal a certain amount of money on a single day); United States v. Haltiwanger, 50 C.M.R. 255 (A.F.C.M.R. 1975).

138. United States v. Soukup, 2 C.M.A. 141, 7 C.M.R. 17 (1953).

139. United States v. Waits, 32 M.J. 274 (C.M.A. 1991) (conduct unbecoming an officer and violation of general regulation involved same conduct were multiplicious for findings); United States v. Scranton, 30 M.J. 322 (C.M.A. 1990) (four offenses of DWI involving injury to four

In *United States v. Baker*,[140] the Court of Appeals attempted to clarify and simplify the rules governing multiplicious pleadings. The court noted that the rules vary slightly depending on whether they are being applied for purposes of charging, for findings of guilt, or for sentencing.[141] For purposes of pleading, the court offered a three-step analysis. First, are the charged offenses based on one transaction or what is substantially one transaction?[142] If not, multiplication of charges is generally not present.[143] If they are, the second step is to determine whether alleging more than one offense constitutes an improper multiplication of charges.[144] In three instances the pleadings will be duplica-

---

persons were multiplicious for findings where the specifications resulted from a single incident of drunk driving and a single accident that resulted); United States v. Beene, 4 C.M.A. 177, 15 C.M.R. 177 (1954). United States v. McCoy, 32 M.J. 907 (A.F.C.M.R. 1991) (charges of false statement and perjury were not multiplicious for findings where they were based on separate statutory provisions, did not require inconsistent findings and had separate elements of proof; they were multiplicious for sentencing, however, because they arose from a singular decision to deceive and were aspects of single transaction); United States v. Crowe, 30 M.J. 1144 (A.F.C.M.R. 1990) (offenses of indecent acts, sodomy, and carnal knowledge were part of single course of criminal conduct but were not multiplicious for findings purposes because they were each based upon a separate statutory provision designed to protect different societal standard. They were multiplicious for sentencing, however); United States v. Lockett, 7 M.J. 753 (A.C.M.R. 1979) (sodomy and communication of threat); United States v. Dearman, 7 M.J. 713 (A.C.M.R. 1979) (sodomy and attempted rape); United States v. Rose, 6 M.J. 754 (N.C.M.R. 1978) (burglary, rape, and sodomy).

140. 14 M.J. 361 (C.M.A. 1983).
141. The court noted that initially unreasonable multiplication of charges was nonprejudicial error unless the accused had received separate sentences. United States v. Baker, 14 M.J. at 365, n.2 (C.M.A. 1983); United States v. Posnick, 8 C.M.A. 201, 24 C.M.R. 11 (1957). However, it has subsequently observed that multiplication might affect an accused's due process rights on findings of guilty. See United States v. Sturdivant, 13 M.J. 323 (C.M.A. 1982) (dismissed *all* charges and specifications); United States v. Krauss, 20 M.J. 741 (N.M.C.M.R. 1985) (the prosecution unreasonably multiplied charges when it took what was essentially two larcenies and charged the accused with over twenty specifications).
142. United States v. Baker, 14 M.J. at 366 (C.M.A. 1983). The court said that the term "transaction" is flexible but that it is "generally construed to embrace a series of occurrences or an aggregate of acts which are logically related to a single course of criminal conduct." *Id.* United States v. Fairly, 27 M.J. 582 (A.F.C.M.R. 1988) (en banc) (offense of stealing ATM and PIN cards was not multiplicious with larceny of funds from ATM machine later the same day and on the next day; the offenses did not arise out of a single impulse or intent and arose from separate acts), overruling United States v. Pulliam, 17 M.J. 1066 (A.F.C.M.R. 1984); United States v. Aquino, 20 M.J. 712 (A.C.M.R. 1985) (successive withdrawals from different accounts by using stolen bank teller machine cards were separate offenses even though they were made at substantially the same time); United States v. Wells, 20 M.J. 513 (A.F.C.M.R. 1985) (if the offenses do not arise from the same act or transaction then no further analysis is necessary).
143. The restriction against multiplication of charges generally focuses on pleading what is basically one offense in a variety of ways. But unreasonable multiplication of charges might still exist where each specification presents a separate, distinguishable offense, but the government has abused its discretion in "stacking" the separate, nonmultiplicious charges.
In United States v. Taylor, 26 M.J. 7 (C.M.A. 1988), the court concluded that the accused was subjected to unreasonable multiplication of charges where he refused to work for six days and was subsequently convicted by general court-martial of 15 specifications of dereliction of duty and 17 specifications of failing to go to his appointed place of duty. The court noted that he should have been charged with six specifications of willful dereliction of all of his duties on that day.
144. United States v. Baker, 14 M.J. at 366 (C.M.A. 1983).

§ 6-1(C)(3) MILITARY CRIMINAL JUSTICE § 6-1(C)(3)

tive as a matter of law: (1) Where the charged offenses "stand in the relationship of greater and lesser;"[145] (2) Where the charged offenses, "as a matter of fact are parts of an indivisible crime as a matter of civilian or military law;"[146] and (3) Where the charged offenses are simply "different aspects of a continuous course of conduct prohibited by one statutory provision."[147]

---

145. Brown v. Ohio, 432 U.S. 161 (1977); United States v. DiBello, 17 M.J. 77 (C.M.A. 1983) (Charge A is not included within Charge B if A contains allegations of an "aggravating circumstance" which is not a necessary element of B and which is not specifically alleged in B). The Court further defined this rule as follows:

> Assuming both offenses arise out of one transaction, one offense may be a lesser-included offense of another offense in two situations: First, where one offense contains only elements of, but not all the elements of the other offense; second, where one offense contains different elements as a matter of law from the other offense, but these different elements are fairly embraced in the factual allegations of the other offense and established by evidence introduced at trial.

United States v. Baker, 14 M.J. at 368 (C.M.A. 1983). *See also* United States v. Phillips, 26 M.J. 963 (A.C.M.R. 1988); United States v. Caldwell, 23 M.J. 748 (A.F.C.M.R. 1987) (fraternization and adultery were not multiplicious). *See also* United States v. Jefferson, 21 M.J. 203 (C.M.A. 1986); United States v. Walker, 21 M.J. 74 (C.M.A. 1985); United States v. McCullar, 20 M.J. 218 (C.M.A. 1985) (specifications of assault and breach of the peace were not multiplicious; the assault specification alleged a battery while the breach of peace specification did not); United States v. Hogan, 20 M.J. 221 (C.M.A. 1985) (specifications alleging possession and use of the same drugs were multiplicious for purposes of findings); United States v. Jennings, 20 M.J. 223 (C.M.A. 1985) (possession with intent to distribute and distribution of marijuana were multiplicious); United States v. Carl, 20 M.J. 216 (C.M.A. 1985) (possession and introduction of drugs specifications were multiplicious for findings purposes); United States v. Zubko, 18 M.J. 378 (C.M.A. 1984) (possession was considered a lesser included offense of the distribution charge and were thus multiplicious); United States v. Rodriquez, 18 M.J. 363 (C.M.A. 1984) (specifications alleging violations of Article 133 were lesser included offenses of specifications alleging violations of Article 134); United States v. Blais, 20 M.J. 781 (A.C.M.R. 1985) (accused was charged with both possession and distribution of drugs in the same specification; because possession is necessarily included within the distribution offense, it was stricken from the specification). *See also* R.C.M. 307(c)(3) Discussion.

146. United States v. Baker, 14 M.J. at 366 (C.M.A. 1983), *citing* Prince v. United States, 352 U.S. 322 (1957); United States v. Carter, 30 M.J. 179 (C.M.A. 1990) (offenses of conspiracy and solicitation were not multiplicious; conspiracy specification did not fairly embrace solicitation specification as lesser-included offense); United States v. Stottlemire, 28 M.J. 477 (C.M.A. 1989) (citing the *Blockburger* rule, the court concluded that the offenses of conspiracy to steal government funds and attempted larceny of the same funds, were not multiplicious; although they constituted a single transaction, the elements of the offenses were different); United States v. Glenn, 20 M.J. 172 (C.M.A. 1985) (offenses of willful damage to government property and arson were multiplicious); United States v. Grubb, 34 M.J. 532 (A.F.C.M.R. 1991) (charged offenses were merely different aspects of indivisible crime).

147. United States v. Baker, 14 M.J. at 366 (C.M.A. 1983), *citing* United States v. Universal C.S.T. Credit Corp., 344 U.S. 218 (1952); United States v. Curry, 35 M.J. 359 (C.M.A. 1992) (charge of solicitation of bribe was multiplicious with violation of regulation which made it illegal); United States v. Edwards, 35 M.J. 351 (C.M.A. 1992) (same acts alleged in rape and assault with intent to commit rape) United States v. Campfield, 20 M.J. 246 (C.M.A. 1985) (under circumstances, a two day unauthorized absence was multiplicious with a breach of restriction specification); United States v. Grasha, 20 M.J. 220 (C.M.A. 1985) (specifications of aggravated arson of a building and simple arson of some items within that building were not multiplicious);

Assuming that the charged offenses arise from one transaction and that they are multiplicious, the third inquiry is whether the exigencies of proof would nonetheless justify letting the pleadings stand until the court has rendered findings on each offense.[148] Whether the *Baker* decision and its progeny will clarify or simplify the problems of multiplicious pleading remains to be seen.[149] Note that *Baker* predates the current Manual for Courts-Martial. The Discussion to R.C.M. 907(b)(3)(B) states that:

> A specification is multiplicious with another if it alleges the same offense, or an offense necessarily included in the other. A specification may also be multiplicious with another if they describe substantially the same misconduct in two different ways.[150] Because the Drafters were obviously aware of *Baker*,[151] it seems safe to assume that continued application of the tests in that case will assist the bench and bar in applying the current *Manual's* definition.[152]

United States v. Grubb, 34 M.J. 532 (A.F.C.M.R. 1991) (charged offenses were merely different aspects of indivisible crime).

United States v. Johnson, 39 M.J. 707 (N.M.C.M.R. 1993) (one transaction should not be made basis for unreasonable multiplication of charges); In United States v. Gill, 37 M.J. 501 (A.F.C.M.R. 1993), the court indicated that the government may decide to use a "course of conduct" approach to charging, i.e., the accused is charged with committing similar criminal acts within a given period; however, a second charge alleging commission of a similar act within that time frame is multiplicious for findings.

United States v. Nagle, 30 M.J. 1229 (A.C.M.R. 1990) (conspiracy and substantive offense were multiplicious for sentencing but not for findings); United States v. Montgomery, 30 M.J. 1118 (N.M.C.M.R. 1989) (offenses of using two different drugs at same time were multiplicious); United States v. Donegan, 27 M.J. 576 (A.F.C.M.R. 1988) (charge of submitting a false claim for overseas housing allowance was multiplicious for findings with charge alleging larceny of the resulting funds; the court noted that "[d]raftsmen need more than a sharp pencil to create specifications which are separate for findings"); United States v. Sheffield, 20 M.J. 957 (A.F.C.M.R. 1985) (specifications alleging involuntary manslaughter of two individuals were not multiplicious; the elements alleging the death of the two persons reflected distinct societal interests).

148. United States v. Baker, 14 M.J. at 369 (C.M.A. 1983). The court concluded that the charged offenses in this case, aggravated assault and communicating a threat, were not multiplicious; thus there was no need to reach this third prong.

149. Testing for multiplicity involves an *ad hoc* analysis in each case. That fact, combined with the "new" *Baker* approach to multiplicity, will undoubtedly muddy the waters for some time. *See generally* Judge Cook's dissenting opinion in United States v. Baker, 14 M.J. at 371-76 (C.M.A. 1983). For example, the court recently addressed the problem of multiplicity in charging absence offenses. United States v. DiBello, 17 M.J. 77 (C.M.A. 1983); United States v. Johnson, 17 M.J. 83 (C.M.A. 1983); United States v. Ridgeway, 19 M.J. 681 (A.F.C.M.R. 1984) (excellent analysis of multiplicity issues).

150. This explanation, in light of *Baker*, may be deceptively simple. *See* Raezer, "Trial Counsel's Guide to Multiplicity," ARMY LAW., Apr. 1985, at 21; Uberman, "Multiplicity Under the New Manual for Courts-Martial," ARMY LAW., June 1985, at 31.

151. *See* R.C.M. 907(b)(3)(B). The Drafters cited *Baker* without comment.

152. The current *Manual* definition generally parallels and reaffirms the basic tests used by the Court in United States v. Baker, 14 M.J. 361 (C.M.A. 1983). In the Discussion to R.C.M. 1003(c)(1)(C), however, the Drafters note that no single test or formula has been developed for deciding multiplicity questions. *Cf.* United States v. Meace, 20 M.J. 972 (N.M.C.M.R. 1985) (citing the 1984 MCM test for multiplicity in R.C.M. 307(c)(4), 907(b)(3)(B), and 1003(c)(1)(C), the court rejected the defense argument that the test in *Baker* should control; that test is unworkable and more complex than the *Blockburger* rule used in civilian courts).

In *United States v. Teters*,[153] the Court of Appeals, however, abandoned the fairly embraced *Baker* test for multiplicity. Citing Supreme Court decisions, and comparing Article 79[154] to Federal Rule of Criminal Procedure 31,[155] the Court held that the true test for multiplicity, under Double Jeopardy analysis, is whether Congress intended for an accused at a single court-martial to be convicted of multiple offenses.[156] The Court applied a three-step inquiry. First, the court should determine whether Congress has expressly stated its intent in the statutes or in the legislative histories.[157] If Congress has not expressly stated its intent, its intent may be inferred or presumed from the elements of the statutes and their possible interrelationship.[158] And finally, using other means of determining congressional intent, the court should determine whether that presumption of separateness (what it called the *Blockburger* presumption) can be overcome by a contrary legislative intent.[159]

In a concurring opinion, Judge Cox expressed the hope that the courts, services, President, and Congress could address the issue of sentencing issues for multiple offenses.[160]

Apparently, the current test for multiplicity, at least for purposes of findings, is what has been referred to as the separate elements test.[161] The ele-

---

In United States v. Jones, 23 M.J. 301 (C.M.A. 1987), the Court of Military Review, in a very short per curiam opinion, rejected *Baker* and applied the *Manual* and *Blockburger* tests, noting that "We see no logical reason which compels the armed forces to follow a rule significantly different than the civilian federal courts." 20 M.J. 602 (N.M.C.M.R. 1985). The Court of Military Appeals affirmed only in the result, holding that generally a Court of Military Review is not free to ignore precedent and stating that the lower court's assertion was based upon "a profound misunderstanding of the legal basis" of the court's decision in *Baker* and was "further exacerbated by an unsupportable reading of the *Manual*."

153. 37 M.J. 370 (C.M.A. 1993).
154. Article 79, U.C.M.J. 37 M.J. at 375-76.
155. Fed. R. Crim. P. 31(c). United States v. Johnson, 38 M.J. 88 (C.M.A. 1993) (acts of adultery with same woman at different times and places are separate offenses; accused failed to show that Congress intended that they be considered multiplicious); United States v. Albrecht, 38 M.J. 627 (A.F.C.M.R. 1993) (making and uttering bad check offenses were not multiplicious).
156. 37 M.J. at 376.
157. *Id.* United States v. Morris, 40 M.J. 792 (A.F.C.M.R. 1994) (court concluded that Congress overtly intended that rape and carnal knowledge are multiplicious).
158. *Id.*
159. *Id.* United States v. Albrecht, 43 M.J. 65 (1995) (court determined that Congress intended to create two different forgery offenses in Article 123; falsely making or altering a writing and uttering that writing).
160. 37 M.J. at 379. *See also* United States v. Lenior, 39 M.J. 751, 753-54 (A.F.C.M.R. 1994) (Heimburg, J., concurring) (discussion of multiplicity vs. cumulative punishments).
161. *See, e.g.*, United States v. Wheeler, 40 M.J. 242 (C.M.A. 1994) (applying elements test, court concluded that adultery and indecent acts were not multiplicious for findings and both were not multiplicious with Article 134 general-disorder findings); United States v. Carter, 39 M.J. 754 (A.F.C.M.R. 1994) (adultery and dereliction of duty are separate offenses; housebreaking and destruction of property are separate offenses); United States v. Lenoir, 39 M.J. 751 (A.F.C.M.R. 1994) (applying different elements test, court concluded that unlawful entry and assault consummated by a battery are separate offenses); United States v. Hancock, 38 M.J. 672 (A.F.C.M.R. 1993) (noting that Teters decision had adopted separate elements test for findings, the court nonetheless applied the "insistent flow and single impulse" tests in finding that charges were multiplicious for purposes of sentencing).

ments test is also used to determine whether an offense is a lesser included offense.[162]

The important point here is that where the issue of multiplicity is raised, the government apparently has more leeway at the pleading stage [163] of the trial than at the findings and sentencing stages. If in fact the charges are multiplicious, however, the defense should move to dismiss one or more of the charges.[164] If the prosecution can show that the exigencies of proof require multiplicious pleading, the judge may defer ruling on the issue until findings have been made.[165] Dismissal is appropriate where the multiplication of charges would unfairly influence the fact-finder [166] or otherwise deny the accused a fair trial or frustrate preparation of a defense.[167]

For further discussions on multiplicious pleadings as they relate to findings and sentencing, see §§ 15-16 and 16-27(D), respectively.

Cf. United States v. Neblock, 40 M.J. 747 (A.F.C.M.R. 1994) (in determining whether multiple prosecutions under general article are multiplicious, the court stated that the court should look at the particular offenses recognized under Article 134, i.e., each paragraph of Part IV of the MCM must be considered a statute for purposes of multiplicity analysis).

162. In United States v. Foster, 40 M.J. 140 (C.M.A. 1994) the court adopted the elements test and concluded that in military jurisprudence, the term "necessarily included" in Article 79 includes derivative offenses under Article 134. The court noted that it would be sound practice to charge both the enumerated offense and any analogous Article 134 offenses as an alternative. The court members would be instructed on the elements and told that the accused could not be convicted of both. If the court convicts him of the greater offense, no findings are entered with regard to the lesser offense and it is dismissed.

Cf. United States v. Weymouth, 43 M.J. 329 (1995) (trial judge did not abuse discretion in granting defense motion to dismiss charges and specifications, without prejudice, which alleged lesser included offenses of attempted murder; the trial court indicated that if the evidence raised the lesser offenses, he would instruct on them; case includes extensive discussion on multiplicity problems; concurring opinion by Judge Crawford labels multiplicity as a "Hydra").

163. *See, e.g.,* United States v. Doss, 15 M.J. 409, 419 (C.M.A. 1983). For a discussion of how multiplicious pleadings may be treated at the various stages of trial, see United States v. Howard, 24 M.J. 897 (C.G.C.M.R. 1987).

164. *See* § 13-3(J). United States v. Abendschein, 19 M.J. 619 (A.C.M.R. 1984) (accused's choice of trial forum does not relieve the judge from sua sponte remedying multiplicious pleadings).

165. *See, e.g.,* United States v. Stegall, 6 M.J. 176 (C.M.A. 1979) (exigency of proof is only justifiable reason for permitting government to proceed on multiplicious offense); United States v. Gibson, 11 M.J. 434, 438 (C.M.A. 1981) (Cook, J., concurring in part, dissenting in part) (judge would be ill-advised to dismiss one or more charges); United States v. Gardner, 36 M.J. 543 (A.C.M.R. 1992), *aff'd on other grounds*, 41 M.J. 189 (C.M.A. 1994) (judge properly denied motion by accused that government choose which of three charges were multiplicious; court indicated it was proper for all three to be submitted to the members with an instruction that they could only find the accused guilty of one of them). *See also* § 13-3(J); United States v. Morris, 18 M.J. 450 (C.M.A. 1984) (multiplicious assault charges could stand until judge could determine from evidence whether either or both charges were proved by prosecution); United States v. Turner, 28 M.J. 536 (C.G.C.M.R. 1989).

166. United States v. Sturdivant, 13 M.J. 323 (C.M.A. 1982).

167. *See* United States v. Baker, 14 M.J. 361, 364, n. 1 (1983).

§ 6-2. Forwarding of Charges.

After the charges are drafted and sworn to, they are forwarded up through the chain of command along with supporting evidence and recommendations of each commander who reviews the charges and the accompanying materials.[1] The discussion here centers on the options and duties of these commanders: the summary court-martial convening authority, the special court-martial convening authority, and the general court-martial convening authority. Appendix 4 presents a graphical demonstration of this forwarding process.

§ 6-2(A). Immediate Commander.

The immediate commander,"[2] the individual who usually prefers the charges, should immediately inform the accused of the charges[3] and note that on the charge sheet.[4] The charge sheet and sworn statements, investigators' reports, and other supporting documentary evidence should be promptly forwarded by transmittal letter[5] to the next higher commander, who is normally the summary court-martial convening authority,[6] with recommendations as to the type of court-martial that should hear the case and whether the accused should be retained in the armed forces.[7] If someone other than the immediate commanding officer prefers charges, they should ordinarily be forwarded to that officer for his consideration. Failure to do so is not jurisdictional error but should be tested for prejudice.[8]

---

1. United States v. Foley, 37 M.J. 822 (A.F.C.M.R. 1993). In *Foley*, the court addressed the question of whether the commanders in the chain must believe that the charges are true before forwarding them. The court concluded that if the commander has any doubts about the charges or their disposition, it is not error to forward them to the next higher commander who will probably have more expertise. The court noted that doing so puts the charges to the test at trial, and the trial is itself the remedy for controversies about the process leading to referral.

2. The "immediate" commander is normally the accused's commanding officer. For example, in the Army that would be the company commander. *Cf.* United States v. Gifford, 16 M.J. 578 (A.C.M.R. 1983) (officer assigned to command "rear detachment" was immediate commander for purposes of forwarding charges, etc.).

3. Article 30(b), U.C.M.J. *See* Appendix 3. *See also* Article 10, U.C.M.J., at Appendix 3, which requires immediate steps to inform an accused who has been incarcerated of the charges. United States v. Wallace, 14 M.J. 869 (C.G.C.M.R. 1982) (further notice not required if accused already knows; issue waived by failing to raise it at trial).

4. *See* Appendix 6. Failure to record this event is not jurisdictional error. United States v. Moore, 6 M.J. 644 (N.C.M.R. 1978).

5. *See* R.C.M. 401(c)(2)(A) Discussion. The actual form of this letter is not crucial and varies among the services.

6. R.C.M. 402 governs action on charges by a commander who is authorized to administer nonjudicial punishment but not authorized to convene a court-martial. This may very well be a commander "between" the immediate commander and the summary court-martial convening authority. According to R.C.M. 402 that commander may dismiss the charges or forward them for action by a superior authority. This sort of situation will be possible where a commander in the chain of command has had his convening powers withheld by a superior commander. *See* R.C.M. 401(a) Discussion.

7. R.C.M. 401(c)(2).

8. United States v. Jones, 15 M.J. 890 (A.C.M.R. 1983).

§ 6-2(B). Summary Court-Martial Convening Authority.

Upon receipt of the charges, the summary court-martial convening authority[9] annotates page two of the charge sheet to reflect the time of receipt and thus tolls the statute of limitations.[10] If in reviewing the charges he notes any minor defects, he may correct them himself, initialing the corrections.[11] The convening authority's options[12] include: (1) dismissing the charges; (2) referring the charges to a summary court-martial; (3) returning the charges to immediate commander for appropriate disposition; (4) forwarding the charges with his recommendations to the special court-martial convening authority; or (5) directing that an Article 32 investigation[13] be held if he feels that the charges may ultimately warrant a general court-martial. In exercising those options the convening authority has substantial discretion and a superior's attempts to control that discretion may constitute unlawful command influence.[14]

§ 6-2(C). Special Court-Martial Convening Authority.

The special court-martial convening authority's[15] options generally parallel those of the summary court-martial convening authority and, in practice, the two functions are usually vested in the same individual. The major difference is the additional power of this convening authority to refer the charges to a

---

9. See Art. 24, U.C.M.J. for a list of who may serve as a summary court-martial convening authority. In United States v. Tucker, 17 M.J. 1004 (N.M.C.M.R. 1984) (en banc) (overruling United States v. Rice, 15 M.J. 605 (N.M.C.M.R. 1982), the court held that U.C.M.J. does not contemplate that only one officer may act as an SCM CA for purposes of receiving sworn charges); but there must be some identifiable nexus between the accused and that convening authority. See also United States v. Milkinevich, 17 M.J. 516 (A.F.C.M.R. 1983); United States v. Centeno, 17 M.J. 642 (N.M.C.M.R. 1983).

10. Art. 43, U.C.M.J.; R.C.M. 907(b)(2)(B); Frage v. Moriarty, 27 M.J. 341 (C.M.A. 1988) (charges sworn to before officer not authorized to administer oaths did not toll statute of limitations).

In United States v. Waller, 24 M.J. 266 (C.M.A. 1987), the court noted that "trial on basis of referral of timely received charge sheet is not barred simply because a second untimely received charge sheet exists." But in this case there was only one charge sheet with an extra page 3 (old form), and the commander had reduced the charge of desertion to absence without leave; there was thus no change in the nature of the originally charged offense. See also § 6-1.

11. R.C.M. 401(a) Discussion. If the changes are major in nature, the charge may have to be repreferred and sworn to. See § 6-1(B)(2).

12. See generally R.C.M. 403.

13. See § 7-2. See also United States v. Lillie, 4 M.J. 907 (N.C.M.R. 1978); United States v. Donaldson, 49 C.M.R. 542 (C.M.A. 1975).

14. R.C.M. 401(a) Discussion. United States v. Wojciechowski, 19 M.J. 577 (N.M.C.M.R. 1984) (fact that subordinate CA said that he was going to send the accused to a GCM did not indicate that he did not make a careful and well-reasoned decision to recommend a GCM). See also § 6-4.

15. Art. 23, U.C.M.J. See Appendix 4; R.C.M. 404. United States v. Nix, 40 M.J. 6 (C.M.A. 1994) (SPCM's authority to forward case with recommendations was called into question; he may have acted for personal reasons rather than official).

§ 6-2(D)   MILITARY CRIMINAL JUSTICE   § 6-3(A)

special court-martial, *i.e.*, the intermediate level of court-martial which may impose a bad-conduct discharge and six months confinement at hard labor.[16]

§ 6-2(D). General Court-Martial Convening Authority.

The general court-martial convening authority's[17] options include those possessed by the subordinate commanders.[18] Thus he could dismiss the charges, or refer the charges to either a summary or special court-martial.[19] If he decides that the charges are serious and that referral of the charges to a general court-martial is the most appropriate disposition, two key procedural criteria must first be met: a formal pretrial investigation into the basis of the charges,[20] and presentation by the staff judge advocate of a written pretrial advice.[21]

PART II
COMMAND INFLUENCE

§ 6-3. Command Influence; In General.

As the next sections point out, one of the pervasive features of the military justice system is the role of the commander in influencing the actions of the participants. While much of the command control of the system is beneficial and insures a well-organized and timely disposition of charges against an accused, there are dangers in the form of unlawful command influence. Although the problem is potentially present at all stages of the court-martial process, it is most likely to appear first in the preferral stage, when subordinate commanders are considering what, if any, charges to prefer. Thus, the topic is included in this chapter.

§ 6-3(A). The Perpetual Problem of Unlawful Command Influence.

One of the most controversial aspects of military justice is the potential influence that a commander and his or her representatives may have on judicial proceedings.[1] Indeed, unlawful command influence has been labelled

---

16. *See supra* § 4-3(B).
17. Art. 22, U.C.M.J.
18. R.C.M. 407.
19. The power to refer to a general court-martial necessarily includes the power to refer a case to the lesser courts.
20. Art. 32, U.C.M.J. *See also infra* § 7-2.
21. Art. 34, U.C.M.J. *See also infra* § 7-3.

1. *See generally* Bower, "Unlawful Command Influence: Preserving the Delicate Balance," 28 M.J. A.F. L. Rev. 65 (1988); DeGiulio, "Command Control: Lawful versus Unlawful Application," 10 SAN DIEGO L. REV. 72 (1972); Gaydos & Warren, "What Commanders Need to Know About Unlawful Command Control," ARMY LAW., Oct. 1986, at 9; Harty, "Unlawful Command Influence and Modern Military Justice," 36 NAVAL L. REV. 231 (1986); Hely, "Command Influence on Military Justice," 15 ST. LOUIS U. L.J. 300 (1970); Johnson, *Unlawful Command Influence: A Question of Balance*, The Judge Advocate General (Navy) Journal 87, 88 (March-April 1965);

"the mortal enemy of military justice."[2] It is ironic that the positive attributes of command control which ensure the military justice system works smoothly, quickly, and justly, can become the bane of the system. The problem of unlawful command influence is specifically mentioned in both the U.C.M.J. and the Manual for Courts-Martial. Article 37, U.C.M.J. prohibits commanders, and others,[3] from unlawfully influencing the action of a court-martial,[4] and Article 98 makes punishable the failure to promptly dispose of charges or to enforce any other provision in the U.C.M.J.[5] To date, there have been no recorded prosecutions under Article 98.[6] The *Manual* also also addresses the problem of command influence and focuses on attempts to influence the actions of counsel, judges, and court members.[7]

Despite prohibitions in the Uniform Code of Military Justice and strong admonitions in case law,[8] unlawful command influence has remained a per-

---

Schwender, "Who's Afraid of Command Influence; or Can the Court of Military Appeals Be This Wrong?" ARMY LAW., April 1992, at 19; Rob, "From *Treakle* to *Thomas*: The Evolution of the Law of Unlawful Command Influence," ARMY LAW., Nov. 1987, at 36; Thwing, "An Appearance of Evil," ARMY LAW., Sept. 1983, at 13; West, "A History of Command Influence on the Military Judicial System," 18 U.C.L.A. L. REV. 1 (1970). Moyer, *Justice and the Military*, Chapter 3 (1972).

2. United States v. Thomas, 22 M.J. 388, 393 (C.M.A. 1986). *See also* United States v. Sullivan, 26 M.J. 442, 444 (C.M.A. 1988) (quoting *Thomas*); United States v. Carlucci, 26 M.J. 328, 332 (C.M.A. 1988) (citing the language in *Thomas*); United States v. Gleason, 39 M.J. 776, 782 (A.C.M.R. 1994), *rev'd*, 43 M.J. 69 (1995) (unlawful command influence is a malignancy that eats away at the fairness of our military justice system).

3. Although most cases of command influence involve commanders, the proscriptions against such influence actually extend to "all persons subject to the code." *See, e.g.*, United States v. Hilow, 32 M.J. 439 (C.M.A. 1991) (court held Article 37 clearly applies to commander's subordinates); United States v. Kitts, 23 M.J. 105 (C.M.A. 1987) (court remanded case for *Dubay* hearing on whether SJA committed unlawful command influence); United States v. Carlson, 21 M.J. 847 (A.C.M.R. 1986) (Article 37 extends to NCO); United States v. Hamilton, 41 M.J. 32 (C.M.A. 1994) (court recognized that actions of SJA might amount to unlawful influence; facts did not support argument that SJA's comments to commander amounted to command influence to prefer court-martial charges).

Cf. United States v. Stombaugh, 40 M.J. 208 (C.M.A. 1994) (court distinguished peer pressure from unlawful command influence and indicated that its decisions on the issue involved some mantle of official authority or rank; dissenting opinion by Chief Judge Sullivan rejected dissection of Article 37 and implication that prejudice standard of United States v. Thomas, is inapplicable where someone other than commander unlawfully influences court-martial).

4. *See* Appendix 3. United States v. Gleason, 43 M.J. 69 (1995) (commander's actions fell squarely within Article 37). Military courts have held that this proscription also extends to attempts to influence witnesses. *See, e.g.*, United States v. Serino, 24 M.J. 848 (A.F.C.M.R.); United States v. Treakle, 18 M.J. 646 (A.C.M.R. 1984), *aff'd*, 23 M.J. 151 (C.M.A. 1986) (summary disposition). *Cf.* United States v. Stombaugh, 40 M.J. 208 (C.M.A. 1994) (court distinguished peer pressure from unlawful command influence and indicated that its decisions on the issue involved some mantle of official authority or rank; dissenting opinion by Chief Judge Sullivan rejected dissection of Article 37 and implication that prejudice standard of United States v. Thomas, is inapplicable where someone other than commander unlawfully influences court-martial).

5. *See* Appendix 3.
6. *Id.*
7. *See* R.C.M. 104.
8. *See* United States v. Thomas, 22 M.J. 388 (C.M.A. 1986) (strong warning about continuing problems of command influence).

petual problem.[9] While most commanders are sensitive enough to the problem to avoid open attempts to influence a court-martial, it is more common for well-intended commanders, or members of their staff, to make passing comments on the merits of past or pending cases.[10] Pragmatically, no matter how well-intentioned or careful the commander or staff officers might be, such comments can be interpreted by subordinates as a "command" or "desire" for a particular result.[11] This appearance or perception of unlawful command influence can be as much of a problem as actual command influence.[12]

§ 6-3(B). Lawful and Unlawful Influence Distinguished.

Because commanders play an important role in administering military justice, the key inquiry in any given case is whether the commander exercised lawful or unlawful influence.[13] The former is permitted, the latter forbidden. In essence, unlawful command influence results from impermissible command control where a superior substitutes (or attempts to substitute) his or her judgment for that of a subordinate who should be allowed to exercise independent judgment.[14] The military courts have repeatedly recognized the difficult responsibility commanders face in maintaining a "delicate balance" between military justice and command discipline.[15] Unfortunately, the fine line that distinguishes lawful command control of a case from unlawful command influence of its disposition is not always easy to draw. The number and types of command influence cases decided by military courts do provide some guidance, however. Some general principles gleaned from the case law are discussed in § 6-4 through § 6-6 and apply to various stages of the trial.

---

9. *See generally* Rob, "From *Treakle* to *Thomas:* The Evolution of the Law of Unlawful Command Influence," ARMY LAW., Nov. 1977, at 36.

10. *See, e.g.*, United States v. Gleason, 39 M.J. 776 (A.C.M.R. 1994), *rev'd*, 43 M.J. 69 (1995) (in most cases, evil of unlawful command influence is shown by overt actions; here, there was no single action on which to hang label of unlawful influence).

11. *See, e.g.*, United States v. Jameson, 33 M.J. 669 (N.M.C.M.R. 1991) (military justice system victimized regardless of whether source of unlawful command influence intended adverse effects on case or not); United States v. Treakle, 18 M.J. 646 (A.C.M.R. 1984), *aff'd*, 23 M.J. 151 (C.M.A. 1986) (summary disposition) (general's command briefings made many listeners feel they shouldn't testify favorably for accused U.C.M.J. offenders); United States v. Pierce, 29 C.M.R. 849 (A.B.R. 1960) (during officers' call, commander jokingly said he wanted to see accused "hanged").

12. This point is discussed in more detail at § 6-3(C).

13. United States v. Lynch, 35 M.J. 579 (C.G.C.M.R. 1992) (Coast Guard Commandant had responsibility to warn officers of dangers associated with navigation of vessels; message did not imply that action should be taken against the accused for loss of vessel). *See generally* Gaydos & Warren, "What Commanders Need to Know About Unlawful Command Control," ARMY LAW., Oct. 1986, at 9.

14. United States v. Wallace, 39 M.J. 284 (C.M.A. 1994) (superior commander's suggestion that company commander reconsider decision to dispose of offenses by nonjudicial punishment was not unlawful command influence; court noted that complete record on issue had facilitated disposition of issue); United States v. Allen, 31 M.J. 572 (N.M.C.M.R. 1990), *aff'd*, 33 M.J. 209 (C.M.A. 1991).

15. *See, e.g.,* United States v. Rosser, 6 M.J. 267 (C.M.A. 1979); United States v. Isbell, 3 C.M.A. 782, 14 C.M.R. 200 (1954); United States v. Littrice, 3 C.M.A. 487, 13 C.M.R. 43 (1953); United States v. Black, 40 M.J. 615 (N.M.C.M.R. 1994) (type of alliance forged between prosecutor, commander, and material witnesses to effect change in testimony ignored the delicate balance between military justice and command discipline).

§ 6-3(C). Actual, Apparent, and Perceived Unlawful Command Influence.

Unlawful command influence can exist in a variety of forms,[16] and it can occur even though the source of the influence did not intend to affect a case.[17] *Actual* unlawful command influence occurs when, under the totality of the circumstances, the evidence would lead a reasonable person to conclude that command influence affected the disposition of a case and prejudiced the accused.[18] One military court has suggested it occurs "when the convening authority has been brought into the deliberation room."[19] After viewing all the evidence describing what "actually" happened, military courts determine if actual command influence occurred based on their expertise in military affairs.[20] In other words, determinations of actual command influence are "based upon considerations from *inside* the military justice system."[21]

In contrast, *apparent* unlawful command influence occurs when reasonable members of the "public"[22] believe command influence prejudiced the accused.[23] Thus, this type of unlawful influence is based upon extrinsic considerations, i.e., those from *outside* the system.[24] The question of whether apparent unlawful influence existed is only relevant when no actual unlawful influence

---

16. *See, e.g.,* United States v. Allen, 31 M.J. 572 (N.M.C.M.R. 1990), *aff'd,* 33 M.J. 209 (C.M.A. 1991) (courts recognize both actual and apparent unlawful command influence); United States v. Johnson, 14 C.M.A. 548, 34 C.M.R. 328 (1964) (unlawful command influence can be actual or apparent); United States v. Hamilton, 41 M.J. 32 (C.M.A. 1994) (term "unlawful command influence" used broadly in military jurisprudence to cover multitude of situations).

17. United States v. Jameson, 33 M.J. 669 (N.M.C.M.R. 1991) (unlawful command influence need not be intentional).

18. *See, e.g.,* United States v. Cruz, 20 M.J. 873 (A.C.M.R. 1985), *rev'd on other grounds,* 25 M.J. 326 (C.M.A. 1987); United States v. Anderson, 26 M.J. 555 (A.C.M.R. 1988). *See also* Bower, "Unlawful Command Influence: Preserving the Delicate Balance," 28 A.F. L. REV. 65, 82 (1988).

19. United States v. Allen, 31 M.J. 572 (N.M.C.M.R. 1990), *aff'd,* 33 M.J. 209 (C.M.A. 1991) (*citing* United States v. Grady, 15 M.J. 275 (C.M.A. 1983)).

20. United States v. Cruz, 20 M.J. 873 (A.C.M.R. 1985), *rev'd on other grounds,* 25 M.J. 326 (C.M.A. 1987).

21. *See, e.g.,* United States v. Allen, 31 M.J. 572 (N.M.C.M.R. 1990), *aff'd,* 33 M.J. 209 (C.M.A. 1991); United States v. Cruz, 20 M.J. 873 (A.C.M.R. 1985), *rev'd on other grounds,* 25 M.J. 326 (C.M.A. 1987).

22. The "public" has been defined to include "not only the civilian population, but also the rank and file of the services because most servicemembers are not directly involved with the military criminal justice system." United States v. Allen, 31 M.J. 572 (N.M.C.M.R. 1990), *aff'd,* 33 M.J. 209 (C.M.A. 1991); United States v. Cruz, 20 M.J. 873 (A.C.M.R. 1985), *rev'd on other grounds,* 25 M.J. 326 (C.M.A. 1987). *See also* Gaydos & Warren, "What Commanders Need to Know About Unlawful Command Control," ARMY LAW., Oct. 1986, at 10.

23. *See, e.g.,* United States v. Rosser, 6 M.J. 267 (C.M.A. 1979); United States v. Campos, 37 M.J. 894 (A.C.M.R. 1993) (definition of apparent command influence); United States v. Lynch, 35 M.J. 579 (C.G.C.M.R. 1992) (evidence failed to show actual or apparent unlawful command influence; Commandant sent message to commands urging safer navigation practices, following incident involving loss of vessel under command of accused); United States v. Cruz, 20 M.J. 873 (A.C.M.R. 1985), *rev'd on other grounds,* 25 M.J. 326 (C.M.A. 1987).

24. United States v. Cruz, 20 M.J. 873 (A.C.M.R. 1985), *rev'd on other grounds,* 25 M.J. 326 (C.M.A. 1987).

exists because remedying any actual influence will most likely remove the appearance of prejudice.[25]

Actual unlawful command influence affects the actual fairness of a trial while the appearance of unlawful command influence merely affects the level of "public" confidence in the military justice system.[26] Although it has no direct impact on the fairness of a trial, the appearance of unlawful command influence is as much to be condemned as its actual existence.[27] Therefore, the template for measuring prejudice from unlawful command influence is not simply whether such influence actually existed, but instead whether there is an appearance of such influence.[28]

Perceived unlawful command influence is another distinct concept of influence that can fall into either category of actual or apparent unlawful command influence.[29] This type of influence focuses on how the recipient of command influence perceives that influence.[30] If the recipient is a court member and his or her independent judgment is affected by the influence or if the recipient is a witness who decides to testify differently or not at all as a result of the influence, actual command influence has occurred. On the other hand, if the recipient is a sufficiently large group of servicemembers (i.e., members of the "public"), and members of that group perceive that the command influence affects the overall fairness of the system, then apparent unlawful command influence has occurred.[31] In all cases, the perception by the recipient must be reasonable in light of the circumstances.[32]

§ 6-4. Pretrial Command Influence.

Unlawful influence on the military justice system can be a problem at virtually every level. The Court of Appeals for the Armed Forces has indicated that in addressing unlawful command influence, there should be a distinction between the accusatorial process and the adjudicative process.[1] Unlawful command influence in the accusatorial process, i.e., preferral, forwarding, and

---

25. *Id.* at 883-84.
26. *Id.* at 873.
27. United States v. Johnson, 14 C.M.A. 548, 34 C.M.R. 328 (1964). *See generally* Gaydos & Warren, "What Commanders Need to Know About Unlawful Command Control," ARMY LAW., Oct. 1986, at 9, 10 (provides brief history and discussion on level of public confidence in military justice system).
28. United States v. Rodriguez, 16 M.J. 740 (A.F.C.M.R. 1983). *See also* United States v. Rosser, 6 M.J. 267 (1979).
29. *See* Bower, "Unlawful Command Influence: Preserving the Delicate Balance," 28 A.F. L. REV. 65, 82, n. 106 (1988). *But see* United States v. Cruz, 20 M.J. 873 (A.C.M.R. 1985), *rev'd on other grounds,* 25 M.J. 326 (C.M.A. 1987) (perception applicable only to actual unlawful command influence).
30. *See* Bower, "Unlawful Command Influence: Preserving the Delicate Balance," 28 A.F. L. REV. 65, 81 (1988).
31. *See* Gaydos & Warren, "What Commanders Need to Know About Unlawful Command Control," ARMY LAW., Oct. 1986, at 9, 10. *Cf.* United States v. Lowery, 18 M.J. 695 (A.F.C.M.R. 1984) (admonishing witness for one trial likely to have a "chilling effect" on judicial system).
32. United States v. Johnson, 14 C.M.A. 548, 34 C.M.R. 328 (1964).
1. United States v. Weasler, 43 M.J. 15 (1995).

referral of charges may generally be waived.[2] The next sections briefly address the impact of such influence on various stages of pretrial processing of a case.

§ 6-4(A). The Preliminary Inquiry and Preferring Charges.

It is a lawful exercise of command influence for commanders to conduct preliminary inquiries whereby they can gather facts and evidence concerning members under their commands who are accused or suspected of committing U.C.M.J. offenses.[3] Problems can arise when the commander conducting the preliminary inquiry is a general or special courts-martial convening authority. If he or she becomes an accuser by deciding to prefer charges based on preliminary inquiry findings,[4] he or she will be disqualified from convening a subsequent court-martial to try those preferred charges.[5] Therefore, command influence during a preliminary inquiry will not usually be unlawful unless the convening authority ordering the inquiry also attempts to prefer and refer the same charges.[6] Attempts by a superior to direct a subordinate to prefer charges may also result in a finding of unlawful command influence.[7] Commanders in the chain of command who are responsible for reviewing the charges and forwarding them with their individual recommendations for disposition, should also be free from unlawful influence.[8]

§ 6-4(B). Command Influence on Article 32 Investigations.

Command influence issues also come into play when a convening authority appoints an investigating officer to conduct a pretrial investigation under Article 32 of the U.C.M.J.[9] Although the convening authority is not required to be neutral and detached, he must appoint an investigating officer who will

---

2. *Id.*
3. *See* R.C.M. 303. United States v. Wallace, 39 M.J. 284 (C.M.A. 1994) (superior commander's suggestion that company commander reconsider decision to dispose of offenses by nonjudicial punishment was not unlawful command influence).
4. *See supra* § 6-1.
5. *See* R.C.M. 504(c)(1). *See also infra* § 6-4(C).
6. *See also* § 6-4(C).
7. United States v. Weasler, 43 M.J. 15 (1995) (captain directed lieutenant how to prefer charges in her absence as commander).
8. United States v. Davis, 37 M.J. 152 (C.M.A. 1993) (commander independently arrived at recommendation that accused be tried by general court-martial; he had originally considered imposing nonjudicial punishment). *Cf.* United States v. Hawthorne, 22 C.M.R. 83 (C.M.A. 1956).
United States v. Drayton, 39 M.J. 871 (A.C.M.R. 1994) (court held that rules governing unlawful command influence govern adjudicary process, not accusatory process; thus attempts by superior to direct particular action in forwarding charges not subject to unlawful command influence; court indicated that relief might be found in showing that superior was de facto accuser or that R.C.M. rules governing processing of charges were not followed).
9. *See, e.g.,* United States v. Brammel, 29 M.J. 958 (A.C.M.R.), *aff'd,* 32 M.J. 3 (C.M.A. 1990) (order from convening authority to investigating officer to use partition between victim of child sexual abuse and accused not unlawful command influence).

be impartial.[10] Because an Article 32 investigation is "judicial in nature"[11] *ex parte* contacts between the investigating officer and those involved in prosecuting the accused may give rise to a presumption of prejudice toward the accused.[12] This presumption would impose a heavy burden on the prosecution to present clear and convincing evidence to the contrary or risk dismissal of the case.[13]

§ 6-4(C). Command Influence on Referral of Charges.

An accuser, usually the commander who prefers charges against an accused, is prohibited from convening a court-martial.[14] Under both the U.C.M.J. and military case law, a convening authority is an "accuser" if he or she "has any interest other than official interest in the prosecution of the accused."[15] Also, a convening authority must remain neutral and free from any influence from the accuser.[16] The test adopted by the military courts for determining if the convening authority is disqualified from referring charges is whether there is a reasonable probability that the convening authority is personally interested in the outcome of the litigation.[17] Therefore, a form of unlawful command influence occurs whenever the accuser also refers the charges to a court-martial.

When a convening authority exercises his or her authority to refer charges to a court-martial, he or she must do so impartially and must not be actually or apparently influenced by superiors.[18] Generally, a superior may announce policies to a convening authority so long as the convening authority understands that he or she can accept or reject such guidance and maintain independent judgment.[19] Once a case is referred to trial, a superior convening

---

10. United States v. Freedman, 23 M.J. 820 (N.M.C.M.R. 1987); United States v. Wojciechowski, 19 M.J. 577 (N.M.C.M.R. 1984).
11. United States v. Davis, 20 M.J. 61 (C.M.A. 1985); United States v. Payne, 3 M.J. 354, 355, n. 5 (C.M.A. 1977).
12. *See, e.g.,* United States v. Dababneh, 28 M.J. 929 (N.M.C.M.R. 1989); *see also* § 6-7.
13. *See, e.g.,* United States v. Payne, 3 M.J. 354 (C.M.A. 1977); United States v. Dababneh, 28 M.J. 929 (N.M.C.M.R. 1989); United States v. Freedman, 23 M.J. 820, (N.M.C.M.R. 1987). *But see* United States v. Bramel, 29 M.J. 958 (A.C.M.R.), aff'd, 32 M.J. 3 (C.M.A. 1990).
14. R.C.M. 504. *See also* Art. 22(a) and Art. 23(a), U.C.M.J. in Appendix 3.
15. Art. 1(9), U.C.M.J. *See also* United States v. Thomas, 22 M.J. 388 (C.M.A. 1986).
16. United States v. LaGrange, 1 C.M.A. 342, 3 C.M.R. 76 (1952) (court-martial not legally convened where convening authority was junior in rank to the accuser); United States v. Lynch, 35 M.J. 579 (C.G.C.M.R. 1992) (no causal connection between message issued by Commandant concerning navigation practices and referral of charges against accused for loss of vessel).
17. *See, e.g.,* United States v. Corcoran, 17 M.J. 137 (C.M.A. 1984); United States v. Crossley, 10 M.J. 376 (C.M.A. 1981); United States v. Gordon, 1 C.M.A. 255, 2 C.M.R. 161 (1952).
18. United States v. Hamilton, 41 M.J. 32 (C.M.A. 1994) (no unlawful command influence exerted on commanders to refer case to court-martial after Article 15 was imposed by unit commander). *See, e.g.,* United States v. Hagen, 25 M.J. 78 (C.M.A. 1987) (Sullivan, J., concurring). In United States v. Allen, 31 M.J. 572 (N.M.C.M.R. 1990), the convening authority testified that he had felt no pressure from Secretary of the Navy in referring accused's national security case to general court-martial.
19. *See, e.g.,* United States v. Rivera, 12 C.M.A. 507, 31 C.M.R. 93 (1961); United States v. Betts, 12 C.M.A. 214, 30 C.M.R. 214 (1961); United States v. Lawson, 33 M.J. 946 (N.M.C.M.R.

authority may intervene and cause the charges to be withdrawn and referred to a higher court-martial.[20] This exercise of authority will not amount to unlawful command influence if the withdrawal is not arbitrary or unfair to the accused and there is good reason for the withdrawal.[21]

§ 6-4(D). Command Influence in Selecting Court Members.

Because a convening authority is responsible for selecting court members to serve on courts-martial he or she convenes,[22] the potential for claims of unlawful command influence is high. Although Article 25(d) of the U.C.M.J. gives the convening authority broad discretion in selecting panel members,[23] the Court of Appeals for the Armed Forces has held this provision means a convening authority must select those he believes to be "experienced, impartial, and fair in fulfilling their adjudicatory responsibilities."[24] Thus, selection of court members to secure a more favorable result to the prosecution amounts to unlawful command influence.[25] Likewise, unlawful command influence may result from the deliberate stacking of the pool of potential courts-martial members by the convening authority's subordinates, even if the convening authority is unaware of such conduct.[26]

§ 6-4(E). Pretrial Comments and Actions.

While the commander has an obligation to assure the community at large that the criminal actions of accuseds will be investigated and, if appropriate, prosecuted, there is always a real danger that such comments will be misconstrued by those participating in the military criminal justice system. Ironically, the higher the rank of the commander making the comments, the greater the danger that those comments will be viewed as a command that a

---

1991) (Marine Corps Commandant issued strong statement about pending case before referral); United States v. Allen, 31 M.J. 572 (N.M.C.M.R. 1990), aff'd, 33 M.J. 209 (C.M.A. 1991). *Cf.* United States v. Kohut, 41 M.J. 565 (N.M.Ct.Crim.App. 1994) (convening authority's failure to obtain prior approval from Judge Advocate General before referring charges to trial, where accused had already been convicted in state court, was not jurisdictional error. The court set out four factors to be considered in determining whether a service regulation has restricted a convening authority's discretion to refer charges: (1) policy is typically not law; (2) accused may only assert regulation only if it is intended to protect an accused's right; (3) a court's duty to enforce agency regulation is clearest where compliance is required by Constitution or federal law; and (4) court has duty to enforce regulation if accused has relied upon it and will suffer substantially if regulation is not followed). *See also* United States v. Brown, 40 M.J. 625 (N.M.C.M.R. 1994) (setting out test).

20. *See, e.g.,* United States v. Blaylock, 15 M.J. 190 (C.M.A. 1983); United States v. Charette, 15 M.J. 197 (C.M.A. 1983). *But see* United States v. Hardy, 4 M.J. 20 (C.M.A. 1977).
21. *See, e.g.,* United States v. Blaylock, 15 M.J. 190 (C.M.A. 1983); United States v. Brown, 22 M.J. 597 (A.C.M.R. 1986). *See also* R.C.M. 604(b) and Chapter 8.
22. *See* Chapter 8.
23. *See* Appendix 3.
24. United States v. Hilow, 32 M.J. 439, 441 (C.M.A. 1991).
25. *See, e.g.,* United States v. Smith, 27 M.J. 242 (C.M.A. 1988); United States v. McClain, 22 M.J. 124 (C.M.A. 1986); United States v. Redman, 33 M.J. 679 (A.C.M.R. 1991).
26. United States v. Hilow, 32 M.J. 439, 441 (C.M.A. 1991).

particular result should be reached in the case.[27] Given the dangers lurking in such pretrial statements or briefings, the better practice is for the commander to avoid making statements about pending cases.[28]

Command influence may also appear when a commander takes particularly strong action against those suspected or accused of committing an offense. For example, in *United States v. Cruz*,[29] the commander held a mass formation, made a strong speech condemning drug activity, publicly stripped the culprits of their unit crests, and had them apprehended. The court concluded that although those actions might have amounted to illegal pretrial punishment under Article 13,[30] they did not affect the findings of guilt in the accused's case.

§ 6-5. Command Influence on Courts-Martial.

§ 6-5(A). Command Influence on Court Members, Judges, and Counsel.

Article 37(a) of the U.C.M.J. states, "no person subject to this chapter may attempt to coerce or, by any unauthorized means, influence the action of a court-martial or any military tribunal or any member thereof."[1] Although Article 37(a) provides some limited exceptions to this mandate,[2] these exceptions have been construed narrowly.[3] Essentially, it is unlawful command

---

27. United States v. Lynch, 35 M.J. 579 (C.G.C.M.R. 1992) (memo by Coast Guard Commandant was not considered unlawful command influence); United States v. Lawson, 33 M.J. 946 (N.M.C.M.R. 1991) (strongly worded statement by Marine Corps Commandant about pending trial; court found no unlawful command influence).
28. United States v. Hagen, 25 M.J. 78 (C.M.A. 1987) (Sullivan, J. concurring); United States v. Dickey, 41 M.J. 637 (N.M.Ct.Crim.App. 1994) (strong speech by CO to command re accuseds charged with rape as low lifes and scumbags was not unlawful command influence; CO was not convening authority and accused failed to show how speech deprived him of fair trial; court noted that the presumption of innocence does not control pretrial functions of commanders, etc. who are charged with concluding that it is more probable than not that an accused committed the offense in authorizing searches, etc.).
29. 25 M.J. 326 (C.M.A. 1987).
30. *See* Chapter 5.
1. *See* Appendix 3.
2. Article 37(a), U.C.M.J., provides that the mandate does not apply to "(1) general instructional or informational courses in military justice if such courses are designed solely for the purpose of instructing members of a command in the substantive and procedural aspects of courts-martial, or (2) to statements and instructions given in open court by the military judge, president of a special court-martial, or counsel."
3. *See, e.g.*, United States v. Brice, 19 M.J. 170 (C.M.A. 1986) (members' attendance at lecture on drug abuse given by convening authority during court-martial involving drugs constituted improper influence upon court); United States v. McCann, 8 C.M.A. 675, 25 C.M.R. 179 (1958) (members' attendance at "justice" lecture given by SJA during trial continuance improper because referred to offense accused charged with as more reprehensible in military than civilian community); United States v. Littrice, 3 C.M.A. 487, 13 C.M.R. 43 (1953) (commander's executive officer meeting with panel immediately prior to trial to give general instructions and policy guidance improper); United States v. Jones, 15 M.J. 967 (A.C.M.R. 1983) (in-court statements by military judge to court members after sentencing regarding his personal views of appropriate sentences improper).

§ 6-5(A)   PREFERRAL AND FORWARDING OF CHARGES   § 6-5(A)

influence if court members are targeted to receive certain comments about desired results or instructions regarding command policy.[4] But as the following discussion points out, command influence can arise during any contact with any participant in the trial. Obviously, not every contact is improper and the difficulty in assessing whether the contact was is not an easy task. In an extensive discussion of command influence, the court in *United States v. Allen*[5] listed six factors that the military courts have considered in deciding whether a commander's contacts were impermissible: (1) the timing of the contact; (2) who made the contact; (3) the type of contact; (4) the content of the contact; (5) who was contacted; and (6) the reasonable likelihood that the accused was prejudiced at trial.[6]

Members may be influenced outside the courtroom through "military justice" lectures and writings[7] or during other meetings where command desires are made known.[8] This type of impermissible influence can also occur, however, inside the courtroom if command policy statements are referred to by counsel[9] or the military judge[10] or when commanders or their representatives maintain an improper "presence" at the trial.[11]

---

4. *See, e.g.*, United States v. Brice, 19 M.J. 170 (C.M.A. 1986) (court members required to attend lecture on drug abuse given during court-martial with drug charges); United States v. Johnson, 14 C.M.A. 548, 34 C.M.R. 328 (1964) (issuing pamphlet entitled "Additional Instructions for Court Members" to court-martial members prejudiced accused); United States v. Zagar, 5 C.M.A. 410, 18 C.M.R. 34 (1955) (SJA lecture regarding accused's probable guilt given to members day before trial was unlawful command influence).

5. 31 M.J. 572 (N.M.C.M.R. 1990), *aff'd*, 33 M.J. 209 (C.M.A. 1991).

6. *See also* United States v. Lynch, 35 M.J. 579 (C.G.C.M.R. 1992) (citing *Allen* factors); United States v. Lawson, 33 M.J. 946 (N.M.C.M.R. 1991) (listing factors to be considered).

7. *See, e.g.*, United States v. Martinez, 42 M.J. 327 (1995) (commander's "We Care" regarding DUI's amounted to improper command influence to the extent that it suggested minimum punishments; court reminded that SJA's should monitor such letters and not be "potted plants" when it comes to avoiding command influence); United States v. Kitchens, 12 C.M.A. 589, 31 C.M.R. 175 (1961) (assistant SJA sent letter to all officers stationed where court-martial was pending and asked them to note the "considerable difference" in sentences imposed during two different periods); United States v. Hollcraft, 17 M.J. 1111 (A.C.M.R. 1984) (court held that pamphlet issued to court members was prohibited but not prejudicial to accused in this case).

8. *See, e.g.*, United States v. Reynolds, 40 M.J. 198 (C.M.A. 1994) (commander's informal comments at meeting concerning his position on drug offenses did not prejudice accused; although such comments were inappropriate, the four members who were present testified that they were not swayed by the comments and the accused later indicated that he did not want to pursue the issue for valid tactical reasons); United States v. Stephens, 21 M.J. 784 (A.C.M.R. 1986) (at NCO call, sergeant major indicated commander wanted anyone convicted of selling hashish to be sentenced to at least 30 years); United States v. Pierce, 29 C.M.R. 849 (A.B.R. 1960) (during officers' call where panel members were present, commander stated desire that accused be convicted and "hanged").

9. *See, e.g.*, United States v. Grady, 15 M.J. 275 (C.M.A. 1983) (sentence set aside because defense counsel referred to policy during voir dire); United States v. Estrada, 7 C.M.A. 635, 23 C.M.R. 99 (1957) (trial counsel read command policy during presentencing); United States v. Fowle, 7 C.M.A. 349, 22 C.M.R. 139 (1956) (trial counsel's reference to SECNAV instruction during trial condemned by court).

10. *See* United States v. Walk, 26 M.J. 665 (A.F.C.M.R. 1987).

11. *See infra* § 6-5(C). United States v. Reynolds, 40 M.J. 198 (C.M.A. 1994) (not clear whether president of panel's comments to junior member exceeded bounds of open and robust discussion during deliberations).

§ 6-5(A)

Contacts with military judges can also result in unlawful command influence.[12] It is a well-established principle that commanders and their representatives may not question or collaterally attack a judge's decision in any particular case.[13] Furthermore, *ex parte* communications from commanders or their representatives to a judge are inappropriate.[14]

In *United States v. Mabe*,[15] the court reiterated that command complaints against the sentences handed down by judges should not be made outside the adversary system and, if they are, they constitute unlawful command influence.[16] In *Mabe* the Chief Judge of the Navy Trial Judiciary sent an informal letter to the chief judge of one of the circuits stating that there was "dissatisfaction and criticism" over sentencing in unauthorized absence courts-martial within that circuit.[17] The court held that the letter constituted unlawful command influence even though it was not specifically directed at the accused's case.[18] In a similar case, the Deputy Judge Advocate General of the Navy called the chief judge of the judiciary to express concern that one of the judges being considered for detail to a case was a "light sentencer."[19] However, the Court held that any purported attempt to influence the selection of a military judge failed and the accused suffered no prejudice because the judge was still assigned to the case, and he had no knowledge of the complaint lodged against him.[20] Even though court-martial panels are more susceptible to unlawful command influence, these two recent cases illustrate that judge-alone sentencing would not necessarily solve the problem of command influence.[21]

Although a commander's directives to the trial counsel, the prosecutor, normally do not cause any problems, the commander could not, however, require the trial counsel to take actions which would be either illegal or unethical. Nor could the commander use the trial counsel as an instrument of unlawful influence on other potential witnesses or participants.[22] Any at-

---

12. *See, e.g.,* United States v. Campos, 42 M.J. 253 (1995) (no indication that trial judge was victim of unlawful command influence; judge had been replaced as senior judge and recognized that local rumors had reflected view that he was replaced because of his lighter sentences. The court added that it condemned calculated carping about judge's sentencing; the tradeoff for a system where judges do not have tenure and professional survival depends on grace, special vigilance is necessary to assure judicial independence); United States v. Allen, 33 M.J. 209 (C.M.A. 1991); United States v. Mabe, 33 M.J. 200 (C.M.A. 1991).
13. *See, e.g.,* United States v. Mabe, 33 M.J. 200 (C.M.A. 1991) (letter from Chief Judge of Navy Trial Judiciary to circuit chief judge voiced concern over "lenient" sentences and court held it was unlawful command influence); United States v. Carlucci, 26 M.J. 328 (C.M.A. 1988); United States v. Ledbetter, 2 M.J. 37 (C.M.A. 1976) (no official inquiries from outside adversary system into judges' decisions unless by independent judicial commission).
14. United States v. Allen, 33 M.J. 209 (C.M.A. 1991); United States v. Foley, 37 M.J. 822 (A.F.C.M.R. 1993) (military judge's brief ex parte communication with Article 32 investigating officer was not sufficient to show bias).
15. 33 M.J. 200 (C.M.A. 1991).
16. *Id.*
17. *Id.* at 202.
18. *Id.* at 206.
19. United States v. Allen, 33 M.J. 209, 211 (C.M.A. 1991).
20. *Id.* at 214.
21. *See infra* § 6-8.
22. In United States v. Sloan, 30 M.J. 741 (A.F.C.M.R. 1990), the court rejected the accused's arguments that the government had exercised unlawful command influence on two government

tempts to improperly pressure the defense counsel into taking, or abandoning a particular course of action could also amount to unlawful influence.[23]

§ 6-5(B). Command Influence on Witnesses.

The Court of Appeals for the Armed Forces has taken a very strong stance against attempts to frustrate the testimony of witnesses and has stated such attempts violate an accused's right to have access to favorable evidence.[24] Military courts have also held that unauthorized influence on witnesses with respect to their testimony violates Article 37 of the U.C.M.J., even though such influence is not specifically addressed in that provision.[25]

Exerting influence on witnesses may also raise constitutional issues. Discouraging witnesses from testifying on behalf of the accused, raises Sixth Amendment concerns in that it threatens the fundamental right to a fair trial, the right to compulsory process, and the right to cross-examine and confront witnesses, and the right to the assistance of counsel.[26] It also potentially violates Article 46 of the Uniform Code of Military Justice which assures the defense equal access to evidence.[27]

While intentional and direct attempts to influence witness testimony in a particular case are clearly prohibited,[28] witnesses can be improperly influ-

---

witnesses by refusing to provide them counsel before interviewing them and then ordering them, under a grant of immunity, to testify against the accused. The court noted that any rights violation that may have occurred were personal to the two witnesses involved and were not transferrable to the accused. The court did not address the issue of whether due process might have prevented use of the witnesses.

23. United States v. Kitts, 23 M.J. 105 (C.M.A. 1987) (court remanded case for *DuBay* hearing on issue of whether SJA had exercised unlawful command influence on witnesses, court members, and defense counsel); United States v. Lynch, 35 M.J. 579 (C.G.C.M.R. 1992) (no evidence that Chief of Military Justice attempted to chill defense counsel's post-trial duties).

24. United States v. Thomas, 22 M.J. 388 (C.M.A. 1986). *See also* United States v. Drayton, 39 M.J. 871 (A.C.M.R. 1994) (court found strong evidence that members in accused's unit were not improperly influenced not to testify against him); United States v. Gleason, 39 M.J. 776 (A.C.M.R. 1994) (court drastically reduced sentence where there was blatant unlawful influence on defense witnesses).

25. United States v. Stombaugh, 40 M.J. 208 (C.M.A. 1994) (pressure on defense witness not to testify was unlawful, but nonprejudicial); United States v. Washington, 42 M.J. 547 (A.F.Ct.Crim.App. 1995) (although accused established first prong of Levite-Stombaugh burden of production-test, he failed to show that commander's actions had resulted in unfair trial); United States v. Serino, 24 M.J. 848 (A.F.C.M.R.); United States v. Treakle, 18 M.J. 646 (A.C.M.R. 1984), aff'd, 23 M.J. 151 (C.M.A. 1986) (summary disposition).

26. United States v. Gleason, 43 M.J. 69 (1995).

27. Art. 46, U.C.M.J. *See also* Chapter 11.

28. *See, e.g.,* Cunningham v. Gilevich, 36 M.J. 94 (C.M.A. 1992) (unlawful command influence where commander told accused to testify before investigating board).

United States v. Stamper, 39 M.J. 1097 (A.C.M.R. 1994) (accused failed to show that former company commander's disparaging remarks amounted to improper influence on potential witnesses); United States v. Gleason, 39 M.J. 776 (A.C.M.R. 1994) (court recounted blatant efforts on part of commander to discourage witnesses to testify on behalf of accused, command sergeant major, who was held in very high regard by command); United States v. Clemons, 35 M.J. 770 (A.C.M.R. 1992) (accused's commander's action of counseling four potential defense witnesses concerning case amounted to unlawful command influence and his actions had chilling effect on

enced if there is an implication or perception that witnesses testifying on behalf of an accused will be cast in a negative light.[29]

The dangers associated with commenting on possible testimony of witnesses were made clear in *United States v. Thomas*,[30] where the court addressed the possibility of massive command influence affecting literally hundreds of cases. In that case, the commanding general had offered his thoughts on the propriety of officers and noncommissioned officers testifying on behalf of defendants. The court ultimately concluded that in cases where unlawful influence has been exercised, the findings and sentence should not be affirmed unless it appears beyond a reasonable doubt that the findings and sentence have been affected by that influence. The court further stated:

> A primary responsibility of this Court in its role as civilian overseer for the military justice system is to ensure that commanders perform their military justice responsibilities properly and that they are provided adequate guidance by their legal advisors in performing those responsibilities. Merely remedying the error in the cases before us is not enough. Instead, we wish to make it clear that incidents of illegal command influence simply must not recur in other commands in the future.
>
> Recognizing that military commanders and judge advocates usually exert themselves in every way to comply with both the spirit and the letter of the law, we are confident that events like those involved here will not be repeated. However, if we have erred in this expectation, this Court "and undoubtedly other tribunals" will find it necessary to consider much more drastic remedies.[31]

Such "drastic remedies" were applied in *United States v. Levite*,[32] where the court reversed the accused's general court-martial conviction for various drug offenses. The command influence in this case was exercised not by the convening authority, but instead by various subordinate unit commanders and noncommissioned officers who attempted to dissuade a number of individuals

---

their testimony; error was cured by judge's remedies at sentencing, *inter alia*, giving defense broad latitude and barring prosecution from calling witnesses in aggravation); United States v. Tucker, 20 M.J. 863 (A.F.C.M.R. 1985) (commander urged members of unit to disassociate themselves from accused); United States v. Saunders, 19 M.J. 763 (A.C.M.R. 1984) (commander spoke with defense witnesses prior to trial concerning Army policy on offense accused charged with and then spoke with witnesses during trial and indicated maximum sentence was warranted); United States v. Charles, 15 M.J. 509 (A.F.C.M.R. 1982) (wing commander suggested squadron commander should modify his views and not give favorable testimony on behalf of the accused).

29. *See, e.g.,* United States v. Thomas, 22 M.J. 388 (C.M.A. 1986); United States v. Hall, 36 M.J. 1043 (N.M.C.M.R. 1993) (trial judge erred in not reopening sentencing hearing to consider evidence of possible command influence on defense witness; trial judge permitted commander to sit in courtroom to hear testimony); United States v. Jones, 33 M.J. 1040 (N.M.C.M.R. 1990) (case remanded for rehearing on sentence where it appeared that commander's adverse actions against defense witnesses in earlier case might have had impact on defense witnesses in accused's case).

30. 22 M.J. 388 (C.M.A. 1986). *See generally* Rob, "Command Influence Update: The Impact of *Cruz* and *Levite*," ARMY LAW., May 1988, at 15.

31. 22 M.J. at 400.

32. 25 M.J. 334 (C.M.A. 1987).

from testifying on behalf of the accused.[33] In reversing the conviction, the court noted that first, there was no post-trial *DuBay* hearing[34] to fully develop the issue of command influence.[35] Second, the pretrial "briefings" that presented the accused as a knife-wielding panderer and assailant polluted the proceedings.[36] Third, the prosecution had not shown that the pretrial and post-trial tampering of the witnesses was harmless.[37] And fourth, the Court of Military Review failed to take any "purging action."[38] The court concluded by stating:

> In summary, the command influence exercised in this case was as pervasive as it was pernicious. Every effort was made by the command to ensure that the court-martial convicted and punished appellant in accordance with its will. Concern for the commands of the Constitution, the Code, and the President was nonexistent. Upon discovery of this fraud on the court, insufficient effort was expended to root out its cause and nullify its effect. We have no confidence as a matter of law in this verdict, and it must be overturned (citations omitted).[39]

The point here is that, first, commanders should take extra care to ensure military members know and understand they have a positive duty to provide any information relevant to an accused's case whether it is favorable or not;[40] and second, commanders must remember that post-trial comments regarding a witness' testimony can still have detrimental and unlawful effects on other witness' testimony, even if no cases are pending when the comments are made.[41]

---

33. 25 M.J. at 338-39. One of the two issues before the court was whether the standard for reversal articulated in *Thomas* also applied to influence exercised by command personnel other than the convening authority. *Id.*

34. *See* § 17-3.

35. 25 M.J. at 339. An informal administrative inquiry that had been conducted (but those findings were not included in the record) was an inadequate substitute according to the court.

36. 25 M.J. at 339. The court noted: "Word travels fast in the military, and these actions, in view of their specificity and content, were so damaging as to render remote the possibility of a fair trial at that time." *Id.*

37. 25 M.J. at 340.

38. *Id.* The court also rejected the Government's argument that the post-trial action of the convening authority in cutting in half the accused's sentence was sufficient. The court said that it was concerned with the fairness of the trial, "not a gratuitous grant of clemency which tends to obfuscate the problem of command influence."

39. 25 M.J. at 340. The court did not address whether the accused in unlawful command influence cases must establish that he has been specifically prejudiced by that influence. In a concurring opinion, Judge Cox expressed the view that it was not necessary to address who carried what burden of proof. In his view, unless he is satisfied beyond a reasonable doubt that the accused has received a fair trial, he will vote for relief. Whether stated or not, it appears that once the issue of command influence has been shown by the accused, the burden rests upon the prosecution to show that the accused nonetheless received a fair trial, beyond a reasonable doubt.

40. *See* United States v. Rodriguez, 16 M.J. 740 (A.F.C.M.R. 1983). *See also* Bower, "Unlawful Command Influence: Preserving the Delicate Balance," 28 A.F. L. Rev. 65, 90 (1988).

41. *See infra* § 6-6.

The Court in *Thomas, supra*, distinguished between character witnesses for the defense and noncharacter witnesses for the defense.[42] In the case of the former, the government may meet its burden of showing that the accused was not deprived of favorable character witnesses in one of several ways. First, the government may present evidence to show that the accused was able to offer extensive favorable character evidence, thus establishing by inference that the command influence did not have much of an effect, if any.[43] Second, the government may show that there was simply no real evidence of good character available to the defense.[44] And third, the government may show that the government evidence was so overwhelming that defense character evidence would have had no impact on the outcome.[45] If the witnesses involved are other than character witnesses, the government may respond by showing first, all persons having relevant information testified at trial and none of them felt pressure to testify in a particular way, or second, if some witnesses did not testify, they would have presented evidence unfavorable to the accused.[46] Applying these templates, the court in *United States v. Gleason*,[47] concluded that the command's unlawful influence had deprived the defense of valuable character evidence which could have been offered on the merits of the case.[48]

§ 6-5(C). Commander's "Presence" at Trial.

Although courts-martial are public trials in most instances, attendance by a commander or his or her representatives may amount to unlawful command influence in and of itself.[49] Such attendance, in or outside the courtroom, can discourage witness testimony or possibly affect the impartiality of judges and court members.[50] Likewise, commander testimony at trial may amount to

---

42. United States v. Thomas 22 M.J. 388, 396-97 (C.M.A. 1986).
43. 22 M.J. at 396.
44. 22 M.J. at 396-97.
45. 22 M.J. at 397.
46. *Id.*
47. 43 M.J. 69 (1995).
48. *Id. See also* United States v. Ayala, 43 M.J. 296 (1995)(accused failed to make threshold showing of improper command influence on his witnesses; Judge Sullivan's separate opinion includes letters signed by President Truman re role of unlawful command influence).
49. *See, e.g.,* United States v. Aurich, 31 M.J. 95 (C.M.A. 1990) (commander testimony at trial may amount to unlawful command influence); United States v. Sanford, 29 M.J. 413 (C.M.A. 1990) (practical effect of commander's testimony about his or her general views can be command influence); United States v. Caritativo, 37 M.J. 175 (C.M.A. 1993) (SJA's presence in courtroom, for purpose of observing effectiveness of counsel, did not prejudice accused).
50. *See, e.g.,* United States v. Singleton, 41 M.J. 200 (C.M.A. 1994) (after hearing evidence that command influence may have been exercised in case, judge barred the chain of command from being present at trial; during even a lengthier post-trial hearing, the trial judge heard extensive evidence on a "reign of terror" conducted by the unit's Sergeant Major); United States v. Rosser, 6 M.J. 267 (C.M.A. 1979) (witnesses observed commander eavesdropping on proceedings and looking into courtroom window during trial); United States v. Levite, 25 M.J. 334 (C.M.A. 1987) (defense witness stated that company commander and first sergeant gave him "strange looks" during his testimony; witnesses also testified that the first sergeant was ranting and raving about the testimony of certain NCOs).

improper influence if the testimony is designed to allow the commander to express his or her general views about the seriousness of the offense or the appropriate sentence to be adjudged.[51] This scenario typically arises when the commander, or someone in the accused's chain of command, testifies about an accused's rehabilitative potential. Such testimony is impermissible if merely a pretext to influence the court members into returning a particular sentence.[52] Unless the commander has direct knowledge of an accused's service performance and character to make a rational basis for his opinions, he may not offer that opinion.[53] The commander's presence in the courtroom may also be indirect when during testimony or instructions, command policies are mentioned. For example, in *United States v. Walk*,[54] the military judge during sentencing proceedings, *sua sponte,* instructed the court members on the impact of Air Force regulations on retention of the accused. The court held that someone should have objected to this instruction because introduction of command policies on drugs into sentencing proceedings constitutes plain error.

§ 6-6. Post-Trial Command Influence.

§ 6-6(A). Clemency Matters.

During the post-trial review of a case, the convening authority must shed his prosecutorial role and take a position similar to an impartial judicial officer.[1] Each accused has a right to an individualized and careful review of his sentence by a convening authority who maintains an impartial and flexible attitude.[2] Any predisposition by the convening authority toward the type of offenses, issues, or parties involved in a particular case will disqualify him from reviewing it.[3] Therefore, policy statements issued by a convening authority or a superior commander that affect the convening authority's impartiality in reviewing clemency matters constitute unlawful command influence.[4]

---

51. *See, e.g.,* United States v. Sanford, 29 M.J. 413 (C.M.A 1990) (commander's general views about appropriateness of punitive discharge improper); United States v. Horner, 22 M.J. 294 (C.M.A. 1986) (battery commander's testimony indicated personal view that accused should be discharged).
52. United States v. Ohrt, 28 M.J. 301 (C.M.A. 1989). *See also* Chapter 17 regarding the propriety of witnesses testifying regarding the rehabilitative potential of an accused.
53. *Id.* at 304.
54. 26 M.J. 665 (A.F.C.M.R. 1987).
1. United States v. Fernandez, 24 M.J. 77 (C.M.A. 1987).
2. 24 M.J. at 78-79.
3. *See, e.g.,* United States v. Conn, 6 M.J. 351 (C.M.A. 1979); United States v. Reed, 2 M.J. 64 (C.M.A. 1976); United States v. Howard, 23 C.M.A. 187, 48 C.M.R. 939 (1974).
4. *See, e.g.,* United States v. Fernandez, 24 M.J. 77 (C.M.A. 1987); United States v. Howard, 23 C.M.A. 187, 48 C.M.R. 939 (1974).

§ 6-6(B). Comments on Outcome of Case.

When commanders and their representatives express personal opinions regarding the result in any particular case or series of cases, their opinions may (and often do) affect the way judges,[5] court members,[6] counsel,[7] and witnesses[8] think and act. Because these opinions have, at the very least, the ability to improperly influence other courts-martial, they constitute actual or apparent unlawful command influence.[9] Article 37 of the U.C.M.J. expressly proscribes the censuring, reprimanding, or admonishing of members, judges, and counsel with respect to findings, sentences, or the functions these persons performed in achieving those results.[10] Furthermore, post-trial comments to or about any witness testimony given during a trial will often raise the issue of unlawful command influence.[11]

§ 6-6(C). Discouraging Witness Testimony in Other Cases.

As one court has recognized, the policy of conducting post-trial lectures to witnesses after they have testified presents a potential chilling effect on the system.[12] The phrase "chilling effect" is often cited in unlawful command influence cases to emphasize the devastating effects that commander statements and actions can have on future cases.[13] Furthermore, such lecturing not only affects the future testimony of those particular witnesses, but also has a direct impact on the testimony of potential witnesses in future cases.[14] This is especially true when comments criticizing witness testimony from a prior court-martial are addressed to groups.[15]

Critical comments, however, are not the only prohibited conduct tending to discourage future testimony. Adverse post-trial actions against witnesses also creates a chilling effect. For instance, in *United States v. Jameson*,[16] two drill

---

5. *See, e.g.,* United States v. Ledbetter, 2 M.J. 37 (C.M.A. 1976). *See also supra* § 6-5(A).
6. United States v. Jones, 15 M.J. 967 (A.C.M.R. 1983). *See also supra* § 6-5(A).
7. *See* R.C.M. 104(b) (restricting commanders from giving less favorable ratings or appraisals to defense counsel because of the zeal with which they represent clients).
8. *See supra* § 6-5(B), and *infra* § 6-6(C).
9. *See generally* Gaydos & Warren, "What Commanders Need to Know About Unlawful Command Control," ARMY LAW., Oct. 1986, at 9, 10-11 (discussion of post-trial "do's and don't's").
10. *See* Appendix 3.
11. *See infra* § 6-6(C).
12. United States v. Lowery, 18 M.J. 695 (A.F.C.M.R. 1983).
13. *See, e.g.,* United States v. Tucker, 20 M.J. 863 (A.F.C.M.R. 1985); United States v. Rodriguez, 16 M.J. 740 (A.F.C.M.R. 1983).
14. *See, e.g.,* United States v. Levite, 25 M.J. 334, 339 (C.M.A. 1987) (lectures and briefings to potential witnesses affect others as well because "[w]ord travels fast in the military").
15. *See, e.g.,* United States v. Jameson, 33 M.J. 669, 677 (N.M.C.M.R. 1991); United States v. Tucker, 20 M.J. 863, 864 (A.F.C.M.R. 1985); United States v. Treakle, 18 M.J. 646 (A.C.M.R. 1984), aff'd, 23 M.J. 151 (C.M.A. 1986) (summary disposition) (this case was only one of the hundreds of cases coming out of the 3rd Armored Division involving a General and certain members of his staff who criticizes those who testify favorably for accused U.C.M.J. offenders).
16. 33 M.J. 669 (N.M.C.M.R. 1991) (noting that process of litigation of command influence issues will benefit if it is possible to decide cases without stigmatizing perpetrators as "military

instructors were relieved of their duties and received unfavorable fitness reports after giving favorable testimony during sentencing of a fellow drill instructor convicted of committing homosexual acts.[17] Not only was the review of that accused's case held to be potentially affected by unlawful command influence,[18] but so was a subsequent court-martial involving similar charges.[19] Therefore, commanders and their representatives must endeavor to choose their words and actions carefully so that members of their commands will not perceive them as discouraging witness testimony.

§ 6-7. Appellate Review of Command Influence.

The issue of unlawful command influence at the trial or appellate stage is not waived merely by failing to raise it.[1] It may be waived, however, by the affirmative actions of the accused.[2] The issue of command influence may be raised through a motion to dismiss,[3] or for appropriate relief, usually in the form of a change of venue.[4] If command influence is introduced at trial through witness testimony[5] or arguments by counsel,[6] the judge has a *sua sponte* duty to restrict such statements and to take corrective action.[7] Regardless of when unlawful command influence occurs or when the issue arises, the court-martial will not be divested of jurisdiction.[8] If the issue of command

---

justice outlaws;" court concluded, however, that adverse actions against two defense witnesses amounted to unlawful command influence).

17. *Id.* at 670-71.
18. *Id.* at 677.
19. United States v. Jones, 30 M.J. 849, 852 (N.M.C.M.R. 1990).
1. *Cf.* United States v. Hamilton, 41 M.J. 32 (C.M.A. 1994) (court concluded that no unlawful command influence had occurred and that accused had waived issue of improper processing of court-martial charges); United States v. Reynolds, 40 M.J. 198 (C.M.A. 1994) (while issue of command influence not considered waived, accused not prejudiced by declining to pursue issue because he feared that a rehearing on sentence would result in imposition of confinement; dissent by Chief Judge Sullivan noted that court should not be in business of encouraging waivers of command influence issues).
2. United States v. Weasler, 43 M.J. 15 (1995) (in case of first impression, court concluded that accused could waive unlawful command influence in preferral of charges in pretrial agreement); United States v. Griffin, 41 M.J. 607 (Army Ct.Crim.App. 1994) (defense affirmatively waived command influence issue; defense used command influence issue to reenter negotiations with convening authority which resulted in drug charge being dropped and stipulation of fact being rewritten).
3. *See generally infra* § 13-3. *See also* United States v. Alexander, 19 M.J. 614 (A.C.M.R. 1984) (judge erred in not hearing evidence on issue of command influence which was reasonably raised by the defense; his simply taking judicial notice of another case and similar facts denied due process).
4. *See infra* § 13-5(C). *See also* United States v. Piatt, 15 M.J. 636 (N.M.C.M.R. 1982) (convening authority's pretrial speeches about offense similar to that with which accused was charged were not unlawful influence and judge did not abuse discretion in denying change of venue).
5. *See supra* § 6-5(C).
6. *See supra* § 6-5(A).
7. United States v. Grady, 15 M.J. 275 (C.M.A. 1983); United States v. Shomaker, 17 M.J. 1122 (N.M.C.M.R. 1984). *See generally* § 16-8. *See also supra* § 6-5.
8. United States v. Blaylock, 15 M.J. 190 (C.M.A. 1983).

influence is raised after trial, a post-trial evidentiary hearing may be held to determine if command influence occurred.[9]

When raising the issue of unlawful command influence, however, an accused must produce more than a generalized and unsupported claim of command control.[10] Instead, the accused must produce evidence that, under the totality of the circumstances, would render a reasonable conclusion that unlawful command influence took place.[11]

While the courts recognize that the threshold is low for triggering additional inquiry into whether unlawful command influence was present, the accused must do more than make a bare assertion or speculate that such occurred.[12] That normally means that the accused has the burden of showing that (1) specific facts, if true, amount to unlawful command influence;[13] (2) the proceedings were unfair;[14] and (3) that the unlawful command influence was the proximate cause of the unfair proceedings.[15]

Once that burden is met, the prosecution must rebut the presumed existence of unlawful influence by clear and convincing evidence.[16] If the prosecu-

---

9. *See, e.g.*, United States v. Ayala, 43 M.J. 296 (1995)(accused failed to meet initial burden of producing sufficient evidence showing that someone with a mantle of authority exercised unlawful command influence against potential witnesses for the accused); United States v. Dykes, 38 M.J. 270 (C.M.A. 1993) (unresolved questions about allegations of unlawful command influence required post-trial evidentiary hearing; court addressed jurisdiction of lower appellate courts to address collateral issues).

10. United States v. Stombaugh, 40 M.J. 208 (C.M.A. 1994) (court discusses burden of production and proof re command influence issues); United States v. Johnston, 39 M.J. 242 (C.M.A. 1994) (accused must raise more than "command influence in the air").

United States v. Dickey, 41 M.J. 637 (N.M.Ct.Crim.App. 1994); United States v. Kelly, 40 M.J. 558 (N.M.C.M.R. 1994) (evidence did not reasonably raise issue of command influence; court noted that affidavits are normally an unsatisfactory means of deciding issue; if issue is reasonably raised, DuBay hearing may be ordered); United States v. Widdekke, 19 C.M.A. 576, 42 C.M.R. 178 (1970). *See also* United States v. Allen, 33 M.J. 209 (C.M.A. 1991) (proof of command influence in the air insufficient to raise issue); United States v. Serino, 24 M.J. 848 (A.F.C.M.R. 1987) (because accused only raised the possibility of unlawful command influence, court did not consider issue justiciable).

11. *See, e.g.*, United States v. Hamilton, 41 M.J. 32 (C.M.A. 1994) (not error for appellate court to decide issue of command influence on basis of affidavits rather than ordering *DuBay* hearing); United States v. Osburn, 33 M.J. 810 (A.F.C.M.R. 1991) (accused failed to show that unlawful command influence prevented squadron commander from testifying for defense or in changing his recommendation concerning possible administrative discharge in lieu of court-martial); United States v. Lawson, 33 M.J. 946 (N.M.C.M.R. 1991); United States v. Jones, 30 M.J. 849 (N.M.C.M.R. 1990); United States v. Cruz, 20 M.J. 873 (A.C.M.R. 1985) (en banc), *rev'd on other grounds*, 25 M.J. 326 (C.M.A. 1987).

12. United States v. Johnson, 39 M.J. 242 (C.M.A. 1994); United States v. Allen, 33 M.J. 209 (C.M.A. 1991); United States v. Maxwell, 42 M.J. 568 (A.F.Ct.Crim.App. 1995) (claim was unsupported by facts).

13. United States v. Stombaugh, 40 M.J. 208, 213 (C.M.A. 1994) (*citing* United States v. Levite, 25 M.J. 334 (C.M.A. 1987)).

14. *Id.*

15. *Id.* United States v. Washington, 42 M.J. 547 (A.F.Ct.Crim.App. 1995) (accused failed to establish second Levite-Stombaugh prong, *i.e.*, that proceedings were unfair).

16. *See, e.g.*, United States v. Rosser, 6 M.J. 267 (C.M.A. 1979); United States v. Adamiak, 4 C.M.A. 412, 15 C.M.R. 412 (1954); United States v. Jones, 30 M.J. 849 (N.M.C.M.R. 1990); United States v. Carlson, 21 M.J. 847 (A.C.M.R. 1986).

tion cannot do so, then it must prove the accused's case was not prejudiced because the reviewing court will not affirm the findings and sentence unless it is persuaded beyond a reasonable doubt that the findings and sentence were not affected by the command influence.[17] If the evidence fails to show that an accused's case was not affected by unlawful command influence, the military courts have an affirmative duty to take all necessary and appropriate remedial and corrective actions to curb any possible prejudice the accused may have suffered.[18]

§ 6-8. Minimizing the Potential for Unlawful Command Influence.

Despite strong language in recent opinions of the Court of Military Appeals (now the Court of Appeals for the Armed Forces), command influence cases continue to appear on the dockets of military appellate courts on a regular basis. In fact, unlawful command influence appears to be emerging as a defense of choice because it need not be timely raised and because commanders are often open to attack by virtue of the roles they must play within the military criminal justice system. The *potential* for unlawful command influence will always exist, however, just as the potential for improper outside influence has always existed in civilian court systems. But the potential for unlawful command influence is perhaps greater in the military system because the system itself, unlike the civilian community, depends on effective command control.

Part of the problem of unlawful command influence is lack of credibility and deterrence. Although cases have been reversed because of unlawful influence, it is difficult to argue convincingly that the system abhors such influence when little, if any, official action is taken against intentional offenders once the military courts find such influence. Indeed, one court has expressed the view that the process of litigating command influence issues will benefit if it is possible to decide the issue without stigmatizing the perpetrators of the influence as "military justice outlaws."[1] The court is correct to a point. Com-

---

17. United States v. Thomas, 22 M.J. 388 (C.M.A. 1986). Cf. United States v. Stombaugh, 40 M.J. 208 (C.M.A. 1994) (court concluded beyond reasonable doubt that unlawful command pressure on defense witness not to testify was nonprejudicial; witness testified, did not appear to be intimated by threats, and testimony was cumulative with other testimony).

18. *Id.* at 400 (court emphasized importance of remedial actions taken in lower courts); United States v. Jones, 30 M.J. 849 (N.M.C.M.R. 1990); United States v. Black, 40 M.J. 615 (N.M.C.M.R. 1994) (appellate court disagreed with trial court that commander's actions had not affected trial proceedings; court noted absence of direct evidence that unlawful command influence affected trial but also noted that it had reasonable doubt on issue; conviction reversed); United States v. Gleason, 39 M.J. 776 (A.C.M.R. 1994) (court noted that a number of persons in military justice system had attempted to stem unlawful actions of commander; two command investigations were conducted on issue and thousands of pages in record were dedicated to issue). Cf. United States v. Sullivan, 26 M.J. 442 (C.M.A. 1988) (court praised trial judges for their actions in remedying the taint of unlawful command influence on the accused's trial).

1. United States v. Jameson, 33 M.J. 669 (N.M.C.M.R. 1991). *See also* United States v. Lawson, 33 M.J. 946 (N.M.C.M.R. 1991) (if courts are too "strident and idealistic" in controlling command influence, their decisions can be debilitating to commanders). Cf. United States v. Gleason, 39 M.J. 776, 783, n.7 (A.C.M.R. 1994) (court noted that commander had been relieved of command

mand influence can arise just as easily from misfeasance as it can from malfeasance. But it is also important to maintain credibility in the system by not turning a blind eye toward the issue. The absence of any visible administrative or judicial action where the case for intentional unlawful influence is clear does not increase the level of credibility. And simply reversing cases in which unlawful command influence has been shown apparently is not in itself sufficient to stem the problem.

Removing commanders from the system is not necessarily the answer.[2] A wholesale removal of commanders from their prosecutorial roles would be virtually impossible given the current structure of the military. Instead, the target areas for scrutiny should be those features of the military criminal justice system that lend themselves to unlawful command influence.

Perhaps the most controversial role a commander must play is that of selecting court members. After determining that there is sufficient evidence to prosecute an accused, the convening authority must select the court members who will decide guilt or innocence and how much punishment to assess. Because the convening authority is most often viewed as a "prosecutor,"[3] the selection process is sometimes viewed with some suspicion. To alleviate this concern, some have suggested adoption of a random selection process.[4]

One counter-argument to such a proposed change is that an accused can choose the trial and sentencing forum if there is a concern that the panel of court members is tainted. However, judge-alone sentences can be greater than those imposed by courts-martial members and, as the cases illustrate, not even judges are immune from the effects of command influence.[5] While tenure for military judges might help shield them from such influence, such a solution is both difficult to implement and largely unnecessary. One court has observed that the answer in protecting judges rests not in granting tenure but rather in taking appropriate action against any lawyer or commander who attempts to exert influence over the trial or appellate judge's independence.[6]

The post-trial review of a case is another suspect feature of the military criminal justice system because the convening authority responsible for prosecuting an accused must then take a position similar to an impartial judicial officer. At the very least, this current practice has the appearance of evil. While it would be simple to suggest that the commander be removed from the post-trial review of the case, it is also generally recognized that while a con-

---

and name had been removed from promotion list for colonels; otherwise no corrective action was taken).

2. Schlueter, "The Twentieth Annual Kenneth J. Hodson Lecture: Military Justice for the 1990's: A Legal System Looking for Respect," 133 MIL. L. REV. 1, 23 (1991).

3. *See, e.g.,* United States v. Lawson, 33 M.J. 946 (N.M.C.M.R. 1991) (convening authority has been described as "partisan prosecutor" in discharging pretrial functions); United States v. Fernandez, 24 M.J. 77 (C.M.A. 1987).

4. *See generally* Remcho, "Military Juries: Constitutional Analysis and the Need for Reform," 47 Ind. L.J. 193 (1973); VanSant, "Trial by Jury of Military Peers," 15 A.F. L. Rev. 185 (1973).

5. *See, e.g.,* United States v. Ralston, 24 M.J. 709, 711 (A.C.M.R. 1987). *See also supra* § 6-5(A).

6. Schlueter, "The Twentieth Annual Kenneth J. Hodson Lecture: Military Justice for the 1990's: A Legal System Looking for Respect," 133 MIL. L. REV. 1, 24-26 (1991).

vening authority may not increase the punishment, he may grant several forms of clemency.[7]

Perhaps the best answer rests not in drastically reforming the structure of the system, but in enforcing those rules and laws which currently proscribe command influence[8] and in ensuring careful appellate review of the often competitive business of prosecuting courts-martial. In *United States v. Thomas*[9] the court published an epilogue attacking the actions of the commander responsible for committing unlawful command influence and criticized his legal advisor for failing to perceive the problem. The court stated, "we wish to make it clear that incidents of illegal command influence must not recur in their commands in the future."[10] The court added that if this expectation could not be met, the court would "find it necessary to consider much more drastic measures."[11] Just over one year later, in *United States v. Levite*,[12] the court cited this language again and expressed its displeasure that command influence was exercised in a manner that flouted both the Constitution and the Code. Consequently, the court felt it appropriate to set aside the findings and sentence.

That sort of review should have a positive, and lawful influence on the military justice system.

---

7. *See* Chapter 17.
8. *See* Articles 37 and 98, U.C.M.J.
9. 22 M.J. 388 (C.M.A. 1986).
10. *Id.* at 400.
11. *Id.*
12. 25 M.J. 334, 338 (C.M.A. 1987).

APPENDIX REFERENCES

Appendix 1. Abbreviations.
Appendix 2. Glossary.
Appendix 3. U.C.M.J.
Appendix 4. Court-Martial Flow Chart.
Appendix 6. Charge Sheet.

ANNOTATED BIBLIOGRAPHY

BOOKS

Byrne, *Military Law* (3d ed. 1981).

This third edition work is a good introductory text to military law. It includes text material, discussion cases, self-quizzes, and appendices that contain forms and tables. The discussion cases, although dated, cover significant areas of courts-martial practice. Chapter 8 includes a discussion of command influence.

Moyer, *Justice and the Military* (1972).

This one volume loose-leaf reference contains detailed discussions of the role of commanders, jurisdiction, military criminal procedure, First Amendment rights, substantive law, and collateral review of courts-martial by the civilian court system. The topic of command influence is discussed in Chapter III.

PERIODICALS

Bower, "Unlawful Command Influence: Preserving the Delicate Balance," 28 A.F. L. REV. 65 (1988).

Noting that unlawful command influence is perhaps the most elusive problem in military justice, the author provides a fine survey of the case law on the subject and analyzing the various ways in which unlawful command influence can affect the court-martial proceedings.

Corrigan, "Prejudicial Joinder: The Crazy-Quilt World of Severances," 68 MIL. L. REV. 1 (1975).

The author generally discusses the law, both constitutional and nonconstitutional standards, relating to joinder of accused. He further categorizes the factual situations giving rise to prejudicial joinder issues (*e.g.*, juror confusion and sentiments against the accused or prosecution) and presents balancing tests that may be applied to both the trial and appellate levels. As a suggested solution to the confusion that often accompanies joinder issues, the author advocates military adoption of the multiple fact-finder forums used by some civilian courts, but generally avoided in military practice.

DeGiulio, "Command Control: Lawful Versus Unlawful Application," 10 SAN DIEGO L. REV. 72 (1972).

This article presents a good review of the permissible and impermissible influence that a superior commander may place upon a subordinate's prosecutorial discretion, addresses command control over court-members, counsel, and judges and briefly addresses some of the proposed legislative changes designed to remove command control from military justice.

Hely, "Command Influence on Military Justice," 15 ST. LOUIS U. L.J. 300 (1970).

This article explores the inherent tendency for command influence in military criminal justice proceedings. In response to this command dilemma, the author suggests establishment of an independent federal judiciary that would have trial jurisdiction over both non-service connected and service connected offenses.

Hollingsworth, "Unlawful Command Influence," 39 A.F. L. REV. 261 (1996).

Noting that unlawful command influence has been repudiated by appellate authorities since 1931, the author notes that the problem is a "significant hurdle to those who would champion the military justice system as one of the best criminal justice systems in the world." After providing some background on the issue, the author focuses on the procedural issues of waiving and raising command influence and urges judge advocates to be proactive in educating new commanders.

McAtamney, "Multiplicity: A Functional Analysis," 106 MIL. L. REV. 115 (1984).

In analyzing the various tests used by the military and civilian courts in determining whether charges are multiplicious, the author advocates a shift in focus to modifying and improving motion practice because no single test will resolve post-trial attacks on multiplicious charges.

Herrington, "Multiplicity in the Military," 134 MIL. L. REV. 45 (1991).

Noting that "multiplicity" in the military has assumed an identity separate from federal law on the topic, the author discusses the various constitutional, Manual for Courts-Martial, and military case law tests used to determine whether the charges are multiplicious. The author concludes that the problems of dealing with the issue can only be solved if the *Manual* rule is rewritten and the Court of Military Appeals follows Supreme Court precedent.

Schiesser & Benson, "Modern Military Justice," 19 CATH. U. L. REV. 489 (1970).

Commending the Military Justice Act of 1968, which amended the U.C.M.J., the authors detail the "modern" practices of military justice, which *inter alia* protect the accused's right to counsel and limit the commander's ability to control the court-martial. Also addressed are discussions of the concept of the military judge—a position first created by the 1968 Act.

Symposium, "Military Law," 10 AM. CRIM. L. REV. 1 (1971).

This symposium issue covers a valuable range of topics pertinent to the practice of military criminal law. Included are articles on jurisdiction over civilian type offenses, plea bargaining, sentencing, discovery, appeals, and an article by General Westmoreland on the commanders perspective of military justice. Also included is a fine bibliography of books, articles, and listings of military law materials.

Symposium, "Military Justice," ARMY LAW., March 1996.

This 127-page symposium contains a Foreword and 11 short articles on a wide range of military justice topics. They are as follows:

Morris, "Foreword."
Barto, "Developments in the Substantive Criminal Law Under the Uniform Code of Military Justice."
Frisk, "New Developments in Pretrial Confinement."
Frisk, "New Developments in Speedy Trial."
Winn, "Recent Developments in Military Pretrial and Trial Procedure."
Masterton, "Recent Developments in Search and Seizure Law."
Masterton, "Recent Developments in Urinalysis Law."
Kohlman, "Are You Ready for Some Changes? Five Fresh Views of the Fifth Amendment."
Wright, "Sex, Lies, and Videotape: Child Sexual Abuse Cases Continue to Create Appellate Issues and Other Developments in the Areas of the Sixth Amendment, Discovery, Mental Responsibility, and Nonjudicial Punishment."
Henley, "Caveat Criminale: The Impact of the New Military Rules of Evidence in Sexual Offense and Child Molestation Cases."
Henley, "Current Developments in Evidence Law."
Morris, "New Developments in Sentencing and Post-Trial Procedure."

West, "A History of Command Influence on the Military Judicial System," 18 U.C.L.A. L. REV. 1 (1970).

The author, a former JAG, takes a comprehensive and somewhat critical look at the commander's ability to direct the outcome of a court-martial. The article presents a historical analysis of this controversial topic, from 1776 to 1970.

Young, "Multiplicity and Lesser-Included Offenses," 39 A.F.L. REV. 159 (1996).

The author briefly addresses the various tests used by the military courts to determine whether specifications are multipicious and in particular the *Teeters-Foster-Weymouth* trilogy of decisions from the Court of Appeals for the Armed Forces. The article contains a helpful appendix of guidelines for determining multiplicity and lesser included offense issues.

CHAPTER 7

THE ARTICLE 32 INVESTIGATION AND THE PRETRIAL ADVICE

§ 7-1. General.
§ 7-2. The Article 32 Investigation.
    § 7-2(A). The Parties to the Investigation.
        § 7-2(A)(1). The Investigating Officer.
        § 7-2(A)(2). Counsel.
    § 7-2(B). The Accused's Rights.
        § 7-2(B)(1). Notice of Charges.
        § 7-2(B)(2). Right to Counsel.
        § 7-2(B)(3). Right to be Present.
        § 7-2(B)(4). Right to Confront Witnesses.
        § 7-2(B)(5). Right to Examine Evidence.
        § 7-2(B)(6). Right to Production of Witnesses.
        § 7-2(B)(7). Right to Present Other Evidence.
        § 7-2(B)(8). Right to Remain Silent.
    § 7-2(C). Article 32 Investigation Procedures.
    § 7-2(D). Investigating Officer's Report.
    § 7-2(E). Defects in the Investigation.
§ 7-3. The Staff Judge Advocate's Pretrial Advice.
    § 7-3(A). Contents of the Pretrial Advice.
    § 7-3(B). Defective Pretrial Advice.
Appendix References.
Annotated Bibliography.

§ 7-1. General.

Before charges may be referred to a general court-martial, the highest court-martial,[1] two statutory criteria must first be met. First, Article 32, U.C.M.J.[2] requires a formal investigation of the charges, and second, Article 34, U.C.M.J.[3] requires the general court-martial convening authority to seek the formal written advice of his staff judge advocate. These two instruments present the general court-martial convening authority with the necessary factual and legal predicates for proceeding. This chapter addresses these two screening devices, which are most often linked together in discussions on military justice because they almost always operate in tandem.

§ 7-2. The Article 32 Investigation.

The Article 32 investigation is the military's counterpart to the civilian grand jury. Both are designed to avoid trials on baseless charges.[1] But the

---

1. *See* § 1-8(D)(3).
2. *See* Appendix 3.
3. *See* Appendix 3.

1. Art. 32(a), U.C.M.J.; Talbot v. Toth, 215 F.2d 22 (D.C. Cir. 1954). *See* Gaydos, "A Comprehensive Guide to the Military Pretrial Investigation," 111 Mɪʟ. L. Rᴇv. 49 (1986). Murphy, "The Formal Pretrial Investigation," 12 Mɪʟ. L. Rᴇv. 1 (1961); Sandell, "The Grand Jury and the

similarity usually ends there. The Article 32 investigation, unlike the grand jury, presents an excellent opportunity for defense discovery[2] and generally provides greater procedural protections for the accused.[3] Another possible use of the Article 32 investigation is the preservation and later use of testimony should a witness be unavailable at trial.[4] The investigation is quasi-judicial in nature and is considered to be a substantial right afforded to the accused.[5] It is clearly intended to be more than a mere formality[6] or a proverbial "rubber stamp" in the pretrial processing of charges.

Note that the accused can waive the investigation.[7] Article 32(c), U.C.M.J. also permits the government to substitute a prior formal investigation or court of inquiry on the same subject matter if the accused does not object and he was present and was afforded the right to counsel, cross-examination and presentation of defense evidence.[8] If the accused demands further investigation, he is entitled to recall witnesses for further cross-examination and offer any new evidence.[9]

Article 32: A Comparison," 1 N. Ky. St. L.F. 25 (1973). *See generally* Bruce, "The Pretrial Investigation: Some Practical Considerations," 26 JAG J. 225 (1972); Duree, "The Defense Counsel and the Pretrial Investigation," 9 A.F. L. Rev. 14 (1967).

2. United States v. Roberts, 10 M.J. 308 (C.M.A. 1981); Hutson v. United States, 19 C.M.A. 437, 42 C.M.R. 39 (1970); United States v. Samuels, 10 C.M.A. 206, 27 C.M.R. 280 (1959); R.C.M. 405(a) Discussion.

Testimony, documents, and other evidence considered by the Article 32 Investigating Officer are available to the defense while the proceedings in a civilian grand jury are usually off-limits. The mere fact that the accused and counsel may attend the Article 32 proceeding is in itself a valuable discovery tool because counsel can observe adverse witnesses and plan trial strategy. *See infra* § 7-2(B).

3. See § 7-2(B) for a discussion on the rights of an accused.

4. The testimony may be admissible under the "former testimony" exception to the hearsay rule. Mil. R. Evid. 804(b)(1). The definition of "unavailability" is set out in Mil. R. Evid. 804(a), and the testimony must have been recorded verbatim and the party against whom the testimony is offered must have had an "opportunity and similar motive to develop the testimony by direct, cross, or redirect examination." *See, e.g.,* United States v. Thornton, 16 M.J. 1011 (A.C.M.R. 1983) (prosecutor must use good faith to make witness available at trial); United States v. Eggers, 3 C.M.A. 191, 11 C.M.R. 191 (1953).

5. United States v. Nichols, 8 C.M.A. 119, 23 C.M.R. 343 (1957).

6. *Id.*

7. R.C.M. 405(c). United States v. Nickerson, 27 M.J. 30 (C.M.A. 1988) (accused failed to show good cause for withdrawing waiver of Article 32 investigation after withdrawing his guilty plea where the waiver was not dependent upon the guilty plea); United States v. Schaffer, 12 M.J. 425 (C.M.A. 1982) (defendant may waive Article 32 investigation as part of a plea bargain with convening authority). *See also* United States v. Czekala, 38 M.J. 566 (A.C.M.R. 1993), *aff'd on other grounds*, 42 M.J. 168 (1995) (accused waived Article 32 investigation; he failed to show good cause for relief from the waiver); United States v. Stone, 37 M.J. 558 (A.C.M.R. 1993), *aff'd on other grounds*, 40 M.J. 420 (C.M.A. 1994) (accused executed valid oral waiver of right to Article 32 investigation; accused unsuccessfully attempted to show good cause for withdrawing waiver); United States v. Frentz, 21 M.J. 813 (N.M.C.M.R. 1985); United States v. Miller, 12 M.J. 836 (A.C.M.R. 1982); United States v. Walls, 8 M.J. 666 (A.C.M.R. 1979).

8. Art. 32(c), U.C.M.J. *See* Appendix 3; R.C.M. 405(b). *See, e.g.,* United States v. Grandy, 9 C.M.A. 355, 26 C.M.R. 135 (1958). *See generally* Hausken, "Article 32(c): A Forgotten Provision Can Assist The Prosecutor," Army Law., Apr. 1988, at 39.

9. Art. 32(c), U.C.M.J.

If during the Article 32 investigation, the evidence indicates that the accused may have committed other, uncharged offenses, the investigating officer may proceed with an investigation of those offenses[10] if (1) the accused is present at the investigation;[11] (2) the accused is apprised of the nature of the uncharged offense being investigated;[12] and (3) the accused is afforded the assistance of counsel, cross-examination, and the opportunity to present evidence.[13]

§ 7-2(A). The Parties to the Investigation.

§ 7-2(A)(1). The Investigating Officer.

The investigating officer, usually appointed by either the summary or special court-martial convening authority,[14] is to be a mature officer, preferably in the grade of at least major or lieutenant commander, or who has "legal training"[15] and who is impartial.[16] The "accuser," the individual who pre-

---

10. *See* Art. 32(d), U.C.M.J. This provision was added by Congress as part of the National Defense Authorization Act for Fiscal Year 1996. Pub. L. No. 104-106, 110 Stat. 186 (1996). Although the change creates the potential for a "runaway" investigation, it clearly saves time; in the past, the Article 32 investigating officer might had had to wait for formal preferral of the offenses and further direction to investigate those offenses. *See generally* "Joint Service Committee on Military Justice Report," ARMY LAW., Mar. 1996, at 138.
11. *Id.*
12. *Id.*
13. *Id.*
14. R.C.M. 405(c) indicates that unless his authority has been limited by a superior commander, any convening authority may direct an Article 32 investigation. As a matter of practice it is usually the summary or special court-martial convening authority who so acts.
In United States v. Bramel, 29 M.J. 958 (A.C.M.R. 1990), the summary court-martial convening authority directed certain procedures to protect a young sodomy victim from being intimidated by her father, the accused. These instructions, which included detailed guidance on erection of a protective screen and producing a verbatim transcript of the testimony, were not considered to be unlawful command influence and did not affect the impartiality of the investigating officer. *See also* R.C.M. 405(c), which provides that the convening authority may give such procedural instructions.
15. Article 32, U.C.M.J. is silent as to the qualifications of the investigating officer. But R.C.M. 405(d)(1) provides that the officer must be commissioned and may not be the "accuser." *See supra* § 6-1. Note that the preference for a higher ranking officer is reduced when the officer has "legal training." The term is ambiguous but arguably might extend to a young officer with some law school experience or perhaps some legal training at one of the service JAG schools.
In United States v. Reynolds, 24 M.J. 261 (C.M.A. 1987), however, the court considered it a "gross breach of military protocol and courtesy to appoint one who is junior in rank [a JAGC captain] to preside over matters involving a person of higher rank [a major]." 24 M.J. at 263.
16. United States v. Davis, 20 M.J. 61 (C.M.A. 1985) (although investigating officer should have recused himself because he was the supervisor to the military defense counsel, no prejudice resulted to the accused. The court emphasized that it did not wish to establish a rule that lawyers should not serve as Art. 32 Officers. The proceeding is judicial and use of lawyers avoids some complaints that are sometimes made about lay investigating officers).
See also United States v. Collins, 6 M.J. 256 (C.M.A. 1979) (court assessed neutrality of officer); United States v. Foley, 37 M.J. 822 (A.F.C.M.R. 1993) (Article 32 I.O. was impartial); United States v. Thorn, 36 M.J. 955 (A.F.C.M.R. 1993) (investigating officer's participation in same capacity in earlier case was not disqualifying; court noted that it had approved appointment of

§ 7-2(A)(1)   MILITARY CRIMINAL JUSTICE   § 7-2(A)(1)

ferred the charges,[17] may not act as the investigating officer.[18] Prior connection with the case may disqualify the officer[19] although the disqualification may be waived.[20] Participation as an investigating officer will later disqualify the officer from serving as a trial counsel, military judge, court member,[21] staff judge advocate, or legal officer[22] to any reviewing authority in the same case. The military courts have viewed the investigating officer as a judicial officer, comparable to a civilian magistrate,[23] and in many commands military lawyers will routinely sit as the investigating officers.

Using military lawyers as investigating officers offers obvious advantages. They are able to quickly identify the legal and factual problems that can arise during an investigation.[24] More importantly they are less likely to need substantive advice from another lawyer which can raise new problems. For example, in *United States v. Payne*,[25] the court ruled that if the investigating officer needs substantive legal advice,[26] he may not receive it *ex parte*,[27] and it

---

single officer in related cases as long as impartiality is preserved); United States v. Spinner, 27 M.J. 892 (A.C.M.R. 1989) (investigating officer's admonishments to defense counsel did not make him partial); United States v. Reynolds, 19 M.J. 529 (A.C.M.R. 1984) (Article 32 Officer was not disqualified simply because he was from the same SJA office as the trial counsel and other individuals who had investigated the accused's false claims); United States v. Wojciechowski, 19 M.J. 577 (N.M.C.M.R. 1984) (it is the investigating officer who is to remain impartial, not the convening authority who ordered the investigation); United States v. Castleman, 11 M.J. 562 (A.F.C.M.R. 1981) (investigating officer should disqualify himself if impartiality might reasonably be questioned; here he was friend of accuser and a principal witness); United States v. Wager, 10 M.J. 546 (N.C.M.R. 1980) (investigating officer who had served as military judge in related case was not disqualified); United States v. Natalello, 10 M.J. 594 (A.F.C.M.R. 1980) (investigating officer had previously expressed an opinion as to the accused's guilt).

17. *See* Chapter 6.
18. *See* R.C.M. 405(d). *See also supra* § 6-1. *Cf.* United States v. Beckermann, 35 M.J. 842 (C.G.C.M.R. 1992) (Article 32 officer not disqualified from preferring charges after completing investigation; court noted that Article 30(a) includes reference to charges being preferred by someone who has investigated allegations).
19. United States v. Parker, 6 C.M.A. 75, 19 C.M.R. 201 (1955) (officer had previously served as a criminal investigator on the case). Mere knowledge of the facts will not be disqualifying. United States v. Clark, 11 M.J. 179 (C.M.A. 1981) (investigating officer read reports from prior Art. 32 investigation); United States v. Schreiber, 16 C.M.R. 639 (A.F.B.R. 1954), *aff'd*, 5 C.M.A. 602, 18 C.M.R. 226 (1955); United States v. Jones, 20 M.J. 919 (N.M.C.M.R. 1985) (investigating officer not disqualified where he sat as the trial judge in the perjury trial of one of the key witnesses to the investigation before he had finished preparing his report).
20. United States v. Lopez, 20 C.M.A. 76, 42 C.M.R. 268 (1970).
21. Articles 26 and 27, U.C.M.J. *Cf.* United States v. Trakowski, 10 M.J. 792 (A.F.C.M.R. 1981), where the officer conducting a pretrial confinement hearing was considered an "investigating officer" and therefore disqualified from serving as trial counsel.
22. Article 6(c), U.C.M.J.; United States v. Jolliff, 22 C.M.A. 95, 46 C.M.R. 95 (1973).
23. *See* United States v. Payne, 3 M.J. 354 (C.M.A. 1977).
24. For example, the investigating officer may find it necessary to determine whether a valid defense exists to a particular offense. He may also need to delve into questions involving searches and seizures and confessions. *See* R.C.M. 405(e) Discussion.
25. 3 M.J. 354 (C.M.A. 1977).
26. Substantive matters, as opposed to procedural matters, generally involve issues concerning

27. Although the advice may not be *ex parte*, *Payne* does not necessarily require that the

must come from a neutral legal advisor.[28] If the investigating officer has received advice *ex parte* or from a source who is not impartial, there is a presumption of prejudice. The prosecution may rebut that presumption with clear and convincing evidence.[29]

§ 7-2(A)(2). Counsel.

Counsel for the accused, as well as a counsel for the government, are permitted in the proceedings. The accused is entitled to be represented at the investigation either by (1) a civilian lawyer provided by the accused at no expense to the government if his appearance will not unduly delay the proceedings;[30] (2) an individually requested military lawyer if reasonably available and whose appearance will not unduly delay the proceedings;[31] or (3) a lawyer appointed by the appropriate authority.[32] Finally, the accused may

---

the elements of the offense, defenses, burdens of proof and evidentiary questions. Arguably, purely procedural or administrative questions can be answered by a partial officer. *Cf.* R.C.M. 405(d)(1) Discussion (legal advice concerning *responsibilities* must come from impartial source; it may not come from counsel for either party).

---

advice be given during the Article 32 investigation itself. The key is that both sides are present when the advice is given. If they are not, the absent party should be fully informed of the advice and given an opportunity to respond. *See generally* United States v. Crumb, 10 M.J. 520 (A.C.M.R. 1980); United States v. Grimm, 6 M.J. 890 (A.C.M.R. 1979).

28. Neutral legal advisor usually means any counsel other than the prosecution or defense. *See* R.C.M. 405(d)(1) Discussion (uses the term "impartial" legal advisor). *Cf.* United States v. Grimm, 6 M.J. 890 (A.C.M.R. 1979) (neutrality means someone other than an individual involved in prosecutorial function).

29. *See* United States v. Payne, 3 M.J. 354 (C.M.A. 1977); United States v. Rushatz, 30 M.J. 525 (A.C.M.R. 1990) (investigating officer's extensive *ex parte* consultations with third parties in an attempt to gain background information did not prejudice the accused).
United States v. Dababneh, 28 M.J. 929 (N.M.C.M.R. 1989) (no prejudice considering that contact was very brief and advice was simply to follow the applicable Rules of Courts-Martial); United States v. Francis, 25 M.J. 614 (A.C.M.R. 1987) (*ex parte* meeting between investigating officer, convening authority, and prosecutor did not give rise to presumption of prejudice); United States v. Ayala, 22 M.J. 777 (A.C.M.R. 1986) (non-prejudicial error); United States v. Whitt, 21 M.J. 658 (A.C.M.R. 1985) (investigating officer committed non-prejudicial error by conducting *ex parte* discussions with witnesses); United States v. Martel, 19 M.J. 917 (A.C.M.R. 1985) (court ruled that government had overcome presumption of prejudice, by clear and convincing evidence, arising from the Art. 32 Officer's *ex parte* discussions with a witness); United States v. Brunson, 15 M.J. 898 (C.G.C.M.R. 1982) (court set aside findings and sentence where investigating officer conducted numerous *ex parte* discussions with prosecution).

30. R.C.M. 405(d)(2)(C). United States v. Maness, 23 C.M.A. 41, 48 C.M.R. 512 (1974); United States v. Freedman, 23 M.J. 820 (N.M.C.M.R. 1987) (convening authority rescinded continuance granted by the investigating officer and thus precluded the accused's civilian counsel from attending the hearing).

31. R.C.M. 405(d)(2)(B). United States v. Courtier, 20 C.M.A. 278, 43 C.M.R. 118 (1971); United States v. Wright, 10 C.M.A. 36, 27 C.M.R. 110 (1958). If the accused selects an individual military counsel, the authority detailing counsel may in his discretion permit the accused to retain his detailed counsel. Note, however, that at a later trial, an accused is in theory entitled to only *one* military counsel. Art. 38(b)(6), U.C.M.J.; R.C.M. 506(a). *Cf.* R.C.M. 506(b)(3).
The definition of "reasonably available" is addressed in R.C.M. 506 and is discussed in § 8-3(B), *infra*.

32. R.C.M. 405(d)(2)(H) indicates that a military counsel will be appointed in all cases. The appointment, which formerly would have been made by the convening authority, will now be

decide to represent himself.[33] Those are the same rights to counsel that he is afforded at trial.[34] The Manual for Courts-Martial permits the presence of a government counsel,[35] although this counsel may not serve as an *ex parte* advisor to the investigating officer.[36]

§ 7-2(B). The Accused's Rights.

Unlike the civilian grand jury system where the defendant's rights are severely limited, the military accused is provided broad rights at the Article 32 investigation. They are stated in Article 32, U.C.M.J., and are briefly discussed here.

§ 7-2(B)(1). Notice of Charges.

First, the accused is to be advised that the charges against him are about to be investigated, the name of the accuser, and the names of witnesses against him.[37] Although this information would generally be previously available on the charge sheet, it would be important for defense counsel to determine that in fact all of the required information has been supplied. The topic of discovery and production of evidence is discussed in more detail in Chapters 10 and 11, *infra*.

§ 7-2(B)(2). Right to Counsel.

The accused has the various rights to counsel noted in § 7-2(A)(2). It is important to note that these rights, along with the right of the accused to actually be present during the hearing,[38] in themselves mark a clear and beneficial departure from civilian practice where counsel is not permitted. Although counsel's exact role is not specifically spelled out in either Article 32 or the *Manual*, it is clear that counsel may be permitted to question (or confront) the witnesses against the accused and to present favorable evidence and

---

made by someone authorized to appoint defense counsel. That will be determined by the applicable service regulations. In the Army, for example, the regional or senior defense counsel will make the appointments. As a practical matter, by the time the Article 32 investigation is held, the accused will already have an attorney-client relationship. *See generally* United States v. Tomaszewski, 8 C.M.A. 266, 24 C.M.R. 76 (1957).

33. *See* United States v. Bramel, 29 M.J. 958 (A.C.M.R. 1990) (no abuse of discretion in denying accused's request to do so where it appeared that he only wanted the opportunity to personally cross-examine his daughter).

34. *See* United States v. Bramel, 29 M.J. 958 (A.C.M.R. 1990). *See also* §§ 8-3(B), 12-2(F).

35. Serving at the Article 32 investigation will not disqualify this counsel from later serving as the trial counsel in the case. *See, e.g.*, United States v. Plaut, 18 C.M.A. 265, 39 C.M.R. 265 (1969).

36. United States v. Payne, 3 M.J. 354 (C.M.A. 1977); United States v. Grimm, 6 M.J. 890 (A.C.M.R. 1979), *petition denied*, 7 M.J. 135 (C.M.A. 1979). *Cf.* United States v. Crumb, 10 M.J. 520 (A.C.M.R. 1980) (investigating officer's discussion with the chief of military justice was nonprejudicial error). *See supra* § 7-2(A)(1).

37. United States v. DeLauder, 8 C.M.A. 656, 25 C.M.R. 160 (1958).

38. *See infra* § 7-2(B)(3).

witnesses on behalf of the accused in hopes of obtaining a favorable recommendation from the investigating officer. At a minimum, counsel should be prepared to treat the proceeding as an excellent opportunity to discover the prosecution's case. Counsel's delicts in representing an accused before the Article 32 investigation may constitute ineffective assistance of counsel.[39]

§ 7-2(B)(3). Right to be Present.

Unlike a civilian grand jury, the servicemember has the right to be present throughout the investigation.[40] This right is not absolute, however, and the accused may forfeit the right when he is voluntarily absent after he has received notice of the time and place of the proceeding.[41] He may also forfeit the right where after ample warning he engages in disruptive conduct and the investigating officer excludes him.[42] Before excluding the accused from the proceeding, the investigating officer may consider other reasonable alternatives to restrain his words or actions.[43] See also § 15-2(A) and R.C.M. 804(b)(2) concerning the accused's presence at trial.

§ 7-2(B)(4). Right to Confront Witnesses.

The accused also has the right to cross-examine and confront[44] the witnesses against him who are "reasonably available."[45] The *Manual* indicates that a witness is reasonably available "if the witness is located within 100 miles of the situs of the investigation and if the investigating officer determines that, on balance, the significance of the witness' testimony and personal appearance outweigh the expense, delay, and effect on military operations of obtaining that witness' personal appearance."[46] Further, a witness

---

39. *See* § 15-2(B)(3).
40. R.C.M. 405(f)(3).
41. R.C.M. 405(h)(4)(A).
42. R.C.M. 405(h)(4)(B).
43. The Discussion to R.C.M. 804(b)(2) notes alternatives such as gagging and/or binding the accused where he becomes disruptive during a trial. The investigating officer, of course, is not required to use any alternatives before excluding the accused.
44. The right is not unlimited, however. *See, e.g.,* United States v. Lewis, 33 M.J. 758 (A.C.M.R. 1991) (investigating officer had authority to restrict repetitive questioning by defense counsel); United States v. Bramel, 29 M.J. 958 (A.C.M.R. 1990) (court concluded that the accused's right of confrontation had not been violated when his minor daughter testified at the Article 32 hearing from behind a partition. The court noted that although the Article 32 investigation is an important right, it is not the equivalent of a trial where the Sixth Amendment confrontation rights would be fully implicated).
45. Article 32(b), U.C.M.J.; R.C.M. 405(g)(1)(A). United States v. Marrie, 43 M.J. 35 (1995) (harmless error for Article 32 officer to conclude that witnesses were not reasonably available); United States v. Douglas, 32 M.J. 694 (A.F.C.M.R. 1991) (witnesses were unavailable at Article 32 because they had claimed their privilege against self-incrimination).
The right apparently does not always extend to face-to-face confrontations. In United States v. Bramel, 28 M.J. 505 (A.C.M.R. 1989), the court concluded that the accused's right to confront the witnesses against him did not prevent placement of a partition between himself and the child abuse victim. *See also* Kentucky v. Stincer, 482 U.S. 730 (1987).
46. R.C.M. 405(g)(1)(A). The 100-mile provision was added in Change 5 (1991) to the *Manual*. *See also* United States v. Marrie, 43 M.J. 35 (1995) (hearing officer and trial judge applied wrong

who is unavailable under Military Rule of Evidence 804 is also not reasonably available for purposes of an Article 32 investigation.[47] If the witness is located more than 100 miles away, the witness may still be produced but that decision would have to be made by the witness' commander if the witness is in the military, or by the authority who ordered the investigation if the witness is a civilian.[48]

Note that the immediate commander of a military witness may veto the investigating officer's initial determination that the witness should be produced.[49] Although that commander's veto cannot be appealed by the defendant, the military judge may later review the decision.[50] Presumably, if he decides that the commander erred, he may grant appropriate relief to the defense.[51] Unfortunately, there is no subpoena power to compel the attendance of civilian witnesses at an Article 32 investigation.[52] However, each of the services, by regulation, may provide for payment of travel and other related expenses.[53] Again, the decision of whether a civilian witness is reasonably available rests with the investigating officer.[54] If the investigating officer decides that any witness is unavailable he must provide a statement of his reasons if the accused objects to the officer's decision.[55]

Although there is a preference for live testimony, the investigating officer may consider alternatives to testimony. R.C.M. 405(g)(4) recognizes that, absent a defense objection, the investigating officer may consider alternatives to live testimony (such as sworn and unsworn statements, depositions, or stipulations) without regard to whether the witness is available.[56] If the witness is not available, he may consider alternatives to testimony over the objection of the defense.[57] During time of war, the investigating officer is permitted to

---

test by concluding that witnesses more than 100 miles away were *per se* unavailable; error was harmless because defense counsel had adequate opportunity to question witnesses before trial); United States v. Cumberledge, 6 M.J. 203 (C.M.A. 1979); United States v. Ledbetter, 2 M.J. 37 (C.M.A. 1976); United States v. Chestnut, 2 M.J. 84 (C.M.A. 1976). Distance alone should not make the witness unavailable.

United States v. Jones, 20 M.J. 919 (N.M.C.M.R. 1985) (Article 32 officer properly balanced the significance of the NIS agents' testimony against the difficulty and expense of obtaining their presence in denying the defense request. Here, the agents were 8,000 miles away and no funding was available. In addition, the defense was able to interview them prior to trial).

47. R.C.M. 405(g)(1)(A). For example, a witness claiming the privilege against self-incrimination under the Fifth Amendment or Article 31, U.C.M.J. is unavailable. United States v. Capel, 15 M.J. 537 (A.F.C.M.R. 1982).

48. R.C.M. 405(g)(1)(A) Analysis.

49. R.C.M. 405(g)(2)(A).

50. Id.

51. See infra § 13-5(D).

52. R.C.M. 405(g)(2)(B) Discussion. See also United States v. Roberts, 10 M.J. 308, 310, n. 1 (C.M.A. 1981) (court declined to address issue of the scope of the military's subpoena power).

53. R.C.M. 405(g)(3). See also Department of Defense Joint Travel Regulations, Vol. 2, paragraphs C3054 and C6000; AR 27-10, para. 5-12.

54. R.C.M. 405(g)(2)(B).

55. R.C.M. 405(g)(2)(D).

56. R.C.M. 405(g)(4)(A). See also United States v. Lassiter, 11 C.M.A. 89, 28 C.M.R. 313 (1959); United States v. Samuels, 10 C.M.A. 206, 27 C.M.R. 280 (1959).

57. R.C.M. 405(g)(4)(B).

consider unsworn statements of an unavailable witness.[58] Similar rules apply to real and documentary evidence. Failure of an available military witness to testify is punishable under the U.C.M.J.[59]

§ 7-2(B)(5). Right to Examine Evidence.

In addition to the right to confront witnesses, the accused has the right to examine real and documentary evidence.[60] In many cases, the real evidence remains with the evidence custodian until the trial.[61] The Manual for Court-Martial provides, however, that the investigating officer may not consider, over defense objection, any alternative forms of evidence, such as testimony describing the evidence, unless the evidence is not reasonably available.[62] According to R.C.M. 405(g)(1)(B), evidence is reasonably available if its significance outweighs the difficulty, expense, delay, and effect on military operations of obtaining the evidence.[63] As with the question of a witness' availability, the investigating officer decides whether the evidence is available.[64] But his decision can apparently be nullified by the evidence custodian if the latter decides that the evidence is not available.[65] That decision may be reviewed by the military judge, usually in a motion for appropriate relief.[66]

§ 7-2(B)(6). Right to Production of Witnesses.

Article 32 and the *Manual* provide that the accused has the right to have available witnesses produced at the investigation, who can give relevant, noncumulative testimony.[67] The rules discussed in § 7-2(B)(4) for determining availability are also applicable here. If an important witness is not available, the defense should consider requesting that the absent witness be deposed.[68]

---

58. R.C.M. 405(g)(4). The Drafters' Analysis to this provision, which was added by Change 5 to the *Manual*, indicates that the Drafters believed that the burdens of war outweigh whatever benefits might result from requiring sworn statements. But it adds that the lack of an oath may be taken into account in assigning the appropriate weight to the witness' statement.
59. *See* Article 134, U.C.M.J.; MCM, Part IV, para. 108.
60. R.C.M. 405(f)(10). United States v. Meadows, 42 M.J. 132 (1995) (version of document produced at Article 32 was not the same as that offered at trial by the prosecution; court concluded beyond a reasonable doubt that substitution did not affect result of trial).
61. In that case, the defense counsel usually will have already examined the real evidence at the evidence room.
62. R.C.M. 405(g)(5)(A), (B).
63. Because in most cases the real and documentary evidence is located on the installation where the investigation is being held, the defense can almost always successfully demand production of the evidence itself. Note that this right exists in addition to other discovery rights. *See* § 10-1 *et seq.*
64. R.C.M. 405(g)(2)(C).
65. *Id.*
66. *See* §§ 13-5(D), (J).
67. Article 32(b), U.C.M.J.; R.C.M. 405(f), (g).
68. *See* United States v. Marrie, 43 M.J. 35 (1995) (hearing officer and trial judge applied wrong test by concluding that witnesses more than 100 miles away were *per se* unavailable; error was harmless because defense counsel had adequate opportunity to question witnesses before trial); United States v. Chuculate, 5 M.J. 143 (C.M.A. 1978). *See also infra* § 11-3.

This request, along with a renewed request at trial may be necessary to avoid waiver of the issue.[69]

§ 7-2(B)(7). Right to Present Other Evidence.

In addition to requesting the presence of witnesses, see § 7-2(B)(6), the accused is permitted to present anything in defense, extenuation, or mitigation.[70] Note that apparently the defense is not limited to presenting evidence that tends to prove that the accused did not commit the alleged offense. The accused may offer evidence that tends to minimize the impact, or seriousness of the offense, in hopes that the investigating officer will make a favorable recommendation concerning disposition of the charges.[71] There is obviously a thin line here for the defense to walk. As noted in the next section, the accused also has the right to remain silent and present no evidence whatsoever. While there are advantages to using the investigation as a one-way discovery device, in an appropriate case it may be beneficial to present a more complete defense and attempt to influence the investigating officer.

§ 7-2(B)(8). Right to Remain Silent.

Finally, the accused may remain silent and present no evidence whatsoever.[72] This obviously reduces the ability of the prosecution to assess the defense's case but in no way limits the full and valuable discovery rights provided to the accused. For additional material on discovery, see R.C.M. 701 and § 10-3 et seq. If the accused decides to make a statement, it may be in any form.[73]

§ 7-2(C). Article 32 Investigation Procedures.

The Article 32 investigation is generally an informal, public proceeding[74] and is completed in a relatively short period of time. Although it may take on the appearance of a quasi-adversary proceeding if counsel for the government is present, only the Military Rules of Evidence governing privileges apply.[75]

---

69. United States v. Cumberledge, 6 M.J. 203 (C.M.A. 1979); United States v. Cruz, 5 M.J. 286 (C.M.A. 1978).
70. Article 32(b), U.C.M.J.; R.C.M. 405(f)(11).
71. See infra § 7-2(C).
72. R.C.M. 405(f)(7); Article 31, U.C.M.J.; MIL. R. EVID. 301.
73. R.C.M. 405(f)(12).
74. See Department of the Army Pamphlet 27-17, Procedural Guide for Article 32(b) Investigating Officer. The proceeding may be closed. McDonald v. Hodson, 19 C.M.A. 582, 42 C.M.R. 184 (1970); R.C.M. 405(h)(3).
75. See Rule 1101(d), Military Rules of Evidence. The investigating officer should take note of objections. McDonald v. Hodson, 19 C.M.A. 582, 42 C.M.R. 184 (1970).
United States v. Martel, 19 M.J. 917 (A.C.M.R. 1985) (no fair risk that Article 32 officer's consideration of privileged testimony materially affected his recommendation or misled the convening authority. Court noted that because this error took place during the hearing where the

The proceedings are conducted in the presence of the accused and his counsel,[76] and begin with the investigating officer advising the accused of his various rights. The investigating officer may examine and consider tangible and documentary evidence, testimony of available witnesses, and alternative forms of evidence and testimony.[77] If the investigating officer considers live testimony, he may either have the statements summarized and sworn to,[78] or he may have a verbatim record made, in which case the Article 32 testimony may be later admissible in a later trial as former testimony[79] and is subject to a Jencks Act request.[80] Counsel for each side may be permitted to question the witnesses, subject to the discretion of the investigating officer.[81]

During the investigation, counsel for the government and for the defense should object promptly[82] to procedures or evidence although the investigating officer is not required to rule upon or resolve the objections.[83] He may require that the objections be in writing.[84] Failure to object will be treated as a waiver unless good cause is shown.[85]

§ 7-2(D). Investigating Officer's Report.

The investigating officer is required to make a formal report of his findings if it appears that the charges may be referred to a general court-martial or if he has been directed to do so. Otherwise an informal report is permitted.[86] The formal report is presented on DD Form 457,[87] with attached exhibits and

---

defense had an opportunity to assess the potential damage, no presumption of prejudice would lie; compare with error occurring outside the presence of the accused or defense counsel).

76. United States v. Matthews, 15 M.J. 622 (N.M.C.M.R. 1982).

77. *See supra* § 7-2(B) and R.C.M. 405(g)(4). United States v. Wood, 36 M.J. 651 (A.C.M.R. 1992) (Article 32 officer admitted copy of videotaped interview of child sexual abuse victim with investigator; it was incorporated into the sworn testimony of the child at the Article 32 hearing and thus became sworn testimony; defense counsel used the tape at trial as a prior inconsistent statement in an attempt to impeach the victim).

78. R.C.M. 405(h)(1)(A) Discussion.

79. Rule 804, MIL. R. EVID. United States v. Spindle, 28 M.J. 35 (C.M.A. 1989) (Article 32 testimony admissible); United States v. Hubbard, 28 M.J. 27 (C.M.A. 1989) (Article 32 testimony of unavailable witness was admissible); United States v. Ortiz, 33 M.J. 549 (A.C.M.R. 1991) (if no objection is made to incorporation of witness's prior statement into Article 32 testimony, the statement is admissible under the former testimony exception to the hearsay rule); United States v. Austin, 35 M.J. 271 (C.M.A. 1992) (prejudicial error where Article 32 testimony taken into deliberation room; court noted commonality between depositions and Article 32 testimony).

80. United States v. Thomas, 7 M.J. 655 (A.C.M.R. 1979); United States v. Scott, 6 M.J. 547 (A.F.C.M.R. 1978). *Cf.* United States v. Giusti, 22 M.J. 733 (C.G.C.M.R. 1986) (failure to record testimony not within Jencks Act). *See also infra* § 10-4(B).

81. *Cf.* United States v. Lewis, 33 M.J. 758 (A.C.M.R. 1991) (Article 32 investigating officer had authority to restrict repetitive questioning by defense counsel).

82. Prompt objections generally permit the investigating officer to take any necessary corrective action when it is most needed. *See* R.C.M. 405(h)(2) Analysis.

83. R.C.M. 405(h)(2).

84. *Id.*

85. *See* R.C.M. 405(k).

86. United States v. Scott, 6 M.J. 547 (A.F.C.M.R. 1978).

87. *See* Appendix 7.

witness statements.[88] The *Manual* requires that the following points be included in the report:[89]

    a. Information as to the name and address of counsel and whether counsel was absent or present during the proceedings;
    b. Statement on the substance of testimony taken;
    c. Any other statements, documents, or matters considered or a description of them;
    d. A statement regarding the mental responsibility and capacity of the accused;
    e. A statement whether essential witnesses will be available for trial and if not, the reasons for their unavailability; and
    f. Recommendation as to disposition of the charges.[90]

A copy of the report is forwarded to the commander who ordered the investigation and to the accused.[91]

While a civilian grand jury has broad investigatory powers to determine what, if any, offenses, have been committed, the Article 32 investigation generally focuses on the alleged charges reflected in the charge sheet,[92] not offenses in general.[93] Thus, if the investigating officer believes that other uncharged offenses may have been committed, he may either recommend the *preferred* of additional charges, if the investigation is still pending, or proceed with an investigation of those offenses.[94] If the investigation has been completed, it may be reopened to consider any additional charges.[95]

Any objections to the report must be made to the commander who ordered the investigation within 5 days of the receipt of the report by the accused. Failure to object constitutes waiver unless good cause is shown.[96]

---

88. The attached materials generally include the charge sheet; sworn statements, or transcripts of witnesses; expected testimony of absent witnesses; documentary and real evidence or a description of it; accused's statement, if any, at the investigation; report of medical or sanity boards, if any; previous convictions; and materials received with the charges but not considered.
89. R.C.M. 405(j)(2).
90. This recommendation is not binding. Green v. Widdecke, 19 C.M.A. 576, 42 C.M.R. 178 (1970).
91. Article 32(b), U.C.M.J.
92. *See* Chapter 6; Appendix 6.
93. *See* United States v. Bender, 32 M.J. 1002 (N.M.C.M.R. 1991) (investigation focuses on charges, not offenses).
94. *See* Art. 32(d), U.C.M.J. This provision was added by Congress as part of the National Defense Authorization Act for Fiscal Year (FY) 1996. Pub. L. No. 104-106, 110 Stat. 186 (1996). The investigating officer may do so, however, only if (1) the accused is present at the investigation; (2) the accused is apprised of the nature of the uncharged offense being investigated; and (3) the accused is afforded the assistance of counsel, cross-examination, and the opportunity to present evidence.
95. *See* United States v. Bender, 32 M.J. 1002 (N.M.C.M.R. 1991) (investigation focuses on charges, not offenses).
96. R.C.M. 405(j)(4).

§ 7-2(E). Defects in the Investigation.

An accused is not entitled to an error-free pretrial investigation. Instead he is entitled to a "thorough and impartial investigation,"[97] and one that is in "substantial compliance" with the Manual for Courts-Martial.[98] Although defects in the investigation are not jurisdictional,[99] they may give rise to appropriate relief in the nature of a new investigation[100] or a continuation of the original investigation. Such relief almost always results in delays. Thus, timely objections are important to insure prompt remedial action.[101]

Assuming that timely objections have been made,[102] uncured defects may be raised in a motion for appropriate relief before the military judge.[103] If the defect has deprived the accused of a substantial pretrial right, he is entitled to judicial relief regardless of whether such relief would benefit him at trial.[104] If no substantial pretrial right is involved, the accused must first demonstrate that he has been, or will be, prejudiced.[105] The military courts have identified the following as substantial pretrial rights: Assistance of effective,[106] qualified[107] defense counsel; production of available witnesses;[108] the investigation must have been ordered by competent authority;[109] and, the accused must be

---

97. Article 32(a), U.C.M.J.
98. R.C.M. 405(a).
99. Article 32(e), U.C.M.J. Humphrey v. Smith, 336 U.S. 695 (1949); United States v. Clark, 11 M.J. 179 (C.M.A. 1981); United States v. Johnson, 7 M.J. 396 (C.M.A. 1979).
100. United States v. Wright, 40 C.M.R. 616 (A.C.M.R. 1969). Granting a new investigation does not void the convening authority's referral of charges to trial. United States v. Clark, 11 M.J. 179 (C.M.A. 1981).
101. See R.C.M. 405(h)(2) Analysis.
102. See §§ 7-2(C), (D). United States v. Cunningham, 21 M.J. 585 (A.C.M.R. 1985) (failure of investigating officer to note defense objection was non-prejudicial error).
103. See § 13-5(D).
104. United States v. Chuculate, 5 M.J. 143 (C.M.A. 1978); United States v. Chestnut, 2 M.J. 84 (C.M.A. 1976); United States v. Donaldson, 23 C.M.A. 293, 49 C.M.R. 542 (1975); United States v. Mickel, 9 C.M.A. 324, 26 C.M.R. 104 (1958); United States v. Miro, 22 M.J. 509 (A.F.C.M.R. 1986).
   Cf. United States v. Freedman, 23 M.J. 820 (N.M.C.M.R. 1987) (convening authority improperly rescinded a continuance granted by the Article 32 investigating officer. Although this clearly constituted error, the court cited United States v. Hasting, 461 U.S. 499 (1983), for the proposition that the standard of review should be the doctrine of constitutional harmless error. The court summarily concluded that the error in this case was harmless).
105. See, e.g., United States v. Payne, 3 M.J. 354 (C.M.A. 1977) (impartiality of Art. 32 officer). See also United States v. Cunningham, 12 C.M.A. 402, 30 C.M.R. 402 (1961); United States v. Lopez, 20 C.M.A. 76, 42 C.M.R. 268 (1970); United States v. Castleman, 11 M.J. 562 (A.F.C.M.R. 1981).
106. United States v. Judson, 3 M.J. 908 (A.C.M.R. 1977).
107. United States v. Mickel, 9 C.M.A. 324, 26 C.M.R. 104 (1958).
108. United States v. Ledbetter, 2 M.J. 37 (C.M.A. 1976); United States v. Chestnut, 2 M.J. 84 (C.M.A. 1976). In United States v. McCarty, 25 M.J. 667 (A.F.C.M.R. 1987), a civilian witness failed to reappear for cross-examination. The court concluded that the right to cross-examine available witnesses is a substantial pretrial right but concluded that the defense counsel had waived the objection for "sound" tactical reasons.
109. United States v. Donaldson, 23 C.M.A. 293, 49 C.M.R. 542 (1975).

mentally competent.[110] Should the Article 32 investigation be reopened, there is no need to re-refer the charges and serve them again on the accused.[111]

Normally, a guilty plea at trial will waive any defects in the Article 32 investigation.[112] If the accused pleaded not guilty but failed to object, the courts have considered the Article 32 defects as having merged with the trial and will grant relief only if the accused can demonstrate that he was prejudiced at trial.[113] In the past, however, the courts have granted relief in the absence of an objection where there has been a gross violation of Article 32[114] or where the accused was denied counsel.[115] *See also* § 13-5(D).

§ 7-3. The Staff Judge Advocate's Pretrial Advice.

The second prong of the two-pronged procedural prerequisite to referral of charges to a general court-martial is the staff judge advocate's (SJA) or legal officer's pretrial advice. Article 34, U.C.M.J.[1] requires the general court-martial convening authority to first obtain the formal written opinion of his chief legal advisor.[2] Thus, the Article 32 pretrial investigation and the Article 34 pretrial advice combine to form an invaluable screening device. The advice, unlike the recommendations of the Article 32 investigating officer, can be binding on the convening authority.[3] In most commands, the draft pretrial advice is prepared by one of the counsel in the legal advisor's office.[4] Nonetheless, the advice that has been labeled a "prosecutorial tool,"[5] constitutes the *personal* advice of the staff judge advocate. Thus, unless he is otherwise disqualified,[6] he is responsible for it and must personally sign it.[7]

Although a pretrial advice is not necessary for charges referred to either a summary or special court-martial, the convening authority may nonetheless receive some sort of written memorandum on the disposition of charges. Note

---

110. United States v. Saunders, 11 M.J. 912 (A.C.M.R. 1981).
111. United States v. Clark, 11 M.J. 179 (C.M.A. 1981); United States v. Packer, 8 M.J. 785 (N.C.M.R. 1980).
112. United States v. Lopez, 20 C.M.A. 76, 42 C.M.R. 268 (1970); United States v. Judson, 3 M.J. 908 (A.C.M.R. 1977); United States v. Griffin, 1 M.J. 884 (A.F.C.M.R. 1976).
113. United States v. Cruz, 5 M.J. 286 (C.M.A. 1978).
114. United States v. Parker, 6 C.M.A. 75, 19 C.M.R. 201 (1955).
115. United States v. McMahan, 6 C.M.A. 709, 21 C.M.R. 31 (1956).
1. *See* Appendix 3. *See generally* Weaver, "Pretrial Advice of the Staff Judge Advocate or Legal Officer Under Article 34, Uniform Code of Military Justice," 19 MIL. L. REV. 37 (1963).
2. R.C.M. 406. United States v. Murray, 25 M.J. 445 (C.M.A. 1988); United States v. Hayes, 24 M.J. 786 (A.C.M.R. 1987) (acting GCM convening authority received legal advice from acting staff judge advocate).
3. United States v. Greenwalt, 6 C.M.A. 569, 20 C.M.R. 285 (1955).
4. United States v. Hardin, 7 M.J. 399 (C.M.A. 1979).
5. *Id.* United States v. Klawuhn, 33 M.J. 941 (N.M.C.M.R. 1991) (extensive discussion of "prosecutorial" tool re pretrial advice).
6. An SJA is disqualified if he has previously acted in the case as an investigating officer, military judge, trial counsel, defense counsel, or court member. *See* Article 6(c), U.C.M.J.; R.C.M. 406(b) Discussion.
7. R.C.M. 406(b) Discussion. *See, e.g.,* United States v. Smith, 33 M.J. 627 (A.F.C.M.R. 1991) (SJA adopted as his own pretrial advice prepared by former assistant trial counsel).

that a formal supplemental pretrial advice is required where charges have been referred to another general court-martial following a mistrial[8] or withdrawal of charges.[9]

§ 7-3(A). Contents of the Pretrial Advice.

Both the U.C.M.J.[10] and *Manual*[11] provisions require the Staff Judge Advocate to include particular matters in his advice. They are as follows:

(1) Conclusion with respect to whether each specification alleges an offense under the code;[12]

(2) Conclusion with respect to whether the allegation of each offense is warranted by the evidence indicated in the report of investigation (if there is such a report);[13]

(3) Conclusion with respect to whether a court-martial would have jurisdiction over the accused and the offense;[14]

(4) Recommendation of the action to be taken by the convening authority.[15]

This "must" list is shorter than that included in the 1969 *Manual*. In addition, there is nothing in either Article 34 or the *Manual* that requires the SJA to discuss exhaustively the four factors. Thus, it is possible to present the required advice without supporting discussion or rationale.[16] On the other hand, an SJA is not limited to these four factors and may include other information such as (1) a brief summary of the evidence,[17] (2) any previous recommendations by those who have forwarded the charges,[18] (3) evidence in extenuation

---

8. R.C.M. 406(a) Discussion. *See also* § 15-4(B).
9. *See infra* § 8-4.
10. Article 34(a), U.C.M.J. Before the 1983 Military Justice Act, Article 34 required the SJA to state whether the charge alleged an offense and whether the charge was warranted by the evidence.
11. R.C.M. 406(b).
12. *See supra* § 6-1. United States v. Harrison, 23 M.J. 907 (N.M.C.M.R. 1987) (SJA was equivocal on whether a specification stated an offense).
13. *See* United States v. Engle, 1 M.J. 387 (C.M.A. 1976) (the standard is that degree of proof that would convince a reasonable, prudent person that there is probable cause to believe a crime was committed and the accused committed it); United States v. Johnson, 40 C.M.R. 451 (A.B.R. 1968). *See also* United States v. Kemp, 7 M.J. 760 (A.C.M.R. 1979) (discussion of available evidence).
14. *See generally* Chapter 4.
15. The SJA's "recommendation" is just that — it is not binding on the convening authority.
16. *See, e.g.*, United States v. Smith, 33 M.J. 968 (A.F.C.M.R. 1991) (pretrial advice need not contain any underlying rationale for conclusions; court noted that advice will rarely be more than one page in length). In a very serious or complicated case, the better practice would be to lay out more than mere conclusions.
17. *See* United States v. Kemp, 7 M.J. 760 (A.C.M.R. 1979).
18. This area has proved to be particularly troublesome. *See, e.g.*, United States v. Rivers, 20 C.M.A. 6, 42 C.M.R. 198 (1970) (unit commander's favorable recommendation omitted); United States v. Lawson, 16 C.M.A. 260, 36 C.M.R. 416 (1966) (investigating officer's favorable recommendation omitted).

or mitigation,[19] and (4) evidence in aggravation.[20] Although the SJA is not required to set out these points, when he does include them, he must insure that the information is accurate.[21]

In addition to the written advice, the SJA will normally forward the charge sheet and the Article 32 investigation report. Within this framework, the legal advisor is free to adopt a variety of formats. But he may not submit an oral advice.[22] For sample pretrial advices (long-form and short-form), see Appendix 8.

While it seems clear that the drafters of the *Manual* intended to keep the pretrial advice short and to the point, that has not always been the case. In *United States v. Smith*,[23] the court addressed the problems associated with an unnecessarily long and legalistic pretrial advice:

> Writers of long and technical advice and recommendations, and the staff judge advocates approving them, lose sight of the reform of the military justice system that occurred with the Military Justice Act of 1983 and the Manual for Courts-Martial, 1984. They do a disservice to the busy commanders they serve by failing to provide these commanders the succinct *conclusions* and *concise information* they need to refer the charges or take action on a case. If the recommendations or advice is too lengthy and filled with unnecessary "legalese," we waste this busy senior officer's time and create a very real possibility that the recommendation or advice will not be read. Finally, such detailed and technical documents only invite a return to the extensive litigation of assertions of error that plagued pre-1984 Manual for Courts-Martial pretrial advice and staff judge advocate reviews (emphasis in original).[24]

If charges are referred to trial, the accused must receive a copy of the SJA's advice.[25]

---

19. The legal advisor may point out the accused's background and his or her character of service. In the past, failure to set out these points was sometimes error. *See, e.g.*, United States v. Foti, 12 C.M.A. 303, 30 C.M.R. 303 (1961) (failure to mention favorable factors); United States v. Greenwalt, 6 C.M.A. 569, 20 C.M.R. 285 (1955) (failure to mention twelve years of unblemished service and family problems). *Cf.* United States v. Green, 37 M.J. 380 (C.M.A. 1993) (racial identifiers should not be used in either pretrial advice or post-trial recommendations; convening authority may not select case for prosecution simply because of race of accused; if such identifiers are used, the defense should challenge the relevance or motivation of such inclusion).

20. This might include, for example, a brief discussion of the impact of the accused's alleged conduct upon the command or upon the victim. *See also* Chapter 16 regarding sentencing evidence.

21. See § 7-3(B) for a discussion of defects in the pretrial advice.

22. United States v. Heaney, 9 C.M.A. 6, 25 C.M.R. 268 (1958).

23. 33 M.J. 968 (A.F.C.M.R. 1991).

24. *Id.* at 970.

25. Article 34(c), U.C.M.J.; R.C.M. 406(c). United States v. Plott, 38 M.J. 735 (A.F.C.M.R. 1993) (R.C.M. 406 includes no requirement that pretrial advice be served at any particular time; court recommended that it be served on accused as early as possible).

§ 7-3(B). Defective Pretrial Advice.

Errors in the pretrial advice, whether procedural or substantive, do not rise to jurisdictional defects[26] and may be waived by either failing to raise the issue[27] or by pleading guilty.[28] Even where there is an error, prejudice must be shown. The courts have adopted a test that inquires whether there is a reasonable likelihood that the convening authority would have disposed of the charges differently had he been presented with a correct pretrial advice.[29] If there is error and it has not been waived, the military judge may require a new advice.[30] If an appellate court determines that relief is warranted, it may reduce the conviction to a lesser included offense,[31] reassess the sentence,[32] or set aside the findings and sentence and order a rehearing.[33]

For a discussion on challenging the pretrial advice in a pretrial motion for appropriate relief, see § 13-5(D).

---

26. United States v. Loving, 41 M.J. 213 (1994) (factual errors in pretrial advice were nonprejudicial and were corrected in supplemental advice); United States v. Allen, 5 C.M.A. 626, 18 C.M.R. 250 (1955).
27. United States v. Jones, 34 M.J. 899 (N.M.C.M.R. 1992) (accused waived defect in pretrial advice, which had been signed by assistant staff judge advocate, by not objecting at trial); United States v. Fleenor, 42 C.M.R. 900 (A.C.M.R. 1970). Cf. United States v. Murray, 22 M.J. 700 (A.C.M.R. 1986) (despite MCM language, requirement of advice cannot be waived). In United States v. Murray, 25 M.J. 445 (C.M.A. 1988), no pretrial advice was prepared and the accused did not raise the issue until appellate review. The Court of Military Review concluded that the requirement of a pretrial advice cannot be waived and failure to submit an advice was *per se* prejudicial error. 22 M.J. 700 (A.C.M.R. 1986). The Court of Appeals concluded that it was nonjurisdictional error not to prepare a written advice and remanded the case for a determination of whether it was waived and, if not, whether the accused had been prejudiced.
   In lengthy dicta, the court in United States v. Hayes, 24 M.J. 786 (A.C.M.R. 1987), concluded that the pretrial advice may not be waived despite the language in R.C.M. 602 to the contrary.
28. *See, e.g.*, United States v. Henry, 50 C.M.R. 685 (A.F.C.M.R. 1975). Cf. United States v. Engle, 1 M.J. 387 (C.M.A. 1976) (plea of guilty did not waive inadequacies going to validity of trial).
29. United States v. Foley, 37 M.J. 822 (A.F.C.M.R. 1993) (SJA's incorrect advice concerning subordinate commander's recommendations was harmless error); United States v. Stark, 19 M.J. 519 (A.C.M.R. 1984) (minor omissions in the pretrial advice for this murder case did not render the advice defective; the court concluded that the irregularities had not misled the convening authority); United States v. Kemp, 7 M.J. 760 (A.C.M.R. 1979); United States v. Henry, 50 C.M.R. 685 (A.F.C.M.R. 1975); United States v. Skaggs, 40 C.M.R. 344 (A.B.R. 1968).
30. In United States v. Harrison, 23 M.J. 907 (N.M.C.M.R. 1987), the SJA equivocated in the pretrial advice on the issue of whether one of the specifications stated an offense. Rather than dismissing the specification on the grounds that it had not been properly referred, the trial judge should have resubmitted the advice to the SJA for a determination of whether he could reach a conclusion on the sufficiency of the specification. Cf. United States v. Klawuhn, 33 M.J. 941 (N.M.C.M.R. 1991) (clearly erroneous pretrial advice entitled accused to relief; trial judge erred in denying motion for appropriate relief).
31. United States v. Lawson, 16 C.M.A. 260, 36 C.M.R. 416 (1966).
32. United States v. Stacy, 42 C.M.R. 547 (A.C.M.R. 1970).
33. United States v. Edwards, 32 C.M.R. 586 (A.B.R. 1962).

APPENDIX REFERENCES

Appendix 1. Abbreviations.
Appendix 2. Glossary.
Appendix 3. U.C.M.J.
Appendix 4. Court-Martial Flow Chart.
Appendix 6. Charge Sheet.
Appendix 7. Investigating Officer's Report.
Appendix 8. Pretrial Advice.

ANNOTATED BIBLIOGRAPHY

BOOKS

Moyer, *Justice and the Military* (1972).

This one-volume loose-leaf reference contains detailed discussions of the role of commanders, jurisdiction, military criminal procedure, First Amendment rights, substantive law, and collateral review of courts-martial by the civilian court system. Chapter II contains a discussion of pretrial investigations.

Saltzburg, Schinasi & Schlueter, *Military Rules of Evidence Manual* (3d ed. 1991).

The authors have compiled the official text of the Military Rules of Evidence and the drafters' analysis to those rules, and have provided an editorial comment for each rule that explains the rule, shows how it might be used, and discusses potential problem areas.

PERIODICALS

Gaydos, "A Comprehensive Guide to the Military Pretrial Investigation," 111 MIL. L. REV. 49 (1986).

This article presents an excellent and comprehensive guide on the law applicable to both the Article 32 Investigation and the Article 34 Pretrial Advice. Although some legal issues under both remain unresolved, the author concludes that a servicemember charged with a felony is provided more due process rights than his civilian counterpart.

Gilley, "Using Counsel to Make Pretrial Procedure More Effective," MIL. L. REV. 45 (1974).

This article contains an excellent general summary of military pretrial procedures and identifies many of the key constitutional issues that relate to the use or nonuse of defense counsel in the pretrial process. It further contrasts the military procedures with the pretrial role of counsel in other American justice systems and suggests proposals to incorporate protections provided in other systems to enhance the efficiency, fairness, and effectiveness of military pretrial procedure.

Moyer, "Procedural Rights of the Military Accused: Advantages Over a Civilian Defendant," 22 ME. L. REV. 105 (1970); 51 MIL. L. REV. 1 (1971).

ARTICLE 32 INVESTIGATION

This forty-page article compares the civilian and military criminal procedures such as pretrial investigation, interrogation, right to witnesses, right to counsel, and appellate review. The author concludes that the military accused enjoys greater procedural and substantive advantages than his or her civilian counterpart.

Murphy, "The Formal Pretrial Investigation," 12 MIL. L. REV. 1 (1961).

The author examines in detail the military's pretrial investigation required by Article 32, U.C.M.J., and discusses the impact of various military case decisions on the procedural and substantive aspects of the military's counterpart to the grand jury.

Sandell, "The Grand Jury and the Article 32: A Comparison," 1 N. KY. ST. L.F. 25 (1973).

This article presents a comparison of the historical background, procedural safeguards, and advantages of the Article 32, U.C.M.J. pretrial investigation with the civilian grand jury system. The author suggests that the Article 32 investigation might be improved by using judges as the hearing officers and making their recommendations binding on the convening authority.

Symposium, "Military Justice," ARMY LAW., March 1996.

This 127-page symposium contains a Foreword and 11 short articles on a wide range of military justice topics. They are as follows:

Morris, "Foreword."
Barto, "Developments in the Substantive Criminal Law Under the Uniform Code of Military Justice."
Frisk, "New Developments in Pretrial Confinement."
Frisk, "New Developments in Speedy Trial."
Winn, "Recent Developments in Military Pretrial and Trial Procedure."
Masterton, "Recent Developments in Search and Seizure Law."
Masterson, "Recent Developments in Urinalysis Law."
Kohlman, "Are You Ready for Some Changes? Five Fresh Views of the Fifth Amendment."
Wright, "Sex, Lies, and Videotape: Child Sexual Abuse Cases Continue to Create Appellate Issues and Other Developments in the Areas of the Sixth Amendment, Discovery, Mental Responsibility, and Nonjudicial Punishment."
Henley, "Caveat Criminale: The Impact of the New Military Rules of Evidence in Sexual Offense and Child Molestation Cases."
Henley, "Current Developments in Evidence Law."
Morris, "New Developments in Sentencing and Post-Trial Procedure."

CHAPTER 8

CONVENING OF A COURT-MARTIAL, DETAILING PARTICIPANTS, AND THE REFERRAL PROCESS

§ 8-1. General.
§ 8-2. Convening the Court-Martial.
    § 8-2(A). The Convening Authority.
    § 8-2(B). The Convening Order.
§ 8-3. Detailing the Participants.
    § 8-3(A). The Military Judge.
    § 8-3(B). Trial and Defense Counsel.
        § 8-3(B)(1). Qualifications of Counsel.
        § 8-3(B)(2). Detailing Military Counsel.
        § 8-3(B)(3). Requests for Individual Military Counsel.
        § 8-3(B)(4). Obtaining Civilian Counsel.
    § 8-3(C). Members of the Court.
        § 8-3(C)(1). Qualifications of Members.
        § 8-3(C)(2). Requests for Enlisted Members.
        § 8-3(C)(3). Constitutional Challenges to Composition.
        § 8-3(C)(4). Selecting the Members.
    § 8-3(D). Changes in Composition of Court.
§ 8-4. Referral of Charges to a Court-Martial.
§ 8-5. Withdrawal of Charges.
§ 8-6. Service of Charges Upon the Accused.
Appendix References.
Annotated Bibliography.

§ 8-1. General.

The court-martial is a temporary creature of statute[1] that hears only a limited number of cases and is then permanently adjourned. Only a court-martial that is properly convened and composed is capable of rendering valid judgments. In addition, the charges must be properly referred to the court for its disposition. Failure to meet these requirements may result in a variety of jurisdictional defects.[2]

In the preceding chapter, the discussion centered on the process of preferring charges and forwarding them up through the chain of command, each commander deciding or recommending what disposition would be appropriate. Here the discussion assumes that a commander has decided that a court-martial should try the case, it addresses the mechanics of convening the court,[3] appointing its participants, and referring the charges to the court.[4] Finally,

---

1. McClaughry v. Deming, 186 U.S. 49 (1902).
2. Runkle v. United States, 122 U.S. 543 (1886); United States v. Marker, 1 C.M.A. 393, 3 C.M.R. 127 (1952). *Cf.* United States v. Glover, 15 M.J. 419 (C.M.A. 1983) (court found no prejudice where the court actually convened was a special court-martial although all parties proceeded under impression that it was a GCM). *See generally* §§ 4-13 to 4-16.
3. *See* § 8-2.
4. *See* §§ 8-3, 8-4.

discussion turns to withdrawal of charges from a court[5] and service of charges upon the accused[6] once referral of the charges is completed.

§ 8-2. Convening the Court-Martial.

A court-martial is created, *convened,* by a properly authorized *convening authority* through means of a *convening order,* which appoints the court members. The following sections address that process.

§ 8-2(A). The Convening Authority.

Congress has delegated to The President the authority to convene courts-martial, and in turn to the Secretaries of the military departments, and certain commanders.[1] Only those so designated, whose authority has not otherwise been restricted[2] and who are not disqualified,[3] may convene courts. The convening authority's powers are two-fold; the power to appoint the court members and the power to refer cases to the court so appointed. Each of these

---

5. *See* § 8-5.
6. *See* § 8-6.
1. *See* Articles 22, 23, 24, U.C.M.J. This would include commanders temporarily assigned. *See, e.g.,* United States v. O'Connor, 19 M.J. 673 (A.F.C.M.R. 1984) (convening authority was properly assigned the position of commander on a temporary basis and was therefore authorized to convene the accused's court-martial even though under the assumption of command regulations he would not have been so authorized). *Cf.* United States v. Guidry, 19 M.J. 984 (A.F.C.M.R. 1985) (substitute convening authority not authorized to convene court because he had not properly assumed command).
2. For example, a superior authority may prohibit a subordinate from convening a court for particular offenses. *See, e.g.,* R.C.M. 401(a) and the Navy's JAGMAN 0107a. United States v. Brown, 39 M.J. 114 (C.M.A. 1994) (court-martial had jurisdiction even though it was convened by temporary successor in command to the officer who was authorized under the regulations to convene court-martial involving national security offenses).
3. *See* § 4-4(A). Convening authority may be disqualified if he is an "accuser." Article 1(a), U.C.M.J. *See, e.g.,* United States v. Jeter, 35 M.J. 442 (C.M.A. 1992) (general who had been blackmailed by accused was considered accuser; nonjurisdictional error to have case referred to trial by subordinate; court held that accused waived issue by putting general in position of having a personal interest in the case).
United States v. Cox, 37 M.J. 543 (N.M.C.M.R. 1993) (convening authority did not become accuser simply because he had ordered restriction which accused was charged with breaking; he had nothing other than official interest in case); United States v. Allen, 31 M.J. 572 (N.M.C.M.R. 1990) (convening authority was not disqualified from acting where Secretary of Navy had provided instructions on handling and disposition of certain national security cases); United States v. Shelton, 26 M.J. 787 (A.F.C.M.R. 1988) (convening authority disqualified where he had ordered subordinate commander to prefer charges against the accused); United States v. Lawrence, 19 M.J. 609 (A.C.M.R. 1984) (CA was not an accuser simply because his superior had awarded medals to prosecution witnesses who had thwarted the accused's attempted rape ... the superior was acting in an official capacity in doing so); United States v. Deachin, 22 M.J. 611 (A.C.M.R. 1986) (defendant waived objection to convening of court by officer who had personal interest in the case; the sexual offense had been committed upon the 12-year-old daughter of his deputy commander); United States v. Beauchamp, 17 M.J. 590 (A.C.M.R. 1983) (convening authority disqualified because accused was charged with violating order (immunity order) given by CA); United States v. Trahan, 11 M.J. 566 (A.F.C.M.R. 1981). *See* § 6-1.

is a personal power and may not be delegated,[4] although the commander's staff and legal advisors may make recommendations throughout the process. Either the absence of authority to convene courts-martial or the improper use of the authority will, as a general rule, result in the court-martial proceedings being declared a nullity.[5]

§ 8-2(B). The Convening Order.

The convening order is a manifestation of the commander's creation of the court, and although it is almost always written, it may be oral.[6] The U.C.M.J. prescribes no particular format, but the *Manual* does provide a sample,[7] and the services have further specified the form to be used for the order itself and any amending orders.[8] Samples are included at Appendix 9. Normally, the order speaks for itself. That is, the order clearly states the type of court-martial being formed (i.e., summary, special, or general) and names the court members. In those cases where the order itself or conflicting orders create doubt about the composition of the court-martial,[9] the courts may attempt to give effect to the convening authority's intent.[10] Normally, minor technical or administrative errors in the convening order will not constitute jurisdictional error.[11] In assessing the validity of court-martial convening orders, the appellate courts will generally apply a presumption of regularity.[12]

---

4. R.C.M. 504(c)(4). United States v. Newcomb, 5 M.J. 4 (C.M.A. 1978); United States v. Ryan, 5 M.J. 97 (C.M.A. 1978) (ministerial acts may be delegated); United States v. Rice, 3 M.J. 1094 (N.C.M.R. 1977), *petition denied*, 4 M.J. 163 (C.M.A. 1977) (SJA selected panels to be submitted to convening authority); United States v. Shearer, 6 M.J. 737 (A.C.M.R. 1978).
5. In United States v. Jette, 25 M.J. 16 (C.M.A. 1987), the court held that a commander was not divested of his statutory authority to convene a court-martial even though he had apparently not resumed command in accordance with Air Force regulations. The court stated that absent congressional intent to the contrary, it would not attach jurisdictional significance to service regulations. United States v. Guidry, 19 M.J. 984 (A.F.C.M.R. 1985); United States v. Cases, 6 M.J. 950 (A.C.M.R. 1979) (commander without authority to convene court-martial).
6. *See, e.g.*, United States v. Ware, 5 M.J. 24 (C.M.A. 1978). But if no written confirmation follows, the members are not properly appointed and a jurisdictional defect exists. *See* United States v. Perkinson, 16 M.J. 400 (C.M.A. 1983).
7. *See* Appendix 6, Manual for Courts-Martial.
8. *See, e.g.*, Army Reg. 27-10, Chapter 12.
9. Note that the government is entitled to rely upon a presumption of regularity. United States v. Saunders, 6 M.J. 731 (A.C.M.R. 1978).
10. *See, e.g.*, United States v. Padilla, 1 C.M.A. 603, 5 C.M.R. 31 (1952).
11. United States v. Otero, 26 M.J. 546 (A.F.C.M.R. 1988) (discrepancy in date on convening order and on charge sheet not jurisdictional defect); United States v. Kellough, 19 M.J. 871 (A.F.C.M.R. 1985) (absence of command line on convening order was only an administrative, nonjurisdictional error). *See also* United States v. Shepardson, 17 M.J. 793 (A.F.C.M.R. 1983) and United States v. O'Connor, 19 M.J. 673 (A.F.C.M.R. 1984).
12. United States v. Jordan, 20 M.J. 977 (A.C.M.R. 1985) (presumption of regularity attaches to evidence of a prior judicial proceeding). *Cf.* United States v. Alston, 11 M.J. 656 (A.F.C.M.R. 1985); United States v. Leahy, 20 M.J. 564 (N.M.C.M.R. 1984) (court presumed regularity of amending order in absence of irregularity or defects on the face of the document; the court declined to rely on appellate defense counsel's off-the-record conversations with the SJA who had signed the order).

§ 8-3. Detailing the Participants.

Under the 1969 Manual for Courts-Martial, the convening authority was technically responsible for "detailing" not only the court members but also the military judge, the prosecutor, and the defense counsel. As a practical matter, however, the convening authority appointed the judge and counsel in accordance with who was available or already working on the case. Thus, the convening authority's appointment of the lawyers to the court was for all practical purposes, a mere formality. The vehicle for detailing all of these participants was the convening order.

The current *Manual* changed all of this. Now the convening authority details only the court members. The other participants are detailed by some other designated authority in accordance with service regulations.

The next sections address the qualifications of each category of participants, the judge, counsel, and members, and the procedures for detailing them to a particular case. The jurisdictional implications of unqualified participants are noted in Chapter 4 and their roles in the conduct of the trial are addressed in Chapter 15.

The accused's specific statutory rights to counsel are discussed in § 8-3(B).

§ 8-3(A). The Military Judge.

The presiding participant at the trial is the military judge, who must be a member of the bar of a federal court or the highest court of a state, and be certified as qualified to perform judicial duties by his or her Judge Advocate General.[1] Article 26(c) also requires that absent special exceptions, a person assigned as a military judge must function primarily in that capacity.[2] And unless the court-martial is convened by the President or the Secretary concerned, neither the convening authority nor a member of his staff is permitted to prepare an efficiency report on the judge.[3]

Article 26 also indicates that the judge will be ineligible if he has previously acted as an accuser,[4] a prosecution witness,[5] investigating officer,[6] magistrate,

---

1. Article 26, U.C.M.J.
2. In United States v. Beckermann, 27 M.J. 334 (C.M.A. 1989), the court discussed at length the requirement in Article 26(c). In an attempt to fill a temporary gap in judges, the convening authority temporarily appointed a JAGC officer to serve as the trial judge in the accused's case. The court held that that was jurisdictional error and noted that it would have been appropriate to appoint a military judge from another service, something that is becoming more commonplace.

In United States v. Mahloch, 29 M.J. 1080 (C.G.C.M.R. 1990), the military judge had previously served as a district legal officer and in that capacity completed an OER on the officer who replaced him and prepared the pretrial advice in this case. In that capacity he was also rated by the officer who eventually became the convening authority in this case; the OER was not finalized until after the trial was completed. The court concluded that this combination of events did not disqualify the judge; the convening authority's rating was only for that period of time when he served in a non-judicial capacity, and the court rejected the argument that the judge was nonetheless subject to the subtle pressures of a pending OER from the convening authority.

3. *See* Article 26(c), U.C.M.J.
4. *See supra* § 6-1.
5. United States v. Conley, 4 M.J. 327 (C.M.A. 1978); United States v. Tomchek, 4 M.J. 66 (C.M.J. 1977).
6. United States v. Goodman, 3 M.J. 1 (C.M.A. 1977). In United States v. Reeves, 12 M.J. 763

or counsel in the same case.[7] Other factors, such as a predisposition against an accused or the case, may later require him to recuse himself.[8] If a new trial or rehearing is ordered in the case, the same military judge may be again appointed.[9]

Military judges are usually not members of the convening authority's command but are instead assigned to an independent trial judiciary command[10] and then attached to a duty station at a particular installation or circuit and, depending on level of experience and rank, designated either as special court-martial or general court-martial judges.

The military judge is detailed in accordance with R.C.M. 503(b)(1):

> (1) By whom detailed. The military judge shall be detailed, in accordance with regulations of the Secretary concerned, by a person assigned as a military judge and directly responsible to the Judge Advocate General or the Judge Advocate General's designee. The authority to detail military judges may be delegated to persons assigned as military judges. If authority to detail military judges has been delegated to a military judge, that military judge may detail himself or herself as military judge for a court-martial.[11]

The order detailing the judge may be either reduced to writing and included in the record of trial or it may be announced orally on the record at the trial.[12] The service secretary may, however, require that in all cases that the order be reduced to writing.[13] Relying only upon an oral announcement at trial is obviously more convenient but that procedure lends itself to problems should the judge fail to note his detail for the record. In that case, failure to note the detail would not be jurisdictional but would instead be measured for specific

---

(A.C.M.R. 1981), the court held that serving as a neutral magistrate to determine pretrial confinement did not necessarily render one an "investigating officer."

7. *See* Article 26(d), U.C.M.J.

8. United States v. Sherrod, 26 M.J. 30 (C.M.A. 1988) (trial judge disqualified because of appearance of impropriety). *See* United States v. Berman, 28 M.J. 615 (A.F.C.M.R. 1989) (court concluded that judge should have recused himself in six cases where he had entered into a personal, sexual relationship with the prosecutor); United States v. Shackleford, 2 M.J. 17 (C.M.A. 1976); United States v. Wilson, 2 M.J. 548 (A.C.M.R. 1976).

9. *See* R.C.M. 810(b) (2); United States v. Mora, 26 M.J. 122 (C.M.A. 1988).

10. For example, Army military judges are assigned to the United States Army Trial Judiciary, United States Army Legal Services Agency.

11. *See, e.g.,* AR 27-10, para. 8-6, which grants the Army's Chief Trial Judge the authority to detail judges. He may delegate that authority to general court-martial judges (a judge who by reason of rank and experience is qualified by the service to preside at general courts-martial) who may detail themselves and also detail the special court-martial judges. United States v. Loving, 41 M.J. 213 (1994) (court rejected argument that accused was denied due process because trial and intermediate judges in peacetime military death-penalty cases do not have the protection of a fixed term of office).

12. R.C.M. 503(b)(2). *See also* § 12-2(G).

13. R.C.M. 503(b)(2).

prejudice.[14] Participation by a military judge who has not been detailed, however, may be jurisdictional error.[15] *See* § 4-15(A).

Although a general court-martial must include a military judge,[16] a judge is needed for a special court-martial only if the convening authority wishes the court to have the power to impose a bad-conduct discharge.[17] In practice, however, military judges preside over all special courts-martial even though the court, for other reasons, may not be empowered to adjudge a discharge. Although it is not common, military judges of one service may preside over the trial of an accused from another service.[18]

Some have suggested that in order to avoid the appearance of impropriety, trial judges (and appellate judges) should be given some form of tenure.[19] The underlying theory, which has some appeal, is that some assurance of job security would at a minimum give the appearance of neutrality. The same result may be reached indirectly, however, by appointing only senior judge advocates who, by reason of their military rank, are guaranteed a minimum number of years on active duty.

---

14. R.C.M. 503(b) Analysis citing S. Rep. No. 53, 98th Cong., 1st Sess. 12 (1983). United States v. Marsh, 19 M.J. 657 (A.C.M.R. 1984) (minor administrative errors in the appointment of the judge did not deprive the court of jurisdiction).

15. *See, e.g.*, United States v. Singleton, 21 C.M.A. 432, 45 C.M.R. 206 (1972).

16. Article 26(a), U.C.M.J.

17. Article 19, U.C.M.J. *See also* § 4-3(B).

18. *See, e.g.*, AR 27-10, para. 8-6e:

e. Cross-servicing.

(1) Nothing in this regulation precludes the detail of a military judge from another armed service who has been made available for detail to either a GCM or SPCM, provided that such military judge has been certified by the Judge Advocate General of his or her armed service. For administrative control, the concurrence of the Chief Trial Judge will be obtained before the judge is detailed.

(2) Army military judges may preside at courts-martial of other services, under R.C.M. 201(e)(4). For administrative control, the concurrence of the Chief Trial Judge should be obtained before the judge is detailed.

19. In United States v. Graf, 35 M.J. 450 (C.M.A. 1992), the court provided an extensive discussion of whether the Fifth Amendment's due process clause requires a fixed term of office for military judges. While it agreed that the due process clause extends to servicemembers and that judicial independence is a necessary component of military justice, the court concluded that the Uniform Code of Military Justice provides the requisite independence for all military judges. The court recognized, however, that a fixed term of office of some type is a fundamental component of the Anglo-American civilian judicial tradition. 35 M.J. at 463. The court also noted, but did not follow, a ruling from the Supreme Court of Canada which indicated that fixed terms are required. Genereux v. Her Majesty The Queen, No. 22103, SCR (Feb. 13, 1992).

United States v. Coffman, 35 M.J. 591 (N.M.C.M.R. 1992) (court rejected accused's argument that lack of fixed terms for military judges denies due process); United States v. Loving, 41 M.J. 213 (A.C.M.R. 1992) (court rejected argument that accused was denied due process because trial and intermediate judges in peace time military death-penalty cases do not have the protection of a fixed term of office). *See also* Fidell, "The Culture of Change in Military Law," 126 MIL. L. REV. 125 (1989).

In *United States v. Weiss*,[20] the Court of Military Appeals, now the Court of Appeals for the Armed Forces, addressed the question of whether the Appointments Clause of the Constitution applied to the appointment of military trial and appellate judges. The Appointments Clause provides that the President:

> [s]hall nominate, and by and with the Advice and Consent of the Senate, shall appoint Ambassadors, other public Ministers and Consuls, Judges of the Supreme Court, and all other Officers of the United States, whose appointments are not herein otherwise provided for, and which shall be established by Law; but the Congress may by Law vest the Appointment of such inferior Officers, as they think proper, in the President alone, in the Courts of Law, or in the Heads of Departments.[21]

A plurality (Judges Gierke and Cox) concluded that the Appointments Clause applies to the military justice system[22] but that a military officer could perform judicial duties without the necessity of a new judicial appointment under that Clause.[23] Thus, neither military trial judges[24] nor military appellate judges required special appointments.[25] In reaching that conclusion the plurality relied, in part, upon the Supreme Court's decision in *Shoemaker v. United States*,[26] where the Court concluded that second appointments of two commissioned officers to a commission created by Congress were not required; the additional duties were germane to the offices they already held under their original appointment as officers in the military service.[27]

Judge Crawford concurred in the result, concluding that in legislating for the armed services, Congress could provide for the designation of military judges in a manner not covered in the Appointments Clause.[28] Chief Judge Sullivan and Judge Wiss dissented. Chief Judge Sullivan, citing Freytag v. Commissioner of Internal Revenue,[29] concluded that both trial and appellate military judges are inferior Officers of the United States under the Appointments Clause and must be appointed to those offices by the President alone,

---

20. 36 M.J. 224 (C.M.A. 1992). *See also* United States v. Coffman, 35 M.J. 91 (N.M.C.M.R. 1992) (court held that Appointments Clause not violated by designation of special court-martial judges; court indicated that all military judges are commissioned officers and a second appointment by the President to serve as a judge is simply not required).

United States v. Carpenter, 37 M.J. 291 (C.M.A. 1993) (appointment of Chief Judge of Coast Guard Court of Military Review by General Counsel of Secretary of Transportation did not satisfy Appointments Clause, but his judicial acts were entitled to de facto validity).

United States v. Kovac, 36 M.J. 521 (C.G.C.M.R. 1992) (lengthy discussion rejecting accused's arguments that assignment of appellate judges violated Appointments Clause); United States v. Prive, 35 M.J. 569 (C.G.C.M.R. 1992) (Congress may provide for designation of appellate military judges in manner not covered in Appointments Clause of Constitution).

21. U.S. CONST., art. II, § 2, para. 2.
22. 36 M.J. at 226.
23. 36 M.J. at 234.
24. 36 M.J. at 230.
25. 36 M.J. at 233.
26. 147 U.S. 282 (1893).
27. 36 M.J. at 240.
28. 501 U.S. 868, 111 S. Ct. 2631 (1991).
29. 36 M.J. at 240.

by the Court of Military Appeals or other Courts of Law, by the Secretary of Defense or one of the Heads of Departments.[30] Judge Wiss concluded that Congress is not exempt from the limitations in the Appointments Clause and because Congress established the distinct office of military judge in Articles 26 and 66, U.C.M.J., the Appointments clause must be satisfied; the prior appointment as a military officer will not satisfy that clause because the specific judicial duties imposed on judges are not germane to the duties of a legally trained military officer.[31]

The Supreme Court granted certiorari review of *Weiss*[32] and concluded that military judges who are already military officers need not have a second appointment before acting in their judicial capacity.[33] Writing for the majority, Chief Justice Rehnquist rejected the argument that Congress intended for a second appointment or that the Appointments Clause, by its own force, required a second appointment.[34] Distinguishing the Court's opinion in *Shoemaker, infra*, he pointed out that even assuming that the principle of germaneness applied, the military justice system remains a highly specialized society and all officers play a role in that system.[35] The Court also rejected the argument that the Due Process Clause requires fixed terms of office for military judges.[36] Recognizing that fair trials depend on a degree of independence, the Court indicated that historically judges had not been tenured in the English military system, and that sufficient protections existed for insuring that military judges were free from unlawful influence.[37]

In *Ryder v. United States*,[38] the Court of Military Appeals concluded that the Appointments Clause had been violated when two civilian judges sat on the Coast Guard Court of Military Review by the appointment of the General Counsel for the Department of Transportation.[39] But the court concluded that the civilians were de facto officers and affirmed the conviction. The Supreme Court reversed, rejecting the argument that the judges were de facto. Rejecting a number of government arguments, the Court concluded that the accused was entitled to have his appeal heard by a properly constituted panel of the service court.

---

30. 36 M.J. at 240.
31. 36 M.J. 262-63.
32. 113 S. Ct. 2412 (1993). *See also* United States v. Rice, 36 M.J. 264 (C.M.A. 1993) (court indicated that it would deny all petitions for review based upon challenge to validity of judges appointments, subject to out-of-time petitions if Supreme Court grants certiorari and grants relief).
33. Weiss v. United States, 114 S. Ct. 752 (1994).
34. 114 S. Ct. at 760.
35. 114 S. Ct. at 759.
36. 114 S. Ct. at 763.
37. 114 S. Ct. at 762-63.
38. 115 S. Ct. 2031 (1995).
39. 39 M.J. 454 (C.M.A. 1994).

§ 8-3(B). Trial and Defense Counsel.

§ 8-3(B)(1). Qualifications of Counsel.

Each court-martial includes initially at least one detailed *trial counsel* (prosecutor) and one detailed *defense counsel*. In addition, assistant trial and defense counsel may be detailed. In a general court-martial, both the detailed trial counsel and the detailed military defense counsel must be "certified" under Article 27(b), U.C.M.J.,[40] by the Judge Advocate General as competent to act as counsel.[41] To be certified, counsel must, at a minimum,[42] be a member of the highest court of a state or a member of the Federal bar.[43] Any commissioned officer may be detailed to serve at a general court-martial as an assistant trial or assistant defense counsel;[44] each is permitted to act under the supervision of either the trial or defense counsel, respectively.[45]

At a special court-martial, the detailed defense counsel must be certified, as discussed *supra*, but any commissioned officer may act as the trial counsel.[46] Again, the assistant counsel need not be certified.[47]

A military counsel is disqualified from acting as counsel in any case in which he has acted as an accuser,[48] investigating officer,[49] military judge, or court member.[50] Note that the accused, however, may expressly waive those disqualifications as to his defense counsel.[51]

The *Manual* also disqualifies any counsel who has acted as counsel for the opposing party.[52] The problem of counsel having served on the opposite side of the case can arise in a number of contents. For example, in *United States v.*

---

40. *See* Appendix 3.
41. R.C.M. 502(d)(1).
42. Each Judge Advocate General may require additional qualifications. R.C.M. 502(d)(1) Discussion.
43. Article 27(b), U.C.M.J.
44. R.C.M. 502(d)(2). But the Secretary of the service may require additional or higher qualifications. *Id.*
45. R.C.M. 502(d)(5), (6).
46. R.C.M. 502(d)(2). United States v. Reynolds, 19 M.J. 529 (A.C.M.R. 1984) (trial counsel was not disqualified from acting on the case, under the ABA Canons (No. 5), simply because he knew that other members of the SJA office were to testify against the accused who was charged with filing a false claim with the SJA claims office; the SJA office is not a "firm" within the meaning of Canon 5).
47. R.C.M. 502(d)(2).
48. *See* § 6-1(A) for a discussion of who is an "accuser."
49. *See* § 7-2(A)(1). *See also* United States v. Trakowski, 10 M.J. 792 (A.F.C.M.R. 1981); United States v. Blanchette, 17 M.J. 512 (A.F.C.M.R. 1983) (trial counsel was not disqualified even though he had served as recorder (prosecutor) in accused's earlier administrative discharge proceeding).
50. R.C.M. 502(d)(4).
51. *Id.*
52. Article 27(a), U.C.M.J.; R.C.M. 502(d)(4). *See also* United States v. Ley, 20 M.J. 814 (N.M.C.M.R. 1985) (nonprejudicial error to detail military defense counsel who was administrative subordinate of the trial counsel). The practice is condemned. *See* United States v. Nicholson, 15 M.J. 436 (C.M.A. 1983).

Rushatz,[53] although the prosecution had been insensitive to issue by placing the accused's former legal assistance counsel on his case, the court concluded that no adverse information had been passed from that counsel to the prosecution team. In *United States v. Smith*,[54] the court concluded that the trial counsel was not disqualified because she had spoken with the defense previously, in her capacity as a member of the trial defense service, about the advisability of the accused taking a polygraph test. There was no actual, nor perceived, impropriety in her later acting as prosecutor where in that meeting she had not acted for the defense. In *United States v. Stubbs*,[55] the court rejected the accused's argument that the entire prosecution staff should have been disqualified because one of the members of the prosecution office had earlier provided him legal advice on the incidents which later resulted in court-martial charges. The court rejected a *per se* disqualification but indicated that:

> [O]nce the accused shows that he entered into an attorney-client relationship with a particular lawyer concerning the same or related matters to those being tried at his court-martial and that his lawyer, after terminating the relationship, has joined the prosecutor's office then prosecuting the accused, the Government has the burden of affirmatively demonstrating that no communication whatsoever has occurred between that lawyer and the prosecution staff regarding any aspect of the accused's case.[56]

In *Stubbs*, the defense apparently agreed that no such conversations had occurred between the lawyer and the prosecution staff. The Discussion to R.C.M. 502(d)(4) indicates that there is a rebuttable presumption that any counsel who has been detailed between referral of charges, *see* § 8-4, and the trial, has acted as counsel for a party.[57] Apparently this disqualification may be waived.[58]

Unlike military justice practices of some years ago, the contemporary court-martial rarely includes a military counsel who is not a JAGC officer.

---

53. 31 M.J. 450 (C.M.A. 1990).
54. 26 M.J. 152 (C.M.A. 1988).
55. 23 M.J. 188 (C.M.A. 1987).
56. *Id.* at 193-94.
57. *See* United States v. Diaz, 9 M.J. 691 (N.C.M.R. 1980); United States v. Fowler, 6 M.J. 501 (A.F.C.M.R. 1978).
58. In United States v. Sparks, 29 M.J. 52 (C.M.A. 1989), the accused was defended by a counsel who had previously acted in the case as the government representative at the Article 32 investigation. The court concluded that the requirements of Article 27(a) are not jurisdictional and that the accused could waive the disqualification if he was fully aware of the potential conflict. The court noted, however, that a military judge would not be required to accept the accused's waiver. *Cf.* United States v. Catt, 1 M.J. 41 (C.M.A. 1975) (accused may expressly elect to be represented by counsel who technically acted for the government). *See also* United States v. Hustwit, 33 M.J. 608 (N.M.C.M.R. 1991) (citing three-pronged test for determining whether a prosecutor is disqualified because he formerly served as defense counsel, the court concluded that although prosecutor had formed attorney-client relationship with accused on Article 15 and that the offense involved was the same as the one at trial, the prosecutor had not assumed an adverse position; even assuming he did, the accused waived the issue by not raising it at trial although he had raised the matter with defense counsel who told him not to worry about it).

Any civilian counsel or individually requested military counsel who represents the accused must either be:

(A) A member of the bar of a Federal court or of the bar of the highest court of a State; or
(B) If not a member of such a bar, a lawyer who is authorized by a recognized licensing authority to practice law and is found by the military judge to be qualified to represent the accused upon a showing to the satisfaction of the military judge that the counsel has appropriate training and familiarity with the general principles of criminal law which apply in a court-martial.[59]

In determining the qualifications of the second category of counsel, the Discussion to R.C.M. 502(d)(3) suggests that the judge consider, *inter alia,* counsel's availability, familiarity of the counsel with spoken English, and the practical alternatives for disciplining such counsel for acts of misconduct.[60] Note that civilian counsel and individual military counsel are not "detailed" to act as counsel. Their representation is arranged through the efforts of the accused, often with the assistance of the detailed military counsel. See the discussion *infra.*

There is no right to detailed counsel at summary courts-martial.[61]

§ 8-3(B)(2). Detailing Military Counsel.

The military counsel are detailed in accordance with service regulations, which generally permit delegation of the authority to detail.[62] For example, the Army has designated the Staff Judge Advocate or his delegate, as the authority to detail the trial counsel, i.e., prosecutors.[63] Defense counsel are to be detailed by the Chief, U.S., Army Trial Defense Service or his delegate.[64] The order of detailing may either be reduced to writing and included in the record or may be orally noted for the record during the trial.[65] Service regulations may require that in all cases the detailing order be reduced to writing.[66] Defects in either the detailing process or in announcing the detail, should be measured for prejudice.[67]

By the time the convening authority directs trial by court-martial, the accused will normally have entered into an attorney-client relationship with a

---

59. R.C.M. 502(d)(3).
60. *See, e.g.,* Soriano v. Hosken, 9 M.J. 221 (C.M.A. 1980) (counsel was not admitted to practice before an American court): United States v. Batts, 3 M.J. 440 (C.M.A. 1977) (Philippine lawyer permitted to represent accused).
61. Middendorf v. Henry, 425 U.S. 25 (1976) (no right to counsel because summary court-martial is not a criminal prosecution).
62. *See* R.C.M. 503(c)(1).
63. AR 27-10, para. 5-3.
64. AR 27-10, para. 5-4.
65. R.C.M. 503(c)(2).
66. R.C.M. 503(c)(2).
67. *See* R.C.M. 503(c) Analysis; Wright v. United States, 2 M.J. 9 (C.M.A. 1976). *See also* § 4-15(B).

military defense counsel.[68] That counsel will normally be detailed to represent the accused at trial.[69] The accused is not limited to the services of a detailed military lawyer, however. He may be represented by civilian counsel and an individually requested military counsel, if that counsel is reasonably available. As noted in the following discussion, if the accused does obtain the services of an individual military counsel, the detailed defense counsel is normally excused from the case.

Where two military counsel have advised the accused prior to trial it would seem appropriate for both to represent the accused: one as individual military counsel and the other as an associate counsel.[70] There is some authority, however, for the proposition that the detailing authority is not required to consider the accused's preferences.[71]

§ 8-3(B)(3). Requests for Individual Military Counsel.

The accused is entitled, under Article 38(b)(3), U.C.M.J., to representation by an individual military counsel who is "reasonably available."[72] The procedure for obtaining such counsel is spelled out in R.C.M. 506(b)(2): The accused or his detailed counsel submits the request through the trial counsel to the convening authority,[73] who in turn determines if the requested counsel is unavailable by virtue of his position, duties, or rank. R.C.M. 506(b) states that the following persons are not reasonably available:

(A) A general or flag officer;
(B) A trial or appellate military judge;
(C) A trial counsel;
(D) An appellate defense or government counsel;

---

68. It should be noted, however, that an accused is not entitled to have a defense counsel permanently assigned to him. Counsel are appointed on a case-by-case basis. United States v. Williams, 27 M.J. 758 (A.F.C.M.R. 1988). *Cf.* United States v. Williams, 40 M.J. 809 (A.C.M.R. 1994) (mere detailing of counsel does not in itself establish attorney-client relationship); United States v. Beckermann, 35 M.J. 842 (C.G.C.M.R. 1992) (court rejected argument that accused was prejudiced by delay in appointing defense counsel for new trial; apparently, appellate counsel had continued to represent the accused).

69. *See* United States v. Kelly, 16 M.J. 244, 247 (C.M.A. 1983), where the court noted that to do so "would seem logical."

70. This would seem especially prudent where attorney-client relationships have been established between both counsel and the accused. *See, e.g.,* United States v. Hanson, 24 M.J. 377 (C.M.A. 1987) (detailed counsel was relieved as counsel by the trial judge when the latter determined that counsel was not being effective; new counsel was detailed but the original counsel remained on the case as assistant defense counsel); United States v. Kelly, 16 M.J. 244 (C.M.A. 1983). The military courts have been particularly sensitive to attempts to sever the attorney-client relationship. United States v. Catt, 1 M.J. 41 (C.M.A. 1975); United States v. Eason, 21 C.M.A. 335, 45 C.M.R. 109 (1972); United States v. Andrews, 21 C.M.A. 165, 44 C.M.R. 219 (1972).

71. United States v. Kelly, 16 M.J. 244 (C.M.A. 1983).

72. *See* Appendix 3.

73. United States v. Cutting, 14 C.M.A. 347, 34 C.M.R. 127 (1964).

§ 8-3(B)(3)   CONVENING OF A COURT-MARTIAL   § 8-3(B)(3)

(E) A principal legal advisor to a command, organization, or agency and, when such command, organization, or agency has general court-martial jurisdiction, the principal assistant of such an advisor;
(F) An instructor or student at a service school or academy;
(G) A student at a college or university;
(H) A member of the staff of the Judge Advocate General of the Army, Navy, or Air Force, the Chief Counsel of the Coast Guard, or the Director, Judge Advocate Division, Headquarters, Marine Corps.

Service regulations may further delineate who is not available.[74] If the convening authority determines that the requested counsel is among those individuals listed in 506(b) or those listed in the service regulations, he will deny the requests[75] unless the accused can demonstrate that the counsel will not be in one of the foregoing categories or that there is an existing attorney-client relationship. In those cases, the convening authority will forward the request to the requested counsel's commander who will decide whether the counsel is reasonably available.[76] In making that administrative decision the commander should consider factors such as the counsel's workload, duty position, possible conflicts of interest, time and distance requirements, and the overall impact of the counsel's participation on the remainder of counsel in the office.[77]

If the request is denied by the counsel's commander, the accused may appeal that decision to the next higher commander.[78] He is not entitled to review by departmental or higher authority, however.[79] If the accused's appeal is unsuccessful he may raise the issue anew before the judge in a motion for appropriate relief.[80] *See* § 13-5(H).

Should the accused obtain an individual military counsel, the detailed military counsel is normally excused[81] because the accused has no statutory right

---

74. *See, e.g.*, AR 27-10, para. 5-7.
75. His decision may be reviewed for abuse of discretion. United States v. Harcrow, 9 M.J. 669 (N.C.M.R. 1980); United States v. Quinones, 1 M.J. 64 (C.M.A. 1975); United States v. Barton, 48 C.M.R. 358 (N.C.M.R. 1973).
76. *See* United States v. Johnson, 23 C.M.A. 148, 48 C.M.R. 764 (1974); United States v. Colton, 23 C.M.A. 152, 48 C.M.R. 768 (1974); United States v. Krajewski, 30 M.J. 995 (N.M.C.M.R. 1990) (counsel's commander committed non-prejudicial error in denying accused's request for counsel with whom he had an attorney-client relationship); United States v. Kelley, 40 M.J. 515 (A.C.M.R. 1994) (no abuse of discretion to deny request for individual military counsel); United States v. Greenwald, 37 M.J. 537 (A.C.M.R. 1993) (no abuse of discretion in denying request to be represented by individual military counsel who was reserve JAGC; court noted that a judge advocate not on active duty will seldom be reasonably available).
77. *See, e.g.*, AR 27-10, para. 5-7; United States v. Harcrow, 9 M.J. 669 (N.C.M.R. 1980) (all circumstances should be considered).
78. *See* R.C.M. 506(b)(2).
79. *Id.*
80. There is some authority that he must do so to preserve the issue for appeal. United States v. Cutting, 14 C.M.A. 347, 34 C.M.R. 127 (1964). *Cf.* United States v. Anderson, 36 M.J. 963 (A.F.C.M.R. 1993) (judge has no authority to overrule convening authority's administrative decision denying individual counsel).
81. R.C.M. 506(b)(3).

to more than one military counsel.[82] Nonetheless, the authority who detailed the military defense counsel may in his discretion permit that counsel to remain on the case as an *associate* defense counsel.[83] An adverse decision is reviewable only on grounds that the detailing authority abused his discretion.[84]

If the detailing authority has abused his discretion the remedy is not dismissal of the charges.[85] Rather, the judge should grant appropriate relief such as a continuance.[86] As noted in the earlier discussion on detailing military counsel, if the accused has already entered into an attorney-client relationship with a detailed military counsel it would seem prudent to permit that counsel to remain on the defense team even if an individual military counsel is provided. Failure to do so may raise substantial questions about whether it was appropriate to sever the attorney-client relationship.[87]

Although the military's system of providing an individual military counsel demonstrates an attribute of fairness, it is not without its drawbacks and potential for abuse. In some cases, the accused's request for individual counsel can be used as leverage against the government, which must bear the costs of providing such counsel. At least one judge on the Court of Military Appeals has urged the removal of the right to individual military counsel.[88]

Once an accused has been represented by an individual military counsel of his choice, generally that counsel will be his counsel at any subsequent rehearing.[89] In *United States v. Beatty*,[90] the accused was represented at trial by an individual military counsel. The convening authority, however, set aside the findings and ordered a rehearing because of defects in the providency inquiry of the accused's guilty plea. The individual military counsel was de-

---

82. R.C.M. 506(a). United States v. Jordan, 22 C.M.A. 164, 46 C.M.R. 164 (1973).

83. R.C.M. 506(b)(3). United States v. Bevacqua, 37 M.J. 996 (C.G.C.M.R. 1993) (SJA interfered with accused's right to counsel by excusing associate defense counsel, who had previously been permitted to remain on case after accused selected individual military counsel; court held that there was no good cause for doing so; accused not required to show prejudice).

84. *Id.* The Discussion to R.C.M. 506(b)(3) indicates that the detailing authority should consider the seriousness and complexity of the case, whether civilian counsel has been obtained, and the detail of an additional trial counsel. United States v. Berry, 30 M.J. 1169 (C.G.C.M.R. 1990) (nonprejudicial error where convening authority denied accused's request to retention of detailed counsel on case).

85. *See* United States v. Redding, 11 M.J. 100 (C.M.A. 1981).

86. R.C.M. 906(b)(2). *See also* § 15-4(A).

87. *See* United States v. Hanson, 24 M.J. 377 (C.M.A. 1987) (military judge relieved counsel of his duties as detailed counsel when it appeared that he was not an effective unnecessary counsel; judge specifically stated that he was not severing the attorney-client relationship and counsel remained on the case as an assistant defense counsel); United States v. Kelly, 16 M.J. 244 (C.M.A. 1983). *Cf.* R.C.M. 506(d) which indicates that representation by an individual military counsel is one justified reason for severing an existing attorney-client relationship between the accused and another military counsel.

88. United States v. Kelly, 16 M.J. 244, 250, n. 5 (C.M.A. 1983) (Fletcher, J., dissenting).

89. United States v. Plott, 38 M.J. 735 (A.F.C.M.R. 1993) (at rehearing accused released counsel who had represented him at trial; later he attempted to renege on release and requested same counsel as IMC; court concluded that release was made knowingly and voluntarily). The same would also be true for other post-trial proceedings. *See infra* § 16-3.

90. 25 M.J. 311 (C.M.A. 1987).

tailed as the accused's counsel and when the accused requested another individual counsel, it was denied. Chief Judge Everett expressed the view that the legislative history of Article 63, which governs rehearings, indicates that the rehearing is a continuation of the earlier trial.[91] Absent special circumstances, such as allegations of ineffective assistance of counsel, an accused should be represented by the same counsel who acted as counsel in that trial.[92] In this case, the addition of charges to those originally tried created a new right to select counsel[93] and reversible error occurred in denying the accused that right.[94] Although he concurred in the disposition of the case, Judge Cox strongly disagreed with the conclusion that adding new charges to a rehearing in itself triggers an additional request for counsel.[95]

§ 8-3(B)(4). Obtaining Civilian Counsel.

As in the case of requests for individual military counsel, *supra*, the burden falls upon the accused to secure representation of a civilian counsel. Unlike requests for individual military counsel, there is little procedural guidance on obtaining civilian counsel. The U.C.M.J. simply states that an accused may be represented by civilian counsel "provided by him."[96] The Manual for Courts-Martial further states that the accused may be represented by civilian counsel "if provided at no expense to the Government."[97] Case law does provide that an accused should be given a reasonable or fair opportunity to obtain civilian counsel,[98] and, generally, there is no problem in obtaining civilian counsel. From time to time it becomes apparent after repeated requests for continuances and "counsel shopping" that the accused may be abusing his entitlement to obtain a civilian counsel. In that case, the judge's decision to move forward with the trial notwithstanding the failure of the accused to obtain counsel will be measured for abuse of discretion.[99] The same standard of re-

---

91. 25 M.J. at 314, *citing* Uniform Code of Military Justice Hearings on H.R. 2498 before a Subcomm. of the House Comm. on Armed Services, 81st Cong., 1st Sess. 1180 (1949).
92. 25 M.J. at 315. Compare United States v. Villines, 9 M.J. 807 (N.C.M.R. 1980) (accused not entitled to request new individual military counsel at second trial) with United States v. Palmer, 44 C.M.R. 608 (A.C.M.R. 1971) (a rehearing is a new, distinct, and separate trial).
93. 25 M.J. at 315.
94. *Id.* at 316.
95. *Id.* at 317-18. Judge Cox concurred in the disposition of the case solely because the case, a special court-martial, had lingered for four years in the appellate channels.
96. Article 38(b)(2), U.C.M.J. *See* Appendix 3.
97. R.C.M. 506(a).
98. United States v. Kinard, 21 C.M.A. 300, 45 C.M.R. 74 (1972); United States v. Brown, 10 M.J. 635 (A.C.M.R. 1980); United States v. Hampton, 50 C.M.R. 531 (N.C.M.R. 1975).
99. United States v. Phillips, 37 M.J. 532 (A.C.M.R. 1993) (no abuse of discretion in denying continuance to obtain civilian counsel; court concluded that purpose of motion was to avoid trial); United States v. Keys, 29 M.J. 920 (A.C.M.R. 1989) (trial court abused discretion in denying request for continuance so that civilian counsel, who had been retained the day before, could prepare for trial); United States v. Gipson, 25 M.J. 781 (A.C.M.R. 1988) (no abuse of discretion in denying request by civilian counsel for continuance where counsel then withdrew and accused had previously been granted delays in several unsuccessful attempts to obtain civilian counsel; even assuming it was error to deny the continuance, detailed military counsel was prepared for

view would apply where civilian counsel has been obtained but the judge rules that counsel is not qualified.[100]

If civilian counsel is obtained, Article 38, U.C.M.J. indicates that any individual military counsel on the case becomes an associate counsel unless excused by the accused.[101] Despite the stated and implied limitations in Article 38 and R.C.M. 506(b),[102] it is theoretically possible that under limited circumstances, the accused might be represented by a civilian counsel, an individual military counsel, a detailed military counsel, and a detailed assistant defense counsel.[103]

For a discussion on the trial judge's inquiry as to who will represent the accused and the accused's right to waive the right to counsel, see § 12-2(F).

§ 8-3(C). Members of the Court.

In selecting individuals to sit as court-members in special and general courts-martial, the convening authority is directed by Article 25, U.C.M.J. to detail those who in his opinion are "best qualified for the duty by reason of age, education, training, experience, length of service, and judicial temperament."[104] That general guidance is tempered by other statutory,[105] *Manual*,[106] and regulatory criteria.[107]

§ 8-3(C)(1). Qualifications of Members.

Article 25 provides the following statutory criteria:

1. The court member must be on active duty.[108]

---

trial); United States v. Brown, 10 M.J. 635 (A.C.M.R. 1980). *See also* § 15-4(A), concerning continuances to obtain counsel.

100. *See* R.C.M. 502(d)(3). Soriano v. Hosken, 9 M.J. 221 (C.M.A. 1980). In United States v. Galinato, 28 M.J. 1049 (N.M.C.M.R. 1989), the court concluded that the defense team, consisting of a civilian and military counsel, were ineffective in not presenting a defense when the judge denied their fourth request for a continuance. Noting that although the civilian counsel may be the chief counsel, the military counsel is nonetheless individually accountable for his own actions. *Id.* at 1054, n.6.

101. *See* Appendix 3.

102. These provisions state that the accused is not entitled to more than one military counsel. But R.C.M. 506(b) specifically recognizes some discretion in the detailing authority to permit more than one military counsel.

103. This theoretical situation might arise where there are pre-existing attorney-client relationships, the case is complicated, and the prosecution team consists of several counsel.

104. *See* Appendix 3. This general guidance usually causes few problems because, on its face, it gives a great deal of discretion to the convening authority. *See generally* Johnson, "In His Opinion—A Convening Authority's Guide to the Selection of Panel Members," ARMY LAW., Apr. 1989, at 43.

105. Article 25, U.C.M.J.

106. R.C.M. 502.

107. *See, e.g.,* AR 27-10, Chapter 7.

108. Article 25(a), (b), (c), U.C.M.J. The Discussion to R.C.M. 502(a) notes that reservists, members of the National Oceanic and Atmospheric Administration and the Public Health Service

§ 8-3(C)(1) CONVENING OF A COURT-MARTIAL § 8-3(C)(1)

2. Commissioned officers may serve as court members in any case.[109]

3. Warrant officers may serve in any case other than one where the accused is a commissioned officer.[110]

4. Enlisted personnel are eligible to serve if the accused has requested that enlisted members be appointed,[111] and the enlisted members are not in the accused's unit. [112]

5. If it can be avoided, no member should be junior in rank or grade to the accused.[113]

6. A court member is ineligible to serve on either a general or special court-martial if he has acted as an accuser,[114] counsel,[115] investigating officer,[116] or prosecution witness, in the same case.[117]

The Manual for Courts-Martial summarizes the first three of the foregoing criteria [118] and also adds in the nonbinding Discussion to R.C.M. 503(a)(1) that the following persons are subject to challenge[119] and should not be detailed: any person who in the case of a rehearing, new trial, or other trial, sat as a member in the first trial[120] and any person who is in arrest or confinement.[121] In appointing members, the convening authority should also be aware of the other grounds for challenge listed in R.C.M. 912(f)(1). *See generally* § 15-10.

Individual service regulations often provide further specific guidance on who should be appointed. For example, Chapter 7 of Army Regulation 27-10

---

are eligible to serve if they are assigned to and serving with an armed force. *See also* Article 2(8), U.C.M.J., which provides for court-martial jurisdiction over those individuals.

109. Article 25(a), U.C.M.J.
110. Article 25(b), U.C.M.J.
111. Article 25(c)(1), U.C.M.J.
112. Article 25(c)(2), U.C.M.J. *See* discussion *infra*.
113. Article 25(d)(1), U.C.M.J. *See also* R.C.M. 503(a)(1) Discussion. For officers this may include the exclusion of a member who is below the accused on a promotion list. *See* United States v. McGee, 15 M.J. 1004 (N.M.C.M.R. 1983) (accused waived error by not objecting).
114. Article 25(d), U.C.M.J. *See also* § 6-1(A) for a discussion of who is an "accuser."
115. Article 25(d), U.C.M.J. This refers to any person who has served as either a trial counsel, United States v. Zamarripa, 1 C.M.R. 432 (A.B.R. 1951), or defense counsel, United States v. Hurt, 8 C.M.A. 224, 24 C.M.R. 34 (1957).
116. Article 25(d)(2), U.C.M.J. United States v. Burkhalter, 17 C.M.A. 266, 38 C.M.R. 64 (1967). *See also* § 7-2(A)(1).
117. The "same case" language may be interpreted to include any rehearing or new trial. *See* R.C.M. 503(a)(1) Discussion.
118. R.C.M. 502(a).
119. *See* § 15-10 for a discussion of challenging court members.
120. United States v. Mora, 26 M.J. 122 (C.M.A. 1988) (because accused had been tried by judge alone in first trial, the convening authority could refer retrial of case to same court-martial consisting of the same members). This provision would probably not apply if the court member had been appointed to the original court but never actually served as a court member.
121. *See generally* Articles 7, 10, U.C.M.J. The wording "arrest or confinement" suggests that charges are pending against the person. But the same underlying rationale that persons charged with offenses should not sit as members would also apply to those already tried and still undergoing some sort of punishment. Note that there is apparently no automatic disqualification for those with a prior conviction or Article 15 punishment. Pragmatically, those persons would probably be challenged at trial on grounds that to permit that person to sit would cast doubt on the impartiality or fairness of the proceeding. *See* R.C.M. 912(f)(1)(N).

notes that members of the Inspector General's Corps, chaplains, veterinarians, doctors,[122] and dentists should normally not serve as members.

The fact that the member may be "eligible" to serve is not the end of the inquiry. Other grounds, discussed in more detail at § 15-10, may cause the member to be challenged at trial. To cover that possibility, the convening authority normally appoints more members than the jurisdictional minimum required for either a special[123] or general court-martial.[124]

§ 8-3(C)(2). Requests for Enlisted Members.

Should an enlisted accused desire that at least one-third of the members be enlisted members,[125] he must make that request in writing or orally on the record.[126] He should personally sign any written request.[127] In the past, failure to make a written request was a jurisdictional defect if enlisted members actually served on the court.[128] A request, however, is not a prerequisite to appointing enlisted members to the court.[129] Thus, in anticipation of a forthcoming request, the convening authority could appoint enlisted members, although the better practice is to wait until a valid request has been presented. Otherwise, there is a real risk that the parties will assume that the necessary request has been executed only to learn after trial that there was a jurisdictional defect.

During the Article 39(a) session preceding trial, the judge is charged with determining whether the enlisted accused is aware of this right to have enlisted members and whether the necessary request has been made.[130] That inquiry usually forecloses the problem. Several courts have struggled with the issue of whether the enlisted court member was in the same "unit" as the

---

122. *See* United States v. Bland, 6 M.J. 565 (N.C.M.R. 1978); United States v. Worrell, 3 M.J. 817 (A.F.C.M.R. 1977) (doctor not *per se* ineligible).
123. Article 16(2), U.C.M.J. requires at least three members for a special court-martial.
124. Article 16(2), U.C.M.J. requires a minimum of five members in a general court-martial.
125. Article 25(c)(1), U.C.M.J.; R.C.M. 503(a)(2). The right to enlisted members may be exercised only by an enlisted accused. *See* R.C.M. 903(a)(2) Discussion.
126. Article 25(c)(1), U.C.M.J. In United States v. Curtis, 28 M.J. 1074 (N.M.C.M.R. 1989) (*en banc*), the court noted that although an accused is not entitled to more than one-third enlisted members, Article 25 does not prohibit such a result. *Id.* at 1089, n. 10. In 1986, Congress amended Article 25 to permit an accused to request orally enlisted members.
127. The language of Article 25(c)(1) requires that the accused "personally" make the request. That language seems to require that the accused personally sign a written request. Further, R.C.M. 903(b)(1) specially requires the accused's signature. *See, e.g.,* United States v. Brookins, 33 M.J. 793 (A.C.M.R. 1991) (defense counsel's written request, on behalf of accused, for enlisted members on the court did not meet jurisdictional requirement that such requests be made personally by an accused).
128. United States v. White, 21 C.M.A. 583, 45 C.M.R. 357 (1972); United States v. Acevedo-Colon, 2 M.J. 969 (A.C.M.R. 1976); United States v. Williams, 50 C.M.R. 219 (A.C.M.R. 1975).
129. United States v. Berlingeri, 35 M.J. 794 (N.M.C.M.R. 1992) (jurisdictional issue of requesting enlisted members only arises where they actually served on court which tried the accused); United States v. Robertson, 7 M.J. 507 (A.C.M.R. 1979).
130. *See* R.C.M. 903. *See also infra* § 12-3.

accused and therefore disqualified.[131] Even assuming they are from the same unit it is not a jurisdictional defect.[132]

The request for enlisted members must be made before the end of the initial Article 39(a) session[133] or if one is not held, before the court is "assembled."[134] A withdrawal of a previously granted request is subject to the same time constraints.[135] Note that the right to enlisted members is not absolute and any requests may be denied by the convening authority if physical conditions or military exigencies prevent appointment.[136] Such denials, however, must be explained in writing and made a part of the record.[137]

If the accused's request is granted, the convening authority may simply add the appropriate number of enlisted members to the existing court with a supplemental convening order or he may withdraw the charges from the existing court and re-refer them to a court that already includes enlisted personnel.[138] As a practical matter, in almost all cases the enlisted persons appointed to the court will be noncommissioned officers with lengthy service.

For a discussion of the potential problems of unlawful command influence on the selection process, see Chapter 6.

---

131. Article 25(c)(1), (2), U.C.M.J. Article 25 defines "unit" as:

> any regularly organized body as defined by the Secretary concerned, but in no case may it be a body larger than a company, squadron, ship's crew, or body corresponding to one of them.

The problem rests not so much with determining the extent of the unit but instead with membership in the unit. For example, either the accused or the enlisted member in question may be a member of the unit for only administrative purposes. Whether they are indeed in the same unit will depend on the circumstances and their duties. *See* United States v. Wilson, 16 M.J. 678 (A.C.M.R. 1983).

132. United States v. Wilson, 21 M.J. 193 (C.M.A. 1986) (not jurisdictional error for enlisted member from same unit as the accused to sit as member of court); United States v. Milam, 33 M.J. 1020 (A.C.M.R. 1991) (members were from same unit and accused did not waive issue; case reversed); United States v. Zengel, 32 M.J. 642 (C.G.C.M.R. 1991) (accused waived objection that enlisted court member was from his unit); United States v. Alexander, 27 M.J. 834 (A.C.M.R. 1988) (accused waived the issue); United States v. Wilson, 16 M.J. 678 (A.C.M.R. 1983) (not jurisdictional defect); United States v. Tagert, 11 M.J. 677 (N.M.C.M.R. 1981) (not jurisdictional defect); United States v. Kimball, 13 M.J. 659 (N.M.C.M.R. 1982) (not jurisdictional defect). *Cf.* United States v. Anderson, 10 M.J. 803 (A.F.C.M.R. 1981).

133. *See* § 12-1.

134. Article 25(c)(1). R.C.M. 903(a)(1). The timing is probably not jurisdictional. *See* the Drafter's Analysis to R.C.M. 903(a). And R.C.M. 903(e) specifically grants the military judge authority to approve untimely requests. *See infra* § 15-9.

135. R.C.M. 903(d). If the request is timely, the accused is entitled to relief as a matter of right. United States v. Stipe, 23 C.M.A. 11, 48 C.M.R. 267 (1974). If his request for withdrawal is untimely, relief may be granted at the judge's discretion. R.C.M. 903(e).

136. Article 25(c)(1), U.C.M.J.; R.C.M. 503(a)(2). Mere inconvenience is not a valid ground.

137. *Id.*

138. *See* R.C.M. 503(a)(2) Discussion.

§ 8-3(C)(3). Constitutional Challenges to Composition.

The Supreme Court has ruled that an accused is denied his Sixth Amendment right to a jury trial when the jury is composed of less than six persons.[139] It has further ruled that where the jury is composed of six persons, their verdict must be unanimous.[140] Despite these rulings, the military system of less than six members in combination with less than a unanimous verdict[141] has not been ruled unconstitutional. The Supreme Court and the service appellate courts have concluded that the Sixth Amendment right to a jury trial is not applicable to the military[142] and that the military "jury" system does not deny due process[143] or otherwise deprive an accused of a trial by persons capable of fairly deciding guilt or innocence.[144] At least one court has observed that the data relied upon by the Supreme Court came not from the military community but rather from the civilian sector.[145]

The Court of Appeals for the Armed Forces has generally declined to review the issue[146] and when presented with the opportunity to do so, the Supreme Court likewise has declined.[147] As a practical matter, in many commands the convening authority appoints more than the jurisdictional minimum.[148]

§ 8-3(C)(4). Selecting the Members.

Although it has been suggested as a means of selecting members,[149] random selection is not required.[150] While systematic exclusion of groups of individ-

---

139. Ballew v. Georgia, 435 U.S. 223 (1978).
140. Burch v. Louisiana, 441 U.S. 130 (1979).
141. See § 15-16.
142. See, e.g., Reid v. Covert, 354 U.S. 1, 37 n. 68 (1957); O'Callahan v. Parker, 395 U.S. 258, 261 (1969); Welchel v. McDonald, 340 U.S. 122, 127 (1950); Kahn v. Anderson, 255 U.S. 1, 8 (1921); Ex parte Milligan, 71 U.S. (4 Wall.) 2 (1866).
United States v. Smith, 27 M.J. 242 (C.M.A. 1988) (Sixth Amendment right to jury trial is not applicable to courts-martial; thus, accused is not entitled to representative cross-section of military community; a convening authority may, however, make good faith attempts to select a cross-section); United States v. Kemp, 22 C.M.A. 152, 46 C.M.R. 152 (1973); United States v. Crawford, 15 C.M.A. 31, 35 C.M.R. 3 (1964); United States v. Allen, 31 M.J. 572 (N.M.C.M.R. 1990).
143. United States v. Allen, 31 M.J. 572 (N.M.C.M.R. 1990) (court briefly noted differences in structure and function of court-martial); United States v. Montgomery, 5 M.J. 832 (A.C.M.R. 1978); United States v. Wolff, 5 M.J. 923 (N.C.M.R. 1978).
144. United States v. Wolff, 5 M.J. 923 (N.C.M.R. 1978).
145. United States v. Corl, 6 M.J. 914 (N.C.M.R. 1979).
146. See United States v. Lamela, 6 M.J. 32 (C.M.A. 1972).
147. United States v. Hutchinson, 17 M.J. 156 (C.M.A. 1984), cert. denied, 105 S. Ct. 384 (1984).
148. See generally Schlueter, "Military Justice in the 1990's: A Legal System in Search of Respect," 133 Mil. L. Rev. 1 (1991) (author suggests examination of possibility of applying Sixth Amendment minimum to courts-martial).
149. See, e.g., Remcho, "Military Juries: Constitutional Analysis and the Need for Reform," 47 Ind. L.J. 193 (1973).
150. See generally Brookshire, "Juror Selection Under the Uniform Code of Military Justice: Fact and Fiction," 58 Mil. L. Rev. 1 (1972); Chmelik, "The Military Justice System and the Right to Trial by Jury: Size and Voting Requirements of the General Court-martial for Service-Con-

uals is prohibited,[151] including particular classes of individuals as members, is usually not error.[152] Any attempts to "stack the court" may constitute unlawful command influence.[153]

---

nected Civilian Offenses," Vol. 8, No. 3 HASTINGS CONST. L.Q. 617 (1981); Remcho, "Military Juries: Constitutional Analysis and the Need for Reform," 47 IND. L.J. 193 (1973); Smallridge, "The Military Jury Selection Reform Movement," 19 A.F. L. REV. 343 (1977); Van Sant, "Trial by Jury of Military Peers," 15 A.F. L. Rev. 185 (1973). Schwender, "One Potato, Two Potato...: A Method to Select Court Members," ARMY LAW., May 1984, at 12.

151. United States v. Loving, 41 M.J. 213 (1994) (no evidence of tokenism and no evidence that qualified females and blacks were improperly excluded from consideration); United States v. McClain, 22 M.J. 124 (C.M.A. 1986) (violation of U.C.M.J. to systematically exclude junior officers and enlisted members below E-7); United States v. Daigle, 1 M.J. 139 (C.M.A. 1975) (improper to use rank as device for deliberate exclusion). Cf. United States v. Yager, 7 M.J. 171 (C.M.A. 1979) (permissible to exclude members below grade E-3 because of demonstrated relation with criteria of Article 25(d) (2), U.C.M.J.).

See also United States v. Nixon, 33 M.J. 433 (C.M.A. 1991) (although convening authority selected only high ranking NCOs because he believed they were the best qualified under Article 25, his testimony established that he had complied with statutory criteria).

United States v. Smith, 37 M.J. 773 (A.C.M.R. 1993) (convening authority's direction to SJA to select only certain ranks of enlisted members from particular units amounted to an impermissible grade-based shortcut to obtain members qualified under Article 25; court thus lacked jurisdiction).

United States v. McLaughlin, 27 M.J. 685 (A.C.M.R. 1988) (convening authority did not impermissibly exclude junior officers where his instructions to SJA were to remove junior officers when accused requested enlisted members).

United States v. James, 24 M.J. 894 (A.C.M.R. 1987) (noting that the selection of members is presumed reliable, the court held that the accused failed to establish that the convening authority had systematically excluded junior officers); United States v. Autrey, 20 M.J. 912 (A.C.M.R. 1985) (selection process of members that deliberately excluded company grade officers was impermissible because it was based upon reasons not justified under Art. 25; here the SJA testified that he recommended that the convening authority not appoint company grade officers because they might know the accused and because senior officers would possess greater attributes noted in Art. 25).

In United States v. Carman, 19 M.J. 932 (A.C.M.R. 1985), the court found no evidence of systematic exclusion of lower ranking officers nor was there any appearance of such. The court noted that the presumption of legality, regularity, and good faith that must be overcome by defense, United States v. Martinez, 19 M.J. 744 (A.C.M.R. 1984). In a footnote, the court observed the potential relationship between Art. 25 and Art. 37.

United States v. Townsend, 12 M.J. 861 (A.F.C.M.R. 1981) (appointing order is not suspect per se simply because it did not include lower grade enlisted personnel).

152. See, e.g., United States v. Smith, 27 M.J. 242 (C.M.A. 1988) (not error for convening authority to make good faith effort to include females on sexual offense cases but under facts it appeared that females were selected because they would favor the prosecution); United States v. Beehler, 35 M.J. 502 (A.F.C.M.R. 1992) (preference for, and intentional inclusion of, commanders on court was not fatal); United States v. Cunningham, 21 M.J. 585 (A.C.M.R. 1985) (not improper for CA to show preference for members holding leadership positions); United States v. Lutz, 18 M.J. 763 (C.G.C.M.R. 1984) (convening authority did not abuse his discretion in selecting members from the local area where child abuse cases arose); United States v. Smith, 18 M.J. 704 (A.C.M.R. 1984) (deliberate inclusion of female court member on cases involving sexual offenses did not violate either Article 25 or the equal protection clause); United States v. Firmin, 8 M.J. 595 (A.C.M.R. 1979), petition denied, 9 M.J. 5 (C.M.A. 1980) (including particular category is not prohibited).

153. See, e.g., United States v. Loving, 41 M.J. 213 (1994) (defense presented no evidence that that members were added or removed for reasons violative of Article 25); United States v. Hilow,

The selection process usually consists of the convening authority personally designating individuals whose names appear in a pool of potential members compiled by the personnel office. The staff judge advocate may assist in the process, but persons serving in a prosecutorial capacity should not.[154] In *United States v. Smith*,[155] members of the prosecution were active in the selection process of "hard-core" females for a case involving indecent assault. The court reiterated that a trial counsel who is prosecuting the accused should not be involved in the selection process. In a concurring opinion, Judge Cox stated:

> Those responsible for nominating court members should reflect upon the importance of this task. It is a solemn and awesome responsibility and not one to be taken lightly or frivolously. It is a responsibility that Congress has entrusted to convening authorities and has not required some other method of selection, such as random choice. Even so, it is the most vulnerable aspect of the court-martial system; the easiest for critics to attack. A fair and impartial court-martial is the most fundamental protection that an accused servicemember has from unfounded or unprovable charges. There is a duty to nominate only fair and impartial members.[156]

The senior member is automatically the president of the court, the equivalent of the jury foreman in a civilian trial, and the convening order need not specify who will fill the position.[157]

Although it is not a common practice, R.C.M. 503(a)(3) recognizes that members from another command or armed force may be appointed to a court. However, the member's commander should concur (oral or written) and, unless exigencies exist, a majority of the sitting members should be of the same armed force as the accused.[158]

The U.C.M.J. envisions that the convening authority will personally select the members. But this does not preclude him from personally selecting a court

---

32 M.J. 439 (C.M.A. 1991) (deliberate stacking of court by division deputy adjunct general violated UCMJ, even if convening authority was unaware of such; court ordered rehearing on sentence; such actions amount to form of unlawful command influence). *See also* § 6-3.

154. *See, e.g.,* United States v. Beehler, 35 M.J. 502 (A.F.C.M.R. 1992) (under facts, there was nothing improper with involvement of SJA in presenting list of five officers to convening authority and briefing him on their qualifications); United States v. Crumb, 10 M.J. 520 (A.C.M.R. 1980) (appearance of evil where chief trial counsel involved in "culling" process of potential members); United States v. Beard, 15 M.J. 768 (A.F.C.M.R. 1983) (winnowing of names by Chief of Military Justice was prejudicial error).

See also United States v. McCall, 26 M.J. 804 (A.C.M.R. 1988) (reversible error for unknown persons to select members for court and then seek approval of convening authority after trial started); United States v. Stafford, 25 M.J. 609 (A.C.M.R. 1987) (no jurisdictional defect occurred when SJA failed to memorialize appointment of alternate members to court-martial).

155. 27 M.J. 242 (C.M.A. 1988).

156. 27 M.J. at 252. *Cf.* United States v. Kroop, 34 M.J. 628 (A.F.C.M.R. 1992), *aff'd on other grounds*, 38 M.J. 470 (C.M.A. 1993) (convening authority suspected of misconduct was not precluded from selecting court members for trial of senior officer accused of similar acts).

157. R.C.M. 502(b). *See* United States v. Pulliam, 3 C.M.A. 95, 11 C.M.R. 95 (1953) (not prejudicial error for other member to serve as president).

158. *See* R.C.M. 503(a)(3) Discussion. United States v. Van Steenwyk, 21 M.J. 795 (N.M.C.M.R. 1985) (accused not entitled to court composed only of naval officers).

convened by another convening authority. For example, in *United States v. England*,[159] the convening authority directed that the accused's case be tried by a general court-martial convened in a specific court-martial order. The court concluded that this particular order reflected an existing court-martial convened by the convening authority's predecessor and that in effect the convening authority had "adopted" the predecessor's selection.[160]

§ 8-3(D). Changes in Composition of Court.

Changes to the composition of the court are effected through oral or written amendments to the original convening or detailing order.[161] The power to make changes in the detailed defense counsel is limited by formation of an attorney-client privilege.[162] Before assembly of the court, the convening authority may add or delete names of court members at his discretion.[163] How-

---

159. 24 M.J. 816 (A.C.M.R. 1987).
160. 24 M.J. at 817. United States v. Allgood, 41 M.J. 492 (1995) (commander of newly created unit referred charges to court convened by commander of predecessor unit through order which indicated that he had "adopted the panel selections by my predecessor." The court noted that at least in the context of the Army, the term adoption means personal evaluation and selection of members as required by Article 25); United States v. Reynolds, 36 M.J. 1128 (A.C.M.R. 1993) (not error for convening authority to refer accused's case for general court-martial to standing panel previously designated for special courts-martial; court noted alternatives for convening authority when faced with disqualified panel); United States v. Gaspard, 35 M.J. 678 (A.C.M.R. 1992) (convening authority adopted selection made by another commander, not his predecessor; court ordered rehearing on issue of whether convening authority had personally selected court); United States v. Bianchi, 25 M.J. 557 (A.C.M.R. 1987); United States v. Alvarez, 5 M.J. 762 (A.C.M.R. 1978). *Cf.* United States v. Yates, 25 M.J. 582 (A.C.M.R. 1987) (convening authority could not ratify substitution of members made by deputy post commander who was not authorized to convene courts-martial).
161. R.C.M. 505(b). *See* Appendix 9.
162. R.C.M. 505(d)(2) specifies that the attorney-client relationship may be severed where the accused or counsel requests such, where an individual military counsel is obtained and the detailed counsel is excused, or where other good cause exists. *See, e.g.*, United States v. Gnibus, 21 M.J. 1 (C.M.A. 1985) (accused's lengthy absence justified appointment of another defense counsel on charges that were withdrawn from SPCM and re-referred to GCM); United States v. Saenz, 18 M.J. 328 (C.M.A. 1984) (good cause existed to terminate attorney-client relationship where the accused's counsel was also an executive officer to a special court-martial convening authority who had investigated the charges); United States v. Hultgren, 40 M.J. 638 (N.M.C.M.R. 1994) (deployment of counsel to Somalia was military exigency and extraordinary circumstance which justified change of defense counsel after attorney-client relationship was formed); United States v. Herod, 21 M.J. 762 (A.F.C.M.R. 1986) (reversible error to remove counsel where accused had waived counsel's potential conflict of interest); United States v. Iverson, 5 M.J. 440 (C.M.A. 1978) (only accused can sever, absent a truly extraordinary circumstance); United States v. Catt, 1 M.J. 41 (C.M.A. 1975).
163. R.C.M. 505(c)(1). United States v. Marsh, 21 M.J. 445 (C.M.A. 1986) (court rejected several arguments re selection of replacement court members); United States v. Larson, 33 M.J. 714 (A.C.M.R. 1991) (no jurisdictional error where convening authority changed members in convening order before the court was assembled and his intent seemed clear to all participants at trial).
See also United States v. Beaulieu, 21 M.J. 528 (C.G.C.M.R. 1985) (error for trial counsel not to disclose to defense the names of members who would be appointed in event original members were challenged); United States v. Cote, 11 M.J. 892 (A.F.C.M.R. 1981).

ever, to prevent removal of a member apparently favorable to the defense,[164] the *Manual* requires that *after assembly* members may only be removed or added for good cause.[165] The trial counsel must affirmatively establish for the record those facts which constitute good cause.[166] As with the initial selection process, the authority to make changes should be exercised personally by the detailing or convening authority. There is an apparent exception in the instance of removal of a court member prior to assembly. In that case, the convening authority may delegate his authority, but the delegee[167] may not excuse more than one-third of the members.[168] If new members are added after evidence has been heard, Article 29(b) requires that the trial may proceed after the recorded evidence has been read to the court in the presence of the accused, counsel, and the judge.[169] In the alternative, the judge may declare a mistrial.[170]

In the case of substitution of military judges, Article 29(d) of the U.C.M.J. envisions that the trial must begin anew unless there is a verbatim record of the evidence introduced to that point or a stipulation thereof is read to the new judge in the presence of the counsel and the accused.[171] But in *United States v. Hawkins*,[172] the court noted that Article 29(d) apparently contemplates that the trial will have begun and evidence will have been introduced. It is not clear that it applies to changes in judges during the preliminary pretrial Article 39(a) sessions. Noting that the critical time for substitution is after assembly of the court,[173] the court concluded that in this particular case, even though the first judge had announced the court assembled, it was not in fact so until after the conclusion of preliminary matters and the presentation

---

164. *See, e.g.,* United States v. Whitley, 5 C.M.A. 786, 19 C.M.R. 82 (1955).
165. Article 29, U.C.M.J.; R.C.M. 505(c)(2). United States v. McGeeney, 41 M.J. 544 (N.M.Ct.Crim.App. 1994) (members removed after three witnesses had testified and reduced number below quorum; testimony was read to new members). *See also infra* § 7-9.
166. United States v. Greenwell, 12 C.M.A. 560, 31 C.M.R. 146 (1961); United States v. Latimer, 30 M.J. 554 (A.C.M.R. 1990) (non-prejudicial error for court to excuse member after assembly so that he could keep medical appointment for physical); United States v. Lindsey, 39 C.M.R. 778 (A.B.R. 1968). "Good cause" contemplates emergency leave, R.C.M. 505(f), assignment to important task, United States v. Geraghty, 40 C.M.R. 499 (A.B.R. 1969) or transfer to combat zone, United States v. Taylor, 41 C.M.R. 749 (N.C.M.R. 1969). Routine transfer does not suffice. United States v. Boysen, 11 C.M.A. 331, 29 C.M.R. 147 (1960). *See also* United States v. Garcia, 15 M.J. 864 (A.C.M.R. 1983).
167. United States v. Barrios, 31 M.J. 750 (A.C.M.R. 1990) (judge's excusing of one-third of members was non-prejudicial error and did not violate military due process); United States v. Ponder, 29 M.J. 782 (A.C.M.R. 1989) (SJA had been delegated authority to excuse court member prior to assembly).
The delegee may be the staff judge advocate, the legal officer, or the convening authority's principal assistant. R.C.M. 505(1)(B)(i).
168. *See* R.C.M. 505(c)(1)(B).
169. Article 29(b), U.C.M.J. United States v. McGeeney, 41 M.J. 544 (N.M.Ct.Crim.App. 1994) (judge had testimony read to new members).
170. R.C.M. 805(d)(1) Discussion. (when number falls below quorum, mistrial may be appropriate).
171. *See* Appendix 3.
172. 24 M.J. 257 (C.M.A. 1987).
173. United States v. Smith, 3 M.J. 490 (C.M.A. 1975).

of evidence. Thus, there was no need to indicate on the record the "good cause" for the substitution.[174]

§ 8-4. Referral of Charges to a Court-Martial.

Charges that have been preferred against an accused are "referred" by the personal order of a qualified convening authority[1] who directs that a particular court-martial will try the accused on these charges.[2] The preferral of charges, and the convening of the court are discussed in § 6-1 and § 8-2, respectively. The referral is effected by completing Part V on the second page of the charge sheet,[3] which is signed by either the convening authority or his delegee acting at the convening authority's direction.[4]

An acting convening authority may also properly refer charges.[5] This endorsement on the charge sheet would also contain any special instructions, such as detail of a court reporter to a special court-martial.[6] The convening authority's decision to refer charges to trial is generally sacrosanct and is usually not questioned.[7] However, where there has been a clear abuse in

---

174. 24 M.J. at 259. The court also noted that the accused had not objected to the substitution and specifically rejected the argument that the substitution amounted to non-waivable jurisdictional error.

1. *See supra* § 8-2(A). *See also* United States v. Carter, 19 M.J. 808 (A.C.M.R. 1985) (command influence issue testimony of commanders did not disqualify CA from referring case to trial).

2. *See* R.C.M. 601(a). United States v. Choy, 33 M.J. 1080, 1082, n. 1 (A.C.M.R. 1992) (referral is order of convening authority that the charges against the accused will be tried by a specified court-martial).

3. *See* Appendix 6 for a sample charge sheet.

4. R.C.M. 601(e). United States v. Plott, 38 M.J. 735 (A.F.C.M.R. 1993) (SJA signed referral portion of charge sheet "For the Commander"; court declined to require convening authorities to personally sign charge sheets, or any other documents, to show decision to refer charges); United States v. Boyle, 30 M.J. 656 (A.F.C.M.R. 1990) (no prejudice where acting staff judge advocate signed Block 14 of charge sheet in capacity as SJA and not as administrative officer acting on behalf of convening authority).

5. *See, e.g.*, United States v. O'Connor, 19 M.J. 673 (A.F.C.M.R. 1984); United States v. Richardson, 5 M.J. 627 (A.C.M.R. 1978).

6. A verbatim record is one of the statutory criteria for imposition of a bad-conduct discharge by a special court-martial. Article 19, U.C.M.J.

7. *See, e.g.*, United States v. Bledsoe, 39 M.J. 691 (N.M.C.M.R. 1993) (commander did not abuse discretion in referring accused's case to trial; accused had not been accepted into Family Advocacy Program which addressed rehabilitation of offenders; court noted that such policies to not otherwise limit referral authority); United States v. Anderson, 36 M.J. 963 (A.F.C.M.R. 1993) (commander who was suspected of misconduct, unlike that with which accused was charged, was replaced by the time case was reviewed; *citing* Kroop, *infra*, court ruled that no relief was required).

United States v. Lewis, 34 M.J. 745 (N.M.C.M.R. 1991) (exercise of convening authority in referring charges is presumed to be regular and there is not requirement that reasons be given for the referral, instead of processing accused for administrative discharge).

But *see* United States v. Kroop, 34 M.J. 628 (A.F.C.M.R. 1992), *aff'd on other grounds*, 38 M.J. 470 (C.M.A. 1993) (court discussed issue of whether charges were improperly referred where the convening authority was arguably guilty of similar conduct. The court said the question was an objective one, i.e., under the facts known, would any reasonable convening authority have believed there was sufficient evidence to refer the charges to trial. The court indicated that the decision to refer the charges to a particular court was not an objective question but that under the

referring charges, such as in a case where there is no evidence offered in the court, corrective action may be in order if the accused was prejudiced.[8] Although there was earlier authority that improper referral could result in the proceedings being declared a nullity,[9] the trend is now toward treating defects in the referral process as non-jurisdictional errors that must be tested for prejudice.[10]

The *Manual* requires that before charges may be referred, the convening authority must have either concluded, or be advised by the staff judge advocate, that there are

> [r]easonable grounds to believe that an offense triable by a court-martial has been committed and that the accused committed it, and that the specification alleges an offense....[11]

There is apparently no requirement in the *Manual* that this decision be reduced to writing, unless the charges are being referred to a general court-martial. In that case, the staff judge advocate must first submit his written pretrial advice.[12] Note that in making his decision, the convening authority may rely upon information from any source.[13] Arguably, this includes information which may not in itself be admissible. In any event, neither the convening authority nor the staff judge advocate are required to resolve legal

---

facts, referring the case of a senior officer to a general court-martial was not an abuse of discretion and a likely decision of any convening authority). United States v. Allen, 31 M.J. 572 (N.M.C.M.R. 1990) (extensive discussion of discretion of convening authority, vis-à-vis guidance from the Secretary of the Navy, in referring national security cases to general court-martial; court concluded that no unlawful influence had been shown by the accused); United States v. Williams, 6 C.M.A. 243, 19 C.M.R. 369 (1955).

8. United States v. Phare, 21 C.M.A. 244, 45 C.M.R. 18 (1972).

9. United States v. Wilkins, 28 M.J. 992 (A.C.M.R. 1989) (court lacked jurisdiction to accept accused's guilty plea to charges that were not properly referred to trial and were not lesser included offenses to those actually referred). See § 6-1(C) (1) for a discussion of the problem of "spill-over effect" of an improperly referred charge on other charges.

Cf. United States v. Cornelius, 29 M.J. 501 (A.C.M.R. 1989) (court distinguished *Wilkins* and held that accused could plead guilty to unreferred charge of adultery; although it was not lesser included offense of rape charge, which had been properly referred, under the facts the accused was fairly apprised of the charge and was prepared to defend against it). *See also* United States v. Hudson, 27 M.J. 734 (A.C.M.R. 1988) (typographical error in referral was administrative and not jurisdictional error).

United States v. Otero, 26 M.J. 546 (A.F.C.M.R. 1988) (discrepancy in date of convening order and date reflected in referral section of charge sheet did not amount to jurisdictional error; court rejected argument that accused's case had been referred to court not yet in existence; accused waived the issue by not objecting); United States v. Duvall, 7 M.J. 832 (N.C.M.R. 1979).

10. *See, e.g.*, United States v. Koke, 32 M.J. 876 (N.M.C.M.R. 1991) (referral errors are nonjurisdictional and are to be measured for prejudice). *See also supra* § 4-16.

11. R.C.M. 601(d). United States v. Howe, 37 M.J. 1062 (N.M.C.M.R. 1993) (although convening authority is not required to screen evidence, government should not have proceeded to trial without evidence corroborating the accused's confession).

12. Article 34, U.C.M.J.; R.C.M. 601(d)(2). United States v. Jones, 34 M.J. 899 (N.M.C.M.R. 1992) (requirement of written pretrial advice, signed by SJA, may be waived by accused). *See* § 7-3.

13. R.C.M. 601(d)(1).

objections or issues before referring the charges to trial.[14] As a practical matter, however, the better (and the normal) practice is for the convening authority and his legal advisor to be reasonably sure that they have a better than even chance of prevailing on the legal issues. Otherwise, there is the appearance of abusing the referral process.

Should a superior convening authority feel that charges are improperly before a court, he may order that those charges be forwarded to him for consideration. Once received, he may personally withdraw them,[15] see § 8-4, and re-refer them to a higher court.[16] This might occur, for example, where a convening authority has referred very serious charges to a special court-martial and a superior convening authority feels that a general court-martial is a more appropriate forum.[17]

§ 8-5. Withdrawal of Charges.

As a general rule a convening authority may withdraw charges that have been referred to a court-martial with a view toward future prosecution.[1] Before trial has commenced, the convening authority may withdraw charges for any reason before findings are announced,[2] as long as the action is not arbitrary nor unfair to the accused.[3] Reasons for the withdrawal should be placed on the record by the prosecution.[4] Withdrawal prior to trial will normally be considered proper where the evidence is insufficient or additional charges are

---

14. *Id.* United States v. Howe, 37 M.J. 1062 (N.M.C.M.R. 1993) (decision to refer charges may be based upon evidence which is incompetent, inadmissible, or tainted).
15. If the superior authority directs that the original convening authority withdraw the charges, there is a real problem with unlawful command influence. *See supra* § 6-4. *Cf.* Satterfield v. Drew, 17 M.J. 269 (C.M.A. 1984) (prosecutor has implied authority to withdraw charges).
16. *See* R.C.M. 601(f). United States v. Blaylock, 15 M.J. 190 (C.M.A. 1983); United States v. Charette, 15 M.J. 197 (C.M.A. 1983).
17. *See, e.g.,* United States v. Blaylock, 15 M.J. 190 (C.M.A. 1983). Such a re-referral to a general court-martial would still require the predicate Article 32 investigation and pretrial advice. *See* §§ 7-2, 7-3.
1. R.C.M. 604. In United States v. Mucthison, 28 M.J. 1113 (N.M.C.M.R. 1989) (*per curiam*), the court discussed the key differences between withdrawing charges and dismissing charges. Once a charge has been preferred, it is pending and remains so until it is dismissed. Withdrawal of a charge from a court-martial is not, said the court, sufficient to dismiss or "unprefer" it. United States v. Brown, 22 M.J. 597 (A.C.M.R. 1986) (withdrawal and re-referral of charges need not be accomplished by same convening authority who originally referred the charges). *See generally* Kates, "Limitations on Power of the Convening Authority to Withdraw Charges," 12 MIL. L. REV. 275 (1961).
2. United States v. Koke, 34 M.J. 313 (C.M.A. 1992) (convening authority withdrew charges after arraignment). *See infra* § 15-16.
3. United States v. Meckler, 6 M.J. 779 (A.C.M.R. 1978), *petition denied,* 7 M.J. 41 (C.M.A. 1979).
4. United States v. Koke, 34 M.J. 313 (C.M.A. 1992) (convening authority withdrew charges after arraignment; trial counsel stated that charges were withdrawn to promote judicial economy, i.e., a desire to join all known charges at single trial); United States v. Hardy, 4 M.J. 20 (C.M.A. 1977). Failure to comply is nonjurisdictional error. United States v. Meckler, 6 M.J. 779 (A.C.M.R. 1978), *petition denied,* 7 M.J. 41 (C.M.A. 1979).

being processed.[5] Improper withdrawal and referral may constitute prejudicial error.[6]

If a superior convening authority believes that charges already referred to trial warrant such, he may withdraw them and re-refer them to a higher court.[7] And where the charges have been withdrawn as part of a pretrial agreement, see Chapter 9, they may later be referred to trial where to do so is not unfair to the accused.[8]

After the trial on the merits has begun there is a heavier burden to show valid reasons for withdrawal and re-referral. The power to withdraw at this point should be exercised only where urgent and unforeseen military necessity requires such.[9] Again, the reasons for the withdrawal must be placed on the record.[10] Reasons such as insufficient evidence, deficient pleadings, a grant of immunity to the accused or mistrial are considered proper.[11] But withdrawal of charges because of inconvenience, fear of a lenient sentence,[12] or a request for defense witnesses are improper motives.[13] In *United States v. Koke*,[14] the court distilled several factors that are indicia of whether withdrawal after arraignment is for proper reason. Included would be those situations where the withdrawal: (1) is undertaken for an articulable reason that genuinely serves a public interest or the interests of justice, or is reactive to an operational exigency; (2) arises because of, or relates to, some event occur-

---

5. United States v. Wells, 9 C.M.A. 509, 26 C.M.R. 289 (1958); United States v. Freeman, 23 M.J. 531 (A.C.M.R. 1986) (withdrawal made to avoid speedy trial problems).
6. See, e.g., United States v. Hardy, 4 M.J. 20 (C.M.A. 1977).
7. United States v. Blaylock, 15 M.J. 190 (C.M.A. 1983); United States v. Charette, 15 M.J. 197 (C.M.A. 1983).
8. United States v. Cook, 12 M.J. 448 (C.M.A. 1982) (withdrawn charges re-referred where charges upon which accused was tried were later improvidenced by appellate court).
9. R.C.M. 604(b).
10. United States v. Hardy, 4 M.J. 20 (C.M.A. 1977).
11. R.C.M. 604(b). See also United States v. Smiley, 17 M.J. 790 (A.F.C.M.R. 1983) (good cause existed where challenges reduced number of court members below jurisdictional minimum, see § 4-3, and convening authority opted to withdraw and re-refer charges rather than adding more members); Dobzynski v. Green, 16 M.J. 84 (C.M.A. 1983) (not error for convening authority to withdraw charges from Navy trial and impose nonjudicial punishment after judge granted defense motion to suppress).
12. United States v. Redman, 33 M.J. 679 (A.C.M.R. 1991) (convening authority's appointment of new court in response to lenient sentences of original court amounted to unlawful command influence but the accused was not prejudiced where he knowingly waived the issue by agreeing to be sentenced by the original panel).
13. Vanover v. Clark, 27 M.J. 345 (C.M.A. 1988) (withdrawal and referral of charges to avoid exclusion of evidence against defendant was improper; military judge's failure to dispel appearance of evil warranted extraordinary relief); United States v. Fleming, 18 C.M.A. 524, 40 C.M.R. 236 (1969); United States v. Williams, 11 C.M.A. 459, 29 C.M.R. 275 (1960); United States v. Mann, 32 M.J. 883 (N.M.C.M.R. 1991) (withdrawal of charges from special court and re-referral of identical charges to general court-martial was reversible error; delayed appreciation of gravity of charges and discovery of additional evidence were not proper reasons for action; trial judge should carefully review convening authority's reasons for withdrawal); United States v. Koke, 32 M.J. 876 (N.M.C.M.R. 1991) (changing court members to adjust sentences, retaliation against defense requested witnesses, and changing venue to avoid witness expenses are improper reasons for withdrawing charges; court listed examples of proper reasons).
14. 32 M.J. 876 (N.M.C.M.R. 1991), aff'd, 34 M.J. 313 (C.M.A. 1992).

ring after arraignment that actually raises a substantial question concerning the appropriateness of the original referral action; (3) is not based on retribution for the assertion of a right by an accused; (4) does not involve harassment of the accused; (5) is not arbitrary or unfair to an accused, considering all of the facts and circumstances of a case and bearing in mind that the mere exposure to potential additional punishment is not controlling; and (6) is invoked in response to an operational exigency. The court added that if re-referral is more onerous to the accused, the convening authority must make an affirmative showing on the record of the reasons for the action.[15]

Former jeopardy considerations may arise if withdrawal and later referral is accomplished over the accused's objection after evidence has been received on the question of guilt or innocence.[16]

When charges are withdrawn, the trial counsel should line out or mask those charges, initial the changes, and renumber any remaining charges.[17] If all of this is accomplished prior to trial, no mention of it should be made to the court members. If they are aware of the withdrawn charges, the judge should instruct them to disregard them for all purposes.[18]

§ 8-6. Service of Charges Upon the Accused.

After charges have been referred to trial, the accused must formally be served with a copy of the charges[1] by the trial counsel or his delegee.[2] In times of peace an accused may not be tried[3] over objection within five days of the service of charges in a general court-martial, or within three days if trial is by special court-martial.[4] The *Manual* indicates that in computing these time requirements, holidays and Sundays are included but the day of the service and the day of trial are excluded.[5] Where major changes are made to the charges and specifications,[6] the new charges must be re-served upon the accused who is again entitled to the three or five-day waiting period.[7]

---

15. *Id.* at 882.
16. *See infra* § 13-3(E).
17. *See* R.C.M. 604(a) Discussion.
18. *Id.*
1. Service must be upon the accused personally. But the defense counsel should be promptly notified. *See* R.C.M. 602 Discussion.
2. Art. 35, U.C.M.J.; R.C.M. 602. In United States v. Desiderio, 31 M.J. 894 (A.F.C.M.R. 1990), the court concluded that the accused was not prejudiced by fact that trial counsel did not personally serve him with the charges. The court indicated that it did not approve of the manner of serving charges and added that even when the trial counsel does not personally serve the charges, he or she should fill in the appropriate blocks on the charge sheet.
3. This includes the Article 39(a) session, which is discussed at Chapter 12. *See* R.C.M. 602.
4. Art. 35, U.C.M.J.; R.C.M. 602.
5. R.C.M. 602.
6. *See* § 6-1 and R.C.M. 603(d).
7. R.C.M. 602 Discussion. *Cf.* United States v. Cruz-Maldonado, 20 M.J. 831 (A.C.M.R. 1985) (accused was not entitled to statutory five-day delay between service of charges and the commencement of trial where the charges had been re-referred without change and the defense did not allege that it needed more time to prepare for trial).

APPENDIX REFERENCES

Appendix 1. Abbreviations.
Appendix 2. Glossary.
Appendix 3. U.C.M.J.
Appendix 4. Court-Martial Flow Chart.
Appendix 6. Charge Sheets.
Appendix 9. Court-Martial Convening Orders.

ANNOTATED BIBLIOGRAPHY

PERIODICALS

Brookshire, "Juror Selection Under the Uniform Code of Military Justice: Fact and Fiction," 58 MIL. L. REV. 71 (1972).

This in-depth article examines the legal requisites for selecting court members under the Uniform Code of Military Justice and also examines the methods actually employed by general court-martial jurisdictions. The author measures these standards and procedures against the civilian models using generally recognized standards of justice. The results of three separate surveys are included along with suggested reforms in the selection process.

Chmelik, "The Military Justice System and the Right to Trial by Jury: Size and Voting Requirements of the General Court-Martial for Service Connected Civilian Offenses," 8 HASTINGS CONST. L.Q. 617 (1981).

The author briefly traces the size and voting requirements of the general court-martial, the Supreme Court's template for jury trials, and the service connection limitations on the ability of the military to try civilian-type offenses. He concludes that in the balance it would be fairer to extend the Sixth Amendment right to jury trial to servicemembers being tried by GCM for non-military offenses.

Cretella & Lynch, "The Military Judge: Military or Judge," CAL. W. L. REV. 57 (1972).

The authors trace the evolution of the military judge's role in the military society as it has evolved and adapted to social changes. Particularly, judges are cast as administrators of justice within a self-contained legal system found in the military services.

Howell, "TDS: The Establishment of the U.S. Army Trial Defense Service," 100 MIL. L. REV. 4 (1983).

The evolution and reasons for the formation of the Trial Defense Service are traced in this article. The author concludes that the birth of this service not only eliminated criticism that defense counsel often were improperly chosen and influenced, but it also ensured the achievement of the need for a fit military fighting force.

Kates, "Limitations on Power of the Convening Authority to Withdraw Charges," 12 MIL. L. REV. 275 (1961).

This short note addresses the convening authority's power to withdraw charges from a court before arraignment under the 1951 Manual for Courts-Martial as interpreted by the Court of Military Appeals in United States v. Williams, 11 C.M.A. 459, 29 C.M.R. 275 (1960).

Lamb, "The Court-Martial Panel Selection Process: A Critical Analysis," 137 MIL. L. REV. 103 (1992).

The author provides an in-depth historical review of the role of juries and court-martial panels. Noting that military case law has encouraged convening authorities to select blue ribbon panels consisting of senior officers and commanders, he recommends that changes be made to the process of selecting panels to reflect a greater cross-section of the community. He recommends the elimination of the variable number of members who sit, repeal of the prerogative of an enlisted panel, establishment of a neutral panel commissioner and random selection, the use of alternate members on the panel, and the establishment of minimum sentences.

Remcho, "Military Juries: Constitutional Analysis and the Need for Reform," 47 IND. L.J. 193 (1973).

This article presents a good review of the constitutional issues involved in the military "jury" selection process. The author addresses several possible alternatives to the current system of selection used under the U.C.M.J. and suggests that there would be little or no loss to discipline if the military adopted a random process of selection.

Schiesser, "Trial by Peers: Enlisted Members on Courts-Martial," 15 CATH. U. L. REV. 171 (1966).

The author reviews the evolution of the "trial by peers" allowed by Art. 25 of the Uniform Code of Military Justice, beginning with the rigid caste system of the Imperial British military justice system, the adoption of that system by the leaders of the American Revolution, and the subsequent realization that the British style of hierarchical justice was incompatible with the American egalitarian ethic. He then describes the contemporary operation of Article 25 and, though making several pointed criticisms, proclaims it a pragmatic and ethical success.

Smallridge, "The Military Jury Selection Reform Movement," 19 A.F. L. REV. 343 (1977).

Noting the calls for reform in the process for selecting court members, this author joins the movement and discusses the "numbers game" often engaged in by counsel in reducing the number of members to gain an advantage in the actual number of members that must vote for a finding of guilty and sentence. The author relies upon statistical analysis to note that the most advantageous number for the prosecution is five, the current minimum number of members that must be appointed to a general court-martial. For the defense, he notes, the number is twelve. The author concludes by offering eight recommended changes.

Stevenson, "The Inherent Authority of the Military Judge," 17 A.F. L. REV. 1 (1975).

The author discusses how the emergence of the military judge has been extremely important in furthering high standards within the military justice system. He concludes that under the U.C.M.J. and the Manual for Courts-Martial, military judges are cloaked with extensive authority. Whether Congress or the courts bless this inherent authority is a function of the judge's wisdom in exercising it.

Symposium, "Military Justice," ARMY LAW., March 1996.

This 127-page symposium contains a Foreword and 11 short articles on a wide range of military justice topics. They are as follows:

> Morris, "Foreword."
> Barto, "Developments in the Substantive Criminal Law Under the Uniform Code of Military Justice."
> Frisk, "New Developments in Pretrial Confinement."
> Frisk, "New Developments in Speedy Trial."
> Winn, "Recent Developments in Military Pretrial and Trial Procedure."
> Masterton, "Recent Developments in Search and Seizure Law."
> Masterton, "Recent Developments in Urinalysis Law."
> Kohlman, "Are You Ready for Some Changes? Five Fresh Views of the Fifth Amendment."
> Wright, "Sex, Lies, and Videotape: Child Sexual Abuse Cases Continue to Create Appellate Issues and Other Developments in the Areas of the Sixth Amendment, Discovery, Mental Responsibility, and Nonjudicial Punishment."
> Henley, "Caveat Criminale: The Impact of the New Military Rules of Evidence in Sexual Offense and Child Molestation Cases."
> Henley, "Current Developments in Evidence Law."
> Morris, "New Developments in Sentencing and Post-Trial Procedure."

VanSant, "Trial by Jury of Military Peers," 15 A.F. L. Rev. 185 (1973).

> The author generally agrees with the principles in the 1970 proposed legislation, introduced by Senator Birch Bayh (S. 4191, 91st Cong., 2d Sess., sec. 825 (1970)), which would have provided for random selection of court members in the military. The author focuses on the issue of whether random selection should also include enlisted personnel and concludes that the arguments in favor of such inclusion outweigh those against such a proposal.

CHAPTER 9

PLEA BARGAINING AND OTHER PRETRIAL NEGOTIATIONS

§ 9-1. General.
§ 9-2. Pretrial Agreements.
    § 9-2(A). Procedures.
        § 9-2(A)(1). Initiation of Negotiations and Terms.
        § 9-2(A)(2). Submission and Acceptance of Offer.
        § 9-2(A)(3). Informal Agreements.
    § 9-2(B). Conditions and Terms.
        § 9-2(B)(1). Valid Conditions.
        § 9-2(B)(2). Invalid Terms.
    § 9-2(C). Withdrawal From the Agreement.
    § 9-2(D). Judicial Review of the Agreement.
§ 9-3. Confessional Stipulations.
§ 9-4. Discharge in Lieu of Court-Martial.
Appendix References.
Annotated Bibliography.

§ 9-1. General.

Throughout the pretrial processing of charges,[1] and in particular after referral of charges to trial,[2] it is common for the defense and government to engage in conversations with a view to disposing of pending charges through means other than a contested trial. This process is most often termed "plea bargaining" and is now a widely accepted facet of military criminal jurisprudence. This chapter addresses not only the formalized military practices surrounding the process of negotiated pleas, but also the related topics of the confessional stipulation and discharges in lieu of court-martial. These latter two topics are discussed here because they may include what amount to admissions of guilt offered in return for a more favorable resolution of the charges or issues.

§ 9-2. Pretrial Agreements.

Negotiated pleas in military practice are embodied in the *pretrial agreement*, an agreement between the accused and the convening authority that the accused will plead guilty or waive certain rights in return for some form of specified relief from the convening authority.[1] Despite the increased use of negotiated pleas in military practice, it was not until the 1984 version of

---

1. *See* Chapter 6.
2. *See* Chapter 8.
1. *See generally* Della Maria, "Negotiating and Drafting the Pretrial Agreement," 25 JAG J. 117 (1971); Gray, "Negotiated Pleas in the Military," 37 FED. B.J. 49 (Winter 1978); Haddenhorst & David, "Guilty Pleas: A Primer for Judge Advocates," 39 A.F.L. REV. 87 (1996); Melhorn, "Negotiating Pleas in Naval Courts-Martial," 16 JAG J. 103 (1962); McMenamin, "Plea Bargaining in the Military," 10 AM. CRIM. L. REV. 93 (1971).

Manual for Courts-Martial[2] that any specific guidance was laid out in either the *Manual* or the U.C.M.J. The U.C.M.J. is still silent on the subject. Thus, the guidelines for pretrial negotiations and agreements in the past came from the military courts and service regulations. Most of this precedent has been captured in R.C.M. 705, which now spells out in detail the applicable procedures.

The widespread use of pretrial agreements is due to the obvious advantages it offers to both the accused and the prosecution. For example, the accused is able to reduce the nature or number of charges against him or obtain sentence relief. The prosecution can obtain a conviction without the risk of an acquittal. The disadvantages are also obvious: The accused usually waives important rights and the government is often limited in the punishment it may impose. Because there are potential dangers in the abuse of this abbreviated method of disposing of charges, a number of safeguards have been included. For example, as the following discussions point out, certain provisions are forbidden,[3] and the judge must conduct a thorough inquiry into any guilty plea and accompanying pretrial agreement.[4]

Although the pretrial agreement takes on the form of a contract, the military courts have been reluctant to apply strict contract rules.[5] Nonetheless, the courts have selectively applied contract principles in interpreting the rights and obligations of the parties. The agreement, which must be *written*,[6] generally consists of an *offer* by the accused to meet certain conditions in return for ameliorative action by the convening authority who registers his acceptance by signing the document.[7]

There is authority for the rule that the convening authority will be strictly bound and that the agreement will be construed in favor of the accused.[8] A sample pretrial agreement is included at Appendix 12.

---

2. *See* R.C.M. 705.
3. *See infra* § 9-2(B)(2).
4. *See infra* § 9-2(D) and § 14-3(C).
5. United States v. Koopman, 20 M.J. 106 (C.M.A. 1985); United States v. Kazena, 11 M.J. 28 (C.M.A. 1981); United States v. Lanzer, 3 M.J. 60 (C.M.A. 1977); United States v. Cox, 22 C.M.A. 69, 46 C.M.R. 69 (1972); United States v. Jacques, 5 M.J. 598 (N.C.M.R. 1978).
6. *See* R.C.M. 705(d)(3). United States v. Troglin, 21 C.M.A. 183, 44 C.M.R. 237 (1972). *See also* United States v. Young, 15 M.J. 857 (A.F.C.M.R. 1983) (AF policy required written agreements); United States v. Stevens, 2 M.J. 488 (A.C.M.R. 1975) (written agreements preferred).
7. United States v. Lanzer, 3 M.J. 60 (C.M.A. 1977). *Cf.* United States v. Kazena, 11 M.J. 28 (C.M.A. 1981), where convening authority was permitted to withdraw from agreement after referring an additional charge to trial.
8. R.C.M. 705(d)(4). *See, e.g.,* United States v. Koopman, 20 M.J. 106 (C.M.A. 1985) (noting that it has enforced oral promises of immunity, the court ruled that upon the accused's failure to keep his end of the bargain "pay off most of his bad checks" the government was free to renege on its promise to send only certain charges to a summary court-martial); United States v. Gooden, 23 M.J. 721 (A.C.M.R. 1986) (convening authority's action set aside where it included a reprimand, a punishment not provided for in the pretrial agreement and which increased the severity of the sentence).

§ 9-2(A). Procedures.

§ 9-2(A)(1). Initiation of Negotiations and Terms.

Either the prosecution or the defense may initiate the plea bargaining process. That was not always so, however. Before R.C.M. 705 was amended in 1991, only the defense could initiate the process and only the defense could suggest terms to be included in the pretrial agreement.[9] That structure led to some difficult analysis and the question of who originated a particular provision was not always clear.[10] Nonetheless, the courts had indicated an inclination to approve pretrial agreements where the government had actually first suggested a particular provision.[11] Now, R.C.M. 705 follows federal practice[12] and specifically recognizes that either side may initiate the plea bargaining procedures.[13] And either side is now free to offer suggested provisions in the agreement,[14] as long as the provisions do not violate regulation, law, or public policy.[15] Apparently the change reflects the view that who originated the process is not as crucial as whether the accused's plea is provident and voluntarily made.[16] That can be determined by a military judge during the providency inquiry, discussed in Chapter 14.

While either the prosecution or the defense may initiate pretrial agreements, the process usually begins with the defense counsel informally determining the amenability of the government to particular terms or conditions. If the defense counsel[17] initiates the negotiation process, the government representative is free to suggest alternative conditions or terms on behalf of the convening authority.[18]

---

9. R.C.M. 705 (1984).
10. In his concurring opinion in United States v. Jones, 23 M.J. 305 (C.M.A. 1987), Judge Cox queried who would be considered the originator once the defense bar realizes that only certain language or provisions will be approved by the convening authority. *Id.* at 308. In his view, there would be no problem with the convening authority "sponsoring, dictating, demanding, etc. 'various provisions and terms because the convening authority's power to absolutely refuse to enter into pretrial agreements is the ultimate command-sponsored limitation.'"
11. *See, e.g.,* United States v. Sanchez, 26 M.J. 564 (C.G.C.M.R. 1988) (pretrial agreement valid although provisions originated with convening authority). In United States v. Huber, 24 M.J. 697 (C.G.C.M.R. 1987), the court approved a provision waiving a trial by members even though the provision apparently originated with the convening authority. The court concluded that the point of origin of a provision was not outcome-dispositive.
12. R.C.M. 705(d) Analysis.
13. R.C.M. 705(d).
14. R.C.M. 705(c)(2).
15. R.C.M. 705(d) Analysis.
16. *Id.*
17. If there is no defense counsel, which would be rare by this point in the pretrial processing, the accused may negotiate and make any formal written offers.
18. R.C.M. 705(d)(2). The government representative is usually the trial counsel but may be the staff judge advocate, or his deputy, or the chief of military justice or chief of criminal law division of the SJA's office.

§ 9-2(A)(2). Submission and Acceptance of Offer.

Although this negotiation process may be, and usually is, informal, the process of submitting the accused's offer is not: the defense offer to enter into an agreement, which may originate with either the government or the accused and his counsel,[19] is reduced to writing[20] with all of the terms and conditions clearly set out,[21] and signed by both the accused and the defense counsel.[22] If the defense initiates the offer, it is normally routed to the convening authority through the staff judge advocate or trial counsel who serves as the legal advisor to the convening authority.[23] The offer may, but need not, include a place for the legal advisor to note his or her recommendation for approval or disapproval. Ultimately, the decision to accept or reject the offer rests solely with the convening authority[24] who signs the offer noting his acceptance or rejection or directs that a delegate sign it.[25] The agreement is "made" when both the accused and the convening authority have signed the agreement.[26] A sample pretrial agreement is at Appendix 12.

Statements made by the accused or his counsel in unsuccessful plea negotiations may be protected from later use at trial under Military Rule of Evidence 410.[27] *See also* § 14-3(B)(2).

---

19. R.C.M. 705(d)(1). As noted above, originally only the defense could initiate terms in the agreement. Change 5 to the MCM, however, removed that limitation from R.C.M. 705. The Drafters recognized the difficulty of determining who had actually originated a particular term.
20. R.C.M. 705(d)(3).
21. *Id.* The exception to this is where the agreement addresses sentence limitations. In that case, the specifics of those limitations are attached as an appendix to the offer. The purpose of this is to permit the judge in a bench trial to review the pretrial agreement separately and sentence the accused without knowing beforehand what limitations have been placed upon the convening authority's power to approve that sentence. *See* § 14-3(C).
22. R.C.M. 705(d)(3).
23. The SJA and trial counsel should not block presentation of the "offer" to the convening authority although they may advise the latter on the legal aspects of accepting the offered terms. The Discussion to R.C.M. 705(d)(4) indicates that the convening authority should consult with his legal advisor before acting on the offer.
24. R.C.M. 705(d)(4). United States v. Caruth, 6 M.J. 184 (C.M.A. 1979); United States v. Walters, 5 M.J. 829 (A.C.M.R. 1978). Should someone other than the convening authority purport to approve the offer in his own right, the convening authority may nonetheless be bound if the accused detrimentally relied on the agreement. Shepardson v. Roberts, 14 M.J. 354 (C.M.A. 1983).

See also United States v. Jones, 26 M.J. 650 (A.C.M.R. 1988) (although decision ultimately rests with convening authority, he must deal in fair manner; not improper to reject pretrial agreement offer by defense that did not include restitution provision); United States v. Upchurch, 23 M.J. 501 (A.F.C.M.R. 1986) (appellate court reduced sentence to conform to terms of agreement offered by the defense but never submitted to the convening authority by the SJA).
25. R.C.M. 705(d)(4). Thus, an absent convening authority could telephonically delegate his SJA or trial counsel to sign the agreement on behalf of the convening authority.
26. *See* United States v. Jacques, 5 M.J. 598 (N.C.M.R. 1978).
27. *See* MIL. R. EVID. 410. United States v. Watkins, 34 M.J. 344 (C.M.A. 1992) (accused's questions of CID agent regarding possible disposition of charges were not made in course of plea bargaining and were not inadmissible under MIL. R. EVID. 410); United States v. Ankeny, 30 M.J. 10 (C.M.A. 1990) (civilian counsel's preliminary overtures to assistant staff judge advocate were part of plea discussions under MIL. R. EVID. 410).

§ 9-2(A)(3). Informal Agreements.

While the temptation may exist to avoid the required formalities and enter into unwritten and informal pretrial agreements, the *Manual* requires the agreements to be in writing[28] and military courts have repeatedly condemned the use of *sub rosa* agreements between the accused and the government.[29] Noting that the existence of a *sub rosa* agreement does not *per se* void the pretrial agreement, the court in *United States v. Corriere*[30] concluded that there had indeed been such an agreement but that the *sub rosa* provisions (waiver of motions) had been conceived by the defense and therefore public policy had not been violated. The court, however, cautioned counsel and staff judge advocates about using such "gentlemen's agreements." In a footnote, the court stated:

> As in this case, this informal practice can lead to misinforming an inquiring military judge that no separate agreements exist, and considerable appellate litigation. Such quibbling conduct speaks ill of the participants' integrity in those cases where such conduct was intended to mislead a trial judge, and may raise questions of competency in those cases where such conduct was inadvertent.[31]

If it appears to the appellate court that a *sub rosa* agreement existed, the case may be returned for a determination of the impact of that agreement on the proceedings.[32]

§ 9-2(B). Conditions and Terms.

With some exceptions, discussed in § 9-2(B)(2), the parties are relatively free to negotiate a wide variety of terms and conditions concerning pleas,[33] charges, and sentence relief. Although the military courts in the past discouraged innovative plea bargaining,[34] more recent decisions[35] and the *Manual*[36] recognize the value of such bargaining.

---

28. R.C.M. 705(d)(3).
29. *See, e.g.*, United States v. Kyle, 32 M.J. 724 (A.F.C.M.R. 1991) (condemned use of oral agreement).
30. 24 M.J. 701 (A.C.M.R. 1987).
31. *Id.* at 708, n. 7.
32. *See, e.g.*, United States v. Corriere, 20 M.J. 905 (A.C.M.R. 1985) (case remanded for hearing on whether there was an undisclosed *sub rosa* agreement between the SJA and the defense concerning what, if any, motions the defense would make).
33. For a discussion on the types of pleas that may be entered see Chapter 14.
34. *See, e.g.*, United States v. Dawson, 10 M.J. 142 (C.M.A. 1981) (innovative provisions run high risk of being ruled invalid).
35. *See, e.g.*, United States v. Jones, 23 M.J. 305 (C.M.A. 1987) (court recognized the permissible growth of a variety of permissible terms in pretrial agreements). *Cf.* United States v. Schaffer, 12 M.J. 425 (C.M.A. 1982); United States v. Dorsey, 25 M.J. 728 (A.F.C.M.R. 1987) (agreement to waive search and seizure issue was void because it did not relate to those rights otherwise

---

36. R.C.M. 705(c) Analysis (accused has substantial latitude as long as agreement is freely and voluntarily entered).

Promises by the convening authority usually relate to withdrawing charges, referring less serious charges, referring charges to a particular court, instructing the prosecutor not to present evidence on certain charges, or providing some sort of sentence relief such as suspension of a portion of the sentence.[37] Most of the litigation on pretrial agreements has centered on the promises made by the accused and whether he improperly bargained away a substantial or valuable right.[38] The following sections focus on both permissible and impermissible terms as set out in R.C.M. 705(c) and in military judicial opinions. It should be readily apparent that the military courts have had ample opportunity to review a variety of conditions.

§ 9-2(B)(1). Valid Conditions.

The following conditions have been deemed valid and may be agreed to by the accused in return for a plea:

1. That the accused enter into a stipulation of fact with the prosecution;[39]

---

specifically waived by the guilty plea and was in violation of Air Force regulation); United States v. Kidwell, 20 M.J. 1020 (A.C.M.R. 1985) (accused was denied effective assistance of counsel where in return for turning in stolen blank ID cards the chief of justice would recommend an administrative discharge but defense counsel never submitted a request for one. He felt that the accused's interests were subordinate to the high national interest in obtaining the remainder of the cards which could be used for terrorist activity. Thus the counsel was representing conflicting interests); United States v. Yost, 20 M.J. 785 (C.G.C.M.R. 1985) (accused was improperly denied the assistance of counsel in signing an agreement with the convening authority that he would waive accrued pay and allowances in return for an administrative discharge, and thus avoid a sentence rehearing. Thus, the agreement was void).

37. *See, e.g.,* R.C.M. 705(b). United States v. Jennings, 36 M.J. 773 (N.M.C.M.R. 1992) (provision requiring suspension of all confinement if punitive discharge was assessed and accused submitted voluntary appellate leave request on day of trial did not violate public policy); United States v. Cassity, 36 M.J. 759 (N.M.C.M.R. 1992) (sentence agreement violated public policy; parties agreed that if more than four months' confinement was adjudged, punitive discharge would be suspended for six months; court agreed with military judge that that agreement was not fair because it, in combination with counsel's arguments, distorted the sentencing process); United States v. Kendra, 31 M.J. 846 (N.M.C.M.R. 1990) (accused and convening authority could agree that suspension of sentence would begin at date sentence was adjudged rather than at time convening authority approved the sentence).

United States v. Gibbs, 30 M.J. 1166 (A.C.M.R. 1990) (convening authority could not convert court's sentence of a fine into forfeitures; where pretrial agreement was silent on possibility of fine, accused could reasonably count on protection from approval of fine). *See also* United States v. Morales-Santana, 32 M.J. 557 (A.F.C.M.R. 1990) (convening authority could not approve fine as part of sentence where pretrial agreement was silent on that possibility); United States v. Penister, 25 M.J. 148 (C.M.A. 1987) (convening authority agreed to refer charges to special instead of general court-martial).

38. The underlying concern is that the accused not bargain away procedures or protections that are designed to ensure that his guilty plea is provident, that his agreement is voluntary, and that sentencing proceedings are satisfactorily met. R.C.M. 705(c) Analysis. United States v. Robinson, 25 M.J. 528 (A.F.C.M.R. 1987) (accused's agreement not to object to videotape of victim during sentencing did not waive important trial right).

39. *See* R.C.M. 705(c)(2)(A). United States v. Allen, 39 M.J. 581 (N.M.C.M.R. 1993) (parties can stipulate to admissibility of evidence); United States v. Klinko, 36 M.J. 840 (A.C.M.R. 1993) (agreement to iron out details in stipulation of fact after offer to plead guilty was accepted was not

§ 9-2(B)(1) PLEA BARGAINING & OTHER PRETRIAL NEGOTIATIONS   § 9-2(B)(1)

2. That the accused enter into a "confessional stipulation" of fact with the prosecution;[40]
3. That the accused testify as a witness or cooperate [41] in other proceedings;[42]
4. That the accused waive the statute of limitations;[43]
5. That the accused meet stated terms of probation;[44]

---

a *sub rosa* agreement; court indicated that stipulations of fact are not truly binding agreements; court recommended that stipulations include statement that the evidence in question is admissible without regard to the rules of evidence); United States v. Sharper, 17 M.J. 803 (A.C.M.R. 1984); United States v. Terrell, 7 M.J. 511 (A.C.M.R. 1979). (not impermissible delegation to authorize trial counsel to determine the terms of the stipulation); United States v. Thomas, 6 M.J. 573 (A.C.M.R. 1978).

Recently there has been some litigation concerning whether the agreement may properly require the accused to stipulate to matters that would otherwise be inadmissible. *See, e.g.*, United States v. Glazier, 26 M.J. 268 (C.M.A. 1988) (parties can agree to stipulation that contains otherwise inadmissible evidence; judge may, however, rule on objections to contents).

United States v. Tompkins, 30 M.J. 1090 (N.M.C.M.R. 1989) (stipulation of expected testimony amounted to confessional stipulation when accused also agreed not to present any evidence or challenge the stipulations on charges to which he was pleading not guilty); United States v. Vargas, 29 M.J. 968 (A.C.M.R. 1990) (stipulation included otherwise inadmissible uncharged misconduct).

United States v. Taylor, 21 M.J. 1016 (A.C.M.R. 1986) (judge should not referee contents of stipulation or rule on admissibility of contents; if parties cannot agree the accused should be advised that he has failed to fulfill agreement); United States v. Rasberry, 21 M.J. 656 (A.C.M.R. 1985) (prosecution may properly require accused to stipulate to aggravating factors; here judge declined to consider defense motion to suppress accused's unwarned statements in stipulation); United States v. Marsh, 19 M.J. 657 (A.C.M.R. 1984) (noting the leeway granted in negotiating pleas, the court held that a stipulation that included damaging information to the accused could be considered on sentencing; the court added that all parties should respect the decision of the parties to the agreement as to what information should be known to the sentencing authority).

40. R.C.M. 705(c)(2)(A). United States v. Bertelson, 3 M.J. 314 (C.M.A. 1977). For a discussion on the confessional stipulations, see § 9-3.

United States v. Tompkins, 30 M.J. 1090 (N.M.C.M.R. 1989) (stipulation of expected testimony amounted to confessional stipulation where accused was not permitted to challenge it; the court declined to address the issue of whether this particular agreement was contrary to public policy or fundamentally unfair).

41. United States v. Phillips, 24 M.J. 812 (A.F.C.M.R. 1987) (the accused agreed to "cooperate" in drug investigations and waive his right against self-incrimination; although waiver of that right is inherent in the case at bar, he should not be required to waive the right in future proceedings; the opinion contains a general discussion of applicable Air Force procedures and regulations governing pretrial agreements); United States v. Tyson, 2 M.J. 583 (N.C.M.R. 1976).

42. R.C.M. 705(c)(2)(B). As long as the clause only requires the accused to testify or testify truthfully, it will be valid. *See* United States v. Scott, 6 M.J. 608 (A.C.M.R. 1978); United States v. Reynolds, 2 M.J. 887 (A.C.M.R. 1976).

But the clause will probably be invalid if it requires the accused to testify in conformity with his pretrial statements, United States v. Conway, 20 C.M.A. 99, 42 C.M.R. 291 (1970), United States v. Stoltz, 14 C.M.A. 461, 34 C.M.R. 241 (1964) (clause here was part of grant of immunity), or if his sentence will be further reduced every time he gives the testimony, United States v. Scoles, 14 C.M.A. 14, 33 C.M.R. 226 (1963).

43. *See, e.g.*, United States v. Clemens, 4 M.J. 791 (N.C.M.R. 1978).

44. R.C.M. 705(c)(2)(D). United States v. Lallande, 22 C.M.A. 170, 46 C.M.R. 170 (1973). The period of suspended sentence should be expressly stated. United States v. Price, 4 M.J. 849 (A.C.M.R. 1978).

6. That upon certain contingencies the agreement may be avoided;[45]
7. That the accused make restitution;[46]
8. That the accused waive an Article 32 investigation;[47]
9. That the accused agree not to engage in post-trial misconduct;[48]
10. That the accused agree to trial by judge alone;[49]

---

45. United States v. Scott, 6 M.J. 608 (A.C.M.R. 1978). These clauses cannot be invoked to relieve the convening authority of limiting punishment on rehearings as required by Article 63(b), U.C.M.J. United States v. Brown, 8 M.J. 559 (N.C.M.R. 1979). Because the 1984 *Manual* specifically provides for withdrawal by either the accused or the convening authority, cancellation clauses may not be necessary.

In an attempt to preclude the defense counsel from attempting to beat the deal by arguing for lengthy confinement, and no punitive discharge, when confinement has been limited by the pretrial agreement, some pretrial agreements to limit the sentence are contingent on imposition of a punitive discharge. *See, e.g.,* United States v. Castleberry, 18 M.J. 826 (A.C.M.R. 1984) (pretrial agreement that hinged upon the imposition of a punitive discharge did not unduly prejudice the accused). *See also* United States v. Hollcraft, 17 M.J. 1111 (A.C.M.R. 1984); United States v. Holmes, 17 M.J. 830 (A.C.M.R. 1984); United States v. Cross, 19 M.J. 973 (A.C.M.R. 1985) (such provisions are not violative of public policy); United States v. Witherspoon, 19 M.J. 978 (A.C.M.R. 1985); United States v. Sanders, 19 M.J. 979 (A.C.M.R. 1985); United States v. Costa, 19 M.J. 980 (A.C.M.R. 1985); United States v. Wordlow, 19 M.J. 981 (A.C.M.R. 1985).

46. R.C.M. 705(c)(2)(C). United States v. Olson, 25 M.J. 293 (C.M.A. 1987) (accused entitled to withdraw from plea agreement where misunderstanding existed with regard to how much money was owed to the government); United States v. Koopman, 20 M.J. 106 (C.M.A. 1985).

United States v. Holstlaw, 41 M.J. 552 (N.M.Ct.Crim.App. 1994) (convening authority erred in releasing himself from pretrial agreement which required accused to make restitution; court cautioned that when agreement requires accused to perform affirmative act post-trial, it is potentially unenforceable unless it includes means for determining whether accused has performed act; if provision requires expenditure of money, it may require consideration of accused's financial status); United States v. Brown, 34 M.J. 1024 (N.M.C.M.R. 1992) (accused agreed to make restitution. Appellate court rejected his argument that agreement's failure to specify time for payment was not fatal; date for performance could be fairly implied).

In United States v. Foust, 25 M.J. 647 (A.C.M.R. 1987), the accused agreed to make restitution and that if it was made in full before arraignment, the maximum imposable punishment would be reduced accordingly. He failed to make full restitution and on appeal argued unsuccessfully that the provision was against public policy because he was indigent. The court noted that the record was devoid of such evidence and that the provision was fully enforceable. Further, the provision had originated with the accused.

United States v. Callahan, 8 M.J. 804 (N.C.M.R. 1980); United States v. Brown, 4 M.J. 654 (A.C.M.R. 1977) (clause valid where only a good faith effort is required).

47. R.C.M. 705(c)(2)(E). United States v. Schaffer, 12 M.J. 425 (C.M.A. 1982); United States v. Bilbo, 13 M.J. 706 (N.M.C.M.R. 1982); United States v. Miller, 12 M.J. 836 (A.C.M.R. 1982). The key here is that the accused has voluntarily waived it; the government cannot demand it. United States v. Walls, 8 M.J. 666 (A.C.M.R. 1979).

48. United States v. Dawson, 10 M.J. 142 (C.M.A. 1981) (dicta). The accused must be guaranteed a post-trial misconduct hearing, however, similar to that afforded accuseds whose suspended sentences are being vacated pursuant to Article 72, U.C.M.J. *See* Appendix 3. *See also* R.C.M. 705(c)(2)(D), R.C.M. 1109. *See generally* United States v. White, 11 M.J. 712 (N.M.C.M.R. 1981); United States v. Connell, 13 M.J. 156 (C.M.A. 1982); Faulkner, "The Pretrial Agreement Misconduct Provision: *United States v. Dawson,*" ARMY LAW., Oct. 1981, at 1.

49. R.C.M. 705(c)(2)(E). United States v. Burnell, 40 M.J. 175 (C.M.A. 1994) (decision to waive trial by members was voluntary and intelligent). In United States v. Zelenski, 24 M.J. 1 (C.M.A. 1987), the court indicated that although it does not condone provisions whereby an accused waives a trial composed of members, it does not intend to invalidate automatically such provisions where it appears that they are a "freely conceived defense product." The court added that

11. That the accused waive the personal appearance of a witness during sentencing.[50]

12. That the accused waive a bar to trial such as former jeopardy,[51] or the statute of limitations;[52]

13. That the accused enter his plea prior to the prosecution's entering of evidence on the merits;[53]

14. That the accused agree to permit the judge to reserve entry of findings until he is about to announce the sentence;[54]

15. That certain motions will survive a guilty plea and be preserved for appellate review;[55]

---

any service or local command policy, through standardized plea agreements, that might undermine the legislative intent to provide the accused with a viable option of being tried by either judge or members would be closely scrutinized.

In United States v. Andrews, 38 M.J. 650 (A.C.M.R. 1993), the court relied upon the 1991 amendments to R.C.M. 705 (Change 5, MCM), which permit either side to propose terms of the pretrial agreement, to approve an agreement where sentence limitation rested on accused waiving right to trial by members. The court added that the provision did not violate public policy.

United States v. Washington, 35 M.J. 774 (A.C.M.R. 1992) (accused requested bench trial pursuant to pretrial agreement); United States v. Young, 35 M.J. 541 (A.C.M.R. 1992) (provision waiving trial by members not enforceable where it was demanded by prosecution).

See also United States v. Baumgart, 23 M.J. 888 (A.C.M.R. 1987); United States v. Ralston, 24 M.J. 709 (A.C.M.R. 1987) (waiver of trial by members originated with accused).

At one point the Air Force prohibited such agreements. United States v. Saulter, 23 M.J. 626 (A.F.C.M.R. 1986) (Air Force Reg. 111-1 specifically prohibits pretrial agreements which contain a waiver of the right to trial with members; *citing* United States v. Russo, 1 M.J. 134 (C.M.A. 1975), the court said that the regulation was binding on the prosecution).

See also United States v. Frierson, 24 M.J. 647 (A.C.M.R. 1987) (because agreement that contains that provision is void, convening authority's action in directing judge to hold hearing on issue of who originated provision was of no effect); United States v. Woodard, 24 M.J. 514 (A.F.C.M.R. 1987) (*per curiam*). The Air Force, however, changed its position on the validity of waiving trial with members and in December 1987 an Interim Message, Change 87-5 eliminated the prohibition that had existed in AF Reg. 111-1, para. 4-5h (Aug. 1984).

See also United States v. Reed, 26 M.J. 891 (A.F.C.M.R. 1988); United States v. Bray, 26 M.J. 661 (N.M.C.M.R. 1988); United States v. Blevins, 22 M.J. 817 (N.M.C.M.R. 1986); United States v. Martin, 4 M.J. 852 (A.C.M.R. 1978); United States v. Schmeltz, 1 M.J. 8 (C.M.A. 1975). *Cf.* United States v. Boyd, 2 M.J. 1014 (A.C.M.R. 1976) (government originated clause); United States v. Cordova, 4 M.J. 604 (A.C.M.R. 1977) (defense counsel erroneously believed government required clause as a matter of policy).

50. R.C.M. 705(c)(2)(E). United States v. Mills, 12 M.J. 1 (C.M.A. 1981); United States v. Callaway, 21 M.J. 770 (A.C.M.R. 1986); United States v. Rodriquez, 12 M.J. 632 (N.M.C.M.R. 1981); United States v. Bradley, 11 M.J. 598 (A.F.C.M.R. 1981); United States v. Krautheim, 10 M.J. 763 (N.C.M.R. 1981); United States v. McDonagh, 10 M.J. 698 (A.C.M.R. 1981).

51. United States v. Troglin, 21 C.M.A. 183, 44 C.M.R. 237 (1972). *See also* § 13-3(E).

52. United States v. Clemens, 4 M.J. 791 (N.C.M.R. 1978). *See also* § 13-3(B).

53. United States v. Elmore, 1 M.J. 262 (C.M.A. 1976). *See* § 15-12.

54. *See, e.g.,* United States v. Arnold, 8 M.J. 806 (N.C.M.R. 1980). The purpose of this clause is to foreclose a double jeopardy bar where the accused pleads guilty to some offenses and is found not guilty on the others when the prosecutor presents no evidence; if the accused should thereafter improvidence his guilty plea, *see* § 14-3(D), the prosecution would be barred from retrying the not guilty findings. *See* United States v. Johnson, 2 M.J. 541 (A.C.M.R. 1976).

55. R.C.M. 910(a)(2) now provides for such conditional guilty pleas. United States v. Schaffer, 12 M.J. 425, 428 (C.M.A. 1982). Earlier cases had rejected such pleas. *See, e.g.,* United States v.

16. That the accused waive motions challenging the admissibility of evidence;[56]

17. That the accused waive challenges to participants in the trial;[57]

18. That the accused will waive rights in any administrative discharge proceeding;[58]

19. That the accused will waive unlawful command influence issues in the pretrial processing of the case;[59] and

20. That the accused agree that any statements he might make during plea discussions may be used to impeach any contradictory statements he might make at trial.[60]

This list is not exhaustive and in view of the current trend to consider favorably innovative terms, a promise approximating any of the foregoing, and not otherwise forbidden, should survive judicial scrutiny.[61] There is some support for this in the Analysis to R.C.M. 705(c), which indicates that matters or issues that can be waived by failing to raise them should be properly subject to a written agreement that affirmatively waives them.

Higa, 12 M.J. 1008 (A.C.M.R. 1982); United States v. Mallett, 14 M.J. 631 (A.C.M.R. 1982). *See* § 14-5.

56. United States v. Gibson, 29 M.J. 379 (C.M.A. 1990) (defense-originated agreement included provision waiving evidentiary objections; trial judge construed it to apply only to confrontation and hearsay objections to out-of-court statements by victims). In United States v. Jones, 23 M.J. 305 (C.M.A. 1987), the court approved terms that provided that the accused would waive search and seizure and eyewitness identification issues. The court noted that such terms are permissible where, first, the term has originated with the defense and, second, the agreement was a "freely conceived defense product." Note that this case preceded the 1991 amendments to R.C.M. 705(c)(2) and (d), which now permit either side to initiate pretrial negotiations and propose provisions. United States v. McKenzie, 39 M.J. 946 (N.M.C.M.R. 1994) (provision requiring accused to waive objections to admissibility of his statements at sentencing was valid provision).

57. *See, e.g.,* United States v. Keyes, 33 M.J. 567 (N.M.C.M.R. 1991) (provision requiring accused to waive challenge to military judge did not deprive accused of fair trial and was not void as against public policy; judge made clear on record that he understood his duty to recuse himself if he believed he could not remain impartial).

58. United States v. Gansemer, 38 M.J. 340 (C.M.A. 1993) (accused's agreement to waive hearing in any subsequent administrative discharge proceeding was valid).

59. United States v. Weasler, 43 M.J. 15 (1995) (accused could waive issue of unlawful command influence regarding preferral of charges). It is not yet clear whether an accused could waive the issue of command influence in what the courts have called the adjudicative process, i.e., unlawful influence on the participants or the trial itself.

60. United States v. Mezzanatto, 115 S. Ct. 797 (1995) (accused may waive Federal Rule of Evidence 410).

61. In United States v. Cantu, 30 M.J. 1088 (N.M.C.M.R. 1989), the defendant agreed to plead guilty to some drug charges and not guilty to two LSD charges. He also agreed to enter into stipulations of expected testimony and stipulations of fact on the LSD charges and agreed not to present any evidence on those charges or challenge the stipulations of expected testimony. Because the court found reversible error in not conducting an inquiry into what it considered confessional stipulations, it declined to address the question of whether this combination of provisions was contrary to public policy or fundamentally unfair.

§ 9-2(B)(2). Invalid Terms.

Any agreement that is not voluntarily entered into by the accused is void[62] and any agreement which deprives the accused of a fair proceeding is likewise impermissible.[63] Few, if any, agreements fall into the first category. Instead, it is more common for a military court to question a clause that ostensibly falls into the second category. Thus, even though the provision may have been voluntarily offered by the accused the clause may be ruled invalid. For example, the following clauses have been considered impermissible: requirements to enter pleas before motions,[64] clauses requiring the accused to waive all motions,[65] clauses that require the accused to waive the right to counsel,[66] speedy trial issues,[67] jurisdiction issues,[68] due process,[69] the right to full sentence proceedings,[70] and appellate and post-trial rights.[71]

Note that the presence of one of these forbidden clauses does not necessarily void the entire agreement. Assuming that neither party wishes to withdraw from the agreement,[72] the appropriate remedy may be fashioned by the judge at trial.[73]

---

62. R.C.M. 705(c)(1)(A). United States v. Care, 18 C.M.A. 535, 40 C.M.R. 247 (1969); United States v. Young, 35 M.J. 541 (A.C.M.R. 1992) (provision waiving trial by members not enforceable where it was demanded by prosecution).
63. United States v. Mills, 12 M.J. 1 (C.M.A. 1981); United States v. Holland, 1 M.J. 58 (C.M.A. 1975).
64. R.C.M. 705(c)(1) Discussion.
65. United States v. Jennings, 22 M.J. 837 (N.M.C.M.R. 1986); United States v. Schaffer, 46 C.M.R. 1089 (A.C.M.R. 1973). Cf. United States v. Jones, 20 M.J. 853 (A.C.M.R. 1985) (court approved the accused's offer to waive search and seizure and eyewitness identification motions as part of a pretrial agreement).
66. R.C.M. 705(c)(1)(B). United States v. Darring, 9 C.M.A. 651, 26 C.M.R. 431 (1958).
67. R.C.M. 705(c)(1)(B). United States v. Cummings, 17 C.M.A. 376, 38 C.M.R. 174 (1968); United States v. Pruitt, 41 M.J. 736 (N.M.Ct.Crim.App. 1994) (provision agreeing to waive speedy trial was invalid; court applied remedy on appeal; accused decided to forego litigating motion to dismiss at rehearing); United States v. Sumbry, 33 M.J. 564 (A.C.M.R. 1991) (provision in pretrial agreement which required accused to waive speedy trial motion was void, without regard to who originated the provision). Cf. United States v. Hobart, 22 M.J. 851 (A.F.C.M.R. 1986) (record did not indicate that waiver of issue was required).
68. R.C.M. 705(c)(1)(B). United States v. Conklan, 41 M.J. 800 (Army Ct.Crim.App. 1995) (court held as matter of law and public policy that the right to litigate good faith claims of lack of jurisdiction and transactional immunity are not proper topics for pretrial agreements, even though such issues may be otherwise waived by accused); United States v. Morales, 12 M.J. 888 (A.C.M.R. 1982); United States v. Peterson, 44 C.M.R. 528 (A.C.M.R. 1971).
69. United States v. Cummings, 17 C.M.A. 376, 38 C.M.R. 174 (1968).
70. United States v. Callahan, 22 C.M.R. 443 (A.B.R. 1956). Cf. United States v. Krautheim, 10 M.J. 763 (N.C.M.R. 1981).
71. R.C.M. 705(c)(1)(B). United States v. Schaller, 9 M.J. 939 (N.C.M.R. 1980); United States v. Ponds, 1 C.M.A. 385, 3 C.M.R. 119 (1952).
72. See infra § 9-2(C).
73. See infra § 9-2(D).

§ 9-2(C). Withdrawal From the Agreement.

Some pretrial agreements include specific contingency clauses that permit withdrawal by either party from the agreement.[74] But even in the absence of such clauses, either the accused or the convening authority may withdraw from the pretrial agreement. The accused may withdraw from the agreement at any time,[75] but his ability to withdraw a guilty plea[76] or a confessional stipulation[77] lies within the trial judge's discretion.[78] The accused's ability to withdraw, according to the Drafters' Analysis for R.C.M. 705(d)(5)(A), reflects another safety valve against prosecutorial abuse. Thus, if at trial, it becomes apparent that the prosecution's reading and planned application of the agreement is not what the accused understood, he may withdraw. As a practical matter, both sides are often willing to re-negotiate or reach some sort of compromise in order to salvage the agreement and avoid a trial on the merits.[79]

The convening authority's ability to withdraw from an agreement depends to some extent on whether the accused has performed, or executed, any of his promises in the agreement. Before the accused does so, the convening authority may withdraw for any reason.[80] After the accused begins performance, the convening authority may withdraw under the following circumstances: (1) where the accused has failed to perform a "material promise or condition" in the pretrial agreement,[81] (2) where the judge determines at trial that there

---

74. *See, e.g.*, Shepardson v. Roberts, 14 M.J. 354 (C.M.A. 1983).
75. R.C.M. 705(d)(5)(A). United States v. Upchurch, 23 M.J. 501 (A.F.C.M.R. 1986) (appellate relief granted where accused's pretrial withdrawal of agreement was based upon misleading representations by representatives of the government).
76. R.C.M. 705(d)(5)(A). *See generally* § 14-3(G).
77. R.C.M. 705(d)(5)(A). *See also* United States v. Romero, 37 M.J. 613 (A.C.M.R. 1993) (if plea agreement falls through, better practice is for judge to announce that stipulation is withdrawn, unless accused affirmatively consents to its use on the record); United States v. Cunningham, 36 M.J. 1011 (A.C.M.R. 1993) (after government withdrew from pretrial agreement, court continued to consider stipulation of fact, which amounted to confessional stipulation, on contested charges; court declined to apply waiver, noting that government received benefit of stipulation without the limitations in the pretrial agreement). *See also* § 9-3.
78. R.C.M. 910(h), 811(d).
79. The prosecutor, however, should obtain the convening authority's approval of any new terms or conditions. *See also* United States v. Olson, 25 M.J. 293 (C.M.A. 1987) (accused entitled to withdraw from agreement to provide restitution where government later took steps to collect funds accused owed; court constructed what it considered to be a fair compromise rather than order a *DuBay* hearing).
80. R.C.M. 705(d)(5)(B). United States v. Pruner, 37 M.J. 573 (A.C.M.R. 1993) (convening authority permitted to withdraw from pretrial agreement before accused had performed or executed provisions in agreement). *See generally* Shepardson v. Roberts, 14 M.J. 354 (C.M.A. 1983); United States v. Jacques, 5 M.J. 598 (N.C.M.R. 1978).
81. R.C.M. 705(d)(5)(B). *See, e.g.*, United States v. Manley, 25 M.J. 346 (C.M.A. 1987) (convening authority could not withdraw after accused had entered into modified stipulation of fact that deleted information affected by the judge's ruling earlier that his plea to a charge referenced in that information was improvident).
United States v. Penister, 25 M.J. 148 (C.M.A. 1987) (convening authority could not withdraw pretrial agreement where accused had entered plea of guilty and due to objection by prosecutor, "his representative," the judge erroneously rejected the plea).

is a disagreement among the parties over the interpretation of a "material term" in the agreement,[82] or (3) where an appellate court later improvidences a guilty plea entered into as a part of the agreement.[83]

§ 9-2(D). Judicial Review of the Agreement.

In order to provide some protection for the accused, the military judge is charged with reviewing at trial the details of any pretrial agreement.[84] He must be satisfied that the terms are not contrary to law or public policy, that the parties mutually agree over the terms, and that the accused has voluntarily entered into the agreement.[85] These points are discussed in more detail at § 14-3(C). But it is important to note that procedure at this point, because the parties involved in the plea negotiations and drafting of the pretrial agreement, must be ever sensitive to the fact that the agreement will be closely scrutinized by both trial and appellate judges.[86]

§ 9-3. Confessional Stipulations.

The confessional stipulation is of fairly recent vintage in military practice.[1] It consists of the defense entering a plea of not guilty and permitting the trial counsel (through prior agreement) to offer into evidence what amounts to an admission of essential facts sufficient to prove guilt.[2]

United States v. Troublefield, 17 M.J. 696 (A.C.M.R. 1983) (accused's voluntary absence before trial materially changed his position and thus justified withdrawal). Other examples of this would be the accused's failure to waive a particular motion or his failure to enter into a stipulation of fact.

82. R.C.M. 705(d)(5)(B). This usually arises during the trial judge's inquiry regarding the agreement. See §§ 9-2(D), 14-3(C).

83. R.C.M. 705(d)(5)(B).

84. United States v. King, 3 M.J. 458 (C.M.A. 1977); United States v. Green, 1 M.J. 453 (C.M.A. 1976).

85. United States v. Care, 18 C.M.A. 535, 40 C.M.R. 247 (1969). Aviz v. Carver, 36 M.J. 1026 (N.M.C.M.R. 1993) (trial judge modified pretrial agreement to reflect mutual understandings of the government and the accused).

86. *Cf.* United States v. Stringer, 34 M.J. 667 (A.C.M.R. 1992) (normally, appellate court will not consider challenges to plea bargaining where military judge has conducted proper inquiry at trial and has determined that agreement was voluntary).

1. *See* United States v. Bertelson, 3 M.J. 314 (C.M.A. 1977); United States v. Kepple, 27 M.J. 773 (A.F.C.M.R. 1988) (extensive discussion and analysis of confessional stipulations in military practice).

Although the Military Rules of Evidence do not address their use, former MCM, para. 154b(1) prohibited their use. *See also* United States v. Long, 3 M.J. 400 (C.M.A. 1977); United States v. Aiello, 7 M.J. 99 (C.M.A. 1979). For a discussion of the admissibility of stipulations at trial, see § 15-21.

2. United States v. Bertelson, 3 M.J. 314 (C.M.A. 1977). In United States v. Kepple, 27 M.J. 773 (A.F.C.M.R. 1988), the court noted the difficulty of determining whether a stipulation is "confessional" in nature and offered the following restatement of the *Bertelson* rule:

> Unless the stipulation itself admits every element and no further evidence is required from the Government for a finding of guilty, the stipulation is not "confessional" and a *Bertelson* inquiry is not mandatory. *Id.* at 779.

Determining whether a stipulation is "confessional" in nature is not always an easy task.[3] The Manual for Courts-Martial defines a confessional stipulation as follows:

> A stipulation practically amounts to a confession when it is the equivalent of a guilty plea, that is, when it establishes, directly or by reasonable inference, every element of the charged offense and when the defense does not present evidence to contest any potential remaining issue on the merits.[4]

This quick disposition of the trial's factual issues is usually employed where defense counsel wishes to preserve issues that would normally be waived by entering a guilty plea.[5] Because the confessional stipulation amounts to an admission of guilt, the military judge must conduct an in-court inquiry of the accused, similar to the inquiry required for guilty pleas, to determine the accused's understanding of the stipulation and its impact on his case.[6] Specifically, the judge must determine:

> (A) from the accused that the accused understands the right not to stipulate and that the stipulation will not be accepted without the accused's consent; that the accused understands the contents and the effect of the stipulation; and that the accused, after consulting with counsel, consents to the stipulation; and
>
> (B) from the accused and counsel for each party whether there are any agreements between the parties in connection with the stipulation, and, if so, what terms of such agreement are.[7]

---

3. United States v. Ballew, 38 M.J. 560 (A.F.C.M.R. 1993) (stipulation of testimony by expert did not amount to confessional stipulation; court noted that the stipulation did not amount to admission of facts). In United States v. Floyd, 31 M.J. 755 (A.C.M.R. 1990), the stipulation was not confessional where the defense contested one of the elements of the offense. The court noted that often stipulations are presented before the defense has indicated how it will proceed. To avoid problems the court should determine first whether the defense will be contesting any of the elements of the offense. If no such evidence will be forthcoming the judge should conduct the *Bertelson* inquiry.

4. R.C.M. 811(c) Discussion. *See also* United States v. Mena, 32 M.J. 937 (N.M.C.M.R. 1991) (presence of permissible inferences arising from stipulation of fact made it confessional in nature and trial court erred in not conducting *Bertelson* inquiry).

5. *Id.* United States v. Curry, 15 M.J. 701 (A.C.M.R. 1983) (confessional stipulation does not waive issues).

6. *See e.g.*, United States v. Banks, 36 M.J. 1003 (A.C.M.R. 1993) (stipulation entered as part of pretrial agreement amounted to confessional stipulation and trial judge should have conducted separate inquiry when stipulation was offered on contested specifications); United States v. Matlock, 35 M.J. 895 (A.C.M.R. 1992) (judge's line-by-line Bertelson inquiry was sufficient); United States v. Snoberger, 26 M.J. 818 (A.C.M.R. 1988) (trial judge properly accepted conditional stipulation that accused offered after judge rejected guilty plea); United States v. Spann, 24 M.J. 508 (A.F.C.M.R. 1987) (judge conducted proper inquiry of confessional stipulation that admitted that lab report showed that drugs were in accused's bloodstream).

United States v. Rivera, 12 M.J. 532 (A.F.C.M.R. 1981); United States v. Corrigan, 11 M.J. 734 (A.F.C.M.R. 1981); United States v. Barden, 9 M.J. 621 (A.C.M.R. 1980); United States v. Krampf, 9 M.J. 593 (A.F.C.M.R. 1980).

7. R.C.M. 811(c) Discussion. In United States v. Enlow, 26 M.J. 940 (A.C.M.R. 1988), the Army Court of Military Review stated that Army judges' inquiry regarding confessional stipulations

Failure to conduct this inquiry may result in reversal,[8] and if during the foregoing inquiry the judge learns that there is a pretrial agreement, *see* § 14-3(C), he must conduct an inquiry into that agreement.[9]

A confessional stipulation will not be used to sustain the findings on appeal where the accused prevails on the legal issue he intended to preserve for appeal and the parties used the stipulation as a means of preserving the error.[10]

Note that in *United States v. Lawrence*,[11] the court overruled its earlier precedent which had permitted the accused to plead not guilty and then, through a confessional stipulation, stipulate to his guilt in order to preserve an issue for appeal should be overruled. The court believed that by specifically permitting conditional guilty pleas in the Manual for Courts-Martial the President had meant to preempt caselaw which permitted that practice. The court did not address the fact that the *Manual* also specifically addresses, and permits, the use of the confessional stipulation to preserve error.[12]

§ 9-4. Discharge in Lieu of Court-Martial.

Service regulations may permit an accused to apply for an administrative discharge in lieu of trial by court-martial. For example, Army Regulation 635-200, Chapter 10, details procedures for obtaining a discharge for "the good of the service" where an enlisted accused is facing charges that could result in the imposition of either a bad-conduct or dishonorable discharge.[1] The application is initiated by the accused, after consulting with counsel and

---

should parallel the *Care* inquiry and the *Green* inquiry, which are both conducted where the accused has pleaded guilty. *See* Chapter 14. To that end, the court provided a detailed explanation of the judge's responsibility.

8. United States v. Wartruba, 35 M.J. 488 (C.M.A. 1992) (confessional stipulation of fact was not knowingly and voluntarily consented to by accused, who failed to conduct thorough inquiry; dissent argued that with changes in military justice, the underlying reasons for the Bertelson rule no longer exist and that military courts should follow the model in the federal courts); United States v. Honeycutt, 29 M.J. 416 (C.M.A. 1990) (judge's failure to conduct inquiry was harmless error); United States v. Cantu, 30 M.J. 1088 (N.M.C.M.R. 1989) (reversible error not to conduct inquiry of stipulations of expected testimony that amounted to a confessional stipulation); United States v. Reagan, 7 M.J. 490 (C.M.A. 1979).

United States v. Thomas, 15 M.J. 528 (A.F.C.M.R. 1982). *Cf.* United States v. Hagy, 12 M.J. 739 (A.F.C.M.R. 1981) (failure to conduct *Bertelson*-type inquiry is not error until the accused, having rested, fails to produce any evidence that is inconsistent with any prima facie admissions of guilt therein).

9. R.C.M. 811(c) Discussion. *See also* R.C.M. 705, 910(f). In United States v. Cantu, 30 M.J. 1088 (N.M.C.M.R. 1989), the defendant agreed to plead guilty to some charges and not guilty to other charges and stipulate to testimony of several witnesses. But he also agreed not to present any evidence on the charges to which he pled not guilty and not to challenge the stipulations of expected testimony. The court concluded that this arrangement amounted to a de facto guilty plea and rendered the stipulations confessional in nature.

10. United States v. Brown, 12 M.J. 420 (C.M.A. 1982).

11. 43 M.J. 677 (A.F.Ct.Crim.App. 1995).

12. R.C.M. 811(c), Analysis.

1. *See generally* Hansen, "Discharge for the Good of the Service: An Historical, Administrative, and Judicial Potpourri," 74 Mil. L. Rev. 99 (1976).

may include an admission of guilt. It is forwarded through the chain of command to the general court-martial convening authority who decides whether to grant the request. Similar provisions govern administrative discharges for officers.[2] Note that statements made by the accused in an attempt to obtain an administrative discharge are probably not admissible against him at any later court-martial.[3]

Potential problems lurk where a request for discharge is processed at the same time that court-martial charges are being tried. That problem was addressed in *United States v. Woods*,[4] where the Court concluded that a service secretary may promulgate a regulation providing for administrative separation of an officer from active duty. In this case, the accused properly submitted his resignation in lieu of trial pursuant to Army regulations, but it was not accepted until after he was convicted by a court-martial. Noting that the Secretary's exercise of his authority should not depend on a race between himself and the convening authority, the court indicated that a court-martial cannot divest the Secretary's powers nor defeat a lawful agreement between the accused and the Secretary. It thus concluded that the court-martial proceedings should be abated. And in *United States v. Shoup*,[5] the court indicated that while failure to follow regulatory provisions in processing an administrative discharge is normally not reviewable by the military courts, the failure to properly process one through to completion, which would abate a court-martial, might be a denial of due process. If the failure to process properly a personnel action that affects the lawfulness of an order, it may be reviewable on due process grounds. Failure to follow regulations may affect the admissibility of a record of administrative action into evidence at trial.

---

2. *See* AR 635-120, para. 5-2. Officers facing general court-martial charges may submit resignations for the good of the service.

See also Slocum, "Officer Resignations in Lieu of Court-Martial," 11 THE REPORTER 136 (Oct. 1982).

3. *See* United States v. Barunas, 23 M.J. 71 (C.M.A. 1986) (*citing* MIL. R. EVID. 410, which is broader than FED. R. EVID. 410).

4. 26 M.J. 372 (C.M.A. 1988).

5. 31 M.J. 819 (A.F.C.M.R. 1990).

APPENDIX REFERENCES

Appendix 1. Abbreviations.
Appendix 2. Glossary.
Appendix 3. U.C.M.J.
Appendix 4. Court-Martial Flow Chart.
Appendix 12. Pretrial Agreement.

ANNOTATED BIBLIOGRAPHY

PERIODICALS

Elling, "Guilty Plea Inquiries: Do We *Care* Too Much?", 134 MIL. L. REV. 195 (1991).

The author notes the differences between guilty plea inquiries in federal and military practice, discusses the history of practice in both systems and focuses on the apparently rigid practice in the military of rejecting pleas where an inconsistency is raised. He concludes that it is time to modernize military practice, by overruling or modifying *United States v. Care* and amending Article 45(a) and R.C.M. 910(h)(2).

Haddenhorst & David, "Guilty Pleas: A Primer for Judge Advocates," 39 A.F. L. REV. 87 (1996).

The authors provide an overview of the pertinent rules and caselaw concerning the entry of provident guilty pleas in courts-martial and include a helpful checklist for counsel on insuring that the plea is properly entered.

Hansen, "Discharge for the Good of the Service: An Historical, Administrative and Judicial Potpourri," 74 MIL. L. REV. 99 (1976).

Building upon the results of a survey, the author presents an extremely thorough analysis of the role of the administrative discharge in meeting criminal justice problems. This fine article, 86 pages in length, covers such topics as the accused's consent to such a discharge, the fairness of the procedures, the efficiency of the practice, and the commander's discretion.

McMenamin, "Plea Bargaining in the Military," 10 AM. CRIM. L. REV. 93 (1971).

This informative article reviews the plea bargaining system in the military, placing special emphasis on the practice of exposing the agreement to the judge and the benefits of placing the agreement in the record. The author also provides some interesting observations on the effects of the underlying relationships between the prosecutorial and defense judge advocates and their common employer.

Melhorn, "Negotiated Pleas in Naval Courts-Martial," 16 JAG J. 103 (1962).

This article contains a discussion of the issues and procedural problems surrounding negotiated pleas in a military context and also contrasts the Navy's system of plea bargaining with the practices employed by other branches of the armed forces.

Thompson, "Constitutional Applications to the Military Criminal Defendant," 66 U. DETROIT L. REV. 221 (1989).

Drawing comparisons between civilian and military practices, the author notes that in order to maintain the requisite good order and discipline needed in the armed forces some modifications to substantive constitutional rights have been made. He concludes that although the military defendant loses protections in the areas of search and seizure and trial by jury, he has enhanced protections in other areas, e.g., negotiated guilty pleas.

Symposium, "Military Law," 10 AM. CRIM. L. REV. 1 (1971).

This symposium issue covers a valuable range of topics pertinent to the practice of military criminal law. Included are articles on jurisdiction over civilian type offenses, plea bargaining, sentencing, discovery, appeals, and an article by General Westmoreland on the commander's perspective of military justice. Also included is a fine bibliography of books, articles, and listings of military law materials.

Symposium, "Military Justice," ARMY LAW., March 1996.

This 127-page symposium contains a Foreword and 11 short articles on a wide range of military justice topics. They are as follows:

Morris, "Foreword."
Barto, "Developments in the Substantive Criminal Law Under the Uniform Code of Military Justice."
Frisk, "New Developments in Pretrial Confinement."
Frisk, "New Developments in Speedy Trial."
Winn, "Recent Developments in Military Pretrial and Trial Procedure."
Masterton, "Recent Developments in Search and Seizure Law."
Masterton, "Recent Developments in Urinalysis Law."
Kohlman, "Are You Ready for Some Changes? Five Fresh Views of the Fifth Amendment."
Wright, "Sex, Lies, and Videotape: Child Sexual Abuse Cases Continue to Create Appellate Issues and Other Developments in the Areas of the Sixth Amendment, Discovery, Mental Responsibility, and Nonjudicial Punishment."
Henley, "Caveat Criminale: The Impact of the New Military Rules of Evidence in Sexual Offense and Child Molestation Cases."
Henley, "Current Developments in Evidence Law."
Morris, "New Developments in Sentencing and Post-Trial Procedure."

CHAPTER 10

NOTICE, DISCLOSURE AND DISCOVERY

§ 10-1. General.
§ 10-2. Notice Requirements.
    § 10-2(A). Notice by the Prosecution.
    § 10-2(B). Notice by the Defense.
§ 10-3. Discovery: General Rules.
    § 10-3(A). Protected Information.
    § 10-3(B). Equal Access to Evidence.
    § 10-3(C). Failure to Call a Witness.
    § 10-3(D). Continuing Duty to Disclose.
    § 10-3(E). Reciprocal Discovery.
    § 10-3(F). The Ethical Duty to Disclose.
§ 10-4. Defense Discovery.
    § 10-4(A). Automatic Prosecutorial Disclosure.
        § 10-4(A)(1). Charges and Allied Papers.
        § 10-4(A)(2). Names of Prosecution Witnesses.
        § 10-4(A)(3). Prior Convictions.
        § 10-4(A)(4). Favorable Evidence: The Constitutional Mandate.
    § 10-4(B). Defense Requests for Discovery.
        § 10-4(B)(1). The *Brady* Request.
        § 10-4(B)(2). Tangibles and Documents.
        § 10-4(B)(3). Reports, Tests, and Results.
        § 10-4(B)(4). Sentencing Evidence.
        § 10-4(B)(5). Jencks Act Materials.
    § 10-4(C). Reciprocal Discovery.
§ 10-5. Prosecution Discovery.
    § 10-5(A). Automatic Defense Disclosure.
        § 10-5(A)(1). Names of Defense Witnesses.
        § 10-5(A)(2). Notice of Alibi Defense.
        § 10-5(A)(3). Notice of Lack of Mental Responsibility Defense.
        § 10-5(A)(4). Notice of Defense of Innocent Ingestion.
    § 10-5(B). Prosecution Requests for Discovery.
    § 10-5(C). Reciprocal Discovery.
§ 10-6. Judicial Control of Discovery: Remedies.
Appendix References.
Annotated Bibliography.

§ 10-1. General.

As the pretrial processing approaches the date of trial it becomes important, for a number of reasons, for each side to evaluate its evidence and tactics and anticipate the evidence it might expect from the other side. This is especially true for the defense, which is entitled under the Constitution to be informed of the nature of the charges against the accused[1] and under the U.C.M.J. to an equal opportunity to obtain witnesses and evidence.[2] The manner in which each side gives or receives the information may be in the form of "notice,"

---

1. *See* Amend. VI, U.S. CONST.
2. Art. 46, U.C.M.J.; United States v. Enloe, 15 C.M.A. 256, 35 C.M.R. 228 (1965); United States v. Franchia, 13 C.M.A. 315, 32 C.M.R. 315 (1962).

"disclosure," or "discovery." Although for all practical purposes the result is the same, i.e., information is transmitted to the opposing counsel, the terms do have separate and technical significance. This chapter examines each of those means of transmitting the information, the applicable rules, and the possible remedies for failure to comply with the rules.

As the following materials amply demonstrate, the military system is particularly generous with its requirements for disclosure and discovery,[3] in an effort to reduce to an absolute minimum the possibility of surprise and trial by ambush.[4]

Although the primary focus of this chapter is on formal disclosure of certain information before trial actually begins, disclosure, notice, and discovery may continue into the actual trial on the merits and beyond; it also includes informal disclosure as well. For example, the defense usually finds the Article 32 investigation and report to be an excellent vehicle for obtaining information with no requirement to reciprocate.[5] Each side may also learn of evidence or the opposing side's tactics during pretrial agreement negotiations,[6] although any statements made by the accused during those discussions are generally inadmissible.[7]

Because there is no general right to discovery in criminal cases,[8] the rules providing for military discovery are found in the U.C.M.J., the Manual for Courts-Martial or service regulations.

§ 10-2. Notice Requirements.

The trend in litigation, and especially in criminal litigation, is to require "notice" to the opposing party of an intent to rely upon a particular defense or to present certain evidence at trial. The underlying rationale historically has been to provide the accused with notice of what he must defend against.[1] This

---

3. In many respects military discovery is broader than discovery in the federal system. R.C.M. 701 Analysis.
4. R.C.M. 701 Analysis. *See generally* Adams, "The Freedom of Information Act and Pretrial Discovery," 43 MIL. L. REV. 1 (1969); Coacher, "Discovery in Courts-Martial," A.F. L. REV. 103 (1996); Coacher, "Discovery in Courts-Martial," 39 A.F. L. REV. 103 (1996); Everett, "Discovery in Criminal Cases—In Search of a Standard," 1964 DUKE L.J. 477; Luedtke, "Open Government and Military Justice," 87 MIL. L. REV. 7 (1980); Melnick, "The Defendant's Right to Obtain Evidence: An Examination of the Military Viewpoint," 29 MIL. L. REV. 1 (1965); Saunders, "Proposed Changes in Military Discovery," 10 AM. CRIM. L. REV. 81 (1971). *See also* Moyer, *Justice and the Military* § 2.440 *et seq.* (1972), and Note, "The Freedom of Information Act—A Potential Alternative to Conventional Criminal Discovery," 14 AM. CRIM. L. REV. 73 (1976).

United States v. Lawrence, 19 M.J. 609 (A.C.M.R. 1984) (no violation of *Brady v. Maryland* where the trial counsel failed to disclose to the defense prior to trial that four prosecution witnesses had been awarded medals prior to trial for their roles in capturing the accused. Citing R.C.M. 701, the court frowned on the gamesmanship of the trial counsel in not revealing the information earlier).

5. *See* § 7-2.
6. *See* Chapter 9.
7. Rule 410, MIL. R. EVID.
8. Weatherford v. Bursey, 429 U.S. 545 (1977).
1. Amend. VI, U.S. CONST.

is particularly true in the case of drafting the charges and specifications.[2] Notice requirements more recently, however, have been extended to include notice by the defense in certain situations.[3] The terms "notice" and "disclosure" are often used interchangeably.[4] But the following discussion focuses on the requirement of one side to give notice to the other side of the intent to use a certain piece of evidence or to follow a particular tactic at trial without necessarily disclosing or producing the evidence.[5]

§ 10-2(A). Notice by the Prosecution.

In addition to providing notice in sworn pleadings of what the accused must be prepared to meet at trial, the prosecution must also ensure that the accused has been informed of the name of his accuser.[6] For a discussion of the pleading requirements, see § 6-1. The prosecution is also required to give notice in a number of other instances. The following notice requirements are located in the Military Rules of Evidence:

(1) *Judicial Notice.* The prosecution must give notice that it intends to ask the court to take judicial notice of a foreign law.[7]

(2) *Undisclosed Evidence.* If the prosecution intends to use previously undisclosed statements by the accused,[8] evidence seized from the accused,[9] or eyewitness evidence[10] that identifies the accused, then it must give timely notice to the judge and the defense counsel of that fact.

(3) *Defendant's Prior Extrinsic Acts.* Upon defense request, the prosecution is required to give reasonable notice of its intention to offer into evidence during trial, prior acts committed by the accused which may be admissible under Military Rule of Evidence 404(b)[11]

(4) *Prior Conviction.* The prosecution is required to give sufficient advance written notice to the defense that it intends to use a prior conviction more that ten years old to impeach a witness.[12]

(5) *Immunity.* If the government has granted immunity[13] or promised clemency to a prosecution witness, the defense must receive notice of that fact

---

2. *See generally* § 6-1.
3. *See* § 10-2(B). *See also* § 10-5(A).
4. *See, e.g.,* R.C.M. 701(b), which uses the term "notice" in listing "disclosure" requirements. *See generally* Thwing, "'Paper Wars': A Prosecutorial Discovery Initiative," ARMY LAW., May 1987, at 23.
5. For example, the prosecution is required to give notice that it intends to use a prior conviction more than ten years old to impeach a witness. *See* § 10-2(A). But the prosecution is not necessarily required to provide a copy of the conviction along with the notice; it must, however, provide the defense an opportunity to inspect it. § 10-4(A)(3).
6. R.C.M. 308(a).
7. Rule 201(A)(a), MIL. R. EVID.
8. Rule 304(d)(2)(B), MIL. R. EVID. United States v. Trimper, 26 M.J. 534 (A.F.C.M.R. 1988) (prosecution not obligated to disclose casual, unofficial statements made by accused).
9. Rule 311(d)(2)(B), MIL. R. EVID.
10. Rule 321(c)(2)(B), MIL. R. EVID.
11. *See* Rule 404(b), MIL. R. EVID.
12. Rule 609, MIL. R. EVID.
13. *See* § 11-2(E).

before arraignment or within a reasonable amount of time before that witness testifies at the accused's trial.[14] Failure to do so may result in a continuance or other appropriate relief.[15] The reasons for the grant need not be revealed,[16] and the notice may be waived.[17]

(6) *Other Notice Requirements.* The prosecution is also required to notify the defense of an intent to use certain hearsay evidence.[18] Notice is also a predicate for using other evidence to establish the contents of an original writing that is in the control of the defense.[19]

Although not all of the foregoing notice provisions require the prosecution to give notice in writing, in most cases it is sound practice to do so.

§ 10-2(B). Notice by the Defense.

Unlike military criminal litigation practices of some years ago, which required little, if any, defense notice or disclosure,[20] more recent requirements place some burdens on the defense to give notice to the prosecution in some circumstances. The following discussion briefly addresses those instances in which the defense must provide notice.

(1) *Alibi Defense.* If the defense intends to rely upon an alibi defense, it must notify the prosecution of that intent before the trial begins.[21] In addition, the defense must inform the prosecution of the names and addresses of the witnesses who will testify on that defense and must provide information as to the specific location where the accused was at the time that the offense was alleged to have occurred.[22]

(2) *Lack of Mental Responsibility Defense.* Before the beginning of the trial on the merits, the defense must notify the prosecution of an intent to use the defense of lack of mental responsibility.[23] Notice must also be given if the defense intends to rely upon expert testimony regarding the mental state of the accused as it relates to his guilt.[24]

---

14. Rule 301(c)(2), MIL. R. EVID. United States v. Webster, 1 M.J. 216 (C.M.A. 1975). The promise must be reduced to writing. What constitutes "reasonable" notice will depend on the circumstances. *See, e.g.,* United States v. Matthews, 13 M.J. 501 (A.C.M.R. 1982) (*en banc*) (nine days' notice was reasonable).
15. United States v. Webster, 1 M.J. 216 (C.M.A. 1975); United States v. Saylor, 6 M.J. 647 (N.C.M.R. 1978).
16. United States v. Webster, 1 M.J. 216 (C.M.A. 1975).
17. United States v. Carroll, 4 M.J. 674 (N.C.M.R. 1977).
18. Rules 803(24), 804(b)(5), MIL. R. EVID.
19. Rule 1004(3), MIL. R. EVID.
20. *See* R.C.M. 701 Analysis.
21. R.C.M. 701(b)(2). *See* Williams v. Florida, 399 U.S. 78 (1970).
22. R.C.M. 701(b)(2). The Discussion to this R.C.M. indicates that if the defense needs more specific information about the particulars of the charged offense, it should request a bill of particulars. *See* R.C.M. 906(b)(6); *infra* § 13-5(F). *See also* § 10-4(A) (disclosure of prosecution rebuttal witnesses).
23. R.C.M. 701(b)(2). In United States v. Walker, 25 M.J. 713 (C.M.A. 1987), the trial court committed reversible error in requiring the defense to provide "notice" at the time of motions, as contemplated by FED. R. CRIM. P. 12.2.
24. *Id. Cf.* Rule 704, MIL. R. EVID., which governs expert opinion testimony on mental responsibility.

(3) *Defense of Innocent Ingestion.* If the defense intends to rely upon the defense of innocent ingestion, it must give notice to the prosecution of the names and addresses of witnesses it intends to call to testify.[25] It must also indicate the place or places where the innocent ingestion occurred.

(4) *Judicial Notice.* If the defense wishes to ask the court to take judicial notice of a foreign law, it is required to give reasonable written notice of that intent.[26]

(5) *Disclosure of Privileged Information.* Under Military Rule of Evidence 505,[27] the defense is required to give written notice to the prosecution of any intent to disclose or cause the disclosure of classified information.[28] The Rule further requires that the notice include a brief description of the information and that a copy should be given to the military judge.[29] Failure to comply with these requirements may prevent the defense from disclosing the information.[30]

(6) *Accused's Testimony.* In moving to suppress evidence of an accused's pretrial statements,[31] evidence seized from the accused,[32] or evidence concerning eyewitness identification of the accused,[33] the defense may present testimony by the accused for the limited purpose of challenging the legality of that evidence. If the defense intends to do so, it must notify the court that the accused is testifying for that limited purpose. Failure to do so should not void that testimony.

(7) *Victim of Sexual Misconduct.* The military has followed the trend to limit the ability of the accused to impeach the testimony of the victim of sexual misconduct.[34] Thus, if the defense wishes to offer evidence of specific acts of the victim's past sexual behavior, it must first give notice[35] and an offer of proof[36] to both the court and the prosecution.

(8) *Prior Conviction.* If the defense intends to impeach a witness with a conviction that is more than ten years old, it must notify the prosecution of that fact, in writing.[37] The conviction will not be admissible unless the notice is given sufficiently far enough in advance to permit the prosecution an oppor-

---

25. R.C.M. 701(b)(2). This provision was added in the 1991 amendments to the *Manual*, i.e., Change 5.
26. Rule 201A(b), MIL. R. EVID.
27. Rule 505, MIL. R. EVID.
28. Rule 505(h), MIL. R. EVID.
29. Rule 505(h)(1), (2), MIL. R. EVID.
30. Rule 505(h)(5), MIL. R. EVID.
31. Rule 304(f), MIL. R. EVID.
32. Rule 311(f), MIL. R. EVID.
33. Rule 321(e), MIL. R. EVID.
34. Rule 412(a), MIL. R. EVID. *See* Saltzburg, Schinasi & Schlueter, *Military Rules of Evidence Manual* 523 (3d ed. 1991).
35. Rule 412, MIL. R. EVID. United States v. Brown, 17 M.J. 544 (A.C.M.R. 1983) (inappropriate to summarily exclude evidence where counsel has failed to comply with notice requirement; judge should grant continuance or evidentiary hearing); United States v. Mahone, 14 M.J. 521 (A.F.C.M.R. 1982) (counsel waived issue of admissibility of evidence by not providing notice and offer of proof).
36. Rule 412(c)(2), MIL. R. EVID.
37. Rule 609(b), MIL. R. EVID.

tunity to challenge the admissibility.[38] Note that these rules also apply where the prosecution intends to use the conviction to impeach a witness. *See* § 10-2(A).

(9) *Other Notice Requirements.* The defense must also give notice if it intends to use secondary evidence of an original writing under the control of the prosecution[39] and of its intent to rely upon the residual hearsay exceptions.[40]

§ 10-3. Discovery: General Rules.

As a prelude to a more detailed discussion of the discovery rules that apply to the defense and prosecution and are discussed in § 10-4 and § 10-5, this section addresses those general rules that tend to apply to both sides.

§ 10-3(A). Protected Information.

Despite the liberalized rules of discovery in military criminal litigation, disclosure is not always required nor is discovery always possible where the information involved is protected. The protected status may arise from an evidentiary privilege specifically spelled out in the Military Rules of Evidence[1] or from statutes or regulations.[2]

A common method of blocking discovery by the opposing counsel is to invoke the time-honored "work-product" rule, which is now specifically recognized in R.C.M. 701(f). Included within the definition of work-product are notes, memoranda, and working papers prepared by counsel or his assistants or representatives. Probably the most common examples of this are the working notes prepared by counsel while interviewing a witness; counsel's impressions and thought processes are normally protected.[3] But in the case of a prosecutor who interviews a prosecution witness and in some way permits that witness to adopt the notes as his statement, the notes may be subject to disclosure[4] under the provisions of the Jencks Act,[5] which is discussed at § 10-4(B)(5). A similar result may occur in the case of the defense under the provisions of R.C.M. 914, which require that after a witness, other than the accused, testifies at trial the opposing counsel is entitled to see any prior statements made by the witness and in the possession of the party that called the witness.[6] Once counsel has the statement, he may attempt to impeach the witness or use its contents to obtain previously undisclosed information.[7]

---

38. Rule 609(b), MIL. R. EVID.
39. Rule 1004(3), MIL. R. EVID.
40. Rules 803(24), 804(b)(5), MIL. R. EVID.
1. R.C.M. 701(f). The evidentiary privileges are set out in Section V of the Military Rules of Evidence. *See also* Rules 301 and 302, MIL. R. EVID.
2. For example, service regulations may bar use of information gathered through drug rehabilitation programs. *See* United States v. Broady, 12 M.J. 963 (A.F.C.M.R. 1982); United States v. Cottle, 11 M.J. 572 (A.F.C.M.R. 1981).
3. *See* United States v. Nobles, 422 U.S. 225 (1975); Hickman v. Taylor, 329 U.S. 495 (1947).
4. Goldberg v. United States, 425 U.S. 94 (1976).
5. 18 U.S.C. § 3500.
6. *See* § 10-4(B)(5).
7. For example, the witness' statement may refer to other statements or documents.

§ 10-3(B). Equal Access to Evidence.

The Manual for Courts-Martial specifically provides that both the defense and prosecution will have an "adequate opportunity" to prepare its case and will have an "equal opportunity" to talk to the witnesses and examine the evidence.[8] It further states that neither counsel may unreasonably impede the other counsel in obtaining access to either a witness or other evidence.[9] Although reasonable minds will obviously differ over what the terms "adequate," "equal," and "unreasonably impede" actually mean, a commonsense reading indicates that counsel may not frustrate the good faith efforts of opposing counsel to obtain information by advising a witness not to submit to an interview by the other counsel,[10] nor may counsel conceal evidence by instructing another not to turn over evidence to the other counsel. This sort of problem may arise where the government assigns a military witness to another duty station without first offering the defense an opportunity to interview or depose that witness.[11]

It is important to note, however, that the *Manual* provision applies to both sides. Thus, the defense counsel should not, even in an effort to zealously represent his client, unreasonably impede the prosecution in its efforts to obtain information. This would include not waiting until just before trial to disclose properly discoverable material that had been requested by the prosecution well in advance of trial.

§ 10-3(C). Failure to Call a Witness.

The rules of disclosure and notice, discussed in § 10-5(A)(2) (alibi defense), § 10-4(A)(2) (names of prosecution witnesses), and § 10-5(A)(1) (names of defense witnesses) require identification of expected witnesses. If for some reason the party disclosing the names of those witnesses decides not to call them at trial, the opponent may not use that as a basis for commenting on the failure to call the witness.[12] Even if the counsel has listed a particular witness without being required to do so, the opposing counsel may not be able to

---

8. R.C.M. 701(e). *See also* Art. 46, U.C.M.J., which provides that the trial counsel, defense counsel, and the court-martial will have an equal opportunity to obtain witnesses and other evidence. *See* United States v. Eshalomi, 23 M.J. 12 (C.M.A. 1986). *See generally* Nortz, "Discovery Under Rule for Courts-Martial 701(e)—Does Equal Really Mean Equal?," ARMY LAW., Aug. 1989, at 21.
9. R.C.M. 701(e).
10. In United States v. Morris, 24 M.J. 93 (C.M.A. 1987), the court rejected the defense argument that the accused had been denied equal access where the trial counsel advised the minor victim's parents that it would be appropriate for a third party to be present when defense counsel interviewed the victim. United States v. Enloe, 15 C.M.A. 256, 35 C.M.R. 228 (1965) (OSI agent was to be accompanied by trial counsel or some other third person). *See also* United States v. Cumberledge, 6 M.J. 203 (C.M.A. 1979); Halfacre v. Chambers, 5 M.J. 1099 (C.M.A. 1976); United States v. Aycock, 15 C.M.A. 158, 35 C.M.R. 130 (1964); United States v. Wysong, 9 C.M.A. 249, 26 C.M.R. 29 (1958).
11. United States v. Killebrew, 9 M.J. 154 (C.M.A. 1980).
12. R.C.M. 701(c).

comment at trial on the failure of counsel to call that witness.[13] A similar prohibition exists if the defense has notified the prosecution before trial that it intends to present an alibi defense, the defense of innocent ingestion, or the defense of lack of mental responsibility and then abandons that course.[14] The prosecutor is barred from commenting on counsel's change of tactics.[15]

§ 10-3(D). Continuing Duty to Disclose.

Both sides have a continuing obligation to disclose any additional or new information that was previously requested by the other side or is subject to automatic disclosure.[16] Thus counsel may not dodge a request for disclosure by arguing that when opposing counsel first requested the information it did not exist. If such a request was made, counsel is apparently under an obligation to disclose it promptly when the information does become available even if the opposing counsel has not renewed his earlier request.[17] This rule should not in itself expand the discovery rules. If the information or evidence in question would not have been discoverable in the first instance, the fact that it came into existence after a discovery request does not in itself require counsel to disclose it.

§ 10-3(E). Reciprocal Discovery.

The mere fact that counsel has disclosed or provided information to the opposing side does not in itself require reciprocity. Some of the discovery rules in the next sections are strictly one-way. For example, the prosecution is required to automatically disclose favorable evidence to the accused[18] but having done so the defense is normally under no obligation to reciprocate and disclose unfavorable evidence against the accused or against the prosecution. The military rules of discovery, however, do specifically provide for some reciprocity which in effect opens the door for prosecution discovery of defense information. Those rules are discussed in more detail in § 10-4(C) and § 10-5(B).

---

13. R.C.M. 701(c).
14. R.C.M. 701(b)(5).
15. R.C.M. 701(b)(5).
16. R.C.M. 701(d).
17. This would be especially true for evidence that is beneficial to the accused. *See infra* § 10-4(A)(4). United States v. Agurs, 427 U.S. 97 (1976). In United States v. Eshalomi, 23 M.J. 12 (C.M.A. 1986), the defense had made a pretrial discovery request for any statements made by the rape victim. After she testified and while the trial was still proceeding, she made additional statements to a CID agent to the effect that she had not told him everything about the offense. The court ruled that the prosecution's failure to provide this statement to the defense amounted to reversible constitutional error. In reviewing the facts, the court noted that decisions concerning what information should be disclosed to the defense are not matters to be determined *ex parte* by the prosecutor, who in this case had decided that the statement was protected by MIL. R. EVID. 412 and a state's physician-patient privilege.
18. *See* § 10-4(A)(4).

§ 10-3(F). The Ethical Duty to Disclose.

In addition to the formalized rules governing discovery, there are ethical considerations applicable to both the prosecution and the defense that require each, for slightly different reasons, to disclose information to either the court or to the opposing counsel.

The Prosecution's Duty. The key provision governing the prosecutor's ethical duty to disclose is Standard 3-3.11 of the ABA Standards for Criminal Justice (Prosecution Function), which provides that:

> (1) It is unprofessional conduct for a prosecutor intentionally to fail to make disclosure to the defense, at the earliest feasible opportunity, of the existence of evidence which tends to negate the guilt of the accused as to the offense charged or which would tend to reduce the punishment of the accused.
>
> (2) The prosecutor should comply in good faith with discovery procedures under the applicable law.

This standard has been captured in R.C.M. 701(a)(6), which places a similar burden on the prosecutor. Note that Disciplinary Rule (DR) 7-103(B) contains similar language. Perhaps because the foregoing "ethical" duties are often specifically noted in more formalized rules, it is easy to forget that such duties, independent of the formalized rules, do exist and do stand on their own.[19]

Defense Counsel's Duty. The defense counsel's ethical duty to disclose any information to either the court or the prosecutor is more difficult to articulate because of the underlying duty of the defense counsel to zealously represent his client within the bounds of the law[20] and because of a duty to keep as confidential that which his client has disclosed to him. Some straightforward rules have been adopted, however. The first is that the defense counsel may not assist his client in perpetrating a fraud upon any person or tribunal. Thus, if counsel learns that his client is doing so he is required to disclose that fact, unless it is privileged information,[21] if the client does not do so after counsel has advised him to do so.[22] The client's stated intent to commit a crime in the future is not privileged and may be disclosed.[23]

If the defense counsel learns that his client intends to commit perjury, the counsel may not associate himself with that crime. But in disassociating himself he may not state to the court why he is doing so.[24] Specific guidance on dealing with the perjurious client is laid out in *United States v. Radford*[25] and is discussed further in § 15-2(B)(4).

---

19. *See* § 10-4(A)(2).
20. ABA Code of Professional Responsibility, EC 7-19.
21. *See* Rule 502, MIL. R. EVID. United States v. Rhea, 33 M.J. 413 (C.M.A. 1991) (information implicating accused was not protected by attorney-client privilege).
22. ABA Code of Professional Responsibility, DR 7-102(B)(2).
23. Rule 502(d), MIL. R. EVID.
24. United States v. Radford, 14 M.J. 322 (C.M.A. 1982); United States v. Winchester, 12 C.M.A. 74, 30 C.M.R. 74 (1961).
25. 14 M.J. 322 (C.M.A. 1982). *See* § 15-2(B)(4).

Finally, there are rules governing disclosure of evidence of a crime that the client has revealed or given to the defense counsel. The general rule is that if the defense counsel comes into possession of evidence of a crime he must disclose it to the prosecution.[26] If he simply hears about it from his client and observes it, then that communication would probably be privileged information and not subject to disclosure.[27]

§ 10-4. Defense Discovery.

As noted in the introductory comments in § 10-1, the military criminal justice system is generous with providing the defense with discoverable information.[1] This section addresses the rules governing defense discovery—rules governing what information the prosecution must disclose to the defense as a matter of course, without any defense request,[2] rules concerning defense requests for information,[3] and finally, rules addressing the issue of reciprocal discovery.[4]

§ 10-4(A). Automatic Prosecutorial Disclosure.

Throughout the pretrial processing of a case, the prosecution, or in some cases the accused's chain of command, is required to disclose to the accused or his counsel certain information without any prior requests to that effect. For example, the accused is entitled to a copy of any Article 32 investigating officer's report.[5] The following discussion briefly addresses several types of information that must be automatically disclosed to the defense.

§ 10-4(A)(1). Charges and Allied Papers.

Under the 1969 version of the Manual for Courts-Martial, the charge sheet automatically reflected the names of the witnesses then known to the prosecution and in some cases a description of any physical or real evidence. The 1984 revision to the *Manual* changed some of that, however. The charge sheet contains none of that information.[6] Instead, the prosecution is required, "as soon as practicable" after the accused has been served with the charges against him, to provide the defense with any papers accompanying the

---

26. *In re* Ryder, 381 F.2d 713 (4th Cir. 1967); United States v. Rhea, 33 M.J. 413 (C.M.A. 1991) (defense counsel acted ethically in turning over to prosecution evidence which accused had given them and which supported prosecution's case).
27. People v. Beige, 41 N.Y.2d 60, 359 N.E.2d 377 (1976). *Cf.* People v. Meredith, 175 Cal. Rptr. 612, 631 P.2d 46 (1981) (evidence may be retained for reasonable time if it is of value to defense; if it is inculpatory it must be turned over to prosecution).
1. United States v. Killebrew, 9 M.J. 154 (C.M.A. 1980).
2. *See* 10-4(A).
3. *See* § 10-4(B).
4. *See* § 10-4(C).
5. *See supra* § 7-2(D).
6. *See* Appendix 6 for a sample charge sheet.

charges when they were referred to trial, the convening order[7] and any amendments to that order, and any signed or sworn statements relating to the charges and which are in the possession of the prosecution.[8] Note that unlike some of the "notice" rules discussed in § 10-2(A), the prosecution is required to actually produce the information, unless it is impractical to do so, and in that case the prosecution is required to provide the defense with an opportunity to inspect the information and, if desired, to copy it.[9]

§ 10-4(A)(2). Names of Prosecution Witnesses.

The prosecution is required, before trial on the merits begins, to disclose to the defense the names and addresses of the witnesses the prosecution intends to call (a) during the presentation of its case-in-chief[10] and (b) in rebuttal to the defense of alibi, insanity, or innocent ingestion,[11] assuming the defense has given timely notice of an intent to rely any of those defenses.[12] This disclosure should be in writing where it is practicable to do so.[13]

§ 10-4(A)(3). Prior Convictions.

The prosecution is also required to disclose to the defense, prior to arraignment, any prior convictions the accused may have of which the prosecution is aware and that may be offered for any purpose during the trial on the merits.[14] If the prosecution has possession of those convictions, which may be either civilian or military, it must permit the defense to inspect them.[15] If the prosecution does not intend to offer the conviction during the merits but does

---

7. *See* § 8-2(B).
8. R.C.M. 701(a)(1). *See* United States v. Murphy, 33 M.J. 323 (C.M.A. 1991) (non-prejudicial error for prosecutor not to give copy of statement of rebuttal witness to defense; military judge granted defense time to review statement and interview witness before cross-examination).
9. R.C.M. 701(a)(1).
10. R.C.M. 701(a)(3)(A). In United States v. Murphy, 33 M.J. 323 (C.M.A. 1991), the court held that the prosecutor's failure to disclose the name of rebuttal witness was error but that granting a continuance to the defense was an appropriate remedy. The court noted that while the prosecution is not required to call any and all witnesses during its case-in-chief and that R.C.M. 701 should not apply to those witnesses that the prosecution only intends to call if some need arises, such as rebuttal witnesses. The court added, however, that doing so presents some risks because the trial judge may ultimately conclude that the witness should have been called during the case-in-chief because the witness does not fulfill the purpose of rebuttal, i.e., "to explain, repel, counteract, or disprove the evidence offered by the opposing party." *Id.* at 328, *citing* United States v. Cleveland, 29 M.J. 361 (C.M.A. 1990).
11. R.C.M. 701(a)(3)(B).
12. *See* § 10-2(B).
13. R.C.M. 701(a)(3) Discussion. United States v. Murphy, 33 M.J. 323 (C.M.A. 1991) (prosecutor's failure to provide defense with copy of statement of rebuttal witness was non-prejudicial error where trial judge granted a short continuance; a copy of the statement was given to the defense who also were given opportunity to interview witness before cross-examining her).
14. R.C.M. 701(a)(4).
15. *Id. See also* Rule 609, MIL. R. EVID.

anticipate offering it during sentencing, arguably this rule does not apply and disclosure is required only after a request from the defense.[16]

§ 10-4(A)(4). Favorable Evidence: The Constitutional Mandate.

Although the formalized rules of discovery and disclosure require the prosecution to disclose any and all evidence that is favorable to the accused, it is important to recognize that the rule may also have a constitutional basis. In *United States v. Agurs*,[17] the Supreme Court ruled that if undisclosed evidence created a reasonable doubt about the accused's guilt then the accused had been denied due process. And in *Brady v. Maryland*,[18] the Court laid out the well-recognized rule that due process would also be denied in those instances where the prosecution had withheld information requested by the defense which was material to the issue of guilt or punishment. Both of these rules have been applied by the military courts and are now memorialized in the Manual for Courts-Martial.[19]

In *United States v. Hart*,[20] the court analyzed Supreme Court and military precedent and concluded that in the military the following "materiality" standards apply: (1) Prosecution use of perjured testimony or similar misconduct will result in reversal unless it is harmless error beyond a reasonable doubt, regardless of whether the prosecution acted in good faith;[21] (2) Where the prosecution has failed to respond to a specific defense request for information, the court must determine if the error was harmless beyond a reasonable doubt;[22] and (3) Failure to disclose information pursuant to all other defense requests, whether regulatory, standing or general in nature is material if there is a reasonable probability that the result would have been different if the evidence had been disclosed.[23] The Court of Military Appeals (now the Court of Appeals for the Armed Forces) agreed with this analysis[24] and con-

---

16. *See* § 10-4(B)(4).
17. 427 U.S. 97 (1976).
18. 373 U.S. 83 (1963). *Cf.* United States v. Trimper, 26 M.J. 534 (A.F.C.M.R. 1988) (there is no constitutional right to evidence that is not exculpatory); United States v. Callara, 21 M.J. 259 (C.M.A. 1986) (sound administration of justice favors disclosure of rebuttal evidence).
19. R.C.M. 701(a)(6). United States v. Watson, 31 M.J. 49 (C.M.A. 1990) (failure to disclose evidence was not error).
20. 27 M.J. 839 (A.C.M.R. 1989).
21. 27 M.J. at 842.
22. 27 M.J. at 842. *See, e.g.,* United States v. Branoff, 38 M.J. 98 (C.M.A. 1993) (military judge did not abuse discretion in denying defense discovery request for AFOSI regulations; the court rejected the argument that the regulations were material under *Brady*; failure to seal and attach regulations to record did not deny due process); United States v. Gabrels, 33 M.J. 622 (A.F.C.M.R. 1991) (prosecutor's failure to disclose impeachment evidence to defense, following request for any information about uncharged misconduct, was reversible error because the undisclosed information raised reasonable doubts about the validity of the proceedings).
23. 27 M.J. at 842. *See, e.g.,* United States v. Simmons, 38 M.J. 376 (C.M.A. 1993) (accused prejudiced by nondisclosure of alleged rape victim's statement to polygrapher); United States v. Romano, 43 M.J. 523 (A.F.Ct.Crim.App. 1995) (no prejudice to accused when prosecution failed to disclose prior inconsistent statement of one of its witnesses).
24. 29 M.J. 407 (C.M.A. 1990).

cluded that the fact that the prosecution had not revealed the results of a laboratory test and the fact that the victim could not identify the accused constituted mere harmless error where the accused had only made a general request for information.[25]

But while the *Brady* information must be generally triggered by a defense request,[26] the *Manual* now requires automatic disclosure of evidence known to the trial counsel that reasonably tends to:

(A) Negate the guilt of the accused of an offense charged;
(B) Reduce the degree of guilt of the accused of an offense charged; or
(C) Reduce the punishment.[27]

§ 10-4(B). Defense Requests for Discovery.

Admittedly much information comes to the defense as a result of automatic prosecutorial disclosure, as discussed in § 10-4(A). But a great deal more is usually available to the defense if it is requested. This section addresses the particular methods by which the defense may obtain further disclosure of information in the hands of the prosecution or other parties.

§ 10-4(B)(1). The *Brady* Request.

What has often been referred to as the *Brady* request[28] is usually a general request for any and all information that may be favorable to the accused, although the better practice is to include requests for disclosure of specific information that the defense has reason to believe exists. As noted in § 10-4(A)(4), the prosecution's failure to respond to such requests when the

---

25. *See also* United States v. Bagley, 473 U.S. 667 (1985) (reversible constitutional error occurs if evidence is material in the sense that its suppression undermines confidence in the outcome of the trial).

26. *See* § 10-4(B)(1). United States v. Eshalomi, 23 M.J. 12 (C.M.A. 1986) (court discusses applicable standards of review where defense has made no request, a general request, or a specific request for information).

27. R.C.M. 701(a)(6). *See generally* United States v. Stone, 40 M.J. 420 (C.M.A. 1994) (harmless error for prosecution not to disclose to defense that government witness was under investigation; failure to disclose did not cast reasonable doubt on validity of trial); United States v. Simmons, 38 M.J. 376 (C.M.A. 1993) (accused prejudiced by nondisclosure of alleged rape victim's statement to polygrapher that she did not believe that she had been raped because she enjoyed the sexual intercourse); United States v. Brickey, 16 M.J. 258 (C.M.A. 1983); United States v. Horsey, 6 M.J. 112 (C.M.A. 1979); United States v. Lucas, 5 M.J. 167 (C.M.A. 1978); United States v. Kinzer, 39 M.J. 559 (A.C.M.R. 1994) (trial counsel's failure to disclose exculpatory evidence amounted to nonprejudicial error); United States v. Marshall, 31 M.J. 712 (A.F.C.M.R. 1990) (there was no intentional secreting of the government witness' prior statement and defense had ample impeaching evidence aliunde the statement in question); United States v. Tebsherany, 30 M.J. 608 (N.M.C.M.R. 1990) (no error in delaying disclosure of evidence that was not clearly exculpatory); United States v. Trimper, 26 M.J. 534 (A.F.C.M.R. 1988) (prosecution's rebuttal evidence is not discoverable under R.C.M. 701 unless it is exculpatory).

United States v. Lawrence, 19 M.J. 609 (A.C.M.R. 1984). *See also* § 10-3(F) for a discussion on the ethical duty to disclose favorable evidence.

28. Brady v. Maryland, 373 U.S. 83 (1963).

requested information is relevant to the case may be a denial of due process.[29] The military courts, in interpreting the requirements of *Brady v. Maryland*,[30] have ruled that that case requires disclosure of only relevant evidence[31] that is "favorable"[32] and that the defense does not already possess.[33] If the government does not have possession of the requested information, then arguably it is under no duty to produce it.

Although the Manual for Courts-Martial specifically includes guidance on defense requests for specific information, such as names of witnesses and access to documentary and physical evidence,[34] the general *Brady* request should still be a viable means of reminding the prosecution to comply with the constitutional mandate to disclose relevant favorable information.

No particular format for the request is required, but it should be in writing in the event the defense wishes to raise the lack of response at trial in the form of a motion for appropriate relief.[35]

§ 10-4(B)(2). Tangibles and Documents.

The defense may request access to various documents, papers, photographs, buildings, and other tangible evidence that are in the possession or control of the government.[36] After the accused is served with a copy of the charges against him, the prosecution is required to grant the defense request if the requested information is (a) material to preparing a defense, (b) intended for use by the prosecution during its case-in-chief, or (c) something belonging to the accused or taken from him.[37] When the defense request is granted the defense has a right to "inspect"[38] the materials. That includes the right to

---

29. United States v. Agurs, 427 U.S. 97 (1976); United States v. Jenkins, 18 M.J. 583 (A.C.M.R. 1984) (government's failure to provide defense with impeaching evidence on key government witness before trial was error).
30. 373 U.S. 83 (1963).
31. United States v. Earl, 9 M.J. 828 (A.F.C.M.R. 1980). *Cf.* United States v. Mouqenel, 6 M.J. 589 (A.F.C.M.R. 1978) (polygraph evidence was inadmissible but would have been of great benefit to defense in preparing for cross-examination).
32. United States v. Brickey, 16 M.J. 258 (C.M.A. 1983); United States v. Horsey, 6 M.J. 112 (C.M.A. 1979); United States v. Trimper, 26 M.J. 534 (A.F.C.M.R. 1988) (prosecution is not required to disclose its rebuttal evidence under R.C.M. 701 unless it is exculpatory); United States v. Alford, 8 M.J. 516 (A.C.M.R. 1979). *Cf.* United States v. Friedman, 593 F.2d 109 (9th Cir. 1979) (mere possibility that evidence might have helped does not establish materiality in constitutional sense).
33. United States v. Lucas, 5 M.J. 167 (C.M.A. 1978).
34. *See* R.C.M. 701(a)(2).
35. *See* § 13-5(J). *See also* United States v. Eshalomi, 23 M.J. 12 (C.M.A. 1986) (discussion of standards of review for specific requests, general requests, and no requests).
36. R.C.M. 701(a)(2)(A). United States v. Meadows, 42 M.J. 132 (1995) (as generous as rule is, it still requires defense to file request).
37. R.C.M. 701(a)(2)(A). United States v. Branoff, 34 M.J. 612 (A.F.C.M.R. 1992) (harmless error where prosecution failed to respond to specific request for production of regulation governing investigations; the defendant never established materiality, i.e., that production of the regulation would have permitted him significantly to alter the quantum of proof in his favor).
38. R.C.M. 701(a)(2)(A).

copy and photograph them.[39] Once the defense request has been granted the prosecution is free to request similar information from the defense.[40]

§ 10-4(B)(3). Reports, Tests, and Results.

During the processing of a case it is likely that at some point a test or examination will have been conducted on the accused or upon evidence associated with the case. For example, in drug prosecutions there is almost always some sort of laboratory report[41] and where there is reason to suspect that the accused is suffering from a mental disease or defect, a sanity report.[42] Where such reports, tests, or examinations have been conducted the defense may request the opportunity to inspect them.[43] As in the case of tangible evidence, discussed in § 10-4(B)(2), the prosecution is required to comply with such requests after charges have been served and the materials are within the custody or control of the government and are known (or should be known) by the prosecution to be in existence and are (a) material to the defense or (b) the prosecution intends to use the materials during its case-in- chief.[44] Again, under reciprocal discovery rules, the prosecution upon complying with such requests is free to ask the defense for similar information.[45]

§ 10-4(B)(4). Sentencing Evidence.

The prosecution is also required upon request by the defense to provide access and the right to inspect written materials that the prosecution will present during the sentencing portion of the trial[46] and also inform the defense of the names and addresses of those witnesses who will testify for the prosecution during sentencing.[47]

---

39. R.C.M. 701(h).
40. *See* § 10-5(B).
41. *See* § 2-7.
42. *See* R.C.M. 706 (inquiry into mental state of accused). *See also* Rule 302, MIL. R. EVID.
43. R.C.M. 701(a)(2)(B). "Inspect" includes photographing or copying. R.C.M. 701(h).
44. R.C.M. 701(a)(2)(B). In United States v. Waldrup, 30 M.J. 1126 (N.M.C.M.R. 1989), the defense requested access to medical reports that it believed had been prepared on the chief government witness but during trial failed to demonstrate that in fact such reports existed.
45. *See* §§ 10-4(C), 10-5(B).
46. R.C.M. 701(a)(5)(A). United States v. Clark, 37 M.J. 1098 (N.M.C.M.R. 1993) (in extensive discussion, court concluded that prosecution was not required to disclose rebuttal letter to defendant; the letter was only made relevant after the defense had presented its case at sentencing). *Cf.* United States v. Trimper, 28 M.J. 460 (C.M.A. 1989) (evidence which was apparently material to the defense case should have been disclosed, even if it was only intended for rebuttal); United States v. Callara, 21 M.J. 259 (C.M.A. 1986) (sound administration of justice favors disclosure of rebuttal evidence). *See generally* Chapter 16 for discussion on sentencing procedures.
47. R.C.M. 701(a)(5)(B).

§ 10-4(B)(5). Jencks Act Materials.

Under the Jencks Act[48] the defense is entitled to see any pretrial statements or reports made by a prosecution witness after that witness has testified at trial.[49] Military decisions have held that the Act applies to witnesses who testify at courts-martial[50] and in the process of applying the rule have adopted several requirements for its use.

First, the government witness must have testified.[51] The defense is not entitled to the witness' pretrial statement under the Jencks Act in anticipation that the witness will testify at trial.[52]

Second, the witness must have made the pretrial statement or in some way adopted it as his own.[53] A problem sometimes arises where an investigator or prosecutor takes a witness's statement but never shows it to the witness, and instead it is intended to serve as working notes. In that case the notes probably do not qualify as the witness's statement.[54] But prior testimony at an Article 32 Investigation would clearly qualify.[55]

---

48. 18 U.S.C. § 3500. Jencks v. United States, 353 U.S. 657 (1957).

49. In effect, the Jencks Act disclosure, and its counterpart in the *Manual*, R.C.M. 914, are not pretrial discovery rules because they are triggered only by testimony at trial. *See* United States v. Ciesialski, 39 C.M.R. 839 (N.B.R. 1968). The Act is probably not triggered by testimony given at Article 32 Investigations. *See* R.C.M. 914 Analysis. *Cf.* United States v. Jackson, 33 C.M.R. 884, 890, nn. 3, 4 (A.F.B.R. 1963).

50. United States v. Jarrie, 5 M.J. 193 (C.M.A. 1978); United States v. Albo, 22 C.M.A. 30, 46 C.M.R. 30 (1972); United States v. Heinel, 9 C.M.A. 259, 26 C.M.R. 39 (1958). *See also* Augenblick v. United States, 377 F.2d 586 (Ct. Cl. 1967), *rev'd on other grounds*, 393 U.S. 348 (1969).

See generally Burnette, "Workshopping the Jencks Act," ARMY LAW., June 1987, at 22. *See generally* Lederer, "Now You See It; Now You Don't—Implicit Repeal of the Jencks Act," 14 THE ADVOCATE 94 (1982). Kesler, "The Jencks Act: An Introductory Analysis," 13 THE ADVOCATE 391 (Nov.-Dec. 1981); Lynch, "Possession Under the Jencks Act," 10 A.F. JAG R. 177 (Dec. 1981); O'Brien, "The Jencks Act—A Recognized Tool for Military Defense Counsel," 11 THE ADVOCATE 20 (Jan.-Feb. 1979); Waldrop, "The Jencks Act," 20 A.F. L. REV. 93 (1978); Bogart, "Jencks Act," 27 JAG J. 427 (1973); West, "Significance of the Jencks Act in Military Law," 30 MIL. L. REV. 83 (1965).

51. 18 U.S.C. § 3500(a). The Act specifies that the testimony must be during direct examination.

52. United States v. Burrell, 5 M.J. 617 (A.C.M.R. 1978) (the Act is not an instrument of pretrial discovery to be used in planning trial strategy).

53. 18 U.S.C. § 3500(e). *See* United States v. Jarrie, 5 M.J. 193 (C.M.A. 1978); United States v. Bosier, 12 M.J. 1010 (A.C.M.R. 1982) (confidential informant's notes were "statements"). Production of the statement or report does not relieve the prosecution from producing the summary which formed the basis for the statement or report. *See* United States v. Dixon, 8 M.J. 149 (C.M.A. 1979). The federal courts have generally held that surveillance notes are not covered. Bosier, *supra* 12 M.J. at 1015. *See, e.g.*, United States v. Bernard, 623 F.2d 551 (9th Cir. 1979).

54. *See, e.g.*, United States v. Vanderweir, 25 M.J. 263 (C.M.A. 1987) (Jencks Act not applicable to interview notes taken by prosecution team but not adopted by witness); United States v. McDaniel, 17 M.J. 553 (A.C.M.R. 1983) (blank cassette tapes and investigation officer's notes on witness' testimony were not "statements"); United States v. Gomez, 15 M.J. 954 (A.C.M.R. 1983) (rough notes by military dispatcher not under Act).

55. United States v. Lewis, 38 M.J. 501 (A.C.M.R. 1993) (Article 32 testimony subject to disclosure); United States v. Crumb, 10 M.J. 520, 528 (A.C.M.R. 1980) (concurring opinion). *See also* United States v. Thomas, 7 M.J. 655 (A.C.M.R. 1979); United States v. Scott, 6 M.J. 547 (A.F.C.M.R. 1978).

Third, the pretrial statement must relate to the subject matter of the witness' trial testimony.[56]

Fourth, the pretrial statement must be in the possession of the government.[57] If the statement was at one time within its possession and is otherwise producible, the prosecution may have to demonstrate that the statement was destroyed or disposed of in good faith.[58] Otherwise, the witness's testimony may be stricken.[59] Where the statement has been destroyed one court has suggested that a balancing test should be used to determine what if any sanctions should be imposed; the court indicated that it would consider the degree of government negligence or bad faith, the importance of the statement that was lost, and other evidence of the accused's guilt that is produced at trial.[60]

The essence of the Jencks Act disclosure has been included in the Manual for Courts-Martial at R.C.M. 914,[61] which provides that after a witness, other

---

56. 18 U.S.C. § 3500(b). United States v. Albo, 22 C.M.A. 30, 46 C.M.R. 30 (1972); United States v. Bosier, 12 M.J. 1010 (A.C.M.R. 1982).

57. 18 U.S.C. § 3500(a). United States v. Longstreath, 42 M.J. 806 (N.M.Ct.Crim.App.1995) (court rejected government's disingenuous argument that it no longer had child abuse victim's transcribed statement; the interview was conducted by NIS and transcribed on NIS letterhead; giving transcript to civilian agency did not end government's obligation under R.C.M. 701 or Jencks); United States v. Ali, 12 M.J. 1018 (A.C.M.R. 1982) (statement in possession of commanding officer). *Cf.* United States v. Paternina-Vergara, 749 F.2d 933 (2d Cir. 1984) (Act not applicable to documents held by foreign government). *See generally* Lynch, "Possession Under the Jencks Act," 10 A.F. JAG Rr. 177 (Dec. 1981).

58. United States v. Roxas, 41 M.J. 727 (N.M.Ct.Crim.App.1994) (no Jencks Act violation where defense conceded that materials, once in the hands of the government, were not lost in bad faith); United States v. Lewis, 38 M.J. 501 (A.C.M.R. 1993) (Article 32 tapes lost in good faith); United States v. Staley, 36 M.J. 896 (A.F.C.M.R. 1993) (prior statements from administrative board proceeding had been destroyed in good faith); United States v. Bosier, 12 M.J. 1010 (A.C.M.R. 1982); United States v. Bufatino, 576 F.2d 446 (2d Cir. 1978). *See* United States v. Durden, 14 M.J. 507 (A.F.C.M.R. 1982) (investigator had no duty to retain rough notes which were incorporated into official records).

59. 18 U.S.C. § 3500(d). That provision also indicates that a failure to produce may result in a mistrial. United States v. Barber, 20 M.J. 678 (A.F.C.M.R. 1985) (the judge committed harmless error in ruling that the government's witness could testify notwithstanding the fact that his pretrial statements were missing and could not be read by the judge to determine whether the statements were within the purview of the Act).

60. United States v. Bosier, 12 M.J. 1010 (A.C.M.R. 1982), *citing* United States v. Bryant, 439 F.2d 642, 653 (D.C. Cir. 1971). *See also* United States v. Pena, 22 M.J. 281 (C.M.A. 1986); United States v. Boyd, 14 M.J. 703 (N.M.C.M.R. 1982) (discussion of sanctions); United States v. Jones, 20 M.J. 919 (N.M.C.M.R. 1985) (balancing the potential prejudice to the accused against the government's culpability in inadvertently destroying an agent's rough notes, the court held that sanctions for the government's "technical" violation of the Jencks Act would be inappropriate).

61. The rule, which is really not a pretrial discovery rule, is based upon Fed. R. Crim. P. 26.2, which in turn is based upon the Jencks Act.

In United States v. White, 23 M.J. 891 (A.C.M.R. 1987), the court noted the differences between material produced under R.C.M. 914 and Mil. R. Evid. 612. Under the latter rule, the material is produced if the witness has relied upon it to refresh his recollection at trial. The R.C.M. is not so limited, and the pretrial statements of the witness should be produced without regard to whether they are used to refresh the witness' memory. In *White*, the defense waived the Jencks-R.C.M. 914 Rule by not pursuing the issue after the judge announced that he was striking the witness's testimony because it was not clear that the witness was testifying from his personal memory.

than the accused, has testified the party not calling the witness may move for the production of any pretrial statements[62] made by the witness that relate to the witness's testimony and are in the possession of the party calling the witness;[63] for the defense this is not really new but for the prosecution this amounts to a reverse Jencks Act disclosure.[64]

The Rule does not apply to Article 32 investigations.[65] If the defense fails to produce the statement, the defense witness's testimony will be stricken.[66] If it is the prosecution that fails to comply, the military judge may declare a mistrial.[67]

§ 10-4(C). Reciprocal Discovery.

Although the topic of reciprocal discovery is also addressed under the following discussions of prosecutorial discovery, it is important to note it here as well because of the impact that it may have on a defense request for information. Where the defense has requested access to tangible items or documents, see § 10-4(B)(2), or access to any reports or tests, see § 10-4(B)(3), the prosecution upon granting the request is entitled to request like disclosure.[68] A request for disclosure of one of the foregoing categories will probably not permit reciprocal discovery requests on the other category. If the defense can obtain discovery of these types of evidence without specifically requesting disclosure then the reciprocal discovery rule will probably not apply. The point here is that a defense request may very well put the defense in the position of disclosing its own evidence.

---

62. "Statement" is defined in R.C.M. 914(f). The entire statement is to be produced if the entire contents relate to the witness's testimony. R.C.M. 914(b). Otherwise, the judge is to review the statement and excise those portions that are not so related. R.C.M. 914(c). United States v. Douglas, 32 M.J. 694 (A.F.C.M.R. 1991) (no prejudice where undercover agent had destroyed notes which amounted to statement); United States v. Hamilton, 27 M.J. 628 (A.F.C.M.R. 1988) (tape recordings of agent's voice were statements but failure to produce the tapes, because they had been erased in good faith, did not require suppression because defense was provided with substantially verbatim transcript of tapes); United States v. Holmes, 25 M.J. 674 (A.F.C.M.R. 1987) (investigator's compilation of information provided by witness was not a pretrial statement of the witness where the information was never adopted by the witness).
63. R.C.M. 914(a)(1), (2). If the "party" is the prosecution the statement must be in the possession of the United States. If it is the defense, the statement must be in the possession of either the accused or the defense counsel. Thus, the Rule would apparently not cover statements held by an agent of the defense team—such as a privately retained psychiatrist or other expert.
64. *See* § 10-5(B).
65. R.C.M. 914(a) Discussion.
66. R.C.M. 914(e).
67. R.C.M. 914(e).
68. R.C.M. 701(b)(3). Reciprocal disclosure under this provision is not automatic. The prosecution must request it.

§ 10-5. Prosecution Discovery.

Until recently military criminal discovery rules generally favored the defense to the extent that very little, if any, information about defense evidence or tactics was available to the prosecution.[1] The 1984 revisions to the *Manual* changed that and specifically opened the door for prosecution discovery. The following sections address those instances in which the defense is required to automatically disclose certain information to the prosecution and those instances in which the prosecution may request information from the defense.

§ 10-5(A). Automatic Defense Disclosure.

In addition to the "notice" requirements noted in § 10-2(B), the defense is required to *disclose*, without any prior request from the prosecution, the names of its witnesses,[2] its intent to use an alibi defense,[3] the defense of lack of mental responsibility,[4] and the defense of innocent ingestion.[5] The purpose of these rules is to reduce the element of surprise that may accompany these defenses and the delays that often result.[6] If the defense has disclosed its intent to rely upon one of these defenses and then later withdraws it, the prosecution is barred from referring to the disclosure by the defense.[7]

§ 10-5(A)(1). Names of Defense Witnesses.

As with the requirement that the prosecution must notify the defense of the names of its witnesses,[8] the defense is also required, before the trial begins,[9] to disclose to the prosecution the names of the witnesses (other than the accused) it intends to call at the trial.[10] Note that this disclosure is automatic. The prosecution need not take any action nor make any requests in order to receive it. Presumably this disclosure extends only to witnesses who will be called during the merits portion of the trial.[11] Another provision explicitly

---

1. *See* R.C.M. 701 Analysis, Introduction.
2. R.C.M. 701(b)(1).
3. R.C.M. 701(b)(2).
4. R.C.M. 701(b)(2).
5. R.C.M. 701(b)(2).
6. *See* R.C.M. 701(b)(2) Analysis.
7. R.C.M. 701(b)(1), (2).
8. R.C.M. 701(a)(3). *See* § 10-4(A)(2).
9. The question of when the "trial" begins may prove problematic. Neither the Rule nor the Analysis for the Rule indicate any more specific time, i.e., assembly of the court, entry of pleas, or arraignment. While it would have been helpful to have the Rule state a more specific time or event, it is probably not crucial as long as the spirit of the Rule is complied with. The closer to the time when the witness actually testifies, the more closely the trial court should examine the timeliness of the disclosure.
10. R.C.M. 701(b)(1)(A). According the Drafters' Analysis for this provision, which was added in 1991, it was included to balance discovery between both sides and thus give meaning to the "equal access" language in Article 46. *See also* § 10-3(B).
11. While the language in R.C.M. 701(a)(3), which requires the prosecution to disclose the names of its witnesses, refers to the prosecution's "case-in-chief," the defense provision in R.C.M. 701(b)(1)(A) is more general and refers to witnesses who will be called "at trial."

addresses disclosure of defense witnesses who will testify during the sentencing portion of the trial.[12] In addition to disclosing the names of its witnesses to be called at trial, the defense must provide all statements made by those witnesses that are known to the defense.[13] The *Manual* does not specify just how this disclosure is to take place. In those instances where the defense witness has made a written statement, that writing should be produced. And where the statement is oral, the disclosure should be specific enough to reasonably inform the prosecution of the circumstances of the making of the statement.[14]

§ 10-5(A)(2). Notice of Alibi Defense.

Before the trial on the merits begins, the defense must notify the prosecution of its intent to rely upon an alibi defense.[15] The prosecution must also be informed of the specific places that the accused will claim to have been when the offense was committed and must also disclose the names and addresses of the defense witnesses who will present the alibi testimony.[16] If the prosecution has received timely notice it must reciprocate with automatic disclosure of any rebuttal witnesses that it will use.[17]

The issue of what, if any, relief should be offered for failure to provide notice was addressed in *United States v. Townsend*.[18] The court indicated that in deciding whether the alibi testimony should nonetheless be permitted, trial judges should consider whether opposing counsel suffered a disadvantage[19] and the reason for counsel's failure to give the required notice.[20]

---

12. R.C.M. 701(b)(1)(B). *See* § 10-5(B).
13. R.C.M. 701(b)(1)(A).
14. *Cf.* FED. R. CRIM. P. 16(a)(1), which provides detailed guidance of production of various types of statements, both oral and written. Because the Drafters apparently used that federal rule as a model for military discovery, any cases applying the federal counterpart should be helpful in determining whether the particular method of disclosure was in substantial compliance with the military version.
15. R.C.M. 701(b)(2). *See generally* Williams v. Florida, 399 U.S. 78 (1970) (upholding constitutionality of state's notice-of-alibi rule).
16. R.C.M. 701(b)(2). Unlike its federal counterpart, Fed. R. Crim. P. 12.1, this Rule does not require the prosecution to first request notice of an alibi defense.
17. *See* § 10-4(A)(2).
18. 23 M.J. 848 (A.F.C.M.R. 1987).
19. *Id.* at 850. United States v. Preuss, 34 M.J. 688 (N.M.C.M.R. 1991) (harmless error for military judge to exclude defense alibi evidence which had not been disclosed prior to trial). *See also* R.C.M. 701(g) Discussion. In this case the court noted that although the civilian defense counsel had told the prosecutor before trial that a particular witness would not serve as an alibi witness, the prosecutor had reason to believe otherwise and had ample opportunity to question the witness before trial.
20. *Id.* at 851. The court concluded that the civilian counsel failed to inform the prosecutor of his intent to use the witness as an alibi witness because of mistake rather than bad faith.

§ 10-5(A)(3). Notice of Lack of Mental Responsibility Defense.

If the defense intends to rely upon the defense of insanity or intends to offer the testimony of an expert on the issue of the accused's mental state, as it relates to his guilt, it must so notify the prosecution.[21] This disclosure must also be made before the trial on the merits begins.[22] If the prosecution intends to offer rebuttal testimony it must automatically reciprocate by disclosing to the defense the names of the witnesses it will call.[23]

§ 10-5(A)(4). Notice of Defense of Innocent Ingestion.

As a result of 1991 amendments to the Manual for Courts-Martial, the defense is also required to give notice to the prosecution of its intent to rely upon the defense of innocent ingestion.[24] That defense is available in those cases where the accused has been charged with use of controlled substances.[25] As with the preceding notice requirements concerning possible defenses, this provision is grounded on the belief that advance notice of the defense will conserve judicial resources and time by taking the surprise out of the case.[26] If the defense, after giving the requisite notice, decides not to pursue that tactic, the prosecution is barred from presenting any evidence of the defense's intentions or disclosures, against either the accused or any witness.[27]

§ 10-5(B). Prosecution Requests for Discovery.

In addition to the avenue of "reciprocal discovery," which is discussed in § 10-5(C), the prosecution has some access to defense sentencing evidence through a request for that information. In 1991, the *Manual* was amended to permit the prosecution to request the defense to provide the names and addresses of the witnesses it would call during the sentencing proceedings.[28] In addition, the prosecution may request that it be permitted to inspect any written materials that the defense intends to offer during sentencing.[29] For a discussion on sentencing procedures, see Chapter 16.

---

21. R.C.M. 701(b)(2). It is not clear from the Rule that this disclosure must include the identities of the defense witnesses. *See generally* FED. R. CRIM. P. 12-2.
22. R.C.M. 701(b)(2).
23. R.C.M. 701(a)(3)(B). *See also* § 10-4(A)(2).
24. R.C.M. 701(b)(2).
25. *See generally* § 2-7.
26. R.C.M. 701(b) Analysis.
27. R.C.M. 701(b)(5). *See also* FED. R. CRIM. P. 12.1 and 12.2.
28. R.C.M. 701(b)(1)(B)(i).
29. R.C.M. 701(b)(1)(B)(ii).

§ 10-5(C). Reciprocal Discovery.

Through rules of reciprocal discovery the prosecution has access to defense evidence that consists of documents and tangible objects or reports or results of examinations or tests, if the defense has first requested and received that type of information from the prosecution.[30] If the prosecution has disclosed that information before the defense requests it, however, the rule of reciprocal discovery will probably not apply. To be discoverable the requested information must be in the custody or control of the defense and must be intended for use by the defense for its case-in-chief.[31]

§ 10-6. Judicial Control of Discovery: Remedies.

As in civilian practice, the fact that discovery or disclosure is permitted or required does not always insure unchallenged compliance. The opposing counsel may resist disclosure on grounds that the requested material is privileged,[1] that it is not relevant to the case,[2] or that it is counsel's work product.[3] Where counsel's attempts to obtain information are frustrated, the *Manual* specifically provides that the military judge may be called upon to resolve the dispute and specify the time, manner, and place for discovery,[4] and lay out any other requirements or conditions for disclosure.[5]

This power to control discovery includes the power to enter any appropriate order that limits access or disclosure.[6] Such orders may be triggered by a motion for denial or deferral of disclosure.[7] Counsel may make a written *ex parte* showing why disclosure should be denied and that any evidence offered by the moving counsel should be sealed and made a part of the record for later appellate review.[8]

If the judge's orders governing disclosure are not followed or if counsel demonstrates that the opposing counsel has not complied with the disclosure, notice, or discovery rules, the judge may (a) order the noncomplying party to permit discovery,[9] (b) grant a continuance,[10] (c) order that the noncomplying party will not be permitted to offer the defense or evidence during trial,[11] or

---

30. R.C.M. 701(b)(3).
31. *Id.* United States v. Stewart, 29 M.J. 621 (C.G.C.M.R. 1989). *See also* § 10-4(C).
1. *See generally* MIL. R. EVID. Section V, Privileges.
2. *See generally* MIL. R. EVID. Section IV, Relevancy.
3. *See* § 10-3(A).
4. R.C.M. 701(g)(1).
5. R.C.M. 701(g)(1).
6. R.C.M. 701(g)(2).
7. R.C.M. 701(g)(2).

8. *Id.* For a helpful discussion on the topic of sealing the materials for appellate review, see United States v. Branoff, 34 M.J. 612 (A.F.C.M.R. 1992). The topic is also discussed at § 13-5(J), *infra*.

9. R.C.M. 701(g)(3)(A). *See generally* FED. R. CRIM. P. 16(d)(2), 12.2(d).
10. R.C.M. 701(g)(3)(B).
11. R.C.M. 701(g)(3)(C). R.C.M. 701(g)(3)(C) was amended by Change 6 to the *Manual* (Dec. 1993) to reflect that an appropriate remedy would be to prohibit the party from introducing evidence, calling a witness, or raising a defense not disclosed. The Drafters' Analysis for the

(d) grant any other relief that may be appropriate.[12] Such relief may not include barring the accused from testifying in his own behalf, however.[13] Thus, although the defense might be prohibited from presenting alibi witnesses because it failed to properly disclose an intent to use that defense to the prosecution, the accused would arguably be able to present that defense during his testimony.

For further discussion on the use of motions to obtain disclosure, see § 13-5(J).

---

amendment indicates that the change was intended to reflect the view that the Sixth Amendment compulsory process clause does not prohibit exclusion of testimony from a material defense witness. Taylor v. Illinois, 484 U.S. 400 (1988). The Analysis points out, however, that the sanction should be reserved for use where the accused has willfully and blatantly violated applicable discovery rules, and alternative sanctions could not have minimized the prejudice to the Government. The Discussion accompanying R.C.M. 701(g)(3)(C) lists the factors the court should consider. The defendant's right to compulsory process should be balanced against the public's interests including: (1) integrity of the adversary process; (2) interest in fair and efficient administration of military justice; and (3) potential prejudice to the truth-finding function of the trial.

12. R.C.M. 701(g)(3)(D).
13. R.C.M. 701(g)(3). *See also* FED. R. CRIM. P. 12.1(d).

APPENDIX REFERENCES

Appendix 1. Abbreviations.
Appendix 2. Glossary.
Appendix 3. U.C.M.J.
Appendix 4. Court-Martial Flow Chart.
Appendix 6. Charge Sheets.
Appendix 7. Investigating Officer's Report.
Appendix 10. Sample Discovery Request.
Appendix 11. Grant of Immunity.
Appendix 19. Disclosure of Section III Evidence.

ANNOTATED BIBLIOGRAPHY

PERIODICALS

Bogart, "Jencks Act: Right of Defense to Criminal Investigators' Notes for Impeachment Purposes," 27 JAG J. 427 (1973).

This article discusses the Court of Military Appeals' interpretation of the Jencks Act in *United States v. Albo,* which allowed defense discovery of notes that prosecution investigators had used to refresh their memories before testifying. The author declares *Albo* to be a sign of the vitality of the Jencks Act as a discovery tool in military practice, and admonishes military judges to give discovery requests under the Act due regard.

Coacher, "Discovery in Courts-Martial," 39 A.F. L. Rev. 103 (1996).

Noting that discovery in military practice is quite liberal, the author briefly discusses key points in military discovery vis-à-vis evidence which must be disclosed even without a prior request, notification of an intent to use certain evidence, and evidence which must be disclosed only upon request.

Paikin, "Problems in Obtaining Evidence in Foreign States for Use in Federal Criminal Prosecutions," 22 Colum. J. Transnat'l L. Rev. 233 (1984).

This informative article considers the barriers that inhibit the procurement of evidence inside another sovereign state. Through a survey of the various devices used to overcome these barriers, the writer analyzes the advantages and disadvantages of possible international and domestic solutions. The results of his analysis suggest the solutions will only be partially successful and the problems inherent in sovereign status will probably persist.

Luedtke, "Open Government and Military Justice," 87 Mil. L. Rev. 7 (1980).

The author presents a thorough discussion of both the Freedom of Information Act and the Privacy Act as they affect the availability of military records. The writer also explores the acts as they relate to military discovery in court-martial proceedings while providing a good review of military discovery law.

Saunders, "Proposed Changes in Military Discovery," 10 Am. Crim. L. Rev. 81 (1971).

Through a comparison with the rules applied in federal courts this article examines the need for a more formalized military discovery system and also evaluates the merits and probable effects of the proposed changes contained in the Military Justice Act of 1971.

Symposium, "Military Justice," ARMY LAW., March 1996.

This 127-page symposium contains a Foreword and 11 short articles on a wide range of military justice topics. They are as follows:

Morris, "Foreword."
Barto, "Developments in the Substantive Criminal Law Under the Uniform Code of Military Justice."
Frisk, "New Developments in Pretrial Confinement."
Frisk, "New Developments in Speedy Trial."
Winn, "Recent Developments in Military Pretrial and Trial Procedure."
Masterton, "Recent Developments in Search and Seizure Law."
Masterton, "Recent Developments in Urinalysis Law."
Kohlman, "Are You Ready for Some Changes? Five Fresh Views of the Fifth Amendment."
Wright, "Sex, Lies, and Videotape: Child Sexual Abuse Cases Continue to Create Appellate Issues and Other Developments in the Areas of the Sixth Amendment, Discovery, Mental Responsibility, and Nonjudicial Punishment."
Henley, "Caveat Criminale: The Impact of the New Military Rules of Evidence in Sexual Offense and Child Molestation Cases."
Henley, "Current Developments in Evidence Law."
Morris, "New Developments in Sentencing and Post-Trial Procedure."

Thompson, "Constitutional Applications to the Military Criminal Defendant," 66 U. DETROIT L. REV. 221 (1989).

Drawing comparisons between civilian and military practices, the author notes that in order to maintain the requisite good order and discipline needed in the armed forces some modifications to substantive constitutional rights have been made. He concludes that although the military defendant loses protections in the areas of search and seizure and trial by jury, he has enhanced protections in other areas, e.g., discovery and witness production.

Waldrop, "The Jencks Act," 20 A.F. L. REV. 93 (1978).

This article is an excellent primer on the Supreme Court's decision in *Jencks v. United States* and the subsequent enactment of the Jencks Act. The author discusses the structure and substance of the Act in detail, and traces its impact on military discovery. Perceiving inconsistency and abuse in the use of the Act by military trial counsel, the author proposes guidelines to minimize these problems and to more fully effectuate the purpose of the Act.

West, "The Significance of the Jencks Act in Military Law," 30 MIL. L. REV. 83 (1965).

Major West argues that the distinct characteristics of military practice restrict the applicability of the Jencks Act to situations where evidence is lost or destroyed or otherwise cannot be produced in compliance with the Act. The author then examines several facets of the Act that have evolved in military practice, such as the good/bad faith issue and the harmless error rule. In conclusion, the author calls for greater sophistication among military defense counsel in the use of the Act.

CHAPTER 11

PRODUCTION OF WITNESSES AND EVIDENCE

§ 11-1. General.
§ 11-2. Production of Witnesses.
    § 11-2(A). General Rules.
        § 11-2(A)(1). Equal Access: The Right to Witnesses.
        § 11-2(A)(2). Unavailable Witnesses.
        § 11-2(A)(3). Employing Expert Witnesses.
        § 11-2(A)(4). Adequate Substitutes for Testimony.
    § 11-2(B). Requests for Witnesses.
        § 11-2(B)(1). Defense Witnesses.
        § 11-2(B)(2). Prosecution Witnesses.
    § 11-2(C). Production of Military Witnesses.
    § 11-2(D). Production of Civilian Witnesses.
        § 11-2(D)(1). General.
        § 11-2(D)(2). Use of the Subpoena.
        § 11-2(D)(3). Sanctions for Failure to Appear.
    § 11-2(E). Immunity for Witnesses.
        § 11-2(E)(1). General.
        § 11-2(E)(2). Immunity for Prosecution Witnesses.
        § 11-2(E)(3). Immunity for Defense Witnesses.
    § 11-2(F). Refusal to Testify.
§ 11-3. Depositions.
    § 11-3(A). In General.
    § 11-3(B). Procedures for Depositions.
        § 11-3(B)(1). In General.
        § 11-3(B)(2). Procedures for Oral Depositions.
        § 11-3(B)(3). Procedures for Written Depositions.
    § 11-3(C). Use of Depositions at Trial.
§ 11-4. Production of Evidence.
Appendix References.
Annotated Bibliography.

§ 11-1. General.

During the process of pretrial notice,[1] disclosure,[2] and discovery,[3] counsel for each side will be able to focus on the evidence and those witnesses who should be obtained for the trial. This chapter will address the general rules that govern the production of witnesses and evidence and the process of preserving a witness' testimony through a deposition. The discussion begins with a review of some of the basic rules that govern the production of witnesses.

---

1. *See* § 10-2.
2. *See* §§ 10-4(A), 10-5(A).
3. *See, e.g.,* §§ 10-4 and 10-5.

§ 11-2. Production of Witnesses.

§ 11-2(A). General Rules.

As a prelude to more detailed discussion of the rules governing the ability of the prosecution and defense to obtain their witnesses, this section will lay out some of the general rules that are applicable to both sides. Particular problems that might be faced by each side are addressed in subsequent sections.

§ 11-2(A)(1). Equal Access: The Right to Witnesses.

The Constitution makes no specific reference to the ability of a party in a criminal proceeding to obtain any particular witness. The Sixth Amendment simply provides the defendant with an opportunity to present a defense and confront the witnesses against him.[1] The U.C.M.J., however, specifically provides that the prosecution, defense, and court-martial will have "equal opportunity to obtain witnesses and other evidence in accordance with such regulations as the President may prescribe."[2] In exercising that authority, the President, in turn, has directed through the Manual for Courts-Martial that counsel and the court shall have equal opportunity to obtain witnesses and evidence, which includes the "benefit of compulsory process."[3] But these provisions do not entitle the parties to all witnesses that might have something to say about the case. The right extends only to those witnesses who, on the merits or on an interlocutory question, would present *relevant and necessary* testimony.[4]

For purposes of witnesses on sentencing, a slightly higher standard must be met. Not only must the witness possess relevant and necessary information, but it must be shown that there is a substantial need for the witness' personal appearance.[5] *See also* § 11-2(B)(1).

The *Manual* standard of "relevant and necessary" varies slightly from the standard used by the military courts in assessing whether a particular witness should have been produced. That standard has been one of materiality.

---

1. Nevertheless, a right of compulsory process has been read into the Sixth Amendment. *See* Washington v. Texas, 388 U.S. 14 (1967) (the defendant's right to present a defense); United States v. Williams, 39 M.J. 555 (A.C.M.R. 1994) (MIL. R. EVID. 707, which excludes any evidence of polygraph results violated accused's Sixth and Fifth Amendment rights to present defense evidence and to a fair trial). *Cf.* United States v. Sceffer, 41 M.J. 683 (A. F. Ct. Crim. App. 1995). *See generally* Gilligan & Lederer, "The Procurement and Presentation of Evidence in Courts-Martial: Compulsory Process and Confrontation," 101 MIL. L. REV. 1 (1983).

2. Art. 46, U.C.M.J. *See* Appendix 3. In an extensive discussion of the issue, the Court in United States v. Irwin, 30 M.J. 87 (C.M.A. 1990), concluded that the convening authority's *ex parte* action that required the presence of a third party when defense counsel interviewed witnesses violated Article 46. United States v. Morris, 24 M.J. 93 (C.M.A. 1987) (no denial of equal access where defense counsel was only able to interview child victim in presence of third party).

3. R.C.M. 703(a).

4. R.C.M. 703(a) Discussion.

5. *See* R.C.M. 1001(e)(2).

That is, the witness's testimony must be material to the case.[6] In effect, the result should be the same. The test is more than a question of whether the testimony is relevant. If the impact of the testimony would be so insignificant as to not have a material bearing on the outcome of the case, then the right to the testimony is not available.[7] The right is also limited if the witness' testimony would be merely cumulative.[8]

Although the foregoing principles apply with equal force to each side, for all practical purposes they have a greater impact on the defense. Because the ability to obtain witnesses tends to favor the government with all of its resources, the guarantee of equal access ensures some benefits to the accused.

All of this assumes that the witness in question is available. Where the witness is unavailable, the course of action depends on just how relevant and necessary the witness is to the case.

---

6. United States v. Valenzuela-Bernal, 458 U.S. 858 (1982); United States v. Fisher, 24 M.J. 358 (C.M.A. 1987) (court concluded that defense witnesses were material and should have been produced; the fact that they might claim the right against self-incrimination was not sufficient to warrant denying the defense request).
United States v. Viola, 26 M.J. 822 (A.C.M.R. 1988); United States v. Menoken, 14 M.J. 10 (C.M.A. 1982); United States v. Jefferson, 13 M.J. 1 (C.M.A. 1982); United States v. Hampton, 7 M.J. 284 (C.M.A. 1979); United States v. Fisher, 17 M.J. 768 (A.F.C.M.R. 1983).

7. United States v. Hampton, 7 M.J. 284 (C.M.A. 1979); United States v. Viola, 26 M.J. 822 (A.C.M.R. 1988) (defense request for character witness did not establish relevancy of expected testimony vis-à-vis MIL. R. EVID. 404. Later, when it became apparent how the witness' testimony would be relevant, the accused failed to renew his request; trial judge is under no duty to *sua sponte* reconsider his rulings).

8. United States v. Harmon, 40 M.J. 107 (C.M.A. 1994) (no constitutional right to cumulative witnesses; court indicated that counsel should have obtained advance ruling on how many witnesses would be permitted at sentencing in order to decide which witnesses to call); United States v. Tangpuz, 5 M.J. 426 (C.M.A. 1978); United States v. Williams, 3 M.J. 239 (C.M.A. 1977); United States v. Allen, 31 M.J. 572 (N.M.C.M.R. 1990) (if court concludes that testimony is cumulative, it should so inform the defense and offer it a choice of witnesses).

In United States v. Tangpuz, 5 M.J. at 429, the court identified four factors that may be considered in determining whether the accused is entitled to the attendance of a witness:

(1) the issues involved in the case and the importance of the requested witness to those issues;
(2) whether the witness was desired on the merits or on sentencing;
(3) whether the witness' testimony would be "merely cumulative"; and
(4) the availability of alternatives to the personal appearance of the witness such as deposition, interrogatories, or previous testimony.

The court in United States v. Jones, 20 M.J. 919 (N.M.C.M.R. 1985) added the following factors:

(a) unavailability of the witness, such as that occasioned by nonamenability to the court's process, United States v. Bennett, 12 M.J. 463 (C.M.A. 1982);
(b) whether or not the requested witness is in the armed forces and/or subject to military orders, United States v. Ciarletta, 7 C.M.A. 606, 23 C.M.R. 70 (1957); United States v. Davis, 19 C.M.A. 217, 41 C.M.R. 217 (1970);
(c) the effect that a military witness' absence will have on his or her unit and whether that absence will adversely affect the accomplishment of an important military mission or cause manifest injury to the service, United States v. Manos, 17 C.M.A. 10, 37 C.M.R. 274 (1967); United States v. Davis, 19 C.M.A. 217, 41 C.M.R. 217 (1970).

§ 11-2(A)(2). Unavailable Witnesses.

The *Manual* indicates that the unavailability of a witness is determined by the template set out in Military Rule of Evidence 804(a),[9] which in turn indicates that an individual (declarant) is unavailable as a witness if he:

(1) is exempted by ruling of the military judge on the ground of privilege from testifying concerning the subject matter of the declarant's statement;[10] or

(2) persists in refusing to testify concerning the subject matter of the declarant's statement despite an order of the military judge to do so; or

(3) testifies to a lack of memory of the subject matter of the declarant's statement; or

(4) is unable to be present or to testify at the hearing because of death or then existing physical or mental illness or infirmity; or

(5) is absent from the hearing and the proponent of the declarant's statement has been unable to procure the declarant's attendance (or in the case of a hearsay exception under [MIL. R. EVID. 804] (b)(2), (3), or (4), the declarant's attendance or testimony) by process or other reasonable means; or

(6) is unavailable within the meaning of Article 49(d)(2).

A declarant is not unavailable as a witness if the declarant's exemption, refusal, claim of lack of memory, inability, or absence is due to the procurement or wrongdoing of the proponent of the declarant's statement for the purpose of preventing the witness from attending or testifying.[11]

If the witness is "unavailable," the party requesting the witness is not entitled to his or her presence.[12] But if the witness's testimony is of "such

---

9. United States v. Burns, 27 M.J. 92 (C.M.A. 1988) (prosecution civilian witness should not have been declared unavailable where the government had not attempted personal service, as required under the 1969 *Manual*, and legal officials had failed to check at other possible locations. R.C.M. 703(e)(2)(D) now only suggests personal service of a subpoena).

10. *See, e.g.*, United States v. Stroup, 24 M.J. 760 (A.F.C.M.R. 1987) (witness held dual citizenship from both United States and Great Britain, and although there was some confusion on which country's law he was relying upon in his refusal to testify, it was clear that he wished not to incriminate himself); United States v. Koistinen, 24 M.J. 676 (A.F.C.M.R. 1987) (witness invoked the Fifth Amendment); United States v. Vega-Cancel, 19 M.J. 899 (A.C.M.R. 1985) (judge erred in not more fully exploring a co-conspirator's decision to invoke the privilege against self-incrimination); United States v. Robinson, 16 M.J. 766 (A.C.M.R. 1983).

11. *See generally* United States v. Barror, 23 M.J. 370 (C.M.A. 1987) (discussion of problem where defendant has discouraged witness from testifying); United States v. Dorgan, 39 M.J. 827 (A.C.M.R. 1994) (government could not argue that civilian witness requested by the defense was unavailable without attempting to deliver subpoena and offer to pay fees and mileage; defense showed how witness could be contacted and judge was under duty to delay trial long enough for government to attempt to serve her with subpoena).

12. R.C.M. 703(b)(3). United States v. Davis, 29 M.J. 357 (C.M.A. 1990) (defense alibi witness was unavailable where government made a number of unsuccessful attempts to have U.S. marshals serve subpoena, and she informed them that she would continue to resist service); United States v. Boswell, 36 M.J. 807 (A.C.M.R. 1993) (two witnesses located in Saudi Arabia were unavailable; defense counsel conceded that their testimony was not central to case); United States

central importance to an issue that it is essential to a fair trial," the military judge may permit the counsel to present an "adequate substitute" for such testimony.[13] Adequate substitutes might include deposition testimony,[14] videotaped statements,[15] or stipulations of expected testimony or of fact.[16]

If no adequate substitute exists, however, the trial judge may then either grant a continuance[17] or other relief in an attempt to obtain the witness's presence or abate the proceedings.[18] If the witness's unavailability was caused or could have been avoided by the counsel who requested the witness's presence,[19] the judge may apparently proceed with the trial even in the absence of the witness.[20]

§ 11-2(A)(3). Employing Expert Witnesses.

The Manual for Courts-Martial specifically provides for employment of expert witnesses when such employment is considered relevant and necessary.[21]

---

v. Minaya, 30 M.J. 1179 (A.F.C.M.R.1990) (Philippine nationals were unavailable witnesses where government had made every reasonable effort to produce them at trial).

13. United States v. Davis, 29 M.J. 357 (C.M.A. 1990) (defense counsel declined to choose an adequate substitute). See § 11-3 for a discussion of depositions.

14. See, e.g., United States v. Baker, 33 M.J. 788 (A.F.C.M.R. 1991) (in order for deposition testimony to be admitted, prosecution must show that it has exhausted every reasonable means of obtaining witness's live testimony; lack of subpoena over foreign witness is not in itself sufficient to establish unavailability). See generally 3 A.L.R.4th 601 (1981). See also § 11-3(C), for a discussion of introducing depositions at trial.

15. See, e.g., United States v. Hampton, 33 M.J. 21 (C.M.A. 1991) (trial judge did not err in admitting videotaped deposition of unavailable victim where it was clear that she would not comply with any attempts to obtain her testimony).

16. See § 11-2(A)(4).

17. See § 15-4(A).

18. R.C.M. 703(b)(3). See United States v. Valenzuela-Bernal, 458 U.S. 858 (1982); United States v. Bennett, 12 M.J. 463 (C.M.A. 1982); United States v. Daniels, 23 C.M.A. 94, 48 C.M.R. 655 (1974). In United States v. Harris, 24 M.J. 622 (A.C.M.R. 1987), the court held that the term "abate" does not mean that the court-martial proceedings are terminated and that charges must therefore be re-referred. The court said that, instead, the term connotes a period of continuance. In this particular case, the trial judge had abated the proceedings while the convening authority decided whether to grant immunity to a defense witness.

19. R.C.M. 703(b)(3).

20. Id. See generally United States v. Cottle, 14 M.J. 260 (C.M.A. 1982) (by waiting to request witness, counsel assumes the risk of unavailability).

21. R.C.M. 703(d). In United States v. Gonzales, 39 M.J. 459 (C.M.A. 1994), citing United States v. Allen, 31 M.J. 572 (N.M.C.M.R. 1990), the court cited three-step test for determining whether defense has shown necessity for employment of expert under Garries v. United States, 22 M.J. 288 (C.M.A. 1988): First, why is expert assistance needed; second, what would requested expert accomplish; and third, what reasons has the defense given for its inability to present evidence that expert would be able to develop.

United States v. Robinson, 39 M.J. 88 (C.M.A. 1994) (accused did not demonstrate necessity for conducting secretor test, at government expense, on urine sample; court indicated that right to expert assistance extends from investigative stage through appeal; in dissent, Judge Cox said that this case represented the golden rule: He who has the gold, rules); United States v. Tharpe, 38 M.J. 8 (C.M.A. 1993) (court rejected argument that accused was entitled to appointment of expert to assist him in showing that defense counsel was ineffective in not presenting evidence that he was abused as a child).

Because the prosecution is generally able to rely on government experts, such as laboratory technicians,[22] the *Manual* provision potentially levels the playing field and equalizes the ability of the defense to obtain its witnesses by employing, at government expense, civilian experts. The defense is always free to incur at its own expense a civilian expert. But the costs of doing so may be assumed by the government if the counsel submits a written request to the convening authority detailing why employment of an expert is necessary and the expected costs involved.[23] If the convening authority declines the request, it may be renewed before the military judge in the form of a motion.[24] If the judge grants the motion or finds that the counsel is entitled to a substitute, the judge may abate the trial if the government fails to comply.[25] Unless the employment has been approved in advance, the government is only required to pay the standard mileage and witness's fees paid to any other civilian witness.[26]

United States v. Thomas, 41 M.J. 873 (N.M.Ct.Crim.App. 1995) (accused failed to show that request for handwriting expert was necessary; counsel had not interviewed government expert, had done only a cursory search of issue, and could not show what any expert assistance would accomplish in case); United States v. Gray, 37 M.J. 730 (A.C.M.R. 1992) (judge did not abuse discretion in denying defense request for funding for an independent investigator; CID agent was assigned to defense team to assist in investigation). *See, e.g.,* United States v. Van Horn, 26 M.J. 434 (C.M.A. 1988) (accused was entitled to expert witness in drug case); United States v. Hagen, 25 M.J. 78 (C.M.A. 1987), *cert. denied,* 108 S. Ct. 1015 (1988) (judge ordered production of defense expert witness who had examined and treated the defendant; government-paid fees usually paid in federal courts to expert witnesses).

United States v. Mustafa, 22 M.J. 165 (C.M.A. 1986) (accused entitled to qualified psychiatrist or psychologist for purpose of presenting insanity defense without regard to indigency); United States v. Johnson, 22 C.M.A. 424, 47 C.M.R. 402 (1973); Hutson v. United States, 19 C.M.A. 437, 42 C.M.R. 39 (1970).

Cf. United States v. Fontenot, 26 M.J. 559 (A.C.M.R. 1988) (request properly denied where accused was examined by competent panel of experts and he failed to show need for additional witness); United States v. Kinsler, 24 M.J. 855 (A.C.M.R. 1987) (counsel's request for an expert witness amounted, in the court's view, to a fishing expedition; counsel was not sure what an expert would say about the evidence and wanted someone to review it to determine if in fact some justiciable problem was present); United States v. Garries, 19 M.J. 845 (A.F.C.M.R. 1985) (request for independent investigator properly denied by trial judge).

See generally Gunn, "Supplementing the Defense Team: A Primer on Requesting and Obtaining Expert Assistance, " 39 A.F. L. REV. 143 (1996). *See generally* Hahn, "Voluntary and Involuntary Expert Testimony in Courts-Martial," 106 MIL. L. REV. 77 (1984).

22. R.C.M. 703(d) on its face applies to both the prosecution and defense. But in practice it will probably almost always involve requests by the defense because the prosecution will normally rely on experts already under federal employment. And the Drafters' Analysis to R.C.M. 703(d) indicates that the provision does not apply to such experts. However, there might conceivably be a case in which the prosecution wishes to employ a civilian expert. In that instance R.C.M. 703(d) should apply.

23. R.C.M. 703(d). The defense must make this request *before* employing the expert. Under the *Manual* there is no provision for the government to ratify previously accomplished employment.

24. United States v. Van Horn, 26 M.J. 434 (C.M.A. 1988). The motion could be in the form of a motion for appropriate relief in the nature of a request for employment of an expert. *See generally* Chapter 13.

25. R.C.M. 703(d).

26. *Id.* The standard travel fees are set out in Department of Defense Travel Regulations.

§ 11-2(A)(3)   PRODUCTION OF WITNESSES AND EVIDENCE   § 11-2(A)(3)

The key here is that the convening authority is free to make available any of the government's resources as an alternative.[27] If the defense is not content with the alternative, it bears the burden of demonstrating that the employment of a civilian expert is *necessary*.[28] Necessity may exist, for example, if the defense can show that the government designated expert is not an adequate substitute because that expert and the one requested by the defense

---

27. R.C.M. 703(d). *See also* United States v. Guitard, 28 M.J. 952 (N.M.C.M.R. 1989) (government's alternative was not adequate where it merely offered the "availability" of its own expert witness). *Cf.* United States v. Robinson, 24 M.J. 649 (N.M.C.M.R. 1987), where the court stated:

We believe that the Sixth Amendment right of an accused to have compulsory process for obtaining witnesses in his favor demands that an "adequate substitute" for a particular requested expert witness at trial not only possess similar professional qualifications as the requested witness, but also be willing to testify to the same conclusions and opinions. To find otherwise would be to effectively foreclose the accused from obtaining favorable expert testimony to counter Government experts testifying against him at trial and would surely amount to a denial of "raw materials integral to the building of an effective defense." Ake v. Oklahoma, 470 U.S. 68, 77 (1985).

24 M.J. at 652. The court did not say, however, that this necessarily means that the government must employ a civilian expert to present this raw material.

28. *Id.* United States v. Kelly, 39 M.J. 235 (C.M.A. 1994) (defense failed to show necessity in light of fact that counsel was well aware of issues in drug case and had expert available for telephonic conference); United States v. Hagen, 25 M.J. 78 (C.M.A. 1987) (expert witness can become necessary after examining and treating accused over period of time); United States v. Ruth, 42 M.J. 730 (Army Ct.Crim.App. 1995) (defense failed to show that assistance of law professor re handwriting analysis was necessary).

United States v. Hargrove, 33 M.J. 515 (A.F.C.M.R. 1991) (testimony from investigator concerning allegations of tampering in urinalysis testing was neither necessary nor relevant; accused was not denied fair trial by failure of judge to order production of that witness); United States v. Gray, 32 M.J. 730 (A.C.M.R. 1991) (accused failed to show need for employment of mental health experts).

United States v. Huerta, 31 M.J. 640 (N.M.C.M.R. 1990) (defense failed to specify as to why expert assistance was required; defense is not entitled to experts of its own choosing at government expense).

United States v. Mann, 30 M.J. 639 (N.M.C.M.R. 1990) (defense failed to show that its requested expert in child abuse case was necessary; court noted that government funds are not required to provide funding to lay groundwork for an expert witness request).

In United States v. True, 28 M.J. 1057 (N.M.C.M.R. 1989), the court distinguished United States v. Robinson, 24 M.J. 649 (N.M.C.M.R. 1987), and relied upon United States v. Garries, 22 M.J. 288 (C.M.A. 1986), in concluding that the trial court erred in denying the defense request for a particular investigative assistant in a drug case. The issue in *Robinson*, said the court, was whether the offered government expert was an adequate substitute, while *Garries* focused on the question of whether due process required appointment of an investigator to prepare for trial. The test is whether the defense can establish on the record that it is unable to prepare for trial without such assistance.

Cf. United States v. Tornowski, 29 M.J. 578 (A.F.C.M.R. 1989) (accused is not entitled to demand that a particular individual be designated).

It is not clear just what sort of a showing the party must make. It will probably not suffice for defense counsel, for example, to simply argue that the government expert is biased toward the government, i.e., his employer. United States v. Garries, 19 M.J. 845 (A.F.C.M.R. 1985), aff'd, 22 M.J. 288 (C.M.A. 1986). *Cf.* Marshall v. United States, 423 F.2d 1315 (10th Cir. 1970).

hold divergent scientific views.[29] An accused, however, is not entitled to the "best witness."[30]

In determining what, if any, communications between the defense counsel, the accused, and the expert may be confidential and privileged, the military courts have drawn a distinction between experts who serve as "consultants" to the defense and experts who will testify as "witnesses."[31] In the case of the former, production of the expert is a matter of due process in order to assist the defense in preparation for trial.[32] This type of expert is considered a part of the defense team and under the attorney-client privilege,[33] any communications between the expert, the accused, and the defense counsel would be privileged.[34] Normally this type of expert may not be interviewed by the prosecution unless he or she will also testify at the trial.[35] An expert witness, whether defense or prosecution, may be called by either side[36] and is subject to pretrial interviews[37] and cross-examination at trial.[38]

§ 11-2(A)(4). Adequate Substitutes for Testimony.

There is clearly a strong preference for live testimony at a trial.[39] A live witness can be observed and otherwise vague answers probed and tested under oath. Even assuming that a witness's testimony is relevant and necessary for the trial, the military courts and the *Manual* recognize that counsel may have to settle for an adequate substitute for the witness's live testimony.[40] Substitutes or alternatives would include depositions,[41] stipulations of fact

---

29. United States v. Van Horn, 26 M.J. 434 (C.M.A. 1988); United States v. Robinson, 43 M.J. 501 (A.F.Ct.Crim.App. 1995) (burden rests on defense to show that experts hold divergent scientific views).
30. United States v. Robinson, 43 M.J. 501 (A.F.Ct.Crim.App. 1995).
31. *See* United States v. Turner, 28 M.J. 487, 489 (C.M.A. 1989); United States v. King, 32 M.J. 709 (A.C.M.R. 1991) (R.C.M. 703 and MIL. R. EVID. 706 contain no privilege).
32. *See, e.g.*, United States v. Langston, 32 M.J. 894 (A.F.C.M.R. 1991) (good discussion of difference, *citing* Article 46 and United States v. Garries, 22 M.J. 288, 290 (C.M.A. 1986)).
33. *See* MIL. R. EVID. 502. *See generally* Saltzburg, Schinasi & Schlueter, *Military Rules of Evidence Manual* 544-55 (3d ed. 1991) (discussion of privilege).
34. *See* United States v. Turner, 28 M.J. 487 (C.M.A. 1989) (prosecutor's conversation with defense expert violated attorney-client privilege rule); United States v. Langston, 32 M.J. 894 (A.F.C.M.R. 1991).
35. United States v. Turner, 28 M.J. 487 (C.M.A. 1989); United States v. Langston, 32 M.J. 894 (A.F.C.M.R. 1991).
36. *See, e.g.*, MIL. R. EVID. 607.
37. United States v. Turner, 28 M.J. 487, n.3 (C.M.A. 1989) (court added in footnote that if expert is to be interviewed, he should be advised to be careful not to divulge any confidential communications between the defense counsel or the accused; further, defense counsel should be present during such interviews to ensure that the prosecutor does not inquire into such matters); United States v. Langston, 32 M.J. 894 (A.F.C.M.R. 1991).
38. *See* United States v. Langston, 32 M.J. 894 (A.F.C.M.R. 1991). MIL. R. EVID. 607, 611.
39. *See, e.g.*, United States v. Scott, 5 M.J. 431 (C.M.A. 1978) (live testimony is normally imperative to a fair proceeding).
40. *See* R.C.M. 703(b)(3). United States v. Courts, 9 M.J. 285 (C.M.A. 1980); United States v. Scott, 5 M.J. 431 (C.M.A. 1978); United States v. Tangpuz, 5 M.J. 426 (C.M.A. 1978).
41. R.C.M. 702. *See also* § 11-3.

and expected testimony,[42] affidavits,[43] and other written instruments that indicate what the witness would say. Unfortunately, there are no hard and fast rules for determining whether any of these alternatives would serve as an *adequate* substitute. In addressing this issue, military cases have indicated that the mode of presenting the evidence may be left to the discretion of the trial judge.[44] The judge in turn should consider whether under the circumstances[45] the proposed alternative diminishes the fairness of the proceedings.[46] For example, a stipulation of expected testimony would probably not be an adequate substitute for the live testimony of the only alibi witness.[47] A deposition or stipulation of fact might be an adequate substitute, however.

§ 11-2(B). Requests for Witnesses.

§ 11-2(B)(1). Defense Witnesses.

Unlike the federal system where the defendant must address a request for a witness to the trial court and establish indigency,[48] the military defendant's request for a witness at government expense is first submitted to the prosecutor.[49] Despite arguments that such a requirement cuts against the "equal opportunity" language of Article 46, U.C.M.J.,[50] the military courts have approved the role of the prosecutor in determining in the first instance whether a particular defense witness should be obtained at government expense.[51]

---

42. R.C.M. 811. *See* § 15-21. Stipulations of fact are preferred over stipulations of expected testimony. *See* United States v. Gonzalez, 16 M.J. 58 (C.M.A. 1983).
43. *See, e.g.,* R.C.M. 1001(c)(3) (proof of character by affidavit). *See also* Mil. R. Evid. 405(c).
44. United States v. Santiago-Davila, 26 M.J. 380 (C.M.A. 1988) (judge may consider the delay, difficulty, and cost involved in obtaining a videotaped deposition against the greater detail and effect of a videotaped deposition); United States v. Courts, 9 M.J. 285 (C.M.A. 1980); United States v. Scott, 5 M.J. 431 (C.M.A. 1978); United States v. Tangpuz, 5 M.J. 426 (C.M.A. 1978). *See also* Rule 611, Mil. R. Evid.
45. Circumstances that the judge might consider would be the issues presented in the case, whether the witness would testify on sentencing or on the merits, and whether the testimony would be merely cumulative or corroborative of other evidence. *See* United States v. Tangpuz, 5 M.J. 426 (C.M.A. 1978). In addition, the court might consider the degree of difficulty in obtaining the witness and the timing of the request. *See* United States v. Courts, 9 M.J. 285 (C.M.A. 1980).
46. United States v. Scott, 5 M.J. 431 (C.M.A. 1978).
47. *See, e.g.,* United States v. Meadow, 14 M.J. 1002 (A.C.M.R. 1982) (court should have ordered live witness to appear and testify about character of accused); United States v. Combs, 20 M.J. 441, 443 n.3 (C.M.A. 1985) (a stipulation of expected testimony is not an adequate substitute for a stipulation of fact). *See* United States v. Gonzalez, 16 M.J. 58 (C.M.A. 1983).
48. Fed. R. Crim. P. 17(b).
49. R.C.M. 703(c)(2)(A). *See, e.g.,* United States v. Johnson, 33 M.J. 855 (A.C.M.R. 1991) (defense counsel did not go through normal channels to request defense expert as a witness; counsel apparently hoped to keep witness's identity concealed until the last minute).
50. *See* § 11-2(A)(1).
51. *See, e.g.,* United States v. Vietor, 10 M.J. 69 (C.M.A. 1980) (ruling that MCM 1969, para. 115a, the precursor to R.C.M. 703, was not inconsistent with Article 46, U.C.M.J.).

The defense request must be written.[52] If the witness is being requested for the merits portion of the trial or will be testifying on an interlocutory matter, the request must include the following information:[53]

a. Name of the witness;
b. Telephone number, if known;
c. Address or location of the witness; and
d. Synopsis of expected testimony sufficient to show why it is relevant and necessary.[54]

If the witness is to testify during sentencing, the defense must add reasons why the personal appearance of the witness is required. Because the rules governing admission of evidence during the sentencing portion of the trial are more liberal,[55] the rules governing the production of defense witnesses at government expense are severely limited. R.C.M. 1001(e)(2) sets out a list of five factors that should be considered in deciding whether the witness should be produced.[56]

---

52. R.C.M. 703(c)(2)(A).
53. R.C.M. 703(c)(2)(B).
54. *Id. See supra* § 11-2(A)(1). United States v. Moore, 32 M.J. 56 (C.M.A. 1991) (request failed to include summary of expected testimony); United States v. Johnson, 36 M.J. 862 (A.C.M.R. 1993) (judge did not abuse discretion in denying request for defense witness; judge indicated that testimony would be cumulative and noted the lateness of the request); United States v. Gans, 23 M.J. 540 (A.C.M.R. 1986) (defense failed to provide identity of witness, provided no synopsis of expected testimony, and failed to demonstrate any efforts to learn of either).
55. Rule 1101(c), MIL. R. EVID.
56. R.C.M. 1001(e)(2) provides:

> (2) Limitations. A witness may be produced to testify during presentence proceeding through a subpoena or travel orders at Government expense only if
> (A) The testimony expected to be offered by the witness is necessary for consideration of a matter of substantial significance to a determination of an appropriate sentence, including evidence necessary to resolve an alleged inaccuracy or dispute as to a material fact;
> (B) The weight or credibility of the testimony is of substantial significance to the determination of an appropriate sentence;
> (C) The other party refuses to enter into a stipulation of fact containing the matters to which the witness is expected to testify, except in an extraordinary case when such a stipulation of fact would be an insufficient substitute for the testimony;
> (D) Other forms of evidence, such as oral depositions, written interrogatories, or former testimony would not be sufficient to meet the needs of the court-martial in the determination of an appropriate sentence; and
> (E) The significance of the personal appearance of the witness to the determination of an appropriate sentence, when balanced against the practical difficulties of producing the witness, the timing of the request for production of the witness, the potential delay in the presentencing proceeding that may be caused by the production of the witness, and the likelihood of significant interference with military operational deployment, mission accomplishment, or essential training.

United States v. Mitchell, 41 M.J. 512 (Army Ct.Crim.App. 1994) (denial of defense request to fund travel for chief of chaplains, a general officer, to testify during sentencing, was not abuse of discretion; court noted that there was no showing that case was extraordinary so that stipulation would not suffice, and that judge permitted defense to draft strong stipulation which set out witness qualifications and fact that government had denied travel funds for witness).

The defense request must be submitted in timely fashion,[57] and failure to do so may result in the denial of a motion to produce the witness on that ground alone.[58]

There is obviously a thin line marking what the defense must show without unfairly disclosing the contents of everything the witness would say. The test should be whether the defense has presented enough information so that a judge reviewing the request could reasonably determine whether the witness' appearance was necessary.[59]

The defense must make a legitimate assertion.[60] Mere representations by the accused as to what the witness will say may not suffice.[61] Likewise, speculation and "hoped-for" testimony will not be adequate.[62] The cases further make clear that the defense must have made some good faith effort to communicate with the witness.[63]

If the prosecutor believes that the witnesses requested are not required and denies the request, the defense may raise the issue with the military judge through a motion.[64] The convening authority need not be involved in this

---

57. R.C.M. 703(c)(2)(C). United States v. Reveles, 41 M.J. 388 (1995) (no abuse of discretion in denying request for military pathologist; where, inter alia, request was untimely); United States v. Johnson, 33 M.J. 855 (A.C.M.R. 1991) (defense counsel did not go through normal channels to request defense expert as a witness; counsel apparently hoped to keep witness's identity quiet until the last minute); United States v. Moore, 32 M.J. 56 (C.M.A. 1991) (judge did not abuse discretion in denying defense request for three sentencing witnesses that was made 5 days before trial and without a summary of each witness' expected testimony); United States v. Brown, 28 M.J. 644 (A.C.M.R. 1989) (trial court committed reversible error in denying accused's request on grounds of timeliness where it was filed almost 48 hours before trial, the witness was a three-hour drive away, and the witness was important to the defense. The court noted that the "touchstone" for determining whether a request is timely is whether it was delayed unnecessarily so as to interfere with the orderly prosecution of the case); United States v. Hawkins, 6 C.M.A. 135, 19 C.M.R. 261, 268 (1955); United States v. Robinson, 24 M.J. 649 (N.M.C.M.R. 1987) (accused's request for expert witness on day of trial was for good cause where defense had just discovered evidence that made expert necessary and where little inconvenience would be caused to the prosecution). The military judge may also set a deadline for submitting witness requests. *See also* United States v. Cottle, 14 M.J. 260 (C.M.A. 1982); United States v. Mitchell, 11 M.J. 907 (A.C.M.R. 1981).

58. R.C.M. 703(c)(2)(C). United States v. Johnson, 36 M.J. 862 (A.C.M.R. 1993) (judge did not abuse discretion in denying request for defense witness; judge noted the lateness of the request); United States v. Ford, 29 M.J. 597 (A.C.M.R. 1989) (court noted that denial of a continuance to obtain a witness should be avoided for good cause shown).

59. United States v. Dehart, 33 M.J. 58 (C.M.A. 1991) (military judge's failure to order presence of defense witness was harmless error where judge asked defense counsel to provide more information about what witness would say and counsel failed to do so).

60. United States v. Fisher, 24 M.J. 358 (C.M.A. 1987) (case reversed where defense denied witnesses who could have testified that accused had not been seen using drugs); United States v. Lucas, 5 M.J. 167 (C.M.A. 1978).

61. United States v. Carey, 1 M.J. 761 (A.F.C.M.R. 1975).

62. United States v. Young, 49 C.M.R. 133 (A.F.C.M.R. 1974). *Cf.* United States v. Christian, 6 M.J. 624 (A.C.M.R. 1978) (parties agreed that if witness had anything to offer he would support one of the parties).

63. *See* United States v. Vietor, 10 M.J. 69 (C.M.A. 1980).

64. R.C.M. 703(c)(2)(D). *See* § 13-5(1). United States v. Allen, 31 M.J. 572 (N.M.C.M.R. 1990) (judge's refusal to require production of high-ranking Navy judge to testify on issue of unlawful command influence was harmless error); United States v. Minaya, 30 M.J. 1179 (A.F.C.M.R.

process unless it appears that high costs would be involved in obtaining the witness.[65] In that case, the prosecutor should so inform the convening authority who may take those costs into consideration in deciding whether to dispose of the charges through some other forum.[66]

If the judge grants the defense motion for production of the witness, the government is bound to produce the witness or face the prospect of the judge abating the proceedings.[67] The trial judge's decision to deny a defense request for a witness will be measured for an abuse of discretion.[68]

For a discussion on granting immunity to defense witnesses, see § 11-(2)(E)(3).

§ 11-2(B)(2). Prosecution Witnesses.

There is no procedure for the prosecution to "request" witnesses. Instead the prosecution is entitled to obtain those witnesses that it considers relevant and necessary.[69] The only check that the defense has on that decision is to object at trial on the grounds that the prosecution witnesses are not relevant and necessary.[70]

§ 11-2(C). Production of Military Witnesses.

Obtaining the presence of a military witness is generally not a problem, especially if the individual is at or near the installation where the court-martial is being held. Normally, all that is required is that the witness's commander be informed of the time and date of trial and asked that any necessary orders be issued to ensure that the witness be present.[71] Failure of a military

---

1990) (judge did not err in ruling that government had made every reasonable good faith effort to produce defense witnesses).

65. R.C.M. 703(c)(2)(D) Discussion.

66. *See supra* § 6-2.

67. R.C.M. 703(c)(2)(D). United States v. Eiland, 39 M.J. 566 (N.M.C.M.R. 1993) (judge did not abuse discretion in abating proceedings and declining to accept government's proposed stipulation of testimony as substitute).

68. United States v. Reveles, 41 M.J. 388 (1995) (no abuse of discretion in denying request for military pathologist; defense was not able to show necessity of witness who was great distance away; request was untimely, and defense failed to show that other, closer, experts could assist); United States v. Dehart, 33 M.J. 58 (C.M.A. 1991) (military judge's failure to order presence of defense witness was harmless error where judge asked defense counsel to provide more information and counsel failed to do so); United States v. Johnson, 36 M.J. 862 (A.C.M.R. 1993) (judge did not abuse discretion in denying request for defense witness; judge indicated that testimony would be cumulative and noted the lateness of the request); United States v. Mow, 22 M.J. 906 (N.M.C.M.R. 1986) (error to deny continuance to obtain important witness); United States v. Jones, 20 M.J. 919 (N.M.C.M.R. 1985) (judge abused his discretion in denying a defense request for a character witness); United States v. Rappaport, 19 M.J. 708 (A.F.C.M.R. 1984) (judge did not abuse discretion in denying defense motion to compel attendance of witness whose statements were vague, uncertain, and not relevant to the issues in the case).

69. R.C.M. 703(c)(1).

70. The defense could raise the issue through a motion *in limine* to block the witness's testimony. *See generally* § 13-5(L).

71. R.C.M. 703(e)(1).

witness to appear may be punishable under either Article 134, U.C.M.J.[72] or for violation of a lawful order if the witness has been specifically ordered to testify.[73] Where the military witness is located at a distant installation, sufficient time, usually 48 hours, should be allowed for travel preparation by the witness.[74] Note that the government generally lacks the power to hold a military witness on active duty who has reached the end of his tour.[75]

§ 11-2(D). Production of Civilian Witnesses.

§ 11-2(D)(1). General.

Production of civilian witnesses for either side may be a little more complicated than obtaining the presence of military witnesses, especially if the witness does not wish to testify before the court-martial. If the witness is agreeable to testifying voluntarily, no subpoena need be issued.[76] At the completion of the testimony the witness will receive standard mileage and witness fees.[77] As a part of their employment, Department of Defense civilian employees may be directed by their supervisors to appear at a court-martial.[78] If the civilian witness will not appear voluntarily, it may be necessary to issue a subpoena and serve it upon the witness.[79] Failure to testify may result in either federal criminal action or issuance of a warrant of attachment.[80]

§ 11-2(D)(2). Use of the Subpoena.

Article 46, U.C.M.J.[81] states that the process to obtain witnesses and evidence shall be similar to that used in federal criminal trials.[82] To that end, the Manual for Courts-Martial lays out specific guidance on the issuance and service of subpoenas to obtain the appearance of civilian witnesses at courts-martial.[83]

Although the prosecutor (trial counsel)[84] prepares the subpoena and issues it for both prosecution and defense witnesses, a summary court-martial[85] may also issue one. Subpoenas may also be issued by an officer detailed to take a

---

72. See MCM, Part IV, para. 108.
73. See supra § 2-4.
74. R.C.M. 703(e)(1) Discussion.
75. United States v. Wheeler, 21 C.M.A. 468, 45 C.M.R. 242 (1972).
76. R.C.M. 703(e)(2)(A) Discussion.
77. The applicable fees are set out in the Department of Defense Pay and Entitlement's Manual.
78. R.C.M. 703(e)(2)(A) Discussion.
79. See infra § 11-2(D)(2).
80. See infra § 11-2(D)(3).
81. See Appendix 3.
82. See FED. R. CRIM. P. 17.
83. R.C.M. 703(e)(2).
84. R.C.M. 703(e)(2)(C).
85. Id.

deposition, see § 11-3, and by the president of a court of inquiry.[86] For a sample subpoena form see Appendix 15. The subpoena may also direct that the witness appear with designated evidence such as records or physical evidence,[87] but subpoenas may not be used to direct a witness to appear at any pretrial interviews with counsel.[88]

The subpoena may be served anywhere within the United States, its territories, and possessions.[89] Thus, a civilian witness residing in the United States could clearly be forced to testify before a court-martial convened within the United States.[90] But military courts do not have the power to order a civilian resident of the United States to appear before a court-martial held abroad.[91] Nor may a foreign national be subpoenaed to testify before a court-martial.[92] In that case military authorities must rely upon international agreements with the host country.[93] It is not clear whether a United States citizen residing abroad may be compelled to appear before a court-martial convened in the United States.[94]

Service of the subpoena is usually informal — the subpoena may be mailed by the prosecutor with a return envelope enclosed.[95] If more formal service is desirable, such as when it appears that the witness may not appear, the subpoena should be personally served by a person subject to the U.C.M.J. along with travel orders and fees.[96]

A witness who feels that compliance with the subpoena would be unreasonable or oppressive may request the convening authority (before referral of charges) or the military judge for relief in the form of modification or withdrawal.[97]

---

86. Id.
87. R.C.M. 703(e)(2)(B).
88. R.C.M. 703(e)(2)(B) (Contents).
89. R.C.M. 703(e)(2)(E).
90. See Art. 46, U.C.M.J.
91. Citing United States v. Tiede, 86 F.R.D. 227 (U.S. Court for Berlin), the court in United States v. Ortiz, 35 M.J. 391 (C.M.A. 1992), held that a civilian witness physically present in Berlin is subject to United States jurisdiction and may be subpoenaed. United States v. Santiago-Davila, 26 M.J. 380 (C.M.A. 1988); United States v. Crockett, 21 M.J. 423 (C.M.A. 1986); United States v. Bennett, 12 M.J. 463 (C.M.A. 1982).
92. See, e.g., United States v. Daniels, 48 C.M.R. 655 (C.M.A. 1974). Cf. R.C.M. 703(e)(2)(E), which provides that in occupied enemy territory, a commander may compel the attendance of a civilian witness.
93. See R.C.M. 703(e)(2)(E).
94. See United States v. Bennett, 12 M.J. 463 (C.M.A. 1982); United States v. Daniels, 48 C.M.R. 655 (C.M.A. 1974). Cf. 28 U.S.C. § 1783, which permits United States courts to obtain the presence of United States residents or citizens residing abroad.
95. R.C.M. 703(e)(2)(D) Discussion.
96. Id. Although the Manual permits informal service, where a witness does not appear, the steps used or not used to obtain the witness will probably have an impact on whether the witness is declared "unavailable." In United States v. Burns, 27 M.J. 92 (C.M.A. 1988), for example, the case was tried under the 1969 Manual. In holding that the prosecution had failed to show sufficient efforts to obtain the witness, the court noted that the 1969 Manual had required personal service.
97. R.C.M. 703(e)(2)(F).

§ 11-2(D)(3). Sanctions for Failure to Appear.

If the civilian witness refuses to appear before the court-martial, the military judge may issue a written *warrant of attachment,* which is a legal order directing an official[98] to bring the witness before the court.[99] Before the judge may issue the warrant, he must be satisfied that probable cause exists to believe that:

    a. The witness was properly served with a properly executed subpoena;
    b. Appropriate fees and mileage were tendered;
    c. The witness is material;
    d. The witness has refused or willfully neglected to appear; and
    e. The witness has no valid excuse.[100]

The official designated to execute the warrant may use force, other than deadly force, to bring the witness to the court.[101]

In lieu of, or in addition to the warrant of attachment, a federal criminal complaint may be filed by a United States Attorney against the witness in accordance with the provisions of Article 47, U.C.M.J.[102]

§ 11-2(E). Immunity for Witnesses.

§ 11-2(E)(1). General.

If it appears that a witness has a legitimate claim to the privilege against self-incrimination,[103] the criminal consequence, which might otherwise face the witness, can be removed by granting immunity. The two commonly recognized types of immunity in military practice are *transactional* immunity and *testimonial* immunity.[104] Under the former, the witness is promised that in

---

98. The warrant may be executed by a United States Marshall or any other individual at least 18 years old. R.C.M. 703(e)(2)(G)(iv).

99. R.C.M. 703(e)(2)(G) Discussion. United States v. Hinton, 21 M.J. 267 (C.M.A. 1986) (judge had power to compel attendance of civilian witness through warrant of attachment). *See generally* Lederer, "Warrants of Attachment—Forcibly Compelling the Attendance of Witnesses," 98 Mil. L. Rev. 1 (1982).

100. R.C.M. 703(e)(2)(G)(ii).

101. R.C.M. 703(e)(2)(G)(iv). United States v. Williams, 23 M.J. 724 (A.F.C.M.R. 1986) (trial judge erred in not issuing warrant of attachment where important defense witness refused to appear after second subpoena was issued).

102. The prosecution rests in the federal courts. Unlike the warrant of attachment, which is used to obtain evidence, the criminal prosecution serves as punishment for failure to appear to produce evidence. *See* R.C.M. 703(e)(2)(G)(i) Discussion. United States v. Hines, 23 M.J. 125 (C.M.A. 1986) (court indicated in footnote 13 that, in some cases, it might be appropriate to incarcerate a recalcitrant witness).

103. In military practice a witness is entitled to self-incrimination protections under the Fifth Amendment, Article 31, U.C.M.J., and Rule 301, Mil. R. Evid. *See supra* § 5-2(B). *See generally* Saltzburg, Schinasi & Schlueter, *Military Rules of Evidence Manual* (3d ed. 1991).

104. R.C.M. 704(a). *See* United States v. Tagert, 11 M.J. 677 (N.M.C.M.R. 1981), for a sample of transactional immunity. *See generally* Green, "Grants of Immunity and Military Law, 1971-1976," 73 Mil. L. Rev. 1 (1976).

return for testimony there will be no prosecution on charges that might otherwise be brought against the witness. This is the broadest form of immunity.

The second type, testimonial immunity, is sometimes referred to as "use plus fruits" or use immunity. It is the constitutional minimum[105] and promises that in return for testimony, the government will not use that testimony against the witness in any later prosecution. Nor will any derivative use be made of the testimony. This is the preferred type of immunity in military practice, because it affords the government the opportunity to obtain otherwise protected testimony and yet retain the option to prosecute the witness. But if the immunized witness is later tried, the prosecution bears a heavy burden of demonstrating that no use or derivative use has been made of the accused's immunized testimony.[106] The safest way for the prosecution to obtain immunized testimony and also prosecute the witness is to prosecute the witness first. An alternative is to obtain all of the evidence that it would use against the witness and then have the evidence certified and sealed *before* the witness testifies under the grant of immunity. At the later hearing to determine whether any derivative use will be made, the prosecution can present the "untainted" evidence it intends to use.

Regardless of the type of immunity, it is usually the general court-martial convening authority who grants the immunity, which is in the form of a written order to testify.[107] If the witness is not subject to the U.C.M.J., the grant of immunity must either come from the United States Attorney General or from the convening authority, who must have obtained explicit approval from the Attorney General to do so.[108] In either event, the prosecution is almost always required to coordinate the grant of immunity with federal authorities[109] in order to ensure that the grant will not jeopardize any federal

---

105. Kastigar v. United States, 406 U.S. 441 (1972). Rule 301(c)(1), MIL. R. EVID.

106. New Jersey v. Portash, 440 U.S. 450 (1979); Kastigar v. United States, 406 U.S. 441 (1972); United States v. Garrett, 24 M.J. 413 (C.M.A. 1987) (prosecution satisfactorily showed that the evidence that it used at accused's retrial was not tainted by his immunized testimony given after the first conviction); United States v. Gardner, 22 M.J. 28 (C.M.A. 1986) (trial not tainted by assistant trial counsel's earlier exposure to accused's immunized testimony); United States v. Whitehead, 5 M.J. 294 (C.M.A. 1978); United States v. Rivera, 1 M.J. 107 (C.M.A. 1975); United States v. Daley, 3 M.J. 541 (A.C.M.R. 1977). *Cf.* United States v. Lucas, 19 M.J. 773 (A.F.C.M.R. 1984) (accused waived issue of challenging the prosecution's use of his prior immunized testimony by not raising it at trial).

107. If anyone in the military is to grant immunity, a general court-martial convening authority is the only official authorized to do so. Any other attempts are void except to the extent that the process may require enforcement that amounts to *de facto* immunity. *See* Cooke v. Orser, 12 M.J. 335 (C.M.A. 1982); United States v. Brown, 13 M.J. 253 (C.M.A. 1982); United States v. Whipple, 4 M.J. 773 (C.G.C.M.R. 1978).

At this point military judges have no authority to grant immunity to a witness. *Cf.* United States v. Villines, 13 M.J. 46 (C.M.A. 1982) (C.J. Everett, dissenting).

The convening authority's power may not be delegated, but it may be limited by a superior commander. R.C.M. 704(c)(3).

For a sample grant of immunity, see Appendix 11.

108. 18 U.S.C. § 6004. R.C.M. 704(c)(2). *See* United States v. Andreas, 14 M.J. 483 (C.M.A. 1983).

109. R.C.M. 704(c)(1). This is especially true where the testimony relates to a federal offense that could be prosecuted in a federal district court. Unless the Department of Justice indicates no

§ 11-2(E)(2)   PRODUCTION OF WITNESSES AND EVIDENCE   § 11-2(E)(2)

plans to prosecute the witness.[110] In some cases it will be necessary also to coordinate the grant with other service officials or the Department of Defense.[111] Because a military or federal grant of immunity will not bar a state prosecution,[112] prior coordination with state authorities is generally not required, although it is desirable in order to maintain good relations with civilian law enforcement and prosecutors.

The grant of immunity removes the threat of incrimination from the witness and thus the witness can be compelled, over objection, to testify. Failure to do so may result in criminal or administrative sanctions.[113] The grant should only require that the witness will testify truthfully. It should not spell out the contents of the testimony that the witness will give.[114]

Note that a grant of immunity does not bar later prosecution for false swearing, perjury, or making false official statements.[115]

§ 11-2(E)(2). Immunity for Prosecution Witnesses.

Where it is necessary to grant immunity to a prosecution witness, the trial counsel will generally accomplish any necessary coordination with federal or state authorities[116] and prepare (1) a memorandum explaining why a grant is necessary[117] and (2) a proposed grant. Assuming that the grant is made, the

---

interest in the matter, the Attorney General should be asked to grant immunity. R.C.M. 704(c)(1) Discussion. *See also* AR 27-10, para. 2-4 for Army procedures for coordination with the Department of Justice.

110. Because federal and military courts are of the same sovereign, military grants of immunity are fully binding on the federal courts. *See* Article 76, U.C.M.J.

111. *See* 704(c)(3) Discussion, which notes that DOD Directive 1355.1 (21 July 1981) requires prior coordination with the DOD general counsel where the proposed grant involves "espionage, subversion, aiding the enemy, sabotage, spying, or violation of rules concerning classified information or the foreign relations of the United States."

See also AR 27-10, para. 2-4 for detailed guidance on the procedures to be used for coordinating with the Department of Justice.

112. The military grant will generally bar use of the immunized testimony in a state trial. Murphy v. Waterfront Comm'n, 378 U.S. 52 (1964).

113. For example, a military witness could be prosecuted under one of several "disobedience" offenses. *See* Chapter 2. There is some limited authority to the effect that the witness could be held in contempt. *See* United States v. Croley, 50 C.M.R. 899 (A.F.C.M.R. 1975).

114. *See* R.C.M. 704(d) Discussion. United States v. Martinez, 19 M.J. 744 (A.C.M.R. 1984) (the accused generally has no standing to object to the CA's grant of immunity to a particular witness even if the grant is defective. An exception exists where the alleged defects create a likelihood that the accused was denied due process, for example, where the witnesses were encouraged not to tell the truth).

115. R.C.M. 705(b). United States v. Olivero, 39 M.J. 246 (C.M.A. 1994) (accused prosecuted for committing perjury at Article 32 Investigation after being granted immunity; conviction reversed for lack of direct evidence of perjury).

116. *See supra* § 11-2(B)(1).

117. The *Manual* indicates that immunity should be

…granted only when testimony or other information from the person is necessary to the public interest, including the needs of good order and discipline, and when the person has refused or is likely to refuse to testify or provide other information on the basis of the privilege against self-incrimination.

prosecution is required to notify the defense of the grant and serve a copy of it before arraignment or within a reasonable time before the witness testifies.[118] The prosecution need not spell out the reasons for the grant of immunity, and the notice may be waived by the defense.[119] If the prosecution fails to provide timely notice, the judge may determine what relief is appropriate.[120]

Although earlier cases had ruled that a grant of immunity or promise of clemency automatically disqualified the convening authority from taking post-trial action on the case,[121] more recent case law has removed that barrier.[122] A similar disability has been removed with regard to any staff judge advocate who may have advised the convening authority on the grant of immunity.[123]

§ 11-2(E)(3). Immunity for Defense Witnesses.

In recent years there has been a growing trend toward granting *testimonial* or *use* immunity to defense witnesses who have evidence to offer in support of the accused but fear that what they say will in some way incriminate them.[124] In effect, the issue of granting such immunity presents a balance of the accused's right to compulsory process and due process, the witness's right not to incriminate himself, and the government's interest in prosecuting the accused and the witness.

The federal courts have split on the standard to be applied in determining whether the government can be required to immunize a defense witness, and thus jeopardize a possible prosecution of that witness. The leading federal case seems to be *Virgin Islands v. Smith*,[125] where the court said that a defense witness could be judicially immunized[126] where it appeared that the government had failed to grant statutory immunity in an attempt to deliberately

---

R.C.M. 704(a) Discussion.

118. Rule 301(c)(2), MIL. R. EVID. United States v. Webster, 1 M.J. 216 (C.M.A. 1975); United States v. Lamar, 29 M.J. 889 (A.C.M.R. 1989) (reversible error not to give notice); United States v. Matthews, 13 M.J. 501 (A.C.M.R. 1982).

119. United States v. Carroll, 4 M.J. 674 (N.C.M.R. 1977).

120. United States v. Saylor, 6 M.J. 647 (N.C.M.R. 1978).

121. United States v. White, 10 C.M.A. 63, 27 C.M.R. 137 (1958); United States v. Hillmon, 2 M.J. 830 (A.C.M.R. 1976); United States v. Espiet-Betancourt, 1 M.J. 91 (C.M.A. 1975) (subordinate's grant disqualified convening authority).

122. United States v. Newman, 14 M.J. 474 (C.M.A. 1983); United States v. Turcsik, 13 M.J. 442; United States v. Walters, 30 M.J. 1290 (N.M.C.M.R. 1990) (convening authority's grant of transactional immunity to prosecution witness did not disqualify him from acting on the case).

123. United States v. Decker, 15 M.J. 416 (C.M.A. 1983).

124. *See generally* Myhre, "Defense Witness Immunity and the Due Process Standard: A Proposed Amendment to the Manual for Courts-Martial," 136 M.I. L. REV. 69 (1992); Western, "The Compulsory Process Clause," 73 MICH. L. REV. 73 (1974); Comment, "Defense Witness Immunity and the Right to a Fair Trial," 129 U. PA. L. REV. 377 (1980); Note, "The Due Process Right to Immunization of Defense Witnesses," 22 B.C. L. REV. 299 (1981); Note, "The Sixth Amendment Right to Have Use Immunity Granted to Defense Witnesses," 91 HARV. L. REV. 1266 (1978).

125. 615 F.2d 964 (3d Cir. 1980).

126. *Cf.* United States v. Lenz, 616 F.2d 960 (6th Cir. 1980) (courts are without power to grant immunity; only the executive possesses that authority).

distort the judicial process or where the accused could show that the witness was available, his proffered testimony was clearly exculpatory and essential, and there was no strong governmental interest against granting immunity.[127]

The military standard set out in the *Manual*,[128] apparently follows the majority federal rule, and not the minority rule in *Virgin Islands v. Smith*. The *Manual* indicates that the decision whether to grant immunity in all cases rests with the general court-martial convening authority[129] and that immunity for a defense witness may be appropriate where certain conditions are met: The defense should be prepared to show that, first, the witness intends to invoke the privilege against self-incrimination, as permitted by law, if called to the stand to testify.[130] Second, the government has engaged in discriminatory use of immunity to obtain a tactical advantage,[131] or the government has, through overreaching, forced the witness to invoke the privilege against self-incrimination.[132] And third, the defense should show that the witness' testimony is clearly exculpatory, noncumulative, cannot be obtained from another source, and would not be offered merely on the issue of another witness' credibility.[133]

---

127. Virgin Islands v. Smith, 615 F.2d at 972.
128. R.C.M. 704(e). The standard finds its genesis in United States v. Villines, 13 M.J. 46 (C.M.A. 1982), which includes a comprehensive discussion of the topic. Although in *Villines* the court could not agree on the extent of the judge's authority to deal with a defense witness who has been refused immunity by the convening authority, in United States v. Zayas, 24 M.J. 132 (C.M.A. 1987), two members of the court agreed that when confronted with a proffer of clearly exculpatory testimony of a witness who will invoke his privilege against self-incrimination if called to testify, he cannot sit idly by, 24 M.J. at 135. He must fashion an appropriate remedy. In this case, which preceded R.C.M. 704(e), the judge declined either to abate the proceedings or grant a defense continuance.
129. *See* R.C.M. 704(e).
130. *See* Art. 31, U.C.M.J., Rule 301, MIL. R. EVID. The key here is that the defense must establish that the witness has firmly indicated an intention to invoke the right against incrimination, and it appears that the claim is legitimate. Several federal cases indicate that a witness' exercise of the privilege should be recognized if it is not perfectly clear that the answers cannot possibly have a tendency to incriminate. See United States v. Nunez, 668 F.2d 1116 (10th Cir. 1981); United States v. D'Apice, 664 F.2d 75 (5th Cir. 1981). Stated another way, the right may be properly invoked where the witness has reasonable cause to believe that he will implicate himself in a criminal offense by answering a question. Hoffman v. United States, 341 U.S. 479, 486 (1951).
131. R.C.M. 704(e)(2). Presumably this would apply where the government has selectively granted immunity to only those witnesses supporting its case and has denied, without any legitimate countervailing reasons, immunity to a defense witness.
132. R.C.M. 704(e)(2). This might arise where the government has overreached by charging, or intimating that it would so charge, the defense witness with committing an offense in the hopes that the witness will invoke the privilege if called by the defense.
133. United States v. Monroe, 42 M.J. 398 (1995) (judge did not abuse discretion in declining to abate proceedings until defense witness was granted immunity; the witness' testimony was neither clearly exculpatory nor of central importance to defense (old standard)); United States v. Thomas, 37 M.J. 302 (C.M.A. 1993) (case remanded for *DuBay* hearing on substance and quality of defense witness for whom immunity was requested by the accused); United States v. Alston, 33 M.J. 370 (C.M.A. 1991) (expected testimony from potential defense witness was not sufficient to entitle accused to grant of immunity for that witness); United States v. Monroe, 42 M.J. 398 (1995) (judge did not abuse discretion in declining to abate proceedings until defense witness was granted immunity; the witness' testimony was neither clearly exculpatory nor of central impor-

Two points should be emphasized. First, under the *Manual* provision, a military judge has no authority to grant immunity.[134] Rather, the judge may entertain a motion for appropriate relief.[135] If the judge believes that the defense is entitled to immunity for one of its witnesses, he may direct that in the absence of a grant of immunity to that witness, by the appropriate authority,[136] the trial will be abated.[137]

Second, there is no clear, explicit mention in the *Manual* of a requirement that the judge consider any countervailing governmental interests.[138] A 1993 change to the *Manual* provision requires the defense to show that the government has either acted in a discriminatory fashion to obtain an advantage or has, in effect, caused the defense witness to invoke the privilege against self-incrimination.[139] That does not seem as clear as saying that the judge should take into account any countervailing government interests in not granting immunity.[140] Nonetheless, those interests should be argued and considered in any motion for appropriate relief.

---

tance to defense (old standard)); United States v. Ratliff, 42 M.J. 797 (N.M.Ct.Crim.App.1995) (no abuse of discretion in ruling that defense witness was not entitled to immunity where it appeared that testimony would not be incriminating).

An example of this would include an eyewitness to the crime who has information which is clearly exculpatory to the defense. United States v. James, 22 M.J. 929 (N.M.C.M.R. 1986) (testimony must be clearly exculpatory). However, it might also be a witness who possesses irrefutable impeachment evidence against a key government witness. *Cf.* R.C.M. 704(e)(3).

Before an amendment in 1993 to R.C.M. 704(e), the test was whether the testimony is of such central importance to the defense that to deny the testimony would deny a fair trial.

134. Only a convening authority or United States Attorney General may grant immunity. R.C.M. 704(c); United States v. Joseph, 11 M.J. 333 (C.M.A. 1981). In theory, however, a military judge, or any other authority, could grant *de facto* immunity by compelling, or inducing, a witness to incriminate himself and promising no adverse consequences. *See* § 5-4(C) and § 11-2(E)(1) *supra*.

135. *See* § 13-5(1) *infra*.

136. *See* § 11-2(E)(1) for a discussion of who may grant immunity.

137. In effect, the judge is ruling that the witness is essential, but unavailable, and that the proceedings should be abated, i.e., indefinitely delayed. *See, e.g.*, United States v. Harris, 24 M.J. 622 (A.C.M.R. 1987) (trial was abated; court held that abatement does not mean termination of the proceedings and there is, therefore, no requirement to re-refer the charges).

138. *See* R.C.M. 704(e). *See* United States v. Zayas, 24 M.J. 132, 138 (C.M.A. 1987) (Cox, J., dissenting).

139. R.C.M. 704(e)(2). The Drafters' Analysis indicates that the amendment was intended to reflect the majority rule in the federal courts and that the judge is required to consider the Government's interest in not granting immunity to a defense witness. The Analysis further indicates that the amendment reflects the view that there is no Sixth Amendment right to immunized defense testimony unless there has been governmental misconduct intended to disrupt the judicial process. Further, the accused is not denied a Fifth Amendment due process right if the government declines to immunize a witness. If the court finds that the defense witness is a target for prosecution, there can be no claim of overreaching or discrimination by the government. United States v. Shandell, 800 F.2d 322 (2d Cir. 1986).

140. *See, e.g.*, United States v. Smith, 17 M.J. 994 (A.C.M.R. 1984) (government had strong countervailing interest). As the court in *Smith* pointed out, the minority federal rule, as reflected in Virgin Islands v. Smith, defense immunity is appropriate where first, the defense witness is available, has clearly exculpatory testimony, and the government has no strong interest in not granting immunity, or second, where there is governmental misconduct. It appears that the language in R.C.M. 704(e), as amended in 1993, reflects the governmental misconduct theory,

§ 11-2(E)(3)   PRODUCTION OF WITNESSES AND EVIDENCE   § 11-2(E)(3)

Although the government is not required to grant anything more than testimonial immunity,[141] the heavy burden of later demonstrating that no derivative use was made of that testimony for all practical purposes bars any later prosecution of the defense witness.[142] Thus, the government's interests could be substantial.

Once the convening authority has granted immunity, the defense witness is required to testify and may be prosecuted for refusing to do so.[143]

This test varies from the *Smith* test in two major respects. First, a military judge has no authority to grant immunity.[144] Rather, he may entertain a motion for appropriate relief.[145] If he feels that the defense is entitled to immunity for one of its witnesses, he may direct that in the absence of a grant of immunity to that witness, by the appropriate authority,[146] the trial will be abated.[147]

Second, there is no mention in the *Manual* of any countervailing governmental interests.[148] Nonetheless, those interests should be argued and considered in any motion for appropriate relief. Although the government is not required to grant anything more than testimonial immunity,[149] the heavy burden of later demonstrating that no derivative use was made of that testimony for all practical purposes bars any later prosecution of the defense witness.[150] Thus, the government's interests could be substantial.

Once the convening authority has granted immunity, the defense witness is required to testify and may be prosecuted for refusing to do so.[151]

---

although the Drafters' Analysis and some military case law reflect the countervailing government interest theory.

141. The constitutional minimum is testimonial immunity. See Rule 301(c)(1), Mɪʟ. R. Evɪᴅ. which follows Kastigar v. United States, 406 U.S. 441 (1972).

142. See § 11-2(E)(1). United States v. Rivera, 1 M.J. 107 (C.M.A 1975); United States v. Whitehead, 5 M.J. 294 (C.M.A. 1978).

143. See § 11-2(F).

144. Only a convening authority or United States Attorney General may grant immunity. R.C.M. 704(c); United States v. Joseph, 11 M.J. 333 (C.M.A. 1981). In theory, however, a military judge, or any other authority, could grant "de facto" immunity by compelling a witness to incriminate himself and promising no adverse consequences. See *supra* § 11-2(E)(1).

145. See *infra* § 13-5(1).

146. See § 11-2(E)(1) for a discussion of who may grant immunity.

147. In effect, the judge is ruling that the witness is essential, but unavailable, and that the proceedings should be abated, i.e., indefinitely delayed. See, e.g., United States v. Harris, 24 M.J. 622 (A.C.M.R. 1987) (trial was abated; court held that abatement does not mean termination of the proceedings and there is, therefore, no requirement to re-refer the charges).

148. See R.C.M. 704(e). See United States v. Zayas, 24 M.J. 132, 138 (C.M.A. 1987) (Cox, J., dissenting).

149. The constitutional minimum is testimonial immunity. See Rule 301(c)(1), Mɪʟ. R. Evɪᴅ. which follows Kastigar v. United States, 406 U.S. 441 (1972).

150. See § 11-2(E)(1). United States v. Rivera, 1 M.J. 107 (C.M.A. 1975); United States v. Whitehead, 5 M.J. 294 (C.M.A. 1978).

151. See § 11-2(F).

§ 11-2(F). Refusal to Testify.

The fact that either side may have successfully obtained the personal appearance of a witness in the courtroom is, of course, no guarantee that the witness will be responsive to questions from either the counsel, judge[152] or court members.[153] Assuming that the witness has no proper reason for refusing to testify, such as invocation of a privilege, several options are available for encouraging the witness to testify.

It is common for the judge or counsel to remind the witness that criminal prosecution for failure to testify may result. This is particularly true for military witnesses who may, in fact at some point, receive a direct order from a superior to testify and thus run the risk of disobeying a lawful order.[154] A military judge could order a witness to testify, but this puts him in the position of being a potential witness in any future prosecution of the witness should the witness disobey the order; the better practice is to have one of the witness' superiors give the order — outside the courtroom. Note that a refusal to testify may also be punished under Article 134, U.C.M.J.[155] In the case of a civilian witness who has been properly subpoenaed,[156] the witness should first be advised that a possible federal prosecution may result under Article 47, U.C.M.J.[157]

Finding a recalcitrant witness in contempt of court is generally not available as an option.[158] The language of Article 48, U.C.M.J. permits a finding of contempt only where a person uses any "menacing word, sign, or gesture in the presence of a court-martial, or disturbs its proceedings by any riot or disorder."[159]

Note that where a witness has testified on direct examination but refuses to answer questions on cross-examination, the direct testimony may be stricken unless the cross-examination dealt with purely collateral matters.[160] Failure to testify may also result in the judge declaring that the witness is "unavailable"[161] and thus open the door for alternate means of producing the evidence. See § 11-2(A)(2).

---

152. See MIL. R. EVID. 614.
153. Id.
154. See Chapter 2.
155. See MCM, Part IV, para. 108.
156. See also § 11-2(D)(3).
157. Id. United States v. Hines, 23 M.J. 125, 133 n. 13 (C.M.A. 1986) (the court noted that "[f]or some offenses, it may not be at all unthinkable for the government to seek to incarcerate victims or close family members of the accused for failing in their societal obligation to present evidence when properly called upon by a court of law"). See also Appendix 3.
158. See R.C.M. 809(a) Discussion.
159. Art. 48, U.C.M.J. See Appendix 3. See also § 15-5, for further discussion on contempts.
160. See, e.g., Rule 301(f)(2), MIL. R. EVID. See generally United States v. Barnes, 8 M.J. 115 (C.M.A. 1979); United States v. Hunter, 17 M.J. 738 (A.C.M.R. 1983); United States v. Lawless, 13 M.J. 943 (A.F.C.M.R. 1982); United States v. Phaneuf, 10 M.J. 831 (A.C.M.R. 1981).
161. United States v. Hines, 23 M.J. 125 (C.M.A. 1986). See supra § 11-2(A)(2). Note that Rule 804(a), MIL. R. EVID. specifically provides that a witness is "unavailable" if he persists in refusing to testify despite an order of the judge to do so.

§ 11-3. Depositions.

§ 11-3(A). In General.

When it appears that a witness may not be available for trial or for an Article 32 Investigation,[1] counsel should consider deposing the witness with a view toward offering the absent witness' sworn answers as evidence. In military practice, the substantive and procedural aspects of taking depositions are governed by Article 49, U.C.M.J.[2] and R.C.M. 702. The latter source defines a deposition as the "out-of-court testimony of a witness under oath in response to questions by the parties, which is reduced to writing or recorded on videotape or audiotape or similar material."[3]

Although the stated purpose of depositions is to preserve the testimony of an unavailable witness,[4] there is some case law which suggests that the deposition may serve as a discovery tool. For example, a deposition may be taken when the government has improperly interfered with the defense's access to a witness[5] or where the discovery purposes of the Article 32 Investigation have been frustrated.[6]

There are two types of depositions in military practice.[7] An *oral deposition* consists of questions being asked of a witness in person and the answers being recorded.[8] A *written deposition* is a deposition taken on written interrogatories prepared by counsel and submitted to the *deposition officer* who in turn questions the witness.[9] The procedures for each type of deposition are discussed in more detail in the following sections.[10]

---

1. *See* Chapter 7.
2. *See* Appendix 3.
3. R.C.M. 702(a) Discussion.
4. *Id.* Limiting the use of depositions to the preservation of evidence criteria would minimize any discovery abuses that now exist in some civilian jurisdictions where use of the deposition is not so limited. *See also* Fed. R. Crim. P. 15 which requires "exceptional circumstances" before a deposition may be taken.
5. United States v. Killebrew, 9 M.J. 154 (C.M.A. 1980); United States v. Cumberledge, 6 M.J. 203, 205, n. 13 (C.M.A. 1979).
6. United States v. Chuculate, 5 M.J. 143 (C.M.A. 1978); United States v. Chestnut, 2 M.J. 84 (C.M.A. 1976).
7. Art. 49, U.C.M.J. R.C.M. 702(a) Discussion. *See generally* McGovern "The Military Oral Deposition and Modern Communications," 45 Mil. L. Rev. 43 (1969); Everett, "The Role of the Deposition in Military Justice," 7 Mil. L. Rev. 131 (1960).
8. R.C.M. 702(a) Discussion. *See generally* Fed. R. Crim. P. 15 (Depositions), which apparently served as a partial model for R.C.M. 702.
9. *Id. See generally* Fed. R. Civ. P. 31 (Deposition on Written Questions).
10. *See infra* §§ 11-3(B)(2), (3).

§ 11-3(B). Procedures for Depositions.

§ 11-3(B)(1). In General.

After charges are preferred[11] either the prosecution or the defense may request that a particular witness be deposed. The request must be in writing[12] and is addressed to either a convening authority or, after referral of charges,[13] to the military judge.[14] It should spell out (1) the name and location of the witness, (2) a statement as to the subject matter of the witness's testimony, (3) reasons for taking the deposition, and (4) a statement as to whether the deposition is to be oral or written.[15] The request should normally be served upon the opposing counsel.[16]

The request may only be denied for good cause[17] such as the fact that the witness will be available for trial[18] or that the counsel has failed to establish the relevance of the witness' testimony.[19]

A request for a *written* deposition may only be approved if the other counsel consents.[20] An exception to that rule lies, however, when the deposition is being taken solely for the purposes of use during sentencing and the approving authority believes that the interests of the court and the parties will be adequately served by a written deposition.[21]

Once the authority approves the request, he should designate a deposition officer[22] and promptly notify the requesting counsel of his decision.[23] If he

---

11. Art. 49(a), U.C.M.J. Depositions taken before charges are preferred are probably void. United States v. Burnom, 35 C.M.R. 908 (A.F.B.R. 1965). *See also* United States v. Vicencio, 44 C.M.R. 323 (A.C.M.R. 1971); United States v. Tatmon, 23 C.M.R. 841 (A.F.B.R. 1957).
12. Art. 49(a), U.C.M.J. R.C.M. 702(c)(1). It should be signed by the party requesting the deposition. United States v. Cantrell, 5 C.M.R. 823 (A.F.B.R. 1952). *See also* United States v. Tatmon, 23 C.M.R. 841 (A.F.B.R. 1957) (Article 32 officer cannot sign).
13. For a discussion on the process of referring charges, see Chapter 8.
14. Art. 49(a), U.C.M.J.; R.C.M. 702(b).
15. R.C.M. 702(c)(2).
16. R.C.M. 702(c) Discussion. The opposing party may object and submit supporting matters in opposition. *See* United States v. Turman, 25 C.M.R. 710 (N.B.R. 1957).
17. *See* Art. 49(a), U.C.M.J., R.C.M. 702(c)(3)(A).
18. The question of "availability" is addressed in Rule 804(a), MIL. R. EVID., which incorporates standards set out in Art. 49(a), U.C.M.J. The topic is discussed in more detail in Chapter 15.

Even though a witness may be available for trial or Article 32 Investigation, however, a deposition may nonetheless be appropriate where the Government has blocked defense attempts to interview the witness or the witness was not able to testify at an Article 32 Investigation. *See* R.C.M. 702(c)(3) Discussion.

19. *See* Rule 401, MIL. R. EVID. for a definition of "relevance."
20. R.C.M. 702(c)(3)(B); United States v. Jacoby, 11 C.M.A. 428, 29 C.M.R. 244 (1960). No consent is required where the request is for an oral deposition. R.C.M. 702(c)(3)(B) Discussion.
21. R.C.M. 702(c)(3)(B).
22. Art. 49(c), U.C.M.J. indicates that a deposition may be taken by any military or civil officer authorized to administer oaths. R.C.M. 702(d)(1) simply states that the authority acting on the request may appoint an officer or appropriate civil officer to serve as a deposition officer without regard to his ability to administer oaths. The possible conflict is resolved by Art. 136(b)(3), U.C.M.J. which authorizes all deposition officers to administer oaths. Thus, the fact that a military officer is otherwise unable to administer oaths is not a disqualifying factor as Art. 49(c) might otherwise indicate. Apparently warrant and noncommissioned officers may not be detailed.
23. *See* R.C.M. 702(c)(3)(C).

§ 11-3(B)(1)   PRODUCTION OF WITNESSES AND EVIDENCE   § 11-3(B)(1)

denies the request he should provide reasons for doing so.[24] Failure to renew a request denied by a convening authority before the military judge will constitute a waiver.[25]

The authority approving the request should also insure that qualified counsel represent each side.[26] If the request has been made after the referral of charges, both counsel will almost always have been assigned to their respective duties.[27]

The parties are free to agree that a deposition should be taken,[28] and in that case, no request need be filed and no order need be issued.[29] The deposition, however, will be taken at no cost to the United States.[30]

The party requesting the deposition is responsible for giving reasonable[31] written notice,[32] which should indicate the time and place of the deposition and the persons to be deposed.[33]

The party receiving the notice may in turn request the deposition officer to reschedule the place or time of the deposition.[34]

The *Manual* sets out specific instructions for the deposition officer, who acts in a ministerial capacity:[35]

(1) Arrange a time and place for taking the deposition and, in the case of an oral deposition, notify the party who requested the deposition accordingly;

(2) Arrange for the presence of any witness whose deposition is to be taken in accordance with the procedures for production of witnesses and evidence under R.C.M. 703(e);

(3) Maintain order during the deposition and protect the parties and witnesses from annoyance, embarrassment, or oppression;

(4) Administer the oath to each witness, the reporter, and interpreter, if any;

(5) In the case of a written deposition, ask the questions submitted by counsel to the witness;

(6) Cause the proceedings to be recorded so that a verbatim record is made or may be prepared;

---

24. *Id.*
25. R.C.M. 702(c)(3)(D). United States v. Cumberledge, 6 M.J. 203 (C.M.A. 1979); United States v. Chuculate, 5 M.J. 143 (C.M.A. 1978).
26. R.C.M. 702(d)(2). See § 8-3(B)(1) for a discussion on the qualifications of counsel.
27. *See* § 8-4.
28. Art. 49(a), U.C.M.J. R.C.M. 702(i).
29. R.C.M. 702(a) Discussion.
30. R.C.M. 702(i).
31. Art. 49(b), U.C.M.J. United States v. Donati, 14 C.M.A. 235, 34 C.M.R. 15 (1963); United States v. Hamilton, 36 M.J. 927 (A.F.C.M.R. 1993) (on appeal by government, court held that defense had reasonable notice where counsel was informed orally on 27 October, and in writing on 29 October, of deposition hearing on 4 November); United States v. Marsh, 35 M.J. 505 (A.F.C.M.R. 1992) (notice to accused and counsel just before deposition was not reasonable written notice of time and place); United States v. Matthews, 31 C.M.R. 620 (A.F.B.R. 1961).
32. Art. 49(b), U.C.M.J. R.C.M. 702(e). United States v. Giles, 42 C.M.R. 880 (A.C.M.R. 1970).
33. R.C.M. 702(e).
34. *Id.*
35. United States v. Riley, 6 C.M.R. 471 (C.G.B.R. 1952).

(7) Record, but not rule upon, objections or motions and the testimony to which they relate;
(8) Authenticate the record of the deposition and forward it to the authority who ordered the deposition; and
(9) Report to the convening authority any substantial irregularity in the proceeding.[36]

In addition to these duties, the authority ordering the deposition may give other instructions to the officer conducting the deposition.[37]

If one of the counsel has an objection to the deposition which, if made in a timely fashion, could have permitted corrective action before the deposition was taken, he should make it. Otherwise, the issue will be considered waived.[38]

More specific rules regarding the presence of counsel and objections during the deposition are noted in the following subsections, which set out the rules for both oral and written depositions.

§ 11-3(B)(2). Procedures for Oral Depositions.

During an oral deposition, the accused has a right in most cases to be present[39] and has a right to the presence and assistance of counsel.[40] The right to counsel entitles the accused to the assistance of (1) a civilian counsel, at no expense to the government, and (2) a detailed military counsel, or (3) a military counsel of the accused's choice if the latter is reasonably available.[41] Counsel need not be sworn,[42] and need not automatically be the same counsel who later represents the accused at trial.[43] Counsel must act in a competent

---

36. R.C.M. 702(f).
37. R.C.M. 702(d)(3).
38. R.C.M. 702(h)(1). *See, e.g.,* United States v. Ciarletta, 7 C.M.A. 606, 23 C.M.R. 70 (1957).
39. R.C.M. 702(g)(1)(A)(i). United States v. Webber, 42 M.J. 675 (A.F.Ct.Crim.App. 1995) (facts demonstrated a conscious intent by accused and his counsel to waive appearance at deposition; an accused or trial counsel who refuses to attend deposition does so at this own peril). The exceptions lie where the accused, after notice, fails to appear or disrupts the proceeding (see R.C.M. 804(b)(2), (3)) or where the deposition is being taken in lieu of production of a sentencing witness and the authority ordering the deposition concludes that the interests of the parties and court can be met without the accused being present at such a deposition. *Id.*
40. R.C.M. 702(g)(1)(A)(ii); United States v. Donati, 14 C.M.A. 235, 34 C.M.R. 15 (1963); United States v. Webber, 42 M.J. 675 (A.F.Ct.Crim.App. 1995) (facts demonstrated a conscious intent by accused and his counsel to waive appearance at deposition; an accused or trial counsel who refuses to attend deposition does so at this own peril); United States v. Johnson, 42 C.M.R. 625 (A.C.M.R. 1970).
41. These rights parallel those available to the accused at an Article 32 Investigation (see Chapter 7) and at the trial itself (see Chapter 15). United States v. Hamilton, 36 M.J. 927 (A.F.C.M.R. 1993) (trial judge did not err in concluding that accused's right to counsel was denied at deposition, but judge did err in not considering deposition itself in determining whether accused had been prejudiced); United States v. Marsh, 35 M.J. 505 (A.F.C.M.R. 1992) (nonprejudicial error to proceed with deposition despite absence of individual military counsel).
42. United States v. Parrish, 7 C.M.A. 337, 22 C.M.R. 127 (1956).
43. United States v. Sutton, 3 C.M.A. 220, 11 C.M.R. 220 (1953).

manner,[44] and the accused is entitled to the assistance of the military counsel detailed to represent him.[45] Counsel's role is limited, however, to examining or cross-examining the witness being deposed and noting any objections.[46]

The procedure for the oral deposition looks very much like a trial in the sense that the witness is sworn by the deposition officer,[47] the witness is asked questions by the counsel seeking the deposition, and the witness is then cross-examined by the opposing counsel.[48] The Military Rules of Evidence generally do not apply to depositions.[49] Military Rule of Evidence 1101 states that the privileges of Section III (Constitutional Rules)[50] and Section V (Privileges) do apply at all stages of all actions, cases, and proceedings,[51] which would include depositions. R.C.M. 702 provides that if the Government has any previous statements of the witness in its possession, it must provide a copy to the accused, if the accused would be entitled to it at trial.[52] The entitlement at trial is generally triggered by the witness first testifying.[53] However, this rule of disclosure apparently does not cover prior statements within the possession of the defense.[54]

If during the deposition a counsel has an objection to the testimony, questions, or evidence, he should make it in a timely manner or risk waiver.[55] Likewise, any appropriate motions should be made.[56] The deposition officer is not to rule on any objections or motions. Instead, the officer is simply directed to note them for the record.[57]

The manner of recording the deposition is within the discretion of the authority who ordered the deposition and may include not only transcription by a reporter, but also by audiotape, videotape, or sound film.[58]

§ 11-3(B)(3). Procedures for Written Depositions.

The procedure for taking a written deposition is quite unlike that for an oral deposition; it more closely approximates civil practice of submitting written interrogatories to the opposing side.[59] In military practice the counsel

---

44. United States v. Ciarletta, 7 C.M.A. 606, 23 C.M.R. 70 (1957).
45. United States v. Brady, 8 C.M.A. 456, 24 C.M.R. 266 (1957).
46. *See* R.C.M. 702(g)(1)(B); United States v. Blackburn, 31 C.M.R. 340 (A.B.R. 1961).
47. *See* R.C.M. 702(f)(4).
48. R.C.M. 702(g)(1)(B). The deposition officer does not conduct the examination. *See* United States v. Riley, 6 C.M.R. 471 (C.G.B.R. 1952).
49. Rule 1101(d), MIL. R. EVID.
50. These privileges include Rule 301, MIL. R. EVID. (right against self-incrimination) and Rule 302, MIL. R. EVID. (privilege concerning mental examination of an accused).
51. Rule 1101(b), MIL. R. EVID.
52. R.C.M. 702(g)(1)(B).
53. *See* § 10-4(B)(5).
54. *Cf.* R.C.M. 914, which provides for reciprocal disclosure after the witness testifies at trial.
55. R.C.M. 702(h)(2).
56. *Id.*
57. R.C.M. 702(f)(7); United States v. Hounshell, 19 C.M.R. 906 (A.F.B.R. 1955).
58. Art. 49, U.C.M.J.; R.C.M. 702(g)(3). *See* United States v. Crockett, 21 M.J. 423 (C.M.A. 1986).
59. The main difference, however, is that the answers in the written deposition are given under oath to a deposition officer. The Federal counterpart is noted in FED. R. CIV. P. 31 (Deposition on Written Questions). *See also* FED. R. CIV. P. 33 (written interrogatories).

wishing to depose a witness prepares written questions to be asked of the witness.[60] The questions are sent to the opposing counsel who may offer any objections or cross-interrogatories to be asked of the witness.[61] The questions, or interrogatories, and any cross-interrogatories are then submitted to the deposition officer.[62]

At the deposition proceeding, the deposition officer places the witness under oath,[63] reads each interrogatory and records each answer.[64] As with the oral deposition, the authority ordering the deposition, see § 11-3(B)(1), decides what form will be used to record the testimony. It may be recorded by a reporter, videotape, audiotape, or sound film.[65]

In those cases where the testimony is transcribed, the deposition officer should normally offer the witness an opportunity to review his answers and offer any additional testimony under oath.[66] If available, the witness should sign the deposition. Otherwise, the deposition officer must indicate why the witness did not sign.[67] In all cases he must execute a certificate of authentication.[68]

Unlike the oral deposition procedures, no party has a right to be present at the written deposition,[69] although the accused is generally entitled to the assistance of counsel.[70] The exception is when the deposition is being taken for a summary court-martial.[71] The accused's choice of counsel is identical to that provided in a general or special court-martial: a civilian lawyer at no expense to the government and either a detailed military counsel or an individually requested military counsel who is reasonably available.[72]

If a counsel has an objection to an interrogatory, he must serve his objection on the counsel who proposed the interrogatory before it is sent to the deposition officer.[73] If the objection is to an answer, the objection may be made at trial.[74]

§ 11-3(C). Use of Depositions at Trial.

The subject of use of a deposition at a court-martial is discussed in more detail in Chapter 15. It is important, however, to point out at this point that the key to admissibility is that before a party may offer a deposition as sub-

---

60. R.C.M. 702(g)(2)(C).
61. Id.
62. R.C.M. 702(g)(2)(C) Discussion.
63. R.C.M. 702(f)(4).
64. R.C.M. 702(f)(5), (g)(2)(D).
65. R.C.M. 702(g)(3).
66. R.C.M. 702(g)(2)(D).
67. Id. For a sample form used for recording written depositions, see Appendix 14.
68. Id.
69. R.C.M. 702(g)(2)(B).
70. R.C.M. 702(g)(2)(A).
71. Id.
72. See §§ 11-3(B)(2) and 8-3(B).
73. R.C.M. 702(h)(3).
74. Id.

stantive evidence and still avoid the hearsay rule, he must establish that the witness is "unavailable" under the criteria set out in Rule 804(a), Military Rule of Evidence.[75] It may also be used to impeach a deponent who has testified at the trial.[76] In either case, the party offering the deposition normally reads it to the fact finder.[77] The trial court's decision to admit or exclude the deposition is reviewed for an abuse of discretion.[78]

§ 11-4. Production of Evidence.

The rules governing the production of evidence are very similar to those that govern the production of witnesses.[1] That is, each party has an equal right to evidence that is both relevant and necessary.[2] This two-prong requirement essentially states that although the requested evidence may address an issue in the case and thus be logically relevant, the evidence may be unnecessary and thus legally irrelevant. An example given in the *Manual* is that cumulative evidence is not necessary.[3] As a rule of thumb, evidence that goes to the core of the case will normally be considered as "necessary".[4]

The fact that a party may demonstrate that the requested evidence is both relevant and necessary does not mean that the trial may not proceed until the evidence is produced. Where the requested evidence is not available because it has been lost, destroyed, or is simply not subject to compulsory process, the military judge should first determine if the evidence in question is of such central importance to the case that its absence will deny a fair trial.[5] If it is,

---

75. United States v. Dieter, 42 M.J. 697 (Army Ct.Crim.App. 1995) (witness not unavailable unless prosecution has made good faith effort to obtain witness; judge abused discretion in admitting oral deposition).
76. *See generally* Rule 613, MIL. R. EVID. and R.C.M. 702(a) Discussion.
77. R.C.M. 702(a) Discussion.
78. United States v. Webber, 42 M.J. 675 (A.F.Ct.Crim.App. 1995).
1. *See supra* § 11-2.
2. R.C.M. 703(f). United States v. Mosley, 42 M.J. 300 (1995) (trial court relied on fundamental fairness and relevance in ordering government to retest accused's urine sample; intermediate appellate court erroneously applied standard of review used for requests for expert assistance for the defense; trial court's decision regarding production of evidence is reviewed for abuse of discretion); United States v. Reece, 25 M.J. 93 (C.M.A. 1987) (treatment records of two minor victims were necessary); United States v. Toledo, 15 M.J. 255 (C.M.A. 1983).
3. R.C.M. 703(f) Discussion. United States v. Jones, 20 M.J. 919 (N.M.C.M.R. 1985) (judge did not abuse discretion in denying a defense request for production of health records and drug rehabilitation records of government witnesses). 42 U.S.C. § 290ee-3 treats these records as confidential but they may be disclosed by a court upon good cause. Here the witnesses admitted that they had used drugs.
4. Even an important matter, however, may not be "in issue" if the parties have stipulated to the matter. *Id.*
5. R.C.M. 703(f)(2). California v. Trombetta, 467 U.S. 479 (1984); United States v. Manuel, 43 M.J. 282 (1995) (service regulations requiring preservation of positive urine samples conferred substantial right on accused to have sample tested and preserved in accordance with those regulations; not abuse of discretion to exclude test as result of failure to follow regulations); United States v. Arguello, 29 M.J. 198 (C.M.A. 1989) (court addressed but did not decide whether government's destruction of urinalysis sample which was determined to be negative was violative of due

the judge should next determine if there is any adequate substitute available. What will constitute an "adequate substitute" will obviously depend upon the individual facts of each case. In most cases, for example, a stipulation of fact will almost always be an adequate substitute.[6]

If an adequate substitute cannot be found, the judge should grant a continuance or other relief in order to provide time and an opportunity to produce the evidence.[7] If that tactic does not produce the evidence, the judge may abate (indefinitely delay) the trial unless it appears that the party requesting the evidence caused the unavailability of the evidence or could have prevented it from becoming unavailable.[8]

If the defense wishes the government to obtain evidence on behalf of the defense or to produce evidence within its control, the defense counsel should present a written request to the trial counsel that sets out:

(1) A list and description of the evidence which sufficiently lays out why the evidence is relevant and necessary;
(2) A statement as to where the evidence can be obtained; and
(3) The name, address, and telephone number of the custodian of the evidence, if that evidence is known.[9]

Assuming that a decision has been made that the evidence should be produced,[10] it is simply a question of notifying the custodian of the time, place, and date that it is needed and requesting the custodian to deliver it.[11] If necessary, a subpoena may be issued to direct a custodian to deliver the

---

process; the court instead ruled that admission of results of test violated due process because it violated government regulations).

United States v. Reece, 25 M.J. 93 (C.M.A. 1987) (defense requested materials in hands of civilian authorities to determine credibility of two victims); United States v. Garries, 22 M.J. 288 (C.M.A. 1986); United States v. Kern, 22 M.J. 49 (C.M.A. 1986) (defense must show that lost evidence was exculpatory and that no adequate substitute exists).

United States v. Gill, 37 M.J. 501 (A.F.C.M.R. 1993) (accused not denied due process by failure of government to preserve evidence where he could not show that evidence was destroyed in bad faith); United States v. Anderson, 36 M.J. 963 (A.F.C.M.R. 1993) (relief denied where accused could not show that evidence had been destroyed in bad faith by government).

In United States v. Mobley, 28 M.J. 1024 (A.F.C.M.R. 1989), the government returned the victim's car, which was, in effect, the "crime scene," to her husband before the defense had had an opportunity to inspect it. The court found no bad faith on the part of the government and concluded that under the facts, the accused had not been denied his rights under either the Sixth Amendment or Article 46. Thus, the trial judge was correct in denying the suppression motion for all of the evidence obtained from the car. The court noted that requiring preservation of the crime scene would generally be impractical. The Court of Military Appeals affirmed. 31 M.J. 273 (C.M.A. 1990). That court indicated that although the vehicle was the crime scene, it also contained at least five critical pieces of evidence. Although Article 46 had been violated, there was no prejudice to the accused.

6. *See* § 11-2(A)(4).
7. R.C.M. 703(f)(2).
8. *Id.*
9. R.C.M. 703(f)(3).
10. United States v. Reece, 21 M.J. 736 (N.M.C.M.R. 1985) (judge did not abuse discretion in denying defense request for subpoena duces tecum for materials held by third parties).
11. R.C.M. 703(f)(4).

evidence.[12] Custodians objecting to an order or subpoena to deliver evidence on grounds that the order is oppressive or unreasonable, may seek relief from either the convening authority or from the military judge.[13] Either authority may, if appropriate, modify or withdraw the order to produce. If necessary, the military judge may conduct an in camera inspection of the evidence to determine if any relief should be granted.[14]

---

12. *See* § 11-2(D)(2).
13. R.C.M. 703(f)(4).
14. *Id.* United States v. Charles, 40 M.J. 414 (C.M.A. 1994) (judge conducted in camera inspection of materials sought by defense); United States v. Reece, 25 M.J. 93 (C.M.A. 1987) (judge abused his discretion in failing to conduct an in camera hearing on requested materials).

APPENDIX REFERENCES

Appendix 1. Abbreviations.
Appendix 2. Glossary.
Appendix 3. U.C.M.J.
Appendix 4. Court-Martial Flow Chart.
Appendix 6. Charge Sheets.
Appendix 11. Grant of Immunity.
Appendix 13. Request to Take Oral Deposition.
Appendix 14. Deposition by Written Interrogatory.
Appendix 15. Subpoena for Civilian Witness.
Appendix 16. Warrant of Attachment.
Appendix 25. Stipulation of Fact.
Appendix 26. Stipulation of Expected Testimony.

ANNOTATED BIBLIOGRAPHY

BOOKS

Saltzburg, Schinasi & Schlueter, *Military Rules of Evidence Manual* (3d ed. 1991).

> The authors have compiled the official text of the Military Rules of Evidence, the drafters' analysis to those rules, and have provided an editorial comment for each rule that explains the rule, shows how it might be used, and discusses potential problem areas. Also included are annotated military cases, a selected bibliography, and selected federal cases.

PERIODICALS

Chute, "Due Process and Unavailable Evidence," 118 MIL. L. REV. 93 (1987).

> This article provides an analysis of the Supreme Court's decision in *California v. Trombetta*, 467 U.S. 479 (1984), the *Manual*'s treatment of discovery and production of evidence, and the Court of Military Appeals' position on the issue of government destruction of evidence useful to the defense. The author notes that military due process considerations may provide more protection for the defense and proposes a number of remedies for such destruction.

Gilligan and Lederer, "The Procurement and Presentation of Evidence in Courts-Martial: Compulsory Process and Confrontation," 101 MIL. L. REV. 1 (1983).

> In the form of an expanded outline, the co-authors of this article provide a thorough and concise overview of the military procedures and constitutional requirements concerning the procurement and presentation of evidence and the due process rights to compulsory process and confrontation. This eighty-two-page article is structured in a very practical form, with a detailed table of contents and excellent documentation.

Green, "Grants of Immunity and Military Law, 1971-1976," 73 MIL. L. REV. 1 (1976).

> This article presents a comprehensive survey of military case law following the enactment in 1970 of the Organized Crime Control Act, 18 U.S.C. § 6001-05 (1970). The author addresses the constitutionality of use immunity, derivative use

of immunized testimony, the exceptions to grants of immunity, and the potential disqualification problems for both the Staff Judge Advocate and the Convening Authority. The article is a sequel to Green, "Grants of Immunity and Military Law," 53 MIL. L. REV. 1 (1971).

Gunn, "Supplementing the Defense Team: A Primer on Requesting and Obtaining Expert Assistance," 39 A.F. L. REV. 143 (1996).

This helpful article notes the advantages and disadvantages of obtaining the assistance of expert assistance at government expense. The author discusses the history of the right to expert assistance, the procedures for requesting such assistance, the necessity standards for obtaining approval of an expert's assistance and whether the courts have adopted an alternate status for deciding whether an expert should be provided. Finally, the author offers some practical advice on the issue.

Hahn, "Voluntary and Involuntary Expert Testimony in Courts-Martial," 106 MIL. L. REV. 77 (1984).

In this article the author examines existing military law concerning the securing of voluntary and involuntary services of military, government employee, and civilian experts. He advocates a change to the Manual for Courts-Martial that will not only align the military with the federal procedures used in securing voluntary and involuntary expert testimony, but that will also enable the military justice system to more effectively handle the increasing use of expert testimony in the courts-martial context.

Lederer, "Warrants of Attachment-Forcibly Compelling the Attendance of Witnesses," 98 MIL. L. REV. 1 (1982).

The author points to the prevalent problem of compelling the attendance of civilian witnesses in military courts-martial. Noting that the military indeed has the authority to order the physical attachment of reluctant civilian witnesses, the author, in great detail, explains the necessary steps in properly obtaining a military warrant of attachment and concludes by observing that this option should be used, in proper situations, to the benefit of both the prosecution and the defense.

Moyer, "Procedural Rights of the Military Accused: Advantages Over a Civilian Defendant," 22 Me. L. Rev. 105 (1970); 51 MIL. L. REV. 1 (1971).

This forty-page article compares the civilian and military criminal procedures such as pretrial investigation, interrogation, right to witnesses, right to counsel, and appellate review. The author concludes that the military accused enjoys greater procedural and substantive advantages than the civilian counterpart.

Myhre, "Defense Witness Immunity and the Due Process Standard: A Proposed Amendment to the Manual for Courts-Martial," 136 MIL. L. REV. 69 (1992).

The author provides a critical analysis of R.C.M. 704 and military caselaw that addresses the ability of the defense to obtain use immunity for a witness who has "clearly exculpatory evidence" to offer. The author questions the underlying rationale for that rule, offers reasons why the rule should be abandoned, and suggests an amendment to the *Manual* that would limit the right of the defense to obtain immunity.

MILITARY CRIMINAL JUSTICE

Symposium, "Military Justice," Army Law., March 1996.

This 127-page symposium contains a Foreword and 11 short articles on a wide range of military justice topics. They are as follows:

Morris, "Foreword."
Barto, "Developments in the Substantive Criminal Law Under the Uniform Code of Military Justice."
Frisk, "New Developments in Pretrial Confinement."
Frisk, "New Developments in Speedy Trial."
Winn, "Recent Developments in Military Pretrial and Trial Procedure."
Masterton, "Recent Developments in Search and Seizure Law."
Masterton, "Recent Developments in Urinalysis Law."
Kohlman, "Are You Ready for Some Changes? Five Fresh Views of the Fifth Amendment."
Wright, "Sex, Lies, and Videotape: Child Sexual Abuse Cases Continue to Create Appellate Issues and Other Developments in the Areas of the Sixth Amendment, Discovery, Mental Responsibility, and Nonjudicial Punishment."
Henley, "Caveat Criminale: The Impact of the New Military Rules of Evidence in Sexual Offense and Child Molestation Cases."
Henley, "Current Developments in Evidence Law."
Morris, "New Developments in Sentencing and Post-Trial Procedure."

Thompson, "Constitutional Applications to the Military Criminal Defendant," 66 U. Detroit L. Rev. 221 (1989).

Drawing comparisons between civilian and military practices, the author notes that in order to maintain the requisite good order and discipline needed in the armed forces some modifications to substantive constitutional rights have been made. He concludes that although the military defendant loses protections in the areas of search and seizure and trial by jury, he has enhanced protections in other areas, e.g., discovery and witness production.

CHAPTER 12

THE ARTICLE 39(a) PRETRIAL SESSION

§ 12-1. Introduction.
§ 12-2. Preliminary Matters.
    § 12-2(A). Calling the Court to Order.
    § 12-2(B). Announcing the Convening Orders, Referral, and Service of Charges.
    § 12-2(C). Accounting for Parties Present and Absent.
    § 12-2(D). Noting the Detail of a Court Reporter and an Interpreter.
    § 12-2(E). Announcing the Detail and Qualifications of the Trial Counsel.
    § 12-2(F). Announcing the Detail and Qualifications of the Defense Counsel and the Judge's Inquiry Concerning the Accused's Rights to Counsel.
        § 12-2(F)(1). Detail and Qualifications of Counsel.
        § 12-2(F)(2). The *Donohew* Inquiry.
        § 12-2(F)(3). The *Breese* Inquiry and Conflicts of Interest.
        § 12-2(F)(4). The *Faretta* Inquiry and Self-Representation.
        § 12-2(F)(5). Accused's Election of Counsel.
    § 12-2(G). Administering the Oaths and Announcing the Detail of the Military Judge.
    § 12-2(H). Challenges for Cause to the Military Judge.
§ 12-3. Military Judge's Inquiries Concerning the Accused's Decisions Regarding Composition of the Court.
    § 12-3(A). Accused's Request for Trial by Judge Alone.
    § 12-3(B). Accused's Request for Enlisted Members on the Court.
§ 12-4. Arraignment.
§ 12-5. Conferences.
Appendix References.
Annotated Bibliography.

§ 12-1. Introduction.

Courts-martial generally include a preliminary pretrial session, usually referred to as the "Article 39(a) pretrial session" or simply, the "Article 39(a) session".[1] This out-of-court proceeding may be held at any time after service of charges,[2] and the Article 35, U.C.M.J. waiting period has elapsed.[3] It is an integral part of the trial[4] and should not be confused with the "pretrial conferences" that are specifically provided for in the Manual for Courts-Martial.[5] The conferences, discussed in § 12-5, are used to dispose of matters in a non-litigation setting. The Article 39(a) pretrial session, on the other hand, is used not only to dispose of administrative and preliminary matters but also to inquire into the accused's understanding of various trial rights, arraign the accused, dispose of pretrial motions, and take the accused's pleas.

---

1. *See* Article 39(a), U.C.M.J. at Appendix 3.
2. See § 8-6 for a discussion on service of charges on the accused.
3. *See supra* § 8-6, and Appendix 3.
4. R.C.M. 803.
5. R.C.M. 803.

The military judge presides over the proceeding, which is attended by the counsel, the accused, the court reporter, and any other necessary personnel, such as the bailiff or interpreter.[6] The court members are not included.[7]

Although the term "Article 39(a) session" is almost always associated with pretrial proceedings, its potential use is broader and denotes any out-of-court session where the members are absent. It may, for example, be used where counsel wishes to litigate an issue out of the hearing of the members or discuss proposed instructions to the court.[8] The *Manual* specifically recognizes that in some circumstances an Article 39(a) session might be an appropriate forum to dispose of post-trial matters following adjournment and before the convening authority takes action on the case.[9] The focus of this chapter, however, is on the pretrial session during which important preliminary issues are resolved or delimited.

The Article 39(a) pretrial session is normally linked with general and special courts-martial, although the summary court-martial may be preceded by a pretrial interview or conference.[10]

The military judge may consider virtually any issue that may affect the trial, but the procedure among the services and from trial to trial is generally uniform and in almost every case adheres to the following format:

1. Calling the court to order.
2. Announcing the convening orders and referral of charges.
3. Accounting for parties present and absent.
4. Noting whether a court reporter is present and has been detailed.
5. Announcing the detail and qualifications of the prosecution counsel.
6. Announcing the detail and qualifications of the defense counsel.
7. Explanation of the accused's rights to counsel and determining who will represent him.
8. Administering any necessary oaths to the participants.
9. Stating the general nature of the charges.
10. Announcing the detail of the military judge.
11. Inquiring into grounds for challenge to the military judge.
12. Inquiring into any request for trial by judge alone.
13. Inquiring into any request for enlisted members on the court.
14. Arraignment.
15. Motions.
16. Pleas and providency inquiry if the accused enters a guilty plea.
17. Entry of findings on a plea of guilty.

To assist counsel and judges in following this format, the Manual for Courts-Martial contains a sample script or "boiler-plate" for pretrial and trial

---

6. R.C.M. 803. *See also* R.C.M. 901.
7. R.C.M. 803, 805.
8. *See* Chapter 15.
9. R.C.M. 803, 1102. *See* Chapter 17.
10. See § 15-25 for a discussion on procedures for summary courts-martial.

proceedings as an appendix. Depending on the particular needs of each service, some minor textual variation may appear.

Depending on the complexity of the case, the number of motions counsel will present, and the accused's pleas, the Article 39(a) session can take anywhere from 15 minutes to several days. Government appeals of a ruling on a motion may further delay completion of the pretrial session.[11] Again, notwithstanding the length or the complexity of the proceedings, the agenda remains fairly constant.

Discussion in this chapter will focus primarily on the preliminary matters covered in the Article 39(a) pretrial session and will generally follow the agenda noted above, from calling the court to order through arraignment. Note that some of the foregoing agenda items have been consolidated for purposes of discussion and that a discussion of pretrial conferences is also included. The topic of pretrial motions will be addressed in Chapter 13, and Chapter 14 will discuss entry of the accused's pleas.

§ 12-2. Preliminary Matters.

In the opening portions of the Article 39(a) pretrial session, a number of preliminary or administrative matters must be dealt with. They generally involve noting that significant steps have been taken or key procedural requirements fulfilled. Failure to note or announce these points does not necessarily invalidate the court-martial, although it can. In some instances, the announcement in open court that a particular procedure has been followed will be the only reflection of that event. For example, under the detailing procedures for military judges it is not necessary that they be appointed by the convening authority in a convening order. Depending on service regulations on the subject, it is possible that the only record of who detailed the judge to the court will be found in the judge's oral announcement of that fact during the Article 39(a) pretrial session.[1]

The following discussion briefly addresses each of the key points in the procedure up to the judge's more specific inquiries concerning the accused's election with regard to forum.

§ 12-2(A). Calling the Court to Order.

The Article 39(a) pretrial proceeding is called into session by the military judge who has been appointed to the case and after charges have been referred[2] and served upon the accused.[3] In addition, Article 35, U.C.M.J.[4] provides a minimum waiting period that may be waived by the accused. For general courts-martial, no session may be called until five days have elapsed

---

11. Government appeals of adverse rulings by the trial judge on motions are addressed in Chapter 13.
1. *See infra* § 12-2(F).
2. *See* Chapter 8.
3. *Id.*
4. *See* Appendix 3.

after service of charges. In the case of a special court-martial, three days must elapse. Although the language of the statutory provision indicates an absolute right to the minimum time,[5] several exceptions have been carved out by the military courts. For example, where the accused was properly served with charges but the charges were later re-referred and re-served without change to the content of the charges, the court held that the accused had no absolute right to the minimum period absent some showing that he needed the time to prepare.[6] Failure to raise the issue waives it.[7] Where it appears, however, that the pretrial session is commencing within the statutory period, the judge should call that fact to the attention of the defense.[8]

Calling the court to order may be accomplished by the judge simply announcing that "the Article 39(a) session is called to order." In some cases, that announcement may be significant insofar as it affects stopping the speedy trial clock. *See* Chapter 13.

§ 12-2(B). Announcing the Convening Orders, Referral, and Service of Charges.

Throughout the pretrial session, the trial counsel generally takes the lead in announcing that certain prerequisites have been met. After the judge calls the session to order, the trial counsel announces which convening order created the court, the fact that the charges against the accused have been properly referred to the court, and the fact that the accused was served with a copy of the charges on a particular date.[9] As noted in § 12-2(A), Article 35, U.C.M.J. may preclude proceeding with the Article 39(a) session until the minimum statutory waiting period has elapsed. At this point the judge should personally examine the charge sheet and other documents to insure that the case has indeed been properly convened and referred. Although that step seems minor, in many cases the jurisdictional defects in convening or referral of charges are not discovered, or raised, until the appellate process has begun. Amendments to the orders should also be stated and if there are minor changes or mistakes in the convening orders, the trial counsel may note those for the record.[10] An example of this would be to note that one of the participants has been promoted in the interim.

---

5. *See also* R.C.M. 803 Discussion.
6. United States v. Cruz-Maldonado, 20 M.J. 831 (A.C.M.R. 1985).
7. United States v. Lumbus, 48 C.M.R. 613 (A.C.M.R. 1974).
8. *See* R.C.M. 901(a) Discussion. *See also* United States v. Perna, 1 C.M.A. 438, 4 C.M.R. 30 (1952); United States v. Pergande, 49 C.M.R. 28 (A.C.M.R. 1974).
9. Referral and service of charges are discussed at Chapter 8.
10. *See* note 7, Guide for General and Special Courts-Martial, MCM, page A8-1.

§ 12-2(C). Accounting for Parties Present and Absent.

The court reporter, if one has been detailed to the court, will usually note which parties are present in his or her notes for the record of trial. However, the trial counsel will also formally announce which parties are present and those which are absent.[11] At each subsequent session of the trial, the judge should insure that the trial counsel notes for the record whether those parties who were present at the time the court was last in session are again present.[12] The Article 39(a) session should not proceed unless the military judge, both counsel, and the accused are present.[13] Under limited circumstances an Article 39(a) session could proceed in the absence of the accused if (1) he was present at the arraignment and was voluntarily absent from subsequent sessions[14] or (2) after proper warnings from the judge, the accused engaged in disruptive courtroom conduct.[15]

As long as one counsel from each side is present, the session may proceed.[16] In cases where more than one counsel represents a party, the absence of an assistant counsel, for instance, should normally not cause delay of the proceedings. However, proceeding without the presence of the lead defense counsel, over objection of the accused, may be improper. If the judge decides to proceed with the pretrial session, he should be prepared to articulate reasons on the record why a continuance was not warranted and why the accused's right to adequate representation was not impaired.[17]

If a military judge has been appointed, he must, of course, be present.[18] In the rare instance where a special court-martial without a military judge has been convened, the President of the Court acts in the stead of the military judge and should follow the same agenda.[19]

---

11. R.C.M. 901(b). United States v. Wheatcraft, 23 M.J. 687 (A.F.C.M.R. 1986) (although record failed to note the court members who were present, the court concluded, by relying in part on logical inferences, that all court members were present throughout the trial). *See also* United States v. Perkinson, 16 M.J. 400 (C.M.A. 1983) (eleventh hour action by prosecution to amend convening order).

R.C.M. 813(a) spells out in detail that the trial counsel is to announce the name and rank of each participant, present or absent. The Drafters Analysis for Rule 901 indicates that the purpose behind this announcement is to ensure that the trial does not inadvertently proceed with one of the necessary parties absent.

12. R.C.M. 813(b). *See also* United States v. Nichelson, 18 C.M.A. 69, 39 C.M.R. 69 (1968).
13. R.C.M. 803, 804, 805.
14. R.C.M. 804(b)(1). For a further discussion on the presence of the accused at the court-martial, see Chapter 15.
15. R.C.M. 804(b)(2).
16. R.C.M. 805(c).
17. R.C.M. 805(c) Discussion. *See also* Ungar v. Sarafite, 376 U.S. 575 (1964); United States v. Morris, 23 C.M.A. 319, 49 C.M.R. 653 (1975); United States v. Kinard, 21 C.M.A. 300, 45 C.M.R. 74 (1972). Under paragraphs 44c and 46c, of the 1969 Manual for Courts-Martial, only the military judge or convening authority could excuse the counsel from attending.
18. R.C.M. 803, 805.
19. R.C.M. 502(b)(2)(C).

§ 12-2(D). Noting the Detail of a Court Reporter and an Interpreter.

In a general court-martial and in a special court-martial in which a punitive discharge is authorized, a court reporter must be detailed in order that a verbatim record might be prepared.[20] Subject to Service regulations, court reporters may be detailed in other cases.[21] In any event, the fact that a court reporter has been detailed must be announced by the trial counsel during the Article 39(a) session.[22] Presumably the purpose of this notation in open session is not only to note for the record who was actually present during the trial but also provides a helpful identification for locating the reporter at some later date and incidentally serves as a reminder to the parties that the trial proceedings will be recorded.

If the court reporter is disqualified for some reason and that fact has not been resolved by the convening authority before the first session has been called to order, the military judge should be advised of the matter at the first opportunity.[23] A reporter may be disqualified if he has served in the same case, as either an accuser, witness, investigating officer, counsel for either party, or a court member of a previous trial and the trial in question is a continuation of that proceeding.[24] If the reporter has not been previously sworn, the oath should be administered at this point by the trial counsel.[25]

In cases where the accused cannot speak or understand English, an interpreter should be detailed to the court.[26] The disqualifications noted for court reporters also apply to interpreters.[27] If the accused desires to obtain a qualified unofficial interpreter he may do so at no cost to the government.[28] Although the *Manual's* suggested script makes no mention of addressing the detail of interpreters at the Article 39(a) session, R.C.M. 902(c) indicates that it should be announced at the same time that the trial counsel announces the detail and identity of the reporter. The oath for interpreters should also be administered by the trial counsel.[29]

---

20. *See generally* R.C.M. 1103. It is not necessary that the convening authority personally appoint the reporter. R.C.M. 501(c).
21. R.C.M. 501(c) Discussion.
22. R.C.M. 901(c).
23. R.C.M. 502(f).
24. R.C.M. 502(e)(2).
25. R.C.M. 901(c). The text of an appropriate oath is set out in R.C.M. 807(b)(2) Discussion.
26. R.C.M. 502(e)(3)(A).
27. R.C.M. 502(e)(2). Noting that there were few military cases addressing the qualifications and use of interpreters, the court in United States v. Ladell, 30 M.J. 672 (A.F.C.M.R. 1990), concluded that a court member who asked that a Spanish-speaking witness speak up so he could hear her statements as well as those of the interpreter did not prejudice the accused; even assuming that the court member was attempting to augment the testimony through his own interpretation, the court noted its reluctance to disqualify a member because of special expertise.
28. R.C.M. 502(e)(2)(A) Discussion. Service regulations generally cover payment of expenses, allowances, and per diem.
29. R.C.M. 901(c). *See* R.C.M. 807(b)(2) for a sample oath for interpreters.

§ 12-2(E). Announcing the Detail and Qualifications of the Trial Counsel.

Because the trial counsel (including assistant trial counsel) are not detailed to a particular court-martial through written convening orders,[30] and generally need not even be detailed in writing, it is critical that trial counsel's appointment be announced orally at the Article 39(a) session.[31] Otherwise, it may be difficult to establish in the record itself that the trial counsel was properly detailed. The *Manual* directs that the detail of trial counsel will be accomplished in accordance with Service regulations.[32] The Army, for example, permits the Staff Judge Advocate or a delegate to detail the trial counsel.[33] The delegate could be the chief trial counsel who would then be authorized to detail himself to the court. For further discussion on the process of detailing counsel to the court, see Chapter 8.

The trial counsel should also announce that all members of the prosecution team are otherwise qualified under Article 27(b) and whether they have previously been sworn under Article 42(a), U.C.M.J.[34] If any trial counsel has not been previously sworn, that may be accomplished after the judge has reviewed the qualifications of the defense counsel.[35] Finally, the trial counsel should announce whether he, or any member of the prosecution team, has acted in any manner which might tend to disqualify him.[36] If it appears that the trial counsel is not qualified, the *Manual* apparently contemplates that the matter will be inquired into and resolved by the military judge before the Article 39(a) session proceeds any further.[37] If necessary, the judge may conduct a hearing on the issue, including the questioning of witnesses and consideration of other evidence.[38] The presence of an unqualified trial counsel is not a jurisdictional defect and presumably may be waived by the accused.[39]

---

30. Before the promulgation of the 1984 revisions to the Manual for Courts-Martial and amendments to Article 27, trial counsel and defense counsel were detailed to a particular court by the convening authority. And that detail was reflected in the convening orders. *See* R.C.M. 503 Analysis.
31. *See* R.C.M. 503(c)(2).
32. *See* R.C.M. 503(c)(1).
33. *See, e.g.,* AR 27-10, para. 5-3.
34. *See* Appendix 3.
35. *See infra* § 12-2(F)(1).
36. R.C.M. 901(d)(1). The qualifications for trial counsel are set out in R.C.M. 502 and are discussed in Chapter 8.
37. R.C.M. 901(d)(3).
38. R.C.M. 901(d)(3) Discussion.
39. Wright v. United States, 2 M.J. 9 (C.M.A. 1976); United States v. Daigneault, 18 M.J. 503 (A.F.C.M.R. 1984) (defects in detailing of trial counsel are procedural in nature and must be tested for prejudice).

§ 12-2(F). Announcing the Detail and Qualifications of the Defense Counsel and the Judge's Inquiry Concerning the Accused's Rights to Counsel.

§ 12-2(F)(1). Detail and Qualifications of Counsel.

After the detail and qualifications of the trial counsel are established for the record, the detailed defense counsel should make a similar announcement with regard to the defense team.[40] Even if the accused does not desire the assistance of the detailed military counsel, that counsel should appear at the initial Article 39(a) pretrial session and remain until the accused's rights to counsel have been explained by the judge and the accused formally excuses his detailed counsel.

Like the trial counsel, the detailed defense counsel should indicate for the record who detailed him, and any assistant defense counsel, to the court.[41] Counsel should also indicate whether the detailed defense counsel are qualified[42] and sworn,[43] under Articles 27(b) and 42(a), respectively. The qualifications of counsel are discussed in Chapter 8. If it appears that a defense counsel is not qualified, the judge should resolve the issue before proceeding further. If the disqualification is not waivable or the accused decides not to waive the disqualification, then the judge should explain the options available to the accused.[44] For example, where the accused has obtained an individual military counsel and it is the detailed military counsel who is disqualified, the accused could simply excuse that counsel and proceed with the trial. In any event, the authority who detailed the counsel should be notified of the problem.[45] In some cases it may be necessary to terminate the attorney-client privilege where the defense counsel is disqualified.[46]

During the course of the Article 39(a) session the judge is charged with conducting several inquiries concerning the right to counsel. The first, which is sometimes referred to as the *Donohew* inquiry, is required in every case. The second and third inquiries, the *Breese* and *Faretta* inquiries respectively, are required only where the circumstances in each trial dictate.

---

40. R.C.M. 901(d)(2).
41. *Id.* R.C.M. 503(c)(2).
42. *See supra* § 8-3(B)(1).
43. United States v. Ponder, 29 M.J. 782 (A.C.M.R. 1989) (nonprejudicial error not to give oath to civilian counsel where it appeared that he had previously practiced before another Army court-martial).

In United States v. Honeycutt, 27 M.J. 863 (A.F.C.M.R. 1989), *aff'd on other grounds,* 29 M.J. 416 (C.M.A. 1990), the court observed that the record of trial failed to show that the civilian defense counsel had taken the necessary oath. Noting that meeting the qualifications to be a counsel does not ensure compliance with Article 42(a), the court indicated that counsel should be administered the oath unless it appears that they were given a "one-time" oath.

44. R.C.M. 901(d)(3) Discussion.
45. *Id.*
46. *See, e.g.,* United States v. Hanson, 24 M.J. 377 (C.M.A. 1987) (military judge "relieved" counsel as detailed defense counsel because he had doubts about counsel's effectiveness; counsel was kept on case as assistant defense counsel); United States v. Saenz, 18 M.J. 328 (C.M.A. 1984).

§ 12-2(F)(2). The *Donohew* Inquiry.

After the defense counsel has announced the detail and qualifications of the defense team, the judge is charged with personally advising the accused of his rights to counsel.[47]

Although the accused's rights are spelled out in both the U.C.M.J.[48] Manual for Courts-Martial,[49] the Court in *United States v. Donohew*[50] held that in order to insure that the accused is properly apprised of those rights and can intelligently select which rights he will invoke, the military judge is required to *sua sponte* advise the accused of those rights and determine his election. This inquiry is required even though the counsel may have already so advised the accused.[51] The judge may not simply rely on the assurances of the counsel and the accused that they have discussed the various rights to counsel and that the accused understands his rights. The *Manual* specifically states what advice the judge must give to the accused. R.C.M. 901(d)(4) requires that the military judge in open session:

(A) Inform the accused of the rights to be represented by military counsel detailed to the defense; or by individual military counsel requested by the accused, if such military counsel is reasonably available; and by civilian counsel, either alone or in association with military counsel, if such civilian counsel is provided at no expense to the United States;[52]

(B) Inform the accused that, if afforded individual military counsel, the accused may request retention of detailed counsel as associate counsel, which request may be granted or denied in the sole discretion of the authority who detailed the counsel;[53] and

(C) Ascertain from the accused whether the accused understands these rights.[54]

---

47. R.C.M. 901(d)(4).
48. *See* Art. 38, U.C.M.J.
49. R.C.M. 502(d), 506, 901(d)(4). See Chapter 8 for a further discussion of the accused's rights to counsel.
50. 18 C.M.A. 149, 39 C.M.R. 149 (1969).
51. *See* United States v. Bowman, 20 C.M.A. 119, 42 C.M.R. 311 (1970).
52. This subsection is based upon the *Donohew* decision.
53. See Article 38(b)(6), U.C.M.J., which indicates that an accused is not entitled to be represented by more than one military counsel, but that if the accused decides to be represented by an individual military defense counsel, the detailing authority may in his sole discretion appoint an assistant military counsel or permit the detailed counsel to remain on the case as associate counsel.

In United States v. Hanson, 24 M.J. 377 (C.M.A. 1987), the military judge "relieved" the detailed defense counsel after ruling that the accused's guilty pleas were improvident, because the judge questioned whether counsel was being effective. In speaking to the accused, he specifically stated that he was not severing the attorney-client relationship. Another defense counsel was detailed to the case, and the original counsel remained as assistant defense counsel.

54. United States v. Donohew, 18 C.M.A. 149, 29 C.M.R. 149 (1969) (accused should personally respond); United States v. Nichols, 38 M.J. 717 (A.C.M.R. 1993) (court condemned practice of military judge explaining counsel and forum rights in en masse proceeding; nonprejudicial error).

Despite these clear and explicit guidelines, a number of cases involve erroneous advice to the accused, especially with regard to the possibility that the detailed military counsel may be retained, at the discretion of the authority who detailed that counsel. In several cases the courts have held that such advice was nonprejudicial error.[55] But in *United States v. Jerasi*,[56] the courts in an *en banc* opinion ruled that the judge's advice that the accused's detailed counsel would be automatically excused was not incorrect advice. The court reached that conclusion by reading Article 38(b), U.C.M.J. to mean that the authority appointing the detailed military counsel probably does not have the discretion to permit that counsel to remain on the case.[57]

Where it appears that the accused had an attorney-client relationship with an absent counsel, it is appropriate for the judge to inquire into whether that relationship was terminated with the consent of the accused.[58]

§ 12-2(F)(3). The *Breese* Inquiry and Conflicts of Interest.

In order to stem the problem of the accused being represented by a counsel with a conflict of interest, especially where one counsel is representing several accuseds, the Court of Appeals for the Armed Forces in *United States v. Breese*[59] required trial judges to conduct a specific inquiry regarding a possible conflict, determine the accused's understanding of the right to have a

---

55. *See, e.g.,* United States v. Johnson, 21 M.J. 211 (C.M.A. 1986) (case remanded for determination whether the accused understood his rights where judge gave incomplete advice; the court declined to overrule its decision in *United States v. Donohew*); United States v. Saul, 26 M.J. 568 (A.F.C.M.R. 1988) (failure to even advise accused of rights to counsel did not amount to plain or prejudicial error); United States v. Carroll, 23 M.J. 766 (A.F.C.M.R. 1987) (the court read United States v. Johnson, 21 M.J. 211 (C.M.A. 1986), to mean that the accused must affirmatively establish that the failure to give a complete *Donohew* advice was prejudicial error).

United States v. Ayala, 21 M.J. 977 (N.M.C.M.R. 1986) (accused failed to establish a colorable claim of prejudice where he was misadvised of his rights to civilian and individual military counsel); United States v. Roberts, 20 M.J. 754 (N.M.C.M.R. 1985) (failure to use exact language of R.C.M. 901 was not error); United States v. Vasquez, 19 M.J. 729 (N.M.C.M.R. 1984) (judge erred in advising the accused that if he selected individual counsel that his detailed counsel would be automatically excused; court expressed chagrin that such errors would occur and noted that counsel should not sit idly by if judge misadvises the accused); United States v. Butler, 19 M.J. 724 (N.M.C.M.R. 1984) (similar misadvice as in *Vasquez*); United States v. Mullen, 18 M.J. 569 (N.M.C.M.R. 1984); United States v. Griffin, 16 M.J. 836 (N.M.C.M.R. 1983) (accused prejudiced by judge's erroneous advice); United States v. Hutchinson, 15 M.J. 1056 (N.M.C.M.R. 1983) (harmless error where judge failed to inquire about accused's desires regarding individual counsel).

The problem in this area, as the courts recognize, is that it is difficult to gauge prejudice where it is not clear from the record what different choices the accused might have made had he been correctly advised of his rights. The fact that he indicates for the record that he is satisfied with his counsel does not usually end the matter if it later develops that he might have chosen another counsel. If the record is unclear, one solution is to order a *DuBay* hearing at the trial level and determine what, if any, effect the judge's erroneous advice had on the accused. For a discussion of *DuBay* hearings, see § 16-3(B).

56. 20 M.J. 719 (N.M.C.M.R. 1985) *(en banc).*
57. 20 M.J. at 734.
58. *See* United States v. Snow, 10 M.J. 742 (N.M.C.M.R. 1981).
59. 11 M.J. 17 (C.M.A. 1981).

conflict-free counsel, and assuming that a conflict exists, obtain the accused's election of counsel on the record. This inquiry and advice have also been specifically incorporated into the *Manual*.[60]

In *Breese*, the court added that in the absence of an inquiry by the judge, where a counsel is representing multiple defendants, there is a presumption that a conflict of interest in fact existed.[61] However, in *United States v. Devitt*,[62] the court indicated that that presumption may be rebutted.[63]

It is important to note that conflicts of interest may arise in a number of settings and not just where multiple representation is involved.[64] In *United States v. Kidwell*,[65] for example, the court found a conflict of interest where the defense counsel failed to follow up on an informal agreement with the chief of military justice that the latter would recommend an administrative discharge in return for the accused's surrender of blank identification cards. Without consulting the accused, the defense counsel decided that society's interest in obtaining additional cards outweighed the accused's interest in obtaining relief on pending charges.

Where the judge is presented with information which would reasonably lead to the conclusion that a conflict might exist, the judge should question counsel about the matter.[66] Where the judge is not presented with any information at

---

60. R.C.M. 901(d)(4)(D). *See also* FED. R. CRIM. P. 44(c), which generally served as the pattern for the *Breese* inquiry.

In United States v. Augusztin, 30 M.J. 707 (N.M.C.M.R. 1990), the court discussed extensively the requirements set out in *Breese* and in other federal cases addressing the issue. The court indicated that it is the judge alone who is responsible for undertaking the accused's attempt to waive any conflict of interests to ensure that such waivers are knowingly and intelligently made. In doing so, the judge should elicit a narrative response from the accused as to his or her understanding of the right to conflict-free counsel.

61. 11 M.J. at 23. *See also* United States v. Smith, 36 M.J. 455 (C.M.A. 1993) (rebuttable presumption of actual conflict where multiple representation has occurred and judge has failed to conduct inquiry; Breese inquiry goes only to question of whether conflict existed; it does not necessarily trigger presumption of prejudice). *See also* United States v. Deifer, 30 M.J. 1038 (A.C.M.R. 1990) (counsel represented accused and compatriot); United States v. Devitt, 22 M.J. 940 (A.F.C.M.R. 1986); United States v. Cote, 11 M.J. 892 (A.F.C.M.R. 1981).

62. 20 M.J. 240 (C.M.A. 1985). On further review in *Devitt*, the Air Force court at 22 M.J. 940, and ultimately the Court of Appeals at 24 M.J. 307 (C.M.A. 1987), concluded that the husband-wife accuseds' representation by the same counsel did not present an actual conflict of interest.

63. *Id.* at 244.

64. United States v. Caritativo, 37 M.J. 175 (C.M.A. 1993) (no conflict of interest where defense counsel's performance ratings were reviewed by Staff Judge Advocate); United States v. Smith, 39 M.J. 587 (A.F.C.M.R. 1994) (counsel had represented government witness against accused at earlier Article 15 proceeding; accused waived conflict; court stated that it is more difficult to show actual conflict where representation is successive rather than simultaneous; in the latter, the conflict arises if the cases are substantially related, if privileged information is revealed, or if counsel's loyalties are divided).

65. 20 M.J. 1020 (A.C.M.R. 1985). In United States v. Whidbee, 28 M.J. 823 (C.G.C.M.R. 1989), the defense counsel was a subordinate of the prosecutor. Following a *DuBay* hearing into the matter, the appellate court concluded that the accused had not been adequately apprised of the nature and extent of the conflict. In lengthy dictum, the court offered its views on the dangers associated with these sorts of arrangements.

66. *See, e.g.*, United States v. Smith, 36 M.J. 455 (C.M.A. 1993) (judge must conduct inquiry); United States v. Jeffries, 33 M.J. 826 (A.F.C.M.R. 1991) (judge was not required to discuss issue of conflict of interest directly with the accused).

§ 12-2(F)(4)

trial that might otherwise indicate a possible conflict of interest, there is some authority for the proposition that no *Breese*-type inquiry is required.[67] Because it is the counsel, especially the defense counsel, who are in the best position to spot initially a possible conflict of interest, an equal, perhaps greater burden rests upon their shoulders to apprise the accused beforehand of the potential conflict. For further discussion on problems of multiple representation, see § 15-2(B)(2).

§ 12-2(F)(4). The *Faretta* Inquiry and Self-Representation.

In the rare case where the accused desires to waive all of his rights to counsel and invoke his right to defend himself, the judge must conduct a thorough inquiry and determine whether the waiver is intentionally and competently made.[68] The inquiry has its genesis in *Faretta v. California*,[69] in which the Supreme Court recognized the accused's Sixth Amendment right to represent himself. The right to self-representation is not absolute, however, and the request may be denied for cause.[70] For example, the right may be denied, or withdrawn, where the accused decides during the trial that he wishes to dismiss counsel and represent himself, where the accused becomes

---

67. United States v. Murphy, 36 M.J. 1137 (A.C.M.R. 1993) (military judge not required to conduct Breese inquiry where he was presented with no information indicating a possible conflict of interest); United States v. Deifer, 30 M.J. 1038 (A.C.M.R. 1990) (questions of multiple representation should be raised in every case, no matter how remote the conflict may appear); United States v. Russaw, 15 M.J. 801 (A.C.M.R. 1983).
In United States v. Mervine, 23 M.J. 801 (N.M.C.M.R. 1986), the accused raised for the first time on appeal the fact that the defense counsel was apparently an administrative subordinate of the prosecutor. The court indicated that, under the facts the trial judge was not put on notice that a potential conflict existed and indicated that it would not presume prejudice.
68. *See* Faretta v. California, 422 U.S. 806 (1975); United States v. Mix, 35 M.J. 283 (C.M.A. 1992) (military judge advised accused of consequences of self-representation); United States v. Proctor, 34 M.J. 549 (A.F.C.M.R. 1992) (judge did not err in granting accused's request to represent himself); United States v. Streater, 32 M.J. 337 (C.M.A. 1991) (judge committed harmless error in failing to question accused closely on his mental competence to represent himself where sanity board was pending; judge should make affirmative finding on the record that accused is competent). *Cf.* United States v. Mix, 32 M.J. 974 (A.C.M.R. 1991) (court rejected argument that there is really a two-tier level of competence to stand trial and that an accused must have a higher level of mental competence to represent himself).
In United States v. Beatty, 25 M.J. 311 (C.M.A. 1987), the judge was apparently not aware of the implications of self-representation and treated the remainder of the trial as any other trial. The court concluded that the judge's failure to conduct a *Faretta* inquiry was harmless error. The court indicated that the test is whether it was satisfied beyond a reasonable doubt that the judge's error did not produce a more adverse result.
United States v. Fox, 31 M.J. 739 (A.F.C.M.R. 1990) (judge conducted inquiry), *repub. at* 32 M.J. 744 (A.F.C.M.R. 1990), *reconsid.*, 32 M.J. 747 (A.F.C.M.R. 1991); United States v. Howell, 11 C.M.A. 712, 29 C.M.R. 528 (1960); United States v. Tanner, 16 M.J. 930 (N.M.C.M.R. 1983) (accused was denied the right). *See also* R.C.M. 506(d).
69. 422 U.S. 806 (1975).
70. *Id.* United States v. Dresen, 36 M.J. 1103 (A.F.C.M.R. 1993), *rev'd on other grounds*, 40 M.J. 462 (C.M.A. 1994) (court rejected argument that degree of mental competency for proceeding pro se is higher than that required for assisting in a defense); United States v. Freeman, 28 M.J. 789 (N.M.C.M.R. 1989) (accused lacked sufficient mental power and understanding to conduct full defense; judge later ordered inquiry into accused's mental capacity).

disruptive and an obstructionist in his tactics, or where it appears that the accused simply does not appreciate the impact of self-representation.[71]

In determining whether the accused is making a knowing and intelligent decision, the judge could apprise the accused:

    1. Of the nature of the charges, maximum punishments, and possible defenses;[72]
    2. That a trial is more than merely telling one's story but includes procedural rules;
    3. That a lawyer with training and experience will be representing the prosecution;
    4. That the accused's inexperience may result in tactical mistakes at the trial, such as failing to object to evidence;
    5. That an accused is generally not permitted to complain on appeal about his inadequacy; and
    6. That his effectiveness may be reduced because he is serving both as an accused and a defense counsel.[73]

There is obviously a thin line demarking where the judge's thorough advice and inquiry ends and becomes a directive to an otherwise competent accused that he should not represent himself. Whether the accused understands the technical rules of court-martial procedure is not dispositive. The test, according to *Faretta*, should be whether the accused is literate, competent, and understanding. Under the circumstances the accused's decision may seem unwise. But it is his constitutional right to make that decision.

Failure to conduct such an inquiry may result in either a denial of effective assistance of counsel, where the request is summarily granted, or denial of the right of self-representation.[74]

Where the request is properly granted, the judge may nonetheless appoint a "standby counsel," over the accused's objection, to assist the accused where the case is complicated or in those cases where the accused requests one.[75] But

---

71. *Id.* R.C.M. 506(d). United States v. Dresen, 36 M.J. 1103 (A.F.C.M.R. 1993), rev'd on other grounds, 40 M.J. 462 (C.M.A. 1994) (accused's actions rejecting military counsel and request for long continuance to obtain another civilian counsel amounted to proceeding pro se. The court indicated that those actions amounted to a knowing and voluntary choice to proceed pro se).

72. *See* Von Moltke v. Gillies, 332 U.S. 708 (1948), where the court laid the groundwork for the subsequent judicial inquiry under *Faretta*.

73. *See* LaFave and Israel, *Criminal Procedure,* at 554 (Student ed. 1992). United States v. Mix, 35 M.J. 283 (C.M.A. 1992) (court noted various inquiries required in federal courts but declined to decide what type of inquiry is required; copy of inquiry is included as appendix to opinion).

74. United States v. Tanner, 16 M.J. 930 (N.M.C.M.R. 1983). The test on appeal is not one of harmless constitutional error. If the judge erred in denying the right, reversal of the conviction follows. Faretta v. California, 422 U.S. 806 (1975). McKaskle v. Wiggins, 465 U.S. 168 (1984). Chapman v. United States, 553 F.2d 886 (5th Cir. 1977). *Cf.* United States v. Beatty, 25 M.J. 311 (C.M.A. 1987) (failure to conduct inquiry was harmless error).

75. McKaskle v. Wiggins, 465 U.S. 168 (1984). R.C.M. 506(d); United States v. Beatty, 25 M.J. 311 (C.M.A. 1987) (individual military counsel remained on the case after the accused indicated a desire to represent himself); United States v. Dresen, 36 M.J. 1103 (A.F.C.M.R. 1993), rev'd on

the standby counsel's advice is not binding on the accused, who retains the right to make any necessary tactical decisions.[76] In addition, too much assistance by the standby counsel may deny the accused his right to self-representation.[77] The appointment of a standby counsel generally does not entitle the accused to a hybrid defense team where the accused acts as co-counsel to the defense counsel.[78]

A point related to the issue of self-representation and standby counsel is the *Manual* provision that permits the accused to have the assistance of a person who is not a lawyer during the trial itself. That person's presence at the defense table is at the discretion of the judge.[79] That does not mean, however, that the nonlawyer assistant may in any way speak for, or "represent," the accused; the right to self-representation does not entitle the accused to delegate that right to a nonlawyer.[80] The general rule remains. Unless an accused is representing himself, he is entitled only to representation by a qualified attorney at a general or special court-martial.[81]

Having made the decision to represent himself, the accused is responsible for any tactical decisions.[82] His errors in making those choices do not necessarily indicate that the trial judge erred in permitting the accused to waive his rights to counsel.[83]

Although the right to self-representation is a constitutional right, there appears to be no requirement that the military judge *sua sponte* apprise the accused of that right before determining who will represent him.[84] Thus, the

---

other grounds, 40 M.J. 462 (C.M.A. 1994) (court required military counsel, who had been released by the accused, to remain at counsel's table over accused's objection).

76. McKaskle v. Wiggins, 465 U.S. 168 (1984).

77. *Id.* The Court in *McKaskle* indicated that test is whether: (1) the standby counsel's representation substantially interfered with the accused's tactical choices or in effect spoke instead of the accused on any matter of importance or (2) assuming the accused presented his case in his own way, whether the standby counsel's actions destroyed the jury's perception that the accused was representing himself.

78. McKaskle v. Wiggins, 465 U.S. 168 (1984) (dictum). *Cf.* United States v. Beatty, 25 M.J. 311 (C.M.A. 1987) (trial was conducted by "stand-by" counsel without objection from accused). *See generally* "Assistance of Counsel: A Right to Hybrid Representation," 57 B.U. L. REV. 570 (1977); Note, "The Accused as Co-Counsel: The Case for the Hybrid Defense," 12 VALPARAISO U. L. REV. 329 (1978).

79. R.C.M. 506(e). *See also* Rule 615, MIL. R. EVID.

80. *See, e.g.,* United States v. Kelley, 539 F.2d 1199 (9th Cir. 1976). *See generally* Comment, "Denial of Defendant's Request for Representation by a Nonattorney Does Not Abuse Sixth Amendment," 26 EMORY L.J. 457 (1977).

81. *See* R.C.M. 502(d). A different rule might apply at a summary court-martial where the accused might provide his own representative or spokesman. *See infra* § 15-28(C).

82. United States v. Fox, 31 M.J. 739 (A.F.C.M.R. 1990) (court rejected argument that pro se defendant was entitled to special treatment by trial and appellate courts), *repub. at* 32 M.J. 744 (A.F.C.M.R. 1990), *reconsid.,* 32 M.J. 747 (A.F.C.M.R. 1991); United States v. Mogavero, 20 M.J. 762 (A.F.C.M.R. 1985).

83. *Id.* United States v. Aponte, 591 F.2d 1247 (9th Cir. 1978).

84. *See* United States v. Bowie, 21 M.J. 453 (C.M.A. 1986) (judge not required to inform accused of the right to self-representation). The right to self-representation is not on the same plane as the right to the assistance of counsel and because most view the former as a poor choice there is little enthusiasm for apprising an accused of that right and perhaps discouraging him from relying upon his detailed or requested counsel.

Faretta inquiry should only be triggered when the accused indicates in some fashion a desire to represent himself. An equivocal statement to that effect should be enough to cause the judge to at least question the accused further. An equivocal request, however, should not be sufficient to support a judge's decision to let the accused represent himself.[85]

§ 12-2(F)(5). Accused's Election of Counsel.

After the judge has explained the accused's various rights to counsel and determined that the accused fully understands those rights, the judge should ask the accused to state for the record who will represent him.[86]

If prior to trial the accused has unsuccessfully sought the assistance of an individual military counsel he should consider renewing that request before the military judge in the Article 39(a) session.[87] If necessary, a continuance may be granted to the defense to obtain either a civilian counsel or individual military counsel.[88]

Finally, the military judge should announce that it appears that all counsel possess the required qualifications. Whether they are qualified is the judges' decision.[89]

§ 12-2(G). Administering the Oaths and Announcing the Detail of the Military Judge.

If any counsel, trial or defense, has not of trial already taken the prescribed oath for counsel at the time, the judge will administer the oath to counsel during the Article 39(a) session.[90] Service regulations usually provide for administering one-time written oaths to military counsel and filing copies of the oath in department headquarters.[91] Thus, in most cases it will not be necessary for any military counsel to be sworn at trial. After the judge has administered any necessary oaths, he should indicate who detailed him to the court.[92] As with both the trial counsel and defense counsel, the judge is no longer appointed to the court by a convening authority through a convening order.[93] Instead, the procedure for detailing judges is determined by each Service.[94]

---

85. *See, e.g.*, United States v. Kennedy, 564 F.2d 1329 (9th Cir. 1977); Meeks v. Craven, 482 F.2d 465 (9th Cir. 1973).
86. *See* R.C.M. 901(d)(4)(E).
87. The topic of requesting individual military counsel before trial is addressed in § 8-3(B).
88. *See, e.g.*, United States v. Kinard, 21 C.M.A. 300, 45 C.M.R. 74 (1972); United States v. Stevens, 27 M.J. 626 (A.F.C.M.R. 1988) (not an abuse of discretion to deny request for continuance so busy civilian counsel could prepare for trial and, because of denial, trial proceeded with detailed defense counsel); United States v. Brown, 10 M.J. 635 (A.C.M.R. 1980).
89. *See* Soriano v. Hosken, 9 M.J. 221 (C.M.A. 1980).
90. R.C.M. 901(d)(5).
91. *See, e.g.*, AR 27-10, Chapter 11, AFI 51-201 para. 5.4.
92. R.C.M. 503(b)(2). United States v. Hutto, 29 M.J. 917 (A.C.M.R. 1989) (trial judge failed to announce who had detailed him to court).
93. See § 8-3(A) for a discussion of the detailing process for military judges.
94. R.C.M. 503(b)(1). *See, e.g.*, AR 27-10, Chapter 8.

Generally, the authority to detail a judge is delegated by the Chief Trial Judge to chief circuit judges or to judges authorized to preside over general courts-martial. Unless there is a Service requirement that the detailing of a judge to a particular court must be in writing,[95] the judge's oral announcement of that fact in the Article 39(a) session is critical. Failure to properly detail a judge may result in jurisdictional error.[96]

§ 12-2(H). Challenges for Cause to the Military Judge.

The trial counsel will normally state for the record the general nature of the charges, and indicate who preferred, forwarded, and investigated the charges. Presumably this information is announced not so much for the benefit of the accused but for the judge who must determine whether there is any just reason for recusing himself. Following the notation of this information, the trial counsel usually asks the judge whether he is aware of any matter that may be a ground for challenge. Depending on the judge's response, each counsel then indicates whether he wishes to challenge the judge for cause. In some cases counsel may wish to question the judge about a particular ground for challenge before deciding whether to lodge a challenge.[97]

The general information that the trial counsel recites serves as a sort of tickler for the judge to recall whether he has had any prior connection with the case. As a practical matter, before trial begins the judge will have already determined some background information on the case. For example, he may be aware that a particular commander has preferred drug charges against the accused. However, to rule properly on any challenges, it may be necessary to present more detailed information about the charges and who processed them. Failure to disclose a ground for challenge may in itself disqualify the judge.[98]

Grounds for Challenging the Judge. There is no peremptory challenge in military practice for removing a military judge from the case. Thus, the burden is on the moving party to establish that some valid reason exists for

---

[95]. R.C.M. 503(b)(2).

[96]. *See* § 4-15(A). *Cf.* United States v. Hutto, 29 M.J. 917 (A.C.M.R. 1989) (failure to identify appointing authority was not jurisdictional error absent evidence to contrary that he was properly detailed); United States v. Marsh, 19 M.J. 657 (A.C.M.R. 1984) (minor administrative errors in appointment are not jurisdictional).

[97]. R.C.M. 902(d)(2). United States v. Foley, 37 M.J. 822 (A.F.C.M.R. 1993) (court noted that no rule in the Manual for Courts-Martial permits a party to challenge a military judge for cause; instead, said the court, a party may move that the military judge determine if he or she is disqualified); United States v. Allen, 31 M.J. 572 (N.M.C.M.R. 1990) (judge permitted extensive voir dire on circumstances of his appointment to case and ex parte private conversation with SJA).

United States v. Smith, 30 M.J. 631 (N.M.C.M.R. 1990) (military judge's restriction on civilian defense counsel's attempt to voir dire the judge on possible grounds of bias against the counsel amounted to abuse of discretion; court held that, under the facts, accused's decision to proceed with bench trial did not amount to waiver). *Cf.* United States v. Small, 21 M.J. 218 (C.M.A. 1986) (judge properly declined to respond to defense counsel's inquiry on voir dire concerning the judge's disposition towards a punitive discharge).

[98]. *See* United States v. Morgan, 44 C.M.R. 699 (A.C.M.R. 1971).

challenging the judge for cause.[99] A number of potential grounds exist for challenging the judge. The following list is a compilation of reasons for disqualification found in Article 26, U.C.M.J. and R.C.M. 502, 503, and 902:

1. The judge's partiality might reasonably be questioned;[100]

---

99. United States v. Allen, 31 M.J. 572 (N.M.C.M.R. 1990); United States v. Elzy, 22 M.J. 640 (A.C.M.R. 1986) (no automatic disqualification where counsel informs judge that accused intends to commit perjury); United States v. Martinez, 19 M.J. 652 (A.C.M.R. 1984).

See generally Cantrell, "Challenging the Military Judge for Cause," 11 THE ADVOCATE 73 (1979); Tyrell, "Piercing the Judicial Veil: Judicial Disqualification in the Federal and Military Systems," ARMY LAW., Apr. 1989, at 46. See also § 15-2(B)(4).

100. R.C.M. 902(a). This broadly stated ground for challenge is the only one listed here that may be waived by the accused. But it may be waived only after the judge has fully disclosed on the record the basis of the possible lack of impartiality. R.C.M. 902(e).

See, e.g., United States v. Sanchez, 37 M.J. 426 (C.M.A. 1993) (judge not disqualified by mere fact that he had previously conducted magistrate's review of commander's decision to confine the accused); United States v. Oakley, 33 M.J. 27 (C.M.A. 1991) (fact that trial judge had denied suppression motions in earlier trials of accused's co-actors did not require recusal in trial with members); United States v. Sherrod, 26 M.J. 30 (C.M.A. 1988) (possible appearance of impropriety existed, and trial judge was therefore disqualified to preside where he lived next door to one of the homes burglarized by the accused and whose daughter was friend of child assaulted during that same burglary).

United States v. Elzy, 25 M.J. 416 (C.M.A. 1988) (trial judge not required to recuse himself where defense counsel's actions indicated that he was disassociating himself from accused who apparently intended to commit perjury if he testified); see also infra § 15-2(B)(4).

United States v. Foley, 37 M.J. 822 (A.F.C.M.R. 1993) (judge's ex parte communication with Article 32 Investigating Officer not disqualifying); United States v. Edmond, 37 M.J. 787 (C.G.C.M.R. 1993), aff'd on other grounds, 41 M.J. 419 (1995) (trial judge not disqualified merely because he had presided at trial of co-accused).

United States v. Aue, 37 M.J. 528 (A.C.M.R. 1993) (reasonable person having full knowledge of facts would not have questioned impartiality of trial judge; mere suspicion is not enough).

United States v. Dudding, 34 M.J. 975 (A.C.M.R. 1992) (military judge's questions did not compare accused to Saddam Hussein; court noted that trial counsel had not objected at trial); Wilson v. Ouelette, 34 M.J. 798 (N.M.C.M.R. 1991) (discussion of disqualification of judges); United States v. Warnock, 34 M.J. 567 (A.C.M.R. 1991) (judge was not biased against the defense although he expressed impatience with counsel and commented on the merits of defense motions).

United States v. Clark, 31 M.J. 721 (A.F.C.M.R. 1990) (noting that the trial judge and the civilian counsel had bickered continuously, the court concluded that the trial judge had not abused his discretion in declining to recuse himself; court provided advice on dealing with unruly counsel). See generally Kuhnell, "Challenging the Military Judge," 17 A.F. L. REV. 50 (Winter 1975).

United States v. Allen, 31 M.J. 572 (N.M.C.M.R. 1990) (although military judge was subject of improper ex parte communication from SJA, he was not subject of unlawful command influence because he did not view it in that light; the test is whether the objective, reasonable man would conclude that a judge's impartiality might reasonably be questioned).

In United States v. Berman, 28 M.J. 615 (A.F.C.M.R. 1989), the court held that the military judge was disqualified from presiding over six trials where he had a sexual relationship with the prosecutor. The court noted that, like Caesar's wife, judges should be above suspicion and observed that normally a judge would not be disqualified by personal or professional relationships. But sometimes, the appearance of partiality is enough to disqualify a judge. Cf. United States v. Anderson, 28 M.J. 895 (A.F.C.M.R. 1989) (cases arising after military judge and prosecutor in Berman discontinued their relationship; court concluded that judge was not disqualified where that prosecutor did not take part in the case).

2. That the judge has a personal bias or prejudice concerning a party;[101]

3. That the judge has personal knowledge of disputed evidence concerning the proceeding;[102]

4. The judge has acted as a counsel,[103] investigating officer,[104] legal officer,[105] staff judge advocate,[106] or convening authority[107] as to any offense in the same case;[108]

United States v. Davis, 27 M.J. 543 (A.C.M.R. 1988) (trial judge did not abuse discretion in not recusing himself where he had previously heard testimony of co-accused and where he had not formed any opinions about credibility and evidence against accused was overwhelming).

United States v. Amos, 26 M.J. 806 (A.C.M.R. 1988) (trial judge not required to recuse himself *sua sponte* where he made comments on record that indicated that it would be hard for him to judge the case fairly because of his prior rulings on the case).

United States v. Wiggers, 25 M.J. 587 (A.C.M.R. 1987) (judge should have recused himself, or granted defense challenge for cause, where he admitted that he would not believe government witness; refusal to do so denied accused right to request trial by judge alone); United States v. Sherrod, 22 M.J. 917 (A.C.M.R. 1986).

101. R.C.M. 902(b)(1). *See* United States v. Ettinger, 36 M.J. 1171 (N.M.C.M.R. 1993) (military judge not disqualified because of racial comments); United States v. Wiggers, 25 M.J. 587 (A.C.M.R. 1987) (military judge was not disqualified under R.C.M. 902(b)(1), which is based upon 28 U.S.C. § 455; that disqualification requires that bias or prejudice be based upon "extrajudicial," not personal, knowledge. In this case, the judge's bias was based upon his determination in a prior case that a witness was not believable); United States v. Rice, 16 M.J. 770 (A.C.M.R. 1983) (pretrial phone call to magistrate concerning the accused's pretrial confinement did not require reversal; judge's disclaimer of bias should be given considerable weight).

102. R.C.M. 902(b)(1). United States v. Conley, 4 M.J. 327 (C.M.A. 1978) (judge possessed handwriting expertise); United States v. Proctor, 34 M.J. 549 (A.F.C.M.R. 1992) (judge's knowledge of facts in case was not disqualifying; knowledge to be disqualifying must be personal in that it comes from an extrajudicial source); United States v. Allen, 31 M.J. 572 (N.M.C.M.R. 1990) (facts learned by judge in judicial capacity cannot serve as basis of disqualification). *Cf.* United States v. Towers, 24 M.J. 143 (C.M.A. 1987) (court member not disqualified to sit in child abuse case even though she had extensive civilian experience as social services counselor); United States v. Jamison, 18 M.J. 540 (A.C.M.R. 1984) (judge possessed specialized knowledge concerning matters in issue on motion to dismiss for lack of jurisdiction).

The fact that the judge presided at a co-accused's trial does not necessarily disqualify him. United States v. Castillo, 18 M.J. 590 (N.M.C.M.R. 1984). *Cf.* United States v. Kratzenberg, 20 M.J. 670 (A.F.C.M.R. 1985) (judge's admission that he had found a co-accused credible indicated that he had personal knowledge of a disputed fact — that person's credibility and that could not be waived); United States v. Scholten, 14 M.J. 939 (A.C.M.R. 1982).

103. R.C.M. 902(b)(2).

104. *Id.* United States v. Goodman, 3 M.J. 1 (C.M.A. 1977). The fact that the judge earlier conducted a pretrial confinement hearing on the accused does not necessarily make the judge an "investigating officer"; United States v. Lynch, 13 M.J. 394 (C.M.A. 1982); United States v. Burrer, 22 M.J. 544 (N.M.C.M.R. 1986) (judge's prior assignment as investigating officer on accused's case was harmless error); United States v. Reeves, 12 M.J. 763 (A.C.M.R. 1981). *Cf.* United States v. Trakowski, 10 M.J. 792 (A.F.C.M.R. 1981) (trial counsel doing so rendered him an investigating officer).

105. R.C.M. 902(b)(2). United States v. Edwards, 20 M.J. 973 (N.M.C.M.R. 1985) (no prejudice to accused where judge had previously served as legal advisor to the command).

106. R.C.M. 902(b)(2).

107. R.C.M. 902(b)(2).

108. This series of disqualifications apparently does not apply to the situation where the judge has previously presided over an earlier trial involving the accused. United States v. Soriano, 20 M.J. 337 (C.M.A. 1985).

5. Where the judge will be a witness in the same case,[109] is an accuser,[110] has forwarded the charges with a personal recommendation,[111] or except in a previous trial, has expressed an opinion as to the guilt of the accused;[112]

6. That the judge is not a commissioned officer;[113]

7. That the judge is not on active duty with one of the armed forces;[114]

8. The judge is not a member of a bar of a federal court or of the highest court of a state;[115]

9. That the judge is not properly certified;[116]

10. In a general court-martial the judge has not been properly designated and assigned;[117] or

11. Where the judge, the judge's spouse, or a person within the third degree of relationship to either is a party to the proceeding, is known by the judge to have an interest that could be substantially affected by the case, or is likely to be a witness.[118]

With the exception of the first ground stated, the lack of impartiality, all other grounds listed may not be waived by the counsel.[119] In the instance where the judge's partiality is alleged, a waiver may follow only where there has been full disclosure of the otherwise disqualifying basis.[120]

Even though the judge has a *sua sponte* duty to recuse himself where one of the foregoing grounds is clearly present,[121] he has an equally compelling duty

---

109. R.C.M. 902(b)(3). United States v. Conley, 4 M.J. 327 (C.M.A. 1978) (judge verified handwriting samples); United States v. Tomchek, 4 M.J. 66 (C.M.A. 1977) (judge was character witness).

United States v. Howard, 33 M.J. 596 (A.C.M.R. 1991) (military judge became de facto witness for prosecution during sentencing when he relied on specialized knowledge regarding types and uses of marijuana in Germany; challenge was not waived and sentencing proceedings were void); United States v. Allen, 31 M.J. 572 (N.M.C.M.R. 1990) (court concluded that military judge would not have been witness); United States v. Griffin, 1 M.J. 784 (A.F.C.M.R. 1976) (judge became witness by telling court members that a witness had been granted immunity).

These cases demonstrate that grounds for disqualification may not arise until the trial is underway. Even so, the judge is disqualified and should not continue to preside. *See also* MIL. R. EVID. 605, which blocks the presiding judge from testifying.

110. R.C.M. 902(b)(3).
111. *Id.*
112. *Id.* United States v. Soriano, 20 M.J. 337 (C.M.A. 1985).
113. Art. 26(b), U.C.M.J.; R.C.M. 502(c).
114. *Id.* The fact that the judge is not in the same Service as the accused would not in itself be a disqualifying factor; service regulations generally permit cross-servicing of military judges. *See also* R.C.M. 201(e)(4).
115. Art. 26(b), U.C.M.J.; R.C.M. 902(b)(4) and 502(c).
116. *Id.* The certification procedures are determined by each service.
117. *Id.*
118. R.C.M. 902(b)(5). This provision is modeled after 28 U.S.C. 455(b)(5), which governs recusal of federal judges.
119. R.C.M. 902(e). *See also* 28 U.S.C. 455(e).
120. R.C.M. 902(e).
121. R.C.M. 902(d)(1). United States v. Sherrod, 26 M.J. 30 (C.M.A. 1988) (once judge is disqualified to sit alone as a judge, he is also disqualified to sit with members).

not to recuse himself unnecessarily.[122] It is therefore important that the judge not recuse himself on the mere suggestion that a disqualifying ground exists.

Although several courts have observed that recusal is not the sole remedy in some cases where the judge might be otherwise disqualified because the judge can always deny a request for trial by judge alone,[123] the better rule is to require recusal and avoid even the appearance of evil.[124]

As with the qualification of counsel, it is important that the ability of the judge to sit be determined at the earliest opportunity in the trial.[125] If at some later point in the trial after evidence has been presented, it becomes apparent that the judge should recuse himself, it will be necessary for the new judge to review, or hear, whatever evidence has already been presented.[126]

§ 12-3. Military Judge's Inquiries Concerning the Accused's Decisions Regarding Composition of the Court.

In a court-martial the accused may exercise one of two options concerning the forum which will hear the case. The first option is to waive his rights to a trial by members and request a trial by judge alone.[1] Assuming first that he decides to proceed with a trial by members and second that he is an enlisted servicemember, he has the additional option of requesting that at least one-third of the members be from the enlisted ranks.[2] At the Article 39(a) session the judge should apprise the accused of these options and determine whether he wishes to exercise either of them.[3] Failure to object to the judge's failure to

---

In United States v. Campos, 42 M.J. 253 (1995), the court held that the trial judge was not required to sua sponte recuse himself where he had been replaced as senior judge, i.e. demoted. The court noted that concerns of RCM 902(a) are met where judge makes full disclosure on record, the defense is given full opportunity to voir dire the judge, and record indicates a lack of prejudice.

See also United States v. Elzy, 25 M.J. 416 (C.M.A. 1988) (trial judge was not required sua sponte to recuse himself where it appeared through defense counsel's comments that accused intended to commit perjury if he testified); United States v. Jones, 15 C.M.R. 967 (A.C.M.R. 1983) (judge has an affirmative duty to avoid the appearance of evil even where there is no challenge).

122. United States v. Proctor, 34 M.J. 549 (A.F.C.M.R. 1992); United States v. Martinez, 19 M.J. 652 (A.C.M.R. 1984); United States v. Montgomery, 16 M.J. 516 (A.C.M.R. 1983); United States v. Stewart, 2 M.J. 423 (A.C.M.R. 1975).

123. See, e.g., United States v. Edmond, 37 M.J. 787 (C.G.C.M.R. 1993), aff'd on other grounds, 41 M.J. 419 (1995) (no evidence in record that denial of challenge to military judge led accused to choose trial by court with members); United States v. Soriano, 15 M.J. 633 (N.M.C.M.R. 1982). Cf. United States v. Sherrod, 26 M.J. 32 (C.M.A. 1988) (judge unsuccessfully attempted to stem appearance of impropriety by denying accused's request for trial by judge alone); United States v. Kratzenberg, 20 M.J. 670 (A.F.C.M.R. 1985) (disqualification cannot be waived by accused's request for bench trial).

124. United States v. Sherrod, 26 M.J. 32 (C.M.A. 1988); United States v. Jones, 15 M.J. 967 (A.C.M.R. 1983) (judge has affirmative duty to avoid even the appearance of evil).

125. 25. R.C.M. 502(f).

126. Art. 29(d), U.C.M.J.; R.C.M. 506(e) and 805(d).

1. Art. 16, U.C.M.J.

2. Art. 25, U.C.M.J.

3. See R.C.M. 903. In United States v. Malone, 29 M.J. 883 (A.C.M.R. 1989), the trial court's failure to inquire was non-prejudicial error where the accused was tried by a court composed of

give this advice and conduct any appropriate inquiries may waive the issue.[4] The next two subsections address the exercise of each of these options during the Article 39(a) session.

§ 12-3(A). Accused's Request for Trial by Judge Alone.

As a general rule the accused is entitled to a bench trial, i.e., trial by judge alone.[5] Exceptions to that general rule exist where the accused's trial is being treated as a capital case,[6] where the court is a special court-martial and no judge has been appointed,[7] or where some other good cause exists for not granting the request.[8]

Article 16, U.C.M.J. requires that the request must be in writing or orally noted on the record,[9] and should be made before the end of the initial Article 39(a) session or in the absence of such a session, before the court is assembled.[10] Unless the accused affirmatively requests trial by judge alone, a military judge is not authorized to sit either as the fact-finder or the sentencing authority.[11] If no such request is made and the judge so acts, the proceedings are normally considered a nullity.[12] The accused may request that the matter

---

officers. Noting that this was a case of first impression, the court distinguished this situation from those where the accused had opted to "waive" a particular forum without the benefit of an inquiry by the judge.

See also United States v. Nichols, 38 M.J. 717 (A.C.M.R. 1993) (court condemned practice of military judge explaining counsel and forum rights in en masse proceeding; nonprejudicial error); United States v. Pettaway, 24 M.J. 589 (N.M.C.M.R. 1987) (the court held that the judge's omission of the inquiry was not prejudicial error where the record otherwise indicated that the accused was aware of his options); United States v. McPhaul, 22 M.J. 808 (A.C.M.R. 1986) (judge failed to question accused).

4. United States v. Hannon, 19 M.J. 726 (N.M.C.M.R. 1984).
5. In United States v. Sherrod, 26 M.J. 32 (C.M.A. 1988), the court stated that "while trial by members is an absolute right, trial by judge alone is not." However, "it is a right nonetheless."
6. Art. 18, U.C.M.J.; R.C.M. 501. See also R.C.M. 201(f)(1)(C).
7. Art. 16(2)(C), U.C.M.J.
8. R.C.M. 903(c)(2)(B) Discussion. United States v. Webster, 24 M.J. 96 (C.M.A. 1987) (denying the request in order to prevent untimely requests in the future was not a good reason for doing so).
9. Art. 16(1)(B), (2)(C), U.C.M.J.; R.C.M. 903(b)(2). The option of submitting the request orally was included in amendments to Article 16 in 1983. Military Justice Act of 1983, Pub. L. No. 98-209, 3(a), 97 Stat. 1393 (1983). Prior to the amendment, the requirement of a written request was jurisdictional. United States v. Dean, 20 C.M.A. 212, 43 C.M.R. 52 (1970); United States v. Hussey, 1 M.J. 804 (A.F.C.M.R. 1976).
10. Art. 16(1)(B), (2)(C); R.C.M. 903(a)(2). United States v. Martinez, 27 M.J. 730 (A.C.M.R. 1988) (accused deferred decision on trial forum at arraignment because his counsel was not present).
11. United States v. Smith, 41 M.J. 817 (N.M.Ct.Crim.App. 1995) (judge may not sit as fact-finder or sentencing authority absent an affirmative request from the accused).
12. United States v. Ginaitt, 43 C.M.R. 56 (C.M.A. 1970); United States v. Smith, 41 M.J. 817 (N.M.Ct.Crim.App. 1995) (judge not authorized to sentence accused where there was no affirmative request on record by accused; sentence was nullity; court noted that judge was authorized to hear guilty pleas and enter findings and until judge began sentencing proceedings, court-martial was properly constituted).

be deferred until any time before assembly.[13] This in effect permits the defense to wait until after the judge has ruled on any defense motions[14] or considered the accused's guilty pleas[15] before deciding whether to have the issue of guilt determined by the judge or court members. Even absent a request by the accused to defer this matter, no prejudicial error should result if the judge fails to address the issue until after pleas have been entered.[16]

Failure to make a timely request will normally be considered a waiver of the right,[17] but the judge in his discretion may consider an otherwise untimely request at any point prior to the introduction of the evidence on the merits of the case.[18] The judge should normally consider an untimely request where it appears that the untimeliness is not merely due to gamesmanship or tactics and little confusion or loss of time will result.[19] Timely submission of the request for trial by judge alone is not a jurisdictional requirement.[20]

Submission of a blank form will not suffice,[21] but unintentional omission of the judge's name is not fatal.[22] There is no statutory requirement that the accused personally sign the request;[23] but the *Manual* indicates that the request should either be in writing *and* signed by the accused or made orally on the record.[24] In any event the failure to sign the form should not be a jurisdictional defect and can be easily remedied by simply noting the oral request on the record.[25] If the request is in writing it will almost always be made on DD Form 1722, Request for Trial Before Military Judge Alone.[26]

The accused is not entitled as a matter of right to a bench trial.[27] Instead, his request is subject to approval by the judge whose decision in turn may be

---

13. R.C.M. 903(a)(2). United States v. Webster, 24 M.J. 96 (C.M.A. 1987) (judge and trial counsel erroneously concluded that request for judge alone was untimely, although it was made just after the beginning of an Article 39(a) session; prejudicial error to deny).
14. See Chapter 13 for a discussion of motions practice.
15. United States v. Cunningham, 6 M.J. 559 (N.C.M.R. 1978) (timely request where it was submitted after pleas and findings but before assembly of the court members). The topic of pleas is addressed in Chapter 14.
16. United States v. Ford, 12 M.J. 636 (N.M.C.M.R. 1981).
17. R.C.M. 903(e)(2).
18. R.C.M. 903(e)(2).
19. *See generally* R.C.M. 903(e) Discussion.
20. R.C.M. 903(a), Drafters' Analysis citing United States v. Morris, 23 C.M.A. 319, 49 C.M.R. 653 (1975).
21. United States v. Brown, 21 C.M.A. 516, 45 C.M.R. 290 (1972).
22. United States v. Stearman, 7 M.J. 13 (C.M.A. 1979).
23. Art. 16, U.C.M.J. United States v. Calhoun, 14 M.J. 588 (N.M.C.M.R. 1982).
24. R.C.M. 903(b)(2).
25. Because under earlier versions of Article 16, U.C.M.J. the requirement of a written request was jurisdictional, greater attention was paid by the appellate courts to issues surrounding the form and substance of the document. The statutory change, which now permits oral requests on the record, should in most cases neutralize any issues concerning defects in the written request. Of course, where there has been no specific oral request on the record, the appellate courts may be left with deciphering the writing as in the past. Because even written requests are usually referred to in the record as the judge explains the accused's rights, that dialogue may suffice for an oral request on the record.
26. A copy of that form is included in this text at Appendix 17.
27. R.C.M. 903(2)(B). United States v. Ward, 3 M.J. 365 (C.M.A. 1977).

reviewed for an abuse of discretion.[28] Grounds for denying the request might be present where it is untimely,[29] where it is clear that the accused is making the request without any comprehension of his actions[30] or where, for example, the judge learns of a fact that might reasonably raise a question about his impartiality.[31]

Before ruling on the request the judge should personally determine if the accused has consulted with counsel on the matter and whether the accused has been informed of his right to be tried by members.[32] The judge should then briefly explain the differences in the two forums.[33] If it appears from the record that the accused was aware of the differences and the ramifications of his choice, the judge's failure to conduct the inquiry will probably not constitute error.[34] Nor will the accused necessarily be prejudiced if the judge's advice is ambiguous.[35] In deciding whether to grant the request the judge may hear arguments of counsel.[36]

Only in rare instances should a request for a trial by judge alone be denied.[37] If the judge denies the request he should state his reasons for doing so on the record.[38] If after his inquiry the judge is satisfied that the accused understands the differences between a trial with members and trial by judge alone, he may approve the request,[39] announce that the court is assembled,[40] and proceed with the trial.[41]

---

28. R.C.M. 903(2)(B) Discussion indicates that a timely request for a bench trial should normally be granted.
29. United States v. Schaffner, 16 M.J. 903 (A.C.M.R. 1983) (last minute request).
30. United States v. Stegall, 6 M.J. 176 (C.M.A. 1979); United States v. Campbell, 47 C.M.R. 965 (A.C.M.R. 1973).
31. United States v. Elzy, 22 M.J. 640 (A.C.M.R. 1986) (learning of accused's plan to commit perjury is not automatically disqualifying); United States v. Roberts, 20 M.J. 689 (A.C.M.R. 1985) (judge should have either refused request or transferred case to another judge when he learned that the accused intended to commit perjury); United States v. Scaife, 48 C.M.R. 290 (A.C.M.R. 1974).
32. R.C.M. 903(c)(2)(A). In United States v. Martinez, 27 M.J. 730 (A.C.M.R. 1988), the court recognized that there is no "constitutional, statutory, or even executive provision" that requires the personal inquiry by the military judge, but commended it as a good practice that avoids potential for error.
33. United States v. Parkes, 5 M.J. 489 (C.M.A. 1978); United States v. Turner, 20 C.M.A. 167, 43 C.M.R. 7 (1970); United States v. Jenkins, 20 C.M.A. 112, 42 C.M.R. 304 (1970); United States v. Daffron, 32 M.J. 912 (A.F.C.M.R. 1991) (trial judge's inquiry into accused's knowledge of the right to elect trial by members does not require advice that any sentence over 10 years requires a three-quarters vote by the members); United States v. Griffin, 18 M.J. 707 (A.C.M.R. 1984). For a sample inquiry, see the Trial Guide at Appendix 24.
34. R.C.M. 903(c)(2)(A) Discussion.
35. United States v. Griffin, 18 M.J. 707 (A.C.M.R. 1984).
36. R.C.M. 903(c)(2)(B) Discussion. United States v. Ward, 3 M.J. 365 (C.M.A. 1977); United States v. Fountain, 2 M.J. 1202 (N.M.C.M.R. 1976).
37. R.C.M. 903(c)(2)(B) Discussion.
38. United States v. Butler, 14 M.J. 72 (C.M.A. 1982).
39. R.C.M. 903(c)(2)(B). Neither the U.C.M.J. nor the *Manual* specify any particular form for

---

40. United States v. Smith, 41 M.J. 817 (N.M.Ct.Crim.App. 1995) (court is ordinarily assembled immediately following granting of request for trial by judge alone). The subject of "assembly" of the court and its significance on the trial is addressed in § 15-9.
41. If members have been waiting for the Article 39(a) session to conclude, they will be excused

Note, however, that the accused has the right to withdraw his request at any time prior to approval of the request.[42] After approval, he has the right to withdraw the request only if there has been a change in judges.[43] Otherwise, it is within the discretion of the trial judge whether the accused will be permitted to withdraw his request at any time prior to the introduction of evidence on the merits.[44] No specific format is required for the withdrawal, although the preferred method would be to do so in writing.[45]

§ 12-3(B). Accused's Request for Enlisted Members on the Court.

Should the accused desire not to be tried by judge alone, the judge must further inquire whether the accused has exercised, or wishes to exercise, his right to request that the court's membership include at least one-third enlisted members.[46] A request to include enlisted personnel may be in writing or orally made on the record. Before Article 25, U.C.M.J. was amended in 1986, the failure to request enlisted members in writing was a jurisdictional defect.[47] Failure of the accused to sign a written request is also a jurisdictional

---

the approval. Where the accused has submitted a written request, the judge will normally annotate or sign the request if he approves it. Either an oral or written approval should suffice as long as the record in some fashion indicates that the judge indeed approved the request. *See generally* United States v. Bowman, 49 C.M.R. 406 (A.C.M.R. 1974); United States v. Campbell, 47 C.M.R. 965 (A.C.M.R. 1973).

---

and the proceedings will continue with the arraignment. *See infra* § 12-4. If there are no motions and the accused pleads not guilty, the trial continues with the case on the merits. In effect, the Article 39(a) pretrial session evolves into a determination of the guilt or innocence of the accused, without the necessity of the judge ever announcing that the Article 39(a) session is concluded or adjourned. As a practical matter, where a break is necessary, the judge will announce the session's adjournment.

42. R.C.M. 903(d)(2).
43. R.C.M. 903(d)(2).
44. R.C.M. 903(e)(3). United States v. Stiner, 30 M.J. 860 (N.M.C.M.R. 1990) (no abuse of discretion for judge to deny accused's request to withdraw request; court rejected accused's argument that judge had predisposition to heavier sentences and noted that prosecution would have borne greater expense in trying case before members).

Note that the right to request a withdrawal of enlisted members, discussed in § 12-3(B), may be made at any time before assembly of the court, which in some cases might be much later in the trial. No similar provision exists with regard to withdrawals of requests for bench trials, presumably because approval of the request for trial by judge alone is followed almost immediately by the judge's announcement that the court is assembled. If for some reason the assembly of the court (judge alone) is delayed, the accused's request to withdraw the approved request is subject to the judge's discretion.

45. *See* United States v. Bryant, 23 C.M.A. 326, 49 C.M.R. 660 (1975) (in a footnote the court indicated that the withdrawal should be in writing; this case preceded the change to Art. 16, which now permits oral requests for trial by judge alone).

46. Art. 25(c)(1), U.C.M.J.; R.C.M. 903(a)(1).

47. United States v. Brandt, 20 M.J. 74 (C.M.A. 1985); United States v. White, 21 C.M.A. 583, 45 C.M.R. 357 (1972); United States v. Acevedo-Colon, 2 M.J. 969 (A.C.M.R. 1980); United States v. Williams, 50 C.M.R. 219 (A.C.M.R. 1975).

See Military Justice Amendments of 1986, tit. VIII, § 803, National Defense Authorization Act for Fiscal Year 1987, Pub. L. No. 99-661, 100 Stat. 3900, (1986).

defect.[48] Unlike the language in Article 16, U.C.M.J., which simply indicates that the request for trial by judge alone must either be written or made orally on the record,[49] Article 25(c)(1) indicates that the accused must *personally* make the request for enlisted members. Further, the *Manual* requires that the accused sign any written request.[50] *See also* Appendix 18.

The request must be submitted at any time before the end of the initial Article 39(a) session.[51] If a 39(a) session is not held, the request should be made before the court is assembled.[52] But these time requirements are not jurisdictional.[53] The judge may permit the accused to defer submission of his request until any time prior to assembly.[54] Because a request for enlisted members may ultimately delay a trial while the convening authority selects the enlisted personnel who will be appointed to the court, the judge should not summarily grant the request for a delay absent some showing of good cause.[55]

An accused has a right to withdraw his request for enlisted members at any time before the initial Article 39(a) session ends or in the absence of a 39(a) session, at any time prior to assembly of the court.[56] As with untimely requests for trial by judge alone, the judge in his discretion may consider an untimely request for enlisted members, or permit the accused to withdraw any such request, at any time before evidence on the merits is introduced.[57] An accused may effectively withdraw his request if, after he submits a request for enlisted members, he also submits a request for trial by judge alone.[58]

Normally, the accused will have submitted his request for enlisted members to the convening authority prior to trial. There is some authority that the requirements of the U.C.M.J. and the Manual for Courts-Martial affect only the ability of the enlisted personnel to "serve" on the court.[59] Thus, their appointment may be effected beforehand in anticipation that a formal request will be submitted.

An otherwise proper request for enlisted members entitles the accused to enlisted members unless the convening authority can establish in a detailed

---

48. United States v. Brandt, 20 M.J. 74 (C.M.A. 1985) (counsel's signature alone was insufficient to meet the requirements of Art. 25).
49. *See supra* § 12-3(B). United States v. Hood, 37 M.J. 784 (A.C.M.R. 1993) (failure of accused to make personal election of enlisted members on court was jurisdictional error).
50. R.C.M. 903(b)(1).
51. Art. 25(c)(1); R.C.M. 903(a)(1).
52. Art. 25(c)(1); R.C.M. 903(a)(1).
53. *See* R.C.M. 903(a) Drafters' Analysis (draws analogy to timing of requests for trial by judge alone).
54. R.C.M. 903(a)(1). United States v. Summerset, 37 M.J. 695 (A.C.M.R. 1993) (trial judge abused discretion when he permitted accused to defer request, but then denied the request because it did not comply with local rules of court; granting request would not have caused unnecessary delay).
55. R.C.M. 903(a)(1) Drafters' Analysis. United States v. Summerset, 37 M.J. 695 (A.C.M.R. 1993) (trial judge abused discretion in denying request because it did not comply with local rules of court; granting request would not have caused unnecessary delay).
56. R.C.M. 903(f)(1). United States v. Stipe, 23 C.M.A. 11, 48 C.M.R. 267 (1974).
57. R.C.M. 903(e).
58. *See, e.g.,* United States v. McDonald, 3 M.J. 1005 (A.C.M.R. 1977).
59. United States v. Robertson, 7 M.J. 507 (A.C.M.R. 1979).

written statement that physical conditions or military exigencies prevent appointment.[60]

The judge's inquiry on the issue of enlisted members on the court need not be as searching or detailed as that required on a request for trial by judge alone. In the latter the accused is waiving a constitutional right to trial by jury and in the case of the former, the accused is invoking a statutory right. Therefore, the accused's interests are protected if the judge inquires whether the accused is aware of the right or if it otherwise appears on the record that the accused understood that he had that option.[61]

For a more detailed discussion of the qualifications of the enlisted members, see Chapter 8.

§ 12-4. Arraignment.

The last major item on the agenda of an Article 39(a) pretrial session is the "arraignment,"[1] if the Service regulations permit it to be conducted at the Article 39(a) session.[2] Although the arraignment usually takes place at the 39(a) session, it could occur with the court members present.[3] That would be the case where the court is a special court-martial and no judge has been detailed to the court.[4]

The arraignment consists simply of (1) the military judge announcing that the accused will be arraigned; (2) trial counsel furnishing all parties with copies of the charges and specifications[5] and determining whether the accused desires the charges to be read, which is usually waived;[6] (3) trial counsel identifying the accuser,[7] the fact that the charges were properly sworn to before a commissioned officer[8] and identifying the convening authority;[9] and finally, (4) the military judge asking the accused how he pleads.[10]

---

60. Art. 25(c)(1), U.C.M.J.; R.C.M. 903(c)(1).
61. *See, e.g.,* United States v. Beard, 7 M.J. 452 (C.M.A. 1979).
1. *See generally* R.C.M. 904, which governs arraignments.
2. *See, e.g.,* AR 27-10, para. 5-22, which permits arraignments in Article 39(a) sessions conducted by a military judge before assembly. Arraignments may not be held at Conferences, discussed at § 12.5, *infra.* R.C.M. 904 Discussion.
3. R.C.M. 904 Discussion.
4. *Id.* Art. 16(2)(A), U.C.M.J.
5. See Chapter 6 for a discussion about preparation of the charge sheet.
6. United States v. Lichtsinn, 32 M.J. 898 (A.F.C.M.R. 1991) (judge's failure to direct reading of charges or to obtain accused's waiver of reading of charges was waived by accused's failure to object; in any event it was harmless error in light of record as a whole, which revealed that accused was aware of charges against him); United States v. Stevens, 25 M.J. 805 (A.C.M.R. 1988) (waiver implied where trial judge asked accused to plead with no reference to reading the charges, the accused pleaded guilty, and there was no objection to the procedure by the defense; even assuming error the accused was not prejudiced where he was served with a copy of the charges and received competent representation).
7. See § 6-1 for a discussion of who is the "accuser."
8. *See* § 6-1.
9. Simply inserting the charge sheet into the record of trial is insufficient. United States v. Perry, 40 C.M.R. 286 (A.C.M.R. 1970).
10. See the Trial Guide at Appendix 8 of the Manual for Courts-Martial.

The accused's plea itself is not a part of the arraignment,[11] and in most cases will not be entered until after the defense has raised any pretrial motions. *See* Chapters 13 and 14. The arraignment serves as a triggering event in two respects.

First, once arraigned, the accused may be tried *in absentia*.[12] Before proceeding with the accused absent, the judge must be satisfied that the accused is voluntarily absent.[13] The burden rests upon the prosecution to demonstrate that fact by a preponderance of the evidence.[14] If it appears that another Article 39(a) session may be necessary to resolve pretrial matters, the trial counsel will almost always urge the court to proceed at least as far as the arraignment and thus protect the government's ability to proceed with the trial should the accused voluntarily absent himself before the next session of court. The issue of the accused's presence at trial is dealt with in Chapter 15.

Second, following arraignment, additional charges may not be joined with the original charges.[15] Any defects in the arraignment procedure will be tested for prejudice.[16]

---

11. United States v. Fleming, 18 C.M.A. 524, 40 C.M.R. 236 (1969).
12. R.C.M. 804(b)(1).
13. *Id.* United States v. Bass, 40 M.J. 220 (C.M.A. 1994) (accused's absence voluntary although trial court had not told him explicitly that trial could proceed in his absence after arraignment; court stated that arraignment constitutes commencement of trial); United States v. Sharp, 38 M.J. 33 (C.M.A. 1993) (not essential that accused be apprised of exact date of trial); no requirement that accused be warned of consequences of being absent after arraignment; court distinguished Crosby v. United States, 113 S.Ct. 748 (1993) (court recognized limited exception to rule that no felony trial may continue with defendant absent where he is present at beginning of trial). United States v. Stewart, 37 M.J. 523 (A.C.M.R. 1993) (failure of judge to advise accused that he could be tried in absentia does not preclude conclusion that his absence was voluntary; he was advised of trial date and that he would be escorted to trial); United States v. Jones, 34 M.J. 899 (N.M.C.M.R. 1992) (fact that accused did not know of specific trial date did not render his absence involuntary; court indicated that while notice of exact date accompanied by a warning of the consequences of not being present are factors to be considered, they are not prerequisites); United States v. Matthews, 19 M.J. 707 (A.F.C.M.R. 1984) (court ruled that accused's absence was voluntary); United States v. Brown, 12 M.J. 728 (N.M.C.M.R. 1981) (error to proceed where no evidence that absence was voluntary); United States v. Knight, 7 M.J. 671 (A.C.M.R. 1979) (accused's civilian confinement was not voluntary). *See also* United States v. Peebles, 3 M.J. 177 (C.M.A. 1977) (accused absent from rehearing due to lack of notice).
14. R.C.M. 804(b)(1) Discussion. United States v. Yarn, 32 M.J. 736 (A.C.M.R. 1991) (once counsel is informed of trial date, accused is deemed to have been advised of that fact; prosecution does not have to show that accused had actual knowledge of date). *Cf.* United States v. Sharp, 38 M.J. 33 (C.M.A. 1993) (burden on the accused to rebut inference that absence is involuntary); United States v. Abilar, 14 M.J. 733 (A.F.C.M.R. 1982) (burden rests on defense).
15. R.C.M. 601(e)(2). *See* Chapter 8.
16. United States v. Napier, 20 C.M.A. 422, 43 C.M.R. 262 (1971); United States v. Jackson, 40 M.J. 620 (N.M.C.M.R. 1994) (nonprejudicial error to proceed with arraignment in absence of counsel; court added that accused's failure to later object waived issue); United States v. Velis, 7 M.J. 699 (N.C.M.R. 1979) (*en masse* arraignments disapproved).

§ 12-5. Conferences.

Before 1984, many military judges routinely relied upon pretrial conferences to resolve informally issues which might otherwise have needlessly consumed time at the initial Article 39(a) session or at the trial on the merits.[1] R.C.M. 802 in the Manual for Courts-Martial specifically provides for "conferences" that may be held either before or during the trial. The Rule is patterned after Federal Rule of Criminal Procedure 17.1 with some modifications for military practice.

Conferences may be ordered by the judge, after referral of charges,[2] either on his own motion or at the request of either side.[3] Before charges have been referred it may be necessary for counsel to meet with the judge but any such meeting would not fall within the coverage of R.C.M. 802.[4] Conferences under Rule 802 may not be held, however, where the accused is not represented by counsel[5] or where the case is being tried by a special court-martial and no judge has been appointed.[6]

There is no set agenda or procedure for these conferences, and they may be held at any time and at any place. Telephonic or radio conferences are permitted[7] and in some cases may be necessary where the judge and the counsel are located at different installations. The purpose of these meetings is to inform the judge of possible issues and resolve matters that can be agreed upon by the parties.[8] The judge can order the parties to meet with him for a conference, although the success of such a meeting may depend on the willingness of both sides to fully cooperate and resolve informally those matters or issues that require their mutual agreement, something the judge cannot, in theory, order the parties to do.[9]

While the original version of R.C.M. 802 required both parties to consent to the conference, an amendment in 1991 dropped that requirement. The *Manual* provision originally indicated that "[t]he conference shall not proceed over the objection of any party."[10] According to the original Drafters' Analysis, that provision was intended to keep the conference from becoming a substitute for an Article 39(a) session.[11] Read narrowly, that could have required the

---

1. *See* R.C.M. 802 Drafters' Analysis.
2. *See* Chapter 8.
3. R.C.M. 802(a).
4. The Rule should not block either the judge or counsel from communicating about matters affecting docketing of cases and other administrative matters. It is simply designed to provide a more formalized setting for resolving pretrial and trial issues without the need for meeting in an Article 39(a) session.
5. For a discussion of the accused's right to proceed *pro se*, see § 12-2(H).
6. Art. 16(2)(A), U.C.M.J.; R.C.M. 802(f).
7. R.C.M. 802(a) Discussion.
8. *Id.* Noting the absence of definitive authority on just what may be considered at R.C.M. 802 conferences, the court in United States v. Stewart, 29 M.J. 621 (C.G.C.M.R. 1989), concluded that discussions of proposed instructions on both findings and sentencing are permitted.
9. R.C.M. 802(c) Drafters' Analysis (1991 Amendment).
10. R.C.M. 802(c).
11. R.C.M. 802(c) Drafters' Analysis.

judge to terminate the conference without any further comments or questions. That has now changed and the current provision gives the judge some latitude in using the conference as an opportunity to spell out those routine administrative matters which are within his control, such as procedures for voir dire and rules of court, even where one of the parties objects to the conference proceeding.[12] This is particularly important where the parties may not be familiar with each other or with local practices and logistics.

In addition to addressing administrative issues, conferences may also be used by the judge to ask counsel to disclose the presence of any particular problem or issue that might be raised in the trial. Assuming that counsel fully inform the judge of such matters, the conference can be used by the judge to reduce the delay and possible confusion that sometimes result from "trial by ambush."

Since the promulgation of R.C.M. 802, the courts have struggled with the issue of whether a particular conversation or session was really a conference under that Rule, or whether it was really part of the trial. While many trial judges have discovered the value of being able to dispose of certain issues quickly and informally, off-the-record, the courts have cautioned trial judges that the conference should not be used as a substitute for the trial itself.[13] Nor should the conferences be used as an opportunity for conducting unrecorded portions of the trial.[14] If it appears that a session was really part of the trial itself, then that session should be recorded verbatim as part of the record. What should be clear is that labels are not always a reliable indicator of whether a session was an R.C.M. 802 conference.[15]

If the parties can agree on major points or issues that would otherwise be litigated at the Article 39(a) session or during the trial on the merits, then those matters can and should be resolved at the conference. These agreements

---

12. *Id.*
13. In United States v. Myers, 25 M.J. 573 (A.F.C.M.R. 1987), the court rejected the argument that because the conference sessions were unrecorded, the record of trial was not verbatim and no punitive discharge could be approved. Citing R.C.M. 802, the court concluded that all matters discussed during the eight conferences were either purely administrative or were later litigated at trial. The court cautioned that the Rule 802 Conference should be used only for administrative matters, and not "central trial issues." United States v. Czekala, 38 M.J. 566 (A.C.M.R. 1993), *aff'd on other grounds*, 42 M.J. 168 (1995) (Rule 802 conferences should not be used to entertain challenges for cause to court member); United States v. Washington, 35 M.J. 774 (A.C.M.R. 1992) (Rule 802 conferences should be limited to their intended purpose and court will closely scrutinize the use of such sessions).
14. In United States v. Garcia, 24 M.J. 518 (A.F.C.M.R. 1987), the court noted that although R.C.M. 802 permits unrecorded conferences, this provision has "occasionally misled judges into allowing substantive portions of the trial to go unrecorded." In this case, the judge had held an unrecorded conference with both counsel in the middle of the plea inquiry and later noted for the record that the conference had been used to discuss issues regarding the providency of the plea. The court noted that the conference should not have been used to discuss the providency of the plea. Because it was impossible to review judicially the components of that conference, the court set aside the findings and sentence.
15. United States v. Thomas, 32 M.J. 1024 (A.F.C.M.R. 1991) (although an off-the-record session between the judge and counsel was not so labelled by the trial participants, the appellate court considered it an 802 Conference; accused waived any objections to fact that it was not recorded).

are off-the-record and must be later noted for the record either in writing or orally.[16] This requirement may be waived by failing to object.[17] Apparently, the absence of a verbatim recording of the conference does not make the record of trial itself a nonverbatim record,[18] which could have an impact on the sentence that could be approved on appeal.[19] The key here is that the parties may agree on an issue, such as whether a particular witness should be obtained, but the parties are not permitted to litigate that issue at the conference nor is the judge permitted to render a decision on the matter.[20] Pragmatically, any indication from the judge as to how he might resolve the issue if it were raised at trial might encourage one of the counsel to reach an agreement with the other side.[21] It is possible that during the conference the parties would go so far as to reach an agreement on disposition of the charges and at least lay the foundation for a plea bargain.[22] If that occurs the judge must be careful not to engage in those negotiations or in any way indicate how such an agreement would affect his view of the merits or possible sentence.[23] The better practice would seem to require that when the discussion appears to be leading to some sort of pretrial agreement, the judge terminate the conference and permit counsel to negotiate further without the judge present.

Although the accused's presence is not required at conferences, he is not prohibited from attending and taking part.[24] Any admissions that the accused or his counsel might make during the conference may not later be used against the accused, unless the admissions have been reduced to writing and signed by both the accused and his counsel.[25]

---

16. R.C.M. 802(b). United States v. Sneed, 32 M.J. 537 (A.F.C.M.R. 1990) (court indicated that an unrecorded ex parte telephone discussion between the judge and the defense counsel, apparently with the permission of the prosecution, did not amount to a Rule 802 conference); United States v. Stewart, 29 M.J. 621 (C.G.C.M.R. 1989) (record of trial was not verbatim simply because it failed to note the proceedings at an R.C.M. 802 conference).

17. Id. United States v. Cordell, 37 M.J. 592 (A.F.C.M.R. 1993) (accused waived issue); United States v. Thomas, 33 M.J. 1024 (A.F.C.M.R. 1991) (accused waived objection); United States v. Stewart, 29 M.J. 621 (C.G.C.M.R. 1989).

18. United States v. Cordell, 37 M.J. 592 (A.F.C.M.R. 1993) (absence of verbatim recording did not render record incomplete); United States v. Leaver, 32 M.J. 995 (C.G.C.M.R. 1991) (verbatim record of conference, during which judge informed counsel of guilty plea concerns, not required). Cf. United States v. Garcia, 24 M.J. 518 (A.F.C.M.R. 1987).

19. See § 17-17-4.

20. R.C.M. 802(a) Discussion and Drafters' Analysis.

21. It could be argued that the Drafters envisioned that practical approach; note that the Discussion to R.C.M. 802(a) indicates that the judge is prohibited only from making a *"binding ruling"* (emphasis added).

22. See Chapter 9 for a discussion on plea bargaining.

23. United States v. Caruth, 6 M.J. 184 (C.M.A. 1979); R.C.M. 802(a) Discussion.

24. R.C.M. 802(d). Where the accused is absent, it may be presumed that his counsel is speaking for him. Id. at the Discussion.

25. R.C.M. 802(e). See also Rule 410, MIL. R. EVID.

APPENDIX REFERENCES

Appendix 1. Abbreviations.
Appendix 2. Glossary.
Appendix 3. U.C.M.J.
Appendix 9. Sample Court-Martial Convening Order.
Appendix 17. Request for Trial Before Military Judge Alone.
Appendix 18. Request for Enlisted Members.

ANNOTATED BIBLIOGRAPHY

PERIODICALS

Cretella & Lynch, "The Military Judge: Military or Judge," CAL. W. L. REV. 57 (1972).

> The authors trace the evolution of the military judge's role in the military society as it has evolved and adapted to social changes. Particularly, judges are cast as administrators of justice within a self-contained legal system found in the military services.

Howell, "TDS: The Establishment of the U.S. Army Trial Defense Service," 100 MIL. L. REV. 4 (1983).

> The evolution and reasons for the formation of the Trial Defense Service are traced in this article. The author, a Deputy Staff Judge Advocate, concludes that the birth of this service not only eliminated criticism that defense counsel often were improperly chosen and influenced, but it also ensured the achievement of the need for a fit military fighting force.

Schiesser, "Trial by Peers: Enlisted Members on Courts-Martial," 15 CATH. U. L. REV. 171 (1966).

> The author reviews the evolution of the "trial by peers" allowed by Art. 25 of the Uniform Code of Military Justice, beginning with the rigid caste system of the Imperial British military justice system, the adoption of that system by the leaders of the American Revolution, and the subsequent realization that the British style of hierarchical justice was incompatible with the American egalitarian ethic. He then describes the contemporary operation of Article 25 and, though making several pointed criticisms, proclaims it a pragmatic and ethical success.

Stevenson, "The Inherent Authority of the Military Judge," 17 A.F. L. REV. 1 (1975).

> The author discusses how the emergence of the military judge has been extremely important in furthering high standards within the military justice system. He concludes that under the U.C.M.J. and the Manual for Courts-Martial, military judges are cloaked with extensive authority; whether Congress or the courts bless this inherent authority is a function of the judge's wisdom in exercising it.

CHAPTER 13

MOTIONS PRACTICE

§ 13-1. Introduction.
§ 13-2. Procedural Aspects of Motions Practice.
    § 13-2(A). Timing of Motions.
    § 13-2(B). Waiver of Motions.
    § 13-2(C). Notice and Service of Motions.
    § 13-2(D). Burden of Proof on Motions.
    § 13-2(E). Rulings on Motions.
    § 13-2(F). Reconsideration of Rulings.
    § 13-2(G). Appeal of Rulings.
        § 13-2(G)(1). Defense Appeals: Extraordinary Writs.
        § 13-2(G)(2). Government Appeals.
§ 13-3. Motions to Dismiss.
    § 13-3(A). Lack of Jurisdiction.
    § 13-3(B). Statute of Limitations.
    § 13-3(C). Speedy Trial.
        § 13-3(C)(1). Sixth Amendment and Due Process Standards.
        § 13-3(C)(2). U.C.M.J. Requirements: The *Burton* 90-Day Rule (1972-1993).
        § 13-3(C)(3). The *Manual's* 120-Day Rule.
        § 13-3(C)(4). Interstate Agreement on Detainers Act (IADA).
        § 13-3(C)(5). Remedies for Speedy Trial Violations.
    § 13-3(D). Lack of Mental Responsibility.
    § 13-3(E). Former Jeopardy.
    § 13-3(F). Failure to Allege an Offense.
    § 13-3(G). Former Punishment.
    § 13-3(H). Grant of Immunity.
    § 13-3(I). Constructive Condonation of Desertion.
    § 13-3(J). Multiplicity.
    § 13-3(K). Defective Specification That Misled the Accused.
    § 13-3(L). Presidential Pardon.
    § 13-3(M). Selective or Vindictive Prosecution; Prosecutorial Misconduct.
    § 13-3(N). Constitutional Challenges to the Underlying Statute, Regulation, or Order.
        § 13-3(N)(1). Equal Protection.
        § 13-3(N)(2). Vagueness: Lack of Fair Notice.
        § 13-3(N)(3). First Amendment: Speech, Religion, and Association.
        § 13-3(N)(4). Rights of Privacy.
        § 13-3(N)(5). *Ex Post Facto* Laws.
§ 13-4. Motions to Suppress.
    § 13-4(A). Pretrial Statements of the Accused.
    § 13-4(B). Illegal Searches and Seizures.
    § 13-4(C). Eyewitness Identification.
§ 13-5. Motions to Grant Appropriate Relief.
    § 13-5(A). Accused Incompetent to Stand Trial.
    § 13-5(B). Pretrial Restraint.
    § 13-5(C). Change of Location of Trial.
    § 13-5(D). Defective Pretrial Investigation or Pretrial Advice.
    § 13-5(E). Defective Pleadings: Motions to Cure or Amend.
    § 13-5(F). Motion for a Bill of Particulars.
    § 13-5(G). Motions to Sever.
        § 13-5(G)(1). Severance of Accused.
        § 13-5(G)(2). Severance of Charges.
        § 13-5(G)(3). Severance of Duplicitous Specification.

§ 13-5(H). Requests Concerning Individual Military Counsel or Retention of Detailed Military Counsel.
§ 13-5(I). Request for Witnesses.
§ 13-5(J). Discovery.
§ 13-5(K). Continuance.
§ 13-5(L). Motions to Obtain Rulings on Evidentiary Matters: Motions *in Limine*.

Appendix References.
Annotated Bibliography.

§ 13-1. Introduction.

"Motions" are defined in the Manual for Courts-Martial as applications to a military judge for particular relief.[1] Those applications may be oral or written[2] and are almost always made at an Article 39(a) pretrial session:[3] after the accused is arraigned[4] but before he enters his pleas.[5] Military practice includes three major categories of motions: (1) motions to dismiss; (2) motions to suppress; and (3) motions for appropriate relief. A fourth type of motion, which could be listed with motions for appropriate relief, is the motion *in limine*. This chapter covers these motions, which are almost always made before the trial on the merits commences; trial motions, such as motions for finding of not guilty, are covered in Chapter 15. The focus here is on the procedural aspects of raising pretrial motions,[6] the various types of motions recognized in the military,[7] and the appellate process that both sides may follow should they decide to appeal the judge's rulings.[8]

§ 13-2. Procedural Aspects of Motions Practice.

Motions in military practice may be oral or written.[1] After referral,[2] counsel may submit a written motion to the military judge and serve a copy on opposing counsel.[3] Unless either side requests a hearing on the matter, the judge may rule on the written motion, before the accused is arraigned, without calling an Article 39(a) session.[4] In some circumstances it might be appropriate to use a conference to discuss the contents of the motion and attempt to bring the parties to some agreement.[5]

---

1. *See* R.C.M. 905(a).
2. R.C.M. 905(a).
3. See Chapter 12 for a discussion of the procedures for an Article 39(a) pretrial session.
4. *See supra* § 12-4.
5. See Chapter 14 for a discussion of the accused's pleas.
6. *See* § 13-2.
7. *See* §§ 13-3 to 13-5.
8. *See* § 13-2(G).
1. R.C.M. 905(a).
2. *See* § 8-4.
3. R.C.M. 905(h).
4. *Id.*
5. *See* § 12-5.

Each motion, whether written or oral, should clearly state what relief is requested and the basis for the request.[6] Failure to put the motion in correct form should not preclude the judge from deciding the matter, however.[7] If a hearing is held on the motion, each side has the right to present evidence and arguments.[8] Note that the Military Rules of Evidence are generally applicable to hearings on motions.[9] Although defense counsel are normally not required to present requests for relief to the convening authority,[10] they may do so either before or after charges have been referred.[11] Doing so does not preclude counsel from raising the matter in a motion to the military judge.[12] Note that there are some matters upon which the convening authority may not act.[13]

§ 13-2(A). Timing of Motions.

As noted in the introduction, most motions are made prior to trial when it is most advantageous, especially for the defense, to obtain favorable rulings on issues that might determine the very outcome of the case. Typically, motions are made at the Article 39(a) session, discussed in Chapter 12, after the accused has been arraigned and before he enters his pleas. In some instances the timing of the motions may be left to the discretion of the parties and the judge.

Aside from the practical aspects of the timing of motions, the subject matter, or nature, of each motion determines that point beyond which the judge is not required to entertain the motion. Three categories of motions emerge: first, those motions addressing issues that *must* be made prior to the plea; second, those that may be made at any time prior to final adjournment; and third, those that may be raised at any time, including the appellate review of the case.

As to the first category, motions addressing the following issues must be made prior to the accused entering his plea:

1. Defects in the charges and specifications;[14]

---

6. R.C.M. 905(a). *See also* FED. R. CRIM. P. 12 and 47, which served as the basis for this Rule.

7. R.C.M. 905(a).United States v. Berry, 24 M.J. 555 (A.C.M.R. 1987) (counsel's statement to judge that accused's restriction had not been subject to magistrate's review was treated by the court as a motion of credit toward sentence; court declined to invoke doctrine of waiver simply because counsel failed to specifically label his request).

8. *See* R.C.M. 905(h). That Rule generally relates to written motions and indicates that upon request either party is entitled to an Article 39(a) session to present evidence and arguments on the motion. That implicitly includes oral motions as well, which would in most cases be made at the Article 39(a) session. The judge of course would have discretion to determine the procedures for hearing the evidence and could limit the time allotted for arguing the motion. *See* United States v. Cooper, 8 C.M.R. 133 (C.M.A. 1953); United States v. Barnard, 32 M.J. 530 (A.C.M.R. 1990) (nonprejudicial error not to permit accused to testify on motion to suppress confession).

9. *See* MIL. R. EVID. 1101. *Cf.* MIL. R. EVID. 104(a).

10. R.C.M. 905(j).

11. *Id.*

12. *Id.*

13. For example, only a military judge may grant a continuance. R.C.M. 906(b)(1).

14. R.C.M. 905(b)(2). § 13-5(E).

§ 13-2(B) MILITARY CRIMINAL JUSTICE § 13-2(B)

2. Defects in the pretrial processing of the charges;[15]
3. Suppression of evidence;[16]
4. Discovery[17] or production of evidence or witnesses;[18]
5. Severance of charges or accuseds;[19]
6. Denial of request for individual military counsel[20] or request for retention of the detailed counsel.[21]

The second category is composed of nonjurisdictional issues, such as release from pretrial confinement[22] and continuances.[23] These must be raised before the trial is over.[24]

The third category of motions, those that may be raised at any time while the case is pending, is composed of those that are considered jurisdictional in nature.[25] Examples would include motions alleging lack of jurisdiction over the accused or the offense, improperly convened court, and failure of the specification to state an offense.[26]

Failure to raise a particular issue in the first two categories in timely fashion may constitute waiver of the issue.[27]

§ 13-2(B). Waiver of Motions.

Failure to comply with the appropriate timeliness requirements noted in § 13-2(A) is generally considered a waiver unless the military judge finds good cause to consider the issue.[28] What constitutes good cause will depend on the facts of each case but in most circumstances a good-faith discovery of information previously undiscovered, or undisclosed, should warrant consideration of a tardy motion. Note that there is some authority for the proposition that failure to raise an issue will not constitute a waiver where the defect amounts to a denial of due process.[29] For a discussion on the matter of when the judge must rule on the motions, see § 13-2(E).

---

15. R.C.M. 905(b)(1). *See infra* § 13-5. United States v. Beehler, 35 M.J. 502 (A.F.C.M.R. 1992) (accused did not waive challenge to selection process for court members by waiting until after entry of plea to lodge objection; it could not reasonably have been raised earlier).
16. R.C.M. 905(b)(3). See § 13-4 for a discussion on motions to suppress.
17. R.C.M. 905(b)(4). *See* Chapter 10.
18. R.C.M. 905(b)(4), 701. *See also* Chapters 10 and 11, and § 13-5(1).
19. R.C.M. 905(b)(5). See § 13-5(F) for a discussion of the various motions for severance.
20. R.C.M. 905(b)(6), 906(b)(2), 506(b). For a discussion of this motion see § 13-5(H).
21. R.C.M. 905(b)(6).
22. *See* United States v. Huelcamp, 21 M.J. 509 (A.C.M.R. 1985) (issue waived where raised for first time on appeal). *See generally* Chapter 5. For a discussion on this motion, see § 13-5(B).
23. *See infra* § 13-5(K).
24. R.C.M. 905(e).
25. *Id.*
26. These jurisdictional matters are discussed in more detail in Chapter 4 and §§ 13-3(A), (F).
27. R.C.M. 905(e).
28. *Id. See* United States v. Nakamura, 21 M.J. 741 (N.M.C.M.R. 1985) (no abuse of discretion in refusing to hear untimely objection to accused's statement).
29. *See, e.g.*, United States v. Addison, 19 M.J. 905 (A.C.M.R. 1985) (issue of command influence); United States v. Scarborough, 49 C.M.R. 580 (A.C.M.R. 1974).

In some instances, a plea of guilty will also waive issues raised in motions. For a discussion of the effects of a guilty plea, see § 14-3(A).

§ 13-2(C). Notice and Service of Motions.

Motions practice in the military places emphasis on prior notice to both counsel and the military judge. Because judges and often counsel are working a circuit, prior notification of possible trial and motion issues can expedite matters. But the practice of giving notice varies among the services and even among military judges. The *Manual* requires that written motions must be served on the opposing party, usually the counsel, but specifies no particular timing requirements.[30] In the past, Uniform Rules of Practice for several of the services have specified as many as three days notice.[31] However, in *United States v. Kelson*[32] the Court ruled that an Army version of those rules that set a three-day notice requirement was invalid because it was inconsistent with a 1969 *Manual* provision that permitted counsel to raise a motion at any time prior to the plea. Thus, failure to comply with any timely notice requirements probably will not preclude raising the motion but may result in delay. Such delays would normally be excluded in computing whether the accused was denied a speedy trial.[33]

§ 13-2(D). Burden of Proof on Motions.

As a general rule the burden of going forward with a motion is upon the moving party who usually also bears the burden of persuasion.[34] In the absence of a special rule setting a higher standard of proof, the moving party must establish any pertinent factual matters necessary for the motion by a preponderance of the evidence.[35]

In several types of motions the burden of persuasion specifically falls upon the prosecution:
1. Motions alleging lack of jurisdiction;[36]
2. Motions alleging denial of a speedy trial;[37]

---

30. *See* R.C.M. 905(i).
31. For a discussion of Uniform Rules, see § 15-6.
32. 3 M.J. 139 (C.M.A. 1977). *See also* United States v. Williams, 23 M.J. 362 (C.M.A. 1987), where the court ruled that a local rule requiring five days' notice of motions was in conflict with Mil. R. Evid. 304(d)(2), which only requires that a motion to suppress be made prior to an accused's plea. It was, therefore, invalid; United States v. Norman, 42 M.J. 501 (Army Ct.Crim.App. 1995) (military judge could not refuse to hear motion to suppress because it did not comply with local notice rules; court noted that although local rules serve laudable purposes, they cannot provide standards which override the MCM).
33. *See generally* § 13-3(C).
34. R.C.M. 905(c)(2)(A).
35. R.C.M. 905(c)(1).
36. R.C.M. 905(c)(2)(B). United States v. Buckingham, 9 M.J. 514 (A.F.C.M.R. 1980). *See also* § 13-3(A).
37. R.C.M. 905(c)(2)(B). *See* § 13-3(C).

3. Motions alleging that the statute of limitations has run;[38]
4. Suppression motions[39] addressing search and seizures, statements by the accused and eyewitness identification of the accused;[40]

§ 13-2(E). Rulings on Motions.

The military judge's ruling on motions are final on questions of law and interlocutory matters.[41] A possible exception lies in the motion to dismiss for lack of mental responsibility, where according to Article 51, U.C.M.J., the judge's ruling is subject to findings by the court members.[42] The *Manual* indicates, however, that motions addressing the accused's mental responsibility are no longer subject to interlocutory rulings.[43] Motions to suppress and procedural questions are purely interlocutory.[44] Motions to dismiss that address purely legal issues are also finally decided by the military judge[45] unless the motion raises a factual issue affecting the merits of the case, in which instance it may be considered by the court members on the merits.[46]

Unless the judge later reconsiders and reverses his own ruling, a judge's provisional ruling is final and may be appealed by the government.[47] The judge should rule on motions at the earliest possible time, although the *Manual* recognizes that in some cases the judge may defer ruling on motions until later in the trial.[48] Generally, motions made prior to the plea should be ruled upon before the accused enters his plea.[49] This not only serves to assist the defense counsel in deciding what plea to enter but also avoids potential double jeopardy problems that may arise if the prosecution appeals a judge's ruling made after jeopardy has attached.[50] A military judge's refusal to rule on a motion is subject to review for abuse of discretion.[51]

---

38. R.C.M. 905(c)(2)(B). *See* § 13-3(B).
39. See § 13-4 for a discussion on the various motions to suppress.
40. *See also* § 5-2.
41. Art. 51(b), U.C.M.J.
42. *See* Appendix 3.
43. R.C.M. 916(k). Motions relating to the accused's capacity to stand trial present interlocutory questions of fact which are finally ruled upon by the judge. R.C.M. 909(c)(1). *See also* § 13-5(A).
44. This is a factor under the *Barker v. Wingo* balancing test discussed at § 13-3(C)(1).
45. Legal effect given to a set of undisputed facts represents a question of law. United States v. Ware, 1 M.J. 282, 284, n.4 (C.M.A. 1976) (speedy trial question). *See also* United States v. Fretwell, 11 C.M.A. 377, 29 C.M.R. 193 (1960) (question of former punishment).
46. *See, e.g.*, United States v. Buckingham, 9 M.J. 514 (A.F.C.M.R. 1980) (question of personal jurisdiction presented factual issues where the accused is charged with an offense where military "status" is underlying element).
47. See § 13-2(G).
48. R.C.M. 905(d). United States v. Helweg, 32 M.J. 129 (C.M.A. 1991) (motion *in limine*). *See, e.g.*, United States v. Lippoldt, 34 M.J. 523 (A.F.C.M.R. 1991) (objection not waived where accused entered unconditional guilty plea to enable judge to develop facts through providence inquiry).
49. R.C.M. 905(d).
50. See § 13-2(G)(2).
51. *See* United States v. Bell, 25 M.J. 676 (A.C.M.R. 1987) (treating the failure of the trial judge to rule on a motion as a question of first impression, the court concluded that failure to rule

Under the Military Rules of Evidence the judge is required to make findings of fact on certain motions to suppress.[52] The *Manual* requires that the judge must state "essential findings" on the record where factual issues are involved in the motion.[53] Note that these findings are not the same as "special findings" that counsel may request in conjunction with a finding of guilty in a bench trial.[54] Failure to state these essential findings is error that may result in reversal.[55]

If the judge's rulings result in dismissal of all of the charges, the court is adjourned and a record of the proceedings is prepared for the convening authority.[56] As discussed in § 13-2(G)(2), the prosecution may in some circumstances appeal the rulings.

§ 13-2(F). Reconsideration of Rulings.

Under former provisions of Article 62, U.C.M.J., the convening authority could request the judge to reconsider his rulings unless they amounted to a finding of not guilty. Rulings on motions for appropriate relief and suppression motions were not covered.[57] The convening authority's action was not considered a direction to change a ruling, but instead was viewed as direction to reconsider.[58] The judge's ruling was to be reached independently and was considered final.

That controversial provision was replaced in the 1983 Military Justice Act by a new Article 62 provision that permits the government to appeal adverse rulings by the judge to the Court of Criminal Appeals.[59]

A reconsideration provision still exists in the *Manual*, however. The judge on his own, or at the request of a party, may reconsider any ruling that does not amount to a finding of not guilty.[60] In theory, if a convening authority is

---

on a motion is an implied denial of the motion); United States v. Covington, 12 M.J. 932 (N.M.C.M.R. 1982) (judge declined to rule on constitutionality of death penalty).

52. See § 13-4.

53. R.C.M. 905(d). United States v. Plott, 38 M.J. 735 (A.F.C.M.R. 1993) (essential findings not required where rulings did not involve factual issues).

54. *See* United States v. Postle, 20 M.J. 632 (N.M.C.M.R. 1985) (comparison of findings required under the Rules of Evidence, rulings on motions, and special findings).

55. United States v. Mayhugh, 41 M.J. 657 (N.M.Ct.Crim.App. 1994) (judge did not enter ruling or essential findings on record; apparently judge informed counsel during an 802 Conference of ruling; court launched what it termed "rescue mission" to resolve issue of whether judge correctly denied motion to suppress); United States v. Butterbaugh, 21 M.J. 1019 (N.M.C.M.R. 1986) (failure to enter essential findings and conclusions of law on speedy trial motion); United States v. Spriddle, 20 M.J. 804 (N.M.C.M.R. 1985).

56. R.C.M. 905(d).

57. *See, e.g.,* United States v. Nivens, 21 C.M.A. 420, 45 C.M.R. 194 (1972) (request for a change of venue); United States v. McElhinney, 21 C.M.A. 436, 45 C.M.R. 210 (1972) (request for witnesses).

58. United States v. Ware, 1 M.J. 282 (C.M.A. 1976).

59. Art. 62(a), U.C.M.J.

60. R.C.M. 905(f). In 1994, R.C.M. 905(f) was changed, by Change 7 to the *Manual*, to expressly permit the judge to reconsider his or her ruling at any time prior to authentication of the record. This clarifies the judge's post-trial authority. *See also* R.C.M. 1102(d). United States v. Copening,

§ 13-2(G)

dissatisfied with a ruling by the judge he could request the trial counsel to request reconsideration. But unlike the former U.C.M.J. provisions, the convening authority is now one step removed from the process and apparently may not directly request the judge to reconsider.

§ 13-2(G). Appeal of Rulings.

Should either side disagree with the judge's ruling on a motion or objection it may consider the possibility of appealing the ruling to the Service's Court of Criminal Appeals. For the defense that will mean seeking extraordinary relief. The prosecution on the other hand has at its disposal a more formalized appeal process to the same court. Both routes are discussed in the next sections.

§ 13-2(G)(1). Defense Appeals: Extraordinary Writs.

There is no formalized channel for the defense to appeal an interlocutory ruling by the military judge. In theory, the defense may contest a trial judge's ruling on any appeal of the court-martial conviction. If there is no conviction, then the adverse ruling is of no effect. For more immediate relief, especially where normal appellate review will be inadequate to protect the rights of the accused, counsel may, however, request a continuance and file a petition for extraordinary relief in the intermediate service appellate courts or the Court Appeals for the Armed Forces (formerly the Court of Military Appeals)[61] under the purview of the All Writs Act.[62] Both of those courts have recognized the validity of this procedure[63] and have granted relief in cases involving illegal pretrial confinement[64] and jurisdictional issues.[65] Further, the Court of Appeals has enjoined an Article 32 Investigation,[66] ordered referral of charges voided,[67] and ordered limited hearings on personal jurisdiction questions.[68] As

---

32 M.J. 512 (A.C.M.R. 1990) (replacement judge did not err in reconsidering motion to suppress that had been previously granted by predecessor judge who recused himself).

61. See United States Navy Marine Corps Court of Military Review v. Carlucci, 26 M.J. 328 (C.M.A. 1988) (court granted request for injunctive relief from N.M.C.M.R. that the Secretary of the Defense Inspector General be limited in his investigation of the court's deliberative process).

See generally Unger v. Ziemniak, 27 M.J. 349 (C.M.A. 1989) (extensive discussion of court's use of extraordinary writ power). For a discussion of the appellate courts in the military justice system, see Chapter 16.

62. 28 U.S.C. 1651(a). See generally Pavlick, "Extraordinary Writs in the Military Justice System: A Different Perspective," 84 MIL. L. REV. 7 (1979); Rankin, "The All Writs Act and the Military Judicial System," 53 MIL. L. REV. 103 (1971); Thorne, "Extraordinary Writs in the Military," ARMY LAW., Aug. 1977, at 8.

63. See, e.g., Dettinger v. United States, 7 M.J. 216 (C.M.A. 1979); United States v. Montcalm, 2 M.J. 787 (A.C.M.R. 1976).

64. See, e.g., Berta v. United States, 9 M.J. 390 (C.M.A. 1980) (misc. docket).

65. Zamora v. Woodson, 19 C.M.A. 403, 42 C.M.R. 5 (1970) (charges against civilian).

66. Petty v. Moriarty, 20 C.M.A. 438, 43 C.M.R. 278 (1971).

67. Vanover v. Clark, 27 M.J. 345 (C.M.A. 1988) (court dismissed additional charges that had been joined with other charges improperly withdrawn and re-referred); Burtt v. Schick, 23 M.J. 140 (C.M.A. 1986) (extraordinary writ sought to dismiss charges on grounds of double jeopardy;

---

68. Barnett v. United States, 3 M.J. 251 (C.M.A. 1977) (misc. docket).

a general rule defense counsel should seek relief first in the service's Court of Criminal Appeals (formerly the Court of Military Review) and then consider an appeal to the Court of Appeals if the lower court fails to grant relief. Finally, an adverse ruling by that court may be appealable to the Supreme Court of the United States.[69]

The test generally employed by the appellate courts in deciding whether extraordinary relief should be granted is whether the trial court has exceeded its authority, or ruled contrary to statute, applicable decisional law, or valid regulation.[70] Stated another way, relief should be granted only in truly extraordinary situations[71] because it is designed to "confine an inferior court to a lawful exercise of its prescribed jurisdiction."[72]

Procedures for seeking extraordinary writs are included in the rules of the Courts of Criminal Appeals and the United States Court of Appeals for the Armed Forces.[73]

§ 13-2(G)(2). Government Appeals.

Before 1983, the only avenue available to the prosecution for appealing a ruling by the trial judge was the extraordinary relief avenues discussed in § 13-2(G)(1).[74] In the Military Justice Act of 1983, however, Article 62, U.C.M.J. was amended specifically to provide for government appeal of a judge's rulings.[75] But the framers of the new provision, and its counterpart in

---

although accused sought relief before trial judge had an opportunity to rule on issue, court noted that unique circumstances of case made extraordinary relief appropriate); Brookins v. Cullins, 23 C.M.A. 216, 49 C.M.R. 5 (1974).

69. The appellate process is addressed in Chapter 17.

70. *See, e.g.,* Evans v. Kilroy, 33 M.J. 730 (A.F.C.M.R. 1991) (court denied accused's mandamus petition based on adverse speedy trial ruling by trial judge; appellate court had ordered stay pending resolution of issue); United States v. Pereira, 13 M.J. 632 (A.F.C.M.R. 1982).

71. *See* United States v. LaBella, 15 M.J. 228 (C.M.A. 1983); Andrews v. Heupel, 29 M.J. 743 (A.F.C.M.R. 1989) (court issued mandamus to trial judge, who had denied motion, to dismiss charges for lack of a speedy trial); Rhea v. Starr, 26 M.J. 683 (A.F.C.M.R. 1988) (extraordinary writ relief is extreme remedy and accused's request for review of trial judge's ruling on suppression motion, although unique, was more appropriate for normal appellate review).

72. Harrison v. United States, 20 M.J. 55, 57 (C.M.A. 1985).

73. See *infra* §§ 17-19 for further discussion on extraordinary relief.

74. *See* Floyd, "Extraordinary Writs in Favor of the Government," 25 JAG J. 3 (1970). Relief was granted to the government in the following cases under the extraordinary writs procedure: United States v. Wholley, 13 M.J. 574 (N.M.C.M.R. 1982) (trial judge abused discretion in dismissing charges on speedy trial grounds); United States v. Redding, 11 M.J. 100 (C.M.A. 1981) (dismissal of charges challenged).

Relief was denied in United States v. LaBella, 14 M.J. 688 (N.M.C.M.R. 1982) (ruling on subject matter jurisdiction); United States v. Pereira, 13 M.J. 632 (A.F.C.M.R. 1982) (ruling on suppression motion); United States v. Bogar, 13 M.J. 768 (A.C.M.R. 1982) (suppression motion).

75. Previously, Article 62 had provided for reconsideration of the ruling at the convening authority's request. *See* § 13-2(F). *See generally,* Hogan, "Government Appeals: A Trial Counsel's Guide," ARMY LAW., June 1989, at 28; Galligan, "Government Appeals: Winning the First Cases," ARMY LAW., Mar. 1985, at 38. Sullivan, "Army Government Appeals: Round Two," ARMY LAW., Dec. 1985, at 30.

§ 13-2(G)(2) MILITARY CRIMINAL JUSTICE § 13-2(G)(2)

the Manual for Courts-Martial[76] were apparently concerned that the right might be abused and placed several limitations on its use.

First, a military judge must be presiding at the court,[77] and it must be a court that may adjudge a punitive discharge.[78] In effect, this rules out appeal of rulings in cases tried before a summary or regular special court-martial,[79] cases usually involving less serious offenses and generally not warranting the lengthy and involved appeals process which may result.[80]

Second, the judge's ruling must either (1) result in *termination* of the proceedings with respect to a charge or specification[81] (2) result in the *exclusion* of evidence that is substantial proof of a fact material in the proceedings[82] or (3) involves specified rulings on disclosure of classified information.[83] These requirements should ensure that the ruling in question in some way includes granting a defense motion to dismiss the charges for lack of jurisdiction[84] or granting a defense motion to suppress the accused's confession[85] when that

---

76. *See* R.C.M. 908.
77. R.C.M. 908(a). See Chapters 4, 8, and 12 for discussions on appointment of a military judge to a court.
78. R.C.M. 908(a). A punitive discharge would consist of either a dishonorable or bad-conduct discharge. See § 15-17(B)(2) for a discussion of the nature and effect of this punishment.
79. *See* §§ 4-3(B), (C).
80. It is generally assumed that in some cases the appellate review of a trial judge's ruling could take months and perhaps even years. Although the appellate rules are designed to speed along the review process, because in theory the Supreme Court of the United States might eventually review the ruling it is not unlikely that lengthy delays would result simply because of the accumulated filing and response time limits.
81. R.C.M. 908(a). In United States v. True, 28 M.J. 1 (C.M.A. 1989), the court concluded that the trial judge's order abating the proceedings when the government failed to comply with an earlier order granting a defense request for appointment of an expert amounted to an appealable order. The court noted that an "abatement" is not a continuance where "intractability has set in." United States v. Laminman, 41 M.J. 518 (C.G.Ct.Crim.App. 1994) (government unsuccessfully appealed trial court's dismissal of charges on speedy trial grounds); United States v. Sepulveda, 40 M.J. 856 (A.F.C.M.R. 1994) (trial court's action in consolidating offenses was equivalent of dismissal of several specifications); United States v. Mahoney, 24 M.J. 911 (A.F.C.M.R. 1987) (judge's ruling on burden of proof re insanity issue was not appealable).
82. R.C.M. 908(a). United States v. Fling, 40 M.J. 847 (A.F.C.M.R. 1994) (appellate court reversed ruling by trial court excluding critical hearsay testimony); United States v. Pacheco, 36 M.J. 530 (A.F.C.M.R. 1992) (requirement is met as long as it is alleged that evidence in question is substantial or as long as essence of appeal indicates substantial nature of evidence; not necessary that evidence in question be only evidence in case); United States v. Scholz, 19 M.J. 837 (N.M.C.M.R. 1984).
83. Article 62(a)(1) was amended in 1996, by adding new subsections (C) through (F) which permit the government to appeal the judge's interlocutory rulings regarding orders or rulings affecting disclosure of classified information. Pub. L. No. 104-106, 110 Stat. 186 (1996), National Defense Authorization Act for Fiscal Year (FY) 1996. *See generally* "Joint Service Committee on Military Justice Report," ARMY LAW., Mar. 1996, at 138.
84. *See, e.g.*, United States v. Ermitano, 19 M.J. 626 (N.M.C.M.R. 1984) (appeal of ruling that specification did not state an offense).
85. *See* United States v. Reinecke, 30 M.J. 1010 (A.F.C.M.R. 1990) (trial judge suppressed results of urinalysis; appellate court reversed); United States v. St. Clair, 19 M.J. 833 (N.M.C.M.R. 1984) (appeal of ruling that accused's statement was inadmissible). *See also* United States v. Scholz, 19 M.J. 837 (N.M.C.M.R. 1984) (appeal of ruling excluding results of urinalysis testing).

piece of evidence is the core of the government's case. An appeal would not be appropriate in most of the examples generally associated with requests for "appropriate relief," such as release from pretrial confinement or severance of charges.[86] Likewise, the government will normally not be able to appeal the judge's denial of a continuance, even though the denial adversely affects the ability of the government to proceed with trial.[87] The issue on appeal of the ruling is whether as a matter of law the judge erred.[88] The appellate court is not likely to reverse a ruling that rests within the sound discretion of the trial judge.[89] On appeal the defense may present alternate arguments for sustaining the trial court's ruling. And the government may respond to those arguments.[90]

Third, the prosecution may *not* appeal a ruling that is a finding of not guilty or a ruling that amounts to such a finding.[91] Note that this limitation existed under the former Article 62 language. Motions for a finding of not guilty are discussed in Chapter 15.

Fourth, each service may designate persons authorized to approve an appeal.[92] The Army, for example, requires that either the Staff Judge Advocate or General Court-Martial Convening Authority must approve any notice of

---

86. United States v. Penn, 21 M.J. 907 (N.M.C.M.R. 1986) (court declined to review trial judge's order for new Article 32 Investigation). *See generally* § 13-5 for discussions on motions for appropriate relief.

87. United States v. Browers, 20 M.J. 356 (C.M.A. 1985).

88. United States v. Berrey, 28 M.J. 714 (N.M.C.M.R. 1989) (*en banc*); United States v. Yingling, 20 M.J. 593 (N.M.C.M.R. 1985) (court declined to review ruling by judge on admissibility of evidence); United States v. Harris, 20 M.J. 795 (N.M.C.M.R. 1985) (appellate court may review factual findings of the trial judge and determine whether they are correct as a matter of law).

89. United States v. Yingling, 20 M.J. 593 (N.M.C.M.R. 1985).

90. United States v. Lincoln, 42 M.J. 315 (1995).

91. R.C.M. 908(a). It is not entirely clear what the drafters meant when they used the term "amounting to a finding of not guilty." Normally, granting a motion to dismiss charges does not amount to a "finding of not guilty" if that term is intended to apply to resolution of the accused's guilt or innocence; the restriction would in most cases apply where the defense successfully moves to terminate the proceedings because of a lack of government proof or evidence, either through a formal motion for a finding of not guilty or some similar motion. *See* § 15-4(C). *See, e.g.*, Smalis v. Penn, 476 U.S. 140 (1986) (granting defense demurrer at close of prosecution case amounted to an acquittal and barred prosecution appeal of the ruling).

In United States v. Hunt, 24 M.J. 723 (A.C.M.R. 1987), the court cited United States v. Scott, 437 U.S. 82 (1978), for the proposition that:

> [a] defendant is acquitted only when the ruling of the judge, whatever its label, actually represents a resolution [in the defendant's favor], correct or not, of some or all of the factual elements of the offense charged. An appeal by the Government is only barred when it is clear that the [trial court] ... evaluated the Government's evidence and determined that it was legally insufficient to sustain a conviction. 24 M.J. at 728.

In United States v. Kinneer, 7 M.J. 974 (N.C.M.R. 1979), defense moved to dismiss the charge on the ground that the order the accused was alleged to have violated was invalid. The judge deferred granting the motion until after the prosecution rested. Under the circumstances the judge's ruling amounted to a finding of not guilty and the accused was protected by the bar against double jeopardy.

92. R.C.M. 908(b)(1).

appeal, which must be in writing.[93] This limitation is apparently designed to provide some supervisory control over appeals that might not be warranted in the context of other pending cases and alternate means of disposing of the charges, such as an administrative discharge.

Assuming that the government decides to pursue an appeal, the procedural steps are spelled out in R.C.M. 908 and in summary are as follows:

Deciding Whether to Appeal. The trial counsel is entitled to no more than 72 hours to decide whether to file a notice of appeal.[94] During that time the court may proceed only with matters unaffected by the judge's order or ruling. The delay offers the trial counsel an opportunity to confer with the SJA or convening authority and with the appellate government counsel in Washington, D.C. who would handle the appeal if it were filed.[95] Once the prosecution requests a delay to consider the possibility of an appeal, the 72-hour continuance is automatic and the judge may not frustrate the purposes behind government appeals by ignoring the request.[96] That of course assumes that the judge's ruling is appealable. If it is not, then the judge may in his discretion proceed with trial.[97] As noted above, the Service Secretary may require initial approval of an appeal at the trial level.

Notice of Appeal. Assuming that the government decides to appeal the judge's ruling, the trial counsel must file a written notice of appeal with the judge within 72 hours of the ruling.[98] The notice must indicate what order or ruling is being appealed,[99] the charges and specifications that are affected,[100]

---

93. *See* AR 27-10, para. 13-3a.

94. R.C.M. 908(b)(2). The rule contemplates that no extension of time will be granted to the trial counsel for making a decision. If for some extraordinary reason an extension was granted, the judge's decision to do so would be measured for prejudice to the accused.

95. For a discussion of the duties of appellate counsel, see § 17-2(A).

96. United States v. Browers, 20 M.J. 542 (A.C.M.R. 1985), *rev'd*, 20 M.J. 356 (C.M.A. 1985).

97. United States v. Browers, 20 M.J. 356 (C.M.A. 1985) (judge's denial of a continuance to obtain government witnesses was not an appealable ruling and judge did not abuse discretion in proceeding with trial).

United States v. Flores-Glaraza, 40 M.J. 900 (N.M.C.M.R. 1994) (timely notice, which is jurisdictional requirement, was untimely; court recommended that in order to avoid confusion about when time begins to run that (1) judge enter essential findings on record contemporaneous with ruling on the motion; (2) judge should state that his or her action is the ruling of the court; (3) the judge should determine on the record if the government intends to appeal; and (4) if the government is going to appeal, the judge should state on the record the time of the ruling, the deadline for notice, and how and where the government may provide the written notice to the judge).

98. R.C.M. 908(b)(3). United States v. Mayer, 21 M.J. 504 (A.F.C.M.R. 1984) (notice was untimely). Because the time for filing the notice of appeal coincides with the 72-hour delay for deciding whether to appeal, the prosecution must allow time for not only reaching a decision on the matter but also for preparation of the written notice and service on the judge. A reasonable reading of this rule would permit the prosecution to make substitute service on the judge who may be at a distant location when the 72-hour time has run.

Service regulations may require additional measures. For example, AR 27-10, para. 13-3b requires the trial counsel to serve a "certificate of notice of appeal" on the military judge that will reflect, inter alia, the date and time of service of the notice of appeal.

99. R.C.M. 908(b)(3). The Manual for Courts-Martial prescribes no particular format for the notice of appeal. As long as the necessary information is relayed to the parties any format should suffice. A suggested sample of a written notice of appeal is included at Appendix 21.

100. R.C.M. 908(b)(3).

§ 13-2(G)(2) MOTIONS PRACTICE § 13-2(G)(2)

that the appeal is not for purposes of delay,[101] and where the judge has excluded evidence, a statement that the evidence in question constitutes substantial proof of a material fact.[102]

Forwarding of Materials Necessary to Appeal. After filing the written notice of appeal the trial counsel must forward, by "expeditious" means, to a person designated by the Judge Advocate General information concerning the appeal, which indicates a statement of the issues appealed and a verbatim copy of the record of proceedings,[103] and any other matters that the service regulations may require.[104] If a verbatim record is not immediately available, the trial counsel should prepare a summary of the evidence and forward the verbatim version within the time limits set by each service.[105]

Appellate Review. Upon review of the file, the person designated by the Judge Advocate General[106] will determine if an appeal should be filed in the Court of Criminal Appeals.[107] If the appeal is filed, the Court is required to give the matter some priority[108] and may rule only on matters of law.[109] That is, the question whether the trial court's ruling is unsupported by the evidence in the record or was clearly erroneous.[110] The test is not whether the appellate

---

101. R.C.M. 908(b)(3). This requirement generally tracks with federal practice governing prosecution appeals.

102. R.C.M. 908(b)(3). What constitutes "substantial proof of a material fact" will turn on the nature of the evidence in question and the relative strength of other evidence. An accused's incriminating statements will, in most cases, fall within this category. However, evidence that might only be used for impeachment purposes would present a closer question; although it would be relevant it would generally not be "substantial" proof. The key here is the intent of the Rule. Although the government has a right to appeal, the right is limited to those instances where its very ability to go forward with the case is substantially threatened because of the judge's ruling.

103. R.C.M. 908(b)(5). The record must be authenticated by the military judge. See R.C.M. 1103(g), (h), (i) and 1104(a). *See also* United States v. Combs, 38 M.J. 741 (A.F.C.M.R. 1993) (government appeal dismissed where it failed to justify delays in forwarding appeal to representative); United States v. Pearson, 33 M.J. 777 (N.M.C.M.R. 1991) (appellate court summarily dismissed government appeal where it failed to "promptly" file the original record of trial with the appellate court).

104. R.C.M. 908(b)(5). The trial judge and Court of Criminal Appeals may specify what additional material should be included.

105. R.C.M. 908(b)(5). *See, e.g.,* AR 27-10, para. 13-3c (must forward within 20 days of the judge's ruling); United States v. Synder, 30 M.J. 662 (A.F.C.M.R. 1990) (prosecutor failed to comply with Air Force Regulation 111-4's 20-day time limit).

106. R.C.M. 908(b)(6). In the Army, that individual is the Chief of the Government Appellate Division who is required to coordinate the matter with the Assistant Judge Advocate General for Military Law. AR 27-10, para. 13-3a.

107. R.C.M. 908(b)(6), (7). If the appeal is not filed the parties at the trial level should be so informed immediately.

108. R.C.M. 908(c)(2).

109. R.C.M. 908(c)(2).The appellate court may review the trial judge's findings of fact to ensure that they are supported by the record and are correct as a matter of law. *Cf.* United States v. Abell, 23 M.J. 99 (C.M.A. 1986) (a de novo ad hoc judgment by the Court of Criminal Appeals on the issue of service connection is within the scope of Article 62, and our review of such a judgment may be equally as broad); United States v. Harris, 20 M.J. 795 (N.M.C.M.R. 1985).

110. United States v. Burris, 21 M.J. 140 (C.M.A. 1985), *citing* Marshall v. Lonberger, 459 U.S. 422 (1983).

court disagrees with the trial court's ruling.[111] Appellate counsel handle the litigation at this stage.[112] Either side may further appeal the ruling of the Court of Criminal Appeals to the Court of Appeals[113] and, in theory, to the Supreme Court of the United States.[114]

Continuation of the Trial Pending Appeal. While the appeal is pending the trial may proceed only as to unaffected charges and specifications that may remain.[115] If trial on the merits has not begun it may be appropriate to sever the charges and specifications.[116] If the trial on the merits has begun, either party may request the judge to grant permission to present further evidence,[117] for example, where a key witness is available and ready to testify. Motions may continue to be litigated.[118] Pending the government appeal, the accused may normally be continued in pretrial confinement.[119] If the ruling being appealed, however, has resulted in dismissal of the charges,[120] continued confinement is probably not appropriate.[121]

§ 13-3. Motions to Dismiss.

A motion to dismiss is a request that the trial judge terminate the proceedings without proceeding to a trial on the merits.[1] The following sections address various motions to dismiss. Because several of the grounds for such a motion are not discussed elsewhere in this book, any pertinent substantive law governing the issue is included here. If the defect that gave rise to the dismissal can be remedied, then the prosecution can generally proceed with new charges and referral.[2]

---

111. United States v. Burris, 21 M.J. 140 (C.M.A. 1985); United States v. Middleton, 10 M.J. 123 (C.M.A. 1981).
112. R.C.M. 908(c)(1).
113. R.C.M. 908(c)(3). United States v. Tucker, 20 M.J. 52 (C.M.A. 1985).
114. Art. 67(h), U.C.M.J.; R.C.M. 908(c)(3). *See also* § 16-17. *See, e.g.*, Solorio v. United States, 483 U.S. 435 (1987).
115. R.C.M. 908(b)(4).
116. R.C.M. 908(b)(4)(B). *See also* § 13-5(F) for a discussion on motions to sever.
117. R.C.M. 908(b)(4)(C).
118. R.C.M. 908(b)(4)(A). Whether additional motions should be litigated lies within the discretion of the trial judge.
119. Frage v. Edington, 26 M.J. 927, 928 (N.M.C.M.R. 1988).
120. For example, the judge may have dismissed the charges for lack of jurisdiction or for lack of a speedy trial.
121. Frage v. Edington, 26 M.J. 927 (N.M.C.M.R. 1988) (*citing* R.C.M. 304(g), the court concluded that if charges have been dismissed, there is no "offense triable by court-martial").
1. R.C.M. 907(a).
2. R.C.M. 907(a) Discussion. This is generally limited to motions to dismiss for lack of jurisdiction or failure to state an offense. *See* §§ 13-3(A), (F).

§ 13-3(A). Lack of Jurisdiction.

Lack of jurisdiction over the accused or the offense or defects in the referral process or detailing of the parties may be raised at any time.[3] It is not waived either by failing to raise it[4] or by pleading guilty.[5] Once raised, the prosecution must establish jurisdiction by a preponderance of the evidence.[6] However, if there is an issue of whether the accused is personally subject to the jurisdiction of the court and military "status" is an element of the charged offense, the prosecution must be prepared to establish the accused's status beyond a reasonable doubt.[7] See Chapter 4 for a more detailed discussion of the jurisdictional prerequisites of a court-martial.

§ 13-3(B). Statute of Limitations.

The statute of limitations, noted in Article 43, U.C.M.J., may bar trial.[8] The issue must be raised or it is considered waived.[9] If there is a *prima facie* issue of whether the statute has run, the military judge must raise the point,[10] and

---

3. *See, e.g.*, United States v. Lockwood, 15 M.J. 1 (C.M.A. 1983). In those cases where the issue is raised for the first time on appeal, the appellate courts necessarily struggle with whether there is any evidence in the record, including allied papers, that jurisdiction existed. Rather than voiding a court-martial, the courts will from time to time order *DuBay* hearings on the issue. And although the appellate courts recognize that the issue may be raised for the first time on appeal, they do not generally appreciate the fact that counsel may have knowingly passed up an opportunity to raise the issue at the trial level where readily available facts might have clarified the issue.
4. R.C.M. 905(e), 907(b)(1) (A). *Cf.* United States v. Hawley, 30 M.J. 1247 (A.C.M.R. 1990) (errors that are not jurisdictional, such as typographical or administrative errors in convening a court, are waivable).
5. United States v. Alef, 3 M.J. 414 (C.M.A. 1977).
6. R.C.M. 905(c)(2)(B). United States v. Buckingham, 9 M.J. 514 (A.F.C.M.R. 1980).
7. United States v. Buckingham, 9 M.J. 514 (A.F.C.M.R. 1980).
8. *See* Appendix 3.
9. R.C.M. 905(e). United States v. Britton, 26 M.J. 24 (C.M.A. 1988) (Court of Military Review is not legally bound to apply waiver rule); United States v. Tunnell, 23 M.J. 110 (C.M.A. 1986) (no waiver where judge failed to apprise accused that statute of limitations might be available); United States v. Troxell, 12 C.M.A. 6, 30 C.M.R. 6 (1960).
United States v. Province, 42 M.J. 821 (N.M. Ct. Crim.App.1995) (military judge did not apprise accused of statute of limitations issue and accused did not waive); United States v. Lee, 32 M.J. 857 (N.M.C.M.R. 1991) (accused may not waive statute of limitations unless record shows that he was aware of the right to plead the statute as a bar to the trial); United States v. Brown, 30 M.J. 907 (A.C.M.R. 1990) (no waiver where counsel erroneously believed that statute of limitations had been tolled; the court indicated that for there to be a waiver, the record must disclose that by reason of advice from the judge or otherwise, the accused was aware of the right to assert the statute of limitations).
United States v. Colley, 29 M.J. 519 (A.C.M.R. 1989) (because trial judge had not apprised accused of right to invoke the statute of limitations, court would not invoke waiver); United States v. Lee, 29 M.J. 516 (A.C.M.R. 1989) (accused was not informed by military judge that statute of limitations was available, thus his plea of guilty in itself was insufficient to waive the issue); United States v. Wesley, 19 M.J. 534 (N.M.C.M.R. 1984) (accused knowingly waived his right to raise the issue).
10. R.C.M. 907(b)(2)(B). United States v. Moore, 32 M.J. 170 (C.M.A. 1991) (no waiver of statute of limitations where judge failed to exercise *sua sponte* duty of inquiring into statute of

the burden falls upon the prosecution to prove by a preponderance of the evidence that the running of the statute has been tolled.[11] The statute of limitations is generally five years[12] and may be tolled by the summary court-martial convening authority receiving the charges[13] at any time within the period of the statute.[14] Once that authority has received the charges, minor changes may be made even after the statute has run.[15] Receipt of properly sworn charges by the summary court-martial convening authority within the statute of limitations will toll the statute, even though a new and untimely charge sheet is prepared.[16] In that case, however, the trial judge should be provided with a copy of the original charge sheet in order to insure that the charges upon which the accused is being tried were properly preferred.[17]

In 1988, Article 43, U.C.M.J. was amended to provide that where charges or specifications have been dismissed for technical defects, the government has an additional 180 days from the date of dismissal to prefer and refer, new charges.[18]

In computing whether the statute of limitations has run, the following rules of construction apply: the statute of limitations begins on the date that the crime is complete;[19] fractions of days should be disregarded;[20] the term "year"

---

limitations issue); United States v. Salter, 20 M.J. 116 (C.M.A. 1985) (case reversed because record devoid of advice by anyone that issue existed); United States v. Jackson, 20 M.J. 83 (C.M.A. 1985) (judge gave proper advice); United States v. Colley, 29 M.J. 519 (A.C.M.R. 1989); United States v. Taylor, 13 M.J. 648 (N.M.C.M.R. 1982).

11. R.C.M. 905(c)(2)(B).
12. The period of time is usually determined by the nature of the offense. There is no limit for offenses for which the death penalty may be imposed and there is a two-year limit on all offenses for purposes of nonjudicial punishment under Article 15, U.C.M.J. *See generally* Chapter 3. Under some circumstances, dismissed charges may be reinstated within six months after the statute has run. *See* Art. 43(b), U.C.M.J. *See* Appendix 3.
13. Frage v. Moriarty, 27 M.J. 341 (C.M.A. 1988) (receipt of charges which had not been sworn to before an officer authorized to administer oaths did not toll statute of limitations).
United States v. Holt, 31 M.J. 758 (A.C.M.R. 1990) (court assumed that officer signing as adjutant for commander did so with proper authority). For a discussion on the process of forwarding the charges to the summary court-martial convening authority, see § 6-2(B).
14. Art. 43(b), (c), U.C.M.J.; R.C.M. 907(b)(2)(B) Discussion. The statute of limitations may in some circumstances be suspended without regard to whether the summary court-martial convening authority has received the charges. *See, e.g.,* Art. 43(f), which permits suspension of the statute for certain offenses committed during wartime.
15. R.C.M. 907(b)(2)(B) Discussion, and R.C.M. 603(d). *See also* § 6-2(B). United States v. Waller, 24 M.J. 266 (C.M.A. 1987).
Cf. United States v. Brown, 30 M.J. 907 (A.C.M.R. 1990), where AWOL charges had been apparently preferred before expiration of statute of limitations but new charges had been preferred after the period of limitation had run without any reference to earlier charges. Under those circumstances, the statute was not tolled. United States v. Glenn, 29 M.J. 696 (A.C.M.R. 1989) (prosecution may not avoid statute of limitations by amending charge to reflect a lesser included offense that is not barred).
16. United States v. Miller, 38 M.J. 121 (C.M.A. 1993), *overruling in part*, United States v. Rodgers, 24 C.M.R. 36 (C.M.A. 1957).
17. *Id.*
18. Article 43(g), U.C.M.J. United States v. Province, 42 M.J. 821 (N.M.Ct.Crim.App.1995).
19. United States v. Lee, 32 M.J. 857 (N.M.C.M.R. 1991) (statute of limitations begins on date that crime is complete).
20. United States v. Tunnell, 23 M.J. 110, 112 (C.M.A. 1986).

in Article 43 refers to an ordinary calendar year of 365 days;[21] and the initial date of the offense and the date that the charges were received by the summary court-martial convening authority should be excluded.[22]

§ 13-3(C). Speedy Trial.

Motions to dismiss for lack of a speedy trial may be waived[23] and must be made before the trial ends.[24] A plea of guilty waives the issue.[25] Once raised, the prosecution must prove by a preponderance of the evidence that it has complied with the applicable time limits.[26] In military practice, speedy trial issues potentially include consideration of the Sixth Amendment, the Uniform Code of Military Justice, specifically Articles 10 and 33, and R.C.M. 707 in the Manual for Courts-Martial. The Federal Speedy Trial Act[27] is not applicable to courts-martial.[28] But the Interstate Agreement on Detainers Act (IADA)[29] is applicable.[30]

The speedy trial requirements also apply to rehearings[31] or "other trials."[32] In those instances, the prosecution's accountability begins when the convening authority is notified of the appellate court's opinion.[33]

---

21. 23 M.J. at 112. United States v. Glenn, 29 M.J. 696 (A.C.M.R. 1989); United States v. Colley, 29 M.J. 519 (A.C.M.R. 1989).
22. 23 M.J. at 117. United States v. Colley, 29 M.J. 519 (A.C.M.R. 1989).
23. R.C.M. 907(b)(2)(A).
24. R.C.M. 905(e).
25. R.C.M. 707(e) (1991 Amendments). United States v. Cornelius, 37 M.J. 622 (A.C.M.R. 1993) (speedy trial issues are waived by guilty plea per R.C.M. 707(e)). *Cf.* United States v. Pierce, 19 C.M.A. 225, 41 C.M.R. 225 (1970); United States v. Schalck, 14 C.M.A. 371, 34 C.M.R. 151 (1964); United States v. Sloan, 48 C.M.R. 211 (A.C.M.R. 1974); R.C.M. 707, 910(j). The issue probably cannot be waived by the accused in a pretrial agreement with the convening authority. *See* § 9-2(B)(2).
26. R.C.M. 905(c)(2)(B). United States v. Cook, 27 M.J. 212 (C.M.A. 1988) (prosecution bears burden of proof); United States v. Burris, 21 M.J. 140 (C.M.A. 1985); United States v. Givens, 28 M.J. 888 (A.F.C.M.R. 1989). Note that under the *Burton* Rule, where the accused has been in pretrial confinement longer than 90 days, the government bears a particularly "heavy" burden.
27. 18 U.S.C. §§ 3161-3174 (1994).
28. United States v. Aragon, 1 M.J. 662 (N.C.M.R. 1975). The federal statute specifically states that it is inapplicable to courts-martial.
Cf. United States v. Greer, 21 M.J. 338 (C.M.A. 1986), where the court apparently concluded that the time requirements of Art. III(A) of the Interstate Agreement on Detainers, 18 U.S.C. App., Pub. L. No. 91-538, § 2, 84 Stat. 1397 (1970), were applicable to the military but that the accused had not activated the Act's protections.
29. 18 U.S.C. app. § 2 (1994).
30. United States v. Bramer, 43 M.J. 538 (N.M. Ct. Crim. App. 1995) (discussing application of act to military).
31. United States v. Flint, 1 M.J. 428 (C.M.A. 1976); United States v. McFarlin, 24 M.J. 631 (A.C.M.R. 1987) (accused denied speedy trial in violation of R.C.M. 707, see § 13-3(C), where trial started 121 days after notification).
32. United States v. Gonda, 27 M.J. 636 (A.C.M.R. 1988) (retrial reset speedy trial clock and time spent in pretrial confinement before first trial was not to be added to time spent in confinement before retrial); United States v. Moreno, 24 M.J. 752 (A.C.M.R. 1987).
33. United States v. McFarlin, 24 M.J. 631 (A.C.M.R. 1987). *See also* United States v. Rivera-Berrios, 24 M.J. 679 (A.C.M.R. 1987).

§ 13-3(C)(1). Sixth Amendment and Due Process Standards.

There are potentially two distinct constitutional arguments that might be advanced where the prosecution has delayed in providing the accused with a speedy trial: First, the guarantee in the Sixth Amendment to a speedy trial, and second, the accused's due process rights to speedy disposition of a pretrial investigation and processing of possible charges.

In *Barker v. Wingo*,[34] the Supreme Court discussed the constitutional significance of providing a speedy trial to an accused. In assessing whether an accused has been denied a Sixth Amendment right to a speedy disposition of the charges against him, the Court listed four factors to be considered by the courts: (1) the length of the delay, (2) reasons for the delay, (3) whether the accused has made a timely assertion of his right to a speedy trial, and (4) whether the accused has suffered specific prejudice.[35] The Court noted that none of these factors was dispositive, although it added that the length of the delay involved would trigger the issue.[36] Under Sixth Amendment analysis the period of accountability runs from the date of the arrest or indictment, whichever comes first.[37] If there have been long delays in the prearrest or preindictment stages, the test is whether the accused was denied due process.[38] See the discussion *infra*.

In several cases the military courts have relied upon the Sixth Amendment template in gauging whether an accused was denied a speedy trial. For example, in *United States v. Grom*,[39] the court used the foregoing analysis in concluding that the accused was not denied a speedy trial under the Sixth Amendment.[40] And in *United States v. Johnson*,[41] the court held that a seventeen-month delay under the circumstances did not amount to a violation of the Sixth Amendment.

---

34. 407 U.S. 514 (1972).

35. 407 U.S. at 530. United States v. Thomas, 43 M.J. 626 (A.F.Ct.Crim.App. 1995) (accused not denied right to Sixth Amendment speedy trial); United States v. Nichols, 42 M.J. 715 (A.F.Ct.Crim.App. 1995) (applying *Barker* factors, court concluded that accused was not denied speedy trial under Sixth Amendment standard); United States v. Nelson, 28 M.J. 922 (N.M.C.M.R. 1988) (no Sixth Amendment violation). The court in United States v. McCallister, 24 M.J. 881 (A.C.M.R. 1987), applied these four factors in conjunction with the *Burton* "demand for trial" rule in determining whether the accused had been denied a speedy trial.

36. 407 U.S. at 530. *Cf.* United States v. Thomas, 43 M.J. 626 (A.F.Ct.Crim.App. 1995) (court indicated that it would give "especially strong weight" to whether a demand for trial was made).

37. United States v. Marion, 404 U.S. 307 (1971); United States v. Vogan, 35 M.J. 32 (C.M.A. 1992) (Sixth Amendment speedy trial rule did not apply where accused was already in confinement at Disciplinary Barracks).

38. United States v. McDonald, 456 U.S. 1 (1982) (four-year delay between dismissal of military charges and federal indictment). *See also* United States v. Rachels, 6 M.J. 232 (C.M.A. 1979); United States v. Reeves, 34 M.J. 1261 (N.M.C.M.R. 1992) (noting split in federal circuits on whether government delay must be intentional to violate due process, court held that Fifth Amendment due process rights of accused were not violated by 462-day delay in preferring charges); United States v. Dorsch, 34 M.J. 1042 (N.M.C.M.R. 1992) (sixth-month delay between report of offense and preferral of charges did not deny due process).

39. 21 M.J. 53 (C.M.A. 1985), *cert. denied*, 475 U.S. 1083 (1986).

40. The *Barker* balancing test was triggered by an eight-month delay from preferral of charges to trial.

41. 17 M.J. 255 (C.M.A. 1984).

A Sixth Amendment analysis, which establishes only the minimum requirements, is generally not required in either military or civilian practice, because the Federal government and many states have enacted speedy trial provisions that set definite time limits. The analysis is useful in understanding the military's statutory requirements, however, which tend to be more rigorous.

Delays in the pretrial processing of a case are generally not measured against the Sixth Amendment template. Instead, the courts will apply a due process test in determining whether the pre-charging delay requires dismissal of the charges. In *United States v. Lovasco*,[42] the Supreme Court set out a two-pronged requirement. First, the defendant must show that the pretrial delay resulted in actual prejudice, such as through the loss of testimony or physical evidence.[43] And second, the courts must determine what, if any, reasons the government has for the delay.[44] While the Court in *Lovasco* declined to list "bad" reasons for pretrial delay,[45] the key here seems to be whether the pretrial delay was intentionally oppressive or demonstrated a complete disregard of the defendant's rights. The Court did indicate that the government is not required to charge an accused at the first available moment and can, for a number of legitimate reasons, delay the charging process while it continues its investigation.[46] But both of the prongs of the test must be met. Thus, a good-faith delay in pretrial processing will not result in a denial of due process, even if the defendant is prejudiced.[47]

§ 13-3(C)(2). U.C.M.J. Requirements: The *Burton* 90-Day Rule (1972-1993).

The Uniform Code of Military Justice contains several statutory provisions addressing the issue of prompt disposition of the charges. The first, Article 33, requires forwarding of general court-martial charges to the general court-martial convening authority within eight days or presenting reasons for failure to do so.[48] Failure to comply with this procedural requirement will nor-

---

42. 431 U.S. 783 (1977). *See also* United States v. Marion, 404 U.S. 307 (1971).
43. 431 U.S. at 790. Mere loss of memory by a witness may not suffice to show actual prejudice. United States v. Reed, 41 M.J. 449 (1995) (accused failed to prove that delays occurring before the preferral of charges resulted in prejudice).
44. 431 U.S. at 790. United States v. Reed, 41 M.J. 449 (1995) (accused failed to prove that delays occurring before the preferral of charges resulted from egregious, intentional, tactical decisions by the prosecution).
45. 431 U.S. at 796-97.
46. 431 U.S. at 792-95.
47. 431 U.S. at 796. The Court noted that few defendants had been able to establish actual prejudice, so that it had been generally unnecessary to review government reasons for delays. *Id.* United States v. Vogan, 35 M.J. 32 (C.M.A. 1992) (eight- or nine-month delay not denial of due process absent showing of egregious pretrial delay or inability to present a defense); United States v. Devine, 36 M.J. 673 (N.M.C.M.R. 1992) (one-year delay in preferral of charges did not amount to denial of due process where only actual prejudice suffered was loss of character witnesses and that was fault of accused, who took no steps to preserve their testimony).
48. *See* Appendix 3.

mally not justify dismissal of the charges unless the accused can demonstrate specific prejudice.[49]

Article 10, U.C.M.J., on the other hand, is more protective than the Sixth Amendment,[50] discussed above, and requires that when an accused is placed in arrest or confinement before trial, immediate steps must be taken to either try him or dismiss the charges and release him.[51] The provisions of Article 10 are triggered by arrest or confinement of some duration,[52] although in some cases the courts have found that severe restriction of the accused amounted to confinement that could trigger the rule.[53] In assessing whether the government has acted with reasonable diligence[54] the courts will consider whether the defense demanded an early trial[55] or requested delays,[56] the length of the delay,[57] the nature of the restraint,[58] and whether there has been a purposeful

---

49. United States v. Rogers, 7 M.J. 274, 275, n.1 (C.M.A. 1979); United States v. Nelson, 5 M.J. 189, 190, n.1 (C.M.A. 1978); United States v. Honican, 27 M.J. 590 (A.C.M.R. 1988) (court found specific prejudice).
Failure to comply may, however, be considered a factor in deciding whether the accused was denied a speedy trial. United States v. Fernandez, 48 C.M.R. 460 (N.M.C.M.R. 1974).

50. United States v. King, 30 M.J. 59, 62, n.5 (C.M.A. 1990); United States v. Marshall, 47 C.M.R. 409 (C.M.A. 1973); United States v. Cole, 3 M.J. 220 (C.M.A. 1977); United States v. Powell, 2 M.J. 6 (C.M.A. 1976). This is due in part to the fact that there is no provision for bail in military practice. See United States v. Mock, 49 C.M.R. 160 (A.C.M.R. 1974).

51. Art. 10, U.C.M.J. See Appendix 3. The period of accountability runs separately on each charge for which the arrest or restraint has been imposed. United States v. Stubbs, 3 M.J. 630 (N.C.M.R. 1977); United States v. Garner, 39 M.J. 721 (N.M.C.M.R. 1993) (Article 10 sets more rigorous standard than Sixth Amendment).

52. United States v. Nelson, 5 M.J. 189 (C.M.A. 1978) (13 days of confinement not sufficient to trigger).

53. United States v. Williams, 16 C.M.A. 589, 37 C.M.R. 209 (1967) (restriction to company area for total of 318 days); United States v. Smith, 39 C.M.R. 315 (A.B.R. 1967), aff'd, 17 C.M.A. 427, 38 C.M.R. 225 (1968).
Withholding an accused's pass privileges may also be tantamount to confinement. United States v. Powell, 2 M.J. 6 (C.M.A. 1976). But simply holding the accused after his enlistment expires, pursuant to regulations, will generally not trigger Article 10. See United States v. Rachels, 6 M.J. 232 (C.M.A. 1979).
The issue of what constitutes "confinement" is also discussed infra with regard to the Burton 90-day rule.

54. United States v. Parish, 17 C.M.A. 411, 38 C.M.R. 209 (1968). The test is one of reasonable diligence, not constant motion. United States v. Tibbs, 15 C.M.A. 350, 35 C.M.R. 322 (1965); United States v. Youngberg, 38 M.J. 635 (A.C.M.R. 1993) (citing United States v. Kossman, appellate court sua sponte considered potential Article 10 compliance and concluded that government acted with reasonable diligence).

55. United States v. Munkus, 15 M.J. 1013 (A.F.C.M.R. 1983) (charges dismissed where the government failed to try the accused after several demands for trial were made); United States v. Mock, 49 C.M.R. 160 (A.C.M.R. 1974).

56. United States v. Roman, 5 M.J. 385 (C.M.A. 1978) (request for counsel). Defense delays are also discussed infra.

57. The length of the delay will in most cases be some indication of the prosecution's resolve to proceed with the case.

58. Aside from the distinctions between restriction and confinement, there is an additional question of whether Article 10 is triggered by civilian restraint. The key is whether the civilian authorities were holding the accused on behalf of the military. If they were, the government is accountable, United States v. Keaton, 18 C.M.A. 500, 40 C.M.R. 212 (1969), but is allowed a reasonable time to pick up the accused and return him to military control. United States v.

or oppressive delay on the part of the government.[59] Although not normally listed as a specific factor in Article 10 speedy trial issues, prejudice to the defense may be considered on the question of the reasonableness of the delay.[60]

The Court of Military Appeals' decision in *United States v. Burton*[61] in 1972 was intended to add teeth to the Article 10 provisions which provide no specific time limits for bringing an accused to trial. In *Burton* the court held that where the accused has been in pretrial confinement for more than 90 days,[62] the prosecution had a heavy burden of showing diligence[63] in bringing the charges to trial.[64] Failure to do so would result in dismissal of the charges.[65] This "*Burton* 90-Day" rule was triggered by military[66] *confinement*,[67] not

---

Marin, 20 C.M.A. 432, 43 C.M.R. 272 (1971). On the other hand, if the civilian authorities are holding the accused for civil charges, the government is not accountable, even if the military initially turned the accused over to the civil authorities. United States v. Reed, 2 M.J. 64 (C.M.A. 1976); United States v. Williams, 12 C.M.A. 81, 30 C.M.R. 81 (1961); United States v. Garner, 39 M.J. 721 (N.M.C.M.R. 1993) (government not accountable for civilian confinement).

Delay in the absence of any restraint may not be considered as raising an Article 10 issue unless the delay is out of the ordinary. In that case, the focus would be on a violation of due process as opposed to denial of a speedy trial.

59. United States v. Parish, 17 C.M.A. 411, 38 C.M.R. 209 (1968).

60. *See, e.g.,* United States v. Smith, 17 C.M.A. 55, 37 C.M.R. 319 (1967) (delay caused defense to lose two witnesses); United States v. Dupree, 42 C.M.R. 681 (A.C.M.R. 1970) (delay forced defense to rely on deposition of alibi witness). However, normal adverse administrative consequences of pretrial delay do not necessarily indicate a denial of a speedy trial. *See, e.g.,* United States v. Amundson, 23 C.M.A. 308, 49 C.M.R. 598 (1975).

61. 21 C.M.A. 112, 44 C.M.R. 166 (1971).

62. The court originally expressed the rule in terms of "three months" but later modified it to read 90 days in United States v. Driver, 23 C.M.A. 243, 49 C.M.R. 376 (1974). In counting the days, the first day of confinement is excluded but the day of trial is included. United States v. Manalo, 1 M.J. 452 (C.M.A. 1976).

63. In expressing the prosecution's burden of proof, the courts did not articulate a specific burden beyond that of preponderance of the evidence. Thus, when a military court speaks in terms of the *Burton* rule placing a "heavy" burden on the prosecution, it, in effect, is setting out a rebuttable presumption that the accused was denied a speedy trial. The prosecution can rebut the presumption by demonstrating by a preponderance of the evidence, the burden of proof normally associated with speedy trial issues, that extraordinary circumstances, prevented an earlier trial date.

64. The *Burton* rule also applied to rehearings on the merits of the case. United States v. Flint, 1 M.J. 428 (C.M.A. 1976). In those instances the government's accountability began when the convening authority receives the opinion of the appellate court. United States v. Cabatic, 7 M.J. 438 (C.M.A. 1979).

65. 21 C.M.A. at 118, 44 C.M.R. at 172. *See, e.g.,* United States v. Henderson, 1 M.J. 421 (C.M.A. 1976) (murder charges dismissed); United States v. Honican, 27 M.J. 590 (A.C.M.R. 1988) (by waiting for fingerprint report on additional forgery charges, which was not required in the court's view, the accused was needlessly subjected to two different trials; court noted that this case demonstrates the practical wisdom of rule that accused has a right to a speedy trial on each set of charges).

66. Civilian confinement might in some circumstances trigger the *Burton* rule. The rules generally applicable to the effect of civilian confinement on Article 10 issues, discussed *supra*, are

---

67. United States v. Howard, 35 M.J. 763 (A.C.M.R. 1992) (speedy trial clock started when accused's post-trial confinement was converted to pretrial confinement for purposes of rehearing ordered by convening authority in his action). *See* § 5-3(B)(4) for a discussion of the prerequisites of placing an accused in pretrial confinement.

§ 13-3(C)(2)   MILITARY CRIMINAL JUSTICE   § 13-3(C)(2)

mere restriction,[68] and was terminated either by the release of the accused from confinement[69] or the beginning of the trial,[70] or its equivalent.[71] Each additional charge began a new and separate accounting by the prosecution.[72] In deciding whether the rule applied, the military courts usually determined the total days of confinement and then deducted any defense delays.[73] If the

---

generally applicable here. That is, the military is not accountable for time spent in civilian confinement unless the civil authorities are holding the accused on behalf of the military. United States v. Keaton, 18 C.M.A. 500, 40 C.M.R. 212 (1969). And in that case the military authorities are given a reasonable period of time to pick him up and return him to military control. *Id.* United States v. Smith, 50 C.M.R. 237 (A.C.M.R. 1975). If the civilian authorities are holding the accused on civil charges, the government is not accountable even if it turned him over to the civilians in the first instance. United States v. Reed, 2 M.J. 64 (C.M.A. 1976); United States v. Frostell, 13 M.J. 680 (N.M.C.M.R. 1982).

68. Military courts have extended the term "confinement" to cover lesser restraints that amount to confinement. *See, e.g.,* United States v. Schilf, 1 M.J. 251 (C.M.A. 1976) (restriction to narrowly defined area constituted confinement); United States v. McDowell, 19 M.J. 937 (A.C.M.R. 1985) (four-month delay and accused's restriction equivalent to confinement); United States v. Acireno, 15 M.J. 570 (A.C.M.R. 1982) (*Burton* triggered where the accused was in an arrest status and restricted to two floors of a four-story building); United States v. Bowman, 13 M.J. 640 (N.M.C.M.R. 1982) (restriction to bar-racks amounted to confinement).

Cf. United States v. Burrell, 13 M.J. 437 (C.M.A. 1982) (restriction to hospital was not equivalent to arrest or confinement); United States v. Buchecker, 13 M.J. 709 (N.M.C.M.R. 1982) (pretrial assignment to Recruit Casual Station was not tantamount to confinement).

69. United States v. Honican, 27 M.J. 590 (A.C.M.R. 1988) (judge erred in deducting 10 days posttrial confinement for earlier conviction from government's accountable time, although ordinarily time spent in such confinement is not included as "pretrial confinement" for subsequent trial). The release from confinement might not actually terminate the period of accountability if the accused is placed in restriction or arrest amounting to confinement, as discussed *supra.* And where the release is followed by inaction by the prosecution to proceed with trial, speedy trial issue may still arise. *See, e.g.,* United States v. Rowsey, 14 M.J. 151 (C.M.A. 1982).

70. This would include the beginning of a rehearing, or retrial, on the merits where the accused is in confinement awaiting resolution of his case. *See* United States v. Flint, 1 M.J. 428 (C.M.A. 1976).

71. An Article 39(a) pretrial session, discussed in Chapter 12, might terminate the running of the *Burton* rule. The key seems to be that that session be tantamount to a trial in the sense that the accused's guilt or innocence has been in some fashion addressed, as opposed to simply handling pretrial motions. *See* United States v. Marell, 23 C.M.A. 240, 49 C.M.R. 373 (1974) (acceptance of guilty plea and findings); United States v. Cole, 3 M.J. 220, 225, n.4 (C.M.A. 1977) (session must address accused's guilt). *Cf.* United States v. Roman, 5 M.J. 385 (C.M.A. 1978) (litigation of speedy trial motion sufficient to toll period).

72. United States v. Talavera, 8 M.J. 14 (C.M.A. 1979); United States v. Honican, 27 M.J. 590 (A.C.M.R. 1988).

73. United States v. Freeman, 23 M.J. 531 (A.C.M.R. 1986) (defense delays consisted of time necessary to translate lengthy German crime report and psychiatric testing; note that this case was tried before the 1984 revisions to the *Manual* took effect. *See* § 13-3(C)(3)). United States v. Stubbs, 3 M.J. 630 (N.C.M.R. 1977); United States v. Boehner, 11 M.J. 658 (A.C.M.R. 1981).

Mere concurrence in a trial date already set is not a defense delay. United States v. Huddelston, 50 C.M.R. 99 (A.C.M.R. 1975). Nor is assertion of the Article 35, service of charges, rights. United States v. Murrell, 50 C.M.R. 793 (A.C.M.R. 1975). *Cf.* United States v. Cherok, 19 M.J. 559 (N.M.C.M.R. 1984) (court castigated defense counsel for using trickery and deceit in creating a speedy trial rule).

Defense counsel's leave or TDY may constitute a delay. *Compare* United States v. Lyons, 50 C.M.R. 804 (A.C.M.R. 1975) *with* United States v. Powell, 2 M.J. 849 (A.C.M.R. 1976).

remainder exceeded ninety days, the prosecution had to demonstrate that "extraordinary circumstances" justified the delay.[74] In dealing with speedy trial issues the judge could urge counsel to stipulate to the pertinent dates in the processing of the case.[75] *United States v. Burton* also laid out a "demand rule" which stated that where the defense requests speedy disposition, the prosecution must either proceed immediately to trial or show good cause for further delay. The request served as "notice" to the government; delays after the demand will be closely examined.[76] The government could respond in both words and actions.[77] The remedy for failure to comply with this rule was usually dismissal of the charges.[78] The Court of Military Appeals abandoned its demand rule in *United States v. McCallister.*[79]

The *Burton* 90-day presumption rule was in doubt following the promulgation of the Manual for Courts-Martial's 120-day and 90-day speedy trial rules in 1984, and then the deletion of the *Manual's* 90-day provision altogether in

---

Delays in obtaining a psychiatric examination of the accused are normally chargeable to the defense in computing the *Burton* rule. United States v. Colon-Angueira, 16 M.J. 20 (C.M.A. 1983); United States v. McClain, 1 M.J. 60 (C.M.A. 1975) (request by Article 32 investigating officer); United States v. Bean, 13 M.J. 970 (A.C.M.R. 1982); United States v. Badger, 7 M.J. 838 (A.C.M.R. 1979); United States v. Jones, 6 M.J. 770 (A.C.M.R. 1978) (defense request); United States v. Hill, 2 M.J. 950 (A.C.M.R. 1976) (ordered by judge). In measuring this sort of delay the courts will permit a reasonable time for conducting the examination. If the government, however, causes unnecessary delays, some or all of the delay will be charged to the prosecution.

Delays in processing a defense request for an administrative discharge is not per se a defense delay. United States v. Bowman, 13 M.J. 640 (N.M.C.M.R. 1982); United States v. Parker, 48 C.M.R. 241 (A.C.M.R. 1973). *Cf.* United States v. Bush, 49 C.M.R. 97 (N.C.M.R. 1974).

If it appears that the delay in question can be attributable to both sides, it will be charged to the defense. United States v. Talavera, 8 M.J. 14 (C.M.A. 1979).

In assessing the delays in question, the court will generally examine the issue of whether the purported defense delay was actually caused by the defense and then whether it actually slowed the prosecution in proceeding to trial. *See, e.g.,* United States v. Cole, 3 M.J. 220, at 225, n.5 (C.M.A. 1977).

74. In United States v. Marshall, 22 C.M.A. 431, 47 C.M.R. 409 (1973), the court drew a distinction between delays caused by operational demands, combat environment, or complex cases and those delays caused by mistakes in drafting, manpower shortages, illnesses, and leave. In addition, the prosecution must establish a clear nexus between the extraordinary reasons and the delay.

See, e.g., United States v. Groshong, 14 M.J. 186 (C.M.A. 1982) (additional charges were considered extraordinary reason for delay under the circumstances); United States v. Johnson, 3 M.J. 143 (C.M.A. 1977) (decision to try co-accused and use his testimony was extraordinary); United States v. Wolzok, 1 M.J. 125 (C.M.A. 1975) (docketing delays not justification); United States v. Miller, 12 M.J. 836 (A.C.M.R. 1982) (prosecution demonstrated several extraordinary reasons).

75. This stipulated chronology is usually marked as an appellate exhibit and included in the record of trial.

76. United States v. Johnson, 1 M.J. 101 (C.M.A. 1975).

77. United States v. Williams, 12 M.J. 894 (A.C.M.R. 1982) (investigating officer appointed next day); United States v. Onstad, 4 M.J. 661 (A.C.M.R. 1977) (Article 39(a) session immediately held); United States v. Tarver, 2 M.J. 1176 (N.C.M.R. 1975).

78. United States v. Morrow, 16 M.J. 328 (C.M.A. 1983); United States v. Rowsey, 14 M.J. 151 (C.M.A. 1982). *Cf.* United States v. Herrington, 2 M.J. 807 (A.C.M.R. 1976) (sentence reassessed).

79. United States v. McCallister, 27 M.J. 138 (C.M.A. 1988).

1991. Initially, the Court of Military Appeals[80] and the Courts of Military Review[81] took the position that *Burton* survived the *Manual* changes. Ultimately, however, the Court of Military Appeals abrogated the *Burton* rule in *United States v. Kossman*.[82] Noting that the speedy trial "landscape" had changed dramatically since *Burton* with the implementation of a military magistrate system and the promulgation of specific speedy trial rules in the Manual for Courts-Martial,[83] the court candidly admitted that the "rough and ready rule of thumb"[84] in *Burton* had lead to mixed results.[85] It also noted that since the promulgation of the *Manual* rules in 1984 and 1991, the government had generally been able to justify its delays in any case where the accused had been in confinement for an excess of 90 days.[86]

In overruling *Burton*, the Court nonetheless left the door open for future litigation regarding the application of Article 10.[87] Noting that it believed that three months, and certainly four months, was a "long time to languish in the brig awaiting to confront one's accusers,"[88] the Court stated:

> [W]here it is established that the Government could readily have gone to trial much sooner than some arbitrarily selected timed demarcation, but negligently or spitefully chose not to, we think an Article 10 motion would lie.[89]

In a footnote, the Court added that the Government should not rely exclusively on the *Manual*'s speedy trial rule as the "know all, be all" rule even though it does provide good guidance.[90] The appropriate Article 10 test to be applied, according to the Court, is whether the Government has acted with "reasonable diligence"—the standard used before adoption of the *Burton* 90-day rule.[91] The Court recognized that its decision might vest military judges

---

80. United States v. Carpenter, 37 M.J. 291 (C.M.A. 1993); United States v. King, 30 M.J. 59, 66 and n.7 (C.M.A. 1990).
   In a memorandum decision in United States v. Harvey, 23 M.J. 280 (C.M.A. 1987) (misc. docket), the court indicated that if the President intended to displace the time requirements of *Burton*, including a speedy trial requirement in the *Manual*, he did not make it clear.
81. *See, e.g.*, United States v. Gray, 37 M.J. 1035 (A.C.M.R. 1993) (*Burton* 90-day rule survived amendments to *Manual*); United States v. Kossman, 37 M.J. 639 (N.M.C.M.R. 1993) (*Burton* remained operative after 1991 amendments; discussion of President's authority to modify U.C.M.J.); United States v. Pascascio, 37 M.J. 1012 (A.C.M.R. 1993) (*Burton* test survived amendments to *Manual*); United States v. Howard, 35 M.J. 763 (A.C.M.R. 1992) (court relied on *Burton* rule but concluded that it was not violated).
   Cf. United States v. Callaway, 23 M.J. 799 (N.M.C.M.R. 1986) (*Burton* superseded by *Manual*); United States v. Ivester, 22 M.J. 933 (N.M.C.M.R. 1986).
82. 38. M.J. 258 (C.M.A. 1993).
83. 38 M.J. at 260.
84. 38 M.J. at 261.
85. 38 M.J. at 260.
86. 38 M.J. at 260.
87. 38 M.J. at 261.
88. 38 M.J. at 261. The references to three and four months apparently refer to the 90-day *Burton* rule and the *Manual*'s 120-day speedy trial provision.
89. 38 M.J. at 261.
90. 38 M.J. at 261, n.3.
91. 38 M.J. at 262. United States v. Thomas, 43 M.J. 626 (A.F.Ct.Crim.App. 1995) (government acted with reasonable diligence in bringing accused to trial 195 days after German authorities

with a discretion on deciding speedy trial issues, but expressed confidence that they could "readily determine whether the Government has been foot-dragging on a given case, under the circumstances then there prevailing."[92]

In a strong dissent, Judge Wiss questioned the wisdom of throwing onto the "legal trash heap" a standard that served the military well for more than two decades.[93] He questioned whether there is now any real speedy trial rule, considering the "lack of ballast" in the *Manual*'s speedy trial rules and a weakening trend for a military accused's right to a speedy trial.[94] Judge Wiss concluded by expressing concern that abrogation of the *Burton* rule would lead to intolerable delays, a trend the Court had noted following abrogation in 1979 of a similar 90-day post-trial delay rule.[95]

Abrogation of the *Burton* 90-day rule clearly resolves the question of whether that rule survived the promulgation of the *Manual* rules. But language in *Kossman* signals that the Court still believes in the viability of motions to dismiss based upon Article 10, aside from whether the accused has been brought to trial within the time required by the *Manual*. To that end, it is important to note that Article 10, as well as the Sixth Amendment, should continue to be viewed as separate speedy trial protections, as they have for years. The fact that they may be seldomly relied upon should not signal to any participants in courts-martial that the *Manual*'s rules are the only measure of protection for servicemembers.[96]

§ 13-3(C)(3). The *Manual*'s 120-Day Speedy Trial Rule.

In 1984, a specific speedy trial provision, which was a hybrid of some of the foregoing principles, was added to the Manual for Courts-Martial. Although the original *Manual* provisions included both a 120-day and 90-day rule, 1991 amendments to the *Manual*[97] dropped the 90-day provision[98] and drastically

---

relinquished jurisdiction); United States v. Laminman, 41 M.J. 518 (C.G.Ct.Crim.App. 1994) (government, under *Kossman*, still bears burden of proving that it has acted with reasonable diligence under Article 10).

92. 38 M.J. at 262. United States v. Collins, 39 M.J. 739 (N.M.C.M.R. 1994) (government's minimal activity for three months was unjustified and required reversal).

93. 38 M.J. at 262.

94. 38 M.J. at 267.

95. 38 M.J. at 269.

96. *See, e.g.*, United States v. Hatfield, 43 M.J. 662 (N.M.Ct.Crim.App. 1995) (government proceeded with reasonable diligence; test is not whether there was constant movement in prosecution); United States v. Scheffer, 41 M.J. 683 (A.F.Ct.Crim.App. 1995) (government prosecuted case within 120-day rule and with reasonable diligence under Article 10); United States v. Youngberg, 38 M.J. 635 (A.C.M.R. 1993) (citing *Kossman*, appellate court sua sponte considered potential Article 10 compliance and concluded that government acted with reasonable diligence).

97. Change 5, Manual for Courts-Martial, Executive Order 12767. The changes were made effective for any trial in which the accused was arraigned on or after 6 July 1991.

United States v. Youngberg, 38 M.J. 635 (A.C.M.R. 1993) (speedy trial clock did not start until German authorities waived jurisdiction and accused was available to military authorities, even though charges had been preferred at an earlier date).

United States v. Vendivel, 37 M.J. 854 (A.F.C.M.R. 1993) (charges dismissed where deserter, who had been originally charged in 1982; no delays were granted by either the military judge or

changed the process of applying the 120-day rule. The amended provision, which is modelled after ABA Standards For Criminal Justice, Speedy Trial, §§ 12-2.1, 12-2.2 (1978), now permits either the convening authority or the military judge to grant delays to either side. Those delays are then excluded by the trial court in determining whether the accused has been brought to trial within the prescribed time of 120 days. The following discussion addresses the key points in the current rule.

Starting the Speedy Trial Clock: R.C.M. 707 requires that the accused must be brought to trial within 120 days of the date that (1) charges are preferred against the accused,[99] (2) pretrial restraint in the form of confinement,[100] arrest,[101] or restriction in lieu of arrest[102] is imposed,[103] or (3) the accused is brought on active duty under R.C.M. 204.[104]

---

the convening authority although statute of limitations had been tolled); United States v. Shim, 36 M.J. 1124 (A.F.C.M.R. 1993) (under literal reading of effective date language, accused had benefit of revised speedy trial rules although he had deserted in 1981). *Cf.*United States v. Powell, 38 M.J. 153 (C.M.A. 1993) (court held that where accused's case straddled the new speedy trial rules, speedy trial clock would run from date of apprehension).

United States v. Patterson, 39 M.J. 678 (N.M.C.M.R. 1993) (court applied R.C.M. 707 as it existed prior to Change 5; speedy trial clock started with accused's return to military control); United States v. Sturgeon, 37 M.J. 1083 (N.M.C.M.R. 1993) (distinguishing *Shim, supra,* court held that accused was not entitled to speedy trial provisions of Change 5 to *Manual.*

98. R.C.M. 707 originally contained a specific provision which indicated that an accused could not be held in pretrial confinement or arrest for more than ninety days. The Rule permitted the judge to extend the period by no more than 10 days, if the prosecution could show extraordinary circumstances. In computing the 90 days the government was entitled to deduct specified periods also applicable to the 120-day rule with the exception of delays attributable to a joint trial.

99. R.C.M. 707(a)(1). United States v. Powell, 38 M.J. 153 (C.M.A. 1993) (court held that where accused's case straddled the 1991 amendments to the *Manual*'s speedy trial rules, speedy trial clock would run from date of apprehension).

100. R.C.M. 707(a)(2), 304(a)(4). United States v. Vogan, 35 M.J. 32 (C.M.A. 1992) (*Manual*'s speedy trial rule was not triggered where accused was already in confinement at Disciplinary Barracks); United States v. Thomas, 41 M.J. 665 (A.F.Ct.Crim.App. 1994) (post-trial confinement did not trigger speedy trial clock); United States v. Garner, 39 M.J. 721 (N.M.C.M.R. 1993) (accused's confinement while awaiting special court-martial on separate charges did not trigger speedy trial rule for subsequent general court-martial).*See generally* § 5-9. United States v. Vogan, 32 M.J. 959 (A.C.M.R. 1991) (accused's status change in preexisting posttrial confinement did not amount to pretrial "confinement" or restraint for purposes of speedy trial analysis).

101. R.C.M. 707(a)(2), 304(a)(3). *See generally* § 5-8.

102. R.C.M. 707(a)(2), 304(a)(2). *See generally* § 5-8. United States v. Camacho, 30 M.J. 644 (N.M.C.M.R. 1990) (restricting accused to base limits triggered 120-day speedy trial rule).

Andrews v. Heupel, 29 M.J. 743 (A.F.C.M.R. 1989) (accused denied speedy trial where he was held in restriction in lieu of arrest for 212 days, even though no charges were then pending); *United States v. Wilkinson, 27 M.J. 645 (A.C.M.R. 1988)* (order restricting accused to barracks area pending trial was restriction in lieu of arrest; conditions on his liberty, *i.e.,* denial of off-post pass was not equivalent of confinement).

United States v. Wilkes, 27 M.J. 571 (N.M.C.M.R. 1988) (accused's transfer from pretrial restriction to liberty risk program did not stop speedy trial clock where the latter status was imposed to ensure his presence at trial); United States v. Miller, 26 M.J. 959 (A.C.M.R. 1988) (five days' restriction in hospital because of accused's attempted suicide was not accountable to government); United States v. Brodin, 25 M.J. 580, 581 n.1 (A.C.M.R. 1987) (restriction in lieu of arrest need not amount to confinement in order to trigger speedy trial rules).

103. R.C.M. 707(a).

104. R.C.M. 204 addresses the issue of jurisdiction over reservists.

§ 13-3(C)(3)   MOTIONS PRACTICE   § 13-3(C)(3)

Pretrial detention by civilian authorities may trigger the speedy trial rule [105] but pretrial restraints that limit the freedom of the accused's movements but do not amount to either confinement, arrest, or restriction in lieu of arrest will usually not trigger the rule.[106]

Originally, R.C.M. 707 provided that the 120-day rule would be triggered by notification to the accused that charges had been preferred against him [107] or some form of pretrial restraint had been imposed upon him, whichever came first.[108] But it appeared that in an attempt to delay the start of the speedy trial clock some commands preferred charges but did not actually notify the accused of that fact until some later date. Several cases addressed the issue of what would properly constitute "notice" and correctly concluded that the practice of deliberately waiting to give actual notice potentially denied the accused of due process.[109] R.C.M. 707 was amended in 1991 to resolve that

---

105. *See, e.g.*, United States v. Thomas, 43 M.J. 626 (A.F.Ct.Crim.App. 1995) (accused's confinement in military facility not accountable to US; confinement was at request of Germans pending their lengthy investigation); United States v. Bramer, 43 M.J. 538 (N.M.C.Ct.Crim.App. 1995) (confinement by civilian authorities, not at the request of the military, did not trigger speedy trial rule); United States v. Youngberg, 38 M.J. 635 (A.C.M.R. 1993) (speedy trial clock did not run from date of preferral of charges where German authorities did not waive jurisdiction until shortly before trial); United States v. McCallister, 24 M.J. 881 (A.C.M.R. 1987) (accountability began when accused was held in civilian jail at request of government); United States v. Asbury, 28 M.J. 595 (N.M.C.M.R. 1989) (detention of deserter by civilian authorities was not accountable to government for speedy trial purposes).

106. *See, e.g.*, United States v. Bradford, 25 M.J. 181 (C.M.A. 1987) (under the facts "liberty risk" status did not automatically convert into pretrial restraint for purposes of speedy trial analysis when accused became prime suspect; the court indicated that whether restriction is administrative or pretrial restraint depends on whether the primary purpose is to restrain the accused for purposes of trial and whether the same conditions would have been imposed even if no trial had been contemplated); United States v. Facey, 26 M.J. 421 (C.M.A. 1988) (general squadron policy that limited accused to travel within the local area did not amount to pretrial restraint for purposes of speedy trial analysis).

United States v. Wagner, 39 M.J. 832 (A.C.M.R. 1994) (restriction in lieu of arrest triggers clock; conditions on liberty do not; ordering married NCO to move into on-post housing, especially in foreign country, might amount to more than condition on liberty); United States v. Reynolds, 36 M.J. 1128 (A.C.M.R. 1993) (conditions on liberty did not trigger speedy trial rule); United States v. Johnson, 24 M.J. 796 (A.C.M.R. 1987) (speedy trial rules were not triggered by cancellation of accused's leave and requirement that he receive permission to leave Frankfurt area); United States v. Orback, 21 M.J. 610 (A.F.C.M.R. 1985) (speedy trial provisions not triggered by "administrative freeze" on the accused).

107. R.C.M. 707(a).

108. R.C.M. 707(a). *See, e.g.*, United States v. Gray, 26 M.J. 16 (C.M.A. 1988) (judges agreed, for different reasons, that the accused was not denied a speedy trial where the accused was held in pretrial confinement for 29 days before being released; charges were preferred one month later, but the accused was not notified of the charges until almost two weeks later).

The government is not accountable under R.C.M. 707 for delays occurring before the effective date of the 1984 changes to the *Manual,* 1 August 1984. United States v. Leonard, 21 M.J. 67 (C.M.A. 1985); United States v. Harrison, 22 M.J. 535 (N.M.C.M.R. 1986).

109. In United States v. Maresca, 28 M.J. 328 (C.M.A. 1989), the court noted that while it is difficult to draw a bright-line rule on the meaning of R.C.M. 308, which requires that an accused be notified of the charges "as soon as practicable," the court believed that under the facts, the speedy trial clock began on the same day the charges were preferred, when the opportunity for notice was apparent. Thomas v. Eddington, 26 M.J. 95 (C.M.A. 1988) (court did not address

problem by focusing on the specific act of preferring charges,[110] which in effect probably means the signing of the charge sheet by the appropriate authority.[111]

The date of either of the three triggering events (preferral of charges, etc.) does not count in computing the 120 days, but the date of the "trial" does count.[112] The accused is considered to have been brought to trial at the time of arraignment.[113] The speedy trial clock runs separately on each charge if multiple charges have been preferred at different times and is started with any of the three triggering events noted supra.[114]

Any delays between the time of the offense and the preferral of charges is not counted in determining whether the *Manual*'s 120-day rule has been followed.[115] Those delays, however, might raise due process[116] or statute of limitations issues.[117]

---

allegation by defendant that in some commands, the accused is not notified of the charges, in contravention of Article 30, U.C.M.J., until the convening authority and the prosecution have decided whether to prosecute; the purpose of this policy is to delay the triggering device for the speedy trial rule). *See also* United States v. Gray, 26 M.J. 16 (C.M.A. 1988).

United States v. Angel, 28 M.J. 600 (N.M.C.M.R. 1989) (in an extensive discussion of the issue, the court concluded that *actual* notice had been given in August 1986 when the defense received a copy of the charge sheet, even though the charge sheet reflected that notice was given in May 1987). *See also* United States v. Voyles, 28 M.J. 831 (N.M.C.M.R. 1989) (in facts almost identical to *Angel,* the court concluded that notice of the charges was given when defense counsel received a copy of an Article 32 appointing order along with a copy of the charges).

United States v. Berrey, 28 M.J. 714 (N.M.C.M.R. 1989) (*en banc*) (court concluded that an intentional and prolonged delay deprived the accused of "military due process" and amounted to reversible error; the topic of "constructive notice" was raised, but not decided. *Id.* at 717, n.3). *Cf.* United States v. Leamer, 29 M.J. 616 (C.G.C.M.R. 1989) (time consumed before charges were preferred was not accountable to government; accused's unintentional sighting of charges was not sufficient to notify him of the charges).

110. R.C.M. 707(a) Drafters' Analysis, *citing* Thomas v. Edington, 26 M.J. 95 (C.M.A. 1988).
111. *See* Chapter 6.
112. R.C.M. 707(b)(1). United States v. Manalo, 1 M.J. 452 (C.M.A. 1976) (court established counting method for speedy review); United States v. Tebsherany, 30 M.J. 608 (N.M.C.M.R. 1990).

See also United States v. Carlisle, 25 M.J. 426 (C.M.A. 1988) (in particularly strong language the court affirmed the C.M.R. decision dismissing the charges where the accused's trial did not occur until after 120 days elapsed. The court noted that "[o]n day number one, everyone associated with a case should know what day will be number 120").

113. R.C.M. 707(b)(1). United States v. Stokes, 39 M.J. 771 (A.C.M.R. 1994) (speedy trial rule met if accused arraigned within 120 days of preferral of charges). *See* § 12-4 for a discussion on arraignments. The original version of R.C.M. 707 indicated that the trial began either when the accused entered a plea of guilty or the prosecution began to present evidence on the merits.

114. R.C.M. 707(b)(4). The problem of applying the speedy trial rules to multiple charges was raised in United States v. Robinson, 28 M.J. 481 (C.M.A. 1989), where the accused was initially placed in pretrial restraint while an indecent solicitation offense was being investigated. But the purpose for the restraint was later tied into drug charges which had been under investigation prior to the solicitation charge. Both charges were then preferred on the same date. The court held that the speedy trial clock on the drug charges did not start until the date that the pretrial restraint was for the purpose of that charge.

United States v. Nelson, 28 M.J. 922 (N.M.C.M.R. 1988) (detailed analysis of various speedy trial rules vis-à-vis multiple charges). *Cf.* United States v. Boden, 21 M.J. 916 (A.C.M.R. 1986).

115. R.C.M. 707(a)(1) Discussion.
116. R.C.M. 707(a)(1) Discussion.
117. R.C.M. 707(a)(1) Discussion. *See also* § 13-3(B).

Stopping and Restarting the Clock: The *Manual* indicates that the 120-day clock may be affected by one of several events: dismissal of the charges, a mistrial, the accused's release from confinement, and government appeals of a trial court's ruling.

First, the clock stops altogether, and a new 120-day clock starts running, when the charges are dismissed[118] or a mistrial is declared,[119] and there is no re-preferral of the charges or the accused is in pretrial restraint.[120] In all other instances, the clock starts anew either on the date of repreferral of charges or the date of imposition of pretrial restraint, whichever occurs first.[121]

The speedy trial clock is also stopped where the accused is released from pretrial restraint for a "significant period."[122] A new 120-day period begins

---

118. United States v. Britton, 26 M.J. 24 (C.M.A. 1988) (withdrawn charges must be dismissed in order to stop speedy trial clock; here convening authority withdrew and immediately re-referred charges to a different court); United States v. Mucthison, 28 M.J. 1113 (N.M.C.M.R. 1989) (per curiam) (convening authority unsuccessfully attempted to create a "limbo" status and stop the speedy trial clock by not referring charges to a court-martial and by not notifying the accused of the charges. The court concluded that once charges are preferred, they remain pending until they are dismissed); United States v. Mickla, 29 M.J. 749 (A.F.C.M.R. 1989) (charges were dismissed in order to avoid problems with amending them and were re-preferred several months later in essentially the same form. The court said that this dismissal was not a dismissal for purposes of stopping the speedy trial clock; the command made it clear that it intended to proceed against the accused).

See also United States v. Weatherspoon, 39 M.J. 762 (A.C.M.R. 1994) (court distinguished dismissal of charges and withdrawal of charges re restarting speedy trial clock; the latter does not restart clock); United States v. Bolado, 34 M.J. 732 (N.M.C.M.R. 1991) (charges against accused were dismissed, and not withdrawn, when it became apparent that key witnesses had been deployed; dismissal stopped speedy trial clock); United States v. Lorenc, 30 M.J. 619 (N.M.C.M.R. 1990) (convening authority's withdrawal of charges amounted to dismissal that stopped speedy trial clock; facts closely parallel to *Mucthison*).

119. R.C.M. 707(b)(3)(A). *See also* § 15-4(B).
120. R.C.M. 707(b)(3)(A).
121. R.C.M. 707(b)(3)(A). United States v. Thomas, 41 M.J. 665 (A.F.Ct.Crim App. 1994) (speedy trial clock restarted with repreferral of charges); United States v. Hayes, 37 M.J. 769 (A.C.M.R. 1993) (speedy trial clock was stopped when convening authority dismissed charges for purposes of obtaining DNA results; court noted that under R.C.M. 707, convening authority could have simply granted government request for delay; clock restarted at time of repreferral); United States v. Gonda, 27 M.J. 636 (A.C.M.R. 1988) (speedy trial clock is reset when new trial or rehearing is ordered). In United States v. Smith, 32 M.J. 586 (A.C.M.R. 1991), the court concluded that the accused's misconduct in breaking arrest stopped the *Burton* 90-day clock.

Cf. United States v. Mickla, 29 M.J. 749 (A.F.C.M.R. 1989) (dismissal of charges did not stop speedy trial clock where it appeared that government intended to reinstitute them).

122. R.C.M. 707(b)(3). United States v. Reynolds, 36 M.J. 1128 (A.C.M.R. 1993) (accused's release from restriction and being placed on restriction for 19 days was sufficient to stop speedy trial clock); United States v. Callinan, 32 M.J. 701 (A.F.C.M.R. 1991) (speedy trial clock stopped when accused was released from pretrial restriction, but conditions on liberty remained in effect; those conditions were more common sense preventative measures).

United States v. Campbell, 32 M.J. 564 (A.C.M.R. 1991) (45-day restriction for Article 15 on unrelated charge interrupted speedy trial clock where no subterfuge was involved).

United States v. Coder, 27 M.J. 650 (A.C.M.R. 1988) (50-day break was significant).

United States v. Evans, 26 M.J. 961 (A.C.M.R. 1988) (significant break occurred where five days after he was restricted (tantamount to confinement) accused was placed on medical restric-

from the date of preferral of charges,[123] entry on active duty under R.C.M. 204,[124] or reimposition of pretrial restraint,[125] whichever occurs first.[126]

The *Manual* also specifies that if the government gives a notice of appeal under R.C.M. 908,[127] the speedy trial clock starts anew when the government gives notice under R.C.M. 908 that it does not intend to appeal a trial court's ruling[128] or the Court of Criminal Appeals decision.[129] It will not stop, however, if it appears that the appeal was filed solely for the purpose of delay, knowing that it was totally frivolous and without merit.[130] And the clock does not stop for those charges that are proceeded on for trial[131] or are severed from those on which the government is appealing.[132]

Finally, if a rehearing is ordered or authorized by an appellate court, a new 120-day period starts on the date when the convening authority receives the opinion of that court along with the record of trial.[133]

Excludable Delays: As originally promulgated, the *Manual*'s 120-day rule provided that specified times would be excluded in calculating whether the 120-day limit had been met.[134] While that approach provided a helpful "cook-

---

tion for five days due to his attempted suicide; the court noted that the five-day break was due to his actions, the hospital, not the unit, imposed the medical restriction, and the break occurred early in the processing without any hint of gamesmanship).

United States v. Britton, 22 M.J. 501 (A.F.C.M.R. 1986) (speedy trial denied on charges withdrawn and immediately re-preferred while government appealed other charges); United States v. Gray, 21 M.J. 1020 (N.M.C.M.R. 1986) (47-day gap was "significant period" which restarted speedy trial clock); United States v. Hulsey, 21 M.J. 717 (A.F.C.M.R. 1985) (release from pretrial confinement for seven days restarted clock).

123. R.C.M. 707(b)(3)(B)(i).
124. R.C.M. 707(b)(3)(B)(iii).
125. R.C.M. 707(b)(3)(B)(ii).
126. R.C.M. 707(b)(3)(B).
127. *See* § 13-2(G)(2).
128. R.C.M. 707(b)(3)(C), 908(b)(8). *See* § 13-2(G)(2).
129. *Id.* R.C.M. 908(c)(3).
130. R.C.M. 707(b)(3)(C). United States v. Reap, 41 M.J. 340 (1995) (appeal was not for frivolous reasons); United States v. Ramsey, 28 M.J. 370 (C.M.A. 1989) (unless government is acting in bad faith, the 72 hours allotted to the government to decide whether to appeal a judge's ruling).
131. R.C.M. 707(b)(3)(C).
132. R.C.M. 707(b)(3)(C).
133. R.C.M. 707(b)(3)(D). United States v. Beckermann, 35 M.J. 842 (C.G.C.M.R. 1992) (120-day time frame commenced with receipt of notification of designation of convening authority). In United States v. Wales, 35 M.J. 501 (A.F.C.M.R. 1992), the rehearing on sentence occurred before the 1991 change to the *Manual*'s 120-day rule. But the court believed that the newer provision, R.C.M. 707(b)(3)(D), does not apply to rehearings on sentence.
134. Key to application of the original 120-day rule was the provision which specifically excluded certain times from computing the delay. R.C.M. 707(c) excluded the following:

  1. Periods of delay incurred in the case including any examination into the competency of the accused to stand trial and any hearings addressing such competency; any time spent on litigating pretrial motions; any time spent by the prosecution appealing a ruling of the judge; and any time spent by either side seeking extraordinary relief.

  2. Periods of delay caused by a judge being unavailable where the reasons for such are extraordinary.

  3. Delays resulting from continuances which are either requested, or consented to, by the defense.

book" approach to determining speedy trial issues, it proved to be problematic. Counsel and the courts struggled with after-the-fact[135] application of the exclusions and whether a particular delay could be attributed to either the prosecution or the defense.[136] As one court observed, it often appeared that the speedy trial issue had become a "mere numbers game."[137]

In 1991, the *Manual* was amended to adopt the principles reflected in the Federal Speedy Trial Act[138] and the ABA Standards for Criminal Justice[139] to

---

4. Any delays caused by failure of the defense to comply with *Manual* provisions regarding timely notice, requests for relief, or submission of any matter.

5. Any prosecution requested delays either in the Article 32 investigation or the trial itself if (a) the prosecution is awaiting relevant and substantial evidence, has exercised due diligence to trying to obtain it, and it will be available in a reasonable time; or (b) "exceptional circumstances" warrant additional time for the prosecution to prepare for trial.

6. Delays resulting from the accused's absence or unavailability.

7. "Reasonable" delays resulting from trying the accused in a joint trial where the co-accused's speedy trial clock has not run and there is no good reason for not granting a severance.

8. Delays for good cause including military exigencies and operational requirements.

See generally Wittmayer, "Rule for Courts-Martial 707: The 1984 Manual for Courts-Martial Speedy Trial Rule," 116 Mɪʟ. L. Rᴇᴠ. 221 (1987) (excellent discussion of application of speedy trial rule).

135. United States v. Maresca, 28 M.J. 328 (C.M.A. 1989), the court observed that the exceptions in R.C.M. 707 catalog principles applied after-the-fact in determining accountability for delays. The court also noted that the rule "has either been amended or changes have been proposed to respond to almost every ruling made by a court which seemed to go against the Government." *Id.* at 333. *See also* United States v. Nichols, 42 M.J. 715 (A.F.Ct.Crim.App. 1995) (court noted that prior methods of calculating delays was method of placing blame on one party or the other).

136. *See, e.g.*, United States v. Longhofer, 29 M.J. 22 (C.M.A. 1989) where the court attempted to clarify the exclusions in the original version of R.C.M. and adopted the following template in an attempt to "articulate simple rules for bench and bar alike":

(1) If the delay fits into one of the exclusions in R.C.M. 707(c)(1) to (8), the prosecution will be relieved from accountability, assuming that the delay is reasonable.
(2) If the delay is occasioned by a specific defense request, in writing or on the record, and the delay is granted by either the military judge, the Article 32 investigating officer, or the convening authority, the prosecution shall be relieved from accountability.
(3) If the delay is occasioned by a specific request for a delay for "good cause" made in writing or on the record by the prosecution and it is granted, the delay shall be excluded. Such delays granted by the convening authority or the Article 32 investigating officer are subject to *de novo* review by the military judge on motion by the defense and are subject to review for abuse of discretion and reasonableness.
(4) If "good cause," including military exigencies and operational requirements, exists, the delay shall not be counted against the government if the delay was reasonable, even if the issue was not previously litigated or no delay was granted. To be excluded, the military judge must have found that the unusual event actually caused a delay in the prosecution's preparation of the case and that it was reasonable for the delay to result. The prosecution need not establish that the delay in question "proximately caused" the trial not to take place within the total time period.

137. United States v. Carlisle, 25 M.J. 426 (C.M.A. 1988) (court expressed concern that the speedy trial rules had been treated as though they were a mere numbers game).
138. 18 U.S.C. §§ 3152-56, 3161-74 (1994).
139. ABA Standards for Criminal Justice, Speedy Trial, § 12-1.3 (1978).

make the 120-day rule more flexibile and yet recognize that unless a competent authority had granted a delay, the government is accountable for the time it takes to bring an accused to trial.[140] Under the rule, either side may seek a delay from the military judge or the convening authority.[141] Before charges are referred to trial[142] the convening authority may grant such requests[143] and the military judge may do so if authorized by Service Regulations.[144] After referral of charges to a court-martial, only the judge may grant such requests.[145] Those delays are then excluded in determining whether the 120-day period has run.[146]

In presenting requests for pretrial delays, counsel must present supporting reasons.[147] This means that counsel should normally not be granted a delay on the mere assurance that one is needed. Rather, counsel should be prepared to articulate specific justifications for the requested delays. Although the *Manual* rule does not specifically require it, the requests should preferably be in writing.[148]

The *Manual* provides no specific guidance on whether counsel are to present their requests in writing or whether they may use electronic means. Presumably, as long as both counsel are heard from, the exact format should not be crucial unless it appears that there is truly a dispute as to the reasonableness of the requested delay and the convening authority or judge wishes to hear personally from both sides. In any event, the requests should not be *ex parte*.[149]

Whether or not a particular delay is reasonable will depend on the surrounding circumstances[150] and should be granted only for as long as necessary.[151] Open-ended delays should be discouraged. A delay is any interval of time between specified events; where a specific date has been set for a particu-

---

140. R.C.M. 707(c) Drafters' Analysis.
141. R.C.M. 707(c). This procedure was first recommended in United States v. Schilf, 1 M.J. 251 (C.M.A. 1976) and later in United States v. Maresca, 28 M.J. 328 (C.M.A. 1989). *See also* United States v. Dies, 42 M.J. 847 (N.M.Ct.Crim.App. 1995) (noting that RCM was ambiguous on which convening authority should grant delays, court concluded that letter from accused's commander was not sufficient).
142. *See* Chapter 8.
143. R.C.M. 707(c)(1).
144. *Id.*
145. *Id.*
146. R.C.M. 707(c).
147. R.C.M. 707(c)(1).
148. In United States v. Longhofer, 29 M.J. 22 (C.M.A. 1989), the court noted that the "primary reason" of written documentation of the requests for delay is to:

> memorialize and litigate questions of delay contemporaneous with the event and to avoid the salvage operation required of military judges and appellate courts faced with trying to allocate periods of delay long after the event occurred.

29 M.J. at 28. *See also* United States v. Dies, 42 M.J. 847 (N.M.Ct.Crim.App. 1995) (court required written request for delay or a motion on the record contemporaneous with event on which request for delay is based).
149. R.C.M. 707(c)(1) Discussion.
150. R.C.M. 707(c) Drafters' Analysis.
151. R.C.M. 707(c) Drafters' Analysis.

lar date and a delay is approved, then the length of the date is measured from that date, and not the date of the request for the delay.[152]

While the rule requires the convening authority and military judge to make an independent judgment on the reasonableness of the requested delays,[153] there is no specific guidance in the rule itself as to what might constitute a reasonable request.[154] To codify specific criteria would undermine the flexibility the Drafters apparently intended to adopt. The Drafters, however, did include in the Discussion to R.C.M. 707(c)(1) a *nonexhaustive* list of illustrative reasons for granting a delay:

1. Time to permit counsel to prepare for a complex case;[155]
2. Time to permit mental examinations of the accused;[156]
3. Time to process an accused reservist who has been activated for purposes of disciplinary action;[157]
4. Delays necessary to complete other proceedings related to the case;[158]
5. Delays requested by the defense;[159]

---

152. United States v. Nichols, 42 M.J. 715 (A.F.Ct.Crim.App. 1995).
153. R.C.M. 707(c) Drafters' Analysis.
154. *Cf.* R.C.M. 707(c)(1) Discussion.
155. R.C.M. 707(c)(1) Discussion.
156. R.C.M. 707(c)(1) Discussion. *See, e.g.,* United States v. Carpenter, 37 M.J. 291 (C.M.A. 1993) (delay for second mental examination was reasonable and not accountable to government under pre-1991 speedy trial rule); United States v. Tebsherany, 32 M.J. 351 (C.M.A. 1991) (defense request for sanity hearing was excludable); United States v. Mahoney, 28 M.J. 865 (A.F.C.M.R. 1989) (68 days needed to complete mental examination was not unreasonable); United States v. Hirsch, 26 M.J. 800 (A.C.M.R. 1988) (under facts lengthy delay for mental evaluation was not unreasonable).

United States v. Demmer, 24 M.J. 731 (A.C.M.R. 1987) (72 days deducted for time spent in mental evaluations of accused); United States v. Pettaway, 24 M.J. 589 (N.M.C.M.R. 1987) (court deducted 36 days for mental exam); United States v. Palumbo, 24 M.J. 512 (A.F.C.M.R. 1987) (court deducted 45 days for competency exams); United States v. Calloway, 23 M.J. 799 (N.M.C.M.R. 1986); United States v. Jones, 21 M.J. 819 (N.M.C.M.R. 1985) (exclusion for mental exams not limited to those conducted under R.C.M. 706).

157. R.C.M. 707(c)(1) Discussion. *See* R.C.M. 204.
158. R.C.M. 707(c)(1) Discussion. *See, e.g.,* United States v. Tebsherany, 32 M.J. 351 (C.M.A. 1991) (defense request to delay Article 32 investigation was excludable); United States v. Martinez, 36 M.J. 291 (C.M.A. 1993) (delay for second mental examination was reasonable and not accountable to government under pre-1991 speedy trial rule); Porter v. Eggers, 32 M.J. 583 (A.C.M.R. 1990) (time spent by defense in contesting jurisdiction in Panamanian court system was excluded); United States v. Pettaway, 24 M.J. 589 (N.M.C.M.R. 1987) (12 days spent on pretrial motions properly excluded without regard to whether that period was reasonable); United States v. Harris, 20 M.J. 795 (N.M.C.M.R. 1985) (delays caused by negotiating a pretrial agreement and requesting an administrative discharge were normal incidents of pretrial processing and thus not accountable to the defense). *See also* United States v. Henderson, 476 U.S. 321 (1986).
159. United States v. Montanino, 40 M.J. 364 (C.M.A. 1994) (defense delay resulting from defense counsel's deployment to Middle East); United States v. Lamer, 32 M.J. 63 (C.M.A. 1990) (delays in conjunction with improperly ordered abatement of trial, while government attempted to obtain defense-requested expert, were attributed to the defense); United States v. Givens, 30 M.J. 294 (C.M.A. 1990) (case remanded where it was not clear whether delays resulting from appointment of replacement defense counsel were excludable); United States v. McKnight, 30

6. Time to secure availability of the accused,[160] substantial witnesses,[161] or other evidence;[162]

M.J. 205 (C.M.A. 1990) (defense request for delay in conducting Article 32 investigation was excludable; defense may not request delay to certain date and then insist that government proceed on that date); United States v. King, 30 M.J. 59 (C.M.A. 1990) (various defense-requested delays should have been excluded; the court added that the speedy trial rule is a shield, not a sword. Defense counsel may not consent to, or request delays, and then attempt to charge those delays to the prosecution); United States v. Cook, 27 M.J. 212 (C.M.A. 1988) (trial judge erroneously deducted 14 days for defense delay in obtaining Article 32 investigation witnesses; this informal after-the-fact deduction was not supported by demands of speedy trial rule).

United States v. Carlisle, 25 M.J. 426 (C.M.A. 1988) (although it was a questionable tactic, defense counsel's suggesting a trial date beyond the 120-day limit did not amount to a defense request for a delay that could be deducted); United States v. Burris, 21 M.J. 140 (C.M.A. 1985) (speedy trial denied where judge erroneously concluded that delays in docketing were attributable to the defense).

In United States v. Giroux, 37 M.J. 553 (A.C.M.R. 1993), the defense submitted a post-trial request for pretrial delay in return for sentence relief. While the court gave effect to the agreement, it strongly recommended that convening authorities and SJA's not execute such agreements because they have "no place in post-trial administration of military justice."

United States v. Wactor, 30 M.J. 821 (A.C.M.R. 1990) (record must show more than mere defense acquiescence; record must show that defense expressly agreed to delay); United States v. Arnold, 28 M.J. 963 (A.C.M.R. 1989) (defense request for delay to consult with civilian counsel and to await response on request for individual military counsel did not delay proceedings); United States v. Nelson, 28 M.J. 922 (N.M.C.M.R. 1988) (defense request for continuance did not stop speedy trial clock on other pending charges); United States v. Givens, 28 M.J. 888 (A.F.C.M.R. 1989) (informal exchanges between counsel cannot be considered delays requested or consented to by the defense); United States v. Raichle, 28 M.J. 876 (A.F.C.M.R. 1989) (defense request for depositions of government witnesses at Article 32 investigation was not a request for a delay).

United States v. Brodin, 25 M.J. 580 (A.C.M.R. 1987) (delay in Article 32 investigation was not defense delay simply because it objected to item of evidence); United States v. Miniclier, 23 M.J. 843 (A.F.C.M.R. 1987) (accused's offer of resignation in lieu of trial did not constitute either an express or implied request for continuance; trial judge was correct in dismissing charges where 162 days elapsed after charges were preferred); United States v. Calloway, 23 M.J. 799 (N.M.C.M.R. 1986) (request to conduct a defense investigation amounted to a request for a continuance); United States v. Turk, 22 M.J. 740 (N.M.C.M.R. 1987), aff'd on other grounds, 24 M.J. 277 (C.M.A. 1987).

160. R.C.M. 707(c)(1) Discussion. United States v. Turk, 24 M.J. 277 (C.M.A. 1987) (time spent in returning accused to ship where charges could be processed was not accountable to government; accused was in effect "unavailable" to the command during that hiatus).

United States v. Bragg, 30 M.J. 1147 (A.F.C.M.R. 1990) (accused's incarceration in civilian jail on civil charges were excludable where military authorities had unsuccessfully attempted to gain his custody); United States v. Brown, 30 M.J. 839 (N.M.C.M.R. 1990) (delay caused by accused's unauthorized absence as well as resulting delays were properly excludable); United States v. Givens, 28 M.J. 888 (A.F.C.M.R. 1989) (court rejected argument that accused was "unavailable" because he was not represented by counsel); United States v. McCallister, 24 M.J. 881 (A.C.M.R. 1987) (government did not act with due diligence in returning accused to post after he was initially apprehended by civilians); United States v. Lilly, 22 M.J. 620 (N.M.C.M.R. 1986) (case remanded for determination on issue of delay caused by accused's absence); United States v. Cummings, 21 M.J. 987 (N.M.C.M.R. 1986) (no denial of speedy trial where accused's confinement within civilian jail was within his control).

161. R.C.M. 707(c)(1) Discussion. United States v. Maresca, 28 M.J. 328 (C.M.A. 1989) (13-day continuance requested by prosecution to obtain presence of two witnesses was properly deducted; the court observed that many speedy trial problems could be avoided by formalizing the requests for delays).

162. R.C.M. 707(c)(1) Discussion. See, e.g., United States v. Byard, 29 M.J. 803 (A.C.M.R. 1989)

7. Time to obtain security clearances for access to classified information[163] or time to declassify evidence[164] or
8. Any other delay for good cause.[165]

While this list bears a close resemblance to the explicitly codified exclusions in the original version of the 120-day rule, counsel should not be required to point to any one particular illustration as grounds for a requested delay. Indeed, the last illustration, delays for good cause, demonstrates that virtually any justifiable reason for delay should be given full consideration.

(prosecution not entitled to exclusion of lengthy delay where it had made tactical decision not to use DOD IG subpoenas to obtain important bank records in defendant's false claim charge; court noted that prosecution could also have used deposition procedure to obtain records); United States v. Raichle, 28 M.J. 876 (A.F.C.M.R. 1989) (delay in obtaining depositions of government witnesses for Article 32 investigation was chargeable to prosecution); United States v. Kuelker, 20 M.J. 715 (N.M.C.M.R. 1985) (prosecution delay in obtaining important evidence from U.S. Treasury was not "delay for good cause").
163. R.C.M. 707(c)(1) Discussion. *See, e.g.*, United States v. Mahoney, 28 M.J. 865 (A.F.C.M.R. 1989) (time needed to obtain approval from AF headquarters to proceed in trial of accused, who has access to highly sensitive classified information, was excludable).
164. R.C.M. 707(c)(1) Discussion. *See generally* MIL. R. EVID. 505 (privilege for classified information).
165. R.C.M. 707(c)(1) Discussion. *See, e.g.*, United States v. Higgins, 27 M.J. 150 (C.M.A. 1988) (request for administrative discharge in lieu of trial that has to be processed outside local command and which results in trial delay without defense protest was good cause for delay); United States v. Camacho, 30 M.J. 644 (N.M.C.M.R. 1990) (six-day delay resulting from death of Article 32 investigating officer's father-in-law amounted to "good cause"; causal connection between emergency leave and delay was clear); Hall v. Thwing, 30 M.J. 583 (A.C.M.R. 1990) (delays in waiting for Germans to decide whether to prosecute the defendant should not have been excluded under original "good cause" provisions of R.C.M. 707); United States v. Givens, 28 M.J. 888 (A.F.C.M.R. 1989) (court declined to apply "residual good cause" exception to speedy trial rule; this exception should be read narrowly; in dicta, the court expressed deep concerns for the future of the speedy trial rule and offered a number of practical pointers for those charged with ensuring that an accused is tried promptly within the military justice system).
United States v. Miniclier, 23 M.J. 843 (A.F.C.M.R. 1987) (accused's tender of resignation in lieu of trial and senator's intercession for accused did not amount to extraordinary circumstances warranting exclusion of time from speedy trial clock).
In an extensive discussion of the issue, the court in United States v. Duncan, 34 M.J. 1232 (A.C.M.R. 1992), concluded that the accused was denied a speedy trial where military authorities delayed prosecution until after the completion of a prosecution of the accused by the Department of Justice. The court concluded that an agreement between DOJ and DOD cannot extinguish court-martial jurisdiction or grant DOJ the authority to delay court-martial proceedings. The court did exclude the time from the date of the federal indictment until the date the accused was convicted. The court agreed that the federal and military prosecutions had to be tried serially. But it also concluded that Article 30 and R.C.M. 401(b) and 707 and the statute of limitations dictated that the military prosecution should have come first. The Court of Military Appeals affirmed, 38 M.J. 476 (C.M.A. 1993). The court indicated that the reasons for the delay are less important than the failure of military authorities to establish at trial good cause for relieving the Government of accountability. *See generally* Jacobson, "*United States v. Duncan*: The United States Court of Military Appeals Frowns on Retroactive 'Pretrial Delays,'" ARMY LAW., May 1994, p. 48.

Any decisions to grant requested delays should be reduced to writing, with reasons and dates being spelled out.[166] Any decisions granting delays are reviewable both for an abuse of discretion and reasonableness of the delay.[167]

Motions to Dismiss: If counsel intends to move for dismissal of some, or all of the charges, on speedy trial grounds, the *Manual* requires submission of a chronology which details the processing of the case.[168] The chronology is to become a part of the appellate record.[169] While the *Manual* is silent as to who carries the responsibility for preparing the chronology, it would usually be prudent for the defense, as the moving party, to be prepared to present one to the court. As under prior practice, it can be assumed that given the nature of the issue, disputes will arise as to whether the chronology accurately reflects all of the delays. Ultimately, the prosecution bears the burden of proving by a preponderance of the evidence that the accused was not denied a speedy trial.[170]

§ 13-3(C)(4). Interstate Agreement on Detainers Act (IADA).

In addition to the foregoing speedy trial rules, other statutory or regulatory provisions may mandate speedy disposition of charges. For example, at one time Army trials in Europe were bound by a 45-day speedy trial rule.[171] If a regulation governs what might be considered speedy trial matters, the threshold question is whether the regulation was intended to benefit the accused.[172] If so, due process principles will require that it be applied, especially if it is more protective of statutory requirements. Failure to comply with those provisions does not always require reversal, however.[173]

As noted in the discussion at § 13-3(C), supra, the Federal Speedy Trial Act does not apply to military trials. But one federal statutory provision that may come into play if a military accused has been charged in another jurisdiction, is the Interstate Agreement on Detainers Act (IADA). That Act,[174] which applies to the military,[175] includes a 180-day speedy trial provision. The Act provides in pertinent part:

> Whenever a person has entered upon a term of imprisonment in a penal or correctional institution of a party State, and whenever during the continuance of the term of imprisonment there is pending in any other

---

166. R.C.M. 707(c)(1) Drafters' Analysis.
167. *Id.* United States v. Longhofer, 29 M.J. 22 (C.M.A. 1989).
168. R.C.M. 707(c)(2).
169. *Id.*
170. R.C.M. 905(c)(2)(B).
171. USAREUR Supplement to Army Reg. 27-10. *See generally* United States v. Dunks, 1 M.J. 254 (C.M.A. 1976). *Cf.* United States v. McGraner, 13 M.J. 408 (C.M.A. 1982) (AFM 111-1 provision requiring expeditious handling of charges did not provide independent, enforceable right to a speedy trial; instead, it was designed for management purposes).
172. United States v. Dunks, 1 M.J. 254 (C.M.A. 1976) (45-day speedy trial rule intended for benefit of accused).
173. United States v. Hutchins, 4 M.J. 190 (C.M.A. 1978).
174. 18 U.S.C. app. § 2 (1988).
175. United States v. Bramer, 43 M.J. 538 (N.M.Ct.Crim.App. 1995) (Act applies to military).

party State any untried indictment, information, or complaint on the basis of which a detainer has been lodged against the prisoner, he shall be brought to trial within one hundred and eighty days after he shall have caused to be delivered to the prosecuting officer and the appropriate court of the prosecuting officer's jurisdiction written notice of the place of his imprisonment and his request for final disposition to be made of the indictment, information, or complaint...[176]

Failure to comply with the provisions of the act may result in a denial of "speedy trial."[177]

§ 13-3(C)(5). Remedies for Speedy Trial Violations.

If the trial court determines that the accused's constitutional rights to a speedy trial have been denied, the trial court must dismiss the charges with prejudice.[178] If the court, on the other hand, concludes that the accused's non-constitutional rights have been violated, the charges must still be dismissed but the trial court may decide to dismiss them with, or without, prejudice.[179] In making that decision the *Manual* indicates that the court should consider:

> [T]he seriousness of the offense; the facts and circumstances of the case that lead to dismissal; the impact of a reprosecution on the administration of justice; and prejudice to the accused resulting from the denial of a speedy trial.[180]

The trial court's decision is reviewable for an abuse of discretion.[181]

§ 13-3(D). Lack of Mental Responsibility.

Normally the issue of the accused's lack of mental responsibility at the time of the offense is raised as a defense at trial[182] and resolved by the fact-

---

176. 18 U.S.C. app. § 2, art. III(a) (1988). United States v. Bramer, 43 M.J. 538 (N.M.Ct.Crim.App. 1995).
177. United States v. Bramer, 43 M.J. 538 (N.M.Ct.Crim.App. 1995).
178. R.C.M. 707(d). See § 13-3(C)(1) for a discussion of the Sixth Amendment right to a speedy trial.
179. R.C.M. 707(d). United States v. Bowles, 37 M.J. 708 (A.C.M.R. 1993) (case returned for determination of whether charge should be dismissed with prejudice).
180. R.C.M. 707(d). *See also* United States v. Dies, 42 M.J. 847 (N.M.Ct.Crim.App. 1995) (dismissal without prejudice appropriate).
181. United States v. Edmond, 41 M.J. 419 (1995) (in case of first impression, court held that under 1991 change to R.C.M. 707 allowing dismissal with prejudice, judge did not abuse discretion in failing to dismiss charges with prejudice; court evaluated facts and circumstances of case, the reasons for the delays, and any prejudice to the accused).
182. In Ellis v. Jacob, 26 M.J. 90 (C.M.A. 1988), the court concluded that Article 50(a), in light of legislative history and federal precedent, should be read to permit evidence of partial lack of mental responsibility notwithstanding the language, Mental disease or defect does not otherwise constitute a defense. The defense must establish the lack of mental responsibility by clear and convincing evidence. *See also* United States v. Massey, 27 M.J. 371 (C.M.A. 1989).
In United States v. Vanderlip, 28 M.J. 1070 (N.M.C.M.R. 1989), the court concluded that the judge committed harmless error when he denied the defense the opportunity to present evidence

finder.[183] Nonetheless, in the past the defense could raise such a motion and obtain an interlocutory ruling from the judge on whether the accused was sane at the time of the offense.[184] However, according to Article 51(b), U.C.M.J., any such ruling is not final and the issue can be litigated before the members.[185] The *Manual* provides that the factual issue of the accused's mental responsibility may not be decided as an interlocutory matter.[186] The Drafters recognized that Article 51 does not forbid consideration of the issue in such a manner but felt that there was no reason for doing so and that in some instances to do so would be detrimental to the accused. In their view, the import of Article 51 was to preserve the factual question of sanity for the fact-finder.[187]

Assuming that the defense determines that it would not be detrimental to raise the issue in a motion to dismiss, especially where trial is by judge alone and it is the judge who will serve as the fact-finder, it should argue that the clear implication of Article 51 is that the issue may be so raised and that the statutory provision should prevail over the conflicting *Manual* provision. Where trial is by members there really is little to gain by obtaining a provisional ruling by the judge on the issue. In any event, the defense would be required to prove by clear and convincing evidence that the accused was not mentally responsible at the time of the offense.[188] The military standard and procedures for determining mental responsibility are spelled out in R.C.M. 706.[189]

Motions addressing the question of whether the accused is competent to stand trial are discussed at § 13-5(A).

---

on partial mental responsibility. *See generally* Becker, "Litigating Mental Responsibility Under Article 50a." 28 A.F. L. Rev. 97 (1988).

183. *See, e.g.*, United States v. Hensler, 40 M.J. 892 (N.M.c.M.R. 1994) (accused must prove absence of mental responsibility by clear and convincing evidence); United States v. Ott, 26 M.J. 542 (A.F.C.M.R. 1988).

184. 1969 Manual for Courts-Martial, para. 67d, 122b(4).

185. *See* Appendix 3.

186. R.C.M. 916(k)(3)(C).

187. R.C.M. 916(k)(3)(C) Analysis.

188. Art. 50a, U.C.M.J., R.C.M. 916(b), (k)(3)(A) Discussion. The burden of proof was shifted from the prosecution to the defense through amendments to Article 50, U.C.M.J. in 1986. See Military Justice Amendments of 1986, tit. VIII, 902, National Defense Authorization Act for Fiscal Year 1987, Pub. L. No. 99-661, 100 Stat. 3816 (1986). The amendments also institute new trial procedures on consideration of the issue by the fact finder. *See* R.C.M. 921.

189. *See* United States v. Massey, 27 M.J. 371 (C.M.A. 1989) (court interpreted R.C.M. 706 to permit inquiries into accused's mental responsibility after case is on appellate review). According to Art. 50a, U.C.M.J. the test for determining whether the accused lacked mental responsibility at the time of the offense is whether the accused as a result of a severe mental disease or defect, was unable to appreciate the nature and quality or wrongfulness of his or her acts. The Rule further states that "Mental disease or defect" does not otherwise constitute a defense.

§ 13-3(E). Former Jeopardy.

Motions to dismiss on the grounds that the accused is being subjected to double jeopardy must be raised before the court adjourns; failure to do so generally constitutes a waiver.[190] The defense bears the burden of proving by a preponderance of the evidence,[191] that the accused is being tried again, without his consent,[192] by the same sovereign for the same offense.[193] The issue is typically raised where the current trial is a rehearing resulting from a successful appeal or a mistrial,[194] or where charges were withdrawn and later re-referred to the current court for trial.[195]

In military practice, courts-martial and federal trials are considered trials by the same sovereign—the federal government.[196] Thus, a state conviction would not, under double jeopardy principles, bar a later military trial.[197] However, evidence of a prior state conviction for the same offense may be introduced as mitigating evidence.[198] And service regulations may, as a policy matter, either block, or require special pretrial handling of, a subsequent court-martial.[199]

---

190. R.C.M. 905(c), 907(b)(2)(C). United States v. Collins, 41 M.J. 428 (1995) (failure to raise double jeopardy grounds waived it); United States v. Schilling, 7 C.M.A. 482, 22 C.M.R. 272 (1957). *Cf.* United States v. Johnson, 2 M.J. 541 (A.C.M.R. 1976); United States v. Florczak, 49 C.M.R. 786 (A.C.M.R. 1975).

191. *See* R.C.M. 905(c).

192. Art. 44(a), U.C.M.J. This implies that the accused has been made aware of the fact that a double jeopardy problem exists. As with the problem of an accused not being aware of a statute of limitations issue, it may be appropriate for a trial judge to raise the issue. *See* § 13-3(B).

193. U.S. CONST., amend. V. Art. 44(a), U.C.M.J. R.C.M. 907(b)(2)(C). United States v. DiAngelo, 31 M.J. 135 (C.M.A. 1990). This would also include lesser included offenses. United States v. Lynch, 47 C.M.R. 143 (A.C.M.R. 1973). *See generally* Annotation, "Modern Status of Doctrine of Res Judicata in Criminal Cases," 9 A.L.R.3d 203 (1966); Weise, "Double Jeopardy: Changes by the Supreme Court and Their Effect on the Military," 11 THE ADVOCATE 28 (1979).

194. The topic of mistrials is also addressed at § 15-4(B).

195. For a discussion on withdrawal of charges, see § 8-5.

196. *See, e.g.,* Abbate v. United States, 359 U.S. 187 (1959); United States v. Blocker, 30 M.J. 1152 (A.C.M.R. 1990) (administrative discharge board findings that resulted in discharge, which was held in abeyance pending court-martial, did not constitute double jeopardy; but court did credit accused with forfeitures that resulted from administrative demotion by board); United States v. Borys, 39 C.M.R. 608 (A.B.R. 1968), *rev'd on other grounds,* 18 C.M.A. 547, 40 C.M.R. 247 (1969).

197. United States v. Schneider, 38 M.J. 387 (C.M.A. 1993) (although military could have prosecuted accused for same offense for which he was tried at state trial, court-martial for conduct unbecoming an officer by testifying falsely before the state tribunal was not a trial on the same charges); *Cf.* United States v. Bordelon, 43 M.J. 531 (Army Ct.Crim.App. 1995) (accused argued that successive military prosecution violated Army regulations concerning double jeopardy; convening authority complied with regulatory guidance on whether accused should be court-martialed following state conviction).

198. United States v. Rosenblatt, 13 C.M.A. 28, 32 C.M.R. 28 (1962).

199. *See* AR 27-10, Chapter 4. In United States v. Stallard, 14 M.J. 933 (A.C.M.R. 1982), the court indicated that failure to follow the provisions of AR 27-10 was non-jurisdictional error.

Trial by a foreign country may, under some circumstances constitute double jeopardy if the United States has a treaty provision governing trials by the foreign state of military accused.[200]

A court-martial is not considered a "trial" for purposes of double jeopardy until there has been a presentation of evidence on the issue of guilt, i.e., the merits portion of the proceedings have begun and the prosecution has offered some evidence, whether it is in the form of testimony or documents.[201] This rule is clearly at odds with the federal standard which, according to *Crist v. Bretz*,[202] states that jeopardy attaches when the jury is impaneled and sworn.[203] In addressing the issue, the Drafters of the *Manual* indicated that the military rule, which places the attachment later in the proceedings, is justified by the differences in the composition of military courts.[204]

If the earlier proceeding resulted in a conviction of the accused, it is not considered a trial for purposes of double jeopardy until appellate review has been completed and the finding of guilty approved.[205] And if a trial is later determined to have lacked jurisdiction, it is generally considered a nullity and will not bar later prosecution for the same offense.[206]

Some additional rules apply if the first proceeding resulted in a mistrial or if the charges were withdrawn from the court. First, a mistrial, which has the effect of "withdrawing" the charges,[207] will not bar a later prosecution unless it was (1) ordered by the judge without the consent of the defense and constituted an abuse of discretion[208] or (2) the mistrial directly resulted from intentional prosecutorial misconduct that was designed to obtain a mistrial.[209]

---

200. *See, e.g.*, para. 8, Art. VII, NATO SOFA, 4 U.S.T. 1792. *See also* United States v. Miller, 16 M.J. 169 (C.M.A. 1983) (no double jeopardy where accused's trial by Korean court was later reversed under provisions of Korean SOFA); United States v. Frostell, 13 M.J. 680 (N.M.C.M.R. 1982) (trial not barred by prior Japanese trial).

201. R.C.M. 907(b)(2)(C)(i). United States v. Browers, 20 M.J. 542, 552 (A.C.M.R. 1985), *rev'd on other grounds*, 20 M.J. 356 (C.M.A. 1985).

202. 437 U.S. 28 (1978).

203. *See also* United States v. Cook, 12 M.J. 448 (C.M.A. 1982).

204. R.C.M. 907(b)(2)(C) Analysis. *Cf.* United States v. Browers, 20 M.J. 542, 552, n.11 (A.C.M.R. 1985) (in jury trial jeopardy attaches when the jury is sworn), *rev'd on other grounds*, 20 M.J. 356 (C.M.A. 1985).

In applying a rule that seems less protective of the accused's rights than the constitution requires, the burden rests upon the government to establish that the rule is required by special needs of the military. Courtney v. Williams, 1 M.J. 267 (C.M.A. 1976).

205. Art. 44(b), U.C.M.J. R.C.M. 907(b)(2)(C)(iii), United States v. Richardson, 21 C.M.A. 54, 44 C.M.R. 108 (1971).

206. R.C.M. 907(b)(2)(C)(iv). Ball v. United States, 163 U.S. 662 (1896). *See, e.g.*, United States v. Jackson, 20 M.J. 83 (C.M.A. 1985) (no trial where judge dismissed charges because charge sheet was untimely under statute of limitations); United States v. Hairston, 15 M.J. 892 (A.C.M.R. 1983) (dismissal of charges for failure to state an offense did not bar later trial on same charges). *Cf.* United States v. Culver, 22 C.M.A. 141, 46 C.M.R. 141 (1973).

207. R.C.M. 915(c)(1). Burtt v. Schick, 23 M.J. 140 (C.M.A. 1986) (trial judge abused discretion in granting government-requested mistrial where it appeared that several alternatives to granting mistrial were available).

208. R.C.M. 915(c)(2)(A). *See generally* Oregon v. Kennedy, 456 U.S. 667 (1982).

209. R.C.M. 915(c)(2)(B).

§ 13-3(F)

As to rules governing withdrawal of charges after jeopardy has attached, subsequent prosecution will not be barred if the prosecution can show that withdrawal was required by "urgent and unforeseen military necessity."[210]

With these rules in mind, it is important to recognize the importance of the timing of the judge's rulings on motions. If the judge unnecessarily delays ruling on motions until after jeopardy attaches, the prosecution's ability to withdraw curable charges may be limited. For example, a successful motion by the defense to suppress evidence would normally not be considered an urgent and unforeseen military necessity.[211] But double jeopardy rules would not prevent the prosecution from appealing the judge's ruling.[212]

If the defense demonstrates that the accused is being subjected to double jeopardy the judge must dismiss the charges.[213] The judge's ruling will be examined for an abuse of discretion.[214]

§ 13-3(F). Failure to Allege an Offense.

If a specification fails to allege an offense,[215] the accused may move to dismiss at any time, even on appeal and does not waive the issue by pleading guilty.[216] The motion presents a question of law for the judge who must determine whether the specification (1) alleges directly or by implication the essential elements of the offense,[217] (2) alleges criminal conduct,[218] (3) apprises the

---

210. R.C.M. 604(b). *See generally* § 8-5.
211. See R.C.M. 905(d), which indicates that normally motions made before pleas should be ruled upon before pleas are entered. *See also* MIL. R. EVID. 304(d)(4), 311(d)(4), and 321(f), which indicate that a judge should not defer ruling on suppression motions if doing so will adversely affect a party's ability to appeal the ruling.
212. *See generally* § 13-2(G)(2).
213. R.C.M. 907(b)(2).
214. United States v. Cole, 31 M.J. 270 (C.M.A. 1990); United States v. Bordelon, 43 M.J. 531 (Army Ct.Crim.App. 1995).
215. *See* § 6-1. *Cf.* United States v. Watkins, 21 M.J. 208 (C.M.A. 1986) (standing to challenge a specification as defective is "considerably less where an accused knowingly and voluntarily pleads guilty to the offense"). *See also* United States v. Simpson, 25 M.J. 865 (A.C.M.R. 1988).
216. R.C.M. 907(b)(1). United States v. Fleig, 16 C.M.A. 444, 37 C.M.R. 64 (1966); United States v. Fout, 3 C.M.A. 565, 13 C.M.R. 121 (1953); United States v. Jefferson, 14 M.J. 806 (A.C.M.R. 1982).
217. United States v. Brecheen, 27 M.J. 67 (C.M.A. 1988) (specification alleging attempted distribution of LSD reasonably included element of wrongfulness); United States v. Davis, 26 M.J. 445 (C.M.A. 1988) (specification alleging that accused, a male, dressed in female clothing, was conduct that was to the prejudice of good order and discipline and of a nature to bring discredit upon the Armed Forces was sufficient to allege criminality); United States v. Mayo, 12 M.J. 286 (C.M.A. 1982) (defective specification is not revived by government's production at trial of evidence of the omitted fact). Note that in *Mayo* the court also ruled that although the specification was insufficient to state an offense under Article 134, citing violation of a civilian statute, it was sufficient to allege an offense prejudicial to good order and discipline. United States v. Woods, 27 M.J. 749 (N.M.C.M.R. 1988) (absence of words of criminality was not fatal in specification alleging that accused, knowing that he had AIDS, engaged in unprotected sexual intercourse); United States v. Brown, 42 C.M.R. 656 (A.C.M.R. 1970). *See* §§ 2-6(A), (C).
218. United States v. Fleig, 16 C.M.A. 444, 37 C.M.R. 64 (1966); United States v. Brown, 25 M.J. 793 (N.M.C.M.R. 1987) (specification of disobedience of order was defective where it failed to allege element of knowledge); United States v. Garcia, 18 M.J. 539 (A.C.M.R. 1984).

accused of what he must defend against,[219] and (4) protects the accused against double jeopardy.[220] The prosecution bears the burden of proving that the specification states an offense.[221] For further discussion on drafting charges see § 6-1. Specifications that state an offense but are still in some way defective may be the subject of a motion for appropriate relief.[222]

§ 13-3(G). Former Punishment.

Imposition of nonjudicial punishment for a minor offense[223] will bar any later prosecution by court-martial for the same offense.[224] Prior nonjudicial punishment for a serious offense, however, will not bar trial but must be considered as a mitigating factor in determining any sentence.[225] Punishment imposed as a result of an administrative action may also be credited.[226]

Punishment imposed in violation of Article 13, U.C.M.J. for minor disciplinary infractions may also bar trial.[227] Although punishment by a foreign gov-

---

219. United States v. Curtiss, 19 C.M.A. 402, 42 C.M.R. 4 (1970); United States v. Brown, 41 M.J. 504 (Army Ct. Crim. App. 1994) (court rejected defense argument that 10 U.S.C. § 976, which prohibits military labor union activities, was impermissibly vague).

220. In United States v. Dear, 40 M.J. 196 (C.M.A. 1994), the court noted that while the double jeopardy prong was important at common law, its relevance might be questioned because the defendant may rely upon the entire record of trial in raising a double jeopardy argument. United States v. Smith, 40 C.M.R. 432 (A.C.M.R. 1969).

221. R.C.M. 907(c)(2)(B). United States v. Jefferson, 14 M.J. 806, 808 (A.C.M.R. 1982).

222. See § 15-3(E).

223. United States v. Hudson, 39 M.J. 958 (N.M.C.M.R. 1994) (NJP for offense of communicating indecent language not minor; accused entitled to credit); United States v. Sorby, 39 M.J. 914 (N.M.C.M.R. 1994) (offense of 23-day unauthorized absence was minor offense; failure of defense counsel to move to dismiss charges waived issue; the court, however, dismissed the specification). An offense is ordinarily considered "minor" if the maximum imposable punishment which could be assessed does not include a dishonorable discharge or confinement for more than one year. See § 3-3(C). However, the question of whether an offense is minor lies within the discretion of the commander imposing the nonjudicial punishment. See generally Chapter 3.

224. MCM, Part V, para. 1(e). R.C.M. 907(b)(2)(D)(iv). United States v. Pierce, 25 M.J. 607 (A.C.M.R. 1987) (prior Article 15 punishment for larceny of $2,000 was not a bar to a later court-martial; judge properly considered the prior punishment, however, in reaching a sentence).

225. Art. 15(f), U.C.M.J.; MCM, Part V, para. 1(e); R.C.M. 1001(c)(1)(B). United States v. Joseph, 11 M.J. 333 (C.M.A. 1981); United States v. Fretwell, 11 C.M.A. 377, 29 C.M.R. 193 (1960); United States v. Flynn, 39 M.J. 774 (A.C.M.R. 1994) (accused must be given credit for prior nonjudicial punishment for same offenses: day for day, dollar for dollar and stripe for stripe); United States v. Bromell, 37 M.J. 978 (A.C.M.R. 1993) (court must give credit for prior Article 15 punishment; appellate court did so because it was not clear that military judge did so); United States v. Strickland, 36 M.J. 569 (A.C.M.R. 1992) (appellate court granted credit for nonjudicial punishment where it was not clear in record that accused had received credit); United States v. Wharton, 33 C.M.R. 729 (A.F.B.R. 1963).

226. United States v. Edwards, 42 M.J. 381 (1995) (military judge may properly grant credit for prior Article 15 punishment; doing so relieved convening authority of need to do so); United States v. Blocker, 33 M.J. 349 (C.M.A. 1991) (administrative imposition of reduction in grade and subsequent court-martial did not result in rare double punishment scenario in United States v. Halper, 490 U.S. 435 (1989)).

227. Art. 13, U.C.M.J. R.C.M. 907(b)(2)(D)(iv). United States v. Nelson, 18 C.M.A. 177, 39 C.M.R. 177 (1969); United States v. Bayhand, 6 C.M.A. 762, 21 C.M.R. 84 (1956). See generally § 5-3(C).

ernment or by a state court will generally not raise a double jeopardy issue,[228] the accused may be able to invoke any statutory or regulatory provisions that are designed to block or discourage subsequent prosecution by military courts.[229]

The accused bears the burden of proving the prior punishment by a preponderance of the evidence.[230] The motion will be considered waived if not raised before the end of the trial.[231] If raised, it is probably not waived by a guilty plea.[232]

§ 13-3(H). Grant of Immunity.

Proper grants of transactional immunity will serve as a bar to trial.[233] The issue is considered waived if it is not raised before the trial is completed,[234] and the burden rests upon the defense to show that a valid grant of immunity was made.[235] The accused must have received the grant from either a general court-martial convening authority or the United States Attorney General.[236] Promises of immunity or clemency from other individuals will generally not block the trial unless due process requires such. For example, in *Cooke v. Orser*,[237] the Court ruled that due process principles required that espionage charges against the accused should be dismissed when it appeared that the accused had reasonably relied upon assurances by the staff judge advocate that he would not be prosecuted if he provided information to investigators.[238]

---

228. *See* § 13-3(G). United States v. Anderson, 36 M.J. 963 (A.F.C.M.R. 1993) (citing Air Force policy of not conducting military prosecution after state prosecution; if military trial is held first, the question of subsequent state prosecution is matter for state to decide); United States v. Olsen, 24 M.J. 669 (A.F.C.M.R. 1987) (conviction reversed where court-martial followed conviction in state court; government failed to follow Air Force Regulation 111-1, para. 2-4, which prohibits court-martial following civilian trial unless the Secretary of the Air Force specifically approves such). *Cf.* United States v. Lorenc, 26 M.J. 793 (A.F.C.M.R. 1988) (court-martial not barred by Air Force Regulation 111-1 where civilian and military offenses were sufficiently dissimilar).

229. *See, e.g.*, AR 27-10, Chapter 4, which places some limitations on the authority of the Army to prosecute service members who have been tried in civilian court.

230. R.C.M. 905(c).

231. R.C.M. 905(e).

232. United States v. Florczak, 49 C.M.R. 786 (A.C.M.R. 1975).

233. Kastigar v. United States, 406 U.S. 441 (1972); United States v. Kirsch, 15 C.M.A. 84, 35 C.M.R. 56 (1964); United States v. Villines, 13 M.J. 46 (C.M.A. 1982). For a general discussion of military grants of immunity, see Green, "Grants of Immunity and Military Law, 1971-1976," 73 MIL. L. REV. 1 (1976).

234. R.C.M. 907(b)(2), 905(e). United States v. Gladdis, 12 M.J. 1005 (A.C.M.R. 1982).

235. R.C.M. 905(c). As noted, however, the burden may rest on the prosecution if a grant of testimonial immunity was made earlier to an accused being tried by court-martial.

236. *See* R.C.M. 704 and Title 11, Organized Crime Control Act of 1970, 18 U.S.C. 6004 (1994). For a discussion on the procedures for granting a witness immunity in military practice, see "Grants of Immunity," ARMY LAW., Dec. 1973, at 22, as amended in ARMY LAW., Feb. 1974, at 14. The services may also provide more detailed guidance on the procedures to be used. *See, e.g.*, AR 27-10, para. 2-4.

237. 12 M.J. 335 (C.M.A. 1982). Clay v. Woodmansee, 29 M.J. 663 (A.C.M.R. 1989) (citing principles of fairness, court enforced convening authority's formal clemency agreement with accused whereby accused received reduction in sentence in return for waiving appellate rights).

238. *See also* United States v. Brown, 13 M.J. 253 (C.M.A. 1982), where the court reviewed an informal clemency agreement between an SJA and a drug informant and noted that fair play and

In any event, a defective grant of transactional immunity will act as a *de facto* grant of testimonial immunity and anything that the accused may have said in reliance upon the grant will not be admissible against him.[239] The same result occurs where the government has promised immunity through drug and alcohol abuse programs that generally permit the accused to turn himself in and submit to treatment in return for immunity from prosecution.[240]

Where the accused has been previously granted testimonial immunity[241] and has testified pursuant to that grant, the government bears a heavy burden in showing that, as a predicate for proceeding with the trial, that its evidence was independently obtained and in no way derived from the accused's immunized testimony.[242] In *United States v. Lucas*,[243] the court held that absent a complaint from the defense, the prosecution is not required to show that it has not used any derivative evidence from the immunized testimony. If the judge, however, is aware that such evidence is being used, he has a duty to intervene.[244]

The military courts have indicated that the practical effects of transactional and testimonial are the same; only on rare occasions will the prosecution be able to proceed successfully against the accused.[245] Whether the prosecution has improperly used immunized testimony is a question of fact.[246] The military courts have also addressed the issue of whether directives or regulations may grant a form of immunity from prosecution under the Uniform Code of Military Justice as incentives for servicemembers to seek assistance. A typical example includes self-identification for treatment in Family Advocacy pro-

---

legitimate law enforcement interests require ungrudging enforcement of such agreements. *See generally* Hoover, "Due Process Immunities in Military Law," 12 THE REPORTER 2 (Feb. 1983).

239. United States v. Caliendo, 13 C.M.A. 405, 32 C.M.R. 405 (1962).

240. United States v. Gladdis, 12 M.J. 1005 (A.C.M.R. 1982) (exemption provisions of AR 600-85 amounted to a grant of immunity).

241. Testimonial or "use" immunity is the constitutional minimum. *See* MIL. R. EVID. 303 and §§ 5-2(B) and 11-2(E).

242. United States v. Whitehead, 5 M.J. 294 (C.M.A. 1978); United States v. McGeeney, 41 M.J. 544 (N.M. Ct. Crim. App. 1994) (court concluded that prosecution had not used accused's immunized statements directly, indirectly, or in a nonevidentiary manner; assistant trial counsel's exposure to statements not grounds for dismissal; court held that there is no per se prohibition that bars knowledge of the statements); United States v. Olivero, 39 M.J. 246 (C.M.A. 1994) (prosecution failed to prove by preponderance of evidence that nonevidentiary use of immunized testimony, i.e., decision to prosecute, was untainted by such testimony; court noted that federal circuits are split on issue).

243. 25 M.J. 9 (C.M.A. 1987), *cert. denied*, 484 U.S. 1026 (1988).

244. *See, e.g.*, United States v. Boyd, 27 M.J. 82 (C.M.A. 1988) (prosecution failed to show lack of derivative use of immunized testimony; prosecution's burden is not limited to negation of taint); United States v. Whitehead, 5 M.J. 294 (C.M.A. 1978); United States v. England, 30 M.J. 1030 (A.F.C.M.R. 1990) (prosecution showed independent basis although officer who had assisted in obtaining grant of testimonial immunity for accused had contact with prosecutor; court indicated that to avoid suggestion of impropriety immunized testimony should be screened from accused's trial team and should have been cataloged or sealed so as to create sanitized paper trail).

245. *See, e.g.*, United States v. Rivera, 1 M.J. 107 (C.M.A. 1975).

246. United States v. Tucker, 20 M.J. 602 (N.M.C.M.R. 1985).

grams.[247] Although servicemembers are encouraged to voluntarily admit their potential for domestic abuse, doing so is normally not a limited form of immunity from prosecution.[248] For further discussion on grants of immunity, see §§ 5-2(B) and 11-2(E).

§ 13-3(I). Constructive Condonation of Desertion.

This bar to trial arises when a general court-martial convening authority unconditionally[249] restores a known deserter[250] to duty without trial.[251] The accused, who bears the burden of proof,[252] must raise the issue before the end of trial or risk waiver.[253] Note that this bar to trial does not apply to the offense of absence without leave.[254]

§ 13-3(J). Multiplicity.

A specification of a charge may be dismissed if the defense can establish that it is multiplicious with another specification.[255] For a general discussion of multiplicious pleadings, see § 6-1(C)(3). If a specification is multiplicious,[256] the judge may dismiss it. Unlike other motions to dismiss, this request for relief rests on "permissible grounds"[257] As a general rule, the judge may decline to dismiss any of the specifications until after the trial on the merits is completed, if the prosecution can show that exigencies of proof require defer-

---

247. *See, e.g.*, United States v. Corcoran, 40 M.J. 478 (C.M.A. 1994) (discussion of DOD and Army's Family Advocacy Programs (FAP)); United States v. Martindale, 40 M.J. 348 (C.M.A. 1994) (Navy Instruction 1752.3 — Family Advocacy Program; any immunity which might otherwise apply to statements not available to accused under facts).
248. United States v. Corcoran, 40 M.J. 478 (C.M.A. 1994) (FAP does not guarantee that servicemember will not be prosecuted).
249. The convening authority's decision must be an informed one. United States v. Scott, 6 C.M.A. 650, 20 C.M.R. 366 (1956).
250. See § 2-2(B) for a discussion of the offense of desertion.
251. R.C.M. 907(b)(2)(D)(iii).
252. R.C.M. 905(c).
253. R.C.M. 905(e), 907(b)(2). United States v. Perkins, 1 C.M.A. 502, 4 C.M.R. 94 (1952).
254. United States v. Minor, 1 C.M.A. 497, 4 C.M.R. 89 (1952); United States v. Pettis, 12 M.J. 616 (N.M.C.M.R. 1981).
255. R.C.M. 907(b)(3)(B). There is some authority that the trial judge may have a duty to *sua sponte* remedy multiplicious pleadings. United States v. Abendschein, 19 M.J. 619, 620, n.1 (A.C.M.R. 1984). *See also* United States v. Zubko, 18 M.J. 378 (C.M.A. 1984); United States v. Baker, 14 M.J. 361 (C.M.A. 1983); United States v. Harclerode, 17 M.J. 981 (A.C.M.R. 1984).
256. The test cited in the Discussion to R.C.M. 907(b)(3)(B) simply indicates that a specification is multiplicious with another if it alleges the same offense or one necessarily included in the other, or if it is simply another way of describing an offense which is already alleged in another specification. As a practical matter, as the discussion of § 6-1(C)(3) demonstrates, the courts are in search of a common, workable test. The point here is that even assuming that the judge agrees with the defense that a specification is multiplicious, he is not required to dismiss it.
257. R.C.M. 907(b)(3)(A). United States v. Howard, 24 M.J. 897 (C.G.C.M.R. 1987) (judge did not abuse discretion in not dismissing multiplicious charges prior to presentation of evidence). In United States v. Hunt, 24 M.J. 725 (A.C.M.R. 1987), the judge dismissed the multiplicious specifications on the condition that the accused's conditional guilty pleas be provident. When he later rejected the accused's plea of guilty, he reinstated the specifications.

ral of that decision.[258] The key here is that problems of proof may result in findings of not guilty being entered on one or more specifications. Rather than requiring the prosecution to choose before trial which specification will go to the fact finder and risk the possibility of picking the wrong one, the appellate courts generally permit delay of the prosecution's selection and dismissal until findings are entered.[259] Indeed, the *Manual* recognizes the possibility that in some cases the dismissal would not take place until appellate review is completed.[260] But it seems clear that dismissal is ultimately required, whether by the trial judge or the appellate court.[261] There is some authority for the proposition that a trial court or appellate court may consolidate the multiplicious charges.[262] Assuming that the judge declines to rule on the motion prior to sentencing, the multiplicious charges should be merged for the purposes of determining the maximum imposable sentence.[263] A guilty plea will not waive this issue.[264] Although there is some authority holding that failure to object will waive the issue,[265] military caselaw has applied the plain error doctrine in granting relief to an accused.[266]

---

258. R.C.M. 907(b)(3)(A). United States v. Fortney, 12 M.J. 987 (A.F.C.M.R. 1982) (judge may decline to dismiss where a genuine issue of proof exists); United States v. Croom, 1 M.J. 635 (A.C.M.R. 1975).

259. United States v. Morris, 18 M.J. 450 (C.M.A. 1984) (multiplicious assault charge could stand until judge could determine from evidence whether either or both charges were proved by the prosecution).

However, there is some authority that dismissal before findings may be appropriate where exigencies of proof are lacking in an inordinate number of specifications, United States v. Hughes, 1 M.J. 346 (C.M.A. 1976), or where one of the specifications is a lesser included offense of the other, United States v. Stegall, 6 M.J. 176 (C.M.A. 1979). In the case of the latter, the prosecution may choose to go to the fact finder with the greater offense and argue that if the proof on that offense is not present that the lesser offense should then be considered in the deliberations.

260. R.C.M. 907(b)(3)(B) Discussion. *See also* United States v. Graves, 12 M.J. 583 (A.F.C.M.R. 1981).

261. United States v. Zupancic, 18 M.J. 387 (C.M.A. 1984). In *Zupancic* the court also indicated that if on appeal it appears that the greater offense must be set aside, the lesser, and multiplicious offense may be reinstated. *Cf.* United States v. Haywood, 6 M.J. 604 (A.C.M.R. 1978).

262. *See, e.g.*, United States v. Boyle, 36 M.J. 326 (C.M.A. 1993) (trial judge consolidated specifications; court noted that doing so does not amount to dismissal); United States v. Sorrell, 23 M.J. 122, n. 1 (C.M.A. 1986) (findings of guilty on consolidated specifications are not affected because they still apply to portions of specifications added to the remaining specification); United States v. Campbell, 22 M.J. 99 (C.M.A. 1986).

263. *See* R.C.M. 1001(c)(1)(C) and § 15-17(A)(1).

264. *See* R.C.M. 910(j). United States v. McMillan, 33 M.J. 257 (C.M.A. 1991) (although appropriate time for making motion to dismiss multiplicious charges in guilty plea case is before pleas are entered, motion may be made after findings and before sentencing); United States v. Thompson, 28 M.J. 769 (A.C.M.R. 1989) (defense request for bill of particulars as to multiplicity issue was sufficient to preserve issue).

265. United States v. Olson, 38 M.J. 597 (A.F.C.M.R. 1993) (accused waived multiplicity issue by not objecting at trial; court found plain error); United States v. Spring, 15 M.J. 669 (A.F.C.M.R. 1983); United States v. Tyler, 14 M.J. 811 (A.C.M.R. 1982); United States v. McGary, 12 M.J. 760 (A.C.M.R. 1981); United States v. Huggins, 12 M.J. 657 (A.C.M.R. 1981). *Cf.* United States v. Warner, 33 M.J. 522 (A.F.C.M.R. 1991) (accused's failure to challenge multiplicity of charges at trial did not waive the issue).

266. United States v. Hendrickson, 16 M.J. 62 (C.M.A. 1983); United States v. Jean, 15 M.J.

§ 13-3(K). Defective Specification That Misled the Accused.

In some cases a particular specification may state an offense[267] but still be so defective as to mislead the accused as to what he is being charged with. As with the multiplicity issue discussed in § 13-3(J), raising this point does not ensure that the judge will dismiss the specification. This is considered a "permissible" ground for dismissal in the *Manual*.[268] The key here is that the trial judge in his discretion may dismiss the specification where the accused has been substantially misled and the judge determines that in the interest of justice, the trial should proceed on the remainder of the charges without further delay.[269] It is not entirely clear just what sort of factual situation the Drafters of the 1984 revisions of the *Manual* envisioned because the Analysis for the pertinent rule only cites the 1969 *Manual* provision, which in turn addressed only the issue of failing to state an offense.[270] Presumably this type of motion would be appropriate where the prosecution could repair the specification only through a bill of particulars[271] or major amendments[272] that would consume valuable trial time. The burden of proof on this motion rests upon the defense[273] and should be raised before pleas are entered.[274] Failure to do so would amount to a waiver of the issue.[275]

§ 13-3(L). Presidential Pardon.

If the President of the United States has issued a pardon to an accused, either individually or through general amnesty, the accused may invoke that grant as a bar to trial.[276] The accused would bear the burden of proof[277] and must raise the issue before the end of trial.[278] There is little case law on this point, although pardons by the President have been granted to service members. For example, following the Viet Nam War, a presidential pardon was extended to individuals who had unlawfully avoided military service.[279] Any

---

433 (C.M.A. 1983); United States v. Olson, 38 M.J. 597 (A.F.C.M.R. 1993) (accused waived multiplicity issue by not objecting at trial; court found plain error); United States v. Juarez, 37 M.J. 779 (A.C.M.R. 1993) (court declined to find waiver where charges were multiplicious on their face, i.e., amounted to plain error).
  267. For discussion on motions to dismiss where the specification fails to state an offense, see § 13-3(F).
  268. R.C.M. 907(b)(3).
  269. R.C.M. 907(b)(3).
  270. Para. 69c(3), MCM 1969.
  271. See § 13-5(F).
  272. See § 6-1(B)(2).
  273. R.C.M. 905(c)(2).
  274. R.C.M. 905(b)(2).
  275. R.C.M. 905(e).
  276. R.C.M. 907(b)(2)(D)(i).
  277. R.C.M. 905(c)(2).
  278. R.C.M. 905(e).
  279. *See* Proclamation 4483 Granting Pardon for Violations of the Selective Service Act, August 4, 1964 to March 28, 1973. 42 FED. REG. 4391 (1-24-77). *See also* EO 11967 at 42 FED. REG.

service or departmental policy of leniency or restraint on prosecuting certain individuals would probably not constitute a "pardon" unless the President had in some fashion ratified or adopted that policy.[280] In the absence of such a ratification, a policy of non-prosecution might be considered, however, in conjunction with an argument that the accused has nonetheless been selectively prosecuted.[281]

§ 13-3(M). Selective or Vindictive Prosecution; Prosecutorial Misconduct.

Under limited circumstances the accused might succeed in obtaining a dismissal of charges on the ground that he has been targeted for selective or vindictive prosecution in violation of his due process and equal protection rights.[282] The applicable Constitutional provision would be the Fifth Amendment to the United States Constitution, which prohibits the federal government from depriving a person of life, liberty, or property without due process of law. Although the Fifth Amendment contains no explicit reference to "equal protection," the Supreme Court has indicated that that concept is part and parcel of due process considerations that require that the government deal with persons in a reasonable fashion, both in substance and in procedure. Thus, the Court has referred to the protection in the Fifth Amendment as the equal protection component of the due process clause.[283]

According to applicable case law from both the federal and military courts, the accused bears a heavy burden of demonstrating that (1) although there are others similarly situated who have not been prosecuted, the accused has been singled out for prosecution and (2) that the government's selection of him has been invidious or in bad faith, in that he has been selected for prosecution

---

4393 (1-24-77), which instructs the United States Attorney General to dismiss pending indictments and investigations.

280. *See* United States v. Garwood, 20 M.J. 148, 154, n.6 (C.M.A. 1985).
281. *See* § 13-3(M).
282. United States v. Nix, 40 M.J. 6 (C.M.A. 1994) (trial court erred in not determining whether SPCM had more than an official interest in recommending GCM); United States v. El-Amin, 38 M.J. 563 (A.F.C.M.R. 1993) (accused's argument of selective prosecution not valid; other actors who were not prosecuted were not similarly situated); United States v. Bradley, 30 M.J. 308 (C.M.A. 1990) (accused failed to establish selective prosecution where he was only member in theft ring to be tried; although the other members received only nonjudicial punishment, he was superior in rank and had a leading role in the ring and his accomplices testified against him).

United States v. Hagen, 25 M.J. 78 (C.M.A. 1987), *cert. denied,* 484 U.S. 1060 (1988) (accused failed to show discriminatory intent; he argued that he had been singled out for prosecution because of attempts to exercise his constitutional right to a trial).

United States v. Fox, 32 M.J. 744 (A.F.C.M.R. 1990) (no evidence of disparate treatment of trying accused officer on charges of fraternization with member of his command), *aff'd on reconsideration,* 32 M.J. 747 (A.F.C.M.R. 1991).

See generally Annotation, 45 A.L.R. Fed. 732 (1988); Kilgallin, "Prosecutorial Power, Abuse, and Misconduct," ARMY LAW., Apr. 1987, at 19.

283. *See* Bolting v. Sharpe, 347 U.S. 497 (1954). *See also* § 13-3(N).

§ 13-3(M)   MOTIONS PRACTICE   § 13-3(M)

for an impermissible reason, such as his race or religion or in an attempt to frustrate his constitutional rights.[284]

An example of a case in which the argument of selective prosecution was addressed is *United States v. Garwood*.[285] Private Garwood was charged with, *inter alia*, communicating with the enemy. The court rejected his arguments that he had been unconstitutionally singled out for prosecution while other American prisoners of war returning from Viet Nam were not prosecuted for making propaganda statements. The court noted the foregoing test and concluded that although there apparently had been a policy of nonprosecution during the administration of President Nixon, that policy had not been carried forward into succeeding administrations. Furthermore, there was no evidence that the government was acting in bad faith.[286]

Normally the convening authority should not be called to the stand to testify on the issue of possible vindictive prosecution[287] unless the defendant presents facts that are "sufficient to raise a reasonable doubt about the prosecutor's purpose."[288]

The military courts have also generally rejected arguments that the command is acting in a vindictive manner where it proceeds with a court-martial after the accused has declined to accept an offered Article 15 punishment.[289]

An accused might also move to dismiss the charges on the grounds of prosecutorial misconduct, i.e., the prosecution has acted in a fashion which has, or will, result in the denial of a fair trial.[290] It should be noted that the actions of the prosecution team or the SJA may also include elements of unlawful command influence, discussed in Chapter 6, and vindictiveness.[291] Indeed, the lines may blur. But a motion to dismiss may be appropriate where the misconduct is not clearly in the nature of "command influence" or where, as discussed *supra*, the accused has not been specifically targeted for selective prosecution or disparate treatment. Examples of possible prosecutorial misconduct

---

284. United States v. Henry, 42 M.J. 231 (1995)(accused did not waive selective prosecution issue by pleading guilty; he made plausible showing on appeal that he was targeted for prosecution because of his race; court remanded case for determination of issue); United States v. Garwood, 20 M.J. 148, 154 (C.M.A. 1985), *citing* United States v. Berrios, 501 F.2d 1207, 1211 (2d Cir. 1974). *See also* Wayte v. United States, 470 U.S. 598 (1985); Oyler v. Boles, 368 U.S. 448 (1962); United States v. Green, 37 M.J. 380 (C.M.A. 1993) (convening authority may not select case for prosecution simply because of race of accused; racial identifiers should not be used in either pretrial advice or post-trial recommendations); United States v. Brown, 41 M.J. 504 (Army Ct. Crim. App. 1994) (no showing that prosecution of black officer was result of intentional or purposeful discrimination); United States v. El-Amin, 38 M.J. 563 (A.F.C.M.R. 1993) (accused's argument of selective prosecution not valid; other actors who were not prosecuted were not similarly situated).
285. 20 M.J. 148 (C.M.A. 1985).
286. 20 M.J. 148 (C.M.A. 1985).
287. United States v. Hagen, 25 M.J. 78 (C.M.A. 1987), *cert. denied*, 484 U.S. 1060 (1988) (military judge denied accused's request to call the convening authority to the stand).
288. *Id.*, *citing* United States v. Falk, 479 F.2d 616, 620-21 (7th Cir. 1973) (*en banc*).
289. *See* United States v. Martino, 18 M.J. 526 (A.F.C.M.R. 1984); United States v. Blanchette, 17 M.J. 512 (A.F.C.M.R. 1983); United States v. Bass, 11 M.J. 545 (A.C.M.R. 1981).
290. *See, e.g.*, United States v. Meek, 40 M.J. 675 (N.M.C.M.R. 1994).
291. *See* § 6-3 *et seq*.

would include intimidation or improper coaching of witnesses, destroying or withholding evidence, or providing false or misleading information to the court, the defense, or other participants.[292]

When the issue is raised, the trial court should determine first, whether in fact misconduct has occurred.[293] What has been alleged as misconduct may be more in the nature of heavy handedness or overly aggressive behavior, which may not rise to the level of misconduct.[294] Second, assuming that actions do amount to misconduct, the court should determine whether the accused has been prejudiced.[295] The test is whether the prosecution's actions are so egregious as to deny the accused a fair trial.[296] Assuming that misconduct has occurred, which does not arise to the level required for dismissal of charges, the trial court may nonetheless impose lesser sanctions or remedies.

Because a motion to dismiss based upon selective prosecution relates to the preferral and referral of charges,[297] there is some authority for the view that if the motion is not made before pleas are entered, the issue will be considered waived.[298]

§ 13-3(N). Constitutional Challenges to the Underlying Statute, Regulation, or Order.

The Constitution of the United States contains a number of provisions designed to protect the individual from various types of government interference.[299] The statute, regulation, or order underlying the accused's prosecution may be challenged in a motion to dismiss on the grounds that it is inconsistent

---

292. *See, e.g.,* United States v. Loving, 41 M.J. 213 (1994) (defense unsuccessfully argued that prosecution had withheld exculpatory evidence and destroyed evidence).
293. United States v. Meek, 40 M.J. 675 (N.M.C.M.R. 1994).
294. *See, e.g.,* United States v. Meek, 40 M.J. 675 (N.M.C.M.R. 1994) (court noted that while some of the prosecutor's actions amounted to misconduct, others were examples of heavy-handedness; court commended trial judge for "thorough and sensitive manner" in which he handled issues; court also noted that counsel's actions left unfavorable impression of JAGs and undermined efforts of "fine young judge advocates to remain true to their representational duties in accordance with the rules of professional conduct").
295. United States v. Meek, 40 M.J. 675 (N.M.C.M.R. 1994).
296. United States v. Meek, 40 M.J. 675 (N.M.C.M.R. 1994); United States v. Sloan, 30 M.J. 741 (A.F.C.M.R. 1990); United States v. Hernandez, 779 F.2d 456 (8th Cir. 1985).
297. *See* R.C.M. 905(e). *See also* Chapters 6 and 8, *supra.*
298. United States v. El-Amin, 38 M.J. 563 (A.F.C.M.R. 1993) (accused's argument of selective prosecution considered waived where he did not raise objection before pleas at trial); United States v. Bradley, 30 M.J. 308, 310-311 (C.M.A. 1990) (suggestion that issue might be waived by not raising at trial).
299. United States v. Stuckey, 10 M.J. 347 (C.M.A. 1981) (Bill of Rights applicable to service members); United States v. Johnson, 21 M.J. 553 (A.F.C.M.R. 1985) (presumption exists that constitutional protections are equally applicable to civilian and military sectors). Whether, and to what extent, constitutional protections apply to service members has been the subject of some debate. *See, e.g.,* Warren, "The Bill of Rights and the Military," 37 N.Y. L. REV. 181 (1962). *See also* Henderson, "Courts-Martial and the Constitution: the Original Understanding," 71 HARV. L. REV. 1 (1957); Weiner, "Courts-Martial and the Bill of Rights: The Original Practice I," 72 HARV. L. REV. 293 (1958); Weiner, "Courts-Martial and the Bill of Rights: The Original Practice II," 72 HARV. L. REV. 266 (1958).

with the Constitution and is therefore invalid. Normally, failure to raise a constitutional challenge at the trial level will preclude appellate review of the issue.[300] This section discusses several of the more common constitutional grounds upon which a motion to dismiss charges may be based, and how such claims are reviewed in the military context.

§ 13-3(N)(1). Equal Protection.

The Fourteenth Amendment requires that states provide "equal protection of the laws" to all persons within their jurisdiction.[301] Although the Fifth Amendment, which is binding on the federal government, does not contain this language, its due process clause[302] does embody the principle that all persons who are similarly situated should be treated similarly by the government.[303] This facet of due process is known as the *equal protection component of the Fifth Amendment's Due Process Clause*,[304] and it establishes Constitutional standards for classifications drawn by the Federal government.[305] The government's motivation for creating classifications may vary from the constitutionally impermissible to the highly compelling.[306] Similarly, the preciseness of the classification may vary from the purely arbitrary distinction to an exact fit between the matter regulated and the persons subject to the regulation.[307]

---

300. *See* Menna v. New York, 423 U.S. 61 (1975). *Cf.* United States v. Hilton, 27 M.J. 323 (C.M.A. 1989) (accused's challenge to regulation could be considered on appeal because it questioned the very power of the government to prosecute him).

301. "No state shall ... deny to any person within its jurisdiction the equal protection of the laws." U.S. CONST. amend. XIV, cl. 1.

302. "No person shall ... be deprived of life, liberty, or property, without due process of law." U.S. CONST. amend. V. United States v. Scott, 32 M.J. 644 (C.G.C.M.R. 1991).

303. Vance v. Bradley, 440 U.S. 93 (1979); Hampton v. Mow Sun Wong, 426 U.S. 88 (1976); Frontiero v. Richardson, 411 U.S. 677 (1973); Bolling v. Sharpe, 347 U.S. 497 (1954); United States v. Means, 10 M.J. 162 (C.M.A. 1981); United States v. Larner, 1 M.J. 371 (C.M.A. 1976); United States v. Curtis, 28 M.J. 1074 (N.M.C.M.R. 1989) (en banc).

304. Vance v. Bradley, 440 U.S. 93 (1979).

305. United States v. Montgomery, 5 M.J. 832 (A.C.M.R. 1978); United States v. Penn, 4 M.J. 879 (N.C.M.R. 1978). The standards created by the principle of equal protection apply not only to laws themselves, but also to the manner in which they are applied. Yick Wo v. Hopkins, 118 U.S. 356 (1886). In the context of a court-martial, a claim that a law, regulation, or order is being enforced in violation of equal protection is known as an arbitrary or selective prosecution defense. United States v. Garwood, 16 M.J. 863 (N.M.C.M.R. 1983). This topic is discussed in § 13-3(M). Equal protection as applied to the states is not identical in all cases to its application as expressed by the Fifth Amendment to the Federal government. *See, e.g.,* Mathews v. Diaz, 426 U.S. 67 (1976) (Federal government has much greater Constitutional latitude in classification of aliens than states).

306. *Compare* Shapiro v. Thompson, 394 U.S. 618 (1969) (proffered interest in discouraging influx of indigents into state not constitutionally permissible) *with* Korematsu v. United States, 323 U.S. 214 (1944) (threat of invasion justified normally invalid interment on basis of ancestry).

307. Logan v. Zimmerman Brush Co., 455 U.S. 422, 443-44 (1982) (Powell, J., concurring) (administrative claims arbitrarily barred by random scheduling of hearings beyond deadline). *See generally* Tussman & ten-Brock, "The Equal Protection of the Laws," 37 CALIF. L. REV. 341 (1949).

The Supreme Court equal protection decisions reflect a "three-tiered" approach to resolving equal protection claims.[308] The bottom tier, often referred to as the *rational basis test*, is traditionally applied to economic and social legislation.[309] This test is characterized by a presumption that the classification in question is valid.[310] The challenger has the burden of proving that the classification is irrational or arbitrary,[311] or that its purpose is constitutionally impermissible.[312] To rebut the equal protection claim the government need only show some conceivably rational basis for the classification.[313]

In certain circumstances, however, courts will discard the traditional deference for acts of the coordinate branches[314] and demand proof from the government that the classification is a necessary means to further some extremely important or compelling government interest.[315] To invoke this highest level of review, the challenger must show that the government has intentionally discriminated[316] on the basis of certain criteria that have been historically used to discriminate against politically vulnerable groups based on stereotypi-

---

308. Dandridge v. Williams, 397 U.S. 471 (1970) (Marshall, J., dissenting) *(de facto* equal protection analysis is non-bracketed balancing of interests); United States v. Lecolst, 4 M.J. 800 (N.M.C.M.R. 1978).

309. City of Cleburne v. Cleburne Living Center, 473 U.S. 432 (1985); Rostker v. Goldberg, 453 U.S. 57 (1981) (criticizing tiered approach, Rehnquist, J., noted: "Announced degrees of 'deference' to legislative judgments, just as levels of 'scrutiny which this Court announces that it applies to particular classifications made by a legislative body, may all too readily become facile abstractions used to justify a result'").

310. City of New Orleans v. Dukes, 427 U.S. 297 (1976); United States v. Gray, 6 M.J. 972 (A.C.M.R. 1979); United States v. Penn, 4 M.J. 879 (N.C.M.R. 1978).

311. United States Dep t of Agriculture v. Moreno, 413 U.S. 528 (1973).

312. Zobel v. Williams, 457 U.S. 55 (1982); United States v. Curtis, 28 M.J. 1074 (N.M.C.M.R. 1989) (en banc) (court found rational basis for military's death penalty provisions; court noted that considering nature of military society it was certainly reasonable for Congress to provide for a heightened punishment for violating military criminal law, even though similar violations are not so punished in the civilian community); United States v. Robinson, 14 M.J. 903 (N.M.C.M.R. 1982).

313. McGowan v. Maryland, 366 U.S. 420 (1961); United States v. Lecolst, 4 M.J. 800 (N.M.C.M.R. 1978).

314. The principle motivation for judicial deference to acts of the legislature and executive is the desire to maintain an appropriate balance and separation between the branches of government and to avoid acting in areas beyond judicial expertise. City of New Orleans v. Dukes, 427 U.S. 297 (1976) (Court seeks to avoid acting as a "super-legislature"); Vance v. Bradley, 440 U.S. 93 (1979) (Court expects "democratic process" to rectify improvident acts of other branches); *cf.* Baker v. Carr, 369 U.S. 186 (1962) (Court discusses separation of powers as grounds for judicial abstention from claims that involve political questions). These concerns are particularly weighty in the sphere of military and foreign affairs. Chappell v. Wallace, 462 U.S. 296 (1983); Rostker v. Goldberg, 453 U.S. 57 (1981); Gilligan v. Morgan, 413 U.S. 1 (1973); Martelon v. Temple, 747 F.2d 1348 (10th Cir. 1984).

315. City of Cleburne v. Cleburne Living Center, 473 U.S. 432 (1985).

316. Official misconduct in the form of discriminatory intent is the evil that offends the principle of equal protection, and is the *sine qua non* of a violation thereof. Washington v. Davis, 426 U.S. 229 (1976); United States v. McGraner, 13 M.J. 408 (C.M.A. 1982). Such intent need not be directly shown, however, but may be inferred from the circumstances. Arlington Heights v. Metropolitan Housing Dev. Corp., 429 U.S. 252 (1977) (discriminatory impact plus evidence of parallel intent as manifested by history of government action and substantive or procedural deviations from the norm may be sufficient to allow inference of unlawful purpose).

§ 13-3(N)(1) MOTIONS PRACTICE § 13-3(N)(1)

cal or antipathic thinking, thus creating a *suspect class*,[317] or that its classification significantly burdens or penalizes the exercise of a fundamental right.[318] For instance, classifications based on suspect criteria such as race,[319] alienage,[320] or national origin,[321] or which interfere with such fundamental rights as procreation[322] or voting[323] or which penalize the exercise of the right to travel[324] are all subject to this highest level of review, often labeled *strict scrutiny*.

---

317. San Antonio School Dist. v. Rodriguez, 411 U.S. 1, 28 (1973) (in rejecting an equal protection claim the Court enumerated the "traditional indicia of suspectness: the class is [not] saddled with such disabilities, or subjected to such a history of purposeful unequal treatment, or relegated to such a position of political powerlessness as to command extraordinary protection from the majoritarian political process"); United States v. Carolene Products Co., 304 U.S. 144, 152-53 n.4 (1938) (Court suggests that official acts that diminish the political fortitude of "discrete and insular minorities" may require "more searching judicial inquiry" than traditionally afforded government classifications). *See also* City of Cleburne v. Cleburne Living Center, 473 U.S. 432 (1985) (classification based on mental retardation not suspect); Plyler v. Doe, 457 U.S. 202 (1982) (Court reviewed various attributes of suspectness); Craig v. Boren, 429 U.S. 190 (1976) (classifications based on sex are subject to higher than traditional deferential review because they are typically based on inaccurate stereotypes and are often not germane to the actual trait sought to be regulated); Massachusetts Bd. of Retirement v. Murgia, 427 U.S. 307 (1976) (classification based on age not suspect). In a case of first impression for the military courts, the court in United States v. Curtis, 28 M.J. 1074 (N.M.C.M.R. 1989) (en banc), held that the death penalty does not infringe a fundamental right so as to trigger strict scrutiny. The Court of Military Appeals later affirmed on other grounds, 32 M.J. 252 (C.M.A. 1991). *See also* 33 M.J. 101 (C.M.A. 1991).

318. Snyder v. Massachusetts, 291 U.S. 97 (1934) (a fundamental right is a "... principle of justice so rooted in the traditions and conscience of our people as to be ranked fundamental"); Palko v. Connecticut, 302 U.S. 319 (1937) (whether or not expressly recognized by the Constitution, fundamental rights are "implicit in the concept of ordered liberty" and are protected by the Constitution); *see also* Shapiro v. Thompson, 394 U.S. 618 (1969) (fundamental right to travel derived from American tradition and implicit in the Constitution as a whole); Zablocki v. Redhail, 434 U.S. 374 (1978); United States v. Rodriguez-Amy, 19 M.J. 177 (C.M.A. 1985); United States v. Penn, 4 M.J. 879 (N.C.M.R. 1978).

319. Palmore v. Sidoti, 466 U.S. 429 (1984); Loving v. Virginia, 388 U.S. 1 (1967); Hirabayashi v. United States, 320 U.S. 81 (1943).

320. Yick Wo v. Hopkins, 118 U.S. 356 (1886) (the Fourteenth Amendment protects all "persons" from discrimination on the basis of race, color, or nationality); Graham v. Richardson, 403 U.S. 365 (1971) (as to the states, aliens are a suspect class); *but see* Mathews v. Diaz, 426 U.S. 67 (1976) (as to federal government, aliens are not a suspect class).

321. Graham v. Richardson, 403 U.S. 365 (1971); Hirabayashi v. United States, 320 U.S. 81 (1943); Yick Wo v. Hopkins, 118 U.S. 356 (1886).

322. Zablocki v. Redhail, 434 U.S. 374 (1978) (classification that "directly and substantially" interfered with fundamental right to marry is invalid as not necessary to achieve asserted state interests); Skinner v. Oklahoma, 316 U.S. 535 (1942) (the right to marry and to procreate are "basic civil rights of man").

323. Lubin v. Panish, 415 U.S. 709 (1974); Harper v. Virginia State Bd. of Elections, 383 U.S. 663 (1966); Reynolds v. Sims, 377 U.S. 533 (1964); Wesberry v. Sanders, 376 U.S. 1 (1964).

324. Shapiro v. Thompson, 394 U.S. 618 (1969) (durational residency requirement struck down as unjustified penalty for exercise of right to migrate into state). *See also* Memorial Hosp. v. Maricopa County, 415 U.S. 250 (1974) (state denials of fundamental political rights, such as franchise, or basic necessities of life, such as medical care or welfare benefits, that penalize migration are subject to strict scrutiny); *but see* Vlandis v. Kline, 412 U.S. 441 (1973) (states may reasonably deny preferred residence status to persons entering state to attend state educational facilities).

The middle-tier standard of review is reserved for those classifications that exhibit some of the indicia of a suspect class,[325] but are more susceptible to permissible government regulation[326] or do not have a history of aggravated government abuse.[327] These quasi-suspect classifications are valid if the government meets its burden of showing that its classification is a narrowly tailored means of achieving some important or substantial government objection.[328] This standard has been most commonly applied to classifications based on gender[329] and illegitimacy.[330]

The courts have generally not altered the civilian equal protection analysis for use in the military.[331] Once the courts have determined the appropriate standard of review, however, the asserted military interests are usually sufficiently important to satisfy any of the three tiers.[332] In *United States v. Courtney*,[333] one of only a few instances of successful equal protection challenges in the military, the defendant prevailed on a claim that his drug prosecution

---

325. Classifications on the basis of sex or illegitimacy are suspect because they are seldom germane to one's ability to perform or contribute to society. Mathews v. Lucas, 427 U.S. 495 (1976); Frontiero v. Richardson, 411 U.S. 677 (1973).

326. *See, e.g.*, Michael M. v. Sonoma County Superior Ct., 450 U.S. 464 (1981) (challenge against statutory rape law that punished only males rejected because with respect to teenage sexual activity males and females are not similarly situated); Rostker v. Goldberg, 453 U.S. 57 (1981) (women may be excluded from duty to register for draft because women and men are not similarly situated with respect to fitness for combat); United States v. Sykes, 11 M.J. 766 (N.M.C.M.R. 1981) (gender-based classification in indecent assault offense not denial of equal protection).

327. Mathews v. Lucas, 427 U.S. 495 (1976) (classifications on the basis of illegitimacy are not subject to the highest level of scrutiny because this "discrimination has never approached the severity or pervasiveness of the historic and political discrimination against women and negroes").

328. Craig v. Boren, 429 U.S. 190 (1976); United States v. Scott, 32 M.J. 644 (C.G.C.M.R. 1991) (court rejected argument that Article 120(b) (carnal knowledge) violated equal protection because it only applies to conduct by males); United States v. Sykes, 11 M.J. 766 (N.M.C.M.R. 1981).

329. Craig v. Boren, 429 U.S. 190 (1976); Reed v. Reed, 404 U.S. 71 (1971); United States v. Harris, 8 M.J. 52 (C.M.A. 1979); United States v. Scott, 32 M.J. 644 (C.G.C.M.R. 1991) (rejected argument that Article 120(b) (carnal knowledge) violated equal protection because it does not apply to females); United States v. Sykes, 11 M.J. 766 (N.M.C.M.R. 1981); *but see* Geduldig v. Aiello, 417 U.S. 484 (1974) (classification based on condition of pregnancy not suspect).

330. Lalli v. Lalli, 439 U.S. 259 (1978).

331. *See, e.g.*, United States v. Rodriguez-Amy, 19 M.J. 177 (C.M.A. 1985); United States v. Means, 10 M.J. 162 (C.M.A. 1981); United States v. Robinson, 14 M.J. 903 (N.M.C.M.R. 1982); United States v. Penn, 4 M.J. 879 (N.C.M.R. 1978); *but see* Goldman v. Weinberger, 475 U.S. 503 (1986) (O'Connor, J., dissenting) (chastises majority for failure to articulate analytical basis for decision and argues that military needs can and should be accommodated within First Amendment jurisprudence developed in civilian sector); Rostker v. Goldberg, 453 U.S. 57 (1981) (Court suggests that due process limitations on federal government may differ as applied to military).

332. *See, e.g.*, Goldman v. Weinberger, 475 U.S. 503 (1986) (Court considered expert testimony that military regulations that prohibit visible religious apparel are counterproductive to military interests to be irrelevant); Rostker v. Goldberg, 453 U.S. 57 (1981) (Court justified exclusion of women from draft on Congressional determination that women are ineligible for combat without consideration of what factors render women unfit); United States v. Young, 1 M.J. 433 (C.M.A. 1976) (court dismissed attack on male/female differential in hair-length regulations, saying "A sound argument can lose its appeal when pushed to unappealing extremes").

333. 1 M.J. 438 (C.M.A. 1976).

under Article 134[334] instead of Article 92[335] was arbitrary and unconstitutional by showing that the vast majority of similar offenses had been prosecuted under Article 92 and that the military authorities lacked any reasonable basis or regulatory guidance for the prosecutorial decision.[336] Similar claims have failed, however, where the authorities have articulated some credible basis for the charging decision[337] or where regulatory or statutory guidance has dispelled the claim of wholly arbitrary enforcement.[338]

§ 13-3(N)(2). Vagueness: Lack of Fair Notice.

The Due Process Clause of the Fifth Amendment requires that laws be drawn with at least a minimum level of specificity.[339] A statute, regulation, or order may be declared *void for vagueness* if (1) it does not provide fair notice to the person within its scope,[340] the conduct prohibited or excluded from prohibition[341] or the penalty to be assessed;[342] (2) its terms by their ambiguity

---

334. Art. 134, U.C.M.J.
335. Art. 92, U.C.M.J.
336. United States v. Courtney, 1 M.J. 438 (C.M.A. 1976).
337. *See, e.g.,* United States v. Means, 10 M.J. 162 (C.M.A. 1981) (officer status may reasonably be taken into account in decision to prosecute); United States v. Lecolst, 4 M.J. 800 (N.M.C.M.R. 1978) (statutory suspension of right to refuse nonjudicial punishment for those attached to a vessel justified by non-feasibility of providing court-martial).
338. *See, e.g.,* United States v. Loving, 34 M.J. 956 (A.C.M.R. 1992) (court rejected argument that accused was denied equal protection because he was subjected to the death penalty; if he had been tried in federal court, he would not have been so subjected); United States v. Casteel, 17 M.J. 713 (N.M.C.M.R. 1983) (regulatory preference for charging under Art. 134 cured potential equal protection violation); United States v. Dillard, 4 M.J. 577 (A.C.M.R. 1977) (regulatory bar on charging heroin offenses under Art. 92 satisfied equal protection concerns expressed in *Courtney*). *See also* United States v. Hoesing, 5 M.J. 355 (C.M.A. 1978) (congressionally created independence between services justifies inter-service disparity in punitive regulations); United States v. Moultak, 21 M.J. 822 (N.M.C.M.R. 1985), *aff'd on other grounds*, 24 M.J. 316 (C.M.A. 1987) (distinctions between missions of services and congressional grant of independent authority to Secretaries of services justifies inter-service disparity in standards of conduct).
339. Connally v. General Constr. Co., 269 U.S. 385, 391 (1926) (the Court declared that "a statute which either forbids or requires the doing of an act in terms so vague that men of common intelligence must necessarily guess at its meaning and differ as to its application" violates the first essential of due process). *See also* Grayned v. City of Rockford, 408 U.S. 104 (1972); Lanzetta v. New Jersey, 306 U.S. 451 (1939).
United States v. Wine, 28 M.J. 688 (A.F.C.M.R. 1989) (although court indicated that vagueness and overbreadth were in issue, it decided that an order to the accused to disassociate himself from a friend's wife was reasonable).
United States v. Johnson, 27 M.J. 798 (A.F.C.M.R. 1988) (void for vagueness argument was not available to accused charged with aggravated assault, transmission of AIDS).
340. United States v. Cardiff, 344 U.S. 174 (1952) (the Court noted that "words which are vague and fluid may be as much a trap for the innocent as the ancient laws of Caligula").
341. Grayned v. City of Rockford, 408 U.S. 104 (1972) (laws must give persons a reasonable opportunity to know what is prohibited so as to steer between lawful and unlawful conduct). *See also* Rose v. Locke, 423 U.S. 48 (1975); Baggett v. Bullitt, 377 U.S. 360 (1964); United States v. Harriss, 347 U.S. 612 (1954); United States v. Cohen Grocery Co., 255 U.S. 81 (1921); Culver v. Secretary of Air Force, 389 F. Supp. 331 (D. D.C. 1975).
342. United States v. Evans, 333 U.S. 483 (1948) (statute void that allowed a "multiple choice" of "possible, yet inconsistent" interpretations of the penalty to be assessed).

§ 13-3(N)(2)

grant unbridled discretion to enforcement authorities;[343] or (3) its imprecision endangers First Amendment rights.[344] This section deals with the first of these types, as the latter two are dealt with in the sections on selective prosecution[345] and the First Amendment,[346] respectively.

Three general rules are applicable to vagueness claims. First, courts favor statutory interpretations that comport with the Constitution, avoiding if possible those readings that raise Constitutional infirmities.[347] Second, laws are not inspected for vagueness in a vacuum, but rather in light of their judicial interpretation and application.[348] Third, absent the situations where the courts have relaxed standing rules to protect First Amendment interests, the defense must show the statute to be incapable of conveying fair notice in any circumstance,[349] or that the statute, as applied, failed to provide to the defendant fair and reasonable notice of the illicit nature of the conduct.[350] It is not enough to show that the statute, though generally ambiguous, might be applied unconstitutionally in a relatively small number of circumstances not before the court.[351]

In *Parker v. Levy*,[352] the Supreme Court stated that laws in the military context need not be as precise as criminal statutes in the civilian sector.[353] Rejecting a vagueness attack on Articles 133 and 134, the Court reasoned that

---

343. Grayned v. City of Rockford, 408 U.S. 104 (1972) (the effect of such discretion is to "impermissibly delegate basic policy matters to policemen, judges, and juries for resolution on an ad hoc and subjective basis"); United States v. Reese, 92 U.S. 214 (1876) (Court analogizes statute that grants such discretion to a "net" that ensnares all possible offenders). *See also* Smith v. Goguen, 415 U.S. 566 (1974); Papchristou v. City of Jacksonville, 405 U.S. 156 (1972).

344. Baggett v. Bullitt, 377 U.S. 360 (1964); NAACP v. Button, 371 U.S. 415 (1963).

345. *See* § 13-3(M).

346. *See* § 13-3(N)(3).

347. United States Civil Service Comm'n v. National Ass'n of Letter Carriers, 413 U.S. 548 (1973) (judicial preference for interpretations that raise no questions of invalidity is an aspect of the general rule of deference to acts of the legislature). *See also* United States v. National Dairy Prod. Corp., 372 U.S. 29 (1963); United States v. Harriss, 347 U.S. 612 (1954); Blodgett v. Holden, 275 U.S. 142 (1927) (Holmes, J., concurring); Culver v. Secretary of Air Force, 389 F. Supp. 331 (D. D.C. 1975).

348. Rose v. Locke, 423 U.S. 48 (1975) (statutory phrase "crime against nature" provides sufficiently ascertainable standard of conduct in light of traditional common-law usage).

349. Such is the challenger's burden when the statute is attacked on its face. Hoffman Estates v. Flipside, 455 U.S. 489 (1982); Smith v. Goguen, 415 U.S. 566 (1974). In United States v. Reed, 24 M.J. 80 (C.M.A. 1987), Chief Judge Everett, in a concurring opinion, discussed at some length the constitutionality of a Navy regulation that required servicemembers to report criminal activity. In his view, that regulation did not adequately apprise the accused that failure to report offenses was criminally punishable.

350. Hoffman Estates v. Flipside, 455 U.S. 489 (1982); Broadrick v. Oklahoma, 413 U.S. 601 (1973); United States v. Mayfield, 21 M.J. 418 (C.M.A. 1986); United States v. Van Steenwyk, 21 M.J. 795 (N.M.C.M.R. 1985).

351. United States v. National Dairy Prod. Corp., 372 U.S. 29 (1963); United States v. Harriss, 347 U.S. 612 (1954).

352. 417 U.S. 733 (1974).

353. Parker v. Levy, 417 U.S. 733 (1974) (proper standard of review for a vagueness challenge to the Articles of the U.C.M.J. is the standard which applies to criminal statutes regulating economic affairs, citing United States v. National Dairy Prod. Corp., 372 U.S. 29 (1963)). *See also* Culver v. Secretary of Air Force, 389 F. Supp. 331 (D. D.C. 1975).

the broad and inexact language of the Articles was necessary to allow military authorities to respond effectively to all possible threats to military discipline, and that the Articles were therefore not facially violative of due process.[354] The Court further found that, as applied, the requisite fair notice could be supplied by military customs, regulations, and other sources that serve to inform servicemen of required behavioral standards.[355] As a result of this approach, only in a few cases have military defendants been able to establish that they were reasonably unaware that their conduct might subject them to prosecution. In *United States v. Johanns*,[356] for instance, the Court of Military Appeals accepted the finding of the Air Force Court of Military Review that due process would not allow a conviction for fornication with a non-subordinate enlisted person under Articles 133 and 134 because historically such relationships had been tolerated by Air Force custom.[357] *See also* § 2-8.

§ 13-3(N)(3). First Amendment: Speech, Religion, and Association.

The most cherished liberty is that provided by the First Amendment:[358] the freedoms of speech, press, and religion, as well as a complement of penumbral rights of association. The language of the amendment, however, does not absolutely proscribe governmental interference with the protected activities.[359] Rather, it establishes guidelines that restrict the power of the Federal government to regulate or prohibit such activity.[360] A statute, regulation, or order may be challenged on the grounds that it is inconsistent with these guidelines. The following sections describe the operation of the First Amendment as it applies to government regulation of speech, religion, and association, respectively, and how these guidelines are altered when translated into the military context.

Government Regulation of Speech. The threshold issue in any First Amendment claim is whether speech is involved at all.[361] Standing alone, spoken and written communication readily qualifies as speech.[362] Most First Amendment

---

354. Parker v. Levy, 417 U.S. 733 (1974). *Cf.* United States v. Reed, 24 M.J. 80 (C.M.A. 1987) (Everett, C.J., concurring) (Navy regulation requiring servicemembers to report offenses violated due process for lack of fair notice). *See also* §§ 2-5 and 2-6.
355. Parker v. Levy, 417 U.S. 733 (1974). *See also* United States v. Adames, 21 M.J. 465 (C.M.A. 1986).
356. 20 M.J. 155 (C.M.A. 1985).
357. 20 M.J. 155 (C.M.A. 1985).
358. West Virginia State Bd. of Educ. v. Barnette, 319 U.S. 624 (1943); Abrams v. United States, 250 U.S. 616 (1919) (Holmes, J., dissenting).
359. Nebraska Press Ass'n v. Stuart, 427 U.S. 539 (1976); Dennis v. United States, 341 U.S. 494 (1951) (Frankfurter, J., concurring); Terminiello v. Chicago, 337 U.S. 1 (1949); Near v. Minnesota, 283 U.S. 697 (1931); *but see* Beauharnais v. Illinois, 343 U.S. 250 (1952) (Black, J., dissenting) (argues that the unqualified language of the amendment should yield absolute protection).
360. *Ex parte* Jackson, 96 U.S. 727 (1878) (First Amendment limits the power of Congress to restrict access to the postal system).
361. United States v. O'Brien, 391 U.S. 367 (1968).
362. Winters v. New York, 333 U.S. 507 (1948) ("sanguinary or salacious publications [are] as much entitled to the protection of free speech as the best of literature").

challenges, however, involve either a mixture of conduct and speech or pure conduct that is claimed to convey protected expression.[363] In general, conduct has a speech component if it is intended to convey a message and is reasonably perceived as conveying such a message.[364] The challenger carries the initial burden of showing that the activity at issue deserves the protection of the First Amendment either because it is speech or because it is closely intertwined with speech.[365]

Once the challenger has implicated the First Amendment by showing that at least a component of the regulated activity is speech, the speech will then be classified according to the degree of constitutional protection it merits.[366] Obscenity,[367] "fighting words,"[368] and defamation,[369] for instance, though un-

---

363. United States v. Eichman, 110 S. Ct. 2404 (1990) (flag burning protected under First Amendment as speech); Texas v. Johnson, 491 U.S. 397 (1989) (burning a U.S. flag was protected speech); Clark v. Community for Creative Non-Violence, 468 U.S. 288 (1984) (Court assumes sleeping in park as part of protest is a form of expression); Tinker v. Des Moines School Dist., 393 U.S. 503 (1969) (wearing protest armbands is a form of "pure speech"); United States v. O'Brien, 391 U.S. 367 (1968) (act of burning draft card included expressive aspect); Brown v. Louisiana, 383 U.S. 131 (1966) (peaceful sit-in demonstration in public library is a form of speech).

364. Spence v. Washington, 418 U.S. 405 (1974) (display of flag where expression was intended and reasonably perceived was protected by the First Amendment); United States v. O'Brien, 391 U.S. 367 (1968) (intention to convey message will not serve to bring all possible varieties of conduct within the protection of the First Amendment).

365. The Supreme Court has fashioned a separate analysis for symbolic speech. United States v. O'Brien, 391 U.S. 367 (1968) (when conduct contains both expressive and non-expressive aspects, the government may regulate the non-speech component if the regulation serves an important or substantial government interest, is not intended to suppress the expressive component, and interfered with that expression only to the extent necessary to achieve its purpose). *See, e.g.,* United States v. McDavid, 37 M.J. 861 (A.F.C.M.R. 1993) (conviction of accused for possessing recipe for making drugs did not violate his First Amendment rights; he was not charged with writing the recipe but instead for possessing it with a criminal intent);United States v. Wilson, 33 M.J. 797 (A.C.M.R. 1991) (accused's First Amendment rights were not violated when he was convicted for blowing nose on American flag while member of detail; while conduct was expressive speech, under *O'Brien* test, the government regulation of that speech was justified).

366. Federal Communications Commission v. Pacifica Foundation, 438 U.S. 726 (1978) (each category of speech must be weighed in light of its value to society); Chaplinski v. New Hampshire, 315 U.S. 568 (1942) (Court singles out categories of speech as deserving of no protection). *Cf.* United States v. Orben, 28 M.J. 172 (C.M.A. 1989) (accused showed non-pornographic pictures to young children; the court noted that the First Amendment right to communicate to young children is less extensive than the right to communicate to adults and concluded that under facts, the accused was guilty of taking indecent liberties).

367. An obscene work is one that portrays sexual conduct in a patently offensive manner, that appeals as a whole to prurient interests, and that lacks any serious literary, artistic, political, or scientific value. Miller v. California, 458 U.S. 747 (1972). Once defined by the factfinder as such, the speech is without constitutional protection. Roth v. United States, 354 U.S. 476 (1957). *But see* Jenkins v. Georgia, 418 U.S. 153 (1974) (film not obscene as a matter of law). *See also* New York v. Ferber, 458 U.S. 747 (1982) (works portraying children engaged in sexual conduct need not be patently offensive or considered as a whole to be defined as obscene).

368. The government may regulate expression that advocates and is likely to produce immediate illegal consequences. Brandenburg v. Ohio, 396 U.S. 444 (1969) (mere advocacy, even of illegal purposes, cannot be prohibited absent likelihood of imminent unlawful result); Chaplinski

---

369. Beauharnais v. Illinois, 343 U.S. 250 (1952) (libel not protected by Constitution); *but see* New York Times Co. v. Sullivan, 376 U.S. 254 (1964) (common law of libel inadequately safeguards the speech of persons who criticize public officials).

questionably forms of expression, receive no protection from the First Amendment.[370] Political speech, on the other hand, is the most highly prized variety of speech.[371] Some categories of speech, such as commercial speech[372] and indecent speech[373] are given only moderate protection from government regulation. Once the challenger has shown that the speech is of a variety that is entitled to some degree of constitutional protection, the courts will balance the First Amendment interests involved against the interests served by the regulation of the speech in light of the nature of the regulation[374] and the degree of accuracy with which the regulation serves those interests.[375]

---

v. New Hampshire, 315 U.S. 568 (1942) (government may limit words which by their very utterance inflict injury or tend to incite an immediate breach of the peace); *but see* United States v. Priest, 21 C.M.A. 564, 45 C.M.R. 338 (1972) (holds *Brandenburg* prohibition against government regulation of mere advocacy inapplicable in military context), *aff'd sub nom.* Priest v. Secretary of Navy, 570 F.2d 1013 (D.C. Cir. 1977).

See also Lewis v. New Orleans, 415 U.S. 130 (1970) (statute that forbade casting "opprobrious" language at police was struck down as overbroad because it allowed punishment of speech which did not of itself cause injury or threaten imminent danger of unlawful disorder); Cohen v. California, 403 U.S. 15 (1971) (wearing of jacket with words "F the Draft" emblazoned on back in courthouse corridor could not be punished because there was no threat of immediate breach of the peace and because offended viewers could simply avert their eyes); Terminiello v. Chicago, 337 U.S. 1 (1949) (central tenet of First Amendment is that society must risk tolerance of colorful or provocative speech); United States v. Davis, 37 M.J. 152 (C.M.A. 1993) (accused guilty of uttering provoking words under Article 117).

370. Chaplinski v. New Hampshire, 315 U.S. 568 (1942).

371. Philadelphia Newspapers, Inc. v. Hepps, 475 U.S. 767 (1986) (constitutional value of publication of matters of public concern requires that private-figure defamation plaintiffs bear the burden of proving the matter at issue false); Connick v. Myers, 461 U.S. 138 (1983) (courts should scrutinize dismissal of public employees for political expression, but should not normally be concerned with dismissals for expression of private matters); New York Times Co. v. Sullivan, 376 U.S. 254 (1964) (public officials pursuing defamation action against publication of statement of public concern must prove higher level of fault). *See also* Blameuser v. Andrews, 630 F.2d 538 (7th Cir. 1980) (ROTC student's views, though abhorrent, were political in nature and thus at the core of speech protected by the First Amendment).

372. Virginia State Bd. of Pharmacy v. Virginia Citizens Consumer Council, Inc., 425 U.S. 748 (1976) (holding that commercial speech is protected by First Amendment); *but see* Dun & Bradstreet, Inc. v. Greenmoss Builders, Inc., 472 U.S. 749 (1985) (commercial speech is hardy because motivated by profit and thus does not require the special protective standards afforded speech on public issues in defamation actions); Bates v. State Bar of Arizona, 433 U.S. 350 (1977) (resilient nature of commercial speech grounds for not extending to it the protection of the overbreadth doctrine).

373. Federal Communications Comm'n v. Pacifica Foundation, 438 U.S. 726 (1978) (because of the lesser value of indecent speech in the eyes of the Constitution it is subject to heightened restriction in its access to the airwaves); *but see* Kingsley Int'l Pictures Corp. v. Regents of the University of New York, 360 U.S. 684 (1959) (advocacy of adultery no less protected by First Amendment than political speech); United States v. Moore, 38 M.J. 490 (C.M.A. 1994) (accused found guilty of communicating indecent speech; court equated indecent and obscene speech); United States v. Gill, 40 M.J. 835 (A.F.C.M.R. 1994) (court rejected argument that conviction for indecent speech violated First Amendment because it was private speech between two consenting adults).

374. Organization for a Better Austin v. Keefe, 402 U.S. 415 (1971) (injunction that forecloses

375. Secretary of State of Maryland v. Joseph H. Munson Co., 467 U.S. 947 (1984) (lack of correlation between breadth of statute regulating speech and breadth of trait being regulated violate First Amendment); Erznoznik v. City of Jacksonville, 422 U.S. 205 (1975) (ordinance that

Because the central purpose of the First Amendment is to protect and promote the dissemination of ideas,[376] regulations that focus on the content of the expression or that foreclose speech before it is exercised are presumptively invalid.[377] Where the regulation is content-neutral, the government can regulate the time, place, or manner of conduct related to expression as long as the regulation only incidentally interferes with the expression, is narrowly-tailored to promote legitimate government interests, and does not unduly foreclose the availability of other avenues of communication.[378] This standard applies to both traditional and designated public forums, that is, public prop-

---

speech in advance of its expression is an impermissible form of government regulation of speech); Secretary of State of Maryland v. Joseph H. Munson Co., 467 U.S. 947 (1984) (ordinance that requires licensure as a predicate to expression is inherently suspect). See also Erznoznik v. City of Jacksonville, 422 U.S. 205 (1975) (sensibilities of passersby not sufficient to justify banning of all outdoor showings of films containing nudity).

---

prohibited outdoor showing of films containing nudity was impermissibly sweeping in application either as a means to protect the sensibilities of passersby or to prevent distraction of motorists because it banned all nudity regardless of the context and applied to films viewed from any public area, not just roadways). Cf. Grayned v. City of Rockford, 408 U.S. 104 (1972) (although antipicketing ordinance was not unconstitutionally vague or overbroad, it violated the Equal Protection Clause by proscribing all but labor picketing).

376. New York Times Co. v. Sullivan, 376 U.S. 254 (1964) (establishing rule that public officials must make elevated showing of culpability to prevail against critics in defamation action); Terminiello v. Chicago, 337 U.S. 1 (1949) (robust exchange of ideas is key to preservation of democracy); Martin v. Struthers, 319 U.S. 141 (1943) (facile dissemination of information is vital to preservation of free society); West Virginia State Bd. of Educ. v. Barnette, 319 U.S. 624 (1943) (expressive diversity prevents establishment of enforced orthodoxy).

377. Carey v. Brown, 447 U.S. 455 (1980) (statute impermissibly hinged on content of speech); Vance v. Universal Amusement Co., 445 U.S. 308 (1980) (government burden of justifying prior restraints is much greater than that imposed for criminal penalties exacted after the fact); Organization for a Better Austin v. Keefe, 402 U.S. 415 (1971) (prior restraint of speech carries a heavy presumption of invalidity). That is not to say, however, that content may not be considered for the purpose of classifying the speech. See New York v. Ferber, 458 U.S. 747 (1982) (libel and child pornography given as examples of speech that may be classified according to content because "within the confines of the given classification, the evil to be restricted so overwhelmingly outweighs the expressive interests, if any, at stake, that no process of case by case adjudication is required"). See also City of Renton v. Playtime Theatres, Inc., 475 U.S. 41 (1986); Carlson v. Schlesinger, 511 F.2d 1327 (D.C. Cir. 1975). Likewise, in special circumstances the prior restraint of speech may be permissible. New York Times Co. v. United States, 403 U.S. 713 (1971) (Brennan, J., concurring) (government must prove that the expression will "inevitably, directly and immediately" cause grave consequences in order to justify restraining order on publication).

The presumption of invalidity that accompanies prior restraints in the civilian sector is less operative in the military sphere. See, e.g., Brown v. Glines, 444 U.S. 348 (1980) (upholding validity of prior approval requirement for distribution); Dash v. Commanding General, 307 F. Supp. 849 (D.S.C. 1969) (upholding right of base commander to prohibit on-base distribution), aff'd per curiam, 429 F.2d 427 (4th Cir. 1970), cert. denied, 401 U.S. 981 (1971); United States v. Voorhees, 4 C.M.A. 509, 16 C.M.R. 83 (C.M.A. 1954) (upholding security clearance restriction on right of military personnel to publish).

378. Perry Educ. Ass'n v. Perry Local Educators Ass'n, 460 U.S. 37 (1983); Carlson v. Schlesinger, 511 F.2d 1327 (D.C. Cir. 1975). See also United States v. Phillips, 38 M.J. 641 (A.C.M.R. 1993), aff'd on other grounds, 42 M.J. 346 (1995) (denial of accused's request for copy of Wiccan "bible" while incarcerated in civilian jail did not infringe impermissibly on First Amendment rights); United States v. Hoard, 12 M.J. 563 (A.C.M.R. 1981) (regulation prohibiting unofficial relationships between training center personnel and trainees did not violate freedom of speech because it was primarily directed at conduct and only incidentally infringed expression).

erty that by "long tradition or government fiat" has been held open for public expression.[379] Public property that has not been so held open, however, may be preserved by the government for its intended purpose, and reasonable restrictions on the time, manner, and place of the expression are permissible if not wholly based on official displeasure with the content of the expression.[380]

Members of the armed forces, by virtue of their status as public employees[381] and the special needs of the military,[382] do not enjoy the degree of protection that the First Amendment affords civilians.[383] The Supreme Court has stated that in the military context, speech loses any constitutional protection that it might otherwise have if it "undermines the effectiveness of response to command,"[384] and that military authorities have wide discretion to

---

379. *See, e.g.,* Hague v. CIO, 307 U.S. 496 (1939) (traditional public forums are those that "have immemorially been held in trust for the use of the public, and, time out of mind, have been used for purpose of assembly, communicating thoughts between citizens, and discussing public questions"); Widmar v. Vincent, 454 U.S. 263 (1981) (university could not deny access to facilities that it had held open for use by diverse student groups, thus designating a public forum). *Compare* Flower v. United States, 407 U.S. 197 (1972) (leafletter could not be prevented from distribution on street on military base because the military had "abandoned" its right to exclude such activity from the environs) *with* Greer v. Spock, 424 U.S. 828 (1976) (prohibition of political speakers from base upheld because the military had not created a public forum by permitting such activity previously).

See also Rosenow, "Open House or Open Forum: When Commanders Invite the Public on Base," 24 A.F. L. Rev. 260 (1984).

380. Los Angeles v. Taxpayers for Vincent, 104 S. Ct. 2118 (1984); Heffron v. Int'l Society for Krishna Consciousness, Inc., 452 U.S. 640 (1981); Greer v. Spock, 424 U.S. 828 (1976). *See also* Cruden & Lederer, "The First Amendment and Military Installations," 1984 Det. C.L. Rev. 845 (1985).

381. Connick v. Myers, 461 U.S. 138 (1983); Kelley v. Johnson, 425 U.S. 238 (1976); United States Civil Service Comm'n v. National Ass'n of Letter Carriers, 413 U.S. 548 (1973); Pickering v. Board of Educ., 391 U.S. 563 (1968); Baron v. Meloni, 602 F. Supp. 614 (D.N.Y. 1984); *but see* Garrity v. New Jersey, 385 U.S. 493 (1967) (public employees receive full constitutional protection).

382. Brown v. Glines, 444 U.S. 348 (1980); Parker v. Levy, 417 U.S. 733 (1974).

383. Parker v. Levy, 417 U.S. 733 (1974); Cortright v. Resor, 447 F.2d 245 (2d Cir. 1971); *contra* Carlson v. Schlesinger, 511 F.2d 1327 (D.C. Cir. 1975) (Bazelon, C.J., dissenting) (argues that courts have abdicated duty to apply meaningful review to First Amendment claims).

See also United States v. Priest, 21 C.M.A. 564, 45 C.M.R. 338 (1972), aff'd sub nom. Priest v. Secretary of Navy, 570 F.2d 1013 (D.C. Cir. 1977). *See generally* Aldrich, "Article 88 of the Uniform Code of Military Justice—Military Muzzle or Just a Restraint on Military Muscle," 33 U.C.L.A. L. Rev. 1189 (1986); Sherman, "The Military Courts and Servicemen's First Amendment Rights," 22 Hast. L.J. 325 (1971); Brown, "Must the Soldier be a Silent Member of Our Society," 43 Mil. L. Rev. 71 (1969); Lewis, "Freedom of Speech—An Examination of the Civilian Test for Constitutionality and its Application to the Military," 41 Mil. L. Rev. 55 (1968); Vigts, "Free Speech in the Armed Forces," 57 Colum. L. Rev. 187 (1957).

384. Parker v. Levy, 417 U.S. 733 (1974); *see also* Brown v. Glines, 444 U.S. 349 (1980) (speech likely to interfere with military effectiveness may be suppressed); Priest v. Secretary of Navy, 570 F.2d 1013 (D.C. Cir. 1977) (speech that presents clear and present danger to military interests may be suppressed); Smith v. United States, 502 F.2d 512 (5th Cir. 1974) (speech that substantially and materially interferes with a service person's military performance may be suppressed); United States v. Hartwig, 39 M.J. 125 (C.M.A. 1994) (court held that clear and present danger test applies to military members, but standard requires different application; in the context of an officer's private speech, the test is whether the speech poses a clear and present danger that the

§ 13-3(N)(3) MILITARY CRIMINAL JUSTICE § 13-3(N)(3)

decide when such is the case.[385] A freedom of speech claim may still be successful, however, if the defense can show that the regulation is irrational or arbitrary, or that its only purpose is to silence officially unpopular expression that does not otherwise threaten legitimate military interests.[386]

A separate type of freedom of speech claim that may be raised is that the law, regulation, or order, by the scope of ambiguity of its language, can be applied to a substantial range of protected expression, and thus has the effect of silencing those who might otherwise exercise their freedom to communicate.[387] Such a law may be held invalid as unconstitutionally overbroad or vague under the First Amendment.[388] In the civilian sector this type of claim merits special standing rules that allow the challenger to attack the statute on the grounds that it infringes on the free expression of others not before the court.[389] The Supreme Court has found, however, that these special rules are much less applicable to First Amendment claims within the military.[390] Thus, a potentially successful overbreadth challenger in the military must be prepared to show not only that the law is substantially overbroad,[391] but also that his own conduct cannot be constitutionally subject to the regulation, either

---

speech will dishonor or disgrace the officer personally and seriously compromise the person's standing as an officer; extensive discussion of the issue).

United States v. Moore, 38 M.J. 490 (C.M.A. 1994) (accused guilty of communicating indecent speech; court noted that need for obedience and discipline necessitates different application of First Amendment within the military).

United States v. Stone, 37 M.J. 558 (A.C.M.R. 1993) (accused's false official speech to high school students while in uniform about his alleged role in Desert Storm violated Article 134).

385. Brown v. Glines, 444 U.S. 348 (1980); Greer v. Spock, 424 U.S. 828 (1976); Carlson v. Schlesinger, 511 F.2d 1327 (1975); United States v. Stuckey, 10 M.J. 347 (C.M.A. 1981); United States v. Howe, 17 C.M.A. 165, 37 C.M.R. 429 (C.M.A. 1967) (contemptuous words directed at the President); cf. Blameuser v. Andrews, 630 F.2d 538 (7'th Cir. 1980) (military interest in securing effective officers grants wide discretion to college R.O.T.C. professor in selecting candidates, including to some extent taking into account the candidate's political affiliations and beliefs).

386. Brown v. Glines, 444 U.S. 348 (1980) (regulation requiring prior command approval for the gathering of petitions is facially valid if it serves substantial government interests and is not intended to silence expression, but such a regulation may not be used to arbitrarily or irrationally restrict right).

387. New York v. Ferber, 458 U.S. 747 (1982); Village of Schauniburg v. Citizens for a Better Environment, 444 U.S. 620 (1980); Erznoznik v. City of Jacksonville, 422 U.S. 205 (1975).

388. A law may be unconstitutionally overbroad if its language infringes on a substantial range of protected expression. United States Civil Service Comm'n v. National Ass'n of Letter Carriers, 413 U.S. 548 (1973); Grayned v. City of Rockford, 408 U.S. 104 (1972). A law may be unconstitutionally vague if its ambiguity threatens a substantial range of protected expression. Smith v. Goguen, 415 U.S. 566 (1974); Broadrick v. Oklahoma, 413 U.S. 601 (1973). See also New York v. Ferber, 458 U.S. 747 (1982) (outside First Amendment, criminal statute may not be attacked as overbroad).

389. Dombrowski v. Pfister, 380 U.S. 479 (1965); Broadrick v. Oklahoma, 413 U.S. 601 (1973).

390. Parker v. Levy, 417 U.S. 733 (1974); United States v. Hoard, 12 M.J. 563 (A.C.M.R. 1981).

391. Broadrick v. Oklahoma, 413 U.S. 601 (1973) (especially where conduct is intermixed with speech, the overbreadth of statute must not only be real, but substantial as well, judged in relation to the statute's plainly legitimate sweep); see also New York v. Ferber, 458 U.S. 747 (1982) (discusses policy grounds for requiring substantial overbreadth and finds the requirement to be generally applicable); Cortright v. Resor, 447 F.2d 245 (2d Cir. 1971).

because of its protected character[392] or because the regulation failed to provide fair notice that the conduct was contrary to military law.[393]

Government Establishment or Interference with Religion. The First Amendment creates two distinct categories of restrictions on the federal government in its dealings with religion, both of which serve to ensure that the government maintains a position of neutrality.[394] First, the government is prohibited by the Establishment Clause[395] from promoting or sponsoring religion. In general, to comport with the Establishment Clause a law must have a secular purpose, must not have the primary effect of promoting or hindering the practice of religion, and must not create an "excessive entanglement" between government and religion.[396] Second, the government is prohibited by the Free Exercise Clause[397] from placing significant burdens on the practice of religion unless the government can demonstrate that it is necessary to do so to protect or further paramount state interests.[398]

Freedom of religion analysis is conducted largely on an ad hoc basis.[399] The government is not required to shun all contact with religious practices, and in many cases may accommodate those practices when there is a legitimate secular reason for doing so.[400] Furthermore, beliefs, to qualify for protection

---

392. *Compare* Tinker v. Des Moines Sch. Dist., 393 U.S. 503 (1969) (wearing armband akin to pure speech) *with* Smith v. United States, 502 F.2d 512 (5th Cir. 1974) (wearing of peace pin). *See also* United States v. Schmidt, 16 C.M.A. 57, 36 C.M.R. 213 (C.M.A. 1966) (recognizing a servicemember's statutory and constitutional right to communicate with his Congressman); United States v. Wolfson, 36 C.M.R. 722 (A.B.R. 1966) (recognizing right of serviceman to "bitch" to superiors).

393. *Cf.* United States v. Johanns, 20 M.J. 155 (C.M.A. 1985), *cert. denied*, 465 U.S. 668 (1985).

394. Engel v. Vitale, 370 U.S. 421 (1962) (discusses difference between two aspects of freedom of religion). *Compare* Everson v. Board of Educ., 330 U.S. 1 (1947) (First Amendment prevents government from supporting religion in general as well as any particular religion) *with* Larson v. Valente, 456 U.S. 228 (1982) (the central tenet of the Establishment Clause is that government shall not favor one religion over others). *See also* Tribe, *American Constitutional Law* 812-23 (1978) (reviews various theories on how the First Amendment's religious guarantees should be interpreted and applied).

395. *See* U.S. CONST. amend. I ("Congress shall make no law respecting an establishment of religion ..."); *see also* Everson v. Board of Educ., 330 U.S. 1 (1947) (Establishment Clause was intended to create a wall of separation between church and state).

396. *See* Wallace v. Jaffree, 105 S. Ct. 2479 (1985); Lemon v. Kurtzman, 403 U.S. 602 (1971).

397. *See* U.S. CONST. amend. I. McDaniel v. Paty, 435 U.S. 618 (1978).

398. Sherbert v. Verner, 374 U.S. 398 (1963) (state interest in preventing filing of fraudulent claims not sufficiently compelling to justify significant burden on religious freedom by denying unemployment benefits on the basis of refusal to work on Sabbath). *See also* Rice, "The Clash Between the Free Exercise of Religion and the Military's Uniform Regulations—*Goldman v. Secretary of Defense*," 58 TEMP. L.Q. 195 (1985).

399. *See, e.g.*, Wisconsin v. Yoder, 406 U.S. 205 (1972) (Court balanced interests of Amish in maintaining ideological and religious contiguity of their order against interest of state in compelling Amish children to attend secondary school).

400. Lynch v. Donnelly, 465 U.S. 668 (1984) (creche could be maintained and displayed by city as a secular remembrance of the origins of Christmas); McGowan v. Maryland, 366 U.S. 420 (1961) (Sunday closing law, though primarily motivated by religious purpose when created, had evolved a legitimate secular purpose and therefore was valid). *See also* Hatheway v. Secretary of Army, 641 F.2d 1376 (9th Cir. 1981) (provision of U.C.M.J. that criminalizes sodomy does not

from the First Amendment, need not be theistic or otherwise part of a recognized religion or ideology. But the beliefs must be sincere.[401] It is also significant that the Free Exercise and Establishment Clauses are often placed in contention because of the tenuous line the government must tread between neutrality and favoritism on the one hand and antipathy on the other.[402]

In the military, freedom of religion claims have been afforded much the same treatment as have freedom of speech claims: religious practices are to be allowed to the extent they do not interfere with military interests. It is largely left up to military authorities to determine what those interests are and when they are threatened.[403] In *Goldman v. Weinberger*,[404] for instance, the Supreme Court accepted the government's contention that the military interest in uniformity was sufficiently important that a Jewish serviceman could be prohibited from wearing a yarmulke in the absence of any showing that the wearing of the apparel otherwise threatened any military interests.[405]

---

violate Establishment Clause, even though originally religiously motivated because it has a legitimate secular purpose).

401. The Court has discussed the definitional problem extensively in cases involving conscientious objectors. United States v. Seeger, 380 U.S. 163 (1965) (in interpreting statute that provides for exemption from service on religious grounds, the Court held that the proper definitional test of religion "in relation to a Supreme Being" is "whether a given belief that is sincere and meaningful occupies a place in the life of its possessor parallel to that filled by the orthodox belief in God of one who clearly qualifies for the exemption"); *but see* Gillete v. United States, 401 U.S. 437 (1971) (Court upheld limitation of exemption to those who oppose all war on religious grounds, not just the war at hand, against both Establishment and Free Exercise claims).

402. Sherbert v. Verner, 374 U.S. 398 (1963) (rejected contention that allowing unemployment benefits to those who refuse on religious grounds to work on a certain day of the week as required by the Free Exercise Clause violated the Establishment Clause).

This tension has often arisen in regard to military chaplains. *See generally Military Chaplains: From a Religious Military to a Military Religion* (H. Cox ed. 1971). *See also* Anderson v. Laird, 466 P.2d 283 (D.C. Cir. 1912) (holding compulsory chapel attendance violative of First Amendment and rejecting finding of lower court that the attendance requirement had a secular training purpose).

403. Brown v. Glines, 444 U.S. 348 (1980); Parker v. Levy, 417 U.S. 733 (1974); United States v. Hoard, 12 M.J. 563 (A.C.M.R. 1981); Carlson v. Schlesinger, 511 F.2d 1327 (D.C. Cir. 1975). *See also* Foreman, "Religion, Conscience and Military Discipline," 52 MIL. L. REV. 77 (1971).

Religious beliefs have been unsuccessfully claimed to justify noncompliance with military requirements. *See, e.g.,* United States v. Wheeler, 12 C.M.A. 387, 30 C.M.R. 387 (1961) (required premarriage consultation with chaplain); United States v. Burry, 36 C.M.R. 829 (C.G.B.R. 1966) (order to work on Saturday); United States v. Chadwell, 36 C.M.R. 741 (N.B.R. 1965) (required inoculation); United States v. Cupp, 24 C.M.R. 565 (A.F.B.R. 1957) (order to salute).

404. Goldman v. Weinberger, 475 U.S. 503 (1986).

405. Goldman v. Weinberger, 475 U.S. 503 (1986). United States v. Reed, 24 M.J. 80 (C.M.A. 1987) (Everett, C.J., concurring) (Navy regulation requiring individuals to report offenses cast a chill on servicemembers' First Amendment rights to associate, by being overbroad; thus the regulation could not be applied to anyone). As noted at § 13-3(N)(3), there is a difference between government interferences with *expressive* associational rights and *intimate* associational rights.

See also United States v. Moultak, 24 M.J. 316 (C.M.A. 1987) (court rejected overbreadth challenge to Navy regulation that forbade officer from making certain pecuniary transactions with enlisted members); United States v. Hawkins, 30 M.J. 682 (A.F.C.M.R. 1990) (assuming that order forbidding accused to talk to various individuals infringed on his First Amendment rights, it passed strict scrutiny test). *See also* Rabinowitz, "*Goldman v. Secretary of Defense:* Restricting the Religious Rights of Military Servicemembers," 34 AM. U. L. REV. 881 (1985).

Penumbral First Amendment Rights: Association. In addition to the right to speak, the First Amendment also protects many other related activities that it does not explicitly mention, such as the right to read, to listen, to distribute literature, and to associate with others for expressive, religious, or political purposes.[406] These several facets of the Constitution's protection of speech and expression form a penumbra of rights that supplement the explicit guarantee of free speech and without which that guarantee would mean little.[407] The standards with which government interference with association protected by the First Amendment must comport are similar to those that apply to individual expressive conduct. That is, the regulation is valid if it serves a compelling or important government interest, is not intended to suppress the content of the group's message, and is not more burdensome to the expression of that message than necessary to achieve its purpose.[408]

It should be noted, however, that not all relations between persons are protected by the First Amendment. Intimate relationships, familial or otherwise, that do not exist for the expression of ideas are not protected by the First

---

406. *See, e.g.*, NAACP v. Claiborne Hardware Co., 458 U.S. 886 (1982) (right to boycott for political change); Abood v. Detroit Bd. of Educ., 431 U.S. 209 (1977) (right not to associate); NAACP v. Button, 371 U.S. 415 (1963) (right to litigate as a group for expressive or political purposes); NAACP v. Alabama, 357 U.S. 449 (1958) (association with others for the purpose of expression and right to refuse to disclose membership); Martin v. Struthers, 319 U.S. 141 (1943) (right to distribute and receive speech).

407. Griswold v. Connecticut, 381 U.S. 479 (1965) (specific guarantees in the Bill of Rights have penumbras, formed by emanations from those guarantees that help give them life and substance. Various guarantees create zones of privacy).

408. Roberts v. United States Jaycees, 468 U.S. 609 (1984); NAACP v. Claiborne Hardware Co., 458 U.S. 886 (1982).

Restrictions on association are generally valid if tailored to military needs. *See, e.g.*, United States v. Pitasi, 20 C.M.A. 601, 44 C.M.R. 31 (1971) (associations between officers and enlisted men that are "palpably and directly prejudicial to the good order and discipline of the service" may be prohibited); United States v. Blevens, 5 C.M.A. 480, 18 C.M.R. 104 (1955) (conviction under general article for affiliation with organization committed to overthrow the United States upheld); United States v. Toomey, 39 C.M.R. 969 (A.F.B.R. 1969) (military necessity justifies punishment of serviceman who engaged in antiwar protest while in uniform).

The military command has broad discretion to exclude persons from the environs under its authority. *See* Greer v. Spock, 424 U.S. 828 (1976) (exclusion of political speakers); Weissman v. United States, 387 F.2d 271 (10th Cir. 1971) (exclusion of journalist seeking to attend court-martial). *But see* Kiiskila v. Nichols, 433 F.2d 745 (7th Cir. 1970) (civilian employee could not be excluded from base for off-base political activities); United States v. Bradley, 418 F.2d 688 (4th Cir. 1969) (conviction for entry for purpose of leafletting disallowed where such activity was not specifically prohibited by post regulations); United States v. Watson, 80 F. Supp. 649 (E.D. Va. 1948) (re-entry contrary to order by driving on public highway through base could not be punished).

The command may also declare areas outside the military environs off-limits to military personnel. *See* Harper v. Jones, 195 F.2d 705 (10th Cir. 1952) (disreputable auto dealership), *cert. denied,* 344 U.S. 821 (1952); Ainsworth v. Barn Ballroom Co., 157 F.2d 97 (4th Cir. 1946) (disreputable dance hall). *See also* Gerwig, "Military Reservations: Forts or Parks?", 12 WM. & MARY L. REV. 51 (1970); Lieberman, "Cafeteria Workers Revisited: Does the Commander Have Plenary Power to Control Access to His Base?", 25 JAG J. 53 (1970).

Amendment, but are protected to some degree by the penumbral privacy rights that flow from the Due Process Clause of the Fifth Amendment.[409]

As in the other possible claims arising out of the First Amendment, a challenge in the military against a statute, regulation, or order on the grounds that it violates an associational guarantee of the First Amendment will not be successful where the government can present substantial military interests that are served by the law in question.[410]

§ 13-3(N)(4). Rights of Privacy.

The Constitution implicitly provides a body of rights generally labelled as privacy.[411] These rights have been derived from long-standing principles of Anglo-American jurisprudence so fundamental that the Framers of the Constitution felt it unnecessary to protect them with explicit language.[412] Examples of such penumbral guarantees include the right to procreate,[413] to marry,[414] to obtain an abortion,[415] and to travel.[416]

---

409. Roberts v. United States Jaycees, 468 U.S. 609 (1984) (Court distinguishes between *intimate* and *expressive* association).

410. *See, e.g.*, United States v. Hoard, 12 M.J. 563 (A.C.M.R. 1981) (prohibition against association between training center staff and trainees); Blameuser v. Andrews, 630 F.2d 538 (7th Cir. 1980) (association of officer candidate with white supremacist group).

411. Roe v. Wade, 410 U.S. 113 (1973) (described various rights of privacy and their possible sources); Griswold v. Connecticut, 381 U.S. 479 (1965) (described the phenomena by which provisions of the Bill of Rights create *zones of privacy*); Meyer v. Nebraska, 262 U.S. 390 (1923) (among a person's liberties implicitly protected by due process are the right of the individual to contract, to engage in any of the common occupations of life, to acquire useful knowledge, to marry, establish a home and bring up children, to worship God according to the dictates of his own conscience, and, generally, to enjoy those privileges long recognized at common law as essential to the orderly pursuit of happiness by free men); People v. Onofre, 415 N.E.2d 936 (N.Y. 1980) (discussion of various possible sources of rights of privacy), *cert. denied*, 451 U.S. 987 (1981).

412. Shapiro v. Thompson, 394 U.S. 618 (1969) (the right to travel is "a right so elementary [that it] was conceived from the beginning to be a necessary concomitant of the stronger Union the Constitution created"); Griswold v. Connecticut, 381 U.S. 479 (1965) (right of marital privacy "older than the Bill of Rights").

413. Skinner v. Oklahoma, 316 U.S. 535 (1942) (sterilization law struck down as infringing on one of the basic civil rights of man in a discriminatory manner); United States v. Gates, 40 M.J. 354 (C.M.A. 1994) (conviction for private, consensual, heterosexual, noncommercial fellatio did not violate due process or equal protection rights under Fifth Amendment). *Cf.* United States v. Henderson, 34 M.J. 174 (C.M.A. 1992) (Article 125 proscription of sodomy was not unconstitutional as applied to consensual heterosexual fellatio); United States v. Fagg, 34 M.J. 179 (C.M.A. 1992) (sodomy statute was constitutional as applied to private heterosexual, noncommercial, consensual oral sex act); United States v. Hall, 34 M.J. 695 (A.C.M.R. 1991) (in lengthy discussion, court held that constitutional right of privacy does not extend to consensual heterosexual sodomy among the unmarried).

414. Zablocki v. Redhail, 434 U.S. 374 (1978) (right to marry fundamental liberty protected by due process).

415. Roe v. Wade, 410 U.S. 113 (1973) (due process guarantees a woman's right to choose to terminate her pregnancy).

416. Shapiro v. Thompson, 394 U.S. 618 (1969) (Court identified implicit right to travel but declined to identify any particular provision as its source).

The effect of these protections is to secure a degree of personal decision-making free from unjustified interference by the government.[417] A law which significantly burdens or penalizes the exercise of one of these fundamental rights is invalid unless the government can show that it is a necessary means to protect or further some compelling interest.[418]

The most common object of privacy challenges in the military are statutes, regulations, or orders that define and proscribe fraternization.[419] The military courts have recognized the right of privacy in the military environment[420] but have concluded that the military's justifications satisfy whatever constitutional standard is imposed.[421] Military proscriptions of fraternization have been found valid in almost all their permutations, especially as applied to public[422] or deviant sexual conduct[423] and undue familiarity in superior-subor-

---

417. Eisenstadt v. Baird, 405 U.S. 438 (1972); Whalen v. Roe, 429 U.S. 589 (1977) (Court noted two varieties of privacy rights: one protecting personal decision making and the other protecting against forced disclosure of private matters).

See also United States v. Womack, 29 M.J. 88 (C.M.A. 1989) (military has compelling reason to ensure that those who defend the nation are healthy; safe sex order given to accused who had AIDS was not constitutionally infirm); United States v. Johnson, 27 M.J. 798 (A.F.C.M.R. 1988) (court accepted without reservation the authority of the Air Force to impose reasonable regulations on sexual relations to servicemembers infected with AIDS).

United States v. Sargeant, 29 M.J. 812 (A.C.M.R. 1989) (whatever privacy interest unmarried defendant had in his private sexual relations were outweighed by the Army's compelling interest in protecting health and welfare of its personnel and the public; safe sex order was therefore not constitutionally infirm. A copy of the written order is included as an appendix to the court's opinion). *See generally* Milhizer, "Legality of the Safe-Sex Order to Soldiers Having AIDS," ARMY LAW., Dec. 1988, at 4; Wells-Petry, "Anatomy of an AIDS Case: Deadly Disease as an Aspect of Deadly Crime," ARMY LAW., Jan. 1988, at 17.

418. Roe v. Wade, 410 U.S. 113 (1973) (Court constructs standards to guide government regulation of abortions based on a timetable of when the various state interests involved become sufficiently compelling to justify burdening that choice).

419. *See generally* Note, "Wrongful Fraternization as an Offense Under the Uniform Code of Military Justice," 33 CLEV. ST. L. REV. 547 (1984-1985).

420. *See, e.g.,* United States v. Jones, 14 M.J. 1008 (C.M.A. 1982); United States v. Scoby, 5 M.J. 160 (C.M.A. 1978); United States v. Adams, 19 M.J. 996 (A.C.M.R. 1985); United States v. McFarlin, 19 M.J. 790 (A.C.M.R. 1985); United States v. Parker, 5 M.J. 923 (N.C.M.R. 1978). *See also* Dronenburg v. Zech, 741 F.2d 1388 (D.C. Cir. 1984); Rich v. Secretary of Army, 735 F.2d 1220 (10th Cir. 1984); West v. Brown, 558 F.2d 757 (5th Cir. 1977).

421. *See, e.g.,* United States v. Jones, 14 M.J. 1008 (C.M.A. 1982); United States v. Scoby, 5 M.J. 160 (C.M.A. 1978); United States v. McFarlin, 19 M.J. 790 (A.C.M.R. 1985); United States v. Parker, 5 M.J. 923 (N.C.M.R. 1978).

422. United States v. Scoby, 5 M.J. 160 (C.M.A. 1978) (sexual conduct is not protected by privacy right when engaged in in public). *Cf.* United States v. Fagg, 33 M.J. 618 (A.F.C.M.R. 1991) (citing right to privacy, court concluded that accused could not be convicted for private, consensual, heterosexual acts of sodomy).

In United States v. Womack, 27 M.J. 630 (A.F.C.M.R. 1988) (en banc), the court concluded that a written order to the accused, who had AIDS, to, *inter alia,* practice safe sex did not implicate constitutional concerns because he was ultimately charged with violating the order by committing forcible sodomy, which in the court's view does not "represent a promising basis for a constitutional challenge."

423. Bowers v. Hardwick, 478 U.S. 186 (1986) (there is no fundamental right to engage in sodomy); *but see* United States v. Fagg, 33 M.J. 618 (A.F.C.M.R. 1991) (in an extensive discussion of constitutional right to privacy issues, court concluded that accused could not be convicted under Article 125 for consensual, adult, heterosexual, private acts of oral sex); New York v. Onofre, 415

dinate relationships.[424] Where, however, the conduct in question is private, consensual, and nondeviate, and where there is no compromise of command integrity, a privacy challenge to a fraternization policy may be successful if the defendant can establish that he received no fair notice of the illicit nature of his conduct from military regulations, custom, or other sources.[425] For further discussion of fraternization, see § 2-8.

Privacy challenges have also occasionally been made against regulations or orders that dictate standards of personal appearance, such as hair length,[426] but the military's interest in uniformity has been found to justify dress regulations against both Fifth Amendment[427] and First Amendment.[428]

§ 13-3(N)(5). *Ex Post Facto* Laws.

The Constitution expressly forbids the federal legislature from enacting criminal laws that operate to the detriment of defendants by retroactively creating or aggravating offenses, altering prescribed punishments, or changing procedural rules to the derogation of substantive rights.[429] The judiciary is precluded from retroactive decision making that has the same effect by operation of the Due Process Clause of the Fifth Amendment.[430] In either its express

---

N.E.2d 936 (N.Y. 1980) (sodomy statute struck down on the grounds that general distaste was insufficient to justify intrusion into the private sphere absent a showing that such activity created a substantial threat to public safety or morality), *cert. denied*, 451 U.S. 987 (1981). *See also* Dronenburg v. Zech, 741 F.2d 1388 (D.C. Cir. 1984); Rich v. Secretary of Army, 735 F.2d 1220 (10th Cir. 1984) (military may exclude homosexuals from entry into service, and may discharge such persons because of their sexual orientation). *See generally* Annotation, "Validity of Statute Making Sodomy a Criminal Offense," 20 A.L.R.4th 1009 (1983).

424. United States v. McFarlin, 19 M.J. 790 (A.C.M.R. 1985) (military has compelling reasons for disallowing sexual relationships between superiors and subordinates).

425. United States v. Johanns, 20 M.J. 155 (C.M.A. 1985), *cert. denied*, 474 U.S. 850 (1985) (accepting finding of lower court that current custom in the Air Force was not such as would provide fair notice that adultery or other private heterosexual liaisons between service people not in a superior/subordinate relationship was prohibited). Indeed, the cases suggest that privacy claims in the military may have no independent vitality apart from the question of fair notice.

426. United States v. Young, 1 M.J. 433 (C.M.A. 1976) (follows *Kelley v. Johnson*, 425 U.S. 238 (1976), and holding that military may dictate rational standards of personal appearance).

427. United States v. Verdi, 5 M.J. 330 (C.M.A. 1978) (hairpiece); United States v. Young, 1 M.J. 433 (C.M.A. 1976) (hairstyle).

428. Goldman v. Weinberger, 106 S. Ct. 1310 (1986) (yarmulke).

429. Calder v. Bull, 3 Dall. 386 (1798) (the Court enumerated the types of *ex post facto* laws: "1st, Every law that makes an action done before the passing of the law, and which was *innocent* when done, criminal. 2d, Every law that *aggravates a crime*, or makes it *greater* than it was when committed. 3d, Every law that *changes the punishment*, and inflicts a *greater punishment*, than the law annexed to the crime, when committed. 4th, Every law that alters the *legal* rules of *evidence*, and receives less, or different testimony, than the law required at the time of the commission of the offense, *in order to convict the offender*") (original emphasis); United States v. Lilly, 34 M.J. 670 (A.C.M.R. 1992) (change in Article 50, U.C.M.J., regarding burden and quantum of proof of insanity was substantive change and *ex post facto* clause required application of earlier standard in accused's rehearing).

430. Bouie v. Columbia, 378 U.S. 347 (1964) (violative of due process for a court to overrule consistent line of procedural decisions or apply an unforeseeable construction in such a way as to

application to the legislature or its implied application to the courts, the underlying purpose of the constitutional proscription of *ex post facto* laws is to prevent the injustice of convicting a defendant under terms of which the defendant had no fair notice at the time of the sanctioned conduct, and to prevent unrestrained discretion in public authorities.[431]

An example of *ex post facto* claims in the military is the 1979 amendment of Article 2 of the U.C.M.J.,[432] in which Congress reversed decisional law that suspended court-martial jurisdiction over defendants that proved recruiter misconduct.[433] In *United States v. McDonagh*,[434] the Court held that the application of this amendment to ensure jurisdiction over defendants whose conduct predated the change was *ex post facto* and unconstitutional, but distinguished between purely military offenses and offenses that are not of such purely military nature.[435] As to the first category, the status of the accused is an element of the crime, and as such cannot be eliminated retroactively so as to ease conviction.[436] As to the latter category, however, the status of the accused is not an element of the crime, and thus the change is merely procedural and not violative of due process.[437]

§ 13-4. Motions to Suppress.

Before adoption of the Military Rules of Evidence[1] in 1980, motions to suppress were not formally recognized in military practice as a separate category of motions. Rather, they were usually labelled as motions for appropriate relief in the nature of a motion to suppress. The Manual for Courts-Martial

---

subject a person to criminal liability for past conduct); *see also* Marks v. United States, 430 U.S. 188 (1977).

431. Bouie v. Columbia, 378 U.S. 347 (1964); United States v. McDonagh, 14 M.J. 415 (C.M.A. 1983); United States v. Lee, 32 M.J. 857 (N.M.C.M.R. 1991) (change in statute of limitations from 2 to 5 years for noncapital offenses did not result in *ex post facto* law simply because offense was committed before the change).

432. Act of November 9, 1979, Pub. L. No. 96-107, 801, 93 Stat. 810; *amending* U.C.M.J. Art. 2.

433. United States v. Russo, 1 M.J. 184 (C.M.A. 1978) (suspended the *in personam* jurisdiction of court-martial over a defendant who established recruiter misconduct).

434. 14 M.J. 415 (C.M.A. 1983).

435. *Compare* United States v. McDonagh, 14 M.J. 415 (C.M.A. 1983) (finding no violation because the offense was drug-related and not particularly military in nature) *with* United States v. Marsh, 15 M.J. 252 (C.M.A. 1983) (finding a violation of due process as the offense, unauthorized absence, was purely military in nature).

436. *See, e.g.*, United States v. McGinnis, 15 M.J. 252 (C.M.A. 1983); United States v. Marsh, 15 M.J. 252 (C.M.A. 1983) (unauthorized absence); United States v. Long, 17 M.J. 661 (N.M.C.M.R. 1983); *cf.* United States v. Gennosa, 11 M.J. 764 (N.M.C.M.R. 1981) (amendment could be applied retroactively as recruiter misconduct involved waivable regulatory defects).

437. *See, e.g.*, United States v. McDonagh, 14 M.J. 415 (C.M.A. 1983); United States v. Andrews, 17 M.J. 717 (N.M.C.M.R. 1983); United States v. Brooks, 17 M.J. 584 (A.C.M.R. 1983) (retroactive application of "rape-shield" rule merely procedural); Chilcott v. Orr, 747 F.2d 39 (1st Cir. 1984). *See also* Dobbert v. Florida, 432 U.S. 282 (1977).

1. *See* § 15-18. *See generally* Saltzburg, Schinasi & Schlueter, *Military Rules of Evidence Manual* (3d ed. 1991); Basham, "Suppression Motions Under the Military Rules of Evidence," ARMY LAW., May 1980, at 17; Castle, "Motion Practice Under Section III of the Military Rules of Evidence," 12 The Advocate 118 (1980).

now recognizes that a motion to suppress is the correct vehicle for challenging admissibility of evidence obtained under the provisions of Section III of the Military Rules of Evidence:[2] an accused's pretrial statements, evidence seized from the accused, pretrial identifications of the accused, and derivative evidence. Motions challenging the admissibility of other types of evidence, such as evidence of an accused's prior conviction for impeachment purposes, would normally be contested through a motion for appropriate relief or more specifically, a motion *in limine*.[3] Thus, the term "motion to suppress" is usually associated only with Section III-type evidence.

The Section III rules of evidence (Rules 301-321) contain a number of common elements for these motions:

> First, the prosecution must disclose to the defense prior to arraignment that it possesses Fourth, Fifth, or Sixth Amendment evidence;[4]
>
> Second, the defense must, prior to the plea, either move to suppress or object. Tardy objections are acceptable only upon a showing of good cause;[5]
>
> Third, the military judge may require the defense to state a specific, rather than general, basis for its motion;[6]
>
> Fourth, unless otherwise noted, the prosecution must prove the legality of the evidence by a preponderance of the evidence;[7]
>
> Fifth, the military judge should enter his rulings prior to the plea and state essential findings of fact on the record;[8] and
>
> Sixth, guilty pleas waive all evidentiary motions and objections.[9]

The following sections briefly address some of the special rules for each of the three separate motions to suppress.

---

2. *See* R.C.M. 905(b)(2).

3. *See* § 13-5(L).

4. Rules 304(d)(1), 311(d)(1), 321(c)(1), MIL. R. EVID. United States v. Trimper, 28 M.J. 460 (C.M.A. 1989) (suppression of evidence was not required even though the prosecution had failed to disclose the evidence as required).

5. Rules 304(d)(2), 311(d)(2), 321(c)(2), MIL. R. EVID. In United States v. Coffin, 25 M.J. 32 (C.M.A. 1987), the court indicated that the requirement of objecting prior to the plea should be liberally construed in order to ensure that the defendant is able to present a "defense."

6. Rules 304(d)(3), 311(d)(3), 321(c)(3), MIL. R. EVID. United States v. Alexander, 32 M.J. 664 (A.F.C.M.R. 1991) (although prosecution is only required to respond to defense's specific objections, it is prudent for prosecution to present any available alternative basis for admitting the evidence).

7. Rules 304(e), 311(e), 321(d), MIL. R. EVID.

8. Rules 304(d)(4), 311(d)(4), 321(f), MIL. R. EVID. United States v. Miller, 31 M.J. 247 (C.M.A. 1990) (defense failure to challenge voluntariness of accused's statements relieved judge from entering findings or instructing the jury); United States v. Doucet, 43 M.J. 656 (A.F.Ct.Crim.App. 1995) (judge erred in not entering essential findings on motion to suppress; court resolved issue as part of its fact-finding function, rather than remanding case).

9. Rules 304(d)(5), 311(d)(5), 321(g), MIL. R. EVID.

§ 13-4(A). Pretrial Statements of the Accused.

Rule 304, Military Rules of Evidence governs the admissibility of an accused's pretrial statements: Involuntary statements are inadmissible. Under the Rule, a statement is involuntary if it resulted from coercion or if it was not preceded by applicable Article 31(b) or right-to-counsel warnings, as required in Rule 305.[10] Although Rule 305(e), as originally promulgated in 1980, also required interrogators to properly notify counsel prior to questioning a suspect or accused,[11] that provision was deleted in 1994.[12] Rule 304 contains several exceptions that permit admission of statements where the only defect was in giving the right-to-counsel warnings[13] or where the statement would have been inevitably discovered.[14]

Rule 304 also provides the procedural framework for moving to suppress those statements. When raised, the issue of admissibility is decided in an out-of-court hearing[15] and the prosecution's burden extends only to those issues specifically raised by the defense motion or objection.[16] The Rule requires the prosecution to disclose to the defense, prior to arraignment, statements by the accused that are (1) relevant to the case, (2) known to the trial counsel, and (3) within the control of the armed forces.[17] If the motion to suppress is de-

---

10. Rules 304(c)(3), 305(a), Mil. R. Evid. In United States v. Steward, 31 M.J. 259 (C.M.A. 1990), the court concluded that the failure to give Article 31(b) warnings to the accused was a "technical violation" of that provision and that the failure in itself did not create a presumptive taint to the statements. The court remanded the case to the lower court to determine if the statements, taken as a whole, were voluntary. In dissent, Chief Judge Everett noted that the presumptive taint rule is simply a commonsense allocation of burdens of proof. When the defense shows that a violation occurred, the burden rests upon the prosecution to show that the statement was not the product of the violation.
United States v. Phillips, 32 M.J. 76 (C.M.A. 1991) (accused's second set of statements were tainted by first unwarned statements, and government failed to show that the subsequent confession was voluntary considering all of the facts and circumstances of the case, including the technical violation of Article 31(b)).
United States v. Vandewoestyne, 41 M.J. 587 (A.F.Ct.Crim.App. 1994) (accused voluntarily waived right to counsel and right to remain silent).
United States v. McCaig, 32 M.J. 751 (A.C.M.R. 1991) (accused's oral statement to military police, following an unwarned statement to his superior, was not voluntary; court listed factors for determining whether such statements are voluntary).
11. Rule 305(e), Mil. R. Evid. See also United States v. McOmber, 1 M.J. 380 (C.M.A. 1976).
12. E.O. 12936 (Nov. 10, 1994).
13. United States v. Sykes, 38 M.J. 669 (A.C.M.R. 1993) (statement taken in violation of accused's rights to counsel could be used for impeachment during his cross-examination, even though the prosecution could not have used it during its case-in-chief).
14. Rule 305(b), Mil. R. Evid. The Rule adopts Harris v. New York, 401 U.S. 222 (1971), and Nix v. Williams, 467 U.S. 431 (1984). See also United States v. Lawless, 18 M.J. 255 (C.M.A. 1984).
15. Rule 104(c), Mil. R. Evid.
16. Rule 304(e), Mil. R. Evid.
17. Rule 304(d)(1), Mil. R. Evid. United States v. Dancy, 38 M.J. 1 (C.M.A. 1993) (error not to disclose letter written by accused to sister; military judge justified in not granting mistrial motion); United States v. Palumbo, 27 M.J. 565 (A.C.M.R. 1988) (judge denied defense request for mistrial where prosecution introduced statements that it had not disclosed to the defense; judge instead instructed members not to consider the statements); United States v. Trimper, 26 M.J.

nied, the defense may nonetheless present relevant evidence to the factfinders who will be instructed to give the admitted statement the weight it deserves.[18] An accused's confession must be corroborated.[19]

Note that Rule 302 creates a sort of privilege for statements made by an accused during a compelled sanity examination.[20] But the procedure for determining the admissibility of those statements is also governed by the procedural mandates of Rule 304.[21]

§ 13-4(B). Illegal Searches and Seizures.

Motions to suppress evidence resulting from illegal searches and seizures are governed by Rule 311, Military Rules of Evidence.[22] A search or seizure is illegal if it does not comport with Rules 312-317.[23] The procedural rules noted in § 13-4 are generally applicable. However, the prosecution need only disclose seized evidence that it intends to offer at trial.[24] The prosecution's burden is by a preponderance of the evidence,[25] except when it is showing the validity of a consent search. In that case it must establish the accused's consent by "clear and convincing evidence."[26] Failure to properly raise the issue or entry of a guilty plea will constitute waiver.[27]

---

534 (A.F.C.M.R. 1988) (prosecution not required to give notice of non-official statements made by accused). Failure to provide timely notice may result in the judge granting appropriate relief. *See* United States v. Reynolds, 15 M.J. 1021 (A.F.C.M.R. 1983) (granted a recess where the failure to disclose was inadvertent).

18. Rule 304(e)(2), (f), Mil. R. Evid. United States v. Miller, 31 M.J. 247 (C.M.A. 1990) (in the absence of a motion to suppress or an objection, the defense waived the issue of voluntariness of the accused's statements); United States v. Everett, 41 M.J. 847 (A.F.C.M.R. 1994) (prejudicial error not to instruct members re voluntariness issue).

19. Rule 304(g), Mil. R. Evid. United States v. Faciane, 40 M.J. 399 (C.M.A. 1994) (testimony of victim's mother and day-care provider were insufficient to corroborate accused's confession that he had committed indecent acts on child); United States v. Rounds, 30 M.J. 76 (C.M.A. 1990).

20. Rule 302(a), Mil. R. Evid. *See generally* Yustas, "Mental Evaluations of an Accused Under the Military Rules of Evidence: An Excellent Balance," Army Law., May 1980, at 4; Ross, "Rule 302 An Unfair Balance," Army Law., Mar. 1981, at 5.

21. Rule 302(e), Mil. R. Evid.
22. Rule 311, Mil. R. Evid.
23. Those Rules generally govern the various Fourth Amendment issues such as probable-cause and nonprobable-cause searches, seizures, and interception of wire and oral communications. *See* Eisenberg, "Fourth Amendment Practice and the Military Rules of Evidence," Army Law., May 1980, at 30.
24. Rule 311(d)(1), Mil. R. Evid.
25. Rule 311(e)(1), Mil. R. Evid.
26. Rule 314(e)(5), Mil. R. Evid.
27. Rule 311(d)(2)(A)(i), Mil. R. Evid. United States v. Evans, 26 M.J. 550 (A.F.C.M.R. 1988) (per curiam) (accused waived issue by not raising it at trial).

§ 13-4(C). Eyewitness Identification.

If the accused has been identified in an out-of-court lineup or similar procedure, litigation on the admissibility of that identification is guided by Military Rule of Evidence 321.[28] An identification procedure may be unlawful if it was unnecessarily suggestive, and thus unreliable,[29] or if the applicable rights to counsel were denied.[30] The prosecution must establish the legality of the identification procedure by a preponderance of the evidence[31] except in those cases where it is attempting to show that subsequent identifications were not tainted by an earlier illegal procedure. In that case it must establish the lack of taint by clear and convincing evidence.[32] See § 13-4 for a general discussion of applicable procedural requirements.

§ 13-5. Motions to Grant Appropriate Relief.

In addition to motions to dismiss and motions to suppress, military practice recognizes a third major category of motions "motions for appropriate relief," a generic term used to describe a host of requests for specific relief from procedural errors or denials of earlier requests to the convening authority. As a general rule, the defense resorts to these motions to cure a defect of form or substance that impedes the accused in properly preparing for trial or conducting his defense.[1] The substance and not the form of the motion will control.[2] The remedies may vary widely and usually fall short of dismissal of the charges.

The more common motions for appropriate relief are briefly noted in the following sections. Discussions of the applicable substantive law underlying each motion in most cases is discussed elsewhere in this book.

In many of the following motions, relief may first be sought from the convening authority.[3] For example, before raising the issue of change of venue before the military judge in the Article 39(a) session,[4] the accused could first request appropriate relief through the convening authority. Raising the issue initially with the convening authority, however, does not preclude renewal of the issue through a motion for appropriate relief. But in some cases doing so may result in relief being granted and negate the need for a motion.

---

28. *See also* Gasperini, "Eyewitness Identification Under the Military Rules of Evidence," ARMY LAW., May 1980, at 42.

29. Rule 321(b)(1), MIL. R. EVID. United States v. Webb, 38 M.J. 62 (C.M.A. 1993) (trial judge did not abuse discretion in permitting evidence of out-of-court identification to go to court members).

United States v. Williams, 35 M.J. 812 (A.F.C.M.R. 1992), *aff'd on other grounds*, 41 M.J. 134 (C.M.A. 1994) (photographic lineup was not impermissibly suggestive).

30. Rule 321(b)(2), MIL. R. EVID.
31. Rule 321(d)(1), (2), MIL. R. EVID.
32. Rule 321(d)(2), MIL. R. EVID.
1. R.C.M. 906(a).
2. R.C.M. 905(a).
3. R.C.M. 905(j).
4. *See* Chapter 12.

§ 13-5(A). Accused Incompetent to Stand Trial.

If there is an indication that the accused is not competent to stand trial, that issue may be raised in a motion for appropriate relief.[5] An accused is considered not competent to stand trial if he does not possess the mental capacity to understand the nature of the proceedings against him and to conduct or cooperate intelligently in his defense.[6] To cooperate, or assist, in his defense generally refers to providing accounts of the facts, identities of witnesses, and similar matters.[7] It does not involve matters that raise legal questions.[8] The accused is presumed to be competent[9] and when the defense raises the issue it carries the burden of proving by a preponderance of the evidence that the accused is not competent to stand trial.[10] This issue can be raised at anytime during the trial and is considered an interlocutory question of fact; the judge's ruling is final.[11] The appropriate remedy is delay of the trial and perhaps dismissal of the charges.[12] Depending on the degree of the accused's incompetence, an administrative (medical) discharge is often an appropriate disposition, although several cases have recognized the difficulty

---

5. United States v. Walker, 20 C.M.A. 241, 43 C.M.R. 81 (1971). As a practical matter this issue will usually be apparent long before trial and the defense counsel or some other authority may have already requested an inquiry into the mental state of the accused. See R.C.M. 706, which governs procedures for inquiries into the mental responsibility or capacity of the accused.

The inquiry may be ordered by the convening authority (before charges are referred and afterwards if a judge is not reasonably available) or by a military judge. A board of one or more physicians, at least one of whom should be a psychiatrist, conducts an inquiry and report on their conclusions. The board is to answer each of the following questions:

1. At the time of the offense did the accused have a severe mental disease or defect?
2. What is the clinical psychiatric diagnosis?
3. Was the accused, at the time of the alleged criminal conduct and as a result of such severe mental disease or defect, unable to appreciate the nature and quality or wrongfulness of his or her conduct?
4. Does the accused have sufficient mental capacity to understand the nature of the proceedings and to conduct or cooperate intelligently in the defense?

Note that much of this information may be privileged and not disclosable to the prosecution. See R.C.M. 706(c)(5) and Rule 302, MIL. R. EVID. See also United States v. Fowler, 30 M.J. 1164 (A.C.M.R. 1990) (psychologist's testimony concerning statements accused had made during sanity board were not admissible where accused had not been informed that his statements could be used against him at sentencing).

6. R.C.M. 909(a). United States v. Thomas, 34 M.J. 768 (A.C.M.R. 1992) (accused incompetent to stand trial); United States v. Proctor, 34 M.J. 549 (A.F.C.M.R. 1992) (under facts, accused was competent to stand trial).

7. United States v. Martinez, 12 M.J. 801 (N.M.C.M.R. 1981).
8. United States v. Martinez, 12 M.J. 801 (N.M.C.M.R. 1981).
9. R.C.M. 909(b).
10. R.C.M. 909(c)(2). As originally written in 1984 the provision placed the burden of proof on the prosecution. It was changed in February 1986 by E.O. 12550, which made other changes to the *Manual*.
11. R.C.M. 909(c)(1). United States v. Proctor, 37 M.J. 330 (C.M.A. 1993) (court will reverse trial court's ruling only if it is clearly erroneous; competency is question of fact); Short v. Chambers, 33 M.J. 49 (C.M.A. 1991).
12. R.C.M. 909(c)(2) Discussion.

of deciding what to do with an incompetent accused.[13] There is also some question about what, if any, actions the government might take to insure that an accused is competent to stand trial.[14]

A related issue is the question of the accused's mental responsibility, or sanity, at the time of the offense. If that issue is raised during the trial the defense may move for appropriate relief in the nature of direction by the judge that the accused undergo mental testing as set out in the *Manual*.[15] For a discussion on the possibility of moving for dismissal on grounds that the accused was insane at the time of the offense, see § 13-3(D).

In 1996, Article 76b, "Lack of Mental Capacity or Mental Responsibility: Commitment of Accused for Examination and Treatment" was added to the Uniform Code of Military Justice.[16] The new article is intended to make specific provision for those servicemembers who are found either incompetent to stand trial or are found not guilty by reason of lack of mental responsibility.[17] Now, the convening authority has specific authority to place the accused in the custody of the Attorney General for treatment and evaluation if the court finds that the accused in incompetent to stand trial.[18] If the accused is found not guilty by reason of lack of mental responsibility, the court is to conduct a hearing on the mental condition of the accused in accordance with 18 U.S.C. § 4243.[19] Article 76b further specifies the appropriate actions to be taken, depending on the court's findings.[20]

---

13. *See, e.g.,* Short v. Chambers, 33 M.J. 49 (C.M.A. 1991) (court noted lack of specific guidance on what the military is supposed to do with an incompetent accused. Here convening authority had transferred the petitioner to a federal correctional facility for follow-up treatment and consultation).

14. Freeman v. Stuart, 33 M.J. 659 (N.M.C.M.R. 1991) (accused filed various petitions for extraordinary relief; in an interesting discussion of the issue the court denied his request for writ of prohibition that would have blocked government medical personnel from administering drug that made him competent to stand trial).

15. R.C.M. 706. United States v. Loving, 41 M.J. 213 (1994) (court concluded in this capital case that requirements of R.C.M. 706 had been met, even though one of the members of the board was not a psychiatrist); United States v. Collins, 41 M.J. 610 (Army Ct. Crim. App. 1994) (not clear from record whether accused was evaluated by board contemplated by R.C.M. 706; case remanded); United States v. Plott, 35 M.J. 512 (A.F.C.M.R. 1992) (nonprejudicial error for trial counsel to continue on case after seeing full report of accused's mental examination board), *on further review on other grounds*, 38 M.J. 735 (A.F.C.M.R. 1993); United States v. Lewis, 34 M.J. 745 (N.M.C.M.R. 1991) (accused waived issue by not raising in timely fashion at trial).

16. Section 1133, Pub. L. No. 104-106, 110 Stat. 186 (1996), National Defense Authorization Act for Fiscal Year (FY) 1996. *See* Appendix 3.

17. *Id. See also* § 15-16(A), *infra*. *See generally* "Joint Service Committee on Military Justice Report," ARMY LAW., Mar. 1996, at 138. The article contains a helpful chart showing the effect of Art. 76b.

18. Art. 76b(a)(1), U.C.M.J. *See* Appendix 3.

19. Art. 76b(b)(2), U.C.M.J.

20. Art. 76b(4), (5), U.C.M.J.

§ 13-5(B). Pretrial Restraint.

Motions relating to an accused's pretrial restraint may take several forms. First, the defense may argue that the accused has been subjected to illegal pretrial restraint; it bears the burden of proof if the conditions of confinement are in issue.[21] The prosecution, on the other hand, bears the burden of proof if the defense is challenging the reasons for the restraint.[22] The nature of the motion is usually a request for administrative credit for any time spent in illegal restraint and where the accused is still restrained, release from that restraint.[23]

As a general rule, the issue of illegal pretrial restraint must be raised at trial[24] and failure to do so may result in a waiver.[25] On occasion, however, the appellate courts have granted relief even though the issue was raised for the first time on appeal.[26]

A related issue is a motion requesting administrative credit for time spent in legal pretrial restraint that amounted to pretrial confinement. In *United States v. Mason*,[27] the Court indicated that such administrative credit was appropriate. The issue is whether the conditions of the restraint were so limited so as to amount to confinement. In an attempt to refine the test for determining an equivalency template, several lower court decisions have indicated that the judge should consider: (1) the nature of the restraint (i.e., was it physical or moral); (2) the area of restraint; (3) the types of duties, if any, that were performed by the accused; and (4) the degree of privacy afforded to the accused.[28] For example, where the accused is restricted to the company area and must be escorted by a guard wherever he goes, or must sign in on some sort of roster every hour, it seems likely that a court will conclude that that amounted to confinement for purposes of administrative credit, and possibly

---

21. *See* Article 13, U.C.M.J., which indicates that restraint shall be no more rigorous than circumstances warrant. *See also* United States v. Heard, 3 M.J. 14 (C.M.A. 1977).

22. United States v. Heard, 3 M.J. 14 (C.M.A. 1977); Courtney v. Williams, 1 M.J. 267 (C.M.A. 1976).

23. For a discussion on the review procedures for pretrial confinement, see § 5-3(B)(4). Note that R.C.M. 305(j) indicates that upon a motion for appropriate relief, the judge shall review the propriety of pretrial confinement; the Rule states specific criteria which the judge should address. The topic of illegal pretrial restraint is also discussed at § 5-3(C).

24. United States v. Martinez, 19 M.J. 744 (A.C.M.R. 1984); United States v. Gambini, 10 M.J. 618 (A.F.C.M.R. 1980).

25. R.C.M. 905(e). United States v. Huffman, 36 M.J. 636 (A.C.M.R. 1992) (accused waived challenge to illegal pretrial punishment by not raising it before military magistrate or military judge); United States v. Martinez, 19 M.J. 744 (A.C.M.R. 1984).

26. *See, e.g.,* United States v. Peacock, 19 M.J. 909 (A.C.M.R. 1985).

27. 19 M.J. 274 (C.M.A. 1985).

28. *See, e.g.,* United States v. Moore, 32 M.J. 774 (A.C.M.R. 1991) (accused's 110-day restriction to company area was not tantamount to confinement); United States v. Russell, 30 M.J. 977 (A.C.M.R. 1990) (under test of totality of circumstances, pretrial restraint to bare barracks room amounted to pretrial confinement for which administrative credit was given because no magisterial review was conducted); United States v. Smith, 20 M.J. 528 (A.C.M.R. 1985) (restraint amounted to confinement); Washington v. Greewald, 20 M.J. 823 (A.C.M.R. 1985) (restraint not equivalent to confinement); United States v. DiMatteo, 19 M.J. 903 (A.C.M.R. 1985) (custody in unit's storage room amounted to pretrial confinement).

confinement for purposes of determining whether the accused has been denied a speedy trial.[29]

Although appellate courts have indicated that such administrative credit may be granted where the issue was raised for the first time on appeal,[30] it would be prudent for counsel to raise it in a pretrial motion.

§ 13-5(C). Change of Location of Trial.

If the accused can show by a preponderance of the evidence that he cannot obtain a fair trial because of a general atmosphere of prejudice at the site of the trial,[31] the judge may rule that the site should be changed, usually to another military installation.[32] This type of motion was formerly labeled as a motion for a change of venue.[33] In 1984 the *Manual* was changed, however, to reflect the fact that in military practice the trial need not be conducted in the same location as where the offense was committed.[34] Consequently, the government has some discretion in choosing the situs of the trial.[35] In most cases the situs will be at the installation where the offense occurred. But the situs may also be changed to accommodate the convenience of the parties and witnesses.[36] For example, it might be appropriate to shift the situs of the trial to a location where key defense witnesses and evidence are located.[37] In turn, that "convenience" should be balanced against the inconveniences to the Government.[38] On the other hand, if the situs is shifted to accommodate only the prosecution, then the test is whether the accused's rights have been prejudiced.[39]

---

29. *See* § 13-3(C).
30. United States v. Cahill, 23 M.J. 544 (A.C.M.R. 1986) (four days of administrative credit where there was increase in conditions of restraint); United States v. Smith, 20 M.J. 528 (A.C.M.R. 1985).
31. R.C.M. 906(b)(11). United States v. Anderson, 36 M.J. 963 (A.F.C.M.R. 1993) (burden rests on accused to show the need for change of location of trial); United States v. Loving, 34 M.J. 956 (A.F.C.M.R. 1992) (accused not entitled to change of location of murder trial; military judge took appropriate steps to shield members from external influence; accused challenged no member on basis of media publicity or knowledge of case); United States v. Smith, 1 M.J. 1204 (N.C.M.R. 1977); United States v. Gravitt, 5 C.M.A. 249, 17 C.M.R. 249 (1954).
32. The choice of sites must be left to the convening authority insofar as his selection is not inconsistent with the ruling of the military judge. R.C.M. 906(b)(11) Discussion. *See generally* United States v. Bennett, 12 M.J. 463 (C.M.A. 1982).
33. 1969 MCM, para. 69e. United States v. Anderson, 36 M.J. 963 (A.F.C.M.R. 1993) (motion for change of place of trial is "near counterpart of venue in civilian practice").
34. Chenoweth v. Van Arsdall, 22 C.M.A. 183, 46 C.M.R. 183 (1973).
35. R.C.M. 906(b)(11) Analysis. The government's interest is both financial and operational.
36. United States v. Bennett, 12 M.J. 463 (C.M.A. 1982).
37. This possibility is implicitly recognized in the Discussion to R.C.M. 906(b)(11) which indicates that the situs may be changed where it is necessary to obtain compulsory process over an essential witness. *See generally* United States v. Carey, 1 M.J. 761 (A.F.C.M.R. 1975); United States v. Cox, 23 C.M.R. 535 (A.B.R. 1957).
38. United States v. Bennett, 12 M.J. 463 (C.M.A. 1982).
39. R.C.M. 906(b)(11).

The judge's ruling is final and may be reversed only for abuse of discretion.[40]

§ 13-5(D). Defective Pretrial Investigation or Pretrial Advice.

An accused may be entitled to a new, or reopened, Article 32 Investigation[41] or a new Article 34 Pretrial Advice[42] if he can show a prejudice to a substantial right[43] by a preponderance of the evidence.[44] The accused is entitled to that relief regardless of whether it will ultimately benefit him at trial.[45] A guilty plea will normally waive the defects.[46] Note that these motions must be raised prior to the accused's plea,[47] and failure to do so will result in waiver absent good cause.[48] For more detailed discussions on the pretrial investigation and advice, see Chapter 7.

§ 13-5(E). Defective Pleadings: Motions to Cure or Amend.

A motion for appropriate relief to cure a defective pleading may be used to make a vague specification more specific, or cause the prosecution to cure duplicious[49] or multiplicious specifications.[50] The motion could be in the form of a bill of particulars, which is discussed in § 13-5(F), or simply in the form of a request to clarify the wording of the specification. A bill of particulars would be more appropriate where the focus of the defense request is not on the legal

---

40. United States v. Loving, 41 M.J. 213 (1994) (judge did not abuse discretion in denying change of venue motion considering that defense failed to challenge any member for cause on the grounds that they had been exposed to pretrial publicity); United States v. Anderson, 36 M.J. 963 (A.F.C.M.R. 1993) (no abuse of discretion to deny accused's motion for change of location where two members had previously reviewed news media reports of incident); United States v. Nivens, 21 C.M.A. 420, 45 C.M.R. 194 (1972); United States v. Geiss, 30 M.J. 678 (A.F.C.M.R. 1990) (judge did not abuse discretion in denying motion for a change of venue from Panama to the United States); United States v. Carey, 1 M.J. 761 (A.F.C.M.R. 1975).
41. Art. 32, U.C.M.J. See Appendix 3. United States v. Donaldson, 23 C.M.A. 293, 49 C.M.R. 542 (1975).
42. Art. 34, U.C.M.J. United States v. Henry, 50 C.M.R. 685 (A.F.C.M.R. 1975).
43. United States v. Johnson, 7 M.J. 396 (C.M.A. 1979); United States v. Mickel, 9 C.M.A. 324, 26 C.M.R. 104 (1958); United States v. Marrie, 39 M.J. 993 (A.F.C.M.R. 1994) (accused not prejudiced by investigating officer's application of incorrect rule for determining witness' availability); United States v. Teeter, 12 M.J. 716 (A.C.M.R. 1981) (accused not denied substantial right of discovery where he was able to depose the witness prior to trial).
    In United States v. Saunders, 11 M.J. 912 (A.C.M.R. 1981), the court granted relief even absent a showing of prejudice where the accused was not mentally competent at the Article 32 investigation.
44. R.C.M. 905(c)(2)(A).
45. *See, e.g.,* United States v. Mickel, 9 C.M.A. 324, 26 C.M.R. 104 (1958).
46. *See, e.g.,* United States v. Packer, 8 M.J. 785 (N.C.M.R. 1980) (waived objection to Art. 32 investigation).
47. R.C.M. 905(b)(1).
48. R.C.M. 905(e).
49. For a discussion on duplicious pleadings, see § 6-1(C)(2). *See also* § 13-5(G)(3), which covers motions to sever duplicitous pleadings.
50. *See* §§ 6-1(C)(2) and 13-3(J) for discussions on multiplicious pleadings.

sufficiency of the specification itself but rather on the details or facts that the prosecution will be using to prove its case.

The burden rests upon the accused[51] who must raise the issue prior to the plea[52] or risk waiver.[53] If the specification is so defective that it does not state an offense, the accused will generally be entitled to relief in the form of dismissal.[54] If the specification states an offense but it is apparent that the defense has been substantially misled, the judge may dismiss the specification in the interest of justice[55] or simply order a continuance.[56]

It is usually the accused that moves for the relief. In theory, however, the government could move to amend its own pleadings.[57] Amendments to the specification itself are usually approved only if the changes are "minor."[58] And in that case the changes may be made over the objection of the accused.[59] If the changes are not minor, the charge and specification will generally have to be resworn, re-referred, and possibly subjected to other pretrial screening rules.[60] For further discussion on amendments to the pleadings, see § 6-1(B)(2). In any event, if the government wishes to amend its pleadings during trial it should first raise the matter with the judge and defense present.

If the pleadings are amended after the accused enters his plea, he should be asked to re-enter his pleas.[61]

§ 13-5(F). Motion for a Bill of Particulars.

The history of using a bill of particulars in military practice is relatively short. Their use has been briefly mentioned in several cases[62] and commentaries,[63] on the subject of pleadings but until recently, the Manual-for-Courts-Martial did not specifically address the issue. Because federal practice was

---

51. R.C.M. 905(c)(2)(A).
52. R.C.M. 905(b)(1).
53. R.C.M. 905(e). United States v. Bucknell, 26 M.J. 523 (A.C.M.R. 1988) (failure to move that AWOL charge be made more specific was "fatal to his belated claim for appellate relief").
54. See § 13-3(F).
55. See R.C.M. 907(b)(3)(A) and § 13-3(F).
56. For a discussion on continuances, see § 13-5(K).
57. R.C.M. 603(c) implies that the prosecution may move to make minor changes in the pleadings so long as a substantial right of the accused is not prejudiced.
58. R.C.M. 906(b)(4). Minor changes are defined in R.C.M. 603(a) and are discussed at § 6-1(B)(2). Such changes would usually include deleting surplusage (irrelevant or redundant details or aggravating circumstances which are not necessary to escalate the punishment), correctly naming the accused, or correcting the designation of the article of the U.C.M.J. allegedly violated. R.C.M. 906(b)(4) Discussion.
59. R.C.M. 906(b)(4).
60. R.C.M. 603(d). In the case of a general court-martial the charges would be subject to another Article 32 investigation and pretrial advice. Id. at the Discussion. See also § 6-1(B)(2).
61. R.C.M. 906(b)(4) Discussion.
62. See, e.g., United States v. Alef, 3 M.J. 414, 419 n.18 (C.M.A. 1977); United States v. Paulk, 13 C.M.A. 456, 32 C.M.R. 456 (1963); United States v. Calley, 46 C.M.R. 1170 (A.C.M.R. 1973).
63. See Dunn, "Military Pleading," 17 A.F. L. Rev. 17 (Fall 1975); James, "Pleadings and Practice under United States v. Alef," 20 A.F. L. Rev. 22 (1978).

used in part in drafting the *Manual* provision,[64] practitioners should feel safe in relying to a great extent on federal case law on the subject. Like its federal counterpart, Federal Rule of Criminal Procedure 7(f), the military version is designed to: (1) inform the accused of the nature of the charge against him so that he may prepare for trial; (2) avoid or reduce the possibility that the accused will be surprised during trial; and (3) protect the accused from double jeopardy.[65]

While a motion to amend or cure a defect in the charges may provide the defense with some additional information about the basis of the pleadings, the bill of particulars, when properly used, should provide more specific factual details. The motion should be in the form of a request that the prosecution answer certain questions relating to the charge. For example, where there is a possible issue of exactly where an offense took place but the specification simply alleges that the offense took place on Range Road, the defense might request that the prosecution specify exactly where on Range Road the crime occurred. The inquiries should be specific and to the point.[66] For a sample motion, see Appendix 20.

Just how much information the prosecution may be required to disclose is not entirely clear from the federal cases. It does seem clear that a bill of particulars may not be used as a general discovery device to gather evidence which the prosecution might use against the defendant.[67] This generally tracks with the *Manual* language that simply says that a bill of particulars should not be used for discovery.[68] However, even where a bill is appropriate, the defense "discovers" some aspect of the prosecution case. Thus, the prosecution is not required to spell out the legal theory of its case[69] nor provide the names of witnesses it will call.[70] As a practical matter, that information can be gleaned from the charge itself or through the generous discovery, notice, and disclosure rules now applicable in military practice.[71] The *Manual* also indicates that a bill of particulars may not be used to "force detailed disclosure of acts underlying a charge...."[72] For example, if the accused is charged with possession of drugs, the prosecution would not be required to disclose the details of the evidence it intended to introduce at trial that would demonstrate that the possession was knowing.

---

64. R.C.M. 906(b)(6).
65. R.C.M. 906(b)(6) Discussion. *See also* United States v. Vesich, 726 F.2d 168 (5th Cir. 1984); United States v. Ilaskins, 345 F.2d 111 (6th Cir. 1965).
66. *See* Morgan v. United States, 380 F.2d 686 (9th Cir. 1967).
67. *See, e.g.,* Nye & Nissen v. United States, 168 F.2d 846 (9th Cir.), aff'd, 336 U.S. 613 (1948).
68. R.C.M. 906(b)(6) Discussion.
69. *See* Rose v. United States, 149 F.2d 755 (9th Cir. 1945). *Cf.* Yeargain v. United States, 314 F.2d 881 (9th Cir. 1963).
70. United States v. Elliott, 266 F. Supp. 318 (S.D.N.Y. 1967). However, the prosecution might be required to disclose this information under other rules governing disclosure or notice. *See* Chapter 10.
71. United States v. Mobley, 31 M.J. 273 (C.M.A. 1990) (accused's receipt of a complete list of witnesses and evidence government intended to offer was functional equivalent of bill of particulars). For a discussion on discovery, notice, and disclosure, see Chapter 10.
72. R.C.M. 906(b)(6).

A bill of particulars may not be used to cure defects in an otherwise void specification, i.e., one that fails to state an offense.[73] In that case the appropriate relief lies not in ordering the prosecution to provide more information but rather in dismissing the specification.[74] If, on the other hand, the requested information can be added through a simple and minor amendment to the specification, that procedure would seem preferable to formally answering a bill of particulars.

In federal practice, the prosecution is bound by its responses in the bill of particulars.[75] Thus, if there is a major variance between the information it supplied in the bill and the evidence it introduced at trial, the accused may be entitled to reversal if he can show prejudice, usually in the form of alleging that he was misled by relying on the bill of particulars.[76] Although the *Manual* indicates that a bill of particulars may not be used to restrict the government's proof at trial,[77] it also recognizes that the government may move to amend its bill of particulars at any time, "subject to such conditions as justice permits."[78] It would seem that the usual reason for amending the bill would be to insure that the bill does comport with the government's evidence. Ultimately, the test should be whether the accused has been misled by the bill of particulars. If he has been, then relief should be granted either in dismissal of the charges, a mistrial, or a continuance to provide the defense with an opportunity to prepare.

Whether to grant the defense motion and order the prosecution to respond to the inquiries lies within the discretion of the judge.[79] If the judge grants the motion he should enter an order, preferably written, which spells out in detail what information the prosecution is to provide. It would also be appropriate to specify a deadline for providing that information. The *Manual* makes no mention of what remedies might be applied if the prosecution is unduly tardy in responding, but at a minimum a continuance would seem appropriate. Because a bill of particulars is not a part of the specification, it need not be sworn.[80] For a sample order see Appendix 20.

---

73. R.C.M. 906(b)(6).
74. *See* § 13-3(F).
75. *See, e.g.,* United States v. Flom, 558 F.2d 1179 (5th Cir. 1977).
76. United States v. Birrell, 447 F.2d 1168 (1971).
77. R.C.M. 906(b)(6) Discussion.
78. R.C.M. 906(b)(6).
79. Wong Tai v. United States, 273 U.S. 77 (1927); United States v. Williams, 40 M.J. 379 (C.M.A. 1994) (judge did not abuse discretion in denying motion for bill of particulars where defense alleged that specification failed to allege specific dates of sexual offenses on child); United States v. Mobley, 31 M.J. 273 (C.M.A. 1990) (judge did not abuse discretion in failing to order a bill of particulars).
80. R.C.M. 906(b)(6) Discussion.

§ 13-5(G). Motions to Sever.

Severances may be an appropriate remedy where: (1) several accused are being tried in a joint or common trial; (2) where the prosecution's joinder of several offenses is prejudicial to the accused; or (3) an accused has been charged with more than one offense in a single specification, i.e., duplicious pleadings. *See* § 6-1(C)(2).

§ 13-5(G)(1). Severance of Accused.

In the case of a joint or common trial, requests for severances are usually liberally granted where the accused are able to show that such proceedings will be prejudicial. A common trial occurs where more than one accused is tried on the same or related charges.[81] In a joint trial a common set of charges and specifications allege identical criminal activity by more than one accused.[82] In both joint and common trials the accused are accorded the same rights as if they were being tried separately. Illustrations of proper grounds for severance include inconsistent defenses,[83] inconsistent pleas,[84] inconsistent requests regarding forum,[85] or instances where the prosecution will be using a pretrial statement of one accused which implicates a co-accused.[86] In the case of a common trial, the *Manual* directs that a severance must be granted where any accused, other than the one requesting the severance, is being tried for charges unrelated to those for which the moving party is being tried.[87]

Where the defense is requesting a severance in a common trial, the *Manual* indicates that the judge, not the prosecution, may decide which accused will be tried first.[88] And in the case of a joint trial, the judge should direct that the

---

81. R.C.M. 601(e)(3). United States v. Mayhugh, 41 M.J. 657 (N.M. Ct. Crim. App. 1994) (accused tried in joint trial). *See generally* Corrigan, "Prejudicial Joinder: The Crazy Quilt World of Severances," 68 MIL. L. REV. 1 (1975).

82. R.C.M. 601(e)(3). In United States v. Evans, 39 M.J. 613 (A.C.M.R. 1994), the court held that an accused does not have standing to object to a convening authority's decision to order separate trials of co-accused. Citing Federal Rule of Criminal Procedure and federal cases on the issue, the court noted that the rules governing joinder of accused do not have as their purpose the protection of personal interests or liberties.

83. For example, in a drug case, one of the accused may defend on the grounds of alibi and another accused defend on grounds of entrapment. *See generally* United States v. Oliver, 14 C.M.A. 192, 33 C.M.R. 404 (1963).

84. United States v. Baca, 14 C.M.A. 76, 33 C.M.R. 288 (1963). The obvious example would be where one accused pleads guilty and the co-accused enters a plea of not guilty. See Chapter 14 for a discussion on pleas.

85. *See* R.C.M. 912 Discussion. As noted in Chapter 12, an accused may choose between trial by court members or trial by judge alone. An enlisted accused has the additional right to request that enlisted personnel be assigned as court members.

86. United States v. Pringle, 3 M.J. 308 (C.M.A. 1977); United States v. Green, 3 M.J. 320 (C.M.A. 1977); United States v. Gooding, 18 C.M.A. 188, 39 C.M.R. 188 (1969); United States v. McHugh, 41 M.J. 657 (N.M.Ct.Crim.App. 1994) (judge did not allow statements of accused in joint trial to be used against the others). *See also* Rule 306, MIL. R. EVID. and Saltzburg, Schinasi & Schlueter, *Military Rules of Evidence Manual* 240-42 (3d ed. 1991).

87. R.C.M. 906(b)(9).

88. R.C.M. 906(b)(9), 801(a)(1).

appropriate amendments be made to the charges to delete references to the severed accused.[89] A judge's denial of a motion to sever will be measured for an abuse of discretion.[90]

§ 13-5(G)(2). Severance of Charges.

If it appears that the government has improperly joined several charges for a trial, the defense may seek relief through a severance of those charges.[91] The fact that the government has joined major and minor offenses is generally not sufficient to justify a severance.[92] The general rule is that all known charges should normally be tried at one time and unless the defense can show some reason why it will be unduly prejudiced by joinder of such offenses, relief will probably be denied.[93] Several examples would include a case where the accused wishes to testify as to one, but not all of the charges or where court members might easily confuse the evidence.[94] A severance of charges might also be appropriate where the prosecution has appealed the judge's ruling with regard to one of the charges and under the circumstances it is appropriate to continue the proceedings as to any remaining charges which are unaffected by the ruling.[95] The *Manual* lists the example of severing a charge where an essential witness to that charge is currently unavailable and to wait

---

89. R.C.M. 906(b)(9) Discussion.
90. United States v. Mayhugh, 41 M.J. 657 (N.M. Ct. Crim.App. 1994) (judge did not abuse discretion in denying defense motion to sever accused being tried jointly).
91. R.C.M. 906(b)(10). In United States v. Haye, 29 M.J. 213 (C.M.A. 1989), the court observed that motions to sever are a rarity in military practice for two reasons: First, they are usually denied and secondly, the unitary sentencing in the military generally favors proceeding on all known charges at one time. See § 6-1(C)(1) for a more complete discussion of this case. Note that this provision suggests that severance of charges is appropriate only where it is necessary to prevent "manifest injustice." United States v. Barrow, 42 M.J. 655 (A.F. Ct. Crim. App. 1995) (judge did not abuse discretion in denying motion to sever charges; court noted that during voir dire the defense counsel specifically asked members about possibility of spillover and members responded that they would consider charges separately).
92. R.C.M. 906(b)(10) Discussion. This changes the former practice of forbidding such combinations. *See* 1969 MCM, para. 26c.
93. R.C.M. 906(b)(10). United States v. Hanson, 39 M.J. 610 (A.C.M.R. 1994) (joinder of unrelated offenses not in itself sufficient ground for severance); United States v. Kirks, 34 M.J. 646 (A.C.M.R. 1992) (severance not required where military judge, in effect, conducted bifurcated trial and instructed court not to consider potential spillover evidence). *Cf.* United States v. Oakley, 33 M.J. 27 (C.M.A. 1991) (trial court properly granted government's motion to sever charges where accused was not willing to waive the five-day service requirement; both sides were prepared to try the case and several witnesses had travelled some distance to attend; court noted possible problems associated with balancing general desire to try all known charges at one trial and accused's right to insist on five-day period).
94. *See* United States v. Curry, 31 M.J. 359 (C.M.A. 1990) (no prejudice from joinder of offenses where evidence of the other crime would have been admissible in each separate prosecution); United States v. Haye, 29 M.J. 213 (C.M.A. 1989) (court concluded that inadmissible evidence on adultery specification had prejudicial spillover effect, despite judge's instructions, on fraternization specification).
95. For a discussion on the effect of a government appeal on a pending trial, see § 13-2(G)(2).

for the witness would deny the accused a speedy trial.[96] Failure to object at trial will normally waive the issue.[97]

§ 13-5(G)(3). Severance of Duplicitous Specification.

Where the defense is alleging that a specification is defective because it is duplicitous,[98] the judge may grant relief by directing the prosecution to sever the defective specification into two or more separate specifications.[99] Where that occurs, the resulting specification may fail to allege an offense, which may result in dismissal[100] or a continuance where it appears that the accused has been mislead and needs additional time to prepare for trial.[101]

Failure to raise the issue of severance prior to entry of a plea will generally constitute waiver.[102]

§ 13-5(H). Requests Concerning Individual Military Counsel or Retention of Detailed Military Counsel.

The convening authority's denial of requests for individual military counsel[103] or retention of detailed counsel (where the accused's request for individual counsel has been granted)[104] may not be overruled or voided by the trial judge.[105] Instead, the defense is left with requesting that the judge note for the record that such requests were made and denied.[106] The judge may consider evidence on the issue and enter findings on the question of whether the convening authority abused his discretion.[107] And the prosecution may request a continuance to inform the convening authority of those findings.[108] It is possi-

---

96. R.C.M. 906(b)(10) Discussion.
97. R.C.M. 905(b)(5), (e). United States v. Hanson, 39 M.J. 610 (A.C.M.R. 1994) (accused waived objection to joinder of offenses by not objecting at trial).
98. R.C.M. 906(b)(5). A specification is duplicitous if it alleges two or more offenses. A specification that alleges a continuous course of conduct at different times is generally not duplicitous. United States v. Adams, 13 M.J. 728 (A.C.M.R. 1982); United States v. Grubbs, 13 M.J. 594 (A.F.C.M.R. 1982). And allegations of a continuing offense are likewise generally not duplicitous. United States v. Aloyian, 16 C.M.A. 333, 36 C.M.R. 489 (1966). *See also* United States v. Davis, 16 C.M.A. 207, 36 C.M.R. 363 (1966) (offenses committed over four-month period were separate).
99. R.C.M. 906(b)(5). Severing the specification is the "sole" remedy. *Id.*
100. *See* § 13-3(F) for a discussion on motions to dismiss for failure to state an offense.
101. For a general discussion on continuances, *see* § 13-5(K).
102. R.C.M. 905(b)(1), (e). United States v. Mincey, 42 M.J. 376 (1995) (accused's failure to move to sever numerous bad-check offenses in one specification waived issue).
103. Requests for individual military counsel are addressed in § 8-3(B). *See* R.C.M. 506(b).
104. *See* R.C.M. 506(b)(3) and §§ 8-3(B), 12-2(F)(2).
105. R.C.M. 906(b)(5). United States v. Anderson, 36 M.J. 963 (A.F.C.M.R. 1993) (judge has no authority to overrule convening authority's administrative decision denying individual counsel). For a discussion on the accused's request for individual military counsel, see § 8-3(B).
106. R.C.M. 906(b)(5).
107. United States v. Redding, 11 M.J. 100 (C.M.A. 1981); United States v. Kelker, 4 M.J. 323 (C.M.A. 1978); United States v. Quinones, 1 M.J. 64 (C.M.A. 1975); United States v. Anderson, 36 M.J. 963 (A.F.C.M.R. 1993) (appellate court found no abuse of discretion in convening authority's denial of request for individual counsel).
108. R.C.M. 906(b)(5).

ble that a judge's "findings" may persuade the convening authority to reconsider his denial and thus avoid an appellate issue. The judge may not, however, dismiss the charges.[109] That relief is reserved for the appellate courts.[110] But in appropriate cases the trial judge may grant other relief, such as a continuance where it appears that the accused's request was denied because the counsel in question is temporarily unavailable.[111] The burden of proof on this issue rests upon the defense, which must demonstrate that the convening authority abused his discretion.[112] There is some authority that the judge need not consider the issue if the defense has not exhausted administrative review or appeal of the convening authority's decision.[113] The accused may waive the denial of a request of counsel by not objecting at trial.[114]

For further discussion on requests for counsel, see § 8-3(B); for a discussion on the judge's inquiries concerning the accused's choice of counsel, see § 12-2(F).

§ 13-5(I). Request for Witnesses.

If defense requests for witnesses have been denied by the convening authority, a motion for appropriate relief is the proper vehicle for raising the issue before the military judge[115] who must determine whether the witness should be produced under the rules discussed in Chapter 11. If the accused meets his burden[116] and the judge orders production of the witness, the government must comply or risk abatement of the trial or dismissal of the charges.[117] This motion may survive a guilty plea[118] and, absent good cause, must be made before a plea is entered.[119] By waiting, the defense runs the risk of the judge denying the request on grounds that the request is untimely.[120] On appeal the issue is whether the judge abused his discretion in declining to order the government to produce the witness.[121]

---

109. R.C.M. 906(b)(5). United States v. Redding, 11 M.J. 100 (C.M.A. 1981).
110. United States v. Redding, 11 M.J. 100 (C.M.A. 1981).
111. R.C.M. 906(b)(5).
112. *See* United States v. Wallace, 14 M.J. 1019 (A.C.M.R. 1982); United States v. Smith, 3 M.J. 912 (A.C.M.R. 1977).
113. United States v. Gray, 14 M.J. 816 (A.C.M.R. 1982); United States v. West, 13 M.J. 800 (A.C.M.R. 1982).
114. United States v. Anderson, 36 M.J. 963 (A.F.C.M.R. 1993) (accused may waive issue by not objecting at trial; although trial court is powerless to overrule convening authority's denial of individual counsel, accused must still object and perfect record).
115. R.C.M. 906(b)(7). *See generally* Gasperini, "Witness Production and the Right to Compulsory Process," ARMY LAW., Sept. 1980, at 22. The judge's ruling is interlocutory and final.
116. R.C.M. 905(c)(2)(A).
117. *See* R.C.M. 703 and § 11-2(B).
118. R.C.M. 910(j).
119. R.C.M. 905(b)(4).
120. *See* United States v. Cottle, 14 M.J. 260 (C.M.A. 1982) (counsel assumes the risk by waiting).
121. *See, e.g.,* United States v. Dorgan, 39 M.J. 827 (A.C.M.R. 1994) (judge abused discretion in denying defense request for production of material civilian witness); United States v. Rust, 38 M.J. 726 (A.F.C.M.R. 1993) (no abuse of discretion to deny defense request for two expert wit-

§ 13-5(J). Discovery.

Motions for discovery or for production of evidence must be made prior to the plea[122] and are usually mooted by pretrial disclosure of the requested materials.[123] The preferred practice is to first request relief from the convening authority or trial counsel, although doing so will not preclude the defense from raising the issue before the military judge.[124] The defense bears the burden of establishing that the requested information is relevant and otherwise discoverable.[125] The judge's ruling is subject to review for abuse of discretion.[126] In deciding a motion concerning discovery, the military judge may examine the materials *in camera*[127] to determine their potential materiality to the case.[128] If the request is denied, the military judge should seal the materials.[129] They should be included as appellate exhibits in the record of trial, thus preserving the movant's right to appeal the ruling and providing the appellate courts with the information denied to the movant.[130] On appeal of the ruling, the sealed materials are accessible only to the judges, not counsel.[131] The topics of disclosure and discovery are discussed in more detail in Chapter 10.

§ 13-5(K). Continuance.

Motions for continuances are generally self-explanatory. The burden rests on the moving party to demonstrate why a delay in the proceedings is required.[132]

---

nesses for reasons of cumulativeness of expected testimony; court noted that although normally two eyewitnesses are not cumulative, these witnesses could only give opinions interpreting what others had done); United States v. Jones, 20 M.J. 919 (N.M.C.M.R. 1985) (Judge abused discretion in denying request to defense character witness; court lists factors to be considered); United States v. Rappaport, 19 M.J. 708 (A.F.C.M.R. 1984) (no abuse of discretion where witness's statements were vague, uncertain, and irrelevant).

122. R.C.M. 905(b)(3).
123. *See* Chapter 10.
124. R.C.M. 905(j).
125. United States v. Franchia, 13 C.M.A. 315, 32 C.M.R. 315 (1962). *See generally* Luedtke, "Open Government and Military Justice," 87 MIL. L. REV. 7 (1980). *See also* Art. 40, U.C.M.J.
126. *See* United States v. Charles, 40 M.J. 414 (C.M.A. 1994) (judge's ruling denying discovery reviewable by appellate court which provides de novo review whether requested materials were material to guilt or punishment and favorable to the defense; here, requested documents were not included in record of trial and Court of Military Review erred in finding harmless error without first reviewing materials in question); United States v. Jones, 20 M.J. 919 (N.M.C.M.R. 1985) (no abuse of discretion in declining to order disclosure of confidential drug records of witnesses where they had admitted using drugs).
127. *See, e.g.*, United States v. Branoff, 34 M.J. 612, 622, n. 19 (A.F.C.M.R. 1992) (*in camera* inspection may proceed with one or more of the parties excluded).
128. United States v. Branoff, 34 M.J. 612 (A.F.C.M.R. 1992).
129. R.C.M. 701(g)(2). United States v. Branoff, 34 M.J. 612 (A.F.C.M.R. 1992).
130. R.C.M. 701(g)(2). United States v. Branoff, 34 M.J. 612 (A.F.C.M.R. 1992).
131. United States v. Branoff, 34 M.J. 612 (A.F.C.M.R. 1992).
132. R.C.M. 905(c)(2)(A). United States v. Dunks, 1 M.J. 254 (C.M.A. 1976).

Where the judge denies a continuance the test should be whether he abused his discretion.[133] But the inquiry may go deeper than that where it appears that failure to grant the continuance denied an important or fundamental trial right.[134] Counsel may also achieve a similar result by filing a motion for abatement of the trial. For example, in *United States v. Anderson*,[135] the defense filed a motion to abate the court-martial until after pending state charges had been resolved.

This motion can be made at any time during the trial and will often be linked with one of the foregoing motions. That is, some delay may be required to effect the judge's ruling or seek appellate relief of a ruling. Note that in *United States v. Browers*[136] the court ruled that denial of a continuance is not the sort of ruling that should be the subject of an appeal under Article 62, U.C.M.J., or its *Manual* counterpart, R.C.M. 908.[137] In that case the trial judge denied the prosecution's request to obtain witnesses important to its case.

§ 13-5(L). Motions to Obtain Rulings on Evidentiary Matters; Motions in *Limine*.

If counsel wants to obtain an early ruling on the admissibility of evidence, the appropriate vehicle is a request that the matter be resolved before trial begins.[138] The request, or motion, may be in the form of (1) a motion to obtain a ruling on a particular piece of evidence,[139] (2) a motion to suppress, which is usually limited to evidence obtained under Section III of the Military Rules of Evidence,[140] or (3) a motion *in limine*, which is like a motion to suppress in that it is an attempt to block introduction of evidence.

The common law motion *in limine* is not formally recognized in the U.C.M.J. nor separately listed by name in the Manual for Courts-Martial among motions for appropriate relief.[141] Nonetheless, use of such motions are

---

133. R.C.M. 906(b)(1). United States v. Sullivan, 26 M.J. 442 (C.M.A. 1988) (judge did not abuse discretion in denying defense request for continuance where the matter had been known and in litigation for several months in other related cases).

United States v. Andrews, 36 M.J. 922 (A.F.C.M.R. 1993) (abuse of discretion standard is strict; challenged action must be arbitrary, clearly erroneous, or clearly unreasonable; in this case judge committed reversible error in denying defense request); United States v. Gipson, 25 M.J. 781 (A.C.M.R. 1988) (no abuse of discretion under facts to deny civilian counsel's request for continuance to prepare for trial); United States v. Garries, 19 M.J. 845 (A.F.C.M.R. 1985). *See also* United States v. Perry, 14 M.J. 856 (A.C.M.R. 1982) (judge should balance the interests of the parties).

134. *See, e.g.*, United States v. Phillips, 37 M.J. 532 (A.C.M.R. 1993) (no abuse of discretion in denying request for continuance to obtain civilian counsel; court concluded that purpose of motion was to avoid trial); United States v. Browers, 20 M.J. 542 (A.C.M.R. 1985) (denial of continuance to obtain witness), *rev'd*, 20 M.J. 356 (C.M.A. 1985).

135. 36 M.J. 963 (A.F.C.M.R. 1993).

136. 20 M.J. 356 (C.M.A. 1985).

137. For a general discussion on government appeals of a judge's rulings, see § 13-2(G)(2).

138. R.C.M. 906(b)(13).

139. R.C.M. 906(b)(13). *See also* Rule 104, Mil. R. Evid.

140. *See* § 13-4 for a discussion on motions to suppress.

141. The term is used, however, in the Drafters Analysis to R.C.M. 906(b)(13) and in the Discussion to R.C.M. 905(b)(3).

firmly planted in current military practice.[142] Although the format of the motion is normally not crucial, the movant should specify what evidence is in question and state the grounds for contesting its admissibility. This type of motion may be effective where the movant's objection is grounded on Military Rule of Evidence 403 (Exclusion of Relevant Evidence on Grounds of Prejudice, Confusion, or Waste of Time).[143] Some pretrial balancing by the military judge may save time and avoid confusion that might otherwise result if raised for the first time during the trial.

Motions *in limine* have often been used to determine before trial whether the government will be permitted to introduce a prior conviction to impeach the accused if he takes the stand.[144] However, in *Luce v. United States*,[145] the Supreme Court indicated that a trial judge would not be required to rule on that issue until the accused took the stand and it was apparent that the government intended to use the prior conviction. In *United States v. Welch*,[146] the Court indicated that the *Luce* case was applicable to courts-martial.[147]

Initially it appeared, however, that the ruling in *Luce* would be read by the military courts to apply only to motions *in limine*to block admission of prior convictions. In *United States v. Gamble*,[148] the court indicated that a trial judge's pretrial ruling on the issue of whether evidence of uncharged misconduct[149] was admissible was sufficient in itself to preserve error for appeal and the defense was not required to renew the objection at trial. Noting the possible inconsistency with *Luce*, the court read R.C.M. 905 to mean that the efficiency of military trials would be enhanced if a judge's rulings on motions *in limine* were given binding effect.[150] But in *United States v. Sutton*,[151] the court held that in the future it would follow the *Luce* decision and any other Supreme Court precedents that addressed the issue of whether the defendant was entitled to an *in limine* ruling on other impeachment evidence before deciding whether to take the stand.[152]

---

142. *See, e.g.,* United States v. Sutton, 31 M.J. 11 (C.M.A. 1990); United States v. Cofield, 11 M.J. 422 (C.M.A. 1981). *See generally* Siano, "Motions in Limine, An Often Neglected Common Law Motion," ARMY LAW., Jan. 1976, at 17. The article contains sample formats for written motions.
143. Rule 403, MIL. R. EVID.
144. *See* Rule 609, MIL. R. EVID.
145. 105 S. Ct. 460 (1984). The *Luce* case is applicable to courts-martial. United States v. Welch, 25 M.J. 23, 26 (C.M.A. 1987); United States v. Cofield, 11 M.J. 422 (C.M.A. 1981).
146. 25 M.J. 23, 26 (C.M.A. 1987).
147. *See also* United States v. Cofield, 11 M.J. 422 (C.M.A. 1981); United States v. Sutton, 27 M.J. 578 (A.F.C.M.R. 1988) (without the evidence in issue being offered later at trial, it is difficult to assess possible prejudice if the judge erred and admitted it).
148. 27 M.J. 298 (C.M.A. 1988).
149. *See* MIL. R. EVID. 404(b).
150. 27 M.J. at 307.
151. 31 M.J. 11 (C.M.A. 1990).
152. *See, e.g.,* United States v. Cannon, 33 M.J. 376 (C.M.A. 1991) (trial judge may properly defer ruling on motion *in limine* regarding admissibility of uncharged misconduct, even if the deferral presents a chilling effect on defense presentation of character evidence); United States v. Rusinskas, 35 M.J. 808 (N.M.C.M.R. 1992) (*Sutton* ruling applies to *in limine* rulings on impeach-

The obvious difficulty with pretrial rulings on evidence is that whether a particular piece of evidence is admissible can often only be determined in the context of other evidence actually offered at trial. Thus, the judge's ruling may be a preliminary or nonbinding ruling that may provide little assistance to the moving party. But there is much to be said for resolving as many evidentiary points before trial as possible, especially where it is apparent that an informed ruling can be made without waiting until trial. In addition to saving time during the trial itself, preliminary rulings also ensure that inadmissible evidence will not be disclosed to the court members.[153]

While motions to suppress must be raised prior to the plea,[154] other motions challenging admissibility of evidence should be permitted throughout the trial. The decision to rule on this motion before trial generally lies within the sound discretion of the judge.[155] If a judge refuses to rule on the motion, his reasons for doing so should be clearly stated for the record.[156]

---

ment evidence; accused's failure to testify following unsuccessful *in limine* motion to block evidence of impeachment evidence statement waived error).

153. *See* R.C.M. 906(b)(13) Discussion.
154. R.C.M. 905(b)(3).
155. R.C.M. 906(b)(13) Discussion. United States v. Helweg, 32 M.J. 129 (C.M.A. 1991) (judge deferred ruling on motion *in limine*); United States v. Cannon, 30 M.J. 886 (A.F.C.M.R. 1990) (judge did not abuse discretion in deferring ruling on motion *in limine* regarding uncharged misconduct).
156. United States v. Gerard, 11 M.J. 440 (C.M.A. 1981).

APPENDIX REFERENCES

Appendix 1. Abbreviations.
Appendix 2. Glossary.
Appendix 3. U.C.M.J.
Appendix 10. Sample Discovery Request.
Appendix 11. Grant of Immunity.
Appendix 19. Disclosure of Section III Evidence.
Appendix 20. Bill of Particulars.
Appendix 21. Notice of Government Appeal.
Appendix 22. Plea Worksheet.
Appendix 23. Entry of Conditional Guilty Plea Form.

ANNOTATED BIBLIOGRAPHY

BOOKS

Moyer, *Justice and the Military* (1972).

  This one volume, 6-chapter, loose-leaf reference contains detailed discussions of the role of commanders, jurisdiction, military criminal procedure, substantive law, and collateral review of courts-martial by the civilian court system. An excellent discussion on First Amendment rights is in Chapter IV.

Saltzburg, Schinasi & Schlueter, *Military Rules of Evidence Manual* (3d ed. 1991).

  The authors have compiled the official text of the 1980 Military Rules of Evidence, with amendments, the drafters' analysis to those rules, and have provided an editorial comment for each rule that explains the rule, shows how it might be used, and discusses potential problem areas.

Zillman, Blaustein & Sherman, *The Military in American Society* (1978).

  This loose-leaf case book represents the efforts of nine individuals familiar with the workings of the military system of justice. Valuable discussions include treatment of the American military establishment, entry into the military, the military Justice system, individual rights of servicemembers, termination of military service and the law of armed conflict. Selected cases are discussed and notes for further reading are located at the end of each chapter.

PERIODICALS

Becker, "Litigating Mental Responsibility Under Article 50a," 28 A.F. L. Rev. 97 (1988).

  The author provides an insightful commentary on the historical aspects of litigating mental responsibility in courts-martial and examines the potential changes in practice which will result from Article 50a.

"Bibliography of Military Law," 10 Am. Crim. L. Rev. 175 (1971).

  This extensive bibliography lists finding aids, books, symposiums, surveys, service publications, and selected writings in legal periodicals. Most entries predate the 1968 amendments to the U.C.M.J.

Cruden & Clederer, "The First Amendment and Military Installations," 1984 DETROIT L. REV. 845 (1984).

Introducing an argument for reversal of *United States v. Albertini* (which recognized and expanded the First Amendment right to expression on military bases) this article provides a thorough discussion of the major cases in this area. The authors are sensitive to the unique position of the military under the Constitution and argue that the power to limit speech on military bases is necessary to preserve the armed forces' traditional political neutrality. The article is well-reasoned and documented and provides an excellent overview of the status of military installations as public forums for First Amendment expression.

Folk, "Military Appearance Requirements and Free Exercise of Religion," 98 MIL. L. REV. 53 (1982).

In this article, the author examines recent cases concerning claims to exemptions from military appearance standards based on the Free Exercise Clause of the First Amendment. The article documents the doctrinal problems encountered in this area and concludes by advocating renewed reliance, in this area, upon United States Supreme Court cases dealing with conscientious objector claims and the analysis utilized in these cases.

Gilligan, "Eyewitness Identification," 58 MIL. L. REV. 183 (1972).

Building on the *Wade-Gilbert-Stovall* trilogy governing eyewitness identification, the author examines the pre-Military Rules of Evidence right to counsel threshold in the civilian and military practice. He also presents a discussion of the trial procedures for moving to suppress such evidence and in conclusion presents a suggested format for service regulations designed to safeguard an accused's rights at a lineup.

Gilligan & Hahn, "Eyewitness Identification in Military Law," 110 MIL. L. REV. 1 (1985).

Noting the special dangers involved in eyewitness identification, the authors comprehensively set out the current state of the law and suggest several solutions to the evidentiary, instructional, and in-court problems inherent in this specialized area of the law.

Hirschhorn, "The Separate Community: Military Uniqueness and Servicemen's Constitutional Rights," 62 N.C. L. REV. 177 (1984).

In this scholarly and massive article (77 pages), the author undertakes an exhaustive critique of the fundamental thesis of civilian/military judicial relations, i.e., that the military is a "separate community" by virtue of its peculiar needs. The author first describes the separate development of civilian and military constitutional jurisprudence, and finds that neither the Supreme Court majority, with its "reflexive" hands-off attitude, nor the minority, which minimizes the distinctiveness of military needs, properly balances all relevant interests. Professor Hirschhorn then delves into the aspects of this doctrine of separation, its relevance to the role and performance of the individual soldier. The author, in conclusion, finds that the "Separate community" doctrine is a necessary and appropriate jurisprudential framework, with adequate political safeguards against abuse.

Kaczynski, "The Admissibility of Illegally Obtained Evidence: American and Foreign Approaches Compared," 101 Mil. L. Rev. 83 (1983).

In this article, the author compares the Exclusionary Rule, as it exists today in the United States, with the exclusionary-type rules currently utilized in other countries. The article concludes with a call for modification of the United States' Exclusionary Rule, and, as a source of possible alternatives, urges a serious analysis of similar laws in other countries.

Nagle, "Demonstrating Prejudice in Speedy Trial Cases," 13 The Advocate 89 (1981).

In addressing what he states to be one of the most frequently litigated motions in military practice, the author provides a good discussion of the requirement of showing prejudice. It categorizes the cases into three sections: (1) cases where pretrial delay is so unreasonable and oppressive that prejudice is irrelevant; (2) cases where prejudice is presumed; and (3) cases where actual prejudice must be shown. Regarding this third category the author does a fine job of discussing specific examples of prejudice (oppressive pretrial incarceration, impairment of the defense, and personal prejudice) and practical guidance on presenting the issue at trial.

Schlueter, "Gays and Lesbians in the Military: A Rationally Based Solution to a Legal Rubik's Cube," 29 Wake Forest L. Rev. 393 (1994).

The author addresses congressional action regarding the ability of gays and lesbians to serve in the armed forces and the potential constitutional law and military justice issues arising under that action.

Shaver, "Restoring the Promise of the Right to Speedy Trial to Service Members in Pretrial Arrent and Confinement," 147 Mil. L. Rev. 84 (1995).

This article presents a well-written and carefully analyzed discussion of the current speedy trial rules. In the author's view, the "teeth" that once existed in the military's rules have been removed, especially for those cases where the accused is in pretrial arrest or confinement.

Symposium, "Military Justice," Army Law., March 1996.

This 127-page symposium contains a Foreword and 11 short articles on a wide range of military justice topics. They are as follows:

Morris, "Foreword."
Barto, "Developments in the Substantive Criminal Law Under the Uniform Code of Military Justice."
Frisk, "New Developments in Pretrial Confinement."
Frisk, "New Developments in Speedy Trial."
Winn, "Recent Developments in Military Pretrial and Trial Procedure."
Masterton, "Recent Developments in Search and Seizure Law."
Masterton, "Recent Developments in Urinalysis Law."
Kohlman, "Are You Ready for Some Changes? Five Fresh Views of the Fifth Amendment."
Wright, "Sex, Lies, and Videotape: Child Sexual Abuse Cases Continue to Create Appellate Issues and Other Developments in the Areas of the Sixth Amendment, Discovery, Mental Responsibility, and Nonjudicial Punishment."

Henley, "Caveat Criminale: The Impact of the New Military Rules of Evidence in Sexual Offense and Child Molestation Cases."
Henley, "Current Developments in Evidence Law."
Morris, "New Developments in Sentencing and Post-Trial Procedure."

"Symposium, The Military Rules of Evidence," ARMY LAW., May 1980.

This fifty-five-page symposium issue contains seven articles on the Military Rules of Evidence. They are as follows:

Schinasi, "The Military Rules of Evidence: An Advocate's Tool."
Basham, "Suppression Motions Under the Military Rules of Evidence."
Yustas, "Mental Evaluations of an Accused Under the Military Rules of Evidence: An Excellent Balance."
Eisenberg, "Fourth Amendment Practice and the Military Rules of Evidence."
Schlueter, "Bodily Evidence and Rule 312, M.R.E."
Gasperini, "Eyewitness Identification Under the Military Rules of Evidence."
Green, "The Military Rules of Evidence and the Military Judge."

Wittmayer, "Rule for Courts-Martial 707: The 1984 Manual for Courts-Martial Speedy Trial Rule," 116 MIL. L. REV. 221 (1987).

This article presents an in-depth review of the original 1984 Manual for Courts-Martial (now simply referred to as the Manual for Courts-Martial) speedy trial rule and some of the problems that have arisen in interpreting its various provisions. The author notes that that rule reflects the view that if the government fails to provide a speedy trial the charges should be dismissed with prejudice. However, that view, he states, is at odds with the Sixth Amendment principle that dismissal should be reserved for those cases where there has been prejudice. The article contains an appendix comparing the various speedy trial provisions.

CHAPTER 14

PLEAS

§ 14-1. Introduction.
§ 14-2. Not Guilty Pleas.
§ 14-3. Guilty Pleas.
    § 14-3(A). Effects of Guilty Plea.
        § 14-3(A)(1). Waiver of Rights.
        § 14-3(A)(2). Waiver of Issues.
        § 14-3(A)(3). Plea as to a Lesser Offense.
        § 14-3(A)(4). Effect of Guilty Plea on Later Proceedings.
    § 14-3(B). The *Care* Providency Inquiry.
        § 14-3(B)(1). Advice Regarding Rights.
        § 14-3(B)(2). Determining the Accuracy of the Plea.
        § 14-3(B)(3). Determining the Voluntariness of the Plea.
        § 14-3(B)(4). Admissibility of Accused's Statements.
    § 14-3(C). The *Green-King* Pretrial Agreement Inquiry.
    § 14-3(D). Improvident Guilty Pleas.
        § 14-3(D)(1). In General.
        § 14-3(D)(2). *Alford* Pleas.
        § 14-3(D)(3). Misunderstanding of Sentence.
        § 14-3(D)(4). Factual and Legal Inconsistencies.
        § 14-3(D)(5). Procedural Consequences of an Improvident Plea.
    § 14-3(E). Entry of Findings.
    § 14-3(F). Informing the Members of the Accused's Plea of Guilty.
    § 14-3(G). Withdrawal of Guilty Plea.
§ 14-4. Conditional Pleas of Guilty.
§ 14-5. Irregular Pleas.
Appendix References.
Annotated Bibliography.

§ 14-1. Introduction.

Following arraignment[1] and consideration of any motions,[2] the military judge asks the accused to plead.[3] There are two basic categories of pleas in military practice: not guilty and guilty.[4] A variation on the guilty plea, the conditional guilty plea, was included in the 1984 revisions to the *Manual*.[5] The following sections will address in more detail these recognized pleas and the applicable rules and procedures for each.

---

1. See § 12-4 for a discussion on the procedural requisites of an arraignment.
2. Motions practice is discussed in Chapter 13.
3. As a practical matter the judge may ask the accused twice how he pleads. The standard language used by trial judges is as follows:

    _____, how do you plead? Before receiving your pleas, I advise you that any motions to dismiss any charge or to grant other relief should be made at this time.

After completing any hearings and arguments on motions, which in some cases may take a considerable amount of time, the judge normally again simply asks the accused to enter his pleas.

4. R.C.M. 910(a)(1). *See also* Art. 45, U.C.M.J. at Appendix 3.
5. R.C.M. 910(a)(2). *See* § 14-3(D).

An accused must enter a plea to both the charge and the specification,[6] and may plead to lesser included offenses through "exceptions" or "exceptions and substitutions."[7] Doing so, however, can lead to confusion for both the parties and the court reporter. In those cases counsel may find it particularly helpful to use a written plea worksheet that can be shown to the judge and reporter. For a sample plea worksheet, see Appendix 22. Note that entry of a plea is not a jurisdictional prerequisite[8] and entry of any plea may waive issues that should have been raised prior to the plea.[9]

The accused's plea is orally announced by the defense counsel, although the decision to enter a particular plea should be made by the accused with the advice of his counsel.[10] A coerced plea may result in reversal, especially where the accused enters a plea of guilty.[11]

As noted in the discussion of arraignments at § 12-4, after the accused has been arraigned, trial may proceed even in his absence. Thus, if the accused has voluntarily absented himself after arraignment but before entering his plea, a plea of not guilty should be entered on his behalf.[12]

§ 14-2. Not Guilty Pleas.

A "not guilty" plea requires the prosecution to prove the accused's guilt beyond a reasonable doubt and places all matters in issue.[1] If the accused has entered a mixed plea, that is, guilty of a lesser included offense[2] but not guilty of the greater offense through exceptions and substitutions, the prosecution's burden may be somewhat lightened. A common example is the case where the accused is charged with desertion[3] and enters a plea of guilty to the lesser

---

6. If the accused pleads guilty to the specification (or at least one of several specifications) but pleads not guilty to the charge, an irregular plea has resulted and the judge should immediately clarify the plea. See R.C.M. 910(b) Discussion.

7. R.C.M. 910(a)(1). The plea must relate to a recognizable offense.

8. United States v. Taft, 21 C.M.A. 68, 44 C.M.R. 122 (1971).

9. For example, as noted in § 13-2(B), failure to raise particular issues before entering a plea usually constitutes waiver. R.C.M. 905(e).

10. See ABA Code of Professional Responsibility, EC 7-8; ABA Standards, The Defense Function, Chapter 4.

11. See, e.g., United States v. Zuis, 49 C.M.R. 150 (A.C.M.R. 1974) (accused alleged that his counsel forced him to plead guilty).

12. Although an absent accused may have wished to plead guilty, without the accused present the judge would be faced with the difficult decision of determining whether the accused voluntarily entered a plea of guilty. Technically, in those situations the accused has failed to enter a plea and a not guilty plea should be entered by the judge. R.C.M. 910(b).

1. Note that the accused has a right to enter a plea of not guilty and require that the prosecution prove guilt beyond a reasonable doubt. Pleading guilty obviously waives this right. See § 14-3.

2. Lesser included offenses are listed with the discussion of each of the punitive articles in Part IV of the Manual. In 1993, R.C.M. 910(a)(1) was amended to permit an accused to plead not guilty to the charged offense but "guilty of a named lesser included offense." The change comports with federal practice. Where that sort of plea is entered, the defense should present the court with a copy of the revised specification and ask that it be included in the record as an appellate exhibit. R.C.M. 910(1)(1) Discussion.

3. Article 85, U.C.M.J. See generally § 2-2.

offense of unauthorized absence[4] and not guilty of the greater offense, i.e., desertion. The prosecution's burden would generally extend only to producing evidence on the issue of the accused's intent to remain away permanently.[5] In that case the judge would defer entering findings on the accused's guilty plea until the prosecution has had an opportunity to present additional evidence.[6]

A not guilty plea may be entered on behalf of the accused by the military judge where the accused enters an "irregular" plea[7] or an improvident guilty plea,[8] stands mute, or pleads guilty to an offense referred to trial as a capital case.[9] A not guilty plea may also be entered where the accused has absented himself after arraignment without entering a plea.[10] In each situation the trial proceeds to the merits with the prosecution carrying the burden as in any other contested case.[11]

In theory an accused who enters a not guilty plea may change that plea to one of guilty at any time before findings are announced by the court.[12] As a practical matter there is little to be gained by such a tactic unless the prosecution is willing to bargain for some relief. A midstream change of pleas might be useful in a hotly contested trial where the outcome is doubtful for both sides.

Note that entering a not guilty plea may act as a waiver of some motions which are to be raised before any plea is entered.[13]

§ 14-3. Guilty Pleas.

An accused may enter a plea of guilty to some or all of the charges and specification, and may enter a plea by exceptions and substitutions,[1] or a plea to a named lesser included offense.[2] However, there is no constitutional right to plead guilty[3] and military practice recognizes limitations on the ability of

---

4. Article 86, U.C.M.J.
5. The issue of the accused's intent is the one distinguishing element between the two offenses. *See* para. 9, Part IV, MCM.
6. R.C.M. 910(g)(2). *See also* § 14-3(F).
7. *See* § 14-5.
8. *See* § 14-3(E).
9. Art. 45(b), U.C.M.J. R.C.M. 910(a)(1).
10. United States v. Amos, 26 M.J. 806 (A.C.M.R. 1988).
11. R.C.M. 910(b).
12. United States v. Jeffries, 33 M.J. 826 (A.F.C.M.R. 1991) (accused changed plea from not guilty to guilty during trial); United States v. Williams, 26 M.J. 644 (A.C.M.R. 1988) (accused changed his plea of not guilty to guilty when the judge denied his motion for mistrial after the last prosecution witness had testified. The court noted that under the circumstances an instruction to the members that a guilty plea is a mitigating factor would not be appropriate).
13. *See generally* § 13-2(B).
1. R.C.M. 910(a)(1).
2. *See* R.C.M. 910(a)(1). This provision was amended in 1993 to comport with federal practice. Where that type of plea is entered, the defense should present the court with a copy of the revised specification and ask that it be included in the record as an appellate exhibit. R.C.M. 910(1)(1) Discussion.
3. Santobello v. New York, 404 U.S. 257 (1971); North Carolina v. Alford, 400 U.S. 25 (1970); United States v. Penister, 25 M.J. 148 (C.M.A. 1987) (although there is no constitutional right to

an accused to do so. A plea of guilty *must* be refused by the military judge if it is improvident,[4] irregular,[5] or is offered in a case referred to trial as a capital case.[6] The *Manual* also indicates that a guilty plea should not be accepted in a general or special court-martial in which the accused is not represented by counsel.[7] Assuming that the accused's plea of guilty does not fit into one of these categories, the judge may exercise discretion in deciding whether to permit the accused's plea to stand.[8] An example would be rejecting a plea that does not appear to be voluntary. Arbitrary rejection of a guilty plea, however, may constitute abuse of discretion.[9]

§ 14-3(A). Effects of Guilty Plea.

Although a guilty plea does not admit jurisdiction, it is the equivalent of a conviction[10] and is the strongest proof of an offense.[11] Because it waives a

---

plead guilty, accused has right to offer plea of guilty under Article 45); United States v. Matthews, 16 M.J. 354 (C.M.A. 1983).

4. R.C.M. 910(b). United States v. Bobroff, 23 M.J. 872 (N.M.C.M.R. 1987) (trial judge rejected guilty plea where factual basis relied upon by accused had nothing to do with government's theory of the crime). *See also* § 14-3(E).

5. R.C.M. 910(b). In United States v. Dock, 26 M.J. 620 (A.C.M.R. 1988) (en banc), *aff'd*, 28 M.J. 117 (C.M.A. 1989) the court, in a case of first impression, concluded that from the four corners of the record, the accused had impermissibly pleaded guilty to a capital offense. The accused pleaded guilty to unpremeditated murder and to robbery and during his opening statement counsel admitted that the accused killed the victim during the robbery. Because no defense was presented to the offense of felony murder, the accused in essence conceded guilt in violation of Article 45. *See also* § 14-5.

6. Art. 45(b), U.C.M.J. R.C.M. 910(a)(1). United States v. Matthews, 16 M.J. 354 (C.M.A. 1983); United States v. Snogdrass, 37 M.J. 844 (A.F.C.M.R. 1993) (in case of first impression, court held that accused's pretrial agreement requiring convening authority to change referral as non-capital case if military judge accepted pleas to premeditated murder, resulted in precluding imposition of death penalty).

7. R.C.M. 910(c)(2) Discussion. By placing this restriction in the nonbinding discussion, the drafters of the *Manual* have apparently recognized that in some cases it might be appropriate for an accused, representing himself, to plead guilty, as long as the judge is assured that the accused realizes the special dangers of waiving not only the right to counsel but also other important trial rights. *See* Brady v. United States, 397 U.S. 742 (1970) (plea of guilty is void if entered by defendant who has neither waived counsel nor been afforded the right to assistance of one). The Analysis to this Rule indicates that it was based in part upon para. 70b(1) of the 1969 *Manual*, which clearly indicated that a guilty plea should be rejected if the accused had not had an opportunity to consult with counsel or if he had refused counsel. If the judge is assured that in fact the accused has been fully apprised by a counsel of his rights, it may be appropriate to entertain a guilty plea; the detailed nature of the providency inquiry further insures that the accused is pleading guilty voluntarily and knowingly. *See also* United States v. Kniess, 264 F.2d 353 (7th Cir. 1969) (accused waived counsel and entered valid guilty plea).

8. *See, e.g.*, United States v. Matthews, 13 M.J. 501, 505 (A.C.M.R. 1982), *rev'd on other grounds*, 16 M.J. 354 (C.M.A. 1983) (the court indicated that it could find no abuse of discretion in the judge's cautious decision to reject the accused's offer to plead guilty to a rape charge).

9. United States v. Williams, 43 C.M.R. 579 (A.C.M.R. 1970).

10. Brady v. United States, 397 U.S. 742 (1970); Kercheval v. United States, 274 U.S. 220 (1926). *See generally* Gray, "The Professional Responsibilities of Defense Counsel in Uncontested Courts-Martial," 13 THE ADVOCATE 318 (1981).

11. Blackledge v. Allison, 431 U.S. 63 (1977); United States v. Joseph, 11 M.J. 333 (C.M.A. 1981).

number of rights,[12] before a guilty plea may be accepted, the military judge must conduct a *providency inquiry* and if a pretrial agreement is involved, an inquiry concerning its validity. Those inquiries are discussed in more detail in §§ 14-3(B) and (C). The following sections address several selected areas in which the effect of a guilty plea may have some special significance.

§ 14-3(A)(1). Waiver of Rights.

A plea of guilty waives a number of important constitutional rights that would otherwise be available to the accused.[13] First, by entering a plea of guilty the accused waives the right against self-incrimination.[14] As noted in § 14-3(B) the judge is required to conduct a searching inquiry of the factual basis of the offense. Thus, the accused is generally required not only to admit that he committed the offense but also to describe the details surrounding the offense.[15] His plea should not, however, waive his right against self-incrimination with regard to other offenses to which he has not pled guilty. The plea should not automatically waive the right with regard to evidence produced at sentencing.[16] For example, in *United States v. Nichols*[17] the accused entered a plea of guilty to unauthorized absences. During sentencing, he declined to respond to the trial judge's questions as to the nature of the drug offenses that had resulted in the imposition of Article 15 punishments.[18] The court indicated that the judge's inquiry into the admissibility of sentencing evidence should not include generalized questioning about uncharged offenses:

> Moreover, the waiver of the privilege against self-incrimination which is implicit in a plea of guilty applies only to the offense with which an accused is charged, and has no bearing on other offenses. Thus—consistent with the accused's right to remain silent, even after findings of guilty have been rendered—the military judge should not have attempted, either directly or indirectly, to compel him to discuss other offenses for which he was not then on trial.[19]

A plea of guilty also waives the right to be tried by court-martial[20] and the right to cross-examine and confront the witnesses against him.[21] In effect, by

---

12. *See* § 14-3(A)(2).
13. McCarthy v. United States, 394 U.S. 459 (1969).
14. R.C.M. 910(c)(3); United States v. Jones, 26 M.J. 632 (A.F.C.M.R. 1988).
15. Additionally, as part of a pretrial agreement the accused will often be required to enter into a stipulation of fact with the prosecution that sets out in detail what occurred. *See* Chapter 9.
16. *See* United States v. Sauer, 15 M.J. 113 (C.M.A. 1983), *citing* Estelle v. Smith, 451 U.S. 454 (1981).
17. 13 M.J. 154 (C.M.A. 1982).
18. *See* § 3-8(B) for a discussion on the admissibility of Article 15 punishments during sentencing at a court-martial.
19. 13 M.J. at 155. United States v. Miller, 23 M.J. 837 (C.G.C.M.R. 1987) (judge erred in questioning the accused further about whether the accused would be willing to identify his drug supplier).
20. R.C.M. 910(c)(3). This would include the panoply of rights concerning the accused's choice of forum and composition of the court. *See* § 12-3.
21. R.C.M. 910(c)(3).

pleading guilty the accused is relieving the prosecution of proving his guilt beyond a reasonable doubt. He is convicting himself and is waiving fundamental trial rights that are designed to ensure a fair proceeding. Because they are important rights, the judge is required to ensure through questioning of the accused that he is fully aware of these rights and is voluntarily waiving them.[22] A plea of guilty does not waive the right to the assistance of counsel. Rather, the assistance of counsel is an important part of the decision to waive these rights, and in the absence of such advice the judge may decline to accept a plea of guilty.[23]

§ 14-3(A)(2). Waiver of Issues.

A plea of guilty will as a general rule waive all objections or issues that are not jurisdictional or deprive an accused of due process. Thus, objections to pretrial statements, evidence obtained through illegal searches or seizures, and eyewitness identifications are waived.[24] And as a general rule, defects in the pretrial processing of a case are also waived.[25] Posttrial defects are not.[26] R.C.M. 910(j) provides:

> Except [where a conditional plea is entered], a plea of guilty which results in a finding of guilty waives any objection, whether or not previously raised, insofar as the objection relates to the factual issue of guilt of the offense(s) to which the plea was made.

Under previous practice the question of waiver generally depended upon the nature of the motion. The language in R.C.M. 910 seems to imply that procedural questions will not be waived by a guilty plea.[27] Whatever the impact of this provision, issues such as jurisdiction[28] and failure to state an offense[29] are

---

22. *See* the discussion at § 14-3(B).
23. *See* R.C.M. 910(c)(2) and § 14-3.
24. United States v. Cooper, 32 M.J. 83 (C.M.A. 1991) (guilty plea to charge waived search and seizure issue with regard to evidence relating to that charge); United States v. King, 30 M.J. 59 (C.M.A. 1990) (accused's voluntary guilty plea waived confession issue); United States v. King, 27 M.J. 664 (A.C.M.R. 1988) (guilty plea waived any error in pretrial representation by counsel). See also § 13-4 for a discussion on motions to suppress. The Military Rules of Evidence specifically state that such issues are waived by a plea of guilty.
25. *See, e.g.*, United States v. Cornelius, 37 M.J. 622 (A.C.M.R. 1993) (speedy trial issues are waived by guilty plea per R.C.M. 707(e)); United States v. Sneed, 32 M.J. 537 (A.F.C.M.R. 1990) (guilty plea waived issue concerning requests for expert witnesses); United States v. Packer, 8 M.J. 785 (N.C.M.R. 1980) (defect in Article 32 investigation). For a listing of issues waived by a plea of guilty, *see* 13 THE ADVOCATE 354 (1981). *See also* Vitaris, "The Guilty Plea's Impact on Appellate Review," 13 THE ADVOCATE 236 (1981).
26. United States v. Barnes, 3 M.J. 406 (C.M.A. 1977).
27. United States v. Lippoldt, 34 M.J. 523 (A.F.C.M.R. 1991) (accused did not waive issue by entering unconditional guilty plea where record indicated intent of parties to use providency inquiry to develop factual basis for issue). *Cf.* United States v. Sneed, 32 M.J. 537 (A.F.C.M.R. 1990) (citing R.C.M. 910(j), court ruled that guilty plea waived issues regarding request for expert witnesses). It seems likely that as in the past the issue of waiver in a particular category of procedural issues will be decided on a case-by-case basis.
28. *See* United States v. Alef, 3 M.J. 414 (C.M.A. 1977).
29. United States v. Fout, 3 C.M.A. 565, 13 C.M.R. 121 (1953); United States v. Arthen, 32 M.J.

not waived by a guilty plea. Entry of a guilty plea generally waives constitutional rights, including the right against self-incrimination.[30]

§ 14-3(A)(3). Plea as to a Lesser Offense.

A provident plea of guilty admits every element of the offense to which the plea relates.[31] Thus, by pleading guilty to a lesser included offense of the offense charged, the accused relieves the prosecution of proving those elements beyond a reasonable doubt.[32] The prosecution may then proceed to offer proof as to those elements which would comprise the greater offense.[33] If the prosecution has separately charged both the greater and the lesser included offense, however, the accused's plea of guilty will not admit the corresponding elements in the specification alleging the greater offense.[34] Similarly, implicit admissions in a plea of guilty to one of several specifications does not relieve the prosecution of proving guilt in the remainder.[35] Note that although an accused may not plead guilty to a capital offense,[36] he may plead guilty to a lesser included offense that is not capital.[37]

As a practical matter, unless the prosecution agrees not to present evidence on the greater offense in return for a guilty plea on the lesser,[38] the usual reason for pleading guilty to a lesser offense is to demonstrate a contrite attitude and a desire to begin rehabilitation.[39]

§ 14-3(A)(4). Effect of Guilty Plea on Later Proceedings.

If during review of the case by the convening authority, or after appellate review, a rehearing is ordered, the accused may change his plea if the rehearing is on the merits;[40] he may not change his plea if the rehearing is only on the sentence.[41] The purpose of the rehearing will generally be determined

---

541 (A.F.C.M.R. 1990) (guilty plea does not waive defective specification).

30. United States v. Jones, 26 M.J. 632 (A.F.C.M.R. 1988).

31. *See* United States v. Care, 18 C.M.A. 535, 541, 40 C.M.R. 247, 253 (1969), which requires the judge to so inform the accused. United States v. Kilgore, 21 C.M.A. 35, 44 C.M.R. 89 (1971); United States v. Guillory, 36 M.J. 952 (A.C.M.R. 1993) (accused's guilty plea to charge of attempted offense may be provident even though his statements during the providency inquiry and stipulation indicate guilty for the greater offense). *See also* § 14-3(B).

32. United States v. Owens, 11 C.M.A. 88, 28 C.M.R. 312 (1959).

33. R.C.M. 910(a)(1) Discussion.

34. United States v. Wahnon, 1 M.J. 144 (C.M.A. 1975).

35. United States v. Caszatt, 11 C.M.A. 705, 29 C.M.R. 521 (1960).

36. Art. 45, U.C.M.J. R.C.M. 910(a)(1).

37. *See, e.g.,* United States v. Matthews, 16 M.J. 354 (C.M.A. 1983).

38. For a discussion on plea bargaining in military practice, *see* Chapter 9.

39. *See* United States v. Matthews, 16 M.J. 354 (C.M.A. 1983) (accused unsuccessfully argued that the judge abused his discretion in not permitting the accused to plead guilty and thereby deprived him of arguing to the court that he recognized the wrong he had done and was on the road to rehabilitation).

40. R.C.M. 810(a)(1).

41. R.C.M. 810(a)(2)(B).

from the order directing the rehearing.[42] Note that the accused's failure to comply with an existing pretrial agreement might affect the maximum punishment that he would be subjected to on the rehearing.[43]

If a post-trial session has been convened, such as a proceeding in revision[44] or an Article 39(a) session,[45] the accused's ability to withdraw a plea would generally be dictated by the nature and purpose of the proceedings. For example, if the session has been convened to consider evidence which might improvidence the guilty plea, or cast doubt on a pretrial agreement, a change of plea may be appropriate.[46]

Where a new trial has been ordered, the accused's plea of guilty in the first proceeding will not bind him in the second.[47] He may enter any of the recognized pleas.[48]

§ 14-3(B). The *Care* Providency Inquiry.

To ensure that the guilty plea is provident the military judge must personally question the accused,[49] in closed session,[50] and must receive personal responses from the accused[51] on a number of matters. The judge must be satisfied that the accused understands that he is waiving important rights, that the accused's plea is voluntary, and that it is accurate. A scenario of a complete providency inquiry is included in the Trial Procedure Guide located at Appendix 8 of the Manual for Courts-Martial.[52] The requirements for a valid inquiry are derived from the *Manual*[53] and *United States v. Care*;[54] thus

---

42. *See generally* United States v. Barfield, 2 M.J. 136 (C.M.A. 1977).

43. Art. 63, U.C.M.J.; R.C.M. 810(d)(2). These provisions indicate that as a general rule the maximum imposable sentence at the rehearing will be the sentence adjudged at the first trial as ultimately reduced by the convening authority or higher appellate authority. However, where the ultimate sentence was affected by a pretrial agreement in the first trial and the accused does not comply with the agreement on the rehearing, the maximum sentence will be determined by the amount of punishment adjudged by the court.

44. *See* R.C.M. 1102(b)(1). Proceedings in revision are usually limited to correcting an error, omission, or inconsistent action of the court. It may be ordered by the judge or the convening authority. This sort of proceeding could be used to inquire into the terms of a pretrial agreement. *Id.* at Discussion.

45. Art. 39(a), U.C.M.J.; R.C.M. 1102(b)(2) indicates that this type of proceeding could be used to inquire into any issue which arises after trial, such as allegations of misconduct by a party.

46. *See generally* United States v. Newkirk, 8 M.J. 684 (N.C.M.R. 1980).

47. R.C.M. 810(a)(1).

48. *See* § 14-1.

49. In United States v. Hook, 20 C.M.A. 516, 43 C.M.R. 356 (1971), the court found error where the defense counsel had conducted large portions of the inquiry.

50. The session is closed to the extent that the court members are not present. The entry of pleas and subsequent plea inquiries are normally conducted during an Article 39(a) session, which precedes any session during which the court members might be present. *See* Chapter 12.

51. R.C.M. 910(c). United States v. Terry, 21 C.M.A. 442, 45 C.M.R. 216 (1972).

52. *See also* United States v. Norris, 33 M.J. 635 (C.G.C.M.R. 1991) (noting that a Navy judge had used an abbreviated plea inquiry in this case, the court cautioned that the Coast Guard Trial Guide sets out a "road map" and that while judges are not required to follow it, failure to do so may invite error).

53. R.C.M. 910(c).

54. 18 C.M.A. 535, 40 C.M.R. 247 (1969).

§ 14-3(B)(1)   PLEAS   § 14-3(B)(1)

the common designation *Care* Inquiry. The three main categories of advice and inquiry are discussed in the following sections.

§ 14-3(B)(1). Advice Regarding Rights.

The military judge should apprise the accused of the impact of his plea and determine that the accused fully understands what rights he is waiving by entering a plea of guilty. Specifically, the judge should determine:

> (a) The accused's understanding of his right to plead not guilty and place the burden of proving his guilt beyond a reasonable doubt on the prosecution, whether or not the accused believes himself to be guilty;[55]
>
> (b) The accused's understanding that he can be convicted on his plea alone, without the necessity of other evidence;[56]
>
> (c) The accused's understanding that he should plead guilty only if he believes he is guilty and should not permit any other consideration to influence him;[57] and
>
> (d) The accused's understanding that he gives up certain rights by his guilty plea:[58] (1) the right against self-incrimination;[59] (2) the right to be tried by a court-martial;[60] and (3) the right to confront and cross-examine witnesses against him;[61]
>
> (e) The accused's understanding that if he pleads guilty he will be placed under oath and questioned by the military judge as to the factual

---

55. United States v. Lilly, 34 M.J. 670 (A.C.M.R. 1992) (for pleas to be provident, military judge must apprise accused of what prosecution would be required to prove in absence of guilty plea; inaccurate statement to accused concerning burden of proof concerning lack of mental responsibility improvidenced guilty plea).The right to plead not guilty is of course not contingent upon the accused's feelings or opinion and the judge is not bound to accept a guilty plea simply because the accused feels that he is guilty. The judge, as noted, must determine that the plea of guilty is indeed accurate, that the accused in fact committed the charged offense.
56. R.C.M. 910(c)(4). United States v. Bowers, 20 M.J. 1003 (A.F.C.M.R. 1985).
57. R.C.M. 910(e). United States v. Caylor, 40 M.J. 786 (A.F.C.M.R. 1994) (court concluded that under the facts the accused's plea was voluntary; court noted that procedures set out in military caselaw have not eliminated post-trial attacks on providence of guilty pleas).
58. United States v. Adams, 28 M.J. 576 (A.C.M.R. 1989) (judge's complete failure to apprise accused of these rights improvidenced the plea).
59. R.C.M. 910(c)(3). *See also* § 14-3(A)(1). Failure to advise the accused of these rights may improvidence the plea. United States v. Serrano, 27 M.J. 611 (A.C.M.R. 1988) (not error for judge to ask defense to state what advice he had given and then to follow up with questions to accused as to whether he understood what rights he was waiving; judges are not prohibited from using different, but adequate, formats for advising an accused of his rights); United States v. Harris, 26 M.J. 729 (A.C.M.R. 1988) (reversible error for trial judge to rely only on assurances from defense counsel that he had advised the accused of these rights); United States v. Bailey, 20 M.J. 703 (A.C.M.R. 1985).
60. *Id. Cf.* United States v. Bingham, 20 C.M.A. 521, 43 C.M.R. 216 (1971) (not prejudicial error to omit).
61. *Id.* Although the practice is commended, it is not necessary that the trial judge inform the accused of his appellate rights. United States v. Dudley, 21 M.J. 615 (A.C.M.R. 1985).

basis of the plea, and that those statements may later be used against him at a later trial on charges of perjury or false statement.[62]

It is normally not necessary, however, for the military judge to apprise an accused of the collateral consequences of his plea of guilty. For example, in *United States v. Berumen*,[63] the court ruled that the military judge was not required to inform the accused, an alien, that as a direct result of his guilty plea he could be deported.[64] The court noted that it would be difficult for a judge to know where to draw the line in notifying an accused of various "collateral" consequences.[65] Nonetheless, the court recognized that in some circumstances such advice might be necessary:

> [W]hen collateral consequences of a court-martial conviction —such as administrative discharge, loss of license or a security clearance, removal from a military program, failure to obtain promotion, deportation, or public derision or humiliation—are relied upon as the basis for contesting the providence of a guilty plea, the appellant is entitled to succeed only when the collateral consequences are major and the appellant's misunderstanding of the consequences (a) results foreseeably and almost inexorably from the language of the pretrial agreement; (b) is induced by the trial judge's comments during the providence inquiry; or (c) is made readily apparent to the judge, who nonetheless fails to correct that misunderstanding.[66]

§ 14-3(B)(2). Determining the Accuracy of the Plea.

Before accepting the plea the judge must also be satisfied that the accused is guilty of the offense charged. This portion of the inquiry begins with placing the accused under oath,[67] a requirement added to the *Manual* in 1984. Arguably, if the accused refuses to take the oath and proceeds with the judge's inquiry, the judge may appropriately decline to accept the plea. The oath is usually given by the trial counsel. The requirement is designed to protect the judicial process from willful deceit, protect the accused from falsely pleading

---

62. R.C.M. 910(c)(5). Failure to give this advice will normally not improvidence the plea but may block the later prosecution. United States v. Serrano, 27 M.J. 611 (A.C.M.R. 1988) (nonprejudicial error for judge not to advise accused that any false statements during the inquiry might later be used against him); United States v. Conrad, 598 F.2d 506 (9th Cir. 1979). *See also* Rule 410, Mil. R. Evid. *See generally* United States v. Mezzanatto, 115 S. Ct. 797 (1995) (accused waived limitations in Fed. R. Evid. 410 as part of plea bargain; he agreed that any statements made during plea discussions could be used for impeachment purposes).
63. 24 M.J. 737 (A.C.M.R. 1987).
64. 24 M.J. at 740.
65. *Id.*
66. 24 M.J. at 740, *citing* United States v. Bedania, 12 M.J. 373, 376 (C.M.A. 1982). In this case the court seems to have depended heavily upon the fact that the judge was not aware that deportation was a possibility.
67. R.C.M. 910(e). United States v. Riley, 35 M.J. 547 (A.C.M.R. 1992) (failure to place accused under oath during providency inquiry was nonprejudicial error).

§ 14-3(B)(2) PLEAS § 14-3(B)(2)

guilty, and reduce the baseless collateral attacks on guilty pleas.[68] The accused need not take the witness stand to take the oath although he should be asked to stand to take the oath; he may answer the judge's inquiries while seated at the defense table.[69]

The judge must apprise the accused of the elements of the offense and determine whether he understands them.[70] Although the practice of specifically listing the elements is the most prudent course, the courts have indicated that it may be sufficient if the record of the inquiry as a whole indicates that the accused understood what the elements were.[71] In some cases it may be necessary for the judge to specifically tailor a description of the elements and describe in more detail the basis of the accused's alleged guilt.[72] Where the accused is charged with violating a regulation,[73] the judge need not deter-

---

68. United States v. Holt, 27 M.J. 57 (C.M.A. 1988); United States v. Daniels, 20 M.J. 648 (N.M.C.M.R. 1985). The court added that those benefits outweigh any possible dampening effect on the accused's willingness to plead guilty. *See also* Rule 410, Mɪʟ. R. Evɪᴅ.

69. *See* R.C.M. 910(e) Discussion.

70. R.C.M. 910(c)(1) Discussion and 910(e) Discussion. Henderson v. Morgan, 426 U.S. 637 (1976); United States v. Kilgore, 21 C.M.A. 35, 44 C.M.R. 89 (1971); United States v. Serrano, 27 M.J. 611 (A.C.M.R. 1988) (inquiry regarding elements of offense where judge asked trial counsel to state elements of each specification; judges are not prohibited from using different, but adequate, formats for advising an accused of his rights).

71. United States v. Bates, 40 M.J. 362 (C.M.A. 1994) (providency inquiry was minimally sufficient where trial court failed to define sexual intercourse; clear from context of plea inquiry, however, that accused admitted an act of carnal knowledge); United States v. Jones, 34 M.J. 270 (C.M.A. 1992) (failure to list elements not fatal where record as a whole indicated that accused had admitted jurisdictional element); United States v. Crouch, 11 M.J. 128 (C.M.A. 1981); United States v. Daffron, 32 M.J. 912 (A.F.C.M.R. 1991) (judge is not required to simply list elements but rather to explain them to accused; technical failure to apprise accused of element was not error under the facts).

United States v. Nystrom, 39 M.J. 698 (N.M.C.M.R. 1993) (failure to read or explain elements of accessory after the fact was error; findings and sentence set aside); United States v. Plante, 36 M.J. 626 (A.C.M.R. 1992) (failure to elicit specific admission on element not fatal where accused unequivocally admitted all elements of offenses); United States v. Dallman, 32 M.J. 624 (A.C.M.R. 1991) (judge not required to list elements separately); United States v. Colley, 29 M.J. 519 (A.C.M.R. 1989) (plea inquiry was sufficient although the trial judge did not define the term "indecent"); United States v. Mervine, 23 M.J. 801 (N.M.C.M.R. 1986) (failure to list elements not fatal where providency inquiry adequately set out elements of the offense); United States v. De Los Santos, 7 M.J. 519 (A.C.M.R. 1979).

Several courts have held that failure to advise the accused of the terminal element of an Article 134 violation, that the accused's conduct was prejudicial to good order and discipline, is not prejudicial because that element is fulfilled as a matter of law if the offense itself is proved or admitted. *See, e.g.,* United States v. Finn, 20 M.J. 696 (N.M.C.M.R. 1985); United States v. Parish, 20 M.J. 696 (N.M.C.M.R. 1985); United States v. Long, 20 M.J. 657 (N.M.C.M.R. 1985); United States v. Arrington, 5 M.J. 756 (A.C.M.R. 1978). *Cf.* United States v. Hein, 23 M.J. 610 (A.F.C.M.R. 1986) (plea improvident where judge failed to advise the accused of the Art. 134 element of "conduct of a nature to bring discredit upon the armed forces").

72. *See, e.g.,* United States v. Craney, 1 M.J. 142 (C.M.A. 1975) (party liability); United States v. Trimble, 30 M.J. 1133 (N.M.C.M.R. 1990) (normally each offense should be subject to individual *Care* inquiry but where offenses arise out of single incident, it is appropriate to inquire into an overview of what occurred to demonstrate whatever relationships exist between the offenses); United States v. Williams, 6 M.J. 611 (A.C.M.R. 1978) (party liability).

73. *See* § 2-2(C).

mine whether the accused knew the specific regulation. It is enough if he knows that he committed a prohibited act.[74]

Having listed the elements, the judge should inquire of the accused whether those elements correctly describe what he did and then ask the accused to state in his own words what took place.[75] This portion of the providency inquiry can prove particularly troublesome where the judge elicits only legal conclusions[76] from the accused or simply receives "yes" and "no" answers to the judge's description of the offense.[77] Most defense counsel realize the problems of determining the necessary factual basis and the possibility that at trial the accused will attempt to mitigate or defend his conduct and thus jeopardize the plea. It is therefore essential that the accused be prepared to clearly articulate for the judge those facts that indicate that he committed the offense. One court has suggested that the accused should use prepared remarks.[78] The key here is that the facts revealed by the accused must objec-

---

74. United States v. Levin, 14 M.J. 814 (A.C.M.R. 1982); United States v. Davis, 13 M.J. 593 (A.F.C.M.R. 1982).

75. *See* United States v. Wright, 25 M.J. 827 (A.C.M.R. 1988) (taken as a whole, the plea inquiry satisfactorily established accused's intent to defraud, although he did not explicitly state such an intent); United States v. Searcy, 24 M.J. 943 (A.C.M.R. 1987) (plea was improvident where inquiry failed to establish adequate factual basis); United States v. Goins, 2 M.J. 458 (A.C.M.R. 1975); United States v. Buske, 2 M.J. 465 (A.C.M.R. 1975).

76. *See, e.g.*, United States v. Tenk, 33 M.J. 765 (A.C.M.R. 1991) (eliciting legal conclusions from accused did not establish factual basis for guilty plea).

77. *See* United States v. Dunning, 40 M.J. 641 (N.M.C.M.R. 1994) (accused's plea improvident where he simply provided affirmative answer to leading question by judge on element of rape charge; decision includes good summary of legal principles of conducting *Care* inquiry); United States v. Vinson, 33 M.J. 1073 (A.C.M.R. 1991) (inquiry was essentially recitation of elements of offense to which accused merely answered in the affirmative; there were no factual admissions); United States v. Duval, 31 M.J. 650 (A.C.M.R. 1990) (judge failed to elicit facts); United States v. Woods, 25 M.J. 916 (N.M.C.M.R. 1988) (record supported providency of the plea, although judge failed to draw out any facts showing wrongfulness of drug use).

In United States v. Frederick, 23 M.J. 561 (A.C.M.R. 1986), the plea was considered improvident where the trial judge failed to elicit more than bare admissions from the accused. The court wisely added in a footnote that:

> [T]rial counsel, who have a continuous duty to protect the record, should remain alert throughout a providence inquiry, and respectfully bring to the military judge's attention any areas which counsel believe have not been sufficiently covered and could result in a plea of guilty subsequently being found improvident.

Id. at 563, n.4. United States v. Harclerode, 17 M.J. 981 (A.C.M.R. 1984) (findings of guilt reversed where judge failed to elicit facts from the accused).

On the other hand, the judge must not venture too far away from the facts of the case. United States v. Miller, 23 M.J. 553 (C.G.C.M.R. 1986) (judge went too far in questioning the accused about his potential cooperation with the government in locating the person who had sold the drugs to him).

78. United States v. Eddy, 41 M.J. 786 (A.F. Ct. Crim. App. 1995) (court recognized problems which arise when accused wishes to take advantage of guilty plea and yet present himself in best light; such puts judge in difficult position and court cautioned about practice of judges trying to save guilty pleas; providence of plea rests on what accused actually admits in the record); United States v. McCann, 11 M.J. 506 (N.C.M.R. 1981).

tively support the plea of guilty.[79] Legal conclusions recited by the accused,[80] or included in a stipulation of fact, will not suffice.[81] And the military judge has a duty to ensure that the accused has entered a plea of guilty to an offense for which he is truly guilty.[82]

If the parties have prepared a stipulation of fact as part of a negotiated plea,[83] the judge may find it helpful to use that document as a guide to garner additional facts from the accused.[84] He should of course first determine that the stipulation has been properly and voluntarily signed by the parties.[85] There is authority for the view that the requirements of *United States v. Care, supra* and its progeny may be met through use of a stipulation of fact.[86] In *United States v. Sweet*,[87] the Navy-Marine Corps Court of Military Review indicated that it is not necessary that the accused admit orally on the record each and every fact comprising the offense, if he has signed a stipulation of fact which relates the facts. The court stated that [e]ssential facts may be established virtually exclusively from the stipulation without questioning the accused about its specific contents.[88] Drawing from federal practice[89] and military law on the subject,[90] the court offered practical guidance to military judges conducting providency inquiries.[91] The Court of Appeals affirmed.[92]

It is not essential that the accused articulate the facts in a way that matches the prosecution's theory of the case.[93] Nor is it essential that the

---

79. United States v. Schwabauer, 37 M.J. 338 (C.M.A. 1993) (facts must objectively establish guilt); United States v. Davenport, 9 M.J. 364 (C.M.A. 1980).
80. United States v. Terry, 45 C.M.R. 216 (C.M.A. 1972); United States v. Davis, 32 M.J. 951 (N.M.C.M.R. 1991); United States v. Armstead, 32 M.J. 1013 (N.M.C.M.R. 1991); United States v. Shields, 39 M.J. 718 (N.M.C.M.R. 1993) (merely requiring accused to stated legal conclusions adds little to inquiry and may mask insufficient factual basis for plea).
81. United States v. Campos, 37 M.J. 1110 (N.M.C.M.R. 1993); United States v. Vinson, 33 M.J. 1073 (A.C.M.R. 1991).
82. United States v. Schwabauer, 37 M.J. 338 (C.M.A. 1993); United States v. Hanson, 24 M.J. 377 (C.M.A. 1987).
83. *See* § 9-2.
84. United States v. Ross, 34 M.J. 338 (C.M.A. 1992) (error for judge to consider stipulation containing uncharged misconduct).*Cf.* United States v. Sawinski, 16 M.J. 808 (N.M.C.M.R. 1983) (stipulation of fact that contained complete admissions of guilt was insufficient to meet *Care* requirement that judge personally question the accused).
85. United States v. Sassaman, 32 M.J. 687 (A.F.C.M.R. 1991) (inquiry was sufficient); United States v. Bright, 32 M.J. 679 (A.F.C.M.R. 1991) (judge's inquiry concerning stipulation was sufficient).
86. United States v. Sweet, 38 M.J. 583 (N.M.C.M.R. 1993) (en banc) (full discussion of issue).
87. 38 M.J. 583 (N.M.C.M.R. 1993).
88. 38 M.J. at 590.
89. *Id.* at 589.
90. *Id.* at 588-89.
91. *Id.* at 592-93.
92. United States v. Sweet, 42 M.J. 183 (1995) (court acknowledged that in many cases it may be advisable or even necessary to conduct a more detailed inquiry; the court took into account the fact that the accused was an officer, represented by competent counsel and that he agreed to stipulation which described his actions in detail).
93. United States v. Penister, 25 M.J. 148 (C.M.A. 1987); United States v. Minor, 11 M.J. 608 (A.C.M.R. 1981).

§ 14-3(B)(2)   MILITARY CRIMINAL JUSTICE   § 14-3(B)(2)

accused personally recall all of the facts.[94] The test is whether the accused is personally convinced of the facts that indicate that he committed the offense.[95] In reaching that conclusion he may rely upon descriptions of the offense by others.[96] Factual admissions implicitly made by an accused during the inquiry cannot be used as evidence against the accused to prove an essential element of a different and separate offense to which he has pleaded not guilty.[97] The admissions made during a guilty plea inquiry may be used, however, for lesser included offenses.[98]

If during the inquiry the accused states facts that appear inconsistent with a factual basis of guilt,[99] or if it appears that a valid defense may exist,[100] the

---

94. United States v. McCline, 32 M.J. 356 (C.M.A. 1991) (accused's plea was provident although he initially asserted loss of memory during providency inquiry).

95. *See, e.g.,* United States v. Phrampus, 34 M.J. 607 (A.F.M.C.R. 1992) (accused's belief in guilt is not sufficient, in itself, to support necessary factual basis for guilty plea); United States v. Wiles, 30 M.J. 1097 (N.M.C.M.R. 1989) (inquiry on drug offense failed to establish any facts relating to offenses; accused simply indicating that his friends had told him that he had used drugs was insufficient to show knowing use of marijuana); United States v. Rios, 24 M.J. 515 (A.F.C.M.R. 1987) (plea inquiry established that accused was convinced of his guilt).

See also United States v. Moglia, 3 M.J. 216 (C.M.A. 1977); United States v. Luebs, 20 C.M.A. 475, 43 C.M.R. 315 (1971); United States v. Butler, 20 C.M.A. 247, 43 C.M.R. 87 (1971); United States v. Kiddo, 16 M.J. 775 (A.C.M.R. 1983); United States v. Whelehan, 10 M.J. 566 (A.F.C.M.R. 1980); United States v. Olson, 7 M.J. 898 (A.F.C.M.R. 1979). *See also* R.C.M. 910(e) Discussion.

96. *See, e.g.,* United States v. Olson, 7 M.J. 898 (A.F.C.M.R. 1979).

97. United States v. Wahnon, 1 M.J. 144 (C.M.A. 1975); United States v. Caszatt, 29 C.M.R. 521 (C.M.A. 1960); United States v. Abdullah, 37 M.J. 692 (A.C.M.R. 1993).

98. United States v. Abdullah, 37 M.J. 692 (A.C.M.R. 1993), citing United States v. Rivera, 23 M.J. 89, 95 (C.M.A. 1986).

99. In United States v. Epps, 25 M.J. 319 (C.M.A. 1987), the court noted that although Article 45 requires accuracy, if during the providency inquiry the accused admits facts during his sworn testimony that support a different but closely related offense having the same maximum punishment, the pleas may be considered provident. *See also* United States v. Felty, 12 M.J. 438 (C.M.A. 1982).

United States v. Byrd, 24 M.J. 286 (C.M.A. 1987) (accused's responses raised possible "voluntary abandonment" defense that the court said would be applicable to the military); United States v. Jennings, 1 M.J. 414 (C.M.A. 1976).

United States v. Dumas, 27 M.J. 676 (A.C.M.R. 1988) (plea improvident where stipulation of fact was inconsistent with accused's statements during inquiry); United States v. Maydwell, 23 M.J. 656 (A.F.C.M.R. 1986) (improper to accept guilty plea without exploring possible defense raised during providency inquiry).

Cf. United States v. Jackson, 23 M.J. 650 (N.M.C.M.R. 1986), where the court stated:

> The military judge is not required by any known authority to embark on a mindless fishing expedition to ferret out or negate all possible defenses or potential inconsistencies. The trial judge is only required to deal with those potential issues raised in the providence inquiry responses or by evidence presented during the trial indicative of inconsistency or defense.

Id. at 652 (citations omitted).

United States v. Burge, 25 M.J. 576 (A.F.C.M.R. 1987) (plea to larceny was improvident where inquiry did not establish necessary intent for all of money allegedly taken); United States v. Borner, 25 M.J. 551 (A.F.C.M.R. 1987) (pleas improvident); United States v. Johnson, 25 M.J. 553 (A.C.M.R. 1987) (plea improvident where facts admitted did not constitute offense charged; decision includes reminders for trial judges conducting plea inquiries).

100. In United States v. Penister, 25 M.J. 148 (C.M.A. 1987), the court concluded that the judge

judge should probe further in an attempt to reconcile the inconsistency or determine if the defense has considered the possibility of a defense. Failure to do so may improvidence the plea. For a further discussion on improvident pleas, see § 14-3(E).

§ 14-3(B)(3). Determining the Voluntariness of the Plea.

Before accepting a guilty plea the judge must be assured that the accused's decision to plead guilty is knowing, intelligent, and voluntary. To meet this requirement the trial judge should give appropriate advice to the accused and determine:

(a) The accused's understanding of the maximum punishment that can be imposed for the offense to which he is pleading guilty;[101]

---

erred in rejecting the accused's plea where after 36 pages of inquiry the trial counsel moved to have the pleas rejected because the use of alcohol had been mentioned. The judge finally, and erroneously, rejected the plea because the accused could not recall all of the incident. The court agreed with the Court of Military Review that there was no inconsistency.

United States v. Williams, 27 M.J. 710 (A.C.M.R. 1988) (plea improvident where accused could have asserted self-incrimination as defense to disclosure requirements in regulation). *See also* United States v. Holman, 28 M.J. 527 (A.C.M.R. 1989) (judge should have obtained formal waiver of right against self-incrimination); United States v. Williams, 27 M.J. 671 (A.C.M.R. 1988) (reversal required where judge failed to explain defense of entrapment to accused, and appellate court was unable to determine from record whether entrapment existed); United States v. Clayton, 25 M.J. 888 (A.C.M.R. 1988) (military judge was too quick to reject guilty plea when the possibility of an entrapment offense was raised; the court emphasized that in order for an accused's responses to rise to the level of improvidency, more than a mere possibility of a defense must exist. They must reasonably raise a defense and, when a defense is raised, the judge should clearly and concisely inquire further); United States v. McMann, 11 M.J. 506 (N.C.M.R. 1981); United States v. Stouffer, 2 M.J. 528 (A.C.M.R. 1976).

The military judge should determine the accused's personal attitude about a potential defense and not rely solely on the defense counsel's conclusions about whether a defense exists. United States v. Collins, 17 M.J. 901 (A.F.C.M.R. 1983).

101. R.C.M. 910(c)(1). This should include an explanation of any applicable escalator clauses. United States v. Zemartis, 10 C.M.A. 353, 27 C.M.R. 427 (1959). R.C.M. 910(c)(1) Analysis. *See also* United States v. Viverito, 34 M.J. 872 (A.C.M.R. 1992) (fine could not be imposed where military judge failed to mention such during providency inquiry and pretrial agreement did not specifically mention it); United States v. Dickens, 30 M.J. 986 (A.C.M.R. 1990) (judge's failure to apprise accused of correct maximum sentence was non-prejudicial error because it appeared that the accused was not substantially misled); United States v. Carroll, 22 M.J. 951 (A.C.M.R. 1986) (harmless error not to advise).

The Court of Military Appeals, now the United States Court of Appeals for the Armed Forces, has held that a combined sentence of total forfeitures and a fine may not be imposed unless: a pretrial agreement specifically mentions that possibility, there is other evidence to indicate that the accused was aware of that possibility, or the judge mentions it in the providency inquiry. United States v. Williams, 18 M.J. 186 (C.M.A. 1984). *See also* United States v. Edwards, 20 M.J. 439 (C.M.A. 1985) (court recognized that the judge's advice on this point may be negated by provisions in the pretrial agreement which may lead the accused to believe that the convening authority would not approve imposition of a fine); United States v. Shirley, 18 M.J. 212 (C.M.A. 1984).

Note that substantial misunderstandings about the maximum authorized punishment may render the plea improvident. *See* § 14-3(E).

(b) The accused's understanding that the maximum punishment can be imposed;[102]

(c) Whether the accused has discussed the meaning and effect of his plea with defense counsel;[103]

(d) The accused's understanding of any pretrial agreement pursuant to which he is pleading guilty;[104]

(e) Whether the decision to negotiate a plea originated with the accused;[105]

(f) Whether anyone has used force or coercion to make the accused plead guilty;[106]

(g) Whether the accused believes it is in his own best interest to plead guilty;[107]

(h) Whether the accused's plea is the product of his own will and a desire to confess his guilt;[108] and

(i) The accused's understanding that he may withdraw his plea at any time before sentence is announced in the discretion of the military judge.[109]

The military judge's decision to accept or reject a plea is interlocutory in nature.[110] In announcing his decision the judge will normally indicate that he is satisfied that the plea has been knowingly and voluntarily entered. However, failure to do so is not necessarily error.[111] If he is satisfied with the

---

102. This element is simply an extension of the preceding advice concerning the maximum punishment; if there is a pretrial agreement affecting the sentence, then the judge should be prepared to clarify this point when he reviews that agreement with the accused. See § 14-3(C).

103. The *Manual* indicates that if the accused is not represented by counsel in a general or special court-martial, a plea of guilty should not be accepted. R.C.M. 910(c)(2) Discussion. This nonbinding guidance, however, although sound, should be read with the Rule it addresses that implies that a plea may be accepted from an uncounselled accused. The key inquiry should be whether the accused has obtained legal advice in deciding whether or not to plead guilty. An appropriate safeguard at this point might be to appoint a standby counsel to assist the accused who insists on pleading guilty. See § 12-2(F)(4).

104. This element is discussed in more detail in § 14-3(C).

105. R.C.M. 910(d), 705.

106. R.C.M. 910(d). In United States v. Stephens, 25 M.J. 171 (C.M.A. 1987), the court rejected the defendant's argument that his defense counsel had coerced him into pleading guilty in return for a job with the counsel's commercial endeavors. The court, however, did conclude that counsel had given incorrect information to the accused concerning the level of court-martial he was facing if he decided to plead not guilty.

United States v. Ortiz, 25 M.J. 840 (N.M.C.M.R. 1988) (sworn statements of voluntariness were more persuasive than appellate unsworn allegations of coercion by counsel to plead guilty).

107. R.C.M. 910(d).

108. R.C.M. 910(d).

109. United States v. Silver, 40 M.J. 351 (C.M.A. 1994) (no requirement that accused be advised of the right to withdraw a guilty plea, although it is better practice to do so): United States v. Acosta, 36 M.J. 1165 (A.C.M.R. 1993) (court held that judge is not required to advise accused of the right to withdraw a guilty plea; court nonetheless advised judges to follow the time-tested provisions of the benchbook to avoid needless appellate litigation); see § 14-3(G).

110. United States v. Care, 18 C.M.A. 535, 40 C.M.R. 247 (1969).

111. United States v. Palos, 20 C.M.A. 104, 42 C.M.R. 296 (1970). Cf. United States v. Lasagni, 8 M.J. 627 (N.C.M.R. 1979) (judge must so announce).

§ 14-2(B)(4)   PLEAS   § 14-2(B)(4)

accused's responses he may proceed to announce his findings, unless the accused has only entered a plea of guilty to a lesser included offense. *See* § 14-3(F). If he is not satisfied that the accused fully understands the meaning and effect of his plea, the military judge may conduct further inquiry or reject the plea.

A plea should not be arbitrarily rejected, however.[112] If the plea is rejected all related matters must be withdrawn. Improvident pleas are discussed in more detail at § 14-3(D).

If the plea is negotiated, i.e., a pretrial agreement exists between the accused and the convening authority, the military judge must continue his inquiry, as noted in the next section.

§ 14-2(B)(4). Admissibility of Accused's Statements.

Although there was some case law that limited the ability of the court to hear and consider on sentencing the statements of the accused made during the providency inquiry with the judge,[113] more recent case law treats the statements as admissions that may be offered against him by the prosecution during sentencing if his guilty plea is accepted.[114] They may be offered either through an authenticated transcript[115] or through the testimony of someone who heard the inquiry.[116] If the inquiry raises matters that are irrelevant or otherwise inadmissible, it may be necessary for the trial judge to strike those portions.[117] The statements may not be used or considered, however, in conjunction with other offenses to which the accused has pleaded not guilty.[118]

---

112. United States v. Williams, 43 C.M.R. 579 (A.C.M.R. 1970). On appeal the test is whether the judge abused his discretion.

See generally Moriarty, "The Providency Inquiry: A Guilty Plea Gauntlet?," 13 THE ADVOCATE 251 (1981); Lukjanowicz, "The Providency Inquiry: An Examination of Judicial Responsibilities," 13 THE ADVOCATE 333 (1981).

113. *See, e.g.,* United States v. Brown, 17 M.J. 987 (A.C.M.R. 1984) (prosecutor improperly referred to accused's testimony given during providency inquiry); United States v. Richardson, 6 M.J. 654 (N.C.M.R. 1978) (error for judge to consider facts elicited from the accused in determining sentencing).

114. United States v. Irwin, 42 M.J. 479 (1995) (prosecution introduced tape of providency inquiry; court indicated that accused's statements amounted to admissible judicial admissions and rejected the argument that he had not received full notice of the effect of his statements during the inquiry); United States v. Holt, 27 M.J. 57 (C.M.A. 1988); United States v. Dukes, 30 M.J. (N.M.C.M.R. 1990). *Cf.* United States v. Peck, 36 M.J. 900 (A.F.C.M.R. 1993) (evidence that accused previously acknowledged dangerousness of LSD not admissible to rebut statements made in accused's guilty plea inquiry). *See generally* Pohl, "Practical Considerations of *United States v. Holt:* Use of Accused's Answers During the Providence Inquiry as Substantive Evidence," ARMY LAW., Nov. 1988, at 20; Prescott, "*United States v. Holt:* The Use of Providence Inquiry Information During Sentencing," ARMY LAW., Apr. 1988, at 34. *See also* MIL. R. EVID. 410.

115. United States v. Holt, 27 M.J. 57, 60 (C.M.A. 1988); United States v. English, 37 M.J. 1107 (N.M.C.M.R. 1993) (judge erred in considering accused's providency inquiry statement during sentencing; he should have waited for them to be offered into evidence). *See, e.g.,* MIL. R. EVID. 902(4)(a).

116. *Id.*

117. For example, the inquiry may have raised evidence about other acts of uncharged misconduct. *See* MIL. R. EVID. 404(b).

118. United States v. Cahn, 31 M.J. 729 (A.F.C.M.R. 1990) (judge properly refused defense

The statements could also be admitted against an accused in a later trial for perjury or false statement.[119] But the statements must have been recorded, under oath, and in the presence of counsel.[120] If the foregoing procedures have been followed those prerequisites will normally be met.

§ 14-3(C). The *Green-King* Pretrial Agreement Inquiry.

In an effort to increase judicial supervision of the widespread practice of negotiated pleas, the Court in *United States v. King*[121] and *United States v. Green*[122] indicated that the military judge must, in those cases involving pretrial agreements, determine whether the accused understands the full meaning and effect of his agreement with the convening authority.[123] Failure to conduct a proper inquiry may result in the plea being improvidenced by an appellate court.[124] The Navy Court of Military Review in *United States v. Williamson*,[125] suggested that to ensure an adequate inquiry the military judge should conduct his inquiry as follows:

> a. Ask the accused and his counsel if there is a pretrial agreement.[126]
> b. If there is an agreement, view it in its entirety before findings when trial is before a court composed of members;[127] otherwise, reserve inquiry into the sentence provisions until after imposition of sentence.[128]

---

request to consider statements made by accused during providency inquiry; permitting such use would deter guilty pleas and present opportunity for accused to garnish the inquiry with favorable statements which could later be placed before the court members without cross-examination). *See also* MIL. R. EVID. 410.

119. *See* Rule 410, MIL. R. EVID.

120. *See* Rule 410, MIL. R. EVID. *See generally* Saltzburg, Schinasi & Schlueter, *Military Rules of Evidence Manual*, 512-17 (3d ed. 1991).

121. 3 M.J. 458 (C.M.A. 1977).

122. 1 M.J. 453 (C.M.A. 1976).

123. United States v. Llewellyn, 27 M.J. 825 (A.C.M.R. 1988) (the trial judge and both counsel have an obligation to ensure that understandings of plea agreement are on record and ambiguous provisions should be interpreted in favor of accused). For a discussion of the plea bargaining process and possible terms in the agreement, see Chapter 9.

124. *See* United States v. King, 3 M.J. 458 (C.M.A. 1977); United States v. Slocumb, 24 M.J. 940 (C.G.C.M.R. 1987) (judge properly conducted inquiry); United States v. Grover-Madrill, 5 M.J. 768 (A.C.M.R. 1978). *Cf.* United States v. Hinton, 10 M.J. 136 (C.M.A. 1981).

125. 4 M.J. 708 (N.C.M.R. 1977). Note that in United States v. Hoaglin, 10 M.J. 769 (N.C.M.R. 1981) (en banc), the court mandated that the *Williamson* points would be applied in all Navy courts-martial where a pretrial agreement is involved.

126. R.C.M. 910(f) Discussion. Note that the *Manual* also places an affirmative obligation upon the parties to inform the military judge of any pretrial agreement. R.C.M. 910(f)(2). Failure of the judge to ask is probably not error. United States v. Cooke, 11 M.J. 257 (C.M.A. 1981).

127. *See* R.C.M. 910(f)(3). Pretrial agreements often consist of severable portions. For example,

---

128. United States v. Green, 1 M.J. 453 (C.M.A. 1976); United States v. Phillipson, 30 M.J. 1019 (A.F.C.M.R. 1990) (judge's failure to recuse himself when he inadvertently learned of sentence limitation was not error where he brought matter to attention of counsel, was available for questioning, and indicated that it would not affect his decision); United States v. Diaz, 30 M.J. 957 (C.G.C.M.R. 1990) (no error where defense counsel informed military judge of sentence limitation and declined to press the point at trial).

§ 14-3(C)   PLEAS   § 14-3(C)

    c. Go over each provision of the agreement with the accused (including, at the appropriate point in the proceedings, the sentence terms), paraphrase each in the judge's own words, and explain in the judge's own words the ramifications of each provision.[129]

    d. Obtain from the accused his statement of concurrence with the judge's explanation or his own understanding, followed by a resolution on the record of any differences.[130]

---

the agreement itself will often make reference to an agreed-to sentence limitation which will appear in a separate, but attached, document which may be marked as an appendix to the agreement. If the accused has not requested trial by judge alone, see § 12-3(A), any sentence would be determined by the court members. Thus the military judge may examine any agreed-to sentence limitation without fear of influencing the members. Once he is aware of a sentence limitation, however, the judge should not inform the members of that limitation. *See* United States v. Massie, 45 C.M.R. 717 (A.C.M.R. 1972) (error to reveal sentence limitation).

As a practical matter, just as civil juries are generally aware that a civil defendant's insurance company will pay damages, most military court members are no doubt aware of the fact that a common plea bargaining chip is a limitation on the sentence. Yet, they are not permitted to speculate as to that possibility and are to impose a sentence that they feel is appropriate based upon the evidence before them.

After sentencing, the judge should inquire of the parties as to their understanding of the impact of the agreement on the adjudged sentence. R.C.M. 910(h)(3) indicates that the judge may, with the consent of the government, conform the agreement to the accused's understanding or permit the accused to withdraw. *Cf.* United States v. Combs, 15 M.J. 743 (A.F.C.M.R. 1983) (responses from the parties should not be used to *modify* the sentencing terms of the agreement).

    United States v. Rondash, 30 M.J. 686 (A.C.M.R. 1990) (agreement to refer case to special court-martial was equivalent to sentence limitation that should not have been revealed to judge until after sentencing).

    United States v. Hall, 26 M.J. 739 (N.M.C.M.R. 1988) (military judge is not authorized to reject plea because the sentence is too lenient).

    In United States v. Jones, 24 M.J. 525 (A.F.C.M.R. 1987), the trial judge committed harmless error by being too thorough in inquiring into the terms of the pretrial agreement before imposing his sentence. The court recognized that in some circumstances it might be appropriate to inquire into the details of the sentence limitation provisions before sentence is announced. It suggested that:

> Before [such an inquiry] is undertaken by a military judge, he should first state the reason or reasons prompting the inquiry. Counsel should be offered an opportunity to comment on or object to the proposed inquiry. If the military judge determines that an inquiry is required, he should thereafter consider the advisability of recusal, depending upon the nature of the information he receives through the inquiry.

24 M.J. at 527. *See also* R.C.M. 910(f)(3).

    129. Inquiry into each clause is recommended but not required by *King* or *Green*. *See* United States v. Winkler, 5 M.J. 835 (A.C.M.R. 1978); United States v. Allen, 39 M.J. 581 (N.M.C.M.R. 1993) (failure to inquire into provision of agreement waiving Article 32 investigation did not render plea improvident). Failure to inquire into the sentence limitation portion of the agreement is error, however. United States v. Wilson, 4 M.J. 687 (N.C.M.R. 1977); United States v. Jackson, 30 M.J. 565 (A.C.M.R. 1990) (judge adequately questioned accused about his understanding of, and agreement with, a stipulation of fact).

    The *Manual* only requires that the judge should explain those terms that the accused apparently does not understand. The key here is that the accused understands the agreement, R.C.M. 910(f)(4)(A), and that the parties agree to the terms, R.C.M. 910(f)(4)(B).

    130. Failure to specifically ask the accused of his understanding of a particular clause is not necessarily error. United States v. Hinton, 10 M.J. 136 (C.M.A. 1981).

e. Strike all provisions, with the consent of the parties, that violate either appellate case law, public policy, or the judge's own notions of fundamental fairness; further, make a statement on the record that the judge considered all remaining provisions to be in accord with appellate case law, not against public policy, and not contrary to his own notions of fundamental fairness.[131]

f. Ask trial and defense counsel if the written agreement encompasses all of the understandings of the parties, and conduct further inquiry into any additional understandings that are revealed.[132]

United States v. Womack, 34 M.J. 876 (A.C.M.R. 1992) (failure to obtain statement from accused concerning his understanding of pretrial agreement was error; remedy was to approve sentence no greater than accused could have received under most favorable interpretation of agreement); United States v. Rascoe, 31 M.J. 544 (N.M.C.M.R. 1990) (court conducted an extensive inquiry into provision that permitted imposition of confinement if accused failed to pay fine; court rejected accused's argument that he was not fully aware of the consequences of the agreement).

United States v. Carter, 27 M.J. 695 (N.M.C.M.R. 1988) (pretrial agreement contained language in the sentence portion that the courts had previously interpreted to mean one thing but the trial judge concluded otherwise; on appeal, the court applied the judge's interpretation); United States v. Gooden, 23 M.J. 721 (A.C.M.R. 1986) (pretrial agreement made no mention of whether the convening authority could impose a reprimand; judge discussed matter with both counsel but left issue unresolved, perhaps in part because defense counsel viewed a reprimand as *de minimis*. Although it was error not to resolve the matter on the record, the judge's omission was harmless error. The convening authority's action in issuing a reprimand constituted plain error, however, because it exceeded the terms of the pretrial agreement).

131. See R.C.M. 910(f)(1), which indicates that a plea agreement may not be accepted if it does not comport with R.C.M. 705, which lists permissible and impermissible terms. The list is not inclusive. See Chapter 9.

The judge may not impose additional terms. United States v. Partin, 7 M.J. 409 (C.M.A. 1979), nor should he involve himself in the plea bargaining process. United States v. Caruth, 6 M.J. 184 (C.M.A. 1979).

132. Failure to inquire about other unwritten or *sub rosa* agreements is not fatal. United States v. Hinton, 10 M.J. 136 (C.M.A. 1981); United States v. Trujillo, 37 M.J. 798 (C.G.C.M.R. 1993) (counsel and accused failed to candidly answer military judge's inquiry concerning existence of other agreements; case remanded for new sentencing proceeding).

In United States v. Stringer, 34 M.J. 667 (A.C.M.R. 1992), the court indicated that while counsel have an obligation to disclose *sub rosa* agreements, they also have a duty to disclose information which may vitiate an important provision in the pretrial agreement. But R.C.M. 910(f) Discussion indicates that counsel have an obligation to *sua sponte* inform the judge of any agreements. *See also* United States v. Dinkel, 13 M.J. 400 (C.M.A. 1982) (recognized modification of *Green-King* rule, i.e., court willing to assume that counsel would advise judge of other agreements); United States v. Kelly, 32 M.J. 835 (N.M.C.M.R. 1991) (trial judges must be alert to possible *sub rosa* agreements between the accused and the convening authority); United States v. Rosario, 13 M.J. 552 (A.C.M.R. 1982) (court accepted posttrial affidavits from counsel that no other agreements existed); United States v. Bilbo, 13 M.J. 706 (N.M.C.M.R. 1982) (judge may rely upon representations by counsel).

In United States v. Muller, 21 M.J. 205 (C.M.A. 1986), the court indicated that where the trial judge receives assurances that there are no *sub rosa* agreements, counsel will not be permitted on appeal to assert that they did exist. United States v. Reed, 26 M.J. 891 (A.F.C.M.R. 1988) (judge's failure to inquire whether pretrial agreement provision waiving trial by members originated with accused was not fatal; court noted language in agreement itself that indicated that it had originated with the accused and the judge inquired into the truthfulness of that statement); United States v. Nebling, 26 M.J. 774 (N.M.C.M.R. 1988) (failure to inquire into whether pretrial agree-

g. Ask trial and defense counsel if the judge's interpretation of the agreement comports with their understanding of the meaning and effect of the plea bargain, and resolve on the record any differences.[133]

An example of a military judge's inquiry is included at Appendix 8 of the Manual for Courts-Martial (Trial Guide). Note that this pretrial agreement inquiry is also conducted out of the court member's presence.[134]

§ 14-3(D). Improvident Guilty Pleas.

§ 14-3(D)(1). In General.

Guilty pleas are generally rendered improvident where the accused attempts to plead guilty and yet maintain his innocence, where there is a substantial misunderstanding of the maximum punishment that may be imposed, or where unresolved, inconsistent matters are raised. This section addresses those grounds and the potential procedural consequences of an improvident guilty plea.

§ 14-3(D)(2). *Alford* Pleas.

A potential ground for finding a guilty plea improvident is entry of an *Alford*-type plea. Although the Supreme Court in *North Carolina v. Alford*[135] permitted entry of a guilty plea by an accused who asserted his innocence, Article 45(a), U.C.M.J., specifically requires rejection of the *Alford*-type plea.[136] As noted in § 14-5, an *Alford* plea is considered an *irregular* plea.

Military courts will sustain acceptance of a guilty plea, however, where the accused has no independent recollection of the offense, but bases his belief on witness accounts and other evidence.[137]

§ 14-3(D)(3). Misunderstanding of Sentence.

The second ground for improvidency, misunderstanding of the maximum punishment, most often arises where the offenses charged may be considered multiplicious for sentencing purposes.[138] Not all misapprehension renders the

---

ment encompassed all agreements was not fatal where posttrial affidavits to that effect were submitted to appellate court).

133. United States v. Griego, 10 M.J. 385 (C.M.A. 1981); Aviz v. Carver, 36 M.J. 1026 (N.M.C.M.R. 1993) (military judge properly modified pretrial agreement to understanding of the parties); United States v. Womack, 34 M.J. 876 (A.C.M.R. 1992) (judge's interpretation of pretrial agreement is not binding on parties; failure to inquire into understanding was not fatal).
134. *See* R.C.M. 803 (sessions without members). *See also* Chapter 12.
135. 400 U.S. 25 (1970).
136. *See* United States v. Reeder, 22 C.M.A. 11, 46 C.M.R. 11 (1972).
137. See the discussion on this point at § 14-3(B)(2).
138. See §§ 6-1(C)(3) and 13-3(J) for discussions on multiplicity. *Cf.* United States v. Tenney, 15 M.J. 779 (A.C.M.R. 1983) (maximum punishment is determined by examining the offenses to which the accused pled guilty, not the offenses that were approved on appeal).

plea improvident, however.[139] The misunderstanding must be "substantial."[140] For example, substantial misunderstanding exists when the accused is told that he faces a bad-conduct discharge and six months confinement at hard labor, when in fact no discharge is authorized and the maximum confinement is only four months.[141] No substantial mistake existed, however, where the military judge advised an accused that the maximum confinement was two years where it was only one.[142] Even where there is a substantial misunderstanding, the appellate courts may find the plea nonetheless provident. For example, in *United States v. Hunt*,[143] the court indicated that it would examine all of the circumstances of the case to determine the impact, if any, of the misunderstanding.[144]

---

139. *See* United States v. McDuffie, 43 M.J. 646 (A.F.Ct.Crim.App. 1995)(error in calculating sentence at 27 years rather than 8½ years not substantial misunderstanding); United States v. Andrade, 32 M.J. 520 (A.C.M.R. 1990) (incorrect information on maximum sentence did not improvidence plea); United States v. English, 25 M.J. 819 (A.F.C.M.R. 1988) (plea provident notwithstanding incorrect advice re maximum punishment—5 years versus 2½ years confinement); United States v. Smith, 21 M.J. 642 (A.C.M.R. 1985).

140. *See, e.g.,* United States v. Mincey, 42 M.J. 376 (1995) (court rejected mathematical formula for determining whether misunderstanding was substantial); United States v. Hemingway, 36 M.J. 349 (C.M.A. 1993) (misunderstanding of sentence was not substantial factor in accused's decision to plead guilty); United States v. Walker, 34 M.J. 264 (C.M.A. 1992) (accused's misunderstanding was substantial where judge advised accused that maximum punishment was 10 years, six months when it was only five years, six months; pretrial agreement placed maximum confinement at five years; court indicated that test for determining whether misunderstanding is substantial is an elastic one); United States v. Castrillon-Moreno, 7 M.J. 414 (C.M.A. 1979) (two years versus ten); United States v. Dowd, 7 M.J. 445 (C.M.A. 1979) (two years versus seven); United States v. Kyle, 32 M.J. 724 (A.F.C.M.R. 1991) (misunderstanding regarding maximum punishment under Assimilative Crimes Act improvidenced plea); United States v. Wirth, 24 M.J. 536 (A.C.M.R. 1987) (case remanded for determination of whether the accused's misunderstanding of the maximum punishment was substantial). On remand the court concluded that the accused's plea was provident. 25 M.J. 863 (A.C.M.R. 1988). United States v. Combs, 15 M.J. 743 (A.F.C.M.R. 1983) (accused not told that a fine could be imposed).

141. United States v. White, 3 M.J. 51 (C.M.A. 1977) (misc. docket).

142. United States v. Muir, 7 M.J. 448 (C.M.A. 1979).

143. 10 M.J. 222 (C.M.A. 1981).

144. *See also* United States v. Hemingway, 36 M.J. 349 (C.M.A. 1993) (task of court is to review all of facts and circumstances in determining whether misapprehension of maximum sentence affected the guilty plea; here, misapprehension was not substantial factor in decision to plead guilty); United States v. Poole, 26 M.J. 272 (C.M.A. 1988) (misapprehension re maximum sentence did not affect guilty plea); United States v. Frangoules, 1 M.J. 467 (C.M.A. 1976) (accused pleaded guilty knowing that some of the offenses might be multiplicious).

United States v. Lewis, 28 M.J. 871 (A.C.M.R. 1989) (accused's plea was not improvident where he was told that maximum punishment was 12 and not 5½ years but evidence of guilt was overwhelming and there was no reasonable likelihood that he would have changed plea); United States v. Smith, 21 M.J. 642 (A.C.M.R. 1985); United States v. Saulter, 1 M.J. 1066 (N.C.M.R. 1976), *rev'd on other grounds,* 5 M.J. 281 (C.M.A. 1978) (no fair risk to accused; he would have pleaded guilty even if he had been correctly advised).

§ 14-3(D)(4). **Factual and Legal Inconsistencies.**

The third possible reason for finding a plea of guilty improvident arises where after the plea has been accepted the accused raises legal or factual matters (often during sentencing) that are substantially inconsistent with that plea.[145] For example, the question of the accused's sanity may be raised[146] or it may become apparent that an affirmative defense may be available.[147]

---

145. Although case law indicates that the inconsistency should be substantial before the plea will be considered improvident, United States v. McCray, 5 M.J. 820 (A.C.M.R. 1978), aff'd, 7 M.J. 191 (C.M.A. 1979), the possibility of an inconsistency should trigger further inquiry by the trial judge.
See also United States v. Rooks, 29 M.J. 291 (C.M.A. 1989) (case remanded to determine providence of plea that raised issue of lack of *mens rea* due to epilepsy).
United States v. Gallion, 36 M.J. 950 (A.C.M.R. 1993) (inconsistency arose during sentencing and judge should have reopened providency inquiry); United States v. Lilly, 34 M.J. 670 (A.C.M.R. 1992) (military judge's inaccurate statement to accused concerning burden of proof concerning lack of mental responsibility improvidenced guilty plea).
United States v. Logan, 31 M.J. 910 (A.F.C.M.R. 1990) (no further inquiry required where evidence of lack of mental responsibility did not reasonably raise defense); United States v. Garcia, 29 M.J. 721 (C.G.C.M.R. 1989) (accused's plea to destruction of property was improvident where he did not admit specific intent); United States v. Sala, 29 M.J. 716 (A.C.M.R. 1989) (plea to charge of conspiracy was improvident); United States v. Pillow, 28 M.J. 1008 (C.G.C.M.R. 1989) (accused's plea of guilty to larceny was improvident where he stated that he did not intend to keep the money; court approved finding of guilty of wrongful appropriation).
United States v. Nichols, 27 M.J. 909 (A.F.C.M.R. 1989) (for plea to be improvident more than a mere possibility of conflict must exist; there must be a substantial indication of a direct conflict between the plea and the inconsistency).
United States v. Brooks, 26 M.J. 933 (A.C.M.R. 1988) (in determining whether an inconsistency has been raised, the sole issue is whether the accused raised an inconsistency, not whether the statement is credible; the judge is still required to conduct a further inquiry of the *accused*).
146. United States v. Batts, 19 C.M.A. 521, 42 C.M.R. 123 (1970); United States v. Leggs, 18 C.M.A. 245, 39 C.M.R. 245 (1969); United States v. Sims, 33 M.J. 684 (A.C.M.R. 1991) (judge erred in not ordering mental examination of accused in determining whether he had requisite mental responsibility at time of offense and thus raised possible affirmative defense to his guilty plea).
147. *See, e.g.,* United States v. Thomas, 31 M.J. 669 (A.C.M.R. 1990) (plea should have been rejected where inconsistency was not resolved); United States v. Duval, 31 M.J. 650 (A.C.M.R. 1990) (judge failed to resolve inconsistencies raised by accused's unsworn statement); United States v. Dukes, 30 M.J. 793 (N.M.C.M.R. 1990) (accused's statements concerning inception of unauthorized absence offense required further inquiry into his possible liberty status at time he left ship); United States v. Allison, 30 M.J. 546 (A.C.M.R. 1990) (judge's inquiry resolved inconsistency).
United States v. Walther, 30 M.J. 829 (N.M.C.M.R. 1990) (accused's plea to offense was improvident where inquiry indicated affirmative defense of voluntary abandonment).
United States v. Advincula, 29 M.J. 676 (A.F.C.M.R. 1989) (accused's plea improvident where his responses failed to remove possibility of defense of duress).
United States v. Rollins, 28 M.J. 803 (A.C.M.R. 1989) (the court observed that although some affirmative defenses admit all of the facts necessary to find the accused guilty of the charged offense but they also interpose new facts which would require a finding of not guilty. The court noted that this can create an impasse because the accused might wish to waive an affirmative defense but is required under oath to disclose the facts necessary to establish such a defense. *Id.* at 806, n.2); United States v. Smith, 27 M.J. 914 (A.C.M.R. 1989) (once accused admitted black market activity, the judge should have inquired into constitutional defense afforded by Fifth Amendment). *See also* United States v. Holman, 28 M.J. 527 (A.C.M.R. 1989); United States v.

Normally, a thorough *Care* inquiry, see § 14-3(B), into the factual basis of the plea will foreclose these inconsistent matters. But if they do arise, the military judge must probe further and determine if the inconsistency actually exists[148] and if it tends to negate any essential element or raise a defense.[149] The military judge should (1) explain the inconsistency to the accused and (2) give the accused an opportunity to explain or withdraw the inconsistency. The judge should do more than merely inquire whether the accused discussed a potential defense with his counsel and whether he believed a defense was available.[150] If the inconsistency is not resolved, the plea is improvident.[151] The key here is that not every possible inconsistency will improvidence a guilty plea.[152] A plea is improvident only if there is evidence which negates the accused's guilt.[153] And the full context of providency inquiry must be

---

Brooks, 26 M.J. 930 (A.C.M.R. 1988) (possible defense of entrapment was raised in accused's unsworn statement during sentencing); United States v. Stouffer, 2 M.J. 528 (A.C.M.R. 1976).

148. *See* R.C.M. 910(h)(2). United States v. Lee, 16 M.J. 278 (C.M.A. 1983); United States v. Logan, 22 C.M.A. 349, 47 C.M.R. 1 (1973); United States v. Daniels, 39 M.J. 789 (N.M.C.M.R 1993) (reversible error not to conduct further inquiry where inconsistency raised during sentencing); United States v. Gunter, 37 M.J. 781 (A.C.M.R. 1993) (military judge obtained satisfactory disclaimers from accused that defense of self-help did not apply).

Only inconsistencies arising after the guilty plea require resolution. There is nothing inconsistent with the loss of a pretrial motion and a later entry of a guilty plea. United States v. Bethke, 13 M.J. 71 (C.M.A. 1982).

149. United States v. Jennings, 1 M.J. 414 (C.M.A. 1976); United States v. Thomas, 39 M.J. 1078 (C.G.C.M.R. 1994) (plea of guilty improvident where judge failed to elicit clarification of possible defense to wrongful appropriation); United States v. Clark, 26 M.J. 589 (A.C.M.R. 1988) (when affirmative defense is raised, the trial judge should direct his inquiry to the accused personally and not the defense counsel as was done in this case. In a concurring opinion, Judge Holdaway stated that only when an inconsistency goes to an element of an offense should it be considered improvident; an accused should be able to waive an affirmative defense).

150. United States v. Randle, 35 M.J. 789 (A.C.M.R. 1992) (judge's inquiry insufficient to determine whether defense was available); United States v. Advincula, 29 M.J. 676 (A.F.C.M.R. 1989) (trial judge should question the accused personally about his attitude concerning the possible defense; he should not base his acceptance of the plea upon only the assertions of counsel that a defense does not exist).

United States v. Brooks, 26 M.J. 933 (A.C.M.R. 1988) (reversible error for trial judge to question only the counsel and not direct his questions to the accused re possible defense of entrapment); United States v. Dejong, 13 M.J. 721 (N.M.C.M.R. 1982); United States v. Collins, 17 M.J. 901 (A.F.C.M.R. 1983). *Cf.* United States v. Matthews, 13 M.J. 501 (A.C.M.R. 1982) (en banc) (judge summarily rejected guilty pleas without conducting factual inquiry).

151. *See, e.g.*, United States v. Adams, 33 M.J. 300 (C.M.A. 1991) (plea improvident where inquiry failed to resolve mistake of fact defense); United States v. Gallion, 36 M.J. 950 (A.C.M.R. 1993) (plea improvident where accused raised inconsistencies during sentencing and judge failed to re-open providency inquiry); United States v. Scofield, 33 M.J. 857 (A.C.M.R. 1991) (accused's guilty plea of assaulting his children by spanking them was improvident); United States v. Ridgeway, 32 M.J. 1006 (A.C.M.R. 1991) (judge failed to resolve inconsistencies in accused's guilty plea to bad check offenses).

152. United States v. Sanders, 33 M.J. 1026 (N.M.C.M.R. 1991) (plea is not improvident simply because mere possibility of conflict exists; record must contain some reasonable ground for finding inconsistency).

153. United States v. Roane, 43 M.J. 93 (1995)(accused's statements were not inconsistent with pleas of guilty); United States v. Reap, 43 M.J. 61 (1995)(accused's statements were more of an

considered in deciding on appeal whether a substantial inconsistency exists.[154]

It is important to note that while a civilian defendant may plead guilty, present inconsistent evidence, and still have his plea accepted,[155] that option, as noted at § 14-3(D)(2), does not exist in military practice.[156] That may sometimes pose a dilemma for an accused who, for whatever valid reason, wishes to plead guilty and at the same time present himself in as sympathetic a posture as possible to the sentencing authority.[157] This also poses problems for the military judge:

> Frequently, the issue of whether a plea of guilty is provident or improvident is anything but clear. The military judge is caught between Scylla and Charybdis and must chart his passage carefully; not only will he be reversed if reviewing authorities decide that he erroneously accepted an improvident plea, but he will suffer the same fate if he arbitrarily rejects a provident plea.[158]

While there is much to be said for the more closely controlled guilty plea inquiry in military practice, which offers protections for the accused against coerced and uninformed guilty pleas, the civilian model on this point offers relief from the dilemmas posed for all of the parties.[159]

§ 14-3(D)(5). Procedural Consequences of an Improvident Plea.

If it becomes apparent to the trial participants that a guilty plea may be improvident, the matter can usually be addressed, and often solved by a short recess, further research or further inquiry of the accused. Normally any discussions between the parties and the military judge concerning the providency of a plea should be entered on the record and not as a part of an

---

attempt to justify his actions and did not raise defense); United States v. Vega, 39 M.J. 79 (C.M.A. 1994) (where accused argues on appeal that plea was improvident, court will not overturn guilty plea unless thee is substantial conflict).

United States v. Kelly, 32 M.J. 813 (N.M.C.M.R. 1991) (sufficient factual basis for plea need not establish accused's guilt; plea is improvident only if there is evidence which negates guilt); United States v. Fahey, 33 M.J. 920 (A.C.M.R. 1991) (mere tactical possibility that a defense exists does not in itself warrant rejection of otherwise valid guilty plea; there must be substantial conflict with the plea).

154. United States v. Little, 43 M.J. 88 (1995) (record of trial raised substantial unresolved question of providency of guilty plea); United States v. Smauley, 42 M.J. 449 (1995)(accused's asserted act of abandonment of attempt to commit carnal knowledge did not raise substantial inconsistency).

155. *See* North Carolina v. Alford, 400 U.S. 25 (1990).

156. Article 45(a), U.C.M.J. See Appendix 3. United States v. Roane, 43 M.J. 93 (1995)(noting distinction in military and federal practice); United States v. Sala, 29 M.J. 716 (A.C.M.R. 1989).

157. United States v. Clark, 28 M.J. 401 (C.M.A. 1989). The court noted that in a borderline case, the military judge could give weight to the defense counsel's evaluation of the evidence. *Id.* at 407.

158. *Id.* at 405, *citing* Judge Carmichael's opinion in United States v. Clark, 26 M.J. 589 (A.C.M.R. 1988).

159. United States v. Clark, 26 M.J. 589 (A.C.M.R. 1988) (in a concurring opinion, Judge Holdaway wisely observed that an accused should be able to waive an affirmative defense in pleading guilty); United States v. Ellerbee, 30 M.J. 517 (A.F.C.M.R. 1990) (accused's unsworn statement reasonably raised discrepancies that should have required rejection of his guilty plea).

R.C.M. 802 conference.[160] If after further discussions or inquiry the inconsistency or misunderstanding is not resolved, the military judge must enter a plea of not guilty, withdraw all related matters, and proceed with the trial.[161]

Rejection of an improvident plea does not automatically require recusal of the military judge or a mistrial.[162] Generally if the trial is by military judge alone and he has heard strong evidence of guilt, he may either recuse himself or grant a defense motion to withdraw the request for trial by military judge alone.[163] In deciding what action to take, it would seem appropriate for the judge to explain the various options available to the defense and permit the accused to put his election, if any, on the record.[164] Failure to challenge the judge may constitute waiver.[165] Either remedy may be appropriate, and the judge's decision will be reviewed only for abuse of discretion.[166] The key here seems to be that mere knowledge of the accused's entry of a plea of guilty is not in itself disqualifying.[167] But if the judge is concerned that he might not be able to judge the accused's guilt free of any bias, recusal is appropriate.[168] This could pose real problems if during the subsequent trial on the merits the accused takes the stand in his defense and makes comments contradictory to those made during the earlier providency inquiry.[169]

Where the court consists of members it may be appropriate to declare a mistrial.[170] If a not guilty plea is entered the parties should be offered a reasonable time to prepare for a trial on the merits.[171]

---

160. *See* Chapter 12.
161. Art. 45, U.C.M.J.; R.C.M. 910(h)(2).
162. United States v. Winter, 35 M.J. 93 (C.M.A. 1992) (judges are not per se disqualified where they have rejected pleas); United States v. Kauffman, 3 M.J. 794 (A.C.M.R. 1977) (not error to omit explanation of right to trial by judge alone); United States v. Jophlin, 3 M.J. 858 (A.C.M.R. 1977).
163. R.C.M. 910(h)(2) Discussion (recusal or withdrawal of judge alone request will "ordinarily be necessary"); United States v. Cooper, 8 M.J. 5 (C.M.A. 1979); United States v. Bradley, 7 M.J. 332 (C.M.A. 1976); United States v. Peterson, 23 M.J. 828 (A.C.M.R. 1986) (judge should have recused himself even after the defense counsel declined to withdraw request for trial by judge alone).
164. United States v. Winter, 35 M.J. 93 (C.M.A. 1992) (preferable for judge to ask accused if he desired to be tried by judge alone after judge rejected guilty plea); United States v. Winter, 32 M.J. 901 (A.F.C.M.R. 1991) (judge did not err in not recusing himself after he rejected accused's guilty plea although he should have explained accused's options when he rejected the pleas).
165. United States v. Melton, 1 M.J. 528 (A.F.C.M.R. 1975).
166. *See, e.g.*, United States v. Haynes, 29 M.J. 610 (A.C.M.R. 1989) (judge did not abuse discretion); United States v. Peterson, 23 M.J. 828 (A.C.M.R. 1986) (judge erred in not recusing himself where he had heard the accused's admissions of guilt and during sentencing had heard about other instances of drug use; both the "fact and the appearance of impurity" were presented by the judge's continued presence on the bench); United States v. Kauffman, 3 M.J. 794 (A.C.M.R. 1977) (judge continued with bench trial).
167. United States v. Cockerell, 49 C.M.R. 567 (A.C.M.R. 1974).
168. *See* United States v. Shackleford, 2 M.J. 17 (C.M.A. 1976) (judge's questioning of accused based upon facts elicited during providency inquiry; case reversed).
169. *Id.*
170. R.C.M. 910(h)(2) Discussion.
171. R.C.M. 910(h)(2) Discussion.

If the potential inconsistency arises after trial, there is apparently no requirement that the convening authority direct a rehearing,[172] although doing so is probably advisable.[173] Where the issue of an improvident plea is raised for the first time on appeal, the appellate court will review the entire record[174] and determine if the plea is improvident.[175] As with other appellate disposition of issues, the court could set aside the plea and remand the case for a possible rehearing or simply reassess the sentence.[176]

§ 14-3(E). Entry of Findings.

Following the providency and pretrial agreement inquiries, the military judge may enter findings of guilt based upon the provident plea.[177] The case then proceeds to the sentencing phase.[178] The exception to this general rule occurs where the accused has pleaded guilty to only a lesser included offense and the prosecution intends to introduce evidence on the charged offense.[179] In

---

172. United States v. Scott, 6 M.J. 608 (A.C.M.R. 1978). *Cf.* United States v. Steck, 10 M.J. 412 (C.M.A. 1981) (a proceeding in revision may be used to correct problems in plea bargaining inquiries).

173. See also R.C.M. 1102 (posttrial sessions), which indicates that posttrial sessions may be used to inquire further into pretrial agreements.

174. United States v. Johnson, 42 M.J. 443 (1995) (uncontroverted that appellate court must consider entire record if providency of plea is in question); United States v. Bester, 42 M.J. 75 (1995) (court will consider entire record); United States v. Martin, 39 M.J. 111 (C.M.A. 1994) (entire record).

175. United States v. Vega, 39 M.J. 79 (C.M.A. 1994) (accused's unsworn statement was not inconsistent with guilty plea); United States v. Vardiman, 35 M.J. 132 (C.M.A. 1992) (accused challenged providency of plea for first time on appeal; court concluded that plea was provident). United States v. Outhier, 42 M.J. 626 (N.M. Ct. Crim. App. 1995) (summary of principles of reviewing factual accuracy of guilty pleas); United States v. Vaughn, 36 M.J. 645 (A.C.M.R. 1992) (accused's guilty plea to AWOL was not improvident where facts showed that NCO was aware of accused's casual presence in unit); United States v. Eischeid, 36 M.J. 561 (N.M.C.M.R. 1992) (court rejected argument that accused's plea could be found provident for closely-related offense; court held that obstruction of justice and violation of an order were different offenses); United States v. Turner, 35 M.J. 787 (A.C.M.R. 1992) (plea was improvident where element missing); United States v. Newsome, 35 M.J. 749 (N.M.C.M.R. 1992) (plea was provident); United States v. Testori, 35 M.J. 745 (N.M.C.M.R. 1992) (plea was provident).

Cf. United States v. McGowan, 41 M.J. 406 (1995) (court will not engage in post-trial speculation about factual basis for plea).

176. United States v. Burnette, 35 M.J. 58 (C.M.A. 1992) (appellate court determined that accused's post-trial renunciations of plea were insufficient to improvidence the plea). *See* Chapter 17.

177. L. R.C.M. 910(g). United States v. Moser, 23 M.J. 568 (A.C.M.R. 1986) (judge's presenting comments to court members was tantamount to his announcing findings of guilt to earlier guilty pleas).

178. *See* Chapter 16.

179. *See* § 14-3(A)(3). In United States v. Boone, 24 M.J. 680 (A.C.M.R. 1987), the trial judge erroneously entered findings of guilty as to the lesser offenses but not guilty as to the greater offense. Following the presentation of evidence by the prosecution, the trial judge found the accused guilty as charged. The court rejected the accused's argument that the first set of findings precluded the judge from considering the evidence on the merits. Distinguishing United States v. Hitchcock, 6 M.J. 188 (C.M.A. 1979), and United States v. Boswell, 23 C.M.R. 369 (C.M.A. 1957), the court concluded that the judge's first announcement was not intended to be his verdict.

that situation, the entry of findings is deferred until the prosecution and defense have presented their evidence.[180] Another possible exception recognized by the *Manual* is where the Secretary of the Service prohibits such.[181]

§ 14-3(F). Informing the Members of the Accused's Plea of Guilty.

Once the judge has entered findings, the trial generally proceeds to the sentencing phase.[182] If the accused has not requested a bench trial,[183] the members are called into the courtroom and in the process of the sentencing proceedings are informed that the accused has entered a plea of guilty; thus the only task before the court is to adjudge an appropriate sentence.[184] However, where the accused has entered pleas of guilty to only some of the charged offenses, or to a lesser charge,[185] it is not always clear whether the court members should be informed of those pleas. Under the 1969 *Manual* it was common practice for the judge to so inform the court members.[186] As one court has noted, however, that practice was an "anachronism" and apparently based upon an earlier requirement in Article 45, U.C.M.J. that the court members vote on a finding of guilty even where the accused had entered a plea of guilty.[187]

The argument against informing the court of partial pleas of guilty is that the court will be influenced to find the accused guilty of the offenses to which he has pleaded not guilty. The safer practice seems to be that informing the court of any pleas of guilty should be reserved until the court has reached a finding on any other offenses. This can be accomplished by not showing the court members the charge sheet but instead preparing a separate sheet listing only those charges and specifications upon which they must reach a finding of guilt. If for some reason the judge does inform the members of a partial plea of guilty, the test should be whether doing so unfairly influenced the members on the remaining charges. Where the charges are sufficiently dissimilar there

---

180. Art. 45(b), U.C.M.J.; R.C.M. 910(g)(2). United States v. Bohl, 3 M.J. 385 (C.M.A. 1977) (misc. docket); United States v. Barnes, 33 M.J. 893 (A.F.C.M.R. 1991) (judge erroneously entered findings by exceptions and substitutions to accused's guilty plea to lesser offense of AWOL although prosecution intended to present evidence on desertion charge to the members; court indicated that proper procedure is to accept the plea to the lesser offense and later instruct the members to enter findings in accordance with those pleas unless they find beyond a reasonable doubt that the accused committed the charged offense); United States v. Baker, 28 M.J. 900 (A.C.M.R. 1989) (harmless error for judge to enter findings on lesser included offense where he knew that the prosecutor intended to present evidence on the greater offense); United States v. Fletcher, 2 M.J. 1252 (N.C.M.R. 1976).

181. *See* R.C.M. 910(g)(1).
182. See Chapter 16 for discussion on sentencing procedures.
183. *See* § 12-3(A).
184. *See* Chapter 16.
185. *See* § 14-3(A)(3).
186. *See* paras. 65a, 39b, 53d(1), and 70b, 1969 MCM.
187. United States v. Nixon, 15 M.J. 1028 (A.C.M.R. 1983). The court noted that this ritualistic provision in Article 45 was removed in the Military Justice Act of 1968, P.L. 90-632. The court encouraged judges to abandon the practice of announcing any findings of guilt until sentencing procedures commenced.

§ 14-3(F)   PLEAS   § 14-3(F)

should usually be no problem.[188] Having so informed the members, it would seem appropriate for the judge to instruct the members that they may draw no adverse inferences against the accused as to the other offenses.[189] It goes without saying that the prosecution must be wary of arguing such an inference. The *Manual* suggests that where such partial pleas of guilty are entered the judge should consult with the parties before deciding whether to announce his findings to the members.[190] Lack of objection by the defense to such announcements would probably constitute waiver of the issue.

In *United States v. Rivera*,[191] the Court agreed that military judges should no longer inform the members that the accused has pleaded guilty to other charges before the members have returned a verdict on other contested charges. The court nonetheless indicated that the prosecution could offer evidence of the charges to which the accused pleaded guilty if such evidence was otherwise admissible as to the contested charges.[192] This may be a distinction without a difference. A key reason for not informing the court members about a guilty plea on other charges is that doing so may cause them to infer that

---

188. *See* United States v. Kyles, 20 M.J. 571 (N.M.C.M.R. 1985) (bigamy and AWOL); United States v. Nixon, 15 M.J. 1028 (A.C.M.R. 1983) (sodomy and AWOL).

189. *Cf.* United States v. Childress, 33 M.J. 602 (A.C.M.R. 1991) (court disagreed with trial judge's instructions to court members that the failure to inform them that the accused had previously entered a plea of guilty amounted to a fraud).

190. R.C.M. 910(g) Discussion. The Drafters' Analysis to this provision recognizes that announcing partial findings of guilty to the members may be "unnecessary and inappropriate." The Analysis cites no arguments or examples supporting such practice. It might be advantageous to the defense where, for example, the accused has entered a plea of guilty to AWOL and not guilty to the greater charge of desertion and intends to take the stand and admit the absence, show remorse for that offense (including references to the plea of guilty), and argue that he always intended to return.

191. 23 M.J. 89 (C.M.A. 1986). A 1990 amendment to R.C.M. 913(a), which addressed preliminary instructions, specifically indicates that the military judge should normally defer informing the members of the guilty plea until after findings on the contested offenses have been entered. The Discussion to that provision indicates that the general rule might not apply in those instances where the defense has requested on the record that the judge so instruct the members and in those instances where the accused entered a plea of guilty to a lesser included offense within the contested offense.

United States v. Davis, 26 M.J. 445 (C.M.A. 1988) (where accused had stipulated to the first two elements of two Article 134 offenses and the only issue was whether the alleged conduct was prejudicial to good order and discipline, his character was not in issue and it was harmless error to inform members of accused's guilty pleas).

In United States v. Staton, 37 M.J. 1047 (N.M.C.M.R. 1993), the judge accepted the accused's plea of guilty to the lesser included offense of absence without leave and entered findings of guilty even though the prosecution intended to present evidence on the greater offense of desertion. Citing *Baker, infra*, court held that the military judge erred by not informing the court members of the accused's plea to the lesser offense before they returned with a guilty verdict on the charge of desertion.

United States v. Hamilton, 36 M.J. 723 (A.C.M.R. 1992) (nonprejudicial error to inform members that accused had entered guilty plea to some offenses).

Cf. United States v. Baker, 28 M.J. 900 (A.C.M.R. 1989) (in a trial with members, military judge should inform members before opening statements about the meaning of the accused's plea of guilty).

192. 23 M.J. at 96.

the accused is also guilty on the contested charges.[193] But that same inference is possible, and equally troublesome, whenever evidence about "uncharged" misconduct is offered by the prosecution.[194] In either event, the judge is required to weigh carefully the probative value of the evidence or information against the possibility of undue prejudice.[195]

§ 14-3(G). Withdrawal of Guilty Plea.

Before the guilty plea is accepted, the accused may withdraw it at any time.[196] After acceptance, but before announcement of the sentence, the plea may be withdrawn only with consent of the judge.[197] Although most judges do so, there is no requirement that the military judge specifically advise an accused of the option of withdrawing a guilty plea before sentence is adjudged.[198] The courts have specifically rejected the argument that the key time is the announcement of findings and that the accused's right to withdraw his plea until that point is not subject to the discretion of the judge. In *United States v. Leonard*,[199] the court indicated that there were practical policy reasons for limiting the right to withdraw: the desirability of having a uniform standard at all stages of the trial and avoiding prejudice to the government that may have released witnesses or evidence in reliance upon the accused's plea of guilty.[200] In any event, the judge should carefully explore the reasons for the requested withdrawal. His decision is subject to review for abuse of discretion.

One court has indicated that a military judge has the authority after the court has adjourned to accept a change in the accused's pleas. In *United States v. Washington*,[201] the accused was convicted pursuant to his pleas of guilty of, *inter alia*, wrongful distribution of cocaine. But six days after the trial, the defense counsel discovered in a laboratory report that the substance that was

---

193. 23 M.J. at 95.
194. *See* MIL. R. EVID. 404(b). *See generally* Saltzburg, Schinasi & Schlueter, *Military Rules of Evidence Manual* 460-64 (3d ed. 1991).
195. In United States v. Smith, 23 M.J. 118 (C.M.A. 1986), the court reversed the conviction where the judge, over the objection of the defense counsel, informed the members of the prior pleas of guilty. The court balanced the apparent absence of useful purpose of that announcement against the risk of substantial prejudice to the accused and concluded that the trial judge erred.
See also United States v. James, 24 M.J. 894 (A.C.M.R. 1987) (no prejudice where government's evidence of guilt was overwhelming); United States v. Jagnandan, 24 M.J. 628 (A.C.M.R. 1987) (prejudicial error for judge to announce findings of guilty to court members where there was apparently no legitimate reason to do so).
196. *See* United States v. Leonard, 16 M.J. 984 (A.C.M.R. 1983) (touchstone is acceptance of the plea under the *Care* inquiry). *See also* United States v. Hayes, 9 M.J. 825 (N.C.M.R. 1980) and R.C.M. 910(h)(1) Drafters' Analysis. *Cf.* United States v. Newkirk, 8 M.J. 684 (N.C.M.R. 1980).
197. R.C.M. 910(h)(1). United States v. Leonard, 16 M.J. 984 (A.C.M.R. 1983). *See also* United States v. Politano. 14 C.M.A. 518, 34 C.M.R. 298 (1964) and Rules 11 and 32(d), FED. R. CRIM. P.
198. United States v. Silver, 40 M.J. 351 (C.M.A. 1994) (judge not required to advise accused of conditional right to withdraw guilty plea).
199. 16 M.J. 984 (A.C.M.R. 1983).
200. 16 M.J. at 986.
201. 23 M.J. 679 (A.C.M.R. 1986).

supposedly the cocaine was actually a mixture of noncontrolled drugs.[202] At the defense counsel's request, the trial judge convened an Article 39(a) session. Although he indicated that he did not have the authority to accept the accused's change of guilty plea to the lesser offense of attempted distribution, he did conduct a further providency inquiry and permitted a change in the sentence limitation on the pretrial agreement. He also heard additional evidence on sentencing but took no further action to change either the findings or the sentence. The convening authority, however, reduced the findings to attempted distribution and reduced the sentence. The court concluded that the convening authority's action was proper but that the military judge also possessed the authority to accept the accused's changed pleas. Citing *United States v. Brickey*,[203] the court indicated that R.C.M. 924(c), which permits a judge to reconsider a finding of guilty at any time before the sentence is announced, must be read in conjunction with R.C.M. 1102(b)(2), which permits posttrial Article 39(a) sessions. However, the court failed to cite or reconcile the possible application of R.C.M. 910(h), which clearly implies that after the sentence is announced the accused may not withdraw his pleas.[204]

§ 14-4. Conditional Pleas of Guilty.

Prior to promulgation of the 1984 revisions to the Manual for Courts-Martial, military practice did not recognize the validity of any attempts to plead guilty and yet preserve issues for appellate review that would normally be considered waived by the plea of guilty.[1] Although attempts by trial participants to do so were rejected by the military appellate courts, the Drafters of the *Manual* officially sanctioned the practice as part of an overall attempt to conform military practices with those used in the federal courts.[2] The vehicle for doing so is through entry of a *conditional plea of guilty*.[3]

By entering a conditional guilty plea the accused is permitted to raise, and preserve for appeal, a variety of issues that are normally considered waived by

---

202. There is nothing in the opinion that indicates why this problem was not discovered prior to trial.

203. 16 M.J. 679 (A.C.M.R. 1986). It should be noted that although *Brickey* was the basis for expanding the posttrial authority of trial judges, that decision was arguably limited to the judge's authority to conduct inquiries into factual matters which might later affect the disposition of the case.

204. *See also* § 16-11.

1. *See* United States v. Schaffer, 12 M.J. 425 (C.M.A. 1982); United States v. Mallett, 14 M.J. 631 (A.C.M.R. 1982); United States v. Higa, 12 M.J. 1008 (A.C.M.R. 1982).

2. *See* R.C.M. 910 Analysis. The *Manual* rule is modeled after Rule 11(a)(2), FED. R. CRIM. P., which was added to federal practice in 1983. The purpose of these rules is to avoid the necessity of conducting a trial on the merits for the sole purpose of preserving an issue for appeal. Unfortunately, there is little federal case law interpreting the federal provision. That is probably due in part to the fact that prosecutors see little advantage in agreeing to conditional pleas of guilty.

Notwithstanding the absence of formal recognition of conditional guilty pleas, defense counsel in the past successfully preserved issues for appeal by entering a plea of not guilty and then agreeing to a confessional stipulation which generally negated the need for an extended trial on the merits. For a discussion of confessional stipulations, see § 9-3.

3. R.C.M. 910(a)(2).

§ 14-4

a guilty plea.[4] The plea is *conditional* in the sense that if the accused prevails on appeal he will be allowed to withdraw his plea of guilty, enter a plea of not guilty, and require the prosecution to present its case.[5] Despite its clear utility to the defense, the military courts have urged sparing use of the conditional guilty plea.[6]

Several key prerequisites must be met before such a plea may be recognized. First, both the trial judge *and* the government must consent to entry of such a plea.[7] Requiring consent of both serves to insure that an accused may not use the conditional plea as a mere delay tactic. That is, the conditional plea is usually appropriate only where the issue being preserved for appeal will dispose of the case.[8] The *Manual* vests the Service Secretaries with authority to designate those who may consent on behalf of the government.[9] In the absence of such designation the trial counsel may consent.[10] The trial judge's decision is reviewable for an abuse of discretion; even if the judge consents to preservation of the issue, the appellate court is not bound to review it.[11] It is important to remember that the accused does not have an enforceable "right" to enter a conditional guilty plea.[12]

Secondly, the accused must state *in writing* that he is reserving the right on further review or appeal to review an adverse ruling by the trial judge of any particular pretrial motion.[13] The *Manual* specifies no particular format for

---

4. See § 14-3(A)(2). *See generally* Note, "Conditional Guilty Pleas," 93 Harv. L. Rev. 564 (1980); Botsford, "Conditional Guilty Pleas: Post-Guilty Plea Appeal of Nonjurisdictional Issues," 26 U.C.L.A. L. Rev. 360 (1978).
5. R.C.M. 910(a)(2). Note that, without regard to a conditional guilty plea, an accused who successfully obtains a rehearing on the merits of the case is normally entitled to change his original plea. *See* § 14-3(A)(4).
6. United States v. Phillips, 32 M.J. 955 (A.F.C.M.R. 1991) (discussion of need to use conditional pleas sparingly; they do nothing to help develop the record and should only be used to preserve issues that would terminate the prosecution).
7. *Id.* United States v. Forbes, 19 M.J. 953 (A.F.C.M.R. 1985). The drafters of both the federal and military versions of the rule recognized that different interests are at stake when the accused attempts to preserve an issue for appeal. The judge would usually be concerned with blocking appeals of issues that could be appropriately resolved by proceeding with a trial; the government, on the other hand, would be concerned with blocking appeal of issues which would not dispose of the case. In the end, the drafters envisioned that requiring consent of both will reduce the possibility of abuse by an accused. *See generally* R.C.M. 910 Analysis. United States v. Burns, 684 F.2d 1066 (2d Cir. 1982).
8. An example would be litigation of an accused's pretrial statement; an issue often critical to the prosecution's case but an issue waived by a plea of guilty. *See* § 13-3(A)(2).
9. R.C.M. 910(a)(2). For example, the Secretary of the Army has designated general courts-martial authorities as the appropriate officials for consenting to conditional guilty pleas. *See* AR 27-10, para. 5-24.
10. R.C.M. 910(a)(2).
11. *See, e.g.*, United States v. Curcio, 712 F.2d 1532 (3d Cir. 1983); United States v. Burns, 684 F.2d 1066 (2d Cir. 1982).
12. United States v. Forbes, 19 M.J. 953 (A.F.C.M.R. 1985) (the discretion granted to the government and the judge is not subject to challenge by the accused); United States v. Fisher, 772 F.2d 371 (7th Cir. 1985) (court rejected arguments that the accused should have been informed of the right to enter a conditional guilty plea).
13. R.C.M. 910(a)(2). United States v. Forbes, 19 M.J. 953 (A.F.C.M.R. 1985) (accused waived challenge to evidence (urinalysis results) by entering conditional guilty plea without first making motion to suppress).

this writing, and any format should do. A sample form is included in this book at Appendix 23. The key is that the accused specify with clarity a particular issue upon which both the judge and government may consent and clearly specify that he has entered a conditional plea. To avoid later disputes it would seem appropriate for both the judge and government representative to register their consent, or lack thereof, on the writing itself, which should be marked and handled as an appellate exhibit. Note that at least one federal court has held that failure of the government to object constitutes consent.[14] It would seem more appropriate for the military courts to adopt a rule that places the burden upon the accused to obtain the affirmative consent of the government, either in writing or on the record.[15]

Once he has specified the issue, the accused should be bound by his assertions on appeal and not be permitted to expand or change the issue ruled upon by the military judge.[16]

If the conditional plea has been part of a plea bargain, the particular issue may properly be indicated in the pretrial agreement.[17] All parties should remember that the judge is not permitted to enter into the negotiation process,[18] even though his consent is still required.

§ 14-5. Irregular Pleas.

As noted in § 14-1, military practice only recognizes pleas of guilty, not guilty, or a combination of the two. *Alford* guilty pleas,[1] *nolo contendere* pleas,[2] and standing mute are considered irregular pleas and will trigger entry by the military judge of a not guilty plea.[3] Another example would include pleading not guilty to the specifications but guilty to the charge.[4] If the accused appears to be unaware of the effect of entering an irregular plea it would seem appropriate for the judge to permit the accused to consult with counsel or seek clarification from counsel or the accused whether an irregular plea is in fact being entered.[5] Upon the entry of the not guilty plea the trial proceeds to the merits portion of the proceedings.[6]

---

14. *See* United States v. Burke, 517 F.2d 377 (2d Cir. 1975).

15. Such a rule lends itself to certainty and less speculation about whether the accused actually complied with the Rule.

16. *See, e.g.*, United States v. Simmons, 763 F.2d 529 (2d Cir. 1985) (court refused to consider issues not reserved by defense); United States v. Alexander, 761 F.2d 1294 (9th Cir. 1985) (defense limited to issues preserved). By reviewing the accused's written assertions, both the trial judge and the government can insure that the specified issue or issues conform to what was actually litigated in the pretrial motions.

17. See Chapter 9 for a discussion of pretrial agreements.

18. *See, e.g.*, United States v. Taylor, 21 M.J. 1016 (A.C.M.R. 1986). See also 10 A.L.R.4th 687 and 56 A.L.R. Fed. 529 for discussions on judicial participation in plea bargaining.

1. North Carolina v. Alford, 400 U.S. 25 (1970). *See* § 14-3(E). *See also* Tesler, "The Guilty Plea Is Innocent: Effects of *North Carolina v. Alford* on Pleading Under the U.C.M.J.," 26 JAG J. 15 (1971).

2. United States v. Davis, 4 C.M.R. 195 (A.B.R. 1952) (plea of *nolo contendere* rejected).

3. R.C.M. 910(b).

4. R.C.M. 910(b) Discussion.

5. R.C.M. 910(b) Discussion.

6. *See* Chapter 15.

APPENDIX REFERENCES

Appendix 1. Abbreviations.
Appendix 2. Glossary.
Appendix 3. U.C.M.J.
Appendix 6. Charge Sheet.
Appendix 12. Pretrial Agreement.
Appendix 22. Plea Worksheet.
Appendix 23. Entry of Conditional Guilty Plea.
Appendix 25. Stipulation of Fact.
Appendix 30. Maximum Punishment Chart.

ANNOTATED BIBLIOGRAPHY

PERIODICALS

Botsford, "Conditional Guilty Pleas: Post-Guilty Plea Appeal of Nonjurisdictional Issues," 26 U.C.L.A. L. REV. 360 (1978).

The author describes the dilemma that faces a defendant whose substantive constitutional claim is rejected at the pretrial stage and who then must make the decision to either plead not guilty and risk a trial in order to preserve the constitutional claim or accept the state's bargain and forgo those claims by pleading guilty. The author describes in detail three techniques that have arisen to circumvent this dilemma, the conditional guilty plea, the stipulation on transcript, and the statutory exemption of specific nonjurisdictional issues, and suggests that the proper solution is an all-inclusive statutory exemption.

Elling, "Guilty Plea Inquiries: Do We *Care* Too Much?" 134 MIL. L. REV. 195 (1991).

The author notes the differences between guilty plea inquiries in federal and military practice, discusses the history of practice in both systems and focuses on the apparently rigid practice in the military of rejecting pleas where an inconsistency is raised. He concludes that it is time to modernize military practice, by overruling or modifying *United States v. Care* and amending Article 45(a) and R.C.M. 910(h)(2).

McGovern, "Guilty Plea—Military Version," 31 FED. B.J. 88 (1972).

This brief article, part of a military law issue, presents a good introduction to the military guilty plea and the requirements imposed by *United States v. Care*, 18 C.M.A. 535, 40 C.M.R. 257 (1969), regarding a providency inquiry. A sample scenario is included at the end of the article.

Note, "Conditional Guilty Pleas," 93 HARV. L. REV. 564 (1980).

Noting that the much increased use of plea bargaining creates constitutionally unacceptable pressure on the defendant to forgo the vindication of rights in exchange for sentencing discounts and other prosecutorial concessions, the author argues that the conditional guilty plea, which allows a defendant to plead guilty yet retain the right to appeal on constitutional grounds the denial of a motion to suppress, is an appropriate compromise between the benefits of the plea bargain system and the need to provide defendants with an adequate forum for the consideration of their constitutional claims.

Saltzburg, "Pleas of Guilty and the Loss of Constitutional Rights: The Current Price of Pleading Guilty," 76 MICH. L. REV. 1265 (1978).

Professor Saltzburg derives from Supreme Court decisions a principle that separates those rights whose vindication is barred by a plea of guilty and those that may be claimed regardless of such a plea; those rights that, if successfully vindicated, would bar further prosecution may be claimed despite a guilty plea. The author describes the Supreme Court's attempts to articulate this distinction and proposes the acceptance of a new rule that would allow a defendant to issue proper notice of his constitutional claims, plead guilty, and claim on appeal the violation of those rights whose vindication would serve to terminate the government's ability to prosecute its charges.

Symposium, "The Guilty Plea," 13 THE ADVOCATE 236 (1981) (Issues 4 & 5).

The symposium consists of four very good articles on various aspects of the guilty plea and a short item on issues waived by a guilty plea:

> Vitaris, "The Guilty Plea's Impact on Appellate Review."
> Moriarty, "The Providence Inquiry: A Guilty Plea Gauntlet?"
> Gray, "The Professional Responsibilities of Defense Counsel in Uncontested Courts-Martial."
> Lukjanowicz, "The Providency Inquiry: An Examination of Judicial Responsibilities." "Issues Waived by Provident Guilty Plea."

Symposium, "Military Law," 10 AM. CRIM. L. REV. 1 (1971).

This symposium issue covers a valuable range of topics pertinent to the practice of military criminal law. Included are articles on jurisdiction over civilian-type offenses, plea bargaining, sentencing, discovery, appeals, and an article by General Westmoreland on the commander's perspective of military justice. Also included is a fine bibliography of books, articles, and listings of military law materials.

Tesler, "The Guilty Plea if Innocent: Effects of *North Carolina v. Alford* on Pleading Under the UCMJ," 26 JAG J. 15 (1971).

The author provides a concise history of the *Alford* decision and its place in the evolution of the theory and treatment of the guilty plea. In recognizing the ability of a defendant to waive his rights to trial on the issue of guilt without conceding such guilt, the author argues that the Supreme Court has clarified a complex and often inconsistent area of criminal law and reduced the occasions for subterfuge in plea determination.

Vickery, "The Providency of Guilty Pleas: Does the Military Really Care?", 58 MIL. L. REV. 209 (1972).

Recognizing that the vast majority of criminal cases are resolved through guilty pleas, the author presents a good discussion of the constitutional standards, as reviewed by the Supreme Court, the statutory standard applicable to military practice, and the potential impact of *North Carolina v. Alford*, 400 U.S. 25 (1970), on military practice.

CHAPTER 15

TRIAL PROCEDURES

Part I
Introduction

§ 15-1.   General.
§ 15-2.   The Participants.
    § 15-2(A). The Accused.
    § 15-2(B). The Defense Counsel.
        § 15-2(B)(1). In General.
        § 15-2(B)(2). Representation of Multiple Accused and Conflicts of Interest.
        § 15-2(B)(3). Ineffective Assistance of Counsel.
        § 15-2(B)(4). Defense Counsel and the Perjurious Client.
    § 15-2(C). The Trial Counsel.
    § 15-2(D). The Military Judge.
    § 15-2(E). The Court Members.
    § 15-2(F). The Court Reporter.
    § 15-2(G). The Interpreter.
§ 15-3.   Courts-Martial and the Media: Public Trials.
§ 15-4.   Motions at Trial.
    § 15-4(A). Continuances.
    § 15-4(B). Mistrial.
    § 15-4(C). Motion for Finding of Not Guilty.
    § 15-4(D). Motions for Inquiring Into Accused's Sanity.
§ 15-5.   Contempts.
§ 15-6.   Trial Procedure Guides—Uniform Rules of Practice.

Part II
Procedures for General and Special Courts-Martial

§ 15-7.   General.
§ 15-8.   Introduction and Swearing of the Participants.
§ 15-9.   Assembly of the Court.
§ 15-10. Voir Dire and Challenges of Court Members.
    § 15-10(A). Voir Dire of Court Members.
    § 15-10(B). Grounds for Challenging Court Members.
    § 15-10(C). Challenges of Court Members.
        § 15-10(C)(1). Challenge of the Selection Process.
        § 15-10(C)(2). Challenges for Cause.
        § 15-10(C)(3). Peremptory Challenges.
§ 15-11. Opening Statements.
§ 15-12. Presentation of the Cases-in-Chief.
    § 15-12(A). Examination of the Witnesses.
    § 15-12(B). Questions by the Court.
    § 15-12(C). Exhibits.
    § 15-12(D). Views and Inspections of Places and Objects.
§ 15-13. Closing Arguments.
§ 15-14. Instructions to the Court Members.
    § 15-14(A). General.
    § 15-14(B). *Sua Sponte* Instructions.
    § 15-14(C). Instructions Upon Request.
    § 15-14(D). Review of Instructions Errors.
§ 15-15. Deliberations.

§ 15-16. Verdict; Announcement of Findings.
  § 15-16(A). General Findings.
  § 15-16(B). Impeaching the Findings.
  § 15-16(C). Special Findings by the Military Judge.
§ 15-17. Sentencing Procedures.

PART III

EVIDENTIARY RULES

§ 15-18. General.
§ 15-19. Military Rules of Evidence.
§ 15-20. Presumptions and Inferences.
§ 15-21. Stipulations.
§ 15-22. Depositions.
§ 15-23. Objections and Preserving Error.
§ 15-24. Evidentiary Instructions During Trial.

PART IV

SUMMARY COURTS-MARTIAL PROCEDURES

§ 15-25. General.
§ 15-26. The Summary Court-Martial Participants.
  § 15-26(A). The Summary Court-Martial Officer.
  § 15-26(B). The Accused.
  § 15-26(C). Counsel.
§ 15-27. Pretrial Conference.
§ 15-28. Trial on the Merits and Sentencing.
§ 15-29. Post-Trial Procedures.
Appendix References.
Annotated Bibliography.

PART I

INTRODUCTION

§ 15-1. General.

The trial on the merits of the case may follow the Article 39(a) pretrial session[1] either immediately or at some later date. The court members who are absent during the pretrial session join the other participants for the formal presentation of evidence and deliberations. This chapter generally addresses the trial procedures of military courts-martial, up to the sentencing portion of the trial, and applicable evidentiary rules. Part I includes a brief examination of the roles of participants and the various trial motions. In Part II, the procedures for general and special courts-martial are discussed; summary courts-martial procedures are noted separately in Part IV. The evidentiary rules, including a discussion of the Military Rules of Evidence, are examined in Part III.

---

1. See § 12-1.

§ 15-2. The Participants.

At the call of the military judge the participants meet.[1] The judge will usually have examined the applicable convening orders beforehand to insure that only proper parties are included.[2] The qualifications of the military judge, counsel, and court members are also addressed in Chapters 4 and 8. What follows are some general comments on the roles and duties of the various participants.

§ 15-2(A). The Accused.

The trial counsel is responsible for the accused's attendance at the court-martial; he should advise the accused's commander of the time and date of trial and should insure that the accused is properly attired.[3] If after arraignment the accused voluntarily absents himself,[4] he may be tried in *absentia*.[5] An accused is deemed to have notice of the trial date once that information has been given to his counsel.[6] In *United States v. Sanders*[7] the court provided a lengthy discussion of the problem of showing the accused's voluntary absence through the statements of his counsel. The court indicated that counsel's averments in this case deprived the accused of his rights to counsel. The

---

1. *See generally* R.C.M. 901.
2. The topics of appointment of the members and convening orders are discussed in more detail in Chapter 8. See also Appendix 9 for sample convening orders.
3. *See, e.g.,* United States v. Taylor, 31 M.J. 905 (A.F.C.M.R. 1990) (no denial of fair trial where judge instructed court not to speculate why accused was not properly attired; court reminded that duty rests upon defense counsel to insure that the accused is properly attired); United States v. Blocker, 30 M.J. 1152 (A.C.M.R. 1990) (accused's presence at court in private's uniform as result of administrative demotion was nonprejudicial and issue was waived); United States v. Whitehead, 27 C.M.R. 875 (N.B.R. 1959) (absence of proper uniform may deprive accused of fair trial).
R.C.M. 804(c)(1) indicates that both the accused and the defense counsel are responsible for the accused's proper attire. The Discussion to that same Rule further states that an accused can be compelled to appear in proper attire before the court.
4. United States v. Sharp, 38 M.J. 33 (C.M.A. 1993) (burden rests upon the defense to rebut the inference that the accused's absence is voluntary); United States v. Sharp, 38 M.J. 33 (C.M.A. 1993) (burden of proof on defense); United States v. Brown, 12 M.J. 728 (N.M.C.M.R. 1981) (error to try *in absentia* where record failed to disclose whether absence was voluntary).
5. United States v. Sharp, 38 M.J. 33 (C.M.A. 1993) (accused could be tried *in absentia* even though he was not apprised of exact date of trial; the court also held that there is no requirement that he be warned of the consequences of his absence). See United States v. Hall, 29 M.J. 786 (A.C.M.R. 1989) (prosecution permitted to present evidence of accused's absence); United States v. Abilar, 14 M.J. 733 (A.F.C.M.R. 1982); United States v. Johnson, 7 M.J. 396 (C.M.A. 1979). *Cf.* United States v. Knight, 7 M.J. 671 (A.C.M.R. 1979) (absence was involuntary). *See also* § 12-4.
It is not error to change composition of the court after the accused absents himself. United States v. Ellison, 13 M.J. 90 (C.M.A. 1982).
6. United States v. Bass, 40 M.J. 220 (C.M.A. 1994) (accused's absence voluntary although trial court had not told him explicitly that trial could proceed in his absence after arraignment; court stated that arraignment constitutes commencement of trial; accused was aware of dates for trial and had gone AWOL); United States v. Yarn, 32 M.J. 736 (A.C.M.R. 1991) (lack of actual knowledge did not preclude trial *in absentia*).
7. 31 M.J. 834 (N.M.C.M.R. 1990).

court indicated that a substitute counsel should be appointed to represent the accused in those cases where it appears that the first counsel will be called upon to give testimony or statements adverse to the client's interest. The accused should be present at all stages of trial,[8] and *ex parte* communications should be avoided.[9] If the accused is absent from trial, the court, in its discretion,[10] may grant a continuance until the accused is present.[11]

The accused's absence may be relevant for determining rehabilitative potential during sentencing, but it has no relevance to the issue of guilt and the judge should *sua sponte* instruct members accordingly.[12]

If an accused becomes disruptive during the trial, the military judge may take reasonable steps to restrain him or remove him from the courtroom.[13] The *Manual* sets out some steps which the court should take when the accused is removed from the courtroom: (1) permit counsel and the absent accused to continue communications through the trial, (2) take reasonable steps to keep the accused informed of the proceedings, (3) continue to offer the accused the opportunity to return to the courtroom, and (4) state the reasons for the removal in the record.[14]

The accused is of course entitled to testify at his or her court-martial. And although this right is constitutionally protected,[15] a trial judge is not required to inform the accused of that right.[16]

§ 15-2(B). The Defense Counsel.

§ 15-2(B)(1). In General.

During the Article 39(a) pretrial session, the military judge will have in-

---

8. United States v. Priest, 19 C.M.A. 446, 42 C.M.R. 48 (1970); United States v. Thrower, 36 M.J. 613 (A.F.C.M.R. 1992) (accused's absence during sentencing was voluntary where he ingested overdose of sleeping pills).
9. United States v. Dean, 13 M.J. 676 (A.F.C.M.R. 1982).
10. United States v. Sharp, 38 M.J. 33 (C.M.A. 1993) (judge did not abuse discretion in denying second defense request for continuance pending the accused's return; counsel had argued that he needed time to talk to the accused before proceeding with trial).
11. See § 15-4(A), *infra*.
12. United States v. Denney, 28 M.J. 521 (A.C.M.R. 1989) (noting that absence is a form of "uncharged misconduct," the court stated that it may not be used to enhance the sentence); United States v. Chapman, 20 M.J. 717 (N.M.C.M.R. 1985) (trial judge could properly consider the accused's voluntary absence as an indication of his rehabilitative potential).
13. Illinois v. Allen, 397 U.S. 337 (1970); United States v. Briggs, 42 M.J. 367 (1995)(accused was restrained while going to and from courtroom; not clear that judge was even aware of restraints; accused waived issue by not objecting at trial); United States v. Gentile, 1 M.J. 69 (C.M.A. 1975) (accused was handcuffed during the trial). *See also* Lancaster, "Disruption in the Courtroom: The Troublesome Defendant," 75 Mil. L. Rev. 35 (1977), for a very good discussion of this problem and possible solutions.
14. *See* R.C.M. 804(b)(2) Discussion.
15. Brooks v. Tennessee, 406 U.S. 605 (1972).
16. United States v. Belizaire, 24 M.J. 183 (C.M.A. 1987) (most persons are aware that they have a right to testify at their own trial).

quired of the accused as to who will represent him.[17] If the accused is being represented by an appointed military counsel and an individual counsel (civilian or military),[18] the appointed military counsel will usually be excused. The accused, however, may request that the detailing authority permit that counsel to act as associate counsel.[19] Although a military counsel may not unilaterally withdraw from representing an accused,[20] if during the trial irreconcilable differences arise between counsel and the accused, or among counsel, one of the counsel may request permission to withdraw from the case.[21] Counsel should also be permitted to withdraw where it appears that he or she will become disqualified[22] or there is some other good reason for severing the attorney-client relationship.[23]

If the excused counsel is an appointed counsel, the detailing authority may appoint a new military defense counsel.[24] The accused's decision to substitute counsel just before or during the trial should be unfettered. But it should not be used to unreasonably delay the proceedings. If in the trial court's view unreasonable delay will result, it may deny a request for a continuance.[25]

The statutory qualifications of defense counsel are noted in § 8-3(B)(1).

§ 15-2(B)(2). Representation of Multiple Accused and Conflicts of Interest.

The military courts have consistently frowned upon attempts of one counsel to represent multiple accused involved in the same offense.[26] Although the opportunity to present a common defense is tempting, and sometimes success-

---

17. *See* § 12-2(F).
18. *See* Article 38(b), U.C.M.J. For additional discussion of the accused's rights to counsel, see § 8-3(B).
19. *See* § 8-3(B)(3). R.C.M. 506(b)(3). United States v. Maness, 23 C.M.A. 41, 48 C.M.R. 512 (1974). The accused may indicate otherwise.
20. United States v. Acton, 38 M.J. 330 (C.M.A. 1993) (although counsel's unilateral withdrawal was improper, no prejudice resulted).
21. R.C.M. 506(c). United States v. Davis, 36 M.J. 702 (A.C.M.R. 1992) (civilian defense requested permission to withdraw when he learned of accused's inability to pay him agreed-upon fee; court said that mere fact that counsel has not been paid is not a sufficient reason to withdraw; here, the dispute had created a conflict); United States v. Harrel, 17 M.J. 675 (A.C.M.R. 1983) (no abuse of discretion in permitting civilian counsel to withdraw). *See generally* A.B.A. Code of Professional Responsibility, DR 2-1, 10.
22. *See, e.g.,* United States v. Smith, 33 M.J. 527 (A.F.C.M.R. 1991) (defense counsel was properly permitted to withdraw from case after trial court ruled that she could be called as witness for prosecution).
23. United States v. Dahood, 32 M.J. 852 (N.M.C.M.R. 1991) (separation of defense counsel from active duty was good cause for severing existing attorney-client relationship).
24. *See generally* § 8-3(B)(2).
25. *See* United States v. Ettleson, 13 M.J. 348 (C.M.A. 1982); United States v. Montoya, 13 M.J. 268 (C.M.A. 1982); United States v. Lambert, 17 M.J. 773 (A.F.C.M.R. 1983) (under facts judge correctly denied request for continuance).
26. In United States v. Newak, 24 M.J. 238 (C.M.A. 1987), the court reversed a portion of the conviction where defense counsel had represented two accuseds, one of whom later testified

§ 15-2(B)(3). MILITARY CRIMINAL JUSTICE § 15-2(B)(3)

ful, such representation more often than not raises the very real possibility of split loyalties and prejudicial trial tactics. If it appears that an accused is being represented by a counsel with such a conflict of interest, the military judge should conduct an inquiry and determine whether the accused is intelligently and voluntarily waiving the right to a conflict-free attorney.[27] In the absence of such an inquiry, there is a rebuttable presumption that a conflict exists.[28] Where the accused has waived counsel's potential conflict of interest, it may be reversible error to remove counsel.[29] *See also* § 12-2(F)(3).

§ 15-2(B)(3). Ineffective Assistance of Counsel.

A military accused is entitled to the effective assistance of counsel during pretrial stages, trial proceedings, and post-trial processing of the court-martial.[30] In testing for effective assistance, the military courts have generally

---

against the defendant. On remand, the Court of Military Review reaffirmed those charges for which the government showed independent evidence which had been derived from the joint representation. 25 M.J. 564 (A.F.C.M.R. 1987); United States v. Devitt, 24 M.J. 307 (C.M.A. 1987). *Cf.* United States v. Smith, 39 M.J. 587 (A.F.C.M.R. 1994) (counsel had represented government witness against accused at earlier Article 15 proceeding; accused waived conflict; court stated that it is more difficult to show actual conflict where representation is successive rather than simultaneous; in the latter, the conflict arises if the cases are substantially related, if privileged information is revealed, or if counsel's loyalties are divided).

See also Cuyler v. Sullivan, 446 U.S. 335 (1980); Holloway v. Arkansas, 435 U.S. 475 (1978); United States v. Blakey, 1 M.J. 247 (C.M.A. 1976); United States v. Evans, 1 M.J. 206 (C.M.A. 1975); United States v. Brewer, 15 M.J. 597 (A.C.M.R. 1983). See § 12-2(F)(3).

27. United States v. Henry, 42 M.J. 231 (1995) (judge's inquiry was insufficient to decide whether defense counsel actively represented conflicting interests or whether an actual conflict interest adversely affected counsel's performance; counsel had also failed to discuss issue with accused until it was raised by judge at trial); United States v. Breese, 11 M.J. 17 (C.M.A. 1981); United States v. Shelby, 40 M.J. 909 (N.M.C.M.R. 1994) (accused, who failed to raise issue of conflict of interest at trial, unsuccessfully attempted to obtain extraordinary relief in the nature of error coram nobis); United States v. Bryant, 35 M.J. 739 (A.C.M.R. 1992) (defense counsel had actual conflict of interest where he believed it was in best interest of Army, but not accused, for accused to select trial by judge alone; the trial was set in Saudi Arabia and counsel believed that combat unit needed every available officer and NCO for combat); United States v. Brakebush, 34 M.J. 1219 (N.M.C.M.R. 1992) (court concluded that no actual conflict existed where defense counsel had previously assisted accused's wife but terminated that relationship before representing accused at court-martial; court encouraged counsel to raise such issues at trial level).

28. *Id.* Where there is an actual conflict of interest, the accused has been denied the effective assistance of counsel and prejudice may be assumed. *See* Cuylar v. Sullivan, 446 U.S. 335, 345-50 (1980). In United States v. Whidbee, 28 M.J. 823 (C.G.C.M.R. 1989), there was no inquiry on the record into the fact that the defense counsel was the subordinate of the prosecutor. Following a *DuBay* hearing, the court concluded that the accused had not been adequately apprised of the conflict and conclusively presumed prejudice. In lengthy dictum, the court addressed the obvious problems of this sort of arrangement. See also § 12-2(F) for a discussion of the military judge's inquiries concerning the accused's choice of counsel.

29. United States v. Herod, 21 M.J. 762 (A.F.C.M.R. 1986).

30. United States v. Rivas, 3 M.J. 282 (C.M.A. 1977). The military's treatment of this issue is traced in United States v. Zuis, 49 C.M.R. 150 (A.C.M.R. 1974). *See generally* Cooper, "United States v. Rivas and United States v. Davis: Effective Representation—Who Bears the Burden,"

relied upon both the Sixth Amendment and the Article 27(a), U.C.M.J., rights to counsel. In *United States v. Rivas*,[31] the court indicated that under Article 27(a) the accused is entitled to a reasonably competent counsel, that is, one who exercises the customary skill and knowledge that normally prevails within the range of competence demanded of criminal defense counsel. Counsel is presumed to have exercised reasonable professional judgment and rendered adequate assistance.[32] The burden rests upon the accused to demonstrate that his counsel did not meet this standard and that he was thus denied effective assistance.[33]

The concomitant Sixth Amendment test for effective counsel was set out by the Supreme Court in *Strickland v. Washington*.[34] First, the defendant must establish that his counsel's performance was deficient—that the performance fell below an objective level of reasonableness—and therefore counsel was not acting as counsel within the meaning of the Sixth Amendment.[35] Second, the defendant must establish prejudice: but for counsel's incompetence, there is a reasonable probability that the results of the trial would have been different.[36]

ARMY LAW., Feb. 1978, at 1; Piatrowski & Taylor, "Competency of Counsel," ARMY LAW., Oct. 1977, at 14.

31. 3 M.J. 282 (C.M.A. 1977). *See also* United States v. DiCupe, 21 M.J. 440 (C.M.A. 1986) where the court applied the *Rivas* standard and did not reach Sixth Amendment test set out in Strickland v. Washington, 466 U.S. 668 (1984) because there was no showing of prejudice. The court did not indicate whether *Rivas* and *Strickland* are thus different.

United States v. Jefferson, 13 M.J. 1 (C.M.A. 1982); United States v. Myles, 7 M.J. 132 (C.M.A. 1979). *See generally* Schaefer, "Current Effective Assistance of Counsel Standards," ARMY LAW., June 1986, at 7; Schaefer, "Effective Assistance of Counsel," ARMY LAW., Oct. 1983, at 25.

32. Strickland v. Washington, 466 U.S. 668 (1984); United States v. Cronic, 466 U.S. 648 (1984); United States v. Scott, 24 M.J. 186 (C.M.A. 1987); United States v. Thomas, 33 M.J. 644 (N.M.C.M.R. 1991) (counsel is presumed to be competent and accused has heavy burden to show otherwise); United States v. Barnard, 32 M.J. 530 (A.F.C.M.R. 1990) (counsel benefits from presumption of competency; court noted that since *Strickland*, the Supreme Court has not identified an instance of attorney dereliction); United States v. Evans, 31 M.J. 927 (A.C.M.R. 1990) (court addressed accused's allegations of ineffectiveness regarding pretrial and trial tactics and concluded that counsel was not ineffective).

33. United States v. Robertson, 39 M.J. 211 (C.M.A. 1994) (defendant failed to meet burden); United States v. Jones, 39 M.J. 815 (A.C.M.R. 1994) (bare allegation of ineffectiveness will not suffice; there is strong presumption that counsel was effective; accused bears heavy burden); United States v. Tyler, 36 M.J. 641 (A.C.M.R. 1992) (counsel is presumed to be competent; mere allegations by accused that counsel was ineffective does not establish that point; if record shows that counsel had strategic or tactical reasons for actions, court will not second-guess counsel); United States v. King, 28 M.J. 855 (A.C.M.R. 1989) (counsel is not ineffective simply because professionally sound tactics were unsuccessful); United States v. Coronado, 15 M.J. 750 (A.F.C.M.R. 1983).

34. 466 U.S. 668 (1984).

35. The Court declined to set out any more specific standards and indicated that appellate courts should give deference to trial counsel's tactical decisions. The ultimate question here is whether the accused was denied a fair trial and thus due process.

36. The Court in *Strickland* indicated that the absence of any prejudice might remove the necessity of addressing the first prong of the two-part test: competency. 466 U.S. at 697. Lockart v. Fretwell, U.S. , 113 S.Ct. 838 (1993); United States v. Murray, 42 M.J. 174 (1995) (reasonable probability existed that result of trial would have been different but for counsel's deficiencies in several areas); United States v. Pierce, 40 M.J. 149 (C.M.A. 1994) (although court could not

Although there was some question as to whether the military courts would follow the *Rivas* template or the *Strickland* Sixth Amendment approach, the Court of Appeals, in *United States v. Scott*,[37] settled the issue when it indicated that the standard for review of claims of ineffectiveness in courts-martial is the test set out by the Supreme Court in *Strickland*.[38]

In *United States v. Polk*,[39] the Court noted that in cases raising ineffectiveness of counsel claims, three questions are pertinent:

> First, are the accused's allegations true and if they are, is there a reasonable explanation for counsel's actions in the case?[40]
>
> Second, if the allegations are true, did the level of advocacy fall measurably below the performance level ordinarily expected of fallible lawyers?[41] and
>
> Third, if ineffectiveness of counsel is found to exist, is there a reasonable probability that absent the errors, the fact finders would have had a reasonable doubt?[42]

The Court noted the difference between federal and state practice, where the appellate courts are usually provided a fairly complete factual record of the accused's allegations and the counsel's response.[43] In the military, the appellate courts are often confronted with post-trial allegations in affidavits and unsworn statements. The Court added that the *DuBay* hearing is a useful tool in assessing counsel's performance.[44]

Notwithstanding these templates, denial of access to counsel,[45] interference with the attorney-client relationship,[46] or representation by counsel with a

---

resolve issue on whether counsel's post-trial actions were reasonable, accused suffered no prejudice).

The "prejudice" test follows the standard used for measuring the materiality of exculpatory evidence that should have been produced by the prosecution. *See* United States v. Agurs, 427 U.S. 97 (1976). *See also* United States v. Valenzuela-Bernal, 458 U.S. 858 (1982).

37. 24 M.J. 186 (C.M.A. 1987).

38. 24 M.J. at 187. The court applied the constitutional test and found the accused's representation wanting. Although there had been some evidence of a sound alibi defense, and the defense counsel recognized it, he failed to investigate the matter properly. *See also* United States v. Mack, 25 M.J. 519 (A.C.M.R. 1987).

39. 32 M.J. 150 (C.M.A. 1991).

40. 32 M.J. at 153.

41. *Id., citing* United States v. DiCupe, 21 M.J. 440 (C.M.A. 1986); United States v. Boone, 39 M.J. 541 (A.C.M.R. 1994) (public reprimand by state bar association of counsel for handling of accused's case did not equate to ineffective assistance of counsel); United States v. Anthony, 37 M.J. 963 (A.C.M.R. 1993) (court rejected accused's arguments that defense counsel's recent brain surgery had resulted in ineffective assistance).

42. *Id., citing* United States v. Scott, 24 M.J. 186 (C.M.A. 1987); United States v. Taylor, 38 M.J. 254 (C.M.A. 1993) (failure to object to inadmissible evidence during sentencing was not prejudicial); United States v. Tharpe, 38 M.J. 8 (C.M.A. 1993) (*Polk* test also applies where accused alleges ineffective assistance of counsel on sentencing).

43. 32 M.J. at 152.

44. 32 M.J. at 153. *See* § 16-3(B).

45. Powell v. Alabama, 287 U.S. 45 (1932); United States v. Galinato, 28 M.J. 1049 (N.M.C.M.R. 1989) (court presumed prejudice when counsel refused to present a defense after trial judge denied their fourth motion for a continuance).

46. Maine v. Moulton, 474 U.S. 159 (1985) (interrogation of accused after indictment); Brewer

conflict of interest,[47] may result in denial of a Sixth Amendment right to effective assistance of counsel, even in the absence of a showing of prejudice.

Where the accused is represented by several counsel, it may be appropriate to test competency of counsel by measuring the combined efforts of the defense "team."[48]

Although claims of ineffective assistance of counsel may cover virtually every area of court-martial practice, most of them can be placed into one of the following categories:

(1) Pretrial preparations,[49]
(2) Plea bargaining,[50] and other preliminary matters;[51]

---

v. Williams, 430 U.S. 387 (1977); United States v. Wattenbarger, 21 M.J. 41 (C.M.A. 1985); United States v. Hultgren, 40 M.J. 638 (N.M.C.M.R. 1994) (deployment of counsel to Somalia was military exigency and extraordinary circumstances which justified change of defense counsel after attorney-client relationship was formed); United States v. Cannon, 39 M.J. 980 (A.F.C.M.R. 1994) (judge's barring of counsel from conferring with accused did not prejudice accused; court indicated that requests to consult with client should be liberally granted).

In United States v. Walker, 38 M.J. 678 (A.F.C.M.R. 1993), the court addressed the issue of whether the government's interception of phone calls had interfered with the accused's right to counsel. The court applied the four-part test in Weatherford v. Bursey, 429 U.S. 545 (1977) in concluding that the accused was not denied effective assistance of counsel.

United States v. Bevacqua, 37 M.J. 996 (C.G.C.M.R. 1993) (SJA interfered with accused's right to counsel by excusing associate defense counsel, who had previously been permitted to remain on case after accused selected individual military counsel; court held that there was no good cause for doing so; accused not required to show prejudice); United States v. Keys, 29 M.J. 920 (A.C.M.R. 1989) (the court concluded that the accused had been denied the effective assistance of counsel when the trial court denied his request for a continuance. His civilian counsel had been retained only the day before trial and had not had an opportunity to prepare for trial).

47. Cuyler v. Sullivan, 446 U.S. 335 (1980); Holloway v. Arkansas, 435 U.S. 475 (1978); United States v. Babbitts, 26 M.J. 157 (C.M.A. 1988) (counsel's emotional and sexual involvement with accused did not amount to an actual conflict of interest); United States v. Washington, 42 M.J. 547 (A.F.Ct.Crim.App. 1995) (court declined to adopt per se rule re sexual relations between defense counsel; under facts, illicit sexual relationship showed poor judgment but was not conflict of interest which adversely affected the accused); United States v. Tripp, 38 M.J. 554 (A.F.C.M.R. 1993) (prejudice presumed in conflict exists; record failed to show that a conflict existed in this case); United States v. Bryant, 35 M.J. 739 (A.C.M.R. 1992) (defense counsel had actual conflict of interest where he believed it was in best interest of Army, but not accused, for accused to select trial by judge alone; the trial was set in Saudi Arabia and counsel believed that combat unit needed every available officer and NCO for combat). *See also* § 15-2(B)(2).

48. United States v. Boone, 39 M.J. 541 (A.C.M.R. 1994) (competency of counsel measured by team efforts where two counsel represented accused); United States v. Jeffries, 33 M.J. 826 (A.F.C.M.R. 1991) (if multiple counsel represent accused, test of ineffectiveness applies to the defense team); United States v. Galinato, 28 M.J. 1049 (N.M.C.M.R. 1989) (court concluded that team of civilian and military counsel was ineffective when it refused to present a defense after trial judge denied its fourth request for a continuance; the court observed that although the civilian counsel may be the lead counsel, the military counsel is still individually accountable); United States v. Urbina, 14 M.J. 962 (A.C.M.R. 1982).

49. United States v. Polk, 32 M.J. 150 (C.M.A. 1991) (counsel was ineffective in not exploring testimony of co-accused); United States v. Saul, 26 M.J. 568 (A.F.C.M.R. 1988) (harmless error for counsel to fail to thoroughly investigate several matters before trial).

50. United States v. Lonetree, 35 M.J. 396 (C.M.A. 1992) (*DuBay* hearing ordered to determine if counsel was ineffective in plea bargaining); United States v. Alomarestrada, 39 M.J. 1068

51. United States v. Sanders, 31 M.J. 834 (N.M.C.M.R. 1990) (accused denied right to counsel

§ 15-2(B)(3) MILITARY CRIMINAL JUSTICE § 15-2(B)(3)

    (3) Locating witnesses;[52]
    (4) Interviewing witnesses;[53]
    (5) Considering possible defenses;[54]
    (6) Obtaining immunity for witnesses;[55]
    (7) Mental examination of accused;[56]
    (8) Representation during Article 32 investigation;[57]
    (9) Pretrial advice to accused concerning options and tactics;[58]
    (10) Motions practice,[59] e.g., motions to dismiss,[60] motions for appropriate

---

(A.C.M.R. 1994) (court rejected argument that counsel was ineffective in not obtaining Spanish-speaking attorney during pretrial discussions).

when his only counsel was called upon to provide evidence that the accused had been informed of the changed trial date); United States v. Ankeny, 28 M.J. 780 (N.M.C.M.R. 1989) (civilian counsel's unauthorized disclosure of accused's confidential statements to government was ineffective assistance of counsel resulting in reversal).

52. United States v. Richardson, 35 M.J. 687 (C.G.C.M.R. 1992) (counsel was not ineffective in not expending further efforts to locate witness and investigate other defense theories); United States v. Barnard, 32 M.J. 530 (A.F.C.M.R. 1990) (counsel made reasonable efforts to locate alibi witness).

53. United States v. Powell, 40 M.J. 1 (C.M.A. 1994) (counsel deficient by not contacting company commander as possible defense witness); United States v. Thomas, 43 M.J. 550 (N.M.Ct.Crim.App.1995) (whether defense actually interviewed potential alibi witness in capital murder case did not really matter because the accused failed to show serious deficiency by defense counsel); United States v. Dickey, 41 M.J. 637 (N.M.Ct.Crim.App. 1994) (failure to interview rape victim not ineffective assistance considering fact that she could not be readily located and fact that counsel had read statements, including accused's confession); United States v. Herd, 29 M.J. 702 (A.C.M.R. 1989) (counsel was not ineffective in not interviewing witnesses where he determined that evidence against accused was overwhelming and that he should plead guilty).

54. United States v. Loving, 41 M.J. 213 (1994) (counsel not deficient in pursuing defense of intoxication); United States v. Morgan, 37 M.J. 407 (C.M.A. 1993) (counsel not ineffective for failing to investigate or present insanity defense); United States v. Scott, 24 M.J. 186 (C.M.A. 1987) (case reversed where counsel failed to investigate alibi defense); United States v. Haston, 21 M.J. 559 (A.C.M.R. 1985) (counsel's failure to investigate a defense did not result in prejudice).

55. United States v. Gilbert, 40 M.J. 652 (N.M.C.M.R. 1994) (counsel was ineffective in not pursuing immunity for defense witness; defendant's credibility was thereby damaged in other charged offenses).

56. United States v. Washington, 29 M.J. 536 (A.F.C.M.R. 1989) (counsel not ineffective in not seeking psychiatric examination of accused when he made gesture toward suicide; court rejected a variety of other claims of ineffective assistance of counsel raised by accused including tactical decision not to challenge admissibility of accused's statements and counsel's decision to disclose anonymous letter, written by the accused, which exonerated the accused).

57. United States v. McCarthy, 34 M.J. 768 (A.C.M.R. 1992) (waiver of Article 32 investigation was not ineffective assistance of counsel); United States v. Stephenson, 30 M.J. 551 (A.C.M.R. 1990) (no ineffective assistance of counsel despite accused's allegations that defense counsel waived Article 32 investigation, conducted no voir dire, challenged no member, and presented no defense; the court concluded that the case was well tried and that counsel had conducted rigorous cross-examination, argued the defense position forcefully and successfully obtained instructions on lesser-included offenses).

58. United States v. Camanga, 38 M.J. 249 (C.M.A. 1993) (counsel failed to relay accused's desire to be represented by civilian counsel to military judge; court treated issue as waiver of right to counsel and not as an ineffectiveness claim).

59. See Chapter 13.

60. United States v. Calloway, 23 M.J. 799 (N.M.C.M.R. 1986) (counsel was not ineffective in not raising speedy trial motion).

relief,[61] motions in limine,[62] and motions to suppress;[63]

(11) Advice and conduct concerning guilty plea;[64]

(12) Challenges to composition of court members[65] and other participants;[66]

(13) Calling, or failing to call expert witnesses[67] and other defense witnesses to testify;[68]

(14) Presenting a case on behalf of the accused;[69]

---

61. United States v. Davis, 30 M.J. 980 (A.C.M.R. 1990) (counsel not ineffective in not challenging pretrial restraint because of lack of credible material presented to counsel before trial); United States v. Huxhold, 20 M.J. 990 (N.M.C.M.R. 1985) (counsel failed to move for change of venue).

62. *See* § 13-5(L) (motions in limine).

63. United States v. Loving, 41 M.J. 213 (1994) (fourth amendment evidence clearly admissible and counsel was not ineffective for failing to object to its admission; court noted that where allegation is made that counsel was ineffective in challenging fourth amendment evidence, accused must show that claim had merit and that verdict would have been different absent the excludable evidence); United States v. Brothers, 30 M.J. 289 (C.M.A. 1990) (counsel not ineffective in not raising suppression motions); United States v. Dumas, 36 M.J. 941 (A.C.M.R. 1993) (counsel not ineffective in failing to move to suppress accused's confession).

64. United States v. King, 30 M.J. 59 (C.M.A. 1990) (counsel's advice to plead guilty and thus waive confession issue was not ineffective assistance); United States v. Tyler, 36 M.J. 641 (A.C.M.R. 1992) (not ineffective to encourage accused to plead guilty in return for reduced confinement); United States v. Gates, 36 M.J. 945 (A.C.M.R. 1993) (not ineffective assistance to urge accused to plead guilty to lesser offense of unpremeditated murder); United States v. Daffron, 32 M.J. 912 (A.F.C.M.R. 1991) (accused failed to show that counsel was ineffective in advising him to plead guilty and thus waive objections to pretrial statements); United States v. Leaver, 32 M.J. 995 (C.G.C.M.R. 1991) (court rejected argument that counsel's actions regarding pretrial agreement and improvidenced guilty plea inquiry amounted to ineffectiveness); United States v. Kelly, 32 M.J. 813 (N.M.C.M.R. 1991) (counsel was ineffective in advising accused to plead guilty where he knew that government could not prove guilt; tactical judgment in securing plea agreement in order to avoid high sentence lacked plausible basis); United States v. Berumen, 24 M.J. 737 (A.C.M.R. 1987) (not ineffective assistance of counsel to fail to advise the accused, an alien, that guilty plea might result in deportation).

65. United States v. Ingham, 42 M.J. 218 (1995) (counsel not ineffective in not noting for record why he was using back-up peremptory challenge against member after court denied challenge for cause); United States v. McMahan, 6 C.M.A. 709, 21 C.M.R. 31 (1956) (voir dire of court members).

66. *See generally* Chapter 8.

67. United States v. Austin, 32 M.J. 757 (A.C.M.R. 1991) (not ineffective to not call expert witness to rebut prosecution witness); United States v. Rios, 24 M.J. 515 (A.F.C.M.R. 1987) (counsel not ineffective in not obtaining services of particular expert witness).

68. United States v. Wright, 42 M.J. 283 (1995) (counsel's failure to call witness was reasonable tactic); United States v. Ingham, 42 M.J. 218 (1995) (failure to call defense witnesses was not ineffective assistance of counsel); United States v. Fluellen, 40 M.J. 96 (C.M.A. 1994) (counsel's decision not to call certain witnesses was valid tactical decision, after weighing pros and cons); United States v. Harris, 36 M.J. 936 (A.C.M.R. 1993) (failure to present documentary evidence and testimony re good soldier defense; counsel had sound tactical reasons for not doing so); United States v. Clark, 32 M.J. 606 (A.C.M.R. 1991) (counsel not ineffective in deciding not to call two witnesses to bolster accused's credibility); United States v. Moses, 26 M.J. 980 (A.F.C.M.R. 1988) (not ineffective for counsel to refrain from calling several alibi witnesses who would have potentially introduced uncharged misconduct when other alibi witnesses were presented).

69. United States v. Galinato, 28 M.J. 1049 (N.M.C.M.R. 1989) (accused's two defense counsel refused to present a defense after the trial judge denied their fourth request for a continuance;

(15) Presenting evidence of defenses;[70]
(16) Manner of presenting[71] or challenging evidence;[72] failing to object;[73]
(17) Calling the accused to testify;[74]
(18) Questionable trial tactics;[75]
(19) Conduct during trial;[76]

---

court, citing United States v. Cronic, 466 U.S. 648, 656 (1984), declared that the Sixth Amendment's requirement of effective assistance of counsel is violated when the trial "loses its character as a confrontation between adversaries...." The net effect was the same as if the government had denied access to counsel).

70. United States v. Lawson, 40 M.J. 475 (C.M.A. 1994) (not ineffective assistance to counsel not to present entrapment defense); United States v. Morgan, 37 M.J. 407 (C.M.A. 1993) (counsel not ineffective for failing to investigate or present insanity defense); United States v. Mansfield, 24 M.J. 611 (A.F.C.M.R. 1987) (accused denied effective assistance of counsel where counsel abandoned defense of insanity halfway through the trial; court noted that problems of representation existed because, of the four counsel working on the case, no one appeared to be in charge and there was poor communication of information between them).

71. United States v. Whitcomb, 34 M.J. 984 (A.C.M.R. 1992) (counsel's questioning of witness which opened door for adverse evidence from prosecution was not ineffective assistance of counsel).

72. United States v. Ryder, 34 M.J. 1077 (C.G.C.M.R. 1992) (defense counsel's failure to enter evidentiary objections was part of trial strategy); United States v. Haston, 21 M.J. 559 (A.C.M.R. 1985) (counsel presented inadmissible evidence against client).

73. United States v. Loving, 41 M.J. 213 (1994) (not ineffective for counsel to not object to Rule 404(b) evidence; such objection would have been without merit): United States v. Purdy, 42 M.J. 666 (Army Ct.Crim.App. 1995) (counsel not ineffective in not objecting to comments by military judge re homosexuals); United States v. Thomas, 38 M.J. 614 (A.F.C.M.R. 1993) (nonprejudicial error not to object to testimony); United States v. Puckett, 32 M.J. 783 (C.G.C.M.R. 1991) (counsel was not ineffective in failing to enter hearsay objections); United States v. King, 27 M.J. 664 (A.C.M.R. 1988) (counsel was not ineffective in failing to argue alternative ground for excluding accused's pretrial statement).

74. United States v. Radford, 14 M.J. 322 (C.M.A. 1982) (counsel ineffective in handling defendant's testimony); United States v. Townsend, 34 M.J. 882 (C.G.C.M.R. 1992) (counsel's statement indicating disbelief of accused's testimony was not ineffective assistance; judge indicated that he would not consider statement); United States v. Henriques, 32 M.J. 832 (N.M.C.M.R. 1991) (counsel ineffective in calling the accused to the stand to testify on charge of desertion); United States v. Tillery, 26 M.J. 799 (A.C.M.R. 1988) (court rejected counsel's argument that he had been ineffective in preparing accused for testifying at trial); United States v. McCarty, 25 M.J. 667 (A.F.C.M.R. 1987) (counsel was not ineffective in deciding not to call accused and other witnesses to testify and offer defense of entrapment).

75. United States v. Donley, 33 M.J. 44 (C.M.A. 1991) (counsel's objection to trial judge's proposed granting of mistrial was not ineffective assistance); United States v. Babbitt, 26 M.J. 157 (C.M.A. 1988) (counsel's strategic decisions did not amount to denial of effective assistance of counsel); United States v. Hennis, 40 M.J. 865 (A.F.C.M.R. 1994) (not ineffective assistance to concede elements of guilt as trial strategy); United States v. Curtis, 38 M.J. 530 (N.M.C.M.R. 1993) (counsel presented reasonable trial strategy under facts available); United States v. Kurz, 20 M.J. 857 (C.G.C.M.R. 1985) (counsel's tactical decisions re admissibility of evidence were consistent with thrust of case).

76. United States v. Hansen, 36 M.J. 599 (A.F.C.M.R. 1992) (counsel not ineffective by conceding accused's guilt on indecent acts charge, failing to cross-examine expert witness, and failing to call defense expert; counsel had discussed trial tactics with accused); United States v. Stephenson, 30 M.J. 551 (A.C.M.R. 1990) (no ineffective assistance of counsel despite accused's allegations that defense counsel waived Article 32 investigation, conducted no voir dire, challenged no member, and presented no defense; the court concluded that the case was well tried and that counsel had conducted rigorous cross-examination, argued the defense position forcefully and successfully

§ 15-2(B)(3)   TRIAL PROCEDURES   § 15-2(B)(3)

(20) Closing arguments;[77]
(21) Presentation of sentencing information[78] *e.g.*, character evidence,[79] service record,[80] evidence regarding sentencing credit for pretrial confinement[81] and prior punishment,[82] and expert testimony;[83]

---

obtained instructions on lesser-included offenses); United States v. Haston, 21 M.J. 559 (A.C.M.R. 1985) (counsel appeared to be asleep during portions of the trial).

77. United States v. Goodman, 33 M.J. 84 (C.M.A. 1991) (counsel was not ineffective in giving confusing sentencing argument); United States v. Burwell, 50 C.M.R. 192 (A.C.M.R. 1975) (counsel should not concede accused's guilt). *See also* § 15-13 for a discussion on closing arguments.

78. United States v. Boone, 42 M.J. 308 (1995) (case remanded to lower court for determination whether counsel's meager presentation of sentencing evidence amounted to ineffective assistance); United States v. Ingham, 42 M.J. 218 (1995 counsel's sentencing efforts were not marred by "serious incompetency"); United States v. Loving, 41 M.J. 213 (1994) (investigation and presentation of defense evidence during sentencing was reasonable; court noted that while use of expert testimony during capital sentencing is often useful, it declined to require such); United States v. Tharpe, 38 M.J. 8 (C.M.A. 1993) (counsel not ineffective in not presenting evidence that accused had been abused as child; court denied accused's argument that an appellate expert should have been appointed to assist him in showing that counsel was ineffective); United States v. Holt, 33 M.J. 400 (C.M.A. 1991) (counsel's nonperformance during sentencing amounted to ineffective assistance of counsel); United States v. Stephenson, 33 M.J. 79 (C.M.A. 1991) (counsel was not ineffective in not calling favorable sentencing witnesses or to produce favorable documents during sentencing; that tactic, although it failed, precluded unfavorable cross-examination and presentation of derogatory information).

United States v. Storts, 35 M.J. 883 (A.C.M.R. 1992) (counsel's failure to *voir dire* members for sentencing was not ineffective; counsel had sound reasons for not highlighting serious offenses); United States v. Newberry, 35 M.J. 777 (A.C.M.R. 1992) (under the facts defense counsel was not ineffective in obtaining government concession for 30-day credit for illegal pretrial punishment, without contesting the issue, where co-accused under similar circumstances received only a three-day credit after presenting motion to court); United States v. Foster, 35 M.J. 700 (N.M.C.M.R. 1992) (counsel not ineffective in sentencing tactics).

United States v. Reddick, 32 M.J. 967 (A.C.M.R. 1991) (court rejected argument that failure of civilian counsel to present sentencing evidence and post-trial submissions amounted to ineffective assistance); United States v. Dorsey, 30 M.J. 1156 (A.C.M.R. 1990) (counsel was ineffective in failing to present favorable sentencing evidence); United States v. Pattugalan, 26 M.J. 762 (A.C.M.R. 1988) (counsel was not ineffective in failing to call two witnesses and in failing to present documentary evidence); United States v. Sadler, 16 M.J. 982 (A.C.M.R. 1983) (ineffective assistance where counsel failed to present favorable evidence and argument on sentencing).

79. United States v. Harris, 34 M.J. 297 (C.M.A. 1992) (counsel's failure to obtain and introduce highly favorable character evidence; case remanded for further review); United States v. Tipton, 34 M.J. 1153 (A.C.M.R. 1992) (counsel was not ineffective in not presenting good soldier defense evidence until sentencing).

80. United States v. Demerse, 37 M.J. 488 (C.M.A. 1993) (counsel's failure to present evidence of accused's Vietnam service nonprejudicial; judge *sua sponte* inquired into accused's awards and decorations).

81. United States v. Brown, 33 M.J. 743 (A.C.M.R. 1991) (counsel was ineffective in not raising issue of credit for pretrial restraint); United States v. Guerrero, 25 M.J. 829 (A.C.M.R. 1988) (court concluded that defense counsel was ineffective in not raising issue of administrative credit for pretrial restriction; no relief was granted, however, because test for ineffectiveness requires evaluation of whole performance of defense counsel, not an episodic critique on non-critical issues). *See* Chapter 5.

82. *See* § 13-3(G) (Former punishment).

83. United States v. Thomas, 33 M.J. 644 (N.M.C.M.R. 1991) (court declined to order government to provide expert psychological background investigation on accused to support his argument that trial counsel had been ineffective during sentencing portion of trial; accused argued

(22) Challenging sentencing evidence;[84]
(23) Presentation of clemency matters to convening authority[85] e.g., clemency letters[86] and recommendations for leniency from the trial court.[87]

---

that study was needed to insure that his appellate counsel would be competent in attacking incompetence of trial counsel).

84. United States v. Bono, 26 M.J. 240 (C.M.A. 1988) (counsel was ineffective in not objecting to uncharged misconduct included within accused's unsworn statement during sentencing and providing other evidence that showed the accused's lack of rehabilitative potential; there was no prejudice, however, where SJA was alert to the problem and convening authority took corrective action).

85. United States v. Pierce, 40 M.J. 149 (C.M.A. 1994) (although court could not resolve issue on whether counsel's post-trial actions were reasonable, accused suffered no prejudice); United States v. Spurlin, 33 M.J. 443 (C.M.A. 1991) (counsel was ineffective in not presenting post-trial matters to convening authority in timely fashion; court remanded for new review and action); United States v. Stephenson, 33 M.J. 79 (C.M.A. 1991) (counsel was ineffective in not presenting clemency material to convening authority where accused had nothing to lose by doing so); United States v. Martinez, 31 M.J. 524 (A.C.M.R. 1990) (counsel was ineffective in not presenting clemency matters to convening authority); United States v. Dorsey, 30 M.J. 1156 (A.F.C.M.R. 1990) (counsel failed to present any matters to convening authority); United States v. Harris, 30 M.J. 580 (A.C.M.R. 1990) (counsel was ineffective in presenting clemency matters to convening authority).

United States v. Cobe, 41 M.J. 654 (N.M.Ct.Crim.App. 1994) (counsel's failure to present, inter alia, clemency matters was prejudicial deficiency); United States v. Aflague, 40 M.J. 501 (A.C.M.R. 1994) (appellate court should act where there is no logical reason for counsel's failure to present matters and record glaringly calls for submission of such matters); United States v. Jackson, 37 M.J. 1045 (N.M.C.M.R. 1993) (counsel failed to present clemency matters or request additional time to do so); United States v. Carmack, 37 M.J. 765 (A.C.M.R. 1993) (accused denied effective assistance of counsel during post-trial processing); United States v. Frueh, 35 M.J. 550 (A.C.M.R. 1992) (defense counsel ineffective in not presenting clemency matters); United States v. Calderon, 34 M.J. 501 (A.F.C.M.R. 1991) (counsel not ineffective; he did all he could do under facts).

United States v. Davis, 20 M.J. 1015 (A.C.M.R. 1985) (in some situations, "extremely grievous situations," a decision not to submit post-trial matters may constitute inadequacy of counsel); United States v. Black, 16 M.J. 507 (A.F.C.M.R. 1983) (counsel failed to clarify desires of accused in clemency report).

Cf. United States v. Peek, 24 M.J. 750 (A.C.M.R. 1987) (counsel was not ineffective in not presenting post-trial matters to convening authority where he decided that it was of little value and instead hoped that convening authority would consider other untimely material from a psychiatrist).

86. United States v. Lewis, 42 M.J. 1 (1995) (nonprejudicial ineffective assistance where counsel declined to submit clemency letter that accused had written and wanted submitted); United States v. Dresen, 40 M.J. 462 (C.M.A. 1994) (relief granted for ineffective assistance where counsel, against accused's wishes, requested in clemency brief that accused should receive sentencing rehearing or in alternative approval of BCD and substantially reduced confinement); United States v. MacCulloch, 40 M.J. 236 (C.M.A. 1994) (ineffective assistance of counsel to enclose in clemency materials a damaging letter written civilian counsel).

87. United States v. Clear, 32 M.J. 658 (A.F.C.M.R. 1991) (counsel not ineffective in not presenting judge's recommendation for rehabilitation to convening authority); United States v. Rich, 26 M.J. 518 (A.C.M.R. 1988) (counsel was ineffective where he failed to inform the convening authority that the trial judge had recommended suspension of a portion of the adjudged sentence); United States v. Cannon, 23 M.J. 676 (A.C.M.R. 1986) (failure to apprise convening authority that trial judge recommended clemency may rise to level of inadequacy of representation).

§ 15-2(B)(3)　　　　　　　　　TRIAL PROCEDURES　　　　　　　　　§ 15-2(B)(3)

   (24) Other post-trial responsibilities;[88] and

   (25) Appellate representation.[89]

Occasionally an accused will argue that defense counsel's prior participation in the case, or another case,[90] or relationship with the prosecution team,[91]

---

   88. United States v. Straight, 42 M.J. 244 (1995) (counsel was ineffective in not seeking post-trial session to determine if court members had engaged in misconduct which might impeach the verdict); United States v. Curry, 31 M.J. 359 (C.M.A. 1990) (counsel not ineffective where accused had told counsel not to present evidence in sentencing and did not specify what matters should have been presented to the convening authority); United States v. Bradford, 28 M.J. 125 (C.M.A. 1989).

   United States v. Beckermann, 35 M.J. 842 (C.G.C.M.R. 1992) (counsel not ineffective in post-trial duties; closer contact and coordination might have alleviated problems); United States v. Jeter, 35 M.J. 674 (A.C.M.R. 1992) (accused denied effective assistance of counsel in post-trial representation; counsel should not have continued to act on behalf of accused after she expressed deep dissatisfaction with him); United States v. Hawkins, 34 M.J. 991 (A.C.M.R. 1992) (under facts, counsel who was deployed to Saudi Arabia was not ineffective in handling post-trial matters; the court declined to decide the issue of whether such deployment constitutes good cause for purposes of terminating a counsel's representation); United States v. Jackson, 34 M.J. 783 (A.C.M.R. 1992) (ineffective assistance where defense counsel unilaterally terminated representation of accused in post-trial processing); United States v. Garner, 34 M.J. 575 (A.C.M.R. 1992) (fair risk that accused received ineffective assistance where counsel, who was deployed to Saudi Arabia, failed to take any post-trial actions and failed to tell superiors that she could not complete duties).

   United States v. Williams, 28 M.J. 911 (A.C.M.R. 1989) (accused was denied effective assistance of counsel where his defense counsel was sent on temporary duty; although counsel was geographically available, his change in primary duty status rendered him unable to effectively represent the accused).

   United States v. Polk, 27 M.J. 812 (A.C.M.R. 1988) (substitute defense counsel was ineffective in representing accused's interests to the convening authority where he failed to determine whether accused had matters to present; court discussed problems associated with releasing defense counsel from active duty before case is final).

   United States v. McClelland, 25 M.J. 903 (A.C.M.R. 1988) (counsel not ineffective simply because he could not remember handling accused's case after trial was over; court noted bald allegations by accused that defense counsel did nothing to help him after the trial).

   89. United States v. Quigley, 35 M.J. 345 (C.M.A. 1992) (accused was denied effective assistance of counsel where appellate counsel did not zealously present hearsay argument to appellate court); United States v. Stinson, 34 M.J. 303 (C.M.A. 1992) (appellate counsel's waiver of appellate argument did not prejudice accused); United States v. Tyler, 34 M.J. 293 (C.M.A. 1992) (court remanded case for determination whether appellate counsel was ineffective in not informing appellate court of accused's protestations of innocence on basis of contradictory evidence); United States v. Baker, 28 M.J. 121 (C.M.A. 1989) (appellate defense counsel was not ineffective in not assigning any errors before the Court of Military Review); United States v. Hullum, 15 M.J. 261 (C.M.A. 1983) (one judge concluded that appellate counsel was ineffective).

   Tillman v. United States, 32 M.J. 962 (A.C.M.R. 1991) (court granted writ of *coram nobis* relief where appellate counsel had been ineffective in raising challenge to pretrial agreement); United States v. Kelly, 32 M.J. 813 (N.M.C.M.R. 1991) (appellate counsel may be constitutionally ineffective if they have a conflict of interest); United States v. Claxton, 25 M.J. 623 (C.G.C.M.R. 1987) (accused not denied effective assistance of appellate counsel simply because counsel was busy with other appellate cases).

   90. *See* United States v. Newak, 24 M.J. 238 (C.M.A. 1987) (conviction reversed where the defense counsel represented both the accused and her homosexual lover who later testified against the accused).

   91. United States v. Caritativo, 37 M.J. 175 (C.M.A. 1993) (no conflict of interest where defense counsel's performance ratings were reviewed by Staff Judge Advocate); United States v. Nichol-

resulted in ineffective assistance of counsel. In those cases the courts have generally tested for specific prejudice.[92] The mere fact that the accused did not get along with his counsel or would have preferred another counsel is not sufficient; there is no constitutional right to a "meaningful" attorney-client relationship.[93] Noting that raising ineffective assistance of counsel claims has become a popular issue,[94] the Court of Appeals has also noted that quibbling over trial tactics is not a sufficient showing.[95]

Where the issue of ineffective counsel manifests itself at trial, the military judge may be placed in the position of balancing the accused's right to preservation of the attorney-client relationship and the right to effective assistance of counsel. This problem was raised in *United States v. Haston*,[96] where the trial judge, after improvidencing the accused's guilty pleas, relieved the defense counsel of his duties and indicated that a new defense counsel should be appointed. The trial judge observed that counsel had apparently failed to speak with his client about a possible defense. A new counsel was detailed and the original counsel remained on the case as the assistant defense counsel.[97] The court noted the high value placed upon an existing attorney-client relationship[98] but also noted that military judges have a "responsibility for the administration of military justice" and that in this case the trial judge had

---

son, 15 M.J. 436 (C.M.A. 1983) (no prejudice where assistant trial counsel was defense counsel's rater on efficiency reports); United States v. Carreiro, 14 M.J. 954 (A.C.M.R. 1982) (no denial of effective assistance where defense counsel was married to prosecutor).

92. United States v. Sparks, 29 M.J. 52 (C.M.A. 1989) (accused could waive statutory disqualification of counsel who had previously been a government counsel; court found no prejudice and concluded that defense counsel's prior association with the case "stood him in stead in defending the accused"); United States v. Nicholson, 15 M.J. 436 (C.M.A. 1983).

93. Morris v. Slappy, 461 U.S. 1 (1983).

94. United States v. Polk, 32 M.J. 150 (C.M.A. 1991) (competency of counsel issue seems to be popular issue for accuseds who have been convicted).

95. In United States v. Carter, 40 M.J. 102 (C.M.A. 1994), the court set out the procedures to be followed where the accused has alleged that his or her counsel is ineffective: the defense counsel should be notified of the allegation; counsel should then determine if his services have been terminated or whether his withdrawal is permissible; he should advise the accused of his options and determine if the accused wishes to be represented by someone else or whether the allegations are merely a sign of frustration; if the accused desires to discharge the counsel, counsel should so inform the appropriate authority and discontinue representation.

United States v. Sanders, 37 M.J. 116 (C.M.A. 1993) (hindsight which suggests that other tactics may have worked better is not measure of ineffectiveness of counsel); United States v. Donley, 33 M.J. 44 (C.M.A. 1991).

96. 24 M.J. 377 (C.M.A. 1987). *Cf.* United States v. Baca, 27 M.J. 110 (C.M.A. 1989) (trial court erred in removing defense counsel from the case on grounds, which court found baseless, that counsel was too emotionally involved in the case; the court stated that the right to continuation of an attorney-client relationship is fundamental; the court concluded that counsel had been far from ineffective).

97. 24 M.J. at 378. In ultimately concluding that the accused was not denied effective assistance of counsel, the court noted that the original counsel had remained on the case and successfully argued for a lenient sentence. Had the original counsel been completely removed from the case, it would have been much more difficult to justify the judge's actions.

98. *Id.* at 379.

acted within his authority to insure a fair trial by insisting that additional counsel be appointed.[99]

If the accused challenges the effectiveness of his trial counsel, caselaw indicates that on appeal, the accused must first overcome the presumption of effectiveness by pointing out clearly the exact manner in which counsel was ineffective, so that the court and the government may evaluate it.[100] Second, the accused must present credible evidence which, together, with the appellate record, indicates that counsel's performance was deficient[101] and that such performance prejudiced the accused.[102] If the presumption of effectiveness is not overcome, then there will generally be no need to require the defense counsel to provide any rebuttal affidavits.[103] On the other hand, if the accused's showing overcomes the presumption of competence, defense counsel may be compelled to explain his or her actions.[104] The appellate court is not required to remand a case for further findings on counsel's competency.[105] It may, in an appropriate case, consider whatever affidavits have been presented by the defense counsel.[106]

It is important to note that in responding to allegations of ineffectiveness, defense counsel may reveal otherwise privileged information in defending his or her actions or tactics.[107] As a general rule, government appellate counsel will coordinate with the trial defense counsel in formulating a response to the accused's accusations.[108] Government counsel, however, may not advise the

---

99. *Id.* at 380. United States v. Galinato, 28 M.J. 1049 (N.M.C.M.R. 1989) (trial judge could have replaced defense counsel when they refused to present a defense after he denied their fourth request for a continuance). *See generally* Schwarzer, "Dealing With Incompetent Counsel—The Trial Judge's Role," 93 HARV. L. REV. 633 (1980).

100. United States v. Walters, 42 M.J. 760 (Army Ct. Crim. App. 1995) (on appeal the accused has a heavy burden of overcoming presumption of effectiveness). *See also* United States v. Jones, 39 M.J. 815 (A.C.M.R. 1994).

101. *Id.* at 762 *citing* Strickland v. Washington, 466 U.S. 668, 687 (1984).

102. *Id.*

103. United States v. Ingham, 42 M.J. 218 (1995) (no need for evidentiary hearing on whether counsel was effective where accused failed to meet threshold burden); United States v. Lewis, 42 M.J. 1, 6 (1995); United States v. Walters, 42 M.J. 760 (Army Ct. Crim. App. 1995).

104. United Stated v. Lewis, 42 M.J. 1 (1995) (trial defense counsel not required to justify actions until court reviews the accused's allegations, the government's response, and the record and decides that there is enough evidence, which if unrebutted, overcomes the presumption of effectiveness); United States v. Walters, 42 M.J. 760 (Army Ct. Crim. App. 1995).

105. United States v. Lewis, 42 M.J. 1 (1995) (court rejected suggestion that evidence on issue of ineffectiveness may be obtained at factfinding *DuBay* hearing; court indicated that Court of Criminal Appeals has discretion to determine how additional evidence will be obtained).

106. United States v. Johnson, 43 M.J. 192 (1995) (court rejected argument that Court of Criminal Appeals erred in not ordering *DuBay* hearing on issue).

107. *See* Rule 502(d)(3), MIL. R. EVID. (Attorney-client privilege not applicable where breach of duty is alleged); United States v. Jones, 39 M.J. 815 (A.C.M.R. 1994) (discussion of procedure on appeal where accused raises claim of ineffective assistance of counsel).

108. United States v. Dupas, 14 M.J. 28 (C.M.A. 1982). *Cf.* United States v. Lewis, 42 M.J. 1 (1995) (court concluded that where accused alleges on appeal that counsel was ineffective, no affidavits should be required until appellate court has determined that evidence has been presented which if uncontroverted would demonstrate incompetence; while court recognized potential problems with government counsel soliciting assistance from the trial defense counsel, the court did not condemn practice).

trial defense counsel to withhold information from appellate defense counsel.[109]

§ 15-2(B)(4). Defense Counsel and the Perjurious Client.

When it appears that the accused intends to take the stand and testify falsely,[110] the defense counsel faces an ethical dilemma: zealously representing his client and acting as an officer to the court. Assuming that the accused cannot be dissuaded from that course, counsel must attempt to withdraw from the case.[111] If the withdrawal is to take place after the trial has started, the judge should determine the accused's position on the issue.[112] If withdrawal is not feasible or is not permitted by the court, counsel must not in any way lend aid to the perjured testimony.[113] That usually means that the counsel may call the accused to the stand, identify him, and ask him to give his version of what happened. He may not question him on those portions of the testimony which are false.[114] Rather, the accused should be permitted only to make his statement in narrative fashion. And on closing arguments counsel should not rely upon nor refer to the false testimony.[115] Although it is normally proper for the prosecution to argue that a testifying accused is not a credible witness, it is not clear that it would be proper to argue that the defense counsel's tactics demonstrated that even counsel did not have faith in his client's testimony.

While the counsel should not reveal to the court that the accused intends to present false testimony, he should in some way make a record of the matter.[116] Improper revelation of the intended perjury may well result in ineffective representation.[117] As a practical matter, counsel's handling of the client will in most cases impliedly telegraph to the judge and trial counsel that the defense counsel is attempting to deal with a perjurious client.[118]

---

109. *Id.*

110. The counsel should be careful to investigate independently the accused's version to insure that in fact the accused's testimony will be false. *See* ABA Standards Relating to Criminal Justice, Defense Function § 4-7.7 [Proposed]. See generally Bowe, "Limiting Defense Counsel's Obligation to Disclose Client Perjury after Adjournment: When Should the 'Conclusion of the Proceedings' Occur?," ARMY LAW., June 1993, p. 27.

111. *Id.* Waiting to withdraw until after the accused has testified may be too late. United States v. Radford, 14 M.J. 322 (C.M.A. 1982). *See generally* Chute, "Client Perjury: Practical Suggestions for Defense Counsel," ARMY LAW., Mar. 1986, at 52; Gaydos, "Client Perjury: A Guide for Military Defense Counsel," ARMY LAW., Sept. 1983, at 13.

112. United States v. Radford, 14 M.J. 322 (C.M.A. 1982).

113. ABA Standards Relating to Criminal Justice, Defense Function § 4-7.7 [Proposed].

114. *Id.*

115. *Id.*

116. *Id.*

117. United States v. Radford, 14 M.J. 322 (C.M.A. 1982); United States v. Winchester, 12 C.M.A. 74, 30 C.M.R. 74 (1961).

118. *See also* United States v. Blanchard, 24 M.J. 803 (N.M.C.M.R. 1987), where the court noted that where a judge has learned that an accused might commit perjury, the case must be examined to determine:

(1) whether counsel through acts or omissions conceded directly or indirectly the guilt or lack of credibility, in whole or in part, of an accused, (2) the context in which and detail and

Refusing to assist the client in his attempts to present false testimony does not constitute ineffective assistance of counsel.[119]

§ 15-2(C). The Trial Counsel.

The trial counsel, whose qualifications are discussed in § 8-3(B)(1), is charged with prosecuting the case on behalf of the United States.[120] In addition to presenting the Government's case, he is tasked with a variety of administrative functions which include: (1) correcting minor errors on the charge sheet;[121] (2) notifying participants of the time, date, and place of trial;[122] (3) arranging for presence of the witnesses;[123] (4) setting up the courtroom;[124] (5) providing the court members with copies of the charges and specifications;[125] and (6) supervising preparation of the record of trial.[126] In some jurisdictions a bailiff or orderly may be appointed and assigned some of the foregoing tasks.[127]

§ 15-2(D). The Military Judge.

The military judge is more than a mere referee; he is an active participant in the court-martial and is tasked with insuring a fair trial.[128] The judge is

---

certainty with which the concession was made, (3) the relationship of the concession to matters materially bearing upon the findings or sentence, (4) the conduct of counsel throughout the trial in representing an accused in relationship to the concession, and (5) the capacity of the fact finder to understand the implications of counsel's conduct and to disregard such concession....

24 M.J. at 806. In this case, the counsel had approached the judge in an R.C.M. 802 Conference, see Chapter 12, with the fact that his client might lie on the stand. The judge then raised the issue on the record, cautioned the accused about the dangers of committing perjury, and determined that the accused did not wish to withdraw his request for trial by judge alone.
United States v. Elzy, 22 M.J. 640 (A.C.M.R. 1986) (judge was not automatically disqualified where he discovered through the defense counsel that the accused might commit perjury).
119. Nix v. Whiteside, 475 U.S. 157 (1986).
120. Article 38(a), U.C.M.J.; R.C.M. 502(d)(5). *See also* United States v. King, 32 M.J. 709 (A.C.M.R. 1991) (prosecutor's interview of defense expert was nonprejudicial error); United States v. Hebert, 32 M.J. 707 (A.C.M.R. 1991) (prosecutor's comments during recess to the effect that the accused was a guilty SOB and that he was going to jail were inappropriate, but they had no impact on the court members); United States v. Chavez, 6 M.J. 615 (A.C.M.R. 1978) (trial counsel is not representative of the Convening Authority).
121. R.C.M. 502(d)(5) Discussion. *See also* R.C.M. 603 and § 6-1(B)(2).
122. R.C.M. 502(d)(5) Discussion.
123. *Id.* See also Chapter 11 for a discussion on the production of witnesses.
124. R.C.M. 502(d)(5) Discussion.
125. *Id.* United States v. Hall, 29 M.J. 786 (A.C.M.R. 1989) (nonprejudicial error for prosecutor to present copy of specifications on which he did not intend to offer any evidence). *Cf.* United States v. Irons, 34 M.J. 807 (N.M.C.M.R. 1992) (prejudicial error for judge to submit uncleansed charge sheet to court members).
126. *Id.* See § 17-4 regarding records of trial.
127. *See, e.g.,* JAGMAN 0153 (bailiff should be present at every court-martial session unless excused by the military judge).
128. United States v. Graves, 1 M.J. 50 (C.M.A. 1975); United States v. Copening, 32 M.J. 512 (A.C.M.R. 1990) (judge's actions in making intemperate remarks to accused and later holding *ex parte* meeting with prosecutor required recusal).

charged with exercising reasonable control over the trial,[129] preventing waste of time,[130] and promoting the ascertainment of truth.[131] Throughout the proceedings, the military judge must insure that his actions and statements reflect impartiality.[132]

As noted in § 15-12(B), *infra*, the military judge may question witnesses and it is during that process that a judge's impartiality may be questioned.[133] However, a judge's conduct during the trial may also indicate partiality.[134] For example, the judge may make comments in front of the members about defense counsel's actions or tactics which indicate a bias against counsel or presentation of the defense case.[135] The judge may have hindered or frustrated the defense,[136] assisted the prosecution in presenting its case[137] or engaged in

---

United States v. Zaccheus, 31 M.J. 766 (A.C.M.R. 1990) (judge was not partisan advocate when he finally asked several questions that established the foundation for relevant and otherwise admissible evidence).

United States v. Hardy, 30 M.J. 757 (A.C.M.R. 1990) (judge is the "most dominant figure" in trial; here judge abandoned impartiality by challenging defense sentencing argument and permitting prosecutor to reopen case and introduce accused's confession); United States v. Wood, 29 M.J. 1075 (A.C.M.R. 1990) (judge entitled to ask clarifying questions of witness).

United States v. Thompson, 29 M.J. 541 (A.F.C.M.R. 1989) (trial judge acted within his discretion in arranging courtroom so that child sodomy victims testified with backs to accused).

United States v. Kershaw, 26 M.J. 723 (A.C.M.R. 1988) (judge should have excluded evidence derived from accused's statements resulting from illegal interrogation even though defense counsel failed to object; judge should have assured himself that offered evidence was admissible).

129. R.C.M. 801(a)(3). United States v. Loving, 41 M.J. 213 (1994) (judge may not abandon impartial role); United States v. Reynolds, 24 M.J. 261 (C.M.A. 1987).

130. R.C.M. 801(a)(3) Discussion.

131. R.C.M. 801(a)(3) Discussion.

132. R.C.M. 801(a)(3). United States v. Ramos, 42 M.J. 392 (1995) (judge must be circumspect in what he says and does); *See generally* Delzompo, "When the Military Judge is No Longer Impartial: A Survey of the Law and Suggestions for Counsel," Army Law., June 1995, at 3.

133. *See* § 15-12(B). *See, e.g.*, United States v. Johnson, 36 M.J. 862 (A.C.M.R. 1993) (nothing in tenor of unusually large number of questions to indicate partiality); United States v. Eckart, 8 M.J. 835 (A.C.M.R. 1980) (judge's vigorous cross-examination of defense witness was prejudicial error); United States v. Beach, 49 C.M.R. 124 (N.M.C.M.R. 1974), *rev'd on other grounds*, 1 M.J. 118 (C.M.A. 1975) (lengthy and thorough questioning was necessary to clarify and develop testimony); United States v. Jordon, 45 C.M.R. 719 (A.C.M.R. 1972) (prejudicial error for judge to call co-conspirator to stand; doing so provided evidence for prosecutor).

134. *See, e.g.*, United States v. Loving, 41 M.J. 213 (1994) (court rejected arguments that judge was biased against defense because he, inter alia, denied a change of venue, accused defense counsel of being unethical and manipulating speedy trial clock, failing to exclude a member who was pro-life, and restricted voir dire of the members).

135. United States v. Loving, 41 M.J. 213 (1994) (judge's comment that defense theory of case was ridiculous in front of members was nonprejudicial); United States v. Thomas, 18 M.J. 545 (A.C.M.R. 1984) (disparaging remarks to counsel).

136. *See, e.g.*, United States v. Thomas, 18 M.J. 545 (A.C.M.R. 1984) (noting that bad blood existed between the judge and defense counsel, the court held that the judge erred in limiting voir dire, preventing presentation of helpful character evidence, and interrupted defense counsel on numerous occasions).

137. United States v. Reynolds, 24 M.J. 261 (C.M.A. 1987) (judge laid foundation for prosecution exhibit; no abandonment of impartiality); United States v. Payne, 31 C.M.R. 41 (C.M.A. 1961) (occasional suggestions are not unusual and mere fact of assistance does not demonstrate partiality).

ex parte communications with the prosecutor which raise questions about the judge's leanings.[138] If it appears that the judge will not be, or is not impartial, counsel may request permission to voir dire the judge, a delicate task in the best circumstances. That process may take place at an initial Article 39(a) session where the defense may challenge the judge for cause,[139] or later during the trial.[140]

Counsel may not simply sit and passively observe the proceedings. In addressing the respective roles of the parties, one court has observed the troubling number of errors of omission and commission in records of trial and noted in part:

> [B]oth trial and defense counsel bear major responsibility for assuring that the military judge properly performs his duty. Counsel must develop their own check lists and closely monitor the military judge's activities and make appropriate suggestions or objections. They cannot be disinterested and unconcerned observers to the manner in which the military judge carries out his duties. If counsel are not active throughout the trial, the trial counsel risks reversal and the defense counsel risks application of the doctrine of waiver. In neither case is the interest of justice served.[141]

In many respects the military judge's powers parallel those of a federal judge. Although the military counterpart has no tenure [142] and the powers are limited to the trial at hand, the military judge may issue search authorizations,[143]

United States v. McGeeney, 41 M.J. 544 (N.M.Ct.Crim.App. 1994) (trial judge's suggestions to trial counsel on how to meet burden of proof on motion was not sufficient in itself to demonstrate bias; court cautioned that a judge may go too far and become a part-time prosecutor); United States v. Masseria, 13 M.J. 868 (N.M.C.M.R. 1982) (not error to instruct trial counsel to present more evidence); United States v. Blackburn, 2 M.J. 929 (A.C.M.R. 1976); United States v. Wilson, 2 M.J. 548 (A.C.M.R. 1976) (numerous actions by judge in assisting prosecution resulted in reversal); United States v. Taylor, 47 C.M.R. 445 (A.C.M.R. 1973) (reversible error for judge to repeatedly assist prosecution).

138. United States v. Ware, 41 M.J. 592 (A.F.Ct.Crim.App. 1994) (conversations between judge and prosecutor occurred during recess in smoking area; court concluded that this ill-advised arrangement resulted in no improper ex parte communications; court recommended that judges who smoke should find a location distant from the masses, lest otherwise innocent exchanges be viewed as reflecting bias).

139. *See* § 12-2(H).

140. *See* R.C.M. 902(d).

141. United States v. Hudson, 16 M.J. 522, 523 (A.C.M.R. 1983).

142. The issue of tenure for military judges was considered by the Advisory Commission formed by the Secretary of Defense under the Military Justice Act of 1983. *See* § 1-6(C). The Commission, three members dissenting, recommended that a proposal to grant military judge's tenure not be adopted. The Commission's report states in part:

> Military judges enjoy judicial independence within the present system. Creating tenure for judges for the sake of appearance would misleadingly suggest that the system does not currently operate with an independent judiciary. Further, the need to maintain assignment flexibility outweighs any possible benefit regarding appearance.

Commission Report at 9.

143. *See* MIL. R. EVID. 315.

declare mistrials,[144] and make interlocutory rulings.[145] He may not, however, suspend a court-martial sentence.[146] The statutory qualifications of the judge are discussed in § 8-3(A).

§ 15-2(E). The Court Members.

The court members comprise the military's counterpart of the civilian jury.[147] If the accused has not requested a bench trial,[148] they serve as factfinders, and if they find the accused guilty,[149] they determine an appropriate sentence.[150] Unlike civilian jurors, military court members may question witnesses.[151] Communications between court members and other participants is restricted;[152] the military courts are sensitive to not only the evil itself, but also the appearance of evil. This is especially true where the communication comes from the convening authority and the spectre of improper command influence is raised.[153]

The "foreman" of the court is the highest ranking officer who is automatically designated as the "president".[154] He or she normally serves as the spokesman for the court[155] and presides over the court members' deliberations.[156] In those rare instances where a military judge is not appointed for a

---

144. See § 15-4(B).
145. R.C.M. 801(e).
146. United States v. Occhi, 2 M.J. 60 (C.M.A. 1976). The issue of whether military judges should have the power to suspend punishments was considered by the 1983 Commission on the U.C.M.J. The Commission recommended that the power to suspend be limited to the Executive Branch.
147. However, the military accused is not entitled to the Sixth Amendment protections of a "jury" trial as that right is applied in the civilian system. See United States v. Corl, 6 M.J. 914 (N.C.M.R. 1979). See also § 8-3(C) for a discussion on the selection process of the members.
148. See § 12-3(A) for a discussion of the accused's option of requesting trial by judge alone.
149. See § 15-16.
150. See Chapter 16. Under the current system there is no provision for the military judge alone to adjudge a sentence if trial has been before members.
151. See Rule 614, MIL. R. EVID. See also § 15-12(B).
152. See United States v. Hamilton, 41 M.J. 22 (C.M.A. 1994) (assistant trial counsel's lengthy social discussion with president of court-martial was improper; trial judge's decision to excuse president from court, but not assistant trial counsel, not abuse of discretion); United States v. Adamiak, 15 C.M.R. 412 (C.M.A. 1954) (communications establish presumption of prejudice that may be rebutted by clear and positive evidence that the communication from third person or witness did not or could not influence the decision); United States v. Knight, 41 M.J. 867 (Army Ct.Crim.App. 1995) (extensive discussions between court members and with driver for one of members amounted to reversible error; the court concluded that the discussions were frequent, extensive, and intended to obtain extrajudicial information); United States v. Elmore, 31 M.J. 678 (N.M.C.M.R. 1990) (government rebutted presumption of prejudice arising from contacts between government expert witness and members).
153. See generally Art. 37, U.C.M.J.; United States v. Rosser, 6 M.J. 267 (C.M.A. 1979); United States v. Almeida, 19 M.J. 874 (A.F.C.M.R. 1985).
154. R.C.M. 502(b). Service by another in that position has been held to be harmless error. United States v. Pulliam, 3 C.M.A. 95, 11 C.M.R. 95 (1953).
155. R.C.M. 502(b)(2).
156. See § 15-15.

special court-martial, the president's powers are much broader.[157]

Any irregular or questionable actions by the court members should be brought to the attention of the military judge. There is authority for the view that where it is shown that a court member was inattentive or sleeping during the trial, reversal is required.[158] Failure to object does not waive the issue.[159]

§ 15-2(F). The Court Reporter.

There are no minimum qualifications for court reporters stated in the U.C.M.J., although the Manual for Courts-Martial indicates that accusers, witnesses, investigating officers, counsel for any party, and court members are disqualified and may not serve as reporters.[160] Individual service regulations may provide further qualifications.[161] Court reporters are normally detailed to a general court-martial, or a special court-martial where the convening authority desires to authorize the court to impose a bad-conduct discharge.[162] Failure to swear the court reporter should not be reversible error[163] and failure of the convening authority to personally appoint the reporter should not constitute jurisdictional error.[164] Note that lack of a verbatim transcript of a court-martial limits the maximum punishment to that which could be imposed by a special court-martial.[165]

§ 15-2(G). The Interpreter.

Article 28, U.C.M.J.[166] permits detail of interpreters to a court-martial but provides no minimum qualifications. That is left to the individual services. As with court reporters, discussed *supra*, the *Manual* does indicate that certain persons are disqualified.[167] The *Manual* also indicates that an interpreter may be detailed as appropriate.[168] Such detailing, which need not be accomplished by the convening authority,[169] would normally be appropriate where the accused does not understand English or where a witness does not understand

---

157. See, e.g., R.C.M. 801(e)(2), for a discussion on the various rulings which may be made by the President of a Special Court-Martial without a military judge appointed.
158. United States v. Groce, 3 M.J. 369 (C.M.A. 1977); United States v. Brown, 3 M.J. 368 (C.M.A. 1977); United States v. Norment, 36 M.J. 1156 (A.C.M.R. 1993).
159. United States v. West, 27 M.J. 223 (C.M.A. 1988).
160. R.C.M. 502(e)(2). United States v. McGee, 13 M.J. 699 (N.M.C.M.R. 1982) (no automatic reversal where nominal accuser served as reporter); United States v. Gloria, 12 M.J. 518 (N.M.C.M.R. 1981).
161. R.C.M. 502(e)(1). See generally AR 27-10, par. 5-11.
162. See AR 27-10, para. 5-11 (reporters will not be detailed to SCMs or SPCMs not authorized to adjudge a BCD).
163. United States v. Stafford, 15 M.J. 866 (A.C.M.R. 1981).
164. United States v. Dionne, 6 M.J. 791 (A.C.M.R. 1978).
165. See United States v. Thompson, 22 C.M.A. 448, 47 C.M.R. 489 (1973). See also § 17-4.
166. See Appendix 3.
167. R.C.M. 502(e)(2) disqualifies accusers, United States v. Martinez, 11 C.M.A. 224, 29 C.M.R. 40 (1960), witnesses, counsel, and court members.
168. R.C.M. 501(c).
169. R.C.M. 501(c) Discussion.

English.[170] Note that interpreters under Rule 604, Military Rules of Evidence, are subject to qualification as expert witnesses and administration of an oath that they will make a true translation.[171]

§ 15-3. Courts-Martial and the Media: Public Trials.

The military accused possesses the same Sixth Amendment right to a public trial as does the civilian accused.[1] Also the public and press media enjoy a First Amendment right of access to military trials.[2] But these rights are not absolute[3] and may be limited under some circumstances.[4] Photographing, recording, or broadcasting of the trial is generally prohibited,[5] and a military judge may restrict or exclude the public to prevent disclosure of classified information[6] or protect the privacy of a witness.[7] The *Manual* indicates a strong preference for public trials[8] and states that servicemembers should be encouraged to attend courts-martial.[9]

In deciding whether to exclude the public, the military judge should apply the balancing test set out in *Press-Enterprise Co. v. Superior Court*:[10] whether the interest in closing the trial outweighs the accused's interest and the pub-

---

170. R.C.M. 502(e)(3) Discussion.
171. *See* Rule 604, MIL. R. EVID.
1. United States v. Short, 41 M.J. 42 (C.M.A. 1994) (Sixth Amendment right to public trial applies to courts-martial); United States v. Hershey, 20 M.J. 433 (C.M.A. 1985); United States v. Brown, 7 C.M.A. 251, 22 C.M.R. 41 (1956). *See also* R.C.M. 806.
2. *See* United States v. Travers, 25 M.J. 61 (C.M.A. 1987) (not error to deny defendant's request for closed sentencing where there was no showing of compelling need to do so); United States v. Story, 35 M.J. 677 (A.C.M.R. 1992) (citing right of public to be present); United States v. Fiske, 28 M.J. 1013 (A.F.C.M.R. 1989); United States v. Czarnecki, 10 M.J. 570 (A.F.C.M.R. 1980) (applying Richmond Newspapers, Inc. v. Virginia, 448 U.S. 555 (1980) to military practice).
3. United States v. Short, 41 M.J. 42 (C.M.A. 1994) (right to public trial not absolute and public may be excused in discretion of the trial judge; exclusion must be used sparingly).
4. Press-Enterprise Co. v. Superior Court, 464 U.S. 501 (1984); Globe Newspapers Co. v. Superior Court, 457 U.S. 596 (1982); United States v. Sombolay, 37 M.J. 647 (A.C.M.R. 1993) (right to public trial is not absolute and can be waived through pretrial agreement).
5. R.C.M. 806(c). *Cf.* Chandler v. Florida, 449 U.S. 560 (1981) (state permitted cameras in courtroom).
6. *See* R.C.M. 806(b). The issue of closing portions of the trial because of classified information was discussed at length in United States v. Lonetree, 31 M.J. 849 (N.M.C.M.R. 1990), where the accused was convicted of passing classified information to Soviet agents. The court concluded that the trial court committed nonprejudicial error in not instructing the members that the fact that some sessions were closed to the public is not itself evidence that the information is classified. *See also* Rules 505 and 506, MIL. R. EVID. United States v. Anzalone, 40 M.J. 658 (N.M.C.M.R. 1994) (court-martial closed only where it appeared that classified information would be revealed).
7. R.C.M. 806(b) Discussion. *See also* United States v. Hershey, 20 M.J. 433 (C.M.A. 1985).
8. R.C.M. 806(a). United States v. Short, 41 M.J. 42 (C.M.A. 1994) (absent overriding interest, court should be open). *See also* Richmond Newspapers, Inc. v. Virginia, 448 U.S. 555 (1980) (presumption of openness).
9. R.C.M. 806(a) Discussion. United States v. Clark, 32 M.J. 606 (A.C.M.R. 1991) (court rejected accused's argument that commander had ordered members of unit to stay away from trial; other evidence showed that commander had indicated that it would be good for unit to observe trial). The Coast Guard has included in its Military Justice Manual (MJM) a sample form for notifying the public of a pending trial.
10. 464 U.S. 501 (1984).

lic's interest in public trials.[11] If it is the accused that is requesting a closed hearing or trial, then the balance should be drawn between his right to nondisclosure against the public's right to access.[12] In any event, the judge should carefully set out for the record how the balance was struck and whether any other reasonable alternatives were considered.[13] If the judge agrees that closure is required, the closure must be closely tailored to protect whatever overriding interest required such.[14]

Occasionally media or public interest in a particular case or accused will provide an opportunity for the participants to comment publicly on the trial. In such cases extreme caution should be exercised to insure that the members, or potential members, are not affected by press interviews. For example, in *United States v. Garwood*[15] the military judge engaged in such interviews. Citing Judicial Canon 3(A)(6), the court chastised the judge for such conduct but concluded that he was not disqualified from presiding at the trial—even though the court members may have been subliminally affected.

Where it appears that press or media coverage may become a problem, the judge may take steps to issue gag orders and otherwise limit or control access of the media to the proceedings and the participants.[16]

As an alternative to closing the trial completely to the public, the Manual for Courts-Martial authorizes a military judge to exclude specific persons from the courtroom in order to maintain the dignity and decorum of the courtroom.[17] Where the trial judge does so, he or she must enter findings on the record which reflect the reason for the exclusion, the judge's belief that exclusion is necessary, and that the order of exclusion is tailored as narrowly and specifically as possible.[18]

---

11. The accused may waive a public trial but the public's interest in the case may outweigh his desires. Gannet Co. v. De Pasquale, 443 U.S. 368 (1979). *See also* R.C.M. 806(b) Discussion.

12. Press-Enterprise Co. v. Superior Court, 478 U.S. 1 (1986); United States v. Travers, 25 M.J. 61 (C.M.A. 1987) (trial judge did not abuse his discretion in denying accused's request to close sentencing to public; court noted that he had not taken other reasonable precautions to protect information he did not want public to hear).

13. United States v. Hershey, 20 M.J. 433 (C.M.A. 1985); United States v. Story, 35 M.J. 677 (A.C.M.R. 1992) (nonprejudicial error for judge to close trial to public without stating reasons); United States v. Fiske, 28 M.J. 1013 (A.F.C.M.R. 1989) (judge's failure to note for record his reasons for closing court-martial was harmless error; court noted that this was only second Air Force court-martial in a decade to be closed to public and observed that that was two too many).

14. *Id. See also* United States v. Grunden, 2 M.J. 116 (C.M.A. 1977) (in excluding, public judge used "ax" instead of judicial "scalpel").

15. 20 M.J. 148 (C.M.A. 1985).

16. Shepherd v. Maxwell, 384 U.S. 333 (1966); United States v. Gray, 37 M.J. 730 (A.C.M.R. 1992) (accused failed to show that pretrial publicity in his murder trial had denied him fair trial). *Cf.* Nebraska Press Ass'n v. Stuart, 427 U.S. 539 (1976) (improper to give orders blocking publication of evidence).

17. R.C.M. 806(b). United States v. Short, 41 M.J. 42 (C.M.A. 1994) (trial judge excluded young children from courtroom).

18. United States v. Short, 41 M.J. 42 (C.M.A. 1994).

§ 15-4. Motions at Trial.

Most motions will be raised and resolved at the Article 39(a) session.[1] Indeed, failure to raise motions for appropriate relief prior to assembly or end of the Article 39(a) session will probably constitute waiver.[2] Of course, motions to dismiss for lack of jurisdiction and motions for discovery may be raised at any time. The discussion here addresses several motions that are by their nature normally raised during trial itself.

§ 15-4(A). Continuances.

Either party may move for a continuance.[3] The moving, or requesting, party must show that its case will be prejudiced if the trial proceeds.[4] Generally, grounds include (1) illness or absence of defense counsel;[5] (2) absence of a key witness;[6] or (3) insufficient time to prepare for trial.[7] The motion presents an

---

1. See Chapter 12.
2. See § 13-2(C), concerning waiver of motions.
3. Art. 40 U.C.M.J. United States v. Price, 41 M.J. 403 (1995) (not abuse of discretion to grant third continuance for purposes of one more competency exam). Note that R.C.M. 906(b)(1) treats a request for a continuance as a motion for appropriate relief.
4. See generally United States v. Dunks, 1 M.J. 254 (C.M.A. 1975).
5. See United States v. Thomas, 22 M.J. 57 (C.M.A. 1986) (no abuse of discretion in granting continuance so that civilian counsel could be present); United States v. Grant, 38 M.J. 684 (A.F.C.M.R. 1993) (no abuse of discretion in denying defense request for continuance to obtain civilian counsel where counsel was under suspension); United States v. Thomas, 33 M.J. 694 (A.C.M.R. 1991) (judge erred in denying continuance so that civilian counsel could be prepared to represent accused; denial affected ability to present defense evidence; error was harmless however as to guilty pleas which were made without civilian counsel present); United States v. Wilson, 28 M.J. 1054 (N.M.C.M.R. 1989) (trial judge abused discretion in denying civilian defense counsel's request for continuance; court presumed prejudice where accused was forced to abandon counsel).
United States v. Galinato, 28 M.J. 1049 (N.M.C.M.R. 1989) (no abuse of discretion to deny request for continuance where three continuances had been granted and counsel provided no further justification). See generally McClleland, "Denial of Delay: A Limitation on the Right to Civilian Counsel in the Military," ARMY LAW., Jan. 1984, at 13; Sandell, "Securing a Continuance to Obtain Civilian Counsel," 11 The ADVOCATE 243 (1979).
6. See United States v. Royster, 42 M.J. 488 (1995) (not abuse of discretion to deny continuance to wait for witness; court noted that court members, military judges, and prosecutors are fungible, but witnesses are not; court noted that a judge will rarely, if ever, be reversed for denying a continuance); United States v. Clark, 35 M.J. 98 (C.M.A. 1992) (no abuse of discretion in denying

7. See United States v. Lopez, 37 M.J. 702 (A.C.M.R. 1993) (no abuse of discretion to deny request for continuance pending transcription of testimony of witnesses in another proceeding); United States v. Andrews, 36 M.J. 922 (A.F.C.M.R. 1993) (reversible error to deny defense request for continuance in order to prepare for trial); United States v. Davis, 36 M.J. 702 (A.C.M.R. 1992) (no abuse of discretion in not sua sponte granting continuance to defense when on day of trial, civilian defense counsel requested permission to withdraw from case in pay dispute; judge determined that appointed military counsel was prepared to proceed); United States v. Keys, 29 M.J. 920 (A.C.M.R. 1989) (court concluded that the defendant had been denied the effective assistance of counsel when the trial court denied civilian counsel's request for a continuance where he had been retained only one day before the trial began. The court noted that the defendant had been required to make several crucial decisions regarding his plea and the forum without his preferred counsel present).

§ 15-4(B)   TRIAL PROCEDURES   § 15-4(B)

interlocutory matter and the judge's ruling is reviewable on appeal for abuse of discretion.[8] The judge's ruling denying a continuance is not appealable by the prosecution, even if it results in dismissal of the charges.[9]

§ 15-4(B). Mistrial.

If during the trial circumstances make a mistrial manifestly necessary in the interests of justice, the military judge may grant a mistrial as to some or all of the charges.[10] Because a mistrial is a drastic remedy, the military judge

---

continuance to defense to obtain presence of accused's wife, who had returned to United States; court concluded that accused's failure to cooperate had made it impossible to secure their attendance in some form); United States v. Wood, 36 M.J. 651 (A.C.M.R. 1992) (accused not entitled to continuance to have child victim tested by clinical psychologist); United States v. Proctor, 34 M.J. 549 (A.F.C.M.R. 1992) (no error in denying continuance to obtain affidavit from medical law consultant); United States v. Browers, 20 M.J. 542 (A.C.M.R. 1985), *rev'd on other grounds*, 21 M.J. 356 (C.M.A. 1985) where the court stated that the judge should consider:

1. Whether the expected testimony is material and noncumulative;
2. Whether the testimony will probably affect the result;
3. Whether the testimony can be obtained;
4. Whether the moving party exercised diligence; and
5. The effect of continuance on other parties.

See also United States v. Johnson, 33 M.J. 855 (A.C.M.R. 1991) (judge abused discretion in denying continuance so defense could obtain presence of expert witness, even though that request was untimely); United States v. Ford, 29 M.J. 597 (A.C.M.R. 1989) (judge abused discretion in denying continuance to obtain defense witness); United States v. Cover, 16 M.J. 800 (N.M.C.M.R. 1983) (judge abused discretion in denying continuance to obtain defense witness).

United States v. Stevens, 27 M.J. 626 (A.F.C.M.R. 1988) (no abuse of discretion in denying continuance so that busy civilian counsel could represent accused, where detailed counsel was ready to proceed); United States v. Gipson, 25 M.J. 781 (A.C.M.R. 1988) (no abuse of discretion to deny civilian counsel's request for continuance to have time to prepare for case where judge had earlier granted multiple requests for delay by the accused); United States v. Garries, 19 M.J. 845 (A.F.C.M.R. 1985) (judge did not abuse discretion in denying defense counsel's request for six months to prepare for a murder case; when judge granted only three months, counsel withdrew from the case).

8. United States v. Royster, 42 M.J. 488 (1995) (unless due process is not being served, said the court, a judge will rarely, if ever, be reversed for denying a continuance); United States v. Menoken, 14 M.J. 10 (C.M.A. 1982); United States v. Andrews, 36 M.J. 922 (A.F.C.M.R. 1993) (abuse of discretion standard is strict; challenged action must be arbitrary, clearly erroneous, or clearly unreasonable; in this case, judge committed reversible error in denying defense request); United States v. Abilar, 14 M.J. 733 (A.F.C.M.R. 1982) (accused had voluntarily absented himself from trial); United States v. Perry, 14 M.J. 856 (A.C.M.R. 1982) (court noted that, in deciding whether to grant a continuance, the judge should balance the interests of the parties).

9. *See* United States v. Browers, 20 M.J. 356 (C.M.A. 1985).

10. R.C.M. 915. United States v. Brice, 19 M.J. 170 (C.M.A. 1985) (mistrial was in order when the court members were excused during the accused's court-martial on drug charges to hear a lecture by the commandant on the topic of drugs in the military); United States v. Donley, 30 M.J. 973 (A.C.M.R. 1990) (judge erred in not declaring mistrial when court member disclosed that he had heard counsel and the judge discussing inadmissible hearsay statements implicating defendant in other offenses); United States v. Ferguson, 29 M.J. 559 (A.F.C.M.R. 1989) (by removing court-martial panel who had been tainted by their reading of Manual for Courts-Martial, military judge erroneously created a hybrid procedure which had effect of declaring a mistrial). *See gener-*

§ 15-4(B)

should normally first consider alternate means of curing the error, such as cautionary instructions.[11]

The trial judge has broad discretion in declaring a mistrial and his decision will bar further prosecution only if he abused his discretion.[12] A defense-re-

---

ally Note, "United States v. Brice: Command Policy or Command Influence," 33 JAG J. 133 (Summer 1984). United States v. Jeanbaptiste, 5 M.J. 374 (C.M.A. 1978); United States v. Thompson, 5 M.J. 28 (C.M.A. 1978). See also Schulhofer, "Jeopardy and Mistrials," 125 U. Pa. L. Rev. 449 (1977).

11. See, e.g., United States v. Balagna, 33 M.J. 54 (C.M.A. 1991) (court reviewed the modern view of granting mistrials and rejected the position of assuming that a mistrial was the only appropriate remedy when the court heard inadmissible evidence. Instead, a curative instruction is the preferred method absent extraordinary circumstances); United States v. Garces, 32 M.J. 345 (C.M.A. 1991) (mistrial is drastic remedy; instruction to disregard unintentional actions by government is preferred to mistrial).

United States v. Rushatz, 31 M.J. 450 (C.M.A. 1990) (preferred remedy is to give a curative instruction rather than declaring a mistrial as long as the instruction avoids prejudice; members are presumed to comply with such instructions); United States v. Evans, 27 M.J. 34 (C.M.A. 1988) (if adequate, cautionary instructions are preferred method of curing error where members have heard inadmissible evidence).

United States v. Mora, 26 M.J. 122 (C.M.A. 1988) (retrial not barred by mere failure of trial judge to consult with defense counsel before declaring mistrial); United States v. Johnson, 23 M.J. 327 (C.M.A. 1987) (judge denied motion for mistrial and gave cautionary instructions when it appeared that one of the members had inadvertently viewed autopsy photos); United States v. Pastor, 8 M.J. 280 (C.M.A. 1980); United States v. Shamlian, 9 C.M.A. 28, 25 C.M.R. 290 (1958) (cautionary instructions).

United States v. Mobley, 34 M.J. 527 (A.F.C.M.R. 1991) (curative instructions preferred over granting motion for mistrial); United States v. Zaccheus, 31 M.J. 766 (A.C.M.R. 1990) (judge did not abuse discretion in denying mistrial where trial counsel noted accused's invocation of the right to remain silent; court struck all of testimony relating to that matter and instructed the court twice on the need to disregard the matter).

United States v. Allen, 31 M.J. 572 (N.M.C.M.R. 1990) (no abuse of discretion in denying defense request for continuance to obtain expert's assistance where counsel failed to show the underlying basis for the request); United States v. Balagna, 31 M.J. 825 (A.C.M.R. 1990) (because mistrial is a drastic remedy, preferred practice where court has heard inadmissible evidence is to strike the evidence and give curative instructions to the court members).

United States v. Seymore, 19 M.J. 608 (A.C.M.R. 1984) (no mistrial required where court members learned of uncharged misconduct and the judge instructed them to disregard such); United States v. Suttles, 15 M.J. 972 (A.C.M.R. 1983) (whether judge had abused discretion depends on prejudicial impact of the inadmissible evidence and quality of curative instructions); United States v. Gore, 14 M.J. 945 (A.C.M.R. 1982) (instead of granting mistrial, judge instructed and questioned members concerning their impartiality after president of court expressed displeasure over delays in trial).

12. R.C.M. 915(c)(2). United States v. Mora, 26 M.J. 122 (C.M.A. 1988) (judge *sua sponte* declared mistrial on sentencing where he concluded that defense counsel was being ineffective); Burtt v. Schick, 23 M.J. 140 (C.M.A. 1986) (trial judge abused discretion in granting government-requested mistrial where alternative steps were available to remedy error); United States v. Jeanbaptiste, 5 M.J. 374 (C.M.A. 1978); United States v. Keenan, 18 C.M.A. 108, 39 C.M.R. 108 (1969).

United States v. Mobley, 34 M.J. 527 (A.F.C.M.R. 1991) (no abuse of discretion in denying motion for mistrial after trial counsel commented on accused's silence; curative instructions are preferred over granting of motion); United States v. Ghent, 21 M.J. 546 (A.F.C.M.R. 1985) (double jeopardy prevented retrial where judge abused discretion in granting mistrial where defense attempted to impeach rape victim by questioning the legitimacy of her child); United States v. Rebuck, 16 M.J. 555 (A.F.C.M.R. 1983) (judge abused discretion in not granting mistrial where

quested mistrial will not bar further prosecution,[13] but a mistrial requested by the prosecution may bar retrial if it appears that the error was induced by the prosecution.[14] In granting the mistrial during sentencing, the military judge may apply his ruling as to the entire proceeding or only the sentencing portion of the trial.[15]

§ 15-4(C). Motion for Finding of Not Guilty.

At the conclusion of the prosecution's case-in-chief or after presenting its case, the defense may move for a finding of not guilty,[16] which is similar in effect to the civilian practice of moving for a judgment of acquittal.[17] The motion should be denied if there is any evidence that together with all applicable inferences and presumptions reasonably tends to establish every element of the offense or a lesser-included offense.[18] The *Manual* specifically recognizes that the defense may limit the motion to a greater charge, as long as a lesser charge remains.[19] The test is not proof beyond a reasonable doubt.[20] The judge may require the defense to specify deficiencies in the evidence,[21]

---

court member's comments could have affected deliberations on verdict). *See also* United States v. Mora, 22 M.J. 719 (A.C.M.R. 1986) (not required to first consult with defense counsel).

13. R.C.M. 915(c)(2). *Cf.* United States v. DiAngelo, 31 M.J. 135 (C.M.A. 1990) (a defendant who obtains a mistrial may invoke the double jeopardy bar if the actions that led to the mistrial were intended, by the court or the prosecution, to provoke the defense into moving for a mistrial).

14. R.C.M. 915(c)(2)(B); Oregon v. Kennedy, 456 U.S. 667 (1982); Gori v. United States, 364 U.S. 917 (1961); United States v. DiAngelo, 31 M.J. 135 (C.M.A. 1990) (prosecutor's failure to disclose evidence was not intended to provoke a mistrial); United States v. Goodyear, 14 M.J. 567 (N.M.C.M.R. 1982) (*citing* Oregon v. Kennedy, court applied "intentional actions" standard).

15. United States v. Mora, 26 M.J. 122 (C.M.A. 1988) (mistrial granted only as to sentencing); Burtt v. Schick, 23 M.J. 140 (C.M.A. 1986); United States v. Goffe, 15 C.M.A. 112, 35 C.M.R. 84 (1964).

16. R.C.M. 917. United States v. Spearman, 23 C.M.A. 31, 48 C.M.R. 405 (1974); United States v. Brown, 15 M.J. 501 (A.F.C.M.R. 1982). *See generally* Hanko, "Motion for a Pretrial Finding of Not Guilty," Army Law., Aug. 1978, at 1.

17. Rule 29(a), Fed. R. Crim. P.

18. R.C.M. 917(d). In United States v. Griffith, 27 M.J. 42 (C.M.A. 1988), the judge denied the defense motion for a finding of not guilty, but after the members had returned a verdict of guilty, he stated for the record that in his view the evidence was insufficient to find the accused guilty beyond a reasonable doubt but took no action because he believed that he had no authority to set aside the findings. In reviewing congressional intent regarding the role of the trial judge, the court concluded that a trial judge may set aside findings where he is convinced that the government's evidence is legally insufficient. But he may not become a "thirteenth juror" and do so based upon his assessment of the credibility of the witnesses.

United States v. Latimer, 30 M.J. 554 (A.C.M.R. 1990) (although trial judge incorrectly noted that the standard was "scintilla of evidence," he correctly denied motion for finding of not guilty).

19. R.C.M. 917(e). Partial grants of such a motion, i.e., granting the motion as to the greater offense but not the lesser, were probably in violation of the 1969 *Manual* provision. *See* United States v. Ureta, 41 M.J. 571 (A.F.Ct.Crim.App. 1994) (judge committed plain error by granting defense motion for finding of not guilty on rape charge in such a way as to fashion new specification alleging carnal knowledge, which was not lesser-included offense of rape); United States v. Brown, 15 M.J. 501 (A.F.C.M.R. 1982).

20. United States v. Gluch, 30 C.M.R. 534 (A.B.R. 1961).

21. R.C.M. 917(b). In United States v. Hunt, 37 M.J. 344 (C.M.A. 1993), the defense moved for a finding of not guilty at the close of the government's case on the ground that there was a variance

and before ruling, may permit the prosecution to reopen its case.[22] His decision is final and is not subject to reconsideration[23] or government appeal.[24] If he grants the motion, the trial ends in an acquittal.[25] If he denies the motion, the defense may waive the issue by presenting evidence during its case-in-chief.[26]

§ 15-4(D). Motions for Inquiring Into Accused's Sanity.

The question of the accused's sanity may be raised at any time,[27] although it is preferable to raise the issue as early as possible. If during the trial itself some evidence is produced which raises the question of the accused's sanity, the military judge may make a ruling, on his own motion or on the motion of counsel, and order that the accused be examined by a sanity board.[28] The results are reported to the court, which may conduct further inquiry or report the matter to the convening authority for his consideration, who may in turn hold the proceedings in abeyance or dismiss the charges.[29] Should the issue of the accused's sanity first arise during sentencing following a guilty plea,[30] the military judge may first treat it as a matter inconsistent with the guilty plea, see § 14-3(E), before setting aside the findings and either ordering further inquiry or granting a mistrial.

§ 15-5. Contempts.

Provision is made in the U.C.M.J. and the Manual for Courts-Martial[1] for holding in contempt any person[2] at trial who "uses any menacing word, sign, or gesture in its presence, or who disturbs its proceedings by any riot or

---

of three weeks in date of offense. The motion was denied and on appeal the court held that the variance was not fatal. The court said that to prevail on a fatal variance claim, the accused must show that the variance was material and the accused was prejudiced.

22. R.C.M. 917(c) Discussion.
23. R.C.M. 917(f). In 1994, R.C.M. 905(f) was amended by Change 7 to permit the judge to reconsider a ruling denying a motion for finding of not guilty at any time before the record of trial is authenticated.The Analysis explains that the judge is limited in deciding whether the evidence adduced is legally sufficient, rather than in assessing the weight of the evidence.
24. Art. 62, U.C.M.J. See also § 13-2(G).
25. R.C.M. 917(f).
26. R.C.M. 917(g). United States v. Wai, 3 C.M.R. 728 (A.F.B.R. 1952). The exception to this is where the defense evidence is comprised of a judicial confession spurred by an inadmissible pretrial statement. See United States v. Bearchild, 17 C.M.A. 598, 38 C.M.R. 396 (1968).
27. United States v. Greer, 41 C.M.R. 582 (1969).
28. R.C.M. 706 and 909. United States v. Thomas, 8 M.J. 661 (A.C.M.R. 1979).
29. R.C.M. 706(c)(3) Discussion.
30. See, e.g., United States v. Trede, 2 C.M.A. 581, 10 C.M.R. 79 (1953).
1. R.C.M. 809(a). Few military cases involving contempts exist. See McHardy, "Military Contempt Law and Procedure," 55 Mil. L. Rev. 131 (1972).
2. In theory, any person appearing before a court-martial may be subject to the jurisdiction of the court to punish for contempt. R.C.M. 809(a) Discussion (excepts military judge, members, and foreign nationals outside United States). Practically, it may be impossible to enforce the punishments.

disorder."[3] Punishment may not exceed thirty days' confinement or a fine of $100.00, or both.[4] The contempt must be direct,[5] and although a warning is advisable, it is not mandatory.[6] These little-used procedures are summary in nature, with no right of appeal except review by the convening authority, and are conducted immediately.

The applicable procedures required to find a person in contempt depend on whether the act was personally witnessed by the court-martial and whether the court-martial includes members.[7]

In bench trials, the military judge may summarily find the person in contempt for actions he personally observed[8] and impose punishment.[9] In trials with members, the members will vote first on the question of whether what they personally observed was a contempt,[10] and if so, what punishment should be assessed.[11] On the other hand, if the act was not personally observed by the court-martial, the person is entitled to notice, assistance of counsel, and a reasonable opportunity to present evidence;[12] in that case the judge, or the members,[13] must be convinced beyond a reasonable doubt that the person is guilty of contempt.[14]

In *United States v. Burnett*,[15] the court discussed extensively the authority of a trial judge to find a person in contempt of court. In this case, the members determined that the civilian defense counsel had acted in contempt of the court. Noting that although a finding of contempt would not be directly reviewable by the court, it would be considered insofar as it might have had an adverse impact on the accused's trial. The court concluded that the *Manual* procedures for requiring a hearing before the members was an anachronism in view of the trial judge's expanded powers, and that a judge could wait until the end of trial to find a person in contempt.

Contempt proceedings are made part of the record and are reviewed by the convening authority, who must approve the punishment before it can be effec-

---

3. Art. 48, U.C.M.J. *See* Appendix 3. In United States v. Galinato, 28 M.J. 1049 (N.M.C.M.R. 1989), the court indicated that the trial court could have found the accused's two counsel in contempt when they refused to present a defense after he denied their request for a continuance. *Id.* at 1054, n.6.
4. Art. 48, U.C.M.J.
5. The Discussion to R.C.M. 809(a) indicates that a "direct" contempt might also include a contempt not actually observed by the court.
6. R.C.M. 809(a) Discussion.
7. R.C.M. 809(b), (c). The procedures are modelled after Rule 42, Fed. R. Crim. P. *See* R.C.M. 809 Analysis.
8. R.C.M. 809(b)(1), (c)(1). The judge must recite the factual basis for his findings and indicate that he personally witnessed the contempt.
9. R.C.M. 809(b)(1). The court-martial proceedings are suspended pending disposition of the contempt.
10. R.C.M. 809(c)(2). The proceedings may be instituted either by the judge or a member of the court.
11. *Id.*
12. R.C.M. 809(b)(2).
13. R.C.M. 809(c)(2).
14. R.C.M. 809(b)(2). It is not clear from the Rule who, if anyone, bears the burden of proof; the procedures should generally not be adversarial in nature.
15. 27 M.J. 99 (C.M.A. 1988).

tive.[16] Pending formal review of the trial, the convening authority may require the party to serve any confinement imposed.[17]

In many cases the court will not be required to rely upon contempt procedures. For example, where the person is subject to the U.C.M.J., the judge or other officer or noncommissioned officer may issue appropriate orders, the violation of which would then be subject to prosecution. See Chapter 2. Failure to testify is not punishable by contempt[18] but may be prosecuted under Article 134 or under Article 47, U.C.M.J.[19]

§ 15-6. Trial Procedure Guides—Uniform Rules of Practice.

Widely used in the individual services, trial procedure guides provide a convenient template for court-martial procedures. They are usually grounded on the trial guide included in Appendix 8 of the Manual for Courts-Martial, but may be fine-tuned to take into account individualized practices.[1] That guide provides the reader with a convenient and predictable guide in understanding the procedures of both general and special courts-martial, the focus of Part II of this Chapter. The military courts have recognized the existence of trial guides and point out that they are only guides. Variances in procedure do not automatically result in prejudicial error.[2]

The services have also promulgated uniform rules of practice before courts-martial. These rules govern a wide variety of trial practices and should be consulted.

PART II
PROCEDURES FOR GENERAL AND SPECIAL COURTS-MARTIAL

§ 15-7. General.

The procedural format for general and special courts-martial is generally the same. The summary court-martial is handled in a much different manner and is discussed separately in Part IV. This part of the Chapter addresses the key procedural bases that will be touched in a court-martial—from assembly of the court to sentencing, which is discussed in Chapter 16.

Prior to formally calling the court to order, the military judge will review the applicable convening orders and determine if the proper parties are present. Because most trials are preceded by an Article 39(a) session,[1] almost all of the preliminary matters will have been disposed of at that session. That

---

16. R.C.M. 809(d). See United States v. Snipes, 19 M.J. 913 (A.C.M.R. 1985) (defense counsel's contempt conviction set aside by convening authority).
17. R.C.M. 809(e).
18. See R.C.M. 809(a) Discussion.
19. Id. See also §§ 11-2(D)(3) and 11-2(F).
1. The Army used to publish its detailed trial guide in DA Pam. 27-15. That publication has been discontinued.
2. See United States v. Dixon, 8 M.J. 858 (N.C.M.R. 1980).
1. See generally Chapter 12.

is, the military judge's inquiries will have settled questions of trial by military judge alone or inclusion of enlisted members on the court, and the qualifications of counsel for both sides.[2] If there have been no changes in the composition of qualifications of the participants, these matters need not be addressed again when the trial begins. Note that if the trial will be with military judge alone, the trial proceeds immediately to the opening statements of counsel.[3]

A trial with court members commences with the judge calling the court to order and the trial counsel announcing the convening orders and the presence of the participants.[4] Failure to announce the presence of the participants is probably not jurisdictional error.[5]

§ 15-8. Introduction and Swearing of the Participants.

The military judge may give preliminary instructions to the court members in introducing the counsel and the court reporter. Following these introductions, the trial counsel will swear the members of the court, the court reporter (if he or she has not been previously sworn),[1] and any interpreters who may take part in the trial. Failure to swear all of the court members is jurisdictional error[2] but absence of an oath for the court reporter is not.[3] If necessary, the military judge will administer the necessary oaths to counsel if they have not previously been sworn. Failure to swear the appointed defense counsel may be reversible error.[4]

---

2. See § 12-3.
3. See Trial Guide at Appendix 8 in Manual for Courts-Martial.
4. United States v. Hayes, 24 M.J. 786 (A.C.M.R. 1987) (court advised that trial counsel should refrain from simply announcing the names of the members who were absent and should also state the names of those actually present).
5. United States v. McElroy, 40 M.J. 368 (C.M.A. 1994) (harmless error not to specifically name court members who were present; accused failed to object and names and ranks of members who served is readily apparent from record of trial); United States v. Fell, 33 M.J. 628 (A.C.M.R. 1991) (failure of judge or trial counsel to personally account for members on the record is not jurisdictional error).
1. See Art. 42, U.C.M.J. The texts of the oaths appear at R.C.M. 807. Military participants will have normally taken a one-time oath.
2. In United States v. Clemons, 35 M.J. 767 (A.C.M.R. 1992), the court held that the failure to give the oath to court members before they were asked questions on voir dire was not fatal. Citing R.C.M. 912(b) Discussion, the court indicated that before questioning the members on voir dire, they should be given the oath, even though the Secretary of the Army has not indicated specifically when the oath should be given. In this case, the members were otherwise apprised of the solemnity of their duties and were sworn before the evidentiary and deliberative portion of the trial began. United States v. Stephenson, 2 C.M.R. 571 (N.B.R. 1951). Cf. United States v. Wilson, 27 M.J. 555 (A.C.M.R. 1988), where the court held that failure to swear two members was not jurisdictional error but was sufficient to cause the sentencing proceedings to be a nullity; thus, the military judge properly conducted a revision proceeding to conduct new sentencing proceedings. The court disavowed its opinion in United States v. Gary, 44 C.M.R. 354 (A.C.M.R. 1970), where it held that failure to take the oath amounted to jurisdictional error.
3. See United States v. Williams, 16 C.M.R. 717 (A.F.B.R. 1954).
4. United States v. Kendall, 17 C.M.A. 561, 38 C.M.R. 359 (1968). Failure to swear a civilian counsel is not. United States v. Danilson, 11 C.M.R. 692 (A.F.B.R. 1953).

§ 15-9. Assembly of the Court.

During the court-martial process certain utterances mark lines of demarcation. *Assembly* of the court is one of those lines. It normally occurs *after* the court members are sworn and before voir dire and challenges. A court is considered assembled when it gathers in the courtroom and is not dependent upon the military judge's formal announcement of assembly.[1] In a trial by military judge alone, the military judge will, upon approving the request for a bench trial, announce that the court is assembled and proceed directly to the merits portion of the trial. The key point here is that *after* assembly, the military judge and court members may be removed only for good cause, the reasons noted on the record by the trial counsel.[2] Assembly may also cut off requests for, or withdrawal of, enlisted personnel on the court[3] and similar actions with regard to bench trials.[4]

If any members are absent, the military judge should establish for the record why they are absent.[5] The absence of members, whether explained or not, is not a jurisdictional defect as long as the minimum number of members are present,[6] five members for a general court-martial and three members for a special court-martial.[7]

Following assembly, the military judge may give preliminary instructions to the court members.[8] Typical instructions could address the general nature of the members' duties,[9] the duties of the military judge,[10] and counsel,[11]

---

1. United States v. Dixon, 18 M.J. 310 (C.M.A. 1984).
2. *See, e.g.,* In United States v. Porter, 36 M.J. 812 (A.C.M.R. 1993), the court held that the military judge acted properly in excusing court member who fell asleep during testimony. The court noted that the judge has a duty to insure that the members are attentive. *See also* United States v. West, 27 M.J. 223 (C.M.A. 1988); United States v. Smith, 3 M.J. 490 (C.M.A. 1975). *See also* R.C.M. 505, 902, 912 and § 8-3(D).
3. R.C.M. 903(a)(1), (d). *See* § 12-3(B).
4. R.C.M. 903(a)(2). *See* § 12-3(A).
5. *See* United States v. Malczewskyj, 26 M.J. 995 (A.F.C.M.R. 1988); United States v. Wheatcraft, 23 M.J. 687 (A.F.C.M.R. 1986).
6. United States v. Colon, 6 M.J. 73 (C.M.A. 1978); United States v. Allen, 5 C.M.A. 626, 18 C.M.R. 250 (1955); United States v. Bouknight, 35 M.J. 671 (A.C.M.R. 1992) (absence of three members was unexplained at trial; nonjurisdictional error which was waived by defense failure to object; court condemned "sloppy pretrial administration and in-court practice that raises unnecessary questions and causes needless delay"); United States v. Malczewskyj, 26 M.J. 995 (A.F.C.M.R. 1988). The absence may be waived by a failure to object. *Id.*

Cf. R.C.M. 805(b), which requires the members to be present except in an Article 39(a) session (*see* Chapter 12), during voir dire, when a member has been excused by the convening authority or military judge, as otherwise provided in R.C.M. 1102 (post-trial sessions).

7. In United States v. Malczewskyj, 26 M.J. 995 (A.F.C.M.R. 1988), six of the eight appointed members were present and no reasons were given for the two absent members. The court concluded that the accused had not been prejudiced because the grade distribution of those present was not substantially affected; there was some communication with the convening authority when the absences were noted, and it was highly unlikely that the presence of the other two members would have affected the outcome of the trial.
8. *See* Appendix 8 to the Manual for Courts-Martial.
9. R.C.M. 502(a)(2), 922, and 1006.
10. R.C.M. 801, 920, 1005; MIL. R. EVID. 104.
11. R.C.M. 502(d)(5) and (6).

procedures for voir dire and determining possible grounds of challenge,[12] the questioning of witnesses,[13] courtroom procedures,[14] and taking notes during the trial.[15] Although these instructions are not required, it is the preferred practice to give them.[16] And doing so is conducive to ensuring a fair trial.[17]

§ 15-10. Voir Dire and Challenges of Court Members.

After the members are sworn[1] and the court is assembled, the military judge and counsel may inquire into possible grounds of challenge to the court members. Inquiry into grounds of challenge against the military judge will normally have been handled at the Article 39(a) pretrial session.[2] This section addresses that inquiry,[3] the possible grounds for disqualification,[4] and finally the process of challenging the members.[5]

§ 15-10(A). Voir Dire of Court Members.

The sole purpose of voir dire is to determine through questioning whether any member is not qualified to sit on the court-martial.[6] And it is improper for counsel to use voir dire to present information that would not be admissible at trial and to attempt to educate the jury about his theory of the case.[7] There is obviously a thin line between thoroughly questioning the members and educating them about the case and possible uses of testimony and other evidence. Prudent counsel should, however, focus primarily on the former and avoid

---

12. R.C.M. 912. *See* § 15-10.
13. MIL. R. EVID. 611, 614. *See* § 15-12(B).
14. MIL. R. EVID. 611. *See* § 15-12.
15. MIL. R. EVID. 611. *See* § 15-15.
16. R.C.M. 913(a); United States v. Brewster, 32 M.J. 591 (A.C.M.R. 1991).
17. United States v. Brewster, 32 M.J. 591 (A.C.M.R. 1991). *See also* United States v. Waggoner, 6 M.J. 77, 79, n.2 (C.M.A. 1978).
1. *See* § 15-8.
2. *See* Chapter 12.
3. *See* § 15-10(A).
4. *See* § 15-10(B).
5. *See* § 15-10(C).
6. *See* R.C.M. 912(d) Discussion. United States v. Smith, 27 M.J. 25 (C.M.A. 1988) (appropriate for trial judge to prevent defense counsel from informing members that if they found the accused guilty, there was a mandatory life sentence; there is no requirement that the trial judge permit counsel to induce "jury nullification").
7. *Id. See, e.g.*, United States v. Credit, 4 M.J. 118 (C.M.A. 1977); United States v. Toro, 34 M.J. 506 (A.F.C.M.R. 1991) (counsel's voir dire was attempt to introduce his case to court members; court recognized that although the practice is widely used, it disapproves of such); United States v. Smith, 24 M.J. 859 (A.C.M.R. 1987) (court held that the trial judge did not abuse his discretion in blocking defense counsel's attempt to inform members during voir dire that a mandatory life sentence would automatically follow conviction of premeditated murder; a possible sentence is not relevant to members' determination on the merits. What the court seemed concerned about was that this information might be used to urge jury nullification.) *Cf.* United States v. Jefferson, 22 M.J. 315, 329 (C.M.A. 1986) (informing members of maximum sentence during arguments is not inappropriate to the extent that it impresses upon them the seriousness of their decision on the findings). ABA Standards for Criminal Justice Relating to Defense Function, Sec. 7-2(c) and Prosecution Function, Sec. 5.3(c).

questions and comments which could reasonably be interpreted as an attempt to influence the court members.

The key to effective voir dire of members is careful pretrial examination of the qualifications and background, or "pedigree," information of the court members.[8] The *Manual* indicates that upon defense request, the prosecution must submit a questionnaire to the members.[9] The written questionnaire, which need not follow any particular format, should contain the following areas of inquiry:

1. Date of birth;
2. Sex;
3. Race;
4. Marital status and sex, age, and number of dependents;
5. Home of record;
6. Civilian and military education;
7. Current assignment;
8. Past assignments;
9. Awards and decorations;
10. Date of rank;
11. Whether the member is disqualified because of prior association with the case, e.g., accuser, counsel, convening authority, etc.[10]

Although this information is normally helpful, in many instances it will be appropriate to request additional information which might reveal bias or predispositions. For example, it would seem appropriate to ask whether the member has been the victim of a particular crime. Upon approval by the military judge, this sort of additional information may be requested.[11] The answers to all the inquiries must be in writing and signed by the member.[12] Using these pretrial questionnaires can greatly expedite the voir dire and should preclude the necessity of repeating the same questions in court.[13] A sample questionnaire is included in this text at Appendix 24.

Defense counsel is also entitled to discovery of whatever written materials were used in selecting court members.[14] But counsel is not entitled to mate-

---

8. United States v. Lake, 36 M.J. 317 (C.M.A. 1993) (counsel should have noted in papers that one member had prior contact with case and that, during voir dire, another member stated that she was the company commander for one of the government's witnesses). *See generally* Ingold, "Discovering and Removing the Biased Court Member," ARMY LAW., Jan. 1986, at 32.

9. R.C.M. 912(a)(1). The use of such questionnaires was approved in United States v. Credit, 4 M.J. 118 (C.M.A. 1977). Such questionnaires have been referred to as *Credit* information. But in United States v. Anderson, 36 M.J. 963 (A.F.C.M.R. 1993), the court indicated that the name was unfortunate and indicated that "[f]ormbooks everywhere should be scrubbed clean of that phrase...." *Id.* at 974, n.22.

10. *Id.* The questionnaire and answers may be attached to the record as an exhibit.

11. R.C.M. 912(a)(1). United States v. Anderson, 36 M.J. 963 (A.F.C.M.R. 1993) (trial court denied accused's request to submit extensive questionnaire to court members; it did not deny accused opportunity to inquire into such matters during voir dire).

12. R.C.M. 912(a)(1).
13. R.C.M. 912(a) Analysis.
14. R.C.M. 912(a)(2).

§ 15-10(A)   TRIAL PROCEDURES   § 15-10(A)

rials on individuals not selected as members unless the military judge, for good cause shown, directs otherwise.[15] This extended discovery may be appropriate where counsel has reason to believe that the entire selection process should be challenged.[16]

Following preliminary instructions concerning the procedures and purposes of voir dire,[17] the court members will be first asked to voluntarily disclose any possible grounds for challenge.[18] The military judge and counsel may then conduct a voir dire of the panel, individually or collectively.[19] The order and manner of voir dire is left to the sound discretion of the military judge.[20] Proper subjects of inquiry include statutory disqualifications, implied or actual bias, or other matters that may have a substantial and direct impact on the accused's right to an impartial court.[21] Although counsel have wide latitude in questioning court members, the military judge is tasked with ensuring that the questions are understandable and pertinent to the trial.[22]

A court member's failure to candidly and fully answer voir dire questions will not in itself deny the accused a fair trial.[23] In an extensive discussion of this issue the court in *United States v. Modesto*,[24] concluded that a prospective

---

15. *Id.*
16. *See* § 15-10(B)(1).
17. DA Pam. 27-9, Military Judge's Benchbook, contains sample instructions.
18. Disclosure is mandatory. United States v. Lackey, 22 C.M.R. 384 (A.B.R. 1956). The members should be instructed to relate only the general nature of the potential ground to minimize the danger of tainting the other members. *See* United States v. Lake, 36 M.J. 317 (C.M.A. 1993), the defense asserted on appeal that the failure of two court members to be completely candid about their involvement with the case had denied him a fair trial. The court concluded that the failure to disclose the information was inadvertent and that the defense should have been able to discern the complained-of grounds by reviewing the papers in the case and in listening to the answers given during voir dire of the entire panel. United States v. Washington, 8 C.M.A. 588, 25 C.M.R. 92 (1958) (member's statement was harmless error).
19. R.C.M. 912(d) Discussion.
20. *See, e.g.*, United States v. Slubowski, 7 M.J. 461 (C.M.A. 1979) (judge required counsel to submit questions in writing). *See also* United States v. Yarborough, 14 M.J. 968 (A.C.M.R. 1982); United States v. Hill, 45 C.M.R. 904 (N.C.M.R. 1972) (defense counsel not entitled to voir dire before assembly). *See generally* Holdaway, "Voir Dire—A Neglected Tool of Advocacy," 40 MIL. L. REV. 1 (1968).
21. *See* § 15-10(B) for a discussion of grounds for challenging court members.
22. United States v. Smith, 27 M.J. 25 (C.M.A. 1988) (judge properly prevented defense counsel from inducing "jury nullification"); United States v. Parker, 6 C.M.A. 274, 19 C.M.R. 400 (1955); United States v. Adams, 36 M.J. 1201 (N.M.C.M.R. 1993) (failure to permit defense counsel to pose voir dire regarding members' view of urinalysis program amounted to reversible error); United States v. Nixon, 30 M.J. 501 (A.F.C.M.R. 1989) (no abuse of discretion to permit prosecutor to inquire of members whether they were opposed to death penalty).

United States v. Smith, 25 M.J. 785 (A.C.M.R. 1988) (trial judge properly cut off voir dire questions by defense that attempted to place members in place of accused; relevance was not apparent from questions or explanations by counsel); United States v. Smith, 24 M.J. 859 (A.C.M.R. 1987) (judge correctly blocked defense counsel from informing members that finding of guilty of premeditated murder charge would require automatic life sentence).

23. *See, e.g.*, United States v. Lake, 36 M.J. 317 (C.M.A. 1993) (member's failure to disclose that he had received and signed accused's charge sheet and another's failure to disclose that he was company commander for government witness and accused's girlfriend were inadvertent; members did not purposefully ignore judge's questions).
24. 43 M.J. 315 (1995).

member did not violate duty of candor and honesty by failing to disclose during voir dire that he had engaged in conduct similar to the accused's. To obtain a new trial on grounds of nondisclosure, the defense must show that the member failed to answer honestly a material question[25] and that a correct response would have given valid basis for challenge for cause.[26] The fact that counsel may have peremptorily challenged the member is not a sufficient to reverse a conviction.[27] The court concluded that defense had failed to ask the question which might have revealed the member's past conduct.[28]

In the process of answering voir dire questions, disclaimers by the court members are not unusual.[29] Even if they are sincere, other facts made known at trial may raise a question of bias, or "implied" bias.[30]

On the other hand, a candid admission by a member that a possible bias or predisposition exists will not result in an automatic removal from the court.[31] For example, in *United States v. Heroit,*[32] the court indicated that a military judge may ask additional questions, or give additional instructions, in a reasonable attempt to rehabilitate the member.[33] If the member retracts an inflexible attitude in a clear and forthright manner, the judge may deny a challenge for cause.[34] Otherwise, the member should be excused.

---

25. *Id.*
26. *Id.*
27. *Id.*
28. *Id.*
29. United States v. Harris, 13 M.J. 288 (C.M.A. 1982) (judge erred in denying challenge for cause of member who was the president, was rater for three other members, and had both a personal and official interest in the case). *Cf.* United States v. Watson, 15 M.J. 784 (A.C.M.R. 1983) (familiarity with accused's past misconduct is not per se a ground for challenge).
30. *See, e.g.,* United States v. Abdelkader, 34 M.J. 605 (A.F.C.M.R. 1992) (court member's perfunctory disclaimer of bias, no matter how sincere, was not enough to remedy a disqualification); United States v. Smart, 21 M.J. 15, 19-20 (C.M.A. 1985); United States v. Carns, 27 M.J. 820 (A.C.M.R. 1988) (concurring in the result, Judge Holdaway observed that when an officer in the Army solemnly states that he will not be biased or predisposed, his word should not lightly be disregarded).
31. United States v. Mack, 41 M.J. 51 (C.M.A. 1994) (court ordered DuBay hearing on whether court member deliberately withheld information that he had been victim of crime during voir dire); United States v. Reynolds, 23 M.J. 292 (C.M.A. 1987) (judge did not abuse his discretion in denying challenges against two members who said they were inclined to be tougher on barracks thieves but expressed a willingness to keep open minds and consider all of the evidence presented; court said that the question of bias is "largely one of demeanor"). *Cf.* United States v. Taylor, 41 M.J. 701 (A.F.Ct.Crim.App. 1995) (in absence of false answers during voir dire or showing of other prejudice, court would not grant relief to accused who showed that president who sat on his case was later convicted of indecent acts). *See generally* McShane, "Questioning and Challenging the 'Brutally' Honest Court Member: Voir Dire in Light of *Smart* and *Heroit*," ARMY LAW., Jan. 1986, at 17.
32. 21 M.J. 11 (C.M.A. 1985) (inflexible attitude on sentencing).
33. *Id.* at 13. United States v. Mayes, 28 M.J. 748 (A.F.C.M.R. 1989) (judge may use leading questions to rehabilitate a challenged member).
34. *Id.* at 14. United States v. Mayes, 28 M.J. 748 (A.F.C.M.R. 1989) (member indicated that he could put aside his general bias against retention and rehabilitation of drug abusers); United States v. Hayden, 17 M.J. 749 (A.C.M.R. 1984) ("inelastic attitude" exists where member's predisposition will not yield to evidence and judge's instructions).

§ 15-10(B). Grounds for Challenging Court Members.

Military practice generally recognizes fourteen disqualifying grounds for court members.[35] Several are listed in the U.C.M.J., while most are noted in the *Manual*. Combined and summarized, they are as follows:

(1) Not competent to serve;[36]
(2) Not properly detailed to the court;[37]
(3) The member was the accuser;[38]
(4) Is a witness;[39]
(5) Served as an investigating officer;[40]
(6) Acted as a counsel for the prosecution or the defense as to any offense charged;[41]
(7) Served as a member of original court on rehearing or new trial;[42]
(8) Is junior in rank or grade to the accused;[43]
(9) Forwarded charges with recommendations for disposition;[44]
(10) Has formed or expressed a positive opinion of the accused's guilt or innocence;[45]

---

35. R.C.M. 912(f)(1).
36. Art. 25, U.C.M.J. R.C.M. 912(f)(1)(A). *See also* § 8-3(C). This includes service by commissioned officers, warrant officers, and a direction that enlisted court members should not be from the accused's unit.
37. R.C.M. 912(f)(1)(B). *See* § 8-3(C).
38. Art. 25(d)(2), U.C.M.J. R.C.M. 912(f)(1)(C). *See* United States v. Miller, 19 M.J. 159 (C.M.A. 1985) (spirit of Art. 25(d)(2) violated where accuser talked to members).
39. Art. 25(d)(2), U.C.M.J. R.C.M. 912(f)(1)(D). "Witness" includes any person whose declaration is admitted for any purpose. *See* R.C.M. 912(i)(2).
See, e.g., United States v. Towers, 24 M.J. 143 (C.M.A. 1987), where court held that a court member who had extensive civilian experience as a social services counselor was not per se disqualified from sitting in a child abuse trial. United States v. Perez, 36 M.J. 1198 (N.M.C.M.R. 1993) (member who was eyewitness to incident should have been excused for cause; court noted that R.C.M. 912 indicates that a member who appears to be disqualified "shall" be excused; public at large would view participation of member-witness as being unfair). *Cf.* United States v. Conley, 4 M.J. 327 (C.M.A. 1978) (trial judge disqualified from sitting where he possessed some expertise in handwriting, which was in issue at trial); United States v. Mansell, 8 C.M.A. 153, 23 C.M.R. 377 (1957).
40. Art. 25(d)(2), U.C.M.J. R.C.M. 912(f)(1)(F). *See also* United States v. Burkhalter, 17 C.M.A. 266, 38 C.M.R. 64 (1967).
41. Art. 25(d)(2), U.C.M.J. R.C.M. 912(f)(1)(E). United States v. Hurt, 8 C.M.A. 224, 24 C.M.R. 34 (1957) (member had served as defense counsel); United States v. Zamarripa, 1 C.M.R. 432 (A.B.R. 1951) (trial counsel).
42. R.C.M. 912(f)(1)(J). There do not appear to be any reported cases on this point.
43. Art. 25(d)(1), U.C.M.J. R.C.M. 912(f)(1)(K). A member may be junior to the accused if it cannot be avoided. United States v. Schneider, 38 M.J. 387 (C.M.A. 1993) (court member was junior to accused; court declined to decide whether defense's delay in disclosing that point to the judge until after findings amounted to waiver; there was no possibility that accused was prejudiced).
44. R.C.M. 912(f)(1)(I). *See, e.g.*, United States v. Lake, 36 M.J. 317 (C.M.A. 1993) (member's routine official involvement as signer of charge sheets did not create substantial doubt about impartiality or fairness); United States v. Strawbridge, 21 C.M.R. 482 (A.B.R. 1955).
45. R.C.M. 912(f)(1)(M). United States v. Coppock, 37 M.J. 145 (C.M.A. 1993) (citing R.C.M. 912(f)(1)(N), court held that although two members had expressed prejudgment of accused's guilt,

(11) Acted as legal officer, staff judge advocate, or convening authority in the case;[46]

(12) Will act as legal officer, staff judge advocate, or convening authority on review of the case;[47]

(13) Is in arrest or confinement;[48] or

(14) Demonstrates other facts showing personal interest or bias. This category is potentially broad and seems to generate the most litigation. It could include religious[49] or racial[50] bias; an inelastic attitude toward a particular sentence,[51] sentencing in general,[52] or an inclination to impose a harsher or lighter sentence for a particular offense;[53] expressing a per-

---

they had not formed opinion on appropriate sentence; not abuse of discretion to deny challenges for cause where members were only seated for purposes of sentencing).

46. R.C.M. 912(f)(1)(G). *See, e.g.,* United States v. Masminster, 7 C.M.R. 593 (A.F.B.R. 1952) (GCM CA appointed himself to court).

47. R.C.M. 912(f)(1)(H). The reported cases on this disqualification have generally centered on the military judge's, or law officer's, ability to serve. *See, e.g.,* United States v. Turner, 9 C.M.A. 124, 25 C.M.R. 386 (1958).

48. R.C.M. 912(f)(1)(L). *See* Chapter 5.

49. *See, e.g.,* United States v. Grittman, 16 C.M.R. 328 (A.B.R. 1954) (prejudice against Jehovah's Witnesses); United States v. Credit, 2 M.J. 631 (A.F.C.M.R. 1976); United States v. Walbert, 32 C.M.R. 945 (A.F.B.R. 1963).

50. Ham v. South Carolina, 409 U.S. 524 (1973); United States v. Parker, 6 C.M.A. 274, 19 C.M.R. 400 (1955); United States v. Credit, 2 M.J. 631 (A.F.C.M.R. 1976).

51. United States v. McLaren, 38 M.J. 112 (C.M.A. 1993) (no abuse of discretion to deny challenge for cause for member who initially indicated that he could not consider a "no punishment" sentence, considering the offenses charged); United States v. Bannwarth, 36 M.J. 265 (C.M.A. 1993) (cumulative effect of member's attitude toward punitive discharge for drug offense, supervisory relationship to another member, and close friendship with accuser was not sufficient to disqualify member).

United States v. Gray, 37 M.J. 730 (A.C.M.R. 1992) (trial judge properly granted government's challenge for cause against two members who opposed death penalty); United States v. Barrios, 31 M.J. 750 (A.C.M.R. 1990) (error not to remove member who expressed inelastic attitude on punitive discharge even after trial counsel attempted to rehabilitate him); United States v. Curtis, 28 M.J. 1074 (N.M.C.M.R. 1989) (en banc) (no abuse of discretion in granting prosecution's challenge for cause against member who stated that upbringing and religious beliefs would preclude him from imposing death penalty in a capital case); United States v. Blevins, 27 M.J. 678 (A.C.M.R. 1988) (trial judge correctly denied challenge to member who initially stated that he would not consider the option of "no punishment" but who later rehabilitated himself by stating that he would listen to all of the evidence).

52. United States v. Heroit, 21 M.J. 11 (C.M.A. 1985) (member initially expressed inelastic attitude about sentencing); United States v. Cosgrove, 1 M.J. 199 (C.M.A. 1975); United States v. Karnes, 1 M.J. 92 (C.M.A. 1975); United States v. Tucker, 16 C.M.A. 318, 36 C.M.R. 474 (1966); United States v. Fort, 16 C.M.A. 86, 36 C.M.R. 242 (1966); United States v. Davis, 29 M.J. 1004 (A.F.C.M.R. 1990) (accused waived challenges for cause against members who admitted inelastic attitude toward sentencing); United States v. Collins, 29 M.J. 778 (A.C.M.R. 1989) (challenge should have been sustained against member who indicated cynical and cavalier attitude toward rehabilitation).

53. *See, e.g.,* United States v. Dale, 42 M.J. 384 (1995) (member's concern about lenient sentence for child abuser in civilian case not disqualifying); United States v. Curtis, 33 M.J. 101 (C.M.A. 1991) (trial judge properly granted prosecutor's challenge for cause against member who expressed reservations about imposing death penalty); United States v. Mayes, 28 M.J. 748 (C.M.A. 1989) (member initially expressed general bias against retention of drug abusers); United States v. Reynolds, 23 M.J. 292 (C.M.A. 1987) (no abuse of discretion in retaining two

§ 15-10(B)   TRIAL PROCEDURES   § 15-10(B)

sonal interest in the case;[54] relationships with other members of the court,[55] the prosecutors,[56] a witness in the trial,[57] the Convening Author-

---

members who expressed inclination to be tougher on barracks thieves. The court noted that bias is largely a question of demeanor and the trial judge is in a better position to judge possible bias of a member. The court also stated that neither side is entitled to a commitment from the members on what they will ultimately do in the case); United States v. Small, 21 M.J. 218 (C.M.A. 1986); United States v. Lenoir, 13 M.J. 452 (C.M.A. 1982) (sentence rehearing required where challenge improperly denied).

United States v. Stewart, 33 M.J. 519 (A.F.C.M.R. 1991) (members saw nothing wrong with order to accused to refrain from drinking alcohol); United States v. Armstrong, 30 M.J. 769 (A.C.M.R. 1990) (court member's distaste for particular type of offense does not per se create disqualifying bias; member's inclination to believe child witnesses was not disqualifying); United States v. Yardley, 24 M.J. 719 (A.C.M.R. 1987) (member's abhorrence of offense of sexual offense on minor was not per se disqualifying; voir dire showed that the member's "emotions would force him to be a 'little tougher' on sentencing but that, he could 'take cognizance' of his emotions"; court noted that under similar facts and circumstances it could ask no more of any Army officer); United States v. Rojas, 15 M.J. 902 (N.M.C.M.R. 1983) (no inelastic attitude re death sentence); United States v. Stennis, 12 M.J. 813 (N.M.C.M.R. 1981) (inelastic attitude towards sentencing on larceny charges); United States v. Goodman, 3 M.J. 1106 (N.C.M.R. 1977) (member felt that drug sale warranted punitive discharge).

54. United States v. Carns, 27 M.J. 820 (A.C.M.R. 1988) (member who took personal as well as professional interest in reducing number of bad checks was not disqualified to sit in trial on bad check charges).

55. United States v. White, 36 M.J. 284 (C.M.A. 1992) (member's position as another member's superior, and rater, was not per se disqualifying); United States v. Bannwarth, 35 M.J. 265 (C.M.A. 1992) (cumulative effect of member's attitude toward punitive discharge for drug offense, supervisory relationship to another member, and close friendship with accuser was not sufficient to disqualify member); United States v. Blocker, 32 M.J. 281 (C.M.A. 1991) (fact that two colonels were involved in rating two different enlisted members did not require their removal; judge was not required to sua sponte inquire into that relationship); United States v. Murphy, 26 M.J. 454 (C.M.A. 1988) (court rejected a per se disqualification of members who were either raters of, or rated by, other court members; court distinguished earlier cases by noting that in those cases in which raters were present in the court, they were disqualified from participating by multiple factors and not simply because they were raters. In his separate opinion, Chief Judge Everett noted that the issue of per se disqualification should be left to each service appellate court).

United States v. Abdelkader, 34 M.J. 605 (A.F.C.M.R. 1992) (trial court erred in denying challenge of member who was installation's vice wing commander, reviewed performance reports of other members, and had prior information about the case through briefings).

United States v. Garcia, 26 M.J. 844 (A.C.M.R. 1988) (court rejected per se rule but indicated that relationship of members should be explored during voir dire; fact that two senior members were raters for two other officers did not provide sufficient cause for removal from court). See also United States v. Harris, 13 M.J. 288 (C.M.A. 1982).

United States v. Eberhardt, 24 M.J. 944 (A.C.M.R. 1987) (the panel consisted of several members who rated other members; court rejected a per se approach and noted that at a small installation it would be extremely difficult to find members who were not in some way connected by the rating process. Nonetheless, trial judge had erred in not excluding a member who was rated by another member and whose wife had been the victim of assault).

56. United States v. Hamilton, 41 M.J. 22 (C.M.A. 1994) (court members who had received legal assistance from assistant trial counsel not disqualified; judge later sustained challenge to president of court who had lengthy discussion with same counsel at officer's club); United States v. Porter, 17 M.J. 377 (C.M.A. 1984) (no implied bias where challenged member was running associate of prosecutor and had been previous victim of larceny).

57. United States v. Lake, 36 M.J. 317 (C.M.A. 1993) (commanding officer of government witness not per se disqualified); United States v. Berry, 34 M.J. 83 (C.M.A. 1992) (petty officer with law enforcement duties knew and on occasion had worked with a special agent who was a

§ 15-10(B)　　　　　MILITARY CRIMINAL JUSTICE　　　　　§ 15-10(B)

ity,[58] the Staff Judge Advocate,[59] someone in the accused's chain of command,[60] or other participants to the trial.[61] The disqualification could also extend to members who have knowledge of the case or evidence;[62] or have had discussions with the convening authority,[63] the accuser,[64] staff judge

---

critical witness in the case); United States v. Huitt, 25 M.J. 136 (C.M.A. 1987) (court members who were casual and social acquaintances with father of one of sexual assault victims was not disqualifying); United States v. Lauzon, 21 M.J. 791 (A.C.M.R. 1986) (no abuse of discretion in denying challenge where court member's children were patients of prosecution witness).

58. United States v. Lake, 36 M.J. 317 (C.M.A. 1993) (merely signing for charge sheet on behalf of summary court-martial convening authority not per se disqualifying); United States v. Thomas, 43 M.J. 550 (N.M.Ct.Crim.App.1995) (fact that member was on convening authority's staff and worked with him on daily basis was not ground for challenge); United States v. Tompkins, 30 M.J. 1090 (N.M.C.M.R. 1989) (no abuse of discretion in denying challenge to member who was second most senior officer on staff of convening authority, who had read through correspondence addressed to staff relating to accused; member gave assurance that he would remain impartial); United States v. Chollet, 30 M.J. 1079 (C.G.C.M.R. 1990) (no abuse of discretion to deny challenge against member who was rated by convening authority, was a rater and supervisor for another court member, had prior knowledge of accused's urinalysis, and had close personal relationship with convening authority; accused eventually used peremptory challenge against the member).

59. United States v. Glenn, 25 M.J. 278 (C.M.A. 1987) (reversible error for acting staff judge advocate not to advise participants that his sister-in-law was member of court, thus precluding inquiry into possible bias of member).

60. United States v. Guthrie, 25 M.J. 808 (A.C.M.R 1988) (member not disqualified because he was close friend of accused's company commander, had a degree in criminology, and whose family had suffered effects of relative with a drug problem).

61. United States v. Huitt, 25 M.J. 136 (C.M.A. 1987) (court members who were casual and social acquaintances with father of one of sexual assault victims was not disqualifying).

62. United States v. Donley, 33 M.J. 44 (C.M.A. 1991) (fact that member had inadvertently overheard inadmissible statements did not render him unqualified to sit on case); United States v. Jobson, 31 M.J. 117 (C.M.A. 1990) (fact that member learned inadvertently of pretrial agreement was not sufficient ground for removal); United States v. Coffin, 25 M.J. 32 (C.M.A. 1987) (member present in the formation during which the defendant was arrested and also knew that a urinalysis test had been performed should not have participated).

United States v. Dock, 35 M.J. 627 (A.C.M.R. 1992) (no error in denying challenge for cause against president of court who had seen artist's sketch of accused in Stars and Stripes and had mentioned retrial); United States v. Abdelkader, 34 M.J. 605 (A.F.C.M.R. 1992) (trial court erred in denying challenge of member who was installation's vice wing commander, reviewed performance reports of other members, and had prior information about the case through briefings); United States v. Sloan, 30 M.J. 741 (A.F.C.M.R. 1990) (members who heard rumors about case were not per se disqualified; there was no evidence that rumors led members to conclude that accused was guilty); United States v. Baum, 30 M.J. 626 (N.M.C.M.R. 1990) (court erred in not removing member who had attended accused's Article 32 investigation and had spoken with NIS investigator and another member who had official interest; he believed that he was in a law enforcement billet); United States v. Carns, 27 M.J. 820 (A.C.M.R. 1988) (member who was aware of accused's uncharged misconduct and a member who had working relationship with superior officer who was a government witness were not disqualified to serve); United States v. Arnold, 26 M.J. 965 (A.C.M.R. 1988) (reversible error not to grant challenge for cause to member who had earlier heard government witness testify at previous trial, he admitted that he found her credible, and the case turned on credibility of witnesses; the court noted that merely having heard testimony from a witness was not in itself disqualifying); United States v. Paige, 23 M.J. 512 (A.F.C.M.R. 1986) (court member knew that absent defense witness was lying about reasons for absence).

63. United States v. Ennis, 15 M.J. 970 (A.C.M.R. 1983) (any member who has discussed the case with the CA, no matter how briefly, should not remain on the court). See generally Note, "United States v. Brice: Command Policy or Command Influence," 33 JAG J. 133 (Summer 1984).

64. United States v. Miller, 19 M.J. 159 (C.M.A. 1985) (the spirit of Art. 25(d)(2) was violated

§ 15-10(B)   TRIAL PROCEDURES   § 15-10(B)

advocate,[65] counsel,[66] or others involved in the case;[67] about the case. Similarly, a member may be disqualified because the member has prior experience as a victim of crime;[68] special expertise or experience;[69] an

---

when the accuser directly communicated with two members of the court); United States v. Bannwarth, 36 M.J. 265 (C.M.A. 1993) (cumulative effect of member's attitude toward punitive discharge for drug offense, supervisory relationship to another member, and close friendship with accuser was not sufficient to disqualify member).

65. United States v. Millender, 27 M.J. 568 (A.C.M.R. 1988) (judge did not abuse discretion in denying challenges for cause against court member who had two contacts with members of SJA office but neither contact resulted in any substantive information being transmitted to member).

66. *Id.* United States v. Ingham, 36 M.J. 990 (A.C.M.R. 1993) (member who was special court-martial convening authority had close professional relationship with trial counsel; no actual or implied bias shown).

67. United States v. Lake, 36 M.J. 317 (C.M.A. 1993) (member was company commander of accused's girlfriend); United States v. White, 36 M.J. 284 (C.M.A. 1993) (innocuous lunch with one of the witnesses was not per se disqualifying); United States v. Elmore, 33 M.J. 387 (C.M.A. 1991) (inadvertent one-hour contact between members and expert witness who later testified did not taint the proceedings where the case was not discussed and members had not formed any strong impressions about witness; prosecution therefore rebutted presumption of prejudice that arises from communications between members and witness); United States v. Brice, 19 M.J. 170 (C.M.A. 1985) (mistrial was in order when the court members were excused during the accused's court-martial on drug charges to hear a lecture by the commandant on the topic of drugs in the military).

68. United States v. Brown, 34 M.J. 105 (C.M.A. 1992) (member in sodomy case not disqualified because son had been victim of homosexual assault; member discussed assault and indicated he could remain impartial); United States v. Reichardt, 28 M.J. 113 (C.M.A. 1989) (accused not entitled to challenge member who had been victim of similar crime); United States v. Smart, 21 M.J. 15 (C.M.A. 1985) (abuse of discretion in not granting challenges to two members who had previously been victims of robbery).

The fact that a member has been a victim is not per se disqualifying. United States v. Porter, 17 M.J. 377 (C.M.A. 1984) (larceny victim not disqualified in a robbery case); United States v. Basnight, 29 M.J. 838 (A.C.M.R. 1989) (court did not err in denying challenge for cause in larceny case against court member who had been victim of two larcenies and whose elderly parents had been victims of three larcenies; ruling was proper in light of his candor and statement that he would consider whole range of punishments); United States v. Campbell, 26 M.J. 970 (A.C.M.R. 1988) (member who had been victim of four separate larcenies akin to barracks larcenies and who gave equivocal answers should have been removed); United States v. Smith, 25 M.J. 785 (A.C.M.R. 1988) (not error to deny challenges for cause where two members had been victims of multiple crimes).

United States v. Barrow, 42 M.J. 655 (A.F.Ct.Crim.App. 1995) (not abuse of discretion to deny challenges to two members who had close relatives who had been victims of child abuse; court noted that issue of implied bias was close call); United States v. Kelley, 40 M.J. 515 (A.C.M.R. 1994) (abuse of discretion not to grant challenge to member whose sister had been rape victim; court noted that once member implies bias the judge should probe further; here, the record was cold on that point); United States v. Nelson, 35 M.J. 716 (N.M.C.M.R. 1992) (member not disqualified in rape case even though his daughter had been rape victim; court member forthrightly stated that her case would not affect his determination).

United States v. Inman, 20 M.J. 773 (A.C.M.R. 1985) (fact that court member in rape trial had in an unrelated incident been the victim of an attempted rape was not automatically disqualifying); United States v. Klingensmith, 17 M.J. 814 (A.C.M.R. 1984) (member's wife had been victim of harassing phone calls; any bias so held was shared by all law-abiding citizens); United States v. Yarborough, 14 M.J. 968 (A.C.M.R. 1982) (husband of assault victim not disqualified in case involving indecent assault).

69. United States v. White, 36 M.J. 284 (C.M.A. 1993) (member who had technical expertise in

inclination not to follow the judge's instructions;[70] holds a law enforcement position,[71] or other factors[72] that would cast doubt on the impartiality of the court.[73]

---

recruiting was not disqualified from serving in case involving fraudulent enlistments); United States v. Towers, 24 M.J. 143 (C.M.A. 1987) (court held that a convening authority could properly consider a court member's prior "experience" as a social services counselor in assigning her to a child abuse case). This case is troublesome. It is difficult to imagine a more dangerous situation of creating at least the appearance of evil in appointing someone to a court with the amount of experience this particular member possessed. The court acknowledged in a footnote that experience is a two-edged sword which may work either to the benefit or detriment of the accused. In either case, that experience denies either the prosecution or the defense of an impartial court member.

United States v. Combs, 35 M.J. 820 (A.F.C.M.R. 1992) (member's casual conversations with wife who ran child care center, concerning child abuse, was not disqualifying in murder and abuse of children). At least one court has recognized the dangers lurking in the appointment of individuals whose experience gives the appearance of evil. United States v. Ladell, 30 M.J. 672 (A.F.C.M.R. 1990) (member's knowledge of the Spanish language did not disqualify him in case where one of the witnesses needed an interpreter to testify, and he asked the witness to speak up so that he could hear what she was telling the interpreter); United States v. Allen, 29 M.J. 1002 (A.F.C.M.R. 1990) (extensive experience with Girl Scouts and Brownies was not disqualifying in child abuse case; court noted that it would be sad if the law were to automatically disqualify those who volunteer their time to worthwhile activities).

70. United States v. Hawks, 19 M.J. 736 (A.F.C.M.R. 1984) (judge abused discretion in not granting challenge for cause of court member who had ignored earlier instructions not to consult with outside sources during trial).

71. United States v. Dale, 42 M.J. 384 (1995) (court should have excused deputy chief of base security from court; court noted that law enforcement officers are not per se disqualified); United States v. Berry, 34 M.J. 83 (C.M.A. 1992) (petty officer was former NIS undercover agent who had recently been assigned to combat drug use; court noted that this factor in itself was not disqualifying); United States v. Dale, 39 M.J. 503 (A.F.C.M.R. 1993) (not error not to exclude security police officer); United States v. McDavid, 37 M.J. 861 (A.F.C.M.R. 1993) (not error to deny challenge for cause to security police officer; he was not assigned to security police squadron on installation and had no law enforcement duties); United States v. Swagger, 16 M.J. 759 (A.C.M.R. 1983) (appearance of evil where provost marshal was president of accused's court-martial; court said that individuals assigned to military police duties should not be appointed to court).

72. The list is nonexhaustive and in any given case more than one of the listed grounds for challenge may be present. *See, e.g.,* United States v. Chollet, 30 M.J. 1079 (C.G.C.M.R. 1990) (multiple grounds).

73. R.C.M. 912(f)(14). United States v. Coppock, 37 M.J. 145 (C.M.A. 1993) (citing R.C.M. 912(f)(1)(N), court held that although two members had been exposed to pretrial coverage of case and expressed prejudgment of accused, they indicated that they had not formed opinion on appropriate sentence; judge did not abuse discretion in denying challenges for cause where members were only seated for purposes of sentencing); United States v. Berry, 34 M.J. 83 (C.M.A. 1992) (in the aggregate, petty officer with law enforcement duties, who knew and on occasion had worked with a special agent who was a critical witness in the case, was disqualified to sit as member); United States v. McQueen, 7 M.J. 281 (C.M.A. 1979) (mere predisposition or abstract bias will not suffice); United States v. Evans, 37 M.J. 867 (A.F.C.M.R. 1993) (members not disqualified simply because commander had issued policy statement registering strong policy against drug offenses); United States v. Anderson, 23 M.J. 894 (A.C.M.R. 1987) (challenge of court member who stated on voir dire that he believed the accused had something to prove should have been sustained); United States v. Carfang, 19 M.J. 739 (A.F.C.M.R. 1984) (member who was deputy base commander was not automatically disqualified). *See also* United States v. Dawdy, 17 M.J. 523 (A.F.C.M.R. 1983).

The accused may waive grounds (2) through (14) by failing to exercise a challenge.[74] But ground (1) may not be waived.[75] Waiver also may be accomplished by either affirmatively declining to challenge the member[76] or by pleading guilty.[77] Also note that these disqualifications may also apply to the military judge.[78]

§ 15-10(C). Challenges of Court Members.

In military practice, each side is entitled to an unlimited number of challenges for cause[79] and one peremptory challenge per accused.[80] In addition, the defense may challenge the selection process used to detail the members.[81] This subsection addresses these three forms of challenging the court members and the applicable rules for each.

§ 15-10(C)(1). Challenge of the Selection Process.

The military does not recognize a "challenge to the array" that is often used in civilian practice. But defense counsel may obtain the same result by challenging the selection process through a motion to stay the proceedings until members are properly selected.[82] Article 41, U.C.M.J. specifically states that the "military judge ... may not receive a challenge to more than one member at a time."[83] A challenge to the selection process technically is not a multiple challenge of the individual members but rather is a challenge to the criteria or procedures used by the convening authority. It is possible that all of the detailed members are otherwise qualified to serve on the court.

---

74. R.C.M. 912(f)(4). *See also* United States v. Lovejoy, 39 C.M.R. 774 (A.B.R. 1968).
75. R.C.M. 912(f)(4).
76. *Id.* United States v. Lake, 36 M.J. 317 (C.M.A. 1993) (accused waived challenges by failing to conduct voir dire and challenge members even though he was not aware of possible grounds of challenge until later in trial; the court indicated that the claim of unfairness dissipates if counsel could have discovered grounds during voir dire); United States v. Beer, 6 C.M.A. 180, 19 C.M.R. 306 (1955).
77. *Cf.* United States v. Lackey, 22 C.M.R. 384 (A.B.R. 1956) (challenges to the partiality of a member on sentencing would not be waived; United States v. McBride, 6 C.M.A. 430, 20 C.M.R. 146 (1955)); United States v. Lake, 36 M.J. 317 (C.M.A. 1993) (list not exhaustive).
78. *See* §§ 4-15(A) and 8-3(A).
79. Art. 41, U.C.M.J.
80. *Id.;* R.C.M. 912(g)(1). Attempt to expand the number of peremptory challenges is error. United States v. Calley, 46 C.M.R. 1131 (A.C.M.R. 1973), aff'd, 22 C.M.A. 534, 48 C.M.R. 19 (1973); United States v. Demeio, 15 M.J. 523 (A.C.M.R. 1982) (error to grant one additional challenge per side). *Cf.* United States v. Harris, 13 M.J. 288 (C.M.A. 1982) (Everett, C.J., dissenting).
81. R.C.M. 912(b). *See also* United States v. Young, 49 C.M.R. 133 (A.F.C.M.R. 1974). Another tack is to challenge the selection process through a motion to dismiss on jurisdictional grounds. *Cf.* United States v. Packer, 8 M.J. 785 (N.C.M.R. 1980).
82. R.C.M. 912(b). In the past, motions for appropriate relief have been used for the same purpose. *See* United States v. Daigle, 1 M.J. 139 (C.M.A. 1975).
83. United States v. Dupree, 45 C.M.R. 456 (A.F.C.M.R. 1972). *See also* United States v. Montgomery, 16 M.J. 516 (A.C.M.R. 1983) (accused's challenge to entire panel was treated as individual challenge to each member).

The defense should be prepared initially to make its challenge through an offer of proof and if it appears that an impropriety exists, the judge should permit further evidence.[84] As noted in § 15-10(A), the defense may be entitled to written materials used during the selection process and in some cases those materials will serve as the basis for the challenge. In other cases it may be necessary to call individuals involved in the selection process, including the convening authority.[85]

This sort of challenge to the entire court may be appropriate where, for example, the convening authority has rejected consideration of an entire class of individuals.[86] Rather than ordering the convening authority to detail a new court, a questionable tactic, the military judge may accomplish the same result by ruling that the trial may not proceed with the detailed panel of members. This approach is similar to abating a trial until a requested defense witness is produced.[87] The defense bears the burden of proof[88] and failure to challenge the selection process may waive the issue[89] unless the court is jurisdictionally defective.[90]

---

84. R.C.M. 912(b). United States v. Curtis, 28 M.J. 1074 (N.M.C.M.R. 1989) (en banc) (defense called expert witness to testify that officers on court could not be objective because they would more readily identify with the officer-murder victim; the court concluded that the expert's "concern" regarding partiality was insufficient to dismiss the members).
United States v. McCall, 26 M.J. 804 (A.C.M.R. 1988) (trial judge should have granted defense challenge to court where offer of proof and evidence showed that two members had been selected by someone other than the convening authority); United States v. Hodge, 26 M.J. 596 (A.C.M.R. 1988) (counsel's offer of proof should contain names and addresses of witnesses on the motion, a summary of their expected testimony, and advise the court that counsel is prepared to call those witnesses); United States v. Chavira, 25 M.J. 705 (A.C.M.R. 1987) (judge's actions in suggesting to trial counsel in *ex parte* discussion to get a new panel because he was concerned about the impartiality of the members was harmless error; he should have raised it either in an R.C.M. 802 conference or at an Article 39(a) session).
85. This may disqualify the convening authority from reviewing the case. See § 17-8(B).
86. See § 8-3(C). United States v. Hilow, 32 M.J. 439 (C.M.A. 1991); United States v. Lynch, 35 M.J. 579 (C.G.C.M.R. 1992) (accused not denied due process by selection of officers who had significant seagoing experience; not improper to select members who have particular experience); United States v. Noxon, 30 M.J. 1210 (A.C.M.R. 1990) (convening authority did not act improperly in selecting only high-ranking NCOs); (selection of members by convening authority tainted where officer charged with preparing list of nominees for court attempted to "stack" the court); United States v. Curtis, 28 M.J. 1074 (N.M.C.M.R. 1989) (en banc) (defense unsuccessfully attempted to have members dismissed on theory that as officers they would more readily identify with the officer-murder victim).
United States v. Hodge, 26 M.J. 596 (A.C.M.R. 1988) (accused, a black servicemember, did not have a right to have black servicemembers appointed to court and failed to establish that black personnel had intentionally been excluded from the court).
87. See § 11-2(A).
88. United States v. McLaughlin, 27 M.J. 685 (A.C.M.R. 1988) (convening authority's actions are presumed to be regular and defense must show violation of Article 25 by clear and convincing evidence); United States v. James, 24 M.J. 894 (A.C.M.R. 1987) (noting that the selection process is presumed legal, the court ruled that the accused had failed to establish that the convening authority had systematically excluded junior officers); United States v. Townsend, 12 M.J. 861 (A.F.C.M.R. 1981) (defense bears burden of showing improper selection process). *Cf.* United States v. Beehler, 35 M.J. 502 (A.F.C.M.R. 1992) (once defense raises issue, burden shifts to government to show by clear and positive evidence that no impropriety occurred).
89. R.C.M. 912(b)(3). United States v. Benoit, 21 M.J. 579 (A.C.M.R. 1985).
90. *Id.* See §§ 4-13 *et seq.* and 8-3.

§ 15-10(C)(2). Challenges for Cause.

Military case law has forged a number of rules governing challenges for cause:

First, the accused has the right to be tried by court members who are free from outside influence.[91]

Second, the challenging party has the burden of proof and must "raise the contention of bias from the realm of speculation to the realm of fact."[92]

Third, challenges for cause should be liberally granted.[93]

Fourth, reversal is appropriate only if the judge clearly abused his discretion in denying a challenge.[94]

Fifth, the possibility of delay while new members are detailed is insufficient cause to deny a challenge for cause.[95]

---

91. United States v. Glenn, 25 M.J. 278 (C.M.A. 1987) (impartiality should not be reasonably open to question); United States v. Brice, 19 M.J. 170 (C.M.A. 1985) (members heard lecture by commandant on topic of drug abuse); United States v. Miller, 19 M.J. 159 (C.M.A. 1985) (accuser spoke with members); United States v. Almeida, 19 M.J. 874 (A.F.C.M.R. 1985) (private conversations between a witness and the court members create a rebuttable presumption of prejudice); United States v. Hawks, 19 M.J. 736 (A.F.C.M.R. 1984); United States v. Ennis, 15 M.J. 970 (A.C.M.R. 1983) (CA discussed case with member).

92. United States v. Dennis, 339 U.S. 162, 168 (1950); R.C.M. 912(f)(3). *See also* United States v. Dawdy, 17 M.J. 523 (A.F.C.M.R. 1983) (appellate courts will not permit defense to create challenge where one does not exist in reality).

93. United States v. White, 36 M.J. 284 (C.M.A. 1993) (court noted that the direction to trial judges to liberally grant challenges for cause is not inconsistent with the view that the appellate courts will defer to the decision to deny the challenge); United States v. Keenan, 39 M.J. 1050 (A.C.M.R. 1994) (liberality does not include challenges which are purely speculative or clearly have no merit); United States v. Glenn, 25 M.J. 278 (C.M.A. 1987) (because there is only one peremptory challenge, challenges for cause should be liberally granted). *Cf.* United States v. Guthrie, 25 M.J. 808 (A.C.M.R. 1988) (although challenges should be liberally granted, judge's decision to deny should be given "special deference" because he is in a position to observe demeanor and judge credibility of member); United States v. Smart, 21 M.J. 15 (C.M.A. 1985); United States v. Miller, 19 M.J. 159 (C.M.A. 1985); United States v. Porter, 17 M.J. 377 (C.M.A. 1984); United States v. Harris, 13 M.J. 288 (C.M.A. 1982).

94. United States v. Smart, 21 M.J. 15 (C.M.A. 1985); United States v. Boyd, 7 M.J. 282 (C.M.A. 1979); United States v. McQueen, 7 M.J. 281 (C.M.A. 1979); United States v. Keenan, 39 M.J. 1050 (A.C.M.R. 1994) (denial of challenge should not be overturned unless record is clear that member had a closed mind about case); United States v. Sloan, 30 M.J. 741 (A.F.C.M.R. 1990) (court did not abuse discretion in denying challenges for cause; court noted earlier reference in *Jobson* to being liberal in granting challenges for cause).

United States v. Moyar, 24 M.J. 635 (A.C.M.R. 1987) (judge abused discretion in denying challenge for cause against member whose sister had been sexually molested under circumstances similar to those in the case; the court indicated that the judge's questioning of the member did not rehabilitate the member); United States v. Paige, 23 M.J. 512 (A.F.C.M.R. 1986) (judge erred in denying defense challenge for cause; the willingness of the prosecution to accept the risk of reversal of judge's ruling is not an "acceptable" criterion); United States v. Lauzon, 21 M.J. 791 (A.C.M.R. 1986); United States v. Cunningham, 21 M.J. 585 (A.C.M.R. 1985).

95. United States v. Smart, 21 M.J. 15 (C.M.A. 1985); United States v. Miller, 19 M.J. 519 (C.M.A. 1984); United States v. Mason, 16 M.J. 455 (C.M.A. 1983).

Sixth, it is important that the court present the image of fairness and integrity.[96]

Challenges for cause may be made at any point during the trial.[97] If a challenge for cause is denied, the defense may waive the issue by failing to exercise its peremptory challenge.[98] To protect the issue for appeal the defense need not exercise its peremptory challenge against the member unsuccessfully challenged for cause.[99] But if it does so, it should state for the record that but for the denied challenge, the peremptory challenge would have been used for another member.[100]

Although the judge may dictate the order of presenting challenges,[101] the normal procedure is as follows: prosecution challenges for cause; prosecution peremptory challenge; defense challenges for cause; and defense peremptory challenge.[102] In *United States v. Newson*,[103] the prosecution conditionally ex-

---

96. R.C.M. 912(f)(1)(N). See United States v. Swagger, 16 M.J. 759 (A.C.M.R. 1983) (appearance of evil where provost marshal was president of accused's court-martial; court said that individuals assigned to military police duties should not be appointed to court); United States v. Brown, 13 M.J. 890 (A.C.M.R. 1982); United States v. Barnes, 12 M.J. 956 (A.F.C.M.R. 1982); United States v. Cockerell, 49 C.M.R. 567 (A.C.M.R. 1974).

97. R.C.M. 912(f)(2)(B). In United States v. Nigro, 28 M.J. 415 (C.M.A. 1989), the court held that the military judge did not abuse his discretion in denying a mid-trial challenge for cause against a member who, against the judge's instructions, consulted an outside source to obtain information about the case. The court determined that the member's efforts had been futile and rejected the defense arguments that the member's failure to follow the judge's instructions established lack of impartiality.

United States v. Paige, 23 M.J. 512 (A.F.C.M.R. 1986) (challenge made during sentencing); United States v. Graham, 14 C.M.R. 645 (A.F.B.R. 1954).

98. R.C.M. 912(g)(4). See, e.g., United States v. Jobson, 31 M.J. 117 (C.M.A. 1990); United States v. Dorsey, 29 M.J. 761 (A.C.M.R. 1989) (where accused unsuccessfully challenges all members of panel, his only alternative is to request a bench trial and doing so does not waive the issue); United States v. Cooper, 8 M.J. 538 (N.C.M.R. 1979).

99. R.C.M. 912(g)(4). See, e.g., United States v. Jobson, 31 M.J. 117 (C.M.A. 1990) (summary of rules governing preserving challenges for cause vis-à-vis peremptory challenges); United States v. Downing, 17 M.J. 636 (N.M.C.M.R. 1983) (accused was forced to use a peremptory challenge when the trial judge erroneously denied two challenges for cause). See also United States v. Dawdy, 17 M.J. 523 (A.F.C.M.R. 1983).

100. R.C.M. 912(g)(4).United States v. Abdelkader, 34 M.J. 605 (A.F.C.M.R. 1992) (challenge for cause preserved when counsel stated for the record that he was using peremptory challenge against member unsuccessfully challenged but would have used it on another member if challenge had been granted); United States v. Dorsey, 29 M.J. 761 (A.C.M.R. 1989) (accused did not waive challenge for cause by requesting trial by judge alone).

In United States v. Jobson, 28 M.J. 844 (A.F.C.M.R. 1989), the court concluded that counsel had preserved the issue for appeal. But by using the peremptory challenge against a member who should have been removed for cause, counsel had purged the error. The court noted the "ancient dilemma" defense counsel face when the court denies a challenge for cause: use the sole peremptory challenge and in effect purge the error and potentially waive the issue. Cf. United States v. Moyar, 24 M.J. 635 (A.C.M.R. 1987); United States v. Anderson, 23 M.J. 894 (A.C.M.R. 1987).

United States v. Campbell, 26 M.J. 970, 971, n.1 (A.C.M.R. 1988); United States v. Eberhardt, 24 M.J. 944 (A.C.M.R. 1987) (counsel indicated that he would have used peremptory challenge on another member). Cf. United States v. Cooper, 8 M.J. 538 (N.C.M.R. 1979).

101. See United States v. Fetch, 17 C.M.R. 836 (A.B.R. 1954).
102. See Art. 41, U.C.M.J.
103. 29 M.J. 17 (C.M.A. 1989).

ercised its peremptory challenge against an enlisted member but when the accused exercised his challenge against another enlisted member, the prosecution withdrew its challenge so as to not reduce the enlisted membership below the minimum one-third. Although the court concluded that there might be situations where the judge might depart from the established procedures, in this case it was error. The court also concluded that the procedure had not prejudiced the accused by providing an "unfavorable" number of court members.

Even in the absence of a challenge for cause from either counsel, the judge may *sua sponte* excuse a member who could have been successfully challenged.[104]

§ 15-10(C)(3). Peremptory Challenges.

Peremptory challenges must normally be made before presentation of evidence,[105] although there is some authority for the proposition that a previously unexercised peremptory challenge may be made following addition or substitution of members.[106] Little or no control should be exercised over this type of challenge.[107] Where the defense has exercised its peremptory challenge and for some reason additional members are thereafter added to the court-martial, the accused is entitled to an additional peremptory challenge.[108]

In *Batson v. Kentucky*,[109] the Supreme Court indicated that a defendant might successfully challenge a prosecutor's exercise of peremptory challenges if they result in dismissal from the panel members of the defendant's race. The Court said that:

---

104. *See* R.C.M. 912(f)(4). *Cf.* United States v. Lopez, 37 M.J. 702 (A.C.M.R. 1993) (judge not required to sua sponte excuse member trial defense counsel did not challenge); United States v. Davis, 29 M.J. 1004 (A.F.C.M.R. 1990), aff'd, 33 M.J. 13 (C.M.A. 1991).

105. R.C.M. 912(g)(2).

106. *Id. See* United States v. Stevenson, 19 M.J. 760 (A.C.M.R. 1984) (judge committed prejudicial error when he denied defense counsel's peremptory challenge which he attempted to make after additional members were added). *See also* R.C.M. 912(g)(2). *Cf.* United States v. Noreen, 48 C.M.R. 228 (A.C.M.R. 1973) *and* United States v. Graham, 14 C.M.R. 645 (A.F.B.R. 1954).

107. United States v. Stevenson, 19 M.J. 760 (A.C.M.R. 1984); *cf.* United States v. Miller, 30 M.J. 960 (N.M.C.M.R. 1990) (any additional peremptory challenges are limited to newly added members).

108. United States v. Carter, 25 M.J. 471 (C.M.A. 1988), *rejecting* United States v. Holley, 17 M.J. 361 (C.M.A. 1984). In his concurring opinion, Judge Cox opined that if additional members are added the trial judge should have the discretion to provide at least one additional challenge. Part of the difficulty in this area arises from the language of Article 41, which indicates that each side has one peremptory challenge but does not specify whether that restriction would apply if new members were added or substituted to the court after the one challenge had been exercised. Note that the *Carter* opinion did not address the issue of whether the prosecution would also benefit from an additional challenge.

Cf. United States v. Banks, 29 M.J. 691 (A.C.M.R. 1989) (when member was added to defense counsel, he was entitled to exercise his additional peremptory challenge against that new member, but not against one of the original members).

109. 476 U.S. 79 (1986). *See generally* Cooper & Milhizer, "Should Preemptory Challenges Be Retained in the Military Justice System in Light of *Batson v. Kentucky* and Its Progeny?," ARMY LAW., October 1992, p. 10.

[The accused] first must show that he is a member of a cognizable racial group ... and that the prosecutor has exercised peremptory challenges to remove from the venire members of the defendant's race. Second, the defendant is entitled to rely on the fact ... that peremptory challenges constitute a jury selection practice that permits "those to discriminate who are of a mind to discriminate." ... Finally, the defendant must show that these facts and any other relevant circumstances raise an inference that the prosecutor used that practice to exclude the veniremen from the petit jury on account of their race.[110]

In *United States v. Santiago-Davila*,[111] the Court of Military Appeals, now the Court of Appeals for the Armed Forces, held that *Batson* is applicable to courts-martial. However, because the accused's trial predated *Batson*, the court ordered a *DuBay* hearing to determine the reasons for the prosecutor's peremptory challenge of the only Hispanic court member.[112]

In *United States v. Moore*,[113] the Army Court of Military Review held that the specific procedures in *Batson* are not applicable to military trials because of both legal and systemic differences between civilian and military trials. Instead the court adopted a per se rule and held that if the accused is a member of a racially identifiable group, the defense need only object[114] to the prosecutor's peremptory challenge of a court member of the same racial group, rather than establish a prima facie case of racial discrimination as required in *Batson*. The prosecutor must then provide an explanation of the challenge even though the defense provides no evidence.[115] The Court of Military Appeals thereafter in its review of *United States v. Moore*[116] adopted the per se rule for all of the services, noting:

> We do so in order to simplify this process for members of courts-martial and, more importantly, to make it fairer for the accused. In military

---

110. *Id.* at 1723, *quoting* Avery v. Georgia, 345 U.S. 559, 562 (1953).
111. 26 M.J. 380 (C.M.A. 1988).
112. Defense counsel at trial, citing People v. Wheeler, 22 Cal.3d 258, 148 Cal. Rptr. 890, 583 P.2d 748 (1978), argued that the challenge violated the accused's rights to a representative cross-section of the community when the only Hispanic was removed from the court. The Court of Military Appeals stated that a servicemember has no right to a cross-section of the community but is entitled to a panel from which no recognizable racial group has been excluded. 26 M.J. at 390.
113. 26 M.J. 692 (A.C.M.R. 1988) (en banc).
114. United States v. Shelby, 26 M.J. 921, 922, n.2 (N.M.C.M.R. 1988) (the objection to the trial counsel's peremptory challenge should be made prior to the member's departure from the courtroom in order to be timely). *See also* United States v. Erwin, 793 F.2d 656, 667 (5th Cir. 1986).
115. United States v. Curtis, 33 M.J. 101 (C.M.A. 1991) (prosecutor provided neutral reason for excluding only black member of the panel); United States v. Shelby, 26 M.J. 921 (N.M.C.M.R. 1988) (challenge of only remaining black member raised inference that prosecutor had challenged him solely on the basis of race; prosecutor, however, provided neutral reason when he explained that he had removed the member for lack of experience); United States v. St. Fort, 26 M.J. 764 (A.C.M.R. 1988) (prosecutor provided racially neutral reason); United States v. Cox, 23 M.J. 808 (N.M.C.M.R. 1986) (without deciding applicability of *Batson*, court concluded that prosecutor had provided racially neutral reason for his challenge; the member's hesitant and deliberate manner of answering counsel's questions indicated an overcautious individual who would hesitate to convict).
116. 28 M.J. 366 (C.M.A. 1989).

trials, it would be difficult to show a "pattern" of discrimination from the use of one peremptory challenge in each court-martial.... After today, every peremptory challenge by the Government of a member of the accused's race, upon objection, must be explained by trial counsel.[117]

The trial judge is then charged with determining whether the trial counsel has "articulated a neutral explanation relative to [the] particular case, giving a clear and reasonably specific explanation of legitimate reasons to challenge [the] member."[118]

Because ordinarily only two-thirds of the members must concur on findings of guilt,[119] counsel for both sides may find it advantageous to use the peremptory challenge in a "numbers game," i.e., reducing the number of members to obtain an advantageous ratio.[120] In computing the required votes, a fraction counts as one. For example, with five or six members sitting, four must vote to convict. Thus, for the defense the most advantageous number of members is 5, 8, or 11. For the prosecution it is more advantageous to have either 6, 9, or 12 members.[121]

---

117. 28 M.J. at 368.
118. 28 M.J. at 369. United States v. Greene, 36 M.J. 274 (C.M.A. 1993) (trial counsel's stated reasons for peremptory challenge of Black-Panamanian were not race-neutral in case involving black accused. Counsel indicated that he believed that member would be antagonistic to him as prosecutor and that as a Panamanian, the member would exhibit an attitude more tolerant of sexual behaviors; court addressed issue of assessing multiple reasons); United States v. Curtis, 33 M.J. 101 (C.M.A. 1991) (prosecutor's peremptory challenge of black member did not violate 14th Amendment in black accused's capital trial); United States v. Cooper, 30 M.J. 201 (C.M.A. 1990) (prosecutor's explanation for striking black court member was racially neutral: duty experience, current position, and review of personnel records); United States v. Thomas, 40 M.J. 726 (N.M.C.M.R. 1994) (member's participation in trial resulting in acquittal and demeanor in answering questions re that prior trial were sufficiently race-neutral; court noted that trial judge may consider trial counsel's credibility, trial counsel's intuition, and matters of common knowledge in community); United States v. Woods, 39 M.J. 1074 (A.C.M.R. 1994) (court member's inattentiveness was race-neutral reason for challenge); United States v. Gray, 37 M.J. 730 (A.C.M.R. 1992) (although trial judge initially indicated that prosecutor was not required to provide race-neutral reasons for challenging black member, prosecutor did so later in the trial); United States v. Lawrence, 30 M.J. 1140 (A.F.C.M.R. 1990) (trial counsel produced racially neutral reason: educational background in criminology); United States v. Chan, 30 M.J. 1028 (A.F.C.M.R. 1990) (prosecutor's reasons for challenging Hispanic member were not sufficient); United States v. Cooper, 28 M.J. 810 (A.C.M.R. 1989) (although court agreed that the prosecutor had provided sufficient reasons for peremptorily challenging a black member, it was harmless error for the judge not to place "formal findings" of that fact on the record).
119. Art. 52, U.C.M.J. A unanimous vote is required for imposition of a death penalty.
120. *See* United States v. Fletch, 17 C.M.R. 836 (A.F.B.R. 1954). *Cf.* United States v. Newson, 29 M.J. 17 (C.M.A. 1989) (court declined to "subscribe to the myth of the numbers game," and concluded that a different mix of members would not have made a difference to the accused). Whether myth or fact, there is no doubt that hundreds of counsel through the years have believed, and will continue to believe, that there is a definite tactical advantage in obtaining a favorable ratio.
121. *Cf.* United States v. Newson, 26 M.J. 719 (A.C.M.R. 1988), *aff'd*, 29 M.J. 17 (C.M.A. 1989) (court-martial is not a chess game and gamesmanship is not encouraged).

§ 15-11. Opening Statements.

Opening statements by counsel may be made immediately before presentation of the counsel's case-in-chief; defense counsel may wish to present his statement immediately after trial counsel's, and before the prosecution's case-in-chief.[1] Counsels opening statements do not constitute evidence.[2] The general proscriptions and errors found in closing arguments are equally applicable to the opening statement, e.g., counsel should not argue facts which will not be placed in evidence and counsel should not place the factfinder in the place of the victim.[3] A more complete discussion of common errors in argument is at § 15-13.

§ 15-12. Presentation of the Cases-in-Chief.

The normal order for presentation of the cases-in-chief is the same as in any other criminal trial. Following optional preliminary instructions by the judge, the prosecution presents its evidence and witnesses, the defense follows, and finally the prosecution is permitted to present rebuttal evidence.[1] The defense may move for a finding of not guilty at the conclusion of the prosecution's case or at the completion of its case, but before findings are rendered.[2] Either side may reopen its case at the discretion of the military judge.[3]

---

1. R.C.M. 913(b).
2. United States v. Turner, 39 M.J. 259 (C.M.A. 1994) (noting that members are also instructed to the effect); United States v. Clifton, 15 M.J. 29 (C.M.A. 1983).
3. *See, e.g.,* United States v. Toro, 34 M.J. 506 (A.F.C.M.R. 1991) (trial counsel's reference to fact that drug offense occurred "on your Air Force Base" was not plain error; court referred to argument as example of forensic adventurism which personalized the charges).

1. *See* R.C.M. 913(c)(1). United States v. Banks, 36 M.J. 150 (C.M.A. 1992) (judge erred as matter of law in precluding important defense rebuttal evidence to government's case); United States v. Wirth, 18 M.J. 214 (C.M.A. 1984) (relevance of government rebuttal must be determined in light of evidence and issues raised by defense); United States v. Rodriguez, 28 M.J. 1016 (A.F.C.M.R. 1989) (trial judge has broad discretion in determining whether rebuttal evidence is admissible); United States v. Hodge, 28 M.J. 883 (A.F.C.M.R. 1989) (prosecutor is entitled to strike hard, but fair, blows in rebuttal and has a right to hope that it will be "devastating").
2. See § 15-4(c) for a discussion on motions for finding of not guilty.
3. R.C.M. 913(c)(5). *See, e.g.,* United States v. Fisiorek, 43 M.J. 244 (1995) (judge erred in not permitting defense to reopen its case during deliberations when the defense learned that person could present evidence exonerating accused; in extensive discussion of issue, court concluded that trial court erroneously applied standard applicable for granting new trial); United States v. Martinsmith, 41 M.J. 343 (1995) (judge denied defense request to reopen case in response to question by court member; without deciding whether judge erred, court held that any error was substantially cured by convening authority's action); United States v. Ray, 26 M.J. 468 (C.M.A. 1988) (no abuse of discretion in permitting prosecution to reopen case after it had rested and defense presented no evidence and rested); United States v. Turner, 30 M.J. 1183 (A.F.C.M.R. 1990) (no abuse of discretion to reopen government's case to deal with court member's question; harmless error not to permit defense to reopen its case to rebut government witnesses); United States v. Walzer, 6 M.J. 856 (N.C.M.R. 1979). *See also* United States v. Kennedy, 8 C.M.A. 251, 24 C.M.R. 61 (1957); United States v. Masseria, 13 M.J. 868 (N.M.C.M.R. 1982) (judge erred in permitting prosecution to reopen after close of all evidence and final argument); United States v. Eason, 49 C.M.R. 844 (N.C.M.R. 1974).

§ 15-12(A). Examination of the Witnesses.

Rule 611, Military Rules of Evidence[4] provides the military judge with a great deal of leeway in controlling the mode and order of interrogating witnesses and presenting evidence.[5] The military judge is charged with making the interrogation effective for determining the truth, avoiding needless consumption of time, and protecting witnesses from harassment or undue embarrassment. The normal flow of examination consists of direct, cross, redirect, and recross.[6] Cross-examination is usually limited to matters raised on direct examination and matters affecting credibility, although the military judge may permit inquiry into new areas.[7] If a witness refuses to answer questions of cross-examination, the court may strike all, or portions of, the witness' direct testimony.[8]

Leading questions are normally not permitted on direct examination unless the witness is hostile or identified with the other side.[9] Although the practice may vary, the trial counsel is usually the only participant who administers the oaths[10] to all witnesses.[11] In some instances he may also ask the typical

---

4. *See* United States v. Vandermark, 14 M.J. 690 (N.M.C.M.R. 1982) (judge properly exercised discretion in striking direct testimony).
5. Rule 611, MIL. R. EVID. United States v. Royster, 42 M.J. 488 (1995) (due to absent witness, court started trial and then continued it two months later; to refresh members' memories', court provided redacted transcripts to members for their review of earlier testimony; court concluded that judge's "resourceful solution, born of necessity," was not an abuse of discretion); United States v. Black, 42 M.J. 505 (Army Ct.Crim.App. 1995) (judge has discretion to determine whether testimony will be cumulative; although defense witnesses are normally determined by defense, accused has no constitutional right to cumulative testimony).
6. R.C.M. 913(c)(2). Circumstances of trial, however, may warrant minor variations. *See, e.g.,* United States v. Johnson, 28 C.M.R. 662, 677 (N.B.R. 1959); United States v. Jackson, 549 F.2d 517 (8th Cir.), *cert. denied,* 438 U.S. 988 (1977).
   For discussion on special problems concerning child witnesses, see Hahn, "Preparing Witnesses for Trial—A Methodology for New Judge Advocates," ARMY LAW., July 1982, at 2; Woods, "Children Can Be Witnesses Too; A Discussion of the Preparation and Utilization of Child-Witnesses in Courts-Martial," ARMY LAW., Mar. 1983, at 2.
7. Rule 611(b), MIL. R. EVID. *See also* Rule 301(e), MIL. R. EVID. (self-incrimination and cross-examination of accused). United States v. Williams, 40 M.J. 216 (C.M.A. 1994) (harmless error to limit accused's cross-examination of key government witness); United States v. Gray, 40 M.J. 77 (C.M.A. 1994) (denial of accused's right to cross-examine witness and present defense was reversible error); United States v. Moore, 36 M.J. 329 (C.M.A. 1993) (striking all of defense witness direct testimony following an invocation of the right to remain silent was harmless error); United States v. Welker, 37 M.J. 1066 (N.M.C.M.R. 1993) (accused's direct testimony opened door on cross-examination to other incidents); United States v. Stavely, 33 M.J. 92 (C.M.A. 1991) (trial judge's limitations of defense cross-examination of prosecution's principal witness was reversible error). *See generally* Saltzburg, Schinasi & Schlueter, *Military Rules of Evidence Manual,* 686-96 (3d ed. 1991).
8. United States v. Longstreath, 42 M.J. 806 (N.M.C.Ct.Crim.App.1995) (judge did not abuse discretion in declining to strike child abuse victim's direct testimony, where counsel had been able to do some cross-examination).
9. Rule 611(c), MIL. R. EVID. United States v. Wood, 36 M.J. 651 (A.C.M.R. 1992) (not abuse of discretion to permit trial counsel to lead child victim).
10. *See* R.C.M. 807(b)(2) Discussion, which implies that trial counsel will normally administer the oaths. See also Art. 136, U.C.M.J. for a list of who may administer oaths.
11. R.C.M. 807(b)(1)(B). *See also* Rule 603, MIL. R. EVID. (the term "oath" includes the word "affirmation").

"pedigree" questions of the defense witnesses. To prevent witnesses from hearing each other's testimony the judge may order witnesses [12] excluded, except the accused, trial counsel's representative, and any other essential party.[13] For a discussion of preserving objections to testimony or other evidence, see § 15-21.

§ 15-12(B). Questions by the Court.

Either the military judge or court members may ask questions of witnesses insofar as they do not become partisan in their questioning; counsel may object to questioning by the court.[14] Questioning by the trial court is normally considered appropriate where the questions are designed to clear up ambiguities in the witness's testimony.[15] There is obviously a fine line between questions propounded for that limited purpose and questions which undermine a witness's testimony or credibility.[16] This is a particularly sensitive problem where the court questions the accused.[17] As one court has noted, has noted, the

---

12. Rule 615, MIL. R. EVID. United States v. Ware, 41 M.J. 592 (A.F.Ct.Crim.App. 1994) (discussion between government and defense witness was nonprejudicial violation of judge's sequestration order); United States v. Gittens, 36 M.J. 594 (A.F.C.M.R. 1992) (defense witness was not a known witness and court declined to find bad faith violation of sequestration order; court noted that the sequestration rule is not an exclusionary rule). *See* Saltzburg, Schinasi & Schlueter, *Military Rules of Evidence Manual*, 713-17 (3d ed. 1991).

13. Rule 615, MIL. R. EVID. United States v. Gittens, 39 M.J. 328 (C.M.A. 1994) (not abuse of discretion to permit witness to testify who had remained in courtroom; prosecutor did not know that person would be a witness until she approached counsel).

14. *See* Rule 614, MIL. R. EVID. *See, e.g.*, United States v. Lents, 32 M.J. 636 (A.C.M.R. 1991) (defense waived objection to trial judge's denial of court-requested witness); United States v. Chavez, 27 M.J. 870 (A.F.C.M.R. 1988) (under facts military judge did not demonstrate bias when he overruled a defense objection to prosecutor's questions); United States v. Cephas, 25 M.J. 832 (A.C.M.R. 1988) (trial judge did not abandon his impartial role by asking NCO to explain inconsistency in his testimony regarding accused's potential for rehabilitation); United States v. Miller, 23 M.J. 553 (C.G.C.M.R. 1986) (judge's questions of accused during providency inquiry came close to the appearance of adversarial cross-examination); United States v. Shackelford, 2 M.J. 17 (C.M.A. 1976); United States v. Morgan, 22 M.J. 959 (C.G.C.M.R. 1986) (harmless error in laying foundation).

15. *See* United States v. Ramos, 42 M.J. 392 (1995) (applying reasonable man standard, questions by judge of witness did not, when taken as a whole in the context of trial, raise doubts about the court-martial's legality, fairness, and impartiality); United States v. Dock, 40 M.J. 112 (C.M.A. 1994) (judge's hypothetical questions of defense's expert witnesses did not tilt toward the prosecution); United States v. Reynolds, 24 M.J. 261 (C.M.A. 1987) (judge does not lay aside impartiality when he asks questions to clarify factual uncertainties); United States v. Bishop, 28 C.M.R. 341 (C.M.A. 1960) (judge is more than mere umpire); United States v. Johnson, 36 M.J. 862 (A.C.M.R. 1993) (although number of questions by judge was unusually large, judge did not abandon impartial role; questions helped neither the prosecution nor the defense); Cf. United States v. Bouie, 18 M.J.529 (A.F.C.M.R. 1984) (no error in bench trial for judge to ask over 300 questions of witnesses; no evidence of prosecutorial bent and defense made no objection).

16. United States v. Hardy, 30 M.J. 757 (A.C.M.R. 1990) (judge abandoned impartiality in challenging defense allegation that accused had not had previous legal problems and permitted prosecution to reopen case to introduce accused's confession).

17. United States v. Shackleford, 2 M.J. 17 (C.M.A. 1976) (judge adopted prosecutorial tone in questioning accused); United States v. Wood, 29 M.J. 1075 (A.C.M.R. 1990) (not error to question accused to clarify ambiguities); United States v. Morgan, 22 M.J. 959 (C.G.C.M.R. 1986) (judge

§ 15-12(C)   TRIAL PROCEDURES   § 15-12(C)

public's confidence in the integrity and impartiality of the judge is sustained largely by the conduct of the judge during the trial.[18]

Military practice also permits either the court members or the military judge to call new witnesses[19] or recall witnesses who have already testified.[20] But the military judge in his discretion may disallow an additional witness called by the members if it appears that the expected testimony is not material or is cumulative. If the court members have questions of a witness, the questions must be first reduced to writing, marked as appellate exhibits, and shown to both counsel who may object to the propriety of the questions.[21] Counsel will normally be permitted to further question the witness based upon answers to the court's inquiries.[22]

§ 15-12(C). Exhibits.

Counsel may find it helpful to mark the exhibits they intend to introduce before the trial begins. Exhibits may be marked without first seeking approval of the judge.[23] Under certain circumstances, premature display of an exhibit to the court members may be prejudicial.[24] Prosecution exhibits gener-

---

erred in questioning accused to lay foundation for knife); United States v. Thomas, 18 M.J. 545 (A.C.M.R. 1984) (reversible error for judge to question accused about information learned in earlier motion to suppress); United States v. Clower, 48 C.M.R. 307 (C.M.A. 1974) (error to question accused in manner approximating impeachment); United States v. Wood, 29 M.J. 1075 (A.C.M.R. 1990) (judge's questions of accused and "cross-examination" of witness were appropriate).

18. United States v. Wood, 29 M.J. 1075 (A.C.M.R. 1990).

19. Rule 614(a), Mil. R. Evid. United States v. Baker, 34 M.J. 559 (A.F.C.M.R. 1992) (military practice does not require that fact-finder be content with evidence presented by parties; judge may ask that additional witnesses be called).

20. Rule 614(a), Mil. R.Evid. See United States v. Martinsmith, 41 M.J. 343 (1995) (during instructions, court member indicated that he would like to ask accused question; trial judge did not permit question because it could have led to additional evidence and response from the government); United States v. Lampani, 14 M.J. 22 (C.M.A. 1982) (members may ask to question witness after they have begun deliberations); United States v. Lents, 32 M.J. 636 (A.C.M.R. 1991) (trial judge committed harmless error in summarily denying court members' request to hear from another witness).

The right to call additional witnesses or recall witnesses who have testified is not absolute, however. United States v. Lampani, 14 M.J. 22 (C.M.A. 1982).

21. Rule 614(b), (c), Mil. R. Evid. United States v. Hill, 42 M.J. 725 (C.G.Ct.Crim.App. 1995) (questions submitted by member and rejected by court, did not exhibit bias of member; court indicated that members should be cautioned not to be advocate of either side in posing questions). Cf. United States v. Miller, 14 M.J. 924 (A.F.C.M.R. 1982) (court noted that following Mil. R. Evid. 614(b) might be more prejudicial to the accused; reading the question aloud, said the court, can dispel speculation about a question).

22. United States v. Campbell, 37 M.J. 1049 (N.M.C.M.R. 1993) (erroneous denial of accused's right to recross-examine victim, who was recalled by court members, was harmless error). See generally Saltzburg, Schinasi & Schlueter, Military Rules of Evidence Manual, 708-12 (3d ed. 1991).

23. See, e.g., United States v. Woodard, 39 M.J. 1022, 1026 n. 6 (A.C.M.R. 1994) (to be admitted, evidence should be marked as either a prosecution or defense exhibit). See generally Schlueter, Saltzburg, Schinasi, & Imwinkelried, Military Evidentiary Foundations § 1-7 (1994).

24. See generally United States v. McDowell, 13 C.M.A. 129, 32 C.M.R. 129 (1962). See also A.B.A. Standards for Criminal Justice, Standards 3-5.6, 4-7.5.

ally bear Arabic numerals (Prosecution Exhibit 1 for Identification). Exhibits for the defense are listed alphabetically (Defense Exhibit A for Identification). Note that all exhibits offered but not admitted are also included in the record of trial. Should exhibits be used in conjunction with interlocutory matters, the military judge may have them marked as Appellate Exhibits (using Roman numerals) and included in the record.[25] Written questions from court members should also be marked as Appellate Exhibits[26] and bulky exhibits may be photographed or extracted for inclusion in the record.

§ 15-12(D). Views and Inspections of Places and Objects.

As an aid to understanding the evidence or the case, it may be appropriate for the court actually to view the scene or object in question. It is important that such a procedure be tightly controlled and viewed as an extension of the courtroom proceedings. All parties must be present including the judge and any members.[27] Because the *Manual* requires that any statements made by the persons present at the scene be made part of the record,[28] it is advisable to have a court reporter or other person present to record accurately what occurred. Conducting such views and inspections lies within the discretion of the judge[29] who may appoint someone familiar with the scene or object to act as an "escort" and explain pertinent features and characteristics.[30] Although personal familiarity of the scene or object should not disqualify a court member,[31] any attempts to personally conduct an informal view or inspection is inappropriate and may be prejudicial error.[32]

§ 15-13. Closing Arguments.

At the completion of the cases-in-chief, both counsel may present closing arguments to the fact-finder.[1] Normally, the prosecution is permitted to open arguments and present a rebuttal argument. Although the trial counsel may waive closing argument, the military courts discourage a similar move by the

---

25. United States v. Maschino, 31 M.J. 841 (N.M.C.M.R. 1990) (in a case involving 80 prosecution exhibits, 16 defense exhibits, and 35 appellate exhibits, the court set out guidance on marking various exhibits to avoid confusion on offered, rejected, or withdrawn exhibits). Appellate exhibits are not normally offered or received into evidence; they are simply appended. *See* Air Force Manual (AFM) 111-1, para. 4-29.
26. *Cf.* United States v. Miller, 14 M.J. 924 (A.F.C.M.R. 1982).
27. *See* R.C.M. 913(c)(3). United States v. Ayala, 22 M.J. 777 (A.C.M.R. 1986).
28. R.C.M. 913(c)(3).
29. *Id.* United States v. Marvin, 24 M.J. 365 (C.M.A. 1987) (judge did not abuse discretion in denying accused's request that members view situs of crime).
30. *Id.* This escort is not to "testify" at the scene although the escort may be a witness who has already testified or will testify about the scene or object.
31. *See* United States v. Bishop, 11 M.J. 7 (C.M.A. 1981).
32. United States v. Witherspoon, 12 M.J. 588 (A.C.M.R. 1981).
1. R.C.M. 919. Note that para. 72a of the 1969 *Manual* permitted an accused to present his argument personally. There are apparently no reported cases on this point. *See generally* Haight, "Argument of Military Counsel of Findings, Sentence, and Motions: Limitations and Abuses," 16 MIL. L. REV. 59 (1962).

defense unless the trial counsel has first waived argument and the defense wishes as a tactical matter to cut off any rebuttal argument by also waiving argument.[2] The military judge may nonetheless require both counsel to argue where justice demands it; the military judge may also limit the length of the arguments, but should not abuse his discretion.[3]

Statutory and *Manual* guidance on proper content of arguments is sparse.[4] Generally, counsel may comment on the testimony, conduct, and motives of witnesses and may argue as though the testimony of his witnesses conclusively establishes certain facts.[5] In arguing, counsel may strike hard blows but not foul blows.[6] Military case law has framed a number of common errors in arguments. They include:

(1) Citing legal authorities;[7]
(2) Comparing factual situations in other cases;[8]
(3) Arguing facts not in evidence or misstating facts in evidence;[9]

---

2. *See* United States v. McMahan, 6 C.M.A. 709, 21 C.M.R. 31 (1956).

3. United States v. Gravitt, 5 C.M.A. 249, 17 C.M.R. 249 (1954); United States v. Dock, 20 M.J. 556 (A.C.M.R. 1985) (no prejudice where court unexpectedly limited defense counsel to only a few more minutes; time constraints should not be imposed in such a manner as to imply that argument is not important).

4. United States v. Causey, 37 M.J. 308 (C.M.A. 1993) (noting that R.C.M. 919(b) provides that arguments may include reasonable comment on the evidence including inferences and that AR 27-10 applies the ABA Standards for Criminal Justice to Army; those provisions provide additional guidance on appropriate arguments).

5. R.C.M. 919.

6. United States v. Doctor, 7 C.M.A. 126, 21 C.M.R. 252 (1956), *citing* Berger v. United States, 295 U.S. 78 (1935); United States v. Thomas, 43 M.J. 550 (N.M.C.Ct.Crim.App.1995) (prosecutor calling accused liar was hard, but fair blow); United States v. Easter, 39 M.J. 876 (A.C.M.R. 1994) (prosecutor's reference to race was measured, nonprejudicial, reference to relevant evidence); United States v. Garland, 39 M.J. 618 (A.C.M.R. 1994) (racial remarks in closing argument exceeded bounds of permissible argument; not plain error); United States v. Thompson, 37 M.J. 1023 (A.C.M.R. 1993) (trial counsel's sentencing argument referring to accused's race amounted to foul blow; court viewed argument as plain, reversible error); United States v. Turner, 17 M.J. 997 (A.C.M.R. 1984) (arguments not required to be sterile or anemic; "blunt and emphatic language is essential to effective advocacy in most cases"); United States v. Zeigler, 14 M.J. 860 (A.C.M.R. 1982) (example of "hard but fair blows."). *See generally* Cargill, "'Hard Blows' Versus 'Fair Ones': Restrictions on Trial Counsel's Closing Argument," ARMY LAW., Jan. 1991, at 20.

7. United States v. Clifton, 15 M.J. 26 (C.M.A. 1983) (counsel cited well-known military treatise); United States v. McCauley, 9 C.M.A. 65, 25 C.M.R. 327 (1958). Citation of legal authorities is permitted in bench trials. R.C.M. 919(b) Discussion.

8. United States v. Bouie, 9 C.M.A. 228, 26 C.M.R. 8 (1958).

9. United States v. Allen, 11 C.M.A. 539, 29 C.M.R. 355 (1960). Counsel may not refer to witnesses who do not testify, United States v. Tackett, 16 C.M.A. 226, 36 C.M.R. 382 (1966) but may comment on facts well-known within the community; United States v. Poteet, 50 C.M.R. 73 (N.C.M.R. 1975) (drug problem).

United States v. Kirk, 41 M.J. 529 (C.G.Ct.Crim.App. 1994) (trial counsel's reference to Bible passage, that people reap what they sow, was permissible as common sense observation of human experience; court noted that if counsel had appealed to member's need to follow higher authority, the argument would have been improper).

United States v. Shoup, 31 M.J. 819 (A.F.C.M.R. 1990) (nonprejudicial error for counsel to refer to earlier drug cases and the fact that 20 people had died in Panama trying to stop drugs from coming into United States); United States v. Carr, 25 M.J. 637 (A.C.M.R. 1987) (error for trial

§ 15-13

(4) Arguing personal opinions;[10]

(5) Commenting on the accused's failure to testify or on pretrial silence;[11] or commenting on an accused's refusal to consent to a search;[12]

---

counsel to argue before sentencing that offense had subjected victim to repeated confrontations and cross-examinations by the accused).

United States v. Brown, 17 M.J. 987 (A.C.M.R. 1984) (prosecutor improperly referred to accused's testimony given during guilty plea inquiry); United States v. Falcon, 16 M.J. 528 (A.C.M.R. 1983) (trial counsel improperly asserted personal knowledge of a fact outside the record; he also improperly insinuated that the accused had committed other offenses not before the court).

United States v. Simmons, 14 M.J. 832 (A.C.M.R. 1982) (prosecutor implied that accused's chain-of-command would have presented adverse testimony against accused).

Trial counsel must also refrain from associating the accused with persons or offenses without supporting evidence. United States v. Nelson, 1 M.J. 235 (C.M.A. 1975).

See also United States v. Bethea, 3 M.J. 526 (A.F.C.M.R. 1977) (error to attribute more serious criminal intent to accused); United States v. Shows, 5 M.J. 892 (A.F.C.M.R. 1978) (misstating facts may be error).

10. Such arguments are tantamount to testimony without the benefit of cross-examination. United States v. Barnack, 10 M.J. 799 (A.F.C.M.R. 1981); United States v. Tanksley, 7 M.J. 573 (A.C.M.R. 1979). There is some authority that counsel may argue personal opinion if he states that the belief is solely based on the evidence. United States v. Knickerbocker, 2 M.J. 128 (C.M.A. 1977). *See also* United States v. Falcon, 16 M.J. 528 (A.C.M.R. 1983) (trial counsel expressed personal opinion about evidence before the court); United States v. Zeigler, 14 M.J. 860 (A.C.M.R. 1982) (prosecutor's repeated use of pronoun "I" was not statement of personal opinion; using the words "I think" would be).

Cf. United States v. Fuentes, 18 M.J. 41 (C.M.A. 1984) (trial counsel's argument that witness' testimony was unbelievable was not expression of personal belief or credibility of the evidence).

11. *See, e.g.,* Doyle v. Ohio, 426 U.S. 610 (1976); Griffin v. California, 380 U.S. 609 (1965); United States v. Webb, 38 M.J. 62 (C.M.A. 1993) (counsel's argument that defense had not presented alibi defense was not impermissible comment on accused's silence; other witnesses could have presented the defense; violation only occurs where accused is only witness who could have contradicted government case); United States v. Mobley, 31 M.J. 273 (C.M.A. 1990) (prosecutor may not comment on failure of defense to call witnesses); United States v. Mills, 7 M.J. 664 (A.C.M.R. 1979); United States v. Albrecht, 4 M.J. 573 (A.C.M.R. 1977). The prosecutor may comment on failure of accused's testimony to address certain matters, United States v. Sims, 5 C.M.A. 115, 17 C.M.R. 115 (1954) but he may *not* argue that the government's evidence is unrebutted when only the accused could offer the rebuttal, United States v. St. John, 23 C.M.A. 20, 48 C.M.R. 312 (1974); United States v. Clifton, 15 M.J. 26 (C.M.A. 1983); United States v. Oatney, 41 M.J. 619 (N.M.Ct.Crim.App.1994) (assuming that prosecutor's argument was impermissible comment on failure of accused to take stand, defense waived the issue by not objecting and such was not plain error).

United States v. Jackson, 40 M.J. 820 (N.M.C.M.R. 1994) (trial counsel's argument re accused's silent remorse at trial, i.e., tears, was harmless error); United States v. Dennis, 39 M.J. 623 (N.M.C.M.R. 1993) (comment that testimony of prosecution's key witness was unrefuted was not intended as comment on accused's failure to testify; court indicated that in determining whether indirect comments are prejudicial, the following factors should be considered: (1) whether language used was manifestly intended to comment on silence or was of such a character that the members would naturally and necessarily consider it as such, (2) whether the improper comments were isolated or extensive, (3) whether evidence of guilty is overwhelming, and (4) whether curative instructions were given).

---

12. United States v. Tuner, 39 M.J. 259 (C.M.A. 1994) (in absence of other factors, evidence or comment upon accused's exercise of Fifth or Fourth Amendment rights is not relevant; court rejected argument that defense's brief comment in opening statement opened door to comment).

(6) Commenting on military-civilian relations;[13]
(7) Arguing to the prejudice of the client;[14]
(8) Placing court members in place of victim;[15]
(9) Appealing to race or class prejudice;[16]

United States v. Weinmann, 37 M.J. 724 (A.F.C.M.R. 1993) (trial counsel's argument did not amount to impermissible comment on accused's right to plead not guilty); United States v. Espronceda, 36 M.J. 535 (A.F.C.M.R. 1992) (prosecutor may not comment on failure of defense to call witnesses; here argument was permitted, however, where defense opened door during arguments).

United States v. Carroll, 34 M.J. 843 (A.C.M.R. 1992) (prosecutor's comment that accused had failed to show remorse in his unsworn statement was proper comment; court cautioned that commenting on something the accused has not said is risky); United States v. Kirks, 34 M.J. 646 (A.C.M.R. 1992) (prosecutor's references to accused as being cold as ice were not plain error. The court noted that commenting on an accused's demeanor is strolling in a minefield and potentially violates, inter alia, the accused's right to remain silent at trial); United States v. Mobley, 34 M.J. 527 (A.F.C.M.R. 1991) (counsel's argument calling attention to accused's silence was harmless error).

Cf. United States v. Heath, 39 M.J. 1101 (C.G.C.M.R. 1994) (prosecutor's sentencing argument that there was no evidence of someone who wanted to repent was not impermissible comment on failure of accused to testify; instead it was fair comment on aggravation evidence); United States v. Zeigler, 14 M.J. 860 (A.C.M.R. 1982) (prosecutor's comment on state of the evidence was not comment on accused's silence).

See also Rules 301 and 512, MIL. R. EVID. *See generally* Saltzburg, Schinasi & Schlueter, *Military Rules of Evidence Manual*, 611-14 (3d ed. 1991).

13. United States v. Boberg, 17 C.M.A. 401, 38 C.M.R. 199 (1968); United States v. Ernst, 17 M.J. 835 (C.G.C.M.R. 1984) (prosecutor improperly and repeatedly referred to civilian-military relations); United States v. Poteet, 50 C.M.R. 73 (N.C.M.R. 1975).

14. Defense counsel's arguments are most often challenged where counsel has argued for a bad-conduct discharge. *See, e.g.,* United States v. McNally, 16 M.J. 32 (C.M.A. 1983) (defense counsel erred in arguing for BCD; the record did not reveal that BCD was inevitable and contains no indication that accused desired one); United States v. Holcomb, 20 C.M.A. 309, 43 C.M.R. 149 (1971) (defense counsel's argument for discharge conflicted with accused's desires).

Cf. United States v. Kadlec, 22 M.J. 571 (A.C.M.R. 1986) (argument for punitive discharge not error even though record did not explicitly reflect accused's desires); United States v. Dotson, 9 M.J. 542 (C.G.C.M.R. 1980) (counsel's argument for discharge was proper because that is what accused wished); United States v. Mosley, 11 M.J. 729 (A.F.C.M.R. 1981) (accused's desire for discharge was implied).

Counsel may not concede guilt, United States v. Burwell, 50 C.M.R. 192 (A.C.M.R. 1975). *Cf.* United States v. Matthews, 13 M.J. 501 (A.C.M.R. 1982) (en banc) (defense counsel's tactic of admitting guilt of rape was realistic and not error). *See generally* Russelburg, "Defense Concession as a Trial Tactic," ARMY LAW., Sept. 1983, at 22.

15. United States v. Shamberger, 1 M.J. 377 (C.M.A. 1976); United States v. Thompson, 37 M.J. 1023 (A.C.M.R. 1993) (trial counsel's sentencing argument referring to accused's race amounted to plain error and reversible error); United States v. Edmonds, 36 M.J. 791 (A.C.M.R. 1993) (trial counsel's argument urging court members to consider fear of robbery victim was permissible; members were not asked to take place of victim); United States v. Williams, 23 M.J. 776 (A.C.M.R. 1987) (referring to court members' daughters as potential rape victims of the accused was not plain error requiring reversal in the absence of a defense objection).

16. United States v. Caldwell, 23 M.J. 748 (A.F.C.M.R. 1987) (trial counsel committed harmless error when he interjected racism into case, apparently unintentionally, by stating during arguments on sentencing that the accused, a black male, was predatory and waited for white, lonely women); United States v. Begley, 38 C.M.R. 488 (A.B.R. 1967).

§ 15-13 MILITARY CRIMINAL JUSTICE § 15-13

(10) Stating specific sentence [17] and command policies; [18]

(11) Making inflammatory arguments. [19]

(12) Diverting the members from their duty to decide the case on the evidence; [20]

(13) Appealing to religious beliefs or impulses. [21]

Although most of the foregoing errors involve arguments by the prosecutor, defense counsel is also under an obligation not to make improper comments. [22] Indeed, doing so may open the door and invite a response in the form of comment or explanation from the prosecutor. [23]

Normally, counsel should not interrupt opposing counsel's closing argument

---

17. United States v. Higdon, 2 M.J. 445 (A.C.M.R. 1975). *Cf.* United States v. Coleman, 41 C.M.R. 953 (A.F.C.M.R. 1970) (prosecutor may argue for maximum punishment); United States v. Wood, 23 C.M.A. 57, 48 C.M.R. 528 (1974) (defense may argue for specific sentence in attempt to beat pretrial agreement).

Cf. United States v. Barus, 16 M.J. 624 (A.F.C.M.R. 1983) (trial counsel's argument that Air Force had drug problem was not error because it did not suggest a certain punishment).

18. *See, e.g.,* United States v. Grady, 15 M.J. 275 (C.M.A. 1983) (military judge has a *sua sponte* duty to restrict arguments addressing command policy); United States v. Schomaker, 17 M.J. 1122 (N.M.C.M.R. 1984) (trial counsel's argument about command's drug policy was improper); United States v. Robertson, 17 M.J. 846 (N.M.C.M.R. 1984) (prosecutor's references to commandant's drug policies were not improper; arguments were made in response to defense contentions and did not operate to inject command influence into deliberations).

19. United States v. Clifton, 15 M.J. 26 (C.M.A. 1983) (conjugation of adultery with heroin and labelling the accused a liar); United States v. Nelson, 1 M.J. 235 (C.M.A. 1975); United States v. McCarthy, 37 M.J. 595 (A.F.C.M.R. 1993) (trial counsel's references to Saddam Hussein came unnecessarily close to improper comment); United States v. Rodriguez, 28 M.J. 1016 (A.F.C.M.R. 1989) (trial counsel's comparison of accused, who was charged with sex offenses, to well-known television evangelist was within the fair bounds of comment).

United States v. Quarles, 25 M.J. 761 (N.M.C.M.R. 1987) (prosecutor's repeated references to accused as sexual deviate and prurient sex fiend inflamed passions of the court members); United States v. White, 3 M.J. 619 (N.C.M.R.), *petition denied,* 3 M.J. 338 (C.M.A. 1977).

See also United States v. Young, 470 U.S. 1 (1985) (prosecutor's arguments, although improper, were an "invited response" to the defense argument that impugned the integrity of the prosecutor).

20. United States v. Causey, 37 M.J. 308 (C.M.A. 1993) (error for counsel to argue that members should reject innocent ingestion defense to drug charges because it would open floodgates for similar arguments; accused waived issue by not objecting and argument did not amount to plain error). *See also* Standard 3-5.8(d), ABA Standards for Criminal Justice, The Prosecution Function (1992). The predecessor to this provision indicated that such diversion could occur by counsel injecting issues which are broader than question of guilt or innocence under the controlling law or by predicting the consequences of the court's verdict. *See* United States v. Causey, 37 M.J. 308, 310 (C.M.A. 1993).

21. Cobb v. Wainwright, 609 F.2d 754 (5th Cir. 1980) (condemns argument based upon Bible or other religious writings); *Cf.* United States v. Kirk, 41 M.J. 529 (C.G.Ct.Crim.App. 1994) (trial counsel's citation to Bible re sowing what one reaps was common sense observation of human experience).

22. *See* United States v. Fisher, 17 M.J. 768 (A.F.C.M.R. 1983) (defense has higher obligation because case will not be reversed because of comments on strength of prosecution's case).

23. United States v. Espronceda, 36 M.J. 535 (A.F.C.M.R. 1992) (prosecutor may not comment on failure of defense to call witnesses; here argument was permitted, however, where defense opened door during arguments). The better practice is for the prosecutor to object and ask for a curative instruction. United States v. Fisher, 17 M.J. 768 (A.F.C.M.R. 1983).

unless it is clearly improper.[24] But the military judge may *sua sponte* stop the argument[25] and take remedial actions which may include instruction to the court,[26] retraction by counsel,[27] or where the error is egregious, declaring a mistrial.[28] In reviewing the argument on appeal, counsel's failure to object may be considered waiver.[29] Failure to object, however, may not constitute waiver where the military judge should have stopped the argument,[30] the failure to object was a flagrant oversight,[31] or waiver would result in a miscarriage of justice.[32] Relief may take the form of a rehearing,[33] reassessment of the sentence, or dismissal of the charges. Some special rules apply to arguments of counsel on sentencing and § 16-8 should be consulted.

§ 15-14. Instructions to the Court Members.

§ 15-14(A). General.

Where the accused is being tried by a court with members, the military judge is required to instruct on the law to be applied to the case.[1] In doing so, he must submit the theories of both parties and provide lucid guideposts

---

24. 1969 *Manual*, para. 72c. *Cf.* United States v. Mobley, 31 M.J. 273 (C.M.A. 1990) (counsel should object as soon as possible to impermissible argument; it is judge's job to determine if the objection has somehow derailed the prosecutor's argument).
25. United States v. Nelson, 1 M.J. 235 (C.M.A. 1975); United States v. Rutherford, 29 M.J. 1030 (A.C.M.R. 1990) (failure of judge to *sua sponte* interrupt improper sentencing argument by prosecutor amounted to plain error; military judge has affirmative duty to interrupt improper argument and give cautionary instructions); United States v. Vanderlip, 28 M.J. 1070 (N.M.C.M.R. 1989) (trial judge properly interrupted defense counsel's argument urging court members to reconsider findings of guilt).
26. United States v. Carpenter, 11 C.M.A. 418, 29 C.M.R. 234 (1960). *See also* R.C.M. 919(c) Discussion.
27. United States v. Lackey, 8 C.M.A. 718, 25 C.M.R. 222 (1958).
28. United States v. O Neal, 16 C.M.A. 33, 36 C.M.R. 189 (1966). *See also* § 15-4(B).
29. R.C.M. 919(c). United States v. Oatney, 41 M.J. 619 (N.M.Ct.Crim.App. 1994) (failure to object waives error; relief only granted if error was plain); United States v. Rodriguez, 28 M.J. 1016 (A.F.C.M.R. 1989) (defense counsel's failure to object lead to "reasonable inference" that nothing was improper in prosecutor's closing argument); United States v. Perry, 12 M.J. 920 (N.M.C.M.R. 1982).
Waiver of improper argument at the trial may give some indication as to how counsel viewed the prejudice. United States v. Grandy, 11 M.J. 270 (C.M.A. 1981); United States v. Poteet, 50 C.M.R. 73 (N.C.M.R. 1975).
30. *See, e.g.*, United States v. Shamberger, 1 M.J. 377 (C.M.A. 1976); United States v. Williams, 23 M.J. 525 (A.C.M.R. 1986).
31. United States v. Boberg, 17 C.M.A. 401, 38 C.M.R. 199 (1968).
32. United States v. Russell, 15 C.M.A. 76, 35 C.M.R. 48 (1964); United States v. Oatney, 41 M.J. 619 (N.M.Ct.Crim.App. 1994) (no relief granted following counsel's silence at trial unless plain error occurred); United States v. Thompson, 37 M.J. 1023 (A.C.M.R. 1993) (trial counsel's sentencing argument referring to accused's race amounted to plain error and reversible error).
33. *See* United States v. Clifton, 15 M.J. 26 (C.M.A. 1983) (curative efforts of trial judge were insufficient where trial counsel violated numerous rules of oral argument).
1. Art. 51(c), U.C.M.J. R.C.M. 920(a). *See generally* Holland, Masterton & Henley, "Annual Review of Developments in Instructions (1995)," ARMY LAW., Feb. 1996, at 1; Holland & Masterson, "Annual Review of Developments in Instructions," ARMY LAW., March 1995, at 3; Holland & Masterson, "Annual Review of Developments in Instructions," ARMY LAW., April 1994, at 3; Green, "Annual Review of Developments in Instructions," ARMY LAW., March 1993, at 3.

§ 15-14(A)

tailored to the facts.[2] In assessing the role of the military judge to properly instruct the members before they deliberate, the Court of Appeals has stated:

> What we do reject is the notion that the legality of a criminal trial may be measured by the same standards applicable to a game of chance. The trial judge is more than a mere referee, and as such he is required to assure that the accused receives a fair trial. Advocacy leaves the proceedings at the junction of instructing the court members. Irrespective of the desires of counsel, the military judge must bear the primary responsibility for assuring that the jury properly is instructed on the elements of the offenses raised by the evidence as well as potential defenses and other questions of law. Simply stated, counsel do not frame issues for the jury; that is the duty of the military judge based upon his evaluation of the testimony related by the witnesses during the trial.[3]

Throughout the trial the military judge will be required to instruct the members on evidentiary issues and points of information.[4] The focus here is on the two basic categories of instructions that must be given before the members deliberate on the findings: *sua sponte* instructions § 15-14(A), and instructions requested by counsel, § 15-14(B).

Before counsel present their closing arguments the military judge will normally call an out-of-court Article 39(a) session[5] to inform counsel of his proposed instructions, consider counsel proposals, and hear arguments on the proposals.[6] Thus, counsel usually know before they argue how the military judge will frame the issues for the court members.[7] The preferred practice is to

---

2. R.C.M. 920(a) Discussion. United States v. Sanders, 41 M.J. 485 (1995) (not plain error for judge not to specifically instruct members that accused had invited victim to strike him: judge did instruct on divestiture).

3. United States v. Graves, 1 M.J. 50, 53 (C.M.A. 1975). Note that several provisions of the Military Rules of Evidence place greater emphasis on the desires of defense counsel with regard to certain instructions. *See, e.g.,* Rules 105, 301(g), Mil. R. Evid. *See generally* Saltzburg, Schinasi & Schlueter, *Military Rules of Evidence Manual,* (3d ed. 1991); Green, "The Military Rules of Evidence and the Military Judge," Army Law., May 1980, at 47.

4. Those are discussed in § 15-24.

5. R.C.M. 920(c) Discussion. In United States v. Sadler, 29 M.J. 370, 373, n.3 (C.M.A. 1990), the court indicated that discussion of instructions should take place on the record, instead of during conferences held pursuant to R.C.M. 802. United States v. Brown-Austin, 34 M.J. 578 (A.C.M.R. 1992) (court strongly urged judges to conduct discussions about proposed instructions on the record, and not during a Rule 802 conference). *See* § 12-5. *Cf.* United States v. Stewart, 29 M.J. 621 (C.G.C.M.R. 1989) (R.C.M. 803 conferences may be used to discuss possible instructions). *See also* § 12-1.

6. R.C.M. 920(c). *See* United States v. Neal, 17 C.M.A. 363, 38 C.M.R. 161 (1968). This approximates the procedure in Federal courts. Rule 30, Fed. R. Crim. P.

7. In 1993, R.C.M. 920(b) was changed to permit the judge to give the instructions before arguments, after arguments, or both. The change was intended to bring military practice in line with federal civilian practice.*See generally* Milhizer & McShane, "Analysis of Change 6 to the 1984 Manual for Courts-Martial," Army Law., May 1994, pp. 40, 44. *Cf.* United States v. Pendry, 29 M.J. 694 (A.C.M.R. 1989) (giving instructions before arguments was nonprejudicial error; court noted that defense counsel may have been aided in his argument by referring to instructions). *See also* Fed. R. Crim. P. 30, which provides that trial judge may give instructions either before or after closing arguments.

§ 15-14(A)   TRIAL PROCEDURES   § 15-14(A)

reduce proposed instructions to writing and include them as appellate exhibits in the record of trial.[8] In reviewing possible instructions, counsel will find it helpful to review one of the several "instructions checklists" used by the services.[9]

Under routine practice, the military judge orally instructs the court, but a written copy of the instructions may also be submitted to the members.[10] In so doing the judge must first orally instruct the members,[11] provide counsel an opportunity to examine them,[12] and finally, have the written instructions marked as an exhibit and handed to the court members.[13] The written copy must contain all of the oral instructions.[14] Several courts have commended use of written instructions[15] because they can reduce the possibility of misunderstandings concerning the applicable law.[16] The written instructions should be attached as an appellate exhibit.

The members may consider only the instructions given by the military judge in the case at bar. It is error for the military judge to incorporate by reference instructions given in an earlier case,[17] and it is improper for the members to rely upon their own research of the law.[18] They are not permitted to consult any books, trial guides, manuals, or pamphlets during their deliberations.[19] If it appears that a court member is not attentive to the instructions, counsel should draw the judge's attention to the problem.[20]

---

8. R.C.M. 920(c) Discussion.

9. See Appendix 27 for a sample list.

10. *See* R.C.M. 920(d). United States v. Ginter, 35 M.J. 799 (N.M.C.M.R. 1992) (failure to provide written copy of instructions not abuse of discretion where there was no indication that court members were confused).

11. United States v. Hillman, 21 C.M.R. 834 (A.F.B.R. 1956).

12. United States v. Helm, 21 C.M.R. 357 (A.B.R. 1956).

13. United States v. Caldwell, 11 C.M.A. 257, 29 C.M.R. 73 (1960).

14. United States v. Sanders, 30 C.M.R. 521 (A.B.R. 1961).

15. *See, e.g.,* United States v. Alford, 31 M.J. 814, 818, n.5 (A.F.C.M.R. 1990) (court commended use of written instructions).

16. United States v. Turner, 30 M.J. 1183, 1185, footnote (A.F.C.M.R. 1990) (using written instructions significantly reduces possibility of misunderstanding instructions and the need for returning to open court for clarification); United States v. Slubowski, 5 M.J. 882 (N.C.M.R. 1978) (erroneous oral instructions saved by written instructions read by the court members), *aff'd,* 7 M.J. 461 (C.M.A. 1979).

17. United States v. Shafer, 17 C.M.A. 456, 38 C.M.R. 254 (1968) (nonprejudicial error under the facts).

18. *See, e.g.,* United States v. Hawks, 19 M.J. 736 (A.F.C.M.R. 1984) (member improperly obtained information from Manual for Courts-Martial); United States v. Bryant, 29 C.M.R. 814 (A.F.B.R. 1960).

19. United States v. Rinehart, 8 C.M.A. 402, 24 C.M.R. 212 (1957).

20. *See, e.g.,* United States v. Brown, 3 M.J. 368 (C.M.A. 1977); United States v. West, 27 M.J. 223 (C.M.A. 1988) (military judge *sua sponte* noted problem and determined for the record that the member was not asleep); United States v. Grace, 3 M.J. 369 (C.M.A. 1977) (counsel may not sow error into record by failing to draw the inattentiveness to the judge's attention); United States v. Boswell, 36 M.J. 807 (A.C.M.R. 1993) (judge acted properly in excusing member who fell asleep during testimony); United States v. Bishop, 21 M.J. 541 (A.F.C.M.R. 1985) (due process denied where member fell asleep during instructions; issue not waived by failing to object).

§ 15-14(B). *Sua Sponte* Instructions.

Certain instructions must be given *sua sponte* by the military judge, and failure of counsel to request them or object to them will normally constitute waiver absent plain error.[21]

Briefly stated, they are as follows:

(1) Instructions as to the elements of the offenses charged[22] and any lesser-included offenses;[23]

---

21. R.C.M. 920(f). United States v. Curry, 38 M.J. 77 (C.M.A. 1993) (plain error not to instruct on defense of accident).

United States v. Thomas, 39 M.J. 626 (N.M.C.M.R. 1993) (court noted that purpose for requiring objections to instruction before members begin deliberation is to provide judge with opportunity to make corrections; failure to timely object will waive issue unless error was plain, i.e., it is clear and obvious and materially prejudices the substantial rights of the accused); United States v. Weinmann, 37 M.J. 724 (A.F.C.M.R. 1993) (defense affirmatively waived instruction on self-defense; failure to give instruction was not plain error); United States v. Davis, 32 M.J. 166 (C.M.A. 1991) (accused waived appellate review of objection on accomplice testimony for defense witness). *Cf.* United States v. Barnes, 39 M.J. 230 (C.M.A. 1994) (right to instruction on affirmative defense is not waived by failure to request; affirmative waiver of issue will); United States v. Mayhugh, 41 M.J. 657 (N.M.Ct.Crim.App. 1994) (accused's failure to request involuntary intoxication instruction not waiver); United States v. Kirk, 41 M.J. 529 (C.G.Ct.Crim.App. 1994) (failure to request instruction did not waive issue); United States v. Birdsong, 40 M.J. 606 (A.C.M.R. 1994) (mere failure to object or request instruction on special defense will not waive; affirmative indication of satisfaction with instructions, which do not include such instructions, will amount to waiver).

22. R.C.M. 920(e)(1). *See, e.g.,* United States v. Crumley, 31 M.J. 21 (C.M.A. 1990) (harmless error not to give instruction on knowledge in drug case; error not waived when instruction affects element of offense); United States v. Sadler, 29 M.J. 370 (C.M.A. 1990) (error not to instruct on elements of state offense alleged as being service discrediting under Article 134(2)); United States v. Mance, 26 M.J. 244 (C.M.A. 1988) (detailed discussion of various instructions necessary on "knowledge" in wrongful possession and drug use cases); *see also* United States v. Brown, 26 M.J. 266 (C.M.A. 1988); United States v. Jackson, 6 M.J. 116 (C.M.A. 1979) (no instructions on elements of offense). *Cf.* United States v. Slubowski, 5 M.J. 882 (N.C.M.R. 1978) (erroneous oral instructions saved by written version read by members), aff'd, 7 M.J. 461 (C.M.A. 1979); United States v. Staten, 6 M.J. 275 (C.M.A. 1979) (lesser-included offense).

United States v. Tarver, 29 M.J. 605 (A.C.M.R. 1989) (judge must *sua sponte* instruct on partial mental responsibility when there is evidence that a mental condition exists that may negate a required mens rea element).

23. R.C.M. 920(e)(2). United States v. Strachan, 35 M.J. 362 (C.M.A. 1992) (judge not required to give instruction on lesser-included offense where defense counsel affirmatively indicated a desire not to have instruction given; absence of instruction was not plain error); United States v. Emmons, 31 M.J. 108 (C.M.A. 1990); United States v. McKinley, 27 M.J. 78 (C.M.A. 1988) (where the *Manual* states that there is no lesser-included offense, the judge rules that there is none, and counsel agree, absent plain error, that ruling becomes the law of the case; here the court concluded that there is no lesser-included offense to obstruction of justice).

United States v. Wilson, 26 M.J. 10 (C.M.A. 1988) (reversible error not to give instruction on lesser offense of involuntary manslaughter); United States v. Rodwell, 20 M.J. 264 (C.M.A. 1985) (prejudicial error in not giving lesser-included offense instruction); United States v. Jackson, 12 M.J. 163 (C.M.A. 1981) (duty to instruct on lesser-included offenses arises whenever some evidence is presented to which court members might attach credit if they desire; evidence may come from accused).

United States v. Cameron, 37 M.J. 1042 (A.C.M.R. 1993) (error not to instruct on lesser-included offense of failure to obey lawful order).

§ 15-14(B) TRIAL PROCEDURES § 15-14(B)

(2) Instructions on special (affirmative) defenses[24] reasonably in issue;[25] this would include the defenses of justification,[26] obedience to orders,[27] self-defense,[28] defense of another,[29] accident,[30] entrapment,[31] coercion or duress,[32] inability,[33] ignorance or mistake of fact,[34] and lack of mental responsibility;[35]

United States v. Arviso, 32 M.J. 616 (A.C.M.R. 1991); United States v. Evans, 28 M.J. 753 (A.F.C.M.R. 1989) (judge failed to instruct on lesser-included offense of absence without leave where accused was charged with attempted desertion); United States v. McCray, 19 M.J. 528 (A.C.M.R. 1984) (instruction not required where evidence did not raise issue of lesser-included offense).

Error in not instructing on lesser-included offense may be corrected on appeal by affirming the lesser offense. United States v. McGee, 1 M.J. 193 (C.M.A. 1975); United States v. Cagle, 12 M.J. 736 (A.F.C.M.R. 1981).

24. R.C.M. 916.; United States v. Taylor, 26 M.J. 127 (C.M.A. 1988) (duty to instruct on affirmative defenses rests primarily on Article 51 and not *Manual* provisions; thus failure to request instruction on affirmative defenses was not waived by failure to request); United States v. Carr, 18 M.J. 300 (C.M.A. 1984).

25. United States v. Brown, 43 M.J. 187 (1995) (duty to instruct is triggered when defense is raised, not by defense theory; any doubt in deciding whether instruction should be given should be resolved in favor of accused); United States v. Barnes, 39 M.J. 230 (C.M.A. 1994) (duty to instruct arises when some evidence is presented to which fact-finders could attach credit); United States v. Van Syoc, 36 M.J. 461 (C.M.A. 1993) (error not to instruct on defense of accident; duty to instruct arises where there is some evidence raising a defense; the evidence need not be compelling or beyond a reasonable doubt); United States v. Yandle, 34 M.J. 890 (N.M.C.M.R. 1992) (judge has duty to instruct on affirmative defenses even if defense does not request).

A defense is "reasonably raised" where record contains some evidence to which the court members could attach some weight if they desired. United States v. Simmelkjaer, 18 C.M.A. 406, 40 C.M.R. 118 (1969). *See also* United States v. Sawyer, 4 M.J. 64 (C.M.A. 1977).

26. R.C.M. 916(c). United States v. McMonagle, 38 M.J. 53 (C.M.A. 1993) (failure to instruct on justification was prejudicial error; duty to instruct is not determined by defense theory of case).

27. R.C.M. 916(d).

28. R.C.M. 916(e). United States v. Martinez, 40 M.J. 426 (C.M.A. 1994) (reversible error not to properly frame instruction on self-defense); United States v. Reid, 32 M.J. 146 (C.M.A. 1991) (self-defense was not reasonably raised); United States v. Rose, 28 M.J. 132 (C.M.A. 1989) (defense of self-defense reasonably in issue); United States v. Bradford, 29 M.J. 829 (A.C.M.R. 1989) (reversible error not to instruct on defense of self-defense that was reasonably raised by evidence, notwithstanding defense requests or theories).

29. R.C.M. 916(e)(5).

30. R.C.M. 916(f). United States v. Curry, 38 M.J. 77 (C.M.A. 1993) (court committed plain error not to instruct on defense of accident); United States v. Van Syoc, 36 M.J. 461 (C.M.A. 1993) (prejudicial error not to give instruction on defense of accident).

31. R.C.M. 916(g).

32. R.C.M. 916(h).

33. R.C.M. 916(i).

34. R.C.M. 916(j). United States v. Gillenwater, 43 M.J. 10 (1995) (mistake-of-fact defense was reasonably in issue); United States v. McMonagle, 38 M.J. 53 (C.M.A. 1993) (failure to instruct on mistake of fact and justification was prejudicial error; duty to instruct is not determined by defense theory of case); United States v. Sellers, 33 M.J. 364 (C.M.A. 1991) (instruction on mistake-of-fact defense in rape trial not required where defense was not reasonably raised); United States v. Peel, 29 M.J. 235 (C.M.A. 1989) (instruction on reasonable mistake of fact in rape and assault trial was not required); United States v. Gamble, 27 M.J. 298 (C.M.A. 1988) (reversible error not to instruct on mistake of fact in rape prosecution); United States v. Taylor,

---

35. R.C.M. 916(k). Voluntary intoxication is not a defense. R.C.M. 916(l).

(3) Instructions that the court consider only matters properly before it;[36]

(4) Instructions that (a) the accused is presumed to be innocent until his guilt is established by legal and competent evidence beyond a reasonable doubt;[37] (b) if there is reasonable doubt as to the accused's guilt, it must be resolved in favor of the accused;[38] (c) if there is reasonable doubt as to the degree of guilt, the finding must be in a lower degree to which there is no reasonable doubt;[39] and (d) the prosecution bears the burden of proof;[40]

(5) Instructions on deliberation and voting procedures.[41]

---

26 M.J. 127 (C.M.A. 1988) (failure to request instruction on reasonable mistake of fact in rape case not waived where evidence raised the defense); United States v. Johnson, 25 M.J. 691 (A.C.M.R. 1987) (reversible error not to give instruction on affirmative defense of mistake of fact in rape case where facts giving rise to that defense were "closely interwoven" with issues of consent and force in a closely contested case); United States v. Daniels, 28 M.J. 743 (A.F.C.M.R. 1989) (mistake of fact instruction was not required on charge of burglary where the evidence did not reasonably raise that defense; it was reasonably raised with regard to the offense of rape).

36. R.C.M. 920(e)(4). United States v. Skerrett, 40 M.J. 331 (C.M.A. 1994) (trial judge gave curative instruction to disregard evidence on charge dismissed at end of government's case).

37. Art. 51(c)(1), U.C.M.J. R.C.M. 920(e)(5)(A). See United States v. Czekala, 42 M.J. 168 (1995) (judge's reasonable doubt instruction; read as a whole the instruction emphasizes that burden was on government); United States v. Robinson, 38 M.J. 30 (C.M.A. 1993) (judge's instruction equating proof beyond a reasonable doubt to proof to a moral certainty was not misleading); United States v. Johnwell, 15 M.J. 32 (C.M.A. 1983) (in highly contested case, "reasonable doubt" *should not* be equated with "substantial doubt"). See also United States v. Salley, 9 M.J. 189 (C.M.A. 1980); United States v. Cherry, 14 M.J. 251 (C.M.A. 1982); United States v. Bins, 38 M.J. 704 (A.C.M.R. 1993) (judge's failure to give verbatim, seriatim instruction on Article 51(c), found in judge's benchbook not error; judge adequately covered key points within four corners of instructions).

38. Art. 51(c)(2), U.C.M.J. R.C.M. 920(e)(5)(B).

39. Art. 51(c)(3), U.C.M.J. R.C.M. 920(e)(5)(C). See, e.g., United States v. Morales, 16 M.J. 503 (A.F.C.M.R. 1983) (judge erred in not instructing under U.C.M.J. art. 51(c)(3); judge erroneously equated the term "degree" with "lesser-included offense." The former term encompasses more than the latter).

40. Art. 51(c)(4), U.C.M.J. R.C.M. 920(e)(5)(D). Note that an inconsistent instruction may arise if an improper mandatory presumption instruction is given that shifts the burden of proof to the accused. See § 15-18.

41. See § 15-15. R.C.M. 920(e)(6). United States v. Greene, 41 M.J. 57 (C.M.A. 1994) (failure to instruct members that they were to vote by secret written ballot was not plain error; defense waived issue by failing to object); United States v. Thomas, 39 M.J. 626 (N.M.C.M.R. 1993) (instruction that members could reconsider at any time and that additional instructions would be given if any member raised the issue was not erroneous; court noted that accepted practice is to inform court that if any member wants to reconsider a finding, additional instructions would be given in open court); United States v. Truitt, 32 M.J. 1010 (A.C.M.R. 1991) (judge's failure to instruct members that junior member should collect the votes and President would count the votes was harmless error, absent any allegation that independence of junior member was affected or that votes were miscounted; the court noted that if the junior member collects the ballots, the senior member is less likely to see how the others voted); United States v. Llewellyn, 32 M.J. 803 (A.C.M.R. 1991) (judge's failure to give instruction that junior member collect and count votes was nonprejudicial because junior member did so; acts of junior member are ministerial in nature; citing legislative history that observed that junior member is "so-called leg-boy"); United States v. Kendrick, 29 M.J. 792 (A.C.M.R. 1989) (nonprejudicial error on instructions regarding procedures for collecting and counting ballots); United States v. Lee, 16 M.J. 532 (A.C.M.R. 1983).

§ 15-14(C) TRIAL PROCEDURES § 15-14(C)

(6) Other instructions offering explanations, definitions, or directions that have been requested or that are *sua sponte* required.[42]

This last category would include definitions of legal terms,[43] instructions on evidence received for a limited purpose,[44] instructions on accomplice testimony,[45] character evidence,[46] and failure of the accused to testify.[47]

§ 15-14(C). Instructions Upon Request.

Requested instructions should be given if the matter is in issue and is not otherwise covered in the judge's instructions.[48] The request places the judge on notice and failure to instruct may be error[49] even if the request is a mis-

---

42. R.C.M. 920(e)(7). *See, e.g.*, United States v. Fleming, 38 M.J. 126 (C.M.A. 1993) (harmless error to fail to instruct court members that security measures necessary because of nature of offenses could not be used to infer accused's guilt); United States v. McLaurin, 22 M.J. 310 (C.M.A. 1986) (no *sua sponte* duty to give eyewitness identification instruction); United States v. Diaz, 39 M.J. 1114 (A.F.C.M.R. 1994) (plain error not to define harass or harassment where latter term was gravamen of offense); United States v. Miller, 34 M.J. 1175 (A.F.C.M.R. 1992) (prejudicial error not to define term custom in fraternization case and in not giving instruction on supervisory relationship); United States v. Combest, 14 M.J. 927 (A.C.M.R. 1982) (court declined to require judges to *sua sponte* instruct on testimony of paid informants; the judge should give an instruction upon request, however).
43. United States v. Sanders, 14 C.M.A. 524, 34 C.M.R. 304 (1964); United States v. Silva, 19 M.J. 501 (A.F.C.M.R. 1984) (nonprejudicial error for judge not to define "felony").
44. United States v. James, 5 M.J. 381 (C.M.A. 1978). *Cf.* Rule 105, Mil. R. Evid.
45. United States v. Gillette, 35 M.J. 468 (C.M.A. 1992) (instruction on accomplice testimony; court indicated that military judge should not label witness as accomplice as matter of law); United States v. Davis, 32 M.J. 166 (C.M.A. 1991) (judge's erroneous instruction on accomplice testimony was not plain error); United States v. McKinnie, 32 M.J. 141 (C.M.A. 1991) (nonprejudicial error for trial court to refuse to give accomplice instruction).
United States v. Devine, 36 M.J. 673 (N.M.C.M.R. 1992) (failure to give accomplice testimony instruction not plain error); United States v. Gittens, 36 M.J. 594 (A.F.C.M.R. 1992) (failure to instruct on accomplice testimony not plain error); United States v. Boswell, 30 M.J. 731 (A.F.C.M.R. 1990) (judge properly instructed court on accomplice testimony; court noted that law may have changed with regard to the need for giving such instructions but did not want to anticipate what Court of Military Appeals would do with the issue); United States v. Gilliam, 23 C.M.A. 4, 48 C.M.R. 260 (1974). *Cf.* United States v. Lee, 6 M.J. 96 (C.M.A. 1978) (not error to omit where the accomplice testimony was not self-contradictory, improbable or uncertain).
See also United States v. Allison, 8 M.J. 143 (C.M.A. 1979); United States v. Oxford, 21 M.J. 963 (N.M.C.M.R. 1986) (plain error not to give); United States v. DuBose, 19 M.J. 877 (A.F.C.M.R. 1985) (no error in refusing to give).
See generally Fischer, "Corroboration of Accomplice Testimony: The Military Rule," Army Law., May 1986, at 48.
46. *See generally*, United States v. Ali, 12 M.J. 1018 (A.C.M.R. 1982).
47. *See* Rule 301(g), Mil. R. Evid. The defense request either to give or not to give this instruction is normally binding. *See also* Carter v. Kentucky, 450 U.S. 288 (1981); Lakeside v. Oregon, 435 U.S. 333 (1978).
48. R.C.M. 920(c) Discussion. United States v. Thompson, 31 M.J. 125 (C.M.A. 1990) (accused was not entitled to instruction on cross-racial identification); United States v. Brooks, 25 M.J. 175 (C.M.A. 1987) (defendant was entitled to instruction on alibi defense).
49. United States v. Brooks, 25 M.J. 175 (C.M.A. 1987) (failure to give alibi defense instruction was reversible error); United States v. Pagel, 40 M.J. 771 (A.F.C.M.R. 1994) (not abuse of discretion to refuse to give sentencing instruction requested by accused); United States v. Ginter, 35

statement of the law or otherwise incorrect.[50] Failure to request an instruction may constitute waiver absent plain error.[51] In giving instructions, the judge should not identify the source of any particular instruction.[52]

§ 15-14(D). Review of Instructions Errors.

On appeal the courts will examine the instructions as a whole to determine if they provided meaningful legal principles for the members' consideration.[53] If there is error, the courts will examine for prejudice. That is, were the court members misled, was the instruction in question necessary, did it address a vital point in the trial, and did counsel lodge an objection at trial?[54] Where the judge has given inconsistent instructions, the courts will generally find prejudice.[55] Prejudice may also arise if the military judge does not tailor his comments on the evidence to the facts of the case,[56] or if he has in any way impermissibly shifted the burden to the accused.[57]

M.J. 799 (N.M.C.M.R. 1992) (test to decide whether failure to give requested instruction is whether the instruction is correct, whether it is substantially covered by other instructions, and whether failure to give it deprived accused of defense or seriously impaired effective presentation of his case); United States v. Sanders, 34 M.J. 1086 (A.F.C.M.R. 1992) (prejudicial not to give requested instruction on accomplice testimony); United States v. Cannon, 26 M.J. 674 (A.F.C.M.R. 1988) (failure to give requested instruction on interracial identification was reversible error where eyewitness identification was primary issue at trial); United States v. Jones, 7 M.J. 441 (C.M.A. 1979). The judge need not use the exact language suggested by counsel. United States v. Baylor, 16 C.M.A. 502, 37 C.M.R. 122 (1967). See also R.C.M. 920(c) Discussion.

50. See, e.g., United States v. Smith, 34 M.J. 341 (C.M.A. 1992) (failure to request instruction on good military character was not plain error and waived issue); United States v. Sellers, 12 C.M.A. 262, 30 C.M.R. 262 (1961) (inaccurate); United States v. Walker, 7 C.M.A. 669, 23 C.M.R. 133 (1957) (incorrect); United States v. Burden, 2 C.M.A. 547, 10 C.M.R. 45 (1953).

51. R.C.M. 920(f). United States v. Gittens, 39 M.J. 328 (C.M.A. 1994) (accused waived error by failing to request accomplice instruction); United States v. Swoape, 21 M.J. 414 (C.M.A. 1986); United States v. Webel, 16 M.J. 64 (C.M.A. 1983) (plain error found only in exceptional circumstances); United States v. Cosby, 14 M.J. 3 (C.M.A. 1982).
United States v. Jursnick, 24 M.J. 504 (A.F.C.M.R. 1987) (counsel failed to request instruction on presumption of continuing entrapment); United States v. Oxford, 21 M.J. 963 (N.M.C.M.R. 1986); United States v. Goetz, 17 M.J. 744 (A.C.M.R. 1983) (no plain error).

52. R.C.M. 920(c) Discussion.

53. United States v. Truman, 19 C.M.A. 504, 42 C.M.R. 106 (1970); United States v. Alford, 31 M.J. 814 (A.F.C.M.R. 1990).

54. United States v. Alford, 31 M.J. 814 (A.F.C.M.R. 1990) (improper instruction on element offense is not waived); United States v. Eckhoff, 27 M.J. 142 (C.M.A. 1988) (failure to give correct instruction on entrapment was plain error); United States v. Wilson, 26 M.J. 10 (C.M.A. 1988) (the fact that the defense was proceeding on an erroneous theory of culpable negligence did not excuse reversible error of judge in not giving instruction on involuntary manslaughter).
United States v. Eck, 28 M.J. 1046 (A.C.M.R. 1989) (judge's error in instructing on the issue of consent in a rape case was nonprejudicial). See generally United States v. Rusterholz, 39 C.M.R. 903 (A.F.B.R. 1968); Hoover, "The Application of the Doctrine of Waiver to Instructional Errors at Trial," 11 The Reporter 46 (Apr. 1982).

55. United States v. Pennington, 21 C.M.A. 461, 45 C.M.R. 235 (1972). Cf. United States v. Cowan, 42 M.J. 475 (1995) (erroneous instruction which contributed to superfluous finding was harmless).

56. E.g., United States v. Grandy, 11 M.J. 270 (C.M.A. 1981); United States v. Rowe, 11 M.J. 11 (C.M.A. 1981).

57. United States v. Fussell, 42 C.M.R. 723 (A.C.M.R. 1970).

In *United States v. Mance*,[58] the court indicated that when a trial judge "omits entirely any instruction on an element of a charged offense," the error may not be tested for harmlessness because the court was prevented from even considering the element.[59] When the judge, however, adequately identifies an element and requires the court to find it beyond a reasonable doubt, an erroneous instruction on that element may be tested for harmlessness.[60]

§ 15-15. Deliberations.

Following delivery of the judge's instructions the members retire for deliberation. They are to enter into full and free discussion of the case[1] in closed session—no other participant may be present.[2] If, during their discussions, they desire further evidence they may, subject to the military judge's interlocutory ruling obtain such evidence.[3] If recesses are necessary, the military judge opens the court and adjourns or recesses the proceedings;[4] the military generally does not follow the practice of sequestering the court members.[5] During their deliberations the members may review and consider any written instructions given by the military judge,[6] admitted exhibits,[7] and any notes they may have taken during trial.[8] They may draw on the knowledge of the

---

58. 26 M.J. 244 (C.M.A. 1988).
59. *Id.* at 255 (emphasis in original). *See* United States v. Brown, 26 M.J. 266 (C.M.A. 1988) (plain error for judge to fail to instruct on the need to find any aspect of knowledge where the accused was charged with use of marihuana).
60. *Id.* at 256 (emphasis in original).
1. United States v. Accordino, 20 M.J. 102 (C.M.A. 1985); United States v. Nash, 5 C.M.A. 550, 18 C.M.R. 174 (1955). *See also* R.C.M. 921(a).
2. R.C.M. 921(a). Error may result if the verdict is not formally arrived at with all members present in this closed session. United States v. Solak, 12 C.M.A. 440, 28 C.M.R. 6 (1959).
3. R.C.M. 921(b). A request for additional evidence is not an announcement of acquittal. United States v. Parker, 7 C.M.A. 182, 21 C.M.R. 308 (1956). Proper announcement of findings as to the specification may save a failure to announce a finding on the charge. *See* United States v. Logan, 15 M.J. 1084 (A.F.C.M.R. 1983).
4. United States v. Jones, 37 M.J. 321 (C.M.A. 1993) (judge erred in not instructing members that they should follow formal procedure for recessing during their deliberations; court noted that that procedure is designed to insure that all members are present and not subject to improper communications).
5. United States v. Cordell, 37 M.J. 592 (A.F.C.M.R. 1993) (discussion of practice; military judge has discretion on instructing members on use of "comfort breaks" during deliberations). *Cf.* United States v. Jones, 37 M.J. 321 (C.M.A. 1993) (error for judge not to instruct court members to return to court for formal recess procedures during sentencing deliberations).
6. *See* R.C.M. 921(b) and § 15-14(A).
7. *See, e.g.,* United States v. Austin, 35 M.J. 271 (C.M.A. 1992) (prejudicial error where Article 32 testimony taken into deliberation room as exhibit; court noted commonality between depositions and Article 32 testimony; Article 32 testimony may be read into evidence by proponent); United States v. Hurt, 9 C.M.A. 735, 27 C.M.R. 3 (1958). However, stipulations of testimony, United States v. Schmitt, 25 C.M.R. 822 (A.F.B.R. 1958) and depositions, United States v. Jakaitis, 10 C.M.A. 41, 27 C.M.R. 115 (1958), are not considered exhibits.
8. United States v. Christensen, 30 C.M.R. 959 (A.F.B.R. 1961); United States v. Turbeville, 32 C.M.R. 745 (C.G.C.M.R. 1962). *See also* United States v. Caldwell, 11 C.M.A. 257, 29 C.M.R. 73 (1960) (clarification in conflicting "notes" must come from military judge in open court).

ways of the world,[9] but they may not consider the expertise of any one of the members on the matter in issue.[10] Nor should superiority of rank be used to sway the other court members during the deliberations.[11]

To assist the members in making their findings, the judge will submit to them a findings worksheet, marked as an appellate exhibit, and previously reviewed by counsel.[12]

Voting on the findings is by secret written ballot.[13] Unless death is a mandatory punishment for the offense charged, a two-thirds vote is required for a finding of guilty; less than that results in an acquittal.[14] There are thus no "hung juries" in military practice. In *United States v. Shroeder*,[15] the court concluded that the requirement of only a two-thirds vote to convict an accused was not inconsistent with the requirement that where the accused has been found guilty of a felony murder, three-fourths of the members must vote to assess a *mandatory* life sentence. The court noted that a vote on the merits only addresses whether the prosecution has proved an accused's guilt beyond a reasonable doubt. On sentencing, the moral judgments of the members are involved.

The President of the Court determines the order in which the charges will be considered.[16] They vote on the specification before voting on the charge[17] and the votes are counted by the junior member of the court.[18]

The finding is fixed by the first ballot[19] but the members may reconsider their vote.[20] Because the rules for reconsideration and reballoting are com-

---

9. United States v. Witherspoon, 16 M.J. 252 (C.M.A. 1983); United States v. Ivey, 37 C.M.R. 626 (A.B.R. 1967); United States v. Worrell, 3 M.J. 817 (A.F.C.M.R. 1977).
10. United States v. Rinehart 8 C.M.A. 402, 24 C.M.R. 212 (1957) (may not use legal references); United States v. Lewandowski, 17 C.M.A. 51, 37 C.M.R. 315 (1967) (member read trial counsel's manual during trial).
11. R.C.M. 921(a). United States v. Accordino, 20 M.J. 102 (C.M.A. 1985).
12. See Appendix 28 for a sample worksheet.
13. Art. 51(a), U.C.M.J. R.C.M. 921(c)(1). United States v. Kendrick, 29 M.J. 792 (A.C.M.R. 1989) (court recounts history of requirement for written ballots); United States v. Martinez, 17 M.J. 916 (N.M.C.M.R. 1984) (prejudicial error occurred where members conducted an *oral* vote).
14. Art. 52, U.C.M.J. United States v. Vidal, 23 M.J. 319 (C.M.A. 1987) (it is not necessary that two-thirds of the court members agree on a particular theory of guilt); United States v. Francis, 15 M.J. 424 (C.M.A. 1983) (failure to reach finding amounts to finding of not guilty); United States v. Lomax, 12 M.J. 1001 (A.C.M.R. 1982). *See also* Mendrano v. Smith, 797 F.2d 1538 (10th Cir. 1986) (court held that the two-thirds requirement does not violate due process).
15. 27 M.J. 87 (C.M.A. 1988).
16. R.C.M. 921(c)(5)(A). The members may, however, object to the president's decision.
17. R.C.M. 921(c)(5)(A).
18. R.C.M. 921(c)(5)(B). United States v. Truitt, 32 M.J. 1010 (A.C.M.R. 1991) (court noted that if the junior member collects the ballots, the senior member is less likely to see how the others voted); United States v. Llewellyn, 32 M.J. 803 (A.C.M.R. 1991) (citing legislative history which observed that junior member is "so-called leg-boy").
19. R.C.M. 921(c)(3) and 924(b) Discussion. *See also* United States v. Thomas, 39 M.J. 626 (N.M.C.M.R. 1993) (judge denied defense request to poll members to determine how many times they had voted on findings; there was no indication that multiple votes had occurred); United States v. Lawson, 16 M.J. 38 (C.M.A. 1983) (although "straw poll" informal, nonbinding votes, are not prohibited by U.C.M.J. or M.C.M., court did not believe the practice should be encouraged).
20. R.C.M. 924.

plex, the members will usually be instructed that if a reballot is desired, the court will be opened and further instructions will be given.[21] A finding of guilty or not guilty[22] may be reconsidered by the court members at any time before the finding is announced in open court.[23] To reconsider a finding of not guilty, a majority of the members must concur in a vote, by secret written ballot, to reconsider.[24] But more than one-third of the members must concur in a vote to reconsider a prior finding of guilty.[25] If the necessary number of members vote to reconsider, they then vote again on the question of guilt.[26]

If during their deliberations the members desire additional evidence or clarification of the judge's instructions,[27] the judge will open the court and consider the members' requests. If the members wish to call additional witnesses, the judge should determine whether under the circumstances, such testimony is required.[28]

§ 15-16. Verdict; Announcement of Findings.

§ 15-16(A). General Findings.

When the court members indicate that they have reached a verdict, the court is opened and the findings are announced.[1] The findings as to specifica-

---

21. *See* United States v. Thomas, 39 M.J. 626 (N.M.C.M.R. 1993) (court noted usual practice of giving more detailed instructions in open court if any member indicates a desire to reballot); United States v. Jones, 15 M.J. 967 (A.C.M.R. 1983) (erroneous instruction on procedures for reconsideration of findings is presumptively prejudicial).
22. R.C.M. 924(a).
23. R.C.M. 924(a). In 1995, R.C.M. 924(a) was amended to reflect that the members could reconsider any finding, whether guilty or not guilty, at any time before the finding was announced in open court. The earlier version permitted the members to reconsider any finding of guilty before a sentence was announced.
The 1995 amendments also changed R.C.M. 924(c) to indicate that if the case is a bench trial, the military judge may reconsider any finding of guilty at any time before sentence is announced and may reconsider a finding of not guilty only by reason of lack of mental responsibility at any time before sentence is announced or authentication of the record in case of a complete acquittal.
24. R.C.M. 924(b).
25. R.C.M. 924(b).
26. R.C.M. 924(b).
27. *See* R.C.M. 921(b). United States v. Westmoreland, 31 M.J. 160 (C.M.A. 1990) (judge was proper in giving additional instructions on aider and abettor theory following court members' questions, even though defense counsel had objected to such); United States v. Higerd, 26 M.J. 848 (A.C.M.R. 1988) (although informal communications between judge and court members may prejudice substantial rights of accused, there was no prejudice where the court opened the door and informally asked judge, in presence of accused and counsel, whether it could adjudge a general discharge).
28. *See* United States v. Carter, 40 M.J. 102 (C.M.A. 1994) (not abuse of discretion to deny court members' request to recall witnesses after court was closed for deliberations); United States v. Lampani, 14 M.J. 22 (C.M.A. 1982) (judge should consider, *inter alia*, problems in obtaining witness, possible delays in proceedings, objections of counsel, materiality of testimony, and whether testimony may be privileged).
1. United States v. Dilday, 47 C.M.R. 172 (A.C.M.R. 1973) (accused has right to announcement in open court). *See also* Art. 53, U.C.M.J. and R.C.M. 922 which require prompt announcement of findings.

§ 15-16(A)   MILITARY CRIMINAL JUSTICE   § 15-16(A)

tions are "guilty," "not guilty," "not guilty of an offense as charged, but guilty of a named lesser-included offense,"[2] "guilty with exceptions, with or without substitutions," "not guilty of the exceptions but guilty of the substitutions, if any," or "not guilty by reason of lack of mental responsibility."[3] A court may not use exceptions and substitutions to create a variance by changing substantially the nature of the offense[4] or to increase the seriousness of the offense or the level of maximum punishment.[5] Findings regarding the *charges* are "guilty," "not guilty," or "not guilty of the listed charge but guilty of another article of the U.C.M.J."[6] The court members are not permitted to make special findings.[7] Under the *Manual* the announcement of the verdict need not refer to the fact that at least two-thirds of the members, voting by secret written ballot, found the accused guilty.[8]

Minor irregularities in form generally will not constitute ground for reversal if the announced verdict conveys the manifest intentions of the members and is free from ambiguity.[9] Where the announcement misstates the wording agreed upon in deliberation, the mistake may be corrected.[10] On the other

---

2. In 1993, R.C.M. 918(a)(1) was amended by Change 6 to the Manual to permit the court to enter a finding for a "named lesser offense" and bring military practice in conformity with federal civilian practice. *See* FED. R. CRIM. P. 31(c). *See generally* Milhizer & McShane, "Analysis of Change 6 to the 1984 Manual for Courts-Martial," ARMY LAW., May 1994, p. 40.

3. *See also* § 13-3(D).

4. *See* R.C.M. 918(a)(1). United States v. Evans, 37 M.J. 468 (C.M.A. 1993) (judge's findings of guilt by exceptions and substitutions were fatal and denied due process because they substantially changed charged offense); United States v. Dailey, 37 M.J. 1078 (N.M.C.M.R. 1993) (judge's findings which varied as to nature of harm caused by accused's assault was not fatal variance; the variance did not change the time, place or means of assault, or identity of victim).

5. R.C.M. 918(a)(1).

6. R.C.M. 918(a)(2).

7. R.C.M. 918(b) Discussion. Cf. United States v. Guron, 37 M.J. 942, 950 n. 8 (A.F.C.M.R. 1993) (military judge did not err in asking court members to announce which theory of larceny they had relied upon; court noted that proscription in Discussion accompanying R.C.M. 918(b) is not binding).

8. *See* R.C.M. 922(a) Analysis. The members are presumed to have followed the judge's instructions on these requirements. United States v. Ricketts, 1 M.J. 78 (C.M.A. 1975).

9. United States v. Harris, 25 M.J. 281 (C.M.A. 1987); United States v. Williams, 21 M.J. 330 (C.M.A. 1986) (absence of specific acts in findings on indecent assault did not amount to an acquittal) (not reversible error for members to return finding of lesser offense of "oral sodomy" instead of using the more precise language of "indecent act").

United States v. Matura, 32 M.J. 671 (A.F.C.M.R. 1991) (challenge to minor variance is waived absent plain error); United States v. Read, 29 M.J. 690 (A.C.M.R. 1989) (noting that the specification is the basis for guilt or innocence, court concluded that failure to announce a finding on the charge was not fatal); United States v. Timmerman, 28 M.J. 531 (A.F.C.M.R. 1989) (president of court announced a finding of guilty of charge but not of three specifications; court concluded that under facts, the members had voted on each of the three specifications); United States v. Dilday, 47 C.M.R. 172 (A.C.M.R. 1973).

10. United States v. Perez, 40 M.J. 373 (C.M.A. 1994) (judge acted correctly in instructing members to return to deliberation room to correct their findings); United States v. Latham, 39 M.J. 841 (A.C.M.R. 1994) (appellate court conformed findings to those intended by judge, even though defense failed to object to judge's omission in announcement); United States v. Mantilla, 36 M.J. 621 (A.C.M.R. 1992) (error was discovered and corrected before court was adjourned; it did not amount to a reconsideration); United States v. Downs, 4 C.M.A. 8, 15 C.M.R. 8 (1954). *See also* R.C.M. 922(b) Discussion.

§ 15-16(A)   TRIAL PROCEDURES   § 15-16(A)

hand, if the verdict itself is defective, the military judge may refuse to give it effect.[11] After findings are announced, the members may still reconsider findings of guilty, but may not reconsider findings of not guilty[12] or findings by exceptions and substitutions that are so defective as to result in an acquittal.[13] This reconsideration must occur before sentence is announced and the same rules apply to reconsideration of findings entered by the military judge.[14] To foreclose many problems in this area the military judge will often review the findings worksheet used by the members before asking the president of the court to announce the verdict.[15] Any statements made by the members of the court during the examination of the worksheet should not be considered the formal announcement of the court's findings.[16]

---

11. *See, e.g.,* United States v. Brooks, 42 M.J. 484 (1995) (military judge entered findings of not guilty after determining that court members had used incorrect voting procedures; court indicated that judge's actions were tantamount to dismissal of charge with prejudice, which was appealable by the government); United States v. Perez, 40 M.J. 373 (C.M.A. 1994) (extensive discussion of options open to judge if court members return an improper finding, e.g., enter a finding of not guilty or ask or direct the court members to reconsider their findings following any additional instructions); United States v. Walker, 39 M.J. 731 (N.M.C.M.R. 1994) (generally an accused is not entitled to relief on an inconsistent verdict because the court may have simply decided to give the accused a break; a verdict is not inherently inconsistent if any grounds exist in record to support judge's findings); United States v. Kelly, 12 M.J. 509 (A.C.M.R. 1981) (judge's authority to enter contrary findings is based upon his power to make rulings of law under Art. 51(b)); in effect this parallels the civilian judge's authority to enter a judgment notwithstanding the verdict.
12. R.C.M. 924(a). *See also* § 15-15. The same rule applies to all lesser included offenses within the offense as to which a not guilty finding was announced. United States v. Boswell, 8 C.M.A. 145, 23 C.M.R. 369 (1957).
13. United States v. Hunt, 37 M.J. 344 (C.M.A. 1993) (variance of three weeks in date of offense was not fatal. The court said that to prevail on a fatal variance claim, the accused must show that the variance was material and the accused was prejudiced); United States v. Lee, 1 M.J. 15 (C.M.A. 1975) (variance not fatal); United States v. Boswell, 8 C.M.A. 145, 23 C.M.R. 369 (1957); United States v. Gowadia, 34 M.J. 714 (A.C.M.R. 1992) (court applied two-pronged test for determining whether the accused was prejudiced by a variance in what was charged and the finding of guilty: (1) whether accused was misled to extent that he could not adequately prepare for trial and (2) whether accused was fully protected against another prosecution for same offense); United States v. Church, 29 M.J. 679 (A.F.C.M.R. 1989) (court determined that variances in the exact dates and locations of the offenses were not fatal variances between pleading and proof).
14. R.C.M. 924(c). United States v. Chatman, 49 C.M.R. 319 (N.C.M.R. 1974).
15. *See* Appendix 28. R.C.M. 921(d) Discussion. *See also* United States v. Johnson, 22 M.J. 945 (A.C.M.R. 1986) (lining out portions amounted to findings).
16. *See* R.C.M. 921(d). United States v. Perez, 40 M.J. 373 (C.M.A. 1994) (president's act of informing judge of finding during latter's examination of the findings worksheet did not amount to the formal announcement of findings; judge instructed members that they had reached an inconsistent finding and ordered them to reconsider); United States v. London, 15 C.M.R. 90 (C.M.A. 1954) (only findings that have effect are those formally and correctly announced in open court).

§ 15-16(B). Impeaching the Findings.

Military courts generally view with disfavor any attempts to impeach the verdict.[17] The military judge may determine whether the minimum number of votes were provided, but he may not poll the members.[18] The internal workings of the court are usually not questioned but may be reviewed if it appears that the members obtained extraneous and prejudicial information[19] or were subjected to external influence[20] or unlawful command influence.[21] In some cases the possibility of such influence will not arise until after trial when one or more members will present information in post-trial affidavits.[22] In any

---

17. United States v. Witherspoon, 16 M.J. 252 (C.M.A. 1983); United States v. Bishop, 11 M.J. 7 (C.M.A. 1981); United States v. Langer, 41 M.J. 780 (A.F.Ct.Crim.App. 1995) (court condemned counsel's attempt to impeach verdict through questionnaire seeking feedback on counsel's performance); United States v. Heimer, 34 M.J. 541 (A.F.C.M.R. 1991) (judicial reluctance to permit inquiry into verdict rests on desire to avoid harassment of court members; if inquiry takes place it must focus on objective manifestations of impropriety. In this case, the use of post-trial questionnaires was improper); United States v. Stone, 23 M.J. 772 (A.F.C.M.R. 1987) (sanctity of deliberation room should not be broken by allegations of eavesdroppers). United States v. Martinez, 17 M.J. 916 (N.M.C.M.R. 1984); See, e.g., Rule 509, MIL. R. EVID. (deliberations are privileged) and Rule 606, MIL. R. EVID. (members usually not permitted to testify). See generally Saltzburg, Schinasi & Schlueter, *Military Rules of Evidence Manual*, 603-605, 631-638 (3d ed. 1991); Stone, "Post-Trial Contact with Court Members: A Critical Analysis," 38 A.F. L. REV. 179 (1994); Dean, "The Deliberative Privilege Under M.R.E. 509," ARMY LAW., Nov. 1981, at 1.
18. R.C.M. 922(e). United States v. Hendon, 6 M.J. 171 (C.M.A. 1970); United States v. Gray, 37 M.J. 751 (A.C.M.R. 1993) (on rehearing) (neither Manual nor U.C.M.J. expressly authorize polling of members). Cf. United States v. Curtis, 33 M.J. 101, 110 (C.M.A. 1991) (Cox, J. concurring) (recommendation that sentence worksheet in death penalty case reflect signatures of members); United States v. Thomas, 39 M.J. 626 (N.M.C.M.R. 1993) (extensive discussion of polling members in death penalty case). Cf. Caldwell, "Polling the Military Jury," 11 The ADVOCATE 53 (1979).
19. R.C.M. 923. United States v. Straight, 42 M.J. 244 (1995) (court member's discussion of the possibility of parole was not extraneous prejudicial information); United States v. Loving, 41 M.J. 213 (1994) (presumption that court members followed instructions of judge; that presumption may be rebutted by competent evidence); United States v. Turner, 42 M.J. 783 (N.M.Ct.Crim.App. 1995) (conviction and sentencing of accused's co-conspirator was extraneous information); United States v. Ezell, 24 M.J. 690 (A.C.M.R. 1987) (deliberations were not affected by fact that several members became aware of dismissed charges when an extra charge sheet "flyer" was erroneously distributed).
    In United States v. Johnson, 23 M.J. 327 (C.M.A. 1987), one of the court members filed an affidavit two years after the trial, which indicated that he had had training in the martial arts and that during the deliberations he had demonstrated how the victim might have been killed with nunchukus, which had been introduced into evidence and taken into the deliberation room. The court concluded that if such a demonstration occurred it was "merely an examination and evaluation of evidence already produced...."
20. R.C.M. 923. United States v. Hargrove, 25 M.J. 68 (C.M.A. 1987) (member's out-of-court experiment with tanks did not prejudice the accused).
21. R.C.M. 923. See also United States v. Loving, 41 M.J. 213 (1994) (defense obtained affidavits from three court members four years after they imposed death sentence; court concluded that under the facts the affidavits were inadmissible under MIL. R. EVID. 606 except for the limited purpose of showing extraneous influence or unlawful command influence; court rejected exception for capital cases); United States v. Accordino, 20 M.J. 102 (C.M.A. 1985), *on remand*, 20 M.J. 870 (A.F.C.M.R. 1985); United States v. Carr, 18 M.J. 297 (C.M.A. 1984).
22. *See, e.g.,* United States v. Hargrove, 25 M.J. 68 (C.M.A. 1987) (court accepted post-trial affidavit but noted that it is normally reluctant to do so); United States v. Accordino, 20 M.J. 102

event the judge may further question the members, in a post-trial proceeding if necessary,[23] and decide whether the findings entered by the members have indeed been impeached.[24] The prosecution in that case must rebut the presumption of prejudice by clear and positive proof.[25] Evidence that indicates that one or more of the court members misunderstood the applicable law or facts will not be sufficient to impeach the verdict.[26] Likewise, attempts to impeach the verdict by showing problems or defects in the deliberative process are not permitted.[27] These same rules would generally apply to impeachment of general findings entered by a military judge.[28]

§ 15-16(C). Special Findings by the Military Judge.

Although court members are not permitted to enter special findings,[29] the military judge is and may find it desirable to do so.[30] He may make them in any case, but must do so if counsel presents a timely request.[31] Counsel's request must be made before the judge makes general findings,[32] must relate to factual matters reasonably in issue,[33] and should specify the matter to be

---

(C.M.A. 1985); United States v. Bishop, 11 M.J. 7 (C.M.A. 1981). *See also* R.C.M. 1102 (post-trial sessions).

23. R.C.M. 923 Discussion. United States v. Straight, 42 M.J. 244 (1995) (court cautioned counsel and court members of obligation to protect secrecy of deliberations; if exceptions to Rule 606 are triggered, disclosure should not extend to impact of extrinsic evidence on deliberations or voting); United States v. Carr, 18 M.J. 297 (C.M.A. 1984) (reversible error for judge not to hold Art. 39(a) session to inquire into merits of letter from court member that command influence had been exerted during court's deliberations); United States v. Thomas, 39 M.J. 626 (N.M.C.M.R. 1993) (detailed discussion of impeaching findings and question of whether could properly order depositions of members); United States v. Stone, 23 M.J. 772 (A.F.C.M.R. 1987) (court concluded that it was harmless error for an allegation of jury misconduct to be handled administratively; such information should be taken to the trial judge. The error was harmless because in this case the letter alleging jury misconduct did not indicate that the members had acted improperly in reaching their verdict).
24. R.C.M. 923 Discussion. United States v. Witherspoon, 16 M.J. 252 (C.M.A. 1983).
25. United States v. Gaston, 45 C.M.R. 837 (A.C.M.R. 1972).
26. R.C.M. 923 Discussion. United States v. Martinez, 17 M.J. 916 (N.M.C.M.R. 1984) (error for judge to inquire into mental processes of members). *See also* United States v. Hance, 10 M.J. 622 (A.C.M.R. 1980).
27. United States v. Brooks, 42 M.J. 484 (1995) (judge erred in questioning members about voting procedures); United States v. Loving, 41 M.J. 213 (1994) (affidavits of members re voting procedures could not be considered except as permitted under Mil.R.Evid. 606(b)).
28. United States v. Perry, 22 M.J. 669 (A.C.M.R. 1986) (judge's finding of assault by means of sexual intercourse was inconsistent with his finding that no rape occurred because the victim consented); United States v. Rice, 20 M.J. 764 (A.F.C.M.R. 1985) (attempted impeachment of sentence imposed by judge).
29. R.C.M. 918(b) Discussion.
30. Art. 51(d), U.C.M.J. R.C.M. 918(b). *See generally* Schinasi, "Special Findings: Their Use at Trial and On Appeal," 87 Mil. L. Rev. 73 (1980).
31. Art. 51(d), U.C.M.J. R.C.M. 918(b). United States v. Gerard, 11 M.J. 440 (C.M.A. 1981); United States v. Falin, 43 C.M.R. 702 (A.C.M.R. 1971). *See also* Rule 23, Fed. R. Crim. P.
32. R.C.M. 918(b). United States v. Pratcher, 14 M.J. 819 (A.C.M.R. 1982).
33. R.C.M. 918(b). United States v. Gerard, 11 M.J. 440 (C.M.A. 1981). The judge need not enter special findings as to any offenses of which the accused was acquitted.

determined.[34] Although the *Manual* indicates that the trial judge may require counsel to submit the request in writing if specific matters are involved, failure to do so will probably not relieve the judge from entering special findings.[35] The format for entering special findings is not crucial as long as the substance is properly presented.[36] Sample special findings are included in Appendix 32. Special findings may be made at any time prior to authentication of the record of trial,[37] but should preferably be made near the time of announcing the general findings.[38] On appeal, the courts will determine the sufficiency of the facts supporting the judge's findings.[39]

These special findings, which relate to the guilt of the accused, should not be confused with other essential factual findings that may be made by the military judge during the course of the trial, such as findings of fact supporting his ruling on the admissibility of certain evidence under the Military Rules of Evidence.[40]

§ 15-17. Sentencing Procedures.

Following an announcement of a finding of guilty, the court-martial usually proceeds directly to sentencing. The topic of sentencing is addressed in Chapter 16.

PART III

EVIDENTIARY RULES

§ 15-18. General.

The evidentiary rules applied at courts-martial include consideration of constitutional standards, various provisions in the U.C.M.J., Chapter XXVII of the Manual for Courts-Martial (The Military Rules of Evidence), rules of evidence generally recognized in criminal cases before federal district courts,

---

When special findings are made, they should address those issues upon which instructions would be required in jury trial. United States v. Ericson, 13 M.J. 725 (N.M.C.M.R. 1982).

See also United States v. Burke, 4 M.J. 530 (N.C.M.R. 1977) (not required where matters were not relevant or material).

34. United States v. Baker, 47 C.M.R. 506 (A.C.M.R. 1973).

35. *Compare* R.C.M. 918(b) *with* United States v. Pratcher, 14 M.J. 819 (A.C.M.R. 1982) (the judge may not refuse to enter special findings simply because counsel failed to submit written request specifying the matter to be decided). *See also* United States v. Gerard, 11 M.J. 440 (C.M.A. 1981).

36. In United States v. Orben, 28 M.J. 172 (C.M.A. 1989), the court indicated that the military judge had properly declined to detail the evidence that he had relied upon in researching certain findings. The court said that he was not required to write a "brief" in support of his findings. R.C.M. 918(b) provides that the special findings may be orally noted for the record.

37. R.C.M. 918(b).

38. United States v. Falin, 43 C.M.R. 702 (A.C.M.R. 1971).

39. United States v. Lohr, 43 C.M.R. 1017 (A.F.C.M.R. 1970).

40. *See* § 13-4.

and finally the rules of evidence at common law.[1] Almost all of the evidentiary rules necessary for trying a military case are included in the Military Rules of Evidence. This part of the chapter addresses not only those Rules but also the topics of presumptions and inferences, stipulations, and depositions, topics not covered in the Rules. Finally the methods of preserving error and the subject of evidentiary instructions are discussed.

§ 15-19. Military Rules of Evidence.

In 1980, Chapter XXVII of the 1969 Manual for Courts-Martial was amended to include 84 new Military Rules of Evidence. In the 1984 revisions to the *Manual* the Rules were placed in Part III and the accompanying Drafters' Analysis is now located in an appendix to the *Manual*. The Rules are for the most part adoptions, with variation, of the Federal Rules of Evidence. The modifications were made to incorporate specialized military practices and terms. Sections I, II, IV, VI-XI generally follow the Federal pattern but Sections III and V are much different. In Section III counsel will find exclusionary rules and in V, specific rules of privilege. The general outline of the Rules is as follows:

    Section I. General Provisions.
    Section II. Judicial Notice.
    Section III. Exclusionary Rules and Related Matters Concerning Self-Incrimination Search and Seizure, and Eyewitness Identification.
    Section IV. Relevancy and Its Limits.
    Section V. Privileges.
    Section VI. Witnesses.
    Section VII. Opinions and Expert Testimony.
    Section VIII. Hearsay.
    Section IX. Authentication and Identification.
    Section X. Contents of Writings, Records and Photographs.
    Section XI. Miscellaneous Rules.

The Rules are applicable to all courts-martial[1] including Article 39(a) sessions, fact-finding proceedings ordered on review, proceedings in revision, and contempt proceedings.[2] They may be relaxed during sentencing proceedings[3] and, with the exception of the privileges, are not applied at Article 32 investigations, proceedings involving search authorizations or pretrial confinement hearings.[4]

---

1. *See* Rule 101, MIL. R. EVID.
1. Rules 101, 1101, MIL. R. EVID.
2. *Id. See* Saltzburg, Schinasi & Schlueter, *Military Rules of Evidence Manual* (3d ed. 1991).
3. Rule 1101(c), MIL. R. EVID. R.C.M. 1003(c)(3). *See generally* United States v. Martin, 20 M.J. 227 (C.M.A. 1985); United States v. Strong, 17 M.J. 263 (C.M.A. 1984).
4. Rule 1101(d), MIL. R. EVID. *See* United States v. Martel, 19 M.J. 917 (A.C.M.R. 1985) (Rules may serve as a "guide" at Article 32 proceeding).

§ 15-20. Presumptions and Inferences.

Although the Military Rules of Evidence do not include discussions of presumptions and inferences in court-martial practice, they are addressed in other parts of the Manual for Courts-Martial and a substantial amount of military case law has engrafted them into courts-martial practice.

The terms *presumption* and *inference* are sometimes confused and used indiscriminately.[1] Both terms describe an evidentiary relationship between predicate facts and the existence, or lack thereof, of another fact. In *Sandstrom v. Montana*,[2] the Supreme Court briefly addressed the differences. Presumptions may be either conclusive[3] or rebuttable;[4] in the either case, the accused's due process rights may be violated if the presumption shifts the burden of *persuasion* to the defendant on an element of the offense.[5] If the presumption, on the other hand, is merely permissive, or if it only reasonably shifts the burden of *production* of evidence, it is normally valid because the burden of persuasion still rests upon the prosecution.[6]

In *Sandstrom*, the Court recognized that permissive inferences are constitutional.[7] That is, the court *may*, but is not required to, conclude that the existence of one fact infers another fact but that the prosecution is still charged with proving each element of the offense beyond a reasonable doubt.[8] The line dividing inferences and presumptions is thin and in many cases what courts call a permissive presumption is really a permissive inference. The label is not crucial as long as the effect of the device is understood.

In military practice the term "presumption" is used in conjunction with (1) the accused's innocence;[9] (2) the accused's sanity at the time of the offense[10] and his mental competency at the time of trial;[11] (3) violation of the

---

1. See Lilly, *An Introduction to the Law of Evidence* (1978) and Hug, "Presumptions and Inferences in Criminal Law," 57 MIL. L. REV. 81 (1972).
2. 442 U.S. 510 (1979).
3. *Id.* at 517, 521. The court observed that this is not really a presumption but more an irrebuttable direction to find the fact in question once the facts triggering the presumption are proved. *See also* Morrissette v. United States, 342 U.S. 246 (1952).
4. 442 U.S. at 524. *See also* Mullaney v. Wilbur, 421 U.S. 684 (1975).
5. 442 U.S. at 523-24. That would conflict with the overriding presumption of innocence. Rose v. Clark, 106 S. Ct. 3101 (1986). *See generally* Jerries & Stephan, "Defenses, Presumptions, and Burden of Proof in Criminal Law," 88 Yale L.J. 1325 (1979).
6. This device is usually labelled as a *defense. See, e.g.,* R.C.M. 916(b) and 916(k)(A) (presumption of sanity remains until evidence to the contrary is admitted).
7. Rose v. Clark, 106 S. Ct. 3101 (1986); Francis v. Franklin, 471 U.S. 307 (1985); Ulster County Court v. Allen, 442 U.S. 140 (1979).
8. *See, e.g.,* United States v. Morton, 15 M.J. 850, 854 (A.F.C.M.R. 1983) where the court said:

   Technically, the term "permissible inference" is simply a description of the general type of logical, relevant, factual deduction that a juror may legitimately draw from one or more general facts introduced at trial as circumstantial evidence when that fact or facts is combined with other evidence admitted at trial and/or the jurors' life experiences.

9. *See* Art. 51(c)(1), U.C.M.J.
10. R.C.M. 916(k)(3).
11. R.C.M. 909.

§ 15-21   TRIAL PROCEDURES   § 15-21

accused's right to a speedy trial where pretrial confinement exceeds ninety days;[12] and (4) a witness' competency to testify.[13]

A number of permissible inferences have been recognized in court-martial litigation. They include inferences that:

(1) A detailed appointed attorney acts on behalf of the client;[14]

(2) Official duties were performed in a proper manner;[15]

(3) An existing condition or relationship continued;[16]

(4) Identity of a name will support an inference of identity of person;[17]

(5) Persons in unexplained possession of recently stolen property stole the property;[18]

(6) Military judges in bench trials considered only competent evidence;[19]

(7) Nonpayment of bad check within five days of notice infers an intent to defraud and knowledge of insufficient funds;[20]

(8) Exclusive and conscious possession of drugs infers wrongful and knowledgeable possession;[21] and

(9) Serviceable Government property has the value stated in the official price lists.[22]

The foregoing inferences may not be substituted for proof as to an element of an offense that must be proved beyond a reasonable doubt.[23] But they may be rebutted by contrary evidence either on the base fact or the fact to be inferred.[24]

§ 15-21. Stipulations.

Stipulations in military practice may be either oral or written and counsel may stipulate to factual matters and expected testimony or the contents of a document.[1] The format used for a written stipulation is not crucial, although it generally includes some information about the style of the case and appro-

---

12. United States v. Burton, 21 C.M.A. 112, 44 C.M.R. 166 (1971), discussed at § 13-3(C).
13. Rule 601, MIL. R. EVID.
14. United States v. Hightower, 5 C.M.A. 385, 18 C.M.R. 9 (1955).
15. *See, e.g.*, United States v. Nault, 4 M.J. 318, 320, n.8 (C.M.A. 1978) (handling of exhibits by laboratory chemists).
16. United States v. Hobbs, 8 M.J. 71 (C.M.A. 1979); United States v. Smith, 14 C.M.A. 405, 34 C.M.R. 185 (1964).
17. United States v. Cramer, 1 C.M.R. 210 (A.B.R. 1951).
18. Rugendorf v. United States, 376 U.S. 528 (1964); United States v. Sparks, 21 C.M.A. 134, 44 C.M.R. 188 (1971); United States v. Morton, 15 M.J. 850 (A.F.C.M.R. 1983).
19. United States v. Weaver, 42 C.M.R. 434 (A.C.M.R. 1970).
20. United States v. Margelony, 14 C.M.A. 55, 33 C.M.R. 267 (1963). *See also* Art. 123(a), U.C.M.J.
21. United States v. Hobbs, 8 M.J. 71 (C.M.A. 1979). *See also* United States v. Harper, 22 M.J. 157 (C.M.A. 1986) (permissive inference of wrongful use of drugs).
22. United States v. Thorton, 8 C.M.A. 57, 23 C.M.R. 281 (1957).
23. United States v. Crowell, 9 C.M.A. 43, 25 C.M.R. 305 (1958).
24. United States v. West, 15 C.M.A. 3, 34 C.M.R. 449 (1964).
1. *See* R.C.M. 811.

priate places for the parties to sign and acknowledge agreement on the contents.[2] Where the parties have orally stipulated, the judge will normally announce that fact to the members of the court.[3]

The military judge is not bound to accept an offered stipulation and may in appropriate cases refuse to permit the parties to stipulate.[4] Rejection of an offered stipulation will normally be appropriate where it is apparent that the parties, especially the accused, have not knowingly consented to the contents.[5]

Although the Rules of Evidence apply to contents of stipulations,[6] the parties should be able to waive the rules, just as if the contents of the stipulation had been offered in some other form of evidence.[7] Some military courts have expressed concern that as part of a pretrial agreement an accused might stipulate to matters that might not be admissible.[8] However, the prevailing view seems to be that the decision to stipulate rests with the accused and that he may waive otherwise valid objections in return for a pretrial agreement.[9] Thus, judges should not in those cases referee the contents of the stipulation.[10]

Either side may withdraw the stipulation before the judge accepts it,[11] although attempts to withdraw after acceptance will be left to the discretion of the judge and may in any event warrant a continuance while the other side garners its proof.[12]

A stipulated fact needs no further proof but the factfinder is free to ignore the stipulation if contrary evidence is available; neither counsel is permitted to offer rebuttal evidence.[13] Written stipulations of fact may be marked as exhibits and presented to the court.[14]

A stipulation of expected testimony of a witness, on the other hand, may be contradicted or impeached as though the witness was present to testify.[15] It may not be shown to the members, but must instead be read to them by counsel; it is marked and made a part of the record, however.[16]

---

2. United States v. Harris, 1 C.M.A. 430, 4 C.M.R. 22 (1952). See Appendices 27 and 28 for sample stipulations.
3. R.C.M. 811(f).
4. R.C.M. 811(b).
5. R.C.M. 811(b) Discussion.
6. R.C.M. 811(e).
7. See Rule 103, MIL. R. EVID.
8. See, e.g., United States v. Sharper, 17 M.J. 803 (A.C.M.R. 1984). See also United States v. Smith, 9 M.J. 537 (A.C.M.R. 1980).
9. See United States v. Rasberry, 21 M.J. 656 (A.C.M.R. 1985); United States v. Keith, 17 M.J. 1078 (A.F.C.M.R. 1984).
10. See United States v. Taylor, 21 M.J. 1016 (A.C.M.R. 1986). Cf. United States v. Cozine, 21 M.J. 581 (A.C.M.R. 1985) (judge may delete portions of confessional stipulation that are inconsistent with accused's oral statements to judge).
11. R.C.M. 811(d).
12. R.C.M. 811(d) Discussion.
13. R.C.M. 811(e). See United States v. Gerlach, 16 C.M.A. 383, 37 C.M.R. 3 (1966).
14. R.C.M. 811(f).
15. R.C.M. 811(e). United States v. Gonzales, 14 M.J. 501 (A.F.C.M.R. 1982).
16. R.C.M. 811(f). See also United States v. Schmitt, 25 C.M.R. 822 (A.F.B.R. 1958) (error to show to members).

§ 15-22   TRIAL PROCEDURES   § 15-22

In all cases the military judge must be satisfied that the accused understands the implications of entering into a stipulation.[17] Stipulations amounting to a confession in a contested case (i.e., confessional stipulations), are permitted but are subject to closer scrutiny.[18] *See* § 9-3.

§ 15-22. Depositions.

As a general rule, depositions (oral or written) may be offered by either side at trial.[1] The substantive and procedural aspects of military depositions are governed by Article 49, U.C.M.J. and R.C.M. 702 in the Manual for Courts-Martial and are discussed in Chapter 11 of this text. Their admissibility at trial, as exceptions to the hearsay rule, are governed by Rule 804, Military Rules of Evidence.[2] Their receipt into evidence is permitted if the accused's confrontation rights were provided, or waived,[3] and the witness is "unavailable."[4]

At trial, the depositions may be read, but not shown,[5] or shown on videotape,[6] to the court members if the substance of the depositions is otherwise competent and relevant to the case.[7] Depositions may not be used by the prosecution in a capital case[8] but their use as substantive evidence during presentencing proceedings is specifically authorized.[9] Failure to object at the deposition hearing to errors which could have been corrected at that time will normally waive the issue.[10] However, the deposition officer is not required to rule on those objections.[11] Thus, if the defect remains counsel should renew the objection and request the judge to rule on the matter. The trial court's

---

17. R.C.M. 811(c). United States v. Cambridge, 3 C.M.A. 377, 12 C.M.R. 133 (1953).
18. R.C.M. 811(c). United States v. Bertelson, 3 M.J. 314 (C.M.A. 1977).
1. The prosecution may not use a deposition in a capital case, i.e., where the death penalty is authorized, unless the accused expressly consents in court or where the accused has opened the door by offering a portion of the deposition. *See* United States v. Aldridge, 4 C.M.A. 107, 15 C.M.R. 107 (1954).
2. Rule 804, Mil. R. Evid.
3. *See* United States v. Jacoby, 11 C.M.A. 428, 29 C.M.R. 244 (1960). *See generally* McGovern, "The Military Oral Deposition and Modern Communications," 45 Mil. L. Rev. 43 (1969); Everett, "The Role of the Deposition in Military Justice," 7 Mil. L. Rev. 131 (1960).
4. "Unavailability" is governed by Article 49, U.C.M.J. and Rule 804(a), Mil. R. Evid. Unavailability is determined at the time of trial—not when the deposition is taken. United States v. Dieter, 42 M.J. 697 (Army Ct.Crim.App. 1995) (witness not unavailable unless prosecution has made good faith effort to obtain witness; judge abused discretion in admitting oral deposition).
5. R.C.M. 702(g)(3). United States v. Austin, 35 M.J. 271 (C.M.A. 1992) (prejudicial error where Article 32 testimony taken into deliberation room; court noted commonality between depositions and Article 32 testimony).
6. *Id.* United States v. Crockett, 21 M.J. 423 (C.M.A. 1986) (noting change in Art. 49, U.C.M.J. which now specifically authorizes use of videotaped depositions); United States v. Kelsey, 14 M.J. 545 (A.C.M.R. 1982) (videotape shown to members).
7. *See, e.g.,* United States v. Shepherd, 9 C.M.A. 90, 25 C.M.R. 352 (1958).
8. *See* Art. 49, U.C.M.J. *See also* § 15-17(B)(1).
9. R.C.M. 1003(b)(4), (5). *See also* § 15-17(C)(1).
10. R.C.M. 702(h). But objections to answers in a written deposition (interrogatories) may be made at trial.
11. R.C.M. 702(f)(7).

§ 15-23   MILITARY CRIMINAL JUSTICE   § 15-24

ruling admitting or excluding a deposition will be measured for an abuse of discretion.[12]

§ 15-23. Objections and Preserving Error.

Rule 103, Military Rules of Evidence governs rulings on evidence at courts-martial.[1] On its face the Rule places a greater burden on the defense to either enter a specific objection[2] or risk waiver of the issue.[3] If the ruling results in exclusion of evidence, counsel should make an offer of proof—a concise statement setting out the substance of the evidence or expected testimony.[4] Appellate relief will normally not be granted unless the error results in prejudice to a substantial right of the accused.[5]

§ 15-24. Evidentiary Instructions During Trial.

Throughout the trial instances may arise when evidence is admitted for a limited purpose or inadmissible evidence or other matters are presented in court. In the first category the military judge should instruct the court members to consider the evidence for the limited purpose for which it was admitted.[1] For example, other acts of misconduct by an accused may be admitted to show motive or plan, but may not be considered as evidence that the accused is a bad person.[2] Likewise, the military judge should instruct the members to

---

12. United States v. Webber, 42 M.J. 675 (A.F.Ct.Crim.App. 1995).
1. See Rule 105, MIL. R. EVID.
2. Rule 103(a)(1). See, e.g., United States v. Owens, 21 M.J. 117 (C.M.A. 1985) (counsel failed to clearly articulate objection). See generally Saltzburg, Schinasi & Schlueter, *Military Rules of Evidence Manual*, 16-43 (2d ed. 1986); Schinasi, "The Military Rules of Evidence: An Advocate's Tool," ARMY LAW., May 1980, at 3.
3. Rule 103(a), MIL. R. EVID. Failure to object will not waive "plain error." Rule 103(d), MIL. R. EVID. See United States v. Ryder, 39 M.J. 454 (C.M.A. 1994) (unobjected to admission of government witness' testimony did not amount to plain error); United States v. Colon-Anqueira, 16 M.J. 20 (C.M.A. 1983) (constitutional error not necessarily plain error).
4. Rule 103(a)(2), (b), MIL. R. EVID.
5. Rule 103(a), MIL. R. EVID. In United States v. Giambra, 38 M.J. 240 (C.M.A. 1993), the court noted a four-part test for determining whether prejudice has resulted from an erroneous ruling: (1) Is the government's case against the accused strong and conclusive? (2) Is the defense's case feeble or implausible? (3) What is the materiality of the proffered testimony (evidence)? and (4) What is the quality of the proferred evidence and is there a substitute for it in the record of trial?
1. See Rule 105, MIL. R. EVID. Upon request the judge must give the limiting instruction. *Id.* Absent a request the judge may do so. See United States v. Jackson, 38 M.J. 106 (C.M.A. 1993) (failure to give adequate limiting instruction on hearsay evidence was not plain error); United States v. Damatta-Olivera, 37 M.J. 474 (C.M.A. 1993) (under facts, not error to refuse to give instruction on inconsistent statement); United States v. Ward, 16 M.J. 341 (C.M.A. 1983) (failure to request does not relieve judge of his responsibilities). See also United States v. Graves, 1 M.J. 50 (C.M.A. 1975) (judge is more than mere referee).
2. Rule 404(b), MIL. R. EVID. See also e United States v. Kick, 7 M.J. 82 (C.M.A. 1979); United States v. Watkins, 17 M.J. 783 (A.F.C.M.R. 1983); United States v. Penn, 5 M.J. 514 (N.C.M.R. 1978).

disregard improper arguments[3] or inadmissible evidence.[4] If the error is not capable of remedy through such an instruction, a mistrial may be required.[5] Finally, the military judge may give informational instructions to the members on matters such as the impact of an offered stipulation[6] or their duties as fact-finders in assessing the evidence.[7]

Part IV

Summary Courts-Martial Procedures

§ 15-25. General.

The summary court-martial is a one-officer court designed to promptly dispose of minor offenses.[1] It is the least formal of the three types of courts-martial and because it offers the least substantive protection to an accused it is permitted to impose only relatively light punishments[2] and may not proceed without the accused's consent.[3] If the accused refuses to be tried by a summary court, the charges may be referred to a special or general court-martial.[4] The jurisdictional limits of the summary court are discussed in § 4-3(C). The discussion in this part of the chapter generally addresses the key participants and procedural steps in summary courts. As with general and special courts-martial, the services normally use summary court-martial trial guides which cover in script form the necessary procedural points.[5]

---

3. See § 15-13 for a discussion on arguments by counsel.

4. *See generally* United States v. Dixon, 17 C.M.A. 423, 38 C.M.R. 221 (1968).

5. On review, the courts will examine for abuse of discretion. United States v. O Neal, 16 C.M.A. 33, 36 C.M.R. 189 (1966).

6. *See* § 15-23.

7. *See, e.g.,* Rule 304(e)(2), Mil. R. Evid. (court members may determine weight to give to accused's pretrial statement).

1. *See* Articles 16 and 20, U.C.M.J. The Supreme Court has labelled this court as a "disciplinary proceeding." *See* Middendorf v. Henry, 425 U.S. 25 (1976) and United States v. Booker, 5 M.J. 238 (C.M.A. 1977). *See generally* Asher, "Reforming the Summary Court-Martial," 79 Col. L. Rev. 173 (1979); Gilbert, "Summary Courts-Martial: Rediscovering the Spumoni of Military Justice," 39 A.F. L. Rev. 119 (1996). *See also* R.C.M. 1301.

2. The maximum punishments include: For those in the grades E-4 and below—30 days confinement at hard labor, 45 days hard labor without confinement, 60 days restriction, forfeiture of two-thirds pay for one month, and reduction to E-1. If the accused is attached to or embarked in a vessel, the maximum sentence is confinement for 24 days (30 days if diminished rations are not adjudged), 3 days on diminished rations, forfeiture of two-thirds pay for one month and reduction to E-1.

For those in grades E-5 and above—60 days restriction, forfeiture of two-thirds of pay for one month, and reduction to next lower pay grade.

3. Art. 20, U.C.M.J. R.C.M. 1303. United States v. Seeber, 22 M.J. 956 (C.G.C.M.R. 1986) (case referred to trial where accused objected to particular summary court officer).

4. *See* § 8-4.

5. *See* Appendix 9 of the *Manual.*

§ 15-26. The Summary Court-Martial Participants.

§ 15-26(A). The Summary Court-Martial Officer.

The officer designated by the convening authority to sit as the court-martial need not be a lawyer but should be of judicial temperament and further qualified because of age, education, training, and experience.[1] The officer should be of the same service as the accused but need not be of the same unit. The fact that the officer is also the "accuser" is not disqualifying.[2] Because he fills a "judicial" position, he should carefully and thoroughly prepare for trial and execute his duties in an impartial manner.[3] During trial, the officer will also act as prosecutor insofar as he presents the case against the accused.[4]

§ 15-26(B). The Accused.

Only enlisted personnel[5] who so consent may be tried by summary courts-martial.[6] The court must have jurisdiction not only over the accused, but also the offense.[7] The various rights of the accused before a summary court are noted in § 15-29.

§ 15-26(C). Counsel.

There is no constitutional or statutory right to counsel before summary courts-martial,[8] although the accused is permitted to have counsel present and act on his behalf.[9] Normally, the accused will at a minimum be afforded the opportunity to consult with counsel before the trial. Both the Supreme Court and the military courts have recognized the absence of the right;[10] the latter court, however, has indicated that the absence of the opportunity to

---

1. *See* R.C.M. 1301(a). These qualifications are implied by Art. 25(d)(2) U.C.M.J.
2. R.C.M. 1302(b).
3. R.C.M. 1301(b).
4. R.C.M. 1304(b)(2)(E).
5. Art. 20, U.C.M.J. R.C.M. 1301(c).
6. Art. 20, U.C.M.J. R.C.M. 1303. The right to object to trial by summary court-martial must be exercised before arraignment.
7. *See* Chapter 4.
8. *See* Middendorf v. Henry, 425 U.S. 25 (1976); United States v. Booker, 5 M.J. 238 (C.M.A. 1977). *See generally* "Military Justice—Right to Counsel—Servicemen Tried Before Summary Courts Have No Constitutional Right to Counsel," 59 Tex. L. Rev. 1471 (1976). But the presence of counsel is not prohibited. *See* R.C.M. 1301(e) Discussion.
9. *See* R.C.M. 1301(e), which indicates that if the accused has civilian counsel, that counsel must be permitted to represent the accused at trial, if counsel's presence will not unduly delay the proceedings and military exigencies do not prevent such presence.
10. Citing United States v. Mack, 9 M.J. 300 (C.M.A. 1980), the Drafters' Analysis for R.C.M. 1301 indicates that there is no right for the accused to consult with counsel. *Cf.* AR 27-10, para. 5-21, which requires the summary court-martial to provide the accused with an opportunity to consult with counsel—unless military exigencies prevent it. DA Form 5111-R (Summary Court-Martial Rights Notification/Waiver Statement) is to be completed and attached to the charge sheet. United States v. Jackson, 12 M.J. 905 (N.M.C.M.R. 1982) (counsel who advised accused of his rights was not "independent").

consult with counsel before consenting to the proceeding may limit the use of the summary court-martial as a "conviction" at a later trial for purposes of impeachment.[11] If counsel does represent the accused, the summary court officer should communicate directly with that counsel.[12]

§ 15-27. Pretrial Conference.

Before trial, the summary court officer will meet with the accused and counsel,[1] if any, in a pretrial proceeding in order to discuss preliminary matters.[2] This is the time for the officer to apprise the accused of the nature of the charges, the name of the accuser, names of adverse witnesses, and of his legal rights.[3] The officer should obtain the names of possible defense witnesses[4] and also set the date for trial.

§ 15-28. Trial on the Merits and Sentencing.

The procedure for trial by summary court-martial generally follows the flow of a general or special court-martial.[1] Before trial proceeds, the court must advise the accused of his rights and inquire into his understanding of those rights.[2] And prior to entering his plea, the accused may enter any motions to dismiss or for appropriate relief.[3] A guilty plea may not be accepted until the court determines that the plea is provident.[4] In contested cases the court presents the prosecution's case in chief, the accused may enter evidentiary objections or cross-examine the witnesses.[5] At the conclusion of the government's case the accused may present defense evidence before the court closes for deliberations.[6] If a verdict of guilty results, the accused may present evi-

---

11. Middendorf v. Henry, 425 U.S. 25 (1976); United States v. Booker, 5 M.J. 238 (C.M.A. 1977).
12. United States v. Booker, 5 M.J. 238 (C.M.A. 1977). *See also* United States v. Syro, 7 M.J. 431 (C.M.A. 1979) (*Booker* applicable to SCM's offered as part of accused's record). See § 15-17(c)(1).
1. This is clearly implied by R.C.M. 1301(e), which recognizes that a counsel may represent the accused, which in turn implies that counsel serves as spokesman, advocate, and intermediary for the accused.
2. R.C.M. 1304(b)(1). This is not the same as the Article 39(a) session discussed in Chapter 12 although it serves a similar purpose—disposing of preliminary matters.
3. R.C.M. 1304(b)(1).
4. The summary court officer may issue subpoenas for witnesses in the same manner as the trial counsel does for general and special courts. *See* § 11-2. Depositions may also be used. Art. 49, U.C.M.J. *See* § 11-3.
1. *See generally* § 15-7 to § 15-19.
2. R.C.M. 1304(b)(1). *See* § 15-29.
3. R.C.M. 1304(b)(2).
4. R.C.M. 1304(b)(2)(D).
5. R.C.M. 1304(b)(2)(E). The Military Rules of Evidence are applicable to summary courts-martial. Rule 1101, MIL. R. EVID.
6. *Id.*

dence in extenuation and mitigation and the court may consider rebuttal evidence to those matters.[7]

§ 15-29. Post-Trial Procedures.

The *Manual* requires that an abbreviated record of trial be prepared.[1] It should contain information concerning the accused's pleas,[2] the findings and sentence,[3] and notations concerning the presence of counsel[4] and whether the summary court-martial was also the convening authority.[5] It should also indicate how many prior convictions were considered and that the accused was properly advised of his various rights.[6]

Each summary court-martial is to receive legal review[7] which is then attached to the record of trial.[8] The accused may, within two years, request that the Judge Advocate General review the case.

---

7. R.C.M. 1304(b)(2)(F).
1. *See* R.C.M. 1305. DA Form 2329.
2. R.C.M. 1305(b)(1).
3. *Id.*
4. *Id.*
5. R.C.M. 1305(b)(3).
6. R.C.M. 1305(b)(2).
7. R.C.M. 1306(c), 1112.
8. R.C.M. 1306(d), 1201(b)(3).

APPENDIX REFERENCES

Appendix 1. Abbreviations.
Appendix 2. Glossary.
Appendix 3. U.C.M.J.
Appendix 9. Court-Martial Convening Orders.
Appendix 13. Request to Take Oral Deposition.
Appendix 14. Interrogatories and Deposition Form.
Appendix 23. Entry of Conditional Guilty Plea.
Appendix 24. Court-Martial Member Questionnaire.
Appendix 25. Stipulation of Fact.
Appendix 26. Stipulation of Expected Testimony.
Appendix 27. Instructions Checklist.
Appendix 28. Findings Worksheet.
Appendix 29. Sentencing Worksheet.
Appendix 30. Maximum Punishment Chart.
Appendix 32. Special Findings.
Appendix 33. Advice on Appellate Rights.

ANNOTATED BIBLIOGRAPHY

BOOKS

Byrne, *Military Law* (3d ed. 1981).

This second edition work is a good introductory text to military law. It includes text material, discussion cases, self-quizzes, and appendices that contain forms and tables. The discussion cases, although dated, cover significant areas of courts-martial practice.

Military Law Reporter.

This loose-leaf service is published by the Public Law Education Institute. The service consists of six bimonthly issues per volume.

Moyer, *Justice and the Military* (1972).

This one volume loose-leaf reference contains detailed discussions of the role of commanders, jurisdiction, military criminal procedure, First Amendment rights, substantive law, and collateral review of courts-martial by the civilian court system.

Saltzburg, Schinasi & Schlueter, *Military Rules of Evidence Manual* (3d ed. 1991).

The authors have compiled the official text of the 1980 Military Rules of Evidence, the Drafters' Analysis to those rules and have provided an editorial comment for each rule which explains the rule, shows how it might be used, and discusses potential problem areas.

Schlueter, Saltzburg, Schinasi & Imwinkelried, *Military Evidentiary Foundations* (1994).

This text discusses how counsel may lay a foundation, or predicate, for a wide variety of evidence. In addressing the mechanics of introducing evidence at courts-martial, the authors present a four-step process for marking exhibits, showing them to opposing counsel, laying the foundation, and offering them into evidence.

PERIODICALS

In General

"Bibliography of Military Law," 10 AM. CRIM. L. REV. 175 (1971).

This extensive bibliography lists finding aids, books, symposiums, surveys, service publications, and selected writings in legal periodicals. Most entries predate the 1968 amendments to the U.C.M.J.

Lancaster, "Disruption in the Courtroom: The Troublesome Defendant," 75 MIL. L. REV. 35 (1977).

The author notes in this well-written article that the burden falls upon the judge to balance the need for an orderly trial against the accused's right to a fair trial. Consequently, he must be aware of what constitutes disruptive behavior and what permissible steps may be taken to remedy the problem. The article addresses these points presenting possible constitutional limitations along the way. Discussed are methods such as warnings, armed guards, shackling, gagging and cooling off periods. In conclusion the author suggests that when disruptive behavior occurs, the judge should call an Article 39(a) session, warn the accused, and provide counsel an opportunity to be heard; removal should only be accomplished after arraignment.

McHardy, "Military Contempt Law and Procedure," 55 MIL. L. REV. 131 (1972).

Although the military Judge's contempt powers in Article 48, U.C.M.J. are seldom used, the powers exist and are discussed in detail in this line work. The author notes the historical development of the power, Congressional intent regarding its use, and the procedural requirements necessary to impose punishment.

Moyer, "Procedural Rights of the Military Accused: Advantages Over a Civilian Defendant," 22 Me. L. Rev. 105 (1970); 51 MIL. L. REV. 1 (1971).

This forty-page article compares the civilian and military criminal procedures such as pretrial investigation, interrogation, right to witnesses, right to counsel, and appellate review. The author concludes that the military accused enjoys greater procedural and substantive advantages than the civilian counterpart.

Swift, "Restraints on Defense Publicity in Criminal Jury Cases," 1984 UTAH L. REV. 45 (1984).

This comprehensive article provides an excellent overview of the constitutional issues surrounding restraints on defense publicity in criminal jury trials and a good discussion of many of the influential cases in this area. The author examines the analytical framework underlying restraints on publicity and explores the invasion on free speech in terms of the various conflicting interests that must be considered and balanced.

Symposium, "Military Justice," ARMY LAW., March 1996.

This 127-page symposium contains a Foreword and 11 short articles on a wide range of military justice topics. They are as follows:

Morris, "Foreword."
Barto, "Developments in the Substantive Criminal Law Under the Uniform Code of Military Justice."
Frisk, "New Developments in Pretrial Confinement."
Frisk, "New Developments in Speedy Trial."
Winn, "Recent Developments in Military Pretrial and Trial Procedure."
Masterton, "Recent Developments in Search and Seizure Law."
Masterton, "Recent Developments in Urinalysis Law."
Kohlman, "Are You Ready for Some Changes? Five Fresh Views of the Fifth Amendment."
Wright, "Sex, Lies, and Videotape: Child Sexual Abuse Cases Continue to Create Appellate Issues and Other Developments in the Areas of the Sixth Amendment, Discovery, Mental Responsibility, and Nonjudicial Punishment."
Henley, "Caveat Criminale: The Impact of the New Military Rules of Evidence in Sexual Offense and Child Molestation Cases."
Henley, "Current Developments in Evidence Law."
Morris, "New Developments in Sentencing and Post-Trial Procedure."

Symposium, "Military Law," 10 AM. CRIM. L. REV. 1 (1971).

This symposium issue covers a valuable range of topics pertinent to the practice of military criminal law. Included are articles on jurisdiction over civilian type offenses, plea bargaining, sentencing, discovery, appeals, and an article by General Westmoreland on the commanders perspective of military justice. Also included is a fine bibliography of books, articles, and listings of military law materials.

Participants

Brookshire, "Juror Selection Under the Uniform Code of Military Justice: Fact and Fiction," 58 MIL. L. REV. 71 (1972).

This in-depth article examines the legal requisites for selecting court members under the Uniform Code of Military Justice and also examines the methods actually employed by general court-martial jurisdictions. The author measures these standards and procedures against the civilian models using generally recognized standards of justice. The results of three separate surveys are included—along with suggested reforms in the selection process.

Cretella & Lynch, "The Military Judge: Military or Judge," CAL. W.L. REV. 57 (1972).

The authors trace the evolution of the military judge's role in the military society as it has evolved and adapted to social changes. Particularly, judges are cast as administrators of justice within a self-contained legal system found in the military services.

Holdaway, "Voir Dire—A Neglected Tool of Advocacy," 40 MIL. L. REV. 1 (1968).

This article analyzes and compares the use of voir dire examination in civilian courts against such examination in the military courts-martial. The author discusses those areas that tend to expose matters such as bias or interest, the extent to which voir dire may be used to develop a theory of defense on the case, and the degree of control which may be exercised over the voir dire by military judges. Practical suggestions for conducting a successful voir dire examination are offered.

Howell, "TDS: The Establishment of the U.S. Army Trial Defense Service," 100 Mɪʟ. L. Rᴇᴠ. 4 (1983).

The evolution and reasons for the formation of the Trial Defense Service are traced in this article. The author, a Deputy Staff Judge Advocate, concludes that the birth of this service not only eliminated criticism that defense counsel often were improperly chosen and influenced, but it also ensured the achievement of the need for a fit military fighting force.

Remcho, "Military Juries: Constitutional Analysis and the Need for Reform," 47 Iɴᴅ. L.J. 193 (1973).

In this article, the author conducts a detailed study of the constitutional guidelines applicable to military juries and the issue of due process in a military context. After a survey of the major cases addressing these issues and on extensive empirical analysis of the exclusive use of officers in military juries, Remcho concludes that the military justice system is best served by incorporating enlisted men into the jury system.

Stevenson, "The Inherent Authority of the Military Judge," 17 Aɪʀ Fᴏʀᴄᴇ L.R. 1 (Summer 1975).

The author discusses how the emergence of the military judge has been extremely important in furthering high standards within the military justice system. He concludes that under the U.C.M.J. and the Manual for Courts-Martial, military judges are cloaked with extensive authority; whether Congress or the courts bless this inherent authority is a function of the judge's wisdom in exercising it.

Stone, "Post-Trial Contact with Court Members: A Critical Analysis," 38 A.F. L. Rᴇᴠ. 179 (1994).

The author indicates that because of the general view that verdicts should not be impeached and that the rules concerning post-trial contact with court-members seems confused, a rule should be devised which prevents such contacts unless a military judge authorizes counsel to speak to the members.

Trial Procedures

Korroch & Davidson, "Jury Nullification: A Call for Justice or An Invitation to Anarchy?" 139 Mɪʟ. L. Rᴇᴠ. 131 (1993).

Noting that the jury (court-martial panel) possesses a general veto power and that jury nullification is not a recognized defense, the authors address the controversial question of whether counsel may urge nullification. They also offer a suggested instruction for informing the court members of their nullification power.

Schinasi, "Special Findings: Their Use at Trial and on Appeal," 87 Mɪʟ. L. Rᴇᴠ. 73 (1980).

The author notes the analogy of special findings to jury instructions (the former being used in bench trials) and encourages military counsel to make use of special findings, as provided for in Art. 51(d), U.C.M.J. This article presents a fine discussion of both the federal practice, under Rule 23(c), Fᴇᴅ. R. Cʀɪᴍ. P., and the few military decisions. Special findings, according to the author, can assist the defense on appeal by uncovering defects in the military judge's reasoning.

TRIAL PROCEDURES

Evidence

Angilvel, "Expert Testimony in Child Sexual Abuse Cases: Avoiding the 'Profile' Trap," 39 A.F. L. Rev. 133 (1996).

This short, but helpful, article addresses some of the evidentiary problems in presenting expert testimony which may impermissibly touch on profile evidence concerning the accused or inadmissible expert testimony regarding the truthfulness of the child victim.

Everett, "The Role of the Deposition in Military Justice," 7 Mil. L. Rev. 131 (1960).

The author presents a good discussion of the use of depositions generally in the military practice and specifically raises questions concerning the different rights available to the defense in both oral and written depositions—the latter being less protective of an accused's Sixth Amendment rights to counsel and confrontation unless it is intended for later use at a court-martial.

Gilligan, "Character Evidence," 109 Mil. L. Rev. 83 (1985).

This article provides an in-depth analysis into character evidence and the related areas of uncharged misconduct evidence, evidence of specific character traits dealing with veracity, rehabilitating a witness via introducing character evidence concerning truthfulness, and, finally, methods of impeachment to show the bad character of the accused.

Martin "Prior Inconsistent Statements and the Military Rules of Evidence," A.F. L. Rev. 207 (1996).

The article provides a good overview of using prior inconsistent statements to impeach a witness. Noting the often confused state of affairs in dealing with such statements during a court-martial, the author addresses key points in technique, tactics, and hearsay concerns.

McGovern, "The Military Oral Deposition and Modern Communications," 45 Mil. L. Rev. 43 (1969).

The author presents a fine discussion of depositions procedures in military practice—detailing both the procedural and substantive requirements. Considering the availability within the military of videotapes, movie cameras, and audio recording devices, the author discusses and proposes wider use of these mediums in the taking of oral depositions. Where all of the parties to the deposition are not present at the same place, recorded telephonic questioning may prove an ingenious solution to sterile written questions and answers.

Hug, "Presumptions and Inferences in Criminal Law," 56 Mil. L. Rev. 81 (1972).

Distinguishing between the oft-confused concepts of "presumptions" and "inferences," the author presents a discussion of both military and civilian case law and specifically addresses the presumption of sanity and the inferences relating to possession of drugs and the five-day rule in bad check offenses.

Symposium, "The Military Rules of Evidence," Army Law., May 1980.

This fifty-five page symposium issue contains seven articles on the Military Rules of Evidence. They are as follows:

Schinasi, "The Military Rules of Evidence: An Advocates' Tool."
Basham, "Suppression Motions Under the Military Rules of Evidence."
Yustas, "Mental Evaluations of an Accused Under the Military Rules of Evidence: An Excellent Balance."
Eisenberg, "Fourth Amendment Practice and the Military Rules of Evidence."
Schlueter, "Bodily Evidence and Rule 312, M.R.E."
Gasperini, "Eyewitness Identification Under the Military Rules of Evidence."
Green, "The Military Rules of Evidence and the Military Judge Sentencing."

Summary Court-Martial

Aher, "Reforming the Summary Court-Martial," 79 COLUM. L. REV. 173 (1979).

After reviewing the inherent tension that exists in the military justice system between protecting servicemembers' Constitutional rights and ensuring discipline, the author examines the dialogue between the Supreme Court and the Court of Military Appeals concerning the right to counsel in summary court-martial proceedings. Concluding that the post-*Booker* summary court-martial fails to serve both justice and military necessity, the author proposes that this procedure be abolished.

Gilbert, "Summary Courts-Martial: Rediscovering the Spumoni of Military Justice," 39 A.F. L. REV. 119 (1996).

The author notes that the summary court-martial is a valuable rehabilitative tool which is too often overlooked. He observes that summary courts are appropriate when the case falls into what he calls a "gray" area—that zone where the accused is worth rehabilitating, an Article 15 punishment is not strong enough and a special court-martial which may be too strong. The article includes general guidance on how a summary court-martial should be handled.

Haight, "Argument of Military Counsel on Findings, Sentence and Motions: Limitations and Abuses," 16 MIL. L. REV. 59 (1962).

Emphasizing that the closing argument can potentially win or lose certain cases, the author provides a useful template to be used by military advocates in preparing their closing arguments. Included in the article is a discussion of relevant case law applicable to closing arguments, along with a proposal for more uniform rules governing this area of the law.

Note, "Military Justice—Right to Counsel— Servicemen Tried Before Summary Courts-Martial Have No Constitutional Right To Counsel," 54 TEX. L. REV. 1471 (1976).

This note critically analyzes the Supreme Court's decision in *Middendorf v. Henry*, and concludes that the Court's holding contravened consistent federal and military court rulings and indeed may have been the deathknell to any Constitutional rights enjoyed by military servicemembers.

Sternlicht, "Military Law—Right to Counsel at a Summary Court-Martial: *Middendorf v. Henry*," 55 N.C. L. REV. 300 (1977).

In analyzing the Supreme Court's decision in *Middendorf,*the author concludes that the Court erred in upholding the Marine Corps' practice of denying counsel to accused individuals during summary courts-martial proceedings. By condoning this denial of counsel, the author fears the Court may have erroneously vested too much faith in the military justice system—at the expense, ultimately, of the military accused's right to counsel.

CHAPTER 16

SENTENCING

§ 16-1. In General.
§ 16-2. Maximum Authorized Punishments.
  § 16-2(A). Jurisdictional Limits on the Sentence.
  § 16-2(B). Nature of Proceeding as Limitation.
  § 16-2(C). Manual for Courts-Martial Limitations.
  § 16-2(D). Multiplicity.
  § 16-2(E). Escalator Provisions.
  § 16-2(F). "Footnote Five" Limitations.
  § 16-2(G). Equivalent Punishments.
§ 16-3. Permissible Punishments.
  § 16-3(A). Death Penalty.
  § 16-3(B). Punitive Separations.
  § 16-3(C). Deprivation of Liberty.
  § 16-3(D). Deprivation of Pay.
  § 16-3(E). Reduction in Grade.
  § 16-3(F). Loss of Numbers.
  § 16-3(G). Reprimand.
§ 16-4. Sentencing Procedures.
  § 16-4(A). In General.
  § 16-4(B). Applicability of Rules of Evidence.
§ 16-5. Prosecution Evidence.
  § 16-5(A). Data From the Charge Sheet.
  § 16-5(B). Data Concerning the Accused's Prior Service.
  § 16-5(C). Evidence of Prior Convictions.
  § 16-5(D). Evidence in Aggravation.
    § 16-5(D)(1). In General.
    § 16-5(D)(2). Evidence of Circumstances Surrounding Offense.
    § 16-5(D)(3). Evidence of Impact of Offense on Victim and Community.
    § 16-5(D)(4). Evidence Addressing Rehabilitative Potential.
    § 16-5(D)(5). Evidence of Uncharged Misconduct.
§ 16-6. Defense Evidence.
§ 16-7. Rebuttal and Surrebuttal.
§ 16-8. Arguments on Sentencing.
  § 16-8(A). In General.
  § 16-8(B). Prosecution Arguments on Sentencing.
  § 16-8(C). Defense Counsel's Argument on Sentencing.
§ 16-9. Instructions on Sentencing.
§ 16-10. Deliberations on Sentencing.
§ 16-11. Announcement of the Sentence.
§ 16-12. Advice on Appellate Rights.
§ 16-13. Adjournment.
Appendix References.
Annotated Bibliography.

§ 16-1. In General.

Unlike most civilian criminal trials, the sentencing at a court-martial involves the factfinder. That is, if the accused has been found guilty by a court with members he will be sentenced by those members. If he has pleaded guilty,[1] he may be sentenced by either the military judge alone or the appointed court members.[2] The sentencing procedure usually begins immediately after the verdict is announced. In fact, in many cases, while the court is deliberating on the findings, the military judge may hold an out-of-court session to review proposed instructions and matters on sentencing.[3] It therefore behooves counsel for both sides to be prepared to move directly into the sentencing phase if a verdict of guilty is rendered.[4] Before examining the sentencing procedures, however, it will be helpful to review briefly the permissible punishments which may be imposed by a court-martial.

§ 16-2. Maximum Authorized Punishments.

Determining the maximum punishment that may be imposed by a court-martial requires consideration of a number of factors and limitations. The maximum permissible punishment will generally be the lowest of the jurisdictional limits of the court-martial hearing the case,[1] the nature of the proceeding,[2] or the maximum punishments authorized in the Manual for Courts-Martial for the offense.[3] If the offense's maximum authorized punishment exceeds the jurisdictional limits of the court-martial, the members may *not* be informed of the maximum authorized punishments.[4] This section examines those limitations, along with other factors, that must be considered in determining the maximum punishment.

§ 16-2(A). Jurisdictional Limits on the Sentence.

As discussed in Chapter 4, Congress has placed limits on the amount and types of punishment that may be imposed by the three types of court-martial.[5] A general court-martial may impose any lawful punishment specified in the Manual for Courts-Martial.[6]

---

1. *See* § 14-3.
2. If an accused has entered a plea of guilty without submitting a request for trial by military judge alone, he will be sentenced by the court members if his plea is accepted by the judge. *See generally* §§ 12-3(A) and 14-3(F).
3. *See, e.g.*, R.C.M. 1005(c) Discussion.
4. Necessary delays may give rise to a valid motion for continuance. *See* § 15-4(A).

1. *See* § 16-2(A).
2. *See* § 16-2(B).
3. United States v. Herd, 29 M.J. 702 (A.C.M.R. 1989); United States v. Lewis, 11 C.M.A. 503, 29 C.M.R. 319 (1960) (court provided an in-depth discussion of the authority of Congress to delegate to the President the authority to promulgate maximum sentences under Article 56, U.C.M.J.; the court concluded that that provision did not violate the constitutional separation of powers). *See generally* Sullivan, "The President's Power to Promulgate Death Penalty Standards," 125 Mil. L. Rev. 143 (1989). United States v. Brown, 15 M.J. 620 (N.M.C.M.R. 1982). *See also* R.C.M. 810(d)(1) Discussion.
4. Para. 127c(6), 1969 MCM.
5. *See* § 4-3 for the jurisdictional limits of a court-martial. *See also* Arts. 18, 19, and 20, U.C.M.J.
6. *See* Article 18, U.C.M.J.; R.C.M. 201(f)(1). *See also* § 4-3(A).

A special court-martial may impose a bad-conduct discharge, confinement for six months, hard labor without confinement for three months, and forfeiture of two-thirds pay per month for six months.[7] A bad-conduct discharge may only be imposed if certain requirements are met: appointment of a trial judge to the court-martial; appointment of a qualified defense counsel; and there is a verbatim record of trial.[8] The Army adds another requirement: the special court must have been convened by a general court-martial convening authority.[9]

A summary court-martial may impose no punishment that exceeds one month confinement, hard labor without confinement for more than forty-five days, restriction for more than two months, or forfeiture of more than two-thirds of one month's pay.[10] Other limits are applicable if more than one form of deprivation of liberty is imposed[11] and if the accused is in the fourth enlisted grade (E-4) or higher.[12]

§ 16-2(B). Nature of Proceeding as Limitation.

The *Manual*[13] limits punishments that may be imposed on rehearings,[14] new trials,[15] and other trials[16] to the lowest of the legal punishments origi-

---

7. Article 19, U.C.M.J.; R.C.M. 201(f)(2). *See also* § 4-3(B).
8. Article 19, U.C.M.J.; R.C.M. 201(f)(2).
9. Army Reg. 27-10, para. 5-25.
10. Article 20, U.C.M.J.; R.C.M. 202(f)(3), 1301(c).
11. The punishments must be apportioned. R.C.M. 1003(b)(6), (7), (9).
12. The court may not impose any form of confinement, hard labor without confinement, or reduction except to the next lowest grade. R.C.M. 1301(d)(2).
13. R.C.M. 810(d)(1).
14. In United States v. Lawson, 34 M.J. 38 (C.M.A. 1992), the accused received a sentence of 14 years confinement in first trial which was later modified by the convening authority who suspended the confinement in excess of seven years. At the rehearing, the judge instructed the members that the maximum sentence was 14 years confinement. The court held that the plain language of Article 66 required the instruction given in the case. Because of the earlier modification to the first sentence, the convening authority in the second case was also required to suspend any portion of the sentence in excess of seven years.
United States v. Turner, 34 M.J. 1123 (A.F.C.M.R. 1992) (judge should have instructed members on rehearing that they could adjudge confinement as lesser punishment instead of punitive discharge); United States v. Frye, 33 M.J. 1075 (A.C.M.R. 1992) (trial court erred in instructing members of maximum sentence which exceeded punishment assessed at first trial); United States v. Ferguson, 27 M.J. 660 (N.M.C.M.R. 1988) (maximum sentence of confinement on rehearing had to be reduced where portion of originally approved sentence *to* confinement had been suspended and later automatically remitted); United States v. Murphy, 23 M.J. 862 (A.C.M.R. 1987) (maximum sentence on rehearing is limited to the lowest amount of punishment approved by a convening authority, court of review, or other authorized officer under the U.C.M.J., unless the reduction is expressly and solely predicated on an erroneous conclusion of law). *See generally* Cargill, "The Article 63 Windfall," ARMY LAW., Dec. 1989, at 26 (discussion of the relationship of the ability of the accused to improvidence his guilty plea on appeal, obtain a rehearing, and take the benefit of Article 63, which sets the ceiling on the punishments which may be imposed on rehearings).
15. *See* Article 73, U.C.M.J., which addresses petitions for new trials. *See also* R.C.M. 810(a).
16. An "other trial" is one where the original proceedings were declared invalid because of lack of jurisdiction or because a charge failed to state an offense. R.C.M. 810(e). There are no sentence limitations for an "other trial" where the original trial was a summary or special court-martial

nally adjudged by the court-martial, as ultimately approved by the convening authority [17] or higher authority, unless the sentence indicated for the particular offense is mandatory.[18] If new charges are added, the maximum punishment equals the sentence originally imposed plus the maximum punishment for the new charges.[19] The court, however, is not required to impose the same *types* of punishment as originally imposed.[20]

If the earlier sentence was approved as part of a pretrial agreement and at a later rehearing the accused does not comply with the earlier agreement, the maximum sentence may not be greater than the one adjudged at the original trial.[21]

§ 16-2(C). Manual for Courts-Martial Limitations.

The 1969 *Manual for Courts-Martial* contained a Table of Maximum Punishments that was the President's prescription of the upper limit of the various punishments.[22] It specifically applied to enlisted members and was used as a guide in assessing punishments for officers.[23] The Table was dropped from the 1984 revision to the *Manual*.[24] Now the maximum punishments of confinement at hard labor, forfeitures, and punitive discharge are listed with the discussion of each punitive article in Part IV of the *Manual*.[25] However, the Drafters wisely included a central listing of the maximum punishments as Appendix 8 in the *Manual* with a caveat—the chart is only a summary of the information in Part IV.

Thus, in determining the maximum punishment for a particular offense, or lesser offense, Part IV of the *Manual* should be consulted. Where the accused has been convicted of an offense, or lesser offense, not listed in Part IV, but it is closely related to an offense which is listed, then the maximum punishment will be the same as that stated for the related offense.[26] If there is no closely related offense listed, then either the United States Code or customs of the

---

that was declared invalid because it tried an offense involving a mandatory punishment or a case considered capital. R.C.M. 810(d)(1).

17. See § 17-9.
18. R.C.M. 810(d)(1). In 1994, R.C.M. 810(d) was amended to conform to changes made to Article 63 in 1993. Pub.L. No. 102-484, 106 Stat. 2315, 2506 (1992). The limits on punishment do not apply in an "other trial" if it was invalid because either a summary or special court-martial improperly tried an offense involving a mandatory punishment or considered capital.
19. R.C.M. 810(d)(1).
20. R.C.M. 810(d)(1) Discussion.
21. R.C.M. 810(d) (as amended in 1995).
22. Para. 127c(6), 1969 MCM.
23. Id. at 126d.
24. The Drafters of the 1984 revisions to the *Manual* also dropped the Table of Equivalent Punishments, see § 16-2(G), which was often used in conjunction with the Table of Maximum Punishments.
25. See the introductory comments to the 1984 version of the *Manual* in § 1-3(B). Punishments of Reprimand, Fine, Loss of Numbers, Reduction in Grade, Restriction, and Hard Labor Without Confinement may be imposed in addition to, or in lieu of, these three types of punishments. See R.C.M. 1003(c)(1)(A)(ii). See also § 16-2(G).
26. R.C.M. 1003(c)(1)(A).

service[27] will set the ceiling.[28] In the case of the United States Code, the specified or prescribed maximum period of confinement for the offense[29] will be the same for purposes of military sentencing.[30] In addition, a specified maximum sentence in the Code of one year or more will permit imposition of a dishonorable discharge[31] and total forfeiture of pay and allowances.[32] A prescribed punishment of six months or more will permit imposition of a bad-conduct discharge[33] and total forfeitures.[34] If less than six months is authorized under the Code,[35] the military court may also impose two-thirds forfeiture[36] for the prescribed period of confinement.[37]

In determining the maximum punishment, other factors such as multiplicious offenses, "escalator" provisions, and other limitations must be considered. These factors are discussed in the following sections.

§ 16-2(D). Multiplicity.

During the trial the prosecution may have avoided dismissal of multiplicious charges in order to meet the exigencies of proof.[38] On sentencing, however, the matter should be reviewed and if the military judge still views them as multiplicious, he should so treat them for punishment purposes.[39] Thus, the punishments merge, the greater including the lesser.[40] The

---

27. The *Manual* does not specifically mention what sorts or amounts of punishments might be appropriately determined by "custom of the service." However, an example would be a punishment of Loss of Numbers, Lineal Position, or Seniority, R.C.M. 1003(b)(4), an authorized punishment only in cases involving officers in the Navy, Marine Corps, and Coast Guard; determining the maximum punishment would generally be determined by those services or department. See § 16-3(F).
28. R.C.M. 1003(c)(1)(B)(i).
29. R.C.M. 1003(c)(1)(B)(ii).
30. *Id. See also* United States v. Walter, 20 C.M.A. 367, 43 C.M.R. 207 (1971).
31. *Id. See* § 16-3(B).
32. *Id. See* § 15-3(D).
33. *Id. See* § 15-17(C).
34. *See* § 15-17(D).
35. R.C.M. 1003(c)(1)(B)(ii).
36. *Id.*
37. *Id.*
38. *See* §§ 6-1(C)(3) and 13-3(J).
39. *See* R.C.M. 1003(c)(1)(C). United States v. Wilson, 35 M.J. 473 (C.M.A. 1992) (judge's failure to announce position on multiplicity of charges was not prejudicial error); United States v. Hyska, 29 M.J. 122 (C.M.A. 1989) (offenses of attempt to distribute marijuana and distribution of marijuana were multiplicious where it appeared that the attempt was part of a continuous course of action); United States v. Wisemore, 32 M.J. 602 (C.G.C.M.R. 1991) (if charges are not multiplicious on their face, military judge is not required to *sua sponte* determine if charges are multiplicious in absence of complaint from the defense); United States v. Morgan, 31 M.J. 535 (A.C.M.R. 1990) (offenses of rape and committing an indecent act were multiplicious for sentencing where they arose from a single act and did not violate separate societal norms).

United States v. Crowe, 30 M.J. 1144 (A.F.C.M.R. 1990) (offenses of indecent acts, sodomy, and carnal knowledge were multiplicious for sentencing purposes when they resulted from single

---

40. R.C.M. 1003(c)(1)(C).

members will be instructed only on the combined punishment.[41] The judge may also dismiss the multiplicious offense.[42] Because the convening authority and service appellate courts have independent fact-finding powers, the judge may decline to do so where any genuine issue as to proof of facts exists.[43]

On the other hand, where the prosecution has alleged multiple offenses in one specification, it may be appropriate to consider each of the offenses separately in determining the maximum punishment.[44]

§ 16-2(E). Escalator Provisions.

The *Manual for Courts-Martial* includes three escalator provisions. In the first, proof of three or more previous final convictions during the year preceding the commission of the charged offense will authorize a dishonorable discharge, forfeiture of all pay and allowances, and confinement at hard labor for one year, if the authorized confinement for the offenses is less than one year.[45] This punishment may only be imposed by a general court-martial.

The second escalator provision permits increase of the maximum punishment stated in the *Manual* if the accused has received two or more convictions within the three years preceding commission of the charged offense. The court, assuming it possesses the requisite jurisdictional limits, could impose a bad-conduct discharge, forfeiture of all pay and allowances, and confinement for three months, if the confinement authorized by the *Manual* is less than three months.[46]

---

impulse and continuous course of action); United States v. Cumbee, 30 M.J. 736 (A.F.C.M.R. 1990) (charges of use and distribution of same drug were not multiplicious, even assuming accused used drug himself whenever he distributed it because the offenses had different elements; charges of distributing legal and tablet Valium were multiplicious).

United States v. Lyons, 30 M.J. 724 (A.F.C.M.R. 1990) (offenses of aggravated assault and carrying a concealed weapon were not multiplicious for sentencing); United States v. Turner, 28 M.J. 556 (C.G.C.M.R. 1989) (court noted the problems associated with dealing with multiplicity problems at sentencing and urged the Code Committee and the Joint Service Committee on Military Justice to closely examine the issue); United States v. Jobes, 20 M.J. 506 (A.F.C.M.R. 1985).

41. *See* R.C.M. 1005(e)(1) Discussion.

42. *See* § 6-1(C)(3). In United States v. Zupancic, 18 M.J. 387 (C.M.A. 1984), the court indicated that the proper procedure is for the military judge or appellate court to dismiss the multiplicious findings. If, on appeal, it appears that the greater offense should be set aside, the lesser, and multiplicious offense, may be reinstated. United States v. Gill, 37 M.J. 501 (A.F.C.M.R. 1993) (trial judge should have treated members' findings on specifications as multiplicious for sentencing purposes). *Cf.* United States v. Haywood, 6 M.J. 604 (A.C.M.R. 1978).

43. United States v. Johnson, 26 M.J. 686 (A.C.M.R. 1988) (three specifications of distributing cocaine were multiplicious; relief granted although defense did not raise issue at trial); United States v. Fortney, 12 M.J. 987 (A.F.C.M.R. 1982).

44. *See, e.g.*, United States v. Mincey, 42 M.J. 376 (1995) (court held that in bad-check offenses, the maximum punishment is determined by number and amount of checks as though they had been charged separately).

45. R.C.M. 1003(d)(1).

46. R.C.M. 1003(d)(2). United States v. Clemons, 39 M.J. 865 (N.M.C.M.R. 1994) (escalator provision not applicable at accused's special court-martial; although accused had been convicted by another special court-martial for three absences, court rejected argument that provisions

In the third provision, the accused may receive a bad-conduct discharge and total forfeitures if convicted of two or more separate offenses and the authorized confinement exceeds six months.[47] Note that a summary court-martial conviction does not apply to any of these escalator provisions[48] and that only convictions that are *final* will trigger the provisions.[49]

In addition to these provisions, the *Manual* may provide for additional punishments where specified aggravating circumstances are present. For example, where the accused is convicted of a drug offense, the maximum period of confinement and forfeiture of pay and allowances may be increased by *five* years if the offense was committed while the accused was: (1) on duty as a sentinel or lookout; (2) on board a vessel or aircraft used by or under the control of the armed forces; (3) in a missile launch facility; (4) in a hostile fire pay zone; or (5) in time of war.[50]

§ 16-2(F). "Footnote Five" Limitations.

Footnote Five to the Table of Maximum Punishments in the 1969 *Manual for Courts-Martial*[51] was one of five notes detailing additional rules for calculating the maximum punishment. It applied to violations of Article 92, U.C.M.J. offenses (disobedience of orders, etc.)[52] and provided that the maximum punishment authorized for violating Article 92 was *not* to be applied where (1) the accused would on the same facts be guilty of an offense with a lesser punishment[53] or (2) the violation or failure to obey was a breach of restraint imposed as a result of the order.[54] Instead the punishment was to be set by the authorized maximum amount specified for that particular offense.

With the removal of the Table of Maximum Punishments in the 1984 revision of the *Manual*, "Footnote Five" also vanished. However, the substance of this limitation on Article 92 offenses is now found in the discussion on Article

---

permit imposition of discharge if accused has been convicted at earlier single trial of three or two offenses).

47. R.C.M. 1003(d)(3) Discussion.
48. *Id.* United States v. Mack, 9 M.J. 300 (C.M.A. 1980); United States v. Booker, 5 M.J. 238 (C.M.A. 1977), *vacated in part,* 5 M.J. 246 (C.M.A. 1978).
49. R.C.M. 1003(d)(3) Discussion.
50. *See* MCM, Part IV, para. 37(e).
51. *See* § 16-2(C).
52. *See* § 2-4. In United States v. Ame, 35 M.J. 592 (N.M.C.M.R. 1992), the court discussed the background of the footnote five limitation (now found in the bracketed note following Para. 16e(2) of the Manual for Courts-Martial) and held that such limitation also applies to a charge of dereliction of duty (under Article 92(3)) which is also properly chargeable under Article 86 as a "'failure to go to,' or 'going from' an appointed place of duty without authority." On appeal, the Court of Military Appeals, 37 M.J. 170 (C.M.A. 1993), reversed, holding that the limitation in the bracketed note following Para. 16e(2) of the Manual for Courts-Martial does not apply to offenses other than wilful disobedience of orders cases.
53. United States v. Timmons, 13 M.J. 431 (C.M.A. 1982) ("gravamen of the offense" test used).
54. *See, e.g.,* para. 102, Part IV, MCM, which discusses the offense of breach of restriction where the maximum punishment is confinement for one month and forfeiture of two-thirds pay per month for one month. If that offense were punished as violation of an order (which is used to place the servicemember in restriction), the maximum punishment might otherwise be a bad-conduct discharge, confinement for six months, and total forfeitures.

92 in Part IV of the *Manual*. The underlying rationale is that an otherwise minor offense should not be treated as a major offense for purposes of punishment simply because it also constituted violation of an order.[55]

In *United States v. Battle*,[56] the court provided an in-depth discussion of the background of the Article 92 punishment limitation and the problems associated with determining what the "ultimate offense" is. It identified several factors to be balanced in determining the "gravamen" of the offense and thus whether the sentence limitation applies: (1) Whether a superior has personally and directly issued an order; (2) Whether the duties imposed by the order were routine in nature; (3) Whether the accused' s violation of the order was marked by defiance; and (4) Whether the order was formulated with an eye to enhancing the punitive consequences of a possible violation.[57] The court noted that some exceptions might apply where a commander must be able to place his full authority behind what would otherwise be a routine duty, and expect that that authority would be recognized at a later court-martial.[58] The court concluded by noting that the *Manual* provision creates a presumption that the punishment will be only for the underlying offense. Thus, said the court, the prosecution bears the burden of raising the issue and showing that the punishment authorized for Article 92 should apply.[59]

§ 16-2(G). Equivalent Punishments.

The *Manual* prescribes the maximum punishments in terms of Punitive Discharge, Forfeitures, and Confinement at Hard Labor. In determining the maximum amounts of punishments of Hard Labor without Confinement,[60] Restriction,[61] and Confinement on Bread and Water or Diminished Rations,[62] the court or reviewing authorities must consult the pertinent *Manual* provision for each of those punishments. Those provisions indicate the conversion formula for changing or substituting one of these three punishments for confinement. For example, the *Manual* indicates that one month of confinement is equivalent to two months of restriction.[63] The 1969 *Manual* contained a

---

55. *See generally* United States v. Quarles, 1 M.J. 231 (C.M.A. 1975); United States v. Showalter, 15 C.M.A. 410, 35 C.M.R. 382 (1965). *See also* United States v. Peaches, 25 M.J. 364 (C.M.A. 1987) (Article 91 should not be used as basis for charging what was essentially a failure to report for routine duty).
56. 27 M.J. 781 (A.F.C.M.R. 1988).
57. 27 M.J. at 786.
58. 27 M.J. at 786. *See, e.g.*, United States v. Loos, 4 C.M.A. 478, 16 C.M.R. 52 (1954); In United States v. Mitchell, 34 M.J. 1252 (A.C.M.R. 1992), the accused was given a written order to join his unit to deploy to Saudi Arabia. The court concluded that the ultimate offense was disobedience of that order and not missing movement. The court indicated that use of the term routine as it relates to duty may be ill-advised. The court said that it would interpret the word in a very broad sense to mean military duty. 34 M.J. at 1255, n.2.
59. 27 M.J.at 787.
60. R.C.M. 1003(b)(7).
61. R.C.M. 1003(b)(6).
62. R.C.M. 1003(b)(9).
63. R.C.M. 1003(b)(6).

Table of Equivalent Punishments[64] that was not carried forward into the 1984 revision of the *Manual* because it was confusing and capable of leading to incorrect results.[65]

§ 16-3. Permissible Punishments.

The common types of permissible court-martial punishments are noted in the following sections. In assessing punishments the court may not impose cruel or unusual punishments,[1] punishments contrary to the customs of the service, or punishments that either result in loss of good time or involve duties usually intended as an honor.[2]

§ 16-3(A). Death Penalty.

Before a court may impose the death penalty, the case must have been referred to trial as a capital case,[3] the U.C.M.J. must authorize the penalty, the case must have been heard by a general court-martial[4] and detailed procedures on sentencing must have been followed.[5] The only offense carrying a mandatory death penalty is wartime spying.[6] All others are permissive.[7] The death penalty may not be imposed where the prosecution has introduced a deposition or portions of a board inquiry as part of its case.[8] Challenges to referral of a case as capital may be waived.[9]

In response to *United States v. Matthews*,[10] the death penalty in military trials may be imposed only if key procedural requirements have been met. First, the prosecution must give written notice to the defense, before arraign-

---

64. Para. 127c(2), 1969 MCM.
65. R.C.M. 1003(b)(6).
1. Para. 127c(2), 1969 MCM.
2. *See* R.C.M. 1003(b) Analysis. *Cf.* United States v. Pierce, 27 M.J. 367 (C.M.A. 1989) (court encouraged services to draft some sort of equivalency table of punishments).
3. *See* R.C.M. 201(f)(2)(C). Capital offenses are defined in R.C.M. 103(3). United States v. Straight, 42 M.J. 244 (1995) (accused waived Eighth Amendment constitutional challenges to referral of rape charges as capital case by failing to raise it).
4. *See* R.C.M. 201(f)(1)(A)(iii).
5. R.C.M. 1004.
6. Art. 106, U.C.M.J. MCM, Part IV, para. 30.
7. *See* Articles 85, 90, 94, 99, 100, 101, 102, 110, 113, 118 and 120.
8. Art. 49, U.C.M.J. R.C.M. 702, 1001(b)(4).
9. United States v. Straight, 42 M.J. 244 (1995) (accused waived Eighth Amendment constitutional challenges to referral of rape charges as capital case by failing to raise it).
10. 16 M.J. 354 (C.M.A. 1983). The court ruled that existing procedures under the 1969 *Manual* were unconstitutional. *See also* United States v. Gay, 16 M.J. 586 (A.F.C.M.R. 1983).

For discussions on those procedures, see generally Dawson, "Is the Death Penalty in the Military Cruel and Unusual?" 31 JAG J. 53 (1980); English, "The Constitutionality of the Court-Martial Death Sentence," 21 A.F. L. Rev. 552 (1979); Pavlick, "The Constitutionality of the U.C.M.J. Death Penalty," 97 Mil. L. Rev. 81 (1982); Pfau and Milhizer, "The Military Death Penalty and the Constitution: There is Life After *Furman*," 97 Mil. L. Rev. 35 (1982); Comment, "The Death Penalty in Military Courts: Constitutionally Imposed?" 30 U.C.L.A. L. Rev. 366 (1982).

ment,[11] that it will be relying upon certain aggravating factors (listed in R.C.M. 1004)[12] in seeking the death penalty. Failure to give timely notice will

---

11. R.C.M. 1004(b)(1).
12. *Id.* The list of aggravating circumstances found at R.C.M. 1004(c), as amended in 1994 (change 7), is as follows:
   (1) That the offense was committed before or in the presence of the enemy; except that this circumstance shall not apply in the case of a violation of Article 118 or 120;
   (2) That in committing the offense the accused:
   (A) Knowingly created a grave risk of substantial damage to the national security of the United States; or
   (B) Knowingly created a grave risk of substantial damage to a mission, system, or function of the United States, provided that this subsection shall apply only if substantial damage to the national security of the United States would have resulted had the intended damage been effected;
   (3) That the offense caused substantial damage to the national security of the United States, whether or not the accused intended such damage, except that this factor shall not apply in the case of a violation of Article 118 or 120;
   (4) That the offense was committed in such a way or under circumstances that the life of one or more persons other than the victim, if any, were unlawfully and substantially endangered, except that this factor shall not apply to a violation of Articles 104, 106a or 120;
   (5) That the accused committed the offense with the intent to avoid hazardous duty;
   (6) That, only in the case of a violation of Article 118 or 120, the offense was committed in time of war and in territory in which the United States or an ally of the United States was then an occupying power or in which the armed forces of the United States were then an occupying power or in which the armed forces of the United States were then engaged in active hostilities;
   (7) That, only in the case of a violation of Article 118(1):
   (A) The accused was serving a sentence of confinement for 30 years or more or for life at the time of the murder;
   (B) The murder was committed: while the accused was engaged in the commission or attempted commission of any robbery, rape, aggravated arson, sodomy, burglary, kidnapping, mutiny, sedition, or piracy of an aircraft or vessel; or while the accused was engaged in the commission or attempted commission of any offense involving the wrongful distribution, manufacture, or introduction or possession with intent to distribute, of a controlled substance; or while the accused was engaged in flight or attempted flight after commission or attempted commission of any such offense.
   (C) The murder was committed for the purpose of receiving money or a thing of value;
   (D) The accused procured another by means of compulsion, coercion, or a promise of an advantage, a service, or a thing of value to commit the murder;
   (E) The murder was committed with the intent to avoid or to prevent lawful apprehension or effect an escape from custody or confinement;
   (F) The victim was the President of the United States, the President-elect, the Vice President, or, if there was no Vice President, the officer next in the order of succession to the office of President of the United States, the Vice-President-elect, or any individual who is acting as President under the Constitution and laws of the United States, any Member of Congress or Member-of-Congress elect, justice or judge of the United States, a chief of state or head of government (or political equivalent) of a foreign nation, or a foreign official (as such term is defined in section 1116(b)(3)(A) of title 18, United States Code), if the official was on official business at the time of the offense and was in the United States or in a place described in Mil. R. Evid. 315(c)(2), 315(c)(3);
   (G) The accused then knew that the victim was any of the following persons in the execution of office: a commissioned, warrant, noncommissioned, or petty officer of the armed services of the United States; a member of any law enforcement or security activity or agency, military or civilian, including correctional custody personnel; or any firefighter;
   (H) The murder was committed with intent to obstruct justice;

not bar the prosecution from relying upon those factors unless the defense can show that a delay in the trial will not be an adequate remedy and that the accused has been specifically prejudiced.[13] Second, during the trial on the merits or sentencing, the prosecution may offer evidence on those aggravating circumstances.[14] The defense is given great leeway in responding to that evidence.[15]

Third, the members must find beyond a reasonable doubt, by unanimous secret ballot,[16] that one or more of the listed aggravating circumstances exists and that any of those circumstances substantially outweighs whatever mitigating and extenuating factors might exist.[17]

Fourth, following their vote on the issue of aggravating circumstances, the court deliberates and votes on the sentence.[18] Again, a sentence of death requires a unanimous vote.[19]

(I) The murder was preceded by the intentional infliction of substantial physical harm or prolonged, substantial mental or physical pain and suffering to the victim. For purposes of this section, substantial physical harm means fractures or dislocated bones, deep cuts, torn members of the body, serious damage to internal organs or other serious bodily injuries. The term substantial physical harm does not mean minor injuries, such as a black eye or bloody nose. The term substantial mental or physical suffering is accorded its common meaning and includes torture.

(J) The accused has been found guilty in the same case of another violation of Article 118;

(8) That, only in the case of a violation of Article 118(4), the accused was the actual perpetrator of the killing;

(9) That, only in the case of a violation of Article 120:

(A) The victim was under the age of 12; or

(B) The accused maimed or attempted to kill the victim; or

(10) That, only in the case of a violation of the law of war, death is authorized under the law of war for the offense.

(11) That in the case of a violation of Article 104 or 106a:

(A) The accused has been convicted of another offense involving espionage or treason for which either a sentence of death or imprisonment for life was authorized by statute; or

(B) That in committing the offense, the accused knowingly created a grave risk of death to a person other than the individual who was the victim. For purposes of this rule, "national security" means the national defense and foreign relations of the United States and specifically includes: a military or defense advantage over any foreign nation or group of nations; a favorable foreign relations position; or a defense posture capable of successfully resisting hostile or destructive action from within or without.

13. R.C.M. 1004(b)(1). United States v. Loving, 41 M.J. 213 (1994) (court rejected defense argument that it had been ambushed by failure of government to specifically set out what evidence it would use to support aggravating factors).

14. R.C.M. 1004(b)(2).

15. R.C.M. 1004(b)(3).

16. R.C.M. 1004(b)(7).

17. R.C.M. 1004(b)(4). In United States v. Curtis, 28 M.J. 1074 (N.M.C.M.R. 1989), aff'd, 32 M.J. 252 (C.M.A. 1981), the court noted that although the sentencing procedures do not explicitly require that members vote on issue of balancing of aggravating and mitigating factors, they are nonetheless required to do so. On remand the court held that improper consideration of double counting of aggravating factors was harmless error 38 M.J. 530.

18. R.C.M. 1004(b)(7).

19. R.C.M. 1006(d)(4)(A).

In *United States v. Curtis*,[20] the Court of Military Appeals, now the Court of Appeals for the Armed Forces, revisited the constitutionality of the death penalty in military practice. In a lengthy opinion, the court concluded that the procedures promulgated by the President in the *Manual for Courts-Martial* did not violate separation of powers because Congress had delegated that authority to the President.[21] The court also rejected defense arguments that R.C.M. 1004 was invalid because it did not require imposition of the death sentence by a 12-person jury, because it did not permit introduction of mitigating factors, and because it lacked any provision to prevent racial bias.[22] In rejecting these arguments, the court observed that in several respects the *Manual* procedures are more protective than some state procedures.[23]

In a second opinion in *Curtis*,[24] the Court of Military Appeals focused on the procedures used in the accused's case and remanded the case for a determination of whether the accused was prejudiced by double counting of two aggravating factors in a double murder. The court suggested that the lower court consider generally similar cases reviewed by the Supreme Court of the United States.[25] Judge Cox noted in a concurring opinion that court members should be required to sign a capital sentencing worksheet or in the alternative be polled by the accused as to whether the sentence reflects each member's vote.[26]

In *Loving v. United States*,[27] the Supreme Court addressed the constitutionality of R.C.M. 1004 and concluded that the rule does not violate the Eighth Amendment or the doctrine of separation of powers. The Court assumed that its death penalty jurisprudence applied to the military and that without the provisions of R.C.M. 1004, Article 118, U.C.M.J. would not pass muster because it does not, standing alone, sufficiently narrow the class of those eligible for the death penalty.[28] Turning to the promulgation of R.C.M. 1004, the Court concluded that Congress has the constitutional power to delegate such matters to the President and that it had done so in Articles 18, 36, and 56, U.C.M.J.[29] It further concluded that the President's promulgation of R.C.M. 1004 did not violate the doctrine of separation of powers.[30] In a concurring

---

20. 32 M.J. 252 (C.M.A. 1991).
21. *Id.* at 260. The court noted that if the aggravating factors relied upon in R.C.M. 1004 were "elements" of a crime, only Congress could prescribe them. The court added that Congress apparently agreed that the President could establish aggravating factors because in a 1985 amendment to the U.C.M.J., Congress specifically recognized the President's authority to do so. *See* Article 106.
22. 32 M.J. at 267-68.
23. *Id.* at 269.
24. 33 M.J. 101 (C.M.A. 1991).
25. 33 M.J. 101 (C.M.A. 1991); United States v. Curtis, 38 M.J. 530 (N.M.C.M.R. 1993) (on remand, court concluded that double counting of aggravating factors was harmless error; court also concluded that penalty was generally proportional to those sentences imposed in similar cases in other jurisdictions).
26. *Id.*
27. 116 S. Ct. 1737 (1996).
28. 116 S. Ct. at 1742.
29. 116 S. Ct. at 1749. The Court relied primarily on Articles 18 and 56, noting that Article 36 "seems further afield from capital aggravating facts than that of Articles 18 and 56." *Id.*
30. 116 S. Ct. at 1751.

opinion, Justice Stevens, joined by three other Justices, observed that the Court had not decided the question of whether the service connection requirement should be extended to military death penalty cases.[31] In his concurring opinion, Justice Thomas questioned whether the extensive death penalty jurisprudence interpreting the Eighth Amendment even applied to capital prosecutions in the military.[32]

Assuming that the court imposes the death penalty, it may not be carried out until the President has approved the sentence.[33] When so approved it will be carried out in accordance with service regulations.[34]

§ 16-3(B). Punitive Separations.

Punitive separations include a dishonorable discharge,[35] a bad-conduct discharge,[36] and dismissal.[37] A dismissal is reserved for officers and warrant officers[38] and may be imposed for any offense by a general court-martial.[39] Warrant officers may receive dishonorable discharges[40] and enlisted accuseds may receive either dishonorable or bad-conduct discharges.[41] Imposition of a dishonorable or bad-conduct discharge may result in an automatic reduction to the lowest enlisted grade.[42] Punitive separations may also result in the loss of veterans' benefits.[43]

§ 16-3(C). Deprivation of Liberty.

The general types of deprivation of liberty punishments include confinement,[44] hard labor without confinement,[45] and restriction.[46] Before 1995, the

---

31. 116 S. Ct. at 1751.
32. 116 S. Ct. at 1753.
33. R.C.M. 1004(e) Discussion.
34. *Id.*
35. R.C.M. 1003(b)(10)(B).
36. R.C.M. 1003(b)(10)(C).
37. R.C.M. 1003(b)(10)(A). It is equivalent to a dishonorable discharge. United States v. Bell, 8 C.M.A. 193, 24 C.M.R. 3 (1957).
38. R.C.M. 1003(b)(10)(A). United States v. Carbo, 35 M.J. 783 (A.C.M.R. 1992) (warrant officers who are commissioned may be dismissed; warrant officers who are not commissioned are subject to dishonorable discharges; because court could not determine status of accused warrant officer, case was returned for DuBay hearing). Cadets and midshipmen are also eligible for dismissals. United States v. Ellman, 9 C.M.A. 549, 26 C.M.R. 329 (1958).
39. R.C.M. 1003(b)(10)(A).
40. R.C.M. 1003(b)(10)(B). The dishonorable discharge should be reserved for what in civilian practice would be felonies.
41. R.C.M. 1003(b)(10)(B), (C).
42. *See* Art. 58, U.C.M.J. and § 15-17(B)(5).
43. United States v. Longhi, 36 M.J. 988 (A.F.C.M.R. 1993) (veteran's benefits do not vest and may be lost for certain offenses).
44. R.C.M. 1003(b)(8). In the past, "confinement at hard labor" was used to describe what is now simply referred to as "confinement." The Drafters suggest that for the sake of uniformity, the words "at hard labor" be dropped from a sentence to confinement. R.C.M. 1003(b)(8) Discussion.
45. R.C.M. 1003(b)(7). The court does not specify the type of labor to be performed; that task is usually left for the accused's commander.
46. R.C.M. 1003(b)(6).

Manual permitted confinement on bread and water or diminished rations.[47] A sentence of life imprisonment is construed to mean confinement at hard labor for life.[48] The *Manual* limits the maximum imposable punishment of hard labor without confinement to three months[49] and restriction to two months.[50] The court should consult the *Manual* if it intends to combine both confinement and other lesser forms of restraint.[51] The punishments of deprivation of liberty run concurrently[52] and may automatically result in a reduction to the lowest enlisted grade.[53] A punishment of correctional custody, a punishment reserved for nonjudicial punishment,[54] may not be imposed by a court-martial.[55]

§ 16-3(D). Deprivation of Pay.

Fines[56] and forfeitures[57] are the two types of court-martial punishments affecting pay. Prior to the 1984 revision of the *Manual for Courts-Martial*,

---

47. 1995 amendments to the Manual deleted R.C.M.1003(b)(9) which provided for confinement on diminished rations. This form of punishment, which remains valid for nonjudicial punishment, had become ineffective; it was originally intended to be an immediate, remedial, punishment. But the delay between the time the sentence was announced and the convening authority's action undercut the intent.
In United States v. Yatchak, 35 M.J. 379 (C.M.A. 1992), the court discussed the background of confinement on bread and water and concluded that imposition of that punishment in this case violated Article 55 and was not authorized because the accused was not attached to or embarked in a vessel, a term found only in Article 15. The court noted that the accused was assigned to the USS Kitty Hawk, a vessel undergoing long-term repairs in a domestic port. The same result was reached in United States v. Lorance, 35 M.J. 382 (C.M.A. 1992). *See also* United States v. Valead, 30 M.J. 634 (N.M.C.M.R. 1990) (confinement on bread and water is not cruel and unusual punishment but was inappropriate in this case), *aff'd,* 32 M.J. 122 (C.M.A. 1991) (court declined to address issue of constitutionality of type of punishment). This punishment may only be imposed upon enlisted members attached to or embarked on a vessel; it may not last more than three days and must be preceded by approval from a medical officer. R.C.M. 1113(d)(5).
48. *See* United States v. Kinder, 14 C.M.R. 742 (A.B.R. 1954). Note that a life sentence may be a mandatory punishment. *See* Article 118, U.C.M.J.
49. R.C.M. 1003(b)(7).
50. R.C.M. 1003(b)(6). United States v. Handy, 26 M.J. 767 (C.G.C.M.R. 1988) (two-month limitation on restriction did not apply to administrative posttrial restriction imposed upon accused for purposes of medical treatment).
51. *See* § 15-17(A)(4).
52. *See* United States v. Brooks, 17 C.M.R. 467 (N.B.R. 1954). However, multiple sentences of confinement will be served consecutively. United States v. Bryant, 12 C.M.A. 133, 30 C.M.R. 133 (1961). *See also* United States v. Ellenson, 19 M.J. 605 (A.F.C.M.R. 1984), where the court, in a case of first impression, ruled that a military and civilian sentence were to be served consecutively. *See* Art. 14(c), U.C.M.J.
53. *See* § 15-17(B)(5).
54. *See* § 3-6(c)(1).
55. United States v. Miller, 17 M.J. 817 (A.C.M.R. 1984). *See also* United States v. Shamel, 22 C.M.A. 361, 47 C.M.R. 116 (1973) (correctional custody is not confinement).
56. R.C.M. 1003(b)(3).
57. R.C.M. 1003(b)(2). But total forfeitures should not be adjudged when there is no sentence including confinement. In United States v. Warner, 25 M.J. 64 (C.M.A. 1987), the court recognized that it had been a long-standing policy not to adjudge more than two-thirds forfeitures if the accused was not sentenced to confinement. *See also* R.C.M. 1107(d)(2) Discussion. The court,

§ 16-3(D)   SENTENCING   § 16-3(D)

detention of pay was also recognized.[58] But it was abandoned as an authorized punishment because it was seldom used and was administratively cumbersome.[59] Total forfeitures should normally not be imposed unless the sentence includes confinement.[60] The customary amount of forfeitures in such cases is limited to two-thirds of the accused's pay per month.[61] An accused may request forfeitures in excess of the two-thirds limit but the request should be clearly spelled out and should expressly refer to R.C.M. 1107(d)(2).[62]

Fines are normally reserved for cases where the accused has been unjustly enriched by his offense.[63] Fines may be imposed by any court-martial in lieu of forfeitures;[64] fines and forfeitures may only be combined in general courts-

---

however, believed that despite the precatory language previously used, there is an obligation not to impose more than two-thirds forfeitures. *See also* United States v. Myers, 25 M.J. 573 (A.F.C.M.R. 1987) (trial judge erred in instructing members on Air Force policy of not approving more than two-thirds forfeitures). In United States v. Hicks, 26 M.J. 935 (A.C.M.R. 1988), the pretrial agreement stated that the convening authority would suspend all confinement adjudged but approved total forfeitures. Noting that R.C.M. 1107(d)(2) Discussion states that an accused may request more than two-thirds forfeitures when he is not in confinement, in this case, the court declined to conclude that the accused's pretrial agreement constituted a request.

R.C.M. 1003(b)(2) was amended in 1994 to include "retired" and "retainer" pay as sources of income subject to forfeiture.

58. Para. 126*h*, 1969 MCM.

59. R.C.M. 1003(b)(3) Analysis.

60. *See* United States v. Warner, 25 M.J. 74 (C.M.A. 1987), where the court noted the prefatory language of R.C.M. 1107(d)(2) but concluded that it is error to impose more than two-thirds forfeitures when confinement is not imposed. United States v. Wright, 35 M.J. 899 (A.C.M.R. 1992) (allowances are not subject to forfeiture unless convening authority's approved sentence includes forfeiture of all pay and allowances).

61. *See* R.C.M. 1107(d)(2).

62. United States v. Santiago, 27 M.J. 688 (A.C.M.R. 1988) (request may be in pretrial agreement or in some other document; in any event, clarification should be obtained from defense counsel).

63. R.C.M. 1003(b)(3). However, fines may be imposed in other cases. *See* United States v. Thomas, 36 M.J. 554 (N.M.C.M.R. 1992) (fine was appropriate even though accused received no unjust enrichment); United States v. Jones, 28 M.J. 939 (N.M.C.M.R. 1989) (in concluding that the fine was legal and appropriate, the court noted that it is not necessary for the trial court to verbalize why a fine was imposed but that it would be helpful to the appellate authorities and would end speculation as to whether the fine was appropriate in the absence of evidence that the accused had been unjustly enriched).

United States v. Czeck, 28 M.J. 563 (N.M.C.M.R. 1989) (whether accused has been unjustly enriched is only one factor to be considered in deciding whether a fine is an appropriate punishment); United States v. Robertson, 27 M.J. 741 (A.C.M.R. 1988) ($5,000 fine to accused officer was not improper where trial judge imposed the fine, not on an unjust enrichment theory but, instead, on fact that military would not have benefit of ROTC scholarship it had paid to the accused).

See also 24 U.S.C. § 44, which provides that fines which are in excess of that due for reimbursement to the government or individuals will be appropriated for support of the Soldiers' and Airmen's Home. United States v. Combs, 15 M.J. 743 (A.F.C.M.R. 1983); United States v. Parini, 12 M.J. 679 (A.C.M.R. 1981).

The Discussion to this Rule notes that fines are appropriate for civilians tried by court-martial. *Cf.* § 4-7. *See also* United States v. Williams, 18 M.J. 186 (C.M.A. 1984) (only limit on fine is prohibition against cruel and unusual punishment).

64. R.C.M. 1003(b)(3). United States v. Harris, 19 M.J. 331 (C.M.A. 1985) (S.P.C.M. may impose fines). *See also* United States v. Sears, 18 M.J. 190 (C.M.A. 1984).

martial[65] and should be stated in specific dollar amounts.[66] Failure to pay a fine adjudged by a court may result in additional confinement if the fine was imposed with a provision that confinement in lieu of the fine will be assessed upon failure to pay.[67] Such confinement, however, may not be imposed where the adjudged sentence did not include confinement[68] or where the confinement portion of the sentence has already been completed.[69] In an extensive discussion of this provision, the court in *United States v. Rascoe*[70] noted the problems of applying and implementing R.C.M. 1003(b)(3) and 1113(d)(3), which permit confinement in lieu of the fine. The court suggested that in the future where the convening authority is "transforming" a fine into confinement, he should include in his action: (1) findings of fact regarding the accused's indigency status, (2) the opportunities given or had by the accused to pay the fine and the accused's efforts to do so, (3) any alternative measures considered, and (4) if those alternatives were inadequate to meet the government's penological interests, a statement why they were.[71]

§ 16-3(E). Reduction in Grade.

In addition to the foregoing punishments, the court may reduce the accused to a lower pay grade.[72] Article 58(a), U.C.M.J.[73] stipulates that unless the service secretaries provide otherwise, a court's imposition of a punitive dis-

---

65. R.C.M. 1003(b)(3).
66. R.C.M. 1003(b)(2), (3). United States v. Hounshell, 7 C.M.A. 3, 21 C.M.R. 129 (1956).
67. R.C.M. 1003(b)(3), 1113(d)(3). United States v. Tuggle, 34 M.J. 89 (C.M.A. 1992) (convening authority erred as matter of law in imposing confinement where accused did not pay fine. The court noted that, under the facts, the accused's financial limitations may have placed him near level of indigence and government had alternative punishments available).
United States v. Blizzard, 34 M.J. 763 (A.C.M.R. 1992) (accused was not denied constitutional rights when confinement was imposed after he failed to pay fine; accused failed to show that he was indigent; the court indicated that the confinement in lieu of the fine is not punishment, but is a tool to enforce collection of fine); United States v. Gerdes, 27 M.J. 587 (A.F.C.M.R. 1988) (court disapproved fine where sentence provided that confinement of one month could be extended up to three months if accused failed to pay fine where period of confinement was served before fine was ordered executed).
If the defendant argues that he has made a good-faith effort to pay the fine but indigency prevents him from doing so, confinement in lieu of the fine may not be imposed unless the accused is provided notice and an opportunity to be heard and there is no other adequate punishment. United States v. Soriano, 22 M.J. 453 (C.M.A. 1986).
See generally Bearden v. Georgia, 461 U.S. 660 (1983); United States v. Vinyard, 3 M.J. 551 (A.C.M.R. 1977); United States v. Martinez, 2 M.J. 1123 (C.G.C.M.R. 1976).
68. United States v. Shada, 28 M.J. 684 (A.F.C.M.R. 1989) (per curiam); United States v. Arnold, 27 M.J. 857 (A.F.C.M.R. 1989) (per curiam); United States v. Carmichael, 27 M.J. 757 (A.F.C.M.R. 1988) (per curiam). *Cf.* United States v. Bevins, 30 M.J. 1149 (A.C.M.R. 1990), where the Army Court of Military Review concluded that confinement could be imposed for failure to pay fine even though sentence did not otherwise include confinement.
69. United States v. Gerdes, 27 M.J. 587 (A.F.C.M.R. 1988).
70. 31 M.J. 544 (N.M.C.M.R. 1990).
71. 31 M.J. at 571.
72. R.C.M. 1003(b)(5). *Cf.* United States v. Sloan, 35 M.J. 4 (C.M.A. 1992) (rank of retiree cannot be reduced by court-martial or operation of law).
73. *See* Appendix 3.

§ 16-3(F)   SENTENCING   § 16-4(A)

charge, confinement, or hard labor without confinement, on an enlisted accused will automatically, as an administrative matter, reduce the accused to the lowest enlisted grade (*i.e.*, E-1).[74] The Secretary of the Navy has indicated that this statutory provision will be given effect in Navy or Marine Corps courts-martial to the extent that a reduction to the lowest enlisted grade will automatically occur where the sentence includes a punitive discharge or confinement in excess of 90 days or 3 months, depending on whether the confinement is expressed in days or months.[75] Convening authorities in the naval service may, in their discretion, suspend the automatic reduction provision.[76]

§ 16-3(F). Loss of Numbers.

A punishment related to reduction in grade is one used in the Navy, Marine Corps, and Coast Guard for officers.[77] The court designates the number of spaces the officer must be moved back on the appropriate seniority lists. Generally this would adversely affect the officer in terms of obtaining quarters and in actual promotion in rank.

§ 16-3(G). Reprimand.

A reprimand may be imposed in addition to any of the foregoing and when imposed as a court-martial punishment constitutes a punitive censure.[78] Although the punishment is imposed by the court-martial, the actual wording is directed by the convening authority;[79] the accused is presented with the original letter of censure and a copy of it is incorporated into the convening authority's post-trial action on the case.[80]

§ 16-4. Sentencing Procedures.

§ 16-4(A). In General.

Assuming that the court has returned a finding of guilty,[1] it turns to the sentencing phase of the trial. Unlike many civilian trials in which sentencing will be by the judge alone and often takes place long after the trial itself, the military sentencing proceedings usually immediately follow the court's an-

---

74. United States v. Young, 24 M.J. 626 (A.C.M.R. 1987) (trial judge erroneously applied the automatic reduction rule of Art. 58a to the sentence he imposed; because trial judge indicated on the record that he did not feel that such a reduction was appropriate, the court corrected the error by approving a sentence which did not include a reduction).
75. JAGMAN 0188a.
76. *Id.*
77. *See* R.C.M. 1003(b)(4).
78. R.C.M. 1003(b)(1).
79. *Id.*
80. See Appendix 36 for a sample promulgating order.
1. *See* R.C.M. 1001(a)(1). If findings of not guilty have been entered on all charges and specifications, the court will be adjourned. *See also* § 15-16.

719

nouncement of the verdict.[2] Although the *Manual* reflects in many respects the procedural rules used in Federal courts,[3] the military sentencing proceedings remain unique. The accused is sentenced by the judge only if he requested that he be tried by the judge[4] and, although more evidence is now likely to be placed before the sentencing authority, the military proceedings remain adversarial. Instead of a sentencing report, both sides are permitted to introduce, and object to, live testimony and documentary evidence that bears on the decision of what sentence is most appropriate.

The sentencing procedures are normally as follows: The prosecution offers evidence concerning the accused's record of service, prior convictions, matters in aggravation, and information on the accused's rehabilitative potential.[5] The defense then responds with evidence in "extenuation and mitigation."[6] Following any rebuttal and surrebuttal,[7] counsel present their arguments,[8] and the judge instructs[9] the court which then begins its deliberations.[10]

Finally, this sentencing procedure is applicable whether or not the accused entered a plea of guilty.[11] The following sections discuss these procedures in more detail. For discussion on special procedures which must be followed to impose a sentence of death, see § 16-3(A).

§ 16-4(B). Applicability of Rules of Evidence.

According to Rule 1101 of the Military Rules of Evidence[12] and R.C.M. 1001 in the *Manual*,[13] the Rules of Evidence are applicable to sentencing.[14] Although the Rules of Evidence may be relaxed for the defense when it presents its evidence on extenuation,[15] the prosecution is apparently bound by them when it initially presents its aggravation evidence.[16] If the judge has relaxed

---

2. *See* § 14-3(E) (judge's findings of guilt following guilty plea and § 15-16 (findings by court)).
3. *See* R.C.M. 1001 Analysis. *See also* United States v. Harrod, 20 M.J. 777, 779 (A.C.M.R. 1985).
4. *See* § 12-3(A).
5. *See* § 16-5.
6. *See* § 16-6.
7. *See* § 16-7.
8. *See* § 16-8.
9. *See* § 16-9.
10. *See* § 16-10.
11. *See* Chapter 14.
12. Rule 1101(c), Mil. R. Evid. *See generally* Saltzburg, Schinasi & Schlueter, *Military Rules of Evidence Manual*, 927-32 (3d ed. 1991).
13. R.C.M. 1001(c)(3), (d), and (e).
14. *See* Rule 1101, Mil. R. Evid.
15. Rule 1101, Mil. R. Evid.; R.C.M. 1001(c)(3). United States v. Eads, 24 M.J. 919 (A.F.C.M.R. 1987) (nothing in Mil. R. Evid. 1101(c) or R.C.M. 1001 overcomes hearsay objection to offered evidence); United States v. Oxford, 23 M.J. 548 (A.C.M.R. 1986) (although Rules of Evidence are relaxed at sentencing, Mil. R. Evid. 412 must be satisfied; here unsworn statement of accused on sentencing concerning marital sexual practices met the rule).
16. R.C.M. 1001(c)(3). *See, e.g.,* United States v. Elrod, 18 M.J. 692 (A.F.C.M.R. 1984) (no authority to relax rules for prosecution as to its initial presentencing evidence).

the rules for the defense, he may also do so for the prosecution during its rebuttal, if any, of the defense evidence.[17]

Even where the Rules of Evidence are relaxed, it does not necessarily mean that otherwise inadmissible evidence will be admitted.[18] For example, the privileges should still apply.[19] The case law instead seems to indicate that the relaxation of the Rules goes more to the question of whether the evidence is authentic and reliable.[20] This seems especially true with regard to prosecution rebuttal evidence.[21]

§ 16-5. Prosecution Evidence.

From the prosecution's perspective, it is important that the court be presented with *as much reliable information as is available,* not only about the surrounding circumstances of the case, but also about the accused's past record and lack of potential for rehabilitation. The prosecution's ability to present evidence in aggravation is the same without regard to whether the accused entered a plea of not guilty or guilty.[1]

Where the trial was contested, some evidence will have already been presented during the trial on the merits and may be referred to by the prosecution. For example, the court will probably already be aware of the circumstances surrounding the crime, or it may already be aware that the accused has a prior conviction.[2] In any event, that type of evidence, and matters not yet before the court, will generally fall into one of the following categories of evidence.

---

17. R.C.M. 1001(c)(3). *See also* § 16-6.
18. United States v. Zakaria, 38 M.J. 280 (C.M.A. 1993) (evidence must tend to prove or disprove existence of fact permitted by sentencing rules); United States v. Elvine, 16 M.J. 14 (C.M.A. 1983) (evidence must still be relevant); United States v. Woodard, 39 M.J. 1022 (A.C.M.R. 1994) (affidavit was inadmissible hearsay; court addressed evidence hurdles for introducing document).
19. *See, e.g.,* United States v. Tipton, 23 M.J. 338 (C.M.A. 1987) (the court rejected the argument that privileged communications were admissible on sentencing because of the relaxation of the Rules of Evidence; privileges, said the court, are applicable at sentencing). *See* Rule 1101(b), MIL. R. EVID.
20. *See, e.g.,* United States v. Wingart, 27 M.J. 128 (C.M.A. 1988).
21. United States v. Gudel, 17 M.J. 1075 (A.F.C.M.R. 1984) (error to admit unreliable hearsay evidence in police report); United States v. McGill, 15 M.J. 242 (C.M.A. 1983) (error to admit accused's Article 15 punishment; government is required to show that its evidence is in some way reliable).
1. United States v. Marshall, 14 M.J. 157 (C.M.A. 1982); *see* United States v. Vickers, 13 M.J. 403 (C.M.A. 1982).
2. *See* Rule 609, MIL. R. EVID., which governs admissibility of prior convictions for purpose of impeachment.

§ 16-5(A). Data From the Charge Sheet.

The sentencing portion of the trial commences with the military judge directing the trial counsel to read the personal data of the accused from the first page of the charge sheet.[3] In lieu of reading the data the prosecutor may reduce the information to writing and present it to the court as an exhibit.[4] The judge may ask the defense counsel to verify the data or register any objections. Failure to object will normally constitute waiver.[5] If the accused does object the judge will determine whether any corrections should be made.[6]

§ 16-5(B). Data Concerning the Accused's Prior Service.

The prosecution is also permitted to introduce information gleaned from the accused's personnel files, including data as to his marital status, efficiency reports, and prior disciplinary action such as letters of reprimand or nonjudicial punishment.[7] This information must have been filed and maintained in accordance with the service regulations[8] and not prepared and filed for the sole purpose of creating adverse information about the accused.[9]

---

3. United States v. Hill, 26 M.J. 836 (A.C.M.R. 1988) (court indicated that when reading the data concerning pretrial confinement from the charge sheet, the trial counsel should inform the trial judge whether timely magisterial review was accomplished and the judge with counsel should then determine any issues regarding that review). See R.C.M. 1001(b)(1) and Appendix 6 for a sample charge sheet. That document should provide information concerning the accused's age, period of service, rank, and information regarding pretrial confinement.

4. R.C.M. 1001(b)(1).

5. Id.

6. Id.

7. R.C.M. 1001(b)(2). United States v. Zakaria, 38 M.J. 280 (C.M.A. 1993) (prejudicial error to admit letter of reprimand re uncharged acts of sexual misconduct; the court noted that trial judges should be particularly sensitive to evidence which includes reference to uncharged misconduct); United States v. Wingart, 27 M.J. 128 (C.M.A. 1989) (the court admitted copies of the accused's Airman Performance Records (APRs) for his 17 years' service as court exhibits because neither the prosecution nor the defense wished to do so for tactical reasons; the prosecution declined because it wanted to use rebuttal evidence and the defense declined because of the possibility of damaging rebuttal evidence).

United States v. Donohue, 30 M.J. 734 (A.F.C.M.R. 1990) (live testimony indicating that accused had had opportunity to respond to administrative document in personnel file; if servicemember refuses to acknowledge administrative matter, entry to that effect should be made on document).

United States v. Shepherd, 30 M.J. 652 (A.F.C.M.R. 1990) (letters of counseling were admissible, letter of reprimand *was not* because accused *had not* been given opportunity to respond to it); United States v. Delaney, 27 M.J. 501 (A.C.M.R. 1988) (admission of accused's enlistment records was impermissible back-door attempt to introduce his civilian arrest record which was not admissible for any purpose).

8. United States v. Boles, 11 M.J. 195 (C.M.A. 1981) (administrative reprimand inadmissible because it was not filed in accord with regulations); United States v. Brown, 11 M.J. 263 (C.M.A. 1981) (Art. 15 improperly in file); United States v. Weatherspoon, 39 M.J. 762 (A.C.M.R. 1994) (Article 15 improperly admitted; not removed from records per Army regulations); United States

9. *See, e.g.,* United States v. Fontenot, 29 M.J. 244 (C.M.A. 1989) (handwritten notes and papers attached to DD Form 508s, disciplinary actions against accused while he was in pretrial confinement, were not properly a part of his military personnel file under Army regulations);

Particularly troublesome are records of nonjudicial punishment.[10] In addition to the requirement that they have properly retained in the accused's files, the court in *United States v. Booker*[11] indicated that such records are not admissible unless the prosecution demonstrates that the accused was given the opportunity to consult with counsel and the opportunity to demand trial by court-martial.[12] The court added, however, that the *Booker* requirements are not applicable where the accused is attached to or embarked on a vessel.[13] A correctly completed copy of the nonjudicial punishment form will normally constitute *prima facie* satisfaction of those two requirements.[14] If the form is

---

v. Edwards, 39 M.J. 528 (A.F.C.M.R. 1994) (record of nonjudicial punishment inadmissible because it did not comport with AF regulations); United States v. Dudley, 34 M.J. 603 (A.F.C.M.R. 1992) (opportunity to respond to proposal to include document in unfavorable information file (UIF) was sufficient to meet requirements of regulations); United States v. Dodds, 11 M.J. 520 (A.F.C.M.R. 1981). Even if it is properly filed, its admissibility rests within the judge's discretion.

See also United States v. Perry, 20 M.J. 1026 (A.C.M.R. 1985) (DD Form 508, which reflects conduct of accused while in pretrial confinement, may be admitted during sentencing under R.C.M. 1001(b)(2)), *overruling* United States v. Paulson, 30 C.M.R. 465 (A.B.R. 1960).

United States v. Goldsmith, 29 M.J. 979 (A.F.C.M.R. 1990) (possibly tardy letter of reprimand concerning accused's failure to inform medical authorities of his HIV status was admissible; it served a legitimate corrective purpose); United States v. Boles, 11 M.J. 195 (C.M.A. 1981) (reprimand prepared for use at trial was inadmissible).

United States v. Smith, 29 M.J. 736 (A.F.C.M.R. 1989) (reprimand not admissible because no showing that accused had opportunity to respond; requirement that only properly maintained personnel records are admissible also applies to prosecution rebuttal); United States v. King, 29 M.J. 535 (A.F.C.M.R. 1989) (letters of reprimand were not admissible due to fact that accused had not been given opportunity to respond to them in accordance with Air Force regulations); United States v. Hopwood, 29 M.J. 530 (A.F.C.M.R. 1989) (letter of reprimand was admissible where court concluded that although it had been issued after charges were preferred, it was not effort to increase sentence); United States v. Williams, 27 M.J. 529 (A.F.C.M.R. 1988) (letter of reprimand was inadmissible where accused's commander indicated that he had prepared the letter so the court would know that the accused was an habitual drug user); United States v. Beaver, 26 M.J. 991 (A.F.C.M.R. 1988) (letter of reprimand for conduct occurring months earlier but prepared days before trial was admissible; the court rejected the argument that the LOR had been "rushed into the record"); United States v. Hagy, 12 M.J. 739 (A.F.C.M.R. 1981); United States v. Dodds, 11 M.J. 520 (A.F.C.M.R. 1981).

10. United States v. Rimmer, 39 M.J. 1083 (A.C.M.R. 1994) (record of nonjudicial punishment not admissible where blocks not filled in; court observed that form indicated slipshod approach to imposition of Article 15); United States v. Sims, 28 M.J. 578 (A.C.M.R. 1989) (court admitted Article 15 punishment that had been imposed more than 10 years earlier; remoteness in time, said the court, goes to weight and not admissibility); United States v. King, 27 M.J. 545 (A.C.M.R. 1988) (accused waived objection to Article 15 punishment which had not been maintained in accordance with regulations); United States v. Shears, 27 M.J. 509 (A.C.M.R. 1988) (nonjudicial punishment forms were properly filed and maintained in unit SMIF, servicemember information files, although such a filing system is not specifically authorized by Army regulations). *See generally* § 3-8(B).

11. 5 M.J. 238 (C.M.A. 1978) (orig. pub. at 3 M.J. 443 (1977)).

12. *Id. Booker* originally required that the accused actually consult with counsel. In United States v. Mack, 9 M.J. 300 (C.M.A. 1980), the court modified the rule to permit a showing that the accused was advised of his right to consult with counsel. United States v. Dailey, 34 M.J. 1039 (N.M.C.M.R. 1992) (not plain error to admit nonjudicial punishment where accused refused such).

13. *See* United States v. Mack, 9 M.J. 300, 320 (C.M.A. 1980).

14. United States v. Wheaton, 18 M.J. 159 (C.M.A. 1984); United States v. Heath, 39 M.J. 1101 (C.G.C.M.R. 1994) (NJP form presumptively completed in presence of responsible officer).

§ 16-5(B)

in some way defective,[15] the prosecution may rely on live testimony[16] or other documentary evidence.[17] In no event should the judge question the accused in determining whether the *Booker* requirements were met.[18]

In addition to the *Booker* limitations, the prosecution will normally not be permitted to introduce evidence of an Article 15 punishment, if the offense which lead to the Article 15 punishment was also the basis of the court-martial charges.[19] If the prosecution offers only a portion of the pertinent document from the personnel file, the defense may rely upon Military Rule of Evidence 106 in requesting presentation of the entire document.[20] This so-called rule of "completeness" has been interpreted to apply not just to individual documents offered by the prosecution. In *United States v. Salgado-Agosto*,[21] the court indicated that the defense could rely upon Rule 106 to require the prosecution to introduce the entire file.[22] Although tactically this may diffuse prosecution rebuttal,[23] it presents a potential problem for the defense where the produced remainder contains further prejudicial information, some or all of which might not have been otherwise admissible if offered by the prosecution.[24] If the prosecution decides not to produce the remainder, it must withdraw its offered evidence.[25]

---

15. *See, e.g.*, United States v. Carmans, 10 M.J. 50 (C.M.A. 1980) (signatures missing); United States v. Gordon, 10 M.J. 31 (C.M.A. 1980). In United States v. Yarbough, 30 M.J. 1114 (N.M.C.M.R. 1990), the court drew an analogy to the requirement of completeness and the requirement that any convictions must be final before they may be offered at sentencing and concluded that an Article 15 still on appeal was not admissible. However, on en banc reconsideration, the court held that the real issue is who has the burden of showing that the document is admissible. The court laid out a rather elaborate scheme for determining whether a document was *prima facie* inadmissible or admissible.

16. *See generally* United States v. McGill, 15 M.J. 242 (C.M.A. 1983).

17. *See* United States v. Wheaton, 18 M.J. 159 (C.M.A. 1984).

18. United States v. Cowles, 16 M.J. 467 (C.M.A. 1983); United States v. Sauer, 15 M.J. 113 (C.M.A. 1983). Doing so violates the accused's rights against self-incrimination.

19. United States v. Pierce, 27 M.J. 367 (C.M.A. 1989) (prior nonjudicial punishment may not be used by prosecutor for any purpose at trial because it has no legal relevance); United States v. Thompson, 41 M.J. 895 (Army Ct.Crim.App. 1995) (trial court erred in permitting prosecutor to exploit Article 15 punishment that accused had already received for same offense).

20. Rule 106, MIL. R. EVID.

21. 20 M.J. 238 (C.M.A. 1985).

22. *Id.* at 239. *See also* United States v. Morgan, 15 M.J. 128 (C.M.A. 1983). *Cf.* R.C.M. 1001(b)(2) Analysis, which indicates that the Drafters intended the rule of completeness to extend to *documents*, not to the entire file. In their view, *Morgan* encouraged gamesmanship.

In United States v. Robbins, 16 M.J. 736 (A.F.C.M.R. 1983), the court ruled that the defense was not entitled to have the prosecution present the accused's complete record until the prosecution introduced a portion.

23. United States v. Morgan, 15 M.J. 128 (C.M.A. 1983) (if favorable evidence produced as requested, prosecution may not offer rebuttal).

24. United States v. Denning, 20 M.J. 935 (N.M.C.M.R. 1985) (although record of Article 15 would have been inadmissible under R.C.M. 1001(b)(2), because it was more than two years old (JAGMAN sec. 0133), it was admissible in rebuttal to defense evidence under R.C.M. 1001(d)). *See also* United States v. Shields, 20 M.J. 174 (C.M.A. 1985).

25. United States v. Goodwin, 21 M.J. 949 (A.F.C.M.R. 1986).

§ 16-5(C)   SENTENCING   § 16-5(C)

Again, the accused's failure to object may constitute waiver of any deficiencies in the offered evidence.[26]

§ 16-5(C). Evidence of Prior Convictions.

The prosecution may also offer any prior military or civilian convictions against the accused.[27] A military "conviction," for purposes of sentencing evidence, results when a general or special court-martial adjudges a sentence.[28] Neither a civilian juvenile conviction[29] nor a nonjudicial punishment is considered a conviction.[30] Whether a particular civilian judicial ruling has amounted to a conviction will generally depend on the law of that jurisdiction.[31]

If the accused was tried by a special court-martial without a military judge or a summary court-martial, a "conviction" is not admissible until it has been reviewed by a judge advocate.[32] In some instances proof of finality, i.e., the fact that the necessary legal review has been completed, will be noted in the

---

26. R.C.M. 1001(b)(2); United States v. Rayford, 33 M.J. 747 (A.C.M.R. 1991) (defense waived objection to introduction of nonjudicial punishment); United States v. Yarbough, 30 M.J. 1114 (N.M.C.M.R. 1989) (no waiver where admission of inadmissible Article 15 was plain error); United States v. Sims, 28 M.J. 578 (A.C.M.R. 1989) (accused raised issue for first time on appeal); United States v. Larkins, 21 M.J. 654 (A.C.M.R. 1985) (failure to object to Article 15).

27. R.C.M. 1001(b)(3).

28. R.C.M. 1001(b)(3). The 1984 revisions to the *Manual* provision discarded the previous rule that to be admissible a prior conviction had to be at least six years old, 1969 MCM, para. 75*b*(3), and that it be "final." In United States v. Caniete, 28 M.J. 426 (C.M.A. 1989), the court distinguished United States v. Krewson, 12 M.J. 157 (C.M.A. 1981) (only offenses occurring prior to the charged offense were admissible), and held that the accused's prior military conviction, which was imposed between the date of the offense and the second trial, was admissible in the second trial as aggravating evidence. United States v. Krewson, 12 M.J. 157 (C.M.A. 1981) (judge erred in permitting evidence of civil conviction not yet final).

See also R.C.M. 1001(b)(4)(A) Discussion.

29. In United States v. Slovacek, 24 M.J. 140 (C.M.A. 1987), the court reversed the Air Force Court of Military Review decision at 21 M.J. 538, and held that a juvenile adjudication is not a conviction for purposes of R.C.M. 1001(b)(3)(A). The court relied in part upon language in Mil. R. Evid. 609(d), which recognizes a difference between a conviction and a juvenile adjudication.

30. United States v. Brown, 23 M.J. 149 (C.M.A. 1987) (Article 15 punishment is not a prior conviction). *See also* Rule 609, Mil. R. Evid. Note that the vacation of a suspended sentence does not amount to another "conviction."

31. R.C.M. 1001(b)(3) Analysis. *See, e.g.,* United States v. Eady, 35 M.J. 15 (C.M.A. 1992) (proof of prior state convictions by letter from local police department, by indictment and offer to plead guilty, and certified copy of records check from local police department); United States v. Browning, 29 M.J. 174 (C.M.A. 1989) (members of court could not agree whether traffic tickets were prior civilian convictions but did agree that the accused suffered no prejudice by their admission); United States v. Hughes, 26 M.J. 119 (C.M.A. 1988) (Texas "Order Deferring Adjudication" was not a conviction).

United States v. Delaney, 27 M.J. 501 (A.C.M.R. 1988) (accused's civilian arrest record was not admissible in sentencing for any purpose); United States v. Evans, 26 M.J. 961 (A.C.M.R. 1988) (accused's probationary status under Georgia First Offender Act was not final conviction); United States v. Hanes, 21 M.J. 647 (A.C.M.R. 1985) (conviction of accused's wife was inadmissible).

32. R.C.M. 1001(b)(4)(B). See Chapter 17 for discussions on legal review of courts-martial. *See also* R.C.M. 1112.

promulgating order.[33] In some cases, the courts have presumed finality if more than a reasonable period of time for such review has elapsed.[34] Where a conflict of information on finality exists, the judge must decide the issue.[35] While it is not necessary that the prior conviction in question precede the offense for which the accused has been tried, it must precede the sentencing portion of the trial.[36]

If the prior conviction is still on appeal,[37] the defense should offer evidence of that fact[38] and argue that little or no weight should be given to the conviction. Before admitting the conviction, the judge should determine that the probative value of the conviction outweighs its prejudicial effect.[39]

In proving the prior conviction, the prosecution may rely either upon testimony or use one of several documents to show the conviction.[40] Examples would include a copy of the promulgating order for the previous case,[41] a copy of DD Form 493 (Extract of Convictions),[42] service forms which register the conviction,[43] or appropriate civilian documentation.[44] Although a transcript of

---

33. See § 17-10 for a discussion on promulgating orders. See also Appendix 36.

34. See, e.g., United States v. Graham, 1 M.J. 308 (C.M.A. 1976) (5-year-old promulgating order); United States v. Hines, 1 M.J. 623 (A.C.M.R. 1975) (8 months). Cf. United States v. Reed, 1 M.J. 166 (C.M.A. 1975) (prima facie showing overcome by lack of entry of final review on DA Form); United States v. Hancock, 12 M.J. 685 (A.C.M.R. 1981).

35. See United States v. Lemieux, 13 M.J. 969 (A.C.M.R. 1982).

36. United States v. Hanes, 21 M.J. 647 (A.C.M.R. 1985) (post-offense conviction); United States v. Allen, 21 M.J. 507 (A.C.M.R. 1985) (post-offense civilian conviction).

37. See Chapter 17 for discussions of the appellate review process.

38. See R.C.M. 1001(b)(3)(B) (evidence of appeal is admissible). Counsel should also address the likelihood of success on appeal.

39. See Rule 403, Mil. R. Evid. and R.C.M. 1001(b)(3) Analysis. See also United States v. Wright, 20 M.J. 518 (A.C.M.R. 1985) (judge properly considered evidence of accused's prior conviction after striking proper balance between the probative value of that evidence, as to the accused's potential for rehabilitation, against possible prejudice).

40. R.C.M. 1001(b)(3)(C) indicates that the prosecution may use "any evidence admissible under the Military Rules of Evidence." Portions of the record of trial may be admitted if they are otherwise relevant. See United States v. Nellum, 24 M.J. 693 (A.C.M.R. 1987) (stipulation of fact in prior special court-martial record of trial was relevant); United States v. Wright, 20 M.J. 518 (A.C.M.R. 1985) (relevant as evidence in aggravation).

In United States v. Nellum, 24 M.J. 693 (A.C.M.R. 1987), the court concluded that the prosecution could properly offer a relevant stipulation of fact which had been introduced in the accused's prior court-martial, which in turn led to the conviction being offered in evidence. The court noted that such stipulations generally explain the circumstances of the earlier conviction. In United States v. Wright, 20 M.J. 518 (A.C.M.R. 1985), the court said that records of trial could be used to prove prior convictions.

41. See Appendix 36.

42. United States v. Lemieux, 13 M.J. 969 (A.C.M.R. 1982); United States v. Hines, 1 M.J. 623 (A.C.M.R. 1975). R.C.M. 1001(b)(3)(C) Discussion.

43. See United States v. Barnes, 33 M.J. 468 (C.M.A. 1992) (DD Form 1966/3, a standard government form for asking recruits about prior legal violations, was permitted. The court indicated that the entries on the form might constitute party admissions under Mil. R. Evid. 801). Cf. United States v. Yeckinevich, 26 M.J. 833 (A.F.C.M.R. 1988) (entries in original enlistment records did not provide sufficient basis to show civilian conviction); United States v. Lemieux, 13 M.J. 969 (A.C.M.R. 1982) (prosecution used DA Form 2-2, Record of Court-Martial Conviction).

44. Trial counsel should pay particular attention to obtaining the necessary authentication of civilian conviction documents. See Rules 901 and 902, Mil. R. Evid. United States v. Prophete, 29

a portion of the record of trial might be admissible, it might be error to introduce the entire record.[45] Normally, the prosecution is not permitted to present the details of the prior conviction during its case-in-chief during sentencing.[46]

As with the introduction of nonjudicial punishment records, discussed above, some special rules apply for introducing records of summary court-martial convictions.[47] In addition to showing that review has been completed, the prosecution must establish that the accused consented to the summary court-martial and that he had the opportunity to consult with legal counsel about whether to demand a trial by special court-martial.[48] If the record of the summary court-martial does not include these elements, the prosecution may rely either upon live testimony or documentary evidence, such as annotated "advice" forms that sometimes accompany the record.[49] The burden of showing the necessary prerequisites for admissibility rests with the prosecution, and the judge may not question the accused in an attempt to lay a foundation.[50]

§ 16-5(D). Evidence in Aggravation.

§ 16-5(D)(1). In General.

The prosecution is permitted to offer evidence in aggravation, that is, evidence as to "any aggravating circumstances directly relating to or resulting from the offenses...."[51] This prescription is potentially broad and would include a wide range of matters that tend to show that the accused's actions should not be viewed in a vacuum. This is particularly important in a case where the court has not heard aggravating evidence because the accused has pleaded guilty or where for various reasons the evidence would not have been relevant in determining guilt. For example, the fact that the victim incurred

---

M.J. 925 (A.F.C.M.R. 1989) (properly authenticated computer printout showing Arkansas conviction of writing hot check was admissible).

45. United States v. Charley, 28 M.J. 903 (A.C.M.R. 1989) (prejudicial error to introduce entire record of accused's prior summary court-martial).

46. United States v. Brogan, 33 M.J. 588 (N.M.C.M.R. 1991) (evidence which explains detailed facts underlying prior conviction inadmissible).

47. See generally Chapter 15 for a discussion of summary courts-martial.

48. United States v. Syro, 7 M.J. 431 (C.M.A. 1979); United States v. Booker, 5 M.J. 238 (C.M.A. 1977).

49. See, e.g., United States v. Alsup, 17 M.J. 166 (C.M.A. 1984) (annotated entries); United States v. Kuehl, 11 M.J. 126 (C.M.A. 1981) (supplemental advice forms).

50. See United States v. Sauer, 15 M.J. 113 (C.M.A. 1983), overruling United States v. Spivey, 10 M.J. 7 (C.M.A. 1980), and United States v. Mathews, 6 M.J. 357 (C.M.A. 1979). See also United States v. Hardy, 21 M.J. 198 (C.M.A. 1986) (because Article 15 and letter of reprimand were not incomplete on their face, judge's questioning of accused was unnecessary to establish admissibility).

51. R.C.M. 1001(b)(4). United States v. Gordon, 31 M.J. 30 (C.M.A. 1990) (prosecutor must show more than mere relevancy; higher standard applies, i.e., aggravating circumstances must directly relate to or result from offense); United States v. Peck, 36 M.J. 900 (A.F.C.M.R. 1993) (standard for admitting evidence in aggravation is more than mere relevancy; enlistment form was inadmissible). Child, "How Aggravating Can You Get? The Expanded Boundaries for Admission of Aggravation Evidence Under R.C.M. 1001(b)(4)," ARMY LAW., Feb. 1986, at 29.

high medical expenses would normally not be admissible on the issue of whether the accused committed the charged assault.[52] But on sentencing, that fact is relevant and important in assessing an appropriate punishment.[53]

In measuring the admissibility of this sort of evidence, the courts generally require that the evidence be admissible under the Rules of Evidence,[54] that it addresses matters directly relating to the offense or the results of the offense,[55] and that in the balance, the probative value of the evidence outweighs its prejudicial impact on the accused.[56]

The prosecution is not limited to offering live testimony and may rely upon both oral and written depositions in offering evidence in aggravation.[57] In cases where the accused has entered a guilty plea, the prosecution will often introduce a stipulation of fact,[58] signed as part of a pretrial agreement,[59] which sets out the aggravating circumstances surrounding the offense.[60] There is some authority for the proposition that where otherwise inadmissible evidence may be included in the stipulation, the military judge is not permitted to excise that information.[61] The alternative is for the defense to not sign

---

52. *See* Rule 401, Mil. R. Evid. *See also* § 16-5(D)(3).
53. R.C.M. 1001(b)(4) Discussion. United States v. Pearson, 17 M.J. 149 (C.M.A. 1984).
54. United States v. Martin, 20 M.J. 227 (C.M.A. 1985); United States v. Witt, 21 M.J. 637 (A.C.M.R. 1985).
55. United States v. Gordon, 31 M.J. 30 (C.M.A. 1990) (commander's testimony relating that offense had reduced soldiers' confidence in each other and had undermined unit's concern for safety did not directly relate to negligent homicide offense; officer was not authorized to lecture members of court on lessons to be drawn from the offense).
United States v. Peck, 36 M.J. 900 (A.F.C.M.R. 1993) (evidence that accused previously acknowledged dangerousness of LSD not admissible to rebut statements made in accused's guilty plea inquiry).
United States v. Hall, 29 M.J. 786 (A.C.M.R. 1989) (uncharged acts of drug offenses were not directly related to charges); United States v. Barber, 27 M.J. 885 (A.C.M.R. 1989) (there must be "reasonable linkage" between offense and effect); United States v. Witt, 21 M.J. 637 (A.C.M.R. 1985).
56. United States v. Yanke, 23 M.J. 144 (C.M.A. 1987) (proper to admit photograph of eight-month-old child that accused had smothered; the photo's probative value—to show that the child was a normal, healthy child who would have struggled—outweighed possible prejudice to the accused); United States v. White, 23 M.J. 84 (C.M.A. 1986) (photos of battered child admissible to explain testimony and illustrations of experts on issue of battered child syndrome); United States v. Hall, 29 M.J. 786 (A.C.M.R. 1989) (prejudicial effect outweighed probative value); United States v. Witt, 21 M.J. 637 (A.C.M.R. 1985); United States v. Green, 21 M.J. 633 (A.C.M.R. 1985). Rule 403, Mil. R. Evid.
57. R.C.M. 1001(b)(4). It may not do so, however, in capital cases. *Id.*
58. *See* § 14-3.
59. *See* § 9-2.
60. *See, e.g.,* United States v. Marsh, 19 M.J. 657 (A.C.M.R. 1984) (explanatory matters); United States v. Sharper, 17 M.J. 803 (A.C.M.R. 1984) (stipulation that accused intended to distribute drugs).
61. *See* United States v. Mullens, 29 M.J. 398 (C.M.A. 1990) (military judge must affirmatively rule on defense objections to stipulations of fact, even if it is signed by the accused and counsel); United States v. DeYoung, 29 M.J. 78 (C.M.A. 1989); United States v. Glazier, 26 M.J. 268 (C.M.A. 1988) (subject to limitations by judge in the interest of justice, counsel may stipulate to otherwise inadmissible evidence, especially in a negotiated plea setting; a military judge may rule upon objections to the contents).

the stipulation and risk losing the benefit of the pretrial agreement.[62]

The following discussion addresses the various types of evidence which are typically considered as "evidence in aggravation."[63]

§ 16-5(D)(2). Evidence of Circumstances Surrounding Offense.

The prosecution is permitted to offer evidence of circumstances surrounding the offense.[64] In guilty plea cases, these can be particularly important in those cases where sentencing will be by court members who will not have heard any detailed factual description of the commission of the offense.[65] To flesh out the facts, the prosecution may introduce a stipulation of fact, as noted in § 16-5(D)(1). A detailed stipulation will generally provide sufficient information about the offense itself.[66] Second, the prosecution may introduce statements made by the accused during the providency inquiry.[67] If, during sentencing, the accused makes statements at odds with his sworn providency statements, the prosecution is probably limited to instituting additional charges.[68]

United States v. Klinko, 36 M.J. 840 (A.C.M.R. 1993) (court indicated that stipulations of fact are not truly binding agreements; court recommended that stipulations include statement that the evidence in question is admissible without regard to the rules of evidence).

United States v. Jackson, 30 M.J. 565 (A.C.M.R. 1990) (uncharged misconduct in stipulation of fact was admissible); United States v. Vargas, 29 M.J. 968 (A.C.M.R. 1990) (otherwise inadmissible uncharged misconduct was admissible as part of a stipulation entered into pursuant to a negotiated plea; court found no overreaching by government); United States v. DeYoung, 27 M.J. 595 (A.C.M.R. 1988) (nonprejudicial error for judge to not rule on defendant's objections to inclusion of uncharged misconduct in stipulation offered as part of a pretrial agreement); United States v. Neil, 25 M.J. 798 (A.C.M.R. 1988) (although accused agreed to inclusion of acts of uncharged misconduct in a stipulation of fact introduced in aggravation, the trial judge erred in assessing punishment for those offenses; the court noted, however, that he could have considered those offenses in deciding what a fair punishment would have been on the offense for which he was found guilty). See also United States v. Mullens, 24 M.J. 745 (A.C.M.R. 1987).

United States v. Taylor, 21 M.J. 1016 (A.C.M.R. 1986) (judge should not referee contents of stipulation); United States v. Rasberry, 21 M.J. 656 (A.C.M.R. 1985) (accused waived challenge of pretrial statements by stipulating to them; no denial of due process); United States v. Sharper, 17 M.J. 803 (A.C.M.R. 1984) (serious doubts about propriety of stipulating to other evidence); United States v. Smith, 9 M.J. 537 (A.C.M.R. 1980).

62. United States v. DeYoung, 29 M.J. 78 (C.M.A. 1989) (accused was not forced to plead guilty or accept stipulation of fact that contained evidence of uncharged misconduct); United States v. Taylor, 21 M.J. 1016 (A.C.M.R. 1986).

63. See R.C.M. 1001(b)(4).

64. See, e.g., United States v. Lawson, 33 M.J. 946 (N.M.C.M.R. 1991) (tally of costs incurred in locating victim and death certificate were related to offense of dereliction of duty which resulted in death of servicemember).

65. See § 14-3.

66. For a discussion about stipulations and plea bargaining, see Chapter 9. The topic is also addressed at § 15-21.

67. See Rule 410, Mil. R. Evid. United States v. Holt, 27 M.J. 57 (C.M.A. 1988) (treating accused's statements during inquiry as admissions). See § 14-3(B)(2).

The statements, however, are not automatically in evidence, and the accused must be given notice of what statements are being offered and an opportunity to object. United States v. Dukes, 30 M.J. 793 (N.M.C.M.R. 1990) (prosecutor referred to accused's providency inquiry statements during closing argument; issue waived).

68. See MCM, Part IV, para. 79 (false swearing) and para. 98 (perjury).

§ 16-5(D)(3)

Evidence falling under this category of prosecution evidence could include testimony concerning the accused's attitude about his activity at the time of the offense.[69] It could also include evidence of uncharged misconduct that helps explain the context of the offense.[70] The topic of admissibility of uncharged misconduct evidence during sentencing is discussed in more detail at § 16-5(D)(6).

§ 16-5(D)(3). Evidence of Impact of Offense on Victim and Community.

In putting the offense in perspective, the prosecution is permitted to introduce evidence of the effect of the offense. While this could include evidence of the effect on the accused, i.e., the potential value of the offense to the accused,[71] the more typical example would also include evidence of the adverse impact of the offense on the victim[72] and the victim's family.[73]

---

69. *See* United States v. Wright, 20 M.J. 518 (A.C.M.R. 1985); United States v. Pooler, 18 M.J. 832 (A.C.M.R. 1984).

70. *See, e.g.*, United States v. Button, 31 M.J. 897 (A.F.C.M.R. 1990); United States v. Hall, 29 M.J. 786 (A.C.M.R. 1989); United States v. Anderson, 25 M.J. 779 (A.C.M.R. 1988).

Cf. United States v. Caro, 20 M.J. 770 (A.F.C.M.R. 1985) (harmless error for prosecution to introduce, under R.C.M. 1001(b)(4), accused's pretrial statement that falsely denied any involvement in a theft; although it might have been admissible as character evidence, it was not relevant for purposes of aggravating evidence). *See also* § 16-5(D)(6).

71. United States v. Hood, 12 M.J. 890 (A.C.M.R. 1982) (black market value of goods); United States v. Witt, 21 M.J. 637 (A.C.M.R. 1985) (street value of drugs).

72. R.C.M. 1001(b)(4) Discussion. *See, e.g.*, United States v. Holt, 33 M.J. 400 (C.M.A. 1991) (prosecution properly presented victim's testimony that she wanted the accused to apologize for crime; another witness testified that such apologies can be important to victims); United States v. Fontenot, 29 M.J. 244 (C.M.A. 1989) (testimony by rape victim's parents regarding impact of offense on their daughter, their family and themselves was admissible); United States v. Fox, 24 M.J. 110 (C.M.A. 1987) (evidence of victim's previous sex life may have been relevant on issue of whether she would have suffered extended trauma); United States v. Hammond, 17 M.J. 218 (C.M.A. 1984) (effect on social life of rape victim).

United States v. Pingree, 39 M.J. 884 (A.C.M.R. 1994) (teacher's testimony that rape victim's behavior had changed was admissible); United States v. Hancock, 38 M.J. 672 (A.F.C.M.R. 1993) (expert testimony on battered wife syndrome admissible as victim impact evidence); United States v. Estrella, 35 M.J. 836 (A.C.M.R. 1992) (evidence that lover of accused had lost her virginity to him when he committed adultery).

United States v. Ringuette, 29 M.J. 527 (A.F.C.M.R. 1989) (accused's uncharged threats to victim were relevant on sentencing); United States v. Groveman, 25 M.J. 796 (A.F.C.M.R. 1988) (murder victim's diary detailing 15-year Air Force career was admissible as "victim impact" evidence; members were not asked to redress wrong done to victim's family but rather to perform their role as "representatives of community at large"); United States v. Snodgrass, 22 M.J. 866 (A.C.M.R. 1986) (child victim).

73. United States v. Reveles, 41 M.J. 388 (1995) (trial judge excluded prosecution videotape prepared on life of victim, showing pictures of victim, family, and interspersed with scenes from Oregon, scripture passages, and music from *Love Story*; the defense argued that the tape was too emotional and was akin to waving a bloody shirt in front of the members); United States v. Wilson, 35 M.J. 473 (C.M.A. 1992) (testimony of father of girl involved in offenses, of frantic search for girl, and of his distress was admissible as victim-impact evidence); United States v. Pearson, 17 M.J. 149 (C.M.A. 1984); United States v. Whitehead, 30 M.J. 1066 (A.C.M.R. 1990) (judge did not abuse discretion in permitting murder victim's family from presenting evidence of

§ 16-5(D)(3) SENTENCING § 16-5(D)(3)

In *United States v. Pearson*,[74] the court ruled that during sentencing it is appropriate for the sentencing authority to hear evidence concerning the *victim*'s character and the magnitude of damages or loss inflicted by the accused. That evidence or testimony, however, may not invade the province of the sentencing authority, such as permitting the desires of society or any particular portion thereof to interfere with the court's independent function.[75]

The prosecution may also present evidence of the impact or effect of the offense on the community[76] and the impact of the offense on the unit,[77] discipline,[78] or the mission of the unit or armed forces.[79]

The key here is that the prosecution must establish some reasonable linkage between the offense and the "effect" or "impact" evidence.[80]

---

impact of crime on them). *Cf.* Booth v. Maryland, 482 U.S. 496 (1987). *See generally* Mickle, "The Army's Victim/Witness Assistance Program," ARMY LAW., Nov. 1994, at 3.

74. 17 M.J. 149 (C.M.A. 1984).

75. *Id.* at 153. *See also* United States v. Marshall, 14 M.J. 157 (C.M.A. 1982) (mental anguish); United States v. Garcia, 18 M.J. 716 (A.F.C.M.R. 1984) (humiliation of trial).

76. *See, e.g.*, United States v. Ferrer, 33 M.J. 96 (C.M.A. 1991) (harmless error for social worker to testify re number of child abuse cases in community); United States v. Bartoletti, 32 M.J. 419 (C.M.A. 1991) (admission of testimony from crime statistics clerk on number of larcenies on base was harmless error where there was no foundational evidence that these crimes had adverse impact on community); United States v. Needham, 23 M.J. 383 (C.M.A. 1987) (proper to admit evidence of excerpts from *Drug Enforcement Magazine* as to the effects of LSD and marijuana); United States v. Sargent, 18 M.J. 331 (C.M.A. 1984) (death from drugs purchased from accused); United States v. Pearson, 17 M.J. 149 (C.M.A. 1984).

United States v. Broussard, 35 M.J. 665 (A.C.M.R. 1992) (testimony of impact of offense on children in neighborhood).

United States v. Eads, 24 M.J. 919 (A.F.C.M.R. 1987) (court noted that there may be a problem with using judicial notice of extracts of government publications dealing with drugs as a means of informing the members of sentencing information); United States v. Sells, 30 M.J. 944 (A.C.M.R. 1990) (testimony by witness with clinical education on effect of drugs in surrounding community was proper evidence in aggravation).

Cf. United States v. Stevens, 21 M.J. 649 (A.C.M.R. 1985) (judge erred in considering impact of offense on United States-Panama relations).

77. R.C.M. 1001(b)(4) Discussion. *See, e.g.*, United States v. Thornton, 32 M.J. 112 (C.M.A. 1991) (testimony by commander gave some insight into impact of offenses on unit by accused who had specialized training and security clearance).

United States v. Krzcuik, 34 M.J. 1002 (A.C.M.R. 1992) (accused's loss of security clearance); United States v. Branoff, 34 M.J. 612 (A.F.C.M.R. 1992) (error to admit testimony that impact of investigating 27 people involved in drug investigation was significant; evidence of impact on unit must directly relate to, or result from, the offenses of which the accused has been found guilty); United States v. Witt, 21 M.J. 637 (A.C.M.R. 1985) (effect of drugs); United States v. Needham, 19 M.J. 614 (A.F.C.M.R. 1984) (effect of drugs); *Cf.* United States v. Sanford, 29 M.J. 413 (C.M.A. 1990) (edifying a court with a commander's general views of impact of offense on unit can have the same effect as other forms of command influence).

78. United States v. Vickers, 13 M.J. 403 (C.M.A. 1982) (disobedience offense aggravated disruption in unit).

79. United States v. Antonitis, 29 M.J. 217 (C.M.A. 1989) (evidence concerning accused's potential loss of security clearance did not show impact on unit's mission); United States v. Fitzhugh, 14 M.J. 595 (A.F.C.M.R. 1982) (offense had effect on mission).

80. United States v. Rust, 41 M.J. 472 (1995) (suicide note by putative father of baby which died as a result of accused-doctor's medical malpractice was not a consequence of the offense nor directly related to it; court noted that an accused is not responsible for never-ending chain of causes and effects); United States v. Barber, 27 M.J. 885 (A.C.M.R. 1989) (court indicated that

§ 16-5(D)(4). Evidence Addressing Rehabilitative Potential.

Evidence of the accused's potential for rehabilitation may also be offered by the prosecution.[81] To some extent, the accused's past conduct, as indicated in prior convictions[82] or disciplinary infractions, whether charged[83] or uncharged,[84] reflects his attitude about improving his future. But the prosecution is not limited to drawing inferences from that evidence and may in addition call witnesses, or use their depositions,[85] to express their opinion on the accused's past conduct and his potential.[86]

---

evidence showing adverse impact on unit must establish a reasonable linkage between the offense and the effect, but testimony implying that unit was waiting to see how the accused would be punished violated the "fundamental sanctity of the court-martial").

81. R.C.M. 1001(b)(5). Evidence of rehabilitative potential relates to the accused's potential to be restored to a useful and constructive place in society, through "vocational, correctional, or therapeutic training, or other corrective measures." R.C.M. 1001(b)(5) (Change 7). Cf. United States v. Antonitis, 29 M.J. 217 (C.M.A. 1989) (accused's potential loss of security clearance was not relevant to issue of rehabilitative potential).

82. See R.C.M. 1001(b)(3).

83. See the discussion above regarding admissibility of records of nonjudicial punishment.

84. See § 16-D(6). United States v. Mullens, 29 M.J. 398 (C.M.A. 1990) (other uncharged sexual acts were admissible because they related directly to charged offenses); United States v. Denney, 28 M.J. 521 (A.C.M.R. 1989) (noting that absence from trial is a form of uncharged misconduct, court held that such evidence is relevant to issue of rehabilitation; court drew analogy to accused giving false testimony at trial). See also United States v. Chapman, 20 M.J. 717 (N.M.C.M.R. 1985), aff'd, 23 M.J. 226 (C.M.A. 1986) (summary disposition).

United States v. Cephas, 25 M.J. 832 (A.C.M.R. 1988) (involvement in other drug offenses was relevant in determining rehabilitative potential); United States v. Anderson, 25 M.J. 779 (A.C.M.R. 1988) (uncharged acts of threatening words and actions related to offense charged and reflected accused's attitude toward rehabilitation).

United States v. Arceneaux, 21 M.J. 571 (A.C.M.R. 1985) (evidence of prior uncharged misconduct, selling drugs, was admissible at sentencing because it had a direct bearing on the accused's rehabilitative potential); United States v. Wright, 20 M.J. 518 (A.C.M.R. 1985) (accused's earlier statements about intent to reform); United States v. Pooler, 18 M.J. 832 (A.C.M.R. 1984) (uncharged misconduct concerning future crimes).

85. R.C.M. 1001(b)(5). See § 11-3.

86. Id. United States v. Davis, 39 M.J. 281 (C.M.A. 1994) (victim's testimony re possibility of accused receiving no punishment was not evidence re rehabilitative potential; the latter relates to the process of restoring an individual to a constructive and useful place in society); United States v. Williams, 41 M.J. 134 (C.M.A. 1994) (forensic psychiatrist testified re predictability of recidivism rates and violence; court said that term "potential for rehabilitation" is broad enough to include expert opinion on future dangerousness); United States v. King, 35 M.J. 337 (C.M.A. 1992) (plain error to permit witness to offer expert opinion on pedophiles; court cautioned against acceptance at face value of any expert testimony); United States v. Stinson, 34 M.J. 233 (C.M.A. 1992) (expert in area of child sexual abuse permitted to offer opinion on accused's prognosis for rehabilitation); United States v. Plott, 35 M.J. 512 (A.F.C.M.R. 1992) (testimony about pedophilia was irrelevant), aff'd on further review on other grounds, 38 M.J. 735 (A.F.C.M.R. 1993); United States v. Claxton, 32 M.J. 159 (C.M.A. 1991) (prosecution is not left to only rebutting defense evidence on rehabilitative potential); United States v. Horner, 22 M.J. 294 (C.M.A. 1986) (commander's opinion was not admissible); United States v. Beno, 24 M.J. 771 (A.F.C.M.R. 1987) (although commander's bare assertion that accused had little rehabilitation potential was admissible, the court observed that it would not have been error to exclude it because it was apparent that, as commander of a large organization, the commander barely knew the accused, if he knew him at all).

§ 16-5(D)(4) SENTENCING § 16-5(D)(4)

Amendments to R.C.M. 1001(b)(5) in 1994 were intended to clarify the admissibility of evidence concerning rehabilitative potential and sets out specific criteria for such evidence.[87] The amendments generally reflect existing case law, *infra,* and in summary provide that the prosecution may present evidence of rehabilitative potential in the form of testimony[88] or oral deposition[89] in the form of opinions regarding the accused's past performance as a servicemember and his potential or rehabilitation.[90] The witness opinion, which must be helpful to the sentencing authority,[91] must be grounded on a rationally-based foundation.[92] The opinion must be based on the accused's personal circumstances[93] but, as the case law has recognized, *infra,* the witness may not base his or her opinion principally on the accused's offense.[94] The witness' opinion is limited to the magnitude or quality of rehabilitative potential[95] and, as noted *infra,* the witness may not offer an opinion on whether the accused should be discharged or returned to his or her unit.[96] Relevant specific instances of conduct may be inquired into on cross-examination.[97] The amendment also provides that, notwithstanding any other provision in R.C.M. 1001, the scope of redirect examination may be expanded, depending on what occurs during cross-examination.[98]

A number of recent cases have addressed the specifics of offering opinion testimony on rehabilitation. The courts have focused on the question of whether the prosecution witness, usually someone in the accused's chain of command, had a sufficient basis for offering an opinion about the accused's potential for rehabilitation.[99] The opinion must be based upon personal knowl-

---

United States v. Lawrence, 22 M.J. 846 (A.C.M.R. 1986) (accused's sworn statement not admissible); United States v. Boughton, 16 M.J. 649 (A.F.C.M.R. 1983) (opinion properly based upon reports).

87. Executive Order 12936, Nov. 10, 1994. The Analysis accompanying the amendments, at Appendix 21, Manual for Courts-Martial, indicates that the changes were based on decision law. *See generally* Borch, "Analysis of Change 7 to the 1984 Manual for Courts-Martial," ARMY LAW., Jan. 1995, at 22.

88. R.C.M. 1001(b)(5)(A).

89. *Id. See also* R.C.M. 702(g)(1) and § 11-3(B).

90. R.C.M. 1001(b)(5) (evidence of rehabilitative potential relates to the accused's potential to be restored to a useful and constructive place in society, through vocational, correctional, or therapeutic training, or other corrective measures).

91. R.C.M. 1001(b)(5)(B). *See also* Rules 701 and 702, MIL. R. EVID.

92. R.C.M. 1001(b)(5)(B) (relevant information includes the accused's character, performance of duty, moral fiber, determination to be rehabilitated, and nature and severity of the offense).

93. R.C.M. 1001(b)(5)(C).

94. *Id.*

95. R.C.M. 1001(b)(5)(D).

96. *Id.*

97. R.C.M. 1001(b)(5)(E). *Cf.* United States v. Sheridan, 43 M.J. 682 (A.F.Ct.Crim.App. 1995) (judge erred in permitting prosecution to elicit during direct examination of its witness that accused had other specific instances of conduct).

98. R.C.M. 1001(b)(5)(F).

99. United States v. Gunter, 29 M.J. 140 (C.M.A. 1989) (supervisor of accused's drug rehabilitation program had sufficient basis for his opinion that accused's potential for rehabilitation was poor); United States v. Sylvester, 38 M.J. 720 (A.C.M.R. 1993) (prosecution witness' opinion that accused did not possess rehabilitative potential was not converted into impermissible opinion re

§ 16-5(D)(4)   MILITARY CRIMINAL JUSTICE   § 16-5(D)(4)

edge about the accused.[100] Thus, an opinion based only upon the nature or severity of the charges will not be permitted.[101] Nor will the witness be permitted to testify, or imply through "euphemisms," that the accused should be discharged.[102] For example, testimony that the accused should not be returned

---

discharge when on cross-examination he admitted that his assessment focused on potential military service).

100. *See* Rule 701, MIL. R. EVID. United States v. Rhoads, 32 M.J. 114 (C.M.A. 1991) (witness may not base opinion on specific acts of misconduct); United States v. Kirk, 31 M.J. 84 (C.M.A. 1990) (record failed to show foundation for commander's opinion); United States v. Malone, 38 M.J. 707 (A.C.M.R. 1993) (not plain error to admit first sergeant to offer opinion on rehabilitative potential without first requiring foundation for opinion); United States v. Grady, 30 M.J. 911 (A.C.M.R. 1990) (witnesses were adequately familiar with accused); United States v. Freeman, 29 M.J. 865 (A.F.C.M.R. 1989).

In United States v. Vega, 29 M.J. 892 (A.F.C.M.R. 1989), the Air Force Court indicated that its reading of the cases indicated that not only must the witness personally know the accused, he must not present an inelastic attitude toward sentencing. This *per se* disqualification was rejected by the Army Court in United States v. Hefner, 29 M.J. 1022 (A.C.M.R. 1990), where the witness was sufficiently familiar with the accused to state an opinion but also possessed an inelastic attitude toward the offenses involved. The court concluded that an otherwise qualified witness may offer an opinion on rehabilitation if the witness's prejudice is only a motivating factor.

101. United States v. Oquendo, 35 M.J. 24 (C.M.A. 1992) (testimony of prosecution witnesses impermissibly based upon severity of charges); United States v. Corraine, 31 M.J. 102 (C.M.A. 1990) (harmless error for NCO to state opinion based on seriousness of charges); United States v. McCanless, 29 M.J. 985 (A.F.C.M.R. 1990) (officer's opinion was improperly based primarily upon nature of charges).

United States v. Lizasuain, 30 M.J. 543 (A.C.M.R. 1990) (accused waived objection and testimony did not amount to plain error); United States v. Stimpson, 29 M.J. 768 (A.C.M.R. 1989) (accused's platoon sergeant relied upon more than mere fact that accused was a "barracks thief"); United States v. Nixon, 29 M.J. 505 (A.C.M.R. 1989) (witness had insufficient basis for expressing opinion on accused's rehabilitative potential); United States v. Savusa, 28 M.J. 1043 (A.C.M.R. 1989) (commander's opinion impermissibly based only on severity of the offense); United States v. Scott, 27 M.J. 889 (A.C.M.R. 1989) (battalion commander should not have been permitted to offer an opinion on rehabilitative potential which was based not on the accused as an individual but instead on the offense).

102. In United States v. Ohrt, 28 M.J. 301 (C.M.A. 1989), the court indicated that a witness could not express an opinion on whether the accused should be retained in the armed forces. That sort of opinion, in the court's view, would usurp the functions of the court. The court recognized that using euphemisms such as "no potential for continued service" was just another way of saying, "Give the accused a punitive discharge." The court also indicated that a punitive discharge can be imposed without regard to the rehabilitative potential of the accused.

See also United States v. Pompey, 33 M.J. 266 (C.M.A. 1991) (there must be rational basis for witness's opinion on rehabilitation even if it is offered in rebuttable to defense sentencing evidence); United States v. Aurich, 31 M.J. 95 (C.M.A. 1990) (if defense opens door by presenting witnesses who indicate that accused is wanted back in his unit, prosecution may respond with contrary testimony; but an accused should not receive a greater punishment simply because his commander does not want him back); United States v. Kirk, 31 M.J. 84 (C.M.A. 1990) (prejudicial error for commander to testify that accused should not be retained); United States v. Cherry, 31 M.J. 1 (C.M.A. 1990) (prejudicial error for commander to suggest that accused should be separated).

United States v. Williams, 35 M.J. 812 (A.F.C.M.R. 1992) (expert's testimony re future dangerousness was not relevant to rehabilitative potential under R.C.M. 1001(b)(5)); United States v. Bolden, 34 M.J. 728 (N.M.C.M.R. 1991) (opinion that accused had no potential for productive military service was not admissible; opinion that he had high potential for continued drug and alcohol abuse might have been admissible if proper witness or evidence had been presented).

to his unit would not suffice.[103] That is apparently a matter solely within the prerogative of the sentencing authority.[104] But Military Rule of Evidence 704 indicates that opinion testimony is not inadmissible simply because it embraces an "ultimate issue to be decided by the trier of fact."[105] The prosecution, however, may not rely upon specific instances of conduct unless the defense first opens the door on cross-examination.[106]

§ 16-5(D)(5). Evidence of Uncharged Misconduct.

One issue that has proved particularly troublesome is the question of whether an accused's acts of uncharged misconduct may be admitted during sentencing.[107] Rule 404(b) of the Military Rules of Evidence generally bars evidence of a person's prior acts if they are introduced to show the propensity of that person to commit a particular act.[108] But the rule also recognizes that such evidence may be admitted for non-character purposes, i.e., motive, lack of accident, or intent.[109] The question addressed here is whether sentencing decisions fall within the category of "non-character purposes."

United States v. Thomas, 31 M.J. 669 (A.C.M.R. 1990) (court permitted testimony by the accused's chain of command that they did not want him back in the unit. That testimony, said the court, falls short of testifying that he should be discharged); United States v. Rogers, 30 M.J. 824 (C.G.C.M.R. 1990) (commander permitted to testify that accused should not be retained where defense had called witness to stand); United States v. Freeman, 29 M.J. 865 (A.F.C.M.R. 1989) (certain words of qualification in terms which express potential for rehabilitation are not impermissible per se); United States v. Stimpson, 29 M.J. 768, 770, n.2. (A.C.M.R. 1989) (any reference by witness to a "discharge, separation from the service, or lack of potential for continued service should be scrupulously avoided"); United States v. Claxton, 29 M.J. 667 (C.G.C.M.R. 1989); United States v. Barber, 27 M.J. 885 (A.C.M.R. 1989) (witness should not express opinion on role of court-martial in sending a signal to the military community through its sentence of the accused).

Cf. United States v. Murphy, 29 M.J. 573 (A.F.C.M.R. 1989) (commander's testimony that he did not want accused back in unit was not an impermissible statement that he should be discharged).

103. *See, e.g.*, United States v. Goodman, 33 M.J. 84 (C.M.A. 1991) (harmless error for prosecution witness to testify that she did not want the accused back in the unit); United States v. St. Romain, 33 M.J. 689 (A.F.C.M.R. 1991) (admission of opinion testimony that accused should not be brought back to unit was harmless error).

104. United States v. Ohrt, 28 M.J. 301 (C.M.A. 1989).

105. United States v. Williams, 41 M.J. 134 (C.M.A. 1994) (term "potential for rehabilitation" is broad enough to include expert opinion on future dangerousness).

106. R.C.M. 1001(b)(5). United States v. Gregory, 31 M.J. 236 (C.M.A. 1990) (questions by court member did not properly open door for government witness to present evidence of accused's uncharged misconduct); United States v. Wingart, 27 M.J. 128, 136 (C.M.A. 1988); United States v. Smith, 23 M.J. 714 (A.C.M.R. 1986) (harmless error to ask for witness's opinion on the rehabilitative potential of the accused where question asked witness to base opinion on the fact that he had been found guilty); United States v. Clarke, 29 M.J. 582 (A.F.C.M.R. 1989).

107. United States v. Martin, 20 M.J. 227 (C.M.A. 1985) (good discussion of determining admissibility). *See generally* Bross, "Uncharged Misconduct on Sentencing: An Update," ARMY LAW., Feb. 1986, at 34.

108. Rule 404(b), MIL. R. EVID. *See generally* Saltzburg, Schinasi & Schlueter, *Military Rules of Evidence Manual*, 457-93 (3d ed. 1991).

109. Rule 404(b), MIL. R. EVID.

§ 16-5(D)(5) MILITARY CRIMINAL JUSTICE § 16-5(D)(5)

What has emerged in the case law are several rules of admissibility. As a general rule, the following rules apply without regard to whether the findings of guilt are based upon a guilty plea.[110]

First, evidence of other acts by the accused that might have been admissible under Rule 404(b) during the merits portion of the trial is not necessarily admissible during sentencing. In an extensive discussion of the issue, the court in *United States v. Wingart*,[111] noted that the *Manual* rules regarding the admissibility of uncharged misconduct as sentencing evidence reflected a rejection of the argument that such evidence would be admissible simply because it would have otherwise been admissible in a contested case to prove that the accused committed the offense.[112]

Second, if evidence of the uncharged misconduct was actually admitted during the merits portion of the trial, it may be considered in determining an appropriate sentence.[113]

Third, evidence of other acts committed by the accused may be admitted if it is properly reflected in the accused's personnel records.[114]

Fourth, evidence of uncharged misconduct is admissible as evidence in aggravation, i.e., aggravating circumstances,[115] if such conduct is directly related to, or has resulted, from the offense.[116] If the acts in question do not satisfy that criteria, they are not admissible as evidence of "aggravating circumstances" under the *Manual*.[117]

---

110. *See, e.g.*, United States v. Silva, 21 M.J. 336 (C.M.A. 1986) (uncharged misconduct not automatically inadmissible where accused pleaded guilty); United States v. Vickers, 13 M.J. 403 (C.M.A. 1982) (court rejected distinctions based upon pleas).
111. 27 M.J. 128 (C.M.A. 1988).
112. 27 M.J. at 135, *citing* R.C.M. 1001(b)(4) Drafters' Analysis. *See also* United States v. Ringuette, 29 M.J. 527 (A.F.C.M.R. 1989).
113. R.C.M. 1001(f)(2).
114. *See* § 16-5(B). *See, e.g.*, United States v. Fontenot, 26 M.J. 559 (A.C.M.R. 1988) (records of accused while in detention facility). *Cf.* United States v. King, 30 M.J. 334 (C.M.A. 1990) (evidence that accused had appeared 19 times before Discipline and Adjustment Boards at Fort Leavenworth was not admissible).
115. R.C.M. 1001(b)(4).
116. R.C.M. 1001(b)(4). *See, e.g.*, United States v. Irwin, 42 M.J. 479 (1995) (accused's admission of threat to victim during providency inquiry was admissible as being directly related to offense, even though judge found him not guilty of making threat); United States v. Shupe, 36 M.J. 431 (C.M.A. 1993) (accused's related drug transactions were admissible to show continuous nature of conduct and impact on community); United States v. Ciulla, 32 M.J. 186 (C.M.A. 1991) (accused's statements to victim of his desire to perform indecent acts on other children was admissible as part of the facts and circumstances of the alleged offenses); United States v. Robinson, 30 M.J. 548 (A.C.M.R. 1990) (uncharged misconduct related to charged offenses); United States v. Moore, 29 M.J. 819 (A.C.M.R. 1989) (trial court erred in admitting evidence of other acts of indecency where they did not grow out of or directly precipitate the charged acts).
United States v. Hall, 29 M.J. 786 (A.C.M.R. 1989) (accused's absence was uncharged misconduct which was admissible as aggravating evidence); United States v. Lynott, 28 M.J. 918 (C.G.C.M.R. 1989) (uncharged misconduct was relevant); United States v. Green, 21 M.J. 633 (A.C.M.R. 1985).
117. *See, e.g.*, United States v. Clabon, 33 M.J. 904 (A.F.C.M.R. 1991) (post-offense uncharged misconduct was inadmissible where it failed to shed light on circumstances of the offense); United States v. Hall, 29 M.J. 786 (A.C.M.R. 1989) (uncharged drug transactions not directly related); United States v. Berger, 23 M.J. 612 (A.F.C.M.R. 1986) (judge erred in admitting stepdaughter's

Fifth, evidence of uncharged misconduct may be admissible on the issue of whether the accused has rehabilitative potential.[118]

Sixth, if the defense presents a witness who offers opinion testimony that the accused has rehabilitative potential,[119] the prosecution may cross-examine that witness by determining whether the witness is aware of the uncharged acts.[120] But the prosecution is probably not free to introduce extrinsic evidence of those acts.[121]

Seventh, evidence of uncharged acts may be admissible in rebuttal to defense evidence presented during sentencing.[122] For example, the prosecution should be able to introduce evidence of uncharged misconduct in response to an accused's assertions that leave the clear, but erroneous, impression that he had never been in trouble before.[123]

---

deposition revealing other uncharged acts of misconduct; court could find no basis for admitting it).

118. *See, e.g.,* United States v. Lawer, 41 M.J. 751(C.G.Ct.Crim.App. 1995) (defense presented expert opinion testimony on rehabilitative potential of accused; proper for prosecution to cross-examine witness re prior uncharged acts of misconduct); United States v. Stone, 37 M.J. 558 (A.C.M.R. 1993), *aff'd on other grounds,* 40 M.J. 420 (C.M.A. 1994) (accused's uncharged misconduct admissible on issue of rehabilitative potential); United States v. Denney, 28 M.J. 521 (A.C.M.R. 1989) (noting that absence from trial is a form of uncharged misconduct, court held that evidence of such is relevant to issue of rehabilitation; court drew analogy to accused giving false testimony at trial); United States v. Chapman, 20 M.J. 717 (N.M.C.M.R. 1985), *aff'd,* 23 M.J. 226 (C.M.A. 1986) (summary disposition).

United States v. Cephas, 25 M.J. 832 (A.C.M.R. 1988) (involvement in other drug offenses was relevant in determining rehabilitative potential); United States v. Anderson, 25 M.J. 779 (A.C.M.R. 1988) (uncharged acts of threatening words and actions related to offense charged and reflected accused's attitude toward rehabilitation).

United States v. Arceneaux, 21 M.J. 571 (A.C.M.R. 1985) (evidence of prior uncharged misconduct, selling drugs, was admissible at sentencing because it had a direct bearing on the accused's rehabilitative potential); United States v. Wright, 20 M.J. 518 (A.C.M.R. 1985) (accused's earlier statements about intent to reform); United States v. Pooler, 18 M.J. 832 (A.C.M.R. 1984) (uncharged misconduct concerning future crimes).

Cf. United States v. Sheridan, 43 M.J. 682 (A.F.Ct.Crim.App. 1995) (prosecutor not permitted to ask witness, offering opinion on rehabilitative potential, about other specific instances of conduct).

119. *See* § 16-6.
120. R.C.M. 1001(b)(5). United States v. Aurich, 31 M.J. 95 (C.M.A. 1990); United States v. Kirk, 31 M.J. 84 (C.M.A. 1990); United States v. Sharp, 29 M.J. 856 (A.F.C.M.R. 1989). *See also* Rule 405(a), MIL. R. EVID.
121. *See* Rule 608(b), MIL. R. EVID.
122. United States v. Hallum, 31 M.J. 254 (C.M.A. 1990) (evidence of good duty performance and recommendation for retention may be rebutted); United States v. Cleveland, 29 M.J. 361 (C.M.A. 1990) (accused's unsworn statement was not statement of fact and could not be rebutted with uncharged misconduct; court concluded that this was merely an attempt to "bootleg" inadmissible evidence into the sentencing hearing under the guise of rebuttal); United States v. Goree, 34 M.J. 1027 (N.M.C.M.R. 1992) (accused's unsworn statement that he had served well did not amount to statement of fact which could be rebutted by uncharged conduct).
123. *See, e.g.,* United States v. Rodgers, 18 M.J. 565 (A.C.M.R. 1984). If the accused makes such statements in an *unsworn* statement, evidence of uncharged misconduct is not admissible to rebut unless the statement amounted to a factual assertion. United States v. Partyka, 30 M.J. 242 (C.M.A. 1990); United States v. Cleveland, 29 M.J. 361 (C.M.A. 1990).

Eighth, evidence of an accused's uncharged misconduct may be included in a stipulation of fact, properly signed and executed by the accused and defense counsel.[124]

Before admitting evidence of the uncharged misconduct, the trial judge must be satisfied that the acts alleged were committed by the accused.[125] Even assuming that the evidence of uncharged misconduct is otherwise relevant and admissible, the court may still exclude the evidence if it determines that the prejudicial dangers in admitting it substantially outweigh the probative value.[126] If the judge admits evidence of uncharged misconduct, it must be made clear to the court members that the sentence may not be increased simply because the uncharged misconduct evidence may imply that the accused is a bad person.[127] Rather, they should be instructed to consider that evidence only for the purpose for which it was offered, e.g., explaining the circumstances of the crime, or to show the lack of rehabilitative potential.[128]

§ 16-6. Defense Evidence.

After the prosecution presents its evidence, the defense is offered the opportunity to present evidence in extenuation[1] or mitigation[2] and may take advantage of the relaxation of the rules of evidence—subject to the discretion of the military judge.[3] Counsel should be aware of the fact that if the judge relaxes the rules for the defense, they may also be relaxed for the prosecution during rebuttal.[4]

---

124. *See, e.g.*, United States v. Mullens, 29 M.J. 398 (C.M.A. 1990); United States v. Glazier, 26 M.J. 268 (C.M.A. 1988); United States v. Silva, 21 M.J. 336 (C.M.A. 1986). *See also* § 16-5.

125. *See, e.g.*, United States v. Williams, 28 M.J. 911 (A.C.M.R. 1989) (no evidence that accused committed acts).

126. Rule 403, MIL. R. EVID. *See, e.g.*, United States v. Anderson, 25 M.J. 779 (A.C.M.R. 1988) (balancing test).

127. Rule 404(b), MIL. R. EVID. United States v. Denney, 28 M.J. 521 (A.C.M.R. 1989) (uncharged misconduct not admissible to increase sentence). This may be distinction without a difference. Having heard the evidence of uncharged misconduct, the court is likely to take that into consideration in arriving at an appropriate sentence. Thus, the evidence almost always has some indirect bearing on the amount of punishment imposed by the court.

128. *See, e.g.*, United States v. Denney, 28 M.J. 521 (A.C.M.R. 1989) (accused's unauthorized absence admissible only on issue of rehabilitative potential and not to increase the sentence).

1. R.C.M. 1001(c)(1). United States v. Fox, 24 M.J. 110 (C.M.A. 1987) (court rejected argument that defense should have been able to introduce indecent assault victim's reputation for chastity, although it might have been relevant to show the lack of trauma to the victim). "Extenuating" evidence is offered to explain the circumstances surrounding the offense which tend to excuse the accused's actions. R.C.M. 1001(c)(A).

2. R.C.M. 1001(c)(1)(B). Mitigation evidence is offered to show why clemency should be extended or the punishment reduced. The *Manual* notes the examples of showing that an Article 15 was previously imposed for the offense, *see* § 3-8, and the accused's prior acts of bravery or fidelity. The accused's financial and personal situations should also be relevant.

3. R.C.M. 1001(c)(3). *Cf.* United States v. Elrod, 18 M.J. 692 (A.F.C.M.R. 1984) (evidentiary rules may not be relaxed as to presentencing aggravation evidence offered by the prosecution).

4. *Id. See* § 16-4(B). United States v. Reveles, 41 M.J. 388 (1995) (judge did not impermissibly chill defense from presenting case during sentencing by indicating that he might reconsider his ruling excluding prosecution videotape of victim, depending on what defense presented. The court

§ 16-6 SENTENCING § 16-6

Before the defense proceeds with its evidence, the judge should personally advise the accused[5] of his "allocution" rights: the right to present an oral sworn statement; the right to make an unsworn statement, either personally or through counsel; and finally the right to remain silent.[6] If the accused makes a sworn statement, he is treated as any other witness and is subject to cross-examination and impeachment.[7]

On the other hand, an unsworn statement, either oral or written, is not evidence[8] and does not subject the accused to cross-examination or impeachment.[9] It may, however, open the door for prosecution rebuttal and may be commented upon in closing argument.[10] The fact that the accused elected to

---

indicated that the defense is not entitled to be free from the chilling effect of legitimate prosecution evidence).

5. *See* United States v. Hawkins, 2 M.J. 23 (C.M.A. 1976); United States v. Grady, 30 M.J. 911 (A.C.M.R. 1990) (judge's failure to advise accused of allocution rights was nonprejudicial error); United States v. Kendrick, 29 M.J. 792 (A.C.M.R. 1989) (failure to apprise accused of his rights was nonprejudicial error where accused presented evidence); United States v. Williams, 23 M.J. 713 (A.C.M.R. 1986) (failure to advise accused of his allocution rights did not specifically prejudice him where the record indicated that he understood those rights and exercised them); United States v. Nelson, 21 M.J. 573 (A.C.M.R. 1985); United States v. Christensen, 12 M.J. 875 (N.M.C.M.R. 1982) (the judge is not required to routinely advise the accused regarding any right to call witnesses).

6. R.C.M. 1001(c)(2). United States v. Provost, 32 M.J. 98 (C.M.A. 1991) (right of allocution is fundamental precept of military justice. The accused may not use an affidavit to make his statement. United States v. Proctor, 34 M.J. 549 (A.F.C.M.R. 1992) (decision to provide sworn statement is accused's to make after being advised of consequences).

7. R.C.M. 1001(c)(2)(B). United States v. Martinsmith, 41 M.J. 343 (1995) (court indicated that the MCM does not technically provide for evidence to be presented in form of sworn statement; concurring opinion notes that term is commonly used by trial practitioners).

8. United States v. Smith, 23 M.J. 744 (A.C.M.R. 1987) (unsworn statement is not evidence).

9. R.C.M. 1001(c)(2)(C). United States v. King, 12 C.M.A. 71, 30 C.M.R. 71 (1960); United States v. Blackmon, 39 M.J. 1091 (A.C.M.R. 1994) (although court member was not permitted to question accused following unsworn statement, judge abused discretion in not showing question to defense counsel; counsel's request was essentially a request to reopen case and judge's denial prevented counsel from knowing how to further proceed); United States v. Thomas, 36 M.J. 638 (A.C.M.R. 1992) (although prosecution was free to offer evidence in rebuttal to unsworn statement, it was not permitted to impeach accused through opinion testimony on character for untruthfulness); United States v. Harris, 13 M.J. 653 (N.M.C.M.R. 1982) (error for prosecution to introduce rebuttal evidence regarding accused's truthfulness after he made unsworn statement).

10. R.C.M. 1001(c)(2)(C). United States v. Partyka, 30 M.J. 242 (C.M.A. 1990) (prosecutor could not rebut accused's unsworn statement with witness who had treated child abuse victim because the accused had not made any factual assertions or statements of fact; the court noted, however, that the prosecutor could have presented the same testimony as evidence in aggravation); United States v. Strong, 17 M.J. 263 (C.M.A. 1984); United States v. Konarski, 8 M.J. 146 (C.M.A. 1979).

United States v. Childress, 33 M.J. 602 (A.C.M.R. 1991) (the prosecution was properly permitted to present rebuttal testimony to accused's unsworn statement of remorse; the testimony, which showed that the accused had threatened the victim after the offense, was also admissible as an aggravating circumstance directly related to the offense); United States v. Campbell, 32 M.J. 580 (A.F.C.M.R. 1990) (prosecution could not rebut accused's carefully worded unsworn statement with evidence of uncharged misconduct; court noted that that evidence could have been admitted as aggravation evidence); United States v. Privette, 31 M.J. 791 (A.F.C.M.R. 1990) (accused presented no statement of facts to be rebutted; trial practitioners may find it hard to define the precise point at which accused steps over the line and presents a false picture); United States v.

make an unsworn statement should not be used against him.[11] Normally, the right of the accused to make an unsworn statement should not be limited.[12] In making his statement, either sworn or unsworn, the accused may limit his comments to a particular matter or a particular element of the offense.[13]

If the judge has relaxed the rules of evidence[14] the defense may be permitted to offer its sentencing evidence through otherwise inadmissible written statements and affidavits from witnesses favorable to the accused.[15] Because during sentencing both sides are given greater leeway in offering evidence through other than live testimony,[16] defense counsel may find it more difficult to obtain witnesses at government expense. The *Manual* now reflects the policy that unless the balance clearly tips toward production of the witness, requests for subpoenas or travel orders should not be authorized.[17]

Britt, 16 M.J. 971 (A.F.C.M.R. 1983) (accused cannot introduce "Dr. Jekyll" and object when prosecution presents "Mr. Hyde"); United States v. Roman, 45 C.M.R. 492 (A.F.C.M.R. 1972).

11. See United States v. King, 12 C.M.A. 71, 30 C.M.R. 71 (1960).

12. United States v. Provost, 32 M.J. 98 (C.M.A. 1991) (accused was entitled to make second unsworn statement to explain uncharged misconduct offered by prosecution); United States v. Rosato, 32 M.J. 93 (C.M.A. 1991) (right to make unsworn statement generally should not be restricted; judge's limitation resulted in prejudice).

13. R.C.M. 1001(c)(2)(A). United States v. Rosato, 32 M.J. 93 (C.M.A. 1991) (military judge improperly limited scope of accused's unsworn statement which raised issues about the administrative consequences of the sentence).

14. See R.C.M. 1001(c)(3).

15. R.C.M. 1001(c)(3). United States v. Taylor, 21 M.J. 840 (A.C.M.R. 1986). *Cf.* United States v. Meade, 19 M.J. 894 (A.C.M.R. 1985) (judge properly excluded transmittal letters from convening authorities concerning recommendations on the disposition of the charges; such evidence was inadmissible opinion evidence).

16. R.C.M. 1001(e)(1).

17. See, e.g., United States v. Harmon, 40 M.J. 107 (C.M.A. 1994) (not abuse of discretion to treat defense witness on sentencing as cumulative; counsel should have sought advance ruling on how many witnesses would be permitted so as to decide which ones to call); United States v. Combs, 20 M.J. 441 (C.M.A. 1985) (although the testimony of the accused's mother would have been material, under the facts the judge did not abuse his discretion in denying a defense request for her production); United States v. Koke, 32 M.J. 876 (N.M.C.M.R. 1991) (accused was not entitled as matter of right to live testimony of his parents; stipulation of fact was adequate substitute).

R.C.M. 1001(e)(2) provides:

> (2) *Limitations.* A witness may be produced to testify during presentence proceedings through a subpoena or travel orders at Government expense only if
> (A) The testimony expected to be offered by the witness is necessary for consideration of a matter of substantial significance to a determination of an appropriate sentence, including evidence necessary to resolve an alleged inaccuracy or dispute as to a material fact;
> (B) The weight or credibility of the witness testimony is of substantial significance to the determination of an appropriate sentence; and
> (C) The other party refuses to enter a stipulation of fact containing the matters to which the witness is expected to testify, except in an extraordinary case when such a stipulation of fact would be an insufficient substitute for the testimony.
> (D) Other forms of evidence, such as oral depositions, written interrogatories, or former testimony would not be sufficient to meet the needs of the court-martial in the determination of an appropriate sentence; and
> (E) The significance of the personal appearance of the witness to the determination of an appropriate sentence, when balanced against the practical difficulties of producing the

During its presentation of evidence the defense is not entitled to relitigate the guilt or innocence of the accused[18] and should be aware of any evidence which might improvidence a guilty plea.[19] Evidence of an accomplice's sentence in a related trial,[20] evidence of a possible administrative discharge,[21] and reference to a pretrial agreement[22] are inadmissible. The defense, however, may introduce evidence that the accused has been previously sentenced in another case.[23] The defense may also present opinion testimony on the accused's rehabilitative potential.[24]

For a discussion on ineffective assistance of counsel claims with regard to sentencing matters, see § 15-2(B)(3).

§ 16-7. Rebuttal and Surrebuttal.

Following the defense evidence, the prosecution may offer relevant rebuttal evidence that contradicts evidence presented by the accused.[1] The defense

---

witness, favors production of the witness. Factors to be considered include the costs of producing the witness, the timing of the request for production of the witness, the potential delay in the presentencing proceeding that may be caused by the production of the witness, and the likelihood of significant interference with military operational deployment, mission accomplishment, or essential training.

18. United States v. Teeter, 16 M.J. 68 (C.M.A. 1983) (counsel urged the court to reconsider its findings); United States v. Brown, 13 M.J. 890 (A.C.M.R. 1982) (accused attempted to resurrect his alibi defense). A potential anomaly exists here. Although the court is free to reconsider its findings until sentence is announced, the defense is generally not permitted to urge reconsideration. And unless extensive reconsideration instructions were actually given before findings were announced, it is possible that the court may not be fully aware of that possibility. See § 15-15. See also United States v. Tobita, 3 C.M.A. 267, 12 C.M.R. 23 (1953).
19. See § 14-3.
20. United States v. Mamaluy, 10 C.M.A. 102, 27 C.M.R. 176 (1959); United States v. McNeece, 30 C.M.R. 453 (A.B.R. 1960).
21. United States v. Pollard, 34 M.J. 1008 (A.C.M.R. 1992) (evidence that disciplinary barracks and correctional brigade have treatment program for sexual offenders was inadmissible collateral information for purposes of aggravation evidence; court recognized that it might be admissible as rebuttal evidence). In United States v. Grady, 30 M.J. 911 (A.C.M.R. 1990), the court indicated that the trial judge erred in constructing a sentence that relied upon collateral matter of which drug programs would be available at the confinement facility. See also United States v. Lapeer, 28 M.J. 189 (C.M.A. 1989); United States v. Jones, 3 M.J. 677 (C.G.C.M.R. 1977); United States v. Lucas, 32 C.M.R. 619 (A.B.R. 1962).
22. United States v. Massie, 45 C.M.R. 717 (A.C.M.R. 1972). See also United States v. Collins, 17 M.J. 901 (A.F.C.M.R. 1983) (defense may not offer).
23. United States v. Maracle, 26 M.J. 431 (C.M.A. 1988).
24. United States v. Lawer, 41 M.J. 751(C.G.Ct.Crim.App. 1995) (defense presented expert opinion testimony on rehabilitative potential of accused; proper for prosecution to cross-examine witness re prior uncharged acts of misconduct).
1. R.C.M. 1001(d). United States v. Blake, 30 M.J. 184 (C.M.A. 1990) (prosecution permitted to offer evidence in rebuttal to defense assertions concerning value of retirement pay to accused); United States v. Peck, 36 M.J. 900 (A.F.C.M.R. 1993) (AF Form 2030 showing accused's acknowledgement of illegal nature of drugs was not admissible in rebuttal on sentencing because at the time it was offered, the defense had not presented any evidence at sentencing; court rejected argument that it could be used to rebut defense evidence presented during merits portion of case); United States v. Campbell, 32 M.J. 580 (A.F.C.M.R. 1990) (prosecution could not rebut carefully

may respond with surrebuttal evidence.[2] Subject to the discretion of the military judge, rebuttal and surrebuttal may continue as appropriate.[3] Note that the normal evidentiary limitations on the prosecution's ability to present a wide range of other aggravating matters[4] may be lifted here if the judge has relaxed the rules of evidence during the defense presentation.[5] For example, where the accused states that he has never been in trouble before, the prosecution may offer otherwise inadmissible specific acts of uncharged misconduct.[6] Or if the judge, for example, permits the defense to offer its evidence through affidavits, the prosecution may be free to rebut in kind.[7]

§ 16-8. Arguments on Sentencing.

§ 16-8(A). In General.

Before counsel proceed with argument the judge will normally conduct an Article 39(a) session to discuss possible instructions for the court.[1] Thus, before making arguments counsel should have in mind what, if any, special instructions will be given to the court.

The order of arguments is left to the military judge who may permit the defense to open and the prosecution to close.[2] In *United States v. McGee*,[3] the

---

worded unsworn statement with evidence of uncharged misconduct that did not refute accused's assertion that except for last year he had good record); United States v. Cleveland, 27 M.J. 530 (A.F.C.M.R. 1988) (prosecution offered rebuttal evidence of nonjudicial punishment and letter of reprimand when accused indicated that although he was not perfect, he had served well); United States v. Evans, 25 M.J. 859 (A.F.C.M.R. 1988) (prosecution offered rebuttal evidence to accused's unsworn statement that left impression that he had not been in trouble before).

2. R.C.M. 1001(d).

3. *Id.* United States v. Driver, 36 M.J. 1020 (N.M.C.M.R. 1993) (evidence of careless driving not relevant rebuttal evidence to accused's statement that he would not drive recklessly or drag race again).

4. *See* United States v. Elrod, 18 M.J. 692 (A.F.C.M.R. 1984) (prosecution bound by Rules of Evidence).

5. R.C.M. 1001(d). *See, e.g.,* United States v. Childress, 33 M.J. 602 (A.C.M.R. 1991) (the prosecution was properly permitted to present testimony that rebutted the accused's unsworn statement of remorse; the testimony, that showed that the accused had threatened the victim after the offense, was also admissible as an aggravating circumstance directly related to the offense); United States v. Smith, 29 M.J. 736 (A.F.C.M.R. 1989) (rebuttal evidence must comply with conditions of admissibility).

6. *See, e.g.,* United States v. Wingart, 27 M.J. 128 (C.M.A. 1988) (prosecutor could not offer evidence of uncharged misconduct where judge had not relaxed rules of evidence; the court noted that the relaxation of the rules of evidence goes to "authenticity and reliability" and not to the scope of the offered evidence); United States v. Strong, 17 M.J. 263 (C.M.A. 1984) (court permitted improperly retained Art. 15 record to be used in rebuttal to defense evidence that accused was exemplary soldier).

7. R.C.M. 1001(c)(3), (d).

1. R.C.M. 1005(c) Discussion.

2. United States v. McGee, 30 M.J. 1086 (N.M.C.M.R. 1989). The *Manual* is silent on the order of arguments. *See* R.C.M. 1001(g).

3. 30 M.J. 1086 (N.M.C.M.R. 1989); United States v. Martin, 39 M.J. 481 (C.M.A. 1994) (court stated that it agreed with lower courts' position that trial counsel should not routinely be permit-

court indicated that as a general rule the prosecution has no right to present a rebuttal argument, and thus the prosecution should not be routinely permitted to present opening and closing arguments on sentencing. Instead, the court should permit the prosecutor to present a rebuttal argument only where it addresses matters newly raised by the defense in its sentencing argument. The same court later indicated that trial counsel should not routinely be permitted to choose whether to argue first or last on sentencing argument when rebuttal is not contemplated.[4]

Regardless of the order of arguments, they must be made before the judge instructs the court.[5] Failure to object to an argument before instructions are given may constitute waiver,[6] unless the error is egregious and the appellate court determines that the trial judge should have interrupted the argument.[7]

§ 16-8(B). Prosecution Arguments on Sentencing.

The rules of counsel's arguments discussed in § 15-13 are equally applicable here except that special attention should be paid to several particular problem areas that may arise during sentencing arguments. The first relates to prosecution general deterrence arguments—using the accused's sentence to deter others from committing offenses. The trial counsel may make such an argument but may not place undue emphasis on that point.[8]

The prosecutor may not suggest ostracism of the court members if they do not impose a heavy sentence,[9] and, although he may suggest a specific sen-

---

ted to choose whether to argue first or last on sentence and should be limited to truly responsive rebuttal).

4. United States v. Budicin, 32 M.J. 795 (N.M.C.M.R. 1990). *See also* United States v. Martin, 36 M.J. 739 (A.F.C.M.R. 1993) (nonprejudicial procedural error to permit trial counsel the option of arguing first or last).

5. United States v. Jones, 6 M.J. 568 (N.C.M.R. 1978) (judge erred by permitting arguments after instructions). *See also* R.C.M. 1005 (instructions to be given after arguments).

6. *See* R.C.M. 1001(g). *See, e.g.,* United States v. Sherman, 32 M.J. 449 (C.M.A. 1991) (accused waived any objections to prosecutor's comments on adverse impact of crime on German-American relations); United States v. Jones, 30 M.J. 898 (A.F.C.M.R. 1990) (failure to object to prosecutor's argument that accused had failed to admit guilt did not amount to waiver where argument was plain error); United States v. Fontenot, 26 M.J. 559 (A.C.M.R. 1988); United States v. Johnson, 24 M.J. 796 (A.C.M.R. 1987) (defense waived objection to prosecutor's sentencing argument that mischaracterized testimony of a witness); United States v. Schwarz, 24 M.J. 823 (A.C.M.R. 1987) (counsel waived objection to prosecutor's argument re propriety of fine as part of the sentence); United States v. Williams, 23 M.J. 776 (A.C.M.R. 1987) (waiver will be strictly enforced).

7. *See, e.g.,* United States v. White, 33 M.J. 555 (A.C.M.R. 1991) (judge should have *sua sponte* interrupted trial counsel's argument that alluded to uncharged misconduct that had not been admitted at trial).

8. United States v. Meeks, 41 M.J. 150 (C.M.A. 1994) (prosecutor's argument asking members to consider message which would be sent to those who did not deploy to Middle East, was fair comment on general deterrence); United States v. Lania, 9 M.J. 100 (C.M.A. 1980). *See generally* Russelburg, "Sentencing Arguments: A View from the Bench," ARMY LAW., Mar. 1986, at 50; Ferrante, "Sentencing Arguments: Defining the Limits of Advocacy," 13 THE ADVOCATE 268 (1981).

9. United States v. Wood, 18 C.M.A. 291, 40 C.M.R. 3 (1969).

§ 16-8(B)   MILITARY CRIMINAL JUSTICE   § 16-8(B)

tence[10] or a sentence that exceeds the limits in a pretrial agreement,[11] he should not in any way suggest any command policy to harshly punish offenders.[12] Counsel should not refer to a level of punishment that the court is not authorized to impose[13] nor refer to sentences imposed in other cases.[14]

The prosecution may refer to the general underlying philosophies for sentencing[15] and under appropriate circumstances the prosecution may address the fact that the accused voluntarily absented himself from trial.[16] And as noted in the discussion on instructions, the prosecution may urge the court to consider the accused's mendacity, where it is apparent that the court must have concluded by its verdict that the accused gave false sworn testimony during the merits portion of the trial.[17]

---

10. R.C.M. 1001(g). United States v. Motsinger, 34 M.J. 255 (C.M.A. 1992) (counsel may not suggest that failure to impose a punitive discharge will also constitute administrative decision whether to retain accused).

11. United States v. Rich, 12 M.J. 661 (A.C.M.R. 1981).

12. *See, e.g.,* United States v. Kropf, 39 M.J. 107 (C.M.A. 1994) (counsel's reference to Navy's zero tolerance toward drugs was not plain error; court noted that this is area where trial counsel must tread lightly); United States v. Sparrow, 33 M.J. 139 (C.M.A. 1991) (prosecutor's reference to convening authority by name and to fact that members had been chosen to do the "right thing" and impose heavy sentence was not plain error); United States v. Grady, 15 M.J. 275 (C.M.A. 1983).

United States v. Martin, 36 M.J. 739 (A.F.C.M.R. 1993) (in context, trial counsel's arguments were not attempt to invoke Air Force policy); United States v. Flynn, 34 M.J. 1183 (A.F.C.M.R. 1992) (any error in trial counsel's argument which might have been interpreted as statement by convening authority was cured through cautionary instructions); United States v. Myers, 14 M.J. 527 (A.F.C.M.R. 1982); United States v. Higdon, 2 M.J. 445 (A.C.M.R. 1975). *Cf.* United States v. Barus, 16 M.J. 624 (A.F.C.M.R. 1983) (trial counsel did not err in arguing that drugs were a problem in the Air Force).

13. United States v. Boese, 13 C.M.A. 131, 32 C.M.R. 131 (1962).

14. United States v. King, 12 C.M.A. 71, 30 C.M.R. 71 (1960); United States v. Schnitzer, 41 M.J. 603 (Army Ct.Crim.App. 1994) (error for prosecutor, in absence of comprehensive limiting instruction, to introduce evidence of pretrial agreement in closely related case where convening authority had agreed to 28-year sentence; court treated the issue as one of command influence); United States v. Jones, 34 C.M.R. 642 (A.C.M.R. 1964).

15. R.C.M. 1001(g). Those philosophies include general deterrence, specific deterrence, and social retribution. *Cf.* United States v. Everett, 33 M.J. 534 (A.F.C.M.R. 1991) (prosecutor could properly argue that members consider NCO's status; that argument was not an allusion to the accused's duties); United States v. Simmons, 31 M.J. 884 (A.F.C.M.R. 1990) (claiming that because of his duties, cleaning airplanes, accused would be menace to Air Force was improper; court noted a number of other problems with closing arguments); United States v. Gruninger, 30 M.J. 1142 (A.F.C.M.R. 1990) (prosecutor may not argue that accused poses a menace to the military because of his or her duty unless there is evidence that an accused's crimes affected his duty); United States v. Lewis, 7 M.J. 958 (A.F.C.M.R. 1979) (duties on flightline).

United States v. Martinez, 30 M.J. 1194 (A.F.C.M.R. 1990) (prosecutor committed reversible error in arguing a theory of culpability (as perpetrator of killing) to the court during sentencing that had been rejected by the military judge in accepting the accused's guilty plea as an aider and abettor).

16. United States v. Hall, 29 M.J. 786 (A.C.M.R. 1989). *Cf.* United States v. Denney, 28 M.J. 521 (A.C.M.R. 1989) (military judge must *sua sponte* instruct the members that an accused's voluntary absence from trial is relevant to issue of rehabilitative potential but it may not be used to enhance the sentence); United States v. Chapman, 20 M.J. 717 (N.M.C.M.R. 1985). *See also* § 15-2(A).

17. United States v. Beaty, 14 M.J. 155 (C.M.A. 1982); United States v. Cabebe, 13 M.J. 303 (C.M.A. 1982); United States v. Warren, 13 M.J. 278 (C.M.A. 1982); United States v. Marsh, 35

§ 16-8(B) SENTENCING § 16-8(B)

The prosecutor may refer to matters that are generally known[18] and may argue any reasonable inference from the aggravating evidence actually admitted at trial[19] and during sentencing[20] such as evidence of the impact of the offense on the victim,[21] the unit,[22] or the mission of the armed forces.[23]

Although the prosecution in a contested trial normally may not argue that the defendant has failed to admit guilt,[24] there is authority for the proposition that the prosecution may argue that the defendant has failed to express remorse for his actions.[25] There is obviously a thin line between the two.[26] In

---

M.J. 505 (A.F.C.M.R. 1992) (trial counsel's argument was acceptable, mendacious, accused argument).

18. United States v. Meeks, 41 M.J. 150 (C.M.A. 1994) (trial counsel's sentencing argument asking members to think of servicemembers who were fighting in the Middle East, unlike accused who had been convicted of refusing to deploy, was fair comment on facts of common knowledge and on preserving good order and discipline and needs of general deterrence); United States v. Long, 17 C.M.A. 323, 38 C.M.R. 121 (1967); United States v. Thompson, 37 M.J. 1023 (A.C.M.R. 1993) (trial counsel's sentencing argument referring to accused's race amounted to plain error and reversible error; counsel had referenced black culture and drug activities); United States v. McCarthy, 37 M.J. 595 (A.F.C.M.R. 1993) (prosecutor's sentencing argument referencing ongoing war with Saddam Hussein bordered on improper comment); United States v. Poteet, 50 C.M.R. 73 (N.M.C.M.R. 1975) (drug problem).

19. United States v. Hampton, 40 M.J. 457 (C.M.A. 1994) (harmless error for prosecutor to misquote stipulation of expected testimony regarding accused's rehabilitative potential); United States v. White, 36 M.J. 306 (C.M.A. 1993) (harmless error for trial counsel to refer to uncharged misconduct during closing argument); United States v. Snodgrass, 37 M.J. 844 (A.F.C.M.R. 1993) (prosecutor's argument on sentencing was plausible inference from facts); United States v. White, 33 M.J. 555 (A.C.M.R. 1991) (judge should have *sua sponte* interrupted trial counsel's argument that alluded to uncharged misconduct that had not been admitted at trial); United States v. Childress, 33 M.J. 449 (A.C.M.R. 1991) (prosecutor's comment on impact of offense on foreign relations was not based upon evidence).

20. *See* § 16-5. United States v. Conway, 40 M.J. 859 (A.F.C.M.R. 1994) (argument by trial counsel re accused as not a decent human being, etc. was fair and reasonably based upon evidence); United States v. Spears, 32 M.J. 934 (A.F.C.M.R. 1991) (error for trial counsel to argue "victim impact" without actually introducing such evidence during sentencing).

21. *See, e.g.,* United States v. Pearson, 17 M.J. 149 (C.M.A. 1984); United States v. Gray, 37 M.J. 730 (A.C.M.R. 1992) (prosecutor could properly argue victim impact); United States v. Edmonds, 36 M.J. 791 (A.C.M.R. 1993) (trial counsel's argument urging court members to consider fear of robbery victim was permissible; members were not asked to take place of victim but were, instead, asked to consider what amounted to victim impact evidence). *Cf.* United States v. Spears, 32 M.J. 934 (A.F.C.M.R. 1991) (error for trial counsel to argue "victim impact" without actually introducing such evidence during sentencing).

22. *See* § 16-5(D)(4).

23. United States v. Sells, 30 M.J. 944 (A.C.M.R. 1990) (impact of drug use on aviators). *Cf.* United States v. Childress, 33 M.J. 602 (A.C.M.R. 1991) (prosecutor's argument that speculated on the impact of the accused's offense on German-American relations was improper where there was no evidence of such).

24. United States v. Johnson, 1 M.J. 213 (C.M.A. 1975); United States v. Gibson, 30 M.J. 1138 (A.F.C.M.R. 1990); United States v. Turner, 30 M.J. 1183 (A.F.C.M.R. 1990) (plain error to argue on sentencing that defendant had not admitted guilt); United States v. Jones, 30 M.J. 898 (A.F.C.M.R. 1990) (prosecutor's argument was plain error).

25. United States v. Toro, 37 M.J. 313 (C.M.A. 1993) (not plain error for prosecutor to argue that accused had failed to show lack of remorse during his unsworn statement).

---

26. United States v. Toro, 37 M.J. 313 (C.M.A. 1993) (not plain error for prosecutor to argue that accused had failed to show lack of remorse during his unsworn statement); United States v.

United States v. Edwards,[27] the court addressed the question of whether a prosecutor may refer to an accused's lack of remorse.[28] Although it declined to set out any bright line rules,[29] the court indicated that if a proper foundation is laid, an accused's recalcitrance in refusing to admit guilt after findings is, in an appropriate case, a factor to be considered in assessing his or her rehabilitative potential.[30] The court added that it might also be relevant as victim-impact evidence.[31] The court noted that normally the predicate for the argument is that the accused has either testified or made an unsworn statement[32] and has either expressed no remorse or his statements of remorse appear to be shallow, artificial, or contrived.[33] An inference of a lack of remorse may not be drawn from his silence at trial.[34]

§ 16-8(C). Defense Counsel's Argument on Sentencing.

The defense counsel may in closing argument on sentencing assist the accused in his desire to receive no punishment other than a punitive discharge.[35] Where counsel intends to argue for a punitive discharge, the accused's desires

---

United States v. Jackson, 40 M.J. 820 (N.M.C.M.R. 1994) (trial counsel's argument re accused's silent remorse at trial, i.e., tears, was harmless error); United States v. Heath, 39 M.J. 1101 (C.G.C.M.R. 1994) (prosecutor's sentencing argument that there was no evidence of someone who wanted to repent was not impermissible comment on failure of accused to testify; instead, it was fair comment on aggravation evidence); United States v. Standifer, 31 M.J. 742 (A.F.C.M.R. 1990) (counsel came dangerously close to arguing that defendant had not admitted his guilt; court treated argument as asserting that accused was "mendacious"; court cautioned trial counsel to choose their words carefully); United States v. Kilbourne, 31 M.J. 731 (A.F.C.M.R. 1990) (not error); United States v. Ryder, 31 M.J. 718 (A.F.C.M.R. 1990) (not error in this case for prosecutor to argue that defendant had failed to show lack of remorse or accept responsibility for his acts); United States v. Minaya, 30 M.J. 1179 (A.F.C.M.R. 1990) (any error in arguing that lack of remorse should be considered by the court was harmless); United States v. Gibson, 30 M.J. 1138 (A.F.C.M.R. 1990) (court held that it was not error for prosecutor to argue that accused had failed to express remorse during his unsworn statement although it would be improper for court to instruct members that they could consider that point).

Standifer, 31 M.J. 742 (A.F.C.M.R. 1990) (court treated the trial counsel's argument as a "mendacious accused" argument, that the accused had lied to the court in his testimony on findings).
27. 35 M.J. 351 (C.M.A. 1992).
28. 35 M.J. at 353 (acknowledging wealth of decisions from service appellate courts on topic).
29. 35 M.J. at 351. The court declined to set out any specific rules because, first, defense counsel should be able to ferret out improper argument and second, it would be impossible to "foresee the myriad of possibilities which arise in a particular trial and make the lack of remorse an issue in sentencing."
30. 35 M.J. at 355.
31. Id.
32. 35 M.J. at 355 See also § 16-6.
33. Id.
34. Id.
35. United States v. Lyons, 36 M.J. 425 (C.M.A. 1993) (defense counsel's argument for punitive discharge was supported by accused's unsworn statement of desire to return to family); United States v. Weikel, 24 M.J. 666 (A.F.C.M.R. 1987) (under the facts, counsel did not commit error in arguing that punitive discharge might be appropriate); United States v. Beckwith, 12 M.J. 939 (N.M.C.M.R. 1982); United States v. Dotson, 9 M.J. 542 (C.G.C.M.R. 1980). See generally Higginbotham, "The Propriety of Argument by Trial Defense Counsel for Bad-Conduct Discharge," 22 A.F.L. Rev. 81 (1980-81).

should be placed in the record. Counsel may do so by requesting an Article 39(a) session or, in the absence of one, the judge should *sua sponte* inquire as to whether the accused indeed desires a discharge.[36] The court is probably not required to conduct a sua sponte hearing in the absence of a conflict in the accused's desires.[37] If an inquiry is conducted, the judge should be careful not to unnecessarily inquire into matters which may be protected by the attorney-client relationship.[38] If the defense counsel's argument for a punitive discharge is contrary to the accused's desires, the court will normally find ineffective assistance.[39]

It is also proper for the defense to argue for a longer period of confinement in lieu of a discharge where a pretrial agreement provides for a shorter period of confinement.[40] In other words, the defense may attempt to beat the pretrial agreement.[41] In anticipation of such arguments, some convening authorities have included a provision in the pretrial agreement which states that the agreement is not binding if no punitive discharge is adjudged.[42] Defense coun-

---

36. United States v. Holcomb, 43 C.M.R. 149 (C.M.A. 1971) (court added that a defense counsel has an obligation to dissuade the accused from seeking a discharge, but if counsel is unsuccessful, he should not inform the court that the accused is acting contrary to counsel's advice); United States v. Blunk, 37 C.M.R. 422 (C.M.A. 1967); United States v. Smith, 34 M.J. 247 (C.M.A. 1992) (counsel submitted BCD Striker Advisement to judge during sentencing; court noted that the term BCD striker is used in the Navy to describe an accused who actively seeks a punitive discharge); United States v. Robinson, 25 M.J. 43 (C.M.A. 1987) (defense counsel's request that court impose a "suspended discharge" was not reversible error in light of gravity of offenses); United States v. Volmar, 15 M.J. 339 (C.M.A. 1983) (court held that because there was no reasonable likelihood that the members would assess a punitive discharge, defense counsel did not err in arguing for a bad-conduct discharge); United States v. Webb, 5 M.J. 406 (C.M.A. 1978).
United States v. Hudson, 37 M.J. 992 (A.C.M.R. 1993) (inquiry by trial judge indicated that the defense counsel had not argued for a punitive discharge); United States v. Butts, 25 M.J. 535 (A.C.M.R. 1987) (record indicated accused's implied consent in counsel's argument for a punitive discharge); United States v. Williams, 21 M.J. 524 (A.C.M.R. 1985) (counsel erred in arguing for punitive discharge where record lacked indication that accused desired such); United States v. Boyce, 12 M.J. 981 (A.F.C.M.R. 1982).
37. United States v. Lyons, 36 M.J. 425 (C.M.A. 1993) (the court held that the trial judge was not required to conduct sua sponte inquiry into accused's desires where there was no conflict in defense counsel's argument for punitive discharge and accused's unsworn statement of desire to return to family; the court noted that where the record is silent on the issue, the defense counsel may not concede that a discharge is appropriate); United States v. Nunes, 39 M.J. 889 (A.F.C.M.R. 1994) ("striker inquiry" not required where judge and counsel did not view argument as request for discharge).
38. United States v. Evans, 35 M.J. 754 (N.M.C.M.R. 1992) (normally the military judge should not make an extended inquiry into the accused's desires for a punitive discharge; in an extended discussion, the court noted that even though it is better practice to conduct a brief inquiry, where the imposition of a punitive discharge is virtually certain and counsel's concession is reasonable, no inquiry is required, even where the accused has not affirmatively indicated a desire for one; court also noted that there may be problems with intruding too deeply into the attorney-client privilege if the judge insists on determining what advice the accused received concerning a punitive discharge).
39. United States v. Volmar, 15 M.J. 339 (C.M.A. 1983).
40. United States v. Wood, 23 C.M.A. 57, 48 C.M.R. 528 (1974); United States v. Rich, 12 M.J. 661 (A.C.M.R. 1981).
41. See Chapter 9.
42. *See, e.g.,* United States v. Castleberry, 18 M.J. 826 (A.C.M.R. 1984) (provision did not unduly prejudice the accused); United States v. Wordlow, 19 M.J. 981 (A.C.M.R. 1985); United

sel should be careful, however, to avoid any references to relitigating the issue of the accused's guilt.[43]

Defense counsel should also refrain from arguing that the accused will be discharged administratively, even if the court does not impose a punitive discharge.[44]

§ 16-9. Instructions on Sentencing.

As with instructions on findings, the military judge should entertain any requests from counsel concerning special instructions during an out-of-court session.[1] The requests should be reduced to writing and marked as an appellate exhibit, whether or not actually given.[2] The judge should not inform the court of the source of any particular instruction.[3] The following instructions must be given by the judge:

(1) A statement as to the maximum punishments;[4]

States v. Costa, 19 M.J. 980 (A.C.M.R. 1985); United States v. Sanders, 19 M.J. 979 (A.C.M.R. 1985); United States v. Witherspoon, 19 M.J. 978 (A.C.M.R. 1985); United States v. Cross, 19 M.J. 973 (A.C.M.R. 1985) (provision does not violate public policy); United States v. Hollcraft, 17 M.J. 1111 (A.C.M.R. 1984); United States v. Holmes, 17 M.J. 830 (A.C.M.R. 1984).

43. United States v. Vanderlip, 28 M.J. 1070 (N.M.C.M.R. 1989) (defense may not argue that members may, or should, reconsider their findings of guilt, although they are free to do so). See United States v. Brown, 13 M.J. 890 (A.C.M.R. 1982); see also § 15-15 and R.C.M. 1001(g).

44. United States v. Keith, 22 C.M.A. 59, 46 C.M.R. 59 (1972).

1. R.C.M. 1005(c) Discussion. United States v. Williams, 26 M.J. 644 (A.C.M.R. 1988) (any error in not calling out-of-court session was waived when defense failed to request one); United States v. Wilson, 26 M.J. 10 (C.M.A. 1988) (court erred in not giving requested instruction to effect that provocation of victim could be considered in sentencing the accused).

2. R.C.M. 1005(c) Discussion.

3. Id.

4. R.C.M. 1005(e)(1). See also § 16-2. See, e.g., United States v. Wilson, 35 M.J. 473 (C.M.A. 1992) (failure to announce position on multiplicity of charges was not prejudicial error); United States v. Motsinger, 34 M.J. 255 (C.M.A. 1992) (failure to give oral instruction re availability of fine as punishment was not fatal where sentence worksheet included reference to fine as possible punishment); United States v. Purdy, 42 M.J. 666 (Army Ct.Crim.App. 1995) (nonprejudicial error for judge to inform members that offenses had merged for sentencing purposes); United States v. Yocom, 17 C.M.A. 270, 38 C.M.R. 68 (1967). A military judge may go further and instruct on the individual maximum punishments for each offense. United States v. Henderson, 11 M.J. 395 (C.M.A. 1981); United States v. Gutierrez, 11 M.J. 122 (C.M.A. 1981). There is no *sua sponte* duty to instruct on all lesser punishments.

See also United States v. Timmons, 13 M.J. 431 (C.M.A. 1982); United States v. Ferguson, 27 M.J. 660 (N.M.C.M.R. 1988) (judge incorrectly instructed on sentence rehearing where he failed to exclude period of confinement that had been suspended by the convening authority pursuant to a pretrial agreement and later remitted); United States v. Brown, 15 M.J. 620 (N.M.C.M.R. 1982) (it is error for the judge to inform the members of the authorized maximum punishment when it exceeds the limits for a special court-martial).

United States v. Holland, 19 M.J. 883 (A.C.M.R. 1985) (judge erred in instructing court members that a BCD was the equivalent of one year's confinement at hard labor because it failed to take into account the variables of an individualized punishment; the judge may comment, however, on the relative severity of the various punishments). See also United States v. Cavalier, 17 M.J. 573 (A.F.C.M.R. 1984).

§ 16-9   SENTENCING   § 16-9

(2) Procedures for deliberating and voting on a sentence;[5]

(3) A statement that the court is solely responsible for the sentence and may not count on any mitigating action by reviewing authorities;[6] and

(4) A reminder to consider all of the matters offered by both the prosecution and the defense that relates to an appropriate sentence.[7]

The judge should be careful to tailor his instructions to the case and to the evidence.[8] He should not allude to any command policies concerning the offense[9] nor should he elaborate on any administrative consequences of the sentence.[10] But he should advise the court concerning consideration of any

---

If the maximum punishment is limited by the jurisdictional limits of the court or by the nature of the proceedings, the members should not be advised of the basis for the limitation. R.C.M. 1005(e)(1) Discussion.

5. R.C.M. 1005(e)(2), 1006. Garrett v. Lowe, 39 M.J. 293 (C.M.A. 1994) (judge erred in instructing members that did not have to vote on the confinement for life portion of the sentence because it was mandatory component of sentence; court noted that R.C.M. 1006(d)(5) requires vote on even mandatory minimum sentences); United States v. Horner, 1 M.J. 227 (C.M.A. 1975); United States v. Wallace, 35 M.J. 897 (A.C.M.R. 1992) (judge's instructions on deliberations on sentence were incorrect when he told members that voting procedures were similar to those used to select candidates running for office); United States v. Harris, 30 M.J. 1150 (A.C.M.R. 1990) (judge's failure to instruct court that junior member should collect and count votes was plain error); United States v. Hutto, 29 M.J. 917 (A.C.M.R. 1989) (although judge's instruction to members regarding counting and verifying ballots on sentencing did not strictly conform with Article 51(a), it did not deprive accused of due process or detract from integrity of proceeding); United States v. Scott, 22 M.J. 646 (A.C.M.R. 1986) (prejudicial error where judge failed to instruct court to begin voting with the lightest proposed sentence). *Cf.* United States v. Fisher, 21 M.J. 327 (C.M.A. 1986) (failure to instruct on correct voting procedures not *per se* plain error).

6. R.C.M. 1005(e)(3), 1002. *See, e.g.,* United States v. Hannan, 17 M.J. 115 (C.M.A. 1984) (judge in bench trial may consider parole guidelines in assessing a sentence); United States v. Grady, 15 M.J. 275 (C.M.A. 1983) (policies impacting on military corrections system).

7. R.C.M. 1005(e)(4). United States v. Chaves, 28 M.J. 691 (A.F.C.M.R. 1989) (judge erred in instructing members that they could consider the fact that the accused during his unsworn statement had not expressed remorse).

8. R.C.M. 1005(a) Discussion. United States v. Loving, 41 M.J. 213 (1994) (instructions on whole demonstrated that judge carefully walked the tightrope). *Cf.* United States v. McLaren, 34 M.J. 926 (A.F.C.M.R. 1992) (judge's explicit instructions on administrative procedures was appropriate where in response to members questions); United States v. Wheeler, 17 C.M.A. 274, 38 C.M.R. 72 (1967).

9. United States v. Kirkpatrick, 33 M.J. 132 (C.M.A. 1991) (reversible error for judge to instruct court during sentencing that it should consider Army's drug policy; court held that although defense counsel did not object, application of waiver doctrine here would be inappropriate).

10. *See, e.g.,* United States v. McElroy, 40 M.J. 368 (C.M.A. 1994) (noting that instructions on administrative consequences should be avoided, the court rejected the defense argument that the instruction was misleading); United States v. Goodwin, 33 M.J. 18 (C.M.A. 1991) (accused waived his objection to the trial judge's failure to instruct members on possible impact of BCD on veterans'benefits; court noted that such an instruction is not mandatory); United States v. Henderson, 29 M.J. 221 (C.M.A. 1989) (accused waived error in judge's instructions re administrative consequences of discharge); United States v. Griffin, 25 M.J. 423 (C.M.A. 1988) (court saw no need to relax the prohibition against instructing the court members on the administrative consequences of a punitive discharge; but it found no error in the judge responding to such questions by the members during their deliberations, especially where defense counsel failed to object); United States v. Ellis, 15 C.M.A. 8, 34 C.M.R. 454 (1964); United States v. Paske, 11 C.M.A. 689, 29 C.M.R. 505 (1960).

§ 16-9 MILITARY CRIMINAL JUSTICE § 16-9

pretrial confinement that may have been imposed.[11] Where the accused has voluntarily absented himself from trial, the judge may also instruct the court on considering that matter.[12]

The judge may also give a "mendacity" instruction. In *United States v. Warren*,[13] the court held that it was proper for the prosecutor to argue that by convicting the accused, the court must have disbelieved the accused's alibi testimony. But the judge's instructions on that point should include three elements. First, the members may not consider this factor unless they conclude that the accused did lie under oath. Not every guilty verdict necessarily raises the spectre of false testimony.[14] Second, the accused's lies must have

---

United States v. Goodwin, 30 M.J. 989 (A.C.M.R. 1990) (no error where judge did not instruct members that punitive discharge would deprive accused of substantial VA benefits); United States v. Maharajh, 28 M.J. 797 (A.F.C.M.R. 1989) (judge erred in instructing court members that if they did not believe that accused should remain in the service they should impose a punitive discharge); United States v. Lenard, 27 M.J. 739 (A.C.M.R. 1988) (failure to give standard instruction that bad-conduct discharge affects VA benefits was not error where accused was nonetheless entitled to such benefits from a prior honorable discharge); United States v. Harris, 26 M.J. 729, 734 (A.C.M.R. 1988); United States v. Hopkins, 25 M.J. 671 (A.F.C.M.R. 1987) (court noted that for several years, Air Force judges have been encouraged to give instruction on VA benefits); United States v. Wheeler, 18 M.J. 823 (A.C.M.R. 1984).

The dangers of elaborating on the administrative consequences were made clear in United States v. Soriano, 20 M.J. 337 (C.M.A. 1985) where the trial judge erred in instructing the members, in accordance with the trial counsel's request, that a punitive discharge *may* adversely affect accused; the court said that the sample instruction indicates that a punitive discharge *will* adversely affect the accused. Thus, the instruction conflicts with the long-standing view of the Court, the Congress, and the President that a punitive discharge is severe and should be viewed as such.

However, there is some authority for the court to consider that a punitive discharge will result in loss of VA benefits. *See* United States v. Chasteen, 17 M.J. 580 (A.F.C.M.R. 1983).

11. United States v. Balboa, 33 M.J. 304 (C.M.A. 1991) (judge's instruction informing members that *Allen*, credit for pretrial confinement would automatically be given by correctional personnel was not error; it did not invite members to impose heavier sentence); United States v. Allen, 17 M.J. 126 (C.M.A. 1984) (administrative credit instructions); United States v. Davidson, 14 M.J. 81 (C.M.A. 1982) (instructions must be given when requested by defense).

See also United States v. Spencer, 32 M.J. 841 (N.M.C.M.R. 1991) (accused is entitled to credit for each day or any part of a day spent in pretrial confinement except where day of confinement is also the date sentence is imposed; this *Allen* credit is not based on R.C.M. 305, or the speedy trial provisions but was instead based on DOD Instruction 1325.4 (Oct. 7, 1968), which implemented the 1966 Bail Reform Act, which requires the Attorney General to give credit for pretrial confinement, but which exempted courts-martial; the DOD instruction was reissued on May 19, 1988 and directs that courts-martial follow applicable and non-conflicting DOD regulations); United States v. Noonan, 21 M.J. 763 (A.F.C.M.R. 1986) (proper for judge to instruct members that accused would receive administrative credit for pretrial confinement); United States v. Stark, 19 M.J. 519 (A.C.M.R. 1984).

12. United States v. Haywood, 19 M.J. 675 (A.F.C.M.R. 1984) (the military judge committed nonprejudicial error when he failed to instruct the court that they could consider the accused's courtroom attire (tennis shoes, robe, and shawl) only insofar as it reflected on her potential for rehabilitation).

13. 13 M.J. 278 (C.M.A. 1982). These requirements also apply in bench trials. United States v. Beaty, 14 M.J. 155 (C.M.A. 1982). The instruction must be given if trial counsel argues the point. United States v. Baxter, 14 M.J. 762 (A.C.M.R. 1982).

14. United States v. Cabebe, 13 M.J. 303 (C.M.A. 1982); United States v. Felton, 31 M.J. 526 (A.C.M.R. 1990) (judge failed to instruct members that they must first find that the accused

§ 16-10 SENTENCING § 16-10

been, in the court's mind, willful and material before they may be considered. And third, this factor should only be considered insofar as it affects the accused's rehabilitative potential. The court may not mete out additional punishment solely for the false testimony.[15] Absent plain error, failure to object to an instruction will constitute waiver.[16]

§ 16-10. Deliberations on Sentencing.

The court members deliberate on the sentence in a closed session[1] and are normally provided with a sentence worksheet to assist them.[2] Because the members have no duty to agree upon a sentence the possibility of a hung jury does exist.[3] In that case the military judge is not free to charge the court to continue deliberations.[4] Instead, he declares a mistrial and the convening authority may order that a sentence of *no punishment* be entered, or it may order a rehearing on the sentence before a different court.[5] Every member is permitted to propose a punishment[6] and voting by secret written ballot[7] begins with the lightest proposed punishment and continues until the required minimum number of votes is reached.[8] Each proposed sentence must be voted on in its entirety.[9] The ballots are collected and counted by the junior member of the court.[10] In death sentences all must concur.[11] For sentences including confinement for life or for more than ten years, three-fourths of the members must concur.[12] In all other punishments, two-thirds of the members must concur.[13]

---

willfully lied); United States v. Smith, 25 M.J. 785 (A.C.M.R. 1988) (judge not required to give mendacity instruction where accused only gave an unsworn statement at trial).

15. United States v. Beaty, 14 M.J. 155 (C.M.A. 1982).
16. R.C.M. 1005(f). *See* United States v. Yanke, 23 M.J. 144 (C.M.A. 1987) (defense waived objections to sentencing instructions by not objecting); United States v. Fisher, 21 M.J. 327 (C.M.A. 1986) (failure to instruct on order of voting was not plain error *per se*); United States v. Webel, 16 M.J. 64 (C.M.A. 1983) (error in sentencing instructions waived by failure to object); United States v. Pauley, 24 M.J. 521 (A.F.C.M.R. 1987) (judge's sentencing instruction to court concerning evidence of uncharged misconduct amounted to plain error where the only reference to such had been raised in trial counsel's questions); United States v. Bolden, 16 M.J. 722 (A.F.C.M.R. 1983) (discussion of plain error). *See also* § 15-14(D).
1. R.C.M. 1006(a). *Cf.* United States v. Martinez, 40 M.J. 82 (C.M.A. 1994) (ex parte communication by bailiff to judge during latter's sentencing deliberations was legal error; court noted that not only must military justice system be fair, it must appear to be fair; the proper procedure, said the court, is for the judge to disclose in open court what the communication has been).
2. *See* Appendix 29. R.C.M. 1005(e)(1) Discussion.
3. United States v. Straukas, 41 C.M.R. 975 (A.F.C.M.R. 1970).
4. *Id.*
5. R.C.M. 1006(d)(6).
6. R.C.M. 1006(b).
7. R.C.M. 1006(d)(2).
8. R.C.M. 1006(d)(3)(A).
9. *Id.* United States v. Allen, 21 M.J. 924 (A.C.M.R. 1986).
10. R.C.M. 1006(d)(3)(B).
11. Art. 52(b)(1), U.C.M.J. R.C.M. 1006(d)(4)(A). For special rules governing imposition of the death penalty see § 16-3(A).
12. Art. 52(b)(2), U.C.M.J. R.C.M. 1006(d)(4)(B). In United States v. Shroeder, 27 M.J. 87

---

13. Art. 52(b)(3), U.C.M.J. R.C.M. 1006(d)(4)(C).

Reballoting, or reconsideration of a sentence, is permitted under limited circumstances and usually requires further detailed instructions by the military judge.[14] After the proper number of members have concurred in a sentence, they may not continue voting on proposed sentences unless they formally reconsider their vote.[15] Any member may request reconsideration of the sentence.[16] Before a reballot may be taken, however, a prescribed number of members, depending on the severity of the sentence originally agreed upon,[17] must agree by secret written ballot to do so.[18] Assuming that the prescribed number concur, the members proceed to vote again on a sentence.[19] Before a sentence is announced,[20] the court may either decrease or increase the sentence.[21] After a sentence is announced, the members may reconsider it at any time before the record of trial is authenticated but may only do so with a view to decreasing it.[22]

If it is necessary for the court members to take a recess during their deliberations, they should return to the courtroom, formally recess, reassemble, and

---

(C.M.A. 1988), the court concluded that there is no inconsistency between Article 118, which requires a mandatory life sentence for a felony murder conviction, and Article 52, which requires that three-fourths of the members must concur in a sentence of 10 or more years. The court also concluded that there is no inconsistency between the requirement that only two-thirds of the members in that situation would have to vote for a finding of guilty.

In United States v. Garrett, 24 M.J. 413 (C.M.A. 1987), the court noted the potential problem arising in a mandatory life sentence situation where the members might have reached a conviction by only a two-thirds majority.

14. See R.C.M. 1009. See United States v. Neeley, 21 M.J. 606 (A.F.C.M.R. 1985) (judge gave incorrect instructions).
15. See R.C.M. 1009(d) Discussion.
16. R.C.M. 1009(c)(1).
17. See R.C.M. 1009(d)(2). To reconsider a sentence for the purpose of increasing the punishment, a majority must agree to a reballot. To decrease the sentence, more than one-fourth of the members must vote to reconsider if sentence included more than 10 years of confinement; if 10 or less years of confinement was included in the sentence, at least one-third must agree to reconsider.

In United States v. Wilson, 18 M.J. 204 (C.M.A. 1984), the court stated that repeated requests for reconsideration may not be used to evade the statutory minimum number of votes on certain matters.

In the past there was some question as to whether the members were required to first vote on whether they should reconsider a sentence when the judge, not the members, have proposed reconsideration. See United States v. King, 13 M.J. 838 (A.C.M.R. 1982) (the court noted the difference in reconsideration initiated by the members and one initiated by a military judge. In the latter instance, procedures for reballoting are not applicable and instructions are unnecessary). However, the Drafters' Analysis to R.C.M. 1009 states that the reconsideration procedures are the same without regard to who initiates such "... since R.C.M. 1006(d)(3)(A) does not permit further voting after a sentence is adopted and there is no authority for the judge to suspend that provision."

18. R.C.M. 1009(d)(2).
19. R.C.M. 1009(d)(4).
20. See § 16-11.
21. R.C.M. 1009(a).
22. R.C.M. 1009(b). United States v. Morero, 41 M.J. 537 (N.M.Ct.Crim.App. 1994) (instruction to court members to start all over during reconsideration of sentence, without regard to increasing or decreasing punishment, was nonprejudicial error).

formally close again to resume deliberations.[23] This process insures that all of the members will be accounted for during the deliberation process and that they are not subject to improper communications.[24]

§ 16-11. Announcement of the Sentence.

The sentence must be promptly announced by the president in open court.[1] Before the sentence is so announced, the military judge should examine the sentence worksheet to insure that it is in order and that the court has not imposed an improper sentence. Examination of this worksheet by the counsel and military judge does not constitute an "announcement."[2] Once the sentence is formally announced the court members may correct any misstatements by the president of the members' intent.[3] On the other hand, if the sentence announced is improper, inconsistent or ambiguous,[4] the judge should ask the court for clarification and possible reconsideration.[5] Any questions of the members should be held in open court with the parties present.[6] If a defect

---

23. R.C.M. 813(b). United States v. Jones, 37 M.J. 321 (C.M.A. 1993) (failure of judge to follow procedure was not plain error; accused waived by not objecting).

24. United States v. Jones, 37 M.J. 321 (C.M.A. 1993) (noting purpose for accounting for members during deliberations).

1. Art. 53, U.C.M.J. R.C.M. 1007. *See* United States v. Washington, 35 M.J. 774 (A.C.M.R. 1992) (in an erroneous procedure the judge tried a co-accused first, determined a sentence but sealed it, tried the accused, reopened the first trial and announced the sentence in the first trial. Citing United States v. Lee, 13 M.J. 181 (C.M.A. 1982), the court concluded that his procedure was nonprejudicial because the accused had expressly consented to it); United States v. Lee, 13 M.J. 181 (C.M.A. 1982) (in an unusual procedure, the judge committed nonprejudicial error by sealing the court's sentence and announcing it outside their presence some time later); United States v. Hemingway, 22 M.J. 939 (A.F.C.M.R. 1986) (recommendation was announcement).

2. United States v. Justice, 3 M.J. 451 (C.M.A. 1977). R.C.M. 1006(e).

3. R.C.M. 1007(b). United States v. Robinson, 4 C.M.A. 12, 15 C.M.R. 12 (1954). This sort of error, often referred to as a "slip-of-the-tongue," may be corrected without reconsideration procedures at any time prior to authentication of the record. R.C.M. 1007(b).

See also United States v. Baker, 32 M.J. 290 (C.M.A. 1991) (after announcement of sentence court may correct upward an otherwise lawful sentence); United States v. Henderson, 21 M.J. 853 (A.C.M.R. 1986) (announcement of sentence was slip of tongue that could have been remedied by either reannouncing the sentence or holding a revision proceeding).

4. United States v. Evans, 35 M.J. 754 (N.M.C.M.R. 1992) (judge erred in explaining sentence of punitive discharge; the explanation made it clear that the judge imposed a punitive discharge primarily because the accused wanted one). For example, the court may not suspend a sentence, *see* United States v. Occhi, 2 M.J. 60 (C.M.A. 1976). Any attempt to impose a punishment other than those authorized by the *Manual* would be considered improper. *See* § 15-17(B). *See also* United States v. Riddick, 19 M.J. 517 (A.F.C.M.R. 1984) (unspecified recommendation for clemency by court members did not make sentence inconsistent or ambiguous).

The defect must be in the announcement of the sentence. A defect or conflict on the sentencing worksheet will not count. United States v. Donnelly, 12 M.J. 503 (A.F.C.M.R. 1981).

5. R.C.M. 1009(c)(2)(B), (3). United States v. Butler, 41 M.J. 211 (C.M.A. 1994) (military judge followed proper procedure in directing court members to reconsider their illegal sentence of a general discharge; court noted that judge could have convened an Article 39(a) session to obtain counsel's views but failure to do so was not error); United States v. Baker, 30 M.J. 594 (A.C.M.R. 1990) (court questioned members about defective announcement of sentence in open court when it was reassembled several days later).

6. United States v. Privette, 31 M.J. 791 (A.F.C.M.R. 1990) (correction made in open court by President of court); United States v. Rainwater, 19 M.J. 545 (N.M.C.M.R. 1984) (where court

in the sentence is discovered after the court has adjourned, either the military judge or the convening authority may direct that the court, in a post-trial session, reconsider its sentence.[7] In the alternative, the convening authority may remedy the problem by simply approving only that portion of the sentence which was properly imposed by the court.[8]

In announcing the sentence, the president should not indicate what fraction of the court voted for the announced sentence[9] nor should he offer any reasons for the sentence.[10]

The rules that bar polling of the members[11] and limit attempts to impeach the verdict[12] are also applicable here.[13]

---

member's announcement of a sentence raises questions, an on-the-record inquiry should be made in open court; here judge's closed door meeting with court members was nonprejudicial error).

7. R.C.M. 1009(c)(2)(B), (3). In United States v. Baker, 32 M.J. 290 (C.M.A. 1991), the court held that after a court-martial has announced its sentence and adjourned, it may not increase its previously announced lawful sentence unless Article 60(e)(2)(C) provides otherwise. The reason for that, said the court, was to avoid the appearance of unlawful command influence. *See also* United States v. Jones, 34 M.J. 270 (C.M.A. 1992) (judge's revision proceeding to correct his failure to announce imposition of confinement was improper).

United States v. Feld, 27 M.J. 537 (A.F.C.M.R. 1988) (revision proceeding was held to determine whether members intended language regarding forfeitures to apply to pay per month, which had been omitted from the announcement of the sentence; the court indicated that failure to use the words "pay per month," means that the amount announced is the total amount of forfeitures).

8. R.C.M. 1009(c)(3). United States v. Haggard, 29 M.J. 905 (A.C.M.R. 1989) (sentence provision requiring accused to "forfeit all pay," amounted to a total forfeiture of pay and thus did not need to be stated in dollar amounts; but it did not extend to forfeiture of allowances); United States v. Riverasoto, 29 M.J. 594 (A.C.M.R. 1989) (failure to state forfeitures in specific dollar amounts is not a jurisdictional defect affecting legality of sentence).

United States v. Frierson, 28 M.J. 501 (A.F.C.M.R. 1989) (court noted problems associated with announcing forfeitures in fractions rather than dollar amounts and in not setting a specific time for such forfeitures); United States v. Bowen, 29 M.J. 779 (A.C.M.R. 1989) (convening authority's action on sentence need not state forfeitures for a specific number of months).

United States v. White, 23 M.J. 859 (A.C.M.R. 1987) (sentence incorrectly failed to state specifically, in whole dollar amounts, the amount of forfeiture of pay; the appellate court remedied the defect by limiting the approved forfeitures to a one-month time period); United States v. Perry, 24 M.J. 557 (A.C.M.R. 1987) (failure to state forfeitures in exact amounts); United States v. Pellman, 24 M.J. 672 (A.F.C.M.R. 1987) (failure to state partial forfeitures in whole dollar amounts).

9. R.C.M. 1006(e) Discussion. This marks a change from the 1969 *Manual*. United States v. Jenkins, 12 M.J. 222 (C.M.A. 1982).

10. United States v. Schultz, 8 C.M.A. 129, 23 C.M.R. 353 (1957) (Latimer, J. concurring) (announcing reasons is inconsistent with the view that deliberations are inviolate). *Cf.* United States v. Harvey, 12 M.J. 626 (N.M.C.M.R. 1981) (one member of appellate court commended judge for stating his reasons for particular punishment on record when he announced sentence). Winthrop, *Military Law and Precedents*, 442-43 (1920 Reprint) (announcing reasons may be done but is more "military and dignified not to").

11. R.C.M. 1007(c). *Cf.* Rule 606, MIL. R. EVID.

12. R.C.M. 1008. That is, a sentence proper on its face may not be impeached unless it appears that outside information or influence or command influence was "brought to bear" upon the members.

In United States v. Stone, 26 M.J. 401 (C.M.A. 1988), the accused's father wrote a letter to the

---

13. *See* § 15-16(B). United States v. Combs, 41 M.J. 400 (1995) (member's statements following trial did not indicate that court had considered extraneous prejudicial information which would be subject of inquiry into validity of sentence).

In 1995, R.C.M. 1009 was amended to prevent a sentencing authority from reconsidering a sentence once it had been announced in open court. The change reflects two exceptions: (1) if the announced sentence is less than the mandatory minimum, the court may reconsider the sentence and increase it; (2) if the announced sentence is greater than the maximum permitted for the offense or more than the jurisdictional limits of the court, the court may reconsider the sentence.

The amendments also clarify what the judge may do if the sentence is ambiguous, at any time before the convening authority acts on the case, using a new procedure specified in R.C.M. 1009(e). Under R.C.M. 1009(d), the convening authority may either return the ambiguous sentence for clarification or act under R.C.M. 1107. If the sentence is apparently illegal, the convening authority may either send it back to the court-martial for reconsideration or approve a sentence no more severe than the legal and unambiguous portions.

§ 16-12. Advice on Appellate Rights.

After the sentence is announced[1] in a general or special court-martial, the military judge is charged with advising the accused, on the record, of his various appellate rights.[2] The advice is to be given after the sentence is announced but before adjournment.[3]

This requirement was added in the 1984 revision to the *Manual for Courts-Martial* at the direction of Congress[4] because changes in the Uniform Code of Military Justice in 1983[5] provided that an accused may in some cases waive appellate review of his conviction.[6] This advice need not be given in the presence of the court members and because other ministerial matters will normally remain, they may be excused after the sentence has been announced and it appears that there are no irregularities in the sentence which require further action by the court.

In summary the judge's advice should cover the following points:

(1) The accused has the right to submit matters to the convening authority before he acts on the case;

(2) The accused has the right to appellate review and the effect of either waiving or withdrawing the appeal;

---

convening authority almost two weeks after trial and complained about laughter and overheard comments of the court members during deliberation on a sentence. The convening authority in turn ordered an administrative hearing that determined that there was nothing to substantiate improper conduct but recommended that a letter of apology be written. The court held that by waiting, the defense had waived the issue but agreed that no improper conduct had occurred, although it recognized that "gallows humor" sometimes accompanies serious situations. Rather than conduct an administrative hearing, the more appropriate method is to conduct a post-trial session before a military judge with counsel present.

See also United States v. Rogan, 19 M.J. 646 (A.F.C.M.R. 1984) (judge did not impeach his sentence by noting that the accused's offense had been an aberration).

1. *See* § 16-11.
2. R.C.M. 1010.
3. *Id.*
4. *See* Senate Report Number 53, 98th Congress, 1st Session 18 (1983).
5. Military Justice Act of 1983, Pub. L. No. 98-209, § 5(a)(1), 97 Stat. 1393 (1983).
6. *See* Art. 61, U.C.M.J.

(3) The accused has a right to seek relief from the Judge Advocate General if the case is not otherwise reviewed by the Court of Military Review; and

(4) The accused has the right to assistance of counsel in exercising or waiving these rights.[7]

As originally written, the *Manual* required the judge to conduct an inquiry of the accused to determine if he understood his rights. In interpreting this provision, the Court of Military Appeals originally stated that the inquiry must be conducted in open court and must provide the accused with the opportunity to ask questions about those rights.[8] In 1986, however, the drafters amended the *Manual* provision by deleting the requirement that the judge conduct the inquiry.[9] In their view, Congress had only mandated the requirement of giving the advice.[10] The judge's inquiry, the drafters indicated, was unnecessary in view of the fact that defense counsel were responsible for advising the accused concerning appellate rights and procedures.[11]

In *United States v. McIntosh*,[12] however, the Court indicated that the *Manual* provision required that the accused receive his rights advisement in some intelligible form at the end of trial and that he should be given the opportunity to ask the judge about those rights on the record.[13] If the advice is in written form, the judge should give both the accused and his counsel ample time to examine and discuss the material.[14] It should be marked as an appellate exhibit and included in the record of trial.[15] Failure to properly advise the accused of his appellate rights will normally be tested for prejudice.[16]

---

7. R.C.M. 1010. United States v. Alford, 29 M.J. 711 (A.C.M.R. 1989) (reversible error for judge to attempt to dissuade accused from seeking assistance of civilian counsel).
8. United States v. Rogers, 21 M.J. 435 (C.M.A. 1986). In a footnote the court noted they had granted petitions in 14 other cases on this issue. In United States v. Homer, 22 M.J. 294 (C.M.A. 1986), the court ruled that written advice was *not* required.
9. Executive Order 12550 (19 Feb. 1986).
10. R.C.M. 1010 Analysis.
11. R.C.M. 1010 Analysis. United States v. McIntosh, 27 M.J. 204 (C.M.A. 1988) (appropriate for judge to provide form containing advisement of rights).
United States v. Carver, 29 M.J. 568 (A.F.C.M.R. 1989) (trial judge's failure to adequately apprise the accused of his post-trial rights was not prejudicial in light of fact that counsel and accused presented post-trial submissions). *See also* Appendix 38, which includes sample forms that the accused should execute when he desires to waive his appellate rights.
12. 27 M.J. 204 (C.M.A. 1988).
13. *Id.* United States v. Diamond, 30 M.J. 902 (A.F.C.M.R. 1990) (the record should establish that the accused in fact read the written appellate rights form; better practice is to have accused sign the advisement acknowledging receipt of advice and then ask if accused has any questions); United State v. Walther, 30 M.J. 829 (N.M.C.M.R. 1990) (better practice is for judge to inquire on the record whether accused understands rights); United State v. Carver, 29 M.J. 568 (A.F.C.M.R. 1989); United State v. Darby, 27 M.J. 761 (A.F.C.M.R. 1988) (the advice of appellate rights should include the opportunity for the accused to ask the judge questions about those rights; here the failure to do so was harmless error).
14. *See* United State v. Rogers, 21 M.J. 435 (C.M.A. 1986) (judge provided written advice to defense counsel prior to the court's deliberation on the sentence).
15. United State v. Grider, 21 M.J. 603 (A.C.M.R. 1985).
16. United State v. Rogers, 21 M.J. 435 (C.M.A. 1986).

§ 16-13. Adjournment.

Adjournment of the court normally marks the end of the trial proceedings and is usually announced by the judge at the end of the trial. But the *Manual* indicates that at the end of the trial the judge may either adjourn the court-martial or proceed with other cases referred to that particular court.[1] In most cases it will not make any difference whether the court was actually adjourned at the close of a particular case or was adjourned after hearing several cases.

But because adjournment of the court in a case, like an arraignment,[2] marks a clear time line for cutting off certain rights or determining how additional proceedings will be handled, it would seem prudent for the judge to mark the end of each trial with a formal adjournment. For example, certain motions and objections are considered waived if not raised prior to the time that "the court-martial is finally adjourned for that case."[3] After adjournment, the ability to conduct post-trial reconsideration of a sentence[4] or other post-trial sessions may be affected.[5] The trial counsel is charged with promptly notifying appropriate authorities of the findings and the sentence after "final adjournment of the court-martial in a case."[6]

Before adjournment, additional matters may be addressed. In addition to the judge's advice of appellate rights,[7] the judge should determine which of several defense counsel will be responsible for responding to the staff judge advocate's recommendation on the case.[8] And in a bench trial where the accused has entered a plea of guilty in return for a pretrial agreement, the judge should review the agreement and determine whether any problems exist with provisions affecting the sentence.[9]

Although adjournment marks the end of the trial, both trial and defense counsel bear continuing duties to process the record and represent the accused. Those duties are discussed in Chapter 17.

---

1. R.C.M. 1011. For example, following completion of one case, the judge may call an Article 39(a) pretrial session in the next case. *See* Chapter 12.
2. *See* § 12-4.
3. R.C.M. 905(e). *See* § 13-2(B).
4. R.C.M. 1009.
5. *See* R.C.M. 1102 and § 17-3(B) *infra*.
6. R.C.M. 1101.
7. *See* § 16-12.
8. *See* United State v. Robinson, 11 M.J. 218 (C.M.A. 1981). *See also* R.C.M. 1106(f)(2) Discussion.
9. R.C.M. 910(f)(3). United State v. Scanlon, 15 M.J. 823 (A.F.C.M.R. 1983). *Cf.* United State v. Combs, 15 M.J. 743 (A.F.C.M.R. 1983) (comments by counsel made between sentencing and adjournment may not be used to modify sentencing terms in the agreement).

APPENDIX REFERENCES

Appendix 1. Abbreviations.
Appendix 2. Glossary.
Appendix 3. U.C.M.J.
Appendix 6. Sample Charge Sheet.
Appendix 25. Stipulation of Fact.
Appendix 26. Stipulation of Expected Testimony.
Appendix 27. Instructions Checklist.
Appendix 29. Sentencing Worksheet.
Appendix 30. Maximum Punishment Chart.
Appendix 33. Advice on Appellate Rights.
Appendix 38. Waiver/Withdrawal of Appellate Rights.

ANNOTATED BIBLIOGRAPHY

BOOKS

Byrne, *Military Law* (3d ed. 1981).

This second edition work is a good introductory text to military law. It includes text material, discussion cases, self-quizzes, and appendices that contain forms and tables. The discussion cases, although dated, cover significant areas of courts-martial practice.

Military Law Reporter.

This loose-leaf service is published by the Public Law Education Institute. The service consists of six bimonthly issues per volume.

Moyer, *Justice and the Military* (1972).

This one volume loose-leaf reference contains detailed discussions of the role of commanders, jurisdiction, military criminal procedure, first amendment rights, substantive law, and collateral review of courts-martial by the civilian court system.

Saltzburg, Schinasi & Schlueter, *Military Rules of Evidence Manual* (3d ed. 1991).

The authors have compiled the official text of the 1980 Military Rules of Evidence, the Drafters' Analysis to those rules and have provided an editorial comment for each rule which explains the rule, shows how it might be used, and discusses potential problem areas.

PERIODICALS

In General

Chilcoat, "Presentencing Procedure in Courts-Martial," 9 MIL. L. REV. 127 (1960).

Although the article predates the 1969 changes to the U.C.M.J., it presents a very good overview of military sentencing. The author discusses the admissibility of both prosecution and defense evidence and also addresses the topic of counsel's arguments on sentence.

Cohen, "The Two-Thirds Verdict: A Surviving Anachronism in an Age of Court-Martial Evolution," 20 CAL. W. L. REV. 9 (1983).

Through a discussion of the differences between the civilian and military requirements for juries and major case law, this article provides an excellent analysis of the constitutionality of the military jury system. Cohen provides a good overview of the background and structure of the military jury system and includes some original research into how individual military judges administer the jury system.

Hemperley, "Looking Beyond the Verdict: An Examination of Prosecution Sentencing Evidence," 39 A.F. L. REV. 185 (1996).

This article is one of 17 articles in "The Master Criminal Law Edition" of the Air Force Law Review. Noting that there is a tendency for prosecutors to relax after a guilty verdict is returned, the author notes that they have a significant opportunity to affect the accused's sentence and to that end provides prosecutors with insight into effective use of the *Manual* provisions concerning admissibility of evidence during sentencing.

Hunt, "Sentencing in the Military," 10 AM. CRIM. L. REV. 107 (1971).

In 17 pages the writer provides an excellent discussion of the many steps and procedures involved in the military sentencing process and also carefully evaluates the effectiveness of the system, both in comparison with its civilian counterpart and in terms of the goals of military justice.

Lovejoy, "Abolition of Court Members Sentencing in the Military," 142 MIL. L. REV. 1 (1994).

Reciting the historical foundations for sentencing by court members, the author notes that while the control of military justice has shifted away from commanders to lawyers and judges, and presents a sort of cost-benefit analysis in support of judge alone sentencing.

Symposium, "Military Justice," ARMY LAW., March 1996.

This 127-page symposium contains a Foreword and 11 short articles on a wide range of military justice topics. They are as follows:

Morris, "Foreword."
Barto, "Developments in the Substantive Criminal Law Under the Uniform Code of Military Justice."
Frisk, "New Developments in Pretrial Confinement."
Frisk, "New Developments in Speedy Trial."
Winn, "Recent Developments in Military Pretrial and Trial Procedure."
Masterton, "Recent Developments in Search and Seizure Law."
Masterton, "Recent Developments in Urinalysis Law."
Kohlman, "Are You Ready for Some Changes? Five Fresh Views of the Fifth Amendment."

Wright, "Sex, Lies, and Videotape: Child Sexual Abuse Cases Continue to Create Appellate Issues and Other Developments in the Areas of the Sixth Amendment, Discovery, Mental Responsibility, and Nonjudicial Punishment."

Henley, "Caveat Criminale: The Impact of the New Military Rules of Evidence in Sexual Offense and Child Molestation Cases."

Henley, "Current Developments in Evidence Law."

Morris, "New Developments in Sentencing and Post-Trial Procedure."

Arguments by Counsel

Haight, "Argument of Military Counsel on Findings, Sentence and Motions: Limitations and Abuses," 16 Mil. L. Rev. 59 (1962).

Emphasizing that the closing argument can potentially win or lose certain cases, the author provides a useful template to be used by military advocates in preparing their closing arguments. Included in the article is a discussion of relevant case law applicable to closing arguments, along with a proposal for more uniform rules governing this area of the law.

Higginbotham, "The Propriety of Argument by Trial Defense Counsel for Bad-Conduct Discharge," 22 A.F. L. Rev. 81 (1980-1981).

The author reviews those cases wherein the appellate courts have examined the propriety of defense counsel's arguments that a punitive discharge is an appropriate sentence for his client. He suggests that to do so is appropriate if counsel places the client's desire to return to civilian life on the record, distinguishes between a bad-conduct and dishonorable discharge, and argues that a discharge is a fair trade-off for other punishments.

Punishments: In General

Herrington, "Multiplicity in the Military," 134 Mil. L. Rev. 45 (1991).

Noting that "multiplicity" in the military has assumed an identity separate from federal law on the topic, the author discusses the various constitutional, *Manual for Courts-Martial,* and military case-law tests used to determine whether the charges are multiplicious. The author concludes that the problems of dealing with the issue can only be solved if the *Manual* rule is rewritten and the Court of Military Appeals follows Supreme Court precedent.

Kunich, "Drumming Out Ceremonies: Historical Relic or Overlooked Tool?," 39 A.F. L. Rev. 47 (1996).

Tracing the history of ceremonies of ignominy, the author briefly discusses applicable legal and prudential concerns and proposes that within appropriate guidelines commanders may be permitted to conduct public ceremonies for removing unit patches, rank, and other unit-related items before the servicemember is escorted off the installation.

Lance, "A Criminal Punitive Discharge—An Effective Punishment?," 79 Mil. L. Rev. 1 (1978).

By examining punitive discharges in terms of the ultimate effect upon the economic and social opportunities of the discharged individual, the author presents a revealing analysis of the usefulness of punitive discharge in accomplishing military justice goals. Through persuasive empirical evidence the author demonstrates that the punitive discharge has lost much of the odious connotation it once carried and may no longer significantly affect employment opportunities when the individual returns to civilian life.

Punishments: Death Penalty

English, "The Constitutionality of the Court-Martial Death Sentence," 21 A.F. L. Rev. 552 (1979).

In concluding that court-martial sentencing procedures in capital cases adhere completely to the due process requirements of the Constitution as laid out by the Supreme Court, the author briefly traces the recent history of the death penalty in the military and examines the Supreme Court's guidance in this area. Also addressed is the question of whether capital punishment may be imposed for offenses such as treason or spying. The author concludes that it may be imposed.

Pavlick, "The Constitutionality of the U.C.M.J. Death Penalty Provisions," 97 Mil. L. Rev. 81 (1982).

While exploring the U.C.M.J. death penalty in constitutional terms, this article also provides in-depth analysis into some of the major recent cases on capital punishment. In a review of the death penalty, Major Pavlick concludes the U.C.M.J. procedures, while tailored to meet military needs, are well within constitutional bounds and that some of the safeguards provided to servicemen exceed the rights afforded in civilian jurisdictions.

Pfau and Milhizer, "The Military Death Penalty and the Constitution: There is Life After Furman," 97 Mil. L. Rev. 35 (1982).

The co-authors analyze the military death in terms of the landmark case *Furman v. Georgia*, paying special attention to the unique needs and purposes behind the use of capital punishment by the armed forces. Also included is a good general survey of the major cases concerning application of the death penalty and those cases bearing directly on its use by the military.

Russelburg, "The UCMJ's Death Penalty: A Constitutional Assessment," 13 The Advocate 74 (1981).

After briefly reviewing the Supreme Court's decisions in *Furman v. Georgia*, 408 U.S. 238 (1972), and *Gregg v. Georgia*, 428 U.S. 153 (1976), the author concludes that the death penalty provisions in the Uniform Code of Military Justice are probably unconstitutional. He reaches this conclusion after noting that similar provisions in the federal rape statute, *United States v. Quinores*, 353 F. Supp. 1325 (D.P.R. 1973), and *United States v. Bohle*, 346 F. Supp. 577 (N.D.N.Y. 1972), have been ruled invalid.

CHAPTER 17

REVIEW OF COURTS-MARTIAL

Part I
General

§ 17-1. Introduction.
§ 17-2. Post-Trial Duties of Counsel.
    § 17-2(A). Trial Counsel's Duties.
    § 17-2(B). Defense Counsel's Duties.
        § 17-2(B)(1). Advice on Appellate Rights.
        § 17-2(B)(2). Request for Deferment of Confinement, Forfeiture of Pay and Reduction in Grade.
        § 17-2(B)(3). Submission of Matters to the Convening Authority.
        § 17-2(B)(4). Review of the Staff Judge Advocate's Post-Trial Recommendation.
§ 17-3. Post-Trial Proceedings.
    § 17-3(A). Revision Proceedings.
    § 17-3(B). Article 39(a) Post-Trial Sessions.
§ 17-4. Records of Trial.
    § 17-4(A). Authentication of the Record.
    § 17-4(B). Service of Record on Accused.
§ 17-5. Confinement Pending Review.
§ 17-6. Military Corrections.

Part II
Initial Review by the Convening Authority

§ 17-7. Introduction.
§ 17-8. Legal Review of Courts-Martial.
    § 17-8(A). General Matters.
    § 17-8(B). Post-Trial Recommendation.
        § 17-8(B)(1). Format and Contents of Recommendation.
        § 17-8(B)(2). Defective Recommendations.
        § 17-8(B)(3). Service of Recommendation on Defense Counsel.
§ 17-9. Convening Authority's Powers.
    § 17-9(A). General Matters.
    § 17-9(B). Qualified and Disqualified Convening Authorities.
    § 17-9(C). Actions and Execution of Sentences.
    § 17-9(D). Power to Suspend.
    § 17-9(E). Other Clemency Powers.
§ 17-10. Promulgating Orders.
§ 17-11. Post-Trial Delays.

Part III
Appellate Review

§ 17-12. General.
§ 17-13. Waiver or Withdrawal of Appeals.
§ 17-14. Appellate Counsel.
§ 17-15. United States Courts of Criminal Appeals.
    § 17-15(A). Jurisdiction.
    § 17-15(B). Scope of Review and Actions.
    § 17-15(C). Procedural Rules.

§ 17-16. The United States Court of Appeals for the Armed Forces.
 § 17-16(A). General.
 § 17-16(B). Jurisdiction.
 § 17-16(C). Scope of Review.
 § 17-16(D). Procedures.
§ 17-17. Review by the Supreme Court of the United States.

PART IV

OTHER FORMS OF REVIEW

§ 17-18. General.
§ 17-19. Extraordinary Writs in the Military Courts.
§ 17-20. Review in the Offices of the Judge Advocates General.
§ 17-21. Petition for New Trial.
§ 17-22. Administrative Relief.
 § 17-22(A). Boards for the Correction of Military Records.
 § 17-22(B). Discharge Review Boards.
§ 17-23. Review in the Federal Courts.
 § 17-23(A). In General.
 § 17-23(B). The Exhaustion of Remedies Requirement.
 § 17-23(C). Forms of Collateral Review.
  § 17-23(C)(1). Habeas Corpus.
  § 17-23(C)(2). *Mandamus.*
Appendix References.
Annotated Bibliography.

PART I

GENERAL

§ 17-1. Introduction.

An accused convicted by a court-martial is entitled to an automatic review of his trial. Depending on the type of court-martial that heard his case and the nature of the approved sentence, the appeal may proceed all the way to the United States Supreme Court. Because there is no common law right to appeal, the accused's right must derive from statutory or regulatory sources.[1] In the military, the statutory provisions are located in Articles 65 to 76, U.C.M.J.[2] This chapter presents the key procedural and substantive facets of the review of courts-martial. Part I discusses general matters of review. Parts II and III address review by the convening authority, the service appellate courts, the United States Court of Appeals for the Armed Forces, and the Supreme Court of the United States. Finally, additional forums for review, e.g., in the federal courts, are noted in Part IV. As with the court-martial procedures, the military review of the trial operates in a predictable and efficient manner. And as in the previous chapters, pertinent post-trial and appellate forms are included in the Appendices.

---

1. *See* United States v. Larneard, 3 M.J. 76 (C.M.A. 1977).
2. *See* Appendix 3.

§ 17-2. Post-Trial Duties of Counsel.

At the conclusion of the trial, both the defense counsel and the trial counsel are tasked with a variety of post-trial duties and responsibilities. In effect, the representation of their respective clients continues into the post-trial procedures and review.

§ 17-2(A). Trial Counsel's Duties.

The prosecutor's duties after trial are largely administrative in nature and center on reporting the results of the trial,[1] ensuring proper preservation of the exhibits, tapes, and stenographic notes and overseeing preparation of the record of trial.[2] In limited circumstances the trial counsel may be required to authenticate the record of trial.[3] Departmental regulations and local directives may impose additional duties.[4]

§ 17-2(B). Defense Counsel's Duties.

Because the defense counsel's responsibility toward the client continues after trial,[5] he should remain attentive to the client's needs and give whatever assistance he can. The relationship should continue until substitute counsel[6] or appellate counsel[7] have been designated and have assumed responsibility

---

1. Art. 60(a), U.C.M.J. *See also* R.C.M. 1101(a) which provides: (a) *Report of the result of trial.* After final adjournment of the court-martial in a case, the trial counsel shall promptly notify the accused's immediate commander, the convening authority or the convening authority's designee, and, if appropriate, the officer in charge of the confinement facility of the findings and sentence.
R.C.M. 1101(a) is silent as to whether the notice must be in writing. But the topic is mentioned in the nonbinding Discussion of R.C.M. 504(d)(5). Note that the services may provide standard forms for accomplishing this. For example, the Army uses DA Form 4930-R, Report of Result of Trial. For a discussion of what constitutes an "adjournment," see § 16-13.
2. *See* Art. 38(a), U.C.M.J. *See also* § 17-4 and R.C.M. 502(d)(5) Discussion. *See also* Ross, "Post-Trial Processing," ARMY LAW., Feb. 1982, at 23.
3. *See* § 17-4.
4. *See, e.g.,* AR 27-10, para. 5-27, which requires the trial counsel to complete a Result of Trial Form, DA Form 4430-R.
5. *See* United States v. Iverson, 5 M.J. 440 (C.M.A. 1978); United States v. Palenius, 2 M.J. 86 (C.M.A. 1977). *See generally* Pardue & Walinsky, "A Compendium of Post-Trial Considerations for Trial Defense Counsel," 14 THE ADVOCATE 160 (1982).
6. United States v. Polk, 27 M.J. 812 (A.C.M.R. 1988) (extensive discussion of problems associated with military defense counsel being released from active duty before case is finalized).
In United States v. Williams, 28 M.J. 911 (A.C.M.R. 1989), the accused's defense counsel was sent on temporary duty to another location to attend military schooling. The court noted that although counsel was "probably geographically available for all practical purposes" his primary duties had changed and he was not able to provide appropriate advocacy. Thus, the accused was denied effective representation of counsel.
7. *See* § 17-13. United States v. Carmack, 37 M.J. 765 (A.C.M.R. 1993) (civilian defense counsel have continuous duty to represent client during post-trial processing, unless released by client); United States v. Starks, 36 M.J. 1160 (A.C.M.R. 1993) (once established, attorney-client relationship continues until appointment of appellate counsel unless accused releases counsel or good cause is shown on record).

for the case.[8] Note that these standards apply to both civilian and military defense counsel.[9] In addition to the five mandatory duties of (1) advising the accused of his appellate rights, (2) advising of the possibility of deferment of any confinement adjudged by the court, (3) reviewing the record of trial for errors, (4) reviewing the post-trial recommendation, and (5) maintaining the attorney-client relationship,[10] the defense counsel may wish to prepare a clemency petition, submit a rebuttal to the post-trial recommendation, if one was prepared, and prepare an Article 38(c) brief. These of course are nonexclusive options, and throughout the review process, counsel should be ever aware of the possibility of other avenues of post-trial relief. Failure to pursue reasonable courses of action may amount to ineffective assistance of counsel.[11]

§ 17-2(B)(1). Advice on Appellate Rights.

During the post-trial processing of the case, the defense counsel must at some point advise the accused of his various appellate rights.[12] As noted in § 16-12, the judge will apprise the accused of his appellate rights, after sentence has been adjudged but before the court is adjourned.[13] In doing so the judge may inquire as to whether the accused has had an opportunity to consult with counsel about his appellate rights. But this additional advice, which will be reflected in the record, does not relieve the defense counsel from going over the various rights and procedures with the accused.[14] If the counsel has not done so prior to the convening authority's "action" on the case,[15] he should certainly do so afterwards when it is finally known what, if any, relief the convening authority might have granted and the case is ripe for further appellate review. At that point counsel should be prepared to provide a realistic assessment of possible appellate relief. Under the Military Justice Act of 1983, an accused may waive appellate review in cases not involving a sentence of death.[16] Thus, it is particularly important that the accused be fully advised of his appellate options.[17]

---

8. United States v. Iverson, 5 M.J. 440 (C.M.A. 1978). In effect this arrangement is designed to ensure that the accused has the continuous services and representation by counsel. This is particularly important because the military defense counsel who represented the accused at trial is not the counsel who will represent him on appeal.
9. United States v. Jeanbaptiste, 5 M.J. 374 (C.M.A. 1978).
10. United States v. Palenius, 2 M.J. 86 (C.M.A. 1977). Cf. United States v. Edwards, 12 M.J. 781 (A.C.M.R. 1982) (absent agreement to the contrary, attorney-client relationship ends with military counsel's separation from the service). See also R.C.M. 504(d)(6) Discussion, which lists several duties of defense counsel.
11. See, e.g., United States v. Davis, 20 M.J. 1015 (A.C.M.R. 1985) (counsel failed to advise convening authority of judge's strong recommendation for suspension of discharge); United States v. Zapata, 12 M.J. 689 (N.M.C.M.R. 1982) (counsel failed to pursue judge's recommendation for suspension of discharge). See also § 15-2(B)(3) for a discussion on ineffective assistance of counsel.
12. See R.C.M. 502(d)(6) Discussion.
13. R.C.M. 1010.
14. R.C.M. 1010 Discussion.
15. See § 17-9(C).
16. See § 17-13.
17. See § 16-12.

§ 17-2(B)(2). Request for Deferment of Confinement, Forfeiture of Pay and Reduction in Grade.

If the sentence of the court-martial includes confinement at hard labor,[18] the accused must be advised that he may request the convening authority[19] to defer the confinement portion of the sentence[20] that has not been executed.[21]

Deferment is not a clemency action[22] but rather a postponement of the confinement.[23] The request, which must be in writing[24] and becomes a part of the record of trial,[25] may be made at any time after the court has adjourned.[26] The burden rests upon the accused to demonstrate that his interest in being released outweighs the public's interest in his confinement.[27]

In deciding whether to grant the request, the convening authority may consider the probability of flight, probability of other offenses, intimidation of witnesses, nature of offenses, sentence adjudged, accused's record, and personal situation, need for the accused in the command, and the impact of deferment on the command. Note that the convening authority may impose conditions on the deferment.[28]

The convening authority's action must also be written and a copy must be served upon the accused.[29] Denied requests and rescinded deferments may be

---

18. *See* § 16-3(C).
19. R.C.M. 502(d)(6) Discussion. If the accused is no longer located under the command of the convening authority, the officer exercising general court-martial jurisdiction over the installation on which the accused is located may defer confinement. R.C.M. 1101(c)(2). By implication a court-martial may not defer confinement. *See also* 1969 MCM, para. 88f.
20. Art. 57a, U.C.M.J.; R.C.M. 1101(c)(2). *See generally* "Securing 'Bail' for a Military Client Pending Appellate Review of a Court-Martial Conviction and Sentence: Litigating under Art. 57(d)," 9 THE ADVOCATE 8 (1977).

Note that in 1996, Article 57 was amended. Pub. L. No. 104-106, 110 Stat. 186 (1996), National Defense Authorization Act for Fiscal Year (FY) 1996. The first two subsections of that article were left as Article 57 which was retitled, "Effective date for forfeiture of pay and allowances and reduction in grade by sentence of court-martial." Subsections (c) and (d) of that Article, which addressed deferment of confinement, were moved to a new Article 57a, titled "Deferment of confinement." In addition, the new Article changed the word "postponed" to "defer" and a new provision was added for deferring confinement where the Judge Advocate General sends a case to the service appellate court for review under Article 67(a)(2), U.C.M.J. *See* Art. 57a(c). As amended in 1992, the former Article 57(e) permitted a convening authority to stop the concurrent running of a court-martial sentence with a state sentence. That provision is now found in Article 57a(b). *See generally* "Joint Service Committee on Military Justice Report," ARMY LAW., Mar. 1996, at 138.

21. *Id. See also* § 17-9(C).
22. R.C.M. 1101(c)(1) Discussion.
23. R.C.M. 1101(c)(1).
24. R.C.M. 1101(c)(2). United States v. Gacioch, 33 M.J. 727 (N.M.C.M.R. 1991) (pretrial provision automatically amounted to valid, timely post-trial written request for deferment). See Appendix 36 for a sample deferment request. *See generally* United States v. Ledbetter, 2 M.J. 37 (C.M.A. 1976) (convening authority may only act on accused's request).
25. R.C.M. 1101(c)(3) Discussion.
26. R.C.M. 1101(c)(2). *See also* § 16-13.
27. R.C.M. 1101(c)(3).
28. R.C.M. 1101(c)(5). Pearson v. Cox, 10 M.J. 317 (C.M.A. 1981).
29. R.C.M. 1101(c)(3). United States v. Dunlap, 39 M.J. 1120 (A.C.M.R. 1994) (convening authority's failure to provide reasons for denial of deferment makes it difficult to assess decision and

reviewed through a petition for extraordinary relief[30] before either the Courts of Criminal Appeals[31] or the Court of Appeals for the Armed Forces.[32]

The convening authority's action in denying the request or rescinding the deferment will be measured for abuse of discretion.[33] Even though a deferment is granted, it is automatically terminated when the convening authority orders the sentence into execution.[34] The convening authority, however, could at that point suspend the confinement.[35]

Counsel may also file a request with the convening authority to defer the imposition of a sentence of forfeiture of pay or allowances and a reduction of grade.[36] In 1996, Article 57, U.C.M.J. was amended regarding the effective dates of those punishments.[37] Now, any forfeiture of pay or allowances[38] or reduction in grade[39] is effective on the earlier of (1) the date 14 days after the date the sentence was adjudged by the court[40] or (2) the date that the convening authority approves the sentence.[41] Because that latter date will almost always be later than 14 days after the sentence is adjudged, punishments of forfeiture and reduction in grade will become effective before the convening authority approves the findings and sentence.[42] The amended Article, however, provides that the accused may apply for a deferment of the forfeiture or reduction in grade which would otherwise be effective before the convening authority acts on the case.[43] The deferment, which is only effective until the

---

may itself be an abuse of discretion); Sullivan v. LaBoa, 34 M.J. 593 (A.C.M.R. 1992) (ex post facto affidavit from convening authority stating reasons for denying deferment may be considered in determining whether there was abuse of discretion).

30. See § 17-19 for a discussion on extraordinary writs.

31. *See* § 17-15. United States v. Dunlap, 39 M.J. 1120 (A.C.M.R. 1994) (by not timely seeking extraordinary relief, passage of time had mooted meaningful remedies for denial of deferment).

32. *See* § 17-16. Pearson v. Cox, 10 M.J. 317 (C.M.A. 1981); Corly v. Thurman, 3 M.J. 192 (C.M.A. 1977).

33. United States v. Sloan, 35 M.J. 4 (C.M.A. 1992) (convening authority's summary denial of request for deferment was harmless error); Trotman v. Haebel, 12 M.J. 27 (C.M.A. 1981) (burden is on the accused to show improbability of flight or lack of likelihood of crime, intimidation of witnesses or interference with the administration of justice); United States v. Brown, 6 M.J. 338 (C.M.A. 1979) (case contains good discussions of the tests to be applied); United States v. Copeland, 14 M.J. 835 (A.F.C.M.R. 1982) (abuse of discretion where only terse denials were given and accused was good candidate for deferment).

34. R.C.M. 1101(c)(6).

35. R.C.M. 1101(c)(6) Discussion.

36. *See* Art. 57(a), U.C.M.J. Appendix 3. *See also* Art. 58b, U.C.M.J. regarding pay for prisoners. *See generally* "Joint Service Committee on Military Justice Report," ARMY LAW., Mar. 1996, at 138.

37. Section 1121, Pub. L. No. 104-106, 110 Stat. 186 (1996), National Defense Authorization Act for Fiscal Year (FY) 1996. *See generally* "Joint Service Committee on Military Justice Report," ARMY LAW., Mar. 1996, at 138.

38. *See* § 16-3(D), *supra*.

39. *See* § 16-3(E), *supra*.

40. Art. 57(a)(1)(A), U.C.M.J. *See* Appendix 3.

41. Art. 57(a)(1)(B), U.C.M.J.

42. *See* § 17-9(C), *infra*.

43. Art. 57(a)(2), U.C.M.J.

convening authority approves the sentence,[44] may be rescinded at any time before that date.[45]

Because of the short time period between the date the sentence is announced and the effective date of those punishments, wise counsel will have a request for deferment, with supporting reasons, ready to present to the convening authority as soon as possible after the trial is over.[46]

§ 17-2(B)(3). Submission of Matters to the Convening Authority.

At any time after the sentence has been announced,[47] the accused may submit written[48] matters to the convening authority that may "reasonably tend" to affect his decision on whether to approve the findings and sentence of the court-martial.[49] Such matters might include: allegations of legal errors in the trial;[50] copies or extracts of documents offered at trial;[51] matters in mitigation which were not available during the trial;[52] or clemency recommendations.[53] Because the Military Rules of Evidence[54] are not applicable to this material,[55] the defense has a great deal of leeway in submitting matters that would not otherwise have been admissible during the trial itself,[56] as long as the submissions are in writing.[57]

---

44. *Id.*
45. *Id.*
46. Amendments have been proposed to the applicable provisions in the Manual for Courts-Martial to implement the statutory changes. *See* 61 Fed. Reg. 15044-15053 (4 Apr. 1996), 61 Fed. Reg. 18123-24 (25 Apr. 1996).
47. *See* § 16-11. R.C.M. 1105(a). *See generally* Effron, "Post-Trial Submissions to the Convening Authority Under the Military Justice Act of 1983," ARMY LAW., July 1984, at 59.
48. Art. 60(b)(1), U.C.M.J. (Submissions must be in writing.)
49. R.C.M. 1105(b). United States v. Moore, 27 M.J. 656, 657, n. 2 (A.C.M.R. 1988) (submission of legal errors in request for appellate counsel did not constitute submission to convening authority; R.C.M. 1105 matters are "customarily" submitted directly to convening authority).
50. R.C.M. 1105(b)(1). United States v. Moore, 27 M.J. 656 (A.C.M.R. 1988) (legal errors asserted).
51. R.C.M. 1105(b)(2).
52. R.C.M. 1105(b)(3). The Discussion notes the example of an accused's exemplary post-trial behavior. In addition, other letters or evidence not received before the end of trial could be submitted.
53. R.C.M. 1105(b)(4). *See also* United States v. Markland, 2 M.J. 356 (A.F.C.M.R. 1977).
54. *See* Part III, Manual for Courts-Martial.
55. R.C.M. 1105(b).
56. United States v. Davis, 33 M.J. 13 (C.M.A. 1991) (accused submitted videotape; court noted that there is no limitation in Article 60(b) as to the format of the materials presented). Even with a relaxation of the Rules of Evidence during sentencing, *see* § 16-4(B), counsel may possess helpful evidence which was rejected by the military judge during trial.
57. In 1996, Article 60(b)(1) was amended specifically to require that submissions to the convening authority be in writing. Pub. L. No. 104-106, 110 Stat. 186 (1996), National Defense Authorization Act for Fiscal Year (FY) 1996. The change was apparently triggered by United States v. Davis, 33 M.J. 13 (C.M.A. 1991) where the court concluded that it was error for the convening authority not to consider the accused's videotape. Although the convening authority is not required to consider non-written matters, he may still consider such matters. *See generally* "Joint Service Committee on Military Justice Report," ARMY LAW., Mar. 1996, at 138.

§ 17-2(B)(3)

The accused's access to the convening authority in this situation is direct and the matters submitted should not be blocked by either the prosecution or the legal advisor to the convening authority.[58] Indeed, there is apparently no requirement that the defense serve copies of the materials upon anyone other than the convening authority. Nonetheless, as in virtually every other area of practice, it is almost always more prudent to do so and take the surprise out of the case. Once received, the convening authority should provide a copy to his legal advisor for assessment and comments.

If matters have been submitted they must be presented to the convening authority[59] who is then charged with considering them before he acts on the case.[60] In theory, if the matters submitted are completely irrelevant to the case, the convening authority could refuse to consider them. But virtually any matter bearing on the accused or the facts of the case would be relevant.[61] Although the convening authority may decide to interview personally the accused before acting on the case, the accused has no right to demand such an audience.[62] Although the convening authority is required by statute[63] to consider matters presented by the accused, there is no specific guidance on how carefully the convening authority must examine those matters.[64]

In the case of a clemency recommendation, counsel should spell out the reasons for the recommendation and the exact nature of the relief requested.[65] If the recommendation comes from a court member it should not in any way reveal information that might disclose any member's opinion or vote during deliberations.[66] Clemency recommendations from members of the court should not in themselves impeach the findings or sentence of the court.[67]

A commonly used vehicle for presenting information to the convening authority is the "Article 38(c) Brief,"[68] which may contain counsel's presentation of mitigating evidence or arguments of law. The military courts have encour-

---

58. See generally R.C.M. 1105(b) Drafters' Analysis.

59. United States v. Siders, 15 M.J. 272 (C.M.A. 1983); United States v. Jaeger, 27 M.J. 620 (A.C.M.R. 1988) (new review and action required where defense counsel had timely submitted clemency matters but SJA failed to mention that fact to the convening authority).

60. R.C.M. 1107(b)(3)(A)(iii). See also § 17-9.

61. United States v. Davis, 33 M.J. 13 (C.M.A. 1991) (concluding that R.C.M. 1105 is inconsistent with Article 60 insofar as it limits accused to presenting only written materials; SJA was incorrect in advising convening authority that he did not have to view accused's videotape; court further held that convening authority in good faith may determine how much consideration to give to any matters submitted by an accused — he is not required to closely examine all of the matters presented).

62. See United States v. Lanford, 6 C.M.A. 371, 20 C.M.R. 87 (1955); United States v. Goode, 1 M.J. 3 (C.M.A. 1975); United States v. Koonce, 16 M.J. 660 (A.C.M.R. 1983).

63. Art. 60, U.C.M.J. United States v. Wilson, 33 M.J. 512 (A.F.C.M.R. 1991) (convening authority has a statutory duty to consider matters submitted by accused).

64. See United States v. Davis, 33 M.J. 13 (C.M.A. 1991) (concluding that convening authority in good faith may determine how much consideration to give to any matters submitted by an accused; he is not required to closely examine all of the matters presented).

65. R.C.M. 1105(b)(4) Discussion.

66. Id. See also Rule 606, Mil. R. Evid.

67. R.C.M. 1105(b)(4) Discussion.

68. Art. 38(c), U.C.M.J. See Appendix 3. See generally Shaw, "The Article 38(c) Brief. A Renewed Vitality," Army Law., June 1975, at 2.

aged the use of this brief,[69] which becomes a part of the record and will be considered at all levels of review.[70] In many cases a well-written brief will serve as invaluable assistance to appellate defense counsel in framing issues for review by the courts. No particular format is required. If the brief raises legal issues, the staff judge advocate or legal officer will be required to address those issues in his post-trial recommendation to the convening authority.[71]

The U.C.M.J. and the Manual for Courts-Martial contain some specific rules regarding the timeliness of submitting matters to the convening authority.[72] As originally written, the rules were complex and administratively difficult to track. In 1986, Congress wisely simplified the rules.[73] In the case of a general court-martial or a special court-martial, the accused must submit his materials within 10 days of receiving an authenticated copy of the record of trial or the recommendation of the staff judge advocate or legal officer, whichever is later.[74] And for summary courts-martial, the accused must submit his materials within 7 days of the announcement of the sentence.[75] The convening authority may grant extensions of time if the accused can show good cause.[76] Conducting post-trial sessions, discussed at § 17-3, will not toll the time periods unless a new sentence is announced.[77] In that case the time starts from that announcement.[78] Failure to submit the matters in a timely fashion waives the right to do so.[79] Although the right to waive submission of matters is the accused's to exercise,[80] failure of counsel to do so may constitute ineffective assistance of counsel.[81] Counsel's representations that the accused did not

---

69. *See* United States v. Fagnan, 12 C.M.A. 192, 30 C.M.R. 192 (1961).

70. Failure to include it in the record may constitute prejudicial error. United States v. Harrison, 16 C.M.A. 484, 37 C.M.R. 104 (1967) (error to omit submitted clemency matters).

71. R.C.M. 1106(d)(4). *See also* § 17-8.

72. Art. 60, U.C.M.J.

73. *See* Military Justice Amendments of 1986, Title VIII, § 802, National Defense Authorization Act for Fiscal Year 1987, Pub. L. No. 99-661, 100 Stat. 3900 (1986).

74. R.C.M. 1105(c).

75. Art. 60(b)(1), U.C.M.J.

76. Art. 60(b)(2), U.C.M.J. United States v. Henry, 37 M.J. 968 (A.C.M.R. 1993) (convening authority did not err in considering accused's untimely submission of clemency matters); United States v. Jackson, 30 M.J. 687 (A.C.M.R. 1990) (convening authority did not abuse discretion in granting accused only an additional seven days); United States v. Derksen, 24 M.J. 818 (A.C.M.R. 1987) (counsel's refusal to accept substitute service of record of trial did not constitute good cause to delay submission of materials); United States v. Pippin, 22 M.J. 806 (A.F.C.M.R. 1986).

77. R.C.M. 1105(c)(3). *See* § 17-3(A).

78. R.C.M. 1105(c)(3).

79. R.C.M. 1105(d)(1). United States v. Euring, 27 M.J. 843 (A.C.M.R. 1989); United States v. Angelo, 25 M.J. 834 (A.C.M.R. 1988) (submission waived). The accused may also affirmatively waive the right in writing. R.C.M. 1105(d)(3). And a partial submission may waive submission of additional matters unless the right to do so is reserved in writing.

80. United States v. Horne, 33 M.J. 575 (N.M.C.M.R. 1991) (defense counsel's indication that accused did not wish to present any matters did not constitute waiver where accused had made it clear that he desired own copy of SJA's recommendation); United States v. Lichtsinn, 32 M.J. 898 (A.F.C.M.R. 1991) (accused waived right to present matters to convening authority although waiver was not endorsed personally by him); United States v. Shaw, 30 M.J. 1033 (A.F.C.M.R. 1990) (waiver of right to submit matters rests with the accused, not his counsel).

81. United States v. Spurlin, 33 M.J. 443 (C.M.A. 1991) (counsel was ineffective in submitting matters to convening authority; court remanded for new advice and action); United States v.

desire to submit matters to the convening authority will normally be presumed to reflect the accused's wishes.[82]

Because the staff judge advocate is no longer required to point out mitigating evidence to the convening authority in his post-trial recommendation,[83] it is even more important for counsel to consider submission of such materials to the convening authority.[84] Failure to raise issues that would reasonably tend to affect the convening authority's decision will probably be waived if not raised first before the convening authority[85] and may result in ineffective assistance of counsel.[86]

There has been a great deal of litigation on the issue of whether the convening authority ever actually received and considered the matters submitted by the accused.[87] In those cases where there has been some real question on that point, the government has generally been successful in creating a paper trail that indicates that the matters were indeed delivered to the convening authority.[88]

All matters submitted by the accused must be included in the record of trial.[89]

Sosebee, 35 M.J. 892 (A.C.M.R. 1992) (counsel was not ineffective in not submitting matters to convening authority; counsel had requested extensions of time, but was told that no further extensions were permitted; court added that SJA, who discourages submissions after 30-day limit but before convening authority acts, is creating needless litigation).

82. United States v. Thomas, 32 M.J. 897 (A.F.C.M.R. 1991) (court applied presumption of regularity to defense counsel's representations that accused would not present any materials to convening authority).

83. R.C.M. 1106(d)(3). See also § 17-8.

84. R.C.M. 1105 Drafters' Analysis. United States v. Davis, 20 M.J. 980 (A.C.M.R. 1985).

85. See, e.g., United States v. Davis, 20 M.J. 980 (A.C.M.R. 1985) (failure of defense to challenge the possible disparity in the punishments adjudged against the accused and a co-actor in a posttrial submission under R.C.M. 1105 or 1106 will normally waive the issue).

86. See, e.g., United States v. Spurlin, 33 M.J. 443 (C.M.A. 1991) (counsel was ineffective in submitting matters to convening authority in timely fashion and court remanded for new advice and action).

87. See, e.g., United States v. Hallums, 26 M.J. 838 (A.C.M.R. 1988) (case points out problems associated with showing that convening authority actually saw clemency matters; court suggested that convening authority could initial and date all documents considered); United States v. Johnson, 26 M.J. 509, 511, n.2 (A.C.M.R. 1988); United States v. McClelland, 25 M.J. 903, 905 (A.C.M.R. 1988). Cf. United States v. Moody, 27 M.J. 683 (A.C.M.R. 1988) (harmless error for SJA to fail to note in his recommendation that clemency matters had been submitted by the defense and that the convening authority considered them).

88. See, e.g., United States v. Kimble, 35 M.J. 904 (A.C.M.R. 1992) (no requirement that posttrial documents contain affirmative statement that convening authority has reviewed matters submitted by defense where SJA's recommendation states that matters have been submitted and are attached; court urged use of Correspondence Manual under AR 25-50); United States v. Komorous, 33 M.J. 907 (A.F.C.M.R. 1991) (government submitted affidavits indicating that convening authority did consider the matters submitted by the defense).

89. See R.C.M. 1103(b)(3)(C). United States v. Hallums, 26 M.J. 838 (A.C.M.R. 1988) (appellate court would not guess whether clemency matters, which were noted but not included within record of trial, were ever submitted to convening authority); United States v. Moore, 27 M.J. 656 (A.C.M.R. 1988).

§ 17-2(B)(4). Review of the Staff Judge Advocate's Post-Trial Recommendation.

In certain cases the Staff Judge Advocate (or legal officer) is required to present a written legal opinion on the case to the convening authority.[90] Where such a recommendation is prepared it must be served[91] on the defense counsel who will be given an opportunity to examine it and prepare a rebuttal, which is attached to the recommendation and considered by the convening authority.[92] Absent an extension of time,[93] failure to note any defects within a period of 10 days[94] of service of the recommendation or receipt of the record of trial, whichever is later, will almost always constitute waiver of those defects.[95] Even where the defense has not been served with a copy of the recommendation before the convening authority acts on the case, the military appellate courts have indicated that the burden rests upon the defense to obtain a copy of the recommendation, raise any objections and ask the appellate court to remand the case to the convening authority for further consideration.[96] For

---

90. *See* § 17-8.
91. The post-trial review should include a certificate of service. *See* Appendix 37. *See generally* Thorne, "SJA Reviews and *United States v. Goode*," ARMY LAW., Nov. 1975, at 17. Service may be by mail. United States v. Kincheloe, 14 M.J. 40 (C.M.A. 1982).
92. R.C.M. 1106(f). The defense is apparently not limited to the contents of the record of trial in responding to the recommendation. United States v. Hawkins, 24 M.J. 257 (C.M.A. 1987). Addendums to the recommendation must also be served. United States v. Ricks, 21 M.J. 569 (A.C.M.R. 1985); United States v. Pryor, 19 M.J. 720 (A.C.M.R. 1984).
93. The convening authority in his discretion may extend the time for up to an additional 20 days for good cause shown. R.C.M. 1106(f)(5). *See, e.g.,* United States v. Jones, 12 M.J. 833 (N.M.C.M.R. 1981) (CA did not abuse discretion in denying defense request for 15 days to respond to SJA review); United States v. Pearson, 15 M.J. 888 (A.C.M.R. 1983) (CA did not abuse discretion in denying extension where DC had 7 days to review it; court suggested that routinely granting such requests might save appellate time).
94. United States v. Goode, 1 M.J. 3 (C.M.A. 1975) (establishing rule for post-trial reviews); United States v. Annis, 5 M.J. 351 (C.M.A. 1978). The *Goode* time limit, later adopted in the 1984 revision of the *Manual*, was 5 days. For a thorough review of this procedure, see Gravelle, "Some *Goode* News and Some Bad News," ARMY LAW., Feb. 1979, at 1. Note that the time period refers to calendar days, not workdays. United States v. Mendoza, 18 M.J. 576 (A.F.C.M.R. 1984).
The 10-day (formerly 5-day) period is a mandatory minimum time span. United States v. Parks, 6 M.J. 11 (C.M.A. 1978) (misc. docket). *See also* United States v. Mercier, 5 M.J. 866 (A.F.C.M.R. 1978) (counsel's tardy rebuttal waived errors).
95. R.C.M. 1106(f)(6). United States v. Goode, 1 M.J. 3 (C.M.A. 1975). The courts have generally followed this doctrine, United States v. Morrison, 3 M.J. 408 (C.M.A. 1977), except where a manifest miscarriage of justice may occur. *See, e.g.,* United States v. Walsh, 36 M.J. 666 (N.M.C.M.R. 1992) (failure to note defect, fact that military judge had ruled that offenses were multiplicious, in recommendation waived issue); United States v. Wilson, 33 M.J. 512 (A.F.C.M.R. 1991) (defense counsel's failure to correct mistake in SJA's advice concerning maximum punishment was waived); United States v. Veney, 6 M.J. 794 (A.C.M.R. 1978). *See also* United States v. Davis, 6 M.J. 874, 879, n.18 (A.C.M.R. 1979) (counsel should provide correct information where review is in error). *Cf.* United States v. Breseman, 21 M.J. 973 (C.G.C.M.R. 1986) (no waiver under "abnormal" circumstances).
96. *See, e.g.,* United States v. Smart, 21 M.J. 15 (C.M.A. 1985) (rejected argument that only service of recommendation will trigger counsel's duty to respond); United States v. Barnette, 21 M.J. 749 (N.M.C.M.R. 1985); United States v. Diamond, 18 M.J. 305 (C.M.A. 1984) (*Goode* rights were denied where the defense counsel was not provided an opportunity to present matters to the

a discussion on the problem of service of the recommendation where the accused has several defense counsel, see § 17-8(B)(3).

If the Staff Judge Advocate prepares an addendum to his or her recommendation,[97] both the defense counsel and the accused are to be served.[98] The defense has ten days to respond unless the Staff Judge Advocate grants an extension of up to 20 days.[99] Only the convening authority may deny such a request.[100]

§ 17-3. Post-Trial Proceedings.

After the court has adjourned it may become necessary to conduct a post-trial proceeding.[1] For example, it may be necessary for the judge to inquire into post-trial allegations of irregularities in the trial or to clarify matters left unresolved at the conclusion of the trial. The nature of these proceedings and the authority to conduct them is the subject of this section. In some instances the lines distinguishing the various types of post-trial proceedings may be dim and inconsequential.[2] In other instances, the purpose of the proceeding may strictly dictate the ability to convene and conduct the proceeding.[3] Post-trial proceedings may be requested by either side or may be *sua sponte* ordered by either the military judge or the convening authority.[4] The judge's authority to order such proceedings ends with his authentication of the record of trial.[5] The

---

convening authority before he took action on the case; once a CA has acted he may not reconsider that action unless the case has been remanded to him); United States v. Babcock, 14 M.J. 34 (C.M.A. 1982); United States v. Kincheloe, 14 M.J. 40 (C.M.A. 1982).

97. See § 17-8(B)(3).
98. R.C.M. 1107(f)(7).
99. R.C.M. 1105(c)(1).
100. R.C.M. 1105(c)(1).

1. R.C.M. 1102. *Cf.* United States v. Reed, 41 M.J. 755 (C.G.Ct.Crim.App. 1995) (court validated post-trial procedure used by judge, prior to authentication of record, to clarify potential inconsistencies between what accused said in providency inquiry and in unsworn statement; judge submitted written questions to accused; judge first conducted R.C.M. 802 Conference by telephone with counsel to determine course of action; opinion includes copies of pertinent documents). *See generally* Peace, "Post-Trial Proceedings," ARMY LAW., Oct. 1985, at 20.

2. *See, e.g.,* United States v. Crowell, 21 M.J. 760 (N.M.C.M.R. 1985) (trial judge held what he called a "rehearing" to re-sentence the accused; but in approving the procedure the court declined to label the proceeding and simply indicated that the judge had the authority to conduct it); United States v. Brickey, 16 M.J. 258 (C.M.A. 1983) (discussion of various post-trial proceedings).

3. For example, if it is necessary to conduct a proceeding that would involve further deliberation by the court members, a revision proceeding rather than an Article 39(a) session should be ordered. It may be that during a post-trial Article 39(a) session it will become apparent that a revision proceeding is required. In that case either the judge or convening authority should formally order that proceeding.

4. R.C.M. 1102(a). *See also* United States v. Roman, 22 C.M.A. 78, 46 C.M.R. 78 (1972).

5. R.C.M. 1102(d). R.C.M. 1102(b)(2), was amended in 1994 to clarify the judge's post-trial authority to call an Article 39(a) session to reconsider a trial ruling which substantially affects the legal sufficiency of a finding of guilty before the record is authenticated, and without waiting for an order from an appellate court. United States v. Toy, 32 M.J. 753 (A.C.M.R. 1991) (military judge may conduct a session after trial before the record is authenticated). *See generally* Woolf, "Post-Trial Authority of the Military Judge," ARMY LAW., Jan. 1991, at 27.

convening authority's power ends when he takes his action on the case.[6] Upon remand from an appellate court or supervisory authority he may regain that power, however.[7]

Presence of the participants will be dictated by the nature and purpose of the proceeding. For example, a post-trial Article 39(a) session would be conducted without the court members being present.[8] But a revision proceeding to reconsider an improper sentence would require the presence of all parties, including the members.[9] The *Manual* recognizes that in some circumstances the delay in conducting post-trial proceedings may result in some of the original parties being absent and provides guidance on absences and substitutions.[10]

Post-trial proceedings may not be used to: (1) reconsider a finding of not guilty on any specification or of a ruling that amounts to a finding of not guilty;[11] (2) reconsider a finding of not guilty on any charge unless the accused has been found guilty under that charge of a specification that alleges a violation of a punitive article;[12] or (3) increase the amount of punishment unless a particular sentence is mandatory.[13]

Post-trial proceedings are to be conducted in open session[14] and recorded, authenticated and served just as with the record of trial on the original proceedings.[15]

§ 17-3(A). Revision Proceedings.

Article 60(e), U.C.M.J. provides that the convening authority may order a proceeding in revision to correct an error or omission, or any other irregularity in the trial.[16] R.C.M. 1102(a) extends similar powers to the military judge until he has authenticated the record of trial.[17] Revision proceedings have been used to conduct a further inquiry into pretrial agreements,[18] correct an

---

6. R.C.M. 1102(d). *See, e.g.*, United States v. McIntosh, 25 M.J. 837 (A.C.M.R. 1988).
7. R.C.M. 1102(d). United States v. Luedtke, 19 M.J. 548 (N.M.C.M.R. 1984).
8. Art. 39(a), U.C.M.J. See also § 12-1 for a discussion of the nature of Article 39(a) sessions.
9. R.C.M. 1102(e)(1)(A).
10. For a revision proceeding, which arguably is an extension or continuation of the trial, absence of some members will not void the proceeding if the jurisdictionally minimum number of members are present, i.e., 5 for a general court-martial and 3 for a special court. R.C.M. 1102(e)(1)(A). The military judge may be replaced if he is not reasonably available. *Id.*
In an Article 39(a) session the judge may be replaced for good cause. R.C.M. 1102(e)(1)(B).
11. Art. 60(e)(2)(A), U.C.M.J.; R.C.M. 1102(c)(1). *Cf.* United States v. Griffith, 27 M.J. 42 (C.M.A. 1988) (trial judge may set aside findings where, after members have returned finding of guilty, he concludes that the government's evidence is legally insufficient to support finding of guilty).
12. Art. 60(e)(2)(B), U.C.M.J.; R.C.M. 1102(c)(2).
13. Art. 60(e)(2)(C), U.C.M.J.; R.C.M. 1102(c)(3). *See, e.g.*, Art. 106 (mandatory sentence of death for accused convicted of spying).
14. *See* R.C.M. 1102(e)(3).
15. R.C.M. 1102(e)(3). United States v. Scaff, 26 M.J. 985 (A.F.C.M.R. 1988). *See also* § 17-4.
16. Art. 60(e)(1), U.C.M.J. R.C.M. 1102(b)(1), (d).
17. R.C.M. 1102(d). *See also* § 17-4(A).
18. *See, e.g.*, United States v. Steck, 10 M.J. 412 (C.M.A. 1981); United States v. Dorsey, 26 M.J. 538 (A.F.C.M.R. 1988) (trial judge *sua sponte* conducted revision proceeding to inquire into propriety of provision in pretrial agreement which violated Air Force policy).

erroneous announcement of findings[19] or sentence,[20] and to reconsider a sentence based in part upon inadmissible evidence.[21]

The proceedings may not be ordered if the correction will result in material prejudice to the substantial rights of the accused.[22] This usually means that revision proceedings may not be used to supply omitted instructions on elements of an offense[23] or on sentencing.[24] Nor may revision proceedings be used to present additional evidence.[25]

If it appears that the record fails to reflect what actually occurred then the proper procedure is to prepare a "certificate of correction" rather than conduct a post-trial revision session.[26] For example, the record may fail to properly reflect that the court members were sworn when in fact they were. Normally it is not necessary to conduct a post-trial session to correct that defect in the record.[27]

§ 17-3(B). Article 39(a) Post-Trial Sessions.

Although the original purpose of Article 39(a), U.C.M.J.[28] was limited to conducting sessions before and during trial to consider various matters that could be resolved without the court members present, the 1984 revisions to the *Manual* extended the utility of such sessions to the post-trial stage.[29] The extension was apparently based upon *United States v. Brickey*,[30] where the court indicated that a military judge possessed the power to conduct, on his

---

19. United States v. Downs, 4 C.M.A. 8, 15 C.M.R. 8 (1954).
20. United States v. Liberator, 14 C.M.A. 499, 34 C.M.R. 279 (1964); United States v. Robinson, 4 C.M.A. 12, 15 C.M.R. 12 (1954); United States v. Jackson, 34 M.J. 1145 (A.C.M.R. 1992) (military judge erred in conducting post-trial revision proceeding where court members ignored his instruction to begin voting on lightest sentence; court held that different sentencing authority should have been used); United States v. Feld, 27 M.J. 537 (A.C.M.R. 1988) (revision proceeding held to determine ambiguity in announcement of forfeiture portion of sentence).
21. United States v. Carpenter, 15 C.M.A. 526, 36 C.M.R. 24 (1965).
22. Art. 60(e)(1), U.C.M.J. R.C.M. 1102(b)(1).
23. United States v. Worsham, 10 C.M.R. 653 (A.F.B.R. 1953); United States v. Evans, 5 C.M.R. 585 (A.F.B.R. 1952); United States v. Stubblefield, 2 C.M.R. 637 (A.F.B.R. 1951).
24. United States v. Roman, 22 C.M.A. 78, 46 C.M.R. 78 (1972).
25. R.C.M. 1102(b)(1) Discussion.
26. *See* R.C.M. 1104(d); United States v. Mosly, 35 M.J. 693 (N.M.C.M.R. 1992) (appellate court has discretion to consider certificate of correction on sentence; court distinguished United States v. Baker, 32 M.J. 290 (C.M.A. 1991), re inability of authorities to correct sentence upward no matter what judge or court members intended).
27. R.C.M. 1104(d)(1) Discussion. However, that same rule recognizes that in some instances it may be necessary to conduct an evidentiary hearing. R.C.M. 1104(d)(2) Discussion. The accused need not be present. *Id.*
28. *See* Appendix 3.
29. R.C.M. 1102(b)(2). R.C.M. 1102(b)(2), was amended in 1994 to clarify the judge's post-trial authority to call an Article 39(a) session to reconsider a trial ruling which substantially affects the legal sufficiency of a finding of guilty before the record is authenticated, and without waiting for an order from an appellate court.
30. 16 M.J. 258 (C.M.A. 1983). *See also* United States v. Griffith, 27 M.J. 42 (C.M.A. 1988) for a discussion of the military judge's post-trial authority to set aside findings of guilt.

own motion, a *Dubay* hearing at any time prior to authentication of the record of trial.[31]

The genesis of *Dubay* hearings is *United States v. Dubay*[32] in which the Court of Military Appeals remanded the case for a limited hearing on the issue of unlawful command control. The trial court was directed to conduct additional hearings and enter findings on specified matters.[33] Typically, the *Dubay* hearings have been ordered by the appellate courts to develop more fully the factual basis for an issue raised on appeal.[34] But R.C.M. 1102 exceeds the normal scope of *Dubay* and authorizes the military judge to inquire into and resolve "any matter which arises after trial and which substantially affects the legal sufficiency of any findings of guilty or the sentence."[35] The Discussion to that Rule indicates that an example would be an inquiry into allegations of misconduct by a member or counsel.[36] But the language of the Rule is obviously broad and would include inquiries into virtually any aspect of the trial.[37] For example, the defense could present additional evidence that the court lacked jurisdiction[38] and R.C.M. 1102 arguably permits the judge to resolve the problem by dismissing the charges.[39] That authority apparently

---

31. 16 M.J. at 265.
32. 17 C.M.A. 147, 37 C.M.R. 411 (1967).
33. The court said:

> He [the law officer] will hear the respective contentions of the parties on the question, permit the presentation of witnesses and evidence in support thereof, and enter findings of fact and conclusions of law based thereon. If he determines the proceedings by which the accused was originally tried were infected with command control, he will set aside the findings or sentence, or both, as the case may require, and proceed with the necessary rehearing. If he determines command control did not exist, he will return the record to the convening authority....

United States v. Dubay, 17 C.M.A. at 149, 37 C.M.R. at 413 (1967); United States v. Sanders, 37 M.J. 1005 (A.C.M.R. 1993) (at *DuBay* hearing, judge is not required to state findings orally in court; they may be made either orally or in writing).

34. United States v. Flint, 1 M.J. 428 (C.M.A. 1976). *See also* United States v. King, 24 M.J. 774 (A.C.M.R. 1987) (*Dubay* hearing had been ordered at 17 M.J. 403 to determine whether accused was insane; the opinion includes an appendix setting out what the hearing was to determine); United States v. Turner, 15 M.J. 754 (A.F.C.M.R. 1983) (*Dubay* hearing on Jencks Act issue).

35. R.C.M. 1102(b)(2). In United States v. Toy, 32 M.J. 753 (A.C.M.R. 1991), the court concluded that the military judge had the authority to hear testimony and make findings of fact and conclusions of law. The court recommended that when such hearings are held at the direction of the convening authority, he should provide specific instructions. *See, e.g.,* United States v. Copening, 32 M.J. 512 (A.C.M.R. 1990).

36. R.C.M. 1102(b)(2) Discussion. United States v. Wallace, 28 M.J. 640 (A.F.C.M.R. 1989) (military judge should have *sua sponte* conducted an Article 39(a) session when he heard allegations that the court had improperly considered the possibility of an administrative discharge). *Cf.* United States v. Boland, 22 M.J. 886 (A.C.M.R. 1986).

37. R.C.M. 1102(b)(2) Analysis, Change 7. The Analysis indicates that the session, which may be called sua sponte by the judge, may be used, inter alia, to inquire into instructional errors, misconduct of counsel, witnesses, or counsel, or legal sufficiency of the evidence.

38. *See* Chapter 4.
39. *See* § 13-3(A).

also extends to considering evidence that might raise some doubt about the accused's guilt.[40]

In *United States v. Scaff*,[41] the court solidified the military judge's authority to take remedial action on a case before the record of trial is authenticated. The court ruled that the trial judge could convene a post-trial Article 39(a) session to consider newly discovered evidence and may, in appropriate cases, set aside the findings and sentence. The government could then appeal that ruling under Article 62.[42] The court also discussed the judge's authority to enforce his rulings that civilian witnesses should be called to testify.[43]

§ 17-4. Records of Trial.

In every court-martial a record of trial must be prepared and authenticated.[1] In cases resulting in acquittals, the record need only establish that there was jurisdiction over the accused and the offenses and that the court was properly convened and constituted.[2] In a case resulting in a conviction the type of court and the sentence adjudged will determine whether the record will be "verbatim"[3] or "summarized." The summary court-martial record is DD Form 2329, a two-page form.[4] The record of a special court-martial may be summarized unless a bad-conduct discharge was adjudged, in which case it

---

40. United States v. Griffith, 27 M.J. 42 (C.M.A. 1988) (trial judge may set aside findings of guilt returned by court members where he believes that government's evidence of guilt was legally insufficient). In United States v. Scaff, 26 M.J. 985 (A.F.C.M.R. 1988), the court distinguished United States v. Washington, 23 M.J. 679 (A.C.M.R. 1986) and held that the trial judge was not authorized to reconsider his findings of guilt at a post-trial session where defense presented additional defense evidence.

In United States v. Washington, 23 M.J. 679 (A.C.M.R. 1986), the court in dicta indicated that a military judge's authority under R.C.M. 1102 includes the power to accept post-trial changes in the accused's guilty plea to a lesser included offense. The court indicated that R.C.M. 924(c), which indicates that a trial judge may reconsider a finding of guilty at any time before the sentence is announced, is not a limitation on that authority. *See also* § 14-3(G).

41. 29 M.J. 60 (C.M.A. 1989). United States v. Williams, 37 M.J. 352 (C.M.A. 1993) (military judge relied upon decision in *Scaff* to hold post-trial hearing on whether to grant defense motion for a rehearing based upon the discovery of new evidence; court concluded that trial court abused its discretion in denying the motion).

United States v. Mahoney, 36 M.J. 679 (A.F.C.M.R. 1992) (in lengthy discussion of the petition for mandamus, instituted by the United States to order circuit military judge to desist involvement in the case, the court concluded that the military judge did not usurp his judicial powers by appointing himself to case and conducting post-trial session to determine if commander had basis for confining accused after predecessor judge ordered him released; the judge did not engage in unlawful command influence by conducting post-trial session). See 1994 amendments to R.C.M. 1102(b)(2) which apparently adopted the court's reasoning in United States v. Griffith, 27 M.J. 42 (C.M.A. 1988) which clarifies the authority of the military judge to conduct Article 39(a) post-trial sessions.

42. Art. 60, U.C.M.J.
43. *See also* Chapter 11.
1. Art. 54, U.C.M.J. *See* Appendix 3. R.C.M. 1103(a).
2. R.C.M. 1103(e).
3. R.C.M. 1103(e). *See also* AR 27-10, para. 5-37 *et seq.* (preparation of records of trial).
4. R.C.M. 1103(d). *See also* Appendix 15 in the Manual for Courts-Martial.

must be verbatim.[5] The record of a general court-martial must be verbatim unless (1) the sentence does not include a discharge, and (2) the sentence does not exceed that which could be imposed by a special court-martial.[6]

Although records of trial are often labelled as being either verbatim or summarized, the terms actually relate to the transcript of the proceedings. The Discussion to R.C.M. 1103(b)(2)(B) specifies the contents of a verbatim transcript. A verbatim transcript includes: all proceedings including sidebar conferences,[7] arguments of counsel,[8] and rulings[9] and instructions by the military judge;[10] matter that the military judge orders stricken from the record or disregarded;[11] and when a record is amended in revision proceedings[12] the part of the original record changed and the changes made, without physical alteration of the original record.[13] Although conferences conducted under R.C.M. 802[14] need not be recorded, any agreements reached during those conferences must be included.[15] If a verbatim transcript is not required, a "summarized report of the proceedings" may be used.[16]

An abbreviated record is also permitted in those cases where the accused has been found not guilty only by reason of lack of mental responsibility[17] or where the case has been terminated by withdrawal of charges, dismissal before findings, or mistrial.[18]

The trial counsel is ultimately responsible for proper preparation,[19] although as a practical matter it is the court reporter who actually prepares the

---

5. R.C.M. 1103(c). *Cf.* Art. 19, U.C.M.J., which requires a "complete" record as a prerequisite. A complete record is not necessarily a verbatim record. United States v. McCullah, 11 M.J. 234 (C.M.A. 1981); United States v. Wynn, 23 M.J. 726 (A.F.C.M.R. 1986) (omission of diagram from record made it incomplete but did not make it nonverbatim; the accused suffered no prejudice from the omission).
6. R.C.M. 1103(b)(2)(B).
7. R.C.M. 1103(b)(2)(B) Discussion. United States v. Eichenlaub, 11 M.J. 239 (C.M.A. 1981) (omission of conversation regarding sentencing); United States v. Sturdivant, 1 M.J. 256 (C.M.A. 1976) (important side bar discussion omitted; not verbatim record of trial); United States v. Martin, 5 M.J. 657 (N.C.M.R. 1978) (verbatim sentencing proceedings not enough to create verbatim record for whole trial). *Cf.* United States v. Velis, 7 M.J. 699 (N.C.M.R. 1979) (insubstantial omission where en masse arraignment not transcribed).
8. R.C.M. 1103(b)(2)(B) Discussion. *See also* § 16-8 (counsel's arguments).
9. R.C.M. 1103(b)(2)(B) Discussion.
10. *Id.*
11. *Id.*
12. *See* R.C.M. 1102.
13. R.C.M. 1103(b)(2)(B) Discussion.
14. *See* Chapter 12.
15. R.C.M. 1103(b)(2)(B) Discussion. *See, e.g.*, United States v. Garcia, 24 M.J. 518 (A.F.C.M.R. 1987) (failure to record a R.C.M. 802 conference, during which counsel and the judge discussed issues concerning the providency of the accused's guilty plea, resulted in nonverbatim record; although the normal remedy is to approve a sentence appropriate for a nonverbatim trial, in this case the court set aside the findings and sentence because the void in the proceedings prevented it from conducting a full judicial review of the trial).
16. R.C.M. 1103(b)(2)(C).
17. R.C.M. 1103(e).
18. *Id.*
19. Art. 38(a), U.C.M.J. R.C.M. 1103(i), 502(d)(5).

record. If portions of the record are missing or incomplete, the trial counsel may attempt to reconstruct it.[20]

Before submitting the record of trial to the military judge for authentication, see § 17-4(A), infra, the defense counsel should be provided with a copy, unless unreasonable delay will result.[21] If the defense counsel discovers errors, counsel may submit an Article 38(c) brief,[22] inform the trial counsel of the errors,[23] or notify the authenticating official of the errors.[24] In reviewing the record for errors, defense counsel should have access to the court reporter's notes and tapes.[25] Failure to provide the record to the defense before authentication will be examined for prejudice.[26]

In reviewing the issue of whether a verbatim record has been prepared, the appellate courts have focused on the question of whether missing exhibits,[27] testimony,[28] transcript of proceedings[29] or other documents[30] have resulted in omissions. Even assuming the record is incomplete, before granting any relief the appellate court must determine that the omissions were "substantial" and thus resulted in a nonverbatim record.[31] If substantial omissions are found in

---

20. *See, e.g.,* United States v. Dornick, 16 M.J. 642 (A.F.C.M.R. 1983).
21. R.C.M. 1103(i)(1)(B). United States v. Anderson, 12 M.J. 195 (C.M.A. 1982); United States v. Bryant, 37 M.J. 668 (A.C.M.R. 1993) (normally defense counsel is entitled to review record before it is authenticated).
22. R.C.M. 1103(i)(1)(B) Discussion. *See also* § 17-2(B)(3).
23. R.C.M. 1103(i)(1)(B) Discussion.
24. *Id.*
25. *Id.*
26. United States v. Bryant, 37 M.J. 668 (A.C.M.R. 1993).
27. United States v. McCullah, 11 M.J. 234 (C.M.A. 1981) (exhibit missing); United States v. Thorn, 36 M.J. 955 (A.F.C.M.R. 1993) (demonstrative exhibits which are not marked nor introduced need not be included in record of trial; exhibits which are marked and referred to but are not introduced into evidence, must be included in record); United States v. Bush, 12 M.J. 647 (A.F.C.M.R. 1981) (failure to enter data on chalkboard into evidence did not make record incomplete where the information was already before the court in the form of testimony).
28. United States v. Cudini, 36 M.J. 572 (A.C.M.R. 1992) (omission of "flyer" as appellate exhibit was not substantial omission); United States v. Brown-Austin, 34 M.J. 578 (A.C.M.R. 1992) (Stipulation of Lost Testimony of missing testimony of four prosecution witnesses not adequate; court cured error by approving a sentence no greater than could be given by a special court-martial. The court noted that a complete record and verbatim record are not synonymous); United States v. Sturkey, 23 M.J. 522 (A.F.C.M.R. 1986) (lack of "meticulous reconstruction" of missing testimony).
29. United States v. Behling, 37 M.J. 637 (A.C.M.R. 1993) (omission of verbatim transcript of instructions was insubstantial; verbatim does not mean exact word for word); United States v. Barney, 23 M.J. 504 (A.F.C.M.R. 1986) (omission of jurisdictional challenge was substantial omission; court offers United States v. Dornick, 16 M.J. 642 (A.F.C.M.R. 1983), as example of how missing testimony can be reconstructed).
30. *See, e.g.,* United States v. Mayville, 32 M.J. 838 (N.M.C.M.R. 1991) (complete record requirement for approving BCD in sentence does not include written conditions of suspension of confinement or proof of service of that writing).
31. United States v. Norris, 33 M.J. 635 (C.G.C.M.R. 1991) (various omissions from the record of trial were insubstantial and court treated it as complete within the requirements of Article 54); United States v. Baker, 21 M.J. 618 (A.C.M.R. 1985) (absence of appellate exhibits not substantial); United States v. Spring, 15 M.J. 669 (A.F.C.M.R. 1983) (reconstructed sentencing arguments not substantial omission); United States v. Barnes, 12 M.J. 614 (N.M.C.M.R. 1981) (a missing exhibit does not render a record nonverbatim).

what is supposed to be a "verbatim record,"[32] prejudice is presumed[33] and the appellate courts may treat it instead as a summarized record and approve only so much of the sentence as could have been imposed by a regular special court-martial[34] or remand the case for reconstruction or clarification of the record.[35]

The *Manual* specifically provides for videotaped or audiotaped records of trial[36] and permits the service secretaries to authorize use of videotape, audio tape, or similar method in lieu of a court reporter. But it must later ultimately be reduced to a written transcript, either verbatim or summarized, as required.[37]

§ 17-4(A). Authentication of the Record.

A general or special[38] court-martial record of trial, according to Article 54(a), U.C.M.J.,[39] is to be authenticated by the military judge unless his death, disability, or absence prevents such.[40] In that case the trial counsel may authenticate it.[41] In the absence of the trial counsel, a court member, or a court reporter (in the case of a bench trial) may authenticate the record.[42]

---

32. *See, e.g.,* United States v. Harper, 25 M.J. 895 (A.C.M.R. 1988) (omission of accused's personnel records from appellate exhibits was not substantial under the facts); United States v. Desciscio, 22 M.J. 684 (A.F.C.M.R. 1986); United States v. Griffin, 17 M.J. 698 (A.C.M.R. 1983) (possibility of prejudice was avoided where eyewitness testified again after recording equipment failed); United States v. Pawis, 12 M.J. 691 (N.M.C.M.R. 1981).
33. United States v. Lashley, 14 M.J. 7 (C.M.A. 1982) (substantial omissions give rise to presumption of prejudice).
34. *See, e.g.,* United States v. Harmon, 29 M.J. 732 (A.F.C.M.R. 1989) (court lacked jurisdiction to impose punitive discharge where omission from record of entire findings portion of trial was presumptively prejudicial and reconstructed portion was not substantially verbatim); United States v. Sturkey, 23 M.J. 522 (A.F.C.M.R. 1986); United States v. Barney, 23 M.J. 504 (A.F.C.M.R. 1986); United States v. King, 45 C.M.R. 466 (A.C.M.R. 1972).
35. United States v. Seal, 38 M.J. 659 (A.C.M.R. 1993) (case returned for preparation of complete record; videotapes of accused in combat were missing); United States v. Alston, 30 M.J. 969 (N.M.C.M.R. 1990) (trial counsel deliberately omitted portions of trial relating to charges on which accused was acquitted; the court determined that these were not insubstantial omissions and sent case to Judge Advocate General for preparation of verbatim transcript); United States v. Williams, 14 M.J. 796 (A.F.C.M.R. 1982) (record returned for possible reconstruction).
36. *See* R.C.M. 1103(j).
37. *Id. Cf.* United States v. Barton, 6 M.J. 16 (C.M.A. 1978) (court rejected videotaped transcriptions as proper substitute).
38. A summary court record is authenticated by the summary court-martial officer. R.C.M. 1104(a)(3).
39. *See* Appendix 3.
40. R.C.M. 1104(a)(2)(A). If more than one judge presided, each judge authenticates his portion of the record. *Id. Cf.* United States v. Gonzales, 13 M.J. 665 (A.F.C.M.R. 1982) (judge presiding at end of trial may authenticate record).
41. R.C.M. 1104(a)(2)(B). An assistant trial counsel may authenticate the record if he has been present throughout the case. United States v. Credit, 4 M.J. 118 (C.M.A. 1977).
42. R.C.M. 1104(a)(2)(B) provides:

(B) *Substitute authentication.* If the military judge cannot authenticate the record of trial because of the military judge's death, disability, or absence, the trial counsel present at the end of the proceedings shall authenticate the record of trial. If the trial counsel cannot authenticate the record of trial because of the trial counsel's death, disability, or absence, a member shall authenticate the record of trial. In a court-martial composed of a military judge

Where a judge's absence is in question, the military courts will be reluctant to accept the trial counsel's substitute authentication unless the trial judge was truly unavailable for a lengthy period.[43]

The authentication of the record is a ministerial act. If the judge is satisfied with its accuracy[44] he has no discretion to refrain from authenticating the record and once accomplished he may not undo it.[45]

Where it is necessary to correct the record before authentication, the military judge may hold a post-trial session.[46] At that session, which may be in the nature of a revision proceeding,[47] an Article 39(a) session,[48] or a *Dubay* hearing,[49] the judge may consider evidence and make rulings of fact and law.

Where after authentication it becomes necessary to propose substantive changes to the record to reflect accurately the trial proceedings, the appropriate vehicle is a Certificate of Correction, where there is no showing of fraud or mistake.[50] The military judge should, however, first give notice to all parties and provide them with an opportunity to be heard on the proposed correction.[51]

§ 17-4(B). Service of Record on Accused.

The accused is entitled to service of a copy of the record of trial as soon as it is authenticated.[52] If the accused is not in the same location as the defense

---

alone, or as to sessions without members, the court reporter shall authenticate the record of trial when this duty would fall upon a member under this subsection. A person authorized to authenticate a record under this subsection may authenticate the record only as to those proceedings at which that person was present.

The Discussion to this rule indicates that substitute authentication may be used only in "emergencies."

43. *See, e.g.*, United States v. Miller, 4 M.J. 207 (C.M.A. 1978) (48-hour absence insufficient); United States v. Batiste, 35 M.J. 742 (A.C.M.R. 1992) (judge's absence was no more than temporary; judge's affidavit was insufficient to authenticate record); United States v. Walker, 20 M.J. 971 (N.M.C.M.R. 1985) (Judge's 30-day absence was the sort of delay that should have triggered the provisions in R.C.M. 1104(a)(2)(B) for substitute authentication).

United States v. White, 12 M.J. 643 (A.F.C.M.R. 1981) (trial counsel may authenticate record where judge has received permanent change assignment orders and his established departure date is imminent); United States v. Cruz-Rijos, 1 M.J. 429 (C.M.A. 1976). *See also* United States v. Andrade, 3 M.J. 757 (A.C.M.R. 1977) (good discussion of this problem).

44. R.C.M. 1104(a)(1).
45. United States v. Eubank, 12 M.J. 752 (A.F.C.M.R. 1981).
46. R.C.M. 1102. United States v. Brickey, 16 M.J. 258 (C.M.A. 1983).
47. *See* R.C.M. 1102(b)(1) Discussion. Additional evidence is usually not received at "revision" proceedings which are corrective in nature.
48. Art. 39(a), U.C.M.J. United States v. Brickey, 16 M.J. 258 (C.M.A. 1983). See § 12-1 for a discussion of using Article 39(a) sessions as a pretrial session.
49. United States v. Brickey, 16 M.J. 258 (C.M.A. 1983) (court held that judge or convening authority could authorize a factual *Dubay* hearing to assist the appellate authorities).
50. R.C.M. 1104(d). United States v. Wilkerson, 1 M.J. 56 (C.M.A. 1975).
51. R.C.M. 1104(d)(2). United States v. Anderson, 12 M.J. 195 (C.M.A. 1982).
52. Art. 54(c), U.C.M.J. R.C.M. 1104(b). United States v. Cruz-Rijos, 1 M.J. 429 (C.M.A. 1976); United States v. Scott, 40 M.J. 914 (A.C.M.R. 1994), *aff'd on other grounds*, 42 M.J. 457 (1995) (failure to serve record on accused where record indicated that counsel had been served, even though no certificate of service was included).

counsel, the government may meet the spirit of the codal requirements by serving a copy of the record on the defense counsel.[53] In any event, the courts have mandated service on the counsel to permit a thorough review for defects that may permit appellate relief.[54] Failure to serve the record of trial may constitute reversible error.[55]

§ 17-5. Confinement Pending Review.

Because sentences of courts-martial are generally not automatically self-executing,[1] no punishment may be imposed until the convening authority has reviewed the case, approved it, and ordered it executed.[2] Pending the convening authority's action, the accused may be required to perform duties unless he is ordered into post-trial confinement. Under the U.C.M.J., an accused may be required to take leave pending appellate review.[3] Although the period of confinement runs from the date the sentence is adjudged,[4] confinement must be independently ordered by a commander or his designee.[5] Post-trial confinement pending review is considered appropriate where confinement is part of the adjudged sentence.[6] While in confinement, an accused may not be required to perform hard labor but may be punished for disciplinary infractions.[7] The commander's decision to impose post-trial restraint is subject to review for abuse of discretion;[8] challenges to post-trial restraint may also be made

---

53. R.C.M. 1104(b)(1)(C). United States v. Diamond, 18 M.J. 305 (C.M.A. 1984) (Art. 54(c) adequately complied with where government informed individual defense counsel that an authenticated copy of the record of trial was available for review); United States v. Cruz-Rios, 1 M.J. 429 (C.M.A. 1976); United States v. Euring, 27 M.J. 843 (A.C.M.R. 1989) (constructive service on counsel permitted).
  In United States v. Derksen, 24 M.J. 818 (A.C.M.R. 1987), the defense counsel refused substitute service on his client who had been transferred to a distant location. The court rejected the argument that the government had failed to demonstrate "impracticability." In the court's view, substitute service is permitted when one of the documented conditions in R.C.M. 1104(b)(1)(C) occurs. The court added that counsel's refusal to accept service of the record was insufficient cause to extend the time for making post-trial submissions to the convening authority.
54. United States v. Palenius, 2 M.J. 86, 92 (C.M.A. 1977). See also R.C.M. 1106(f)(3) (counsel may request copy of record).
55. United States v. Beard, 15 M.J. 768 (A.F.C.M.R. 1983).
1. See generally Art. 57, U.C.M.J. In 1996, Article 57(a) U.C.M.J., was amended to indicate that any forfeiture of pay or allowances or reduction in grade takes effect on the earlier of the date that is 14 days after the date sentence is adjudged or the date that the sentence is approved by the convening authority. National Defense Authorization Act for Fiscal Year (FY) 1996, § 1121.
2. See § 17-9(C).
3. Art. 76a, U.C.M.J. permits the services to require "appellate leave" where the sentence, as approved by the general court-martial convening authority, includes an unsuspended discharge or dismissal.
4. Art. 57(b), U.C.M.J.
5. R.C.M. 1101(b)(2). See, e.g., Reed v. Ohman, 19 C.M.A. 110, 41 C.M.R. 110 (1969); Levy v. Resor, 17 C.M.A. 135, 37 C.M.R. 399 (1967).
6. See also United States v. Petroff-Tachomakoff, 5 C.M.A. 824, 19 C.M.R. 120 (1955); United States v. Teague, 3 C.M.A. 317, 12 C.M.R. 73 (1953) (arrest was appropriate). R.C.M. 1101(b)(2) Discussion.
7. See Art. 13, U.C.M.J.
8. Reed v. Ohman, 19 C.M.A. 110, 41 C.M.R. 110 (1969). See also United States v. Phelps, 40 M.J. 550 (A.C.M.R. 1994) (appellate court granted relief where accused remained in post-trial

through extraordinary writs to the service Courts of Criminal Appeals or the Court of Appeals for the Armed Forces.[9] See § 17-19. At any time after the sentence is adjudged and before execution of the sentence, the accused may request deferment, i.e., postponement, of the confinement portion of the sentence.[10]

§ 17-6. Military Corrections.

The Department of Defense maintains a policy of rehabilitating convicted servicemembers who receive sentences including confinement.[1] Short-term sentences of confinement are normally served at the service's confinement or retraining centers.[2] Longer term sentences are usually served at the United States Disciplinary Barracks (USDB) at Fort Leavenworth, Kansas or other federal penal institutions.[3] Each service provides more detailed guidance on disposition of convicted servicemembers in regulations.[4] In acting on a case, the convening authority may direct where confinement will be served, in accordance with those regulations. Although an appellate court may determine whether confinement was legal, it may not interfere with the commander's determination of the place of confinement.[5]

PART II

INITIAL REVIEW BY THE CONVENING AUTHORITY

§ 17-7. Introduction.

The first step in the military's appellate process is review by the convening authority, that is, the commander who appointed the participants and referred the accused's case to trial.[1] The initial review, which is mandatory and

---

confinement six days longer than necessary due to administrative oversight; court noted that "incidents of poor administration reflect adversely on ... military justice system"); United States v. Keith, 36 M.J. 518 (A.C.M.R. 1992) (court disapproved forfeiture of all pay and allowances because of administrative error); United States v. Martinez, 19 M.J. 744 (A.C.M.R. 1984) (not cruel and unusual punishment to segregate homosexual accused from rest of prisoners).

9. *See, e.g.*, Walker v. Commanding Officer, 19 C.M.A. 247, 41 C.M.R. 247 (1970).
10. *See* § 17-2(B)(2).
1. *See* 10 U.S.C. § 951(b)(2) (1994).
2. *E.g.*, The Army's Retraining Brigade (ARB) at Fort Riley, Kansas. *See* AR 190-47, Military Police, The United States Army Correctional System; AR 633-30, Apprehension and Confinement, Military Sentences to Confinement. *See also* AFI 31-205 which governs the Air Force correctional system. Women prisoners are sometimes placed in local civilian facilities where the military facilities are limited to males only. Such discrimination may deny such female prisoners equal protection. *See* United States v. Houston, 12 M.J. 907 (N.M.C.M.R. 1982).
3. This institution has been established under the authority of 10 U.S.C. § 951. *See generally* Herrod, "The United States Disciplinary Barracks System," 8 MIL. L. REV. 35 (1960); Birnbaum, "Who Goes to Leavenworth?" 11 THE REPORTER 97 (Aug. 1982).
4. *See, e.g.*, Army Regulations 190-47 and 633-30 and United States v. Schmit, 13 M.J. 934 (A.F.C.M.R. 1982) (good discussion of Air Force provisions and procedures).
5. United States v. Krenn, 12 M.J. 594 (A.C.M.R. 1981).
1. Art. 60, U.C.M.J. *See* Appendix 3. *See also* § 8-2(A).

nondelegable,[2] may also be taken by the temporary convening authority,[3] the successor in command,[4] or any general court-martial convening authority.[5] This part of the chapter focuses on this first important step of review and specifically includes examination of the convening authority's powers and legal review of courts-martial.

§ 17-8. Legal Review of Courts-Martial.

§ 17-8(A). General Matters.

At some point in the initial post-trial processing of a court-martial, an attorney at the trial level will review the case for legal sufficiency. Depending on the type of case and the sentence adjudged, the legal review may take place before or after the convening authority acts on the case, and may consist of either an informal review for legal sufficiency or a formal, written, post-trial review.

Summary courts-martial are first reviewed and acted upon by the convening authority.[1] After he has acted, the convening authority forwards the case to a judge advocate for review.[2] This legal review will determine whether the proceedings, findings, and sentence, as approved by the convening authority, are correct in fact and law.[3] If the proceedings meet those criteria, the case becomes final.[4] If not, the judge advocate forwards the case to the general court-martial convening authority for corrective action.[5]

Special courts-martial not authorized to adjudge a bad conduct discharge are reviewed in generally the same manner as that used for the summary court.[6] The legal review will normally be presented in a standard format and made part of the record.[7]

The more complete legal review of general courts-martial and special courts-martial where a bad conduct discharge was adjudged is discussed in the next section.

---

2. R.C.M. 1107(a) Discussion.
3. Art. 60, U.C.M.J. R.C.M. 1107(a).
4. Id.
5. Art. 60, U.C.M.J.; R.C.M. 1107(a). Referral of the case to another convening authority should be accomplished by a letter of transmittal. United States v. Walker, 7 M.J. 976 (N.C.M.R. 1979); United States v. James, 12 M.J. 944 (N.M.C.M.R. 1982) (no error where transmittal letter not attached to record; good discussion of situation where original convening authority defers to another authorized reviewer). Reasons for the referral should be included in the record. R.C.M. 1107(a) Discussion.

1. R.C.M. 1107.
2. R.C.M. 1111.
3. Art. 64, U.C.M.J. R.C.M. 1112(a)(3).
4. R.C.M. 1112(e).
5. R.C.M. 1112(e). If the convening authority declines to take necessary corrective action at least as favorable as that recommended by the judge advocate, the case will be referred to the Judge Advocate General for review.
6. Art. 64, U.C.M.J. R.C.M. 1112(2).
7. See Appendix 35.

§ 17-8(B). Post-Trial Recommendation.

A written post-trial recommendation to the convening authority is required in all general courts-martial and in special courts-martial where a bad conduct discharge was adjudged.[8] In general courts-martial resulting in acquittal of all charges and specification, no recommendation is required.[9]

This formal legal recommendation is prepared and presented to the court-martial convening authority *before* he acts on the case[10] and is prepared by his[11] staff judge advocate or the legal officer, unless prior association with the case renders him disqualified to do so.[12] A reviewer is disqualified if he has acted in the same case as a court member,[13] military judge,[14] trial or assistant trial counsel,[15] defense or assistant defense counsel,[16] or investigating officer.[17] He is also disqualified if he testified as a witness,[18] has other than an official interest in the case,[19] or will be reviewing the legality of his own

---

8. Art. 60(d), U.C.M.J. R.C.M. 1106(a).
9. R.C.M. 1106(e). This is a change from an earlier version of Art. 61, U.C.M.J. which required review of question of whether the court had jurisdiction.
10. Art. 60(d), U.C.M.J. R.C.M. 1106(a).
11. United States v. Reilly, 36 M.J. 887 (N.M.C.M.R. 1993) (error for convening authority to rely on predecessor's Staff Judge Advocate's recommendation); United States v. Simpson, 33 M.J. 1063 (A.C.M.R. 1991) (clear that Congress intended that convening authority receive advice of his or her most seasoned military lawyer).
12. R.C.M. 1106(b). United States v. Hall, 39 M.J. 593 (A.C.M.R. 1994) (preparation of post-trial recommendation by SJA of convening authority was error); United States v. Gavitt, 37 M.J. 761 (A.C.M.R. 1993) (recommendation prepared by an SJA not on the convening authority's staff was improper where such preparation was not requested or coordinated by convening authority).
13. Art. 6(c), U.C.M.J. R.C.M. 1106(b).
14. Art. 6(c), U.C.M.J.
15. Article 6(c), U.C.M.J. United States v. Holt, 38 M.J. 682 (A.F.C.M.R. 1993) (court presumed prejudice where trial counsel prepared addendum to SJA recommendation and defense counsel had no opportunity to raise error); United States v. Felix, 36 M.J. 903 (A.F.C.M.R. 1993) (en banc), *aff'd on other grounds*, 40 M.J. 356 (C.M.A. 1994) (accused waived error in post-trial recommendation being prepared by assistant trial counsel; SJA also signed recommendation and certified that he had reviewed recommendation and concurred); United States v. McCormick, 34 M.J. 752 (N.M.C.M.R. 1992) (drafter of post-trial recommendation had previously served as trial counsel in case; even though draft was filtered through two Staff Judge Advocates, new recommendation was required); In United States v. Siders, 17 M.J. 986 (A.C.M.R. 1984), the court ruled that the SJA who made post-appellate review recommendations to the convening authority was disqualified because he had previously served as a government appellate counsel in the case when it was before the appellate courts.
16. Article 6(c), U.C.M.J. *See* United States v. Thompson, 3 M.J. 966 (N.C.M.R. 1977) (counsel in companion case), *rev'd on other grounds*, 6 M.J. 106 (C.M.A. 1979).
17. *Id.* United States v. Grinter, 28 M.J. 840 (A.F.C.M.R. 1989) (nonprejudicial error for post-trial recommendation to be prepared by officer who had also been appointed to serve as an Article 32 investigating officer). *See also* § 7-2(A)(1).
18. United States v. Rice, 33 M.J. 451 (C.M.A. 1991) (plain error for legal officer who testified at sentencing to prepare post-trial recommendation); United States v. Choice, 23 C.M.A. 329, 49 C.M.R. 663 (1975); United States v. Cansdale, 7 M.J. 143 (C.M.A. 1979); United States v. Reynolds, 36 M.J. 1128 (A.C.M.R. 1993) (SJA not disqualified where he testified at trial for government on issue of appointment of court members; court said that merely testifying is not per se disqualification). RCM 1106(b) Discussion.
19. United States v. Conn, 6 M.J. 351 (C.M.A. 1979); United States v. Bygrave, 40 M.J. 839 (N.M.C.M.R. 1994) (while mere contact with media following case did not indicate improper disposition of SJA, court ordered new review and action in order to avoid the appearance of evil).

pretrial actions when such have been contested.[20] He may also be disqualified if he recommended that a prosecution witness be granted immunity or clemency.[21] If he is disqualified the case should be forwarded to another staff judge advocate or legal officer for action.[22] Failure to object to a disqualified SJA preparing the recommendation, may waive the issue.[23]

In all cases the recommendation should be signed by an unbiased and impartial staff judge advocate or legal officer,[24] and must not be signed before the military judge properly authenticates the record of trial.[25] As a practical matter, someone other than the staff judge advocate or legal officer will prepare a first draft of the recommendation[26] for later personal adoption and signing by the appropriate officer.[27] After signing, the review is served upon the defense counsel who has 10 days to submit comments or rebuttal before it is submitted to the convening authority for action.[28] If his action varies from that recommended by his legal advisor in the review the convening authority

---

20. United States v. Lynch, 39 M.J. 223 (C.M.A. 1994) (SJA disqualified because material factual dispute existed between defense counsel and SJA concerning latter's pretrial conduct); United States v. Caritativo, 37 M.J. 175 (C.M.A. 1993) (SJA not disqualified from preparing post-trial recommendation even though his pretrial advice had been challenged at trial; the advice was correct in all material respects); United States v. Collins, 6 M.J. 256 (C.M.A. 1979); United States v. Engle, 1 M.J. 387 (C.M.A. 1976); United States v. Hill, 32 M.J. 940 (N.M.C.M.R. 1991) (SJA was "accuser" and thus disqualified from acting where he had earlier given direct, personal order disobeyed by accused and subject of charge against him). *Cf.* United States v. Price, 15 M.J. 628 (N.M.C.M.R. 1982).
21. *See, e.g.,* United States v. Decker, 15 M.J. 416 (C.M.A. 1983); United States v. Newman, 14 M.J. 474 (C.M.A. 1983); United States v. Johnson, 4 M.J. 8 (C.M.A. 1977).
22. R.C.M. 1106(c)(1). United States v. Hall, 39 M.J. 593 (A.C.M.R. 1994) (if SJA is disqualified the convening authority should request assignment of SJA to review record and prepare recommendation or forward record for action to general court-martial convening authority; court recognized that there is confusion over the procedures to be used).
23. United States v. Zaptin, 41 M.J. 877 (N.M.Ct.Crim.App. 1995) (issue waived; court determined that nominal accuser's preparation of recommendation was not plain error; SJA did not have anything other than an official interest in the case).
24. United States v. Curry, 28 M.J. 419 (C.M.A. 1989) (legal officer authorized to prepare post-trial recommendation; although Congress has stated a preference that SJA prepare the review, the review is no longer "legal" and preparation by a lawyer is not compulsory); United States v. Jolliff, 22 C.M.A. 95, 46 C.M.R. 95 (1973); United States v. Felix, 36 M.J. 903 (A.F.C.M.R. 1993), *aff'd on other grounds,* 40 M.J. 356 (C.M.A. 1994) (en banc) (accused waived error in post-trial recommendation being prepared by assistant trial counsel; SJA also signed recommendation and certified that he had reviewed recommendation and concurred); United States v. Smith, 34 M.J. 894 (N.M.C.M.R. 1992) (recommendation by someone not a commissioned officer was plain error; accused could challenge on appeal despite lack of defense objection).
25. United States v. King, 44 C.M.R. 680 (A.C.M.R. 1971).
26. *See* United States v. Moultak, 21 M.J. 822 (N.M.C.M.R. 1985) (not improper for superior command to adopt draft of disqualified SJA).
27. Before it was amended in 1983, Article 61, U.C.M.J. required a signature. United States v. Gray, 14 M.J. 816 (A.C.M.R. 1982) (review signed by deputy SJA did not meet requirements of Art. 61, which required that SJA sign; "acting" SJA may do so, however). The Code is now silent on the subject. *See also* United States v. Reed, 19 M.J. 764 (A.C.M.R. 1984) (nonprejudicial error for SJA not to personally sign an addendum to his post-trial review. Purpose of signature is to authenticate review and is a procedural requirement. Court left open question of whether signature is currently required).
28. R.C.M. 1106(f). *See also* §§ 17-2(B)(4) and 17-8(B)(3).

need not state his reasons for doing so.[29] Failure of the convening authority to read the recommendation may not be error where the staff judge advocate or legal officer orally advises him and personally gives his recommendation.[30]

§ 17-8(B)(1). Format and Contents of Recommendation.

The Military Justice Act of 1983[31] and the 1984 revisions to the *Manual*[32] greatly simplified the contents and format of the post-trial recommendation. Under earlier practice, considerable time and expense were expended on preparation of lengthy and complex post-trial reviews that discussed in great detail the trial itself, including a summary of the evidence and discussion of legal issues and defenses raised by the defense. The move toward simplification was accelerated by the consternation of the appellate courts in finding an error in the review and in remanding the case to the trial level for a new review and action.[33] Some relief was realized with the decision in *United States v. Goode*[34] where the court placed the burden on the defense counsel to either raise or waive defects in the post-trial review before the convening authority took his action on the case.[35] But that case offered little relief to the staff judge advocates and legal officers who were still charged with preparation of detailed post-trial reviews. The 1983 amendments to the U.C.M.J. and the 1984 revisions to the *Manual* reduced that burden.

The *Manual* notes that the purpose of the recommendation of the staff judge advocate or legal officer is to "assist the convening authority to decide what action to take on the sentence in the exercise of command prerogative."[36] In effect, this removes from the convening authority the burden of independently reviewing the legal sufficiency of the findings.[37] This abbreviated process is

---

29. R.C.M. 1106(e). This is a change from prior law. *See, e.g.,* United States v. McKnight, 30 M.J. 205 (C.M.A. 1990) (convening authority not required to explain why he did not follow legal advice); United States v. Harris, 10 M.J. 276 (C.M.A. 1981); United States v. Keller, 1 M.J. 159 (C.M.A. 1975); United States v. Shanaham, 16 M.J. 654 (A.F.C.M.R. 1983).
30. United States v. Curry, 15 M.J. 701 (A.C.M.R. 1983).
31. *See* Art. 60(d), U.C.M.J.
32. R.C.M. 1106(d).
33. *See, e.g.,* United States v. Morrison, 3 M.J. 408 (C.M.A. 1977) (C.J. Fletcher, concurring) ("proposed" abbreviated post-trial review). *Cf.* United States v. Sankey, 6 M.J. 790 (A.C.M.R. 1978); United States v. Davis, 6 M.J. 874 (A.C.M.R. 1979).
34. 1 M.J. 3 (C.M.A. 1975).
35. *See* § 17-8(B)(3) *infra*.
36. R.C.M. 1106(d)(1). *See, e.g.,* United States v. Ralbovsky, 32 M.J. 921 (A.F.C.M.R. 1991) (discussion of convening authority's changed role in post-trial review procedures); United States v. Blodgett, 20 M.J. 756 (A.F.C.M.R. 1985) (court indicated that under the new procedures the "convening authority's action now serves the primary function, not of protecting the accused, but of protecting and maintaining the military commander's unique interest in discipline, morale, and his organization's ability to perform its mission").

In a separate opinion in United States v. Johnson, 26 M.J. 686, 692, n.3 (A.C.M.R. 1988), Senior Judge Felder correctly noted that the above quote failed to mention the commander's interest in "justice" and that where there is "injustice, discipline, morale and mission performance will certainly suffer."
37. R.C.M. 1106(d) Drafters' Analysis.

implied in use of the term "recommendation" rather than "review," which connotes a more exhaustive study and analysis of the trial proceedings.[38] The recommendation must include only the following elements:

1. The findings and sentence adjudged by the court.[39]
2. A summary of the accused's military record which should include the length and character of his service, any decorations or awards, records of nonjudicial punishment or prior convictions.[40]
3. A statement concerning the length and nature of pretrial restraint.[41]
4. If there is a pretrial agreement, a statement as to what action the convening authority is required to take or reasons why he is not bound by that agreement.[42]
5. A specific recommendation as to what action the convening authority should take on the sentence.[43]
6. Any recommendation for clemency made by the sentencing authority in conjunction with the sentence.[44]

The foregoing elements should be set out in concise language.[45] In most cases this will mean that a post-trial recommendation can be presented in one or two pages rather than the long documents that were previously required.[46]

---

38. Despite the change in terminology in the *Manual*, the courts have continued to refer to the document as a "review."

39. R.C.M. 1106(d)(3)(A). United States v. Beaudin, 35 M.J. 385 (C.M.A. 1992) (nonprejudicial error for SJA not to include information that military judge had merged offenses for purpose of sentencing). *Cf.* United States v. Russett, 40 M.J. 184 (C.M.A. 1994) (Beaudin did not establish uniform rule that SJA's recommendation must include specification recitation of fact that judge made findings re multiplicity).

United States v. Shiftic, 36 M.J. 1193 (N.M.C.M.R. 1993) (nonprejudicial plain error for SJA to omit information that military judge had treated offenses as being multiplicious).

40. R.C.M. 1106(d)(3)(C). United States v. Demerse, 37 M.J. 488 (C.M.A. 1993) (SJA's failure to include information on accused's Vietnam service amounted to plain error; sentence and action set aside); United States v. Thomas, 39 M.J. 1078 (C.G.C.M.R. 1994) (SJA should include reference to medals and awards which may be found in the record of trial or an accused's written service record book; R.C.M. does not require SJA to search further).

41. R.C.M. 1106(d)(3)(D). United States v. Holman, 23 M.J. 565 (A.C.M.R. 1986) (SJA's recommendation failed to note pretrial restraint; issue waived). *See also* Chapter 5.

42. R.C.M. 1106(d)(3)(E). *See also* Chapter 9.

43. R.C.M. 1106(d)(3)(F). United States v. Elliott, 23 M.J. 1 (C.M.A. 1986) (not reasonable for different government officials to take different positions on accused's unsworn statement at sentencing; prosecutor had argued that the statement implied an admission of guilt, and SJA, in post-trial recommendation, had advised CA that same statement lacked an admission of guilt necessary for rehabilitation). *See also* § 16-8(B).

44. R.C.M. 1106(d)(3)(B). This requirement was added in Change 7 to the Manual for Courts-Martial, in 1994. The provision was inserted as a new subsection (B), and the existing subsections (B) through (E) were redesignated (C) through (F). The Analysis accompanying the amendment indicates that the accused may request in writing that the information not be included, although that specific language does not appear in the rule itself.

45. R.C.M. 1106(d)(2).

46. United States v. Smith, 33 M.J. 968 (A.F.C.M.R. 1991) (post-trial advice will rarely exceed two or three pages in length; court included strong language about keeping the recommendation short and to the point).

In some circumstances the recommendation must address legal errors.[47] If the defense has raised legal issues in its submission of matters to the convening authority,[48] the recommendation must state whether corrective action should be taken on either the findings or sentence.[49] But the recommendation need only present a statement of agreement or disagreement.[50] It need not contain any analysis of the issue.[51] In any event, the recommendation may address legal issues where in the view of the staff judge advocate or legal officer considers it is advisable to do so.[52]

It is important to note that the foregoing discussion indicates the minimum requirements for the post-trial recommendation.[53] The recommendation may consist of other optional matters considered appropriate, including matters from outside the record.[54] But if such matters are included, the defense must be given an opportunity to rebut them.[55]

---

47. R.C.M. 1106(d)(4). In United States v. Hill, 27 M.J. 293 (C.M.A. 1988), the Court of Military Appeals concluded that the President intended in the Manual for Courts-Martial to require the Staff Judge Advocate to respond to any allegations of legal error asserted by the defense after service of the recommendation but still within the time limits of R.C.M. 1105(c)(1). The court further noted that where the SJA has failed to do so, the appellate court should normally remand the case back to the convening authority unless it appears that the defense allegation of error "would not foreseeably have led to a favorable recommendation by the staff judge advocate." See also United States v. Craig, 28 M.J. 321 (C.M.A. 1989) (defense did not raise legal issues in response); United States v. Williams-Oatman, 38 M.J. 602 (A.C.M.R. 1993) (nonprejudicial error for SJA not to advise convening authority with regard to legal issues raised by defense counsel); United States v. Williamson, 28 M.J. 660 (N.M.C.M.R. 1989) (harmless error for SJA not to address legal errors raised by the defense); United States v. Allen, 28 M.J. 610 (N.M.C.M.R. 1989) (error for SJA not to address legal errors raised by defense counsel); United States v. Johnson, 26 M.J. 686 (A.C.M.R. 1988) (harmless error where SJA failed to address legal error raised by defense counsel in his clemency petition to the effect that trial judge erred in ruling on multiplicity issue).

48. See § 17-2(B)(3). United States v. Williams-Oatman, 38 M.J. 602 (A.C.M.R. 1993) (court noted that defense counsel should be as clear as possible about what legal issues they are raising).

49. Id. United States v. Williams-Oatman, 38 M.J. 602 (A.C.M.R. 1993) (SJA's comment need only consist of statement of agreement or disagreement); United States v. Moore, 27 M.J. 656 (A.C.M.R. 1988) (new review and action required where SJA did not respond to accused's asserted legal errors); United States v. Keck, 22 M.J. 755 (N.M.C.M.R. 1986) (no error where SJA failed to respond).

50. Id.

51. Id. The Drafters apparently followed the proverbial advice to trial judges: Make your ruling without giving reasons because you might be making the right ruling for the wrong reasons. The trend has been to encourage judges to explain their rulings on some evidentiary matters. Although the recommendation need not present the SJA's legal analysis, a detailed and comprehensive nonfrivolous argument by the defense should normally merit something more than a one sentence rejection of the argument.

52. R.C.M. 1106(c)(4).

53. R.C.M. 1106(d). United States v. Carroll, 30 M.J. 598 (C.G.C.M.R. 1990) (SJA is not required to address matters raised by defense in clemency request to convening authority). Cf. United States v. McLemore, 30 M.J. 605 (N.M.C.M.R. 1990) (SJA is obligated to provide convening authority with necessary clemency information; court noted that while it was not establishing a per se rule, in most cases the failure to do so would result in plain error); United States v. Brown, 21 M.J. 780 (A.C.M.R. 1985).

54. R.C.M. 1106(d)(5). United States v. Drayton, 40 M.J. 447 (C.M.A. 1994) (harmless error for

---

55. R.C.M. 1107(b)(3)(B)(iii). United States v. Cassell, 33 M.J. 448 (C.M.A. 1991) (although

The net effect of this abbreviated recommendation on the defense is that counsel now bears a much heavier burden of ensuring that the convening authority is aware of those matters that indicate that clemency may be warranted.[56] In the past, counsel could count on the post-trial review to present those clemency matters. Indeed, the failure to do so often resulted in a new post-trial review and action.[57] As noted in § 17-2(B)(3), the accused is permitted to present clemency matters directly to the convening authority.[58] It would seem prudent then for counsel in virtually every case to present nonfrivolous matters to the convening authority or at least draw his attention to clemency evidence presented at trial.[59]

§ 17-8(B)(2). Defective Recommendations.

In the past, the post-trial review, now labelled "recommendation," provided a fertile ground for defects and appellate relief. However, not all errors rendered the review invalid. The key inquiry was whether, assuming there was an error, there was a reasonable likelihood that the omitted or misstated matter might have been considered by the convening authority.[60] The *Goode* rebuttal,[61] discussed in § 17-8(B)(3), removed much of the former appellate consternation with returning cases to the trial level for preparation of a new review. Most errors are noted and corrected before the convening authority acts on the case[62] and only prejudicial errors, not waived, will require appel-

---

SJA to include matters from Article 32 investigation in attempt to sustain sufficiency of evidence); United States v. Groves, 30 M.J. 811 (A.C.M.R. 1990) (SJA included evidence of uncharged misconduct which was not in record; accused had opportunity to respond). *Cf.* United States v. Holmes, 33 M.J. 750 (A.C.M.R. 1991) (evidence admitted for limited purpose at trial may not be used for any purpose during post-trial review unless SJA clearly indicates its limited nature).

SJA did not include new adverse matters, per se, into recommendation, but referred to unidentified "other matter" that denied accused a "meaningful" opportunity to respond).

56. R.C.M. 1105(b) Drafters' Analysis. *See also* § 17-2(B)(3). *Cf.* United States v. Clear, 34 M.J. 129 (C.M.A. 1992) (court held that normally it is plain error for Staff Judge Advocate not to tell convening authority that military judge recommended clemency; the court noted that it would not second-guess defense counsel's tactical decision not to bring clemency recommendation to attention of convening authority).

57. *See, e.g.*, United States v. Rivera, 20 C.M.A. 6, 42 C.M.R. 198 (1970) (prejudice may occur where review is misleading, erroneous, or inaccurate).

58. *See* R.C.M. 1105.

59. Failure to do so may constitute ineffective assistance of counsel. *See, e.g.*, United States v. Davis, 20 M.J. 1015 (A.C.M.R. 1985).

60. *See, e.g.*, United States v. Clear, 34 M.J. 129 (C.M.A. 1992) (court held that normally it is plain error for Staff Judge Advocate not to tell convening authority that military judge recommended clemency); United States v. Arnold, 21 C.M.A. 151, 44 C.M.R. 205 (1972); United States v. Latimer, 35 M.J. 736 (A.C.M.R. 1992) (new action required where it was not clear that SJA presented clemency information to convening authority); United States v. Davis, 6 M.J. 874 (A.C.M.R. 1979).

61. United States v. Goode, 1 M.J. 3 (C.M.A. 1975).

62. United States v. Ruiz, 30 M.J. 867 (N.M.C.M.R. 1990) (SJA incorrectly advised convening authority on number of convictions); United States v. Tu, 30 M.J. 587 (A.C.M.R. 1990) (SJA incorrectly advised convening authority of clemency matters submitted by defendant); United States v. Huffman, 25 M.J. 758 (N.M.C.M.R. 1987) (court concluded that the SJA erred in advis-

late relief, i.e., prejudice may be found where the error adversely affects a substantial right.[63] Even where the defense makes no objection to the recommendation at the time it is submitted, appellate relief may also be granted if the court finds that the defect amounted to plain error.[64] In making that decision the courts may consider whether the error is an omission or affirmative misstatement, whether matter is material and substantial, and whether there is reasonable likelihood that convening authority was misled by error.[65]

Simplification of the contents of the post-trial recommendation should further reduce the risk of errors or deficiencies.[66] If the appellate court agrees with the defense that relief is required, the court should not return the case to the convening authority. The *Manual* indicates that the appropriate corrective action will be taken by the appellate court.[67]

---

ing the convening authority of what offense the accused was convicted; the court treated this as plain error and set aside the convening authority's action and expressed concern for the growing number of defective post-trial recommendations and the failure of defense counsel to challenge the defects); United States v. Leininger, 25 M.J. 746 (A.C.M.R. 1987) (reversible error for SJA to include incorrect information in his addendum that mischaracterized the company commander's testimony concerning the impact of a punitive discharge and which suggested that the convening authority need not consider sentence disparity in deciding what sentence to approve).

63. R.C.M. 1106(f)(6). United States v. Martinsmith, 37 M.J. 665 (A.C.M.R. 1993) (accused waived defect in post-trial recommendation). Only "plain errors" will not be waived. *See, e.g.,* United States v. Ruiz, 30 M.J. 867 (N.M.C.M.R. 1990) (SJA's incorrect advice on number of convictions was not plain error; accused waived issue by not responding to SJA's post-trial recommendation).

United States v. Lohrman, 26 M.J. 610 (A.C.M.R. 1988) (staff judge advocate's erroneous advice that accused had pleaded guilty to certain charges and that he had been convicted of those charges, which had been dismissed, was not plain error); United States v. Holman, 23 M.J. 565 (A.C.M.R. 1986) (defect waived); United States v. Breseman, 21 M.J. 973 (C.G.C.M.R. 1986) (no waiver under "abnormal" circumstances).

64. United States v. Clear, 34 M.J. 129 (C.M.A. 1992) (normally plain error for Staff Judge Advocate not to call convening authority's attention to military judge's recommendation of clemency); United States v. Lowry, 33 M.J. 1035 (N.M.C.M.R. 1991) (discussion of what amounts to plain error regarding mistakes in post-trial recommendation); United States v. Ford, 33 M.J. 1046 (N.M.C.M.R. 1991) (mistakes in post-trial recommendation were plain error, citing three-pronged test in *Lowry*).

65. United States v. Demerse, 37 M.J. 488 (C.M.A. 1993) (SJA's failure to include information on accused's Vietnam service amounted to plain error; sentence and action set aside); United States v. Bernier, 42 M.J. 521 (C.G.Ct.Crim.App. 1995) (SJA erroneous description of guilty finding was not plain error); United States v. Lowry, 33 M.J. 1035 (N.M.C.M.R. 1991).

66. As noted in the discussion in § 17-8(B)(1), the SJA can usually avoid errors by not volunteering additional information. But in appropriate cases, fairness may dictate a more thorough recommendation even at the risk of error.

67. R.C.M. 1106(e)(6). *Cf.* United States v. Reed, 33 M.J. 98 (C.M.A. 1991) (accused entitled to new post-trial advice and action where SJA failed to provide any guidance to convening authority on options for correcting trial defect); United States v. Tu, 30 M.J. 587 (A.C.M.R. 1990) (court concluded that SJA had incorrectly advised convening authority in post-trial recommendation and returned case to Judge Advocate General for new review and action).

§ 17-8(B)(3). Service of Recommendation on Defense Counsel.

The recommendation must be presented to the defense counsel for review *prior* to submission to the convening authority.[68] Prejudice may result if the service is made after the convening authority receives a copy.[69]

Counsel is given a minimum of 10 days to closely examine the recommendation and present comments or rebuttal.[70] Failure to respond, present a timely response, or note defects will normally constitute waiver.[71] If incorrect information is contained in the recommendation, the defense counsel should present the correct information.[72]

There has been a great deal of litigation in those cases where the staff judge advocate or legal officer has included new comments or matters to the recommendation following the defense response.[73] Assuming the matter is *new*,[74] the defense should again be served.[75] Where there is some question as to

---

68. R.C.M. 1106(f)(1). United States v. Moseley, 35 M.J. 481 (C.M.A. 1992) (case returned to convening authority where defense counsel was not served at all with recommendation); United States v. Miller, 41 M.J. 647 (N.M.Ct.Crim.App. 1994) (failure to serve counsel who actually had attorney-client relationship was nonprejudicial error; counsel who received recommendation did not establish attorney-client relationship); United States v. Diaz-Carrero, 31 M.J. 920 (A.C.M.R. 1990) (absence of receipt for copy of recommendation does not establish failure to serve both accused and defense counsel because affirmative proof of service is not required; but accused's affidavit indicating nonreceipt of recommendation rebutted presumption of regularity).

See Morgan, "*Goode* Response—Seven Years Later," 12 THE REPORTER 32 (Apr. 1983). *See also* § 17-2(B)(4).

69. United States v. Funk, 29 M.J. 692 (A.C.M.R. 1989) (failure to serve defense counsel before submission to convening authority was prejudicial error).

70. R.C.M. 1106(f)(5). United States v. Johnson, 23 M.J. 327 (C.M.A. 1987) (convening authority took action on the case only seven days after the defense counsel had been served and after counsel had requested several extensions of time; assuming this was error, no prejudice occurred because the response, which was eventually filed two months later, merely summarized issues raised at trial). The time may be extended up to 20 additional days. *Id.*

71. R.C.M. 1106(f)(6). United States v. Lugo, 32 M.J. 719 (C.G.C.M.R. 1991).

72. United States v. Davis, 6 M.J. 874, 879, n.18 (A.C.M.R. 1979).

73. *See* R.C.M. 1106(f)(7). United States v. Godfrey, 36 M.J. 629 (A.C.M.R. 1992) (addendum to recommendation did not raise new matters which should have been served on defense counsel); United States v. Blodgett, 20 M.J. 756 (A.F.C.M.R. 1985) (SJA's failure to respond to the defense counsel's R.C.M. 1106(f)(4) response to the SJA review was nonprejudicial error).

74. *See, e.g.,* United States v. Norment, 34 M.J. 224 (C.M.A. 1992) (SJA's response to defense response raised new matters which should have been served on defense counsel); United States v. Heirs, 29 M.J. 68 (C.M.A. 1989) (SJA's addendum to posttrial recommendation raised new matter and should have been served on defense counsel); United States v. Anderson, 25 M.J. 342 (C.M.A. 1987) (SJA's reference in supplemental recommendation to convening authority to fact that accused's misconduct had given rise to five-million-dollar claim against the government was a nontrivial "new matter" that should have been served on the defense; case returned for new recommendation and action); United States v. Thompson, 25 M.J. 662 (A.F.C.M.R. 1987) (change in SJA's recommendation regarding place of posttrial confinement was new matter); United States v. Wixon, 23 M.J. 570 (A.C.M.R. 1986) (response to defense comment was not new matter requiring service on defense counsel); United States v. Clark, 22 M.J. 708 (A.C.M.R. 1986) (SJA rebuttal to defense response was not new matter).

75. R.C.M. 1106(f)(7). United States v. Narine, 14 M.J. 55 (C.M.A. 1982); United States v. Yates, 39 M.J. 737 (N.M.C.M.R. 1994) (failure to submit new matter to defense counsel required corrective action). R.C.M.1106(f)(7) was amended in 1994 to provide that where the SJA ad-

whether the matter is new, the more prudent course seems to be that it be served on the defense.[76] Failure to do so will be measured for prejudice.[77]

The issue of which counsel should be served, where several were involved in the case, has generated a good deal of litigation. The problem generally arises where the defense counsel, who represented the accused at trial, is no longer available and service is made upon a "substitute" counsel. In *United States v. Iverson*,[78] the court stated:

> Absent truly extraordinary circumstances rendering virtually impossible the continuation of the established [attorney-client] relationship only the accused may terminate the existing affiliation with his trial defense counsel prior to the case reaching the appellate level (footnotes omitted).[79]

Recognizing a multitude of problems involving service of the review upon the wrong counsel, the court in *United States v. Robinson*[80] set out several suggestions: (1) At the trial's conclusion, the judge should attempt to determine which defense counsel will prepare the *Goode* response. (2) If civilian defense counsel is involved, the judge should apprise him of the *Goode* response. (3) The staff judge advocate or legal officer should determine, if it is not clear from the record, who will be served and address that point in his review. (4) When in doubt, all defense counsel should be served.

The *Manual* indicates that the accused may designate counsel either at trial or in writing to the staff judge advocate or legal officer.[81] Otherwise, service should be made in the following order of preference: civilian counsel, individual military counsel, or detailed defense counsel.[82] If none of these is reason-

---

dresses new matters in an addendum, the addendum must be served on both the defense counsel and the accused; United States v. Ricks, 21 M.J. 569 (A.C.M.R. 1985); United States v. Pryor, 19 M.J. 720 (A.C.M.R. 1984).

In United States v. Scott, 15 M.J. 589 (A.C.M.R. 1983), the court declined to hold that the addendum must in all cases be served. Here, however, it contained extensive factual and legal matters not presented in the SJA's review. Failure to serve it was therefore error.

76. United States v. Haynes, 28 M.J. 881 (A.F.C.M.R. 1989) (court noted that if there is any doubt that the SJA's addendum contains new matter, the SJA should err on the side of giving the defense additional time and opportunity to respond).

77. United States v. Harris, 43 M.J. 652 (Army Ct.Crim.App. 1995) (court did not apply harmless error analysis; action set aside where SJA raised new matters and failed to serve counsel); United States v. Haire, 40 M.J. 530 (C.G.C.M.R. 1994) (accused prejudiced where defense not served with addendum including new matter); United States v. Komorous, 33 M.J. 907 (A.F.C.M.R. 1991) (noting that errors in submission of posttrial recommendations remained a "bogeyman," court held that inclusion of new matter in recommendation without service on defense counsel was error); United States v. Ortiz, 33 M.J. 549 (A.C.M.R. 1991) (failure to serve addendum to SJA posttrial recommendation, which included new material, was harmless error); United States v. Torres, 25 M.J. 555 (A.C.M.R. 1987) (reversible error not to serve defense with response and rebuttal including new matter by prosecutor to defense clemency petition).

78. 5 M.J. 440 (C.M.A. 1978).

79. 5 M.J. at 449. *See also* United States v. Zarate, 5 M.J. 219 (C.M.A. 1978) (misc. docket) (counsel left service); United States v. Annis, 5 M.J. 351 (C.M.A. 1978) (leave in conjunction with reassignment not sufficient grounds).

80. 11 M.J. 218 (C.M.A. 1981).

81. R.C.M. 1106(f)(2).

82. R.C.M. 1106(f)(2). *Cf.* United States v. Thompson, 26 M.J. 512 (A.C.M.R. 1988) where the recommendation was erroneously served on the detailed rather than the civilian counsel but the

ably available, service may be made on a substitute counsel who must enter into an attorney-client relationship before reviewing the recommendation and preparing a response.[83]

Use of a substitute counsel may be required for post-trial processing in those instances where the accused has alleged counsel's ineffectiveness.[84] In those instances, a potential conflict of interest arises[85] and the defense counsel should be notified of the allegation.[86] Counsel should then determine if his services have been terminated or whether his withdrawal is permissible;[87] he should advise the accused of his options and determine if the accused wishes to be represented by someone else or whether the allegations are merely a sign of frustration;[88] if the accused desires to discharge the counsel, counsel should so inform the appropriate authority and discontinue representation.[89]

In any event, using a substitute counsel should be viewed as a last resort and should be saved for truly extraordinary circumstances.[90] Where substitute counsel is appointed or retained, there should be some documentation of that fact.[91]

---

court concluded that no harm occurred because the detailed counsel had been present during the entire trial, the accused apparently acquiesced in counsel's posttrial representation, and civilian counsel also presented a response to the recommendation. The court added that service on the detailed counsel is service on the defense team.

83. R.C.M. 1106(f)(2) United States v. Miller, 41 M.J. 647 (N.M.Ct.Crim.App. 1994) (failure to serve counsel who actually had attorney-client relationship was nonprejudicial error; counsel who received recommendation did not establish attorney-client relationship); United States v. Richter, 37 M.J. 615 (A.C.M.R. 1993) (nonprejudicial error for substitute counsel to represent accused although no attorney-client relationship had been established). United States v. Leaver, 32 M.J. 995 (C.G.C.M.R. 1991) (failure to appoint substitute counsel where accused was alleging ineffective assistance of counsel and had severed relationship amounted to harmless error); United States v. Mix, 29 M.J. 956 (A.C.M.R. 1990) (action of convening authority was set aside where record failed to indicate that defense counsel who represented pro se accused in posttrial proceedings did so with approval of accused). It would seem prudent for this substitute counsel to determine from the accused whether the accused has previously designated a particular counsel. *See* United States v. Antonio, 20 M.J. 828 (A.C.M.R. 1985) (accused waived his right to challenge the appointment of substitute counsel to review and respond to the SJA review; in this case the counsel had specifically contacted the accused to determine his wishes with regard to counsel).

84. United States v. Carter, 40 M.J. 102 (C.M.A. 1994). *See also* § 15-2(B)(3).

85. 40 M.J. at 105, *citing* United States v. Clark, 22 M.J. 708 (A.C.M.R. 1986) (attorney-client conflict due to allegation of ineffectiveness arises upon notification to counsel). In *Carter*, the defense counsel was unaware of the allegations at the time he prepared his post-trial submissions; thus, he was "mentally free of competing interests". *See also* United States v. Leaver, 36 M.J. 133 (C.M.A. 1992) (prejudicial error not to provide substitute counsel to accused after he expressed intent to sever attorney-client relationship; accused was denied right to conflict-free counsel).

86. United States v. Carter, 40 M.J. 102 (C.M.A. 1994).

87. 40 M.J. at 105 (citing ABA Model Rules of Professional Conduct).

88. 40 M.J. at 105.

89. *Id.*

90. United States v. Iverson, 5 M.J. 440, 449 (C.M.A. 1978).

91. United States v. Dahood, 32 M.J. 852 (N.M.C.M.R. 1991) (there should be documentation in record of trial that substitute counsel has been appointed or retained).

At least one court has recommended that because there may be questions as to whether the recommendation has been served, some sort of certificate of service should be executed.[92]

Even where the defense is not served with a copy of the posttrial recommendation there is some case law that indicates that the defense should take steps to obtain a copy and raise objections before the appellate courts.[93]

In 1990, R.C.M. 1106(f)(1) was amended to require service of the SJA's recommendation on *both* the defense counsel and the accused. In a case of first impression, the court in *United States v. Roland*,[94] concluded that the 1990 amendment was not intended to create a new substantive right but instead was made to provide a procedural protection to an existing right. The amendment, said the court, conforms the *Manual* with Article 60(d) of the U.C.M.J., which requires service of the recommendation on the accused.[95] The court indicated that in the absence of evidence to the contrary, it would assume that the staff judge advocate complied with the Rule.[96] The court applied the same presumption to the defense counsel.

The service requirement apparently does not apply to those situations where the SJA or legal officer is not offering a legal review of a trial, new trial, or rehearing.[97]

§ 17-9. Convening Authority's Powers.

§ 17-9(A). General Matters.

It is well-recognized that it is during the initial review by the convening authority that the accused has the best opportunity for relief.[1] This is due in

---

92. United States v. Lowery, 37 M.J. 1038, 1041 n.1 (A.C.M.R. 1993) (court recommended that service should be proved by contemporaneously prepared certificates of service, not through affidavits, presumptive assertions in post-trial documents, or presumptions of regularity). Noting that the issue of whether counsel was ever served with the posttrial recommendation of the SJA is often litigated, the court in United States v. McClelland, 25 M.J. 903 (A.C.M.R. 1988), urged Army-wide adoption of a certificate of service form. Such certificates were used prior to the 1984 amendments to the Manual for Courts-Martial. No particular method of service or proof of service is prescribed in the *Manual*, R.C.M. 1106(f)(1) Discussion, although some proof of service is clearly implied. *See* R.C.M. 1103(b)(3)(G). *Cf.* United States v. St. Romain, 33 M.J. 689 (A.F.C.M.R. 1991) (proof of service of SJA's recommendation is not required, service is required).
93. *See, e.g.*, United States v. Smart, 21 M.J. 15 (C.M.A. 1985); United States v. Barnette, 21 M.J. 749 (N.M.C.M.R. 1985).
94. 31 M.J. 747 (A.C.M.R. 1990).
95. United States v. Smith, 37 M.J. 583 (N.M.C.M.R. 1993) (nonprejudicial error not to serve accused with copy of recommendation; court concluded that it is not impracticable to send an accused copy of recommendation when he and convening authority are in United States and accused has provided mailing address); United States v. Watkins, 35 M.J. 709 (N.M.C.M.R. 1992) (nonprejudicial error not to serve accused with copy of recommendation). *See* Appendix 3.
96. 31 M.J. at 750. United States v. Jackson, 36 M.J. 757 (A.C.M.R. 1993) (accused's unrebutted affidavit that he had not been served overcame any presumption of regularity; failure to serve copy of recommendation was prejudicial error).
97. United States v. Dowell, 12 M.J. 768 (A.C.M.R. 1981), *rev'd on other grounds*, 15 M.J. 351 (C.M.A. 1983) (court noted that even though it was not going to institute a new "service" requirement, it would be wise for SJAs to serve DCs first with copies of decision papers, etc.).
1. United States v. Rivera, 20 C.M.A. 6, 42 C.M.R. 198 (1970).

large part to the convening authority's broad powers to act on a case; those powers are not always shared with the military appellate courts. For example, the convening authority may suspend all or a portion of the adjudged sentence a power not possessed by either the Courts of Criminal Appeals or the Court of Appeals for the Armed Forces.[2]

If the convening authority is convinced that the evidence establishes the accused's guilt beyond a reasonable doubt, he may approve all, or a portion of, the findings and sentence.[3] Note that even where the evidence clearly points to guilt, he may in his discretion nonetheless disapprove both the findings and the sentence.[4] If in reviewing the case, error is discovered, the convening authority may order a revision proceeding, if the error is minor,[5] or order a rehearing where the error goes to the core of the case.[6] His decisions regarding approval or disapproval of the proceedings are reflected in his action.[7] Depending on the amount and types of punishment in the sentence, he may order it into execution when he takes his initial action.[8]

In lieu of approving the sentence as adjudged by the court, the convening authority may suspend,[9] mitigate, or commute it.[10] He may not increase it, however.[11]

---

2. United States v. Darville, 5 M.J. 1 (C.M.A. 1978). *See also* § 17-9(D).

3. Art. 60, U.C.M.J. R.C.M. 1107. In a lengthy discussion of the issue, the Court of Military Appeals in United States v. Diaz, 40 M.J. 335 (C.M.A. 1994), indicated that although the convening authority is not required to act expressly on the findings, he is not prevented from doing so. When the convening authority explicitly approves the sentence, he implicitly approves the findings as well. But if the SJA has incorrectly stated the trial court's findings and the convening authority impliedly approves those incorrect findings, error has occurred; he may not attempt to approve a guilty finding that was not adjudged by the court-martial.

See also United States v. Drayton, 40 M.J. 447 (C.M.A. 1994) (convening authority's purported implicit approval of SJA's inaccurate report of findings was nullity; but accused waived issue by not noting defect in response to SJA recommendation). United States v. Mann, 22 M.J. 279 (C.M.A. 1986) (CA may consider sentences in other cases).

4. *Id.* This rarely exercised clemency power is grounded on the rationale that even though guilty, the servicemember's service may be important enough to warrant posttrial dismissal of the charges and/or disapproval of the sentence. *See generally* Hearings on H.R. 2498 Before a Subcomm. of the House Comm. on Armed Services; 81st Cong., 1st Sess. 1182-85 (1949).

5. *See* Art. 60(e), U.C.M.J. R.C.M. 1102(D). *See also* § 17-3(A).

6. Art. 60(e), 63, U.C.M.J. R.C.M. 1102. *See also* § 17-3(B), and United States v. Noonan, 21 M.J. 763 (A.F.C.M.R. 1986).

7. *See* § 17-9(c).

8. Art. 67, U.C.M.J.

9. R.C.M. 1108. *See also* § 17-9(D).

10. R.C.M. 1107(d)(1). Waller v. Swift, 30 M.J. 139 (C.M.A. 1990)(in lengthy discussion comparing relative severity of punitive discharges and confinement, the court granted extraordinary relief to accused where convening authority improperly commuted BCD to 12 months' confinement); United States v. Carter, 42 M.J. 745 (A.F.Ct.Crim.App. 1995) (convening authority could commute bad conduct discharge to 24 months additional confinement; accused and counsel had specifically requested additional confinement in lieu of discharge); United States v. Barratt, 42 M.J. 734 (Army Ct.Crim.App. 1995) (convening authority lacked authority to commute confinement to punitive discharge, even if accused consented); United States v. Jordan, 32 M.J. 672 (A.F.C.M.R. 1991) (convening authority could take corrective action on sentence where SJA informed him that judge had incorrectly found the accused guilty of offenses).

11. R.C.M. 1107(d)(1). Waller v. Swift, 30 M.J. 139 (C.M.A. 1990) (commuting BCD to 12

If the accused was temporarily released by a state or foreign country to military authorities for purposes of a court-martial,[12] the convening authority may postpone any adjudged confinement, without the accused's consent, until after the accused has been permanently released to the military by the state[13] or foreign government.[14] That decision should normally be reflected in the convening authority's action.[15]

The convening authority's powers with regard to the sentence may also be limited by a pretrial agreement he made with the accused.[16] For example, in return for a conviction based upon the accused's provident plea of guilty[17] the convening authority may have agreed to a limitation on the amount of confinement he would approve.[18] Or he may have agreed to suspend a portion of the adjudged punishment.[19]

---

months' confinement was an increase in the punishment); United States v. Foster, 40 M.J. 552 (A.C.M.R. 1994) (ambiguity in convening authority's action re length of time of forfeitures; court held that where action is ambiguous, convening authority may correct and clarify action and is not limited to duration of only one month for forfeitures); United States v. Coleman, 31 M.J. 653 (C.G.C.M.R. 1990) (converting dishonorable discharge to 18 additional months of confinement to 18 imposed by court and then suspending any confinement in excess of 18 months for 15 months was not an increase in the punishment); United States v. Petty, 30 M.J. 1237 (A.C.M.R. 1990) (increase in partial forfeiture of pay to total forfeiture is permissible if sentence as a whole is made less severe).

12. R.C.M. 1107(d)(3). The Rule was changed in 1995 amendments to the *Manual* by adding a new subsection (3) and renumbering existing subsection (3) as (4). The provision was based upon Article 57(e) which was added in 1992. Pub. L. No. 102-484, 106 Stat. 2315, 2505 (1992). *See also* Interstate Agreement of Detainers Act, 18 U.S.C. App. III. In effect, the change permits a court-martial sentence to run consecutively with a civilian or foreign sentence.

13. The term "state" refers to a state of the United States, the District of Columbia, a territory, and a possession of the United States. R.C.M. 1107(d)(3)(C).

14. R.C.M. 1107(d)(3)(A).

15. R.C.M. 1107(d)(3) Discussion.

16. United States v. Gooden, 23 M.J. 721 (A.C.M.R. 1986) (court set aside convening authority's action where it included a reprimand, a punishment which exceeded the terms of the pretrial agreement). *See* Chapter 9 for a discussion of pretrial agreements and plea bargaining.

17. *See* § 14-3. This assumes that the accused has been convicted following the judge's acceptance of his guilty plea and that there are no other reasons for not meeting the terms of the agreement. *See* § 9-2(C).

See also United States v. Cabral, 20 M.J. 269 (C.M.A. 1985) (although the convening authority may agree in a pretrial agreement to take lawful administrative action, hereby automatically reducing the accused to an E-1, he was arguably violating the provisions of the agreement which indicated that he would approve any reduction, as adjudged by the court ... in this case reduction to E-3. The court said that any ambiguities would be resolved in favor of the accused); United States v. Christian, 20 M.J. 966 (A.C.M.R. 1985) (accused waived objections to potential latent ambiguity in his pretrial agreement where he did not respond to the SJA's post-trial recommendation). R.C.M. 1105 and 1106.

18. *See* § 9-2(B)(1). United States v. Albert, 30 M.J. 331 (C.M.A. 1990) (convening authority's approval of sentence to conform to pretrial agreement that included provision for suspension of forfeitures was not affected by the collateral consequences that the accused was not otherwise entitled to any forfeitures); United States v. Gibbs, 30 M.J. 1166 (A.C.M.R. 1990) (convening authority could not convert fine adjudged by court into forfeitures where pretrial agreement did not include provision for approving any fine). *See also* § 17-9(D) for a discussion of the convening authority's power to suspend a punishment.

19. *See* §§ 9-2(B)(1) and 17-9(D). United States v. Koppen, 39 M.J. 897 (A.C.M.R. 1994) (parties

Before exercising his review powers the convening authority must consider any posttrial clemency matters submitted by the accused[20] and any legal recommendations submitted by the staff judge advocate or legal officer.[21] In the case of the former, the convening authority may not take action on the case until the minimum time for submitting clemency matters has expired[22] or the accused has waived the right to submit those matters.[23]

Notwithstanding the fact that the accused may have presented matters to the convening authority for consideration, there is often a real question of whether the convening authority received, and considered, them.[24] In *United States v. Foy*,[25] the court noted the continuing problem of determining whether convening authority had considered defense's post-trial clemency matters and set out a procedure designed to create presumption that such matters were considered: The SJA should include an addendum to his post-trial recommendation which (1) informs the convening authority that the accused has submitted matters and that they are attached to the addendum; (2) informs the convening authority that he must consider those matters before acting on the case; and (3) lists as attachments the matters submitted by the accused.

---

may agree as to beginning date of suspension of sentence; any ambiguity in effective date will be resolved in favor of accused); United States v. Jenkins, 30 M.J. 1101 (N.M.C.M.R. 1989) (accused was entitled to sentence relief where the convening authority's original action failed to comply with a pretrial agreement with the accused, and he unsuccessfully attempted to correct the matter with an improperly executed "supplemental" action); United States v. Hicks, 26 M.J. 935 (A.C.M.R. 1988).

20. *See* R.C.M. 1107(b)(3)(A)(iii) and 1105. This would also include any responses filed by the defense to the post-trial recommendation.

United States v. Espinoza, 27 M.J. 551 (C.G.C.M.R. 1988) (court noted that convening authority granted clemency and distinguished clemency measures from determining sentence appropriateness at the appellate level). *See* §§ 17-8(B)(3), 17-2(B)(3).

21. *See* § 17-8(B). *See* United States v. Murphy, 26 M.J. 658 (N.M.C.M.R. 1988) (failure to take action without obtaining legal recommendation was procedural and not substantive error); United States v. Hughes, 22 M.J. 609 (A.C.M.R. 1986) (case remanded for further review by convening authority).

22. Art. 60(b), U.C.M.J. *See also* § 17-2(B)(3). Failure to let the time run may be error. *See, e.g.,* United States v. DeGrocco, 23 M.J. 146 (C.M.A. 1987) (convening authority acted prematurely, but defense waived the issue by not showing that it would have offered any information to the convening authority for his consideration); United States v. Skaar, 20 M.J. 836 (N.M.C.M.R. 1985) (en banc) (accused suffered no specific prejudice when the convening authority acted before the period required by R.C.M. 1105 had run; important here was the fact that the accused had not intended to offer any materials to the convening authority for his consideration).

23. *See* R.C.M. 1105(d)(3), which indicates that the accused can expressly waive the right to submit materials to the convening authority. United States v. Scott, 39 M.J. 769 (A.C.M.R. 1994) (accused waived opportunity to present additional matters where he timely submitted some materials but did not reserve right to submit additional matters).

24. *See, e.g.,* United States v. Craig, 28 M.J. 321 (C.M.A. 1989) (court declined to guess whether convening authority had received and considered clemency matters and remanded case); United States v. Ericson, 37 M.J. 1011 (A.C.M.R. 1993) (must be tangible proof that convening authority considered submitted clemency matters); United States v. Miller, 35 M.J. 882 (A.C.M.R. 1992) (absent showing to contrary, court will presume that convening authority considered clemency matters submitted to him); United States v. Crawford, 34 M.J. 758 (A.F.C.M.R. 1992) (court examined entire record to determine that convening authority had considered post-trial clemency submissions).

25. 30 M.J. 664 (A.F.C.M.R. 1990).

In *United States v. Godreau*,[26] the court addressed the issue of showing that the convening authority considered the matter when no addendum is prepared. In those cases there must still be a statement in the posttrial recommendation which informs the convening authority that he is required to consider all matters submitted by the accused[27] and second, there must be some means of determining that, in fact, those matters were considered.[28] It approved the procedure whereby the convening authority initials and dates each item submitted in a clearly indicated fashion. If all else fails, an affidavit from the convening authority must be submitted.[29]

If the convening authority considers matters that are adverse to the accused but were not in the record of trial, he must give the accused an opportunity to rebut those materials.[30]

§ 17-9(B). Qualified and Disqualified Convening Authorities.

Normally, the convening authority who authorized the court-martial[31] acts on the case[32] even if the accused is no longer a member of his command.[33] In no case may he delegate his authority.[34] But he may transfer the case to another convening authority where it is impractical for him to act on the case[35] or where he is disqualified.[36]

---

26. 31 M.J. 809 (A.F.C.M.R. 1990).
27. United States v. Godreau, 31 M.J. 809 (A.F.C.M.R. 1990); United States v. Ericson, 37 M.J. 1011 (A.C.M.R. 1993).
28. *Cf.* United States v. Ericson, 37 M.J. 1011 (A.C.M.R. 1993) (when the recommendation or addendum clearly indicates matters submitted by the accused and those matters are attached, there is no requirement for affirmative statement by convening authority that he considered them); United States v. Kimble, 35 M.J. 904 (A.C.M.R. 1992).
29. United States v. Gardner, 29 M.J. 673 (A.F.C.M.R. 1989) (government was permitted to provide "paper trail" that showed that convening authority had considered the clemency materials; to foreclose problems, court suggested that SJA "close out" his recommendation with a brief comment regarding the submission of clemency matters).
30. R.C.M. 1107(b)(3)(B)(iii). United States v. Logan, 29 M.J. 1072 (A.C.M.R. 1990) (although convening authority apparently considered information included in the allied papers, the court held that the accused was on notice that they might be considered because the "entire record" includes allied papers).
31. *See* § 8-2.
32. Art. 60(a), U.C.M.J.; R.C.M. 1107(a). United States v. Delp, 31 M.J. 645 (A.F.C.M.R. 1990) (same convening authority, or authorized substitute, must both convene (including referral) and take initial action on a court-martial).
33. R.C.M. 1107(a) Discussion. *See, e.g.,* United States v. Kloese, 24 M.J. 783 (A.C.M.R. 1987).
34. R.C.M. 1107(a) Discussion.
35. United States v. Watson, 37 M.J. 166 (C.M.A. 1993) (court concluded that transfer of case from one Marine Corps convening authority to another, pursuant to a memorandum of understanding, was not error; the new convening authority was acting de facto).
United States v. Solnick, 39 M.J. 930 (N.M.C.M.R. 1994) (error to forward case to different convening authority where subordinate commander, convening authority, was available to act; the rule is designed to prevent a superior commander from plucking a case out of the hands of a convening authority for an improper reason). R.C.M. 1107(a) Discussion indicates that it may be "impractical" to act on the case where the command has been deactivated or the command is under alert for overseas movement.
36. R.C.M. 1107(a) Discussion.

A convening authority may be disqualified where he has (1) appeared as a witness in the case,[37] (2) granted immunity or clemency to a government witness in the case,[38] (3) shown more than an official interest in the case,[39] or (4) has expressed an inflexible attitude toward the sentence.[40] Where a disqualification exists, the case should be forwarded to the next higher command or laterally to another command.[41] If a disqualified convening authority acts on the case, the action is a nullity.[42]

---

37. *See* United States v. Reed, 2 M.J. 64 (C.M.A. 1976); United States v. Ward, 1 M.J. 18 (C.M.A. 1975).

38. United States v. Vith, 34 M.J. 277 (C.M.A. 1992) (convening authority not disqualified to review accused's case where he had earlier granted immunity to accused to testify in another case; accused unsuccessfully argued that convening authority learned of adverse information he would not otherwise have known had he not granted immunity); United States v. Newman, 14 M.J. 474 (C.M.A. 1983) (the court ruled that a grant of testimonial immunity to either a defense or prosecution witness does not affect the impartiality of the convening authority and his ability to review a court-martial. The court declined to consider under what circumstances a convening authority might be disqualified for granting transactional immunity or sentence reduction); United States v. Turcsik, 13 M.J. 442 (C.M.A. 1982) (there must be direct unattenuated causal relationship between grant and convening authority's subsequent action); United States v. Andreas, 14 M.J. 483 (C.M.A. 1983) (the convening authority was not disqualified by an ineffectual promise of transactional immunity to a civilian witness); United States v. Walters, 30 M.J. 1290 (N.M.C.M.R. 1990) (convening authority's grant of *transactional* immunity to prosecution witness was not disqualifying). Under earlier authority, such grants were almost always disqualifying. *See, e.g.*, United States v. Smith, 1 M.J. 83 (C.M.A. 1975); United States v. Dickerson, 22 C.M.A. 489, 47 C.M.R. 790 (1973). *Cf.* United States v. Lochausen, 8 M.J. 262 (C.M.A. 1980). Grants of immunity to defense witnesses are not disqualifying, however. United States v. Griffin, 8 M.J. 66 (C.M.A. 1979).

39. United States v. Crossley, 10 M.J. 376 (C.M.A. 1981) (reasonable probability that convening authority had a personal interest in outcome); United States v. Jackson, 3 M.J. 153 (C.M.A. 1977) (CA's involvement in pretrial processing was personal and therefore disqualifying); United States v. Allen, 31 M.J. 572 (N.M.C.M.R. 1990) (Secretary of the Navy's actions regarding national security cases were official and not personal, and convening authority did not act solely as alter ego of Secretary); United States v. Joyner, 25 M.J. 700 (A.C.M.R. 1987) (convening authority not disqualified by earlier comments he made in accused officer's efficiency report). *Cf.* United States v. Kroop, 34 M.J. 628 (A.F.C.M.R. 1992) (convening authority was disqualified from reviewing conviction for sexual acts where he was suspected of sexual misconduct).

40. *See* United States v. Lacey, 23 C.M.A. 334, 49 C.M.R. 738 (1975) (policy regarding larceny offenses); United States v. Howard, 23 C.M.A. 187, 48 C.M.R. 939 (1974) (policy regarding drug offenses). In United States v. Fernandez, 24 M.J. 77 (C.M.A. 1987), the court distinguished the role of the convening authority in referring cases to trial and in providing a post-trial review of the cases. In the former, he is acting in a prosecutorial capacity and in the latter, as a judicial officer. In this case, the convening authority was not disqualified from reviewing the accused's case simply because he had issued a command letter revealing his serious concerns about drugs. In the court's view, that letter "taken as a whole indicates a flexible mind regarding the legally appropriate ways in which to deal with drug dealers." For a discussion on command influence in the referral of charges, see Chapter 6.

41. *See* R.C.M. 1107(a) Discussion. The reasons for forwarding the case should be explained. *Id.* Service regulations may govern the transfer or forwarding process.

42. *See, e.g.*, United States v. McGuire, 32 M.J. 871 (N.M.C.M.R. 1991) (commander action on case was nullity where he was not authorized to act as convening authority).

§ 17-9(C). Actions and Execution of Sentences.

The vehicle for approving of the court-martial and execution of the sentence is the convening authority's written *action*.[43] The format is standard and is included in the promulgating order.[44] Although a convening authority may approve the findings and sentence,[45] his authority to order the sentence into execution may be limited. The U.C.M.J. limits the convening authority's power to execute any portion of a sentence which includes death or dismissal and an unsuspended punitive charge.[46] Execution of such sentences are deferred until after appellate review by the military courts and any necessary Presidential or Secretarial approval is accomplished.[47] In the interim, the convening authority must decide whether to impose post-trial confinement,[48] whether to suspend any portion of the sentence,[49] or whether to grant requests for deferment of the confinement or forfeiture or reduction in grade.[50] If the sentence does not include any of the above listed elements, the convening authority at the time of approval may order the sentence executed.[51] In doing so he may designate the place of confinement,[52] order forfeitures,[53] and grant credit for any pretrial confinement served.[54] The "action," which normally terminates the convening authority's jurisdiction over the case,[55] must be

---

43. See *generally* R.C.M. 1107.
44. See Appendix 36.
45. See § 17-9(B).
46. Art. 57, U.C.M.J. R.C.M. 1113.
47. Art. 74, U.C.M.J. United States v. McCarthy, 28 M.J. 887 (A.F.C.M.R. 1989) (convening authority's attempt to execute punitive discharge was premature).
48. See § 17-4.
49. See § 17-9(D).
50. See Art. 51(a), U.C.M.J. R.C.M. 1107(f)(4)(E) and § 17-2(B)(2). In 1996, Article 57(a) U.C.M.J., was amended to indicate that any forfeiture of pay or allowances or reduction in grade takes effect on the earlier of the date that is 14 days after the date sentence is adjudged or the date that the sentence is approved by the convening authority. National Defense Authorization Act for Fiscal Year (FY) 1996, § 1121. But Congress also included a provision which permits the convening authority to defer forfeiture of pay or allowances or reduction in grade until the date on which the sentence is approved by the convening authority. Art. 57(a)(2), U.C.M.J. The convening authority may rescind the deferment at any time.
51. Art. 71(d), U.C.M.J.
52. See R.C.M. 1107(f)(4)(C), 1113(d)(2)(C).
53. See Art. 57(a), U.C.M.J. Article 57(a) U.C.M.J., was amended to indicate that any forfeiture of pay or allowances or reduction in grade takes effect on the earlier of the date that is 14 days after the date sentence is adjudged or the date that the sentence is approved by the convening authority. National Defense Authorization Act for Fiscal Year (FY) 1996, § 1121.
54. See § 5-3(C). United States v. Stanford, 37 M.J. 388 (C.M.A. 1993) (nonprejudicial error where convening authority's action failed to reference pretrial confinement credited by military judge; although evidence indicated that appropriate credit was given, court remanded for correction of action). See *also* United States v. Davis, 22 M.J. 557 (A.C.M.R. 1986) (credit for pretrial confinement in civilian jail); United States v. Huelskamp, 21 M.J. 509 (A.C.M.R. 1985) (civilian pretrial confinement).
55. See R.C.M. 1102 (post-trial sessions) and 1107(f)(2). See *also* United States v. Luedtke, 19 M.J. 548 (N.M.C.M.R. 1984) (once CA has acted and has published it or the accused is officially notified of his action; he may not act further on the case unless the case is remanded to him).

served on the accused.[56] In the 1995 amendments to the Manual for Courts-Martial, R.C.M. 1107(f)(2) (modification of initial action) was changed. The new provision now permits the convening authority to recall and modify any action at any time prior to forwarding the record for review, as long as the modification does not result in an action less favorable to the accused than the earlier action. The original provision, which permitted any modification before the action was published or the accused was officially notified, remains in the Rule. In reviewing a convening authority's action, the appellate court will usually interpret it to give effect to his intentions.[57]

§ 17-9(D). Power to Suspend.

The convening authority's power to suspend is a function of his executive powers[58] and courts-martial[59] and the military appellate courts do not have the power to suspend.[60] The suspension provides a probationary period for the

---

In United States v. Jenkins, 30 M.J. 1101 (N.M.C.M.R. 1989), the convening authority's original action failed to comply with a pretrial agreement with the accused and later an improperly executed "supplemental" action was signed. In noting that the first action terminated the convening authority's jurisdiction over the case, the court noted:

> While it may indeed be tedious to pay attention to detail, to read one's own agreements, or to consult the Manual for Court-Martial, failure to do so when the rights of a servicemember are at stake cannot be condoned.

United States v. Murphy, 26 M.J. 658 (N.M.C.M.R. 1988) (convening authority had no power to modify published action without direction from higher authority); United States v. McIntosh, 25 M.J. 837 (A.C.M.R. 1988) (action by acting commander precluded later action by commander).
56. R.C.M. 1107(h).
57. United States v. Nastro, 7 C.M.A. 373, 22 C.M.R. 163 (1956); United States v. Simpson, 25 M.J. 865 (A.C.M.R. 1988).
58. Art. 74(a), U.C.M.J. United States v. Cowan, 34 M.J. 258 (C.M.A. 1992) (convening authority has inherent powers to suspend forfeitures contingent on providing for financial support for minor child; court indicated that even though there is no express authority to do so, a convening authority has the power to suspend all of an adjudged sentence or any part thereof).
United States v. Wendlandt, 39 M.J. 810 (A.C.M.R. 1994) (convening authority's power to suspend is function of position and may not be delegated; a sentence may be suspended, however, by persons designated in Article 60, U.C.M.J.; attempt to delegate authority to medical treatment facility was improper).
59. United States v. Clark, 16 M.J. 239 (C.M.A. 1983); United States v. Occhi, 2 M.J. 60 (C.M.A. 1976).
60. R.C.M. 1108(b) Discussion. See United States v. Darville, 5 M.J. 1 (C.M.A. 1978). The Advisory Commission established under the 1983 Military Justice Act considered the possibility of permitting military trial judges and appellate courts to grant suspension. The Commission concluded that in the balance granting such power was not advisable. In its report, the Commission cited the testimony of Major General Robert C. Oaks, Director of Personnel Plans, USAF, and a former convening authority:

> Military judges are not in a position to assess the effect on discipline, morale and good order that retaining a convicted military member would have on the command. Only the commander can determine this. As opposed to civilian court jurisdictions, the military judge does not exercise supervisory control over the member serving a suspended sentence or over the person administering the convicted member's probation. This is the responsibility of the commander and, as such, only the commander should have the authority to suspend sen-

accused on any unexecuted portions of the punishment[61] and must (1) run for a definite time, not beyond the accused's current enlistment,[62] (2) provide for automatic remission of the suspension at the end of the suspension,[63] and (3) spell out any conditions of the suspension.[64] Neither the U.C.M.J. nor the Manual for Courts-Martial state any specific time limits on the length of the suspension, the *Manual* does indicate that the period of suspension should not be "unreasonably long."[65] Acts of misconduct during the period of suspension[66] may lead to vacation of the suspension.[67] The procedural requirements for such a procedure are dictated by the type of court-martial that imposed the original sentence. Although the period of suspension may begin immediately

---

tences. Specifically in the civilian community as opposed to military, there is not a single person responsible for the overall conduct of life and good order and discipline such as the commander, and so the commander possesses an option, an opportunity, that is not available in civilian jurisdictions.

Commission Report at page 6.

61. United States v. Carter, 32 M.J. 830 (N.M.C.M.R. 1991) (error to attempt to suspend period of confinement that had already run).

62. R.C.M. 1108(d). The suspension may run until an anticipated event. *Id.* Service regulations may further limit the length of suspension. *See* AR 27-10, para. 5-31 (specific limits set in regulation). Spriggs v. United States, 40 M.J. 158 (C.M.A. 1994) (period of suspension was indefinite, i.e., until accused completed rehabilitation program; court limited time to five years).
United States v. Leonard, 41 M.J. 900 (C.G.Ct.Crim.App. 1995) (any error in imposing suspension which exceed Coast Guard regulation limitation of 18 months absent extraordinary circumstances was waived by failure to object). *See also* United States v. Bernier, 42 M.J. 521 (C.G.Ct.Crim.App. 1995); United States v. Merritte, 42 M.J. 519 (C.G.Ct.Crim.App. 1995); United States v. Robertson, 21 M.J. 1105 (A.C.M.R. 1986) (3-year suspension violated AR 27-10). *Cf.* United States v. Kinney, 22 M.J. 872 (A.C.M.R. 1986) (36-month suspension not in violation); United States v. Snodgrass, 22 M.J. 866 (A.C.M.R. 1986) (90-month suspension approved).

63. R.C.M. 1108(d). *See also* 1108(e), which provides:

(e) *Termination of suspension by remission.* Expiration of the period provided in the action suspending a sentence or part of a sentence shall remit the suspended portion unless the suspension is sooner vacated. Death or separation which terminates status as a person subject to the code shall result in remission of the suspended portion of the sentence.

64. R.C.M. 1108(c). United States v. Cowan, 34 M.J. 258 (C.M.A. 1992) (convening authority suspended forfeitures contingent on accused initiating and maintaining allotment to her sister in order to care for the accused's minor child). That Rule requires that the suspension authority shall (a) specify in writing the conditions, (b) cause a copy of that writing to be served upon the servicemember (probationer), and (c) obtain a receipt upon service; United States v. Myrick, 24 M.J. 792 (A.C.M.R. 1987) (court ruled that failure to follow these requirements was not fatal where the accused had been made aware of the conditions, which were included in the pretrial agreement, and the trial judge inquired into the matter at trial); United States v. Cowan, 32 M.J. 1041 (A.C.M.R. 1991) (convening authority could require accused to provide financial support for family in return for suspension of forfeitures).

65. R.C.M. 1108(d). *Cf.* United States v. Ratliff, 42 M.J. 797 (N.M.Ct.Crim.App.1995) (placing accused on probation for entire period of confinement is reasonable, in this case, for eleven years).

66. R.C.M. 1109(B)(1). United States v. Schwab, 30 M.J. 842 (N.M.C.M.R. 1990) (vacation of suspension was improper where convening authority had not yet acted to suspend required portion of sentence pursuant to pretrial agreement). *Cf.* United States v. Kendra, 31 M.J. 846 (N.M.C.M.R. 1990) (accused and convening authority agreed that suspension would begin at date sentence was adjudged; misconduct occurring before action could thus be used to vacate suspension). *See also* AR 27-10, para. 5-31 (specific limits established).

67. *See* R.C.M. 1109(a).

after trial, actual suspension does not exist until the convening authority acts on the case.[68]

Where the sentence was imposed by a general or special court-martial authorized to impose a bad-conduct discharge, the vacation hearing, similar to the Article 32 investigation,[69] must be personally conducted by the special court-martial convening authority,[70] who must be neutral and detached.[71] The accused is entitled to representation by counsel.[72] DD Form 455 is used to report the vacation proceedings and is forwarded with recommendations to the general court-martial convening authority.[73] His action vacating the suspension is reflected in a supplemental court-martial order that must state the evidence relied upon to support the vacation.[74] Failure to do so may invalidate the proceedings.[75]

The procedures for cases where the sentence was imposed by either a special or summary court-martial are generally the same as above.[76] Again, the accused is entitled to the assistance of counsel[77] and the hearing is conducted by the special or summary court-martial convening authority who may personally vacate the suspension.[78] His reasons should be recorded.[79]

§ 17-9(E). Other Clemency Powers.

In addition to suspending the sentence or portions of it,[80] the convening authority may mitigate the sentence by reducing it in quantity[81] or by commuting it, i.e., changing the nature of the punishment.[82] A commutation, however, may not be used to increase the punishment.[83] For example, a convening authority may not convert a punishment of confinement at hard labor

---

68. United States v. Saylor, 40 M.J. 715 (N.M.C.M.R. 1994).

69. *Id.* (decision to vacate suspension was technically void where witnesses' unsworn statements were considered over objections of accused). *See generally* § 7-2.

70. Art. 72, U.C.M.J. R.C.M. 1109(d). United States v. Rozycki, 3 M.J. 127 (C.M.A. 1977); United States v. Bingham, 3 M.J. 119 (C.M.A. 1977). *See generally* "Defending the Vacation of a Suspended Sentence," 9 THE ADVOCATE 11 (1977).

71. United States v. Connell, 42 M.J. 462 (1995) (without deciding broader constitutional issue, court concluded that special court-martial convening authority who heard accused's vacation proceeding was neutral and detached).

72. R.C.M. 1109(c)(4)(A).

73. *See* Appendix 39.

74. *See* R.C.M. 1109(d)(2)(A). United States v. Englert, 42 M.J. 827 (N.M.Ct.Crim.App. 1995) (error for convening authority not to make required findings; court approved pretrial agreement by not affirming discharge).

75. United States v. Hurd, 7 M.J. 18 (C.M.A. 1979); United States v. Lynch, 10 M.J. 764 (N.M.C.R. 1981) (vacation proceedings are integral parts of court-martial sentence).

76. *See* R.C.M. 1109(e).

77. R.C.M. 1109(e)(2).

78. R.C.M. 1109(e)(1).

79. R.C.M. 1109(e)(5). United States v. Bingham, 3 M.J. 119 (C.M.A. 1977).

80. *See* § 17-9(D).

81. R.C.M. 1107(d)(1).

82. *Id.*

83. *Id.*

into a punitive discharge.[84] And the approved sentence must be within the jurisdictional limits of the court that adjudged the sentence.[85] Determining what clemency to grant rests within the sound discretion of the convening authority[86] who may consider sentences imposed in similar cases.[87]

§ 17-10. Promulgating Orders.

The result of trial and actions by the convening authority and any higher authorities are recorded in court-martial orders; the convening authority of a general or special court-martial issues what is called the initial "promulgating order."[1] No promulgating order is needed for a summary court-martial.[2] The convening authority's initial action in that type of case is noted on the record of trial.[3] Subsequent actions by a reviewing authority in any court-martial are noted in supplemental promulgating orders.[4] Note that before the initial promulgating order is published or the accused is officially notified of the convening authority's action, the convening authority may recall and modify this action.[5]

§ 17-11. Post-Trial Delays.

Long delays in the post-trial processing of a case will not normally in themselves give rise to appellate relief [1] especially where it appears that under the

---

84. *See* R.C.M. 1107(d)(1) Discussion. United States v. Johnson, 12 C.M.A. 640, 31 C.M.R. 226 (1962).

85. *Id.* Jones v. Ignatius, 18 C.M.A. 7, 39 C.M.R. 7 (1968). *See also* § 4-3, concerning the jurisdictional limits of the court-martial.

86. R.C.M. 1107(b)(1). United States v. Mitchell, 15 M.J. 238 (C.M.A. 1983) (convening authority abused his clemency powers by stating in the referral statement that he would grant clemency if the trial was completed within 15 days; no appellate relief was granted however where there was no indication that the defense was in any way curtailed); United States v. Brown, 40 M.J. 625 (N.M.C.M.R. 1994) (Navy's family advocacy program re child abuse was not law requiring specified action by convening authority; convening authority who views such programs as requiring particular action abdicates responsibility to exercise discretion).

87. *See* United States v. Snelling, 14 M.J. 267 (C.M.A. 1982). *Cf.* United States v. Feagans, 15 M.J. 667 (A.F.C.M.R. 1983) (CA may not compare cases where there is no "direct relationship" between them).

1. R.C.M. 1114(a). *See* Appendix 36.
2. R.C.M. 1114(a)(3).
3. R.C.M. 1306(b)(2).
4. R.C.M. 1114(b)(2).
5. R.C.M. 1107(f)(2). United States v. Jenkins, 30 M.J. 1101 (N.M.C.M.R. 1989) (convening authority's original action which failed to comply with a pretrial agreement with the accused terminated his control of the case and he could not issue "supplemental" action); United States v. Luedtke, 19 M.J. 548 (N.M.C.M.R. 1984).

1. United States v. Burns, 2 M.J. 78 (C.M.A. 1976); United States v. Williams, 42 M.J. 791 (N.M.Ct.Crim.App.1995) (unexplained five-year delay resulted in reduction of approved sentence); United States v. Henry, 40 M.J. 722 (N.M.C.M.R. 1994) (8-year delay resulting from unexplained loss of record of trial not per se prejudicial; court expressed great frustration over such cases).

Cf. United States v. Thomas, 41 M.J. 873 (N.M.Ct.Crim.App. 1995) (expressing concern about unacceptable post-trial delays in naval service, court set aside bad conduct discharge, where SJA

circumstances the delay was reasonable.[2] Extremely long delays, however, might violate due process.[3]

The accused must demonstrate either that a prejudicial error occurred at trial which would require a hearing[4] or that prejudicial error has occurred because of post-trial delays.[5] If no prejudicial error occurred at trial, the court may nonetheless find prejudice because of the delay and reduce or disapprove the sentence.[6] Such prejudice might result, for example, where the accused

---

did not submit four-page recommendation until 10 months after the trial and took another 9 months to respond to defense counsel's concerns about post-trial delay); United States v. Olivari, 33 M.J. 933 (C.G.C.M.R. 1991) (180-day post-trial delay in guilty plea case did not result in prejudice to accused); United States v. Carter, 32 M.J. 830 (N.M.C.M.R. 1991) (no corrective action taken where convening authority did not act on case until 9 months after trial); United States v. Boldon, 17 M.J. 1046 (N.M.C.M.R. 1984) (628-day delay did not in itself create prejudice although the post-trial handling of the case was characterized by "administrative bungling, passive inattention, and divisible responsibility"); United States v. Rose, 16 M.J. 568 (A.C.M.R. 1983) (no prejudice although delay between convening authority's action and forwarding of record was unreasonably long); United States v. Riemer, 12 M.J. 915 (N.M.C.M.R. 1982) (10-month delay, although "inordinate, deplorable, and unexplained," did not require dismissal); United States v. Curry, 15 M.J. 701 (A.C.M.R. 1983) (8-month delay not prejudicial).

2. *See, e.g.*, United States v. Mansfield, 33 M.J. 972 (A.F.C.M.R. 1991) (423-day post-trial delay after 5-month trial was reasonable given record's size and complexity); United States v. Solorio, 29 M.J. 510 (C.G.C.M.R. 1989) (272-day delay from sentencing to action by convening authority was not unreasonable under the circumstances).

3. *See* United States v. Madison, 20 M.J. 860 (C.G.C.M.R. 1985) (appellate delay of three years resulted in disapproval of the entire sentence); United States v. Ward, 48 C.M.R. 588 (C.G.C.M.R. 1974) (774-day delay resulted in dismissal).

4. United States v. DeLello, 8 M.J. 777 (A.F.C.M.R. 1980).

5. United States v. Jenkins, 38 M.J. 287 (C.M.A. 1993) (accused failed to show substantial prejudice resulting from four-year delay); United States v. Dupree, 37 M.J. 1089 (N.M.C.M.R. 1993) (two-year, post-trial delay did not prejudice accused); United States v. Stombugh, 36 M.J. 1180 (N.M.C.M.R. 1993) (one-year, post-trial delay did not prejudice accused). In United States v. Hock, 31 M.J. 334 (C.M.A. 1990), the Court addressed the question of whether denial of speedy appellate review had prejudiced fifteen different accuseds. When it was discovered that the accuseds in hundreds of Navy cases had not been informed of the decisions of the Navy-Marine Corps Court of Military Review, the Court appointed a Special Master to conduct an inquiry into the matter. Based upon the conclusions and recommendations of the Master, the Court set aside the punitive discharge in one case, but affirmed the remainder.

See also United States v. Dunbar, 31 M.J. 70 (C.M.A. 1990) (three-year delay from sentencing docketing of case in Court of Military Review did not warrant dismissal where accused had failed to show specific prejudice); United States v. Shely, 16 M.J. 431 (C.M.A. 1983) (439-day post-trial processing was marked by administrative bungling and indifference; charges dismissed because of prejudice).

United States v. Hobbs, 30 M.J. 1095 (N.M.C.M.R. 1989) (court set aside punitive discharge where government could not account for 400-day post-trial delay in case); United States v. Bourgette, 27 M.J. 904 (A.F.C.M.R. 1989) (accused could show no prejudice resulting from post-trial delays); United States v. Ray, 24 M.J. 657 (A.F.C.M.R. 1987) (court rejected the argument that there was no jurisdiction over the accused where he committed additional offenses during a long post-trial delay after the Court of Military Review approved his punitive discharge in an earlier case).

United States v. Echols, 17 M.J. 856 (N.M.C.M.R. 1984) (accused suffered prejudice from 14-month delay); United States v. Williams, 14 M.J. 994 (N.M.C.M.R. 1982) (302-day delay was prejudicial); United States v. Ellis, 2 M.J. 616 (N.C.M.R. 1977); United States v. Owens, 2 M.J. 1286 (C.G.C.M.R. 1976).

6. United States v. Matias, 25 M.J. 356 (C.M.A. 1987) (13-month delay in appellate review by CMR did not result in prejudice); United States v. Halcomb, 25 M.J. 750 (N.M.C.M.R. 1987)

has lost civilian employment opportunities[7] or military benefits because of the delay.[8] Even where the accused is in post-trial confinement, he must be prepared to establish prejudice.[9]

PART III

APPELLATE REVIEW

§ 17-12. General.

As noted in § 17-7, every court-martial is initially reviewed by the convening authority. The review process may continue, however, into other appellate forums under automatic appeal provisions in the U.C.M.J.[1] Depending on the type and amounts of the sentence approved by the convening authority, a court-martial may be reviewed by a service Court of Criminal Appeals[2] and under more limited circumstances the United States Court of Appeals for the Armed Forces[3] and the Supreme Court of the United States.[4] Those forums serve as the keystone for the discussion in this part of the chapter.

§ 17-13. Waiver or Withdrawal of Appeals.

The Military Justice Act of 1983[1] and the 1984 revisions to the *Manual*[2] changed the rules regarding the ability of an accused to waive or withdraw otherwise automatic appellate review by the military appellate courts. Under earlier rules the accused's conviction was automatically sent to the service appellate court for review without regard for whether the accused desired further appeal. Continued appellate review of a case often meant that an

---

(absent prejudicial error in trial proceedings, appellate delay does not warrant relief; court nonetheless reduced the sentence where delay from convening authority action until filing with CMR was over one year in length); United States v. Amparo, 25 M.J. 722 (C.G.C.M.R. 1987) (accused not prejudiced by 322-day delay between sentencing and referral to CMR); United States v. King, 18 M.J. 535 (A.F.C.M.R. 1984) (seven-month delay prejudiced the accused); United States v. Simmons, 20 M.J. 567 (N.M.C.M.R. 1985) (court commended the supervisory authority for holding an evidentiary hearing to investigate appellate delays).

7. United States v. Bruton, 18 M.J. 156 (C.M.A. 1984) (unexplained six-month delay in conducting post-trial supervisory review, when linked with prejudice to the accused who could not obtain civilian employment, resulted in reversal); United States v. Sutton, 15 M.J. 235 (C.M.A. 1983) (321-day delay was prejudicial; inability to find employment); United States v. Clevidence, 14 M.J. 17 (C.M.A. 1982) (charges dismissed where convening authority acted 313 days after sentence was adjudged; delay frustrated the accused's attempts to find civilian employment).

8. *See, e.g.,* United States v. Berry, 33 M.J. 570 (N.M.C.M.R. 1991) (accused was prejudiced by 133-day post-trial delay; he was denied an opportunity to return to duty and obtain any resulting benefits).

9. United States v. Banks, 7 M.J. 92 (C.M.A. 1979).

1. *See* Arts. 66, 67, U.C.M.J.
2. *See* § 17-5.
3. *See* § 17-6.
4. *See* § 17-17.

1. *See* Art. 61, U.C.M.J., which was amended by Pub. L. No. 98-209, § 5(b)(1), 97 Stat. 1393 (1983).
2. *See* R.C.M. 1110.

accused who had no desire to remain in the armed forces had to await final appellate action before the convening authority could order the execution of a punitive discharge. Under the new rules the accused may now waive or withdraw appellate review and in doing so avoid delays in execution of any adjudged punitive discharges.[3]

The right to waive or withdraw an appeal is limited to only those cases that would otherwise be automatically reviewed by the Court of Criminal Appeals: where the sentence approved by the convening authority includes death, dismissal, a punitive discharge, or confinement for one or more years.[4] Appellate review may not be waived where the accused has been sentenced to death.[5] In effect, the waiver and withdrawal rules do not apply to summary or regular special courts-martial. In these cases and in those in which the accused has waived appellate review, a judge advocate nonetheless reviews the cases.[6] Those cases may also be reviewed by the Judge Advocate General.[7]

Before waiving or withdrawing the appellate review, the accused is entitled to the advice of counsel.[8] If the counsel who represented the accused at trial[9] has been excused or is not "immediately available," an associate counsel will be detailed if requested by the accused.[10] That counsel in turn is charged with communicating with both the accused and the trial defense counsel before advising the accused on the matter of waiver.[11] If necessary, a substitute counsel may be appointed to advise the accused.[12] Although face-to-face consultation is encouraged,[13] it is not required and may be accomplished, for example, over the telephone.[14] The key is that the accused has the opportunity to obtain legal advice on the wisdom of waiving appellate review and that the resulting waiver or withdrawal be free from coercion.[15]

A waiver of appellate review must be in writing[16] and signed by both the defense counsel and the accused.[17] It must indicate that they have discussed the latter's right to an appellate review[18] and the effect of waiving or withdrawing such review,[19] and that the waiver or withdrawal is being made

---

3. *See* Art. 71(c)(2), U.C.M.J., which indicates that where appellate review has been waived or withdrawn, a punitive discharge may be executed after a legal review by a judge advocate, *see* § 17-8, has been completed. Otherwise, appellate review must first be completed.
4. *See* Art. 61, U.C.M.J. R.C.M. 1110. *See also* § 17-15.
5. Art. 61(a), U.C.M.J. R.C.M. 1110(a).
6. *See* R.C.M. 1110 Discussion, and R.C.M. 1112. *See also* § 17-8(A).
7. R.C.M. 1110 Discussion, 1201(b)(3). *See* § 17-20.
8. R.C.M. 1110(b).
9. R.C.M. 1110(b)(2)(A), (3)(A).
10. R.C.M. 1110(b)(2)(B), (3)(B).
11. *Id.*
12. R.C.M. 1110(b)(2)(C), (3)(C).
13. R.C.M. 1110 Drafters' Analysis.
14. *Id.*
15. R.C.M. 1110(c).
16. R.C.M. 1110(d)(1).
17. Art. 61(a), U.C.M.J. R.C.M. 1110(d)(4). United States v. Rohrig, 19 M.J. 876 (A.F.C.M.R. 1985) (waiver was faulty because counsel failed to sign).
18. R.C.M. 1110(d)(2).
19. *Id.*

voluntarily.[20] The services provide standard forms for accomplishing this waiver; a sample is included at Appendix 38.

If the accused is waiving appellate review, the necessary document must be filed with the convening authority[21] within 10 days of his action on the case,[22] unless an extension of time (not more than 30 days) has been granted for good cause shown.[23] In a lengthy discussion of the issue, the court in *United States v. Hernandez*,[24] concluded that an accused's waiver of his appellate rights *before* the convening authority had acted was ineffective. The court explained that good reasons undergirded Article 61 and R.C.M. 1110(f) provisions that waiver must be filed within 10 days *after* action. First, the delay provides for a sort of "cooling off" period for the accused who has just been convicted.[25] Second, an accused's decision should be based on knowledge of what convening authority did with the case.[26] Finally, there is a danger that a waiver may be improvident if it is too easily accomplished.[27]

Where the accused is withdrawing appellate review, the document may be filed directly with the Judge Advocate General or with the general court-martial convening authority who has jurisdiction over the accused, who then forwards it to the Judge Advocate General.[28] The individual services may further specify how the withdrawal will be handled by the appellate court.[29] A withdrawal of appellate review may be filed at any time before that review is finished.[30]

Once accomplished, a waiver or withdrawal that is in substantial compliance with the *Manual* may not be withdrawn.[31]

§ 17-14. Appellate Counsel.

Qualifications for appellate counsel are the same before both the Courts of Criminal Appeals[1] and the Court of Appeals for the Armed Forces (CAAF):[2] Counsel must be qualified within the terms of Article 27(b)(1), U.C.M.J.[3] The

---

20. R.C.M. 1110(d)(3).
21. *See* R.C.M. 1110(e)(1).
22. R.C.M. 1110(f)(1). United States v. Smith, 34 M.J. 247 (C.M.A. 1992) (premature waiver of right to be represented by appellate counsel amounted to a premature wavier of appeal).
23. R.C.M. 1110(f)(1).
24. 33 M.J. 145 (C.M.A. 1991). *Cf.* United States v. Kaminski, 32 M.J. 808 (N.M.C.M.R. 1990) (waiver of appellate rights executed before date of delivery of convening authority's action is effective on that date). *See also* United States v. Williams, 32 M.J. 1060 (N.M.C.M.R. 1991) (accused's waiver of appellate review was effective even though it was filed before accused was served with copy of convening authority's initial action).
25. 33 M.J. at 148.
26. *Id.*
27. 33 M.J. at 149.
28. R.C.M. 1110(e)(2).
29. R.C.M. 1110(g)(3).
30. R.C.M. 1110(f)(2).
31. R.C.M. 1110(g)(1).
1. *See* § 17-15.
2. *See* § 17-16.
3. Art. 70, U.C.M.J. United States v. Thomas, 33 M.J. 768 (N.M.C.M.R. 1991) (in an extensive discussion court concluded that there is no per se rule that military accused is entitled to specially

Judge Advocates General of each service will appoint appellate counsel and assign them to "government" or "defense" appellate divisions. Appellate defense counsel will assume responsibility for the case on appeal and represent the convicted servicemember before the military's appellate courts.[4] Additionally, the accused is permitted to obtain civilian counsel, at no expense to the government.[5] Defense counsel will be appointed to represent the accused when (1) requested by him; (2) the United States is represented by counsel; or (3) the Judge Advocate General has certified the case to the Court of Appeals.[6] The military courts encourage continuation of the trial defense counsel's representation of the servicemember until appellate counsel has been designated and to that end,[7] trial defense counsel are encouraged to contact the appellate defense counsel.[8] If the appellant becomes dissatisfied with his or her appellate counsel, it is apparently incumbent upon the appellant to show good cause to the appellate court why counsel should be substituted.[9]

Appellate defense counsel must raise all arguable issues that are not, in his professional opinion, frivolous.[10] If an accused urges counsel to raise an issue

---

qualified counsel in capital case although military due process entitles accused to show necessity of need for counsel with such qualifications); United States v. Gray, 32 M.J. 730 (A.C.M.R. 1991) (court rejected the argument that Army appellate counsel were not qualified to represent him on appeal of his murder conviction because they were not qualified under the ABA Guidelines concerning death penalty cases. The court noted that those guidelines specifically exempt military counsel).

4. Art. 70, U.C.M.J.

5. *Id.*; R.C.M. 1202(b) Discussion. Martindale v. Campbell, 25 M.J. 755 (N.M.C.M.R. 1987) (court denied request for *mandamus* relief that Judge Advocate General appoint appellate counsel from outside appellate defense division because trial judge had presided at accused's trial; court found no actual conflict of interest). The accused does not have a right to an individual military appellate counsel. *Id.* United States v. Patterson, 22 C.M.A. 157, 46 C.M.R. 157 (1973).

6. Art. 70(c), U.C.M.J.; R.C.M. 1202(b)(2). *See, e.g.,* United States v. Sink, 27 M.J. 920 (A.C.M.R. 1989) (appellate counsel appointed even though accused had not requested one; court noted that appellate representation may take place even in absence of accused's knowledge or participation); United States v. Evans, 25 M.J. 699 (A.C.M.R. 1987) (court discussed reasons for denying accused's request to appear *pro se* in oral argument); United States v. Matthews, 19 M.J. 707 (A.F.C.M.R. 1984) (accused waived representation by appellate counsel when he voluntarily absented himself and was not available to sign the request for appellate counsel form).

7. United States v. Iverson, 5 M.J. 440 (C.M.A. 1978); United States v. Palenius, 2 M.J. 86 (C.M.A. 1977).

8. *See generally* Clark, "Defense Appellate Division and the Trial Defense Counsel: The Defense Team," 10 THE ADVOCATE 26 (1978).

9. United States v. Jennings, 42 M.J. 764 (C.G.Ct.Crim.App. 1995). *See also* United States v. Leaver, 36 M.J. 133 (C.M.A. 1992).

10. United States v. Baker, 28 M.J. 121 (C.M.A. 1989) (appellate defense counsel was not ineffective in not assigning any errors before the Court of Military Review). *See also* United States v. Bradford, 28 M.J. 125 (C.M.A. 1989); United States v. Grostefon, 12 M.J. 431 (C.M.A. 1982); United States v. Knight, 15 M.J. 202 (C.M.A. 1983). *Cf.* Jones v. Barnes, 463 U.S. 745 (1983) (counsel does not have a constitutional duty to raise every nonfrivolous issue requested by the defendant).

In United States v. Arroyo, 17 M.J. 224 (C.M.A. 1984), the court noted that *Grostefon* rests not on the Sixth Amendment but rather upon Articles 66 and 70 of the U.C.M.J. It also noted that the issue of whether an issue is frivolous should be left to the judgment of appellate counsel. *See also* United States v. Williams, 22 M.J. 584 (A.C.M.R. 1986) (appellate counsel should determine what information is relevant).

which would be counterproductive, counsel should try to have the accused withdraw it. If he refuses to do so, counsel may simply list the issue without briefing it.[11]

§ 17-15. United States Courts of Criminal Appeals.

The four service Courts of Criminal Appeals (Air Force, Army, Coast Guard and Navy-Marine Corps), formerly Courts of Military Review,[1] and before that Boards of Review,[2] are located in the Washington, D.C. area and consist of senior judge advocates, although the U.C.M.J. does provide that civilian judges may be appointed.[3] Each court may consist of one or more panels of three judges[4] and includes a clerk and other necessary administrative personnel. The courts review the cases referred to them by the Judge Advocates General.[5] After appellate counsel have submitted their written briefs, the

---

11. United States v. Quigley, 35 M.J. 345 (C.M.A. 1992) (accused was denied effective assistance of counsel where appellate counsel did not zealously present hearsay argument to appellate court); United States v. Grostefon, 12 M.J. 431 (C.M.A. 1982); United States v. Arroyo, 17 M.J. 224 (C.M.A. 1984); United States v. Bell, 34 M.J. 937 (A.F.C.M.R. 1992) (counsel submitted accused's 31 issues pursuant to Grostefon; extensive discussion of problems caused by repeated filings in case); United States v. Burdine, 29 M.J. 834 (A.C.M.R. 1989) (court indicated that when the accused has alleged that trial counsel was ineffective, appellate counsel should contact the accused and determine with as much specificity as possible how counsel was ineffective; counsel should also advise the accused that it would help the case to file an affidavit spelling out the details of the allegation).
1. The names of the courts were changed, effective October 5, 1994, by Pub. L. No. 103-337, § 924, 108 Stat. 2663. That same act changed the name of the United States Court of Military Appeals to the United States Court of Appeals for the Armed Forces.
2. Art. 66, U.C.M.J. The change occurred on August 1, 1968, the effective date of the Military Justice Act of 1968. *See* Currier and Kent, "The Boards of Review of the Armed Services," 6 VAND. L. REV. 241 (1953). *See also* § 1-3(D) for a discussion on locating and citing the opinions of these courts.
3. Art. 66(a), U.C.M.J. In an extensive discussion of the issue, the Court of Military Appeals, in United States v. Mitchell, 39 M.J. 131 (C.M.A. 1994), held that the fact that the Judge Advocate General of the Navy prepares and signs the fitness reports for the judges of the Navy-Marine Corps Court of Military Review did not deprive court of independence. Nor did it deprive the court of the appearance of fairness. Noting that the appellate judges seemed dissatisfied with the arrangement, the Court declined to legislate a change in the manner of rating the judges.
In Ryder v. United States, 115 S. Ct. 2031 (1995), the Court of Military Appeals concluded that the Appointments Clause had been violated when two civilian judges sat on the Coast Guard Court of Military Review by the appointment of the General Counsel for the Department of Transportation. 39 M.J. 454 (C.M.A. 1994). But the court concluded that the civilians were de facto officers and confirmed the conviction. The Supreme Court reversed, rejecting the argument that the judges were de facto. Rejecting a number of government arguments, the Court concluded that the accused was entitled to have his appeal heard by a properly constituted panel of the service court.
4. *Id.* The judges may sit en banc. *Id. See also* United States v. Vines, 15 M.J. 247 (C.M.A. 1983), for a discussion on the procedures for assigning cases to the various panels; there are no restrictions on the authority of the court's Chief Judge to assign cases to panels as he wishes. In United States v. Elliott, 15 M.J. 347 (C.M.A. 1983), the court reversed the CMR's decision because only two judges were actually members of the particular panel hearing the case.
5. Art. 66(b), U.C.M.J. *See also* § 17-15(A).

court may hear oral arguments at request of counsel before rendering their opinions.[6]

§ 17-15(A). Jurisdiction.

The Courts of Criminal Appeals hear cases referred by the respective Judge Advocates General, who must, in the absence of a waiver,[7] do so in all cases in which the approved sentence includes a penalty of death, a punitive discharge, dismissal, or confinement for one or more years.[8]

Article 66 was amended in 1983 to remove automatic appeal for cases involving general or flag officers. The Report from the Senate Committee on Armed Services for the Military Justice Act of 1983[9] stated in part:

> Section 7(c) amends Article 66(b) to remove from the mandatory appellate jurisdiction of the Courts of Military Review cases affecting a general or flag officer that are not otherwise within the jurisdiction of the court. As amended, Court of Military Review jurisdiction over a case affecting such officers will be the same as jurisdiction over all military personnel. Only a handful of cases have involved general or flag officers since the UCMJ was enacted over 30 years ago; the requirement of mandatory appellate review of all cases affecting such officers, however, may lead to a perception that the Code provides rights to flag and general officers that are not available to other service personnel. Although there are situations where military life requires distinctions based upon rank, this is not such a case.[10]

The Judge Advocates General may refer a court-martial, not otherwise reviewable by the Court of Criminal Appeals, where they determine that any part of the findings or sentence are unsupported in law, or if they otherwise so direct.[11] It now seems settled that these military courts have authority to issue extraordinary writs,[12] and may, where the case is pending before it, consider a petition for new trial.[13] The courts' jurisdiction continues[14] until

---

6. For the applicable procedural rules for the Courts, see 22 M.J. CXXVII (1986). See also United States v. Rodriguez-Amy, 19 M.J. 177 (C.M.A. 1985) (no denial of equal protection for CMR to deny oral argument on issue of sentence appropriateness).

7. See § 17-13.

8. Art. 66, U.C.M.J. R.C.M. 1201(a). See also United States v. Wilson, 20 M.J. 335 (C.M.A. 1985) (CMR was not deprived of jurisdiction to further review of a case that it had remanded for further proceedings, and as a result the accused's sentence had been reduced below the jurisdictional level of punishment applicable to the CMR; in such cases, the appellate courts have an interest in determining whether their earlier mandates have been followed). See, e.g., United States v. Grow, 3 C.M.A. 77, 11 C.M.R. 77 (1953).

9. Report No. 98-53, Apr. 5, 1983.

10. Id. at 28.

11. Art. 69, U.C.M.J.; R.C.M. 1201(b). See also § 17-20.

12. See § 17-19.

13. See § 17-21.

14. See United States v. Engle, 28 M.J. 299 (C.M.A. 1989) (per curiam) (execution of discharge does not in itself deprive court of considering accused's petition for review); United States v. Lange, 18 M.J. 162 (C.M.A. 1984) (accused's death during the 30-day period provided for filing a

the accused places any petition to the Court of Appeals for the Armed Forces appropriate channels.[15]

For a discussion of the authority of the Courts of Criminal Appeals to review government appeals of trial court rulings, see § 13-2(G)(2).

§ 17-15(B). Scope of Review and Actions.

The powers of the Courts of Criminal Appeals generally mirror those possessed by the convening authority; they may only act with regard to the findings and sentences as approved by the convening authority.[16] The courts do have fact-finding powers:[17] they may affirm only those findings and sen-

---

petition of review with the Court of Military Appeals did not deprive the ACMR of jurisdiction to abate the proceedings); United States v. Roettger, 17 M.J. 453 (C.M.A. 1984) (death of defendant during appellate proceedings did not abate jurisdiction).

United States v. Ross, 32 M.J. 715 (C.G.C.M.R. 1991) (accused was not entitled to withdraw case from appellate review); United States v. Johnson, 29 M.J. 1065 (C.G.C.M.R. 1990) (once jurisdiction has attached, accused is not entitled as a matter of right to withdraw the case); United States v. Boudreaux, 26 M.J. 879 (N.M.C.M.R. 1988) (court concluded that Article 69 review in the Office of the Judge Advocate General was not precluded in a remanded case that had previously been reviewed by the court under Article 66; but it also concluded that where the sentence on remand did not otherwise meet the jurisdictional requirement for Article 66 review by the court, the court could under its "ancillary" jurisdiction review the case if it desired. Here, the original mandate did not specify that the case should be returned to the court, the case was reviewed pursuant to Article 69, and there appeared no good reason to disturb that review); United States v. Montesinos, 24 M.J. 682 (A.C.M.R. 1987) (court had remanded the case to the convening authority for a possible rehearing on the sentence. Instead, he accepted a request from the accused for a discharge in lieu of trial. The court held that the convening authority's powers were limited by the court and that he could not terminate the jurisdiction of the court by discharging the accused. The court noted that there is contrary authority, United States v. Wilson, 20 M.J. 335 (C.M.A. 1985), but observed that a different rule would permit the convening authority to avoid the directives of the court by reducing the sentence or, as in this case, simply discharging the accused through administrative means); United States v. Woods, 21 M.J. 856 (A.C.M.R. 1986) (accused's administrative discharge did not terminate CMR's jurisdiction).

15. R.C.M. 1203(d)(2) Discussion. See also § 17-16.
16. See R.C.M. 1203(b) Discussion. In United States v. Murphy, 23 M.J. 862 (A.C.M.R. 1987), the court said:

> The action by the [court of review] is always taken on behalf of the accused and in his own interest. An accused may never be prejudiced by this appellate review; consequently, he cannot be tried for an offense greater than that charged at the first trial, nor can he receive a sentence greater than that adjudged at the first trial as approved by the convening authority.

23 M.J. at 862, citing United States v. Dean, 23 C.M.R. 185, 189 (C.M.A. 1957). This view may have become tempered by the 1984 Manual which permits prosecution appeal of some rulings by the trial judge. See § 13-2(G)(2). See also § 17-9.

17. R.C.M. 1203(b) Discussion. United States v. Cole, 31 M.J. 270 (C.M.A. 1990) (Court of Military Appeals described the power as "awesome, plenary, de novo power of review" that allows the court to substitute its judgment for that of the trial court); United States v. Turner, 25 M.J. 324 (C.M.A. 1987) (case remanded to CMR to determine factual sufficiency of the evidence). Cf. United States v. Hogan, 20 M.J. 221 (C.M.A. 1985) (Court of Military Review was bound by the factual conclusions of the military judge in concluding that the amount of LSD possessed by the accused was the same as that used by the accused). Cf. United States v. Smith, 39 M.J. 448

§ 17-15(B) REVIEW OF COURTS-MARTIAL § 17-15(B)

tences that are correct in law and fact.[18] In doing so, they may review the record,[19] judge the credibility of the witnesses,[20] and determine questions of controverted facts.[21] A finding or sentence of the trial court may not be held incorrect on an error of law unless the error is constitutional[22] or materially prejudices the substantial rights of the accused.[23] The Courts of Criminal Appeals do not have the power to suspend a sentence[24] nor may they order deferment of confinement.[25] They do, however, have the power to reduce the period of suspension imposed by the convening authority.[26] They may review a denial of a request for deferment of confinement.[27]

(C.M.A. 1994) (fact finding powers do not permit court to make findings of fact which contradict findings of not guilty reached by court-martial).
18. R.C.M. 1203(b) Discussion. United States v. Stidman, 29 M.J. 999 (A.F.C.M.R. 1990) (court determined that evidence did not support finding of guilty); United States v. Carlos, 25 M.J. 812 (C.G.C.M.R. 1988) (court concluded that under the facts, a punitive discharge was an excessive penalty for unauthorized absence of 72 days by accused with 18 years of service).
19. In United States v. Grostefon, 12 M.J. 431 (C.M.A. 1982), the court stated that the CMRs have a responsibility to read the entire record and independently decide whether the findings and sentence are correct in law and fact. *See also* United States v. Teeter, 12 M.J. 716 (A.C.M.R. 1981); United States v. Mitchell, 20 M.J. 350 (C.M.A. 1985) (CMR erred in not considering a signed, unsworn, letter from the accused that appellate counsel had submitted through a motion to file supplemental assignments of error).
Cf. Longhofer v. Hilbert, 23 M.J. 755 (A.C.M.R. 1987) (where the court declined to review an "appellate exhibit" that government counsel filed in an attempt to show that the convening authority had acted properly in denying the accused's request for deferment of post-trial confinement. The court noted that it has indicated a desire to curtail sharply appellate litigation through use of affidavits); *See also* United States v. Hurd, 7 M.J. 18 (C.M.A. 1979) (court declined to consider post facto documents); United States v. McCarthy, 24 M.J. 841 (A.F.C.M.R. 1987) (court set out case law that supports denying appellate consideration of various matters submitted to the court which were not a part of the record); United States v. Williams, 22 M.J. 584 (A.C.M.R. 1986); United States v. Brundidge, 20 M.J. 1028 (A.C.M.R. 1985) (court would not consider extra-record information concerning the death of the accused's father as a matter to be considered in approving an appropriate sentence).
20. Art. 66(c), U.C.M.J., R.C.M. 1203(b) Discussion. United States v. Lips, 22 M.J. 679 (A.F.C.M.R. 1986).
21. *Id. See, e.g.,* United States v. Clayborne, 7 M.J. 528 (A.C.M.R. 1979); United States v. Taliau, 7 M.J. 845 (A.C.M.R. 1979).
22. *See, e.g.,* United States v. Barnes, 8 M.J. 115 (C.M.A. 1979); United States v. Brown, 7 M.J. 815 (N.C.M.R. 1979).
23. Art. 59(a), U.C.M.J. A decision by a service's appellate court on a rule of law is binding upon all courts-martial within that service absent a contrary ruling by the Court of Appeals for the Armed Forces. United States v. Gutierrez, 11 M.J. 122 (C.M.A. 1981).
24. R.C.M. 1203(b) Discussion. United States v. Clark, 16 M.J. 239 (C.M.A. 1983); United States v. Darville, 5 M.J. 1 (C.M.A. 1978); United States v. Hallums, 26 M.J. 838 (A.C.M.R. 1988).
25. R.C.M. 1203(b). *See also* § 17-2(B)(2).
26. United States v. Darville, 5 M.J. 1 (C.M.A. 1978). The court may also decide that an unsuspended punishment is inappropriate and remand the case to the convening authority with a suggestion to reconsider. United States v. Clark, 16 M.J. 239, 243 (C.M.A. 1983) (Everett, C.J., concurring). *See, e.g.,* United States v. Millsap, 17 M.J. 980 (A.C.M.R. 1984).
27. R.C.M. 1203(b) Discussion. United States v. Brown, 6 M.J. 338 (C.M.A. 1979); United States v. Hilbert, 23 M.J. 755 (A.C.M.R. 1986) (court concluded that convening authority had abused his discretion in denying accused's request for deferment of confinement).

§ 17-15(B)

In acting on the case, the courts may (1) approve the findings and sentence;[28] (2) set aside all or portions of the findings or sentence,[29] and order a rehearing or order dismissal;[30] (3) order what is referred to as a *DuBay* hearing on specified issues,[31] or (4) reassess the sentence.[32] In assessing the appro-

---

28. R.C.M. 1203(b) Discussion.
29. *Id.* This assumes that the court has concluded that prejudicial error has occurred. In other words, it may not set aside the conviction for no reason, as can the convening authority. *See* § 17-9(A).
30. R.C.M. 1203(b) Discussion. United States v. Taylor, 25 M.J. 697 (A.C.M.R. 1987) (noting that it could not issue administrative discharge, the court set aside the findings and sentence in order to enable the convening authority to do so).
31. United States v. Dubay, 17 C.M.A. 147, 37 C.M.R. 411 (1967) (limited hearing by trial court to determine specified issue of command control). These hearings are now employed to examine a variety of issues that are normally raised for the first time on appeal. *See, e.g.,* Washington v. Edwards, 38 M.J. 501 (A.F.C.M.R. 1993) (court reiterated 7-pronged test in Tripp for determining whether to order post-trial hearing); United States v. Tripp, 38 M.J. 554 (A.F.C.M.R. 1993); United States v. King, 24 M.J. 774 (A.C.M.R. 1987); United States v. Turner, 15 M.J. 754 (A.F.C.M.R. 1983) (court returned case for *Dubay* hearing on Jencks Act issue). *See also* § 17-3.
32. United States v. Jones, 39 M.J. 315 (C.M.A. 1994) (good discussion of scope of court's powers to reassess sentence); United States v. Baker, 29 M.J. 126 (C.M.A. 1989) (court noted distinction between clemency and sentence appropriateness and remanded to Court of Military Review for determination of whether material it had not considered, because it seemed to be a matter of clemency, might also legitimately affect the issue of rehabilitative potential); United States v. Sories, 22 M.J. 305 (C.M.A. 1986) (reassessment does not require reduction); United States v. Suzuki, 20 M.J. 248 (C.M.A. 1985) (in reassessing the appropriateness of a sentence, the CMR must insure that the sentence is no greater than that which would have been given in the absence of the error).

United States v. Keith, 36 M.J. 518 (A.C.M.R. 1992) (court fashioned remedy where record showed that accused was held in confinement past release date); United States v. Rapolla, 34 M.J. 1268 (A.F.C.M.R. 1992) (power over sentence appropriateness is broad, although it does not include pure clemency power).

United States v. Tucker, 29 M.J. 915 (A.C.M.R. 1989) (court may consider sentence limitation in plea agreement in determining appropriate sentence; but fact that accused has agreed to particular sentence does not mean that he necessarily believes that that sentence is appropriate); United States v. Bell, 28 M.J. 1062 (N.M.C.M.R. 1989) (court reduced a dishonorable discharge to bad conduct discharge).

Garcia v. United States, 28 M.J. 917 (C.G.C.M.R. 1989) (petition for early release was based upon clemency, rather than appropriateness of sentence, and was therefore more properly within the prerogative of the Executive); United States v. Holt, 28 M.J. 835 (A.F.C.M.R. 1989) (court noted that its function was not to grant clemency through suspension of a sentence but rather to determine appropriateness of the sentence).

See also United States v. Smith, 28 M.J. 863 (A.F.C.M.R. 1989); United States v. Hardin, 29 M.J. 801 (C.G.C.M.R. 1989) (difference between sentence appropriateness and clemency); United States v. Conley, 28 M.J. 210 (C.M.A. 1989) (on petition for reconsideration, the court of review found a punitive discharge to be an appropriate sentence although on its initial hearing it had concluded that a discharge was not appropriate); United States v. Espinoza, 27 M.J. 551 (C.G.C.M.R. 1988) (court distinguished clemency measures, which are acts of leniency beyond jurisdiction of Courts of Military Review, and the authority to reassess a sentence); United States v. Harden, 14 M.J. 598 (A.F.C.M.R. 1982); United States v. Cowan, 13 M.J. 906 (N.M.C.M.R. 1982) (court declined to approve punitive discharge even where accused had requested one).

In United States v. Smith, 15 M.J. 948 (A.F.C.M.R. 1983), the court noted that comparing sentences might be appropriate if certain requirements were met.

priateness of the sentence, the appellate court may, but is not required to, consider sentences imposed in other cases.[33]

§ 17-15(C). Procedural Rules.

Article 66, U.C.M.J.[34] requires the Judge Advocates General to promulgate uniform rules of procedure for the service appellate courts, i.e., the Courts of Criminal Appeals.[35] Those rules govern such items as the format of pleadings, procedures for obtaining extensions of time to file pleadings, and procedures for obtaining reconsideration of the courts' opinions. In rendering their decisions the courts may issue opinions, which are normally published in the *Military Justice Reporter*,[36] or issue memorandum opinions which are not published.[37] Notice of the opinions, which are not self-executing,[38] are served upon the accused,[39] or his appellate counsel (constructive service),[40] who has sixty days to file a petition in the Court of Appeals for the Armed Forces. *See* § 17-16(B).

---

33. United States v. Henry, 42 M.J. 231 (1995) (appellate court did not abuse discretion in declining to equate accused's sentence with those of co-conspirators; court notes that purpose of Article 66 was to establish uniformity of sentences); United States v. Ballard, 20 M.J. 282 (C.M.A. 1985) (appellate court may, but is not required to, consider the sentences given in other cases).
United States v. Schnitzer, 41 M.J. 603 (Army Ct.Crim.App. 1994) (under facts, 14 years' difference in sentences of co-actors in closely related cases was not inappropriate); United States v. Gill, 40 M.J. 835 (A.F.C.M.R. 1994) (not appropriate to compare sentences in other cases unless cases are closely related and sentences are highly disparate); United States v. Kelly, 40 M.J. 558 (N.M.C.M.R. 1994) (extensive discussion of authority of court to compare similar cases in deciding whether sentence was appropriate; here, court concluded that accused in a similar case had received preferential treatment); United States v. Hawkins, 37 M.J. 718 (A.F.C.M.R. 1993) (sentence comparison with other cases deserved little weight under facts); United States v. Thorn, 36 M.J. 955 (A.F.C.M.R. 1993) (disparate sentences imposed on co-accuseds should be reviewed carefully; when there is a direct relationship between the accuseds and their offenses, the sentences are highly disparate, and there appear to be no reasons for the disparity); United States v. Ciulla, 29 M.J. 868 (A.F.C.M.R. 1989) (court reduced 40-year sentence to 30 years noting that it had found no other Air Force case in which such a heavy punishment had been given for similar offenses); United States v. Reeder, 29 M.J. 563 (A.F.C.M.R. 1989) (court compared sentence of co-actor); United States v. Anderson, 28 M.J. 895 (A.F.C.M.R. 1989) (court declined to engage in comparing sentences from different bases belonging to different commands); United States v. Lomax, 12 M.J. 1001 (A.C.M.R. 1982) (court considered sentences of co-actors in reassessing accused's sentence).
34. *See* Appendix 3.
35. *See* Art. 66(f), U.C.M.J. *See generally* Ghent, "Military Appellate Process," 10 The Am. Crim. L. Rev. 125 (1971); Miller, "Procedure in the Appellate Court," 9 THE ADVOCATE 1 (1977).
36. *See* § 1-3(D)(2).
37. *See* United States v. Clifton, 35 M.J. 79 (C.M.A. 1992) (lengthy opinion on Court of Military Review's practice of publishing unwritten opinions; lower court is not required to address specifically in writing all of accused's assignments of error as long as court indicates that judges considered issues and found them without merit); United States v. Pooler, 13 M.J. 786 (A.C.M.R. 1982) (court addressed issue of why it may affirm without an opinion).
38. *See* United States v. Kraffa, 11 M.J. 453 (C.M.A. 1981).
39. Art. 67(c)(1), U.C.M.J. R.C.M. 1203(d)(1).
40. Art. 67(c)(2), U.C.M.J. R.C.M. 1203(d)(1) Discussion. Service may be made, after appellate counsel has been served, by certified mail to the accused's last known address.

§ 17-16. The United States Court of Appeals for the Armed Forces.

§ 17-16(A). General.

The Court of Appeals for the Armed Forces,[1] originally called the Court of Military Appeals and first convened in 1951,[2] sits as a civilian appellate forum in Washington, D.C. It is composed of five civilian judges appointed by the President for fifteen-year terms; no more than two may be from the same political party.[3] For administrative purposes the Court is attached to the Department of Defense.[4] Article 67, U.C.M.J.[5] details the structure and powers of the Court, but in no way captures the broad powers exercised by the Court in providing the civilian review deemed so necessary by the drafters of the Uniform Code of Military Justice.[6]

---

1. The name of the court was changed, effective on October 5, 1994. See Pub.L. No. 103-337, § 924, 108 Stat. 2663. The same law changed the names of the Courts of Military Review to Courts of Criminal Appeals.

2. The court, originally called the "Court of Military Appeals," was created by the enactment of the Uniform Code of Military Justice in 1950. 64 Stat. 108 (1950). The effective date of the Act was May 31, 1951. The name of the court was changed to "United States Court of Military Appeals" in 1968 to reflect the fact that it was not an administrative court.

The organization, operations, and internal structure of the court were extensively reviewed in 1987-89 by a court committee appointed by the court in 1987. 25 M.J. at p. XCIX (Announcement of Court). The committee consisted of: Assoc. Dean James Taylor (Chairman), Mr. Wayne Carroll, Mr. Robert Duncan, Prof. A. Leo Levin, Prof. Daniel Meador, Mr. Russell Rourke, Prof. Stephen Saltzburg, Mr. Henry Steenstra, Prof. David Schlueter (Reporter), and Mrs. Linda Michalski (Administrative Asst.). The committee presented its report to the court in January 1989 and in its conclusion stated:

> The Court merits praise for much excellent judicial work and for its sponsorship of this independent examination and critique. Although the Committee offers a number of suggested changes, it believes that the Court has performed its tasks with determination and purpose. The recommended changes are offered in the spirit that their adoption will serve to improve not only the Court, but also the public's confidence in the military justice system.

The committee recommended a number of changes to the internal operations of the court to expedite appellate processing times and structure of the staff. It also recommended that the court be logistically separated from the Department of Defense, its membership be increased to five judges, that judges be appointed for terms without years (with retirement at age 70), that the chief judge be appointed for five-year terms, and that the "same political party" limitation be removed. The Committee's Recommendations are reported at 28 M.J. 99-102 and several of them were enacted as amendments to the U.C.M.J. in November 1989. One of the most significant was the addition of two new members to the Court, effective October 1, 1990. See Appendix 3.

3. Art. 67(a), U.C.M.J. In its 1989 report, the court committee, see note 1 supra, recommended that Article 67 be amended to remove this limitation, which now appears to be an anachronism.

4. See generally Art. 67(g), U.C.M.J. which authorizes a committee to review on an annual basis the operation of the U.C.M.J. and offer proposed changes.

5. See Appendix 3.

6. For an excellent discussion of the court, see Cooke, "The United States Court of Military Appeals, 1975-77: Judicializing the Military Justice System," 78 MIL. L. REV. 43 (1977).

§ 17-16(B). Jurisdiction.

There are three avenues of review before the Court. First, automatic appeal from the Courts of Criminal Appeals is provided for cases in which the affirmed sentence extends to death.[7] Second, the Judge Advocates General may certify issues raised in cases before the Courts of Criminal Appeals.[8] And third, the accused may petition the Court for review of the lower court's decision, clearly the most common method of review.[9] Filing the petition, which must be placed in channels within sixty days of receiving actual or constructive notice of the lower court's opinion,[10] terminates the jurisdiction of the Court of Criminal Appeals.[11] The official notice contains instructions to the accused and the necessary forms.[12] The petition is forwarded directly to the court, appellate counsel is assigned, and a brief in support of the petition is prepared.[13] The Court's extraordinary writ powers are addressed in § 17-19, and the ability of the accused to waive or withdraw appellate review is addressed in § 17-13.

---

7. Art. 67(b)(1), U.C.M.J.; R.C.M. 1204(a)(1). Articles 66 and 67 were amended in 1983 to remove automatic appeal for cases involving general or flag officers. *See* the Report from the Senate Committee on Armed Services for the Military Justice Act of 1983 (Report No. 98-53, Apr. 5, 1983). *See, e.g.,* United States v. Grow, 3 C.M.A. 77, 11 C.M.R. 77 (1953).

8. Art. 67(b)(2), U.C.M.J.; R.C.M. 1204(a)(2). United States v. Russett, 40 M.J. 184 (C.M.A. 1994) (it is important that court answer certified questions where lower courts are misinterpreting its decisions); United States v. Schoof, 37 M.J. 96 (C.M.A. 1993) (accused lacked standing to argue that he was denied equal treatment under provision which permits Judge Advocate General to certify question to Court of Military Appeals for automatic review; accused failed to request certification). In effect, this provision provides the government with further appellate review. In United States v. Caprio, 12 M.J. 30 (C.M.A. 1981), the court noted that the government could seek review of adverse C.M.R. decision regarding an extraordinary writ via a petition for review. *See generally* Mummey, "Judicial Limitations upon a Statutory Right: The Power of the Judge Advocate General to certify Under Article 67(b)(2)," 12 Mil. L. Rev. 193 (1961).

9. Art. 67(b)(3), U.C.M.J.; R.C.M. 1204(a)(3).

10. Art. 67(c), U.C.M.J. The Court has accepted untimely petitions on motions to file. *See, e.g.,* United States v. Hock, 31 M.J. 334 (C.M.A. 1990) (court disposed of many cases in which Navy had failed to provide procedures for determining whether accused had been served with decision); United States v. Myers, 28 M.J. 191 (C.M.A. 1989) (discussion and sample forms for informing the accused of the decision of the Court of Military Review); United States v. Ortiz, 24 M.J. 323 (C.M.A. 1987) (court indicated that in showing good cause for a late filing the counsel must assign meritorious issues for possible review); United States v. Sumpter, 22 M.J. 33 (C.M.A. 1986).

11. United States v. Hernandez, 33 M.J. 145 (C.M.A. 1991) (filing of petition in Court of Military Appeals divested Court of Military Review of jurisdiction). *See also* United States v. Boudreaux, 33 M.J. 649 (N.M.C.M.R. 1991) (accused was originally tried in 1975; extensive discussion of authority to conduct rehearing at trial level where accused apparently filed a petition for review with Court of Appeals).

12. *See, e.g.,* AR 27-10, para. 13-9 which details the process of providing the necessary service and forms on the accused.

13. United States v. Larneard, 3 M.J. 76 (C.M.A. 1977). *See* the rules of the Court at 44 M.J. XLVII (1996).

§ 17-16(C). Scope of Review.

Unlike the service appellate courts,[14] the Court of Appeals does not possess fact-finding powers. Its review is limited to examining questions of law.[15] The line between the two is often fine and in several cases evidentiary matters have been treated as a question of law.[16] Review is normally limited to issues certified by the Judge Advocate General or granted by the Court on petition by the accused although the Court may specify issues to be briefed and argued.[17] The practice of specifying issues has generated commentary and debate. One view is that the Court should exercise independent review powers, which are not always reactive to issues raised by appellate counsel.[18] Others argue that specifying issues demonstrates little confidence in the appellate review process and rarely results in meaningful relief.[19]

The Court may neither reassess[20] nor suspend, a court-martial sentence.[21] Nor may it defer confinement.[22] However, it can order a Court of Criminal Appeals to reassess an improper sentence[23] and it may review a denial of a request of deferment for abuse of discretion by the convening authority.[24] If the Court determines that the findings or sentences are not correct in law, it may direct the Judge Advocate General to order a dismissal of the charges or order a rehearing.[25]

---

14. See § 17-15.
15. Art. 67(d), U.C.M.J. United States v. Sanders, 37 M.J. 116 (C.M.A. 1993) (Court of Military Appeals has no authority to assess credibility of witnesses; court may determine whether there is some evidence supporting conviction); United States v. Dukes, 5 M.J. 71 (C.M.A. 1978); United States v. Brown, 3 M.J. 402 (C.M.A. 1977); United States v. McCrary, 1 C.M.A. 1, 1 C.M.R. 1 (1951).
16. See, e.g., United States v. Doran, 9 M.J. 385 (C.M.A. 1980) (admissibility of nonjudicial punishment was question of law); United States v. Brown, 3 M.J. 402 (C.M.A. 1977).
17. See Rule 5, Rules of Practice and Procedure—United States Court of Appeals for the Armed Forces, 40 M.J. LIX (1994) ("The Court may specify or act on any issue concerning a matter of law which materially affects the rights of the parties").
18. See, e.g., Early, Longstreet, and Richardson, "USCMA and the Specified Issue: The Current Practice," 123 MIL. L. REV. 9 (1989); Everett, "Specified Issues in the United States Court of Military Appeals: A Rationale," 123 MIL. L. REV. 1 (1989).
19. See Fidell & Greenhouse, "A Roving Commission: Specified Issues and the Function of the United States Court of Military Appeals," 122 MIL. L. REV. 117 (1988); Fidell, "The Specification of Appellate Issues By the United States Court of Military Appeals," 31 JAG J. 99 (1980).
20. See, e.g., United States v. Olinger, 12 M.J. 458 (C.M.A. 1982) (doing so might involve factfinding); United States v. Dukes, 5 M.J. 71 (C.M.A. 1978).
21. E.g., United States v. Darville, 5 M.J. 1 (C.M.A. 1978) (military courts are not empowered to suspend sentences).
22. Art. 57(d), U.C.M.J. R.C.M. 1103(c). The authority to defer confinement rests solely within the discretion of the convening authority.
23. See, e.g., United States v. Suzuki, 14 M.J. 491 (C.M.A. 1983), where court remanded with directions to provide meaningful relief. On remand, the Court of Military Review reaffirmed the sentence, 16 M.J. 621 (A.F.C.M.R. 1983), and a further review the Court of Military Appeals determined that the most equitable action would be to set aside all forfeitures. 20 M.J. 248 (C.M.A. 1985).
24. See, e.g., United States v. Brown, 6 M.J. 338 (C.M.A. 1978).
25. R.C.M. 1204(c)(1).

§ 17-16(D). Procedures.

The Court's procedural rules are set out at 40 M.J. LXI (1995).[26] In summary, after the Court grants a petition and specifies the issues it will consider, appellate counsel prepare final briefs and present oral arguments at the call of the Court. Opinions rendered by the Court are published in the Military Justice Reporter.[27]

§ 17-17. Review by the Supreme Court of the United States.

Before 1984, any hope by an accused of having his court-martial conviction reviewed by the Supreme Court rested solely within the lengthy process of collateral review in the federal courts.[1] For the government, there was no further appeal.[2] The Military Justice Act of 1983 changed that.[3] Both the accused and the government may now petition the Supreme Court for a writ of certiorari to the Court of Appeals for the Armed Forces.[4]

The applicable statute, however, provides that this direct review is limited to *decisions* of the United States Court of Appeals for the Armed Forces in:

(1) Cases reviewed by the Court of Appeals for the Armed Forces under [Article 67(b)(1), U.C.M.J.].

(2) Cases certified to the Court of Appeals for the Armed Forces by the Judge Advocate General under [Article 67(b)(2), U.C.M.J.].

---

26. Amendments to the rules are located at 43 M.J. LXI (1996). For a good discussion of these rules, see Fidell, "Guide to the Rules of Practice and Procedure of the United States Court of Military Appeals, Second Edition," 131 MIL. L. REV. (1991).

27. *See* § 1-3(D)(2).

1. *See* § 17-23.

2. The lack of government appeal was of some concern to the Senate Committee on Armed Services which in its Report on the 1983 Act (Report No. 98-53, dated Apr. 5, 1983) stated:

> The Court of Military Appeals is an independent judicial tribunal. It has demonstrated a willingness to strike down provisions of the Manual for Court-Martial and departmental regulations, and to interpret provisions of the UCMJ to require procedural requirements or to impose limitations. Such a development is a natural outgrowth of the creation of a civilian tribunal. When the Court overturns a rule or interprets a statute on nonconstitutional grounds, the President can amend the rule or seek an amendment of the statute. However, the absence of Supreme Court review means that the government cannot obtain judicial review of a decision by the Court of Military Appeals. This means that the Court of Military Appeals can render a decision as a matter of constitutional law interpreting a rule or statute in a manner that the President, on an issue vital to military discipline, might consider inconsistent with the intent of Congress or the views of the Supreme Court, but he could not obtain Supreme Court review. There is no other agency or government whose regulations can be ruled to be unconstitutional by a judicial body that is not subject to review by the Supreme Court.

Id. at p. 9.

3. Pub. L. No. 98-209, 97 Stat. 1393 (1983).

4. *See* Art. 67(h), U.C.M.J. 28 U.S.C. § 1259. *See generally* Effron, "Supreme Court of Review of Decisions by the Court of Military Appeals: The Legislative Background," ARMY LAW., Jan. 1985, at 59; Boskey & Grossman, "The Supreme Court's New Certiorari Jurisdiction Over Military Appeals." 105 S. Ct. at XCII (1984).

(3) Cases in which the Court of Appeals for the Armed Forces granted a petition for review under [Article 67(b)(3), U.C.M.J.].

(4) Cases, other than those described in paragraphs (1), (2), and (3) of this subsection, in which the Court of Appeals for the Armed Forces.[5] Review by the Supreme Court is not available for actions by the Court of Appeals in denying a petition for review.[6]

The intent of the drafters of this legislation was to limit the possibility of Supreme Court review to only those cases in which the Court of Appeals has affirmatively acted on a particular court-martial. But it appears that subsection (4) above provides a sort of catch-all which would include a case in which the Court of Appeals granted extraordinary relief on petition by either side while the case was still at the trial stage.[7] It is important to remember that Supreme Court review of military cases is entirely discretionary.[8]

And if the past several years are any indication, such review will be rare. It was not until 1986, almost two years after the effective date of the 1983 Act, that the Supreme Court granted plenary review of a decision by the military's highest court.[9] In *United States v. Solorio,*[10] the Supreme Court granted certiorari on the question of whether the Court of Military Appeals correctly ap-

---

5. 28 U.S.C. § 1259 (as amended in 1994).
6. Art. 67(h)(l), U.C.M.J.
7. *See* § 17-19.
8. In formulating possible issues for a petition for certiorari, counsel should consult Rule 10 of the Rules of the Supreme Court:

Rule 10. Considerations Governing Review on Certiorari

Review on a writ of certiorari is not a matter of right, but of judicial discretion. A petition for a writ of certiorari will be granted only for compelling reasons. The following, although neither controlling nor fully measuring the Court's discretion, indicate the character of the reasons the Court considers:

(a) a United States court of appeals has entered a decision in conflict with the decision of another United States court of appeals on the same important matter; has decided an important federal question in a way that conflicts with a decision by a state court of last resort; or has so far departed from the accepted and usual course of judicial proceedings, or sanctioned such a departure by a lower court, as to call for an exercise of this Court's supervisory power;

(b) a state court of last resort has decided an important federal question in a way that conflicts with the decision of another state court of last resort or of a United States court of appeals;

(c) a state court or a United States court of appeals has decided an important question of federal law that has not been, but should be, settled by this Court, or has decided an important federal question in a way that conflicts with relevant decisions of this Court.

A petition for a writ of certiorari is rarely granted when the asserted error consists of erroneous factual findings or the misapplication of a properly stated rule of law.

9. In *United States v. Goodson,* the Supreme Court granted certiorari, vacated, and remanded the case to the Court of Military Appeals for consideration in light of its decision in Illinois v. Smith, 469 U.S. 91 (1984). Goodson v. United States, 471 U.S. 1063 (1985). The court did so and reversed. 22 M.J. 22 (C.M.A. 1986).
10. 483 U.S. 435 (1987).

plied the service-connection requirement in determining subject matter jurisdiction and ultimately overruled its earlier cases on the subject.[11]

In an attempt to control the flow of petitions for certiorari the services may institute procedures for deciding which cases the government may pursue. As a general rule, the Solicitor General of the United States ultimately decides which cases will be filed on behalf of the government.[12] For the defense bar, the decision by military counsel to proceed with a petition to the Court may involve consultations in the respective Defense Appellate Divisions.[13] Note that a military accused is exempted from paying the necessary filing fees.[14] The jurisdiction of the Supreme Court, its scope of review, and the applicable procedures are beyond the scope of this book. Suffice it to say, the Court expects strict adherence to its procedural rules which may be found in 28 U.S.C.A.

PART IV

OTHER FORMS OF REVIEW

§ 17-18. General.

Exhaustion of the military appellate channels is not always the end of the review of a court-martial.[1] There are a variety of additional avenues of review available to the convicted servicemember, including internal military administrative review of the proceedings[2] and external collateral, review by the Federal courts.[3] Brief discussion of some of these forums comprises the final part of this chapter. Counsel seeking collateral review of the court-martial must be ever aware that the sought relief may be denied on the time-honored concept of "exhaustion of remedies." This may be particularly true in the Federal courts and in administrative review for correction of military records.

§ 17-19. Extraordinary Writs in the Military Courts.

The discussion of the military courts' rapidly expanding power to entertain petitions for extraordinary relief from servicemembers is included here[1] because it is more in the nature of a non-appellate avenue of relief although military appellate courts provide the forum. The authority of the military

---

11. *See* Chapter 4.
12. *See* House Report No. 98-599, p. 17; 1983 U.S. Code Congressional and Administrative News, Vol. 3, p. 2182.
13. *See also* Art. 70, U.C.M.J.
14. Art. 67(h)(2), U.C.M.J.
1. *See generally* Reardon & Carroll, "After the Dust Settles: Other Modes of Relief," 10 THE ADVOCATE 274 (1978).
2. *See* §§ 17-17, 17-20, 17-22.
3. *See* § 17-23.
1. *See also* § 13-2(G)(1).

appellate courts to issue writs[2] is derived from the All Writs Act which provides:

> The Supreme Court and all courts established by act of Congress may issue all writs necessary or appropriate in aid of their respective jurisdictions and agreeable to the usages and principles of law.[3]

To date, most of the activity in this form of review has taken place in the Court of Appeals, which has indicated that the language "in aid of [its] jurisdiction" may extend beyond actual jurisdiction.[4] That is, the court's writ powers are not necessarily limited to post-conviction relief because Congress intended the court to have general supervisory powers over the military justice system.[5]

Over the years, the debate has centered on the issue of just how broadly the courts, especially the Court of Appeals, should read the term "supervisory authority."[6] While the Court of Appeals has generally declined to review imposition of nonjudicial punishments[7] and other administrative matters,[8] it has exercised its extraordinary writ powers broadly where the military appellate process is in question.

For example, the court may have signalled an expanded view of its supervisory powers in *United States Navy Marine Corps Court of Military Review v. Carlucci*,[9] where it granted a protective order insulating the judges of the Navy Marine Corps Court of Military Review from being questioned by the Inspector General regarding allegations of impropriety in the court's decision

---

2. The five writs are Writ of Certiorari, Writ of Mandamus, Writ of Prohibition, Writ of Habeas Corpus, and Writ of Coram Nobis. *See* United States v. Biondi, 27 M.J. 830 (A.F.C.M.R. 1988) (discussion of *writ of coram nobis*).

3. 28 U.S.C. § 1651(a) (1994). *See generally* Floyd, "Extraordinary Writs in Favor of the Government," 25 JAG J. 3 (1970); Pavlick, "Extraordinary Writs in the Military Justice System: A Different Perspective," 84 MIL. L. REV. 7 (1979); Rankin, "The All Writs Act and the Military Judicial System," 53 MIL. L. REV. 103 (1971); Wacker, "The 'Unreviewable' Court-Martial Conviction: Supervisory Relief Under the All Writs Act from the United States Court of Military Appeals," 10 Harv. Civ. Rights Civ. Lib. L. Rev. 33 (1975); Winter, "Putting on the Writs: Extraordinary Relief in a Nutshell," ARMY LAW., May 1988, at 20. Note, "Building A System of Military Justice Through the All Writs Act," 52 Ind. L.J. 189 (1976).

4. *See* Robinson v. Abbott, 23 C.M.A. 219, C.M.R. 8 (1974) (writ powers extend to cases that will potentially come before the court). The limits of actual jurisdiction are prescribed in Articles 66 and 67, U.C.M.J. *See also* §§ 17-15(A) and 17-15(B).

5. *See* Gale v. United States, 17 C.M.A. 40, 37 C.M.R. 304 (1967).

6. McPhail v. United States, 1 M.J. 457 (C.M.A. 1976) (the court granted relief in a case that had been finally reviewed by the Air Force Judge Advocate General under Article 69, U.C.M.J.).

7. Stewart v. Stevens, 5 M.J. 220 (C.M.A. 1978) (court declined review of nonjudicial punishment procedures; Judge Cook indicated that he had been wrong in McPhail v. United States, 1 M.J. 457 (C.M.A. 1976) and acknowledged that certain areas of military justice must be left exclusively to the service Judge Advocates General). *Cf.* Fletcher v. Covington, 42 M.J. 215 (1995) (misc. docket) (court stayed imposition of Article 15 punishment by respondent).

8. Keys v. Cole, 31 M.J. 228 (C.M.A. 1990) (court declined to grant accused mandamus relief regarding his pay status and instead deferred to the Court of Claims). *See also* Vorbeck v. Commanding Officer, 11 M.J. 480 (C.M.A. 1981) (court declined to provide relief where OTJAG had not yet reviewed). *Cf.* United States v. Jackson, 5 M.J. 223 (C.M.A. 1978).

9. 26 M.J. 328 (C.M.A. 1988).

in *United States v. Billig*.[10] The court reasoned that Congress has indicated through its enactments, e.g., direct certiorari by the Supreme Court, that litigants within the military justice system not be required first to seek assistance from Article III courts. The court appointed Judge Cox as a special master to determine whether judicial misconduct had occurred in the *Billig* case.[11] And in *Unger v. Ziemniak*,[12] the court reiterated its broad powers under the All Writs Act, noting that Congress has had a number of opportunities to limit the court's jurisdiction but had instead enacted legislation that expressed confidence in the court. The court added that:

> Congress never intended that this Court sit by helplessly while courts-martial are misused in disregard of an accused servicemember's rights under the Constitution or the Uniform Code.[13]

Only recently was the question of the service appellate courts' writ powers settled; it is now clear that they too may issue any necessary writs.[14] The current philosophy is not to require exhaustion of remedies before seeking extraordinary relief at either of the appellate courts,[15] although counsel should consider first raising the issue at the trial level.[16] Denial of a petition for relief at a service appellate court may be appealed to the Court of Appeals.[17] Generally, extraordinary writs are used in situations involving juris-

---

10. 26 M.J. 744 (N.M.C.M.R. 1988) (*en banc*).
11. In 1989, Congress amended the U.C.M.J. by adding Article 6(a), which specifically authorizes the President to promulgate appropriate rules and procedures for investigating allegations against a military trial or appellate judge. *See* Appendix 3 for the text of the implementing legislation.
12. 27 M.J. 349 (C.M.A. 1989). Davis v. United States, 35 M.J. 640 (A.C.M.R. 1992) (*citing Unger*, court held that it had jurisdiction to consider petition for mandamus in case reviewed under Article 69(a); concurring opinion noted that extraordinary writ power involving cases not otherwise coming before the court if the petitioner's claim involves a constitutional issue).
13. 27 M.J. at 355.
14. In United States v. Montesinos, 28 M.J. 38 (C.M.A. 1989), the court indicated in a footnote that the Courts of Military Review could on their own motion issue an extraordinary writ where the integrity of its orders was at stake. Dukes v. Smith, 34 M.J. 803 (N.M.C.M.R. 1991) (court had no jurisdiction over nonjudicial punishment proceeding). *Cf.* In re Clifton, 28 M.J. 614 (A.F.C.M.R. 1989) (court held that it did not have jurisdiction to entertain extraordinary writ petition for review of servicemember's administrative discharge); Dettinger v. United States, 7 M.J. 216 (C.M.A. 1979).
15. *E.g.*, Garrett v. Mahoney, 39 M.J. 299 (C.M.A. 1994) (petitioner not required to first seek extraordinary relief in lower appellate court). *Cf.* United States v. Lemoine, 34 M.J. 1120 (A.F.C.M.R. 1992) (petitioner failed to exhaust available alternative remedies). Pearson v. Cox, 10 M.J. 317 (C.M.A. 1981); Kelly v. United States, 1 M.J. 172 (C.M.A. 1975).
16. *See* R.C.M. 1204(a) Discussion.
17. *See, e.g.*, Spriggs v. United States, 40 M.J. 158 (C.M.A. 1994) (petitioner servicemember successfully appealed); United States v. Pruner, 33 M.J. 272 (C.M.A. 1991) (writ appeal to review lower court's denial of petition for extraordinary relief regarding declassification of documents); United States v. LaBella, 15 M.J. 228 (C.M.A. 1983) (court considered the trial judge's appeal of a ruling by the Navy-Marine Corps Court of Military Review granting mandamus relief to the prosecution; noting that mandamus relief was not warranted, the court reversed); United States v. Redding, 11 M.J. 100 (C.M.A. 1981) (government appealed adverse ruling by N.C.M.R. to C.M.A. via certificate of review under Art. 67(b)(2)); United States v. Caprio, 12 M.J. 30 (C.M.A.

dictional issues,[18] speedy trial issues,[19] enforcement of pretrial agreements,[20] pretrial[21] or post-trial confinement,[22] grants of immunity,[23] command influence,[24] or in those instances where writs are necessary to ensure the lawful

---

1981) (government permitted to petition C.M.A. for reversal of adverse C.M.R. decision). See Rule 27, Rules of Practice and Procedure, Court of Appeals.

18. Sands v. Colby, 35 M.J. 620 (A.C.M.R. 1992) (court rejected mandamus petition from civilian employee who was retired from active duty). Woodrick v. Divich, 24 M.J. 147 (C.M.A. 1987) (court granted accused's request to stay court-martial proceedings until it could be administratively determined whether he was entitled to relief from an order to involuntary active duty); Wickham v. Hall, 12 M.J. 145 (C.M.A. 1981) (personal jurisdiction); Lwin v. Cooper, 33 M.J. 666 (N.M.C.M.R. 1991) (court denied habeas corpus relief; accused had argued that his conviction was based on illegal reserve call-up procedures); Spiller v. Vest, 32 M.J. 792 (N.M.C.M.R. 1990) (determined that court-martial jurisdiction existed over accused who had not been finally discharged).

19. Sands v. Colby, 35 M.J. 620 (A.C.M.R. 1992) (court rejected mandamus petition on speedy trial issue; writ will lie only for usurpation of judicial power or recurring legal error); Pascascio v. Fischer, 34 M.J. 996 (A.C.M.R. 1992) (in extensive discussion of issue, court concluded that accused was not entitled to mandamus relief because judge had denied speedy trial motion; court also rejected argument that a writ was required because the government had no right to try him at all). Hall v. Thwing, 30 M.J. 583 (A.C.M.R. 1990) (using its extraordinary writ powers, court ordered dismissal of charges for lack of a speedy trial even though no charges had been preferred with 120 days of imposition of restraint).

20. Spriggs v. United States, 40 M.J. 158 (C.M.A. 1994) (court granted requested relief enforcing provisions of pretrial agreement re suspension of sentence); Aviz v. Carver, 36 M.J. 1026 (N.M.C.M.R. 1993) (appellate court declined to grant mandamus relief; accused failed to show that he was indisputably entitled to relief on interpretation of pretrial agreement). In Shepardson v. Roberts, 14 M.J. 354 (C.M.A. 1983), the court agreed to exercise its extraordinary writ jurisdiction and review the propriety of a convening authority withdrawing from a pretrial agreement. The court ultimately denied relief.

21. See, e.g., Short v. Chambers, 33 M.J. 49 (C.M.A. 1991) (court denied accused's request to be released from civilian facility where he was being evaluated for mental competency to stand trial); Berta v. United States, 9 M.J. 390 (C.M.A. 1980) (misc. docket).

22. Waller v. Swift, 30 M.J. 139 (C.M.A. 1990) (court ordered accused released from post-trial confinement where convening authority improperly commuted BCD to 12 months' confinement); McCray v. Grande, 38 M.J. 657 (A.C.M.R. 1993) (court granted habeas corpus relief for improperly imposed post-trial confinement); Collazo v. Welling, 34 M.J. 793 (C.G.C.M.R. 1992) (accused granted habeas corpus relief by ordering him released from confinement and mandamus relief to compel the respondent to timely consider his deferment request); Longhofer v. Hilbert, 23 M.J. 755 (A.C.M.R. 1986) (noting the inadequacy of normal appellate channels, court granted extraordinary relief to convicted servicemember whose request for deferment of confinement had been denied by convening authority); Trotman v. Haebel, 12 M.J. 27 (C.M.A. 1981); Pearson v. Cox, 10 M.J. 317 (C.M.A. 1981); Bouler v. United States, 1 M.J. 299 (C.M.A. 1976).

23. Cunningham v. Gilevich, 36 M.J. 94 (C.M.A. 1992) (petition for relief granted to extent that although accused was not granted de facto tenure where commander told him to testify before investigating board, court indicated that coerced statements could not be used against him at trial). Cooke v. Orser, 12 M.J. 335 (C.M.A. 1982) (request to dismiss charges where government granted de facto immunity); United States v. Thomas, 33 M.J. 768 (N.M.C.M.R. 1991) (accused petitioned appellate court to order government to provide funds to hire death-qualified attorney to represent him in appeal of capital case); Clay v. Woodmansee, 29 M.J. 663 (A.C.M.R. 1989) (court granted extraordinary relief enforcing convening authority's formal clemency agreement whereby accused waived appellate rights in return for reduction in his sentence).

24. Hamilton v. DeGiulio, 35 M.J. 829 (A.C.M.R. 1992) (court denied mandamus relief to seek granting of motions to appellate court concerning issue of unlawful command influence); Davis v.

and orderly administration of justice.[25]

The five recognized writs are: (1) the writ of habeas corpus,[26] (2) the writ of *mandamus*,[27] (3) the writ of *coram nobis*,[28] (4) the writ of prohibition,[29] and (5) the writ of certiorari.[30] The military courts have generally followed prevailing federal law in determining whether a particular writ should be granted. The procedures governing petitions for extraordinary relief, which is not considered a substitute for an appeal,[31] are included in the rules for each of the appellate courts.[32]

United States, 35 M.J. 640 (A.C.M.R. 1992) (court had jurisdiction to consider allegation of unlawful command influence).

25. *See, e.g.*, Davis v. United States, 35 M.J. 640 (A.C.M.R. 1992) (court had jurisdiction to consider allegation of unlawful command influence); United States v. Lemoine, 34 M.J. 1120 (A.F.C.M.R. 1992) (court concluded that writ of mandamus requesting relief from active duty would not aid the court's jurisdiction); Wilson v. Ouelette, 34 M.J. 798 (N.M.C.M.R. 1991) (court denied accused's mandamus petition designed to disqualify judge from trying case); United States v. Bullington, 12 M.J. 570 (A.C.M.R. 1981) (to prevent frustration of prior orders in a case).

26. Collazo v. Welling, 34 M.J. 793 (C.G.C.M.R. 1992) (habeas corpus relief granted). Addis v. Thorsen, 32 M.J. 777 (C.G.C.M.R. 1991) (court considered but rejected accused's habeas corpus challenge to convening authority's denial of his request for deferment of confinement). *See also* 28 U.S.C. § 2441 (1988) (authority of Article III court to grant writ of habeas corpus).

27. *See, e.g.*, Collazo v. Welling, 34 M.J. 793 (C.G.C.M.R. 1992) (mandamus relief granted). Coffey v. Commanding Officer, 33 M.J. 938 (N.M.C.M.R. 1991) (petition for *writ of mandamus* is not appropriate where other normal appeal process is available for reviewing order vacating suspended sentence); Andrews v. Heupel, 29 M.J. 743 (A.F.C.M.R. 1989) (court issued *mandamus* to trial judge to dismiss charges for lack of a speedy trial).

28. Garrett v. Lowe, 39 M.J. 293 (C.M.A. 1994) (*coram nobis* granted in part re instructional error; court noted that although writ had earlier been limited to errors of fact, it now covers constitutional and other fundamental errors); United States v. Shelby, 40 M.J. 909 (N.M.C.M.R. 1994) (accused, who failed to raise issue of conflict of interest at trial, unsuccessfully attempted to obtain extraordinary relief in the nature of error *coram nobis*). Tillman v. United States, 32 M.J. 962 (A.C.M.R. 1991) (court had jurisdiction to rule on accused's petition for writ of error *coram nobis* alleging ineffective assistance of appellate counsel; the writ is not substitute for appeal but is remedy based upon exceptional circumstances not apparent to court in its initial consideration of case); United States v. Biondi, 27 M.J. 830 (A.F.C.M.R. 1988) (court refused to grant request for a writ of error *coram nobis* where the accused's petition essentially raised issues of law that had already been resolved against him during appellate review of his conviction).

29. *See, e.g.*, Gray v. Mahoney, 39 M.J. 299 (C.M.A. 1994) (writ of prohibition granted re trial judge's ultra vires order regarding disposition of videotapes belonging to accused). Freeman v. Stuart, 33 M.J. 659 (N.M.C.M.R. 1991) (accused filed various petitions for extraordinary relief; in an interesting discussion of the issue the court denied his request for writ of prohibition that would have blocked government medical personnel from administering drug that made him competent to stand trial); Pearson v. Bloss, 28 M.J. 764 (A.F.C.M.R. 1989) (although court ultimately denied relief, it considered accused's application for a writ of prohibition because it raised the "extraordinary" issue of whether court-martial had jurisdiction over him as a retired master sergeant).

30. The writ of certiorari is a discretionary writ for granting appellate review of a lower court's holding and in the military context is usually associated with military appeals to the Supreme Court of the United States. *See* § 17-17.

31. Mastropietro v. Nix, 12 M.J. 759 (A.C.M.R. 1981); *cf.* Andrews v. Heupel, 29 M.J. 743 (A.F.C.M.R 1989) (court granted extraordinary relief where it observed that the normal appellate process might be bypassed).

32. United States v. Lemoine, 34 M.J. 1120 (A.F.C.M.R. 1992) (under court's rules of procedure, petitioner's request for mandamus relief was untimely; rule required that petition for extraordinary relief be filed within 20 days of event complained of). *See also* § 13-2(G) for use of extraordinary writs for appealing rulings on motions at trial.

§ 17-20. Review in the Offices of the Judge Advocates General.

The Services' Judge Advocates General are vested with various supervisory powers over the military justice system.[1] One example, and the subject of discussion here, is what is commonly referred to as "Article 69" review of courts-martial.[2] That article of the U.C.M.J. contains two key provisions. The first, briefly addressed in § 17-15(A), requires the appropriate Judge Advocate General to review all general courts-martial that are not otherwise reviewed by the Court of Criminal Appeals and appellate review has not been waived.[3] If he finds any part of the findings or sentence unsupported in law or that the sentence is inappropriate he may modify the findings or sentence or both.[4] If he otherwise so directs, the case will be reviewed by the Court of Appeals for the Armed Forces.[5]

The second provision is much broader and provides that:

> (b) The findings or sentence, or both, in a court-martial not reviewed under subsection (a) [discussed *supra*] or [Article 66, U.C.M.J.] may be modified or set aside, in whole or in part, by the Judge Advocate General on the ground of newly discovered evidence, fraud on the court, lack of jurisdiction over the accused or the offense, error prejudicial to the substantial rights of the accused, or the appropriateness of the sentence. If such a case is considered upon application of the accused, the application must be filed in the office of the Judge Advocate General by the accused on or before the last day of the two-year period beginning on the date the sentence is approved under [Article 60, U.C.M.J.], unless the accused establishes good cause for failure to file within that time.[6]

Relief under this provision, which is not appellate relief, is requested through formal applications to the Office of Judge Advocate General.[7] Note that there is a statutory "exhaustion" requirement here; the conviction must have been finally reviewed, but not by a Court of Criminal Appeals.[8] And review must be sought, absent good cause for delay, within two years. The practical effect of this provision is that it provides an avenue of relief for persons convicted by a summary or a regular special court-martial.[9] The service regulations should

---

1. *See, e.g.*, Stewart v. Stevens, 5 M.J. 220 (C.M.A. 1978) (misc. docket).
2. Art. 69, U.C.M.J. *See* Appendix 3.
3. *See* Art. 69(a), U.C.M.J. R.C.M. 1201(b)(3)(A).
4. Art. 69(a), U.C.M.J. R.C.M. 1201(b)(3)(A).
5. *See, e.g.*, United States v. Mayhugh, 41 M.J. 657 (N.M.Ct.Crim.App. 1994) (case submitted to court by Navy Judge Advocate General under Article 69). The case may only be further reviewed by the Court of Military Appeals if the Judge Advocate General certifies the case to that court. Art. 69(a), 67(b)(2), U.C.M.J.
6. Art. 69(b), U.C.M.J. In Smithee v. Vorbach, 25 M.J. 561 (C.G.C.M.R. 1987), the accused failed to file his petition within the two-year limit and then unsuccessfully sought a writ of mandamus from the Court of Military Review to order the Article 69(b) review of his conviction.
7. See Appendix 40 for a sample form to accomplish this.
8. *See generally* § 17-14.
9. The results of these two types of court will have been finally reviewed at the trial level. *See* § 17-8(A).

be consulted for any further guidance on preparation and submission of the request for relief.[10]

§ 17-21. Petition for New Trial.

Petitions for new trials may be made to the service's Judge Advocate General at anytime within two years after the court-martial sentence is approved by the convening authority.[1] The two statutory grounds are (1) newly discovered evidence, and (2) fraud on the court.[2] If the petitioner proceeds on the first ground he must demonstrate that the evidence has been discovered since the trial, exercise of due diligence would not have permitted discovery at the time of trial, and finally, in light of this new evidence, trial by court-martial would probably produce a substantially more favorable result for the accused.[3]

---

10. *See* AR 27-10, Ch. 14. Slocum, "The Article 69 (UCMJ) Application: Jurisdiction and Use," 12 The Reporter 41 (Apr. 1983) (Air Force Procedures). *See generally* Glidden "Article 69 Appeals 'The Little Understood Remedy,'" 10 THE ADVOCATE 177 (1978).
1. Art. 73, U.C.M.J. R.C.M. 1210(a). United States v. Van Tessel, 38 M.J. 91 (C.M.A. 1993) (court rejected argument that filing of petition for new trial 37 months after action was not untimely; during much of that time, legal proceedings had been stayed by Court of Military Review because medical findings indicated that accused could not participate in them). *See generally* Carle, "New Trial Petitions Under Article 73, U.C.M.J.," 13 THE ADVOCATE 2 (1981).
2. Art. 73, U.C.M.J. United States v. Bacon, 12 M.J. 489 (C.M.A. 1982) (requests for new trial are not regarded with favor and should be "granted only with great caution"). *See also* United States v. Williams, 37 M.J. 352 (C.M.A. 1993) (military judge erred in not granting defense post-trial motion for a new trial (rehearing) which was grounded on discovery of new evidence); United States v. Evans, 26 M.J. 550 (A.C.M.R. 1988) (*per curiam*) (court denied pro se petition for new trial).
3. R.C.M. 1210(f)(1). United States v. Sztuka, 43 M.J. 261 (1995) (lower appellate court erred in denying petition for new trial based upon newly discovered evidence which supported defense theory that accused had innocently ingested drugs); United States v. Young, 43 M.J. 196 (1995) (if accused raises mental condition as newly discovered evidence, he must first make a showing that something brings into question his competence or mental responsibility); United States v. Singleton, 41 M.J. 200 (C.M.A. 1994) (trial judge erred in not granting new trial where defense showed that witness had lied out of fear of command influence); United States v. Williams, 37 M.J. 352 (C.M.A. 1993) (military judge erred in not granting defense post-trial motion for a new trial (rehearing) which was grounded on discovery of new evidence); United States v. Parker, 36 M.J. 269 (C.M.A. 1993) (affidavit which impeached testimony of victim was "new evidence" but did not entitle accused to new trial; Court of Military Review properly refused to accept affidavit); United States v. Bacon, 12 M.J. 489 (C.M.A. 1982) (good discussion on use of this ground to obtain new trial); United States v. Thomas, 11 M.J. 315 (C.M.A. 1981).

United States v. Zaiss, 42 M.J. 586 (Army.Ct.Crim.App. 1995) (requests for new trial are not regarded with favor and should normally be granted only if manifest injustice would result absent a new trial); United States v. Black, 42 M.J. 505 (Army Ct.Crim.App. 1995) (new trial not warranted where accused failed to show that evidence would have resulted in a substantially more favorable result); United States v. Good, 39 M.J. 615 (A.C.M.R. 1994) (accused entitled to new trial where post-trial evidence indicated that key prosecution witness suffered from mental disease); United States v. Hanson, 39 M.J. 610 (A.C.M.R. 1994) (noting that courts disfavor petitions for new trial based upon witness' change in testimony, court denied petition; witness' trial testimony was more credible than *ex parte* post-trial recantation); United States v. Bell, 38 M.J. 523 (A.C.M.R. 1993) (although evidence could have been discovered prior to trial, it did not affect findings of guilt or sentence); United States v. Brosius, 37 M.J. 652 (A.C.M.R. 1993) (petition for new trial denied by appellate court); United States v. Dyer, 22 M.J. 578 (A.C.M.R. 1986)

Fraud on the court will only be good cause for a new trial where it had a substantial contributing effect on the finding of guilty or sentence.[4]

If the case is not pending before one of the military appellate courts, the Judge Advocate General acts on the petition.[5] Otherwise, he must forward it to the court considering the case.[6] Counsel may submit a written request for oral argument to the authority acting on the petition and that authority may in its discretion grant the request.[7] It may also order further investigation or ask for additional matters.[8] Even though relief may not be provided in the form of a new trial, the Judge Advocate General may take appropriate action under Article 69, U.C.M.J.[9] or under Article 74, U.C.M.J., which permits certain authorities to remit (cancel) sentences and substitute administrative discharges for punitive discharges.[10] The format for the petition is set out in the Manual for Courts-Martial.[11]

(discovery of impeaching evidence not sufficient); United States v. Garries, 19 M.J. 845 (A.F.C.M.R. 1985) (court denied request for new trial on grounds of newly discovered evidence and fraud upon the court); United States v. Dyer, 16 M.J. 894 (A.C.M.R. 1983) (the accused was granted a new trial where it was discovered that the government psychiatrist who refuted his insanity defense and engaged in acts parallel in nature to those allegedly committed by the accused); United States v. Papageorgiou, 13 M.J. 584 (N.M.C.M.R. 1982) (accused seeking new trial has heavier burden than accused in normal course of appellate review); United States v. Peterson, 7 M.J. 981 (A.C.M.R. 1979).

4. R.C.M. 1210(f)(3). *See* United States v. Kennedy, 8 M.J. 877 (A.C.M.R. 1979).
5. R.C.M. 1210(e).
6. *Id. See* United States v. Van Tassel, 38 M.J. 91 (C.M.A. 1993) (Court of Military Review should have granted new trial based upon evidence that accused was probably insane). Holodinski v. McDowell, 7 M.J. 921 (N.C.M.R. 1979).
7. R.C.M. 1210(g)(1).
8. R.C.M. 1210(g)(1). United States v. Giambra, 38 M.J. 240 (C.M.A. 1993) (court remanded case for evidentiary hearing on whether victim had actually recanted testimony and accused was entitled to new trial; on further review, court held that victim had not recanted).
United States v. Niles, 39 M.J. 878 (A.C.M.R. 1994) (court ordered *Dubay* evidentiary hearing to obtain additional information on petition for new trial); United States v. Taylor, 30 M.J. 1008 (A.F.C.M.R. 1990) (in lieu of granting new trial, appellate court ordered *Dubay* hearing on issue of whether rape victim had truthfully recanted testimony which led to accused's conviction). *See* § 17-20.
9. *See* Appendix 3. R.C.M. 1210(g)(3).
10. R.C.M. 1210(g)(3).
11. R.C.M. 1210(c) provides:

> (c) *Form of petition.* A petition for a new trial shall be written and shall be signed under oath or affirmation by the accused, by a person possessing the power of attorney of the accused for that purpose, or by a person with the authorization of an appropriate court to sign the petition as the representative of the accused. The petition shall contain the following information, or an explanation why such matters are not included:
>
> (1) The name, service number, and current address of the accused;
> (2) The date and location of the trial;
> (3) The type of court-martial and the title or position of the convening authority;
> (4) The request for the new trial;
> (5) The sentence or a description thereof as approved or affirmed, with any later reduction thereof by clemency or otherwise;
> (6) A brief description of any finding or sentence believed to be unjust;

§ 17-22. Administrative Relief.

There are two statutory forums for correcting military records: Boards for Correction of Military Records, and Discharge Review Boards. These bodies are not within the appellate review chain of courts-martial and in most instances, the Boards will not grant relief unless the servicemember has exhausted his remedies. The review is collateral; the servicemember's request normally goes to the issue of correction of his records. In assessing whether "correction" is warranted, the Boards may no longer review the legality of the court-martial conviction that blemished the military record.[1] Applicable service regulations should be consulted for more detailed procedural guidelines.[2]

§ 17-22(A). Boards for the Correction of Military Records.

Each service is authorized under 10 U.S.C. § 1552 to establish civilian Boards for Correction of Military Records (BCMRs), which may review applications from servicemembers seeking correction of their military records and any related monetary claims against the United States. The Board may (1) correct any record where it considers such action necessary to reflect correctly the disposition of the case by reviewing authorities under the U.C.M.J. or (2) grant clemency on the sentence.[3] The application must be filed, unless otherwise provided by the Board, within three years of the discovery of the error.[4] The Board in its discretion may hold a hearing[5] and its recommendations are forwarded to the service Secretary for action. Examples of relief would include upgrading of a punitive discharge, reinstatement, or providing for retroactive pay. The Board, before granting relief, may require the servicemember to exhaust his administrative remedies.[6] The Board's decisions may be judicially reviewed in the Federal courts.[7]

---

(7) A full statement of the newly discovered evidence or fraud on the court-martial which is relied upon for the remedy sought;

(8) Affidavits pertinent to the matters in subsection (c)(6) of this rule; and

(9) The affidavit of each person whom the accused expects to present as a witness in the event of a new trial. Each such affidavit should set forth briefly the relevant facts within the personal knowledge of the witness.

1. Brown v. United States, 365 F. Supp. 328 (E.D. Pa. 1973), aff'd in part and remanded in part on other grounds, 508 F.2d 618 (3d Cir. 1975), cert. denied, 422 U.S. 1027 (1975) (establishment of Boards was not for purpose of reviewing courts-martial convictions). This point was made clear when Congress amended 10 U.S.C. § 1552 in the Military Justice Act of 1983 to reflect that the Board's authority extended only to correction of records to reflect actions taken by reviewing authorities under the U.C.M.J. or to extend clemency on court-martial sentences.

2. *See generally* 32 CFR Part 581 (Army); 32 CFR Part 723 (Navy); 32 CFR Part 865 (Air Force); and 32 CFR Part 52 (Coast Guard).

3. 10 U.S.C. § 1552(f) (1994).

4. 10 U.S.C. § 1552(b) (1994). *See also* Yonan v. Seamans, 380 F. Supp. 505 (N.C. 1974). The application is made on DD Form 149.

5. *See* Newman v. United States, 185 Ct. Cl. 269 (1968).

6. *See* Horn v. Schlesinger, 514 F.2d 549 (8th Cir. 1975); Champagne v. Schlesinger, 506 F.2d 979 (7th Cir. 1974).

7. *See* Midgett v. United States, 603 F.2d 835 (Ct. Cl. 1979).

§ 17-22(B). Discharge Review Boards.

Under the provisions of 10 U.S.C. § 1553, the services are authorized to establish Discharge Review Boards.[8] These Boards are normally composed of five senior military officers who may, with regard to review of courts-martial, examine bad-conduct discharges imposed by special courts-martial. The application is made on DD Form 293 and must be initiated within fifteen years of the discharge or dismissal.[9] The procedures for proceeding before the Boards are detailed in applicable regulations and should be consulted.[10] This review Board, which does hold hearings,[11] may upgrade a punitive discharge for purposes of clemency[12] but it may not reinstate the servicemember.

§ 17-23. Review in the Federal Courts.

§ 17-23(A). In General.

Once the servicemember's military remedies have been exhausted, the federal courts may collaterally review the court-martial.[1] But as a general rule, federal court review of military decisions, especially in the review of courts-martial convictions, has historically been very deferential. Most federal courts are reluctant to intrude into military decisionmaking, particularly in light of the military's internal appellate system.[2]

Collateral review seeks a declaration that a judgment is void. The Supreme Court in *Schlesinger v. Councilman*[3] explained:

> Collateral attack seeks, as a necessary incident to relief otherwise within the court's power to grant, a declaration that a judgment is void. A judgment, however, is not rendered void merely by error, nor does the granting of collateral relief necessarily mean that the judgment is invalid for all purposes. On the contrary, it means only that for purposes of the matter at hand the judgment must be deemed without res judicata effect:

---

8. 10 U.S.C. § 1553(a) (1994) specifically exempts review of discharges or dismissals imposed by general courts-martial.
9. 10 U.S.C. 1553(a) (1994).
10. *See* 32 CFR Part 581 (Army); 32 CFR Part 723 (Navy); 32 CFR Part 865 (Air Force); and 32 CFR Part 52 (Coast Guard).
11. The hearing, however, is not a *de novo* determination. Van Bourg v. Nitze, 388 F.2d 557 (D.C. Cir. 1967).
12. 10 U.S.C. § 1553(b) (1994).
1. *See generally* Rosen, "Civilian Courts and the Military Justice System: Collateral Review of Courts-Martial," 108 MIL. L. REV. 5 (1985); Peck, "The Justices and the Generals: The Supreme Court and Judicial Review of Military Activities," 70 MIL. L. REV. 1 (1975); Weckstein, "Federal Court Review of Courts-Martial Proceedings: A Delicate Balance of Individual Rights and Military Responsibilities," 54 MIL. L. REV. 1 (1971).
2. Chappell v. Wallace, 462 U.S. 296 (1983). *See also* Orloff v. Willoughby, 345 U.S. 83, 93 (1953) (civilian judges are not given the task of running the military); Parker v. Levy, 417 U.S. 733 (1974) (the need for a separate jurisprudence for the military is necessary to promote the purposes of the armed forces).
3. 420 U.S. 738 (1975).

because of lack of jurisdiction or some other equally fundamental defect, the judgment neither justifies not bars relief from its consequences.[4]

For example, a servicemember may seek monies for back pay in the Court of Claims on the argument that the military tribunal was without jurisdiction.[5] Thus, the threshold question is to determine whether a fundamental defect exists which would justify holding the conviction void.[6]

§ 17-23(B). **The Exhaustion of Remedies Requirement.**

As a general rule, before a servicemember may seek collateral review by a federal court, all available military remedies must be exhausted.[7] In adopting the exhaustion of remedies doctrine, the Supreme Court analogized federal collateral review of military courts-martial to a petition for habeas corpus in the federal court challenging the jurisdiction of a state court.[8] In *Gusik v. Schilder*[9] the Court stated:

> If the state procedure provides a remedy, which though available has not been exhausted, the federal courts will not interfere.... The policy underlining that rule is as pertinent to the collateral attack of military judgments as it is to collateral attack of judgments rendered in state courts. If an available procedure has not been employed to rectify the alleged error which the federal court is asked to correct, any interference by the federal court may be wholly needless.[10]

The Court concluded that the accused servicemember did not exhaust all available military remedies, and therefore the federal court lacked jurisdiction to adjudicate his claim.[11] Although *Gusik* was a collateral review pursuant to a writ of habeas corpus, the prerequisite of exhaustion of remedies generally applies to nearly all other remedies as well.[12]

---

4. 420 U.S. at 747. *See generally* Bishop, "Civilian Judges and Military Justice: Collateral Review of Court-Martial Convictions," 61 Col. L. Rev. 40 (1961).
5. Schlesinger v. Councilman, 420 U.S. at 749.
6. Hatheway v. Secretary of Army, 641 F.2d 1376 (9th Cir. 1971).
7. *See* Gusik v. Schilder, 340 U.S. 128, 131-32 (1975); Williams v. Secretary of Navy, 787 F.2d 552 (Fed. Cir. 1986); Bowman v. Wilson, 672 F.2d 1145 (3d Cir. 1982). *See generally* Rosen, "Civilian Courts and the Military Justice System: Collateral Review of Courts-Martial," 108 MIL. L. REV. 5, 67 (1985).
8. *See, e.g.,* Gusik v. Schilder, 340 U.S. 128 (1950); Noyd v. Bond, 395 U.S. 683 (1969).
9. 340 U.S. 128 (1950).
10. 340 U.S. at 132.
11. *Id.*
12. *See, e.g.,* Artis v. United States, 506 F.2d 1387 (Ct. Cl. 1974) (action for back pay brought in claims court); Williams v. Secretary of the Navy, 787 F.2d 552 (Fed. Cir. 1986) (mandamus action under 28 U.S.C. § 1361 dismissed because servicemember failed to exhaust his military remedies under 10 U.S.C. § 869(b) [Appeal to Judge Advocate General] and through the Board for Correction of Naval Records); Hooper v. Hartman, 274 F.2d 429 (9th Cir. 1959) (action for declaratory and injunctive relief); Williamson v. Secretary of the Navy, 395 F. Supp. 146 (D.C. 1975) (declaratory judgment).

There are exceptions to the exhaustion of remedies requirement, however. For example, under Article 66, U.C.M.J.,[13] a servicemember is entitled to an automatic appeal to a military appellate court in certain situations.[14] And under Article 69, the Judge Advocate General may direct a Court of Criminal Appeals to review certain cases that would not otherwise be subject to scrutiny by the military appellate courts.[15] But if the servicemember's punishment does not fall into those categories of case reviewable in the Courts of Criminal Appeals and the Judge Advocate General refuses to direct a court to review the case, the requirement of exhaustion of remedies is not required.[16] It is important to remember that even though Article 69 review is discretionary with the Judge Advocate General, the servicemember must still seek such relief before civil collateral review may be sought.[17]

Another example of an exception to the general rule that remedies must have been exhausted is where the remedy sought is unavailable through the military.[18] In *Parisi v. Davidson*,[19] the Supreme Court held that even though a court-martial proceeding was pending, the servicemember was entitled to collateral review because the military courts could not grant the requested relief.[20]

§ 17-23(C). Forms of Collateral Review.

Assuming that the servicemember has exhausted whatever military remedies exist for reviewing his court-martial conviction,[21] he may seek collateral review through one of several avenues. The review can take a number of forms, but is usually undertaken where the servicemember is seeking monetary claims or damages, i.e., in the United States Court of Claims, or relief in the nature of habeas corpus, injunctive relief,[22] *mandamus*, or a declaratory judgment.[23] The focus here will be on habeas corpus and *mandamus* relief.

---

13. *See* Appendix 3.
14. *See* § 17-12.
15. *See* §§ 17-17 to 20.
16. *See* Cole v. Laird, 468 F.2d 829 (5th Cir. 1972) (in addition to Art. 66, U.C.M.J. being inapplicable and Art. 69 relief being denied, any administrative relief, *e.g.*, Board of Correction of Military Records, would be ineffective).
17. Allen v. VanCantfort, 420 F.2d 525-26 (1st Cir. 1970).
18. Parisi v. Davidson, 404 U.S. 34 (1972).
19. 404 U.S. 34 (1972).
20. In *Parisi*, the Court noted that the petitioning servicemember sought a discharge from the service based upon a conscientious objector status and that the military courts were powerless to grant a separation from the service.
21. *See* § 17-23(B).
22. *See, e.g.*, Schlesinger v. Councilman, 420 U.S. 738 (1975). *See also* Rule 65, FED. R. CIV. P., which provides for injunctive relief.
23. *See* 29 U.S.C. § 2201 (1994) (Declaratory Judgments Act); Homcy v. Resor, 455 F.2d 1345 (D.C. Cir. 1971).

§ 17-23(C)(1). Habeas Corpus.

Convicted servicemembers may seek immediate release from the "custody" of the armed forces through a petition for habeas corpus in Federal district courts.[24] The servicemember does not necessarily have to be in actual confinement or restraint.[25] In determining whether the petitioner is in unlawful custody, the federal courts will collaterally review the court-martial and may consider arguments that the court-martial was without jurisdiction, that due process was lacking, or that the trial did not afford all the procedural safeguards necessary for a fair trial under military law.[26] In almost all cases, the courts will require exhaustion of military appeals—both automatic and discretionary.[27]

§ 17-23(C)(2). *Mandamus.*

This avenue of relief is normally employed by servicemembers seeking correction of military records. That is, the federal district courts are empowered under 28 U.S.C. § 1361 to order United States officers and employees to perform duties owed the petitioner, e.g., change military records[28] if a mistake has been made in completing the records. Again, in considering the petition the court may collaterally review the court-martial that led to the adverse military record.[29]

---

24. *See* 28 U.S.C. § 2441 (1994).
25. *See, e.g.,* Kauffman v. Secretary of Air Force, 415 F.2d 991 (D.C. Cir. 1969).
26. *See, e.g.,* Burnes v. Wilson, 346 U.S. 137 (1953); Calley v. Callaway, 519 F.2d 184 (5th Cir. 1975), *cert. denied,* 425 U.S. 911 (1976); Gorko v. Commanding Officer, 314 F.2d 858 (10th Cir. 1963).
27. *See* Gusik v. Schilder, 340 U.S. 128 (1950); Woodrick v. Hungerford, 800 F.2d 1413 (5th Cir. 1986), *cert. denied,* 481 U.S. 1036 (1987); Woodrick v. Divich, 24 M.J. 147 (C.M.A. 1987).
28. *See, e.g.,* 10 U.S.C. § 1552 (1994) and § 17-22.
29. Ashe v. McNamara, 355 F.2d 277 (1st Cir. 1965).

APPENDIX REFERENCES

Appendix 1. Abbreviations.
Appendix 2. Glossary.
Appendix 3. U.C.M.J.
Appendix 35. Sample Post-Trial Recommendation.
Appendix 36. Promulgating Orders.
Appendix 37. Judge Advocate Legal Review.
Appendix 38. Waiver/Withdrawal of Appellate Review.
Appendix 39. Vacation Proceedings.
Appendix 40. Application for Relief Under Article 69, U.C.M.J.

ANNOTATED BIBLIOGRAPHY

BOOKS

Addlestone, Kosloske, Milford, Snyder, & Stichman *Military Discharge Upgrading* (1982).

This loose-leaf practice manual provides an exhaustive survey of the sometimes complex procedural and substantive rules governing the upgrading of military discharges. The book is divided into 28 chapters and covers virtually every issue associated with the topic, including practice before the Boards of Correction of Military Records (BCMR), the Discharge Review Board (DRB), and the Veterans Administration.

Fidell, *Guide to the Rules of Practice and Procedure of the United States Court of Military Appeals* (1978).

The author presents in this short book the text of the rules and brief comments on the intent of the rules and how they might affect practice before the military's "supreme court."

PERIODICALS

The Military Appellate Process: In General

Ghent, "Military Appellate Processes," 10 AM. CRIM. L. REV. 125 (1971).

This short article presents a good, brief review of the appellate process from action by the convening authority, through the Court of Military Review, and finally the Court of Military Appeals. Based upon this review, the author concludes that the military's appellate structure provides "a greater panoply of protective remedies" than does the civilian system, i.e., automatic appeals, at no expense whatsoever, at several levels.

Jividen, "Will the Dike Burst? Plugging the Unconstitutional Hole in Article 66(c) U.C.M.J.," 38 A.F. L. REV. 63 (1994).

The author explains that the unique powers of the service appellate courts under Article 66(c), U.C.M.J. to render independent factual findings may be abused where the courts rely on post-trial affidavits rather than ordering *Dubay* rehearings which might be better able to determine disputes on a wide range of issues which arise post-trial, e.g., effectiveness of counsel.

Karlen, "Civilian and Military Justice at the Appellate Level," 3 Wis. L. Rev. 786 (1968).

This interesting article builds on the premise that the civilian courts can learn much from an examination of the military appellate system with its range of benefits and protections fro the accused. The work presents a review of not only operation of the military system before the codal changes in 1969, but also makes comparisons with the operation of United States Court of Appeals, specifically the Second Circuit Court. In conclusion the author raises questions regarding automatic appeal, mandatory retirement of judges, and the number of opinions published.

Lurie, "Presidential Preferences and Aspiring Appointees: Selections to the U.S. Court of Military Appeals 1951-1968," 29 Wake Forest L. Rev. 521 (1994).

The author presents an insightful survey of presidential appointments to the United States Court of Military Appeals since its inception in 1951. Relying upon primary evidence, the author highlights a trend to place political considerations over the substantive issues in naming judges to the court.

Moyer, "Procedural Rights of the Military Accused: Advantages Over a Civilian Defendant," 22 Me. L. Rev. 105 (1970); 51 Mil. L. Rev. 1 (1971).

This forty-page article compares the civilian and military criminal procedures such as pretrial investigation, interrogation, right to witnesses, right to counsel, and appellate review. The author concludes that the military accused enjoys greater procedural and substantive advantages than the civilian counterpart.

Powers, "Fact Finding in the Courts of Military Review," 44 Baylor L. Rev. 457 (1992).

This article provides an excellent discussion of the fact-finding powers allocated to the Courts of Military Review under Article 66, U.C.M.J. The author addresses the difficult question of differentiating between questions of fact and questions of law and the further distinctions in the military appellate courts' authority to determine legal sufficiency and factual sufficiency. He concludes that what occurs now in the military appellate courts is not bona fide, traditional, fact-finding.

The Court of Appeals for the Armed Forces (The Court of Military Appeals)

Symposium, "Military Law," 10 Am. Crim. L. Rev. 1 (1971).

This symposium issue covers a valuable range of topics pertinent to the practice of military criminal law. Included are articles on jurisdiction over civilian type offenses, plea bargaining, sentencing, discovery, appeals, and an article by General Westmoreland on the commander's perspective of military justice. Also included is a fine bibliography of books, articles, and listings of military law materials.

Thompson, "Constitutional Applications to the Military Criminal Defendant," 66 U. Detroit L. Rev. 221 (1989).

Drawing comparisons between civilian and military practices, the author notes that in order to maintain the requisite good order and discipline needed in the armed forces some modifications to substantive constitutional rights have been made. He concludes that although the military defendant loses protections in the areas of search and seizure and trial by jury, he has enhanced protections in other areas, e.g., post-trial appellate review.

Federal Review of Courts-Martial

Sullivan, "The Last Line of Defense: Federal Habeas Review of Military Death Penalty Cases," 144 Mil. L. Rev. 1 (1994).

Noting that under current law, review of courts-martial by habeas corpus does not provide a meaningful analysis of whether constitutional error occurred at the court-martial. The author believes that the reason for that rests in the narrow scope of review provided by federal courts and in the fact that counsel are not readily available. This is particularly a problem, he asserts, in military death penalty cases. The author includes suggested legislation to remedy the problems.

Post-Trial Confinement

Wilberding, "The Progressive Penal System at the United States Disciplinary Barracks," 31 Fed. B.J. 44 (1972).

This short but informative article examines how the military penal system achieves its goals through an emphasis on correction rather than retribution. By using innovative techniques such as mandatory educational programs, counseling, and selective reinstatement to honorable duty, the military penal system has been increasingly successful in correcting some of the fundamental problems experiences by many other penal institutions.

Suspension of Sentence

Young, "Due Process in Military Probation Revocation: Has *Morrissey* Joined the Service?" 65 Mil. L. Rev. 1 (1974).

This article provides a good analysis of the due process requirements prescribed in *Morrissey v. Brewer* and *Gagnon v. Scarpelli* as they relate to military probation revocation procedures. The author explores the policy rationale behind the *Morrissey* decision and also provides a detailed overview of existing procedures under the U.C.M.J. After an analysis of these procedures in terms of the new due process requirements, Young concludes that changes are needed and presents an extensive proposal to amend the U.C.M.J.

Suspension of Sentence

Young, "Due Process in Military Probation Revocation: Has *Morrissey* Joined the Service?" 65 Mil. L. Rev. 1 (1974).

This article provides a good analysis of the due process requirements prescribed in *Morrissey v. Brewer* and *Gagnon v. Scarpelli* as they relate to military probation revocation procedures. The author explores the policy rationale behind the *Morrissey* decision and also provides a detailed overview of existing procedures under the U.C.M.J. After an analysis of these procedures in terms of the new due process requirements, Young concludes that changes are needed and presents an extensive proposal to amend the U.C.M.J.

The Court of Military Appeals

Cooke, "The United States Court of Military Appeals, 1975-1977: Judicializing the Military Justice System," 76 MIL. L. REV. 43 (1977).

The author carefully catalogs and analyzes key decisions from the Court of Military Appeals during a crucial two-year period in the Court's history. Between 1975 and 1977, the Court made significant first steps to shift, in the author's view, the center of authority from the commander to military judges and lawyers, thus judicializing military justice. The author notes that in the midst of questioning, and in some cases discarding, traditional rules of military justice, the Court established itself as a supervisory authority in the system. In retrospect, this well-written article is a chronicle of controversial case law that ultimately served as the genesis for Supreme Court review of the Court's decisions.

Early, Longstreet, and Richardson, "USCMA and the Specified Issue: The Current Practice," 123 MIL. L. REV. 9 (1989).

The authors, members of the Central Legal Staff of the Court of Military Appeals, provide an in-depth review of the practice of identifying specifying issues that appear to have merit but have not been raised by appellate counsel. They assert three reasons for continuing the practice: judicial economy, judicial consistency, and the role of the court as the final arbiter of ensuring protection of the accused's rights.

Everett, "Specified Issues in the United States Court of Military Appeals: A Rationale," 123 MIL. L. REV. 1 (1989).

Chief Judge Everett briefly reviews the practice of the Court of Military Appeals specifying issues for appellate review and concludes that the practice is some protection against "command control" over what issues defense counsel will raise. It presents the perception of justice to the public. Noting that although "paternalism" is on the wane and the doctrine of waiver on the rise, the unique requirements of military justice, in his view, require independent review of the records of trial by the Court.

Fidell, "Guide to the Rules of Practice and Procedure of the United States Court of Military Appeals, Second Edition" 131 MIL. L. REV. 169 (1991).

This lengthy and helpful article on practice before the Court of Military Appeals is a second edition of an earlier work by the same author. The article includes the text of each of the court's rules of practice (See Appendix 42) along with a discussion on each rule, which in turn includes insight into how the rule works, how the Court has applied it, and citations of pertinent authority.

Fidell, "The Specification of Appellate Issues by the United States Court of Military Appeals," 31 JAG J. 99 (1980).

The author discusses the historical basis of the Court of Military Appeals' practice of granting review on issues not assigned by the petitioner and compares this with practices before the Supreme Court and Court of Appeals. He proposes a hard look at the current practice and urges sparing use of granting of such *sua sponte* issues.

Fidell and Greenhouse, "A Roving Commission: Specified Issues and the Function of the United States Court of Military Appeals," 122 MIL. L. REV. 117 (1988).

The authors present several arguments against the Court of Military Appeals' practice of specifying for appellate review issues not raised by the appellate defense counsel. To support their argument that the practice rarely results in meaningful relief they catalog the various cases in which the Court has specified issues.

Goodwin, "Military Law — The Role of the Military Judiciary—The United States Court of Military Appeals Strengthens Judicial Control of Courts-Martial and Expands Its Scope of Appellate Review," 38 VANDERBILT L. REV. 891 (1977).

This article surveys several significant cases in the Court of Military Appeals that signal a trend towards greater independence of the military judicial system. By limitation of the traditional doctrine of Accession (the power of a commander or other convening authority to reverse a dismissal of charges referred for court-martial) and an increased assertion of appellate review power, the Court of Military Appeals has strengthened its supervisory functions over the administration of military justice.

Jewell and Williams, "COMA Watch 1989," 128 MIL. L. REV. 115 (1990).

The authors provide a synopsis of significant 1989 developments and decisions from the Court of Military Appeals. The article includes a brief analysis of a wide variety of criminal issues decided by that Court.

"Significant Decisions of the Court of Military Appeals: 1982-1983," 103 MIL. L. REV. 79 (1984).

This insightful survey-type article analyzes significant decisions from the Court of Military Appeals rendered between 1 October 1982 and 30 September 1983. The cases are organized in trial chronology (i.e., pretrial practice through post-trial procedures).

Willis, "The United States Court of Military Appeals: Its Origin, Operation, and Future," 55 MIL. L. REV. 39 (1972).

This work serves as a good introduction to the military's "Supreme Court" and is one of several articles by the same author on the work of the Court. *See also* Willis, "The Constitution, The United States Court of Military Appeals and the Future," 57 MIL. L. REV. 27 (1972).

Extraordinary Writs

Brown, "Building a System of Military Justice Through the All Writs Act," 52 IND. L.J. 184 (1976).

This note explores two key decisions by the Court of Military Appeals: *United States v. McPhail* and *Courtney v. Williams,* in which the court demonstrated its willingness to employ its supervisory powers over the military justice system. The author concludes that the manner in which the court addressed its powers indicates a broad "legislative" move by the court to change the system.

Pavlick, "Extraordinary Writs in the Military Justice System: A Different Perspective," 84 Mil. L. Rev. 7 (1979).

This short article presents a brief history of use of extraordinary writs by the Court of Military Appeals and an analysis of that court's use of that power in an attempt to exercise its supervisory authority over the military justice system. The author observes that in its attempts to broaden its authority the court has not developed a unified theory of application of the All Writs Act.

Rankin, "The All Writs Act and the Military Judicial System," 53 Mil. L. Rev. 103 (1971).

The author presents an examination of the common law writs (*mandamus*, prohibition, *coram nobis*, and habeas corpus), the All Writs Act, 28 U.S.L. SS 1651a, and the application, or the lack thereof, by the Court of Military Appeals and the lower military courts. The article focuses on the cases where writs have been granted in aid of jurisdiction, a much more limited scope than that now held by the military courts.

Wacker, The "'Unreviewable' Court-Martial Conviction: Supervisory Relief under the All Writs Act from the United States Court of Military Appeals," 10 Harv. Civ. Rights-Civ. Lib. L. Rev. 33 (1975).

In a well-written article detailing use of extraordinary writs, the author discusses the potential use of such writs as an instrument for supervising the operation of the military justice system. Particular emphasis is placed upon use of extraordinary writs in those cases which might not otherwise be reviewed by the military appellate courts. The Court of Military Appeals made such use of its writ powers in *United States v. McPhail*.

Administrative Review of Courts-Martial

Berkowitz, "Project: The Administrative Consequences of Courts-Martial," 14 The Advocate 218 (1982).

In this special issue of The Advocate, the author provides an invaluable guide to the administrative consequences of a court-martial conviction. Topics covered include discharge upgrading; clemency; pay, allowances, and entitlements; and collateral attack of convictions. Helpful charts and directories are included.

Russell, "The Effect of the Privacy Act on Correction of Military Records," 79 Mil. L. Rev. 135 (1978).

While reviewing the remedies available to those unable to obtain administrative corrections in their military records, this article also evaluates those opportunities and the usefulness of the Privacy Act. The writer compares the limited remedies created by the Privacy Act with the broad authority of the Army Board of Correction of Military Records and provides a good overview of each.

Federal Review of Courts-Martial

Burris & Jones, "Civilian Courts and Courts-Martial — The Civilian Attorney's Perspective," 10 AM. CRIM. L. REV. 139 (1971).

This helpful article explores various remedies that servicemembers have used in attempting to secure relief from adverse court-martial determinations and discusses the scope of review applied by the civilian courts.

Levinci, "The Doctrine of Military Necessity in the Federal Courts," 89 MIL. L. REV. 3 (1980).

The Supreme Court has in recent years recognized the controlling principle of "military necessity" in assessing the lawfulness of military regulations, orders, and laws. *See, e.g.,* Brown v. Glines, 444 U.S. 348 (1980). The author discusses the doctrine, as noted in dictum in *Parker v. Levy,* 417 U.S. 733 (1974), and notes its application by the Supreme Court in subsequent decisions such as *Schlesinger v. Councilman,* 420 U.S. 738 (1975), where the Court applied the doctrine in assessing court-martial jurisdiction.

Rosen, "Civilian Courts and the Military Justice System: Collateral Review of Courts-Martial," 108 MIL. L. REV. 5 (1985).

The author examines the relationship between civilian and military courts, emphasizing current legal developments. In response to the divergence in collateral review of military decisions by military courts, the author proposes a standard of collateral review that would define and equalize the roles of the federal judiciary and the military courts.

Sherman, "Judicial Review of Military Determinations and the Exhaustion of Remedies Requirement," 55 VA. L. REV. 483 (1969).

Traditionally, the federal courts have for a number of reasons limited their review of military activities in general and courts-martial proceedings in particular. However, review is available. This article discusses the historical basis for limited review and addresses those cases, particularly Supreme Court decisions where a servicemember's court-martial conviction has been reviewed. E.g., *Burns v. Wilson,* 346 U.S. 137 (1953) and its progeny.

Sillman, "The Supreme Court and Its Impact on the Court of Military Appeals," 18 A.F. L. REV. 81 (Summer 1976).

In an analysis of the interrelation between the U.S. Supreme Court and the Court of Military Appeals, the author comments on the "philosophy" of each court and the extent to which the Supreme Court and other sources of commentary have influenced the Court of Military Appeals' perception of its function and identity.

Strassburg, "Civilian Judicial Review of Military Criminal Justice," 66 MIL. L. REV. 1 (1974).

Clearly one of the leading articles on this topic, it presents an excellent discussion of the role of civilian courts in reviewing military courts-martial. Included are discussions of the historical development of the review, the expansion of collateral review, pretrial relief, the view of Federal Judges' view of review, and the propriety of broad collateral review by the Federal courts.

Weckstein, "Federal Court Review of Courts-Martial Proceedings: A Delicate Balance of Individual Rights and Military Responsibilities," 54 MIL. L. REV. 1 (1971).

This article provides an excellent overview of the important area of federal court review of courts-martial decisions. The author examines the traditional deference paid by the federal courts to unique military needs in the sensitive areas of due process and constitutional rights and also proposes guidelines to determine when federal review of military proceedings is necessary that is specifically tailored to the unique needs of military justice.

APPENDICES

1. Abbreviations 846
2. Glossary 850
3. Uniform Code of Military Justice (U.C.M.J.) 864
4. Court-Martial Flow Chart 927
5. Sample Nonjudicial Punishment Form 928
6. Charge Sheet 930
7. Investigating Officer's Report 932
8. Sample Pretrial Advice 934
9. Sample Court-Martial Convening Order 937
10. Sample Discovery Request 938
11. Grant of Immunity 940
12. Pretrial Agreement 942
13. Request to Take Oral Deposition 945
14. Interrogatories and Deposition Form 946
15. Subpoena for Civilian Witness 950
16. Warrant of Attachment 951
17. Request for Trial Before Military Judge Alone 953
18. Request for Enlisted Members 954
19. Disclosure of Section III Evidence 955
20. Bill of Particulars 956
21. Notice of Government Appeal 958
22. Plea Worksheet 959
23. Entry of Conditional Guilty Plea 960
24. Court-Martial Member Questionnaire 961
25. Stipulation of Fact 962
26. Stipulation of Expected Testimony 963
27. Instructions Checklist 964
28. Findings Worksheet 966
29. Sentencing Worksheet 967
30. Maximum Punishment Chart 968
31. Punishments Chart 976
32. Special Findings 978
33. Advice on Appellate Rights 981
34. Application for Deferment 982
35. Sample Post-Trial Recommendation 984
36. Promulgating Orders 986
37. Judge Advocate Legal Review 988
38. Waiver/Withdrawal of Appellate Rights 991
39. Vacation Proceedings 993
40. Sample Application for Relief Under Article 69 997

APPENDIX 1

ABBREVIATIONS

ABF	Accessory Before the Fact
ABCMR	Army Board for Correction of Military Records
ABR	Army Board of Review
ACC	Accused
ACMR	Army Court of Military Review
ADC	Assistant Defense Counsel
ADC	Area Defense Counsel
AF	Air Force
AFBR	Air Force Board of Review
AFCMR	Air Force Court of Military Review
AFDW	Air Force District of Washington
AFI	Air Force Instruction
AFM	Air Force Manual
AFP	Air Force Pamphlet
AFR	Air Force Regulation
AFOSI	Air Force Office of Special Investigations
AFRES	Air Force Reserve
ALMR	General message from the Commandant of the Marine Corps to all Marine Corps activities
ALNAV	General message from the Secretary of the Navy to all Naval activities
ANG	Air National Guard
AR	Army Regulation
ARNG	Army National Guard
ARPERCEN	Army Reserve Personnel Center
ART	Article, Uniform Code of Military Justice
ASD	Assistant Secretary of Defense
ATC	Assistant Trial Counsel
AWOL	Absent Without Leave
BCD	Bad Conduct Discharge
BCNR	Board for Correction of Naval Records
BOR	Board of Review
BUPERSMAN	Bureau of Naval Personnel Manual
CA	Convening Authority
CAAF	Court of Appeals for the Armed Forces
CC	Correctional Custody
CCDC	Chief Circuit Defense Counsel
CCF	Correctional Custody Facility
CCTC	Chief Circuit Trial Counsel
CDC	Circuit Defense Counsel
CDO	Command Duty Officer
CFR	Code of Federal Regulations
CG	Commanding General; Coast Guard
CGBR	Coast Guard Board of Review
CGCMR	Coast Guard Court of Military Review
CGR	Coast Guard Regulation
CH	Charge

APP. 1 — ABBREVIATIONS

CHAMPUS	Civilian Health and Medical Program of the Uniformed Services
CHL	Confinement at Hard Labor
CHNAVPERS	Chief of Naval Personnel
CID	Criminal Investigation Division (Army)
CMA	United States Court of Military Appeals
CMC	Commandant of the Marine Corps
CMDR	Commander
CMO	Court-Martial Order
CMR	Court of Military Review; Court-Martial Reports
CNO	Chief of Naval Operations
CO	Commanding Officer; Conscientious Objector
COMA	United States Court of Military Appeals
CONUS	Continental United States
CPO	Chief Petty Officer
CTC	Circuit Trial Counsel
CWO	Chief Warrant Officer
DAD	Defense Appellate Division
DAF	Department of the Air Force
DA PAM	Department of the Army Pamphlet
DC	Defense Counsel
DD	Dishonorable Discharge
DIG. OPS	Digest of Opinions of the Judge Advocate General of the Armed Forces
DOD	Department of Defense
ED	Extra Duty
EER	Enlisted Evaluation Report
EMI	Extra Military Instruction
E & M	Extenuation and Mitigation
ETS	Expiration Term of Service
FAX	Data Facsimile
FBI	Federal Bureau of Investigation
FM	Field Manual (Army)
FOIA	Freedom of Information Act
FORF; FF	Forfeiture
FSC	Family Support Center
G	Guilty
GAD	Government Appellate Division
GCM	General Court-Martial
GCMCA	General Court-Martial Convening Authority
HL w/o C	Hard Labor without Confinement
IC	Individual Counsel
IG	Inspector General
IMC	Individual Military Counsel
IMDC	Individual Military Defense Counsel
INST	Instruction
IO	Investigating Officer
ITO	Invitational Travel Order
JAG	Judge Advocate General
JAGC	Judge Advocate General's Corps
JAGMAIL	Judge Advocate General Department's Electronic Mail (AF)

JAGMAN	JAG Manual; Manual of the Judge Advocate General of the Navy
LEGALADMINMAN	Manual for Legal Administration (Marine Corps)
LIO	Lesser-Included Offense
LO	Legal Officer
LRO	Local Responsible Official
MAJCOM	Major Command
MC	Marine Corps
Mil. R. Evid.	Military Rules of Evidence
MCM	Manual for Courts-Martial, United States, 1969 (Rev.)
MFNG	Motion for a finding of not guilty
MJ	Military Judge
MJM	Military Justice Manual (Coast Guard)
MP	Military Police
MPRJ	Military Personnel Records Jacket
MRE	Military Rules of Evidence
N/A	Not Applicable
NBR	Navy Board of Review
NCIS	Naval Criminal Investigative Service
NCMR	Navy Court of Military Review
NCO	Noncommissioned Officer
NG	Not Guilty
NIS	Naval Investigative Service (now NCIS)
NJP	Nonjudicial Punishment
NLSO	Naval Legal Service Office
NMCMR	Navy-Marine Corps Court of Military Review
NMPC	Naval Military Personnel Command
NAVY REGS	U.S. Naval Regulations, 1973
OINC; OIC	Officer in Charge
OJAG	Office of the Judge Advocate General
OD	Officer of the Day
OOD	Officer of the Deck/Day
OPNAV	Office of the Chief of Naval Operations
OSI	Office of Special Investigations (Air Force)
OTH	Discharge under Other Than Honorable Conditions
PA	Privacy Act
PAO	Public Affairs Officer
PCRO	Pretrial Confinement Reviewing Officer
PCS	Permanent Change of Station
PIF	Personnel Information File
PIO	Preliminary Inquiry Officer
PO	Petty Officer
PTA	Pretrial Agreement
PTI	Pretrial Investigation
PTIO	Pretrial Investigating Officer
RCM	Rule of Court-Martial
RED	Reduction
REST.; R	Restriction
RO	Responsible Official
ROT	Record of Trial
RTDP	Return to Duty Program

ABBREVIATIONS

SA	Supervisory Authority
SAF	Secretary of the Air Force
SCM	Summary Court-Martial
SCMCA	Summary Court-Martial Convening Authority
SECNAV	Secretary of the Navy
SIDPERS	Standard Installation/Division Personnel System
SJA	Staff Judge Advocate
S/L	Statute of Limitations
SLO	Staff Legal Officer
SOFA	Status of Forces Agreement
SNCO	Staff Noncommissioned Officer
SP	Shore Patrol
SPCM	Special Court-Martial
SPCMCA	Special Court-Martial Convening Authority
SPEC.	Specification
SRB	Service Record Book
TAD	Temporary Additional Duty
TC	Trial Counsel
TDY	Temporary Duty
TENP	Table of Equivalent Nonjudicial Punishments
TEP	Table of Equivalent Punishments
TJAG	The Judge Advocate General
TMP	Table of Maximum Punishments
TR	Transportation Request
UA	Unauthorized Absence
UCMJ	Uniform Code Military Justice
USA	United States Army
USACID	US Army Criminal Investigation Division
USAF	United States Air Force
USALSA	US Army Legal Services Agency
USAR	US Army Reserve
USAREUR	US Army, Europe
USATDS	US Army Trial Defense Service
USC	United States Code
USCA	United States Code Annotated
USCG	United States Coast Guard
USCMA	United States Court of Military Appeals (1951-1994)
USMC	United States Marine Corps
USN	United States Navy
USSS	United States Secret Service
VA	Veterans Administration
WO	Warrant Officer
VWAP	Victim Witness Assistance Program
VWL	Victim/Witness Liaison
XO	Executive Officer

APPENDIX 2
GLOSSARY

A

ABATEMENTS — a. Good conduct time—any deductions from the term of a sentence for good conduct.

b. Extra good—time any deductions from the term of a sentence which may be earned for actual employment in assignments for which extra good time has been approved.

ABET — To encourage, incite, or set another on to commit a crime. Art. 77, U.C.M.J.

ACCESSORY AFTER THE FACT — Any person subject to the Code who, knowing that an offense punishable by this Code has been committed, receives, comforts, or assists the offender in order to hinder or prevent his apprehension, trial, or punishment. NOTE: Art. 78, U.C.M.J. deals with accessories after the fact.

ACCESSORY BEFORE THE FACT — One who counsels, commands, procures, or causes another to commit an offense, whether present or absent at the commission of the offense.

ACCUSED — One who is charged with an offense under the Code.

ACCUSER — Any person who signs and swears to charges, any person who directs that charges normally be signed and sworn to by another, and any other person who has an interest other than an official interest in the prosecution of the accused. Art. 1(9), U.C.M.J.

ACTIVE DUTY — The status of being in the active Federal Service of any of the Armed Forces under a competent appointment or enlistment or pursuant to a competent muster, order, call or induction.

ACTUAL KNOWLEDGE — A state wherein the person in fact knows of the existence of an order, regulation, fact, etc., in question.

ADDITIONAL CHARGES — New and separate charges preferred against an accused who has other charges that are still pending against him.

ADJUDGED PRISONER — An enlisted or civilian person in confinement pursuant to a sentence adjudged by a court-martial which has not been ordered executed.

ADMISSION — A self-incriminatory statement falling short of a complete acknowledgement of guilt.

AFFIRMATION — A solemn and formal external pledge, binding upon one's conscience, that the truth will be stated.

AIDER AND ABETTOR — One who shares the criminal intent or purpose of the perpetrator, and hence is liable as a principal. Art. 77, U.C.M.J.

ALIBI — A defense that the accused *could not* have committed the offense alleged because he was somewhere else when the crime was committed.

ALLEGE — To assert or state in a pleading; to plead in a specification.

ALLEGATION — The assertion, declaration, or statement of a party in a pleading of what he expects to prove.

ALL WRITS ACT — A Federal statute, 28 USC 1651(a), which empowers all courts established by Act of Congress, including the Court of Military Appeals and the Courts of Military Review, to issue such extraordinary writs as are necessary or appropriate in aid of their respective jurisdictions and agreeable to the usages and principles of law.

APPEAL — A complaint to a superior court of an injustice done or error committed by an inferior one whose judgment or decision the court above is called upon to correct or reverse.

APPELLATE REVIEW — Automatic reconsideration of the records of cases tried by court-martial. Reviewing authorities include the convening authority, GCM authority, the Court of Military Review, and the Court of Military Appeals. The level to which a case proceeds for review is determined by the Code. *See* Arts. 65, 66, and 67, U.C.M.J.

APPREHENSION — The taking of a person into custody.

APPROVED ADJUDGED PRISONER — An enlisted member or civilian person in confinement pursuant to a sentence adjudged by a court-martial and approved by a convening authority but which has not yet been ordered executed.

AREA CONFINEMENT FACILITY — An Army facility providing confinement service on an area basis for military service personnel awaiting court-martial or trial by a foreign court, for those individuals returned to military control from a dropped from roll status for whom confinement is directed, and for post-trial prisoners, to include those post-trial prisoners pending transfer to a correctional facility.

ARRAIGNMENT — The reading of the charges and specifications to the accused or the waiver of their reading, coupled with the request that the accused plead thereto.

ARREST — Moral restraint imposed upon a person by oral or written orders of competent authority limiting the persons personal liberty pending disposition of charges. Arrest is *not* imposed as punishment for an offense.

ARREST IN QUARTERS — A moral restraint limiting an officer's liberty, imposed as a nonjudicial punishment by a flag or general officer in command.

ARTICLE 15 — See Nonjudicial Punishment.

ARTICLE 39a SESSION — A session of a court-martial called by the military judge, either before or after assembly of the court, without the members of the court being present, to dispose of matters not amounting to a trial of the accused's guilt or innocence. *See* Art. 39. U.C.M.J.

ASSAULT — An attempt, or offer with unlawful force or violence, to do bodily harm to another, whether or not the attempt or offer is consummated. Art. 128, U.C.M.J.

ATTEMPT — An act, or acts, done with a specific intent to commit an offense under the Code, amounting to more than mere preparation, and tending, but failing, to effect the commission of such offense.

B

BAD CONDUCT DISCHARGE — One of two types of punitive discharges that may be awarded an enlisted man; designed as a punishment for bad conduct, rather than as a punishment for serious offenses of either a civil or military nature; may be awarded by GCM or SPCM.

BATTERY — An unlawful and intentional or culpably negligent application of force to the person of another by a material agency used directly or indirectly. Art. 218, U.C.M.J.

BENCH TRIAL — A trial before a judge alone.

BEYOND A REASONABLE DOUBT — The degree of persuasion based upon proof such as to exclude not every hypothesis or possibility of innocence, but any fair and rational hypothesis except that of guilt; not an absolute or mathematical certainty but a moral certainty.

BONA FIDE — In good faith.

BREACH OF ARREST — Going beyond the limits of arrest as set by orders. Art. 95, U.C.M.J.

BREACH OF PEACE — An unlawful disturbance of the peace by an outward demonstration of a violent or turbulent nature. Art. 116, U.C.M.J.

BREAKING ARREST — Going beyond the limits of arrest before being released by proper authority.

BURGLARY — The breaking and entering in the nighttime of the dwelling of another with intent to commit murder, manslaughter, rape, carnal knowledge, larceny and wrongful appropriation, robbery, forgery, maiming, sodomy, arson, extortion, or assault. Art. 129, U.C.M.J.

C

CAPITAL OFFENSE — An offense for which the maximum punishment includes the death penalty.

CAPTAIN'S MAST — The term applied, through tradition and usage in the Navy and Coast Guard, to nonjudicial punishment proceedings under Art. 15, U.C.M.J.

CARNAL KNOWLEDGE — An act of sexual intercourse, under circumstances not amounting to rape, by a person with a female who is not his wife, and who has not attained the age of 16 years. Art. 120, U.C.M.J.

CASUAL PRISONER — A prisoner who is held in confinement pending disposition instructions from other commands or is awaiting transportation to a designated confinement facility or return to parent unit.

CHALLENGE — A formal objection to a member of a court or the military judge continuing as such in subsequent proceedings. May be either (1) a challenge for cause such objections based on a fact or circumstance which has the effect of disqualifying the person challenged from further participation in the proceedings, or (2) peremptory challenge such objection permitted without a showing of grounds or basis, except that the military judge cannot be peremptorily challenged.

CHARGE — A formal statement of the Article of the U.C.M.J. which the accused is alleged to have violated.

CHARGE AND SPECIFICATION — A description in writing of the offense which the accused is alleged to have committed; each specification, together with the charge under which it is placed, constitutes a separate accusation.

CHIEF WARRANT OFFICER — A warrant officer of the Armed Forces who holds a commission or warrant in warrant officer grades W-2 through W-4.

CIRCUMSTANTIAL EVIDENCE — Evidence which tends directly to prove or disprove not a fact in issue, but a fact or circumstance from which, either alone or in connection with other facts, a court may, according to the common experience of mankind, reasonable infer the existence or nonexistence of another fact which is in the issue; sometimes called indirect evidence.

CLASSIFICATION — The evaluation of individual prisoners to determine custody grade, employment, training, and other correctional treatment requirements.

CLEMENCY — Discretionary action by proper authority to reduce the severity of a punishment.

COLLATERAL ATTACK — An attempt to impeach or challenge the integrity of a court judgment in a proceeding other than that in which the judgment was rendered and outside the normal chain of appellate review.

COMMAND — (1) The authority which a commander in the military service lawfully exercises over his subordinates by virtue of rank or assignment; (2) a unit or units, an organization, or an area under the authority of one individual; (3) an order given by one person to another who, because of the relationship of the parties, is under an obligation or sense of duty to obey the order, including demanding of another to do an act towards commission of a crime.

COMMANDING OFFICER — A commissioned officer in command of a unit or units, an organization, or an area of the Armed Forces.

COMMISSIONED OFFICER — An officer who holds a commission issued by the President.

COMMON TRIAL — A trial in which two or more persons are charged with the commission of an offense or offenses which, although not jointly committed, were committed at the same time and place and are provable by the same evidence.

CONCURRENT JURISDICTION — Jurisdiction which is possessed over the same parties or subject matter at the same time by two or more separate tribunals.

CONCURRENT SERVICE OF PUNISHMENTS — Two or more punishments being served at the same time.

CONFESSION — An acknowledgement of guilt of an offense.

CONFINEMENT — The physical restraint of a person, imposed by either oral or written orders of competent authority, depriving him of freedom.

CONFINEMENT FACILITY — Facility for the confinement of military prisoners. It applies to transient confinement facilities, installation confinement facilities, area confinement facilities, and hospitalized prisoner wards.

CONFINEMENT OFFICER — The officer assigned to a stockade and charged with the custody, control, correctional treatment, and administration of prisoners.

CONSPIRACY — A combination of two or more persons who have agreed to accomplish, by concerted action, an unlawful purpose or some purpose not in itself unlawful but accomplished by unlawful means, and the doing of some act by one or more of the conspirators to effect the object of that agreement.

CONSTRUCTIVE ENLISTMENT — A valid enlistment arising in a situation where the initial enlistment was void but the enlistee unconditionally continues in the military and accepts military benefits.

CONSTRUCTIVE KNOWLEDGE — Knowledge which may be found to have existed because the regulation, notice, fact or directive, etc., at issue was of so notorious a nature, or was so conspicuously posted or distributed, that the particular accused ought to have known of its existence; knowledge is constructive when it is shown that the accused would in the ordinary course of events, or by the exercise of ordinary care, have secured knowledge of the order, notice of movement, etc.

CONTEMPT — The use of any menacing words, signs, or gestures in the presence of the court, or the disturbance of its proceedings by any riot or disorder; the refusal of a duly subpoenaed civilian witness to qualify, appear, or to testify before a court-martial, court of inquiry, or military commission.

CONTRABAND — Items, the possession of which is in itself illegal.

CONVENING AUTHORITY — The officer having authority to convene a court-martial and who convened the court-martial in question, or his successor in command.

CONVENING ORDER — The document by which a court-martial is created; which specifies the type of court; and which lists the time and place of meeting, the names of the members, trial and defense counsel and, in the case of a general court-martial, the name of the ruling officer and, when appropriate, the authority by which the court is created.

CORPUS DELICTI — The body of a crime; facts or circumstances showing that the crime alleged has been committed by someone.

CORRECTIONAL FACILITY — A facility providing correctional treatment to military prisoners to motivate and retrain them for return to military duty or return to civilian life as better citizens. It applies to retraining brigades and disciplinary barracks.

CORRECTIONAL OFFICER — An officer assigned to a confinement/correctional facility who assists in the custody, control, administration, and correctional treatment of military prisoners.

CORRECTIONAL TREATMENT — Individualized program designed to enhance and accomplish behavior and attitude change by the prisoner. Includes medical and/or mental health treatment programs, educational and vocational training, useful and constructive employment, recreational activities, religious affiliation, mature supervision, and counseling and guidance.

COUNSELING — Directly or indirectly advising or encouraging another to commit an offense. Art. 77, U.C.M.J.

COURT-MARTIAL — A military tribunal composed of one or more eligible members of the Armed Forces (the number depending on the kind of court), the functions of which are to decide whether a person subject to military law has committed a violation of the Uniform Code and, if it finds him guilty, to adjudge punishment for the offense.

COURT-MARTIAL ORDERS — May be either a convening order or a promulgating order. *See* respective definitions.

COURT OF INQUIRY — The most formal fact-finding body convened in the Armed Forces, governed by Art. 135, U.C.M.J.

COURT OF APPEALS FOR THE ARMED FORCES — A civilian court consisting of five judges appointed from civilian life by the President, by and with the advice and consent of the Senate, for a term of fifteen years the highest appellate court under the U.C.M.J. *See* Art. 67, U.C.M.J. (called the "Court of Military Appeals" from 1951-1994).

COURT OF MILITARY APPEALS — A civilian court consisting of five judges appointed from civilian life by the President, by and with the advice and consent of the Senate, for a term of fifteen years the highest appellate court under the U.C.M.J. *See* Art. 67, U.C.M.J. (renamed the Court of Appeals for the Armed Forces in 1994).

COURT OF CRIMINAL APPEALS — A military court composed of not less than three officers or civilians, each of whom shall be a member of the bar of a Federal court or of the highest court of a State of the United States, constituted to review the records of certain courts-martial. *See* Art. 66, U.C.M.J. (called "Court of Military Review" from 1969-1994).

COURT OF MILITARY REVIEW — A military court composed of not less than three officers or civilians, each of whom shall be a member of the bar of a Federal court or of the highest court of a State of the United States, constituted to review the records of certain courts-martial. *See* Art. 66, U.C.M.J. (renamed "Court of Criminal Appeals in 1994).

CREDIBILITY OF WITNESS — His or her worthiness of belief.

CULPABLE — Deserving blame.

CULPABLE NEGLIGENCE — A degree of carelessness greater than simple negligence; a negligent act or omission accompanied by a flagrant or reckless disregard for the foreseeable consequences to others of such act or omission.

CUSTODIAL INTERROGATION — Questioning initiated by law enforcement officers or others in authority after a subject has been taken into custody or otherwise deprived of his freedom of action in any significant way.

CUSTODY — That restraint of free movement which is imposed by lawful apprehension.

CUSTODY CLASSIFICATION — Degree of custodial supervision designated by custody grade (installation parolee, minimum, medium, or maximum) appropriate for the individual prisoner.

CUSTOM — A practice which fulfills the following conditions: (a) it must be long continued; (b) it must be certain or uniform; (c) it must be compulsory; (d) it must be consistent; (e) it must be general; (f) it must be known; (g) it must not be in opposition to the terms and provisions of a statute or lawful regulation or order.

D

DANGEROUS WEAPON — A weapon used in such a manner that it is likely to produce death or grievous bodily harm.

DEFERMENT OF CONFINEMENT — Discretionary action by proper authority, postponing the running of the confinement portion of a sentence, together with a lack of any post-trial restraint.

DEPOSITION — The testimony of a witness taken out of court, reduced to writing, under oath or affirmation, before a person empowered to administer oaths, in answer to interrogatories (questions) and cross-interrogatories submitted by the party desiring the deposition and the opposite party, or based on oral examination by counsel for accused and the prosecution.

DERELICTION IN THE PERFORMANCE OF DUTIES — Willfully or negligently failing to perform assigned duties, or performing them in a culpably inefficient manner.

DESIGN — Specifically intended; inferred from conduct so shockingly and grossly devoid of care as to leave room for no reasonable inference but that the result was contemplated as a probable result of the course of conduct followed.

DESTROYED — (As used in Art. 108, U.C.M.J.). Not completely demolished or annihilated, but only sufficiently injured to be useless for the purpose for which it was intended.

DETAILED PRISONER — Any enlisted military person or civilian in confinement awaiting filing of charges, disposition of charges, trial by courts-martial, or trial by a foreign court.

DETAINER — A writ for the future detention of a person already in custody.

DETENTION OF PAY — A less severe form of punishment than a forfeiture in that the amount detained is ultimately returned to the accused when he is separated from service, or within specified period of one year or less.

DIRECT EVIDENCE — Evidence which tends directly to prove or disprove a fact in issue.

DISHONORABLE DISCHARGE — The most severe punitive discharge, reserved for those who should be separated under conditions of dishonor, after having been convicted of offenses usually recognized by the civil law as felonies, or of offenses of military nature requiring severe punishment.

DISORDERLY CONDUCT — Behavior of such a nature as to affect the peace and quiet of persons who may witness the same and who may be disturbed or provoked to resentment thereby.

DISRESPECT — Words, acts, or omissions that are synonymous with contempt and amount to behavior or language which detracts from the respect due to authority and person of a superior.

DOMINION — Control of property; possession of property with the ability to exercise control over it.

DRUNKENNESS — (1) As an offense under the Code, intoxication which is sufficient sensibly to impair the rational and full exercise of the mental and physical faculties; may be caused by liquor or drugs.

(2) As a defense in rebuttal of the existence of specific intent or knowledge, intoxication which amounts to loss of reason preventing the accused from knowing the nature of his act or the natural and probable consequences thereof.

DUE PROCESS — A course of legal proceedings according to those rules and principles which have been established in our system of jurisprudence for the enforcement and protection of private rights; such as exercise of the powers of the government as the settled maxims of law permit and sanction, and under such safeguards for the protection of the individual rights as those maxims prescribe.

DURESS — Unlawful constraint of a person where he is forced to do some act that he otherwise would not have done.

E

ELEMENTS — The essential ingredients of an offense which are to be proved at the trial; the acts or omissions which form the basis of any particular offense.

ENTRAPMENT — A defense available when actions of an agent of the government intentionally instill in the mind of the accused an intent to commit a criminal offense and when the accused had no notion, predisposition, or intent to commit the offense and was not engaged in an unlawful business which the agent was trying to detect.

ESCAPED PRISONER — A prisoner who has cast off the restraint of confinement before he has been set at liberty by proper authority.

EVIDENCE — Information admissible before a court of law which tends to prove or disprove any matter in question or to influence belief respecting it.

EXECUTION OF OFFICE — Engaged in any act or service required or authorized to be done by statute, regulation, the order of a superior, or military usage.

EX POST FACTO LAW — A law passed after the occurrence of a fact or commission of an act which makes the act punishable, imposes additional punishment, or changes the rules of evidence by which less or different testimony is sufficient to convict.

EXTRA MILITARY INSTRUCTION — Extra tasks assigned to one exhibiting behavioral or performance deficiencies for the purpose of correcting those deficiencies through the performance of the assigned tasks; also known as Additional Military Duty or Additional Military Instruction.

F

FACILITY COMMANDER — An officer appointed by appropriate orders as the commanding officer (Commandant, USDB) of a confinement/correctional facility, who is charged with the custody, control, administration, and correctional treatment of military prisoners.

FIELD STOCKADE — Any area or facility so designated which is under the jurisdiction of a division, corps, field army, or communications zone commander in the field used for the confinement of military prisoners. AR 190-2 and AR 190-4.

FINE — A type of punishment making the accused liable to the United States for the specified amount of money.

FORMER JEOPARDY — The rule of law that no person shall be tried for the same offense by the same sovereign a second time without his consent. Art. 44, U.C.M.J.

FORMER PUNISHMENT — The rule of law that nonjudicial punishment for a minor offense may be interposed as a bar to trial for same offense.

FORFEITURE OF PAY — A type of punishment depriving the accused of all or part of his pay.

G

GRIEVOUS BODILY HARM — Serious bodily injury; does not include minor injuries, such as a black eye or a bloody nose, but does include fractured or dislocated bones, deep cuts, torn members of the body, serious damage to internal organs, and other serious bodily injuries.

GROSS NEGLIGENCE — A wanton, careless and reckless disregard of the rights and safety of others; an utter indifference to the consequences of one's actions; a total abandonment of the standard of reasonable care coupled with a wanton disregard for the safety of others; that degree of negligence that is substantially higher in magnitude than simple inadvertence, but falls short of intentional wrong.

H

HABEAS CORPUS — An order from a court which causes the custodian of a prisoner to appear before a court to show cause why the prisoner is confined or detained.

HARMLESS ERROR — Error of such quantity and quality that a court of reasonable and conscientious men would have reached the same result had the error not been committed.

HAZARD A VESSEL — To put a vessel in danger of damage or loss.

I

INFERENCE — A deduction based upon reason from a fact or facts proved.

INITIAL CUSTODY CLASSIFICATION — The initial assignment of a custody grade to a prisoner which is based on a comprehensive evaluation.

INSANITY — *See* mental capacity, mental responsibility.

INSPECTION — An official examination of persons or property to determine the fitness or readiness of a person, organization or equipment, not made with a view to any criminal action.

INSTALLATION COMMANDER — Commanding officer of a post, camp, or station.

INSTALLATION CONFINEMENT FACILITY — A facility providing pretrial confinement services for prisoners awaiting court-martial at the installation or trial by a foreign court, short-term post-trial prisoners, and acting as a transfer point for other prisoners pending movement to an area confinement facility or correctional facility.

INSTALLATION PAROLEE — Post-trial prisoner considered to require little custodial supervision.

INTRACTABLE PRISONER — A prisoner who consistently refuses to cooperate with competent authority and who poses a threat to the safety, security, or well-being of other prisoners, staff, or the efficient operation of the facility. Prisoners who are suicidal or destructive may also be considered as intractable.

IPSO FACTO — By the very fact itself.

J

JOINT OFFENSE — One committed by two or more persons acting together in pursuance of a common intent.

JOINT TRIAL — The trial of two or more persons charged with committing a joint offense.

JURISDICTION — The power of a court to hear and decide on a case and to impose any appropriate punishment.

K

KNOWINGLY — With knowledge; consciously, intelligently.

L

LEGAL OFFICER — Any commissioned officer of the Navy, Marine Corps, or Coast Guard designated to perform legal duties of a command.

LESSER-INCLUDED OFFENSE — An offense necessarily included in the offense charged; an offense containing some, but not all, of the elements of the offense charged, so that, if one or more of the elements of the offense charged is not proved, the evidence may still support a finding of guilty of the included offense.

M

MATTER IN AGGRAVATION — Any circumstance attending the commission of a crime which increases its enormity.

MATTER IN EXTENUATION — Any circumstance serving to explain the commission of the offense, including the reasons that actuated the accused, but not extending to a legal justification. Opposite of aggravation.

MATTER IN MITIGATION — Any circumstance having for its purpose the lessening of the punishment to be awarded by the court and the furnishing of grounds for a recommendation of clemency.

MAXIMUM CUSTODY — Classification assigned to a prisoner considered to require special control because of established characteristics of a dangerous, violent, or troublesome nature, or who is considered an escape risk.

MEDIUM CUSTODY — Classification assigned to a prisoner considered to require continuous correctional supervision, but whose potential for escape or conduct while supervised does not present a threat to life, limb, or property.

MENTAL CAPACITY — The ability of the accused at the time of trial to understand the nature of the proceedings against him and to conduct or cooperate intelligently in his defense.

MENTAL RESPONSIBILITY — The condition of the accused at the time of the commission of an offense; that he was so far free from mental defect, disease, or derangement as to be able, concerning the particular act charged, both to distinguish right from wrong and to adhere to the right.

MILITARY DUE PROCESS — Due process under protections and rights granting military personnel by the Constitution or laws enacted by Congress.

MILITARY JUDGE — An official of a general or special court-martial detailed in accordance with Art. 26, U.C.M.J.

MINIMUM CUSTODY — Classification assigned to a prisoner considered to be sufficiently dependable as to require little correctional supervision.

MINOR OFFENSE — An offense for which confinement for less than one year is authorized; generally also misconduct not involving moral turpitude or any greater degree of criminality than is involved in the average offense tried by summary court-martial.

MISTRIAL — Discretionary action of the military judge, or the president of a special court-martial without a military judge, in withdrawing the charges from the court where such action appears manifestly necessary in the interest of justice because of circumstances arising during the proceedings which cast substantial doubt upon the fairness of the trial.

MORAL TURPITUDE — An act of baseness, vileness, or depravity in private or social duties contrary to the accepted and customary rule of right and duty between man and man.

MOTION TO DISMISS — A motion raising any defense or objection in bar or trial.

MOTION TO GRANT APPROPRIATE RELIEF — A motion made to cure a defect of form or substance that impedes the accused in properly preparing for trial or conducting his defense.

MOTION TO SEVER — A motion by one or more of two co-accused that he be tried separately from the other or others.

N

NEGLECT — Omission or failure to do an act or perform a duty due to want of due care or attention.

NEGLIGENCE — The omission to do something which a reasonable man, guided by those ordinary considerations which ordinarily regulate human affairs, would do, or the doing of something which a reasonable and prudent man would not do; the absence of due care; the legal standard that defines what would have been done by a reasonable, prudent man in the same or similar circumstances; as used in the U.C.M.J., the failure to exercise the care, prudence, or attention to duties which the interests of the government require to be exercised by a prudent and reasonable person under the circumstances.

NONJUDICIAL PUNISHMENT — Punishment imposed under Article 15 for minor offenses, without the intervention of a court-martial.

O

ON-DUTY — As used in Article 112, U.C.M.J., the exercise of duties of routine or detail in garrison, at a station, or in the field. Does not relate to those periods when, no duty being required of them by order or regulations, officers and men occupy the status of leisure known as off-duty or on liberty.

OFFICER HOURS — The term applied, through tradition and usage in the Marine Corps, to nonjudicial punishment proceedings.

OFFICER — Any commissioned or warrant officer of the Armed Forces, Warrant Officer (W-1) and above.

OFFICER IN CHARGE — A member of the Armed Forces designated as such by appropriate authority.

OFFICER PRISONER — A commissioned or warrant officer of the military services on active duty as a commissioned officer or warrant officer who is confined in a military confinement facility.

P

PER CURIAM — By the court; a phrase used in the report of the opinion of a court to distinguish an opinion of the whole court from an opinion written by any one judge.

PER SE — Taken alone; in and of itself; by itself.

PLEADING — The written, formal indictment by which an accused is charged with an offense; in military law, the pleadings are called charges and specifications.

POSSESSION — Physical control over an item of property.

PREFERRAL OF CHARGES — The formal accusation against an accused by an accuser signing and swearing to the charges and specifications.

PREJUDICIAL ERROR — An error of law which materially affects the substantial rights of the accused and requiring corrective action.

PRESUMPTION — A justifiable inference; a well-recognized example of the use of circumstantial evidence, the weight or effect of which should be measured only in terms of its logical value.

PRETRIAL INVESTIGATION — An investigation pursuant to Article 32, U.C.M.J., that is required before convening a GCM, unless waived by the accused.

PRIMA FACIE CASE — Introduction of substantial evidence which, together with all proper inferences to be drawn therefrom and all applicable presumptions, reasonably tends to establish every essential element of an offense charged or included in any specification.

PRINCIPAL — (1) One who aids, abets, counsels, commands, or procures another to commit an offense which is subsequently perpetrated in consequence of such counsel, command or procuring, whether he is present or absent at the commission of the offense; (2) The perpetrator.

PROBABLE CAUSE — (1) For apprehension, a reasonable grounds for believing that an offense has been committed and that the person apprehended committed it; (2) for pretrial restraint, reasonable grounds for believing that an offense was committed by the person being restrained; and (3) for search, a reasonable grounds for believing that items connected with criminal activity are located in the place or on the person to be searched.

PROCEDURAL LAW — The rules of pleading and practice by which rights are accorded and enforced.

PROMULGATING ORDERS — a. *Initial promulgating orders.* In all cases, the convening authority will issue an order promulgating the results of the trial by a general special, or summary court-martial.

b. *Supplementary promulgating orders.* Action taken on the findings or sentence of a general, special, or summary court-martial subsequent to the initial action thereon by the convening authority shall be promulgated, as appropriate, by the convening authority who took the initial action in the case, the commanding officer of the accused who is authorized to take the action being promulgated, an officer exercising general court-martial jurisdiction over the accused at the time of the action, or the Secretary.

c. *Designation.* Initial and supplementary promulgating orders in general, special, and summary court-martial are designated GENERAL COURT-MARTIAL ORDER, SPECIAL COURT-MARTIAL ORDER, or SUMMARY COURT-MARTIAL ORDER, respectively.

PROXIMATE CAUSE — That which, in natural and continuous sequence, unbroken by any efficient intervening cause, produces the injury, and without which the results would not have occurred.

PUNITIVE ARTICLES — Articles 77 through 134, U.C.M.J., which generally describe various crimes and offenses and state how they may be punished.

PUNITIVE DISCHARGE — A bad conduct discharge or dishonorable discharge from the Armed Forces.

PUNITIVE-DISCHARGE PRISONER — A prisoner whose sentence as initially promulgated, regardless of whether the sentence has been ordered executed, includes confinement and punitive discharge (suspended or executed), confinement and dismissal, or death.

R

RECKLESSLY — With disregard for the probable destructive results of some voluntary act; with culpable negligence.

RECONSIDERATION — The action of the convening authority in returning the record of trial to the court for renewed consideration of a ruling of the court dismissing a specification on motion, where the ruling of the court does not amount to a finding of not guilty.

REFERRAL OF CHARGES — The action of a convening authority in directing that a particular case be tried by a particular court-martial previously created.

RELEVANCY — The quality of evidence which renders it properly applicable in proving or disproving any matter in issue; a tendency in logic to prove or disprove a fact which is in issue in the case. Rule 401, MIL. R. EVID.

REMEDIAL ACTION — Action taken by proper reviewing authorities to correct an error or errors in the proceedings or to offset the adverse impact of an error.

REMISSION — Action by proper authority interrupting the execution of a punishment and cancelling out the punishment remaining to be served, while *not* restoring any right, privilege, or property already affected by the executed portion of the punishment.

RESISTING APPREHENSION — An active resistance to the restraint attempted to be imposed by the person apprehending.

RESTORATION TO DUTY — Term used to describe procedures taken in connection with an individual who was sentenced to confinement and a punitive discharge or dismissal by court-martial.

RESTRICTION IN LIEU OF ARREST — Moral restraint, less severe than arrest, imposed upon a person by oral or written orders, limiting him to specified areas of a military command, with the further provision that he will participate in all military duties and activities of his organization while under such restriction.

RESTRICTION TO LIMITS — Restriction imposed as punishment.

RETURN TO DUTY — Term used to describe procedures taken in connection with a prisoner whose sentence(s) include(s) confinement without a punitive discharge or whose punitive discharge has been remitted or suspended by the convening authority or appellate review agencies, or who is still pending the appellate process and whose discharge has not yet been executed.

REVISION — A procedure to correct an apparent error or omission or improper or inconsistent action of a court-martial with respect to a finding or a sentence.

S

SELF-INCRIMINATION — The giving of evidence against oneself which tends to establish guilt of an offense.

SENTENCED PRISONER — A prisoner whose sentence to confinement has been ordered into execution.

SET ASIDE — Action by proper authority voiding the proceedings and the punishment awarded and restoring all rights, privileges, and property lost by virtue of the punishment imposed.

SPECIFICATION — A formal statement of specific acts and circumstances relied upon as constituting the offense charged.

STATUTE OF LIMITATIONS — The rule of law which establishes the time within which an accused must be charged with an offense to be tried successfully.

STRAGGLE — To wander away, to rove, to stray, to become separated from or to lag or linger behind.

SUBPOENA — A formal written instrument or legal process that serves to summon a witness to appear before a certain tribunal and to give testimony.

SUBSTANTIVE LAW — That portion of the body of law which contains rights and duties and regulations of the government, as opposed to that part which contains the rules and remedies by which the substantive law is administered.

SUPERVISORY AUTHORITY — An officer normally exercising general court-martial jurisdiction who acts on summary court-martial and special court-martial records after the Convening Authority has acted.

SUSPENSION — Action by proper authority to withhold the execution of a punishment for a probationary period pending good behavior on the part of the accused.

T

TOLL — To suspend or interrupt the running of.

TRAINEE — (1) An individual undergoing initial military training; (2) An individual undergoing correctional treatment and training at the US Army Retraining Brigade. This term applies to prisoners as well as to those individuals whose sentence to confinement has expired, been suspended, or remitted at the Retraining Brigade.

TRANSIENT INSTALLATION CONFINEMENT FACILITY — Short-term confinement of installation and casual prisoners. This is a confinement facility with a fluctuating prisoner population and part-time cadre staff which is operated in accordance with exceptions to Department of the Army policies governing confinement facilities.

TRUE OWNER — The person, who, at the time of the taking, obtaining or withholding or property, had the superior right to possession of the property involved in the light of all conflicting interests therein involved in the particular case.

U

UNITED STATES ARMY RETRAINING BRIGADE (USARB) — Provides an intensive motivational and retraining program to prisoners whose sentences include no punitive discharge, or a suspended punitive discharge and no more than six months confinement. Prisoners with executed punitive discharges must be assigned by direction of the Secretary of the Army. The program is designed to prepare prisoners for return to honorable military service or to rapidly identify and eliminate from military service, through administrative or legal actions, those prisoners who do not have the desire or ability to serve honorably.

UNITED STATES DISCIPLINARY BARRACKS (USDB) — Provides a place of confinement for prisoners with punitive discharges, or those with a sentence in excess of six months confinement and no punitive discharges. Provides an extensive vocational and academic training program to improve prisoner attitudes and motivation for either return to duty or release to civilian life as useful citizens.

USAGE — A general habit, mode, or course of procedure.

V

VERBATIM — In the exact words; word for word.

W

WANTON — Includes reckless but, in describing the operation of a vehicle, may in a proper case mean willfulness or a gross disregard of probable consequences, and thus describe a more aggravated offense.

WARRANT OFFICER — An officer of the Armed Forces who holds a commission or warrant in a warrant officer grade, pay grades W-1 through W-4.

WILLFUL — Deliberate, voluntary, and intentional, as distinguished from acts committed through inadvertence, accident, or ordinary negligence.

WRONGFUL — Contrary to law, regulation, lawful order, or custom.

APPENDIX 3

UNIFORM CODE OF MILITARY JUSTICE

Chapter 47. Uniform Code of Military Justice

Subchapter	Sec.	Art.
I. General Provisions	801	1
II. Apprehension and Restraint	807	7
III. Non-Judicial Punishment	815	15
IV. Court-Martial Jurisdiction	816	16
V. Composition of Courts-Martial	822	22
VI. Pre-Trial Procedure	830	30
VII. Trial Procedure	836	36
VIII. Sentences	855	55
IX. Post-Trial Procedure and Review of Courts-Martial	859	59
X. Punitive Articles	877	77
XI. Miscellaneous Provisions	935	135
XII. Court of Military Appeals	941	141

Subchapter 1. GENERAL PROVISIONS

§ 801. Art. 1. Definitions

In this chapter:

(1) The term "Judge Advocate General" means, severally, the Judge Advocates General of the Army, Navy, and Air Force and, except when the Coast Guard is operating as a service in the Navy, the General Counsel of the Department of Transportation.

(2) The Navy, the Marine Corps, and the Coast Guard when it is operating as a service in the Navy, shall be considered as one armed force.

(3) The term "commanding officer" includes only commissioned officers.

(4) The term "officer in charge" means a member of the Navy, the Marine Corps, or the Coast Guard designated as such by appropriate authority.

(5) The term "superior commissioned officer" means a commissioned officer superior in rank or command.

(6) The term "cadet" means a cadet of the United States Military Academy, the United States Air Force Academy, or the United States Coast Guard Academy.

(7) The term "midshipman" means a midshipman of the United States Naval Academy and any other midshipman on active duty in the naval service.

(8) The term "military" refers to any or all of the armed forces.

(9) The term "accuser" means a person who signs and swears to charges, any person who directs that charges nominally be signed and sworn to by another, and any other person who has an interest other than an official interest in the prosecution of the accused.

(10) The term "military judge" means an official of a general or special court-martial detailed in accordance with section 826 of this title (article 26).

(11) The term "law specialist" means a commissioned officer of the Coast Guard designated for special duty (law).

(12) The term "legal officer" means any commissioned officer of the Navy, Marine Corps, or Coast Guard designated to perform legal duties for a command.

(13) The term "judge Advocate" means

(A) an officer of the Judge Advocate General's Corps of the Army or the Navy;

(B) an officer of the Air Force or the Marine Corps who is designated as a judge advocate; or

(C) an officer of the Coast Guard who is designated as a law specialist.

(14) The term "record", when used in connection with the proceedings of a court-martial, means

(A) an official written transcript, written summary, or other writing relating to the proceedings; or

(B) an official audiotape, videotape, or similar material from which sound, or sound and visual images, depicting the proceedings may be reproduced.

(15) The term 'classified information' means (A) any information or material that has been determined by an official of the United States pursuant to law, an Executive Order, or regulation to require protection against unauthorized disclosure for reasons of national security, and (B) any restricted data, as defined in section 11(y) of the Atomic Energy Act of 1954 (42 U.S.C. 2014(y)).

(16) The term 'national security' means the national defense and foreign relations of the United States.

§ 802. Art. 2. Persons subject to this chapter

(a) The following persons are subject to this chapter.

(1) Members of a regular component of the armed forces, including those awaiting discharge after expiration of their terms of enlistment; volunteers from the time of their muster or acceptance into the armed forces; inductees from the time of their actual induction into the armed forces; and other persons lawfully called or ordered into, or to duty in or for training in, the armed forces, from the dates when they are required by the terms of the call or order to obey it.

(2) Cadets, aviation cadets, and midshipmen.

(3) Members of a reserve component while on inactive duty training, but in the case of members of the Army National Guard of the United States or the Air National Guard of the United States only when in Federal service.

(4) Retired members of a regular component of the armed forces who are entitled to pay.

(5) Retired members of a reserve component who are receiving hospitalization from an armed force.

(6) Members of the Fleet Reserve and Fleet Marine Corps Reserve.

(7) Persons in custody of the armed forces serving a sentence imposed by a court-martial.

(8) Members of the National Oceanic and Atmospheric Administration, Public Health Service, and other organizations, when assigned to and serving with the armed forces.

(9) Prisoners of war in custody of the armed forces.

(10) In time of war, persons serving with or accompanying an armed force in the field.

(11) Subject to any treaty or agreement to which the United States is or may be a party or to any accepted rule of international law, person serving with, employed by, or accompanying the armed forces outside the United States and outside the Commonwealth of Puerto Rico, Guam, and the Virgin Islands.

(12) Subject to any treaty or agreement to which the United States is or may be a party or to any accepted rule of international law, persons within an area leased by or otherwise reserved or acquired for the use of the United States which is under the

control of the Secretary concerned and which is outside the United States and outside the Commonwealth of Puerto Rico, Guam, and the Virgin Islands.

(b) The voluntary enlistment of any person who has the capacity to understand the significance of enlisting in the armed forces shall be valid for purposes of jurisdiction under subsection (a) and a change of status from civilian to member of the armed forces shall be effective upon the taking of the oath of enlistment.

(c) Notwithstanding any other provision of law, a person serving with an armed force who

(1) submitted voluntarily to military authority;

(2) met the mental competency and minimum age qualifications of sections 504 and 505 of this title at the time of voluntary submission to military authority;

(3) received military pay or allowances; and

(4) performed military duty is subject to this chapter until such person's active service has been terminated in accordance with law or regulations promulgated by the Secretary concerned.

(d)(1) A member of a reserve component who is not on active duty and who is made the subject of proceedings under section 815 (article 15) or section 830 (article 30) with respect to an offense against this chapter may be ordered to active duty involuntarily for the purpose of

(A) investigation under section 832 of this title (article 32);

(B) trial by court-martial; or

(C) nonjudicial punishment under section 815 of this title (article 15).

(2) A member of a reserve component may not be ordered to active duty under paragraph (1) except with respect to an offense committed while the member was

(A) on active duty; or

(B) on inactive-duty training, but in the case of members of the Army National Guard of the United States or the Air National Guard of the United States only when in Federal service.

(3) Authority to order a member to active duty under paragraph (1) shall be exercised under regulations prescribed by the President.

(4) A member may be ordered to active duty under paragraph (1) only by a person empowered to convene general court-martial in a regular component of the armed forces.

(5) A member ordered to active duty under paragraph (1), unless the order to active duty was approved by the Secretary concerned, may not

(A) be sentenced to confinement; or

(B) be required to serve a punishment consisting of any restriction on liberty during a period other than a period of inactive-duty training or active duty (other than active duty ordered under paragraph (1)).

§ 803. Art. 3. Jurisdiction to try certain personnel

(a) Subject to section 843 of this title (article 43), a person who is in a status in which the person is subject to this chapter and who committed an offense against this chapter while formerly in a status in which the person was subject to this chapter is not relieved from amenability to the jurisdiction of this chapter for that offense by reason of a termination of that person's former status.

(b) Each person discharged from the armed forces who is later charged with having fraudulently obtained his discharge is, subject to section 843 of this title (article 43), subject to trial by court-martial on that charge and is after apprehension subject to this chapter while in the custody of the armed forces for that trial. Upon conviction of that charge he is subject to trial by court-martial for all offenses under this chapter committed before the fraudulent discharge.

(c) No person who has deserted from the armed forces may be relieved from amenability to the jurisdiction of this chapter by virtue of a separation from any later period of service.

(d) A member of a reserve component who is subject to this chapter is not, by virtue of the termination of a period of active duty or inactive-duty training, relieved from amenability to the jurisdiction of this chapter for an offense against this chapter committed during such period of active duty or inactive-duty training.

§ 804. Art. 4. Dismissed officer's right to trial by court-martial

(a) If any commissioned officer, dismissed by order of the President, makes a written application for trial by court-martial setting forth, under oath, that he has been wrongfully dismissed, the President, as soon as practicable, shall convene a general court-martial to try that officer on the charges on which he was dismissed. A court-martial so convened has jurisdiction to try the dismissed officer on those charges, and he shall be considered to have waived the right to plead any statute of limitations applicable to any offense with which he is charged. The court-martial may, as part of its sentence, adjudge the affirmance of the dismissal, but if the court-martial acquits the accused or if the sentence adjudged, as finally approved or affirmed, does not include dismissal or death, the Secretary concerned shall substitute for the dismissal ordered by the President a form of discharge authorized for administrative issue.

(b) If the President fails to convene a general court-martial within six months from the presentation of an application for trial under this article, the Secretary concerned shall substitute for the dismissal order by the President a form of discharge authorized for administrative issue.

(c) If a discharge is substituted for a dismissal under this article, the President alone may reappoint the officer to such commissioned grade and with such rank as, in the opinion of the President, that former officer would have attained had he not been dismissed. The reappointment of such a former officer shall be without regard to the existence of a vacancy and shall affect the promotion status of other officers only insofar as the President may direct. All time between the dismissal and the reappointment shall be considered as actual service for all purposes, including the right to pay and allowances.

(d) If an officer is discharged from any armed force by administrative action or is dropped from the rolls by order of the President, he has no right to trial under this article.

§ 805. Art. 5. Territorial applicability of this chapter

This chapter applies in all places.

§ 806. Art. 6. Judge Advocates and legal officers

(a) The assignment for duty of judge advocates of the Army, Navy, Air Force, and Coast Guard shall be made upon the recommendation of the Judge Advocate General of the armed force of which they are members. The assignment for duty of judge advocates of the Marine Corps shall be made by direction of the Commandant of the Marine Corps. The Judge Advocate General or senior members of his staff shall make frequent inspection in the field in supervision of the administration of military justice.

(b) Convening authorities shall at all times communicate directly with their staff judge advocates or legal officers in matters relating to the administration of military justice; and the staff judge advocate or legal officer of any command is entitled to communicate directly with the staff judge advocate or legal officer of a superior or subordinate command, or with the Judge Advocate General.

(c) No person who has acted as member, military judge, trial counsel, assistant trial counsel, defense counsel, assistant defense counsel, or investigating officer in any case may later act as a staff judge advocate or legal officer to any reviewing authority upon the same case.

(d)(1) A judge advocate who is assigned or detailed to perform the functions of a civil office in the Government of the United States under section 973(b)(2)(B) of this title may perform such duties as may be requested by the agency concerned, including representation of the United States in civil and criminal cases.

(2) The Secretary of Defense, and the Secretary of Transportation with respect to the Coast Guard when it is not operating as a service in the Navy, shall prescribe regulations providing that reimbursement may be a condition of assistance by judge advocates assigned or detailed under section 973(b)(2)(B) of this title.

§ 806a. Art. 6a. Investigation and disposition of matters pertaining to the fitness of military judges

(a) The President shall prescribe procedures for the investigation and disposition of charges, allegations, or information pertaining to the fitness of a military judge or military appellate judge to perform the duties of the judge's position. To the extent practicable, the procedures shall be uniform for all armed forces.

(b) The President shall transmit a copy of the procedures pursuant to this section to the Committees on Armed Services of the Senate and the House of Representatives.

Subchapter II. APPREHENSION AND RESTRAINT

§ 807. Art. 7. Apprehension

(a) Apprehension is the taking of a person into custody.

(b) Any person authorized under regulations governing the armed forces to apprehend persons subject to this chapter or to trial thereunder may do so upon reasonable belief that an offense has been committed and that the person apprehended committed it.

(c) Commissioned officers, warrant officers, petty officers, and noncommissioned officers have authority to quell quarrels, frays and disorders among persons subject to this chapter and to apprehend persons subject to this chapter who take part therein.

§ 808. Art. 8. Apprehension of deserters

Any civil officer having authority to apprehend offenders under the laws of the United States or of a State, Territory, Commonwealth, or possession, or the District of Columbia may summarily apprehend a deserter from the armed forces and deliver him into the custody of those forces.

§ 809. Art. 9. Imposition of restraint

(a) Arrest is the restraint of a person by an order, not imposed as a punishment for an offense, directing him to remain within certain specified limits. Confinement is the physical restraint of a person.

(b) An enlisted member may be ordered into arrest or confinement by any commissioned officer by an order, oral or written, delivered in person or through other persons subject to this chapter. A commanding officer may authorize warrant officers, petty officers, or noncommissioned officers to order enlisted members of his command or subject to his authority into arrest or confinement.

(c) A commissioned officer, a warrant officer, or a civilian subject to this chapter or to trial thereunder may be ordered into arrest or confinement only by a commanding officer to whose authority he is subject, by an order, oral or written, delivered in person or by another commissioned officer. The authority to order such persons into arrest or confinement may not be delegated.

(d) No person may be ordered into arrest or confinement except for probable cause.

(e) Nothing in this article limits the authority of persons authorized to apprehend offenders to secure the custody of an alleged offender until proper authority may be notified.

§ 810. Art. 10. Restraint of persons charged with offenses

Any person subject to this chapter charged with an offense under this chapter shall be ordered into arrest or confinement, as circumstances may require; but when charged only with an offense normally tried by a summary court-martial, he shall not ordinarily be placed in confinement. When any person subject to this chapter is placed in arrest or confinement prior to trial, immediate steps shall be taken to inform him of the specific wrong of which he is accused and to try him or to dismiss the charges and release him.

§ 811. Art. 11. Reports and receiving of prisoners

(a) No provost marshall, commander of a guard, or master at arms may refuse to receive or keep any prisoner committed to his charge by a commissioned officer of the armed forces, when the committing officer furnishes a statement, signed by him, of the offense charged against the prisoner.

(b) Every commander of a guard or master at arms to whose charge a prisoner is committed shall, within twenty-four hours after that commitment or as soon as he is relieved from guard, report to the commanding officer the name of the prisoner, the offense charged against him, and the name of the person who ordered or authorized the commitment.

§ 812. Art. 12. Confinement with enemy prisoners prohibited

No member of the armed forces may be placed in confinement in immediate association with enemy prisoners or other foreign nationals not members of the armed forces.

§ 813. Art. 13. Punishment prohibited before trial

No person, while being held for trial, may be subjected to punishment or penalty other than arrest or confinement upon the charges pending against him, nor shall the arrest or confinement imposed upon him be any more rigorous than the circumstances required to insure his presence, but he may be subjected to minor punishment during that period for infractions of discipline.

§ 814. Art. 14. Delivery of offenders to civil authorities

(a) Under such regulations as the Secretary concerned may prescribe, a member of the armed forces accused of an offense against civil authority may be delivered, upon request, to the civil authority for trial.

(b) When delivery under this article is made to any civil authority of a person undergoing sentence of a court-martial, the delivery, if followed by conviction in a civil tribunal, interrupts the execution of the sentence of the court-martial, and the offender after having answered to the civil authorities for his offense shall, upon the request of competent military authority, be returned to military custody for the completion of his sentence.

Subchapter III. NON-JUDICIAL PUNISHMENT

§ 815. Art. 15. Commanding officer's non-judicial punishment

(a) Under such regulations as the President may prescribe, and under such additional regulations as may be prescribed by the Secretary concerned, limitations may be placed on the powers granted by this article with respect to the kind and amount of punishment authorized, the categories of commanding officers and warrant officers exercising command authorized to exercise those powers, the applicability of this article to an accused who demands trial by court-martial, and the kinds of courts-martial to which the case may be referred upon such a demand. However, except in the case of a member attached to or embarked in a vessel, punishment may not be imposed upon any member of the armed forces under this article if the member has, before the imposition of such punishment, demanded trial by court-martial in lieu of such punishment. Under similar regulations, rules may be prescribed with respect to the suspension of punishments authorized hereunder. If authorized by regulations of the Secretary concerned, a commanding officer exercising general court-martial jurisdiction or an officer of general or flag rank in command may delegate his powers under this article to a principal assistant.

(b) Subject to subsection (a), any commanding officer may, in addition to or in lieu of admonition or reprimand, impose one or more of the following disciplinary punishments for minor offenses without the intervention of a court-martial—

(1) upon officers of his command—

(A) restriction to certain specified limits, with or without suspension from duty, for not more than 30 consecutive days;

(B) if imposed by an officer exercising general court-martial jurisdiction or an officer of general or flag rank in command—

(i) arrest in quarters for not more than 30 consecutive days;

(ii) forfeiture of not more than one-half of one month's pay per month for two months;

(iii) restriction to certain specified limits, with or without suspension from duty, for not more than 60 consecutive days;

(iv) detention of not more than one-half of one month's pay per month for three months;

(2) upon other personnel of his command—

(A) if imposed upon a person attached to or embarked in a vessel, confinement on bread and water or diminished rations for not more than three consecutive days;

(B) correctional custody for not more than seven consecutive days;

(C) forfeiture of not more than seven days' pay;

(D) reduction to the next inferior pay grade, if the grade from which demoted is within the promotion authority of the officer imposing the reduction or any officer subordinate to the one who imposes the reduction;

(E) extra duties, including fatigue or other duties, for not more than 14 consecutive days;

(F) restriction to certain specific limits, with or without suspension from duty, for not more than 14 consecutive days;

(G) detention of not more than 14 days' pay;

(H) if imposed by an officer of the grade of major or lieutenant commander, or above—

(i) the punishment authorized under clause (A);

(ii) correctional custody for not more than 30 consecutive days;

(iii) forfeiture of not more than one-half of one month's pay per month for two months;

(iv) reduction to the lowest or intermediate pay grade, if the grade from which demoted is within the promotion authority of the officer imposing the reduction or any officer subordinate to the one who imposes the reduction, but an enlisted member in a pay grade above E-4 may not be reduced more than two pay grades;

(v) extra duties, including fatigue or other duties, for not more than 45 consecutive days;

(vi) restriction to certain specified limits, with or without suspension from duty, for not more than 60 consecutive days;

(vii) detention of not more than one-half of one month's pay per month for three months.

Detention of pay shall be for a stated period of not more than one year but if the offender's term of service expires earlier, the detention shall terminate upon that expiration. No two or more of the punishments of arrest in quarters, confinement on bread and water or diminished rations, correctional custody, extra duties, and restriction may be combined to run consecutively in the maximum amount imposable for each. Whenever any of those punishments are combined to run consecutively, there must be an apportionment. In addition, forfeiture of pay may not be combined with detention of pay without an apportionment. For the purpose of this subsection, "correctional custody" is the physical restraint of a person during duty or nonduty hours and may include extra duties, fatigue duties, or hard labor. If practicable, correctional custody will not be served in immediate association with persons awaiting trial or held in confinement pursuant to trial by court-martial.

(c) An officer in charge may impose upon enlisted members assigned to the unit of which he is in charge such of the punishment authorized under subsection (b)(2)(A)-(G) as the Secretary concerned may specifically prescribe by regulation.

(d) The officer who imposes the punishment authorized in subsection (b), or his successor in command, may, at any time, suspend probationally any part or amount of the unexecuted punishment imposed and may suspend probationally a reduction in grade or a forfeiture imposed under subsection (b), whether or not executed. In addition, he may, at any time, remit or mitigate any part or amount of the unexecuted punishment imposed and may set aside in whole or in part the punishment, whether executed or unexecuted, and restore all rights, privileges and property affected. He may also mitigate reduction in grade to forfeiture or detention of pay. When mitigating—

(1) arrest in quarters to restriction;
(2) confinement on bread and water or diminished rations to correctional custody;
(3) correctional custody or confinement on bread and water or diminished rations to extra duties or restriction, or both; or
(4) extra duties to restriction;

the mitigated punishment shall not be for a greater period than the punishment mitigated. When mitigating forfeiture of pay to detention of pay, the amount of the detention shall not be greater than the amount of the forfeiture. When mitigating reduction in grade to forfeiture or detention of pay, the amount of the forfeiture or detention shall not be greater than the amount that could have been imposed initially under this article by the officer who imposed the punishment mitigated.

(e) A person punished under this article who considers his punishment unjust or disproportionate to the offense may, through the proper channel, appeal to the next superior authority. The appeal shall be promptly forwarded and decided, but the person punished may in the meantime be required to undergo the punishment adjudged. The superior authority may exercise the same powers with respect to the punishment imposed as may be exercised under subsection (d) of the officer who imposed the punishment. Before acting on an appeal from a punishment of—

(1) arrest in quarters for more than seven days;
(2) correctional custody for more than seven days;
(3) forfeiture of more than seven days' pay;
(4) reduction of one or more pay grades from the fourth or a higher pay grade;
(5) extra duties for more than 14 days;
(6) restriction for more than 14 days; or
(7) detention of more than 14 days' pay;

the authority who is to act on the appeal shall refer the case to a judge advocate or a lawyer of the Department of Transportation for consideration and advice, and may so refer the case upon appeal from any punishment imposed under subsection (b).

(f) The imposition and enforcement of disciplinary punishment under this article for any act or omission is not a bar to trial by court-martial for a serious crime or offense growing out of the same act or omission, and not properly punishable under this article; but the fact that a disciplinary punishment has been enforced may be shown by the accused upon trial, and when so shown shall be considered in determining the measure of punishment to be adjudged in the event of a finding of guilty.

(g) The Secretary concerned may, by regulation, prescribe the form of records to be kept of proceedings under this article and may also prescribe that certain categories of those proceedings shall be in writing.

Subchapter IV. COURT-MARTIAL JURISDICTION

§ 816. Art. 16. Courts-martial classified

The three kinds of courts-martial in each of the armed forces are
(1) general courts-martial, consisting of—

    (A) a military judge and not less than five members; or
    (B) only a military judge, if before the court is assembled the accused, knowing the identity of the military judge and after consultation with defense counsel, requests orally on the record or in writing a court composed only of a military judge and the military judge approves;

(2) special courts-martial, consisting of—

    (A) not less than three members; or
    (B) a military judge and not less than three members; or
    (C) only a military judge, if one has been detailed to the court, and the accused under the same conditions as those prescribed in clause (1)(B) so requests; and

(3) summary courts-martial, consisting of one commissioned officer.

§ 817. Art. 17. Jurisdiction of courts-martial in general

(a) Each armed force has court-martial jurisdiction over all persons subject to this chapter. The exercise of jurisdiction by one armed force over personnel of another armed force shall be in accordance with regulations prescribed by the President.

(b) In all cases, departmental review after that by the officer with authority to convene a general court-martial for the command which held the trial, where that review is required under this chapter, shall be carried out by the department that includes the armed force of which the accused is a member.

§ 818. Art. 18. Jurisdiction of general courts-martial

Subject to section 817 of this title (article 17), general courts-martial have jurisdiction to try persons subject to this chapter for any offense made punishable by this chapter and may, under such limitations as the President may prescribe, adjudge any punishment not forbidden by this chapter, including the penalty of death when specifically authorized by this chapter. General courts-martial also have jurisdiction to try any person who by the law of war is subject to trial by a military tribunal and may adjudge any punishment permitted by the law of war. However, a general court-martial of the kind specified in section 816(1)(B) of this title (Article 16(1)(B)) shall not have jurisdiction to try any person for any offense for which the death penalty may be adjudged unless the case has been previously referred to trial as a noncapital case.

§ 819. Art. 19. Jurisdiction of special courts-martial

Subject to section 817 of this title (article 17), special courts-martial have jurisdiction to try persons subject to this chapter for any noncapital offense made punishable by this chapter and, under such regulations as the President may prescribe, for capital offenses. Special courts-martial may, under such limitations as the President may prescribe, adjudge any punishment not forbidden by this chapter except death, dishonorable discharge, dismissal, confinement for more than six months, hard labor without confinement for more than three months, forfeiture of pay exceeding two-thirds pay per month, or forfeiture of pay for more than six months. A bad-conduct discharge may not be adjudged unless a complete record of the proceedings and testimony has been made, counsel having the qualifications prescribed under section 827(b) of this title (article 27(b)) was detailed to represent the accused, and a military judge was detailed to the trial, except in any case in which a military judge could not be detailed to the trial because of physical conditions or military exigencies. In any such case in which a military judge was not detailed to the trial, the convening authority shall make a detailed written statement, to be appended to the record, stating the reason or reasons a military judge could not be detailed.

§ 820. Art. 20. Jurisdiction of summary courts-martial

Subject to section 817 of this title (article 17), summary courts-martial have jurisdiction to try persons subject to this chapter, except officers, cadets, aviation cadets, and midshipmen, for any noncapital offense made punishable by this chapter. No person with respect to whom summary courts-martial have jurisdiction may be brought to trial before a summary court-martial if he objects thereto. If objection to trial by summary court-martial is made by an accused, trial may be ordered by special or general court-martial as may be appropriate. Summary courts-martial may, under such limitations as the President may prescribe, adjudge any punishment not forbidden by this chapter except death, dismissal, dishonorable or bad-conduct discharge, confinement for more than one month, hard labor without confinement for more than 45 days, restriction to specified limits for more than two months, or forfeiture of more than two-thirds of one month's pay.

§ 821. Art. 21. Jurisdiction of courts-martial not exclusive

The provisions of this chapter conferring jurisdiction upon courts-martial do not deprive military commissions, provost courts, or other military tribunals of concurrent jurisdiction with respect to offenders or offenses that by statute or by the law of war may be tried by military commission, provost courts, or other military tribunals.

Subchapter V. COMPOSITION OF COURTS-MARTIAL

§ 822. Art. 22. Who may convene general courts-martial

(a) General courts-martial may be convened by—

(1) the President of the United States;
(2) the Secretary of Defense;
(3) the Commanding officer of a unified or specified combatant command;
(4) the Secretary concerned;
(5) the commanding officer of a Territorial Department, an Army Group, an Army, an Army Corps, a division, a separate brigade, or a corresponding unit of the Army or Marine Corps;
(6) the commander-in-chief of a fleet; the commanding officer of a naval station or larger shore activity of the Navy beyond the United States;
(7) the commanding officer of an air command, an air force, an air division, or a separate wing of the Air Force or Marine Corps;
(8) any other commanding officer designated by the Secretary concerned; or
(9) any other commanding officer in any of the armed forces when empowered by the President.

(b) If any such commanding officer is an accuser, the court shall be convened by superior competent authority, and may in any case be convened by such authority if considered desirable by him.

§ 823. Art. 23. Who may convene special courts-martial

(a) Special courts-martial may be convened by—

(1) any person who may convene a general court-martial;
(2) the commanding officer of a district, garrison, fort, camp, station, Air Force base, auxiliary airfield, or other place where members of the Army or the Air Force are on duty;
(3) the commanding officer of a brigade, regiment, detached battalion, or corresponding unit of the Army;
(4) the commanding officer of a wing, group, or separate squadron of the Air Force;
(5) the commanding officer of any naval or Coast Guard vessel, shipyard, base, or station; the commanding officer of any Marine brigade, regiment, detached battalion, or corresponding unit; the commanding officer of any Marine barracks, wing, group, separate squadron, station, base, auxiliary airfield, or other place where members of the Marine Corps are on duty;
(6) the commanding officer of any separate or detached command or group of detached units of any of the armed forces placed under a single commander for this purpose; or
(7) the commanding officer or officer in charge of any other command when empowered by the Secretary concerned.

(b) If any such officer is an accuser, the court shall be convened by superior competent authority, and may in any case be convened by such authority if considered advisable by him.

§ 824. Art. 24. Who may convene summary courts-martial

(a) Summary courts-martial may be convened by—

(1) any person who may convene a general or special court-martial;
(2) the commanding officer of a detached company or other detachment of the Army;
(3) the commanding officer of a detached squadron or other detachment of the Air Force; or
(4) the commanding officer or officer in charge of any other command when empowered by the Secretary concerned.

(b) When only one commissioned officer is present with a command or detachment he shall be the summary court-martial of that command or detachment and shall hear and determine all summary court-martial cases brought before him. Summary courts-martial may, however, be convened in any case by superior competent authority when considered desirable by him.

§ 825. Art. 25. Who may serve on courts-martial

(a) Any commissioned officer on active duty is eligible to serve on all courts-martial for the trial of any person who may lawfully be brought before such courts for trial.

(b) Any warrant officer on active duty is eligible to serve on general and special courts-martial for the trial of any person, other than a commissioned officer, who may lawfully be brought before such courts for trial.

(c)(1) Any enlisted member of an armed force on active duty who is not a member of the same unit as the accused is eligible to serve on general and special courts-martial for the trial of any enlisted member of an armed force who may lawfully be brought before such courts for trial, but he shall serve as a member of a court only if, before the conclusion of a session called by the military judge under section 839(a) of this title (article 39(a)) prior to trial or, in the absence of such a session, before the court is assembled for the trial of the accused, the accused personally has requested orally on the record or in writing that enlisted members serve on it. After such a request, the accused may not be tried by a general or special court-martial the membership of which does not include enlisted members in a number comprising at least one-third of the total membership of the court, unless eligible enlisted members cannot be obtained on account of physical conditions or military exigencies. If such members cannot be obtained, the court may be assembled and the trial held without them, but the convening authority shall make a detailed written statement, to be appended to the record, stating why they could not be obtained.

(2) In this article, "unit" means any regularly organized body as defined by the Secretary concerned, but in no case may it be a body larger than a company, squadron, ship's crew, or body corresponding to one of them.

(d)(1) When it can be avoided, no member of an armed force may be tried by a court-martial any member of which is junior to him in rank or grade.

(2) When convening a court-martial, the convening authority shall detail as members thereof such members of the armed forces as, in his opinion, are best qualified for the duty by reason of age, education, training, experience, length of service, and judicial temperament. No member of an armed force is eligible to serve as a member of a general or special court-martial when he is the accuser or a witness for the prosecution or has acted as investigating officer or as counsel in the same case.

(e) Before a court-martial is assembled for the trial of a case, the convening authority may excuse a member of the court from participating in the case. Under such regulations as the Secretary concerned may prescribe, the convening authority may delegate his authority under this subsection to his staff judge advocate or legal officer or to any other principal assistant.

§ 826. Art. 26. Military judge of a general or special court-martial

(a) A military judge shall be detailed to each general court-martial. Subject to regulations of the Secretary concerned, a military judge may be detailed to any special court-martial. The Secretary concerned shall prescribe regulations providing for the manner in which military judges are detailed for such courts-martial and for the persons who are authorized to detail military judges for such courts-martial. The military judge shall preside over each open session of the court-martial to which he has been detailed.

(b) A military judge shall be a commissioned officer of the armed forces who is a member of the bar of a Federal court or a member of the bar of the highest court of a

State and who is certified to be qualified for duty as a military judge by the Judge Advocate General of the armed force of which such military judge is a member.

(c) The military judge of a general court-martial shall be designated by the Judge Advocate General, or his designee, of the armed force of which the military judge is a member for detail in accordance with regulations prescribed under subsection (a). Unless the court-martial was convened by the President or the Secretary concerned, neither the convening authority nor any member of his staff shall prepare or review any report concerning the effectiveness, fitness, or efficiency of the military judge so detailed, which relates to his performance of duty as a military judge. A commissioned officer who is certified to be qualified for duty as a military judge of a general court-martial may perform such duties only when he is assigned and directly responsible to the Judge Advocate General, or his designee, of the armed force of which the military judge is a member and may perform duties of a judicial or nonjudicial nature other than those relating to his primary duty as a military judge of a general court-martial when such duties are assigned to him by or with the approval of that Judge Advocate General or his designee.

(d) No person is eligible to act as military judge in a case if he is the accuser or a witness for the prosecution or has acted as investigating officer or a counsel in the same case.

(e) The military judge of a court-martial may not consult with the members of the court except in the presence of the accused, trial counsel, and defense counsel, nor may he vote with the members of the court.

§ 827. Art. 27. Detail of trial counsel and defense counsel

(a)(1) Trial counsel and defense counsel shall be detailed for each general and special court-martial. Assistant trial counsel and assistant and associate defense counsel may be detailed for each general and special court-martial. The Secretary concerned shall prescribe regulations providing for the manner in which counsel are detailed for such courts-martial and for the persons who are authorized to detail counsel for such courts-martial.

(2) No person who has acted as investigating officer, military judge, or court member in any case may act later as trial counsel, assistant trial counsel, or, unless expressly requested by the accused, as defense counsel or assistant or associate defense counsel in the same case. No person who has acted for the prosecution may act later in the same case for the defense, nor may any person who has acted for the defense act later in the same case for the prosecution.

(b) Trial counsel or defense counsel detailed for a general court-martial—

(1) must be a judge advocate who is a graduate of an accredited law school or is a member of the bar of a Federal court or of the highest court of a State; or must be a member of the bar of a Federal court or of the highest court of a State; and

(2) must be certified as competent to perform such duties by the Judge Advocate General of the armed force of which he is a member.

(c) In the case of a special court-martial—

(1) the accused shall be afforded the opportunity to be represented at the trial by counsel having the qualifications prescribed under section 827(b) of this title (article 27(b)) unless counsel having such qualifications cannot be obtained on account of physical conditions or military exigencies. If counsel having such qualifications cannot be obtained, the court may be convened and the trial held but the convening authority shall make a detailed written statement, to be appended to the record, stating why counsel with such qualifications could not be obtained;

(2) if the trial counsel is qualified to act as counsel before a general court-martial, the defense counsel detailed by the convening authority must be a person similarly qualified; and

(3) if the trial counsel is a judge advocate or a member of the bar of a Federal court or the highest court of a State, the defense counsel detailed by the convening authority must be one of the foregoing.

§ 828. Art. 28. Detail or employment of reporters and interpreters

Under such regulations as the Secretary concerned may prescribe, the convening authority of a court-martial, military commission, or court of inquiry shall detail or employ qualified court reporters, who shall record the proceedings of and testimony taken before the court or commission. Under like regulations the convening authority of a court-martial, military commission, or court of inquiry may detail or employ interpreters who shall interpret for the court or commission.

§ 829. Art. 29. Absent and additional members

(a) No member of a general or special court-martial may be absent or excused after the court has been assembled for the trial of the accused unless excused as a result of a challenge, excused by the military judge for physical disability or other good cause, or excused by order of the convening authority for good cause.

(b) Whenever a general court-martial, other than a general court-martial composed of a military judge only, is reduced below five members, the trial may not proceed unless the convening authority details new members sufficient in number to provide not less than five members. The trial may proceed with the new members present after the recorded evidence previously introduced before the members of the court has been read to the court in the presence of the military judge, the accused, and counsel for both sides.

(c) Whenever a special court-martial, other than a special court-martial composed of a military judge only, is reduced below three members, the trial may not proceed unless the convening authority details new members sufficient in number to provide not less than three members. The trial shall proceed with the new members present as if no evidence had previously been introduced at the trial, unless a verbatim record of the evidence previously introduced before the members of the court or a stipulation thereof is read to the court in the presence of the military judge, if any, the accused, and counsel for both sides.

(d) If the military judge of a court-martial composed of a military judge only is unable to proceed with the trial because of physical disability, as a result of a challenge, or for other good cause, the trial shall proceed, subject to any applicable conditions of section 816(1)(B) or (2)(C) of this title (article 16(1)(B) or (2)(C)), after the detail of a new military judge as if no evidence had previously been introduced, unless a verbatim record of the evidence previously introduced or a stipulation thereof is read in court in the presence of the new military judge, the accused, and counsel for both sides.

Subchapter VI. PRETRIAL PROCEDURE

§ 830. Art. 30. Charges and specifications

(a) Charges and specifications shall be signed by a person subject to this chapter under oath before a commissioned officer of the armed forces authorized to administer oaths and shall state—

(1) that the signer has personal knowledge of, or has investigated, the matters set forth therein; and
(2) that they are true in fact to the best of his knowledge and belief.

(b) Upon the preferring of charges, the proper authority shall take immediate steps to determine what disposition should be made thereof in the interest of justice and discipline, and the person accused shall be informed of the charges against him as soon as practicable.

§ 831. Art. 31. Compulsory self-incrimination prohibited

(a) No person subject to this chapter may compel any person to incriminate himself or to answer any question the answer to which may tend to incriminate him.

(b) No person subject to this chapter may interrogate or request any statement from an accused or a person suspected of an offense without first informing him of the nature of the accusation and advising him that he does not have to make any statement regarding the offense of which he is accused or suspected and that any statement made by him may be used as evidence against him in a trial by court-martial.

(c) No person subject to this chapter may compel any person to make a statement or produce evidence before any military tribunal if the statement or evidence is not material to the issue and may tend to degrade him.

(d) No statement obtained from any person in violation of this article, or through the use of coercion, unlawful influence, or unlawful inducement may be received in evidence against him in a trial by court-martial.

§ 832. Art. 32. Investigation

(a) No charge or specification may be referred to a general court-martial for trial until a thorough and impartial investigation of all the matters set forth therein has been made. The investigation shall include inquiry as to the truth of the matter set forth in the charges, consideration of the form of charges, and a recommendation as to the disposition which should be made of the case in the interest of justice and discipline.

(b) The accused shall be advised of the charges against him and of his right to be represented at that investigation by counsel. The accused has the right to be represented at that investigation as provided in section 838 of this title (article 38) and in regulations prescribed under that section. At that investigation, full opportunity shall be given to the accused to cross-examine witnesses against him if they are available and to present anything he may desire in his own behalf, either in defense or mitigation, and the investigating officer shall examine available witnesses requested by the accused. If the charges are forwarded after the investigation, they shall be accompanied by a statement of the substance of the testimony taken on both sides and a copy thereof shall be given to the accused.

(c) If an investigation of the subject matter of an offense has been conducted before the accused is charged with the offense, and if the accused was present at the investigation and afforded the opportunities for representation, cross-examination, and presentation prescribed in subsection (b), no further investigation of that charge is necessary under this article unless it is demanded by the accused after he is informed of the charge. A demand for further investigation entitles the accused to recall witnesses for further cross-examination and to offer any new evidence in his own behalf.

(d) If evidence adduced in an investigation under this article indicates that the accused committed an uncharged offense, the investigating officer may investigate the subject matter of such offense without the accused having first been charged with the offense, if the accused—

(1) is present at the investigation;
(2) is informed of the nature of each uncharged offense investigated; and
(3) is afforded the opportunities for representation, cross-examination, and presentation prescribed in subsection (b)."

(e) The requirements of this article are binding on all persons administering this chapter but failure to follow them does not constitute jurisdictional error.

§ 833. Art. 33. Forwarding of charges

When a person is held for trial by general court-martial the commanding officer shall, within eight days after the accused is ordered into arrest or confinement, if practicable, forward the charges, together with the investigation and allied papers, to the officer exercising general court-martial jurisdiction. If that is not practicable, he shall report in writing to that officer the reasons for delay.

§ 834. Art. 34. Advice of staff judge advocate and reference for trial

(a) Before directing the trial of any charge by general court-martial, the convening authority shall refer it to his staff judge advocate for consideration and advice. The convening authority may not refer a specification under a charge to a general court-martial for trial unless he has been advised in writing by the staff judge advocate that—

(1) the specification alleges an offense under this chapter;
(2) the specification is warranted by the evidence indicated in the report of investigation under section 832 of this title (article 32) (if there is such a report); and
(3) a court-martial would have jurisdiction over the accused and the offense.

(b) The advice of the staff judge advocate under subsection (a) with respect to a specification under a charge shall include a written and signed statement by the staff judge advocate—

(1) expressing his conclusion with respect to each matter set forth in subsection (a); and
(2) recommending action that the convening authority take regarding the specification.

If the specification is referred for trial, the recommendation of the staff judge advocate shall accompany the specification.

(c) If the charges or specifications are not formally correct or do not conform to the substance of the evidence contained in the report of the investigating officer, formal corrections, and such changes in the charges and specifications as are needed to make them conform to the evidence, may be made.

§ 835. Art. 35. Service of charges

The trial counsel to whom court-martial charges are referred for trial shall cause to be served upon the accused a copy of the charges upon which trial is to be had. In time of peace no person may, against his objection, be brought to trial or be required to participate by himself or counsel in a session called by the military judge under section 839(a) of this title (article 39(a)), in a general court-martial case within a period of five days after the service of charges upon him or in a special court-martial within a period of three days after the service of charges upon him.

Subchapter VII. TRIAL PROCEDURE

§ 836. Art. 36. President may prescribe rules

(a) Pretrial, trial, and posttrial procedures, including modes of proof, for cases arising under this chapter triable in courts-martial, military commissions and other military tribunals, and procedures for courts of inquiry, may be prescribed by the President by regulations which shall, so far as he considers practicable, apply the principles of law and the rules of evidence generally recognized in the trial of criminal cases in the United States district courts, but which may not be contrary to or inconsistent with this chapter.

(b) All rules and regulations made under this article shall be uniform insofar as practicable and shall be reported to Congress.

§ 837. Art. 37. Unlawfully influencing action of court

(a) No authority convening a general, special, or summary court-martial, nor any other commanding officer, may censure, reprimand, or admonish the court or any member, military judge, or counsel thereof, with respect to the findings or sentence adjudged by the court, or with respect to any other exercises of its or his functions in the conduct of the proceedings. No person subject to this chapter may attempt to coerce or, by any unauthorized means, influence the action of a court-martial or any other military tribunal or any member thereof, in reaching the findings or sentence in any case, or the action of any convening, approving, or reviewing authority with respect to his judicial acts. The foregoing provisions of the subsection shall not apply with respect to (1) general instructional or informational courses in military justice if such courses are designed solely for the purpose of instructing members of a command in the substantive and procedural aspects of courts-martial, or (2) to statements and instructions given in open court by the military judge, president of a special court-martial, or counsel.

(b) In the preparation of an effectiveness, fitness, or efficiency report or any other report or document used in whole or in part for the purpose of determining whether a member of the armed forces is qualified to be advanced in grade, or in determining the assignment or transfer of a member of the armed forces or in determining whether a member of the armed forces should be retained on active duty, no person subject to this chapter may, in preparing any such report (1) consider or evaluate the performance of duty of any such member of a court-martial, or (2) give a less favorable rating or evaluation of any member of the armed forces because of the zeal with which such member, as counsel, represented any accused before a court-martial.

§ 838. Art. 38. Duties of trial counsel and defense counsel

(a) The trial counsel of a general or special court-martial shall prosecute in the name of the United States, and shall, under the direction of the court, prepare the record of the proceedings.

(b) (1) The accused has the right to be represented in his defense before a general or special court-martial or at an investigation under section 832 of this title (article 32) as provided in this subsection.

(2) The accused may be represented by civilian counsel if provided by him.

(3) The accused may be represented—

(A) by military counsel detailed under section 827 of this title (article 27); or
(B) by military counsel of his own selection if that counsel is reasonably available (as determined under regulations prescribed under paragraph (7)).

(4) If the accused is represented by civilian counsel, military counsel detailed or selected under paragraph (3) shall act as associate counsel unless excused at the request of the accused.

(5) Except as provided under paragraph (6), if the accused is represented by military counsel of his own selection under paragraph (3)(B), any military counsel detailed under paragraph (3)(A) shall be excused.

(6) The accused is not entitled to be represented by more than one military counsel. However, the person authorized under regulations prescribed under section 827 of this title (article 27) to detail counsel in his sole discretion—

(A) may detail additional military counsel as assistant defense counsel; and
(B) if the accused is represented by military counsel of his own selection under paragraph (3)(B), may approve a request from the accused that military counsel detailed under paragraph (3)(A) act as associate defense counsel.

(7) The Secretary concerned shall, by regulation, define reasonably available for the purpose of paragraph (3)(B) and establish procedures for determining whether the military counsel selected by an accused under that paragraph is reasonably available. Such regulations may not prescribe any limitation based on the reasonable availability of counsel solely on the grounds that the counsel selected by the accused is from an armed force other than the armed force of which the accused is a member. To the maximum extent practicable, such regulations shall establish uniform policies among the armed forces while recognizing the differences in the circumstances and needs of the various armed forces. The Secretary concerned shall submit copies of regulations prescribed under this paragraph to the Committees on Armed Services of the Senate and House of Representatives.

(c) In any court-martial proceeding resulting in a conviction, the defense counsel—

(1) may forward for attachment to the record of proceedings a brief of such matters as he determines should be considered in behalf of the accused on review (including any objection to the contents of the record which he considers appropriate);

(2) may assist the accused in the submission of any matter under section 860 of this title (article 60); and

(3) may take other action authorized by this chapter.

(d) An assistant trial counsel of a general court-martial may, under the direction of the trial counsel or when he is qualified to be a trial counsel as required by section 827 of this title (article 27), perform any duty imposed by law, regulation, or the custom of the service upon the trial counsel of the court. An assistant trial counsel of a special court-martial may perform any duty of the trial counsel.

(e) An assistant defense counsel of a general or special court-martial may, under the direction of the defense counsel or when he is qualified to be the defense counsel as required by section 827 of this title (article 27), perform any duty imposed by law, regulation, or the custom of the service upon counsel for the accused.

§ 839. Art. 39. Sessions

(a) At any time after the service of charges which have been referred for trial to a court-martial composed of a military judge and members, the military judge may, subject to section 835 of this title (article 35), call the court into session without the presence of the members for the purpose of—
(1) hearing and determining motions raising defenses or objections which are capable of determination without trial of the issues raised by a plea of not guilty;
(2) hearing and ruling upon any matter which may be ruled upon by the military judge under this chapter, whether or not the matter is appropriate for later consideration or decision by the members of the court;
(3) if permitted by regulations of the Secretary concerned, holding the arraignment and receiving the pleas of the accused; and
(4) performing any other procedural function which may be performed by the military judge under this chapter or under rules prescribed pursuant to section 836 of this title (article 36) and which does not require the presence of the members of the court. These proceedings shall be conducted in the presence of the accused, the defense counsel, and the trial counsel and shall be made a part of the record.

(b) When the members of a court-martial deliberate or vote, only the members may be present. All other proceedings, including any other consultation of the members of the court with counsel or the military judge, shall be made a part of the record and shall be in the presence of the accused, the defense counsel, the trial counsel, and in cases in which a military judge has been detailed to the court, the military judge.

§ 840. Art. 40. Continuances

The military judge or a court-martial without a military judge may, for reasonable cause, grant a continuance to any party for such time, and as often, as may appear to be just.

§ 841. Art. 41. Challenges

(a) The military judge and members of a general or special court-martial may be challenged by the accused or the trial counsel for cause stated to the court. The military judge, or, if none, the court, shall determine the relevance and validity of challenges for cause, and may not receive a challenge to more than one person at a time. Challenges by the trial counsel shall ordinarily be presented and decided before those by the accused are offered.

(b) Each accused and the trial counsel is entitled to one peremptory challenge, but the military judge may not be challenged except for cause.

§ 842. Art. 42. Oaths

(a) Before performing their respective duties, military judges, members of general and special courts-martial, trial counsel, assistant trial counsel, defense counsel, assistant or associate defense counsel, reporters, and interpreters shall take an oath to perform their duties faithfully. The form of the oath, the time and place of the taking thereof, the manner of recording the same, and whether the oath shall be taken for all cases in which these duties are to be performed or for a particular case, shall be as prescribed in regulations of the Secretary concerned. These regulations may provide that an oath to perform faithfully duties as a military judge, trial counsel, assistant trial counsel, defense counsel, or assistant or associate defense counsel may be taken at any time by any judge advocate or other person certified to be qualified or competent for the duty, and if such an oath is taken it need not again be taken at the time the judge advocate or other person is detailed to that duty.

(b) Each witness before a court-martial shall be examined on oath.

§ 843. Art. 43. Statute of limitations

(a) A person charged with absence without leave or missing movement in time of war, or with any offense punishable by death, may be tried and punished at any time without limitation.

(b)(1) Except as otherwise provided in this section (article), a person charged with an offense is not liable to be tried by court-martial if the offense was committed more than five years before the receipt of sworn charges and specifications by an officer exercising summary court-martial jurisdiction over the command.

(2) A person charged with an offense is not liable to be punished under section 815 of this title (article 15) if the offense was committed more than two years before the imposition of punishment.

(c) Periods in which the accused is absent without authority or fleeing from justice shall be excluded in computing the period of limitation prescribed in this section (article).

(d) Periods in which the accused was absent from territory in which the United States has the authority to apprehend him, or in the custody of civil authorities, or in the hands of the enemy, shall be excluded in computing the period of limitation prescribed in this article.

(e) For an offense the trial of which in time of war is certified to the President by the Secretary concerned to be detrimental to the prosecution of the war or inimical to the national security, the period of limitation prescribed in this article is extended to six months after the termination of hostilities as proclaimed by the President or by a joint resolution of Congress.

(f) When the United States is at war, the running of any statute of limitations applicable to any offense under this chapter—

(1) involving fraud or attempted fraud against the United States or any agency thereof in any manner, whether by conspiracy or not;

(2) committed in connection with the acquisition, care, handling, custody, control, or disposition of any real or personal property of the United States; or

(3) committed in connection with the negotiation, procurement, award, performance, payment, interim financing, cancellation, or other termination or settlement, of any contract, subcontract, or purchase order which is connected with or related to the prosecution of the war, or with any disposition of termination inventory by any war

contractor or Government agency; is suspended until three years after the termination of hostilities as proclaimed by the President or by a joint resolution of Congress.

(g)(1) If charges or specifications are dismissed as defective or insufficient for any cause and the period prescribed by the applicable statute of limitations—

(A) has expired; or

(B) will expire within 180 days after the date of dismissal of the charges and specifications,

trial and punishment under new charges and specifications are not barred by the statute of limitations if the conditions specified in paragraph (2) are met.

(2) The conditions referred to in paragraph (1) are that the new charges and specifications must—

(A) be received by an officer exercising summary court-martial jurisdiction over the command within 180 days after the dismissal of the charges or specifications; and

(B) allege the same acts or omissions that were alleged in the dismissed charges or specifications (or allege acts or omissions that were included in the dismissed charges or specifications).

§ 844. Art. 44. Former jeopardy

(a) No person may, without his consent, be tried a second time for the same offense.

(b) No proceeding in which an accused has been found guilty by court-martial upon any charge or specification is a trial in the sense of this article until the finding of guilty has become final after review of the case has been fully completed.

(c) A proceeding which, after the introduction of evidence but before a finding, is dismissed or terminated by the convening authority or on motion of the prosecution for failure of available evidence or witnesses without any fault of the accused is a trial in the sense of this article.

§ 845. Art. 45. Pleas of the accused

(a) If an accused after arraignment makes an irregular pleading, or after a plea of guilty sets up matter inconsistent with the plea, or if it appears that he has entered the plea of guilty improvidently or through lack of understanding of its meaning and effect, or if he fails or refuses to plead, a plea of not guilty shall be entered in the record, and the court shall proceed as though he had pleaded not guilty.

(b) A plea of guilty by the accused may not be received to any charge or specification alleging an offense for which the death penalty may be adjudged. With respect to any other charge or specification to which a plea of guilty has been made by the accused and accepted by the military judge or by a court-martial without a military judge, a finding of guilty of the charge or specification may, if permitted by regulations of the Secretary concerned, be entered immediately without vote. This finding shall constitute the finding of the court unless the plea of guilty is withdrawn prior to announcement of the sentence, in which event the proceedings shall continue as though the accused had pleaded not guilty.

§ 846. Art. 46. Opportunity to obtain witnesses and other evidence

The trial counsel, the defense counsel, and the court-martial shall have equal opportunity to obtain witnesses and other evidence in accordance with such regulations as the President may prescribe. Process issued in court-martial cases to compel witnesses to appear and testify and to compel the production of other evidence shall be similar to that which courts of the United States having criminal jurisdiction may lawfully issue and shall run to any part of the United States, or the Territories, Commonwealths, and possessions.

§ 847. Art. 47. Refusal to appear or testify

(a) Any person not subject to this chapter who—
(1) has been duly subpoenaed to appear as a witness before a court-martial, military commission, court of inquiry, or any other military court or board, or before any military or civil officer designated to take a deposition to be read in evidence before such a court, commission, or board;
(2) has been duly paid or tendered the fees and mileage of a witness at the rates allowed to witnesses attending the courts of the United States; and
(3) willfully neglects or refuses to appear, or refuses to qualify as a witness or to testify or to produce any evidence which that person may have been legally subpoenaed to produce; is guilty of an offense against the United States.

(b) Any person who commits an offense named in subsection (a) shall be tried on indictment or information in a United States district court or in a court of original criminal jurisdiction in any of the Territories, Commonwealths, or possessions of the United States, and jurisdiction is conferred upon those courts for that purpose. Upon conviction, such a person shall be fined or imprisoned, or both, at the court's discretion.

(c) The United States attorney or the officer prosecuting for the United States in any such court of original criminal jurisdiction shall, upon the certification of the facts to him by the military court, commission, court of inquiry, or board, file an information against and prosecute any person violating this article.

(d) The fees and mileage of witnesses shall be advanced or paid out of the appropriations for the compensation of witnesses.

§ 848. Art. 48. Contempts

A court-martial, provost court, or military commission may punish for contempt any person who uses any menacing word, sign, or gesture in its presence, or who disturbs its proceedings by any riot or disorder. The punishment may not exceed confinement for 30 days or a fine of $100, or both.

§ 849. Art. 49. Depositions

(a) At any time after charges have been signed as provided in section 830 of this title (article 30), any party may take oral or written depositions unless the military judge or court-martial without a military judge hearing the case or, if the case is not being heard, an authority competent to convene a court-martial for the trial or those charges forbids it for good cause. If a deposition is to be taken before charges are referred for trial, such an authority may designate commissioned officers to represent the prosecution and the defense and may authorize those officers to take the deposition of any witness.

(b) The party at whose instance a deposition is to be taken shall give to every other party reasonable written notice of the time and place for taking the deposition.

(c) Depositions may be taken before and authenticated by any military or civil officer authorized by the laws of the United States or by the laws of the place where the deposition is taken to administer oaths.

(d) A duly authenticated deposition taken upon reasonable notice to the other parties, so far as otherwise admissible under the rules of evidence, may be read in evidence or, in the case of audiotape, videotape, or similar material, may be played in evidence before any military court or commission in any case not capital, or in any proceeding before a court of inquiry or military board, if it appears—

(1) that the witness resides or is beyond the State, Territory, Commonwealth, or District of Columbia in which the court, commission, or board is ordered to sit, or beyond 100 miles from the place of trial or hearing;

(2) that the witness by reason of death, age, sickness, bodily infirmity, imprisonment, military necessity, nonamenability to process, or other reasonable cause, is unable or refuses to appear and testify in person at the place of trial or hearing; or

(3) that the present whereabouts of the witness is unknown.

(e) Subject to subsection (d), testimony by deposition may be presented by the defense in capital cases.

(f) Subject to subsection (d), a deposition may be read in evidence or, in the case of audiotape, videotape, or similar material, may be played in evidence in any case in which the death penalty is authorized but is not mandatory, whenever the convening authority directs that the case be treated as not capital, and in such a case a sentence of death may not be adjudged by the court-martial.

§ 850. Art. 50. Admissibility of records of courts of inquiry

(a) In any case not capital and not extending to the dismissal of a commissioned officer, the sworn testimony, contained in the duly authenticated record of proceedings of a court of inquiry, of a person whose oral testimony cannot be obtained, may, if otherwise admissible under the rules of evidence, be read in evidence by any party before a court-martial or military commission if the accused was a party before the court of inquiry and if the same issue was involved or if the accused consents to the introduction of such evidence.

(b) Such testimony may be read in evidence only by the defense in capital cases or cases extending to the dismissal of a commissioned officer.

(c) Such testimony may also be read in evidence before a court of inquiry or a military board.

§ 850a. Art. 50a. Defense of lack of mental responsibility

(a) It is an affirmative defense in a trial by court-martial that, at the time of the commission of the acts constituting the offense, the accused, as a result of a severe mental disease or defect, was unable to appreciate the nature and quality or the wrongfulness of the acts. Mental disease or defect does not otherwise constitute a defense.

(b) The accused has the burden of proving the defense of lack of mental responsibility by clear and convincing evidence.

(c) Whenever lack of mental responsibility of the accused with respect to an offense is properly at issue, the military judge, or the president of a court-martial without a military judge, shall instruct the members of the court as to the defense of lack of mental responsibility under this section and charge them to find the accused—

(1) guilty;
(2) not guilty; or
(3) not guilty only by reason of lack of mental responsibility.

(d) Subsection (c) does not apply to a court-martial composed of a military judge only. In the case of a court-martial composed of a military judge only, whenever lack of mental responsibility of the accused with respect to an offense is properly at issue, the military judge shall find the accused—

(1) guilty;
(2) not guilty; or
(3) not guilty only by reason of lack of mental responsibility.

(e) Notwithstanding the provisions of section 852 of this title (article 52), the accused shall be found not guilty only by reason of lack of mental responsibility if—

(1) a majority of the members of the court-martial present at the time the vote is taken determines that the defense of lack of mental responsibility has been established; or
(2) in the case of a court-martial composed of a military judge only, the military judge determines that the defense of lack of mental responsibility has been established.

§ 851. Art. 51. Voting and rulings

(a) Voting by members of a general or special court-martial on the findings and on the sentence, and by members of a court-martial without a military judge upon questions of challenge, shall be by secret written ballot. The junior member of the court shall count the votes. The count shall be checked by the president, who shall forthwith announce the result of the ballot to the members of the court.

(b) The military judge and, except for questions of challenge, the president of a court-martial without a military judge shall rule upon all questions of law and all interlocutory questions arising during the proceedings. Any such ruling made by the military judge upon any question of law or any interlocutory question other than the factual issue of mental responsibility of the accused, or by the president of a court-martial without a military judge upon any question of law other than a motion for a finding of not guilty, is final and constitutes the ruling of the court. However, the military judge or the president of a court-martial without a military judge may change his ruling at any time during the trial. Unless the ruling is final, if any member objects thereto, the court shall be cleared and closed and the question decided by a voice vote as provided in section 852 of this title (article 52), beginning with the junior in rank.

(c) Before a vote is taken on the findings, the military judge or the president of a court-martial without a military judge shall, in the presence of the accused and counsel, instruct the members of the court as to the elements of the offense and charge them—

(1) that the accused must be presumed to be innocent until his guilt is established by legal and competent evidence beyond reasonable doubt;
(2) that in the case being considered, if there is a reasonable doubt as to the guilt of the accused, the doubt must be resolved in favor of the accused and he must be acquitted;

(3) that, if there is a reasonable doubt as to the degree of guilt, the finding must be in a lower degree as to which there is no reasonable doubt; and

(4) that the burden of proof to establish the guilt of the accused beyond reasonable doubt is upon the United States.

(d) Subsections (a), (b), and (c) do not apply to a court-martial composed of a military judge only. The military judge of such a court-martial shall determine all questions of law and fact arising during the proceedings and, if the accused is convicted, adjudge an appropriate sentence. The military judge of such a court-martial shall make a general finding and shall in addition on request find the facts specially. If an opinion or memorandum of decision is filed, it will be sufficient if the findings of fact appear therein.

§ 852. Art. 52. Number of votes required

(a)(1) No person may be convicted of an offense for which the death penalty is made mandatory by law, except by the concurrence of all the members of the court-martial present at the time the vote is taken.

(2) No person may be convicted of any other offense, except as provided in section 845(b) of this title (article 45(b)) or by the concurrence of two-thirds of the members present at the time the vote is taken.

(b)(1) No person may be sentenced to suffer death, except by the concurrence of all the members of the court-martial present at the time the vote is taken and for an offense in this chapter expressly made punishable by death.

(2) No person may be sentenced to life imprisonment or to confinement for more than ten years, except by the concurrence of three-fourths of the members present at the time the vote is taken.

(3) All other sentences shall be determined by the concurrence of two-thirds of the members present at the time the vote is taken.

(c) All other questions to be decided by the members of a general or special court-martial shall be determined by a majority vote, but a determination to reconsider a finding of guilty or to reconsider a sentence, with a view toward decreasing it, may be made by any lesser vote which indicates that the reconsideration is not opposed by the number of votes required for that finding or sentence. A tie vote on a challenge disqualifies the member challenged. A tie vote on a motion for a finding of not guilty or on a motion relating to the questions of the accused's sanity is a determination against the accused. A tie vote on any other question is a determination in favor of the accused.

§ 853. Art. 53. Court to announce action

A court-martial shall announce its findings and sentence to the parties as soon as determined.

§ 854. Art. 54. Record of trial

(a) Each general court-martial shall keep a separate record of the proceedings in each case brought before it, and the record shall be authenticated by the signature of the military judge. If the record cannot be authenticated by the military judge by reason of his death, disability, or absence, it shall be authenticated by the signature of the trial counsel or by that of a member if the trial counsel is unable to authenticate it by reason of his death, disability, or absence. In a court-martial consisting of only a military judge the record shall be authenticated by the court reporter under the same conditions which would impose such a duty on a member under this subsection.

(b) Each special and summary court-martial shall keep a separate record of the proceedings in each case, and the record shall be authenticated in the manner required by such regulations as the President may prescribe.

(c)(1) A complete record of the proceedings and testimony shall be prepared—

(A) in each general court-martial case in which the sentence adjudged includes death, a dismissal, a discharge, or (if the sentence adjudged does not include a discharge) any other punishment which exceeds that which may otherwise be adjudged by a special court-martial; and

(B) in each special court-martial case in which the sentence adjudged includes a bad-conduct discharge.

(2) In all other court-martial cases, the record shall contain such matters as may be prescribed by regulations of the President.

(d) A copy of the record of the proceedings of each general and special court-martial shall be given to the accused as soon as it is authenticated.

Subchapter VIII. SENTENCES

§ 855. Art. 55. Cruel and unusual punishments prohibited

Punishment by flogging, or by branding, marking, or tattooing on the body, or any other cruel or unusual punishment, may be not adjudged by a court-martial or inflicted upon any person subject to this chapter. The use of irons, single or double, except for the purpose of safe custody, is prohibited.

§ 856. Art. 56. Maximum limits

The punishment which a court-martial may direct for an offense may not exceed such limits as the President may prescribe for that offense.

§ 857. Art. 57. Effective date of sentences

(a)(1) Any forfeiture of pay or allowances or reduction in grade that is included in a sentence of a court-martial takes effect on the earlier of—

(A) the date that is 14 days after the date on which the sentence is adjudged; or
(B) the date on which the sentence is approved by the convening authority.

(2) On application by an accused, the convening authority may defer a forfeiture of pay or allowance or reduction in grade that would otherwise become effective under paragraph (1)(A) until the date on which the sentence is approved by the convening authority. Such a deferment may be rescinded at any time by the convening authority.

"(3) A forfeiture of pay or allowances shall be applicable to pay and allowances accruing on and after the date on which the sentence takes effect.

"(4) In this subsection, the term 'convening authority', with respect to a sentence of a court-martial, means any person authorized to act on the sentence under section 869 of this title (article 60).

(b) Any period of confinement included in a sentence of a court-martial begins to run from the date the sentence is adjudged by the court-martial, but periods during which the sentence to confinement is suspended or deferred shall be excluded in computing the service of the term of confinement.

(c) All other sentences of courts-martial are effective on the date ordered executed.

§ 857a. Art. 57a. Deferment of sentences

(a) On application by an accused who is under sentence to confinement that has not been ordered executed, the convening authority or, if the accused is no longer under his jurisdiction, the officer exercising general court-martial jurisdiction over the command to which the accused is currently assigned, may in his sole discretion defer service of the sentence to confinement. The deferment shall terminate when the sentence is ordered executed. The deferment may be rescinded at any time by the officer who granted it or, if the accused is no longer under his jurisdiction, by the officer exercising general court-martial jurisdiction over the command to which the accused is currently assigned.

(b)(1) In any case in which a court-martial sentences a person referred to in paragraph (2) to confinement, the convening authority may postpone the service of the sentence to confinement, without the consent of that person, until after the person has been permanently released to the armed forces by a state or foreign country referred to in that paragraph.

(2) Paragraph (1) applies to a person subject to this chapter who—

(A) While in the custody of a state or foreign country is temporarily returned by that state or foreign country to the armed forces for trial by court-martial; and

(B) After the court-martial, is returned to that state or foreign country under the authority of a mutual agreement or treaty, as the case may be.

(3) In this subsection, the term 'state' means a state of the United States, the District of Columbia, a territory, or a possession of the United States.

(c) In any case in which a court-martial sentences a person to confinement and the sentence to confinement has been ordered executed, but in which review of the case under section 867(a)(2) of this title (article 67(a)(2)) is pending, the Secretary concerned may defer further service of the sentence to confinement while that review is pending.

§ 858. Art. 58. Execution of confinement

(a) Under such instructions as the Secretary concerned may prescribe, a sentence of confinement adjudged by a court-martial or other military tribunal, whether or not the sentence includes discharge or dismissal, and whether or not the discharge or dismissal has been executed, may be carried into execution by confinement in any place of confinement under the control of any of the armed forces or in any penal or correctional institution under the control of the United States, or which the United States may be allowed to use. Persons so confined in a penal or correctional institution not under his control of one of the armed forces are subject to the same discipline and treatment as persons confined or committed by the courts of the United States or of the State, Territory, District of Columbia, or place in which the institution is situated.

(b) The omission of the words hard labor from any sentence of a court-martial adjudging confinement does not deprive the authority executing that sentence of the power to require hard labor as a part of the punishment.

§ 858a. Art. 58a. Sentences; reduction in enlisted grade upon approval

(a) Unless otherwise provided in regulations to be prescribed by the Secretary concerned, a court-martial sentence of an enlisted member in a pay grade above E-1, as approved by the convening authority, that includes—

   (1) a dishonorable or bad-conduct discharge;
   (2) confinement; or
   (3) hard labor without confinement;

reduces that member to pay grade E-1, effective on the date of that approval.

(b) If the sentence of a member who is reduced in pay grade under subsection (a) is set aside or disapproved, or, as finally approved, does not include any punishment named in subsection (a)(1), (2), or (3), the rights and privileges of which he was deprived because of that reduction shall be restored to him and he is entitled to the pay and allowances to which he would have been entitled for the period the reduction was in effect, had he not been so reduced.

§ 858b. Art. 58b. Sentences: forfeiture of pay and allowances during confinement

(a)(1) A court-martial sentence described in paragraph (2) shall result in the forfeiture of pay and allowances due that member during any period of confinement or parole. The forfeiture pursuant to this section shall take effect on the date determined under section 857(a) of this title (article 57(a)) and may be deferred as provided in that section. The pay and allowances forfeited, in the case of a general court-martial, shall be all pay and allowances due that member during such period and, in the case of a special court-martial, shall be two-thirds of all pay and allowances due that member during such period.

(2) A sentence covered by this section is any sentence that includes—

   (A) confinement for more than six months or death; or
   (B) confinement for six months or less and a dishonorable or bad-conduct discharge or dismissal.

(b) In a case involving an accused who has dependents, the convening authority or other person acting under section 860 of this title (article 60) may waive any or all of the forfeitures of pay and allowances required by subsection (a) for a period not to exceed six months. Any amount of pay or allowances that, except for a waiver under this subsection, would be forfeited shall be paid, as the convening authority or other person taking action directs, to the dependents of the accused.

(c) If the sentence of a member who forfeits pay and allowances under subsection (a) is set aside or disapproved or, as finally approved, does not provide for a punishment referred to in subsection (a)(2), the member shall be paid the pay and allowances which the member would have been paid, except for the forfeiture, for the period during which the forfeiture was in effect.

Subchapter IX. POST-TRIAL PROCEDURE AND REVIEW OF COURTS-MARTIAL

§ 859. Art. 59. Error of law; lesser-included offense

(a) A finding or sentence of a court-martial may not be held incorrect on the ground of an error of law unless the error materially prejudices the substantial rights of the accused.

(b) Any reviewing authority with the power to approve or affirm a finding of guilty may approve or affirm, instead, so much of the finding as includes a lesser-included offense.

§ 860. Art. 60. Action by the convening authority

(a) The findings and sentence of a court-martial shall be reported promptly to the convening authority after the announcement of the sentence.

(b)(1) The accused may submit to the convening authority matters for consideration by the convening authority with respect to the findings and the sentence. Any such submissions shall be in writing. Except in a summary court-martial case, such a submission shall be made within 10 days after the accused has been given an authenticated record of trial and, if applicable, the recommendation of the staff judge advocate or legal officer under subsection (d). In a summary court-martial case, such a submission shall be made within seven days after the sentence is announced.

(2) If the accused shows that additional time is required for the accused to submit such matters, the convening authority or other person taking action under this section, for good cause, may extend the applicable period under paragraph (1) for not more than an additional 20 days.

(3) In a summary court-martial case, the accused shall be promptly provided a copy of the record of trial for use in preparing a submission authorized by paragraph (1).

(4) The accused may waive his right to make a submission to the convening authority under paragraph (1). Such a waiver must be made in writing and may not be revoked. For the purposes of subsection (c)(2), the time within which the accused may make a submission under this section shall be deemed to have expired upon the submission of such a waiver to the convening authority.

(c)(1) The authority under this section to modify the findings and sentence of a court-martial is a matter of command prerogative involving the sole discretion of the convening authority. Under regulations of the Secretary concerned, a commissioned officer commanding for the time being, a successor in command, or any person exercising general court-martial jurisdiction may act under this section in place of the convening authority.

(2) Action on the sentence of a court-martial shall be taken by the convening authority or by another person authorized to act under this section. Subject to regulations of the Secretary concerned, such action may be taken only after consideration of any matters submitted by the accused under subsection (b) or after the time for submitting such matters expires, whichever is earlier. The convening authority or other person taking such action, in his sole discretion, may approve, disapprove, commute, or suspend the sentence in whole or in part.

(3) Action on the findings of a court-martial by the convening authority or other person acting on the sentence is not required. However, such person, in his sole discretion, may—

(A) dismiss any charge of specification by setting aside a finding of guilty thereto; or

(B) change a finding of guilty to a charge or specification to a finding of guilty to an offense that is a lesser-included offense of the offense stated in the charge or specification.

(d) Before acting under this section on any general court-martial case or any special court-martial case that includes a bad-conduct discharge, the convening authority or other person taking action under this section shall obtain and consider the written recommendation of the staff judge advocate or legal officer. The convening authority or other person taking action under this section shall refer the record of trial to his staff judge advocate or legal officer, and the staff judge advocate or legal officer shall use such record in the preparation of his recommendation. The recommendation of the staff judge advocate or legal officer shall include such matters as the President may prescribe by regulation and shall be served on the accused, who may submit any matter in response under subsection (b). Failure to object in the response to the recommendation or to any matter attached to the recommendation waives the right to object thereto.

(e)(1) The convening authority or other person taking action under this section, in his sole discretion, may order a proceeding in revision or a rehearing.

(2) A proceeding in revision may be ordered if there is an apparent error or omission in the record or if the record shows improper or inconsistent action by a court-martial with respect to the findings or sentence that can be rectified without material prejudice to the substantial rights of the accused. In no case, however, may a proceeding in revision—

(A) reconsider a finding of not guilty of any specification or a ruling which amounts to a finding of not guilty;

(B) reconsider a finding of not guilty of any charge, unless there has been a finding of guilty under a specification laid under that charge, which sufficiently alleges a violation of some article of this chapter; or

(C) increase the severity of some article of the sentence unless the sentence prescribed for the offense is mandatory.

(3) A rehearing may be ordered by the convening authority or other person taking action under this section if he disapproves the findings and sentence and states the reasons for disapproval of the findings. If such person disapproves the findings and sentence does not order a rehearing, he shall dismiss the charges. A rehearing as to the findings may not be ordered where there is a lack of sufficient evidence in the record to support the findings. A rehearing as to the sentence may be ordered if the convening authority or other person taking action under this subsection disapproves the sentence.

§ 861. Art. 61. Waiver or withdrawal of appeal

(a) In each case subject to appellate review under section 866 or 869(a) of this title (article 66 or 69(a)), except a case in which the sentence as approved under section 860(c) of this title (article 60(c)) includes death, the accused may file with the convening authority a statement expressly waiving the right of the accused to such review. Such a waiver shall be signed by both the accused and by defense counsel and must be filed within 10 days after the action under section 860(c) of this title (article 60(c)) is served on the accused or on defense counsel. The convening authority or other person taking such action, for good cause, may extend the period for such filing by not more than 30 days.

(b) Except in a case in which the sentence as approved under section 860(c) of this title (article 60(c)) includes death, the accused may withdraw an appeal at any time.

(c) A waiver of the right to appellate review or the withdrawal of an appeal under this section bars review under section 866 or 869(a) of this title (article 66 or 69(a)).

§ 862. Art. 62. Appeal by the United States

(a)(1) In a trial by court-martial in which a military judge presides and in which a punitive discharge may be adjudged, the United States may appeal the following (other than an order or ruling that is, or that amounts to, a finding of not guilty with respect to the charge or specification):

(A) An order or ruling of the military judge which terminates the proceedings with respect to a charge or specification.
(B) An order or ruling which excludes evidence that is substantial proof of a fact material in the proceeding.
(C) An order or ruling which directs the disclosure of classified information.
(D) An order or ruling which imposes sanctions for nondisclosure of classified information.
(E) A refusal of the military judge to issue a protective order sought by the United States to prevent the disclosure of classified information.
(F) A refusal by the military judge to enforce an order described in subparagraph (E) that has previously been issued by appropriate authority.

(2) An appeal of an order or ruling may not be taken unless the trial counsel provides the military judge with written notice of appeal from the order or ruling within 72 hours of the order or ruling. Such notice shall include a certification by the trial counsel that the appeal is not taken for the purpose of delay and (if the order or ruling appealed is one which excludes evidence) that the evidence excluded is substantial proof of a fact material in the proceeding.

(3) An appeal under this section shall be diligently prosecuted by appellate Government counsel.

(b) An appeal under this section shall be forwarded by a means prescribed under regulations of the President directly to the Court of Criminal Appeals and shall, whenever practicable, have priority over all other proceedings before that court. In ruling on an appeal under this section, the Court of Criminal Appeals may act only with respect to matters of law, notwithstanding section 866(c) of this title (article 66(c)).

(c) Any period of delay resulting from an appeal under this section shall be excluded in deciding any issue regarding denial of a speedy trial unless an appropriate authority determines that the appeal was filed solely for the purpose of delay with the knowledge that it was totally frivolous and without merit.

§ 863. Art. 63. Rehearings

Each rehearing under this chapter shall take place before a court-martial composed of members not members of the court-martial which first heard the case. Upon a rehearing the accused may be tried for any offense of which he was found not guilty by the first court-martial, and no sentence in excess of or more severe than the original sentence may be approved, unless the sentence is based upon a finding of guilty of an offense not considered upon the merits in the original proceeding, or unless the sentence prescribed for the offense is mandatory. If the sentence approved after the first court-martial was in accordance with a pretrial agreement and the accused at the rehearing changes his plea with respect to the charges or specifications upon which the pretrial agreement was based, or otherwise does not comply with the pretrial agreement, the approved sentence as to those charges or specifications may include any punishment not in excess of that lawfully adjudged at the first court-martial.

§ 864. Art. 64. Review by a judge advocate

(a) Each case in which there has been a finding of guilty that is not reviewed under section 866 or 869(a) of this title (article 66 or 69(a)) shall be reviewed by a judge advocate under regulations of the Secretary concerned. A judge advocate may not review a case under this subsection if he has acted in the same case as an accuser, investigating officer, member of the court, military judge, or counsel or has otherwise acted on behalf of the prosecution or defense. The judge advocate's review shall be in writing and shall contain the following:
(1) conclusions as to whether—

(A) the court had jurisdiction over the accused and the offense;
(B) the charge and specification stated an offense; and
(C) the sentence was within the limits prescribed as a matter of law.

(2) A response to each allegation of error made in writing by the accused.
(3) If the case is sent for action under subsection (b), a recommendation as to the appropriate action to be taken and an opinion as to whether corrective action is required as a matter of law.
(b) The record of trial and related documents in each case reviewed under subsection (a) shall be sent for action to the person exercising general court-martial jurisdiction over the accused at the time the court was convened (or to that person's successor in command) if—

(1) the judge advocate who reviewed the case recommends corrective action;
(2) the sentence approved under section 860(c) of this title (article 60(c)) extends to dismissal, a bad conduct or dishonorable discharge, or confinement for more than six months; or
(3) such action is otherwise required by regulations of the Secretary concerned.

(c)(1) The person to whom the record of trial and related documents are sent under subsection (b) may—

(A) disapprove or approve the findings or sentence, in whole or in part;
(B) remit, commute, or suspend the sentence in whole or in part;
(C) except where the evidence was insufficient at the trial to support the findings, order a rehearing on the findings, on the sentence, or on both; or
(D) dismiss the charges.

(2) If a rehearing is ordered by the convening authority finds a rehearing impracticable, he shall dismiss the charges.
(3) If the opinion of the judge advocate in the judge advocate's review under subsection (a) is that corrective action is required as a matter of law and if the person required to take action under subsection (b) does not take action that is at least as favorable to the accused as that recommended by the judge advocate, the record of trial and action thereon shall be sent to the Judge Advocate General for review under section 869(b) of this title (article 69(b)).

§ 865. Art. 65. Disposition of records

(a) In a case subject to appellate review under section 866 or 869(a) of this title (article 66 or 69(a)) in which the right to such review is not waived, or an appeal is not withdrawn, under section 861 of this title (article 61), the record of trial and action thereon shall be transmitted to the Judge Advocate General for appropriate action.

(b) Except as otherwise required by this chapter, all other records of trial and related documents shall be transmitted and disposed of as the Secretary concerned may prescribe by regulation.

§ 866. Art. 66. Review by Court of Criminal Appeals

(a) Each Judge Advocate General shall establish a Court of Criminal Appeals which shall be composed of one or more panels, and each such panel shall be composed of not less than three appellate military judges. For the purpose of reviewing court-martial cases, the court may sit in panels or as a whole in accordance with rules prescribed under subsection (f). Any decision of a panel may be reconsidered by the court sitting as a whole in accordance with such rules. Appellate military judges who are assigned to a Court of Criminal Appeals may be commissioned officers or civilians, each of whom must be a member of a bar of a Federal court or the highest court of a State. The Judge Advocate General shall designate as chief judge one of the appellate military judges of the Court of Criminal Appeals established by him. The chief judge shall determine on which panels of the court the appellate judges assigned to the court will serve and which military judge assigned to the court will act as the senior judge on each panel.

(b) The Judge Advocate General shall refer to a Court of Criminal Appeals the record in each case of trial by court-martial—

(1) in which the sentence, as approved, extends to death, dismissal of a commissioned officer, cadet, or midshipman, dishonorable or bad-conduct discharge, or confinement for one year or more; and

(2) except in the case of a sentence extending to death, the right to appellate review has not been waived or an appeal has not been withdrawn under section 861 of this title (article 61).

(c) In a case referred to it, the Court of Criminal Appeals may act only with respect to the findings and sentence as approved by the convening authority. It may affirm only such findings of guilty, and the sentence or such part or amount of the sentence, as it finds correct in law and fact and determines, on the basis of the entire record, should be approved. In considering the record, it may weigh the evidence, judge the credibility of witnesses, and determine controverted questions of fact, recognizing that the trial court saw and heard the witnesses.

(d) If the Court of Criminal Appeals sets aside the findings and sentence, it may, except where the setting aside is based on lack of sufficient evidence in the record to support the findings, order a rehearing. If it sets aside the findings and sentence and does not order a rehearing, it shall order that the charges be dismissed.

(e) The Judge Advocate General shall, unless there is to be further action by the President, the Secretary concerned, the Court of Appeals for the Armed Forces, or the Supreme Court, instruct the convening authority to take action in accordance with the decision of the Court of Criminal Appeals. If the Court of Criminal Appeals has ordered a rehearing but the convening authority finds a rehearing impracticable, he may dismiss the charges.

(f) The Judge Advocates General shall prescribe uniform rules of procedure for Courts of Criminal Appeals and shall meet periodically to formulate policies and procedure in regard to review of court-martial cases in the offices of the Judge Advocates General and by the Courts of Criminal Appeals.

(g) No member of a Court of Criminal Appeals shall be required, or on his own initiative be permitted, to prepare, approve, disapprove, review, or submit, with respect to any other member of the same or another Court of Criminal Appeals, an effectiveness, fitness, or efficiency report, or any other report documents used in whole or in part for the purpose of determining whether a member of the armed forces is qualified to be advanced in grade, or in determining the assignment or transfer of a member of the armed forces, or in determining whether a member of the armed forces shall be retained on active duty.

(h) No member of a Court of Criminal Appeals shall be eligible to review the record of any trial if such member served as investigating officer in the case or served as a member of the court-martial before which such trial was conducted, or served as military judge, trial or defense counsel, or reviewing officer of such trial.

§ 867. Art. 67. Review by the Court of Appeals for the Armed Forces

(a) The Court of Appeals for the Armed Forces shall review the record in—

(1) all cases in which the sentence, as affirmed by a Court of Criminal Appeals, extends to death;

(2) all cases reviewed by a Court of Criminal Appeals which the Judge Advocate General orders sent to the Court of Appeals for the Armed Forces for review; and

(3) all cases reviewed by a Court of Criminal Appeals in which, upon petition of the accused and on good cause shown, the Court of Appeals for the Armed Forces has granted a review.

(b) the accused may petition the Court of Appeals for the Armed Forces for review of a decision of a Court of Criminal Appeals within 60 days from the earlier of—

(1) the date on which the accused is notified of the decision of the Court of Criminal Appeals; or

(2) the date on which a copy of the decision of the Court of Criminal Appeals, after being served on appellate counsel of record for the accused (if any), is deposited in the United States mails for delivery by first class certified mail to the accused at an address provided by the accused or, if no such address has been provided by the accused, at the latest address listed for the accused in his official service record. The Court of Appeals for the Armed Forces shall act upon such a petition promptly in accordance with the rules of the court.

(c) In any case reviewed by it, the Court of Appeals for the Armed Forces may act only with respect to the findings and sentence as approved by the convening authority and as affirmed or set aside as incorrect in law by the Court of Criminal Appeals. In a case which the Judge Advocate General orders sent to the Court of Appeals for the Armed Forces, that action need be taken with respect to the issues raised by him. In a case reviewed upon petition of the accused, that action need be taken only with respect to issues specified in the grant of review. The Court of Appeals for the Armed Forces shall take action only with respect to matters of law.

(d) If the Court of Appeals for the Armed Forces sets aside the findings and sentence, it may, except where the setting aside is based on lack of sufficient evidence in the record to support the findings, order a rehearing. If it sets aside the findings and sentence and does not order a rehearing, it shall order that the charges be dismissed.

(e) After it has acted on a case, the Court of Appeals for the Armed Forces may direct the Judge Advocate General to return the record to the Court of Criminal Appeals for further review in accordance with the decision of the Court. Otherwise, unless there is to be further action by the President or the Secretary concerned, the Judge Advocate General shall instruct the convening authority to take action in accordance with that decision. If the court ordered a rehearing, but the convening authority finds a rehearing impracticable, he may dismiss the charges.

§ 867a. Art. 67a. Review by the Supreme Court

(a) Decisions of the United States Court of Appeals for the Armed Forces are subject to review by the Supreme Court by writ of certiorari as provided in section 1259 of title 28. The Supreme Court may not review by a writ of certiorari under this section any action of the Court of Appeals for the Armed Forces in refusing to grant a petition for review.

(b) The accused may petition the Supreme Court for a writ of certiorari without prepayment of fees and costs or security therefor and without filing the affidavit required by section 1915(a) of title 28.

§ 868. Art. 68. Branch offices

The Secretary concerned may direct the Judge Advocate General to establish a branch office with any command. The branch office shall be under an Assistant Judge Advocate General who, with the consent of the Judge Advocate General, may establish a Court of Criminal Appeals with one or more panels. That Assistant Judge Advocate General and any Court of Criminal Appeals established by him may perform for that command under the general supervision of the Judge Advocate General, the respective duties which the Judge Advocate General and a Court of Criminal Appeals established by the Judge Advocate General would otherwise be required to perform as to all cases involving sentences not requiring approval by the President.

§ 869. Art. 69. Review in the office of the Judge Advocate General

(a) The record of trial in each general court-martial that is not otherwise reviewed under section 866 of this title (article 66) shall be examined in the office of the Judge Advocate General if there is a finding of guilty and the accused does not waive or withdraw his right to appellate review under section 861 of this title (article 61). If any part of the findings or sentence is found to be unsupported in law or if reassessment of the sentence is appropriate, the Judge Advocate General may modify or set aside the findings or sentence or both.

(b) The findings or sentence, or both, in a court-martial case not reviewed under subsection (a) or under section 866 of this title (article 66) may be modified or set aside, in whole or in part, by the Judge Advocate General on the ground of newly discovered evidence, fraud on the court, lack of jurisdiction over the accused or the offense, error prejudicial to the substantial rights of the accused, or the appropriateness of the sentence. If such a case is considered upon application of the accused, the application must be filed in the office of the Judge Advocate General by the accused on or before the last day of the two-year period beginning on the date the sentence is approved under section 860(c) of this title (article 60(c)), unless the accused establishes good cause for failure to file within that time.

(c) If the Judge Advocate General sets aside the findings or sentence, he may, except when the setting aside is based on lack of sufficient evidence in the record to support the findings, order a rehearing. If he sets aside the findings and sentence and does not order a rehearing, he shall order that the charges be dismissed. If the Judge Advocate General orders a rehearing but the convening authority finds a rehearing impractical, the convening authority shall dismiss the charges.

(d) A Court of Criminal Appeals may review, under section 866 of this title (article 66)—

(1) any court-martial case which (A) is subject to action by the Judge Advocate General under this section, and (B) is sent to the Court of Criminal Appeals by order of the Judge Advocate General; and,

(2) any action taken by the Judge Advocate General under this section in such case.

(e) Notwithstanding section 866 of this title (article 66), in any case reviewed by a Court of Criminal Appeals under this section, the Court may take action only with respect to matters of law.

§ 870. Art. 70. Appellate counsel

(a) The Judge Advocate General shall detail in his office one or more commissioned officers as appellate Government counsel, and one or more commissioned officers as appellate defense counsel, who are qualified under section 827(b)(1) of this title (article 27(b)(1)).

(b) Appellate Government counsel shall represent the United States before the Court of Criminal Appeals or the Court of Appeals for the Armed Forces when directed to do so by the Judge Advocate General. Appellate Government counsel may represent the United States before the Supreme Court in cases arising under this chapter when requested to do so by the Attorney General.

(c) Appellate defense counsel shall represent the accused before the Court of Criminal Appeals, the Court of Appeals for the Armed Forces, or the Supreme Court—

(1) when requested by the accused;
(2) when the United States is represented by counsel; or
(3) when the Judge Advocate General has sent the case to the Court of Appeals for the Armed Forces.

(d) The accused has the right to be represented before the Court of Criminal Appeals, the Court of Appeals for the Armed Forces, or the Supreme Court by civilian counsel if provided by him.

(e) Military appellate counsel shall also perform such other functions in connection with the review of court-martial cases as the Judge Advocate General directs.

§ 871. Art. 71. Execution of sentence; suspension of sentence

(a) If the sentence of the court-martial extends to death, that part of the sentence providing for death may not be executed until approved by the President. In such a case, the President may commute, remit, or suspend the sentence, or any part thereof, as he sees fit. The part of the sentence providing for death may not be suspended.

(b) If in the case of a commissioned officer, cadet, or midshipman, the sentence of a court-martial extends to dismissal, that part of the sentence providing for dismissal may not be executed until approved by the Secretary concerned or such Under Secretary or Assistant Secretary as may be designated by the Secretary concerned. In such a case, the Secretary, Under Secretary or Assistant Secretary, as the case may be, may commute, remit, or suspend the sentence, or any part of the sentence, as he sees fit. In time or war or national emergency he may commute a sentence of dismissal to reduction to any enlisted grade. A person so reduced may be required to serve for the duration of the war or emergency and six months thereafter.

(c)(1) If a sentence extends to death, dismissal, or a dishonorable or bad-conduct discharge and if the right of the accused to appellate review is not waived, and an appeal is not withdrawn, under section 861 of this title (article 61), that part of the sentence extending to death, dismissal, or a dishonorable or bad-conduct discharge may not be executed until there is a final judgment as to the legality of the proceedings (and with respect to death or dismissal, approval under subsection (a) or (b), as appropriate). A judgment as to legality of the proceedings is final in such cases when review is completed by a Court of Military Review and—

(A) the time for the accused to file a petition for review by the Court of Military Appeals has expired and the accused has not filed a timely petition for such review and the case is not otherwise under review by that Court;

(B) such a petition is rejected by the Court of Military Appeals; or

(C) review is completed in accordance with the judgment of the Court of Military Appeals and—

(i) a petition for a writ of certiorari is not filed within the time limits prescribed by the Supreme Court;

(ii) such a petition is rejected by the Supreme Court; or

(iii) review is otherwise completed in accordance with the judgment of the Supreme Court.

(2) If a sentence extends to dismissal or a dishonorable or bad-conduct discharge and if the right of the accused to appellate review is waived, or an appeal is withdrawn, under section 861 of this title (article 61), that part of the sentence extending to dismissal or a bad-conduct or dishonorable discharge may not be executed until review of the case by a judge advocate (and any action on that review) under section 864 of this title (article 64) is completed. Any other part of a court-martial sentence may be ordered executed by the convening authority or other person acting on the case under section 860 of this title (article 60) when approved by him under that section.

(d) The convening authority or other person acting on the case under section 860 of this title (article 60) may suspend the execution of any sentence or part thereof, except a death sentence.

§ 872. Art. 72. Vacation of suspension

(a) Before the vacation of the suspension of a special court-martial sentence which as approved includes a bad-conduct discharge, or of any general court-martial sentence, the officer having special court-martial jurisdiction over the probationer shall hold a hearing on the alleged violation of probation. The probationer shall be represented at the hearing by counsel if he so desires.

(b) The record of the hearing and the recommendation of the officer having special court-martial jurisdiction shall be sent for action to the officer exercising general court-martial jurisdiction over the probationer. If he vacates the suspension, any unexecuted part of the sentence, except a dismissal, shall be executed, subject to applicable restrictions in section 871(c) of this title (article 71(c)). The vacation of the suspension of a dismissal is not effective until approved by the Secretary concerned.

(c) The suspension of any other sentence may be vacated by any authority competent to convene, for the command in which the accused is serving or assigned, a court of the kind that imposed the sentence.

§ 873. Art. 73. Petition for a new trial

At any time within two years after approval by the convening authority of a court-martial sentence, the accused may petition the Judge Advocate General for a new trial on the grounds of newly discovered evidence or fraud on the court. If the accused's case is pending before a Court of Criminal Appeals or before the Court of Appeals for the Armed Forces, the Judge Advocate General shall refer the petition to the appropriate court for action. Otherwise the Judge Advocate General shall act upon the petition.

§ 874. Art. 74. Remission and suspension

(a) The Secretary concerned and, when designated by him, any Under Secretary, Assistant Secretary, Judge Advocate General, or commanding officer may remit or suspend any part or amount of the unexecuted part of any sentence, including all uncollected forfeitures other than a sentence approved by the President.

(b) The Secretary concerned may, for good cause, substitute an administrative form of discharge for a discharge or dismissal executed in accordance with the sentence of a court-martial.

§ 875. Art. 75. Restoration

(a) Under such regulations as the President may prescribe, all rights, privileges, and property affected by an executed part of a court-martial sentence which has been set aside or disapproved, except an executed dismissal or discharge, shall be restored unless a new trial or rehearing is ordered and such executed part is included in a sentence imposed upon the new trial or rehearing.

(b) If a previously executed sentence of dishonorable or bad-conduct discharge is not imposed on a new trial, the Secretary concerned shall substitute therefor a form of discharge authorized for administrative issuance unless the accused is to serve out the remainder of this enlistment.

(c) If a previously executed sentence of dismissal is not imposed on a new trial, the Secretary concerned shall substitute therefor a form of discharge authorized for administrative issue, and the commissioned officer dismissed by the sentence may be reappointed by the President alone to such commissioned grade and with such rank as in the opinion of the President that former officer would have attained had he not been dismissed. The reappointment of such a former officer shall be without regard to the existence of a vacancy and shall affect the promotion status of other officers only insofar as the President may direct. All time between the dismissal and the reappointment shall be considered as actual service for all purposes, including the right to pay and allowances.

§ 876. Art. 76. Finality of proceedings, findings, and sentences

The appellate review of records of trial provided by this chapter, the proceedings, findings, and sentences of courts-martial as approved, reviewed, or affirmed as required by this chapter, and all dismissals and discharges carried into execution under sentences by courts-martial following approval, review, or affirmation as required by this chapter, are final and conclusive. Orders publishing the proceedings of courts-martial and all action taken pursuant to those proceedings are binding upon all departments, courts, agencies, and officers of the United States, subject only to action upon a petition for a new trial as provided in section 873 of this title (article 73) and to action by the Secretary concerned as provided in section 874 of this title (article 74), and the authority of the President.

§ 876a. Art. 76a. Leave required to be taken pending review of certain court-martial convictions

Under regulations prescribed by the Secretary concerned, an accused who has been sentenced by a court-martial may be required to take leave pending completion of action under this subchapter if the sentence, as approved under section 860 of this title (article 60), includes an unsuspended dismissal or an unsuspended dishonorable or bad-conduct discharge. The accused may be required to begin such leave on the date on which the sentence is approved under section 860 of this title (article 60) or at any time after such date, and such leave may be continued until the date which action under this subchapter is completed or may be terminated at any earlier time.

§ 876b. Art. 76b. Lack of mental capacity or mental responsibility; commitment of accused for examination and treatment

(a) PERSONS INCOMPETENT TO STAND TRIAL.—

(1) In the case of a person determined under this chapter to be presently suffering from a mental disease or defect rendering the person mentally incompetent to the extent that the person is unable to understand the nature of the proceedings against that person or to conduct or cooperate intelligently in the defense of the case, the general court-martial convening authority for that person shall commit the person to the custody of the Attorney General.

(2) The Attorney General shall take action in accordance with section 4241(d) of title 18.

(3) If at the end of the period for hospitalization provided for in section 4241(d) of title 18, it is determined that the committed person's mental condition has not so improved as to permit the trial to proceed, action shall be taken in accordance with section 4246 of such title.

(4)(A) When the director of a facility in which a person is hospitalized pursuant to paragraph (2) determines that the person has recovered to such an extent that the person is able to understand the nature of the proceedings against the person and to conduct or cooperate intelligently in the defense of the case, the director shall promptly transmit a notification of that determination to the Attorney General and to the general court-martial convening authority for the person. The director shall send a copy of the notification to the person's counsel.

(B) Upon receipt of a notification, the general court-martial convening authority shall promptly take custody of the person unless the person covered by the notification is no longer subject to this chapter. If the person is no longer subject to this chapter, the Attorney General shall take any action with authority of the Attorney General that the Attorney General considers appropriate regarding the person.

(C) The director of the facility may retain custody of the person for not more than 30 days after transmitting the notifications required by subparagraph (A).

(5) In the application of section 4246 of title 18 to a case under this subsection, references to the court that ordered the commitment of a person, and to the clerk of such court, shall be deemed to refer to the general court-martial convening authority for that person. However, if the person is no longer subject to this chapter at a time relevant to the application of such section to the person, the United States district court for the district where the person is hospitalized or otherwise may be found shall be considered as the court that ordered the commitment of the person.

(b) PERSONS FOUND NOT GUILTY BY REASON OF LACK OF MENTAL RESPONSIBILITY.—

(1) If a person is found by a court-martial not guilty only by reason of lack of mental responsibility, the person shall be committed to a suitable facility until the person is eligible for release in accordance with this section.

(2) The court-martial shall conduct a hearing on the mental condition in accordance with subsection (c) of section 4243 of title 18. Subsections (b) and (d) of that section shall apply with respect to the hearing.

(3) A report of the results of the hearing shall be made to the general court-martial convening authority for the person.

(4) If the court-martial fails to find by the standard specified in subsection (d) of section 4243 of title 18 that the person's release would not create a substantial risk of bodily injury to another person or serious damage of property of another due to a present mental disease or defect—

(A) the general court-martial convening authority may commit the person to the custody of the Attorney General; and

(B) the Attorney General shall take action in accordance with subsection (e) of section 4243 of title 18.

(5) Subsections (f), (g), and (h) of section 4243 of title 18 shall apply in the case of a person hospitalized pursuant to paragraph (4)(B), except that the United States district court for the district where the person is hospitalized shall be considered as the court that ordered the person's commitment.

(c) GENERAL PROVISIONS.—

(1) Except as otherwise provided in this subsection and subsection (d)(1), the provisions of section 4247 of title 18 apply in the administration of this section.

(2) In the application of section 4247(d) of title 18 to hearings conducted by a court-martial under this section or by (or by order of) a general court-martial convening authority under this section, the reference in that section to section 3006A of such title does not apply.

(d) APPLICABILITY.—

(1) The provisions of chapter 313 of title 18 referred to in this section apply according to the provisions of this section notwithstanding section 4247(j) of title 18.

(2) If the status of a person as described in section 802 of this title (article 2) terminates while the person is, pursuant to this section, in the custody of the Attorney General, hospitalized, or on conditional release under a prescribed regimen of medical, psychiatric, or psychological care or treatment, the provisions of this section establish-

ing requirements and procedures regarding a person no longer subject to this chapter shall continue to apply to that person notwithstanding the change of status.

Subchapter X. PUNITIVE ARTICLES

§ 877. Art. 77. Principals

Any person punishable under this chapter who—

(1) commits an offense punishable by this chapter, or aids, abets, counsels, commands, or procures its commission; or

(2) causes an act to be done which if directly performed by him would be punishable by this chapter;

is a principal.

§ 878. Art. 78. Accessory after the fact

Any person subject to this chapter who, knowing that an offense punishable by this chapter has been committed, receives, comforts, or assists the offender in order to hinder or prevent his apprehension, trial, or punishment shall be punished as a court-martial may direct.

§ 879. Art. 79. Conviction of lesser-included offense

An accused may be found guilty of an offense necessarily included in the offense charged or of an attempt to commit either the offense charged or an offense necessarily included therein.

§ 880. Art. 80. Attempts

(a) An act, done with specific intent to commit an offense under this chapter, amounting to more than mere preparation and tending, even though failing, to effect its commission, is an attempt to commit that offense.

(b) Any person subject to this chapter who attempts to commit any offense punishable by this chapter shall be punished as a court-martial may direct, unless otherwise specifically prescribed.

(c) Any person subject to this chapter may be convicted of an attempt to commit an offense although it appears on the trial that the offense was consummated.

§ 881. Art. 81. Conspiracy

Any person subject to this chapter who conspires with any other person to commit an offense under this chapter shall, if one or more of the conspirators does an act to effect the object of the conspiracy, be punished as a court-martial may direct.

§ 882. Art. 82. Solicitation

(a) Any person subject to this chapter who solicits or advises another or others to desert in violation of section 885 of this title (article 85) or mutiny in violation of section 894 of this title (article 94) shall, if the offense solicited or advised is attempted or committed, be punished with the punishment provided for the commission of the offense, but, if the offense solicited or advised is not committed or attempted, he shall be punished as a court-martial may direct.

(b) Any person subject to this chapter who solicits or advises another or others to commit an act of misbehavior before the enemy in violation of section 899 of this title (article 99) or sedition in violation of section 894 of this title (article 94) shall, if the offense solicited or advised is committed, be punished with the punishment provided for the commission of the offense, but, if the offense solicited or advised is not committed, he shall be punished as a court-martial may direct.

§ 883. Art. 83. Fraudulent enlistment, appointment, or separation

Any person who—

(1) procures his own enlistment or appointment in the armed forces by knowingly false representation or deliberate concealment as to his qualifications for the enlistment or appointment and receives pay or allowances thereunder; or

(2) procures his own separation from the armed forces by knowingly false representation or deliberate concealment as to his eligibility for that separation;
shall be punished as a court-martial may direct.

§ 884. Art. 84. Unlawful enlistment, appointment, or separation

Any person subject to this chapter who effects an enlistment or appointment in or a separation from the armed forces of any person who is known to him to be ineligible for that enlistment, appointment, or separation because it is prohibited by law, regulation, or order shall be punished as a court-martial may direct.

§ 885. Art. 85. Desertion

(a) Any member of the armed forces who—

(1) without authority goes or remains absent from his unit, organization, or place of duty with intent to remain away therefrom permanently;

(2) quits his unit, organization, or place of duty with intent to avoid hazardous duty or to shirk important service; or

(3) without being regularly separated from one of the armed forces enlists or accepts an appointment in the same or another one of the armed forces without fully disclosing the fact that he has not been regularly separated, or enters any foreign armed service except when authorized by the United States; is guilty of desertion.

(b) Any commissioned officer of the armed forces who, after tender of his resignation and before notice of its acceptance, quits his post or proper duties without leave and with intent to remain away therefrom permanently is guilty of desertion.

(c) Any person found guilty of desertion or attempt to desert shall be punished, if the offense is committed in time of war, by death or such other punishment as a court-martial may direct, but if the desertion or attempt to desert occurs at any other time, by such punishment, other than death, as a court-martial may direct.

§ 886. Art. 86. Absence without leave

Any member of the armed forces who, without authority—

(1) fails to go to his appointed place of duty at the time prescribed;
(2) goes from that place; or
(3) absents himself or remains absent from his unit, organization, or place of duty at which he is required to be at the time prescribed;

shall be punished as a court-martial may direct.

§ 887. Art. 87. Missing movement

Any person subject to this chapter who through neglect or design misses the movement of a ship, aircraft, or unit with which he is required in the course of duty to move shall be punished as a court-martial may direct.

§ 888. Art. 88. Contempt toward officials

Any commissioned officer who uses contemptuous words against the President, the Vice President, Congress, the Secretary of Defense, the Secretary of a military department, the Secretary of Transportation, or the Governor or legislature of any State, Territory, Commonwealth, or possession in which he is on duty or present shall be punished as a court-martial may direct.

§ 889. Art. 89. Disrespect toward superior commissioned officer

Any person subject to this chapter who behaves with disrespect toward his superior commissioned officer shall be punished as a court-martial may direct.

§ 890. Art. 90. Assaulting or willfully disobeying superior commissioned officer

Any person subject to this chapter who—

(1) strikes his superior commissioned officer or draws or lifts up any weapon or offers any violence against him while he is in the execution of his office; or
(2) willfully disobeys a lawful command of his superior commissioned officer; shall be punished, if the offense is committed in time of war, by death or such other punishment as a court-martial may direct, and if the offense is committed at any other time, by such punishment, other than death, as a court-martial may direct.

§ 891. Art. 91. Insubordinate conduct toward warrant officer, noncommissioned officer, or petty officer

Any warrant officer or enlisted member who—

(1) strikes or assaults a warrant officer, noncommissioned officer, or petty officer, while that officer is in the execution of his office;
(2) willfully disobeys the lawful order of a warrant officer, noncommissioned officer, or petty officer; or
(3) treats with contempt or is disrespectful in language or deportment toward a

warrant officer, noncommissioned officer, or petty officer while that officer is in the execution of his office;

shall be punished as a court-martial may direct.

§ 892. Art. 92. Failure to obey order or regulation

Any person subject to this chapter who—

(1) violates or fails to obey any lawful general order or regulation;
(2) having knowledge of any other lawful order issued by a member of the armed forces, which it is his duty to obey, fails to obey the order; or
(3) is derelict in the performance of his duties;

shall be punished as a court-martial may direct.

§ 893. Art. 93. Cruelty and maltreatment

Any person subject to this chapter who is guilty of cruelty toward, or oppression or maltreatment of, any person subject to his orders shall be punished as a court-martial may direct.

§ 894. Art. 94. Mutiny or sedition

(a) Any person subject to this chapter who—

(1) with intent to usurp or override lawful military authority, refuses, in concert with any other person, to obey orders or otherwise do his duty or creates any violence or disturbance is guilty of mutiny;
(2) with intent to cause the overthrow or destruction of lawful civil authority, creates, in concert with any other person, revolt, violence, or other disturbance against that authority is guilty of sedition;
(3) fails to do his utmost to prevent and suppress a mutiny or sedition being committed in his presence, or fails to take all reasonable means to inform his superior commissioned officer or commanding officer of a mutiny or sedition which he knows or has reason to believe is taking place, is guilty of a failure to suppress or report a mutiny or sedition.

(b) A person who is found guilty of attempted mutiny, mutiny, sedition, or failure to suppress or report a mutiny or sedition shall be punished by death or such other punishment as a court-martial may direct.

§ 895. Art. 95. Resistance, flight, breach of arrest, and escape

Any person subject to this chapter who—
(1) resists apprehension;
(2) flees from apprehension;
(3) breaks arrest; or
(4) escapes from custody or confinement;
shall be punished as a court-martial may direct.

§ 896. Art. 96. Releasing prisoner without proper authority

Any person subject to this chapter who, without proper authority, releases any prisoner committed to his charge, or who through neglect or design suffers any such prisoner to escape, shall be punished as a court-martial may direct, whether or not the prisoner was committed in strict compliance with law.

§ 897. Art. 97. Unlawful detention

Any person subject to this chapter who, except as provided by law, apprehends, arrests, or confines any person shall be punished as a court-martial may direct.

§ 898. Art. 98. Noncompliance with procedural rules

Any person subject to this chapter who—

(1) is responsible for unnecessary delay in the disposition of any case of a person accused of an offense under this chapter; or
(2) knowingly and intentionally fails to enforce or comply with any provision of this chapter regulating the proceedings before, during, or after trial of an accused;
shall be punished as a court-martial may direct.

§ 899. Art. 99. Misbehavior before the enemy

Any person subject to this chapter who before or in the presence of the enemy—

(1) runs away;
(2) shamefully abandons, surrenders, or delivers up any command, unit, place, or military property which it is his duty to defend;
(3) through disobedience, neglect, or intentional misconduct endangers the safety of any such command, unit, place, or military property;
(4) casts away his arms or ammunition;
(5) is guilty of cowardly conduct;
(6) quits his place of duty to plunder or pillage;
(7) causes false alarms in any command, unit, or place under control of the armed forces;
(8) willfully fails to do his utmost to encounter, engage, capture, or destroy any enemy troops, combatants, vessels, aircraft, or any other thing, which it is his duty so to encounter, engage, capture, or destroy; or
(9) does not afford all practicable relief and assistance to any troops, combatants, vessels, or aircraft of the armed forces belonging to the United States or their allies when engaged in battle;

shall be punished by death or such other punishment as a court-martial may direct.

§ 900. Art 100. Subordinate compelling surrender

Any person subject to this chapter who compels or attempts to compel the commander of any place, vessel, aircraft, or other military property, or of any body of members of the armed forces, to give it up to an enemy or to abandon it, or who strikes the colors or flag to any enemy without proper authority, shall be punished by death or such other punishment as a court-martial may direct.

§ 901. Art. 101. Improper use of countersign

Any person subject to this chapter who in time of war discloses the parole or countersign to any person not entitled to receive it or who gives to another who is entitled to receive and use the parole or countersign a different parole or countersign from that which, to his knowledge, he was authorized and required to give, shall be punished by death or such other punishment as a court-martial may direct.

§ 902. Art. 102. Forcing a safeguard

Any person subject to this chapter who forces a safeguard shall suffer death or such other punishment as a court-martial may direct.

§ 903. Art. 103. Captured or abandoned property

(a) All persons subject to this chapter shall secure all public proper taken from the enemy for the service of the United States, and shall give notice and turn over to the proper authority without delay all captured or abandoned property in their possession, custody, or control.
(b) Any person subject to this chapter who—
(1) fails to carry out the duties prescribed in subsection (a);
(2) buys, sells, trades, or in any way deals in or disposes of captured or abandoned property, whereby he receives or expects any profit, benefit, or advantage to himself or another directly or indirectly connected with himself; or
(3) engages in looting or pillaging;

shall be punished as a court-martial may direct.

§ 904. Art. 104. Aiding the enemy

Any person who—

(1) aids, or attempts to aid, the enemy with arms, ammunition, supplies, money, or other things; or
(2) without proper authority, knowingly harbors or protects or gives intelligence to or communicates or corresponds with or holds any intercourse with the enemy, either directly or indirectly;

shall suffer death or such other punishment as a court-martial or military commission may direct.

§ 905. Art. 105. Misconduct as prisoner

Any person subject to this chapter who, while in the hands of the enemy in time of war—
(1) for the purpose of securing favorable treatment by his captors acts without proper authority in a manner contrary to law, custom, or regulation, to the detriment of others of whatever nationality held by the enemy as civilian or military prisoners; or
(2) while in a position of authority over such persons maltreats them without justifiable cause;

shall be punished as a court-martial may direct.

§ 906. Art. 106. Spies

Any person who in time of war is found lurking as a spy or acting as a spy in or about any place, vessel, or aircraft, within the control or jurisdiction of any of the armed forces, or in or about any shipyard, any manufacturing or industrial plant, or any other place or institution engaged in work in aid of the prosecution of the war by the United States, or elsewhere, shall be tried by a general court-martial or by a military commission and on conviction shall be punished by death.

§ 906a. Art. 106a. Espionage

(a)(1) Any person subject to this chapter who, with intent or reason to believe that it is to be used to the injury of the United States or to the advantage of a foreign nation, communicates, delivers, or transmits, or attempts to communicate, deliver, or transmit, to any entity described in paragraph (2), either directly or indirectly, any thing described in paragraph (3) shall be punished as a court-martial may direct, except that if the accused is found guilty of an offense that directly concerns (A) nuclear weaponry, military spacecraft or satellites, early warning systems, or other means of defense or retaliation against large scale attack, (B) war plans, (C) communications intelligence or cryptographic information, or (D) any other major weapons system or major element of defense strategy, the accused shall be punished by death or such other punishment as a court-martial may direct.

(2) An entity referred to in paragraph (1) is—

(A) a foreign government;
(B) a faction or party or military or naval force within a foreign country, whether recognized or unrecognized by the United States; or
(C) a representative, officer, agent, employee, subject, or citizen of such a government, faction, party, or force.

(3) A thing referred to in paragraph (1) is a document, writing, code book, signal book, sketch, photograph, photographic negative, blueprint, plan, map, model, note, instrument, appliance, or information relating to the national defense.

(b)(1) No person may be sentenced by court-martial to suffer death for an offense under this section (article) unless—

(A) the members of the court-martial unanimously find at least one of the aggravating factors set out in subsection (c); and
(B) the members unanimously determine that any extenuating or mitigating circumstances are substantially outweighed by any aggravating circumstances, including the aggravating factors set out under subsection (c).

(2) Findings under this subsection may be based on—

(A) evidence introduced on the issue of guilt or innocence;
(B) evidence introduced during the sentencing proceeding; or
(C) all such evidence.

(3) The accused shall be given broad latitude to present matters in extenuation and mitigation.

(c) A sentence of death may be adjudged by a court-martial for an offense under this section (article) only if the members unanimously find, beyond a reasonable doubt, one or more of the following aggravating factors:

(1) The accused has been convicted of another offense involving espionage or treason for which either a sentence of death or imprisonment for life was authorized by statute.

(2) In the commission of the offense, the accused knowingly created a grave risk of substantial damage to the national security.

(3) In the commission of the offense, the accused knowingly created a grave risk of death to another person.

(4) Any other factor that may be prescribed by the President by regulations under section 836 of this title (Article 36).

§ 907. Art. 107. False official statements

Any person subject to this chapter who, with intent to deceive, signs any false record, return, regulation, order, or other official document, knowing it to be false, or makes any other false-official statement knowing it to be false;
shall be punished as a court-martial may direct.

§ 908. Art. 108. Military property of United States Loss, damage, destruction, or wrongful disposition

Any person subject to this chapter who, without proper authority—

(1) sells or otherwise disposes of;

(2) willfully or through neglect damages, destroys, or loses; or

(3) willfully or through neglect suffers to be lost, damaged, sold, or wrongfully disposed of;

any military property of the United States, shall be punished as a court-martial may direct.

§ 909. Art. 109. Property other than military property of United States Waste, spoilage, or destruction

Any person subject to this chapter who willfully or recklessly wastes, spoils, or otherwise willfully and wrongfully destroys or damages any property other than military property of the United States shall be punished as a court-martial may direct.

§ 910. Art. 110. Improper hazarding of vessel

(a) Any person subject to this chapter who willfully and wrongfully hazards or suffers to be hazarded any vessel of the armed forces shall suffer death or such punishment as a court-martial may direct.

(b) Any person subject to this chapter who negligently hazards or suffers to be hazarded any vessel of the armed forces shall be punished as a court-martial may direct.

§ 911. Art. 111. Drunken or reckless operation of a vehicle, aircraft, or vessel

Any person subject to this chapter who—

(1) operates or physically controls any vehicle, aircraft, or vessel in a reckless or wanton manner or while impaired by a substance described in section 912a(b) of this title (article 112a(b)), or

(2) operates or is in actual physical control of any vehicle, aircraft, or vessel while drunk or when the alcohol concentration in the person's blood or breath is 0.10 grams or more of alcohol per 100 milliliters of blood or 0.10 grams or more of alcohol per 210 liters of breath, as shown by chemical analysis,

shall be punished as a court-martial may direct.

§ 912. Art. 112. Drunk on duty

Any person subject to this chapter other than a sentinel or lookout, who is found drunk on duty, shall be punished as a court-martial may direct.

§ 912a. Art. 112a. Wrongful use, possession, etc., of controlled substances

(a) Any person subject to this chapter who wrongfully uses, possesses, manufactures, distributes, imports into the customs territory of the United States, exports from the United States, or introduces into an installation, vessel, vehicle, or aircraft used by or under the control of the armed forces a substance described in subsection (b) shall be punished as a court-martial may direct.

(b) The substances referred to in subsection (a) are the following:

(1) Opium, heroin, cocaine, amphetamine, lysergic acid diethylamide, methamphetamine, phencyclidine, barbituric acid, and marijuana and any compound or derivative of any such substance.

(2) Any substance not specified in clause (1) that is listed on a schedule of controlled substances prescribed by the President for the purposes of this article.

(3) Any other substance not specified in clause (1) or contained on a list prescribed by the President under clause (2) that is listed in schedules I through V of section 202 of the Controlled Substances Act (21 U.S.C. 812).

§ 913. Art. 113. Misbehavior of sentinel

Any sentinel or look-out who is found drunk or sleeping upon his post, or leaves it before he is regularly relieved, shall be punished, if the offense is committed in time of war, by death or such other punishment as a court-martial may direct, but if the offense is committed at any other time, by such punishment other than death as a court-martial may direct.

§ 914. Art. 114. Dueling

Any person subject to this chapter who fights or promotes, or is concerned in or connives at fighting a duel, or who, having knowledge of a challenge sent or about to be sent, fails to report the fact promptly to the proper authority, shall be punished as a court-martial may direct.

§ 915. Art. 115. Malingering

Any person subject to this chapter who for the purpose of avoiding work, duty, or service—

(1) feigns illness, physical disablement, mental lapse or derangement; or
(2) intentionally inflicts self-injury;

shall be punished as a court-martial may direct.

§ 916. Art. 116. Riot or breach of peace

Any person subject to this chapter who causes or participates in any riot or breach of the peace shall be punished as a court-martial may direct.

§ 917. Art. 117. Provoking speeches or gestures

Any person subject to this chapter who uses provoking or reproachful words or gestures towards any other person subject to this chapter shall be punished as a court-martial may direct.

§ 918. Art. 118. Murder

Any person subject to this chapter who, without justification or excuse, unlawfully kills a human being, when he—

(1) has a premeditated design to kill;
(2) intends to kill or inflict great bodily harm;
(3) is engaged in an act which is inherently dangerous to another and evinces a wanton disregard of human life; or
(4) is engaged in the perpetration or attempted perpetration of burglary, sodomy, rape, robbery, or aggravated arson;

is guilty of murder, and shall suffer such punishment as a court-martial may direct, except that if found guilty under clause (1) or (4), he shall suffer death or imprisonment for life as a court-martial may direct.

§ 919. Art. 119. Manslaughter

(a) Any person subject to this chapter who, with an intent to kill or inflict great bodily harm, unlawfully kills a human being in the heat of sudden passion caused by adequate provocation is guilty of voluntary manslaughter and shall be punished as a court-martial may direct.

(b) Any person subject to this chapter who, without an intent to kill or inflict great bodily harm, unlawfully kills a human being—

(1) by culpable negligence; or
(2) while perpetrating or attempting to perpetrate an offense, other than those named in clause (4) of section 918 of this title (article 118), directly affecting the person;

is guilty of involuntary manslaughter and shall be punished as a court-martial may direct.

§ 920. Art. 120. Rape and carnal knowledge

(a) Any person subject to this chapter who commits an act of sexual intercourse by force and without her consent, is guilty of rape and shall be punished by death or such other punishment as a court-martial may direct.

(b) Any person subject to this chapter who, under circumstances not amounting to rape, commits an act of sexual intercourse with a person—

(1) who is not that person's spouse; and
(2) who has not attained the age of sixteen years;

is guilty of carnal knowledge and shall be punished as a court-martial may direct.

(c) Penetration, however slight, is sufficient to complete either of these offenses.

(d)(1) In a prosecution under subsection (b), it is a defense that—

(A) the person with whom the accused committed the act of sexual intercourse had at the time of the alleged offense attained the age of twelve years; and

(B) the accused reasonably believed that the person had at the time of the alleged offense attained the age of sixteen years.

(2) The accused has the burden of proving a defense under paragraph (1) by a preponderance of evidence.

§ 921. Art. 121. Larceny and wrongful appropriation

(a) Any person subject to this chapter who wrongfully takes, obtains, or withholds, by any means, from the possession of the owner or of any other person any money, personal property, or article of value of any kind—

(1) with intent permanently to deprive or defraud another person of the use and benefit of property or to appropriate it to his own use or the use of any person other than the owner, steals that property and is guilty of larceny; or

(2) with intent temporarily to deprive or defraud another person of the use and benefit of property or to appropriate it to his own use or the use of any person other than the owner, is guilty of wrongful appropriation.

(b) Any person found guilty of larceny or wrongful appropriation shall be punished as a court-martial may direct.

§ 922. Art. 122. Robbery

Any person subject to this chapter who with intent to steal takes anything of value from the person or in the presence of another, against his will, by means of force or violence or fear of immediate or future injury to his person or property or to the person or property of a relative or member of his family or of anyone in his company at the time of the robbery, is guilty of robbery and shall be punished as a court-martial may direct.

§ 923. Art. 123. Forgery

Any person subject to this chapter who, with intent to defraud—

(1) falsely makes or alters any signature, to, or any part of, any writing which would, if genuine, apparently impose a legal liability on another or change his legal right or liability to his prejudice; or

(2) utters, offers, issues, or transfers such a writing, known by him to be so made or altered;

is guilty of forgery and shall be punished as a court-martial may direct.

§ 923a. Art. 123a. Making, drawing, or uttering check, draft, or order without sufficient funds

Any person subject to this chapter who—

(1) for the procurement of any article or thing of value, with intent to defraud; or
(2) for the payment of any past due obligation, or for any other purpose, with intent to deceive;

makes, draws, utters, or delivers any check, draft, or order for the payment of money upon any bank or other depository, knowing at the time that the maker or drawer has not or will not have sufficient funds in, or credit with, the bank or other depository for the payment of that check, draft, or order in full upon its presentment, shall be punished as a court-martial may direct. The making, drawing, uttering, or delivering by a maker or drawer of a check, draft or order, payment of which is refused by the drawee because of insufficient funds of the maker or drawer in the drawee's possession or control, is prima facie evidence of his intent to defraud or deceive and of his knowledge of insufficient funds in, or credit with, that bank or other depository, unless the maker or drawer pays the holder the amount due within five days after receiving notice, orally or in writing, that the check, draft, or order was not paid on presentment. In this section, the word credit means an arrangement or understanding, express or implied, with the bank or other depository for the payment of the check, draft, or order.

§ 924. Art. 124. Maiming

Any person subject to this chapter who, with intent to injure, disfigure, or disable, inflicts upon the person of another an injury which—

(1) seriously disfigures his person by a mutilation thereof;
(2) destroys or disables any member or organ of his body; or
(3) seriously diminishes his physical vigor by the injury of any member or organ;

is guilty of maiming and shall be punished as a court-martial may direct.

§ 925. Art. 125. Sodomy

(a) Any person subject to this chapter who engages in unnatural carnal copulation with another person of the same or opposite sex or with an animal is guilty of sodomy. Penetration, however slight, is sufficient to complete the offense.

(b) Any person found guilty of sodomy shall be punished as a court-martial may direct.

§ 926. Art. 126. Arson

(a) Any person subject to this chapter who willfully and maliciously burns or sets on fire an inhabited dwelling, or any other structure, movable or immovable, wherein to the knowledge of the offender there is at the time a human being, is guilty of aggravated arson and shall be punished as court-martial may direct.

(b) Any person subject to this chapter who willfully and maliciously burns or sets fire to the property of another, except as provided in subsection (a), is guilty of simple arson and shall be punished as a court-martial may direct.

§ 927. Art. 127. Extortion

Any person subject to this chapter who communicates threats to another person with the intention thereby to obtain anything of value or any acquittance, advantage, or immunity is guilty of extortion and shall be punished as a court-martial may direct.

§ 928. Art. 128. Assault

(a) Any person subject to this chapter who attempts or offers with unlawful force or violence to do bodily harm to another person, whether or not the attempt or offer is consummated, is guilty of assault and shall be punished as a court-martial may direct.
(b) Any person subject to this chapter who—

(1) commits an assault with a dangerous weapon or other means or force likely to produce death or grievous bodily harm; or
(2) commits an assault and intentionally inflicts grievous bodily harm with or without a weapon;

is guilty of aggravated assault and shall be punished as a court-martial may direct.

§ 929. Art. 129. Burglary

Any person subject to this chapter who, with intent to commit an offense punishable under section 918-928 of this title (article 118-128), breaks and enters, in the nighttime, the dwelling house of another, is guilty of burglary and shall be punished as a court-martial may direct.

§ 930. Art. 130. Housebreaking

Any person subject to this chapter who unlawfully enters the building or structure of another with intent to commit a criminal offense therein is guilty of housebreaking and shall be punished as a court-martial may direct.

§ 931. Art. 131. Perjury

Any person subject to this chapter who in a judicial proceeding or in a course of justice willfully and corruptly—

(1) upon a lawful oath or in any form allowed by law to be substituted for an oath, gives any false testimony material to the issue or matter of inquiry; or
(2) in any declaration, certificate, verification, or statement under penalty or perjury as permitted under section 1746 of title 28. United States Code, subscribes any false statement material to the issue or matter of inquiry;

is guilty of perjury and shall be punished as a court-martial may direct.

§ 932. Art. 132. Frauds against the United States

Any person subject to this chapter—
(1) who, knowing it to be false or fraudulent—

(A) makes any claim against the United States or any officer thereof; or

(B) presents to any person in the civil or military service thereof, for approval or payment, any claim against the United States or any officer thereof;

(2) who, for the purpose of obtaining the approval, allowance, or payment of any claim against the United States or any officer thereof—

(A) makes or uses any writing or other paper knowing it to contain any false or fraudulent statements;

(B) makes any oath to any fact or to any writing or other paper knowing the oath to be false; or

(C) forges or counterfeits any signature upon any writing or other paper, or uses any such signature knowing it to be forged or counterfeited;

(3) who, having charge, possession, custody, or control of any money, or other property or the United States, furnished or intended for the armed forces thereof, knowingly delivers to any person having authority to receive it, any amount thereof less than that for which he receives a certificate or receipt; or

(4) who, being authorized to make or deliver any paper certifying the receipt of any property of the United States furnished or intended for the armed forces thereof, makes or delivers to any person such writing without having full knowledge of the truth of the statements therein contained and with intent to defraud the United States;

shall, upon conviction, be punished as a court-martial may direct.

§ 933. Art. 133. Conduct unbecoming an officer and a gentleman

Any commissioned officer, cadet, or midshipman who is convicted of conduct unbecoming an officer and a gentleman shall be punished as a court-martial may direct.

§ 934. Art. 134. General article

Though not specifically mentioned in this chapter, all disorders and neglects to the prejudice of good order and discipline in the armed forces, all conduct of a nature to bring discredit upon the armed forces, and crimes and offenses not capital, of which persons subject to this chapter may be guilty, shall be taken cognizance of by a general, special or summary court-martial, according to the nature and degree of the offense, and shall be punished at the discretion of that court.

Subchapter XI. MISCELLANEOUS PROVISIONS

§ 935. Art. 135. Courts of inquiry

(a) Courts of inquiry to investigate any matter may be convened by any person authorized to convene a general court-martial or by any other person designated by the Secretary concerned for that purpose, whether or not the persons involved have requested such an inquiry.

(b) A court of inquiry consists of three or more commissioned officers. For each court of inquiry the convening authority shall also appoint counsel for the court.

(c) Any person subject to this chapter whose conduct is subject to inquiry shall be designated as a party. Any person subject to this chapter or employed by the Department of Defense who has a direct interest in the subject of inquiry has the right to be designated as a party upon request to the court. Any person designated as a party shall be given due notice and has the right to be present, to be represented by counsel, to cross-examine witnesses, and to introduce evidence.

(d) Members of a court of inquiry may be challenged by a party, but only for cause stated to the court.

(e) The members, counsel, the reporter, and interpreters of courts of inquiry shall take an oath to faithfully perform their duties.

(f) Witnesses may be summoned to appear and testify and be examined before courts of inquiry, as provided for courts-martial.

(g) Courts of inquiry shall make findings of fact but may not express opinions or make recommendations unless required to do so by the convening authority.

(h) Each court of inquiry shall keep a record of its proceedings, which shall be authenticated by the signatures of the president and counsel for the court and forwarded to the convening authority. If the record cannot be authenticated by the president, it shall be signed by a member in lieu of the president. If the record cannot be authenticated by the counsel for the court, it shall be signed by a member in lieu of the counsel.

§ 936. Art. 136. Authority to administer oaths and to act as notary

(a) The following persons on active duty or performing inactive-duty training may administer oaths for the purposes of military administration, including military justice:

(1) All judge advocates.
(2) All summary courts-martial.
(3) All adjutants, assistant adjutants, acting adjutants, and personnel adjutants.
(4) All commanding officers of the Navy, Marine Corps, and Coast Guard.
(5) All staff judge advocates and legal officers, and acting or assistant staff judge advocates and legal officers.
(6) All other persons designated by regulations of the armed forces or by statute.

(b) The following persons on active duty or performing inactive-duty training may administer oaths necessary in the performance of their duties:

(1) The president, military judge, trial counsel, and assistant trial counsel for all general and special courts-martial.
(2) The president and the counsel for the court of any court of inquiry.
(3) All officers designated to take a deposition.
(4) All persons detailed to conduct an investigation.
(5) All recruiting officers.
(6) All other persons designated by regulations of the armed forces or by statute.

§ 937. Art. 137. Articles to be explained

(a)(1) The sections of this title (articles of the Uniform Code of Military Justice) specified in paragraph (3) shall be carefully explained to each enlisted member at the time of (or within six days after)—

(A) the member's initial entrance on active duty; or
(B) the member's initial entrance into a duty status with a reserve component.

(2) Such sections (articles) shall be explained again—

(A) after the member has completed six months of active duty or, in the case of a member of a reserve component, after the member has completed basic or recruit training; and

(B) at the time when the member reenlists.

(3) This subsection applies with respect to sections 802, 803, 807-815, 825, 827, 831, 837, 838, 855, 877-934, and 937-939 of this title (articles 2, 3, 7-15, 25, 27, 31, 37, 38, 55, 77-134, and 137-139).

(b) The text of the Uniform Code of Military Justice and of the regulations prescribed by the President under such Code shall be made available to a member on active duty or to a member of a reserve component, upon request by the member, for the member's personal examination.

§ 938. Art. 138. Complaints of wrongs

Any member if the armed forces who believes himself wronged by his commanding officer, and who, upon due application to that commanding officer, is refused redress, may complain to any superior commissioned officer, who shall forward the complaint to the officer exercising general court-martial jurisdiction over the officer against whom it is made. The officer exercising general court-martial jurisdiction shall examine into the complaint and take proper measures for redressing the wrong complained of; and he shall, as soon as possible, send to the Secretary concerned a true statement of that complaint, with the proceedings had thereon.

§ 939. Art. 139. Redress of injuries to property

(a) Whenever complaint is made to any commanding officer that willful damage has been done to the property of any person or that his property has been wrongfully taken by members of the armed forces, he may, under such regulations as the Secretary concerned may prescribe, convene a board to investigate the complaint. The board shall consist of from one to three commissioned officers and, for the purpose of that investigation, it has power to summon witnesses and examine them upon oath, to receive depositions or other documentary evidence, and to assess the damages sustained against the responsible parties. The assessment of damages made by the board is subject to the approval of the commanding officer, and in the amount approved by him shall be charged against the pay of the offenders. The order of the commanding officer directing charges herein authorized is conclusive on any disbursing officer for the payment by him to the injured parties of the damages as assessed and approved.

(b) If the offenders cannot be ascertained, but the organization or detachment to which they belong is known, charges totaling the amount of damages assessed and approved may be made in such proportion as may be considered just upon the individual members thereof who are shown to have been present at the scene at the time the damages complained of were inflicted, as determined by the approved findings of the board.

§ 940. Art. 140. Delegation by the President

The President may delegate any authority vested in him under this chapter, and provide for the subdelegation of any such authority.

Subchapter XII. UNITED STATES COURT OF APPEALS FOR THE ARMED FORCES

§ 941. Art. 141. Status.

There is a court of record known as the United States Court of Appeals for the Armed Forces. The court is established under Article I of the Constitution. The court is located for administrative purposes only in the Department of Defense.

§ 942. Art. 142. Judges

(a) *Number.* The United States Court of Appeals for the Armed Forces consists of five judges.
(b) *Appointment; qualification.*
(1) Each judge of the court shall be appointed from civil life by the President, by and with the advice and consent of the Senate, for a specified term determined under paragraph (2). A judge may serve as a senior judge as provided in subsection (e).
(2) The term of a judge shall expire as follows:

(A) In the case of a judge who is appointed after September 30 of any year and before April 1 of the following year, the term shall expire fifteen years after such September 30.

(B) In the case of a judge who is appointed after September 30 of any year and before April 1 of the following year, the term shall expire fifteen years after such September 30.

(3) Not more than three of the judges of the court may be appointed from the same political party, and no person may be appointed to be a judge of the court unless the person is a member of the bar of a Federal court or the highest court of a State.
(c) *Removal.* Judges of the court may be removed from office by the President, upon notice and hearing for—

(1) neglect of duty;
(2) misconduct; or
(3) mental or physical disability. A judge may not be removed by the President for any other cause.

(d) *Pay and allowances.* Each judge of the court is entitled to the same salary and travel allowances as are, and from time to time may be, provided for judges of the United States Courts of Appeals.
Senior judges.—(1) (A) A former judge of the court who is receiving retired pay or an annuity under section 945 of this title (article 145) or under subchapter III of chapter 83 or chapter 84 of title 5 shall be a senior judge. The chief judge of the court may call upon an individual who is a senior judge of the court under this subparagraph, with the consent of the senior judge, to perform judicial duties with the court—
(i) during a period a judge of the court is unable to perform his duties because of illness or other disability;
(ii) during a period in which a position of judge of the court is vacant; or
(iii) in any case in which a judge of the court recuses himself.

(B) If, at the time the term of a judge expires, no successor to that judge has been appointed, the chief judge of the court may call upon that judge (with that judge's consent) to continue to perform judicial duties with the court until the vacancy is filled.

A judge who, upon the expiration of the judge's term, continues to perform judicial duties with the court without a break in service under this subparagraph shall be a senior judge while such service continues.

(2) A senior judge shall be paid for each day on which he performs judicial duties with the court an amount equal to the daily equivalent of the annual rate of pay provided for a judge of the court. Such pay shall be in lieu of retired pay and in lieu of an annuity under section 945 of this title (Article 145), subchapter III of chapter 83 or subchapter II of chapter 84 of title 5, or any other retirement system for employees of the Federal Government.

(3) A senior judge, while performing duties referred to in paragraph (1), shall be provided with such office space and staff assistance as the chief judge considers appropriate and shall be entitled to the per diem, travel allowances, and other allowances provided for judges of the court.

(4) A senior judge shall be considered to be an officer or employee of the United States with respect to his status as a senior judge, but only during periods the senior judge is performing duties referred to in paragraph (1). For the purposes of section 205 of title 18, a senior judge shall be considered to be a special Government employee during such periods. Any provision of law that prohibits or limits the political or business activities of an employee of the United States shall apply to a senior judge only during such periods.

(5) The court shall prescribe rules for the use and conduct of senior judges of the court. The chief judge of the court shall transmit such rules, and any amendments to such rules, to the Committees on Armed Services of the Senate and the House of Representatives not later than 15 days after the issuance of such rules or amendments, as the case may be.

(6) For purposes of subchapter III of chapter 83 of title 5 (relating to the Civil Service Retirement and Disability System) and chapter 84 of such title (relating to the Federal Employees Retirement System) and for purposes of any other Federal Government retirement system for employees of the Federal Government—

(A) a period during which a senior judge performs duties referred to in paragraph (2) shall not be considered creditable service;

(B) no amount shall be withheld from the pay of a senior judge as a retirement contribution under section 8334, 8343, 8422, or 8432 of title 5 or under other such retirement system for any period during which the senior judge performs duties referred to in paragraph (1);

(C) no contribution shall be made by the Federal Government to any retirement system with respect to a senior judge for any period during which the senior judge performs duties referred to in paragraph (1); and

(D) a senior judge shall not be considered to be a reemployed annuitant for any period during which the senior judge performs duties referred to in paragraph (1).

(f) *Service of Article III judges.*

(1) The Chief Justice of the United States, upon the request of the chief judge of the court, may designate a judge of the United States court of appeals or of a United States district court to perform the duties of judge of the United States Court of Appeals for the Armed Forces—

(A) during a period a judge of the court is unable to perform his duties because of illness or other disability; or

(B) in any case in which a judge of the court recuses himself.

(C) during a period when there is a vacancy on the court and in the opinion of the chief judge of the court such a designation is necessary for the proper dispatch of the business of the court.

(2) The chief judge of the court may not request that a designation be made under paragraph (1) unless the chief judge has determined that no person is available to perform judicial duties with the court as a senior judge under subsection (e).

(3) A designation under paragraph (1) may be made only with the consent of the designated judge and the concurrence of the chief judge of the court of appeals or district court concerned.

(4) Per diem, travel allowances, and other allowances paid to the designated judge in connection with the performance of duties for the court shall be paid from funds available for the payment of per diem and such allowances for judges of the court.

(g) *Effect of vacancy on court.* A vacancy on the court does not impair the right of the remaining judges to exercise the powers of the court.

§ 943. Art. 143. Organization and employees

(a) **Chief judge.**—(1) The chief judge of the United States Court of Appeals for the Armed Forces shall be the judge of the court in regular active service who is senior in commission among the judges of the court who—

(A) have served for one or more years as judges of the court; and
(B) have not previously served as chief judge.

(2) In any case in which there is no judge of the court in regular active service who has served as a judge of the court for at least one year, the judge of the court in regular active service who is senior in commission and has not served previously as chief judge shall act as the chief judge.

(3) Except as provided in paragraph (4), a judge of the court shall serve as the chief judge under paragraph (1) for a term of five years. If no other judge is eligible under paragraph (1) to serve as chief judge upon the expiration of that term, the chief judge shall continue to serve as chief judge until another judge becomes eligible under that paragraph to serve as chief judge.

(4)(A) The term of a chief judge shall be terminated before the end of five years if—
(i) the chief judge leaves regular active service as a judge of the court; or
(ii) the chief judge notifies the other judges of the court in writing that such judge desires to be relieved of his duties as chief judge.

(B) The effective date of a termination of the term under subparagraph (A) shall be the date on which the chief judge leaves regular active service or the date of the notification under subparagraph (A)(ii), as the case may be.

(5) If a chief judge is temporarily unable to perform his duties as a chief judge, the duties shall be performed by the judge of the court in active service who is present, able and qualified to act, and is next in precedence.

(b) *Precedence of judges.* The chief judge of the court shall have precedence and preside at any session that he attends. The other judges shall have precedence and preside according to the seniority of their original commissions. Judges whose commissions bear the same date shall have precedence according to seniority in age.

(c) *Status of attorney positions.*

(1) Attorney positions of employment under the Court of Appeals for the Armed Forces are excepted from the competitive service. Appointments to such positions shall

be made by the court, without the concurrence of any other officer or employee of the executive branch, in the same manner as appointments are made to other executive branch positions of a confidential or policy-determining character for which it is not practicable to examine or to hold a competitive examination. Such positions shall not be counted as positions of that character for purposes of any limitation on the number of positions of that character provided in law.

(2) In making appointments to the positions described in paragraph (1), preference shall be given, among equally qualified persons, to persons who are preference eligibles (as defined in section 2108(3) of title 5).

§ 944. Art. 144. Procedure

The United States Court of Appeals for the Armed Forces may prescribe its rules of procedure and may determine the number of judges required to constitute a quorum.

§ 945. Art. 145. Annuities for judges and survivors

(a) *Retirement annuities for judges.*
(1) A person who has completed a term of service for which he was appointed as a judge of the United States Court of Appeals for the Armed Forces is eligible for an annuity under this section upon separation from civilian service in the Federal Government. A person who continues service with the court as a senior judge under section 942(e)(1)(B) of this title (article 142(e)(1)(B)) upon the expiration of the judge's term shall be considered to have been separated from civilian service in the Federal Government only upon the termination of that continuous service.

(2) A person who is eligible for any annuity under this section shall be paid that annuity if, at the time he becomes eligible to receive that annuity, he elects to receive that annuity in lieu of any other annuity for which he may be eligible at the time of such election (whether an immediate or a deferred annuity) under subchapter III of chapter 83 or subchapter II of chapter 84 of title 5 or any other retirement system for civilian employees of the Federal Government. Such an election may not be revoked.

(3) (A) The Secretary of Defense shall notify the Director of the Office of Personnel Management whenever an election under paragraph (2) is made affecting any right or interest under subchapter III of chapter 83 or subchapter II of chapter 85 of title 5 based on service as a judge of the United States Court of Military Appeals.

(B) Upon receiving any notification under subparagraph (A) in the case of a person making an election under (2), the Director shall determine the amount of the person's lump-sum credit under subchapter III of chapter 83 or subchapter II of chapter 84 of title 5, as applicable, and shall request the Secretary of the Treasury to transfer such amount from the Civil Service Retirement and Disability Fund to the Department of Defense Military Retirement Fund. The Secretary of the Treasury shall make any transfer so requested.

(C) In determining the amount of a lump-sum credit under section 8331(8) of title 5 for purposes of this paragraph—

   (i) interest shall be computed using the rates under section 8334(e) of such title; and
   (ii) the completion of 5 years of civilian service (no longer) shall not be a basis for excluding interest.

(b) *Amount of annuity.* The annuity payable under this section to a person who makes an election under subsection (a)(2) is 80 percent of the rate of pay for a judge in active service on the United States Court of Military Appeals as of the date on which the person is separated from civilian service.

(c) *Relation to thrift savings plan.* Nothing in this section affects any right of any person to participate in the thrift savings plan under section 8351 of subchapter III of chapter 84 of such title.

(d) *Survivor annuities.* The Secretary of Defense shall prescribe by regulation a program to provide annuities for survivors and former spouses of persons receiving annuities under this section by reason of elections made by such persons under subsection (a)(2). That program shall, to the maximum extent practicable, provide benefits and establish terms and conditions that are similar to those provided under survivor and former spouse annuity programs under other retirement systems for civilian employees of the Federal Government. The program may include provisions for the reduction in the annuity paid the person as a condition for the survivor annuity. An election by a judge (including a senior judge) or former judge to receive an annuity under this section terminates any right or interest which any other individual may have to a survivor annuity under any other retirement system for civilian employees of the Federal Government based on the service of that judge or former judge as a civilian officer or employee of the Federal Government (except with respect to an election under subsection (g)(1)(B)).

(e) *Cost-of-living increases.* The Secretary of Defense shall periodically increase annuities and survivor annuities paid under this section in order to take account of changes in the cost of living. The Secretary shall prescribe by regulation procedures for increases in annuities under this section. Such system shall, to the maximum extent appropriate, provide cost-of-living adjustments that are similar to those that are provided under other retirement systems for civilian employees of the Federal Government.

(f) *Dual compensation.* A person who is receiving an annuity under this section by reason of service as a judge of the court and who is appointed to a position in the Federal Government shall, during the period of such person's service in such position, be entitled to receive only the annuity under this section or the pay for that position, whichever is higher.

(g) *Election of judicial retirement benefits.*

(1) A person who is receiving an annuity under this section by reason of service as a judge of the court and who later is appointed as a justice or judge of the United States, to hold office during good behavior and who retires from that office, or from regular active service in that office, shall be paid either

(A) the annuity under this section, or

(B) the annuity or salary to which he is entitled by reason of his service as such a justice or judge of the United States, as determined by an election by that person at the time of his retirement from the office, or from regular active service in the office, of justice or judge of the United States. Such an election may not be revoked.

(i) Eligibility to elect between retirement systems.—(1) This subsection applies with respect to any person who—

(A) prior to being appointed as a judge of the United States Court of Appeals for the Armed Forces, performed civilian service of a type making such person subject to the Civil Service Retirement System; and

(B) would be eligible to make an election under section 301(a)(2) of the Federal Employees' Retirement System Act of 1986, by virtue of being appointed as such a judge, but for the fact that such person has not had a break in service of sufficient duration to be considered someone who is being reemployed by the Federal Government.

(2) Any person with respect to whom this subsection applies shall be eligible to make an election under section 301(a)(2) of the Federal Employees' Reitrement System Act of 1986 to the same extent and in the same manner (including subject to the condition set forth in section 301(d) of such Act) as if such person's appointment constituted reemployment with the Federal Government.

(2) An election by a person to be paid an annuity or salary pursuant to paragraph (1)(B) terminates (A) any election previously made by such person to provide a survivor annuity pursuant to section (d), and (B) any right of any individual to receive a survivor annuity pursuant to section (d) on the basis of the service of that person.

(h) *Source of payment of annuities.* Annuities and survivor annuities paid under this section shall be paid out of the Department of Defense Military Retirement Fund.

§ 946. Art. 146. Code committee

(a) *Annual survey.* A committee shall meet at least annually and shall make an annual comprehensive survey of the operation of this chapter.

(b) *Composition of committee.* The committee shall consist of—

(1) the judges of the United States Court of Appeals for the Armed Forces;
(2) the Judge Advocates General of the Army, Navy, and Air Force, the Chief Counsel of the Coast Guard, and the Staff Judge Advocate to the Commander of the Marine Corps; and
(3) two members of the public appointed by the Secretary of Defense.

(c) *Reports.*
(1) After each such survey, the committee shall submit a report

(A) to the Committees on Armed Services of the Senate and House of Representatives; and
(B) to the Secretary of Defense, the Secretaries of the military departments, and the Secretary of Transportation.

(2) Each report under paragraph (1) shall include the following:

(A) Information on the number and status of pending cases.
(B) Any recommendation of the committee relating to

(i) uniformity of policies as to sentences;
(ii) amendments to this chapter; and
(iii) any other matter the committee considers appropriate.

(d) *Qualifications and terms of appointed members.* Each member of the committee appointed by the Secretary of Defense under subsection (B)(3) shall be a recognized authority in military justice or criminal law. Each such member shall be appointed for a term of three years.

(e) *Applicability of Federal Advisory Committee Act.* The Federal Advisory Committee Act (5 U.S.C. App. I) shall not apply to the committee.

APPENDIX 4
COURT-MARTIAL FLOW CHART

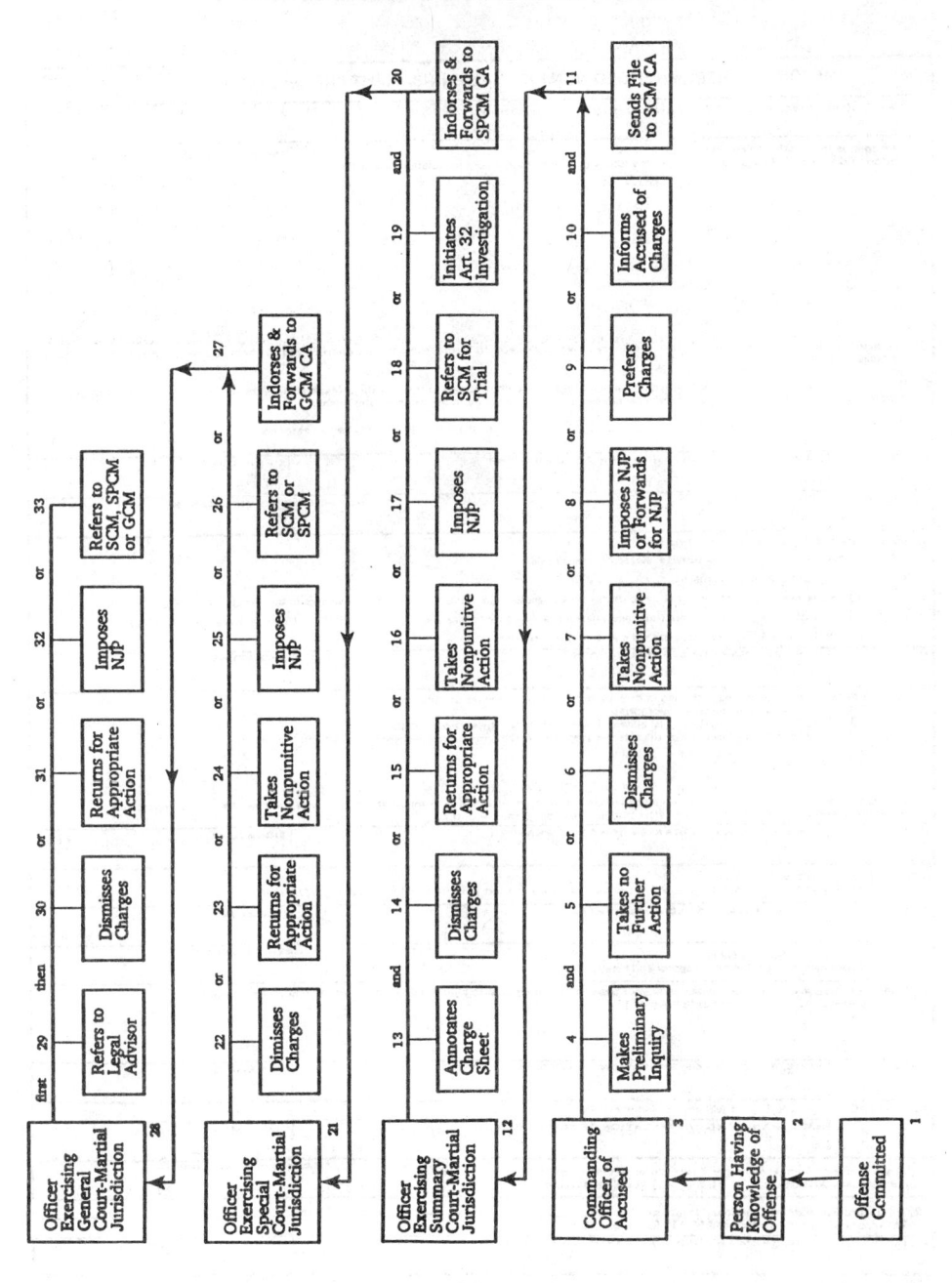

```
                                                                                                    11
                                                                                              Sends File
                                                                                              to SCM CA
                                                                                                   ↑
                                                                                                  and
                                                                                                   
                              20                                                               10
                        Indorses &                                                         Informs
                        Forwards to                                                        Accused of
                        SPCM CA                                                            Charges
                             ↑                                                                 ↑
                            and                                                                or
                                                                                                
                              19                                                               9
                        Initiates                                                          Prefers
                        Art. 32                                                            Charges
                        Investigation                                                          ↑
                             ↑                                                                 or
                             or                                                                 
                                                                                               8
                              18                                                           Imposes NJP
                        Refers to                                                          or Forwards
                        SCM for                                                            for NJP
                        Trial                                                                  ↑
                             ↑                                                                 or
                             or                                                                 
              27                                                                               7
       Indorses &             17                                                           Takes
       Forwards to      Imposes                                                            Nonpunitive
       GCM CA           NJP                                                                Action
             ↑               ↑                                                                 ↑
            or               or                                                                or
                                                                                                
              26              16                                                               6
       Refers to        Takes                                                              Dismisses
       SCM or           Nonpunitive                                                        Charges
       SPCM             Action                                                                 ↑
             ↑               ↑                                                                 or
            or               or                                                                 
                                                                                               5
              25              15                                                           Takes no
       Imposes          Returns for                                                        Further
       NJP              Appropriate                                                        Action
             ↑          Action
            or               ↑
                             or
              24
       Takes                  14
       Nonpunitive      Dismisses
       Action           Charges
             ↑               ↑
            or              and
                                                                                               4
              23              13                                                           Makes
       Returns for      Annotates                                                          Preliminary
       Appropriate      Charge                                                             Inquiry
       Action           Sheet
             ↑               ↑                                                                 ↑
            or               ↑                                                                 
                                                                                               3
              22             12                                                            Commanding
       Dismisses                                                                           Officer of
       Charges                                                                             Accused
```

Officer Exercising General Court-Martial Jurisdiction — 28: first — 29 Refers to Legal Advisor — then — 30 Dismisses Charges — or — 31 Returns for Appropriate Action — or — 32 Imposes NJP — or — 33 Refers to SCM, SPCM or GCM

Officer Exercising Special Court-Martial Jurisdiction — 21

Officer Exercising Summary Court-Martial Jurisdiction — 12

2 Person Having Knowledge of Offense

1 Offense Committed

927

APPENDIX 5

SAMPLE NONJUDICIAL PUNISHMENT FORM

RECORD OF RECOMMENDED NONJUDICIAL PUNISHMENT PROCEEDINGS	ATCH(S)

TO: *(Name, Rank, Organization, SSAN, and Major Command of Service Member)* | THRU:

1. I am considering whether to recommend to[1] that you be punished under Article 15, Uniform Code of Military Justice *(UCMJ)* for the following alleged misconduct in violation of Article(s) _____, _____, _____, UCMJ:[2]

2. You have the rights listed on the reverse side. A military lawyer is available to further explain these rights to you and help you decide what to do. You may contact:

3. If you accept nonjudicial punishment proceedings, and if I find you committed one or more of the offenses alleged, the maximum punishment I could impose upon you is listed on the reverse side in paragraph _____ under maximum permissible punishments.

4. You will notify me of your decision by _____, _____ *(3 duty days)*, unless I grant you an extension.
   (time)   (date)

DATE	NAME, RANK, AND ORGANIZATION OF COMMANDER	SIGNATURE

DATE/TIME SERVED ON MEMBER	SIGNATURE OF PERSON SERVING MEMBER *(If not Commander)*

5. I understand the rights listed on the reverse side:[3]
   I [ ] have [ ] have not consulted a lawyer. My decisions are:
   a. [ ] I demand trial by court-martial.
   b. [ ] I waive my right to demand trial by court-martial and accept nonjudicial punishment proceedings under Article 15, UCMJ.
      (1) I [ ] do [ ] do not request to make a personal appearance before you. I [ ] do [ ] do not desire that it be public.
      (2) I [ ] have [ ] have not attached a written presentation.[4]

DATE	NAME AND RANK OF SERVICE MEMBER	SIGNATURE

6. I have considered any matters you presented in defense, mitigation, or extenuation, and find that:
   a. [ ] Nonjudicial punishment is not appropriate.
   b. [ ] You did not commit the offense(s) alleged. I hereby terminate these proceedings.
   c. [ ] You did commit one or more of the offenses alleged.[5] I hereby impose the following punishment:[6]

7. This punishment is effective immediately unless otherwise stated. If you decide not to appeal at this time, you still have the right to appeal this punishment within 5 days. An appeal made after that time may be rejected as untimely.[7]

DATE	NAME, RANK, AND ORGANIZATION OF COMMANDER	SIGNATURE

8. [ ] I do not appeal
   [ ] I appeal and [ ] will [ ] will not submit additional matters in writing within 3 duty days. *(72 hours)*

DATE	NAME AND RANK OF SERVICE MEMBER	SIGNATURE

| [ ] I hereby withdraw my appeal. | DATE | MEMBER'S SIGNATURE |
| [ ] I withdraw my decision not to appeal and hereby appeal. | | |

9. After consideration of all matters presented in your appeal and after referral to a judge advocate, I have decided that your appeal is:
   [ ] Denied   [ ] Granted as follows:

DATE	NAME, RANK, AND ORGANIZATION OF APPELLATE AUTHORITY	SIGNATURE

10. Article 15 [ ] will [ ] will not be filed in member's UIF.

DATE	NAME, RANK, AND ORGANIZATION OF COMMANDER	SIGNATURE

11. I have seen the action taken on my appeal and/or was informed of my commander's decision to [ ] file [ ] not file this record in a UIF.	DATE	MEMBER'S SIGNATURE

12. This record was examined and found legally sufficient on _____. A copy was received by CBPO on _____ and AFO on _____. The record is being forwarded per AFR 111-9.

DATE	NAME, RANK, AND ORGANIZATION OF JUDGE ADVOCATE	SIGNATURE

AF FORM 3071   PREVIOUS EDITIONS ARE OBSOLETE

APP. 5 SAMPLE NONJUDICIAL PUNISHMENT FORM APP. 5

RIGHTS

1. In making your decision whether to accept nonjudicial punishment, you are entitled to be provided with a brief summary of the information upon which the allegations of misconduct are based or you may request to examine the available statements and evidence.

2. If you demand trial by court-martial, charges could be preferred against you and referred for trial by a summary, special, or general court-martial. However you may not be tried by summary court-martial if you object to that proceeding. If charges are referred for trial by special or general court-martial, you may be tried over your objection. In a trial by court-martial, you have the right to be represented by a lawyer.

3. If you elect to accept nonjudicial punishment, you are entitled to make a full presentation in writing or in person or both. Your presentation may include matters of defense, mitigation, or extenuation. You do not have to give any information or say anything about the offense(s) alleged. If you do, it may be used against you in either this action or in a trial by court-martial.

   (a) If you elect a personal presentation, you may appear before the commander who will be imposing nonjudicial punishment, except when such appearance is prevented by unavailability of the commander or by extraordinary circumstances, in which case you may appear before a person designated by that commander. You would be entitled to be informed orally or in writing of the evidence against you relating to the misconduct alleged, and be allowed to examine any documents or physical objects on which the commander intends to rely in deciding whether or how much punishment to impose. At a personal appearance: (1) you may have present relevant witnesses who are reasonably available and can be presented without legal process (that is, without subpoena or payment of witness fees); (2) you may present evidence; and (3) you may be accompanied by a person to speak on your behalf. However, there is no requirement that a lawyer be made available to accompany you. If you request the personal appearance be made open to the public, it will be, unless military exigencies or security considerations prevent. If you do not request that it be open to the public, your commander is authorized to open it anyway at his or her discretion.

   (b) If you make either a written presentation appearance, or both, the final decision as to whether to impose punishment and, if so, the amount of punishment will be decided only after the imposing commander considers the matters you present.

   (c) If your commander recommends nonjudicial punishment, he or she will forward any written presentation and a summary of any personal appearance to the commander who would impose punishment.

4. You must reply to this notification. Initial the appropriate blocks in paragraph 5, attach any written presentation you desire to be considered, and return it along with this notification within 3 duty days (72 hours) of the time and date you received it. If you desire more time, you must make a written request to your commander.

NOTES

1. Insert designation of the commander who would impose nonjudicial punishment.

2. If the space provided in Item 1 is insufficient for all offenses considered, insert the following after that item: "that you committed the offenses listed in Attachment 1," and state them in full in a "List of Offenses" appended as Attachment 1.

3. The member will indicate his or her decision by initialing the block in front of the option chosen. The member then will sign at the bottom of paragraph 5.

4. The initiating commander will forward by separate indorsement a summary of matters presented in any personal appearance by the member, with copies of all documents presented, to the commander who would impose punishment. AFR 111-9, paragraph 6i(5).

5. Offenses determined not to have been committed will be lined out and initialed by the commander. If the imposing commander decides not to impose any punishment, the member will be notified.

6. See Format of Nonjudicial Punishments, Attachment 4, AFR 111-9.

7. After being informed of the punishment, the member will elect whether to appeal by initialing the block in front of the option chosen. The member then will sign at the bottom of block 8. If the member appeals, this form, all written evidence considered by the imposing commander, and any written matters submitted by the member will be forwarded to the superior authority through the staff judge advocate by an indorsement to this form. The indorsement may state the imposing commander's rationale for imposing punishment and the commander's recommendation for action on the appeal.

If the member refuses to sign or make his or her elections in blocks 4, 5, 8, or 11, the commander, or his designee, will write "Member refused to sign (or elect)" in that block and sign and date underneath.

If additional space is needed, use 8½ x 11" bond sheets, and identify the item expanded by the item number.

MAXIMUM PERMISSABLE PUNISHMENTS

If the commander imposing punishment is a:

1. General Court-Martial Convening Authority or General Officer and you are:

   a. An officer – The commander may impose a reprimand; 30 days arrest in quarters or 60 days restriction; and, forfeiture of one-half of one month's pay per month for two months.

   b. Enlisted – The commander may impose a reprimand; 30 days correctional custody or 45 days extra duties and/or 60 days restriction; forfeiture of one-half of one month's pay per month for two months; and, if serving in the grade of E-4 (Sgt) through E-9, reduction to the next inferior grade, or if serving in the grade of E-2 through E-4 (SrA), reduction to the lowest grade. (If serving in the grade of E-8 or E-9, reduction may be imposed only by MAJCOM commanders or commanders to whom promotion authority has been delegated IAW AFR 39-29.)

2. Special Court-Martial Convening Authority, Colonel or Lieutenant Colonel and you are:

   a. An officer – The commander may impose a reprimand and 30 days restriction.

   b. Enlisted – The commander may impose a reprimand; 30 days correctional custody or 45 days extra duties and/or 60 days restriction; forfeiture of one-half of one month's pay per month for two months; and, if serving in the grade of E-4 (Sgt) through E-7, reduction to the next inferior grade, or if serving in the grade of E-2 through E-4 (SrA), reduction to the lowest enlisted grade.

3. Major and you are serving in the grade of E-1 through E-7, the commander may impose a reprimand; 30 days correctional custody or 45 days extra duties and/or 60 days restriction; forfeiture of one-half of one month's pay per month for two months; and, if serving in the grade of E-4 (Sgt) through E-6, reduction to the next inferior grade, or if serving in the grade of E-2 through E-4 (SrA), reduction to the lowest enlisted grade.

4. Company Grade Officer and you are serving in the grade of E-1 through E-7, the commander may impose a reprimand; 7 days correctional custody or 14 days restriction and/or 14 days extra duties; forfeiture of 7 days pay; and, if serving in the grade of E-2 through E-5, reduction to the next inferior grade.

Restriction and extra duties may be combined to run concurrently, but the combination may not exceed the maximum imposable for extra duties.

AF FORM 3071, JUN 85 (Reverse)

APPENDIX 6
CHARGE SHEET

CHARGE SHEET

I. PERSONAL DATA

1. NAME OF ACCUSED (Last, First, MI)	2. SSN	3. GRADE OR RANK	4. PAY GRADE

5. UNIT OR ORGANIZATION	6. CURRENT SERVICE	
	a. INITIAL DATE	b. TERM

7. PAY PER MONTH			8. NATURE OF RESTRAINT OF ACCUSED	9. DATE(S) IMPOSED
a. BASIC	b. SEA/FOREIGN DUTY	c. TOTAL		

II. CHARGES AND SPECIFICATIONS

10. CHARGE: VIOLATION OF THE UCMJ, ARTICLE

SPECIFICATION:

III. PREFERRAL

11a. NAME OF ACCUSER (Last, First, MI)	b. GRADE	c. ORGANIZATION OF ACCUSER

d. SIGNATURE OF ACCUSER	e. DATE

AFFIDAVIT: Before me, the undersigned, authorized by law to administer oaths in cases of this character, personally appeared the above named accuser this _____ day of _____, 19 _____, and signed the foregoing charges and specifications under oath that he/she is a person subject to the Uniform Code of Military Justice and that he/she either has personal knowledge of or has investigated the matters set forth therein and that the same are true to the best of his/her knowledge and belief.

_____ _____
Typed Name of Officer   Organization of Officer

_____ _____
Grade   Official Capacity to Administer Oath
                                 (See R.C.M. 307(b)—must be commissioned officer)

_____
Signature

DD FORM 458, 84 AUG   EDITION OF OCT 69 IS OBSOLETE.

CHARGE SHEET

12.
On _____, 19 ___, the accused was informed of the charges against him/her and of the name(s) of the accuser(s) known to me *(See R.C.M. 308 (a)). (See R.C.M. 308 if notification cannot be made.)*

_____ _____
Typed Name of Immediate Commander *Organization of Immediate Commander*

_____
Grade

_____
Signature

IV. RECEIPT BY SUMMARY COURT-MARTIAL CONVENING AUTHORITY

13.
The sworn charges were received at _____ hours, _____ 19 ___ at _____
                                                                    Designation of Command or
_____
Officer Exercising Summary Court-Martial Jurisdiction (See R.C.M. 403)

FOR THE[1] _____

_____ _____
Typed Name of Officer *Official Capacity of Officer Signing*

_____
Grade

_____
Signature

V. REFERRAL; SERVICE OF CHARGES

14a. DESIGNATION OF COMMAND OF CONVENING AUTHORITY	b. PLACE	c. DATE

Referred for trial to the _____ court-martial convened by _____

_____, _____ 19 ___, subject to the following instructions:[2] _____

_____ By _____ of _____
                    Command or Order

_____ _____
Typed Name of Officer *Official Capacity of Officer Signing*

_____
Grade

_____
Signature

15.
On _____, 19 ___, I (caused to be) served a copy hereof on (each of) the above named accused.

_____ _____
Typed Name of Trial Counsel *Grade or Rank of Trial Counsel*

_____
Signature

FOOTNOTES: 1 — *When an appropriate commander signs personally, inapplicable words are stricken.*
2 — *See R.C.M. 601(e) concerning instructions. If none, so state.*

GPO : 1985 O - 489-158

APPENDIX 7

INVESTIGATING OFFICER'S REPORT

INVESTIGATING OFFICER'S REPORT
(Of Charges Under Article 32, UCMJ and R.C.M. 405, Manual for Courts-Martial)

1a. FROM: *(Name of Investigating Officer — Last, First, MI)*	b. GRADE	c. ORGANIZATION		d. DATE OF REPORT
2a. TO: *(Name of Officer who directed the Investigation — Last, First, MI)*	b. TITLE		c. ORGANIZATION	
3a. NAME OF ACCUSED *(Last, First, MI)*	b. GRADE	c. SSN	d. ORGANIZATION	e. DATE OF CHARGES

(Check appropriate answer) — YES / NO

4. IN ACCORDANCE WITH ARTICLE 32, UCMJ, AND R.C.M. 405, MANUAL FOR COURTS-MARTIAL, I HAVE INVESTIGATED THE CHARGES APPENDED HERETO (Exhibit 1)
5. THE ACCUSED WAS REPRESENTED BY COUNSEL (If not, see 9 below)
6. COUNSEL WHO REPRESENTED THE ACCUSED WAS QUALIFIED UNDER R.C.M. 405(d)(2), 502(d)

7a. NAME OF DEFENSE COUNSEL *(Last, First, MI)*	b. GRADE	8a. NAME OF ASSISTANT DEFENSE COUNSEL *(If any)*	b. GRADE
c. ORGANIZATION *(If appropriate)*		c. ORGANIZATION *(If appropriate)*	
d. ADDRESS *(If appropriate)*		d. ADDRESS *(If appropriate)*	

9. *(To be signed by accused if accused waives counsel. If accused does not sign, investigating officer will explain in detail in Item 21.)*

a. PLACE	b. DATE

I HAVE BEEN INFORMED OF MY RIGHT TO BE REPRESENTED IN THIS INVESTIGATION BY COUNSEL, INCLUDING MY RIGHT TO CIVILIAN OR MILITARY COUNSEL OF MY CHOICE IF REASONABLY AVAILABLE. I WAIVE MY RIGHT TO COUNSEL IN THIS INVESTIGATION.

c. SIGNATURE OF ACCUSED

10. AT THE BEGINNING OF THE INVESTIGATION I INFORMED THE ACCUSED OF: *(Check appropriate answer)* — YES / NO
   a. THE CHARGE(S) UNDER INVESTIGATION
   b. THE IDENTITY OF THE ACCUSER
   c. THE RIGHT AGAINST SELF-INCRIMINATION UNDER ARTICLE 31
   d. THE PURPOSE OF THE INVESTIGATION
   e. THE RIGHT TO BE PRESENT THROUGHOUT THE TAKING OF EVIDENCE
   f. THE WITNESSES AND OTHER EVIDENCE KNOWN TO ME WHICH I EXPECTED TO PRESENT
   g. THE RIGHT TO CROSS-EXAMINE WITNESSES
   h. THE RIGHT TO HAVE AVAILABLE WITNESSES AND EVIDENCE PRESENTED
   i. THE RIGHT TO PRESENT ANYTHING IN DEFENSE, EXTENUATION, OR MITIGATION
   j. THE RIGHT TO MAKE A SWORN OR UNSWORN STATEMENT, ORALLY OR IN WRITING

11a. THE ACCUSED AND ACCUSED'S COUNSEL WERE PRESENT THROUGHOUT THE PRESENTATION OF EVIDENCE *(If the accused or counsel were absent during any part of the presentation of evidence, complete b below.)*

b. STATE THE CIRCUMSTANCES AND DESCRIBE THE PROCEEDINGS CONDUCTED IN THE ABSENCE OF ACCUSED OR COUNSEL

NOTE: If additional space is required for any item, enter the additional material in Item 21 or on a separate sheet. Identify such material with the proper numerical and, if appropriate, lettered heading *(Example: "7c".)* Securely attach any additional sheets to the form and add a note in the appropriate item of the form: "See additional sheet."

DD FORM 457, 84 AUG

EDITION OF OCT 69 IS OBSOLETE.

APP. 7 — INVESTIGATING OFFICER'S REPORT — APP. 7

12a. THE FOLLOWING WITNESSES TESTIFIED UNDER OATH: *(Check appropriate answer)*					
NAME *(Last, First, MI)*	GRADE *(If any)*	ORGANIZATION/ADDRESS *(Whichever is appropriate)*	YES	NO

b. THE SUBSTANCE OF THE TESTIMONY OF THESE WITNESSES HAS BEEN REDUCED TO WRITING AND IS ATTACHED.

13a. THE FOLLOWING STATEMENTS, DOCUMENTS, OR MATTERS WERE CONSIDERED; THE ACCUSED WAS PERMITTED TO EXAMINE EACH.

DESCRIPTION OF ITEM	LOCATION OF ORIGINAL *(If not attached)*

b. EACH ITEM CONSIDERED, OR A COPY OR RECITAL OF THE SUBSTANCE OR NATURE THEREOF, IS ATTACHED

14. THERE ARE GROUNDS TO BELIEVE THAT THE ACCUSED WAS NOT MENTALLY RESPONSIBLE FOR THE OFFENSE(S) OR NOT COMPETENT TO PARTICIPATE IN THE DEFENSE. *(See R.C.M. 909, 916(k).)*

15. THE DEFENSE DID REQUEST OBJECTIONS TO BE NOTED IN THIS REPORT *(If Yes, specify in Item 21 below.)*

16. ALL ESSENTIAL WITNESSES WILL BE AVAILABLE IN THE EVENT OF TRIAL

17. THE CHARGES AND SPECIFICATIONS ARE IN PROPER FORM

18. REASONABLE GROUNDS EXIST TO BELIEVE THAT THE ACCUSED COMMITTED THE OFFENSE(S) ALLEGED

19. I AM NOT AWARE OF ANY GROUNDS WHICH WOULD DISQUALIFY ME FROM ACTING AS INVESTIGATING OFFICER. *(See R.C.M. 405(d)(1).)*

20. I RECOMMEND:
a. TRIAL BY ☐ SUMMARY ☐ SPECIAL ☐ GENERAL COURT-MARTIAL
b. ☐ OTHER *(Specify in Item 21 below)*

21. REMARKS *(Include, as necessary, explanation for any delays in the investigation, and explanation for any "no" answers above.)*

22a. TYPED NAME OF INVESTIGATING OFFICER	b. GRADE	c. ORGANIZATION
d. SIGNATURE OF INVESTIGATING OFFICER		e. DATE

☆U.S. G.P.O. 1984-421-646/17045

APPENDIX 8
SAMPLE PRETRIAL ADVICE

Sample A Short Form, Referral

DEPARTMENT OF THE ARMY
HEADQUARTERS, FORT BLANK
Fort Blank, Missouri 77777

AKPS-JA   10 June 199X

MEMORANDUM FOR COMMANDING GENERAL

SUBJECT: Advice on Disposition of Court-Martial Charges

1. I have reviewed the attached charges, allied papers, and report of investigation in the case of Private E-1 Willie E. Smith, 429-86-4916, U.S. Army, Headquarters Company, 1st Battalion, 69th Infantry, Fort Blank, Missouri, and render this advice in accordance with the provisions of Article 34, Uniform Code of Military Justice, and R.C.M. 406, Manual for Courts-Martial.

2. <u>Legal Conclusions.</u> After reviewing the attached charges, allied papers, and report of the Article 32 investigation I have reached the following legal conclusions:

   a. Each specification alleges an offense under the Uniform Code of Military Justice.

   b. The allegations in each specification are warranted by the evidence indicated in the report of the Article 32 investigation.

   c. There is court-martial jurisdiction over the accused and all charged offenses.

3. <u>Recommendations.</u> I recommend that all charged offenses be tried by general court-martial and that the case be referred to trial by General Court-Martial Convening Order Number 14, Headquarters, Fort Blank, Missouri, dated 1 May 199X.

/s/
DONALD S. DOE
Colonel, JAGC
Staff Judge Advocate

DIRECTION OF THE CONVENING AUTHORITY;

All recommendations of the Staff Judge Advocate are (approved) (disapproved).

JAMES E. RYDER
Major General, USA
Commanding

Note: Derived from ARMY LAW., July 1984.

APP. 8   SAMPLE PRETRIAL ADVICE   APP. 8

Sample B Long Form With Optional Information

DEPARTMENT OF THE ARMY
HEADQUARTERS, FORT BLANK
Fort Blank, Missouri 77777

AKPS-JA   10 August 199x

MEMORANDUM FOR COMMANDING GENERAL

SUBJECT: Advice on Disposition of Court-Martial Charges

1. I have received the attached charges, allied papers, and report of investigation in the case of Private E-1 Willie E. Smith, 429-86-4916, U.S. Army, Headquarters Company, 1st Battalion, 69th Infantry, Fort Blank, Missouri, and render this advice in accordance with the provisions of Article 34, Uniform Code of Military Justice, and R.C.M. 406, Manual for Courts-Martial.
2. (OPTIONAL) Personal Data Concerning Accused
    a. Date of Birth: 8 May 198X
    b. Marital Status: Married
    c. Number of Dependents: 1
    d. Prior Military Service:

Dates	Service	Discharge
14 March 19XX—14 March 19XX	U.S. Army	Honorable

    e. Current Service: 15 April 19XX for 4 years.
    f. Aptitude Area GT Score: 87
    g. Education: High School Graduate
    h. Prior Disciplinary Record: Article 15 Assault 15 May 199X.
    i. Prior Convictions: None
    j. Restraint: Restriction to company area, 24 June 199X.
3. (OPTIONAL) Summary of Charges

Charge	Art. UCMJ	Spec	Gist of Offense	Maximum Punishment Authorized
I	86	1	AWOL 6 June 19XX-XX June 1984	DD, Conf. 1 yr, TF, RLEG
		2	AWOL 7 June 19XX-XX June 19XX	DD, Conf. 1 yr, TF, RLEG

4. (OPTIONAL) Summary of Available Evidence:
    a. On 6 June 199X the accused, without authority, absented himself from his unit and remained absent until 3 June 199X when he was apprehended by civilian authorities in St. Louis, Missouri.
    b. On 7 June 199X, after being in military control for only four days, the accused again absented himself from his unit without authority. He remained absent until he voluntarily turned himself in to the Fort Blank military police station on 24 June 199X.
5. (OPTIONAL) Extenuating and Mitigating Factors:
    a. In an unsworn statement given at the Article 32 investigation the accused stated that he went AWOL because his mother was ill and had financial problems. PVT Smith is the sole source of support for his mother.
    b. The accused is qualified as a sharpshooter with the M-16 rifle.
6. (OPTIONAL) Recommendations:
    a. Unit Commander: General Court-Martial.
    b. Battalion Commander: General Court-Martial.
    c. Brigade Commander: General Court-Martial.
    d. Article 32 Investigating Officer: General Court-Martial.
7. Legal Conclusions. After reviewing the charges, allied papers, and report of the Article 32 investigation I have reached the following legal conclusions:
    a. Each specification alleges an offense under the Uniform Code of Military Justice.

b. The allegations in each specification are warranted by the evidence indicated in the report of the Article 32 investigation.

c. There is court-martial jurisdiction over the accused and all charged offenses.

8. <u>Staff Judge Advocate Recommendation:</u> I recommend that all charged offenses be tried by general court-martial and that the case be referred to trial by Court-Martial Convening Order Number 14, Headquarters, Fort Blank, Missouri, dated 1 May 199X.

/s/
DONALD S. DOE
Colonel, JAGC
Staff Judge Advocate

DIRECTION OF THE CONVENING AUTHORITY:

All recommendations of the Staff Judge Advocate are (approved) (disapproved)

JAMES E. RYDER
Major General, USA
Commanding

Note: Derived from ARMY LAW., July 1984.

APPENDIX 9

SAMPLE COURT-MARTIAL CONVENING ORDER

DEPARTMENT OF THE ARMY
Headquarters, 20th Infantry Division and Fort Blank
Fort Blank, Missouri 77777

COURT MARTIAL CONVENING ORDER 27 August 199X
NUMBER 30

Pursuant to authority contained in paragraph 63, General Order No. 26, DA, dated 24 October 199X, a general court-martial is hereby convened. It may proceed at this HQ to try such persons as may be properly brought before it. The court will be constituted as follows:

MEMBERS

COL JOHN K. GREER, 441-46-3212, Arty, 20th Inf Div Arty
LTC SAMUEL T. GOLDEN, 907-44-6930, Inf, 1st Bn, 73d Inf
LTC M. JERRY TAYLOR, 076-62-5931, Armor, 1st Bn, 2d Recon
MAJ JOHN O. BINNS III, 527-14-1623, MSC, 20th Med Bn
MAJ GLENN T. GOODMAN, 664-16-9531, QMC, 20th S&T Bn
CPT DWAYNE S. CARR, 155-54-3622, Inf, 1st Bn, 70th Inf
1LT LAWRENCE L. LaVALLE, 677-67-8940, CE, 20th Eng Bn
1LT TOBY F. HARRIS, 146-24-9766, SigC, 20th Sig Bn

BY COMMAND OF MAJOR GENERAL BLUNT:

/s/ James S. Slade

DISTRIBUTION:
1 - Ea Off Conc
1 - Record of Trial
1 - Record Set
1 - Reference Set
50 - SJA, 20th Inf Div
    and Ft Blank

JAMES S. SLADE
CW2, USA
Acting Asst Adjutant

APPENDIX 10
SAMPLE DISCOVERY REQUEST

UNITED STATES   )
)
v.   )   REQUEST FOR DISCOVERY
)
Name, Rank   )
SSN   )
Unit   )
APO 09165, U.S. Army)

1. The accused requests the government to produce for the use, inspection and copying by the accused, through his/her attorney, the following:

   a. Any handwritten, typed or recorded statements by the accused or any other potential witness in connection with the investigation of this case, to representatives of the government to include summaries of conversations with representatives of the government, which were not attached as allied papers at the time the charges were referred and served.

   b. The contents of *all* statements, *oral or written,* made *by the accused* that are relevant to the case, known to the trial counsel, and within control of the armed forces. Disclosure is requested *prior to arraignment* pursuant to MIL. R. EVID. 304(d)(1).

   c. Disclosure of all evidence seized from the person or property of the accused, or believed to be owned by the accused, that the prosecution intends to offer into evidence against the accused at trial. Disclosure is requested prior to arraignment pursuant to MIL. R. EVID. 311(d)(1).

   d. Disclosure of all evidence of prior identification of the accused at a lineup or other identification process that the prosecution intends to offer into evidence against the accused at trial. Disclosure is requested *prior to arraignment* pursuant to MIL. R. EVID. 321(d)(1).

   e. Pursuant to MIL. R. EVID. 612, any writing or document used by a witness to prepare for trial.

   f. Any matter which the prosecution seeks to have judicially noticed. *See* MIL. R. EVID. 201.

   g. Pursuant to MIL. R. EVID. 301(c)(2) and *United States v. Webster,* 1 M.J. 216 (C.M.A. 1975), disclosure of *any* immunity or leniency pertaining to witnesses or to potential witnesses.

   h. Any known evidence tending to diminish credibility of witnesses including, but not limited to, prior convictions under MIL. R. EVID. 609, evidence of other character, conduct, or bias bearing on witness credibility under MIL. R. EVID. 608. *See Brady v. Maryland,* 373 U.S. 83 (1963); *United States v. Agurs,* 427 U.S. 97 (1976).

   i. Names of all witnesses and potential witnesses interviewed in this case.

   j. The names of all government investigators who have participated or are presently participating in the investigation of the instant case.

   k. All personal or business notes, memoranda, and writings prepared by investigators in said case which are not furnished pursuant to any other provisions of this request.

   l. The military status of all witnesses. As to those presently in civilian status, I request the date of separation from the Army, the discharge provisions used to effect such discharge, and a summary of circumstances explaining any discharges for other than completion of the obligated term of service.

m. Access to all personnel and medical records of all potential witnesses whether they are presently in the Army or have been discharged at an earlier date.

n. The names and locations of witnesses and potential witnesses used in developing the case against the accused.

o. A written list of material which includes names of witnesses (to include business address and phone), documents and other items of real evidence (and their locations) intended to be used on the findings and sentence portions of the government case. Request compliance ASAP by the government trial counsel.

p. Any evidence of prior Article 15 action, civilian or military convictions, and adverse administrative actions in the government's possession relating to any of the government's witnesses.

q. Any other matters not previously mentioned contained in files held by the government as provided by Rule 36 of the *Rules of Court* dated 1 December 199X.

r. Access to the 201 personnel file of the prospective court members.

s. Any and all evidence in the possession of the government favorable to the accused.

2. This request is made on the grounds that the accused cannot properly prepare for trial without production and inspection of the documents and items requested in advance of trial.

3. Request the government inform the defense counsel if it does not intend to comply with any of the provisions of this request.

4. It is understood that this is a continuing request.

Note: Derived from DA Pam 27-10 (1982).

APPENDIX 11
GRANT OF IMMUNITY

GRANT OF IMMUNITY)
IN THE MATTER OF)
_____)
_____)   GRANT OF IMMUNITY
_____)   (TRANSACTIONAL)
)

To: (Witness to whom immunity is to be granted)

1. It appears that you are a material witness for the (Government) (Defense) in the matter of [*if charges have been preferred, set forth a full identification of the accused and the substance of all specifications preferred.*]

2. In consideration of your testimony as a witness for the (Government) (Defense) in the foregoing matter, you are hereby granted immunity (as provided for in R.C.M. 704, MCM, 1984) from prosecution for any offense or offenses arising out of the matters therein involved concerning which you may be required to testify under oath.

3. It is understood that this grant of immunity from prosecution is effective only upon the condition that you actually testify as a witness for the (Government) (Defense). It is further understood that this grant of immunity from prosecution extends only to the offense or offenses in which you were implicated in the matter herein set forth and concerning which you testify under oath.

_____
Signature

_____
Grade, Title
Officer Exercising General
Court-Martial Jurisdiction

Note: These sample grants of immunity are taken from the Coast Guard's Military Justice Manual.

APP. 11   GRANT OF IMMUNITY   APP. 11

GRANT OF IMMUNITY

IN THE MATTER OF   )
)
_____)   GRANT OF IMMUNITY
_____)   (TESTIMONIAL)
_____)

To: (Witness to whom immunity is to be granted)

1. It appears that you are a material witness for the (Government) (Defense) in the matter of (if charges have been preferred, set forth a full identification of the accused and the substance of all specifications preferred.)

2. In consideration of your testimony as a witness for the (Government) (Defense) in the foregoing matter, you are hereby granted immunity (as provided for in R.C.M. 704, MCM), from the use of your testimony or other information given by you (or any information directly or indirectly derived from such testimony or other information) against you in (a trial by court-martial) except a prosecution for perjury, giving a false statement, or otherwise failing to comply with an order to testify in this matter.

3. It is understood that this grant of immunity from the use of your testimony or other information given by you (or other information directly or indirectly derived from such testimony or other information) against you in (a trial by court-martial) is effective only upon the condition that you testify under oath as a witness for the (Government) (Defense).

_____
Signature

_____
Grade, Title
Officer Exercising General
Court-Martial Jurisdiction

APPENDIX 12

PRETRIAL AGREEMENT

UNITED STATES   )
)
v.   )
)   Place:
)
Grade, Name, SSN, Organization)

OFFER FOR PRETRIAL AGREEMENT

I, (grade, name, SSN), am presently the accused under court-martial charge(s) dated _____ (and _____). I have read the charge(s) and specification(s) alleged against me and they have been explained to me by my defense counsel, (rank, if military, and name). I understand the charge(s) and specification(s) and I am aware that I have a legal and moral right to plead Not Guilty and to place upon the prosecution the burden of proving my guilt beyond a reasonable doubt by legal and competent evidence. For these reasons and under the conditions set forth below, and in consideration of agreement by the convening authority to approve a sentence in accord with the limitations set forth in Appendix A (and to) (withdraw Charge _____, Specification _____) (modify Specification _____ of Charge _____ to the lesser offense of _____) (refer the case to a special court-martial), I offer to plead Guilty

    To all Charge(s) and Specification(s)
or
    To the Charge(s) and Specification(s)
or
    To the following Charge(s) and Specification(s):

(set forth by number or in full the charge(s) and specification(s) to which the guilty plea will apply. If the plea is to be a lesser included offense as to one or more specifications, set forth the exceptions and substitutions correctly and in full; see MCM, Appendix 10.)

I understand that this offer, when accepted by the convening authority, will constitute a binding agreement. I assert that I am in fact guilty of the offense(s) to which I am offering to plead guilty and I understand that this agreement will permit the government to avoid presentation in court of sufficient evidence to prove my guilt. I offer to plead guilty only because it will be in my best interest that the convening authority grant me the relief set forth above and in Appendix A. I understand that I waive my right to a trial of the facts and to be confronted by the witnesses against me, and my right to avoid self-incrimination so far as a plea of guilty will incriminate me.

In making this offer, I state that:

1. I am satisfied with the defense counsel who has advised me with respect to this offer and consider him or her competent to represent me in this court-martial.

2. This offer to plead guilty originated with me and my counsel, and no person or persons have made any attempt to force or coerce me into making this offer or to plead guilty.

3. My counsel has fully advised me of the nature of the charges against me, the possibility of my defending against them, any defense which might apply, and the effect of the guilty plea which I am offering to make, and I fully understand his or her advice and the meaning, effect, and consequences of this plea.

APP. 12   PRETRIAL AGREEMENT   APP. 12

4. I understand that the signature of the convening authority to this offer and to Appendix A, or to any modified version of Appendix A which I also sign, will transform this offer into an agreement binding upon me and the government.

5. I understand that I may withdraw my plea of guilty at any time before sentence but not after sentence is announced and that, if I do so, this agreement is cancelled and of no effect. This agreement will also be cancelled and of no effect if any of the following occurs:

    a. Refusal of the court to accept my plea of guilty, as set forth above, or modification of the plea by anyone during the trial to not guilty or to a lesser degree of guilt.

    b. Withdrawal by either party to the agreement before the trial.

    c. My failure to agree with the trial counsel on stipulations concerning facts and circumstances.

6. I understand this agreement will be cancelled and of no effect if I (fail to provide restitution to ____ in the amount of ____ or fail to return ____) (commit any offenses chargeable under the UCMJ between the date of this agreement and the convening authority's approval of my sentence or the completion of any period of suspension of my sentence, whichever is later) (fail to refrain from ____ between the date of this agreement and the convening authority's approval of my sentence or the completion of any period of suspension of my sentence, whichever is later).

I understand that, if this agreement is cancelled for any reason stated above, this offer for an agreement cannot be used against me in any way at any time to establish my guilt of the offense(s), and the limitations upon disposition of my case set forth in Appendix A will have no effect.

This document and Appendix A include all of the terms of this pretrial agreement and no other inducements have been made by the convening authority or any other person which affect my offer to plead guilty.

_____   _____
Date   Signature

I certify that I have given the accused the advice referred to above, that I have explained to him or her the elements of the offense(s) and that I have witnessed his or her voluntary signature to this offer for a pretrial agreement. (I am a member of the bar of ____) (I am a judge advocate) (certified/not certified under Article 27(b)).

_____   _____
Date   Defense Counsel

I recommend (acceptance) (rejection) of this offer.

_____   _____
Date   Name, Grade, Staff Judge Advocate to the Convening Authority

The foregoing instrument, including Appendix A dated ____, is (approved and accepted) (disapproved).

_____   _____
Date   Name, Grade, and Title of Convening Authority

UNITED STATES   )   Place:
       v.   )
Grade, Name, SSN, Organization)   Date:

APPENDIX A TO OFFER FOR PRETRIAL AGREEMENT

As consideration for the offer of the accused to plead guilty as set forth in the Offer for Pretrial Agreement dated ____, the Convening Authority will undertake that:
  (The approved sentence will not exceed _____)
                                    or
  (No punitive discharge will be approved.)
(This is the original Appendix A submitted with the Offer for Pretrial Agreement.)
                                    or
(This Appendix A replaced the original submitted with the Offer for Pretrial Agreement.)

_____   _____
Date   Signature

I certify that I have advised the accused of the effect of the foregoing and that I have witnessed his or her voluntary signature to this Appendix A.

_____   _____
Date   Name, Rank (if applicable)
                                 Defense Counsel

I recommend (acceptance) (rejection) of this Appendix A.

_____   _____
Date   Name, Grade, Staff Judge Advocate to
                                 the Convening Authority

The foregoing Appendix A is approved in conjunction with the Pretrial Agreement dated as shown above.
The foregoing Appendix A is approved in conjunction with the Pretrial Agreement dated as shown above.

_____   _____
Date   Name, Grade, and Title of Convening
                                 Authority

_____
Note: Taken from AFR 111-1(1984).

APPENDIX 13

REQUEST TO TAKE ORAL DEPOSITION

DEPARTMENT OF THE ARMY
Headquarters, Fort Hood
Fort Hood, Texas 76544

AZBSJA [DATE]

SUBJECT: Request to take Deposition, *United States vs. Thomas Sublette*, 123-45-6789, Headquarters Company, 20th Maintenance Battalion, Fort Hood, Texas

Commanding General
Fort Hood
ATTN: SJA
Fort Hood, Texas 76544

1. Pursuant to the provisions of R.C.M. 702, Manual for Courts-Martial, the prosecution requests permission to take the oral deposition of Master Sergeant Henry J. Simms, Headquarters Company, 20th Maintenance Battalion, at the Office of the Staff Judge Advocate, Fort Hood, Texas, at 0900, 10 August 1996. The deposition is to be taken in connection with the charges and specifications in the pending General Court-Martial against Private Thomas Sublette, Headquarters Company, 20th Maintenance Battalion, alleging the willful disobedience of Master Sergeant Simms' order.

2. Master Sergeant Simms has been ordered to depart his present station on 12 August 1996 and to proceed to Headquarters, United States Army Europe, APO New York 09403, on a permanent change of station. The pretrial investigation indicates that he will be a necessary prosecution witness concerning the specifications and charge alleging willful disobedience of orders. It is anticipated that on oral deposition Master Sergeant Simms will testify that:

On the afternoon of 6 August 1996, while he was First Sergeant of Headquarters Company, 20th Maintenance Battalion, he gave an order to Private Sublette to mow the lawn in front of the company dayroom (Bldg. T-400). This order was given in the presence of Lieutenant Ferguson. He and Lieutenant Ferguson then left the accused who said nothing concerning the order. When he returned about five minutes later Private Sublette had disappeared without mowing the lawn. He did not see Private Sublette again until the following day.

CPT, JAGC
Trial Counsel

Note: Derived from DA Pam 27-10 (1982).

APPENDIX 14

INTERROGATORIES AND DEPOSITION FORM

INTERROGATORIES AND DEPOSITION [1]

UNITED STATES)
v.)
)
In the Matter of [2])
_____)

[1] This form to be used when a deposition is taken on written interrogatories. It may be appropriately modified when used for an oral deposition. (See generally, RCM 702, MCM, 1984.)

[2] Strike out words not applicable.

[3] General, special, or summary court-martial, military commission, court of inquiry, or military board.

[4] Insert name or title of person who is requested to authorize the taking of the deposition. A separate letter complying with RCM 702(c)(2) should be enclosed.

[5] To be subscribed by the trial counsel or other person requesting the deposition with name, rank, unit/command name, and official title, as "trial counsel," "defense counsel," "summary court," "recorder," etc. Describe legal qualifications, as "certified in accordance with Article 27(b)," "member of the bar of the Supreme Court of _____" etc.; if none, so state.

[6] If it is desired to give special instructions, there should be added "special instructions attached."

Deposition of _____ (stationed) (residing) [2]
at _____ to be read in evidence before a [3]
_____ of the United States,
convened to meet at _____ by _____
_____ dated _____, 19 ___.

TO: [4] _____

It is requested that you authorize the deposition of the above-named witness to be taken on the following interrogatories.

TRIAL COUNSEL OR OTHER PERSON REQUESTING DEPOSITION [5]

a. TYPED NAME (Last, First, Middle Initial)	b. OFFICIAL TITLE	
c. UNIT/COMMAND NAME	d. LEGAL QUALIFICATIONS	
e. SIGNATURE	f. RANK	g. DATE SIGNED

_____
_____, _____, 19 ___,

TO: _____,

You will take or cause to be taken the deposition of the above-named witness on the following interrogatories, cross-interrogatories, and additional interrogatories, if any. [6]

By _____ of _____ .

PERSON ORDERING DEPOSITION OR PERSON SIGNING THEREFOR

a. TYPED NAME (Last, First, Middle Initial)	b. RANK	c. SIGNATURE
d. UNIT/COMMAND NAME		e. OFFICIAL TITLE

DD Form 456, OCT 84, Page 1   *Previous editions are obsolete.*

APP. 14 INTERROGATORIES AND DEPOSITION FORM APP. 14

[1] The officer taking the deposition shall administer the following oath to the deponent prior to deposing: "You (swear) (affirm) that the evidence you give shall be the truth, the whole truth, and nothing but the truth, so help you God?"

[2] If the spaces for answers are not sufficient, extra sheets may be inserted by the officer taking the deposition. In such case, he/she will rewrite the interrogatories, writing the answers immediately below the respective interrogatories.

Interrogatories propounded by the above-named person requesting the deposition are as follows: [1]

First Interrogatory: Are you in the military service of the United States? If so, what is your full name, rank, unit/command name, and station? If not, what is your full name, occupation, and residence?

Answer: [2]

Second interrogatory: Do you know the accused? If so, how long have you know him/her?

Answer:

Third interrogatory:

Answer:

DD Form 456, OCT 84, Page 2

APP. 14 — MILITARY CRIMINAL JUSTICE — APP. 14

[1] To be subscribed by the defense counsel or other person with name, pay grade, unit/command name, and official title. Describe legal qualifications, as "certified in accordance with Article 27(b)," "member of the bar of the Supreme Court of _____" etc.; if none, so state. When deposition is requested by the defense, the trial counsel propounds the cross-interrogatories.	**The following cross-interrogatories are propounded by:**
	PERSON PROPOUNDING CROSS-INTERROGATORIES [1]
	a. TYPED NAME (Last, First, Middle Initial) b. OFFICIAL TITLE
	c. UNIT/COMMAND NAME d. LEGAL QUALIFICATIONS
	e. SIGNATURE f. RANK g. DATE SIGNED
	First cross-interrogatory: [2]
[2] If none, so state.	Answer:
[3] Insert "court," "commission," "board," if appropriate. If not applicable, or if no interrogatories are propounded, so state.	Additional interrogatories by the _____ are as follows: [3]
	Answer:

DD Form 456, OCT 84, Page 3

APP. 14   INTERROGATORIES AND DEPOSITION FORM   APP. 14

My answers to the foregoing interrogatories, cross-interrogatories, if any, are indicated above.

WITNESS

a. TYPED NAME (Last, First, Middle Initial)	b. SIGNATURE	c. DATE SIGNED

CERTIFICATE OF PERSON TAKING DEPOSITION

I certify that the above deposition was duly taken by me on the _____ day of _____, 19 ___; the above-named witness, having been first sworn by me, gave the foregoing answers to the several interrogatories; that the above-named witness was given an opportunity to read his/her testimony after it was reduced to writing, and all corrections desired by the above-named witness were made; and the above-named witness subscribed the foregoing deposition in my presence at _____, this _____ day of _____, 19 ___. I further certify that the detailed reporter was duly sworn by me and that said reporter signed in my presence the reporter's certificate appearing below.

OFFICER TAKING DEPOSITION

a. TYPED NAME (Last, First, Middle Initial)	b. RANK	c. SIGNATURE	d. DATE SIGNED
e. UNIT/COMMAND NAME		f. OFFICIAL TITLE	

REPORTER'S CERTIFICATION

I certify that the foregoing interrogatories and answers thereto are a true, complete and accurate transcription of the interrogatories propounded to and the answers by the above-named witness.

REPORTER

a. TYPED NAME (Last, First, Middle Initial)	b. SIGNATURE	c. DATE SIGNED
d. UNIT/COMMAND NAME		

DD Form 456, OCT 84, Page 4   ☆ GPO : 1984 O - 461-033 (27029)

APPENDIX 15
SUBPOENA FOR CIVILIAN WITNESS

SUBPOENA

The President of the United States, to _____
(Name and Title of Person being Subpoenaed)

You are hereby summoned and required to appear on the _____ day of _____, 19____, at _____ o'clock _____ .M., at _____, (before _____
(Place of Proceeding) (Name and Title of Deposition Officer)

designated to take your deposition) (a _____ court-martial of the United States) (a court of inquiry), appointed by _____, dated _____
(Identification of Convening Order or Convening Authority)

19____, to testify as a witness in the matter of _____
(Name of Case)

(and bring with you _____).
(Specific Identification of Documents or Other Evidence)

Failure to appear and testify is punishable by a fine of not more than $500 or imprisonment for a period not more than six months, or both. 10 U.S.C. § 847. Failure to appear may also result in your being taken into custody and brought before the court-martial (_____) under a Warrant of Attachment (DD Form 454). Manual for Courts-Martial R.C.M. 703(e)(2)(G).

Bring this subpoena with you and do not depart from the proceeding without proper permission.

Subscribed at _____ this _____ day of _____ 19____

_____
(Signature (See R.C.M. 703(e)(2)(C))

The witness is requested to sign one copy of this subpoena and to return the signed copy to the person serving the subpoena.

I hereby accept service of the above subpoena.

_____
Signature of Witness

NOTE: If the witness does not sign, complete the following:

Personally appeared before me, the undersigned authority, _____,

who, being first duly sworn according to law, deposes and says that at _____, on _____,

19____, he personally delivered to _____ in person a duplicate of this subpoena.

_____   _____
Grade   Signature

Subscribed and sworn to before me at _____, this _____ day of

_____ 19____.

_____   _____
Grade

_____   _____
Official Status   Signature

DD FORM 453
84 AUG   EDITION OF OCT 69 IS OBSOLETE.

APPENDIX 16
WARRANT OF ATTACHMENT

WARRANT OF ATTACHMENT

_____ Court-Martial of the United States

_____

UNITED STATES)
v.   )
)
_____)
)
_____)

The President of the United States, to _____
(United States marshal or such other person as may be directed,
_____ :

RCM 703(e)(2)(G)(iv), MCM, 1984)

WHEREAS, _____, of _____, was on the _____ day of _____, 19_____, at _____, duly subpoenaed to appear and attend at _____, on the _____ day of _____, 19_____, at _____ o'clock _____.m., before a _____ court-martial duly convened by _____, dated _____, 19_____, to testify on the part of the _____ in the above-entitled case; and whereas he/she has willfully neglected or refused (to appear and attend)[1] (to produce documentary evidence which he/she was legally subpoenaed to produce) before said _____ court-martial, as by said subpoena required, although sufficient time has elapsed for that purpose; and whereas he/she has offered no valid excuse for his/her failure to appear; and whereas he/she is a necessary and material witness in behalf of the _____ _____ in the above-entitled case:

[1] Line out inappropriate words.

DD Form 454, OCT 84   Previous editions are obsolete.

NOW, THEREFORE, by virtue of the power vested in me, the undersigned, as military judge [1] of said _____ court-martial, by Article 46 of the Uniform Code of Military Justice (10 USC 846), you are hereby commanded and empowered to apprehend and attach the said _____ wherever he/she may be found within the United States, its Territories and possessions, and forthwith bring him/her before the said _____ court-martial at _____ to testify as required by said subpoena.

_____

_____
Military judge of said [1] _____ COURT-MARTIAL

Dated at _____
_____, 19_____

[1] *If there is no military judge, line out the words "military judge" and enter "convening authority."*

DD Form 454 Reverse, OCT 84

☆ GPO : 1984 O - 461-033 (27028)

APPENDIX 17

REQUEST FOR TRIAL BEFORE MILITARY JUDGE ALONE

REQUEST FOR TRIAL BEFORE MILITARY JUDGE ALONE
(Article 16, UCMJ)

UNITED STATES
v.

_____

1. ACCUSED

I have been informed that _____ is the military judge detailed to the court-martial to which the charges and specifications pending against me have been referred for trial. After consulting with my defense counsel, I hereby request that the court be composed of the military judge alone. I make this request with full knowledge of my right to be tried by a court-martial composed of (commissioned)[1] officers (and, if I so request, enlisted personnel).[2]

a. TYPED NAME (Last, First, Middle Initial)	b. RANK	c. SIGNATURE	d. DATE SIGNED

2. DEFENSE COUNSEL

Prior to the signing of the foregoing request, I fully advised the above accused of his/her right to trial before a court-martial composed of (commissioned)[1] officers (and of his/her right to have such court consist of at least one-third enlisted members not of his/her unit, upon his/her request).[2]

a. TYPED NAME (Last, First, Middle Initial)	b. RANK	c. SIGNATURE	d. DATE SIGNED

3. TRIAL COUNSEL

Argument is (not) requested.

a. TYPED NAME (Last, First, Middle Initial)	b. RANK	c. SIGNATURE	d. DATE SIGNED

4. MILITARY JUDGE

The foregoing request for trial before me alone is hereby: (X one) ☐ APPROVED   ☐ DISAPPROVED[3]

a. TYPED NAME (Last, First, Middle Initial)	b. RANK	c. SIGNATURE	d. DATE SIGNED

[1] Delete when the accused is a warrant officer or enlisted member
[2] Delete when the accused is a commissioned officer or warrant officer.
[3] When request is disapproved, the basis for denial must be put on the record. (See MCM, 1984 RCM 903(c))

DD Form 1722, OCT 84   Replaces edition of 1 OCT 69 which may be used until supply is exhausted
☆ U.S. Government Printing Office: 1985—461-033/27153

APPENDIX 18
REQUEST FOR ENLISTED MEMBERS

DEPARTMENT OF THE ARMY
Headquarters, Fort Blank
Fort Blank, Missouri 63899

AXBSJA   19 December 199X

SUBJECT: Request for Enlisted Members in the Case of United States v. Joe E. Brown

Commander
1st Support Brigade
Fort Blank, Missouri 63899

I request that the Convening Authority detail at least one-third enlisted members to my special court-martial.

                                        JOE E. BROWN
                                        PV2, US Army
                                        Accused

                                        FRED C. CUMMINGS
                                        CPT, JAGC
                                        Defense Counsel

Note: Derived from DA Pam 27-10.

APPENDIX 19

DISCLOSURE OF SECTION III EVIDENCE

UNITED STATES   )   Fort Blank, Texas
)
    v.   )
)   DISCLOSURE OF
William Q. Fiberbored   )   SECTION III EVIDENCE
Private (E-1), US Army   )
139-36-5941   )
(Unit)   )

Pursuant to Section III of the Military Rules of Evidence the defense is hereby notified:

A. Rule 304(d)(1). There are (no) relevant statements, oral or written, by the accused in this case, presently known to the trial counsel (and they are appended hereto as appendix ____).

B. Rule 311(d)(1). There is (no) evidence seized from the person or property of the accused or believed to be owned by the accused that the prosecution intends to offer into evidence against the accused at trial [(and it is described with particularity in appendix ____) (and described as follows _____

_____)].

C. Rule 321(d)(1). There is (no) evidence of a prior identification of the accused at a lineup or other identification process, which the prosecution intends to offer against the accused at trial [(and it is described with particularity in appendix _____) (and described as follows

_____)].

A copy of this disclosure has been provided to the military judge.

Date   ALFRED P. JONES
                                                           Captain, JAGC
                                                             Trial Counsel

---

Note: Derived from DA Pam 27-10 (1982).

APPENDIX 20
BILL OF PARTICULARS

UNITED STATES)	
)	
v.)	MOTION FOR
)	
John Q. Rogers)	BILL OF PARTICULARS
460-55-1111)	
P.F.C., U.S. Army)	
B Co., 96th Sig. Bn.)	

Private First Class John Q. Rogers, the defendant, moves the Court for an order directing the Prosecution to furnish him with a Bill of Particulars with respect to the following matters alleged in Charge I, particularly setting forth the following:

1. The exact location, including the street address, where the government claims the defendant made the illegal sale of the narcotic drug.
2. The exact time when the alleged illegal sale occurred.
3. The name and address of the person[s] to whom the government claims the defendant sold and transferred the narcotic drug.
4. Whether such person[s] was at the time of the alleged illegal sale and transfer employed by the government, either directly or indirectly.
5. Whether such person[s] was acting at the instance of the government at the time of the alleged illegal sale and transfer.
6. The precise manner in which the government claims that the alleged illegal sale and transfer occurred.
7. The name and address of any other person[s] who was present at the scene and time of the alleged illegal sale and transfer.

This motion is made on the grounds that Charge I fails to state with particularity the location or time of, the participant in, or any witnesses to the alleged offense, all of which information is within the particular knowledge of the Trial Counsel and is essential to enable the defendant to prepare for and to avoid surprise at trial. The motion is based on all the papers, pleadings, and files of this action.

Dated: 23 July 199X.

Anastasio G. Lamente
Cpt., JAGC
Defense Counsel

APP. 20　　　　　　　BILL OF PARTICULARS　　　　　　　APP. 20

UNITED STATES　　　　　　　　)
　　　　　　　　　　　　　　　)
　　　　v.　　　　　　　　　　)　　ORDER FOR
　　　　　　　　　　　　　　　)
John Q. Rogers　　　　　　　　)　　BILL OF PARTICULARS
460-55-1111　　　　　　　　　)
P.F.C., U.S. Army　　　　　　)
B Co., 96th Sig. Bn.　　　　　)

The motion of the defendant for a Bill of Particulars having been heard on 23 July, 1996, and the Court having read the moving papers and affidavits submitted, and the memoranda of points and authorities submitted by the parties;

IT IS ORDERED that the motion is granted, and that the Prosecution is directed, within 10 days after service of a copy of this order, to serve and file a Bill of Particulars, showing with particularity the following:

1. The exact location, including the street address, where the government claims the defendant made the illegal sale of the narcotic drug.

2. The exact time when the alleged illegal sale occurred.

3. The name[s] and address[es] of the person[s] to whom the government claims the defendant sold and transferred the narcotic drug.

4. Whether such person[s] were at the time of the alleged illegal sale and transfer employed by the government, either directly or indirectly.

5. Whether such person[s] were acting at the instance of the government at the time of the alleged illegal sale and transfer.

6. The precise manner in which the government claims that the alleged illegal sale and transfer occurred.

7. The name[s] and address[es] of any other person[s] who were present at the scene and time of the alleged illegal sale and transfer.

Dated: 29 July 199X.

　　　　　　　　　　　　　　　　　　Aloysius P. Quagmire
　　　　　　　　　　　　　　　　　　Col., JAGC
　　　　　　　　　　　　　　　　　　Military Judge

APPENDIX 21
NOTICE OF GOVERNMENT APPEAL

United States)
)
v.) NOTICE OF
) GOVERNMENT APPEAL
John Q. Rogers)
460-55-1111)
P.F.C., U.S. Army)
B. Co., 96th Sig. Bn.)

1. On 18 Nov. 199X at approximately 1100 hrs, this Court in an Article 39(a) pretrial session ordered the suppression of a pretrial statement made by the accused on 17 Sept. 199X to C.I.D. Agent Rapp. The Prosecution intended to offer that statement in support of Charge II and its specification.

2. In accordance with R.C.M. 908(b)(3), the Prosecution hereby gives timely notice that it intends to appeal that ruling to the Army Court of Criminal Appeals.

3. The Prosecution certifies that the appeal is not being taken for the purpose of delay and that the accused's statement is substantial proof of a fact material to the proceeding.

Dated: 20 Nov. 199X
Time: 1000 hours

Ray N. Kwist
Cpt., JAGC
Trial Counsel

APPENDIX 22

PLEA WORKSHEET

Your Honor, the accused _____ (Rank) _____ (Name) _____
pleads as follows:

1. To (all) the Specification(s) and the Charge(s): Guilty.
2. To Specification _____, Charge _____: Guilty. To Specification _____, Charge _____: Not Guilty. To the Charge: Guilty.
3. To the Specification: Guilty except the word(s): "_____
_____"

To the excepted word(s):
Not Guilty. To the Charge: (Guilty) (Not Guilty but Guilty of a violation of Article _____).
4. To the Specification: Guilty except the word(s): "_____
_____" and "_____
_____"

substituting therefor, respectively, the word(s): "_____
_____"
and "_____"
of the excepted word(s): Not Guilty; to the substituted word(s): Guilty. To the Charge: (Guilty) (Not Guilty, but Guilty of a violation of Article _____).

APPENDIX 23

ENTRY OF CONDITIONAL GUILTY PLEA

UNITED STATES)	
)	
v.)	ENTRY OF CONDITIONAL
)	
LESTER J. TUDBAHL)	GUILTY PLEA
616-16-1616)	
PFC (E-3))	

1. The accused, PFC Lester J. Tudbahl, 616-16-1616, pleads guilty to the Charge and Specification on the condition that the following issue be preserved for appellate review and appeal:

> Whether the military judge correctly ruled that cocaine found in the accused's footlocker on 6 December 199X by Sergeant Brown was the product of a lawful inspection under Military Rule of Evidence 313(b)?

2. The United States consents to the entry of this conditional guilty plea.
3. The military judge consents to the entry of this conditional guilty plea.
4. All parties understand that if the accused prevails on appellate review or appeal of this specified issue, he will be permitted to withdraw this guilty plea.

Lester J. Tudbahl
Accused

Ted D. Smith
LTC, JAGC
Military Judge

Joan S. Worthy
CPT, JAGC
Defense Counsel

Roger D. Jones
BG, USA
General Court-Martial
Convening Authority

APPENDIX 24

COURT-MARTIAL MEMBER QUESTIONNAIRE

The *voir dire* examination of court members can be very time consuming. As a prospective member of a court-martial, you can substantially assist in lessening the time spent in court by voluntarily completing this questionnaire without delay. The questions asked herein are in no way an attempt to pry into your personal life, and they are in no way an attempt to embarrass or discredit you. These questions are fairly standard questions asked of all prospective members of courts-martial in order to provide some basis for determining their qualifications to sit fairly and impartially as a member of a court-martial.

1. NAME:_____ RANK:_____ AGE:_____

2. PRESENT DUTY ASSIGNMENT (Specifically):

3. BRIEF SUMMARY OF COAST GUARD CAREER AND DUTY ASSIGNMENTS:

4. NATURE OF ANY LAW ENFORCEMENT ASSIGNMENTS (If any):

5. MARITAL STATUS: AGE AND SEX OF CHILDREN:

6. HAVE YOU OR ANY MEMBER OF YOUR FAMILY BEEN THE VICTIM OF OR INVOLVED WITH ANY CRIME? (If YES, please describe briefly):

7. HAVE YOU EVER SERVED AS A MEMBER OF A COURT-MARTIAL? (If YES, state how many times; the type of court-martial; and the general nature of the case(s)):

8. ARE YOU A: (a) High School Graduate? ____
                 (b) College Graduate? ____

(If you are a college graduate, please state the name of the college and the degree attained.)

9. DO YOU HOLD A POST GRADUATE DEGREE? (If YES, state the field and the degree held):

10. HAVE YOU EVER ATTENDED A LAW SCHOOL OR TAKEN ANY LAW COURSES? (If YES, state the school attended, courses taken, and the length of school or courses taken):

11. HAVE YOU EVER TAKEN ANY COURSES IN PSYCHIATRY OR PSYCHOLOGY? (If YES, briefly describe the courses taken and the school from which taken):

_____
SIGNATURE OF PROSPECTIVE MEMBER

Note: Taken from Coast Guard Military Justice Manual.

APPENDIX 25
STIPULATION OF FACT

UNITED STATES	)	
v.	)	
	)	STIPULATION OF FACT
A1C ADAM A. ADAMSON	)	
21 CSG	)	
Wilson AFB, AK	)	

It is hereby stipulated and agreed by and between the trial counsel and defense counsel, with the express consent of the accused, that:

The loudspeaker at Base Operations, Building 176, Wilson Air Force Base, Alaska, was in proper working order on 22 June 199X, between the period of 0800 hours and 1700 hours, and that no complaint was received by the work order section to repair it.

JAMES J. JAMES, First Lieutenant, USAF
Trial Counsel

DANIEL T. GALLWORTHY,
Captain, USAF
Defense Counsel

ADAM A. ADAMSON, A1C, USAF
Accused

APPENDIX 26

STIPULATION OF EXPECTED TESTIMONY

UNITED STATES)
)
v.)
) STIPULATION OF
A1C ADAM A. ADAMS) EXPECTED TESTIMONY
21 CSG)
Wilson AFB, AK)

It is hereby stipulated and agreed by and between the trial counsel and defense counsel, with the express consent of the accused, that if Master Sergeant John S. Mitchell, FR 567-60-7330, 21 TFW, Wilson AFB, Alaska, were present and testifying under oath, he would testify as follows:

I have known Airman First Class Adam A. Adams for approximately 3½ years; we were overseas in Thailand together and I was his immediate supervisor, etc.

PETER N. JAMESON, Lieutenant,
USAF
Trial Counsel

DANIEL T. GALLWORTHY, Captain,
USAF
Defense Counsel

ADAM A. ADAMS, A1C, USAF
Accused

APPENDIX 27

INSTRUCTIONS CHECKLIST

I. Prior to Findings .... ( )
   A. Preliminary Remarks
      1. Prefatory Instructions on Findings .... ( )
      2. Other General Introductory Explanations .... ( )
         a. Joint Offenders .... ( )
         b. .... ( )
   B. Elements of Offenses Charged .... ( )
      1. Including definition of terms having
         special legal connotation .... ( )
      2. Law of Principals .... ( )
   C. Lesser-Included Offenses .... ( )
     (Including definition of terms having
     special legal connotation)
   D. Special and Other Defenses
      1. Self-Defense .... ( )
      2. Defense of Another .... ( )
      3. Accident .... ( )
      4. Duress .... ( )
      5. Entrapment .... ( )
      6. Agency .... ( )
      7. Obedience to Orders .... ( )
      8. Physical Impossibility or Inability .... ( )
      9. Financial and Other Inability .... ( )
     10. Ignorance or Mistake of Fact or Law .... ( )
     11. Voluntary Intoxication .... ( )
     12. Alibi .... ( )
     13. Character Evidence .... ( )
     14. Mental Responsibility at Time of Offense .... ( )
     15. Partial Mental Responsibility .... ( )
     16. Personality (Character or Behavior) Disorders .... ( )
     17. Voluntary Abandonment .... ( )
     18. Parental Discipline .... ( )
     19. Evidence Negating Mens Rea .... ( )
     20. Self-Help Under a Claim of Right .... ( )
     21. Lack of Causation .... ( )
     22. Other .... ( )
   E. Evidentiary and Other Matters
      1. Pretrial Statements .... ( )
      2. Law of Principals .... ( )
      3. Joint Offenders .... ( )
      4. Circumstantial Evidence .... ( )
         a. Proof of intent by circumstantial evidence .... ( )
         b. Proof of knowledge by circumstantial evidence .... ( )
      5. Stipulations .... ( )
      6. Depositions .... ( )
      7. Judicial Notice .... ( )
      8. Credibility of Witness .... ( )

INSTRUCTIONS CHECKLIST

      9. Character Evidence .... ( )
     10. Expert Testimony .... ( )
     11. Accomplice Testimony .... ( )
     12. Prior Statements by Witness .... ( )
     13. Excited Utterance .... ( )
     14. Statement of Mental, Emotional or Physical Condition .... ( )
     15. Statements for Purpose of Medical Diagnosis .... ( )
     16. Accused's Failure to Testify .... ( )
     17. Other Offenses or Acts of Misconduct by Accused .... ( )
     18. Past Sexual Behavior of Nonconsensual Sex Victim .... ( )
     19. Interracial Identification .... ( )
     20. Have You Heard Impeachment Questions .... ( )
     21. Grant of Immunity .... ( )
     22. Variance Findings by Exceptions and Substitutions .... ( )
     23. Value, Damage or Amount .... ( )
  F. Continuing (Closing) Instructions on Findings .... ( )

II. Prior to Sentencing
  A. Introductory Instructions on Sentence .... ( )
  B. Maximum Punishment .... ( )
  C. Extenuation, Mitigation, and Aggravation .... ( )
      1. Summary of Evidence in Extenuation Mitigation .... ( )
      2. Effect of Guilty Plea .... ( )
      3. Unsworn Statement by Accused .... ( )
      4. Mendacity .... ( )
      5. Argument for Specific Sentence .... ( )
      6. Other .... ( )
  D. Procedural and Concluding Instructions .... ( )

NOTE: Derived from DA. Pam. 27-9, Military Judge's Benchbook.

APPENDIX 28

FINDINGS WORKSHEET

IN CASE OF AN ACQUITTAL:

_____ it is my duty as president of this court to advise you that the court in closed session and upon secret written ballot has found you not guilty of (the) (all) Specification(s) and Charge(s). (Rank & Last Name of Accused)

IN CASE OF A CONVICTION:

_____ it is my duty as president of this court to inform you that the court in closed session and upon secret written ballot, two-thirds of the members present at the time the vote was taken concurring in each finding of guilty, finds you: (Rank & Last Name of Accused)

1. Of (the) (all) Specification(s) and Charge(s): _____
2. Of Specification _____, of Charge _____: (Guilty) (Not Guilty)
   Of Specification _____, of Charge _____: (Guilty) (Not Guilty)
   Of Charge _____: (Guilty) (Not Guilty)
   Of Specification _____, of Charge _____: (Guilty) (Not Guilty)
   Of Specification _____, of Charge _____: (Guilty) (Not Guilty)
   Of Charge _____: (Guilty) (Not Guilty)
3. Of the Specification _____, of Charge _____:
Guilty except the word(s) "And with the intent to remain away therefrom permanently 'and' in desertion."
Of the excepted word(s); Not Guilty.
   Of the Charge _____: (Not Guilty, but Guilty of violation of Article 86).
4. Of (the) Specification _____, of (the) Charge _____:
Guilty except the words "_____" and "_____" substituting therefor, respectively, the words "_____" and "_____," of the excepted words:
Not Guilty, of the substituted words: Guilty.
   Of (the) Charge _____: (Guilty) (Not Guilty, but Guilty of a violation of Article _____).

APPELLATE EXHIBIT____

APPENDIX 29

SENTENCING WORKSHEET
(SPECIAL COURT-MARTIAL)

Note: After the court has determined its sentence, the president should strike out the inapplicable material, and announce:

_____, it is my duty as president of this court to inform you that the court in closed session and upon secret written ballot two-thirds of the members present at the time the vote was taken concurring, sentences you: (Rank & Last Name of Accused)

1. To no punishment. (Admonition or Reprimand)
2. To be admonished.
3. To be reprimanded. (Reduction of Enlisted Personnel)
4. To be reduced to the grade of _____. (Forfeitures, etc.)
5. To forfeit $_____ pay per month for _____ month(s). (Restraint and Hard Labor)
6. To be restricted to the limits of _____ for _____ (day(s)) (month(s)).
7. To perform hard labor without confinement for _____ (day(s)) (month(s)).
8. To be confined at hard labor for _____ (day(s)) (month(s)). (Punitive Discharge)
9. To be discharged from the Service with a Bad Conduct Discharge.

APPELLATE EXHIBIT____

APPENDIX 30

MAXIMUM PUNISHMENT CHART

This chart was compiled for convenience purposes only and is not the authority for specific punishments. *See* Part IV and R.C.M. 1003 for specific limits and additional information concerning maximum punishments.

Article	Offense	Discharge	Confinement	Forfeitures
77	Principals (*see* Part IV, ¶ 1 and pertinent offenses)			
78	Accessory after the fact (*see* Part IV, ¶ 3.e.)			
79	Lesser included offenses (*see* Part IV, ¶ 2 and pertinent offenses)			
80	Attempts (*see* Part IV, ¶ 4.e.)			
81	Conspiracy (*see* Part IV, ¶ 5.e.)			
82	Solicitation			
	If solicited offense committed, or attempted, *see* Part IV, ¶ 6.e.			
	If solicited offense not committed:			
	Solicitation to desert [1]	DD, BCD	3 yrs. [1]	Total
	Solicitation to mutiny [1]	DD, BCD	10 yrs. [1]	Total
	Solicitation to commit act of misbehavior before enemy [1]	DD, BCD	10 yrs. [1]	Total
	Solicitation to commit act of sedition [1]	DD, BCD	10 yrs. [1]	Total
83	Fraudulent enlistment, appointment	DD, BCD	2 yrs.	Total
	Fraudulent separation	DD, BCD	5 yrs.	Total
84	Effecting unlawful enlistment, appointment, separation	DD, BCD	5 yrs.	Total
85	Desertion			
	Intent to avoid hazardous duty, shirk important service [1]	DD, BCD	5 yrs. [1]	Total
	Other cases			
	Terminated by apprehension	DD, BCD	3 yrs. [1]	Total
	Otherwise terminated	DD, BCD	2 yrs. [1]	Total
86	Absence without leave, etc.			
	Failure to go, going from place of duty	None	1 mo.	2/3 1 mo.
	Absence from unit, organization, etc.			
	Not more than 3 days	None	1 mo.	2/3 1 mo.
	More than 3, not more than 30 days	None	6 mos.	2/3 6 mos.
	More than 30 days	DD, BCD	1 yr.	Total
	More than 30 days and terminated by apprehension	DD, BCD	1 yr., 6 mos.	Total
	Absence from guard or watch	None	3 mos.	2/3 3 mos.
	Absence from guard or watch with intent to abandon	BCD	6 mos.	Total
	Absence with intent to avoid maneuvers, field exercises	BCD	6 mos.	Total
87	Missing movement			
	Through design	DD, BCD	2 yrs.	Total
	Through neglect	BCD	1 yr.	Total
88	Contempt toward officials	Dismissal	1 yr.	Total
89	Disrespect toward superior commissioned officer	BCD	1 yr.	Total
90	Assaulting, willfully disobeying superior commissioned officer			
	Striking, drawing or lifting up any weapon or offering any violence toward superior commissioned officer execution of duty [1]	DD, BCD	10 yrs. [1]	Total

APP. 30   MAXIMUM PUNISHMENT CHART   APP. 30

This chart was compiled for convenience purposes only and is not the authority for specific punishments. *See* Part IV and R.C.M. 1003 for specific limits and additional information concerning maximum punishments.

Article	Offense	Discharge	Confinement	Forfeitures
	Willfully disobeying lawful order of superior commissioned officer [1]	DD, BCD	5 yrs. [1]	Total
91	Insubordinate conduct toward warrant, noncommissioned, petty officer			
	Striking or assaulting:			
	Warrant officer	DD, BCD	5 yrs.	Total
	Superior noncommissioned officer	DD, BCD	3 yrs.	Total
	Other noncommissioned or petty officer	DD, BCD	1 yr.	Total
	Willfully disobeying:			
	Warrant officer	DD, BCD	2 yrs.	Total
	Noncommissioned or petty officer	BCD	1 yr.	Total
	Contempt, disrespect toward:			
	Warrant Officer	BCD	9 mos.	Total
	Superior noncommissioned or petty officer	BCD	6 mos.	Total
	Other noncommissioned or petty officer	None	3 mos.	2/3 3 mos.
92	Failure to obey order, regulation			
	Violation, failure to obey general order or regulation [2]	DD, BCD	2 yrs.	Total
	Violation, failure to obey other order [2]	BCD	6 mos.	Total
	Dereliction in performance of duties			
	Through neglect, culpable inefficiency	None	3 mos.	2/3 3 mos.
	Willful	BCD	6 mos.	Total
93	Cruelty, maltreatment of subordinates	DD, BCD	1 yr.	Total
94	Mutiny & sedition	Death, DD, BCD	Life	Total
95	Resisting apprehension, breach of arrest; escape			
	Resisting apprehension	BCD	1 yr.	Total
	Breaking arrest	BCD	6 mos.	Total
	Escape from custody, pretrial confinement, or confinement on bread and water or diminished rations	DD, BCD	1 yr.	Total
	Escape from post-trial confinement	DD, BCD	5 yrs.	Total
96	Releasing prisoner without proper authority	DD, BCD	2 yrs.	Total
	Suffering prisoner to escape through neglect	BCD	1 yr.	Total
	Suffering prisoner to escape through design	DD, BCD	2 yrs.	Total
97	Unlawful detention	DD, BCD	3 yrs.	Total
98	Noncompliance with procedural rules, etc.			
	Unnecessary delay in disposition of case	BCD	6 mos.	Total
	Knowingly, intentionally failing to comply, enforce code	DD, BCD	5 yrs.	Total
99	Misbehavior before enemy	Death, DD, BCD	Life	Total
100	Subordinate compelling surrender	Death, DD, BCD	Life	Total
101	Improper use of countersign	Death, DD, BCD	Life	Total
102	Forcing safeguard	Death, DD, BCD	Life	Total
103	Captured, abandoned property; failure to secure, etc.			
	Of value of $100.00 or less	BCD	6 mos.	Total
	Of value of more than $100.00	DD, BCD	5 yrs.	Total
	Looting, pillaging	DD, BCD	Life	Total
104	Aiding the enemy	Death, DD, BCD	Life	Total
105	Misconduct as prisoner	DD, BCD	Life	Total

This chart was compiled for convenience purposes only and is not the authority for specific punishments. *See* Part IV and R.C.M. 1003 for specific limits and additional information concerning maximum punishments.

Article	Offense	Discharge	Confinement	Forfeitures
106	Spying	Mandatory Death, DD, BCD	Not applicable	Total
106a	Espionage			
	Cases listed in Art. 106a(a)(1)(A)–(D)	Death, DD, BCD	Life	Total
	Other cases	DD, BCD	Life	Total
107	False official statements	DD, BCD	5 yrs.	Total
108	Military property; loss, damage, destruction, disposition			
	Selling, otherwise disposing			
	Of value of $100 or less	BCD	1 yr.	Total
	Of value of more than $100.00	DD, BCD	10 yrs.	Total
	Any firearm, explosive or incendiary device	DD, BCD	10 yrs.	Total
	Damaging, destroying, losing or suffering to be lost, damaged, destroyed, sold, or wrongfully disposed:			
	Through neglect, of a value of:			
	$100.00 or less	None	6 mos.	2/3 6 mos.
	More than $100.00	BCD	1 yr.	Total
	Willfully, of a value of			
	$100.00 or less	BCD	1 yr.	Total
	More than $100.00	DD, BCD	10 yrs.	Total
	Any firearm, explosive, or incendiary device	DD, BCD	10 yrs.	Total
109	Property other than military property of U.S.: loss, damage, destruction, disposition:			
	Wasting, spoiling, destroying, or damaging property of a value of:			
	$100.00 or less	BCD	1 yr.	Total
	More than $100.00	DD, BCD	5 yrs.	Total
110	Hazarding a vessel			
	Willfully and wrongfully	Death, DD, BCD	Life	Total
	Negligently	DD, BCD	2 yrs.	Total
111	Drunken driving			
	Resulting in personal injury	DD, BCD	1 yr., 6 mos.	Total
	Other cases	BCD	6 mos.	Total
112	Drunk on duty	BCD	9 mos.	Total
112a	Wrongful use, possession, etc. of controlled substances [3]			
	Wrongful use, possession, manufacture, or introduction of:			
	Amphetamine, cocaine, heroin, lysergic acid diethylamide, marijuana (except possession of less than 30 grams or use), methamphetamine, opium, phencyclidine, secobarbital, and Schedule I, II, and III controlled substances	DD, BCD	5 yrs.	Total
	Marijuana (possession of less than 30 grams or use), phenobarbital, and Schedule IV and V controlled substances	DD, BCD	2 yrs.	Total
	Wrongful distribution of, or, with intent to distribute, wrongful possession, manufacture, introduction, or wrongful importation of or exportation of:			
	Amphetamine, cocaine, heroin, lysergic acid diethylamide,			

MAXIMUM PUNISHMENT CHART

This chart was compiled for convenience purposes only and is not the authority for specific punishments. *See* Part IV and R.C.M. 1003 for specific limits and additional information concerning maximum punishments.

Article	Offense	Discharge	Confinement	Forfeitures
	marijuana, methamphetamine, opium, phencyclidine, secobarbital,			
	and Schedule I, II, and III controlled substances	DD, BCD	15 yrs.	Total
	Phenobarbital and Schedule IV and V controlled substances	DD, BCD	10 yrs.	Total
113	Misbehavior of sentinel or lookout			
	In time of war	Death, DD, BCD	Life	Total
	In other time:			
	While receiving special pay under 37 U.S.C. 310	DD, BCD	10 yrs.	Total
	Other places	DD, BCD	1 yr.	Total
114	Dueling	DD, BCD	1 yr.	Total
115	Malingering			
	Feigning illness, etc.			
	In time of war, or while receiving special pay under 37 U.S.C. 310	DD, BCD	3 yrs.	Total
	Other	DD, BCD	1 yr.	Total
	Intentional self-inflicted injury			
	In time of war, or while receiving special pay under 37 U.S.C. 310	DD, BCD	10 yrs.	Total
	Other	DD, BCD	5 yrs.	Total
116	Riot	DD, BCD	10 yrs.	Total
	Breach of peace	None	6 mos.	2/3 6 mos.
117	Provoking speech, gestures	None	6 mos.	2/3 6 mos.
118	Murder			
	Article 118(1) or (4)	Death, mandatory minimum life, DD, BCD	Life	Total
	Article 118(2) or (3)	DD, BCD	Life	Total
119	Manslaughter			
	Voluntary	DD, BCD	10 yrs.	Total
	Involuntary	DD, BCD	3 yrs.	Total
120	Rape	Death, DD, BCD	Life	Total
	Carnal knowledge	DD, BCD	15 yrs.	Total
121	Larceny			
	Of military property of a value of $100.00 or less	BCD	1 yr.	Total
	Of property other than military property of a value of $100.00 or less	BCD	6 mos.	Total
	Of military property of a value of more than $100.00 or of any military motor vehicle, aircraft, vessel, firearm, or explosive	DD, BCD	10 yrs.	Total
	Of property other than military property of a value of more than $100.00 or any motor vehicle, aircraft, vessel, firearm, or explosive	DD, BCD	5 yrs.	Total
	Wrongful appropriation			
	Of value of $100.00 or less	None	3 mos.	2/3 3 mos.
	Of value of more than $100.00	BCD	6 mos.	Total
	Of vehicle, aircraft, vessel	DD, BCD	2 yrs.	Total
122	Robbery			
	Committed with a firearm	DD, BCD	15 yrs.	Total
	Other cases	DD, BCD	10 yrs.	Total
123	Forgery	DD, BCD	5 yrs.	Total

This chart was compiled for convenience purposes only and is not the authority for specific punishments. *See* Part IV and R.C.M. 1003 for specific limits and additional information concerning maximum punishments.

Article	Offense	Discharge	Confinement	Forfeitures
123a	Checks, etc., insufficient funds, intent to deceive			
	To procure anything of value of:			
	$100.00 or less	BCD	6 mos.	Total
	More than $100.00	DD, BCD	5 yrs.	Total
	For payment of past due obligation, and other cases	BCD	6 mos.	Total
124	Maiming	DD, BCD	7 yrs.	Total
125	Sodomy			
	By force and without consent	DD, BCD	20 yrs.	Total
	With child under age of 16 years	DD, BCD	20 yrs.	Total
	Other cases	DD, BCD	5 yrs.	Total
126	Arson			
	Aggravated	DD, BCD	20 yrs.	Total
	Other cases, where property value is:			
	$100.00 or less	DD, BCD	1 yr.	Total
	More than $100.00	DD, BCD	5 yrs.	Total
127	Extortion	DD, BCD	3 yrs.	Total
128	Assaults			
	Simple assault	None	3 mos.	2/3 3 mos.
	Assault consummated by battery	BCD	6 mos.	Total
	Assault upon commissioned officer of U.S. or friendly power not in execution of office	DD, BCD	3 yrs.	Total
	Assault upon warrant officer, not in execution of office	DD, BCD	1 yr., 6 mos.	Total
	Assault upon noncommissioned or petty officer not in execution of office	BCD	6 mos.	Total
	Assault upon, in execution of office, person serving as sentinel, lookout, security policeman, military policeman, shore patrol, master at arms, or civil law enforcement	DD, BCD	3 yrs.	Total
	Assault consummated by battery upon child under age of 16 years	DD, BCD	2 yrs.	Total
	Assault with dangerous weapon or means likely to produce grievous bodily harm or death:			
	Committed with loaded firearm	DD, BCD	8 yrs.	Total
	Other cases	DD, BCD	3 yrs.	Total
	Assault in which grievous bodily harm is intentionally inflicted:			
	With a loaded firearm	DD, BCD	10 yrs.	Total
	Other cases	DD, BCD	5 yrs.	Total
129	Burglary	DD, BCD	10 yrs.	Total
130	Housebreaking	DD, BCD	5 yrs.	Total
131	Perjury	DD, BCD	5 yrs.	Total
132	Frauds against the United States			
	Offenses under article 132(1) or (2)	DD, BCD	5 yrs.	Total
	Offenses under article 132(3) or (4)			
	$100.00 or less	BCD	6 mos.	Total
	More than $100.00	DD, BCD	5 yrs.	Total
133	Conduct unbecoming officer (*see* Part IV, para. 59e)	Dismissal	1 yr. or as prescribed	Total

APP. 30 — MAXIMUM PUNISHMENT CHART

This chart was compiled for convenience purposes only and is not the authority for specific punishments. *See* Part IV and R.C.M. 1003 for specific limits and additional information concerning maximum punishments.

Article	Offense	Discharge	Confinement	Forfeitures
134	Abusing public animal	None	3 mos.	2/3 3 mos.
	Adultery	DD, BCD	1 yr.	Total
	Assault, indecent	DD, BCD	5 yrs.	Total
	Assault			
	With intent to commit murder or rape	DD, BCD	20 yrs.	Total
	With intent to commit voluntary manslaughter, robbery, sodomy, arson, or burglary	DD, BCD	10 yrs.	Total
		DD, BCD	5 yrs.	Total
	With intent to commit housebreaking	DD, BCD	2 yrs.	Total
	Bigamy	DD, BCD	5 yrs.	Total
	Bribery	DD, BCD	3 yrs.	Total
	Graft	DD, BCD	10 yrs.	Total
	Burning with intent to defraud			
	Check, worthless, making and uttering—by dishonorably failing to maintain funds	BCD	6 mos.	Total
	Cohabitation, wrongful	None	4 mos.	2/3 4 mos.
	Correctional custody, escape from	DD, BCD	1 yr.	Total
	Correctional custody, breach of	BCD	6 mos.	Total
	Debt, dishonorably failing to pay	BCD	6 mos.	Total
	Disloyal statements	DD, BCD	3 yrs.	Total
	Disorderly conduct			
	Under such circumstances as to bring discredit	None	4 mos.	2/3 4 mos.
	Other cases	None	1 mo.	2/3 1 mo.
	Drunkenness			
	Aboard ship or under such circumstances as to bring discredit	None	3 mos.	2/3 3 mos.
	Other cases	None	1 mo.	2/3 1 mo.
	Drunk and disorderly			
	Aboard ship	BCD	6 mos.	Total
	Under such circumstances as to bring discredit	None	6 mos.	2/3 6 mos.
	Other cases	None	3 mos.	2/3 3 mos.
	Drinking liquor with prisoner	None	3 mos.	2/3 3 mos.
	Drunk prisoner	None	3 mos.	2/3 3 mos.
	Drunkenness—incapacitating oneself for performance of duties through prior indulgence in intoxicating liquor or drugs	None	3 mos.	2/3 3 mos.
	False or unauthorized pass offenses			
	Possessing or using with intent to defraud or deceive, or making, altering, counterfeiting, tampering with, or selling	DD, BCD	3 yrs.	Total
	All other cases	BCD	6 mos.	Total
	False pretenses, obtaining services under			
	Of a value of $100.00 or less	BCD	6 mos.	Total

This chart was compiled for convenience purposes only and is not the authority for specific punishments. *See* Part IV and R.C.M. 1003 for specific limits and additional information concerning maximum punishments.

Article	Offense	Discharge	Confinement	Forfeitures
	Of a value of more than $100.00	DD, BCD	5 yrs.	Total
	False swearing	DD, BCD	3 yrs.	Total
	Firearm, discharging—through negligence	None	3 mos.	2/3 3 mos.
	Firearm, discharging—willfully, under such circumstances as to endanger human life	DD, BCD	1 yr.	Total
	Fleeing scene of accident	BCD	6 mos.	Total
	Fraternization	Dismissal	2 yrs.	Total
	Gambling with subordinates	None	3 mos.	2/3 3 mos.
	Homicide, negligent	BCD	1 yr.	Total
	Impersonation			
	With intent to defraud	DD, BCD	3 yrs.	Total
	All other cases	BCD	6 mos.	Total
	Indecent act, liberties with child	DD, BCD	7 yrs.	Total
	Indecent exposure	BCD	6 mos.	Total
	Indecent language			
	Communicated to child under 16 yrs	DD, BCD	2 yrs.	Total
	Other cases	BCD	6 mos.	Total
	Indecent acts with another	DD, BCD	5 yrs.	Total
	Jumping from vessel into the water	BCD	6 mos.	Total
	Kidnapping	DD, BCD	Life	Total
	Mail, taking, opening, secreting, destroying, or stealing	DD, BCD	5 yrs.	Total
	Mails, depositing or causing to be deposited obscene matters in	DD, BCD	5 yrs.	Total
	Misprision of serious offense	DD, BCD	3 yrs.	Total
	Obstructing justice	DD, BCD	5 yrs.	Total
	Wrongful interference with an adverse administrative proceeding	DD, BCD	5 yrs.	Total
	Pandering	DD, BCD	5 yrs.	Total
	Prostitution	DD, BCD	1 yr.	Total
	Parole, violation of	BCD	6 mos.	2/3 6 mos.
	Perjury, subornation of	DD, BCD	5 yrs.	Total
	Public record, altering, concealing, removing, mutilating, obliterating, or destroying	DD, BCD	3 yrs.	Total
	Quarantine, breaking	None	6 mos.	2/3 6 mos.
	Restriction, breaking	None	1 mo.	2/3 1 mo.
	Seizure, destruction, removal, or disposal of property to prevent	DD, BCD	1 yr.	Total
	Self-injury without intent to avoid service			
	In time of war, or in a hostile fire pay zone	DD	5 yrs.	Total
	Other	DD	2 yrs.	Total
	Sentinel, lookout			
	Disrespect to	None	3 mos.	2/3 3 mos.
	Loitering or wrongfully sitting on post by			
	In time of war or while receiving special pay	DD, BCD	2 yrs.	Total
	Other cases	BCD	6 mos.	Total
	Soliciting another to commit an offense (*see* Part IV, para. 105e)			

APP. 30 — MAXIMUM PUNISHMENT CHART

This chart was compiled for convenience purposes only and is not the authority for specific punishments. *See* Part IV and R.C.M. 1003 for specific limits and additional information concerning maximum punishments.

Article	Offense	Discharge	Confinement	Forfeitures
134	Stolen property, knowingly receiving, buying, concealing			
	Of a value of $100.00 or less	BCD	6 mos.	Total
	Of a value of more than $100.00	DD, BCD	3 yrs.	Total
	Straggling	None	3 mos.	2/3 3 mos.
	Testify, wrongfully refusing to	DD, BCD	5 yrs.	Total
	Threat, bomb, or hoax	DD, BCD	5 yrs.	Total
	Threat, communicating	DD, BCD	3 yrs.	Total
	Unlawful entry	BCD	6 mos.	Total
	Weapon, concealed, carrying	BCD	1 yr.	Total
	Wearing unauthorized insignia, decoration, badge, ribbon, device, or lapel button	BCD	6 mos.	Total

Notes:
1. Suspended in time of war.
2. *See* paragraph 16e(1) & (2) Note, Part IV
3. When any offense under paragraph 37, Part IV, is committed: while the accused is on duty as a sentinel or lookout; on board a vessel or aircraft used by or under the control of the armed forces; in or at a missile launch facility used by or under the control of the armed forces; while receiving special pay under 37 U.S.C. sec. 310; in time of war; or in a confinement facility used by or under the control of the armed forces, the maximum period of confinement authorized for such offense shall be increased by 5 years.

APPENDIX 31
PUNISHMENTS CHART
JURISDICTIONAL LIMITS

Type	CHL	Forfeitures	Punitive Discharge
Summary	1 Month[1]	2/3 per month (1 month)	None
Special	6 Months[2]	2/3 per month (6 months)	None
BCD Special	6 Months[3]	2/3 per month (6 months)	BCD[3]
General[4]	See Table of Maximum Punishments	Total Forfeitures	BCD DD Dismissal

[1] A Summary Court-Martial may only impose CHL and hard labor without confinement on persons in the grade of E-4 and below.

[2] A Special Court-Martial may only impose CHL on enlisted persons.

[3] In order to impose a BCD, a Special Court-Martial must:
  (1) Be convened by a General Court-Martial Convening Authority (Army)
  (2) Have a Military Judge detailed
  (3) Have a Defense Counsel within the meaning of Article 27(b) detailed
  (4) Have a verbatim Record of Trial

[4] A General Court-Martial may impose the death penalty when authorized and when referred to trial as a capital case by the Convening Authority.

NOTE: Chart derived from DA Pam 27-18.

PUNISHMENTS CHART
(TYPES OF PUNISHMENTS)

Type of punishment	Persons	Limitations as to type of court	Other limitations
Admonition and Reprimand	Anyone	Any court	None
Restriction	Anyone	Any court	60 days maximum regardless of court
Hard Labor w/o Confinement	Anyone	Any court	Summary: 45 days Special and General: 3 months
Confinement at Hard Labor	Enlisted persons only	Officers and Warrant Officers[1] GCM Only Enlisted persons: Any court	See Chart on Court-Martial punishment limitations
Bad Conduct Discharge	Enlisted persons only	Special Court (BCD) or General Court	None
Dishonorable Discharge	Warrant officers and enlisted persons	General court only	None
Dismissal	Officers only[2]	Any court	None
Reduction in Grade	Enlisted persons only	Any court	General & Special: to lowest enlisted grade Summary: E-5 and above, 1 grade; E-4 and below: to lowest enlisted grade
Forfeiture of Pay[3]	Anyone	Any court	See Chart on Court-Martial Punishment Limitations
Fine[4]	Anyone	Any court	Special and Summary: in lieu of forfeiture General: in addition to forfeiture

[1] Will not exceed maximum authorized by MCM.
[2] Includes Commissioned Officers and Commissioned Warrant Officers.
[3] May not exceed 2/3 pay per month by any court if no confinement is adjudged.
[4] Normally used where the accused is unjustly enriched or to punish contempt.

APPENDIX 32
SPECIAL FINDINGS

FORMAT A

United States of America	)	Headquarters, III Corps, Fort Hood
v.	)	
Sergeant Jean Birdbath 234-56-789, US Army Co A, 2d Bn, 2d Inf	)	SPECIAL AND GENERAL FINDINGS

On 14 January 199X charges were preferred against the accused, Sergeant Jean Birdbath, 234-56-789, alleging desertion on or about 15 August 199X from his organization, to wit: Company A, 2d Battalion, 2d Infantry, located at Fort Hood, Texas, until he was apprehended on or about 28 December 199X in violation of Article 85, UCMJ.

On 15 January 199X the accused was served with a copy of the charges, which were referred to trial by general court-martial by the Commanding General, III Corps, on 12 February 199X. Thereafter, the accused, after consultation with counsel and knowing the identity of the military judge, requested in writing under Article 16(1)(B), UCMJ, that he be tried by a court composed only of a military judge.

On 20 February 199X the accused having appeared with counsel, entered a plea of not guilty to desertion but guilty to the lesser-included offense of absence without leave, in violation of Article 86, UCMJ.

The issues raised by said pleading were duly heard before this court on 20 February 199X and evidence received from the government and the accused.

This court decides and finds as follows:

1. The accused, Sergeant Jean Birdbath, at all the times herein mentioned was and now is a member of the United States Army.

2. The accused, Sergeant Jean Birdbath, did on 15 August 199X, absent himself without proper authority from his organization, to wit: Company A, 2d Battalion, 2d Infantry, located at Fort Hood, Texas.

3. The accused, Sergeant Jean Birdbath, intended at the time of absenting himself, to remain away permanently from his organization.

4. The accused, Sergeant Jean Birdbath, remained so absent until 28 December 199X, when he was apprehended at San Francisco, California.

5. The testimony of Sergeant Richard Roe, a witness for the defense, was unworthy of belief. Sergeant Roe, a friend of the accused, stated that the accused told him he intended to return to his unit after a short absence. Sergeant Roe's answers were given in a halting, hesitant, and evasive manner. His friendship for the accused, his demeanor on the stand, and inconsistencies in his testimony convinced me that he was not telling the truth.

6. Prosecution evidence supporting the element of intent to remain absent permanently was most compelling. It was shown that the accused attempted to dispose of his uniform at the time he absented himself; that he used an assumed name during his unlawful absence; that he accepted permanent civilian employment, and that he expressed dissatisfaction with military service.

7. Upon the evidence in this case the accused is guilty beyond reasonable doubt of desertion terminated by apprehension as charged in the specification of the charge.

APP. 32   SPECIAL FINDINGS   APP. 32

Sergeant Birdbath, it is my duty as military judge to inform you that this court finds you of the specification and charge: Guilty.

Dated: _____   _____
                                             Military Judge

FORMAT B

United States of America	)	Fort Blank, Missouri
	)	
v.	)	
	)	
PVT (E-2) Roger Holliday 000-00-000,	)	SPECIAL AND GENERAL
U.S. Army Company B, 20th Signal	)	FINDINGS
Battalion, 20th Infantry Division	)	
Dated: 23 August 199X	)	

Pursuant to Article 51(d), UCMJ, the following findings are made:

SPECIAL FINDINGS: CHARGE I

1. On 2 August 199X PVT Holliday had in his possession .02 ounces more or less of marijuana.

2. PVT Holliday's possession of such marijuana was knowing.

3. The chain of custody established by the prosecution was sufficient to show beyond a reasonable doubt that the substance seized from PVT Holliday was the substance later identified as marijuana by CWO Komura of the CID Laboratory.

4. The testimony of PVT Holliday that he was unaware that the substance found on him was marijuana was not credible. The marijuana was found in a package in PVT Holliday's footlocker. He also admitted that he did tell PVTs Dale and Elk that he had some grass, although he testified that he was just joking.

5. Upon the evidence in this case the accused is guilty beyond reasonable doubt of wrongful possession of marijuana as alleged in the specification of Charge I.

APPENDIX 33

ADVICE ON APPELLATE RIGHTS

UNITED STATES	)	
	)	
v.	)	STATEMENTS REGARDING
	)	APPELLATE RIGHTS
_____	)	

I hereby certify that I have advised the defendant of his appellate rights in accordance with R.C.M. 502(d)(6), Manual for Courts-Martial.

_____
(Signature of Counsel)

_____
(Date)

STATEMENT OF DEFENDANT

Having been advised of my appellate rights, including that in the event my case is referred to the Coast Guard Court of Criminal Appeals I have the right to be represented before that Court by appellate defense counsel detailed by the Chief Counsel or by civilian counsel provided by me, or by both, pursuant to Article 70, UCMJ, I state the following:

_____ I desire to be represented before the Court of Criminal Appeals by appellate defense counsel detailed by the Chief Counsel of the Coast Guard.

_____ I intend to retain civilian counsel whose name and address will be furnished to the Chief Counsel of the Coast Guard. (If name and address of counsel are currently available, so state: _____).

_____ I do not desire to be represented by appellate defense counsel before the Court of Criminal Appeals.

_____
(Signature of Defendant)

_____
(Date)

Note: Taken from Coast Guard Military Justice Manual.

APPENDIX 34

APPLICATION FOR DEFERMENT

UNITED STATES   )
)   Fort Blank, Missouri
)
v.   )   APPLICATION FOR
)   DEFERMENT
)
)

THRU: Staff Judge Advocate
      Fort Blank, Missouri
To: Commander
      Fort Blank, Missouri

1. Under the provisions of Article 57(a), Uniform Code of Military Justice, the accused requests that the confinement portion of (his)(her) sentence adjudged on ____ 19 ____ by the (General) (Special) (Summary) Court-Martial convened by Court-Martial Convening Order Number ____, Headquarters, Fort Blank, Missouri, dated _____ 19____, be deferred until (*specified date*) (*the date the sentence is ordered into execution*) (_____).

2. The accused submits:

   a. that the purpose of the deferment provision of Article 57(d), UCMJ, is to increase the post-conviction safeguards and remedies available to the accused, p. 4504, Senate Report Number 1601, 90th Congress, Second Session, and to remedy the situation of an accused serving his sentence of confinement before appellate review, which may result in reversal, is completed. *United States v. Corley*, 5 M.J. 558, 568 (A.C.M.R. 1978);

   b. that (he)(she) is not a danger to the community;

   c. that there is no likelihood that (he)(she) may repeat the offense(s) of which (he)(she) has been convicted;

   d. that there is no substantial risk that (he)(she) will commit a serious crime;

   e. that there is no likelihood that (he)(she) will flee to avoid the service of (his)(her) sentence and that there is no substantial risk that (he)(she) will not appear to answer the judgment following the conclusion of appellate proceedings; and

   f. that there is no likelihood that (he)(she) will intimidate witnesses or otherwise interfere with the administration of justice.

3. The following establishes that the accused is not a danger to the community and that (he)(she) will not flee the jurisdiction:

   a. The offenses of which the accused was convicted are nonviolent;

   b. The accused has never previously been convicted of a crime nor has (he)(she) been punished under the provisions of Article 15, UCMJ;

   c. The offense was one of impulse which will not be repeated;

   d. The accused's first sergeant, company commander, and supervisor all testified at trial that the accused is a hard worker and a nonviolent person. All testified they would like (him)(her) back in the unit immediately;

   e. The accused was not in any restraint during the investigation of the offenses prior to preferral of charges nor during the pretrial proceedings after preferral of charges;

   f. The accused made no attempt to flee the jurisdiction prior to trial;

g. The accused (has custody of (his)(her) minor daughter who lives with (him)(her)) (is the sole support for his wife and children who live with him in off-post quarters). Said quarters are owned by the accused subject to a home mortgage for which the accused must make monthly payments) (_____).

h. The accused has substantial investments in the local area to wit: (home improvement loan) (loan secured by personal property) the security for which may be forfeited if the accused flees.

i....

4. The following errors which substantially prejudiced the accused were committed at trial:

a. The military judge improperly admitted into evidence Prosecution Exhibits 1, 2, and 3 which were obtained as a result of an illegal search and seizure;

b. The military judge improperly admitted into evidence a pretrial statement of the accused (Prosecution Exhibit 7) which was obtained in violation of Article 31, UCMJ;

c. The military judge improperly permitted a prosecution witness (name of witness) to testify as to an ultimate issue in the case in violation of Military Rules of Evidence 702, 704; and

d. The military judge improperly permitted a prosecution witness (name of witness) to refresh his memory in violation of Military Rule of Evidence 612.

JOHN SMITH
PFC, US Army
Accused

SAMUEL FREUM
CPT, JAGC
Defense Counsel

Dated: _____

NOTE: This form was derived from DA Pam 27-10. Paragraph 3 should be tailored to those facts and circumstances of the particular case which tend to prove that the accused is not a danger to the community and is not a risk to flee the jurisdiction. For example, the fact that an accused had sole custody of his minor daughter and had substantial personal property in the local community may be sufficient to establish the absence of a flight risk. *United States v. Brown*, 6 M.J. 338 (C.M.A. 1978). On the other hand, merely setting forth conclusions that the accused will not flee nor commit a serious offense is insufficient to establish the accused's entitlement to deferment. *United States v. Thomas*, 7 M.J. 763 (A.C.M.R. 1979). Similarly, indicating that the accused had twenty-six months creditable service, was promoted to the grade of SP4, was being considered for promotion to E-5, was the distinguished graduate in his AIT class at Fort Dix for which he had received a letter of commendation, that his superiors and peers in the motor pool regarded him as trustworthy and reliable, that he graduated at the top of his class at the Primary Noncommissioned Officer Course and that he would submit a petition for clemency may establish grounds for clemency but does not adequately ... [allege] ... facts relevant to deferment of confinement. *United States v. Alicea-Baez*, 7 M.J. 989, 991 (A.C.M.R. 1979).

APPENDIX 35

SAMPLE POST-TRIAL RECOMMENDATION

**Recommendation of the
Staff Judge Advocate**
United States v. Orwell

(date)

SUBJECT: Staff Judge Advocate's Recommendation in the (General) (Special) Court-Martial Case of *United States v. James Orwell*.
Commander
1984th Division
Fort Farm, MO 12345

1. This is my recommendation under R.C.M. 1106 in the (General) (Special) court-martial case of *United States v. James Orwell*, Specialist Four, U.S. Army, 123-45-6789, Headquarters and Headquarters Company, 1984th Division.

2. In accordance with his plea the accused was found guilty of the following offense(s): (brief statement of each offense; *e.g.*, wrongful possession of marijuana on 13 Aug 84; wrongful distribution of marijuana on 13 Aug 84; aggravated assault on a military policeman on 13 Aug 84). [The accused was found not guilty of the following offense(s): (brief statement of each offense).] The court-martial adjudged the following sentence: (brief description of sentence; *e.g.*, dishonorable discharge, confinement for four years, forfeiture of all pay and allowances, and reduction to the lowest enlisted grade). [*This paragraph could be done in a chart format.*] [The following is a summary of the charges, specifications, pleas, findings and sentence in this case:

CH.	ART.	SPEC.	GIST OF OFFENSE	PLEA	FIND
I	112(a)	1	Possession of marijuana on 13 Aug 84	G	G
I	112(a)	2	Distribution of marijuana on 13 Aug 84	G	G
II	128		Aggravated assault on 13 Aug 84	G	G
Sentence adjudged:			DD, Conf. 30 months, TF, RED-LEG]		

3. The accused has been in the Army for 32 months. His MOS is 91T, animal care specialist. He has received the Army Service Ribbon. He has one prior conviction by a summary court-martial for a 3-day AWOL and one instance of nonjudicial punishment. [*This paragraph may be a more extensive resumé of the service member's career when appropriate.*]

4. The accused was not subject to any pretrial restraint. [The accused was in (pretrial confinement) (restriction) for 36 days before trial.]

5. The accused pleaded guilty pursuant to a pretrial agreement in which you agreed to approve a sentence no greater than a bad-conduct discharge, confinement for 30 months, forfeiture of all pay and allowances and reduction to the lowest enlisted grade.

Accordingly, you cannot approve any sentence in excess of the terms of the agreement. [The accused's plea of guilty was entered pursuant to a pretrial agreement in which you agreed to limit the maximum punishment to a bad-conduct discharge, confinement for 30 months, forfeiture of all pay and allowances, and reduction to the lowest enlisted grade. The agreement also obligated the accused to testify in the court-martial of SSG Farmer, a suspected drug dealer. The accused refused to testify at that trial on 30 September 1984. Accordingly, you are not bound by the sentence limitation contained in the pretrial agreement.] [*If the accused has not submitted matters under R.C.M. 1105 which allege legal error and the staff judge advocate does not deem it appropriate for the convening authority to take corrective action on the findings or sentence, the following paragraph is unnecessary.*]

6. The accused submitted a memorandum (attached at Tab A) pursuant to R.C.M. 1105(b)(1) alleging that testimony was improperly admitted in presentencing proceedings and asking you to reduce the severity of the sentence. I disagree. [The accused's offenses consisted of selling some marijuana from the front seat of the commander's official car to an undercover police agent. When the military policeman then apprehended the accused, the accused assaulted him with the car. The military judge properly allowed the accused's commander to describe these offenses. Such misconduct merits a severe sentence. Accordingly, no corrective action is necessary.] [*The following paragraph is only used when the staff judge advocate deems it appropriate to call additional matters to the convening authority's attention. Such matters may be from outside the record of trial. But see R.C.M. 1107(b)(3)(B)(iii).*]

7. In a stipulation of expected testimony your predecessor condemned the accused's misconduct but added that SP4 Orwell was a competent driver and had rehabilitation potential. [*This paragraph could also call the convening authority's attention to matters other than legal errors, if any, in the accused's matters submitted under R.C.M. 1105. Such matters need not be discussed in the post-trial recommendation.*]

8. I recommend that you approve only so much of the sentence adjudged as provides for a bad-conduct discharge, confinement for 30 months, forfeiture of all pay and allowances, and reduction to the lowest enlisted grade. [The accused's motive for not testifying was a threat to his life made by SSG Farmer. Under these circumstances, I think he should retain the benefit of his pretrial agreement.] [I recommend that you approve the sentence as adjudged.] If you agree with this recommendation an action designed to accomplish the foregoing is attached at Tab B.

9. This recommendation has been served on the defense counsel who then had five days to submit a response. If the defense counsel submitted a response, it is attached at Tab A for your consideration.

AL S. BABYLON
LTC. JAGC
Staff Judge Advocate

Note: Taken from ARMY LAW., July 1984.

APPENDIX 36
PROMULGATING ORDERS

DEPARTMENT OF THE ARMY
Headquarters, 20th Infantry Division
Fort Blank, Missouri 63889

GENERAL COURT-MARTIAL ORDER 2 September 1992
NUMBER 3

Before a general court-martial which convened at Fort Blank, Missouri, pursuant to Court-Martial Convening Order Number 1, this headquarters, dated 1 August 1992, was arraigned and tried: Private (E2) John Doe, 102-23-3446, US Army, Company A, 1st Battalion, 66th Infantry, Fort Blank, Missouri 63889.

The accused was arraigned on the following offenses and the following findings or other dispositions were reached:

Charge I. Article 86. (Guilty).
Specification 1: Unauthorized absence from unit from 1 April 1992 to 31 May 1992. (Guilty).
Specification 2: Failure to repair on 18 March 1984. (Dismissed on motion of defense for failure to state an offense).
Charge II. Article 91. (Not guilty).
Specification: Disrespect to superior noncommissioned officer on 30 March 1992 by saying to him Stick it in your ear. (Not guilty).
Charge III. Article 112a. (Guilty).
Specification 1: Wrongful possession of 150 grams of marijuana on 24 March 1992. (Guilty).
Specification 2: Wrongful use of marijuana while on duty as a sentinel on 24 March 1992. (Guilty).
Specification 3: Wrongful possession of heroin with intent to distribute on 24 March 1992. (Guilty).
Charge IV. Article 121. (Guilty).
Specification 1: Larceny of property of a value of $150.00 on 26 March 1992. (Guilty).
Specification 2: Larceny of property of a value of $125.00 on 27 March 1992. (Not guilty of larceny, but Guilty of wrongful appropriation).
Charge V: Article 134 (Guilty; Article 128).
Specification: Assault on 25 March 1992 with intent to commit robbery. (Not guilty, but Guilty of assault and battery).
Additional Charge. Article 121. (Guilty).
Specification 1: (Redesignated the Specification). Larceny of property of a value of $150.00 on 1 June 1992. (By consolidation with Specification 2, Guilty of larceny of property of a value of $350.00 on 1 June 1992).
Specification 2: Larceny of property of a value of $200.00 on 1 June 1984. (Dismissed upon consolidation with Specification 1 by the military judge).
The findings of guilty as to Charge I, Specification 1 and Charge IV, Specification 2 were based on accused's pleas of guilty. The accused pleaded not guilty to the remaining charges and specifications.

SENTENCE

The military judge adjudged the following sentence on 29 August 1992. Dishonorable discharge, forfeiture of all pay and allowances, confinement for 2 years, and reduction to the lowest enlisted grade.

APP. 36   PROMULGATING ORDERS   APP. 36

ACTION

DEPARTMENT OF THE ARMY
Headquarters, 20th Infantry Division
Fort Blank, Missouri 63889

2 September 1992

In the case of Private (E2) John Doe, 102-23-3446, US Army, Company A, 1st Battalion, 66th Infantry, Fort Blank, Missouri, the sentence is approved and, except for the part of the sentence extending to dishonorable discharge, will be executed. The service of the sentence to confinement was deferred 29 August 1992 and the deferment is rescinded this date.

                                    /s/   John T. Blunt
                                    /t/   JOHN T. BLUNT
                                            Major General, USA
                                            Commanding

BY COMMAND OF MAJOR GENERAL BLUNT:
                                    (Signature)
DISTRIBUTION: JAMES S. SLADE
                                    CW2, USA
                                    Legal Administrator

Note: Derived from AR 27-10.

APPENDIX 37

JUDGE ADVOCATE LEGAL REVIEW

Review of a Court-Martial
by a Judge Advocate
[In Cases Forwarded to the
GCMCA Under R.C.M. 1112(e)]

(Date)

SUBJECT: Review of the (General) (Special) (Summary) Court-Martial Case of *United States v. Orwell*.
Commander
1984th Division
Fort Farm, Missouri 12345

1. Pursuant to R.C.M. 1112(a), the attached record of trial in the (general) (special) (summary) court-martial case of *United States v. James Orwell,* Specialist Four, U.S. Army, 123-45-6789, Headquarters and Headquarters Company, 1984th Division, has been reviewed by the undersigned judge advocate.

2. Based upon my review of the record (and the matters submitted by the accused under R.C.M. 1105, [1106(f)], [and 1112(d)(2)], I have concluded that:

    a. The court-martial had jurisdiction over the accused and each offense as to which there is a finding of guilty which has not been disapproved [The court-martial lacked jurisdiction over the accused] [The court-martial had jurisdiction over the accused but lacked jurisdiction over all the offenses as to which findings of guilty have been approved] [The court-martial had jurisdiction over the accused but lacked jurisdiction as to (specify which charges and specifications, e.g., charge I, specification 1). The court-martial had jurisdiction over the remaining offenses as to which there are findings of guilty which have not been disapproved];

    b. Each specification [None of the specifications] as to which there is a finding of guilty which has not been disapproved states an offense [The only specification on which there is a finding of guilty which has not been disapproved fails to state an offense] [The (specify which specification, *e.g.,* specification of charge I or first and third specifications of charge I) fail to state offenses. The remaining specifications as to which there are findings of guilty which have not been disapproved state offenses]; and

    c. The sentence is legal [The sentence is not legal].

[*These following paragraphs are only necessary if the accused has submitted written allegations of error pursuant to R.C.M. 1105, 1106(f), or 1112(d)(2)*].

3. In a memorandum submitted pursuant to R.C.M. 1105 the accused alleged that it was error for the military judge not to suppress the marijuana seized from the accused. [The military judge, in my opinion, properly ruled that the accused was lawfully apprehended at the time the marijuana was seized and, therefore, the seizure was lawful. The accused's allegation of error merits no relief.] [I agree that the seizure of the marijuana from the accused was unlawful in this case. The accused should be given appropriate relief.]

In response to the post-trial recommendation in this case, the accused alleged that the testimony of his immediate commander was improperly admitted at trial and that this inadmissible evidence was prejudicial to the accused by causing the members to impose an unduly harsh sentence. [In my opinion the military judge properly admitted the commander's testimony during the presentencing portion of the trial as evidence in aggravation (*see* R.C.M. 1001(b)(4). No sentence relief is warranted.] [I agree that the commander's testimony was under the circumstances unfairly prejudicial and should have been excluded by the judge (*see* M.R.E. 403). The accused is entitled to appropriate relief by decreasing the terms of the approved sentence.]

The accused submitted a memorandum to me during the course of my review of his record of trial. In it he alleged that it was error for the convening authority to not reduce his sentence in conformity with the pretrial agreement. [In my opinion, the failure of the accused to testify in the court-martial trial of SSG Farmer, as required by an express condition in the pretrial agreement, justified the convening authority's decision not to be bound by the terms of agreement. Accordingly, no relief is warranted.] [In my opinion the accused should have been given the benefit of his pretrial agreement. His failure to testify as required by the pretrial agreement is excusable in light of the threat made against his life by SSG Farmer. Therefore, the accused's sentence should be reduced to the terms of the agreement.] [*In cases forwarded to the GCMCA for action on a specific recommendation as to appropriate corrective action, if any, and an opinion as to whether corrective action is required by law must be stated.*]

4. In light of the foregoing discussion, I recommend that [you take no corrective action in this case as none is appropriate or required by law. Accordingly, the initially approved sentence should be approved, and, as it is thus finally affirmed, the bad-conduct discharge should be executed. If you agree with this recommendation, a form of action designed to accomplish the foregoing is attached as Tab A.] [you take corrective action in this case by disapproving the finding of guilty of charge I, specification 1 (wrongful possession of marijuana on (Date). This action is required as a matter of law because of the violation of the servicemember's constitutional rights under the 4th Amendment. If you agree with this recommendation, it would be appropriate to reduce the accused's sentence. I recommend a reduction to a bad-conduct discharge, confinement for eighteen months, forfeiture of all pay and allowances, and reduction to the lowest enlisted grade. This reduction in sentence is not required as a matter of law because the sentence as approved is not in excess of the maximum sentence which could have been adjudged for the remaining offenses. An action designed to accomplish the foregoing is attached at Tab A.] [*you take corrective action in this case by reducing the accused's sentence to a bad-conduct discharge, confinement for eighteen months, forfeiture of all pay and allowances, and reduction to the grade of Private E-1. Corrective action to reduce the sentence is required by law because the military judge improperly admitted testimony in aggravation of the accused's offenses during the presentencing stage of the trial. No specific quantity of reduction in sentence is required but in my opinion the improperly admitted evidence probably had a substantial impact on the sentence adjudged by the members. Accordingly, the substantial relief recommended is appropriate. If you agree with this recommendation an action designed to accomplish the foregoing is attached at Tab A.*] [you take corrective action in this case by reducing the accused's sentence to the agreed upon level in the pretrial agreement, to wit: a bad-conduct discharge, confinement for thirty months, forfeiture of all pay and allowances, and reduction to the lowest enlisted grade. This corrective action, although appropriate in my opinion, is not required by law. Because the accused did not fulfill his obligations under the pretrial agreement the convening authority was not bound by the sentence limitation agreed upon therein, but I think the accused's reason for not testifying as he agreed to do was a legitimate and compelling concern for his personal safety. He should

retain the benefit of his pretrial agreement. If you agree with this recommendation an action designed to accomplish the foregoing is attached at Tab A].

AL S. BABYLON
LTC, JAGC
Staff Judge Advocate

Note: Derived from the ARMY LAW., July 1984.

APPENDIX 38
WAIVER/WITHDRAWAL OF APPELLATE RIGHTS

WAIVER/WITHDRAWAL OF APPELLATE RIGHTS IN GENERAL AND SPECIAL COURTS—MARTIAL SUBJECT TO REVIEW BY A COURT OF MILITARY REVIEW

NOTE: See R.C.M. 1203(b) concerning which cases are subject to review by a Court of Military Review. See R.C.M. 1110 concerning waiver or withdrawal of appellate review.

I have read the attached action dated ——————————————————————————.

I have consulted with ————————————————————, my (associate) defense counsel concerning my appellate rights and I am satisfied with his/her advice.

I understand that:

1. If I do not waive or withdraw appellate review —

    a. My court-martial will be reviewed by the ——————————— Court of Military Review.

    b. The Court of Military Review will review my case to determine whether the findings and sentence are correct in law and fact and whether the sentence is appropriate.

    c. After review by the Court of Military Review, my case could be reviewed for legal error by the United States Court of Military Appeals, on petition by me or on request of the Judge Advocate General.

    d. If the Court of Military Appeals reviews my case, my case could be reviewed for legal error by the United States Supreme Court on petition by me or the Government.

    e. I have the right to be represented by military counsel, at no cost to me, or by civilian counsel, at no expense to the United States, or both, before the Court of Military Review, the Court of Military Appeals, and the Supreme Court.

2. If I waive or withdraw appellate review —

    a. My case will not be reviewed by the Court of Military Review, or be subject to further review by the Court of Military Appeals, or by the Supreme Court under 28 U.S.C. 1259.

    b. My case will be reviewed by a judge advocate for legal error, and I may submit in writing allegations of legal error for consideration by the judge advocate.

    c. After review by the judge advocate and final action in my case, I may petition the Judge Advocate General for correction of legal errors under Article 69(b). Such a petition must be filed within 2 years of the convening authority's action, unless I can show good cause for filing later.

    d. A waiver or withdrawal, once filed, cannot be revoked, and bars further appellate review.

Understanding the foregoing, I (waive my rights to appellate review) (withdraw my case from appellate review). I make this decision freely and voluntarily. No one has made any promises that I would receive any benefits from this waiver/withdrawal, and no one has forced me to make it.

TYPED NAME OF ACCUSED	RANK OF ACCUSED
SIGNATURE OF ACCUSED	DATE

DD FORM 2330
84 AUG

STATEMENT OF COUNSEL

(Check appropriate block)

☐ 1. I represented the accused at his/her court-martial.

☐ 2. I am associate counsel detailed under R.C.M. 1110(b). I have communicated with the accused's (detailed) (individual military) (civilian) (appellate) defense counsel concerning the accused's waiver/withdrawal and discussed this communication with the accused.

☐ 3. I am substitute counsel detailed under R.C.M. 1110(b).

☐ 4. I am a civilian counsel whom the accused consulted concerning this matter. I am a member in good standing of the bar of _____.

☐ 5. I am appellate defense counsel for the accused.

I have advised the accused of his/her appellate rights and of the consequences of waiving or withdrawing appellate review. The accused has elected to (waive) (withdraw) appellate review.

TYPED NAME OF COUNSEL	UNIT OF COUNSEL
RANK OF COUNSEL	BUSINESS ADDRESS *(If Civilian Counsel)*
SIGNATURE OF COUNSEL	DATE

☆ GPO : 1984 O - 421-646 (17050)

APPENDIX 39

VACATION PROCEEDINGS

REPORT OF PROCEEDINGS TO VACATE SUSPENSION OF A GENERAL COURT-MARTIAL SENTENCE OR OF A SPECIAL COURT-MARTIAL SENTENCE INCLUDING A BAD—CONDUCT DISCHARGE UNDER ARTICLE 72, UCMJ, and R.C.M. 1109

1a. TO: (Name of Officer exercising general court-martial jurisdiction — Last, First, MI)	2a. FROM: (Name of Officer exercising special court-martial jurisdiction — Last, First, MI)
Rabino, Arthur K.	Roberts, Leonard E.
b. TITLE Commander	**b. TITLE** Commander
c. ORGANIZATION 5000th Support Wing APO AP 99999	**c. ORGANIZATION** 5001st Support Group APO AP 99999

3a. NAME OF PROBATIONER (Last, First, MI)	b. RANK	c. SSN	d. ORGANIZATION
Dice, Morris L.	Airman	000-00-0000	5001st Support Group

4. DATA AS TO TRIAL BY COURT-MARTIAL. ATTACH A COPY OF THE COURT-MARTIAL ORDER AND ANY SUPPLEMENTARY ORDERS OR, IF NO COURT-MARTIAL ORDER HAS BEEN PROMULGATED OR IS AVAILABLE, ATTACH A SUMMARY OF THE CHARGES AND SPECIFICATIONS, FINDINGS, SENTENCE, INITIAL ACTION, AND ANY SUPPLEMENTARY ACTIONS. ATTACH A COPY OF THE WRITTEN NOTICE OF SUSPENSION (see R.C.M. 1108(c)).

5. ALLEGED VIOLATION(S) OF THE CONDITIONS OF SUSPENSION. (BRIEF STATEMENT AND DATE. See R.C.M. 1108(c) AND 1109(a) CONCERNING THE CONDITIONS OF SUSPENSION.)

Assault on Master Sgt Vic Timm, while in the execution of duties on 15 September 1993, in violation of Article 91.

(Check appropriate answer)	YES	NO
6. PURSUANT TO THE PROVISIONS OF ARTICLE 72, UCMJ, AND R.C.M. 1109, A HEARING WAS HELD ON THE ALLEGED VIOLATION(S) OF THE CONDITIONS OF SUSPENSION.	X	
7. BEFORE THE HEARING THE AUTHORITY CONDUCTING THE HEARING CAUSED THE PROBATIONER TO BE NOTIFIED OF (see R.C.M. 1109(d)(1)(B)):		
a. THE TIME, PLACE, AND PURPOSE OF THE HEARING.	X	
b. THE RIGHT TO BE PRESENT AT THE HEARING.	X	
c. THE ALLEGED VIOLATION(S) OF THE CONDITIONS OF SUSPENSION AND THE EVIDENCE EXPECTED TO BE RELIED ON.	X	
d. THE RIGHT TO BE REPRESENTED AT THE HEARING BY CIVILIAN COUNSEL PROVIDED BY THE PROBATIONER OR, UPON REQUEST, BY MILITARY COUNSEL DETAILED FOR THIS PURPOSE.	X	
e. THE OPPORTUNITY TO BE HEARD, TO PRESENT WITNESSES AND OTHER EVIDENCE, AND THE RIGHT TO CONFRONT AND CROSS-EXAMINE ADVERSE WITNESSES UNLESS THE HEARING OFFICER DETERMINES THAT THERE IS GOOD CAUSE FOR NOT ALLOWING CONFRONTATION AND CROSS-EXAMINATION.	X	
8a. THE PROBATIONER REQUESTED DETAILED MILITARY COUNSEL.	X	

b. NAME OF DETAILED COUNSEL (Last, First, MI)	c. RANK	d. ORGANIZATION
Young, Louise	Captain	Area Defense Counsel, APO AP 99999

| e. DETAILED COUNSEL WAS QUALIFIED WITHIN THE MEANING OF ARTICLE 27(b), UCMJ, and R.C.M. 502(d). | X | |

NOTE: If this form is used and additional space is required for any item, enter the additional material in Block 18 or on a separate sheet. Identify such material with the proper heading (Example: "3d"). Securely attach any additional sheet(s) and add a note in the appropriate item: "See Block 18" or "See additional sheet." This form may be used to vacate a suspended special court-martial sentence not including a bad-conduct discharge or a suspended summary court-martial sentence under R.C.M. 1109(e) by lining through or altering the form, as appropriate.

DD FORM 455, 84 AUG   EDITION OF OCT 69 IS OBSOLETE.

APP. 39   MILITARY CRIMINAL JUSTICE   APP. 39

	(Check appropriate answer)	YES	NO
9a.	THE PROBATIONER INDICATED THAT HE/SHE WOULD BE REPRESENTED BY CIVILIAN COUNSEL PROVIDED BY HIM/HER.		X
b.	NAME OF CIVILIAN COUNSEL *(Last, First, MI)* c. ADDRESS OF CIVILIAN COUNSEL		
d.	ENTRY OF APPEARANCE BY PROBATIONER'S CIVILIAN COUNSEL. I HEREBY ENTER MY APPEARANCE FOR THE ABOVE NAMED PROBATIONER AND REPRESENT THAT I AM A MEMBER IN GOOD STANDING OF THE FOLLOWING BAR(S) (LIST) OR LICENSED OR OTHERWISE AUTHORIZED TO PRACTICE LAW (EXPLAIN) *(see R.C.M. 502(d)(3) CONCERNING QUALIFICATIONS)*:		
e.	SIGNATURE OF COUNSEL f. DATE		
10a.	DETAILED COUNSEL OR CIVILIAN COUNSEL WAS PRESENT THROUGHOUT THE PROCEEDINGS. *(If probationer waives the right to have counsel present throughout part or all of the proceedings after requesting detailed counsel or employing civilian counsel, complete b below.)*	X	
b.	STATE CIRCUMSTANCES AND SPECIFIC PROCEEDINGS CONDUCTED IN ABSENCE OF COUNSEL.		
11.	*(To be signed by probationer if answer to items 8 or 9 was "No." If probationer fails to sign, the hearing officer shall explain in Item 18.)* I have been informed and understand my right under R.C.M. 1109(d) to representation at this hearing by civilian counsel provided by me or, upon request, by detailed military counsel. I hereby knowingly waive my right to such: a. ☐ Detailed Counsel b. ☒ Civilian Counsel		
c.	SIGNATURE OF PROBATIONER d. DATE 1 October 1993		
12a.	THE PROBATIONER WAS AFFORDED THE RIGHT TO OBTAIN WITNESSES AND PRODUCE EVIDENCE *(see R.C.M. 405(g))*.	X	
b.	IN THE PRESENCE OF PROBATIONER I QUESTIONED UNDER OATH ALL AVAILABLE WITNESSES AND EXAMINED DOCUMENTARY AND REAL EVIDENCE FOR BOTH SIDES. ANY DOCUMENTS AND REAL EVIDENCE WERE SHOWN TO THE PROBATIONER.	X	
c.	THE PROBATIONER WAS AFFORDED THE RIGHT TO CROSS-EXAMINE ALL AVAILABLE WITNESSES.	X	
d.	I HAVE SUMMARIZED THE EVIDENCE CONSIDERED IN EXHIBIT ___1___	X	
e.	THE FOLLOWING WITNESSES REQUESTED BY THE ACCUSED WERE NOT AVAILABLE UNDER R.C.M. 405(g) FOR THE REASONS INDICATED. *(Explain why requested witnesses were unavailable and any alternatives to testimony under R.C.M. 405(g)(4) used.)*		

NAME *(Last, First, MI)*	REASON UNAVAILABLE	ALTERNATIVES

		YES	NO
13.	AFTER HAVING BEEN INFORMED OF THE RIGHT TO REMAIN SILENT OR MAKE A STATEMENT, THE PROBATIONER		
a.	INDICATED THAT HE/SHE DID NOT WISH TO MAKE A STATEMENT.		X
b.	MADE A STATEMENT SUMMARIZED IN EXHIBIT ___2___	X	

APP. 39 — VACATION PROCEEDINGS

(Check appropriate answer)	YES	NO
14a. THERE ARE REASONABLE GROUNDS TO BELIEVE THAT THE PROBATIONER NOW OR AT THE TIME OF THE ALLEGED VIOLATION WAS NOT MENTALLY RESPONSIBLE (see R.C.M. 916(k)) OR IS NOW INCOMPETENT TO PARTICIPATE IN THE VACATION PROCEEDING (see R.C.M. 909).		X
b. INDICATE THE GROUNDS FOR SUCH BELIEF AND THE ACTION TAKEN.		
c. A REPORT OF MEDICAL OFFICERS UNDER R.C.M. 706 IS ATTACHED IN EXHIBIT _____.		X
15. IF PROBATIONER WAS CONFINED PENDING VACATION PROCEEDINGS UNDER R.C.M. 1109(c):		
a. I FIND THAT THERE IS PROBABLE CAUSE TO BELIEVE THAT THE PROBATIONER VIOLATED THE CONDITIONS OF SUSPENSION.	X	
b. I DO NOT FIND THAT THERE IS PROBABLE CAUSE TO BELIEVE THAT THE PROBATIONER VIOLATED THE CONDITIONS OF SUSPENSION AND ORDER HIS/HER RELEASE UNDER R.C.M. 1109(d)(1)(E).		
16. RECOMMENDATION OF THE OFFICER EXERCISING SPECIAL COURT-MARTIAL JURISDICTION OVER THE PROBATIONER.		
a. I RECOMMEND THAT THE SUSPENSION OF THE SENTENCE BE VACATED. (Indicate type and amount of punishment, if any, to be vacated.) Bad-Conduct Discharge	X	
b. I RECOMMEND THAT THE PROCEEDINGS TO VACATE SUSPENSION BE DROPPED.		
c. I RECOMMEND (state other recommendation):		

17a. NAME OF OFFICER EXERCISING SPECIAL COURT MARTIAL JURISDICTION OVER PROBATIONER	b. RANK	c. ORGANIZATION
Leonard E. Roberts	LTC	5001st Support Group

d. SIGNATURE: *Leonard E. Roberts*
e. DATE: 1 October 1993

18. REMARKS

Airman Basic Dice struck Master Sgt Timm in the face twice with a closed fist after Timm directed Dice to clean up his living area. Although Airman Dice testified that Timm was prejudiced against him because he was a probationer, no evidence of such bias was offered. Dice offered no other extenuating or mitigating evidence and the record reveals none. Dice had served under the suspended sentence for 2 weeks before this offense without previous incident. Dice was previously convicted by a special court-martial of disrespect and disobedience toward superior NCOs on two different occasions. I am satisfied that Dice is guilty of the offense of assaulting a superior NCO in the execution of office. I recommend that the suspension of the bad-conduct discharge be vacated.

REMARKS (Continued)

(Check appropriate answer)	YES	NO
19. DECISION OF THE OFFICER EXERCISING GENERAL COURT-MARTIAL JURISDICTION OVER PROBATIONER.		
a. VACATE SUSPENSION OF THE SENTENCE TO *(specify type/amount of punishment to be vacated)*: Suspension of bad-conduct discharge vacated.	X	
b. NOT TO VACATE.		
c. OTHER *(specify)*:		

d. IF DECISION IS TO VACATE, INDICATE EVIDENCE RELIED ON:
Testimony of Master Sgt Timm and Airman I.C. Nitt and Warren Teed established Airman Dice assaulted Timm, without provocation, while Timm was in the execution of his office. Medical report reflects Timm was bruised on check and forehead, Dice therefore violated conditions of suspension.

e. IF DECISION IS TO VACATE, INDICATE REASONS FOR VACATING:
Airman Dice's offense strikes at the heart of military discipline and reflects his failure to adapt despite second chance. Bad-conduct discharge is appropriate.

20a. NAME OF OFFICER EXERCISING GENERAL COURT-MARTIAL JURISDICTION OVER PROBATIONER Arthur K. Rubino	b. RANK MG	c. ORGANIZATION Commander 5000th Support Wing APO AP 99999
d. SIGNATURE */s/ Arthur K. Rubino*		e. DATE 30 October 1983

APPENDIX 40

SAMPLE APPLICATION FOR RELIEF UNDER ARTICLE 69, UCMJ

APPLICATION FOR RELIEF FROM COURT-MARTIAL FINDINGS AND/OR SENTENCE UNDER THE PROVISIONS OF TITLE 10, UNITED STATES CODE, SECTION 869 For use of this form, see AR 27-10; the proponent agency is TJAG.	DOCKET NUMBER (For TJAG Use)

(Read Instructions on Reverse BEFORE Completing Application)

DATA REQUIRED BY THE PRIVACY ACT OF 1974

AUTHORITY: 10 USC 869 AND 3037.
PRINCIPAL PURPOSES: To appeal your court-martial findings and/or sentence to The Judge Advocate General under the provisions of Article 69(b), UCMJ.
ROUTINE USES: To evaluate your appeal and aid in determining whether the relief sought is appropriate.
DISCLOSURE: Disclosure of the requested information is voluntary. Failure to provide complete information may delay evaluation of your appeal and may result in incomplete evaluation of your appeal.

1. NAME OF CONVICTED PERSON *(Last, First, MI)*
2. SSN
3. PRESENT GRADE OR STATUS
4. DATE OF TRIAL
5. PLACE OF TRIAL
6. COMMAND CONVENING COURT-MARTIAL
7. TYPE OF COURT-MARTIAL
   ☐ GENERAL ☐ SUMMARY ☐ SPECIAL
8. OFFENSE(S) CHARGED *(Article(s) and brief description of offense(s))*
9. PLEA(S)
10. FINDINGS OF THE COURT-MARTIAL, SENTENCE ADJUDGED, AND LATER MODIFICATIONS, IF ANY:
11. I BELIEVE RELIEF IN THE ABOVE NAMED COURT-MARTIAL IS JUSTIFIED BECAUSE: *(State fully the reasons you believe relief should be granted. The reasons must relate to at least one of the five grounds set forth in Article 69(b), UCMJ.)*
12. RELIEF REQUESTED
13. NAME AND ADDRESS OF COUNSEL ASSISTING WITH APPLICATION, IF ANY: *(Include ZIP Code)*

DA FORM 3499, AUG 84   EDITION OF MAY 69 IS OBSOLETE.

APP. 40 MILITARY CRIMINAL JUSTICE APP. 40

14. ENCLOSED ARE:

☐ A COPY OF COURT-MARTIAL ORDER(S) PROMULGATING RESULT OF TRIAL, AND LATER MODIFICATION(S), IF ANY.

☐ SWORN AFFIDAVITS, DOCUMENTS, OR OTHER MATTERS IN SUPPORT OF APPLICATION.

15. PRESENT ADDRESS OF APPLICANT *(Include ZIP Code) (Forward notification of any change)*

16. OATH OR AFFIRMATION: *(See instruction 5)*

I DO SOLEMNLY [SWEAR] [AFFIRM AND DECLARE] THAT TO THE BEST OF MY KNOWLEDGE AND BELIEF, THE STATEMENTS CONTAINED IN THIS APPLICATION *(including accompanying matters submitted)* ARE TRUE [SO HELP ME GOD]. I MAKE THIS ASSERTION UNDER THE PAINS AND PENALTIES OF FALSE SWEARING. *(Title 18, U.S. Code, Section 1001 provides a penalty of not more than $10,000 fine, five years imprisonment, or both, for knowingly making false statement in connection with this application.)*

_____
SIGNATURE OF APPLICANT

_____
NAME OF APPLICANT

SWORN TO BEFORE ME AND SUBSCRIBED IN MY PRESENCE THIS _____ DAY OF _____ 19 _____

(Seal)

INSTRUCTIONS
(Read ALL Instructions Before Completing Form)

1. Application for relief from the findings or sentence, or both, of a court-martial case which has been finally reviewed, but has not been reviewed by the United States Army Court of Military Review *(formerly Board of Review)* is governed by Chapter 14, Army Regulation 27-10, which is summarized in these instructions.

2. Article 69(b) of the Uniform Code of Military Justice *(Title 10, US Code, Section 869(b))* provides that: "The findings or sentence, or both, in a court-martial case not reviewed under subsection (a) or under section 866 of this title (Article 66) may be modified or set aside, in whole or in part, by the Judge Advocate General on the ground of newly discovered evidence, fraud on the court, lack of jurisdiction over the accused or the offense, error prejudicial to the substantial rights of the accused, or the appropriateness of the sentence."

3. Relief is authorized only when (1) the post-trial process of legal review of the case has been completed, and (2) at least one of the five grounds set forth in paragraph 2 above has been established to the satisfaction of The Judge Advocate General. Application for relief on the ground of sentence appropriateness normally will not be considered if the application is based solely on the quality of the behavior or duty performance of the convicted member after trial, or on any evidence of personal hardship not admitted at trial. For other avenues of relief, see Title 10, U.S. Code, Section 874 (Article 74, UCMJ) or 32 CFR 581.3 *(Army Board for the Correction of Military Records)*.

4. Except as provided in this paragraph, the application must be signed by the individual convicted by court-martial. In those cases where the individual is deceased, incapable of making application, or whose whereabouts are unknown, The Judge Advocate General may permit application to be made by such person as he/she determines to be competent and suitable, and to have a proper interest therein, including, but not limited to, a spouse, parent, or relative of the person convicted by court-martial substantially affected as a result of the findings or sentence, or both, which the applicant maintains should be vacated or modified. If application is not signed by the individual convicted, full explanation should be made and attached.

5. The application must be submitted under oath or affirmation executed before an official authorized to administer oaths. A notary public is usually authorized to perform this function. Military personnel on active duty may execute the application before a judge advocate or other officer authorized by Article 136(a) of the Uniform Code of Military Justice to administer oaths. Knowingly making a false statement in connection with an application for relief can be punished by a $10,000 fine, five years imprisonment, or both.

6. Applicant's entry in Item 11 should describe the reasons for the request for relief. Relevant facts which support the applicant's contentions should be included. Legal authorities may be presented in this section, or may be attached in the form of a legal brief, if applicant desires. Other matters tending to support applicant's allegations of error or impropriety, including but not limited to, sworn affidavits, official records, and other documents, may be attached. The applicant bears the burden of establishing an alleged impropriety. Unsupported allegations of matters outside the record of trial will seldom be sufficient to warrant relief.

7. A copy of the court-martial order *(or the record of trial in the case of a summary court-martial)* promulgating the findings, sentence, and action of the convening authority in the case, and a copy of any later modifying order(s), if available to the applicant, should be submitted with the application.

8. A copy of the record of trial in cases other than summary courts-martial should not be submitted.

9. If the applicant is a member of the command which convened the court-martial, or of a unit within the same general court-martial jurisdiction, the application should be submitted through the Office of the Staff Judge Advocate of that general court-martial jurisdiction. In all other cases, applications will be submitted directly to HQDA (JALS-ED), Nassif Building, 5611 Columbia Pike, Falls Church, VA 22041 and must be received on or before the last day of the 2-year period beginning on the date the sentence was approved by the convening authority. Failure to file within the prescribed time may be excused by The Judge Advocate General for good cause established by the applicant.

10. Submit only the original of this form.

11. Type, or print all entries in ink.

12. If space allotted is insufficient, attach additional sheet(s), indicating item number continued thereon.

13. Complete all items, if inapplicable, enter "None".

14. Applicant should send notice of change in address while application is pending to The Judge Advocate General at the address shown in instruction 9 above.

15. Applicant will be notified of receipt of application by The Judge Advocate General, and the result of review, when completed.

Reverse of DA Form 3499, Aug 84

☆ GPO : 1984 O - 421-646 (17044)

TABLE OF CASES

A

Abbate v. United States, 359 U.S. 187 (1959) — § 13-3(E), n. 196
Abbott, Robinson v.
Abdelkader, United States v.
Abdullah, United States v.
Abell, United States v.
Abendschein, United States v.
Abernathy, United States v.
Abilar, United States v.
Abood v. Detroit Bd. of Educ., 431 U.S. 209 (1977) — § 13-3(N)(3), n. 406
Abrams v. United States, 250 U.S. 616 (1919) — § 13-3(N)(3), n. 358
Abrecht, United States v.
Accordino, United States v.
Acemoglu, United States v.
Acevedo-Colon, United States v.
Acireno, United States v.
Acosta, United States v.
Acton, United States v.
Adam, United States v.
Adames, United States v.
Adamiak, United States v.
Adams, United States v.
Addis v. Thorsen, 32 M.J. 777 (C.G.C.M.R. 1991) — § 17-19, n. 26
Addison, United States v.
Adolph, United States v.
Advincula, United States v.
Aflague, United States v.
Aguilar v. Texas, 378 U.S. 108 (1964) — § 5-3(B), n. 37
Agurs, United States v.
Aiello, Geduldig v.
Aiello, United States v.
Aikens, United States v.
Ainsworth v. Barn Ballroom Co., 157 F.2d 97 (4th Cir. 1946) — § 13-3(N)(3), n. 408
Airhart, United States v.
Ake v. Oklahoma, 470 U.S. 68 (1985) — § 11-2(A)(3), n. 27
Alabama, NAACP v.
Albert, United States v.
Albo, United States v.
Albrecht, United States v.
Aldridge, United States v.
Alef, United States v.
Alexander, United States v.
Alford, North Carolina v.
Alford, United States v.
Ali, United States v.
Alicea-Baez, United States v.
Allen, Illinois v.

TABLE OF CASES

Allen, Ulster County Court v.
Allen, United States v.
Allen v. VanCantfort, 420 F.2d 525 (1st Cir. 1970) — § 5-10(D), n. 34; § 17-23(B), n. 17
Allgood, United States v.
Allison, Blackledge v.
Allison, United States v.
Almeida, United States v.
Almy, United States v.
Alomarestrada, United States v.
Aloyian, United States v.
Alston, United States v.
Alsup, United States v.
Alvarez, United States v.
Ame, United States v.
Amos, United States v.
Amparo, United States v.
Amundson, United States v.
Anderson, Jenkins v.
Anderson, Kahn v.
Anderson v. Laird, 466 P.2d 283 (D.C. Cir. 1912) — § 13-3(N)(3), n. 402
Anderson, United States v.
Andrade, United States v.
Andreas, United States v.
Andrews, Blameuser v.
Andrews v. Heupel, 29 M.J. 743 (A.F.C.M.R. 1989) — § 13-2(G)(1), n. 71; § 13-3(C)(3), n. 102
Andrews, United States v.
Angel, United States v.
Angelo, United States v.
Ankeny, United States v.
Annis, United States v.
Anthony, United States v.
Antonio, United States v.
Antonitis, United States v.
Anzalone, United States v.
Aponte, United States v.
Appel, United States v.
Applewhite, United States v.
Aquino, United States v.
Aragon, United States v.
Arbic, United States v.
Arceneaux, United States v.
Argersinger v. Hamlin, 407 U.S. 25 (1972) — § 3-6(C)(1), n. 9; § 3-8(B)
Arguello, United States v.
Arizona, Edwards v.
Arizona v. Hicks, 480 U.S. 321 (1987) — § 5-3(E), n. 7
Arizona, Miranda v.
Arizona v. Roberson, 486 U.S. 675 (1988) — § 5-4(B), n. 50
Arkansas, Holloway v.
Arlington Heights v. Metropolitan Housing Dev. Corp., 429 U.S. 252 (1977) — § 13-3(N)(1), n. 316

TABLE OF CASES

Armstead, United States v.
Armstrong, United States v.
Arnold, United States v.
Arrington, United States v.
Arroyo, United States v.
Arsneault, United States v.
Arthen, United States v.
Arthur, United States v.
Artis v. United States, 506 F.2d 1387 (Ct. Cl. 1974) — § 17-23(B), n. 12
Arviso, United States v.
Asbury, United States v.
Asfeld, United States v.
Ash, United States v.
Ashe v. McNamara, 355 F.2d 277 (1st Cir. 1965) — § 17-23(C)(2), n. 29
Atchison, United States v.
Atkinson, United States v.
Aue, United States v.
Augenblick v. United States, 377 F.2d 586 (Ct. Cl. 1967) — § 10-4(B)(5), n. 50
Augusztin, United States v.
Aurich, United States v.
Austin, United States v.
Autrey, United States v.
Averette, United States v.
Avery v. Georgia, 345 U.S. 559 (1953) — § 15-10(C)(3), n. 110
Avery, United States v.
Avila, United States v.
Aviz v. Carver, 36 M.J. 1026 (N.M.C.M.R. 1993) — § 9-2(D), n. 85; § 14-3(C), n. 133
Ayala, United States v.
Aycock, United States v.
Azevedo, United States v.

B

Babbitt, United States v.
Babcock, United States v.
Baca, United States v.
Bachand, United States v.
Bacon, United States v.
Badger, United States v.
Baggett v. Bullitt, 377 U.S. 360 (1964) — § 13-3(N)(2), nn. 341, 344
Bagley, United States v.
Bailey, United States v.
Baird, Eisenstadt v.
Baker v. Carr, 369 U.S. 186 (1962) — § 13-3(N)(1), n. 314
Baker, United States v.
Balagna, United States v.
Balboa, United States v.
Balcom, United States v.
Baldwin, United States v.
Ball v. United States, 163 U.S. 662 (1896) — § 13-3(E), n. 206
Ballard, United States v.

TABLE OF CASES

Ballesteros, United States v.
Ballew v. Georgia, 435 U.S. 223 (1978) — § 8-3(C)(3), n. 139
Ballew, United States v.
Baltimore City Dep't of Social Services v. Bouknight, 100 S. Ct. 900 (1990) — § 5-4(A)(2), n. 15
Banks, United States v.
Bannwarth, United States v.
Barbeau, United States v.
Barber, United States v.
Barden, United States v.
Barfield, United States v.
Barker v. Wingo, 407 U.S. 514 (1972) — § 13-3(C)(1), nn. 34, 35, 40
Barn Ballroom Co., Ainsworth v.
Barnack, United States v.
Barnard, United States v.
Barnes, Jones v.
Barnes, United States v.
Barnett v. United States, 3 M.J. 251 (C.M.A. 1977) — § 13-2(G)(1), n. 68
Barnette, United States v.
Barnette, West Virginia State Bd. of Educ. v.
Barney, United States v.
Baron v. Meloni, 602 F. Supp. 614 (D.N.Y. 1984) — § 13-3(N)(3), n. 381
Barratt, United States v.
Barraza, United States v.
Barrios, United States v.
Barror, United States v.
Barrow, United States v.
Bartell, United States v.
Bartlett, United States v.
Bartole, United States v.
Bartoletti, United States v.
Barton, United States v.
Barunas, United States v.
Barus, United States v.
Bashaw, United States v.
Basnight, United States v.
Bass, United States v.
Bassano, United States v.
Batchelder, Illinois v.
Batchelder, United States v.
Bates v. State Bar of Arizona, 433 U.S. 350 (1977) — § 13-3(N)(3), n. 372
Bates, United States v.
Batiste, United States v.
Batson v. Kentucky, 476 U.S. 79 (1986) — § 15-10(C)(3), nn. 109, 110
Battle, United States v.
Battles, United States v.
Batts, United States v.
Batzel, United States v.
Baum, United States v.
Baumgart, United States v.
Baxter, United States v.

1002

TABLE OF CASES

Bayhand, United States v.
Baylor, United States v.
Beach, United States v.
Bean, United States v.
Bearchild, United States v.
Beard, United States v.
Bearden v. Georgia, 461 U.S. 660 (1983) — § 16-3(D), n. 67
Beattie, United States v.
Beatty, United States v.
Beaty, United States v.
Beauchamp, United States v.
Beaudin, United States v.
Beauharnais v. Illinois, 343 U.S. 250 (1952) — § 13-3(N)(3), nn. 359, 369
Beaulieu, United States v.
Beaver, United States v.
Becker, United States v.
Beckermann, United States v.
Beckwith, United States v.
Bedania, United States v.
Beehler, United States v.
Beeker, United States v.
Beeks, United States v.
Beene, United States v.
Beer, United States v.
Beerey, United States v.
Begley, United States v.
Behling, United States v.
Beige, People v.
Belizaire, United States v.
Bell, United States v.
Bell v. Wolfish, 441 U.S. 520 (1979) — § 5-3(C)(4), n. 79; § 5-10(A), n. 3; § 5-10(C), nn. 15, 18
Bellett, United States v.
Belmont, United States v.
Beloney, United States v.
Belton, New York v.
Bement, United States v.
Bemis v. Whalen, 341 F. Supp. 1289 (S.D. Cal. 1912) — § 4-5(A), n. 7
Bender, United States v.
Bennett v. Tarquin, 466 F. Supp. 257 (D. Hawaii 1979) — § 3-4, n. 3; § 3-7, n. 5
Bennett, United States v.
Beno, United States v.
Benoit, United States v.
Berger, United States v.
Berger v. United States, 295 U.S. 78 (1935) — § 15-13, n. 6
Berlingeri, United States v.
Berman, United States v.
Bermudez, United States v.
Bernard, United States v.
Berner, United States v.
Bernier, United States v.

TABLE OF CASES

Berrey, United States v.
Berrigan, United States v.
Berrios, United States v.
Berry, United States v.
Berta v. United States, 9 M.J. 390 (C.M.A. 1980) — § 5-9(A), n. 5; § 5-9(E), n. 53; § 13-2(G)(1), n. 64
Bertelson, United States v.
Berue, In re
Berumen, United States v.
Bester, United States v.
Bethea, United States v.
Bethke, United States v.
Betts, United States v.
Bevacqua, United States v.
Bevins, United States v.
Beyers, California v.
Bianchi, United States v.
Bickel, United States v.
Bierley, United States v.
Biggers, Neil v.
Bilbo, United States v.
Bilby, United States v.
Billig, United States v.
Billings v. Truesdell, 311 U.S. 541 (1944) — § 4-5, n. 1; § 4-5(B), nn. 19, 20
Bindley, United States v.
Bingham, United States v.
Bins, United States v.
Birbeck, United States v.
Birdsong, United States v.
Birrell, United States v.
Bishop, United States v.
Bisser, United States v.
Biswell, United States v.
Black, United States v.
Blackburn, United States v.
Blackledge v. Allison, 431 U.S. 63 (1977) — § 14-3(A), n. 11
Blackmon, United States v.
Blair, United States v.
Blais, United States v.
Blake, United States v.
Blakey, United States v.
Blameuser v. Andrews, 630 F.2d 538 (7th Cir. 1980) — § 13-3(N)(3), nn. 371, 385, 410
Blanchard, United States v.
Blanchette, United States v.
Bland, United States v.
Blanton, United States v.
Blascak, United States v.
Blaylock, United States v.
Bledsoe, United States v.
Blevens, United States v.
Blevins, United States v.

1004

TABLE OF CASES

Blizzard, United States v.
Blockburger v. United States, 284 U.S. 299 (1931) — § 6-1(C)(3), nn. 133, 146, 152, 159
Blocker, United States v.
Blodgett v. Holden, 275 U.S. 142 (1927) — § 13-3(N)(2), n. 347
Bloss, Pearson v.
Blucker, United States v.
Bluitt, United States v.
Blunk, United States v.
Blye, United States v.
Board of Educ., Everson v.
Board of Educ., Pickering v.
Boberg, United States v.
Bobroff, United States v.
Boden, United States v.
Boehner, United States v.
Boese, United States v.
Bogar, United States v.
Bohl, United States v.
Bohle, United States v.
Bohlender, Wilson v.
Bolado, United States v.
Boland, United States v.
Bolden, United States v.
Boldon, United States v.
Boles, Oyler v.
Boles, United States v.
Bolling v. Sharpe, 347 U.S. 497 (1954) — § 13-3(M), n. 283; § 13-3(N)(1), n. 303
Bonar, United States v.
Bond, Noyd v.
Bono, United States v.
Booker, United States v.
Boone, United States v.
Booth v. Maryland, 482 U.S. 496 (1987) — § 16-5(D)(3), n. 73
Bordelon, United States v.
Boren, Craig v.
Borner, United States v.
Borys, United States v.
Bosier, United States v.
Boswell, United States v.
Boudreaux, United States v.
Boughton, United States v.
Bouie v. Columbia, 378 U.S. 347 (1964) — § 13-3(N)(5), nn. 430, 431
Bouie, United States v.
Bouknight, Baltimore City Dep't of Social Services v.
Bouknight, United States v.
Boulden, United States v.
Bouler v. United States, 1 M.J. 299 (C.M.A. 1976) — § 17-19, n. 22
Bourgette, United States v.
Bowen, United States v.
Bowerman, United States v.

1005

TABLE OF CASES

Bowers v. Hardwick, 478 U.S. 186 (1986) — § 2-9(C)(2); § 2-9(C)(2), n. 43; § 2-8(D), n. 37; § 2-9(D), nn. 59, 63
Bowers, United States v.
Bowie, United States v.
Bowler v. Wood, 1 M.J. 191 (C.M.A. 1975) — § 5-9(E), n. 53
Bowles, United States v.
Bowman, United States v.
Bowman v. Wilson, 672 F.2d 1145 (3d Cir. 1982) — § 17-23(B), n. 7
Boyce, United States v.
Boyd, United States v.
Boyett, United States v.
Boyle, United States v.
Boysen, United States v.
Brabant, United States v.
Bradford, United States v.
Bradley, United States v.
Bradley, Vance v.
Bradshaw, Oregon v.
Brady v. Maryland, 373 U.S. 83 (1963) — § 10-4(A)(4), nn. 18, 22; § 10-4(B)(1), nn. 28, 30
Brady, United States v.
Brady v. United States, 397 U.S. 742 (1970) — § 14-3, n. 7; § 14-3(A), n. 10
Bragg, United States v.
Brakebush, United States v.
Bramel, United States v.
Bramer, United States v.
Brammel, United States v.
Brandenburg v. Ohio, 396 U.S. 444 (1969) — § 13-3(N)(3), n. 368
Brandt, United States v.
Branford, United States v.
Branoff, United States v.
Bratcher, United States v.
Brathwaite, Manson v.
Brauchler, United States v.
Bray, United States v.
Breault, United States v.
Brecheen, United States v.
Breese, United States v.
Breland, United States v.
Brenton, United States v.
Breseman, United States v.
Bretz, Crist v.
Brewer, Morrisey v.
Brewer, United States v.
Brewer v. Williams, 430 U.S. 387 (1977) — § 5-4(B), nn. 30, 46
Brewster, United States v.
Brice, United States v.
Brickey, United States v.
Bridges, United States v.
Briggs, United States v.
Bright, United States v.

TABLE OF CASES

Briley, United States v.
Brinston, United States v.
Britcher, United States v.
Britt, United States v.
Britton, United States v.
Broadnax, United States v.
Broadrick v. Oklahoma, 413 U.S. 601 (1973) — § 13-3(N)(2), n. 350; § 13-3(N)(3), nn. 388, 389, 391
Broadus, United States v.
Broady, United States v.
Brodin, United States v.
Brogan, United States v.
Bromell, United States v.
Brookins v. Cullins, 23 C.M.A. 216, 49 C.M.R. 5 (1974) — § 4-14(A)(2), n. 12; § 13-2(G)(1), n. 67
Brookins, United States v.
Brooks v. Tennessee, 406 U.S. 605 (1972) — § 15-2(A), n. 15
Brooks, United States v.
Brosius, United States v.
Brothers, United States v.
Broussard, United States v.
Browers, United States v.
Brown, Carey v.
Brown v. Glines, 444 U.S. 348 (1980) — § 13-3(N)(3), nn. 377, 382, 384-386, 403; § 17-23(C)(2)
Brown, Hiatt v.
Brown v. Illinois, 422 U.S. 590 (1975) — § 5-3(F), nn. 18, 21
Brown v. Louisiana, 383 U.S. 131 (1966) — § 13-3(N)(3), n. 363
Brown v. Ohio, 432 U.S. 161 (1977) — § 6-1(C)(3), n. 145
Brown, United States v.
Brown v. United States, 365 F. Supp. 328 (E.D. Pa. 1973) — § 17-22, n. 1
Brown, West v.
Brown-Austin, United States v.
Browning, United States v.
Brownlow, United States v.
Bruce, United States v.
Brundidge, United States v.
Brunson, United States v.
Brunton, United States v.
Bruton, United States v.
Bryant, United States v.
Bubonics, United States v.
Buchecker, United States v.
Buckingham, United States v.
Bucknell, United States v.
Budicin, United States v.
Bufatino, United States v.
Buie, Maryland v.
Bull, Calder v.
Bullington, United States v.
Bullitt, Baggett v.

TABLE OF CASES

Bunting, United States v.
Burch v. Louisiana, 441 U.S. 130 (1979) — § 8-3(C)(3), n. 140
Burden, United States v.
Burdine, United States v.
Burge, United States v.
Burger, New York v.
Burgess, United States v.
Burke, United States v.
Burkhalter, United States v.
Burl, United States v.
Burnell, United States v.
Burnett, United States v.
Burnette, United States v.
Burney, United States v.
Burnom, United States v.
Burns, United States v.
Burns v. Wilson, 346 U.S. 137 (1953) — § 1-7, n. 6; § 17-23(C)(1), n. 26; § 17-23(C)(2)
Burrell, United States v.
Burrer, United States v.
Burris, United States v.
Burry, United States v.
Bursey, Weatherford v.
Burton, United States v.
Burtt v. Schick, 23 M.J. 140 (C.M.A. 1986) — § 13-2(G)(1), n. 67; § 13-3(E), n. 207; § 15-4(B), nn. 12, 15
Burwell, United States v.
Bush, United States v.
Buske, United States v.
Bustamonte, Schneckloth v.
Butler, United States v.
Butner, United States v.
Butterbaugh, United States v.
Button, NAACP v.
Button, United States v.
Butts, United States v.
Byard, United States v.
Byers, United States v.
Bygrave, United States v.
Byrd, United States v.

C

Caballero, United States v.
Cabatic, United States v.
Cabebe, United States v.
Cabral, United States v.
Cadenhead, United States v.
Cage, United States v.
Cagle, United States v.
Cahill, United States v.
Cahn, United States v.

TABLE OF CASES

Cain, United States v.
Calder v. Bull, 3 Dall. 386 (1798) — § 13-3(N)(5), n. 429
Calderon, United States v.
Caldwell, United States v.
Calhoun, United States v.
Caliendo, United States v.
California v. Beyers, 402 U.S. 424 (1971) — § 5-4(A)(2), n. 15
California v. Carney, 471 U.S. 386 (1985) — § 5-3(A), n. 19
California, Chimel v.
California, Cohen v.
California, Faretta v.
California, Griffin v.
California, Miller v.
California v. Trombetta, 467 U.S. 479 (1984) — § 11-4, n. 5
Callahan, United States v.
Callara, United States v.
Callaway, Calley v.
Callaway, United States v.
Calley v. Callaway, 519 F.2d 184 (5th Cir. 1975) — § 1-1, n. 2; § 17-23(C)(1), n. 26
Calley, United States v.
Callinan, United States v.
Calloway, United States v.
Camacho, United States v.
Camanga, United States v.
Cambridge, United States v.
Camero v. United States, 345 F.2d 798 (Ct. Cl. 1965) — § 2-8(A), n. 6
Cameron, United States v.
Campbell, Martindale v.
Campbell, United States v.
Campfield, United States v.
Campos, United States v.
Canatelli, United States v.
Caniete, United States v.
Cannon, United States v.
Cansdale, United States v.
Cantrell, United States v.
Cantu, United States v.
Capel, United States v.
Caputo, United States v.
Carbo, United States v.
Cardiff, United States v.
Care, United States v.
Carey v. Brown, 447 U.S. 455 (1980) — § 13-3(N)(3), n. 377
Carey, United States v.
Carfang, United States v.
Caritativo, United States v.
Carl, United States v.
Carlisle, United States v.
Carlos, United States v.
Carlson v. Schlesinger, 511 F.2d 1327 (1975) — § 13-3(N)(3), nn. 377, 378, 383, 385, 403

TABLE OF CASES

Carlson, United States v.
Carlucci, United States v.
Carlucci, United States Navy-Marine Corps Court of Military Review v.
Carmack, United States v.
Carman, United States v.
Carmans, United States v.
Carmichael, United States v.
Carney, California v.
Carns, United States v.
Caro, United States v.
Carolene Products Co., United States v.
Carpenter, United States v.
Carr, Baker v.
Carr, United States v.
Carreiro, United States v.
Carroll, United States v.
Carrott, United States v.
Carter v. Kentucky, 450 U.S. 288 (1981) — § 15-14(B), n. 47
Carter, United States v.
Caruth, United States v.
Carver, Aviz v.
Carver, United States v.
Cases, United States v.
Cashwell, United States v.
Cassell, United States v.
Cassity, United States v.
Casteel, United States v.
Castillo, United States v.
Castleberry, United States v.
Castleman, United States v.
Castrillon-Moreno, United States v.
Castro, United States v.
Caszatt, United States v.
Catlow, United States v.
Caton, United States v.
Catt, United States v.
Causey, United States v.
Cavalier, United States v.
Caver, United States v.
Caylor, United States v.
Centeno, United States v.
Cephas, United States v.
Chadwell, United States v.
Chadwick, United States v.
Chafee, Wallace v.
Chambers, Halfacre v.
Chambers, Short v.
Chambers v. Sir John Jennings, 7 Mod. 127 — § 1-5(B), n. 12
Chambers, United States v.
Champagne v. Schlesinger, 506 F.2d 979 (7th Cir. 1974) — § 17-22(A), n. 6

TABLE OF CASES

Chan, United States v.
Chandler v. Florida, 449 U.S. 560 (1981) — § 15-3, n. 5
Chandler, United States v.
Chaplinski v. New Hampshire, 315 U.S. 568 (1942) — § 13-3(N)(3), nn. 366, 368, 370
Chapman, United States v.
Chapman v. United States, 553 F.2d 886 (5th Cir. 1977) — § 12-2(F)(4), n. 74
Chappell v. Wallace, 462 U.S. 296 (1983) — § 1-1, n. 6; § 13-3(N)(1), n. 314
Chapple, United States v.
Charette, United States v.
Charles, United States v.
Charley, United States v.
Chasteen, United States v.
Chatman, United States v.
Chattin, United States v.
Chaves, United States v.
Chavez, United States v.
Chavira, United States v.
Cheeks, United States v.
Chenoweth v. Van Arsdall, 22 C.M.A. 183, 46 C.M.R. 183 (1973) — § 13-5(C), n. 34
Cherok, United States v.
Cherry, United States v.
Chestnut, United States v.
Chicago, Terminiello v.
Chick, United States v.
Chilcott v. Orr, 747 F.2d 39 (1st Cir. 1984) — § 13-3(N)(5), n. 437
Childress, United States v.
Chimel v. California, 395 U.S. 752 (1969) — § 5-3(C)(7), nn. 99, 100
Chisholm, United States v.
Chitwood, United States v.
Chodara, United States v.
Choice, United States v.
Chollet, United States v.
Choy, United States v.
Christensen, United States v.
Christian, United States v.
Chuculate, United States v.
Church, United States v.
Ciarletta, United States v.
Ciesialski, United States v.
CIO, Hague v.
Cisler, United States v.
Citizens for a Better Environment, Village of Schauniburg v.
City of Cleburne v. Cleburne Living Center, 473 U.S. 432 (1985) — § 13-3(N)(1), nn. 309, 315, 317
City of Jacksonville, Erznoznik v.
City of Jacksonville, Papchristou v.
City of New Orleans v. Dukes, 427 U.S. 297 (1976) — § 13-3(N)(1), nn. 310, 314
City of Renton v. Playtime Theatres, Inc., 475 U.S. 41 (1986) — § 13-3(N)(3), n. 377
City of Rockford, Grayned v.
Ciulla, United States v.
Clabon, United States v.

TABLE OF CASES

Claiborne Hardware Co., NAACP v.
Clardy, United States v.
Clark v. Community for Creative Non-Violence, 468 U.S. 288 (1984) — § 13-3(N)(3), n. 363
Clark, Rose v.
Clark, United States v.
Clark, Vanover v.
Clarke, United States v.
Claussen, United States v.
Claxton, United States v.
Clay v. Woodmansee, 29 M.J. 663 (A.C.M.R. 1989) — § 13-3(H), n. 237
Clayborne, United States v.
Clayton, United States v.
Claytor, United States v.
Clear, United States v.
Cleburne Living Center, City of Cleburne v.
Clemens, United States v.
Clemons, United States v.
Cleveland, United States v.
Clevidence, United States v.
Clifton, In re
Clifton, United States v.
Cline, United States v.
Clow, United States v.
Clower, United States v.
Clowser, United States v.
Cloyd, United States v.
Coates, United States v.
Cobb v. Wainwright, 609 F.2d 754 (5th Cir. 1980) — § 15-13, n. 21
Cobe, United States v.
Coburn, United States v.
Cockerell, United States v.
Coder, United States v.
Coffey v. Commanding Officer, 33 M.J. 938 (N.M.C.M.R. 1991) — § 17-19, n. 27
Coffin, United States v.
Coffman, United States v.
Cofield, United States v.
Coglin, United States v.
Cohen v. California, 403 U.S. 15 (1971) — § 13-3(N)(3), n. 368
Cohen Grocery Co., United States v.
Colby, Sands v.
Cole, Keys v.
Cole v. Laird, 468 F.2d 829 (5th Cir. 1972) — § 17-23(B), n. 16
Cole, United States v.
Coleman v. Tennessee, 97 U.S. 509 (1879) — § 1-7, n. 17
Coleman, United States v.
Collazo v. Welling, 34 M.J. 793 (C.G.C.M.R. 1992) — § 17-19, nn. 22, 26, 27
Colley, United States v.
Collier, United States v.
Collins, United States v.
Colon, United States v.

1012

TABLE OF CASES

Colon-Angueira, United States v.
Colonnade Catering Corp. v. United States, 397 U.S. 73 (1970) — § 5-3(D)(1), n. 122
Colton, United States v.
Columbia, Bouie v.
Combest, United States v.
Combs, United States v.
Commandant, Relford v.
Commander, United States v.
Commander, Naval Air Force, Jones v.
Commanding General, Dash v.
Commanding Officer, Coffey v.
Commanding Officer, Gorko v.
Commanding Officer, Vorbeck v.
Commanding Officer, Walker v.
Commissioner of Internal Revenue, Freytag v.
Community for Creative Non-Violence, Clark v.
Conklan, United States v.
Conley, United States v.
Conlon, United States v.
Conn, United States v.
Connally v. General Constr. Co., 269 U.S. 385 (1926) — § 13-3(N)(2), n. 339
Connecticut, Griswold v.
Connecticut, Palko v.
Connell, United States v.
Connick v. Myers, 461 U.S. 138 (1983) — § 13-3(N)(3), nn. 371, 381
Conrad, United States v.
Conway, United States v.
Cook, United States v.
Cooke v. Orser, 12 M.J. 335 (C.M.A. 1982) — § 5-4(C), nn. 57, 59; § 11-2(E)(1), n. 107; § 13-3(H), n. 237
Cooke, United States v.
Cooley, United States v.
Cooper, Lwin v.
Cooper, United States v.
Cooper-Tyson, United States v.
Copeland, United States v.
Copening, United States v.
Copper, United States v.
Coppock, United States v.
Corcoran, United States v.
Cordell, United States v.
Cordero, United States v.
Cordova, United States v.
Corl, United States v.
Corley, United States v.
Corly v. Thurman, 3 M.J. 192 (C.M.A. 1977) — § 17-2(B)(2), n. 32
Cornelius, United States v.
Coronado, United States v.
Corraine, United States v.
Corriere, United States v.
Corrigan, United States v.

TABLE OF CASES

Cortes, United States v.
Cortright v. Resor, 447 F.2d 245 (2d Cir. 1971) — § 13-3(N)(3), nn. 383, 391
Cortte, United States v.
Cosby, United States v.
Cosgrove, United States v.
Costa, United States v.
Costello, United States v.
Cote, United States v.
Cottle, United States v.
Cottrell, United States v.
Councilman, Schlesinger v.
County of Riverside v. McLaughlin — § 5-9(D), nn. 21, 22
Court, United States v.
Courtier, United States v.
Courtney, United States v.
Courtney v. Williams, 1 M.J. 267 (C.M.A. 1976) — § 1-1(B), n. 26; § 5-3, n. 2; § 5-9(A), nn. 2, 5; § 13-3(E), n. 204; § 13-5(B), n. 22; § 17-23(C)(2)
Courts, United States v.
Couser, United States v.
Cover, United States v.
Covert, Reid v.
Covington, Fletcher v.
Covington, United States v.
Cowan, United States v.
Cowles, United States v.
Cox, Pearson v.
Cox, Pickens v.
Cox, Ragan v.
Cox, United States v.
Cozine, United States v.
Craig v. Boren, 429 U.S. 190 (1976) — § 13-3(N)(1), nn. 317, 328, 329
Craig, United States v.
Cramer, United States v.
Craney, United States v.
Craven, Meeks v.
Crawford, United States v.
Credit, United States v.
Crist v. Bretz, 437 U.S. 28 (1978) — § 13-3(E), n. 202
Crockett, United States v.
Croley, United States v.
Cronic, United States v.
Cronier, United States v.
Croom, United States v.
Crosby v. United States, 113 S. Ct. 748 (1993) — § 12-4, n. 13
Cross, United States v.
Crossley, United States v.
Crouch, United States v.
Crowe, United States v.
Crowell, United States v.
Crumb, United States v.
Crumley, United States v.

TABLE OF CASES

Cruz, United States v.
Cruz-Maldonado, United States v.
Cruz-Rijos, United States v.
Cruz-Rios, United States v.
Cudini, United States v.
Cuevas-Orvalle, United States v.
Cuffee, United States v.
Cullins, Brookins v.
Culver v. Secretary of Air Force, 389 F. Supp. 331 (D.D.C. 1975) — § 13-3(N)(2), nn. 341, 347, 353
Culver, United States v.
Cumbee, United States v.
Cumberledge, United States v.
Cummings, United States v.
Cunningham v. Gilevich, 36 M.J. 94 (C.M.A. 1992) — § 5-4(C), nn. 56, 59; § 6-5(B), n. 28
Cunningham, United States v.
Cupp, United States v.
Curcio, United States v.
Curry v. Secretary of Army, 595 F.2d 873 (D.C. Cir. 1979) — § 1-1, n. 7; § 1-7, n. 14
Curry, United States v.
Curtin, United States v.
Curtis, United States v.
Curtiss, United States v.
Cutting, United States v.
Cuylar v. Sullivan, 446 U.S. 335 (1980) — § 15-2(B)(2), nn. 26, 28; § 15-2(B)(3), n. 47
Czarnecki, United States v.
Czeck, United States v.
Czekala, United States v.

D

Dababneh, United States v.
Daffron, United States v.
Dahood, United States v.
Daigle, United States v.
Daigneault, United States v.
Dailey, United States v.
Dale, United States v.
Daley, United States v.
Dallman, United States v.
Dalton, Murphy v.
Damatta-Olivera, United States v.
Dancy, United States v.
Dandridge v. Williams, 397 U.S. 471 (1970) — § 13-3(N)(1), n. 308
Daniel, United States v.
Daniels, United States v.
Danilson, United States v.
D'Apice, United States v.
Darby, United States v.
Darring, United States v.

TABLE OF CASES

Darville, United States v.
Dash v. Commanding General, 307 F. Supp. 849 (D.S.C. 1969) — § 13-3(N)(3), n. 377
Daskam, United States v.
Davenport, United States v.
Davidson, Parisi v.
Davidson, United States v.
Davis, Dickenson v.
Davis, United States v.
Davis v. United States, 35 M.J. 640 (A.C.M.R. 1992) — § 17-19, nn. 12, 24, 25
Davis, Washington v.
Davis, United States v.
Dawdy, United States v.
Dawson, United States v.
Daye, United States v.
Dayton, United States v.
De Los Santos, United States v.
De Pasquale, Gannet Co. v.
Deachin, United States v.
Dean, United States v.
Dear, United States v.
Dearman, United States v.
DeBarrows, United States v.
Decker, United States v.
DeGiulio, Hamilton v.
DeGrocco, United States v.
Dehart, United States v.
Deifer, United States v.
Dejong, United States v.
DeJonge, United States v.
Delaney, United States v.
DeLauder, United States v.
DeLello, United States v.
Dellarosa, United States v.
Deller, United States v.
DeLoatch, United States v.
Delp, United States v.
Demeio, United States v.
Demerse, United States v.
Deming, McClaughry v.
Demmer, United States v.
Denney, United States v.
Denning, United States v.
Dennis, United States v.
Dennis v. United States, 341 U.S. 494 (1951) — § 13-3(N)(3), n. 359
Dent, United States v.
Derksen, United States v.
Des Moines Sch. Dist., Tinker v.
Desciscio, United States v.
Deserano, United States v.
Desiderio, United States v.
Destefano, United States v.

TABLE OF CASES

Detroit Bd. of Educ., Abood v.
Dettinger v. United States, 7 M.J. 216 (C.M.A. 1979) — § 13-2(G)(1), n. 63
Devine, United States v.
Devitt, United States v.
Dewey, Donovan v.
DeYoung, United States v.
Diamond, United States v.
DiAngelo, United States v.
Diaz, Mathews v.
Diaz, United States v.
Diaz-Carrero, United States v.
DiBartolo, In re
DiBello, United States v.
Dick, United States v.
Dickens, United States v.
Dickenson v. Davis, 245 F.2d 317 (10th Cir. 1951) — § 4-5(A), n. 9
Dickerson, United States v.
Dickey, United States v.
DiCupe, United States v.
Dienst, United States v.
Dies, United States v.
Dieter, United States v.
Dilday, United States v.
Dillard, United States v.
DiMatteo, United States v.
Dinkel, United States v.
Dionne, United States v.
Divich, Woodrick v.
Dixon, United States v.
Dobbert v. Florida, 432 U.S. 282 (1977) — § 13-3(N)(5), n. 437
Dobzynski v. Green, 16 M.J. 84 (C.M.A. 1983) — § 3-3(C), nn. 23, 30, 32-34; § 3-4, n. 9; § 6-1, n. 24; § 8-5, n. 11
Dock, United States v.
Doctor, United States v.
Dodds, United States v.
Doe, Plyler v.
Dohle, United States v.
Dombrowski v. Pfister, 380 U.S. 479 (1965) — § 13-3(N)(3), n. 389
Domingue, United States v.
Donaldson, United States v.
Donati, United States v.
Donegan, United States v.
Donley, United States v.
Donnelly, Lynch v.
Donnelly, United States v.
Donohew, United States v.
Donohue, United States v.
Donovan v. Dewey, 452 U.S. 594 (1981) — § 5-3(D)(1), n. 122
Doran, United States v.
Dorgan, United States v.
Dornick, United States v.

1017

TABLE OF CASES

Dorsch, United States v.
Dorsey, United States v.
Doss, United States v.
Dotson, United States v.
Doucet, United States v.
Dougal, United States v.
Douglas, United States v.
Douse, United States v.
Dowd, United States v.
Dowell, United States v.
Dowlat, United States v.
Downing, United States v.
Downs, United States v.
Doyle v. Ohio, 426 U.S. 610 (1976) — § 5-4(A)(3), n. 19; § 15-13, n. 11
Drayton, United States v.
Dresen, United States v.
Drew, Satterfield v.
Driver, United States v.
Dronenburg v. Zech, 741 F.2d 1388 (D.C. Cir. 1984) — § 2-8(D), n. 37
Dubay, United States v.
DuBose, United States v.
Dubry, United States v.
Dudding, United States v.
Dudley, United States v.
Duga, United States v.
Duke, United States v.
Dukes, City of New Orleans v.
Dukes v. Smith, 34 M.J. 803 (N.M.C.M.R. 1991) — § 17-19, n. 14
Dukes, United States v.
Dulus, United States v.
Dumas, United States v.
Dumford, United States v.
Dunaway v. New York, 439 U.S. 979 (1979) — § 5-4(B), n. 38
Dunbar, United States v.
Duncan, United States v.
Duncan v. Usher, 23 M.J. 29 (C.M.A. 1986) — § 4-6, nn. 5, 12
Duncan, United States v.
Dunks, United States v.
Dunlap, United States v.
Dunn, United States v.
Dunn & Bradstreet v. Greenmoss Builders, Inc., 472 U.S. 749 (1985) — § 13-3(N)(3), n. 372
Dunning, United States v.
Dupas, United States v.
Dupree, United States v.
Durden, United States v.
Durham, United States v.
Duval, United States v.
Duvall, United States v.
Dyer, United States v.
Dykes, United States v.

TABLE OF CASES

Dynes v. Hoover, 61 U.S. 659 (1857) — § 1-6(A), n. 27

E

Eads, United States v.
Eady, United States v.
Earl, United States v.
Earnesty, United States v.
Eason, United States v.
Easter, United States v.
Ebanks, United States v.
Eberhardt, United States v.
Echols, United States v.
Eck, United States v.
Eckart, United States v.
Eckhoff, United States v.
Ecoffey, United States v.
Eddington, Thomas v.
Eddy, United States v.
Edington, Frage v.
Edmond, United States v.
Edmonds, United States v.
Edwards v. Arizona, 451 U.S. 477 (1981) — § 5-4(B), n. 50
Edwards, United States v.
Edwards, Washington v.
Eggers, Porter v.
Eggers, United States v.
Eichenlaub, United States v.
Eichman, United States v.
Eiland, United States v.
Eischeid, United States v.
Eisenstadt v. Baird, 405 U.S. 438 (1972) — § 2-9(D), n. 58
El-Amin, United States v.
Eldridge, Matthews v.
Ellenson, United States v.
Ellerbee, United States v.
Elliott, United States v.
Ellis v. Jacob, 26 M.J. 90 (C.M.A. 1988) — § 13-3(D), n. 182
Ellis, United States v.
Ellison, United States v.
Ellman, United States v.
Ellsey, United States v.
Elmore, United States v.
Elrod, United States v.
Elstad, Oregon v.
Elvine, United States v.
Elzy, United States v.
Emerson, United States v.
Emmons, United States v.
Engel v. Vitale, 370 U.S. 421 (1962) — § 13-3(N)(3), n. 394
England, United States v.

TABLE OF CASES

Engle, United States v.
Englert, United States v.
English, United States v.
Enloe, United States v.
Enlow, United States v.
Ennis, United States v.
Epps, United States v.
Ericson, United States v.
Erie, United States v.
Ermitano, United States v.
Ernest, United States v.
Ernst, United States v.
Erwin, United States v.
Erznoznik v. City of Jacksonville, 422 U.S. 205 (1975) — § 13-3(N)(3), nn. 374, 375, 387
Escobar, United States v.
Eshalomi, United States v.
Espiet-Betancourt, United States v.
Espinoza, United States v.
Espronceda, United States v.
Estelle v. Smith, 451 U.S. 454 (1981) — § 3-8(B), n. 15; § 14-3(A)(1), n. 16
Estrada, United States v.
Estrella, United States v.
Ettinger, United States v.
Ettleson, United States v.
Eubank, United States v.
Euring, United States v.
Evans v. Kilroy, 33 M.J. 730 (A.F.C.M.R. 1991) — § 13-2(G)(1), n. 70
Evans, United States v.
Everett, United States v.
Everson v. Board of Educ., 330 U.S. 1 (1947) — § 13-3(N)(3), nn. 394, 395
Everson, United States v.
Ex parte Milligan, 71 U.S. (4 Wall.) 2 (1866) — § 8-3(C)(3), n. 142
Ex parte Quirin, 317 U.S. 1 (1942) — § 4-1, n. 1
Ezell, United States v.

F

Facey, United States v.
Faciane, United States v.
Fagan, United States v.
Fagg, United States v.
Fagnan, United States v.
Fahey, United States v.
Fairchild, United States v.
Fairly, United States v.
Falcon, United States v.
Falin, United States v.
Falk, United States v.
Fals, United States v.
Faretta v. California, 422 U.S. 806 (1975) — § 12-2(F)(1), nn. 68-70, 72, 74
Fassler, United States v.

TABLE OF CASES

Feagans, United States v.
Federal Communications Comm'n v. Pacifica Foundation, 438 U.S. 726 (1978) — § 13-3(N)(3), nn. 366, 373
Feld, United States v.
Felix, United States v.
Fell, United States v.
Felton, United States v.
Felty, United States v.
Fenno, United States v.
Ferber, New York v.
Ferenczi, United States v.
Ferguson, United States v.
Fernandez, United States v.
Ferrer, United States v.
Fessenden, Ponzi v.
Fetch, United States v.
Fielder, United States v.
Fields, United States v.
Fields, Wyrick v.
Figueroa, United States v.
Fimmano, United States v.
Finn, United States v.
Finsel, United States v.
Firmin, United States v.
First, United States v.
Fischer, Pascascio v.
Fish, United States v.
Fisher, States v.
Fisher, United States v.
Fisiorek, United States v.
Fiske, United States v.
Fitten, United States v.
Fitzhugh, United States v.
Fitzpatrick, United States v.
Fitzsimmons, United States v.
Fleenor, United States v.
Fleig, United States v.
Fleming, United States v.
Fletch, United States v.
Fletcher v. Covington, 42 M.J. 215 (1995) — § 3-3(C), n. 32; § 3-7, n. 1
Fletcher, United States v.
Fletcher v. Weir, 455 U.S. 603 (1982) — § 5-4(A)(3), n. 20
Fling, United States v.
Flint, United States v.
Flipside, Hoffman Estates v.
Flom, United States v.
Florczak, United States v.
Flores-Glaraza, United States v.
Florida, Chandler v.
Florida, Dobbert v.
Florida, Williams v.

TABLE OF CASES

Flowers v. United States, 407 U.S. 197 (1972) — § 5-8(A), n. 22; § 13-3(N)(3), n. 379
Flowers, United States v.
Floyd, United States v.
Fluellen, United States v.
Flynn, United States v.
Fogarty, United States v.
Foley, United States v.
Folk, United States v.
Fontenot, United States v.
Forbes, United States v.
Ford, United States v.
Forehand, United States v.
Forester, United States v.
Fors, United States v.
Fort, United States v.
Fortney, United States v.
Foster, United States v.
Foti, United States v.
Fountain, United States v.
Foust, United States v.
Fout, United States v.
Fowle, United States v.
Fowler, United States v.
Fox, United States v.
Foy, United States v.
Frage v. Edington, 26 M.J. 927 (N.M.C.M.R. 1988) — § 13-2(G)(2), nn. 119, 121
Frage v. Moriarty, 27 M.J. 341 (C.M.A. 1988) — § 6-1, n. 37; § 6-2(B), n. 10; § 13-3(B), n. 13
Frage, United States v.
Franchia, United States v.
Francis v. Franklin, 471 U.S. 307 (1985) — § 15-20, n. 7
Francis, United States v.
Frangoules, United States v.
Franklin, Francis v.
Franklin, United States v.
Frazier, United States v.
Frederick, United States v.
Free, United States v.
Freedman, United States v.
Freeman v. Stuart, 33 M.J. 659 (N.M.C.M.R. 1991) — § 13-5(A), n. 14
Freeman, United States v.
French, United States v.
Frentz, United States v.
Fretwell, Lockart v.
Fretwell, United States v.
Freytag v. Commissioner of Internal Revenue, 36 M.J. 240 — § 8-3(A), nn. 27, 29-31
Friedman, United States v.
Frierson, United States v.
Fritz, United States v.
Froehlke, Hoersch v.
Frontiero v. Richardson, 411 U.S. 677 (1973) — § 13-3(N)(1), nn. 303, 325

TABLE OF CASES

Frost, United States v.
Frostell, United States v.
Frueh, United States v.
Fruscella, United States v.
Frye, United States v.
Fuentes, United States v.
Funk, United States v.
Furman v. Georgia, 408 U.S. 238 (1972) — § 16-13
Fussell, United States v.

G

Gabrels, United States v.
Gacioch, United States v.
Gaither, United States v.
Gale v. United States, 17 C.M.A. 40, 37 C.M.R. 304 (1967) — § 17-19, n. 5
Galinato, United States v.
Gallion, United States v.
Galloway, United States v.
Gambini, United States v.
Gamble, United States v.
Gannet Co. v. De Pasquale, 443 U.S. 368 (1979) — § 15-3, n. 11
Gans, United States v.
Gansemer, United States v.
Garces, United States v.
Garcia, United States v.
Garcia v. United States, 28 M.J. 917 (C.G.C.M.R. 1989) — § 17-15(B), n. 32
Gardner, United States v.
Garland, United States v.
Garner, United States v.
Garrett v. Lowe, 39 M.J. 293 (C.M.A. 1994) — § 16-9, n. 5
Garrett v. Mahoney, 39 M.J. 299 (C.M.A. 1994) — § 17-19, n. 15
Garrett, Murphy v.
Garrett, United States v.
Garries, United States v.
Garries v. United States, 22 M.J. 288 (C.M.A. 1988) — § 11-2(A)(3), n. 21
Garrity v. New Jersey, 385 U.S. 493 (1967) — § 13-3(N)(3), n. 381
Garvin, United States v.
Garwood, United States v.
Gary, United States v.
Gaskins, United States v.
Gaspard, United States v.
Gaston, United States v.
Gates, Illinois v.
Gates, United States v.
Gavitt, United States v.
Gay, United States v.
Geary, United States v.
Gebhart, United States v.
Geduldig v. Aiello, 417 U.S. 484 (1974) — § 13-3(N)(1), n. 329
Geiss, United States v.

TABLE OF CASES

General Constr. Co., Connally v.
Genereux v. Her Majesty The Queen, No. 22103, SCR (Feb. 13, 1992) — § 8-3(A), n. 19
Genesee, United States v.
Gennosa, United States v.
Gentile, United States v.
George, United States v.
Georgia, Avery v.
Georgia, Ballew v.
Georgia, Bearden v.
Georgia, Furman v.
Georgia, Gregg v.
Georgia, Jenkins v.
Geraghty, United States v.
Gerard, United States v.
Gerdes, United States v.
Gerlach, United States v.
Gerstein v. Pugh, 420 U.S. 103 (1975) — § 5-9(C), n. 18; § 5-9(D), nn. 21, 25, 43
Ghent, United States v.
Ghiglieri, United States v.
Giambra, United States v.
Gibbs, United States v.
Gibson, United States v.
Gifford, United States v.
Gilbert, United States v.
Giles, United States v.
Gilevich, Cunningham v.
Gill, United States v.
Gillespie, United States v.
Gillete v. United States, 401 U.S. 437 (1971) — § 13-3(N)(3), n. 401
Gillette, United States v.
Gilliam, United States v.
Gillies, Von Moltke v.
Gilligan v. Morgan, 413 U.S. 1 (1973) — § 13-3(N)(1), n. 314
Ginaitt, United States v.
Ginter, United States v.
Ginyard, United States v.
Gipson, United States v.
Girard, Wilson v.
Girard v. Wilson, 354 U.S. 524 (1957) — § 4-12(B), n. 16
Giroux, United States v.
Gittens, United States v.
Giusti, United States v.
Givens, United States v.
Gladdis, United States v.
Gladue, United States v.
Glazier, United States v.
Gleason, United States v.
Glenn, United States v.
Glines, Brown v.
Globe Newspapers Co. v. Superior Court, 457 U.S. 596 (1982) — § 15-3, n. 4
Gloria, United States v.

TABLE OF CASES

Glover, United States v.
Gluch, United States v.
Gnibus, United States v.
Godfrey, United States v.
Godreau, United States v.
Goetz, United States v.
Goffe, United States v.
Goguen, Smith v.
Goins, United States v.
Goldberg, Rostker v.
Goldberg v. United States, 425 U.S. 94 (1976) — § 10-3(A), n. 4
Goldman v. Secretary of Defense — § 13-3(N)(3), nn. 398, 405
Goldman v. Weinberger, 106 S. Ct. 1310 (1986) — § 13-3(N)(5), n. 428
Goldman v. Weinberger, 475 U.S. 503 (1986) — § 4-11(C), n. 55; § 13-3(N)(1), nn. 331, 332; § 13-3(N)(3), nn. 404, 405
Goldsmith, United States v.
Gomez, United States v.
Gonda, United States v.
Gonzales, United States v.
Gonzalez, United States v.
Good, United States v.
Goode, United States v.
Gooden, United States v.
Gooding, United States v.
Goodman, United States v.
Goodson v. United States, 471 U.S. 1063 (1985) — § 17-17, n. 9
Goodson, United States v.
Goodwin, United States v.
Goodyear, United States v.
Goosby, United States v.
Gordon, United States v.
Gore, United States v.
Goree, United States v.
Gori v. United States, 364 U.S. 917 (1961) — § 15-4(B), n. 14
Gorko v. Commanding Officer, 314 F.2d 858 (10th Cir. 1963) — § 17-23(C)(1), n. 26
Gosa v. Mayden, 413 U.S. 665 (1973) — § 4-10, n. 4
Goudy, United States v.
Gowadia, United States v.
Grace, United States v.
Grady, United States v.
Graf, United States v.
Graham v. Richardson, 403 U.S. 365 (1971) — § 13-3(N)(1), nn. 320, 321
Graham, United States v.
Granda, United States v.
Grande, McCray v.
Grandy, United States v.
Grant, United States v.
Grasha, United States v.
Graves, United States v.
Gravitt, United States v.
Gray v. Mahoney, 39 M.J. 299 (C.M.A. 1994) — § 17-19, n. 29

TABLE OF CASES

Gray, United States v.
Grayned v. City of Rockford, 408 U.S. 104 (1972) — § 13-3(N)(2), nn. 339, 341, 343; § 13-3(N)(3), nn. 375, 388
Green, Dobzynski v.
Green, United States v.
Greene, United States v.
Greenmoss Builders, Inc., Dunn & Bradstreet v.
Greenwald, United States v.
Greenwald, Wiggins v.
Greenwalt, United States v.
Greenwell, United States v.
Greer v. Spock, 424 U.S. 828 (1976) — § 13-3(N)(3), nn. 379, 380, 385, 408
Greer, United States v.
Greewald, Washington v.
Gregg v. Georgia, 428 U.S. 153 (1976) — § 16-13
Gregorio, United States v.
Gregory, United States v.
Grider, United States v.
Griego, United States v.
Griffin v. California, 380 U.S. 609 (1965) — § 15-13, n. 11
Griffin, United States v.
Griffith, United States v.
Grimley, In re
Grimm, United States v.
Grinter, United States v.
Grisham v. Hagan, 361 U.S. 278 (1960) — § 4-7(B), nn. 12, 13
Griswold v. Connecticut, 381 U.S. 479 (1965) — § 2-9(D), nn. 57-59, 62; § 13-3(N)(3), nn. 407, 411, 412
Grittman, United States v.
Groce, United States v.
Groh, United States v.
Grom, United States v.
Grooters, United States v.
Groshong, United States v.
Grosskreutz, United States v.
Grostefon, United States v.
Groveman, United States v.
Grover, United States v.
Grover-Madrill, United States v.
Groves, United States v.
Grow, United States v.
Grubb, United States v.
Grubbs, United States v.
Grunden, United States v.
Gruninger, United States v.
Guaglione, United States v.
Gudaitis, United States v.
Gudel, United States v.
Guerrero, United States v.
Guerro, United States v.
Guidry, United States v.

TABLE OF CASES

Guillory, United States v.
Guitard, United States v.
Gunter, United States v.
Guron, United States v.
Gusik v. Schilder, 340 U.S. 128 (1950) — § 17-23(B), nn. 7-11; § 17-23(C)(1), n. 27
Gussen, United States v.
Guthrie, United States v.
Gutierrez, United States v.
Guzman, United States v.

H

Haebel, Trotman v.
Hagan, Grisham v.
Hagan, United States v.
Hagarty v. United States, 449 F.2d 352 (Ct. Cl. 1971) — § 3-3(C), n. 29
Hagen, United States v.
Haggard, United States v.
Hague v. CIO, 307 U.S. 496 (1939) — § 13-3(N)(3), n. 379
Hagy, United States v.
Haire, United States v.
Hairston, United States v.
Halcomb, United States v.
Haldeman, Murray v.
Halfacre v. Chambers, 5 M.J. 1099 (C.M.A. 1976) — § 10-3(B), n. 10
Hall v. Thwing, 30 M.J. 583 (A.C.M.R. 1990) — § 13-3(C)(3), n. 165
Hall, United States v.
Hall, Wickham v.
Hallum, United States v.
Hallums, United States v.
Halper, United States v.
Haltiwanger, United States v.
Ham v. South Carolina, 409 U.S. 524 (1973) — § 15-10(B), n. 50
Hamilton v. DeGiulio, 35 M.J. 829 (A.C.M.R. 1992) — § 17-19, n. 24
Hamilton, United States v.
Hamlin, Argersinger v.
Hamm, United States v.
Hammond, United States v.
Hammork, United States v.
Hampton v. Mow Sun Wong, 426 U.S. 88 (1976) — § 13-3(N)(1), n. 303
Hampton, United States v.
Hance, United States v.
Hancock, United States v.
Handy, United States v.
Hanes, United States v.
Hanna, United States v.
Hannan, United States v.
Hannon, United States v.
Hansen, United States v.
Hanson, United States v.
Happel, United States v.

TABLE OF CASES

Harclerode, United States v.
Harcrow, United States v.
Harden, United States v.
Hardin, United States v.
Hardwick, Bowers v.
Hardy, United States v.
Hargrove, United States v.
Harmon, United States v.
Harper v. Jones, 195 F.2d 705 (10th Cir. 1952) — § 13-3(N)(3), n. 408
Harper, United States v.
Harper v. Virginia State Bd. of Elections, 383 U.S. 663 (1966) — § 13-3(N)(1), n. 323
Harrel, United States v.
Harrington, United States v.
Harris, New York v.
Harris v. New York, 401 U.S. 222 (1971) — § 5-4(B), n. 31; § 13-4(A), n. 14
Harris, United States v.
Harrison, United States v.
Harrison v. United States, 20 M.J. 55 (C.M.A. 1985) — § 13-2(G)(1), n. 72
Harriss, United States v.
Harrod, United States v.
Harry, United States v.
Hart, United States v.
Hartman, Hooper v.
Hartsock, United States v.
Hartwig, United States v.
Harvey, United States v.
Haskins, United States v.
Hasting, United States v.
Haston, United States v.
Hatfield, United States v.
Hatheway v. Secretary of Army, 641 F.2d 1376 (9th Cir. 1981) — § 13-3(N)(3), n. 400
Hatley, United States v.
Havens, United States v.
Hawkins, United States v.
Hawks, United States v.
Hawley, United States v.
Hawthorne, United States v.
Hay, United States v.
Hayden, United States v.
Haye, United States v.
Hayes, United States v.
Haynes, United States v.
Haywood, United States v.
Healy, United States v.
Heaney, United States v.
Heard, United States v.
Heath, United States v.
Hebert, United States v.
Hecker, United States v.
Hedlund, United States v.

TABLE OF CASES

Heffron v. Int'l Society for Krishna Consciousness, Inc., 452 U.S. 640 (1981) — § 13-3(N)(3), n. 380
Heflebower, Mayborn v.
Hefner, United States v.
Heimer, United States v.
Hein, United States v.
Heinel, United States v.
Heirs, United States v.
Helm, United States v.
Helweg, United States v.
Hemingway, United States v.
Henderson v. Morgan, 426 U.S. 637 (1976) — § 14-3(B)(2), n. 70
Henderson, United States v.
Hendon, United States v.
Hendrickson, United States v.
Hennis, United States v.
Henriques, United States v.
Henry, Middendorf v.
Henry, United States v.
Hensler, United States v.
Hepps, Philadelphia Newspapers, Inc. v.
Her Majesty The Queen, Genereux v.
Herd, United States v.
Hernandez, United States v.
Herod, United States v.
Heroit, United States v.
Herrin, United States v.
Herring, United States v.
Herrington, United States v.
Herron, United States v.
Hershey, United States v.
Heupel, Andrews v.
Heyward, United States v.
Hiatt v. Brown, 339 U.S. 103 (1950) — § 1-7, n. 6
Hiatt, United States v.
Hickman v. Taylor, 329 U.S. 495 (1947) — § 10-3(A), n. 3
Hicks, Arizona v.
Hicks, United States v.
Higa, United States v.
Higdon, United States v.
Higerd, United States v.
Higgins, United States v.
Hightower, United States v.
Hilbert, United States v.
Hill, United States v.
Hillman, United States v.
Hillmon, United States v.
Hilow, United States v.
Hilton, United States v.
Hines v. Mikell, 259 F. 28 (4th Cir. 1919) — § 4-7(A), n. 5
Hines, United States v.

TABLE OF CASES

Hinton, United States v.
Hirabayashi v. United States, 320 U.S. 81 (1943) — § 13-3(N)(1), nn. 319, 321
Hirsch, United States v.
Hitchcock, United States v.
Hitchman, United States v.
Hoaglin, United States v.
Hoard, United States v.
Hobart, United States v.
Hobbs, United States v.
Hock, United States v.
Hocker, United States v.
Hodge, United States v.
Hodges, United States v.
Hodson, McDonald v.
Hoersch v. Froehlke, 382 F. Supp. 1235 (E.D. Pa. 1974) — § 4-6, n. 20
Hoesing, United States v.
Hoffman v. United States, 341 U.S. 479 (1951) — § 11-2(E)(3), n. 130
Hoffman Estates v. Flipside, 455 U.S. 489 (1981) — § 2-7(A), n. 8; § 13-3(N)(2), nn. 349, 350
Hogan, United States v.
Holcomb, United States v.
Holden, Blodgett v.
Holder, United States v.
Holland, United States v.
Hollcraft, United States v.
Holley, United States v.
Holliday, United States v.
Holloway v. Arkansas, 435 U.S. 475 (1978) — § 15-2(B)(2), n. 26; § 15-2(B)(3), n. 47
Holloway, United States v.
Holman, United States v.
Holmes, United States v.
Holodinski v. McDowell, 7 M.J. 921 (N.C.M.R. 1979) — § 17-21, n. 6
Holstlaw, United States v.
Holt, United States v.
Homcy v. Resor, 455 F.2d 1345 (D.C. Cir. 1971) — § 17-23(C), n. 23
Homer, United States v.
Honeycutt, United States v.
Honican, United States v.
Hood, United States v.
Hook, United States v.
Hooper v. Hartman, 274 F.2d 429 (9th Cir. 1959) — § 4-8(D), nn. 60, 61; § 17-23(B), n. 12
Hooper, United States v.
Hoover, Dynes v.
Hoover, United States v.
Hopkins, United States v.
Hopkins, Yick Wo v.
Hopwood, United States v.
Horn v. Schlesinger, 514 F.2d 549 (8th Cir. 1975) — § 17-22(A), n. 6
Horne, United States v.
Horner, United States v.

TABLE OF CASES

Horsey, United States v.
Horton, United States v.
Hosford, United States v.
Hosken, Soriano v.
Hoskins, United States v.
Hounshell, United States v.
Householder, United States v.
Houston, United States v.
Hout, United States v.
Howard, United States v.
Howe, United States v.
Howell, United States v.
Hoxsey, United States v.
Hubbard, United States v.
Huber, United States v.
Huddelston, United States v.
Hudson, United States v.
Huelcamp, United States v.
Huelsman, United States v.
Huerta, United States v.
Huet-Vaughn, United States v.
Huff, United States v.
Huffman, United States v.
Huggins, United States v.
Hughes, United States v.
Huitt, United States v.
Hullum, United States v.
Hulsey, United States v.
Hultgren, United States v.
Humphrey v. Smith, 336 U.S. 695 (1949) — § 7-2(E), n. 99
Hungerford, Woodrick v.
Hunt, United States v.
Hunter, United States v.
Hurd, United States v.
Hurt, United States v.
Hussey, United States v.
Hustwit, United States v.
Hutchins, United States v.
Hutchinson, United States v.
Hutson v. United States, 19 C.M.A. 437, 42 C.M.R. 39 (1970) — § 7-2, n. 2; § 11-2(A)(3), n. 21
Hutto, United States v.
Huxhold, United States v.
Hypolite, United States v.
Hyska, United States v.

I

Ignatius, Jones v.
Ignatius, Latney v.
Ignatko, United States v.

TABLE OF CASES

Ilaskins, United States v.
Illinois v. Allen, 397 U.S. 337 (1970) — § 15-2(A), n. 13
Illinois v. Batchelder, 463 U.S. 1112 (1983) — § 1-1(B), n. 17
Illinois, Beauharnais v.
Illinois, Brown v.
Illinois v. Gates, 462 U.S. 213 (1983) — § 5-3(B), nn. 37, 38
Illinois, James v.
Illinois v. Krull, 480 U.S. 340 (1987) — § 5-3(F), n. 23
Illinois v. Lafayette, 462 U.S. 640 (1983) — § 5-3(D)(1), n. 133
Illinois v. Rodriguez, 110 S.Ct. 2793 (1990) — § 5-3(C)(6), n. 90
Illinois v. Smith, 469 U.S. 91 (1984) — § 17-17, n. 9
Illinois, Taylor v.
Imler, United States v.
In re Berue, 54 F. Supp. 252 (S.D. Ohio 1944) — § 4-7(A), n. 5
In re Clifton, 28 M.J. 614 (A.F.C.M.R. 1989) — § 17-19, n. 14
In re DiBartolo, 50 F. Supp. 929 (S.D.N.Y. 1943) — § 4-7(A), n. 6
In re Grimley, 137 U.S. 147 (1890) — § 4-5(A), nn. 4, 5; § 4-5(A)(1), n. 11; § 4-5(A)(2), n. 6
In re Ryder, 381 F.2d 713 (4th Cir. 1967) — § 10-3(F), n. 26
In re Taylor, 160 F. Supp. 932 (W.D. Mo. 1958) — § 4-6, n. 25
In re Yamashita, 327 U.S. 1 (1946) — § 4-1, n. 1
Ingham, United States v.
Inman, United States v.
Innis, Rhode Island v.
Int'l Society for Krishna Consciousness, Inc., Heffron v.
Irons, United States v.
Irvin, United States v.
Irving, United States v.
Irwin, United States v.
Isbell, United States v.
Isler, United States v.
Iverson, United States v.
Ivester, United States v.
Ivey, United States v.

J

Jack, United States v.
Jackson, United States v.
Jacob, Ellis v.
Jacobs, United States v.
Jacobson v. Massachusetts, 197 U.S. 11 (1905) — § 2-9(B), n. 21
Jacoby, United States v.
Jacques, United States v.
Jaeger, United States v.
Jaffree, Wallace v.
Jagnandan, United States v.
Jakaitis, United States v.
James v. Illinois, 493 U.S. 307 (1990) — § 5-3(F), n. 25
James, United States v.
James Orwell, United States v.

TABLE OF CASES

Jameson, United States v.
Jamison, United States v.
Jarrell, United States v.
Jarrie, United States v.
Jasper, United States v.
Jean, United States v.
Jeanbaptiste, United States v.
Jefferson, United States v.
Jeffries, United States v.
Jemmings, United States v.
Jencks v. United States, 353 U.S. 657 (1957) — § 10-4(B)(5), n. 48; § 10-6
Jenkins v. Anderson, 447 U.S. 231 (1980) — § 5-4(A)(3), n. 20
Jenkins v. Georgia, 418 U.S. 153 (1974) — § 13-3(N)(3), n. 367
Jenkins, United States v.
Jennings, United States v.
Jerasi, United States v.
Jessie, United States v.
Jeter, United States v.
Jette, United States v.
Jobes, United States v.
Jobson, United States v.
Johanns, United States v.
Johhnson, United States v.
Johnson, Kelley v.
Johnson, Texas v.
Johnson, United States v.
Johnston, United States v.
Johnwell, United States v.
Jolliff, United States v.
Jones v. Barnes, 463 U.S. 745 (1983) — § 17-14, n. 10
Jones v. Commander, Naval Air Force, 18 M.J. 198 (C.M.A. 1984) — § 3-3(C) n. 32
Jones, Harper v.
Jones v. Ignatius, 18 C.M.A. 7, 39 C.M.R. 7 (1968) — § 17-9(E), n. 85
Jones, United States v.
Jophlin, United States v.
Jordan, United States v.
Jordon, United States v.
Joseph, United States v.
Joseph H. Munson Co., Secretary of State of Maryland v.
Joslin, United States v.
Joyner, United States v.
Juarez, United States v.
Judson, United States v.
Julian, United States v.
Jursnick, United States v.
Justice, United States v.

K

Kabelka, United States v.
Kadlec, United States v.

TABLE OF CASES

Kahn v. Anderson, 255 U.S. 1 (1921) — § 4-8(C)(3), nn. 36, 49, 56; § 8-3(C)(3), n. 142
Kaliski, United States v.
Kalscheuer, United States v.
Kaminski, United States v.
Kamrath, Slater v.
Kapple, United States v.
Karnes, United States v.
Kastigar v. United States, 406 U.S. 441 (1972) — § 5-4(C), n. 55; § 11-2(E)(1), nn. 105, 106; § 11-2(E)(3), nn. 141, 149; § 13-3(H), n. 233
Kauffman v. Secretary of Air Force, 415 F.2d 991 (D.C. Cir. 1969) — § 17-23(C)(1), n. 25
Kauffman, United States v.
Kazena, United States v.
Kazmierczak, United States v.
Keaton, United States v.
Keck, United States v.
Keefe, Organization for a Better Austin v.
Keenan, United States v.
Keith, United States v.
Kelker, United States v.
Keller, United States v.
Kelley v. Johnson, 425 U.S. 238 (1976) — § 13-3(N)(3), nn. 381, 426
Kelley, United States v.
Kelliher, United States v.
Kellough, United States v.
Kelly, United States v.
Kelly v. United States, 1 M.J. 172 (C.M.A. 1975) — § 17-19, n. 15
Kelsey, United States v.
Kelson, United States v.
Kemp, United States v.
Kendall, United States v.
Kendig, United States v.
Kendra, United States v.
Kendrick, United States v.
Kennedy, Oregon v.
Kennedy, United States v.
Kentucky, Batson v.
Kentucky, Carter v.
Kentucky v. Stincer, 482 U.S. 730 (1987) — § 7-2(B)(4), n. 45
Kepple, United States v.
Kercheval v. United States, 274 U.S. 220 (1926) — § 14-3(A), n. 10
Kern, United States v.
Kersh, United States v.
Kershaw, United States v.
Kessinger, United States v.
Keyes, United States v.
Keys v. Cole, 31 M.J. 228 (C.M.A. 1990) — § 17-19, n. 8
Keys, United States v.
Kick, United States v.
Kiddo, United States v.
Kidwell, United States v.

TABLE OF CASES

Kiiskila v. Nichols, 433 F.2d 745 (7th Cir. 1970) — § 13-3(N)(3), n. 408
Kilbourne, United States v.
Kilbreth, United States v.
Kilgore, United States v.
Killebrew, United States v.
Kilpatrick, McCune v.
Kilroy, Evans v.
Kim, United States v.
Kimball, United States v.
Kimble, United States v.
Kimbrell, United States v.
Kinane, United States v.
Kinard, United States v.
Kincheloe, United States v.
Kinder, United States v.
King, United States v.
Kingsley Int'l Pictures Corp. v. Regents of the Univ. of New York, 360 U.S. 684 (1959)
 — § 13-3(N)(3), n. 373
Kinneer, United States v.
Kinney, United States v.
Kinsella v. Krueger, 359 U.S. 1 (1957) — § 4-7(B), n. 13
Kinsella, Madsen v.
Kinsella v. United States ex rel. Singleton, 361 U.S. 234 (1960) — § 4-7(B), n. 14
Kinsler, United States v.
Kinzer, United States v.
Kirk, United States v.
Kirkpatrick, United States v.
Kirks, United States v.
Kirsch, United States v.
Kitchen, United States v.
Kitchens, United States v.
Kitts, United States v.
Klawuhn, United States v.
Klein, United States v.
Kline, United States v.
Kline, Vlandis v.
Klingensmith, United States v.
Klink, United States v.
Klinko, United States v.
Kloese, United States v.
Klunk, United States v.
Knickerbocker, United States v.
Kniess, United States v.
Knight, United States v.
Kochan, United States v.
Koepke, United States v.
Kohlman, United States v.
Kohut, United States v.
Koistinen, United States v.
Koke, United States v.
Komorous, United States v.

1035

TABLE OF CASES

Konarski, United States v.
Konieczka, United States v.
Koonce, United States v.
Koopman, United States v.
Koppen, United States v.
Korda, United States v.
Korematsu v. United States, 323 U.S. 214 (1944) — § 13-3(N)(1), n. 306
Korte v. United States, 260 F.2d 633 (9th Cir. 1958) — § 4-5(B), n. 24
Kossman, United States v.
Kovac, United States v.
Kozak, United States v.
Kraffa, United States v.
Krajewski, United States v.
Kramer, United States v.
Krampf, United States v.
Kratzenberg, United States v.
Krauss, United States v.
Krautheim, United States v.
Krenn, United States v.
Kretchmer, United States v.
Krewson, United States v.
Kroop, United States v.
Kropf, United States v.
Krueger, Kinsella v.
Krull, Illinois v.
Krutsinger, United States v.
Krzcuik, United States v.
Kuczaj, United States v.
Kuehl, United States v.
Kuelker, United States v.
Kunkle, United States v.
Kurtzman, Lemon v.
Kurz, United States v.
Kyle, United States v.
Kyles, United States v.

L

LaBella, United States v.
LaBoa, Sullivan v.
Lacey, United States v.
Lackey, United States v.
Ladell, United States v.
Lafayette, Illinois v.
LaGrange, United States v.
Lahman, United States v.
Laird, Anderson v.
Laird, Cole v.
Lake, United States v.
Lakeside v. Oregon, 435 U.S. 333 (1978) — § 15-14(B), n. 47
Lallande, United States v.

TABLE OF CASES

Lalli v. Lalli, 439 U.S. 259 (1978) — § 13-3(N)(1), n. 330
Lamar, United States v.
Lambert, United States v.
Lamela, United States v.
Lamer, United States v.
Laminman, United States v.
Lampani, United States v.
Lancaster, United States v.
Landwehr, United States v.
Lane, United States v.
Lanford, United States v.
Lange, United States v.
Langer, United States v.
Langford, United States v.
Langston, United States v.
Lania, United States v.
Lanphear, United States v.
Lanzer, United States v.
Lanzetta v. New Jersey, 306 U.S. 451 (1939) — § 13-3(N)(2), n. 339
Lapeer, United States v.
Larkins, United States v.
Larneard, United States v.
Larner, United States v.
Larson, United States v.
Larson v. Valente, 456 U.S. 228 (1982) — § 13-3(N)(3), n. 394
Lasagni, United States v.
Lashley, United States v.
Lassiter, United States v.
Latham, United States v.
Latimer, United States v.
Latney v. Ignatius, 416 F.2d 821 (D.D.C. 1969) — § 4-7(A), n. 7
Latta, United States v.
Lauzon, United States v.
Lavalla, United States v.
Lavine, United States v.
Lawer, United States v.
Lawless, United States v.
Lawrence, United States v.
Laws, United States v.
Lawson, United States v.
Lazenby, United States v.
Lazzaro, United States v.
Leahy, United States v.
Leamer, United States v.
Leaver, United States v.
Lecolst, United States v.
Ledbetter, United States v.
Ledbetter v. United States, 170 U.S. 606 (1898) — § 6-1(C), n. 96
Lee, United States v.
Leggs, United States v.
Leiffer, United States v.

TABLE OF CASES

Leiker, United States v.
Leininger, United States v.
LeMaster, United States v.
LeMasters, United States v.
Lemieux, United States v.
Lemley, United States v.
Lemoine, United States v.
Lemon v. Kurtzman, 403 U.S. 602 (1971) — § 13-3(N)(3), n. 396
Lemon, United States v.
Lenard, United States v.
Lenior, United States v.
Lenoir, United States v.
Lents, United States v.
Lenz, United States v.
Leonard, United States v.
Leon, United States v.
Levin, United States v.
Levite, United States v.
Levy, Parker v.
Levy v. Resor, 17 C.M.A. 135, 37 C.M.R. 399 (1967) — § 17-5, n. 5
Lewandowski, United States v.
Lewis v. New Orleans, 415 U.S. 130 (1970) — § 13-3(N)(3), n. 368
Lewis, United States v.
Ley, United States v.
Liberator, United States v.
Lichtenhan, United States v.
Lichtsinn, United States v.
Light, United States v.
Lightfoot, United States v.
Lillie, United States v.
Lilly, United States v.
Lincoln, United States v.
Lindsay, United States v.
Lindsey, United States v.
Lippoldt, United States v.
Lips, United States v.
Lipscomb, United States v.
Little, United States v.
Littrice, United States v.
Lizasuain, United States v.
Llewellyn, United States v.
Lloyd, United States v.
Lochausen, United States v.
Lockart v. Fretwell, 113 S. Ct. 838 (1993) — § 15-2(B)(3), n. 36
Locke, Rose v.
Lockett, United States v.
Lockwood, United States v.
Logan, United States v.
Logan v. Zimmerman Brush Co., 455 U.S. 422 (1982) — § 13-3(N)(1), n. 307
Lohr, United States v.
Lohrman, United States v.

TABLE OF CASES

Lomax, United States v.
Lonberger, Marshall v.
London, United States v.
Lonetree, United States v.
Long, United States v.
Longhi, United States v.
Longhofer, United States v.
Longmire, United States v.
Longstreath, United States v.
Loos, United States v.
Lopez, United States v.
Lorance, United States v.
Lorenc, United States v.
Los Angeles v. Taxpayers for Vincent, 104 S. Ct. 2118 (1984) — § 13-3(N)(3), n. 380
Louder, United States v.
Louisiana, Brown v.
Louisiana, Burch v.
Loukas, United States v.
Lovasco, United States v.
Lovejoy, United States v.
Lovell, United States v.
Loving, United States v.
Loving v. United States, 116 S. Ct. 1737 (1996) — § 1-1(B), n. 21; § 1-6, n. 1; § 4-11(C)(1), n. 61; § 16-3(A), nn. 27-32
Loving v. Virginia, 388 U.S. 1 (1967) — § 13-3(N)(1), n. 319
Lovisi v. Slayton, 363 F. Supp. 620 (E.D. Va. 1973) — § 2-9(D), n. 63
Lowe, Garrett v.
Lowery, United States v.
Lowry, United States v.
Lubin v. Panish, 415 U.S. 709 (1974) — § 13-3(N)(1), n. 323
Lubitz, United States v.
Lucas, Mathews v.
Lucas, United States v.
Luce v. United States, 105 S. Ct. 460 (1984) — § 13-5(L), n. 97
Ludlum, United States v.
Luebs, United States v.
Luedtke, United States v.
Lugo, United States v.
Lumagui, United States v.
Lumbus, United States v.
Lusk, United States v.
Lutz, United States v.
Lwin v. Cooper, 33 M.J. 666 (N.M.C.M.R. 1991) — § 17-19, n. 18
Lwin, United States v.
Lynch v. Donnelly, 465 U.S. 668 (1984) — § 13-3(N)(3), n. 400
Lynch, United States v.
Lynott, United States v.
Lyons, United States v.

M

Mabe, United States v.

TABLE OF CASES

Mabie, United States v.
MacCulloch, United States v.
Mack, United States v.
Mackey, United States v.
Maderia, United States v.
Madison, United States v.
Madsen v. Kinsella, 343 U.S. 341 (1952) — § 4-1, n. 1
Maglito, United States v.
Maharajh, United States v.
Mahloch, United States v.
Mahone, United States v.
Mahoney, Garrett v.
Mahoney, Gray v.
Mahoney, United States v.
Maine v. Moulton, 474 U.S. 159 (1985) — § 15-2(B)(3), n. 46
Malczewskyj, United States v.
Malia, United States v.
Malik, United States v.
Mallett, United States v.
Malone, United States v.
Mamaluy, United States v.
Manalo, United States v.
Mance, United States v.
Mancini, United States v.
Maness, United States v.
Mangsen v. Snyder, 1 M.J. 287 (C.M.A. 1976) — § 4-14(A), n. 2
Manley, United States v.
Mann, United States v.
Manos, United States v.
Mansbarger, United States v.
Mansell, United States v.
Mansfield, United States v.
Manson v. Brathwaite, 432 U.S. 98 (1977) — § 5-5, n. 9
Mantilla, United States v.
Manuel, United States v.
Maracle, United States v.
Marcy, United States v.
Marell, United States v.
Maresca, United States v.
Margelony, United States v.
Marin, United States v.
Marion, United States v.
Marker, United States v.
Markland, United States v.
Marks v. United States, 430 U.S. 188 (1977) — § 13-3(N)(5), n. 430
Marler, United States v.
Marquardt, United States v.
Marrie, United States v.
Marsh, United States v.
Marshall v. Lonberger, 459 U.S. 422 (1983) — § 13-2(G)(2), n. 110
Marshall, United States v.

TABLE OF CASES

Marshall v. United States, 423 F.2d 1315 (10th Cir. 1970) — § 11-2(A)(3), n. 28
Marston, United States v.
Martel, United States v.
Martelon v. Temple, 747 F.2d 1348 (10th Cir. 1984) — § 13-3(N)(1), n. 314
Martin v. Struthers, 319 U.S. 141 (1943) — § 13-3(N)(3), nn. 376, 406
Martin, United States v.
Martindale v. Campbell, 25 M.J. 755 (N.M.C.M.R. 1987) — § 17-14, n. 5
Martindale, United States v.
Martinez, United States v.
Martino, United States v.
Martinsmith, United States v.
Marvin, United States v.
Maryland, Booth v.
Maryland, Brady v.
Maryland v. Buie, 494 U.S. 325 (1990) — § 5-3(C)(7), n. 105
Maryland, McGowan v.
Maschino, United States v.
Maslanich, United States v.
Masminster, United States v.
Mason, United States v.
Massachusetts, Jacobson v.
Massachusetts, Snyder v.
Massachusetts Bd. of Retirement v. Murgia, 427 U.S. 307 (1976) — § 13-3(N)(1), n. 317
Massengill, United States v.
Masseria, United States v.
Massey, United States v.
Massie, United States v.
Mastropietro v. Nix, 12 M.J. 759 (A.C.M.R. 1981) — § 17-19, n. 31
Mathews v. Diaz, 426 U.S. 67 (1976) — § 13-3(N)(1), nn. 305, 320
Mathews v. Lucas, 427 U.S. 495 (1976) — § 13-3(N)(1), nn. 325, 327
Mathews, United States v.
Mathiason, Oregon v.
Mathieu, United States v.
Mathis, United States v.
Matias, United States v.
Matlock, United States v.
Matthews v. Eldridge, 424 U.S. 319 (1976) — § 1-1(B), n. 17
Matthews, United States v.
Matura, United States v.
Mauck, United States v.
Maxwell, Shepherd v.
Maxwell, United States v.
May, United States v.
Mayborn v. Heflebower, 145 F.2d 864 (5th Cir. 1944) — § 4-5(B), nn. 19, 20
Mayden, Gosa v.
Maydwell, United States v.
Mayer, United States v.
Mayes, United States v.
Mayfield, United States v.
Mayhugh, United States v.
Mayne, United States v.

TABLE OF CASES

Mayo, United States v.
Mayville, United States v.
McBride, United States v.
McCaig, United States v.
McCall, United States v.
McCallister, United States v.
McCanless, United States v.
McCann, United States v.
McCants, United States v.
McCarthy, United States v.
McCarthy v. United States, 394 U.S. 459 (1969) — § 14-3(A)(1), n. 13
McCarty, United States v.
McCauley, United States v.
McClain, United States v.
McClaughry v. Deming, 186 U.S. 49 (1902) — § 4-2(A), n. 7; § 4-13, n. 4; § 8-1, n. 1
McClelland, United States v.
McClendon, United States v.
McCline, United States v.
McCollum, United States v.
McCormick, United States v.
McCoy, United States v.
McCrary, United States v.
McCray v. Grande, 38 M.J. 657 (A.C.M.R. 1993) — § 17-19, n. 22
McCray, United States v.
McCreight, United States v.
McCullah, United States v.
McCullar, United States v.
McCullom, United States v.
McCullough, United States v.
McCune v. Kilpatrick, 53 F. Supp. 80 (E.D. Va. 1943) — § 4-7(A), nn. 5, 7
McDaniel v. Paty, 435 U.S. 618 (1978) — § 13-3(N)(3), n. 397
McDaniel, United States v.
McDavid, United States v.
McDonagh, United States v.
McDonald v. Hodson, 19 C.M.A. 582, 42 C.M.R. 184 (1970) — § 7-2(C), n. 75
McDonald, United States v.
McDonald, Welchel v.
McDowell, Holodinski v.
McDowell, United States v.
McDuffie, United States v.
McElhinney, United States v.
McElroy, United States v.
McElroy v. United States ex rel. Guagliardo, 361 U.S. 281 (1960) — § 4-7(B), n. 14
McElyea, United States v.
McFaddon, Schooner Exchange v.
McFarlin, United States v.
McFatrich, United States v.
McGary, United States v.
McGee, United States v.
McGeeney, United States v.
McGill, United States v.

TABLE OF CASES

McGinnis, United States v.
McGowan v. Maryland, 366 U.S. 420 (1961) — § 13-3(N)(1), nn. 313, 400
McGowan, United States v.
McGraner, United States v.
McGuinness, United States v.
McGuire, United States v.
McHugh, United States v.
McIntosh, United States v.
McKaskle v. Wiggins, 465 U.S. 168 (1984) — § 12-2(F)(4), nn. 74-78
McKenzie, United States v.
McKillop, United States v.
McKinley, United States v.
McKinney, United States v.
McKinnie, United States v.
McKnight, United States v.
McLaren, United States v.
McLaughlin, County of Riverside v.
McLaughlin, United States v.
McLaurin, United States v.
McLemore, United States v.
McLeod, United States v.
McMahan, United States v.
McMann, United States v.
McMillan, United States v.
McMonagle, United States v.
McNally, United States v.
McNamara, Ashe v.
McNeece, United States v.
McNeill, United States v.
McNett, United States v.
McOmber, United States v.
McPhail, United States v.
McPhaul, United States v.
McQueen, United States v.
Meace, United States v.
Meade, United States v.
Meadow, United States v.
Meadows, United States v.
Means, United States v.
Mechanics' & Traders' Bank v. Union Bank, 89 U.S. (22 Wall.) 276 (1875) — § 4-1, n. 1
Meckler, United States v.
Medley, United States v.
Meek, United States v.
Meeks v. Craven, 482 F.2d 465 (9th Cir. 1973) — § 12-2(F)(4), n. 85
Meeks, United States v.
Meloni, Baron v.
Melton, United States v.
Memorial Hosp. v. Ma, 415 U.S. 250 (1974) — § 13-3(N)(1), n. 324
Mena, United States v.
Mendoza, United States v.
Mendrano v. Smith, 797 F.2d 1538 (10th Cir. 1986) — § 15-15, n. 14

1043

TABLE OF CASES

Menna v. New York, 423 U.S. 61 (1975) — § 13-3(N), n. 300
Menoken, United States v.
Mercier, United States v.
Meredith, People v.
Merrill, United States v.
Merritt, United States v.
Merritte, United States v.
Merriweather, United States v.
Merrow, United States v.
Mervine, United States v.
Messiah v. United States, 377 U.S. 201 (1964) — § 5-4(B), n. 30
Metropolitan Housing Dev. Corp., Arlington Heights v.
Meyer v. Nebraska, 262 U.S. 390 (1923) — § 13-3(N)(4), n. 411
Mezzanatto, United States v.
Michael M. v. Sonoma County Superior Ct., 450 U.S. 464 (1981) — § 13-3(N)(1), n. 326
Michaels, United States v.
Michigan v. Mosley, 423 U.S. 96 (1975) — § 5-4(B), n. 48
Mickel, United States v.
Mickla, United States v.
Middendorf v. Henry, 411 U.S. 25 (1976) — § 4-3(C), n. 11
Middendorf v. Henry, 425 U.S. 25, 96 S. Ct. 1281, 47 L. Ed. 2d 566 (1976) — § 1-1, n. 6; § 1-1(B), n. 17; § 1-8(D)(1), n. 13; § 8-3(B)(1), n. 61; § 15-25, n. 1; § 15-26(C), nn. 8, 11; § 15-29
Middleton, United States v.
Midgett v. United States, 603 F.2d 835 (Ct. Cl. 1979) — § 17-22(A), n. 7
Mikell, Hines v.
Milam, United States v.
Milkinevich, United States v.
Millender, United States v.
Miller v. California, 458 U.S. 747 (1972) — § 13-3(N)(3), n. 367
Miller, United States v.
Milligan, Ex parte
Mills, United States v.
Millsap, United States v.
Minaya, United States v.
Mincey, United States v.
Miner, United States v.
Miniclier, United States v.
Minnesota, Near v.
Minor, United States v.
Miranda v. Arizona, 384 U.S. 436 (1966) — § 5-4(B), nn. 24, 26
Miro, United States v.
Mitchell, United States v.
Mix, United States v.
Mobley, United States v.
Mock, United States v.
Modesto, United States v.
Mogavero, United States v.
Moglia, United States v.
Monroe, United States v.
Mons, United States v.

TABLE OF CASES

Montana, Sandstrom v.
Montanino, United States v.
Montcalm, United States v.
Montesinos, United States v.
Montford, United States v.
Montgomery, United States v.
Montoya, United States v.
Moody, United States v.
Moore, United States v.
Moorer, United States v.
Moore, United States v.
Mora, United States v.
Morales, United States v.
Morales-Santana, United States v.
Moreno, United States v.
Moreno, United States Dep't of Agriculture v.
Morero, United States v.
Morgan, Gilligan v.
Morgan, Henderson v.
Morgan, United States v.
Morgan v. United States, 380 F.2d 686 (9th Cir. 1967) — § 13-5(F), n. 18
Moriarty, Frage v.
Moriarty, Petty v.
Morris v. Slappy, 461 U.S. 1 (1983) — § 15-2(B)(3), n. 93
Morris, United States v.
Morrisey v. Brewer, 408 U.S. 471 (1972) — § 5-9(D), n. 39; § 17-23(C)(2)
Morrisey v. Perry, 137 U.S. 157 (1890) — § 4-5(A)(2), n. 1
Morrison, United States v.
Morrissette v. United States, 342 U.S. 246 (1952) — § 15-20, n. 3
Morrow, United States v.
Morse, United States v.
Morton, United States v.
Moseley, United States v.
Mosely, United States v.
Moser, United States v.
Moses, United States v.
Mosley, Michigan v.
Mosley, United States v.
Mosly, United States v.
Moss, United States v.
Motsinger, United States v.
Moultak, United States v.
Moulton, Maine v.
Mountain, United States v.
Mouqenel, United States v.
Mow, United States v.
Mow Sun Wong, Hampton v.
Moyar, United States v.
Mucthison, United States v.
Mueller, United States v.
Muir, United States v.

TABLE OF CASES

Mullaney v. Wilbur, 421 U.S. 684 (1975) — § 15-20, n. 4
Mullen, United States v.
Mullens, United States v.
Muller, United States v.
Muniz, United States v.
Munkus, United States v.
Murgia, Massachusetts Bd. of Retirement v.
Murphy v. Dalton, 81 F.3d 343 (3rd Cir. 1996) — § 4-6, nn. 18, 19
Murphy v. Garrett, 29 M.J. 469 (C.M.A. 1990) — § 4-6, n. 16; § 4-8(C)(3), n. 31
Murphy, United States v.
Murphy v. Waterfront Comm'n, 378 U.S. 52 (1964) — § 5-4(C), n. 62; § 11-2(E)(1), n. 112
Murray v. Haldeman, 16 M.J. 74 (C.M.A. 1983) — § 2-4(A), n. 16; § 4-11(B), n. 40; § 5-3(C)(9), n. 114; § 5-3(D)(1), nn. 131, 132; § 5-4(A)(1), n. 6
Murray, United States v.
Murray v. United States, 487 U.S. 533 (1988) — § 5-4(B), n. 33
Murrell, United States v.
Musguire, United States v.
Mustafa, United States v.
Myers, Connick v.
Myers, United States v.
Myhre, United States v.
Myles, United States v.
Myrick, United States v.

N

NAACP v. Alabama, 357 U.S. 449 (1958) — § 13-3(N)(3), n. 406
NAACP v. Button, 371 U.S. 415 (1963) — § 13-3(N)(2), n. 344; § 13-3(N)(3), n. 406
NAACP v. Claiborne Hardware Co., 458 U.S. 886 (1982) — § 13-3(N)(3), nn. 406, 408
Naar, United States v.
Nagle, United States v.
Nakamura, United States v.
Napier, United States v.
Nardell, United States v.
Nardone v. United States, 308 U.S. 338 (1939) — § 5-4(B), n. 34
Narine, United States v.
Nash, United States v.
Nastro, United States v.
Natalello, United States v.
National Ass'n of Letter Carriers, United States Civil Service Comm'n v.
National Dairy Prod. Corp., United States v.
National Treasury Employees Union v. Von Raab, 489 U.S. 656 (1989) — § 2-9(B), n. 17
Nault, United States v.
Neal, United States v.
Near v. Minnesota, 283 U.S. 697 (1931) — § 13-3(N)(3), n. 359
Nebling, United States v.
Neblock, United States v.
Nebraska, Meyer v.

TABLE OF CASES

Nebraska Press Ass'n v. Stuart, 427 U.S. 539 (1976) — § 15-3, n. 16; § 13-3(N)(3), n. 359
Needham, United States v.
Neeley, United States v.
Negron, United States v.
Negrone, United States v.
Neil v. Biggers, 409 U.S. 188 (1972) — § 5-5, n. 9
Neil, United States v.
Nellum, United States v.
Nelson, United States v.
New, United States v.
New Hampshire, Chaplinski v.
New Jersey, Garrity v.
New Jersey, Lanzetta v.
New Jersey v. Portash, 440 U.S. 450 (1979) — § 5-4(C), n. 56; § 11-2(E)(1), n. 106
New Jersey v. T.L.O., 105 S. Ct. 733 (1985) — § 5-10(D)
New Orleans, Lewis v.
New York v. Belton, 453 U.S. 454 (1981) — § 5-3(C)(7), n. 102
New York, Dunaway v.
New York v. Ferber, 458 U.S. 747 (1982) — § 13-3(N)(3), nn. 367, 377, 387, 388, 391
New York, Harris v.
New York v. Harris, 110 S. Ct. 1640 (1990) — § 5-3(F), nn. 20, 21
New York, Menna v.
New York v. Onofre, 415 N.E.2d 936 (N.Y. 1980) — § 13-3(N)(4), n. 423
New York, Payton v.
New York, Santobello v.
New York, Winters v.
New York Times Co. v. Sullivan, 376 U.S. 254 (1964) — § 13-3(N)(3), nn. 369, 371, 376
New York Times Co. v. United States, 403 U.S. 713 (1971) — § 13-3(N)(3), n. 377
Newak, United States v.
Newberry, United States v.
Newcomb, United States v.
Newkirk, United States v.
Newman, United States v.
Newman v. United States, 185 Ct. Cl. 269 (1968) — § 17-22(A), n. 5
Newsome, United States v.
Newson, United States v.
Nichelson, United States v.
Nichols, Kiiskila v.
Nichols, United States v.
Nichols v. United States, 114 S. Ct. 1921 (1994) — § 3-8(B), n. 8
Nicholson, United States v.
Nickaboine, United States v.
Nickels, United States v.
Nickerson, United States v.
Nigro, United States v.
Niles, United States v.
Nitze, Van Bourg v.
Nivens, United States v.
Nix, Mastropietro v.
Nix, United States v.

1047

TABLE OF CASES

Nix v. Whiteside, 475 U.S. 157 (1986) — § 15-2(B)(4), n. 119
Nix v. Williams, 467 U.S. 431 (1984) — § 5-3(F), n. 26; § 13-4(A), n. 14
Nixon, United States v.
Nobles, United States v.
Noel, United States v.
Noonan, United States v.
Noreen, United States v.
Norfleet, United States v.
Norman, United States v.
Norment, United States v.
Norris, United States v.
North Carolina v. Alford, 400 U.S. 25 (1970) — § 14-3, n. 3; § 14-3(D)(2), n. 135; § 14-3(D)(4), n. 155; § 14-5, n. 1
Northern, United States v.
Northrup, United States v.
Norvell, United States v.
Novak v. Rumsfeld, 423 F. Supp. 971 (N.D. Cal. 1976) — § 4-5(A), n. 8
Noxon, United States v.
Noyd v. Bond, 395 U.S. 683 (1969) — § 17-23(B), n. 8
Nunes, United States v.
Nunez, United States v.
Nye & Nissen v. United States, 168 F.2d 846 (9th Cir. 1948) — § 13-5(F), n. 19
Nystrom, United States v.

O

O'Brien, United States v.
O'Callahan v. Parker, 395 U.S. 258 (1969) — § 1-1(B), n. 30; § 4-10, nn. 2, 4; § 4-11; § 4-11(A), n. 28; § 4-11(B), n. 38; § 4-11(C); § 4-11(C), nn. 47, 55; § 4-11(C)(1); § 4-16; § 8-3(C)(3), n. 142
O'Connor, United States v.
O'Neal, United States v.
O'Quin, United States v.
Oakley, United States v.
Oates, United States v.
Oatney, United States v.
Occhi, United States v.
Odegard, United States v.
Ohio, Brandenburg v.
Ohio, Brown v.
Ohio, Doyle v.
Ohio, Terry v.
Ohman, Reed v.
Ohrt, United States v.
Oklahoma, Ake v.
Oklahoma, Broadrick v.
Oldaker, United States v.
Olinger, United States v.
Olivari, United States v.
Oliver, United States v.
Oliver v. United States, 466 U.S. 170 (1984) — § 5-3(A), n. 23

TABLE OF CASES

Olivero, United States v.
Olsen, United States v.
Olson, United States v.
Onofre, New York v.
Onofre, People v.
Onstad, United States v.
Opperman, South Dakota v.
Oquendo, United States v.
Orback, United States v.
Orben, United States v.
Oregon v. Bradshaw, 462 U.S. 1039 (1983) — § 5-4(B), n. 50
Oregon v. Elstad, 470 U.S. 298 (1985) — § 5-4(B), n. 34
Oregon v. Kennedy, 456 U.S. 667 (1982) — § 13-3(E), n. 208; § 15-4(B), n. 14
Oregon, Lakeside v.
Oregon v. Mathiason, 429 U.S. 492 (1977) — § 5-4(B), n. 37
Organization for a Better Austin v. Keefe, 402 U.S. 415 (1971) — § 13-3(N)(3), nn. 374, 377
Orloff v. Willoughby, 345 U.S. 83 (1953) — § 2-5, nn. 1, 2
Ornelas, United States v.
Orr, Chilcott v.
Orser, Cooke v.
Ortiz, United States v.
Ortiz-Vergara, United States v.
Osborne, United States v.
Osburn, United States v.
Otero, United States v.
Ott, United States v.
Ouelette, Wilson v.
Outhier, United States v.
Overton, United States v.
Owens, United States v.
Oxford, United States v.
Oyler v. Boles, 368 U.S. 448 (1962) — § 13-3(M), n. 284

P

Pabon, United States v.
Pacheco, United States v.
Pacifica Foundation, Federal Communications Comm'n v.
Packer, United States v.
Padilla, United States v.
Pagel, United States v.
Paige, United States v.
Painter, United States v.
Palenius, United States v.
Palko v. Connecticut, 302 U.S. 319 (1937) — § 13-3(N)(1), n. 318
Palmer, United States v.
Palmiter, United States v.
Palmore v. Sidoti, 466 U.S. 429 (1984) — § 13-3(N)(1), n. 319
Palos, United States v.
Palumbo, United States v.

TABLE OF CASES

Panish, Lubin v.
Papageorgiou, United States v.
Papchristou v. City of Jacksonville, 405 U.S. 156 (1972) — § 13-3(N)(2), n. 343
Pappas, United States v.
Parini, United States v.
Parish, United States v.
Parisi v. Davidson, 404 U.S. 34 (1972) — § 17-23(B), nn. 18-20
Parker v. Levy, 417 U.S. 733 (1974) — § 2-1, n. 1; § 2-3, n. 1; § 2-4(A), n. 18; § 2-6, n. 2; § 2-8(B), n. 14; § 2-9(D), n. 66; § 13-3(N)(2), nn. 352-355; § 13-3(N)(3), nn. 382, 383, 384, 390, 403; § 17-23(C)(2)
Parker, O'Callahan v.
Parker, O'Callahan v.
Parker, United States v.
Parkes, United States v.
Parks, United States v.
Parrillo, United States v.
Parrish, United States v.
Partin, United States v.
Partyka, United States v.
Pascascio v. Fischer, 34 M.J. 996 (A.C.M.R. 1992) — § 17-19, n. 19
Pascascio, United States v.
Paske, United States v.
Pastor, United States v.
Paternina-Vergara, United States v.
Patterson, United States v.
Patton, United States v.
Pattugalan, United States v.
Paty, McDaniel v.
Pauley, United States v.
Paulk, United States v.
Paulson, United States v.
Pawis, United States v.
Payne, United States v.
Payton v. New York, 445 U.S. 573 (1980) — § 5-7, n. 13
Peaches, United States v.
Peacock, United States v.
Pearson v. Bloss, 28 M.J. 764 (A.F.C.M.R. 1989) — § 4-8(D), n. 64
Pearson v. Cox, 10 M.J. 317 (C.M.A. 1981) — § 17-2(B)(2), nn. 28, 32
Pearson, United States v.
Peck, United States v.
Peebles, United States v.
Peek, United States v.
Peel, United States v.
Pellman, United States v.
Pena, United States v.
Pendry, United States v.
Penister, United States v.
Penn, Smalis v.
Penn, United States v.
Pennington, United States v.
People v. Beige, 41 N.Y.2d 60, 359 N.E.2d 377 (1976) — § 10-3(F), n. 27

TABLE OF CASES

People v. Meredith, 175 Cal. Rptr. 612, 631 P.2d 46 (1981) — § 10-3(F), n. 27
People v. Onofre, 415 N.E.2d 936 (N.Y. 1980) — § 13-3(N)(4), n. 411
People v. Wheeler, 22 Cal.3d 258, 148 Cal. Rptr. 890, 583 P.2d 748 (1978) — § 15-10(C)(3), n. 112
Peoples, United States v.
Pereira, United States v.
Perez, United States v.
Pergande, United States v.
Perkinson, United States v.
Perna, United States v.
Perry, Morrisey v.
Perry, United States v.
Perry Educ. Ass'n v. Perry Local Educators Ass'n, 460 U.S. 37 (1983) — § 13-3(N)(3), n. 378
Perry Local Educators Ass'n, Perry Educ. Ass'n v.
Peszynski, United States v.
Peterson, United States v.
Petroff-Tachomakoff, United States v.
Pettaway, United States v.
Pettersen, United States v.
Petterson, United States v.
Pettigrew, United States v.
Pettis, United States v.
Petty v. Moriarty, 20 C.M.A. 438, 43 C.M.R. 278 (1971) — § 13-2(G)(1), n. 66
Petty, United States v.
Pfister, Dombrowski v.
Phaneuf, United States v.
Phare, United States v.
Phelps, United States v.
Philadelphia Newspapers, Inc. v. Hepps, 475 U.S. 767 (1986) — § 13-3(N)(3), n. 371
Phillips, United States v.
Phillipson, United States v.
Phrampus, United States v.
Piatt, United States v.
Pickens v. Cox, 181 F.2d 784 (10th Cir. 1960) — § 4-5(B), n. 25
Pickering v. Board of Educ., 391 U.S. 563 (1968) — § 13-3(N)(3), n. 381
Picotte, United States v.
Pierce, United States v.
Pillow, United States v.
Pingree, United States v.
Pinkston, United States v.
Pippin, United States v.
Pirraglia, United States v.
Pitasi, United States v.
Pitt, United States v.
Pittman, United States v.
Place, United States v.
Plante, United States v.
Plaut, United States v.
Playtime Theatres, Inc., City of Renton v.
Plott, United States v.

TABLE OF CASES

Plyler v. Doe, 457 U.S. 202 (1982) — § 13-3(N)(1), n. 317
Politano, United States v.
Polk, United States v.
Pollack, United States v.
Pollard, United States v.
Pompey, United States v.
Pond, United States v.
Ponder, United States v.
Ponds, United States v.
Ponzi v. Fessenden, 258 U.S. 254 (1922) — § 4-12(B), n. 17
Poole, United States v.
Pooler, United States v.
Portash, New Jersey v.
Porter v. Eggers, 32 M.J. 583 (A.C.M.R. 1990) — § 4-12(B), n. 16; § 13-3(C)(3), n. 158
Porter v. Richardson, 50 C.M.R. 910 (C.M.A. 1975) — § 5-9(E), n. 53
Porter, United States v.
Posnick, United States v.
Postle, United States v.
Poteet, United States v.
Potter, United States v.
Powell v. Alabama, 287 U.S. 45 (1932) — § 15-2(B)(3), n. 45
Powell, United States v.
Power, United States v.
Pownall, United States v.
Pratcher, United States v.
Pratt, United States v.
Press-Enterprise Co. v. Superior Court, 464 U.S. 501 (1984) — § 15-3, nn. 4, 10
Press-Enterprise Co. v. Superior Court, 478 U.S. 1 (1986) — § 15-3, n. 12
Preuss, United States v.
Price, United States v.
Priest v. Secretary of Navy, 570 F.2d 1013 (D.C. Cir. 1977) — § 13-3(N)(3), nn. 368, 383, 384
Priest, United States v.
Prince v. United States, 352 U.S. 322 (1957) — § 6-1(C)(3), n. 146
Pringle, United States v.
Prive, United States v.
Privette, United States v.
Proctor, United States v.
Prophete, United States v.
Province, United States v.
Provost, United States v.
Pruitt, United States v.
Pruner, United States v.
Pryor, United States v.
Puckett, United States v.
Pugh, Gerstein v.
Pullen, United States v.
Pulliam, United States v.
Purdy, United States v.

Q

Quarles, Toth v.

TABLE OF CASES

Quarles, United States v.
Quarles, United States ex rel. Toth v.
Queen, United States v.
Quezada, United States v.
Quigley, United States v.
Quillen, United States v.
Quinones, United States v.
Quinores, United States v.
Quintana, United States v.
Quirin, Ex parte

R

Rachel, United States v.
Rachels, United States v.
Radford, United States v.
Radimecky, United States v.
Ragan v. Cox, 320 F.2d 815 (10th Cir. 1963) — § 4-8(C)(5), n. 57
Raichle, United States v.
Rainwater, United States v.
Ralbovsky, United States v.
Ralston, United States v.
Ramos, United States v.
Ramsey, United States v.
Randle, United States v.
Rankins, United States v.
Rapolla, United States v.
Rappaport, United States v.
Rasberry, United States v.
Rascoe, United States v.
Ratliff, United States v.
Ravenel, United States v.
Ravine, United States v.
Ray, United States v.
Rayford, United States v.
Rayle, United States v.
Raymond, United States v.
Read, United States v.
Reagan, United States v.
Reap, United States v.
Rebuck, United States v.
Reddick, United States v.
Redding, United States v.
Redhail, Zablocki v.
Redman, United States v.
Reece, United States v.
Reed v. Ohman, 19 C.M.A. 110, 41 C.M.R. 110 (1969) — § 17-5, nn. 5, 8
Reed v. Reed, 404 U.S. 71 (1971) — § 13-3(N)(1), n. 329
Reed, United States v.
Reeder, United States v.
Reese, United States v.

TABLE OF CASES

Reeves, United States v.
Regan, United States v.
Regents of the Univ. of New York, Kingsley Int'l Pictures Corp. v.
Reichardt, United States v.
Reichenbach, United States v.
Reid v. Covert, 354 U.S. 1 (1957) — § 4-7(A), n. 10; § 4-7(B), n. 13; § 8-3(C)(3), n. 142
Reid, United States v.
Reilly, United States v.
Reinecke, United States v.
Reister, United States v.
Relford v. Commandant, 401 U.S. 355 (1971) — § 4-10, nn. 2, 6; § 4-11, n. 1; § 4-11(A), n. 35; § 4-11(B), nn. 38, 45; § 4-11(C), nn. 48, 57, 58
Repp, United States v.
Resor, Cortright v.
Resor, Homcy v.
Resor, Levy v.
Respess, United States v.
Reveles, United States v.
Rexroat, United States v.
Reynolds v. Sims, 377 U.S. 533 (1964) — § 13-3(N)(1), n. 323
Reynolds, United States v.
Rhea v. Starr, 26 M.J. 683 (A.F.C.M.R. 1988) — § 13-2(G)(1), n. 71
Rhea, United States v.
Rhoads, United States v.
Rhode Island v. Innis, 440 U.S. 934 (1980) — § 5-4(B), n. 44
Rhodes, United States v.
Rice, United States v.
Rich v. Secretary of Army, 735 F.2d 1220 (10th Cir. 1984) — § 13-3(N)(4), nn. 420, 423
Rich, United States v.
Richardson, Frontiero v.
Richardson, Graham v.
Richardson, Porter v.
Richardson, United States v.
Richmond Newspapers, Inc. v. Virginia, 448 U.S. 555 (1980) — § 15-3, nn. 2, 8
Richter, United States v.
Ricketts, United States v.
Ricks, United States v.
Riddick, United States v.
Ridgeway, United States v.
Ridley, United States v.
Riemer, United States v.
Riggins, United States v.
Riley, United States v.
Rimmer, United States v.
Rinehart, United States v.
Ringer, United States v.
Ringuette, United States v.
Rios, United States v.
Rivas, United States v.
Rivera, United States v.
Rivera-Berrios, United States v.

TABLE OF CASES

Riverasoto, United States v.
Rivers, United States v.
Roa, United States v.
Roach, United States v.
Roane, United States v.
Robbins, United States v.
Roberson, Arizona v.
Roberts, Shepardson v.
Roberts, United States v.
Roberts v. United States Jaycees, 468 U.S. 609 (1984) — § 13-3(N)(3), nn. 408, 409
Robertson, United States v.
Robinson v. Abbott, 23 C.M.A. 219 (1974) — § 17-19, n. 4
Robinson, United States v.
Rodgers, United States v.
Rodriguez, Illinois v.
Rodriguez, San Antonio School Dist. v.
Rodriguez, United States v.
Rodriguez-Amy, United States v.
Rodriquez, United States v.
Rodwell, United States v.
Roe v. Wade, 410 U.S. 113 (1973) — § 2-9(D), n. 57
Roe, Whalen v.
Roettger, United States v.
Rogan, United States v.
Rogers, United States v.
Rohrig, United States v.
Rojas, United States v.
Rolfe, United States v.
Rollins, United States v.
Roman, United States v.
Romano, United States v.
Romero, United States v.
Rondash, United States v.
Rooks, United States v.
Roppolo, United States v.
Rosario, United States v.
Rosato, United States v.
Rose v. Clark, 106 S. Ct. 3101 (1986) — § 15-20, nn. 5, 7
Rose v. Locke, 423 U.S. 48 (1975) — § 13-3(N)(2), nn. 341, 348
Rose, United States v.
Rose v. United States, 149 F.2d 755 (9th Cir. 1945) — § 13-5(F), n. 21
Rosen, United States v.
Rosenblatt, United States v.
Ross, United States v.
Rosser, United States v.
Rostker v. Goldberg, 453 U.S. 57 (1981) — § 13-3(N)(1), nn. 309, 314, 326, 331, 332
Roth v. United States, 354 U.S. 476 (1957) — § 13-3(N)(3), n. 367
Rounds, United States v.
Rowe, United States v.
Rowsey, United States v.
Roxas, United States v.

1055

TABLE OF CASES

Royster, United States v.
Rozier, United States v.
Rozycki, United States v.
Rubenstein, United States v.
Rugendorf v. United States, 376 U.S. 528 (1964) — § 15-20, n. 18
Ruiz, United States v.
Rumsfeld, Novak v.
Runkle v. United States, 122 U.S. 543 (1886) — § 8-1, n. 2
Rupert, United States v.
Rushatz, United States v.
Rushing, United States v.
Rusinskas, United States v.
Russaw, United States v.
Russell, United States v.
Russett, United States v.
Russo, United States v.
Rust, United States v.
Rusterholz, United States v.
Ruth, United States v.
Rutherford, United States v.
Ryan, United States v.
Ryder, In re
Ryder, United States v.
Ryder v. United States, 115 S. Ct. 2031 (1995) — § 8-3(A), n. 38; § 17-15, n. 3

S

Sadler, United States v.
Saenz, United States v.
Sager, United States v.
Sala, United States v.
Salgado-Agosto, United States v.
Salley, United States v.
Salter, United States v.
Samples v. Vest, 38 M.J. 482 (C.M.A. 1994) — § 5-4(C), n. 59
Samuels, United States v.
San Antonio School Dist. v. Rodriguez, 411 U.S. 1 (1973) — § 13-3(N)(1), n. 317
Sanchez, United States v.
Sanders, United States v.
Sanders, Wesberry v.
Sands v. Colby, 35 M.J. 620 (A.C.M.R. 1992) — § 4-8(D), n. 58
Sandstrom v. Montana, 442 U.S. 510 (1979) — § 15-20, nn. 2-5
Sanford, United States v.
Sankey, United States v.
Santiago, United States v.
Santiago-Davila, United States v.
Santobello v. New York, 404 U.S. 257 (1971) — § 14-3, n. 3
Sarafite, Ungar v.
Sargeant, United States v.
Sargent, United States v.
Sartin, United States v.

1056

TABLE OF CASES

Sassaman, United States v.
Satterfield v. Drew, 17 M.J. 269 (C.M.A. 1984) — § 8-4, n. 15
Sauer, United States v.
Saul, United States v.
Saulter, United States v.
Saunders, United States v.
Savusa, United States v.
Sawinski, United States v.
Sawyer, United States v.
Saylor, United States v.
Scaff, United States v.
Scaife, United States v.
Scanlon, United States v.
Scarborough, United States v.
Sceffer, United States v.
Schaffer, United States v.
Schaffner, United States v.
Schake, United States v.
Schalck, United States v.
Schaller, United States v.
Scheffer, United States v.
Scheunemann, United States v.
Schick, Burtt v.
Schilder, Gusik v.
Schilf, United States v.
Schilling, United States v.
Schlesinger, Carlson v.
Schlesinger, Champagne v.
Schlesinger v. Councilman, 420 U.S. 738 (1975) — § 4-10, n. 5; § 4-11, nn. 3-7; § 17-23(C), n. 22
Schlesinger, Horn v.
Schmeltz, United States v.
Schmidt, United States v.
Schmit, United States v.
Schmitt, United States v.
Schneckloth v. Bustamonte, 412 U.S. 218 (1973) — § 5-3(C)(6), n. 83
Schneider, United States v.
Schnitzer, United States v.
Scholten, United States v.
Scholz, United States v.
Schomaker, United States v.
Schoof, United States v.
Schoolfield, United States v.
Schooner Exchange v. McFaddon, 11 U.S. (7 Cranch) 116 (1812) — § 4-12(B), n. 11
Schreiber, United States v.
Schroeder, United States v.
Schuering, United States v.
Schultz, United States v.
Schumacher, United States v.
Schuring, United States v.
Schwab, United States v.

TABLE OF CASES

Schwabauer, United States v.
Schwarz, United States v.
Scoby, United States v.
Scofield, United States v.
Scoles, United States v.
Scott, United States v.
Scranton, United States v.
Seal, United States v.
Seamans, Yonan v.
Searcy, United States v.
Sears, United States v.
Seay, United States v.
Secretary of Air Force, Culver v.
Secretary of Air Force, Kauffman v.
Secretary of Army, Curry v.
Secretary of Army, Hatheway v.
Secretary of Army, Rich v.
Secretary of Defense, Goldman v.
Secretary of Navy, Priest v.
Secretary of Navy, Williams v.
Secretary of State of Maryland v. Joseph H. Munson Co., 467 U.S. 947 (1984) —
  § 13-3(N)(3), nn. 374, 375
Secretary of the Navy, Williams v.
Secretary of the Navy, Williamson v.
Seeber, United States v.
Seeger, United States v.
Seivers, United States v.
Self, United States v.
Sellers, United States v.
Sells, United States v.
Selman, United States v.
Sennett, United States v.
Sepulveda, United States v.
Serino, United States v.
Serrano, United States v.
Seymore, United States v.
Shackelford, United States v.
Shada, United States v.
Shafer, United States v.
Shamberger, United States v.
Shamel, United States v.
Shamlian, United States v.
Shanaham, United States v.
Shandell, United States v.
Shapiro v. Thompson, 394 U.S. 618 (1969) — § 13-3(N)(1), nn. 306, 318, 324
Sharkey, United States v.
Sharp, United States v.
Sharpe, Bolling v.
Sharper, United States v.
Sharrock, United States v.
Shaw, United States v.

TABLE OF CASES

Shearer, United States v.
Shears, United States v.
Sheehan, United States v.
Sheffield, United States v.
Shelby, United States v.
Shell, United States v.
Shelton, United States v.
Shely, United States v.
Shepard, United States v.
Shepardson v. Roberts, 14 M.J. 354 (C.M.A. 1983) — § 9-2(A)(2), n. 24; § 9-2(C), nn. 74, 80
Shepardson, United States v.
Shepherd v. Maxwell, 384 U.S. 333 (1966) — § 15-3, n. 16
Shepherd, United States v.
Sherbert v. Verner, 374 U.S. 398 (1963) — § 13-3(N)(3), nn. 398, 402
Sheridan, United States v.
Sherman, United States v.
Sherrod, United States v.
Shields, United States v.
Shiftic, United States v.
Shim, United States v.
Shiner, United States v.
Shirley, United States v.
Shober, United States v.
Shoemaker v. United States, 147 U.S. 282 (1893) — § 8-3(A), n. 26
Shomaker, United States v.
Short v. Chambers, 33 M.J. 49 (C.M.A. 1991) — § 13-5(A), nn. 11, 13
Short, United States v.
Shorte, United States v.
Shoup, United States v.
Shover, United States v.
Showalter, United States v.
Shows, United States v.
Shroeder, United States v.
Shull, United States v.
Shupe, United States v.
Siders, United States v.
Sidney, United States v.
Sidoti, Palmore v.
Silva, United States v.
Silver, United States v.
Silvis, United States v.
Simmelkjaer, United States v.
Simmons, United States v.
Simpson, United States v.
Sims, Reynolds v.
Sims, United States v.
Singleton, United States v.
Sink, United States v.
Sir John Jennings, Chambers v.
Skaar, United States v.

TABLE OF CASES

Skaggs, United States v.
Skerrett, United States v.
Skinner v. Oklahoma, 316 U.S. 535 (1942) — § 13-3(N)(1), n. 322
Slappy, Morris v.
Slater v. Kamrath, 33 M.J. 491 (C.M.A. 1991) — § 3-3(C), n. 32
Slayton, Lovisi v.
Sloan, United States v.
Slocumb, United States v.
Slovacek, United States v.
Slubowski, United States v.
Smalis v. Penn, 476 U.S. 140 (1986) — § 13-2(G)(2), n. 91
Small, United States v.
Smalls, United States v.
Smart, United States v.
Smauley, United States v.
Smiley, United States v.
Smith, Dukes v.
Smith, Estelle v.
Smith v. Goguen, 415 U.S. 566 (1974) — § 13-3(N)(2), nn. 343, 349; § 13-3(N)(3), n. 388
Smith, Humphrey v.
Smith, Illinois v.
Smith, Mendrano v.
Smith, United States v.
Smith v. United States, 502 F.2d 512 (5th Cir. 1974) — § 13-3(N)(3), nn. 384, 392
Smith, Virgin Islands v.
Smithee v. Vorbach, 25 M.J. 561 (C.G.C.M.R. 1987) — § 17-20, n. 6
Smythe, United States v.
Sneed, United States v.
Snelling, United States v.
Snipes, United States v.
Snoberger, United States v.
Snodgrass, United States v.
Snow, United States v.
Snyder, Mangsen v.
Snyder v. Massachusetts, 291 U.S. 97 (1934) — § 13-3(N)(1), n. 318
Snyder, United States v.
Solak, United States v.
Solnick, United States v.
Solorio, United States v.
Solorio v. United States, 483 U.S. 435 (1987) — § 1-8(D)(3); § 4-8(C)(3), n. 51; § 4-10, n. 8; § 4-11(B), n. 46; § 4-11(C), nn. 49, 59; § 4-11(C)(1); § 4-11(C)(2); § 6-1(B)(1), n. 72; § 13-2(G)(2), n. 114
Sombolay, United States v.
Sonnenfeld, United States v.
Sonoma County Superior Ct., Michael M. v.
Sorby, United States v.
Soriano v. Hosken, 9 M.J. 221 (C.M.A. 1980) — § 8-3(B)(1), n. 60; § 8-3(B)(4), n. 100; § 12-2(F)(5), n. 89
Soriano, United States v.
Sories, United States v.
Sorrell, United States v.

TABLE OF CASES

Sorrells, United States v.
Sosebee, United States v.
Soukup, United States v.
South Carolina, Ham v.
South Dakota v. Opperman, 428 U.S. 364 (1976) — § 5-3(D)(1), n. 133
Southers, United States v.
Spann, United States v.
Sparks, United States v.
Sparrow, United States v.
Spearman, United States v.
Spears, United States v.
Spence v. Washington, 418 U.S. 405 (1974) — § 13-3(N)(3), n. 364
Spencer, United States v.
Spiller v. Vest, 32 M.J. 792 (N.M.C.M.R. 1990) — § 17-19, n. 18
Spindle, United States v.
Spinner, United States v.
Spivey, United States v.
Spock, Greer v.
Spradley, United States v.
Sprague, United States v.
Spriddle, United States v.
Spriggs v. United States, 40 M.J. 158 (C.M.A. 1994) — § 17-9(D), n. 62
Spring, United States v.
Spurlin, United States v.
St. Clair, United States v.
St. Fort, United States v.
St. John, United States v.
St. Romain, United States v.
Stacy, United States v.
Stafford, United States v.
Staley, United States v.
Stallard, United States v.
Stamper, United States v.
Standifer, United States v.
Stanford, United States v.
Stark, United States v.
Starks, United States v.
Starr, Rhea v.
State Bar of Arizona, Bates v.
Staten, United States v.
States v. Fisher, 37 M.J. 812 (N.M.C.M.R. 1993) — § 1-3(B), n. 5
Staton, United States v.
Stavely, United States v.
Stearman, United States v.
Steck, United States v.
Stegald v. United States, 451 U.S. 204 (1981) — § 5-7, n. 14
Stegall, United States v.
Steinruck, United States v.
Stennis, United States v.
Stephens, United States v.
Stephenson, United States v.

TABLE OF CASES

Stevens, Stewart v.
Stevens, United States v.
Stevenson, United States v.
Steward, United States v.
Stewart v. Stevens, 5 M.J. 220 (C.M.A. 1978) — § 3-7, n. 1
Stewart, United States v.
Stidman, United States v.
Stimpson, United States v.
Stincer, Kentucky v.
Stiner, United States v.
Stinson, United States v.
Stipe, United States v.
Stocken, United States v.
Stockman, United States v.
Stokes, United States v.
Stoltz, United States v.
Stombaugh, United States v.
Stombugh, United States v.
Stone, United States v.
Storts, United States v.
Story, United States v.
Stottlemire, United States v.
Stouffer, United States v.
Stovall, United States v.
Strachan, United States v.
Straight, United States v.
Strangstalien, United States v.
Straukas, United States v.
Strawbridge, United States v.
Streater, United States v.
Strickland, United States v.
Strickland v. Washington, 466 U.S. 668 (1984) — § 15-2(B)(3), nn. 31, 32, 34, 36, 38, 101, 102
Stringer, United States v.
Stringfellow, United States v.
Strong, United States v.
Stroud, United States v.
Stroup, United States v.
Strozier, United States v.
Struckman, United States v.
Struthers, Martin v.
Stuart, Freeman v.
Stuart, Nebraska Press Ass'n v.
Stuart, United States v.
Stubblefield, United States v.
Stubbs, United States v.
Stuckey, United States v.
Sturdivant, United States v.
Sturgeon, United States v.
Sturkey, United States v.
Sullivan, Cuylar v.

TABLE OF CASES

Sullivan v. LaBoa, 34 M.J. 593 (A.C.M.R. 1992) — § 17-2(B)(2), n. 29
Sullivan, New York Times Co. v.
Sullivan, United States v.
Sumbry, United States v.
Summerset, United States v.
Sumpter, United States v.
Superior Court, Globe Newspapers Co. v.
Superior Court, Press-Enterprise Co. v.
Sutherland, United States v.
Suttles, United States v.
Sutton, United States v.
Suzuki, United States v.
Swagger, United States v.
Swanholm, United States v.
Sweet, United States v.
Sweitzer, United States v.
Swift, Waller v.
Swoape, United States v.
Sykes, United States v.
Sylvester, United States v.
Synder, United States v.
Syro, United States v.
Sztuka, United States v.

T

Tackett, United States v.
Taft, United States v.
Tagert, United States v.
Talavera, United States v.
Taliau, United States v.
Tallon, United States v.
Tangpuz, United States v.
Tanksley, United States v.
Tanner, United States v.
Tarquin, Bennett v.
Tarver, United States v.
Tassos, United States v.
Tatmon, United States v.
Tatum, United States v.
Taxpayers for Vincent, Los Angeles v.
Taylor, Hickman v.
Taylor v. Illinois, 484 U.S. 400 (1988) — § 10-6, n. 11
Taylor, In re
Taylor, United States v.
Teague, United States v.
Tebsherany, United States v.
Tedder, United States v.
Teeter, United States v.
Tempia, United States v.
Temple, Martelon v.

TABLE OF CASES

Tena, United States v.
Tenk, United States v.
Tennessee, Brooks v.
Tennessee, Coleman v.
Tenney, United States v.
Terminiello v. Chicago, 337 U.S. 1 (1949) — § 13-3(N)(3), nn. 359, 368, 376
Terrell, United States v.
Terry v. Ohio, 392 U.S. 1 (1968) — § 5-3(C)(8), nn. 109, 110
Terry, United States v.
Testori, United States v.
Teters, United States v.
Texas, Aguilar v.
Texas v. Johnson, 491 U.S. 397 (1989) — § 13-3(N)(3), n. 363
Tharpe, United States v.
Thatch, United States v.
Thatcher, United States v.
Thomas v. Eddington, 26 M.J. 95 (C.M.A. 1988) — § 6-1, n. 16; § 13-3(C)(3), nn. 109, 110
Thomas, United States v.
Thompson, Shapiro v.
Thompson, United States v.
Thorn, United States v.
Thornton, United States v.
Thorsen, Addis v.
Thorton, United States v.
Thrower, United States v.
Thun, United States v.
Thurman, Corly v.
Thwing, Hall v.
Tibbetts, United States v.
Tibbs, United States v.
Tiede, United States v.
Tiede & Rusk, United States v.
Tiggs, United States v.
Tillery, United States v.
Tillman v. United States, 32 M.J. 962 (A.C.M.R. 1991) — § 15-2(B)(3), n. 89
Timberlake, United States v.
Timmerman, United States v.
Timmons, United States v.
Timoney, United States v.
Tinker v. Des Moines Sch. Dist., 393 U.S. 503 (1969) — § 13-3(N)(3), nn. 363, 392
Tinker, United States v.
Tipton, United States v.
T.L.O., New Jersey v.
Tobita, United States v.
Toledo, United States v.
Tolkach, United States v.
Tomaszewski, United States v.
Tomchek, United States v.
Tomlinson, United States v.
Tompkins, United States v.

TABLE OF CASES

Toomey, United States v.
Tornowski, United States v.
Toro, United States v.
Torres, United States v.
Toth v. Quarles, 350 U.S. 11 (1950) — § 4-4, n. 4; § 4-8(C)(2), n. 24; § 4-8(C)(3), nn. 30, 37, 41, 44-46; § 4-10, nn. 1, 5
Towers, United States v.
Townsend, United States v.
Toy, United States v.
Trahan, United States v.
Trakowski, United States v.
Travers, United States v.
Traxler, United States v.
Treakle, United States v.
Trede, United States v.
Trimble, United States v.
Trimper, United States v.
Tripp, United States v.
Troglin, United States v.
Trombetta, California v.
Trotman v. Haebel, 12 M.J. 27 (C.M.A. 1981) — § 17-2(B)(2), n. 33
Trottier, United States v.
Troublefield, United States v.
Troxell, United States v.
True, United States v.
Truesdell, Billings v.
Truitt, United States v.
Trujillo, United States v.
Truman, United States v.
Tu, United States v.
Tubbs, United States v.
Tucker, United States v.
Tuggle, United States v.
Tuner, United States v.
Tunnell, United States v.
Turbeville, United States v.
Turcsik, United States v.
Turk, United States v.
Turman, United States v.
Turner, United States v.
Tyler, United States v.
Tyson, United States v.

U

Ulster County Court v. Allen, 442 U.S. 140 (1979) — § 15-20, n. 7
Ungar v. Sarafite, 376 U.S. 575 (1964) — § 12-2(C), n. 17
Unger v. Ziemniak, 27 M.J. 349 (C.M.A. 1989) — § 2-4(A), nn. 2, 3; § 13-2(G)(1), n. 61
Union Bank, Mechanics' & Traders' Bank v.
United States, Abbate v.

TABLE OF CASES

United States v. Abdelkader, 34 M.J. 605 (A.F.C.M.R. 1992) — § 15-10(A), n. 30; § 15-10(B), nn. 55, 62; § 15-10(C)(2), n. 1

United States v. Abdullah, 37 M.J. 692 (A.C.M.R. 1993) — § 14-3(B)(2), nn. 97, 98

United States v. Abell, 23 M.J. 99 (C.M.A. 1986) — § 13-2(G)(2), n. 109

United States v. Abendschein, 19 M.J. 619 (A.C.M.R. 1984) — § 6-1(C)(3), n. 164; § 13-3(J), n. 255

United States v. Abernathy, 48 C.M.R. 205 (C.G.C.M.R. 1974) — § 3-3(B), n. 15; § 4-6, nn. 4, 5, 7

United States v. Abilar, 14 M.J. 733 (A.F.C.M.R. 1982) — § 12-4, n. 14; § 15-2(A); § 15-2(A), n. 5; § 15-4(A), n. 8

United States, Abrams v.

United States v. Abrecht, 4 M.J. 573 (A.C.M.R. 1977) — § 5-4(A)(3), n. 21

United States v. Accordino, 20 M.J. 102 (C.M.A. 1985) — § 15-15, nn. 1, 11; § 15-16(B), nn. 21, 22

United States v. Acemoglu, 21 C.M.A. 561, 45 C.M.R. 335 (1972) — § 2-2(C)(3), n. 47

United States v. Acevedo-Colon, 2 M.J. 969 (A.C.M.R. 1976) — § 8-3(C)(2), n. 128; § 12-3(B), n. 47

United States v. Acireno, 15 M.J. 570 (A.C.M.R. 1982) — § 13-3(C)(2), n. 68

United States v. Acosta, 11 M.J. 307 (C.M.A. 1981) — § 5-3(C)(7), n. 101; § 5-7, n. 7; § 5-8(A), n. 9; § 14-3(B)(3), n. 109

United States v. Acton, 38 M.J. 330 (C.M.A. 1993) — § 15-2(B)(1), n. 20

United States v. Adam, 20 M.J. 681 (A.F.C.M.R. 1985) — § 2-7(B), n. 20

United States v. Adames, 21 M.J. 465 (C.M.A. 1986) — § 2-8(B), n. 16; § 13-3(N)(2), n. 355

United States v. Adamiak, 15 C.M.R. 412 (C.M.A. 1954) — § 15-2(E), n. 152

United States v. Adamiak, 4 C.M.A. 412, 15 C.M.R. 412 (1954) — § 6-7, n. 16

United States v. Adams, 13 M.J. 728 (A.C.M.R. 1982) — § 4-11(A), n. 31; § 6-1(B)(1), n. 76; § 6-1(C)(2), n. 126; § 13-5(G)(3), n. 50

United States v. Adams, 19 M.J. 996 (A.C.M.R. 1985) — § 2-8(A), n. 5; § 2-8(D), n. 37; § 14-3(B)(1), n. 58

United States v. Adams, 33 M.J. 300 (C.M.A. 1991) — § 14-3(D)(4), n. 151

United States v. Adams, 36 M.J. 1201 (N.M.C.M.R. 1993) — § 15-10(A), n. 22

United States v. Addison, 19 M.J. 905 (A.C.M.R. 1985) — § 13-2(B), n. 29

United States v. Adolph, 13 M.J. 775 (A.C.M.R. 1982) — § 3-8(B), n. 14

United States v. Advincula, 29 M.J. 676 (A.F.C.M.R. 1989) — § 14-3(D)(4), nn. 147, 150

United States v. Aflague, 40 M.J. 501 (A.C.M.R. 1994) — § 15-2(B)(3), n. 85

United States v. Agurs, 427 U.S. 97 (1976) — § 10-3(D), n. 17; § 10-4(A)(4), n. 17; § 10-4(B)(1), n. 29; § 15-2(B)(3), n. 36; § 946

United States v. Aiello, 7 M.J. 99 (C.M.A. 1979) — § 9-3, n. 1

United States v. Aikens, 16 M.J. 821 (N.M.C.M.R. 1983) — § 5-4(B), n. 48

United States v. Airhart, 23 C.M.A. 124, 48 C.M.R. 685 (1974) — § 4-15(A), n. 1

United States v. Albert, 30 M.J. 331 (C.M.A. 1990) — § 17-9(A), n. 18

United States v. Albo, 22 C.M.A. 30, 46 C.M.R. 30 (1972) — § 10-4(B)(5), nn. 50, 56; § 10-6

United States v. Albrecht, 4 M.J. 573 (A.C.M.R. 1977) — § 15-13, n. 11

United States v. Albrecht, 38 M.J. 627 (A.F.C.M.R. 1993) — § 6-1(C)(3), nn. 155, 157

United States v. Albrecht, 43 M.J. 65 (1995) — § 6-1(C)(3), n. 159

United States v. Aldridge, 4 C.M.A. 107, 15 C.M.R. 107 (1954) — § 15-22, n. 1

United States v. Alef, 3 M.J. 414 (C.M.A. 1977) — § 4-9, n. 1; § 4-11(A), nn. 32-34; § 6-1(B), n. 68; § 6-1(B)(1), n. 73; § 6-1(B)(2), n. 77; § 13-3(A), n. 5; § 13-5(F), n. 14; § 14-3(A)(2), n. 28

TABLE OF CASES

United States v. Alexander, 19 M.J. 614 (A.C.M.R. 1984) — § 6-7, n. 3
United States v. Alexander, 761 F.2d 1294 (9th Cir. 1985) — § 14-4, n. 16
United States v. Alexander, 26 M.J. 796 (A.F.C.M.R. 1988) — § 2-4(F), n. 50
United States v. Alexander, 27 M.J. 834 (A.C.M.R. 1988) — § 8-3(C)(2), n. 132
United States v. Alexander, 29 M.J. 877 (A.F.C.M.R. 1989) — § 6-1, n. 19
United States v. Alexander, 32 M.J. 664 (A.F.C.M.R. 1991) — § 5-3(D)(1), n. 128; § 13-4, n. 6
United States v. Alexander, 34 M.J. 121 (C.M.A. 1992) — § 5-3(A), n. 30; § 5-3(D)(1), n. 129
United States v. Alford, 8 M.J. 516 (A.C.M.R. 1979) — § 10-4(B)(1), n. 32
United States v. Alford, 29 M.J. 711 (A.C.M.R. 1989) — § 16-12, n. 7
United States v. Alford, 31 M.J. 814 (A.F.C.M.R. 1990) — § 15-14(A), n. 15; § 15-14(D), nn. 53, 54
United States v. Alford, 32 M.J. 596 (A.C.M.R. 1991) — § 2-6(A), n. 17
United States v. Ali, 12 M.J. 1018 (A.C.M.R. 1982) — § 10-4(B)(5), n. 57; § 15-14(B), n. 46
United States v. Alicea-Baez, 7 M.J. 989 (A.C.M.R. 1979) — § 946
United States v. Allen, 5 C.M.A. 626, 18 C.M.R. 250 (1955) — § 4-15(C), n. 19; § 7-3(B), n. 26; § 15-9, n. 6
United States v. Allen, 11 C.M.A. 539, 29 C.M.R. 355 (1960) — § 15-13, n. 9
United States v. Allen, 6 M.J. 633 (C.G.C.M.R. 1978) — § 1-3(D)(2), n. 22
United States v. Allen, 10 M.J. 576 (A.C.M.R. 1980) — § 2-3(C), n. 25
United States v. Allen, 17 M.J. 126 (C.M.A. 1984) — § 5-9(D), n. 26; § 5-10(D), n. 34; § 16-9, n. 11
United States v. Allen, 21 M.J. 507 (A.C.M.R. 1985) — § 16-5(C), n. 36
United States v. Allen, 21 M.J. 924 (A.C.M.R. 1986) — § 16-10, n. 9
United States v. Allen, 28 M.J. 610 (N.M.C.M.R. 1989) — § 17-8(B)(1), n. 47
United States v. Allen, 31 M.J. 572 (N.M.C.M.R. 1990) — § 5-3(B), n. 41; § 6-1, n. 15; § 6-3(B), n. 14; § 6-3(C), nn. 16, 19, 21, 22; § 6-4(C), nn. 18, 19; § 6-5(A), nn. 5, 6; § 8-2(A), n. 3; § 8-3(C)(3), nn. 142, 143; § 8-4, n. 7; § 11-2(A)(1), n. 8; § 11-2(A)(3), n. 21; § 11-2(B)(1), n. 64; § 12-2(H), nn. 97, 99, 100, 102, 109; § 15-4(B), n. 11
United States v. Allen, 33 M.J. 209 (C.M.A. 1991) — § 4-8(D), n. 58; § 5-10(A), n. 2; § 6-5(A), nn. 12, 14, 19, 20; § 6-7, nn. 10, 12
United States v. Allen, 34 M.J. 228 (C.M.A. 1992) — § 5-3(F), n. 26
United States v. Allen, 39 M.J. 581 (N.M.C.M.R. 1993) — § 14-3(C), n. 129
United States v. Allgood, 41 M.J. 492 (1995) — § 4-13, n. 4; § 4-14(A)(3), n. 15; § 4-16, n. 1; § 8-3(C)(4), n. 160
United States v. Allison, 8 M.J. 143 (C.M.A. 1979) — § 15-14(B), n. 45
United States v. Allison, 30 M.J. 546 (A.C.M.R. 1990) — § 14-3(D)(4), n. 147
United States v. Almeida, 19 M.J. 874 (A.F.C.M.R. 1985) — § 15-2(E), n. 153; § 15-10(C)(2), n. 91
United States v. Almy, 34 M.J. 1082 (C.G.C.M.R. 1992) — § 4-14(A)(1), n. 4
United States v. Almy, 37 M.J. 465 (C.M.A. 1993) — § 4-14(A), n. 3
United States v. Alomarestrada, 39 M.J. 1068 (A.C.M.R. 1994) — § 15-2(B)(3), n. 50
United States v. Aloyian, 16 C.M.A. 333, 36 C.M.R. 489 (1966) — § 13-5(G)(3), n. 50
United States v. Alston, 11 M.J. 656 (A.F.C.M.R. 1985) — § 8-2(B), n. 12
United States v. Alston, 30 M.J. 969 (N.M.C.M.R. 1990) — § 17-4, n. 35
United States v. Alston, 33 M.J. 370 (C.M.A. 1991) — § 11-2(E)(3), n. 133
United States v. Alsup, 17 M.J. 166 (C.M.A. 1984) — § 16-5(C), n. 49
United States v. Alvarez, 5 M.J. 762 (A.C.M.R. 1978) — § 8-3(C)(4), n. 160
United States v. Ame, 35 M.J. 592 (N.M.C.M.R. 1992) — § 16-2(F), n. 52

TABLE OF CASES

United States v. Amos, 22 M.J. 798 (A.C.M.R. 1986) — § 5-10(D), n. 38
United States v. Amos, 26 M.J. 806 (A.C.M.R. 1988) — § 12-2(H), n. 100; § 14-2, n. 10
United States v. Amparo, 25 M.J. 722 (C.G.C.M.R. 1987) — § 17-11, n. 6
United States v. Amundson, 23 C.M.A. 308, 49 C.M.R. 598 (1975) — § 13-3(C)(2), n. 60
United States v. Anderson, 17 C.M.A. 588, 38 C.M.R. 386 (1968) — § 2-2(E)(6), n. 96; § 4-7(A), n. 9
United States v. Anderson, 1 M.J. 688 (N.C.M.R. 1975) — § 2-2(C)(3), n. 46
United States v. Anderson, 10 M.J. 803 (A.F.C.M.R. 1981) — § 8-3(C)(2), n. 132
United States v. Anderson, 12 M.J. 195 (C.M.A. 1982) — § 17-4, n. 21; § 17-4(A), n. 51
United States v. Anderson, 23 M.J. 894 (A.C.M.R. 1987) — § 15-10(B), n. 73; § 15-10(C)(2), n. 100
United States v. Anderson, 25 M.J. 779 (A.C.M.R. 1988) — § 16-5(D)(2), n. 70; § 16-5(D)(4), n. 84; § 16-5(D)(5), nn. 118, 126
United States v. Anderson, 26 M.J. 555 (A.C.M.R. 1988) — § 6-1, n. 15; § 6-3(C), n. 18
United States v. Anderson, 28 M.J. 895 (A.F.C.M.R. 1989) — § 12-2(H), n. 100
United States v. Anderson, 36 M.J. 963 (A.F.C.M.R. 1993) — § 8-3(B)(3), n. 80; § 8-4, n. 7; § 11-4, n. 5; § 13-3(G), n. 228; § 13-5(C), nn. 31, 33, 40; § 13-5(H), nn. 57, 59, 66; § 13-5(K), n. 87; § 15-10(A), nn. 9-11
United States v. Andrade, 3 M.J. 757 (A.C.M.R. 1977) — § 17-4(A), n. 43
United States v. Andrade, 32 M.J. 520 (A.C.M.R. 1990) — § 14-3(D)(3), n. 139
United States v. Andreas, 14 M.J. 483 (C.M.A. 1983) — § 5-4(C), n. 54; § 11-2(E)(1), n. 108
United States v. Andrews, 21 C.M.A. 165, 44 C.M.R. 219 (1972) — § 8-3(B)(2), n. 70
United States v. Andrews, 17 M.J. 717 (N.M.C.M.R. 1983) — § 4-5(A)(3), n. 12
United States v. Andrews, 36 M.J. 922 (A.F.C.M.R. 1993) — § 13-5(K), n. 85; § 15-4(A), nn. 7, 8
United States v. Andrews, 38 M.J. 650 (A.C.M.R. 1993) — § 9-2(B)(1), n. 49
United States v. Angel, 28 M.J. 600 (N.M.C.M.R. 1989) — § 13-3(C)(3), n. 109
United States v. Angelo, 25 M.J. 834 (A.C.M.R. 1988) — § 17-2(B)(3), n. 79
United States v. Ankeny, 28 M.J. 780 (N.M.C.M.R. 1989) — § 15-2(B)(3), n. 51
United States v. Ankeny, 30 M.J. 10 (C.M.A. 1990) — § 9-2(A)(2), n. 27
United States v. Annis, 5 M.J. 351 (C.M.A. 1978) — § 17-2(B)(4), nn. 79, 94
United States v. Anthony, 37 M.J. 963 (A.C.M.R. 1993) — § 15-2(B)(3), nn. 41, 42
United States v. Antonio, 20 M.J. 828 (A.C.M.R. 1985) — § 17-8(B)(3), n. 83
United States v. Antonitis, 29 M.J. 217 (C.M.A. 1989) — § 16-5(D)(3), n. 79; § 16-5(D)(4), n. 81
United States v. Anzalone, 40 M.J. 658 (N.M.C.M.R. 1994) — § 2-7(B), n. 24; § 5-4(A)(2), n. 11; § 15-3, n. 6
United States v. Aponte, 591 F.2d 1247 (9th Cir. 1978) — § 12-2(F)(4), n. 83
United States v. Appel, 31 M.J. 314 (C.M.A. 1990) — § 2-8(B), nn. 19, 23
United States v. Applewhite, 23 M.J. 196 (C.M.A. 1986) — § 5-4(B), n. 50
United States v. Aquino, 20 M.J. 712 (A.C.M.R. 1985) — § 6-1(C)(3), n. 142
United States v. Aragon, 1 M.J. 662 (N.C.M.R. 1975) — § 13-3(C), n. 28
United States v. Arbic, 16 C.M.A. 292, 36 C.M.R. 448 (1966) — § 2-2(E)(6), n. 98; § 6-1(B)(2), n. 81
United States v. Arceneaux, 21 M.J. 571 (A.C.M.R. 1985) — § 16-5(D)(4), n. 84; § 16-5(D)(5), n. 118
United States v. Arguello, 29 M.J. 198 (C.M.A. 1989) — § 11-4, n. 5
United States v. Armstead, 32 M.J. 1013 (N.M.C.M.R. 1991) — § 14-3(B)(2), n. 80
United States v. Armstrong, 9 M.J. 374 (C.M.A. 1980) — § 2-4(A), n. 16; § 5-4(A)(1), n. 5

TABLE OF CASES

United States v. Armstrong, 30 M.J. 769 (A.C.M.R. 1990) — § 15-10(B), n. 53
United States v. Arnold, 21 C.M.A. 151, 44 C.M.R. 205 (1972) — § 17-8(B)(2), n. 60
United States v. Arnold, 8 M.J. 806 (N.C.M.R. 1980) — § 9-2(B)(1), n. 54
United States v. Arnold, 26 M.J. 965 (A.C.M.R. 1988) — § 15-10(B), n. 62
United States v. Arnold, 27 M.J. 857 (A.F.C.M.R. 1989) — § 16-3(D), n. 68
United States v. Arnold, 28 M.J. 963 (A.C.M.R. 1989) — § 13-3(C)(3), n. 159
United States v. Arrington, 5 M.J. 756 (A.C.M.R. 1978) — § 14-3(B)(2), n. 71
United States v. Arroyo, 17 M.J. 224 (C.M.A. 1984) — § 17-14, nn. 10, 11
United States v. Arsneault, 6 M.J. 182 (C.M.A. 1979) — § 2-2(E)(6), n. 98
United States v. Arthen, 32 M.J. 541 (A.F.C.M.R. 1990) — § 2-8(B), nn. 10, 25; § 14-3(A)(2), n. 29
United States v. Arthur, 2 M.J. 481 (A.C.M.R. 1975) — § 4-6, n. 20
United States, Artis v.
United States v. Arviso, 32 M.J. 616 (A.C.M.R. 1991) — § 15-14(B), n. 23
United States v. Asbury, 28 M.J. 595 (N.M.C.M.R. 1989) — § 2-2(C)(3), n. 45; § 2-2(E)(5), n. 92; § 13-3(C)(3), n. 105
United States v. Asfeld, 30 M.J. 917 (A.C.M.R. 1990) — § 2-4(C), n. 32; § 6-1, n. 15
United States v. Ash, 413 U.S. 300 (1973) — § 5-5, n. 5
United States v. Atchison, 13 M.J. 798 (A.C.M.R. 1982) — § 3-8(B), n. 14
United States v. Atkinson, 39 M.J. 462 (C.M.A. 1994) — § 2-2(C)(3), n. 35
United States v. Aue, 37 M.J. 528 (A.C.M.R. 1993) — § 6-1, nn. 7, 31, 36; § 12-2(H), n. 100
United States, Augenblick v.
United States v. Augusztin, 30 M.J. 707 (N.M.C.M.R. 1990) — § 12-2(F)(3), n. 60
United States v. Aurich, 31 M.J. 95 (C.M.A. 1990) — § 6-5(C), n. 49; § 16-5(D)(4), n. 102; § 16-5(D)(5), n. 120
United States v. Austin, 25 M.J. 639 (A.C.M.R. 1987) — § 5-10(C), n. 14
United States v. Austin, 27 M.J. 227 (C.M.A. 1988) — § 2-4(A), n. 19; § 2-4(B), n. 26
United States v. Austin, 32 M.J. 757 (A.C.M.R. 1991) — § 15-2(B)(3), n. 67
United States v. Austin, 35 M.J. 271 (C.M.A. 1992) — § 7-2(C), n. 79; § 15-15, n. 7; § 15-22, nn. 5, 6
United States v. Autrey, 12 M.J. 547 (A.C.M.R. 1981) — § 6-1, n. 33
United States v. Autrey, 20 M.J. 912 (A.C.M.R. 1985) — § 8-3(C)(4), n. 151
United States v. Averette, 19 C.M.A. 363, 41 C.M.R. 363 (1970) — § 4-7(A), nn. 8, 9
United States v. Avery, 40 M.J. 325 (C.M.A. 1994) — § 5-3(C)(6), n. 85
United States v. Avila, 24 M.J. 501 (A.F.C.M.R. 1987) — § 4-11(C), n. 52
United States v. Avila, 27 M.J. 62 (C.M.A. 1988) — § 4-11(C), n. 59
United States v. Ayala, 22 M.J. 777 (A.C.M.R. 1986) — § 7-2(A)(1), n. 29; § 15-12(D), n. 27
United States v. Ayala, 21 M.J. 977 (N.M.C.M.R. 1986) — § 12-2(F)(2), n. 55
United States v. Ayala, 26 M.J. 190 (C.M.A. 1988) — § 5-3(A), n. 28
United States v. Ayala, 43 M.J. 296 (1995) — § 5-3(C)(3), n. 75; § 6-5(B), n. 48; § 6-7, n. 9;
United States v. Aycock, 15 C.M.A. 158, 35 C.M.R. 130 (1964) — § 10-3(B), n. 10
United States v. Azevedo, 24 M.J. 559 (C.G.C.M.R. 1987) — § 4-14(A)(2), n. 10; § 6-1, n. 9
United States v. Babbitt, 26 M.J. 157 (C.M.A. 1988) — § 15-2(B)(3), nn. 47, 75
United States v. Babcock, 14 M.J. 34 (C.M.A. 1982) — § 17-2(B)(4), n. 96
United States v. Baca, 14 C.M.A. 76, 33 C.M.R. 288 (1963) — § 13-5(G)(1), n. 36
United States v. Baca, 27 M.J. 110 (C.M.A. 1989) — § 15-2(B)(3), n. 96
United States v. Bachand, 16 M.J. 896 (A.C.M.R. 1983) — § 4-5(A)(2), n. 3

TABLE OF CASES

United States v. Bacon, 12 M.J. 489 (C.M.A. 1982) — § 17-21, nn. 2, 3
United States v. Badger, 7 M.J. 838 (A.C.M.R. 1979) — § 13-3(C)(2), n. 73
United States v. Bagley, 473 U.S. 667 (1985) — § 10-4(A)(4), n. 25
United States v. Bailey, 6 M.J. 965 (N.C.M.R. 1979) — § 4-9, nn. 4, 5
United States v. Bailey, 20 M.J. 703 (A.C.M.R. 1985) — § 14-3(B)(1), n. 59
United States v. Baker, 17 C.M.A. 346, 38 C.M.R. 144 (1967) — § 2-4(C), n. 35
United States v. Baker, 47 C.M.R. 506 (A.C.M.R. 1973) — § 15-16(C), n. 34
United States v. Baker, 14 M.J. 361 (C.M.A. 1983) — § 6-1, nn. 15, 17, 21, 23; § 6-1(C)(3), nn. 140-142, 144-149, 151, 152, 167; § 13-3(J), n. 255
United States v. Baker, 21 M.J. 618 (A.C.M.R. 1985) — § 17-4, n. 31
United States v. Baker, 28 M.J. 121 (C.M.A. 1989) — § 15-2(B)(3), n. 89; § 17-14, n. 10
United States v. Baker, 28 M.J. 900 (A.C.M.R. 1989) — § 5-3(A), n. 14; § 14-3(E), nn. 180, 191
United States v. Baker, 29 M.J. 126 (C.M.A. 1989) — § 17-15(B), n. 32
United States v. Baker, 30 M.J. 262 (C.M.A. 1990) — § 5-3(A), n. 33
United States v. Baker, 30 M.J. 594 (A.C.M.R. 1990) — § 16-11, n. 5
United States v. Baker, 32 M.J. 290 (C.M.A. 1991) — § 16-11, nn. 3, 7
United States v. Baker, 33 M.J. 788 (A.F.C.M.R. 1991) — § 11-2(A)(2), n. 14
United States v. Baker, 34 M.J. 559 (A.F.C.M.R. 1992) — § 15-12(B), n. 19
United States v. Balagna, 31 M.J. 825 (A.C.M.R. 1990) — § 15-4(B), n. 11
United States v. Balagna, 33 M.J. 54 (C.M.A. 1991) — § 15-4(B), n. 11
United States v. Balboa, 33 M.J. 304 (C.M.A. 1991) — § 16-9, n. 11
United States v. Balcom, 20 M.J. 558 (A.C.M.R. 1985) — § 3-8(B), n. 17
United States v. Baldwin, 49 C.M.R. 814 (A.C.M.R. 1975) — § 2-2(C)(1), n. 28
United States, Ball v.
United States v. Ballard, 20 M.J. 282 (C.M.A. 1985) — § 17-15(B), n. 33
United States v. Ballesteros, 29 M.J. 14 (C.M.A. 1989) — § 5-9(D), n. 22; § 5-10(D), n. 32
United States v. Ballew, 38 M.J. 560 (A.F.C.M.R. 1993) — § 9-3, n. 3
United States v. Banks, 7 M.J. 92 (C.M.A. 1979) — § 17-11, n. 9
United States v. Banks, 29 M.J. 691 (A.C.M.R. 1989) — § 15-10(C)(3), n. 108
United States v. Banks, 36 M.J. 150 (C.M.A. 1992) — § 15-12, n. 1
United States v. Banks, 36 M.J. 1003 (A.C.M.R. 1993) — § 2-9(C), n. 24; § 9-3, n. 6
United States v. Banks, 37 M.J. 700 (A.C.M.R. 1993) — § 2-2(E)(3), n. 79
United States v. Bannwarth, 36 M.J. 265 (C.M.A. 1992) — § 15-10(B), nn. 51, 55, 64
United States v. Barbeau, 9 M.J. 569 (A.F.C.M.R. 1980) — § 4-8(B), n. 13
United States v. Barber, 8 M.J. 153 (C.M.A. 1979) — § 2-3(B), n. 19
United States v. Barber, 20 M.J. 678 (A.F.C.M.R. 1985) — § 10-4(B)(5), n. 59
United States v. Barber, 23 M.J. 751 (A.F.C.M.R. 1987) — § 4-11(C), n. 52
United States v. Barber, 27 M.J. 885 (A.C.M.R. 1989) — § 16-5(D)(1), n. 55; § 16-5(D)(3), n. 80; § 16-5(D)(4), n. 102
United States v. Barden, 9 M.J. 621 (A.C.M.R. 1980) — § 9-3, n. 6
United States v. Barfield, 2 M.J. 136 (C.M.A. 1977) — § 14-3(A)(4), n. 42
United States v. Barnack, 10 M.J. 799 (A.F.C.M.R. 1981) — § 15-13, n. 10
United States v. Barnard, 32 M.J. 530 (A.C.M.R. 1990) — § 13-2, n. 8; § 15-2(B)(3), nn. 32, 52
United States v. Barnes, 3 M.J. 406 (C.M.A. 1977) — § 14-3(A)(2), n. 26
United States v. Barnes, 8 M.J. 115 (C.M.A. 1979) — § 11-2(F), n. 160
United States v. Barnes, 12 M.J. 614 (N.M.C.M.R. 1981) — § 17-4, n. 31
United States v. Barnes, 12 M.J. 956 (A.F.C.M.R. 1982) — § 15-10(C)(2), n. 96
United States v. Barnes, 33 M.J. 893 (A.F.C.M.R. 1991) — § 14-3(E), n. 180

TABLE OF CASES

United States v. Barnes, 33 M.J. 468 (C.M.A. 1992) — § 16-5(C), n. 43
United States v. Barnes, 39 M.J. 230 (C.M.A. 1994) — § 2-2(E)(1), n. 72; § 15-14(B), nn. 21, 25
United States, Barnett v.
United States v. Barnette, 21 M.J. 749 (N.M.C.M.R. 1985) — § 17-2(B)(4), nn. 93, 96
United States v. Barney, 23 M.J. 504 (A.F.C.M.R. 1986) — § 17-4, nn. 29, 34
United States v. Barratt, 42 M.J. 734 (Army Ct.Crim.App. 1995) — § 17-9(A), n. 10
United States v. Barraza, 5 M.J. 230 (C.M.A. 1978) — § 4-6, n. 22
United States v. Barrios, 31 M.J. 750 (A.C.M.R. 1990) — § 8-3(D), n. 167; § 15-10(B), n. 51
United States v. Barror, 23 M.J. 370 (C.M.A. 1987) — § 11-2(A)(2), n. 11
United States v. Barrow, 42 M.J. 655 (A.F. Ct. Crim. App. 1995) — § 15-10(B), n. 68; § 13-5(G)(2), n. 43
United States v. Bartell, 32 M.J. 295 (C.M.A. 1991) — § 2-4(C), n. 31
United States v. Bartlett, 12 M.J. 880 (A.F.C.M.R. 1981) — § 4-15(B), n. 11
United States v. Bartole, 21 M.J. 234 (C.M.A. 1986) — § 2-6(A), n. 17
United States v. Bartoletti, 32 M.J. 419 (C.M.A. 1991) — § 16-5(D)(3), n. 76
United States v. Barton, 48 C.M.R. 358 (N.C.M.R. 1973) — § 8-3(B)(3), n. 75
United States v. Barton, 6 M.J. 16 (C.M.A. 1978) — § 17-4, n. 37
United States v. Barunas, 23 M.J. 71 (C.M.A. 1986) — § 9-4, n. 3
United States v. Barus, 16 M.J. 624 (A.F.C.M.R. 1983) — § 15-13, n. 17
United States v. Bashaw, 6 M.J. 179 (C.M.A. 1979) — § 6-1(C)(3), n. 135
United States v. Basnight, 29 M.J. 838 (A.C.M.R. 1989) — § 15-10(B), n. 68
United States v. Bass, 11 M.J. 545 (A.C.M.R. 1981) — § 3-4, n. 10; § 13-3(M), n. 289
United States v. Bass, 40 M.J. 220 (C.M.A. 1994) — § 12-4, n. 13; § 15-2(A), n. 6
United States v. Bassano, 23 M.J. 661 (A.F.C.M.R. 1986) — § 2-7(C), n. 43
United States v. Batchelder, 442 U.S. 114 (1979) — § 2-7(A), n. 5
United States v. Batchelder, 41 M.J. 337 (1994) — § 4-8(B), n. 14
United States v. Bates, 40 M.J. 362 (C.M.A. 1994) — § 14-3(B)(2), n. 71
United States v. Batiste, 35 M.J. 742 (A.C.M.R. 1992) — § 17-4(A), n. 43
United States v. Battle, 27 M.J. 781 (A.F.C.M.R. 1988) — § 2-4(F), n. 51; § 16-2(F), nn. 56-59
United States v. Battles, 25 M.J. 58 (C.M.A. 1987) — § 5-3(A), n. 26
United States v. Batts, 19 C.M.A. 521, 42 C.M.R. 123 (1970) — § 14-3(D)(4), n. 146
United States v. Batts, 3 M.J. 440 (C.M.A. 1977) — § 8-3(B)(1), n. 60
United States v. Batzel, 15 M.J. 640 (N.M.C.M.R. 1982) — § 5-5, n. 9
United States v. Baum, 30 M.J. 626 (N.M.C.M.R. 1990) — § 15-10(B), n. 62
United States v. Baumgart, 23 M.J. 888 (A.C.M.R. 1987) — § 9-2(B)(1), n. 49
United States v. Baxter, 14 M.J. 762 (A.C.M.R. 1982) — § 16-9, n. 13
United States v. Bayhand, 6 C.M.A. 762, 21 C.M.R. 84 (1956) — § 5-10(A), n. 1; § 5-10(C), n. 15; § 13-3(G), n. 227
United States v. Baylor, 16 C.M.A. 502, 37 C.M.R. 122 (1967) — § 15-14(C), n. 49
United States v. Beach, 49 C.M.R. 124 (N.M.C.M.R. 1974) — § 15-2(D), n. 133
United States v. Bean, 13 C.M.A. 203, 32 C.M.R. 203 (1962) — § 4-5(A)(2), n. 1
United States v. Bean, 13 M.J. 970 (A.C.M.R. 1982) — § 13-3(C)(2), n. 73
United States v. Bearchild, 17 C.M.A. 598, 38 C.M.R. 396 (1968) — § 15-4(C), n. 26
United States v. Beard, 7 M.J. 452 (C.M.A. 1979) — § 4-8(A), n. 8; § 12-3(B), n. 61
United States v. Beard, 15 M.J. 768 (A.F.C.M.R. 1983) — § 8-3(C)(4), n. 154
United States v. Beattie, 17 M.J. 537 (A.C.M.R. 1983) — § 2-4(B), n. 24; § 2-4(F), n. 50
United States v. Beatty, 25 M.J. 311 (C.M.A. 1987) — § 8-3(B)(3), nn. 90-95; § 12-2(F)(4), nn. 68, 74, 75, 78

TABLE OF CASES

United States v. Beaty, 14 M.J. 155 (C.M.A. 1982) — § 16-8(B), n. 17; § 16-9, nn. 13, 15
United States v. Beauchamp, 17 M.J. 590 (A.C.M.R. 1983) — § 8-2(A), n. 3; § 4-14(A)(2), nn. 10, 12
United States v. Beaudin, 35 M.J. 385 (C.M.A. 1992) — § 17-8(B)(1), n. 39
United States v. Beaulieu, 21 M.J. 528 (C.G.C.M.R. 1985) — § 8-3(D), n. 163
United States v. Beaver, 26 M.J. 991 (A.F.C.M.R. 1988) — § 16-5(B), n. 9
United States v. Becker, 5 M.J. 244 (C.M.A. 1978) — § 3-8(B), n. 9
United States v. Beckermann, 35 M.J. 842 (C.G.C.M.R. 1992) — § 6-1, n. 3; § 7-2(A)(1), n. 18; § 8-3(A), n. 2; § 8-3(B)(2), n. 68; § 13-3(C)(3), n. 133; § 15-2(B)(3), n. 88
United States v. Beckwith, 12 M.J. 939 (N.M.C.M.R. 1982) — § 16-8(C), n. 35
United States v. Bedania, 12 M.J. 373 (C.M.A. 1982) — § 14-3(B)(1), n. 66
United States v. Beehler, 35 M.J. 502 (A.F.C.M.R. 1992) — § 8-3(C)(4), nn. 152, 154; § 13-2(A), n. 15; § 15-10(C)(1), n. 88
United States v. Beeker, 18 C.M.A. 563, 40 C.M.R. 275 (1969) — § 4-11(A), n. 9
United States v. Beeks, 9 C.M.R. 743 (A.F.B.R. 1953) — § 4-15(C), n. 15
United States v. Beene, 4 C.M.A. 177, 15 C.M.R. 177 (1954) — § 6-1(C)(3), n. 139
United States v. Beer, 6 C.M.A. 180, 19 C.M.R. 306 (1955) — § 15-10(B), n. 76
United States v. Beerey, 28 M.J. 714 (N.M.C.M.R. 1989) — § 6-1, n. 45
United States v. Begley, 38 C.M.R. 488 (A.B.R. 1967) — § 15-13, n. 16
United States v. Behling, 37 M.J. 637 (A.C.M.R. 1993) — § 17-4, n. 29
United States v. Belizaire, 24 M.J. 183 (C.M.A. 1987) — § 15-2(A), n. 16
United States v. Bell, 8 C.M.A. 193, 24 C.M.R. 3 (1957) — § 16-3(B), n. 37
United States v. Bell, 25 M.J. 676 (A.C.M.R. 1987) — § 5-9(D), n. 39; § 13-2(E), n. 51
United States v. Bell, 28 M.J. 1062 (N.M.C.M.R. 1989) — § 17-15(B), n. 32
United States v. Bell, 34 M.J. 937 (A.F.C.M.R. 1992) — § 17-14, n. 11
United States v. Bell, 38 M.J. 358 (C.M.A. 1993) — § 2-7(B), n. 24
United States v. Bell, 38 M.J. 523 (A.C.M.R. 1993) — § 17-21, n. 3
United States v. Bellett, 36 M.J. 563 (A.F.C.M.R. 1992) — § 4-14(A), n. 3; § 4-14(B), n. 17
United States v. Belmont, 27 M.J. 516 (N.M.C.M.R. 1988) — § 5-10(D), n. 34
United States v. Beloney, 32 M.J. 639 (A.C.M.R. 1991) — § 5-9(C), n. 20
United States v. Bement, 34 C.M.R. 648 (A.B.R. 1964) — § 2-2(C)(3), n. 33
United States v. Bender, 32 M.J. 1002 (N.M.C.M.R. 1991) — § 7-2(D), n. 93
United States v. Bennett, 12 M.J. 463 (C.M.A. 1982) — § 11-2(A)(1), n. 8; § 11-2(A)(2), n. 18; § 11-2(D)(2), nn. 91, 94; § 13-5(C), nn. 32, 36, 38
United States v. Bennett, 23 M.J 664 (A.C.M.R. 1986) — § 5-10(D), n. 39
United States v. Beno, 24 M.J. 771 (A.F.C.M.R. 1987) — § 16-5(D)(4), n. 86
United States v. Benoit, 21 M.J. 579 (A.C.M.R. 1985) — § 15-10(C)(1), nn. 89, 90
United States, Berger v.
United States v. Berger, 23 M.J. 612 (A.F.C.M.R. 1986) — § 16-5(D)(5), n. 117
United States v. Berlingeri, 35 M.J. 794 (N.M.C.M.R. 1992) — § 8-3(C)(2), n. 129
United States v. Berman, 28 M.J. 615 (A.F.C.M.R. 1989) — § 8-3(A), n. 8; § 12-2(H), n. 100
United States v. Bermudez, 47 C.M.R. 68 (A.F.C.M.R. 1973) — § 2-2(E)(1), n. 72
United States v. Bernard, 623 F.2d 551 (9th Cir. 1979) — § 10-4(B)(5), n. 53
United States v. Berner, 32 M.J. 570 (A.C.M.R. 1991) — § 6-1(C), n. 104
United States v. Bernier, 42 M.J. 521 (C.G.Ct.Crim.App. 1995) — § 1-3(D)(2), nn. 62, 65
United States v. Berrey, 28 M.J. 714 (N.M.C.M.R. 1989) — § 1-1(B), n. 17; § 13-2(G)(2), n. 88; § 13-3(C)(3), n. 109

TABLE OF CASES

United States v. Berrigan, 283 F. Supp. 336 (D. MD. 1968) — § 2-2(E)(7), n. 107; § 2-4(F), n. 61
United States v. Berrios, 501 F.2d 1207 (2d Cir. 1974) — § 13-3(M), n. 284
United States v. Berry, 24 M.J. 555 (A.C.M.R. 1987) — § 13-2, n. 7
United States v. Berry, 30 M.J. 134 (C.M.A. 1990) — § 2-7(C), n. 34; § 17-11, n. 8
United States v. Berry, 30 M.J. 1169 (C.G.C.M.R. 1990) — § 8-3(B)(3), n. 84
United States v. Berry, 34 M.J. 83 (C.M.A. 1992) — § 15-10(B), nn. 57, 71, 73
United States, Berta v.
United States v. Bertelson, 3 M.J. 314 (C.M.A. 1977) — § 9-2(B)(1), n. 40; § 9-3, nn. 1, 2, 3, 8; § 15-21, n. 18
United States v. Berumen, 24 M.J. 737 (A.C.M.R. 1987) — § 15-2(B)(3), n. 64
United States v. Bester, 42 M.J. 75 (1995) — § 14-3(D)(5), n. 174
United States v. Bethea, 2 M.J. 892 (A.C.M.R. 1976) — § 2-4(F), n. 53
United States v. Bethea, 3 M.J. 526 (A.F.C.M.R. 1977) — § 15-13, n. 9
United States v. Bethke, 13 M.J. 71 (C.M.A. 1982) — § 14-3(D)(4), n. 148
United States v. Betts, 12 C.M.A. 214, 30 C.M.R. 214 (1961) — § 6-4(C), n. 19
United States v. Bevacqua, 37 M.J. 996 (C.G.C.M.R. 1993) — § 8-3(B)(3), nn. 83, 84; § 15-2(B)(3), n. 46
United States v. Bevins, 30 M.J. 1149 (A.C.M.R. 1990) — § 16-3(D), n. 68
United States v. Bianchi, 25 M.J. 557 (A.C.M.R. 1987) — § 4-15(C), n. 18; § 8-3(C)(4), n. 160
United States v. Bickel, 30 M.J. 277 (C.M.A. 1990) — § 5-3(D)(1), n. 125
United States v. Bierley, 23 M.J. 557 (A.F.C.M.R. 1986) — § 4-14(A)(1), n. 7
United States v. Bilbo, 13 M.J. 706 (N.M.C.M.R. 1982) — § 9-2(B)(1), n. 47; § 14-3(C), n. 132
United States v. Bilby, 34 M.J. 1191 (A.F.C.M.R. 1992) — § 2-5, n. 2
United States v. Bilby, 39 M.J. 467 (C.M.A. 1994) — § 2-5, n. 4
United States v. Billig, 26 M.J. 744 (N.M.C.M.R. 1988) — § 17-19, n. 10
United States v. Bindley, 23 M.J. 658 (A.F.C.M.R. 1986) — § 2-2(B), n. 14
United States v. Bingham, 20 C.M.A. 521, 43 C.M.R. 216 (1971) — § 14-3(B)(1), n. 60
United States v. Bingham, 3 M.J. 119 (C.M.A. 1977) — § 17-9(D), nn. 70, 79
United States v. Bins, 38 M.J. 704 (A.C.M.R. 1993) — § 15-14(B), n. 37
United States v. Birbeck, 35 M.J. 519 (A.F.C.M.R. 1992) — § 2-7(B), n. 13
United States v. Birdsong, 40 M.J. 606 (A.C.M.R. 1994) — § 15-14(B), n. 21
United States v. Birrell, 447 F.2d 1168 (1971) — § 13-5(F), n. 28
United States v. Bishop, 28 C.M.R. 341 (C.M.A. 1960) — § 15-12(B), n. 15
United States v. Bishop, 11 M.J. 7 (C.M.A. 1981) — § 15-12(D), n. 31; § 15-16(B), nn. 17, 22
United States v. Bishop, 21 M.J. 541 (A.F.C.M.R. 1985) — § 15-14(A), n. 20
United States v. Bisser, 27 M.J. 692 (N.M.C.M.R. 1988) — § 2-2(D), n. 64
United States v. Biswell, 406 U.S. 311 (1972) — § 5-3(D)(1), n. 122
United States v. Black, 1 M.J. 340 (C.M.A. 1976) — § 4-11(A), n. 30
United States v. Black, 16 M.J. 507 (A.F.C.M.R. 1983) — § 15-2(B)(3), n. 85
United States v. Black, 40 M.J. 615 (N.M.C.M.R. 1994) — § 6-3(B), n. 15; § 6-7, n. 18
United States v. Black, 42 M.J. 505 (Army Ct.Crim.App. 1995) — § 15-12(A), n. 5; § 17-21, n. 3
United States v. Blackburn, 31 C.M.R. 340 (A.B.R. 1961) — § 11-3(B)(2), n. 46
United States v. Blackburn, 2 M.J. 929 (A.C.M.R. 1976) — § 15-2(D), n. 137
United States v. Blackmon, 39 M.J. 1091 (A.C.M.R. 1994) — § 16-6, n. 9
United States v. Blair, 10 M.J. 54 (C.M.A. 1980) — § 3-8(B), n. 17
United States v. Blair, 21 M.J. 981 (N.M.C.M.R. 1986) — § 6-1(B)(2), n. 82

TABLE OF CASES

United States v. Blair, 24 M.J. 879 (A.C.M.R. 1987) — § 2-2(D), nn. 65, 67
United States v. Blair, 29 M.J. 862 (A.F.C.M.R. 1989) — § 2-4(A), n. 16
United States v. Blais, 20 M.J. 781 (A.C.M.R. 1985) — § 6-1(C)(3), n. 145
United States v. Blake, 20 M.J. 614 (A.F.C.M.R. 1985) — § 4-11(B), n. 42
United States v. Blake, 30 M.J. 184 (C.M.A. 1990) — § 16-7, n. 1
United States v. Blake, 35 M.J. 539 (A.C.M.R. 1992) — § 2-8(B), nn. 21, 26
United States v. Blakey, 1 M.J. 247 (C.M.A. 1976) — § 15-2(B)(2), n. 26
United States v. Blanchard, 19 M.J. 196 (C.M.A. 1985) — § 2-4(C), n. 32
United States v. Blanchard, 24 M.J. 803 (N.M.C.M.R. 1987) — § 15-2(B)(4), n. 118
United States v. Blanchette, 17 M.J. 512 (A.F.C.M.R. 1983) — § 3-4, n. 10; § 8-3(B)(1), n. 49; § 13-3(M), n. 289
United States v. Bland, 6 M.J. 565 (N.C.M.R. 1978) — § 4-15(C), n. 16; § 8-3(C)(1), n. 122
United States v. Bland, 39 M.J. 921 (N.M.C.M.R. 1994) — § 5-4(A)(2), n. 16
United States v. Blanton, 7 C.M.A. 664, 23 C.M.R. 128 (1957) — § 4-5(A), n. 6; § 4-5(A)(2), n. 1
United States v. Blascak, 17 M.J. 1081 (A.F.C.M.R. 1984) — § 4-14(B), n. 21
United States v. Blaylock, 15 M.J. 190 (C.M.A. 1983) — § 6-4(C), nn. 20, 21; § 6-7, n. 8; § 8-4, nn. 16, 17; § 8-5, n. 7
United States v. Bledsoe, 39 M.J. 691 (N.M.C.M.R. 1993) — § 8-4, n. 7
United States v. Blevens, 5 C.M.A. 480, 18 C.M.R. 104 (1955) — § 13-3(N)(3), n. 408
United States v. Blevins, 22 M.J. 817 (N.M.C.M.R. 1986) — § 9-2(B)(1), n. 49
United States v. Blevins, 27 M.J. 678 (A.C.M.R. 1988) — § 15-10(B), n. 51
United States v. Blizzard, 34 M.J. 763 (A.C.M.R. 1992) — § 16-3(D), n. 67
United States, Blockburger v.
United States v. Blocker, 30 M.J. 1152 (A.C.M.R. 1990) — § 13-3(E), n. 196; § 15-2(A), n. 3
United States v. Blocker, 32 M.J. 281 (C.M.A. 1991) — § 15-10(B), n. 55
United States v. Blocker, 33 M.J. 349 (C.M.A. 1991) — § 13-3(G), n. 226
United States v. Blucker, 30 M.J. 690 (A.C.M.R. 1990) — § 6-1(C)(2), n. 131
United States v. Bluitt, 50 C.M.R. 675 (A.C.M.R. 1975) — § 6-1(C), n. 95
United States v. Blunk, 37 C.M.R. 422 (C.M.A. 1967) — § 16-8(C), n. 36
United States v. Blye, 37 M.J. 92 (C.M.A. 1993) — § 2-4(A), n. 13
United States v. Boberg, 17 C.M.A. 401, 38 C.M.R. 199 (1968) — § 15-13, nn. 13, 31
United States v. Bobroff, 23 M.J. 872 (N.M.C.M.R. 1987) — § 6-1(B)(2), n. 81; § 14-3, n. 4
United States v. Boden, 21 M.J. 916 (A.C.M.R. 1986) — § 13-3(C)(3), n. 114
United States v. Boehner, 11 M.J. 658 (A.C.M.R. 1981) — § 13-3(C)(2), n. 73
United States v. Boese, 13 C.M.A. 131, 32 C.M.R. 131 (1962) — § 16-8(B), n. 13
United States v. Bogar, 13 M.J. 768 (A.C.M.R. 1982) — § 13-2(G)(2), n. 74
United States v. Bohl, 3 M.J. 385 (C.M.A. 1977) — § 14-3(E), n. 180
United States v. Bohle, 346 F. Supp. 577 (N.D.N.Y. 1972) — § 16-13
United States v. Bolado, 34 M.J. 732 (N.M.C.M.R. 1991) — § 13-3(C)(3), n. 118
United States v. Boland, 22 M.J. 886 (A.C.M.R. 1986) — § 17-3(B), n. 36
United States v. Bolden, 40 C.M.R. 758 (A.C.M.R. 1969) — § 6-1(B), n. 62
United States v. Bolden, 16 M.J. 722 (A.F.C.M.R. 1983) — § 16-9, n. 16
United States v. Bolden, 34 M.J. 728 (N.M.C.M.R. 1991) — § 16-5(D)(4), n. 102
United States v. Boldon, 17 M.J. 1046 (N.M.C.M.R. 1984) — § 17-11, n. 1
United States v. Boles, 11 M.J. 195 (C.M.A. 1981) — § 16-5(B), nn. 8, 9
United States v. Bonar, 40 C.M.R. 482 (A.B.R. 1969) — § 2-5, n. 3
United States v. Bono, 26 M.J. 240 (C.M.A. 1988) — § 15-2(B)(3), n. 84

TABLE OF CASES

United States v. Booker, 5 M.J. 238 (C.M.A. 1978) — § 3-8(B), nn. 6, 7, 10, 11; § 15-25, n. 1; § 15-26(C), nn. 8, 11, 12; § 16-2(E), n. 48; § 16-5(B), nn. 11, 12; § 16-5(C), n. 48
United States v. Boone, 10 M.J. 715 (A.C.M.R. 1981) — § 4-5(A)(4), n. 18
United States v. Boone, 24 M.J. 680 (A.C.M.R. 1987) — § 14-3(E), n. 179
United States v. Boone, 39 M.J. 541 (A.C.M.R. 1994) — § 15-2(B)(3), nn. 41, 48
United States v. Boone, 42 M.J. 308 (1995) — § 15-2(B)(3), n. 78
United States v. Bordelon, 43 M.J. 531 (Army Ct.Crim.App. 1995) — § 13-3(E), nn. 197, 214
United States v. Borner, 25 M.J. 551 (A.F.C.M.R. 1987) — § 14-3(B)(2), n. 99
United States v. Borys, 39 C.M.R. 608 (A.B.R. 1968) — § 13-3(E), n. 196
United States v. Bosier, 12 M.J. 1010 (A.C.M.R. 1982) — § 10-4(B)(5), nn. 53, 56, 58, 60
United States v. Boswell, 23 C.M.R. 369 (C.M.A. 1957) — § 14-3(E), n. 179
United States v. Boswell, 8 C.M.A. 145, 23 C.M.R. 369 (1957) — § 15-16(A), nn. 12, 13
United States v. Boswell, 45 C.M.R. 742 (A.C.M.R. 1972) — § 6-1(B), n. 66
United States v. Boswell, 30 M.J. 731 (A.F.C.M.R. 1990) — § 15-14(B), n. 45
United States v. Boswell, 36 M.J. 807 (A.C.M.R. 1993) — § 11-2(A)(2), n. 12; § 15-14(A), n. 20
United States v. Boudreaux, 26 M.J. 879 (N.M.C.M.R. 1988) — § 17-15(A), n. 14
United States v. Boudreaux, 33 M.J. 649 (N.M.C.M.R. 1991) — § 17-16(B), n. 11
United States v. Boughton, 16 M.J. 649 (A.F.C.M.R. 1983) — § 16-5(D)(4), n. 86
United States v. Bouie, 9 C.M.A. 228, 26 C.M.R. 8 (1958) — § 15-13, n. 8
United States v. Bouie, 18 M.J.529 (A.F.C.M.R. 1984) — § 15-12(B), n. 15
United States v. Bouknight, 35 M.J. 671 (A.C.M.R. 1992) — § 15-9, n. 6
United States v. Boulden, 29 M.J. 44 (C.M.A. 1989) — § 2-7(C), n. 40
United States, Bouler v.
United States v. Bourgette, 27 M.J. 904 (A.F.C.M.R. 1989) — § 17-11, n. 5
United States v. Bowen, 29 M.J. 779 (A.C.M.R. 1989) — § 16-11, n. 8
United States v. Bowerman, 39 M.J. 219 (C.M.A. 1994) — § 5-4(B), n. 42
United States v. Bowers, 47 C.M.R. 516 (A.C.M.R. 1973) — § 4-11(A), n. 11
United States v. Bowers, 20 M.J. 1003 (A.F.C.M.R. 1985) — § 14-3(B)(1), n. 56
United States v. Bowie, 14 C.M.A. 631, 34 C.M.R. 411 (1964) — § 4-8(D), n. 60
United States v. Bowie, 21 M.J. 453 (C.M.A. 1986) — § 12-2(F)(4), n. 84
United States v. Bowles, 37 M.J. 708 (A.C.M.R. 1993) — § 13-3(C)(5), n. 179
United States v. Bowman, 20 C.M.A. 119, 42 C.M.R. 311 (1970) — § 12-2(F)(2), n. 51
United States v. Bowman, 49 C.M.R. 406 (A.C.M.R. 1974) — § 4-15(A), n. 5; § 12-3(A), n. 39
United States v. Bowman, 9 M.J. 676 (A.C.M.R. 1980) — § 4-8(A), n. 8
United States v. Bowman, 13 M.J. 640 (N.M.C.M.R. 1982) — § 13-3(C)(2), nn. 68, 73
United States v. Boyce, 12 M.J. 981 (A.F.C.M.R. 1982) — § 16-8(C), n. 36
United States v. Boyd, 21 C.M.R. 395 (A.B.R. 1956) — § 1-3(D)(1), n. 18
United States v. Boyd, 2 M.J. 1014 (A.C.M.R. 1976) — § 9-2(B)(1), n. 49
United States v. Boyd, 7 M.J. 282 (C.M.A. 1979) — § 15-10(C)(2), n. 94
United States v. Boyd, 14 M.J. 703 (N.M.C.M.R. 1982) — § 10-4(B)(5), n. 60
United States v. Boyd, 27 M.J. 82 (C.M.A. 1988) — § 5-4(C), n. 56; § 13-3(H), n. 244
United States v. Boyett, 42 M.J. 150 (1995) — § 2-8(B), nn. 13, 17, 18
United States v. Boyle, 30 M.J. 656 (A.F.C.M.R. 1990) — § 8-4, n. 4
United States v. Boyle, 36 M.J. 326 (C.M.A. 1993) — § 13-3(J), n. 262
United States v. Boysen, 11 C.M.A. 331, 29 C.M.R. 147 (1960) — § 8-3(D), n. 166
United States v. Brabant, 29 M.J. 259 (C.M.A. 1989) — § 5-4(B), n. 50
United States v. Bradford, 25 M.J. 181 (C.M.A. 1987) — § 5-8(B), n. 29; § 13-3(C)(3), n. 106

TABLE OF CASES

United States v. Bradford, 28 M.J. 125 (C.M.A. 1989) — § 15-2(B)(3), n. 88; § 17-14, n. 10
United States v. Bradford, 29 M.J. 829 (A.C.M.R. 1989) — § 15-14(B), n. 28
United States v. Bradley, 418 F.2d 688 (4th Cir. 1969) — § 13-3(N)(3), n. 408
United States v. Bradley, 7 M.J. 332 (C.M.A. 1976) — § 14-3(D)(5), n. 163
United States v. Bradley, 11 M.J. 598 (A.F.C.M.R. 1981) — § 9-2(B)(1), n. 50
United States v. Bradley, 30 M.J. 308 (C.M.A. 1990) — § 13-3(M), nn. 282, 298
United States, Brady v.
United States v. Brady, 8 C.M.A. 456, 24 C.M.R. 266 (1957) — § 11-3(B)(2), n. 45
United States v. Bragg, 30 M.J. 1147 (A.F.C.M.R. 1990) — § 13-3(C)(3), n. 160
United States v. Brakebush, 34 M.J. 1219 (N.M.C.M.R. 1992) — § 15-2(B)(2), nn. 27, 28
United States v. Bramel, 28 M.J. 505 (A.C.M.R. 1989) — § 7-2(B)(4), n. 45
United States v. Bramel, 29 M.J. 958 (A.C.M.R. 1990) — § 6-4(B), n. 13; § 7-2(A)(1), n. 14; § 7-2(A)(2), nn. 33, 34; § 7-2(B)(4), n. 44
United States v. Bramer, 43 M.J. 538 (N.M.Ct.Crim.App. 1995) — § 13-3(C), n. 30; § 13-3(C)(3), n. 105; § 13-3(C)(4), nn. 175-177
United States v. Brammel, 29 M.J. 958 (A.C.M.R. 1990) — § 6-4(B), n. 9
United States v. Brandt, 20 M.J. 74 (C.M.A. 1985) — § 4-15(C), n. 15; § 12-3(B), nn. 47, 48
United States v. Branford, 2 C.M.R. 489 (A.B.R. 1952) — § 6-1(C)(2), n. 130
United States v. Branoff, 34 M.J. 612 (A.F.C.M.R. 1992) — § 5-4(B), n. 52; § 10-4(B)(2), n. 37; § 10-6, n. 8; § 13-5(J), nn. 79-83; § 16-5(D)(3), n. 77
United States v. Branoff, 38 M.J. 98 (C.M.A. 1993) — § 10-4(A)(4), n. 22
United States v. Bratcher, 19 C.M.A. 125, 39 C.M.R. 125 (1969) — § 2-4(F), n. 51
United States v. Brauchler, 15 M.J. 755 (A.F.C.M.R. 1983) — § 4-11(A), n. 12
United States v. Bray, 26 M.J. 661 (N.M.C.M.R. 1988) — § 9-2(B)(1), n. 49
United States v. Breault, 30 M.J. 833 (N.M.C.M.R. 1990) — § 2-4(C), n. 30
United States v. Brecheen, 27 M.J. 67 (C.M.A. 1988) — § 6-1(C), nn. 94, 102; § 13-3(F), n. 217
United States v. Breese, 11 M.J. 17 (C.M.A. 1981) — § 12-2(F)(1); 12-2(F)(3), nn. 59-61; § 15-2(B)(2), n. 27
United States v. Breland, 32 M.J. 801 (A.C.M.R. 1991) — § 3-3(C), n. 27
United States v. Brenton, 24 M.J. 562 (A.F.C.M.R. 1987) — § 4-11(C), n. 52
United States v. Breseman, 21 M.J. 973 (C.G.C.M.R. 1986) — § 17-2(B)(4), n. 95
United States v. Breseman, 26 M.J. 398 (C.M.A. 1988) — § 5-3(B), n. 39
United States v. Brewer, 15 M.J. 597 (A.C.M.R. 1983) — § 15-2(B)(2), n. 26
United States v. Brewster, 32 M.J. 591 (A.C.M.R. 1991) — § 6-1(B)(2), n. 81; § 6-1(C), n. 95; § 15-9, nn. 16, 17
United States v. Brice, 48 C.M.R. 368 (N.C.M.R. 1973) — § 6-1(B), n. 68
United States v. Brice, 19 M.J. 170 (C.M.A. 1985) — § 6-5(A), nn. 3, 4; § 15-4(B), n. 10; § 15-10(B), nn. 63, 67; § 15-10(C)(2), n. 91
United States v. Brickey, 16 M.J. 258 (C.M.A. 1983) — § 10-4(A)(4), n. 27; § 10-4(B)(1), nn. 30-32; § 17-3, n. 2; § 17-4(A), nn. 46, 48, 49
United States v. Brickey, 16 M.J. 679 (A.C.M.R. 1986) — § 14-3(G), n. 203
United States v. Bridges, 9 C.M.A. 121, 25 C.M.R. 383 (1958) — § 2-2(D), n. 68
United States v. Briggs, 39 M.J. 600 (A.C.M.R. 1994) — § 5-4(B), n. 52
United States v. Briggs, 42 M.J. 367 (1995) — § 15-2(A), n. 13
United States v. Bright, 20 M.J. 661 (N.M.C.M.R. 1985) — § 2-4(C), n. 32
United States v. Bright, 32 M.J. 679 (A.F.C.M.R. 1991) — § 14-3(B)(2), n. 85
United States v. Briley, 26 M.J. 977 (A.F.C.M.R. 1988) — § 5-4(B), n. 23
United States v. Brinston, 28 M.J. 631 (A.F.C.M.R. 1989) — § 4-14(A)(1), n. 4

TABLE OF CASES

United States v. Britcher, 41 M.J. 806 (C.G.Ct.Crim.App. 1995) — § 5-4(B), n. 41
United States v. Britt, 16 M.J. 971 (A.F.C.M.R. 1983) — § 16-6, n. 10
United States v. Britton, 22 M.J. 501 (A.F.C.M.R. 1986) — § 13-3(C)(3), n. 122
United States v. Britton, 26 M.J. 24 (C.M.A. 1988) — § 13-3(B), n. 9; § 13-3(C)(3), n. 118
United States v. Britton, 33 M.J. 238 (C.M.A. 1991) — § 5-3(A), n. 14
United States v. Broadnax, 23 M.J. 389 (C.M.A. 1987) — § 2-7(C), n. 35
United States v. Broadus, 2 M.J. 438 (A.C.M.R. 1975) — § 4-14(B), n. 19
United States v. Broady, 12 M.J. 963 (A.F.C.M.R. 1982) — § 10-3(A), n. 2
United States v. Brodin, 25 M.J. 580 (A.C.M.R. 1987) — § 13-3(C)(3), nn. 102, 159
United States v. Brogan, 33 M.J. 588 (N.M.C.M.R. 1991) — § 16-5(C), n. 46
United States v. Bromell, 37 M.J. 978 (A.C.M.R. 1993) — § 13-3(G), n. 225
United States v. Brookins, 33 M.J. 793 (A.C.M.R. 1991) — § 4-15(C), n. 15; § 8-3(C)(2), n. 127
United States v. Brooks, 17 C.M.R. 467 (N.B.R. 1954) — § 16-3(C), n. 52
United States v. Brooks, 44 C.M.R. 873 (A.C.M.R. 1971) — § 2-3(B), n. 18
United States v. Brooks, 17 M.J. 584 (A.C.M.R. 1983) — § 13-3(N)(5), n. 437
United States v. Brooks, 25 M.J. 175 (C.M.A. 1987) — § 15-14(C), nn. 48, 49
United States v. Brooks, 26 M.J. 930 (A.C.M.R. 1988) — § 14-3(D)(4), nn. 145, 147, 150
United States v. Brooks, 42 M.J. 484 (1995) — § 15-16(A), n. 11; § 15-16(B), n. 27
United States v. Brosius, 37 M.J. 652 (A.C.M.R. 1993) — § 5-4(B), nn. 23, 49; § 17-21, n. 3
United States v. Brothers, 30 M.J. 289 (C.M.A. 1990) — § 15-2(B)(3), n. 63
United States v. Broussard, 35 M.J. 665 (A.C.M.R. 1992) — § 6-1, n. 15; § 16-5(D)(3), n. 76
United States v. Browers, 20 M.J. 356 (C.M.A. 1985) — § 13-5(K), n. 88; § 15-4(A), n. 9; § 13-2(G)(2), nn. 87, 97
United States v. Browers, 20 M.J. 542 (A.C.M.R. 1985) — § 13-3(E), nn. 210, 204; § 13-3(G)(2), n. 96; § 13-5(K), n. 86; § 15-4(A), n. 6
United States, Brown v.
United States v. Brown, 4 C.M.A. 683, 16 C.M.R. 257 (1954) — § 6-1(C), n. 96
United States v. Brown, 7 C.M.A. 251, 22 C.M.R. 41 (1956) — § 15-3, n. 1
United States v. Brown, 24 C.M.R. 585 (A.B.R. 1957) — § 2-2(C)(3), n. 33
United States v. Brown, 31 C.M.R. 279 (C.M.A. 1962) — § 4-8(C)(2), n. 26
United States v. Brown, 42 C.M.R. 656 (A.C.M.R. 1970) — § 6-1(B), n. 60; § 13-3(F), n. 217
United States v. Brown, 21 C.M.A. 516, 45 C.M.R. 290 (1972) — § 12-3(A), n. 21
United States v. Brown, 13 C.M.A. 162, 48 C.M.R. 778 (1974) — § 4-5(A)(4), n. 17
United States v. Brown, 3 M.J. 368 (C.M.A. 1977) — § 15-2(E), n. 158; § 15-14(A), n. 20
United States v. Brown, 4 M.J. 654 (A.C.M.R. 1977) — § 9-2(B)(1), n. 46
United States v. Brown, 1 M.J. 1151 (N.C.M.R. 1977) — § 2-2(E)(6), n. 101
United States v. Brown, 6 M.J. 338 (C.M.A. 1978) — § 946; § 17-2(B)(2), n. 33
United States v. Brown, 8 M.J. 501 (A.F.C.M.R. 1979) — § 4-11(A), nn. 22, 23
United States v. Brown, 7 M.J. 815 (N.C.M.R. 1979) — § 17-15(B), n. 22
United States v. Brown, 8 M.J. 559 (N.C.M.R. 1979) — § 9-2(B)(1), n. 45
United States v. Brown, 10 M.J. 635 (A.C.M.R. 1980) — § 8-3(B)(4), nn. 98, 99; § 12-2(F)(5), n. 88
United States v. Brown, 11 M.J. 263 (C.M.A. 1981) — § 16-5(B), n. 8
United States v. Brown, 11 M.J. 769 (N.M.C.M.R. 1981) — § 4-8(A), n. 8
United States v. Brown, 12 M.J. 728 (N.M.C.M.R. 1981) — § 12-4, n. 13; § 15-2(A), n. 4
United States v. Brown, 12 M.J. 420 (C.M.A. 1982) — § 5-3(D)(1), nn. 120, 124; § 9-3, n. 10

1077

TABLE OF CASES

United States v. Brown, 13 M.J. 253 (C.M.A. 1982) — § 5-4(C), nn. 53, 59; § 11-2(E)(1), n. 107; § 13-3(H), n. 238
United States v. Brown, 13 M.J. 890 (A.C.M.R. 1982) — § 15-10(C)(2), n. 96; § 16-6, n. 18; § 16-8(C), n. 43
United States v. Brown, 15 M.J. 501 (A.F.C.M.R. 1982) — § 5-10(D), n. 44; § 15-4(C), nn. 16, 19
United States v. Brown, 15 M.J. 620 (N.M.C.M.R. 1982) — § 16-2, n. 3; § 16-9, n. 4
United States v. Brown, 17 M.J. 544 (A.C.M.R. 1983) — § 10-2(B), n. 35
United States v. Brown, 17 M.J. 987 (A.C.M.R. 1984) — § 14-2(B)(4), n. 113; § 15-13, n. 9
United States v. Brown, 19 M.J. 63 (C.M.A. 1984) — § 2-7(B), n. 20
United States v. Brown, 19 M.J. 826 (N.M.C.M.R. 1984) — § 4-11(B), n. 40
United States v. Brown, 21 M.J. 780 (A.C.M.R. 1985) — § 17-8(B)(1), n. 53
United States v. Brown, 21 M.J. 995 (A.C.M.R. 1986) — § 6-1(B)(2), n. 82
United States v. Brown, 22 M.J. 597 (A.C.M.R. 1986) — § 6-4(C), n. 21; § 8-5, n. 1
United States v. Brown, 23 M.J. 149 (C.M.A. 1987) — § 3-8(B), n. 5; § 16-5(C), n. 30
United States v. Brown, 25 M.J. 793 (N.M.C.M.R. 1987) — § 2-4(D), n. 44; § 6-1(C), nn. 94, 96; § 13-3(F), n. 218
United States v. Brown, 26 M.J. 266 (C.M.A. 1988) — § 15-14(B), n. 22; § 15-14(D), nn. 59, 60
United States v. Brown, 27 M.J. 614 (A.C.M.R. 1988) — § 5-4(B), n. 50
United States v. Brown, 28 M.J. 644 (A.C.M.R. 1989) — § 11-2(B)(1), n. 57
United States v. Brown, 30 M.J. 907 (A.C.M.R. 1990) — § 13-3(B), nn. 9, 15
United States v. Brown, 30 M.J. 839 (N.M.C.M.R. 1990) — § 13-3(C)(3), n. 160
United States v. Brown, 33 M.J. 706 (A.C.M.R. 1991) — § 2-7(C), n. 40; § 15-2(B)(3), n. 81
United States v. Brown, 34 M.J. 105 (C.M.A. 1992) — § 6-1(B)(2), n. 81; § 15-10(B), n. 68
United States v. Brown, 35 M.J. 877 (A.F.C.M.R. 1992) — § 5-3(D)(1), n. 131
United States v. Brown, 34 M.J. 1024 (N.M.C.M.R. 1992) — § 9-2(B)(1), n. 46
United States v. Brown, 38 M.J. 696 (A.F.C.M.R. 1993) — § 5-4(B), n. 42
United States v. Brown, 39 M.J. 114 (C.M.A. 1994) — § 8-2(A), n. 2
United States v. Brown, 40 M.J. 152 (C.M.A. 1994) — § 4-12(A), n. 10; § 5-4(B), nn. 23
United States v. Brown, 40 M.J. 625 (N.M.C.M.R; § 6-4(C), n. 19; § 17-9(E), n. 86
United States v. Brown, 41 M.J. 504 (Army Ct. Crim. App. 1994) — § 13-3(F), n. 219; § 13-3(M), n. 284
United States v. Brown, 43 M.J. 187 (1995) — § 15-14(B), n. 25
United States v. Brown-Austin, 34 M.J. 578 (A.C.M.R. 1992) — § 15-14(A), n. 5; § 17-4, n. 28
United States v. Browning, 29 M.J. 174 (C.M.A. 1989) — § 16-5(C), n. 31
United States v. Brownlow, 39 M.J. 484 (C.M.A. 1994) — § 2-4(F), n. 51
United States v. Bruce, 14 M.J. 254 (C.M.A. 1982) — § 5-10(A), n. 1; § 5-10(D), n. 40
United States v. Bruce, 17 M.J. 1083 (A.F.C.M.R. 1984) — § 5-10(D), n. 28
United States v. Brundidge, 20 M.J. 1028 (A.C.M.R. 1985) — § 17-15(B), n. 19
United States v. Brunson, 15 M.J. 898 (C.G.C.M.R. 1982) — § 7-2(A)(1), n. 29
United States v. Brunson, 30 M.J. 766 (A.C.M.R. 1990) — § 2-5, n. 3
United States v. Brunton, 24 M.J. 566 (N.M.C.M.R. 1987) — § 4-8(B), n. 11; § 5-4(A)(2), n. 16
United States v. Bruton, 18 M.J. 156 (C.M.A. 1984) — § 17-11, n. 7
United States v. Bryant, 29 C.M.R. 814 (A.F.B.R. 1960) — § 15-14(A), n. 18
United States v. Bryant, 12 C.M.A. 133, 30 C.M.R. 133 (1961) — § 16-3(C), n. 52

TABLE OF CASES

United States v. Bryant, 439 F.2d 642 (D.C. Cir. 1971) — § 10-4(B)(5), n. 60
United States v. Bryant, 23 C.M.A. 326, 49 C.M.R. 660 (1975) — § 12-3(A), n. 45
United States v. Bryant, 27 M.J. 811 (A.C.M.R. 1988) — § 5-10(D), n. 39
United States v. Bryant, 28 M.J. 504 (A.C.M.R. 1989) — § 6-1(C), n. 94
United States v. Bryant, 30 M.J. 72 (C.M.A. 1990) — § 6-1(C), nn. 101-103
United States v. Bryant, 35 M.J. 739 (A.C.M.R. 1992) — § 15-2(B)(2), n. 27; § 15-2(B)(3), n. 47
United States v. Bryant, 37 M.J. 668 (A.C.M.R. 1993) — § 17-4, nn. 21, 26
United States v. Bubonics, 40 M.J. 734 (N.M.C.M.R. 1994) — § 5-4(B), n. 52
United States v. Buchecker, 13 M.J. 709 (N.M.C.M.R. 1982) — § 13-3(C)(2), n. 68
United States v. Buckingham, 9 M.J. 514 (A.F.C.M.R. 1980) — § 4-9, nn. 4, 7; § 13-2(D), n. 36; § 13-2(E), n. 46; § 13-3(A), nn. 6, 7
United States v. Buckingham, 11 M.J. 184 (C.M.A. 1981) — § 4-5(A)(3), n. 12
United States v. Bucknell, 26 M.J. 523 (A.C.M.R. 1988) — § 13-5(E), n. 5
United States v. Budicin, 32 M.J. 795 (N.M.C.M.R. 1990) — § 16-8(A), n. 4
United States v. Bufatino, 576 F.2d 446 (2d Cir. 1978) — § 10-4(B)(5), n. 58
United States v. Bullington, 12 M.J. 570 (A.C.M.R. 1981) — § 5-3, n. 9
United States v. Bunting, 4 C.M.A. 84, 15 C.M.R. 84 (1954) — § 4-14(A)(1), n. 7
United States v. Burden, 2 C.M.A. 547, 10 C.M.R. 45 (1953) — § 2-6, n. 7; § 15-14(C), n. 50
United States v. Burden, 1 M.J. 89 (C.M.A. 1975) — § 4-5(B), n. 28
United States v. Burdine, 29 M.J. 834 (A.C.M.R. 1989) — § 17-14, n. 11
United States v. Burge, 25 M.J. 576 (A.F.C.M.R. 1987) — § 14-3(B)(2), n. 99
United States v. Burgess, 32 M.J. 446 (C.M.A. 1991) — § 5-7, n. 22
United States v. Burke, 517 F.2d 377 (2d Cir. 1975) — § 14-4, n. 14
United States v. Burke, 4 M.J. 530 (N.C.M.R. 1977) — § 15-16(C), n. 33
United States v. Burkhalter, 17 C.M.A. 266, 38 C.M.R. 64 (1967) — § 8-3(C)(1), n. 116; § 15-10(B), n. 40
United States v. Burl, 10 M.J. 48 (C.M.A. 1980) — § 3-8(B), n. 17
United States v. Burnell, 40 M.J. 175 (C.M.A. 1994) — § 9-2(B)(1), n. 49
United States v. Burnett, 27 M.J. 99 (C.M.A. 1988) — § 15-5, n. 15
United States v. Burnette, 35 M.J. 58 (C.M.A. 1992) — § 14-3(D)(5), n. 176
United States v. Burney, 21 C.M.A. 71, 44 C.M.R. 125 (1971) — § 6-1(C)(3), nn. 136, 137
United States v. Burnom, 35 C.M.R. 908 (A.F.B.R. 1965) — § 11-3(B)(1), n. 11
United States v. Burns, 2 M.J. 78 (C.M.A. 1976) — § 17-11, n. 1
United States v. Burns, 684 F.2d 1066 (2d Cir. 1982) — § 14-4, nn. 7, 11
United States v. Burns, 27 M.J. 92 (C.M.A. 1988) — § 11-2(A)(2), n. 9; § 11-2(D)(2), n. 96
United States v. Burns, 33 M.J. 316 (C.M.A. 1991) — § 5-3(C)(6), n. 98
United States v. Burrell, 5 M.J. 617 (A.C.M.R. 1978) — § 10-4(B)(5), n. 52
United States v. Burrell, 13 M.J. 437 (C.M.A. 1982) — § 13-3(C)(2), n. 68
United States v. Burrer, 22 M.J. 544 (N.M.C.M.R. 1986) — § 12-2(H), n. 104
United States v. Burris, 21 M.J. 140 (C.M.A. 1985) — § 13-2(G)(2), nn. 110, 111; § 13-3(C), n. 26; § 13-3(C)(3), n. 159
United States v. Burris, 25 M.J. 846 (A.F.C.M.R. 1988) — § 5-3(D)(1), n. 124
United States v. Burry, 36 C.M.R. 829 (C.G.B.R. 1966) — § 13-3(N)(3), n. 403
United States v. Burton, 21 C.M.A. 112, 44 C.M.R. 166 (1971) — § 1-1(B), n. 29; § 13-3(C), n. 26; § 13-3(C)(2), nn. 53, 66, 68, 73, 80, 81; § 13-3(C)(3), n. 121; § 15-20, n. 12

TABLE OF CASES

United States v. Burwell, 50 C.M.R. 192 (A.C.M.R. 1975) — § 15-2(B)(3), n. 77; § 15-13, n. 14
United States v. Bush, 49 C.M.R. 97 (N.C.M.R. 1974) — § 13-3(C)(2), n. 73
United States v. Bush, 12 M.J. 647 (A.F.C.M.R. 1981) — § 17-4, n. 27
United States v. Bush, 18 M.J. 685 (N.M.C.M.R. 1984) — § 2-2(C)(3), n. 53
United States v. Buske, 2 M.J. 465 (A.C.M.R. 1975) — § 14-3(B)(2), n. 75
United States v. Butler, 20 C.M.A. 247, 43 C.M.R. 87 (1971) — § 14-3(B)(2), n. 95
United States v. Butler, 14 M.J. 72 (C.M.A. 1982) — § 12-3(A), n. 38
United States v. Butler, 19 M.J. 724 (N.M.C.M.R. 1984) — § 12-2(F)(2), n. 55
United States v. Butler, 23 M.J. 702 (A.F.C.M.R. 1986) — § 5-9(D), nn. 39, 43
United States v. Butler, 41 M.J. 211 (C.M.A. 1994) — § 16-11, n. 5
United States v. Butner, 15 M.J. 139 (C.M.A. 1983) — § 5-4(B), nn. 44, 52
United States v. Butterbaugh, 21 M.J. 1019 (N.M.C.M.R. 1986) — § 13-2(E), n. 55
United States v. Button, 31 M.J. 897 (A.F.C.M.R. 1990) — § 2-4(A), n. 17; § 16-5(D)(2), n. 70
United States v. Butts, 25 M.J. 535 (A.C.M.R. 1987) — § 16-8(C), n. 36
United States v. Byard, 29 M.J. 803 (A.C.M.R. 1989) — § 13-3(C)(3), n. 162
United States v. Byers, 26 M.J. 132 (C.M.A. 1988) — § 5-4(B), n. 44
United States v. Byers, 34 M.J. 923 (A.C.M.R. 1992) — § 4-14(A)(2), n. 11
United States v. Byers, 40 M.J. 321 (C.M.A. 1994) — § 2-4(B), n. 25
United States v. Bygrave, 40 M.J. 839 (N.M.C.M.R. 1994) — § 2-9(C)(1), n. 35; § 17-8(B), n. 19
United States v. Byrd, 24 M.J. 286 (C.M.A. 1987) — § 14-3(B)(2), n. 99
United States v. Caballero, 49 C.M.R. 594 (C.M.A. 1975) — § 2-7(A), n. 8
United States v. Cabatic, 7 M.J. 438 (C.M.A. 1979) — § 13-3(C)(2), n. 64
United States v. Cabebe, 13 M.J. 303 (C.M.A. 1982) — § 16-8(B), n. 17; § 16-9, n. 14
United States v. Cabral, 20 M.J. 269 (C.M.A. 1985) — § 17-9(A), n. 17
United States v. Cadenhead, 14 C.M.A. 271, 34 C.M.R. 51 (1963) — § 4-12(B), n. 14
United States v. Cage, 42 M.J. 139 (1995) — § 1-3(D)(2)
United States v. Cagle, 12 M.J. 736 (A.F.C.M.R. 1981) — § 15-14(B), n. 23
United States v. Cahill, 23 M.J. 544 (A.C.M.R. 1986) — § 5-10(D), n. 37; § 13-5(B), n. 30
United States v. Cahn, 31 M.J. 729 (A.F.C.M.R. 1990) — § 14-2(B)(4), n. 118
United States v. Cain, 5 M.J. 844 (A.C.M.R. 1978) — § 5-4(A)(1), n. 9
United States v. Calderon, 34 M.J. 501 (A.F.C.M.R. 1991) — § 5-10(D), n. 37; § 15-2(B)(3), n. 85
United States v. Caldwell, 11 C.M.A. 257, 29 C.M.R. 73 (1960) — § 15-14(A), n. 13; § 15-15, n. 8
United States v. Caldwell, 16 M.J. 575 (A.C.M.R. 1983) — § 4-15(C), n. 15
United States v. Caldwell, 23 M.J. 748 (A.F.C.M.R. 1987) — § 2-8(D), n. 41; § 6-1(C)(3), n. 145; § 15-13, n. 16
United States v. Calhoun, 13 M.J. 322 (C.M.A. 1982) — § 4-8(C)(1), n. 16
United States v. Calhoun, 14 M.J. 588 (N.M.C.M.R. 1982) — § 12-3(A), n. 23
United States v. Caliendo, 13 C.M.A. 405, 32 C.M.R. 405 (1962) — § 13-3(H), n. 239
United States v. Callahan, 22 C.M.R. 443 (A.B.R. 1956) — § 9-2(B)(2), n. 70
United States v. Callahan, 8 M.J. 804 (N.C.M.R. 1980) — § 9-2(B)(1), n. 46
United States v. Callara, 21 M.J. 259 (C.M.A. 1986) — § 10-4(A)(4), n. 18; § 10-4(B)(4), n. 46
United States v. Callaway, 21 M.J. 770 (A.C.M.R. 1986) — § 2-8(C), n. 32; § 6-1(C), n. 94; § 9-2(B)(1), n. 50
United States v. Callaway, 23 M.J. 799 (N.M.C.M.R. 1986) — § 13-3(C)(2), n. 81

TABLE OF CASES

United States v. Calley, 46 C.M.R. 1131 (A.C.M.R. 1973) — § 13-5(F), n. 14; § 15-10(C), n. 80
United States v. Calley, 22 C.M.A. 534, 48 C.M.R. 19 (1973) — § 1-1, n. 2
United States v. Callinan, 32 M.J. 701 (A.F.C.M.R. 1991) — § 13-3(C)(3), n. 122
United States v. Calloway, 23 M.J. 799 (N.M.C.M.R. 1986) — § 13-3(C)(3), nn. 156, 159; § 15-2(B)(3), n. 60
United States v. Camacho, 30 M.J. 644 (N.M.C.M.R. 1990) — § 13-3(C)(3), nn. 102, 165
United States v. Camanga, 38 M.J. 249 (C.M.A. 1993) — § 15-2(B)(3), n. 58; § 5-3(C)(6), n. 89; § 5-3(F), n. 27; § 5-7, n. 7
United States v. Cambridge, 3 C.M.A. 377, 12 C.M.R. 133 (1953) — § 15-21, n. 17
United States, Cameron v.
United States v. Cameron, 37 M.J. 1042 (A.C.M.R. 1993) — § 15-14(B), n. 23
United States v. Campbell, 47 C.M.R. 965 (A.C.M.R. 1973) — § 12-3(A), nn. 30, 39
United States v. Campbell, 22 M.J. 99 (C.M.A. 1986) — § 13-3(J), n. 262
United States v. Campbell, 26 M.J. 970 (A.C.M.R. 1988) — § 15-10(B), n. 68; § 15-10(C)(2), n. 100
United States v. Campbell, 32 M.J. 580 (A.F.C.M.R. 1990) — § 16-6, n. 10; § 16-7, n. 1
United States v. Campbell, 32 M.J. 564 (A.C.M.R. 1991) — § 13-3(C)(3), n. 122
United States v. Campbell, 37 M.J. 1049 (N.M.C.M.R. 1993) — § 15-12(B), n. 22
United States v. Campbell, 41 M.J. 177 (C.M.A. 1994) — § 5-3(F), n. 26; § 5-3(D)(1), n. 131
United States v. Campfield, 17 M.J. 715 (N.M.C.M.R. 1983) — § 2-2(E)(3), n. 78
United States v. Campfield, 20 M.J. 246 (C.M.A. 1985) — § 6-1(C)(3), n. 147
United States v. Campos, 37 M.J. 894 (A.C.M.R. 1993) — § 6-3(C), n. 23
United States v. Campos, 37 M.J. 1110 (N.M.C.M.R. 1993) — § 14-3(B)(2), n. 81
United States v. Campos, 42 M.J. 253 (1995) — § 6-5(A), n. 12; § 12-2(H), n. 121
United States v. Canatelli, 5 M.J. 838 (A.C.M.R. 1978) — § 2-6(C), n. 35
United States v. Caniete, 28 M.J. 426 (C.M.A. 1989) — § 16-5(C), n. 28
United States v. Cannon, 5 M.J. 198 (C.M.A. 1978) — § 3-8(B), n. 6
United States v. Cannon, 29 M.J. 549 (A.F.C.M.R. 1980) — § 5-3(C)(6), n. 98
United States v. Cannon, 13 M.J. 777 (A.C.M.R. 1982) — § 2-7(A), n. 8
United States v. Cannon, 23 M.J. 676 (A.C.M.R. 1986) — § 15-2(B)(3), n. 87
United States v. Cannon, 26 M.J. 674 (A.F.C.M.R. 1988) — § 15-14(C), n. 49
United States v. Cannon, 30 M.J. 886 (A.F.C.M.R. 1990) — § 13-5(L), n. 107
United States v. Cannon, 33 M.J. 376 (C.M.A. 1991) — § 13-5(L), n. 104
United States v. Cannon, 39 M.J. 980 (A.F.C.M.R. 1994) — § 15-2(B)(3), n. 46
United States v. Cansdale, 7 M.J. 143 (C.M.A. 1979) — § 17-8(B), n. 18
United States v. Cantrell, 5 C.M.R. 823 (A.F.B.R. 1952) — § 11-3(B)(1), n. 12
United States v. Cantu, 30 M.J. 1088 (N.M.C.M.R. 1989) — § 9-2(B)(1), n. 61; § 9-3, nn. 8, 9
United States v. Capel, 15 M.J. 537 (A.F.C.M.R. 1982) — § 7-2(B)(4), n. 47
United States v. Caputo, 18 M.J. 259 (C.M.A. 1984) — § 4-6, nn. 5, 9, 12, 13; § 4-8(C)(2), n. 26
United States v. Carbo, 35 M.J. 783 (A.C.M.R. 1992) — § 16-3(B), n. 38
United States v. Cardiff, 344 U.S. 174 (1952) — § 13-3(N)(2), n. 340
United States v. Care, 18 C.M.A. 535, 40 C.M.R. 247 (1969) — § 2-2(B), n. 14; § 9-2(D), n. 85; § 9-3, n. 7; § 9-4; § 14-3(A)(3), n. 31; § 14-3(B), n. 54; § 14-3(B)(2), nn. 72, 77, 84; § 14-3(B)(3), n. 110; § 14-3(D)(4); § 14-5
United States v. Carey, 1 M.J. 761 (A.F.C.M.R. 1975) — § 11-2(B)(1), n. 61; § 13-5(C), nn. 37, 40
United States v. Carfang, 19 M.J. 739 (A.F.C.M.R. 1984) — § 15-10(B), n. 73

TABLE OF CASES

United States v. Caritativo, 37 M.J. 175 (C.M.A. 1993) — § 6-5(C), n. 49; § 12-2(F)(3), n. 64; § 15-2(B)(3), n. 91; § 17-8(B), n. 20
United States v. Carl, 20 M.J. 216 (C.M.A. 1985) — § 6-1(C)(3), n. 145
United States v. Carlisle, 25 M.J. 426 (C.M.A. 1988) — § 13-3(C)(3), nn. 112, 137, 159
United States v. Carlos, 25 M.J. 812 (C.G.C.M.R. 1988) — § 17-15(B), n. 18
United States v. Carlson, 21 M.J. 847 (A.C.M.R. 1986) — § 6-3(A), n. 3; § 6-7, n. 16
United States v. Carlucci, 26 M.J. 328 (C.M.A. 1988) — § 6-3(A), n. 2; § 6-5(A), n. 13
United States v. Carmack, 37 M.J. 765 (A.C.M.R. 1993) — § 17-2(B), n. 7; § 15-2(B)(3), n. 85
United States v. Carman, 19 M.J. 932 (A.C.M.R. 1985) — § 8-3(C)(4), n. 151
United States v. Carmans, 10 M.J. 50 (C.M.A. 1980) — § 3-8(B), n. 17; § 16-5(B), n. 15
United States v. Carmichael, 27 M.J. 757 (A.F.C.M.R. 1988) — § 16-3(D), n. 68
United States v. Carns, 27 M.J. 820 (A.C.M.R. 1988) — § 15-10(A), n. 30; § 15-10(B), nn. 54, 62
United States v. Caro, 20 M.J. 770 (A.F.C.M.R. 1985) — § 16-5(D)(2), n. 70
United States v. Carolene Products Co., 304 U.S. 144 (1938) — § 13-3(N)(1), n. 317
United States v. Carpenter, 11 C.M.A. 418, 29 C.M.R. 234 (1960) — § 15-13, n. 26
United States v. Carpenter, 37 M.J. 291 (C.M.A. 1993) — § 8-3(A), nn. 20, 21; § 13-3(C)(2), n. 80; § 13-3(C)(3), n. 156
United States v. Carr, 18 M.J. 297 (C.M.A. 1984) — § 15-14(B), n. 24; § 15-16(B), nn. 21, 23
United States v. Carr, 25 M.J. 637 (A.C.M.R. 1987) — § 15-13, n. 9
United States v. Carr, 28 M.J. 661 (N.M.C.M.R. 1989) — § 2-6(B), n. 31
United States v. Carr, 37 M.J. 987 (A.C.M.R. 1993) — § 5-10(C), n. 13; § 5-10(D), n. 28
United States v. Carreiro, 14 M.J. 954 (A.C.M.R. 1982) — § 15-2(B)(3), n. 91
United States v. Carroll, 4 M.J. 674 (N.C.M.R. 1977) — § 10-2(A), n. 17; § 11-2(E)(2), n. 119
United States v. Carroll, 22 M.J. 951 (A.C.M.R. 1986) — § 14-3(B)(3), n. 101
United States v. Carroll, 23 M.J. 766 (A.F.C.M.R. 1987) — § 12-2(F)(2), n. 55
United States v. Carroll, 30 M.J. 598 (C.G.C.M.R. 1990) — § 17-8(B)(1), n. 53
United States v. Carroll, 34 M.J. 843 (A.C.M.R. 1992) — § 15-13, n. 11
United States v. Carrott, 25 M.J. 823 (A.F.C.M.R. 1988) — § 2-7(C), n. 34
United States v. Carter, 19 M.J. 808 (A.C.M.R. 1985) — § 8-4, n. 1
United States v. Carter, 21 M.J. 665 (A.C.M.R. 1985) — § 6-1(C)(2), n. 126
United States v. Carter, 23 M.J. 683 (N.M.C.M.R. 1986) — § 2-8(B), n. 26
United States v. Carter, 25 M.J. 471 (C.M.A. 1988) — § 15-10(C)(3), n. 108
United States v. Carter, 26 M.J. 1002 (A.F.C.M.R. 1988) — § 5-4(B), n. 42
United States v. Carter, 27 M.J. 695 (N.M.C.M.R. 1988) — § 14-3(C), n. 130
United States v. Carter, 30 M.J. 179 (C.M.A. 1990) — § 6-1(C)(3), n. 146
United States v. Carter, 31 M.J. 502 (C.M.A. 1990) — § 5-7, n. 15
United States v. Carter, 32 M.J. 830 (N.M.C.M.R. 1991) — § 17-9(D), n. 61; § 17-11, n. 1
United States v. Carter, 39 M.J. 754 (A.F.C.M.R. 1994) — § 6-1(C)(3), n. 161
United States v. Carter, 40 M.J. 102 (C.M.A. 1994) — § 15-2(B)(3), nn. 84-89, 95; § 15-15, n. 28;
United States v. Carter, 42 M.J. 745 (A.F.Ct.Crim.App. 1995) — § 17-9(A), n. 10
United States v. Caruth, 6 M.J. 184 (C.M.A. 1979) — § 9-2(A)(2), n. 24; § 12-5, n. 23; § 14-3(C), n. 131
United States v. Carver, 29 M.J. 568 (A.F.C.M.R. 1989) — § 16-12, nn. 11, 13
United States v. Cases, 6 M.J. 950 (A.C.M.R. 1979) — § 8-2(A), n. 5
United States v. Cashwell, 45 C.M.R. 748 (A.C.M.R. 1972) — § 6-1(C)(3), n. 133
United States v. Cassell, 33 M.J. 448 (C.M.A. 1991) — § 17-8(B)(1), n. 55

1082

TABLE OF CASES

United States v. Cassity, 36 M.J. 759 (N.M.C.M.R. 1992) — § 9-2(B), n. 37
United States v. Casteel, 17 M.J. 713 (N.M.C.M.R. 1983) — § 13-3(N)(1), n. 338
United States v. Castillo, 18 M.J. 590 (N.M.C.M.R. 1984) — § 12-2(H), n. 102
United States v. Castillo, 29 M.J. 145 (C.M.A. 1989) — § 5-4(A)(3), n. 21
United States v. Castillo, 34 M.J. 1160 (N.M.C.M.R. 1992) — § 1-8(D)(2), n. 20
United States v. Castleberry, 18 M.J. 826 (A.C.M.R. 1984) — § 16-8(C), n. 42; § 9-2(B)(1), n. 45
United States v. Castleman, 11 M.J. 562 (A.F.C.M.R. 1981) — § 7-2(E), n. 105; § 7-2(A)(1), n. 16
United States v. Castrillon-Moreno, 7 M.J. 414 (C.M.A. 1979) — § 14-3(D)(3), n. 140
United States v. Castro, 23 C.M.A. 166, 48 C.M.R. 782 (1974) — § 5-3(C)(1), n. 61
United States v. Caszatt, 29 C.M.R. 521 (C.M.A. 1960) — § 14-3(B)(2), n. 97
United States v. Caszatt, 11 C.M.A. 705, 29 C.M.R. 521 (1960) — § 14-3(A)(3), n. 35
United States v. Catlow, 23 C.M.A. 142, 48 C.M.R. 758 (1974) — § 4-5(A)(2); § 4-5(A)(2), n. 3
United States v. Caton, 23 M.J. 691 (A.F.C.M.R. 1986) — § 2-4(F), n. 51
United States v. Catt, 1 M.J. 41 (C.M.A. 1975) — § 8-3(D), n. 162; § 8-3(B)(1), n. 58; § 8-3(B)(2), n. 70
United States v. Causey, 37 M.J. 308 (C.M.A. 1993) — § 15-13, nn. 4, 20
United States v. Cavalier, 17 M.J. 573 (A.F.C.M.R. 1984) — § 16-9, n. 4
United States v. Caver, 41 M.J. 556 (N.M.Ct.Crim.App.1994) — § 5-7, n. 2
United States v. Caylor, 40 M.J. 786 (A.F.C.M.R. 1994) — § 14-3(B)(1), n. 57
United States v. Centeno, 17 M.J. 642 (N.M.C.M.R. 1983) — § 6-2(B), n. 9
United States v. Cephas, 25 M.J. 832 (A.C.M.R. 1988) — § 15-12(B), n. 14; § 16-5(D)(4), n. 84; § 16-5(D)(5), n. 118
United States v. Chadwell, 36 C.M.R. 741 (N.B.R. 1965) — § 2-9(B), n. 21
United States v. Chadwick, 433 U.S. 1 (1977) — § 5-3(C)(7), n. 101
United States v. Chambers, 7 M.J. 24 (C.M.A. 1979) — § 4-11(A), n. 14
United States v. Chambers, 24 M.J. 586 (N.M.C.M.R. 1987) — § 2-7(B), n. 15
United States v. Chambers, 31 M.J. 776 (A.C.M.R. 1990) — § 2-6(B), n. 29
United States v. Chan, 30 M.J. 1028 (A.F.C.M.R. 1990) — § 15-10(C)(3), n. 118
United States v. Chandler, 23 C.M.A. 193, 48 C.M.R. 945 (1974) — § 2-2(D), n. 70
United States v. Chandler, 17 M.J. 678 (A.C.M.R. 1983) — § 5-4(A)(1), n. 8
United States, Chapman v.
United States v. Chapman, 20 M.J. 717 (N.M.C.M.R. 1985) — § 15-2(A), n. 12; § 16-8(B), n. 16; § 16-5(D)(4), n. 84; § 16-5(D)(5), n. 118
United States v. Chapman, 26 M.J. 515 (A.C.M.R. 1988) — § 5-10(D), n. 32
United States v. Chapple, 36 M.J. 410 (C.M.A. 1993) — § 5-3, n. 8; § 5-3(B), n. 43
United States v. Charette, 15 M.J. 197 (C.M.A. 1983) — § 6-4(C), n. 20; § 8-4, n. 16; § 8-5, n. 7
United States v. Charles, 15 M.J. 509 (A.F.C.M.R. 1982) — § 6-5(B), n. 28
United States v. Charles, 40 M.J. 414 (C.M.A. 1994) — § 11-4, n. 14; § 13-5(J), n. 78
United States v. Charley, 28 M.J. 903 (A.C.M.R. 1989) — § 16-5(C), n. 45
United States v. Chasteen, 17 M.J. 580 (A.F.C.M.R. 1983) — § 16-9, n. 10
United States v. Chatman, 49 C.M.R. 319 (N.C.M.R. 1974) — § 15-16(A), n. 14
United States v. Chattin, 33 M.J. 802 (N.M.C.M.R. 1991) — § 2-6(C), n. 36
United States v. Chaves, 28 M.J. 691 (A.F.C.M.R. 1989) — § 16-9, n. 7
United States v. Chavez, 6 M.J. 615 (A.C.M.R. 1978) — § 4-12(A), n. 8; § 15-2(C), n. 120
United States v. Chavez, 27 M.J. 870 (A.F.C.M.R. 1988) — § 15-12(B), n. 14
United States v. Chavira, 25 M.J. 705 (A.C.M.R. 1987) — § 15-10(C)(1), n. 84
United States v. Cheeks, 43 C.M.R. 1013 (A.F.C.M.R. 1971) — § 2-3(C), n. 25

TABLE OF CASES

United States v. Cherok, 19 M.J. 559 (N.M.C.M.R. 1984) — § 13-3(C)(2), n. 73
United States v. Cherry, 14 M.J. 251 (C.M.A. 1982) — § 15-14(B), n. 37
United States v. Cherry, 31 M.J. 1 (C.M.A. 1990) — § 16-5(D)(4), n. 102
United States v. Chestnut, 2 M.J. 84 (C.M.A. 1976) — § 7-2(E), nn. 6, 104, 108; § 11-3(A), n. 6; § 7-2(B)(4), n. 46
United States v. Chick, 30 M.J. 658 (A.F.C.M.R. 1990) — § 5-3(F), n. 26
United States v. Childress, 33 M.J. 449 (A.C.M.R. 1991) — § 14-3(F), n. 189; § 16-6, n. 10; § 16-7, n. 5; 16-8(B), n. 19
United States v. Childress, 33 M.J. 602 (A.C.M.R. 1991) — § 16-8(B), n. 23
United States v. Chisholm, 10 M.J. 795 (A.F.C.M.R. 1981) — § 6-1(C)(3), n. 132
United States v. Chitwood, 12 M.J. 535 (A.F.C.M.R. 1981) — § 4-11(B), n. 45
United States v. Chodara, 29 M.J. 943 (A.C.M.R. 1990) — § 4-11(C)(2), n. 64
United States v. Choice, 23 C.M.A. 329, 49 C.M.R. 663 (1975) — § 17-8(B), n. 18
United States v. Chollet, 30 M.J. 1079 (C.G.C.M.R. 1990) — § 15-10(B), nn. 58, 72
United States v. Choy, 33 M.J. 1080 (A.C.M.R. 1992) — § 4-16, n. 17; § 8-4, n. 2
United States v. Christensen, 30 C.M.R. 959 (A.F.B.R. 1961) — § 15-15, n. 8
United States v. Christensen, 12 M.J. 875 (N.M.C.M.R. 1982) — § 16-6, n. 5
United States v. Christian, 6 M.J. 624 (A.C.M.R. 1978) — § 11-2(B)(1), n. 62
United States v. Christian, 20 M.J. 966 (A.C.M.R. 1985) — § 17-9(A), n. 17
United States v. Chuculate, 5 M.J. 143 (C.M.A. 1978) — § 7-2(E), n. 104; § 11-3(A), n. 6; § 7-2(B)(6), n. 68; § 11-3(B)(1), n. 25
United States v. Church, 29 M.J. 679 (A.F.C.M.R. 1989) — § 15-16(A), n. 13
United States v. Ciarletta, 7 C.M.A. 606, 23 C.M.R. 70 (1957) — § 11-2(A)(1), n. 8; § 11-3(B)(1), n. 38; § 11-3(B)(2), n. 44
United States v. Ciesialski, 39 C.M.R. 839 (N.B.R. 1968) — § 10-4(B)(5), n. 49
United States v. Cisler, 33 M.J. 503 (A.F.C.M.R. 1991) — § 2-8(B), n. 12
United States v. Ciulla, 29 M.J. 868 (A.F.C.M.R. 1989) — § 17-15(B), n. 33
United States v. Ciulla, 32 M.J. 186 (C.M.A. 1991) — § 16-5(D)(5), n. 116
United States v. Clabon, 33 M.J. 904 (A.F.C.M.R. 1991) — § 16-5(D)(5), n. 117
United States v. Clardy, 13 M.J. 308 (C.M.A. 1982) — § 4-8(C)(1), n. 16
United States v. Clark, 49 C.M.R. 192 (A.C.M.R. 1974) — § 4-16, nn. 5, 6; § 6-1, n. 35
United States v. Clark, 11 M.J. 179 (C.M.A. 1981) — § 7-2(E), nn. 99, 100, 111; § 7-2(A)(1), n. 19
United States v. Clark, 15 M.J. 594 (A.C.M.R. 1983) — § 2-5, n. 3
United States v. Clark, 16 M.J. 239 (C.M.A. 1983) — § 17-9(D), n. 59
United States v. Clark, 26 M.J. 589 (A.C.M.R. 1988) — § 14-3(D)(4), nn. 149, 158, 159
United States v. Clark, 28 M.J. 401 (C.M.A. 1989) — § 14-3(D)(4), nn. 157-159
United States v. Clark, 31 M.J. 721 (A.F.C.M.R. 1990) — § 12-2(H), n. 100
United States v. Clark, 32 M.J. 606 (A.C.M.R. 1991) — § 15-3, n. 9; § 15-2(B)(3), n. 68
United States v. Clark, 35 M.J. 730 (A.F.C.M.R. 1992) — § 15-4(A), n. 6; § 4-8(C)(1), n. 17
United States v. Clark, 37 M.J. 1098 (N.M.C.M.R. 1993) — § 10-4(B)(4), n. 46
United States v. Clarke, 13 M.J. 566 (A.C.M.R. 1982) — § 2-7(A), n. 8
United States v. Clarke, 23 M.J. 519 (A.F.C.M.R. 1986) — § 4-11(B), n. 42; § 4-11(C), n. 52
United States v. Clarke, 25 M.J. 631 (A.C.M.R. 1987) — § 2-8(B), n. 26
United States v. Clarke, 29 M.J. 582 (A.F.C.M.R. 1989) — § 16-5(D)(4), n. 106
United States v. Claussen, 15 M.J. 660 (N.M.C.M.R. 1983) — § 2-2(C)(3), n. 48
United States v. Claxton, 25 M.J. 623 (C.G.C.M.R. 1987) — § 15-2(B)(3), n. 89
United States v. Claxton, 29 M.J. 667 (C.G.C.M.R. 1989) — § 16-5(D)(4), n. 102
United States v. Claxton, 32 M.J. 159 (C.M.A. 1991) — § 16-5(D)(4), n. 86

TABLE OF CASES

United States v. Clayborne, 7 M.J. 528 (A.C.M.R. 1979) — § 17-15(B), n. 21
United States v. Clayton, 25 M.J. 888 (A.C.M.R. 1988) — § 14-3(B)(2), n. 100
United States v. Claytor, 34 M.J. 1030 (N.M.C.M.R. 1992) — § 2-4(B), n. 24
United States v. Clear, 32 M.J. 658 (A.F.C.M.R. 1991) — § 15-2(B)(3), n. 87
United States v. Clemens, 4 M.J. 791 (N.C.M.R. 1978) — § 9-2(B)(1), nn. 43, 52
United States v. Clemons, 35 M.J. 767 (A.C.M.R. 1992) — § 6-5(B), n. 28; § 15-8, n. 2
United States v. Clemons, 39 M.J. 865 (N.M.C.M.R. 1994) — § 16-2(E), n. 46
United States v. Cleveland, 27 M.J. 530 (A.F.C.M.R. 1988) — § 16-7, n. 1
United States v. Cleveland, 29 M.J. 361 (C.M.A. 1990) — § 10-4(A)(2), n. 10; § 16-5(D)(5), nn. 122, 123
United States v. Clevidence, 14 M.J. 17 (C.M.A. 1982) — § 17-11, n. 7
United States v. Clifton, 15 M.J. 26 (C.M.A. 1983) — § 15-11, n. 2; § 15-13, nn. 7, 11, 19, 33
United States v. Clifton, 35 M.J. 79 (C.M.A. 1992) — § 17-15(C), n. 37
United States v. Cline, 29 M.J. 83 (C.M.A. 1989) — § 4-5, n. 1; § 4-6, n. 1
United States v. Clow, 26 M.J. 176 (C.M.A. 1988) — § 5-3(C)(6), n. 89
United States v. Clower, 48 C.M.R. 307 (C.M.A. 1974) — § 15-12(B), n. 17
United States v. Clowser, 16 C.M.R. 543 (A.F.B.R. 1954) — § 2-4(B), n. 28
United States v. Cloyd, 25 C.M.R. 908 (A.F.B.R. 1958) — § 5-4(A)(3), n. 19
United States v. Coates, 2 C.M.A. 625, 10 C.M.R. 123 (1953) — § 2-2(C)(3), n. 43
United States v. Cobe, 41 M.J. 654 (N.M.Ct.Crim.App. 1994) — § 15-2(B)(3), n. 85
United States v. Coburn, 42 M.J. 609 (N.M.Ct.Crim.App. 1995) — § 5-9(B), n. 14; § 5-9(D), nn. 29, 30, 31, 39; § 5-10(D), n. 30
United States v. Cockerell, 49 C.M.R. 567 (A.C.M.R. 1974) — § 14-3(D)(5), n. 167; § 15-10(C)(2), n. 96
United States v. Coder, 27 M.J. 650 (A.C.M.R. 1988) — § 5-10(B), n. 12; § 13-3(C)(3), n. 122
United States v. Coffin, 25 M.J. 32 (C.M.A. 1987) — § 13-4, n. 5; § 15-10(B), n. 62
United States v. Coffman, 35 M.J. 591 (N.M.C.M.R. 1992) — § 8-3(A), nn. 19, 20
United States v. Cofield, 11 M.J. 422 (C.M.A. 1981) — § 13-5(L), nn. 94, 97, 99, 105
United States v. Coglin, 10 M.J. 670 (A.C.M.R. 1981) — § 2-2(C)(3), n. 41
United States v. Cohen Grocery Co., 255 U.S. 81 (1921) — § 13-3(N)(2), n. 341
United States v. Cole, 3 M.J. 220 (C.M.A. 1977) — § 13-3(C)(2), nn. 50, 71, 73
United States v. Cole, 24 M.J. 18 (C.M.A. 1987) — § 4-8(C)(3), n. 31
United States v. Cole, 31 M.J. 270 (C.M.A. 1990) — § 13-3(E), n. 214
United States v. Coleman, 41 C.M.R. 953 (A.F.C.M.R. 1970) — § 15-13, n. 17
United States v. Coleman, 26 M.J. 451 (C.M.A. 1988) — § 5-4(B), n. 50
United States v. Coleman, 32 M.J. 508 (A.C.M.R. 1990) — § 2-7(C), n. 40
United States v. Coleman, 31 M.J. 653 (C.G.C.M.R. 1990) — § 17-9(A), n. 11
United States v. Coleman, 34 M.J. 1020 (A.C.M.R. 1992) — § 2-2(C)(3), n. 47
United States v. Colley, 29 M.J. 519 (A.C.M.R. 1989) — § 13-3(B), nn. 9, 10, 21, 22
United States v. Collier, 27 M.J. 806 (A.C.M.R. 1988) — § 2-3(C), nn. 23, 25; § 2-4(F), n. 54
United States v. Collier, 36 M.J. 501 (A.F.C.M.R. 1992) — § 5-4(B), nn. 30, 42, 46, 47
United States v. Collins, 6 M.J. 256 (C.M.A. 1979) — § 17-8(B), n. 20; § 7-2(A)(1), n. 16
United States v. Collins, 17 M.J. 901 (A.F.C.M.R. 1983) — § 16-6, n. 22; § 14-3(B)(2), n. 100; § 14-3(D)(4), n. 150
United States v. Collins, 29 M.J. 778 (A.C.M.R. 1989) — § 15-10(B), n. 52
United States v. Collins, 30 M.J. 991 (A.C.M.R. 1990) — § 3-3(C), n. 27 Art. 15(f)
United States v. Collins, 37 M.J. 1072 (N.M.C.M.R. 1993) — § 2-2(E)(3), n. 83
United States v. Collins, 39 M.J. 739 (N.M.C.M.R. 1994) — § 13-3(C)(2), n. 92

TABLE OF CASES

United States v. Collins, 41 M.J. 610 (Army Ct. Crim. App. 1994) — § 13-5(A), n. 15
United States v. Collins, 41 M.J. 428 (1995) — § 13-3(E), n. 190
United States v. Colon, 6 M.J. 73 (C.M.A. 1978) — § 4-15(C), n. 19; § 15-9, n. 6
United States v. Colon-Angueira, 16 M.J. 20 (C.M.A. 1983) — § 15-23, n. 3; § 13-3(C)(2), n. 73
United States, Colonnade Catering Corp. v.
United States v. Colton, 23 C.M.A. 152, 48 C.M.R. 768 (1974) — § 8-3(B)(3), n. 76
United States v. Combest, 14 M.J. 927 (A.C.M.R. 1982) — § 15-14(B), n. 42
United States v. Combs, 15 M.J. 743 (A.F.C.M.R. 1983) — § 14-3(C), n. 127; § 16-3(D), n. 63; § 16-13, n. 9; § 14-3(D)(3), n. 140
United States v. Combs, 20 M.J. 441 (C.M.A. 1985) — § 16-6, n. 17; § 11-2(A)(4), n. 47
United States v. Combs, 35 M.J. 820 (A.F.C.M.R. 1992) — § 15-10(B), n. 69
United States v. Combs, 38 M.J. 741 (A.F.C.M.R. 1993) — § 13-2(G)(2), n. 103
United States v. Combs, 41 M.J. 400 (1995) — § 16-11, n. 13
United States v. Commander, 39 M.J. 972 (A.F.C.M.R. 1994) — § 2-7(B), n. 13
United States v. Conklan, 41 M.J. 800 (Army Ct.Crim.App. 1995) — § 9-2(B)(2), n. 68
United States v. Conley, 4 M.J. 327 (C.M.A. 1978) — § 8-3(A), n. 5; § 12-2(H), nn. 102, 109; § 15-10(B), n. 39
United States v. Conley, 28 M.J. 210 (C.M.A. 1989) — § 17-15(B), n. 32
United States v. Conlon, 41 M.J. 800 (Army Ct.Crim.App. 1995) — § 5-4(C), n. 59
United States v. Conn, 6 M.J. 351 (C.M.A. 1979) — § 4-11(A), n. 20; § 6-6(A), n. 3; § 17-8(B), n. 19
United States v. Connell, 13 M.J. 156 (C.M.A. 1982) — § 9-2(B)(1), n. 48
United States v. Connell, 42 M.J. 462 (1995) — § 17-9(D), n. 71
United States v. Conrad, 598 F.2d 506 (9th Cir. 1979) — § 14-3(B)(1), n. 62
United States v. Conway, 20 C.M.A. 99, 42 C.M.R. 291 (1970) — § 9-2(B)(1), n. 42
United States v. Conway, 40 M.J. 859 (A.F.C.M.R. 1994) — § 16-8(B), n. 20
United States v. Cook, 12 M.J. 448 (C.M.A. 1982) — § 8-5, n. 8; § 13-3(E), n. 203
United States v. Cook, 27 M.J. 212 (C.M.A. 1988) — § 13-3(C), n. 26; § 13-3(C)(3), n. 159
United States v. Cook, 27 M.J. 858 (A.F.C.M.R. 1989) — § 5-3(C)(6), nn. 85, 97
United States v. Cooke, 11 M.J. 257 (C.M.A. 1981) — § 14-3(C), n. 126
United States v. Cooley, 21 M.J. 968 (A.C.M.R. 1986) — § 6-1(C), n. 94
United States v. Cooper, 8 C.M.R. 133 (C.M.A. 1953) — § 13-2, n. 8
United States v. Cooper, 16 C.M.R. 390, 37 C.M.R. 10 (1966) — § 2-2(E)(6), n. 101
United States v. Cooper, 8 M.J. 5 (C.M.A. 1979) — § 14-3(D)(5), n. 163
United States v. Cooper, 8 M.J. 538 (N.C.M.R. 1979) — § 15-10(C)(2), nn. 98, 100
United States v. Cooper, 28 M.J. 810 (A.C.M.R. 1989) — § 15-10(C)(3), n. 118
United States v. Cooper, 30 M.J. 201 (C.M.A. 1990) — § 15-10(C)(3), n. 118
United States v. Cooper, 32 M.J. 83 (C.M.A. 1991) — § 14-3(A)(2), n. 24
United States v. Cooper, 33 M.J. 356 (C.M.A. 1991) — § 2-7(B), n. 24
United States v. Cooper-Tyson, 37 M.J. 481 (C.M.A. 1993) — § 4-16, n. 11
United States v. Copeland, 14 M.J. 835 (A.F.C.M.R. 1982) — § 17-2(B)(2), n. 33
United States v. Copening, 32 M.J. 512 (A.C.M.R. 1990) — § 13-2(F), n. 60; § 15-2(D), n. 128
United States v. Copper, 35 M.J. 417 (C.M.A. 1992) — § 2-7(B), n. 24
United States v. Coppock, 37 M.J. 145 (C.M.A. 1993) — § 15-10(B), nn. 45, 73
United States v. Corcoran, 17 M.J. 137 (C.M.A. 1984) — § 6-1, nn. 8, 9; § 6-4(C), n. 17; § 4-14(A)(2), n. 10
United States v. Corcoran, 40 M.J. 478 (C.M.A. 1994) — § 13-3(H), nn. 247, 248

TABLE OF CASES

United States v. Cordell, 37 M.J. 592 (A.F.C.M.R. 1993) — § 12-5, nn. 17, 18; § 15-15, n. 5
United States v. Cordero, 11 M.J. 210 (C.M.A. 1981) — § 5-3(B), n. 41
United States v. Cordova, 4 M.J. 604 (A.C.M.R. 1977) — § 9-2(B)(1), n. 49
United States v. Corl, 6 M.J. 914 (N.C.M.R. 1979) — § 15-2(E), n. 147; § 8-3(C)(3), n. 145
United States v. Corley, 5 M.J. 558 (A.C.M.R. 1978) — § 946
United States v. Cornelius, 29 M.J. 501 (A.C.M.R. 1989) — § 4-16, n. 12; § 8-4, n. 9
United States v. Cornelius, 37 M.J. 622 (A.C.M.R. 1993) — § 13-3(C), n. 25; § 14-3(A)(2), n. 25
United States v. Coronado, 15 M.J. 750 (A.F.C.M.R. 1983) — § 15-2(B)(3), n. 33
United States v. Corraine, 31 M.J. 102 (C.M.A. 1990) — § 16-5(D)(4), n. 101
United States v. Corriere, 20 M.J. 905 (A.C.M.R. 1985) — § 5-7, n. 2; § 9-2(A)(3), n. 32
United States v. Corriere, 24 M.J. 701 (A.C.M.R. 1987) — § 9-2(A)(3), nn. 30, 31
United States v. Corrigan, 11 M.J. 734 (A.F.C.M.R. 1981) — § 9-3, n. 6
United States v. Cortes, 29 M.J. 946 (A.C.M.R. 1990) — § 2-7(B), n. 24
United States v. Cortte, 36 M.J. 767 (N.M.C.M.R. 1992) — § 4-8(B), n. 13
United States v. Cosby, 14 M.J. 3 (C.M.A. 1982) — § 15-14(C), n. 51
United States v. Cosgrove, 1 M.J. 199 (C.M.A. 1975) — § 15-10(B), n. 52
United States v. Costa, 19 M.J. 980 (A.C.M.R. 1985) — § 9-2(B)(1), n. 45; § 16-8(C), n. 42
United States v. Costello, 20 M.J. 659 (N.M.C.M.R. 1985) — § 6-1(C), n. 95
United States v. Cote, 11 M.J. 892 (A.F.C.M.R. 1981) — § 8-3(D), n. 163; § 12-2(F)(3), n. 61
United States v. Cottle, 11 M.J. 572 (A.F.C.M.R. 1981) — § 10-3(A), n. 2
United States v. Cottle, 14 M.J. 260 (C.M.A. 1982) — § 11-2(A)(2), n. 20; § 11-2(B)(1), n. 57; § 13-5(I), n. 72
United States v. Cottrell, 32 M.J. 675 (A.F.C.M.R. 1991) — § 2-8(B), n. 21
United States v. Court, 25 M.J. 507 (A.F.C.M.R. 1987) — § 2-5, n. 7
United States v. Courtier, 20 C.M.A. 278, 43 C.M.R. 118 (1971) — § 7-2(A)(2), n. 31
United States v. Courtney, 1 M.J. 438 (C.M.A. 1976) — § 2-7(A), n. 4; § 13-3(N)(1), nn. 333, 336, 338
United States v. Courts, 9 M.J. 285 (C.M.A. 1980) — § 11-2(A)(4), nn. 40, 44, 45
United States v. Couser, 3 M.J. 561 (A.C.M.R. 1977) — § 2-4(F), n. 50
United States v. Cover, 16 M.J. 800 (N.M.C.M.R. 1983) — § 15-4(A), n. 6
United States v. Covington, 10 M.J. 64 (C.M.A. 1980) — § 3-5(C)(4), n. 65
United States v. Covington, 12 M.J. 932 (N.M.C.M.R. 1982) — § 13-2(E), n. 51
United States v. Cowan, 13 M.J. 906 (N.M.C.M.R. 1982) — § 17-15(B), n. 32
United States v. Cowan, 32 M.J. 1041 (A.C.M.R. 1991) — § 17-9(D), n. 64
United States v. Cowan, 34 M.J. 258 (C.M.A. 1992) — § 17-9(D), nn. 58, 64
United States v. Cowan, 42 M.J. 475 (1995) — § 15-14(D), n. 55
United States v. Cowles, 16 M.J. 467 (C.M.A. 1983) — § 16-5(B), n. 18
United States v. Cox, 23 C.M.R. 535 (A.B.R. 1957) — § 13-5(C), n. 37
United States v. Cox, 22 C.M.A. 69, 46 C.M.R. 69 (1972) — § 9-2, n. 5
United States v. Cox, 23 M.J. 808 (N.M.C.M.R. 1986) — § 15-10(C)(3), n. 115
United States v. Cox, 37 M.J. 543 (N.M.C.M.R. 1993) — § 8-2(A), n. 3; § 4-14(A)(2), n. 12
United States v. Cox, 42 M.J. 647 (A.F.Ct.Crim.App. 1995) — § 1-3(D)(2)
United States v. Cozine, 21 M.J. 581 (A.C.M.R. 1985) — § 15-21, n. 10
United States v. Craig, 8 C.M.A. 218, 24 C.M.R. 28 (1957) — § 6-1(C), n. 97
United States v. Craig, 28 M.J. 321 (C.M.A. 1989) — § 17-8(B)(1), n. 47; § 17-9(A), n. 24

TABLE OF CASES

United States v. Craig, 32 M.J. 614 (A.C.M.R. 1991) — § 5-3(A), n. 27
United States v. Cramer, 1 C.M.R. 210 (A.B.R. 1951) — § 15-20, n. 17
United States v. Craney, 1 M.J. 142 (C.M.A. 1975) — § 14-3(B)(2), n. 72
United States v. Crawford, 15 C.M.A. 31, 35 C.M.R. 3 (1964) — § 8-3(C)(3), n. 142
United States v. Crawford, 34 M.J. 758 (A.F.C.M.R. 1992) — § 17-9(A), n. 24
United States v. Credit, 2 M.J. 631 (A.F.C.M.R. 1976) — § 15-10(B), nn. 49, 50
United States v. Credit, 4 M.J. 118 (C.M.A. 1977) — § 15-10(A), nn. 7, 9; § 17-4(A), n. 41
United States v. Crockett, 21 M.J. 423 (C.M.A. 1986) — § 15-22, n. 6; § 11-2(D)(2), n. 91; § 11-3(B)(2), n. 58
United States v. Croley, 50 C.M.R. 899 (A.F.C.M.R. 1975) — § 11-2(E)(1), n. 113
United States v. Cronic, 466 U.S. 648 (1984) — § 15-2(B)(3), nn. 32, 69
United States v. Cronier, 14 M.J. 1 (C.M.A. 1982) — § 4-5(A)(3), n. 11
United States v. Croom, 1 M.J. 635 (A.C.M.R. 1975) — § 13-3(J), n. 258
United States, Crosby v.
United States v. Cross, 10 M.J. 34 (C.M.A. 1980) — § 3-8(B), n. 17
United States v. Cross, 19 M.J. 973 (A.C.M.R. 1985) — § 16-8(C), n. 42; § 9-2(B)(1), n. 45
United States v. Crossley, 10 M.J. 376 (C.M.A. 1981) — § 6-4(C), n. 17
United States v. Crouch, 11 M.J. 128 (C.M.A. 1981) — § 14-3(B)(2), n. 71
United States v. Crowe, 30 M.J. 1144 (A.F.C.M.R. 1990) — § 16-2(D), n. 39; § 6-1(C)(3), n. 139
United States v. Crowell, 9 C.M.A. 43, 25 C.M.R. 305 (1958) — § 15-20, n. 23
United States v. Crowell, 21 M.J. 760 (N.M.C.M.R. 1985) — § 17-3, n. 2
United States v. Crumb, 10 M.J. 520 (A.C.M.R. 1980) — § 7-2(A)(1), n. 27; § 8-3(C)(4), n. 154; § 10-4(B)(5), n. 55
United States v. Crumley, 31 M.J. 21 (C.M.A. 1990) — § 15-14(B), n. 22
United States v. Cruz, 5 M.J. 286 (C.M.A. 1978) — § 7-2(E), n. 113; § 7-2(B)(6), n. 69
United States v. Cruz, 20 M.J. 873 (A.C.M.R. 1985) — § 6-3(C), nn. 18, 20-26, 29; § 6-7, n. 11
United States v. Cruz, 25 M.J. 326 (C.M.A. 1987) — § 5-10(B), n. 7; § 5-10(D), nn. 36, 41; § 6-4(E), n. 29
United States v. Cruz-Maldonado, 20 M.J. 831 (A.C.M.R. 1985) — § 8-6, n. 7; § 12-2(A), n. 6
United States v. Cruz-Rijos, 1 M.J. 429 (C.M.A. 1976) — § 17-4(B), nn. 52, 53; § 17-4(A), n. 43
United States v. Cudini, 36 M.J. 572 (A.C.M.R. 1992) — § 17-4, n. 28
United States v. Cuevas-Orvalle, 6 M.J. 284 (A.C.M.R. 1979) — § 2-6(C), n. 39
United States v. Cuffee, 10 M.J. 381 (C.M.A. 1981) — § 2-4(C), n. 39; § 2-7(B), n. 18
United States v. Culver, 22 C.M.A. 141, 46 C.M.R. 141 (1973) — § 6-1(B), n. 64; § 13-3(E), n. 206
United States v. Cumbee, 30 M.J. 736 (A.F.C.M.R. 1990) — § 16-2(D), n. 39
United States v. Cumberledge, 6 M.J. 203 (C.M.A. 1979) — § 10-3(B), n. 10; § 7-2(B)(4), n. 46; § 7-2(B)(6), n. 69; § 11-3(A), n. 5; § 11-3(B)(1), n. 25
United States v. Cummings, 17 C.M.A. 376, 38 C.M.R. 174 (1968) — § 9-2(B)(2), nn. 67, 69
United States v. Cummings, 21 M.J. 987 (N.M.C.M.R. 1986) — § 13-3(C)(3), n. 160
United States v. Cunningham, 12 C.M.A. 402, 30 C.M.R. 402 (1961) — § 7-2(E), n. 105
United States v. Cunningham, 6 M.J. 559 (N.C.M.R. 1978) — § 12-3(A), n. 15
United States v. Cunningham, 21 M.J. 585 (A.C.M.R. 1985) — § 7-2(E), n. 102; § 8-3(C)(4), n. 152; § 15-10(C)(2), n. 94

TABLE OF CASES

United States v. Cunningham, 36 M.J. 1011 (A.C.M.R. 1993) — § 9-2(C), n. 77
United States v. Cupp, 24 C.M.R. 565 (A.F.B.R. 1957) — § 13-3(N)(3), n. 403
United States v. Curcio, 712 F.2d 1532 (3d Cir. 1983) — § 14-4, n. 11
United States v. Curry, 15 M.J. 701 (A.C.M.R. 1983) — § 9-3, n. 5; § 17-8(B), n. 30; § 17-11, n. 1
United States v. Curry, 28 M.J. 419 (C.M.A. 1989) — § 17-8(B), n. 24
United States v. Curry, 31 M.J. 359 (C.M.A. 1990) — § 6-1(C)(1), nn. 114-115; § 13-5(G)(2), n. 46; § 15-2(B)(3), n. 88
United States v. Curry, 35 M.J. 359 (C.M.A. 1992) — § 6-1(C)(3), n. 147
United States v. Curry, 38 M.J. 77 (C.M.A. 1993) — § 15-14(B), nn. 21, 30
United States v. Curtin, 9 C.M.A. 427, 26 C.M.R. 207 (1958) — § 2-4(D), n. 44
United States v. Curtis, 28 M.J. 1074 (N.M.C.M.R. 1989) — § 15-10(B), n. 51; § 16-3(A), n. 17; § 8-3(C)(2), n. 126; § 13-3(N)(1), nn. 303, 312, 317; § 15-10(C)(1), nn. 84, 86
United States v. Curtis, 32 M.J. 252 (C.M.A. 1991) — § 16-3(A), nn. 20-23
United States v. Curtis, 33 M.J. 101 (C.M.A. 1991) — § 15-16(B), n. 18
United States v. Curtis, 33 M.J. 101 (C.M.A. 1991) — § 15-10(B), n. 53; § 16-3(A), nn. 24, 25; § 15-10(C)(3), nn. 115, 118
United States v. Curtis, 38 M.J. 530 (N.M.C.M.R. 1993) — § 16-3(A), nn. 25, 26; § 15-2(B)(3), n. 75
United States v. Curtiss, 19 C.M.A. 402, 42 C.M.R. 4 (1970) — § 6-1(B), n. 61; § 13-3(F), n. 219
United States v. Cutting, 14 C.M.A. 347, 34 C.M.R. 127 (1964) — § 8-3(B)(3), nn. 73, 80
United States v. Czarnecki, 10 M.J. 570 (A.F.C.M.R. 1980) — § 15-3, n. 2
United States v. Czeck, 28 M.J. 563 (N.M.C.M.R. 1989) — § 16-3(D), n. 63
United States v. Czekala, 38 M.J. 566 (A.C.M.R. 1993) — § 2-5, n. 2; § 7-2, n. 7; § 12-5, n. 13
United States v. Czekala, 42 M.J. 168 (1995) — § 15-14(B), n. 37
United States v. Dababneh, 28 M.J. 929 (N.M.C.M.R. 1989) — § 6-4(B), nn. 12, 13; § 7-2(A)(1), n. 29
United States v. Daffron, 32 M.J. 912 (A.F.C.M.R. 1991) — § 12-3(A), n. 33; § 14-3(B)(2), n. 71; § 15-2(B)(3), n. 64
United States v. Dahood, 32 M.J. 852 (N.M.C.M.R. 1991) — § 15-2(B)(1), n. 23; § 17-8(B)(3), n. 91
United States v. Daigle, 1 M.J. 139 (C.M.A. 1975) — § 8-3(C)(4), n. 151; § 15-10(C)(1), n. 82
United States v. Daigneault, 18 M.J. 503 (A.F.C.M.R. 1984) — § 4-15(B), n. 11; § 12-2(E), n. 39
United States v. Dailey, 34 M.J. 1039 (N.M.C.M.R. 1992) — § 16-5(B), n. 12
United States v. Dailey, 37 M.J. 1078 (N.M.C.M.R. 1993) — § 15-16(A), n. 4
United States v. Dale, 23 M.J. 598 (A.F.C.M.R. 1986) — § 4-11(C), nn. 52, 53
United States v. Dale, 39 M.J. 503 (A.F.C.M.R. 1993) — § 15-10(B), n. 71
United States v. Dale, 42 M.J. 384 (1995) — § 15-10(B), nn. 53, 71
United States v. Daley, 3 M.J. 541 (A.C.M.R. 1977) — § 5-4(C), n. 56; § 11-2(E)(1), n. 106
United States v. Dallman, 32 M.J. 624 (A.C.M.R. 1991) — § 2-5, n. 2; § 2-6(C), n. 38; § 14-3(B)(2), n. 71
United States v. Dallman, 34 M.J. 274 (C.M.A. 1992) — § 2-4(E), n. 46
United States v. Damatta-Olivera, 37 M.J. 474 (C.M.A. 1993) — § 15-24, n. 1
United States v. Dancy, 38 M.J. 1 (C.M.A. 1993) — § 13-4(A), n. 17
United States v. Daniel, 42 M.J. 802 (N.M.Ct.Crim.App. 1995) — § 2-4(C), n. 32
United States v. Daniels, 48 C.M.R. 655 (C.M.A. 1974) — § 11-2(D)(2), nn. 92, 94

TABLE OF CASES

United States v. Daniels, 23 C.M.A. 34, 48 C.M.R. 655 (1974) — § 11-2(A)(2), n. 18
United States v. Daniels, 20 M.J. 648 (N.M.C.M.R. 1985) — § 14-3(B)(2), n. 68
United States v. Daniels, 23 M.J. 867 (A.C.M.R. 1987) — § 5-10(C), nn. 21, 22
United States v. Daniels, 28 M.J. 743 (A.F.C.M.R. 1989) — § 15-14(B), n. 34
United States v. Daniels, 39 M.J. 789 (N.M.C.M.R 1993) — § 14-3(D)(4), n. 148
United States v. Danilson, 11 C.M.R. 692 (A.F.B.R. 1953) — § 15-8, n. 4
United States v. D'Apice, 664 F.2d 75 (5th Cir. 1981) — § 11-2(E)(3), n. 130
United States v. Darby, 27 M.J. 761 (A.F.C.M.R. 1988) — § 16-12, n. 13
United States v. Darring, 9 C.M.A. 651, 26 C.M.R. 431 (1958) — § 9-2(B)(2), n. 66
United States v. Darville, 5 M.J. 1 (C.M.A. 1978) — § 17-9(A), n.2; § 17-9(D), n. 60; § 17-15(B), nn. 24, 26; § 17-16(C), n. 21
United States v. Daskam, 31 M.J. 77 (C.M.A. 1990) — § 5-3(D)(1), nn. 118, 125
United States v. Davenport, 9 M.J. 364 (C.M.A. 1980) — § 5-4(A)(1), n. 8; § 14-3(B)(2), n. 79
United States v. Davidson, 14 M.J. 81 (C.M.A. 1982) — § 5-9(A), n. 1; § 5-10(A), n. 1; § 16-9, n. 11
United States, Davis v.
United States v. Davis, 4 C.M.R. 195 (A.B.R. 1952) — § 14-5, n. 2
United States v. Davis, 16 C.M.A. 207, 36 C.M.R. 363 (1966) — § 6-1(C)(2), n. 129; § 13-5(G)(3), n. 50
United States v. Davis, 19 C.M.A. 217, 41 C.M.R. 217 (1970) — § 11-2(A)(1), n. 8
United States v. Davis, 22 C.M.A. 241, 46 C.M.R. 241 (1973) — § 2-2(E)(4), n. 85
United States v. Davis, 6 M.J. 874 (A.C.M.R. 1979) — § 17-2(B)(4), n. 95; § 17-8(B)(1), n. 33; § 17-8(B)(2), n. 60; § 17-8(B)(3), n. 72
United States v. Davis, 8 M.J. 575 (A.C.M.R. 1979) — § 4-5(A), n. 9; § 4-5(C), n. 32
United States v. Davis, 13 M.J. 593 (A.F.C.M.R. 1982) — § 2-4(C), n. 38; § 14-3(B)(2), n. 74
United States v. Davis, 16 M.J. 225 (C.M.A. 1983) — § 2-4(C), n. 38
United States v. Davis, 20 M.J. 61 (C.M.A. 1985) — § 6-4(B), n. 11; § 7-2(A)(1), n. 16
United States v. Davis, 20 M.J. 980 (A.C.M.R. 1985) — § 17-2(B)(3), nn. 84, 85
United States v. Davis, 20 M.J. 1015 (A.C.M.R. 1985) — § 17-2(B), n. 11; § 15-2(B)(3), n. 85; § 17-8(B)(1), n. 59
United States v. Davis, 22 M.J. 557 (A.C.M.R. 1986) — § 17-9(C), n. 54
United States v. Davis, 26 M.J. 445 (C.M.A. 1988) — § 2-6(A), n. 17; § 2-6(B), n. 29; § 13-3(F), n. 217; § 14-3(F), n. 191
United States v. Davis, 27 M.J. 543 (A.C.M.R. 1988) — § 12-2(H), n. 100
United States v. Davis, 29 M.J. 896 (A.F.C.M.R. 1989) — § 5-10(D), n. 29
United States v. Davis, 29 M.J. 357 (C.M.A. 1990) — § 11-2(A)(2), nn. 12, 13
United States v. Davis, 29 M.J. 1004 (A.F.C.M.R. 1990) — § 15-10(B), n. 52; § 15-10(C)(2), n. 104
United States v. Davis, 30 M.J. 718 (A.F.C.M.R. 1990) — § 5-7, n. 11
United States v. Davis, 30 M.J. 980 (A.C.M.R. 1990) — § 5-10(A), n. 1; § 15-2(B)(3), n. 61
United States v. Davis, 32 M.J. 166 (C.M.A. 1991) — § 15-14(B), nn. 21, 45
United States v. Davis, 33 M.J. 13 (C.M.A. 1991) — § 17-2(B)(3), nn. 56, 57, 61, 64
United States v. Davis, 32 M.J. 951 (N.M.C.M.R. 1991) — § 2-7(A), n. 6; § 14-3(B)(2), n. 80
United States v. Davis, 36 M.J. 702 (A.C.M.R. 1992) — § 15-4(A), n. 7; § 15-2(B)(1), n. 21
United States v. Davis, 36 M.J. 337 (C.M.A. 1993) — § 5-4(B), n. 23
United States v. Davis, 37 M.J. 152 (C.M.A. 1993) — § 6-4(A), n. 8; § 13-3(N)(3), n. 368

TABLE OF CASES

United States v. Davis, 39 M.J. 281 (C.M.A. 1994) — § 16-5(D)(4), n. 86
United States v. Davis, 114 S. Ct. 2350 (1994) — § 5-4(B), n. 49
United States v. Dawdy, 17 M.J. 523 (A.F.C.M.R. 1983) — § 15-10(B), n. 73; § 15-10(C)(2), nn. 92, 99
United States v. Dawson, 10 M.J. 142 (C.M.A. 1981) — § 9-2(B), n. 34; § 9-2(B)(1), n. 48
United States v. Daye, 17 M.J. 555 (A.C.M.R. 1983) — § 4-11(A), n. 12
United States v. Dayton, 29 M.J. 6 (C.M.A. 1989) — § 2-7(B), n. 24
United States v. De Los Santos, 7 M.J. 519 (A.C.M.R. 1979) — § 14-3(B)(2), n. 71
United States v. Deachin, 22 M.J. 611 (A.C.M.R. 1986) — § 8-2(A), n. 3; § 4-14(A)(2), n. 10
United States v. Dean, 23 C.M.R. 185 (C.M.A. 1957) — § 17-15(B), n. 16
United States v. Dean, 20 C.M.A. 212, 43 C.M.R. 52 (1970) — § 4-15(A), n. 5; § 12-3(A), n. 9
United States v. Dean, 13 M.J. 676 (A.F.C.M.R. 1982) — § 15-2(A), n. 9
United States v. Dear, 40 M.J. 196 (C.M.A. 1994) — § 6-1(C), n. 94; § 13-3(F), n. 220
United States v. Dearman, 7 M.J. 713 (A.C.M.R. 1979) — § 6-1(C)(3), n. 139
United States v. DeBarrows, 41 M.J. 710 (C.G. Ct. Crim. App. 1995) — § 4-14(A)(1), n. 4
United States v. Decker, 15 M.J. 416 (C.M.A. 1983) — § 17-8(B), n. 21; § 11-2(E)(2), n. 123
United States v. DeGrocco, 23 M.J. 146 (C.M.A. 1987) — § 17-9(A), n. 22
United States v. Dehart, 33 M.J. 58 (C.M.A. 1991) — § 11-2(B)(1), nn. 59, 68
United States v. Deifer, 30 M.J. 1038 (A.C.M.R. 1990) — § 12-2(F)(3), nn. 61, 67
United States v. Dejong, 13 M.J. 721 (N.M.C.M.R. 1982) — § 14-3(D)(4), n. 150
United States v. DeJonge, 16 M.J. 974 (A.F.C.M.R. 1983) — § 6-1(C)(2), n. 131
United States v. Delaney, 27 M.J. 501 (A.C.M.R. 1988) — § 16-5(B), n. 7; § 16-5(C), n. 31
United States v. DeLauder, 8 C.M.A. 656, 25 C.M.R. 160 (1958) — § 7-2(B)(1), n. 37
United States v. DeLello, 8 M.J. 777 (A.F.C.M.R. 1980) — § 17-11, n. 4
United States v. Dellarosa, 27 M.J. 860 (A.F.C.M.R. 1989) — § 2-4(B), n. 28
United States v. Dellarosa, 30 M.J. 255 (C.M.A. 1990) — § 3-6(G), n. 31; § 3-6(C)(2), n. 10
United States v. Deller, 3 C.M.A. 409, 12 C.M.R. 165 (1953) — § 2-2(B), n. 10
United States v. DeLoatch, 25 M.J. 718 (A.C.M.R. 1987) — § 5-9(D), n. 22; § 5-10(D), n. 35
United States v. Delp, 31 M.J. 645 (A.F.C.M.R. 1990) — § 17-9(B), n. 32
United States v. Demeio, 15 M.J. 523 (A.C.M.R. 1982) — § 15-10(C), n. 80
United States v. Demerse, 37 M.J. 488 (C.M.A. 1993) — § 15-2(B)(3), n. 80; § 17-8(B)(1), nn. 40, 65
United States v. Demmer, 24 M.J. 731 (A.C.M.R. 1987) — § 13-3(C)(3), n. 156
United States v. Denney, 28 M.J. 521 (A.C.M.R. 1989) — § 15-2(A), n. 12; § 16-8(B), n. 16; § 16-5(D)(4), n. 84; § 16-5(D)(5), nn. 118, 127, 128
United States v. Denning, 20 M.J. 935 (N.M.C.M.R. 1985) — § 16-5(B), n. 24
United States, Dennis v.
United States v. Dennis, 339 U.S. 162 (1950) — § 15-10(C)(2), n. 92
United States v. Dennis, 39 M.J. 623 (N.M.C.M.R. 1993) — § 15-13, n. 11
United States v. Dent, 26 M.J. 968 (A.C.M.R. 1988) — § 5-9(D), n. 22; § 5-10(D), n. 32
United States v. Derksen, 24 M.J. 818 (A.C.M.R. 1987) — § 17-2(B)(3), n. 76; § 17-4(B), n. 53
United States v. Desciscio, 22 M.J. 684 (A.F.C.M.R. 1986) — § 17-4, n. 32

TABLE OF CASES

United States v. Deserano, 41 M.J. 678 (A.F.Ct.Crim.App. 1995) — § 2-6(A), n. 26; § 2-7(A), n. 7
United States v. Desiderio, 31 M.J. 894 (A.F.C.M.R. 1990) — § 8-6, n. 2
United States v. Destefano, 20 M.J. 347 (C.M.A. 1985) — § 5-10(C), n. 19
United States, Dettinger v.
United States v. Devine, 36 M.J. 673 (N.M.C.M.R. 1992) — § 15-14(C), n. 45; § 13-3(C)(1), n. 47
United States v. Devitt, 20 M.J. 240 (C.M.A. 1985) — § 12-2(F)(3), n. 62
United States v. Devitt, 22 M.J. 940 (A.F.C.M.R. 1986) — § 12-2(F)(3), nn. 61, 62
United States v. Devitt, 24 M.J. 307 (C.M.A. 1987) — § 15-2(B)(2), n. 26
United States v. DeYoung, 27 M.J. 595 (A.C.M.R. 1988) — § 16-5(D)(1), n. 61
United States v. DeYoung, 29 M.J. 78 (C.M.A. 1989) — § 16-5(D)(1), nn. 61, 62
United States v. Diamond, 18 M.J. 305 (C.M.A. 1984) — § 17-2(B)(4), n. 96; § 17-4(B), n. 53
United States v. Diamond, 30 M.J. 902 (A.F.C.M.R. 1990) — § 16-12, n. 13
United States v. DiAngelo, 31 M.J. 135 (C.M.A. 1990) — § 13-3(E), n. 193; § 15-4(B), nn. 13, 14
United States v. Diaz, 9 M.J. 691 (N.C.M.R. 1980) — § 8-3(B)(1), n. 57
United States v. Diaz, 30 M.J. 957 (C.G.C.M.R. 1990) — § 5-10(D), n. 39; § 14-3(C), n. 128
United States v. Diaz, 39 M.J. 1114 (A.F.C.M.R. 1994) — § 15-14(B), n. 42
United States v. Diaz, 40 M.J. 335 (C.M.A. 1994) — § 17-9(A), n. 3
United States v. Diaz-Carrero, 31 M.J. 920 (A.C.M.R. 1990) — § 17-8(B)(3), n. 68
United States v. DiBello, 17 M.J. 77 (C.M.A. 1983) — § 2-2(C)(3), n. 39; § 6-1(C)(3), nn. 145, 149
United States v. Dick, 9 M.J. 869 (N.C.M.R. 1980) — § 5-9(E), nn. 55, 58, 61
United States v. Dickens, 30 M.J. 986 (A.C.M.R. 1990) — § 14-3(B)(3), n. 101
United States v. Dickerson, 22 C.M.A. 489, 47 C.M.R. 790 (1973) — § 17-9(B), n. 38
United States v. Dickey, 41 M.J. 637 (N.M.Ct.Crim.App. 1994) — § 6-4(E), n. 28; § 6-7, n. 10; § 15-2(B)(3), n. 53
United States v. DiCupe, 21 M.J. 440 (C.M.A. 1986) — § 15-2(B)(3), nn. 31, 41
United States v. Dienst, 16 M.J. 727 (A.F.C.M.R. 1983) — § 2-2(E)(6), n. 96
United States v. Dies, 42 M.J. 847 (N.M.Ct.Crim.App.1995) — § 13-3(C)(3), nn. 141, 148; § 13-3(C)(5), n. 180
United States v. Dieter, 42 M.J. 697 (Army Ct.Crim.App. 1995) — § 11-3(C), n. 75; § 15-22, n. 4
United States v. Dilday, 47 C.M.R. 172 (A.C.M.R. 1973) — § 15-16(A), nn. 1, 9
United States v. Dillard, 4 M.J. 577 (A.C.M.R. 1977) — § 13-3(N)(1), n. 338
United States v. DiMatteo, 19 M.J. 903 (A.C.M.R. 1985) — § 5-10(D), n. 37; § 13-5(B), n. 28
United States v. Dinkel, 13 M.J. 400 (C.M.A. 1982) — § 14-3(C), n. 132
United States v. Dionne, 6 M.J. 791 (A.C.M.R. 1978) — § 15-2(F), n. 164
United States v. Dixon, 17 C.M.A. 423, 38 C.M.R. 221 (1968) — § 15-24, n. 4
United States v. Dixon, 8 M.J. 149 (C.M.A. 1979) — § 10-4(B)(5), n. 53
United States v. Dixon, 8 M.J. 858 (N.C.M.R. 1980) — § 15-6, n. 2
United States v. Dixon, 18 M.J. 310 (C.M.A. 1984) — § 4-15(A), n. 9; § 15-9, n. 1
United States v. Dock, 20 M.J. 556 (A.C.M.R. 1985) — § 15-13, n. 3
United States v. Dock, 26 M.J. 620 (A.C.M.R. 1988) — § 14-3, n. 5
United States v. Dock, 35 M.J. 627 (A.C.M.R. 1992) — § 15-10(B), n. 62
United States v. Dock, 40 M.J. 112 (C.M.A. 1994) — § 5-4(B), n. 49; § 15-12(B), n. 15
United States v. Doctor, 7 C.M.A. 126, 21 C.M.R. 252 (1956) — § 15-13, n. 6

TABLE OF CASES

United States v. Dodds, 11 M.J. 520 (A.F.C.M.R. 1981) — § 16-5(B), nn. 8, 9
United States v. Dohle, 1 M.J. 223 (C.M.A. 1975) — § 5-4(B), n. 42
United States v. Domingue, 24 M.J. 766 (A.F.C.M.R. 1987) — § 2-7(B), n. 19
United States v. Donaldson, 49 C.M.R. 542 (C.M.A. 1975) — § 6-2(B), n. 13
United States v. Donaldson, 23 C.M.A. 293, 49 C.M.R. 542 (1975) — § 7-2(E), nn. 104, 109; § 13-5(D), n. 41
United States v. Donati, 14 C.M.A. 235, 34 C.M.R. 15 (1963) — § 11-3(B)(1), n. 31; § 11-3(B)(2), n. 40
United States v. Donegan, 27 M.J. 576 (A.F.C.M.R. 1988) — § 6-1(C)(3), n. 147
United States v. Donley, 30 M.J. 973 (A.C.M.R. 1990) — § 15-4(B), n. 10
United States v. Donley, 33 M.J. 44 (C.M.A. 1991) — § 15-10(B), n. 62; § 15-2(B)(3), nn. 75, 95
United States v. Donnelly, 12 M.J. 503 (A.F.C.M.R. 1981) — § 16-11, n. 4
United States v. Donohew, 18 C.M.A. 149, 29 C.M.R. 149 (1969) — § 12-2(F)(2), nn. 50, 54
United States v. Donohue, 30 M.J. 734 (A.F.C.M.R. 1990) — § 16-5(B), n. 7
United States v. Doran, 9 M.J. 385 (C.M.A. 1980) — § 17-16(C), n. 16
United States v. Dorgan, 39 M.J. 827 (A.C.M.R. 1994) — § 13-5(I), n. 73; § 11-2(A)(2), n. 11
United States v. Dornick, 16 M.J. 642 (A.F.C.M.R. 1983) — § 2-3(A), n. 13; § 17-4, nn. 20, 29
United States v. Dorsch, 34 M.J. 1042 (N.M.C.M.R. 1992) — § 13-3(C)(1), n. 38
United States v. Dorsey, 25 M.J. 728 (A.F.C.M.R. 1987) — § 9-2(B), n. 35
United States v. Dorsey, 26 M.J. 538 (A.F.C.M.R. 1988) — § 17-3(A), n. 18
United States v. Dorsey, 29 M.J. 761 (A.C.M.R. 1989) — § 15-10(C)(2), nn. 98, 100
United States v. Dorsey, 30 M.J. 1156 (A.C.M.R. 1990) — § 15-2(B)(3), nn. 78, 85
United States v. Doss, 15 M.J. 409, 419 (C.M.A. 1983) — § 6-1(C)(3), n. 163
United States v. Dotson, 9 M.J. 542 (C.G.C.M.R. 1980) — § 15-13, n. 14; § 16-8(C), n. 35
United States v. Doucet, 43 M.J. 656 (A.F.Ct.Crim.App. 1995) — § 5-4(B), n. 48; § 13-4, n. 8
United States v. Dougal, 32 M.J. 863 (N.M.C.M.R. 1991) — § 6-1(C)(3), n. 136
United States v. Douglas, 1 M.J. 354 (C.M.A. 1976) — § 1-1(B), n. 25
United States v. Douglas, 32 M.J. 694 (A.F.C.M.R. 1991) — § 6-1, nn. 40, 41; § 7-2(B)(4), n. 45; § 10-4(B)(5), n. 62
United States v. Douse, 12 M.J. 473 (C.M.A. 1982) — § 4-8(A), nn. 5, 9
United States v. Dowd, 7 M.J. 445 (C.M.A. 1979) — § 14-3(D)(3), n. 140
United States v. Dowell, 10 M.J. 36 (C.M.A. 1980) — § 5-4(B), n. 44
United States v. Dowell, 12 M.J. 768 (A.C.M.R. 1981) — § 17-8(B)(3), n. 97
United States v. Dowlat, 28 M.J. 958 (A.F.C.M.R. 1989) — § 2-8(C), n. 30
United States v. Downing, 17 M.J. 636 (N.M.C.M.R. 1983) — § 15-10(C)(2), n. 99
United States v. Downs, 4 C.M.A. 8, 15 C.M.R. 8 (1954) — § 15-16(A), n. 10; § 17-3(A), n. 19
United States v. Drayton, 39 M.J. 871 (A.C.M.R. 1994) — § 6-4(A), n. 8; § 6-5(B), n. 24
United States v. Drayton, 40 M.J. 447 (C.M.A. 1994) — § 17-8(B)(1), n . 54; § 17-9(A), n. 3
United States v. Dresen, 36 M.J. 1103 (A.F.C.M.R. 1993) — § 12-2(F)(4), nn. 70, 71, 75
United States v. Dresen, 40 M.J. 462 (C.M.A. 1994) — § 15-2(B)(3), n. 86
United States v. Driver, 23 C.M.A. 243, 49 C.M.R. 376 (1974) — § 13-3(C)(2), n. 62
United States v. Driver, 36 M.J. 1020 (N.M.C.M.R. 1993) — § 16-7, n. 3
United States v. Dubay, 17 C.M.A. 147, 37 C.M.R. 411 (1967) — § 9-2(C), n. 79; § 12-2(F)(2), n. 55; § 12-2(F)(3), n. 65; § 15-2(B)(2), n. 28; § 15-2(B)(3), nn. 50, 105, 106; § 15-10(C)(3); § 17-3(B), nn. 32-34; § 17-21, n. 8

TABLE OF CASES

United States v. DuBose, 19 M.J. 877 (A.F.C.M.R. 1985) — § 15-14(B), n. 45
United States v. Dubry, 12 M.J. 36 (C.M.A. 1981) — § 2-2(C)(3), n. 47; § 2-2(E)(5), n. 92
United States v. Dudding, 34 M.J. 975 (A.C.M.R. 1992) — § 12-2(H), n. 100
United States v. Dudley, 21 M.J. 615 (A.C.M.R. 1985) — § 14-3(B)(1), n. 61
United States v. Dudley, 34 M.J. 603 (A.F.C.M.R. 1992) — § 16-5(B), n. 8
United States v. Dudley, 42 M.J. 528 (N.M.Ct.Crim.App. 1995) — § 5-4(B), n. 42
United States v. Duga, 10 M.J. 206 (C.M.A. 1981) — § 5-4(B), n. 42
United States v. Duke, 23 M.J. 710 (A.F.C.M.R. 1986) — § 5-9(D), n. 39
United States v. Dukes, 5 M.J. 71 (C.M.A. 1978) — § 17-16(C), nn. 15, 20
United States v. Dukes, 30 M.J. 793 (N.M.C.M.R. 1990) — § 14-2(B)(4), n. 114; § 14-3(D)(4), n. 147; § 16-5(D)(2), n. 67
United States v. Dulus, 16 M.J. 324 (C.M.A. 1983) — § 5-3(D)(1), n. 133
United States v. Dumas, 27 M.J. 676 (A.C.M.R. 1988) — § 14-3(B)(2), n. 99
United States v. Dumas, 36 M.J. 941 (A.C.M.R. 1993) — § 15-2(B)(3), n. 63
United States v. Dumford, 30 M.J. 137 (C.M.A. 1990) — § 2-9(A), nn. 3, 4; § 2-9(B), nn. 13, 18, 20, 21; § 2-9(D), n. 60
United States v. Dunbar, 31 M.J. 70 (C.M.A. 1990) — § 17-11, n. 5
United States v. Duncan, 34 M.J. 1232 (A.C.M.R. 1992) — § 4-12(A), n. 6; § 13-3(C)(3), n. 165
United States v. Duncan, 34 M.J. 1232 (A.C.M.R. 1992) — § 13-3(C)(3), n. 165
United States v. Dunks, 1 M.J. 254 (C.M.A. 1975) — § 15-4(A), n. 4
United States v. Dunks, 1 M.J. 254 (C.M.A. 1976) — § 13-5(K), n. 84; § 13-3(C)(4), nn. 171, 172
United States v. Dunlap, 39 M.J. 1120 (A.C.M.R. 1994) — § 17-2(B)(2), nn. 29, 31
United States v. Dunn, 480 U.S. 294 (1987) — § 5-3(A), n. 23
United States v. Dunning, 40 M.J. 641 (N.M.C.M.R. 1994) — § 14-3(B)(2), n. 77
United States v. Dupas, 14 M.J. 28 (C.M.A. 1982) — § 15-2(B)(3), n. 108
United States v. Dupree, 42 C.M.R. 681 (A.C.M.R. 1970) — § 13-3(C)(2), n. 60
United States v. Dupree, 45 C.M.R. 456 (A.F.C.M.R. 1972) — § 15-10(C)(1), n. 83
United States v. Dupree, 24 M.J. 319 (C.M.A. 1987) — § 2-4(E), n. 46
United States v. Dupree, 25 M.J. 659 (A.F.C.M.R. 1987) — § 2-4(E), n. 46
United States v. Dupree, 37 M.J. 1089 (N.M.C.M.R. 1993) — § 17-11, n. 5
United States v. Durden, 14 M.J. 507 (A.F.C.M.R. 1982) — § 10-4(B)(5), n. 58
United States v. Durham, 21 M.J. 232 (C.M.A. 1986) — § 6-1(C), n. 98
United States v. Duval, 31 M.J. 650 (A.C.M.R. 1990) — § 14-3(B)(2), n. 77; § 14-3(D)(4), n. 147
United States v. Duvall, 7 M.J. 832 (N.C.M.R. 1979) — § 8-4, n. 9
United States v. Dyer, 16 M.J. 894 (A.C.M.R. 1983) — § 17-21, n. 3
United States v. Dyer, 22 M.J. 578 (A.C.M.R. 1986) — § 17-21, n. 3
United States v. Dykes, 38 M.J. 270 (C.M.A. 1993) — § 6-7, n. 9
United States v. Eads, 24 M.J. 919 (A.F.C.M.R. 1987) — § 16-4(B), n. 15; § 16-5(D)(3), n. 76
United States v. Eady, 35 M.J. 15 (C.M.A. 1992) — § 16-5(C), n. 31
United States v. Earl, 9 M.J. 828 (A.F.C.M.R. 1980) — § 10-4(B)(1), n. 31
United States v. Earnesty, 34 M.J. 1179 (A.F.C.M.R. 1992) — § 5-4(A)(3), n. 19
United States v. Eason, 21 C.M.A. 335, 45 C.M.R. 109 (1972) — § 8-3(B)(2), n. 70
United States v. Eason, 49 C.M.R. 844 (N.C.M.R. 1974) — § 15-12, n. 3
United States v. Easter, 39 M.J. 876 (A.C.M.R. 1994) — § 15-13, n. 6
United States v. Ebanks, 29 M.J. 926 (A.F.C.M.R. 1989) — § 2-4(F), n. 51; § 2-9(C), n. 22; § 5-10(D), n. 34

TABLE OF CASES

United States v. Eberhardt, 417 F.2d 1009 (4th Cir. 1969) — § 2-4(F), n. 61; § 2-2(E)(7), n. 107
United States v. Eberhardt, 24 M.J. 944 (A.C.M.R. 1987) — § 15-10(B), n. 55; § 15-10(C)(2), n. 100
United States v. Echols, 17 M.J. 856 (N.M.C.M.R. 1984) — § 17-11, n. 5
United States v. Eck, 28 M.J. 1046 (A.C.M.R. 1989) — § 15-14(D), n. 54
United States v. Eckart, 8 M.J. 835 (A.C.M.R. 1980) — § 15-2(D), n. 133
United States v. Eckhoff, 23 M.J. 875 (N.M.C.M.R. 1987) — § 2-7(B), n. 24
United States v. Eckhoff, 27 M.J. 142 (C.M.A. 1988) — § 15-14(D), n. 54
United States v. Ecoffey, 23 M.J. 629 (A.C.M.R. 1986) — § 5-10(D), n. 39
United States v. Eddy, 41 M.J. 786 (A.F. Ct. Crim. App. 1995) — § 14-3(B)(2), n. 78
United States v. Edmond, 37 M.J. 787 (C.G.C.M.R. 1993) — § 12-2(H), nn. 100, 123
United States v. Edmond, 41 M.J. 419 (1995) — § 13-3(C)(5), n. 181
United States v. Edmonds, 36 M.J. 791 (A.C.M.R. 1993) — § 15-13, n. 15; § 16-8(B), n. 21
United States v. Edwards, 43 M.J. 619 — § 3-4, n. 3
United States v. Edwards, 32 C.M.R. 586 (A.B.R. 1962) — § 7-3(B), n. 33
United States v. Edwards, 12 M.J. 781 (A.C.M.R. 1982) — § 17-2(B), n. 10
United States v. Edwards, 20 M.J. 439 (C.M.A. 1985) — § 14-3(B)(3), n. 101
United States v. Edwards, 20 M.J. 973 (N.M.C.M.R. 1985) — § 12-2(H), n. 105
United States v. Edwards, 35 M.J. 351 (C.M.A. 1992) — § 16-8(B), nn. 27-34; § 6-1(C)(3), n. 147
United States v. Edwards, 39 M.J. 528 (A.F.C.M.R. 1994) — § 3-8(B), n. 5; § 16-5(B), n. 8
United States v. Edwards, 42 M.J. 381 (1995) — § 13-3(G), n. 226
United States v. Eggers, 3 C.M.A. 191, 11 C.M.R. 191 (1953) — § 7-2, n. 4
United States v. Eichenlaub, 11 M.J. 239 (C.M.A. 1981) — § 17-4, n. 7
United States v. Eichman, 110 S. Ct. 2404 (1990) — § 13-3(N)(3), n. 363
United States v. Eiland, 39 M.J. 566 (N.M.C.M.R. 1993) — § 11-2(B)(1), n. 67
United States v. Eischeid, 36 M.J. 561 (N.M.C.M.R. 1992) — § 14-3(D)(5), n. 175
United States v. El-Amin, 38 M.J. 563 (A.F.C.M.R. 1993) — § 13-3(M), nn. 282, 284, 298
United States v. Ellenson, 19 M.J. 605 (A.F.C.M.R. 1984) — § 16-3(C), n. 52
United States v. Ellerbee, 30 M.J. 517 (A.F.C.M.R. 1990) — § 14-3(D)(4), n. 159
United States v. Elliott, 266 F. Supp. 318 (S.D.N.Y. 1967) — § 13-5(F), n. 22
United States v. Elliott, 15 M.J. 347 (C.M.A. 1983) — § 17-15, n. 4
United States v. Elliott, 23 M.J. 1 (C.M.A. 1986) — § 17-8(B)(1), n. 43
United States v. Ellis, 15 C.M.A. 8, 34 C.M.R. 454 (1964) — § 16-9, n. 10
United States v. Ellis, 2 M.J. 616 (N.C.M.R. 1977) — § 17-11, n. 5
United States v. Ellis, 24 M.J. 370 (C.M.A. 1987) — § 5-3(D)(1), n. 124
United States v. Ellison, 13 M.J. 90 (C.M.A. 1982) — § 15-2(A), n. 5
United States v. Ellman, 9 C.M.A. 549, 26 C.M.R. 329 (1958) — § 16-3(B), n. 38
United States v. Ellsey, 16 C.M.A. 455, 37 C.M.R. 75 (1966) — § 5-9(A), n. 3
United States v. Elmore, 1 M.J. 262 (C.M.A. 1976) — § 9-2(B)(1), n. 53
United States v. Elmore, 31 M.J. 678 (N.M.C.M.R. 1990) — § 15-2(E), n. 152
United States v. Elmore, 33 M.J. 387 (C.M.A. 1991) — § 15-10(B), n. 67
United States v. Elrod, 18 M.J. 692 (A.F.C.M.R. 1984) — § 16-4(B), n. 16; § 16-6, n. 3; § 16-7, n. 4
United States v. Elvine, 16 M.J. 14 (C.M.A. 1983) — § 16-4(B), n. 18
United States v. Elzy, 22 M.J. 640 (A.C.M.R. 1986) — § 12-2(H), n. 99; § 12-3(A), n. 31; § 15-2(B)(4), n. 118

TABLE OF CASES

United States v. Elzy, 25 M.J. 416 (C.M.A. 1988) — § 12-2(H), nn. 100, 121
United States v. Emerson, 1 C.M.A. 43, 1 C.M.R. 43 (1951) — § 4-13, n. 4
United States v. Emerson, 12 M.J. 512 (N.M.C.M.R. 1981) — § 4-14(B), n. 20; § 4-15(C), n. 17
United States v. Emmons, 31 M.J. 108 (C.M.A. 1990) — § 15-14(B), n. 23
United States v. England, 24 M.J. 816 (A.C.M.R. 1987) — § 8-3(C)(4), nn. 159, 160
United States v. England, 30 M.J. 1030 (A.F.C.M.R. 1990) — § 13-3(H), n. 244
United States v. England, 33 M.J. 37 (C.M.A. 1991) — § 5-4(C), n. 56
United States v. Engle, 1 M.J. 387 (C.M.A. 1976) — § 7-3(A), n. 13; § 7-3(B), n. 28; § 17-8(B), n. 20
United States v. Engle, 28 M.J. 299 (C.M.A. 1989) — § 17-15(A), n. 14
United States v. Englert, 42 M.J. 827 (N.M.Ct.Crim.App. 1995) — § 17-9(D), n. 74
United States v. English, 25 M.J. 819 (A.F.C.M.R. 1988) — § 14-3(D)(3), n. 139
United States v. English, 37 M.J. 1107 (N.M.C.M.R. 1993) — § 14-2(B)(4), n. 115
United States v. Enloe, 15 C.M.A. 256, 35 C.M.R. 228 (1965) — § 10-3(B), n. 10
United States v. Enlow, 26 M.J. 940 (A.C.M.R. 1988) — § 9-3, n. 7
United States v. Ennis, 15 M.J. 970 (A.C.M.R. 1983) — § 15-10(B), n. 63; § 15-10(C)(2), n. 91
United States v. Epps, 25 M.J. 319 (C.M.A. 1987) — § 14-3(B)(2), n. 99
United States v. Ericson, 13 M.J. 725 (N.M.C.M.R. 1982) — § 15-16(C), n. 33
United States v. Ericson, 37 M.J. 1011 (A.C.M.R. 1993) — § 17-9(A), nn. 24, 27, 28
United States v. Erie, 29 M.J. 1008 (A.C.M.R. 1990) — § 5-4(B), nn. 26, 28, 52
United States v. Ermitano, 19 M.J. 626 (N.M.C.M.R. 1984) — § 13-2(G)(2), n. 84
United States v. Ernest, 32 M.J. 135 (C.M.A. 1991) — § 4-5(A)(4), n. 18
United States v. Ernst, 17 M.J. 835 (C.G.C.M.R. 1984) — § 15-13, n. 13
United States v. Erwin, 793 F.2d 656 (5th Cir. 1986) — § 15-10(C)(3), n. 114
United States v. Escobar, 7 M.J. 197 (C.M.A. 1979) — § 4-11(A), n. 15
United States v. Eshalomi, 23 M.J. 12 (C.M.A. 1986) — § 1-1(B), n. 25; § 10-3(B), n. 8; § 10-3(D), n. 17; § 10-4(A)(4), n. 26; § 10-4(B)(1), n. 35
United States v. Espiet-Betancourt, 1 M.J. 91 (C.M.A. 1975) — § 11-2(E)(2), n. 121
United States v. Espinoza, 27 M.J. 551 (C.G.C.M.R. 1988) — § 17-9(A), n. 20; § 17-15(B), n. 32
United States v. Espronceda, 36 M.J. 535 (A.F.C.M.R. 1992) — § 5-4(B), n. 49; § 15-13, nn. 11, 23
United States v. Estrada, 7 C.M.A. 635, 23 C.M.R. 99 (1957) — § 6-5(A), n. 9
United States v. Estrella, 35 M.J. 836 (A.C.M.R. 1992) — § 2-4(D), n. 40; § 16-5(D)(3), n. 72
United States v. Ettinger, 36 M.J. 1171 (N.M.C.M.R. 1993) — § 12-2(H), n. 101
United States v. Ettleson, 13 M.J. 348 (C.M.A. 1982) — § 2-7(A), n. 1; § 15-2(B)(1), n. 25
United States v. Eubank, 12 M.J. 752 (A.F.C.M.R. 1981) — § 17-4(A), n. 45
United States v. Euring, 27 M.J. 843 (A.C.M.R. 1989) — § 17-2(B)(3), n. 79; § 17-4(B), n. 53
United States v. Evans, 333 U.S. 483 (1948) — § 13-3(N)(2), n. 342
United States v. Evans, 5 C.M.R. 585 (A.F.B.R. 1952) — § 17-3(A), n. 23
United States v. Evans, 1 M.J. 206 (C.M.A. 1975) — § 15-2(B)(2), n. 26
United States v. Evans, 6 M.J. 577 (A.C.M.R. 1978) — § 4-12(B), n. 17
United States v. Evans, 16 M.J. 951 (A.F.C.M.R. 1983) — § 2-7(C), n. 33
United States v. Evans, 25 M.J. 699 (A.C.M.R. 1987) — § 17-14, n. 6
United States v. Evans, 25 M.J. 859 (A.F.C.M.R. 1988) — § 16-7, n. 1
United States v. Evans, 26 M.J. 550 (A.F.C.M.R. 1988) — § 13-4(B), n. 27; § 17-21, n. 2

TABLE OF CASES

United States v. Evans, 26 M.J. 961 (A.C.M.R. 1988) — § 16-5(C), n. 31; § 13-3(C)(3), n. 122
United States v. Evans, 27 M.J. 34 (C.M.A. 1988) — § 15-4(B), n. 11
United States v. Evans, 28 M.J. 753 (A.F.C.M.R. 1989) — § 15-14(B), n. 23
United States v. Evans, 31 M.J. 927 (A.C.M.R. 1990) — § 15-2(B)(3), n. 32
United States v. Evans, 33 M.J. 309 (C.M.A. 1991) — § 2-6(C), n. 35
United States v. Evans, 32 M.J. 1016 (N.M.C.M.R. 1991) — § 5-3(F), n. 24
United States v. Evans, 35 M.J. 306 (C.M.A. 1992) — § 5-3(B), n. 53
United States v. Evans, 35 M.J. 754 (N.M.C.M.R. 1992) — § 16-8(C), n. 38; § 16-11, n. 4
United States v. Evans, 37 M.J. 468 (C.M.A. 1993) — § 15-16(A), n. 4
United States v. Evans, 37 M.J. 867 (A.F.C.M.R. 1993) — § 15-10(B), n. 73; § 5-3(D)(1), nn. 118, 125
United States v. Evans, 39 M.J. 613 (A.C.M.R. 1994) — § 13-5(G)(1), n. 34
United States v. Everett, 33 M.J. 534 (A.F.C.M.R. 1991) — § 16-8(B), n. 15
United States v. Everett, 41 M.J. 847 (A.F.C.M.R. 1994) — § 13-4(A), n. 18
United States v. Everson, 19 C.M.A. 70, 41 C.M.R. 70 (1969) — § 4-11(A), n. 9
United States v. Ezell, 6 M.J. 307 (C.M.A. 1979) — § 5-3, n. 1; § 5-3(B), n. 41
United States v. Ezell, 24 M.J. 690 (A.C.M.R. 1987) — § 15-16(B), n. 19
United States v. Facey, 26 M.J. 421 (C.M.A. 1988) — § 13-3(C)(3), n. 106
United States v. Faciane, 40 M.J. 399 (C.M.A. 1994) — § 13-4(A), n. 19
United States v. Fagan, 24 M.J. 865 (N.M.C.M.R. 1987) — § 5-4(B), n. 40
United States v. Fagan, 28 M.J. 64 (C.M.A. 1989) — § 5-3, n. 2; § 5-3(A), n. 22
United States v. Fagg, 33 M.J. 618 (A.F.C.M.R. 1991) — § 13-3(N)(4), nn. 422, 423
United States v. Fagg, 34 M.J. 179 (C.M.A. 1992) — § 13-3(N)(4), n. 413
United States v. Fagnan, 12 C.M.A. 192, 30 C.M.R. 192 (1961) — § 17-2(B)(3), n. 69
United States v. Fahey, 33 M.J. 920 (A.C.M.R. 1991) — § 6-1, n. 19; § 14-3(D)(4), n. 153
United States v. Fairchild, 16 M.J. 746 (A.F.C.M.R. 1983) — § 4-8(A), n. 7
United States v. Fairchild, 33 M.J. 970 (A.F.C.M.R. 1991) — § 4-8(C)(1), n. 17
United States v. Fairly, 27 M.J. 582 (A.F.C.M.R. 1988) — § 6-1(C)(3), n. 142
United States v. Falcon, 16 M.J. 528 (A.C.M.R. 1983) — § 15-13, nn. 9, 10
United States v. Falin, 43 C.M.R. 702 (A.C.M.R. 1971) — § 15-16(C), nn. 31, 38
United States v. Falk, 479 F.2d 616 (7th Cir. 1973) — § 13-3(M), n. 288
United States v. Fals, 6 M.J. 713 (A.F.C.M.R. 1978) — § 5-9(D), n. 23
United States v. Fassler, 29 M.J. 193 (C.M.A. 1989) — § 5-4(B), n. 50
United States v. Feagans, 15 M.J. 667 (A.F.C.M.R. 1983) — § 17-9(E), n. 87
United States v. Feld, 27 M.J. 537 (A.F.C.M.R. 1988) — § 16-11, n. 7; § 17-3(A), n. 20
United States v. Felix, 36 M.J. 903 (A.F.C.M.R. 1993) — § 2-4(D), n. 40; § 17-8(B), nn. 15, 24; § 3-6(C)(1), nn. 6, 9
United States v. Fell, 33 M.J. 628 (A.C.M.R. 1991) — § 15-7, n. 5
United States v. Felton, 31 M.J. 526 (A.C.M.R. 1990) — § 16-9, n. 14
United States v. Felty, 12 M.J. 438 (C.M.A. 1982) — § 5-7, n. 23; § 14-3(B)(2), n. 99
United States v. Fenno, 167 F.2d 593 (2d Cir. 1948) — § 4-8(D), n. 60
United States v. Ferenczi, 10 C.M.A. 3, 27 C.M.R. 77 (1958) — § 2-3(A), n. 14; § 2-4(B), n. 27
United States v. Ferguson, 12 C.M.R. 570 (A.B.R. 1953) — § 2-4(E), n. 48
United States v. Ferguson, 27 M.J. 660 (N.M.C.M.R. 1988) — § 16-2(B), n. 14; § 16-9, n. 4
United States v. Ferguson, 29 M.J. 559 (A.F.C.M.R. 1989) — § 15-4(B), n. 10
United States v. Ferguson, 40 M.J. 823 (N.M.C.M.R. 1994) — § 2-4(E), n. 47
United States v. Fernandez, 48 C.M.R. 460 (N.M.C.M.R. 1974) — § 13-3(C)(2), n. 49

TABLE OF CASES

United States v. Fernandez, 24 M.J. 77 (C.M.A. 1987) — § 6-6(A), nn. 1, 4; § 6-8, n. 3; § 17-9(B), n. 40
United States v. Ferrer, 33 M.J. 96 (C.M.A. 1991) — § 16-5(D)(3), n. 76
United States v. Fetch, 17 C.M.R. 836 (A.B.R. 1954) — § 15-10(C)(2), n. 101
United States v. Fielder, 21 M.J. 544 (A.F.C.M.R. 1985) — § 2-2(C)(3), n. 40
United States v. Fields, 17 M.J. 1070 (A.F.C.M.R. 1984) — § 4-14(B), n. 21
United States v. Figueroa, 35 M.J. 54 (C.M.A. 1992) — § 5-3(B), n. 39
United States v. Fimmano, 8 M.J. 197 (C.M.A. 1980) — § 1-3(D)(2), n. 22
United States v. Finn, 20 M.J. 696 (N.M.C.M.R. 1985) — § 14-3(B)(2), n. 71
United States v. Finsel, 33 M.J. 739 (A.C.M.R. 1991) — § 2-4(C), n. 33
United States v. Firmin, 8 M.J. 595 (A.C.M.R. 1979) — § 8-3(C)(4), n. 152
United States v. First, 2 M.J. 1266 (A.C.M.R. 1976) — § 6-1(B)(3), n. 91
United States v. Fish, 25 M.J. 732 (A.F.C.M.R. 1987) — § 5-3(C)(6), n. 89
United States v. Fisher, 17 M.J. 768 (A.F.C.M.R. 1983) — § 15-13, nn. 22, 23; § 11-2(A)(1), n. 6
United States v. Fisher, 772 F.2d 371 (7th Cir. 1985) — § 14-4, n. 12
United States v. Fisher, 21 M.J. 327 (C.M.A. 1986) — § 16-9, nn. 5, 16
United States v. Fisher, 24 M.J. 358 (C.M.A. 1987) — § 11-2(A)(1), n. 6; § 11-2(B)(1), n. 60
United States v. Fisher, 37 M.J. 812 (N.M.C.M.R. 1993) — § 5-9(D), n. 37; § 5-10(D), n. 25
United States v. Fisiorek, 43 M.J. 244 (1995) — § 15-12, n. 3
United States v. Fiske, 28 M.J. 1013 (A.F.C.M.R. 1989) — § 15-3, nn. 2, 13, 14
United States v. Fitten, 42 M.J. 179 (1995) — § 5-3(D)(2), n. 140
United States v. Fitzhugh, 14 M.J. 595 (A.F.C.M.R. 1982) — § 16-5(D)(3), n. 79
United States v. Fitzpatrick, 14 M.J. 394 (C.M.A. 1983) — § 4-8(A), n. 8; § 5-4(A)(3), n. 19
United States v. Fitzsimmons, 33 M.J. 710 (A.C.M.R. 1991) — § 5-10(D), n. 34
United States v. Fleenor, 42 C.M.R. 900 (A.C.M.R. 1970) — § 7-3(B), n. 27
United States v. Fleig, 16 C.M.A. 444, 37 C.M.R. 64 (1966) — § 13-3(F), nn. 216, 218
United States v. Fleming, 18 C.M.A. 524, 40 C.M.R. 236 (1969) — § 8-5, n. 13; § 12-4, n. 11
United States v. Fleming, 38 M.J. 126 (C.M.A. 1993) — § 15-14(B), n. 42
United States v. Fletch, 17 C.M.R. 836 (A.F.B.R. 1954) — § 15-10(C)(3), n. 120
United States v. Fletcher, 2 M.J. 1252 (N.C.M.R. 1976) — § 14-3(E), n. 180
United States v. Fling, 40 M.J. 847 (A.F.C.M.R. 1994) — § 13-2(G)(2), n. 82
United States v. Flint, 1 M.J. 428 (C.M.A. 1976) — § 13-3(C), n. 31; § 13-3(C)(2), nn. 64, 70; § 17-3(B), n. 34
United States v. Flom, 558 F.2d 1179 (5th Cir. 1977) — § 13-5(F), n. 27
United States v. Florczak, 49 C.M.R. 786 (A.C.M.R. 1975) — § 13-3(E), n. 190; § 13-3(G), n. 232
United States v. Flores-Glaraza, 40 M.J. 900 (N.M.C.M.R. 1994) — § 13-2(G)(2), n. 97
United States, Flowers v.
United States v. Flowers, 26 M.J. 463 (C.M.A. 1988) — § 5-3(D)(1), n. 118
United States v. Floyd, 31 M.J. 755 (A.C.M.R. 1990) — § 9-3, n. 3
United States v. Fluellen, 40 M.J. 96 (C.M.A. 1994) — § 15-2(B)(3), n. 68
United States v. Flynn, 28 M.J. 218 (C.M.A. 1989) — § 6-1(C)(3), n. 137
United States v. Flynn, 34 M.J. 1183 (A.F.C.M.R. 1992) — § 2-4(A), nn. 6, 17; § 5-4(B), n. 50; § 16-8(B), n. 12
United States v. Flynn, 39 M.J. 774 (A.C.M.R. 1994) — § 13-3(G), n. 225

TABLE OF CASES

United States v. Fogarty, 35 M.J. 885 (A.C.M.R. 1992) — § 5-10(A), n. 2; § 5-10(B), n. 8; § 5-10(C), n. 15
United States v. Foley, 12 M.J. 826 (N.M.C.M.R. 1981) — § 5-4(B), n. 46
United States v. Foley, 37 M.J. 822 (A.F.C.M.R. 1993) — § 6-2, n. 1; § 6-5(A), n. 14; § 7-2(A)(1), n. 16; § 7-3(B), n. 29; § 12-2(H), nn. 97, 100
United States v. Folk, 37 M.J. 851 (A.F.C.M.R. 1993) — § 5-10(D), n. 41
United States v. Fontenot, 26 M.J. 559 (A.C.M.R. 1988) — § 16-8(A), n. 6; § 11-2(A)(3), n. 21; § 16-5(D)(5), n. 114
United States v. Fontenot, 29 M.J. 244 (C.M.A. 1989) — § 16-5(B), n. 9; § 16-5(D)(3), n. 72
United States v. Forbes, 19 M.J. 953 (A.F.C.M.R. 1985) — § 14-4, nn. 7, 12, 13
United States v. Ford, 12 M.J. 636 (N.M.C.M.R. 1981) — § 12-3(A), n. 16
United States v. Ford, 23 M.J. 331 (C.M.A. 1987) — § 2-7(C), n. 42
United States v. Ford, 29 M.J. 597 (A.C.M.R. 1989) — § 15-4(A), n. 6; § 11-2(B)(1), n. 58
United States v. Ford, 33 M.J. 1046 (N.M.C.M.R. 1991) — § 17-8(B)(2), n. 64
United States v. Ford, 34 F.3d 992 (11th Cir. 1994) — § 5-3(A), n. 31
United States v. Forehand, 8 C.M.R. 564 (N.B.R. 1953) — § 4-15(C), n. 17
United States v. Forester, 8 M.J. 560 (N.C.M.R. 1979) — § 3-4, n. 3
United States v. Fors, 10 M.J. 367 (C.M.A. 1981) — § 5-5, n. 9
United States v. Fort, 16 C.M.A. 86, 36 C.M.R. 242 (1966) — § 15-10(B), n. 52
United States v. Fortney, 12 M.J. 987 (A.F.C.M.R. 1982) — § 13-3(J), n. 258; § 16-2(D), n. 43
United States v. Foster, 13 M.J. 789 (A.C.M.R. 1982) — § 2-6(A), n. 27
United States v. Foster, 14 M.J. 246 (C.M.A. 1982) — § 2-4(C), n. 38
United States v. Foster, 35 M.J. 700 (N.M.C.M.R. 1992) — § 5-10(D), n. 41; § 15-2(B)(3), n. 78
United States v. Foster, 40 M.J. 140 (C.M.A. 1994) — § 2-6, n. 15; § 6-1(C)(3), n. 162
United States v. Foster, 40 M.J. 552 (A.C.M.R. 1994) — § 17-9(A), n. 11
United States v. Foti, 12 C.M.A. 303, 30 C.M.R. 303 (1961) — § 7-3(A), n. 19
United States v. Fountain, 2 M.J. 1202 (N.M.C.M.R. 1976) — § 12-3(A), n. 36
United States v. Foust, 17 M.J. 85 (C.M.A. 1983) — § 5-3(A), n. 24
United States v. Foust, 25 M.J. 647 (A.C.M.R. 1987) — § 9-2(B)(1), n. 46
United States v. Fout, 3 C.M.A. 565, 13 C.M.R. 121 (1953) — § 2-2(C)(3), n. 37; § 6-1(B), n. 65; § 6-1(C), n. 94; § 13-3(F), n. 216; § 14-3(A)(2), n. 29
United States v. Fowle, 7 C.M.A. 349, 22 C.M.R. 139 (1956) — § 6-5(A), n. 9
United States v. Fowler, 6 M.J. 501 (A.F.C.M.R. 1978) — § 8-3(B)(1), n. 57
United States v. Fowler, 30 M.J. 1164 (A.C.M.R. 1990) — § 13-5(A), n. 5
United States v. Fox, 24 M.J. 110 (C.M.A. 1987) — § 16-6, n. 1; § 16-5(D)(3), n. 72
United States v. Fox, 31 M.J. 739 (A.F.C.M.R. 1990) — § 12-2(F)(4), nn. 68, 82
United States v. Fox, 32 M.J. 747 (A.F.C.M.R. 1990) — § 2-8(B), n. 16; § 2-8(D), n. 40; § 13-3(M), n. 282
United States v. Fox, 34 M.J. 99 (C.M.A. 1992) — § 2-8(B), nn. 21, 22
United States v. Foy, 30 M.J. 664 (A.F.C.M.R. 1990) — § 17-9(A), n. 25
United States v. Frage, 26 M.J. 924 (N.M.C.M.R. 1988) — § 6-1, n. 35
United States v. Franchia, 13 C.M.A. 315, 32 C.M.R. 315 (1962) — § 13-5(J), n. 77
United States v. Francis, 15 M.J. 424 (C.M.A. 1983) — § 15-15, n. 14; § 2-2(C)(3), nn. 39, 51, 53
United States v. Francis, 25 M.J. 614 (A.C.M.R. 1987) — § 7-2(A)(1), n. 29
United States v. Frangoules, 1 M.J. 467 (C.M.A. 1976) — § 14-3(D)(3), n. 144
United States v. Franklin, 4 M.J. 635 (A.F.C.M.R. 1977) — § 2-2(E)(1), n. 71
United States v. Frazier, 30 M.J. 1231 (A.C.M.R. 1990) — § 2-7(B), n. 24

TABLE OF CASES

United States v. Frazier, 34 M.J. 135 (C.M.A. 1992) — § 5-3(C)(6), n. 87
United States v. Frazier, 34 M.J. 194 (C.M.A. 1992) — § 2-5, n. 2
United States v. Frederick, 23 M.J. 561 (A.C.M.R. 1986) — § 14-3(B)(2), n. 77
United States v. Free, 14 C.M.R. 466 (N.B.R. 1953) — § 2-8(A), n. 3; § 2-8(B), n. 9
United States v. Freedman, 23 M.J. 820 (N.M.C.M.R. 1987) — § 6-4(B), nn. 10, 13; § 7-2(E), n. 104; § 7-2(A)(2), n. 30
United States v. Freeman, 23 M.J. 531 (A.C.M.R. 1986) — § 8-5, n. 5; § 13-3(C)(2), n. 73
United States v. Freeman, 24 M.J. 547 (A.C.M.R. 1987) — § 5-9(C), n. 18; § 5-9(D), nn. 38, 39
United States v. Freeman, 29 M.J. 865 (A.F.C.M.R. 1989) — § 16-5(D)(4), nn. 100, 102
United States v. Freeman, 28 M.J. 789 (N.M.C.M.R. 1989) — § 12-2(F)(4), nn. 70, 71
United States v. Freeman, 42 M.J. 239 (1995) — § 5-3(B), n. 40
United States v. French, 10 C.M.A. 171, 27 C.M.R. 245 (1959) — § 2-6(C), n. 35
United States v. French, 14 M.J. 510 (A.F.C.M.R. 1982) — § 5-4(A)(2), n. 15
United States v. French, 31 M.J. 57 (C.M.A. 1990) — § 6-1(C), n. 104
United States v. French, 38 M.J. 420 (C.M.A. 1993) — § 5-3, n. 1; § 5-4(B), n. 43
United States v. Frentz, 21 M.J. 813 (N.M.C.M.R. 1985) — § 7-2, n. 7
United States v. Fretwell, 11 C.M.A. 377, 29 C.M.R. 193 (1960) — § 3-3(C), nn. 23, 25; § 13-2(E), n. 45; § 13-3(G), n. 225
United States v. Friedman, 593 F.2d 109 (9th Cir. 1979) — § 10-4(B)(1), n. 32
United States v. Frierson, 24 M.J. 647 (A.C.M.R. 1987) — § 9-2(B)(1), n. 49
United States v. Frierson, 28 M.J. 501 (A.F.C.M.R. 1989) — § 16-11, n. 8
United States v. Fritz, 31 M.J. 661 (N.M.C.M.R. 1990) — § 2-2(C)(3), nn. 42, 46
United States v. Frost, 19 M.J. 509 (A.F.C.M.R. 1984) — § 4-11(B), n. 40
United States v. Frostell, 13 M.J. 680 (N.M.C.M.R. 1982) — § 13-3(E), n. 200; § 13-3(C)(2), n. 66
United States v. Frueh, 35 M.J. 550 (A.C.M.R. 1992) — § 15-2(B)(3), n. 85
United States v. Fruscella, 21 C.M.A. 26, 44 C.M.R. 80 (1971) — § 2-7(B), n. 25
United States v. Frye, 33 M.J. 1075 (A.C.M.R. 1992) — § 16-2(B), n. 14
United States v. Fuentes, 18 M.J. 41 (C.M.A. 1984) — § 15-13, n. 10
United States v. Funk, 29 M.J. 692 (A.C.M.R. 1989) — § 17-8(B)(3), n. 69
United States v. Fussell, 42 C.M.R. 723 (A.C.M.R. 1970) — § 15-14(D), n. 57
United States v. Gabrels, 33 M.J. 622 (A.F.C.M.R. 1991) — § 10-4(A)(4), n. 22
United States v. Gacioch, 33 M.J. 727 (N.M.C.M.R. 1991) — § 17-2(B)(2), n. 24
United States v. Gaither, 41 M.J. 774 (A.F.Ct.Crim.App. 1995) — § 5-9(E), n. 54
United States, Gale v.
United States v. Galinato, 28 M.J. 1049 (N.M.C.M.R. 1989) — § 15-4(A), n. 5; § 15-5, n. 3; § 8-3(B)(4), n. 100; § 15-2(B)(3), nn. 45, 48, 69, 99
United States v. Gallion, 36 M.J. 950 (A.C.M.R. 1993) — § 14-3(D)(4), nn. 145, 151
United States v. Galloway, 34 M.J. 1017 (A.C.M.R. 1992) — § 2-2(B), n. 10
United States v. Gambini, 10 M.J. 618 (A.F.C.M.R. 1980) — § 13-5(B), n. 24
United States v. Gamble, 27 M.J. 298 (C.M.A. 1988) — § 13-5(L), nn. 100, 102; § 15-14(B), n. 34
United States v. Gans, 23 M.J. 540 (A.C.M.R. 1986) — § 11-2(B)(1), n. 54
United States v. Gansemer, 38 M.J. 340 (C.M.A. 1993) — § 9-2(B)(1), n. 58
United States v. Garces, 32 M.J. 345 (C.M.A. 1991) — § 15-4(B), n. 11
United States, Garcia v.
United States v. Garcia, 15 M.J. 864 (A.C.M.R. 1983) — § 8-3(D), n. 166
United States v. Garcia, 18 M.J. 539 (A.C.M.R. 1984) — § 6-1(C), n. 94; § 13-3(F), n. 218
United States v. Garcia, 18 M.J. 716 (A.F.C.M.R. 1984) — § 16-5(D)(3), n. 75
United States v. Garcia, 21 M.J. 127 (C.M.A. 1985) — § 2-4(C), n. 37

TABLE OF CASES

United States v. Garcia, 24 M.J. 518 (A.F.C.M.R. 1987) — § 12-5, nn. 14, 18; § 17-4, n. 15
United States v. Garcia, 26 M.J. 844 (A.C.M.R. 1988) — § 15-10(B), n. 55
United States v. Garcia, 29 M.J. 721 (C.G.C.M.R. 1989) — § 14-3(D)(4), n. 145
United States v. Gardner, 22 M.J. 28 (C.M.A. 1986) — § 5-4(C), n. 56; § 11-2(E)(1), n. 106
United States v. Gardner, 29 M.J. 673 (A.F.C.M.R. 1989) — § 2-7(B), n. 13; § 17-9(A), n. 29
United States v. Gardner, 36 M.J. 543 (A.C.M.R. 1992) — § 6-1(C)(3), n. 165
United States v. Gardner, 41 M.J. 189 (C.M.A. 1994) — § 5-3(D)(1), n. 131
United States v. Garland, 39 M.J. 618 (A.C.M.R. 1994) — § 15-13, n. 6
United States v. Garner, 7 C.M.A. 578, 23 C.M.R. 42 (1957) — § 2-2(C)(3), n. 42
United States v. Garner, 34 M.J. 575 (A.C.M.R. 1992) — § 15-2(B)(3), n. 88
United States v. Garner, 39 M.J. 721 (N.M.C.M.R. 1993) — § 13-3(C)(2), nn. 51, 58; § 13-3(C)(3), n. 100
United States v. Garrett, 15 M.J. 601 (N.M.C.M.R. 1982) — § 5-3(C)(8), n. 110
United States v. Garrett, 17 M.J. 907 (A.F.C.M.R. 1984) — § 6-1(B)(2), n. 84
United States v. Garrett, 24 M.J. 413 (C.M.A. 1987) — § 16-10, n. 12; § 5-4(A)(3), n. 20; § 11-2(E)(1), n. 106
United States, Garries v.
United States v. Garries, 19 M.J. 845 (A.F.C.M.R. 1985) — § 13-5(K), n. 85; § 15-4(A), n. 7; § 17-21, n. 3; § 11-2(A)(3), nn. 21, 28
United States v. Garries, 22 M.J. 288 (C.M.A. 1986) — § 11-2(A)(3), nn. 28, 32; § 11-4, n. 5
United States v. Garvin, 26 M.J. 194 (C.M.A. 1988) — § 4-8(B), n. 12
United States v. Garwood, 16 M.J. 863 (N.M.C.M.R. 1983) — § 1-1, n. 4; § 13-3(N)(1), n. 305
United States v. Garwood, 20 M.J. 148 (C.M.A. 1985) — § 13-3(L), n. 280; § 13-3(M), nn. 284-286; § 15-3, n. 15
United States v. Gary, 44 C.M.R. 354 (A.C.M.R. 1970) — § 15-8, n. 2
United States v. Gaskins, 5 M.J. 772 (A.C.M.R. 1978) — § 5-9(B), n. 9
United States v. Gaspard, 35 M.J. 678 (A.C.M.R. 1992) — § 8-3(C)(4), n. 160
United States v. Gaston, 45 C.M.R. 837 (A.C.M.R. 1972) — § 15-16(B), n. 25
United States v. Gates, 36 M.J. 945 (A.C.M.R. 1993) — § 15-2(B)(3), n. 64
United States v. Gates, 40 M.J. 354 (C.M.A. 1994) — § 13-3(N)(4), n. 413
United States v. Gavitt, 37 M.J. 761 (A.C.M.R. 1993) — § 17-8(B), n. 12
United States v. Gay, 16 M.J. 586 (A.F.C.M.R. 1983) — § 16-3(A), n. 10
United States v. Gay, 24 M.J. 304 (C.M.A. 1987) — § 5-4(B), n. 45
United States v. Geary, 30 M.J. 855 (N.M.C.M.R. 1990) — § 2-6(C), n. 38
United States v. Gebhart, 32 M.J. 634 (A.C.M.R. 1991) — § 4-15(C), n. 15
United States v. Gebhart, 34 M.J. 189 (C.M.A. 1992) — § 4-15(C), n. 15
United States v. Geiss, 30 M.J. 678 (A.F.C.M.R. 1990) — § 13-5(C), n. 40
United States v. Genesee, 26 C.M.R. 845 (A.F.B.R. 1958) — § 4-13, n. 5
United States v. Gennosa, 11 M.J. 764 (N.M.C.M.R. 1981) — § 13-3(N)(5), n. 436
United States v. Gentile, 1 M.J. 69 (C.M.A. 1975) — § 15-2(A), n. 13
United States v. George, 14 M.J. 990 (N.M.C.M.R. 1982) — § 4-11(A), n. 34
United States v. Geraghty, 40 C.M.R. 499 (A.B.R. 1969) — § 8-3(D), n. 166
United States v. Gerard, 11 M.J. 440 (C.M.A. 1981) — § 13-5(L), n. 108; § 15-16(C), nn. 31, 33, 35
United States v. Gerdes, 27 M.J. 587 (A.F.C.M.R. 1988) — § 16-3(D), nn. 67, 69
United States v. Gerlach, 16 C.M.A. 383, 37 C.M.R. 3 (1966) — § 15-21, n. 13

TABLE OF CASES

United States v. Ghent, 21 M.J. 546 (A.F.C.M.R. 1985) — § 15-4(B), n. 12
United States v. Ghiglieri, 25 M.J. 687 (A.C.M.R. 1987) — § 4-5(A)(2); § 4-5(A)(2), n. 3; § 4-5(A)(4), n. 14
United States v. Giambra, 38 M.J. 240 (C.M.A. 1993) — § 15-23, n. 5; § 17-21, n. 8
United States v. Gibbs, 30 M.J. 1166 (A.C.M.R. 1990) — § 9-2(B), n. 37; § 17-9(A), n. 18
United States v. Gibson, 11 M.J. 434 (C.M.A. 1981) — § 6-1(C)(3), nn. 132, 165
United States v. Gibson, 17 M.J. 143 (C.M.A. 1984) — § 2-2(D), n. 67
United States v. Gibson, 29 M.J. 379 (C.M.A. 1990) — § 9-2(B)(1), n. 56
United States v. Gibson, 30 M.J. 1138 (A.F.C.M.R. 1990) — § 16-8(B), nn. 24, 25
United States v. Gifford, 16 M.J. 578 (A.C.M.R. 1983) — § 6-2(A), n. 2
United States v. Gilbert, 23 C.M.R. 914 (A.F.B.R. 1957) — § 2-2(C)(1), n. 25; § 2-2(C)(2), n. 30
United States v. Gilbert, 40 M.J. 652 (N.M.C.M.R. 1994) — § 15-2(B)(3), n. 55
United States v. Giles, 42 C.M.R. 880 (A.C.M.R. 1970) — § 11-3(B)(1), n. 32
United States v. Gill, 37 M.J. 501 (A.F.C.M.R. 1993) — § 5-4(B), n. 52; § 11-4, n. 5; § 16-2(D), n. 42; § 6-1(C)(3), n. 147
United States v. Gill, 40 M.J. 835 (A.F.C.M.R. 1994) — § 13-3(N)(3), n. 373; § 17-15(B), n. 33
United States v. Gillenwater, 43 M.J. 10 (1995) — § 15-14(B), n. 34
United States v. Gillespie, 3 M.J. 721 (A.C.M.R. 1977) — § 5-5, n. 5
United States, Gillete v.
United States v. Gillette, 35 M.J. 468 (C.M.A. 1992) — § 15-14(B), n. 45
United States v. Gilliam, 23 C.M.A. 4, 48 C.M.R. 260 (1974) — § 15-14(B), n. 45
United States v. Ginaitt, 43 C.M.R. 56 (C.M.A. 1970) — § 12-3(A), n. 12
United States v. Ginter, 35 M.J. 799 (N.M.C.M.R. 1992) — § 15-14(A), n. 10; § 15-14(C), n. 49
United States v. Ginyard, 16 C.M.A. 512, 37 C.M.R. 132 (1967) — § 4-16; § 4-8(C)(1), nn. 15, 16
United States v. Gipson, 25 M.J. 781 (A.C.M.R. 1988) — § 13-5(K), n. 85; § 15-4(A), n. 7; § 8-3(B)(4), n. 99
United States v. Giroux, 37 M.J. 553 (A.C.M.R. 1993) — § 13-3(C)(3), n. 159
United States v. Gittens, 36 M.J. 594 (A.F.C.M.R. 1992) — § 15-12(A), n. 12; § 15-14(B), n. 45
United States v. Gittens, 39 M.J. 328 (C.M.A. 1994) — § 15-12(A), n. 13; § 15-14(C), n. 51
United States v. Giusti, 22 M.J. 733 (C.G.C.M.R. 1986) — § 7-2(C), n. 80
United States v. Givens, 28 M.J. 888 (A.F.C.M.R. 1989) — § 13-3(C), n. 26; § 13-3(C)(3), nn. 159, 160, 165
United States v. Givens, 30 M.J. 294 (C.M.A. 1990) — § 13-3(C)(3), n. 159
United States v. Gladdis, 12 M.J. 1005 (A.C.M.R. 1982) — § 13-3(H), nn. 234, 240
United States v. Gladue, 4 M.J. 1 (C.M.A. 1977) — § 4-8(C)(2), n. 21
United States v. Glazier, 26 M.J. 268 (C.M.A. 1988) — § 9-2(B)(1), n. 39; § 16-5(D)(1), n. 61; § 16-5(D)(5), n. 124
United States v. Gleason, 39 M.J. 776 (A.C.M.R. 1994) — § 6-3(A), nn. 2, 10; § 6-5(B), nn. 24, 28; § 6-7, n. 18; § 6-8, n. 1
United States v. Gleason, 43 M.J. 69 (1995) — § 6-3(A), n. 4; § 6-5(B), nn. 26, 47, 48
United States v. Glenn, 20 M.J. 172 (C.M.A. 1985) — § 6-1(C)(3), n. 146
United States v. Glenn, 25 M.J. 278 (C.M.A. 1987) — § 15-10(B), n. 59; § 15-10(C)(2), nn. 91, 93
United States v. Glenn, 29 M.J. 696 (A.C.M.R. 1989) — § 13-3(B), nn. 15, 21; § 6-1(B)(2), n. 82

TABLE OF CASES

United States v. Gloria, 12 M.J. 518 (N.M.C.M.R. 1981) — § 15-2(F), n. 160
United States v. Glover, 15 M.J. 419 (C.M.A. 1983) — § 4-16, n. 17; § 8-1, n. 2
United States v. Gluch, 30 C.M.R. 534 (A.B.R. 1961) — § 15-4(C), n. 20
United States v. Gnibus, 21 M.J. 1 (C.M.A. 1985) — § 8-3(D), n. 162
United States v. Godfrey, 36 M.J. 629 (A.C.M.R. 1992) — § 17-8(B)(3), n. 73
United States v. Godreau, 31 M.J. 809 (A.F.C.M.R. 1990) — § 17-9(A), nn. 26, 27
United States v. Goetz, 17 M.J. 744 (A.C.M.R. 1983) — § 15-14(C), n. 51
United States v. Goffe, 15 C.M.A. 112, 35 C.M.R. 84 (1964) — § 15-4(B), n. 15
United States v. Goins, 2 M.J. 458 (A.C.M.R. 1975) — § 14-3(B)(2), n. 75
United States v. Goins, 20 M.J. 673 (A.F.C.M.R. 1985) — § 4-11(A), n. 15
United States, Goldberg v.
United States v. Goldsmith, 29 M.J. 979 (A.F.C.M.R. 1990) — § 5-4(B), n. 23; § 16-5(B), n. 9
United States v. Gomez, 15 M.J. 954 (A.C.M.R. 1983) — § 10-4(B)(5), n. 54
United States v. Gonda, 27 M.J. 636 (A.C.M.R. 1988) — § 13-3(C), n. 32; § 13-3(C)(3), n. 121
United States v. Gonzales, 12 M.J. 747 (A.F.C.M.R. 1981) — § 4-8(C)(2), n. 21
United States v. Gonzales, 13 M.J. 665 (A.F.C.M.R. 1982) — § 17-4(A), n. 40
United States v. Gonzales, 14 M.J. 501 (A.F.C.M.R. 1982) — § 15-21, n. 15
United States v. Gonzales, 19 M.J. 951 (A.F.C.M.R. 1985) — § 2-4(E), n. 49
United States v. Gonzales, 39 M.J. 459 (C.M.A. 1994) — § 11-2(A)(3), n. 21
United States v. Gonzales, 42 M.J. 469 (1995) — § 2-2(B), n. 10
United States v. Gonzalez, 16 M.J. 58 (C.M.A. 1983) — § 11-2(A)(4), nn. 42, 47
United States v. Good, 32 M.J. 105 (C.M.A. 1991) — § 5-4(B), nn. 23, 42
United States v. Good, 39 M.J. 615 (A.C.M.R. 1994) — § 4-14(B), n. 21; § 4-16, n. 14; § 17-21, n. 3
United States v. Goode, 1 M.J. 3 (C.M.A. 1975) — § 17-2(B)(3), n. 62; § 17-2(B)(4), nn. 91, 94, 95, 96
United States v. Gooden, 23 M.J. 721 (A.C.M.R. 1986) — § 9-2, n. 8; § 14-3(C), n. 130; § 17-9(A), n. 16
United States v. Gooden, 37 M.J. 1055 (N.M.C.M.R. 1993) — § 5-4(B), n. 43
United States v. Gooding, 18 C.M.A. 188, 39 C.M.R. 188 (1969) — § 13-5(G)(1), n. 38
United States v. Goodman, 3 M.J. 1 (C.M.A. 1977) — § 8-3(A), n. 6; § 12-2(H), n. 104
United States v. Goodman, 3 M.J. 1106 (N.C.M.R. 1977) — § 15-10(B), n. 53
United States v. Goodman, 33 M.J. 84 (C.M.A. 1991) — § 15-2(B)(3), n. 77; § 16-5(D)(4), n. 103
United States, Goodson v.
United States v. Goodwin, 21 M.J. 949 (A.F.C.M.R. 1986) — § 16-5(B), n. 25
United States v. Goodwin, 30 M.J. 989 (A.C.M.R. 1990) — § 16-9, n. 10
United States v. Goodwin, 33 M.J. 18 (C.M.A. 1991) — § 16-9, n. 10
United States v. Goodwin, 37 M.J. 606 (A.C.M.R. 1993) — § 2-4(C), n. 32
United States v. Goodyear, 14 M.J. 567 (N.M.C.M.R. 1982) — § 15-4(B), n. 14
United States v. Goosby, 36 M.J. 512 (A.F.C.M.R. 1992) — § 2-5, n. 2
United States v. Gordon, 1 C.M.A. 255, 2 C.M.R. 161 (1952) — § 6-4(C), n. 17; § 4-14(A)(2), n. 11
United States v. Gordon, 10 M.J. 31 (C.M.A. 1980) — § 3-8(B), n. 17; § 16-5(B), n. 15
United States v. Gordon, 31 M.J. 30 (C.M.A. 1990) — § 16-5(D)(1), nn. 51, 55
United States v. Gore, 14 M.J. 945 (A.C.M.R. 1982) — § 15-4(B), n. 11
United States v. Goree, 34 M.J. 1027 (N.M.C.M.R. 1992) — § 16-5(D)(5), n. 122
United States, Gori v.
United States v. Goudy, 32 M.J. 88 (C.M.A. 1991) — § 5-3(C)(6), nn. 86, 87

TABLE OF CASES

United States v. Gowadia, 34 M.J. 714 (A.C.M.R. 1992) — § 15-16(A), n. 13
United States v. Grace, 3 M.J. 369 (C.M.A. 1977) — § 15-14(A), n. 20
United States v. Grady, 15 M.J. 275 (C.M.A. 1983) — § 6-3(C), n. 19; § 6-5(A), n. 9; § 6-7, n. 7; § 15-13, n. 18; § 16-8(B), n. 12; § 16-9, n. 6
United States v. Grady, 30 M.J. 911 (A.C.M.R. 1990) — § 16-6, nn. 5, 21; § 16-5(D)(4), n. 100
United States v. Graf, 35 M.J. 450 (C.M.A. 1992) — § 8-3(A), n. 19
United States v. Graham, 14 C.M.R. 645 (A.F.B.R. 1954) — § 15-10(C)(2), n. 97; § 15-10(C)(3), n. 106
United States v. Graham, 1 M.J. 308 (C.M.A. 1976) — § 16-5(C), n. 34
United States v. Graham, 9 M.J. 556 (N.C.M.R. 1980) — § 2-5, n. 5; § 4-11(A), nn. 21, 35
United States v. Graham, 16 M.J. 460 (C.M.A. 1983) — § 2-2(D), n. 66
United States v. Graham, 37 M.J. 603 (A.C.M.R. 1993) — § 2-2(C)(3), n. 34
United States v. Granda, 29 M.J. 771 (A.C.M.R. 1989) — § 5-4(B), n. 50
United States v. Grandy, 9 C.M.A. 355, 26 C.M.R. 135 (1958) — § 7-2, n. 8
United States v. Grandy, 11 M.J. 270 (C.M.A. 1981) — § 15-13, n. 29; § 15-14(D), n. 56
United States v. Grant, 38 M.J. 684 (A.F.C.M.R. 1993) — § 15-4(A), n. 5
United States v. Grasha, 20 M.J. 220 (C.M.A. 1985) — § 6-1(C)(3), n. 147
United States v. Graves, 1 M.J. 50 (C.M.A. 1975) — § 15-2(D), n. 128; § 15-14(A), n. 3; § 15-24, n. 1
United States v. Graves, 12 M.J. 583 (A.F.C.M.R. 1981) — § 13-3(J), n. 260
United States v. Gravitt, 5 C.M.A. 249, 17 C.M.R. 249 (1954) — § 4-2, n. 4; § 13-5(C), n. 31; § 15-13, n. 3
United States v. Gray, 6 C.M.A. 615, 20 C.M.R. 331 (1956) — § 2-4(A), n. 4
United States v. Gray, 6 M.J. 972 (A.C.M.R. 1979) — § 13-3(N)(1), n. 310
United States v. Gray, 14 M.J. 816 (A.C.M.R. 1982) — § 13-5(H), n. 65; § 17-8(B), n. 27
United States v. Gray, 21 M.J. 1020 (N.M.C.M.R. 1986) — § 13-3(C)(3), n. 122
United States v. Gray, 26 M.J. 16 (C.M.A. 1988) — § 13-3(C)(3), n. 108
United States v. Gray, 32 M.J. 730 (A.C.M.R. 1991) — § 17-14, n. 3; § 11-2(A)(3), n. 28
United States v. Gray, 37 M.J. 730 (A.C.M.R. 1992) — § 15-3, n. 16; § 15-10(B), n. 51; § 16-8(B), n. 21; § 11-2(A)(3), n. 21; § 15-10(C)(3), n. 118
United States v. Gray, 37 M.J. 751 (A.C.M.R. 1993) — § 15-16(B), n. 18
United States v. Gray, 37 M.J. 1035 (A.C.M.R. 1993) — § 13-3(C)(2), n. 81
United States v. Gray, 40 M.J. 77 (C.M.A. 1994) — § 15-12(A), n. 7
United States v. Green, 47 C.M.R. 727 (A.F.C.M.R. 1973) — § 2-4(E), n. 49
United States v. Green, 1 M.J. 453 (C.M.A. 1976) — § 9-2(D), n. 84; § 9-3, n. 7; § 14-3(C), nn. 122, 128, 129
United States v. Green, 3 M.J. 320 (C.M.A. 1977) — § 13-5(G)(1), n. 38
United States v. Green, 14 M.J. 461 (C.M.A. 1983) — § 4-12(B), n. 14
United States v. Green, 21 M.J. 633 (A.C.M.R. 1985) — § 16-5(D)(1), nn. 56, 57; § 16-5(D)(5), n. 116
United States v. Green, 22 M.J. 711 (A.C.M.R. 1986) — § 2-4(A), n. 13
United States v. Green, 33 M.J. 918 (A.C.M.R. 1991) — § 2-6(A), n. 24
United States v. Green, 37 M.J. 380 (C.M.A. 1993) — § 7-3(A), n. 19; § 13-3(M), n. 284
United States v. Green, 39 M.J. 606 (A.C.M.R. 1994) — § 2-6(A), nn. 17, 25
United States v. Greene, 8 M.J. 796 (N.C.M.R. 1980) — § 2-4(F), n. 53
United States v. Greene, 34 M.J. 713 (A.C.M.R. 1992) — § 2-6(A), n. 18
United States v. Greene, 36 M.J. 274 (C.M.A. 1993) — § 15-10(C)(3), n. 118
United States v. Greene, 41 M.J. 57 (C.M.A. 1994) — § 15-14(B), n. 41
United States v. Greenwald, 37 M.J. 537 (A.C.M.R. 1993) — § 8-3(B)(3), n. 76

TABLE OF CASES

United States v. Greenwalt, 6 C.M.A. 569, 20 C.M.R. 285 (1955) — § 7-3, n. 3; § 7-3(A), n. 19
United States v. Greenwell, 12 C.M.A. 560, 31 C.M.R. 146 (1961) — § 8-3(D), n. 166
United States v. Greer, 41 C.M.R. 582 (1969) — § 15-4(D), n. 27
United States v. Greer, 21 M.J. 338 (C.M.A. 1986) — § 13-3(C), n. 28
United States v. Gregorio, 32 M.J. 401 (C.M.A. 1991) — § 5-4(A)(2), n. 14
United States v. Gregory, 21 M.J. 952 (A.C.M.R. 1986) — § 5-10(D), n. 38
United States v. Gregory, 31 M.J. 236 (C.M.A. 1990) — § 16-5(D)(4), n. 106
United States v. Grider, 21 M.J. 603 (A.C.M.R. 1985) — § 16-12, n. 15
United States v. Griego, 10 M.J. 385 (C.M.A. 1981) — § 14-3(C), n. 133
United States v. Griffin, 13 C.M.A. 213, 32 C.M.R. 213 (1962) — § 4-14(B), n. 21
United States v. Griffin, 1 M.J. 884 (A.F.C.M.R. 1976) — § 7-2(E), n. 112; § 12-2(H), n. 109
United States v. Griffin, 8 M.J. 66 (C.M.A. 1979) — § 17-9(B), n. 38
United States v. Griffin, 17 M.J. 698 (A.C.M.R. 1983) — § 17-4, n. 32
United States v. Griffin, 16 M.J. 836 (N.M.C.M.R. 1983) — § 12-2(F)(2), n. 55
United States v. Griffin, 18 M.J. 707 (A.C.M.R. 1984) — § 12-3(A), nn. 33, 35
United States v. Griffin, 25 M.J. 423 (C.M.A. 1988) — § 16-9, n. 10
United States v. Griffin, 41 M.J. 607 (Army Ct.Crim.App. 1994) — § 6-7, n. 2
United States v. Griffith, 27 M.J. 42 (C.M.A. 1988) — § 15-4(C), n. 18; § 17-3, n. 11; § 17-3(B), nn. 30, 40, 41
United States v. Grimm, 6 M.J. 890 (A.C.M.R. 1979) — § 7-2(A)(1), nn. 27, 28; § 7-2(A)(2), n. 36
United States v. Grinter, 28 M.J. 840 (A.F.C.M.R. 1989) — § 17-8(B), n. 17
United States v. Grittman, 16 C.M.R. 328 (A.B.R. 1954) — § 15-10(B), n. 49
United States v. Groce, 3 M.J. 369 (C.M.A. 1977) — § 15-2(E), n. 158
United States v. Groh, 24 M.J. 767 (A.F.C.M.R. 1987) — § 5-4(B), n. 50
United States v. Grom, 21 M.J. 53 (C.M.A. 1985) — § 13-3(C)(1), n. 39
United States v. Grooters, 35 M.J. 659 (A.C.M.R. 1992) — § 5-4(B), n. 50
United States v. Groshong, 14 M.J. 186 (C.M.A. 1982) — § 13-3(C)(2), n. 74
United States v. Grosskreutz, 5 M.J. 344 (C.M.A. 1978) — § 5-3(D)(1), n. 129
United States v. Grostefon, 12 M.J. 431 (C.M.A. 1982) — § 17-14, nn. 10, 11; § 17-15(B), n. 19
United States v. Groveman, 25 M.J. 796 (A.F.C.M.R. 1988) — § 16-5(D)(3), n. 72
United States v. Grover, 10 C.M.A. 91, 27 C.M.R. 165 (1958) — § 2-2(E)(5), n. 88
United States v. Grover-Madrill, 5 M.J. 768 (A.C.M.R. 1978) — § 14-3(C), n. 124
United States v. Groves, 30 M.J. 811 (A.C.M.R. 1990) — § 17-8(B)(1), n. 54
United States v. Grow, 3 C.M.A. 77, 11 C.M.R. 77 (1953) — § 2-4(E), n. 48; § 17-15(B), nn. 7, 8
United States v. Grubb, 34 M.J. 532 (A.F.C.M.R. 1991) — § 6-1(C)(3), nn. 146, 147
United States v. Grubbs, 13 M.J. 594 (A.F.C.M.R. 1982) — § 6-1(C)(2), n. 126; § 13-5(G)(3), n. 50
United States v. Grunden, 2 M.J. 116 (C.M.A. 1977) — § 15-3, n. 14
United States v. Gruninger, 30 M.J. 1142 (A.F.C.M.R. 1990) — § 16-8(B), n. 15
United States v. Guaglione, 27 M.J. 268 (C.M.A. 1988) — § 2-5, n. 3
United States v. Gudaitis, 18 M.J. 816 (A.F.C.M.R. 1984) — § 2-2(C)(3), n. 44
United States v. Gudel, 17 M.J. 1075 (A.F.C.M.R. 1984) — § 16-4(B), n. 21
United States v. Guerrero, 25 M.J. 829 (A.C.M.R. 1988) — § 5-10(D), n. 39; § 15-2(B)(3), n. 81
United States v. Guerrero, 31 M.J. 692 (N.M.C.M.R. 1990) — § 2-6(A), n. 17
United States v. Guerrero, 33 M.J. 295 (C.M.A. 1991) — § 2-6(B), n. 29

TABLE OF CASES

United States v. Guerro, 10 M.J. 52 (C.M.A. 1980) — § 3-8(B), n. 17
United States v. Guidry, 19 M.J. 984 (A.F.C.M.R. 1985) — § 8-2(A), nn. 1, 5; § 4-14(A)(1), n. 7
United States v. Guillory, 36 M.J. 952 (A.C.M.R. 1993) — § 14-3(A)(3), n. 31
United States v. Guitard, 28 M.J. 952 (N.M.C.M.R. 1989) — § 11-2(A)(3), n. 27
United States v. Gunter, 29 M.J. 140 (C.M.A. 1989) — § 16-5(D)(4), n. 99
United States v. Gunter, 37 M.J. 781 (A.C.M.R. 1993) — § 14-3(D)(4), n. 148
United States v. Guron, 37 M.J. 942 (A.F.C.M.R. 1993) — § 5-4(B), n. 44; § 15-16(A), n. 7
United States v. Gussen, 33 M.J. 736 (A.C.M.R. 1991) — § 2-4(D), n. 41
United States v. Guthrie, 25 M.J. 808 (A.C.M.R 1988) — § 15-10(B), n. 60; § 15-10(C)(2), n. 93
United States v. Gutierrez, 11 M.J. 122 (C.M.A. 1981) — § 16-9, n. 4; § 17-8(B)(3), n. 23
United States v. Guzman, 3 M.J. 740 (N.C.M.R. 1977) — § 2-2(E)(3), n. 81
United States v. Ha, 26 M.J. 838 (A.C.M.R. 1, 26
United States v. Hagan, 24 M.J. 571 (N.M.C.M.R. 1987) — § 2-7(C), nn. 39, 40
United States, Hagarty v.
United States v. Hagen, 25 M.J. 78 (C.M.A. 1987) — § 6-1, n. 15; § 6-4(C), n. 18; § 6-4(E), n. 28; § 13-3(M), nn. 282, 287, 288; § 11-2(A)(3), nn. 21, 28
United States v. Haggard, 29 M.J. 905 (A.C.M.R. 1989) — § 16-11, n. 8
United States v. Hagy, 12 M.J. 739 (A.F.C.M.R. 1981) — § 9-3, n. 8; § 16-5(B), n. 9
United States v. Haire, 40 M.J. 530 (C.G.C.M.R. 1994) — § 17-8(B)(3), n. 77
United States v. Hairston, 15 M.J. 892 (A.C.M.R. 1983) — § 13-3(E), n. 206
United States v. Halcomb, 25 M.J. 750 (N.M.C.M.R. 1987) — § 17-11, n. 6
United States v. Hall, 17 C.M.A. 88, 37 C.M.R. 352 (1967) — § 4-5(B), n. 22
United States v. Hall, 26 M.J. 739 (N.M.C.M.R. 1988) — § 14-3(C), n. 128
United States v. Hall, 29 M.J. 786 (A.C.M.R. 1989) — § 15-2(A), n. 5; § 15-2(C), n. 125; § 16-8(B), n. 16; § 16-5(D)(1), nn. 55, 56; § 16-5(D)(2), n. 70; § 16-5(D)(5), nn. 116, 117
United States v. Hall, 34 M.J. 695 (A.C.M.R. 1991) — § 13-3(N)(4), n. 413
United States v. Hall, 36 M.J. 770 (N.M.C.M.R. 1992) — § 3-3(C), n. 27
United States v. Hall. 36 M.J. 1043 (N.M.C.M.R. 1993) — § 6-5(B), n. 29
United States v. Hall, 39 M.J. 593 (A.C.M.R. 1994) — § 17-8(B), nn. 12, 22
United States v. Hallum, 31 M.J. 254 (C.M.A. 1990) — § 16-5(D)(5), n. 122
United States v. Hallums, 26 M.J. 838 (A.C.M.R. 1988) — § 17-2(B)(3), nn. 87, 89
United States v. Halper, 490 U.S. 435 (1989) — § 13-3(G), n. 226
United States v. Haltiwanger, 50 C.M.R. 255 (A.F.C.M.R. 1975) — § 6-1(C)(3), n. 137
United States v. Hamilton, 27 M.J. 628 (A.F.C.M.R. 1988) — § 10-4(B)(5), n. 62
United States v. Hamilton, 36 M.J. 723 (A.C.M.R. 1992) — § 3-3(C), nn. 25, 27; § 3-8(B), n. 5; § 14-3(F), n. 191
United States v. Hamilton, 36 M.J. 927 (A.F.C.M.R. 1993) — § 11-3(B)(1), n. 31; § 11-3(B)(2), n. 41
United States v. Hamilton, 41 M.J. 22 (C.M.A. 1994) — § 15-2(E), n. 152; § 15-10(B), n. 56
United States v. Hamilton, 41 M.J. 32 (C.M.A. 1994) — § 6-3(A), n. 3; § 6-3(C), n. 16; § 6-4(C), n. 18; § 6-7, nn. 1, 11
United States v. Hamm, 36 C.M.R. 656 (A.B.R. 1966) — § 4-8(B), n. 14
United States v. Hammond, 17 M.J. 218 (C.M.A. 1984) — § 16-5(D)(3), n. 72
United States v. Hammork, 13 C.M.R. 385 (A.B.R. 1953) — § 4-14(A)(2), n. 13
United States v. Hampton, 50 C.M.R. 531 (N.C.M.R. 1975) — § 8-3(B)(4), n. 98
United States v. Hampton, 7 M.J. 284 (C.M.A. 1979) — § 11-2(A)(1), nn. 6, 7
United States v. Hampton, 33 M.J. 21 (C.M.A. 1991) — § 11-2(A)(2), n. 15

TABLE OF CASES

United States v. Hampton, 40 M.J. 457 (C.M.A. 1994) — § 16-8(B), n. 19
United States v. Hance, 10 M.J. 622 (A.C.M.R. 1980) — § 15-16(B), n. 26
United States v. Hancock, 12 M.J. 685 (A.C.M.R. 1981) — § 16-5(C), n. 34
United States v. Hancock, 38 M.J. 672 (A.F.C.M.R. 1993) — § 6-1(C)(3), n. 161; § 16-5(D)(3), n. 72
United States v. Handy, 14 M.J. 202 (C.M.A. 1982) — § 4-8(A), n. 8
United States v. Handy, 26 M.J. 767 (C.G.C.M.R. 1988) — § 16-3(C), n. 50
United States v. Hanes, 21 M.J. 647 (A.C.M.R. 1985) — § 16-5(C), nn. 31, 36
United States v. Hanes, 34 M.J. 1168 (N.M.C.M.R. 1992) — § 5-9(D), n. 43
United States v. Hanna, 2 M.J. 69 (C.M.A. 1976) — § 5-4(B), n. 28
United States v. Hannan, 17 M.J. 115 (C.M.A. 1984) — § 16-9, n. 6
United States v. Hannon, 19 M.J. 726 (N.M.C.M.R. 1984) — § 12-3, n. 4
United States v. Hansen, 36 M.J. 599 (A.F.C.M.R. 1992) — § 15-2(B)(3), n. 76
United States v. Hanson, 24 M.J. 377 (C.M.A. 1987) — § 8-3(B)(2), n. 70; § 8-3(B)(3), n. 87; § 12-2(F)(1), n. 46; § 12-2(F)(2), n. 53; § 14-3(B)(2), n. 82
United States v. Hanson, 39 M.J. 610 (A.C.M.R. 1994) — § 17-21, n. 3; § 13-5(G)(2), nn. 45, 49
United States v. Happel, 5 M.J. 908 (A.C.M.R. 1978) — § 1-3(D)(2), n. 22
United States v. Harclerode, 17 M.J. 981 (A.C.M.R. 1984) — § 13-3(J), n. 255; § 14-3(B)(2), n. 77
United States v. Harcrow, 9 M.J. 669 (N.C.M.R. 1980) — § 8-3(B)(3), nn. 75, 77
United States v. Harden, 14 M.J. 598 (A.F.C.M.R. 1982) — § 17-15(B), n. 32
United States v. Harden, 18 M.J. 81 (C.M.A. 1984) — § 5-4(A)(1), n. 7
United States v. Hardin, 7 M.J. 399 (C.M.A. 1979) — § 4-11(A), n. 14; § 7-3, nn. 4, 5
United States v. Hardin, 29 M.J. 801 (C.G.C.M.R. 1989) — § 17-15(B), n. 32
United States v. Hardy, 4 M.J. 20 (C.M.A. 1977) — § 6-4(C), n. 20; § 8-5, nn. 4, 6, 10
United States v. Hardy, 21 M.J. 198 (C.M.A. 1986) — § 16-5(C), n. 50
United States v. Hardy, 30 M.J. 757 (A.C.M.R. 1990) — § 15-2(D), n. 128; § 15-12(B), n. 16
United States v. Hargrove, 25 M.J. 68 (C.M.A. 1987) — § 15-16(B), nn. 20, 22
United States v. Hargrove, 33 M.J. 515 (A.F.C.M.R. 1991) — § 11-2(A)(3), n. 28
United States v. Harmon, 29 M.J. 732 (A.F.C.M.R. 1989) — § 17-4, n. 34
United States v. Harmon, 40 M.J. 107 (C.M.A. 1994) — § 16-6, n. 17; § 11-2(A)(1), n. 8
United States v. Harper, 22 M.J. 157 (C.M.A. 1986) — § 2-6(A), n. 17; § 15-20, n. 21
United States v. Harper, 25 M.J. 895 (A.C.M.R. 1988) — § 17-4, n. 32
United States v. Harper, 32 M.J. 620 (A.C.M.R. 1991) — § 2-7(C), nn. 35, 40
United States v. Harrel, 17 M.J. 675 (A.C.M.R. 1983) — § 15-2(B)(1), n. 21
United States v. Harrington, 23 M.J. 788 (A.C.M.R. 1987) — § 4-14(A)(1), n. 7
United States v. Harris, 1 C.M.A. 430, 4 C.M.R. 22 (1952) — § 15-21, n. 2
United States v. Harris, 5 M.J. 44 (C.M.A. 1978) — § 5-3(C)(3), n. 74; § 5-3(D)(1), n. 124
United States v. Harris, 8 M.J. 52 (C.M.A. 1979) — § 13-3(N)(1), n. 329
United States v. Harris, 10 M.J. 276 (C.M.A. 1981) — § 17-8(B), n. 29
United States v. Harris, 13 M.J. 288 (C.M.A. 1982) — § 15-10(A), n. 29; § 15-10(B), n. 55; § 15-10(C), n. 80; § 15-10(C)(2), n. 93
United States v. Harris, 13 M.J. 653 (N.M.C.M.R. 1982) — § 16-6, n. 9
United States v. Harris, 16 M.J. 562 (A.C.M.R. 1983) — § 5-4(B), n. 50
United States v. Harris, 19 M.J. 331 (C.M.A. 1985) — § 16-3(D), n. 64
United States v. Harris, 20 M.J. 795 (N.M.C.M.R. 1985) — § 13-2(G)(2), nn. 88, 109; § 13-3(C)(3), n. 158
United States v. Harris, 24 M.J. 622 (A.C.M.R. 1987) — § 11-2(A)(2), n. 18; § 11-2(E)(3), nn. 137, 147

TABLE OF CASES

United States v. Harris, 25 M.J. 281 (C.M.A. 1987) — § 15-16(A), n. 9
United States v. Harris, 26 M.J. 729 (A.C.M.R. 1988) — § 16-9, n. 10; § 14-3(B)(1), n. 59
United States v. Harris, 27 M.J. 681 (A.C.M.R. 1988) — § 2-6(C), n. 38
United States v. Harris, 29 M.J. 169 (C.M.A. 1989) — § 5-7, nn. 4-6
United States v. Harris, 30 M.J. 580 (A.C.M.R. 1990) — § 15-2(B)(3), n. 85
United States v. Harris, 30 M.J. 1150 (A.C.M.R. 1990) — § 16-9, n. 5
United States v. Harris, 34 M.J. 297 (C.M.A. 1992) — § 15-2(B)(3), n. 79
United States v. Harris, 36 M.J. 936 (A.C.M.R. 1993) — § 15-2(B)(3), n. 68
United States v. Harris, 41 M.J. 433 (1995) — § 2-7(B), n. 24
United States v. Harris, 43 M.J. 652 (Army Ct.Crim.App. 1995) — § 17-8(B)(3), n. 77
United States, Harrison v.
United States v. Harrison, 16 C.M.A. 484, 37 C.M.R. 104 (1967) — § 17-2(B)(3), n. 70
United States v. Harrison, 4 M.J. 332 (C.M.A. 1978) — § 6-1(C)(3), n. 133
United States v. Harrison, 22 M.J. 535 (N.M.C.M.R. 1986) — § 13-3(C)(3), n. 108
United States v. Harrison, 23 M.J. 907 (N.M.C.M.R. 1987) — § 7-3(A), n. 12; § 7-3(B), n. 30
United States v. Harriss, 347 U.S. 612 (1954) — § 13-3(N)(2), nn. 341, 347, 351
United States v. Harrod, 20 M.J. 777 (A.C.M.R. 1985) — § 16-4(A), n. 3
United States v. Harry, 25 M.J. 513 (A.F.C.M.R. 1987) — § 4-8(C)(5), n. 56
United States v. Hart, 27 M.J. 839 (A.C.M.R. 1989) — § 10-4(A)(4), nn. 20-22
United States v. Hart, 30 M.J. 1176 (C.M.A. 1990) — § 2-5, n. 10
United States v. Hart, 32 M.J. 101 (C.M.A. 1991) — § 6-1(C)(2), n. 125
United States v. Hartsock, 14 M.J. 837 (A.C.M.R. 1982) — § 5-4(B), n. 44
United States v. Hartwig, 39 M.J. 125 (C.M.A. 1994) — § 2-5, n. 2; § 13-3(N)(3), n. 384
United States v. Harvey, 12 M.J. 626 (N.M.C.M.R. 1981) — § 16-11, n. 10
United States v. Harvey, 23 M.J. 280 (C.M.A. 1987) — § 13-3(C)(2), n. 80
United States v. Harvey, 37 M.J. 140 (C.M.A. 1993) — § 5-4(B), nn. 37, 42
United States v. Haskins, 11 C.M.A. 365, 29 C.M.R. 181 (1960) — § 5-4(A)(1), n. 10
United States v. Hasting, 461 U.S. 499 (1983) — § 7-2(E), n. 104
United States v. Haston, 21 M.J. 559 (A.C.M.R. 1985) — § 15-2(B)(3), nn. 54, 72, 76
United States v. Haston, 24 M.J. 377 (C.M.A. 1987) — § 15-2(B)(3), nn. 96-99
United States v. Hatfield, 43 M.J. 662 (N.M.Ct.Crim.App. 1995) — § 13-3(C)(2), n. 96
United States v. Hatley, 14 M.J. 890 (N.M.C.M.R. 1982) — § 4-9, n. 3
United States v. Havens, 444 U.S. 962 (1980) — § 5-3(F), n. 25
United States v. Hawkins, 6 C.M.A. 135, 19 C.M.R. 261, 268 (1955) — § 11-2(B)(1), n. 57
United States v. Hawkins, 2 M.J. 23 (C.M.A. 1976) — § 16-6, n. 5
United States v. Hawkins, 24 M.J. 257 (C.M.A. 1987) — § 4-15(A), n. 7; § 17-2(B)(4), n. 92
United States v. Hawkins, 172 24 M.J. 257 (C.M.A. 1987) — § 8-3(D), n. 172
United States v. Hawkins, 30 M.J. 682 (A.F.C.M.R. 1990) — § 13-3(N)(3), n. 405
United States v. Hawkins, 34 M.J. 991 (A.C.M.R. 1992) — § 15-2(B)(3), n. 88
United States v. Hawkins, 37 M.J. 718 (A.F.C.M.R. 1993) — § 17-15(B), n. 33
United States v. Hawks, 19 M.J. 736 (A.F.C.M.R. 1984) — § 15-10(B), n. 70; § 15-14(A), n. 18; § 15-10(C)(2), n. 91
United States v. Hawley, 30 M.J. 1247 (A.C.M.R. 1990) — § 13-3(A), n. 4
United States v. Hawthorne, 22 C.M.R. 83 (C.M.A. 1956) — § 6-4(A), n. 8
United States v. Hay, 3 M.J. 654 (A.C.M.R. 1977) — § 5-4(A)(1), n. 3
United States v. Hayden, 17 M.J. 749 (A.C.M.R. 1984) — § 15-10(A), n. 34
United States v. Haye, 29 M.J. 213 (C.M.A. 1989) — § 6-1(C)(1), nn. 105, 111-114; § 13-5(G)(2), nn. 43, 46

TABLE OF CASES

United States v. Hayes, 9 M.J. 825 (N.C.M.R. 1980) — § 14-3(G), n. 196
United States v. Hayes, 24 M.J. 786 (A.C.M.R. 1987) — § 7-3, n. 2; § 7-3(B), n. 27; § 15-7, n. 4
United States v. Hayes, 37 M.J. 769 (A.C.M.R. 1993) — § 13-3(C)(3), n. 121
United States v. Haynes, 28 M.J. 881 (A.F.C.M.R. 1989) — § 17-8(B)(3), n. 76
United States v. Haynes, 29 M.J. 610 (A.C.M.R. 1989) — § 14-3(D)(5), n. 166
United States v. Haywood, 6 M.J. 604 (A.C.M.R. 1978) — § 13-3(J), n. 261; § 16-2(D), n. 42
United States v. Haywood, 19 M.J. 675 (A.F.C.M.R. 1984) — § 16-9, n. 12
United States v. Healy, 39 C.M.R. 636 (A.B.R. 1968) — § 6-1, n. 18; § 6-1(C)(1), n. 107
United States v. Heaney, 9 C.M.A. 6, 25 C.M.R. 268 (1958) — § 7-3(A), n. 22
United States v. Heard, 3 M.J. 14 (C.M.A. 1977) — § 5-8(B), n. 27; § 5-9(A), n. 5; § 5-9(B), n. 9; § 5-9(D), n. 43; § 13-5(B), nn. 21, 22
United States v. Heath, 39 M.J. 1101 (C.G.C.M.R. 1994) — § 15-13, n. 11; § 16-5(B), n. 14; § 16-8(B), n. 25
United States v. Hebert, 32 M.J. 707 (A.C.M.R. 1991) — § 15-2(C), n. 120
United States v. Hecker, 42 M.J. 640 (A.F.Ct.Crim.App. 1995) — § 2-4(C), n. 32
United States v. Hedlund, 2 M.J. 11 (C.M.A. 1976) — § 4-11(A), nn. 10, 11
United States v. Hefner, 29 M.J. 1022 (A.C.M.R. 1990) — § 16-5(D)(4), n. 100
United States v. Heimer, 34 M.J. 541 (A.F.C.M.R. 1991) — § 15-16(B), n. 17
United States v. Hein, 23 M.J. 610 (A.F.C.M.R. 1986) — § 14-3(B)(2), n. 71
United States v. Heinel, 9 C.M.A. 259, 26 C.M.R. 39 (1958) — § 10-4(B)(5), n. 50
United States v. Heirs, 29 M.J. 68 (C.M.A. 1989) — § 17-8(B)(3), n. 74
United States v. Helm, 21 C.M.R. 357 (A.B.R. 1956) — § 15-14(A), n. 12
United States v. Helweg, 32 M.J. 129 (C.M.A. 1991) — § 13-2(E), n. 48; § 13-5(L), n. 107
United States v. Hemingway, 22 M.J. 939 (A.F.C.M.R. 1986) — § 16-11, n. 1
United States v. Hemingway, 36 M.J. 349 (C.M.A. 1993) — § 14-3(D)(3), nn. 140, 144
United States v. Henderson, 1 M.J. 421 (C.M.A. 1976) — § 13-3(C)(2), n. 65
United States v. Henderson, 7 M.J. 817 (N.C.M.R. 1979) — § 3-8(B), n. 8
United States v. Henderson, 11 M.J. 395 (C.M.A. 1981) — § 16-9, n. 4
United States v. Henderson, 21 M.J. 853 (A.C.M.R. 1986) — § 16-11, n. 3
United States v. Henderson, 476 U.S. 321 (1986) — § 13-3(C)(3), n. 158
United States v. Henderson, 23 M.J. 860 (A.C.M.R. 1987) — § 4-11(B), n. 42
United States v. Henderson, 29 M.J. 221 (C.M.A. 1989) — § 16-9, n. 10
United States v. Henderson, 32 M.J. 941 (N.M.C.M.R. 1991) — § 2-6(B), n. 30
United States v. Henderson, 34 M.J. 174 (C.M.A. 1992) — § 13-3(N)(4), n. 413
United States v. Hendon, 6 M.J. 171 (C.M.A. 1970) — § 15-16(B), n. 18
United States v. Hendrickson, 16 M.J. 62 (C.M.A. 1983) — § 13-3(J), n. 266
United States v. Hennis, 40 M.J. 865 (A.F.C.M.R. 1994) — § 15-2(B)(3), n. 75
United States v. Henriques, 32 M.J. 832 (N.M.C.M.R. 1991) — § 15-2(B)(3), n. 74
United States v. Henry, 50 C.M.R. 685 (A.F.C.M.R. 1975) — § 7-3(B), nn. 28, 29; § 13-5(D), n. 42
United States v. Henry, 444 U.S. 824 (1980) — § 5-4(B), n. 30
United States v. Henry, 37 M.J. 968 (A.C.M.R. 1993) — § 17-2(B)(3), n. 76
United States v. Henry, 40 M.J. 722 (N.M.C.M.R. 1994) — § 17-11, n. 1
United States v. Henry, 42 M.J. 231 (1995) — § 13-3(M), n. 284; § 15-2(B)(2), n. 27; § 17-15(B), n. 33
United States v. Henry, 42 M.J. 593 (Army Ct. Crim. App. 1995) — § 1-3(D)(2)
United States v. Hensler, 40 M.J. 892 (N.M.C.M.R. 1994) — § 13-3(D), n. 183
United States v. Herd, 29 M.J. 702 (A.C.M.R. 1989) — § 16-2, n. 3; § 15-2(B)(3), n. 53
United States v. Hernandez, 3 M.J. 916 (A.C.M.R. 1977) — § 4-14(A)(2), n. 13

TABLE OF CASES

United States v. Hernandez, 779 F.2d 456 (8th Cir. 1985) — § 13-3(M), n. 296
United States v. Hernandez, 33 M.J. 145 (C.M.A. 1991) — § 17-16(B), n. 11
United States v. Herod, 21 M.J. 762 (A.F.C.M.R. 1986) — § 8-3(D), n. 162; § 15-2(B)(2), n. 29
United States v. Heroit, 21 M.J. 11 (C.M.A. 1985) — § 15-10(A), nn. 31, 32; § 15-10(B), n. 52
United States v. Herrin, 32 M.J. 983 (A.C.M.R. 1991) — § 5-10(C), n. 17
United States v. Herring, 20 M.J. 1002 (A.F.C.M.R. 1985) — § 4-11(A), n. 24
United States v. Herrington, 33 C.M.R. 814 (A.F.B.R. 1963) — § 4-12(A), n. 5
United States v. Herrington, 2 M.J. 807 (A.C.M.R. 1976) — § 13-3(C)(2), n. 78
United States v. Herron, 39 M.J. 860 (N.M.C.M.R. 1994) — § 2-6(A), n. 17
United States v. Hershey, 20 M.J. 433 (C.M.A. 1985) — § 15-3, nn. 1, 7, 13
United States v. Heyward, 22 M.J. 35 (C.M.R. 1986) — § 2-4(E), n. 46; § 5-4(A)(2), n. 16
United States v. Hiatt, 27 M.J. 818 (A.C.M.R. 1988) — § 6-1(C)(2), nn. 124, 131
United States v. Hicks, 26 M.J. 935 (A.C.M.R. 1988) — § 16-3(D), n. 57; § 17-9(A), n. 19
United States v. Higa, 12 M.J. 1008 (A.C.M.R. 1982) — § 14-4, n. 1; § 9-2(B)(1), n. 55
United States v. Higdon, 2 M.J. 445 (A.C.M.R. 1975) — § 15-13, n. 17; § 16-8(B), n. 12
United States v. Higerd, 26 M.J. 848 (A.C.M.R. 1988) — § 15-15, n. 27
United States v. Higgins, 27 M.J. 150 (C.M.A. 1988) — § 13-3(C)(3), n. 165
United States v. Hightower, 5 C.M.A. 385, 18 C.M.R. 9 (1955) — § 15-20, n. 14
United States v. Hilbert, 23 M.J. 755 (A.C.M.R. 1986) — § 17-15(B), n. 27
United States v. Hill, 45 C.M.R. 904 (N.C.M.R. 1972) — § 15-10(A), n. 20
United States v. Hill, 2 M.J. 950 (A.C.M.R. 1976) — § 13-3(C)(2), n. 73
United States v. Hill, 26 M.J. 836 (A.C.M.R. 1988) — § 5-10(D), n. 32; § 16-5(A), n. 3
United States v. Hill, 27 M.J. 293 (C.M.A. 1988) — § 17-8(B)(1), n. 47
United States v. Hill, 26 M.J. 876 (N.M.C.M.R. 1988) — § 2-4(A), nn. 20, 22
United States v. Hill, 32 M.J. 940 (N.M.C.M.R. 1991) — § 17-8(B), n. 20
United States v. Hill, 42 M.J. 725 (C.G.Ct.Crim.App. 1995) — § 15-12(B), n. 21
United States v. Hillman, 21 C.M.R. 834 (A.F.B.R. 1956) — § 15-14(A), n. 11
United States v. Hillmon, 2 M.J. 830 (A.C.M.R. 1976) — § 11-2(E)(2), n. 121
United States v. Hilow, 32 M.J. 439 (C.M.A. 1991) — § 6-3(A), n. 3; § 6-4(D), nn. 24, 26; § 8-3(C)(4), n. 153; § 15-10(C)(1), n. 86
United States v. Hilton, 27 M.J. 323 (C.M.A. 1989) — § 13-3(N), n. 300
United States v. Hilton, 29 M.J. 1036 (A.F.C.M.R. 1990) — § 5-4(A)(1), n. 10
United States v. Hilton, 32 M.J. 393 (C.M.A. 1991) — § 5-4(A)(2), n. 14
United States v. Hines, 1 M.J. 623 (A.C.M.R. 1975) — § 16-5(C), nn. 34, 42
United States v. Hines, 23 M.J. 125 (C.M.A. 1986) — § 11-2(F), nn. 157, 161; § 11-2(D)(3), n. 102
United States v. Hinton, 10 M.J. 136 (C.M.A. 1981) — § 14-3(C), nn. 124, 130, 132
United States v. Hinton, 21 M.J. 267 (C.M.A. 1986) — § 11-2(D)(3), n. 99
United States, Hirabayashi v.
United States v. Hirsch, 26 M.J. 800 (A.C.M.R. 1988) — § 4-5(A)(2), nn. 2; § 4-5(A)(4), n. 14; § 13-3(C)(3), n. 156
United States v. Hitchcock, 6 M.J. 188 (C.M.A. 1979) — § 14-3(E), n. 179
United States v. Hitchman, 29 M.J. 951 (A.C.M.R. 1990) — § 5-9(E), n. 54
United States v. Hoaglin, 10 M.J. 769 (N.C.M.R. 1981) — § 14-3(C), n. 125
United States v. Hoard, 12 M.J. 563 (A.C.M.R. 1981) — § 2-4(A), n. 17; § 2-8(C), nn. 29, 34; § 2-8(D), n. 36; § 13-3(N)(3), nn. 378, 390, 403, 410
United States v. Hobart, 22 M.J. 851 (A.F.C.M.R. 1986) — § 9-2(B)(2), n. 67
United States v. Hobbs, 8 M.J. 71 (C.M.A. 1979) — § 15-20, nn. 16, 21
United States v. Hobbs, 30 M.J. 1095 (N.M.C.M.R. 1989) — § 17-11, n. 5

TABLE OF CASES

United States v. Hock, 31 M.J. 334 (C.M.A. 1990) — § 17-11, n. 5; § 17-16(B), n. 10
United States v. Hocker, 32 M.J. 594 (A.C.M.R. 1991) — § 2-2(B), n. 10
United States v. Hodge, 26 M.J. 596 (A.C.M.R. 1988) — § 15-10(C)(1), nn. 84, 86
United States v. Hodge, 28 M.J. 883 (A.F.C.M.R. 1989) — § 15-12, n. 1
United States v. Hodges, 27 M.J. 754 (A.F.C.M.R. 1988) — § 5-3(A), n. 35
United States v. Hoesing, 5 M.J. 355 (C.M.A. 1978) — § 13-3(N)(1), n. 338
United States, Hoffman v.
United States v. Hogan, 20 M.J. 71 (C.M.A. 1985) — § 6-1(C)(1), n. 116
United States v. Hogan, 20 M.J. 221 (C.M.A. 1985) — § 6-1(C)(3), n. 145; § 17-15(B), n. 17
United States v. Holcomb, 43 C.M.R. 149 (C.M.A. 1971) — § 16-8(C), n. 36
United States v. Holcomb, 20 C.M.A. 309, 43 C.M.R. 149 (1971) — § 15-13, n. 14
United States v. Holder, 7 C.M.A. 213, 22 C.M.R. 3 (1956) — § 2-2(B), n. 7; § 2-2(E)(4), n. 86
United States v. Holland, 1 M.J. 58 (C.M.A. 1975) — § 9-2(B)(2), n. 63
United States v. Holland, 19 M.J. 883 (A.C.M.R. 1985) — § 16-9, n. 4
United States v. Hollcraft, 17 M.J. 1111 (A.C.M.R. 1984) — § 6-5(A), n. 7; § 16-8(C), n. 42; § 9-2(B)(1), n. 45
United States v. Holley, 17 M.J. 361 (C.M.A. 1984) — § 15-10(C)(3), n. 108
United States v. Holliday, 24 M.J. 686 (A.C.M.R. 1987) — § 5-4(B), nn. 50, 51
United States v. Holloway, 38 M.J. 302 (C.M.A. 1993) — § 5-9(D), n. 21
United States v. Holman, 19 M.J. 784 (A.C.M.R. 1984) — § 4-11(A), n. 30
United States v. Holman, 23 M.J. 565 (A.C.M.R. 1986) — § 2-7(C), n. 35; § 17-18(B)(1), n. 41; § 17-8(B)(2), n. 63
United States v. Holman, 28 M.J. 527 (A.C.M.R. 1989) — § 14-3(B)(2), n. 100; § 14-3(D)(4), n. 147
United States v. Holmes, 43 C.M.R. 446 (A.C.M.R. 1970) — § 2-2(C)(3), n. 35
United States v. Holmes, 17 M.J. 611 (N.M.C.M.R. 1983) — § 4-14(B), n. 20
United States v. Holmes, 17 M.J. 830 (A.C.M.R. 1984) — § 16-8(C), n. 42; § 9-2(B)(1), n. 45
United States v. Holmes, 25 M.J. 674 (A.F.C.M.R. 1987) — § 10-4(B)(5), n. 62
United States v. Holmes, 33 M.J. 750 (A.C.M.R. 1991) — § 17-8(B)(1), n. 54
United States v. Holstlaw, 41 M.J. 552 (N.M.Ct.Crim.App. 1994) — § 9-2(B)(1), n. 46
United States v. Holt, 27 M.J. 57 (C.M.A. 1988) — § 14-2(B)(4), nn. 114, 115; § 14-3(B)(2), n. 68; § 16-5(D)(2), n. 67
United States v. Holt, 28 M.J. 835 (A.F.C.M.R. 1989) — § 17-15(B), n. 32
United States v. Holt, 31 M.J. 758 (A.C.M.R. 1990) — § 13-3(B), n. 13
United States v. Holt, 33 M.J. 400 (C.M.A. 1991) — § 15-2(B)(3), n. 78; § 16-5(D)(3), n. 72
United States v. Holt, 38 M.J. 682 (A.F.C.M.R. 1993) — § 17-8(B), n. 15
United States v. Homer, 22 M.J. 294 (C.M.A. 1986) — § 16-12, n. 8
United States v. Honeycutt, 27 M.J. 863 (A.F.C.M.R. 1989) — § 12-2(F)(1), n. 43
United States v. Honeycutt, 29 M.J. 416 (C.M.A. 1990) — § 9-3, n. 8
United States v. Honican, 27 M.J. 590 (A.C.M.R. 1988) — § 6-1, n. 20; § 13-3(C)(2), nn. 49, 65, 69, 72
United States v. Hood, 12 M.J. 890 (A.C.M.R. 1982) — § 16-5(D)(3), n. 71
United States v. Hood, 37 M.J. 784 (A.C.M.R. 1993) — § 4-15(C), n. 15; § 12-3(B), n. 49
United States v. Hook, 20 C.M.A. 516, 43 C.M.R. 356 (1971) — § 14-3(B), n. 49
United States v. Hooper, 9 C.M.A. 637, 26 C.M.R. 417 (1958) — § 4-8(D), nn. 61, 62
United States v. Hoover, 24 M.J. 874 (A.C.M.R. 1987) — § 5-10(A), n. 1; § 5-10(D), nn. 28, 43

TABLE OF CASES

United States v. Hopkins, 4 M.J. 260 (C.M.A. 1978) — § 4-11(A), n. 16
United States v. Hopkins, 25 M.J. 671 (A.F.C.M.R. 1987) — § 16-9, n. 10
United States v. Hopwood, 29 M.J. 530 (A.F.C.M.R. 1989) — § 16-5(B), n. 9
United States v. Horne, 33 M.J. 575 (N.M.C.M.R. 1991) — § 17-2(B)(3), n. 80
United States v. Horner, 1 M.J. 227 (C.M.A. 1975) — § 16-9, n. 5
United States v. Horner, 22 M.J. 294 (C.M.A. 1986) — § 6-5(C), n. 51; § 16-5(D)(4), n. 86
United States v. Horner, 32 M.J. 576 (C.G.C.M.R. 1991) — § 2-2(B), n. 14; § 2-4(A), nn. 5, 10
United States v. Horsey, 6 M.J. 112 (C.M.A. 1979) — § 10-4(A)(4), n. 27; § 10-4(B)(1), n. 32
United States v. Horton, 17 M.J. 1131 (N.M.C.M.R. 1984) — § 2-4(C), n. 32
United States v. Horton, 36 M.J. 1039 (N.M.C.M.R. 1993) — § 2-2(C)(3), n. 33
United States v. Hosford, 11 M.J. 762 (N.M.C.M.R. 1981) — § 4-5(A)(2); § 4-5(A)(2), n. 3
United States v. Hoskins, 17 M.J. 134 (C.M.A. 1984) — § 6-1(C), n. 94
United States v. Hounshell, 19 C.M.R. 906 (A.F.B.R. 1955) — § 11-3(B)(2), n. 57
United States v. Hounshell, 7 C.M.A. 3, 21 C.M.R. 129 (1956) — § 16-3(D), n. 66
United States v. Householder, 21 M.J. 613 (A.F.C.M.R. 1985) — § 4-11(B), n. 42
United States v. Houston, 12 M.J. 907 (N.M.C.M.R. 1982) — § 17-6, n. 2
United States v. Hout, 19 C.M.A. 299, 41 C.M.R. 299 (1970) — § 4-8(A), n. 9
United States v. Howard, 7 M.J. 962 (A.C.M.R. 1970) — § 3-8(B), n. 11
United States v. Howard, 23 C.M.A. 187, 48 C.M.R. 939 (1974) — § 6-6(A), nn. 3, 4; § 17-9(B), n. 40
United States v. Howard, 20 M.J. 353 (C.M.A. 1985) — § 4-8(B), nn. 11, 13; § 4-8(C)(3), nn. 32, 40
United States v. Howard, 24 M.J. 897 (C.G.C.M.R. 1987) — § 13-3(J), n. 257; § 6-1(C)(3), n. 163
United States v. Howard, 33 M.J. 596 (A.C.M.R. 1991) — § 12-2(H), n. 109
United States v. Howard, 35 M.J. 763 (A.C.M.R. 1992) — § 13-3(C)(2), nn. 67, 81
United States v. Howe, 17 C.M.A. 165, 37 C.M.R. 429 (C.M.A. 1967) — § 13-3(N)(3), n. 385
United States v. Howe, 37 M.J. 1062 (N.M.C.M.R. 1993) — § 8-4, nn. 11, 14
United States v. Howell, 11 C.M.A. 712, 29 C.M.R. 528 (1960) — § 12-2(F)(4), n. 68
United States v. Howell, 36 M.J. 354 (C.M.A. 1993) — § 2-7(B), n. 24
United States v. Hoxsey, 17 M.J. 964 (A.F.C.M.R. 1984) — § 2-3(A), n. 10
United States v. Hubbard, 28 M.J. 27 (C.M.A. 1989) — § 7-2(C), n. 79
United States v. Huber, 24 M.J. 697 (C.G.C.M.R. 1987) — § 9-2(A)(1), n. 11
United States v. Huddelston, 50 C.M.R. 99 (A.C.M.R. 1975) — § 13-3(C)(2), n. 73
United States v. Hudson, 5 M.J. 413 (C.M.A. 1978) — § 4-6, n. 26
United States v. Hudson, 16 M.J. 522 (A.C.M.R. 1983) — § 15-2(D), n. 141
United States v. Hudson, 27 M.J. 734 (A.C.M.R. 1988) — § 4-16, n. 14; § 8-4, n. 9
United States v. Hudson, 37 M.J. 992 (A.C.M.R. 1993) — § 16-8(C), n. 36
United States v. Hudson, 39 M.J. 958 (N.M.C.M.R. 1994) — § 3-3(C), n. 27; § 13-3(G), n. 223
United States v. Huelcamp, 21 M.J. 509 (A.C.M.R. 1985) — § 13-2(A), n. 22; § 17-9(C), n. 54
United States v. Huelcamp, 27 M.J. 511 (A.C.M.R. 1988) — § 5-4(B) n. 26
United States v. Huerta, 31 M.J. 640 (N.M.C.M.R. 1990) — § 11-2(A)(3), n. 28
United States v. Huet-Vaughn, 43 M.J. 105 (1995) — § 2-2(B), nn. 13, 14; § 2-4(F), nn. 56, 60, 61; § 2-2(E)(2), n. 77; § 2-2(E)(7), nn. 103-107
United States v. Huff, 7 C.M.A. 247, 22 C.M.R. 37 (1956) — § 4-8(C)(4), n. 55

TABLE OF CASES

United States v. Huff, 4 M.J. 731 (A.F.C.M.R. 1978) — § 3-8(B), n. 11
United States v. Huffman, 25 M.J. 758 (N.M.C.M.R. 1987) — § 17-8(B)(2), n. 62
United States v. Huffman, 36 M.J. 636 (A.C.M.R. 1992) — § 13-5(B), n. 25
United States v. Huffman, 40 M.J. 225 (C.M.A. 1994) — § 5-10(C), n. 15; § 5-10(D), n. 40
United States v. Huggins, 12 M.J. 657 (A.C.M.R. 1981) — § 13-3(J), n. 265
United States v. Hughes, 1 M.J. 346 (C.M.A. 1976) — § 13-3(J), n. 259; § 6-1(C)(3), n. 132
United States v. Hughes, 22 M.J. 609 (A.C.M.R. 1986) — § 17-9(A), n. 21
United States v. Hughes, 26 M.J. 119 (C.M.A. 1988) — § 16-5(C), n. 31
United States v. Huitt, 25 M.J. 136 (C.M.A. 1987) — § 15-10(B), nn. 57, 61
United States v. Hullum, 15 M.J. 261 (C.M.A. 1983) — § 2-2(E)(3), n. 78; § 15-2(B)(3), n. 89
United States v. Hulsey, 21 M.J. 717 (A.F.C.M.R. 1985) — § 13-3(C)(3), n. 122
United States v. Hultgren, 40 M.J. 638 (N.M.C.M.R. 1994) — § 8-3(D), n. 162; § 15-2(B)(3), n. 46
United States v. Hunt, 10 M.J. 222 (C.M.A. 1981) — § 14-3(D)(3), n. 143
United States v. Hunt, 24 M.J. 723 (A.C.M.R. 1987) — § 13-2(G)(2), n. 91; § 13-3(J), n. 257
United States v. Hunt, 33 M.J. 345 (C.M.A. 1991) — § 2-7(C), n. 32
United States v. Hunt, 34 M.J. 765 (A.C.M.R. 1992) — § 2-7(B), n. 24
United States v. Hunt, 37 M.J. 344 (C.M.A. 1993) — § 6-1(C), n. 96; § 15-4(C), n. 21; § 15-16(A), n. 13
United States v. Hunter, 17 M.J. 738 (A.C.M.R. 1983) — § 11-2(F), n. 160
United States v. Hurd, 7 M.J. 18 (C.M.A. 1979) — § 17-9(D), n. 75; § 17-15(B), n. 19
United States v. Hurd, 8 M.J. 555 (N.C.M.R. 1979) — § 4-5(A)(2); § 4-5(A)(2), n. 3
United States v. Hurt, 8 C.M.A. 224, 24 C.M.R. 34 (1957) — § 15-10(B), n. 41; § 8-3(C)(1), n. 115
United States v. Hurt, 9 C.M.A. 735, 27 C.M.R. 3 (1958) — § 15-15, n. 7
United States v. Hussey, 1 M.J. 804 (A.F.C.M.R. 1976) — § 12-3(A), n. 9
United States v. Hustwit, 33 M.J. 608 (N.M.C.M.R. 1991) — § 8-3(B)(1), n. 58
United States v. Hutchins, 4 M.J. 190 (C.M.A. 1978) — § 4-8(A), nn. 8, 9; § 13-3(C)(4), n. 173
United States v. Hutchinson, 15 M.J. 1056 (N.M.C.M.R. 1983) — § 12-2(F)(2), n. 55
United States v. Hutchinson, 17 M.J. 156 (C.M.A. 1984) — § 8-3(C)(3), n. 147
United States, Hutson v.
United States v. Hutto, 29 M.J. 917 (A.C.M.R. 1989) — § 12-2(G), nn. 92, 96; § 16-9, n. 5
United States v. Huxhold, 20 M.J. 990 (N.M.C.M.R. 1985) — § 15-2(B)(3), n. 61
United States v. Hypolite, 39 C.M.R. 830 (N.B.R. 1969) — § 6-1, n. 18; § 6-1(C)(1), n. 107
United States v. Hyska, 29 M.J. 122 (C.M.A. 1989) — § 16-2(D), n. 39; § 6-1(C)(3), n. 134
United States v. Ignatko, 33 M.J. 571 (N.M.C.M.R. 1991) — § 6-1(C)(3), n. 137
United States v. Ilaskins, 345 F.2d 111 (6th Cir. 1965) — § 13-5(F), n. 17
United States v. Imler, 17 M.J. 1021 (N.M.C.M.R. 1984) — § 4-5(A), n. 9
United States v. Ingham, 36 M.J. 990 (A.C.M.R. 1993) — § 15-10(B), n. 66; § 6-1(C)(3), n. 132
United States v. Ingham, 42 M.J. 218 (1995) — § 15-2(B)(3), nn. 65, 68, 78, 103
United States v. Inman, 20 M.J. 773 (A.C.M.R. 1985) — § 15-10(B), n. 68
United States v. Irons, 34 M.J. 807 (N.M.C.M.R. 1992) — § 15-2(C), nn. 125, 126

TABLE OF CASES

United States v. Irvin, 21 M.J. 184 (C.M.A. 1986) — § 2-6, n. 4
United States v. Irving, 2 M.J. 967 (A.C.M.R. 1976) — § 2-2(E)(1), n. 72
United States v. Irving, 3 M.J. 6 (C.M.A. 1977) — § 6-1(C)(3), n. 135
United States v. Irwin, 30 M.J. 87 (C.M.A. 1990) — § 11-2(A)(1), n. 2
United States v. Irwin, 42 M.J. 479 (1995) — § 14-2(B)(4), n. 114; § 16-5(D)(5), n. 116
United States v. Isbell, 3 C.M.A. 782, 14 C.M.R. 200 (1954) — § 6-3(B), n. 15
United States v. Isler, 36 M.J. 1061 (A.F.C.M.R. 1993) — § 5-10(C), n. 20
United States v. Iverson, 5 M.J. 440 (C.M.A. 1978) — § 8-3(D), n. 162; § 17-2(B), n. 5; § 17-8(B)(3), n. 90; § 17-14, n. 7
United States v. Ivester, 22 M.J. 933 (N.M.C.M.R. 1986) — § 13-3(C)(2), n. 81
United States v. Ivey, 37 C.M.R. 626 (A.B.R. 1967) — § 15-15, n. 9
United States v. Jack, 7 C.M.A. 235, 22 C.M.R. 25 (1956) — § 2-2(C)(3), n. 34
United States v. Jackson, 33 C.M.R. 884, 890, nn. 3, 4 (A.F.B.R. 1963) — § 10-4(B)(5), n. 49
United States v. Jackson, 46 C.M.R. 1128 (A.C.M.R. 1973) — § 2-4(C), n. 32
United States v. Jackson, 3 M.J. 153 (C.M.A. 1977) — § 17-9(B), n. 39
United States v. Jackson, 549 F.2d 517 (8th Cir. 1977) — § 15-12(A), n. 6
United States v. Jackson, 5 M.J. 223 (C.M.A. 1978) — § 5-9(D), n. 40; § 17-19, n. 8
United States v. Jackson, 6 M.J. 116 (C.M.A. 1979) — § 15-14(B), n. 22
United States v. Jackson, 12 M.J. 163 (C.M.A. 1981) — § 15-14(B), n. 23
United States v. Jackson, 12 M.J. 905 (N.M.C.M.R. 1982) — § 15-26(C), n. 10
United States v. Jackson, 20 M.J. 83 (C.M.A. 1985) — § 13-3(B), n. 10; § 13-3(E), n. 206; § 2-2(C)(3), n. 39
United States v. Jackson, 23 M.J. 650 (N.M.C.M.R. 1986) — § 14-3(B)(2), n. 99
United States v. Jackson, 23 M.J. 841 (A.F.C.M.R. 1987) — § 5-4(A)(3), n. 19
United States v. Jackson, 30 M.J. 565 (A.C.M.R. 1990) — § 14-3(C), n. 129; § 16-5(D)(1), n. 61
United States v. Jackson, 30 M.J. 687 (A.C.M.R. 1990) — § 17-2(B)(3), n. 76
United States v. Jackson, 34 M.J. 783 (A.C.M.R. 1992) — § 15-2(B)(3), n. 88
United States v. Jackson, 34 M.J. 1145 (A.C.M.R. 1992) — § 5-7, n. 12; § 5-3(C)(5), n. 81; § 17-3(A), n. 20
United States v. Jackson, 36 M.J. 757 (A.C.M.R. 1993) — § 17-8(B)(3), n. 96
United States v. Jackson, 38 M.J. 106 (C.M.A. 1993) — § 15-24, n. 1
United States v. Jackson, 37 M.J. 1045 (N.M.C.M.R. 1993) — § 15-2(B)(3), n. 85
United States v. Jackson, 40 M.J. 620 (N.M.C.M.R. 1994) — § 12-4, n. 16
United States v. Jackson, 40 M.J. 820 (N.M.C.M.R. 1994) — § 15-13, n. 11; § 16-8(B), n. 25
United States v. Jacobs, 31 M.J. 138 (C.M.A. 1990) — § 5-3(A), n. 32; § 5-3(E), n. 7
United States v. Jacoby, 11 C.M.A. 428, 29 C.M.R. 244 (1960) — § 1-1(B), n. 25; § 5-3, n. 1; § 15-22, n. 3; § 11-3(B)(1), n. 20
United States v. Jacques, 5 M.J. 598 (N.C.M.R. 1978) — § 9-2, n. 5; § 9-2(C), n. 80; § 9-2(A)(2), n. 26
United States v. Jaeger, 27 M.J. 620 (A.C.M.R. 1988) — § 17-2(B)(3), n. 59
United States v. Jagnandan, 24 M.J. 628 (A.C.M.R. 1987) — § 14-3(F), n. 195
United States v. Jakaitis, 10 C.M.A. 41, 27 C.M.R. 115 (1958) — § 15-15, n. 7
United States v. James, 5 M.J. 381 (C.M.A. 1978) — § 15-14(B), n. 44
United States v. James, 12 M.J. 944 (N.M.C.M.R. 1982) — § 17-7, n. 5
United States v. James, 22 M.J. 929 (N.M.C.M.R. 1986) — § 11-2(E)(3), n. 133
United States v. James, 24 M.J. 894 (A.C.M.R. 1987) — § 14-3(F), n. 195; § 8-3(C)(4), n. 151; § 15-10(C)(1), n. 88
United States v. James, 28 M.J. 214 (C.M.A. 1989) — § 5-10(C), n. 20

TABLE OF CASES

United States v. Jameson, 33 M.J. 669 (N.M.C.M.R. 1991) — § 6-3(A), n. 11; § 6-3(C), n. 17; § 6-6(C), nn. 15-18; § 6-8, n. 1
United States v. Jamison, 18 M.J. 540 (A.C.M.R. 1984) — § 12-2(H), n. 102
United States v. Jarrell, 12 M.J. 917 (N.M.C.M.R. 1982) — § 4-5(A)(2); § 4-5(A)(2), n. 3
United States v. Jarrie, 5 M.J. 193 (C.M.A. 1978) — § 10-4(B)(5), nn. 50, 53
United States v. Jasper, 16 M.J. 786 (A.C.M.R. 1983) — § 5-3(D)(1), nn. 134, 136
United States v. Jean, 15 M.J. 433 (C.M.A. 1983) — § 13-3(J), n. 266
United States v. Jeanbaptiste, 5 M.J. 374 (C.M.A. 1978) — § 15-4(B), nn. 10, 12; § 17-2(B), n. 9
United States v. Jefferson, 13 M.J. 1 (C.M.A. 1982) — § 11-2(A)(1), n. 6; § 15-2(B)(3), n. 31
United States v. Jefferson, 14 M.J. 806 (A.C.M.R. 1982) — § 13-3(F), nn. 216, 221
United States v. Jefferson, 21 M.J. 203 (C.M.A. 1986) — § 2-8(D), n. 41; § 6-1(C)(3), n. 145
United States v. Jefferson, 22 M.J. 315 (C.M.A. 1986) — § 15-10(A), n. 7
United States v. Jeffries, 33 M.J. 826 (A.F.C.M.R. 1991) — § 14-2, n. 12; § 12-2(F)(3), n. 66; § 15-2(B)(3), n. 48
United States v. Jemmings, 1 M.J. 414 (C.M.A. 1976) — § 2-2(E)(3), n. 79
United States, Jencks v.
United States v. Jenkins, 20 C.M.A. 112, 42 C.M.R. 304 (1970) — § 12-3(A), n. 33
United States v. Jenkins, 12 M.J. 222 (C.M.A. 1982) — § 16-11, n. 9
United States v. Jenkins, 18 M.J. 583 (A.C.M.R. 1984) — § 10-4(B)(1), n. 29
United States v. Jenkins, 24 M.J. 846 (A.F.C.M.R. 1987) — § 5-3(C)(6), n. 96
United States v. Jenkins, 30 M.J. 1101 (N.M.C.M.R. 1989) — § 17-9(A), n. 19; § 17-9(C), n. 55; § 17-10, n. 5
United States v. Jenkins, 38 M.J. 287 (C.M.A. 1993) — § 17-11, n. 5
United States v. Jenkins, 39 M.J. 843 (A.C.M.R. 1994) — § 2-5, n. 3
United States v. Jennings, 1 M.J. 414 (C.M.A. 1976) — § 14-3(B)(2), n. 99; § 14-3(D)(4), n. 149
United States v. Jennings, 20 M.J. 223 (C.M.A. 1985) — § 6-1(C)(3), n. 145
United States v. Jennings, 22 M.J. 837 (N.M.C.M.R. 1986) — § 9-2(B)(2), n. 65
United States v. Jennings, 36 M.J. 773 (N.M.C.M.R. 1992) — § 9-2(B), n. 37
United States v. Jennings, 42 M.J. 764 (C.G.Ct.Crim.App. 1995) — § 17-14, n. 9
United States v. Jerasi, 20 M.J. 719 (N.M.C.M.R. 1985) — § 1-1(B), n. 17; § 12-2(F)(2), nn. 56, 57
United States v. Jessie, 5 M.J. 573 (A.C.M.R. 1978) — § 4-9, n. 4
United States v. Jeter, 35 M.J. 442 (C.M.A. 1992) — § 8-2(A), n. 3; § 4-14(A)(2), nn. 8-10
United States v. Jeter, 35 M.J. 674 (A.C.M.R. 1992) — § 15-2(B)(3), n. 88
United States v. Jette, 25 M.J. 16 (C.M.A. 1987) — § 8-2(A), n. 5; § 4-14(A)(1), n. 7
United States v. Jobes, 20 M.J. 506 (A.F.C.M.R. 1985) — § 16-2(D), n. 39
United States v. Jobson, 28 M.J. 844 (A.F.C.M.R. 1989) — § 15-10(C)(2), n. 100
United States v. Jobson, 31 M.J. 117 (C.M.A. 1990) — § 15-10(B), n. 62; § 15-10(C)(2), nn. 94, 98, 99
United States v. Johanns, 20 M.J. 155 (C.M.A. 1985) — § 2-8(A) n. 8; § 2-8(B), nn. 13, 15; § 2-8(D), n. 39; § 13-3(N)(2), nn. 356, 357; § 13-3(N)(3), n. 393; § 13-3(N)(4), n. 425
United States v. Johnson, 3 C.M.A. 174, 11 C.M.R. 174 (1953) — § 2-2(D), n. 66
United States v. Johnson, 28 C.M.R. 662 (N.B.R. 1959) — § 15-12(A), n. 6
United States v. Johnson, 12 C.M.A. 640, 31 C.M.R. 226 (1962) — § 17-9(E), nn. 84, 85
United States v. Johnson, 14 C.M.A. 548, 34 C.M.R. 328 (1964) — § 6-3(C), nn. 16, 27, 32; § 6-5(A), n. 4

TABLE OF CASES

United States v. Johnson, 40 C.M.R. 451 (A.B.R. 1968) — § 7-3(A), n. 13
United States v. Johnson, 42 C.M.R. 625 (A.C.M.R. 1970) — § 11-3(B)(2), n. 40
United States v. Johnson, 19 C.M.A. 464, 42 C.M.R. 66 (1970) — § 3-8(B), n. 5
United States v. Johnson, 22 C.M.A. 424, 47 C.M.R. 402 (1973) — § 11-2(A)(3), n. 21
United States v. Johnson, 49 C.M.R. 477 (A.C.M.R. 1974) — § 6-1, n. 18; § 6-1(C)(1), n. 106
United States v. Johnson, 23 C.M.A. 148, 48 C.M.R. 764 (1974) — § 8-3(B)(3), n. 76
United States v. Johnson, 1 M.J. 101 (C.M.A. 1975) — § 13-3(C)(2), n. 76
United States v. Johnson, 1 M.J. 213 (C.M.A. 1975) — § 16-8(B), n. 24
United States v. Johnson, 2 M.J. 541 (A.C.M.R. 1976) — § 13-3(E), n. 190; § 9-2(B)(1), n. 54
United States v. Johnson, 3 M.J. 143 (C.M.A. 1977) — § 13-3(C)(2), n. 74
United States v. Johnson, 4 M.J. 8 (C.M.A. 1977) — § 17-8(B), n. 21
United States v. Johnson, 3 M.J. 623 (N.C.M.R. 1977) — § 6-1, n. 30; § 2-2(E)(6), n. 98
United States v. Johnson, 4 M.J. 770 (A.C.M.R. 1978) — § 2-6(A), n. 27
United States v. Johnson, 7 M.J. 396 (C.M.A. 1979) — § 7-2(E), n. 99; § 13-5(D), n. 43; § 15-2(A), n. 5
United States v. Johnson, 14 M.J. 710 (N.M.C.M.R. 1982) — § 6-1(B)(3), n. 92
United States v. Johnson, 17 M.J. 83 (C.M.A. 1983) — § 6-1(C)(3), n. 149
United States v. Johnson, 17 M.J. 255 (C.M.A. 1984) — § 13-3(C)(1), n. 41
United States v. Johnson, 18 M.J. 76 (C.M.A. 1984) — § 2-7(B), n. 24
United States v. Johnson, 21 M.J. 553 (A.F.C.M.R. 1985) — § 13-3(N), n. 299
United States v. Johnson, 21 M.J. 211 (C.M.A. 1986) — § 12-2(F)(2), n. 55
United States v. Johnson, 22 M.J. 945 (A.C.M.R. 1986) — § 15-16(A), n. 15
United States v. Johnson, 23 M.J. 209 (C.M.A. 1987) — § 5-3(B), n. 37
United States v. Johnson, 23 M.J. 327 (C.M.A. 1987) — § 15-4(B), n. 11; § 15-16(B), n. 19; § 17-8(B)(3), n. 70
United States v. Johnson, 24 M.J. 796 (A.C.M.R. 1987) — § 16-8(A), n. 6; § 13-3(C)(3), n. 106
United States v. Johnson, 25 M.J. 553 (A.C.M.R. 1987) — § 14-3(B)(2), n. 99
United States v. Johnson, 25 M.J. 691 (A.C.M.R. 1987) — § 15-14(B), n. 34
United States v. Johnson, 26 M.J. 509 (A.C.M.R. 1988) — § 17-2(B)(3), n. 87
United States v. Johnson, 26 M.J. 686 (A.C.M.R. 1988) — § 16-2(D), n. 43; § 17-8(B)(3) nn. 36, 47
United States v. Johnson, 27 M.J. 798 (A.F.C.M.R. 1988) — § 13-3(N)(2), n. 339; § 13-3(N)(4), n. 417
United States v. Johnson, 30 M.J. 53 (C.M.A. 1990) — § 2-9(A), n. 3; § 2-9(C), n. 24; § 2-9(C)(1), nn. 34, 36, 37; § 2-9(C)(2), n. 43
United States v. Johnson, 30 M.J. 930 (A.C.M.R. 1990) — § 6-1(C), n. 102
United States v. Johnson, 29 M.J. 1065 (C.G.C.M.R. 1990) — § 17-15(B), n. 14
United States v. Johnson, 33 M.J. 855 (A.C.M.R. 1991) — § 15-4(A), n. 6; § 11-2(B)(1), nn. 49, 57
United States v. Johnson, 36 M.J. 862 (A.C.M.R. 1993) — § 15-2(D), n. 133; § 15-12(B), n. 15; § 11-2(B)(1), nn. 54, 58, 68
United States v. Johnson, 37 M.J. 982 (A.C.M.R. 1993) — § 2-2(B), n. 10
United States v. Johnson, 38 M.J. 88 (C.M.A. 1993) — § 6-1(C)(3), n. 155
United States v. Johnson, 39 M.J. 707 (N.M.C.M.R. 1993) — § 6-1(C)(3), n. 147
United States v. Johnson, 39 M.J. 242 (C.M.A. 1994) — § 6-7, n. 12
United States v. Johnson, 39 M.J. 1033 (A.C.M.R. 1994) — § 2-6(A), nn. 18, 19
United States v. Johnson, 42 M.J. 443 (1995) — § 14-3(D)(5), n. 174
United States v. Johnson, 43 M.J. 192 (1995) — § 15-2(B)(3), n. 106

TABLE OF CASES

United States v. Johnston, 24 M.J. 271 (C.M.A. 1987) — § 5-3(D)(1), nn. 124, 128
United States v. Johnston, 39 M.J. 242 (C.M.A. 1994) — § 6-1, n. 10; § 6-7, n. 10
United States v. Johnwell, 15 M.J. 32 (C.M.A. 1983) — § 15-14(B), n. 37
United States v. Jolliff, 22 C.M.A. 95, 46 C.M.R. 95 (1973) — § 17-8(B), n. 24; § 7-2(A)(1), n. 22
United States v. Jones, 1 C.M.A. 276, 3 C.M.R. 10 (1952) — § 2-2(D), n. 62
United States v. Jones, 15 C.M.R. 664 (A.B.R. 1954) — § 6-1(C)(2), n. 126
United States v. Jones, 34 C.M.R. 642 (A.C.M.R. 1964) — § 16-8(B), n. 14
United States v. Jones, 50 C.M.R. 92 (A.C.M.R. 1975) — § 4-5(A)(2), n. 2
United States v. Jones, 50 C.M.R. 724 (A.C.M.R. 1975) — § 6-1(B)(2), n. 86
United States v. Jones, 3 M.J. 677 (C.G.C.M.R. 1977) — § 16-6, n. 21
United States v. Jones, 5 M.J. 579 (A.C.M.R. 1978) — § 2-6, n. 13
United States v. Jones, 6 M.J. 770 (A.C.M.R. 1978) — § 13-3(C)(2), n. 73
United States v. Jones, 6 M.J. 568 (N.C.M.R. 1978) — § 16-8(A), n. 5
United States v. Jones, 7 M.J. 441 (C.M.A. 1979) — § 15-14(C), n. 49
United States v. Jones, 12 M.J. 833 (N.M.C.M.R. 1981) — § 17-2(B)(4), n. 93
United States v. Jones, 14 M.J. 1008 (C.M.A. 1982) — § 13-3(N)(4), nn. 420, 421
United States v. Jones, 15 M.J. 890 (A.C.M.R. 1983) — § 6-2(A), n. 8
United States v. Jones, 15 M.J. 967 (A.C.M.R. 1983) — § 6-5(A), n. 3; § 6-6(B), n. 6; § 12-2(H), nn. 121, 124; § 15-15, n. 21
United States v. Jones, 20 M.J. 853 (A.C.M.R. 1985) — § 9-2(B)(2), n. 65
United States v. Jones, 20 M.J. 919 (N.M.C.M.R. 1985) — § 11-4, n. 3; § 13-5(I), n. 73; § 13-5(J), n. 78; § 7-2(A)(1), n. 19; § 7-2(B)(4), n. 46; § 10-4(B)(5), n. 60; § 11-2(A)(1), n. 8; § 11-2(B)(1), n. 68
United States v. Jones, 21 M.J. 819 (N.M.C.M.R. 1985) — § 13-3(C)(3), n. 156
United States v. Jones, 23 M.J. 305 (C.M.A. 1987) — § 6-1(C)(3), n. 152; § 9-2(A)(1), n. 10; § 9-2(B), n. 35; § 9-2(B)(1), n. 56
United States v. Jones, 24 M.J. 294 (C.M.A. 1987) — § 5-3(B), n. 39; § 5-3(D)(1), n. 124
United States v. Jones, 24 M.J. 367 (C.M.A. 1987) — § 5-4(B), n. 42
United States v. Jones, 24 M.J. 525 (A.F.C.M.R. 1987) — § 14-3(C), n. 128
United States v. Jones, 26 M.J. 353 (C.M.A. 1988) — § 5-4(B), nn. 47, 52
United States v. Jones, 26 M.J. 632 (A.F.C.M.R. 1988) — § 14-3(A)(1), n. 14; § 14-3(A)(2), n. 30
United States v. Jones, 26 M.J. 650 (A.C.M.R. 1988) — § 9-2(A)(2), n. 24
United States v. Jones, 26 M.J. 1009 (A.C.M.R. 1988) — § 2-2(C)(3), n. 39
United States v. Jones, 28 M.J. 939 (N.M.C.M.R. 1989) — § 16-3(D), n. 63
United States v. Jones, 30 M.J. 898 (A.F.C.M.R. 1990) — § 16-8(A), n. 6; § 16-8(B), n. 24
United States v. Jones, 31 M.J. 189 (C.M.A. 1990) — § 5-4(A)(1), n. 10
United States v. Jones, 30 M.J. 849 (N.M.C.M.R. 1990) — § 6-6(C), n. 19; § 6-7, nn. 11, 16, 18
United States v. Jones, 33 M.J. 1040 (N.M.C.M.R. 1990) — § 6-5(B), n. 29
United States v. Jones, 34 M.J. 270 (C.M.A. 1992) — § 16-11, n. 7; § 14-3(B)(2), n. 71
United States v. Jones, 34 M.J. 899 (N.M.C.M.R. 1992) — § 5-4(B), n. 52; § 7-3(B), n. 27; § 8-4, nn. 12, 14; § 12-4, n. 13
United States v. Jones, 37 M.J. 321 (C.M.A. 1993) — § 15-15, nn. 4, 5; § 16-10, nn. 23, 24
United States v. Jones, 39 M.J. 315 (C.M.A. 1994) — § 17-15(B), n. 32
United States v. Jones, 39 M.J. 815 (A.C.M.R. 1994) — § 15-2(B)(3), nn. 33, 100, 101, 107
United States v. Jophlin, 3 M.J. 858 (A.C.M.R. 1977) — § 14-3(D)(5), n. 162
United States v. Jordan, 21 C.M.R. 627 (A.F.B.R. 1955) — § 2-4(D), n. 44

TABLE OF CASES

United States v. Jordan, 22 C.M.A. 164, 46 C.M.R. 164 (1973) — § 8-3(B)(3), n. 82
United States v. Jordan, 20 M.J. 977 (A.C.M.R. 1985) — § 8-2(B), n. 12
United States v. Jordan, 32 M.J. 672 (A.F.C.M.R. 1991) — § 17-9(A), n. 10
United States v. Jordan, 38 M.J. 346 (C.M.A. 1993) — § 5-4(B), n. 49
United States v. Jordon, 45 C.M.R. 719 (A.C.M.R. 1972) — § 15-2(D), n. 133
United States v. Joseph, 11 M.J. 333 (C.M.A. 1981) — § 3-3(C), n. 25; § 13-3(G), n. 225; § 14-3(A), n. 11; § 11-2(E)(3), nn. 134, 144
United States v. Joseph, 36 M.J. 846 (A.C.M.R. 1993) — § 5-4(B), n. 49
United States v. Joseph, 37 M.J. 392 (C.M.A. 1993) — § 2-9(C)(1), nn. 35, 38
United States v. Joslin, 47 C.M.R. 271 (A.F.C.M.R. 1973) — § 3-8(B), n. 5
United States v. Joyner, 25 M.J. 700 (A.C.M.R. 1987) — § 17-9(B), n. 39
United States v. Juarez, 37 M.J. 779 (A.C.M.R. 1993) — § 13-3(J), n. 266
United States v. Judson, 3 M.J. 908 (A.C.M.R. 1977) — § 7-2(E), nn. 106, 112
United States v. Julian, 45 C.M.R. 876 (N.C.M.R. 1971) — § 4-5(A)(2), n. 2
United States v. Jursnick, 24 M.J. 504 (A.F.C.M.R. 1987) — § 15-14(C), n. 51
United States v. Justice, 3 M.J. 451 (C.M.A. 1977) — § 16-11, n. 2
United States v. Justice, 32 M.J. 599 (A.C.M.R. 1991) — § 5-9(D), nn. 22, 23
United States v. Kabelka, 30 M.J. 1136 (A.F.C.M.R. 1990) — § 5-3(B), n. 37
United States v. Kadlec, 22 M.J. 571 (A.C.M.R. 1986) — § 15-13, n. 14
United States v. Kaliski, 37 M.J. 105 (C.M.A. 1993) — § 5-3(A), n. 18
United States v. Kalscheuer, 11 M.J. 373 (C.M.A. 1981) — § 5-3(B), n. 55
United States v. Kaminski, 32 M.J. 808 (N.M.C.M.R. 1990) — § 17-13, n. 24
United States v. Kapple, 36 M.J. 1119 (A.F.C.M.R. 1993) — § 2-2(E)(1), n. 73
United States v. Kapple, 40 M.J. 472 (C.M.A. 1994) — § 2-2(D), n. 67
United States v. Karnes, 1 M.J. 92 (C.M.A. 1975) — § 15-10(B), n. 52
United States, Kastigar v.
United States v. Kauffman, 14 C.M.A. 283, 34 C.M.R. 63 (1963) — § 5-4(A)(2), n. 11
United States v. Kauffman, 3 M.J. 794 (A.C.M.R. 1977) — § 14-3(D)(5), nn. 162, 166
United States v. Kazena, 11 M.J. 28 (C.M.A. 1981) — § 9-2, nn. 5, 7
United States v. Keaton, 18 C.M.A. 500, 40 C.M.R. 212 (1969) — § 13-3(C)(2), nn. 58, 66
United States v. Keck, 22 M.J. 755 (N.M.C.M.R. 1986) — § 17-8(B)(1), nn. 49-51
United States v. Keenan, 18 C.M.A. 108, 39 C.M.R. 108 (1969) — § 15-4(B), n. 12
United States v. Keenan, 39 M.J. 1050 (A.C.M.R. 1994) — § 15-10(C)(2), nn. 93, 94
United States v. Keith, 22 C.M.A. 59, 46 C.M.R. 59 (1972) — § 16-8(C), n. 44
United States v. Keith, 17 M.J. 1078 (A.F.C.M.R. 1984) — § 15-21, n. 9
United States v. Keith, 36 M.J. 518 (A.C.M.R. 1992) — § 17-5, n. 8; § 17-15(B), n. 32
United States v. Kelker, 4 M.J. 323 (C.M.A. 1978) — § 13-5(H), n. 59
United States v. Keller, 1 M.J. 159 (C.M.A. 1975) — § 17-8(B), n. 29
United States v. Kelley, 539 F.2d 1199 (9th Cir. 1976) — § 12-2(F)(4), n. 80
United States v. Kelley, 40 M.J. 515 (A.C.M.R. 1994) — § 15-10(B), n. 68; § 8-3(B)(3), n. 76
United States v. Kelliher, 31 M.J. 701 (N.M.C.M.R. 1990) — § 5-4(B), n. 30; § 5-4(A)(2), n. 11
United States v. Kelliher, 35 M.J. 320 (C.M.A. 1992) — § 5-4(A)(2), n. 11
United States v. Kellough, 19 M.J. 871 (A.F.C.M.R. 1985) — § 8-2(B), n. 11
United States, Kelly v.
United States v. Kelly, 12 M.J. 509 (A.C.M.R. 1981) — § 15-16(A), n. 11
United States v. Kelly, 16 M.J. 244 (C.M.A. 1983) — § 8-3(B)(2), nn. 69, 70, 71; § 8-3(B)(3), nn. 87, 88

TABLE OF CASES

United States v. Kelly, 32 M.J. 813 (N.M.C.M.R. 1991) — § 14-3(D)(4), n. 153; § 15-2(B)(3), nn. 64, 89
United States v. Kelly, 32 M.J. 835 (N.M.C.M.R. 1991) — § 14-3(C), n. 132
United States v. Kelly, 39 M.J. 235 (C.M.A. 1994) — § 11-2(A)(3), n. 28
United States v. Kelly, 40 M.J. 558 (N.M.C.M.R. 1994) — § 6-7, n. 10; § 17-15(B), n. 33
United States v. Kelly, 41 M.J. 833 (N.M.Ct.Crim.App. 1995) — § 1-1(B), n. 16; § 3-8(B), n. 8; § 3-5(B)(2), n. 14
United States v. Kelsey, 14 M.J. 545 (A.C.M.R. 1982) — § 15-22, n. 6
United States v. Kelson, 3 M.J. 139 (C.M.A. 1977) — § 13-2(C), n. 32
United States v. Kemp, 22 C.M.A. 152, 46 C.M.R. 152 (1973) — § 8-3(C)(3), n. 142
United States v. Kemp, 7 M.J. 760 (A.C.M.R. 1979) — § 7-3(A), nn. 13, 17; § 7-3(B), n. 29
United States v. Kemp, 42 M.J. 839 (N.M. Ct. Crim. App. 1995) — § 2-7(B), n. 24
United States v. Kendall, 17 C.M.A. 561, 38 C.M.R. 359 (1968) — § 15-8, n. 4
United States v. Kendig, 36 M.J. 291 (C.M.A. 1993) — § 5-4(B), nn. 23, 46, 51; § 3-5(B)(2), n. 14; § 3-5(C)(2), n. 38; § 3-5(D)(2), n. 74; § 3-5(E)(2), n. 105
United States v. Kendra, 31 M.J. 846 (N.M.C.M.R. 1990) — § 9-2(B), n. 37; § 17-9(D), n. 66
United States v. Kendrick, 29 M.J. 792 (A.C.M.R. 1989) — § 15-14(B), n. 41; § 15-15, n. 13; § 16-6, n. 5
United States v. Kennedy, 8 C.M.A. 251, 24 C.M.R. 61 (1957) — § 15-12, n. 3
United States v. Kennedy, 564 F.2d 1329 (9th Cir. 1977) — § 12-2(F)(4), n. 85
United States v. Kennedy, 8 M.J. 877 (A.C.M.R. 1979) — § 17-21, n. 4
United States v. Kepple, 27 M.J. 773 (A.F.C.M.R. 1988) — § 9-3, nn. 1, 2
United States, Kercheval v.
United States v. Kern, 22 M.J. 49 (C.M.A. 1986) — § 11-4, n. 5
United States v. Kersh, 34 M.J. 913 (N.M.C.M.R. 1992) — § 5-10(D), n. 34
United States v. Kershaw, 26 M.J. 723 (A.C.M.R. 1988) — § 5-4(C), n. 59; § 15-2(D), n. 128
United States v. Kessinger, 9 C.M.R. 261 (A.B.R. 1952) — § 2-2(E)(1), n. 73
United States v. Keyes, 33 M.J. 567 (N.M.C.M.R. 1991) — § 9-2(B)(1), n. 57
United States v. Keys, 29 M.J. 920 (A.C.M.R. 1989) — § 15-4(A), n. 7; § 8-3(B)(4), n. 99; § 15-2(B)(3), n. 46
United States v. Kick, 7 M.J. 82 (C.M.A. 1979) — § 15-24, n. 2
United States v. Kiddo, 16 M.J. 775 (A.C.M.R. 1983) — § 14-3(B)(2), n. 95
United States v. Kidwell, 20 M.J. 1020 (A.C.M.R. 1985) — § 9-2(B), n. 35; § 12-2(F)(3), n. 65
United States v. Kilbourne, 31 M.J. 731 (A.F.C.M.R. 1990) — § 16-8(B), n. 25
United States v. Kilbreth, 22 C.M.A. 390, 47 C.M.R. 327 (1973) — § 4-6, n. 21
United States v. Kilgore, 21 C.M.A. 35, 44 C.M.R. 89 (1971) — § 14-3(A)(3), n. 31; § 14-3(B)(2), n. 70
United States v. Killebrew, 9 M.J. 154 (C.M.A. 1980) — § 10-3(B), n. 11; § 10-4, n. 1; § 11-3(A), n. 5
United States v. Kim, 35 M.J. 553 (A.C.M.R. 1992) — § 2-2(B), n. 10; § 6-1(C)(2), nn. 124, 131
United States v. Kimball, 50 C.M.R. 337 (A.C.M.R. 1975) — § 5-10(D), n. 28
United States v. Kimball, 13 M.J. 659 (N.M.C.M.R. 1982) — § 8-3(C)(2), n. 132
United States v. Kimble, 33 M.J. 284 (C.M.A. 1991) — § 5-4(C), n. 59
United States v. Kimble, 35 M.J. 904 (A.C.M.R. 1992) — § 17-2(B)(3), n. 88; § 17-9(A), n. 28
United States v. Kimbrell, 28 M.J. 542 (A.F.C.M.R. 1989) — § 2-2(C)(3), nn. 39, 41

TABLE OF CASES

United States v. Kinane, 1 M.J. 309 (C.M.A. 1976) — § 5-4(A)(1), n. 3; § 5-7, n. 5
United States v. Kinard, 21 C.M.A. 300, 45 C.M.R. 74 (1972) — § 12-2(C), n. 17; § 8-3(B)(4), n. 98; § 12-2(F)(5), n. 88
United States v. Kincheloe, 14 M.J. 40 (C.M.A. 1982) — § 17-2(B)(4), nn. 91, 96
United States v. Kinder, 14 C.M.R. 742 (A.B.R. 1954) — § 16-3(C), n. 48
United States v. King, 11 C.M.A. 19, 28 C.M.R. 243 (1959) — § 4-5(A)(4), n. 14
United States v. King, 12 C.M.A. 71, 30 C.M.R. 71 (1960) — § 16-6, nn. 9, 11; § 16-8(B), n. 14
United States v. King, 44 C.M.R. 680 (A.C.M.R. 1971) — § 17-8(B), n. 25
United States v. King, 45 C.M.R. 466 (A.C.M.R. 1972) — § 17-4, n. 34
United States v. King, 3 M.J. 458 (C.M.A. 1977) — § 9-2(D), n. 84; § 14-3(C), nn. 121, 124, 129
United States v. King, 13 M.J. 838 (A.C.M.R. 1982) — § 16-10, n. 17
United States v. King, 18 M.J. 535 (A.F.C.M.R. 1984) — § 17-11, n. 6
United States v. King, 20 M.J. 706 (A.C.M.R. 1985) — § 6-1(C)(2), n. 127
United States v. King, 24 M.J. 774 (A.C.M.R. 1987) — § 17-4, n. 34; § 17-15(B), n. 31
United States v. King, 27 M.J. 545 (A.C.M.R. 1988) — § 16-5(B), n. 10
United States v. King, 27 M.J. 664 (A.C.M.R. 1988) — § 14-3(A)(2), n. 24; § 15-2(B)(3), n. 73
United States v. King, 27 M.J. 327 (C.M.A. 1989) — § 4-8(B), n. 13; § 2-2(E)(4), n. 86; § 4-8(C)(1), n. 18
United States v. King, 28 M.J. 397 (C.M.A. 1989) — § 4-16, nn. 15-17
United States v. King, 28 M.J. 855 (A.C.M.R. 1989) — § 15-2(B)(3), n. 33
United States v. King, 29 M.J. 535 (A.F.C.M.R. 1989) — § 16-5(B), n. 9
United States v. King, 29 M.J. 885 (A.C.M.R. 1989) — § 2-4(F), n. 54
United States v. King, 30 M.J. 59 (C.M.A. 1990) — § 13-3(C)(2), nn. 50, 80; § 13-3(C)(3), n. 159; § 14-3(A)(2), n. 24; § 15-2(B)(3), n. 64
United States v. King, 30 M.J. 334 (C.M.A. 1990) — § 16-5(D)(5), n. 114
United States v. King, 32 M.J. 588 (A.C.M.R. 1991) — § 6-1(C), n. 104
United States v. King, 32 M.J. 709 (A.C.M.R. 1991) — § 15-2(C), n. 120; § 11-2(A)(3), n. 31
United States v. King, 35 M.J. 337 (C.M.A. 1992) — § 16-5(D)(4), n. 86
United States v. King, 42 M.J. 79 (1995) — § 4-8(B), nn. 11, 13
United States v. Kinneer, 7 M.J. 974 (N.C.M.R. 1979) — § 13-2(G)(2), n. 91
United States v. Kinney, 22 M.J. 872 (A.C.M.R. 1986) — § 17-9(D), n. 62
United States v. Kinsler, 24 M.J. 855 (A.C.M.R. 1987) — § 11-2(A)(3), n. 21
United States v. Kinzer, 39 M.J. 559 (A.C.M.R. 1994) — § 10-4(A)(4), n. 27
United States v. Kirk, 31 M.J. 84 (C.M.A. 1990) — § 16-5(D)(4), nn. 100, 102; § 16-5(D)(5), n. 120
United States v. Kirk, 41 M.J. 529 (C.G.Ct.Crim.App. 1994) — § 15-13, nn. 9, 21; § 15-14(B), n. 21
United States v. Kirkpatrick, 33 M.J. 132 (C.M.A. 1991) — § 16-9, n. 9
United States v. Kirks, 34 M.J. 646 (A.C.M.R. 1992) — § 15-13, n. 11; § 6-1(C)(1), n. 115; § 13-5(G)(2), n. 45
United States v. Kirsch, 15 C.M.A. 84, 35 C.M.R. 56 (1964) — § 13-3(H), n. 233
United States v. Kitchen, 5 C.M.A. 541, 18 C.M.R. 165 (1955) — § 2-2(C)(3), n. 44
United States v. Kitchens, 12 C.M.A. 589, 31 C.M.R. 175 (1961) — § 6-5(A), n. 7
United States v. Kitts, 23 M.J. 105 (C.M.A. 1987) — § 6-3(A), n. 3; § 6-5(A), n. 23
United States v. Kitts, 43 M.J. 23 (1995) — § 5-3(C)(6), n. 86
United States v. Klawuhn, 33 M.J. 941 (N.M.C.M.R. 1991) — § 7-3, n. 5; § 7-3(B), n. 30
United States v. Klein, 42 C.M.R. 671 (A.C.M.R. 1970) — § 2-3(B), n. 19

TABLE OF CASES

United States v. Kline, 21 M.J. 366 (C.M.A. 1986) — § 2-6(C), n. 40
United States v. Kline, 35 M.J. 329 (C.M.A. 1992) — § 5-4(B), n. 31
United States v. Klingensmith, 17 M.J. 814 (A.C.M.R. 1984) — § 15-10(B), n. 68
United States v. Klink, 5 M.J. 404 (C.M.A. 1978) — § 4-11(A), n. 12
United States v. Klinko, 36 M.J. 840 (A.C.M.R. 1993) — § 9-2(B)(1), n. 39; § 16-5(D)(1), n. 61
United States v. Kloese, 24 M.J. 783 (A.C.M.R. 1987) — § 17-9(B), n. 33
United States v. Klunk, 3 C.M.A. 92, 11 C.M.R. 92 (1953) — § 4-8(A), n. 5
United States v. Knickerbocker, 2 M.J. 128 (C.M.A. 1977) — § 15-13, n. 10
United States v. Kniess, 264 F.2d 353 (7th Cir. 1969) — § 14-3, n. 7
United States v. Knight, 7 M.J. 671 (A.C.M.R. 1979) — § 12-4, n. 13; § 15-2(A), n. 5
United States v. Knight, 15 M.J. 202 (C.M.A. 1983) — § 17-14, n. 10
United States v. Knight, 33 M.J. 896 (A.F.C.M.R. 1991) — § 4-16, n. 17
United States v. Knight, 41 M.J. 867 (Army Ct.Crim.App. 1995) — § 15-2(E), n. 152
United States v. Kochan, 27 M.J. 574 (N.M.C.M.R. 1988) — § 2-4(A), n. 13
United States v. Koepke, 15 C.M.A. 542, 36 C.M.R. 40 (1965) — § 6-1, n. 32
United States v. Kohlman, 21 C.M.R. 793 (A.B.R. 1956) — § 2-2(C)(3), n. 36
United States v. Kohut, 41 M.J. 565 (N.M.Ct.Crim.App. 1994) — § 4-12(A), n. 10; § 6-4(C), n. 19
United States v. Koistinen, 24 M.J. 676 (A.F.C.M.R. 1987) — § 11-2(A)(2), n. 10
United States v. Koke, 32 M.J. 876 (N.M.C.M.R. 1991) — § 8-4, n. 10; § 8-5, nn. 13-15; § 16-6, n. 17
United States v. Koke, 34 M.J. 313 (C.M.A. 1992) — § 8-5, nn. 2, 4
United States v. Komorous, 33 M.J. 907 (A.F.C.M.R. 1991) — § 17-2(B)(3), n. 88; § 17-8(B)(3), n. 77
United States v. Konarski, 8 M.J. 146 (C.M.A. 1979) — § 16-6, n. 10
United States v. Konieczka, 31 M.J. 289 (C.M.A. 1990) — § 5-3(D)(1), n. 128
United States v. Koonce, 16 M.J. 660 (A.C.M.R. 1983) — § 17-2(B)(3), n. 62
United States v. Koopman, 20 M.J. 106 (C.M.A. 1985) — § 9-2, nn. 5, 8; § 9-2(B)(1), n. 46
United States v. Koppen, 39 M.J. 897 (A.C.M.R. 1994) — § 17-9(A), n. 19
United States v. Korda, 36 M.J. 578 (A.F.C.M.R. 1992) — § 5-3(C)(5), n. 81
United States, Korematsu v.
United States, Korte v.
United States v. Kossman, 38. M.J. 258 (C.M.A. 1993) — § 13-3(C)(2), nn. 82-96
United States v. Kossman, 37 M.J. 639 (N.M.C.M.R. 1993) — § 13-3(C)(2), nn. 54, 81
United States v. Kossman — § 13-3(C)(2), n. 54
United States v. Kovac, 36 M.J. 521 (C.G.C.M.R. 1992) — § 8-3(A), n. 20
United States v. Kozak, 12 M.J. 389 (C.M.A. 1982) — § 5-3(F), n. 26
United States v. Kraffa, 11 M.J. 453 (C.M.A. 1981) — § 17-15(C), n. 38
United States v. Krajewski, 30 M.J. 995 (N.M.C.M.R. 1990) — § 8-3(B)(3), n. 76
United States v. Kramer, 30 M.J. 805 (A.F.C.M.R. 1990) — § 5-4(B), n. 44
United States v. Krampf, 9 M.J. 593 (A.F.C.M.R. 1980) — § 9-3, n. 6
United States v. Kratzenberg, 20 M.J. 670 (A.F.C.M.R. 1985) — § 12-2(H), nn. 102, 123
United States v. Krauss, 20 M.J. 741 (N.M.C.M.R. 1985) — § 6-1(C)(3), n. 141
United States v. Krautheim, 10 M.J. 763 (N.C.M.R. 1981) — § 9-2(B)(1), n. 50; § 9-2(B)(2), n. 70
United States v. Krenn, 12 M.J. 594 (A.C.M.R. 1981) — § 17-6, n. 5
United States v. Kretchmer, 33 M.J. 617 (A.F.C.M.R. 1991) — § 5-4(A)(2), n. 14
United States v. Krewson, 12 M.J. 157 (C.M.A. 1981) — § 16-5(C), n. 28

TABLE OF CASES

United States v. Kroop, 34 M.J. 628 (A.F.C.M.R. 1992) — § 8-4, n. 7; § 8-3(C)(4), n. 156; § 17-9(B), n. 39

United States v. Kropf, 39 M.J. 107 (C.M.A. 1994) — § 16-8(B), n. 12

United States v. Krutsinger, 15 C.M.A. 235, 35 C.M.R. 207 (1965) — § 2-2(C)(3), n. 55; § 6-1(B)(2), n. 82

United States v. Krzcuik, 34 M.J. 1002 (A.C.M.R. 1992) — § 16-5(D)(3), n. 77

United States v. Kuczaj, 29 M.J. 604 (A.C.M.R. 1989) — § 5-10(D), n. 32

United States v. Kuehl, 11 M.J. 126 (C.M.A. 1981) — § 16-5(C), n. 49

United States v. Kuelker, 20 M.J. 715 (N.M.C.M.R. 1985) — § 13-3(C)(3), n. 162

United States v. Kunkle, 23 M.J. 213 (C.M.A. 1987) — § 2-7(B), n. 19

United States v. Kurz, 20 M.J. 857 (C.G.C.M.R. 1985) — § 15-2(B)(3), n. 75

United States v. Kyle, 32 M.J. 724 (A.F.C.M.R. 1991) — § 9-2(A)(3), n. 29; § 14-3(D)(3), n. 140

United States v. Kyles, 20 M.J. 571 (N.M.C.M.R. 1985) — § 4-11(A), n. 18; § 14-3(F), n. 188

United States v. LaBella, 14 M.J. 688 (N.M.C.M.R. 1982) — § 13-2(G)(2), n. 74

United States v. LaBella, 15 M.J. 228 (C.M.A. 1983) — § 13-2(G)(1), n. 71; § 17-19, n. 17

United States v. Lacey, 23 C.M.A. 334, 49 C.M.R. 738 (1975) — § 17-9(B), n. 40

United States v. Lackey, 22 C.M.R. 384 (A.B.R. 1956) — § 15-10(A), n. 18; § 15-10(B), n. 77

United States v. Lackey, 8 C.M.A. 718, 25 C.M.R. 222 (1958) — § 15-13, n. 27

United States v. Ladell, 30 M.J. 672 (A.F.C.M.R. 1990) — § 12-2(D), n. 27; § 15-10(B), n. 69

United States v. LaGrange, 1 C.M.A. 342, 3 C.M.R. 76 (1952) — § 6-4(C), n. 16

United States v. Lahman, 12 M.J. 513 (N.M.C.M.R. 1981) — § 4-2, n. 4; § 1-3(D)(2), n. 22

United States v. Lake, 36 M.J. 317 (C.M.A. 1993) — § 15-10(A), nn. 8, 18, 23; § 15-10(B), nn. 44, 57, 58, 67, 76, 77

United States v. Lallande, 22 C.M.A. 170, 46 C.M.R. 170 (1973) — § 9-2(B)(1), n. 44

United States v. Lamar, 29 M.J. 889 (A.C.M.R. 1989) — § 11-2(E)(2), n. 118

United States v. Lambert, 17 M.J. 773 (A.F.C.M.R. 1983) — § 15-2(B)(1), n. 25

United States v. Lamela, 6 M.J. 32 (C.M.A. 1972) — § 8-3(C)(3), n. 146

United States v. Lamer, 32 M.J. 63 (C.M.A. 1990) — § 13-3(C)(3), n. 159

United States v. Laminman, 41 M.J. 518 (C.G.Ct.Crim.App. 1994) — § 13-2(G)(2), n. 81; § 13-3(C)(2), n. 91

United States v. Lampani, 14 M.J. 22 (C.M.A. 1982) — § 15-12(B), n. 20; § 15-15, n. 28

United States v. Lancaster, 36 M.J. 1115 (A.F.C.M.R. 1993) — § 2-7(B), n. 14

United States v. Landwehr, 18 M.J. 355 (C.M.A. 1984) — § 2-4(F), n. 53

United States v. Lane, 28 C.M.R. 749 (A.F.B.R. 1959) — § 2-6(A), n. 23

United States v. Lanford, 6 C.M.A. 371, 20 C.M.R. 87 (1955) — § 17-2(B)(3), n. 62

United States v. Lange, 15 C.M.A. 486, 35 C.M.R. 458 (1965) — § 5-3(D)(1), n. 118

United States v. Lange, 18 M.J. 162 (C.M.A. 1984) — § 17-15(A), n. 14

United States v. Langer, 41 M.J. 780 (A.F.Ct.Crim.App. 1995) — § 5-4(B), n. 30; § 15-16(B), n. 17

United States v. Langford, 15 M.J. 1090 (A.C.M.R. 1983) — § 5-4(A)(3), nn. 19, 21

United States v. Langston, 32 M.J. 894 (A.F.C.M.R. 1991) — § 11-2(A)(3), nn. 32, 34, 35, 37, 38

United States v. Lania, 9 M.J. 100 (C.M.A. 1980) — § 16-8(B), n. 8

United States v. Lanphear, 23 C.M.A. 338, 49 C.M.R. 742 (1975) — § 2-2(C)(3), n. 45; § 2-2(E)(5), n. 91

TABLE OF CASES

United States v. Lanzer, 3 M.J. 60 (C.M.A. 1977) — § 9-2, nn. 5, 7
United States v. Lapeer, 28 M.J. 189 (C.M.A. 1989) — § 16-6, n. 21
United States v. Larkins, 21 M.J. 654 (A.C.M.R. 1985) — § 16-5(B), n. 26
United States v. Larneard, 3 M.J. 76 (C.M.A. 1977) — § 17-1, n. 1; § 17-16(B), n. 13
United States v. Larner, 1 M.J. 371 (C.M.A. 1976) — § 13-3(N)(1), n. 303
United States v. Larson, 33 M.J. 714 (A.C.M.R. 1991) — § 8-3(D), n. 163
United States v. Lasagni, 8 M.J. 627 (N.C.M.R. 1979) — § 14-3(B)(3), n. 111
United States v. Lashley, 14 M.J. 7 (C.M.A. 1982) — § 17-4, n. 33
United States v. Lassiter, 11 C.M.A. 89, 28 C.M.R. 313 (1959) — § 7-2(B)(4), n. 56
United States v. Lassiter, 35 M.J. 831 (A.C.M.R. 1992) — § 5-10(D), n. 37
United States v. Latham, 39 M.J. 841 (A.C.M.R. 1994) — § 15-16(A), n. 10
United States v. Latimer, 30 M.J. 554 (A.C.M.R. 1990) — § 8-3(D), n. 166; § 15-4(C), n. 18
United States v. Latimer, 35 M.J. 736 (A.C.M.R. 1992) — § 17-8(B)(2), n. 60
United States v. Latta, 34 M.J. 596 (A.C.M.R. 1992) — § 5-10(B), n. 8; § 5-10(D), n. 36
United States v. Lauzon, 21 M.J. 791 (A.C.M.R. 1986) — § 15-10(B), n. 57; § 15-10(C)(2), n. 94
United States v. Lavalla, 24 M.J. 593 (A.F.C.M.R. 1987) — § 5-9(E), n. 54; § 5-10(D), n. 29
United States v. Lavine, 13 M.J. 150 (C.M.A. 1982) — § 5-4(B), n. 23
United States v. Lawer, 41 M.J. 751 (C.G.Ct.Crim.App. 1995) — § 16-5(D)(5), n. 118; § 16-6, n. 24
United States v. Lawless, 13 M.J. 943 (A.F.C.M.R. 1982) — § 11-2(F), n. 160
United States v. Lawless, 18 M.J. 255 (C.M.A. 1984) — § 5-3(F), n. 26; § 13-4(A), n. 14
United States v. Lawrence, 19 M.J. 609 (A.C.M.R. 1984) — § 8-2(A), n. 3; § 10-4(A)(4), n. 27
United States v. Lawrence, 22 M.J. 846 (A.C.M.R. 1986) — § 16-5(D)(4), n. 86
United States v. Lawrence, 30 M.J. 1140 (A.F.C.M.R. 1990) — § 15-10(C)(3), n. 118
United States v. Lawrence, 43 M.J. 677 (A.F.Ct.Crim.App. 1995) — § 9-3, n. 11
United States v. Laws, 11 M.J. 475 (C.M.A. 1981) — § 4-9, n. 7
United States v. Lawson, 16 C.M.A. 260, 36 C.M.R. 416 (1966) — § 7-3(A), n. 18; § 7-3(B), n. 31
United States v. Lawson, 16 M.J. 38 (C.M.A. 1983) — § 15-15, n. 19
United States v. Lawson, 33 M.J. 946 (N.M.C.M.R. 1991) — § 6-4(C), n. 19; § 6-4(E), n. 27; § 6-5(A), n. 6; § 6-7, n. 11; § 6-8, nn. 1, 3; § 16-5(D)(2), n. 64
United States v. Lawson, 34 M.J. 38 (C.M.A. 1992) — § 16-2(B), n. 14
United States v. Lawson, 36 M.J. 415 (C.M.A. 1993) — § 2-4(E), n. 48
United States v. Lawson, 40 M.J. 475 (C.M.A. 1994) — § 15-2(B)(3), n. 70
United States v. Lazenby, 42 M.J. 702 (C.G.Ct.Crim.App. 1995) — § 5-3(B), n. 40
United States v. Lazzaro, 2 M.J. 76 (C.M.A. 1976) — § 4-11(A), n. 30
United States v. Leahy, 20 M.J. 564 (N.M.C.M.R. 1984) — § 8-2(B), n. 12
United States v. Leamer, 29 M.J. 616 (C.G.C.M.R. 1989) — § 6-1, n. 45; § 13-3(C)(3), n. 109
United States v. Leaver, 32 M.J. 995 (C.G.C.M.R. 1991) — § 12-5, n. 18; § 15-2(B)(3), n. 64; § 17-8(B)(3), n. 83
United States v. Leaver, 36 M.J. 133 (C.M.A. 1992) — § 17-14, n. 9; § 17-8(B)(3), n. 85
United States v. Lecolst, 4 M.J. 800 (N.M.C.M.R. 1978) — § 3-4, n. 1; § 13-3(N)(1), nn. 308, 313, 337
United States, Ledbetter v.
United States v. Ledbetter, 2 M.J. 37 (C.M.A. 1976) — § 6-5(A), n. 13; § 6-6(B), n. 5; § 7-2(E), n. 108; § 7-2(B)(4), n. 46; § 17-2(B)(2), n. 24

TABLE OF CASES

United States v. Lee, 1 M.J. 15 (C.M.A. 1975) — § 15-16(A), n. 13
United States v. Lee, 6 M.J. 96 (C.M.A. 1978) — § 15-14(B), n. 45
United States v. Lee, 13 M.J. 181 (C.M.A. 1982) — § 16-11, n. 1
United States v. Lee, 14 M.J. 633 (A.C.M.R. 1982) — § 2-2(E)(1), n. 73
United States v. Lee, 14 M.J. 983 (N.M.C.M.R. 1982) — § 6-1(B)(3), n. 89
United States v. Lee, 16 M.J. 278 (C.M.A. 1983) — § 14-3(D)(4), n. 148
United States v. Lee, 16 M.J. 532 (A.C.M.R. 1983) — § 15-14(B), n. 41
United States v. Lee, 25 M.J. 457 (C.M.A. 1988) — § 5-4(B), n. 42
United States v. Lee, 29 M.J. 516 (A.C.M.R. 1989) — § 13-3(B), n. 9
United States v. Lee, 32 M.J. 857 (N.M.C.M.R. 1991) — § 13-3(B), nn. 9, 19; § 13-3(N)(5), n. 431
United States v. Leggs, 18 C.M.A. 245, 39 C.M.R. 245 (1969) — § 14-3(D)(4), n. 146
United States v. Leiffer, 13 M.J. 337 (C.M.A. 1982) — § 5-4(B), n. 23
United States v. Leiker, 37 M.J. 418 (C.M.A. 1993) — § 5-4(B), n. 44
United States v. Leininger, 25 M.J. 746 (A.C.M.R. 1987) — § 17-8(B)(2), n. 62
United States v. LeMaster, 40 M.J. 178 (C.M.A. 1994) — § 2-7(B), n. 24
United States v. LeMasters, 39 M.J. 490 (C.M.A. 1994) — § 5-4(B), n. 51
United States v. Lemieux, 13 M.J. 969 (A.C.M.R. 1982) — § 16-5(C), nn. 35, 42, 43
United States v. Lemley, 2 M.J. 1196 (N.C.M.R. 1976) — § 2-2(D), n. 65
United States v. Lemoine, 34 M.J. 1120 (A.F.C.M.R. 1992) — § 17-19, nn. 15, 25, 32
United States v. Lemon, 5 M.J. 750 (A.F.C.M.R. 1978) — § 3-8(B), n. 12
United States v. Lenard, 27 M.J. 739 (A.C.M.R. 1988) — § 16-9, n. 10
United States v. Lenoir, 13 M.J. 452 (C.M.A. 1982) — § 15-10(B), n. 53
United States v. Lenoir, 39 M.J. 751 (A.F.C.M.R. 1994) — § 6-1(C)(3), nn. 160, 161
United States v. Lents, 32 M.J. 636 (A.C.M.R. 1991) — § 15-12(B), nn. 14, 20
United States v. Lenz, 616 F.2d 960 (6th Cir. 1980) — § 11-2(E)(3), n. 126
United States v. Leonard, 16 M.J. 984 (A.C.M.R. 1983) — § 14-3(G), nn. 196, 197, 199
United States v. Leonard, 21 M.J. 67 (C.M.A. 1985) — § 13-3(C)(3), n. 108
United States v. Leonard, 41 M.J. 900 (C.G.Ct.Crim.App. 1995) — § 17-9(D), n. 62
United States v. Leon, 468 U.S. 897 (1984) — § 5-3(F), n. 23
United States v. Levin, 14 M.J. 814 (A.C.M.R. 1982) — § 14-3(B)(2), n. 74
United States v. Levite, 25 M.J. 334 (C.M.A. 1987) — § 6-5(B), nn. 32, 33, 35-37, 39; § 6-5(C), n. 50; § 6-6(C), n. 14; § 6-7, nn. 13-15; § 6-8, n. 12
United States v. Lewandowski, 17 C.M.A. 51, 37 C.M.R. 315 (1967) — § 15-15, n. 10
United States v. Lewis, 11 C.M.A. 503, 29 C.M.R. 319 (1960) — § 16-2, n. 3
United States v. Lewis, 1 M.J. 904 (A.F.C.M.R. 1976) — § 1-3(D)(2), n. 22
United States v. Lewis, 5 M.J. 712 (A.C.M.R. 1978) — § 4-11(A), n. 35; § 6-1(B)(1), n. 75
United States v. Lewis, 7 M.J. 348 (C.M.A. 1979) — § 2-3(C), n. 27
United States v. Lewis, 7 M.J. 958 (A.F.C.M.R. 1979) — § 16-8(B), n. 15
United States v. Lewis, 12 M.J. 205 (C.M.A. 1982) — § 5-4(B), n. 23
United States v. Lewis, 23 M.J. 508 (A.F.C.M.R. 1986) — § 5-4(B), n. 51
United States v. Lewis, 28 M.J. 179 (C.M.A. 1989) — § 2-5, n. 3
United States v. Lewis, 28 M.J. 871 (A.C.M.R. 1989) — § 14-3(D)(3), n. 144
United States v. Lewis, 33 M.J. 758 (A.C.M.R. 1991) — § 5-4(B), n. 51; § 7-2(C), n. 81; § 7-2(B)(4), n. 44
United States v. Lewis, 34 M.J. 745 (N.M.C.M.R. 1991) — § 8-4, n. 7; § 13-5(A), n. 15
United States v. Lewis, 36 M.J. 299 (C.M.A. 1993) — § 5-4(B), n. 51
United States v. Lewis, 38 M.J. 501 (A.C.M.R. 1993) — § 10-4(B)(5), nn. 55, 58
United States v. Lewis, 42 M.J. 1 (1995) — § 15-2(B)(3), nn. 86, 103, 104, 105, 108, 109
United States v. Ley, 20 M.J. 814 (N.M.C.M.R. 1985) — § 8-3(B)(1), n. 52
United States v. Liberator, 14 C.M.A. 499, 34 C.M.R. 279 (1964) — § 17-3(A), n. 20

TABLE OF CASES

United States v. Lichtenhan, 40 M.J. 466 (C.M.A. 1994) — § 5-4(B), n. 46
United States v. Lichtsinn, 32 M.J. 898 (A.F.C.M.R. 1991) — § 12-4, n. 6; § 17-2(B)(3), n. 80
United States v. Light, 36 C.M.R. 579 (A.B.R. 1965) — § 2-8(A), n. 2
United States v. Lightfoot, 4 M.J. 262 (C.M.A. 1978) — § 4-5(A)(2), n. 4
United States v. Lillie, 4 M.J. 907 (N.C.M.R. 1978) — § 6-2(B), n. 13
United States v. Lilly, 22 M.J. 620 (N.M.C.M.R. 1986) — § 13-3(C)(3), n. 160
United States v. Lilly, 34 M.J. 670 (A.C.M.R. 1992) — § 14-3(B)(1), n. 55; § 14-3(D)(4), n. 145; § n. 429
United States v. Lincoln, 40 M.J. 679 (N.M.C.M.R. 1994) — § 5-4(B), nn. 30, 52
United States v. Lincoln, 42 M.J. 315 (1995) — § 5-4(B), n. 30; § 13-2(G)(2), n. 90
United States v. Lindsay, 11 M.J. 550 (A.C.M.R. 1981) — § 5-4(A)(2), n. 15
United States v. Lindsey, 39 C.M.R. 778 (A.B.R. 1968) — § 8-3(D), n. 166
United States v. Lippoldt, 34 M.J. 523 (A.F.C.M.R. 1991) — § 13-2(E), n. 48; § 14-3(A)(2), n. 27
United States v. Lips, 22 M.J. 679 (A.F.C.M.R. 1986) — § 17-15(B), nn. 20, 21
United States v. Lipscomb, 38 M.J. 608 (C.G.C.M.R. 1993) — § 5-9(B), n. 7
United States v. Little, 1 M.J. 476 (C.M.A. 1976) — § 4-5(A)(3), n. 11
United States v. Little, 43 M.J. 88 (1995) — § 14-3(D)(4), n. 154
United States v. Littrice, 3 C.M.A. 487, 13 C.M.R. 43 (1953) — § 6-3(B), n. 15; § 6-5(A), n. 3
United States v. Lizasuain, 30 M.J. 543 (A.C.M.R. 1990) — § 16-5(D)(4), n. 101
United States v. Llewellyn, 27 M.J. 825 (A.C.M.R. 1988) — § 14-3(C), n. 123
United States v. Llewellyn, 32 M.J. 803 (A.C.M.R. 1991) — § 15-14(B), n. 41; § 15-15, n. 18
United States v. Lloyd, 10 M.J. 172 (C.M.A. 1981) — § 2-4(A), n. 16
United States v. Lochausen, 8 M.J. 262 (C.M.A. 1980) — § 17-9(B), n. 38
United States v. Lockett, 7 M.J. 753 (A.C.M.R. 1979) — § 6-1(C)(3), n. 139
United States v. Lockwood, 15 M.J. 1 (C.M.A. 1983) — § 4-11(A), n. 16; § 4-11(B), nn. 41-44; § 13-3(A), n. 3
United States v. Lockwood, 31 M.J. 514 (A.C.M.R. 1990) — § 5-4(B), n. 50
United States v. Logan, 22 C.M.A. 349, 47 C.M.R. 1 (1973) — § 14-3(D)(4), n. 148
United States v. Logan, 15 M.J. 1084 (A.F.C.M.R. 1983) — § 15-15, n. 3
United States v. Logan, 18 M.J. 606 (A.F.C.M.R. 1984) — § 2-2(B), n. 14
United States v. Logan, 29 M.J. 1072 (A.C.M.R. 1990) — § 17-9(A), n. 30
United States v. Logan, 31 M.J. 910 (A.F.C.M.R. 1990) — § 14-3(D)(4), n. 145
United States v. Lohr, 43 C.M.R. 1017 (A.F.C.M.R. 1970) — § 15-16(C), n. 39
United States v. Lohrman, 26 M.J. 610 (A.C.M.R. 1988) — § 17-8(B)(2), n. 63
United States v. Lomax, 12 M.J. 1001 (A.C.M.R. 1982) — § 15-15, n. 14; § 17-15(B), n. 33
United States v. London, 15 C.M.R. 90 (C.M.A. 1954) — § 15-16(A), n. 16
United States v. Lonetree, 31 M.J. 849 (N.M.C.M.R. 1990) — § 5-4(B), nn. 37, 43; § 15-3, n. 6
United States v. Lonetree, 35 M.J. 396 (C.M.A. 1992) — § 5-4(B), nn. 43, 52; § 15-2(B)(3), n. 50
United States v. Long, 17 C.M.A. 323, 38 C.M.R. 121 (1967) — § 16-8(B), n. 18
United States v. Long, 3 M.J. 400 (C.M.A. 1977) — § 9-3, n. 1
United States v. Long, 17 M.J. 661 (N.M.C.M.R. 1983) — § 4-5(A)(3), n. 12; § 13-3(n)(5), n. 436
United States v. Long, 20 M.J. 657 (N.M.C.M.R. 1985) — § 14-3(B)(2), n. 71
United States v. Longhi, 36 M.J. 988 (A.F.C.M.R. 1993) — § 16-3(B), n. 43

TABLE OF CASES

United States v. Longhofer, 29 M.J. 22 (C.M.A. 1989) — § 13-3(C)(3), nn. 136, 148, 167
United States v. Longmire, 39 M.J. 536 (A.C.M.R. 1994) — § 4-16, n. 11; § 6-1(B)(2), nn. 84, 85
United States v. Longstreath, 42 M.J. 806 (N.M.C.Ct.Crim.App. 1995) — § 15-12(A), n. 8; § 10-4(B)(5), n. 57
United States v. Loos, 4 C.M.A. 478, 16 C.M.R. 52 (1954) — § 16-2(F), n. 58
United States v. Lopez, 20 C.M.A. 76, 42 C.M.R. 268 (1970) — § 7-2(E), nn. 105, 112; § 7-2(A)(1), n. 20
United States v. Lopez, 32 M.J. 924 (A.F.C.M.R. 1991) — § 5-3(F), n. 24
United States v. Lopez, 35 M.J. 35 (C.M.A. 1992) — § 5-3(F), n. 24
United States v. Lopez, 37 M.J. 702 (A.C.M.R. 1993) — § 15-4(A), n. 7; § 15-10(C)(2), n. 104
United States v. Lorance, 35 M.J. 382 (C.M.A. 1992) — § 16-3(C), n. 47; § 3-6(C)(5), n. 16
United States v. Lorenc, 26 M.J. 793 (A.F.C.M.R. 1988) — § 4-12(A), n. 7; § 13-3(G), n. 228
United States v. Lorenc, 30 M.J. 619 (N.M.C.M.R. 1990) — § 13-3(C)(3), n. 118
United States v. Louder, 7 M.J. 548 (A.F.C.M.R. 1979) — § 6-1(B)(2), n. 84
United States v. Loukas, 29 M.J. 385 (C.M.A. 1990) — § 5-4(B), n. 42
United States v. Lovasco, 431 U.S. 783 (1977) — § 13-3(C)(1), nn. 42-47
United States v. Lovejoy, 39 C.M.R. 774 (A.B.R. 1968) — § 15-10(B), nn. 74, 76
United States v. Lovejoy, 20 C.M.A. 18, 42 C.M.R. 210 (1971) — § 2-8(A), n. 3
United States v. Lovell, 7 C.M.A. 445, 22 C.M.R. 235 (1956) — § 2-2(C)(3), n. 39
United States, Loving v.
United States v. Loving, 34 M.J. 956 (A.F.C.M.R. 1992) — § 13-5(C), n. 31; § 13-3(N)(1), n. 338
United States v. Loving, 41 M.J. 213 (A.C.M.R. 1992) — § 8-3(A), n. 19
United States v. Loving, 41 M.J. 213 (1994) — § 7-3(B), n. 26; § 8-3(A), n. 11; § 13-3(M), n. 292; § 13-5(A), n. 15; § 13-5(C), n. 40; § 15-2(D), nn. 129, 134, 135; § 15-16(B), nn. 19, 21, 27; § 16-3(A), n. 13; § 16-9, n. 8; § 6-1(B)(2), n. 81; § 8-3(C)(4), nn. 151, 153; § 15-2(B)(3), nn. 54, 63, 73, 78
United States v. Lowery, 18 M.J. 695 (A.F.C.M.R. 1984) — § 6-3(C), n. 31; § 6-6(C), n. 12
United States v. Lowery, 21 M.J. 998 (A.C.M.R. 1986) — § 2-8(B), n. 18
United States v. Lowery, 37 M.J. 1038 (A.C.M.R. 1993) — § 17-8(B)(3), n. 92
United States v. Lowry, 33 M.J. 1035 (N.M.C.M.R. 1991) — § 17-8(B)(2), nn. 64, 65
United States v. Lubitz, 40 M.J. 165 (C.M.A. 1994) — § 2-7(B), n. 24
United States v. Lucas, 32 C.M.R. 619 (A.B.R. 1962) — § 16-6, n. 21
United States v. Lucas, 5 M.J. 167 (C.M.A. 1978) — § 10-4(A)(4), n. 27; § 10-4(B)(1), n. 33; § 11-2(B)(1), n. 60
United States v. Lucas, 19 M.J. 773 (A.F.C.M.R. 1984) — § 11-2(E)(1), n. 106
United States v. Lucas, 25 M.J. 9 (C.M.A. 1987) — § 5-4(C), n. 56; § 13-3(H), n. 243
United States, Luce v.
United States v. Ludlum, 20 M.J. 954 (A.F.C.M.R. 1985) — § 2-7(B), n. 20
United States v. Luebs, 20 C.M.A. 475, 43 C.M.R. 315 (1971) — § 14-3(B)(2), n. 95
United States v. Luedtke, 19 M.J. 548 (N.M.C.M.R. 1984) — § 17-3, n. 7; § 17-9(C), n. 55; § 17-10, n. 5
United States v. Lugo, 32 M.J. 719 (C.G.C.M.R. 1991) — § 17-8(B)(3), n. 71
United States v. Lumagui, 31 M.J. 789 (A.F.C.M.R. 1990) — § 2-4(A), n. 14
United States v. Lumbus, 48 C.M.R. 613 (A.C.M.R. 1974) — § 12-2(A), n. 7
United States v. Lusk, 21 M.J. 695 (A.C.M.R. 1985) — § 2-3(B), n. 17

TABLE OF CASES

United States v. Lutz, 18 M.J. 763 (C.G.C.M.R. 1984) — § 8-3(C)(4), n. 152
United States v. Lwin, 42 M.J. 279 (1995) — § 4-6, n. 1
United States v. Lynch, 47 C.M.R. 143 (A.C.M.R. 1973) — § 13-3(E), n. 193
United States v. Lynch, 22 C.M.A. 457, 47 C.M.R. 498 (1973) — § 2-2(C)(3), nn. 40, 50
United States v. Lynch, 10 M.J. 764 (N.M.C.R. 1981) — § 17-9(D), n. 75
United States v. Lynch, 13 M.J. 394 (C.M.A. 1982) — § 5-9(D), n. 35; § 12-2(H), n. 104
United States v. Lynch, 35 M.J. 579 (C.G.C.M.R. 1992) — § 6-3(B), n. 13; § 6-3(C), n. 23; § 6-4(C), n. 16; § 6-4(E), n. 27; § 6-5(A), nn. 6, 23; § 15-10(C)(1), n. 86
United States v. Lynch, 39 M.J. 223 (C.M.A. 1994) — § 17-8(B), n. 20
United States v. Lynott, 28 M.J. 918 (C.G.C.M.R. 1989) — § 16-5(D)(5), n. 116
United States v. Lyons, 50 C.M.R. 804 (A.C.M.R. 1975) — § 13-3(C)(2), n. 73
United States v. Lyons, 30 M.J. 724 (A.F.C.M.R. 1990) — § 16-2(D), n. 39
United States v. Lyons, 33 M.J. 543 (A.F.C.M.R. 1991) — § 6-1(C)(3), n. 134
United States v. Lyons, 36 M.J. 425 (C.M.A. 1993) — § 16-8(C), nn. 35, 37
United States v. Mabe, 33 M.J. 200 (C.M.A. 1991) — § 6-5(A), nn. 12, 13, 15-18
United States v. Mabie, 24 M.J. 711 (A.C.M.R. 1987) — § 2-6(B), n. 30
United States v. MacCulloch, 40 M.J. 236 (C.M.A. 1994) — § 15-2(B)(3), n. 86
United States v. Mack, 9 M.J. 300 (C.M.A. 1980) — § 16-5(B), n. 13
United States v. Mack, 9 M.J. 300 (C.M.A. 1980) — § 3-8(B), n. 13; § 15-26(C), n. 10; § 16-2(E), n. 48; § 16-5(B), n. 12
United States v. Mack, 25 M.J. 519 (A.C.M.R. 1987) — § 15-2(B)(3), n. 38
United States v. Mack, 33 M.J. 251 (C.M.A. 1991) — § 2-7(C), n. 40
United States v. Mack, 41 M.J. 51 (C.M.A. 1994) — § 15-10(A), n. 31
United States v. Mackey, 46 C.M.R. 754 (N.C.M.R. 1972) — § 2-2(B), n. 15
United States v. Maderia, 38 M.J. 494 (C.M.A. 1994) — § 2-5, n. 2
United States v. Madison, 20 M.J. 860 (C.G.C.M.R. 1985) — § 17-11, n. 3
United States v. Maglito, 20 C.M.A. 456, 43 C.M.R. 296 (1971) — § 5-3(C)(4), n. 77
United States v. Maharajh, 28 M.J. 797 (A.F.C.M.R. 1989) — § 16-9, n. 10
United States v. Mahloch, 29 M.J. 1080 (C.G.C.M.R. 1990) — § 8-3(A), n. 2
United States v. Mahone, 14 M.J. 521 (A.F.C.M.R. 1982) — § 10-2(B), n. 35
United States v. Mahoney, 27 C.M.R. 898 (N.B.R. 1959) — § 3-3(C), n. 23
United States v. Mahoney, 24 M.J. 911 (A.F.C.M.R. 1987) — § 13-2(G)(2), n. 81
United States v. Mahoney, 28 M.J. 865 (A.F.C.M.R. 1989) — § 13-3(C)(3), nn. 156, 163
United States v. Mahoney, 36 M.J. 679 (A.F.C.M.R. 1992) — § 17-3(B), n. 41
United States v. Malczewskyj, 26 M.J. 995 (A.F.C.M.R. 1988) — § 4-15(C), n. 19; § 15-9, nn. 5-7
United States v. Malia, 6 M.J. 65 (C.M.A. 1978) — § 5-9(A), n. 5; 5-9(D), n. 43
United States v. Malik, 23 M.J. 607 (A.F.C.M.R. 1986) — § 4-11(B), n. 40
United States v. Mallett, 14 M.J. 631 (A.C.M.R. 1982) — § 14-4, n. 1; § 9-2(B)(1), n. 55
United States v. Malone, 29 M.J. 883 (A.C.M.R. 1989) — § 12-3, n. 3
United States v. Malone, 29 M.J. 1027 (A.C.M.R. 1990) — § 6-1(C)(3), n. 134
United States v. Malone, 38 M.J. 707 (A.C.M.R. 1993) — § 16-5(D)(4), n. 100
United States v. Mamaluy, 10 C.M.A. 102, 27 C.M.R. 176 (1959) — § 16-6, n. 20
United States v. Manalo, 1 M.J. 452 (C.M.A. 1976) — § 13-3(C)(2), n. 62; § 13-3(C)(3), n. 112
United States v. Mance, 26 M.J. 244 (C.M.A. 1988) — § 2-7(B), nn. 21, 22; § 15-14(B), n. 22; § 15-14(D), nn. 58, 59
United States v. Mancini, 8 F.3d 104 (1st Cir. 1993) — § 5-3(A), n. 16
United States v. Maness, 23 C.M.A. 41, 48 C.M.R. 512 (1974) — § 7-2(A)(2), n. 30; § 15-2(B)(1), n. 19
United States v. Manley, 25 M.J. 346 (C.M.A. 1987) — § 9-2(C), n. 81

TABLE OF CASES

United States v. Mann, 12 C.M.R. 367 (A.B.R. 1953) — § 2-2(E)(1), n. 73
United States v. Mann, 22 M.J. 279 (C.M.A. 1986) — § 17-9(A), nn. 3, 4
United States v. Mann, 30 M.J. 639 (N.M.C.M.R. 1990) — § 11-2(A)(3), n. 28
United States v. Mann, 32 M.J. 883 (N.M.C.M.R. 1991) — § 8-5, n. 13
United States v. Manos, 17 C.M.A. 10, 37 C.M.R. 274 (1967) — § 11-2(A)(1), n. 8
United States v. Mansbarger, 20 C.M.R. 449 (A.B.R. 1955) — § 4-8(B), n. 14
United States v. Mansell, 8 C.M.A. 153, 23 C.M.R. 377 (1957) — § 15-10(B), n. 39
United States v. Mansfield, 24 M.J. 611 (A.F.C.M.R. 1987) — § 15-2(B)(3), n. 70
United States v. Mansfield, 33 M.J. 972 (A.F.C.M.R. 1991) — § 17-11, n. 2
United States v. Mantilla, 36 M.J. 621 (A.C.M.R. 1992) — § 2-4(B), n. 24; § 15-16(A), n. 10
United States v. Manuel, 43 M.J. 282 (1995) — § 11-4, n. 5
United States v. Maracle, 26 M.J. 431 (C.M.A. 1988) — § 16-6, n. 23
United States v. Marcy, 1 C.M.A. 176, 2 C.M.R. 82 (1952) — § 6-1, nn. 35, 36
United States v. Marell, 23 C.M.A. 240, 49 C.M.R. 373 (1974) — § 13-3(C)(2), n. 71
United States v. Maresca, 28 M.J. 328 (C.M.A. 1989) — § 6-1, n. 45; § 13-3(C)(3), nn. 109, 135, 141, 161
United States v. Margelony, 14 C.M.A. 55, 33 C.M.R. 267 (1963) — § 15-20, n. 20
United States v. Marin, 20 C.M.A. 432, 43 C.M.R. 272 (1971) — § 13-3(C)(2), n. 58
United States v. Marion, 404 U.S. 307 (1971) — § 13-3(C)(1), nn. 37, 42
United States v. Marker, 1 C.M.A. 393, 3 C.M.R. 127 (1952) — § 8-1, n. 2
United States v. Markland, 2 M.J. 356 (A.F.C.M.R. 1977) — § 17-2(B)(3), n. 53
United States, Marks v.
United States v. Marler, 7 M.J. 629 (A.F.C.M.R. 1979) — § 5-9(D), n. 48
United States v. Marquardt, 39 M.J. 239 (C.M.A. 1994) — § 5-4(B), n. 34
United States v. Marrie, 39 M.J. 993 (A.F.C.M.R. 1994) — § 1-1(B), n. 34; § 13-5(D), n. 43
United States v. Marrie, 43 M.J. 35 (1995) — § 7-2(B)(4), nn. 45, 46; § 7-2(B)(6), n. 68
United States v. Marsh, 3 C.M.A. 48, 11 C.M.R. 48 (1953) — § 4-14(A)(2), n. 11
United States v. Marsh, 15 M.J. 252 (C.M.A. 1983) — § 4-5(A)(2), n. 5; § 13-3(N)(5), nn. 435, 436
United States v. Marsh, 19 M.J. 657 (A.C.M.R. 1984) — § 8-3(A), n. 14; § 12-2(G), n. 96; § 6-1(B)(3), n. 90; § 9-2(B)(1), n. 39; § 16-5(D)(1), n. 60
United States v. Marsh, 21 M.J. 616 (A.F.C.M.R. 1985) — § 2-4(C), n. 38
United States v. Marsh, 21 M.J. 445 (C.M.A. 1986) — § 8-3(D), n. 163
United States v. Marsh, 35 M.J. 505 (A.F.C.M.R. 1992) — § 16-8(B), n. 17; § 11-3(B)(1), n. 31; § 11-3(B)(2), n. 41
United States, Marshall v.
United States v. Marshall, 47 C.M.R. 409 (C.M.A. 1973) — § 13-3(C)(2), n. 50
United States v. Marshall, 22 C.M.A. 431, 47 C.M.R. 409 (1973) — § 13-3(C)(2), n. 74
United States v. Marshall, 14 M.J. 157 (C.M.A. 1982) — § 16-5, n. 1; § 16-5(D)(3), n. 75
United States v. Marshall, 31 M.J. 712 (A.F.C.M.R. 1990) — § 10-4(A)(4), n. 27
United States v. Marston, 22 M.J. 850 (A.F.C.M.R. 1986) — § 5-10(C), n. 14
United States v. Martel, 19 M.J. 917 (A.C.M.R. 1985) — § 15-19, n. 4; § 7-2(A)(1), n. 29
United States v. Martin, 1 C.M.A. 674, 5 C.M.R. 102 (1952) — § 2-4(A), n. 7
United States v. Martin, 9 C.M.A. 568, 26 C.M.R. 348 (1958) — § 4-5(B), n. 24
United States v. Martin, 4 M.J. 852 (A.C.M.R. 1978) — § 9-2(B)(1), n. 49
United States v. Martin, 5 M.J. 657 (N.C.M.R. 1978) — § 17-4, n. 7
United States v. Martin, 9 M.J. 731 (N.C.M.R. 1979) — § 5-4(A)(1), n. 9
United States v. Martin, 20 M.J. 227 (C.M.A. 1985) — § 15-19, n. 3; § 16-5(D)(1), n. 54; § 16-5(D)(5), n. 107

TABLE OF CASES

United States v. Martin, 33 M.J. 599 (A.C.M.R. 1991) — § 5-7, n. 7
United States v. Martin, 36 M.J. 315 (C.M.A. 1993) — § 6-1(C)(3), n. 134
United States v. Martin, 36 M.J. 739 (A.F.C.M.R. 1993) — § 16-8(A), n. 4; § 16-8(B), n. 12
United States v. Martin, 39 M.J. 111 (C.M.A. 1994) — § 14-3(D)(5), n. 174
United States v. Martin, 39 M.J. 481 (C.M.A. 1994) — § 16-8(A), n. 3
United States v. Martindale, 40 M.J. 348 (C.M.A. 1994) — § 13-3(H), n. 247
United States v. Martinez, 11 C.M.A. 224, 29 C.M.R. 40 (1960) — § 15-2(G), n. 167
United States v. Martinez, 2 M.J. 1123 (C.G.C.M.R. 1976) — § 16-3(D), n. 67
United States v. Martinez, 12 M.J. 801 (N.M.C.M.R. 1981) — § 13-5(A), nn. 7, 8
United States v. Martinez, 19 M.J. 652 (A.C.M.R. 1984) — § 12-2(H), nn. 99, 122
United States v. Martinez, 19 M.J. 744 (A.C.M.R. 1984) — § 5-10(D), n. 41; § 13-5(B), nn. 24, 25; § 17-5, n. 8; § 8-3(C)(4), n. 151; § 11-2(E)(1), n. 114
United States v. Martinez, 17 M.J. 916 (N.M.C.M.R. 1984) — § 15-15, n. 13; § 15-16(B), nn. 17, 26
United States v. Martinez, 27 M.J. 730 (A.C.M.R. 1988) — § 12-3(A), nn. 10, 32
United States v. Martinez, 30 M.J. 1194 (A.F.C.M.R. 1990) — § 16-8(B), n. 15
United States v. Martinez, 31 M.J. 524 (A.C.M.R. 1990) — § 15-2(B)(3), n. 85
United States v. Martinez, 36 M.J. 291 (C.M.A. 1993) — § 13-3(C)(3), n. 158
United States v. Martinez, 38 M.J. 82 (C.M.A. 1993) — § 5-4(B), n. 52
United States v. Martinez, 40 M.J. 82 (C.M.A. 1994) — § 16-10, n. 1
United States v. Martinez, 40 M.J. 426 (C.M.A. 1994) — § 15-14(B), n. 28
United States v. Martinez, 42 M.J. 327 (1995) — § 2-6(A), n. 21; § 6-5(A), n. 7
United States v. Martino, 18 M.J. 526 (A.F.C.M.R. 1984) — § 3-4, n. 10; § 13-3(M), n. 289
United States v. Martinsmith, 37 M.J. 665 (A.C.M.R. 1993) — § 17-8(B)(2), n. 63
United States v. Martinsmith, 41 M.J. 343 (1995) — § 15-12, n. 3; § 15-12(B), n. 20; § 16-6, n. 7
United States v. Marvin, 24 M.J. 365 (C.M.A. 1987) — § 15-12(D), nn. 29, 30
United States v. Maschino, 31 M.J. 841 (N.M.C.M.R. 1990) — § 15-12(C), n. 25
United States v. Maslanich, 13 M.J. 611 (A.F.C.M.R. 1982) — § 2-2(B), n. 8
United States v. Masminster, 7 C.M.R. 593 (A.F.B.R. 1952) — § 15-10(B), n. 46
United States v. Mason, 16 M.J. 455 (C.M.A. 1983) — § 15-10(C)(2), n. 95
United States v. Mason, 19 M.J. 274 (C.M.A. 1985) — § 5-10(D), n. 37; § 13-5(B), n. 27
United States v. Massengill, 30 M.J. 800 (A.F.C.M.R. 1990) — § 2-7(B), n. 24
United States v. Masseria, 13 M.J. 868 (N.M.C.M.R. 1982) — § 15-2(D), n. 137; § 15-12, n. 3
United States v. Massey, 27 M.J. 371 (C.M.A. 1989) — § 13-3(D), nn. 182, 189
United States v. Massie, 45 C.M.R. 717 (A.C.M.R. 1972) — § 14-3(C), n. 127; § 16-6, n. 22
United States v. Mathews, 6 M.J. 357 (C.M.A. 1979) — § 3-8(B), n. 14; § 16-5(C), n. 50
United States v. Mathieu, 29 M.J. 823 (A.C.M.R. 1989) — § 5-10(D), n. 32
United States v. Mathis, 31 M.J. 726 (A.F.C.M.R. 1990) — § 5-4(B), n. 50
United States v. Matias, 25 M.J. 356 (C.M.A. 1987) — § 17-11, n. 6
United States v. Matlock, 35 M.J. 895 (A.C.M.R. 1992) — § 9-3, n. 6
United States v. Matthews, 31 C.M.R. 620 (A.F.B.R. 1961) — § 11-3(B)(1), n. 31
United States v. Matthews, 13 M.J. 501 (A.C.M.R. 1982) — § 4-5(A)(3), n. 12; § 10-2(A), n. 14; § 11-2(E)(2), n. 118; § 14-3, n. 8; § 15-13, n. 14
United States v. Matthews, 15 M.J. 622 (N.M.C.M.R. 1982) — § 7-2(C), n. 76
United States v. Matthews, 16 M.J. 354 (C.M.A. 1983) — § 14-3, nn. 3, 6; § 16-3(A), n. 10; § 14-3(A)(3), nn. 37, 39

TABLE OF CASES

United States v. Matthews, 19 M.J. 707 (A.F.C.M.R. 1984) — § 12-4, n. 13; § 17-14, n. 6
United States v. Matura, 32 M.J. 671 (A.F.C.M.R. 1991) — § 15-16(A), n. 9
United States v. Mauck, 17 M.J. 1033 (A.C.M.R. 1984) — § 2-4(B), n. 28; § 4-11(A), n. 12
United States v. Maxwell, 38 M.J. 148 (C.M.A. 1993) — § 5-3(D)(2), n. 142
United States v. Maxwell, 42 M.J. 568 (A.F.Ct.Crim.App. 1995) — § 5-3(A), n. 14; § 6-7, n. 12
United States v. May, 3 C.M.A. 703, 14 C.M.R. 121 (1954) — § 6-1(C), n. 98
United States v. Maydwell, 23 M.J. 656 (A.F.C.M.R. 1986) — § 14-3(B)(2), n. 99
United States v. Mayer, 21 M.J. 504 (A.F.C.M.R. 1984) — § 13-2(G)(2), n. 98
United States v. Mayes, 28 M.J. 748 (A.F.C.M.R. 1989) — § 15-10(A), nn. 33, 34; § 15-10(B), n. 53
United States v. Mayfield, 21 M.J. 418 (C.M.A. 1986) — § 2-8(B), n. 17; § 13-3(N)(2), n. 350
United States v. Mayhugh, 41 M.J. 657 (N.M.Ct.Crim.App.1994) — § 5-4(B), n. 43; § 13-2(E), n. 55; § 15-14(B), n. 21; § 13-5(G)(1), nn. 33, 42; § 17-20, n. 5
United States v. Mayne, 39 C.M.R. 628 (A.B.R. 1968) — § 2-8(A), n. 2
United States v. Mayo, 12 M.J. 286 (C.M.A. 1982) — § 2-6(C), n. 41; § 13-3(F), n. 217
United States v. Mayville, 32 M.J. 838 (N.M.C.M.R. 1991) — § 17-4, n. 30
United States v. McBride, 6 C.M.A. 430, 20 C.M.R. 146 (1955) — § 15-10(B), n. 77
United States v. McCaig, 32 M.J. 751 (A.C.M.R. 1991) — § 13-4(A), n. 10
United States v. McCall, 26 M.J. 804 (A.C.M.R. 1988) — § 8-3(C)(4), n. 154; § 15-10(C)(1), n. 84
United States v. McCallister, 24 M.J. 881 (A.C.M.R. 1987) — § 13-3(C)(1), n. 35; § 13-3(C)(3), nn. 105, 160
United States v. McCallister, 27 M.J. 138 (C.M.A. 1988) — § 13-3(C)(2), n. 79
United States v. McCanless, 29 M.J. 985 (A.F.C.M.R. 1990) — § 16-5(D)(4), n. 101
United States v. McCann, 8 C.M.A. 675, 25 C.M.R. 179 (1958) — § 6-5(A), n. 3
United States v. McCann, 11 M.J. 506 (N.C.M.R. 1981) — § 14-3(B)(2), n. 78
United States v. McCants, 39 M.J. 91 (C.M.A. 1994) — § 5-10(D), nn. 32, 39
United States, McCarthy v.
United States v. McCarthy, 2 M.J. 26 (C.M.A. 1976) — § 4-11(A), n. 10
United States v. McCarthy, 24 M.J. 841 (A.F.C.M.R. 1987) — § 17-15(B), n. 19
United States v. McCarthy, 28 M.J. 887 (A.F.C.M.R. 1989) — § 17-9(C), n. 47
United States v. McCarthy, 34 M.J. 768 (A.C.M.R. 1992) — § 15-2(B)(3), n. 57
United States v. McCarthy, 37 M.J. 595 (A.F.C.M.R. 1993) — § 5-4(B), n. 37; § 15-13, n. 19; § 16-8(B), n. 18
United States v. McCarthy, 38 M.J. 398 (C.M.A. 1993) — § 5-3, nn. 2, 7; § 5-3(A), n. 26; § 5-7, n. 10
United States v. McCarty, 25 M.J. 667 (A.F.C.M.R. 1987) — § 7-2(E), n. 108; § 15-2(B)(3), n. 74
United States v. McCauley, 9 C.M.A. 65, 25 C.M.R. 327 (1958) — § 15-13, n. 7
United States v. McClain, 1 M.J. 60 (C.M.A. 1975) — § 13-3(C)(2), n. 73
United States v. McClain, 10 M.J. 271 (C.M.A. 1981) — § 2-4(A), n. 15
United States v. McClain, 22 M.J. 124 (C.M.A. 1986) — § 1-6(B), n. 39; § 6-4(D), n. 25; § 8-3(C)(4), n. 151
United States v. McClain, 31 M.J. 130 (C.M.A. 1990) — § 5-3(C)(6), n. 85
United States v. McClelland, 25 M.J. 903 (A.C.M.R. 1988) — § 15-2(B)(3), n. 88; § 17-2(B)(3), n. 87; § 17-8(B)(2), n. 92
United States v. McClendon, 41 M.J. 882 (A.F.Ct.Crim.App. 1994) — § 5-3(C)(6), n. 85
United States v. McCline, 32 M.J. 356 (C.M.A. 1991) — § 14-3(B)(2), n. 94

TABLE OF CASES

United States v. McCollum, 6 M.J. 224 (C.M.A. 1979) — § 4-11(A), nn. 13, 14
United States v. McCollum, 13 M.J. 127 (C.M.A. 1982) — § 6-1(C), n. 94
United States v. McCormick, 13 M.J. 900 (N.M.C.M.R. 1982) — § 5-3(D)(1), n. 136
United States v. McCormick, 34 M.J. 752 (N.M.C.M.R. 1992) — § 17-8(B), n. 15
United States v. McCoy, 31 M.J. 323 (C.M.A. 1990) — § 5-4(B), n. 31
United States v. McCoy, 32 M.J. 907 (A.F.C.M.R. 1991) — § 6-1(C)(3), n. 139
United States v. McCrary, 1 C.M.A. 1, 1 C.M.R. 1 (1951) — § 17-16(C), n. 15
United States v. McCray, 5 M.J. 820 (A.C.M.R. 1978) — § 14-3(D)(4), n. 145
United States v. McCray, 643 F.2d 323 (5th Cir. 1981) — § 5-4(B), n. 26
United States v. McCray, 19 M.J. 528 (A.C.M.R. 1984) — § 15-14(B), n. 23
United States v. McCreight, 39 M.J. 530 (A.F.C.M.R. 1994) — § 2-8(B), n. 17
United States v. McCullah, 8 M.J. 697 (A.F.C.M.R. 1981) — § 3-5(B)(2), n. 12
United States v. McCullah, 11 M.J. 234 (C.M.A. 1981) — § 17-4, nn. 5, 27
United States v. McCullar, 20 M.J. 218 (C.M.A. 1985) — § 6-1(C)(3), n. 145
United States v. McCullom, 13 M.J. 127 (C.M.A. 1982) — § 6-1(B), n. 60
United States v. McCullough, 33 M.J. 595 (A.C.M.R. 1991) — § 5-10(D), n. 34
United States v. McDaniel, 7 M.J. 522 (A.C.M.R. 1979) — § 2-3(C), n. 28
United States v. McDaniel, 17 M.J. 553 (A.C.M.R. 1983) — § 10-4(B)(5), n. 54
United States v. McDavid, 37 M.J. 861 (A.F.C.M.R. 1993) — § 5-4(B), n. 50; § 15-10(B), n. 71; § 13-3(N)(3), n. 365
United States v. McDonagh, 10 M.J. 698 (A.C.M.R. 1981) — § 4-5(A)(4), n. 18; § 9-2(B)(1), n. 50
United States v. McDonagh, 14 M.J. 415 (C.M.A. 1983) — § 4-9, n. 7; § 4-5(A)(2), n. 5; § 13-3(N)(5), nn. 431, 434, 435, 437
United States v. McDonald, 3 M.J. 1005 (A.C.M.R. 1977) — § 12-3(B), n. 58
United States v. McDonald, 456 U.S. 1 (1982) — § 13-3(C)(1), n. 38
United States v. McDowell, 13 C.M.A. 129, 32 C.M.R. 129 (1962) — § 15-12(C), n. 24
United States v. McDowell, 19 M.J. 937 (A.C.M.R. 1985) — § 13-3(C)(2), n. 68
United States v. McDowell, 34 M.J. 719 (N.M.C.M.R. 1992) — § 4-8(A), n. 9
United States v. McDuffie, 43 M.J. 646 (A.F.Ct.Crim.App. 1995) — § 14-3(D)(3), n. 139
United States v. McElhinney, 21 C.M.A. 436, 45 C.M.R. 210 (1972) — § 13-2(F), n. 57
United States v. McElroy, 40 M.J. 368 (C.M.A. 1994) — § 15-7, n. 5; § 16-9, n. 10
United States v. McElyea, 22 M.J. 863 (A.C.M.R. 1986) — § 5-10(D), n. 37
United States v. McFarlin, 19 M.J. 790 (A.C.M.R. 1985) — § 2-8(D), n. 37; § 13-3(N)(4), nn. 420, 421, 424
United States v. McFarlin, 24 M.J. 631 (A.C.M.R. 1987) — § 13-3(C), nn. 31, 33
United States v. McFatrich, 32 M.J. 1039 (A.C.M.R. 1991) — § 2-4(A), n. 13
United States v. McGary, 12 M.J. 760 (A.C.M.R. 1981) — § 3-8(B), n. 14; § 13-3(J), n. 265
United States v. McGee, 1 M.J. 193 (C.M.A. 1975) — § 15-14(B), n. 23
United States v. McGee, 13 M.J. 699 (N.M.C.M.R. 1982) — § 15-2(F), n. 160
United States v. McGee, 15 M.J. 1004 (N.M.C.M.R. 1983) — § 4-15(C), n. 17; § 8-3(C)(1), n. 113
United States v. McGee, 30 M.J. 1086 (N.M.C.M.R. 1989) — § 16-8(A), nn. 2, 3
United States v. McGeeney, 41 M.J. 544 (N.M.Ct.Crim.App. 1994) — § 8-3(D), nn. 165, 169; § 13-3(H), n. 242; § 15-2(D), n. 137
United States v. McGill, 15 M.J. 242 (C.M.A. 1983) — § 16-4(B), n. 21; § 16-5(B), n. 16
United States v. McGinnis, 15 M.J. 252 (C.M.A. 1983) — § 13-3(N)(5), n. 436
United States v. McGinnis, 15 M.J. 345 (C.M.A. 1983) — § 4-5(A)(2), n. 5
United States v. McGowan, 41 M.J. 406 (1995) — § 14-3(D)(5), n. 175

TABLE OF CASES

United States v. McGraner, 13 M.J. 408 (C.M.A. 1982) — § 13-3(C)(4), n. 171; § 13-3(N)(1), n. 316
United States v. McGuinness, 35 M.J. 149 (C.M.A. 1992) — § 2-6(C), n. 37
United States v. McGuire, 32 M.J. 871 (N.M.C.M.R. 1991) — § 17-9(B), n. 42
United States v. McHugh, 41 M.J. 657 (N.M. Ct. Crim. App. 1994) — § 13-5(G)(1), n. 38
United States v. McIntosh, 12 27 M.J. 204 (C.M.A. 1988) — § 16-12, nn. 12, 13
United States v. McIntosh, 25 M.J. 837 (A.C.M.R. 1988) — § 17-3, n. 6; § 17-9(C), n. 55
United States v. McIntosh, 27 M.J. 204 (C.M.A. 1988) — § 16-12, n. 11
United States v. McKenzie, 39 M.J. 946 (N.M.C.M.R. 1994) — § 9-2(B)(1), n. 56
United States v. McKillop, 38 M.J. 701 (A.C.M.R. 1993) — § 4-14(A)(1), n. 5
United States v. McKinley, 27 M.J. 78 (C.M.A. 1988) — § 15-14(B), n. 23
United States v. McKinney, 40 C.M.R. 1013 (A.F.B.R. 1969) — § 6-1(C), n. 96
United States v. McKinnie, 32 M.J. 141 (C.M.A. 1991) — § 15-14(B), n. 45
United States v. McKnight, 30 M.J. 205 (C.M.A. 1990) — § 17-8(B), n. 29; § 13-3(C)(3), n. 159
United States v. McLaren, 34 M.J. 926 (A.F.C.M.R. 1992) — § 16-9, n. 8
United States v. McLaren, 38 M.J. 112 (C.M.A. 1993) — § 5-4(B), n. 49; § 15-10(B), n. 51
United States v. McLaughlin, 14 M.J. 908 (N.M.C.M.R. 1982) — § 2-4(B), n. 24; § 2-4(D), n. 42
United States v. McLaughlin, 27 M.J. 685 (A.C.M.R. 1988) — § 8-3(C)(4), n. 151; § 15-10(C)(1), n. 88
United States v. McLaurin, 22 M.J. 310 (C.M.A. 1986) — § 15-14(B), n. 42
United States v. McLemore, 30 M.J. 605 (N.M.C.M.R. 1990) — § 17-8(B)(1), n. 53
United States v. Mcleod, 39 M.J. 278 (C.M.A. 1994) — § 5-9(D), nn. 23, 36
United States v. McMahan, 6 C.M.A. 709, 21 C.M.R. 31 (1956) — § 7-2(E), n. 115; § 15-2(B)(3), n. 65; § 15-13, n. 2;
United States v. McMann, 11 M.J. 506 (N.C.M.R. 1981) — § 14-3(B)(2), n. 100
United States v. McMillan, 33 M.J. 257 (C.M.A. 1991) — § 13-3(J), n. 264
United States v. McMonagle, 34 M.J. 852 (A.C.M.R. 1992) — § 2-4(A), nn. 13, 17
United States v. McMonagle, 38 M.J. 53 (C.M.A. 1993) — § 15-14(B), nn. 26, 34
United States v. McNally, 16 M.J. 32 (C.M.A. 1983) — § 15-13, n. 14
United States v. McNeece, 30 C.M.R. 453 (A.B.R. 1960) — § 16-6, n. 20
United States v. McNeill, 2 C.M.A. 383, 9 C.M.R. 13 (1953) — § 4-5(B), nn. 26, 27
United States v. McNett, 21 M.J. 969 (A.C.M.R. 1986) — § 6-1(C)(2), n. 128
United States v. McOmber, 1 M.J. 380 (C.M.A. 1976) — § 5-4(B), n. 51; § 13-4(A), n. 11
United States v. McPhaul, 22 M.J. 808 (A.C.M.R. 1986) — § 12-3, n. 3
United States v. McQueen, 7 M.J. 281 (C.M.A. 1979) — § 15-10(B), n. 73; § 15-10(C)(2), n. 94
United States v. Meace, 20 M.J. 972 (N.M.C.M.R. 1985) — § 6-1(C)(3), n. 152
United States v. Meade, 19 M.J. 894 (A.C.M.R. 1985) — § 16-6, n. 15
United States v. Meadow, 14 M.J. 1002 (A.C.M.R. 1982) — § 11-2(A)(4), n. 47
United States v. Meadows, 13 M.J. 165 (C.M.A. 1982) — § 4-8(B), nn. 13, 14
United States v. Meadows, 42 M.J. 132 (1995) — § 7-2(B)(5), n. 60; § 10-4(B)(2), n. 36
United States v. Means, 12 C.M.A. 290, 30 C.M.R. 290 (1961) — § 6-1(C)(2), n. 126
United States v. Means, 10 M.J. 162 (C.M.A. 1981) — § 6-1, n. 22; § 13-3(N)(1), nn. 303, 331, 337
United States v. Meckler, 6 M.J. 779 (A.C.M.R. 1978) — § 8-5, nn. 3, 4
United States v. Medley, 30 M.J. 879 (A.F.C.M.R. 1990) — § 5-4(A)(2), n. 13
United States v. Medley, 33 M.J. 75 (C.M.A. 1991) — § 5-4(A)(2), n. 16
United States v. Meek, 40 M.J. 675 (N.M.C.M.R. 1994) — § 13-3(M), nn. 290, 293-296

TABLE OF CASES

United States v. Meeks, 41 M.J. 150 (C.M.A. 1994) — § 5-4(B), n. 23; § 16-8(B), nn. 8, 18
United States v. Melton, 1 M.J. 528 (A.F.C.M.R. 1975) — § 14-3(D)(5), n. 165
United States v. Mena, 32 M.J. 937 (N.M.C.M.R. 1991) — § 9-3, nn. 4, 5
United States v. Mendoza, 18 M.J. 576 (A.F.C.M.R. 1984) — § 17-2(B)(4), n. 94
United States v. Menoken, 14 M.J. 10 (C.M.A. 1982) — § 15-4(A), n. 8; § 11-2(A)(1), n. 6
United States v. Mercier, 5 M.J. 866 (A.F.C.M.R. 1978) — § 17-2(B)(4), n. 94
United States v. Merrill, 25 M.J. 501 (A.F.C.M.R. 1987) — § 3-8(B), n. 17
United States v. Merritt, 23 M.J. 654 (N.M.C.M.R. 1986) — § 2-7(C), n. 43
United States v. Merritte, 42 M.J. 519 (C.G.Ct.Crim.App. 1995) — § 17-9(D), n. 62
United States v. Merriweather, 13 M.J. 605 (A.F.C.M.R. 1982) — § 2-3(A), n. 9
United States v. Merrow, 14 C.M.A. 265, 34 C.M.R. 45 — § 2-2(B), n. 10
United States v. Mervine, 23 M.J. 801 (N.M.C.M.R. 1986) — § 12-2(F)(3), n. 67; § 14-3(B)(2), n. 71
United States, Messiah v.
United States v. Mezzanatto, 115 S. Ct. 797 (1995) — § 9-2(B)(1), n. 60; § 14-3(B)(1), n. 62
United States v. Michaels, 3 M.J. 846 (A.C.M.R. 1977) — § 4-16, n. 5
United States v. Mickel, 9 C.M.A. 324, 26 C.M.R. 104 (1958) — § 7-2(E), nn. 104, 107; § 13-5(D), nn. 43, 45
United States v. Mickla, 29 M.J. 749 (A.F.C.M.R. 1989) — § 13-3(C)(3), nn. 118, 121
United States v. Middleton, 10 M.J. 123 (C.M.A. 1981) — § 5-3, n. 2; § 5-3(B), n. 42; § 5-3(D)(1), nn. 118, 128, 129; § 13-2(G)(2), n. 111
United States v. Middleton, 36 M.J. 835 (A.C.M.R. 1993) — § 2-3(C), n. 23
United States, Midgett v.
United States v. Milam, 33 M.J. 1020 (A.C.M.R. 1991) — § 8-3(C)(2), n. 132
United States v. Milkinevich, 17 M.J. 516 (A.F.C.M.R. 1983) — § 6-2(B), n. 9
United States v. Millender, 27 M.J. 568 (A.C.M.R. 1988) — § 15-10(B), nn. 65, 66
United States v. Miller, 48 C.M.R. 446 (N.C.M.R. 1973) — § 6-1(B)(2), n. 77
United States v. Miller, 4 M.J. 207 (C.M.A. 1978) — § 17-4(A), n. 43
United States v. Miller, 12 M.J. 836 (A.C.M.R. 1982) — § 7-2, n. 7; § 9-2(B)(1), n. 47; § 13-3(C)(2), n. 74
United States v. Miller, 14 M.J. 924 (A.F.C.M.R. 1982) — § 15-12(B), n. 21; § 15-12(C), n. 26
United States v. Miller, 16 M.J. 169 (C.M.A. 1983) — § 4-12(B), n. 14; § 13-3(E), n. 200
United States v. Miller, 17 M.J. 817 (A.C.M.R. 1984) — § 16-3(C), n. 55
United States v. Miller, 19 M.J. 519 (C.M.A. 1984) — § 15-10(C)(2), n. 95
United States v. Miller, 19 M.J. 159 (C.M.A. 1985) — § 15-10(B), nn. 38, 64; § 15-10(C)(2), nn. 91, 93
United States v. Miller, 23 M.J. 553 (C.G.C.M.R. 1986) — § 15-12(B), n. 14; § 14-3(B)(2), n. 77
United States v. Miller, 23 M.J. 837 (C.G.C.M.R. 1987) — § 14-3(A)(1), n. 19
United States v. Miller, 26 M.J. 959 (A.C.M.R. 1988) — § 13-3(C)(3), n. 102
United States v. Miller, 30 M.J. 703 (A.C.M.R. 1990) — § 5-4(B), nn. 25, 30
United States v. Miller, 31 M.J. 247 (C.M.A. 1990) — § 13-4, n. 8; § 13-4(A), n. 18
United States v. Miller, 30 M.J. 960 (N.M.C.M.R. 1990) — § 15-10(C)(3), n. 107
United States v. Miller, 33 M.J. 235 (C.M.A. 1991) — § 6-1, n. 7
United States v. Miller, 34 M.J. 1175 (A.F.C.M.R. 1992) — § 15-14(B), n. 42
United States v. Miller, 35 M.J. 882 (A.C.M.R. 1992) — § 17-9(A), n. 24
United States v. Miller, 36 M.J. 124 (C.M.A. 1992) — § 5-4(B), n. 43
United States v. Miller, 37 M.J. 133 (C.M.A. 1993) — § 2-5, n. 2

TABLE OF CASES

United States v. Miller, 38 M.J. 121 (C.M.A. 1993) — § 13-3(B), n. 16
United States v. Miller, 41 M.J. 647 (N.M.Ct.Crim.App.1994) — § 17-8(B)(3), nn. 68, 83
United States v. Mills, 7 M.J. 664 (A.C.M.R. 1979) — § 15-13, n. 11
United States v. Mills, 12 M.J. 1 (C.M.A. 1981) — § 9-2(B)(1), n. 50; § 9-2(B)(2), n. 63
United States v. Millsap, 17 M.J. 980 (A.C.M.R. 1984) — § 17-9(A), n. 26
United States v. Minaya, 30 M.J. 1179 (A.F.C.M.R. 1990) — § 16-8(B), n. 25; § 11-2(A)(2), n. 12; § 11-2(B)(1), n. 64
United States v. Mincey, 42 M.J. 376 (1995) — § 16-2(D), n. 44; § 6-1(C)(2), nn. 125, 131; § 13-5(G)(3), n. 54; § 14-3(D)(3), n. 140
United States v. Miner, 23 M.J. 694 (A.F.C.M.R. 1986) — § 4-14(A)(1), n. 7
United States v. Miniclier, 23 M.J. 843 (A.F.C.M.R. 1987) — § 13-3(C)(3), nn. 159, 165
United States v. Minor, 1 C.M.A. 497, 4 C.M.R. 89 (1952) — § 13-3(I), n. 254
United States v. Minor, 11 M.J. 608 (A.C.M.R. 1981) — § 14-3(B)(2), n. 93
United States v. Minor, 25 M.J. 898 (A.C.M.R. 1988) — § 6-1(C), n. 94
United States v. Miro, 22 M.J. 509 (A.F.C.M.R. 1986) — § 7-2(E), n. 104
United States v. Mitchell, 6 C.M.A. 579, 20 C.M.R. 295 (1955) — § 2-4(B), n. 24
United States v. Mitchell, 7 C.M.A. 238, 22 C.M.R. 28 (1956) — § 2-2(C)(3), n. 38
United States v. Mitchell, 3 M.J. 641 (A.C.M.R. 1977) — § 2-2(D), n. 69
United States v. Mitchell, 11 M.J. 907 (A.C.M.R. 1981) — § 11-2(B)(1), n. 57
United States v. Mitchell, 15 M.J. 238 (C.M.A. 1983) — § 17-9(E), n. 86
United States v. Mitchell, 20 M.J. 350 (C.M.A. 1985) — § 17-15(B), n. 19
United States v. Mitchell, 34 M.J. 970 (A.C.M.R. 1992) — § 2-2(E)(3), nn. 78, 83
United States v. Mitchell, 34 M.J. 1252 (A.C.M.R. 1992) — § 2-4(F), n. 51; § 16-2(F), n. 58
United States v. Mitchell, 36 M.J. 882 (N.M.C.M.R. 1993) — § 2-6(C), nn. 35, 40
United States v. Mitchell, 39 M.J. 131 (C.M.A. 1994) — § 17-15; § 17-15, n. 3
United States v. Mitchell, 41 M.J. 512 (Army Ct.Crim.App. 1994) — § 11-2(B)(1), n. 56
United States v. Mix, 29 M.J. 956 (A.C.M.R. 1990) — § 17-8(B)(3), n. 83
United States v. Mix, 32 M.J. 974 (A.C.M.R. 1991) — § 5-3(B), n. 39; § 5-3(F), n. 24; § 12-2(F)(4), n. 68
United States v. Mix, 35 M.J. 283 (C.M.A. 1992) — § 5-3(B), n. 39; § 5-3(E), n. 7; § 5-3(C)(4), n. 77; § 12-2(F)(4), nn. 68, 73
United States v. Mobley, 28 M.J. 1024 (A.F.C.M.R. 1989) — § 11-4, n. 5; § 6-1(C)(2), n. 125
United States v. Mobley, 31 M.J. 273 (C.M.A. 1990) — § 13-5(F), nn. 23, 31; § 15-13, nn. 11, 24
United States v. Mobley, 34 M.J. 527 (A.F.C.M.R. 1991) — § 15-4(B), nn. 11, 12; § 15-13, n. 11
United States v. Mock, 49 C.M.R. 160 (A.C.M.R. 1974) — § 13-3(C)(2), nn. 50, 55
United States v. Modesto, 39 M.J. 1055 (A.C.M.R. 1994) — § 5-3(B), n. 45
United States v. Mogavero, 20 M.J. 762 (A.F.C.M.R. 1985) — § 12-2(F)(4), nn. 82, 83
United States v. Moglia, 3 M.J. 216 (C.M.A. 1977) — § 14-3(B)(2), n. 95
United States v. Monroe, 42 M.J. 398 (1995) — § 11-2(E)(3), n. 133
United States v. Mons, 14 M.J. 575 (N.M.C.M.R. 1982) — § 5-3(D)(1), n. 133
United States v. Montanino, 40 M.J. 364 (C.M.A. 1994) — § 13-3(C)(3), n. 159
United States v. Montcalm, 2 M.J. 787 (A.C.M.R. 1976) — § 13-2(G)(1), n. 63
United States v. Montesinos, 24 M.J. 682 (A.C.M.R. 1987) — § 17-15(A), n. 14
United States v. Montesinos, 28 M.J. 38 (C.M.A. 1989) — § 17-19, n. 14
United States v. Montford, 13 M.J. 829 (A.C.M.R. 1982) — § 5-9(E), nn. 55, 58
United States v. Montgomery, 11 C.M.R. 308 (A.B.R. 1953) — § 2-3(A), n. 13; § 2-3(B), n. 18

TABLE OF CASES

United States v. Montgomery, 5 M.J. 832 (A.C.M.R. 1978) — § 8-3(C)(3), n. 143; § 13-3(N)(1), n. 305
United States v. Montgomery, 16 M.J. 516 (A.C.M.R. 1983) — § 12-2(H), n. 122; § 15-10(C)(1), n. 83
United States v. Montgomery, 30 M.J. 1118 (N.M.C.M.R. 1989) — § 6-1(C)(3), n. 147
United States v. Montoya, 13 M.J. 268 (C.M.A. 1982) — § 15-2(B)(1), n. 25
United States v. Moody, 10 M.J. 845 (N.C.M.R. 1981) — § 4-2, n. 4
United States v. Moody, 27 M.J. 683 (A.C.M.R. 1988) — § 17-2(B)(3), n. 87
United States v. Moore, 21 C.M.R. 544 (N.B.R. 1956) — § 2-4(E), n. 46
United States v. Moore, 1 M.J. 448 (C.M.A. 1976) — § 4-11(A), n. 18
United States v. Moore, 6 M.J. 644 (N.C.M.R. 1978) — § 6-2(A), n. 4
United States v. Moore, 22 M.J. 523 (N.M.C.M.R. 1986) — § 4-8(C)(1), n. 17
United States v. Moore, 23 M.J. 295 (C.M.A. 1987) — § 5-3(A), n. 17; § 5-3(B), n. 37; § 5-3(D)(1), n. 118
United States v. Moore, 26 M.J. 692 (A.C.M.R. 1988) — § 15-10(C)(3), n. 113
United States v. Moore, 27 M.J. 656 (A.C.M.R. 1988) — § 17-2(B)(3), nn. 49, 50, 89
United States v. Moore, 29 M.J. 819 (A.C.M.R. 1989) — § 5-9(D), n. 23; § 16-5(D)(5), n. 116
United States v. Moore, 32 M.J. 56 (C.M.A. 1991) — § 5-4(B), n. 42; § 5-9(B), n. 9; § 11-2(B)(1), nn. 54, 57
United States v. Moore, 32 M.J. 170 (C.M.A. 1991) — § 13-3(B), n. 10
United States v. Moore, 32 M.J. 774 (A.C.M.R. 1991) — § 3-3(C), n. 27; § 13-5(B), n. 28
United States v. Moore, 36 M.J. 329 (C.M.A. 1993) — § 15-12(A), n. 7; § 5-4(A)(3), n. 21
United States v. Moore, 36 M.J. 795 (A.C.M.R. 1993) — § 4-16, nn. 11, 12
United States v. Moore, 38 M.J. 644 (A.F.C.M.R. 1993) — § 5-4(B), n. 49
United States v. Moore, 38 M.J. 490 (C.M.A. 1994) — § 5-3(A), n. 14; § 13-3(N)(3), nn. 373, 384
United States v. Moore, 41 M.J. 812 (N.M.Ct.Crim.App. 1995) — § 5-3(D)(1), n. 127
United States v. Moorer, 15 M.J. 520 (A.C.M.R. 1983) — § 2-8(B), n. 16
United States v. Moore, 28 M.J. 366 (C.M.A. 1989) — § 15-10(C)(3), n. 116
United States v. Mora, 22 M.J. 719 (A.C.M.R. 1986) — § 15-4(B), n. 12
United States v. Mora, 26 M.J. 122 (C.M.A. 1988) — § 8-3(A), n. 9; § 15-4(B), nn. 11, 12, 15; § 8-3(C)(1), n. 120
United States v. Morales, 12 M.J. 888 (A.C.M.R. 1982) — § 9-2(B)(2), n. 68
United States v. Morales, 16 M.J. 503 (A.F.C.M.R. 1983) — § 15-14(B), n. 39
United States v. Morales-Santana, 32 M.J. 557 (A.F.C.M.R. 1990) — § 9-2(B), n. 37
United States v. Moreno, 23 M.J. 622 (A.F.C.M.R. 1986) — § 5-3, n. 9
United States v. Moreno, 24 M.J. 752 (A.C.M.R. 1987) — § 13-3(C), n. 32
United States v. Moreno, 31 M.J. 935 (A.C.M.R. 1990) — § 5-4(B), n. 43
United States v. Moreno, 36 M.J. 107 (C.M.A. 1992) — § 5-4(B), n. 43
United States v. Morero, 41 M.J. 537 (N.M.Ct.Crim.App. 1994) — § 16-10, n. 22
United States, Morgan v.
United States v. Morgan, 44 C.M.R. 699 (A.C.M.R. 1971) — § 12-2(H), n. 98
United States v. Morgan, 15 M.J. 128 (C.M.A. 1983) — § 1-1(B), n. 32; § 16-5(B), nn. 22, 23
United States v. Morgan, 22 M.J. 959 (C.G.C.M.R. 1986) — § 15-12(B), nn. 14, 17
United States v. Morgan, 31 M.J. 535 (A.C.M.R. 1990) — § 16-2(D), n. 39
United States v. Morgan, 37 M.J. 407 (C.M.A. 1993) — § 15-2(B)(3), nn. 54, 70
United States v. Morgan, 40 M.J. 389 (C.M.A. 1994) — § 5-4(B), n. 49
United States v. Morris, 9 C.M.R. 786 (A.F.B.R. 1953) — § 4-15(C), n. 16
United States v. Morris, 11 C.M.A. 16, 28 C.M.R. 240 (1959) — § 2-2(E)(6), n. 102

TABLE OF CASES

United States v. Morris, 23 C.M.A. 319, 49 C.M.R. 653 (1975) — § 12-2(C), n. 17; § 12-3(A), n. 20
United States v. Morris, 13 M.J. 297 (C.M.A. 1982) — § 5-4(B), n. 23
United States v. Morris, 18 M.J. 450 (C.M.A. 1984) — § 13-3(J), n. 259; § 6-1(C)(3), n. 165
United States v. Morris, 24 M.J. 93 (C.M.A. 1987) — § 10-3(B), n. 10; § 11-2(A)(1), n. 2
United States v. Morris, 28 M.J. 8 (C.M.A. 1989) — § 5-3(F), n. 24
United States v. Morris, 30 M.J. 1221 (A.C.M.R. 1990) — § 2-7(C), n. 34; § 2-9(C), n. 25; § 2-9(D), nn. 64, 65, 67; § 6-1(C), n. 102; § 2-9(C)(3), n. 55
United States v. Morris, 40 M.J. 792 (A.F.C.M.R. 1994) — § 6-1(C)(3), nn. 157, 158
United States v. Morrison, 3 M.J. 408 (C.M.A. 1977) — § 17-2(B)(4), n. 95; § 17-8(B)(1), n. 33
United States v. Morrison, 22 M.J. 743 (N.M.C.M.R. 1986) — § 4-8(A), n. 8
United States, Morrissette v.
United States v. Morrow, 16 M.J. 328 (C.M.A. 1983) — § 13-3(C)(2), n. 78
United States v. Morse, 34 M.J. 677 (A.C.M.R. 1992) — § 2-4(A), n. 20
United States v. Morton, 15 M.J. 850 (A.F.C.M.R. 1983) — § 15-20, nn. 8, 18
United States v. Moseley, 35 M.J. 481 (C.M.A. 1992) — § 17-8(B)(3), n. 68
United States v. Mosely, 14 M.J. 852 (A.C.M.R. 1982) — § 4-8(C)(2), n. 21
United States v. Moser, 23 M.J. 568 (A.C.M.R. 1986) — § 14-3(E), n. 177
United States v. Moses, 26 M.J. 980 (A.F.C.M.R. 1988) — § 15-2(B)(3), n. 68
United States v. Mosley, 11 M.J. 729 (A.F.C.M.R. 1981) — § 15-13, n. 14
United States v. Mosley, 42 M.J. 300 (1995) — § 11-4, n. 2
United States v. Mosly, 35 M.J. 693 (N.M.C.M.R. 1992) — § 17-3(A), n. 26
United States v. Moss, 44 C.M.R. 298 (A.C.M.R. 1971) — § 2-2(B), n. 10
United States v. Motsinger, 34 M.J. 255 (C.M.A. 1992) — § 16-8(B), n. 10; § 16-9, n. 4
United States v. Moultak, 21 M.J. 822 (N.M.C.M.R. 1985) — § 2-8(B), n. 18; § 2-8(D), n. 38; § 17-8(B), n. 26; § 6-1(B)(2), n. 82; § 13-3(N)(1), n. 338
United States v. Moultak, 24 M.J. 316 (C.M.A. 1987) — § 13-3(N)(3), n. 405
United States v. Mountain, 20 C.M.A. 319, 43 C.M.R. 159 (1971) — § 1-3(D)(1), n. 19
United States v. Mouqenel, 6 M.J. 589 (A.F.C.M.R. 1978) — § 10-4(B)(1), n. 31
United States v. Mow, 22 M.J. 906 (N.M.C.M.R. 1986) — § 11-2(B)(1), n. 68
United States v. Moyar, 24 M.J. 635 (A.C.M.R. 1987) — § 15-10(C)(2), nn. 94, 100
United States v. Mucthison, 28 M.J. 1113 (N.M.C.M.R. 1989) — § 8-5, n. 1; § 13-3(C)(3), n. 118
United States v. Mueller, 40 M.J. 708 (A.C.M.R. 1994) — § 5-5, n. 9
United States v. Muir, 7 M.J. 448 (C.M.A. 1979) — § 14-3(D)(3), n. 142
United States v. Mullen, 18 M.J. 569 (N.M.C.M.R. 1984) — § 12-2(F)(2), n. 55
United States v. Mullens, 24 M.J. 745 (A.C.M.R. 1987) — § 16-5(D)(1), n. 61
United States v. Mullens, 29 M.J. 398 (C.M.A. 1990) — § 16-5(D)(1), n. 61; § 16-5(D)(4), n. 84; § 16-5(D)(5), n. 124
United States v. Muller, 21 M.J. 205 (C.M.A. 1986) — § 14-3(C), n. 132
United States v. Muniz, 1 M.J. 151 (C.M.A. 1975) — § 4-5(A)(3), n. 11
United States v. Muniz, 23 M.J. 201 (C.M.A. 1987) — § 5-3(A), n. 27; § 5-3(C)(2), n. 67
United States v. Munkus, 15 M.J. 1013 (A.F.C.M.R. 1983) — § 13-3(C)(2), n. 55
United States v. Murphy, 18 M.J. 220 (C.M.A. 1984) — § 4-12(B), n. 13; § 5-4(B), n. 52
United States v. Murphy, 23 M.J. 310 (C.M.A. 1987) — § 2-7(C), n. 38
United States v. Murphy, 23 M.J. 862 (A.C.M.R. 1987) — § 16-2(B), n. 14; § 17-15(B), n. 16
United States v. Murphy, 26 M.J. 454 (C.M.A. 1988) — § 15-10(B), n. 55
United States v. Murphy, 26 M.J. 658 (N.M.C.M.R. 1988) — § 17-9(A), nn. 21, 55

TABLE OF CASES

United States v. Murphy, 28 M.J. 758 (A.F.C.M.R. 1989) — § 5-3(D)(1), n. 128
United States v. Murphy, 29 M.J. 573 (A.F.C.M.R. 1989) — § 16-5(D)(4), n. 102
United States v. Murphy, 30 M.J. 1040 (A.C.M.R. 1990) — § 4-4, nn. 2, 3; § 4-12(B), nn. 16, 17
United States v. Murphy, 33 M.J. 248 (C.M.A. 1991) — § 2-7(C), n. 40
United States v. Murphy, 33 M.J. 323 (C.M.A. 1991) — § 10-4(A)(1), n. 8; § 10-4(A)(2), nn. 10, 13
United States v. Murphy, 36 M.J. 1137 (A.C.M.R. 1993) — § 4-12(B), n. 16; § 12-2(F)(3), n. 67
United States v. Murphy, 39 M.J. 486 (C.M.A. 1994) — § 5-3(C)(6), n. 98
United States, Murray v.
United States v. Murray, 16 M.J. 914 (N.M.C.M.R. 1983) — § 5-10(D), n. 40
United States v. Murray, 22 M.J. 700 (A.C.M.R. 1986) — § 7-3(B), n. 27
United States v. Murray, 25 M.J. 445 (C.M.A. 1988) — § 7-3, n. 2; § 7-3(B), n. 27
United States v. Murray, 42 M.J. 174 (1995) — § 15-2(B)(3), n. 36
United States v. Murray, 43 M.J. 507 (A.F.Ct.Crim.App. 1995) — § 5-10(D), n. 34
United States v. Murrell, 50 C.M.R. 793 (A.C.M.R. 1975) — § 13-3(C)(2), n. 73
United States v. Musguire, 9 C.M.A. 67, 25 C.M.R. 329 (1958) — § 2-4(A), n. 16
United States v. Mustafa, 22 M.J. 165 (C.M.A. 1986) — § 11-2(A)(3), n. 21
United States v. Myers, 14 M.J. 527 (A.F.C.M.R. 1982) — § 16-8(B), n. 12
United States v. Myers, 25 M.J. 573 (A.F.C.M.R. 1987) — § 12-5, n. 13; § 16-3(D), n. 57
United States v. Myers, 28 M.J. 191 (C.M.A. 1989) — § 17-16(B), n. 10
United States v. Myhre, 9 C.M.A. 32, 25 C.M.R. 294 (1958) — § 2-2(E)(1), n. 72; § 2-2(E)(5), n. 90
United States v. Myles, 7 M.J. 132 (C.M.A. 1979) — § 15-2(B)(3), n. 31
United States v. Myrick, 24 M.J. 792 (A.C.M.R. 1987) — § 17-9(D), n. 64
United States v., Naar, 2 C.M.R. 739 (A.F.B.R. 1951) — § 4-1, n. 3
United States v. Nagle, 30 M.J. 1229 (A.C.M.R. 1990) — § 6-1(C)(3), n. 147
United States v. Nakamura, 21 M.J. 741 (N.M.C.M.R. 1985) — § 13-2(B), n. 28
United States v. Napier, 20 C.M.A. 422, 43 C.M.R. 262 (1971) — § 4-14(B), n. 18; § 12-4, n. 16
United States v. Nardell, 21 C.M.A. 327, 45 C.M.R. 101 (1972) — § 2-4(C), n. 33
United States, Nardone v.
United States v. Narine, 14 M.J. 55 (C.M.A. 1982) — § 17-8(B)(3), n. 75
United States v. Nash, 5 C.M.A. 550, 18 C.M.R. 174 (1955) — § 15-15, n. 1
United States v. Nastro, 7 C.M.A. 373, 22 C.M.R. 163 (1956) — § 17-9(C), n. 57
United States v. Natalello, 10 M.J. 594 (A.F.C.M.R. 1980) — § 7-2(A)(1), n. 16
United States v. National Dairy Prod. Corp., 372 U.S. 29 (1963) — § 13-3(N)(2), nn. 347, 351, 353
United States v. Nault, 4 M.J. 318 (C.M.A. 1978) — § 15-20, n. 15
United States v. Neal, 17 C.M.A. 363, 38 C.M.R. 161 (1968) — § 15-14(A), n. 6
United States v. Neal, 41 M.J. 855 (A.F.Ct.Crim.App. 1994) — § 5-3(D)(1), n. 128
United States v. Nebling, 26 M.J. 774 (N.M.C.M.R. 1988) — § 14-3(C), n. 132
United States v. Neblock, 40 M.J. 747 (A.F.C.M.R. 1994) — § 6-1(C)(3), n. 161
United States v. Needham, 19 M.J. 614 (A.F.C.M.R. 1984) — § 16-5(D)(3), n. 77
United States v. Needham, 23 M.J. 383 (C.M.A. 1987) — § 16-5(D)(3), n. 76
United States v. Neeley, 21 M.J. 606 (A.F.C.M.R. 1985) — § 16-10, n. 14
United States v. Negron, 28 M.J. 775 (A.C.M.R. 1989) — § 2-9(B), n. 13; § 2-9(D), nn. 56, 60
United States v. Negrone, 9 M.J. 171 (C.M.A. 1980) — § 3-8(B), n. 17
United States v. Neil, 25 M.J. 798 (A.C.M.R. 1988) — § 16-5(D)(1), n. 61

TABLE OF CASES

United States v. Nellum, 24 M.J. 693 (A.C.M.R. 1987) — § 16-5(C), n. 40
United States v. Nelson, 18 C.M.A. 177, 39 C.M.R. 177 (1969) — § 5-10(A), n. 1; § 5-10(D), n. 28; § 13-3(G), n. 227
United States v. Nelson, 1 M.J. 235 (C.M.A. 1975) — § 15-13, nn. 9, 19, 25
United States v. Nelson, 5 M.J. 189 (C.M.A. 1978) — § 13-3(C)(2), nn. 49, 52
United States v. Nelson, 21 M.J. 573 (A.C.M.R. 1985) — § 16-6, n. 5
United States v. Nelson, 28 M.J. 922 (N.M.C.M.R. 1988) — § 13-3(C)(1), n. 35; § 13-3(C)(3), nn. 114, 159
United States v. Nelson, 35 M.J. 716 (N.M.C.M.R. 1992) — § 15-10(B), n. 68
United States v. New, 23 M.J. 889 (A.C.M.R. 1987) — § 5-10(D), n. 35
United States, New York Times Co. v.
United States v. Newak, 15 M.J. 541 (A.F.C.M.R. 1982) — § 1-1, n. 6
United States v. Newak, 24 M.J. 238 (C.M.A. 1987) — § 15-2(B)(2), n. 26; § 15-2(B)(3), n. 90
United States v. Newberry, 35 M.J. 777 (A.C.M.R. 1992) — § 5-10(D), n. 28; § 15-2(B)(3), n. 78
United States v. Newcomb, 5 M.J. 4 (C.M.A. 1978) — § 4-15(A), n. 2; § 8-2(A), n. 4; § 4-14(A)(1), n. 6
United States v. Newkirk, 8 M.J. 684 (N.C.M.R. 1980) — § 14-3(G), n. 196; § 14-3(A)(4), n. 46
United States, Newman v.
United States v. Newman, 14 M.J. 474 (C.M.A. 1983) — § 17-8(B), n. 21; § 11-2(E)(2), n. 122; § 17-9(B), n. 38
United States v. Newsome, 35 M.J. 749 (N.M.C.M.R. 1992) — § 14-3(D)(5), n. 175
United States v. Newson, 26 M.J. 719 (A.C.M.R. 1988) — § 15-10(C)(3), n. 121
United States v. Newson, 29 M.J. 17 (C.M.A. 1989) — § 15-10(C)(2), n. 103; § 15-10(C)(3), n. 120
United States v. Nichelson, 18 C.M.A. 69, 39 C.M.R. 69 (1968) — § 12-2(C), n. 12
United States, Nichols v.
United States v. Nichols, 8 C.M.A. 119, 23 C.M.R. 343 (1957) — § 7-2, nn. 5, 6
United States v. Nichols, 13 M.J. 154 (C.M.A. 1982) — § 3-8(B), n. 16; § 14-3(A)(1), nn. 17, 19
United States v. Nichols, 27 M.J. 909 (A.F.C.M.R. 1989) — § 14-3(D)(4), n. 145
United States v. Nichols, 38 M.J. 717 (A.C.M.R. 1993) — § 12-3, n. 3; § 12-2(F)(2), n. 54
United States v. Nichols, 42 M.J. 715 (A.F.Ct.Crim.App. 1995) — § 13-3(C)(1), n. 35; § 13-3(C)(3), nn. 135, 152
United States v. Nicholson, 15 M.J. 436 (C.M.A. 1983) — § 8-3(B)(1), n. 52; § 15-2(B)(3), nn. 91, 92
United States v. Nickaboine, 3 C.M.A. 152, 11 C.M.R. 152 (1953) — § 2-2(B), n. 18
United States v. Nickels, 20 M.J. 225 (C.M.A. 1985) — § 2-4(E), n. 48
United States v. Nickerson, 27 M.J. 30 (C.M.A. 1988) — § 7-2, n. 7
United States v. Nigro, 28 M.J. 415 (C.M.A. 1989) — § 15-10(C)(2), n. 97
United States v. Niles, 39 M.J. 878 (A.C.M.R. 1994) — § 17-21, n. 8
United States v. Nivens, 21 C.M.A. 420, 45 C.M.R. 194 (1972) — § 13-2(F), n. 57; § 13-5(C), n. 40
United States v. Nix, 40 M.J. 6 (C.M.A. 1994) — § 6-1, n. 2; § 6-2(C), n. 15; § 13-3(M), n. 282
United States v. Nixon, 15 M.J. 1028 (A.C.M.R. 1983) — § 14-3(F), nn. 187, 188
United States v. Nixon, 29 M.J. 505 (A.C.M.R. 1989) — § 16-5(D)(4), n. 101
United States v. Nixon, 30 M.J. 501 (A.F.C.M.R. 1989) — § 15-10(A), n. 22
United States v. Nixon, 33 M.J. 433 (C.M.A. 1991) — § 8-3(C)(4), n. 151

TABLE OF CASES

United States v. Nobles, 422 U.S. 225 (1975) — § 10-3(A), n. 3
United States v. Noel, 3 M.J. 328 (C.M.A. 1977) — § 5-4(A)(3), n. 20
United States v. Noonan, 21 M.J. 763 (A.F.C.M.R. 1986) — § 16-9, n. 11; § 17-9(A), n. 6
United States v. Noreen, 48 C.M.R. 228 (A.C.M.R. 1973) — § 15-10(C)(3), n. 106
United States v. Norfleet, 36 M.J. 129 (C.M.A. 1992) — § 5-4(B), n. 52
United States v. Norman, 9 M.J. 355 (C.M.A. 1980) — § 4-11(A), n. 27
United States v. Norman, 42 M.J. 501 (Army Ct.Crim.App. 1995) — § 13-2(C), n. 32
United States v. Norment, 34 M.J. 224 (C.M.A. 1992) — § 17-8(B)(3), n. 74
United States v. Norment, 36 M.J. 1156 (A.C.M.R. 1993) — § 15-2(E), n. 158
United States v. Norris, 33 M.J. 635 (C.G.C.M.R. 1991) — § 14-3(B), n. 52; § 17-4, n. 31
United States v. Northern, 42 M.J. 638 (N.M.Ct.Crim.App. 1995) — § 2-2(C)(3), n. 57
United States v. Northrup, 12 C.M.A. 487, 31 C.M.R. 73 (1961) — § 2-2(E)(5), n. 87
United States v. Norvell, 26 M.J. 477 (C.M.A. 1988) — § 2-5, n. 3
United States v. Noxon, 30 M.J. 1210 (A.C.M.R. 1990) — § 15-10(C)(1), n. 86
United States v. Nunes, 39 M.J. 889 (A.F.C.M.R. 1994) — § 2-8(B), n. 25; § 2-8(D), n. 40; § 16-8(C), n. 37
United States v. Nunez, 668 F.2d 1116 (10th Cir. 1981) — § 11-2(E)(3), n. 130
United States, Nye & Nissen v.
United States v. Nystrom, 39 M.J. 698 (N.M.C.M.R. 1993) — § 14-3(B)(2), n. 71
United States v. O' Connor, 19 M.J. 673 (A.F.C.M.R. 1984) — § 8-2(A), n. 1; § 8-2(B), n. 11; § 8-4, n. 5
United States v. O'Neal, 16 C.M.A. 33, 36 C.M.R. 189 (1966) — § 15-13, n. 28; § 15-24, n. 5
United States v. Oakley, 33 M.J. 27 (C.M.A. 1991) — § 5-4(B), n. 43; § 12-2(H), n. 100; § 13-5(G)(2), n. 45
United States v. Oates, 560 F.2d 45 (2d Cir. 1977) — § 2-7(C), n. 35
United States v. Oatney, 41 M.J. 619 (N.M.Ct.Crim.App.1994) — § 15-13, nn. 11, 29, 32
United States v. O'Brien, 391 U.S. 367 (1968) — § 13-3(N)(3), nn. 361, 363-365
United States v. Occhi, 2 M.J. 60 (C.M.A. 1976) — § 15-2(D), n. 146; § 16-11, n. 4; § 17-9(D), n. 59
United States v. Odegard, 25 M.J. 140 (C.M.A. 1987) — § 4-4, n. 6
United States v. Ohrt, 28 M.J. 301 (C.M.A. 1989) — § 6-5(C), nn. 52, 53; § 16-5(D)(4), nn. 102, 104
United States v. Oldaker, 41 C.M.R. 497 (A.C.M.R. 1969) — § 2-4(F), n. 50
United States v. Olinger, 12 M.J. 458 (C.M.A. 1982) — § 17-16(C), n. 20
United States v. Olivari, 33 M.J. 933 (C.G.C.M.R. 1991) — § 17-11, n. 1
United States, Oliver v.
United States v. Oliver, 14 C.M.A. 192, 33 C.M.R. 404 (1963) — § 13-5(G)(1), n. 35
United States v. Olivero, 39 M.J. 246 (C.M.A. 1994) — § 5-4(C), n. 56; § 13-3(H), n. 242; § 11-2(E)(1), n. 115
United States v. Olsen, 24 M.J. 669 (A.F.C.M.R. 1987) — § 4-12(A), n. 7; § 13-3(G), n. 228
United States v. Olson, 7 M.J. 898 (A.F.C.M.R. 1979) — § 14-3(B)(2), nn. 95, 96
United States v. Olson, 25 M.J. 293 (C.M.A. 1987) — § 9-2(C), n. 79; § 9-2(B)(1), n. 46
United States v. Olson, 38 M.J. 597 (A.F.C.M.R. 1993) — § 2-5, n. 6; § 13-3(J), nn. 265, 266
United States v. Onstad, 4 M.J. 661 (A.C.M.R. 1977) — § 13-3(C)(2), n. 77
United States v. Oquendo, 35 M.J. 24 (C.M.A. 1992) — § 16-5(D)(4), n. 101
United States v. O'Quin, 16 M.J. 650 (A.F.C.M.R. 1983) — § 4-13, n. 4; § 4-14(A)(2), n. 10

TABLE OF CASES

United States v. Orback, 21 M.J. 610 (A.F.C.M.R. 1985) — § 5-8(B), n. 29; § 13-3(C)(3), n. 106

United States v. Orben, 28 M.J. 172 (C.M.A. 1989) — § 15-16(C), n. 36; § 13-3(N)(3), n. 366

United States v. Ornelas, 2 C.M.A. 96, 6 C.M.R. 96 (1952) — § 4-5(B), nn. 20, 21; § 4-9, n. 6

United States v. Ortiz, 24 M.J. 323 (C.M.A. 1987) — § 17-16(B), n. 10

United States v. Ortiz, 25 M.J. 840 (N.M.C.M.R. 1988) — § 14-3(B)(3), n. 106

United States v. Ortiz, 33 M.J. 549 (A.C.M.R. 1991) — § 7-2(C), n. 79; § 17-8(B)(3), n. 77

United States v. Ortiz, 35 M.J. 391 (C.M.A. 1992) — § 11-2(D)(2), n. 91

United States v. Ortiz-Vergara, 24 C.M.R. 315 (A.B.R. 1957) — § 5-4(A)(3), n. 19

United States v. Osborne, 31 M.J. 842 (N.M.C.M.R. 1990) — § 6-1(B), n. 68

United States v. Osburn, 23 M.J. 903 (N.M.C.M.R. 1987) — § 4-11(B), n. 40

United States v. Osburn, 33 M.J. 810 (A.F.C.M.R. 1991) — § 6-7, n. 11

United States v. Otero, 5 M.J. 781 (A.C.M.R. 1978) — § 5-9(B), n. 10

United States v. Otero, 26 M.J. 546 (A.F.C.M.R. 1988) — § 4-14(B), n. 21; § 8-2(B), n. 11; § 8-4, n. 9

United States v. Ott, 26 M.J. 542 (A.F.C.M.R. 1988) — § 13-3(D), n. 183

United States v. Outhier, 42 M.J. 626 (N.M. Ct. Crim. App. 1995) — § 14-3(D)(5), n. 175

United States v. Overton, 20 M.J. 998 (N.M.C.M.R. 1985) — § 4-8(D), n. 60

United States v. Overton, 24 M.J. 309 (C.M.A. 1987) — § 4-8(D), n. 65

United States v. Owens, 11 C.M.A. 88, 28 C.M.R. 312 (1959) — § 14-3(A)(3), n. 32

United States v. Owens, 2 M.J. 1286 (C.G.C.M.R. 1976) — § 17-11, n. 5

United States v. Owens, 21 M.J. 117 (C.M.A. 1985) — § 15-23, n. 2

United States v. Oxford, 23 M.J. 548 (A.C.M.R. 1986) — § 16-4(B), n. 15

United States v. Oxford, 21 M.J. 963 (N.M.C.M.R. 1986) — § 15-14(B), n. 45; § 15-14(C), n. 51

United States v. Pabon, 37 M.J. 836 (A.F.C.M.R. 1993) — § 5-3(C)(6), n. 85

United States v. Pacheco, 36 M.J. 530 (A.F.C.M.R. 1992) — § 13-2(G)(2), n. 82

United States v. Packer, 8 M.J. 785 (N.C.M.R. 1980) — § 5-9(D), n. 41; § 7-2(E), n. 111; § 13-5(D), n. 46; § 15-10(C), n. 81; § 14-3(A)(2), n. 25

United States v. Padilla, 1 C.M.A. 603, 5 C.M.R. 31 (1952) — § 8-2(B), n. 10

United States v. Pagel, 40 M.J. 771 (A.F.C.M.R. 1994) — § 4-15(A), n. 8; § 15-14(C), n. 49

United States v. Paige, 23 M.J. 512 (A.F.C.M.R. 1986) — § 15-10(B), n. 62; § 15-10(C)(2), nn. 94, 97

United States v. Painter, 39 M.J. 578 (N.M.C.M.R. 1993) — § 2-7(A), n. 1

United States v. Palenius, 2 M.J. 86 (C.M.A. 1977) — § 17-2(B), nn. 5, 10; § 17-14(B), n. 54; § 17-14, n. 7

United States v. Palmer, 44 C.M.R. 608 (A.C.M.R. 1971) — § 8-3(B)(3), n. 92

United States v. Palmer, 41 M.J. 747 (N.M. Ct. Crim. App. 1994) — § 4-16, n. 14

United States v. Palmiter, 20 M.J. 90 (C.M.A. 1985) — § 5-10(C), nn. 15, 16; § 5-10(D), n. 40

United States v. Palos, 20 C.M.A. 104, 42 C.M.R. 296 (1970) — § 14-3(B)(3), n. 111

United States v. Palumbo, 24 M.J. 512 (A.F.C.M.R. 1987) — § 13-3(C)(3), n. 156

United States v. Palumbo, 27 M.J. 565 (A.C.M.R. 1988) — § 4-8(B), n. 11; § 13-4(A), n. 17

United States v. Papageorgiou, 13 M.J. 584 (N.M.C.M.R. 1982) — § 17-21, n. 3

United States v. Pappas, 30 M.J. 513 (A.F.C.M.R. 1990) — § 5-3(D)(1), n. 125

United States v. Parini, 12 M.J. 679 (A.C.M.R. 1981) — § 16-3(D), n. 63

TABLE OF CASES

United States v. Parish, 17 C.M.A. 411, 38 C.M.R. 209 (1968) — § 13-3(C)(2), nn. 54, 59
United States v. Parish, 20 M.J. 696 (N.M.C.M.R. 1985) — § 14-3(B)(2), n. 71
United States v. Parker, 3 C.M.A. 541, 13 C.M.R. 97 (1953) — § 6-1(C)(2), n. 131
United States v. Parker, 6 C.M.A. 75, 19 C.M.R. 201 (1955) — § 7-2(E), n. 114; § 7-2(A)(1), n. 19
United States v. Parker, 6 C.M.A. 274, 19 C.M.R. 400 (1955) — § 15-10(A), n. 22; § 15-10(B), n. 50
United States v. Parker, 7 C.M.A. 182, 21 C.M.R. 308 (1956) — § 15-15, n. 3
United States v. Parker, 48 C.M.R. 241 (A.C.M.R. 1973) — § 13-3(C)(2), n. 73
United States v. Parker, 5 M.J. 923 (N.C.M.R. 1978) — § 13-3(N)(4), nn. 420, 421
United States v. Parker, 27 M.J. 522 (A.F.C.M.R. 1988) — § 5-3(D)(1), n. 132
United States v. Parker, 36 M.J. 269 (C.M.A. 1993) — § 17-21, n. 3
United States v. Parkes, 5 M.J. 489 (C.M.A. 1978) — § 12-3(A), n. 33
United States v. Parks, 6 M.J. 11 (C.M.A. 1978) — § 17-2(B)(4), n. 94
United States v. Parrillo, 31 M.J. 886 (A.F.C.M.R. 1990) — § 2-8(B), n. 10; § 5-4(B), n. 42
United States v. Parrillo, 34 M.J. 112 (C.M.A. 1992) — § 5-3, n. 4
United States v. Parrish, 7 C.M.A. 337, 22 C.M.R. 127 (1956) — § 11-3(B)(2), n. 42
United States v. Parrish, 20 M.J. 665 (N.M.C.M.R. 1985) — § 6-1(C), nn. 94, 95
United States v. Partin, 7 M.J. 409 (C.M.A. 1979) — § 14-3(C), n. 131
United States v. Partyka, 30 M.J. 242 (C.M.A. 1990) — § 16-6, n. 10; § 16-5(D)(5), n. 123
United States v. Pascascio, 37 M.J. 1012 (A.C.M.R. 1993) — § 13-3(C)(2), n. 81
United States v. Paske, 11 C.M.A. 689, 29 C.M.R. 505 (1960) — § 16-9, n. 10
United States v. Pastor, 8 M.J. 280 (C.M.A. 1980) — § 15-4(B), n. 11
United States v. Paternina-Vergara, 749 F.2d 933 (2d Cir. 1984) — § 10-4(B)(5), n. 57
United States v. Patterson, 22 C.M.A. 157, 46 C.M.R. 157 (1973) — § 17-14, n. 5
United States v. Patterson, 39 M.J. 678 (N.M.C.M.R. 1993) — § 5-3(D)(1), n. 125; § 13-3(C)(3), n. 97
United States v. Patton, 41 C.M.R. 572 (A.C.M.R. 1969) — § 2-4(A), n. 21
United States v. Pattugalan, 26 M.J. 762 (A.C.M.R. 1988) — § 15-2(B)(3), n. 78
United States v. Pauley, 24 M.J. 521 (A.F.C.M.R. 1987) — § 16-9, n. 16
United States v. Paulk, 13 C.M.A. 456, 32 C.M.R. 456 (1963) — § 13-5(F), n. 14; § 6-1(C)(2), n. 124
United States v. Paulson, 30 C.M.R. 465 (A.B.R. 1960) — § 16-5(B), n. 8
United States v. Pawis, 12 M.J. 691 (N.M.C.M.R. 1981) — § 17-4, n. 32
United States v. Payne, 31 C.M.R. 41 (C.M.A. 1961) — § 15-2(D), n. 137
United States v. Payne, 3 M.J. 354 (C.M.A. 1977) — § 6-4(B), nn. 11, 13; § 7-2(E), n. 105; § 7-2(A)(1), nn. 23, 25, 29; § 7-2(A)(2), n. 36
United States v. Payne, 29 M.J. 899 (A.C.M.R. 1989) — § 2-4(B), n. 26; § 2-4(D), n. 44
United States v. Peaches, 25 M.J. 364 (C.M.A. 1987) — § 2-4(F), n. 51; § 16-2(F), n. 55
United States v. Peacock, 19 M.J. 909 (A.C.M.R. 1985) — § 5-10(D), n. 41; § 13-5(B), n. 26
United States v. Pearson, 13 M.J. 140 (C.M.A. 1982) — § 4-6, n. 28
United States v. Pearson, 15 M.J. 888 (A.C.M.R. 1983) — § 17-2(B)(4), n. 93
United States v. Pearson, 17 M.J. 149 (C.M.A. 1984) — § 16-8(B), n. 21; § 16-5(D)(1), n. 53; § 16-5(D)(3), nn. 73, 76
United States v. Pearson, 74 17 M.J. 149 (C.M.A. 1984) — § 16-5(D)(3), nn. 74, 75
United States v. Pearson, 33 M.J. 777 (N.M.C.M.R. 1991) — § 13-2(G)(2), n. 103
United States v. Peck, 36 M.J. 900 (A.F.C.M.R. 1993) — § 16-7, n. 1; § 14-2(B)(4), n. 114; § 16-5(D)(1), nn. 51, 55

TABLE OF CASES

United States v. Peebles, 3 M.J. 177 (C.M.A. 1977) — § 12-4, n. 13
United States v. Peek, 24 M.J. 750 (A.C.M.R. 1987) — § 15-2(B)(3), n. 85
United States v. Peel, 4 M.J. 28 (C.M.A. 1977) — § 4-6, n. 26
United States v. Peel, 29 M.J. 235 (C.M.A. 1989) — § 15-14(B), n. 34
United States v. Pellman, 24 M.J. 672 (A.F.C.M.R. 1987) — § 16-11, n. 8; § 5-3(C)(6), nn. 85, 96, 97
United States v. Pena, 22 M.J. 281 (C.M.A. 1986) — § 10-4(B)(5), n. 60
United States v. Pendry, 29 M.J. 694 (A.C.M.R. 1989) — § 15-14(A), n. 7
United States v. Penister, 25 M.J. 148 (C.M.A. 1987) — § 9-2(B), n. 37; § 9-2(C), n. 81; § 14-3, n. 3; § 14-3(B)(2), nn. 93, 100
United States v. Penn, 18 C.M.A. 194, 39 C.M.R. 194 (1969) — § 5-4(B), n. 43
United States v. Penn, 4 M.J. 879 (N.C.M.R. 1978) — § 3-4, n. 1; § 13-3(N)(1), nn. 305, 310, 318, 331
United States v. Penn, 5 M.J. 514 (N.C.M.R. 1978) — § 15-24, n. 2
United States v. Penn, 21 M.J. 907 (N.M.C.M.R. 1986) — § 13-2(G)(2), n. 86
United States v. Pennington, 21 C.M.A. 461, 45 C.M.R. 235 (1972) — § 15-14(D), n. 55
United States v. Peoples, 6 M.J. 904 (A.C.M.R. 1979) — § 2-3(A), n. 11
United States v. Peoples, 28 M.J. 686 (A.F.C.M.R. 1989) — § 5-3(F), n. 26; § 5-3(C)(6), n. 85
United States v. Pereira, 13 M.J. 632 (A.F.C.M.R. 1982) — § 13-2(G)(1), n. 70; § 13-2(G)(2), n. 74
United States v. Perez, 33 M.J. 1050 (A.C.M.R. 1991) — § 2-9(C)(1), n. 34
United States v. Perez, 36 M.J. 1198 (N.M.C.M.R. 1993) — § 15-10(B), n. 39
United States v. Perez, 40 M.J. 373 (C.M.A. 1994) — § 15-16(A), nn. 10, 11, 16
United States v. Pergande, 49 C.M.R. 28 (A.C.M.R. 1974) — § 12-2(A), n. 8
United States v. Perkinson, 16 M.J. 400 (C.M.A. 1983) — § 8-2(B), n. 6; § 12-2(C), n. 11
United States v. Perna, 1 C.M.A. 438, 4 C.M.R. 30 (1952) — § 12-2(A), n. 8
United States v. Perry, 40 C.M.R. 286 (A.C.M.R. 1970) — § 12-4, n. 9
United States v. Perry, 14 M.J. 856 (A.C.M.R. 1982) — § 13-5(K), n. 85; § 15-4(A), n. 8
United States v. Perry, 12 M.J. 920 (N.M.C.M.R. 1982) — § 15-13, n. 29
United States v. Perry, 20 M.J. 1026 (A.C.M.R. 1985) — § 16-5(B), n. 8
United States v. Perry, 22 M.J. 669 (A.C.M.R. 1986) — § 15-16(B), n. 28
United States v. Perry, 24 M.J. 557 (A.C.M.R. 1987) — § 16-11, n. 8
United States v. Peszynski, 40 M.J. 874 (N.M.C.M.R. 1994) — § 2-6, n. 2
United States v. Peterson, 44 C.M.R. 528 (A.C.M.R. 1971) — § 9-2(B)(2), n. 68
United States v. Peterson, 7 M.J. 981 (A.C.M.R. 1979) — § 17-21, n. 3
United States v. Peterson, 23 M.J. 828 (A.C.M.R. 1986) — § 14-3(D)(5), nn. 163, 166
United States v. Peterson, 30 M.J. 946 (A.C.M.R. 1990) — § 5-7, n. 24; § 5-10(D), n. 34
United States v. Petroff-Tachomakoff, 5 C.M.A. 824, 19 C.M.R. 120 (1955) — § 17-5, n. 6
United States v. Pettaway, 24 M.J. 589 (N.M.C.M.R. 1987) — § 12-3, n. 3; § 13-3(C)(3), nn. 156, 158
United States v. Pettersen, 14 M.J. 608 (A.F.C.M.R. 1982) — § 2-2(C)(3), n. 41
United States v. Pettersen, 15 M.J. 934 (N.M.C.M.R. 1983) — § 2-7(B), n. 25
United States v. Petterson, 17 M.J. 69 (C.M.A. 1983) — § 2-4(F), n. 51
United States v. Pettigrew, 19 C.M.A. 191, 41 C.M.R. 191 (1970) — § 2-4(B), n. 26
United States v. Pettis, 12 M.J. 616 (N.M.C.M.R. 1981) — § 13-3(I), n. 254
United States v. Petty, 30 M.J. 1237 (A.C.M.R. 1990) — § 17-9(A), n. 11
United States v. Phaneuf, 10 M.J. 831 (A.C.M.R. 1981) — § 11-2(F), n. 160
United States v. Phare, 21 C.M.A. 244, 45 C.M.R. 18 (1972) — § 8-4, n. 8
United States v. Phelps, 40 M.J. 550 (A.C.M.R. 1994) — § 17-5, n. 8

TABLE OF CASES

United States v. Phillips, 24 M.J. 812 (A.F.C.M.R. 1987) — § 9-2(B)(1), n. 41
United States v. Phillips, 26 M.J. 963 (A.C.M.R. 1988) — § 6-1(C)(3), n. 145
United States v. Phillips, 28 M.J. 599 (N.M.C.M.R. 1989) — § 2-2(C)(3), n. 32
United States v. Phillips, 32 M.J. 76 (C.M.A. 1991) — § 13-4(A), n. 10
United States v. Phillips, 32 M.J. 955 (A.F.C.M.R. 1991) — § 14-4, nn. 6, 7; § 5-3(C)(6), n. 84
United States v. Phillips, 37 M.J. 532 (A.C.M.R. 1993) — § 13-5(K), n. 86; § 8-3(B)(4), n. 99
United States v. Phillips, 38 M.J. 641 (A.C.M.R. 1993) — § 5-10(C), n. 20; § 13-3(N)(3), n. 378
United States v. Phillips, 38 M.J. 593 (N.M.C.M.R. 1993) — § 5-3(A), n. 25; § 5-3(B), n. 52
United States v. Phillips, 42 M.J. 346 (1995) — § 5-10(C), n. 20
United States v. Phillipson, 30 M.J. 1019 (A.F.C.M.R. 1990) — § 14-3(C), n. 128
United States v. Phrampus, 34 M.J. 607 (A.F.M.C.R. 1992) — § 14-3(B)(2), n. 95
United States v. Piatt, 15 M.J. 636 (N.M.C.M.R. 1982) — § 6-7, n. 4
United States v. Picotte, 12 C.M.A. 196, 30 C.M.R. 196 (1961) — § 2-6(C), n. 40
United States v. Pierce, 29 C.M.R. 849 (A.B.R. 1960) — § 6-3(A), n. 11; § 6-5(A), n. 8
United States v. Pierce, 19 C.M.A. 225, 41 C.M.R. 225 (1970) — § 13-3(C), n. 25
United States v. Pierce, 25 M.J. 607 (A.C.M.R. 1987) — § 13-3(G), n. 224
United States v. Pierce, 27 M.J. 367 (C.M.A. 1989) — § 3-3(C), nn. 25, 27; § 3-8(B), n. 5; § 16-3, n. 2; § 16-5(B), n. 19
United States v. Pierce, 40 M.J. 149 (C.M.A. 1994) — § 15-2(B)(3), nn. 36, 85
United States v. Pillow, 28 M.J. 1008 (C.G.C.M.R. 1989) — § 14-3(D)(4), n. 145
United States v. Pingree, 39 M.J. 884 (A.C.M.R. 1994) — § 16-5(D)(3), n. 72
United States v. Pinkston, 32 M.J. 555 (A.F.C.M.R. 1991) — § 2-7(C), n. 32
United States v. Pippin, 22 M.J. 806 (A.F.C.M.R. 1986) — § 17-2(B)(3), n. 76
United States v. Pirraglia, 24 M.J. 671 (A.F.C.M.R. 1987) — § 4-11(B), n. 42
United States v. Pitasi, 20 C.M.A. 601, 44 C.M.R. 210 (1970) — § 2-8(D), n. 40
United States v. Pitasi, 20 C.M.A. 601, 44 C.M.R. 31 (1971) — § 2-8(A), n. 3; § 13-3(N)(3), n. 408
United States v. Pitt, 35 M.J. 478 (C.M.A. 1992) — § 2-7(A), n. 10
United States v. Pittman, 36 M.J. 404 (C.M.A. 1993) — § 5-4(B), n. 43
United States v. Place, 457 U.S. 1104 (1983) — § 5-3(A), n. 30
United States v. Plante, 36 M.J. 626 (A.C.M.R. 1992) — § 14-3(B)(2), n. 71
United States v. Plaut, 18 C.M.A. 265, 39 C.M.R. 265 (1969) — § 7-2(A)(2), n. 35
United States v. Plott, 35 M.J. 512 (A.F.C.M.R. 1992) — § 13-5(A), n. 15; § 16-5(D)(4), n. 86
United States v. Plott, 38 M.J. 735 (A.F.C.M.R. 1993) — § 7-3(A), n. 25; § 8-4, n. 4; § 13-2(E), n. 53; § 8-3(B)(3), n. 89
United States v. Politano, 14 C.M.A. 518, 34 C.M.R. 298 (1964) — § 14-3(G), n. 197
United States v. Polk, 27 M.J. 812 (A.C.M.R. 1988) — § 17-2(B), n. 6; § 15-2(B)(3), n. 88
United States v. Polk, 32 M.J. 150 (C.M.A. 1991) — § 15-2(B)(3), nn. 39, 49, 94
United States v. Pollack, 7 M.J. 627 (A.F.C.M.R. 1979) — § 4-11(A), n. 17
United States v. Pollard, 26 M.J. 947 (C.G.C.M.R. 1988) — § 5-3(D)(1), n. 131
United States v. Pollard, 34 M.J. 1008 (A.C.M.R. 1992) — § 16-6, n. 21
United States v. Pompey, 32 M.J. 547 (A.F.C.M.R. 1990) — § 5-3(D)(1), n. 118
United States v. Pompey, 33 M.J. 266 (C.M.A. 1991) — § 16-5(D)(4), n. 102
United States v. Pond, 36 M.J. 1050 (A.F.C.M.R. 1993) — § 5-3(A), n. 15; § 5-3(F), n. 24; § 5-4(B), n. 37; § 5-3(C)(5), n. 82; § 5-3(C)(7), n. 99; § 5-3(D)(2), n. 140

TABLE OF CASES

United States v. Ponder, 29 M.J. 782 (A.C.M.R. 1989) — § 8-3(D), n. 167; § 12-2(F)(1), n. 43
United States v. Ponds, 1 C.M.A. 385, 3 C.M.R. 119 (1952) — § 9-2(B)(2), n. 71
United States v. Poole, 20 M.J. 598 (N.M.C.M.R. 1985) — § 4-6, n. 11
United States v. Poole, 24 M.J. 539 (A.C.M.R. 1987) — § 6-1(C)(2), n. 126
United States v. Poole, 26 M.J. 272 (C.M.A. 1988) — § 14-3(D)(3), n. 144
United States v. Poole, 30 M.J. 149 (C.M.A. 1990) — § 4-8(A), n. 10
United States v. Poole, 30 M.J. 271 (C.M.A. 1990) — § 5-3(B), n. 37
United States v. Poole, 39 M.J. 819 (A.C.M.R. 1994) — § 2-6(A), nn. 19, 20, 25
United States v. Pooler, 13 M.J. 786 (A.C.M.R. 1982) — § 17-15(C), n. 37
United States v. Pooler, 18 M.J. 832 (A.C.M.R. 1984) — § 16-5(D)(2), n. 69; § 16-5(D)(4), n. 84; § 16-5(D)(5), n. 118
United States v. Porter, 50 C.M.R. 508 (N.C.M.R. 1975) — § 6-1, n. 41
United States v. Porter, 17 M.J. 377 (C.M.A. 1984) — § 15-10(B), nn. 56, 68; § 15-10(C)(2), n. 93
United States v. Porter, 36 M.J. 812 (A.C.M.R. 1993) — § 5-3(A), n. 34; § 15-9, n. 2; § 5-3(C)(5), n. 82
United States v. Posnick, 8 C.M.A. 201, 24 C.M.R. 11 (1957) — § 6-1(C)(3), n. 141
United States v. Postle, 20 M.J. 632 (N.M.C.M.R. 1985) — § 1-1(B), n. 33; § 13-2(E), n. 54
United States v. Poteet, 50 C.M.R. 73 (N.C.M.R. 1975) — § 15-13, nn. 9, 13, 29; § 16-8(B), n. 18
United States v. Potter, 15 C.M.A. 271, 35 C.M.R. 243 (1965) — § 2-6(A), n. 22
United States v. Powell, 2 M.J. 6 (C.M.A. 1976) — § 13-3(C)(2), nn. 50, 53
United States v. Powell, 2 M.J. 849 (A.C.M.R. 1976) — § 13-3(C)(2), n. 73
United States v. Powell, 8 M.J. 260 (C.M.A. 1980) — § 5-3(B), n. 42
United States v. Powell, 32 M.J. 117 (C.M.A. 1991) — § 2-4(E), nn. 45, 46
United States v. Powell, 38 M.J. 153 (C.M.A. 1993) — § 13-3(C)(3), nn. 97, 99
United States v. Powell, 40 M.J. 1 (C.M.A. 1994) — § 5-4(B), n. 46; § 15-2(B)(3), n. 53
United States v. Power, 20 M.J. 275 (C.M.A. 1985) — § 2-7(B), n. 26
United States v. Pownall, 42 M.J. 682 (Army Ct.Crim.App. 1995) — § 5-4(B), nn. 23, 42
United States v. Pratcher, 14 M.J. 819 (A.C.M.R. 1982) — § 2-3(C), n. 29; § 15-16(C), nn. 32, 35
United States v. Pratcher, 17 M.J. 388 (C.M.A. 1984) — § 2-3(C), n. 29
United States v. Pratt, 34 C.M.R. 731 (C.G.B.R. 1963) — § 2-4(E), n. 47
United States v. Preuss, 34 M.J. 688 (N.M.C.M.R. 1991) — § 10-5(A)(2), nn. 19, 20
United States v. Price, 4 M.J. 849 (A.C.M.R. 1978) — § 9-2(B)(1), n. 44
United States v. Price, 15 M.J. 628 (N.M.C.M.R. 1982) — § 17-8(B), n. 20
United States v. Price, 41 M.J. 403 (1995) — § 15-4(A), n. 3
United States v. Priest, 19 C.M.A. 446, 42 C.M.R. 48 (1970) — § 15-2(A), n. 8
United States v. Priest, 21 C.M.A. 564, 45 C.M.R. 338 (1972) — § 2-4(A), n. 18; § 13-3(N)(3), nn. 368, 383
United States, Prince v.
United States v. Pringle, 19 C.M.A. 324, 41 C.M.R. 324 (1970) — § 5-10(C), n. 15; § 5-10(D), n. 28
United States v. Pringle, 3 M.J. 308 (C.M.A. 1977) — § 13-5(G)(1), n. 38
United States v. Prive, 35 M.J. 569 (C.G.C.M.R. 1992) — § 8-3(A), n. 20
United States v. Privette, 31 M.J. 791 (A.F.C.M.R. 1990) — § 16-6, n. 10; § 16-11, n. 6
United States v. Proctor, 34 M.J. 549 (A.F.C.M.R. 1992) — § 12-2(H), nn. 102, 122; § 13-5(A), n. 6; § 15-4(A), n. 6; § 16-6, n. 6; § 12-2(F)(4), n. 68
United States v. Proctor, 37 M.J. 330 (C.M.A. 1993) — § 13-5(A), n. 11

TABLE OF CASES

United States v. Prophete, 29 M.J. 925 (A.F.C.M.R. 1989) — § 16-5(C), n. 44
United States v. Province, 42 M.J. 821 (N.M.C.Ct.Crim.App.1995) — § 6-1(C), n. 104; § 13-3(B), nn. 9, 18
United States v. Provost, 32 M.J. 98 (C.M.A. 1991) — § 16-6, nn. 6, 12
United States v. Pruitt, 17 C.M.A. 438, 38 C.M.R. 236 (1968) — § 2-6, n. 10
United States v. Pruitt, 41 M.J. 736 (N.M.Ct.Crim.App. 1994) — § 9-2(B)(2), n. 67
United States v. Pruner, 33 M.J. 272 (C.M.A. 1991) — § 17-19, n. 17
United States v. Pruner, 37 M.J. 573 (A.C.M.R. 1993) — § 2-2(B), n. 10; § 9-2(C), n. 80
United States v. Pryor, 19 M.J. 720 (A.C.M.R. 1984) — § 17-2(B)(4), n. 92; § 17-8(B)(3), n. 75
United States v. Puckett, 32 M.J. 783 (C.G.C.M.R. 1991) — § 15-2(B)(3), n. 73
United States v. Pullen, 41 M.J. 886 (A.F.Ct.Crim.App. 1995) — § 2-6(C), n. 39
United States v. Pulliam, 3 C.M.A. 95, 11 C.M.R. 95 (1953) — § 15-2(E), n. 154; § 8-3(C)(4), n. 157
United States v. Pulliam, 17 M.J. 1066 (A.F.C.M.R. 1984) — § 6-1(C)(3), n. 142
United States v. Purdy, 42 M.J. 666 (Army Ct.Crim.App. 1995) — § 16-9, n. 4; § 15-2(B)(3), n. 73
United States v. Quarles, 1 M.J. 231 (C.M.A. 1975) — § 16-2(F), n. 55
United States v. Quarles, 50 C.M.R. 514 (N.C.M.R. 1975) — § 6-1(B), nn. 60, 67
United States v. Quarles, 25 M.J. 761 (N.M.C.M.R. 1987) — § 15-13, n. 19
United States v. Queen, 26 M.J. 136 (C.M.A. 1988) — § 5-3(F), n. 24
United States v. Quezada, 40 M.J. 109 (C.M.A. 1994) — § 2-2(D), n. 62
United States v. Quigley, 35 M.J. 345 (C.M.A. 1992) — § 17-14, n. 11; § 15-2(B)(3), n. 89
United States v. Quillen, 27 M.J. 312 (C.M.A. 1988) — § 5-4(B), n. 43
United States v. Quinones, 1 M.J. 64 (C.M.A. 1975) — § 13-5(H), n. 59; § 8-3(B)(3), n. 75
United States v. Quinores, 353 F. Supp. 1325 (D.P.R. 1973) — § 16-13
United States v. Quintana, 5 M.J. 484 (C.M.A. 1978) — § 5-4(B), n. 26
United States v. Rachel, 32 M.J. 669 (A.F.C.M.R. 1991) — § 5-3(C)(6), n. 85
United States v. Rachels, 6 M.J. 232 (C.M.A. 1979) — § 13-3(C)(1), n. 38; § 13-3(C)(2), n. 53
United States v. Radford, 14 M.J. 322 (C.M.A. 1982) — § 10-3(F), nn. 24, 25; § 15-2(B)(3), n. 74; § 15-2(B)(4), nn. 111, 112, 117
United States v. Radimecky, 25 M.J. 505 (A.F.C.M.R. 1987) — § 4-14(A)(1), n. 7
United States v. Raichle, 28 M.J. 876 (A.F.C.M.R. 1989) — § 13-3(C)(3), nn. 159, 162
United States v. Rainwater, 19 M.J. 545 (N.M.C.M.R. 1984) — § 16-11, n. 6
United States v. Ralbovsky, 32 M.J. 921 (A.F.C.M.R. 1991) — § 17-8(B)(1), n. 36
United States v. Ralston, 24 M.J. 709 (A.C.M.R. 1987) — § 1-1, n. 6; § 6-8, n.5; § 9-2(B)(1), n. 49
United States v. Ramos, 42 M.J. 392 (1995) — § 15-2(D), n. 132 R.C.M. 80; § 15-12(B), n. 15
United States v. Ramsey, 28 M.J. 370 (C.M.A. 1989) — § 13-3(C)(3), n. 130
United States v. Randle, 35 M.J. 789 (A.C.M.R. 1992) — § 4-16, n. 17; § 14-3(D)(4), n. 150
United States v. Rankins, 34 M.J. 326 (C.M.A. 1992) — § 2-2(E)(3), nn. 78, 83
United States v. Rapolla, 34 M.J. 1268 (A.F.C.M.R. 1992) — § 17-15(B), n. 32
United States v. Rappaport, 19 M.J. 708 (A.F.C.M.R. 1984) — § 13-5(I), n. 73; § 11-2(B)(1), n. 68
United States v. Rasberry, 21 M.J. 656 (A.C.M.R. 1985) — § 15-21, n. 9; § 9-2(B)(1), n. 39; § 16-5(D)(1), n. 61
United States v. Rascoe, 31 M.J. 544 (N.M.C.M.R. 1990) — § 14-3(C), n. 130

TABLE OF CASES

United States v. Ratliff, 42 M.J. 797 (N.M.Ct.Crim.App.1995) — § 17-9(D), n. 65; § 11-2(E)(3), n. 133
United States v. Ravenel, 26 M.J. 344 (C.M.A. 1988) — § 5-4(B), n. 52
United States v. Ravine, 11 M.J. 325 (C.M.A. 1981) — § 5-3(F), n. 21
United States v. Ray, 24 M.J. 657 (A.F.C.M.R. 1987) — § 17-11, n. 5
United States v. Ray, 26 M.J. 468 (C.M.A. 1988) — § 15-12, n. 3
United States v. Ray, 37 M.J. 1052 (N.M.C.M.R. 1993) — § 2-2(D), n. 67
United States v. Rayford, 33 M.J. 747 (A.C.M.R. 1991) — § 16-5(B), n. 26
United States v. Rayle, 6 M.J. 836 (N.C.M.R. 1979) — § 2-2(C)(3), n. 45
United States v. Raymond, 38 M.J. 136 (C.M.A. 1993) — § 5-4(B), n. 43
United States v. Read, 29 M.J. 690 (A.C.M.R. 1989) — § 15-16(A), n. 9
United States v. Reagan, 7 M.J. 490 (C.M.A. 1979) — § 9-3, n. 8
United States v. Reap, 41 M.J. 340 (1995) — § 13-3(C)(3), n. 130
United States v. Reap, 43 M.J. 61 (1995) — § 14-3(D)(4), n. 153
United States v. Rebuck, 16 M.J. 555 (A.F.C.M.R. 1983) — § 15-4(B), n. 12
United States v. Reddick, 32 M.J. 967 (A.C.M.R. 1991) — § 15-2(B)(3), n. 78
United States v. Redding, 11 M.J. 100 (C.M.A. 1981) — § 13-5(H), nn. 59, 61, 62; § 8-3(B)(3), n. 85; § 13-2(G)(2), n. 74; § 17-19, n. 17
United States v. Redman, 33 M.J. 679 (A.C.M.R. 1991) — § 6-4(D), n. 25; § 8-5, n. 12
United States v. Reece, 21 M.J. 736 (N.M.C.M.R. 1985) — § 11-4, n. 10
United States v. Reece, 25 M.J. 93 (C.M.A. 1987) — § 11-4, nn. 2, 5, 14
United States v. Reed, 1 M.J. 166 (C.M.A. 1975) — § 16-5(C), n. 34
United States v. Reed, 2 M.J. 64 (C.M.A. 1976) — § 6-6(A), n. 3; § 13-3(C)(2), nn. 58, 66; § 17-9(B), n. 37
United States v. Reed, 19 M.J. 764 (A.C.M.R. 1984) — § 17-8(B), n. 27
United States v. Reed, 24 M.J. 80 (C.M.A. 1987) — § 5-4(A)(2), n. 16; § 13-3(N)(2), nn. 349, 354; § 13-3(N)(3), n. 405
United States v. Reed, 26 M.J. 891 (A.F.C.M.R. 1988) — § 14-3(C), n. 132; § 9-2(B)(1), n. 49
United States v. Reed, 33 M.J. 98 (C.M.A. 1991) — § 17-8(B)(2), n. 67
United States v. Reed, 41 M.J. 449 (1995) — § 13-3(C)(1), nn. 43, 44
United States v. Reed, 41 M.J. 755 (C.G.Ct.Crim.App. 1995) — § 17-3, n. 1
United States v. Reeder, 22 C.M.A. 11, 46 C.M.R. 11 (1972) — § 2-2(C)(3), nn. 49, 50; § 14-3(D)(2), n. 136
United States v. Reeder, 29 M.J. 563 (A.F.C.M.R. 1989) — § 17-15(C), n. 33
United States v. Reese, 92 U.S. 214 (1876) — § 13-3(N)(2), n. 343
United States v. Reeves, 49 C.M.R. 841 (A.C.M.R. 1975) — § 2-2(E)(6), nn. 98, 99; § 6-1(B)(2), n. 86
United States v. Reeves, 12 M.J. 763 (A.C.M.R. 1981) — § 8-3(A), n. 6; § 12-2(H), n. 104
United States v. Reeves, 34 M.J. 1261 (N.M.C.M.R. 1992) — § 13-3(C)(1), n. 38
United States v. Regan, 7 M.J. 600 (N.C.M.R. 1979) — § 4-11(A), n. 25
United States v. Regan, 11 M.J. 745 (A.C.M.R. 1981) — § 2-6(A), n. 17
United States v. Reichardt, 28 M.J. 113 (C.M.A. 1989) — § 15-10(B), n. 68
United States v. Reichenbach, 29 M.J. 128 (C.M.A. 1989) — § 2-7(A), nn. 1, 6-8
United States v. Reid, 32 M.J. 146 (C.M.A. 1991) — § 15-14(B), n. 28
United States v. Reilly, 36 M.J. 887 (N.M.C.M.R. 1993) — § 17-8(B), n. 11
United States v. Reinecke, 30 M.J. 1010 (A.F.C.M.R. 1990) — § 13-2(G)(2), n. 85
United States v. Reister, 40 M.J. 666 (N.M.C.M.R. 1994) — § 2-9(C)(1), n. 34; § 5-3(C)(6), n. 88
United States v. Repp, 23 M.J. 589 (A.F.C.M.R. 1986) — § 5-3(A), n. 22
United States v. Respess, 7 M.J. 566 (A.C.M.R. 1979) — § 4-11(A), n. 24

TABLE OF CASES

United States v. Reveles, 41 M.J. 388 (1995) — § 16-6, n. 4; § 11-2(B)(1), nn. 57, 68; § 16-5(D)(3), n. 73
United States v. Rexroat, 36 M.J. 708 (A.C.M.R. 1992) — § 5-9(D), n. 23
United States v. Rexroat, 38 M.J. 292 (C.M.A. 1993) — § 5-9(B), n. 7; § 5-9(C), n. 18; § 5-9(D), nn. 21, 22
United States v. Reynolds, 2 M.J. 887 (A.C.M.R. 1976) — § 9-2(B)(1), n. 42
United States v. Reynolds, 15 M.J. 1021 (A.F.C.M.R. 1983) — § 13-4(A), n. 17
United States v. Reynolds, 19 M.J. 529 (A.C.M.R. 1984) — § 7-2(A)(1), n. 16; § 8-3(B)(1), n. 46
United States v. Reynolds, 23 M.J. 292 (C.M.A. 1987) — § 15-10(A), n. 31; § 15-10(B), n. 53
United States v. Reynolds, 24 M.J. 261 (C.M.A. 1987) — § 15-2(D), nn. 129, 137; § 15-12(B), n. 15; § 7-2(A)(1), n. 15
United States v. Reynolds, 36 M.J. 1128 (A.C.M.R. 1993) — § 17-8(B), n. 18; § 8-3(C)(4), n. 160; § 13-3(C)(3), nn. 106, 122
United States v. Reynolds, 40 M.J. 198 (C.M.A. 1994) — § 6-5(A), nn. 8, 11; § 6-7, n. 1
United States v. Rhea, 33 M.J. 413 (C.M.A. 1991) — § 10-3(F), nn. 21, 26
United States v. Rhoads, 32 M.J. 114 (C.M.A. 1991) — § 16-5(D)(4), n. 100
United States v. Rhodes, 42 M.J. 287 (1995) — § 5-5, n. 9
United States v. Rice, 3 M.J. 1094 (N.C.M.R. 1977) — § 8-2(A), n. 4
United States v. Rice, 16 M.J. 770 (A.C.M.R. 1983) — § 12-2(H), n. 101
United States v. Rice, 20 M.J. 764 (A.F.C.M.R. 1985) — § 15-16(B), n. 28
United States v. Rice, 33 M.J. 451 (C.M.A. 1991) — § 17-8(B), n. 18
United States v. Rice, 36 M.J. 264 (C.M.A. 1993) — § 8-3(A), n. 32
United States v. Rich, 12 M.J. 661 (A.C.M.R. 1981) — § 16-8(B), n. 11; § 16-8(C), n. 40
United States v. Rich, 26 M.J. 518 (A.C.M.R. 1988) — § 15-2(B)(3), n. 87
United States v. Richardson, 21 C.M.A. 54, 44 C.M.R. 108 (1971) — § 13-3(E), n. 205
United States v. Richardson, 5 M.J. 627 (A.C.M.R. 1978) — § 8-4, n. 5
United States v. Richardson, 6 M.J. 654 (N.C.M.R. 1978) — § 14-2(B)(4), n. 113
United States v. Richardson, 7 M.J. 320 (C.M.A. 1979) — § 2-3(C), n. 26
United States v. Richardson, 34 M.J. 1015 (A.C.M.R. 1992) — § 5-10(D), n. 37
United States v. Richardson, 35 M.J. 687 (C.G.C.M.R. 1992) — § 15-2(B)(3), n. 52
United States v. Richter, 37 M.J. 615 (A.C.M.R. 1993) — § 17-8(B)(3), n. 83
United States v. Ricketts, 1 M.J. 78 (C.M.A. 1975) — § 15-16(A), n. 8
United States v. Ricks, 21 M.J. 569 (A.C.M.R. 1985) — § 17-2(B)(4), n. 92; § 17-8(B)(3), n. 75
United States v. Riddick, 19 M.J. 517 (A.F.C.M.R. 1984) — § 16-11, n. 4
United States v. Ridgeway, 19 M.J. 681 (A.F.C.M.R. 1984) — § 6-1(C)(3), n. 149
United States v. Ridgeway, 32 M.J. 1006 (A.C.M.R. 1991) — § 14-3(D)(4), n. 151
United States v. Ridley, 22 M.J. 43 (C.M.A. 1986) — § 4-14(A)(1), n. 5
United States v. Riemer, 12 M.J. 915 (N.M.C.M.R. 1982) — § 17-11, n. 1
United States v. Riggins, 2 C.M.A. 451, 9 C.M.R. 81 (1953) — § 6-1(C)(2), n. 125
United States v. Riley, 6 C.M.R. 471 (C.G.B.R. 1952) — § 11-3(B)(1), n. 35; § 11-3(B)(2), n. 48
United States v. Riley, 35 M.J. 547 (A.C.M.R. 1992) — § 14-3(B)(2), n. 67
United States v. Rimmer, 39 M.J. 1083 (A.C.M.R. 1994) — § 16-5(B), n. 10
United States v. Rinehart, 8 C.M.A. 402, 24 C.M.R. 212 (1957) — § 15-14(A), n. 19; § 15-15 n. 10
United States v. Ringer, 14 M.J. 979 (N.M.C.M.R. 1982) — § 2-2(C)(3), n. 41
United States v. Ringuette, 29 M.J. 527 (A.F.C.M.R. 1989) — § 16-5(D)(3), n. 72; § 16-5(D)(5), n. 112

TABLE OF CASES

United States v. Rios, 24 M.J. 515 (A.F.C.M.R. 1987) — § 14-3(B)(2), n. 95; § 15-2(B)(3), n. 67
United States v. Rios, 24 M.J. 809 (A.F.C.M.R. 1987) — § 5-9(B), n. 9; § 5-9(E), n. 54
United States v. Rivas, 3 M.J. 282 (C.M.A. 1977) — § 15-2(B)(3), nn. 30, 31
United States v. Rivera, 12 C.M.A. 507, 31 C.M.R. 93 (1961) — § 6-4(C), n. 19
United States v. Rivera, 20 C.M.A. 6, 42 C.M.R. 198 (1970) — § 17-8(B)(1), n. 57; § 17-9(A), n. 1
United States v. Rivera, 45 C.M.R. 582 (A.C.M.R. 1972) — § 3-3(C), n. 24
United States v. Rivera, 1 M.J. 107 (C.M.A. 1975) — § 5-4(C), n. 56; § 13-3(H), n. 245; § 11-2(E)(1), n. 106; § 11-2(E)(3), n. 150
United States v. Rivera, 1 M.J. 107 (C.M.A. 1975) — § 11-2(E)(3), n. 142
United States v. Rivera, 4 M.J. 215 (C.M.A. 1978) — § 5-3(C)(3), n. 75
United States v. Rivera, 10 M.J. 55 (C.M.A. 1980) — § 5-3(B), n. 41
United States v. Rivera, 12 M.J. 532 (A.F.C.M.R. 1981) — § 9-3, n. 6
United States v. Rivera, 23 M.J. 89 (C.M.A. 1986) — § 14-3(B)(2), n. 98; § 14-3(F), nn. 191-193
United States v. Rivera-Berrios, 24 M.J. 679 (A.C.M.R. 1987) — § 13-3(C), n. 33
United States v. Riverasoto, 29 M.J. 594 (A.C.M.R. 1989) — § 16-11, n. 8
United States v. Rivers, 20 C.M.A. 6, 42 C.M.R. 198 (1970) — § 7-3(A), n. 18
United States v. Roa, 20 M.J. 867 (A.F.C.M.R. 1985) — § 4-11(A), n. 19
United States v. Roa, 24 M.J. 297 (C.M.A. 1987) — § 5-3(F), n. 26; § 5-4(B), n. 50
United States v. Roach, 29 M.J. 33 (C.M.A. 1989) — § 2-4(A), n. 13
United States v. Roane, 43 M.J. 93 (1995) — § 14-3(D)(4), nn. 153, 156
United States v. Robbins, 16 M.J. 736 (A.F.C.M.R. 1983) — § 16-5(B), n. 22
United States v. Roberts, 2 M.J. 31 (C.M.A. 1976) — § 5-3(D)(1), n. 117
United States v. Roberts, 10 M.J. 308 (C.M.A. 1981) — § 7-2, n. 2; § 7-2(B)(4), n.52
United States v. Roberts, 14 M.J. 671 (N.M.C.M.R. 1982) — § 2-2(E)(3), nn. 78, 79
United States v. Roberts, 20 M.J. 689 (A.C.M.R. 1985) — § 12-3(A), n. 31
United States v. Roberts, 20 M.J. 754 (N.M.C.M.R. 1985) — § 12-2(F)(2), n. 55
United States v. Roberts, 32 M.J. 681 (A.F.C.M.R. 1991) — § 2-6(C), n. 38; § 5-3(C)(6), n. 84
United States v. Robertson, 17 C.M.R. 684 (A.F.B.R. 1954) — § 1-8(B), n. 7
United States v. Robertson, 7 M.J. 507 (A.C.M.R. 1979) — § 12-3(B), n. 59; § 8-3(C)(2), n. 129
United States v. Robertson, 17 M.J. 846 (N.M.C.M.R. 1984) — § 15-13, n. 18
United States v. Robertson, 21 M.J. 747 (N.M.C.M.R. 1985) — § 4-5(A)(2), n. 5
United States v. Robertson, 21 M.J. 1105 (A.C.M.R. 1986) — § 17-9(D), n. 62
United States v. Robertson, 27 M.J. 741 (A.C.M.R. 1988) — § 16-3(D), n. 63
United States v. Robertson, 39 M.J. 211 (C.M.A. 1994) — § 15-2(B)(3), n. 33
United States v. Robinson, 4 C.M.A. 12, 15 C.M.R. 12 (1954) — § 16-11, n. 3; § 17-3(A), n. 20
United States v. Robinson, 11 M.J. 218 (C.M.A. 1981) — § 16-13, n. 8
United States v. Robinson, 11 M.J. 218 (C.M.A. 1981) — § 17-8(B)(3), n. 80
United States v. Robinson, 14 M.J. 903 (N.M.C.M.R. 1982) — § 13-3(N)(1), nn. 312, 331
United States v. Robinson, 16 M.J. 766 (A.C.M.R. 1983) — § 11-2(A)(2), n. 10
United States v. Robinson, 25 M.J. 43 (C.M.A. 1987) — § 16-8(C), n. 36
United States v. Robinson, 25 M.J. 528 (A.F.C.M.R. 1987) — § 9-2(B), n. 38
United States v. Robinson, 24 M.J. 649 (N.M.C.M.R. 1987) — § 11-2(A)(3), nn. 27, 28; § 11-2(B)(1), n. 57
United States v. Robinson, 26 M.J. 361 (C.M.A. 1988) — § 5-4(B), n. 52
United States v. Robinson, 28 M.J. 481 (C.M.A. 1989) — § 13-3(C)(3), n. 114

TABLE OF CASES

United States v. Robinson, 30 M.J. 548 (A.C.M.R. 1990) — § 16-5(D)(5), n. 116
United States v. Robinson, 37 M.J. 588 (A.F.C.M.R. 1993) — § 2-4(C), n. 33
United States v. Robinson, 38 M.J. 30 (C.M.A. 1993) — § 15-14(B), n. 37
United States v. Robinson, 39 M.J. 88 (C.M.A. 1994) — § 11-2(A)(3), n. 21
United States v. Robinson, 43 M.J. 501 (A.F. Ct. Crim. App. 1995) — § 4-15(A), nn. 8, 10; § 11-2(A)(3), nn. 29, 30
United States v. Rodgers, 24 C.M.R. 36 (C.M.A. 1957) — § 13-3(B), nn. 16, 17
United States v. Rodgers, 18 M.J. 565 (A.C.M.R. 1984) — § 16-5(D)(5), n. 123
United States v. Rodriguez, 2 C.M.A. 101, 6 C.M.R. 101 (1952) — § 4-5(B), n. 22
United States v. Rodriguez, 16 M.J. 740 (A.F.C.M.R. 1983) — § 6-3(C), n. 28; § 6-5(B), n. 40; § 6-6(C), n. 13
United States v. Rodriguez, 28 M.J. 1016 (A.F.C.M.R. 1989) — § 15-12, n. 1; § 15-13, nn. 19, 29
United States v. Rodriguez, 31 M.J. 150 (C.M.A. 1990) — § 6-1(C)(1), n. 116
United States v. Rodriguez-Amy, 19 M.J. 177 (C.M.A. 1985) — § 17-15, n. 6; § 13-3(N)(1), nn. 318, 331
United States v. Rodriquez, 12 M.J. 632 (N.M.C.M.R. 1981) — § 9-2(B)(1), n. 50
United States v. Rodriquez, 18 M.J. 363 (C.M.A. 1984) — § 2-5, n. 7; § 6-1(C)(3), n. 145
United States v. Rodriquez, 23 M.J. 896 (A.C.M.R. 1987) — § 5-3(D)(1), n. 128
United States v. Rodwell, 20 M.J. 264 (C.M.A. 1985) — § 15-14(B), n. 23
United States v. Roettger, 17 M.J. 453 (C.M.A. 1984) — § 17-15(A), n. 14
United States v. Rogan, 19 M.J. 646 (A.F.C.M.R. 1984) — § 16-11, n. 12
United States v. Rogers, 7 M.J. 274 (C.M.A. 1979) — § 4-11(A), n. 11; § 13-3(C)(2), n. 49
United States v. Rogers, 21 M.J. 435 (C.M.A. 1986) — § 16-12, nn. 8, 14, 16
United States v. Rogers, 30 M.J. 824 (C.G.C.M.R. 1990) — § 16-5(D)(4), n. 102
United States v. Rohrig, 19 M.J. 876 (A.F.C.M.R. 1985) — § 17-13, n. 17
United States v. Rojas, 15 M.J. 902 (N.M.C.M.R. 1983) — § 15-10(B), n. 53
United States v. Rolfe, 24 M.J. 756 (A.F.C.M.R. 1987) — § 5-9(E), n. 59
United States v. Rollins, 7 M.J. 125 (C.M.A. 1979) — § 4-11(A), n. 37
United States v. Rollins, 23 M.J. 729 (A.F.C.M.R. 1986) — § 5-4(B), n. 44
United States v. Rollins, 28 M.J. 803 (A.C.M.R. 1989) — § 14-3(D)(4), n. 147
United States v. Roman, 45 C.M.R. 492 (A.F.C.M.R. 1972) — § 16-6, n. 10
United States v. Roman, 22 C.M.A. 78, 46 C.M.R. 78 (1972) — § 17-3, n. 4; § 17-3(A), n. 24
United States v. Roman, 5 M.J. 385 (C.M.A. 1978) — § 13-3(C)(2), nn. 56, 71
United States v. Romano, 43 M.J. 523 (A.F.Ct.Crim.App. 1995) — § 10-4(A)(4), n. 23
United States v. Romero, 37 M.J. 613 (A.C.M.R. 1993) — § 9-2(C), n. 77
United States v. Rondash, 30 M.J. 686 (A.C.M.R. 1990) — § 14-3(C), n. 128
United States v. Rooks, 29 M.J. 291 (C.M.A. 1989) — § 14-3(D)(4), n. 145
United States v. Roppolo, 34 M.J. 820 (A.F.C.M.R. 1992) — § 3-5(A), n. 3
United States v. Rosario, 13 M.J. 552 (A.C.M.R. 1982) — § 14-3(C), n. 132
United States v. Rosato, 32 M.J. 93 (C.M.A. 1991) — § 16-6, nn. 12, 13
United States, Rose v.
United States v. Rose, 6 M.J. 754 (N.C.M.R. 1978) — § 6-1(C)(3), n. 139
United States v. Rose, 16 M.J. 568 (A.C.M.R. 1983) — § 17-11, n. 1
United States v. Rose, 28 M.J. 132 (C.M.A. 1989) — § 15-14(B), n. 28
United States v. Rosen, 9 C.M.A. 175, 25 C.M.R. 437 (1958) — § 6-1(C)(3), n. 134
United States v. Rosenblatt, 13 C.M.A. 28, 32 C.M.R. 28 (1962) — § 13-3(E), n. 198
United States v. Ross, 40 C.M.R. 718 (A.C.M.R. 1969) — § 2-3, n. 7; § 2-3(A), n. 12; § 2-3(B), n. 17; § 2-3(C), n. 30
United States v. Ross, 9 M.J. 726 (A.C.M.R. 1980) — § 4-11(A), n. 36

TABLE OF CASES

United States v. Ross, 32 M.J. 715 (C.G.C.M.R. 1991) — § 17-15(A), n. 14
United States v. Ross, 34 M.J. 338 (C.M.A. 1992) — § 14-3(B)(2), n. 84
United States v. Rosser, 6 M.J. 267 (C.M.A. 1979) — § 6-3(B), n. 15; § 6-3(C), nn. 23, 28; § 6-5(C), n. 50; § 6-7, n. 16; § 15-2(E), n. 153
United States, Roth v.
United States v. Rounds, 30 M.J. 76 (C.M.A. 1990) — § 13-4(A), n. 19
United States v. Rowe, 11 M.J. 11 (C.M.A. 1981) — § 2-7(B), n. 20; § 15-14(D), n. 56
United States v. Rowsey, 14 M.J. 151 (C.M.A. 1982) — § 13-3(C)(2), nn. 69, 78
United States v. Roxas, 41 M.J. 727 (N.M.Ct.Crim.App.1994) — § 10-4(B)(5), n. 58
United States v. Royster, 42 M.J. 488 (1995) — § 15-4(A), nn. 6, 8; § 15-12(A), n. 5
United States v. Rozier, 41 M.J. 707 (Army Ct.Crim.App. 1995) — § 5-10(D), n. 25
United States v. Rozycki, 3 M.J. 127 (C.M.A. 1977) — § 17-9(D), n. 70
United States v. Rubenstein, 7 C.M.A. 523, 36 C.M.R. 313 (1957) — § 4-6, n. 12
United States, Rugendorf v.
United States v. Ruiz, 23 C.M.A. 181, 48 C.M.R. 797 (1974) — § 2-4(A), n. 16; § 5-4(A)(1), n. 1
United States v. Ruiz, 30 M.J. 867 (N.M.C.M.R. 1990) — § 17-8(B)(2), nn. 62, 63
United States, Runkle v.
United States v. Rupert, 25 M.J. 531 (A.C.M.R. 1987) — § 6-1(C)(2), n. 126
United States v. Rushatz, 30 M.J. 525 (A.C.M.R. 1990) — § 7-2(A)(1), n. 29
United States v. Rushatz, 31 M.J. 450 (C.M.A. 1990) — § 15-4(B), n. 11; § 8-3(B)(1), n. 53
United States v. Rushing, 11 M.J. 95 (C.M.A. 1981) — § 6-1(C)(3), n. 132
United States v. Rusinskas, 35 M.J. 808 (N.M.C.M.R. 1992) — § 13-5(L), n. 104
United States v. Russaw, 15 M.J. 801 (A.C.M.R. 1983) — § 12-2(F)(3), n. 67
United States v. Russell, 15 C.M.A. 76, 35 C.M.R. 48 (1964) — § 15-13, n. 32
United States v. Russell, 30 M.J. 977 (A.C.M.R. 1990) — § 5-10(D), n. 37; § 13-5(B), n. 28
United States v. Russett, 40 M.J. 184 (C.M.A. 1994) — § 17-8(B)(1), n. 39; § 17-16(B), n. 39
United States v. Russo, 1 M.J. 134 (C.M.A. 1975) — § 4-5(A)(3), nn. 9, 10, 13; § 4-5(B), n. 29; § 9-2(B)(1), n. 49
United States v. Russo, 1 M.J. 184 (C.M.A. 1978) — § 13-3(N)(5), n. 433
United States v. Rust, 38 M.J. 726 (A.F.C.M.R. 1993) — § 13-5(I), n. 73
United States v. Rust, 41 M.J. 472 (1995) — § 2-4(E), nn. 45; § 16-5(D)(3), n. 80
United States v. Rusterholz, 39 C.M.R. 903 (A.F.B.R. 1968) — § 15-14(D), n. 54
United States v. Ruth, 42 M.J. 730 (Army Ct.Crim.App. 1995) — § 11-2(A)(3), n. 28
United States v. Rutherford, 29 M.J. 1030 (A.C.M.R. 1990) — § 15-13, n. 25
United States v. Ryan, 5 M.J. 97 (C.M.A. 1978) — § 4-16, n. 17; § 8-2(A), n. 4; § 4-14(A)(3), nn. 15, 16
United States, Ryder v.
United States v. Ryder, 31 M.J. 718 (A.F.C.M.R. 1990) — § 16-8(B), n. 25
United States v. Ryder, 34 M.J. 1077 (C.G.C.M.R. 1992) — § 15-2(B)(3), n. 72
United States v. Ryder, 39 M.J. 454 (C.M.A. 1994) — § 15-23, n. 3
United States v. Sadler, 16 M.J. 982 (A.C.M.R. 1983) — § 15-2(B)(3), n. 78
United States v. Sadler, 29 M.J. 370 (C.M.A. 1990) — § 2-6(B), n. 32; § 15-14(A), n. 5; § 15-14(B), n. 22
United States v. Saenz, 18 M.J. 328 (C.M.A. 1984) — § 8-3(D), n. 162; § 12-2(F)(1), n. 46
United States v. Sager, 30 M.J. 777 (A.C.M.R. 1990) — § 5-7, n. 11
United States v. Sager, 32 M.J. 968 (A.C.M.R. 1991) — § 5-4(B), n. 49
United States v. Sager, 36 M.J. 137 (C.M.A. 1992) — § 5-4(B), nn. 49, 51

TABLE OF CASES

United States v. Sala, 29 M.J. 716 (A.C.M.R. 1989) — § 14-3(D)(4), nn. 145, 156
United States v. Salgado-Agosto, 20 M.J. 238 (C.M.A. 1985) — § 16-5(B), nn. 21, 22
United States v. Salley, 9 M.J. 189 (C.M.A. 1980) — § 15-14(B), n. 37
United States v. Salter, 20 M.J. 116 (C.M.A. 1985) — § 13-3(B), n. 10
United States v. Samuels, 10 C.M.A. 206, 27 C.M.R. 280 (1959) — § 7-2, n. 2; § 7-2(B)(4), n. 56
United States v. Sanchez, 11 C.M.A. 216, 29 C.M.R. 32 (1960) — § 2-6(B), n. 30
United States v. Sanchez, 26 M.J. 564 (C.G.C.M.R. 1988) — § 9-2(A)(1), n. 11
United States v. Sanchez, 37 M.J. 426 (C.M.A. 1993) — § 12-2(H), n. 100
United States v. Sanders, 30 C.M.R. 521 (A.B.R. 1961) — § 15-14(A), n. 14
United States v. Sanders, 14 C.M.A. 524, 34 C.M.R. 304 (1964) — § 15-14(B), n. 43
United States v. Sanders, 19 M.J. 979 (A.C.M.R. 1985) — § 16-8(C), n. 42; § 9-2(B)(1), n. 45
United States v. Sanders, 31 M.J. 834 (N.M.C.M.R. 1990) — § 15-2(A), n. 7; § 15-2(B)(3), n. 51
United States v. Sanders, 33 M.J. 1026 (N.M.C.M.R. 1991) — § 14-3(D)(4), n. 152
United States v. Sanders, 34 M.J. 1086 (A.F.C.M.R. 1992) — § 15-14(C), n. 49
United States v. Sanders, 36 M.J. 1013 (A.C.M.R. 1993) — § 5-10(D), n. 41
United States v. Sanders, 37 M.J. 116 (C.M.A. 1993) — § 15-2(B)(3), n. 95; § 17-16(C), n. 15
United States v. Sanders, 37 M.J. 628 (A.C.M.R. 1993) — § 2-3(C), n. 25
United States v. Sanders, 37 M.J. 1005 (A.C.M.R. 1993) — § 17-3(B), n. 33
United States v. Sanders, 41 M.J. 485 (1995) — § 15-14(A), n. 2
United States v. Sanford, 12 M.J. 170 (C.M.A. 1981) — § 5-3(A), n. 20
United States v. Sanford, 29 M.J. 413 (C.M.A. 1990) — § 6-5(C), nn. 49, 51; § 16-5(D)(3), n. 77
United States v. Sankey, 6 M.J. 790 (A.C.M.R. 1978) — § 17-8(B)(1), n. 33
United States v. Santiago, 1 C.M.R. 365 (A.B.R. 1951) — § 4-5(A)(4), n. 15
United States v. Santiago, 27 M.J. 688 (A.C.M.R. 1988) — § 16-3(D), n. 62
United States v. Santiago-Davila, 26 M.J. 380 (C.M.A. 1988) — § 11-2(A)(4), n. 44; § 11-2(D)(2), n. 91; § 15-10(C)(3), nn. 111, 112
United States v. Sargeant, 29 M.J. 812 (A.C.M.R. 1989) — § 13-3(N)(4), n. 417
United States v. Sargeant, 29 M.J. 813 (A.C.M.R. 1989) — § 2-9(B), n. 18; § 2-9(D), n. 60
United States v. Sargent, 18 M.J. 331 (C.M.A. 1984) — § 16-5(D)(3), n. 76
United States v. Sartin, 24 M.J. 873 (A.C.M.R. 1987) — § 2-8(C), n. 31
United States v. Sassaman, 32 M.J. 687 (A.F.C.M.R. 1991) — § 4-4, n. 6; § 14-3(B)(2), n. 85
United States v. Sauer, 15 M.J. 113 (C.M.A. 1983) — § 3-8(B), n. 14; § 16-5(B), n. 18; § 16-5(C), n. 50; § 14-3(A)(1), n. 16
United States v. Saul, 26 M.J. 568 (A.F.C.M.R. 1988) — § 12-2(F)(2), n. 55; § 15-2(B)(3), n. 49
United States v. Saulter, 1 M.J. 1066 (N.C.M.R. 1976) — § 14-3(D)(3), n. 144
United States v. Saulter, 5 M.J. 281 (C.M.A. 1978) — § 4-11(A), n. 20
United States v. Saulter, 23 M.J. 626 (A.F.C.M.R. 1986) — § 9-2(B)(1), n. 49
United States v. Saunders, 6 M.J. 731 (A.C.M.R. 1978) — § 4-14(B), n. 20; § 8-2(B), n. 9
United States v. Saunders, 11 M.J. 912 (A.C.M.R. 1981) — § 7-2(E), n. 110; § 13-5(D), n. 43
United States v. Saunders, 19 M.J. 763 (A.C.M.R. 1984) — § 6-5(B), n. 28
United States v. Savusa, 28 M.J. 1043 (A.C.M.R. 1989) — § 16-5(D)(4), n. 101
United States v. Sawinski, 16 M.J. 808 (N.M.C.M.R. 1983) — § 14-3(B)(2), n. 84

TABLE OF CASES

United States v. Sawyer, 4 M.J. 64 (C.M.A. 1977) — § 15-14(B), n. 25
United States v. Saylor, 6 M.J. 647 (N.C.M.R. 1978) — § 10-2(A), n. 15; § 11-2(E)(2), n. 120
United States v. Saylor, 40 M.J. 715 (N.M.C.M.R. 1994) — § 17-9(D), nn. 68, 69
United States v. Scaff, 26 M.J. 985 (A.F.C.M.R. 1988) — § 17-3, n. 15; § 17-3(B), n. 40
United States v. Scaff, 29 M.J. 60 (C.M.A. 1989) — § 17-3(B), n. 41
United States v. Scaife, 48 C.M.R. 290 (A.C.M.R. 1974) — § 12-3(A), n. 31
United States v. Scanlon, 15 M.J. 823 (A.F.C.M.R. 1983) — § 16-13, n. 9
United States v. Scarborough, 49 C.M.R. 580 (A.C.M.R. 1974) — § 13-2(B), n. 29
United States v. Sceffer, 41 M.J. 683 (A. F. Ct. Crim. App. 1995) — § 11-2(A)(1), n. 1
United States v. Schaffer, 46 C.M.R. 1089 (A.C.M.R. 1973) — § 9-2(B)(2), n. 65
United States v. Schaffer, 12 M.J. 425 (C.M.A. 1982) — § 7-2, n. 7; § 9-2(B), n. 35; § 14-4, n. 1; § 9-2(B)(1), nn. 47, 55
United States v. Schaffner, 16 M.J. 903 (A.C.M.R. 1983) — § 12-3(A), n. 29
United States v. Schake, 30 M.J. 314 (C.M.A. 1990) — § 5-4(B), nn. 37, 44
United States v. Schalck, 14 C.M.A. 371, 34 C.M.R. 151 (1964) — § 13-3(C), n. 25
United States v. Schaller, 9 M.J. 939 (N.C.M.R. 1980) — § 9-2(B)(2), n. 71
United States v. Scheffer, 41 M.J. 683 (A.F.Ct.Crim.App. 1995) — § 5-9(D), n. 26; § 13-3(C)(2), n. 96
United States v. Scheunemann, 14 C.M.A. 479, 34 C.M.R. 259 (1964) — § 4-5(B), nn. 19, 20; § 2-2(E)(4), n. 84
United States v. Schilf, 1 M.J. 251 (C.M.A. 1976) — § 13-3(C)(2), n. 68; § 13-3(C)(3), n. 141
United States v. Schilling, 7 C.M.A. 482, 22 C.M.R. 272 (1957) — § 13-3(E), n. 190
United States v. Schmeltz, 1 M.J. 8 (C.M.A. 1975) — § 9-2(B)(1), n. 49
United States v. Schmidt, 16 C.M.A. 57, 36 C.M.R. 213 (1966) — § 13-3(N)(3), n. 392
United States v. Schmit, 13 M.J. 934 (A.F.C.M.R. 1982) — § 17-6, n. 4
United States v. Schmitt, 25 C.M.R. 822 (A.F.B.R. 1958) — § 15-15, n. 7; § 15-21, n. 16
United States v. Schmitt, 33 M.J. 24 (C.M.A. 1991) — § 5-3(E), n. 7
United States v. Schneider, 14 M.J. 189 (C.M.A. 1982) — § 5-4(B), nn. 37, 39, 40
United States v. Schneider, 38 M.J. 387 (C.M.A. 1993) — § 13-3(E), n. 197; § 15-10(B), n. 43; § 6-1(C)(1), n. 115
United States v. Schnitzer, 41 M.J. 603 (Army Ct.Crim.App. 1994) — § 16-8(B), n. 14; § 17-15(C), n. 33
United States v. Scholten, 14 M.J. 939 (A.C.M.R. 1982) — § 12-2(H), n. 102
United States v. Scholz, 19 M.J. 837 (N.M.C.M.R. 1984) — § 13-2(G)(2), nn. 82, 85
United States v. Schomaker, 17 M.J. 1122 (N.M.C.M.R. 1984) — § 15-13, n. 18
United States v. Schoof, 37 M.J. 96 (C.M.A. 1993) — § 17-15(C), n. 8
United States v. Schoolfield, 36 M.J. 545 (A.C.M.R. 1992) — § 2-9(B), n. 12; § 5-3(B), n. 54; § 5-4(B), n. 42
United States v. Schoolfield, 40 M.J. 132 (C.M.A. 1994) — § 2-9(C)(1), n. 34
United States v. Schreiber, 16 C.M.R. 639 (A.F.B.R. 1954) — § 7-2(A)(1), n. 19
United States v. Schroeder, 39 M.J. 471 (C.M.A. 1994) — § 5-4(B), n. 49
United States v. Schuering, 16 C.M.A. 314, 36 C.M.R. 480 (1966) — § 4-6, n. 8
United States v. Schuering, 16 C.M.A. 324, 36 C.M.R. 480 (1966) — § 4-6, nn. 5, 12
United States v. Schultz, 8 C.M.A. 129, 23 C.M.R. 353 (1957) — § 16-11, n. 10
United States v. Schumacher, 11 M.J. 612 (A.C.M.R. 1981) — § 2-5, n. 3
United States v. Schuring, 16 M.J. 664 (A.C.M.R. 1983) — § 5-4(B), n. 52
United States v. Schwab, 30 M.J. 842 (N.M.C.M.R. 1990) — § 17-9(D), n. 66
United States v. Schwabauer, 34 M.J. 709 (A.C.M.R. 1992) — § 2-4(B), n. 28
United States v. Schwabauer, 37 M.J. 338 (C.M.A. 1993) — § 14-3(B)(2), nn. 79, 82

TABLE OF CASES

United States v. Schwarz, 15 M.J. 109 (C.M.A. 1983) — § 6-1(B), n. 65
United States v. Schwarz, 24 M.J. 823 (A.C.M.R. 1987) — § 16-8(A), n. 6
United States v. Scoby, 5 M.J. 160 (C.M.A. 1978) — § 13-3(N)(4), nn. 420-422
United States v. Scofield, 33 M.J. 857 (A.C.M.R. 1991) — § 14-3(D)(4), n. 151
United States v. Scoles, 14 C.M.A. 14, 33 C.M.R. 226 (1963) — § 9-2(B)(1), n. 42
United States v. Scott, 6 C.M.A. 650, 20 C.M.R. 366 (1956) — § 13-3(I), n. 249
United States v. Scott, 11 C.M.A. 646, 29 C.M.R. 462 (1960) — § 4-5(A)(2), n. 1; § 4-8(B), n. 13
United States v. Scott, 41 C.M.R. 773 (N.C.M.R. 1969) — § 6-1(B), n. 60
United States v. Scott, 5 M.J. 431 (C.M.A. 1978) — § 11-2(A)(4), nn. 39, 40, 44, 46
United States v. Scott, 6 M.J. 547 (A.F.C.M.R. 1978) — § 7-2(C), n. 80; § 7-2(D), n. 86; § 10-4(B)(5), n. 55
United States v. Scott, 6 M.J. 608 (A.C.M.R. 1978) — § 9-2(B)(1), nn. 42, 45; § 14-3(D)(5), n. 172
United States v. Scott, 437 U.S. 82 (1978) — § 13-2(G)(2), n. 91 R.C.M. 908
United States v. Scott, 15 M.J. 589 (A.C.M.R. 1983) — § 4-11(A), n. 13; § 17-8(B)(3), n. 75
United States v. Scott, 21 M.J. 345 (C.M.A. 1986) — § 4-11(C), n. 52
United States v. Scott, 22 M.J. 297 (C.M.A. 1986) — § 5-4(B), n. 40
United States v. Scott, 22 M.J. 646 (A.C.M.R. 1986) — § 16-9, n. 5
United States v. Scott, 24 M.J. 186 (C.M.A. 1987) — § 15-2(B)(3), nn. 32, 37, 42, 54
United States v. Scott, 24 M.J. 578 (N.M.C.M.R. 1987) — § 4-11(B), n. 42
United States v. Scott, 27 M.J. 889 (A.C.M.R. 1989) — § 16-5(D)(4), n. 101
United States v. Scott, 32 M.J. 644 (C.G.C.M.R. 1991) — § 13-3(N)(1), nn. 302, 328, 329
United States v. Scott, 39 M.J. 769 (A.C.M.R. 1994) — § 17-9(A), n. 23
United States v. Scott, 40 M.J. 914 (A.C.M.R. 1994) — § 17-4(B), n. 52
United States v. Scranton, 30 M.J. 322 (C.M.A. 1990) — § 6-1(C)(3), n. 139
United States v. Seal, 38 M.J. 659 (A.C.M.R. 1993) — § 17-4, n. 35
United States v. Searcy, 24 M.J. 943 (A.C.M.R. 1987) — § 14-3(B)(2), n. 75
United States v. Sears, 18 M.J. 190 (C.M.A. 1984) — § 16-3(D), n. 64
United States v. Seay, 1 M.J. 201 (C.M.A. 1975) — § 5-4(B), n. 42
United States v. Seeber, 22 M.J. 956 (C.G.C.M.R. 1986) — § 15-25, n. 3
United States v. Seeger, 380 U.S. 163 (1965) — § 13-3(N)(3), n. 401
United States v. Seivers, 8 M.J. 63 (C.M.A. 1979) — § 4-11(A), n. 15
United States v. Self, 35 C.M.R. 557 (A.B.R. 1965) — § 2-2(C)(3), n. 48
United States v. Self, 13 M.J. 132 (C.M.A. 1982) — § 4-6, nn. 25, 27; § 4-8(A), n. 8
United States v. Sellers, 12 C.M.A. 262, 30 C.M.R. 262 (1961) — § 15-14(C), n. 50; § 5-4(A)(1), n. 10
United States v. Sellers, 33 M.J. 364 (C.M.A. 1991) — § 15-14(B), n. 34
United States v. Sells, 30 M.J. 944 (A.C.M.R. 1990) — § 16-8(B), n. 23; § 16-5(D)(3), n. 76
United States v. Selman, 28 M.J. 627 (A.F.C.M.R. 1989) — § 2-4(B), n. 25; § 2-4(D), n. 43
United States v. Sennett, 42 M.J. 787 (N.M. Ct. Crim. App. 1995) — § 5-4(B), n. 52
United States v. Sepulveda, 40 M.J. 856 (A.F.C.M.R. 1994) — § 13-2(G)(2), n. 81
United States v. Serino, 24 M.J. 848 (A.F.C.M.R. 1987) — § 2-8(D), n. 40; § 6-3(A), n. 4; § 6-5(B), n. 25; § 6-7, n. 10
United States v. Serrano, 27 M.J. 611 (A.C.M.R. 1988) — § 14-3(B)(1), nn. 59, 62; § 14-3(B)(2), n. 70
United States v. Seymore, 19 M.J. 608 (A.C.M.R. 1984) — § 15-4(B), n. 11

TABLE OF CASES

United States v. Shackleford, 2 M.J. 17 (C.M.A. 1976) — § 8-3(A), n. 8; § 15-12(B), nn. 14, 17; § 14-3(D)(5), nn. 168, 169
United States v. Shada, 28 M.J. 684 (A.F.C.M.R. 1989) — § 16-3(D), n. 68
United States v. Shafer, 17 C.M.A. 456, 38 C.M.R. 254 (1968) — § 15-14(A), n. 17
United States v. Shamberger, 1 M.J. 377 (C.M.A. 1976) — § 15-13, nn. 15, 30
United States v. Shamel, 22 C.M.A. 361, 47 C.M.R. 116 (1973) — § 3-8(B); § 16-3(C), n. 55; § 3-6(C)(1), n. 9
United States v. Shamlian, 9 C.M.A. 28, 25 C.M.R. 290 (1958) — § 15-4(B), n. 11
United States v. Shanaham, 16 M.J. 654 (A.F.C.M.R. 1983) — § 17-8(B), n. 29
United States v. Shandell, 800 F.2d 322 (2d Cir. 1986) — § 11-2(E)(3), n. 139
United States v. Sharkey, 19 C.M.A. 26, 41 C.M.R. 26 (1969) — § 4-11(A), n. 29
United States v. Sharp, 29 M.J. 856 (A.F.C.M.R. 1989) — § 16-5(D)(5), n. 120
United States v. Sharp, 38 M.J. 33 (C.M.A. 1993) — § 12-4, nn. 13, 14; § 15-2(A), nn. 4, 5, 10
United States v. Sharper, 17 M.J. 803 (A.C.M.R. 1984) — § 15-21, n. 8; § 9-2(B)(1), n. 39; § 16-5(D)(1), nn. 60, 61
United States v. Sharrock, 30 M.J. 1003 (A.F.C.M.R. 1990) — § 5-3(F), n. 24; § 5-9(B), nn. 9, 10
United States v. Sharrock, 32 M.J. 326 (C.M.A. 1991) — § 5-10(D), n. 23
United States v. Shaw, 30 M.J. 1033 (A.F.C.M.R. 1990) — § 17-2(B)(3), n. 80
United States v. Shearer, 6 M.J. 737 (A.C.M.R. 1978) — § 8-2(A), n. 4
United States v. Shears, 27 M.J. 509 (A.C.M.R. 1988) — § 16-5(B), n. 10
United States v. Sheehan, 15 M.J. 724 (A.C.M.R. 1983) — § 2-5, n. 3
United States v. Sheffield, 20 M.J. 957 (A.F.C.M.R. 1985) — § 6-1(C)(3), n. 147
United States v. Shelby, 26 M.J. 921 (N.M.C.M.R. 1988) — § 15-10(C)(3), nn. 114, 115
United States v. Shelby, 40 M.J. 909 (N.M.C.M.R. 1994) — § 15-2(B)(2), n. 27; § 17-19, n. 28
United States v. Shell, 7 C.M.A. 646, 23 C.M.R. 110 (1957) — § 2-2(E)(6), n. 96
United States v. Shelton, 26 M.J. 787 (A.F.C.M.R. 1988) — § 6-1, nn. 8, 9; § 8-2(A), n. 3; § 4-14(A)(2), n. 10
United States v. Shelton, 27 M.J. 540 (A.C.M.R. 1988) — § 5-9(B), n. 9; § 5-9(C), n. 18; § 5-9(D), n. 22; § 5-10(D), n. 31
United States v. Shely, 16 M.J. 431 (C.M.A. 1983) — § 17-11, n. 5
United States v. Shepard, 38 M.J. 408 (C.M.A. 1993) — § 5-4(B), nn. 46, 47
United States v. Shepardson, 17 M.J. 793 (A.F.C.M.R. 1983) — § 4-14(B), n. 21; § 8-2(B), n. 11
United States v. Shepherd, 9 C.M.A. 90, 25 C.M.R. 352 (1958) — § 15-22, n. 7
United States v. Shepherd, 24 M.J. 596 (A.F.C.M.R 1987) — § 5-3(D)(1), n. 123
United States v. Shepherd, 30 M.J. 652 (A.F.C.M.R. 1990) — § 16-5(B), n. 7
United States v. Sheridan, 43 M.J. 682 (A.F.Ct.Crim.App. 1995) — § 16-5(D)(4), n. 97; § 16-5(D)(5), n. 118
United States v. Sherman, 32 M.J. 449 (C.M.A. 1991) — § 16-8(A), n. 6
United States v. Sherrod, 22 M.J. 917 (A.C.M.R. 1986) — § 12-2(H), n. 100
United States v. Sherrod, 26 M.J. 30 (C.M.A. 1988) — § 8-3(A), n. 8; § 12-2(H), nn. 100, 121
United States v. Sherrod, 26 M.J. 32 (C.M.A. 1988) — § 12-2(H), nn. 123, 124; § 12-3(A), n. 5
United States v. Shields, 20 M.J. 174 (C.M.A. 1985) — § 16-5(B), n. 24
United States v. Shields, 39 M.J. 718 (N.M.C.M.R. 1993) — § 14-3(B)(2), n. 80
United States v. Shiftic, 36 M.J. 1193 (N.M.C.M.R. 1993) — § 17-8(B)(1), n. 39
United States v. Shim, 36 M.J. 1124 (A.F.C.M.R. 1993) — § 13-3(C)(3), n. 97

TABLE OF CASES

United States v. Shiner, 40 M.J. 155 (C.M.A. 1994) — § 4-14(A)(2), nn. 9, 10
United States v. Shirley, 18 M.J. 212 (C.M.A. 1984) — § 14-3(B)(3), n. 101
United States v. Shober, 26 M.J. 501 (A.F.C.M.R. 1986) — § 2-5, n. 3
United States, Shoemaker v.
United States v. Shomaker, 17 M.J. 1122 (N.M.C.M.R. 1984) — § 6-7, n. 7
United States v. Short, 41 M.J. 42 (C.M.A. 1994) — § 15-3, nn. 1, 3, 8, 17, 18
United States v. Shorte, 18 M.J. 518 (A.F.C.M.R. 1984) — § 4-11(A), n. 23
United States v. Shoup, 31 M.J. 819 (A.F.C.M.R. 1990) — § 9-4, n. 5; § 15-13, n. 9
United States v. Shover, 42 M.J. 753 (A.F.Ct.Crim.App. 1995) — § 5-3(D)(1), n. 128
United States v. Showalter, 15 C.M.A. 410, 35 C.M.R. 382 (1965) — § 16-2(F), n. 55
United States v. Shows, 5 M.J. 892 (A.F.C.M.R. 1978) — § 15-13, n. 9
United States v. Shroeder, 27 M.J. 87 (C.M.A. 1988) — § 15-15, n. 15; § 16-10, n. 12
United States v. Shull, 1 C.M.A. 177, 2 C.M.R. 83 (1952) — § 2-2(B), n. 10
United States v. Shupe, 36 M.J. 431 (C.M.A. 1993) — § 16-5(D)(5), n. 116
United States v. Siders, 15 M.J. 272 (C.M.A. 1983) — § 17-2(B)(3), n. 59
United States v. Siders, 17 M.J. 986 (A.C.M.R. 1984) — § 17-8(B), n. 15
United States v. Sidney, 23 C.M.A. 185, 48 C.M.R. 801 (1974) — § 2-4(F), n. 51
United States v. Silva, 19 M.J. 501 (A.F.C.M.R. 1984) — § 15-14(B), n. 43
United States v. Silva, 21 M.J. 336 (C.M.A. 1986) — § 16-5(D)(5), nn. 110, 124
United States v. Silver, 40 M.J. 351 (C.M.A. 1994) — § 14-3(G), n. 198; § 14-3(B)(3), n. 109
United States v. Silvis, 31 M.J. 707 (N.M.C.M.R. 1990) — § 6-1(C)(1), n. 115
United States v. Simmelkjaer, 18 C.M.A. 406, 40 C.M.R. 118 (1969) — § 15-14(B), n. 25
United States v. Simmons, 3 M.J. 398 (C.M.A. 1977) — § 2-2(C)(3), n. 40
United States v. Simmons, 14 M.J. 832 (A.C.M.R. 1982) — § 15-13, n. 9
United States v. Simmons, 763 F.2d 529 (2d Cir. 1985) — § 14-4, n. 16
United States v. Simmons, 20 M.J. 567 (N.M.C.M.R. 1985) — § 17-11, n. 6
United States v. Simmons, 26 M.J. 667 (A.F.C.M.R. 1988) — § 5-3(C)(6), n. 85
United States v. Simmons, 31 M.J. 884 (A.F.C.M.R. 1990) — § 16-8(B), n. 15
United States v. Simmons, 38 M.J. 376 (C.M.A. 1993) — § 10-4(A)(4), nn. 23, 27
United States v. Simpson, 25 M.J. 865 (A.C.M.R. 1988) — § 6-1(C), n. 94; § 13-3(F), n. 215; § 17-9(C), n. 57
United States v. Simpson, 33 M.J. 1063 (A.C.M.R. 1991) — § 17-8(B), n. 11
United States v. Sims, 5 C.M.A. 115, 17 C.M.R. 115 (1954) — § 15-13, n. 11
United States v. Sims, 2 M.J. 109 (C.M.A. 1977) — § 4-11(A), n. 16
United States v. Sims, 28 M.J. 578 (A.C.M.R. 1989) — § 16-5(B), nn. 10, 26
United States v. Sims, 33 M.J. 684 (A.C.M.R. 1991) — § 14-3(D)(4), n. 146
United States v. Singleton, 21 C.M.A. 432, 45 C.M.R. 206 (1972) — § 4-15(A), n. 6; § 8-3(A), n. 15
United States v. Singleton, 15 M.J. 579 (A.C.M.R. 1983) — § 4-12(B), n. 11
United States v. Singleton, 41 M.J. 200 (C.M.A. 1994) — § 6-5(C), n. 50; § 17-21, n. 3
United States v. Sink, 27 M.J. 920 (A.C.M.R. 1989) — § 3-8(B), n. 17; § 17-14, n. 6
United States v. Skaar, 20 M.J. 836 (N.M.C.M.R. 1985) — § 17-9(A), n. 22
United States v. Skaggs, 40 C.M.R. 344 (A.B.R. 1968) — § 7-3(B), n. 29
United States v. Skerrett, 40 M.J. 331 (C.M.A. 1994) — § 15-14(B), n. 36
United States v. Sloan, 48 C.M.R. 211 (A.C.M.R. 1974) — § 13-3(C), n. 25
United States v. Sloan, 30 M.J. 741 (A.F.C.M.R. 1990) — § 5-3(B), n. 41; § 6-5(A), n. 22; § 13-3(M), n. 296; § 15-10(B), n. 62; § 15-10(C)(2), n. 94
United States v. Sloan, 35 M.J. 4 (C.M.A. 1992) — § 4-8(D), n. 58; § 4-12(A), n. 9; § 16-3(E), n. 72; § 17-2(B)(2), n. 33
United States v. Slocumb, 24 M.J. 940 (C.G.C.M.R. 1987) — § 14-3(C), n. 124

TABLE OF CASES

United States v. Slovacek, 24 M.J. 140 (C.M.A. 1987) — § 16-5(C), n. 29
United States v. Slubowski, 5 M.J. 882 (N.C.M.R. 1978) — § 15-14(A), n. 16; § 15-14(B), n. 22
United States v. Slubowski, 7 M.J. 461 (C.M.A. 1979) — § 15-10(A), n. 20
United States v. Small, 21 M.J. 218 (C.M.A. 1986) — § 12-2(H), n. 97; § 15-10(B), n. 53
United States v. Smalls, 30 M.J. 666 (A.F.C.M.R. 1990) — § 5-4(A)(1), n. 10
United States v. Smalls, 32 M.J. 398 (C.M.A. 1991) — § 5-4(A)(2), n. 14
United States v. Smart, 21 M.J. 15 (C.M.A. 1985) — § 15-10(A), nn. 30, 31; § 15-10(B), n. 68; § 15-10(C)(2), nn. 93-95; § 17-2(B)(4), n. 96; § 17-8(B)(3), n. 93
United States v. Smauley, 42 M.J. 449 (1995) — § 14-3(D)(4), n. 154
United States v. Smiley, 17 M.J. 790 (A.F.C.M.R. 1983) — § 4-14(B), n. 21; § 8-5, n. 11
United States, Smith v.
United States v. Smith, 8 C.M.A. 178, 23 C.M.R. 402 (1957) — § 6-1, n. 9
United States v. Smith, 9 C.M.A. 240, 26 C.M.R. 20 (1958) — § 5-4(A)(2), n. 12
United States v. Smith, 14 C.M.A. 405, 34 C.M.R. 185 (1964) — § 15-20, n. 16
United States v. Smith, 39 C.M.R. 315 (A.B.R. 1967) — § 13-3(C)(2), n. 53
United States v. Smith, 17 C.M.A. 55 C.M.R. 319 (1967) — § 13-3(C)(2), n. 60
United States v. Smith, 39 C.M.R. 46 (C.M.A. 1968) — § 2-2(B), n. 9
United States v. Smith, 40 C.M.R. 432 (A.C.M.R. 1969) — § 13-3(F), n. 220
United States v. Smith, 21 C.M.A. 231, 45 C.M.R. 5 (1972) — § 2-4(A), n. 2
United States v. Smith, 1 M.J. 83 (C.M.A. 1975) — § 17-9(B), n. 38
United States v. Smith, 3 M.J. 490 (C.M.A. 1975) — § 4-15(A), n. 4; § 8-3(D), n. 173; § 15-9, n. 2
United States v. Smith, 2 M.J. 566 (A.C.M.R. 1976) — § 2-2(D), n. 63; § 5-5, n. 6
United States v. Smith, 3 M.J. 912 (A.C.M.R. 1977) — § 13-5(H), n. 64
United States v. Smith, 1 M.J. 1204 (N.C.M.R. 1977) — § 13-5(C), n. 31
United States v. Smith, 4 M.J. 265 (C.M.A. 1978) — § 4-8(B), n. 14
United States v. Smith, 9 M.J. 359 (C.M.A. 1980) — § 4-11(A), n. 29
United States v. Smith, 9 M.J. 537 (A.C.M.R. 1980) — § 15-21, n. 8; § 16-5(D)(1), n. 61
United States v. Smith, 15 M.J. 948 (A.F.C.M.R. 1983) — § 17-15(B), n. 32
United States v. Smith, 16 M.J. 694 (A.F.C.M.R. 1983) — § 2-5, n. 3
United States v. Smith, 17 M.J. 994 (A.C.M.R. 1984) — § 11-2(E)(3), n. 140
United States v. Smith, 18 M.J. 704 (A.C.M.R. 1984) — § 8-3(C)(4), n. 152
United States v. Smith, 18 M.J. 786 (N.M.C.M.R. 1984) — § 2-8(C), n. 32
United States v. Smith, 20 M.J. 528 (A.C.M.R. 1985) — § 5-10(D), n. 37; § 13-5(B), nn. 28, 30
United States v. Smith, 21 M.J. 642 (A.C.M.R. 1985) — § 14-3(D)(3), nn. 139, 144
United States v. Smith, 23 M.J. 118 (C.M.A. 1986) — § 14-3(F), n. 195
United States v. Smith, 23 M.J. 714 (A.C.M.R. 1986) — § 16-5(D)(4), n. 106
United States v. Smith, 23 M.J. 744 (A.C.M.R. 1987) — § 16-6, n. 8
United States v. Smith, 24 M.J. 859 (A.C.M.R. 1987) — § 15-10(A), nn. 7, 22
United States v. Smith, 25 M.J. 545 (A.C.M.R. 1987) — § 2-4(A), n. 8; § 2-6(A), n. 17
United States v. Smith, 25 M.J. 785 (A.C.M.R. 1988) — § 15-10(A), n. 22; § 15-10(B), n. 68; § 16-9, n. 14
United States v. Smith, 26 M.J. 152 (C.M.A. 1988) — § 8-3(B)(1), n. 54
United States v. Smith, 26 M.J. 276 (C.M.A. 1988) — § 2-2(D), n. 67
United States v. Smith, 27 M.J. 25 (C.M.A. 1988) — § 15-10(A), nn. 6, 22
United States v. Smith, 27 M.J. 242 (C.M.A. 1988) — § 6-4(D), nn. 25
United States v. Smith, 50 C.M.R. 237 (A.C.M.R 1989); § 8-3(C)(3), n. 142; § 8-3(C)(4), nn. 152, 155; § 13-3(C)(2), n. 66
United States v. Smith, 27 M.J. 914 (A.C.M.R. 1989) — § 14-3(D)(4), n. 147

TABLE OF CASES

United States v. Smith, 28 M.J. 863 (A.F.C.M.R. 1989) — § 17-15(B), n. 32
United States v. Smith, 29 M.J. 736 (A.F.C.M.R. 1989) — § 16-5(B), n. 9; § 16-7, n. 5
United States v. Smith, 30 M.J. 694 (A.C.M.R. 1990) — § 5-4(B), n. 50
United States v. Smith, 30 M.J. 631 (N.M.C.M.R. 1990) — § 12-2(H), n. 97
United States v. Smith, 32 M.J. 586 (A.C.M.R. 1991) — § 13-3(C)(3), n. 121
United States v. Smith, 33 M.J. 527 (A.F.C.M.R. 1991) — § 15-2(B)(1), n. 22
United States v. Smith, 33 M.J. 627 (A.F.C.M.R. 1991) — § 7-3, n. 7
United States v. Smith, 33 M.J. 968 (A.F.C.M.R. 1991) — § 7-3(A), nn. 16, 23, 24; § 17-8(B)(1), n. 46
United States v. Smith, 34 M.J. 247 (C.M.A. 1992) — § 16-8(C), n. 36; § 17-13, n. 22
United States v. Smith, 34 M.J. 341 (C.M.A. 1992) — § 15-14(C), n. 50
United States v. Smith, 34 M.J. 1005 (A.C.M.R. 1992) — § 2-2(D), n. 63; § 2-2(E)(1), n. 71
United States v. Smith, 34 M.J. 894 (N.M.C.M.R. 1992) — § 17-8(B), n. 24
United States v. Smith, 36 M.J. 455 (C.M.A. 1993) — § 12-2(F)(3), nn. 61, 66
United States v. Smith, 36 M.J. 754 (A.C.M.R. 1993) — § 6-1(C), n. 102
United States v. Smith, 37 M.J. 773 (A.C.M.R. 1993) — § 4-15(C), n. 15; § 8-3(C)(4), n. 151
United States v. Smith, 37 M.J. 583 (N.M.C.M.R. 1993) — § 2-2(C)(3), n. 32; § 17-8(B)(3), n. 95
United States v. Smith, 39 M.J. 448 (C.M.A. 1994) — § 17-15(B), n. 17
United States v. Smith, 39 M.J. 587 (A.F.C.M.R. 1994) — § 12-2(F)(3), n. 64; § 15-2(B)(2), n. 26
United States v. Smith, 41 M.J. 817 (N.M.Ct.Crim.App. 1995) — § 12-3(A), nn. 11, 12, 40
United States v. Smythe, 37 M.J. 804 (C.G.C.M.R. 1993) — § 6-1(C), n. 102
United States v. Sneed, 32 M.J. 537 (A.F.C.M.R. 1990) — § 12-5, n. 16; § 14-3(A)(2), nn. 25, 27
United States v. Snelling, 14 M.J. 267 (C.M.A. 1982) — § 17-9(E), n. 87
United States v. Snipes, 19 M.J. 913 (A.C.M.R. 1985) — § 15-5, n. 16
United States v. Snoberger, 26 M.J. 818 (A.C.M.R. 1988) — § 9-3, n. 6
United States v. Snodgrass, 22 M.J. 866 (A.C.M.R. 1986) — § 17-9(D), n. 62; § 16-5(D)(3), n. 72
United States v. Snogdrass, 37 M.J. 844 (A.F.C.M.R. 1993) — § 14-3, n. 6; § 16-8(B), n. 19
United States v. Snow, 10 M.J. 742 (N.M.C.M.R. 1981) — § 12-2(F)(2), n. 58
United States v. Snyder, 1 C.M.A. 423, 4 C.M.R. 15 (1952) — § 2-6(B), n. 29
United States v. Solak, 12 C.M.A. 440, 28 C.M.R. 6 (1959) — § 15-15, n. 2
United States v. Solnick, 39 M.J. 930 (N.M.C.M.R. 1994) — § 17-9(B), n. 35
United States, Solorio v.
United States v. Solorio, 483 U.S. 435 (1987) — § 17-17, n. 10
United States v. Solorio, 29 M.J. 510 (C.G.C.M.R. 1989) — § 4-11(C), n. 50; § 17-11, n. 2
United States v. Sombolay, 37 M.J. 647 (A.C.M.R. 1993) — § 15-3, n. 4
United States v. Sonnenfeld, 41 M.J. 765 (N.M. Ct. Crim. App. 1994) — § 4-15(C), n. 15
United States v. Sorby, 39 M.J. 914 (N.M.C.M.R. 1994) — § 3-3(C), n. 26 R.C.M. 907; § 13-3(G), n. 223
United States v. Soriano, 15 M.J. 633 (N.M.C.M.R. 1982) — § 12-2(H), n. 123
United States v. Soriano, 20 M.J. 337 (C.M.A. 1985) — § 12-2(H), nn. 108, 112; § 16-9, n. 10
United States v. Soriano, 22 M.J. 453 (C.M.A. 1986) — § 16-3(D), n. 67
United States v. Sories, 22 M.J. 305 (C.M.A. 1986) — § 17-15(B), n. 32

TABLE OF CASES

United States v. Sorrell, 20 M.J. 684 (A.C.M.R. 1985) — § 2-7(B), n. 20
United States v. Sorrell, 23 M.J. 122, n. 1 (C.M.A. 1986) — § 13-3(J), n. 262
United States v. Sorrells, 49 C.M.R. 44 (A.C.M.R. 1974) — § 2-3(C), n. 22
United States v. Sosebee, 35 M.J. 892 (A.C.M.R. 1992) — § 17-2(B)(3), n. 81
United States v. Soukup, 2 C.M.A. 141, 7 C.M.R. 17 (1953) — § 6-1(C)(3), n. 138
United States v. Southers, 12 M.J. 924 (N.M.C.M.R. 1982) — § 5-10(A), n. 1
United States v. Spann, 24 M.J. 508 (A.F.C.M.R. 1987) — § 2-7(C), nn. 41, 43; § 9-3, n. 6; § 5-3(C)(6), n. 85
United States v. Sparks, 21 C.M.A. 134, 44 C.M.R. 188 (1971) — § 15-20, n. 18
United States v. Sparks, 29 M.J. 52 (C.M.A. 1989) — § 8-3(B)(1), n. 58; § 15-2(B)(3), n. 92
United States v. Sparrow, 33 M.J. 139 (C.M.A. 1991) — § 16-8(B), n. 12
United States v. Spearman, 23 C.M.A. 31, 48 C.M.R. 405 (1974) — § 15-4(C), n. 16
United States v. Spears, 32 M.J. 934 (A.F.C.M.R. 1991) — § 16-8(B), nn. 20, 21
United States v. Spencer, 29 M.J. 740 (A.F.C.M.R. 1989) — § 2-4(A), n. 6
United States v. Spencer, 32 M.J. 841 (N.M.C.M.R. 1991) — § 16-9, n. 11
United States v. Spindle, 28 M.J. 35 (C.M.A. 1989) — § 7-2(C), n. 79
United States v. Spinner, 27 M.J. 892 (A.C.M.R. 1989) — § 7-2(A)(1), n. 16
United States v. Spivey, 10 M.J. 7 (C.M.A. 1980) — § 3-8(B), n. 14; § 16-5(C), n. 50
United States v. Spradley, 41 M.J. 827 (N.M.Ct.Crim.App. 1995) — § 4-8(C)(3), n. 28
United States v. Sprague, 25 M.J. 743 (A.C.M.R. 1987) — § 2-2(E)(1), n. 71
United States v. Spriddle, 20 M.J. 804 (N.M.C.M.R. 1985) — § 13-2(E), n. 55
United States, Spriggs v.
United States v. Spring, 15 M.J. 669 (A.F.C.M.R. 1983) — § 13-3(J), n. 265; § 17-4, n. 31
United States v. Spurlin, 33 M.J. 443 (C.M.A. 1991) — § 15-2(B)(3), n. 85; § 17-2(B)(3), nn. 81, 86
United States v. St. Clair, 19 M.J. 833 (N.M.C.M.R. 1984) — § 13-2(G)(2), n. 85
United States v. St. Fort, 26 M.J. 764 (A.C.M.R. 1988) — § 15-10(C)(3), n. 115
United States v. St. John, 23 C.M.A. 20, 48 C.M.R. 312 (1974) — § 15-13, n. 11
United States v. St. Romain, 33 M.J. 689 (A.F.C.M.R. 1991) — § 16-5(D)(4), n. 103; § 17-8(B)(3), n. 92
United States v. Stacy, 42 C.M.R. 547 (A.C.M.R. 1970) — § 7-3(B), n. 32
United States v. Stafford, 15 M.J. 866 (A.C.M.R. 1981) — § 15-2(F), n. 163
United States v. Stafford, 25 M.J. 609 (A.C.M.R. 1987) — § 4-15(C), n. 17; § 8-3(C)(4), n. 154
United States v. Staley, 36 M.J. 896 (A.F.C.M.R. 1993) — § 10-4(B)(5), n. 58
United States v. Stallard, 14 M.J. 933 (A.C.M.R. 1982) — § 13-3(E), n. 199
United States v. Stamper, 39 M.J. 1097 (A.C.M.R. 1994) — § 5-10(B), n. 8; § 6-5(B), n. 28
United States v. Standifer, 31 M.J. 742 (A.F.C.M.R. 1990) — § 16-8(B), nn. 25, 26
United States v. Stanford, 37 M.J. 388 (C.M.A. 1993) — § 17-9(C), n. 54
United States v. Stark, 19 M.J. 519 (A.C.M.R. 1984) — § 7-3(B), n. 29; § 16-9, n. 11
United States v. Stark, 24 M.J. 381 (C.M.A. 1987) — § 5-4(B), n. 52
United States v. Starks, 24 M.J. 857 (A.C.M.R. 1987) — § 4-11(C), n. 59
United States v. Starks, 36 M.J. 1160 (A.C.M.R. 1993) — § 17-2(B), n. 7
United States v. Staten, 6 M.J. 275 (C.M.A. 1979) — § 15-14(B), n. 22
United States v. Staton, 37 M.J. 1047 (N.M.C.M.R. 1993) — § 14-3(F), n. 191
United States v. Stavely, 33 M.J. 92 (C.M.A. 1991) — § 15-12(A), n. 7
United States v. Stearman, 7 M.J. 13 (C.M.A. 1979) — § 12-3(A), n. 22
United States v. Steck, 10 M.J. 412 (C.M.A. 1981) — § 14-3(D)(5), n. 172; § 17-3(A), n. 18

TABLE OF CASES

United States, Stegald v.
United States v. Stegall, 6 M.J. 176 (C.M.A. 1979) — § 12-3(A), n. 30; § 13-3(J), n. 259; § 6-1(C)(3), n. 165
United States v. Steinruck, 11 M.J. 322 (C.M.A. 1981) — § 2-7(B), n. 25
United States v. Stennis, 12 M.J. 813 (N.M.C.M.R. 1981) — § 15-10(B), n. 53
United States v. Stephens, 21 M.J. 784 (A.C.M.R. 1986) — § 6-5(A), n. 8
United States v. Stephens, 25 M.J. 171 (C.M.A. 1987) — § 14-3(B)(3), n. 106
United States v. Stephenson, 2 C.M.R. 571 (N.B.R. 1951) — § 15-8, n. 2
United States v. Stephenson, 30 M.J. 551 (A.C.M.R. 1990) — § 15-2(B)(3), nn. 57, 76
United States v. Stephenson, 33 M.J. 79 (C.M.A. 1991) — § 15-2(B)(3), nn. 78, 85
United States v. Stevens, 2 M.J. 488 (A.C.M.R. 1975) — § 9-2, n. 6
United States v. Stevens, 21 M.J. 649 (A.C.M.R. 1985) — § 16-5(D)(3), n. 76
United States v. Stevens, 25 M.J. 805 (A.C.M.R. 1988) — § 12-4, n. 6
United States v. Stevens, 27 M.J. 626 (A.F.C.M.R. 1988) — § 15-4(A), n. 7; § 12-2(F)(5), n. 88
United States v. Stevenson, 19 M.J. 760 (A.C.M.R. 1984) — § 15-10(C)(3), nn. 106, 107
United States v. Steward, 31 M.J. 259 (C.M.A. 1990) — § 13-4(A), n. 10
United States v. Stewart, 2 M.J. 423 (A.C.M.R. 1975) — § 2-4(C), n. 33; § 12-2(H), n. 122
United States v. Stewart, 29 M.J. 92 (C.M.A. 1989) — § 2-9(C), n. 24; § 2-9(C)(1), n. 34
United States v. Stewart, 29 M.J. 621 (C.G.C.M.R. 1989) — § 10-5(C), n. 31; § 12-5, nn. 8, 16, 17; § 15-14(A), n. 5
United States v. Stewart, 33 M.J. 519 (A.F.C.M.R. 1991) — § 2-4(A), n. 13; § 15-10(B), n. 53
United States v. Stewart, 37 M.J. 523 (A.C.M.R. 1993) — § 12-4, n. 13
United States v. Stidman, 29 M.J. 999 (A.F.C.M.R. 1990) — § 17-15(B), n. 18
United States v. Stimpson, 29 M.J. 768 (A.C.M.R. 1989) — § 16-5(D)(4), nn. 101, 102
United States v. Stiner, 30 M.J. 860 (N.M.C.M.R. 1990) — § 12-3(A), n. 44
United States v. Stinson, 34 M.J. 233 (C.M.A. 1992) — § 4-16, n. 3; § 16-5(D)(4), n. 86
United States v. Stinson, 34 M.J. 303 (C.M.A. 1992) — § 15-2(B)(3), n. 89
United States v. Stipe, 23 C.M.A. 11, 48 C.M.R. 267 (1974) — § 12-3(B), n. 56; § 8-3(C)(2), n. 135
United States v. Stocken, 17 M.J. 826 (A.C.M.R. 1984) — § 2-8(B), n. 26
United States v. Stockman, 17 M.J. 530 (A.C.M.R. 1983) — § 2-1, n. 1
United States v. Stokes, 12 M.J. 229 (C.M.A. 1982) — § 4-12(B), n. 14
United States v. Stokes, 39 M.J. 771 (A.C.M.R. 1994) — § 13-3(C)(3), n. 113
United States v. Stoltz, 14 C.M.A. 461, 34 C.M.R. 241 (1964) — § 9-2(B)(1), n. 42
United States v. Stombaugh, 40 M.J. 208 (C.M.A. 1994) — § 6-3(A), nn. 3, 4; § 6-5(B), n. 25; § 6-7, nn. 10, 13, 17, 18
United States v. Stombugh, 36 M.J. 1180 (N.M.C.M.R. 1993) — § 17-11, n. 5
United States v. Stone, 8 M.J. 140 (C.M.A. 1979) — § 4-5(A)(3), n. 12
United States v. Stone, 23 M.J. 772 (A.F.C.M.R. 1987) — § 15-16(B), nn. 17, 23
United States v. Stone, 26 M.J. 401 (C.M.A. 1988) — § 16-11, n. 12
United States v. Stone, 37 M.J. 558 (A.C.M.R. 1993) — § 7-2, n. 7; § 13-3(N)(3), n. 384; § 16-5(D)(5), n. 118
United States v. Stone, 40 M.J. 420 (C.M.A. 1994) — § 2-6(B), n. 30; § 10-4(A)(4), n. 27
United States v. Storts, 35 M.J. 883 (A.C.M.R. 1992) — § 15-2(B)(3), n. 78
United States v. Story, 35 M.J. 677 (A.C.M.R. 1992) — § 15-3, nn. 2, 13
United States v. Stottlemire, 28 M.J. 477 (C.M.A. 1989) — § 6-1(C)(3), n. 146
United States v. Stouffer, 2 M.J. 528 (A.C.M.R. 1976) — § 14-3(B)(2), n. 100; § 14-3(D)(4); § 14-3(D)(4), n. 147

TABLE OF CASES

United States v. Stovall, 44 C.M.R. 576 (A.F.C.M.R. 1971) — § 2-4(D), n. 42
United States v. Strachan, 35 M.J. 362 (C.M.A. 1992) — § 15-14(B), n. 23
United States v. Straight, 42 M.J. 244 (1995) — § 15-16(B), nn. 19, 23; § 16-3(A), nn. 3, 9; § 15-2(B)(3), n. 88
United States v. Strangstalien, 7 M.J. 225 (C.M.A. 1979) — § 2-7(C), n. 35; § 4-11(A), n. 14
United States v. Straukas, 41 C.M.R. 975 (A.F.C.M.R. 1970) — § 16-10, nn. 3, 4
United States v. Strawbridge, 21 C.M.R. 482 (A.B.R. 1955) — § 15-10(B), n. 44
United States v. Streater, 32 M.J. 337 (C.M.A. 1991) — § 12-2(F)(4), n. 68
United States v. Strickland, 36 M.J. 569 (A.C.M.R. 1992) — § 3-3(C), n. 27; § 13-3(G), n. 225
United States v. Stringer, 34 M.J. 667 (A.C.M.R. 1992) — § 9-2(D), n. 86; § 14-3(C), n. 132
United States v. Stringer, 37 M.J. 120 (C.M.A. 1993) — § 5-3(C)(3), n. 73
United States v. Stringfellow, 32 M.J. 335 (C.M.A. 1991) — § 2-7(B), nn. 22, 23
United States v. Strong, 17 M.J. 263 (C.M.A. 1984) — § 15-19, n. 3; § 16-6, n. 10; § 16-7, n. 6
United States v. Stroud, 27 M.J. 765 (A.F.C.M.R. 1988) — § 2-2(D), n. 67; § 5-10(C), n. 14; § 2-2(C)(3), n. 35
United States v. Stroup, 24 M.J. 760 (A.F.C.M.R. 1987) — § 11-2(A)(2), n. 10
United States v. Strozier, 31 M.J. 283 (C.M.A. 1990) — § 5-3(B), n. 37
United States v. Struckman, 20 C.M.A. 493, 43 C.M.R. 333 (1971) — § 2-3(C), n. 24
United States v. Stuart, 36 M.J. 746 (A.C.M.R. 1993) — § 5-9(D), n. 22
United States v. Stubblefield, 2 C.M.R. 637 (A.F.B.R. 1951) — § 17-3(A), n. 23
United States v. Stubbs, 3 M.J. 630 (N.C.M.R. 1977) — § 13-3(C)(2), nn. 51, 73
United States v. Stubbs, 23 M.J. 188 (C.M.A. 1987) — § 8-3(B)(1), nn. 55, 56
United States v. Stuckey, 10 M.J. 347 (C.M.A. 1981) — § 5-3(B), n. 51; § 13-3(N), n. 299; § 13-3(N)(3), n. 385
United States v. Sturdivant, 1 M.J. 256 (C.M.A. 1976) — § 17-4, n. 7
United States v. Sturdivant, 13 M.J. 323 (C.M.A. 1982) — § 6-1(C)(3), nn. 141, 166
United States v. Sturgeon, 37 M.J. 1083 (N.M.C.M.R. 1993) — § 13-3(C)(3), n. 97
United States v. Sturkey, 50 C.M.R. 110 (A.C.M.R. 1975) — § 2-2(C)(1), n. 24
United States v. Sturkey, 23 M.J. 522 (A.F.C.M.R. 1986) — § 17-4, nn. 28, 34
United States v. Sullivan, 26 M.J. 442 (C.M.A. 1988) — § 6-3(A), n. 2; § 6-7, n. 18; § 13-5(K), n. 85
United States v. Sullivan, 38 M.J. 746 (A.C.M.R. 1993) — § 5-3(A), n. 29; § 6-1(B)(2), n. 77
United States v. Sullivan, 42 M.J. 360 (1995) — § 5-3(A), n. 35; § 6-1(B)(2), n. 81
United States v. Sumbry, 33 M.J. 564 (A.C.M.R. 1991) — § 9-2(B)(2), n. 67
United States v. Summerset, 37 M.J. 695 (A.C.M.R. 1993) — § 12-3(B), nn. 54, 55
United States v. Sumpter, 22 M.J. 33 (C.M.A. 1986) — § 17-16(B), n. 10
United States v. Sutherland, 16 M.J. 338 (C.M.A. 1983) — § 5-4(B), n. 51
United States v. Suttles, 15 M.J. 972 (A.C.M.R. 1983) — § 15-4(B), n. 11
United States v. Sutton, 3 C.M.A. 220, 11 C.M.R. 220 (1953) — § 11-3(B)(2), n. 43
United States v. Sutton, 23 C.M.A. 231, 49 C.M.R. 248 (1974) — § 2-3(B), n. 18
United States v. Sutton, 15 M.J. 235 (C.M.A. 1983) — § 17-11, n. 7
United States v. Sutton, 27 M.J. 578 (A.F.C.M.R. 1988) — § 13-5(L), n. 99
United States v. Sutton, 31 M.J. 11 (C.M.A. 1990) — § 13-5(L), nn. 94, 103, 104
United States v. Suzuki, 14 M.J. 491 (C.M.A. 1983) — § 17-16(C), n. 23
United States v. Suzuki, 20 M.J. 248 (C.M.A. 1985) — § 17-16(C), n. 32

TABLE OF CASES

United States v. Swagger, 16 M.J. 759 (A.C.M.R. 1983) — § 15-10(B), n. 71; § 15-10(C)(2), n. 96
United States v. Swanholm, 36 M.J. 743 (A.C.M.R. 1992) — § 2-2(B), n. 10
United States v. Sweet, 38 M.J. 583 (N.M.C.M.R. 1993) — § 14-3(B)(2), nn. 86-91
United States v. Sweet, 42 M.J. 183 (1995) — § 14-3(B)(2), n. 92
United States v. Sweitzer, 14 C.M.A. 39, 33 C.M.R. 251 (1963) — § 2-4(C), n. 36
United States v. Swoape, 21 M.J. 414 (C.M.A. 1986) — § 15-14(C), n. 51
United States v. Sykes, 11 M.J. 766 (N.M.C.M.R. 1981) — § 13-3(N)(1), nn. 326, 328, 329
United States v. Sykes, 32 M.J. 791 (N.M.C.M.R. 1990) — § 1-8(D)(2), n. 20
United States v. Sykes, 38 M.J. 669 (A.C.M.R. 1993) — § 13-4(A), n. 13
United States v. Sylvester, 38 M.J. 720 (A.C.M.R. 1993) — § 16-5(D)(4), n. 99
United States v. Synder, 30 M.J. 662 (A.F.C.M.R. 1990) — § 13-2(G)(2), n. 105
United States v. Syro, 7 M.J. 431 (C.M.A. 1979) — § 15-26(C), n. 12; § 16-5(C), n. 48
United States v. Sztuka, 43 M.J. 261 (1995) — § 17-21, n. 3
United States v. Tackett, 16 C.M.A. 226, 36 C.M.R. 382 (1966) — § 15-13, n. 9
United States v. Taft, 21 C.M.A. 68, 44 C.M.R. 122 (1971) — § 14-1, n. 8
United States v. Tagert, 11 M.J. 677 (N.M.C.M.R. 1981) — § 5-4(C), n. 55; § 8-3(C)(2), n. 132; § 11-2(E)(1), n. 104
United States v. Talavera, 8 M.J. 14 (C.M.A. 1979) — § 13-3(C)(2), nn. 72, 73
United States v. Taliau, 7 M.J. 845 (A.C.M.R. 1979) — § 17-15(B), n. 21
United States v. Tallon, 28 M.J. 635 (A.F.C.M.R. 1989) — § 5-3(F), n. 26; § 6-1(C), n. 94
United States v. Tangpuz, 5 M.J. 426 (C.M.A. 1978) — § 11-2(A)(1), n. 8; § 11-2(A)(4), nn. 40, 44, 45
United States v. Tanksley, 7 M.J. 573 (A.C.M.R. 1979) — § 15-13, n. 10
United States v. Tanksley, 36 M.J. 428 (C.M.A. 1993) — § 2-4(E), n. 46
United States v. Tanner, 16 M.J. 930 (N.M.C.M.R. 1983) — § 12-2(F)(4), nn. 68, 74
United States v. Tarver, 2 M.J. 1176 (N.C.M.R. 1975) — § 13-3(C)(2), n. 77
United States v. Tarver, 29 M.J. 605 (A.C.M.R. 1989) — § 15-14(B), n. 22
United States v. Tassos, 18 C.M.A. 12, 39 C.M.R. 12 (1968) — § 2-4(C), n. 34
United States v. Tatmon, 23 C.M.R. 841 (A.F.B.R. 1957) — § 11-3(B)(1), nn. 11, 12
United States v. Tatum, 34 M.J. 1115 (N.M.C.M.R. 1992) — § 2-6, n. 13
United States v. Taylor, 13 C.M.R. 201 (A.B.R. 1953) — § 6-1(C)(2), n. 129
United States v. Taylor, 41 C.M.R. 749 (N.C.M.R. 1969) — § 8-3(D), n. 166
United States v. Taylor, 47 C.M.R. 445 (A.C.M.R. 1973) — § 15-2(D), n. 137
United States v. Taylor, 13 M.J. 648 (N.M.C.M.R. 1982) — § 13-3(B), n. 10
United States v. Taylor, 21 M.J. 840 (A.C.M.R. 1986) — § 16-6, n. 15
United States v. Taylor, 21 M.J. 1016 (A.C.M.R. 1986) — § 14-4, n. 18; § 15-21, n. 10; § 9-2(B)(1), n. 39; § 16-5(D)(1), nn. 61, 62
United States v. Taylor, 23 M.J. 314 (C.M.A. 1987) — § 2-5, nn. 4, 7; § 2-6, n. 4
United States v. Taylor, 25 M.J. 697 (A.C.M.R. 1987) — § 17-15(B), n. 30
United States v. Taylor, 26 M.J. 7 (C.M.A. 1988) — § 6-1(C)(3), n. 143
United States v. Taylor, 26 M.J. 127 (C.M.A. 1988) — § 15-14(B), nn. 24, 34
United States v. Taylor, 26 M.J. 816 (A.C.M.R. 1988) — § 6-1, n. 17; § 6-1(B)(2), n. 81
United States v. Taylor, 30 M.J. 1008 (A.F.C.M.R. 1990) — § 17-21, n. 8
United States v. Taylor, 31 M.J. 905 (A.F.C.M.R. 1990) — § 15-2(A), n. 3
United States v. Taylor, 36 M.J. 1166 (A.C.M.R. 1993) — § 5-9(D), n. 21
United States v. Taylor, 38 M.J. 254 (C.M.A. 1993) — § 15-2(B)(3), n. 42
United States v. Taylor, 41 M.J. 168 (C.M.A. 1994) — § 5-3(D)(1), n. 131
United States v. Taylor, 41 M.J. 701 (A.F.Ct.Crim.App. 1995) — § 15-10(A), n. 31
United States v. Teague, 3 C.M.A. 317, 12 C.M.R. 73 (1953) — § 17-5, n. 6

TABLE OF CASES

United States v. Tebsherany, 30 M.J. 608 (N.M.C.M.R. 1990) — § 10-4(A)(4), n. 27; § 13-3(C)(3), n. 112
United States v. Tebsherany, 32 M.J. 351 (C.M.A. 1991) — § 13-3(C)(3), nn. 156, 158
United States v. Tedder, 24 M.J. 176 (C.M.A. 1987) — § 2-8(B), n. 17
United States v. Teeter, 12 M.J. 716 (A.C.M.R. 1981) — § 13-5(D), n. 43; § 17-15(B), n. 19
United States v. Teeter, 16 M.J. 68 (C.M.A. 1983) — § 16-6, n. 18
United States v. Tempia, 16 C.M.A. 629, 37 C.M.R. 249 (1967) — § 5-4(B), n. 24
United States v. Tena, 15 M.J. 728 (A.C.M.R. 1983) — § 5-3(D)(1), n. 120
United States v. Tenk, 33 M.J. 765 (A.C.M.R. 1991) — § 14-3(B)(2), n. 76
United States v. Tenney, 15 M.J. 779 (A.C.M.R. 1983) — § 14-3(D)(3), n. 138
United States v. Terrell, 7 M.J. 511 (A.C.M.R. 1979) — § 9-2(B)(1), n. 39
United States v. Terry, 45 C.M.R. 216 (C.M.A. 1972) — § 14-3(B)(2), n. 80
United States v. Terry, 21 C.M.A. 442, 45 C.M.R. 216 (1972) — § 14-3(B), n. 51
United States v. Testori, 35 M.J. 745 (N.M.C.M.R. 1992) — § 14-3(D)(5), n. 175
United States v. Teters, 37 M.J. 370 (C.M.A. 1993) — § 6-1(C)(3), nn. 153, 160
United States v. Tharpe, 38 M.J. 8 (C.M.A. 1993) — § 11-2(A)(3), n. 21; § 15-2(B)(3), nn. 42, 78
United States v. Thatch, 30 M.J. 623 (N.M.C.M.R. 1990) — § 2-6(A), n. 17
United States v. Thatcher, 28 M.J. 20 (C.M.A. 1989) — § 5-3(A), n. 17; § 5-3(D)(1), n. 128
United States v. Thomas, 1 M.J. 397 (C.M.A. 1976) — § 5-3(D)(1), n. 117
United States v. Thomas, 6 M.J. 573 (A.C.M.R. 1978) — § 9-2(B)(1), n. 39
United States v. Thomas, 7 M.J. 655 (A.C.M.R. 1979) — § 7-2(C), n. 80; § 10-4(B)(5), n. 55
United States v. Thomas, 7 M.J. 763 (A.C.M.R. 1979) — § 946
United States v. Thomas, 8 M.J. 661 (A.C.M.R. 1979) — § 15-4(D), n. 28
United States v. Thomas, 11 M.J. 315 (C.M.A. 1981) — § 17-21, n. 3
United States v. Thomas, 15 M.J. 528 (A.F.C.M.R. 1982) — § 9-3, n. 8
United States v. Thomas, 18 M.J. 545 (A.C.M.R. 1984) — § 15-2(D), nn. 135, 136; § 15-12(B), n. 17
United States v. Thomas, 22 M.J. 57 (C.M.A. 1986) — § 15-4(A), n. 5
United States v. Thomas, 22 M.J. 388 (C.M.A. 1986) — § 6-3(A), nn. 2, 4, 8; § 6-4(C), n. 15; § 6-5(B), nn. 24, 29-31, 42-46; § 6-7, n. 17; § 6-8, nn. 9-11
United States v. Thomas, 31 M.J. 669 (A.C.M.R. 1990) — § 14-3(D)(4), n. 147; § 16-5(D)(4), n. 102
United States v. Thomas, 32 M.J. 897 (A.F.C.M.R. 1991) — § 17-2(B)(3), n. 82
United States v. Thomas, 32 M.J. 1024 (A.F.C.M.R. 1991) — § 12-5, n. 15
United States v. Thomas, 33 M.J. 694 (A.C.M.R. 1991) — § 15-4(A), n. 5
United States v. Thomas, 33 M.J. 1024 (A.F.C.M.R. 1991) — § 12-5, n. 17
United States v. Thomas, 33 M.J. 644 (N.M.C.M.R. 1991) — § 15-2(B)(3), nn. 32, 83
United States v. Thomas, 33 M.J. 768 (N.M.C.M.R. 1991) — § 17-14, n. 3; § 17-19, n. 23
United States v. Thomas, 34 M.J. 768 (A.C.M.R. 1992) — § 13-5(A), n. 6
United States v. Thomas, 36 M.J. 638 (A.C.M.R. 1992) — § 16-6, n. 9
United States v. Thomas, 36 M.J. 554 (N.M.C.M.R. 1992) — § 16-3(D), n. 63
United States v. Thomas, 37 M.J. 302 (C.M.A. 1993) — § 11-2(E)(3), n. 133
United States v. Thomas, 38 M.J. 614 (A.F.C.M.R. 1993) — § 15-2(B)(3), n. 73
United States v. Thomas, 39 M.J. 626 (N.M.C.M.R. 1993) — § 15-14(B), nn. 21, 41; § 15-15, nn. 19, 21; § 15-16(B), nn. 18, 23
United States v. Thomas, 39 M.J. 1094 (A.C.M.R. 1994) — § 5-4(B), n. 52
United States v. Thomas, 40 M.J. 726 (N.M.C.M.R. 1994) — § 15-10(C)(3), n. 118

TABLE OF CASES

United States v. Thomas, 39 M.J. 1078 (C.G.C.M.R. 1994) — § 14-3(D)(4), n. 149; § 17-8(B)(1), n. 40
United States v. Thomas, 41 M.J. 665 (A.F.Ct.Crim.App. 1994) — § 13-3(C)(3), nn. 100, 121
United States v. Thomas, 41 M.J. 873 (N.M.Ct.Crim.App. 1995) — § 17-11, n. 1; § 11-2(A)(3), n. 21
United States v. Thomas, 43 M.J. 550 (N.M.Ct.Crim.App.1995) — § 15-10(B), n. 58; § 15-13, n. 6; § 15-2(B)(3), n. 53
United States v. Thomas, 43 M.J. 626 (A.F.Ct.Crim.App. 1995) — § 13-3(C)(1), nn. 35, 36; § 13-3(C)(2), n. 91; § 13-3(C)(3), n. 105
United States v. Thompson, 2 C.M.A. 460, 9 C.M.R. 90 (1953) — § 2-2(D), n. 68
United States v. Thompson, 39 C.M.R. 537 (A.B.R. 1968). R.C.M. 916(b) — § 2-2(E)(4), n. 84
United States v. Thompson, 22 C.M.A. 448, 47 C.M.R. 489 (1973) — § 15-2(F), n. 165
United States v. Thompson, 1 M.J. 692 (N.C.M.R. 1975) — § 6-1(B), n. 63
United States v. Thompson, 3 M.J. 966 (N.C.M.R. 1977) — § 17-8(B), nn. 16, 17
United States v. Thompson, 5 M.J. 28 (C.M.A. 1978) — § 15-4(B), n. 10
United States v. Thompson, 21 M.J. 854 (A.C.M.R. 1986) — § 4-8(B), n. 13
United States v. Thompson, 22 M.J. 40 (C.M.A. 1986) — § 2-4(E), n. 46
United States v. Thompson, 25 M.J. 662 (A.F.C.M.R. 1987) — § 17-8(B)(3), n. 74
United States v. Thompson, 26 M.J. 512 (A.C.M.R. 1988) — § 17-8(B)(3), n. 82
United States v. Thompson, 28 M.J. 769 (A.C.M.R. 1989) — § 13-3(J), n. 264
United States v. Thompson, 29 M.J. 541 (A.F.C.M.R. 1989) — § 15-2(D), n. 128
United States v. Thompson, 30 M.J. 577 (A.C.M.R. 1990) — § 5-3(F), n. 24
United States v. Thompson, 31 M.J. 125 (C.M.A. 1990) — § 15-14(C), n. 48
United States v. Thompson, 31 M.J. 667 (A.C.M.R. 1990) — § 4-16, n. 17; § 6-1, n. 36; § 6-1(B)(2), n. 84
United States v. Thompson, 31 M.J. 781 (A.C.M.R. 1990) — § 5-4(B), n. 42
United States v. Thompson, 33 M.J. 218 (C.M.A. 1991) — § 5-3(F), n. 13
United States v. Thompson, 34 M.J. 287 (C.M.A. 1992) — § 2-7(C), n. 42
United States v. Thompson, 37 M.J. 601 (A.C.M.R. 1993) — § 4-16, n. 14
United States v. Thompson, 37 M.J. 1023 (A.C.M.R. 1993) — § 15-13, nn. 6, 15, 32; § 16-8(B), n. 18
United States v. Thompson, 41 M.J. 895 (Army Ct.Crim.App. 1995) — § 3-3(C), n. 27 Art. 15(f); § 16-5(B), n. 19
United States v. Thorn, 36 M.J. 955 (A.F.C.M.R. 1993) — § 17-4, n. 27; § 7-2(A)(1), n. 16; § 17-15(B), n. 33
United States v. Thornton, 16 M.J. 1011 (A.C.M.R. 1983) — § 7-2, n. 4
United States v. Thornton, 32 M.J. 112 (C.M.A. 1991) — § 16-5(D)(3), n. 77
United States v. Thorton, 8 C.M.A. 57, 23 C.M.R. 281 (1957) — § 15-20, n. 22
United States v. Thrower, 36 M.J. 613 (A.F.C.M.R. 1992) — § 5-4(B), n. 52; § 15-2(A), n. 8
United States v. Thun, 36 M.J. 468 (C.M.A. 1993) — § 2-2(B), nn. 10, 15
United States v. Tibbetts, 1 M.J. 1024 (N.C.M.R. 1976) — § 5-4(B), n. 23
United States v. Tibbs, 15 C.M.A. 350, 35 C.M.R. 322 (1965) — § 13-3(C)(2), n. 54
United States v. Tiede & Rusk, 86 F.R.D. 227 (U.S. Court for Berlin) — § 4-11(A), n. 31; § 11-2(D)(2), n. 91
United States v. Tiggs, 40 C.M.R. 352 (A.B.R. 1968) — § 2-4(A), n. 3; § 2-4(F), n. 53
United States v. Tillery, 26 M.J. 799 (A.C.M.R. 1988) — § 15-2(B)(3), n. 74
United States, Tillman v.
United States v. Timberlake, 7 18 M.J. 371 (C.M.A. 1984) — § 2-5, n. 7

TABLE OF CASES

United States v. Timberlake, 18 M.J. 371 (C.M.A. 1984) — § 2-5, n. 5
United States v. Timmerman, 28 M.J. 531 (A.F.C.M.R. 1989) — § 15-16(A), n. 9
United States v. Timmons, 13 M.J. 431 (C.M.A. 1982) — § 16-2(F), n. 53; § 16-9, n. 4
United States v. Timoney, 34 M.J. 1108 (A.C.M.R. 1992) — § 5-3(F), n. 17
United States v. Tinker, 10 C.M.A. 292, 27 C.M.R. 366 (1959) — § 2-4(C), n. 38
United States v. Tipton, 23 M.J. 338 (C.M.A. 1987) — § 16-4(B), n. 19
United States v. Tipton, 34 M.J. 1153 (A.C.M.R. 1992) — § 15-2(B)(3), n. 79
United States v. Tobita, 3 C.M.A. 267, 12 C.M.R. 23 (1953) — § 16-6, n. 18
United States v. Toledo, 15 M.J. 255 (C.M.A. 1983) — § 11-4, n. 2
United States v. Toledo, 25 M.J. 270 (C.M.A. 1987) — § 5-4(B), n. 42
United States v. Tolkach, 14 M.J. 239 (C.M.A. 1982) — § 2-4(C), n. 38
United States v. Tomaszewski, 8 C.M.A. 266, 24 C.M.R. 76 (1957) — § 7-2(A)(2), n. 32
United States v. Tomchek, 4 M.J. 66 (C.M.J. 1977) — § 8-3(A), n. 5; § 12-2(H), n. 109
United States v. Tomlinson, 7 M.J. 667 (A.C.M.R. 1979) — § 4-11(A), n. 26
United States v. Tompkins, 30 M.J. 1090 (N.M.C.M.R. 1989) — § 15-10(B), n. 58; § 9-2(B)(1), nn. 39, 40
United States v. Toomey, 39 C.M.R. 969 (A.F.B.R. 1969) — § 13-3(N)(3), n. 408
United States v. Tornowski, 29 M.J. 578 (A.F.C.M.R. 1989) — § 11-2(A)(3), n. 28
United States v. Toro, 34 M.J. 506 (A.F.C.M.R. 1991) — § 15-10(A), n. 7; § 15-11, n. 3
United States v. Toro, 37 M.J. 313 (C.M.A. 1993) — § 16-8(B), nn. 25, 26
United States v. Torres, 7 M.J. 102 (C.M.A. 1979) — § 4-5(A)(3), n. 11
United States v. Torres, 25 M.J. 555 (A.C.M.R. 1987) — § 17-8(B)(3), n. 77
United States v. Towers, 24 M.J. 143 (C.M.A. 1987) — § 12-2(H), n. 102; § 15-10(B), nn. 39, 69
United States v. Townsend, 12 M.J. 861 (A.F.C.M.R. 1981) — § 8-3(C)(4), n. 151; § 15-10(C)(1), n. 88
United States v. Townsend, 23 M.J. 848 (A.F.C.M.R. 1987) — § 10-5(A)(2), n. 18
United States v. Townsend, 34 M.J. 882 (C.G.C.M.R. 1992) — § 15-2(B)(3), n. 74
United States v. Toy, 32 M.J. 753 (A.C.M.R. 1991) — § 17-3, n. 5; § 17-3(B), n. 35
United States v. Trahan, 11 M.J. 566 (A.F.C.M.R. 1981) — § 8-2(A), n. 3
United States v. Trakowski, 10 M.J. 792 (A.F.C.M.R. 1981) — § 12-2(H), n. 104; § 7-2(A)(1), n. 21; § 8-3(B)(1), n. 49
United States v. Travers, 25 M.J. 61 (C.M.A. 1987) — § 15-3, nn. 2, 12
United States v. Traxler, 39 M.J. 476 (C.M.A. 1994) — § 2-4(F), n. 51
United States v. Treakle, 18 M.J. 646 (A.C.M.R. 1984) — § 6-3(A), nn. 4, 11; § 6-5(B), n. 25; § 6-6(C), n. 15
United States v. Trede, 2 C.M.A. 581, 10 C.M.R. 79 (1953) — § 15-4(D), n. 30
United States v. Trimble, 30 M.J. 1133 (N.M.C.M.R. 1990) — § 14-3(B)(2), n. 72
United States v. Trimper, 26 M.J. 534 (A.F.C.M.R. 1988) — § 13-4(A), n. 17; § 10-4(A)(4), nn. 18, 27; § 10-4(B)(1), n. 32
United States v. Trimper, 28 M.J. 460 (C.M.A. 1989) — § 13-4, n. 4; § 10-4(B)(4), n. 46
United States v. Tripp, 38 M.J. 554 (A.F.C.M.R. 1993) — § 15-2(B)(3), n. 47; § 17-15(B), n. 31
United States v. Troglin, 21 C.M.A. 183, 44 C.M.R. 237 (1972) — § 9-2, n. 6; § 9-2(B)(1), n. 51
United States v. Trottier, 9 M.J. 337 (C.M.A. 1980) — § 1-8(D)(3); § 4-11(B), nn. 38-40; § 4-16
United States v. Troublefield, 17 M.J. 696 (A.C.M.R. 1983) — § 9-2(C), n. 81
United States v. Troxell, 12 C.M.A. 6, 30 C.M.R. 6 (1960) — § 13-3(B), n. 9; § 2-2(E)(6), n. 100
United States v. True, 28 M.J. 1 (C.M.A. 1989) — § 13-2(G)(2), n. 81

TABLE OF CASES

United States v. True, 28 M.J. 1057 (N.M.C.M.R. 1989) — § 11-2(A)(3), n. 28
United States v. Truitt, 32 M.J. 1010 (A.C.M.R. 1991) — § 15-14(B), n. 41; § 15-15, n. 18
United States v. Trujillo, 37 M.J. 798 (C.G.C.M.R. 1993) — § 14-3(C), n. 132
United States v. Truman, 19 C.M.A. 504, 42 C.M.R. 106 (1970) — § 15-14(D), n. 53
United States v. Tu, 30 M.J. 587 (A.C.M.R. 1990) — § 17-8(B)(2), nn. 62, 67
United States v. Tubbs, 34 M.J. 654 (A.C.M.R. 1992) — § 5-4(B), n. 46
United States v. Tucker, 16 C.M.A. 318, 36 C.M.R. 474 (1966) — § 15-10(B), n. 52
United States v. Tucker, 1 M.J. 463 (C.M.A. 1976) — § 4-11(A), n. 10
United States v. Tucker, 17 M.J. 1004 (N.M.C.M.R. 1984) — § 6-2(B), n. 9
United States v. Tucker, 20 M.J. 52 (C.M.A. 1985) — § 13-2(G)(2), n. 113
United States v. Tucker, 20 M.J. 863 (A.F.C.M.R. 1985) — § 6-5(B), n. 28; § 6-6(C), nn. 13, 15
United States v. Tucker, 20 M.J. 602 (N.M.C.M.R. 1985) — § 13-3(H), n. 246
United States v. Tucker, 29 M.J. 915 (A.C.M.R. 1989) — § 17-15(B), n. 32
United States v. Tuggle, 34 M.J. 89 (C.M.A. 1992) — § 16-3(D), n. 67
United States v. Tuner, 39 M.J. 259 (C.M.A. 1994) — § 15-13, n. 12
United States v. Tunnell, 23 M.J. 110 (C.M.A. 1986) — § 13-3(B), nn. 9, 20-22
United States v. Turbeville, 32 C.M.R. 745 (C.G.C.M.R. 1962) — § 15-15, n. 8
United States v. Turcsik, 13 M.J. 442 (C.M.A. 1982) — § 11-2(E)(2), n. 122; § 17-9(B)n. 38
United States v. Turk, 24 M.J. 277 (C.M.A. 1987) — § 13-3(C)(3), n. 160
United States v. Turk, 22 M.J. 740 (N.M.C.M.R. 1987) — § 13-3(C)(3), n. 159
United States v. Turman, 25 C.M.R. 710 (N.B.R. 1957) — § 11-3(B)(1), n. 16
United States v. Turner, 9 C.M.A. 124, 25 C.M.R. 386 (1958) — § 15-10(B), n. 47
United States v. Turner, 20 C.M.A. 167, 43 C.M.R. 7 (1970) — § 12-3(A), n. 33
United States v. Turner, 15 M.J. 754 (A.F.C.M.R. 1983) — § 17-3(B), n. 34; § 17-15(B), n. 31
United States v. Turner, 17 M.J. 997 (A.C.M.R. 1984) — § 15-13, n. 6
United States v. Turner, 25 M.J. 324 (C.M.A. 1987) — § 17-15(B), n. 17
United States v. Turner, 28 M.J. 487 (C.M.A. 1989) — § 11-2(A)(3), nn. 31, 34, 35, 37
United States v. Turner, 28 M.J. 536 (C.G.C.M.R. 1989) — § 6-1(C)(3), n. 165
United States v. Turner, 28 M.J. 556 (C.G.C.M.R. 1989) — § 16-2(D), n. 39
United States v. Turner, 30 M.J. 1183 (A.F.C.M.R. 1990) — § 15-12, n. 3; § 15-14(A), n. 16; § 16-8(B), n. 24
United States v. Turner, 33 M.J. 40 (C.M.A. 1991) — § 5-3(D)(1), n. 118
United States v. Turner, 34 M.J. 1123 (A.F.C.M.R. 1992) — § 16-2(B), n. 14
United States v. Turner, 35 M.J. 787 (A.C.M.R. 1992) — § 14-3(D)(5), n. 175
United States v. Turner, 39 M.J. 259 (C.M.A. 1994) — § 15-11, n. 2
United States v. Turner, 42 M.J. 783 (N.M.Ct.Crim.App. 1995) — § 15-16(B), n. 19
United States v. Tyler, 145 U.S. 244 (1882) — § 4-8(D), n. 63
United States v. Tyler, 14 M.J. 811 (A.C.M.R. 1982) — § 13-3(J), n. 265
United States v. Tyler, 34 M.J. 293 (C.M.A. 1992) — § 15-2(B)(3), n. 89
United States v. Tyler, 36 M.J. 641 (A.C.M.R. 1992) — § 15-2(B)(3), nn. 33, 64
United States v. Tyson, 2 M.J. 583 (N.C.M.R. 1976) — § 9-2(B)(1), n. 41
United States v. Universal C.S.T. Credit Corp., 344 U.S. 218 (1952) — § 6-1(C)(3), n. 147
United States v. Upchurch, 23 M.J. 501 (A.F.C.M.R. 1986) — § 9-2(C), n. 75; § 9-2(A)(2), n. 24
United States v. Urbina, 14 M.J. 962 (A.C.M.R. 1982) — § 15-2(B)(3), n. 48
United States v. Ureta, 41 M.J. 571 (A.F.Ct.Crim.App. 1994) — § 15-4(C), n. 19

TABLE OF CASES

United States v. Valead, 30 M.J. 634 (N.M.C.M.R. 1990) — § 16-3(C), n. 47
United States v. Valenzuela, 24 M.J. 934 (A.C.M.R. 1987) — § 5-3(D)(1), n. 131
United States v. Valenzuela-Bernal, 458 U.S. 858 (1982) — § 11-2(A)(1), n. 6; § 11-2(A)(2), n. 18; § 15-2(B)(3), n. 36
United States v. Vallenthine, 2 M.J. 1170 (N.C.M.R. 1975) — § 2-3(C), n. 28
United States v. Van Beek, 47 C.M.R. 98 (A.C.M.R. 1973) — § 2-3, n. 7; § 2-3(A), n. 10
United States v. Van Horn, 26 M.J. 434 (C.M.A. 1988) — § 11-2(A)(3), nn. 21, 24, 29
United States v. Van Metre, 29 M.J. 765 (A.C.M.R. 1989) — § 5-10(A), n. 1; § 5-10(B), n. 10
United States v. Van Slate, 14 M.J. 872 (N.M.C.M.R. 1982) — § 5-9(E), n. 55
United States v. Van Steenwyk, 21 M.J. 795 (N.M.C.M.R. 1985) — § 2-5, n. 2; § 2-8(A), n. 8; § 8-3(C)(4), n. 158; § 13-3(N)(2), n. 350
United States v. Van Syoc, 36 M.J. 461 (C.M.A. 1993) — § 15-14(B), nn. 25, 30
United States v. Van Tessel, 38 M.J. 91 (C.M.A. 1993) — § 17-21, nn. 1, 6
United States v. Vanderlip, 28 M.J. 1070 (N.M.C.M.R. 1989) — § 13-3(D), n. 182; § 15-13, n. 25; § 16-8(C), n. 43
United States v. Vandermark, 14 M.J. 690 (N.M.C.M.R. 1982) — § 15-12(A), n. 4
United States v. Vanderweir, 25 M.J. 263 (C.M.A. 1987) — § 10-4(B)(5), n. 54
United States v. Vandewoestyne, 41 M.J. 587 (A.F. Ct. Crim. App. 1994) — § 13-4(A), n. 10
United States v. Vanzandt, 14 M.J. 332 (C.M.A. 1982) — § 2-7(B), n. 24
United States v. Vardiman, 35 M.J. 132 (C.M.A. 1992) — § 14-3(D)(5), n. 175
United States v. Vargas, 29 M.J. 968 (A.C.M.R. 1990) — § 9-2(B)(1), n. 39; § 16-5(D)(1), n. 61
United States v. Varraso, 15 M.J. 793 (A.C.M.R. 1983) — § 5-4(B), n. 51
United States v. Vasquez, 19 M.J. 729 (N.M.C.M.R. 1984) — § 12-2(F)(2), n. 55
United States v. Vaughn, 36 M.J. 645 (A.C.M.R. 1992) — § 14-3(D)(5), n. 175
United States v. Vaughters, 42 M.J. 564 (A.F.Ct.Crim.App. 1995) — § 5-4(B), n. 49
United States v. Vega, 29 M.J. 892 (A.F.C.M.R. 1989) — § 2-7(B), n. 19; § 16-5(D)(4), n. 100
United States v. Vega, 39 M.J. 79 (C.M.A. 1994) — § 14-3(D)(4), n. 153; § 14-3(D)(5), n. 175
United States v. Vega-Cancel, 19 M.J. 899 (A.C.M.R. 1985) — § 11-2(A)(2), n. 10
United States v. Velis, 7 M.J. 699 (N.C.M.R. 1979) — § 12-4, n. 16; § 17-4, n. 7
United States v. Vendivel, 37 M.J. 854 (A.F.C.M.R. 1993) — § 13-3(C)(3), n. 97
United States v. Ventura, 36 M.J. 832 (A.C.M.R. 1993) — § 2-6, n. 4
United States v. Verdi, 5 M.J. 330 (C.M.A. 1978) — § 2-4(A), n. 12; § 2-4(C), n. 39; § 13-3(N)(4), n. 427
United States v. Vesich, 726 F.2d 168 (5th Cir. 1984) — § 13-5(F), n. 17
United States v. Vicencio, 44 C.M.R. 323 (A.C.M.R. 1971) — § 11-3(B)(1), n. 11
United States v. Vickers, 13 M.J. 403 (C.M.A. 1982) — § 16-5, n. 1; § 16-5(D)(3), n. 78; § 16-5(D)(5), n. 110
United States v. Victorian, 31 M.J. 830 (N.M.C.M.R. 1990) — § 2-4(B), n. 24
United States v. Vidal, 45 C.M.R. 540 (A.C.M.R. 1972) — § 2-2(C)(3), n. 34
United States v. Vidal, 23 M.J. 319 (C.M.A. 1987) — § 5-4(B), n. 50; § 6-1(B), n. 69; § 15-15, n. 14
United States v. Vietor, 10 M.J. 69 (C.M.A. 1980) — § 11-2(B)(1), nn. 51, 63
United States v. Vigilito, 22 C.M.A. 394, 47 C.M.R. 331 (1973) — § 6-1(C)(2), n. 127
United States v. Villamil-Perez, 32 M.J. 341 (C.M.A. 1991) — § 5-10(A), n. 1; § 5-10(B), n. 11
United States v. Villamonte-Marquez, 462 U.S. 579 (1983) — § 5-3(C)(3), n. 72

TABLE OF CASES

United States v. Villines, 9 M.J. 807 (N.C.M.R. 1980) — § 8-3(B)(3), n. 92
United States v. Villines, 13 M.J. 46 (C.M.A. 1982) — § 13-3(H), n. 233; § 11-2(E)(1), n. 107; § 11-2(E)(3), n. 128
United States v. Vincent, 15 M.J. 613 (N.M.C.M.R. 1982) — § 5-3(D)(1), n. 128
United States v. Vines, 15 M.J. 247 (C.M.A. 1983) — § 17-15, n. 4
United States v. Vinson, 33 M.J. 1073 (A.C.M.R. 1991) — § 14-3(B)(2), nn. 77, 81
United States v. Vinyard, 3 M.J. 551 (A.C.M.R. 1977) — § 16-3(D), n. 67
United States v. Viola, 26 M.J. 822 (A.C.M.R. 1988) — § 11-2(A)(1), nn. 6, 7
United States v. Visser, 40 M.J. 86 (C.M.A. 1994) — § 5-3(A), n. 28; § 5-3(B), n. 45
United States v. Vitale, 34 M.J. 210 (C.M.A. 1992) — § 5-4(B), n. 46
United States v. Vith, 34 M.J. 277 (C.M.A. 1992) — § 5-4(C), n. 56; § 17-9(B), n. 38
United States v. Viverito, 34 M.J. 872 (A.C.M.R. 1992) — § 14-3(B)(3), n. 101
United States v. Vogan, 32 M.J. 959 (A.C.M.R. 1991) — § 13-3(C)(3), n. 100
United States v. Vogan, 35 M.J. 32 (C.M.A. 1992) — § 13-3(C)(1), nn. 37, 47; § 13-3(C)(3), n. 100
United States v. Volmar, 15 M.J. 339 (C.M.A. 1983) — § 16-8(C), nn. 36, 39
United States v. Voorhees, 4 C.M.A. 509, 16 C.M.R. 83 (C.M.A. 1954) — § 13-3(N)(3), n. 377
United States v. Voyles, 28 M.J. 831 (N.M.C.M.R. 1989) — § 6-1, n. 44; § 13-3(C)(3), n. 109
United States v. Vuitch, 402 U.S. 62 (1971) — § 2-4(C), n. 39
United States v. Wactor, 30 M.J. 821 (A.C.M.R. 1990) — § 13-3(C)(3), n. 159
United States v. Wade, 388 U.S. 218 (1967) — § 5-5, n. 8
United States v. Wager, 10 M.J. 546 (N.C.M.R. 1980) — § 7-2(A)(1), n. 16
United States v. Waggoner, 6 M.J. 77 (C.M.A. 1978) — § 15-9, n. 17
United States v. Wagner, 5 M.J. 461 (C.M.A. 1978) — § 4-5(A)(2); § 4-5(A)(2), nn. 3, 4
United States v. Wagner, 35 M.J. 721 (A.F.C.M.R. 1992) — § 5-4(C), n. 59
United States v. Wagner, 39 M.J. 832 (A.C.M.R. 1994) — § 13-3(C)(3), n. 106
United States v. Wahnon, 1 M.J. 144 (C.M.A. 1975) — § 14-3(A)(3), n. 34; § 14-3(B)(2), n. 97
United States v. Wai, 3 C.M.R. 728 (A.F.B.R. 1952) — § 15-4(C), n. 26
United States v. Waits, 32 M.J. 274 (C.M.A. 1991) — § 6-1(C)(3), n. 139
United States v. Wakeman, 25 M.J. 644 (A.C.M.R. 1987) — § 6-1(C)(2), n. 131
United States v. Walbert, 32 C.M.R. 945 (A.F.B.R. 1963) — § 15-10(B), n. 49
United States v. Waldrup, 30 M.J. 1126 (N.M.C.M.R. 1989) — § 10-4(B)(3), n. 44
United States v. Wales, 31 M.J. 301 (C.M.A. 1990) — § 2-8(B), nn. 16, 19
United States v. Wales, 35 M.J. 501 (A.F.C.M.R. 1992) — § 13-3(C)(3), n. 133
United States v. Walk, 26 M.J. 665 (A.F.C.M.R. 1987) — § 6-5(A), n. 10; § 6-5(C), n. 54
United States v. Walker, 7 C.M.A. 669, 23 C.M.R. 133 (1957) — § 15-14(C), n. 50
United States v. Walker, 20 C.M.A. 241, 43 C.M.R. 81 (1971) — § 13-5(A), n. 5
United States v. Walker, 7 M.J. 976 (N.C.M.R. 1979) — § 17-7, n. 5
United States v. Walker, 21 M.J. 74 (C.M.A. 1985) — § 2-8(D), n. 41; § 6-1(C)(3), n. 145
United States v. Walker, 20 M.J. 971 (N.M.C.M.R. 1985) — § 17-4(A), n. 43
United States v. Walker, 23 M.J. 740 (A.C.M.R. 1987) — § 4-11(B), n. 40
United States v. Walker, 25 M.J. 713 (C.M.A. 1987) — § 10-2(B), n. 23
United States v. Walker, 26 M.J. 886 (A.F.C.M.R. 1988) — § 2-2(B), n. 10
United States v. Walker, 27 M.J. 878 (A.C.M.R. 1989) — § 5-10(D), n. 39
United States v. Walker, 34 M.J. 264 (C.M.A. 1992) — § 14-3(D)(3), n. 140
United States v. Walker, 38 M.J. 678 (A.F.C.M.R. 1993) — § 15-2(B)(3), n. 46
United States v. Walker, 39 M.J. 731 (N.M.C.M.R. 1994) — § 15-16(A), n. 11
United States v. Walker, 41 M.J. 462 (1995) — § 2-2(B), n. 10

TABLE OF CASES

United States v. Wall, 15 M.J. 531 (A.F.C.M.R. 1982) — § 5-10(D), n. 44
United States v. Wallace, 19 C.M.A. 146, 41 C.M.R. 146 (1969) — § 2-2(B), n. 16
United States v. Wallace, 2 M.J. 1 (C.M.A. 1976) — § 5-8(A), n. 12
United States v. Wallace, 14 M.J. 1019 (A.C.M.R. 1982) — § 13-5(H), n. 64
United States v. Wallace, 14 M.J. 869 (C.G.C.M.R. 1982) — § 5-9(B), n. 12; § 6-2(A), n. 3
United States v. Wallace, 28 M.J. 640 (A.F.C.M.R. 1989) — § 17-3(B), n. 36
United States v. Wallace, 33 M.J. 561 (A.C.M.R. 1991) — § 2-6(B), n. 34
United States v. Wallace, 34 M.J. 353 (C.M.A. 1992) — § 5-7, nn. 7, 18; § 5-3(C)(7), n. 101
United States v. Wallace, 35 M.J. 897 (A.C.M.R. 1992) — § 16-9, n. 5
United States v. Wallace, 39 M.J. 284 (C.M.A. 1994) — § 6-3(B), n. 14; § 6-4(A), n. 3
United States v. Waller, 24 M.J. 266 (C.M.A. 1987) — § 6-2(B), n. 10; § 13-3(B), n. 15
United States v. Walls, 1 M.J. 734 (A.F.C.M.R. 1975) — § 2-2(C)(3), n. 35
United States v. Walls, 8 M.J. 666 (A.C.M.R. 1979) — § 7-2, n. 7; § 9-2(B)(1), n. 47
United States v. Walsh, 36 M.J. 666 (N.M.C.M.R. 1992) — § 17-2(B)(4), n. 95
United States v. Walter, 20 C.M.A. 367, 43 C.M.R. 207 (1971) — § 16-2(C), nn. 30-33
United States v. Walter, 39 M.J. 1067 (A.C.M.R. 1994) — § 5-10(D), nn. 37, 39
United States v. Walters, 5 M.J. 829 (A.C.M.R. 1978) — § 9-2(A)(2), n. 24
United States v. Walters, 30 M.J. 1290 (N.M.C.M.R. 1990) — § 11-2(E)(2), n. 122; § 17-9(B), n. 38
United States v. Walters, 42 M.J. 760 (Army Ct. Crim. App. 1995) — § 15-2(B)(3), nn. 100, 103, 104
United States v. Walther, 30 M.J. 829 (N.M.C.M.R. 1990) — § 16-12, n. 13; § 14-3(D)(4), n. 147
United States v. Walzer, 6 M.J. 856 (N.C.M.R. 1979) — § 15-12, n. 3
United States v. Ward, 48 C.M.R. 588 (C.G.C.M.R. 1974) — § 17-11, n. 3
United States v. Ward, 1 M.J. 18 (C.M.A. 1975) — § 17-9(B), n. 37
United States v. Ward, 1 M.J. 21 (C.M.A. 1975) — § 6-1(B)(3), n. 91
United States v. Ward, 3 M.J. 365 (C.M.A. 1977) — § 12-3(A), nn. 27, 36
United States v. Ward, 16 M.J. 341 (C.M.A. 1983) — § 15-24, n. 1
United States v. Ware, 1 M.J. 282, 284, n. 4 (C.M.A. 1976) — § 13-2(E), n. 45
United States v. Ware, 1 M.J. 282 (C.M.A. 1976) — § 13-2(F), n. 58
United States v. Ware, 5 M.J. 24 (C.M.A. 1978) — § 8-2(B), n. 6
United States v. Ware, 41 M.J. 592 (A.F.Ct.Crim.App. 1994) — § 15-2(D), n. 138; § 15-12(A), n. 12
United States v. Wargo, 11 M.J. 501 (N.C.M.R. 1981) — § 2-2(C)(3), n. 32
United States v. Warner, 25 M.J. 64 (C.M.A. 1987) — § 16-3(D), nn. 57, 60
United States v. Warner, 33 M.J. 522 (A.F.C.M.R. 1991) — § 5-9(E), n. 51; § 13-3(J), n. 265
United States v. Warnock, 34 M.J. 567 (A.C.M.R. 1991) — § 2-6(A), n. 17; § 12-2(H), n. 100
United States v. Warren, 13 M.J. 160 (C.M.A. 1982) — § 2-4(B), n. 24
United States v. Warren, 13 M.J. 278 (C.M.A. 1982) — § 16-8(B), n. 17; § 16-9, n. 13
United States v. Warren, 24 M.J. 656 (A.F.C.M.R. 1987) — § 5-4(B), n. 51
United States v. Wartruba, 35 M.J. 488 (C.M.A. 1992) — § 9-3, n. 8
United States v. Wartsbaugh, 21 C.M.A. 535, 45 C.M.R. 309 (1972) — § 2-4(A), n. 11; § 2-4(B), n. 25; § 2-4(D), n. 43; § 2-4(F), n. 51
United States v. Washington, 8 C.M.A. 588, 25 C.M.R. 92 (1958) — § 15-10(A), n. 18
United States v. Washington, 23 M.J. 679 (A.C.M.R. 1986) — § 14-3(G), n. 201; § 17-3(B), n. 40

TABLE OF CASES

United States v. Washington, 24 M.J. 527 (A.F.C.M.R. 1987) — § 2-2(B), n. 18

United States v. Washington, 29 M.J. 536 (A.F.C.M.R. 1989) — § 15-2(B)(3), n. 56

United States v. Washington, 35 M.J. 774 (A.C.M.R. 1992) — § 12-5, n. 13; § 16-11, n. 1; § 9-2(B)(1), n. 49

United States v. Washington, 39 M.J. 1014 (A.C.M.R. 1994) — § 5-3(B), nn. 38, 41; § 5-3(F), nn. 18, 24

United States v. Washington, 42 M.J. 547 (A.F.Ct.Crim.App. 1995) — § 5-4(B), n. 52; § 5-10(B), n. 8; § 6-5(B), n. 25; § 6-7, n. 15; § 15-2(B)(3), n. 47

United States v. Wasson, 26 M.J. 894 (A.F.C.M.R. 1988) — § 2-3(B), n. 19; § 2-3(C), n. 22

United States v. Watkins, 17 M.J. 783 (A.F.C.M.R. 1983) — § 15-24, n. 2

United States v. Watkins, 21 M.J. 208 (C.M.A. 1986) — § 6-1(C), nn. 94, 102; § 13-3(F), n. 215; § 2-2(C)(3), n. 37

United States v. Watkins, 32 M.J. 1054 (A.C.M.R. 1991) — § 5-3(A), n. 26; § 5-4(B), n. 50

United States v. Watkins, 34 M.J. 344 (C.M.A. 1992) — § 5-4(B), n. 48; § 9-2(A)(2), n. 27

United States v. Watkins, 35 M.J. 709 (N.M.C.M.R. 1992) — § 17-8(B)(3), n. 95

United States v. Watson, 80 F. Supp. 649 (E.D. Va. 1948) — § 13-3(N)(3), n. 408

United States v. Watson, 40 C.M.R. 571 (A.B.R. 1969) — § 2-4(C), n. 35

United States v. Watson, 15 M.J. 784 (A.C.M.R. 1983) — § 15-10(A), n. 29

United States v. Watson, 31 M.J. 49 (C.M.A. 1990) — § 10-4(A)(4), n. 19

United States v. Watson, 37 M.J. 166 (C.M.A. 1993) — § 17-9(B), n. 35

United States v. Wattenbarger, 21 M.J. 41 (C.M.A. 1985) — § 15-2(B)(3), n. 46

United States v. Watts, 36 M.J. 748 (A.C.M.R. 1993) — § 5-10(D), nn. 40, 41

United States, Wayte v.

United States v. Weasler, 43 M.J. 15 (1995) — § 6-4, nn. 1, 2; — § 6-4(A), n. 7; § 6-7, n. 2; § 9-2(B)(1), n. 59

United States v. Weatherspoon, 39 M.J. 762 (A.C.M.R. 1994) — § 16-5(B), n. 8; § 13-3(C)(3), n. 118

United States v. Weaver, 42 C.M.R. 434 (A.C.M.R. 1970) — § 15-20, n. 19

United States v. Weaver, 20 C.M.A. 58, 42 C.M.R. 250 (1970) — § 6-1(C)(3), n. 134

United States v. Webb, 5 M.J. 406 (C.M.A. 1978) — § 16-8(C), n. 36

United States v. Webb, 38 M.J. 62 (C.M.A. 1993) — § 13-4(C), n. 29; § 15-13, n. 11

United States v. Webber, 42 M.J. 675 (A.F.Ct.Crim.App. 1995) — § 11-3(C), n. 78; § 15-22, n. 12; § 11-3(B)(2), nn. 39, 40

United States v. Webel, 16 M.J. 64 (C.M.A. 1983) — § 15-14(C), n. 51; § 16-9, n. 16

United States v. Webster, 1 M.J. 216 (C.M.A. 1975) — § 946; § 10-2(A), nn. 14-16; § 11-2(E)(2), n. 118

United States v. Webster, 24 M.J. 96 (C.M.A. 1987) — § 12-3(A), nn. 8, 13

United States v. Webster, 37 M.J. 670 (C.G.C.M.R. 1993) — § 2-4(C), n. 30

United States v. Weddle, 28 M.J. 649 (A.C.M.R. 1989) — § 5-10(D), n. 35

United States v. Weems, 13 M.J. 609 (A.F.C.M.R. 1982) — § 6-1(B), n. 62

United States v. Weikel, 24 M.J. 666 (A.F.C.M.R. 1987) — § 16-8(C), n. 35

United States v. Weinmann, 37 M.J. 724 (A.F.C.M.R. 1993) — § 15-13, n. 11; § 15-14(B), n. 21

United States v. Weise, 7 M.J. 993 (A.C.M.R. 1979) — § 4-8(A), n. 8

United States, Weiss v.

United States v. Weiss, 36 M.J. 224 (C.M.A. 1992) — § 8-3(A), n. 20

United States v. Weiss, 114 S. Ct. 752 (1994) — § 1-1(B), n. 17

United States, Weissman v.

TABLE OF CASES

United States v. Welch, 25 M.J. 23 (C.M.A. 1987) — § 13-5(L), nn. 97, 98, 105
United States v. Welker, 37 M.J. 1066 (N.M.C.M.R. 1993) — § 15-12(A), n. 7
United States v. Wells, 4 C.M.R. 501 (C.G.B.R. 1952) — § 4-15(C), n. 15
United States v. Wells, 9 C.M.A. 509, 26 C.M.R. 289 (1958) — § 8-5, n. 5
United States v. Wells, 20 M.J. 513 (A.F.C.M.R. 1985) — § 6-1(C)(3), n. 142
United States v. Wendlandt, 39 M.J. 810 (A.C.M.R. 1994) — § 17-9(D), n. 58
United States v. Wentzel, 50 C.M.R. 690 (A.F.C.M.R. 1975) — § 4-11(A), n. 29
United States v. Weshenfelder, 20 C.M.A. 416, 43 C.M.R. 256 (1971) — § 5-3(C)(2), n. 66
United States v. Wesley, 19 M.J. 534 (N.M.C.M.R. 1984) — § 13-3(B), n. 9
United States v. West, 15 C.M.A. 3, 34 C.M.R. 449 (1964) — § 15-20, n. 24
United States v. West, 13 M.J. 800 (A.C.M.R. 1982) — § 13-5(H), n. 65
United States v. West, 27 M.J. 223 (C.M.A. 1988) — § 15-2(E), n. 159; § 15-9, n. 2; § 15-14(A), n. 20
United States v. Westmoreland, 31 M.J. 160 (C.M.A. 1990) — § 15-15, n. 27
United States v. Weymouth, 43 M.J. 329 (1995) — § 6-1(B), n. 58; § 6-1(C)(3), n. 162
United States v. Whalen, 15 M.J. 872 (A.C.M.R. 1983) — § 5-3(C)(2), n. 66
United States v. Wharton, 33 C.M.R. 729 (A.F.B.R. 1963) — § 3-3(C), n. 23; § 6-1, n. 13; § 13-3(G), n. 225
United States v. Whatley, 5 M.J. 39 (C.M.A. 1978) — § 4-11(A), n. 19
United States v. Wheatcraft, 23 M.J. 687 (A.F.C.M.R. 1986) — § 12-2(C), n. 11; § 15-9, n. 5
United States v. Wheaton, 18 M.J. 159 (C.M.A. 1984) — § 3-8(B), n. 9; § 16-5(B), nn. 14, 17
United States v. Wheeler, 28 C.M.R. 212 (C.M.A. 1959) — § 4-8(C)(2), n. 26
United States v. Wheeler, 12 C.M.A. 387, 30 C.M.R. 387 (1961) — § 2-4(A), n. 17; § 13-3(N)(3), n. 403
United States v. Wheeler, 17 C.M.A. 274, 38 C.M.R. 72 (1967) — § 16-9, n. 8
United States v. Wheeler, 21 C.M.A. 468, 45 C.M.R. 242 (1972) — § 11-2(C), n. 75
United States v. Wheeler, 18 M.J. 823 (A.C.M.R. 1984) — § 16-9, n. 10
United States v. Wheeler, 22 M.J. 76 (C.M.A. 1986) — § 5-4(B), n. 52
United States v. Wheeler, 40 M.J. 242 (C.M.A. 1994) — § 6-1(C)(3), n. 161
United States v. Wheeley, 6 M.J. 220 (C.M.A. 1979) — § 4-8(A), n. 8
United States v. Whelehan, 10 M.J. 566 (A.F.C.M.R. 1980) — § 14-3(B)(2), n. 95
United States v. Whidbee, 28 M.J. 823 (C.G.C.M.R. 1989) — § 12-2(F)(3), n. 65; § 15-2(B)(2), n. 28
United States v. Whipple, 4 M.J. 773 (C.G.C.M.R. 1978) — § 5-4(C), n. 59; § 5-4(A)(1), n. 3; § 11-2(E)(1), n. 107
United States v. Whipple, 28 M.J. 314 (C.M.A. 1989) — § 5-3(C)(6), n. 85
United States v. Whitcomb, 34 M.J. 984 (A.C.M.R. 1992) — § 15-2(B)(3), n. 71
United States v. White, 10 C.M.A. 63, 27 C.M.R. 137 (1958) — § 11-2(E)(2), n. 121
United States v. White, 17 C.M.A. 211, 38 C.M.R. 9 (1967) — § 5-9(D), n. 48
United States v. White, 21 C.M.A. 583, 45 C.M.R. 357 (1972) — § 1-7, n. 19; § 12-3(B), n. 47; § 8-3(C)(2), n. 128
United States v. White, 3 M.J. 51 (C.M.A. 1977) — § 14-3(D)(3), n. 141
United States v. White, 3 M.J. 619 (N.C.M.R. 1977) — § 15-13, n. 19
United States v. White, 12 M.J. 643 (A.F.C.M.R. 1981) — § 17-4(A), n. 43
United States v. White, 11 M.J. 712 (N.M.C.M.R. 1981) — § 9-2(B)(1), n. 48
United States v. White, 19 M.J. 662 (C.G.C.M.R. 1984) — § 6-1(C)(1), n. 110
United States v. White, 23 M.J. 84 (C.M.A. 1986) — § 16-5(D)(1), n. 56
United States v. White, 23 M.J. 859 (A.C.M.R. 1987) — § 16-11, n. 8

TABLE OF CASES

United States v. White, 23 M.J. 891 (A.C.M.R. 1987) — § 10-4(B)(5), n. 61
United States v. White, 27 M.J. 264 (C.M.A. 1988) — § 5-3(C)(6), n. 85
United States v. White, 33 M.J. 555 (A.C.M.R. 1991) — § 16-8(A), n. 7; § 16-8(B), n. 19
United States v. White, 36 M.J. 284 (C.M.A. 1993) — § 15-10(B), nn. 55, 67, 69; § 15-10(C)(2), n. 93
United States v. White, 36 M.J. 306 (C.M.A. 1993) — § 16-8(B), n. 19
United States v. White, 40 M.J. 257 (C.M.A. 1994) — § 5-3(C)(6), n. 90
United States v. White, 39 M.J. 796 (N.M.C.M.R. 1994) — § 2-3(A), n. 9; § 2-3(B), n. 18; § 2-6(C), n. 40
United States v. Whitehead, 27 C.M.R. 875 (N.B.R. 1959) — § 15-2(A), n. 3
United States v. Whitehead, 5 M.J. 294 (C.M.A. 1978) — § 5-4(C), n. 56; § 13-3(H), nn. 242, 244; § 11-2(E)(1), n. 106; § 11-2(E)(3), nn. 142, 150
United States v. Whitehead, 30 M.J. 1066 (A.C.M.R. 1990) — § 16-5(D)(3), n. 73
United States v. Whitfield, 35 M.J. 535 (A.C.M.R. 1992) — § 4-16, n. 14; § 6-1, n. 19
United States v. Whiting, 12 M.J. 253 (C.M.A. 1982) — § 5-3, n. 9
United States v. Whitley, 5 C.M.A. 786, 19 C.M.R. 82 (1955) — § 8-3(D), n. 164
United States v. Whitt, 21 M.J. 658 (A.C.M.R. 1985) — § 6-1(B)(2), n. 82; § 7-2(A)(1), n. 29
United States v. Whittier, 14 M.J. 606 (A.F.C.M.R. 1982) — § 5-10(D), n. 28
United States v. Whittle, 34 M.J. 206 (C.M.A. 1992) — § 2-7(B), n. 24
United States v. Wholley, 13 M.J. 574 (N.M.C.M.R. 1982) — § 13-2(G)(2), n. 74
United States v. Wickersham, 14 M.J. 404 (C.M.A. 1983) — § 2-6(A), n. 17
United States v. Widdekke, 19 C.M.A. 576, 42 C.M.R. 178 (1970) — § 6-7, n. 10
United States v. Wiegand, 23 M.J. 644 (A.C.M.R. 1986) — § 2-6, n. 4
United States v. Wierzba, 11 M.J. 742 (A.F.C.M.R. 1981) — § 4-11(A), n. 17
United States v. Wiggers, 25 M.J. 587 (A.C.M.R. 1987) — § 3-8(B), n. 13; § 12-2(H), nn. 100, 101
United States v. Wiles, 30 M.J. 1097 (N.M.C.M.R. 1989) — § 14-3(B)(2), n. 95
United States v. Wiley, 37 M.J. 885 (A.C.M.R. 1993) — § 2-2(B), n. 10
United States v. Wilkerson, 1 M.J. 56 (C.M.A. 1975) — § 17-4(A), n. 50
United States v. Wilkes, 27 M.J. 571 (N.M.C.M.R. 1988) — § 13-3(C)(3), n. 102
United States v. Wilkins, 28 M.J. 992 (A.C.M.R. 1989) — § 4-16, nn. 3, 7-12; § 8-4, n. 9
United States v. Wilkinson, 27 M.J. 645 (A.C.M.R. 1988) — § 13-3(C)(3), n. 102
United States v. Willeford, 5 M.J. 634 (A.F.C.M.R. 1978) — § 5-4(B), nn. 26, 46
United States v. Williams, 2 C.M.A. 430, 9 C.M.R. 60 (1953) — § 5-4(B), n. 27
United States v. Williams, 16 C.M.R. 717 (A.F.B.R. 1954) — § 15-8, n. 3
United States v. Williams, 6 C.M.A. 243, 19 C.M.R. 369 (1955) — § 8-4, n. 7; § 4-14(A)(1), n. 5
United States v. Williams, 11 C.M.A. 459, 29 C.M.R. 275 (1960) — § 8-5, n. 13; § 8-6
United States v. Williams, 12 C.M.A. 81, 30 C.M.R. 81 (1961) — § 13-3(C)(2), n. 58
United States v. Williams, 16 C.M.A. 589, 37 C.M.R. 209 (1967) — § 13-3(C)(2), n. 53
United States v. Williams, 39 C.M.R. 471 (A.B.R. 1968) — § 4-5(A)(4), n. 15
United States v. Williams, 43 C.M.R. 579 (A.C.M.R. 1970) — § 14-3, n. 9; § 14-3(B)(3), n. 112
United States v. Williams, 50 C.M.R. 219 (A.C.M.R. 1975) — § 12-3(B), n. 47; § 8-3(C)(2), n. 128
United States v. Williams, 3 M.J. 155 (C.M.A. 1977) — § 2-4(C), n. 37
United States v. Williams, 3 M.J. 239 (C.M.A. 1977) — § 11-2(A)(1), n. 8
United States v. Williams, 6 M.J. 611 (A.C.M.R. 1978) — § 14-3(B)(2), n. 72
United States v. Williams, 12 M.J. 894 (A.C.M.R. 1982) — § 13-3(C)(2), n. 77
United States v. Williams, 14 M.J. 796 (A.F.C.M.R. 1982) — § 17-4, n. 35

TABLE OF CASES

United States v. Williams, 14 M.J. 994 (N.M.C.M.R. 1982) — § 17-11, n. 5
United States v. Williams, 17 M.J. 207 (C.M.A. 1984) — § 2-6(C), n. 38; § 4-11(A), n. 12
United States v. Williams, 18 M.J. 186 (C.M.A. 1984) — § 16-3(D), n. 63; § 14-3(B)(3), n. 101
United States v. Williams, 21 M.J. 524 (A.C.M.R. 1985) — § 4-8(A), n. 8; § 16-8(C), n. 36
United States v. Williams, 21 M.J. 330 (C.M.A. 1986) — § 15-16(A), n. 9
United States v. Williams, 21 M.J. 360 (C.M.A. 1986) — § 2-2(E)(1), n. 73
United States v. Williams, 22 M.J. 584 (A.C.M.R. 1986) — § 17-14, n. 10; § 17-15(B), n. 19
United States v. Williams, 23 M.J. 525 (A.C.M.R. 1986) — § 15-13, n. 30
United States v. Williams, 23 M.J. 713 (A.C.M.R. 1986) — § 16-6, n. 5
United States v. Williams, 23 M.J. 724 (A.F.C.M.R. 1986) — § 11-2(D)(3), n. 101
United States v. Williams, 23 M.J. 582 (N.M.C.M.R. 1986) — § 2-7(C), n. 43
United States v. Williams, 23 M.J. 362 (C.M.A. 1987) — § 5-4(B), n. 31; § 13-2(C), n. 32
United States v. Williams, 23 M.J. 776 (A.C.M.R. 1987) — § 15-13, n. 15; § 16-8(A), n. 6
United States v. Williams, 26 M.J. 606 (A.C.M.R. 1988) — § 2-6, n. 4; § 2-6(A), n. 17; § 6-1(B)(2), n. 81
United States v. Williams, 26 M.J. 644 (A.C.M.R. 1988) — § 14-2, n. 12; § 16-9, n. 1
United States v. Williams, 27 M.J. 529 (A.F.C.M.R. 1988) — § 16-5(B), n. 9
United States v. Williams, 27 M.J. 671 (A.C.M.R. 1988) — § 14-3(B)(2), n. 100
United States v. Williams, 27 M.J. 710 (A.C.M.R. 1988) — § 14-3(B)(2), n. 100
United States v. Williams, 27 M.J. 758 (A.F.C.M.R. 1988) — § 8-3(B)(2), n. 68
United States v. Williams, 28 M.J. 911 (A.C.M.R. 1989) — § 17-2(B), n. 6; § 15-2(B)(3), n. 88; § 16-5(D)(5), n. 125
United States v. Williams, 29 M.J. 112 (C.M.A. 1989) — § 5-4(A)(2), n. 14
United States v. Williams, 29 M.J. 504 (A.C.M.R. 1989) — § 2-2(C)(3), n. 47
United States v. Williams, 29 M.J. 570 (A.F.C.M.R. 1989) — § 5-9(D), nn. 42, 43, 45; § 5-10(D), n. 32
United States v. Williams, 32 M.J. 1060 (N.M.C.M.R. 1991) — § 17-13, n. 24
United States v. Williams, 35 M.J. 323 (C.M.A. 1992) — § 5-3(D)(1), n. 131
United States v. Williams, 35 M.J. 812 (A.F.C.M.R. 1992) — § 13-4(C), n. 29; § 16-5(D)(4), n. 102
United States v. Williams, 37 M.J. 352 (C.M.A. 1993) — § 17-21, nn. 2, 3; § 17-3(B), n. 41
United States v. Williams, 37 M.J. 972 (A.C.M.R. 1993) — § 2-7(B), n. 23
United States v. Williams, 39 M.J. 555 (A.C.M.R. 1994) — § 11-2(A)(1), n. 1
United States v. Williams, 39 M.J. 758 (A.C.M.R. 1994) — § 5-4(B), n. 42
United States v. Williams, 40 M.J. 216 (C.M.A. 1994) — § 15-12(A), n. 7
United States v. Williams, 40 M.J. 379 (C.M.A. 1994) — § 6-1(C), n. 96; § 13-5(F), n. 31
United States v. Williams, 40 M.J. 809 (A.C.M.R. 1994) — § 8-3(B)(2), n. 68
United States v. Williams, 41 M.J. 134 (C.M.A. 1994) — § 16-5(D)(4), nn. 86, 105
United States v. Williams, 42 M.J. 791 (N.M.Ct.Crim.App.1995) — § 17-11, n. 1
United States v. Williams-Oatman, 38 M.J. 602 (A.C.M.R. 1993) — § 17-8(B)(1), nn. 47-49
United States v. Williamson, 4 M.J. 708 (N.C.M.R. 1977) — § 14-3(C), n. 125
United States v. Williamson, 26 M.J. 835 (A.C.M.R. 1988) — § 5-10(D), n. 34
United States v. Williamson, 28 M.J. 511 (A.C.M.R. 1989) — § 5-3(C)(9), n. 115
United States v. Williamson, 28 M.J. 660 (N.M.C.M.R. 1989) — § 17-15(B)(1), n. 47
United States v. Williamson, 42 M.J. 613 (N.M.Ct.Crim.App. 1995) — § 1-3(D)(2)
United States v. Willingham, 2 C.M.A. 590, 10 C.M.R. 88 (1953) — § 2-2(B), n. 10

TABLE OF CASES

United States v. Willis, 7 M.J. 827 (C.G.C.M.R. 1979) — § 2-2(C)(3), n. 36
United States v. Wills, 20 C.M.A. 8, 42 C.M.R. 200 (1970) — § 4-11(A), n. 8
United States v. Wilson, 30 C.M.R. 630 (N.B.R. 1960) — § 2-2(E)(3), n. 80
United States v. Wilson, 2 M.J. 548 (A.C.M.R. 1976) — § 8-3(A), n. 8; § 15-2(D), n. 137
United States v. Wilson, 4 M.J. 687 (N.C.M.R. 1977) — § 14-3(C), n. 129
United States v. Wilson, 16 M.J. 678 (A.C.M.R. 1983) — § 4-15(C), n. 16; § 8-3(C)(2), nn. 131, 132
United States v. Wilson, 18 M.J. 204 (C.M.A. 1984) — § 16-10, n. 17
United States v. Wilson, 20 M.J. 335 (C.M.A. 1985) — § 17-15(A), nn. 8, 14
United States v. Wilson, 21 M.J. 193 (C.M.A. 1986) — § 8-3(C)(2), n. 132
United States v. Wilson, 26 M.J. 10 (C.M.A. 1988) — § 15-14(B), n. 23; § 15-14(D), n. 54; § 16-9, n. 1
United States v. Wilson, 27 M.J. 555 (A.C.M.R. 1988) — § 15-8, n. 2
United States v. Wilson, 28 M.J. 1054 (N.M.C.M.R. 1989) — § 15-4(A), n. 5
United States v. Wilson, 33 M.J. 512 (A.F.C.M.R. 1991) — § 17-2(B)(3), n. 63; § 17-2(B)(4), n. 95
United States v. Wilson, 33 M.J. 797 (A.C.M.R. 1991) — § 2-4(E), n. 46; § 13-3(N)(3), n. 365
United States v. Wilson, 35 M.J. 473 (C.M.A. 1992) — § 16-2(D), n. 39; § 16-9, n. 4; § 16-5(D)(3), n. 73
United States v. Winchester, 12 C.M.A. 74, 30 C.M.R. 74 (1961) — § 10-3(F), n. 24; § 15-2(B)(4), n. 117
United States v. Wine, 28 M.J. 688 (A.F.C.M.R. 1989) — § 2-4(A), n. 17; § 13-3(N)(2), n. 339
United States v. Wingart, 27 M.J. 128 (C.M.A. 1988) — § 16-4(B), n. 20; § 16-5(D)(4), n. 106; § 16-7, n. 6
United States v. Wingart, 27 M.J. 128 (C.M.A. 1989) — § 16-5(B), n. 7; § 16-5(D)(5), nn. 111, 112
United States v. Winkler, 5 M.J. 835 (A.C.M.R. 1978) — § 14-3(C), n. 129
United States v. Winter, 32 M.J. 901 (A.F.C.M.R. 1991) — § 14-3(D)(5), n. 164
United States v. Winter, 35 M.J. 93 (C.M.A. 1992) — § 14-3(D)(5), nn. 162, 164
United States v. Wirth, 18 M.J. 214 (C.M.A. 1984) — § 15-12, n. 1
United States v. Wirth, 24 M.J. 536 (A.C.M.R. 1987) — § 14-3(D)(3); § 14-3(D)(3), n. 140 See
United States v. Wisemore, 32 M.J. 602 (C.G.C.M.R. 1991) — § 16-2(D), n. 39
United States v. Witherspoon, 12 M.J. 588 (A.C.M.R. 1981) — § 15-12(D), n. 32
United States v. Witherspoon, 16 M.J. 252 (C.M.A. 1983) — § 15-15, n. 9; § 15-16(B), nn. 17, 24
United States v. Witherspoon, 19 M.J. 978 (A.C.M.R. 1985) — § 16-8(C), n. 42; § 9-2(B)(1), n. 45
United States v. Witt, 21 M.J. 637 (A.C.M.R. 1985) — § 16-5(D)(1), nn. 54-56; § 16-5(D)(3), nn. 71, 77
United States v. Wixon, 23 M.J. 570 (A.C.M.R. 1986) — § 5-10(D), n. 41; § 17-8(B)(3), n. 74
United States v. Wojciechowski, 19 M.J. 577 (N.M.C.M.R. 1984) — § 6-2(B), n. 14; § 6-4(B), n. 10; § 7-2(A)(1), n. 16
United States v. Wolff, 5 M.J. 923 (N.C.M.R. 1978) — § 8-3(C)(3), nn. 143, 144
United States v. Wolff, 25 M.J. 752 (N.M.C.M.R. 1987) — § 2-2(B), n. 10
United States v. Wolfson, 36 C.M.R. 722 (A.B.R. 1966) — § 13-3(N)(3), n. 392
United States v. Wolfson, 21 C.M.A. 549, 45 C.M.R. 323 (1972) — § 4-11(A), n. 9
United States v. Woltmann, 22 C.M.R. 737 (C.G.C.B.R. 1956) — § 2-3(B), n. 19

TABLE OF CASES

United States v. Wolzok, 1 M.J. 125 (C.M.A. 1975) — § 13-3(C)(2), n. 74
United States v. Womack, 27 M.J. 630 (A.F.C.M.R. 1988) — § 13-3(N)(4), n. 422
United States v. Womack, 29 M.J. 88 (C.M.A. 1989) — § 2-9(B), nn. 13-17; § 2-9(D), n. 56; § 2-9(C)(2), n. 44; § 13-3(N)(4), n. 417
United States v. Womack, 34 M.J. 876 (A.C.M.R. 1992) — § 14-3(C), nn. 130, 133
United States, Wong Tai v.
United States v. Wood, 18 C.M.A. 291, 40 C.M.R. 3 (1969) — § 16-8(B), n. 9
United States v. Wood, 23 C.M.A. 57, 48 C.M.R. 528 (1974) — § 15-13, n. 17; § 16-8(C), n. 40
United States v. Wood, 29 M.J. 1075 (A.C.M.R. 1990) — § 15-2(D), n. 128; § 15-12(B), nn. 17, 18
United States v. Wood, 36 M.J. 651 (A.C.M.R. 1992) — § 7-2(C), n. 77; § 15-4(A), n. 6; § 15-12(A), n. 9
United States v. Woodard, 24 M.J. 514 (A.F.C.M.R. 1987) — § 9-2(B)(1), n. 49
United States v. Woodard, 39 M.J. 1022 (A.C.M.R. 1994) — § 15-12(C), n. 23; § 16-4(B), n. 18
United States v. Woodley, 20 C.M.A. 357, 43 C.M.R. 197 (1971) — § 2-4(B), n. 28; § 2-4(D), n. 43
United States v. Woods, 21 M.J. 856 (A.C.M.R. 1986) — § 17-15(A), n. 14
United States v. Woods, 26 M.J. 372 (C.M.A. 1988) — § 9-4, n. 4
United States v. Woods, 25 M.J. 916 (N.M.C.M.R. 1988) — § 14-3(B)(2), n. 77
United States v. Woods, 27 M.J. 749 (N.M.C.M.R. 1988) — § 13-3(F), n. 217
United States v. Woods, 28 M.J. 318 (C.M.A. 1989) — § 2-6(A), n. 17; § 2-9(C), n. 25; § 2-9(D), nn. 64, 67; § 2-9(C)(3), n. 54
United States v. Woods, 39 M.J. 1074 (A.C.M.R. 1994) — § 15-10(C)(3), n. 118
United States v. Wooten, 34 M.J. 141 (C.M.A. 1992) — § 5-3(A), n. 21; § 5-3(F), n. 13
United States v. Wordlow, 19 M.J. 981 (A.C.M.R. 1985) — § 16-8(C), n. 42; § 9-2(B)(1), n. 45
United States v. Worrell, 3 M.J. 817 (A.F.C.M.R. 1977) — § 15-15, n. 9; § 8-3(C)(1), n. 122
United States v. Worsham, 10 C.M.R. 653 (A.F.B.R. 1953) — § 17-3(A), n. 23
United States v. Wrenn, 36 M.J. 1188 (N.M.C.M.R. 1993) — § 6-1(C), n. 102
United States, Wright v.
United States v. Wright, 10 C.M.A. 36, 27 C.M.R. 110 (1958) — § 7-2(A)(2), n. 31
United States v. Wright, 40 C.M.R. 616 (A.C.M.R. 1969) — § 7-2(E), n. 100
United States v. Wright, 2 M.J. 9 (C.M.A. 1976) — § 4-15(B), n. 11
United States v. Wright, 5 M.J. 106 (C.M.A. 1978) — § 2-6(A), n. 17
United States v. Wright, 20 M.J. 518 (A.C.M.R. 1985) — § 16-5(C), nn. 39, 40; § 16-5(D)(2), n. 69; § 16-5(D)(4), n. 84; § 16-5(D)(5), n. 118
United States v. Wright, 25 M.J. 827 (A.C.M.R. 1988) — § 14-3(B)(2), n. 75
United States v. Wright, 35 M.J. 899 (A.C.M.R. 1992) — § 16-3(D), n. 60
United States v. Wright, 42 M.J. 283 (1995) — § 15-2(B)(3), n. 68
United States v. Wynn, 23 M.J. 726 (A.F.C.M.R. 1986) — § 17-4, n. 5; § 5-4(A)(3), n. 20
United States v. Wysong, 9 C.M.A. 249, 26 C.M.R. 29 (1958) — § 10-3(B), n. 10
United States v. Yager, 7 M.J. 171 (C.M.A. 1979) — § 4-15(C), n. 12; § 8-3(C)(4), n. 151
United States v. Yancey, 36 M.J. 859 (A.C.M.R. 1993) — § 2-6(B), n. 33
United States v. Yandell, 13 M.J. 616 (A.F.C.M.R. 1982) — § 5-3(C)(8), n. 110
United States v. Yandle, 34 M.J. 890 (N.M.C.M.R. 1992) — § 15-14(B), n. 25
United States v. Yanke, 23 M.J. 144 (C.M.A. 1987) — § 16-9, n. 16; § 16-5(D)(1), n. 56
United States v. Yarborough, 50 C.M.R. 149 (A.F.C.M.R. 1975) — § 5-3(C)(5), n. 81

TABLE OF CASES

United States v. Yarborough, 14 M.J. 968 (A.C.M.R. 1982) — § 15-10(A), n. 20; § 15-10(B), n. 68
United States v. Yarbough, 30 M.J. 1114 (N.M.C.M.R. 1989) — § 16-5(B), nn. 15, 26
United States v. Yarbough, 33 M.J. 122 (C.M.A. 1991) — § 3-8(B), n. 17
United States v. Yardley, 24 M.J. 719 (A.C.M.R. 1987) — § 15-10(B), n. 53
United States v. Yarn, 32 M.J. 736 (A.C.M.R. 1991) — § 12-4, n. 14; § 15-2(A), n. 6
United States v. Yatchak, 35 M.J. 379 (C.M.A. 1992) — § 16-3(C), n. 47
United States v. Yates, 25 M.J. 582 (A.C.M.R. 1987) — § 4-15(C), n. 18; § 8-3(C)(4), n. 160
United States v. Yates, 28 M.J. 60 (C.M.A. 1989) — § 4-14(A)(1), n. 7
United States v. Yates, 39 M.J. 737 (N.M.C.M.R. 1994) — § 17-8(B)(3), n. 75
United States, Yeargain v.
United States v. Yeckinevich, 26 M.J. 833 (A.F.C.M.R. 1988) — § 16-5(C), n. 43
United States v. Yelverton, 40 C.M.R. 655 (A.B.R. 1969) — § 6-1, n. 18; § 6-1(C)(1), nn. 105, 108
United States v. Yeoman, 25 M.J. 1 (C.M.A. 1987) — § 5-4(B), n. 52
United States v. Yingling, 20 M.J. 593 (N.M.C.M.R. 1985) — § 13-2(G)(2), nn. 88, 89
United States v. Yocom, 17 C.M.A. 270, 38 C.M.R. 68 (1967) — § 16-9, n. 4
United States v. Yost, 20 M.J. 785 (C.G.C.M.R. 1985) — § 9-2(B), n. 35
United States v. Young, 18 C.M.A. 324, 40 C.M.R. 36 (1969) — § 2-4(B), n. 27
United States v. Young, 44 C.M.R. 670 (A.F.C.M.R. 1971) — § 5-5, n. 7
United States v. Young, 49 C.M.R. 133 (A.F.C.M.R. 1974) — § 15-10(C), n. 81; § 11-2(B)(1), n. 62
United States v. Young, 1 M.J. 433 (C.M.A. 1976) — § 2-4(A), n. 12; § 13-3(N)(1), n. 332; § 13-3(N)(4), nn. 426, 427
United States v. Young, 15 M.J. 857 (A.F.C.M.R. 1983) — § 9-2, n. 6
United States v. Young, 470 U.S. 1 (1985) — § 15-13, n. 19
United States v. Young, 24 M.J. 626 (A.C.M.R. 1987) — § 16-3(E), n. 74
United States v. Young, 35 M.J. 541 (A.C.M.R. 1992) — § 9-2(B)(1), n. 49; § 9-2(B)(2), n. 62
United States v. Young, 43 M.J. 196 (1995) — § 17-21, n. 3
United States v. Youngberg, 38 M.J. 635 (A.C.M.R. 1993) — § 13-3(C)(2), nn. 54, 96; § 13-3(C)(3), nn. 97, 105
United States v. Yunque-Burgos, 3 C.M.A. 498, 13 C.M.R. 54 (1953) — § 2-4(A), n. 11
United States v. Zaccheus, 31 M.J. 766 (A.C.M.R. 1990) — § 15-2(D), n. 128; § 15-4(B), n. 11
United States v. Zachary, 10 M.J. 628 (A.C.M.R. 1980) — § 5-3(C)(3), n. 69
United States v. Zagar, 5 C.M.A. 410, 18 C.M.R. 34 (1955) — § 6-5(A), n. 4
United States v. Zaiss, 42 M.J. 586 (Army.Ct.Crim.App. 1995) — § 17-21, n. 3
United States v. Zakaria, 38 M.J. 280 (C.M.A. 1993) — § 16-4(B), n. 18; § 16-5(B), n. 7
United States v. Zamarripa, 1 C.M.R. 432 (A.B.R. 1951) — § 15-10(B), n. 41; § 8-3(C)(1), n. 115
United States v. Zammit, 14 M.J. 554 (N.C.M.R. 1982) — § 2-2(C)(3), n. 44
United States v. Zapata, 12 M.J. 689 (N.M.C.M.R. 1982) — § 17-2(B), n. 11
United States v. Zaptin, 41 M.J. 877 (N.M.Ct.Crim.App. 1995) — § 17-8(B), n. 23
United States v. Zarate, 5 M.J. 219 (C.M.A. 1978) — § 17-8(B)(3), n. 79
United States v. Zayas, 24 M.J. 132 (C.M.A. 1987) — § 11-2(E)(3), nn. 128, 138, 148
United States v. Zeigler, 14 M.J. 860 (A.C.M.R. 1982) — § 15-13, nn. 6, 10, 11
United States v. Zelenski, 24 M.J. 1 (C.M.A. 1987) — § 9-2(B)(1), n. 49
United States v. Zemartis, 10 C.M.A. 353, 27 C.M.R. 427 (1959) — § 14-3(B)(3), n. 101
United States v. Zengel, 32 M.J. 642 (C.G.C.M.R. 1991) — § 8-3(C)(2), n. 132

TABLE OF CASES

United States v. Zickefoose, 17 M.J. 449 (C.M.A. 1984) — § 2-7(B), n. 24
United States v. Zubko, 18 M.J. 378 (C.M.A. 1984) — § 13-3(J), n. 255; § 6-1(C)(3), n. 145
United States v. Zuis, 49 C.M.R. 150 (A.C.M.R. 1974) — § 14-1, n. 11; § 15-2(B)(3), n. 30
United States v. Zupan, 17 M.J. 1039 (A.C.M.R. 1984) — § 2-6(C), n. 38
United States v. Zupancic, 18 M.J. 387 (C.M.A. 1984) — § 13-3(J), n. 261; § 16-2(D), n. 42
United States v. Zupkosfska, 34 M.J. 537 (A.F.C.M.R. 1991) — § 5-4(C), n. 59
United States Civil Service Comm'n v., national Ass'n of Letter Carriers, 413 U.S. 548 (1973) — § 13-3(N)(2), n. 347; § 13-3(N)(3), nn. 381, 388
United States Dep't of Agriculture v. Moreno, 413 U.S. 528 (1973) — § 13-3(N)(1), n. 311
United States ex rel. Guagliardo, McElroy v.
United States ex rel. Singleton, Kinsella v.
United States ex rel. Toth v. Quarles, 350 U.S. 11 (1955) — § 1-1, n. 11
United States Jaycees, Roberts v.
United States, Navy-Marine Corps Court of Military Review v. Carlucci, 26 M.J. 328 (C.M.A. 1988) — § 1-1, n. 10; § 13-2(G)(1), n. 61
Universal Amusement Co., Vance v.
Universal C.S.T. Credit Corp., United States v.
Upchurch, United States v.
Urbina, United States v.
Ureta, United States v.
Usher, Duncan v.

V

Valead, United States v.
Valente, Larson v.
Valenzuela, United States v.
Valenzuela-Bernal, United States v.
Vallenthine, United States v.
Van Arsdall, Chenoweth v.
Van Beek, United States v.
Van Bourg v. Nitze, 388 F.2d 557 (D.C. Cir. 1967) — § 17-22(B), n. 11
Van Horn, United States v.
Van Metre, United States v.
Van Slate, United States v.
Van Steenwyk, United States v.
Van Syoc, United States v.
Van Tassel, United States v.
Van Tessel, United States v.
VanCantfort, Allen v.
Vance v. Bradley, 440 U.S. 93 (1979) — § 13-3(N)(1), nn. 303, 304, 314
Vance v. Universal Amusement Co., 445 U.S. 308 (1980) — § 13-3(N)(3), n. 377
Vanderlip, United States v.
Vandermark, United States v.
Vanderweir, United States v.
Vandewoestyne, United States v.
Vanover v. Clark, 27 M.J. 345 (C.M.A. 1988) — § 8-5, n. 13; § 13-2(G)(1), n. 67
Vanzandt, United States v.

TABLE OF CASES

Vardiman, United States v.
Vargas, United States v.
Varraso, United States v.
Vasquez, United States v.
Vaughn, United States v.
Vaughters, United States v.
Vega, United States v.
Vega-Cancel, United States v.
Velis, United States v.
Vendivel, United States v.
Ventura, United States v.
Verdi, United States v.
Verner, Sherbert v.
Vesich, United States v.
Vest, Spiller v.
Vicencio, United States v.
Vickers, United States v.
Victorian, United States v.
Vidal, United States v.
Vietor, United States v.
Vigilito, United States v.
Village of Schauniburg v. Citizens for a Better Environment, 444 U.S. 620 (1980) —
  § 13-3(N)(3), n. 387
Villamil-Perez, United States v.
Villamonte-Marquez, United States v.
Villines, United States v.
Vincent, United States v.
Vincent, Widmar v.
Vines, United States v.
Vinson, United States v.
Vinyard, United States v.
Viola, United States v.
Virgin Islands v. Smith, 615 F.2d 964 (3d Cir. 1980) — § 11-2(E)(3), nn. 125, 127, 140
Virginia, Loving v.
Virginia, Richmond Newspapers, Inc. v.
Virginia Citizens Consumer Council, Inc., Virginia State Bd. of Pharmacy v.
Virginia State Bd. of Elections, Harper v.
Virginia State Bd. of Pharmacy v. Virginia Citizens Consumer Council, Inc., 425 U.S.
  748 (1976) — § 13-3(N)(3), n. 372
Visser, United States v.
Vitale, Engel v.
Vitale, United States v.
Vith, United States v.
Viverito, United States v.
Vlandis v. Kline, 412 U.S. 441 (1973) — § 13-3(N)(1), n. 324
Vogan, United States v.
Volmar, United States v.
Von Moltke v. Gillies, 332 U.S. 708 (1948) — § 12-2(F)(4), n. 72
Von Raab, National Treasury Employees Union v.
Voorhees, United States v.
Vorbach, Smithee v.

TABLE OF CASES

Vorbeck v. Commanding Officer, 11 M.J. 480 (C.M.A. 1981) — § 17-19, n. 8
Voyles, United States v.
Vuitch, United States v.

W

Wactor, United States v.
Wade, Roe v.
Wade, United States v.
Wager, United States v.
Waggoner, United States v.
Wagner, United States v.
Wahnon, United States v.
Wai, United States v.
Wainwright, Cobb v.
Waits, United States v.
Wakeman, United States v.
Walbert, United States v.
Waldrup, United States v.
Wales, United States v.
Walk, United States v.
Walker v. Commanding Officer, 19 C.M.A. 247, 41 C.M.R. 247 (1970) — § 17-5, n. 9
Walker, United States v.
Wall, United States v.
Wallace v. Chafee, 451 F.2d 1374 (9th Cir. 1911) — § 4-6, n. 8; § 4-16
Wallace, Chappell v.
Wallace v. Jaffree, 105 S. Ct. 2479 (1985) — § 13-3(N)(3), n. 396
Wallace, United States v.
Waller v. Swift, 30 M.J. 139 (C.M.A. 1990) — § 17-9(A), nn. 10, 11; § 17-19, n. 22
Waller, United States v.
Walls, United States v.
Walsh, United States v.
Walter, United States v.
Walters, United States v.
Walther, United States v.
Walzer, United States v.
Ward, United States v.
Ware, United States v.
Wargo, United States v.
Warner, United States v.
Warnock, United States v.
Warren, United States v.
Wartruba, United States v.
Wartsbaugh, United States v.
Washington v. Davis, 426 U.S. 229 (1976) — § 13-3(N)(1), n. 316
Washington v. Edwards, 38 M.J. 501 (A.F.C.M.R. 1993) — § 17-15(B), n. 31
Washington v. Greewald, 20 M.J. 823 (A.C.M.R. 1985) — § 13-5(B), n. 28
Washington, Spence v.
Washington, Strickland v.
Washington, United States v.
Wasson, United States v.

TABLE OF CASES

Waterfront Comm'n, Murphy v.
Watkins, United States v.
Watson, United States v.
Wattenbarger, United States v.
Watts, United States v.
Wayte v. United States, 470 U.S. 598 (1985) — § 13-3(M), n. 284
Weasler, United States v.
Weatherford v. Bursey, 429 U.S. 545 (1977) — § 10-1, n. 8; § 15-2(B)(3), n. 46
Weatherspoon, United States v.
Weaver, United States v.
Webb, United States v.
Webber, United States v.
Webel, United States v.
Webster, United States v.
Weddle, United States v.
Weems, United States v.
Weikel, United States v.
Weinberger, Goldman v.
Weinmann, United States v.
Weir, Fletcher v.
Weise, United States v.
Weiss, United States v.
Weiss v. United States, 114 S. Ct. 752 (1994) — § 8-3(A), nn. 33-37
Weissman v. United States, 387 F.2d 271 (10th Cir. 1971) — § 13-3(N)(3), n. 408
Welch, United States v.
Welchel v. McDonald, 340 U.S. 122 (1950) — § 8-3(C)(3), n. 142
Welker, United States v.
Welling, Collazo v.
Wells, United States v.
Wendlandt, United States v.
Wentzel, United States v.
Wesberry v. Sanders, 376 U.S. 1 (1964) — § 13-3(N)(1), n. 323
Weshenfelder, United States v.
Wesley, United States v.
West v. Brown, 558 F.2d 757 (5th Cir. 1977) — § 13-3(N)(4), n. 420
West, United States v.
West Virginia State Bd. of Educ. v. Barnette, 319 U.S. 624 (1943) — § 13-3(N)(3), nn. 358, 376
Westmoreland, United States v.
Weymouth, United States v.
Whalen, Bemis v.
Whalen v. Roe, 429 U.S. 589 (1977) — § 13-3(N)(4), n. 417
Whalen, United States v.
Wharton, United States v.
Whatley, United States v.
Wheatcraft, United States v.
Wheaton, United States v.
Wheeler, People v.
Wheeler, United States v.
Wheeley, United States v.
Whelehan, United States v.

TABLE OF CASES

Whidbee, United States v.
Whipple, United States v.
Whitcomb, United States v.
White, United States v.
Whitehead, United States v.
Whiteside, Nix v.
Whitfield, United States v.
Whiting, United States v.
Whitley, United States v.
Whitt, United States v.
Whittier, United States v.
Whittle, United States v.
Wholley, United States v.
Wickersham, United States v.
Wickham v. Hall, 12 M.J. 145 (C.M.A. 1981) — § 4-8(C)(3), n. 29; § 17-19, n. 18
Wickham v. Hall, 706 F.2d 713 (5th Cir. 1983) — § 4-8(C)(3), n. 29
Widdekke, United States v.
Widmar v. Vincent, 454 U.S. 263 (1981) — § 13-3(N)(3), n. 379
Wiegand, United States v.
Wierzba, United States v.
Wiggers, United States v.
Wiggins v. Greenwald, 20 M.J. 823 (A.C.M.R. 1985) — § 5-10(D), n. 37
Wiggins, McKaskle v.
Wilbur, Mullaney v.
Wiles, United States v.
Wiley, United States v.
Wilkerson, United States v.
Wilkes, United States v.
Wilkins, United States v.
Wilkinson, United States v.
Willeford, United States v.
Williams, Brewer v.
Williams, Courtney v.
Williams, Dandridge v.
Williams v. Florida, 399 U.S. 78 (1970) — § 10-2(B), n. 21; § 10-5(A)(2), n. 15
Williams, Nix v.
Williams v. Secretary of the Navy, 787 F.2d 552 (Fed. Cir. 1986) — § 17-23(B), nn. 7, 12
Williams, United States v.
Williams, Zobel v.
Williams-Oatman, United States v.
Williamson v. Secretary of the Navy, 395 F. Supp. 146 (D.C. 1975) — § 17-23(B), n. 12
Williamson, United States v.
Willingham, United States v.
Willis, United States v.
Willoughby, Orloff v.
Wills, United States v.
Wilson v. Bohlender, 361 U.S. 281 (1960) — § 4-7(B), n. 14
Wilson, Bowman v.
Wilson, Burns v.
Wilson, Girard v.
Wilson v. Girard, 354 U.S. 524 (1957) — § 4-12(B), n. 13

TABLE OF CASES

Wilson v. Ouelette, 34 M.J. 798 (N.M.C.M.R. 1991) — § 17-19, n. 25
Wilson, United States v.
Winchester, United States v.
Wine, United States v.
Wingart, United States v.
Wingo, Barker v.
Winkler, United States v.
Winter, United States v.
Winters v. New York, 333 U.S. 507 (1948) — § 13-3(N)(3), n. 362
Wirth, United States v.
Wisconsin v. Yoder, 406 U.S. 205 (1972) — § 13-3(N)(3), n. 399
Wisemore, United States v.
Witherspoon, United States v.
Witt, United States v.
Wixon, United States v.
Wojciechowski, United States v.
Wolff, United States v.
Wolfish, Bell v.
Wolfson, United States v.
Woltmann, United States v.
Wolzok, United States v.
Womack, United States v.
Wong Tai v. United States, 273 U.S. 77 (1927) — § 13-5(F), n. 31
Wood, Bowler v.
Wood, United States v.
Woodard, United States v.
Woodley, United States v.
Woodmansee, Clay v.
Woodrick v. Divich, 24 M.J. 147 (C.M.A. 1987) — § 4-4, n. 6; § 4-5(A), nn. 8, 9, 13; § 17-23(C)(1), n. 27; § 17-19, n. 18
Woodrick v. Hungerford, 800 F.2d 1413 (5th Cir. 1986) — § 17-23(C)(1), n. 27
Woods, United States v.
Woodson, Zamora v.
Wooten, United States v.
Wordlow, United States v.
Worrell, United States v.
Worsham, United States v.
Wrenn, United States v.
Wright, United States v.
Wright v. United States, 2 M.J. 9 (C.M.A. 1976) — § 12-2(E), n. 39; § 8-3(B)(2), n. 67
Wynn, United States v.
Wyrick v. Fields, 459 U.S. 42 (1982) — § 5-4(B), n. 50
Wysong, United States v.

Y

Yager, United States v.
Yamashita, In re
Yancey, United States v.
Yandell, United States v.
Yandle, United States v.

TABLE OF CASES

Yanke, United States v.
Yarborough, United States v.
Yarbough, United States v.
Yardley, United States v.
Yarn, United States v.
Yatchak, United States v.
Yates, United States v.
Yeargain v. United States, 314 F.2d 881 (9th Cir. 1963) — § 13-5(F), n. 21
Yeckinevich, United States v.
Yelverton, United States v.
Yeoman, United States v.
Yick Wo v. Hopkins, 118 U.S. 356 (1886) — § 13-3(N)(1), nn. 305, 320, 321
Yingling, United States v.
Yocom, United States v.
Yoder, Wisconsin v.
Yonan v. Seamans, 380 F. Supp. 505 (N.C. 1974) — § 17-22(A), n. 4
Yost, United States v.
Young, United States v.
Youngberg, United States v.
Yunque-Burgos, United States v.

Z

Zablocki v. Redhail, 434 U.S. 374 (1978) — § 13-3(N)(1), nn. 318, 322; § 13-3(N)(4), n. 414
Zaccheus, United States v.
Zachary, United States v.
Zagar, United States v.
Zaiss, United States v.
Zakaria, United States v.
Zamarripa, United States v.
Zammit, United States v.
Zamora v. Woodson, 19 C.M.A. 403, 42 C.M.R. 5 (1970) — § 13-2(G)(1), n. 65
Zapata, United States v.
Zaptin, United States v.
Zarate, United States v.
Zayas, United States v.
Zech, Dronenburg v.
Zeigler, United States v.
Zelenski, United States v.
Zemartis, United States v.
Zengel, United States v.
Zickefoose, United States v.
Ziemniak, Unger v.
Zimmerman Brush Co., Logan v.
Zobel v. Williams, 457 U.S. 55 (1982) — § 13-3(N)(1), n. 312
Zubko, United States v.
Zuis, United States v.
Zupan, United States v.
Zupancic, United States v.
Zupkosfska, United States v.

INDEX

A

ABBREVIATIONS, Appx. 1.

ABSENCE OFFENSES, §§2-2(A) to 2-2(E)(7).

ABSENCE WITHOUT LEAVE, §§2-2(C), 2-2(C)(3).
Defenses.
  Civilian detention, §2-2(E)(5).
  Duress, §2-2(E)(3).
  Impossibility, §2-2(E)(1).
  Justification or necessity, §2-2(E)(2).
  Mistake of fact, §2-2(E)(4).
  Moral grounds or beliefs, §2-2(E)(7).
  Statute of limitations, §2-2(E)(6).
Failing to go to place of duty, §2-2(C)(1).
Leaving place of duty, §2-2(C)(2).

ACCUSED.
Article 32 investigations.
  Accused's rights.
    See ARTICLE 32 INVESTIGATIONS.
Disruptive behavior, §15-2(A).
In absentia.
  Tried in absentia, §15-2(A).
Interrogation, §5-4(B).
Limited testimony.
  Notice by defense, §10-2(B).
Oral depositions.
  Rights, §11-3(B)(2).
Presence at all stages of trial, §15-2(A).
Pretrial statements.
  Motions to suppress, §13-4(A).
Self-incrimination.
  See SELF-INCRIMINATION.
Self-representation.
  Faretta inquiry, §12-2(F)(4).
Service of charges upon, §8-6.
Severance, §13-5(G)(1).
Summary courts-martial procedures, §15-26(B).
Trial participants, §15-2(A).
Written depositions.
  Rights, §11-3(B)(3).

ACCUSER.
Nominal accuser, §6-1.
Preferral of charges, §6-1.

ACQUITTAL.
Motion for finding of not guilty, §15-4(C).

ACTS OF GOD.
Defense to absence without leave, §2-2(E).

ADDITIONAL CHARGES.
Pleading, §6-1(B)(3).

ADMINISTRATIVE CREDIT.
Pretrial restraint amounting to pretrial confinement, §5-10(D).

ADMINISTRATIVE DEDUCTIONS IN RANK.
Nonpunitive option of commander, §1-8(B).

ADMINISTRATIVE DISCHARGE.
In lieu of trial, §9-4.
Nonpunitive option of commander, §1-8(B).

ADMINISTRATIVE REVIEW OF COURTS-MARTIAL, §17-22.
Boards for correction of military records, §17-22(A).
Discharge review boards, §17-22(B).

ADMISSIONS.
Confessional stipulations, §9-3.

ADMONITION.
Censure as nonjudicial punishment, §3-6(E).

AFFIDAVIT OF EXPECTED TESTIMONY.
Substitute for live testimony, §11-2(A)(4).

AGGRAVATED ASSAULT.
HIV-related offenses.
  Prosecuting under Article 128 of UCMJ, §2-9(C)(1).

AIDS AND HIV-RELATED OFFENSES.
Assault, §2-9(C)(1).
Catch-all offenses under Articles 133 and 134, §2-9(C)(3).
Constitutionality of prosecuting conduct, §2-9(D).
Generally, §2-9(A).
Manslaughter, §2-9(C)(1).
Murder, §2-9(C)(1).
Rape, §2-9(C)(2).
Safe sex order violations, §2-9(B).
Sodomy, §2-9(C)(2).

AIR FORCE LAW REVIEW.
Legal periodicals, §1-3(e).

1183

AIR FORCE NONJUDICIAL PUNISHMENT PROCEDURES, §§3-5(C) to 3-5(C)(4).

ALFORD PLEAS, §14-3(D)(2).

ALIBI.
Notice by defense, §10-2(B).
Automatic defense disclosure, §10-5(A)(2).

ALL WRITS ACT.
Defense appeals on motion rulings, §13-2(G)(1).

AMENDMENTS TO PLEADINGS, §6-1(B)(2).

APPEALS.
Appellate rights advice.
Duties of defense counsel, §17-2(B)(1).
Form, Appx. 33.
Command influence, §6-7.
Counsel.
Generally, §17-14.
Post-trial duties of counsel.
See COUNSEL.
Court of appeals for the armed forces.
Generally, §17-16(A).
Jurisdiction, §17-16(B).
Procedures, §17-16(D).
Scope of review, §17-16(C).
Courts-martial.
Generally, §§17-1 to 17-23.
See REVIEW OF COURTS-MARTIAL.
Courts of criminal appeals, §17-15.
Jurisdiction, §17-15(A).
Procedural rules, §17-15(C).
Scope of review and actions, §17-15(B).
First amendment challenges, §13-3(N)(3).
Generally, §17-12.
Government appeals.
Notice, Appx. 21.
Individually requested counsel.
Denial, §8-3(B)(3).
Motions, §13-2(G).
Defense appeals, §13-2(G)(1).
Government appeals, §13-2(G)(2).
Nonjudicial punishment.
Air force procedures, §3-5(C)(4).
Army procedures, §3-5(B)(4).
Coast guard procedures, §3-5(E)(4).
Navy and marine corps procedures, §3-5(D)(4).
Notice.
Government appeals, §13-2(G)(2).
Pretrial agreements.
Judicial review, §9-2(D).

APPEALS —Cont'd
Pretrial confinement.
Judicial review, §5-9(E).
Remedy for unlawful confinement, §5-10(D).
Sentencing.
Advice on appellate rights, §16-12.
Supreme court, §17-17.
Waiver or withdrawal, §§17-13; Appx. 38.

APPOINTED OFFICERS.
Inception of personal jurisdiction, §4-5(C).

APPREHENSION.
Pretrial restraints.
See PRETRIAL RESTRAINTS.
Searches and seizures.
Searches incident to apprehension, §5-3(C)(7).

ARGUMENTS OF COUNSEL.
Closing arguments, §15-13.
Opening statements, §15-11.
Sentencing arguments.
Defense counsel argument, §16-8(C).
Generally, §16-8(A).
Prosecution arguments, §16-8(B).

ARMY LAWYER.
Legal periodicals, §1-3(E).

ARMY NONJUDICIAL PUNISHMENT PROCEDURES, §§3-5(B) to 3-5(B)(4).

ARRAIGNMENT, §12-4.

ARREST.
Apprehension, §5-7.
Generally, §5-8(D).
In quarters, §3-6(C)(4).
Pretrial restraints.
See PRETRIAL RESTRAINTS.
Unlawful arrest, §5-10(D).

ARREST IN QUARTERS.
Nonjudicial punishment, §3-6(C)(4).

ARTICLE 2.
Jurisdiction over persons generally.
See JURISDICTION.

ARTICLE 3(A).
Personal jurisdiction.
Discharge terminates status.
Article 3(a) offenses as exceptions to general rules, §4-8(C)(2).

ARTICLE 10.
Speedy trial provisions, §13-3(C)(2).

ARTICLE 13.
Illegal pretrial punishment and restraint.
See PRETRIAL RESTRAINTS.

INDEX

ARTICLE 15.
Nonjudicial punishment.
  See NONJUDICIAL PUNISHMENT.

ARTICLES 22, 23 AND 24.
Statutory authorization to convene courts-martial, §4-14(A)(1).

ARTICLE 25.
Selecting court members generally.
  See COURT MEMBERS.

ARTICLE 26.
Grounds for challenging judge, §12-2(H).

ARTICLE 27.
Ineffective assistance of counsel, §15-2(B)(3).

ARTICLE 32 INVESTIGATIONS, §7-2.
Accused's rights, §7-2(B).
  Notice of charges, §7-2(B)(1).
  Right to be present, §7-2(B)(3).
  Right to confront witnesses, §7-2(B)(4).
  Right to counsel, §7-2(B)(2).
  Right to examine evidence, §7-2(B)(5).
  Right to present other evidence, §7-2(B)(7).
  Right to production of witnesses, §7-2(B)(6).
  Right to remain silent, §7-2(B)(8).
Counterpart to grand jury, §7-2.
Defective investigations, §§7-2(E), 13-5(D).
Generally, §7.1.
Parties.
  Counsel, §7-2(A)(2).
  Investigating officer, §7-2(A)(1).
Pretrial command influence, §6-4(B).
Procedures, §7-2(C).
Report of investigating officer, §7-2(D).

ARTICLE 34.
Pretrial advice by staff judge advocate.
  See PRETRIAL ADVICE BY STAFF JUDGE ADVOCATE.

ARTICLE 39(A) POST-TRIAL SESSION, §17-3(B).

ARTICLE 39(A) PRETRIAL SESSION.
Accused represented by counsel with conflict of interest.
  Breese inquiry, §12-2(F)(3).
Accused's election of counsel, §12-2(F)(5).
Accused's invoking right to defend self.
  Faretta inquiry, §12-2(F)(4).
Advising accused of rights to counsel.
  Donohew inquiry, §12-2(F)(2).
Arraignment, §12-4.

ARTICLE 39(A) PRETRIAL SESSION
  —Cont'd
Breese inquiry, §12-2(F)(3).
Calling court to order, §12-2(A).
Challenges for cause to military judge, §12-2(H).
Composition of court.
  Inquiries concerning accused decisions, §§12-3 to 12-3(B).
Conferences, §12-5.
Convening orders, referral and service of charges.
  Announcing, §12-2(B).
Detail and qualifications of defense counsel.
  Announcing, §12-2(F)(1).
Detail and qualifications of trial counsel.
  Announcing, §12-2(E).
Detail of court reporter and interpreter.
  Noting, §12-2(D).
Detail of military judge.
  Announcing, §12-2(G).
Donohew inquiry, §12-2(F)(2).
Enlisted members on court.
  Accused's request, §12-3(B).
Faretta inquiry, §12-2(F)(4).
Introduction, §12-1.
Military judge presides, §12-1.
Oaths.
  Administering, §12-2(G).
Parties present and absent.
  Accounting for, §12-2(C).
Preliminary matters generally, §12-2.
Procedure generally, §12-1.
Trial by judge alone.
  Accused's request, §12-3(A).

ARTICLE 54.
Authentication of trial records, §17-4(A).

ARTICLE 60.
Revision proceedings, §17-3(A).

ARTICLE 69.
Sample application for relief under, Appx. 40.

ARTICLES 85 TO 87.
Absence offenses, §§2-2(A) to 2-2(E)(7).

ARTICLE 89.
Disrespect toward superior commissioned officers, §2-3(A).

ARTICLES 90, 91 AND 92.
Disobedience offenses, §§2-4(A) to 2-4(E).

ARTICLE 97.
Unlawful apprehension, arrest or confinement of person, §5-10(D).

1185

ARTICLE 112A.
Drug offenses, §§2-7(A) to 2-7(C).

ARTICLE 133.
Conduct unbecoming officer and gentleman, §2-5.
   Fraternization and general articles, §2-8(B).
   HIV-related offenses prosecuted under, §2-9(C)(3).

ARTICLE 134, GENERAL ARTICLE.
Conduct bringing discredit upon armed forces, §2-6(B).
Disorders and neglects to prejudice of good order and discipline, §2-6(A).
Fraternization and general articles, §2-8(B).
Generally, §2-6.
HIV-related offenses prosecuted under, §2-9(C)(3).
Noncapital crimes and offenses, §2-6(C).

ASSAULT.
HIV-related offenses.
   Prosecuting under Article 128 of UCMJ, §2-9(C)(1).

ASSEMBLY OF COURT, §15-9.

ASSIGNMENT TRANSFER.
Nonpunitive option of commander, §1-8(B).

ATTACHMENT WARRANT.
Failure of civilian witness to appear, §11-2(D)(3).
Form, Appx. 16.

ATTORNEY-CLIENT PRIVILEGE.
Changes in detailed defense counsel limited by formation of, §8-3(D).

ATTORNEYS.
See COUNSEL.

AUTHENTICATION OF TRIAL RECORDS, §17-4(A).

AWOL, §§2-2(C), 2-2(C)(3).
Defenses.
   Civilian detention, §2-2(E)(5).
   Duress, §2-2(E)(3).
   Impossibility, §2-2(E)(1).
   Justification or necessity, §2-2(E)(2).
   Mistake of fact, §2-2(E)(4).
   Moral grounds or beliefs, §2-2(E)(7).
   Statute of limitations, §2-2(E)(6).
Failing to go to place of duty, §2-2(C)(1).
Leaving place of duty, §2-2(C)(2).

B

BAD-CONDUCT DISCHARGE.
Post-trial recommendation, §§17-8(B) to 17-8(B)(3).

BAD-CONDUCT DISCHARGE
—Cont'd
Punitive separation, §16-3(B).

BCMRS.
Boards for correction of military records, §17-22(A).

BILL OF PARTICULARS.
Form, Appx. 20.
Motions, §13-5(F).

BOARDS FOR CORRECTION OF MILITARY RECORDS, §17-22(A).

BOARDS OF REVIEW.
See COURTS OF CRIMINAL APPEALS.

BODY CAVITY SEARCHES, §5-3(D)(2).

BORDER SEARCHES, §5-3(C)(3).

BRADY REQUEST.
Defense request for discovery, §10-4(B)(1).

BREAD AND WATER CONFINEMENT.
Deprivation of liberty, §16-3(C).
Nonjudicial punishment, §3-6(C)(5).

BREESE INQUIRY.
Accused represented by counsel with conflict of interest, §12-2(F)(3).

BRITISH SYSTEM.
Constable's court, §1-5(B).
Council of war, §1-5(C).
Court of chivalry, §1-5(B).
Generally, §1-5(A).
Mutiny act, §1-5(D).

BURDEN OF PROOF.
Challenging court member selection process, §15-10(C)(1).
Command influence, §6-7.
Drug offenses, §2-7(B).
Former jeopardy, §13-3(E).
Incompetence to stand trial, §13-5(A).
Motions, §13-2(D).
Not guilty pleas, §14-2.

C

CAPITAL PUNISHMENT, §16-3(A).

CAPTAIN'S MAST.
Nonjudicial punishment.
   See NONJUDICIAL PUNISHMENT.

CASE-IN-CHIEF.
Presentation, §§15-12 to 15-12(D).

CASE LAW.
Citator, §1-3(D)(3).
Court-martial reports, §1-3(D)(1).

INDEX

CASE LAW —Cont'd
Military justice reporter, §1-3(D)(2).

CENSURE.
Nonjudicial punishment, §3-6(E).

CERTIORARI.
Extraordinary writs in military courts, §17-19.
Review by supreme court, §17-17.

CHALLENGES TO MILITARY JUDGE, §12-2(H).

CHALLENGING COURT MEMBERS, §15-10(C).
Cause, §15-10(C)(2).
Grounds, §15-10(B).
Peremptory challenges, §15-10(C)(3).

CHANGE OF VENUE.
Motion, §13-5(C).

CHARGES AND SPECIFICATIONS.
Article 32 investigations.
  See ARTICLE 32 INVESTIGATIONS.
Defective specification misleading accused.
  Motion to dismiss, §13-3(K).
Disclosure.
  Automatic prosecutorial disclosures, §10-4(A)(1).
Duplicity.
  More than one offense alleged, §6-1(C)(2).
  Severance of duplicitous specifications, §13-5(G)(3).
Failure to allege offense.
  Motions to dismiss, §13-3(F).
Formal investigation of charges.
  See ARTICLE 32 INVESTIGATIONS.
Forwarding of charges.
  General court-martial convening authority, §6-2(D).
  Generally, §6-2.
  Immediate commander, §6-2(A).
  Special court-martial convening authority, §6-2(C).
  Summary court-martial convening authority, §6-2(B).
Jurisdiction.
  Charges properly referred, §4-16.
Multiplicity, §6-1(C)(3).
  Motion to dismiss, §13-3(J).
Notice of charges.
  Accused's rights at Article 32 investigations, §7-2(B)(1).
Pleading.
  See PLEADING CHARGES AND SPECIFICATIONS.

CHARGES AND SPECIFICATIONS —Cont'd
Preferring sworn charges.
  Accuser, §6-1.
  Charge sheet, §6-1(A).
  Defective pleadings, §6-1(C).
    Duplicity, §6-1(C)(2).
    Misjoinder, §6-1(C)(1).
    Multiplicity, §6-1(C)(3).
  Generally, §6-1.
  Guidance on preferral, §6-1.
  Nominal accuser, §6-1.
  Pretrial command influence, §6-4(A).
  Rules of pleading, §6-1(B).
    Additional charges, §6-1(B)(3).
    Amendments, §6-1(B)(2).
    Jurisdiction, §6-1(B)(1).
  Sworn charges requirement.
    Critical, §6-1.
Pretrial advice by staff judge advocate.
  See PRETRIAL ADVICE BY STAFF JUDGE ADVOCATE.
Referral of charges.
  Announcing, §12-2(B).
  Charges properly referred, §4-16.
  Pretrial command influence, §6-4(C).
  To court-martial, §8-4.
Service of charges, §8-6.
  Announcing, §12-2(B).
Severance of charges, §13-5(G)(2).
Withdrawal of charges, §8-5.

CHARGE SHEET, §6-1(A).
Form, Appx. 6.
Sentencing.
  Data from, §16-5(A).

CIVILIAN COUNSEL.
Obtaining, §8-3(B)(4).
Qualifications, §8-3(B)(1).

CIVILIAN DETENTION.
Defense to absence without leave, §2-2(E)(5).

CIVILIANS, JURISDICTION OVER.
Generally, §4-7.
Peacetime, §4-7(B).
Wartime, §4-7(A).

CIVILIAN WITNESSES.
Production.
  See WITNESSES.
Subpoenas.
  Form, Appx. 15.

CLEMENCY.
Notice by prosecution, §10-2(A).
Post-trial command influence, §6-6(A).
Powers of convening authority, §§17-9(A), 17-9(E).

CLOSING ARGUMENTS, §15-13.

COAST GUARD NONJUDICIAL PUNISHMENT PROCEDURES, §§3-5(E) to 3-5(E)(4).

COLLATERAL REVIEW IN FEDERAL COURTS.
Exhaustion of remedies requirements, §17-23(B).
Forms generally, §17-23(C).
Generally, §17-23(A).
Habeas corpus, §17-23(C)(1).
Mandamus, §17-23(C)(2).

COMBINING CHARGES.
Misjoinder, §6-1(C)(1).

COMMANDER'S INVESTIGATION, §§5-1, 5-2.

COMMANDER'S OPTIONS.
Court-martial, §§1-8(d) to 1-8(D)(3).
Generally, §1-8(A).
Nonjudicial punishment, §1-8(C).
Nonpunitive measures, §1-8(B).

COMMAND INFLUENCE.
Appellate review, §6-7.
Courts-martial.
  Commander's presence at trial, §6-5(C).
  Court members, judges and counsel, §6-5(A).
  Witnesses, §6-5(B).
Generally, §6-3.
Lawful command influence.
  Distinguished from unlawful influence, §6-3(B).
Post-trial command influence.
  Clemency matters, §6-6(A).
  Comments on outcome of case, §6-6(B).
  Discouraging witness testimony in other cases, §6-6(C).
Pretrial command influence, §6-4.
  Article 32 investigation, §6-4(B).
  Comments and actions, §6-4(E).
  Preliminary inquiry in preferring charges, §6-4(A).
  Referral of charges, §6-4(C).
  Selecting court members, §6-4(D).
Unlawful command influence.
  Actual, apparent and perceived, §6-3(C).
  Distinguished from lawful influence, §6-3(B).
  Minimizing potential, §6-8.
  Problem of, §6-3(A).

COMMANDING OFFICER.
Fowarding of charges.
  Immediate commanders, §6-2(A).

COMMANDING OFFICER —Cont'd
Nonjudicial punishment.
  Authority to impose, §3-3(A).
Preferring sworn charges, §6-1.

COMMENTS ON OUTCOME OF CASE.
Post-trial command influence, §6-6(B).

COMMISSIONED OFFICERS.
Disrespect toward superior commissioned officer, §2-3(A).

COMMUNITY IMPACT OF OFFENSE.
Evidence on sentencing, §16-5(D)(3).

COMPOSITION OF COURTS-MARTIAL.
Changes in, §8-3(B).
Inquiries concerning accused's decisions, §12-3.
  Request for enlisted members on court, §12-3(B).
  Request for trial by judge alone, §12-3(A).
Proper composition, §4-15.
  Counsel, §4-15(B).
  Court members, §4-15(C).
  Military judge, §4-15(A).

CONDITIONAL GUILTY PLEA, §14-4.
Entry, Appx. 23.

CONDITIONS ON LIBERTY.
Pretrial restraints, §5-8(B).

CONDUCT BRINGING DISCREDIT UPON ARMED FORCES, §2-6(B).

CONDUCT UNBECOMING OFFICER AND GENTLEMAN, §2-5.
Fraternization and general articles, §2-8(B).
HIV-related offenses prosecuted under Article 133, §2-9(C)(3).

CONFERENCES, §12-5.

CONFESSIONAL STIPULATIONS, §9-3.

CONFINEMENT.
Bread and water confinement, §3-6(C)(5).
Deferment of confinement request.
  Application, Appx. 34.
  Post-trial duties of defense counsel, §17-2(B)(2).
Deprivation of liberty, §16-3(C).
Pending review, §17-5.
Pretrial confinement.
  See PRETRIAL CONFINEMENT.
Pretrial restraints.
  See PRETRIAL RESTRAINTS.

INDEX

CONFINEMENT —Cont'd
Punishments generally.
　See SENTENCING AND PUNISHMENT.
Remedy for unlawful confinement, §5-10(D).
Served at service confinement or retaining centers, §17-6.
Unlawful confinement, §5-10(D).

CONFLICTS OF INTEREST.
Breese inquiry and conflicts of interest, §12-2(F)(3).
Counsel.
　Breese inquiry, §12-2(F)(3).
　Multiple representation by defense counsel, §15-2(B)(2).

CONSENT SEARCHES, §5-3(C)(6).

CONSTABLE'S COURT.
British system, §1-5(B).

CONSTITUTIONAL CHALLENGES.
Motions to dismiss, §§13-3(N) to 13-3(N)(5).

CONSTITUTIONALITY OF FRATERNIZATION PROSECUTIONS, §2-8(D).

CONSTITUTIONALITY OF PROSECUTING HIV-RELATED CONDUCT, §2-9(D).

CONSTITUTIONAL UNDERPINNINGS, §1-1(A).
Military due process, §1-1(B).

CONTEMPTS, §15-5.

CONTINUANCE.
Motions, §13-5(K).
　At trial, §15-4(A).

CONVENING AUTHORITY, §4-14(A).
Authority to convene, §4-14.
　Delegation, §4-14(A)(3).
　Disqualifications, §4-14(A)(2).
　Statutory authorization, §4-14(A)(1).
Courts-martial, §8-2(A).
　Generally.
　　See CONVENING OF COURTS-MARTIAL.
Detailing participants, §8-3.
Disqualifications, §4-14(A)(2).
Forwarding of charges.
　General court-martial convening authority, §6-2(D).
　Special court-martial convening authority, §6-2(C).
　Summary court-martial convening authority, §6-2(B).

CONVENING AUTHORITY —Cont'd
Immunity granted to witness, §11-2(E)(1).
Powers, §8-2(A).
Pretrial agreements.
　Acceptance or rejection, §9-2(A)(2).
Referral of charges to court-martial, §8-4.
Review of courts-martial.
　Clemency powers, §17-9(E).
　Execution of sentence.
　　Approving, §17-9(C).
　General matters, §17-8(A).
　Introduction, §17-7.
　Post-trial delays, §17-11.
　Post-trial recommendation, §17-8(B).
　　Defective recommendation, §17-8(B)(2).
　　Format and contents, §17-8(B)(1).
　　Service on defense counsel, §17-8(B)(3).
　Powers generally, §17-9(A).
　Promulgating orders, §17-10; Appx. 36.
　Qualified authority, §17-9(B).
　Suspension of sentence power, §17-9(D).
Submission of matters to post-trial duties of defense counsel, §17-2(B)(3).
Withdrawal of charges, §8-5.

CONVENING OF COURTS-MARTIAL, §§8-1, 8-2.
Detailing the participants, §8-3.
　Court members, §§8-3(C)(1) to 8-3(C)(4).
　Military judge, §8-3(A).
　Trial and defense counsel, §§8-3(B)(1) to 8-3(B)(4).
Jurisdictional elements.
　Authority to convene, §4-14.
　　Convening authority, §4-14(A).
　　　Delegation, §4-14(A)(3).
　　　Disqualification, §4-14(A)(2).
　　　Statutory authorization, §4-14(A)(1).
　　Convening orders, §4-14(B).
　　Generally, §4-13.

CONVENING ORDER, §§4-14(B), 8-2(B).
Announcing, §12-2(B).
Changes in composition of court, §8-3(D).
Creation of court, §8-2(B).
Sample, Appx. 9.

CORAM NOBIS.
Extraordinary writs in military courts, §17-19.

CORRECTIONAL CUSTODY.
Nonjudicial punishment, §3-6(C)(1).

COUNCIL OF WAR.
British system, §1-5(C).

COUNSEL.
Accused's rights.
  Advising accused, §12-2(F)(2).
Appellate counsel, §17-14.
Appointment, §4-15(B).
Arguments of counsel.
  See ARGUMENTS OF COUNSEL.
Article 32 investigations.
  Parties to investigation, §7-2(A)(2).
  Right to counsel, §7-2(B)(2).
Breese inquiry and conflicts of interest, §12-2(F)(3).
Certification, §8-3(B)(1).
Changes in detailed defense counsel, §8-3(D).
Civilian counsel.
  Obtaining, §8-3(B)(4).
  Qualifications, §8-3(B)(1).
Command influence on courts-martial, §6-5(A).
Conflict of interest.
  Breese inquiry, §12-2(F)(3).
  Multiple representation by defense counsel, §15-2(B)(2).
Defense counsel generally, §15-2(B)(1).
Detailing military counsel, §8-3(B)(2).
  Announcing, §§12-2(E), 12-2(F)(1).
Disqualification, §8-3(B)(1).
Donohew inquiry.
  Advising accused of rights to counsel, §12-2(F)(2).
Election of counsel, §12-2(F)(5).
Individually requested military counsel.
  Qualifications, §8-3(B)(1).
  Request for, §8-3(B)(3).
Ineffective assistance of defense counsel, §15-2(B)(3).
Miranda right to counsel warnings.
  Interrogation of suspects, §5-4(B).
Motions concerning requests, §13-5(H).
Multiple representation by defense counsel, §15-2(B)(2).
Oral depositions.
  Right of accused, §11-3(B)(2).
Perjurious clients and defense counsel, §15-2(B)(4).
Photographic identification.
  Right to, §5-5.
Post-trial duties, §17-2.
  Defense counsel, §17-2(B).
    Appellate rights advice, §17-2(B)(1).

COUNSEL —Cont'd
Post-trial duties —Cont'd
  Defense counsel —Cont'd
    Confinement deferment request, §17-2(b)(2); Appx. 34.
    Staff judge advocate's post-trial recommendation review, §17-2(B)(4).
    Submission of matters to convening authority, §17-2(B)(3).
  Trial counsel, §17-2(A).
Qualifications, §8-3(B)(1).
  Announcing, §§12-2(E), 12-2(F)(1).
Self-representation by accused.
  Faretta inquiry, §12-2(F)(4).
Standby counsel.
  Assistance to accused representing self, §12-2(F)(4).
Summary courts-martial, §15-26(C).
Swearing, §15-8.
Trial counsel generally, §15-2(c).
Written depositions.
  Right of accused, §11-3(B)(3).

COURT-MARTIAL FLOW CHART,
Appx. 4.

COURT-MARTIAL REPORTS.
Military case law, §1-3(D)(1).

COURT MEMBERS, §15-2(E).
Adding or deleting names, §8-3(D).
Challenging, §15-10(C).
  Cause, §15-10(C)(2).
  Composition, §8-3(C)(3).
  Grounds, §15-10(B).
  Peremptory challenges, §15-10(C)(3).
  Selection process, §15-10(C)(1).
Command influence on courts-martial, §6-5(A).
Competence to serve, §4-15(C).
Composition challenges, §8-3(C)(3).
Deliberations, §15-15.
  Sentencing, §16-10.
Detailing generally, §8-3(C).
Enlisted members.
  Accused's request for, §§8-3(C)(2), 12-3(B).
  Form of request for, Appx. 18.
Equivalent of civil jury, §4-15(C).
Generally, §15-2(E).
Guilty pleas.
  Informing, §14-3(F).
Instructions to.
  Checklist, Appx. 27.
  Evidentiary instructions during trial, §15-24.
  Generally, §15-14(A).

INDEX

COURT MEMBERS —Cont'd
Instructions to —Cont'd
  Requests, §15-14(C).
  Review of errors, §15-14(D).
  Sentencing instructions, §16-9.
  Sua sponte instructions, §15-14(B).
Pretrial command influence on selecting, §6-4(D).
Qualifications, §8-3(C)(1).
Selecting, §8-3(C)(4).
  Challenges, §15-10(C)(1).
Swearing, §15-8.
Verdict and announcement of findings.
  Findings worksheet, Appx. 28.
  General findings, §15-16(A).
  Impeaching findings, §15-16(B).
  Special findings by military judge, §15-16(C); Appx. 32.
View or inspection of places and objects.
  General and special courts-martial, §15-12(D).
Voir dire, §15-10(A).
  Court-martial member questionnaire, Appx. 24.

COURT OF APPEALS FOR THE ARMED FORCES.
Appeals generally.
  See APPEALS.
Extraordinary writs, §17-19.
Generally, §17-16(A).
Jurisdiction, §17-16(B).
Procedures, §17-16(D).
Scope of review, §17-16(C).

COURT OF CHIVALRY.
British system, §1-5(B).

COURT REPORTER, §15-2(F).
Detail, §12-2(D).
Swearing, §15-8.

COURTS-MARTIAL JURISDICTION.
See JURISDICTION.

COURTS OF CRIMINAL APPEALS.
Appeals generally.
  See APPEALS.
Generally, §17-15.
Jurisdiction, §17-15(A).
Procedural rules, §17-15(C).
Scope of review and actions, §17-15(B).

CRIMES, §2-1.
Absence offenses.
  Absence without leave, §§2-2(C), 2-2(C)(3).
    Defenses, §§2-2(e)(1) to 2-2(e)(7).
  Desertion, §2-2(B).
  Failing to go to place of duty, §2-2(C)(1).

CRIMES —Cont'd
Absence offenses —Cont'd
  Generally, §2-2(A).
  Leaving place of duty, §2-2(C)(2).
  Missing movement, §2-2(D).
AIDS and HIV-related offenses.
  Catch-all offenses under Articles 133 and 134, §2-9(C)(3).
  Constitutionality of prosecuting HIV-related conduct, §2-9(D).
  Generally, §2-9(A).
  Murder, manslaughter and assault, §2-9(C)(1).
  Prosecuting under other UCMJ provisions, §2-9(C).
  Rape and sodomy, §2-9(C)(2).
  Safe sex order violations, §2-9(B).
Article 133, conduct unbecoming officer and gentleman, §2-5.
Article 134, the general article.
  Conduct bringing discredit upon armed services, §2-6(B).
  Disorders and neglects to prejudice of good order and discipline, §2-6(A).
  Federal crimes, §2-6(C).
  Generally, §2-6.
  Noncapital crimes, §2-6(C).
Defenses.
  Absence without leave, §§2-2(E)(1) to 2-2(E)(7).
  Disobedience of orders offenses, §2-4(F).
  Disrespect offenses, §2-3(C).
  Drug offenses, §2-7(B).
  Notice by defense, §10-2(B).
Disobedience offenses.
  Defenses, §2-4(F).
  Dereliction of duty, §2-4(E).
  Disobedience of other orders, §2-4(D).
  Disobedience of superior officer's orders, §2-4(B).
  Generally, §2-4(A).
  Violation of general orders or regulations, §2-4(C).
Disrespect offenses.
  Defenses, §2-3(C).
  Disrespect toward officers, §2-3(A).
  Generally, §2-3.
  Insubordination toward petty, warrant or noncommissioned officers, §2-3(B).
Drug offenses.
  Charging, §2-7(A).
  Defenses, §2-7(B).
  Evidentiary issues, §2-7(C).
  Identity of the drugs.
    Proving, §2-7(C).
  Proving wrongfulness, §2-7(B).

CRIMES —Cont'd
Federal crimes, §2-6(C).
Fraternization.
  Fraternization and constitution, §2-8(D).
  Fraternization and general articles, §2-8(B).
  Fraternization and regulations or orders, §2-8(C).
  Generally, §2-8(A).
Jurisdiction over offense generally.
  See JURISDICTION.
Unlawful apprehension, arrest or confinement, §5-10(D).

D

DEATH PENALTY, §16-3(A).

DEFECTIVE PLEADINGS, §§6-1(C) to 6-1(C)(3).

DEFENSE COUNSEL.
Generally.
  See COUNSEL.

DEFENSE NOTICE, §10-2(B).

DEFENSES.
Absence without leave, §§2-2(E)(1) to 2-2(E)(7).
Disobedience of orders offenses, §2-4(F).
Disrespect offenses, §2-3(C).
Drug offenses, §2-7(B).
Notice by defense, §10-2(B).

DEFINED TERMS.
Glossary, Appx. 2.

DELIBERATIONS OF COURT MEMBERS, §15-15.
Sentencing deliberations, §16-10.

DEPOSITIONS.
Adequate substitute for live testimony, §11-2(A)(4).
Discovery generally.
  See DISCOVERY.
Generally, §11-3(A).
Interrogatories and deposition forms, Appx. 14.
Oral depositions, §11-3(A).
  Form of request to take, Appx. 13.
  Procedure, §11-3(B)(2).
Procedure generally, §11-3(B)(1).
Use at trial, §§11-3(C), 15-22.
Written depositions, §§11-3(A), 11-3(B)(3).

DEPRIVATION OF LIBERTY, §16-3(C).
Nonjudicial punishment, §§3-6(C) to 3-6(C)(4).

DEPRIVATION OF PAY, §16-3(D).

DERELICTION OF DUTY, §2-4(E).

DESERTION, §2-2(B).
Defenses to absence without leave, §§2-2(E)(1) to 2-2(E)(7).
Discharge not relieving service member of accountability, §4-8(C)(4).
Motion to dismiss for constructive condonation, §13-3(I).

DIMINISHED RATIONS.
Confinement on bread and water, §3-6(C)(5).
Deprivation of liberty, §16-3(C).

DISCHARGE.
Administrative discharge.
  Nonpunitive option of commander, §1-8(B).
Enlistment generally.
  See ENLISTMENT.
In lieu of court-martial, §9-4.
Punitive separations, §16-3(B).
Termination of personal jurisdiction.
  Discharge terminates status, general rule, §4-8(B).
  Exceptions to general rule.
    Article 3(a) offenses, §4-8(C)(2).
    Deserters, §4-8(C)(4).
    Fraudulent discharge, §4-8(C)(3).
    Generally, §4-8(C).
    Persons in custody, §4-8(C)(5).
    Re-enlistment discharges, §4-8(C)(1).

DISCHARGE REVIEW BOARDS, §17-22(B).

DISCLOSURE.
Automatic defense disclosure, §§10-5(A) to 10-5(A)(4).
Automatic prosecutorial disclosure, §§10-4(A) to 10-4(A)(4).
Continuing duty to disclose, §10-3(D).
Disclosure of section III evidence, Appx. 19.
Ethical duty, §10-3(F).
Generally, §10-1.
Judicial control, §10-6.
Remedies for noncompliance, §10-6.

DISCOVERY.
Continuing duty to disclose, §10-3(D).
Defense discovery, §10-4.
  Automatic prosecutorial disclosure, §10-4(A).
  Charges and allied papers, §10-4(A)(1).
  Favorable evidence, §10-4(A)(4).

INDEX

DISCOVERY —Cont'd
Defense discovery —Cont'd
  Automatic prosecutorial disclosure —Cont'd
    Names of prosecution witnesses, §10-4(A)(2).
    Prior convictions, §10-4(A)(3).
  Defense request for discovery, §10-4(B).
    Brady request, §10-4(B)(1).
    Jencks act materials, §10-4(B)(5).
    Reciprocal discovery, §10-4(C).
    Reports, tests and results, §10-4(B)(3).
    Sentencing evidence, §10-4(B)4).
    Tangibles and documents, §10-4(B)(2).
Depositions.
  See DEPOSITIONS.
Disclosure of section III evidence, Appx. 19.
Equal access to evidence, §10-3(B).
Ethical duty to disclose, §10-3(F).
Generally, §10-1.
General rules, §§10-3 to 10-3(F).
Identification of expected witnesses.
  Failure to call witness, §10-3(C).
Judicial control, §10-6.
Motions, §13-5(J).
Production of witnesses generally.
  See WITNESSES.
Prosecution discovery, §10-5.
  Automatic defense disclosure, §10-5(A).
    Names of defense witnesses, §10-5(A)(1).
    Notice of alibi defense, §10-5(A)(2).
    Notice of defense of innocent ingestion, §10-5(A)(4).
    Notice of lack of mental responsibility defense, §10-5(A)(3).
  Prosecutor's request for discovery, §10-5(B).
  Reciprocal discovery, §10-5(C).
Protected information, §10-3(A).
Reciprocal discovery, §§10-3(E), 10-4(C), 10-5(C).
Remedies for noncompliance, §10-6.
Sample request, Appx. 10.
Work product rule, §10-3(A).

DISCREDIT UPON ARMED FORCES.
Conduct bringing, §2-6(B).

DISHONORABLE DISCHARGE.
Punitive separation, §16-3(B).

DISMISSAL FROM SERVICE.
Punitive separation, §16-3(B).

DISOBEDIENCE OFFENSES.
Defenses, §2-4(F).
Dereliction of duty, §2-4(E).
Generally, §2-4(A).
General orders or regulations violations, §2-4(C).
Other orders, §2-4(D).
Superior's orders, §2-4(B).

DISORDERS AND NEGLECTS TO PREJUDICE OF GOOD ORDER AND DISCIPLINE, §2-6(A).

DISRESPECT OFFENSES.
Defenses, §2-3(C).
Generally, §2-3.
Insubordination, §2-3(B).
Towards officers, §2-3(A).

DONOHEW INQUIRY.
Advising accused of rights to counsel, §12-2(F)(2).

DOUBLE JEOPARDY, §13-3(E).
Motion to dismiss, §13-3(E).
Withdrawal and later referral of charges, §8-5.

DRAFTED PERSONNEL.
Inception of personal jurisdiction, §4-5(B).

DRUG OFFENSES.
Charging, §2-7(A).
Defenses, §2-7(B).
Evidentiary issues, §2-7(C).
Identity of drugs.
  Proving, §2-7(C).
Proving wrongfulness, §2-7(B).

DUE PROCESS.
Constitutional challenges, §§13-3(N) to 13-3(N)(5).
Constitutionality of prosecuting HIV-related conduct, §2-9(D).
Military due process, §1-1(B).
Speedy trial standards, §13-3(C)(1).

DUPLICITY.
Severance of duplicitous specifications, §13-5(G)(3).
Specifications alleging more than one offense, §6-1(C)(2).

DURESS.
Defense to absence without leave, §2-2(E)(3).

E

EMERGENCY SEARCHES, §5-3(C)(5).

ENLISTMENT.
Court members.
  Request for enlisted members, §§8-3(C)(2), 12-3(B).
    Form, Appx. 18.
Discharge generally.
  See DISCHARGE.
Inception of personal jurisdiction.
  Constructive enlistment, §4-5(A)(4).
  Incompetents, §4-5(A)(2).
  Involuntary, §4-5(A)(2).
  Minors, §4-5(A)(2).
  Recruiter misconduct effect, §4-5(A)(3).
  Valid enlistments, §4-5(A)(1).
  Void enlistments, §4-5(A)(2).
  Voluntary entry generally, §4-5(A).

EQUAL PROTECTION.
Challenges to classifications, §13-3(N)(1).
Fraternization and constitution, §2-8(D).

EQUIVALENT PUNISHMENTS, §16-2(G).

ESCALATOR PROVISION.
Punishments, §16-2(E).

EUROPEAN MODELS.
History of courts-martial.
  Early European models, §1-4.

EVIDENCE.
Article 32 investigations.
  Accused's rights.
    Right to examine, §7-2(B)(5).
    Right to present other evidence, §7-2(B)(7).
Depositions.
  Use at trial, §15-22.
Disclosure.
  See DISCLOSURE.
Discovery.
  See DISCOVERY.
Drug offenses, §2-7(C).
Errors.
  Objections and preserving, §15-23.
Examination by accused.
  Accused's rights at Article 32 investigations, §7-2(B)(5).
Exclusionary rule, §5-3(F).
  Motions to suppress, §§13-4 to 13-4(C).
Exhibits, §15-12(C).
Eyewitness identification, §5-5.
Generally, §15-18.
Guilty pleas.
  Admissibility of accused's statements, §14-3(B)(4).
Hearsay.
  Depositions as exceptions, §15-22.
  Notice by prosecution, §10-2(A).

EVIDENCE —Cont'd
Immunity grants, §5-4(C).
Inferences, §15-20.
Instructions during trials, §15-24.
Lineups, §5-5.
Military rules of evidence.
  See MILITARY RULES OF EVIDENCE.
Motion in limine, §13-5(L).
Motions to obtain rulings, §13-5(L).
Motions to suppress, §13-4.
  Eyewitness identification, §13-4(C).
  Illegal searches and seizures, §13-4(B).
  Pretrial statements, §13-4(A).
  Unlawful confinement, remedies, §5-10(D).
Nonjudicial punishment used at court-martial or administrative proceedings, §3-8(B).
Notice, §§10-2 to 10-2(B).
Presumptions, §15-20.
Pretrial agreements.
  Statements made by accused or counsel in unsuccessful negotiations, §9-2(A)(2).
Production of witnesses and evidence, §§11-1 to 11-4.
Rebuttal.
  Sentencing, §16-7.
Rules of evidence.
  See MILITARY RULES OF EVIDENCE.
Searches and seizures generally.
  See SEARCHES AND SEIZURES.
Self-incrimination.
  See SELF-INCRIMINATION.
Sentencing.
  See SENTENCING AND PUNISHMENT.
Suppression.
  Motions, §§13-4 to 13-4(C).
  Unlawful confinement, remedies, §5-10(D).
Surrebuttal.
  Sentencing, §16-7.
Undisclosed evidence.
  Notice by prosecution, §10-2(A).
Views and inspections of places and objects, §15-12(D).
Witnesses generally.
  See WITNESSES.

EXCLUSIONARY RULE, §5-3(F).
Motions to suppress, §§13-4 to 13-4(C).
  Unlawful confinement remedies, §5-10(D).

EXECUTION OF SENTENCES.
Powers of convening authority, §17-9(C).

INDEX

EXHAUSTION OF REMEDIES.
Collateral review in federal courts, §17-23(B).

EXHIBITS, §15-12(C).

EXPERT WITNESSES.
Employing, §11-2(A)(3).

EX POST FACTO LAWS.
Constitutional challenges, §13-3(N)(5).

EXTRA DUTIES.
Nonjudicial punishment, §3-6(C)(2).

EXTRAORDINARY WRITS.
Defense appeals on motion rulings, §13-2(G)(1).
Review of courts-martial, §17-19.

EXTRA TRAINING.
Nonpunitive option of commander, §1-8(B).

EYEWITNESS IDENTIFICATION, §5-5.
Motion to suppress, §13-4(C).

F

FAILING TO GO TO PLACE OF DUTY, §2-2(C)(1).

FAILURE TO ALLEGE OFFENSE.
Motions to dismiss, §13-3(F).

FARETTA INQUIRY.
Self-representation, §12-2(F)(4).

FEDERAL COURTS.
Collateral review of courts-martial.
　Exhaustion of remedies requirements, §17-23(B).
　Forms generally, §17-23(C).
　Generally, §17-23(A).
　Habeas corpus, §17-23(C)(1).
　Mandamus, §17-23(C)(2).
Concurrent jurisdiction over offenses, §4-12(A).

FEDERAL NONCAPITAL OFFENSES.
Article 134 prosecutions, §2-6(C).

FINDING OF NOT GUILTY.
Motion, §15-4(C).

FINES, §16-3(D).

FIRST AMENDMENT.
Constitutional challenges, §13-3(N)(3).
Public and press access to trials, §15-3.

FOOTNOTE FIVE LIMITATION.
Punishments, §16-2(F).

FOREIGN COURTS.
Reciprocal jurisdiction over offenses, §4-12(B).

FORFEITURES, §16-3(D).
Pay, §3-6(D).

FORMAL INVESTIGATION OF CHARGES.
See ARTICLE 32 INVESTIGATIONS.

FORMER JEOPARDY, §13-3(E).
Withdrawal and later referral of charges, §8-5.

FORMER PUNISHMENT, §13-3(G).

FORMS.
Appellate rights advice, Appx. 33.
Appellate's rights waived or withdrawn, Appx. 38.
Article 69.
　Sample application for relief under, Appx. 40.
Bill of particulars, Appx. 20.
Charge sheet, Appx. 6.
Conditional guilty plea.
　Entry, Appx. 23.
Convening order sample, Appx. 9.
Court-martial member questionnaire, Appx. 24.
Deferment application, Appx. 34.
Depositions.
　Interrogatories and depositions, Appx. 14.
　Request to take oral deposition, Appx. 13.
Disclosure of section III evidence, Appx. 19.
Discovery request sample, Appx. 10.
Enlisted members.
　Request for, Appx. 18.
Findings worksheet, Appx. 28.
Government appeals.
　Notice, Appx. 21.
Immunity grant, Appx. 11.
Investigating officer's report, Appx. 7.
Judge advocate legal review, Appx. 37.
Nonjudicial punishment, Appx. 5.
Plea worksheet, Appx. 22.
Post-trial recommendation sample, Appx. 35.
Pretrial advice sample, Appx. 8.
Pretrial agreement, Appx. 12.
Promulgating orders, Appx. 36.
Sentencing worksheet, Appx. 29.
Special findings, Appx. 32.
Stipulation of expected testimony, Appx. 26.

FORMS —Cont'd
Stipulation of fact, Appx. 25.
Subpoena for civilian witness, Appx. 15.
Trial before military judge alone.
  Request for, Appx. 17.
Vacation proceedings, Appx. 39.
Warrant of attachment, Appx. 16.

FORWARDING OF CHARGES.
See CHARGES AND SPECIFICATIONS.

FRATERNIZATION.
Constitution, §2-8(D).
General article, §2-8(B).
Generally, §2-8(A).
Regulations or orders, §2-8(C).

FRAUDULENT DISCHARGE,
  §4-8(C)(3).

FREEDOM OF ASSOCIATION.
First amendment challenges,
  §13-3(N)(3).

FREEDOM OF RELIGION.
First amendment challenges,
  §13-3(N)(3).

FREEDOM OF SPEECH.
First amendment challenges,
  §13-3(N)(3).
Fraternization and constitution, §2-8(D).

G

GATE SEARCHES, §5-3(C)(3).

GCM.
See GENERAL COURTS-MARTIAL.

GENERAL ARTICLE, 134.
Conduct bringing discredit upon armed forces, §2-6(B).
Disorders and neglects to prejudice of good order and discipline, §2-6(A).
Fraternization and general articles, §2-8(B).
Generally, §2-6.
HIV-related offenses prosecuted under, §2-9(C)(3).
Noncapital crimes and offenses, §2-6(C).

GENERAL COURTS-MARTIAL.
Disqualifications of convening authority, §4-14(A)(2).
Forwarding of charges.
  Convening authority, §6-2(D).
Generally, §1-8(D)(3).
Jurisdictional limits on sentence, §16-2(A).
Limits of jurisdiction, §4-3(A).

GENERAL COURTS-MARTIAL —Cont'd
Qualifications of detailed counsel, §8-3(B)(1).
Trial procedures.
  General and special courts-martial.
  See TRIAL PROCEDURES.

GENERAL ORDERS.
Violations, §2-4(C).

GENERAL REGULATIONS.
Violations, §2-4(C).

GLOSSARY, Appx. 2.

GOOD ORDER.
Disorders and neglects to prejudice of, §2-6(A).

GOVERNMENT APPEALS.
Notice, Appx. 21.

GOVERNMENT PROPERTY.
Nonprobable cause searches, §5-3(C)(2).

GRADE REDUCTION, §16-3(E).
Nonjudicial punishment, §3-6(B).

GRAND JURY.
Article 32 investigations counterpart to, §7-2.

GREEN-KING PRETRIAL AGREEMENT INQUIRY, §14-3(C).

GUIDES FOR TRIAL PROCEDURE, §15-6.

GUILTY PLEAS, §14-3.
Care providency inquiry, §14-3(B).
  Accuracy determination, §14-3(B)(2).
  Admissibility of accused's statements, §14-3(B)(4).
  Advice regarding rights, §14-3(B)(1).
  Voluntariness, §14-3(B)(3).
Conditional guilty plea, §14-4.
  Entry, Appx. 23.
Effect, §14-3(A).
  Guilty plea on later proceedings, §14-3(A)(4).
  Plea as to lesser offense, §14-3(A)(3).
  Waiver of issues, §14-3(A)(2).
  Waiver of rights, §14-3(A)(1).
Entry of findings, §14-3(E).
Green-King pretrial agreement inquiry, §14-3(C).
Improvident pleas.
  Alford pleas, §14-3(D)(2).
  Factual and legal inconsistencies, §14-3(D)(4).
  Generally, §14-3(D)(1).
  Misunderstanding of sentence, §14-3(D)(3).

INDEX

GUILTY PLEAS —Cont'd
Improvident pleas —Cont'd
  Procedural consequences, §14-3(D)(5).
Informing members, §14-3(F).
Pretrial agreements.
  Green-King pretrial agreement inquiry, §14-3(C).
Withdrawal, §14-3(G).

H

HABEAS CORPUS.
Collateral review in federal courts, §17-23(C)(1).
Extraordinary writs in military courts, §17-19.

HARD LABOR.
Deprivation of liberty, §16-3(C).

HEARINGS.
Nonjudicial punishment.
  Air force procedures, §3-5(C)(3).
  Army procedures, §3-5(B)(3).
  Coast guard procedures, §3-5(E)(3).
  Navy and marine corps procedures, §3-5(D)(3).
Trial procedures generally.
  See TRIAL PROCEDURES.

HEARSAY.
Depositions as exceptions, §15-22.
Notice by prosecution, §10-2(A).

HISTORY OF COURTS-MARTIAL.
American system.
  Generally, §1-6.
  1775 to 1800, the formative years, §1-6(A).
  1800 to 1900, quiet growth, §1-6(B).
  1900 to present, rapid change, §1-6(C).
British system.
  Constable's court, §1-5(B).
  Council of war, §1-5(C).
  Court of chivalry, §1-5(B).
  Generally, §1-5(A).
  Mutiny act, §1-5(D).
European models.
  Early European models, §1-4.

HIV-RELATED OFFENSES.
See AIDS AND HIV-RELATED OFFENSES.

I

IADA.
Speedy trial, applicability, §13-3(C)(4).

IDENTIFICATION BY EYEWITNESS, §5-5.
Motion to suppress, §13-4(C).

IMMUNITY.
Grants of, §5-4(C).
  Form, Appx. 11.
Motion to dismiss for grant of, §13-3(H).
Notice by prosecution, §§10-2(A), 11-2(E)(2).
Witnesses, §11-2(E)(1).
  Defense witnesses, §11-2(E)(3).
  Prosecution witnesses, §11-2(E)(2).

IMPEACHING FINDINGS, §15-16(B).

IMPOSSIBILITY.
Defense to absence without leave, §2-2(E)(1).

INCOMPETENCE TO STAND TRIAL, §13-5(A).

INCOMPETENTS, ENLISTMENT OF.
Void for purposes of personal jurisdiction, §4-5(A)(2).

INDIVIDUALLY REQUESTED COUNSEL.
Qualifications, §8-3(B)(1).
Request for, §8-3(B)(3).

INDUCTION.
Inception of personal jurisdiction, §4-5(B).

INEFFECTIVE ASSISTANCE OF COUNSEL, §15-2(B)(3).

INFERENCES, §15-20.

INFLUENCE OF COMMANDERS.
See COMMAND INFLUENCE.

IN LIMINE MOTIONS, §13-5(L).

INNOCENCE OF ACCUSED.
Presumption, §15-20.

INNOCENT INGESTION DEFENSE.
Notice by defense, §10-2(B).
  Automatic defense disclosure, §10-5(A)(4).

INSANITY OF ACCUSED.
Incompetence to stand trial, §13-5(A).
Lack of mental responsibility defense.
  See LACK OF MENTAL RESPONSIBILITY DEFENSE.
Motions at trial for inquiring into, §15-4(D).
Presumption of sanity, §15-20.

INSPECTION OF PERSONS AND PROPERTY, §5-3(D)(1).

INSPECTION OF PLACES AND OBJECTS, §15-12(D).

INSTRUCTIONS TO COURT MEMBERS.
Checklist, Appx. 27.
Error review, §15-14(D).
Evidentiary instructions during trial, §15-24.
Generally, §15-14(A).
Requests, §15-14(C).
Sentencing instructions, §16-9.
Sua sponte instructions, §15-14(B).

INSUBORDINATION TOWARD PETTY, WARRANT OR NONCOMMISSIONED OFFICERS, §2-3(B).

INTERPRETER, §15-2(G).
Detail, §12-2(D).
Swearing, §15-8.

INTERROGATION OF SUSPECTS, §5-4(B).

INTERROGATORIES.
Written depositions.
  Form of interrogatories and depositions, Appx. 14.
  Procedures, §§11-3(B)(1), 11-3(B)(3).

INTERSTATE AGREEMENT ON DETAINERS ACT.
Speedy trial.
  Applicability, §13-3(C)(4).

INVENTORY OF PROPERTY, §5-3(D)(1).

INVESTIGATING OFFICER.
Article 32 investigations.
  Parties to investigations, §7-2(A)(1).
  Report, §7-2(D); Appx. 7.

INVESTIGATION BY COMMANDER, §§5-1, 5-2.

IRREGULAR PLEAS, §14-5.

J

JAIL AND RESTRICTED AREA SEARCHES, §5-3(C)(4).

JENCKS ACT MATERIALS.
Defense request for discovery, §10-4(B)(5).

JOINDER OF CHARGES.
Misjoinder, §6-1(C)(1).

JUDGE.
See MILITARY JUDGE.

JUDGE ADVOCATE.
Legal review, Appx. 37.
New trial petitions made to judge advocate general, §17-21.
Pretrial advice by staff judge advocate, §§7-3 to 7-3(B).
Review in office of judge advocate general, §17-20.

JUDICIAL NOTICE.
Notice by defense, §10-2(B).
Notice by prosecution, §10-2(A).

JURISDICTION.
Appointed officers.
  Inception of personal jurisdiction, §4-5(C).
Change of status from civilian to servicemember.
  Inception of personal jurisdiction, §§4-5 to 4-5(C).
Charges and specifications.
  Pleading, §6-1(B)(1).
Civilians, §§4-7 to 4-7(B).
Composition of courts-martial.
  Counsel, §4-15(B).
  Court members, §4-15(C).
  Military judge, §4-15(A).
  Properly composed generally, §4-15.
Convening of courts-martial.
  Authority to convene, §4-14.
    Convening authority, §4-14(A).
      Delegation of authority, §4-14(A)(3).
      Disqualification, §4-14(A)(2).
      Statutory authorization, §4-14(A)(1).
    Convening orders, §4-14(B).
  Generally, §4-13.
Court of appeals for the armed forces, §17-16(B).
Courts of criminal appeals, §17-15(A).
Creature of statute, §4-2(A).
Discharge terminates status, §4-8(B).
  Exceptions to general rule, §§4-8(C) to 4-8(C)(5).
Enlistment.
  Inception of personal jurisdiction, §§4-5(A) to 4-5(A)(4).
Exclusive, reciprocal and concurrent jurisdiction, §§4-12 to 4-12(B).
Federal courts.
  Concurrent jurisdiction over offenses, §4-12(A).
Foreign courts.
  Reciprocal jurisdiction over offenses, §4-12(B).
Generally, §4-1.

INDEX

JURISDICTION —Cont'd
Induction.
  Inception of personal jurisdiction, §4-5(B).
Lack of jurisdiction.
  Motion to dismiss, §13-3(A).
Limits of courts-martial jurisdiction.
  General court-martial, §4-3(A).
  Generally, §4-3.
  Special court-martial, §4-3(B).
  Summary court-martial, §4-3(C).
Motion to dismiss for lack of jurisdiction, §13-3(A).
National guard members, §4-6.
Nature of court-martial jurisdiction.
  Creature of statute, §4-2(A).
  Generally, §4-2.
  Requisites, §4-2(B).
Over offense.
  Exclusive, reciprocal and concurrent jurisdiction.
    Foreign courts, §4-12(B).
    Generally, §4-12.
    State and federal courts, §4-12(A).
  Introduction, §4-10.
  Service connection requirement, §4-11.
    Demise, §4-11(C).
      Constitutional implications, §4-11(C)(1).
      Practical implications, §4-11(C)(2).
    Relford factors, §4-11(A).
    Retreat from, §4-11(B).
Personal jurisdiction.
  Appointed officers, §4-5(C).
  Change of status from civilian to servicemember.
    Inception of jurisdiction, §§4-5 to 4-5(C).
  Civilians.
    Generally, §4-7.
    Peacetime, §4-7(B).
    Wartime, §4-7(A).
  Continuing jurisdiction, §4-8(A).
  Discharge terminates status, §4-8(B).
    Exceptions.
      Article 3(a) offenses, §4-8(C)(2).
      Deserters, §4-8(C)(4).
      Fraudulent discharge, §4-8(C)(3).
      Generally, §4-8(C).
      Persons in custody, §4-8(C)(5).
      Re-enlistment discharges, §4-8(C)(1).
  Enlistment.
    Constructive enlistment, §4-5(A)(4).
    Recruiter misconduct, §4-5(A)(3).
    Valid enlistments, §4-5(A)(1).

JURISDICTION —Cont'd
Personal jurisdiction —Cont'd
  Enlistment —Cont'd
    Void enlistments, §4-5(A)(2).
    Voluntary entry generally, §4-5(A).
  Generally, §4-4.
  Inception of jurisdiction.
    Change of status from civilian to servicemember, §§4-5 to 4-5(C).
  Involuntary entry.
    Induction, §4-5(B).
  National guard members, §4-6.
  Pleading and proving, §4-9.
  Reservists, §4-6.
  Retired members, §4-8(D).
  Termination.
    Continuing jurisdiction, §4-8(A).
    Discharge terminates status, §4-8(B).
    Exceptions to general rule, §§4-8(C) to 4-8(C)(5).
    Generally, §4-8.
  Voluntary entry.
    Enlistment generally, §§4-5(A) to 4-5(A)(4).
Punishment.
  Jurisdictional limits, §16-2(A).
Referral of charges.
  Charges properly referred to court-martial, §4-16.
Requisites, §4-2(B).
Reservists, §4-6.
Retired members, §4-8(D).
Service connection requirement, §§4-11 to 4-11(C)(2).
State courts.
  Concurrent jurisdiction over offenses, §4-12(A).

JURY.
See COURT MEMBERS.

JUSTIFICATION.
Defense to absence without leave, §2-2(E)(2).

L

LACK OF MENTAL RESPONSIBILITY DEFENSE.
Motions to dismiss, §13-3(D).
Notice by defense, §10-2(B).
  Automatic defense disclosure, §10-5(A)(3).

LEADING QUESTIONS, §15-12(A).

LEAVING PLACE OF DUTY, §2-2(C)(2).

LEGAL PERIODICALS, §1-3(e).
LEGAL SERVICES-MILITARY JUSTICE.
Army service supplement to manual for courts-manual, §1-3(C).
LESSER INCLUDED OFFENSES.
Guilty pleas.
   Effect as to lesser offense, §14-3(A)(2).
LIBERTY CONDITIONS.
Pretrial restraints, §5-8(B).
LIBERTY DEPRIVATION, §16-3(C).
LIBERTY PUNISHMENTS.
Nonjudicial punishment, §§3-6(C) to 3-6(C)(4).
LINEUPS.
Eyewitness identification, §5-5.

M

MANDAMUS.
Collateral review in federal courts, §17-23(C)(2).
Extraordinary writs in military courts, §17-19.
MANSLAUGHTER.
HIV-related offenses.
   Prosecuting under Articles 118 and 119 of UCMJ, §2-9(C)(1).
MANUAL FOR COURTS-MARTIAL.
Researching issues, §1-3(B).
Rules binding, §1-3(B).
Service supplements to, §1-3(C).
Table of maximum punishments, §16-2(C).
MANUAL OF THE JUDGE ADVOCATE GENERAL.
Navy and marine corps service supplement to manual for courts-martial, §1-3(C).
MARINE CORPS NONJUDICIAL PUNISHMENT PROCEDURES, §§3-5(D) to 3-5(D)(4).
MAXIMUM PUNISHMENT.
See SENTENCING AND PUNISHMENT.
MEDIA.
Courts-martial and media, §15-3.
MENTAL ILLNESS OF ACCUSED.
Incompetence to stand trial, §13-5(A).
Lack of mental responsibility defense.
   See LACK OF MENTAL RESPONSIBILITY DEFENSE.

MENTAL ILLNESS OF ACCUSED
—Cont'd
Motions at trial for inquiring into sanity, §15-4(D).
Presumption of sanity, §15-20.
MILITARY CORRECTIONS, §17-6.
MILITARY CRIMES.
See CRIMES.
MILITARY DUE PROCESS, §1-1(B).
MILITARY JUDGE, §15-2(D).
Active participant at trials, §15-2(D).
Challenges for cause, §12-2(H).
Command influence on courts-martial, §6-5(A).
Detailing, §8-3(A).
   Announcing, §12-2(G).
Ineligibility, §8-3(A).
Peremptory challenge, §12-2(H).
Presiding participant, §8-3(A).
Qualifications, §§4-15(A), 8-3(A).
Questions by court, §15-12(B).
Special findings by, §15-16(C).
Substitution, §8-3(D).
Trial by judge alone.
   Accused's request, §12-3(A).
   Form of request, Appx. 17.
MILITARY JUSTICE GUIDE.
Air force service supplement to manual for courts-martial, §1-3(C).
MILITARY JUSTICE MANUAL.
Coast guard service supplement to manual for courts-martial, §1-3(C).
MILITARY JUSTICE REPORTER.
Researching issues, §1-3(D)(2).
MILITARY LAW REVIEW.
Legal periodicals, §1-3(e).
MILITARY RULES OF EVIDENCE, §15-19.
Body cavity searches, §5-3(D)(2).
Depositions as exception to hearsay rule.
   Rule 804, §15-22.
Evidence generally.
   See EVIDENCE.
Examination of witnesses.
   Rule 611, §15-12(A).
Exclusionary rule.
   Rule 311, §5-3(F).
Inspections and inventories.
   Rule 313, §5-3(D)(1).
Lineups.
   Rule 321, §5-5.
Motions to suppress evidence resulting from illegal searches and seizures.
   Rule 311, §13-4(B).

INDEX

MILITARY RULES OF EVIDENCE —Cont'd
Motion to suppress pretrial statements.
 Rule 304, §13-4(A).
Nonprobable cause searches, §5-3(C)(1).
Notice requirements, §10-2(A).
Pretrial agreement statements made by accused or counsel.
 Rule 410, §9-2(A)(2).
Rulings on.
 Rule 103, §15-23.
Sentencing, §16-4(B).
Unavailable witnesses.
 Rule 804, §11-2(A)(2).

MINOR OFFENSES.
Nonjudicial punishment, §3-3(C).

MINORS.
Enlistment.
 Void for purposes of personal jurisdiction, §4-5(A)(2).

MIRANDA RIGHT TO COUNSEL WARNINGS.
Interrogation of suspects, §5-4(B).

MISJOINDER.
Combining charges, §6-1(C)(1).

MISSING MOVEMENT, §2-2(D).

MISTAKE OF FACT.
Defense to absence without leave, §2-2(E)(4).

MISTRIAL.
Guilty pleas.
 Procedural consequences of improvident plea, §14-3(D)(5).
Motion at trial, §15-4(B).

MIXED PLEAS, §14-2.

MORAL BELIEFS.
Defense to absence without leave, §2-2(E)(7).

MOTION FOR RELEASE FROM PRETRIAL CONFINEMENT, §5-10(D).

MOTIONS AT TRIAL, §15-4.
Continuances, §15-4(A).
Finding of not guilty, §15-4(C).
Mistrial, §15-4(B).

MOTIONS IN LIMINE, §13-5(L).

MOTIONS PRACTICE.
Appeal of rulings, §13-2(G).
 Defense appeals, §13-2(G)(1).
 Government appeals, §13-2(G)(2).
Burden of proof, §13-2(D).

MOTIONS PRACTICE —Cont'd
Categories of motions, §13-2(A).
Extraordinary writs.
 Defense appeals, §13-2(G)(1).
Finality of rulings, §13-2(E).
Introduction, §13-1.
Motions required to be made prior to accused's entering plea, §13-2(A).
Notice, §13-2(C).
Procedural aspects generally, §13-2.
Rulings, §13-2(E).
 Appeal, §§13-2(G) to 13-2(G)(2).
 Reconsideration, §13-2(F).
Service, §13-2(C).
Timing, §13-2(A).
Waiver, §13-2(B).

MOTIONS TO DISMISS.
Command influence, §6-7.
Constitutional challenges, §§13-3(N) to 13-3(N)(5).
Defective specification misleading accused, §13-3(K).
Desertion.
 Constructive condonation, §13-3(I).
Equal protection challenges, §13-3(N)(1).
Ex post facto laws, §13-3(N)(5).
Failure to allege offense, §13-3(F).
First amendment challenges, §13-3(N)(3).
Former jeopardy, §13-3(E).
Former punishment, §13-3(G).
Grant of immunity, §13-3(H).
Jurisdiction.
 Lack of jurisdiction, §13-3(A).
Lack of fair notice, §13-3(N)(2).
Lack of mental responsibility, §13-3(D).
Multiplicity, §13-3(J).
Presidential pardon, §13-3(L).
Privacy rights, §13-3(N)(4).
Selective or vindictive prosecution, §13-3(M).
Speedy trial, §§13-3(C) to 13-3(C)(5).
Statute of limitations, §13-3(B).
Vagueness, §13-3(N)(2).

MOTIONS TO GRANT APPROPRIATE RELIEF, §13-5.
Abatement, §13-5(K).
Bill of particulars, §13-5(F).
Change of venue, §13-5(C).
Continuance, §13-5(K).
Counsel.
 Requests concerning, §13-5(H).
Discovery, §13-5(J).
Evidentiary matters.
 Rulings on, §13-5(L).
Incompetence to stand trial, §13-5(A).

MOTIONS TO GRANT APPROPRIATE RELIEF —Cont'd
Motions in limine, §13-5(L).
Pleadings defective, §13-5(E).
Pretrial investigation or pretrial advice.
  Defective, §13-5(D).
Pretrial restraint, §13-5(B).
Severance, §13-5(G).
  Accused, §13-5(G)(1).
  Charges, §13-5(G)(2).
  Duplicitous specifications, §13-5(G)(3).
Witnesses.
  Requests for, §13-5(I).

MOTIONS TO SUPPRESS, §13-4.
Accused's limited testimony.
  Notice by defense, §10-2(B).
Eyewitness identification, §13-4(C).
Illegal searches and seizures, §13-4(B).
Pretrial statements of accused, §13-4(A).

MULTIPLICITY.
Motion to dismiss, §13-3(J).
Punishments, §16-2(D).
Single criminal transaction alleged in more than one specification, §6-1(C)(3).

MURDER.
HIV-related offenses.
  Prosecuting under Articles 118 and 119 of UCMJ, §2-9(C)(1).

MUTINY ACT.
British act, §1-5(D).

N

NATIONAL GUARD.
Personal jurisdiction over members, §4-6.

NAVAL LAW REVIEW.
Military legal periodicals, §1-3(e).

NAVY NONJUDICIAL PUNISHMENT PROCEDURES, §§3-5(D) to 3-5(D)(4).

NECESSITY.
Defense to absence without leave, §2-2(E)(2).

NEGLIGENCE.
Dereliction of duty, §2-4(E).

NEGOTIATED PLEAS.
Pretrial agreements generally.
  See PRETRIAL AGREEMENTS.

NEW TRIAL.
Limitation of punishment imposed on, §16-2(B).

NEW TRIAL —Cont'd
Petition for, §17-21.

NOMINAL ACCUSER, §6-1.

NONCAPITAL FEDERAL CRIMES.
Article 134 prosecutions, §2-6(C).

NONCOMMISSIONED OFFICERS.
Insubordination toward, §2-3(B).

NONJUDICIAL PUNISHMENT.
Air force procedures.
  Appeals, §3-5(C)(4).
  Generally, §3-5(C).
  Hearing, §3-5(C)(3).
  Notice, §3-5(C)(2).
  Preliminary inquiry, §3-5(C)(1).
Applicable policies, §3-2.
Army procedures.
  Appeals, §3-5(B)(4).
  Generally, §3-5(B).
  Hearings, §3-5(B)(3).
  Notice, §3-5(B)(2).
  Preliminary inquiry, §3-5(B)(1).
Authority to impose.
  General rule, §3-3.
  Minor offenses, §3-3(C).
  Who may be punished, §3-3(B).
  Who may impose, §3-3(A).
Censure, §3-6(E).
Coast guard procedures.
  Appeals, §3-5(E)(4).
  Generally, §3-5(E).
  Hearing, §3-5(E)(3).
  Notice, §3-5(E)(2).
  Preliminary inquiry, §3-5(E)(1).
Combination of punishments, §3-6(F).
Consequences.
  Military career, §3-8(A).
  Use at court-martial or administrative proceedings, §3-8(B).
Corrective or rehabilitative in design, §3-2.
Deprivation of liberty.
  Arrest in quarters, §3-6(C)(4).
  Bread and water confinement, §3-6(C)(5).
  Correctional custody, §3-6(C)(1).
  Extra duties, §3-6(C)(2).
  Generally, §3-6(C).
  Restriction, §3-6(C)(3).
Effective date of punishments, §3-6(G).
Errors in imposition, §3-7.
Forfeiture of pay, §3-6(D).
Former punishment, §13-3(G).
  Motion to dismiss, §13-3(G).
Forms, Appx. 5.
Introduction, §3-1.

INDEX

NONJUDICIAL PUNISHMENT
—Cont'd
Limitations on combination of punishments, §3-6(F).
Military career effect, §3-8(A).
Minor offenses, §3-3(C).
Navy and marine corps procedures.
  Appeals, §3-5(D)(4).
  Generally, §3-5(D).
  Hearing, §3-5(D)(3).
  Notice, §3-5(D)(2).
  Preliminary inquiry, §3-5(D)(1).
Option of commander, §1-8(C).
Procedural rules generally, §3-5(A).
Punishments generally, §3-6(A).
Reduction in grade, §3-6(B).
Trial by court-martial.
  Right to demand, §3-4.
Use at court-martial or administrative proceedings, §3-8(B).
Who may be punished, §3-3(B).
Who may impose, §3-3(A).

NONPROBABLE CAUSE SEARCHES, §5-3(C).

NONPUNITIVE MEASURES.
Commander's options, §1-8(B).

NOT GUILTY PLEAS, §14-2.

NOTICE.
Charges.
  Accused's rights at Article 32 investigations, §7-2(B)(1).
Defense notice, §10-2(B).
Generally, §10-1.
Government appeals, §13-2(G)(2); Appx. 21.
Lack of fair notice challenges, §13-3(N)(2).
Motions, §13-2(C).
Nonjudicial punishment.
  Air force procedures, §3-5(C)(2).
  Army procedures, §3-5(B)(2).
  Coast guard procedures, §3-5(E)(2).
  Navy and marine corps procedures, §3-5(D)(2).
Prosecution notice, §10-2(A).
Requirements, §10-2.
Service of charges upon accused, §8-6.

NUREMBURG DEFENSE.
Absence without leave, §2-2(E)(7).

O

OATHS.
Administering, §12-2(G).
Trial participants, §15-8.

OBJECTIONS.
Military rules of evidence, §15-23.

OFFICE HOURS.
Nonjudicial punishment.
  See NONJUDICIAL PUNISHMENT.

OFFICERS' LOSS OF NUMBERS.
Permissible punishments, §16-3(F).

120-DAY SPEEDY TRIAL RULE, §13-3(C)(3).

ON-THE-SCENE IDENTIFICATIONS, §5-5.
Motion to suppress eyewitness identification, §13-4(C).

OPENING STATEMENTS, §15-11.

OPTIONS OF COMMANDER.
Court-martial, §§1-8(D) to 1-8(D)(3).
Generally, §1-8(A).
Nonjudicial punishment, §1-8(C).
Nonpunitive measures, §1-8(B).

ORDERS.
Constitutional challenges.
  Motions to dismiss, §§13-3(N) to 13-3(N)(5).
Convening order.
  See CONVENING ORDER.
Disobedience offenses, §§2-4(A) to 2-4(E).
Fraternization, §2-8(C).
General orders, violation, §2-4(c).
Lawful orders generally, §2-4(A).
Promulgating orders, §17-10; Appx. 36.
Safe sex order violations, §2-9(B).

OVERVIEW TO PRESENT SYSTEM, §1-7.

P

PARDONS.
Motion to dismiss for presidential pardons, §13-3(L).

PARTICIPANTS AT TRIAL.
See TRIAL PROCEDURES.

PAY DEPRIVATION, §16-3(D).

PAY FORFEITURE.
Nonjudicial punishment, §3-6(D).

PEREMPTORY CHALLENGE FOR REMOVING JUDGE, §12-2(H).

PEREMPTORY CHALLENGES TO COURT MEMBERS, §15-10(C)(3).

PERJURY.
Defense counsel and perjurious clients, §15-2(B)(4).

PERSONAL JURISDICTION.
See JURISDICTION.

PETTY OFFICERS.
Insubordination toward, §2-3(B).

PHOTOGRAPHIC IDENTIFICATIONS, §5-5.

PLACE OF DUTY.
Failing to go to, §2-2(C)(1).
Leaving, §2-2(C)(2).

PLEA BARGAINING, §9-1.
Pretrial agreements generally.
  See PRETRIAL AGREEMENTS.

PLEADING CHARGES AND SPECIFICATIONS.
Defective pleadings, §6-1(C).
  Duplicity, §6-1(C)(2).
  Misjoinder, §6-1(C)(1).
  Motion to cure or amend, §13-5(E).
  Multiplicity, §6-1(C)(3).
General rules, §6-1(B).
  Additional charges, §6-1(B)(3).
  Amendments, §6-1(B)(2).
  Jurisdiction, §6-1(B)(1).

PLEADING PERSONAL JURISDICTION, §4-19.

PLEAS.
Conditional guilty plea, §14-4.
  Entry, Appx. 23.
Confessional stipulations, §9-3.
Guilty pleas, §14-3.
  Care providency inquiry, §§14-3(B) to 14-3(B)(4).
  Effects, §§14-3(A) to 14-3(A)(4).
  Entry of findings, §14-3(E).
  Green-King pretrial agreement inquiry, §14-3(C).
  Improvident pleas, §§14-3(D)(1) to 14-3(D)(5).
  Informing members of plea, §14-3(F).
  Withdrawal, §14-3(G).
Introduction, §14-1.
Irregular pleas, §14-5.
Mixed plea.
  Guilty of lesser included offense but not guilty of greater offense, §14-2.
Negotiated pleas.
  Pretrial agreements generally.
    See PRETRIAL AGREEMENTS.
Not guilty pleas, §14-2.
  Confessional stipulations, §9-3.
Worksheet, Appx. 22.

POST-TRIAL COMMAND INFLUENCE.
See COMMAND INFLUENCE.

POST-TRIAL DUTIES OF COUNSEL.
See COUNSEL.

POST-TRIAL PROCEEDINGS, §17-3.
Article 39(a) post-trial sessions, §17-3(B).
Revision proceedings, §17-3(A).

POST-TRIAL RECOMMENDATION, §17-8(B).
Defense counsel to review staff judge advocate's recommendations, §17-2(B)(4).
Effective recommendations, §17-8(B)(2).
  Service on defense counsel, §17-8(B)(3).
Format and contents, §17-8(B)(1).
Sample, Appx. 35.

PREFERRING SWORN CHARGES.
See CHARGES AND SPECIFICATIONS.

PRELIMINARY INQUIRIES.
Nonjudicial punishment.
  Air force procedures, §3-5(C)(1).
  Army procedures, §3-5(B)(1).
  Coast guard procedures, §3-5(E)(1).
  Navy and marine corps procedures, §3-5(D)(1).
Pretrial command influence, §6-4(A).

PRESENCE AT ARTICLE 32 INVESTIGATIONS.
Accused's rights, §7-2(B)(3).

PRESENCE AT TRIAL.
Accused, §15-2(A).
Commander's presence, §6-5(C).
Court members, §15-2(E).

PRESERVATION OF TESTIMONY.
See DEPOSITIONS.

PRESIDENTIAL PARDON.
Motion to dismiss, §13-3(L).

PRESS.
Courts-martial and media, §15-3.

PRESUMPTIONS, §15-20.
Lawfulness of orders and regulations, §2-4(A).

PRETRIAL ADVICE BY STAFF JUDGE ADVOCATE.
Contents, §7-3(A).
Defective advice, §§7-3(B), 13-5(D).
Generally, §§7-1, 7-3.
Sample advice, Appx. 8.

PRETRIAL AGREEMENTS.
Conditions and terms generally, §9-2(B).
Confessional stipulations, §9-3.
Contract principles, §9-2.
Discharge in lieu of court-martial, §9-4.

PRETRIAL AGREEMENTS —Cont'd
Form, Appx. 12.
Generally, §9-2.
Guilty pleas.
  Green-King pretrial agreement inquiry, §14-3(C).
Informal agreements, §9-2(A)(3).
Initiation of negotiations and terms, §9-2(A)(1).
Invalid terms, §9-2(B)(2).
Judicial review, §9-2(D).
Submission and acceptance of offer, §9-2(A)(2).
Valid conditions, §9-2(B)(1).
Withdrawal from, §9-2(C).

PRETRIAL COMMAND INFLUENCE.
See COMMAND INFLUENCE.

PRETRIAL CONFERENCES, §12-5.
Summary courts-martial, §15-27.

PRETRIAL CONFINEMENT.
Generally, §5-9(A).
Initial decision to confine, §5-9(B).
Judicial review, §5-9(E).
Review by commander, §5-9(C).
Review of commander's decision, §5-9(D).

PRETRIAL INVESTIGATION, ARTICLE 32.
See ARTICLE 32 INVESTIGATIONS.

PRETRIAL MOTIONS.
Motions practice.
  See MOTIONS PRACTICE.
Motions to dismiss.
  See MOTIONS TO DISMISS.
Motions to grant appropriate relief.
  See MOTIONS TO GRANT APPROPRIATE RELIEF.
Motions to suppress.
  See MOTIONS TO SUPPRESS.

PRETRIAL RESTRAINTS.
Apprehension, §5-7.
  Unlawful apprehension, §5-10(D).
Arrest, §§5-8(A), 5-8(D).
  Restriction in lieu of, §5-8(C).
Conditions on liberty, §5-8(B).
Confinement.
  Generally, §5-9(A).
  Initial decision, §5-9(B).
  Judicial review, §5-9(E).
  Remedy for unlawful confinement, §5-10(D).
  Review by commander, §5-9(C).
  Review of commander's decision, §5-9(D).

PRETRIAL RESTRAINTS —Cont'd
Generally, §§5-6, 5-8(A).
Illegal pretrial punishment and restraint.
  Generally, §5-10(A).
  Pretrial punishment other than restraint, §5-10(B).
  Pretrial restraints constituting illegal punishment, §5-10(C).
  Remedies, §5-10(D).
Imposition generally, §5-8(A).
Motions relating to, §13-5(B).
Probable cause.
  Basis for forms of restraint, §5-8(A).
Punishment.
  Illegal pretrial punishment and restraint, §§5-10(A) to 5-10(D).
  Pretrial restraint may not constitute, §5-8(A).
Remedy for unlawful confinement, §5-10(D).
Restriction in lieu of arrest, §5-8(C).

PRETRIAL SESSION.
See ARTICLE 39(A) PRETRIAL SESSION.

PRETRIAL STATEMENTS.
Defense request for discovery.
  Jencks act materials, §10-4(B)(5).
Motion to suppress, §13-4(A).

PRIOR CONVICTIONS.
Automatic prosecutorial disclosure, §10-4(A)(3).
Notice by defense, §10-2(B).
Notice by prosecution, §10-2(A).
Sentencing.
  Evidence of, §16-5(C).

PRIOR EXTRINSIC ACTS.
Notice by prosecution, §10-2(A).

PRIOR SERVICE.
Evidence during sentencing, §16-5(B).

PRIVACY RIGHTS.
Constitutional challenges, §13-3(N)(4).
Constitutionality of prosecuting HIV-related conduct, §2-9(D).
Fraternization and constitution, §2-8(D).
Searches and seizures, §5-3(A).

PRIVILEGED INFORMATION.
Disclosure.
  Notice by defense, §10-2(B).

PROBABLE CAUSE.
Apprehension, §5-7.
Pretrial restraints.
  Basis for forms of restraint, §5-8(A).
Searches, §5-3(B).

PROBABLE CAUSE —Cont'd
Warrant of attachment, §11-2(D)(3).

PRODUCTION OF EVIDENCE, §11-4.

PRODUCTION OF WITNESSES.
See WITNESSES.

PROFANITY.
Defense to disrespect offenses, §2-3(C).

PROHIBITION.
Extraordinary writs in military courts, §17-19.

PROSECUTION NOTICE, §10-2(A).

PROSECUTORIAL DISCRETION.
Court-martial, §§1-8(D) to 1-8(D)(3).
Generally, §1-8(A).
Nonjudicial punishment, §1-8(C).
Nonpunitive measures, §1-8(B).

PROSECUTOR, TRIAL COUNSEL.
Counsel generally.
  See COUNSEL.

PUBLIC TRIALS, §15-3.

PUNISHMENT.
See SENTENCING AND PUNISHMENT.

PUNITIVE SEPARATIONS, §16-3(B).

Q

QUESTIONS BY COURT, §15-12(B).

R

RACIAL SLURS.
Defense to disrespect offenses, §2-3(C).

RAPE.
HIV-related offenses.
  Prosecuting under Article 120 of UCMJ, §2-9(C)(2).

RAPE SHIELD LAW.
Past sexual behavior of victim.
  Notice by defense, §10-2(B).

REBUTTAL EVIDENCE.
Sentencing, §16-7.

RECORDS OF TRIAL, §17-4.
Authentication, §17-4(A).
Service on accused, §17-4(B).

REDUCTION IN GRADE OR RANK, §16-3(E).
Administrative reduction, §1-8(B).
Nonjudicial punishment, §3-6(B).

REFERRAL OF CHARGES.
Article 32 investigations generally.
  See ARTICLE 32 INVESTIGTIONS.
Generally.
  See CHARGES AND SPECIFICATIONS.

REGULATIONS.
Constitutional challenges.
  Motions to dismiss, §§13-3(N) to 13-3(N)(5).
Disobedience offenses, §§2-4(A) to 2-4(E).
Fraternization, §2-8(C).
Lawfulness of regulations, §2-4(A).

REHABILITATION.
Evidence during sentencing, §16-5(D)(4).

REHEARING.
Limitation of punishment imposed on, §16-2(B).

RELIGIOUS FREEDOM.
First amendment challenges, §13-3(N)(3).

REPORT OF INVESTIGATING OFFICERS.
Article 32 investigations, §7-2(D); Appx. 7.

REPRIMAND.
Nonjudicial punishment.
  Censure, §3-6(E).
Nonpunitive option of commander, §1-8(B).
Permissible punishment generally, §16-3(G).

REQUESTS FOR WITNESSES AT GOVERNMENT EXPENSE.
Defense witnesses, §11-2(B)(1).

RESEARCHING ISSUES, §1-3.
Manual for courts-martial (MCM), §1-3(B).
  Service supplements to, §1-3(C).
Military case law.
  Citator, §1-3(D)(3).
  Court-martial reports, §1-3(D)(1).
  Military justice reporter, §1-3(D)(2).
Military legal periodicals, §1-3(E).
Uniform code of military justice, §1-3(A).

RESERVISTS.
Personal jurisdiction, §4-6.

RESTRICTION.
Deprivation of liberty, §16-3(C).
In lieu of arrest.
  Pretrial restraints, §5-8(C).
Nonjudicial punishment, §3-6(C)(3).

INDEX

RETIRED MEMBERS.
Personal jurisdiction, §4-8(D).

REVIEW OF COURTS-MARTIAL.
Administrative relief, §17-22.
  Boards for correction of military records, §17-22(A).
  Discharge review boards, §17-22(B).
Appellate review generally.
  See APPEALS.
Automatic review, §17-1.
Collateral relief in federal courts.
  Exhaustion of remedies requirement, §17-23(B).
  Forms of review generally, §17-23(C).
  Generally, §17-23(A).
  Habeas corpus, §17-23(C)(1).
  Mandamus, §17-23(C)(2).
Confinement pending review, §17-5.
Convening authority.
  Initial review.
    See CONVENING AUTHORITY.
Extraordinary writs in military courts, §17-19.
Introduction, §17-1.
Judge advocate general review, §17-20; Appx. 37.
New trial petition, §17-21.
Other forms generally, §17-18.
Post-trial duties of counsel.
  See COUNSEL.
Post-trial proceedings, §17-3.
  Article 39(a) post-trial sessions, §17-3(B).
  Revision proceedings, §17-3(A).
Post-trial recommendation.
  Sample, Appx. 35.
Records of trial, §17-4.
  Authentication, §17-4(A).
  Service on accused, §17-4(B).

REVISION PROCEEDINGS.
Correction of errors or omissions, §17-3(A).

RIGHTS OF PRIVACY.
See PRIVACY RIGHTS.

RIGHTS WARNINGS.
Interrogation of suspects, §5-4(B).

RULES OF EVIDENCE.
See MILITARY RULES OF EVIDENCE.

S

SAFE SEX ORDERS.
Violating, §2-9(B).

SCM.
See SUMMARY COURTS-MARTIAL.

SEARCHES AND SEIZURES.
Apprehension.
  Searches incident to apprehension, §5-3(C)(7).
Body views and intrusions, §5-3(D)(2).
Border searches, §5-3(C)(3).
Consent searches, §5-3(C)(6).
Drug offense evidentiary issues, §2-7(C).
Emergency searches, §5-3(C)(5).
Exclusionary rule, §5-3(F).
Gate searches, §5-3(C)(3).
Generally, §5-3(A).
Inspections and inventories, §5-3(D)(1).
Jails or other restricted areas, §5-3(C)(4).
Motions to suppress.
  Illegal searches and seizures, §13-4(B).
Nonprobable cause searches, §5-3(C).
  Other nonprobable cause searches, §5-3(C)(9).
Probable cause searches, §5-3(B).
Right to privacy, §5-3(A).
Seizures generally, §5-3(E).
Stop and frisk, §5-3(C)(8).

SELECTIVE PROSECUTION.
Motion to dismiss, §13-3(M).

SELF-INCRIMINATION.
Article 32 investigations.
  Accused's right to remain silent, §7-2(B)(8).
Generally, §5-4(A)(1).
Immunity, §§5-4(C), 11-2(E)(1) to 11-2(E)(3).
Interrogation of suspects, §5-4(B).
Invoking right, §5-4(A)(3).
Reporting contacts with agents of foreign government, accidents, etc., §5-4(A)(2).

SELF-REPRESENTATION.
Faretta inquiry, §12-2(F)(4).

SENTENCING AND PUNISHMENT.
Adjournment of court, §16-13.
Announcement of sentence, §16-11.
Appellate rights advice, §16-12.
Arguments on sentencing.
  Defense arguments, §16-8(C).
  Generally, §16-8(A).
  Prosecution arguments, §16-8(B).
Charge sheet.
  Data from, §16-5(A).
Charts.
  Maximum amount, Appx. 30.
  Types and jurisdictional limits, Appx. 31.

SENTENCING AND PUNISHMENT
—Cont'd
Confinement generally.
  See CONFINEMENT.
Deliberations on sentencing, §16-10.
Discovery.
  Defense request for discovery, §10-4(B)(4).
Evidence.
  Aggravation evidence generally, §16-5(D)(1).
  Applicability of rules of evidence, §16-4(B).
  Charge sheet data, §16-5(A).
  Circumstances surrounding offenses, §16-5(D)(2).
  Defense evidence, §16-6.
  Prior convictions, §16-5(C).
  Prior service of accused, §16-5(B).
  Prosecution evidence generally, §16-5.
  Rebuttal and surrebuttal, §16-7.
  Rehabilitative potential, §16-5(D)(4).
  Uncharged misconduct, §16-5(D)(5).
  Victim and community impact, §16-5(D)(3).
Execution of sentence.
  Powers of convening authority, §17-9(C).
General and special courts-martial procedures, §15-17.
Generally, §16-1.
Illegal pretrial punishment and restraint.
  Generally, §5-10(A).
  Pretrial punishment other than restraint, §5-10(B).
  Pretrial restraints constituting illegal punishment, §5-10(C).
  Pretrial restraints may not constitute punishment, §5-8(A).
  Remedies, §5-10(D).
Instructions on sentencing, §16-9.
Maximum punishment, §16-2.
  Chart, Appx. 30.
  Equivalent punishments, §16-2(G).
  Escalator provisions, §16-2(E).
  Jurisdictional limits, §16-2(A).
    Chart, Appx. 31.
  Limitation on punishments.
    Footnote five, §16-2(F).
    Manual for courts-martial limitations, §16-2(C).
    Nature of proceeding as limitation, §16-2(B).
  Multiplicity, §16-2(D).
Nonjudicial punishment.
  See NONJUDICIAL PUNISHMENT.

SENTENCING AND PUNISHMENT
—Cont'd
Permissible punishments, §16-3.
  Death penalty, §16-3(A).
  Deprivation of liberty, §16-3(C).
  Deprivation of pay, §16-3(D).
  Loss of numbers, §16-3(F).
  Punitive separations, §16-3(B).
  Reduction in grade, §16-3(E).
  Reprimand, §16-3(G).
Prior convictions.
  Evidence of, §16-5(C).
Procedures generally, §16-4(A).
Summary courts-martial procedures, §15-28.
Suspension of sentence.
  Powers of convening authority, §17-9(D).
  Vacation, Appx. 39.
Types of punishment.
  Chart, Appx. 31.
Worksheet, Appx. 29.

SEPARATE SYSTEM, §1-1.

SERVICE CONNECTION REQUIREMENT.
Jurisdiction over offense, §4-11.
  Demise, §4-11(C).
    Constitutional implications, §4-11(C)(1).
    Practical implications, §4-11(C)(2).
  Relford factors, §4-11(A).
  Retreat from, §4-11(B).

SERVICE OF CHARGES UPON ACCUSED, §8-6.

SERVICE OF MOTIONS, §13-2(C).

SERVICE OF POST-TRIAL RECOMMENDATION, §17-8(B)(3).

SERVICE OF RECORD OF TRIAL ON ACCUSED, §17-4(B).

SERVICE OF SUBPOENAS, §11-2(D)(2).

SEVERANCE.
Motions, §13-5(G).
  Accused, §13-5(G)(1).
  Charges, §13-5(G)(2).
  Duplicitous specifications, §13-5(G)(3).

SEXUAL CONDUCT.
AIDS and HIV-related offenses, §§2-9 to 2-9(D).

SEXUAL MISCONDUCT VICTIMS.
Past sexual behavior.
  Notice by defense, §10-2(B).

SHEPARD'S MILITARY JUSTICE CITATIONS.
Researching issues, §1-3(D)(3).

SIXTH AMENDMENT.
Ineffective assistance of counsel, §15-2(B)(3).
Public trial, §15-3.
Speedy trial, §13-3(C)(1).

SODOMY.
HIV-related offenses.
  Prosecuting under Article 125 of UCMJ, §2-9(C)(2).

SPCM.
See SPECIAL COURTS-MARTIAL.

SPECIAL COURTS-MARTIAL.
Disqualifications of convening authority, §4-14(A)(2).
Forwarding of charges.
  Convening authority, §6-2(C).
Generally, §1-8(D)(2).
Jurisdictional limits on sentence, §16-2(A).
Limits of jurisdiction, §4-3(B).
Qualifications of detailed counsel, §8-3(B)(1).
Trial procedures.
  General and special courts-martial. See TRIAL PROCEDURES.

SPECIAL FINDINGS BY MILITARY JUDGE, §15-16(C); Appx. 32.

SPEECH.
First amendment challenges, §13-3(N)(3).

SPEEDY TRIAL.
Burton 90-day rule, §13-3(C)(2).
Interstate agreement on detainers act.
  Applicability, §13-3(C)(4).
Manual for courts-martial 120-day rule, §13-3(C)(3).
Motions to dismiss for lack of, §13-3(C).
Presumption, §15-20.
Remedies for violations, §13-3(C)(5).
Sixth amendment and due process standards, §13-3(C)(1).
UCMJ requirements, §13-3(C)(2).

STAFF JUDGE ADVOCATE'S POST-TRIAL RECOMMENDATION.
Review by defense counsel, §17-2(B)(4).

STAFF JUDGE ADVOCATE'S PRETRIAL ADVICE, §§7-3 to 7-3(B).

STANDBY COUNSEL.
Assistance to accused representing self, §12-2(F)(4).

STATE COURTS.
Concurrent jurisdiction over offenses, §4-12(A).

STATUTE OF LIMITATIONS.
Defense to absence without leave, §2-2(E)(6).
Motions to dismiss, §13-3(B).

STIPULATIONS, §15-21.
Adequate substitute for live testimony, §11-2(A)(4).
Confessional stipulations, §9-3.
Stipulation of expected testimony, Appx. 26.
Stipulation of fact, Appx. 25.

STOP AND FRISK.
Searches incident to lawful stop, §5-3(C)(8).

SUBPOENAS.
Form, Appx. 15.
Production of civilian witnesses, §11-2(D)(2).

SUMMARY COURTS-MARTIAL.
Accused, §15-26(B).
Counsel, §15-26(C).
Forwarding of charges.
  Convening authority, §6-2(B).
Generally, §1-8(D)(1).
Limits of jurisdiction, §4-3(C).
  Sentencing, §16-2(A).
No right to detailed counsel, §8-3(B)(1).
Post-trial procedures, §15-29.
Pretrial conferences, §15-27.
Procedures generally, §15-25.
Summary court-martial officer, §15-26(A).
Trial on merits and sentencing, §15-28.

SUPERIOR COMMISSIONED OFFICERS.
Disrespect toward, §2-3(A).

SUPERIOR'S ORDERS.
Disobedience, §2-4(b).

SUPPRESSION OF EVIDENCE.
Exclusionary rule, §5-3(F).
Motions to suppress, §§13-4 to 13-4(C).

SUPREME COURT.
Review by, §17-17.

SURREBUTTAL EVIDENCE.
Sentencing, §16-7.

SUSPENSION OF SENTENCE.
Powers of convening authority, §17-9(D).
Vacation proceedings, Appx. 39.

T

TANGIBLES.
Defense request for discovery, §10-4(B)(2).

TESTIMONIAL IMMUNITY, §11-2(E)(1).

TESTS AND RESULTS.
Defense request for discovery, §10-4(B)(3).

THE ADVOCATE.
Legal periodicals, §1-3(E).

THE GENERAL ARTICLE.
Article 134 crimes, §§2-6 to 2-6(C).

THE REPORTER.
Legal periodicals, §1-3(E).

THIRD PARTY ACTS.
Impossibility as defense to absence without leave, §2-2(E).

TRANSACTIONAL IMMUNITY, §11-2(E)(1).

TRIAL BY JUDGE ALONE.
Accused's request, §12-3(A).
  Form of request, Appx. 17.

TRIAL COUNSEL.
Counsel generally.
  See COUNSEL.

TRIAL PROCEDURES.
Contempts, §15-5.
Evidence.
  See EVIDENCE.
General and special courts-martial.
  Assembly of court, §15-9.
  Case-in-chief.
    Presentation generally, §15-12.
  Challenging court members, §§15-10, 15-10(C).
    Cause, §15-10(C)(2).
    Grounds, §15-10(B).
    Peremptory challenges, §15-10(C)(3).
    Selection process, §15-10(C)(1).
  Closing arguments, §15-13.
  Deliberations by court members, §15-15.
  Exhibits, §15-12(C).
  Generally, §15-7.
  Instructions to court members.
    Generally, §15-14(A).
    Review of errors, §15-14(D).
    Sua sponte instructions, §15-14(B).
    Upon request, §15-14(C).
  Oaths of participants, §15-8.

TRIAL PROCEDURES —Cont'd
General and special courts-martial —Cont'd
  Opening statements, §15-11.
  Participants.
    Introduction and swearing, §15-8.
  Sentencing procedure, §15-17.
  Verdict.
    General findings announced, §15-16(A).
    Impeaching findings, §15-16(B).
    Special findings by military judge, §15-16(C).
  Views and inspections of places and objects, §15-12(D).
  Voir dire of court members, §§15-10, 15-10(A).
  Witness examination, §15-12(A).
    Questions by court, §15-12(B).
Generally, §15-1.
Guides, §15-6.
Media and courts-martial, §15-3.
Motions at trial, §15-4.
  Continuances, §15-4(A).
  Finding of not guilty, §15-4(C).
  Insanity inquiry of accused, §15-4(D).
  Mistrial, §15-4(B).
Participants, §15-2.
  Accused, §15-2(A).
  Court members, §15-2(E).
  Court reporter, §15-2(F).
  Defense counsel.
    Generally, §15-2(B)(1).
    Ineffective assistance, §15-2(B)(3).
    Multiple accused representation and conflicts of interest, §15-2(B)(2).
    Perjurious client, §15-2(B)(4).
  General and special courts-martial.
    Introduction and swearing, §15-8.
  Interpreter, §15-2(G).
  Military judge, §15-2(D).
  Summary courts-martial.
    Accused, §15-26(B).
    Counsel, §15-26(C).
    Summary court-martial officer, §15-26(A).
  Trial counsel, §15-2(C).
Rules of evidence.
  See MILITARY RULES OF EVIDENCE.
Summary courts-martial.
  Generally, §15-25.
  Participants.
    Accused, §15-26(B).
    Counsel, §15-26(C).
    Summary court-martial officer, §15-26(A).

INDEX

TRIAL PROCEDURES —Cont'd
Summary courts-martial —Cont'd
Post-trial procedure, §15-29.
Pretrial conference, §15-27.
Trial on merits and sentencing, §15-28.
Uniform rules of practice, §15-6.
Witnesses.
See WITNESSES.

U

UNIFORM CODE OF MILITARY JUSTICE, Appx. 3.
Researching issues, §1-3(A).

UNIFORM RULES OF PRACTICE, §15-6.

UNIQUE LEGAL SYSTEM, §1-1.

UNITED STATES COURTS OF CRIMINAL APPEALS, §17-15.

UNLAWFUL COMMAND INFLUENCE.
See COMMAND INFLUENCE.

USE IMMUNITY, §11-2(E)(1).

USE PLUS FRUITS.
Immunity for witnesses, §11-2(E)(1).

USING BOOK, §§1-2 to 1-2(F).

V

VACATION OF SUSPENSION, Appx. 39.

VENUE.
Change of venue.
Command influence, §6-7.
Motion, §13-5(C).

VERDICT.
Findings worksheet, Appx. 28.
General findings, §15-16(A).
Impeaching findings, §15-16(B).
Special findings by military judge, §15-16(C); Appx. 32.

VICTIM IMPACT OF OFFENSE.
Evidence on sentencing, §16-5(D)(3).

VICTIMS OF SEXUAL MISCONDUCT.
Past sexual behavior.
Notice by defense, §10-2(B).

VIEWS OF PLACES AND OBJECTS, §15-12(D).

VINDICTIVE PROSECUTION.
Motion to dismiss, §13-3(M).

VOID FOR VAGUENESS, §13-3(N)(2).

VOIR DIRE, §15-10(A).
Court-martial member questionnaire, Appx. 24.

W

WARRANT OF ATTACHMENT.
Failure of civilian witness to appear, §11-2(D)(3).
Form, Appx. 16.

WARRANT OFFICERS.
Insubordination toward, §2-3(B).
Nonjudicial punishment.
Authority to impose, §3-3(A).

WITHDRAWAL OF APPEALS, §17-13.

WITHDRAWAL OF CHARGES, §8-5.

WITHDRAWAL OF GUILTY PLEA, §14-3(G).

WITHDRAWAL OF PRIVILEGES OR PASSES.
Nonpunitive option of commander, §1-8(B).

WITNESSES.
Adequate substitute, §11-2(A)(4).
Unavailable witnesses, §11-2(A)(2).
Article 32 investigations.
Accused's right, §7-2(B)(6).
Civilian witness production.
Generally, §11-2(D)(1).
Sanctions for failure to appear, §11-2(D)(3).
Subpoenas, §11-2(D)(2); Appx. 15.
Clemency.
Notice by prosecution, §10-2(A).
Command influence on, §6-5(B).
Discouraging witness testimony in other cases, §6-6(C).
Competency.
Presumption, §15-20.
Confrontation.
Accused's rights at Article 32 investigations, §7-2(B)(4).
Depositions.
See DEPOSITIONS.
Equal access to, §§10-3(B), 11-2(A)(1).
Examination, §15-12(A).
Questions by court, §15-12(B).
Experts.
Employing, §11-2(A)(3).
Failure to call identified witness.
Comment on failure, §10-3(C).
General rules concerning production, §§11-2(A) to 11-2(A)(4).

WITNESSES —Cont'd
Immunity, §5-4(C).
  Defense witnesses, §11-2(E)(3).
  Generally, §11-2(E)(1).
  Notice by prosecution, §10-2(A).
  Prosecution witnesses, §11-2(E)(2).
Jencks act materials.
  Defense request for discovery, §10-4(B)(5).
Military witness production, §11-2(C).
Names of defense witnesses.
  Automatic defense disclosure, §10-5(A)(1).
Names of prosecution witnesses.
  Automatic prosecutorial disclosure, §10-4(A)(2).
Preservation of testimony.
  See DEPOSITIONS.

WITNESSES —Cont'd
Pretrial statements or reports.
  Defense request for discovery, §10-4(B)(5).
Production of witnesses and evidence, §§11-1 to 11-4.
Refusal to testify, §11-2(F).
Requests for.
  Defense witnesses, §11-2(B)(1).
  Motions, §13-5(I).
  Prosecution witnesses, §11-2(B)(2).
Right to witness, §§10-3(B), 11-2(A)(1).
Self-incrimination.
  See SELF-INCRIMINATION.
Unavailable witnesses, §11-2(A)(2).
  Depositions.
    See DEPOSITIONS.

WORK-PRODUCT RULE, §10-3(A).

MILITARY CRIMINAL JUSTICE: PRACTICE AND PROCEDURE

FOURTH EDITION

1998 CUMULATIVE SUPPLEMENT

DAVID A. SCHLUETER

Professor of Law
St. Mary's University
San Antonio, Texas

Place in pocket of bound volume
and recycle previous supplement.

LEXIS® LAW PUBLISHING
CHARLOTTESVILLE, VIRGINIA

COPYRIGHT © 1998
by
LEXIS® Law Publishing
A Division of Reed Elsevier Inc.

All rights reserved.

ISBN # 0-327-00491-6

The views of the author do not purport to reflect the views
of the Departments of the Air Force, Army, Navy or Transportation
or the Department of Defense.

6692914

TABLE OF CONTENTS

Page

CHAPTER 1. THE MILITARY CRIMINAL JUSTICE SYSTEM............ 1

PART I. INTRODUCTION

§ 1-1. A Separate System: Justice or Discipline?...................................... 1
§ 1-1(B). Military Due Process: The Hierarchy...................................... 1

PART II. HISTORICAL ROOTS OF THE COURT-MARTIAL

§ 1-4. The Early European Models 2
§ 1-6. The American Court-Martial 2
§ 1-6(C). From 1900 to Present: Rapid Change................................... 2

PART III. THE PRESENT SYSTEM: A PROLOGUE

§ 1-7. An Overview.. 2
Annotated Bibliography.. 2

CHAPTER 2. MILITARY CRIMES 7

§ 2-2. Absence Offenses 7
§ 2-2(B). Desertion 7
§ 2-2(E). Defenses to Absence Offenses 7
§ 2-2(E)(5). Civilian Detention.. 7
§ 2-2(E)(7). Moral Grounds or Beliefs 8
§ 2-4. Disobedience Offenses 8
§ 2-4(A). General 8
§ 2-4(B). Disobedience of Superior's Orders 9
§ 2-4(C). Violation of General Orders or Regulations 9
§ 2-4(E). Dereliction of Duty.. 9
§ 2-4(F). Defenses to Disobedience Offenses................................... 9
§ 2-5. Article 133: Conduct Unbecoming an Officer and a Gentleman 10
§ 2-6. Article 134: The General Article... 10
§ 2-6(A). Disorders and Neglects to the Prejudice of Good Order
    and Discipline 10
§ 2-6(B). Conduct Bringing Discredit Upon the Armed Forces.............. 10
§ 2-6(C). Crimes and Offenses Not Capital: Federal Crimes 11
§ 2-7. Drug Offenses 11
§ 2-7(B). Proving Wrongfulness; Defenses 11
§ 2-8. Fraternization... 11
§ 2-8(A). In General.. 11
§ 2-8(B). Fraternization and the General Article 11
§ 2-9. AIDS and HIV-Related Offenses... 12

TABLE OF CONTENTS

Page

§ 2-9(D). Constitutionality of Prosecuting HIV-Related Conduct 12
Annotated Bibliography 12

CHAPTER 3.   NONJUDICIAL PUNISHMENT: A COMPARATIVE ANALYSIS 15
§ 3-3. Authority to Impose Punishment 15
§ 3-3(C). "Minor" Offenses 15
§ 3-4. The Right to Demand Trial 15
§ 3-5. Procedural Rules for Imposing Nonjudicial Punishment 16
§ 3-5(B). Army Procedures 16
§ 3-5(B)(2). Notice 16
§ 3-5(C). Air Force Procedures 16
§ 3-5(C)(2). Notice 16
§ 3-5(D). Navy and Marine Corps Procedures 17
§ 3-5(D)(2). Notice 17
§ 3-5(E). Coast Guard Procedures 17
§ 3-5(E)(2). Notice 17
§ 3-7. Effect of Errors in Imposition 17
§ 3-8. Consequences of Nonjudicial Punishment 17
§ 3-8(B). Use at Court-Martial or Administrative Proceedings 17
Annotated Bibliography 18

CHAPTER 4.   JURISDICTION 21

PART II. PERSONAL JURISDICTION

§ 4-6. Jursidiction Over Reservists and Members of National Guard 21
§ 4-8. Termination of Personal Jurisdiction 21
§ 4-8(A). Continuing Jurisdiction 21
§ 4-8(B). General Rule: Discharge Terminates Status 21
§ 4-8(C). Exceptions to the General Rule 22
§ 4-8(C)(3). Fraudulent Discharge 22

PART III. JURISDICTION OVER THE OFFENSE

§ 4-12. Exclusive, Reciprocal, and Concurrent Jurisdiction 22
§ 4-12(A). State and Federal Courts 22

PART IV. CONVENING AND COMPOSITION OF COURTS-MARTIAL;
REFERRAL OF CHARGES

§ 4-15. Properly Composed Court-Martial 23
§ 4-15(A). Military Judge 23
§ 4-15(C). Court Members 23
Annotated Bibliography 24

TABLE OF CONTENTS

Page

CHAPTER 5. THE COMMANDER'S INVESTIGATION, PRETRIAL RESTRAINTS, AND CONFINEMENT 27

PART I. THE COMMANDER'S INVESTIGATION

§ 5-3. Searches and Seizures 27
   § 5-3(A). The Servicemember's Reasonable Expectation of Privacy 28
   § 5-3(B). Probable Cause Searches 28
   § 5-3(C). Nonprobable Cause Searches 28
      § 5-3(C)(5). Emergency Searches 28
      § 5-3(C)(6). Consent Searches 28
      § 5-3(C)(7). Searches Incident to Apprehension 29
      § 5-3(C)(8). Searches Incident to Lawful Stop 29
   § 5-3(D). Other Reasonable Searches 29
      § 5-3(D)(1). Inspections and Inventories 29
   § 5-3(F). Exclusionary Rule; Exceptions 29
§ 5-4. The Right Against Self-Incrimination, Interrogation, and Immunity 29
   § 5-4(A). The Right Against Self-Incrimination 29
      § 5-4(A)(2). Reporting Requirements 29
      § 5-4(A)(3). Comments on Invoking the Right 29
   § 5-4(B). Interrogation of Suspects; Rights Warnings 30
   § 5-4(C). Grants of Immunity 31

PART II. PRETRIAL RESTRAINTS AND CONFINEMENT

§ 5-8. Pretrial Restraints 31
§ 5-9. Pretrial Confinement 31
   § 5-9(A). In General 31
   § 5-9(C). Review by Commander 31
   § 5-9(D). Review of Commander's Decision to Confine 32
   § 5-9(E). Judicial Review 33
§ 5-10. Illegal Pretrial Punishment and Restraints 33
   § 5-10(A). In General 33
   § 5-10(C). Pretrial Restraints Constituting Illegal Punishment 34
   § 5-10(D). Remedies; Waiver 34
Annotated Bibliography 34

CHAPTER 6. PREFERRAL AND FORWARDING OF CHARGES; COMMAND INFLUENCE 37

PART I. PREFERRAL AND FORWARDING OF CHARGES

§ 6-1. Preferring Sworn Charges 37
   § 6-1(B). General Rules of Pleading 37

TABLE OF CONTENTS

                                 Page

  § 6-1(B)(2). Amendments to Pleadings 38
  § 6-1(B)(3). Additional Charges 38
 § 6-1(C). Defective Pleadings 38
  § 6-1(C)(3). Multiplicity 38
§ 6-2. Forwarding of Charges 39
 § 6-2(B). Summary Court-Martial Convening Authority 39
 § 6-2(C). Special Court-Martial Convening Authority 39

PART II. COMMAND INFLUENCE

§ 6-3. Command Influence; In General 39
 § 6-3(C). Actual, Apparent, and Perceived Unlawful Command
     Influence 39
§ 6-4. Pretrial Command Influence 39
 § 6-4(A). The Preliminary Inquiry and Preferring Charges 39
 § 6-4(C). Command Influence on Referral of Charges 40
 § 6-4(E). Pretrial Comments and Actions 40
§ 6-5. Command Influence on Courts-Martial 40
 § 6-5(A). Command Influence on Court Members, Judges, and
     Counsel 40
 § 6-5(B). Command Influence on Witnesses 40
 § 6-5(C). Commander's "Presence" at Trial 40
§ 6-7. Appellate Review of Command Influence 40
Annotated Bibliography 42

**CHAPTER 7. THE ARTICLE 32 INVESTIGATION AND THE
       PRETRIAL ADVICE** 45
§ 7-2. The Article 32 Investigation 45
 § 7-2(A). The Parties to the Investigation 45
  § 7-2(A)(1). The Investigating Officer 45
 § 7-2(B). The Accused's Rights 45
  § 7-2(B)(4). Right to Confront Witnesses 45
  § 7-2(B)(6). Right to Production of Witnesses 46
 § 7-2(C). Article 32 Investigation Procedures 46
 § 7-2(D). Investigating Officer's Report 46
§ 7-3. The Staff Judge Advocate's Pretrial Advice 47
 § 7-3(B). Defective Pretrial Advice 47
Annotated Bibliography 47

**CHAPTER 8. CONVENING OF A COURT-MARTIAL, DETAILING
       PARTICIPANTS, AND THE REFERRAL PROCESS** 49
§ 8-2. Convening the Court-Martial 49

TABLE OF CONTENTS

Page

§ 8-2(A). The Convening Authority 49
§ 8-3. Detailing the Participants...49
  § 8-3(B). Trial and Defense Counsel 49
    § 8-3(B)(1). Qualifications of Counsel..49
  § 8-3(C). Members of the Court..49
    § 8-3(C)(2). Requests for Enlisted Members..................................49
    § 8-3(C)(3). Constitutional Challenges to Composition.....................49
    § 8-3(C)(4). Selecting the Members 50
  § 8-3(D). Changes in the Composition of the Court............................50
§ 8-5. Withdrawal of Charges...50
Annotated Bibliography..50

CHAPTER 9. PLEA BARGAINING AND OTHER PRETRIAL NEGOTIATIONS 53
§ 9-2. Pretrial Agreements 53
  § 9-2(A). Procedures..53
    § 9-2(A)(3). Informal Agreements...53
  § 9-2(B). Conditions and Terms 53
    § 9-2(B)(1). Valid Conditions...54
    § 9-2(B)(2). Invalid Terms..54
  § 9-2(D). Judicial Review of the Agreement 54
§ 9-3. Confessional Stipulations 55
Annotated Bibliography..55

CHAPTER 10. NOTICE, DISCLOSURE, AND DISCOVERY 57
§ 10-4. Defense Discovery..57
  § 10-4(A). Automatic Prosecutorial Disclosure....................................57
    § 10-4(A)(4). Favorable Evidence: The Constitutional Mandate........57
  § 10-4(B). Defense Request for Discovery...57
    § 10-4(B)(1). The *Brady* Request 57
    § 10-4(B)(5). Jencks Act Materials..57
Annotated Bibliography..58

CHAPTER 11. PRODUCTION OF WITNESSES AND EVIDENCE..........61
§ 11-2. Production of Witnesses 61
  § 11-2(A). General Rules..61
    § 11-2(A)(1). Equal Access: The Right to Witnesses........................61
    § 11-2(A)(3). Employing Expert Assistants and Witnesses 61
  § 11-2(B). Requests for Witnesses..62
    § 11-2(B)(1). Defense Witnesses..62
§ 11-3. Depositions 63

TABLE OF CONTENTS

	Page
§ 11-3(B). Procedures for Depositions	63
§ 11-3(B)(1). In General	63
§ 11-4. Production of Evidence	63
Annotated Bibliography	64

CHAPTER 12. THE ARTICLE 39(A) PRETRIAL SESSION 67

§ 12-1. Introduction	67
§ 12-2. Preliminary Matters	67
§ 12-2(C). Accounting for Parties Present and Absent	67
§ 12-2(F). Announcing the Detail and Qualifications of the Defense Counsel and the Judge's Inquiry Concerning the Accused's Rights to Counsel	67
§ 12-2(F)(2). The *Donohew* Inquiry	67
§ 12-2(H). Challenges for Cause to the Military Judge	68
§ 12-3. Military Judge's Inquiries Concerning the Accused's Decisions Regarding Composition of the Court	68
§ 12-3(A). Accused's Request for Trial by Judge Alone	68
§ 12-4. Arraignment	68
§ 12-5. Conferences	68
Annotated Bibliography	69

CHAPTER 13. MOTIONS PRACTICE 71

§ 13-2. Procedural Aspects of Motions Practice	71
§ 13-2(E). Rulings on Motions	71
§ 13-2(G). Appeal of Rulings	72
§ 13-2(G)(2). Government Appeals	72
§ 13-3. Motions to Dismiss	72
§ 13-3(B). Statute of Limitations	72
§ 13-3(C). Speedy Trial	72
§ 13-3(C)(2). U.C.M.J. Requirements: The *Burton* 90-Day Rule (1972-1993)	73
§ 13-3(C)(3). The *Manual*'s 120-Day Speedy Trial Rule	73
§ 13-3(C)(4). Interstate Agreement on Detainers Act (IADA)	75
§ 13-3(D). Lack of Mental Responsibility	75
§ 13-3(H). Grant of Immunity	75
§ 13-3(J). Multiplicity	76
§ 13-3(M). Selective or Vindictive Prosecutions; Prosecutorial Misconduct	77
§ 13-3(N). Constitutional Challenges to the Underlying Statute, Regulation, or Order	77

TABLE OF CONTENTS

Page

§ 13-3(N)(2). Vagueness: Lack of Fair Notice 77
§ 13-3(N)(3). First Amendment, Speech, Religion, and
    Association 78
§ 13-3(N)(4). Rights of Privacy 78
§ 13-4. Motions to Suppress 79
§ 13-4(A). Pretrial Statements of the Accused 79
§ 13-5. Motions to Grant Appropriate Relief 79
§ 13-5(A). Accused Incompetent to Stand Trial 79
§ 13-5(C). Change of Location of Trial 79
§ 13-5(E). Defective Pleadings: Motions to Cure or Amend 79
§ 13-5(G). Motions to Sever 80
§ 13-5(G)(1). Severance of Accused 80
§ 13-5(G)(2). Severance of Charges 80
§ 13-5(K). Continuance 80
§ 13-5(L). Motions to Obtain Rulings on Evidentiary Matters;
    Motions *in Limine* 80
Annotated Bibliography 81

CHAPTER 14. PLEAS 83
§ 14-2. Not Guilty Pleas 83
§ 14-3. Guilty Pleas 83
§ 14-3(B). The *Care* Providency Inquiry 83
§ 14-3(B)(2). Determining the Accuracy of the Plea 83
§ 14-3(B)(3). Determining the Voluntariness of the Plea 84
§ 14-3(B)(4). Admissibility of Accused's Statements 84
§ 14-3(C). The *Green-King* Pretrial Agreement Inquiry 84
§ 14-3(D). Improvident Guilty Pleas 85
§ 14-3(D)(4). Factual and Legal Inconsistencies 85
§ 14-3(D)(5). Procedural Consequences of an Improvident Plea 86
§ 14-3(E). Entry of Findings 86
§ 14-4. Conditional Pleas of Guilty 86
Annotated Bibliography 86

CHAPTER 15. TRIAL PROCEDURES 89

PART I. INTRODUCTION

§ 15-2. The Participants 90
§ 15-2(A). The Accused 90
§ 15-2(B). The Defense Counsel 90
§ 15-2(B)(2). Representation of Multiple Accused and
    Conflicts of Interest 90

TABLE OF CONTENTS

Page

 § 15-2(B)(3). Ineffective Assistance of Counsel 90
 § 15-2(D). The Military Judge 96
 § 15-2(E). The Court Members 96
§ 15-3. Courts-Martial and the Media: Public Trials 96
§ 15-4. Motions at Trial 96
 § 15-4(A). Continuances 96
§ 15-5. Contempts 97

PART II. PROCEDURES FOR GENERAL AND SPECIAL COURTS-MARTIAL

§ 15-10. *Voir Dire* and Challenges of Court Members 97
 § 15-10(A). *Voir Dire* of Court Members 97
 § 15-10(B). Grounds for Challenging Court Members 98
 § 15-10(C). Challenges of Court Members 101
  § 15-10(C)(1). Challenge of the Selection Process 101
  § 15-10(C)(2). Challenges for Cause 101
  § 15-10(C)(3). Peremptory Challenges 101
§ 15-12. Presentation of the Case-in-Chief 102
 § 15-12(A). Examination of the Witnesses 102
 § 15-12(B). Questions by the Court 103
§ 15-13. Closing Arguments 103
§ 15-14. Instructions to the Court Members 104
 § 15-14(A). General 104
 § 15-14(B). *Sua Sponte* Instructions 104
 § 15-14(C). Instructions Upon Request 104
 § 15-14(D). Review of Instructions Errors 105
§ 15-15. Deliberations 105
§ 15-16. Verdict; Announcement of Findings 105
 § 15-16(A). General Findings 105
 § 15-16(B). Impeaching the Findings 106

PART III. EVIDENTIARY RULES

§ 15-23. Objections and Preserving Error 106
Annotated Bibliography 106

CHAPTER 16. SENTENCING 109
§ 16-2. Maximum Authorized Punishments 109
 § 16-2(D). Multiplicity 109
§ 16-3. Permissible Punishments 109
 § 16-3(A). Death Penalty 109
 § 16-3(B). Punitive Separations 110
 § 16-3(C). Deprivation of Liberty 111

TABLE OF CONTENTS

	Page
§ 16-3(D). Deprivation of Pay	111
§ 16-5. Prosecution Evidence	111
§ 16-5(B). Data Concerning the Accused's Prior Service	111
§ 16-5(C). Evidence of Prior Convictions	111
§ 16-5(D). Evidence in Aggravation	112
§ 16-5(D)(1). In General	112
§ 16-5(D)(2). Evidence of Circumstances Surrounding Offense	112
§ 16-5(D)(3). Evidence of Impact on Victim and Community	112
§ 16-5(D)(4). Evidence Addressing Rehabilitative Potential	112
§ 16-5(D)(5). Evidence of Uncharged Misconduct	112
§ 16-6. Defense Evidence	113
§ 16-7. Rebuttal and Surrebuttal	113
§ 16-8. Arguments on Sentencing	113
§ 16-8(B). Prosecution Arguments on Sentencing	113
§ 16-8(C). Defense Counsel's Argument on Sentencing	114
§ 16-9. Instructions on Sentencing	114
§ 16-10. Deliberations on Sentencing	114
§ 16-11. Announcement of the Sentence	115
§ 16-13. Adjournment	115
Annotated Bibliography	115

CHAPTER 17. REVIEW OF COURTS-MARTIAL 119

PART I. GENERAL

§ 17-2. Post-Trial Duties of Counsel	120
§ 17-2(B). Defense Counsel's Duties	120
§ 17-2(B)(2). Request for Deferment of Confinement, Forfeiture of Pay and Reduction in Grade	120
§ 17-2(B)(3). Submission of Matters to the Convening Authority	120
§ 17-2(B)(4). Review of the Staff Judge Advocate's Post-Trial Recommendation	121
§ 17-2(B)(5). Requesting a Waiver of Automatic Forfeitures	121
§ 17-2(B)(6). Negotiating a Post-Trial Agreement	122
§ 17-3. Post-Trial Proceedings	124
§ 17-4. Records of Trial	124
§ 17-4(A). Authentication of Record	124
§ 17-4(B). Service of Record on Accused	124
§ 17-5. Confinement Pending Review	124

PART II. INITIAL REVIEW BY THE CONVENING AUTHORITY

§ 17-8. Legal Review of Courts-Martial	124

TABLE OF CONTENTS

Page

§ 17-8(B). Post-Trial Recommendation 124
   § 17-8(B)(1). Format and Contents of Recommendation 125
   § 17-8(B)(2). Defective Recommendations 126
   § 17-8(B)(3). Service of Recommendation on Defense Counsel 126
§ 17-9. Convening Authority's Powers 128
§ 17-9(A). General Matters 128
§ 17-9(B). Qualified and Disqualified Convening Authorities 130
§ 17-9(C). Actions and Executions of Sentences 130
§ 17-9(D). Power to Suspend 130
§ 17-9(E). Other Clemency Powers 130
§ 17-11. Post-Trial Delays 130

PART III. APPELLATE REVIEW

§ 17-13. Waiver or Withdrawal of Appeals 131
§ 17-14. Appellate Counsel 131
§ 17-15. United States Courts of Criminal Appeals 131
§ 17-15(B). Scope of Review and Actions 131
§ 17-16. The United States Court of Appeals for the Armed Forces 132
§ 17-16(C). Scope of Review 132

PART IV. OTHER FORMS OF REVIEW

§ 17-19. Extraordinary Writs in the Military Courts 132
§ 17-21. Petition for New Trial 135
Annotated Bibliography 136

APPENDIX 3. UNIFORM CODE OF MILITARY JUSTICE 139

Subchapter VIII. SENTENCES 139
§ 858. Article 58. Execution of Confinement 139
Subchapter XII. UNITED STATES COURT OF APPEALS FOR
               THE ARMED FORCES 139
§ 943. Article 143. Organization and Employees 139

Table of Cases 141
Index 165

CHAPTER 1

THE MILITARY CRIMINAL JUSTICE SYSTEM

PART I.

INTRODUCTION

§ 1-1. A Separate System: Justice or Discipline?
   § 1-1(B). Military Due Process: The Hierarchy.

PART II.

HISTORICAL ROOTS OF THE COURT-MARTIAL

§ 1-4. The Early European Models.
§ 1-6. The American Court-Martial.
   § 1-6(C). From 1900 to Present: Rapid Change.

PART III.

THE PRESENT SYSTEM: A PROLOGUE

§ 1-7. An Overview.

PART I.

INTRODUCTION

§ 1-1. A Separate System: Justice or Discipline?

§ 1-1(B). Military Due Process: The Hierarchy.

Page 6, n. 16. The Court of Appeals ultimately reversed *Kelly* on other grounds. United States v. Kelly, 45 M.J. 259 (1996). United States v. Sargeant, 47 M.J. 367 (1997) (using term "military due process" regarding absence of court member from trial).

Page 7. Add footnote 18.1 at the end of the second full sentence at the top of the page:

[18.1] United States v. Guess, 48 M.J. 69 (1998) (noting hierarchy of protections; President's narrowing construction of statute was more protective for accused); United States v. Romano, 46 M.J. 269 (1997) (discussion of hierarchy of protections for servicemembers); United States v. Lopez, 35 M.J. 35 (C.M.A. 1992).

Page 9, n. 34. United States v. Davis, 47 M.J. 484 (1998) (noting President's authority *re Manual* provision concerning dangerous weapon; that provision gives greater rights than higher sources).

1

Part II.
Historical Roots of the Court-Martial

§ 1-4. The Early European Models.

Page 15, n. 1. *See generally* Loving v. United States, 517 U.S. 748 (1996) (discussion of history of court-martial procedures, especially those relating to military's death penalty procedures).

§ 1-6. The American Court-Martial.

§ 1-6(C). From 1900 to Present: Rapid Change.

Page 34, n. 62. LURIE, ARMING MILITARY JUSTICE: THE ORIGINS OF THE UNITED STATES COURT OF MILITARY APPEALS, 1775-1950, 46 et. seq. (1992) (excellent discussion of the debates concerning military justice reform).

Page 35, n. 70. *See generally* LURIE, ARMING MILITARY JUSTICE: THE ORIGINS OF THE UNITED STATES COURT OF MILITARY APPEALS, 1775-1950, 127 et. seq. (1992).

Part III.
The Present System: A Prologue

§ 1-7. An Overview.

Page 38, n. 11. United States v. Curtis, 44 M.J. 106 (1996) (discussion of system for selecting members).

ANNOTATED BIBLIOGRAPHY

BOOKS

Filbert & Kaufman, *Naval Law: Justice and Procedure in the Sea Services* (3d ed. 1998)

  Designed to serve as an introduction to military naval law, the text presents a combination of actual cases, regulations, and statutes in a format intended for classroom use.

Lurie, *Arming Military Justice: The Origins of the United States Court of Military Appeals, 1775-1950* (1992).

  This text (the first of two volumes) provides an extremely inciteful historical view of the origins of the United States Court of Military Appeals (now the United States Court of Appeals for the Armed Forces) from 1775 to 1950. The book traces the issue of independent review of courts-martial convictions and the controversy stirred by question of whether any military or civilian court should be permitted, or required, to review military justice convictions.

Lurie, *Pursuing Military Justice: The History of the United States Court of Appeals for the Armed Forces, 1951-1980* (1997).

The focus of this volume, the second in a set of two, is on first three decades of what is often referred to as the supreme court of the miltary justice system. The author notes the political and legal struggles faced by the Court of Appeals in reviewing courts-martial convictions.

Schlueter, Jansen, Barry & Arnold, *Military Criminal Procedure Forms* (1997).

This book presents a variety of sample forms, letters, pleadings, checklists, briefs, and motions for military criminal justice practitioners. The text, which provides coverage for processing a case from pretrial investigation through appellate disposition, demonstrates how formats may vary among the services.

PERIODICALS

In General

Cooke, "The Twenty-Sixth Annual Kenneth J. Hodson Lecture: Manual for Courts-Martial 20X," 156 MIL. L. REV. 1 (1998).

The author, a senior judge advocate, provides a helpful analysis on the history and trends of military justice, and proposes several areas of amendment to the Manual, including tenure for military judges, judge alone sentencing, and jurisdiction over civilians overseas.

Dordal, "The Military Criminal Justice System: A Commander's Perspective," THE REP., June 1997, at 3.

This short article, written by a senior Air Force commander, presents the view of the "client" in the military justice system and discusses four particular problem areas facing commanders: lack of flexibility for commanders after an investigation is initiated, the relative speed of military justice, unlawful command influence, and public scrutiny. He concludes that the current system is healthy and that it provides commanders with a vital tool for accomplishing their duties.

Green, "Military Justice and Discipline: The Role of Punishment in the Military," THE REP., June 1997, at 9.

Observing that "discipline" is the *sine qua non* of an effective fighting force, the author presents a wide range of thoughts and perspectives on the role of military justice and punishment. Although the article was originally published in 1980, it rings of current debates about the proper role of the military justice system.

Hoskins, "One Tin Soldier: A New Look at the Constitutionality of Placing United States Soldiers Under the Command of the United Nations," 22 U. DAYTON L. REV. 125 (1996).

Drawing from the court-martial of Specialist Michael New for refusing to wear the UN insignia on his uniform, the author discusses the constitutionality of placing United States servicemembers under foreign command and concludes that the President's authority to place United States troops under the temporary command of foreign commanders should be validated.

Symposia

Symposium, "Military Justice Under Scrutiny: Exploring the Conflict Between Society's Norms and the Military's Needs," THE REP., June 1998, at 3.

This short piece is a collection of the remarks of three speakers at the Air Force Judge Advocate General's School Foundation Symposium in January 1998. The speakers, Colonels Swanson and Pribyla and Mr. Spinner, addressed the question of responding to challenges to the military justice system.

Symposium, "Military Justice Symposium—Volume I," ARMY LAW., April 1998.

This 128-page symposium is the first of two volumes and includes seven short articles on a range of military justice topics; it was authored by the faculty members of the Criminal Law Division at the Army's Judge Advocate School:

>   Stitler, "The Power to Prosecute: New Developments in Courts-Martial Jurisdiction," at 1.
>   Lovejoy, "Re-interpreting the Rules: Recent Developments in Speedy Trial and Pretrial Restraint," at 10.
>   Einwechter, "New Developments in Substantive Criminal Law Under the Uniform Code of Military Justice (1997)," at 20.
>   Coe, "'Something Old, Something New, Something Borrowed, Something Blue': Recent Developments in Pretrial and Trial Procedure," at 44.
>   Pede, "New Developments in Search and Seizure and Urinalysis," at 80.
>   Stitler, "Widening the Door: Recent Developments in Self-Incrimination Law," at 93.
>   Moran, "Pyrrhic Victories and Permutations: New Developments in the Sixth Amendment, Discovery, and Mental Responsibility," at 106.

Symposium, "Military Justice Symposium—Volume II," ARMY LAW., May 1998.

This 68-page symposium consists of four articles on a range of military justice topics; it was authored by the faculty members of the Criminal Law Division at the Army's Judge Advocate School:

>   Henley, "Developments in Evidence III—The Final Chapter," at 1.
>   Lovejoy, "The CAAF at a Crossroads: New Developments in Post-Trial Processing," at 25.

Allen, "Recent Developments in Sentencing Under the Uniform Code of Military Justice," at 39.

Morris, "'This Better Be Good': The Courts Continue to Tighten the Burden in Unlawful Command Influence Cases," at 49.

Symposium, "Military Justice Symposium I," ARMY LAW., April 1997.

This 149-page symposium, which presents a series of short articles on a range of military justice topics, was authored by the faculty members of the Criminal Law Division at the Army's Judge Advocate School:

Morris, Foreword.
Frisk, "The Long Arm of Military Justice: Court-Martial Jurisdiction and the Limits of Power," at 5.
Frisk, "Walking the Fine Line Between Promptness and Haste: Recent Developments in Speedy Trial and Pretrial Restraint Jurisprudence," at 14.
Coe, "Restating Some Old Rules and Limiting Some Landmarks: Recent Developments in Pretrial and Trial Procedure," at 25.
Barto, "Recent Developments in the Substantive Criminal Law Under the Uniform Code of Military Justice," at 50.
Wright, "'An Old Fashioned Crazy Quilt': New Developments in the Sixth Amendment, Discovery, Mental Responsibility, and Nonjudicial Punishment," at 72.
Henley, "Postcards from the Edge: Privileges, Profiles, Polygraphs, and Other Developments in the Military Rules of Evidence," at 92.
Allen, "New Developments in Sentencing," at 116.
Morris, "'Just One More Thing...' and Other Thoughts on Recent Developments in Post-Trial Processing," at 129.

Affirmation of Military Justice

Moorman, "Answering the Critics of the Military Justice System: Staff Judge Advocates Take Note," THE REP., June 1997, at 7.

This short article responds to recent high-visibility military cases which have raised questions about the strength of the military justice system. The author, a senior judge advocate, addresses his remarks primarily to Staff Judge Advocates, who are particularly charged with exercising tremendous influence in the system. He charges them to exercise daily leadership skills in order to strengthen the system — not just maintain it.

CHAPTER 2

MILITARY CRIMES

§ 2-2. Absence Offenses.
   § 2-2(B). Desertion.
   § 2-2(E). Defenses to Absence Offenses.
      § 2-2(E)(5). Civilian Detention.
      § 2-2(E)(7). Moral Grounds or Beliefs.
§ 2-4. Disobedience Offenses.
   § 2-4(A). General.
   § 2-4(B). Disobedience of Superior's Orders.
   § 2-4(C). Violation of General Orders or Regulations.
   § 2-4(E). Dereliction of Duty.
   § 2-4(F). Defenses to Disobedience Offenses.
§ 2-5. Article 133: Conduct Unbecoming an Officer and a Gentleman.
§ 2-6. Article 134: The General Article.
   § 2-6(A). Disorders and Neglects to the Prejudice of Good Order and Discipline.
   § 2-6(B). Conduct Bringing Discredit Upon the Armed Forces.
   § 2-6(C). Crimes and Offenses Not Capital: Federal Crimes.
§ 2-7. Drug Offenses.
   § 2-7(B). Proving Wrongfulness; Defenses.
§ 2-8. Fraternization.
   § 2-8(A). In General.
   § 2-8(B). Fraternization and the General Article.
§ 2-9. AIDS and HIV-Related Offenses.
   § 2-9(D). Constitutionality of Prosecuting HIV-Related Conduct.

§ 2-2. Absence Offenses.

§ 2-2(B). Desertion.

Page 57, n. 10: replace citation to *United States v. Johnson*, 37 M.J. 982 with: United States v. Johnson, 45 M.J. 88 (1996) (pending application for conscientious objector status, or alleged procedural problems with considering the application, is not a defense to charges for missing movement or disobeying otherwise valid orders).

§ 2-2(E). Defenses to Absence Offenses.

§ 2-2(E)(5). Civilian Detention.

Page 66, n. 87. United States v. Williams, 49 C.M.R. 12 (C.M.A. 1974) (accused authorized to attend state court proceeding which resulted in his immediate confinement in state facility); United States v. Urban, 45 M.J. 528 (N.M.Ct.Crim.App. 1996) (accused's guilty plea to absence without leave was improvident where charged offense resulted from his civilian two-day detention following conviction of civilian traffic offense; he had been given liberty from military duties to deal with civilian charges).

§ 2-2(E)(7). Moral Grounds or Beliefs.

Page 68, n. 104. United States v. Johnson, 45 M.J. 88 (1996) (pending application for conscientious objector status, or alleged procedural problems with considering the application, is not a defense to charges for missing movement or disobeying otherwise valid orders).

§ 2-4. Disobedience Offenses.

§ 2-4(A). General.

Page 71, n. 2. United States v. Hughey, 46 M.J. 152 (1997) (general regulation issued over signature of person authorized to do so is presumed lawful; accused has burden to show otherwise); United States v. Nieves, 44 M.J. 96 (1996) (superior's order is presumed to be lawful).

Page 71, n. 3. *Cf.* United States v. Hughey, 46 M.J. 152 (1997) (general regulation issued over signature of person authorized to do so is presumed lawful; accused has burden to show otherwise).

Page 72, n. 5. United States v. Nieves, 44 M.J. 96 (1996) (order to accused not to talk to witnesses involved in administrative investigation was related to valid military purpose and was sufficiently narrow).

Page 73, n. 17. United States v. Hill, 46 M.J. 567 (A.F.Ct.Crim.App. 1997) (order not to associate with lover); United States v. Padgett, 45 M.J. 520 (C.G. Ct.Crim.App. 1996) (order to accused not to have any association with 14-year-old civilian girl did not have sufficient nexus to proper military objectives and purposes; order was result of girl's mother's complaints to military authorities; court noted that orders to cease all contact with another person are not necessarily per se illegal).

Page 73, n. 18. United States v. Swan, 48 M.J. 551 (N.M.Ct.Crim.App. 1998) (Secretary of the Navy Instruction prohibiting sexual harassment did not violate accused's free speech rights).

Page 73. Add the following text after last sentence on page:

The same would hold true for any orders which prevent an accused from speaking to witnesses;[18.1] in that case the order might be unlawful to the extent that it prevents the accused from preparing a defense.[18.2]

[18.1] United States v. Nieves, 44 M.J. 96 (1996) (citing cases).

[18.2] *Id.* (commander's order to accused not to discuss pending administrative investigation with witnesses did not frustrate his ability to prepare a defense; commander would have entertained requests from defense counsel and accused for permission to discuss case with witnesses); United States v. Aycock, 35 C.M.R. 130 (C.M.A. 1964) (order prohibiting accused from contacting witnesses was unlawful); United States v. Wysong, 26 C.M.R. 29 (C.M.A. 1958) (order not to discuss case with persons was overly broad and thus unlawful).

§ 2-4(B). Disobedience of Superior's Orders.

Page 74, n. 23. United States v. Hill, 46 M.J. 567 (A.F.Ct.Crim.App. 1997) (accused disobeyed lawful order by NCO; validity of NCO's order is not conditioned on command relationship to person being given order).

Page 75, n. 28. *Cf.* United States v. Jenkins, 44 M.J. 596 (N.M.Ct.Crim.App. 1996) (accused's begrudging compliance with command under Article 90 which was repeated three times was not a defense to disobedience of order).

§ 2-4(C). Violation of General Orders or Regulations.

Page 75, n. 30. United States v. Townsend, 46 M.J. 517 (C.G.Ct.Crim.App. 1997) (lack of commandant's signature on general regulation did not make it invalid; as long as it is signed by person with authority to do so, regulation is facially valid; under facts, regulation in question was valid).

Page 76, n. 33. United States v. Hode, 44 M.J. 816 (A.F.Ct.Crim.App. 1996) (AF instruction governing alcoholic beverage program was not punitive; instruction's purpose statement contained no notice that it might be enforceable under Article 92).

§ 2-4(E). Dereliction of Duty.

Page 77, n. 45. United States v. Sojfer, 44 M.J. 603 (N.M.Ct.Crim.App. 1996) (accused's conducting of authorized physical exams was not dereliction of duty; those actions were actually willful acts which exceeded his prescribed duties).

Page 77, n. 46. United States v. Long, 46 M.J. 783 (Army Ct.Crim.App. 1997) (accused guilty of dereliction of duty by unauthorized use of American Express card).

§ 2-4(F). Defenses to Disobedience Offenses.

Page 78, n. 51. United States v. Henderson, 44 M.J. 232 (1996) (failure to comply with NCO's order to get dressed and report for formation was offense of failure to report, not disobedience of order).

Page 79, n. 55. United States v. Rockwood, 48 M.J. 501 (Army Ct.Crim.App. 1998) (trial judge did not err in refusing to give instruction on defense of justification; accused had violated orders by conducting independent inspection of Haitian penitentiary; court rejected argument that he was justified in those actions by the stated intent of the President or by international law principles).

Page 80. Add following text after sentence ending with footnote 61:

In *United States v. Johnson*,[61.1] the Court of Appeals for the Armed Forces held that a pending application for conscientious objector status, or alleged procedural problems with considering the application, is not a defense to charges for missing movement or disobeying otherwise valid orders.[61.2] The court stated:

> Action by the Secretary of a military department on [an application for conscientious objector status], even if erroneous, does not end the

obligation of a member of the armed forces to obey orders that are otherwise lawful. The discipline and obedience to facially lawful orders that are critical to military mission accomplishment can tolerate no less.[61.3]

The court indicated that an accused's remedy is civil in nature — either by seeking an injunction or in filing a petition for habeas corpus.[61.4]

[61.1] 45 M.J. 88 (1996).
[61.2] *Id.* at 91.
[61.3] *Id.* at 92.
[61.4] *Id.* at 92.

§ 2-5. Article 133: Conduct Unbecoming an Officer and a Gentleman.

Page 80, n. 2. United States v. Page, 43 M.J. 804 (A.F.Ct.Crim.App. 1995) (court observed that conduct of officer which substantially denigrates marital relationship of an enlisted subordinate or exhibits flagrant disrespect for an enlisted man's family severely erodes confidence in command and thus clearly constitutes conduct unbecoming an officer; even though enlisted man was not in direct chain of command, he was bound to follow lawful orders of accused officer).

Page 80, n. 3. United States v. Zander, 46 M.J. 558 (N.M.Ct.Crim.App. 1997) (officer misrepresented himself in 20 courts-martial as officer fully qualified to serve as defense counsel).

§ 2-6. Article 134: The General Article.

§ 2-6(A). Disorders and Neglects to the Prejudice of Good Order and Discipline.

Page 84, n. 25. *See generally*, Barto, "The Scarlet Letter and the Military Justice System," ARMY LAW., August 1997, at 3.

Page 84. Add the following text mid-sentence, after footnote 25:

pandering,[25.1] solicitation of another to commit prostitution,[25.2]

[25.1] United States v. Miller, 47 M.J. 352 (A.F.Ct.Crim.App. 1996) (court found that accused's acts did not constitute pandering because they did not involve third person).

[25.2] *Id.* (although government charged accused with pandering, court concluded that in effect, accused had committed solicitation of another to commit prostitution).

§ 2-6(B). Conduct Bringing Discredit Upon the Armed Forces.

Page 85, n. 33. United States v. Agosto, 46 M.J. 705 (A.F.Ct.Crim.App. 1997) (accused may waive evidentiary proof of whether location of assimilated crime falls within area of federal jurisdiction)

Page 87, n. 40. United States v. Clinkenbeard, 44 M.J. 577 (A.F.Ct.Crim.App. 1996) (accused may not be punished under Assimilative Crimes Act if state has decriminalized charged behavior; in this case, accused had been improperly charged with violating state's traffic laws which were not considered "criminal" under state law). *Cf.* United States v. White, 39 M.J. 796 (N.M.C.M.R. 1994) (accused may be prosecuted under Assimilative Crimes Act for state non-criminal conduct).

§ 2-6(C). Crimes and Offenses Not Capital: Federal Crimes.

Page 86, n. 38. United States v. Agosto, 46 M.J. 705 (A.F.Ct.Crim.App. 1997) (accused must prove beyond reasonable doubt that act occurred in area under federal jurisdiction; under facts, accused waived evidentiary proof).

§ 2-7. Drug Offenses.

§ 2-7(B). Proving Wrongfulness; Defenses.

Page 90, n. 24. United States v. Fegurgur, 43 M.J. 871 (Army Ct.Crim.App. 1996) (accused not entrapped where agent merely asked her if she could obtain drugs).

Page 90. Add the following text after sentence ending with footnote 24:

The military courts also recognize entrapment where the law enforcement officers have acted in an outrageous fashion which resulted in a lack of due process.[24.1]

[24.1] *See, e.g.*, Jacobson v. United States, 503 U.S. 540 (1992); United States v. Bell, 38 M.J. 358 (C.M.A. 1993); United States v. Fegurgur, 43 M.J. 871 (Army Ct.Crim.App. 1996) (actions of officers were not outrageous).

Page 92, n. 42. *See also* United States v. Bond, 46 M.J. 86 (1997).

§ 2-8. Fraternization.

§ 2-8(A). In General.

Page 93, n. 5. United States v. Page, 43 M.J. 804 (A.F.Ct.Crim.App. 1995) (court observed that conduct of officer which substantially denigrates marital relationship of an enlisted subordinate or exhibits flagrant disrespect for an enlisted man's family severely erodes confidence in command).

Page 94, n. 8. United States v. McCreight, 43 M.J. 483 (1996) (offense of fraternization found in non-sexual relationship where accused showed partiality to enlisted member).

§ 2-8(B). Fraternization and the General Article.

Page 95, n. 12. United States v. Goddard, 47 M.J. 581 (N.M.Ct.Crim.App. 1997) (fraternization on terms of military equality between noncommissioned officers and other enlisted Marines or petty officers and non-rates, regardless of position, is contrary to custom and traditions of sea services).

§ 2-9. AIDS and HIV-Related Offenses.

§ 2-9(D). Constitutionality of Prosecuting HIV-Related Conduct.

Page 106, n. 61. United States v. Pritchard, 45 M.J. 126 (1996) (court noted, but did not decide, constitutional implications of finding accused guilty of violating safe-sex order involving spouse; accused conceded issue at trial and court found no plain error).

Page 106, n. 63. United States v. Pritchard, 45 M.J. 126 (1996) (court noted, but did not decide, constitutional implications of finding accused guilty of violating safe-sex order involving spouse; accused conceded issue at trial).

ANNOTATED BIBLIOGRAPHY

BOOKS

Byrne, *Military Crimes: Desertion* (1997).

This 400-page text provides a comprehensive discussion on the subject of desertion. It contains an exhaustive list of citations and references and covers virtually every aspect of the crime. The text is one of two volumes, the remaining volume serves as a "quickfinder" reference to the cases.

PERIODICALS

Hoskins, "One Tin Soldier: A New Look at the Constitutionality of Placing United States Soldiers Under the Command of the United Nations," 22 U. OF DAYTON L. REV. 125 (1996).

Drawing from the court-martial of Specialist Michael New for refusing to wear the UN insignia on his uniform, the author discusses the constitutionality of placing United States servicemembers under foreign command and concludes that the President's authority to place United States troops under the temporary command of foreign commanders should be validated.

Symposia

Symposium, "Military Justice Symposium—Volume I," ARMY LAW., April 1998.

This 128-page symposium is the first of two volumes and includes seven short articles on a range of military justice topics; it was authored by the faculty members of the Criminal Law Division at the Army's Judge Advocate School:

Stitler, "The Power to Prosecute: New Developments in Courts-Martial Jurisdiction," at 1.

Lovejoy, "Re-interpreting the Rules: Recent Developments in Speedy Trial and Pretrial Restraint," at 10.

Einwechter, "New Developments in Substantive Criminal Law Under the Uniform Code of Military Justice (1997)," at 20.

Coe, "'Something Old, Something New, Something Borrowed, Something Blue': Recent Developments in Pretrial and Trial Procedure," at 44.

Pede, "New Developments in Search and Seizure and Urinalysis," at 80.

Stitler, "Widening the Door: Recent Developments in Self-Incrimination Law," at 93.

Moran, "Pyrrhic Victories and Permutations: New Developments in the Sixth Amendment, Discovery, and Mental Responsibility," at 106.

Symposium, "Military Justice Symposium—Volume II," ARMY LAW., May 1998.

This 68-page symposium consists of four articles articles on a range of military justice topics; it was authored by the faculty members of the Criminal Law Division at the Army's Judge Advocate School:

Henley, "Developments in Evidence III—The Final Chapter," at 1.

Lovejoy, "The CAAF at a Crossroads: New Developments in Post-Trial Processing," at 25.

Allen, "Recent Developments in Sentencing Under the Uniform Code of Military Justice," at 39.

Morris, "'This Better Be Good': The Courts Continue to Tighten the Burden in Unlawful Command Influence Cases," at 49.

Symposium, "Military Justice Symposium I," ARMY LAW., April 1997.

This 149-page symposium, which presents a series of short articles on a range of military justice topics, was authored by the faculty members of the Criminal Law Division at the Army's Judge Advocate School:

Morris, Foreword.

Frisk, "The Long Arm of Military Justice: Court-Martial Jurisdiction and the Limits of Power," at 5.

Frisk, "Walking the Fine Line Between Promptness and Haste: Recent Developments in Speedy Trial and Pretrial Restraint Jurisprudence," at 14.

Coe, "Restating Some Old Rules and Limiting Some Landmarks: Recent Developments in Pretrial and Trial Procedure," at 25.

Barto, "Recent Developments in the Substantive Criminal Law Under the Uniform Code of Military Justice," at 50.

Wright, "'An Old Fashioned Crazy Quilt': New Developments in the Sixth Amendment, Discovery, Mental Responsibility, and Nonjudicial Punishment," at 72.

Henley, "Postcards from the Edge: Privileges, Profiles, Polygraphs, and Other Developments in the Military Rules of Evidence," at 92.

Allen, "New Developments in Sentencing," at 116.

Morris, "'Just One More Thing...' and Other Thoughts on Recent Developments in Post-Trial Processing," at 129.

CHAPTER 3

NONJUDICIAL PUNISHMENT: A COMPARATIVE ANALYSIS

§ 3-3. Authority to Impose Punishment.
    § 3-3(C). "Minor" Offenses.
§ 3-4. The Right to Demand Trial.
§ 3-5. Procedural Rules for Imposing Nonjudicial Punishment.
    § 3-5(B). Army Procedures.
        § 3-5(B)(2). Notice.
    § 3-5(C). Air Force Procedures.
        § 3-5(C)(2). Notice.
    § 3-5(D). Navy and Marine Corps Procedures.
        § 3-5(D)(2). Notice.
    § 3-5(E). Coast Guard Procedures.
        § 3-5(E)(2). Notice.
§ 3-7. Effect of Errors in Imposition.
§ 3-8. Consequences of Nonjudicial Punishment.
    § 3-8(B). Use at Court-Martial or Administrative Proceedings.

§ 3-3. Authority to Impose Punishment.

§ 3-3(C). "Minor" Offenses.

Page 119, n. 27. United States v. Dire, 46 M.J. 804 (C.G. Ct.Crim.App. 1997) (accused waived issue by not requesting that his prior nonjudicial punishment for same offenses be considered in adjudging a sentence; court nonetheless adjusted the sentence to remove any doubt about credit for the prior punishment); United States v. Gammons, 47 M.J. 766 (C.G. Ct.Crim.App. 1997) (en banc) (distinguishing *Dire, supra,* court concluded that accused did not waive issue of credit for prior NJP for charged offense; accused entitled to dollar for dollar credit for the prior punishment; case remanded for rehearing on sentence); *Cf.* United States v. Zamberlan, 45 M.J. 491 (1997) (not error not to instruct members to consider the reimposition of NJP against accused on different charge; *Pierce* distinguished).

§ 3-4. The Right to Demand Trial.

Page 121, n. 1. *See* Sullivan, "Overhauling the Vessel Exception," 43 NAVAL L. REV. 57 (1996) (criticizing *Penn* decision).

Page 121. n. 3, delete the reference to *Edwards***, 43 M.J. 619 and add:** *See also* Sullivan, "Overhauling the Vessel Exception," 43 NAVAL L. REV. 57 (1996) (extensive discussion on vessel exception).

Page 121. Add the following text after sentence ending with footnote 3:

In *United States v. Edwards*,[3.1] the Court of Appeals for the Armed Forces addressed the vessel exception in the context of the admissibility of a nonjudicial punishment during sentencing.[3.2] At trial, the defense had unsuccessfully argued that the accused's Article 15 punishment was inadmissible because he had been denied the right to demand trial and consult with counsel.[3.3] The vessel exception did not apply, counsel argued, because the accused was not assigned to a vessel which was in "operational status."[3.4] The Court of Appeals agreed with that logic. Citing the legislative history of Article 15,[3.5] the court concluded that Congress intended to limit the vessel exception to those cases where the servicemember is "aboard a vessel, in the immediate vicinity and in the process or boarding, or attached to vessels and absent without authority in foreign ports."[3.6] Turning to the definition of "vessel" in 1 U.S.C. § 3, the court also concluded that whether a vessel is in "operational status" is relevant to determining whether the vessel is — in the words of that definition — "used or capable of being used, as a means of transportation on water."[3.7] The court remanded the case for a determination whether in this case the vessel, which had been in long-term overhaul, was a vessel within that definition.[3.8]

[3.1] 46 M.J. 41(1997).

[3.2] The court was careful to note that the question was not whether the Article 15 punishment was legal and that the court's jurisdiction did not extend to direct review of nonjudicial punishment proceedings. *Id.* at 43. *See also* §§ 3-8(B) and 16-5(B), *infra*.

[3.3] 46 M.J. at 42.

[3.4] *Id.*

[3.5] *Id.* at 44-45. *See also* Sullivan, "Overhauling the Vessel Exception," 43 NAVAL L. REV. 57 (1996) (discussion of legislative history of vessel exception).

[3.6] 46 M.J. at 45. The court cited the "Schlei" memorandum which indicated that the Executive intended to read the exception more narrowly. A copy of that memorandum is included as an appendix at Sullivan, "Overhauling the Vessel Exception," 43 NAVAL L. REV. 57 (1996).

[3.7] 46 M.J. at 45.

[3.8] *Id.*

§ 3-5. Procedural Rules for Imposing Nonjudicial Punishment.

§ 3-5(B). Army Procedures.

§ 3-5(B)(2). Notice.

Page 124, n. 8. *Cf.* United States v. Marshall, 45 M.J. 268 (1996) (court assumed that a servicemember has a Sixth Amendment right to the effective assistance of counsel during Article 15 proceedings; court also noted that service regulations governing right to consult with counsel were apparently intended to be meaningful in their own right; under the facts, the accused was not denied the effective assistance of counsel where counsel advised him to demand trial — which resulted in punitive discharge).

§ 3-5(C). Air Force Procedures.

§ 3-5(C)(2). Notice.

Page 128, n. 33. *See also* United States v. Marshall, 45 M.J. 268 (1996) (court assumed that a servicemember has a Sixth Amendment right to the effective assistance of counsel during Article 15 proceedings; court also noted that service regulations governing right to consult with counsel were apparently intended to be meaningful in their own right; under the facts, the accused was not denied the effective assistance of counsel where counsel advised him to demand trial — which resulted in punitive discharge).

§ 3-5(D). Navy and Marine Corps Procedures.

§ 3-5(D)(2). Notice.

Page 133, n. 75. *See also* United States v. Marshall, 45 M.J. 268 (1996) (court assumed that a servicemember has a Sixth Amendment right to the effective assistance of counsel during Article 15 proceedings; court also noted that service regulations governing right to consult with counsel were apparently intended to be meaningful in their own right; under the facts, the accused was not denied the effective assistance of counsel where counsel advised him to demand trial — which resulted in punitive discharge).

§ 3-5(E). Coast Guard Procedures.

§ 3-5(E)(2). Notice.

Page 136, n. 105. *Cf.* United States v. Marshall, 45 M.J. 268 (1996) (court assumed that a servicemember has a Sixth Amendment right to the effective assistance of counsel during Article 15 proceedings; court also noted that service regulations governing right to consult with counsel were apparently intended to be meaningful in their own right; under the facts, the accused was not denied the effective assistance of counsel where counsel advised him to demand trial — which resulted in punitive discharge).

§ 3-7. Effect of Errors in Imposition.

Page 143, n. 1. *See also* Sullivan, "Overhauling the Vessel Exception," 43 NAVAL L. REV. 57 (1996).

§ 3-8. Consequences of Nonjudicial Punishment.

§ 3-8(B). Use at Court-Martial or Administrative Proceedings.

Page 145, n. 8. The Court of Appeals reversed the decision in *Kelly*. 45 M.J. 259 (1996). The court indicated that the Navy court was bound to follow the prior holdings of the Court of Appeals on the *Booker* issue. Re-examining its rationale, the court concluded that the *Booker* rule was still binding.

Page 146, n. 13. United States v. Kelly, 45 M.J. 259 (1996) (court reaffirmed its holding in *Booker* and *Mack*).

ANNOTATED BIBLIOGRAPHY

BOOKS

Schlueter, Jansen, Barry & Arnold, *Military Criminal Procedure Forms* (1997).

This book presents a variety of sample forms, letters, pleadings, checklists, briefs, and motions for military criminal justice practitioners. The text, which provides coverage for processing a case from pretrial investigation through appellate disposition, demonstrates how formats may vary among the services.

PERIODICALS

Sullivan, "Overhauling the Vessel Exception," 43 NAVAL L. REV. 57 (1996).

This excellent article traces the historical basis of the "vessel exception" in Article 15, U.C.M.J., and chronicles some of the problems generally associated with application of that exception. Noting that the drafters of the exception did not expect it to be applied in a broad fashion, the author proposes several modifications to the Manual which would, *inter alia*, limit the exception to those situations where nonjudicial punishment is being imposed aboard a vessel. The article includes a copy of the 1963 "Schlei" memorandum which clearly sets out the intent of the drafters.

Symposia

Symposium, "Military Justice Symposium—Volume I," ARMY LAW., April 1998.

This 128-page symposium is the first of two volumes and includes seven short articles on a range of military justice topics; it was authored by the faculty members of the Criminal Law Division at the Army's Judge Advocate School:

- Stitler, "The Power to Prosecute: New Developments in Courts-Martial Jurisdiction," at 1.
- Lovejoy, "Re-interpreting the Rules: Recent Developments in Speedy Trial and Pretrial Restraint," at 10.
- Einwechter, "New Developments in Substantive Criminal Law Under the Uniform Code of Military Justice (1997)," at 20.
- Coe, "'Something Old, Something New, Something Borrowed, Something Blue': Recent Developments in Pretrial and Trial Procedure," at 44.
- Pede, "New Developments in Search and Seizure and Urinalysis," at 80.
- Stitler, "Widening the Door: Recent Developments in Self-Incrimination Law," at 93.
- Moran, "Pyrrhic Victories and Permutations: New Developments in the Sixth Amendment, Discovery, and Mental Responsibility," at 106.

Symposium, "Military Justice Symposium—Volume II," ARMY LAW., May 1998.

This 68-page symposium consists of four articles articles on a range of military justice topics; it was authored by the faculty members of the Criminal Law Division at the Army's Judge Advocate School:

> Henley, "Developments in Evidence III—The Final Chapter," at 1.
> Lovejoy, "The CAAF at a Crossroads: New Developments in Post-Trial Processing," at 25.
> Allen, "Recent Developments in Sentencing Under the Uniform Code of Military Justice," at 39.
> Morris, "'This Better Be Good': The Courts Continue to Tighten the Burden in Unlawful Command Influence Cases," at 49.

Symposium, "Military Justice Symposium I," ARMY LAW., April 1997.

This 149-page symposium, which presents a series of short articles on a range of military justice topics, was authored by the faculty members of the Criminal Law Division at the Army's Judge Advocate School:

> Morris, Foreword.
> Frisk, "The Long Arm of Military Justice: Court-Martial Jurisdiction and the Limits of Power," at 5.
> Frisk, "Walking the Fine Line Between Promptness and Haste: Recent Developments in Speedy Trial and Pretrial Restraint Jurisprudence," at 14.
> Coe, "Restating Some Old Rules and Limiting Some Landmarks: Recent Developments in Pretrial and Trial Procedure," at 25.
> Barto, "Recent Developments in the Substantive Criminal Law Under the Uniform Code of Military Justice," at 50.
> Wright, "'An Old Fashioned Crazy Quilt': New Developments in the Sixth Amendment, Discovery, Mental Responsibility, and Nonjudicial Punishment," at 72.
> Henley, "Postcards from the Edge: Privileges, Profiles, Polygraphs, and Other Developments in the Military Rules of Evidence," at 92.
> Allen, "New Developments in Sentencing," at 116.
> Morris, "'Just One More Thing...' and Other Thoughts on Recent Developments in Post-Trial Processing," at 129.

CHAPTER 4

JURISDICTION

PART II.
PERSONAL JURISDICTION

§ 4-6. Jurisdiction Over Reservists and Members of National Guard.
§ 4-8. Termination of Personal Jurisdiction.
   § 4-8(A). Continuing Jurisdiction.
   § 4-8(B). General Rule: Discharge Terminates Status.
   § 4-8(C). Exceptions to the General Rule.
      § 4-8(C)(3). Fraudulent Discharge.

PART III.
JURISDICTION OVER THE OFFENSE

§ 4-12. Exclusive, Reciprocal, and Concurrent Jurisdiction.
   § 4-12(A). State and Federal Courts.

PART IV.
CONVENING AND COMPOSITION OF COURTS-MARTIAL: REFERRAL OF CHARGES

§ 4-15. Properly Composed Court-Martial.
   § 4-15(A). Military Judge.
   § 4-15(C). Court Members.

PART II.
PERSONAL JURISDICTION

§ 4-6. Jurisdiction Over Reservists and Members of National Guard.

Page 164, n. 25. Wilson v. Courter, 46 M.J. 745 (A.F.Ct.Crim.App. 1997) (guardsman subject to jurisdiction for AWOL committed while on active duty).

§ 4-8. Termination of Personal Jurisdiction.

§ 4-8(A). Continuing Jurisdiction.

Page 167, n. 8. United States v. Lee, 43 M.J. 794 (N.M.Ct.Crim.App. 1995) (list in R.C.M. 202(c)(2) of actions sufficient to continue jurisdiction is not all-inclusive; investigatory actions are sufficient; magnitude of thefts signaled that court-martial would follow).

§ 4-8(B). General Rule: Discharge Terminates Status.

Page 168, n. 11. Smith v Vanderbush, 47 M.J. 56 (1997) (delivery of discharge certificate to accused cut off court-martial jurisdiction even though he had already been arraigned on offenses; in an extensive discussion of the issue, the court distinguished other cases involving continuing jurisdiction after a person's period of enlistment expires; the court also rejected the arguments that the discharge was invalid because of mistakes of facts or law or because of fraud; case includes extensive discussion of the topic of continuing jurisdiction).

Page, 168, n. 12. United States v. Guest, 46 M.J. 778 (Army Ct.Crim.App. 1997) (delivery of courtesy copy of DD 214 was not a valid discharge for purposes of terminating jurisdiction); Wilson v. Courter, 46 M.J. 745 (A.F.Ct.Crim.App. 1997) (simply delivering discharge certificate is not in itself sufficient; the discharge it represents must be valid; unauthorized issuance of certificate by Master Sergeant did not effectively end jurisdiction).

Page 168, n. 13. United States v. Pou, 43 M.J. 778 (A.F.Ct.Crim.App. 1995) (accused's being declared dead by Air Force was not equivalent of discharge; military thus had jurisdiction over offenses he committed after faking his own death and when he was apprehended five years later).

§ 4-8(C). Exceptions to the General Rule.

§ 4-8(C)(3). Fraudulent Discharge.

Page 170, n. 27. United States v. Pou, 43 M.J. 778 (A.F.Ct.Crim.App. 1995) (accused's faking of own death and being declared dead by Air Force was not fraudulent discharge contemplated by statute; military thus had jurisdiction over offenses he committed after faking death and before time of apprehension five years later).

Page 170, n. 28. In United States v. Reid, 46 M.J. 236 (1997) the court concluded that jurisdiction under Article 3(b) does not exist until there is a conviction for the fraudulent discharge. And that, the court said, means that the accused must have been convicted and sentenced. The court noted that a fraudulent discharge is voidable, and not void, and that Article 3(b) contemplates a two-stepped process. The first trial is for the fraudulent discharge. And if the accused is convicted and sentenced on that charge, the accused may be tried by another court-martial on any charges occurring before that discharge. *See also* Frisk, "The Long Arm of Military Justice: Court-Martial Jurisdiction and the Limits of Power," ARMY LAW., April 1997, at 5; Smith v. Vanderbush, 47 M.J. 56 (1997) (delivery of discharge certificate to accused cut off court-martial jurisdiction even though he had already been arraigned on offenses; in an extensive discussion of the issue, the court distinguished other cases involving continuing jurisdiction after a person's period of enlistment expires; the court also rejected the arguments that the discharge was invalid because of fraud).

PART III.

JURISDICTION OVER THE OFFENSE

§ 4-12. Exclusive, Reciprocal, and Concurrent Jurisdiction.

§ 4-12(A). State and Federal Courts.

Page 189, n. 5. United States v. Kohut, 44 M.J. 245 (1996) (regulations governing subsequent prosecution by military courts are matter of comity and may include language which specifically indicates that there is no intent to confer additional rights on an accused). *See also* Frisk, "The Long Arm of Military Justice: Court-Martial Jurisdiction and the Limits of Power," ARMY LAW., April 1997, at 5.

Page 189, n. 7. United States v. Kohut, 44 M.J. 245 (1996) (not jurisdictional error to try accused by court-martial in violation of Section 0124, JAGMAN, JAGINST 5800.7C (Change 1, 1992)).

Page 190. Add the following text after sentence ending with footnote 9:

If the court-martial follows a completed state trial, the defense should be able to introduce evidence at sentencing that the accused has already received punishment from the state court for the same acts.[9.1]

[9.1] United States v. Simmons, 48 M.J. 193 (1998) (court concluded that the trial court erred in not admitting defense evidence that the accused had already been sentenced in state court for the underlying conduct).

Page 190, n. 10. The Court of Appeals affirmed *Kohut*. United States v. Kohut, 44 M.J. 245 (1996). The court noted that unless Congress indicates otherwise, it is assumed that service regulations are not jurisdictional. Additionally, the Navy regulation in question was clearly policy, not law, and specifically indicated that it was not intended to confer any additional rights on an accused; thus the accused had no standing to complain about the government's violation of the regulation.

PART IV.

CONVENING AND COMPOSITION OF COURTS-MARTIAL: REFERRAL OF CHARGES

§ 4-15. Properly Composed Court-Martial.

§ 4-15(A). Military Judge.

Page 196, n. 5. *Cf.* United States v. Turner, 47 M.J. 348 (1997) (court-martial did not lack jurisdiction where record contained no personal request from accused that he be tried by judge alone); United States v. Mayfield, 45 M.J. 176 (1996) (sentencing by military judge alone following guilty plea was not jurisdictionally defective where there was no request for judge alone sentencing where accused in post-trial session personally confirmed his desire for judge alone trial; court indicated that before trial the accused had presented "pretrial paperwork" for trial by judge alone). *See also* Coe, "Restating Some Old Rules and Limiting Some Landmarks: Recent Developments in Pretrial and Trial Procedure," ARMY LAW., April 1997, at 25.

§ 4-15(C). Court Members.

Page 199, n. 20. United States v. Sargent, 47 M.J. 367 (1997) (unexplained absence of member from trial was not jurisdictional error; nine members remained and absence did not frustrate power of convening authority to convene court or deny accused right to military due process).

ANNOTATED BIBLIOGRAPHY

BOOKS

Schlueter, Jansen, Barry & Arnold, *Military Criminal Procedure Forms* (1997).

This book presents a variety of sample forms, letters, pleadings, checklists, briefs, and motions for military criminal justice practitioners. The text, which provides coverage for processing a case from pretrial investigation through appellate disposition, demonstrates how formats may vary among the services.

PERIODICALS

Symposia

Symposium, "Military Justice Symposium—Volume I," ARMY LAW., April 1998.

This 128-page symposium is the first of two volumes and includes seven short articles on a range of military justice topics; it was authored by the faculty members of the Criminal Law Division at the Army's Judge Advocate School:

- Stitler, "The Power to Prosecute: New Developments in Courts-Martial Jurisdiction," at 1.
- Lovejoy, "Re-interpreting the Rules: Recent Developments in Speedy Trial and Pretrial Restraint," at 10.
- Einwechter, "New Developments in Substantive Criminal Law Under the Uniform Code of Military Justice (1997)," at 20.
- Coe, "'Something Old, Something New, Something Borrowed, Something Blue': Recent Developments in Pretrial and Trial Procedure," at 44.
- Pede, "New Developments in Search and Seizure and Urinalysis," at 80.
- Stitler, "Widening the Door: Recent Developments in Self-Incrimination Law," at 93.
- Moran, "Pyrrhic Victories and Permutations: New Developments in the Sixth Amendment, Discovery, and Mental Responsibility," at 106.

Symposium, "Military Justice Symposium—Volume II," ARMY LAW., May 1998.

This 68-page symposium consists of four articles articles on a range of military justice topics; it was authored by the faculty members of the Criminal Law Division at the Army's Judge Advocate School:

- Henley, "Developments in Evidence III—The Final Chapter," at 1.
- Lovejoy, "The CAAF at a Crossroads: New Developments in Post-Trial Processing," at 25.
- Allen, "Recent Developments in Sentencing Under the Uniform Code of Military Justice," at 39.
- Morris, "'This Better Be Good': The Courts Continue to Tighten the Burden in Unlawful Command Influence Cases," at 49.

Symposium, "Military Justice Symposium I," ARMY LAW., April 1997.

This 149-page symposium, which presents a series of short articles on a range of military justice topics, was authored by the faculty members of the Criminal Law Division at the Army's Judge Advocate School:

> Morris, Foreword.
> Frisk, "The Long Arm of Military Justice: Court-Martial Jurisdiction and the Limits of Power," at 5.
> Frisk, "Walking the Fine Line Between Promptness and Haste: Recent Developments in Speedy Trial and Pretrial Restraint Jurisprudence," at 14.
> Coe, "Restating Some Old Rules and Limiting Some Landmarks: Recent Developments in Pretrial and Trial Procedure," at 25.
> Barto, "Recent Developments in the Substantive Criminal Law Under the Uniform Code of Military Justice," at 50.
> Wright, "'An Old Fashioned Crazy Quilt': New Developments in the Sixth Amendment, Discovery, Mental Responsibility, and Nonjudicial Punishment," at 72.
> Henley, "Postcards from the Edge: Privileges, Profiles, Polygraphs, and Other Developments in the Military Rules of Evidence," at 92.
> Allen, "New Developments in Sentencing," at 116.
> Morris, "'Just One More Thing...' and Other Thoughts on Recent Developments in Post-Trial Processing," at 129.

CHAPTER 5

THE COMMANDER'S INVESTIGATION, PRETRIAL RESTRAINTS, AND CONFINEMENT

PART I.

THE COMMANDER'S INVESTIGATION

§ 5-3. Searches and Seizures.
  § 5-3(A). The Servicemember's Reasonable Expectation of Privacy.
  § 5-3(B). Probable Cause Searches.
  § 5-3(C). Nonprobable Cause Searches.
    § 5-3(C)(5). Emergency Searches.
    § 5-3(C)(6). Consent Searches.
    § 5-3(C)(7). Searches Incident to Apprehension.
    § 5-3(C)(8). Searches Incident to Lawful Stop.
  § 5-3(D). Other Reasonable Searches.
    § 5-3(D)(1). Inspections and Inventories.
  § 5-3(F). Exclusionary Rule; Exceptions.
§ 5-4. The Right Against Self-Incrimination, Interrogation, and Immunity.
  § 5-4(A). The Right Against Self-Incrimination.
    § 5-4(A)(2). Reporting Requirements.
    § 5-4(A)(3). Comments on Invoking the Right.
  § 5-4(B). Interrogation of Suspects; Rights Warnings.
  § 5-4(C). Grants of Immunity.

PART II.

PRETRIAL RESTRAINTS AND CONFINEMENT

§ 5-8. Pretrial Restraints.
§ 5-9. Pretrial Confinement.
  § 5-9(A). In General.
  § 5-9(C). Review by Commander.
  § 5-9(D). Review of Commander's Decision to Confine.
  § 5-9(E). Judicial Review.
§ 5-10. Illegal Pretrial Punishment and Restraints.
  § 5-10(A). In General.
  § 5-10(C). Pretrial Restraints Constituting Illegal Punishment.
  § 5-10(D). Remedies; Waiver.

PART I.

THE COMMANDER'S INVESTIGATION

§ 5-3. Searches and Seizures.

Page 211, n. 8. United States v. Moore, 45 M.J. 652 (A.F.Ct.Crim.App. 1996) (under facts, medical group commander was authorized to order urinalysis test for accused).

§ 5-3(A). The Servicemember's Reasonable Expectation of Privacy.

Page 212, n. 14, replace citation to *Maxwell* with: United States v. Maxwell, 45 M.J. 406 (1996) (court held that accused had reasonable expectation of privacy in e-mail messages stored in America On-Line computers).

§ 5-3(B). Probable Cause Searches.

Page 214, n. 38. United States v. Hester, 47 M.J. 461 (1998) (sufficient probable cause based upon informant's tip; court noted that although tip would satisfy *Gates* test, it would also satisfy earlier *Aguilar-Spinelli* two-pronged test as well); United States v. DuFour, 43 M.J. 772 (N.M.Ct.Crim.App. 1995) (probable cause existed to search accused's quarters based upon tip, officers' observations, and statement by participant); United States v. Agosto, 43 M.J. 745 (A.F.Ct.Crim.App. 1995) (probable cause to search accused's quarters existed even though information was several months old; information was not stale in light of other information).

Page 215, n. 49. United States v. Claypoole, 46 M.J. 786 (C.G.Ct.Crim.App. 1997) (search of accused's vehicle was valid).

§ 5-3(C). Nonprobable Cause Searches.

§ 5-3(C)(5). Emergency Searches.

Page 218, n. 81. United States v. Curry, 48 M.J. 115 (1998) (accused's suicide notes admissible as product of emergency search; Fourth Amendment issues are reviewed de novo on appeal).

§ 5-3(C)(6). Consent Searches.

Page 218, n. 85. United States v. Radvansky, 45 M.J. 226 (1996) (accused's consent to urinalysis was voluntary even though superior mentioned possibility of commanding direct testing if accused did not consent); United States v. Baker, 45 M.J. 538 (A.F.Ct.Crim.App. 1996) (accused's consent to urinalysis testing was voluntary).

Page 218, n. 86. United States v. DuFour, 43 M.J. 772 (N.M.Ct.Crim.App. 1995) (accused voluntarily signed consent form for search of his home).

Page 218, n. 87. United States v. Rodriguez, 44 M.J. 766 (N.M.Ct.Crim.App. 1996) (accused consented to search of his car).

Page 218, n. 88, replace citation to *Reister* with: United States v. Reister, 44 M.J. 409 (1996) (house sitter had authority to consent to search of accused's quarters).

Page 219, n. 96. United States v. Salazar, 44 M.J. 464 (1996) (consent search invalid where officers used deception to get accused's wife to turn over contraband to them; case returned for *DuBay* hearing; the dissent argued that deception does not amount to coercion).

§ 5-3(C)(7). Searches Incident to Apprehension.

Page 219, n. 99. United States v. Curtis, 44 M.J. 106 (1996) (officers authorized to search murder defendant's clothing despite delay between apprehension and search), *rev'd on other grounds on reconsideration*, 46 M.J. 129 (1997) (per curiam).

§ 5-3(C)(8). Searches Incident to Lawful Stop.

Page 220, n. 108. United States v. Rodriguez, 44 M.J. 766 (N.M.Ct.Crim.App. 1996) (civilian officers lawfully stopped accused's car).

Page 220, n. 111. United States v. Rodriguez, 44 M.J. 766 (N.M.Ct.Crim.App. 1996) (officers had sufficient cause to look for weapons in accused's car after it was stopped).

§ 5-3(D). Other Reasonable Searches.

§ 5-3(D)(1). Inspections and Inventories.

Page 221, n. 119. United States v. Shover, 45 M.J. 119 (1996) (primary purpose of urinalysis was valid inspection to end low morale in unit).

Page 223, n. 131. United States v. Streetman, 43 M.J. 752 (A.F.Ct.Crim.App. 1995) (commander's second order to provide urine sample was not invalidated by accused's refusal to submit sample following the original, valid, order to produce a sample).

§ 5-3(F). Exclusionary Rule; Exceptions.

Page 226, n. 161. United States v. Hall, 45 M.J. 546 (Army Ct.Crim.App. 1997) (in deciding whether evidence has been tainted, first question is whether the underlying act was illegal).

§ 5-4. The Right Against Self-Incrimination, Interrogation, and Immunity.

§ 5-4(A). The Right Against Self-Incrimination.

§ 5-4(A)(2). Reporting Requirements.

Page 228. Add in second sentence, following footnote 13:

possession of controlled documents or information,[13.1]

[13.1] United States v. Oxfort, 44 M.J. 337 (1996) (court applied required reports doctrine to accused who had unauthorized possession of classified documents).

§ 5-4(A)(3). Comments on Invoking the Right.

Page 229, n. 19. United States v. Riley, 47 M.J. 276 (1997) (admission of investigator's testimony that accused had invoked his right to silence constituted plain, reversible, error); United States v. Wright, 47 M.J. 555 (N.M.Ct.Crim.App. 1997) (testimony concerning accused's lack of surprise during search; comment was not directed at accused's silence).

§ 5-4(B). Interrogation of Suspects; Rights Warnings.

Page 230, n. 23. United States v. Miller, 48 M.J. 49 (1998) (accused was not suspect at time he was questioned by agents); United States v. Muirhead, 48 M.J. 527 (N.M.Ct.Crim.App. 1998) (accused was not suspect at time of questioning; mere hunch does not trigger requirement to warn).

Page 230, n. 26. United States v. Rogers, 47 M.J. 135 (1997) (accused received adequate notice of offense being investigated).

Page 231. In first full sentence at top of page, add new footnote as follows:

servicemember has been placed in custody[29.1]

[29.1] United States v. Miller, 46 M.J. 80 (1997) (accused not in custody when questioned by public safety officer); United States v. Moses, 45 M.J. 132 (1996) (accused was not entitled to *Miranda* warnings during prearrest questioning; he was not in custody during 24-hour standoff outside Naval housing unit).

Page 231, n. 30. United States v. Miller, 48 M.J. 49 (1998) (accused not subjected to custodial interrogation while being briefly detained).

Page 232, n. 42. United States v. Moses, 45 M.J. 132 (1996) (accused was not entitled to Article 31 warnings before questioning by officers who were attempting to bring peaceful end to accused's 24-hour standoff outside Naval housing unit); United States v. Price, 44 M.J. 430 (1996) (officer not required to give Article 31 warnings to his technical supervisor where he was not acting in law enforcement capacity); United States v. Bradley, 47 M.J. 715 (A.F.Ct.Crim.App. 1997) (although acting commander was acting in official capacity, his questions related to security clearance, not investigation of offense; thus, no warnings required); United States v. Rios, 45 M.J. 558 (A.F.Ct.Crim.App. 1997) (accused not entitled to rights warnings before making statements to daughter during pretext phone call coordinated by AFOSI; accused's statements were voluntary).

Page 233, n. 43. United States v. Rios, 45 M.J. 558 (A.F.Ct.Crim.App. 1997) (no warnings required before questioning by state social worker); United States v. Rodriguez, 44 M.J. 766 (N.M.Ct.Crim.App. 1996) (civilian law enforcement officers not required to give Article 31 warnings where they were conducting independent investigation).

Page 234, n. 44. United States v. Turner, 48 M.J. 513 (Army Ct.Crim.App. 1998) (no interrogation occurred where agents informed accused that he was suspected of being AWOL and that he would be turned over to CID); United States v. Warren, 47 M.J. 649 (Army Ct.Crim.App. 1997) (interrogation did not occur when agents asked accused to write out account of how he had come into possession of victim's items).

Page 234, n. 46. United States v. Warren, 47 M.J. 649 (Army Ct.Crim.App. 1997) (accused's comments were spontaneous).

Page 234, n. 49. United States v. Nadel, 46 M.J. 682 (N.M.Ct.Crim.App. 1997) (accused invoked right to counsel only as to one offense and agreed to talk about others).

Page 235, n. 50. United States v. Faisca, 46 M.J. 276 (1997) (not denial of right to counsel where investigators asked accused, who had invoked right to counsel six months earlier, whether he obtained counsel); United States v. Vaughters, 44 M.J. 377 (1996) (reinitiation of interrogation not barred by *Edwards* where accused had been released from custody for 19 days and had been provided meaningful opportunity to consult with counsel); United States v. Young, 46 M.J. 768 (Army Ct.Crim.App. 1997) (investigator's comment to accused that he had missed opportunity to talk was not reasonably likely to elicit retraction of request for counsel).

Page 236, n. 52, remove reference to *United States v. Bubonics*, 40 M.J. 734 and add: United States v. Sojfer, 47 M.J. 425 (1998) (accused's statement was voluntary); United States v. Payne, 47 M.J. 37 (1997) (under facts, the accused's statements during polygraph examination were voluntary); United States v. Cottrill, 45 M.J. 485 (1997) (accused's confession was voluntary); United States v. Bubonics, 45 M.J. 93 (1996) (accused's confession was involuntary where officers used "Mutt and Jeff" routine); United States v. Murray, 45 M.J. 554 (N.M.Ct.Crim.App. 1996) (confession voluntary even though accused was told that if he did not do it, his wife must have and she would be charged in state court); United States v. Morris, 44 M.J. 841 (Army Ct.Crim.App. 1996) (appeal to accused's membership in fraternal organization and its principles was lawful.

§ 5-4(C). Grants of Immunity.

Page 237, n. 56. United States v. McGeeney, 44 M.J. 418 (1996) (initial investigation and decision to prosecute accused were not tainted by his earlier immunized testimony in previous case).

PART II.

PRETRIAL RESTRAINTS AND CONFINEMENT

§ 5-8. Pretrial Restraints.

Page 243, n. 9. *Cf.* United States v. Perez, 45 M.J. 323 (1996) (probable cause hearing not required for pretrial restriction).

§ 5-9. Pretrial Confinement.

§ 5-9(A). In General.

Page 245, n. 1. In United States v. Tilghman, 44 M.J. 493 (1996), the Court of Appeals indicated that pretrial confinement includes any period of confinement prior to completion of the trial. Thus, the period of confinement imposed on the accused between findings and sentencing was pretrial confinement. Because there was no showing that the accused was a flight risk, that period was illegal. *See also* R.C.M. 304(g) (pretrial confinement terminates when accused is sentenced or acquitted, or the charges are dismissed).

§ 5-9(C). Review by Commander.

Page 248, n. 18. United States v. Roberson, 43 M.J. 732 (A.F.Ct.Crim.App. 1995) (commander not disqualified from reviewing own decision to confine accused simply because he was aware of prior nonjudicial punishments or because he ultimately became accuser in case).

Page 248. Add the following paragraph after the last sentence of the section:

In 1998, R.C.M. 305 was finally amended to recognize the constitutional requirement that a neutral and detached person must review a defendant's pretrial confinement within 48 hours of the time it was imposed.[20.1] The *Manual* now reflects that the current requirement for a review within 72 hours may satisfy that requirement if the reviewing officer is indeed neutral and detached and the review is conducted within the 48-hour period.[20.2] The new language also notes that nothing prevents the neutral and detached reviewer from conducting either the 48-hour or 72-hour review right after confinement has been imposed.[20.3]

[20.1] R.C.M. 305(h)(2)(A). County of Riverside v. McLaughlin, 500 U.S. 44 (1991); United States v. Rexroat, 38 M.J. 292 (C.M.A. 1993).
[20.2] R.C.M. 305(h)(2)(A).
[20.3] *Id.*

§ 5-9(D). Review of Commander's Decision to Confine.

Pages 248-49. Replace the first paragraph in the section with the following:

Military case law[21] and the Manual for Courts-Martial[21.1] require that within 48 hours pretrial confinement begins,[22] a "neutral and detached" reviewing officer[23] must decide whether continued confinement is warranted.[24] This is the equivalent of a *Gerstein v. Pugh,* probable cause hearing conducted by civilian magistrates or judges. The *Manual* now clarifies the differences in the 48-hour review set out in R.C.M. 305(i)(1),[24.1] the 72-hour review set out in R.C.M. 305(h)(2)[24.2] and the seven-day review required in R.C.M. 305(i)(2).[24.3]

---

[21] United States v. Rexroat, 38 M.J. 292 (C.M.A. 1993) (*applying* County of Riverside v. McLaughlin, 500 U.S. 44 (1991) to military practice); United States v. Bell, 44 M.J. 677 (N.M.Ct.Crim.App. 1996) (requirement to review decision to confine was satisfied by ship command duty officer's initial decision to confine the accused).
[21.1] R.C.M. 305(i), as amended by Executive Order 13086, 27 May 1998.
[22] [Same as bound volume.]
[23] [Same as bound volume.]
[24] R.C.M. 305(i). *Cf.* United States v. Perez, 45 M.J. 323 (1996) (48-hour probable cause hearing not required for pretrial restriction).
[24.1] R.C.M. 305(i)(1), as amended by Executive Order 13086, 27 May 1998.
[24.2] R.C.M. 305(h)(2), as amended by Executive Order 13086, 27 May 1998.
[24.3] R.C.M. 305(i)(2), as amended by Executive Order 13086, 27 May 1998.

Page 249, n. 26. United States v. Lamb, 47 M.J. 384 (1997) (accused failed to show that he had been confined by civilian authorities solely for military offense and failed to show lack of compliance with *County of Riverside v. McLaughlin,* upon which *United States v. Rexrot* was based).

§ 5-9(E). Judicial Review.

Page 252, n. 54, delete reference to *United States v. Gaither*, 41 M.J. 774.

Page 252. Add the following text after the last sentence on the page:

The military courts have recognized that there are two aspects to the judicial review of pretrial confinement by a military judge.[54.1] First, the military judge may be called upon to determine whether the accused should be released from pretrial confinement.[54.2] In deciding this issue, the military judge should determine if the magistrate abused his or her discretion in approving the pretrial confinement.[54.3] That in turn requires the judge to limit his or her review to the information available to the magistrate when the latter made the decision to continue the confinement.[54.4] On the other hand, the question about whether the accused should be kept in pretrial confinement should be decided de novo by the judge.[54.5] In that instance, the judge may consider new information.[54.6]

In a second scenario, the military judge may be called upon to decide whether the confinement served was legal.[54.7] In that case, the judge conducts a review of the information available to the magistrate at the time he or she made the decision.[54.8]

[54.1] United States v. Gaither, 45 M.J. 349 (1996) (discussion of two scenarios). *See also* Frisk, "Walking the Fine Line Between Promptness and Haste: Recent Developments in Speedy Trial and Pretrial Restraint Jurisprudence," ARMY LAW., April 1997, at 14.

[54.2] R.C.M. 305(j), Drafter's Analysis. United States v. Gaither, 45 M.J. 349, 351 (1996).

[54.3] R.C.M. 305(j)(1)(A). United States v. Gaither, 45 M.J. 349, 351 (1996).

[54.4] United States v. Gaither, 45 M.J. 349, 351 (1996).

[54.5] R.C.M. 305(j)(1)(B). United States v. Gaither, 45 M.J. 349, 351 (1996).

[54.6] United States v. Gaither, 45 M.J. 349, 351 (1996).

[54.7] *Id.*

[54.8] *Id.*

Page 253, n. 60. United States v. Williams, 47 M.J. 621 (Army Ct.Crim.App. 1997) (accused was illegally ordered back into pretrial confinement by supervising military judge following government "appeal" of magistrate's decision to release accused).

Page 253, n. 61. Keaton v. Marsh, 43 M.J. 757 (Army Ct.Crim.App. 1996) (judge's decision to reconfine accused in absence of new information was not authorized under R.C.M. 305(l) even though AR 27-10 indicated that such reconfinement might be appropriate; *Manual* provision controls).

§ 5-10. Illegal Pretrial Punishment and Restraints.

§ 5-10(A). In General.

Page 254, n. 1. United States v. Combs, 47 M.J. 330 (1997) (Article 13 acts on limit on any confinement imposed while awaiting trial or retrial or rehearing; court granted 20 months credit after authorities reduced his rank following court-martial which was set aside).

Page 255, n. 6. United States v. Combs, 47 M.J. 330 (1997) (court granted 20 months credit after authorities reduced his rank following court-martial which was set aside).

§ 5-10(C). Pretrial Restraints Constituting Illegal Punishment.

Page 257, n. 16. United States v. McCarthy, 47 M.J. 162 (1997) (no intent to impose illegal pretrial punishment where government placed accused in maximum confinement for a variety of non-punishment purposes).

§ 5-10(D). Remedies; Waiver.

Page 258, n. 28. United States v. Tilghman, 44 M.J. 493 (1996) (accused received 10-for-one credit for less than 24 hours in illegal pretrial confinement, i.e., period between findings and sentencing).

Page 258, n. 29. Coyle v. Commander, 21st Theatre Army Area Command, 47 M.J. 626 (Army Ct.Crim.App. 1997) (remedy for illegal pretrial confinement is "confinement credit" which is to be applied administratively against the approved sentence; remedy for illegal pretrial punishment is "punishment credit" which must at a minimum be applied against the adjudged sentence).

Page 259, n. 32. United States v. Lamb, 44 M.J. 779 (N.M.Ct.Crim.App. 1996) (accused not entitled to *Rexroat* credit for failure to review his pretrial confinement in civilian jail).

Page 260, n. 36. Coyle v. Commander, 21st Theatre Army Area Command, 47 M.J. 626 (Army Ct.Crim.App. 1997) (remedy for illegal pretrial confinement is "confinement credit" which is to be applied administratively against the approved sentence; remedy for illegal pretrial punishment is "punishment credit" which must at a minimum be applied against the adjudged sentence).

Page 260, n. 37. United States v. Ruppel, 45 M.J. 578 (A.F.Ct.Crim.App. 1997) (accused not entitled to credit for time spent in inpatient psychiatric unit).

Page 261, n. 39. United States v. Swan, 45 M.J. 672 (N.M.Ct.Crim.App. 1996) (accused's restriction did not amount to pretrial confinement).

ANNOTATED BIBLIOGRAPHY

BOOKS

Schlueter, Jansen, Barry & Arnold, *Military Criminal Procedure Forms* (1997).

This book presents a variety of sample forms, letters, pleadings, checklists, briefs, and motions for military criminal justice practitioners. The text, which provides coverage for processing a case from pretrial investigation through appellate disposition, demonstrates how formats may vary among the services.

PERIODICALS

McQuillen, "Article 31(b) Triggers: Re-examining the 'Officiality Doctrine,'" 150 MIL. L. REV. 1 (1995).

Noting that Article 31(b) serves as a guardian of the citizen soldier's privilege against self-incrimination, the author provides an historical overview of the rights warnings requirement in that statutory provision. The author notes that over the years the various tests applied by the military courts in deciding when those warnings are required have proved to be confusing and tangled. He recommends that the courts adopt a new test which would focus on the objective perceptions of the servicemember being questioned.

Symposia

Symposium, "Military Justice Symposium—Volume I," ARMY LAW., April 1998.

This 128-page symposium is the first of two volumes and includes seven short articles on a range of military justice topics; it was authored by the faculty members of the Criminal Law Division at the Army's Judge Advocate School:

- Stitler, "The Power to Prosecute: New Developments in Courts-Martial Jurisdiction," at 1.
- Lovejoy, "Re-interpreting the Rules: Recent Developments in Speedy Trial and Pretrial Restraint," at 10.
- Einwechter, "New Developments in Substantive Criminal Law Under the Uniform Code of Military Justice (1997)," at 20.
- Coe, "'Something Old, Something New, Something Borrowed, Something Blue': Recent Developments in Pretrial and Trial Procedure," at 44.
- Pede, "New Developments in Search and Seizure and Urinalysis," at 80.
- Stitler, "Widening the Door: Recent Developments in Self-Incrimination Law," at 93.
- Moran, "Pyrrhic Victories and Permutations: New Developments in the Sixth Amendment, Discovery, and Mental Responsibility," at 106.

Symposium, "Military Justice Symposium—Volume II," ARMY LAW., May 1998.

This 68-page symposium consists of four articles articles on a range of military justice topics; it was authored by the faculty members of the Criminal Law Division at the Army's Judge Advocate School:

- Henley, "Developments in Evidence III—The Final Chapter," at 1.
- Lovejoy, "The CAAF at a Crossroads: New Developments in Post-Trial Processing," at 25.
- Allen, "Recent Developments in Sentencing Under the Uniform Code of Military Justice," at 39.
- Morris, "'This Better Be Good': The Courts Continue to Tighten the Burden in Unlawful Command Influence Cases," at 49.

MILITARY CRIMINAL JUSTICE

Symposium, "Military Justice Symposium I," ARMY LAW., April 1997.

This 149-page symposium, which presents a series of short articles on a range of military justice topics, was authored by the faculty members of the Criminal Law Division at the Army's Judge Advocate School:

> Morris, Foreword.
> Frisk, "The Long Arm of Military Justice: Court-Martial Jurisdiction and the Limits of Power," at 5.
> Frisk, "Walking the Fine Line Between Promptness and Haste: Recent Developments in Speedy Trial and Pretrial Restraint Jurisprudence," at 14.
> Coe, "Restating Some Old Rules and Limiting Some Landmarks: Recent Developments in Pretrial and Trial Procedure," at 25.
> Barto, "Recent Developments in the Substantive Criminal Law Under the Uniform Code of Military Justice," at 50.
> Wright, "'An Old Fashioned Crazy Quilt': New Developments in the Sixth Amendment, Discovery, Mental Responsibility, and Nonjudicial Punishment," at 72.
> Henley, "Postcards from the Edge: Privileges, Profiles, Polygraphs, and Other Developments in the Military Rules of Evidence," at 92.
> Allen, "New Developments in Sentencing," at 116.
> Morris, "'Just One More Thing...' and Other Thoughts on Recent Developments in Post-Trial Processing," at 129.

CHAPTER 6

PREFERRAL AND FORWARDING OF CHARGES; COMMAND INFLUENCE

PART I.
PREFERRAL AND FORWARDING OF CHARGES

§ 6-1. Preferring Sworn Charges.
   § 6-1(B). General Rules of Pleading.
      § 6-1(B)(2). Amendments to Pleadings.
      § 6-1(B)(3). Additional Charges.
   § 6-1(C). Defective Pleadings.
      § 6-1(C)(3). Multiplicity.
§ 6-2. Forwarding of Charges.
   § 6-2(B). Summary Court-Martial Convening Authority.
   § 6-2(C). Special Court-Martial Convening Authority.

PART II.
COMMAND INFLUENCE

§ 6-3. Command Influence; In General.
   § 6-3(C). Actual, Apparent, and Perceived Unlawful Command Influence.
§ 6-4. Pretrial Command Influence.
   § 6-4(A). The Preliminary Inquiry and Preferring Charges.
   § 6-4(C). Command Influence on Referral of Charges.
   § 6-4(E). Pretrial Comments and Actions.
§ 6-5. Command Influence on Courts-Martial.
   § 6-5(A). Command Influence on Court Members, Judges, and Counsel.
   § 6-5(B). Command Influence on Witnesses.
   § 6-5(C). Commander's "Presence" at Trial.
§ 6-7. Appellate Review of Command Influence.

PART I.

PREFERRAL AND FORWARDING OF CHARGES

§ 6-1. Preferring Sworn Charges.

Page 271, n. 10. McKinney v. Jarvis, 46 M.J. 870 (Army Ct.Crim.App. 1997) (in case of first impression court denied writ of prohibition where commander, who was normally both the summary and special court-martial convening authority, was disqualified from appointing Article 32 officer because he had become the accuser in the case).

§ 6-1(B). General Rules of Pleading.

Page 276, n. 60. United States v. Russell, 47 M.J. 412 (1997) (allegation that accused wrongfully possessed and received pornographic information was sufficient to allege that he acted knowingly).

§ 6-1(B)(2). Amendments to Pleadings.

Page 277, n. 81. United States v. Moreno, 46 M.J. 216 (1997) (changing allegation of overt act in conspiracy specification did not amount to major change resulting in unsworn charge).

Page 278, n. 82. United States v. Page, 43 M.J. 804 (A.F.Ct.Crim.App. 1995) (amendment which changed ending date of conduct unbecoming officer and other amendments which merely narrowed court's focus on separate offenses of fraternization and conduct unbecoming were minor changes; court cautioned government to tread softly when amending specifications without reswearing).

§ 6-1(B)(3). Additional Charges.

Page 278, n. 90. *Cf.* United States v. Hayward, 47 M.J. 381 (1997) (protection in RCM 601(e)(2) *re* post-arraignment referral of additional charge is important but is not a statutory or constitutional right; any error must be examined for prejudice, which in this case was missing).

§ 6-1(C). Defective Pleadings.

Page 280, n. 104, add following citation to *Province:* , *aff'd on other grounds,* 45 M.J. 359 (1996).

§ 6-1(C)(3). Multiplicity.

Page 288, n. 153. In *United States v. Neblock,* 45 M.J. 191 (1996), the court noted that its decision in *Teters* did not purport to address all multiplicity issues; instead, it addressed only the "method of discerning Congress' intent on multiple convictions under two different statutes at a single trial where those two statutes were violated by a single act."

Page 288, n. 161. *Neblock* was reversed at 45 M.J. 191 (1996) (the court noted that its decision in *Teters* did not purport to address all multiplicity issues; instead, it addressed only the "method of discerning Congress' intent on multiple convictions under two different statutes at a single trial where those two statutes were violated by a single act"); United States v. Carroll, 43 M.J. 487 (1996) (court applied elements test and concluded that solicitation and conspiracy were not multiplicious).

Page 289, n. 162. United States v. Oatney, 45 M.J. 185 (1996) (communicating threat offense was not lesser included offense of obstruction of justice offense).

Page 289, n. 165. United States v. Earle, 46 M.J. 823 (A.F.Ct.Crim.App. 1997) (if charges or specifications are multiplicious, the conviction cannot stand for both even if sentencing relief was given); United States v. Swango, 44 M.J. 686 (Army Ct.Crim.App. 1996) (prosecution may allege desertion in alternative theories; after findings, court should dismiss one of them; court consolidated two specifications).

Page 289. Add the following text after footnote 162:

The Court apparently modified the "elements" test slightly in *United States v. Weymouth*[162.1] and adopted a "elements/pleadings" approach to deciding if charges are multiplicious.[162.2] That test is intended to recognize the historical significance of pleadings in the military, the policy of trying all known charges at a single trial, and the incentive to multiply charges because of the military's sentencing scheme.[162.3]

[162.1] 43 M.J. 329 (1995).
[162.2] United States v. Britton, 47 M.J. 195 (1997) (Effron, J. concurring); United States v. Weymouth, 43 M.J. 329 (1995).
[162.3] United States v. Britton, 47 M.J. 195 (1997).

§ 6-2. Forwarding of Charges.

§ 6-2(B). Summary Court-Martial Convening Authority.

Page 291, n. 13. McKinney v. Jarvis, 46 M.J. 870 (Army Ct.Crim.App. 1997) (in case of first impression, court held that commander who preferred charges and was normally both the summary and special court-martial convening authority, was not disqualified from appointing Article 32 officer).

§ 6-2(C). Special Court-Martial Convening Authority.

Page 291. Add new footnote at end of first sentence in section, as follows:

are usually vested in the same individual."[15.1]

[15.1] McKinney v. Jarvis, 46 M.J. 870 (Army Ct.Crim.App. 1997) (officer, who was normally both the summary and special court-martial convening authority, was not disqualified from appointing Article 32 officer because he had become the accuser in the case).

PART II.

COMMAND INFLUENCE

§ 6-3. Command Influence; In General.

§ 6-3(C). Actual, Apparent, and Perceived Unlawful Command Influence.

Page 295, n. 23. *See e.g.*, United States v. Plumb, 47 M.J. 771 (A.F.Ct.Crim.App. 1997) (noting issue of apparent unlawful influence, court reversed accused's conviction where command encouraged defense witnesses to avoid the accused and his trial; court noted that it had never seen such a flagrant case of government misconduct and egregious acts of command influence).

§ 6-4. Pretrial Command Influence.

§ 6-4(A). The Preliminary Inquiry and Preferring Charges.

Page 297, n. 8. *Drayton* was affirmed at 45 M.J. 180 (1996) (accused waived unlawful command influence challenge to preferral of charges by not raising it at trial).

§ 6-4(C). Command Influence on Referral of Charges.

Page 298, n. 18. United States v. Gerlich, 45 M.J. 309 (1996) (government failed to overcome presumption that unlawful command influence had existed in referral of charges to court-martial; accused had previously received Article 15 but it was set aside and charges referred after SPCM received letter from GCM authority).

§ 6-4(E). Pretrial Comments and Actions.

Page 300, n. 28. United States v. Newbold, 45 M.J. 109 (1996) (evidence that commander made numerous negative references about accused and his offenses in front of unit at "all hands" formation; accused failed to show that such conduct had affected the proceedings).

§ 6-5. Command Influence on Courts-Martial.

§ 6-5(A). Command Influence on Court Members, Judges, and Counsel.

Page 300, n. 1. United States v. Fisher, 45 M.J. 159 (1996) (Article 37 violated and new action ordered where convening authority told defense counsel during recess that he was unethical because he had attempted to suppress results of urinalysis testing).

Page 301, n. 8. United States v. Witham, 44 M.J. 664 (N.M.Ct.Crim.App. 1996) (president of court-martial was not influenced by comments of Provost Marshal Officer that accused was guilty).

Page 303, n. 23. United States v. Fisher, 45 M.J. 159 (1996) (Article 37 violated and case returned for new post-trial action where convening authority told defense counsel during recess that he was unethical because he had attempted to suppress results of urinalysis testing); United States v. Crawford, 46 M.J. 771 (C.G.Ct.Crim.App. 1997) (commander's comments to defense counsel amounted to a violation of Article 37 and justified his removal as convening authority in accused's case).

§ 6-5(B). Command Influence on Witnesses.

Page 303, n. 24. *Drayton* was affirmed at 45 M.J. 180 (1996) (accused failed to establish that any witnesses were actually discouraged from testifying on his behalf).

Page 303, n. 28. United States v. Plumb, 47 M.J. 771 (A.F.Ct.Crim.App. 1997) (case reversed where command encouraged defense witnesses to avoid the accused and his trial; court noted that it had never seen such a flagrant case of government misconduct and egregious acts of command influence).

§ 6-5(C). Commander's "Presence" at Trial.

Page 307, n. 54. United States v. Schnitzer, 44 M.J. 380 (1996) (members' learning of pretrial agreement in government witness' case was not equivalent of informing them of command policies on sentencing).

§ 6-7. Appellate Review of Command Influence.

Page 309, n. 1. United States v. Fisher, 45 M.J. 159 (1996) (accused did not waive issue of unlawful command influence by convening authority where record did not indicate whether she was actually aware of his conduct). *Cf.* United States v. Brown, 45 M.J. 389 (1996) (court drew distinction between allegations of command influence at accusatorial and adjudicative stages; in the case of the former, the accused may waive the issue by failing to raise it at trial).

Page 309, n. 2. United States v. Brown, 45 M.J. 389 (1996) (court drew distinction between allegations of command influence at accusatorial and adjudicative stages; in the case of the former, the accused may waive the issue by failing to raise it at trial); United States v. Witham, 44 M.J. 664 (N.M.Ct.Crim.App. 1996) (accused affirmatively waived issue of command influence when he declined to challenge member who had heard provost marshal officer's comments implying that accused was guilty).

Page 309, n. 7. United States v. Denier, 47 M.J. 253 (1997) (trial judge did not err in concluding that court members had not been subjected to unlawful command influence; accused had argued that someone acting under mantle of command authority had attempted to draw connection between accused's trial and Tail Hook incident; opinion includes copies of documents used by trial judge to conduct inquiry of members); United States v. Plumb, 47 M.J. 771 (A.F.Ct.Crim.App. 1997) (case reversed where command encouraged defense witnesses to avoid the accused and his trial; court held that trial court had failed to take sufficient measures to purge command influence from case; it had merely relied on willingness of witnesses to testify; court noted that it had never seen such a flagrant case of government misconduct and egregious acts of command influence).

Page 310, n. 9. United States v. Bradley, 47 M.J. 715 (A.F.Ct.Crim.App. 1997) (appellate court ordered *DuBay* hearing to determine if unlawful command influence occurred in case); United States v. Denier, 43 M.J. 693 (A.F.Ct.Crim.App. 1995) (accused raised issue of command influence in motion for new trial after judge denied claim in post-trial Article 39(a) session).

Page 310, n. 11. United States v. Johnson, 46 M.J. 253 (1997) (under uncontested facts, accused officer presented inferences supporting claim that action in his case had been inappropriately influenced by higher command); United States v. Newbold, 45 M.J. 109 (1996) (evidence that commander made numerous negative references about accused and his offenses in front of unit at "all hands" formation; accused failed to show that such conduct had affected the proceedings).

Page 310, n. 12. *Maxwell* was affirmed on other grounds, 45 M.J. 406 (1996).

Page 310, n. 13. United States v. Schlarb, 46 M.J. 708 (N.M.Ct.Crim.App. 1997) (although accused showed that she was unpopular with command, she offered no evidence that unlawful command influence had occurred, not even that it was in the "air"); United States v. Denier, 43 M.J. 693 (A.F.Ct.Crim.App. 1995) (accused failed to show that affidavit from witness established that person in position of command had attempted to influence court members).

Page 310, n. 16. United States v. Plumb, 47 M.J. 771 (A.F.Ct.Crim.App. 1997) (case reversed where case was replete with unlawful command influence; court noted that it had never seen such a flagrant case of government misconduct and egregious acts of command influence). *Cf.* United States v. Gerlich, 45 M.J. 309 (1996) (court noted but did not decide what government's burden of proof should be; it noted that it has not delineated any distinction between the government's burden of overcoming the presumption of the existence of command influence and overcoming the existence of prejudice).

ANNOTATED BIBLIOGRAPHY

BOOKS

Schlueter, Jansen, Barry & Arnold, *Military Criminal Procedure Forms* (1997).

This book presents a variety of sample forms, letters, pleadings, checklists, briefs, and motions for military criminal justice practitioners. The text, which provides coverage for processing a case from pretrial investigation through appellate disposition, demonstrates how formats may vary among the services.

PERIODICALS

Barto, "Alexander the Great, the Gordian Knot, and the Problem of Multiplicity in the Military Justice System," 152 MIL. L. REV. 1 (1996).

The author observes that the military justice system has its own "Gordian Knot" which is formed by the intersection of double jeopardy, multiplicity and lesser included offenses — a knot which seems to confound all who confront it. The article presents an analysis of this multiplicity problem and includes recommended changes, including promulgation of a table of equivalent offenses.

Symposia

Symposium, "Military Justice Symposium—Volume I," ARMY LAW., April 1998.

This 128-page symposium is the first of two volumes and includes seven short articles on a range of military justice topics; it was authored by the faculty members of the Criminal Law Division at the Army's Judge Advocate School:

- Stitler, "The Power to Prosecute: New Developments in Courts-Martial Jurisdiction," at 1.
- Lovejoy, "Re-interpreting the Rules: Recent Developments in Speedy Trial and Pretrial Restraint," at 10.
- Einwechter, "New Developments in Substantive Criminal Law Under the Uniform Code of Military Justice (1997)," at 20.
- Coe, "'Something Old, Something New, Something Borrowed, Something Blue': Recent Developments in Pretrial and Trial Procedure," at 44.
- Pede, "New Developments in Search and Seizure and Urinalysis," at 80.
- Stitler, "Widening the Door: Recent Developments in Self-Incrimination Law," at 93.
- Moran, "Pyrrhic Victories and Permutations: New Developments in the Sixth Amendment, Discovery, and Mental Responsibility," at 106.

Symposium, "Military Justice Symposium—Volume II," ARMY LAW., May 1998.

This 68-page symposium consists of four articles articles on a range of military justice topics; it was authored by the faculty members of the Criminal Law Division at the Army's Judge Advocate School:

- Henley, "Developments in Evidence III—The Final Chapter," at 1.
- Lovejoy, "The CAAF at a Crossroads: New Developments in Post-Trial Processing," at 25.
- Allen, "Recent Developments in Sentencing Under the Uniform Code of Military Justice," at 39.
- Morris, "'This Better Be Good': The Courts Continue to Tighten the Burden in Unlawful Command Influence Cases," at 49.

Symposium, "Military Justice Symposium I," ARMY LAW., April 1997.

This 149-page symposium, which presents a series of short articles on a range of military justice topics, was authored by the faculty members of the Criminal Law Division at the Army's Judge Advocate School:

- Morris, Foreword.
- Frisk, "The Long Arm of Military Justice: Court-Martial Jurisdiction and the Limits of Power," at 5.
- Frisk, "Walking the Fine Line Between Promptness and Haste: Recent Developments in Speedy Trial and Pretrial Restraint Jurisprudence," at 14.
- Coe, "Restating Some Old Rules and Limiting Some Landmarks: Recent Developments in Pretrial and Trial Procedure," at 25.
- Barto, "Recent Developments in the Substantive Criminal Law Under the Uniform Code of Military Justice," at 50.
- Wright, "'An Old Fashioned Crazy Quilt': New Developments in the Sixth Amendment, Discovery, Mental Responsibility, and Nonjudicial Punishment," at 72.
- Henley, "Postcards from the Edge: Privileges, Profiles, Polygraphs, and Other Developments in the Military Rules of Evidence," at 92.
- Allen, "New Developments in Sentencing," at 116.
- Morris, "'Just One More Thing...' and Other Thoughts on Recent Developments in Post-Trial Processing," at 129.

CHAPTER 7

THE ARTICLE 32 INVESTIGATION AND THE PRETRIAL ADVICE

§ 7-2. The Article 32 Investigation.
　§ 7-2(A). The Parties to the Investigation.
　　§ 7-2(A)(1). The Investigating Officer.
　§ 7-2(B). The Accused's Rights.
　　§ 7-2(B)(4). Right to Confront Witnesses.
　　§ 7-2(B)(6). Right to Production of Witnesses.
　§ 7-2(C). Article 32 Investigation Procedures.
　§ 7-2(D). Investigating Officer's Report.
　§ 7-2(E). Defective Pretrial Advice.
§ 7-3. The Staff Judge Advocate's Pretrial Advice.

§ 7-2. The Article 32 Investigation.

§ 7-2(A). The Parties to the Investigation.

§ 7-2(A)(1). The Investigating Officer.

Page 319, n. 14. McKinney v. Jarvis, 46 M.J. 870 (Army Ct.Crim.App. 1997) (officer, who was normally both the summary and special court-martial convening authority, was not disqualified from appointing Article 32 officer because he had become the accuser in the case).

Page 319, n. 16. United States v. Willis, 43 M.J. 889 (A.F.Ct.Crim.App. 1996) (fact that IO was an SJA for a wing under the command of the convening authority was not disqualifying; court rejected argument that IO's rulings showed partiality), *aff'd on other grounds*, 46 M.J. 258 (1997).

Page 321, n. 29. United States v. Argo, 46 M.J. 454 (1997) (SJA's *ex parte* discussions with Article 32 investigating officer were improper but did not result in prejudice).

Page 321. Add the following text after sentence ending with footnote 29.

Likewise, the investigating officer should not abandon his or her quasi-judicial role by providing *ex parte* information to either the government counsel or defense counsel.[29.1]

[29.1] United States v. Holt, 46 M.J. 853 (N.M.Ct.Crim.App. 1997) (investigating officer's action of giving information only to trial counsel following completion of investigation gave appearance of officer being adjunct for prosecution; investigating officers must be scrupulously attentive to requirement that they play no role in post-investigation administration of case).

§ 7-2(B). The Accused's Rights.

§ 7-2(B)(4). Right to Confront Witnesses.

Page 323, n. 46. United States v. Burfitt, 43 M.J. 815 (A.F.Ct.Crim.App. 1996) (100-mile rule is not *per se* rule of unavailability; investigating officer must be given some latitude in determining availability of witnesses).

Page 324, n. 56. United States v. Burfitt, 43 M.J. 815 (A.F.Ct.Crim.App. 1996) (IO set up telephonic questioning of witnesses who were placed under oath and cross-examined by defense counsel).

§ 7-2(B)(6). Right to Production of Witnesses.

Page 326, n. 69. United States v. Simoy, 46 M.J.592 (A.F.Ct.Crim.App. 1996) (any error in not producing witnesses was harmless in view of fact that the defense did not attempt to depose those witnesses).

§ 7-2(C). Article 32 Investigation Procedures.

Page 326, n. 74. In *ABC, Inc. v. Powell*, 47 M.J. 363 (1997), the Court of Appeals held that absent reasons outweighing the value of openness, the accused is entitled to a public Article 32 investigation hearing. In that case, a news organization sought a writ of mandamus ordering the convening authority to open an Article 32 being conducted on the Sergeant Major of the Army. The government had argued that it was necessary to close the hearing in order to protect the privacy rights of the female victims. The court indicated that the decision to close a hearing must be made on a case by case, circumstance by circumstance, and witness by witness analysis.

Page 327. Add the following text after sentence ending with footnote 81:

The decision to open the Article 32 hearing to the public will normally rest within the discretion of the investigating officer.[81.1] In making that decision, the officer should consider the same factors the judge would consider in deciding whether to close the trial itself [81.2] along with the possibility that broad disclosure of the proceedings might infect or taint the potential pool of court members.[81.3]

If during the proceeding it appears that a witness may be incriminating himself or herself, the Investigating Officer is not required to give rights warnings.[81.4] For purposes of determining whether the Fifth Amendment applies, the Court of Appeals for the Armed Forces has indicated that the Article 32 investigation is the military equivalent of a grand jury.[81.5]

[81.1] San Antonio Express-News v. Morrow, 44 M.J. 706 (A.F.Ct.Crim.App. 1996). *Cf.* MacDonald v. Hodson, 42 C.M.R. 184 (C.M.A. 1970) (Article 32 hearing is not trial within meaning of Sixth Amendment and public hearing is not required).

[81.2] *See* § 15-3, *infra*.

[81.3] San Antonio Express-News v. Morrow, 44 M.J. 706 (A.F.Ct.Crim.App. 1996) (Article 32 IO considered impact of opening hearing on potential pool of members). *See also* § 5-10(B), *supra*.

[81.4] United States v. Bell, 44 M.J. 403 (1996) (Article 31 warnings do not apply at trial and Article 32 investigation is judicial in nature).

[81.5] *Id.*

§ 7-2(D). Investigating Officer's Report.

Page 328, n. 94. *See also* R.C.M. 405(e) (as amended by E.O. 13086, effective 27 May 1998); "Amendments to the Manual for Courts-Martial," ARMY LAW., July 1998, at 1.

§ 7-3. The Staff Judge Advocate's Pretrial Advice.

§ 7-3(B). Defective Pretrial Advice.

Page 333, n. 30. United States v. Plumb, 47 M.J. 771 (A.F.Ct.Crim.App. 1997) (military judge required new pretrial advice because it misstated a material fact; SJA later disqualified from signing post-trial recommendation).

ANNOTATED BIBLIOGRAPHY

BOOKS

Schlueter, Jansen, Barry & Arnold, *Military Criminal Procedure Forms* (1997).

This book presents a variety of sample forms, letters, pleadings, checklists, briefs, and motions for military criminal justice practitioners. The text, which provides coverage for processing a case from pretrial investigation through appellate disposition, demonstrates how formats may vary among the services.

PERIODICALS

Symposia

Symposium, "Military Justice Symposium—Volume I," ARMY LAW., April 1998.

This 128-page symposium is the first of two volumes and includes seven short articles on a range of military justice topics; it was authored by the faculty members of the Criminal Law Division at the Army's Judge Advocate School:

> Stitler, "The Power to Prosecute: New Developments in Courts-Martial Jurisdiction," at 1.
> Lovejoy, "Re-interpreting the Rules: Recent Developments in Speedy Trial and Pretrial Restraint," at 10.
> Einwechter, "New Developments in Substantive Criminal Law Under the Uniform Code of Military Justice (1997)," at 20.
> Coe, "'Something Old, Something New, Something Borrowed, Something Blue': Recent Developments in Pretrial and Trial Procedure," at 44.
> Pede, "New Developments in Search and Seizure and Urinalysis," at 80.
> Stitler, "Widening the Door: Recent Developments in Self-Incrimination Law," at 93.
> Moran, "Pyrrhic Victories and Permutations: New Developments in the Sixth Amendment, Discovery, and Mental Responsibility," at 106.

Symposium, "Military Justice Symposium—Volume II," ARMY LAW., May 1998.

This 68-page symposium consists of four articles articles on a range of military justice topics; it was authored by the faculty members of the Criminal Law Division at the Army's Judge Advocate School:

Henley, "Developments in Evidence III—The Final Chapter," at 1.

Lovejoy, "The CAAF at a Crossroads: New Developments in Post-Trial Processing," at 25.

Allen, "Recent Developments in Sentencing Under the Uniform Code of Military Justice," at 39.

Morris, "'This Better Be Good': The Courts Continue to Tighten the Burden in Unlawful Command Influence Cases," at 49.

Symposium, "Military Justice Symposium I," ARMY LAW., April 1997.

This 149-page symposium, which presents a series of short articles on a range of military justice topics, was authored by the faculty members of the Criminal Law Division at the Army's Judge Advocate School:

Morris, Foreword.

Frisk, "The Long Arm of Military Justice: Court-Martial Jurisdiction and the Limits of Power," at 5.

Frisk, "Walking the Fine Line Between Promptness and Haste: Recent Developments in Speedy Trial and Pretrial Restraint Jurisprudence," at 14.

Coe, "Restating Some Old Rules and Limiting Some Landmarks: Recent Developments in Pretrial and Trial Procedure," at 25.

Barto, "Recent Developments in the Substantive Criminal Law Under the Uniform Code of Military Justice," at 50.

Wright, "'An Old Fashioned Crazy Quilt': New Developments in the Sixth Amendment, Discovery, Mental Responsibility, and Nonjudicial Punishment," at 72.

Henley, "Postcards from the Edge: Privileges, Profiles, Polygraphs, and Other Developments in the Military Rules of Evidence," at 92.

Allen, "New Developments in Sentencing," at 116.

Morris, "'Just One More Thing...' and Other Thoughts on Recent Developments in Post-Trial Processing," at 129.

CHAPTER 8

CONVENING OF A COURT-MARTIAL, DETAILING PARTICIPANTS, AND THE REFERRAL PROCESS

§ 8-2. Convening the Court-Martial.
   § 8-2(A). The Convening Authority.
§ 8-3. Detailing the Participants.
   § 8-3(B). Trial and Defense Counsel.
      § 8-3(B)(1). Qualifications of Counsel.
   § 8-3(C). Members of the Court.
      § 8-3(C)(2). Requests for Enlisted Members.
      § 8-3(C)(3). Constitutional Challenges to Composition.
      § 8-3(C)(4). Selecting the Members.
   § 8-3(D). Changes in the Composition of the Court.
§ 8-5. Withdrawal of Charges.

§ 8-2. Convening the Court-Martial.

§ 8-2(A). The Convening Authority.

Page 338, n. 3. McKinney v. Jarvis, 46 M.J. 870 (Army Ct.Crim.App. 1997) (in case of first impression court held that commander, who was normally both the summary and special court-martial convening authority, was not disqualified from appointing Article 32 officer because he had become the accuser in the case).

§ 8-3. Detailing the Participants.

§ 8-3(B). Trial and Defense Counsel.

§ 8-3(B)(1). Qualifications of Counsel.

Page 345, n. 43. United States v. Harness, 44 M.J. 593 (N.M.Ct.Crim.App. 1996) (no *per se* violation of Sixth Amendment right to counsel where military counsel was not properly licensed to practice law; accused was also represented by qualified civilian counsel; combined efforts of counsel were more than adequate under *Strickland*).

§ 8-3(C). Members of the Court.

§ 8-3(C)(2). Requests for Enlisted Members.

Page 355, n. 131. United States v. Curtis, 44 M.J. 106 (1996) (exclusion of enlisted members from accused's unit was proper exercise of congressional discretion in designing military justice system), *rev'd on other grounds on reconsideration*, 46 M.J. 129 (1997) (per curiam).

§ 8-3(C)(3). Constitutional Challenges to Composition.

Page 356, n. 142. United States v. Curtis, 44 M.J. 106 (1996) (accused does not have right to be tried by civilian jury), *rev'd on other grounds on reconsideration*, 46 M.J. 129 (1997) (per curiam). *See also* Solorio v. United States, 483 U.S. 435 (1987) (Marshall, J., dissenting).

Page 356, n. 143. United States v. Curtis, 44 M.J. 106 (1996), *rev'd on other grounds on reconsideration*, 46 M.J. 129 (1997) (per curiam).

§ 8-3(C)(4). Selecting the Members.

Page 357, n. 153. United States v. Lewis, 46 M.J. 338 (1997) (accused failed to show that convening authority had stacked the court with females or that he had engaged in improper actions or motives; court noted that there is no prohibition from convening authority directing that no important segment of military community be excluded from panel).

Page 359, n. 160. United States v. Brewick, 47 M.J. 730 (N.M.Ct.Crim.App. 1997) (charge was referred to court-martial convened by predecessor-in-command; no requirement that convening authority explicitly adopt prior court); United States v. Vargas, 47 M.J. 552 (N.M.Ct.Crim.App. 1997) (court was properly convened where convening authority referred case to court selected by earlier convening authority in same billet).

§ 8-3(D). Changes in the Composition of the Court.

Page 360, n. 173. United States v. Miller, 44 M.J. 582 (A.F.Ct.Crim.App. 1996), *rev'd on other grounds*, 47 M.J. 352 (1997) (substitution of trial judge following remand from appellate court on first judge's rulings on motions to suppress was based on good cause; first judge had been assigned to appellate court).

Page 361. Add the following text after the sentence ending with footnote 174:

If the accused does not object to the substitution of judges and requests a bench trial before the new judge, he waives all possible objections to the change of judges.[174.1]

[174.1] United States v. Kosek, 46 M.J. 349 (1997) (court reiterated rule that an accused's failure to object to change of trial judge and request for bench trial in front of new judge "irrevocably" waives all objections to the change in judges); United States v. Hawkins, 24 M.J. 257 (1987).

§ 8-5. Withdrawal of Charges.

Page 363, n. 3. United States v. Underwood, 48 M.J. 805 (A.F.Ct.Crim.App. 1997) (convening authority's reason for withdrawing and re-referring charges was proper in face of judge's refusal to grant delay in start of trial).

ANNOTATED BIBLIOGRAPHY

BOOKS

Schlueter, Jansen, Barry & Arnold, *Military Criminal Procedure Forms* (1997).

This book presents a variety of sample forms, letters, pleadings, checklists, briefs, and motions for military criminal justice practitioners. The text, which provides coverage for processing a case from pretrial investigation through appellate disposition, demonstrates how formats may vary among the services.

PERIODICALS

Symposia

Symposium, "Military Justice Symposium—Volume I," ARMY LAW., April 1998.

This 128-page symposium is the first of two volumes and includes seven short articles on a range of military justice topics; it was authored by the faculty members of the Criminal Law Division at the Army's Judge Advocate School:

> Stitler, "The Power to Prosecute: New Developments in Courts-Martial Jurisdiction," at 1.
> Lovejoy, "Re-interpreting the Rules: Recent Developments in Speedy Trial and Pretrial Restraint," at 10.
> Einwechter, "New Developments in Substantive Criminal Law Under the Uniform Code of Military Justice (1997)," at 20.
> Coe, "'Something Old, Something New, Something Borrowed, Something Blue': Recent Developments in Pretrial and Trial Procedure," at 44.
> Pede, "New Developments in Search and Seizure and Urinalysis," at 80.
> Stitler, "Widening the Door: Recent Developments in Self-Incrimination Law," at 93.
> Moran, "Pyrrhic Victories and Permutations: New Developments in the Sixth Amendment, Discovery, and Mental Responsibility," at 106.

Symposium, "Military Justice Symposium—Volume II," ARMY LAW., May 1998.

This 68-page symposium consists of four articles articles on a range of military justice topics; it was authored by the faculty members of the Criminal Law Division at the Army's Judge Advocate School:

> Henley, "Developments in Evidence III—The Final Chapter," at 1.
> Lovejoy, "The CAAF at a Crossroads: New Developments in Post-Trial Processing," at 25.
> Allen, "Recent Developments in Sentencing Under the Uniform Code of Military Justice," at 39.
> Morris, "'This Better Be Good': The Courts Continue to Tighten the Burden in Unlawful Command Influence Cases," at 49.

Symposium, "Military Justice Symposium I," ARMY LAW., April 1997.

This 149-page symposium, which presents a series of short articles on a range of military justice topics, was authored by the faculty members of the Criminal Law Division at the Army's Judge Advocate School:

> Morris, Foreword.
> Frisk, "The Long Arm of Military Justice: Court-Martial Jurisdiction and the Limits of Power," at 5.
> Frisk, "Walking the Fine Line Between Promptness and Haste: Recent Developments in Speedy Trial and Pretrial Restraint Jurisprudence," at 14.

Coe, "Restating Some Old Rules and Limiting Some Landmarks: Recent Developments in Pretrial and Trial Procedure," at 25.

Barto, "Recent Developments in the Substantive Criminal Law Under the Uniform Code of Military Justice," at 50.

Wright, "'An Old Fashioned Crazy Quilt': New Developments in the Sixth Amendment, Discovery, Mental Responsibility, and Nonjudicial Punishment," at 72.

Henley, "Postcards from the Edge: Privileges, Profiles, Polygraphs, and Other Developments in the Military Rules of Evidence," at 92.

Allen, "New Developments in Sentencing," at 116.

Morris, "'Just One More Thing...' and Other Thoughts on Recent Developments in Post-Trial Processing," at 129.

CHAPTER 9

PLEA BARGAINING AND OTHER PRETRIAL NEGOTIATIONS

§ 9-2. Pretrial Agreements.
   § 9-2(A). Procedures.
      § 9-2(A)(3). Informal Agreements.
   § 9-2(B). Conditions and Terms.
      § 9-2(B)(1). Valid Conditions.
      § 9-2(B)(2). Invalid Terms.
   § 9-2(D). Judicial Review of the Agreement.
§ 9-3. Confessional Stipulations.

§ 9-2. Pretrial Agreements.

Page 369, n. 1. Although the discussion here focuses on *pretrial* agreements, the parties may enter *post-trial* agreements, which usually affect the sentence to be approved by the convening authority. *See* United States v. Pilkington, 48 M.J. 523 (N.M.Ct.Crim.App. 1998) (discussion of post-trial agreements).

§ 9-2(A). Procedures.

§ 9-2(A)(3). Informal Agreements.

Page 373, n. 29. United States v. Forester, 48 M.J. 1 (1998) (government erroneously attempted to include agreement provision in stipulation of fact); United States v. Mooney, 47 M.J. 496 (1998) (error to accept guilty plea where judge learned that parties had reached oral pretrial agreement; nonprejudicial); United States v. Bartley, 47 M.J. 182 (1997) (noting problems of *sub rosa* agreements; case remanded for determination whether unlawful command influence had played role in accused's decision to plead guilty and waive motion alleging such influence); United States v. Mitchell, 46 M.J. 840 (N.M.Ct.Crim.App. 1997) (purpose of pretrial agreements is to prevent informal understandings).

§ 9-2(B). Conditions and Terms.

Page 373, n. 35. United States v. Davis, 46 M.J. 551 (N.M.Ct.Crim.App. 1997) (in case of first impression, court held that accused could agree to plead not guilty, present no evidence, and sign a confessional stipulation in return for a sentence limitation); United States v. Rivera, 44 M.J. 527 (A.F.Ct.Crim.App. 1996) (court noted that field of permissible pretrial agreement provisions is growing as military justice system becomes less paternalistic; courts are beginning to confront novel and inventive clauses and must take steps to discuss them with counsel at trial), *aff'd*, 46 M.J. 52 (1997). *See also* Coe, "Restating Some Old Rules and Limiting Some Landmarks: Recent Developments in Pretrial and Trial Procedure," ARMY LAW., April 1997, at 25.

Page 374. Add the following text after full paragraph at top of page:

Although pretrial agreements usually involve a promise by the accused to plead guilty, there is nothing to prevent the parties from reaching an agreement involving a plea of not guilty or even a conditional plea of guilty. In a case of first impression, the court in *United States v. Davis*[38.1] held that accused could agree to plead not guilty, present no evidence, and sign a confessional stipulation in return for a sentence limitation.[38.2] The court observed that while it was concerned that the parties may have entered into this sort of agreement merely to avoid a *Care* providency inquiry,[38.3] it nonetheless affirmed the case because it was satisfied that the judge in fact had conducted an inquiry substantively similar to that required for a guilty plea.[38.4]

[38.1] 46 M.J. 551 (N.M.Ct.Crim.App. 1997).
[38.2] *Id.* at 554.
[38.3] *Id.* at 556. Apparently the accused was not attempting to preserve any issues for appeal and even in that case, he would have sought to enter a conditional plea of guilty.
[38.4] *Id.* at 556.

§ 9-2(B)(1). Valid Conditions.

Page 375, n. 40. United States v. Davis, 46 M.J. 551 (N.M.Ct.Crim.App. 1997) (in what the court called a case of first impression, it held that accused could agree to plead not guilty, present no evidence, and sign a confessional stipulation in return for a sentence limitation).

Page 375, n. 42. United States v. Rivera, 46 M.J. 52 (1997) (accused agreed to testify in any related trials without benefit of immunity).

Page 376, n. 46. United States v. Mitchell, 46 M.J. 840 (N.M.Ct.Crim.App. 1997) (court rejected argument that accused's promise to provide thirty thousand dollars in restitution was substantially unfair because he was unable to make the payment; court indicated that it would violate public policy to let the accused off the hook).

Page 378, n. 59. *See generally* Klein, "United States v. Weasler and the Bargained Waiver of Unlawful Command Influence Motions: Common Sense or Heresy," ARMY LAW., Feb. 1998, at 3.

§ 9-2(B)(2). Invalid Terms.

Page 379, n. 65. United States v. Forester, 48 M.J. 1 (1998) (requirement that accused waive any and all defenses was invalid; government may not avoid scrutiny of such provisions by including them in stipulation of fact; accused showed no prejudice). *Cf.* United States v. Rivera, 46 M.J. 52 (1997) (on its face, agreement to waive all motions was too broad and could violate prohibition against waivers of right to challenge, *inter alia*, jurisdiction and lack of speedy trial; under facts, however, there was no evidence of government coercion or overreaching).

§ 9-2(D). Judicial Review of the Agreement.

Page 381, n. 85. United States v. Mitchell, 46 M.J. 840 (N.M.Ct.Crim.App. 1997) (court reviewed pretrial agreement to determine if agreement to provide thirty thousand dollars in restitution was violative of public policy where accused was unable to pay).

Page 381, n. 86. United States v. Acevedo, 46 M.J. 830 (C.G.Ct.Crim.App. 1997) (court reviewed alleged ambiguities in pretrial agreements and indicated that it would attempt to determine mutual understandings of the parties).

§ 9-3. Confessional Stipulations.

Page 382, n. 4. United States v. Dixon, 45 M.J. 104 (1996) (stipulation was not confessional because accused actually contested one of the elements of the alleged offense; therefore, no *Bertelson* inquiry was required).

Page 382, n. 6. United States v. Craig, 48 M.J. 77 (1998) (judge's inquiry was sufficient concerning factual predicate but committed harmless error in advising defendant that acceptance of the confessional stipulation would result in waiving her constitutional right of the privilege against self-incrimination, the right to confrontation and cross-examination, and the right to present a defense).

ANNOTATED BIBLIOGRAPHY

BOOKS

Schlueter, Jansen, Barry & Arnold, *Military Criminal Procedure Forms* (1997).

This book presents a variety of sample forms, letters, pleadings, checklists, briefs, and motions for military criminal justice practitioners. The text, which provides coverage for processing a case from pretrial investigation through appellate disposition, demonstrates how formats may vary among the services.

PERIODICALS

Symposia

Symposium, "Military Justice Symposium—Volume I," ARMY LAW., April 1998.

This 128-page symposium is the first of two volumes and includes seven short articles on a range of military justice topics; it was authored by the faculty members of the Criminal Law Division at the Army's Judge Advocate School:

> Stitler, "The Power to Prosecute: New Developments in Courts-Martial Jurisdiction," at 1.
> Lovejoy, "Re-interpreting the Rules: Recent Developments in Speedy Trial and Pretrial Restraint," at 10.
> Einwechter, "New Developments in Substantive Criminal Law Under the Uniform Code of Military Justice (1997)," at 20.
> Coe, "'Something Old, Something New, Something Borrowed, Something Blue': Recent Developments in Pretrial and Trial Procedure," at 44.
> Pede, "New Developments in Search and Seizure and Urinalysis," at 80.
> Stitler, "Widening the Door: Recent Developments in Self-Incrimination Law," at 93.

Moran, "Pyrrhic Victories and Permutations: New Developments in the Sixth Amendment, Discovery, and Mental Responsibility," at 106.

Symposium, "Military Justice Symposium—Volume II," ARMY LAW., May 1998.

This 68-page symposium consists of four articles articles on a range of military justice topics; it was authored by the faculty members of the Criminal Law Division at the Army's Judge Advocate School:

Henley, "Developments in Evidence III—The Final Chapter," at 1.
Lovejoy, "The CAAF at a Crossroads: New Developments in Post-Trial Processing," at 25.
Allen, "Recent Developments in Sentencing Under the Uniform Code of Military Justice," at 39.
Morris, "'This Better Be Good': The Courts Continue to Tighten the Burden in Unlawful Command Influence Cases," at 49.

Symposium, "Military Justice Symposium I," ARMY LAW., April 1997.

This 149-page symposium, which presents a series of short articles on a range of military justice topics, was authored by the faculty members of the Criminal Law Division at the Army's Judge Advocate School:

Morris, Foreword.
Frisk, "The Long Arm of Military Justice: Court-Martial Jurisdiction and the Limits of Power," at 5.
Frisk, "Walking the Fine Line Between Promptness and Haste: Recent Developments in Speedy Trial and Pretrial Restraint Jurisprudence," at 14.
Coe, "Restating Some Old Rules and Limiting Some Landmarks: Recent Developments in Pretrial and Trial Procedure," at 25.
Barto, "Recent Developments in the Substantive Criminal Law Under the Uniform Code of Military Justice," at 50.
Wright, "'An Old Fashioned Crazy Quilt': New Developments in the Sixth Amendment, Discovery, Mental Responsibility, and Nonjudicial Punishment," at 72.
Henley, "Postcards from the Edge: Privileges, Profiles, Polygraphs, and Other Developments in the Military Rules of Evidence," at 92.
Allen, "New Developments in Sentencing," at 116.
Morris, "'Just One More Thing...' and Other Thoughts on Recent Developments in Post-Trial Processing," at 129.

CHAPTER 10

NOTICE, DISCLOSURE, AND DISCOVERY

§ 10-4. Defense Discovery.
  § 10-4(A). Automatic Prosecutorial Disclosure.
    § 10-4(A)(4). Favorable Evidence: The Constitutional Mandate.
  § 10-4(B). Defense Request for Discovery.
    § 10-4(B)(1). The *Brady* Request.
    § 10-4(B)(5). Jencks Act Materials.

§ 10-4. Defense Discovery.

§ 10-4(A). Automatic Prosecutorial Disclosure.

§ 10-4(A)(4). Favorable Evidence: The Constitutional Mandate.

Page 398, n. 23. United States v. Morris, 47 M.J. 695 (N.M.Ct.Crim.App. 1997) (denial of discovery of rape victim's medical, psychological, and counseling records was not prejudicial; material was marginally relevant to impeach victim and there was no reasonable probability that result of trial would have been different).

Page 399, n. 27. United States v. Morris, 47 M.J. 695 (N.M.Ct.Crim.App. 1997) (denial of discovery of rape victim's medical, psychological, and counseling records was not prejudicial; material was marginally relevant to impeach victim); United States v. Williams, 47 M.J. 621 (Army Ct.Crim.App. 1997) (prosecutor had no duty to discover evidence located in an unrelated investigative file); United States v. Sebring, 44 M.J. 805 (N.M.Ct.Crim.App. 1996) (trial counsel had obligation to search for favorable evidence in drug lab's files which showed some mistakes in handling drug samples). *See also* Kyles v. Whitley, 514 U.S. 419 (1995) (prosecutor has duty to learn of any favorable evidence known to others acting on government's behalf, including police).

§ 10-4(B). Defense Request for Discovery.

§ 10-4(B)(1). The *Brady* Request.

Page 399, n. 28. In Kyles v. Whitley, 514 U.S. 419 (1995), the Supreme Court indicated that evidence is material if there is a reasonable probability that, had the evidence been disclosed to the defense, the result of the proceeding would have been different. That does not mean that the accused would have been acquitted. The test is not one of sufficiency of the evidence but whether in the evidence's absence the accused received a fair trial, understood as a trial resulting in a verdict worthy of confidence. *Id.* at 1566; United States v. Romano, 46 M.J. 269 (1997) (accused was prejudiced by government failure to disclose *Brady* material, i.e., statements by witnesses supporting defense case); United States v. Sebring, 44 M.J. 805 (N.M.Ct.Crim.App. 1996) (failure to provide defense with quality control tests of drug lab did not permit fair trial).

See generally SCHLUETER, JANSEN, BARRY & ARNOLD, MILITARY CRIMINAL PROCEDURE FORMS § 7-3 (1997) (sample forms for defense requests for discovery).

§ 10-4(B)(5). Jencks Act Materials.

Page 403, n. 57. *Longstreath* was affirmed on other grounds at 45 M.J. 366 (1996).

ANNOTATED BIBLIOGRAPHY

BOOKS

Schlueter, Jansen, Barry & Arnold, *Military Criminal Procedure Forms* (1997).

This book presents a variety of sample forms, letters, pleadings, checklists, briefs, and motions for military criminal justice practitioners. The text, which provides coverage for processing a case from pretrial investigation through appellate disposition, demonstrates how formats may vary among the services.

PERIODICALS

Symposia

Symposium, "Military Justice Symposium—Volume I," ARMY LAW., April 1998:

This 128-page symposium is the first of two volumes and includes seven short articles on a range of military justice topics; it was authored by the faculty members of the Criminal Law Division at the Army's Judge Advocate School:

> Stitler, "The Power to Prosecute: New Developments in Courts-Martial Jurisdiction," at 1.
> Lovejoy, "Re-interpreting the Rules: Recent Developments in Speedy Trial and Pretrial Restraint," at 10.
> Einwechter, "New Developments in Substantive Criminal Law Under the Uniform Code of Military Justice (1997)," at 20.
> Coe, "'Something Old, Something New, Something Borrowed, Something Blue': Recent Developments in Pretrial and Trial Procedure," at 44.
> Pede, "New Developments in Search and Seizure and Urinalysis," at 80.
> Stitler, "Widening the Door: Recent Developments in Self-Incrimination Law," at 93.
> Moran, "Pyrrhic Victories and Permutations: New Developments in the Sixth Amendment, Discovery, and Mental Responsibility," at 106.

Symposium, "Military Justice Symposium—Volume II," ARMY LAW., May 1998:

This 68-page symposium consists of four articles articles on a range of military justice topics; it was authored by the faculty members of the Criminal Law Division at the Army's Judge Advocate School:

> Henley, "Developments in Evidence III—The Final Chapter," at 1.
> Lovejoy, "The CAAF at a Crossroads: New Developments in Post-Trial Processing," at 25.
> Allen, "Recent Developments in Sentencing Under the Uniform Code of Military Justice," at 39.
> Morris, "'This Better Be Good': The Courts Continue to Tighten the Burden in Unlawful Command Influence Cases," at 49.

Symposium, "Military Justice Symposium I," ARMY LAW., April 1997.

This 149-page symposium, which presents a series of short articles on a range of military justice topics, was authored by the faculty members of the Criminal Law Division at the Army's Judge Advocate School:

> Morris, Foreword.
>
> Frisk, "The Long Arm of Military Justice: Court-Martial Jurisdiction and the Limits of Power," at 5.
>
> Frisk, "Walking the Fine Line Between Promptness and Haste: Recent Developments in Speedy Trial and Pretrial Restraint Jurisprudence," at 14.
>
> Coe, "Restating Some Old Rules and Limiting Some Landmarks: Recent Developments in Pretrial and Trial Procedure," at 25.
>
> Barto, "Recent Developments in the Substantive Criminal Law Under the Uniform Code of Military Justice," at 50.
>
> Wright, "'An Old Fashioned Crazy Quilt': New Developments in the Sixth Amendment, Discovery, Mental Responsibility, and Nonjudicial Punishment," at 72.
>
> Henley, "Postcards from the Edge: Privileges, Profiles, Polygraphs, and Other Developments in the Military Rules of Evidence," at 92.
>
> Allen, "New Developments in Sentencing," at 116.
>
> Morris, "'Just One More Thing...' and Other Thoughts on Recent Developments in Post-Trial Processing," at 129.

CHAPTER 11

PRODUCTION OF WITNESSES AND EVIDENCE

§ 11-2. Production of Witnesses.
   § 11-2(A). General Rules.
      § 11-2(A)(1). Equal Access: The Right to Witnesses.
      § 11-2(A)(3). Employing Expert Assistants and Witnesses.
   § 11-2(B). Requests for Witnesses.
      § 11-2(B)(1). Defense Witnesses.
§ 11-3. Depositions.
   § 11-3(B). Procedures for Depositions.
      § 11-3(B)(1). In General.
§ 11-4. Production of Evidence.

§ 11-2. Production of Witnesses.

§ 11-2(A). General Rules.

§ 11-2(A)(1). Equal Access: The Right to Witnesses.

Page 415, n. 6. United States v. Miller, 47 M.J. 352 (1997) (judge abused discretion in denying accused's request for witness at *DuBay* hearing; testimony of witness was both relevant and necessary).

Page 417. Change heading to read:

§ 11-2(A)(3). Employing Expert Assistants and Witnesses.

Page 417. Add the following text after the sentence with footnote 21:

Technically, there are two rights here: First, the right to have expert *assistance* in the preparation of the case,[21.1] and second, the right to have an expert appear as a *witness* for the defense at trial.[21.2] The first right is based on case law,[21.3] and the second is grounded on R.C.M. 703(d).[21.4] Both are grounded on a showing of "necessity." In determining whether an accused is entitled to expert assistance in preparing his or her case, the court will apply a three-pronged test adopted in *United States v. Gonzales*:[21.5]

> There are three aspects to showing necessity. First, why the expert assistance is needed. Second, what would the expert assistance accomplish for the accused. Third, why is the defense counsel unable to gather and present the evidence that the expert assistant would be able to develop.[21.6]

The courts have reminded that "an indigent is not entitled to all the assistance that a wealthier counterpart might buy, but only to the basic and integral tools."[21.7] As noted, *infra*, the test for deciding whether an accused is entitled to employment of an expert witness at government expense is whether the expert's testimony is "relevant and necessary."[21.8] Although the two rights may at some

§ 11-2(B)   MILITARY CRIMINAL JUSTICE   § 11-2(B)(1)

point merge, the fact that an accused may be entitled to one of those rights will not necessarily mean that he or she is automatically entitled to the other.

[21.1] United States v. Ndanyi, 45 M.J. 315 (1996) (noting differences).

[21.2] *Id.*

[21.3] *Id.* (noting differences); United States v. Kelly, 39 M.J. 235 (C.M.A. 1994); United States v. Robinson, 39 M.J. 88 (C.M.A. 1994); United States v. Burnette, 29 M.J. 473 (C.M.A. 1990); United States v. Garries, 22 M.J. 288 (C.M.A. 1986); United States v. Mustafa, 22 M.J. 165 (C.M.A. 1986); United States v. Johnson, 47 C.M.R. 402 (C.M.A. 1973).

[21.4] R.C.M. 703(d).

[21.5] 39 M.J. 459 (C.M.A. 1994). United States v. Anderson, 47 M.J. 576 (N.M.Ct.Crim.App. 1997) (accused failed to show the necessity for having the assistance of an additional expert; one expert had already been assigned to case and accused requested one more when prosecutor obtained its expert).

[21.6] *Gonzales* at 461; United States v. Washington, 46 M.J. 477 (1997) (defense failed to justify need for expert assistance; court noted that defense is not entitled to expert assistance merely because the prosecution has employed expert assistance in preparing its case); United States v. Ndanyi, 45 M.J. 315 (1996) (applying test court held that defense failed to show third prong — government had offered to provide assistance of DNA experts at CID lab).

[21.7] United States v. Ndanyi, 45 M.J. 315, 319 (1996), *citing* Britt v. North Carolina, 404 U.S. 226, 227 (1971).

[21.8] R.C.M. 703(d)(B)(i); United States v. Ndanyi, 45 M.J. 315 (1996).

Page 418, n. 24. United States v. Ndanyi, 45 M.J. 315, 319 (1996) (judge did not abuse discretion in denying defense request for expert witness where request had not been properly filed with convening authority or the trial judge in a timely fashion).

Page 418. Add the following text after sentence ending with footnote 24:

In an unusual case, the court may hear the motion *ex parte*.[24.1]

[24.1] United States v. Garries, 22 M.J. 288, 291 (1986); United States v. Kaspers, 47 M.J. 176 (1997) (accused failed to show need for *ex parte* hearing; counsel had argued that stating the reasons for the expert on the record would disclose otherwise privileged information; not abuse of discretion to require counsel to make preliminary showing of need for expert on the record).

Page 419, n. 28, delete reference to *Ruth*, 42 M.J. 730.

§ 11-2(B). Requests for Witnesses.

§ 11-2(B)(1). Defense Witnesses.

Page 423, n. 59. United States v. Ruth, 46 M.J. 1 (1997) (court noted that it had not adopted a bright line rule for determining whether requested defense witness should be provided; trial judge properly deferred ruling on defense request for expert witness until after government expert had testified, but defense failed to renew request).

Page 423, n. 61. United States v. Miller, 44 M.J. 549 (A.F.Ct.Crim.App. 1996), *rev'd on other grounds*, 47 M.J. 352 (defense counsel had apparently not spoken to requested defense witness; court denied request on ground that witness would have been cumulative).

Page 424, n. 68. United States v. Breeding, 44 M.J. 345 (1996) (not abuse of discretion to deny accused's requests for character witnesses; facts indicated that witnesses had not known accused long enough to be reputation witnesses; court noted that even where defense offers to pay for witness, judge still serves as gatekeeper).

§ 11-3. Depositions.

§ 11-3(B). Procedures for Depositions.

§ 11-3(B)(1). In General.

Page 437, n. 35. United States v. Washington, 46 M.J. 477 (1997) (deposition officer's role is ministerial).

Page 438: Add the following text after the sentence ending with footnote 37:

Although neither the *Code* nor the *Manual* specifically require that the deposition officer be impartial, the court in *United States v. Washington*,[37.1] held that the language of Article 46(c) is broad enough to incorporate the impartiality requirements of the *Federal Rules of Criminal Procedure*.[37.2] Thus, in appointing a deposition officer, the command should insure that the officer has not had any prior role or personal interest in the case.[37.3]

[37.1] 46 M.J. 477 (1997).

[37.2] *See Fed.R.Civ. P.* 28(c) and *Fed.R.Crim.P.* 15(d).

[37.3] *See e.g.*, United States v. Washington, 46 M.J. 477 (1997) (deposition officer had originally served as SJA at the time of investigation and had been apprised of the progress of the investigation by the OSI; that disqualification, however, had ceased by the time he was appointed deposition officer).

§ 11-4. Production of Evidence.

Page 441, n. 4. United States v. Briggs, 48 M.J. 143 (1998) (general description of medical records was insufficient to compel production).

Page 443, n. 12. United States v. Curtin, 44 M.J. 439 (1996) (subpoena issued by trial counsel is judicial subpoena, not administrative subpoena, even though trial counsel acts as ministerial or administrative arm of the court-martial).

ANNOTATED BIBLIOGRAPHY

BOOKS

Schlueter, Jansen, Barry & Arnold, *Military Criminal Procedure Forms* (1997).

This book presents a variety of sample forms, letters, pleadings, checklists, briefs, and motions for military criminal justice practitioners. The text, which provides coverage for processing a case from pretrial investigation through appellate disposition, demonstrates how formats may vary among the services.

PERIODICALS

Symposia

Symposium, "Military Justice Symposium—Volume I," ARMY LAW., April 1998.

This 128-page symposium is the first of two volumes and includes seven short articles on a range of military justice topics; it was authored by the faculty members of the Criminal Law Division at the Army's Judge Advocate School:

> Stitler, "The Power to Prosecute: New Developments in Courts-Martial Jurisdiction," at 1.
> Lovejoy, "Re-interpreting the Rules: Recent Developments in Speedy Trial and Pretrial Restraint," at 10.
> Einwechter, "New Developments in Substantive Criminal Law Under the Uniform Code of Military Justice (1997)," at 20.
> Coe, "'Something Old, Something New, Something Borrowed, Something Blue': Recent Developments in Pretrial and Trial Procedure," at 44.
> Pede, "New Developments in Search and Seizure and Urinalysis," at 80.
> Stitler, "Widening the Door: Recent Developments in Self-Incrimination Law," at 93.
> Moran, "Pyrrhic Victories and Permutations: New Developments in the Sixth Amendment, Discovery, and Mental Responsibility," at 106.

Symposium, "Military Justice Symposium—Volume II," ARMY LAW., May 1998.

This 68-page symposium consists of four articles articles on a range of military justice topics; it was authored by the faculty members of the Criminal Law Division at the Army's Judge Advocate School:

> Henley, "Developments in Evidence III—The Final Chapter," at 1.
> Lovejoy, "The CAAF at a Crossroads: New Developments in Post-Trial Processing," at 25.
> Allen, "Recent Developments in Sentencing Under the Uniform Code of Military Justice," at 39.
> Morris, "'This Better Be Good': The Courts Continue to Tighten the Burden in Unlawful Command Influence Cases," at 49.

Symposium, "Military Justice Symposium I," ARMY LAW., April 1997.

This 149-page symposium, which presents a series of short articles on a range of military justice topics, was authored by the faculty members of the Criminal Law Division at the Army's Judge Advocate School:

Morris, Foreword.
Frisk, "The Long Arm of Military Justice: Court-Martial Jurisdiction and the Limits of Power," at 5.
Frisk, "Walking the Fine Line Between Promptness and Haste: Recent Developments in Speedy Trial and Pretrial Restraint Jurisprudence," at 14.
Coe, "Restating Some Old Rules and Limiting Some Landmarks: Recent Developments in Pretrial and Trial Procedure," at 25.
Barto, "Recent Developments in the Substantive Criminal Law Under the Uniform Code of Military Justice," at 50.
Wright, "'An Old Fashioned Crazy Quilt': New Developments in the Sixth Amendment, Discovery, Mental Responsibility, and Nonjudicial Punishment," at 72.
Henley, "Postcards from the Edge: Privileges, Profiles, Polygraphs, and Other Developments in the Military Rules of Evidence," at 92.
Allen, "New Developments in Sentencing," at 116.
Morris, "'Just One More Thing...' and Other Thoughts on Recent Developments in Post-Trial Processing," at 129.

CHAPTER 12

THE ARTICLE 39(A) PRETRIAL SESSION

§ 12-1. Introduction.
§ 12-2. Preliminary Matters.
　§ 12-2(C). Accounting for Parties Present and Absent.
　§ 12-2(F). Announcing the Detail and Qualifications of the Defense Counsel and the Judge's Inquiry Concerning the Accused's Rights to Counsel.
　　§ 12-2(F)(2). The *Donohew* Inquiry.
　§ 12-2(H). Challenges for Cause to the Military Judge.
§ 12-3. Military Judge's Inquiries Concerning the Accused's Decisions Regarding Composition of the Court.
　§ 12-3(A). Accused's Request for Trial by Judge Alone.
§ 12-4. Arraignment.
§ 12-5. Conferences.

§ 12-1. Introduction.

Page 448, n. 6. In United States v. Reynolds, 44 M.J. 726 (Army Ct.Crim.App. 1996), the court concluded that the trial judge erred in holding an Article 39(a) session via speaker phones with counsel and the accused on a different installation. Citing various provisions in the U.C.M.J. and the *Manual for Courts-Martial* concerning the presence of the participants and the accused, the court indicated that the clear intent of those sources is that the accused be personally present before the judge. The court also concluded, however, that the error was harmless because the accused had consented to the procedure.

§ 12-2. Preliminary Matters.

§ 12-2(C). Accounting for Parties Present and Absent.

Page 451, n. 11. United States v. Reynolds, 44 M.J. 726 (Army Ct.Crim.App. 1996) (trial judge erred in holding an Article 39(a) session via speaker phones with counsel and the accused on a different installation; citing various provisions in the U.C.M.J. and the *Manual for Courts-Martial* concerning the presence of the participants and the accused, the court indicated that the clear intent of those sources is that the accused be personally present before the judge).

§ 12-2(F). Announcing the Detail and Qualifications of the Defense Counsel and the Judge's Inquiry Concerning the Accused's Rights to Counsel.

§ 12-2(F)(2). The *Donohew* Inquiry.

Page 456, n. 58. United States v. Miller, 44 M.J. 549 (A.F.Ct.Crim.App. 1996), *rev'd on other grounds*, 47 M.J. 376 (1997) (court examined record as whole to determine whether accused had consented to changes of several military counsel before trial; during inquiry with accused, judge had failed to determine status of one of those counsel).

§ 12-2(H). Challenges for Cause to the Military Judge.

Page 463, n. 100 . United States v. Cornett, 47 M.J. 128 (1997) (judge did not err in refusing to recuse himself after the accused argued that the judge had demonstrated his attitude toward sentencing); United States v. Alis, 47 M.J. 817 (A.F.Ct.Crim.App. 1998) (numerous *ex parte* contacts between judge and prosecutor were not sufficient grounds for judge to recuse himself from case).

Page 464, n. 101. Liteky v. United States, 510 U.S. 540 (1994); United States v. Horne, 44 M.J. 216 (1996) (per curiam) (accused was not denied due process as result of disagreements with trial judge; judge did not abandon role of impartiality).

§ 12-3. Military Judge's Inquiries Concerning the Accused's Decisions Regarding Composition of the Court.

§ 12-3(A). Accused's Request for Trial by Judge Alone.

Page 467, n. 11. *Cf.* United States v. Tuner, 47 M.J. 348 (1997) (accused's failure to request bench trial, either in writing or orally on the record, was nonprejudicial error; court noted that judge had obtained oral statement requesting trial by judge alone from defense counsel on the record); United States v. Mayfield, 45 M.J. 176 (1996) (under facts, accused's failure to orally request trial by judge alone before assembly of court was nonjurisdictional, technical, error; accused had prepared paperwork for bench trial, raised no objection during trial, and confirmed desires in post-trial session).

§ 12-4. Arraignment.

Page 472, n. 10. United States v. Price, 48 M.J. 181 (1998) (reversible error to try accused in absentia where arraignment was defective because accused had not been called upon to enter his pleas).

Page 473, n. 12. United States v. Price, 48 M.J. 181 (1998) (reversible error to try accused in absentia where arraignment was defective because accused had not been called upon to enter his pleas).

Page 473, n. 16. United States v. Price, 48 M.J. 181 (1998) (reversible error to try accused in absentia where arraignment was defective because accused had not been called upon to enter his pleas)

§ 12-5. Conferences.

Page 475, n. 14. United States v. McQuinn, 47 M.J. 736 (N.M.Ct.Crim.App. 1997) (no requirement for verbatim record for pretrial conferences, conducted with parties consent, to discuss providency of plea).

ANNOTATED BIBLIOGRAPHY

BOOKS

Schlueter, Jansen, Barry & Arnold, *Military Criminal Procedure Forms* (1997).

This book presents a variety of sample forms, letters, pleadings, checklists, briefs, and motions for military criminal justice practitioners. The text, which provides coverage for processing a case from pretrial investigation through appellate disposition, demonstrates how formats may vary among the services.

PERIODICALS

Symposia

Symposium, "Military Justice Symposium—Volume I," ARMY LAW., April 1998.

This 128-page symposium is the first of two volumes and includes seven short articles on a range of military justice topics; it was authored by the faculty members of the Criminal Law Division at the Army's Judge Advocate School:

- Stitler, "The Power to Prosecute: New Developments in Courts-Martial Jurisdiction," at 1.
- Lovejoy, "Re-interpreting the Rules: Recent Developments in Speedy Trial and Pretrial Restraint," at 10.
- Einwechter, "New Developments in Substantive Criminal Law Under the Uniform Code of Military Justice (1997)," at 20.
- Coe, "'Something Old, Something New, Something Borrowed, Something Blue': Recent Developments in Pretrial and Trial Procedure," at 44.
- Pede, "New Developments in Search and Seizure and Urinalysis," at 80.
- Stitler, "Widening the Door: Recent Developments in Self-Incrimination Law," at 93.
- Moran, "Pyrrhic Victories and Permutations: New Developments in the Sixth Amendment, Discovery, and Mental Responsibility," at 106.

Symposium, "Military Justice Symposium—Volume II," ARMY LAW., May 1998.

This 68-page symposium consists of four articles articles on a range of military justice topics; it was authored by the faculty members of the Criminal Law Division at the Army's Judge Advocate School:

- Henley, "Developments in Evidence III—The Final Chapter," at 1.
- Lovejoy, "The CAAF at a Crossroads: New Developments in Post-Trial Processing," at 25.
- Allen, "Recent Developments in Sentencing Under the Uniform Code of Military Justice," at 39.
- Morris, "'This Better Be Good': The Courts Continue to Tighten the Burden in Unlawful Command Influence Cases," at 49.

Symposium, "Military Justice Symposium I," ARMY LAW., April 1997.

This 149-page symposium, which presents a series of short articles on a range of military justice topics, was authored by the faculty members of the Criminal Law Division at the Army's Judge Advocate School:

> Morris, Foreword.
> Frisk, "The Long Arm of Military Justice: Court-Martial Jurisdiction and the Limits of Power," at 5.
> Frisk, "Walking the Fine Line Between Promptness and Haste: Recent Developments in Speedy Trial and Pretrial Restraint Jurisprudence," at 14.
> Coe, "Restating Some Old Rules and Limiting Some Landmarks: Recent Developments in Pretrial and Trial Procedure," at 25.
> Barto, "Recent Developments in the Substantive Criminal Law Under the Uniform Code of Military Justice," at 50.
> Wright, "'An Old Fashioned Crazy Quilt': New Developments in the Sixth Amendment, Discovery, Mental Responsibility, and Nonjudicial Punishment," at 72.
> Henley, "Postcards from the Edge: Privileges, Profiles, Polygraphs, and Other Developments in the Military Rules of Evidence," at 92.
> Allen, "New Developments in Sentencing," at 116.
> Morris, "'Just One More Thing...' and Other Thoughts on Recent Developments in Post-Trial Processing," at 129.

CHAPTER 13

MOTIONS PRACTICE

§ 13-2. Procedural Aspects of Motions Practice.
    § 13-2(E). Rulings on Motions.
    § 13-2(G). Appeal of Rulings.
        § 13-2(G)(2). Government Appeals.
§ 13-3. Motions to Dismiss.
    § 13-3(B). Statute of Limitations.
    § 13-3(C). Speedy Trial.
        § 13-3(C)(2). U.C.M.J. Requirements: The *Burton* 90-Day Rule (1972-1993).
        § 13-3(C)(3). The *Manual*'s 120-Day Speedy Trial Rule.
        § 13-3(C)(4). Interstate Agreement on Detainers Act (IADA).
    § 13-3(D). Lack of Mental Responsibility.
    § 13-3(H). Grant of Immunity.
    § 13-3(J). Multiplicity.
    § 13-3(M). Selective or Vindictive Prosecutions; Prosecutorial Misconduct.
    § 13-3(N). Constitutional Challenges to the Underlying Statute, Regulation, or Order.
        § 13-3(N)(2). Vagueness: Lack of Fair Notice.
        § 13-3(N)(3). First Amendment: Speech, Religion, and Association.
        § 13-3(N)(4). Rights of Privacy.
§ 13-4. Motions to Suppress.
    § 13-4(A). Pretrial Statements of the Accused.
§ 13-5. Motions to Grant Appropriate Relief.
    § 13-5(A). Accused Incompetent to Stand Trial.
    § 13-5(C). Change of Location of Trial.
    § 13-5(E). Defective Pleadings: Motions to Cure or Amend.
    § 13-5(G). Motions to Sever.
        § 13-5(G)(1). Severance of Accused.
        § 13-5(G)(2). Severance of Charges.
    § 13-5(K). Continuance.
    § 13-5(L). Motions to Obtain Rulings on Evidentiary Matters; Motions *in Limine*.

§ 13-2. Procedural Aspects of Motions Practice.

Page 481, n. 7. United States v. Underwood, 48 M.J. 805 (A.F.Ct.Crim.App. 1997) (substance, not form, of motion governs; phrasing motion as motion to dismiss did not preclude judge or court from treating it as a motion for appropriate relief).

§ 13-2(E). Rulings on Motions.

Page 485, n. 53. United States v. Calloway, 47 M.J. 782 (N.M.Ct.Crim.App. 1998) (appellate court took issue with trial court's essential findings; such findings were conclusory and did not address relevant facts in speedy trial motion).

§ 13-2(G). Appeal of Rulings.

§ 13-2(G)(2). Government Appeals.

Page 490. Add following the partial paragraph at the top of the page:

The fact that the government may appeal certain rulings of a trial court does not preclude the appellate courts from reviewing those rulings during an appeal of a conviction.[93.1]

[93.1] United States v. Hall, 45 M.J. 546 (Army Ct.Crim.App. 1997) (court rejected defense argument that establishment of government right to appeal precludes court from reviewing trial court's rulings).

Page 491, n. 108. United States v. Dowty, 46 M.J. 845 (N.M.Ct.Crim.App. 1997), *aff'd on other grounds*, 48 M.J. 102 (1998) (court provided expedited consideration of government appeal of trial court's dismissal of charge).

§ 13-3. Motions to Dismiss.

§ 13-3(B). Statute of Limitations.

Page 493, n. 8. United States v. Gonzales, 46 M.J. 667 (N.M.Ct.Crim.App. 1997) (statute of limitations did not bar rape trial; offense of rape can be punished by death penalty; statute cannot be avoided by referring case as non-capital).

Page 493, n. 9. Add following citation to *Province*: , *aff'd on other grounds*, 45 M.J. 359 (1996).

Page 494, n. 11. United States v. Pou, 43 M.J. 778 (A.F.Ct.Crim.App. 1995) (accused's period of desertion tolled statute of limitations regarding offense he committed during period of desertion).

Page 494. Add the following text after sentence ending with footnote 17.

The statute of limitations may also be tolled by other statutory provisions.[17.1]

[17.1] United States v. Dowty, 48 M.J. 845 (1998) (delay caused by accused's invocation of right to challenge subpoena under Right to Financial Privacy Act tolled U.C.M.J. statute of limitations).

Page 494, n. 18. Add following citation to *Province*: , *aff'd on other grounds*, 45 M.J. 359 (1996).

§ 13-3(C). Speedy Trial.

Page 495, n. 23. United States v. Flarity, 48 M.J. 545 (N.M.Ct.Crim.App. 1998) (accused waived speedy trial claims).

Page 495, n. 30. *Bramer* was affirmed in part and set aside in part, on other grounds, 45 M.J. 296.

§ 13-3(C)(2). U.C.M.J. Requirements: The *Burton* 90-Day Rule (1972-1993).

Page 502, n. 87. United States v. Calloway, 47 M.J. 782 (N.M.Ct.Crim.App. 1998) (accused denied speedy trial in violation of Article 10; accused not brought to trial until 115 days after being placed in pretrial confinement; judge-granted delays insufficient to excuse government delays).

Page 502, n. 89. United States v. Hatfield, 44 M.J. 22 (1996) (court concluded that under facts, accused was denied speedy trial rights under Article 10).

Page 502, n. 90. United States v. Calloway, 47 M.J. 782 (N.M.Ct.Crim.App. 1998) (115-day delay was violation of Article 10; court noted that trial judge had focused on R.C.M. 707 instead of Article 10).

Page 502, n. 91. United States v. Calloway, 47 M.J. 782 (N.M.Ct.Crim.App. 1998) (115-day delay denied speedy trial in violation of Article 10; trial judge is not authorized to relieve government of burden of proving that it acted with reasonable diligence).

Page 503, n. 92. United States v. Hatfield, 44 M.J. 22 (1996) (court concluded that trial judge had properly granted motion to dismiss charges for lack of a speedy trial under Article 10; court noted that trial judge had given due consideration for factors indicated in *Kossman*).

Page 503, n. 96. United States v. Hatfield, 44 M.J. 22 (1996) (court concluded that under facts, accused was denied speedy trial rights under Article 10, noting that *Manual* rules are not the only rules governing speedy trials in the military).

§ 13-3(C)(3). The *Manual*'s 120-Day Speedy Trial Rule.

Page 505, n. 105. *Bramer* was affirmed in part and set aside in part, on other grounds, 45 M.J. 296.

Page 507, n. 118. United States v. Robinson, 47 M.J. 506 (N.M.Ct.Crim.App. 1997) (dismissal of charges on day 120 and reprefferral five days later was a subterfuge which was done only to stop speedy trial clock; the appellate court set aside the findings and sentence and dismissed the charge).

Page 508, n. 125. United States v. Ruffin, 48 M.J. 211 (1998) (speedy trial clock started with preferral of charges which occurred one day after accused was released from 67-day restriction and there was no reimposition of confinement; trial took place 195 days after preferral of charges but convening authority had approved 127 days' worth of delays).

Page 508, n. 133. United States v. Olinger, 45 M.J. 644 (N.M.Ct.Crim.App. 1996) (R.C.M. 707 does not apply to sentencing-only rehearings).

Page 508. Insert the following text after sentence ending with footnote 133:

As amended in 1998,[133.1] R.C.M. 707(b) now provides that any periods during which an incompetent accused has been in the custody of the Attorney General will be excluded when deciding whether the 120-day period has run.[133.2] And if at the end of the confinement, the accused is returned to the custody of the general court-martial convening authority, a new 120-day period begins on the date of that return.[133.3]

[133.1] *See generally,* "Amendments to the Manual for Courts-Martial," ARMY LAW., July 1998, at 1.
[133.2] R.C.M. 707(b)(3)(E).
[133.3] R.C.M. 707(b)(3)(E).

Page 510, n. 141, delete reference to *United States v. Dies.*

Page 510, n. 143. United States v. Thompson, 46 M.J. 472 (1997) (defense delays approved by Article 32 Investigating Officer were properly excluded where they were later ratified by Special Court-Martial Convening Authority; the court noted that Rule 707 does not specifically indicate that a convening authority must approve the delays before the fact; the court declined to decide whether an Article 32 IO has the inherent authority to grant delays); United States v. Anderson, 46 M.J. 540 (N.M.Ct.Crim.App. 1997) ("appointing authority," i.e., commander who appointed Article 32 investigating officer, approved defense delay).

Page 510. Add the following text after sentence ending with footnote 146:

In 1998, R.C.M. 707(c) was amended to permit exclusion of any time periods during which the accused was "hospitalized due to incompetence, or is otherwise in the custody of the Attorney General."[146.1] According to the Analysis accompanying this change, Congress mandated in Article 76b[146.2] that any incompetent accused be remanded to the custody of the Attorney General and thus is beyond the control of the military during that period. As written, however, the amendment would cover any other period of time during which the accused was in the custody of the Attorney General for reasons other than incompetence.

[146.1] *See* R.C.M. 707(c). *See generally,* "Amendments to the Manual for Courts-Martial," ARMY LAW., July 1998, at 1.
[146.2] Article 76b, U.C.M.J. at Appendix 3.

Page 510, n. 148. *Dies* was reversed at 45 M.J. 644 (1996) (prosecution not required to make written request to exclude time during which accused was absent without authority).

Page 511. In last sentence of first full paragraph, add new footnote as follows:

a *nonexhaustive*[154.1]

[154.1] United States v. Dies, 45 M.J. 376 (1996) (court created what amounted to a judicially created exclusion of time for unauthorized absence of the accused).

Page 513. Add following the last sentence on the page:

In *United States v. Dies*,[165.1] the Court of Appeals created what amounted to a judicially created exclusion of time for unauthorized absence of the accused. The court noted that R.C.M. 707(c) merely indicates that certain delays are excluded; it does not indicate that only those delays and stays approved by the courts and the convening authority are excluded.[165.2] The court further held that an accused is estopped from asserting a denial of speedy trial during the period of his or her absence, at a minimum; thus, the government is not required to request a delay from the convening authority.[165.3]

[165.1] 45 M.J. 376 (1996). *See also* Frisk, "Walking the Fine Line Between Promptness and Haste: Recent Developments in Speedy Trial and Pretrial Restraint Jurisprudence," ARMY LAW., April 1997, at 14.
[165.2] 45 M.J. at 378.
[165.3] *Id.* at 378.

§ 13-3(C)(4). Interstate Agreement on Detainers Act (IADA).

Page 514, n. 175. *Bramer* was affirmed in part and set aside in part, on other grounds, 45 M.J. 296.

Page 515, n. 176. *Bramer* was affirmed in part and set aside in part, on other grounds, 45 M.J. 296.

Page 515, n. 177. *Bramer* was affirmed in part and set aside in part, on other grounds, 45 M.J. 296.

Page 515, n. 180, delete reference to *United States v. Dies*, **42 M.J. 847.**

§ 13-3(D). Lack of Mental Responsibility.

Page 516, n. 188. United States v. DuBose, 47 M.J. 386 (1998) (accused must prove lack of mental responsibility by clear and convincing objective evidence that at the time of the offense he did not know what he was doing or that he did not know that what he was doing was wrong).

§ 13-3(H). Grant of Immunity.

Page 522, n. 242, replace the citation to *McGeeney* **with the following:** United States v. McGeeney, 44 M.J. 418 (1996) (prosecution had not used accused's immunized testimony directly, indirectly, or in nonevidentiary manner; trial counsel was sufficiently insulated — he had no conversations with predecessor about such statements and did not discuss facts with investigator; decision to prosecute was made before immunized testimony was given).

Page 522, n. 242. United States v. Youngman, 48 M.J. 123 (1998) (conviction reversed where government failed to show that prosecution of accused was based upon information independent of his prior immunized testimony in another case; decision includes review of applicable principles).

Page 522, n. 243. United States v. Christian, 43 M.J. 763 (N.M.Ct.Crim.App. 1995) (accused waived issue by not raising it at trial).

Page 522, n. 244. United States v. Christian, 43 M.J. 763 (N.M.Ct.Crim.App. 1995) (judge not required to intervene where nothing in record indicated that government was using immunized testimony).

§ 13-3(J). Multiplicity.

Page 524, n. 261. United States v. Earle, 46 M.J. 823 (A.F.Ct.Crim.App. 1997) (if charges or specifications are multiplicious, the conviction cannot stand for both even if sentencing relief was given).

Page 524, n. 263. *Cf.* United States v. Lloyd, 43 M.J. 886 (A.F.Ct.Crim.App. 1996) (citing *United States v. Morrison*, 41 M.J. 482 (1995), court noted that after 1995, concept of multiplicity for sentencing does not exist under current law), *aff'd on other grounds*, 46 M.J. 19 (1997).

Page 524. Replace the sentence with footnote 264 with the following:

An unconditional plea of guilty will waive a multiplicity issue,[264] unless the specifications and charges are facially duplicative.[264.1] If they are facially duplicative, the court may apply the plain error doctrine.[264.2]

[264.] United States v. Lloyd, 46 M.J. 19 (1997).

[264.1] *Id.* 46 M.J. 19 (1997), *citing* United States v. Boce, 488 U.S. 563 (1989); United States v. Harwood, 46 M.J. 26 (1997) (charges were facially duplicative; thus, court applied plain error doctrine); United States v. Earle, 46 M.J. 823 (A.F.Ct.Crim.App. 1997) (even though accused did not challenge multiplicity at trial, court granted relief because charges were facially duplicative).

[264.2] United States v. Harwood, 46 M.J. 26 (1997) (charges were facially duplicative; thus, court applied plain error doctrine); United States v. Roberson, 46 M.J. 826 (A.F.Ct.Crim.App. 1997) (because accused pleaded guilty court applied test for plain error and found none in multiple charging of possession and transportation of shotgun; decision addresses four pronged requirement for finding plain error).

Page 524, n. 265. United States v. Britton, 47 M.J. 195 (1997) (failure to raise issue in motion to dismiss constitutes waiver).

Page 524, n. 266. United States v. Britton, 47 M.J. 195 (1997).

§ 13-3(M). Selective or Vindictive Prosecutions; Prosecutorial Misconduct.

Page 527, n. 284. United States v. Argo, 46 M.J. 454 (1997) (no showing of vindictive prosecution where officer prosecuted for adultery and another officer was not); United States v. Gargaro, 45 M.J. 99 (1996) (accused — charged with various offenses relating to smuggling AK-47s into country — failed to show that he had been subjected to improper selective prosecution).

Page 527, n. 290. United States v. Argo, 46 M.J. 454 (1997) (discussion of what constitutes prosecutorial misconduct); United States v. Meek, 44 M.J. 1 (1996) (prosecutorial misconduct generally defined as prosecutorial action or inaction which violates some legal norm or standard, such as constitutional provision, statute, manual rule or professional ethical standard).

Page 527, n. 291. United States v. Argo, 46 M.J. 454 (1997) (case included allegations of both proescutorial misconduct and unlawful command influence).

Page 528, n. 292. United States v. Meek, 44 M.J. 1 (1996) (prosecutor attempted pretrial to intimidate defense witness; no *per se* reversal; court will evaluate record as whole to determine if prejudice occurred).

Page 528, n. 293. United States v. Argo, 46 M.J. 454 (1997) (SJA's *ex parte* discussions with Article 32 investigating officer was improper; but no prejudice resulted; discussion of subordinate officers' Article 32 testimony was not improper); United States v. Meek, 44 M.J. 1 (1996) (prosecutor attempted, *inter alia*, to intimidate defense witness and denounced defense counsel in accused's presence; court indicated that number of violations is not determinative of appropriate remedy for prosecutorial misconduct).

Page 528, n. 295. United States v. Meek, 44 M.J. 1 (1996) (court found no prejudice from prosecutor's pretrial attempt to intimidate defense witness; court indicated that if issue of prosecutorial misconduct is raised, court must consider trial record as a whole).

Page 528. Add the following text after sentence ending with footnote 298:

On appeal, the court will review the military judge's findings of fact under the "clearly erroneous" standard of review.[298.1] If the military judge has concluded that there has been prosecutorial misconduct and that prejudice has resulted, the court will treat those issues as matters of law and will conduct a *de novo* review.[298.2]

[298.1] United States v. Argo, 46 M.J. 454 (1997) (stating standard of review).
[298.2] United States v. Argo, 46 M.J. 454 (1997).

§ 13-3(N). Constitutional Challenges to the Underlying Statute, Regulation, or Order.

§ 13-3(N)(2). Vagueness: Lack of Fair Notice.

Page 533, n. 341. United States v. Swan, 48 M.J. 551 (N.M.Ct.Crim.App. 1998) (Secretary of the Navy Instruction prohibiting sexual harassment was not unconstitutionally vague).

Page 534, n. 344. United States v. Swan, 48 M.J. 551 (N.M.Ct.Crim.App. 1998) (Secretary of the Navy Instruction prohibiting sexual harassment did not violate accused's free speech rights).

Page 534, n. 353. United States v. Swan, 48 M.J. 551 (N.M.Ct.Crim.App. 1998) (noting different standards for measuring precision of military orders and regulations).

§ 13-3(N)(3). First Amendment: Speech, Religion, and Association.

Page 536, n. 367. United States v. Maxwell, 45 M.J. 406 (1996) (improper to instruct members to apply community standard of society at large; test should have been the "Air Force community standard").

Page 539, n. 383. United States v. Brown, 45 M.J. 389 (1996) (plurality opinion noted that servicemembers' First Amendment rights may be limited); United States v. Zimmerman, 43 M.J. 782 (Army Ct.Crim.App. 1996) (noting that First Amendment rights of servicemembers may be limited).

Page 540, n. 386. United States v. Zimmerman, 43 M.J. 782 (Army Ct.Crim.App. 1996) (as general proposition, defendant's abstract beliefs may not be taken into consideration by sentencing authority, no matter how obnoxious the beliefs may be).

Page 540, n. 388. United States v. Brown, 45 M.J. 389 (1996) (plurality opinion held that federal "anti-union" statute was not fatally overbroad).

Page 544, n. 410. United States v. Zimmerman, 43 M.J. 782 (Army Ct.Crim.App. 1996) (citing Army regulation which states that activities of extremist organizations are inconsistent with responsibilities of military service).

§ 13-3(N)(4). Rights of Privacy.

Page 544. Add new text and footnote to last sentence of last paragraph, following footnote 415:

to engage in intimate associations,[415.1]

[415.1] Roberts v. United States Jaycees, 468 U.S. 609 (1984) (discussion of freedom of association in certain intimate human associations); United States v. Padgett, 45 M.J. 520 (C.G. Ct.Crim.App. 1996) (order to accused to cease all contact with minor girlfriend was not the sort of intimate association contemplated by Supreme Court in *Roberts*; order was nonetheless invalid because it lacked nexus to valid military purpose).

Page 545, n. 418. United States v. Bygrave, 46 M.J. 491 (1997) (even assuming that accused had fundamental privacy right to engage in heterosexual intercourse, the government had a compelling interest in proscribing unprotected sexual intercourse between HIV-infected servicemember and uninfected, unmarried, noncivilian partners).

§ 13-4. Motions to Suppress.

§ 13-4(A). Pretrial Statements of the Accused.

Page 550, n. 18. United States v. Duvall, 47 M.J. 189 (1997) (error to exclude corroborating evidence for court members' consideration which they could have considered in assigning weight to accused's statement).

Page 550, n. 19. United States v. Duvall, 47 M.J. 189 (1997) (confession must be corroborated); United States v. Cottrill, 45 M.J. 485 (1997) (corroboration does not require independent evidence of all elements of offense or corpus delicti of offense; reliability of essential facts need not be proved beyond reasonable doubt or preponderance of the evidence); United States v. Schap, 44 M.J. 512 (Army Ct.Crim.App. 1996) (confession corroborated).

§ 13-5. Motions to Grant Appropriate Relief.

Page 551, n. 1. For sample motions for appropriate relief, *see* SCHLUETER, JANSEN, BARRY & ARNOLD, MILITARY CRIMINAL PROCEDURE FORMS § 8-4 et seq. (Michie 1997).

§ 13-5(A). Accused Incompetent to Stand Trial.

Page 552, n. 5, change the fourth question posed to the board to:

4. Is the accused presently suffering from a mental disease or defect rendering the accused unable to understand the nature of the proceedings against the accused or to conduct or cooperate intelligently in the defense of the case?

That provision was changed as a result of the 1998 amendments to R.C.M. 706(c)(2)(D). *See generally,* "Amendments to the Manual for Courts-Martial," ARMY LAW., July 1998, at 18.

Page 552, n. 5. *See generally* Wright, "'Though this be madness, yet there is a method in it:' A Practitioner's Guide to Mental Responsibility and Competency to Stand Trial," ARMY LAW., Sept. 1997, at 3.

Page 553, n. 15. United States v. English, 47 M.J. 215 (1997) (reversible error not to grant defense motion for R.C.M. 706 mental examination; prior examination of accused was not an adequate substitute); United States v. James, 47 M.J. 641 (Army Ct.Crim.App. 1997) (trial judge erred in denying defense request for a R.C.M. 706 sanity board; court set out criteria for determining if such a board should be convened).

§ 13-5(C). Change of Location of Trial.

Page 555, n. 31. United States v. Curtis, 44 M.J. 106 (1996) (showing of actual prejudice is usually required before motion is granted; here, murder case was not so permeated with pretrial publicity that defense was left with mere promises from members to disregard what they had heard), *rev'd on other grounds on reconsideration,* 46 M.J. 129 (1997) (per curiam).

§ 13-5(E). Defective Pleadings: Motions to Cure or Amend.

Page 557, n. 59. United States v. Page, 43 M.J. 804 (A.F.Ct.Crim.App. 1995) (amendment which changed ending date of conduct unbecoming officer and other amendments which merely narrowed court's focus on separate offenses of fraternization and conduct unbecoming were minor changes).

Page 557, n. 60. United States v. Page, 43 M.J. 804 (A.F.Ct.Crim.App. 1995) (although changes to specifications were minor, court cautioned government to tread softly when amending specifications without re-swearing).

§ 13-5(G). Motions to Sever.

§ 13-5(G)(1). Severance of Accused.

Page 561, n. 90. United States v. Mayhugh, 44 M.J. 363 (1996) (judge did not abuse discretion in denying motion to sever accuseds).

§ 13-5(G)(2). Severance of Charges.

Page 561, n. 93. United States v. Underwood, 48 M.J. 805 (A.F.Ct.Crim.App. 1997) (judge did not abuse discretion in denying defense motion to sever charges).

§ 13-5(K). Continuance.

Page 565, n. 133. United States v. Miller, 47 M.J. 352 (1997) (judge abused discretion in denying accused's request for continuance to have civilian defense counsel present at *DuBay* hearing; if judge denies continuance for purpose of obtaining civilian counsel, prejudice is likely).

§ 13-5(L). Motions to Obtain Rulings on Evidentiary Matters; Motions in Limine.

Page 566. Add following partial paragraph at top of page:

There is authority for the proposition that a pretrial motion *in limine* may not in itself preserve error.[143.1] Such motions may address hypothetical issues that may not actually arise at trial; thus, counsel should be prepared to renew his or her objection at trial. A motion *in limine* may, on the other hand, preserve an issue for appeal if it concerns a matter which can be definitively decided before trial. In *United States v. Dollente*,[143.2] the Court of Appeals cited a three-part test articulated by the Court of Appeals for the Tenth Circuit:

> First, we ask whether the matter was adequately presented to the district court... Second, we determine whether the issue is of the type that can be finally decided in a pretrial hearing. That is, some evidentiary issues are akin to questions of law, and the decision to admit such evidence is not dependent upon the character of the other evidence admitted at trial... [Finally,] the district court's ruling must be definitive.[143.3]

[143.1] United States v. Dollente, 45 M.J. 234 (1996); United States v. Johnson, 35 M.J. 17 (C.M.A. 1992).

[143.2] *Dollente*, 45 M.J. 234 (1996).

[143.3] *Id.* at 240, *citing* United States v. Mejia-Alarcon, 995 F.2d 982, 987-88 (10th Cir. 1993).

ANNOTATED BIBLIOGRAPHY

BOOKS

Schlueter, Jansen, Barry & Arnold, *Military Criminal Procedure Forms* (1997).

This book presents a variety of sample forms, letters, pleadings, checklists, briefs, and motions for military criminal justice practitioners. The text, which provides coverage for processing a case from pretrial investigation through appellate disposition, demonstrates how formats may vary among the services.

PERIODICALS

Barto, "Alexander the Great, the Gordian Knot, and the Problem of Multiplicity in the Military Justice System," 152 MIL. L. REV. 1 (1996).

The author observes that the military justice system has its own "Gordian Knot" which is formed by the intersection of double jeopardy, multiplicity and lesser included offenses — a knot which seems to confound all who confront it. The article presents an analysis of this multiplicity problem and includes recommended changes, including promulgation of a table of equivalent offenses.

Hoskins, "One Tin Soldier: A New Look at the Constitutionality of Placing United States Soldiers Under the Command of the United Nations," 22 U. DAYTON L. REV. 125 (1996).

Drawing from the court-martial of Specialist Michael New for refusing to wear the UN insignia on his uniform, the author discusses the constitutionality of placing United States servicemembers under foreign command and concludes that the President's authority to place United States troops under the temporary command of foreign commanders should be validated.

Symposia

Symposium, "Military Justice Symposium—Volume I," ARMY LAW., April 1998.

This 128-page symposium is the first of two volumes and includes seven short articles on a range of military justice topics; it was authored by the faculty members of the Criminal Law Division at the Army's Judge Advocate School:

Stitler, "The Power to Prosecute: New Developments in Courts-Martial Jurisdiction," at 1.
Lovejoy, "Re-interpreting the Rules: Recent Developments in Speedy Trial and Pretrial Restraint," at 10.
Einwechter, "New Developments in Substantive Criminal Law Under the Uniform Code of Military Justice (1997)," at 20.

Coe, "'Something Old, Something New, Something Borrowed, Something Blue': Recent Developments in Pretrial and Trial Procedure," at 44.

Pede, "New Developments in Search and Seizure and Urinalysis," at 80.

Stitler, "Widening the Door: Recent Developments in Self-Incrimination Law," at 93.

Moran, "Pyrrhic Victories and Permutations: New Developments in the Sixth Amendment, Discovery, and Mental Responsibility," at 106.

Symposium, "Military Justice Symposium—Volume II," ARMY LAW., May 1998.

This 68-page symposium consists of four articles articles on a range of military justice topics; it was authored by the faculty members of the Criminal Law Division at the Army's Judge Advocate School:

Henley, "Developments in Evidence III—The Final Chapter," at 1.

Lovejoy, "The CAAF at a Crossroads: New Developments in Post-Trial Processing," at 25.

Allen, "Recent Developments in Sentencing Under the Uniform Code of Military Justice," at 39.

Morris, "'This Better Be Good': The Courts Continue to Tighten the Burden in Unlawful Command Influence Cases," at 49.

Symposium, "Military Justice Symposium I," ARMY LAW., April 1997.

This 149-page symposium, which presents a series of short articles on a range of military justice topics, was authored by the faculty members of the Criminal Law Division at the Army's Judge Advocate School:

Morris, Foreword.

Frisk, "The Long Arm of Military Justice: Court-Martial Jurisdiction and the Limits of Power," at 5.

Frisk, "Walking the Fine Line Between Promptness and Haste: Recent Developments in Speedy Trial and Pretrial Restraint Jurisprudence," at 14.

Coe, "Restating Some Old Rules and Limiting Some Landmarks: Recent Developments in Pretrial and Trial Procedure," at 25.

Barto, "Recent Developments in the Substantive Criminal Law Under the Uniform Code of Military Justice," at 50.

Wright, "'An Old Fashioned Crazy Quilt': New Developments in the Sixth Amendment, Discovery, Mental Responsibility, and Nonjudicial Punishment," at 72.

Henley, "Postcards from the Edge: Privileges, Profiles, Polygraphs, and Other Developments in the Military Rules of Evidence," at 92.

Allen, "New Developments in Sentencing," at 116.

Morris, "'Just One More Thing...' and Other Thoughts on Recent Developments in Post-Trial Processing," at 129.

CHAPTER 14

PLEAS

§ 14-2. Not Guilty Pleas.
§ 14-3. Guilty Pleas.
    § 14-3(B). The *Care* Providency Inquiry.
        § 14-3(B)(2). Determining the Accuracy of the Plea.
        § 14-3(B)(3). Determining the Voluntariness of the Plea.
        § 14-3(B)(4). Admissibility of Accused's Statements.
    § 14-3(C). The *Green-King* Pretrial Agreement Inquiry.
    § 14-3(D). Improvident Guilty Pleas.
        § 14-3(D)(4). Factual and Legal Inconsistencies.
        § 14-3(D)(5). Procedural Consequences of an Improvident Plea.
    § 14-3(E). Entry of Findings.
§ 14-4. Conditional Pleas of Guilty.

§ 14-2. Not Guilty Pleas.

Page 575, n. 12. United States v. Fricke, 48 M.J. 547 (N.M.Ct.Crim.App. 1998) (accused changed not guilty plea to guilty plea near end of government's case-in-chief to avoid death penalty; court held that plea was not invalid simply because accused changed plea to avoid possibility of death penalty).

§ 14-3. Guilty Pleas.

§ 14-3(B). The *Care* Providency Inquiry.

§ 14-3(B)(2). Determining the Accuracy of the Plea.

Page 583, n. 70. United States v. Ray, 44 M.J. 835 (Army Ct.Crim.App. 1996) (failure to discuss meaning of term "grievous bodily harm" with accused did not improvidence plea).

Page 585, n. 79. United States v. Shearer, 44 M.J. 330 (1996); United States v. Higgins, 40 M.J. 67 (1994).

Page 585, n. 82. United States v. Keith, 48 M.J. 563 (C.G. Ct.Crim.App. 1998) (simply eliciting statements *re* identity of LSD was sufficient to support accused's plea of guilty to drug offense; court observed that it would have been better to inquire into accused's reason for believing that substance was in fact LSD).

Page 585. Add after sentence ending with footnote 82:

The inquiry must establish more than just the fact that the accused believes, or thinks, that he is guilty of the charged offense.[82.1] It must show that the objective facts revealed by the accused objectively support his plea of guilty.[82.2] Recitation by the accused of mere conclusions of law will not be a sufficient factual basis.[82.3] In short, under military practice, "the providence of a guilty plea depends on what the accused actually admits on the record."[82.4]

[82.1] United States v. Higgins, 40 M.J. 67, 68 (C.M.A. 1994). *See also* R.C.M. 910(c)-(e).

[82.2] United States v. Shearer, 44 M.J. 330 (1996) ("inquiry must establish factual circumstances admitted by the accused which 'objectively supports' his plea"); United States v. Higgins, 40 M.J. 67, 68 (C.M.A. 1994). *See also* R.C.M. 910(c)-(e).

[82.3] United States v. Outhier, 45 M.J. 326 (1996); United States v. Terry, 45 C.M.R. 216 (C.M.A. 1972).

[82.4] United States v. Adams, 33 M.J. 300 (C.M.A. 1991).

Page 585, n. 84. United States v. Anderson, 46 M.J. 728 (Army Ct.Crim.App. 1997) (court observed that contents of stipulation of expected testimony do not reflect facts properly before the court in support of a guilty plea).

Page 586, n. 100. United States v. Lark, 47 M.J. 435 (1998) (accused's responses did not raise affirmative defense); United States v. Biscoe, 47 M.J. 398 (1997) (judge made sufficient inquiry into whether accused had defense of sexual harassment for unauthorized absence); United States v. Smith, 44 M.J. 387 (1996) (accused's guilty plea responses reflected that he was aware of possible defenses and that they were precluded).

§ 14-3(B)(3). Determining the Voluntariness of the Plea.

Page 587, n. 101. United States v. Williams, 46 M.J. 820 (A.F.Ct.Crim.App. 1997) (judge need not advise accused of direct and indirect consequences of all possible amendments to U.C.M.J.; here the accused had unsuccessfully argued that the judge should have advised her of the impact of the amendments to Articles 57 and 58 *re* forfeiture of pay).

Page 589. Change section heading to:

§ 14-3(B)(4). Admissibility of Accused's Statements.

Page 589, n. 114. United States v. Figura, 44 M.J. 308 (1996) (statements admitted during sentencing).

Page 589, n. 116. United States v. Figura, 44 M.J. 308 (1996) (spectator called as sentencing witness to relate what accused had said during providency inquiry; judge also included in his instructions a summary of what the accused had said; court noted that there is no demonstrative right or wrong way to introduce such evidence and that judge had not made any backdoor summation of evidence; in a concurring opinion, Judge Sullivan suggested that judges use R.C.M. 20 to give the members a "good, exhaustive, accurate, and fair view of the facts").

Page 589, n. 118. United States v. Ramelb, 44 M.J. 625 (Army Ct.Crim.App. 1996) (court cited long-standing policy of not using accused's statements during providency inquiry against him for charges to which he pleaded not guilty).

§ 14-3(C). The *Green-King* Pretrial Agreement Inquiry.

Page 590, n. 123. United States v. Bartley, 47 M.J. 182 (1997) (noting problems of *sub rosa* agreements, court reiterated reasons for the *King-Green* inquiry—to prevent agreements that would violate public policy; case remanded for determination whether unlawful command influence had played role in accused's decision to plead guilty and waive motion alleging such influence).

Page 590, n. 125. United States v. Pilkington, 48 M.J. 523 (N.M.Ct.Crim.App. 1998) (noting that the *Williamson* elements had been incorporated into the NAVY-MARINE CORPS TRIAL JUDICIARY'S TRIAL GUIDE (1996) and that it rarely sees any violation of those requirements).

Page 591, n. 130. United States v. Acevedo, 46 M.J. 830 (C.G.Ct.Crim.App. 1997) (in reviewing alleged ambiguities in pretrial agreements, court noted that at trial the judge had obtained the concurrence of the defendant in interpreting the provisions).

§ 14-3(D). Improvident Guilty Pleas.
§ 14-3(D)(4). Factual and Legal Inconsistencies.

Page 595, n. 145. United States v. Greig, 44 M.J. 356 (1996) (no substantial basis for rejecting guilty plea); United States v. Eberle, 44 M.J. 374 (1996) (judge did not abuse discretion in accepting pleas to indecent acts).

Page 595, n. 146. United States v. Handy, 48 M.J. 590 (A.F.Ct.Crim.App. 1997) (establishes requirement that if issue of accused's sanity arises, judge must question defense counsel on whether an R.C.M. 706 board has examined the accused and also ask both the counsel if mental responsibility has been explored as a possible defense, etc).

Page 595. Add following footnote 146:

that an element of the charged offense is missing,[146.1] that the accused lacks the requisite *mens rea*,[146.2] that there is variance between the alleged offense and the offense pleaded to,[146.3]

[146.1] United States v. Sunden, 45 M.J. 508 (Army Ct.Crim.App. 1996) (plea improvident where accused had no legal duty to account for erroneously transferred property).

[146.2] *Id.* (plea improvident where it failed to establish requisite *mens rea*). United States v. Willis, 46 M.J. 258 (1997) (accused's plea to attempted murder was provident under either transferred-intent or concurrent-intent theory).

[146.3] United States v. Harris, 8 M.J. 52 (C.M.A. 1979); United States v. Pritchard, 45 M.J. 126 (1996) (plea not improvident where offense pleaded is closely related to offense charged; accused's plea to committing sodomy without condom was closely related to alleged offense of violating safe-sex order which referred to "sexual intercourse").

Page 595, n. 147. United States v. Lark, 47 M.J. 435 (1998) (accused's responses did not raise alleged affirmative defense of usury); United States v. Thomas, 45 M.J. 661 (Army Ct.Crim.App. 1997) (plea improvident where judge failed to inquire into possible defense of mistake of fact).

Page 596, n. 148. United States v. Hanson, 24 M.J. 377 (C.M.A. 1987) (military judge has *sua sponte* duty to make sure that an accused does not plead guilty to offense for which he or she is not guilty); United States v. Ellis, 47 M.J. 801 (N.M.Ct.Crim.App. 1998) (judge has *sua sponte* duty to clarify ambiguities).

Page 596, n. 152. United States v. Peterson, 47 M.J. 231 (1997) (accused's statements during sentencing did not improvidence guilty plea).

§ 14-3(D)(5). Procedural Consequences of an Improvident Plea.

Page 597, n. 157. United States v. Peele, 46 M.J. 866 (Army Ct.Crim.App. 1997) (accused's attempt to plead guilty and at same time mitigate his guilt resulted in improvident plea).

Page 599, n. 175, delete reference to *United States v. Outhier*, **42 M.J. 626.**

Page 599. Add the following text after sentence ending with footnote 176:

Or the court may simply approve any lesser included offense for which the accused's plea is provident.[176.1]

[176.1] United States v. Hoskins, 29 M.J. 402 (C.M.A. 1990); United States v. Bivens, 45 M.J. 501 (A.F.Ct.Crim.App. 1996) (court may affirm lesser offense if it is not persuaded that the guilty plea to the charged offense was provident).

§ 14-3(E). Entry of Findings.

Page 599, n. 177. United States v. Rhodes, 47 M.J. 790 (Army Ct.Crim.App. 1998) (judge is not permitted to enter alternative or conjunctive findings); United States v. Jones, 46 M.J. 815 (N.M.Ct.Crim.App. 1997) (failure to announce findings was technical, nonprejudicial, error; judge corrected problem by convening post-trial Article 39(a) session).

§ 14-4. Conditional Pleas of Guilty.

Page 604, n. 13. United States v. Tarleton, 47 M.J. 170 (1997) (accused failed to preserve challenge to results of urinalysis test by not specifying issue in conditional plea).

ANNOTATED BIBLIOGRAPHY

BOOKS

Schlueter, Jansen, Barry & Arnold, *Military Criminal Procedure Forms* (1997).

This book presents a variety of sample forms, letters, pleadings, checklists, briefs, and motions for military criminal justice practitioners. The text, which provides coverage for processing a case from pretrial investigation through appellate disposition, demonstrates how formats may vary among the services.

PERIODICALS

Symposia

Symposium, "Military Justice Symposium—Volume I," ARMY LAW., April 1998.

This 128-page symposium is the first of two volumes and includes seven short articles on a range of military justice topics; it was authored by the faculty members of the Criminal Law Division at the Army's Judge Advocate School:

> Stitler, "The Power to Prosecute: New Developments in Courts-Martial Jurisdiction," at 1.
> Lovejoy, "Re-interpreting the Rules: Recent Developments in Speedy Trial and Pretrial Restraint," at 10.
> Einwechter, "New Developments in Substantive Criminal Law Under the Uniform Code of Military Justice (1997)," at 20.
> Coe, "'Something Old, Something New, Something Borrowed, Something Blue': Recent Developments in Pretrial and Trial Procedure," at 44.
> Pede, "New Developments in Search and Seizure and Urinalysis," at 80.
> Stitler, "Widening the Door: Recent Developments in Self-Incrimination Law," at 93.
> Moran, "Pyrrhic Victories and Permutations: New Developments in the Sixth Amendment, Discovery, and Mental Responsibility," at 106.

Symposium, "Military Justice Symposium—Volume II," ARMY LAW., May 1998.

This 68-page symposium consists of four articles articles on a range of military justice topics; it was authored by the faculty members of the Criminal Law Division at the Army's Judge Advocate School:

> Henley, "Developments in Evidence III—The Final Chapter," at 1.
> Lovejoy, "The CAAF at a Crossroads: New Developments in Post-Trial Processing," at 25.
> Allen, "Recent Developments in Sentencing Under the Uniform Code of Military Justice," at 39.
> Morris, "'This Better Be Good': The Courts Continue to Tighten the Burden in Unlawful Command Influence Cases," at 49.

Symposium, "Military Justice Symposium I," ARMY LAW., April 1997.

This 149-page symposium, which presents a series of short articles on a range of military justice topics, was authored by the faculty members of the Criminal Law Division at the Army's Judge Advocate School:

> Morris, Foreword.
> Frisk, "The Long Arm of Military Justice: Court-Martial Jurisdiction and the Limits of Power," at 5.
> Frisk, "Walking the Fine Line Between Promptness and Haste: Recent Developments in Speedy Trial and Pretrial Restraint Jurisprudence," at 14.

Coe, "Restating Some Old Rules and Limiting Some Landmarks: Recent Developments in Pretrial and Trial Procedure," at 25.

Barto, "Recent Developments in the Substantive Criminal Law Under the Uniform Code of Military Justice," at 50.

Wright, "'An Old Fashioned Crazy Quilt': New Developments in the Sixth Amendment, Discovery, Mental Responsibility, and Nonjudicial Punishment," at 72.

Henley, "Postcards from the Edge: Privileges, Profiles, Polygraphs, and Other Developments in the Military Rules of Evidence," at 92.

Allen, "New Developments in Sentencing," at 116.

Morris, "'Just One More Thing...' and Other Thoughts on Recent Developments in Post-Trial Processing," at 129.

CHAPTER 15

TRIAL PROCEDURES

PART I.
INTRODUCTION

§ 15-2. The Participants.
    § 15-2(A). The Accused.
    § 15-2(B). The Defense Counsel.
        § 15-2(B)(2). Representation of Multiple Accused and Conflicts of Interest.
        § 15-2(B)(3). Ineffective Assistance of Counsel.
    § 15-2(D). The Military Judge.
    § 15-2(E). The Court Members.
§ 15-3. Courts-Martial and the Media: Public Trials.
§ 15-4. Motions at Trial.
    § 15-4(A). Continuances.
§ 15-5. Contempts.

PART II.
PROCEDURES FOR GENERAL AND SPECIAL COURTS-MARTIAL

§ 15-10. *Voir Dire* and Challenges of Court Members.
    § 15-10(A). *Voir Dire* of Court Members.
    § 15-10(B). Grounds for Challenging Court Members.
    § 15-10(C). Challenges of Court Members.
        § 15-10(C)(1). Challenge of the Selection Process.
        § 15-10(C)(2). Challenges for Cause.
        § 15-10(C)(3). Peremptory Challenges.
§ 15-12. Presentation of the Case-in-Chief.
    § 15-12(A). Examination of the Witnesses.
    § 15-12(B). Questions by the Court.
§ 15-13. Closing Arguments.
§ 15-14. Instructions to the Court Members.
    § 15-14(A). General.
    § 15-14(B). *Sua Sponte* Instructions.
    § 15-14(C). Instructions Upon Request.
    § 15-14(D). Review of Instructions Errors.
§ 15-15. Deliberations.
§ 15-16. Verdict; Announcement of Findings.
    § 15-16(A). General Findings.
    § 15-16(B). Impeaching the Findings.

PART III.
EVIDENTIARY RULES

§ 15-23. Objections and Preserving Error.

Part I.
Introduction

§ 15-2. The Participants.

§ 15-2(A). The Accused.

Page 611. Add at beginning of the subsection:

The accused has a constitutional and statutory right to be present at his or her court-martial[2.1] unless the accused becomes disruptive or is voluntarily absent.

[2.1] *See, e.g.,* United States v. Staten, 45 C.M.R. 267 (C.M.A. 1972); United States v. Peebles, 3 M.J. 177 (C.M.A. 1977); United States v. Rembert, 43 M.J. 837 (Army Ct.Crim.App. 1996) (reversible error to exclude accused, against his wishes, from courtroom during testimony of child victim).

§ 15-2(B). The Defense Counsel.

§ 15-2(B)(2). Representation of Multiple Accused and Conflicts of Interest.

Page 614, n. 26, replace the citation to *Smith*, 39 M.J. 587 with the following: United States v. Smith, 44 M.J. 459 (1996) (although there was an actual conflict of interest where counsel had earlier represented a government witness, the accused knowingly and intelligently waived right to conflict-free counsel; there was no evidence that conflict adversely affected counsel's representation).

§ 15-2(B)(3). Ineffective Assistance of Counsel.

Page 614, n. 28. United States v. Calhoun, 47 M.J. 520 (A.F.Ct.Crim.App. 1997) (counsel created a conflict of interest where he made his continued representation of the accused contingent upon government payment of his fees).

Page 615, n. 33. United States v. Simoy, 46 M.J. 592 (A.F.Ct.Crim.App. 1996) (counsel's effectiveness is not measured by quantity of evidence offered; instead, focus is on quality of representation); United States v. Clark, 45 M.J. 613 (Army Ct.Crim.App. 1996) (accused failed to present enough evidence to overcome presumption that counsel was effective).

Page 615, n. 36. United States v. Walters, 45 M.J. 165 (1996) (accused failed to show prejudice; court indicated that it had little patience for appellate calls for a penalty flag from an accused who was mugged by his own lack of candor with counsel).

Page 615. Add the following text after sentence ending with footnote 36:

In several recent cases, the Court of Appeals for the Armed Forces has indicated that the second prong of the *Strickland* test is whether the counsel's errors were so serious as to deprive the accused of a "fair trial, a trial whose result is reliable."[36.1] The Supreme Court in *Strickland* used both the "outcome" language[36.2] and the "lack of fair trial" language[36.3] in describing the second prong of the two-pronged test. But it clearly focused on the "outcome" test when it stated that:

> [The] appropriate test for prejudice finds its roots in the test for materiality of exculpatory information not disclosed to the defense by the prosecution and in the test for materiality of testimony made unavailable to the defense by Government deportation of a witness. The defendant must show that there is a reasonable probability that, but for counsel's unprofessional errors, the result of the proceeding would have been different. A reasonable probability is a probability sufficient to undermine confidence in the outcome.[36.4]

The Court of Appeals, however, has apparently relied on more recent language in *Lockhart v. Fretwell*,[36.5] which seems to indicate that the real focus may be on the question of whether the accused received a fair trial. In *Lockhart*, the Supreme Court indicated that:

> [F]ocusing solely on the mere outcome determination, without attention to whether the result of the proceeding was fundamentally unfair or unreliable, is defective. To set aside a conviction or sentence solely because the outcome would have been different but for counsel's error may grant the defendant a windfall to which the law does not entitle him.[36.6]

In a concurring opinion, Justice O'Connor indicated that the original test articulated in *Strickland* for determining prejudice, i.e., outcome analysis, was still intact.[36.7] In her view, the Supreme Court was merely identifying another factor which may not be used to inform the prejudice determination — the effect of an objection it knows to be wholly meritless under contemporary law.[36.8]

[36.1] *See, e.g.*, United States v. Gibson, 46 M.J. 77, 78 (1997); United States v. Christy, 46 M.J. 47 (1997) (court should not set aside conviction solely because the outcome would have been different but for counsel's error; that might provide a windfall to the accused; the test is whether the accused was deprived of a fair trial).

[36.2] Strickland v. Washington, 466 U.S. 668, 694 (1984).

[36.3] *Id.* at 687.

[36.4] *Id.* (citations omitted). The Supreme Court also referred to this prong as the "strict outcome-determinative test." *Id.* at 697.

[36.5] 506 U.S. 364 (1993).

[36.6] *Id.* at 369.

[36.7] *Id.* at 373-74.

[36.8] *Id.*

Page 616, n. 45. United States v. Harness, 44 M.J. 593 (N.M.Ct.Crim.App. 1996) (no *per se* violation of Sixth Amendment right to counsel where military counsel was not properly licensed to

§ 15-2(B)(3)   MILITARY CRIMINAL JUSTICE   § 15-2(B)(3)

practice law; accused was also represented by qualified civilian counsel; combined efforts of counsel were more than adequate under *Strickland*).

Page 617, n. 48. United States v. Harness, 44 M.J. 593 (N.M.Ct.Crim.App. 1996) (no *per se* violation of Sixth Amendment right to counsel where military counsel was not properly licensed to practice law; accused was also represented by qualified civilian counsel; combined efforts of counsel were more than adequate under *Strickland*).

Page 617. In first sentence of the second full paragraph, add new footnote as follows:

may cover virtually every area of court-martial practice."[48.1]

[48.1] In *United States v. Marshall*, 45 M.J. 268 (1996), the court assumed that a servicemember has a Sixth Amendment right to the effective assistance of counsel during Article 15 proceedings. Although it had earlier indicated in *United States v. Kendig*, 36 M.J. 291, 296 (C.M.A. 1993), that there is normally no Sixth Amendment right to counsel, the court was apparently persuaded (at least in this case) that the option of demanding a court-martial may remain open until the first day of trial and thus the accused's decision to forego nonjudicial punishment — upon the advice of counsel — fell within the purview of the Sixth Amendment. The court also noted that service regulations governing the right to consult with counsel were apparently intended to be meaningful in their own right. Under the facts, the accused was not denied the effective assistance of counsel where counsel advised him to demand trial — which resulted in punitive discharge.

Page 618, n. 58. United States v. Sorbera, 43 M.J. 818 (A.F.Ct.Crim.App. 1996) (in case of first impression in the military, the court held that defense counsel was constitutionally deficient when he gave advice to accused which amounted to obstruction of justice on other charges; accused could thus not be convicted of obstruction of justice).

See also United States v. Marshall, 45 M.J. 268 (1996) (court assumed that a servicemember has a Sixth Amendment right to the effective assistance of counsel in deciding whether to forego Article 15 proceedings and demand a trial; under the facts, the accused was not denied the effective assistance of counsel where counsel advised him to demand trial — which resulted in punitive discharge).

Page 618, n. 59. United States v. Lorenzen, 47 M.J. 8 (1997) (counsel not ineffective for not making bill of particulars).

Page 619, n. 63. United States v. McCastle, 43 M.J. 438 (1996) (counsel not ineffective by failing to move to suppress confession which followed command-directed urinalysis).

Page 619, n. 65. United States v. Curtis, 44 M.J. 106 (1996) (counsel not ineffective in conducting *voir dire*), *rev'd on other grounds on reconsideration*, 46 M.J. 129 (1997) (per curiam); United States v. Travels, 47 M.J. 596 (A.F.Ct.Crim.App. 1997) (counsel not ineffective in failing to challenge five members on grounds that they had been victims and two other members on grounds that they had medical expertise).

Page 619. Add to the text mid-sentence, after footnote 67:

, character witnesses,[67.1]

[67.1] United States v. Simoy, 46 M.J.592 (A.F.Ct.Crim.App. 1996) (counsel had tactical reasons for not presenting character evidence; he was concerned about possible rebuttal evidence).

Page 619, n. 68. United States v. Sojfer, 44 M.J. 603 (N.M.Ct.Crim.App. 1996), aff'd on other grounds, 47 M.J. 425 (1998) (counsel's decision not to call defense character witnesses was reasonable tactical decision).

Page 620, n. 71. United States v. Lorenzen, 47 M.J. 8 (1997) (counsel not ineffective for not presenting unsworn letter); United States v. Gillespie, 47 M.J. 750 (A.F.Ct.Crim.App. 1997) (counsel not ineffective by opening door to Rule 404(b) evidence after successfully obtaining *in limine* ruling).

Page 620, n. 72. United States v. Flack, 47 M.J. 415 (1997) (counsel not ineffective by not claiming psychotherapist-patient privilege; at time of trial that privilege was not recognized in military practice); United States v. Lorenzen, 47 M.J. 8 (1997) (counsel not ineffective for not challenging prosecution exhibits).

Page 620, n. 76. United States v. Lorenzen, 47 M.J. 8 (1997) (counsel not ineffective for not making opening statement).

Page 621, n. 77. In United States v. Curtis, 46 M.J. 129 (1997), the Court of Appeals in a short *per curiam* opinion granted reconsideration and reversed its earlier decision, as to sentence, that the defense counsel had not been inadequate in sentencing arguments. 44 M.J. 106. In the Court's view, there was a reasonable probability that the result of the case — imposition of the death penalty — would have been different if "all available mitigating evidence had been exploited by the defense." On further review, the Court ultimately concluded that the accused had been deprived of the effective assistance of counsel during sentencing. United States v. Curtis, 46 M.J. 129 (1997) (per curiam).

Page 621: Change text accompanying footnote 78 to read as follows:

(21) Advice and presentation of sentencing information,[78] ...

Page 621, n. 78. United States v. Davis, 47 M.J. 707 (N.M.Ct.Crim.App. 1997) (counsel not ineffective in not advising accused, a LCDR, that sentence might result in inability to retire from service); United States v. Simoy, 46 M.J.592 (A.F.Ct.Crim.App. 1996) (not ineffective assistance not to retain "mitigation specialist" in death penalty case).

Page 621, n. 79. United States v. Boone, 44 M.J. 742 (Army Ct.Crim.App. 1996) (counsel ineffective in not presenting character witnesses on behalf of accused).

Page 621. Add the following text mid-sentence, after footnote 82:

sentencing arguments,[82.1]

[82.1] United States v. Wean, 45 M.J. 461 (1997) (counsel was ineffective in commenting during sentencing argument that the accused was suffering from an illness of mind that compelled him to commit the offense; accused had contested guilt throughout trial; the court noted that counsel should normally not concede guilt during sentencing arguments because the defense may wish to move for reconsideration of the findings at any time before sentence is announced).

Page 622, n. 85. United States v. Sylvester, 47 M.J. 390 (1997) (counsel not ineffective in not filing written materials with convening authority); United States v. Hood, 47 M.J 95 (1997) (accused not prejudiced by counsel's actions, *inter alia*, in failing to consult with accused re submission of post-trial matters); United States v. Hicks, 47 M.J. 90 (1997) (accused was not prejudiced by counsel's deficiency in representing accused re post-trial matters); United States v. Ellis, 47 M.J. 20 (1997) (accused not denied effective post-trial representation by not submitting certain matters to convening authority).

Page 623, n. 88. United States v. Wiley, 47 M.J. 158 (1997) (counsel's failure to object to characterization of evidence was nonprejudicial error); United States v. Cornett, 47 M.J. 128 (1997) (counsel was ineffective in unilaterally withdrawing from the case; no prejudice, however).

Page 625, n. 99. United States v. Lindsey, 48 M.J. 93 (1998) (no error in not replacing defense counsel where accused, during unsworn statement at sentencing, stated that his counsel had been ineffective).

Page 625. Add the following text after sentence ending with footnote 99:

If the accused raises concerns about the effectiveness of his defense counsel during post-trial process of his conviction, steps should be taken to determine if in fact there are any possible conflicts which would interfere with counsel's continued representation.[99.1] That would include, for example, a determination by the defense counsel if the accused wishes to have him or her continue to represent the accused.[99.2] And if the Staff Judge Advocate is aware of any complaints of ineffectiveness, he or she should notify the defense counsel of the problem and providing counsel with an opportunity to determine whether another counsel should handle the post-trial duties.[99.3]

[99.1] United States v. Cornelious, 41 M.J. 397 (1995) (counsel has obligation to resolve issue); United States v. Carter, 40 M.J. 102 (C.M.A. 1994); United States v. Cavan, 48 M.J. 567 (A.F.Ct.Crim.App. 1997).

[99.2] United States v. Cavan, 48 M.J. 567 (A.F.Ct.Crim.App. 1997).

[99.3] United States v. Cornelious, 41 M.J. 397 (1995) (counsel has obligation to resolve issue); United States v. Carter, 40 M.J. 102 (C.M.A. 1994); United States v. Cavan, 48 M.J. 567 (A.F.Ct.Crim.App. 1997).

Page 625, n. 100, replace the citation to *Walters* with the following: United States v. Walters, 45 M.J. 165 (1996).

Page 625, n. 100. United States v. Ellis, 47 M.J. 20 (1997) (court must indulge strong presumption that counsel's actions were within range of reasonable professional assistance).

Page 625, n. 101. United States v. Moulton, 47 M.J. 227 (1997) (accused failed to establish first prong of *Strickland* two-pronged test); United States v. Ellis, 47 M.J. 20 (1997) (burden on accused to prove why he is entitled to relief). *Cf.* United States v. Wiley, 47 M.J 158 (1997) (counsel's failure to object to characterization of evidence in SJA review was nonprejudicial error; court noted that in an appropriate case it is permissible to avoid deciding whether the first prong of *Strickland*, showing some deficiency, if the accused cannot show prejudice).

The test is not whether the counsel lost or that a number of options were not pursued or could have been pursued differently. United States v. Kilber, 43 M.J. 725 (Army Ct.Crim.App. 1995).

Page 625, n. 102. United States v. Wiley, 47 M.J. 158 (1997) (counsel's failure to object to characterization of evidence in SJA review was nonprejudicial error; court noted that in an appropriate case it is permissible to avoid deciding whether the first prong of *Strickland*, showing some deficiency, if the accused cannot show prejudice); United States v. Hicks, 47 M.J. 90 (1997) (accused was not prejudiced by counsel's deficiency in representing accused re post-trial matters); United States v. Calhoun, 47 M.J. 520 (A.F.Ct.Crim.App. 1997) (court concluded that prejudice to accused was clear where counsel unilaterally withdrew from case).

Page 625, n. 103. In *United States v. Walters*, 45 M.J. 165 (1996), the court affirmed 42 M.J. 760 (Army Ct.Crim.App. 1995).

Page 625, n. 104. *Walters* was affirmed in *United States v. Walters*, 45 M.J. 165 (1996).

Page 625. Add the following text after last sentence in first full paragraph:

The court may also order a *DuBay* hearing[106.1] if the facts on the record are clear and the accused can show that such a hearing is likely to be effective in determining whether counsel was ineffective.[106.2] In *United States v. Ginn*,[106.3] the Court of Appeals held that a service Court of Criminal Appeals does not have the authority to make findings of fact regarding post-trial claims of ineffectiveness of counsel based partially on post-trial submissions.[106.4] Instead, it may use such submissions, e.g., affidavits, to decide if a *DuBay* hearing is required.[106.5]

[106.1] United States v. DuBay, 37 C.M.R. 411 (C.M.A. 1967).

[106.2] United States v. Curtis, 44 M.J. 106 (1996) (discussion of when *DuBay* hearing is appropriate to determine ineffectiveness), *rev'd on other grounds on reconsideration*, 46 M.J. 129 (1997) (per curiam).

[106.3] 47 M.J. 236 (1997).

[106.4] *Id.*

[106.5] *Id.*

Page 625, n. 107. United States v. Lorenzen, 47 M.J. 8 (1997) (attorney-client privilege waived as to matters reasonably related to claim of ineffective assistance of counsel).

§ 15-2(D). The Military Judge.

Page 628, n. 133. United States v. Goddard, 47 M.J. 581 (N.M.Ct.Crim.App. 1997) (judge's clarification of witness' testimony regarding customs of service did not constitute abandonment of impartial role); United States v. Acosta, 46 M.J. 670 (N.M.Ct.Crim.App. 1997) (judge crossed line in asking 89 questions which introduced evidence of the accused's predisposition to commit a drug offense and appeared to help the prosecution; error was nonprejudicial).

Page 628, n. 137. United States v. Acosta, 46 M.J. 670 (N.M.Ct.Crim.App. 1997) (judge's 89 questions appeared to help the prosecution).

Page 629, n. 139. United States v. Acosta, 46 M.J. 670 (N.M.Ct.Crim.App. 1997) (nonprejudicial error for judge to deny defense counsel's request for Article 39(a) session during extensive questioning of witness by judge).

§ 15-2(E). The Court Members.

Page 630, n. 152. United States v. Miller, 44 M.J. 549, *rev'd on other grounds*, 47 M.J. 352 (1997) (A.F.Ct.Crim.App. 1996) (contact between court member and third party during trial is presumptively prejudicial; here, president's conversation with SJA concerning security measures did not influence outcome of case).

§ 15-3. Courts-Martial and the Media: Public Trials.

Page 632, n. 8. San Antonio Express-News v. Morrow, 44 M.J. 706 (A.F.Ct.Crim.App. 1996) (court noted that normally Article 32 hearings should be open to the public). *Cf.* MacDonald v. Hodson, 42 C.M.R. 184 (C.M.A. 1970) (Article 32 hearing is not trial within meaning of Sixth Amendment and need not be open to public).

Page 633, n. 12. United States v. Anderson, 46 M.J. 728 (Army Ct.Crim.App. 1997) (judge erred in closing trial on grounds that testimony of witness would have been embarrassing to accused).

Page 633, n. 16. United States v. Rockwood, 48 M.J. 501 (Army Ct.Crim.App. 1998) (accused was not denied fair trial because of media attention on his case; court concluded that much of the publicity had been actively and intentionally generated by the defense; court indicated that it would not be sympathetic to charges of unfair publicity where the defense has made tactical decision to try its case in the media).

§ 15-4. Motions at Trial.

§ 15-4(A). Continuances.

Page 634, n. 5. United States v. Miller, 47 M.J. 352 (1997) (judge abused discretion in denying accused's request for continuance to have civilian defense counsel present at *DuBay* hearing; if judge denies continuance for purpose of obtaining civilian counsel, prejudice is likely; court noted that normally continuances granted for a reasonable opportunity to obtain counsel).

Page 634, n. 6. United States v. Weisbeck, 48 M.J. 570 (Army Ct.Crim.App. 1998) (not abuse of discretion to deny continuance to obtain testimony of defense expert witness; defense was partially responsible for problem).

§ 15-5. Contempts.

Page 639. Delete the first, second, and third full paragraphs and replace them with the following:

The applicable procedures vary slightly depending on whether the contempt was directly witnessed by the military judge in presence of the court-martial.[7] If the act was directly witnessed by the judge, the judge may summarily punish the actor.[8] If, on the other hand, the act is not directly witnessed by the military judge, then the actor is entitled to notice, assistance of counsel, and reasonable opportunity to present evidence, and may be punished only if the evidence shows beyond a reasonable doubt that the contempt occurred.[9]

As amended in 1998,[10] the *Manual for Courts-Martial* now indicates that in all cases, the military judge will determine whether the conduct constituted contempt and if so, what the punishment should be.[11] The timing of the judge's determination is left to his or her discretion.[12] If the judge has personally witnessed the contempt in the presence of the court-martial, he or she may summarily punish for contempt only if that fact is noted for the record along with the facts as to what occurred.[13] If the court is composed of members, then the judge must conduct the contempt proceedings out of their presence.[14]

---

[7] R.C.M. 809(b).

[8] R.C.M. 809(b)(1).

[9] R.C.M. 809(b)(2).

[10] *See generally*, "Amendments to the Manual for Courts-Martial," ARMY LAW., July 1998, at 1 (noting change to R.C.M. 809.)

[11] R.C.M. 809(c). The amendments to 809(c) were, in part, a response to *United States v. Burnett*, 27 M.J. 99 (C.M.A. 1988), where the court indicated that the *Manual* requirement that the members decide whether a contempt had occurred was an anachronism.

[12] *Id*.

[13] *Id*.

[14] *Id*.

PART II.

PROCEDURES FOR GENERAL AND SPECIAL COURTS-MARTIAL

§ 15-10. *Voir Dire* and Challenges of Court Members.

§ 15-10(A). *Voir Dire* of Court Members.

Page 643, n. 6. United States v. Jefferson, 44 M.J. 312 (1996) (discussion of history and purposes of *voir dire*).

Page 645, n. 19. United States v. Williams, 44 M.J. 482 (1996) (judge did not abuse discretion in denying defense request to conduct individual *voir dire*; judge did not preclude defense from asking questions collectively and issue as to one of members was mooted when court granted challenge for cause); United States v. DeNoyer, 44 M.J. 619 (Army Ct.Crim.App. 1996) (judge's summary rejection of defense counsel's request to conduct individual *voir dire* of members regarding supervisory or rating relationships; court noted that it did not endorse trial judge's actions). *See generally* Coe, "Restating Some Old Rules and Limiting Some Landmarks: Recent Developments in Pretrial and Trial Procedure," ARMY LAW., April 1997, at 25.

Page 645, n. 20. United States v. Jefferson, 44 M.J. 312 (1996) (error to cut off *voir dire* of members who may have been victims; *DuBay* hearing ordered on issue; the court, however, indicated that the judge did not abuse his discretion in not permitting the defense counsel to "tag team" on *voir dire*); United States v. Bradley, 47 M.J. 715 (A.F.Ct.Crim.App. 1997) (court will not reverse judge's decision to limit *voir dire* unless there has been clear abuse of discretion which prejudices the accused).

Page 645, n. 21. United States v. Thomas, 44 M.J. 667 (N.M.Ct.Crim.App. 1996) (nonprejudicial error for prosecutor to refer to policy of zero tolerance during *voir dire*).

Page 645, n. 22. United States v. Jefferson, 44 M.J. 312 (1996) (discussion about judge's role in controlling *voir dire*; the right to *voir dire* is fundamental and judge can be both "efficient and business-like while being patient and deliberate" in permitting individual *voir dire* of members).

Page 645, n. 23. McDonough Power Equip. Inc. v. Greenwood, 464 U.S. 548 (1984); United States v. Miles, 47 M.J. 683 (N.M.Ct.Crim.App. 1997) (accused was not entitled to new trial on grounds that member failed to disclose that the NCIS was attempting to interview him about rape charges; court was convinced that had he been asked directly about the matter he would have answered it honestly; accused under facts was not denied fair trial).

Page 646, n. 25. United States v. Taylor, 44 M.J. 475 (1996) (no evidence that president of court failed to honestly answer material question; at time of *voir dire*, he apparently was not aware that he was under investigation for same type of offenses for which he was later convicted).

Page 646, n. 30. United States v. Napoleon, 46 M.J. 279 (1997) (noting that challenge may be based upon actual or implied bias); United States v. Lavender, 46 M.J. 485 (1997) (noting distinction between actual and implied bias in assessing ability of member to serve).

Page 646, n. 31, delete reference to *United States v. Taylor*, 41 M.J. 701.

§ 15-10(B). Grounds for Challenging Court Members.

Page 648. Add additional text and new footnote to first sentence in (14):

(14) Demonstrates other facts showing personal interest or bias — actual or implied.[48.1]

[48.1] There is some authority for the proposition that there is a distinction between "implied" and "actual" bias. The latter type of bias focuses on whether or not the member being challenged for cause is actually biased; the former type of bias rests on the assumption that if a challenged member is permitted to serve, "the system's appearance of fairness is necessarily implicated." United States v. Daulton, 45 M.J. 212 (1996) (implied bias present; member whose mother and sister had been sexual abuse victims should have been removed; it would require too much of both her and the system). *See also* United States v. Rome, 47 M.J. 467 (1998) (noting distinctions between actual

§ 15-10(B) 1998 CUMULATIVE SUPPLEMENT § 15-10(B)

and implied bias; member should have been excused where, in aggregate of factors, public would view implied bias on part of member; it would have been too much to ask of him and the system); United States v. Youngblood, 47 M.J. 338 (1997) (judge erred in not excusing members on grounds of implied bias; members had received briefing from commanding general and SJA regarding status of discipline in the command and heard general's views on career potential of commander who under-reacted to discipline problem); United States v. Napoleon, 46 M.J. 279 (1997) (discussion of difference between actual and implied bias; the test for actual bias is whether any bias is such that it will not yield to evidence presented and the judge's instructions; that is a essentially a question of credibility and demeanor; the test for implied bias is objective standard, viewed through eyes of the public); United States v. Dinatale, 44 M.J. 325 (1996) (president of court who had previously reviewed sanity board hearing on accused did not exhibit either actual or implied bias); United States v. Denier, 43 M.J. 693, 701 (A.F.Ct.Crim.App. 1995) (*citing* United States v. Dale, 42 M.J. 384 (1995)); United States v. Barrow, 42 M.J. 655 (A.F.Ct.Crim.App. 1995) (discussing two general forms of court-member bias), *aff'd on other grounds*, 45 M.J. 478 (1997).

Page 648, n. 51. United States v. Giles, 48 M.J. 60 (1998) (error not to strike court member who demonstrated actual bias through his inelastic attitude toward sentencing).

Page 649, n. 57. United States v. Napoleon, 46 M.J. 279 (1997) (not error to reject challenge to court member who knew prosecution witness and told court that he would "automatically" believe that witness).

Page 650, n. 62. United States v. Curtis, 44 M.J. 106 (1996) (members not disqualified by prior knowledge of facts in murder case; court discussed two types of prejudice which may be implicated in pretrial publicity cases: prejudice *per se* and actual prejudice), *rev'd on other grounds on reconsideration*, 46 M.J. 129 (1997) (per curiam).

Page 651, n. 66. United States v. Smith, 43 M.J. 390 (1996) (under facts, there was no reason to believe that member's discussion with trial counsel resulted in unfair proceedings; court cautioned all trial personnel to be circumspect in interpersonal dealings and that even casual conversations between counsel and members may give appearance of impropriety).

Page 651, n. 67. United States v. Minyard, 46 M.J. 229 (1997) (error not to remove court member who was wife of OSI investigator who had worked on case; court noted although she might have exhibited actual bias, this was an example of implied bias, i.e., in the public's view there would be substantial doubt about her impartiality; the court declined to hold that law enforcement personnel and their spouses are ineligible *per se*); United States v. Mosqueda, 43 M.J. 491 (1996) (trial court abused discretion in not removing member when it learned during trial that member had discussed issue of victim's credibility with Force Surgeon).

Page 651, n. 68. United States v. Lavender, 46 M.J. 485 (1997) (court did not err in denying defense challenge to entire panel on grounds of implied bias after several members had items stolen from them during the trial; the two victims were removed); United States v. Fulton, 44 M.J. 100 (1996) (member not disqualified by fact that he had been robbery victim 20 years earlier); United States v. Travels, 47 M.J. 596 (A.F.Ct.Crim.App. 1997) (victims are not *per se* unqualified to serve); United States v. Jones, 46 M.J. 815 (N.M.Ct.Crim.App. 1997) (not error to deny challenge to members who had spouses who had been rape victims).

Page 651, n. 69. United States v. Travels, 47 M.J. 596 (A.F.Ct.Crim.App. 1997) (no *per se* rule disqualifying members who have some expertise related to case).

Page 652, n. 71. United States v. Minyard, 46 M.J. 229 (1997) (error not to remove court member who was wife of OSI investigator who had worked on case; court declined to hold that law enforcement personnel and their spouses are ineligible *per se*); United States v. Fulton, 44 M.J. 100 (1996) (officer not disqualified although he had law enforcement duties which required only minimal involvement with local security police unit); United States v. Alis, 47 M.J. 817 (A.F.Ct.Crim.App. 1998) (member's prior status as policeman and experience in working sexual investigations were not sufficient grounds for challenge). *See also* Coe, "Restating Some Old Rules and Limiting Some Landmarks: Recent Developments in Pretrial and Trial Procedure," ARMY LAW., April 1997, at 25.

Page 652, n. 72. United States v. Daulton, 45 M.J. 212 (1996) (member who was medical doctor and had treated abused children was not disqualified even though she had distaste for such cases).

Page 652, n. 73. United States v. Ovando-Moran, 44 M.J. 753 (N.M.Ct.Crim.App. 1996) (member's initial indication that he would hold against the accused if he did not testify was not disqualified where he later agreed to follow judge's instructions).

Page 653. Add the following text after sentence ending with footnote 78:

In reviewing the trial judge's decision to grant or deny a challenge for cause on the grounds of bias, the appellate court will apply an abuse of discretion standard and will generally be deferential to the trial court if the grounds for challenge focused on the member's actual bias.[78.1] In that instance, the trial judge is considered to be in a good position to assess the member's answers and demeanor on *voir dire* by counsel and the court.[78.2] On the other hand, if the grounds for challenge focus on the member's implied bias, the court will be less deferential.[78.3] Implied bias is reviewed through the eyes of the public and focuses on the question of whether the public would view the service of the member as being fair.[78.4]

[78.1] United States v. Youngblood, 47 M.J. 338 (1997) (regarding questions of actual bias, reviewing court gives trial judge great deference); United States v. Napoleon, 46 M.J. 279 (1997); United States v, Minyard, 46 M.J. 229 (1997); United States v. Daulton, 45 M.J. 212 (1996); United States v. Harris, 13 M.J. 288 (C.M.A. 1982).

[78.2] United States v. Lavender, 46 M.J. 485 (1997); United States v. Napoleon, 46 M.J. 279 (1997).

[78.3] United States v. Youngblood, 47 M.J. 338 (1997); United States v. Lavender, 46 M.J. 485 (1997); United States v. Napoleon, 46 M.J. 279 (1997).

[78.4] United States v. Dale, 42 M.J. 384 (1995); United States v. Lavender, 46 M.J. 485 (1997) (court did not err in denying defense challenge to entire panel on grounds of implied bias after several members had items stolen from them during the trial); United States v. Napoleon, 46 M.J. 279 (1997).

§ 15-10(C). Challenges of Court Members.

§ 15-10(C)(1). Challenge of the Selection Process.

Page 654, n. 85. United States v. Ruiz, 46 M.J. 503 (A.F.Ct.Crim.App. 1997) (government demonstrated by clear and convincing evidence that error did not occur in not selecting any members from accused's unit, the Medical Group).

Page 654, n. 88. *Cf.* United States v. Ruiz, 46 M.J. 503 (A.F.Ct.Crim.App. 1997) (defense bears initial burden of raising issue of institutional bias in selection of members to reach particular result; then, burden shifts to government to present clear and positive evidence that no improprieties took place).

§ 15-10(C)(2). Challenges for Cause.

Page 655, n. 91. Art. 41, U.C.M.J.

Page 655, n. 94. United States v. Mosqueda, 43 M.J. 491 (1996) (trial court abused discretion in not removing member who had discussed issue of victim's credibility with Force Surgeon).

Page 656, n. 97. United States v. Mosqueda, 43 M.J. 491 (1996) (trial court abused discretion in not removing member when it learned during trial that member had discussed issue of victim's credibility with Force Surgeon; trial court held hearing on issue).

Page 656, n. 99. United States v. Eby, 44 M.J. 425 (1996) (accused must exercise peremptory challenge against member unsuccessfully challenged for cause).

Page 656, n. 100. United States v. Eby, 44 M.J. 425 (1996) (to preserve error, the defense must peremptorily challenge the member who was unsuccessfully challenged for cause and must state on the record that he or she would have used the peremptory challenge on another member).

§ 15-10(C)(3). Peremptory Challenges.

Page 657, n. 108. Article 41(c), U.C.M.J.; United States v. Pritchett, 48 M.J. 609 (N.M.Ct.Crim.App. 1998) (reversible error to deny accused statutory right to exercise additional peremptory challenge when additional members were added to the court).

Page 659, n. 118. United States v. Williams, 44 M.J. 482 (1996) (prosecutor provided race-neutral reason — fact that challenged member and accused belonged to same fraternal organization — the Masons).

Page 659. Add the following text after the sentence ending with footnote 118:

In a case of first impression, the court in *United States v. Witham*[118.1] held that an accused could not exercise his sole peremptory challenge against a member on the basis of the member's gender.[118.2] The court cited *J.E.B. v. Alabama*[118.3] and Article 25 for the proposition that race and gender may not be used for peremptorily challenging members.[118.4] If counsel (either prosecution or defense) objects to the court-martial on the basis of gender and makes a *prima facie* showing of intentional gender discrimination,[118.5] the counsel exercising the peremptory challenge must provide a gender-neutral reason for the strike.[118.6]

The Supreme Court has concluded that counsel is not required to give a persuasive, or even plausible, reason for the peremptory strikes;[118.7] any race-neutral reason is permissible and there is no requirement that the reason stated makes any sense.[118.8] The Court of Appeals for the Armed Forces has, however, rejected that approach.[118.9] In military practice, counsel may not strike a court member for reasons that are "unreasonable, implausible, or that otherwise make no sense."[118.10]

Although it is the prosecutor who must state a race-neutral reason, the ultimate burden of persuading the court that purposeful discrimination has occurred rests on the defense.[118.11] That burden never shifts to the government.[118.12] The judge's decision whether a race neutral reason has been provided is reviewed under an abuse of discretion standard.[118.13] There is authority for the position that once counsel has cited a neutral reason for challenging the member, the court is not required to permit additional *voir dire* by opposing counsel.[118.14]

[118.1] 47 M.J. 297 (1997) (accused is considered a "state actor" for purposes of applying Fifth Amendment due process clause). *See also* United States v. Ruiz, 46 M.J. 503 (A.F.Ct.Crim.App. 1997).

[118.2] *Witham*, 47 M.J. at 303.

[118.3] 511 U.S. 127 (1994).

[118.4] *Witham*, 47 M.J. at 303.

[118.5] United States v. Ruiz, 46 M.J. 503 (A.F.Ct.Crim.App. 1997).

[118.6] *Id.*

[118.7] Purkett v. Elem, 514 U.S. 765 (1995).

[118.8] *Id.* at 769 (1995).

[118.9] United States v. Tulloch, 47 M.J. 283 (1997).

[118.10] *Id.* (prosecutor's stated reason that member seemed uncomfortable was not sufficiently race-neutral).

[118.11] Batson v. Kentucky, 476 U.S. 79, 97-98 (1986); United States v. Clemente, 46 M.J. 715 (A.F.Ct.Crim.App. 1997) (ultimate burden rests on defense).

[118.12] Purkett v. Elem, 514 U.S. 765 (1995); United States v. Greene, 36 M.J. 274 (C.M.A. 1993); United States v. Clemente, 46 M.J. 715 (A.F.Ct.Crim.App. 1997).

[118.13] Hernandez v. New York, 500 U.S. 352 (1991); United States v. Greene, 36 M.J. 274 (C.M.A. 1993); United States v. Clemente, 46 M.J. 715 (A.F.Ct.Crim.App. 1997).

[118.14] United States v. Bradley, 47 M.J. 715 (A.F.Ct.Crim.App. 1997) (judge not required to permit additional *voir dire*).

§ 15-12. Presentation of the Case-in-Chief.

§ 15-12(A). Examination of the Witnesses.

Page 661, n. 7, replace citation to *Welker* with: United States v. Welker, 44 M.J. 85 (1996) (trial counsel's cross-examination of complaining witness was within scope of direct examination).

Page 661, n. 8, replace citation to *Longstreath* with: United States v. Longstreath, 45 M.J. 366 (1996) (judge did not abuse discretion in deciding not to strike victim's direct examination where she answered some of defense counsel's cross-examination questions).

Page 662, n. 13. United States v. Spann, 48 M.J. 586 (N.M.Ct.Crim.App. 1998) (provision in 42 U.S.C. § 10606 regarding ability of victims to remain in courtroom takes priority over Mil. R. Evid. 615).

§ 15-12(B). Questions by the Court.

Page 663, n. 21, replace reference to *United States v. Hill*, 42 M.J. 725 with the following: United States v. Hill, 45 M.J. 245 (1996) (large number of questions from court members in themselves was not sufficient to reflect lack of impartiality; one member's question of defense witness about gang activity in an attempt to objectively explore credibility may have been improper under rules of evidence but did not demonstrate lack of impartiality).

§ 15-13. Closing Arguments.

Page 665, n. 5. United States v. Mance, 47 M.J. 742 (N.M.Ct.Crim.App. 1997) (trial counsel's arguments were proper comment on the evidence).

Page 665, n. 9. United States v. Cook, 48 M.J. 64 (1998) (trial counsel erred in commenting on fact that accused had yawned during trial; that information was not in evidence and was not relevant to the issue of guilt or innocence); United States v. Robles-Ramos, 47 M.J. 474 (1998) (argument based on fair inferences from evidence admitted at trial); United States v. Adams, 44 M.J. 251 (1996) (harmless error for prosecutor to mention evidence which was not presented at trial).

Page 666, n. 11. *Cf.* United States v. Cook, 48 M.J. 64 (1998) (trial counsel erred in commenting on fact that non-testifying accused had yawned during trial, in an attempt to inform members that accused did not take his murder case seriously; assuming that amounted to comment on his right not to testify, the issue was waived).

Page 667, n. 16. United States v. Lawrence, 47 M.J. 572 (N.M.Ct.Crim.App. 1997) (trial counsel's reference to accused's "Jamaican brothers" was unmistakably pejorative and amounted to racial stereotype; accused's failure to object did not waive plain error).

Page 668, n. 18. United States v. Thomas, 44 M.J. 667 (N.M.Ct.Crim.App. 1996) (non-prejudicial error for prosecutor to refer to policy of zero tolerance during closing arguments).

Page 668, n. 19. United States v. Mance, 47 M.J. 742 (N.M.Ct.Crim.App. 1997) (prosecutor's comments concerning gravity of theft of variable housing allowance was not impermissibly inflammatory).

Page 669, n. 32. United States v. Lawrence, 47 M.J. 572 (N.M.Ct.Crim.App. 1997) (trial counsel's reference to accused's "Jamaican brothers" was amounted to racial stereotype and constituted plain error).

§ 15-14. Instructions to the Court Members.

§ 15-14(A). General.

Page 669, n. 1. Wright & Cuculic, "Annual Review of Developments in Instructions—1997," ARMY LAW., July 1998, at 39.

§ 15-14(B). *Sua Sponte* Instructions.

Page 673, n. 26. United States v. Rockwood, 48 M.J. 501 (Army Ct.Crim.App. 1998) (trial judge did not err in refusing to give instruction on defense of justification; accused had violated orders by conducting independent inspection of Haitian penitentiary; court rejected argument that he was justified in those actions by the stated intent of the President or by international law principles).

Page 673, n. 28. United States v. Curtis, 44 M.J. 106 (1996) (evidence did not raise issue of self-defense in murder charge), *rev'd on other grounds on reconsideration*, 46 M.J. 129 (1997) (per curiam).

Page 673. Add text mid-sentence, following footnote 34:

involuntary intoxication,[34.1]

___

[34.1] United States v. Hensler, 44 M.J. 184 (1996) (involuntary intoxication is treated like legal insanity).

Page 674, n. 41. United States v. Fitzgerald, 44 M.J. 434 (1996) (accused waived any error in judge's instructions on voting procedures by not objecting).

Page 675, n. 45. United States v. Gillespie, 47 M.J. 750 (A.F.Ct.Crim.App. 1997) (accomplice instruction not sufficiently tailored to facts of case; no prejudice).

§ 15-14(C). Instructions Upon Request.

Page 676. Add the following text after sentence ending with footnote 52:

In an extensive discussion of the issue, the Court of Appeals in *United States v. Hardy*[52.1] concluded that the court members do "not have the right to nullify the lawful instructions of a military judge."[52.2] Thus, it was not error for the military judge to refuse to give an instruction on jury nullification.[52.3] Citing civilian authority and noting unique features of the role of court-members, the court stated:

> The fact that a jury has the power to acquit (as well as convict) by disregarding the instructions of the judge on matters of law does not mean that the panel must be told that it is permissible for them to ignore the law. That raw power is the result of the premium our legal tradition places on the prohibition against double jeopardy, the virtues of a general verdict in criminal cases, and the protections that are accorded to a jury's deliberative process. That raw power, however, does not equate to a legal right.

Congress and the President have made similar judgments with respect to the rules governing the military justice system. This does not mean that they want or expect court-martial panel members to disregard the law; only that they have determined that the values of a general verdict, the prohibition against double jeopardy, and the protection of the deliberative process outweigh the consequences of an occasional disregard of the law by a court-martial panel.[52.4]

[52.1] 46 M.J. 67 (1997).
[52.2] *Id.* at 75.
[52.3] *Id.*
[52.4] *Id.* at 74 (citation omitted).

§ 15-14(D). Review of Instructions Errors.

Page 676, n. 50. *Cf.* United States v. Poole, 47 M.J. 17 (1997) (denial of requested instruction is error is the requested instruction is correct, it is not substantially covered in the main charge, and it is on such a vital point that failure to give it deprived defense of defense or seriously impaired its effective presentation).

Page 676, n. 54. United States v. Fitzgerald, 44 M.J. 434 (1996) (accused waived any error in judge's instructions on voting procedures by not objecting).

§ 15-15. Deliberations.

Page 677, n. 2. United States v. Thompson, 47 M.J. 378 (1997) (nonprejudicial error for judge and court reporter to enter deliberation room to answer court members' questions about findings worksheet); United States v. Baker, 43 M.J. 734 (A.F.Ct.Crim.App. 1995) (judge did not err in failing to question court members about fact that they had ordered lunch during deliberations and determining whether anyone had entered or left deliberation room; there was no evidence that any of the exceptions in Mil. R. Evid. § 606(b) had been triggered.)

Page 677, n. 7. United States v. Ureta, 44 M.J. 290 (1996) (harmless error to permit court members to take Article 32 transcript of testimony into deliberations).

§ 15-16. Verdict; Announcement of Findings.

§ 15-16(A). General Findings.

Page 680, n. 6. United States v. Rhodes, 47 M.J. 790 (Army Ct.Crim.App. 1998) (judge or court members are not permitted to enter alternative or conjunctive findings).

Page 681. Add the following text after sentence ending with footnote 11:

For example, the findings may be defective where there is a variance between the offense alleged and the offense proved.[11.1]

[11.1] *See, e.g.,* United States v. Pritchard, 45 M.J. 126 (1996) (in guilty plea case, court noted potential problem of variance where accused had been given order to use safe sex in having sexual intercourse with his spouse, but was charged with violating order by not using condom while committing sodomy).

§ 15-16(B). Impeaching the Findings.

Page 682, n. 21. United States v. Ovando-Moran, 44 M.J. 753 (N.M.Ct.Crim.App. 1996) (accused failed to show that members improperly considered extraneous information; members submitted affidavits which indicated that they had considered their own life experiences in measuring evidence; court cautioned services against routinely using post-trial surveys to question court members about their deliberative process — that might invade the confidentiality of the deliberations).

Page 683, n. 27. United States v. Baker, 43 M.J. 734 (A.F.Ct.Crim.App. 1995) (judge did not err in failing to question court members about fact that they had ordered lunch during deliberations and determining whether anyone had entered or left deliberation room; inquiry into process not permitted where there was no evidence that any of the exceptions in Mil. R. Evid. 606(b) had been triggered).

PART III.
EVIDENTIARY RULES

§ 15-23. Objections and Preserving Error.

Page 690, n. 1. United States v. Jones, 43 M.J. 708 (A.F.Ct.Crim.App. 1995) (error not preserved where accused failed to obtain "ruling" from military judge).

ANNOTATED BIBLIOGRAPHY

BOOKS

Schlueter, Jansen, Barry & Arnold, *Military Criminal Procedure Forms* (1997).

This book presents a variety of sample forms, letters, pleadings, checklists, briefs, and motions for military criminal justice practitioners. The text, which provides coverage for processing a case from pretrial investigation through appellate disposition, demonstrates how formats may vary among the services.

PERIODICALS

Symposia

Symposium, "Military Justice Symposium—Volume I," ARMY LAW., April 1998.

This 128-page symposium is the first of two volumes and includes seven short articles on a range of military justice topics; it was authored by the faculty members of the Criminal Law Division at the Army's Judge Advocate School:

Stitler, "The Power to Prosecute: New Developments in Courts-Martial Jurisdiction," at 1.

> Lovejoy, "Re-interpreting the Rules: Recent Developments in Speedy Trial and Pretrial Restraint," at 10.
> Einwechter, "New Developments in Substantive Criminal Law Under the Uniform Code of Military Justice (1997)," at 20.
> Coe, "'Something Old, Something New, Something Borrowed, Something Blue': Recent Developments in Pretrial and Trial Procedure," at 44.
> Pede, "New Developments in Search and Seizure and Urinalysis," at 80.
> Stitler, "Widening the Door: Recent Developments in Self-Incrimination Law," at 93.
> Moran, "Pyrrhic Victories and Permutations: New Developments in the Sixth Amendment, Discovery, and Mental Responsibility," at 106.

Symposium, "Military Justice Symposium—Volume II," ARMY LAW., May 1998.

This 68-page symposium consists of four articles articles on a range of military justice topics; it was authored by the faculty members of the Criminal Law Division at the Army's Judge Advocate School:

> Henley, "Developments in Evidence III—The Final Chapter," at 1.
> Lovejoy, "The CAAF at a Crossroads: New Developments in Post-Trial Processing," at 25.
> Allen, "Recent Developments in Sentencing Under the Uniform Code of Military Justice," at 39.
> Morris, "'This Better Be Good': The Courts Continue to Tighten the Burden in Unlawful Command Influence Cases," at 49.

Symposium, "Military Justice Symposium I," ARMY LAW., April 1997.

This 149-page symposium, which presents a series of short articles on a range of military justice topics, was authored by the faculty members of the Criminal Law Division at the Army's Judge Advocate School:

> Morris, Foreword.
> Frisk, "The Long Arm of Military Justice: Court-Martial Jurisdiction and the Limits of Power," at 5.
> Frisk, "Walking the Fine Line Between Promptness and Haste: Recent Developments in Speedy Trial and Pretrial Restraint Jurisprudence," at 14.
> Coe, "Restating Some Old Rules and Limiting Some Landmarks: Recent Developments in Pretrial and Trial Procedure," at 25.
> Barto, "Recent Developments in the Substantive Criminal Law Under the Uniform Code of Military Justice," at 50.
> Wright, "'An Old Fashioned Crazy Quilt': New Developments in the Sixth Amendment, Discovery, Mental Responsibility, and Nonjudicial Punishment," at 72.
> Henley, "Postcards from the Edge: Privileges, Profiles, Polygraphs, and Other Developments in the Military Rules of Evidence," at 92.

Allen, "New Developments in Sentencing," at 116.

Morris, "'Just One More Thing...' and Other Thoughts on Recent Developments in Post-Trial Processing," at 129.

CHAPTER 16

SENTENCING

§ 16-2. Maximum Authorized Punishments.
  § 16-2(D). Multiplicity.
§ 16-3. Permissible Punishments.
  § 16-3(A). Death Penalty.
  § 16-3(B). Punitive Separations.
  § 16-3(C). Deprivation of Liberty.
  § 16-3(D). Deprivation of Pay.
§ 16-5. Prosecution Evidence.
  § 16-5(B). Data Concerning the Accused's Prior Service.
  § 16-5(C). Evidence of Prior Convictions.
  § 16-5(D). Evidence in Aggravation.
    § 16-5(D)(1). In General.
    § 16-5(D)(2). Evidence of Circumstances Surrounding Offense.
    § 16-5(D)(3). Evidence of Impact on Victim and Community.
    § 16-5(D)(4). Evidence Addressing Rehabilitative Potential.
    § 16-5(D)(5). Evidence of Uncharged Misconduct.
§ 16-6. Defense Evidence.
§ 16-7. Rebuttal and Surrebuttal.
§ 16-8. Arguments on Sentencing.
  § 16-8(B). Prosecution Arguments on Sentencing.
  § 16-8(C). Defense Counsel's Argument on Sentencing.
§ 16-9. Instructions on Sentencing.
§ 16-10. Deliberations on Sentencing.
§ 16-11. Announcement of the Sentence.
§ 16-13. Adjournment.

§ 16-2. Maximum Authorized Punishments.

§ 16-2(D). Multiplicity.

Page 707, n. 39. *Cf.* United States v. Oatney, 45 M.J. 185 (1996) (judge did not abuse discretion in treating non-multiplicious offenses as separate for purposes of sentencing).

Page 708, n. 42. United States v. Morrison, 41 M.J. 482 (1995); United States v. Dolbow, 44 M.J. 814 (A.F.Ct.Crim.App. 1996) (if offenses merge for sentencing, they merge for findings); United States v. Swango, 44 M.J. 686 (Army Ct.Crim.App. 1996) (prosecution may allege desertion in alternative theories; after findings, court should dismiss one of them; court consolidated two specifications).

§ 16-3. Permissible Punishments.

§ 16-3(A). Death Penalty.

Page 711, n. 3. *See generally* Loving v. United States, 517 U.S. 748 (1996) (discussion of military's death penalty procedures).

Page 713, n. 14. Loving v. United States, 517 U.S. 748 (1996) (discussion of military's death penalty procedures); Loving v. Hart, 47 M.J. 438 (1998) (denying mandamus relief to accused's whose death penalty conviction had been upheld by Supreme Court; aggravating factor in RCM 1004(c)(8), that accused was actual perpetrator, was constitutionally valid on its face).

Page 713, n. 18. United States v. Thomas, 46 M.J. 311 (1997) (plain error to instruct jury to consider sentence of life sentence before sentence of death; new sentencing proceeding ordered).

Page 714, n. 24. Following a remand to the Court of Criminal Appeals, *see* 38 M.J. 530, the Court of Appeals for the Armed Forces again affirmed the conviction at United States v. Curtis, 44 M.J. 106 (1996). On reconsideration, the Court set aside the death sentence because it found defense counsel's representation to be inadequate. 46 M.J. 129 (1997) (per curiam).

Page 715. Add the following text after sentence ending with footnote 32:

Following the Supreme Court's decision, the accused unsuccessfully sought mandamus relief from the Court of Appeals for the Armed Forces.[32.1]

[32.1] Loving v. Hart, 47 M.J. 438 (1998) (denying mandamus relief to accused's whose death penalty conviction had been upheld by Supreme Court; aggravating factor in RCM 1004(c)(8), that accused was actual perpetrator, was constitutionally valid on its face).

Page 715. Add the following text after sentence ending with footnote 34:

The Court of Appeals for the Armed Forces has held that an accused in a death penalty case is not entitled to representation by a defense counsel who is qualified under the *American Bar Association Guidelines for the Appointment and Performance of Counsel in Death Penalty Cases* (1989).[34.1] Those guidelines specifically indicate that they may be subject to "exceptions as may be appropriate in the military...."[34.2]

[34.1] United States v. Curtis, 44 M.J. 106 (1996) (not error that accused was represented by counsel who was not qualified under ABA Guidelines), *rev'd on other grounds on reconsideration*, 46 M.J. 129 (1997) (per curiam).

[34.2] United States v. Curtis, 44 M.J. 106, 126 (1996), *rev'd on other grounds on reconsideration*, 46 M.J. 129 (1997) (per curiam).

§ 16-3(B). Punitive Separations.

Page 715. Change second sentence of section to read:

A dismissal is reserved for commissioned officers and commissioned warrant officers,[38] and may be imposed for any offense by a general court-martial.[39]

Page 715, n. 38, add: United States v. Stockman, 43 M.J. 856 (N.M.Ct.Crim.App. 1996) (dishonorable discharge and dismissal are different only in terminology; commissioned warrant officers may be dismissed; non-commissioned warrant officers may be dishonorably discharged). For a discussion on the impact of a dismissal on an officer's loss of retirement pay, *see* United States v. Sumrall, 45 M.J. 207 (1996) (officer's loss of over $600,000.00 in retirement pay as result of dismissal did not violate due process).

§ 16-3(C). Deprivation of Liberty.

Page 716. Add the following text after sentence ending with footnote 55:

In 1996, Congress amended Article 58, U.C.M.J. to provide in part that an accused who is sentenced to confinement for more than six months, or to any period of confinement and a punitive discharge, must forfeit two-thirds pay.[55.1] As noted in § 17-2(B)(2), the accused may request the convening authority to defer such forfeitures.[55.2]

[55.1] National Defense Authorization Act for Fiscal Year (FY) 1996, § 1122(a)(1) of P.L. 104-106. *Cf.* United States v. Gorski, 47 M.J. 370 (1997) (court held that amendments violated ex post facto law as applied to accused; statute applied to offenses committed before effective date of act and operated to increase the minimum punishment by requiring total forfeitures for any accused receiving specified sentence).

[55.2] *See* Article 57(a)(2), U.C.M.J.; R.C.M. 1101(c). *See generally,* "Amendments to the Manual for Courts-Martial, ARMY LAW," July 1998, at 1. Specific guidance on deferment procedures is set out in R.C.M. 1101(c).

§ 16-3(D). Deprivation of Pay.

Page 716, n. 57. United States v. Gorski, 47 M.J. 370 (1997) (forfeitures are punishment rather than administrative matters).

Page 717, n. 63. United States v. Martinez, 42 M.J. 327 (1996) (accused fined $1,000.00 in negligent homicide case).

Page 718, n. 71. United States v. Lee, 43 M.J. 794 (N.M.Ct.Crim.App. 1995) (commuting forfeiture to fine is not necessarily increase in punishment).

§ 16-5. Prosecution Evidence.

§ 16-5(B). Data Concerning the Accused's Prior Service.

Page 723, n. 10. United States v. Godden, 44 M.J. 716 (A.F.Ct.Crim.App. 1996) (NJP proceedings were properly completed even though there was no typed signature block of reviewing officer; omissions did not affect any procedural due process rights of accused and were administrative trivia; under facts, failure of government to disclose NJP did not require exclusion).

Page 724, n. 19. *Cf.* United States v. Zamberlan, 45 M.J. 491 (1997) (not error not to instruct members to consider that reimposition of NJP against accused on different charge; *Pierce* distinguished).

§ 16-5(C). Evidence of Prior Convictions.

Page 725, n. 27. United States v. Tillar, 48 M.J. 541 (1998) (accused's prior conviction admitted at sentencing; court noted that Mil.R.Evid 609 was inapplicable because it was not admitted on issue of credibility); United States v. Cantrell, 44 M.J. 711 (A.F.Ct.Crim.App. 1996) (evidence of prior conviction sheds light on character of the accused).

Page 726, n. 39. United States v. Tillar, 48 M.J. 541 (1998) (accused's prior 18-year-old conviction admitted at sentencing; court noted that Mil.R.Evid 609 was inapplicable; trial judge applied Rule 403 balancing test).

§ 16-5(D). Evidence in Aggravation.

§ 16-5(D)(1). In General.

Page 728, n. 55. United States v. Gargaro, 45 M.J. 99 (1996) (assuming that it was error to admit evidence that one of guns accused help smuggle into country was sold to drug dealer, it was nonprejudicial error).

Page 728, n. 58. United States v. Zimmerman, 43 M.J. 782 (Army Ct.Crim.App. 1996) (permissible to introduce evidence through stipulation that accused has transferred firearms to white supremacy organizations; court noted that ordinarily the First Amendment prohibits introduction of the defendant's abstract beliefs).

§ 16-5(D)(2). Evidence of Circumstances Surrounding Offense.

Page 729, n. 64. *See, e.g.*, United States v. Zimmerman, 43 M.J. 782 (Army Ct.Crim.App. 1996) (permissible to introduce evidence through stipulation that accused has transferred firearms to white supremacy organizations; court noted that ordinarily the First Amendment prohibits introduction of the defendant's abstract beliefs but here it was evidence of accused's motives).

§ 16-5(D)(3). Evidence of Impact on Victim and Community.

Page 730, n. 72. United States v. Wilson, 47 M.J. 152 (1997) (evidence of impact of accused's disrespectful words on officer-victim); United States v. Sanchez, 47 M.J. 794 (N.M.Ct.Crim.App. 1998) (victim's testimony regarding the severity of the assault and impact and photographs of injuries were properly admitted as evidence in aggravation).

§ 16-5(D)(4). Evidence Addressing Rehabilitative Potential.

Page 733, n. 92. United States v. Yerich, 47 M.J. 615 (Army Ct.Crim.App. 1997) (opinion testimony of commander and four senior NCO's *re* rehabilitative potential was rationally based).

Page 733, n. 97. United States v. Powell, 45 M.J. 637 (N.M.Ct.Crim.App. 1997) (trial counsel improperly elicited evidence of specific conduct; no prejudice because conduct did not amount to uncharged misconduct and was benign).

§ 16-5(D)(5). Evidence of Uncharged Misconduct.

Page 736, n. 114. United States v. Clemente, 46 M.J. 715 (A.F.Ct.Crim.App. 1997) (two LOR's admissible to show accused's military character even though they reflected child neglect and spouse abuse).

Page 736, n. 116. United States v. Hollingsworth, 44 M.J. 688 (C.G.Ct.Crim.App. 1996) (uncharged act of indecency with teenage daughter was admissible aggravating evidence). *See also* Allen, "New Developments in Sentencing," ARMY LAW., April 1997, at 116.

§ 16-6. Defense Evidence.

Page 740, n. 12. In an extensive discussion of the history of considering an accused's "unsworn statement," the court in *United States v. Britt*, 44 M.J. 731 (A.F.Ct.Crim.App. 1996), held that the trial judge did not err in preventing the accused from commenting about the possibility of an administrative discharge in his unsworn statement. The unsworn statement, said the court, should be limited to evidence in extenuation, mitigation, and matters in rebuttal to the prosecution, as provided for in R.C.M. 1001(c)(2). *See also* United States v. Grill, 48 M.J. 131 (1998) (judge erred in denying accused opportunity to refer to civilian disposition of accused's co-conspirators; right to make unsworn statement may involve reference to evidence which might not otherwise be admissible on sentencing); United States v. Simoy, 46 M.J. 592 (A.F.Ct.Crim.App. 1996) (judge did not err in preventing accused from mentioning co-actor's sentence in unsworn statement).

Page 741. Add the following text after sentence ending with footnote 23:

That would include a prior sentence imposed by a state court for essentially the same conduct alleged in the court-martial.[23.1]

_____

[23.1] United States v. Simmons, 48 M.J. 193 (1998) (court concluded that the trial erred in not admitting defense evidence that the accused had already been sentenced in state court for the underlying conduct).

Page 741. Add the following text after sentence ending with footnote 24:

And there is authority for the proposition that the defense may offer evidence of the projected loss of retirement benefits which might result from a discharge or dismissal.[24.1]

_____

[24.1] United States v. Becker, 46 M.J. 141 (1997) (judge erred in excluding defense evidence of projected loss of retirement benefits where accused was within months of being eligible for retirement).

§ 16-7. Rebuttal and Surrebuttal.

Page 742, n. 3. United States v. Tilly, 44 M.J. 851 (N.M.Ct.Crim.App. 1996) (judge could permit parties to reopen case after having started deliberating on sentence).

§ 16-8. Arguments on Sentencing.

§ 16-8(B). Prosecution Arguments on Sentencing.

Page 744, n. 13. United States v. Weisbeck, 48 M.J. 570 (Army Ct.Crim.App. 1998) (error for assistant trial counsel to urge court members to sentence accused for uncharged acts of misconduct which were properly admitted at trial).

Page 745, n. 19. United States v. Cantrell, 44 M.J. 711 (A.F.Ct.Crim.App. 1996) (proper for prosecutor to argue that accused's prior convictions showed that he was "absolutely not influenced" by previous punishments).

§ 16-8(C). Defense Counsel's Argument on Sentencing.

Page 746, n. 35. United States v. Strauss, 47 M.J. 739 (N.M.Ct.Crim.App. 1997) (during unsworn statement, accused requested punitive discharge; on appeal, court set that punishment aside as being too severe).

§ 16-9. Instructions on Sentencing.

Page 749, n. 5, change reference from R.C.M. 1005(e)(2) to: 1005(e)(3).

Page 749, n. 5. United States v. Thomas, 46 M.J. 311 (1997) (plain error to instruct jury to consider sentence of life sentence before sentence of death; new sentencing proceeding ordered).

Page 749, n. 6, change reference from R.C.M. 1005(e)(3) to: 1005(e)(4).

Page 749, n. 7, change reference from R.C.M. 1005(e)(4) to: 1005(e)(5).

Page 749. Add the following after list item (4):

(5) A statement informing the members of the effect that a sentence which includes a punitive discharge and confinement, or confinement in excess of six months, will have on the accused's entitlement to pay and allowances.[7.1]

[7.1] R.C.M. 1005(e)(2). The change was added in 1998 to reflect amendments to Articles 58b, U.C.M.J. which provide for automatic forfeitures if those punishments are imposed. *See generally,* "Amendments to the Manual for Courts-Martial," ARMY LAW., July 1998, at 1.

Page 749, n. 10. United States v. Greaves, 46 M.J. 133 (1997) (whether instruction on collateral consequences is appropriate depends on facts of case; here, failure to answer court members' questions about impact of discharge on retirement benefits was reversible error; accused was within months of being eligible for retirement). *See also* United States v. Becker, 46 M.J. 141 (1997) (error to exclude relevant defense evidence of projected loss from retirement benefits); United States v. Hall, 46 M.J. 145 (1997) (although instructions re collateral consequences of conviction should normally not be given, not error to do so in response to court members' questions and accused agrees). *Cf.* United States v. Thompson, 43 M.J. 703 (A.F.Ct.Crim.App. 1995) (not abuse of discretion for trial judge to answer court member's question concerning administrative consequence of sentence and convening authority's discretion to defer confinement; court noted that under the facts, the judge properly addressed issue; court members are forced to flounder along in ignorance unless they ask questions; a judge should not be faulted for answering the mail).

§ 16-10. Deliberations on Sentencing.

Page 751, n. 8. United States v. Thomas, 46 M.J. 311 (1997) (plain error to instruct jury to consider sentence of life sentence before sentence of death; new sentencing proceeding ordered).

§ 16-11. Announcement of the Sentence.

Page 754. Add text following sentence ending with footnote 13:

Although a court does not have the authority to adjudge a suspended sentence, the court-martial may recommend clemency contemporaneously with announcement of the sentence.[13.1] Absent such an announcement that the court recommends clemency, the court members, either individually or collectively, may indicate their recommendations in communications with the convening authority.[13.2] In *United States v. Weatherspoon*,[13.3] the Court of Appeals for the Armed Forces noted that the current *Manual for Courts-Martial* does not provide specific guidance for the practice, specifically how the members are to determine during their deliberations whether to recommend clemency; the court assumed that to do so collectively as part of the announcement of the sentence, at least a majority of the members would have to concur in the recommendation.[13.4]

If necessary, the judge may reopen the court-martial to permit the parties to present additional evidence.[13.5]

[13.1] United States v. Weatherspoon, 44 M.J. 211 (1996) (noting long-standing practice).

[13.2] *See* SCHLUETER, JANSEN, BARRY & ARNOLD, MILITARY CRIMINAL PROCEDURE FORMS § 11-6(b) (1997) (sample request for clemency recommendation).

[13.3] 44 M.J. 211 (1996).

[13.4] *Id.* at 213-14.

[13.5] R.C.M. 1006(b); United States v. Tilly, 44 M.J. 851 (N.M.Ct.Crim.App. 1996) (not error for judge to interrupt his deliberations on sentencing to hear additional evidence).

§ 16-13. Adjournment.

Page 757, n. 4. United States v. Dodd, 46 M.J. 864 (Army Ct.Crim.App. 1997) (trial court erred in conducting revision proceedings after court adjourned to correct announced sentence; action resulted in upward correction); United States v. Jones, 34 M.J. 270 (1992).

ANNOTATED BIBLIOGRAPHY

BOOKS

Schlueter, Jansen, Barry & Arnold, *Military Criminal Procedure Forms* (1997).

This book presents a variety of sample forms, letters, pleadings, checklists, briefs, and motions for military criminal justice practitioners. The text, which provides coverage for processing a case from pretrial investigation through appellate disposition, demonstrates how formats may vary among the services.

PERIODICALS

Punishments: Death Penalty

Daniels, "Capital Punishment and the Courts-Martial: Questions Surface Following *Loving v. United States,*" 55 WASH. & LEE L. REV. 577 (1998).

This article addresses the Supreme Court's decision in *Loving v. United States*, 116 S. Ct. 1737 (1996), which held that Congress could delegate to the President the authority to spell out the aggravating factors to be considered in imposing the death penalty. The author focuses specifically on two issues that were not addressed by the Court: First, the question of whether there should be court-martial jurisdiction over common-law capital crimes committed during peacetime. And second, the question of whether courts-martial are bound by the same English Amendment requirements as applied to civilian courts.

Symposia

Symposium, "Military Justice Symposium—Volume I," ARMY LAW., April 1998.

This 128-page symposium is the first of two volumes and includes seven short articles on a range of military justice topics; it was authored by the faculty members of the Criminal Law Division at the Army's Judge Advocate School:

- Stitler, "The Power to Prosecute: New Developments in Courts-Martial Jurisdiction," at 1.
- Lovejoy, "Re-interpreting the Rules: Recent Developments in Speedy Trial and Pretrial Restraint," at 10.
- Einwechter, "New Developments in Substantive Criminal Law Under the Uniform Code of Military Justice (1997)," at 20.
- Coe, "'Something Old, Something New, Something Borrowed, Something Blue': Recent Developments in Pretrial and Trial Procedure," at 44.
- Pede, "New Developments in Search and Seizure and Urinalysis," at 80.
- Stitler, "Widening the Door: Recent Developments in Self-Incrimination Law," at 93.
- Moran, "Pyrrhic Victories and Permutations: New Developments in the Sixth Amendment, Discovery, and Mental Responsibility," at 106.

Symposium, "Military Justice Symposium—Volume II," ARMY LAW., May 1998.

This 68-page symposium consists of four articles articles on a range of military justice topics; it was authored by the faculty members of the Criminal Law Division at the Army's Judge Advocate School:

- Henley, "Developments in Evidence III—The Final Chapter," at 1.
- Lovejoy, "The CAAF at a Crossroads: New Developments in Post-Trial Processing," at 25.
- Allen, "Recent Developments in Sentencing Under the Uniform Code of Military Justice," at 39.

Morris, "'This Better Be Good': The Courts Continue to Tighten the Burden in Unlawful Command Influence Cases," at 49.

Symposium, "Military Justice Symposium I," ARMY LAW., April 1997.

This 149-page symposium, which presents a series of short articles on a range of military justice topics, was authored by the faculty members of the Criminal Law Division at the Army's Judge Advocate School:

Morris, Foreword.
Frisk, "The Long Arm of Military Justice: Court-Martial Jurisdiction and the Limits of Power," at 5.
Frisk, "Walking the Fine Line Between Promptness and Haste: Recent Developments in Speedy Trial and Pretrial Restraint Jurisprudence," at 14.
Coe, "Restating Some Old Rules and Limiting Some Landmarks: Recent Developments in Pretrial and Trial Procedure," at 25.
Barto, "Recent Developments in the Substantive Criminal Law Under the Uniform Code of Military Justice," at 50.
Wright, "'An Old Fashioned Crazy Quilt': New Developments in the Sixth Amendment, Discovery, Mental Responsibility, and Nonjudicial Punishment," at 72.
Henley, "Postcards from the Edge: Privileges, Profiles, Polygraphs, and Other Developments in the Military Rules of Evidence," at 92.
Allen, "New Developments in Sentencing," at 116.
Morris, "'Just One More Thing...' and Other Thoughts on Recent Developments in Post-Trial Processing," at 129.

CHAPTER 17

REVIEW OF COURTS-MARTIAL

PART I.
GENERAL

§ 17-2. Post-Trial Duties of Counsel.
  § 17-2(B). Defense Counsel's Duties.
    § 17-2(B)(2). Request for Deferment of Confinement, Forfeiture of Pay and Reduction in Grade.
    § 17-2(B)(3). Submission of Matters to the Convening Authority.
    § 17-2(B)(4). Review of the Staff Judge Advocate's Post-Trial Recommendation.
    § 17-2(B)(5). Requesting a Waiver of Automatic Forfeitures.
    § 17-2(B)(6). Negotiating a Post-Trial Agreement.
§ 17-3. Post-Trial Proceedings.
§ 17-4. Records of Trial.
  § 17-4(A). Authentication of Record.
  § 17-4(B). Service of Record on Accused.
§ 17-5. Confinement Pending Review.

PART II.
INITIAL REVIEW BY THE CONVENING AUTHORITY

§ 17-8. Legal Review of Courts-Martial.
  § 17-8(B). Post-Trial Recommendation.
    § 17-8(B)(1). Format and Contents of Recommendation.
    § 17-8(B)(2). Defective Recommendations.
    § 17-8(B)(3). Service of Recommendation on Defense Counsel.
§ 17-9. Convening Authority's Powers.
  § 17-9(A). General Matters.
  § 17-9(B). Qualified and Disqualified Convening Authorities.
  § 17-9(C). Actions and Executions of Sentences.
  § 17-9(D). Power to Suspend.
  § 17-9(E). Other Clemency Powers.
§ 17-11. Post-Trial Delays.

PART III.
APPELLATE REVIEW

§ 17-13. Waiver or Withdrawal of Appeals.
§ 17-14. Appellate Counsel.
§ 17-15. United States Courts of Criminal Appeals.
  § 17-15(B). Scope of Review and Actions.
§ 17-16. United States Court of Appeals for the Armed Forces
  § 17-16(C). Scope of Review.

PART IV.
OTHER FORMS OF REVIEW

§ 17-19. Extraordinary Writs in the Military Courts.
§ 17-21. Petition for New Trial.

PART I.

GENERAL

§ 17-2. Post-Trial Duties of Counsel.

§ 17-2(B). Defense Counsel's Duties.

Page 766, n. 11. United States v. Miller, 45 M.J. 149 (1996) (substitute defense counsel's failure to contact accused and establish attorney-client relationship amounted to error which could be tested for prejudice).

§ 17-2(B)(2). Request for Deferment of Confinement, Forfeiture of Pay and Reduction in Grade.

Page 767, n. 24. *See, e.g.*, SCHLUETER, JANSEN, BARRY & ARNOLD, MILITARY CRIMINAL PROCEDURE FORMS § 11-10 (1997) (sample request for deferment).

Page 768, n. 36. *See* R.C.M. 1101(c) (Specific guidance on deferment procedures). *See generally*, "Amendments to the Manual for Courts-Martial", ARMY LAW., July 1998, at 1.

Page 768, n. 40. *Cf.* United States v. Gorski, 47 M.J. 370 (1997) (court held that amendments violated ex post facto law as applied to accused; statute applied to offenses committed before effective date of act and operated to increase the minimum punishment by requiring total forfeitures for any accused receiving specified sentence).

Page 768, n. 43. R.C.M. 1001(c).

§ 17-2(B)(3). Submission of Matters to the Convening Authority.

Page 769, n. 49. *See generally* Faculty, TJAGSA, "The Art of Trial Advocacy: The Art of Clemency", ARMY LAW., March 1998, at 31.

Page 769, n. 57. *Cf.* R.C.M. 1105(b). This provision was added as part of the 1998 amendments to the *Manual*. *See generally*, "Amendments to the Manual for Courts-Martial", ARMY LAW., July 1998, at 1. The Discussion for that Rule now states:

> Although only written submissions must be considered, the convening authority may consider any submission by the accused, including, but not limited to, videotapes, photographs, and oral presentations.

Page 770, n. 58. United States v. Green, 44 M.J. 93 (1996) (even if brig officials wrongfully kept accused's clemency materials from reaching convening authority, there was no actual prejudice).

Page 770, n. 67. United States v. Haire, 44 M.J. 520 (C.G.Ct.Crim.App. 1996) (convening authority not obligated to consider videotape submitted by accused; case decided before change to Article 60).

Page 770, n. 68. *See generally* SCHLUETER, JANSEN, BARRY & ARNOLD, MILITARY CRIMINAL PROCEDURE Forms § 11-6 (1997) (sample clemency matters).

Page 771, n. 80. United States v. Hollingsworth, 44 M.J. 688 (C.G.Ct.Crim.App. 1996) (defense counsel waived right to present clemency matters to convening authority).

Page 772, n. 86. United States v. Hood, 47 M.J 95 (1997) (accused not prejudiced by counsel's actions, *inter alia*, in failing to consult with accused *re* submission of post-trial matters); United States v. Hicks, 47 M.J. 90 (1997) (accused was not prejudiced by counsel's deficiency in representing accused re post-trial matters); United States v. Ellis, 47 M.J. 20 (1997) (accused not denied effective post-trial representation by not submitting certain matters to convening authority).

Page 772. Add the following text after sentence ending with footnote 86:

The primary responsibility for making strategic and tactical decisions regarding whether to submit materials to the convening authority, rests with defense counsel—after consulting with the accused.[86.1] Counsel should not, however, offer matters over the objection of the accused, or refuse to offer matters that the accused wants submitted.[86.2] The courts have analogized this process to the question of who decides whether an accused should take the stand during trial; that is, counsel should provide the necessary information for the accused to make the decision.[86.3] But the final decision on what should be submitted to the convening authority rests with the accused.[86.4]

[86.1] United States v. Hood, 47 M.J. 95, 97 (1997).

[86.2] 47 M.J. at 97 (1997); United States v. Hicks, 47 M.J. 90 (1997).

[86.3] United States v. Hood, 47 M.J. 95 (1997); United States v. Hicks, 47 M.J. 90 (1997) (analogy to decision whether to testify); United States v. Lewis, 42 M.J. 1 (1995) (final decision rests with accused).

[86.4] United States v. Hood, 47 M.J. 95 (1997) (final decision rests with accused).

Page 772, n. 88. United States v. Garcia, 44 M.J. 748 (C.G.Ct.Crim.App. 1996) (SJA's affidavit indicated that accused's materials were submitted to convening authority).

§ 17-2(B)(4). Review of the Staff Judge Advocate's Post-Trial Recommendation.

Page 773, n. 95. United States v. Strange, 45 M.J. 642 (N.M.Ct.Crim.App. 1997) (defense waived defect in recommendation which erroneously indicated that judge had not made any clemency recommendations at sentencing).

Page 774: Add new sections:

§ 17-2(B)(5). Requesting a Waiver of Automatic Forfeitures.

As a result of amendments in 1996 to the *Uniform Code of Military Justice,* an accused *automatically* forfeits all pay and allowances if the accused received an adjudged sentence of either (1) confinement for more than six months or death or (2) confinement of six months or less of confinement and a punitive discharge (BCD or DD).[100.1] These forfeitures are applied by operation of law, without regard to whether any forfeitures were actually a part of the adjudged sentence.[100.2] As noted in § 17-2(B)(2), *supra*, an accused may request the convening authority to defer the imposition of any forfeitures which were adjudged by the court-martial until the convening authority takes action on the case.[100.3] Although there is no provision for deferring the imposition of automatic forfeitures, an accused may request the convening authority to "waive" all of some of such forfeitures for six months and direct that they be paid to the accused's dependents.[100.4] In effect, this amounts to a temporary allotment to those who may have a financial need resulting from the accused's conviction.[100.5] Such waivers are intended for the benefit of the dependents, not the accused.[100.6]

Neither the U.C.M.J nor the *Manual for Courts-Martial* provide any specific guidance on the exact procedures to be used in obtaining such waivers.[100.7] Indeed, their is no requirement that the accused actually make the requested waiver. The *Manual* does indicate that in considering whether to grant a waiver, the convening authority should consider, *inter alia*, the length of the accused's confinement, the number and ages of the dependents, the accused's debts, and the ability of the accused's family to find employment.[100.8] Most importantly, the convening authority may consider whether the accused has requested the waiver.[100.9] To that end, counsel should consider advising the accused to make such a request. The request should be in writing and should be directed to the convening authority. It should spell out in careful detail the factors listed in the *Manual* in addition to any other matters which counsel believes will demonstrate concern for the welfare of the accused's dependents.[100.10]

There is currently no requirement that the convening authority provide any reasons for denying a requested waiver.[100.11]

§ 17-2(B)(6). Negotiating a Post-Trial Agreement.

Following the trial, defense counsel may wish to negotiate a post-trial agreement with the convening authority.[100.12] A post-trial agreement might include reduction in the adjudged sentence in return for assistance in other investigations[100.13] or trials,[100.14] or modification to an existing pretrial agreement.[100.15] Although post-trial agreements are not used frequently in military practice, the military courts have generally recognized that such agreements exist.[100.16] But they have not set out specific guidance or procedures for determining whether a post-trial agreement is valid.[100.17] In *United States v. Pilkington*,[100.18] the accused and convening authority entered into a post-trial agreement which modified their pretrial agreement; the convening authority approved a sentence conforming to the post-trial agreement.[100.19] The court rejected the accused's argument that the agreement was void because the trial judge had not been given the opportunity to conduct a *King-Green* inquiry.[100.20] The Court of Criminal Appeals indicated that post-trial agreements could be reviewed at the appellate level,[100.21] or if necessary, at a post-trial Article 39(a) session.[100.22] As with any analysis of pretrial agreements, a key inquiry here would be whether the agreement was knowingly, voluntarily, and intelligently entered into the by the accused.[100.23]

[100.1] Art. 58b, U.C.M.J. *See* Appendix 3. R.C.M. 1101(d). *See generally*, "Amendments to the Manual for Courts-Martial," ARMY LAW., July 1998, at 1.

[100.2] *Id.*

[100.3] Art. 57a, U.C.M.J.

[100.4] Art. 58b(b), U.C.M.J.

[100.5] *Id.*

[100.6] *Id.* United States v. Clemente, 46 M.J. 715 (A.F.Ct.Crim.App. 1997) (court concluded that Article 57(a) is for the benefit of the accused's dependents, and not the accused; thus, an accused does not have standing to challenge the convening authority's decision not to defer forfeitures).

[100.7] United States v. Clemente, 46 M.J. 715 (A.F.Ct.Crim.App. 1997) (court noted that there is no guidance in the *Manual for Courts-Martial* on the procedures to be used for requesting a deferment of forfeitures).

[100.8] R.C.M. 1001(d). This provision was added in the 1998 amendments to the *Manual*. *See generally*, "Amendments to the Manual for Courts-Martial," ARMY LAW., July 1998, at 1.

[100.9] R.C.M. 1001(d).

[100.10] *Id.*

[100.11] *Id. See* United States v. Quintin, 47 M.J. 798 (N.M.Ct.Crim.App. 1998) (no requirement that convening authority state reasons for denying accused's request for waiver of forfeiture of pay under Article 58b(b)).

[100.12] *See, e.g.*, United States v. Pilkington, 48 M.J. 523 (N.M.Ct.Crim.App. 1998). Ironically, the defense counsel in *Pilkington* had strongly advised the accused not to enter into the agreement. 48 M.J. at 525, n. 2.

[100.13] *See, e.g.*, United States v. Lonetree, 31 M.J. 849 (N.M.C.M.R. 1990) (post-trial agreement to submit to polygraph in return for reduction of sentence).

[100.14] *See, e.g.*, United States v. Stantas, 45 C.M.R. 765 (N.C.M.R. 1971) (agreement to reduce confinement in return for testimony in other cases).

[100.15] United States v. Pilkington, 48 M.J. 523 (N.M.Ct.Crim.App. 1998) (convening authority could approve bad conduct discharge as long as approved confinement did not exceed 90 days; pretrial agreement would have permitted convening authority to suspend bad-conduct discharge).

[100.16] United States v. Cassell, 33 M.J. 448, 450 (C.M.A. 1991) (referring to post-trial agreement); United States v. Pilkington, 48 M.J. 523 (N.M.Ct.Crim.App. 1998) (citing cases); United States v. Giroux, 37 M.J. 553 (A.C.M.R. 1993) (noting such agreements); United States v. Rascoe, 31 M.J. 544 (N.M.C.M.R. 1990) (offer to enter into post-trial agreement); United States v. Nutter, 22 M.J. 727 (A.C.M.R. 1986) (noting existence of agreement which resulted in reduction of approved sentence); United States v. Cooper, 17 M.J. 1062 (A.F.C.M.R. 1984) (noting absence of post-trial agreement).

[100.17] *Cf.* § 14-3(C) (discussion of detailed inquiry necessary for pretrial agreements), *supra*.

[100.18] 48 M.J. 523 (N.M.Ct.Crim.App. 1998).

[100.19] *Id..* at 524.

[100.20] *Id.* at 526. For a discussion of the *King-Green* inquiry, see § 14-3(C), *supra*.

[100.21] 48 M.J. at 526.
[100.22] *Id.* at 526, n. 5. *See also* § 17-3(B), *infra*.
[100.23] In *Pilkington*, the court reminded counsel that the precision used in drafting pretrial agreements would also apply to drafting post-trial agreements. 48 M.J. at 527, n. 6.

§ 17-3. Post-Trial Proceedings.

Page 774, n. 4. *See, e.g.*, SCHLUETER, JANSEN, BARRY & ARNOLD, MILITARY CRIMINAL PROCEDURE FORMS § 11-9 (1997) (sample request for post-trial proceeding).

§ 17-4. Records of Trial.

Page 781, n. 33. United States v. Santoro, 46 M.J. 344 (1997) (substantial omissions give rise to presumption of prejudice which must be rebutted by government; here action by lower appellate court had removed whatever prejudice may have existed).

§ 17-4(A). Authentication of Record.

Page 781, n. 41. United States v. Galaviz, 46 M.J. 548 (N.M.Ct.Crim.App. 1997) (trial counsel authenticated portion of record of trial; court found that failure to explain why the judge could not authenticate the record was harmless error).

§ 17-4(B). Service of Record on Accused.

Page 783, n. 55. United States v. Diamond, 18 M.J. 305 (C.M.A. 1984) (nonprejudicial error not to serve copy of record; defense counsel had been notified that copy was available for inspection); United States v. Duckworth, 45 M.J. 549 (C.G. Ct.Crim.App. 1996) (nonprejudicial error not to serve accused with copy of record of trial until after convening authority had taken action on the case).

§ 17-5. Confinement Pending Review.

Page 783, n. 4. United States v. Bramer, 45 M.J. 296 (1996) (under facts, convening authority's attempt to treat military sentence and civilian sentence as running consecutively was not authorized).

PART II.

INITIAL REVIEW BY THE CONVENING AUTHORITY

§ 17-8. Legal Review of Courts-Martial.

§ 17-8(B). Post-Trial Recommendation.

Page 786, n. 10. United States v. Jones, 47 M.J. 725 (A.F.Ct.Crim.App. 1997) (several standard documents were missing from SJA post-trial recommendation; court declined to presume that matters were properly presented to convening authority; court also declined to find waiver).

Page 786, n. 12. United States v. Dresen, 47 M.J. 122 (1997) (SJA not disqualified to prepare review even though his office had prior connection with the appellate review of the case; in lengthy appellate consideration of the case the accused had never requested the courts to require a new SJA to review the case).

Page 786, n. 15. United States v. Johnson-Saunders, 48 M.J. 74 (1998) (plain error where SJA drafted recommendation in a case where she had acted as assistant trial counsel); United States v. Hamilton, 47 M.J. 32 (1997) (court did not decide whether preparation of draft recommendation by acting SJA who was wife of prosecutor was error because such action did not materially prejudice the accused; new SJA prepared final draft and submitted it to convening authority); United States v. Edwards, 45 M.J. 114 (1996) (plain error where legal officer was disqualified from preparing post-trial recommendation where he had assumed prosecutorial role by preferring charges, conducted videotaped interrogation of accused, and acted as evidence custodian in early stage of trial).

Page 786, n. 17. United States v. Edwards, 45 M.J. 114 (1996) (plain error where legal officer was disqualified from preparing post-trial recommendation where he had assumed prosecutorial role by conducting videotaped interrogation of accused which led to confession).

Page 786, n. 19. United States v. Sorrell, 47 M.J. 432 (1998) (court did not answer question of whether SJA was disqualified from preparing post-trial recommendation where officer who drafted it had been member of prosecution team and had promised clemency to accused; assuming it was error, there was no prejudice to accused); United States v. Wansley, 46 M.J. 335 (1997) (SJA was not disqualified where prosecutor wrote article for base newsletter condemning accused's actions; accused did not make prima facie case of disqualification; officer was not assigned to convening authority's command and was not speaking on behalf of convening authority or SJA).

Page 787, n. 23. United States v. Edwards, 45 M.J. 114 (1996) (plain error where legal officer was clearly disqualified from preparing post-trial recommendation; he had assumed prosecutorial role by preferring charges, conducting videotaped interrogation of accused, and acting as evidence custodian in early stage of trial).

Page 787, n. 24. United States v. Plumb, 47 M.J. 771 (A.F.Ct.Crim.App. 1997) (SJA disqualified from preparing post-trial recommendation where he had prepared faulty pretrial advice); United States v. Cunningham, 44 M.J. 758 (N.M.Ct.Crim.App. 1996) (plain error for enlisted legal officer to sign post-trial recommendation; court noted that although person signing recommendation need not be a lawyer, he or she must be an officer; court noted that this seems to be recurring problem in Navy).

§ 17-8(B)(1). Format and Contents of Recommendation.

Page 788, n. 33. United States v. Thompson, 43 M.J. 703 (A.F.Ct.Crim.App. 1995) (court noted increase in post-trial processing errors; court noted that laying out foolproof appellate guidance and returning cases for new reviews and actions has not solved problem).

Page 789, n. 40. United States v. Williams, 47 M.J. 593 (N.M.Ct.Crim.App. 1997) (omission of information *re* character of accused's service was not plain error and resulted in no prejudice).

Page 790, n. 47. United States v. Jennings, 44 M.J. 658 (C.G.Ct.Crim.App. 1996) (SJA should have responded to defense issue concerning announcement of sentence). *Cf.* United States v. Welker, 44 M.J. 85 (1996) (not error for SJA not to address legal issue raised by defense where record failed to demonstrate any deficiency at trial).

Page 790, n. 50. United States v. Casey, 45 M.J. 623 (N.M.Ct.Crim.App. 1996) (SJA only required to register agreement or disagreement).

§ 17-8(B)(2). Defective Recommendations.

Page 792, n. 63. United States v. Griffaw, 46 M.J. 791 (A.F.Ct.Crim.App. 1997) (prejudicial error to incorrectly inform convening authority that his action in reducing sentence to comport with pretrial agreement amounted to a form of clemency); United States v. Barnes, 44 M.J. 680 (N.M.Ct.Crim.App. 1996) (error not to include information that accused had received Navy Commendation Medal for meritorious service); United States v. Jennings, 44 M.J. 658 (C.G.Ct.Crim.App. 1996) (prejudicial error for SJA not to respond to legal issue raised by defense).

Page 792, n. 67. *Cf.* United States v. Barnes, 44 M.J. 680 (N.M.Ct.Crim.App. 1996) (court set aside action and returned case for new recommendation).

§ 17-8(B)(3). Service of Recommendation on Defense Counsel.

Page 793. Substitute the following for the second sentence in the second paragraph:

Failure to respond, present a timely response, or note defects will normally constitute waiver,[71] absent plain error.[71.1]

[71.1] United States v. Stallworth, 44 M.J. 785 (N.M.Ct.Crim.App. 1996) (test for plain error is whether first, there has been an error, second, the error was plain or obvious, and third, the error affected a substantial right of the accused).

Page 793, n. 73. United States v. Leal, 44 M.J. 235 (1996) (discussion of problems associated with SJA failing to provide copy of new matter to defense counsel; court indicated that essence of post-trial practice is fair play, including notice and an opportunity to respond).

Page 793, n. 74. United States v. Leal, 44 M.J. 235 (1996) (SJA's mention of reprimand for prior drug use which had been ruled inadmissible by trial judge was new matter; court rejected government argument that matter was not new because it had been between the "blue covers" of the record; the dissenting judges viewed the matter as not new and as proper rebuttal information to issues raised by the defense in its response to the SJA's original recommendation); United States v. Jones, 44 M.J. 242 (1996) (description of post-trial authentication process constituted new matter and should have been served on defense).

Cf. United States v. Graham, 46 M.J. 583 (A.F.Ct.Crim.App. 1997) (SJA's disagreeing with accused's assertions, without more, was not new matter).

Page 793, n. 75. United States v. Leal, 44 M.J. 235 (1996) (noting that government can avoid unnecessary appellate litigation, SJA construes the term "new matter" liberally); United States v. Thompson, 43 M.J. 703 (A.F.Ct.Crim.App. 1995).

Page 794, n. 76. United States v. Leal, 44 M.J. 235 (1996) (case returned for new review and action); United States v. Jones, 44 M.J. 242 (1996) (violation of rule was so trivial as to be nonprejudicial; court noted that normally this sort of error is presumptively prejudicial); United States v. Gonyea, 44 M.J. 811 (A.F.Ct.Crim.App. 1996) (under facts, interjection of new matter was not prejudicial). *See also* Morris, "'Just One More Thing...' and Other Thoughts on Recent Developments in Post-Trial Processing", ARMY LAW., April 1997, at 129.

Page 794, n. 77. United States v. Buller, 46 M.J. 467 (1997) (assuming that SJA failed to provide notice of new matter, accused suffered no prejudice where SJA's comments were neutral responses to matters raised by defense and accused failed to show that comments were erroneous, misleading, or inadequate); United States v. Catalani, 46 M.J. 325 (1997) (accused entitled to new action by convening authority where SJA submitted new and erroneous information without providing defense counsel with notice); United States v. Haney, 45 M.J. 447 (1996) (failure of SJA to serve defense counsel with new matter was presumptively prejudicial; case remanded); United States v. Jones, 44 M.J. 242 (1996) (injection of new matter is presumptively prejudicial); United States v. Jordon, 44 M.J. 847 (N.M.Ct.Crim.App. 1996) (accused prejudiced by SJA's failure to provide defense with copy of new matter until after convening authority had acted; discussion of tests for determining whether relief is due when defense counsel is not served with new matter).

Page 794. Add the following text after sentence ending with footnote 77:

Regarding the showing of prejudice, the Court of Appeals for the Armed Forces has indicated that if the accused asserts that the defense counsel was not served with the addendum containing new matter, the accused must demonstrate prejudice by showing the court what information, if any, would have been submitted to the convening authority to "deny, counter, or explain" that new matter.[77.1] The court added that the threshold for the accused is low and that if he or she makes some colorable claim of possible prejudice, the accused will be given the benefit of the doubt.[77.2] That is, the court will not speculate on what the convening authority might have done if the defense had been given an opportunity to respond.[77.3]

[77.1] United States v. Chatman, 46 M.J. 321 (1997) (SJA included new matter in addendum by referring to accused's second urinalysis which was matter outside record).

[77.2] *Id.* at 321, 323 (1997).

[77.3] *Id.* at 321, 324 (1997); United States v. Jones, 44 M.J. 242 (1996).

Page 794, n. 79. United States v. Tyson, 44 M.J. 588 (N.M.Ct.Crim.App. 1996) (defense counsel may not unilaterally withdraw from representing accused whom he cannot locate).

Page 794, n. 81. United States v. Washington, 45 M.J. 497 (1997) (government's service of recommendation on civilian counsel rather than military counsel, as the accused had directed, was nonprejudicial error).

Page 795, n. 83. United States v. Howard, 47 M.J. 104 (1997) (accused showed that he never entered into attorney-client relationship with substitute counsel; accused made colorable showing of prejudice in counsel's failure to submit matters to convening authority); United States v. Miller, 45 M.J. 149 (1996) (substitute defense counsel's failure to contact accused and establish attorney-client relationship amounted to error which could be tested for prejudice).

Page 795. Add text following sentence ending with footnote 83:

If the defense counsel (or authorized substitute counsel) is "absent"[83.1] for purposes of accepting service of the post-trial recommendation and responding to it, the accused has been deprived of his or her right to the assistance of counsel. In those cases, the courts will apparently treat the error as requiring *per se* reversal.[83.2] On the other hand, if counsel charged with representing the accused is present, then any error in connection with that counsel's performance of duties, or from procedural errors affecting counsel's ability to meet his or her responsibilities, will be measured for prejudice.[83.3]

[83.1] United States v. Hickok, 45 M.J. 142 (1996) (court clarified standard of review on post-trial processing issues; accused not represented by counsel when defense counsel left active duty). *See also* Morris, "'Just One More Thing...' and Other Thoughts on Recent Developments in Post-Trial Processing", ARMY LAW., April 1997, at 129 (noting philosophical division on post-trial review).

[83.2] *Hickok*, 45 M.J. at 146 (case remanded for new post-trial action).

[83.3] *Id.* at 145; United States v. Washington, 45 M.J. 497 (1997) (government's service of recommendation on civilian counsel rather than military counsel, as the accused had directed, was nonprejudicial error); United States v. Miller, 45 M.J. 149 (1996) (substitute defense counsel's failure to contact accused and establish attorney-client relationship amounted to error which could be tested for prejudice); United States v. Pierce, 40 M.J. 149 (C.M.A. 1994); United States v. Spurlin, 33 M.J. 443 (C.M.A. 1991); United States v. Smart, 21 M.J. 15 (C.M.A. 1985).

Page 795, n. 90. United States v. Hardy, 44 M.J. 507 (A.F.Ct.Crim.App. 1996) (defense counsel's unilateral withdrawal as counsel was justified; counsel sensed that his continued representation of accused would create impermissible conflict of interest).

Page 796, n. 93. *See also* United States v. Tyson, 44 M.J. 588 (N.M.Ct.Crim.App. 1996) (defense counsel obligated to provide effective assistance even if he or she is unable to contact the accused).

Page 796, n. 96. *Cf.* United States v. Mark, 47 M.J. 99 (1997) (because record did not contain copy of SJA recommendation, the court declined to presume regularity in the service of the recommendation).

§ 17-9. Convening Authority's Powers.

§ 17-9(A). General Matters.

Page 797, n. 10. United States v. Carter, 45 M.J. 168 (1996) (convening authority could properly commute bad-conduct discharge to additional confinement for two years; under facts, change in punishment did not result in increase in sentence); United States v. Lee, 43 M.J. 794 (N.M.Ct.Crim.App. 1995) (commuting forfeiture to fine is not necessarily increase in punishment).

Page 797, n. 11. United States v. Barraza, 44 M.J. 622 (N.M.Ct.Crim.App. 1996) (sentence not increased where convening authority increased suspension by two years and reduced actual amount of confinement; the aggregate still totaled less than period in pretrial agreement); United States v.

Lee, 43 M.J. 794 (N.M.Ct.Crim.App. 1995) (commuting forfeiture to fine is not necessarily increase in punishment).

Page 799. Add the following text after sentence ending with footnote 23:

Although the matter is not explicitly addressed in the *Manual for Courts-Martial*, the military courts have recognized that in exercising his or her command prerogative, the convening authority may consider information or advice from persons other than the Staff Judge Advocate, the defense counsel, or the accused.[23.1] For example, the convening authority might conceivably seek or receive comments or advice from members in the chain of command, or perhaps even the victim or other interested persons.[23.2] And R.C.M. 1103 requires that any recommendations and other papers related to clemency are supposed to be attached to the record of trial, which in turn will be served on the defense counsel and accused.[23.3] The courts normally do not consider it error not to provide the accused with an opportunity to rebut such evidence;[23.4] it might be prejudicial error, however, not to provide the accused with an opportunity to respond where those matters contain substantive information not included in the record of trial and the accused makes a colorable showing of possible prejudice.[23.5] Given that possibility, the safer course would be for the convening authority to relate such information to the legal office, the defense counsel, and the accused for comment, when the information is received.

[23.1] *See, e.g.,* United States v. Trosper, 47 M.J. 728 (N.M.Ct.Crim.App. 1997) (Division Sergeant Major submitted written comments to convening authority urging approval of sentence; accused was not given opportunity to respond).

[23.2] United States v. McCloskey, 31 C.M.R. 207 (C.M.A. 1962) (commanders can solicit opinions of others); United States v. Trosper, 47 M.J. 728 (N.M.Ct.Crim.App. 1997) (Division Sergeant Major submitted written comments to convening authority);

[23.3] *See* R.C.M. 1103(b)(3)(I).

[23.4] *See* § 17-4(B), supra.

[23.5] United States v. Chatman, 46 M.J. 321 (1997); United States v. Trosper, 47 M.J. 728, 730 (N.M.Ct.Crim.App. 1997) (Division Sergeant Major submitted written comments to convening authority urging approval of sentence; accused was not given opportunity to respond; no prejudice, however).

Page 799, n. 25. United States v. Garcia, 44 M.J. 748 (C.G. Ct.Crim.App. 1996) (SJA's affidavit indicated that accused's materials were submitted to convening authority).

Page 800, n. 30. United States v. Bright, 44 M.J. 749 (C.G. Ct.Crim.App. 1996) (convening authority could consider adverse letter from accused's wife; accused was served with copy and was provided with time to respond).

§ 17-9(B). Qualified and Disqualified Convening Authorities.

Page 801, n. 42. United States v. Fisher, 45 M.J. 159 (1996) (case reversed where convening authority told defense counsel during recess that he was unethical because he had attempted to suppress results of urinalysis testing; such actions violated Article 37).

§ 17-9(C). Actions and Executions of Sentences.

Page 802, n. 53. United States v. Pedrazoli, 45 M.J. 567 (A.F.Ct.Crim.App. 1997) (1995 amendments to Article 57 do not violate *ex post facto* clause).

Page 803. Add new footnote at end of second sentence in partial paragraph at top of page, as follows:

was changed.[56.1]

[56.1] R.C.M. 1107. United States v. Smith, 44 M.J. 788 (N.M.Ct.Crim.App. 1996) (convening authority lacked authority to modify action after it had been forwarded to appellate court).

Page 803, n. 57. United States v. Schiaffo, 43 M.J. 835 (Army Ct.Crim.App. 1996) (court returned record of trial and substituted a corrected action; record indicated that convening authority clearly intended to impose bad-conduct discharge).

§ 17-9(D). Power to Suspend.

Page 804, n. 64. United States v. Mitchell, 46 M.J. 840 (N.M.Ct.Crim.App. 1997) (confinement suspended on condition that accused make restitution in amount of over thirty thousand dollars).

Page 805, n. 73. United States v. Smith, 46 M.J. 263 (1997) (regardless of whether accused's post-trial misconduct preceded or followed convening authority's action, SPCM authority is required to forward report of vacation proceedings to GCM authority); United States v. Perlman, 44 M.J. 615 (N.M.Ct.Crim.App. 1996) (vacation of suspension was invalid where special court-martial convening authority failed to forward recommendation to general court-martial convening authority).

Page 805, n. 75. United States v. Smith, 46 M.J. 263 (1997) (failure of SPCM authority to forward report of vacation proceedings to GCM authority was error).

§ 17-9(E). Other Clemency Powers.

Page 805, n. 81. United States v. Griffaw, 46 M.J. 791 (A.F.Ct.Crim.App. 1997) (approving sentence to comport with sentence cap in pretrial agreement is not exercise of command prerogative amounting to clemency action).

§ 17-11. Post-Trial Delays.

Page 807, n. 5. United States v. Hudson, 46 M.J. 226 (1997) (839-day delay not sufficient in itself to warrant relief; accused was unable to show any real harm or prejudice caused by the delay); United States v. Nelson, 46 M.J. 764 (A.F.Ct.Crim.App. 1997) (171-day post-trial delay was unreasonable but did not result in prejudice to accused).

Page 807, n. 6. United States v. Schlarb, 46 M.J. 708 (N.M.Ct.Crim.App. 1997) (19-month post-trial delay was unacceptable but nonprejudicial).

Page 808. Add the following text after sentence ending with footnote 9:

Despite arguments that the Court of Appeals for the Armed Forces should adopt a rule that sends a strong signal that gross delays in post-trial processing will not be tolerated, that Court has declined to so.[9.1] It has, however, indicated concern about unexplained and lengthy delays in post-trial processing of cases.[9.2]

[9.1] *See e.g.*, United States v. Santoro, 46 M.J. 344 (1997) (court declined to adopt rule or measure; court believed that lower courts' actions of adjusting sentences would provide enough incentive to correct problems of delays).

[9.2] *See e.g.*, United States v. Bell, 46 M.J. 351 (1997) (court expressed concern for delays).

PART III.

APPELLATE REVIEW

§ 17-13. Waiver or Withdrawal of Appeals.

Page 810, n. 24. United States v. Smith, 44 M.J. 387 (1996) (accused's waiver invalid where it was filed before convening authority's action).

§ 17-14. Appellate Counsel.

Page 812. Add the following text after sentence ending with footnote 11:

As discussed at § 15-2(B)(3), *supra*, counsel's actions, or inaction, at the appellate level may also result in an assessment of whether the accused was denied the right to the effective assistance of counsel.[11.1]

[11.1] *See, e.g.*, United States v. May, 47 M.J. 478 (1998) (accused denied assistance of counsel where retained civilian counsel failed to file any briefs with Court of Criminal Appeals and that court failed to take any action enforcing its order; court notes options where counsel fails to file brief).

§ 17-15. United States Courts of Criminal Appeals.

Page 812, n. 3. On remand in *United States v. Ryder*, 44 M.J. 9 (1996), the Court of Appeals for the Armed Forces (formerly the Court of Military Appeals) held that Congress has authorized the Secretary of Transportation to appoint civilian judges to the Coast Guard Court of Criminal Appeals.

§ 17-15(B). Scope of Review and Actions.

Page 814, n. 17. United States v. Ginn, 47 M.J. 236 (1997) (service Court of Criminal Appeals does not have the authority to make findings of fact regarding post-trial claims of ineffectiveness of counsel based partially on post-trial submissions. Instead, it may use such submissions, e.g., affidavits, to decide if a *DuBay* hearing is required).

Page 816, n. 31. United States v. Ginn, 47 M.J. 236 (1997) (service Court of Criminal Appeals does not have the authority to make findings of fact regarding post-trial claims of ineffectiveness of counsel based partially on post-trial submissions. Instead, it may use such submissions, e.g., affidavits, to decide if a *DuBay* hearing is required).

Page 816, n. 32. United States v. Taylor, 47 M.J. 322 (1997) (in reassessing sentence, court must determine what original sentence would have been absent the error; the test is not what sentence might be imposed on a rehearing); United States v. Collins, 44 M.J. 830 (Army Ct.Crim.App. 1996) (court provided relief for accused who had been held in post-trial confinement beyond release date).

Page 817, n. 33. United States v. Clack, 48 M.J. 813 (A.F.Ct.Crim.App. 1998) (court declined to compare sentence to other cases and reduced sentence as being too severe); United States v. Swan, 43 M.J. 788 (N.M.Ct.Crim.App. 1995) (discussion of *Navy JAG Manual* which requires convening authority to list in action on court-martial whether separate trial was ordered in companion case; Navy uses information for possible comparison of sentences).

§ 17-16. The United States Court of Appeals for the Armed Forces.

§ 17-16(C). Scope of Review.

Page 820, n. 15. United States v. Miller, 46 M.J. 248 (1997) (court declined to review legality of post-trial confinement because the accused had failed to exhaust his administrative remedies); United States v. Barrow, 45 M.J. 478 (1996) (unlike Courts of Criminal Appeals, the Court of Appeals for the Armed Forces reviews only for legal sufficiency of evidence, not factual sufficiency).

Page 820, n. 23. United States v. Brock, 46 M.J. 11 (1997) (case remanded for court to consider sentence appropriateness).

PART IV.

OTHER FORMS OF REVIEW

§ 17-19. Extraordinary Writs in the Military Courts.

Page 824, n. 5. Goldsmith v. Clinton, 48 M.J. 84, 86-87 (1998) (noting that Congress intended for the Court of Appeals "to have broad responsibility with respect to administration of military justice").

Page 825. Add the following text after sentence ending with footnote 13:

That expansive reading of the Court's powers under the All Writs Act was continued in *Goldsmith v. Clinton*,[13.1] where the confined petitioner challenged the ability of the government to drop him from the rolls as a member of the armed forces. The petitioner, an HIV-infected officer, had been convicted of violating a safe sex order.[13.2] His conviction was affirmed by the Court of Criminal Appeals but he did not seek any further direct review at the Air Force Court of Appeals for the Armed Forces.[13.3] However, he later sought extraordinary relief from the Court of Criminal Appeals, arguing that the government had improperly cut off his medication while serving his sentence. When that court denied his petition, he sought extraordinary relief from the Court of Appeals seeking relief, *inter alia*, on grounds that the government was unlawfully dropping him from the rolls under a newly enacted statute.[13.4] Addressing the question of its authority under the All Writs Act, the Court noted that it had previously held that it could review a court-martial conviction that would have never been subject to direct review before the Court.[13.5] Accordingly, the Court continued, it could review the lawfulness of a conviction which was subject to such review, and in fact had been reviewed by a service appellate court.[13.6] The fact that the accused had initially waived direct review did not affect the Court's extraordinary writ jurisdiction.[13.7] Although the Court doubted that Congress intended for it to review the details of prison administration, it was not convinced that every aspect of an accused's service of a court-martial sentence would be immune from review under the All Writs Act.[13.8] The Court recognized that the power to grant extraordinary relief to servicemembers serving court-martial sentences should be "exercised sparingly" because there are often more efficient ways of providing simpler remedies, e.g., filing an Article 138 complaint.[13.9] Turning the merits of the case, the Court concluded that the medication issue had been mooted and that the government's contemplated action of dropping him from the rolls, under a statute enacted after he committed the charged offenses, violated the *ex post facto* clause because it had the effect of increasing his punishment.[13.10]

[13.1] Goldsmith v. Clinton, 48 M.J. 84 (1998).
[13.2] 48 M.J. at 85.
[13.3] *Id.*
[13.4] *Id.* at 85-86.
[13.5] *Id.* at 86, *citing* Unger v. Ziemniak, 27 M.J. 349 (C.M.A. 1989).
[13.6] *Id.* at 87.
[13.7] *Id.*
[13.8] *Id.*
[13.9] *Id. See* Article 138, U.C.M.J. at Appendix 3.
[13.10] 48 M.J. at 90.

Page 825, n. 14. San Antonio Express-News v. Morrow, 44 M.J. 706 (A.F.Ct.Crim.App. 1996) (discussion of court's supervisory authority over Article 32 investigations and ability to issue extraordinary writs).

Page 825, n. 15. McKinney v. Jarvis, 46 M.J. 870 (Army Ct.Crim.App. 1997) (court determined that it had extraordinary writ powers to decide if convening authority had properly appointed Article 32 investigating officer).

Page 826, n. 18. Wilson v. Courter, 46 M.J. 745 (A.F.Ct.Crim.App. 1997) (habeas corpus petition challenged lack of personal jurisdiction over member of National Guard). *See also* Frisk, "The Long Arm of Military Justice: Court-Martial Jurisdiction and the Limits of Power," ARMY LAW., April 1997, at 5.

Page 826. Add text mid-sentence, following footnote 18:

vacation proceedings,[18.1] Article 32 investigations,[18.2]

[18.1] Hobdy v. United States, 46 M.J. 653 (N.M.Ct.Crim.App. 1997); United States v. Ward, 5 M.J. 685 (N.C.M.R. 1978).

[18.2] San Antonio Express-News v. Morrow, 44 M.J. 706 (A.F.Ct.Crim.App. 1996) (court indicated that it had authority to issue extraordinary writ to Article 32 investigating officer involving highly publicized murder case, but declined to do so in an area which the court considered to be a developing area of law).

Page 826, n. 21. Coyle v. Commander, 21st Theatre Army Area Command, 47 M.J. 626 (Army Ct.Crim.App. 1997) (court denied mandamus relief where accused failed to show clear and indisputable right to additional credit for illegal pretrial punishment); Keaton v. Marsh, 43 M.J. 757 (Army Ct.Crim.App. 1996) (accused's writ of habeas corpus granted where court concluded that judge's decision to reconfine accused in absence of new information was not authorized under R.C.M. 305(l)).

Page 827, n. 25. McKinney v. Jarvis, 46 M.J. 870 (Army Ct.Crim.App. 1997) (in case of first impression court denied writ of prohibition where officer, who was normally both the summary and special court-martial convening authority, became accuser and also appointed the Article 32 officer).

Page 827, n. 27. Loving v. Hart, 47 M.J. 438 (1998) (petitioner's request for mandamus challenging his death penalty was denied); Wean v. Holder, 47 M.J. 540 (Army Ct.Crim.App. 1997) (accused not entitled to writ of mandamus where accused failed to show that he was not provided pay for which he was due).

Page 827, n. 28. Ross v. United States, 43 M.J. 770 (N.M.Ct.Crim.App. 1995) (court granted writ of error *coram nobis* to accused who sought to have his case reviewed by court 10 years after it was originally filed; because government could not find authenticated record of trial, court set aside findings and sentence and dismissed the charges).

Page 827, n. 29. McKinney v. Jarvis, 46 M.J. 870 (Army Ct.Crim.App. 1997) (in case of first impression court denied writ of prohibition where officer, who was normally both the summary and special court-martial convening authority, preferred charges and also appointed Article 32 officer; the court indicated that a writ of prohibition is process where superior court prevents an inferior court or tribunal from exceeding its jurisdiction); Smith v. Vanderbush, 47 M.J. 56 (1997) (accused successful in obtaining writ of prohibition for lack of jurisdiction where accused was discharged while pending charges).

Page 827. Add the following text after sentence ending with footnote 32:

In determining whether to grant an extraordinary writ, the courts will normally view that relief as a drastic remedy which should only be invoked in those situations which are truly extraordinary.[32.1] That is, in the courts' view, such relief is not appropriate in the typical case.[32.2] The courts also view extraordinary writs with some hesitation because they can disrupt the normal and orderly trial and appellate procedures.[32.3] Given that view, the petitioner bears a heavy burden of showing a need for extraordinary review of the case[32.4] and that the alleged errors amounted to gross error and constituted judicial usurpation of power.[32.5] And that in turn normally requires that the petitioner show that the complained of action was contrary to statute, settled case law, or valid regulation."[32.6]

[32.1] Coyle v. Commander, 21st Theatre Army Area Command, 47 M.J. 626 (Army Ct.Crim.App. 1997) (petition for extraordinary relief requests court to take exceptional measures); McKinney v. Jarvis, 46 M.J. 870 (Army Ct.Crim.App. 1997); Aviz v. Carter, 36 M.J. 1026 (N.M.C.M.R. 1993); Pearson v. Bloss, 28 M.J. 764 (A.F.C.M.R. 1989).

[32.2] McKinney v. Jarvis, 46 M.J. 870 (Army Ct.Crim.App. 1997).

[32.3] Will v. Calvert Fire Ins. Co., 437 U.S. 655 (1978); McKinney v. Jarvis, 46 M.J. 870 (Army Ct.Crim.App. 1997); Ross v. United States, 43 M.J. 770 (N.M.Ct.Crim.App. 1995).

[32.4] McKinney v. Jarvis, 46 M.J. 870 (Army Ct.Crim.App. 1997); United States v. Mahoney, 36 M.J. 679 (A.F.C.M.R. 1992).

[32.5] San Antonio Express News v. Morrow, 44 M.J. 706 (A.F.Ct.Crim.App. 1996).

[32.6] McKinney v. Jarvis, 46 M.J. 870 (Army Ct.Crim.App. 1997); Evans v. Kilroy, 33 M.J. 730 (A.F.C.M.R. 1991).

§ 17-21. Petition for New Trial.

Page 829, n. 3. United States v. Niles, 45 M.J. 455 (1996) (Court of Criminal Appeals erred in denying petition for new trial based on newly discovered evidence; case remanded for new trial or dismissal of charges).

Page 829. Add the following text after sentence ending with footnote 3:

The *Manual for Courts-Martial* explicitly states, however, that an accused may not use the "newly discovered" ground for seeking a new trial when he or she was found guilty following a plea of guilty.[3.1]

[3.1] *See* R.C.M. 1210(a). This provision was added in the 1998 amendments to the *Manual*. *See generally*, "Amendments to the Manual for Courts-Martial," ARMY LAW., July 1998, at 1. The reasons for the limitation are spelled out in the R.C.M. 1210 Analysis in Appendix 21 to the *Manual for Courts-Martial*.

Page 830. Add the following text after the sentence-ending with footnote 4:

Petitions for new trials are generally disfavored and will not be granted absent a "manifest injustice."[4.1] Thus, the servicemember bears the heavy burden of showing that a new trial is an appropriate remedy.[4.2]

[4.1] United States v. Niles, 45 M.J. 435 (1996) (petitions for new trials are disfavored); United States v. Williams, 37 M.J. 352 (C.M.A. 1993).

[4.2] United States v. Niles, 45 M.J. 435 (1996); United States v. Giambra, 38 M.J. 240 (C.M.A. 1993).

Page 830, n. 6. United States v. Denier, 43 M.J. 693 (A.F.Ct.Crim.App. 1995) (accused filed motion for new trial on issue of command influence after judge denied relief at post-trial Article 39(a) session; court indicated that because judge had already considered substance of motion, it would review decision for abuse of discretion; motion for new trial is not intended as means to relitigate issues raised and ruled upon by trial court).

ANNOTATED BIBLIOGRAPHY

BOOKS

Lurie, *Arming Military Justice: The Origins of the United States Court of Military Appeals, 1775-1950* (1992).

This text (the first of two volumes) provides an extremely insightful historical view of the origins of the United States Court of Military Appeals (now the United States Court of Appeals for the Armed Forces) from 1775 to 1950. The book traces the issue of independent review of courts-martial convictions and the controversy stirred by question of whether any military or civilian court should be permitted, or required, to review military justice convictions.

Lurie, *Pursuing Military Justice: The History of the United States Court of Appeals for the Armed Forces, 1951-1980* (1997).

The focus of this volume, the second in a set of two, is on first three decades of what is often referred to as the supreme court of the miltary justice system. The author notes the political and legal struggles faced by the Court of Appeals in reviewing court-martial convictions.

Schlueter, Jansen, Barry & Arnold, *Military Criminal Procedure Forms* (1997).

This book presents a variety of sample forms, letters, pleadings, checklists, briefs, and motions for military criminal justice practitioners. The text, which provides coverage for processing a case from pretrial investigation through appellate disposition, demonstrates how formats may vary among the services.

PERIODICALS

Symposia

Symposium, "Military Justice Symposium—Volume I," ARMY LAW., April 1998.

This 128-page symposium is the first of two volumes and includes seven short articles on a range of military justice topics; it was authored by the faculty members of the Criminal Law Division at the Army's Judge Advocate School:

> Stitler, "The Power to Prosecute: New Developments in Courts-Martial Jurisdiction," at 1.
> Lovejoy, "Re-interpreting the Rules: Recent Developments in Speedy Trial and Pretrial Restraint," at 10.
> Einwechter, "New Developments in Substantive Criminal Law Under the Uniform Code of Military Justice (1997)," at 20.
> Coe, "'Something Old, Something New, Something Borrowed, Something Blue': Recent Developments in Pretrial and Trial Procedure," at 44.
> Pede, "New Developments in Search and Seizure and Urinalysis," at 80.
> Stitler, "Widening the Door: Recent Developments in Self-Incrimination Law," at 93.
> Moran, "Pyrrhic Victories and Permutations: New Developments in the Sixth Amendment, Discovery, and Mental Responsibility," at 106.

Symposium, "Military Justice Symposium—Volume II," ARMY LAW., May 1998.

This 68-page symposium consists of four articles articles on a range of military justice topics; it was authored by the faculty members of the Criminal Law Division at the Army's Judge Advocate School:

> Henley, "Developments in Evidence III—The Final Chapter," at 1.
> Lovejoy, "The CAAF at a Crossroads: New Developments in Post-Trial Processing," at 25.
> Allen, "Recent Developments in Sentencing Under the Uniform Code of Military Justice," at 39.
> Morris, "'This Better Be Good': The Courts Continue to Tighten the Burden in Unlawful Command Influence Cases," at 49.

Symposium, "Military Justice Symposium I," ARMY LAW., April 1997.

This 149-page symposium, which presents a series of short articles on a range of military justice topics, was authored by the faculty members of the Criminal Law Division at the Army's Judge Advocate School:

> Morris, Foreword.
> Frisk, "The Long Arm of Military Justice: Court-Martial Jurisdiction and the Limits of Power," at 5.
> Frisk, "Walking the Fine Line Between Promptness and Haste: Recent Developments in Speedy Trial and Pretrial Restraint Jurisprudence," at 14.

Coe, "Restating Some Old Rules and Limiting Some Landmarks: Recent Developments in Pretrial and Trial Procedure," at 25.

Barto, "Recent Developments in the Substantive Criminal Law Under the Uniform Code of Military Justice," at 50.

Wright, "'An Old Fashioned Crazy Quilt': New Developments in the Sixth Amendment, Discovery, Mental Responsibility, and Nonjudicial Punishment," at 72.

Henley, "Postcards from the Edge: Privileges, Profiles, Polygraphs, and Other Developments in the Military Rules of Evidence," at 92.

Allen, "New Developments in Sentencing," at 116.

Morris, "'Just One More Thing...' and Other Thoughts on Recent Developments in Post-Trial Processing," at 129.

APPENDIX 3

UNIFORM CODE OF MILITARY JUSTICE

Subchapter VIII. SENTENCES

§ 858. Article 58. Execution of confinement.

Subchapter XII. UNITED STATES COURT OF APPEALS FOR THE ARMED FORCES

§ 943. Article 143. Organization and employees.

Subchapter VIII. SENTENCES

§ 858. Article 58. Execution of confinement.

[**Note**: Article 58 was amended in 1996 by Pub. L. 104-201, § 1068(a)(1), which added the words "(if adjudged by a general court-martial)" following the words "all pay and" and substituted the words "two-thirds of all pay" for the words "two-thirds of all pay and allowances." As the court in *United States v. Pedrazoli*, 45 M.J. 567 (A.F.Ct.Crim.App. 1997), noted, as originally written the words "and allowances" in conjunction with references to special courts-martial, created the possibility that the sentence might exceed the jurisdictional limits of a special court-martial.]

Subchapter XII. UNITED STATES COURT OF APPEALS FOR THE ARMED FORCES

§ 943. Article 143. Organization and employees.

[**Note**: An amendment was made in 1996 to the title of subsection (c). The word "Certain" was substituted for the word "Attorney." Subsection (c)(1) was amended by adding a provision after the first sentence which reads: "A position of employment under the Court that is provided primarily for the service of one judge of the court, reports directly to the judge, and is a position of a confidential character is excepted from the competitive service." Pub. L. 104-201, § 1068(b).]

TABLE OF CASES

A

ABC, Inc. v. Powell, 47 M.J. 363 (1997), — § 7-2(C), n. 74
Acevedo, United States v.
Acosta, United States v.
Adams, United States v.
Agosto, United States v.
Alabama, J.E.B. v.
Alis, United States v.
Anderson, United States v.
Argo, United States v.
Aviz v. Carter, 36 M.J. 1026 (N.M.C.M.R. 1993) — § 17-19, n. 32.1
Aycock, United States v.

B

Baker, United States v.
Barnes, United States v.
Barraza, United States v.
Barrow, United States v.
Bartley, United States v.
Batson v. Kentucky, 476 U.S. 79, 97-98 (1986) — § 15-10 (C)(3), n. 118.11
Becker, United States v.
Bell, United States v.
Biscoe, United States v.
Bivens, United States v.
Bloss, Pearson v.
Bond, United States v.
Boone, United States v.
Bradley, United States v.
Bramer, United States v.
Breeding, United States v.
Brewick, United States v.
Briggs, United States v.
Bright, United States v.
Britt v. North Carolina, 404 U.S. 226, 227 (1971) — § 11-2(A)(3), n. 21.7
Britt, United States v.
Britton, United States v.
Brock, United States v.
Brown, United States v.
Bubonics, United States v.
Buller, United States v.
Burfitt, United States v.

TABLE OF CASES.

Burnette, United States v.
Bygrave, United States v.

C

Calhoun, United States v.
Calloway, United States v.
Calvert Fire Ins. Co., Will v.
Cantrell, United States v.
Carroll, United States v.
Carter, Aviz v.
Carter, United States v.
Casey, United States v.
Cassell, United States v.
Catalani, United States v.
Cavan, United States v.
Chatman, United States v.
Christian, United States v.
Christy, United States v.
Clack, United States v.
Clark, United States v.
Claypoole, United States v.
Clemente, United States v.
Clinkenbeard, United States v.
Clinton, Goldsmith v.
Collins, United States v.
Combs, United States v.
Commander, 21st Theatre Army Area Command, Coyle v.
Cook, United States v.
Cooper, United States v.
Cornelious, United States v.
Cornett, United States v.
Cottrill, United States v.
County of Riverside v. McLaughlin, 500 U.S. 44 (1991) — § 5-9(C), n. 20.1
Courter, Wilson v.
Coyle v. Commander, 21st Theatre Army Area Command, 47 M.J. 626 (Army Ct.Crim.App. 1997) — § 5-10–, nn. 29, 36; § 17-19, nn. 21, 32.1
Craig, United States v.
Crawford, United States v.
Cunningham, United States v.
Curry, United States v.
Curtin, United States v.
Curtis, United States v.

TABLE OF CASES

D

Dale, United States v.
Daulton, United States v.
Davis, United States v.
Denier, United States v.
DeNoyer, United States v.
Diamond, United States v.
Dies, United States v.
Dinatale, United States v.
Dire, United States v.
Dixon, United States v.
Dodd, United States v.
Dolbow, United States v.
Dollente, United States v.
Dowty, United States v.
Drayton, United States v.
Dresen, United States v.
DuBay, United States v.
DuBose, United States v.
Duckworth, United States v.
DuFour, United States v.
Duvall, United States v.

E

Earle, United States v.
Eberle, United States v.
Eby, United States v.
Edwards, United States v.
Elem, Purkett v.
Ellis, United States v.
English, United States v.
Evans v. Kilroy, 33 M.J. 730 (A.F.C.M.R. 1991) § 17-19, n. 32.6

F

Faisca, United States v.
Fegurgur, United States v.
Figura, United States v.
Fisher, United States v.
Fitzgerald, United States v.
Flack, United States v.
Flarity, United States v.
Forester, United States v.

TABLE OF CASES

Fretwell, Lockhart v.
Fricke, United States v.
Fulton, United States v.

G

Gaither, United States v.
Galaviz, United States v.
Gammons, United States v.
Garcia, United States v.
Gargaro, United States v.
Garries, United States v.
Gerlich, United States v.
Giambra, United States v.
Gibson, United States v.
Giles, United States v.
Gillespie, United States v.
Ginn, United States v.
Giroux, United States v.
Goddard, United States v.
Godden, United States v.
Goldsmith v. Clinton, 48 M.J. 84 (1998) — § 17-19, nn. 13.1-13.10
Gonyea, United States v.
Gonzales, United States v.
Gorski, United States v.
Graham, United States v.
Greaves, United States v.
Green, United States v.
Greene, United States v.
Greenwood, McDonough Power Equip., Inc. v.
Greig, United States v.
Griffaw, United States v.
Guess, United States v.
Guest, United States v.

H

Haire, United States v.
Hall, United States v.
Hamilton, United States v.
Handy, United States v.
Haney, United States v.
Hanson, United States v.
Hardy, United States v.
Harness, United States v.

TABLE OF CASES

Harris, United States v.
Hart, Loving v.
Harwood, United States v.
Hatfield, United States v.
Hawkins, United States v
Hayward, United States v.
Heard, United States v.
Henderson, United States v.
Hensler, United States v.
Hernandez v. New York, 500 U.S. 352 (1991) — § 15-10 (C)(3), n. 118.13
Hester, United States v.
Hickok, United States v.
Hicks, United States v.
Higgins, United States v.
Hill, United States v.
Hobdy v. United States, 46 M.J. 653 (N.M.Ct.Crim.App. 1997) — § 17-19, n. 18.1
Hode, United States v.
Hodson, MacDonald v.
Hollingsworth, United States v.
Holt, United States v.
Hood, United States v.
Horne, United States v.
Hoskins, United States v.
Howard, United States v.
Hudson, United States v.
Hughey, United States v.

J

James, United States v.
Jarvis, McKinney v.
Jacobson v. United States, 503 U.S. 540 (1992) — § 2-7(B), n. 24.1
Jefferson, United States v.
Jenkins, United States v.
Jennings, United States v.
Johnson, United States v.
Johnson-Saunders, United States v.
Jones, United States v.
Jordon, United States v.

K

Keaton v. Marsh, 43 M.J. 757 (Army Ct.Crim.App. 1996) — § 5-9(E), n. 61; § 17-19, n. 21
Keith, United States v.

TABLE OF CASES

Kelly, United States v.
Kendig, United States v.
Kentucky, Batson v.
Kilber, United States v.
Kilroy, Evans v.
Kohut, United States v.
Kosek, United States v.
Kyles v. Whitley, 514 U.S. 419 (1995) — § 10-4(A)(4), n. 27; § 10-4(B)(1), n. 28

L

Lamb, United States v.
Lark, United States v.
Lavender, United States v.
Lawrence, United States v.
Leal, United States v.
Lee, United States v.
Lewis, United States v.
Lindsey, United States v.
Liteky v. United States, 510 U.S. 540 (1994) — § 12-2(H), n. 101
Lloyd, United States v.
Lockhart v. Fretwell, 506 U.S. 364 (1993) — § 15-2(B)(3), nn. 36.5-36.8
Lonetree, United States v.
Long, United States v.
Longstreath, United States v.
Lorenzen, United States v.
Loving v. Hart, 47 M.J. 438 (1998) — § 16-3(A), nn. 14, 32.1; § 17-19, n. 27
Loving v. United States, 517 U.S. 748 (1996) — § 1-4, n. 1; § 16-3(A), nn. 3, 14

M

MacDonald v. Hodson, 42 C.M.R. 184 (C.M.A. 1970) — § 7-2(C), n. 81.1; § 15-3, n. 8
Mahoney, United States v.
Mance, United States v.
Mark, United States v.
Marsh, Keaton v.
Marshall, United States v.
Martinez, United States v.
Maxwell, United States v.
May, United States v.
Mayfield, United States v.
Mayhugh, United States v.
McCarthy, United States v.
McCastle, United States v.
McCloskey, United States v.

TABLE OF CASES

McCreight, United States v.
McDonough Power Equip., Inc. v. Greenwood, 464 U.S. 548 (1984) — § 15-10(A), n. 23
McGeeney, United States v.
McKinney v. Jarvis, 46 M.J. 870 (Army Ct.Crim.App. 1997) — § 6-1, n. 10; § 6-2, n. 13; § 6-2(C), n. 15.1; § 7-2(A)(1), n. 14; § 8-2(A), n. 3; § 17-19, nn. 15, 25, 29, 32.1-32.4, 32.6
McLaughlin, County of Riverside v.
Meek, United States v.
Mejia-Alarcon, United States v.
Miles, United States v.
Miller, United States v.
Minyard, United States v.
Mitchell, United States v.
Moore, United States v.
Moreno, United States v.
Morris, United States v.
Morrison, United States v.
Morrow, San Antonio Express-News v.
Moses, United States v.
Mosqueda, United States v.
Moulton, United States v.
Muirhead, United States v.
Murray, United States v.
Mustafa, United States v.

N

Nadel, United States v.
Napoleon, United States v.
Ndanyi, United States v.
Neblock, United States v.
Nelson, United States v.
New York, Hernandez v.
Newbold, United States v.
Nieves, United States v.
Niles, United States v.
North Carolina, Britt v.
Nutter, United States v.

O

Oatney, United States v.
Olinger, United States v.
Outhier, United States v.
Ovando-Moran, United States v.

TABLE OF CASES

Oxfort, United States v.

P

Padgett, United States v.
Page, United States v.
Pearson v. Bloss, 28 M.J. 764 (A.F.C.M.R. 1989) — § 17-19, n. 32.1
Pedrazoli, United States v.
Peebles, United States v.
Peele, United States v.
Perez, United States v.
Perlman, United States v.
Peterson, United States v.
Pierce, United States v.
Pilkington, United States v.
Plumb, United States v.
Poole, United States v.
Pou, United States v.
Powell, ABC, Inc. v.
Powell, United States v.
Price, United States v.
Pritchard, United States v.
Pritchett, United States v.
Province, United States v.
Purkett v. Elem, 514 U.S. 765 (1995) — § 15-10 (C)(3), nn. 118.7, 118.8, 118.12

Q

Quintin, United States v.

R

Radvansky, United States v.
Ramelb, United States v.
Rascoe, United States v.
Ray, United States v.
Reid, United States v.
Reister, United States v.
Rembert, United States v.
Rexroat, United States v.
Reynolds, United States v.
Rhodes, United States v.
Riley, United States v.
Rios, United States v.
Rivera, United States v.
Roberson, United States v.

TABLE OF CASES

Roberts v. United States Jaycees, 468 U.S. 609 (1984) — § 13-3(N)(4), n. 415.1
Robinson, United States v.
Robles-Ramos, United States v.
Rockwood, United States v.
Rodriguez, United States v.
Rogers, United States v.
Romano, United States v.
Rome, United States v.
Ross v. United States, 43 M.J. 770 (N.M.Ct.Crim.App. 1995) — § 17-19, nn. 28, 32.3
Ruffin, United States v.
Ruiz, United States v.
Ruppel, United States v.
Russell, United States v.
Ruth, United States v.
Ryder, United States v.

S

Salazar, United States v.
San Antonio Express-News v. Morrow, 44 M.J. 706 (A.F.Ct.Crim.App. 1996) — § 7-2(C), nn. 81.1, 81.3; § 15-3, n. 8; § 17-19, nn. 14, 18.2, 32.5
Sanchez, United States v.
Santoro, United States v.
Sargeant, United States v.
Schap, United States v.
Schiaffo, United States v.
Schlarb, United States v.
Schnitzer, United States v.
Sebring, United States v.
Shearer, United States v.
Shover, United States v.
Simmons, United States v.
Simoy, United States v.
Smart, United States v.
Smith v Vanderbush, 47 M.J. 56 (1997) — § 4-8(B), n. 11; § 4-8(C)(3), n. 28; § 17-19, n. 29
Smith, United States v.
Smith, Vanderbush v.
Sojfer, United States v.
Solorio v. United States, 483 U.S. 435 (1987) — § 8-3(C)(3), n. 142
Sorbera, United States v.
Sorrell, United States v.
Spann, United States v.
Spurlin, United States v.
Stallworth, United States v.

TABLE OF CASES

Stantas, United States v.
Staten, United States v.
Stockman, United States v.
Strange, United States v.
Strauss, United States v.
Strickland v. Washington, 466 U.S. 668, 694 (1984) — § 15-2(B)(3), nn. 36.2-36.4
Sumrall, United States v.
Sunden, United States v.
Swan, United States v.
Swango, United States v.
Sylvester, United States v.

T

Tarleton, United States v.
Taylor, United States v.
Terry, United States v.
Thomas, United States v.
Thompson, United States v.
Tillar, United States v.
Tilghman, United States v.
Tilly, United States v.
Townsend, United States v.
Travels, United States v.
Trosper, United States v.
Tulloch, United States v.
Tuner, United States v.
Turner, United States v.
Tyson, United States v.

U

Underwood, United States v.
United States v. Acevedo, 46 M.J. 830 (C.G.Ct.Crim.App. 1997) — § 9-2(B)(2), n. 86; § 14-3(C), n. 130
United States v. Acosta, 46 M.J. 670 (N.M.Ct.Crim.App. 1997) — § 15-2(D), nn. 133, 137, 139
United States v. Adams, 33 M.J. 300 (C.M.A. 1991) — § 14-3(B)(2), n. 82.4
United States v. Adams, 44 M.J. 251 (1996) — § 15-13, n. 9
United States v. Agosto, 46 M.J. 705 (A.F.Ct.Crim.App. 1997) — § 2-6(B), n. 33; § 2-6(C), n. 38
United States v. Alis, 47 M.J. 817 (A.F.Ct.Crim.App. 1998) — § 12-2(H), n. 100; § 15-10(B), n. 71
United States v. Anderson, 46 M.J. 540 (N.M.Ct.Crim.App. 1997) — § 13-3(C)(3), n. 143

TABLE OF CASES

United States v. Anderson, 47 M.J. 576 (N.M.Ct.Crim.App. 1997) — § 11-2(A)(3), n. 21.5

United States v. Anderson, 46 M.J. 728 (Army Ct.Crim.App. 1997) — § 14-3(B)(2), n. 84; § 15-3, n. 12

United States v. Argo, 46 M.J. 454 (1997) — § 7-2(A)(1), n. 29; § 13-3(M), nn. 284, 290, 291, 293

United States v. Aycock, 35 C.M.R. 130 (C.M.A. 1964) — § 2-4(A), n. 18.2

United States v. Baker, 43 M.J. 736 (A.F.Ct.Crim.App. 1995) — § 15-15, n. 2; § 15-16(B), n. 27

United States v. Baker, 45 M.J. 538 (A.F.Ct.Crim.App. 1996) — § 5-3(C)(6), n. 85

United States v. Barnes, 44 M.J. 680 (N.M.Ct.Crim.App. 1996) — § 17-8(B)(2), nn. 63, 67

United States v. Barraza, 44 M.J. 622 (N.M.Ct.Crim.App. 1996) — § 17-9(A), n. 11

United States v. Barrow, 42 M.J. 655 (A.F.Ct.Crim.App. 1995), *aff'd on other grounds*, 45 M.J. 478 (1997) — § 15-10(B), n. 48.1; § 17-16(C), n. 15

United States v. Bartley, 47 M.J. 182 (1997) — § 9-2(A)(3), n. 29; § 14-3(C), n. 123

United States v. Becker, 46 M.J. 141 (1997) — § 16-5(D)(5), n. 24.1; § 16-9, n. 10

United States v. Bell, 38 M.J. 358 (C.M.A. 1993) — § 2-7(B), n. 24.1

United States v. Bell, 44 M.J. 403 (1996) — § 7-2(C), nn. 81.4, 81.5

United States v. Bell, 44 M.J. 677 (N.M.Ct.Crim.App. 1996) — § 5-9(D), n. 21

United States v. Bell, 46 M.J. 351 (1997) — § 17-11, n. 9.2

United States v. Biscoe, 47 M.J. 398 (1997) — § 14-3(B)(2), n. 100

United States v. Bivens, 45 M.J. 501 (A.F.Ct.Crim.App. 1996) — § 14-3(D)(4), n. 176.1

United States v. Boce, 488 U.S. 563 (1989) — § 13-3(J), n. 264.2

United States v. Bond, 46 M.J. 86 (1997) — § 2-7(B), n. 42

United States v. Boone, 44 M.J. 742 (Army Ct.Crim.App. 1996) — § 15-2(B)(3), n. 79

United States v. Bradley, 47 M.J. 715 — § 15-10(A), n. 20; — § 6-7, n. 9; § 15-10(C)(3), n. 118.14

United States v. Bramer, 43 M.J. 538 (N.M.Ct.Crim. App. 1995), 45 M.J. 296 — § 13-3(C), n. 30; § 13-3(C)(3), n. 105

United States v. Bramer, 45 M.J. 296 (1996) — § 13-3(C)(4), nn. 175-177; § 17-5, n. 4

United States v. Breeding, 44 M.J. 345 (1996) — § 11-2(B)(1), n. 68

United States v. Brewick, 47 M.J. 730 (N.M.Ct.Crim.App. 1997) — § 8-3(C)(4), n. 160

United States v. Briggs, 48 M.J. 143 (1998) — § 11-4, n. 4

United States v. Bright, 44 M.J. 749 (C.G. Ct.Crim.App. 1996) — § 17-9(A), n. 30

United States v. Britt, 44 M.J. 731 (A.F.Ct.Crim.App. 1996) — § 16-6, n. 12

United States v. Britton, 47 M.J. 195 (1997) — § 6-1(C)(3), nn. 162.2, 162.3; § 13-3(J), nn. 265, 266

United States v. Brock, 46 M.J. 11 (1997) — § 17-16(C), n. 23

United States v. Brown, 45 M.J. 389 (1996) — § 6-7, n. 2; § 13-3(N)(4), nn. 383, 388

United States v. Bubonics, 45 M.J. 93 (1996) — § 5-4(B), n. 52

United States v. Buller, 46 M.J. 467 (1997) — § 17-8(B)(3), n. 77

United States v. Burfitt, 43 M.J. 815 (A.F.Ct.Crim.App. 1996) — § 7-2(B)(4), nn. 46, 56

United States v. Burnette, 29 M.J. 473 (C.M.A. 1990) — § 11-2(A)(3), n. 21.3

United States v. Bygrave, 46 M.J. 491 (1997) — § 13-3(N)(4), n. 418

United States v. Calhoun, 47 M.J. 520 (A.F.Ct.Crim.App. 1997) — § 15-2(B)(3), nn. 28, 102

TABLE OF CASES

United States v. Calloway, 47 M.J. 782 (N.M.Ct.Crim.App. 1998) — § 13-2(E), n. 53; § 13-3(C)(2), nn. 87, 90, 91

United States v. Cantrell, 44 M.J. 711 (A.F.Ct.Crim.App. 1996) — § 16-5(C), n. 27; § 16-8(B), n. 19

United States v. Carroll, 43 M.J. 487 (1996) — § 6-1(C)(3), n. 161

United States v. Carter, 45 M.J. 168 (1996) — § 17-9(A), n. 10

United States v. Carter, 40 M.J. 102 (C.M.A. 1994) — § 15-2(B)(3), nn. 99.1, 99.3

United States v. Casey, 45 M.J. 623 (N.M.Ct.Crim.App. 1996) — § 17-8(B)(1), n. 50

United States v. Cassell, 33 M.J. 448, 450 (C.M.A. 1991) — § 17-2(B)(5), n. 100.16

United States v. Catalani, 46 M.J. 325 (1997) — § 17-8(B)(3), n. 77

United States v. Cavan, 48 M.J. 567 (A.F.Ct.Crim.App. 1997) — § 15-2(B)(3), n. 99.1, 99.2, 99.3

United States v. Chatman, 46 M.J. 321 (1997) — § 17-8(B)(3), nn. 77.1-77.3; § 17-9(A), n. 23.5

United States v. Christian, 43 M.J. 763 (N.M.Ct.Crim.App. 1995) — § 13-3(H), nn. 243, 244

United States v. Christy, 46 M.J. 47 (1997) — § 15-2(B)(3), n. 36.1

United States v. Clack, 48 M.J. 813 (A.F.Ct.Crim.App. 1998) — § 17-15(B), n. 33

United States v. Clark, 45 M.J. 613 (Army Ct.Crim.App. 1996) — § 15-2(B)(3), n. 33

United States v. Claypoole, 46 M.J. 786 (C.G.Ct.Crim.App. 1997) — § 5-3(B), n. 49

United States v. Clemente, 46 M.J. 715 (A.F.Ct.Crim.App. 1997) — § 15-10 (C)(3), nn. 118.11-118.13; § 16-5(D)(5), n. 114; § 17-2(B)(5), nn. 100.6, 100.7

United States v. Clinkenbeard, 44 M.J. 577 (A.F.Ct.Crim.App. 1996) — § 2-6(B), n. 40

United States v. Collins, 44 M.J. 830 (Army Ct.Crim.App. 1996) — § 17-15(B), n. 32

United States v. Combs, 47 M.J. 330 (1997) — § 5-10(A), nn. 1, 6

United States v. Cook, 48 M.J. 64 (1998) — § 15-13, nn. 9, 11

United States v. Cooper, 17 M.J. 1062 (A.F.C.M.R. 1984) — § 17-2(B)(5), n. 100.16

United States v. Cornelious, 41 M.J. 397 (1995) — § 15-2(B)(3), nn. 99.1, 99.3

United States v. Cornett, 47 M.J. 128 (1997) — § 12-2(H), n. 100; § 15-2(B)(3), n. 88

United States v. Cottrill, 45 M.J. 485 (1997) — § 5-4(B), n. 52; § 13-4(A), n. 19

United States v. Craig, 48 M.J. 77 (1998) — § 9-3, n. 6

United States v. Crawford, 46 M.J. 771 (C.G.Ct.Crim.App. 1997) — § 6-5(A), n. 23

United States v. Cunningham, 44 M.J. 758 (N.M.Ct.Crim.App. 1996) — § 17-8(B), n. 24

United States v. Curtin, 44 M.J. 439 (1996) — § 11-4, n. 12

United States v. Curry, 48 M.J. 115 (1998) — § 5-3(C)(5), n. 81

United States v. Curtis, 38 M.J. 530 (N.M.C.M.R. 1993) — § 16-3(A), n. 24

United States v. Curtis, 44 M.J. 106 (1996), *rev'd on other grounds on reconsideration*, 46 M.J. 129 (1997) (per curiam) — § 1-7, n. 7; § 5-3(C)(7), n. 99; § 8-3(C)(2), n. 131; § 8-3(C)(3), nn. 142, 143; § 13-5(C), n. 31; § 15-2(B)(3), nn. 65, 77, 106.2;§ 15-10(B), n. 62; § 15-14(B), n. 28; § 16-3(A), nn. 24, 34.1, 34.2

United States v. Dale, 42 M.J. 384 (1995) — § 15-10(B), nn. 48.1, 78.4

United States v. Daulton, 45 M.J. 212 (1996) — § 15-10(B), nn. 48.1, 72, 78.1

United States v. Davis, 46 M.J. 551 (N.M.Ct.Crim.App. 1997) — § 9-2(B), nn. 35, 38.1-38.4; § 9-2(B)(1), n. 40

United States v. Davis, 47 M.J. 707 (N.M.Ct.Crim.App. 1997) — § 15-2(B)(3), n. 78

United States v. Davis, 47 M.J. 484 (1998) — § 1-1(B), n. 34

TABLE OF CASES

United States v. Denier, 43 M.J. 693 (A.F.Ct.Crim.App. 1995) — § 6-7, nn. 9, 13; § 15-10(B), nn. 48.1; § 17-21, n. 6
United States v. Denier, 47 M.J. 253 (1997) — § 6-7, n. 7
United States v. DeNoyer, 44 M.J. 619 (Army Ct.Crim.App. 1996) — § 15-10(A), n. 19
United States v. Diamond, 18 M.J. 305 (C.M.A. 1984) — § 17-4(B), n. 55
United States v. Dies, 42 M.J. 847 (N.M.Ct.Crim. App. 1995), *reversed at* 45 M.J. 644 (1996) — § 13-3(C)(3), n. 148
United States v. Dies, 45 M.J. 376 (1996) — § 13-3(C)(3), nn. 154.1, 165.1-165.3
United States v. Dinatale, 44 M.J. 325 (1996) — § 15-10(B), n. 48.1
United States v. Dire, 46 M.J. 804 (C.G. Ct.Crim.App. 1997) — § 3-3(C), n. 27
United States v. Dixon, 45 M.J. 104 (1996) — § 9-3, n. 4
United States v. Dodd, 46 M.J. 864 (Army Ct.Crim.App. 1997) — § 16-13, n. 4
United States v. Dolbow, 44 M.J. 814 (A.F.Ct.Crim.App. 1996) — § 16-2(D), n. 42
United States v. Dollente, 45 M.J. 234 (1996) — § 13-5(L), nn. 143.1-143.3
United States v. Dowty, 46 M.J. 845 (N.M.Ct.Crim.App. 1997) — § 13-2(G)(2), n. 108; § 13-3(B), n. 17.1
United States v. Drayton, 45 M.J. 180 (1996) — § 6-4(A), n. 8; 6-5(B), n. 24
United States v. Dresen, 47 M.J. 122 (1997) — § 17-8(B), n. 12
United States v. DuBay, 37 C.M.R. 411 (C.M.A. 1967) — § 15-2(B)(3), n. 106.1
United States v. DuBose, 47 M.J. 386 (1998) — § 13-3(D), n. 188
United States v. Duckworth, 45 M.J. 549 (C.G. Ct.Crim.App. 1996) — § 17-4(B), n. 55
United States v. DuFour, 43 M.J. 772 (N.M.Ct.Crim.App. 1995) — § 5-3(B), n. 38; § 5-3(C)(6), n. 86
United States v. Duvall, 47 M.J. 189 (1997) — § 13-4(A), nn. 18, 19
United States v. Earle, 46 M.J. 823 (A.F.Ct.Crim.App. 1997) — § 6-1(C)(3), n. 165; § 13-3(J), nn. 261, 264.1
United States v. Eberle, 44 M.J. 374 (1996) — § 14-3(D)(4), n. 145
United States v. Eby, 44 M.J. 425 (1996) — § 15-10(C)(2), nn. 99, 100
United States v. Edwards, 43 M.J. 619 (N.M.Ct.Crim.App. 1995) — § 3-4, n. 3
United States v. Edwards, 45 M.J. 114 (1996) — § 17-8(B), nn. 15, 17, 23
United States v. Edwards, 46 M.J. 41 (1997) — § 3-4, nn. 3.1-3.7
United States v. Ellis, 47 M.J. 801 (N.M.Ct.Crim.App. 1998) — § 14-3(D)(4), n. 148
United States v. Ellis, 47 M.J. 20 (1997) — § 15-2(B)(3), nn. 85; 100, 101; § 17-2(B)(3), n. 86
United States v. English, 47 M.J. 215 (1997) — § 13-5(A), n. 15
United States v. Faisca, 46 M.J. 276 (1997) — § 5-4(B), n. 50
United States v. Fegurgur, 43 M.J. 871 (Army Ct.Crim.App. 1996) — § 2-7(B), nn. 24, 24.1
United States v. Figura, 44 M.J. 308 (1996) — § 14-3(B)(4), n. 114, n. 116
United States v. Fisher, 45 M.J. 159 (1996) — § 6-5(A), nn. 1, 23; § 6-7, n. 1; § 17-9(B), n. 42
United States v. Fitzgerald, 44 M.J. 434 (1996) — § 15-14(B), n. 41; § 15-14(D), n. 54
United States v. Flack, 47 M.J. 415 (1997) — § 15-2(B)(3), n. 72
United States v. Flarity, 48 M.J. 545 (N.M.Ct.Crim.App. 1998) — § 13-3(C), n. 23
United States v. Forester, 48 M.J. 1 (1998) — § 9-2(A)(3), n. 29; § 9-2(B)(2), n. 65
United States v. Fricke, 48 M.J. 547 (N.M.Ct.Crim.App. 1998) — § 14-2, n. 12

TABLE OF CASES

United States v. Fulton, 44 M.J. 100 (1996) — § 15-10(B), nn. 68, 71
United States v. Gaither, 45 M.J. 349, 351 (1996) — § 5-9(E), nn. 54.1-54.8
United States v. Galaviz, 46 M.J. 548 (N.M.Ct.Crim.App. 1997) — § 17-4(A), n. 41
United States v. Gammons, 47 M.J. 766 (C.G. Ct.Crim.App. 1997) — § 3-3(C), n. 27
United States v. Garcia, 44 M.J. 748 (C.G.Ct.Crim.App. 1996) — § 17-2(B)(3), n. 88; § 17-9(A), n. 25
United States v. Gargaro, 45 M.J. 99 (1996) — § 13-3(M), n. 284; § 16-5(D)(1), n. 55
United States v. Garries, 22 M.J. 288 (C.M.A. 1986) — § 11-2(A)(3), nn. 21.3, 24.1
United States v. Gerlich, 45 M.J. 309 (1996) — § 6-4(C), n. 18; § 6-7, n. 16
United States v. Giambra, 38 M.J. 240 (C.M.A. 1993) — § 17-21, n. 4.2
United States v. Gibson, 46 M.J. 77, 78 (1997) — § 15-2(B)(3), n. 36.1
United States v. Giles, 48 M.J. 60 (1998) — § 15-10(B), n. 51
United States v. Gillespie, 47 M.J. 750 (A.F.Ct.Crim.App. 1997) — § 15-2(B)(3), n. 71; 15-14(B), n. 45
United States v. Ginn, 47 M.J. 236 (1997) — § 15-2(B)(3), nn. 106.3-106.5; § 17-15(B), nn. 17, 31
United States v. Giroux, 37 M.J. 553 (A.C.M.R. 1993) — § 17-2(B)(5), n. 100.16
United States v. Goddard, 47 M.J. 581 (N.M.Ct.Crim.App. 1997) — § 2-8(B), n. 12; § 15-2(D), n. 133
United States v. Godden, 44 M.J. 716 (A.F.Ct.Crim.App. 1996) — § 16-5(B), n. 10
United States v. Gonyea, 44 M.J. 811 (A.F.Ct.Crim.App. 1996) — § 17-8(B)(3), n. 76
United States v. Gonzales, 39 M.J. 459 (C.M.A. 1994) — § 11-2(A)(3), nn. 21.5, 21.6
United States v. Gonzales, 46 M.J. 667 (N.M.Ct.Crim.App. 1997) — § 13-3(B), n. 8
United States v. Gorski, 47 M.J. 370 (1997) — § 16-3(C), n. 55.1; § 16-3(D), n. 57; § 17-2(B)(2), n. 40
United States v. Graham, 46 M.J. 583 (A.F.Ct.Crim.App. 1997) — § 17-8(B)(3), n. 74
United States v. Greaves, 46 M.J. 133 (1997) — § 16-9, n. 10
United States v. Green, 44 M.J. 93 (1996) — § 17-2(B)(3), n. 58
United States v. Greene, 36 M.J. 274 (C.M.A. 1993) — § 15-10 (C)(3), nn. 118.12, 118.13
United States v. Greig, 44 M.J. 356 (1996) — § 14-3(D)(4), n. 145
United States v. Griffaw, 46 M.J. 791 (A.F.Ct.Crim.App. 1997) — § 17-8(B)(2), n. 63; § 17-9(E), n. 81
United States v. Guess, 48 M.J. 69 (1998) — § 1-1(B), n. 18.1
United States v. Guest, 46 M.J. 778 (Army Ct.Crim.App. 1997) — § 4-8(B), n. 12
United States v. Haire, 44 M.J. 520 (C.G.Ct.Crim.App. 1996) — § 17-2(B)(3), n. 67
United States v. Hall, 45 M.J. 546 (Army Ct.Crim.App. 1997) — § 5-3(F), n. 161; § 13-2(G)(2), n. 93.1
United States v. Hall, 46 M.J. 145 (1997) — § 16-9, n. 10
United States v. Hamilton, 47 M.J. 32 (1997) — § 17-8(B), n. 15
United States v. Handy, 48 M.J. 590 (A.F.Ct.Crim.App. 1997) — § 14-3(D)(4), n. 146
United States v. Haney, 45 M.J. 447 (1996) — § 17-8(B)(3), n. 77
United States v. Hanson, 24 M.J. 377 (C.M.A. 1987) — § 14-3(D)(4), n. 148
United States v. Hardy, 44 M.J. 507 (A.F.Ct.Crim.App. 1996) — § 17-8(B)(3), n. 90
United States v. Hardy, 46 M.J. 67 (1997) — § 15-14(C), nn. 52.1-52.4

TABLE OF CASES

United States v. Harness, 44 M.J. 593 (N.M.Ct.Crim.App. 1996) — § 8-3(B)(1), n. 43; § 15-2(B)(3), nn. 45, 48
United States v. Harris, 8 M.J. 52 (C.M.A. 1979) — § 14-3(D)(4), n. 146.3
United States v. Harris, 13 M.J. 288 (C.M.A. 1982) — § 15-10(B), n. 78.1
United States v. Harwood, 46 M.J. 26 (1997) — § 13-3(J), n. 264.2, n. 264.3
United States v. Hatfield, 44 M.J. 22 (1996) — § 13-3(C)(2), nn. 89, 92, 96
United States v. Hawkins, 24 M.J. 257 (1987) — § 8-3(D), n. 174.1
United States v. Hayward, 47 M.J. 381 (1997) — § 6-1(B)(3), n. 90
United States v. Henderson, 44 M.J. 232 (1996) — § 2-4(F), n. 51
United States v. Hensler, 44 M.J. 184 (1996) — § 15-14(B), n. 34.1
United States v. Hester, 47 M.J. 461 (1998) — § 5-3(B), n. 38
United States v. Hickok, 45 M.J. 142 (1996) — § 17-8(B)(3), nn. 83.1-83.3
United States v. Hicks, 47 M.J. 90 (1997) — § 15-2(B)(3), nn. 85, 102; § 17-2(B)(3), nn. 86, 86.2, 86.3
United States v. Higgins, 40 M.J. 67 (1994) — § 14-3(B)(2), nn. 82.1, 82.2
United States v. Hill, 45 M.J. 245 (1996) — § 15-12(B), n. 21
United States v. Hill, 46 M.J. 567 (A.F.Ct.Crim.App. 1997) — § 2-4(A), n. 17; § 2-4(B), n. 23
United States v. Hode, 44 M.J. 816 (A.F.Ct.Crim.App. 1996) — § 2-4(C), n. 33
United States v. Hollingsworth, 44 M.J. 688 (C.G.Ct.Crim.App. 1996) — § 16-5(D)(5), n. 116; § 17-2(B)(3), n. 80
United States v. Holt, 46 M.J. 853 (N.M.Ct.Crim.App. 1997) — § 7-2(A)(1), n. 29.1
United States v. Hood, 47 M.J 95 (1997) — § 15-2(B)(3), n. 85; § 17-2(B)(3), nn. 86, 86.1, 86.3, 86.4
United States v. Horne, 44 M.J. 216 (1996) — § 12-2(H), n. 101
United States v. Hoskins, 29 M.J. 402 (C.M.A. 1990) — § 14-3(D)(4), n. 176.1
United States v. Howard, 47 M.J. 104 (1997) — § 17-8(B)(3), n. 83
United States v. Hudson, 46 M.J. 226 (1997) — § 17-11, n. 5
United States v. Hughey, 46 M.J. 152 (1997) — § 2-4(A), nn. 2, 3
United States v. James, 47 M.J. 641 (Army Ct.Crim.App. 1997) — § 13-5(A), n. 15
United States v. Jefferson, 44 M.J. 312 (1996) — § 15-10(A), nn. 6, 20, 22
United States v. Jenkins, 44 M.J. 596 (N.M.Ct.Crim.App. 1996) — § 2-4(B), n. 28
United States v. Jennings, 44 M.J. 658 (C.G.Ct.Crim.App. 1996) — § 17-8(B)(1), n. 47; § 17-8(B)(2), n. 63
United States v. Johnson, 35 M.J. 17 (C.M.A. 1992) — § 13-5(L), n. 143.1
United States v. Johnson, 45 M.J. 88 (1996) — § 2-2(B), n. 10; § 2-2(E)(7), n. 104; § 2-4(F), nn. 61.1, 61.2, 61.3, 61.4
United States v. Johnson, 47 C.M.R. 402 (C.M.A. 1973) — § 11-2(A)(3), n. 21.3
United States v. Johnson, 46 M.J. 253 (1997) — § 6-7, n. 11
United States v. Johnson-Saunders, 48 M.J. 74 (1998) — § 17-8(B), n. 15
United States v. Jones, 43 M.J. 708 (A.F.Ct.Crim.App. 1995) — § 15-23 n. 1
United States v. Jones, 44 M.J. 242 (1996) — § 17-8(B)(3), nn. 74, 76, 77, 77.3
United States v. Jones, 46 M.J. 815 (N.M.Ct.Crim.App. 1997) — § 14-3(E), n. 177; § 15-10(B), n. 68
United States v. Jones, 47 M.J. 725 (A.F.Ct.Crim.App. 1997) — § 17-8(B), n. 10
United States v. Jordon, 44 M.J. 847 (N.M.Ct.Crim.App. 1996) — § 17-8(B)(3), n. 77

TABLE OF CASES

United States v. Keith, 48 M.J. 563 (C.G. Ct.Crim.App. 1998) — § 14-3(B)(2), n. 82
United States v. Kelly, 39 M.J. 235 (C.M.A. 1994) — § 11-2(A)(3), n. 21.3
United States v. Kelly, 45 M.J. 259 (1996) — § 1-1(B), n. 16; § 3-8(B), nn. 8, 13
United States v. Kendig, 36 M.J. 291, 296 (C.M.A. 1993) — § 15-2(B)(3), n. 48.1
United States v. Kilber, 43 M.J. 725 (Army Ct.Crim.App. 1995) — § 15-2(B)(3), n. 101
United States v. Kohut, 44 M.J. 245 (1996) — § 4-12(A), nn. 5, 7, 10
United States v. Kosek, 46 M.J. 349 (1997) — § 8-3(D), n. 174.1
United States v. Lamb, 44 M.J. 779 (N.M.Ct.Crim.App. 1996) — § 5-10(D), n. 32
United States v. Lamb, 47 M.J. 384 (1997) — § 5-9(D), n. 26
United States v. Lark, 47 M.J. 435 (1998) — § 14-3(B)(2), n. 100; § 14-3(D)(4), n. 147
United States v. Lavender, 46 M.J. 485 (1997) — § 15-10(A), n. 30; § 15-10(B), nn. 68, 78.2-78.4
United States v. Lawrence, 47 M.J. 572 (N.M.Ct.Crim.App. 1997) — § 15-13, nn. 16, 32
United States v. Leal, 44 M.J. 235 (1996) — § 17-8(B)(3), nn. 73-76
United States v. Lee, 43 M.J. 794 (N.M.Ct.Crim.App. 1995) — § 4-8(A), n. 8; § 16-3(D), n. 71; § 17-9(A), n. 10, n. 11
United States v. Lewis, 46 M.J. 338 (1997) — § 8-3(C)(4), n. 153
United States v. Lewis, 42 M.J. 1 (1995) — § 17-2(B)(3), n. 86.3
United States v. Lindsey, 48 M.J. 93 (1998) — § 15-2(B)(3), n. 99
United States v. Lloyd, 43 M.J. 886 (A.F.Ct.Crim.App. 1996), *aff'd on other grounds*, 46 M.J. 19 (1997) — § 13-3(J), nn. 263, 264.1, 264.2
United States v. Lonetree, 31 M.J. 849 (N.M.C.M.R. 1990) — § 17-2(B)(5), n. 100.13
United States v. Long, 46 M.J. 783 (Army Ct.Crim.App. 1997) — § 2-4(E), n. 46
United States v. Longstreath, 42 M.J. 806 (N.M.Ct.Crim. App. 1995), *aff'd on other grounds*, 45 M.J. 366 (1996) — § 10-4(B)(5), n. 57
United States v. Longstreath, 45 M.J. 366 (1996) — § 15-12(A), n. 8
United States v. Lorenzen, 47 M.J. 8 (1997) — § 15-2(B)(3), nn. 59, 71, 72, 76, 107
United States v. Mahoney, 36 M.J. 679 (A.F.C.M.R. 1992) — § 17-19, n. 32.4
United States v. Mance, 47 M.J. 742 (N.M.Ct.Crim.App. 1997) — § 15-13, nn. 5, 19
United States v. Mark, 47 M.J. 99 (1997) — § 17-8(B)(3), n. 96
United States v. Marshall, 45 M.J. 268 (1996) — § 3-5(B)(2), n. 8; § 3-5(C)(2), n. 33; § 3-5(D)(2), n. 75; § 3-5(E)(2), n. 105; § 15-2(B)(3), nn. 48.1, 58
United States v. Martinez, 42 M.J. 327 (1996) — § 16-3(D), n. 63
United States v. Maxwell, 45 M.J. 406 (1996) — § 5-3(A), n. 14; § 6-7, n. 12; § 13-3(N)(4), n. 367
United States v. May, 47 M.J. 478 (1998) — 17-14, n. 11.1
United States v. Mayfield, 45 M.J. 176 (1996) — § 4-15(A), n. 5; § 12-3(A), n. 11
United States v. Mayhugh, 44 M.J. 363 (1996) — § 13-5(G)(1), n. 90
United States v. McCarthy, 47 M.J. 162 (1997) — § 5-10(C), n. 16
United States v. McCloskey, 31 C.M.R. 207 (C.M.A. 1962) — § 17-9(A), n. 23.2
United States v. McCastle, 43 M.J. 438 (1996) — § 15-2(B)(3), n. 63
United States v. McCreight, 43 M.J. 483 (1996) — § 2-8(B), n. 8
United States v. McGeeney, 44 M.J. 418 (1996) — § 5-4(C), n. 56; § 13-3(H), n. 242
United States v. Meek, 44 M.J. 1 (1996) — § 13-3(M), n. 290, nn. 292-293, n. 295
United States v. Mejia-Alarcon, 995 F.2d 982, 987-88 (10th Cir. 1993) — § 13-5(L), n. 143.3

TABLE OF CASES

United States v. Miles, 47 M.J. 683 (N.M.Ct.Crim.App. 1997) — § 15-10(A), n. 23
United States v. Miller, 44 M.J. 549 (A.F.Ct.Crim.App. 1996) — § 11-2(B)(1), n. 61; § 12-2(F)(2), n. 58; § 15-2(E), n. 152
United States v. Miller, 44 M.J. 582 (A.F.Ct.Crim.App. 1996) — § 8-3(D), n. 173
United States v. Miller, 45 M.J. 149 (1996) — § 17-2(B), n. 11; § 17-8(B)(3), nn. 83, 83.3
United States v. Miller, 46 M.J. 80 (1997) — § 5-4(B), n. 29.1
United States v. Miller, 47 M.J. 352 (1997) — § 2-6(A), nn.25.1, 25.2; § 11-2(A)(1), n. 6; § 11-2(B)(1), n. 61; § 12-2(F)(2), n. 58; § 13-5(K), n. 133; § 15-2(E), n. 152; § 15-4(A), n. 5
United States v. Miller, 46 M.J. 248 (1997) — § 17-16(C), n. 15
United States v. Miller, 48 M.J. 49 (1998) — § 5-4(B), nn. 23, 30
United States v. Minyard, 46 M.J. 229 (1997) — § 15-10(B), nn. 67, 71, 78.1
United States v. Mitchell, 46 M.J. 840 (N.M.Ct.Crim.App. 1997) — § 9-2(A)(3), n. 29; § 9-2(B)(1), n. 46; § 9-2(D), n. 85; § 17-9(D), n. 64
United States v. Moore, 45 M.J. 652 (A.F.Ct.Crim.App. 1996) — § 5-3, n. 8
United States v. Moreno, 46 M.J. 216 (1997) — § 6-1(B)(2), n. 81
United States v. Morris, 47 M.J. 695 (N.M.Ct.Crim.App. 1997) — § 10-4(A)(4), nn. 23, 27
United States v. Morris, 44 M.J. 841 (Army Ct.Crim.App. 1996) — § 5-4(B), n. 52
United States v. Morrison, 41 M.J. 482 (1995) — § 13-3(J), n. 263; 16-2(D), n. 42
United States v. Moses, 45 M.J. 132 (1996) — § 5-4(B), n. 42
United States v. Mosqueda, 43 M.J. 491 (1996) — § 15-10(B), n. 67; § 15-10(C)(2), nn. 94, 97
United States v. Moulton, 47 M.J. 227 (1997) — § 15-2(B)(3), n. 101
United States v. Mustafa, 22 M.J. 165 (C.M.A. 1986) — § 11-2(A)(3), n. 21.3
United States v. Muirhead, 48 M.J. 527 (N.M.Ct.Crim.App. 1998) — § 5-4(B), n. 23
United States v. Murray, 45 M.J. 554 (N.M.Ct.Crim.App. 1996) — § 5-4(B), n. 52
United States v. Nadel, 46 M.J. 682 (N.M.Ct.Crim.App. 1997) — § 5-4(B), n. 49
United States v. Napoleon, 46 M.J. 279 (1997) — § 15-10(A), n. 30; § 15-10(B), nn. 48.1, 57, 78.1-78.4
United States v. Ndanyi, 45 M.J. 315 (1996) — § 11-2(A)(3), nn. 21.1-21.3, 21.7, 21.8, 24
United States v. Neblock, 45 M.J. 191 (1996) — § 6-1(C)(3), n. 153, n. 161
United States v. Nelson, 46 M.J. 764 (A.F.Ct.Crim.App. 1997) — § 17-11, n. 5
United States v. Newbold, 45 M.J. 109 (1996) — § 6-4(E), n. 28; § 6-7, n. 11
United States v. Nieves, 44 M.J. 96 (1996) — § 2-4(A), nn. 2, 5, 18.1
United States v. Niles, 45 M.J. 455 (1996) — § 17-21, n. 3, n. 4.1
United States v. Nutter, 22 M.J. 727 — § 17-2(B)(5), n. 100.16
United States v. Oatney, 45 M.J. 185 (1996) — § 6-1(C)(3), n. 162; § 16-2(D), n. 39
United States v. Olinger, 45 M.J. 644 (N.M.Ct.Crim.App. 1996) — § 13-3(C)(3), n. 133
United States v. Outhier, 45 M.J. 326 (1996) — § 14-3(B)(2), n. 82.3
United States v. Ovando-Moran, 44 M.J. 753 (N.M.Ct.Crim.App. 1996) — § 15-10(B), n. 73; § 15-16(B), n. 21
United States v. Oxfort, 44 M.J. 337 (1996) — § 5-4(A)(2), n. 13.1
United States v. Padgett, 45 M.J. 520 (C.G. Ct.Crim.App. 1996) — § 2-4(A), n. 17; § 13-3(N)(4), n. 415.1

TABLE OF CASES

United States v. Page, 43 M.J. 804 (A.F.Ct.Crim.App. 1995) — § 2-5, n. 2; § 2-8(B), n. 5; § 6-1(B)(2), n. 82; § 13-5(E), n. 59, n. 60
United States v. Pedrazoli, 45 M.J. 567 (A.F.Ct.Crim.App. 1997) — § 16-3(C), n. 55.1; § 17-9(C), n. 53; App. 3, § 858
United States v. Peebles, 3 M.J. 177 (C.M.A. 1977) — § 15-2(A), n. 2.1
United States v. Peele, 46 M.J. 866 (Army Ct.Crim.App. 1997) — § 14-3(D)(5), n. 157
United States v. Perez, 45 M.J. 323 (1996) — § 5-8, n. 9; § 5-9(D), n. 24
United States v. Perlman, 44 M.J. 615 (N.M.Ct.Crim.App. 1996) — § 17-9(D), n. 73
United States v. Peterson, 47 M.J. 231 (1997) — § 14-3(D)(4), n. 152
United States v. Pierce, 40 M.J. 149 (C.M.A. 1994) — § 17-8(B)(3), n. 83.3
United States v. Pilkington, 48 M.J. 523 (N.M.Ct.Crim.App. 1998) — § 9-2, n. 1; § 14-3(C), n. 123; § 17-2(B)(5), nn. 100.12, 100.15, 100.16, 100.18-100.23
United States v. Plumb, 47 M.J. 771 (A.F.Ct.Crim.App. 1997) — § 6-3(C), n. 23; § 6-5(B), n. 28; § 6-7, nn. 7, 16; § 7-3(B), n. 30; § 17-8(B), n. 24
United States v. Poole, 47 M.J. 17 (1997) — § 15-14(D), n. 50
United States v. Pou, 43 M.J. 778 (A.F.Ct.Crim.App. 1995) — § 4-8(B), n. 13; § 4-8(C)(3), n. 27; § 13-3(B), n. 11
United States v. Powell, 45 M.J. 637 (N.M.Ct.Crim.App. 1997) — § 16-5(D)(4), n. 97
United States v. Price, 48 M.J. 181 (1998) — § 12-4, nn. 10, 12, 16
United States v. Price, 44 M.J. 430 (1996) — § 5-4(B), n. 42
United States v. Pritchard, 45 M.J. 126 (1996) — § 2-9(D), n. 61, n. 63; § 14-3(D)(4), n. 146.3; § 15-16(A), n. 11.1
United States v. Pritchett, 48 M.J. 609 (N.M.Ct.Crim.App. 1998) — § 15-10(C)(3), n. 108
United States v. Province, 42 M.J. 821 (N.M.C.Ct.Crim.App. 1995), *aff'd on other grounds*, 45 M.J. 359 (1996) — § 6-1(C), n. 104; § 13-3(B), n. 9, n. 18
United States v. Quintin, 47 M.J. 798 (N.M.Ct.Crim.App. 1998) — § 17-2(B)(5), n. 100.11
United States v. Radvansky, 45 M.J. 226 (1996) — § 5-3(C)(6), n. 85
United States v. Ramelb, 44 M.J. 625 (Army Ct.Crim.App. 1996) — § 14-3(B)(4), n. 118
United States v. Rascoe, 31 M.J. 544 (N.M.C.M.R. 1990) — § 17-2(B)(5), n. 100.16
United States v. Ray, 44 M.J. 835 (Army Ct.Crim.App. 1996) — § 14-3(B)(2), n. 70
United States v. Reid, 46 M.J. 236 (1997) — § 4-8(C)(3), n. 28
United States v. Reister, 44 M.J. 409 (1996) — § 5-3(C)(6), n. 88
United States v. Rembert, 43 M.J. 837 (Army Ct.Crim.App. 1996) — § 15-2(A), n. 2.1
United States v. Rexroat, 38 M.J. 292 (C.M.A. 1993) — § 5-9(C), n. 20.1; §5-9(D), n. 21
United States v. Reynolds, 44 M.J. 726 (Army Ct.Crim.App. 1996) — § 12-1, n. 6; § 12-2(C), n. 11
United States v. Rhodes, 47 M.J. 790 (Army Ct.Crim.App. 1998) — § 14-3(E), n. 177; § 15-16(A), n. 6
United States v. Riley, 47 M.J. 276 (1997) — § 5-4(A)(3), n. 19
United States v. Rios, 45 M.J. 558 (A.F.Ct.Crim.App. 1997) — § 5-4(B), n. 42, n. 43
United States v. Rivera, 44 M.J. 527 (A.F.Ct.Crim.App. 1996), *aff'd*, 46 M.J. 52 (1997)— § 9-2(A)(3), n. 35; § 9-2(B)(1), n. 42
United States v. Rivera, 46 M.J. 52 (1997) — § 9-2(B)(1), n. 42; § 9-2(B)(2), n. 65
United States v. Roberson, 43 M.J. 732 (A.F.Ct.Crim.App. 1995) — § 5-9(C), n. 18
United States v. Roberson, 46 M.J. 826 (A.F.Ct.Crim.App. 1997) — § 13-3(J), n. 264.2

TABLE OF CASES

United States v. Robinson, 39 M.J. 88 (C.M.A. 1994) — § 11-2(A)(3), n. 21.3
United States v. Robinson, 47 M.J. 506 (N.M.Ct.Crim.App. 1997) — § 13-3(C)(3), n. 118
United States v. Robles-Ramos, 47 M.J. 474 (1998) — § 15-13, n. 9
United States v. Rockwood, 48 M.J. 501 (Army Ct.Crim.App. 1998) — § 15-3, n. 16; 15-14(B), n. 26
United States v. Rodriguez, 44 M.J. 766 (N.M.Ct.Crim.App. 1996) — § 5-3(C)(6), n. 87; § 5-3(C)(8), nn. 108, 111; § 5-4(B), n. 43
United States v. Rogers, 47 M.J. 135 (1997) — § 5-4(B), n. 26
United States v. Romano, 46 M.J. 269 (1997) — § 1-1(B), n. 18.1; § 10-4(B)(1), n. 28
United States v. Rome, 47 M.J. 467 (1998) — § 15-10(B), n. 48.1
United States v. Ruffin, 48 M.J. 211 (1998) — § 13-3(C)(3), n. 125
United States v. Ruiz, 46 M.J. 503 (A.F.Ct.Crim.App. 1997) — § 15-10(C)(1), nn. 85, 88; § 15-10(C)(3), nn. 118.1, 118.5, 118.6
United States v. Ruppel, 45 M.J. 578 (A.F.Ct.Crim.App. 1997) — § 5-10(D), n. 37
United States v. Russell, 47 M.J. 412 (1997) — § 6-1(B), n. 60
United States v. Ruth, 46 M.J. 1 (1997) — § 11-2(B)(1), n. 59
United States v. Ryder, 44 M.J. 9 (1996) — § 17-15, n. 3
United States v. Salazar, 44 M.J. 464 (1996) — § 5-3(C)(6), n. 96
United States v. Sanchez, 47 M.J. 794 (N.M.Ct.Crim.App. 1998) — § 16-5(D)(3), n. 72
United States v. Santoro, 46 M.J. 344 (1997) — § 17-4, n. 33; § 17-11, n. 9.1
United States v. Sargeant, 47 M.J. 367 (1997) — § 1-1(B), n. 16
United States v. Schap, 44 M.J. 512 (Army Ct.Crim.App. 1996) — § 13-4(A), n. 19
United States v. Schiaffo, 43 M.J. 835 (Army Ct.Crim.App. 1996) — § 17-9(C), n. 57
United States v. Schlarb, 46 M.J. 708 (N.M.Ct.Crim.App. 1997) — § 6-7, n. 13; § 17-11, n. 6
United States v. Schnitzer, 44 M.J. 380 (1996) — § 6-5(C), n. 54
United States v. Sebring, 44 M.J. 805 (N.M.Ct.Crim.App. 1996) — § 10-4(A)(4), n. 27; § 10-4(B)(1), n. 28
United States v. Shearer, 44 M.J. 330 (1996) — § 14-3(B)(2), n. 79, n. 82.2
United States v. Shover, 45 M.J. 119 (1996) — § 5-3(D)(1), n. 119
United States v. Simmons, 48 M.J. 193 (1998) — § 4-12(A), n. 9.1; § 16-6, n. 23.1
United States v. Simoy, 46 M.J. 592 (A.F.Ct.Crim.App. 1996) — § 7-2(B)(6), n. 69; § 16-6, n. 12; § 15-2(B)(3), n. 33, n. 67.1, n. 78
United States v. Smart, 21 M.J. 15 (C.M.A. 1985) — § 17-8(B)(3), n. 83.3
United States v. Smith, 43 M.J. 390 (1996) — § 15-10(B), n. 66
United States v. Smith, 44 M.J. 387 (1996) — § 14-3(B)(2), n. 100; § 17-13, n. 24
United States v. Smith, 44 M.J. 459 (1996) — § 15-2(B)(2), n. 26
United States v. Smith, 44 M.J. 788 (N.M.Ct.Crim.App. 1996) — § 17-9(C), n. 56.1
United States v. Smith, 46 M.J. 263 (1997) — § 17-9(D), nn. 73, 75
United States v. Sojfer, 44 M.J. 603 (N.M.Ct.Crim.App. 1996) — § 2-4(E), n. 45; § 15-2(B)(3), n. 68
United States v. Sojfer, 47 M.J. 425 (1998) — § 5-4(B), n. 52; § 15-2(B)(3), n. 68
United States v. Sorbera, 43 M.J. 818 (A.F.Ct.Crim.App. 1996) — § 15-2(B)(3), n. 58
United States v. Sorrell, 47 M.J. 432 (1998) — § 17-8(B), n. 19
United States v. Spann, 48 M.J. 586 (N.M.Ct.Crim.App. 1998) — § 15-12(A), n. 13

TABLE OF CASES

United States v. Spurlin, 33 M.J. 443 (C.M.A. 1991) — § 17-8(B)(3), n. 83.3
United States v. Stallworth, 44 M.J. 785 (N.M.Ct.Crim.App. 1996) — § 17-8(B)(3), n. 71.1
United States v. Stantas, 45 C.M.R. 765 (N.C.M.R. 1971) — § 17-2(B)(5), n. 100.14
United States v. Staten, 45 C.M.R. 267 (C.M.A. 1972) — § 15-2(A), n. 2.1
United States v. Stockman, 43 M.J. 856 (N.M.Ct.Crim.App. 1996) — § 16-3(B), n. 38
United States v. Strange, 45 M.J. 642 (N.M.Ct.Crim.App. 1997) — § 17-2(B)(4), n. 95
United States v. Strauss, 47 M.J. 739 (N.M.Ct.Crim.App. 1997) — § 16-8(C), n. 35
United States v. Streetman, 43 M.J. 752 (A.F.Ct.Crim.App. 1995) — § 5-3(D)(1), n. 131
United States v. Sumrall, 45 M.J. 207 (1996) — § 16-3(B), n. 38
United States v. Sunden, 45 M.J. 508 (Army Ct.Crim.App. 1996) — § 14-3(D)(4), nn. 146.1, 146.2
United States v. Swan, 43 M.J. 788 (N.M.Ct.Crim.App. 1995) — § 17-15(B), n. 33
United States v. Swan, 45 M.J. 672 (N.M.Ct.Crim.App. 1996) — § 5-10(D), n. 39
United States v. Swan, 48 M.J. 551 (N.M.Ct.Crim.App. 1998) — § 2-4(A), n. 18; § 13-3(N)(2), nn. 341, 344, 353
United States v. Swango, 44 M.J. 686 (Army Ct.Crim.App. 1996) — § 6-1(C)(3), n. 165; § 16-2(D), n. 42
United States v. Sylvester, 47 M.J. 390 (1997) — § 15-2(B)(3), n. 85
United States v. Tarleton, 47 M.J. 170 (1997) — § 14-4, n. 13
United States v. Taylor, 44 M.J. 475 (1996) — § 15-10(A), n. 25
United States v. Taylor, 47 M.J. 322 (1997) — § 17-15(B), n. 32
United States v. Terry, 45 C.M.R. 216 (C.M.A. 1972) — § 14-3(B)(2), n. 82.3
United States v. Thomas, 44 M.J. 667 (N.M.Ct.Crim.App. 1996) — § 15-10(A), n. 21; § 15-13, n. 18
United States v. Thomas, 45 M.J. 661 (Army Ct.Crim.App. 1997) — § 14-3(D)(4), n. 147
United States v. Thomas, 46 M.J. 311 (1997) — § 16-3(A), n. 18; § 16-9, n. 5; § 16-10, n. 8
United States v. Thompson, 43 M.J. 703 (A.F.Ct.Crim.App. 1995) — § 16-9, n. 10; § 17-8(B)(1), n. 33; § 17-8(B)(3), n. 75
United States v. Thompson, 46 M.J. 472 (1997) — § 13-3(C)(3), n. 143
United States v. Thompson, 47 M.J. 378 (1997) — § 15-15, n. 2
United States v. Tilghman, 44 M.J. 493 (1996) — § 5-9(A), n. 1; § 5-10(D), n. 28
United States v. Tillar, 48 M.J. 541 (1998) — § 16-5(C), nn. 27, 39
United States v. Tilly, 44 M.J. 851 (N.M.Ct.Crim.App. 1996) — § 16-7, n. 3; § 16-11, n. 13.5
United States v. Townsend, 46 M.J. 517 (C.G.Ct.Crim.App. 1997) — § 2-4(C), n. 30
United States v. Travels, 47 M.J. 596 (A.F.Ct.Crim.App. 1997) — § 15-2(B)(3), n. 65; § 15-10(B), nn. 68, 69
United States v. Trosper, 47 M.J. 728 (N.M.Ct.Crim.App. 1997) — § 17-9(A), nn. 23.1, 23.2, 23.5
United States v. Tulloch, 47 M.J. 283 (1997) — § 15-10 (C)(3), nn. 118.9, 118.10
United States v. Tuner, 47 M.J. 348 (1997) — § 4-15(A), n. 5; § 12-3(A), n. 11
United States v. Turner, 48 M.J. 513 (Army Ct.Crim.App. 1998) — § 5-4(B), n. 44

TABLE OF CASES

United States v. Tyson, 44 M.J. 588 (N.M.Ct.Crim.App. 1996) — § 17-8(B)(3), nn. 79, 93
United States v. Underwood, 48 M.J. 805 (A.F.Ct.Crim.App. 1997) — § 8-5, n. 3; § 13-2, n. 7; § 13-5(G)(2), n. 93
United States v. Urban, 45 M.J. 528 (N.M.Ct.Crim.App. 1996) — § 2-2(E)(5), n. 87
United States v. Ureta, 44 M.J. 290 (1996) — § 15-15, n. 7
United States v. Vargas, 47 M.J. 552 (N.M.Ct.Crim.App. 1997) — § 8-3(C)(4), n. 160
United States v. Vaughters, 44 M.J. 377 (1996) — § 5-4(B), n. 50
United States v. Walters, 42 M.J. 760 (Army Ct.Crim.App. 1995), *aff'd* 45 M.J. 165 (1996) — § 15-2(B)(3), nn. 103, 104
United States v. Walters, 45 M.J. 165 (1996) — § 15-2(B)(3), nn. 36, 100, 103, 104.
United States v. Wansley, 46 M.J. 335 (1997) — § 17-8(B), n. 19
United States v. Ward, 5 M.J. 685 (N.C.M.R. 1978) — § 17-19, n. 18.1
United States v. Warren, 47 M.J. 649 (Army Ct.Crim.App. 1997) — § 5-4(B), nn. 44, 46
United States v. Washington, 45 M.J. 497 (1997) — § 17-8(B)(3), nn. 81, 83.3
United States v. Washington, 46 M.J. 477 (1997) — § 11-2(A)(3), n. 21.6; § 11-3(B)(1), nn. 35, 37.1, 37.3
United States v. Wean, 45 M.J. 461 (1997) — § 15-2(B)(3), n. 82.1
United States v. Weatherspoon, 44 M.J. 211 (1996) — § 16-11, nn. 13.1, 13.3, 13.4
United States v. Weisbeck, 48 M.J. 570 (Army Ct.Crim.App. 1998) — § 15-4(A), n. 6; § 16-8(B), n. 13
United States v. Welker, 44 M.J. 85 (1996) — § 15-12(A), n. 7; § 17-8(B)(1), n. 47
United States v. Weymouth, 43 M.J. 329 (1995) — § 6-1(C)(3), nn. 162.1, 162.2
United States v. White, 39 M.J. 796 (N.M.C.M.R. 1994) — § 2-6(B), n. 40
United States v. Wiley, 47 M.J. 158 (1997) — § 15-2(B)(3), nn. 88, 101, 102
United States v. Williams, 37 M.J. 352 (C.M.A. 1993) — § 17-21, nn. 4.1, 4.2
United States v. Williams, 44 M.J. 482 (1996) — § 15-10(A), n. 19; § 15-10(C)(3), n. 118.
United States v. Williams, 49 C.M.R. 12 (C.M.A. 1974) — § 2-2(E)(5), n. 87
United States v. Williams, 47 M.J. 621 (Army Ct.Crim.App. 1997) — § 5-9(E), n. 60; § 10-4(A)(4), n. 27
United States v. Williams, 46 M.J. 820 (A.F.Ct.Crim.App. 1997) — § 14-3(B)(3), n. 101
United States v. Williams, 47 M.J. 593 (N.M.Ct.Crim.App. 1997) — § 17-8(B)(1), n. 40
United States v. Willis, 43 M.J. 889 (A.F.Ct.Crim.App. 1996), *aff'd on other grounds*, 46 M.J. 258 (1997) — § 7-2(A)(1), n. 16; § 14-3(D)(4), n. 146.2
United States v. Wilson, 47 M.J. 152 (1997) — § 16-5(D)(3), n. 72
United States v. Witham, 44 M.J. 664 (N.M.Ct.Crim.App. 1996) — § 6-5(A), n. 8; § 6-7, n. 2
United States v. Witham, 47 M.J. 297 (1997) — § 15-10 (C)(3), nn. 118.1, 118.2, 118.4
United States v. Wright, 47 M.J. 555 (N.M.Ct.Crim.App. 1997) — § 5-4(A)(3), n. 19
United States v. Wysong, 26 C.M.R. 29 (C.M.A. 1958) — § 2-4(A), n. 18.2
United States v. Yerich, 47 M.J. 615 (Army Ct.Crim.App. 1997) — § 16-5(D)(4), n. 92
United States v. Young, 46 M.J. 768 (Army Ct.Crim.App. 1997) — § 5-4(B), n. 50
United States v. Youngblood, 47 M.J. 338 (1997) — § 15-10(B), nn. 48.1, 78.1, 78.3
United States v. Youngman, 48 M.J. 123 (1998) — § 13-3(H), n. 242

TABLE OF CASES

United States v. Zamberlan, 45 M.J. 491 (1997) — § 3-3(C), n. 27; § 16-5(B), n. 19
United States v. Zander, 46 M.J. 558 (N.M.Ct.Crim.App. 1997) — § 2-5, n.3
United States v. Zimmerman, 43 M.J. 782 (Army Ct.Crim.App. 1996) — § 13-3(N)(4), nn. 383, 386, 410; § 16-5(D)(1), n. 58; § 16-5(D)(2), n. 64
United States, Hobdy v.
United States, Jacobson v.
United States, Liteky v.
United States, Ross v.
United States, Solorio v.
United States Jaycees, Roberts v.
Urban, United States v.
Ureta, United States v.

V

Vanderbush, Smith v.
Vargas, United States v.
Vaughters, United States v.

W

Walters, United States v.
Wansley, United States v.
Ward, United States v.
Warren, United States v.
Washington, Strickland v.
Wean, United States v.
Weatherspoon, United States v.
Weisbeck, United States v.
Welker, United States v.
Weymouth, United States v.
White, United States v.
Whitley, Kyles v.
Wiley, United States v.
Will v. Calvert Fire Ins. Co., 437 U.S. 655 (1978) — § 17-19, n. 32.3
Williams, United States v.
Willis, United States v.
Wilson v. Courter, 46 M.J. 745 (A.F.Ct.Crim.App. 1997) — § 4-6, n. 25; § 4-8(B), n. 12; § 17-19, n. 15
Witham, United States v.
Wright, United States v.
Wysong, United States v.

TABLE OF CASES

Y

Yerich, United States v.
Young, United States v.
Youngblood, United States v.
Youngman, United States v.

Z

Zamberlan, United States v.
Zander, United States v.
Zimmerman, United States v.

INDEX

A

APPEALS.
Counsel.
　Generally, §17–14.
Government appeals, §13–2(G)(2).
Pretrial confinement.
　Judicial review, §5–9(E).

ARTICLE 32 INVESTIGATIONS.
Procedures, §7–2(C).

AUTOMATIC FORFEITURES.
Requesting a waiver of, §17–2(B)(5).

C

CHARGES AND SPECIFICATIONS.
Forwarding of charges.
　Special court-martial convening authority, §6–2(B).

CONSCIENTIOUS OBJECTORS.
Defenses to disobedience offenses, §2–4(F).

CONTEMPTS, §15–5.

COUNSEL.
Appellate counsel, §17–14.
Ineffective assistance, §15–2(B)(3).

D

DEATH PENALTY, §16–3(A).

DEPOSITIONS.
Procedure generally, §11–3(B)(1).

DEPRIVATION OF LIBERTY, §16–3(C).

DISMISSAL FROM SERVICE.
Punitive separation, §16–3(B).

E

EXPERT ASSISTANCE IN PREPARING CASE, §11–2(A)(3).

EXPERT WITNESSES.
Employing, §11–2(A)(3).

F

FORFEITURES.
Automatic forfeitures.
　Requesting a waiver of, §17–2(B)(5).

G

GENDER.
Peremptory challenges to be gender-neutral, §15–10(C)(3).

GUILTY PLEAS.
Care providency inquiry.
　Accuracy determination, §14–3(B)(2).
Improvident pleas.
　Factual and legal inconsistencies, §14–3(D)(4).
　Procedural consequences, §14–3(D)(5).

I

INEFFECTIVE ASSISTANCE OF COUNSEL, §15–2(B)(3).

INSTRUCTIONS TO COURT MEMBERS.
Requests, §15–14(C).

J

JURISDICTION.
Federal courts.
　Concurrent jurisdiction over offenses, §4–12(A).

M

MOTIONS TO GRANT APPROPRIATE RELIEF.
Evidentiary matters.
　Rulings on, §13–5(L).

INDEX

N

NEW TRIAL.
Petition for, §17–21.

P

PEREMPTORY CHALLENGES TO COURT MEMBERS, §15–10(C)(3).

PLEAS.
Conditional guilty plea.
    Pretrial agreement, §9–2(B).

POST-TRIAL AGREEMENT.
Negotiating, §17–2(B)(6).

S

SENTENCING AND PUNISHMENT.
Announcement of sentence, §16–11.

SERVICE OF POST-TRIAL RECOMMENDATION, §17–8(B)(3).

SPEEDY TRIAL.
Manual for courts-martial 120-day rule, §13–3(C)(3).

T

TRIAL PROCEDURES.
Right to demand trial, §3–4.